TCLC Cumulative Title Index, Vols. 1-197

"A Andrea Sperelli" (D'Annunzio) **6**:143
A. B. '. . . a Minor Marginal Note' (Smith) **25**:389
"À chacun son serpent" (Vian) **9**:537
"A Charles Mauras" (Moréas) **18**:288
"a- / float on some" (Cummings) **137**:63-64
"A histeria" (Lugones) **15**:285
"A la deriva" (Quiroga) **20**:210, 212, 214-15, 217-19, 221
À la grande nuit; ou, le bluff surréaliste (Artaud) **36**:23-4
À la mystérieuse (Desnos) **22**:60-1, 72
A la orilla del mar (Echegaray) **4**:101
"À la recherche" (Radnóti) **16**:411-12, 419-20
À la recherche du temps perdu (Proust) **7**:519-30, 532-43, 545-53; **13**:401, 403-04, 406-07, 412-13, 415-23, 425-27, 430-31; **33**:252-91; **161**:123, 128-34, 142-44, 148-49, 153-58, 162-63, 165, 173-74, 178-79, 185-87, 189, 193, 196, 199-202, 204-5
"À la Russie libre et libératrice" (Rolland) **23**:271
"À la santé" (Apollinaire) **3**:35; **51**:14, 57, 59-60
"À l'intérieur de l'armure" (Péret) **20**:185
"À l'Italie" (Apollinaire) **8**:28
À l'ombre des jeunes filles en fleurs (Proust) **7**:519, 525, 527, 540; **13**:405; **33**:254, 256, 258, 274; **161**:135, 142, 149, 154, 156
A los piés de Venus (Blasco Ibáñez) **12**:43, 47
"A mi hermano Miguel" (Vallejo) **3**:531; **56**:288-89, 294
"À Nîmes" (Apollinaire) **51**:35
A. O. Barnabooth, ses oeuvres complètes, c'est-à-dire: Un conte, ses poèmes, et son journal intime (Larbaud) **9**:196-98, 200-02, 205-07
"A peine défigurée" (Éluard) **7**:252
A propos de la campagne "antisuperstitieuse" (Roumain) **19**:342, 346
"À propos du style de Flaubert" (Proust) **161**:179
A quelle heure un train partira-t-il pour Paris? (Apollinaire) **8**:25-7
"À quoi bon dire?" (Mew) **8**:299
"A Raymond de La Tailhède" (Moréas) **18**:288
A rebours (Huysmans) **7**:405-07, 409-10, 412-13, 416-18; **69**:2-3, 6-7, 9, 11, 17-23, 25-32, 35, 37-9, 43, 47-50, 54-63, 65-66, 68-71
"A Roosevelt" (Darío) **4**:59, 61, 64
"A secreto agravio" (Pardo Bazán) **189**:226-27
"A tus imperfecciones" (Lugones) **15**:285
"A un angelo del Costa" (Campana) **20**:83
"A. V. Laider" (Beerbohm) **24**:101, 118
"Aa! Silimela!" (Mqhayi) **25**:327
Aandens Stadier (Jensen) **41**:294
"Aanun" (Bjoernson) **37**:33
"Aaron Hatfield" (Masters) **25**:299
"Aaron Stark" (Robinson) **101**:111, 119
Aaron's Rod (Lawrence) **2**:346-47, 350, 358, 371; **9**:215-16; **16**:323; **33**:188; **48**:117, 121, 126; **93**:23, 97, 103
Aarstiderne (Jensen) **41**:294
"Abandoned Church (Ballad of the Great War)" (García Lorca) **49**:81; **197**:184, 267, 270
"The Abandoned Rifle" (Morgenstern)
See "Die weggeworfene Flinte"
"The Abandoned Woman" (Kolmar) **40**:177
"The Abasement of the Northmores" (James) **47**:201
"Abashiri made" (Shiga) **172**:201, 203
L'Abbé C (Bataille) **155**:14, 89
L'Abbé Jules (Mirbeau) **55**:280, 283, 289-93
Abbey Church; or, Self-control and Self-conceit (Yonge)
See *Abbeychurch*
"Abbey Walks 8,000 Miles by Adroit Use of Thumb" (Abbey) **160**:57
Abbeychurch (Yonge) **48**:366, 373, 387
Abbey's Road (Abbey) **160**:3, 11-12, 31, 34, 36, 39, 42-44, 48, 51, 87, 90, 94
Abbots Verney (Macaulay) **7**:420, 422, 426; **44**:120
"The Abducted Woman" (Kolmar) **40**:175
"Abe ichizoku" (Mori Ogai) **14**:378, 380
Abe Lincoln in Illinois (Sherwood) **3**:412-16, 418-19
"Abeille" (France) **9**:40
"L'abeille" (Valéry) **15**:460
Abel Sánchez (Unamuno)
See *Abel Sánchez: Una historia de pasión*
Abel Sánchez, and Other Stories (Unamuno)
See *Abel Sánchez: Una historia de pasión*
Abel Sánchez: Una historia de pasión (Unamuno) **2**:564, 567, 569; **9**:513, 515-16; **148**:231, 239, 253, 256, 261, 265, 287
Abelard and Heloise (Torrence) **97**:152, 156-57, 159
"Abencaján el Bojarí, muerto en su laberinto" (Borges) **109**:37-8, 40, 88
"Abend in Skåne" (Rilke) **195**:183
Abenddammerung (Kandinsky) **92**:49
"Abenjacán el-Bokhari, Dead in His Labryrinth" (Borges)
See "Abencaján el Bojarí, muerto en su laberinto"
"Abenjacán the Bojarí, Dead in His Labyrinth" (Borges)
See "Abencaján el Bojarí, muerto en su laberinto"
"Abenjacán the Buckharian, Dead in His Labyrinth" (Borges)
See "Abencaján el Bojarí, muerto en su laberinto"
"Das Abenteuer" (Böll) **185**:18, 50
"Abenteuer" (Kandinsky) **92**:67
Abenteuer in Japan (Brod) **115**:110
"Der Abenteurer und die Sängerin" (Hofmannsthal) **11**:292, 303
Abhāgīr swarga (Chatterji) **13**:81
Ab-i zindigi (Hedāyat) **21**:75
Abie's Irish Rose (Mankiewicz) **85**:111
"Les Abîmes, par Ernest Clouët" (Swinburne) **8**:439
Abinger Harvest (Forster) **125**:162-63
"Abisag" (Rilke) **195**:228
"Abji khanum" (Hedāyat) **21**:71
The Abortion: An Historical Romance, 1966 (Brautigan) **133**:3-10, 28
"About a Willow Trees" (Hagiwara) **60**:302
"About Beata Beatrice and the Mamma of Sampietro" (Rolfe) **12**:272
"About Censorship" (Galsworthy) **45**:33
"About Divinamore and the Maiden Anima" (Rolfe) **12**:272
About Fiction: Reverent Reflections on the Nature of Fiction with Irreverent Observations on Writers, Readers, and Other Abuses (Morris) **107**:120, 173
"About Influenza" (Péguy)
See "De la grippe"
"About Mr Cogito's Two Legs" (Herbert) **168**:8, 10, 18
"About My Story Reishō" (Nagai) **51**:89
"About Myself and about Something Else" (Zoshchenko) **15**:496
About Myself and Others (Couperus)
See *Van en over mijzelf en anderen*
About Norway (Hansen)
See *Kringen*
"About Papa Feretti and the Blest Heresiarch" (Rolfe) **12**:266
"About Play-Acting" (Twain) **161**:240; **185**:234
"About Popular Culture" (Jarrell) **177**:222
About Pushkin (Khodasevich) **15**:203
"About Socialist Realism" (Fadeyev) **53**:58
"About Some Friends" (Rolfe) **12**:272
"About That" (Mayakovski) **4**:291; **18**:266-70
About the Depot (Bergelson) **81**:16
"About the Holy Duchess and the Wicked King" (Rolfe) **12**:266
About the Last Things (Weininger)
See *Über die letzten Dinge*
"About the Original Fritter of Sangiuseppe" (Rolfe) **12**:272
"About the Siskin Who Lied and the Woodpecker Who Loved the Truth" (Gorky)
See "O chizhe, kotoryi lgal, i o diatle liubitele istiny"
About the Understanding (Rozanov)
See *O ponimanii*
"About Those Colored Movies" (Childress) **116**:36
"About Time" (Nemerov) **124**:218
About Understanding (Rozanov)
See *O ponimanii*
"About What? About This" (Mayakovski) **4**:297
"Above" (Nemerov) **124**:256
"Above Corn Tassels" (Wright) **136**:301
"Above the Gaspereau" (Carman) **7**:139
"Above the Ravine" (Pilnyak) **23**:203
"Above These Cares" (Millay) **49**:225
Abracadabra, and Other Stories (Galsworthy) **45**:33
"Abraham and Isaac" (Lasker-Schueler)
See "Abraham und Isaak"
Abraham and Isaac (Housman) **7**:360

"Abraham Carew" (Lee-Hamilton) **22**:187, 189
Abraham Lincoln (Drinkwater) **57**:124-26, 128-33, 135-38, 140-43, 146, 148
Abraham Lincoln (Griffith) **68**:169, 177, 220
"Abraham Lincoln Walks at Midnight" (Lindsay) **17**:230-31, 236
"Abraham Men" (Powys) **9**:365
"Abraham und Isaak" (Lasker-Schueler) **57**:301, 332, 336
"Abrigo" (Sá-Carneiro) **83**:401
Abrojos (Darío) **4**:58-60
"Abrupt Decisions" (McAlmon) **97**:113
Absalom, Absalom! (Faulkner) **141**:30-32, 34, 36, 39, 57-59, 62, 101, 107-10, 112, 128, 133, 135-36, 151-52, 159-61, 168, 172-74, 193, 202; **170**:109, 127-29, 132, 143, 145-48, 150-51, 160-65, 171-75, 183, 185, 193-96, 208-09, 212, 214, 223-24, 234, 237, 242, 244
"Abschied" (Kolmar) **40**:174
"Abschied" (Lasker-Schueler) **57**:304, 309, 320, 326
"Abschied" (Raabe) **45**:189
"Der Abschied" (Sarton) **120**:303
Abschied (Kandinsky) **92**:49
"Abschied und Wiederkehr" (Kraus) **5**:292
"Abschied vom Jazz" (Adorno) **111**:84-5, 132, 134, 139-40
Abschied von den Eltern: Erzählung (Weiss) **152**:246-47, 249, 251-52, 285, 293-94, 309
"Abschied von England" (Bachmann) **192**:108-9, 112-13
"Abschied von Stuttgart" (Raabe) **45**:191
"An Absence" (Ginzburg)
See "Un assenza"
The Absence of Myth (Bataille) **155**:88-89, 92-94, 109, 114
"The Absence of Religion in Shakespeare" (Santayana) **40**:388
"The Absent" (Muir) **2**:485
"The Absent One" (Villaurrutia) **80**:458
"Absent With Official Leave" (Jarrell) **177**:193-94
Absent without Leave (Böll)
See *Entfernung von der Truppe*
Absentee Ownership (Veblen) **31**:350, 362
"Absent-Minded Professor" (Nemerov) **124**:178
"The Absinthe Drinker" (Symons) **11**:427, 439
"Absinthia taetra" (Dowson) **4**:92
"Absoluta" (Vallejo) **56**:289
"The Absolute Answers" (Hardy) **143**:200
The Absolute at Large (Čapek)
See *Továrna na absolutno*
The Absolute Gravedigger (Nezval)
See *Absolutní hrobař*
Absolute Love (Jarry)
See *L'amour absolu*
"Absolute Peace" (Balmont) **11**:42
"Absolute Prosa" (Benn) **3**:110
"Absolution" (Fitzgerald) **1**:241, 262-63; **6**:169-71; **14**:179, 182-83; **55**:191; **157**:124, 126, 142, 204
Absolutní hrobař (Nezval) **44**:245
"Absorbed in Letters" (Akutagawa Ryūnosuke) **16**:23
The Absorbent Mind (Montessori)
See *La menta del bambino*
Abu Casem's Slippers (Strindberg)
See *Abu Casems tofflor*
Abu Casems tofflor (Strindberg) **47**:369
Abu Telfan (Raabe) **45**:160, 162, 164, 168-70, 172, 174-75, 178-80, 194, 200
"Abuela Julieta" (Lugones) **15**:292
El abuelo (Pérez Galdós) **27**:248, 250, 254-56, 268
El abuelo del rey (Miro) **5**:338-39, 341
"Abu-Hasan" (Caragiale) **76**:159, 170
"The Abuse of Woman's Strength" (Key) **65**:236
The Abysmal Brute (London) **9**:261
The Abyss (Andreyev) **3**:24, 26
The Abyss (Yourcenar)
See *L'Oeuvre au noir*
"The Abyss of Mr. Cogito" (Herbert) **168**:9
"Acaba" (Aleixandre) **113**:8
"Acabó el Amor" (Aleixandre) **113**:49
Academic Freedom: An Essay in Definition (Kirk) **119**:253, 256, 275
"The Academic Horse" (Bataille) **155**:111
"An Academic Question" (Fisher) **87**:73
"Accalmie" (Moréas) **18**:280, 282, 285
"An Accident" (Chesterton) **6**:109
"An Accident" (Coppee) **25**:121
Accident (Bennett) **5**:37
Accident (Kandinsky) **92**:48
An Accidental Man (Murdoch) **171**:307, 323
"Acción" (Jiménez) **183**:269
"Accompagnement" (Garneau) **13**:195, 203
Accompagnés de la Flûte (Giono) **124**:91
"According to Meredith" (Lowndes) **12**:200
According to Plan of a One-Eyed Mystic (Dent) **72**:24
"According to the Pattern" (Evans) **85**:27-8, 33
Account of the Dialect of the Southern Counties of Scotland (Murray) **117**:280, 283
"An Account of Yesterday" (Tolstoy) **11**:464
"Accountability" (Dunbar) **12**:108, 110
"Accounting" (Radnóti) **16**:419
The Accumulation of Capital, Or What the Epigones Have Made of Marxian Theory: A Countercriticism (Luxemburg)
See *Die Akkumulation des Kapitals, oder Was die Epigonen aus der Marxschen Theorie gemacht haben: Eine Antikritik*
The Accursed Share (Bataille)
See *La part maudite*
"Aceldama" (Crowley) **7**:208
"Acéphale" (Bataille) **155**:97, 113
"El acercamiento a Almotásim" (Borges) **109**:21
"Ach, der Erhabene" (Benn) **3**:107
"Ach, nicht getrennt sein" (Rilke) **195**:256
Achalāyatan (Tagore) **3**:486
The Achievement of T. S. Eliot: An Essay on the Nature of Poetry (Matthiessen) **100**:158, 166, 168, 170, 186, 203, 213, 218, 221-22, 225, 238, 242
"Achille ou le mensonge" (Yourcenar) **193**:355
"Achilles at the Altar" (Bryusov) **10**:80, 88
"Achilles or the Lie" (Yourcenar)
See "Achille ou le mensonge"
"La achirana del Inca" (Palma) **29**:256
Het achterhuis (Frank) **17**:101, 104, 107-08, 111, 113-14, 116-17, 119
"Achtung, Die Schweiz!" (Frisch) **121**:232
"Acorn, Yom Kippur" (Nemerov) **124**:320-21
"Acquaintance" (Popa) **167**:175, 177, 179
Acquainted with Grief (Gadda)
See *La cognizione del dolore*
Acquainted with the Night (Böll)
See *Und sagte kein einziges Wort*
Acque turbate (Betti) **5**:60, 63-6
"Acquiescence" (Gurney) **33**:85
"An Acre of Grass" (Yeats) **1**:580; **18**:447; **116**:343
"The Acrobat" (Nezval) **44**:239
"The Acropolis" (Merezhkovsky) **29**:246
Acropolis (Sherwood) **3**:414, 418
"Across Graves" (Talvik) **87**:319
Across Spoon River (Masters) **25**:302, 310, 316
Across the Board on Tomorrow Morning (Saroyan) **137**:155
Across the Borderline (Tammsaare)
See *Üle piiri*
Across the Plains (Ince) **89**:9
"Across the River" (Frye) **165**:184
Across the Smiling Meadow and Other Stories (Aldrich) **125**:10, 18
Across the Stream (Benson) **27**:19
Across the Wide Missouri (De Voto) **29**:124, 127-29
Act of Darkness (Bishop) **103**:14, 20, 25, 27, 30-7, 40-2, 46-7, 49
"An Act of God" (Post) **39**:338
"An Act of Redress" (Caragiale)
See "O reparatie"
"An Act of Reparation" (Warner) **131**:323
Act without Words (Beckett)
See *Acte sans paroles I*
Act without Words I (Beckett)
See *Acte sans paroles I*
"Actaeon" (Erskine) **84**:174
"Actaeon" (Roberts) **8**:313-14, 320
Actaeon and Other Poems (Erskine) **84**:160
"Acte héraldique" (Jarry) **147**:311, 314
Acte sans paroles I (Beckett) **145**:143, 158
"Acte Terreste" (Jarry) **147**:311
Acteon (Gumilev) **60**:265
"Acting Captain" (Lewis) **3**:288
"Acting Intuition" (Nishida)
See "Koiteki chokkan"
Acting: The First Six Lessons (Stanislavsky) **167**:337
"Action and the Pursuit of Happiness" (Arendt) **193**:75-6, 177
The Action and the World (Matthews) **95**:253, 272, 276-7
Active Service (Crane) **11**:125, 128, 137, 160, 162, 166-67
L'Activité rationaliste de la physique contemporaine (Bachelard) **128**:28, 52-3
Activities: India and Cambridge, 1906-14 (Keynes) **64**:240
Activities: The Treasury and Versailles, 1914-19 (Keynes) **64**:241
"The Actor" (Zoshchenko) **15**:499
Actor and Self (Stanislavsky)
See *Actor and Self: Personal Work in the Creative Process of Re-Living*
Actor and Self: Personal Work in the Creative Process of Re-Living (Stanislavsky) **167**:247-48
"The Actor Forest Guard" (Quiroga)
See "El guardabosque comediante"
Actor from Vienna (Molnár) **20**:171
An Actor Prepares (Stanislavsky) **167**:240, 243, 247, 251, 253, 264, 267-68, 271, 273, 276-79, 282-83, 294-95, 300, 303-8, 310-12, 319, 328-32, 334, 337-40
Actors and Sin (Hecht) **101**:77
"Actor's Blood" (Hecht) **101**:77
An Actor's Handbook (Stanislavsky) **167**:305
An Actor's Work on a Role: Materials Toward a Book (Stanislavsky) **167**:279, 306-7, 331
The Actor's Work on Himself (Stanislavsky) **167**:304, 306, 326, 328-29, 332, 335-36, 340
The Actor's Work on Himself in the Creative Process of Embodying (Stanislavsky) **167**:253, 279
The Actor's Work on Himself in the Creative Process of Experiencing (Stanislavsky) **167**:252, 279, 304-6
The Actor's Work on Himself in the Creative Process of Incarnation (Stanislavsky) **167**:306
The Actor's Work on Himself, Part I (Stanislavsky) **167**:340
The Actor's Work on Himself Part II: Physical Characterization (Stanislavsky) **167**:305-6
"The Actress" (Mann)
See "Schauspielerin"
"The Actress" (Tolstoy) **18**:377
The Actress Nana (Nagai)
See *Joyū nana*
The Acts of Saint Peter (Bottomley) **107**:8-10
Actually Comedies (Bacovia) **24**:64
Açvaghosha's Discourse on the Awakening of Faith in the Mahayana (Suzuki) **109**:387
"Ad Astra" (Faulkner) **170**:174
"Ad az isten" (Ady) **11**:18
"Ad Cinarem" (Manning) **25**:277
Ad matrem (Gray) **19**:154
Ad Me Ipsum (Hofmannsthal) **11**:300
"Ad Olam" (Agnon) **151**:11-12, 18-19, 36

Ad Ora Incerta (Levi) **109**:287, 289
Ada (Nabokov) **189**:76, 81, 154, 174, 179, 187
"Ada" (Stein) **1**:428; **48**:256-57, 260-63
Ada; or, Ardor: A Family Chronicle (Nabokov) **108**:59, 63, 65, 73, 77, 86-89, 92, 101-04, 107, 113, 145, 147, 178, 183-85, 191, 224
"Adagia" (Stevens) **3**:463-64, 474; **12**:384-85, 387; **45**:278, 286, 293, 295, 298, 302, 314, 317, 324-26, 337
"L'adagio" (Coppee) **25**:124
"Adagio" (Scott) **6**:389
L'adalgisa, disegni milanesi (Gadda) **144**:116, 131
"Adam" (García Lorca) **49**:91, 93; **181**:26-27
Adam (Huidobro)
See *Adán*
"Adam and Eve" (Lin) **149**:326
"Adam and Eve" (Machado de Assis)
See "Adão e Eva"
"Adam and Eve" (Prishvin) **75**:215
Adam and Eve (Bulgakov) **16**:85, 111-12
Adam and Eve (Rebreanu)
See *Adam şi Eva*
Adam and Eve and Pinch Me: Tales (Coppard) **5**:175-76, 179, 181
Adam and the Serpent (Fisher) **140**:156, 186
Adam Cast Forth (Doughty) **27**:53-4, 59, 62-3, 65-6, 68-9, 74, 84-5
Adam et Eve (Lemonnier) **22**:197, 199
Adam et Eve (Ramuz) **33**:302
"Ádám, hol vagy?" (Ady) **11**:15, 17
Adam Johnstone's Son (Crawford) **10**:141, 151
"Adam, One Afternoon" (Calvino)
See "Un pomeriggio Adamo"
Adam, One Afternoon (Calvino)
See *Romanzi e racconti*
Adam, One Afternoon, and Other Stories (Calvino)
See *Ultimo viene il corvo*
Adam Schrader (Lie) **5**:324, 326, 332
Adam şi Eva (Rebreanu) **28**:272
Adam stvořitel (Čapek) **6**:85, 90; **37**:53, 55, 59, 61; **192**:193, 201-2, 228
Adam the Creator (Čapek)
See *Adam stvořitel*
"Adam, Where Art Thou?" (Ady)
See "Ádám, hol vagy?"
Adam, Where Art Thou? (Böll)
See *Wo warst du, Adam?*
Adamastor (Campbell) **5**:117, 120, 122-23, 126
Adame miroire (Genet) **128**:139, 141
"Adams" (Douglas) **40**:71, 76
Adam's Breed (Hall) **12**:184, 190-91, 195
"Adam's Curse" (Yeats) **1**:581; **11**:527, 533; **93**:348
"Adam's Dream" (Muir) **2**:485; **87**:159
Adán (Huidobro) **31**:122, 133, 137, 145
Adán y Eva (Pardo Bazán) **189**:249, 313
"Adão e Eva" (Machado de Assis) **10**:290-91
"Adaptations" (Villa)
See "New Poems and Adaptations"
"Add This to Rhetoric" (Stevens) **45**:283, 331
"Addenda" (Čapek) **192**:189
The Adder (Abercrombie) **141**:10-12, 21
The Adding Machine: Collected Essays (Burroughs) **121**:137, 144
"Addolorata's Intervention" (Fuller) **103**:85
Address (Faulkner) **141**:115
"Address Delivered at Seneca Falls" (Stanton) **73**:271
"Address of President Woodrow Wilson, Accepting the Lincoln Homestead at Hodgenville" (Wilson) **79**:488
"Address on Nietzsche" (Mann) **44**:165
"Address to the Legislature of New York on Women's Rights" (Stanton) **73**:272
"Address to the Raven, Jefferson, and ODK Societies of the University of Virginia" (Faulkner) **170**:240
"Address to the Swedish Peace Congress" (Tolstoy) **79**:430
Addresses on Religion (Gentile)
See *Discoursi di religione*
Adela Cathcart (MacDonald) **9**:291; **113**:210, 213-14, 314, 327
"Adelina de paseo" (García Lorca) **181**:179
Aden, Arabie (Nizan) **40**:288-90, 294, 299, 310-11, 314-15, 320, 324
"Ades!" (Buchanan) **107**:14
"Adieu" (Apollinaire) **51**:6, 61
"Adieu" (Obstfelder) **23**:179
Adiós a mamá (Arenas) **191**:216, 220
"Adiós a mamá" (Arenas) **191**:193, 216-17, 219
Los adioses (Onetti) **131**:133, 135, 153, 155-56, 162, 175-77, 191, 194-95, 203-4, 217-18, 232, 234, 263-67, 282-83, 285-86, 288
Adjutantenritte und Andere Gedichte (Liliencron) **18**:212-14
"Adjutantentrite" (Liliencron) **18**:206-08, 211
"Adlestrop" (Thomas) **10**:452, 455, 463, 467
The Admirable Bashville (Shaw) **45**:260
The Admirable Bashville; or, Constancy Unrewarded (Shaw)
See *Cashel Byron's Profession*
The Admirable Crichton (Barrie) **2**:40, 42-4, 48-9; **164**:7, 37, 39, 80
Admiral Guinea (Henley) **8**:99, 102, 108
Admiral Hornblower in the West Indies (Forester) **152**:134-35, 139-40
"The Admiral Seeks a House for Rent" (Tzara) **168**:238
"The Admiral's Ghost" (Noyes) **7**:503, 512
"Admiral's Night" (Machado de Assis) **10**:306
Admiralteiskaia igla (Nabokov) **108**:146
"The Admiralty Spire" (Nabokov)
See *Admiralteiskaia igla*
"Admiring the Scenery" (O'Faolain) **143**:253
"An Admonishment to All Buddhist Disciples" (Su Man-shu) **24**:455
"Admonition" (Bell) **43**:91
"Adobe House in a Provincial Garden" (Platonov)
See "Glinyanyy dom v uyezdnom sadu"
"Adoescence" (Aleixandre)
See "Adolescencia"
Adolescence (Tolstoy)
See *Otrochestvo*
"Adolescencia" (Aleixandre) **113**:3
"Adolescencia" (Jiménez) **183**:298
"The Adolescent" (Jiménez)
See "Adolescencia"
"Adolescent" (Tsvetaeva)
See "Otrok"
L'adolescent (Rolland) **23**:261
The Adolescent Diaries of Karen Horney (Horney) **71**:252, 263
"The Adolescent Marriage" (Fitzgerald) **6**:167
"Adolphe van Bever" (Léautaud) **83**:207
Adonis, Attis, Osiris: Studies in the History of Oriental Religion (Frazer) **32**:221
"The Adopted Daughter" (Post) **39**:339
Adorable Clio (Giraudoux) **2**:163
"Adoration" (Nemerov) **124**:298
"The Adoration of the Magi" (Yeats) **31**:407, 415; **93**:363
"L'Adoration perpétuelle" (Proust) **161**:143-44
The Adored One (Barrie) **164**:39
"Adown the Lesbian Vales" (Field) **43**:178
Adrea (Belasco) **3**:85, 90
Adrian et Jusemina (Ghelderode) **187**:5
Adrian Rome (Dowson) **4**:89, 92
"Adrien Brauwer" (Huysmans) **69**:8
Adrienne Ambrossat (Kaiser) **9**:176
Adrienne Lecouvreur (Schoenberg) **75**:19, 25, 52, 59
"Adrift" (Quiroga)
See "A la deriva"
Adrift from Marx and Freud (Lyotard)
See *Dérive à partir de Marx et Freud*
"Adult Epigram" (Stevens) **12**:365
The Adult Life of Toulouse Lautrec by Henri Toulouse Lautrec (Acker) **191**:33, 42, 67, 69-70, 127
"Adultery" (Dickey) **115**:111, 121, 199, 212
"The Advanced Lady" (Mansfield) **2**:456; **8**:282; **164**:269-70, 293
The Advanced Montessori Method (Montessori) **103**:289, 291
"Advances in Methods of Teaching" (Boas) **56**:105
"The Advantage of Having One Leg" (Chesterton) **1**:184
"The Advantages of Civilization" (Gray) **19**:158
"Advent" (Fletcher) **35**:106, 108
Advent (Rilke) **195**:258
Advent (Strindberg) **1**:456, 460; **8**:414-15; **21**:353
"Advent: Late Customer" (Radnóti) **16**:418
"Adventure" (Anderson) **10**:54, 56; **24**:34, 45, 48, 52, 56; **123**:14, 38, 76-7, 82-3, 85
"The Adventure" (Bojer) **64**:349
"The Adventure" (Böll)
See "Das Abenteuer"
Adventure (London) **9**:266, 276
An Adventure (Tsvetaeva)
See *Prikliuchenie*
"An Adventure at Brownville" (Bierce)
See "An Occurrence at Brownville"
"An Adventure from a Work in Progress" (Thomas) **105**:299-301, 325-26
"The Adventure of a Bather" (Calvino) **183**:93
"The Adventure of a Clerk" (Calvino) **183**:191
"The Adventure of a Near-sighted Man" (Calvino) **183**:93
"The Adventure of a Night Driver" (Calvino) **183**:93
"The Adventure of a Poet" (Calvino)
See "L'avventura di un poeta"
"The Adventure of a Reader" (Calvino) **183**:191
"The Adventure of a Soldier" (Calvino)
See "L'Avventura di un soldato"
"The Adventure of a Swimmer" (Calvino)
See "L'Avventura di una bagnante"
"The Adventure of a Traveler" (Calvino) **183**:93
"The Adventure of a Wife" (Calvino)
See "L'Avventura di una moglie"
"The Adventure of Charles Augustus Milverton" (Doyle) **7**:241
The Adventure of Lady Ursula (Hope) **83**:170
"The Adventure of Life" (Bourne) **16**:60
"An Adventure of Mrs. Mackenzie's" (Scott) **6**:398-99
"The Adventure of Stasio" (Prus)
See "Przygoda Stasia"
"The Adventure of the Broken Mirror" (Hecht) **101**:44
"The Adventure of the Cardboard Box" (Doyle) **7**:240
The Adventure of the Dying Detective (Doyle) **7**:223
"The Adventure of the Empty House" (Doyle) **7**:231
"The Adventure of the Engineer's Thumb" (Doyle) **7**:216
"The Adventure of the Norwood Builder" (Doyle) **7**:240
"The Adventure of the Red-Headed League" (Doyle) **7**:216, 219, 231
"The Adventure of the Reigate Puzzle" (Doyle) **7**:228
"The Adventure of the Retired Colourman" (Doyle) **7**:236
"The Adventure of the Silver Blaze" (Doyle) **7**:223, 228
"The Adventure of the Speckled Band" (Doyle) **7**:216, 223, 230
"The Adventure of the Veiled Lodger" (Doyle) **7**:235
"The Adventure of the Yellow Face" (Doyle) **7**:231, 241
"The Adventure of Two Spouses" (Calvino)
See "L'avventura di due sposi"
The Adventurer (Osbourne) **93**:132
Adventures among Birds (Hudson) **29**:138, 144
Adventures and Enthusiasms (Lucas) **73**:162

Adventures and Misgivings (Lucas) **73**:174
Adventures in Contentment (Baker) **47**:2-3, 17, 20, 22-3, 27
Adventures in Friendship (Baker) **47**:27-8
Adventures in Phunniland (Baum) **132**:80
Adventures in Solitude (Baker) **47**:23
"Adventures in the Skin Trade" (Thomas) **105**:325
Adventures in the Skin Trade, and Other Stories (Thomas) **45**:374, 390, 395-96; **105**:296, 307-8, 311, 316, 325-28, 334, 347, 350, 352, 356-58
Adventures in Understanding (Baker) **47**:24
Adventures, Inventions, and Hoaxes of Silvestre Paradox (Baroja)
See *Aventuras, inventos, y mixtificaciones de Silvestre Paradox*
The Adventures of a Modest Man (Chambers) **41**:95
"Adventures of a Monkey" (Zoshchenko) **15**:496, 502, 506, 509-10
Adventures of a Young Man (Reed) **9**:388
The Adventures of Aimé Lebeuf (Kuzmin) **40**:191, 193
"The Adventures of Ann, the Bound Girl of Samuel Wales, of Braintree, in the Province of Massachusetts Bay" (Freeman) **9**:72
The Adventures of Captain Hatteras (Verne)
See *Les aventures du Capitaine Hatteras*
The Adventures of Captain Horn (Stockton) **47**:317, 321, 325
"The Adventures of Chichikov" (Bulgakov) **2**:64; **16**:84
Adventures of Elizabeth in Rügen (Elizabeth) **41**:122-23, 130, 132
The Adventures of François (Mitchell) **36**:272
Adventures of Gerard (Doyle) **7**:232-33, 239
The Adventures of Harry Richmond (Meredith) **17**:269, 273, 278, 290-91, 293; **43**:259, 275
The Adventures of Huckleberry Finn (Twain) **6**:454-7, 459-61, 463-70, 473-6, 478, 480, 482-5; **12**:427-9, 431, 434-7, 439-45, 448, 451, 454; **19**:351-69, 372-6, 378-88, 391; **36**:352, 354-5, 358-63, 366, 369, 372, 375, 379, 381-7, 392; **48**:334, 336, 339, 341-9, 351-2, 356, 359, 361; **59**:168, 173-7, 181-9, 196, 201-3, 208-10; **161**:208-351; **185**:243, 249, 256, 259, 307, 310, 320, 328
Adventures of Ideas (Whitehead) **97**:206, 211, 215, 219-20, 238
The Adventures of Marco Polo (Sherwood) **3**:417
Adventures of Martin Hewitt (Morrison) **72**:363
The Adventures of Menakhem-Mendl (Aleichem) **1**:32; **35**:306-08, 310, 327
"The Adventures of Mercurius" (van Ostaijen) **33**:409
The Adventures of Monsieur de Mailly (Lindsay) **15**:221-22, 232-33
Adventures of Mottel, the Cantor's Son (Aleichem)
See *Motl Peysi dem khazns*
"The Adventures of Mr Cogito with Music" (Herbert) **168**:21, 57
Adventures of Rasteghin (Tolstoy) **18**:373
The Adventures of Romney Pringle (Freeman) **21**:54
The Adventures of Seumas Beg (Stephens) **4**:415, 419
The Adventures of Sherlock Holmes (Doyle) **7**:215-16, 220, 238
"The Adventures of the Black Girl in Her Search for God" (Shaw) **3**:387
"The Adventures of the Bruce-Partington Plans" (Doyle) **7**:229
The Adventures of Tom Sawyer (Twain) **6**:455-56, 460-61, 463-66, 468-70, 473-76, 480, 483-84; **12**:427, 431-32, 437-38, 440, 451-53; **19**:351-58, 361-63, 366-67, 369, 371-72, 407, 409, 411; **36**:354-55, 358, 384, 394, 401, 404, 409; **48**:330, 334-35, 339, 357; **59**:159-212; **161**:210, 214-17, 223, 236, 255, 257, 259, 276, 289, 292, 337; **185**:259, 307
The Adventures of Wesley Jackson (Saroyan) **137**:168, 170, 181, 186
Adventures, Rhymes, and Designs (Lindsay) **17**:239
Adventures While Preaching the Gospel of Beauty (Lindsay) **17**:223, 239
"Adventures with the Eldest Daughter Eight Years Old" (Lindsay) **17**:241
"The Adventurous Exploit of the Cave of Ali Baba" (Sayers) **15**:379
"Advertencia" (Vallejo) **56**:316
"Advertisement" (Bachmann) **192**:81
"Advertisement" (Henley) **8**:109
Advice (Bodenheim) **44**:59, 67-8
"Advice to a Beauty" (Cullen) **37**:160
"Advice to a Bluebird" (Bodenheim) **44**:62, 64
"Advice to a Man" (Bodenheim) **44**:66
"Advice to a Poet" (Dobson) **79**:30
"Advice to a Street Pavement" (Bodenheim) **44**:59, 68
"Advice to a Young Critic" (Nathan) **18**:308
"Advice to the Little Peyton Girl" (Parker) **143**:285, 331, 333-35, 340
"Advice to Young Men" (Mencken) **13**:365
"Advice to Youth" (Cullen) **37**:154, 164, 167
"The Advisability of Not Being Brought Up in a Handbag: A Trivial Tragedy for Wonderful People" (Leverson) **18**:199
Advisory Ben: A Story (Lucas) **73**:159, 162
Aelita (Tolstoy) **18**:359, 373, 378, 383-86
"Aemilius, l'arbre laisse" (Moréas) **18**:288
"Aepyornis Island" (Wells) **19**:443
"Aeroplano" (Huidobro) **31**:125
Aërt (Rolland) **23**:257, 260
"Aesop's Last Fable" (March) **96**:252
"Aesthetic" (Collingwood) **67**:179
Aesthetic as Science of Expression and General Linguistic (Croce)
See *Estetica come scienza dell' espressione e linguistica generale*
"The Aesthetic Infinite" (Valéry) **15**:460
Aesthetic Studies (Brandes)
See *Aesthetiske studier*
Aesthetic Theory (Adorno)
See *Asthetische Theorie*
"Aesthetic Weasel" (Morgenstern) **8**:308
Aesthetica in Nuce (Croce) **37**:127
"Aesthetics of Gogol's 'Dead Souls' and Its Legacy" (Annensky) **14**:29
The Aesthetics of Resistance (Weiss) **152**:282-83, 285-87, 289
Aesthetiske studier (Brandes) **10**:60; **11**:70
"Aeternae memoriae patris" (Fargue) **11**:199
"Aether" (Ginsberg) **120**:9, 38, 77
Aferhønen (Hansen) **32**:249, 251
"The Affair at Coulter's Notch" (Bierce) **7**:88; **44**:12, 44-7
"The Affair at Ysterspruit" (Bosman) **49**:19
"Affair of Honor" (Rohmer) **28**:286
"An Affair of Outposts" (Bierce) **44**:12, 22, 44-5
"The Affair of the -th of July" (Remington) **89**:306
L'affaire Crainquebille (France) **9**:43, 47, 51-2
Une affaire de viol (Himes) **139**:246, 248, 250, 252
"L'Affaire est l'Affaire" (Jarry) **147**:278-79
Les affaires sont les affaires (Mirbeau) **55**:281-82
Affairs of the Heart (Hunt) **53**:191
Affairs of the Heart (Muggeridge) **120**:186
Die Affenhochzeit (Zuckmayer) **191**:302, 304
L'affiche (Epstein) **92**:11
Affinities (Rinehart) **52**:282
Affinities in Literature (Su Man-shu) **24**:458
Affirmations (Ellis) **14**:108, 111, 114, 116, 119, 127, 131-34, 142
"The Afghans" (Ingamells) **35**:137
Afield and Afloat (Stockton) **47**:326-27
Afiny i Ierusalim (Shestov)
See *Athènes et Jérusalem: un essai de philosophie religieuse*
"Afonka Bida" (Babel) **171**:7, 10-11, 18, 24, 37, 84-85
Afoot in England (Hudson) **29**:138, 162
Aforismos (Sarduy) **167**:205
"Afra" (Pardo Bazán) **189**:228
"Africa" (Zamyatin) **37**:427, 430
"The African Coast" (Tomlinson) **71**:381, 400
African Game Trails (Roosevelt) **69**:181, 266-67
"African Moonrise" (Campbell) **5**:117
"African Night" (Gumilev)
See "Afrikanskaja noč'"
The African Queen (Forester) **152**:141, 144, 147-48, 152, 164
African Religions in Western Scholarship (p'Bitek) **149**:7-8, 108, 120, 124-25, 131
African Secret (Martin du Gard)
See *Confidence Africaine*
The African Witch (Cary) **1**:144; **29**:63-4, 66, 68, 71, 79, 85-6, 92, 98, 101, 104, 106-07; **196**:172, 214-15
Africa's Cultural Revolution (p'Bitek) **149**:70, 108, 110, 112-13
"Afrika" (Zamyatin) **8**:553-54
"Afrikanskaja noč'" (Gumilev) **60**:282
"Afrique j'ai gardé ta mémoire" (Roumain) **19**:347
"The Afro-American in Literature" (Wells-Barnett) **125**:335
Afsana-yi Afarinish (Hedāyat) **21**:72
"Afsked" (Ekelund) **75**:95
Aftenrøde (Hamsun) **2**:202, 204; **14**:244, **49**:127
"After" (Benét) **28**:7
After 1903—What? (Benchley) **1**:81; **55**:18
"After 1984" (Muir) **87**:174
"After a Hypothetical War" (Muir) **2**:489; **87**:175
"After a Journey" (Hardy) **4**:164; **53**:94-6, 111, 114-5; **143**:190, 193
"After a May Shower" (Ady) **11**:13
"After a Visit" (Dunbar) **2**:128; **12**:108
"After a Visit (At Padraic Colum's Where There Were Irish Poets)" (Cullen) **37**:158
"After a Walk" (García Lorca) **197**:267
"After All" (Lawson) **27**:140
After All (Day) **25**:137
"After All These Years" (Sarton) **120**:270
"After All, What Else is There to Say" (Ginsberg) **120**:8
"After Anointing" (Field) **43**:160
"After Commencement" (Nemerov) **124**:221
"After Dead Souls" (Ginsberg) **120**:35, 68
"After Death" (Aleixandre) **113**:42
"After Death" (Swinburne) **36**:299
After Death: Letters from Julia (Stead)
See *Letters from Julia*
"After Dinner" (Söderberg) **39**:438
"After Drought" (Montgomery) **51**:207
After Euripides' 'Electra' (Baring) **8**:32
"After Exile" (Knister) **56**:156
"After Four Years" (Sarton) **120**:267
After Hearing a Waltz by Bartok (Lowell) **1**:373
After Hierarchy (Trambley) **163**:306
"After His Own Heart" (Williams) **89**:375
"After Holbein" (Wharton) **129**:364
The After House (Rinehart) **52**:284, 289-91, 303
"After Lalon" (Ginsberg) **120**:74
"After Long Silence" (Yeats) **18**:463; **116**:338
"After Love" (Middleton) **56**:173
After Many Years (Griffith) **68**:141, 150, 203
"After Me Deluge" (Kerouac) **117**:214, 253
"After My Last Song" (Ledwidge) **23**:115-16
"After Night" (Manning) **25**:277
After Office Hours (Mankiewicz) **85**:163-4
"After Publication of Under the Volcano" (Lowry) **40**:222
"After Rain" (Thomas) **10**:451, 454

After Russia (Tsvetaeva)
See *Posle Rossii*
After Such Pleasures (Parker) **143**:287, 342
"After the Ball" (Tolstoy) **173**:349
After the Banquet (Mishima)
See *Utage no ato*
"After the Battle" (Babel)
See "Posle boia"
"After the Cards Are Dealt" (Jozsef) **22**:165
After the Death of Don Juan (Warner) **131**:308, 326, 331-36, 362-63
"After the Defeat at Manilla" (Jensen) **41**:292
"After the Deluge" (Benchley) **55**:26
After the Divorce (Deledda)
See *Dopo il divorzio*
"After the Fair" (Hardy) **143**:169
"After the Fair" (Thomas) **45**:408; **105**:296, 316, 320, 332, 353
"After the Fire" (Merrill) **173**:228
After the Fire (Strindberg)
See *Brända tomten*
After the Flood (Porter) **21**:277
"After the Funeral: In Memory of Anne Jones" (Thomas) **1**:466, 470; **8**:450, 459-61; **45**:362, 382, 389, 400-02; **105**:314, 338
"After the Gleaning" (George) **14**:215-16
After the Great War (Raabe) **45**:202
"After the Last Breath" (Hardy) **143**:109, 111
"After the Parade" (Wright) **136**:300
"After the Party" (Slesinger) **10**:441-42, 446
"After the Race" (Joyce) **8**:170; **16**:232; **35**:147-48, 163, 166-67, 193-97; **159**:299
"After the Rain" (Reese) **181**:347
"After the Revolution" (Talvik) **87**:319
"After the Sermon" (Wright) **136**:302
After the Stroke: A Journal (Sarton) **120**:319
"After the Suspension of Gold" (Keynes) **64**:244
After the Tea (Nagai)
See *Kōcha no ato*
"After the Tiger" (Sarton) **120**:293
After the Wedding (Bjoernson)
See *De nygifte*
"After the Winter" (McKay) **41**:344
After Thirty Years: The Daring Young Man on the Flying Trapeze (Saroyan) **137**:193
"After Thoughts" (Ginsberg) **120**:39
"After You Speak" (Thomas) **10**:454
"After-Glow" (Gurney) **33**:102
"Aftergrowth" (Bialik) **25**:60, 66
Aftermath (Churchill) **113**:102, 105, 148
"Afternnon at a Ranch" (Foote) **108**:34
"Afternoon" (Davidson) **24**:164
"An Afternoon" (Heym)
See "Ein Nachmittag"
"Afternoon" (Parker) **143**:323
"An Afternoon Dream" (Csáth) **13**:149, 153
The Afternoon Landscape (Higginson) **36**:170
"An Afternoon Miracle" (Henry) **19**:190
"Afternoon of an Author" (Fitzgerald) **6**:172
"An Afternoon of Spring on Fifth Avenue" (Jiménez) **183**:330
"Afternoon on a Hill" (Millay) **4**:307; **49**:224-25
"An Afternoon Party" (Leverson) **18**:198
"The Afternoon Sun" (Cavafy) **7**:164
"Afternoon Tea" (Mew) **8**:301
"Afternoon Tickertape" (Burroughs) **121**:143
Afternoons (Hecht)
See *1001 Afternoons in Chicago*
Afternoons in Mid-America (Caldwell) **117**:27
"After-Pain" (Lasker-Schueler) **57**:328
"Afterthought" (Du Bois) **169**:81, 90-91, 94
Afterthought (Bowen) **148**:4-5
"Afterward" (Wharton) **3**:578; **129**:362, 364-65
"Afterwards" (Hardy) **53**:97-8; **143**:113, 157, 159, 189
"Afterwards" (Leverson) **18**:202
"Afterwards" (Scott) **6**:394
Afterwhiles (Riley) **51**:285
"De aftocht" (van Ostaijen) **33**:421-22
Aftonland (Lagerkvist) **144**:181, 201, 204, 211, 215
"Aftonvandring" (Södergran) **31**:291
"Agadat HaSofer" (Agnon) **151**:35-36
"Agadat sheloshah ve'arba'ah" (Bialik) **25**:53-7
"Agafia" (Chekhov) **163**:77
"Again" (Nemerov) **124**:227, 258, 292
"Again Concerning the Freedom of the Reader" (Rilke) **195**:310
"Again the Sea" (Gumilev)
See "Snoya more"
Again the Three (Wallace) **57**:408
Again to the North (Mackenzie)
See *The North Wind of Love*
"Against Abstract Expressionism" (Jarrell) **177**:190, 240
"Against Being Convinced" (Muir) **87**:252
"Against Dryness: A Polemical Sketch" (Murdoch) **171**:309, 315, 318, 330
Against Epistemology (Adorno) **111**:53
"Against Juliette" (Moréas) **18**:281
Against Nature (Huysmans)
See *A rebours*
"Against Superficiality" (Fadeyev)
See "Protiv verkhoglyadstva"
"Against Temptation" (Brecht) **1**:114
"Against the Current" (Fadeyev) **53**:51
Against the Current: Essays in the History of Ideas (Berlin) **105**:21, 23, 35, 50, 53, 71
Against the Grain (Huysmans)
See *A rebours*
Against the Stream (Dazai Osamu)
See *Gyakkō*
Against This Age (Bodenheim) **44**:69
Against This and That (Unamuno)
See *Contra esto y aquello*
"Against Unworthy Praise" (Yeats) **93**:349
"Against your will" (Arp) **115**:23
"Agape" (Vallejo) **56**:295
"Agarian Art: An Outline" (Miyazawa) **76**:280, 282, 287-88
"Agatha Christie: An Unlikely Obituary" (Ibarguengoitia)
See "Resuélvame este caso"
Agatha Webb (Green) **63**:151
"Agathon" (Woodberry) **73**:367
"Age" (de la Mare) **4**:79
"The Age" (Mandelstam) **2**:409; **6**:266
L'Age d'homme (Sarraute) **145**:306
"L'âge l'éclair la main et lafeuille" (Arp) **115**:41
"The Age of a Dream" (Johnson) **19**:243
"The Age of Criticism" (Jarrell) **177**:184
The Age of Enlightenment (Berlin) **105**:71
"The Age of Genius" (Schulz) **51**:309, 316, 324
The Age of Innocence (Wharton) **3**:558-59, 563, 567-69, 572-74, 576, 579-80; **9**:544, 546, 548-51; **27**:385, 396; **53**:360-414; **129**:349, 351, 362; **149**:142, 144-46, 148, 168, 234, 245, 250, 259, 270, 283
"The Age of Miracles" (Post) **39**:338
Age of Shakespeare (Swinburne) **8**:430
The Age of Suspicion: Essays on the Novel (Sarraute)
See *L'ere du soupçon: Essais sur le roman*
The Age of the Fish (Horvath)
See *Jugend ohne Gott*
"Age Romantic" (Bierce) **44**:24
Agee on Film: Five Film Scripts (Agee) **1**:15; **19**:22
L'Agence Thompson and Co. (Verne) **52**:359
"Agenda for President Roosevelt" (Keynes) **64**:243
"Agesilaus Santander" (Benjamin) **39**:45, 49
"Aggei Korovin" (Tolstoy) **18**:355, 377
Aglavaine et Sélysette (Maeterlinck) **3**:318, 321, 323, 327, 332
Agnete (Kaiser) **9**:192
An Agnostic's Apology, and Other Essays (Stephen) **23**:304, 311, 313
El agonía del Cristianismo (Unamuno) **2**:559; **9**:511, 514, 522; **148**:243, 299
Las agonias de nuestro tiempo (Baroja) **8**:51
"Agony" (Obstfelder) **23**:188
Agony (Lagerkvist)
See *Angest*
The Agony Column (Biggers) **65**:4, 9
The Agony of Christianity (Unamuno)
See *El agonía del Cristianismo*
The Agony of Flies (Canetti)
See *Die Fliegenpein*
"Agosto" (Aleixandre) **113**:3
Agosto (Pereda) **16**:372
"Agraphon" (Sikelianos) **39**:408, 419, 421-23
Die Agraverhaltnisse im Altertum (Weber) **69**:384
"Agreement with Bung Karno" (Anwar)
See "Persetudjuan dengan Bung Karno"
"The Agricultural Show" (McKay) **41**:329-30
Agriculture and the War (Baker) **10**:22
"Agrippe i Menakheme, syne Iegudy" (Korolenko) **22**:175
Agua (Arguedas) **147**:7-8, 12, 23, 76, 92-93, 99
Agua Dulce (Adams) **56**:10
Aguafuertes (Arlt) **29**:57
"Águeda" (Lugones) **15**:293
"Las águilas" (Aleixandre) **113**:14
"Agunot: A Tale" (Agnon) **151**:27-30, 72, 81
Die Ägyptische Helena (Hofmannsthal) **11**:301
"Ah, Are You Digging on My Grave?" (Hardy) **53**:100
Ah, but Your Land Is Beautiful (Paton) **165**:298
"Ah Kolue" (Rosenberg) **12**:313
"Ah, My Mushroom, Dear White Mushroom!" (Tsvetaeva) **35**:395
"Ah, not to be cut off" (Rilke)
See "Ach, nicht getrennt sein"
Ah Sin (Harte) **25**:217-18
Ah Sin (Twain) **12**:445
Ah, Wilderness! (O'Neill) **1**:386, 390, 400; **6**:329, 331; **49**:243, 264
Ahab (Crowley) **7**:208
"Ahabansangit" (Tagore) **53**:339
"Ahana" (Aurobindo) **63**:7
"Ahasuerus" (Nemerov) **124**:284
Ahasverus (Heijermans) **24**:292-93
Ahasverus död (Lagerkvist) **144**:204, 212, 215, 217, 220, 235, 240-41
"Ahmet" (Campbell) **9**:32
"Die Ahnfrau" (Carossa) **48**:24
"Aholibah" (Swinburne) **36**:299
Ahven ja kultakalat (Leino) **24**:372
Ai no Kawaki (Mishima) **161**:30, 51-52
"Aidemémoire" (Barthes) **135**:184
"Aids" (Sarton) **120**:305
"Les aïeules" (Coppee) **25**:124
L'aigle à deux têtes (Cocteau) **119**:75, 82
L'aiglon (Rostand) **6**:375-78, 382; **37**:281-84, 286-89, 293, 297-300, 304-05
L'aiguille creuse (Leblanc) **49**:193, 196-97
"Aika" (Leino) **24**:368-70
"Aileen" (Sharp) **39**:374-75
Les ailes de la guerre (Verhaeren) **12**:470-71
"An Ailing Face at the Bottom of the Earth" (Hagiwara) **60**:296
"Ailleurs ici partout" (Éluard) **41**:153
Ailsa Paige (Chambers) **41**:95-7
"The Aim" (Roberts) **8**:318
Aimé Pache, peintre vaudois (Ramuz) **33**:294-95, 312
"Aimless Journey" (Tagore)
See "Niruddesh yatra"
"Aims and Autographs" (Chopin) **127**:201
Aims and Objects (Housman) **7**:358
The Aims of Education (Whitehead) **97**:238
"The Aims of Ethnology" (Boas) **56**:92, 105
"The Aims of the Poets" (Croce) **37**:109
"Ain't You Mad?" (Childress) **116**:34
"Air!" (Jozsef) **22**:163
"Air" (Toomer) **172**:273
Air at High Altitude (Rilke) **6**:369-70
Air Current (Bergelson) **81**:19-20
"Air de sémiramis" (Valéry) **4**:496
"L'Air est une Racine" (Arp) **115**:28, 48

L'Air et les Songes: Essai sur l'imagination du mouvement (Bachelard) **128**:5, 10, 19, 21-2, 32-4, 36-41, 45, 47, 55-6, 63-7, 69-70, 73-4
"Air Mexicain" (Péret) **20**:198, 202
"Airde danse" (Moréas) **18**:286
"Aire" (Villaurrutia) **80**:477
"Airen" (Hagiwara) **60**:313
Aires nacionales (Valle-Inclán) **5**:479
"The Airman's Death" (Stevens) **12**:364
Aissa Saved (Cary) **1**:144; **29**:63, 66, 68, 71, 75, 80, 84, 86, 91-2, 101, 103-08; **196**:214
Aitei Tsūshin (Kunikida Doppo) **99**:297
L'aiuola bruciata (Betti) **5**:55-8, 60, 62, 66-7
Ajaiyi and His Inherited Poverty (Tutuola) **188**:289-90, 301-2, 304, 306-8
"Ajan aalloilla" (Leino) **24**:368
"Ajan kirja" (Leino) **24**:368
"El ajedrez y el tresillo" (Unamuno) **148**:308
"Ajisai" (Nagai) **51**:96
Akage no An (Montgomery) **140**:309
"El Akalde de Zalamea" (Valle-Inclán) **5**:478
"Akanishi Kakita" (Shiga) **172**:229
Akarumie (Yosano) **59**:346
Ākāś pradīp (Tagore) **3**:487, 489
Akatsuki no tera (Mishima) **161**:3-4, 51, 55, 67-68, 70-71, 75
"Akemi's Poetry" (Masaoka) **18**:230
Akila (Tolstoy) **18**:382
Akin to Anne: Tales of Other Orphans (Montgomery) **51**:212
"Akkan" (Nagai) **51**:99
Die Akkumulation des Kapitals, oder Was die Epigonen aus der Marxschen Theorie gemacht haben: Eine Antikritik (Luxemburg) **63**:163, 166, 172, 178, 180-82, 194-96, 198-99, 200, 202, 205
Akli Miklós (Mikszath) **31**:172
Akogare (Ishikawa) **15**:130
Akritika (Sikelianos) **39**:404, 408
Die Akten des Vogelsangs (Raabe) **45**:165-66, 169-70, 172-74, 176-78, 181
Aktualitat der Philosophie (Adorno) **111**:72
"Aku" (Anwar) **22**:19, 25
"Akwarel" (van Ostaijen) **33**:417
"Al" (Engel) **137**:113
"Al amor" (Aleixandre) **113**:15
Al amor de los tizones (Pereda) **16**:373
"Al centro rayeante" (Jiménez) **183**:259, 264
"Al fin, un monte" (Vallejo) **56**:287
"'Al ha-shehitah" (Bialik) **25**:63-4
"Al hombre" (Aleixandre) **113**:75
"Al horizonte de un suburbio" (Borges) **109**:11
"Al oído de una muchacha" (García Lorca) **181**:183
Al primer vuelo (Pereda) **16**:379
"Al rescoldo" (Güiraldes) **39**:176
"Al skabningens sukker" (Obstfelder) **23**:177
"Al tal vez lector" (Borges) **109**:11
Alabama (Thomas) **97**:126-29, 140
"Alabaster" (Naidu) **80**:291
An Alabaster Box (Freeman) **9**:74
"El alacrán de Fray Gómez" (Palma) **29**:259
Alafroiskiotos (Sikelianos) **39**:402-03, 406, 410-13, 417-18, 420
Alain on Happiness (Alain)
See *Propos sur le bonheur*
Alain und Elise (Kaiser) **9**:176, 180-81, 192
"El alambre de pua" (Quiroga) **20**:213
Alamein to Zem Zem (Douglas) **40**:55-8, 62, 69-72, 74, 76-7, 79, 82, 86, 88, 90, 93-4
"Los álamos de plata" (García Lorca) **181**:121
Alaric Spenceley; or, A High Ideal (Riddell) **40**:335
"The Alarm" (Hardy) **4**:152
"Alarums and Excursions" (Grahame) **64**:55
"Al-arwāh al-mutamarridah" (Gibran) **1**:326; **9**:90
"Alas" (Lugones) **15**:286
"Alasdair the Proud" (Sharp) **39**:377
"Alatyr" (Zamyatin) **8**:541-42, 544, 551; **37**:427
Alaviyeh Khanom (Hedāyat) **21**:67, 72
Al-'awāsif (Gibran) **9**:89
"Alba" (Aleixandre) **113**:4
"Alba" (García Lorca) **181**:123, 198
"Alba" (Villaurrutia) **80**:478
"Alba festiva" (Pascoli) **45**:156
"Al-bahr" (Gibran) **9**:89
The Albany Depot (Howells) **7**:387-88
"L'albatross" (Campbell) **5**:123
Un albergo sul porto (Betti) **5**:58
"Albert" (Tolstoy) **11**:464
Albert Einstein: Philosopher-Scientist (Einstein) **65**:81, 100, 126
"Albert F. McComb" (Fuller) **103**:67
Albertine Disparue (Proust) **7**:527; **13**:425; **33**:272, 287; **161**:123, 139, 142, 158, 162-64
"Der Albino" (Meyrink) **21**:223
"The Album" (Nezval) **44**:243
"El álbum" (Onetti) **131**:194
The Album (James) **11**:339-40
The Album (Rinehart) **52**:290, 293, 300, 302
Album de vers anciens, 1890-1900 (Valéry) **4**:498; **15**:447, 468
"Alcestis" (Rilke) **195**:243
"Alcestis to Admetus" (Coleridge) **73**:13
"Alchak" (Khlebnikov) **20**:130
"The Alchemist" (Crowley) **7**:208
The Alchemist's House (Meyrink)
See *Das Haus des Alchimisten*
"Alcidor" (Beer-Hofmann) **60**:38
"Alcinos et Rhodope" (Moréas) **18**:288
Alcione (D'Annunzio) **6**:136, 139; **40**:11, 13-14, 20, 36, 43, 45
"La alcoba solitaria" (Lugones) **15**:285
"Alcohol and Me" (Fields) **80**:253
"An Alcoholic Case" (Fitzgerald) **6**:172
"An Alcoholic's Death" (Hagiwara)
See "Death of an Alcoholic"
Alcools (Apollinaire) **3**:33, 35-41, 45; **8**:16, 18, 20, 22; **51**:2-5, 7, 9, 13-14, 17, 24, 29-30, 32, 35, 38, 49-50, 53-61
L'alcòva d'acciaio (Marinetti) **10**:321-24
"Alcune applicazioni del Mimete" (Levi) **109**:295-96
Alcyone (D'Annunzio)
See *Alcione*
Aldea ilusoria (Martinez Sierra and Martinez Sierra) **6**:286
"Al'debaran" (Olesha) **136**:76, 154-55
"Aldebaron at Dusk" (Sterling) **20**:374, 385-86
"Ale" (Tsvetaeva) **7**:568
Alec Forbes of Howglen (MacDonald) **9**:287, 290-92, 295-96, 302, 309; **113**:282
Aleksandr Nevskii (Eisenstein) **57**:158, 161, 167, 169, 179, 181, 190-91, 193-97
"Além-Tédio" (Sá-Carneiro) **83**:397, 411
"Alenushka" (Remizov) **27**:339
"The Aleph" (Borges)
See "El aleph"
"El aleph" (Borges) **109**:17, 37, 49, 57-8, 66, 144
El aleph (Borges) **109**:17, 19-21, 24, 32-3, 42, 47, 49-50, 61-4, 66-7, 98, 109, 126, 151, 161
The Aleph, and Other Stories, 1933-1969 (Borges)
See *El aleph*
"Alere Flammam" (Gosse) **28**:142
"Alerta" (Huidobro) **31**:125
"Ales and Dialogues" (Calvino) **183**:234
"Aleš iz Razora" (Cankar) **105**:157
"Alësha Gorshók" (Tolstoy) **11**:464
Alex Haley's Queen: The Story of an American Family (Haley) **147**:216, 219-20
Alexander I (Merezhkovsky) **29**:231
Alexander, and Three Small Plays (Dunsany) **2**:145; **59**:13-14, 26
Alexander Pope (Stephen) **23**:340
"Alexander Throckmorten" (Masters) **25**:313
Alexanderplatz, Berlin: The Story of Franz Biberkopf (Döblin)
See *Berlin Alexanderplatz: Die Geschichte vom Franz Biberkopf*
Alexander's Bridge (Cather) **1**:153, 155-59, 165; **11**:93, 95-6, 104; **31**:25, 47-8, 59, 62; **99**:173, 245; **132**:125, 132, 137, 140, 148, 152, 154; **152**:16, 26, 32-33, 44, 67-69, 76, 78, 93-94, 96-97, 112
"Alexander's Masquerade" (Cather) **132**:132
"Alexandra" (Cather) **132**:126; **152**:13, 20-21, 33, 36, 44, 76-77
"Alexandrian Kings" (Cavafy) **2**:88-9; **7**:153
Alexandrian Songs (Kuzmin)
See *Alexandryskie pesni*
"Alexandrian Tale" (Machado de Assis)
See "Conto alexandrino"
Alexandryskie pesni (Kuzmin) **40**:190-92, 194, 196-99, 201, 207-08, 210, 216
Alexis, ou le Traité du vain combat (Yourcenar) **193**:256, 271, 302, 321-22, 354-55
Alfonso XIII desenmascarado (Blasco Ibáñez) **12**:40
Alfonso XIII Unmasked: The Military Terror in Spain (Blasco Ibáñez)
See *Alfonso XIII desenmascarado*
Alfred Jarry, or The Supermale of Lettres (Vallette)
See *Alfred Jarry ou le surmale de lettres*
Alfred Jarry ou le surmale de lettres (Vallette) **67**:270, 300, 303
Algabal (George) **2**:149-50; **14**:196, 203-05, 207-08, 210, 212
Algae, an Anthology of Phrases (Baring) **8**:44
Algeria (Acker) **191**:102, 104
"Algeria Unveiled" (Fanon) **188**:36, 65, 67, 71-3, 92
"The Algerian Family" (Fanon) **188**:71-3
"L'Algérie se dévoile" (Fanon) **188**:139
"Algernon Charles Swinburne" (Cotter) **28**:43
"Algernon, Who Played with a Loaded Gun, and, on Missing His Sister, Was Reprimanded by His Father" (Belloc) **18**:40
"Algo te identifica" (Vallejo) **56**:285, 311
"De alguien a nadie" (Borges) **109**:92, 97
"Alguien se ha ido" (Gonzalez Martinez) **72**:152
Alguma poesia (Drummond de Andrade) **139**:223-24, 228, 231-33
Algunas cosillas de Pito Pérez que se me quedaron en el tintero (Romero) **14**:442
"Algunos caracteres de la nueva poesía española" (Aleixandre) **113**:66
El alhajadito (Asturias) **184**:10-11, 15-16
"Ali Baba of the Sierras" (Harte) **25**:217
"Alibi Ike" (Lardner) **14**:291, 293, 304-05, 317, 319-20
Alice Adams (Tarkington) **9**:455, 457-60, 463, 468, 473-75
Alice: An Adultery (Crowley) **7**:209
Alice Lorraine (Blackmore) **27**:28-9, 36, 39-41, 44-5
Alice Sit-by-the-Fire (Barrie) **2**:40, 42-3; **164**:36
"Alice Trubner" (Lasker-Schueler) **57**:331
Alice Who Was Afraid of Mice (Kuzmin)
See *Alisa, kotoraia boialas' myshei*
"Alice's Godmother" (de la Mare) **4**:78; **53**:16, 23
"The Alien" (Fuller) **103**:102, 107
Alien Skies (Gumilev)
See *Chuzhoe nebo*
"The Aliens" (Tarkington) **9**:466
"Alike and Unlike" (Strindberg) **21**:365
Aline (Ramuz) **33**:294-96
Alisa, kotoraia boialas' myshei (Kuzmin) **40**:201
Alison Hepburn's Exploit (Davidson) **24**:193
Alison's House (Glaspell) **55**:247, 258, 266, 270, 275; **175**:59, 62, 69-75, 85, 87, 89-90, 108, 114-16, 147
"Alix's Refusal" (Colette) **16**:139
Alkibiades (Leino) **24**:372
Alkibiades Saved (Kaiser)
See *Der gerettete Alkibiades*
All Aboard (Cobb) **77**:129

All Aboard for Ararat (Wells) **133**:236
"All about Miss Tubman" (Childress) **116**:37
"All about My Job" (Childress) **116**:36
"All All and All" (Thomas) **45**:372
All and Everything: An Objectively Impartial Criticism of the Life of Man (Gurdjieff) **71**:177, 205
"All around the Lagoon" (Papadiamantis) **29**:272-73
"All at One Point" (Calvino) **183**:227
All at Sea (Wells) **35**:422
All Bloods (Arguedas)
See *Todas las sangres*
"All Creation Sighs" (Obstfelder) **23**:188-89
All Flanders (Verhaeren)
See *Toute la Flandre*
"All for a Pinch of Snuff" (Peretz) **16**:393
All God's Chillun Got Wings (O'Neill) **1**:382, 384-85, 387, 390, 400; **6**:329-30; **49**:238, 257, 260, 264-65
"All Hallows" (de la Mare) **4**:80; **53**:14-16, 19-21, 26-7, 29, 33 37-8
"All Hallow's Eve" (Ledwidge) **23**:122
All Hallow's Eve (Williams) **1**:517, 519, 524; **11**:486-88, 494, 499, 502
"All Horse Players Die Broke" (Runyon) **10**:429-30, 437
"All in the Day's Hunt" (Adams) **56**:8
"All in White" (Hearn) **9**:136
All Ireland (O'Grady) **5**:349, 351
"All Is Illusion" (Kuttner) **10**:268
"All Is Stone" (Khodasevich) **15**:209
"All Last Night" (Abercrombie) **141**:19
"All Life in a Life" (Masters) **25**:288
All Men Are Brothers (Gandhi) **59**:61
All My Melodies (Bryusov) **10**:80, 87
All on the Irish Shore (Somerville & Ross) **51**:331
All Our Yesterdays (Ginzburg)
See *Tutti i nostri ieri*
All Our Yesterdays (Tomlinson) **71**:400, 405
All Quiet on the Western Front (Anderson) **144**:72
All Roads Lead to Calvary (Jerome) **23**:89-90
All Shot Up (Himes) **139**:255-56, 258-59, 283-84, 321
All Sorts of Folks (Vazov)
See *Pustur svet*
"All Souls'" (Wharton) **3**:572; **9**:547
All Souls (Heijermans) **24**:288, 292-93
"All Souls' Night" (Yeats) **1**:580
All Souls' Night (Walpole) **5**:504
All Strange Away (Beckett) **145**:92-98
"All suddenly the Wind comes soft" (Brooke) **7**:122
"All Sunday" (Stein) **48**:235
"All That Could Have Been, Although It Was" (Arenas)
See "Todo lo que pudo ser, aunque haya sido"
All That Fall (Beckett) **145**:177
All That Matters (Guest) **95**:208
"All That Messuage" (Morrison) **72**:376
All That Rises Must Converge (O'Connor)
See *Everything That Rises Must Converge*
All That Swagger (Franklin) **7**:267-71, 274
All the Brothers Were Valiant (Williams) **89**:360, 363, 372, 385
"All the Dark and Beautiful Warriors" (Hansberry) **192**:275
"All the Dead Pilots" (Faulkner) **170**:138
All the Dogs of My Life (Elizabeth) **41**:131
All the Sad Young Men (Fitzgerald) **6**:162; **55**:191
"All the Same" (Hippius) **9**:159
All the Way Home (Agee) **180**:26, 77
All the Way Home (Riggs) **56**:215, 218
All Things Are Possible (Shestov)
See *Apofeoz bezpochvennosti*
"All We" (Muir) **87**:256
"Alla croce di Savoia" (Carducci) **32**:84, 90
Alla kasvon Kaikkivallan (Leino) **24**:372
"Alla mensa dell' amico" (Carducci) **32**:102
"Alla rima" (Carducci) **32**:101
"Alla Stazione in una Mattina d'Autunno" (Carducci) **32**:94, 96
"Alla sua donna" (Dowson) **4**:85
"An All-American Almanac and Prophetic Messenger" (Millay) **169**:238
Allan and the Holy Flower (Haggard) **11**:250
Allan Quatermain (Haggard) **11**:239-41, 244, 248, 253-54
Allan's Wife (Haggard) **11**:239, 250, 254
"All'Aurora" (Carducci) **32**:87
"Alle fonti del Clitumno" (Carducci) **32**:84, 96, 98, 102-05, 109
Alle Galgenlieder (Morgenstern) **8**:307
"Alle Milchgeschäfte heissen Hinsch" (Borchert) **5**:109
"Alle Tage" (Bachmann) **192**:56
"Allégories" (Giraudoux) **2**:163, 166
"Allegro sentimentale" (Obstfelder) **23**:185
L'Alléluiah (Bataille) **155**:17, 127
Les allemands à Paris (Rod) **52**:325
Allen (Larbaud) **9**:208
Allen Adair (Mander) **31**:151, 154, 157, 160-62
Allen Verbatim (Ginsberg) **120**:80
"Allen's Alley" (Allen) **87**:13, 28-32, 37, 41, 53
"Alles" (Bachmann) **192**:10-12, 69, 137-38
"Alles oder nichts" (Huch) **13**:253
"The Alley" (Wakefield) **120**:343, 349, 358
"Allez!" (Kuprin) **5**:300
All-Fellows (Housman) **7**:352
"The All-Golden" (Riley) **51**:284
The Allinghams (Sinclair) **11**:411, 414
"Allô" (Péret) **20**:184, 187
"Allt hvila under Herrens hand" (Lagerkvist) **144**:181
All'uscita (Pirandello) **29**:283, 294, 317, 320
Den allvarsamma leken (Söderberg) **39**:428
Allzumenschliches (Nietzsche) **18**:342-43
"El alma bajo el agua" (Aleixandre) **113**:6
"El alma que sufrió de ser su cuerpo" (Vallejo) **56**:286, 318, 321, 323
Alma triunfante (Benavente) **3**:94
Almaide d'Etremont, ou l'Histoire d'une jeune fille passionnee (Jammes) **75**:105, 115, 117-18
Almanachs du Père Ubu (Jarry) **14**:286; **147**:265, 272, 275-78, 280
"Almas agradecidas" (Machado de Assis) **10**:294
Almas ausentes (Martinez Sierra and Martinez Sierra) **6**:279, 285
Almas de violeta (Jiménez) **4**:216
"Las almas muertas" (Gonzalez Martinez) **72**:152
Almas que pasan (Nervo) **11**:394
Al-mawakib (Gibran) **9**:88-9
Almayer's Folly (Conrad) **1**:202-03, 215; **6**:117-19; **13**:113; **25**:84; **43**:115
"Almenut" (Bialik) **25**:53
"Almighty Man" (Stephens) **4**:409
"El almohadón de pluma" (Quiroga) **20**:212, 218-21
"Almond Blossom" (Lawrence) **93**:58, 80
"The Almond Tree" (de la Mare) **4**:74, 78, 80; **53**:27, 41
Almost (Sá-Carneiro)
See *Quase*
"Almost a Gentleman" (Lewis) **3**:288
"Almost a Gentleman" (Remizov)
See "Bez piati minut barin"
Almost a Gentleman (Osborne) **153**:339
The Almost Perfect State (Marquis) **7**:439-40, 445
Alnilam (Dickey) **151**:153-58, 165, 173, 176, 203, 207, 210, 225
The Aloe (Mansfield) **164**:250-54, 332, 334-35
"Alone" (Bialik) **25**:50
"Alone" (Joyce) **3**:255
"Alone" (Obstfelder) **23**:188
Alone (Douglas) **68**:3, 5-7, 21, 37, 39-40, 43
Alone (Strindberg) **21**:351
"Alone at the foot of the Rigi" (Arp) **115**:16
Alone in London (Buchanan) **107**:31
"Alone in the Canyon" (Noguchi) **80**:380
Alone on a Mountaintop (Kerouac) **117**:266
"Along Came Ruth" (Lardner) **14**:303, 319
"Along Shore" (Montgomery) **51**:209
Along the Cornices (Remizov)
See *Po karnizam*
"Along the Flowery Path" (Martinez Sierra and Martinez Sierra) **6**:286
Along This Way: The Autobiography of James Weldon Johnson (Johnson) **3**:246; **19**:208-09; **175**:165-67, 176, 185-86, 191, 198, 200-201, 205, 224-27, 233, 237, 239-40, 244-48
"Alonzo Grout" (Fuller) **103**:106-08
L'alouette (Anouilh) **195**:18, 25, 30-3, 35, 47, 50-2, 60
"Alp" (Toller) **10**:490
An Alphabet of Economics (Orage) **157**:264
"Alphabetical Catalogue of Saints Connected with Cornwall, with an Epitome of Their Lives and List of Churches and Chapels Dedicated to Them" (Baring-Gould) **88**:21
Alphabets and Birthdays (Stein) **48**:235
"Alpine Noontime" (Carducci)
See "Mezzogiorno alpino"
The Alpine Path: The Story of My Career (Montgomery) **51**:186; **140**:302, 306-8, 330
Alps and Sanctuaries of Piedmont and the Canton Ticino (Butler) **33**:29, 42, 52, 59
The Alps in Winter (Stephen) **23**:310
Alraune (Ewers) **12**:133-35, 137
"Already Evening" (Esenin) **4**:114
Als der Krieg ausbrach (Böll) **185**:52
"Als der Krieg zu Ende war" (Böll) **185**:52-4
Als der Krieg zu Ende war (Frisch) **121**:229
Als wär's ein Stück von mir (Zuckmayer) **191**:300, 303, 311, 331, 338, 348
Alsino (Prado) **75**:192-94, 197, 201, 211
Alta California (Twain) **185**:289
"Alta quies" (Housman) **10**:255
"The Altar at Midnight" (Kornbluth) **8**:216-17
An Altar in the Fields (Lewisohn) **19**:273, 278
"The Altar of Hagar" (Ady)
See "A hágár oltára"
"The Altar of the Dead" (James) **2**:246, 248, 272; **11**:321
"An Altar of the West" (Sterling) **20**:372, 385
The Altar Steps (Mackenzie) **116**:206-07, 209, 212, 214-17, 231, 234
The Altars (Palamas) **5**:385, 388
"Altarwise by Owl-light" (Thomas) **1**:475; **8**:459; **45**:362, 364, 372, 380, 399-400, 402, 406; **105**:347
Altazor o el viaje en paracaídos (Huidobro) **31**:123, 125, 127, 129, 131-32, 137-39, 145
"Der alte Brunnen" (Carossa) **48**:21
"Die alte Frau" (Kolmar) **40**:178
Alte Meister (Bernhard) **165**:11-13, 43-45, 79, 85-89, 96, 102, 108-9, 111
Alte Nester (Raabe) **45**:169-70, 172, 176, 178, 181, 192, 200, 203
"Das Alte Spiel vom Jedermann" (Hofmannsthal) **11**:301
"Der alte Taschenspieler" (Carossa) **48**:24
"Der alte Tibetteppich" (Lasker-Schueler) **57**:296, 330
Alte und neue Götter, 1848: Die Revolution des neunzehnten Jahrunderstsin in Deutschland (Huch) **13**:245
"Alter Ego" (Baker) **10**:27
"Ein alter Tibetteppich" (Lasker-Schueler) **57**:302
Alterhausen (Raabe) **45**:169, 173, 199
"Das Altern der Neuen Musik" (Adorno) **111**:34
Althea (Lee) **5**:311, 315-16
Altneuland (Herzl) **36**:128-30, 135, 142, 148-49, 154-56, 158-61
L'altra metà (Papini) **22**:280-81, 287
Altri scritti (Campana) **20**:88

L'altro figlio (Pirandello) **29**:297
L'altrui mestiere (Levi) **109**:286-88, 301, 314, 316
"The Aluminum Dagger" (Freeman) **21**:55
"Alvdrottningens spira" (Södergran) **31**:295
Always Comes Evening (Howard) **8**:137
Always Ridiculous (Echegaray)
See *Siempre en ridículo*
Aly mech (Hippius) **9**:161
Alyi mak (Sologub) **9**:444
"Am I a Liberal?" (Keynes) **64**:217, 219, 245
"Am I A Snob?" (Woolf) **128**:374
Am Ziel (Bernhard) **165**:75, 96
El ama de la casa (Martinez Sierra and Martinez Sierra) **6**:286
La amada inmóvil (Nervo) **11**:399, 401
"Amagama omcebisi" (Mqhayi) **25**:320
"Amai" (Saba) **33**:368, 370
Amal'eZulu (Vilakazi) **37**:403, 405, 407, 409
"Amām 'arsh al-jamāl" (Gibran) **9**:88
"Amanda" (Scott) **6**:394
Amanecer (Martinez Sierra and Martinez Sierra) **6**:277
"Amanecer y repique" (García Lorca) **181**:65
"Amante" (Aleixandre) **113**:3
"L'amante di Gramigna" (Verga) **3**:539, 543, 547
"Los Amantes enterrados" (Aleixandre) **113**:49
"Gli amanti" (Calvino) **183**:211-12
Amanto (Mirbeau)
See *Les amants*
Les amants (Mirbeau) **55**:281
"Amants, heureux amants" (Larbaud) **9**:198, 200-01, 207
"Amar-Amaro" (Drummond de Andrade) **139**:226, 230
Amaranth (Robinson) **101**:100, 105, 184-85, 187-89
"Amarga boca" (Aleixandre) **113**:51
"Amarina's Roses" (Freeman) **9**:73
"Amaryllis" (Robinson) **101**:197
L'amata alla finestra (Alvaro) **60**:2
The Amateur Cracksman (Hornung) **59**:112, 114, 120
Un amateur d'âmes (Barrès) **47**:57, 62
"Amateur poet" (Service) **15**:412
"The Amateur Rider" (Paterson) **32**:373
"Amateur Theatricals" (Benchley) **55**:3
Amateurs at War (Williams) **89**:389-90
"The Amateurs of Heaven" (Nemerov) **124**:232, 300-01
The Amazed Evangelist: A Nightmare (Bridie) **3**:139-40
The Amazing Adventures of Letitia Carberry (Rinehart) **52**:281, 300
"The Amazing Hat Mystery" (Wodehouse) **108**:335
The Amazing Interlude (Rinehart) **52**:283, 288, 295
"The Amazing Magician" (Nezval)
See "Podivuhodny kouzelnik"
The Amazing Marriage (Meredith) **17**:269, 286, 291-95, 297; **43**:260, 290, 296
The Amazons (Pinero) **32**:398, 406, 411-12
"Ambarvalia" (Brooke) **7**:121
The Ambassadors (James) **2**:244-45, 252, 254, 258-59, 263-64, 266, 270-71; **11**:322-24, 327, 341, 346; **40**:105-06, 133, 140, 169; **47**:161-62, 164-65, 172-75, 177, 194-96, 207; **64**:184; **171**:119-201
"Amber Preserved" (Balmont) **11**:40
"The Amber Witch" (Moody) **105**:236
Ambit (Aleixandre)
See *Ambito*
"Ambition" (Thomas) **10**:463
Ambition (Nagai)
See *Yashin*
"The Ambitious Violet" (Gibran) **1**:327; **9**:94
Ambito (Aleixandre) **113**:2, 4, 6-7, 19, 30, 38, 41, 44-47, 58-59, 61-64, 68, 70, 72-77
Ambrose Holt and Family (Glaspell) **175**:59, 62, 149
"L'ame de la ville" (Verhaeren) **12**:470
L'âme de Napoléon (Bloy) **22**:45
"L'ame de Victor Hugo" (Roussel) **20**:234, 240, 244
"L'âme du monde" (Teilhard de Chardin) **9**:492
L'ame enchantée (Rolland) **23**:262
"L'âme et la danse" (Valéry) **15**:445
L'ame française et la guerre (Barrès) **47**:45
"L'ame paysanne" (Verhaeren) **12**:471
"Ame Shōshō" (Nagai) **51**:95
"America" (Drummond de Andrade) **139**:232
"America" (Ginsberg) **120**:35-6, 99
America (Asch)
See *Amerika*
America (Griffith) **68**:135, 169
America (Kafka)
See *Amerika*
"America, 1918" (Reed) **9**:385
"America and the Future" (Abbey) **160**:57
América antes de Colón (Sender) **136**:209
"America del este" (Jiménez) **4**:225
America, I Like You (Wodehouse) **108**:353-54, 369
America, I Presume (Lewis) **2**:391
"America in 1804" (Masters) **2**:470
"America in 1904" (Masters) **2**:470
America in Literature (Woodberry) **73**:365
America in Mid-Passage (Beard) **15**:28
America Is Worth Saving (Dreiser) **10**:184, 195
"America Journal" (Obstfelder)
See "Amerikansk juleaften"
The America of George Ade (Shepherd) **177**:293, 295, 298, 302
"The American" (Papadiamantis) **29**:272-73, 277
The American (James) **2**:246, 255-57, 262; **11**:325-26, 338; **24**:343; **40**:102, 108, 122, 125, 133, 161; **47**:150-51, 205-7; **64**:171-72, 175; **171**:150-51, 158, 180
"American Art: A Possible Future" (Rourke) **12**:318, 320, 330
"American Authors and British Pirates" (Matthews) **95**:256, 270
The American Cause (Kirk) **119**:253, 275
"American Change" (Ginsberg) **120**:86
"American Character in American Fiction" (Matthews) **95**:266
"An American Citizen" (Fisher) **87**:112
The American Claimant (Twain) **6**:461-62; **12**:432, 447-48; **48**:351
"The American County Fair" (Anderson) **10**:45
"The American Cowboy" (Adams) **56**:21
"The American Credo" (Mencken) **13**:363
The American Credo (Nathan) **18**:306
The American Democracy (Laski) **79**:95, 106, 145, 148, 153
American Diaries, 1902-1926 (Dreiser) **18**:63; **35**:60
American Diary, 1898 (Webb and Webb) **22**:419
The American Diary of a Japanese Girl (Noguchi) **80**:360
"The American Eagle" (Lawrence) **93**:103
American Fairy Tales (Baum) **7**:14, 16; **132**:30, 103
"American Family" (Hecht) **101**:36
American Foreign Policy in the Making, 1932-1940: A Study in Responsibilities (Beard) **15**:27
"The American Form of the Novel" (Austin) **25**:34
American Ghosts and Old World Wonders (Carter) **139**:99, 138-39
"An American Girl" (Matthews) **95**:236
An American Girl in London (Duncan) **60**:177, 197, 206-7, 209, 226, 228, 230, 232
American Government and Politics (Beard) **15**:33-4, 37
"American Humor" (Harte) **25**:220
American Humor: A Study of the National Character (Rourke) **12**:319-25, 327-29, 331-32
American Hunger (Wright) **136**:223-28, 278-79, 284, 315-16; **180**:303, 309, 313
The American Idea (Cohan) **60**:157
American Ideals and Other Essays (Roosevelt) **69**:177
"American Influence on Canadian Thought" (Duncan) **60**:211
"The American James" (Howells) **41**:266
American Labour (Laski) **79**:106
The American Language (Mencken) **13**:359-60, 364, 367, 379, 382, 386-87, 392, 394
American Leviathan (Beard) **15**:33
"American Literary Tradition and the Negro" (Locke) **43**:236
American Literature (Van Doren) **18**:399, 405
"American Names" (Benét) **7**:79
American Notes (Williams) **89**:399
The American Novel (Van Doren) **18**:389-90, 393, 404-05
"American Novels" (Bodenheim) **44**:74
American Outpost: A Book of Reminiscences (Sinclair) **160**:252, 293
An American Politician (Crawford) **10**:150
American Portraits, 1875-1900 (Bradford) **36**:52, 57
The American Presidency (Laski) **79**:148, 151, 154
The American Renaissance: Art and Expression in the Age of Emerson and Whitman (Matthiessen) **100**:158, 160, 162-63, 165-68, 170-71, 173, 176-77, 179-80, 182, 184-87, 189-95, 197, 201-02, 205, 209-16, 218-19, 223, 227-34, 250-54, 257-63, 267-71, 275, 283-88, 290-94, 297-300, 304-08
The American Rhythm (Austin) **25**:19, 23, 27, 29, 33, 35-7
The American Scene (James) **2**:254, 275-76; **47**:173; **171**:133
"The American School of Fiction" (Fuller) **103**:110, 117
"An American School of Fiction" (Norris) **24**:450; **155**:339
"American Social Conditions" (Rölvaag) **17**:333
American Stories (Nagai)
See *Amerika monogatari*
"An American to Mother England" (Lovecraft) **22**:241
An American Tragedy (Dreiser) **10**:171-74, 176-79, 183, 185-95, 198; **18**:52-4, 59, 61, 63-5, 72-5; **35**:32-3, 36, 39, 52, 57-60, 62-8, 71, 76-7, 79, 84-5; **83**:2-123
An American Visitor (Cary) **1**:144; **29**:66, 68, 79-80, 84-6, 92, 101, 104-07; **196**:159, 214
"American Wives and English Husbands" (Atherton) **2**:18
Americanas (Machado de Assis) **10**:279
"Americanism" (Matthews) **95**:264
"Americanism in Literature" (Higginson) **36**:178
"Americanisms and Briticisms" (Matthews) **95**:254, 257
Americanisms and Briticisms, with Other Essays on Other Isms (Matthews) **95**:223, 225, 227-8, 254
The Americanization of Edward Bok (Bok) **101**:21
"Americans and Their Cars" (Shepherd) **177**:316
"The American's Tale" (Doyle) **7**:238
America's Economic Supremacy (Adams) **80**:5, 12, 14, 27, 36, 38, 55-6
Amerigo (Zweig) **17**:457-58
Amerika (Asch) **3**:66
Amerika (Kafka) **2**:302-03, 307-08; **6**:219-20, 223, 225-26; **29**:213; **47**:232; **53**:203; **112**:69, 83; **179**:238-331
"Amerika ist anders" (Zuckmayer) **191**:300, 303, 305
Amerika monogatari (Nagai) **51**:87
Amerika-breve fra P. A. Smevik til hans for og bror i Norge (Rölvaag) **17**:338, 344, 346

"Amerikansk juleaften" (Obstfelder) **23**:182, 192
Les ames fortes (Giono) **124**:54, 84, 106, 115
Les ames mortes (Adamov) **189**:31-2, 34, 36-7
The Amethyst Ring (France)
See *L'anneau d'améthyste*
"L'Ami d'Amienne" (Léautaud) **83**:204
"Un Ami dort" (Cocteau) **119**:76
Amica America (Giraudoux) **2**:163
L'amica delle mogli (Pirandello) **29**:299, 318
"De amicitia" (Johnson) **19**:256
L'amico del vincitore (Brancati) **12**:84
Amid These Storms (Churchill) **113**:115
Amida Butsu (Suzuki) **109**:387
"Amiel and Some Others" (Barbellion) **24**:90
El amigo Manso (Pérez Galdós) **27**:250, 261, 266-67, 283
Amîndoi (Rebreanu) **28**:272
"L'amitié de l'homme et de la bête" (Bataille) **155**:114
Les amitiés françaises (Barrès) **47**:65-6, 69
"Ammonizione" (Saba) **33**:372
"Ammonoosuc" (Morley) **87**:144
Amnesia (Nervo) **11**:403
El amo del mundo (Storni) **5**:449, 453-54
Amok (Zweig) **17**:454-55, 457
"Among Emigrants" (Bergelson) **81**:19
"Among Our Foreign Residents" (Gilman) **117**:137
"Among School Children" (Nemerov) **124**:284
"Among School Children" (Yeats) **1**:566, 583; **11**:529, 533; **18**:446-47, 452; **31**:402, 410; **116**:281, 290
Among Strangers (Gorky) **8**:74
"Among the Aspens" (Carman) **7**:138
"Among the Corn Rows" (Garland) **3**:190
"Among the Ferns" (Carpenter) **88**:54
"Among the Leaves" (Wetherald) **81**:409
"Among the Paths to Eden" (Capote) **164**:99-100, 104-5
Among the Ruins (Mizoguchi)
See *Haikyo no naka*
"Among Those Killed in the Dawn Raid Was a Man Aged a Hundred" (Thomas) **105**:348
Among Women Only (Pavese)
See *Tra donne solo*
"Amor" (García Lorca) **181**:181-82
"Amor" (Gogarty) **15**:101
"¡Amor!" (Jiménez) **183**:290
"El amor asesinado" (Pardo Bazán) **189**:226
El amor brujo (Arlt) **29**:45, 52-4, 57-9
El amor cardrático (Martinez Sierra and Martinez Sierra) **6**:279
"Amor condusee noi ad una morte" (Villaurrutia) **80**:463-4
Amor de Don Perlimplín (García Lorca) **181**:17, 22, 35-39, 41, 45
Amor de Don Perlimplín con Belisa en su jardín (García Lorca) **1**:315-16, 318, 320; **7**:292-94, 300; **9**:292; **49**:76, 85, 87, 105, 108-09
"Amor de madre" (Palma) **29**:259
"Amor de nieve" (Lugones) **15**:292
"Amor en Stendhal" (Ortega y Gasset) **9**:351-53
"El amor iracundo" (Aleixandre) **113**:16
Amor Mundo y todos los cuentos de Arguedos (Arguedas) **147**:99, 107-8
"El amor no es relieve" (Aleixandre) **113**:5, 46
"El amor padecido" (Aleixandre) **113**:6, 46
"Amor prohibido" (Vallejo) **3**:532
Amor y pedagogía (Unamuno) **2**:558, 564; **9**:513, 515; **148**:245, 250-54, 256, 338, 340-41
Les amorandes (Benda) **60**:63
"De amore" (Dowson) **4**:87
L'amore (Tozzi) **31**:314
"Amore e morte" (Papini) **22**:272
Amores (Lawrence) **2**:343; **93**:3, 6, 9, 22, 43, 44, 45, 67, 70
Gli amori difficili (Calvino) **183**:93, 95, 97, 145, 147, 190-92, 221, 223-24, 237
Amori et dolori sacrum (Barrès) **47**:41, 48, 81, 94
Amori senza amore (Pirandello) **4**:332
Amoris victima (Symons) **11**:428-29, 431-32, 434, 439, 445-46
L'amorosa spina (Saba) **33**:369, 373
Amos Killbright: His Adscititious Experiences, with Other Stories (Stockton) **47**:314
"L'amour" (Schwob) **20**:321, 328
L'amour absolu (Jarry) **14**:274, 278-82, 287; **147**:231, 265-67, 270, 290, 305
"L'amour de Dieu et le malheur" (Weil) **23**:379
"Un amour de Swann" (Proust) **7**:539, 547; **161**:189, 201
L'amour du monde (Ramuz) **33**:296, 302
"Amour dure" (Lee) **5**:320
L'amour en visites (Jarry) **14**:278-79, 281; **147**:244, 262-66, 268, 307
"Amour et cinéma" (Desnos) **22**:65
Amour et piano (Feydeau) **22**:90-1
"Amour immaculé" (Nelligan) **14**:392
L'amour la poésie (Éluard) **7**:248, 250, 253; **41**:150
"L'amour, le Dédain et l'Espérance" (Apollinaire) **51**:6
L'Amour, les Muses, et la chasse (Jammes) **75**:119
L'Amour maladroit (Jarry) **147**:271
Amour sublime (Péret) **20**:186
"L'amoureuse" (Éluard) **41**:154
"Amours" (Léautaud) **83**:190
"Les Amours Étiques, par Félicen Cossu" (Swinburne) **8**:439
"Amparo" (García Lorca) **181**:196
Amphitryon Thirty-Eight (Giraudoux) **2**:157-58, 165, 173; **7**:321, 327-28
"Amphora" (Sologub) **9**:437
"Amplificaciones" (Villaurrutia) **80**:477
"Amplifications" (Villaurrutia)
See "Amplificaciones"
Amras (Bernhard) **165**:19-20, 95
"Amuck in the Bush" (Callaghan) **145**:255
"The Amulet" (Naidu) **80**:315
The Amulet (Rosenberg) **12**:293, 300, 310
Amurath to Amurath (Bell) **67**:3-5, 16-18
The Amusements of Khan Kharada (Dunsany) **2**:144
"Amycus célestin" (France) **9**:52
L'An V de la révolution algérienne (Fanon) **188**:12, 65, 71-4, 79, 81-2, 85, 92, 96-7, 100, 120, 128, 147
"An alle Gegangen" (Toller) **10**:491
"An Apollon" (Lasker-Schueler) **57**:300, 307, 312
"An den Bürger" (Kraus) **5**:285
"An den Gralprinzen" (Lasker-Schueler) **57**:298
"An den Knaben Elis" (Trakl) **5**:464
"An die Dichter" (Toller) **10**:490
"An die Musik" (Rilke) **195**:202, 255
"An einen Frühverstorbenen" (Trakl) **5**:458
"An Ihn" (Lasker-Schueler) **57**:312
"An mein Kind" (Lasker-Schueler) **57**:299, 305, 334, 336
"An Stephen George" (Rilke) **195**:260
Ana María (Martinez Sierra and Martinez Sierra)
See *Túeres la paz*
"The Anachronism" (Brennan) **124**:7
"Anaconda" (Quiroga) **20**:208, 212-15, 218-19
"Anactoria" (Swinburne) **8**:424, 437, 442, 446; **36**:294, 297, 317-18, 322-23, 328-29
"Anagram" (Thomas) **105**:336
Anales de la inquisición de Lima (Palma) **29**:255
"Analogue" (Nemerov) **124**:255, 306
"L'analyse schématique" (Roumain) **19**:346
"Analysis of a Theme" (Stevens) **45**:285
"The Analytical Language of John Wilkins" (Borges) **109**:72
Anaphora ston Gkreko (Kazantzakis) **33**:151-52, 154, 163-64, 166, 170; **181**:236, 243, 277-78, 313, 322, 324-26
"Anapæsts" (Flecker) **43**:188
"Anarchism" (Goldman) **13**:224
Anarchism, and Other Essays (Goldman) **13**:208-09, 212, 220
"Anarchism and the Morality of Violence" (Abbey) **160**:12, 29, 83, 93
Anarchism or Socialism? (Stalin) **92**:183
"The Anarchist" (Stringer) **37**:328
"Anarchist Communism" (Kropotkin) **36**:211
"The Anarchist: His Dog" (Glaspell) **175**:94
Anarchist Morality (Kropotkin) **36**:204, 222
"Anarchy" (McCrae) **12**:210
"Anashuya and Vijaya" (Yeats) **11**:511
"Anastacio Lucena" (Graham) **19**:130
Anastomòsi (Gadda) **144**:126, 128
Anatéma (Andreyev) **3**:18-20, 22, 25
"Anathema" (Kuprin) **5**:300
Anathema (Andreyev)
See *Anatéma*
Anatol (Schnitzler) **4**:385-91, 397, 399
The Anatomist, and Other Plays (Bridie) **3**:133, 136-37
Anatomy of Criticism (Frye) **165**:141-46, 149-54, 161, 164-69, 171, 173-74, 179-80, 188, 192-93, 208-9, 226-30, 233-38, 243-44, 256-57, 260-61
"The Anatomy of Fiction" (Woolf) **101**:269
The Anatomy of Frustration: A Modern Synthesis (Wells) **12**:513
The Anatomy of Negation (Saltus) **8**:342, 345-49, 351-53, 355
"Anaxagoras" (Lawrence) **93**:26
Anaximander and the Indeterminate (Vaihinger) **71**:416
"The Ancestors" (Bishop) **103**:9
Ancestors (Atherton) **2**:14-15
"Ancestral Houses" (Yeats) **11**:534-36; **31**:400, 423
Ancestral Poems (Lugones)
See *Poemas solariegos*
"An Ancestry of Genius" (Ellis) **14**:132
"Anch'io cerco di dire la mia" (Calvino) **183**:153
"The Anchored Angel" (Villa) **176**:94
The Anchored Angel: Selected Writings by José Garcia Villa (Villa) **176**:115
"The Anchorite" (Balmont)
See "Otshel'nik"
"Anchors" (Robinson) **101**:111
L'Ancienne et la nouvelle metaphysique (Sorel) **91**:321
The Ancient Allan (Haggard) **11**:242, 254
"Ancient Experiments in Cooperation" (Wells) **133**:262
The Ancient Gerfalcons (Valle-Inclán) **5**:486
"An Ancient Gesture" (Millay) **49**:222; **169**:250
"The Ancient Gods" (Webb) **24**:473
"The Ancient Gulf" (Roberts) **68**:305, 337
"Ancient Irish Sagas" (Roosevelt) **69**:255-56, 264
Ancient Judaism (Weber) **69**:297, 330
"Ancient Lament" (Carducci)
See "Pianto antico"
"The Ancient Landmark" (Williams) **89**:395
The Ancient Law (Glasgow) **2**:180, 185, 188
Ancient Lights and Certain New Reflections (Ford) **172**:56, 97, 124
"Ancient Memory" (Gumilev)
See "Prapamjat'"
"Ancient Sorceries" (Blackwood) **5**:69-70, 73
Ancient Tales of God and Emperors, Poets and Courtesans (Couperus)
See *Antieke Verhalen van Goden en Keizers, van Dichters en Hetaeren*
"An Ancient to Ancients" (Hardy) **53**:93, 107, 115; **143**:147
The Ancient Tragedy (Lindsay) **15**:230
"The Ancient World in Contemporary French Poetry" (Annensky) **14**:17
& (Cummings) **137**:19-21, 34, 41, 44-45, 47
And (Cummings)
See *&*

And a Threefold Cord (La Guma) **140**:196, 199, 201-2, 205, 209, 212, 224-25, 233-34, 239-40, 245-47, 249, 256, 262, 272-73
And Again? (O'Faolain) **143**:271, 273
"And Death Shall Have No Dominion" (Thomas) **8**:459-60; **45**:372, 409
"And Even Beyond" (Peretz) **16**:395
And Even Now (Beerbohm) **1**:66-7, 69; **24**:102, 104, 117, 123, 125
"And If the Angel Asks" (Bialik)
See "We-'im yish' al ha-malach"
And It Came to Pass (Bialik)
See *Vayehi Hayom*
. . . And Ladies of the Club (Santmyer) **133**:210-16, 218-19
And Long Remember (Fisher) **87**:105
And Most of All Man (Mais) **8**:245
"And No Bird Sings" (Benson) **27**:16-17
And No Man's Wit (Macaulay) **7**:427; **44**:124
And Now Good-Bye (Hilton) **21**:92-3
"And Once Again—the Negro" (Heyward) **59**:92, 102
"And Pass" (Toomer) **172**:273
And So Ad Infinitum (Čapek)
See *Ze života hmyzu*
"And So Cervantes Was Maimed" (Arenas)
See "De modo que Cervantes era manco"
And the Crooked Shall Be Made Straight (Agnon)
See *Ve-Haya he-Akov le-Mishor*
"And the Dead Spake—" (Benson) **27**:16
"And the Head Began to Burn" (Storni)
See "Y la cabeza comenzó a arder"
And Then (Natsume)
See *Sorekara*
"And Then They Were None" (Babel) **171**:14
"And There Was a Great Calm" (Hardy) **143**:157, 201-2, 212
And Tomorrow, Monday (Pirandello)
See *E domani lunedi*
"And What, Dear Heart" (Roberts) **68**:337
"And When the Net Was Unwound Venus Was Found Ravelled With Mars" (Bishop) **103**:3, 5-6
"And Who Shall Say—?" (Middleton) **56**:175
And Yet They Go (Mizoguchi) **72**:322, 324
"Andaluzas" (García Lorca) **181**:177, 179, 182
"A & W Root Beer Stand" (Shepherd) **177**:316
"Andante" (Coppard) **5**:177-78
"Andante" (Gray) **19**:158
Andanzas y visiones Españolas (Unamuno) **9**:512, 514
Andarse por las ramas (Garro) **153**:9, 12, 14-18, 28, 71, 90
"Ande desnudo" (Vallejo) **56**:312
Der andere Prozeß (Canetti) **157**:80, 101
Die andere Seite (Kubin) **23**:93-100, 103
"Anders" (Kandinsky) **92**:67
"Andersen's Swan" (Miyazawa) **76**:292
"¿Para quién escribo?" (Aleixandre) **113**:34
Andor (Molnár) **20**:164, 175, 177
Andorra (Frisch) **121**:205, 230, 232, 236, 240, 248, 250, 252, 254-55
"Andraitix, Pomengranate Flowers" (Lawrence) **93**:21
André (Molnár)
See *Andor*
"André Chénier Died by the Guillotine" (Tsvetaeva) **35**:394
Andrea Delfin (Heyse) **8**:121, 123, 125
Andreas; oder, Die Vereinigten (Hofmannsthal) **11**:302, 306, 310
"Andreas Olufsen" (Jensen) **41**:308
Andreas; or, The United (Hofmannsthal)
See *Andreas; oder, Die Vereinigten*
Andrés Pérez, maderista (Azuela) **3**:75, 77, 79; **145**:14, 17
"Andrew Johnson Swinging Around the Circle" (Bell) **43**:89
Androcles and the Lion (Shaw) **3**:392, 395-96, 400
"Androgin" (Gumilev) **60**:280
"The Androgyne" (Gumilev)
See "Androgin"
Andromeda (Buchanan) **107**:87
"Andromeda over Tewkesbury" (Gurney) **33**:97
Androvar (Prado) **75**:192
"Andy's Gone with Cattle" (Lawson) **27**:138, 140
"Andy's Return" (Lawson) **27**:134
"Anecdote" (Jacob) **6**:191
"Anecdote" (Parker) **143**:320-21
"Anecdote for Fathers" (Quiller-Couch) **53**:289
"Anecdote of Canna" (Stevens) **45**:304
"Anecdote of the Abnormal" (Stevens) **12**:382
"Anecdote of the Jar" (Stevens) **3**:475; **45**:297, 299, 304, 310, 327-28, 334
"Anedota pecuniária" (Machado de Assis) **10**:290
"Anemone" (Benn) **3**:113
"Anfang und Ende" (Heyse) **8**:119
"L'ange du méridien" (Rilke) **6**:366
"Angel" (Brodkey) **123**:200-1, 275, 227
"El ángel" (Miro) **5**:335
Angel (Heyward) **59**:86, 94, 100
"Angel and Stone" (Nemerov) **124**:177-78, 195, 315
"The Angel and the Sweep" (Coppard) **5**:176
"The Angel at the Grave" (Wharton) **3**:571; **9**:541; **129**:360
The Angel at the Western Window (Meyrink)
See *Der Engel vom westlichen Fenster*
"El ángel de la sombra" (Lugones) **15**:286
"Angel extraviado" (Salinas) **17**:358
"An Angel Flew in the Midnight Sky" (Platonov) **14**:410
Angel guerra (Pérez Galdós) **27**:247, 249-52, 255-58, 263-64, 267
"Angel in the House" (Mansfield) **164**:239
"Angel Levine" (Malamud) **184**:167, 237, 278-80, 283, 310-13
Angel Making Music (Molnár)
See *A zenélő angyal*
"Angel of Annunciation" (Tynan) **3**:502
"The Angel of Mons" (Machen)
See "The Bowmen"
The Angel of Pain (Benson) **27**:17
The Angel of Terror (Wallace) **57**:394
"The Angel of the Lord" (Post) **39**:338
"Angel or Earthly Creature" (Merrill) **173**:172
"Angel Surrounded by Paysans" (Stevens) **45**:302, 334, 350
"The Angel Was a Yankee" (Benét) **7**:81
"Angelfish" (Dent) **72**:28-31
"Angelic Butterfly" (Levi)
See "Angelica Farfalla"
"Angelic Greeting" (Vallejo)
See "Salutación angélica"
"Angelica Farfalla" (Levi) **109**:294
"Angelina" (Dunbar) **12**:122
Angelo (Giono) **124**:38, 50, 54-55, 83-84, 88, 97, 115
Angels and Earthly Creatures (Wylie) **8**:529-30, 532, 534
Angels and Minister (Housman) **7**:354, 357
"The Angels at Hamburg" (Jarrell) **177**:195
Angels Over Broadway (Hecht) **101**:75, 89
"The Angel's Visit" (Forten) **16**:147, 150
Angel's Wings: A Series of Essays on Art and Its Relation to Life (Carpenter) **88**:97, 107
"Angel's-Eye View" (Coffin) **95**:11-2
"Angelus" (Coppee) **25**:124
"The Angelus" (Cram) **45**:12
Anger (Sarton) **120**:246, 248
"The Anger of a Jewish Woman" (Peretz) **16**:399
"The Anger of Samson" (Gurney) **33**:87
Angest (Lagerkvist) **144**:181, 194, 196-97, 210, 213, 222, 230
"Angest, angest är min arvedel" (Lagerkvist) **144**:179-80, 194
"Angina" (Dickey) **151**:97, 109
"Anglais Mort à Florence" (Stevens) **45**:282
"Angleterre" (Verhaeren) **12**:471
L'Angleterre en 1815 (Halévy)
See *Histoire du peuple anglais au xlxe siècle. iv. Le milieu du siècle, 1841-52*
The Anglican Career of Cardinal Newman (Abbott) **139**:32, 34-40
Anglické listy (Čapek) **6**:85; **192**:179
Anglore (Mistral)
See *Lou pouèma dóu Rose*
Anglo-Saxony: A League That Works (Lewis) **9**:240
L'angoisse de Pascal (Barrès) **47**:62, 66
"Angry Love" (Aleixandre) **113**:24
The Angry Toy (Arlt)
See *El juguete rabioso*
"Angst" (Zweig) **17**:454, 456-57
Angst (Lagerkvist)
See *Angest*
"Angst, angst is my inheritance" (Lagerkvist)
See "Angest, angest är min arvedel"
"The Anguish" (Millay) **49**:210; **169**:267
Anguish (Lagerkvist)
See *Angest*
Anguish (Ramos)
See *Angústia*
"Anguish of Transitoriness" (Annensky)
See "Toska mimolet-nosti"
"Angulo" (Sá-Carneiro) **83**:401
Angústia (Ramos) **32**:419-20, 422-32, 434-35, 437-39
"Anielka" (Prus) **48**:182
"Anika's Times" (Andrić)
See "Anikina vremena"
"Anikina vremena" (Andrić) **135**:11-12, 54, 79, 85, 90, 94, 96
"The Anilin Inn" (Herzl) **36**:141
"De Anima" (Nemerov) **124**:204, 250-51, 304, 306
Anima Celtica (Sharp) **39**:394
"Anima hominis" (Yeats) **11**:521; **93**:338, 339
"Anima mundi" (Yeats) **11**:520; **93**:338, 339, 353, 354; **116**:269, 271
"The Animal" (Kolmar) **40**:176
"Animal Consciousness" (Orage) **157**:275
Animal de fondo (Jiménez) **4**:216-18, 221; **183**:256-64, 276-82, 284, 288, 290-91, 293, 300, 304, 306-12, 319, 321
"Animal Dynamo Velocity" (McAlmon) **97**:93
Animal Fairy Tales (Baum) **132**:80
The Animal Family (Jarrell) **177**:153, 155-58, 210
Animal Farm (Orwell) **2**:497-98, 500-01, 504-07, 510-12, 514; **6**:344-45, 348, 351, 353; **15**:299-300, 302, 308, 319, 321-23, 325-26, 329-30, 333-35, 343, 353-54, 364; **31**:176-80; **51**:221, 227, 237, 242-43, 246, 264-65; **128**:258-62, 264-67, 270-72, 278-79, 286, 290, 293, 296, 298, 307, 310-11; **129**:223, 225, 228, 235, 244, 246-47, 251, 255, 259, 261, 264
Animal Heroes (Seton) **31**:266-67, 269, 272
"Animal Intelligence: An Experimental Study of the Associative Process in Animals" (Thorndike) **107**:370, 382, 390-92, 395-99, 403, 408, 415, 423, 426
The Animal Kingdom (Barry) **11**:54-6, 61, 64, 67-8
Animal of Depth (Jiménez)
See *Animal de fondo*
Animal of Inner Depths (Jiménez)
See *Animal de fondo*
"Animal Psychology" (Weininger) **84**:306
"The Animal Story" (Roberts) **8**:322
"The Animal Trainer" (Gumilev)
See "Ukrotitel' zverej"
"Animal Woods" (Calvino) **183**:92
"Los animales malditos" (Lugones) **15**:293
"Animals" (Lawrence) **93**:98
"The Animals" (Muir) **2**:483, 486; **87**:168, 172
Animals and Men (Clark) **147**:125-26
Animals, and Other People (Bromfield) **11**:81, 84

Animals and Their Masters, Masters and Their Animals (Éluard)
See *Les animaux et leurs hommes, les hommes et leurs animaux*
"The Animals in the Case" (Wakefield) **120**:352
"Animals in the Nursery" (Carter) **139**:206, 209, 211
"The Animals of Nineveh" (Kolmar) **40**:178
Les animaux et leurs hommes, les hommes et leurs animaux (Éluard) **7**:250; **41**:152-53
Anime oneste (Deledda) **23**:37-8
"Animula vagula" (Graham) **19**:129, 136
Anjelica (Bradford) **36**:62
"Ankor Wat" (Ginsberg) **120**:22, 121
"Ankunft" (Lasker-Schueler) **57**:313, 315
"Ankunft" (Rilke) **195**:308
"Anmutiger Vertrag" (Morgenstern) **8**:309
"Ann Garner" (Agee) **19**:23
Ann Veronica (Wells) **19**:440
Ann Vickers (Lewis) **4**:251, 255, 257; **13**:337-38, 343, 350-51; **23**:148; **39**:247
"Anna" (Baker) **47**:20
Anna (Hauptmann) **4**:202
"An Anna Blume" (Schwitters) **95**:297, 302, 314-5, 322-5, 330, 341, 350-1
An Anna Blume (Arp) **115**:7
Anna Blume und ich (Schwitters) **95**:315, 317
Anna Christie (O'Neill) **1**:384, 402; **6**:324-26, 329-30, 334; **49**:252, 265-66, 270, 282
Anna Karenina (Tolstoy) **4**:447-9, 451, 453, 457-8, 460-3, 466, 468-69, 471-72, 474-83; **11**:459-60, 463, 465, 469-70, 473-76, 478-80; **17**:373-418; **28**:349, 352, 365-66, 368, 37; **44**:335, 352-55, 363; **79**:325-6, 328-9, 334-5, 353, 359, 363, 365, 368, 374-7, 380, 386, 388-90, 394, 398, 402, 406-7, 415-7, 421, 424, 436-40, 442-3, 445-52, 454; **173**:280, 292-93, 301, 305
Anna of the Five Towns (Bennett) **5**:24, 26, 33, 40-3, 47; **20**:35-41; **197**:11, 17, 31, 94-95, 97, 100, 102-3, 106, 108, 125-30, 133-35, 141, 15
"Anna on the Neck" (Chekhov) **3**:166
Anna Sophie Hedvig (Abell) **129**:69, 75, 112, 159-61, 164, 184-85
Anna, soror . . . (Yourcenar) **193**:279, 302, 304-05, 317, 343
Anna Svärd (Lagerloef) **4**:235; **36**:244
"Anna Tellwright" (Bennett) **197**:125
Anna Tellwright (Bennett) **197**:127, 135
Anna-Anna (Brecht)
See *Die sieben Todsünden der Kleinburger*
Annalena Bilsini (Deledda) **23**:40
Annals of a Quiet Neighborhood (MacDonald) **9**:292
Annan Water (Buchanan) **107**:84-5
"Anna's Marriage" (Smith) **25**:399
"Anne Donne" (Warner) **131**:311
Anne Frank: The Diary of a Young Girl (Frank)
See *Het achterhuis*
Anne of Avonlea (Montgomery) **51**:199, 201; **140**:278-80, 288
Anne of Green Gables (Montgomery) **51**:175-87, 190, 193-94, 202, 204-05, 207, 210-12, 215; **140**:276-346
Anne of Ingleside (Montgomery) **51**:180, 216; **140**:278
Anne of the Island (Montgomery) **140**:278-79, 323, 325, 334
Anne of the Thousand Days (Anderson) **2**:7-8, 10-11; **144**:3-7, 17-18, 35, 39, 71
Anne of Windy Poplars (Montgomery) **140**:278
"Anne Rutledge" (Masters) **25**:304
Anne Severn and the Fieldings (Sinclair) **3**:436; **11**:411-12, 414
L'anneau d'améthyste (France) **9**:47
"Annelid Dancer" (Miyazawa) **76**:301
"Anner Lizer's Stumblin' Block" (Dunbar) **2**:133; **12**:120
Anne's House of Dreams (Montgomery) **51**:196, 198-200, 215; **140**:278-79, 334
Anne's Terrible Good Nature and Other Stories for Children (Lucas) **73**:158
Annette et Sylvie (Rolland) **23**:262-64
Gli anni perduti (Brancati) **12**:84-5, 87-8, 91
"Annie" (Moore) **7**:487
Annie Besant: An Autobiography (Besant) **9**:13-14
"Annie Hill's Grave" (Merrill) **173**:257
Annie Kilburn (Howells) **7**:371, 376, 378-79, 386, 393, 397; **17**:178, 185-86; **41**:269
"The Annir Choile" (Sharp) **39**:372, 376-77
"An Anniversary" (de la Mare) **53**:35
"Anniversary" (Lardner) **14**:313
"The Anniversary" (Lowell) **8**:227, 229, 234
The Anniversary (Chekhov)
See *Zhubilei*
Anniversary Dinner (Molnár) **20**:171
"Anniversary Ode" (Moody) **105**:267
"Anniversary Poem" (Mayakovski) **18**:268
"Anniversary Poem" (Oppen) **107**:267
"An Anniversary Poem Entitled 'The Progress of Liberty': Delivered January 1st, 1886 . . . at the Celebration of the Third Anniversary of President Lincon's Proclamation" (Bell) **43**:91, 93
Anno 1915 giornale di campagna (Gadda) **144**:144
Anno dada (Kandinsky) **92**:72
L'annonce faite à Marie (Claudel) **2**:99, 101, 106, 108; **10**:122, 123, 128
L'annonce faite à Marie (Giraudoux) **2**:167
The Annotated Lolita (Nabokov) **108**:89-92, 228; **189**:74, 116
"The Annunciation" (Muir) **2**:483; **87**:161, 168
"L'annunzio" (D'Annunzio) **40**:40-1, 45
Año cristiano (Pardo Bazán) **189**:247
"Ano jibun" (Kunikida Doppo) **99**:295
"Año nuevo" (Huidobro) **31**:124
"Anodyne" (Mansfield) **39**:314
"The Anointed Man" (Sharp) **39**:375
Anomalies (Bourget) **12**:69
"An Anonymous Story" (Chekhov) **3**:117; **163**:11
The Anonymous Work (Witkiewicz) **8**:513
Años y leguas (Miro) **5**:338-39, 342-45
"Another Acteon" (Bishop) **103**:9-10
"Another Boaster" (Lindsay) **17**:240
Another Book of Verses for Children (Lucas) **73**:158
Another Book on the Theatre (Nathan) **18**:294, 296
Another Caesar (Neumann) **100**:315
"Another Face" (Agnon)
See "Panim aherot"
"Another Heroic Beginning" (Wright) **136**:265
Another Language (Mankiewicz) **85**:163
"Another Man's Poison" (Williams) **89**:371
Another Part of the Forest (Hellman) **119**:132-35, 138-140, 142-43, 164, 166-67, 171-21, 175, 177-78, 183-87, 228, 235
Another Part of the Wood (Clark) **147**:123-24, 126
"Another Patriot" (Abbey) **160**:57
Another Sheaf (Galsworthy) **45**:34-5
"Another Tale" (Orage) **157**:282
"Another Weeping Woman" (Stevens) **45**:269
Another's Crime (Quiroga)
See *El crimen del otro*
"Anregungen zur Erlangung einer Systemschrift" (Schwitters) **95**:304
Anrufung des Grossen Bären (Bachmann) **192**:5, 9, 53-54, 63, 66
"Ans Werk" (Raabe) **45**:188
Anschauung und Begriff (Brod) **115**:87, 89
Die Anschauung vom heiligen Geiste bei Luther (Otto) **85**:313
Ansichten eines Clowns (Böll) **185**:10, 18-19, 21-2, 25, 27, 29, 36, 40, 44, 51, 58, 65, 69, 98, 105, 129-30, 144-46, 148-49, 151, 172, 176, 179, 181-82
"Ansiedad para el día" (Aleixandre) **113**:6, 47
"Answer" (Baker) **10**:19
"Answer" (Capote) **164**:171
"The Answer" (Kipling) **17**:196
"An Answer" (Tynan) **3**:503
"Answer from Norway" (Bjoernson) **7**:110
"The Answer on the Magnolia Tree" (Slesinger) **10**:441-42, 446
"Answer to a Letter from Charles Walter Stetson" (Gilman) **117**:147
"Answer to an Inquiry" (Babel) **13**:27
"Answer to Dunbar's 'After a Visit'" (Cotter) **28**:43
"An Answer to Various Bards" (Paterson) **32**:369
Answered Prayers (Capote) **164**:123, 134, 151, 170, 199, 204
"Ant" (Jozsef) **22**:161
Antant en emport e le vent (Moréas) **18**:279
An Antarctic Mystery (Verne)
See *Le Sphinx des glaces*
"Ante Um Nu De Bianco" (Drummond de Andrade) **139**:231
"An Antebellum Sermon" (Dunbar) **12**:110
"Antek" (Prus) **48**:157, 161
"The Antelope People" (Fisher) **140**:165-67
"Antes" (Villaurrutia) **80**:477
Antes que anochezca (Arenas) **191**:144-46, 149-53, 160, 175, 178, 186-87, 216-17, 219-20, 225, 229-30, 233-34, 239, 248-49, 251-53, 265
"Anthem for Doomed Youth" (Owen) **5**:359, 364-69, 371-72; **27**:199, 203, 208, 212, 217-18, 226, 230, 232
"Anthem of Earth" (Thompson) **4**:434-35
"An Anthem of Love" (Naidu) **80**:289
Anthologie de la Commune (Adamov) **189**:50
Anthologie des mythes, légendes, et contes populaires d'Amérique (Péret) **20**:192, 198, 203
Anthology (Jiménez)
See *Antolojía poética (1898-1953)*
An Anthology of Pure Poetry (Moore) **7**:479, 488, 490-91
An Anthology of World Prose (Van Doren) **18**:399, 401
Anthology of Writings on Art (Éluard)
See *Ecrits sur l'art*
Anthony Comstock; roundsman Of The Lord (Broun) **104**:98
Anthony John (Jerome) **23**:89-90
Anthony Wilding (Sabatini) **47**:303
Anthropogenie oder Entwickelungs-geschichte des Menschens (Haeckel) **83**:128, 130, 133, 143, 147
"The Anthropologist at Large" (Freeman) **21**:49
Anthropology and Modern Life (Boas) **56**:61, 63, 67-68, 94
"Anthropology and the Abnormal" (Benedict) **60**:127, 150
"Anthropology and the Humanities" (Benedict) **60**:121
L'Anti-Œdipe (Deleuze) **116**:57-9, 61, 67, 77, 79-84, 87-8, 90-3, 95, 100, 107, 109, 123, 155-56, 174
"Antichrist" (Einstein) **65**:169
"The Anti-Christ" (George) **14**:214
"Antichrist" (Muir) **87**:168
Antichrist (Merezhkovsky)
See *Peter and Alexis*
Der Antichrist (Nietzsche) **18**:342, 351-52; **55**:354-55
The Antichrist (Nietzsche)
See *Der Antichrist*
Der Antichrist (Roth) **33**:338
Anticipación a la muerte (Romero) **14**:434, 442
"Anticipation" (Lowell) **1**:372; **8**:233
"Anticipation" (Rilke)
See "Vorgefühl"
Anticipations of the Reaction of Mechanical and Scientific Progress upon Human Life and Thought (Wells) **6**:525, 535, 542, 552; **12**:487-88, 509; **19**:450; **133**:284
"Anti-Climax" (Patton) **79**:300

Antiek toerisme (Couperus) **15**:47
Antieke Verhalen van Goden en Keizers, van Dichters en Hetaeren (Couperus) **15**:47
Antigone (Anouilh) **195**:19-23, 25, 30-1, 33, 36, 38, 42-3, 47-8, 50-2, 55-7, 59-60, 64, 67-74
"Antigone" (Nemerov) **124**:143
Antigone (Cocteau) **119**:67, 74, 81
Antigone, and Other Portraits of Women (Bourget)
See *Voyageuses*
Die Antigone Des Sophokles (Brecht) **169**:7
"Antigone or the Choice" (Yourcenar)
See "Antigone ou le choix"
"Antigone ou le choix" (Yourcenar) **193**:333, 335, 337, 339
La antigua retórica (Reyes) **33**:316, 323
"Antiguo sentimiento" (García Lorca) **181**:183
The Antihead (Tzara)
See *L'Antitête*
Antikrists mirakler (Lagerloef) **4**:229, 231, 234, 240; **36**:230, 242, 246-47
"Antillais et Africains" (Fanon) **188**:147, 149
Antinous, and Other Poems (Summers) **16**:430
Anti-Oedipe (Deleuze)
See *L'Anti-Œdipe*
The Anti-Oedipus (Deleuze)
See *L'Anti-Œdipe*
Anti-Oedipus: Capitalism and Schizophrenia (Deleuze)
See *L'Anti-Œdipe*
"Antiope" (Field) **43**:166
Antiquamania (Roberts) **23**:238
Antisemitism (Arendt) **193**:145
"Anti-Semitism in Britain" (Orwell) **128**:286
L'Antitête (Tzara) **168**:229, 231, 279-83, 322-23
"L'anti-tradition futuriste" (Apollinaire) **8**:26; **51**:22
"Anti-Vietnam War Peace Mobilization" (Ginsberg) **120**:79
Antoine Bloyé (Nizan) **40**:289-91, 297-99, 302, 308, 311, 313-19, 321-23
Antoinette (Rolland) **23**:261
Antologia personal (Borges) **109**:156
Antolojía poética (1898-1953) (Jiménez) **4**:213
Anton Chekhov, and Other Essays (Shestov)
See *Nachala i kontsy*
Ántonia (Cather)
See *My Ántonia*
Antonia (Dujardin) **13**:189, 191
Antonin Artaud: Selected Writings (Artaud) **36**:32
Antonio, the Great Lover (Brancati)
See *Il bell'Antonio*
"Antranik of Armenia" (Saroyan) **137**:187-88, 193
"The Ant's Wedding" (Levi) **109**:302
"Antwerp" (Ford) **15**:72
Antwort aus der Stille (Frisch) **121**:211-13
"L'Anus solaire" (Bataille) **155**:129
"The Anvil of Souls" (Benét) **28**:2, 5
Anxieties (Andrić) **135**:8, 14, 23, 33
"Anxiety" (Lawrence) **93**:45
The Anxiety of the Rose (Storni)
See *La inquietud del rosal*
"The Anxious Dead" (McCrae) **12**:208, 211
"any april" (Engel) **137**:113
"Any Human to Another" (Cullen) **37**:158
"Any Lover, Any Lass" (Middleton) **56**:175
"Any Saint" (Thompson) **4**:435, 438
Anya Kōro (Shiga) **172**:202, 207, 214-17, 221-28, 231-35, 237-43, 245
"Anyám nagybátyja réji pap" (Babits) **14**:39
"anyone lived in a pretty how town" (Cummings) **137**:56
Anything Goes (Wodehouse) **108**:367, 392
Aoneko (Hagiwara) **60**:287, 289, 295, 297-99
Apache Devil (Burroughs) **2**:79, 85-6
Apache Drums (Lewton) **76**:201, 210
Apariencias (Gamboa) **36**:74-5
Apartheid: A Collection of Writings on South African Racism by South Africans (La Guma) **140**:262
Apartheid and the Archbishop: The Life and Times of Geoffrey Clayton, Archbishop of Cape Town (Paton) **165**:295, 298
"An Apartment House Anthology" (Parker) **143**:281
Apéndice a mis últimas tradiciones (Palma) **29**:257, 259
"Apes and Ivory" (Noyes) **7**:502
The Apes of God (Lewis) **2**:384-89, 391, 395, 398; **9**:237, 239-40, 242-46, 249; **104**:179, 181, 187-89, 201, 205-08, 210, 212, 214, 226, 231, 238, 243, 245-48, 250-51, 278, 283-84, 288, 290, 292
"Aphorism" (Gogarty) **15**:100, 113, 115
Aphorismen (Canetti) **157**:73
"Aphorisms" (George) **2**:148
"Aphorisms" (Villa) **176**:94, 106-7
"Aphorisms and Notes" (Bishop) **103**:6,
"Aphrodite" (Platonov) **14**:411-12, 414-15, 424
"Aphrodite and the King's Prisoners" (Hearn) **9**:134
Aphrodite in Aulis (Moore) **7**:497-98
Aphrodite Urania (Sikelianos) **39**:418
Apice (Sá-Carneiro) **83**:400
"A-Playin' of Old Sledge at the Settlemint" (Murfree) **135**:201, 204, 219, 227
"Apocalíptica" (Palma) **29**:262
Apocalypse (Lawrence) **2**:358, 368, 372; **48**:101, 121, 134-35, 139, 147, 149; **61**:209, 229; **93**:25, 72, 74, 104
"L'Apocalypse de Saint-sever" (Bataille) **155**:139
The Apocalypse of Our Times (Rozanov)
See *Apokalipsis nashego vremeni*
"An Apocryph" (Čapek) **192**:186
Apocrypha (Čapek)
See *Apokryfy*
"Apocryphal Songbook" (Machado)
See "Cancionero apócrifo"
Apocryphal Stories (Čapek)
See *Kniha apokryfů*
Apofeoz bezpochvennosti (Shestov) **56**:247-48, 252, 254, 259-260
Apokalipsis nashego vremeni (Rozanov) **104**:305, 315-19, 326, 345, 348-49, 354-57, 360, 371, 381, 384-87, 394
Apokryfy (Čapek) **192**:183
"Apollo" (Dickey) **151**:104, 113, 144, 170
"Apollo" (Lasker-Schueler) **57**:312
"Apollo and Marsyas" (Field) **43**:166
"Apollo and Marsyas" (Herbert)
See "Apollo i marsjasz"
"Apollo and Marsyas" (Lee-Hamilton) **22**:193
Apollo and Marsyas, and Other Poems (Lee-Hamilton) **22**:187-89, 193-94
"Apollo at Pheræ" (Masters) **25**:289
"Apollo i marsjasz" (Herbert) **168**:46, 62-63, 65-66, 78
The Apollo of Bellac (Giraudoux)
See *L'Apollon de Bellac*
Apollo of Tyrus (Remizov) **27**:334
L'Apollon de Bellac (Giraudoux) **2**:170; **7**:329
"Apollon tragique" (Yourcenar) **193**:335-38
"Apollo's Written Grief" (Field) **43**:177
"Apologia" (Tynan) **3**:501
Apologia (Abbott) **139**:12-15
"Apologia manzoniana" (Gadda) **144**:98
"Apologia Pro Mente Sua" (Santayana) **40**:389
"Apologia pro poemate meo" (Owen) **5**:358, 367, 372, 374; **27**:201, 206, 208-10, 212, 217, 222, 236
"Apology" (Hardy) **143**:212
"Apology" (Lowell) **1**:372
"An Apology for Crudity" (Anderson) **1**:43, 62; **10**:50
"Apology of Solon" (Sikelianos) **39**:419
"The Apostate" (London) **15**:262, 270-71
The Apostate (Belasco) **3**:86
"The Apostate of Chego-Chegg" (Cahan) **71**:12, 27, 29, 65, 68
The Apostle (Asch)
See *Paulus*
Los apostólicos (Pérez Galdós) **27**:256, 287
"Apostrophe to Man" (Millay) **169**:232, 250, 268
"The Apostrophe to Vincentine" (Stevens) **3**:445; **45**:348
apoteose (Sá-Carneiro) **83**:412
The Apothecary (Bromfield) **11**:82
The Apotheosis of Groundlessness (Shestov)
See *Apofeoz bezpochvennosti*
"Appalachia" (Abbey) **160**:58
Appalachian Wilderness (Abbey) **160**:56, 58-59, 70
"Apparation" (Bishop) **103**:4, 9,
"Apparition" (Rosenberg) **12**:311
L'apparition de l'homme (Teilhard de Chardin) **9**:479, 483
"The Apparitions" (Yeats) **31**:395, 397
Les apparus dans mes chemins (Verhaeren) **12**:466, 469
Appassionata (Villa) **176**:119
"An Appeal by the Presidents of Planet Earth" (Khlebnikov) **20**:151
"An Appeal for Death" (Gurney) **33**:98
"Appeal to All Art Lovers" (Hartmann) **73**:138
"Appeal to Every Briton" (Gandhi) **59**:52-3
"An Appeal to My Countrywomen" (Harper) **14**:264
"An Appeal to the American People" (Harper) **14**:260, 263
"Appeal to the Authorities" (Dazai Osamu) **11**:186-87
"An Appeal to the Intelligentsia" (Garvey) **41**:198
An Appeal to the Soul of White America (Garvey) **41**:179
The Appearance of Man (Teilhard de Chardin)
See *L'apparition de l'homme*
"Appearances" (Ginsberg) **120**:130
"Appel" (Roumain) **19**:339, 344
L'appel au soldat (Barrès) **47**:37, 42, 49, 51-2, 64, 70, 79, 94
"An Appendix on a Tender Theme" (Mencken) **13**:363
Appendix to My Latest Traditions (Palma)
See *Apéndice a mis últimas tradiciones*
"An Apple Blossom" (Wright) **136**:302
"The Apple Blossom Snow Blues" (Lindsay) **17**:228
The Apple Cart (Shaw) **3**:391, 393; **21**:324
"The Apple Tree" (Bowen) **148**:20
"The Apple Tree" (Galsworthy) **45**:39, 48
"The Apple Tree" (Mansfield) **39**:293
"The Apple Tree" (Parker) **143**:325
"The Apple Trees" (Trambley) **163**:337
"The Apples" (Trambley) **163**:316
Apples and Pears (Ellis) **14**:106
"The Apple's Guilt" (Bialik) **25**:50
"Apples of Hesperides" (Lowell) **1**:372
"The Applicant" (Bierce) **44**:45, 50
"An Application" (Caragiale)
See "Petitie"
"Appointment With Fire" (Wakefield) **120**:352
Appreciation (Graham) **19**:111
The Appreciation of Literature (Woodberry) **73**:365, 377
"The Apprentice" (Bambara) **116**:2-5
"The Approach to al Mu'tasim" (Borges)
See "El acercamiento a Almotásim"
"The Approach to Almotasim" (Borges)
See "El acercamiento a Almotásim"
"Approaches" (Balmont)
See "Priblizheniia"
"Approaches to Canadian Economic History" (Innis) **77**:338
"Approaching Prayer" (Dickey) **151**:180
Approximate Man and Other Writings (Tzara)
See *L'homme approximatif*
"Appuldurcombe Park" (Lowell) **8**:236

"Appunti" (Saba) **33**:370
"Aprel" (Zamyatin) **8**:548, 552
"Après le Ballet" (Engel) **137**:114
"Après les plus vieux vertiges" (Garneau) **13**:201
"L'Apres-Midi d'un Faune" (Faulkner) **141**:92
"April" (Colette) **16**:125
"April" (Roth) **33**:362
"April" (Thomas) **10**:467
"April" (Zamyatin)
See "Aprel"
"April 19" (Howe) **21**:113
April: A Fable of Love (Fisher) **140**:147-48, 151-52, 155, 166, 170, 175, 178-79, 182
April Airs (Carman) **7**:143, 147
The April Baby's Book of Tunes (Elizabeth) **41**:122
"April Dance-Song" (Manning) **25**:277
"April Days" (Higginson) **36**:175, 186
"April Fool" (Caragiale) **76**:164
"An April Ghost" (Reese) **181**:347
April Hopes (Howells) **7**:376, 393; **41**:286
"An April Masque" (Fisher) **87**:73
"April Showers" (Wharton) **129**:360
April Twilights (Cather) **11**:93; **99**:207; **132**:123, 128, 131, 149; **152**:16, 73
Apropos of Dolores (Wells) **6**:548; **12**:515
"Apróságok a házból" (Mikszath) **31**:169
Apuntes (Unamuno) **148**:252
"Apuntes autobiográficos" (Pardo Bazán) **189**:259, 261
Apuntes de un lugareño (Romero) **14**:432, 434
"Apuntes para un estudio" (Vallejo) **56**:319
"Aquae Sulis" (Hardy) **53**:101; **143**:169
Aquazzoni in montagna (Giacosa) **7**:310
"Aqueducts" (Gray) **19**:158
"Aquél" (Borges) **109**:5-6
Aquila de blason (Valle-Inclán) **5**:471, 473-74, 486
'Arī' is al-muruj (Gibran) **1**:327; **9**:84, 90-1
"Det är vackrast när det skymmer" (Lagerkvist) **144**:181, 210
"Arab Love Song" (Thompson) **4**:440
"Arabel" (Masters) **2**:461; **25**:288
Arabella (Hofmannsthal) **11**:310
Arabesques (Bely) **7**:59
"Arabia" (de la Mare) **4**:74
Arabia Deserta (Doughty)
See *Travels in Arabia Deserta*
"Arabian Nights' Entertainments" (Henley) **8**:110
Arabische Reiterei (Kandinsky) **92**:49
"Araby" (Joyce) **8**:166, 170-71; **35**:143-44, 146, 156, 159-60, 162-63, 165, 167-74, 176-83, 190-93, 197; **159**:276-77, 297-99, 304, 307-14, 316
"Arachné" (Schwob) **20**:323
L'araignee de cristal (Vallette) **67**:270, 278
Araksanīyā (Chatterji) **13**:80
The Aran Islands (Synge) **6**:431-32, 439-40; **37**:380, 388
"Arano" (Pascoli) **45**:154-55
The Arawak Girl (De Lisser) **12**:97-8
Arbeidsfolk (Kielland) **5**:275-77, 279
Arbeitsjournal (Brecht) **169**:9, 57-58, 62-63
"Arbejderen" (Jensen) **41**:303
"El árbol" (Aleixandre) **113**:15, 27
El Árbol (Garro) **153**:17, 19-20, 72
El árbol de la ciencia (Baroja) **8**:48, 51-5, 61-5
Arbol de pólvora (Reyes) **33**:324
"Arbolé arbolé" (García Lorca) **181**:83
"L'arboscello" (Saba) **33**:369
"Arbre" (Apollinaire) **51**:32
Arcades (Benjamin) **39**:10-11
Arcadian Adventures with the Idle Rich (Leacock) **2**:380
"Arcadie, Arcadie!" (Giono) **124**:124
L'Arc-en-ciel des amours (Jammes) **75**:119
"Archaeology of the Skin" (Sarduy) **167**:200
"Archaic Torso of Apollo" (Rilke)
See "Archaïscher Torso Apollos"
"Archaïscher Torso Apollos" (Rilke) **195**:202, 253, 260, 312, 316-17
L'arche (Lemonnier) **22**:198
"The Archer" (Sharp) **39**:366
"The Archetype" (Mistral)
See "Lou parangoun"
"Archibald Higbie" (Masters) **25**:297
Archibald Malmaison (Hawthorne) **25**:235, 238-41, 249-53
The Archibishop (Cather)
See *Death Comes for the Archbishop*
"The Archimedean Point" (Arendt) **193**:182
"Archimedes' Point" (Söderberg) **39**:438
"The Archipelagoes" (Bishop) **103**:21
"The Architectonics of Answerability" (Bakhtin) **160**:152
"The Architecture of Theories" (Peirce) **81**:290
Archives du Nord (Yourcenar) **193**:257, 266-68, 280, 302
Les archontes; ou, La liberté religieuse (Larbaud) **9**:205
Archy and Mehitabel (Marquis) **7**:448, 451-52
Archy Does His Part (Marquis) **7**:448
Archy's Life of Mehitabel (Marquis) **7**:448
"Arckép" (Radnóti) **16**:412
Arctic Poems (Huidobro)
See *Poemas árticos*
"Arctic Seas" (Huidobro)
See "Mares árticos"
Arctic Summer, and Other Fiction (Forster) **125**:126
Ardath: The Story of a Dead Self (Corelli) **51**:66-7, 72, 79-80, 82
Ardèle; ou, La marguerite (Anouilh) **195**:6-7, 14-15, 17, 26, 38, 48
Arden of Feversham (Artaud) **36**:32
"Ardid de guerra" (Pardo Bazán) **189**:236
Ardis Claverden (Stockton) **47**:321, 324-25
"Are History and Science Different Kinds of Knowledge?" (Collingwood) **67**:155
"Are We Downhearted? No!" (Rinehart) **52**:282
"Are We Hegelians?" (Croce)
See "Siamo noi hegeliani?"
"Are You Better Off Than You Were Last Year?" (Roosevelt) **93**:184
"Are You Too Late or Was I Too Early" (Collier) **127**:261
Are Your Teeth White? Then Laugh! (p'Bitek)
See *Lak tar miyo kinyero wi lobo*
Ärenlese (Hauptmann) **4**:200
"Arethusa" (Freeman) **9**:75-6
Arethusa (Crawford) **10**:148
"Argamak" (Babel) **2**:29; **13**:38; **171**:8, 25, 45, 70, 73, 88
"L'argent" (Péguy) **10**:404, 409
L'argent (Zola) **1**:597; **6**:563, 566; **41**:412, 439, 448-49
"L'argent dans la littérature" (Zola) **6**:561
"L'argent suite" (Péguy) **10**:409
"The Argentine Ant" (Calvino)
See "La formica Argentina"
"The Argentine Writer and Tradition" (Borges)
See "El escritor argentino y la tradición"
"Argo and his Master" (Svevo)
See "Argo e il suo padrone"
"Argo e il suo padrone" (Svevo) **2**:541
Los argonautas (Blasco Ibáñez) **12**:37
"The Argonauts" (Lawrence) **93**:59, 73
The Argonauts (Blasco Ibáñez)
See *Los argonautas*
The Argonauts (Crowley) **7**:208
"The Argonauts of North Liberty" (Harte) **25**:200
"The Argo's Chanty" (Benét) **28**:2, 5
Aria da capo (Millay) **4**:307, 312, 314, 317-18; **169**:234, 249, 282, 302
"Ariadna" (Chekhov)
See "Ariadne"
Ariadna (Tsvetaeva) **7**:565; **35**:393, 415-16
"Ariadne" (Chekhov) **55**:66; **163**:128
"Ariadne" (Roberts) **8**:313, 319, 328-30
Ariadne (Tsvetaeva)
See *Ariadna*
Ariadne: A Story of a Dream (Ouida) **43**:339, 347, 349-50, 355, 369-70
Ariadne auf Naxos (Hofmannsthal) **11**:301
"Ariadne in Naxos" (Baring) **8**:37
Arias tristes (Jiménez) **4**:213; **183**:298
"Arina" (Pilnyak) **23**:211, 213
Aristo, Shakespeare, Corneille (Croce) **37**:127, 131
"The Aristocrat" (Davidson) **24**:164, 186
"Aristocrats" (Douglas) **40**:61, 65, 74, 76, 88
"Aristotle on Wealth and Property" (Wallas) **91**:404
Aristotle's Bellows (Gregory) **1**:334; **176**:34, 39-40
"Arithmetic of Love" (Hippius) **9**:166
Arizona (Thomas) **97**:125-27, 139-40
The Ark Sakura (Abe)
See *Hakobune sakura maru*
Arkansas (Fletcher) **35**:106
"Arkansas Red Haw" (Fletcher) **35**:111
"Arkhip" (Tolstoy) **18**:367-68, 377
The Arm of Gold (Connor) **31**:115-16
"Armada" (Dobson) **79**:37
"The Armadillo" (Bishop) **121**:9, 42, 84
"Der arme Heinrich" (Huch) **13**:249, 252
Der Arme Heinrich (Hauptmann) **4**:196
Der arme Vetter (Barlach) **84**:74-5, 86
"Armed for War" (Davies) **5**:209
Armed with Madness (Butts) **77**:71-2, 75-8, 80, 82-3, 86, 90-2, 94-8, 100, 103-5, 108
Die Armen (Mann) **9**:319, 323, 325, 327-29
"Armenak of Bitlis" (Saroyan) **137**:171
"Armenia" (Mandelstam) **2**:408
"The Armenian & the Armenian" (Saroyan) **137**:187-88, 193
"Armenian Writers" (Saroyan) **137**:151
"Les armes de la douleur" (Éluard) **7**:251; **41**:168
"Les armes des Dieux" (Moréas) **18**:288
"Armistice" (Malamud) **129**:159
"Armod" (Lagerkvist) **144**:221-22
"Armonia" (García Lorca) **181**:65
Armonías, libro de un desterrado (Palma) **29**:254
Armored Cruiser Potemkin (Eisenstein)
See *Bronenosets "Potyomkin"*
"Armorel" (Pickthall) **21**:251-52
"The Armour of Constable Crake" (Warung) **45**:418
Armour Wherein He Trusted (Webb) **24**:468-70, 475, 482-83
"The Armpit" (Huysmans) **69**:25
"Arms and the Boy" (Owen) **5**:363, 366; **27**:206, 210, 212, 217-18
Arms and the Man (Shaw) **3**:387-88, 400-01, 405, 407; **9**:412-13, 420; **21**:309, 311
Armut (Rilke) **195**:179
Army Beef (Adams) **56**:7-8
"The Army Ensign" (Kuprin) **5**:300
Army Life in a Black Regiment (Higginson) **36**:165, 168-71, 173-74
"The Army of a Dream" (Kipling) **17**:212
"The Army of the Rear" (Lawson) **27**:122, 133, 135-36
"Arnaux" (Seton) **31**:259
Arne (Bjoernson) **7**:100-02, 105-07, 110, 112-13, 117-18; **37**:6, 17, 23
Arne's Treasure (Lagerloef) **36**:231, 238, 241, 244, 247-48
Arnljot Gelline (Bjoernson) **7**:100, 102-03, 109; **37**:10, 18, 23, 25
"Arnljot's Yearning for the Ocean" (Bjoernson) **7**:102
Arnold Beer: Das Schicksal eines Juden (Brod) **115**:107-08, 114
Arnold Bennett: Sketches for Autobiography (Bennett) **197**:128, 130, 133
Arnold Waterlow (Sinclair) **11**:414
Ārogya (Tagore) **3**:488-89; **53**:343

Aromas y leyenda (Valle-Inclán) **5**:471-72, 476-77
"Der aromat" (Morgenstern) **8**:305
Around About America (Caldwell) **117**:24-5,
"Around an empty grave" (Calvino)
See "Introno a una fossa vuota"
"Around the Birches Weaves the Spring, and Even the Elder Feels Its Spell" (Barlach) **48**:124
Around the Cape of the Good Hope: Poems of the Sea (Grieg)
See *Rundt Kap det Gode Haab: Vers fra sjøen*
Around the Moon (Verne)
See *Autour de la lune*
Around the Walls of the Temple (Rozanov) **104**:314
Around the World in Eighty Days (Verne)
See *Le tour du monde en quatre-vingt jours*
Around Theatres (Beerbohm) **24**:112
El arquero divino (Nervo) **11**:395, 402-03
"Arqueros" (García Lorca) **181**:199
"Arrabal" (Borges) **109**:10
"Arrabalera" (Güiraldes) **39**:176
"L'arrabiata" (Heyse) **8**:113-14, 119-21
L'arrache-coeur (Vian) **9**:529, 532-33, 535-37
"Arracombe Wood" (Mew) **8**:296, 298, 300
"Arrangement in Black and White" (Parker) **143**:297, 331-32
Los arrecifes de coral (Quiroga) **20**:211
"An Arrest" (Bierce) **44**:45
"Arrest of Antoñito the Camborio" (García Lorca)
See "Prendimiento de Antoñito el Camborio"
The Arrest of Arsène Lupin (Leblanc)
See *Arsène Lupin contre Herlock Sholmès*
Arrière-saison (Coppee) **25**:124
"The Arrival" (Fletcher) **35**:96
"The Arrival" (Palamas) **5**:384
"Arrival" (Rilke)
See "Ankunft"
"Arrival in Hades" (Södergran) **31**:287
"Arrival in the Country" (Guro)
See "Priezd v derevnju"
The Arrow (Morley) **87**:125
Arrow Forms (Kandinsky) **92**:147
The Arrow Maker (Austin) **25**:18, 23
The Arrow of Gold (Conrad) **1**:202, 218; **6**:121; **13**:113; **25**:77; **43**:116
"The Arrow of Heaven" (Chesterton) **6**:100
Arrowsmith (Lewis) **4**:248-50, 252-55, 257; **13**:328-30, 332-33, 335, 338-40, 346-48, 350-52; **39**:215, 234, 246-47
Arroz y gallo muerto (Pereda) **16**:373
Arroz y tartana (Blasco Ibáñez) **12**:30, 35, 39, 41, 44-5, 47-9
"Ars" (Cavafy) **7**:162
"Ars poetica" (Jozsef) **22**:159, 163-64
"Ars Victrix" (Dobson) **79**:19, 27
Arsène Lupin contre Herlock Sholmès (Leblanc) **49**:193, 196-97
Arsène Lupin, Gentleman-Burglar (Leblanc)
See *Arsène Lupin, gentleman-cambrioleur*
Arsène Lupin, gentleman-cambrioleur (Leblanc) **49**:192, 196
Arsène Lupin versus Holmlock Shears (Leblanc)
See *Arsène Lupin contre Herlock Sholmès*
"Art" (Rosenberg) **12**:308
Art and a Changing Civilisation (Gill) **85**:89
"Art and Answerability" (Bakhtin) **160**:144, 188
Art and Answerability: Early Philosophical Essays (Bakhtin) **160**:152
Art and Artist (Rank)
See *Dev Künstler*
Art and Conscience Today (Pirandello)
See *Arte e coscienza d'oggi*
Art and Death (Artaud) **3**:57-8
"Art and How to Fake It: Advice to the Art-Lorn" (Millay) **169**:237
"Art and Ideas" (Yeats) **116**:319-20
"Art and Morality" (Stephen) **23**:333
Art and Morality (Nishida)
See *Geijutsu to dotoku*
"Art and Morals" (James) **2**:252
Art and Nature (Alexander) **77**:36-7
Art and Reality (Cary) **1**:146; **29**:93, 102; **196**:136-41, 143-44, 149, 154-55, 157, 174, 177
"Art and Revolution" (Gill) **85**:77
"Art and the Individual" (Lawrence) **48**:140-41
"Art and the State" (Keynes) **64**:253
Art as Experience (Dewey) **95**:36, 49, 52-6, 61, 192
"Art as Salvation for Its Characters" (James) **2**:252
"An Art Critic's Estimate of Alfred Stieglitz" (Hartmann) **73**:128
L'Art du theatre (Bernhardt) **75**:38, 46, 70
"L'art et la science" (Jarry) **2**:284
"L'art et l'amour" (Sully Prudhomme) **31**:302
"L'Art et le refuge . . ." (Genet) **128**:167
"Art, etc." (Akutagawa Ryūnosuke) **16**:25
"Art for What's Sake?" (Agee) **180**:89, 91
Art Forms in Nature (Haeckel) **83**:145, 147
"Art in America" (Fuller) **103**:63, 106, 108, 113
"Art in Education" (Collingwood) **67**:125
"Art in the Light of Conscience" (Tsvetaeva) **7**:570-71; **35**:406
Art in the Light of Mystery Wisdom (Steiner)
See *Die kunst der rezitation und deklamation*
"Art, Life, and the Ideal" (James) **2**:252
L'art moderne (Huysmans) **7**:405, 412; **69**:6, 9-10, 27, 32
The Art of Being Ruled (Lewis) **2**:391; **9**:237, 240-42; **104**:162-65, 175, 186-87, 189, 192, 194-98, 201, 203-04, 211-12, 226, 231, 233-39, 241, 243-44, 250-51, 299
"The Art of Biography" (Bradford) **36**:60
"The Art of Biography" (Woolf) **56**:381
"The Art of Building up Free Men" (Iqbal) **28**:182
The Art of Comedy (de Filippo) **127**:290
The Art of Creation: Essays on the Self and Its Powers (Carpenter) **88**:80-1, 101, 108-9
The Art of Criticism (James) **171**:146
"The Art of Cutting Metals" (Taylor) **76**:343-44, 358
The Art of Decorating Dry Goods Windows (Baum) **132**:24, 29-30, 75, 107
"The Art of Donald McGill" (Orwell) **51**:221-22, 247-49; **128**:285
The Art of Fiction (Gardner) **195**:144, 149
"The Art of Fiction" (James) **40**:116, 143, 148, 160-61; **47**:152
"Art of Fiction" (Kerouac) **117**:205, 270
"The Art of Fiction" (Woolf) **20**:430; **43**:394
The Art of Fiction (James) **171**:179
Art of Love (Anderson) **144**:72
Art of Morals (Ellis) **14**:109
"Art of Murder" (Chandler)
See "The Simple Art of Murder"
Art of Murder (Chandler)
See *The Simple Art of Murder*
The Art of Poetry (Valéry) **15**:454-55
The Art of Reading (Orage) **157**:239, 243, 246, 253
"The Art of Reading Myths" (Campbell) **140**:70
The Art of Spiritual Harmony (Kandinsky)
See *Über das Geistige in der Kunst*
"The Art of the Detective Story" (Freeman) **21**:62
"The Art of the Great Race" (Lewis) **104**:157
The Art of the Moving Picture (Lindsay) **17**:236
Art of the Night (Nathan) **18**:308
The Art of the Novel (James) **11**:329; **24**:336
The Art of the Theatre (Bernhardt)
See *L'Art du theatre*
The Art of Thomas Hardy (Johnson) **19**:227, 230, 232-33, 235, 257
The Art of Thought (Wallas) **91**:357, 359, 361, 372, 380-1, 390, 398, 401
The Art of Versification (Sully Prudhomme) **31**:307
"The Art of Writing" (Becker) **63**:76, 79, 82
"Art Photography and Its Relationship to Painting" (Hartmann) **73**:126
Art poétique (Claudel) **2**:109; **10**:121, 130
Art poétique (Jacob) **6**:194-95, 201
"Art That Tries to Depart from Nature" (Natsume) **2**:495
"An Art Wrangler's Aftermath" (Hartmann) **73**:145-46
The Artamonov Business (Gorky)
See *Delo Artmunovykh*
"Artaud le Momo" (Artaud) **3**:51, 58
Arte e coscienza d'oggi (Pirandello) **29**:309, 320
"El arte narrativo y la magia" (Borges) **109**:42, 148
"Arte poética" (Huidobro) **31**:125-26, 136-37, 144
El arte y el revolución (Vallejo) **56**:314
Artemis to Actaeon and Other Verse (Wharton) **129**:361
"An Artesian Well" (Sarton) **120**:304
"Arthur A. Grammar" (Stein) **48**:255
"Arthur Jermyn" (Lovecraft)
See "Facts concerning the Late Arthur Jermyn and His Family"
"Arthur roi passé roi futur" (Apollinaire) **51**:20
"The Artificial Nigger" (O'Connor) **132**:229-30, 232, 239-40, 244, 246, 248, 266, 271-73, 276, 280, 283, 324, 326, 357
The Artificial Nigger, and Other Tales (O'Connor)
See *A Good Man Is Hard to Find and Other Stories*
"Artificial Populations" (Stevens) **45**:349
The Artificial Princess (Firbank) **1**:227
"The Artisan's Prayer" (Gumilev) **60**:272
"Artist" (Andrade) **43**:3
"The Artist" (Blok) **5**:84
"The Artist" (Mencken) **13**:386
The Artist (Fisher) **87**:73
The Artist (Rank)
See *Dev Künstler*
"The Artist and Politics" (Woolf) **43**:395
"The Artist and the Disease of Time" (Ball)
See "De Künstler and die Zietkrankheit"
"The Artist as Cuckold" (Faulkner) **141**:173
Artist, the Ruler: Essays on Art, Culture, and Values (p'Bitek) **149**:90-91
"Un artista" (Pereda) **16**:367
"Artist-Devil" (Balmont) **11**:30, 40
"The Artistic Career of Corky" (Wodehouse) **108**:372
"Artistik" (Benn) **3**:106
"The Artist's Model" (Bennett) **197**:77
"An Artist's Story" (Chekhov) **3**:160; **10**:108
"The Artless Age" (Glasgow) **7**:343
Art-Nonsense and Other Essays (Gill) **85**:53, 78, 89
"Arts de fête et de cérémonie" (Péret) **20**:198
Arturo, la estrella más brillante (Arenas) **191**:161, 170-71, 219, 225-26, 228-32
"Aru ahō no isshō" (Akutagawa Ryūnosuke) **16**:32
"Aru asa" (Shiga) **172**:201-2
Aru otoko, sono ane no shi (Shiga) **172**:202, 207, 214-15
Arum Vokzal (Bergelson) **81**:30
"Arunacala-aksara-mana-malai" (Ramana Maharshi) **84**:260, 272
Arunacala-astakam (Ramana Maharshi) **84**:255, 260
Arunacala-pancakam (Ramana Maharshi) **84**:260, 274
Arunacala-pancaratnam (Ramana Maharshi) **84**:274
Arunakala-padigam (Ramana Maharshi) **84**:255, 260

Arundel (Roberts) **23**:228-30, 232-33, 235-36, 238-39, 241-43
"Arusak-i pust-i parda" (Hedāyat) **21**:71, 81
"Arv kyoju no taishoku no ji" (Nishida) **83**:214
Árvácska (Moricz) **33**:243-44, 247, 251
Árvalányok (Moricz) **33**:242
Arvat (Myers) **59**:150
"Arvie Aspinall's Alarm Clock" (Lawson) **27**:119
"Arxierej" (Chekhov) **3**:160; **10**:111, 114-15; **55**:64-5
The Aryan (Ince) **89**:20, 22-3
"Aryeh the Gross" (Bialik) **25**:60
Der Arzt Gion (Carossa) **48**:19-20, 22, 27-8, 30
"As a Bird Out of the Snare" (Fisher) **87**:73
As a Man Grows Older (Svevo)
See *Senilità*
As a Man Thinks (Thomas) **97**:132-34, 139-40
As a Thief in the Night (Freeman) **21**:49-50, 58
"As a Wife Has a Cow: A Love Story" (Stein) **48**:237
"As a World Would Have It" (Robinson) **5**:400
"As between Friends" (Runyon) **10**:435
As Does New Hampshire (Sarton) **120**:303-04
"As Down the Woodland Ways" (Roberts) **8**:321, 326
"As Easy as A B C" (Kipling) **8**:196, 201; **17**:208
"As Far as Abashiri" (Shiga)
See "Abashiri made"
"A's from Propolis" (Khlebnikov)
See "Azy iz uzy"
As God Made Them: Portraits of Some Nineteenth-Century Americans (Bradford) **36**:64
As Husbands Go (Crothers) **19**:73, 78, 80
As I Lay Dying (Faulkner) **141**:38-39, 41, 62, 86-87, 97, 111-12, 139, 190-91; **170**:127-29, 131-32, 144, 164, 234, 247-48, 252-53
"As I Please" (Orwell) **51**:246, 256; **128**:258-60, 263, 286-88; **129**:241, 246
As I Remember It (Cabell) **6**:78
As I Was Going Down Sackville Street (Gogarty) **15**:102, 104, 115, 117-19
"As I Went Down to Havre de Grace" (Wylie) **8**:538
"As, Imperceptibly" (Radnóti) **16**:419
As Impurezas do Branco (Drummond de Andrade) **139**:230
"As in the Good Old Days" (Čapek) **192**:187-88
"As Is the Needle to the Pole" (Rhodes) **53**:316
"As It Was in the Beginning" (Benét) **7**:81
"As Long as It Remains in My Power to Prevent, There Will Be No Blackout of Peace in the United States" (Roosevelt) **93**:184
"As My Anger Ebbs" (Wright) **136**:303
"As One Woman to Another" (Stockton) **47**:313
As Sad as She Is (Onetti)
See *Tan triste como ella*
As the Bee Sucks (Lucas) **73**:166
As the Leaves (Giacosa)
See *Come le foglie*
"As the Team's Head Brass" (Warner) **131**:311
"As the Team's Head-Brass" (Thomas) **10**:450, 461, 463, 469
"As the World Sees" (Wright) **183**:352
"As They Draw to a Close" (Gurney) **33**:96, 98, 103
"As toward Immortality" (Lowell) **8**:236
"As toward One's Self" (Lowell) **8**:236
"As toward War" (Lowell) **8**:236
As We Are (Benson) **27**:12
As We Are Now (Sarton) **120**:219-222, 227, 231-33, 237-40, 242, 247-53, 279-84, 306, 309, 311, 314-15
As We Were (Benson) **27**:12
As We Were (Adamov)
See *Comme nous avons été*
As Well as Before, Better than Before (Pirandello)
See *Come prima, meglio di prima*
As You Desire Me (Pirandello)
See *Come tu mi vuoi*
"As You Like It" (Chopin) **127**:215
El asalto (Arenas) **191**:158-59, 161-62, 199-202, 204-09, 217-19
"Asaph" (Stockton) **47**:327
Asas (Sá-Carneiro) **83**:401
"Ascent" (Morgenstern)
See "Auffahrt"
"The Ascent of the Spear" (Williams) **1**:512
Ascents (Sologub)
See *Voskhozhdeniia*
Asclepigenia (Valera y Alcala-Galiano) **10**:503, 505, 508
"The Ascrean" (Palamas) **5**:377, 380, 383, 385, 387
"Ascription" (Roberts) **8**:318
"Ascuas" (Vallejo) **56**:294
"The Ash of Generations and the Eternal Fire" (Gibran) **9**:91
The Ash Tree (Balmont)
See *Iasen'*
Ash Wednesday (Csáth) **13**:147, 149
Ash Wednesday (Erskine) **84**:160
Ashe of Rings (Butts) **77**:70-1, 103, 105
Ashes (Bely)
See *Pepel'*
Ashes (Deledda)
See *Cenere*
"Ashes of Descending Incense: First Brazier" (Chang) **184**:106, 108, 139
"Ashes of Descending Incense: Second Brazier" (Chang) **184**:106-10, 138
Ashes of Empire (Chambers) **41**:91
"Ashes of Life" (Millay) **4**:307
"Ashes of the Beacon" (Bierce) **44**:7-9, 14
Die Äshetik des Widerstands (Weiss) **152**:276-80
"Ashoka Blossoms" (Naidu) **80**:272, 280
"Ashputtle or The Mother's Ghost" (Carter) **139**:99
"The Ash-Tree" (James) **6**:213, 215
Así que pasen cinco años (García Lorca) **1**:309, 314, 320; **9**:292-93, 300; **49**:88, 105, 117; **181**:17, 41, 44-45, 123, 137-38, 140, 142, 146-48
"Así y todo . . ." (Pardo Bazán) **189**:226-27
"Asides on the Oboe" (Stevens) **12**:383-84; **45**:269-73, 296
"Ašikovanje" (Andrić) **135**:85
"Asir-i faransaui" (Hedāyat) **21**:72
Ask for Ronald Standish (Sapper) **44**:317
"Ask That Man" (Benchley) **55**:13, 17
"Aska and the Wolf" (Andrić)
See "Aska i vuk"
"Aska i vuk" (Andrić) **135**:24, 52, 62, 89
"Asked and Answered" (Cullen) **37**:169
Asketeke (Kazantzakis) **33**:148
Askitikí (Kazantzakis)
See *Salvatores Dei: Asketike*
Asklipios (Sikelianos) **39**:419
"Asleep" (Owen) **5**:372; **27**:206, 212, 217-18, 222
"Asmodel" (Crowley) **7**:203
"Asobi" (Mori Ogai) **14**:369-70, 379
"Aspasia" (Dowson) **4**:85
"An Aspect of My Twenties" (Shiga)
See "Nijudai ichimen"
Aspectos da literatura brasileira (Andrade) **43**:9-10, 12-14, 16
Aspects of Fiction and other Ventures in Criticism (Matthews) **95**:263
Aspects of Jewish Power in the United States (Ford) **73**:93
Aspects of Literature (Murry) **16**:332, 338, 340, 343, 355
Aspects of Sociology (Adorno) **111**:53
Aspects of the Novel (Forster) **125**:32, 118, 128-31, 133, 162-64, 166-67, 183
"Aspens" (Thomas) **10**:464, 468
The Aspern Papers (James) **11**:342-44; **24**:327; **47**:171, 195, 200
The Aspirant (Dreiser) **10**:196
"Aspirations" (Rosenberg) **12**:292
The Aspirations of Jean Servien (France)
See *Le désirs de Jean Servien*
"Asra" (Strindberg) **8**:407
Asrar-i khudi (Iqbal) **28**:180-84, 193-94
"The Ass" (Lawrence) **93**:58
"The Assassination of Escovedo" (Lang) **16**:254
L'assassinio di via Belpoggio (Svevo) **2**:539; **35**:364
The Assault (Arenas)
See *El asalto*
"Assault" (Millay) **4**:306; **49**:225-27
"Assault Convoy" (Lewis) **3**:289-90
"Un assenza" (Ginzburg) **156**:14, 63, 73, 112
Assez (Beckett) **145**:94-95, 97
"Assisi" (D'Annunzio) **6**:139
The Assistant (Malamud) **129**:63, 66-7, 69, 71, 73-4, 84, 87-8, 91-2, 94-5, 99, 106, 111-12, 116-17, 120, 123-25, 142, 159, 167, 175-83, 187, 189, 193, 195, 197, 205-8; **184**:158-60, 164-68, 171, 173-75, 177-78, 183-84, 186, 198, 203, 221, 223-25, 236-38, 244, 259, 264-69, 271, 275, 278, 281-83, 285-87, 290-92, 299-300
The Associate Hermits (Stockton) **47**:327
L'Assomoir (Pardo Bazán) **189**:237
L'assommoir (Zola) **41**:408-09, 413, 415, 422, 425-29, 431, 435-39, 444, 448-49, 451, 453; **1**:587-88, 591-96; **6**:558-59, 561-64, 567-68, 570; **21**:414-16, 418-21, 424-26, 428, 430, 437, 442-46, 449-52; **41**:408-09, 413, 415, 422, 425-29, 431, 435-
"Assonances" (Moréas) **18**:286
"Assumptia Maria" (Thompson) **4**:435
"Assunta" (Tozzi) **31**:325
"The Assyrian" (Saroyan) **137**:181, 187
The Assyrian (Saroyan) **137**:157-58
Az asszony beleszól (Moricz) **33**:242-43
"Astern" (Benn) **3**:113
Asthetische Theorie (Adorno) **111**:27-33, 36,42-3, 53-4, 65-8, 73, 75, 84, 88-94, 98-104, 120, 140, 178, 196
"Das ästhetische Wiesel" (Morgenstern) **8**:305
El astillero (Onetti) **131**:133, 135, 140, 143, 148-49, 153, 157-60, 162, 166, 178, 181-83, 195, 205-11, 214, 218, 231, 245, 263, 290, 294, 296
"Astræa" (Guiney) **41**:215, 222, 229
"Astrid" (Noyes) **7**:503
"Astro" (Huidobro) **31**:135
"Astrology" (Crowley) **7**:208
"Astrology" (Lasker-Schueler) **57**:331
"Astros" (Jiménez) **183**:263
"At a Bridal" (Hardy) **53**:81
"At a Calvary near the Ancre" (Owen) **5**:367, 372-73; **27**:203, 211-12, 215-16, 236
"At a Country Hotel" (Nemerov) **124**:180, 249-51
"At a Lunar Eclipse" (Hardy) **143**:145
"At a Month's End" (Swinburne) **8**:441; **36**:319-20
"At a Mountain Resort" (Anwar)
See "Puntjak"
"At a Pantomine" (Gilbert) **3**:217
"At a Parting" (Cullen) **4**:43; **37**:168
"At Abdul Ali's Grave" (Benson) **27**:19
"At Algeciras—A Meditation upon Death" (Yeats) **116**:336
"At Apollinaire's Grave" (Ginsberg) **120**:35
"At Assisi" (Moody) **105**:220
"At Batko Makhno's" (Babel)
See "U bat'ki nashego Makhno"
"At Carmel" (Austin) **25**:34
"At Castle Boterel" (Hardy) **53**:93, 95, 111-2; **143**:145
"At Charing Cross" (Stringer) **37**:329, 343
"At Chênière Caminada" (Chopin) **127**:9
"At Cheshire Cheese" (Dunbar) **12**:105
"At Dalmary" (Graham) **19**:131
"At Darien Bridge" (Dickey) **151**:169
"At Dawn" (Naidu) **80**:343

"At Daybreak" (Calvino) **183**:128
"At Dead of Night" (Coleridge) **73**:13
"At Delphi" (Sarton) **120**:304
"At Dusk" (Naidu) **80**:343
"At Dusk" (Reese) **181**:344
At Eighty-Two: A Journal (Sarton) **120**:318-19
"At Eleusis" (Swinburne) **36**:299, 332-33
"At Entering the New Year" (Hardy) **53**:101
"At Fathpur Sikir" (Sarton) **120**:265
At Fault (Chopin) **5**:141-42, 144-45, 150; **14**:60, 62, 65-8, 80-1; **127**:75, 128, 165, 167-69, 171-72, 175-76, 194, 216-17
"At First Sight" (de la Mare) **53**:17, 27, 35
At First Sight (de la Mare) **53**:16
"At Friends with Life" (Markham) **47**:286
"At Galway Races" (Yeats) **93**:351
"At Geisenheimer's" (Wodehouse) **108**:394
"At Gibraltar" (Woodberry) **73**:368
"At Gull Lake: August, 1810" (Scott) **6**:394, 396
At Home Again (Grieg) **10**:205
"At Home in Auschwitz" (Borowski)
See "Auschwitz, Our Home"
"At Home in the Ozarks" (Lane) **177**:282
"At Home with Nature" (Eastman) **55**:164
"At Home With the Editor" (Bok) **101**:22
"At Howli Thana" (Kipling) **8**:185
"At Kinosaki" (Shiga)
See "Kinosaki nite"
"At Laban's Well" (Coppard) **5**:180
"At Lehmann's" (Mansfield) **8**:282; **39**:297-98, 300; **164**:325
"At les eboulements" (Scott) **6**:393
"At Melville's Tomb" (Crane) **2**:125; **5**:184; **80**:182
"At Midnight" (Teasdale) **4**:428
"At Monastery Gates" (Meynell) **6**:294
"At Newport" (Forten) **16**:150
"At Night" (Korolenko) **22**:170, 173
"At Night" (Rosenberg) **12**:299-300, 311
"At Night" (Santos) **156**:310
At Night (Kraus)
See *Nachts*
At Night in the Old Market Place (Peretz) **16**:398, 400
"At Nikola's" (Pilnyak)
See "U Nikoly, čto na Belyx Kolodezjax"
At One's Goal (Bernhard)
See *Am Ziel*
"At Peles" (Caragiale) **76**:156
"At Plangeant's Locks" (Scott) **6**:398
"At Pozzuoli" (Roberts) **8**:319
"At Rest" (Kuprin) **5**:298
"At Saint Judas's" (Fuller) **103**:63, 88-89
"At Scarboro Beach" (Scott) **6**:385
"At Sea" (Percy) **84**:203
"At Sea" (Toomer) **172**:277
"At Sea" (Welch) **22**:456
At Seventy, Journal of a Solitude (Sarton) **120**:245-47, 268, 280, 283-85, 319-21
"At Shaft 11" (Dunbar) **2**:128; **12**:107, 109, 120, 122
"At St. Valentine's Church" (Babel)
See "U sviatogo Valenta"
At Storhove (Bjoernson)
See *På Storhove*
"At Sugar Camp" (Guest) **95**:205
"At Sunrise" (Bialik) **25**:50
At Sunset (Howe) **21**:109-10
"At Sunwich Port" (Jacobs) **22**:107
"At Teague Poteet's: A Sketch of the Hog Mountain Range" (Harris) **2**:209
"At the Airport" (Nemerov) **124**:180
"At the Aquatic Sports" (Hardy) **53**:117
At the Back of Beyond (Zamyatin)
See *Na kulichkakh*
At the Back of the North Wind (MacDonald) **9**:290, 292, 300, 306-08; **113**:212-14, 217, 221, 225, 259, 261-63, 265-66, 279-80, 286-88, 290-91, 301, 313-28
"At the Bay" (Mansfield) **2**:446, 450-51, 458; **8**:275, 280-81, 285, 292-93; **39**:295, 301, 303-08, 318-19, 322-24, 329-30; **164**:241, 248-49, 253, 255, 266-68, 270-71, 273-74, 295-97, 299-302, 309, 326-28, 332-37, 340
"At the Bedside of a Dying Man" (Peretz)
See "By a Dying Man's Pillow"
"At the Blacksmith's House" (Shimazaki Toson) **5**:439
At the Boundary (Ingamells) **35**:129
At the Brink (Artsybashev)
See *Breaking Point*
"At the Burial of Cardinal Manning" (Johnson) **19**:246
"At the Burnt Stump" (Prishvin) **75**:214
"At the 'Cadian Ball" (Chopin) **14**:64-5; **127**:23, 206-7
"At the Café Door" (Cavafy) **2**:98
At the Campfire (Lagerkvist)
See *Vid lägereld*
"At the Cavour" (Symons) **11**:445
"At the Cedars" (Scott) **6**:388-89, 393, 396-97
"At the Circus" (Kuprin) **5**:304-05
"At the Coffin" (Annensky)
See "U groba"
"At the Death of a Philosopher" (Babits)
See "Egy filozófus halálára"
At the Depot (Bergelson)
See *About the Depot*
At the Dnieper (Bergelson)
See *Baym Dnieper*
At the Dnieper: Young Years (Bergelson)
See *Baym Dnieper*
"At the Doctors" (Andrić)
See "Kod lekara"
At the Earth's Core (Burroughs) **2**:81
At the Edge of Life (Kubin) **23**:95
"At the End of the Passage" (Kipling) **8**:191, 195, 198
At the Exit (Pirandello)
See *All'uscita*
"At the Fair" (Kielland) **5**:275-76
At the Feet of Venus (Blasco Ibáñez)
See *A los piés de Venus*
"At the Ferry" (Scott) **6**:389
"At the Fireside" (Gumilev)
See "U kamina"
"At the Fishhouses" (Bishop) **121**:3, 5, 21-2, 27, 56
"At the Foot of Hemlock Mountain" (Fisher) **87**:72
"At the Forks" (Agee) **180**:5, 33, 36
"At the Fox's Ball" (Remizov) **27**:351
At the Gate (Pirandello)
See *All'uscita*
"At the Gate of the Valley" (Herbert) **168**:27, 46
At the Gates of the Kingdom (Hamsun)
See *La vie de Michel-Ange*
At the German Meetingplace (Éluard)
See *Au rendez-vous allemand*
"At the Great Release" (Carman) **7**:137, 139
At the Hawk's Well (Yeats) **1**:562, 570-71; **93**:341, 364
"At the Hazy Dawn of Youth" (Platonov)
See "Na zare tumannoy yunosti"
"At the House of Suddhoo" (Kipling) **8**:176, 185
"At the Lattice" (Scott) **6**:385
"At the Meeting of Seven Valleys" (Markham) **47**:278
At the Mermaid Inn (Campbell) **9**:33-6
"At the Mosque" (Anwar)
See "Dimesjid"
"At the Mountains of Madness" (Lovecraft) **4**:267-68, 274; **22**:215, 219, 238
"At the Palace Tonight" (Barthes)
See "Au Palais ce soir"
"At the Piano" (Green) **63**:135
"At the Piano" (Scott) **6**:387, 389
"At the Portagee's" (La Guma) **140**:205, 238
"At the Railroad Station on an Autumn Morning" (Carducci)
See "Alla Stazione in una Mattina d'Autunno"
"At the Sea" (Przybyszewski) **36**:282
At the Shrine of St. Charles: Stray Papers on Lamb Brought Together for the Centenary of His Death in 1834 (Lucas) **73**:173
At the Sign of the Eagle (Vallette) **67**:271
At the Sign of the Lyre (Dobson) **79**:2-3, 5, 24
"At the Sign of the Savage" (Howells) **17**:179
"At the Source" (Glaspell) **175**:144
"At the Sources of the Clitumnus" (Carducci)
See "Alle fonti del Clitumno"
"At the Station on an Autumn Morning" (Carducci)
See "Alla Stazione in una Mattina d'Autunno"
"At the Table" (Coppee) **25**:121
"At the Theatre" (Cavafy) **2**:98
"At the Threshold" (Ivanov) **33**:138
"At the Top of the Voice" (Mayakovski) **4**:298-300; **18**:246, 248, 262, 267, 271
At the Turn of the Century (Bely) **7**:49
"At the Turn of the Road" (Glaspell) **175**:53-54
"At the Urn of Percy Bysshe Shelley" (Carducci)
See "By the Urn of P. B. Shelley"
"At the Wailing Wall in Jerusalem" (Cullen) **37**:155
At the Walls of the Unseen City (Prishvin) **75**:215
"At the Water" (Roberts) **68**:336
"At the Window" (Wetherald) **81**:408
"At the World's End" (Zamyatin)
See *Na kulichkakh*
"At the Zoo" (Carter) **139**:206
"At the Zoo" (Hagiwara) **60**:299
"At This Time When the World Is Threatened by Forces of Destruction, It Is My Resolve and Yours to Build Up Our Armed Defenses" (Roosevelt) **93**:184
"At Tide Water" (Roberts) **8**:318, 325
"At Twilight: On the Way to Golconda" (Naidu) **80**:275
"At Venerable Upsala" (Heidenstam) **5**:252
"At Waking" (Wetherald) **81**:411
Atalanta in Calydon (Swinburne) **8**:423, 425-26, 430-31, 434-38, 441, 445-46; **36**:295, 300-01, 308, 311-14, 316, 320-21, 331-32, 341
Atalanta in Wimbledon (Dunsany) **59**:23
"Atama Narabi ni Hara" (Yokomitsu) **47**:390, 395
"Atavism" (Stringer) **37**:343
"Atavism" (Wylie) **8**:521, 533-34
"An Atavist Rat" (Jozsef) **22**:163
"At-Davan" (Korolenko) **22**:170, 174, 182
Der Atem (Bernhard) **165**:60
Der Atem (Mann) **9**:326
Der Atem: Eine Entscheidung (Bernhard)
See *Der Atem*
"Atenea política" (Reyes) **33**:323
El atentado (Ibarguengoitia) **148**:201-8, 214, 216
"The Athanor" (Crowley) **7**:208
"Athassel Abbey" (Guiney) **41**:205
"Athénaïse" (Chopin) **5**:142, 147, 153, 158; **14**:61, 70-2, 81-2; **127**:110-11, 113, 187-90, 194, 198, 227, 229
Athènes et Jérusalem: un essai de philosophie religieuse (Shestov) **56**:254-56, 259-260, 262-64
"Athens" (Quiller-Couch) **53**:290
Athens and Jerusalem (Shestov)
See *Athènes et Jérusalem: un essai de philosophie religieuse*
Atheological Summa (Bataille)
See *La somme athéologique*
"Atherton's Gambit" (Robinson) **5**:404; **101**:112
Atilla (Zamyatin) **8**:549; **37**:429, 433

"Atlanta Blues" (Handy) **97**:42, 44
Atlanta Offering Poems (Harper) **14**:263
Atlanterhavet (Grieg) **10**:206, 209
The Atlantic (Grieg)
See *Atlanterhavet*
"Atlantic City Waiter" (Cullen) **4**:40, 45, 50; **37**:141, 152-53
Atlantic Essays (Higginson) **36**:170
"The Atlantic Ocean" (Mayakovski) **18**:258
"Atlantica" (Leino) **24**:370
"Atlantis" (Bottomley) **107**:7
"Atlantis" (Crane) **2**:112, 121; **5**:186-88, 190; **80**:82-3, 87, 89, 92, 96, 100, 103, 113, 117, 125-6,134-5, 139-40, 142-3, 147, 157, 162-7, 172, 178, 186, 191-2, 199
"Atlantis" (Spitteler) **12**:339
Atlantis (Hauptmann) **4**:195-96
Atlas (Borges) **109**:117-18
"Atlas and Gazetteer of the West China Shore" (Engel) **137**:123
"Atomo verde número cinco" (Donoso) **133**:149, 151-52, 154-55
"Atrophy" (Wharton) **129**:364
"Att döda ett barn" (Dagerman) **17**:89
"The Attack" (Gumilev)
See "Nastuplenie"
"An Attack of Nerves" (Chekhov)
See "Pripadok"
"The Attack on Western Morality" (Benda) **60**:51
"Attacks" (Stein) **48**:234
"Attaque du moulin" (Zola) **6**:568
"Attente" (Roumain) **19**:339
L'attente de Dieu (Weil) **23**:371, 373, 380, 393-94, 404
"Attentiveness and Obedience" (Nemerov) **124**:291-92
"Attic" (Sikelianos) **39**:419
Attila, My Attila (Field) **43**:173-74
Atto unico (Svevo) **35**:369, 371
"Attorney Sneak" (Buchanan) **107**:79
"Atys, the Land of Biscay" (Housman) **10**:247
"Au 125 du boulevard Saint Germain" (Péret) **20**:201
Au Bonheur des dames (Pardo Bazán) **189**:237
Au bonheur des dames (Zola) **1**:589; **6**:559, 563-64; **41**:412, 438, 451
Au bord de l'eau (Kandinsky) **92**:48
Au coeur frais de la forêt (Lemonnier) **22**:199-200
Au juste (Lyotard) **103**:151, 157, 159-65, 167-68, 175, 198, 201, 206, 219, 232, 241, 260
"Au Maroc" (Loti) **11**:361
Au milieu du chemin (Rod) **52**:309-10, 312, 324
"Au mocassin le verbe" (Desnos) **22**:60
"Au Palais ce soir" (Barthes) **135**:162, 174
"Au petit jour" (Desnos) **22**:61
"Au peuple allemand" (Verhaeren) **12**:471
"Au platane" (Valéry) **15**:468
"Au prolétaire" (Apollinaire) **3**:43
"Au reichstag" (Verhaeren) **12**:471
Au rendez-vous allemand (Éluard) **7**:246, 248-49, 251, 257
"Au Revoir" (Dobson) **79**:27
Au service de l'Allemagne (Barrès) **47**:38, 45, 70
"Au sujet d'euréka" (Valéry) **4**:494
"L'aube" (Manning) **25**:277
L'aube (Rolland) **23**:261
L'Auberge rouge (Epstein) **92**:2-3
Les aubes (Verhaeren) **12**:458, 464, 469, 472, 478-83
Aucassin and Nicolete (Lang) **16**:265
Auch ich habe in Arkadien gelebt (Bachmann) **192**:144
The Auctioneer (Belasco) **3**:90
"Auction-Model 1934" (Fitzgerald) **52**:56
Audacity (Williams) **89**:360
El audaz (Pérez Galdós) **27**:265, 282, 288
"L'au-delà du sérieux" (Bataille) **155**:88
"Au-dessus de la mêlée" (Rolland) **23**:262, 279
"Audi alteram partem" (Gray) **19**:145
"The Audience" (Meynell) **6**:296
The Audience (García Lorca)
See *El público*
Audrey Craven (Sinclair) **11**:407, 413
Audubon (Rourke) **12**:321, 323
"Auf das Opfer darf keiner sich berufen" (Bachmann) **192**:70
Auf der Erde und in der Holle (Bernhard) **165**:95
"Auf der Galerie" (Kafka) **112**:111
"Auf der Marschinsel" (Liliencron) **18**:213
"Auf meinem Gute" (Liliencron) **18**:217
Auf vielen Wegen (Morgenstern) **8**:309
"Aufarbeitung der Vergangenheit" (Adorno) **111**:51
"Auferstehung" (Mann) **9**:320-21, 331
"Auferstehung des Gewissens" (Böll) **185**:189
Auferstehung des Gewissens (Böll) **185**:158
"Auffahrt" (Morgenstern) **8**:309
"Die Auffahrt" (Spitteler) **12**:350
Der aufhaltsame aifstieg des Arturo Ui (Brecht) **1**:104; **6**:37
Der aufhaltsame Augstieg des Arturo Ui (Brecht) **169**:26
Auf'n opgrunt (Asch) **3**:68, 72
"Die Aufnahme in den Orden" (George) **14**:209
"Aufruf (ein Epos)" (Schwitters) **95**:326, 330-1
Aufsatze zur Gesellschaftstheorie (Adorno) **111**:52
Aufstieg und Fall der Stadt Mahagonny (Brecht) **1**:107, 114-15, 122; **6**:31, 36; **169**:37, 52-53, 55
Aufzeichnungen (Canetti) **157**:96, 98, 100-101
Die Aufzeichnungen des Malte Laurids Brigge (Rilke) **1**:409, 412, 417-18, 421, 423; **6**:359, 364, 366-68; **19**:299-312, 316, 318-27; **195**:163, 167, 179-80, 183, 193, 195-98, 221, 259, 265, 285, 290-91, 298-99, 320-22, 326-28
Die Augen des Ewigen Bruders (Zweig) **17**:434, 436-37
"Augenblink" (Sarton) **120**:271
Das Augenspiel: Lebensgeschichte 1931-1937 (Canetti) **157**:20-21, 23, 35, 37, 63, 68, 77, 80, 83, 97, 107, 110
"The Augsburg Adoration" (Jarrell) **177**:162
"Auguries" (Rosenberg) **12**:299
"Auguries of Experience" (Frye) **165**:226
"August" (Babits)
See "Augusztus"
"August" (Belloc) **18**:40
"August" (Pasternak) **188**:189-90, 194
"August" (Riley) **51**:294, 297
"August" (Schulz) **5**:422; **51**:308, 311, 319
"August" (Wylie) **8**:532-34
August (Hamsun) **14**:241; **49**:130
"August, 1914" (Rosenberg) **12**:302-03, 307, 312
"August, 1945" (Nemerov) **124**:182
"August Heat" (Tynan) **3**:506
August Holiday (Pavese)
See *Feria d'agosto*
"An August Midnight" (Hardy) **53**:94-5; **143**:144
"August Night" (Roberts) **68**:302, 336
"An August Reverie" (Campbell) **9**:29
"Auguste Rodin. Zweiter Teil" (Rilke) **195**:285, 292
"August Third" (Sarton) **120**:305
"An August Wood Rood" (Roberts) **8**:321
Auguste Bolte (Schwitters) **95**:302, 352-3
Auguste Strindberg (Adamov) **189**:58
Augustus (Buchan) **41**:59-60, 63-4
"Augusztus" (Babits) **14**:39
Augzeichnungen (Canetti) **157**:69
Auld Licht Idylls (Barrie) **2**:45, 47; **164**:14-15, 61-62
L'aumonyme (Desnos) **22**:59-60, 72
"Aunt Cynthy Dallett" (Jewett) **22**:142
"Aunt Ellen" (Kipling) **8**:202-03
"Aunt Hagars Children" (Handy) **97**:40, 42
"Aunt Imogen" (Robinson) **101**:119, 125, 130
Aunt Jane's Nieces (Baum) **7**:26
"Aunt Mandy's Investment" (Dunbar) **12**:120
"Aunt Mary" (McAlmon) **97**:89
"Aunt Mary's Pie Plant" (Gilman) **117**:77-8
"Aunt Sonya's Sofa" (Kuzmin) **40**:203
"Aunt Tempy's Triumph" (Dunbar) **12**:106-07
Aunts Aren't Gentlemen (Wodehouse) **108**:342, 344, 356
The Aunt's Story (White) **176**:125, 127-29, 131, 142-44, 171, 175-79, 183-86, 189, 199, 219, 228, 235, 238-40, 248, 272, 275, 296, 306-7
"The Aurelian" (Nabokov) **108**:52
"Auringon hyvästijättö" (Leino) **24**:371, 378
"La aurora" (García Lorca) **49**:94; **181**:28; **197**:238-39, 247, 261
Aurora Floyd (Braddon) **111**:210-11, 215, 230-32, 238, 240-43, 262-63, 285, 305
Aurora roja (Baroja) **8**:48, 50, 52
"The Auroras of Autumn" (Stevens) **12**:365; **45**:285, 299-300, 307, 311, 337, 350
"Aus Bimbos Seelenwanderungen" (Huch) **13**:249
Aus dem bürgerlichen Heldenleben (Sternheim) **8**:373, 377-78, 382
"Aus der Ferne" (Lasker-Schueler) **57**:315
Aus der Triumphgasse: Lebensskizzen (Huch) **13**:240-41, 243-44, 246, 252
"Aus der Welt Merz, a dialogue with interventions of the public" (Schwitters) **95**:339
Aus einem Lesebuch für Städtebewohner gehörige Gedichte (Brecht) **169**:37
"Aus einem Tagebuch des Jahres 1920" (Hesse) **196**:324
"Aus einer Sturmnacht" (Rilke) **195**:181, 267
Aus Indien (Hesse) **196**:259
Aus Insulinde (Haeckel) **83**:147
Aus Marsch und Geest (Liliencron) **18**:213
Ausbreitung und Verfall der Romantik (Huch) **13**:244, 247, 253
"Auschwitz, Our Home" (Borowski) **9**:21-2, 26-7
"Die Ausdehnung" (Simmel) **64**:323
"La ausencia" (Quiroga) **20**:214
"Ausgang" (Kandinsky) **92**:68
"Die Ausgelieferten" (Borchert) **5**:104
Auslöschung (Bernhard) **165**:21, 89-90, 96, 98, 102, 108-9, 111, 119
"Auspicious Look" (Tagore) **3**:483
"Aussatz" (Böll) **185**:130
Aussatz (Böll) **185**:107, 184
"Aussi bien que les cigales" (Apollinaire) **8**:17-18, 28; **51**:34-5
"The Aussolas Martin Cat" (Somerville & Ross) **51**:385
Austin Friars (Riddell) **40**:335
Australia Felix (Richardson) **4**:372-73, 381-82
Australia for the Australians (Paterson) **32**:371, 380
"Auszug der Erstlinge" (George) **14**:201
"Autarkia" (Manning) **25**:279
The Author (Strindberg) **47**:362
"Author and Hero in Aesthetic Activity" (Bakhtin) **160**:127-28, 144-46, 152, 157
"The Author as Producer" (Benjamin) **39**:42, 51
Author! Author! (Wodehouse) **108**:365, 371, 373
"The Author of Beltraffio" (James) **24**:350; **47**:206
"The Author to His Body on Their Fifteenth Birthday, 29 ii 80" (Nemerov) **124**:277
The Authoress of the 'Odyssey' (Butler) **1**:134; **33**:29, 34
The Authoritarian Personality (Adorno) **111**:49, 51, 54, 134
Authority in the Modern State (Laski) **79**:77, 104, 106
"An Author's Answer to His Critics" (Dixon) **163**:196
The Author's Craft (Bennett) **5**:46; **20**:38; **197**:14, 21, 36, 38, 52, 66, 88-92, 108

"Author's Introduction" (Abbey) **160**:20, 49
"Author's Note" (Paton) **165**:305
"Author's Outline" (McCullers) **155**:233, 237
"Author's Prologue" (Thomas) **8**:454; **45**:362-63, 381, 401, 405; **105**:322, 336
Autobiografia (Saba) **33**:370, 373
"Autobiografija" (Andrić) **135**:57-59, 61
"An Autobiographical Essay: Family and Childhood" (Borges) **109**:18, 57, 130, 154
"Autobiographical Note" (Bataille) **155**:104
Autobiographical Notes (Einstein)
See *Autobiographisches*
"Autobiographical Poem of the Author at Forty" (Lin) **149**:346
An Autobiographical Sketch (Lawrence) **93**:32, 60
Autobiographical Writings (Hesse) **148**:172, 181
Autobiographies (Yeats) **1**:555, 564, 567; **11**:520; **18**:443, 453; **31**:399, 409; **93**:363, 366, 369, 401; **116**:222-34
Autobiographisches (Einstein) **65**:92, 122-26
"The Autobiography" (Andrić)
See "Autobiografija"
"Autobiography" (Moore) **89**:195
Autobiography (Bradford) **36**:69
Autobiography (Bryan) **99**:30
Autobiography (Chesterton) **6**:103; **64**:32, 44, 49
Autobiography (Collingwood) **67**:98-100, 102, 106, 124, 131-32, 139, 146, 152, 154, 171-72, 182, 194
An Autobiography (Croce) **37**:123-24
Autobiography (Gill) **85**:60, 68-77, 88-9
Autobiography (James) **171**:197
Autobiography (Milne) **88**:229
An Autobiography (Muir) **87**:154-55, 161-63, 170, 183, 185, 187, 191, 194-98, 201, 206, 214-15, 217, 233, 242, 253-54, 274, 281, 284, 286-89, 294-96, 299-300, 306
Autobiography (Sinclair) **160**:247, 261, 276-77
Autobiography (Twain) **185**:233, 298
An Autobiography (Wright) **95**:394, 397, 402-3, 405, 411
Autobiography of a Damned Fool (Twain) **161**:289
"The Autobiography of a Quack" (Mitchell) **36**:264
The Autobiography of a Super-Tramp (Davies) **5**:198, 200, 205-08
The Autobiography of Alice B. Toklas (Stein) **1**:430-31, 434, 442; **6**:404-06, 410, 412, 415; **28**:313-14, 318, 320, 324, 326, 333-34, 342; **48**:209, 214, 218-22, 236, 240, 245-49, 251-52, 255-56, 258, 260-61, 263
"Autobiography of an American Jew" (Cahan) **71**:44
The Autobiography of an American Novelist (Wolfe) **13**:496
The Autobiography of an Attitude (Nathan) **18**:324
The Autobiography of an Ex-Colored Man (Johnson) **3**:240-42, 247-49; **19**:204, 209, 212, 214-17, 220-21, 223-24; **175**:165, 167, 169-70, 173, 176-85, 188-91, 195, 197, 200, 203, 205-7, 210-11, 213-20, 222-28, 230, 232, 234, 238-48, 251
"The Autobiography of Aureola" (Phelps) **113**:342
The Autobiography of Lincoln Steffens (Steffens) **20**:338-52, 354, 364-65
The Autobiography of Malcolm X (Haley) **147**:152, 213, 219-20
The Autobiography of Mark Rutherford, Dissenting Minister (Rutherford) **25**:334-35, 337-40, 342, 345-46, 350, 353, 355-56, 358-59, 361-64
The Autobiography of W. E. B. Du Bois (Du Bois) **169**:84-85, 96-97, 208, 213
The Autobiography of W. E. B. Du Bois: A Soliloquy on Viewing My Life from the Last Decade of Its First Century (Du Bois)
See *The Autobiography of W. E. B. Du Bois*
The Autobiography of Will Rogers (Rogers) **8**:334
The Autobiography of William Butler Yeats (Yeats) **31**:391; **93**:387
Autobiography; or, The Story of My Experiments with Truth (Gandhi) **59**:41, 44, 67, 70, 74, 79
"Ha'Autobus ha'Aharon" (Agnon) **151**:22
"Autochthon" (Masters) **25**:298
"Autochthon" (Roberts) **8**:318, 320-21
"Autoclète" (Jarry) **2**:284
"Autocracy and War" (Conrad) **25**:87
The Autocracy of Mr. Parham: His Remarkable Adventures in This Changing World (Wells) **6**:532; **12**:500
Auto-da-Fé (Canetti)
See *Die Blendung*
"Autoepitafio" (Arenas) **191**:196
Automat svet (Hrabal) **155**:150
"Automatism of Taste" (Tzara) **168**:228
"Automne" (Nelligan) **14**:398
L'automne à Pékin (Vian) **9**:528, 532, 536
"Automne malade" (Apollinaire) **3**:36
Automne régulier (Huidobro) **31**:123, 125, 132
El automóvil (Benavente) **3**:97
"El automóvil de la muerte" (Nervo) **11**:395
"Autopsia del superrealismo" (Vallejo) **56**:319
Autopsias (Ibarguengoitia) **148**:202-3, 207, 217
L'autopsie du Docteur Z. et autres nouvelles (Rod) **52**:309
"Der Autor und das Theater" (Frisch) **121**:232
Autos profanos (Villaurrutia) **80**:466-8
"Autour de la Bible" (Jacob) **6**:191
Autour de la lune (Verne) **6**:493, 499-500; **52**:331-32, 355
"L'Autre Alceste" (Jarry) **147**:263-64
"Autres temps" (Wharton) **9**:546-47; **53**:380; **129**:362, 365; **149**:245
"Autumn" (Campbell) **9**:29
"Autumn" (Davidson) **24**:161
"Autumn" (Davies) **5**:201
"Autumn" (Gumilev) **60**:270
"Autumn" (Hulme) **21**:145
"Autumn" (Lasker-Schueler) **57**:328, 334
"Autumn" (Ledwidge) **23**:112
"Autumn" (Pasternak) **188**:186, 194
"Autumn" (Södergran)
See "Höst"
"Autumn" (Strindberg) **8**:407
"Autumn" (Stringer) **37**:343
"Autumn" (Sudermann) **15**:428
"Autumn" (Wen I-to) **28**:417
Autumn (Reymont) **5**:390-91
"Autumn II" (Mansfield)
See "The Wind Blows"
"Autumn at Taos" (Lawrence) **93**:103
"Autumn Colors" (Wen I-to) **28**:409, 420
"Autumn Day" (Rilke)
See "Herbsttag"
The Autumn Dream (Guro)
See *Osennii son*
"Autumn Elegy" (Merrill) **173**:173
"Autumn Evening in Serbia" (Ledwidge) **23**:121
"Autumn Fields" (Roberts) **68**:336
"Autumn Flowers" (Kuprin) **5**:301
"Autumn Garden" (Campana)
See "Giardino autunnale"
The Autumn Garden (Hellman) **119**:134-35, 140, 142, 144, 164-66, 235
"An Autumn Idyll" (Dobson) **79**:5, 31
An Autumn in Italy (O'Faolain) **143**:233, 239
Autumn Journey (Molnár)
See *Őszi utazás*
Autumn Love (Bradford) **36**:63
"The Autumn Mountain" (Akutagawa Ryūnosuke)
See "Shūzan zu"
"The Autumn of the Flesh" (Yeats) **11**:539
"Autumn on the Riviera" (Levi) **109**:296
"An Autumn Penitent" (Callaghan) **145**:255
"Autumn Refrain" (Stevens) **45**:275, 281-82
"Autumn Song" (Coppard) **5**:177
"Autumn Song" (Naidu) **80**:293, 348
"The Autumn Sonnets" (Sarton) **120**:271-72, 286, 305
"An Autumn Stroll" (Barbellion) **24**:76
"An Autumn Sunset" (Wright) **136**:301
"An Autumn Thrush" (Sterling) **20**:386
"Autumn Valentine" (Parker) **143**:326
Autumn Wind (Natsume)
See *Nowaki*
"Autumn Wisdom" (Percy) **84**:198
"Autumnal" (Dowson) **4**:91
Autumnal Lakes (Kuzmin)
See *Osennie ozera*
Autumnal Roses (Benavente) **3**:94
"Auvergnat" (Belloc) **7**:32
"Aux champs" (Zola) **6**:567
Aux couleurs de Rome (Larbaud) **9**:208
"Aux morts de la république" (Claudel) **10**:122
"Aux sources mêmes de l'espérance" (Giono) **124**:33
"Gli avanguardisti a Mentone" (Calvino) **183**:96
"Avant-Propos" (Adamov) **189**:31
"Avanti! Avanti!" (Carducci) **32**:90, 106
Avanzada (Azuela) **3**:78; **145**:12, 17-18
The Avatars: A Futurist Fantasy (Baker) **10**:22
"Avatars of the Tortoise" (Borges) **109**:74
"Ave" (Carducci) **32**:101
Ave: An Ode for the Centenary of the Birth of Percy Bysshe Shelley, August 4, 1792 (Roberts) **8**:318, 320
"Ave atque Vale" (Swinburne) **36**:320, 329, 337
"Ave Maria" (Crane) **2**:123; **5**:187; **80**:81, 83, 94, 97, 103, 106, 109, 118, 126-7, 139-40, 144, 147, 166-7, 186-7, 202
Ave Ogden!: Nash in Latin (Nash) **109**:356
Ave, sol! (Rainis) **29**:392
Ave Vergil (Bernhard) **165**:95-97
Les aveaux (Bourget) **12**:57, 74
"Avec le coeur du Chêne" (Desnos) **22**:61
The Avenger (Oppenheim) **45**:132, 134
The Avenger (Wallace) **57**:402
Avengers in Space (Kuttner) **10**:268
The Avenging Conscience (Griffith) **68**:203, 217, 236
"L'avenir" (Apollinaire) **51**:37
L'avenir de l'homme (Teilhard de Chardin) **9**:488-89
L'avenir socialiste des syndicats (Sorel) **91**:332
"Una aventura amorosa del Padre Chuecas" (Palma) **29**:262
"Una aventura del rey poeta" (Palma) **29**:256
"Aventuras idiotas del capitán John" (García Lorca) **197**:247
Aventuras, inventos, y mixtificaciones de Silvestre Paradox (Baroja) **8**:61-2
L'Aventure sémiologique (Barthes) **135**:162
Aventures de Jérôme Bardini (Giraudoux) **2**:156, 165; **7**:320, 326
Les Aventures de la dialectique (Merleau-Ponty) **156**:127, 142, 144, 164, 183, 185-86, 213-14
Les aventures du Capitaine Hatteras (Verne) **6**:500, 504; **52**:338, 352
"Aventures d'un orteil" (Péret) **20**:184
"The Avenue" (Shimazaki Toson)
See "Namiki"
"Averroes's Search" (Borges)
See "La busca de Averroes"
"The Averted Strike" (Chesnutt) **39**:98
Avery (Phelps) **113**:337-39
Averyan Myshin's Good Luck (Tolstoy) **18**:378
L'aveu (Adamov) **189**:4, 9, 14-15, 17-18, 48
"L'aveugle" (Desnos) **22**:61

Les aveugles (Maeterlinck) **3**:317, 320, 322, 331-32
"Avevo" (Saba) **33**:368
"Avey" (Toomer) **172**:256, 258, 285
"Avi" (Bialik) **25**:53
"L'Aviateur" (Saint-Exupéry) **169**:335
"Avice" (Dobson) **79**:5
Aviraneta, o la vida de un conspirador (Baroja) **8**:63
Aviraneta; or, The Life of a Conspirator (Baroja)
See *Aviraneta, o la vida de un conspirador*
"Avis" (Scott) **6**:388-89, 393
"Avondgeluiden" (van Ostaijen) **33**:418
Avon's Harvest (Robinson) **5**:415; **101**:110, 134
"Avons-nous changé tout cela" (Strachey) **12**:400
Avonturiers (van Schendel) **56**:241
Avowals (Moore) **7**:480, 491, 496-97
Avril (Belloc) **7**:38
"Avtor i geroi v esteticheskoi deiatel nosti" (Bakhtin) **160**:128
"Avunculus" (Fisher) **87**:73
"L'avventura di due sposi" (Calvino) **183**:214
L'avventura di Maria (Svevo) **35**:353, 370
"L'Avventura di un fotografo" (Calvino) **183**:147, 191
"L'avventura di un poeta" (Calvino) **183**:92-93, 191, 213
"L'Avventura di un soldato" (Calvino) **183**:92-93, 159, 224
"Le Avventure di tre orologiai e di tre automi" (Calvino) **183**:105
"Awake" (Naidu) **80**:287
Awake and Rehearse (Bromfield) **11**:81
"An Awakening" (Anderson) **10**:33; **24**:20, 34, 42, 48-9, 54, 59; **123**:33-4, 40
"Awakening" (Babel)
See "Probuzhdenie"
"Awakening" (Baker) **10**:21
"The Awakening" (Dunsany) **59**:28
The Awakening (Benson) **17**:32
The Awakening (Chopin) **5**:142-59; **14**:57, 59, 61-3, 65, 68-73, 76, 78-83; **127**:3-17, 23-4, 29, 32-3, 35-43, 45-6, 48-50, 52-3, 55, 56, 58, 61, 66-7, 72, 74-7, 79, 81-3, 92, 96, 98, 101, 103, 107-12, 115, 117-20, 123-28, 131, 134, 136-41, 145, 147, 150, 152, 158, 162, 164, 167, 173, 180-81, 183-86, 190, 192, 195, 197-98, 201-2, 207, 209, 211-13, 219, 221, 223, 227, 230
The Awakening of the Waterfall (Tagore)
See *Nirjharer svapnabhanga*
"Aware no otoko" (Shiga) **172**:215
"The Awareness of Mysteries" (Balmont) **11**:29
"Away" (McAlmon) **97**:97
"Away" (Riley) **51**:284
"Away it soars, away it soars" (Arp) **115**:24-5
The Awkward Age (James) **2**:257, 270, 272; **11**:320, 328, 347-48; **40**:149, 169
The Axe (Undset) **3**:511, 519
Axël (Maeterlinck) **3**:328
The Axis of the Earth (Bryusov) **10**:78
Ayesha: The Return of She (Haggard) **11**:246, 255-56
"Ayina-yi shikasta" (Hedāyat) **21**:72
"Azabu Miscellany" (Nagai)
See *Azabu zakki*
Azabu zakki (Nagai) **51**:104
Azamuzakaru no ki (Kunikida Doppo) **99**:296
Azbuka (Tolstoy) **173**:294
"Azef" (Tolstoy) **18**:382
"Azélie" (Chopin) **127**:9, 191
"L'azione parlata" (Pirandello) **172**:175, 188
Aziyadé (Loti) **11**:351, 353-54, 356, 358-60, 363-67
Azrael and Other Poems (Warner) **131**:310-12
Azul (Darío) **4**:57-8, 60, 62, 64-6, 68
"Azure Beavers" (Prishvin) **75**:216
Azure Mountains (Sologub)
See *Lazurnye gory*
"Azy iz uzy" (Khlebnikov) **20**:137
"Baa, Baa, Black Sheep" (Kipling) **8**:182-83, 187-88, 201; **17**:215
Baal (Brecht) **1**:104, 108-09, 118; **6**:35-6, 40-1; **169**:25
Bab: A Sub-Deb (Rinehart) **52**:282
The "Bab" Ballads: Much Sound and Little Sense (Gilbert) **3**:207, 209-10, 212-13, 217
"Baba oğul" (Sait Faik) **23**:294
Babbitt (Lewis) **4**:246-47, 249, 253-55, 257-59, 261; **13**:327-30, 332-33, 335, 338-47, 350, 352-53; **23**:132, 135-37, 139, 151-52; **39**:199-258
The Babe, B. A. (Benson) **27**:8, 12
"Bab'e carstuo" (Chekhov) **3**:159; **10**:108; **163**:10, 129
"Bab'e carstvo" (Chekhov)
See "Bab'e carstuo"
"Babeau" (Giono) **124**:126
Babel (Couperus) **15**:46
"The Babel: Gate of the God" (Bottomley) **107**:5, 7
Babel to Byzantium (Dickey) **151**:93, 95-96, 98-99, 120, 131-33, 145, 164, 200, 203
Babes in the Darkling Wood (Wells) **6**:550
"Babette" (Service) **15**:412
"Babies" (Jerome) **23**:77
"The Baby" (Nash) **109**:362
"Baby" (Remizov)
See "Bebka"
Baby Bullet (Osbourne) **93**:132
The Baby Camels of the Sky (Guro)
See *Nebesye verblyuzhata*
"Baby, I Don't Care" (Holly) **65**:138
"Baby, It's Love" (Holly) **65**:149
"The Baby of the Family" (McAlmon) **97**:114
"The Baby Party" (Fitzgerald) **28**:97
Baby Sister (Himes) **139**:253
"Baby Sketches" (Crane) **11**:140
"The Baby Sorceress" (Higginson) **36**:179
"Baby Sylvester" (Harte) **25**:218
"Baby Tortoise" (Lawrence) **9**:230; **93**:55
"A Baby Tramp" (Bierce) **44**:8, 13, 15, 45
"The Baby Who Was Three-Fourths Good" (Wetherald) **81**:411
"Baby, Won't You Come Out Tonight" (Holly) **65**:148
"Babylon" (Crevel)
See *Babylone*
Babylon (Fitzgerald) **157**:204
"The Babylon Lottery" (Borges)
See "La lotería en Babilonia"
"Babylon Revisited" (Fitzgerald) **1**:261-62; **6**:171-72; **28**:97, 120
Babylone (Crevel) **112**:7-11, 18
"Baby's Breath" (Bambara) **116**:15
"Bacchanal" (Rosenberg) **12**:310
"Bacchanals" (Nagai)
See "Kanraku"
Bacchus (Cocteau) **119**:61
Bacchus and Ariadne (Bradford) **36**:62
"Bachelor Days" (Milne) **88**:249
Bachelors Anonymous (Wodehouse) **108**:372
The Bachelors' Club (Zangwill) **16**:439, 444, 462
El bachiller (Nervo) **11**:403-04
"The Back Bay Fens" (Lowell) **8**:236
"Back for Christmas" (Collier) **127**:258, 261
"Back from a Walk" (García Lorca)
See "Vuelta de paseo"
"Back from the Country" (Gogarty) **15**:109, 114
Back Home (Cobb) **77**:244
Back of Beyond (Moricz)
See *Az Isten háta mögött*
Back of God's Country (Moricz)
See *Az Isten háta mögött*
Back of the Beyond (Leacock) **2**:378
"Back on Times Square, Dreaming of Times Square" (Ginsberg) **120**:111
Back to Africa (Himes)
See *Retour en Afrique*
Back to Bool Bool (Franklin) **7**:264-71, 273
"Back to Boston" (Bishop) **121**:27-8, 30-1
Back to Methuselah (Shaw) **3**:385-86, 392-93, 397, 404, 406-07; **9**:426; **21**:323, 338, 340; **45**:210, 218, 221-22
Back to the Stone Age (Burroughs) **2**:79, 81; **32**:58
"Back Yards" (Baring-Gould) **88**:22
"Backbone" (Dixon) **163**:166
"The Backbone Flute" (Mayakovski) **18**:250-51, 261, 270
"Background" (Lovecraft) **22**:241
"The Backslider" (Fisher) **11**:209, 214
"Backslider" (McAlmon) **97**:115
"Backstage" (Zamyatin)
See "Zakulisy"
A Backward Glance (Liliencron)
See *Rückblick*
A Backward Glance (Wharton) **3**:581; **9**:544, 548; **27**:397; **53**:388, 399-400; **129**:364; **149**:149-50, 154, 174, 182, 248, 253-58, 260, 266, 268, 272, 275
"The Backward Look" (Nemerov) **124**:260
"A Backward Look" (Riley) **51**:294
"A Backward Spring" (Hardy) **53**:81
"The Backward View" (Jewett) **22**:132
Backwater (Richardson) **3**:346, 356, 358
"The Backwoods" (Kuprin) **5**:304
"The Bacterial War" (Nemerov) **124**:153
The Bad (Mann)
See *Der bösen*
The Bad Child's Book of Beasts (Belloc) **7**:42; **18**:18, 28, 39, 42
"Bad Company" (de la Mare) **53**:34, 36
Bad Dreams (Sologub)
See *Tyazhelye sny*
"The Bad Music" (Jarrell) **177**:155, 222
"Bad Ol' Stagolee" (Walker) **129**:272, 330-31
"Bad Roads in Spring" (Pasternak) **188**:183
Bad Seed (Anderson) **144**:34, 39, 74
The Bad Seed (March) **96**:236, 238, 248, 251-52, 259, 264, 266-67, 269-70
"Bad Sir Brian Botany" (Milne) **6**:315, 319; **88**:241
Baden Didactic Play on Acquiescence (Brecht) **1**:107
"The Badge of Men" (Davidson) **24**:164
"The Badger" (Akutagawa Ryūnosuke) **16**:21
"Badly Done!" (Mayakovski) **18**:248
"Bad-Man Stagolee" (Walker)
See "Bad Ol' Stagolee"
"A Baffled Ambuscade" (Bierce) **44**:45
"Bagarre de Fruits" (Arp) **115**:28
Les baglioni (Rolland) **23**:256
Bagrovyi ostrov (Bulgakov) **16**:85, 110; **159**:165
Bags of Gold (Bradford) **36**:63
"Bahnhof" (Schwitters) **95**:301
"Bahnofstrasse" (Joyce) **159**:279
The Baikie Charivari; or, The Seven Prophets (Bridie) **3**:133-35, 137-42
Bailado (Sá-Carneiro) **83**:397
Bailén (Pérez Galdós) **27**:256-57
The Bailiff Jernej and his Rights (Cankar)
See *Hlapec Jernej in njegova pravica*
Bailiff Yerney and his Rights (Cankar)
See *Hlapec Jernej in njegova pravica*
"Bains Turcs" (Mansfield) **39**:297-300
The Bait (Merrill) **173**:183, 255
"Der Bajazzo" (Mann) **35**:209, 258
Baji Prabhou (Aurobindo) **63**:6, 36
"Bajka o gwozdziu" (Herbert) **168**:45
Bajky a podpovídky (Čapek) **37**:45
"Bajo en siglio de la luna" (Villaurrutia) **80**:477
"Bajo la tierra" (Aleixandre) **113**:15
"Bajron u Sintri" (Andrić) **135**:95
Baker Eddy (Hartmann) **73**:116, 134
"The Baker of Barnbury" (Stockton) **47**:324, 330
"The Baker's Wife" (Giono) **124**:37, 39, 113
"A Baking of Gingersnaps" (Montgomery) **51**:200-01
"Bakmandens Hund" (Jensen) **41**:308

"Le Bal de têtes" (Proust) **161**:143-44
Le bal des voleurs (Anouilh) **195**:10, 16, 18, 25, 35, 38-40, 46-7, 50
Le bal du comte d'Orgel (Radiguet) **29**:348-56, 361, 367-68, 370, 373-75
"Bal Macabre" (Meyrink) **21**:231
Bal Masque (Kandinsky) **92**:49
"Balaam" (Harris) **2**:209
"Balada para el Marqués de Bradomín" (Huidobro) **31**:124
"Balada triste" (García Lorca) **181**:41-42, 121, 189
"La balada triste del largo camino" (Huidobro) **31**:124, 132
Baladas de primavera (Jiménez) **4**:213, 224
La Balade du grand macabre (Ghelderode) **187**:4
"Baladilla de los tres ríos" (García Lorca) **181**:192, 194
Balaganchik (Blok) **5**:84, 86
Balākā (Tagore) **3**:491-92, 496; **53**:335, 341-42
"Bālakkāl" (Devkota) **23**:49
"Balance der Welt" (Werfel) **8**:477
"The Balance Sheet of the Intelligence" (Valéry) **15**:447
"Balandro" (Huidobro) **31**:134
Balaoo (Leroux) **25**:260
"Balcón" (García Lorca) **181**:199
Le balcon (Genet) **128**:123-28, 131-32, 134-53, 155, 168, 171-72, 177-78, 187, 189
"Balconies" (Nezval)
See "Balkony"
"Les Balcons Qui Rêent" (Bishop) **103**:5
"The Balcony" (Sarton) **120**:305
The Balcony (Genet)
See *Le balcon*
Balder the Beautiful (Buchanan) **107**:40, 66, 69, 73
Balder the Beautiful (Frazer) **32**:211
Baldwin (Lee) **5**:311, 315-16
"Baleia" (Ramos) **32**:424
"Balek Scales" (Böll) **185**:54
"Balgarskijat ezik" (Vazov) **25**:456
"Balgarskijat vojnik" (Vazov) **25**:455
"Balgrummo's Hell" (Kirk) **119**:281, 335, 338, 341
Bal-i Jibril (Iqbal) **28**:182
"Balikcisini bulan olta" (Sait Faik) **23**:293
Balisand (Hergesheimer) **11**:270-71, 273-74, 276
"The Balking of Christopher" (Freeman) **9**:74
"Balkony" (Nezval) **44**:247
"The Ball" (Akutagawa Ryūnosuke)
See "Butōkai"
The Ball and the Cross (Chesterton) **1**:184; **6**:102-04, 108; **64**:35, 38
"Ball Gown" (Prus)
See "Sukienka balowa"
"Ballad" (Buchanan) **107**:23
"Ballad" (Khodasevich)
See "Ballada"
"Ballad" (Oppen) **107**:306, 309
"Ballad about the Bureaucrat and the Worker-Correspondent" (Mayakovski) **18**:268
"Ballad from the Mountains of the Sauerland" (Lasker-Schueler) **57**:329
"A Ballad in Blank Verse on the Making of a Poet" (Davidson) **24**:160-61, 163, 175, 186-87, 191
"A Ballad of a Coward" (Davidson) **24**:164
"Ballad of a Dream" (Zweig) **17**:424
"Ballad of a Grandfather" (Coffin) **95**:2
"A Ballad of a Nun" (Davidson) **24**:160, 162-64, 175
"A Ballad of a Workman" (Davidson) **24**:164, 191
"Ballad of an Artist's Wife" (Davidson) **24**:164
"Ballad of Another Ophelia" (Lawrence) **93**:120
"The Ballad of Beau Brocade" (Dobson) **79**:6, 9, 26-7
"The Ballad of Blasphemous Bill" (Service) **15**:406
"A Ballad of Burdens" (Swinburne) **36**:299
"The Ballad of Camden Town" (Flecker) **43**:186, 194, 199
"A Ballad of Death" (Swinburne) **8**:429, 436, 446; **36**:298
"The Ballad of East and West" (Kipling) **8**:177, 201; **17**:196, 203, 212, 214
"The Ballad of East and West" (Rhodes) **53**:316
"The Ballad of Eternal Life" (Muir) **87**:152, 207
"A Ballad of Euthanasia" (Davidson) **24**:164
"The Ballad of Everyman" (Muir) **87**:175
"The Ballad of Father O'Hart" (Yeats) **11**:512
"The Ballad of Hampstead Heath" (Flecker) **43**:186, 194
"Ballad of Heaven" (Davidson) **24**:160, 164
"Ballad of Hector in Hades" (Muir) **2**:488; **87**:167
"A Ballad of Hell" (Davidson) **24**:164
"The Ballad of Iskander" (Flecker) **43**:191, 194
"The Ballad of Judas Iscariot" (Buchanan) **107**:24-5, 35, 39-40, 65
The Ballad of Judas Iscariot (Buchanan) **107**:72
"A Ballad of Kenelm" (Guiney) **41**:205, 207, 214
"The Ballad of Launcelot and Elaine" (Masters) **25**:288
"A Ballad of Life" (Swinburne) **8**:429, 436, 446; **36**:298, 314-15, 336
"Ballad of Mazeppa" (Brecht) **1**:114
"The Ballad of Melicertes" (Swinburne) **36**:343
"A Ballad of Metz" (Guiney) **41**:206
"Ballad of New York, New York" (Morley) **87**:142
"The Ballad of One-Eyed Mike" (Service) **15**:405
"Ballad of Purchase Moneys" (Owen) **27**:218
"The Ballad of Reading Gaol" (Wilde) **1**:509; **8**:492, 495-96, 499; **175**:317
The Ballad of Reading Gaol, and Other Poems (Wilde) **1**:499, 502, 504, 507; **8**:490-91; **41**:358, 397
"The Ballad of Ruby" (Sarton) **120**:261
"A Ballad of Sark" (Swinburne) **36**:342
"Ballad of Shop-Windows in the High" (Morley) **87**:141
"Ballad of St. John of Nepomuk" (Sterling) **20**:386
"The Ballad of the Black Fox Skin" (Service) **15**:405-06
"Ballad of the Black Sorrow" (García Lorca)
See "Romance de la pena negra"
The Ballad of the Brown Girl: An Old Ballad Retold (Cullen) **4**:43, 45, 51; **37**:143-45, 147, 154, 156-57, 167
"Ballad of the Calliope" (Paterson) **32**:372
"Ballad of the Dark Trouble" (García Lorca)
See "Romance de la pena negra"
"The Ballad of the Emeu" (Harte) **25**:190
"A Ballad of the Exodus from Houndsditch" (Davidson) **24**:161, 163
"Ballad of the Flood" (Muir) **87**:163, 204
"Ballad of the Gallows Bird" (Markham) **47**:295
"Ballad of the Gods" (Kuttner) **10**:267
"The Ballad of the Harp-Weaver" (Millay) **4**:308; **49**:214, 222; **169**:295
The Ballad of the Harp-Weaver (Millay) **169**:245, 255
"The Ballad of the King's Jest" (Kipling) **17**:196
"The Ballad of the King's Mercy" (Kipling) **17**:196
"Ballad of the Little Square" (García Lorca)
See "Ballada de la Placeta"
"The Ballad of the Long-Legged Bait" (Thomas) **45**:364, 377-78; **105**:299, 301, 322, 337, 347
"The Ballad of the Northern Lights" (Service) **15**:405, 407
"A Ballad of the Poet Born" (Davidson) **24**:164
"The Ballad of the Poet's Thought" (Roberts) **8**:313
"The Ballad of the Quick and Dead" (Kaye-Smith) **20**:106
The Ballad of the Sad Café (McCullers)
See *The Ballad of the Sad Cafe: The Novels and Stories of Carson McCullers*
The Ballad of the Sad Cafe: The Novels and Stories of Carson McCullers (McCullers) **155**:174-75, 180, 183, 189, 209-10, 216, 225
"Ballad of the Sixties" (Sarton) **120**:261
"The Ballad of the Skeletons" (Ginsberg) **120**:89
"Ballad of the Soul" (Muir)
See "The Ballad of Eternal Life"
"Ballad of the Spanish Civil Guard" (García Lorca)
See "Romance de la Guardia Civil Española"
"The Ballad of the Student in the South" (Flecker) **43**:186, 192-94, 199
"A Ballad of the Upper Thames" (Gosse) **28**:132
"Ballad of the Veil of Iris" (Babits)
See "Ballada Irisz fátyoláról"
The Ballad of the White Horse (Chesterton) **1**:178, 180, 186; **6**:98-99, 102, 109
"A Ballad of Three Mistresses" (Roberts) **8**:313
"Ballad of Two Seas" (Sterling) **20**:386
"The Ballad of Villon and Fat Madge" (Swinburne) **8**:439
"Ballad of Whitechapel" (Rosenberg) **12**:307, 312
"The Ballad of William Sycamore, 1790-1880" (Benét) **7**:78-9
"Ballada" (Khodasevich) **15**:204, 207, 212-13
Ballada a nema ferfiakrol (Karinthy) **47**:269
"Ballada de la Placeta" (García Lorca) **49**:83; **197**:202
"Ballada Irisz fátyoláról" (Babits) **14**:39
"Ballade" (Gumilev) **60**:269
"Ballade des äusseren Lebens" (Hofmannsthal) **11**:293, 295
"La ballade du Mal Aimé" (Apollinaire)
See "La chanson du mal-aimé"
"Ballade d'une grande dame" (Chesterton) **1**:186
"Ballade of a Not Insupportable Loss" (Parker) **143**:337
"Ballade of a Talked-off Ear" (Parker) **143**:325
"Ballade of Autumn" (Coleridge) **73**:18
"Ballade of Imitation" (Dobson) **79**:7, 37
"Ballade of Prose and Rhyme" (Dobson) **79**:7, 37
"A Ballade of Suicide" (Chesterton) **1**:186
"The Ballade of the Bank-Teller" (Fuller) **103**:116
"The Ballade of the Tourists" (Fuller) **103**:116
"Ballade of Unfortunate Mammals" (Parker) **143**:325
"Ballade of Unsuccessful Men" (Belloc) **7**:33
"The Ballade of Wild Bees" (Rhodes) **53**:316
"Ballade to Our Lady of Czestochowa" (Belloc) **7**:33
"Ballade vom Imker" (Broch) **20**:54
Balladen (Spitteler) **12**:339, 348, 350
Ballades (Jacob) **6**:193
"Ballad-Maker" (Buchanan) **107**:16, 25
"Ballads" (Roberts) **8**:321
Ballads and Lyrics (Tynan) **3**:501-04
"Ballads and Lyrics of Old France" (Lang) **16**:251
Ballads and Poems (Noyes) **7**:508
Ballads and Songs (Davidson) **24**:160, 163, 175-76, 191
Ballads for Sale (Lowell) **8**:228, 237-38
Ballads of a Bohemian (Service) **15**:400, 402, 411, 413
Ballads of a Cheechako (Service) **15**:399-400, 403-04, 406, 413
Ballads of Lost Haven (Carman) **7**:135, 138

Ballads of Spring (Jiménez)
See *Baladas de primavera*
Ballads of Square-Toed Americans (Coffin) **95**:2-3
The Ballard of New York, New York, and Other Poems (Morley) **87**:144
"Ballet" (Bishop) **103**:3, 17
"Ballet of the Nations" (Lee) **5**:312
"The Balloon" (Lagerloef) **36**:241, 244
"A Balloon Journey" (Verne)
See "Un Voyage en ballon (réponse à l'enigme de juillet)"
"The Ballroom at Sandover" (Merrill) **173**:249
"Balls" (Lowell) **8**:230
"Balstemning" (Kielland) **5**:275
"Balthasar" (France) **9**:53
The Balwhinnie Bomb (Tey) **14**:459
Balzac (Zweig) **17**:429, 457
"Bamberg" (Jarrell) **177**:143, 162
"Bamboo" (Hagiwara)
See "Take"
"Bamboos" (Hagiwara) **60**:296
Bāmunēr mēyē (Chatterji) **13**:79, 81
"Banal Dance" (van Ostaijen) **33**:422
Banalité (Fargue) **11**:200
"Banal'nostjam" (Hippius) **9**:164
Banana Bottom (McKay) **7**:457-59, 461, 464-65, 469, 471; **41**:322-25, 328, 330, 335, 340-43
"The Bandits" (Akutagawa Ryūnosuke)
See "Chūtō"
"The Bandog" (de la Mare) **4**:74
The Bane (Caragiale) **76**:162, 168
"Bang Went the Chance of a Lifetime" (Rohmer) **28**:293
Bang-i-dara (Iqbal) **28**:182, 198
"Bangiku" (Hayashi) **27**:106
"Bangle-Sellers" (Naidu) **80**:292
"Banished" (Lagerloef) **36**:240
"Banished" (Lasker-Schueler) **57**:325
"The Banished King" (Stockton) **47**:329
"Banishment of Man from the Garden of the Lord" (Bell) **43**:90
Banjo (McKay) **7**:456-59, 464-66, 468; **41**:317-18, 320-23, 325, 328-29, 335, 338-40, 342
"A Banjo Song" (Dunbar) **12**:121
"A Banjo Song" (Johnson) **19**:210
The Bank Dick (Fields) **80**:226-231, 240-1, 244, 252
"A Bank Fraud" (Kipling) **8**:198
"Bank Holiday" (Mansfield) **39**:303
"Bank ka diwala" (Premchand) **21**:297
"Banking Coal" (Toomer) **172**:273
The Bankrupt (Bjoernson)
See *En fallit*
Bannen (Dazai Osamu) **11**:175-77, 181, 187-88
The Banner and the Gusla (Vazov) **25**:450
"Banner of Men Who Were Free" (Masters) **2**:470
The Banner of the Bull: Three Episodes in the Career of Cesare Borgia (Sabatini) **47**:303
Bannertail: The Story of a Gray Squirrel (Seton) **31**:260
"The Banquet of Crow" (Parker) **143**:285, 314
"Bansheng yuan" (Chang) **184**:138
Bansheng yuan (Chang) **184**:123-25
"Banshu" (Shiga) **172**:214
Banshū Heiya (Miyamoto) **37**:268-70, 275
The Banshu Plan (Miyamoto)
See *Banshū Heiya*
"Bantams in Pine-Woods" (Stevens) **3**:446, 454; **45**:290, 295, 299, 328, 348
"Banya" (Zoshchenko)
See "The Bath"
Banya (Mayakovski) **4**:302; **18**:243, 248, 254, 259, 262-63
"The Baptism" (Bishop) **121**:48-9
"Baptism" (Talvik)
See "Ristimine"
"The Baptism of Dobsho" (Bierce) **44**:45
Baptist Lake (Davidson) **24**:159, 169, 177, 192, 194
"The Bar Sinister" (Davis) **24**:204
"Bar Titanic" (Andrić)
See "Bife titanik"
"Barabal" (Sharp) **39**:375
Barabbas (Ghelderode) **187**:5, 8, 14, 19, 22
Barabbas (Grieg) **10**:206, 208
Barabbas (Lagerkvist) **144**:168-72, 174, 189, 191, 194, 202-4, 207, 211, 215, 235, 237, 239-41
Barabbas: A Dream of the World's Tragedy (Corelli) **51**:66-7
Baradidi (Chatterji) **13**:75, 80
"Barb Wire" (Adams) **56**:10
Barb Wire (Adams) **56**:7, 10, 22-23
Barbara (Jerome) **23**:82
Barbara Baynton (Baynton) **57**:14, 16, 25, 30
Barbara Blomberg (Zuckmayer) **191**:280, 282, 284, 298
"Barbara Bobs Her Hair" (Fitzgerald)
See "Bernice Bobs Her Hair"
Barbara Ladd (Roberts) **8**:324
Barbara; oder, Die Frömmigkeit (Werfel) **8**:467, 470, 477, 480-82
Barbara Rebell (Lowndes) **12**:201
Barbara Who Came Back (Haggard) **11**:256
Barbarian in the Garden (Herbert)
See *Barbarzyńca w ogrodzie*
"The Barbarians" (Gumilev)
See "Varvary"
"Barbarians" (Stephens) **4**:415
The Barbarians (Gorky)
See *Varvary*
Barbarians (Moricz)
See *Barbárok*
Barbaric Odes (Carducci)
See *Odi barbare*
Barbaric Tales (Sharp) **39**:359, 363, 374
"Barbarism and Civilization" (Higginson) **36**:175
Barbárok (Moricz) **33**:238, 243, 251
Barbarous Odes (Carducci)
See *Odi barbare*
Barbary Coast (Hecht) **101**:62
The Barbary Pirates (Forester) **152**:141
Barbary Sheep (Hichens) **64**:124, 129, 131
Barbarzyńca w ogrodzie (Herbert) **168**:7, 13, 27, 39, 71, 73
"Barbed Wire" (Quiroga)
See "El alambre de pua"
"The Barber" (Gray) **19**:141-42, 149-52, 157
The Barber Shop (Fields) **80**:235-6
"The Barber's Apprentice" (Saroyan) **137**:191
The Barber's Clock: A Conversation Piece (Lucas) **73**:160, 165
"Barcarole" (Obstfelder) **23**:189
Bardelys the Magnificent (Sabatini) **47**:300, 303-04
Bardic History of Ireland (O'Grady) **5**:349, 351-52
"Bare Almond-Trees" (Lawrence) **93**:55, 58
"Bare Fig-Trees" (Lawrence) **93**:55
"The Bare Line of the Hill" (Gurney) **33**:97
Bare Souls (Bradford) **36**:52, 55, 57, 64, 67-8
Barefoot in Athens (Anderson) **144**:4, 6, 17, 39
"The Bargain" (Muir) **87**:278
"Baring the Method" (Prishvin) **75**:215
The Barker (Mankiewicz) **85**:111
"Barker's Luck" (Harte) **25**:199, 222
"The Barking" (Bachmann)
See "Das Gebell"
Barking at the Moon (Hagiwara)
See *Tsuki ni hoeru*
"Barking Hall: A Year After" (Swinburne) **36**:345
"Barks that Lure to Death" (Quiroga)
See "Buques suicidantes"
"The Barn" (Coffin) **95**:3
"The Barn" (Thomas) **10**:468
"The Barn" (Welch) **22**:445-46, 456, 458
"Barn Burning" (Faulkner) **141**:203-10, 212; **170**:127, 134, 138
Barnets arhundrade (Key) **65**:223-26, 233, 237-38
Barnharrow (Tey) **14**:459
Ett barns memoarer (Lagerloef) **36**:235
"Barnstorming for Poetry" (Dickey) **151**:94
"Barnum Had the Right Idea" (Cohan) **60**:68
"The Barometer" (Hunt) **53**:190
"The Baron" (Mansfield) **164**:293
"The Baron Baedeker, Blew His Nose and, Sighing, Departed" (Nemerov) **124**:277
The Baron in the Trees (Calvino)
See *Il barone rampante*
The Baron of Ratzeburg (Barlach)
See *Der Graf von Ratzburg*
"The Baron Starkheim" (Post) **39**:343
Il barone rampante (Calvino) **183**:4-6, 32, 96-97, 113-14, 117, 130, 157, 159, 164-66, 179, 188-89, 197, 200-5, 212, 220-21, 224-25, 227, 238, 240-41
The Barque "Future"; or, Life in the Far North (Lie)
See *Tremasteren "fremtiden"; eller, Liv nordpaa*
La barraca (Blasco Ibáñez) **12**:28-33, 35, 37-8, 41-6, 48-9, 51
Barrack Room Ballads and Other Verses (Kipling) **8**:176-79, 205; **17**:197, 200
Barranca abajo (Sánchez) **37**:311-13, 315-20, 322, 324
"Barre fixe" (Fondane) **159**:240, 243-44, 247
"The Barred Door" (Rhodes) **53**:314
"The Barrel" (Millay) **169**:234
"The Barrel Organ" (Noyes) **7**:502-03, 507, 510, 512, 515
The Barrel Organ (Platonov) **14**:423-25
"The Barrel-Organ" (Prus)
See "Katarynka"
"The Barrel-Organ" (Symons) **11**:435
Barren Ground (Glasgow) **2**:177, 182-84, 186-91; **7**:337-38, 340-41, 343-44, 346-47
"The Barren Mare" (Adams) **56**:8
La barricade (Bourget) **12**:69, 74-5
Barroco (Sarduy) **167**:191
Bar-Room Ballads (Service) **15**:409, 411, 413
Barry Lyndon (Kubrick) **112**:137-38, 140-41, 148, 151-52, 173, 178, 188-89, 205-08, 213, 225, 233, 240, 251, 259, 263, 269-70, 279
The Barsac Mission (Verne)
See *L'etonnante aventure de la mission Barsac*
"Bartek the Conqueror" (Sienkiewicz) **3**:425, 427, 430
"Barter" (Teasdale) **4**:428
The Bartered Bride (Brod) **115**:87
The Bartered Bride (Tolstoy) **18**:383
"Bartleby, ou la Formule" (Deleuze) **116**:86
"Baruch Spinoza" (Borges) **109**:27-31
"Barzoi" (Kolmar) **40**:178
"Le bas matérialisme et la gnose" (Bataille) **155**:97, 110, 139
"Basantayapan" (Tagore) **3**:496
"Base Materialism and Gnosticism" (Bataille)
See "Le bas matérialisme et la gnose"
"Baseball Game" (Bodenheim) **44**:71
"Basement Blues" (Handy) **97**:41
Bases of Yoga (Aurobindo) **63**:33
Bashkir Folk Tales (Platonov) **14**:420
Bashō zatsudan (Masaoka) **18**:235
"Bashoteki ronri to shuyoteki sekaikan" (Nishida) **83**:226, 243, 252, 313, 329, 343, 354-6, 359
Basic Concepts in Sociology (Weber)
See *Wirtschaft und Gesellschaft*
Basic Montessori (Montessori) **103**:336
"Basilica" (Bierce) **7**:97
"The Basis of Artistic Creation in Literature" (Anderson) **144**:45
"The Basis of Realism" (Alexander) **77**:49-50
"The Basket" (Lowell) **1**:375; **8**:235
The Basket Woman (Austin) **25**:31, 34, 38
Basketful Two (Rozanov)
See *Opavshie list'ia. Korob vtoroj*

Básně noci (Nezval) **44**:245
Basque People (Fisher) **83**:105
"Bassoon" (Kandinsky) **92**:74
"Un bastimento carico di granchi" (Calvino) **183**:208
"Basundhara" (Tagore) **3**:496
"Bat" (Lawrence) **93**:20
"The Bat" (Pirandello)
See "Il pipistrello"
The Bat (Rinehart) **52**:301
The Bat Flies Low (Rohmer) **28**:285
Bat Wing (Rohmer) **28**:282
"La Bataille de Morsang" (Jarry) **147**:267
La bataille invisible (Leroux) **25**:260
Les batailles (Péguy) **10**:410-11
Batailles dans la montagne (Giono) **124**:45, 53-4, 56, 72-3, 96, 104, 113, 115
La batalla de los Arapiles (Pérez Galdós) **27**:249, 287-88
"Batallas II" (Vallejo) **56**:307, 313
"Batard" (London) **9**:269; **15**:273
"Bateese de Lucky Man" (Drummond) **25**:151
"The Bath" (Zoshchenko) **15**:504
The Bathhouse (Mayakovski)
See *Banya*
"The Bathing Boy" (Middleton) **56**:180, 187, 189
"The Bathing Maids" (Leino) **24**:376
Les bâtisseurs d'empire; ou, Le schmürz (Vian) **9**:529-35, 537
"The Bat-Poet" (Jarrell) **177**:152-56, 159
"The Battalion" (Devkota)
See "Paltān"
"Batte botte" (Campana) **20**:84
A Battery Shelled (Lewis) **104**:210
"The Battle" (Norris) **155**:331-32
"Battle Ardour" (Baker) **10**:21
The Battle Cry (Thomas) **97**:140
"The Battle Eucharist" (Howe) **21**:113
"Battle for Honour" (La Guma) **140**:238-39
"The Battle Hymn of the Republic" (Howe) **21**:108-09, 113-14
"The Battle of Brains" (Strindberg) **47**:362
The Battle of Cowpens: The Great Morale Builder (Roberts) **23**:237-38
"The Battle of Drumliemoor" (Buchanan) **107**:16, 25
The Battle of Gettysburg (Ince) **89**:10, 17
"The Battle of Grünwald" (Borowski) **9**:22
"The Battle of Magnesia" (Cavafy) **7**:157, 163
"The Battle of Perryville" (Roberts) **68**:338
The Battle of Ravana and Jatayu (Devkota)
See *Rāvan-Jatāyu-Yuddha*
"The Battle of the Century" (Lardner) **14**:319-20
Battle of the Red Men (Ince) **89**:9
"Battledore" (Gray) **19**:157
The Battle-Ground (Glasgow) **2**:176-77; **7**:333
The Battleground: Syria and Palestine, the Seedbed of Religion (Belloc) **18**:24, 45
Battles in the Mountain (Giono)
See *Batailles dans la montagne*
Battleship Potemkin (Eisenstein)
See *Bronenosets "Potyomkin"*
Batum (Bulgakov) **16**:86
"Der bau" (Kafka) **2**:307; **13**:285; **29**:208, 210; **47**:222, 245; **53**:221; **112**:95
Der Bau (Kafka) **179**:275, 326, 328
"Der Bau des epischen Werks" (Döblin) **13**:166
Baudelaire et l'Experience du Gouffre (Fondane) **159**:239
"Baudelaire-Prybszewski" (Ekelund) **75**:94
Der Bauer aus dem Taunus und andere Geschichten (Zuckmayer) **191**:321
"Der Baum" (Heym) **9**:142
Baumeister der Welt (Zweig) **17**:426, 448, 458
"Bavarian Gentians" (Lawrence) **2**:367-68; **48**:121-22; **93**:17, 19, 22,54, 55, 62, 71, 72, 75, 76, 96
"Baxter's Procrustes" (Chesnutt) **39**:89-93
"Bay City Blues" (Chandler) **179**:127-28
"Bay Rum" (Huidobro) **31**:125
"The Bayaderes" (Leino) **24**:370
Baym Dnieper (Bergelson) **81**:20-1,24,31
"Bayn al-kharā'ib" (Gibran) **9**:89
Bayou Folk (Chopin) **5**:142, 144-46, 157; **14**:56, 58, 60, 63; **127**:20, 122-23, 126, 186, 212, 216, 218
Bays (Lawrence) **93**:22
Baza de espadas: El ruedo Ibérico III (Valle-Inclán) **5**:487-88
The Bazalgettes (Delafield) **61**:133
"Be Brief" (Villaurrutia) **80**:458
"Be Careful of Stones that You Throw" (Williams) **81**:423
Be Faithful unto Death (Moricz)
See *Légy jó mindhalálig*
Be Good til You Die (Moricz)
See *Légy jó mindhalálig*
"Be 'ir ha-haregah" (Bialik) **25**:64
"Be Quiet, Wind" (Roberts) **8**:321
"Be This Her Memorial" (Evans) **85**:11, 25, 41
The Beach (Pavese)
See *La spiagga*
The Beach of Falesá (Thomas) **105**:296, 303-04, 318, 320, 359
The Beadle (Smith) **25**:378-79, 381-82, 384-92, 394-404
"Beads of Quicksilver" (Wright) **136**:300
Bealby (Wells) **6**:528; **12**:494-95
"Beale Street" (Dunbar) **2**:128
"Beale Street Blues" (Handy) **97**:40, 42-43, 45
Béâle-Gryne (Bosschere) **19**:52-3, 55, 61-6
"Beams" (Lorde) **173**:143
"Beans and Rice and Mustard Greens" (Devkota)
See "Dāl-Bhāt-Dukū"
"The Beanstalk" (Millay) **4**:306, 309; **49**:226, 228
"The Bear" (Faulkner) **141**:103, 112-13, 160-63; **170**:162-63, 166, 175, 208
"The Bear" (Warner) **131**:331
The Bear (Chekhov)
See *Medved*
Bear (Engel) **137**:71, 73-78, 81-83, 85-86, 89-90, 95-103, 105-7, 117, 123-26, 129-30, 133, 138
"The Bear Story" (Riley) **51**:286
Bear's Dance (Jozsef) **22**:165
"The Bears of Mt. Nametko" (Miyazawa) **76**:278, 302
"The Beast in the Cave" (Lovecraft) **22**:218
"The Beast in the Jungle" (James) **40**:133; **2**:272; **40**:133
The Beast in the Jungle (James) **47**:185, 199; **64**:177
The Beast of Krutoyarsk (Prishvin) **75**:215
Beasts (Tozzi)
See *Bestie*
Beasts and Super-Beasts (Saki) **3**:363, 370, 373
The Beasts of Tarzan (Burroughs) **32**:62, 79
Beat Around the Bush (Garro)
See *Andarse por las ramas*
"Beat the Ghost" (Devkota)
See "Bhūtlāī jhatāro"
Beat to Quarters (Forester) **152**:129, 131, 135-38, 160-63
"Beat Up the Rain" (Engel) **137**:109, 115-16
"Beati Mortui" (Guiney) **41**:215
"Beatrice" (Patton) **79**:298
"Béatrice" (Schwob) **20**:323
"Beatrice" (Teasdale) **4**:424
Beatrice (Haggard) **11**:256
Beatrice (Schnitzler)
See *Frau Beate und ihr Sohn*
Beatrix Randolph (Hawthorne) **25**:238, 241, 249
"Beattock for Moffat" (Graham) **19**:104, 112, 131
Beau Austin (Henley) **8**:97, 99-100, 102, 107-08
"Beau Brocade" (Dobson)
See "The Ballad of Beau Brocade"
"Un beau film" (Apollinaire) **51**:20
Beauchamp's Career (Meredith) **17**:269, 275-76, 278, 287-88, 290, 293; **43**:258-59, 290
Beaumaroy Home from the Wars (Hope) **83**:170
"La beauté" (Sully Prudhomme) **31**:302
Beauté, mon beau souci (Larbaud) **9**:196-97, 207
La beauté sur la terre (Ramuz) **33**:296, 302
"The Beauties of Nature" (Gray) **19**:156
The Beautiful and Damned (Fitzgerald) **1**:234-36, 242, 244-45, 247-48, 254, 258, 261, 264-67, 269-71; **6**:161, 167; **14**:148, 176, 183-84; **28**:86, 106, 110, 120; **55**:191; **157**:123, 131, 147, 182, 187, 190, 195
The Beautiful Blonde from Bashful Bend (Sturges) **48**:275, 283, 291, 294, 309
"A Beautiful Child" (Capote) **164**:200
"The Beautiful City" (Trakl) **5**:466
"A Beautiful Lady" (Roberts) **68**:336
"Beautiful Lofty Things" (Yeats) **1**:580; **18**:463
The Beautiful People (Saroyan) **137**:170, 196, 201, 204-5
"Beautiful Rosalinda" (Herzl) **36**:141
"The Beautiful Stranger" (Jackson) **187**:237, 281
"The Beautiful Suit" (Wells) **133**:257
"Beauty" (Hagiwara) **60**:305
"Beauty" (Södergran) **31**:286
"Beauty" (Thomas) **10**:452, 463
"Beauty" (Wylie) **8**:521
Beauty (Jiménez)
See *Belleza*
Beauty and Life (Scott) **6**:386, 388, 394-95
"Beauty and Love" (Wen I-to) **28**:416
"Beauty and the Barge" (Jacobs) **22**:107
"Beauty and the Beast" (Kuttner) **10**:268
Beauty and the Beast (Cocteau)
See *La belle et la bête*
"Beauty and the Commonplace" (Gale) **7**:284
Beauty and the Jacobin (Tarkington) **9**:460
"Beauty Instead of Ashes" (Locke) **43**:236
Beauty Looks After Herself (Gill) **85**:101
Beauty on the Earth (Ramuz)
See *La beauté sur la terre*
"Beauty Spots" (Kipling) **8**:202
"Beauty That Is Never Old" (Johnson) **3**:241
Les beaux quartiers (Aragon) **123**:143
The Beaver Coat (Hauptmann)
See *Der Biberpelz*
"Beaver Up" (Wylie) **8**:522
"Bébée, or The Two Little Wooden Shoes" (Ouida) **43**:347
Bebee; or, Two Little Wooden Shoes (Ouida)
See *Two Little Wooden Shoes*
"Bebka" (Remizov) **27**:338, 340
"En Beboer af Jorden" (Jensen) **41**:307
"Because I Love You" (Holly) **65**:148
"Because I Was Not Able to Restrain Your Hands" (Mandelstam) **2**:407
"Because It's Real" (Sarduy) **167**:200
"Because the Pleasure-Bird Whistles" (Thomas)
See "January, 1939"
"Because What I Want Most is Permanence" (Sarton) **120**:259-60, 302
"Because You Asked about the Line between Prose and Poetry" (Nemerov) **124**:266, 307
"Because . . . You Say" (Vilakazi)
See "Ngoba . . . sewuthi"
El becerro de metal (Pardo Bazán) **189**:199
Becket (Anouilh) **195**:26-7, 30-3, 38-40, 47
"Becky" (Toomer) **172**:256, 328
Becky Sharp (Hichens) **64**:131
Becq (Coleridge) **73**:24
"The Bed by the Window" (Benson) **27**:17
"the bed is not very big" (Cummings) **137**:20-21
The Bedbug, and Selected Poetry (Mayakovski)
See *Klop*
Die Bedeutung der Psychoanalyse fu< umlr die Geisteswissenschaften (Rank) **115**:247

Die Bedeutung des Leides (von Hartmann) **96**:206
"Bedlam" (Dowson) **4**:88
Bedlam (Lewton) **76**:202, 204
Bednyi rystar (Guro) **56**:132, 145-47
Bedouins (Huneker) **65**:170, 179, 185, 187-88, 195
"Bedovaia dolia" (Remizov) **27**:347
"The Bedquilt" (Fisher) **87**:72
"Bedreigde stad" (van Ostaijen) **33**:418, 420-21
"The Bedridden Peasant to an Unknowing God" (Hardy) **53**:86
"Bedrock and Paradox" (Abbey) **160**:21
Bedtime Stories (Dazai Osamu)
See *Otogi zōshi*
"Bedtime Story" (Molnár) **20**:173
Bee Time Vine (Stein) **48**:234-35
"Bee Wise" (Gilman) **117**:78
"Beehive" (Toomer) **172**:258, 274-75, 329-30
"The Beekeeper Speaks" (Nemerov) **124**:177, 186, 253
Beelzebub's Tales to His Grandson (Gurdjieff) **71**:186, 189, 191-193, 195, 197-203, 205
"The Bee-Man of Orn" (Stockton) **47**:328-29
The Bee-Man of Orn, and Other Fanciful Tales (Stockton) **47**:314, 328
"Been There Before" (Paterson) **32**:372
"Beeny Cliff" (Hardy) **53**:96, 109
"Beethoven" (Gurney) **33**:87
Beethoven (Rolland) **23**:260, 262, 282
"Beethoven's Ninth Symphony and the King Cobra" (Masters) **25**:316
Beffe della morte e della vita (Pirandello) **4**:332
"Before a Bookshelf" (Bengtsson) **48**:13
"Before a Crucifix" (Swinburne) **8**:437; **36**:318
Before Adam (London) **9**:261, 266, 283; **39**:270
Before and After the Rains (Nagai)
See *Tsuyu no atosaki*
"Before Breakfast" (Cather) **132**:137-38
Before Dawn (Hauptmann)
See *Vor Sonnenaufgang*
"Before Easter" (Babits) **14**:42
"Before Her Portrait in Youth" (Thompson) **4**:440
"Before I Knocked and Flesh Let Enter" (Thomas) **1**:471; **45**:361-62, 379-80, 383, 406
Before Night Falls (Arenas)
See *Antes que anochezca*
Before Retirement (Bernhard)
See *Vor dem Ruhestand*
"Before San Guido" (Carducci)
See "Davanti San Guido"
"Before Sedan" (Dobson) **79**:23
"Before Spring" (Guro)
See "Pered vesnoi"
"Before Storm" (Montgomery) **51**:209
Before Sunrise (Zoshchenko)
See *Pered voskhodom solntsa*
"Before the Altar" (Lowell) **8**:232, 235
"Before the Baths of Caracalla" (Carducci)
See "Walking through Meadows . . ."
"Before the Bookcase" (Bialik)
See "Lifne'aron ha-sefarim"
"Before the Break of Day" (Matthews) **95**:250-1, 273
"Before the Cloister" (Johnson) **19**:244
Before the Dawn (Shimazaki Toson)
See *Yoaké maé*
Before the Face of the Almighty (Leino)
See *Alla kasvon Kaikkivallan*
Before the Flowers of Friendship Faded Friendship Faded (Stein) **48**:253, 255
Before the Gates of the Kingdom (Hamsun)
See *Ved rigets port: Forspil*
"Before the Law" (Kafka)
See "Vor dem gesetz"
"Before the Mirror" (Khodasevich) **15**:209
"Before the Mirror" (Swinburne) **36**:315
"Before the Rain" (Reese) **181**:345
"Before the Tears" (Ledwidge) **23**:115, 119
"Before the War of Cooley" (Ledwidge) **23**:109, 116-17
Die Befristeten (Canetti) **157**:39, 42-43, 63, 68, 77, 82-83, 85-87
Beg (Bulgakov) **16**:81-2, 94-5, 109-11; **159**:139
"Beg Karčić's Dream" (Andrić)
See "San bega Karčića"
"Bega" (Pickthall) **21**:245, 250-51, 257
"Bégaya-t-il" (Deleuze) **116**:86
"The Begetter" (Remizov)
See "Rozhanitsa"
The Beggar (Devkota)
See *Bhikhārī*
"Beggar and the Angel" (Scott) **6**:394
"The Beggars" (Pavese) **3**:340
"The Beggars" (Rilke)
See "Die Bettler"
Beggars (Davies) **5**:206-07
Beggars (Dunsany) **2**:143
"Beggars in Velvet" (Kuttner) **10**:274
"Beggar's Soliloquy" (Meredith) **17**:254
The Begging Bowl (Santoka)
See *Hachi no ko*
"Begin, Ephebe, by Perceiving" (Stevens) **3**:448
Begin Here (Sayers) **15**:374, 387
"Beginner's Guide" (Nemerov) **124**:197, 211, 214, 256
"The Beginning" (Brooke) **2**:58
A Beginning (de la Mare) **53**:35, 38
"The Beginning of the Parade" (Arenas)
See "Comienza el Desfile"
The Beginning of Wisdom (Benét) **7**:69, 80
"Beginnings" (Coleridge) **73**:7
"Beginnings" (Engel) **137**:107
Beginnings and Ends (Shestov)
See *Nachala i kontsy*
The Beginnings of the American People (Becker) **63**:64, 75
"Begone, Sweet Ghost" (Gogarty) **15**:100, 103
Der Begrabene Leuchter (Zweig) **17**:433, 457
Die Begriffsform im mythischen Denken (Cassirer) **61**:115
The Begum's Fortune (Verne)
See *Les cinq cents millions de la Begúm, suivi de les revoltés de la "Bounty"*
"Behavior of the Sun" (Bishop) **103**:4, 7-8
"Behaviour of Fish in an Egyptian Tea Garden" (Douglas) **40**:56, 65, 76, 89
"Beheaded" (Kahanovitsch)
See "Gekept"
"The Beheaded Chicken" (Quiroga)
See "La gallina degollada"
"The Beheaded Hen" (Quiroga)
See "La gallina degollada"
"Beheading of the Baptist" (García Lorca)
See "Degollación del Bautista"
Behind Closed Doors (Green) **63**:148, 151
Behind God's Back (Moricz)
See *Az Isten háta mögött*
"Behind Smichov" (Rilke)
See "Hinter Smichov"
Behind That Curtain (Biggers) **65**:5, 9
"Behind the Arras" (Carman) **7**:135, 141-42, 146
"Behind the Burning Town" (Bergelson) **81**:19
"Behind the Closed Eye" (Ledwidge) **23**:108, 120
"Behind the Fence" (Bialik) **25**:60
"Behind the Line" (Gurney) **33**:86
"Behind the Prison" (Nagai)
See "Kangokusho no ura"
"Behind the Scenes" (Zamyatin)
See "Zakulisy"
"Behind the Shade" (Morrison) **72**:353, 376
"Behind the Stumps" (Kirk) **119**:279-81, 291, 335
"Behind Time" (Lowell) **8**:231
"Behold, I am not one who goes to lectures" (Quiller-Couch) **53**:290
"Behold the Key" (Malamud) **184**:237
Behold, This Dreamer! (de la Mare) **4**:78, 81
"The Beholders" (Dickey) **151**:163
"Bei Hennef" (Lawrence) **93**:55
Der Beichtvater (Hesse) **148**:160-61, 164, 166
Beim Bau der Chinesischen Mauer (Kafka) **2**:297, 306; **47**:245; **53**:216
Beinakht oifn Altn Mark (Peretz) **16**:391
"Being" (Coffin) **95**:14
"being as to timelessness as it's to time" (Cummings) **137**:55
Being Geniuses Together: 1920-1930 (McAlmon) **97**:97, 101, 111, 115, 118, 121-22
"Being in Love" (Jerome) **23**:77
"The Being in Love" (Nabokov)
See "Vlyublyonnost"
"Being of Hope and Rain" (Aleixandre) **113**:41
"Being Young and Green" (Millay) **49**:226
"Beitraege zur Variationsrechnung" (Husserl) **100**:39
"Bekenntnis zu Deutschland" (Roth) **33**:336
"Das Bekenntnis zum Übernationalen" (Mann) **9**:329
Bekenntnisse des Hochstaplers Felix Krull (Mann) **2**:423-24, 431, 436, 441; **8**:254; **14**:326, 354; **21**:279; **44**:165, 170; **168**:156
Bekenntnisse des Hochstaplers Felix Krull. Der Memoiren erster Teil (Mann)
See *Bekenntnisse des Hochstaplers Felix Krull*
"Bekenntnis zur Trümmerliteratur" (Böll) **185**:26, 57
Bekenntnis zur Trümmerliteratur (Böll) **185**:4
A Bekkersdal Marathon (Bosman) **49**:8, 13-14, 16
"Bela lada" (Popa) **167**:164
"Belagerte Stadt" (Raabe) **45**:188
Belaia gvardiia (Bulgakov) **2**:63-4; **16**:74-78, 80-83, 85-86, 91, 94-95, 97-98, 105, 109-11; **159**:5, 23, 59, 92, 138-39, 153
Belaia gvardiia: Dni Turbinykh (Bulgakov)
See *Belaia gvardiia*
"Belaja noč'" (Zabolotsky) **52**:367, 376-78
"Belated Lament" (Jozsef) **22**:164
"Belaya bashnya" (Remizov) **27**:338
Belcaro (Lee) **5**:310, 314
Belenky (Glaspell) **175**:158
The Belfry (Sinclair)
See *Tasker Jevons: The Real Story*
"Belgian Cemeteries" (Quiroga)
See "Los cementerios Belgas"
"The Belgian Congo: A Preliminary Report on Its Land, Its History and Its People" (Hansberry) **192**:276
Belgium's Agony: L'allemagne incivilisable (Verhaeren) **12**:471
Belief (Kandinsky) **92**:48
Belinda (Belloc) **18**:27, 45
Belinda (Milne) **6**:306, 310
"Belitis Sings (From the French of Pierre Louys)" (Cullen) **37**:158
"The Bell" (de la Mare)
See "Out of the Deep"
The Bell (Murdoch) **171**:221, 224, 243, 247, 283, 309, 317, 319, 323
Bell, Book, and Candle (Van Druten) **2**:574
"De Bell of Saint Michel" (Drummond) **25**:151
Bella (Giraudoux) **2**:163-65; **7**:317, 325-26
Una bella domenica di settembre (Betti) **5**:61-2
Bella Donna (Hichens) **64**:121, 125-27, 129, 131
La bella durmiente (Salinas) **17**:362
La bella estate (Pavese) **3**:342-43
"Bella vista" (Colette) **16**:129-31, 133-34
Belladonna (Balmont) **11**:32
Il bell'Antonio (Brancati) **12**:80-1, 83, 85, 87-8, 90-2
"The Bellbo Heritage" (Heidenstam) **5**:252
"La Belle au Bois Dormant" (Jarrell) **177**:128
"belle époque" inaspettata" (Calvino) **183**:102
La belle et la bête (Cocteau) **119**:45, 50, 55-6, 74, 76, 83, 85-9, 93, 101-2, 104
"Le belle lettere e i contributi espressivi delle tecniche" (Gadda) **144**:148-49

Une belle matinée (Yourcenar) **193**:302, 305
The Belle of Toorak (Hornung) **59**:113
La belle saison (Martin du Gard) **24**:394, 397
"La Belle Zoraïde" (Chopin) **14**:61, 68; **127**:9, 20-3, 111, 167, 172-3, 175-6, 206-7, 223, 226-7
"The Belled Buzzard" (Cobb) **77**:119, 123, 136, 139, 142
"Bellerophon" (Leino) **24**:371
Bellerophôn (Field) **43**:155, 177
Bellerophon (Kaiser) **9**:177-78, 192
"Belles Demoiselles Plantation" (Cable) **4**:32
Belles saisons (Colette) **5**:169, 173
Belleza (Jiménez) **4**:218-19; **183**:257-64, 290-91, 294
"The Bellringer" (D'Annunzio) **6**:144
"Bells" (Naidu) **80**:292
The Bells of Basel (Aragon)
See *Les cloches de bâle*
"The Bells of the Church" (Vilakazi)
See "Izinsimbi zesonto"
Belmoro (Alvaro) **60**:12
"The Belokonsky Estate" (Pilnyak)
See "Imenie Belokonskoe"
The Beloved Returns (Mann)
See *Lotte in Weimar*
"Below the Battle" (Bourne) **16**:44
Belphégor (Benda) **60**:41, 46-7
Belshazzar's feast (Fondane)
See *Le Festin de Balthazar*
Belt of Suspicion (Wakefield) **120**:355
"Belutak" (Popa) **167**:155, 177, 179
"Belye klaviši" (Bryusov) **10**:92
"Belye, serye, černye, krasnye" (Sologub) **9**:449
"Belyi zayats" (Remizov) **27**:339
Belyi zodchii (Balmont) **11**:37-8
"Ben Jonson Entertains a Man from Stratford" (Robinson) **5**:403-04, 413, 417; **101**:111, 175, 180
"Ben sete 'arim" (Agnon) **151**:21-23
Ben Tobit (Andreyev) **3**:22
"Ben Trovato" (Robinson) **101**:192
"The Bench of Desolation" (James) **40**:140; **47**:199, 201
The Benchley Roundup (Benchley) **55**:10, 16
Bend Sinister (Nabokov) **108**:55, 66-68, 82-83, 85-88, 92, 115, 118-19, 144, 154-55, 157, 173, 175-78, 180, 200-01, 218; **189**:93, 117
"Bendigo Jones—his Tree" (Sapper) **44**:307
The Bending of the Bough (Moore) **7**:498
"Bendy's Sermon" (Doyle) **7**:221
Beneath the Iron of the Moon (Bernhard)
See *Unter dem Eisen des Mondes*
"Beneath the Sign of the Moon" (Balmont) **11**:40
Beneath the Wheel (Hesse) **196**:271, 278, 339
"La bénédiction" (Coppee) **25**:124
"Benediction" (Fitzgerald) **1**:262
"Benediction" (Lu Hsun) **3**:297
The Benefactor (Ford) **1**:283
The Benefactor: A Tale of a Small Circle (Ford) **172**:5, 8
The Benefactress (Elizabeth) **41**:122, 130
Bénéfice d'Inventaire (Yourcenar) **193**:270
"Benefit Day" (Adams) **56**:8
"Benefit of Clergy: Some Notes on Salvador Dali" (Orwell) **51**:223, 239; **128**:288
"The Benefit of the Doubt" (London) **15**:259
The Benefit of the Doubt (Pinero) **32**:389, 393, 396, 398, 400-05
"The Bengali Doctor's Skinny Jackass" (Devkota) **23**:50
Benia Krik: Kino-Povest' (Babel) **171**:57, 73
"Benighted" (de la Mare) **53**:36
Benigna Machiavelli (Gilman) **9**:114
"Benítez entra en el juego" (Arenas) **191**:157
Benito Fernández (Garro) **153**:72, 86-89, 91
Benito Mussolini: Memoirs 1942-1943 (Mussolini) **96**:282
"The Bênitou's Slave" (Chopin) **14**:82; **127**:20, 167
Benjamin Franklin (Van Doren) **18**:407-08, 410-12
Benoni (Hamsun) **2**:202, 205; **14**:221, 223, 237; **49**:128, 133-34, 153, 159
The Benson Murder Case (Van Dine) **23**:351, 353-54, 359-61
"Bent over the Map, Unsleeping" (Tsvetaeva) **35**:394
The Bent Twig (Fisher) **87**:72
"Benvolio" (James) **64**:163
Benya Krik the Gangster, and Other Stories (Babel) **2**:36; **13**:19
"Beograd" (Popa) **167**:158
"Beowulf: The Monsters and the Critics" (Tolkien) **137**:329
"Beppo" (Borges) **109**:4
Berecche and the War (Pirandello)
See *Berecche e la guerra*
Berecche e la guerra (Pirandello) **29**:291
"Bereft" (Hardy) **53**:117
Berendey's Kingdom (Prishvin) **75**:217-19
"Berestechko" (Babel) **2**:31; **13**:22, 33; **171**:10-11, 13, 19-21, 39, 45, 61, 74-75, 81, 84, 88
Der Berg (Bernhard) **165**:122
De berg van licht (Couperus) **15**:46-7
Die Bergbahn (Horvath) **45**:76, 96, 98, 106
Berge, Meere, und Giganten (Döblin) **13**:160, 162, 175, 180
Bergsonism (Deleuze)
See *Bergsonisme*
Bergsonisme (Deleuze) **116**:113
"Das Bergwerk zu Falun" (Hofmannsthal) **11**:292, 296, 300, 309
Bericht anderswohin (Brecht) **169**:43
Bericht über Einrichtungen und Gebräuche in den Siedlungen der Grauhäute (Weiss) **152**:295-96
Berichte zur Gesinnungslage der Nation (Böll) **185**:60, 94, 97, 153, 155
"Ein Beriht für eine Akademie" (Kafka) **2**:293, 303; **13**:276; **29**:188
"Berkeley at the Crossroads" (Borges) **109**:14
"Berlin" (Khodasevich) **15**:209
Berlin (Hergesheimer) **11**:275, 282-84
Berlin Alexanderplatz: Die Geschichte vom Franz Biberkopf (Döblin) **13**:158-59, 161-71, 175, 177, 179-80
A Berlin Childhood Around the Turn of the Century (Benjamin)
See *Berliner Kindheit um Neunzehnhundert*
A Berlin Chronicle (Benjamin) **39**:38-9, 44-5, 47-8
Berlin oder Juste Milieu (Sternheim) **8**:368, 372, 380
"Berlin Revisited" (Lewis) **104**:212
Berliner Kindheit um Neunzehnhundert (Benjamin) **39**:20, 39, 44-5, 48, 55-9
"Berliner Salon" (Arendt) **193**:143
"El bermejino prehistórico" (Valera y Alcala-Galiano) **10**:508
Bernal Diaz del Castillo (Graham) **19**:111, 124
Bernard Barton and His Friends (Lucas) **73**:158, 161, 173
"Bernard, le faible Bernard" (Giraudoux) **7**:324
Bernard Shaw's Rhyming Picture Guide to Ayot St. Lawrence (Shaw) **3**:396-97
Bernarda Alba (García Lorca)
See *La casa de Bernarda Alba*
Bernarda Alba's Family (García Lorca)
See *La casa de Bernarda Alba*
"Bernardo del Carpio" (Bryan) **99**:5, 34
"Bernice" (Moore) **7**:487
Bernice (Glaspell) **55**:233-34, 236-41, 247, 258-59, 275; **175**:69-73, 75, 108, 112-13, 144-53
"Bernice Bobs Her Hair" (Fitzgerald) **1**:234; **6**:169
Il berretto a sonagli (Pirandello) **4**:331, 353; **29**:283, 285-86, 297
Bertha (Bradford) **36**:62
Bertie Wooster Sees It Through (Wodehouse)
See *Jeeves and the Feudal Spirit*
Bertie's Escapade (Grahame) **64**:96; **136**:18, 37
Bertram Cope's Year (Fuller) **103**:59-60, 63, 65, 88-89, 122-23
"Der Beruf des Dichters" (Canetti) **157**:59, 75, 90, 95
"Beruhigung" (Raabe) **45**:187
Die Berühmten (Bernhard) **165**:74
"The Beryl Coronet" (Doyle) **7**:235
"Beryl, the Croucher and the Rest of England" (Burke) **63**:121
"Die Beschenkten" (Beer-Hofmann) **60**:37
Beschreibung eines Kampfes: Novellen, Skizzen, Aphorismen aus dem Nachlas (Kafka) **179**:261
"Beseda s chitateliami" (Olesha) **136**:182-83
"Bešenoe vino" (Kuprin) **5**:303
Die Besessenen (Ewers) **12**:136
"Beside Hazlitt's Grave" (Guiney) **41**:216
"Beside the Bed" (Mew) **8**:296-97
"Beside the Brandy Still" (Andrić)
See "Kod kazana"
"Beside the Winter Sea" (Roberts) **8**:325-26
Die Besiegten (Weiss) **152**:283-85, 289, 294
Besovskoe deistvo (Remizov) **27**:328, 335, 345
A Bess Streeter Aldrich Reader (Aldrich) **125**:10
"The Best for the Poorest" (Gilman) **117**:139-41
"Best Friend" (Kornbluth) **8**:215
Best Ghost Stories of H. R. Wakefield (Wakefield) **120**:344
"The Best Man" (Wharton) **129**:361
The Best of Edward Abbey (Abbey) **160**:58-59
"The Best of Friends" (Pirandello) **4**:350
The Best of Henry Kuttner (Kuttner) **10**:272
The Best of Lamb (Lucas) **73**:173
The Best of Runyon (Runyon) **10**:425
"The best of School" (Lawrence) **93**:23
The Best of Will Rogers (Rogers) **8**:340
Best SF Stories of C. M. Kornbluth (Kornbluth) **8**:217
The Best Short Stories of M. P. Shiel (Shiel) **8**:364
The Best Short Stories of Theodore Dreiser (Dreiser) **10**:180; **35**:71, 75
The Best Stories of Sarah Orne Jewett (Jewett) **1**:361
The Best Supernatural Tales of Arthur Conan Doyle (Doyle) **7**:237
"The Best Years" (Cather) **132**:137
"Bestiaire" (Apollinaire) **51**:56
Le bestiaire (Lemonnier) **22**:203
Le bestiaire; ou, Cortège d'Orphée (Apollinaire) **3**:33, 39, 42, 45; **51**:2, 61
"Bestial entre las flores" (Arenas) **191**:241
"bestial Marj" (Cummings) **137**:42
"Bestiarires sans Prénoms" (Arp) **115**:31
Bestie (Tozzi) **31**:312-14, 317-19, 321-22, 332-33
"Bestre" (Lewis) **9**:246
"Best-Seller" (Henry) **19**:174
"Der Besuch aus dem Elysium" (Werfel) **8**:479
Besuch aus Indien (Hesse) **196**:324
"Besvärjelsen" (Södergran) **31**:292-93
Beszterce ostroma (Mikszath) **31**:168, 170-73
Bet Mashber (Kahanovitsch)
See *Di mishpoke Mashber*
La bête humaine (Zola) **1**:586, 593; **6**:562-64, 566, 569; **21**:431, 441; **41**:414, 422, 436, 439, 451
"Bête Noire" (Douglas) **40**:62-3, 80, 83, 87
"Beth Marie" (Percy) **84**:198
Bethel Merriday (Lewis) **4**:256
"Bethlehem" (Čapek)
See "Betlém"
Bethlehem (Housman) **7**:353, 358-59
"Bethmoora" (Dunsany) **59**:20
"Betlém" (Čapek) **37**:59
Beton (Bernhard) **165**:96, 98, 111, 117-18, 119119
Betrachtung (Kafka) **2**:304; **47**:239
Betrachtungen (Hesse) **196**:251
Betrachtungen eines Unpolitischen (Mann) **2**:429-30, 436; **8**:255-56, 270; **14**:323,338; **44**:165, 168, 179, 192, 228; **60**:328, 347,

353; **168**:91, 115, 118-19, 154, 160, 175-76, 180, 189-93, 204, 208
"Betrayal" (Babel) **13**:33
"Betrayal" (Muir) **87**:153, 219
The Betrayal (Micheaux) **76**:248, 253, 274
"The Betrayal of Christ by the Churches" (Murry) **16**:340
"The Betrayal of Sir Walter Raleigh" (Sabatini) **47**:300
Die Betrogene (Mann) **2**:431, 433; **21**:179; **168**:209
"The Betrothal" (Apollinaire)
See "Les fiançailles"
The Betrothal: A Sequel to The Blue Bird (Maeterlinck)
See *Les fiançailles*
"Betrothed" (Agnon) **151**:45
"The Betrothed" (Chekhov)
See "Nevesta"
"The Betrothed" (Remizov) **27**:328
"The Betrothed" (Roberts) **68**:325-26, 348, 352
"Bet's Bravery" (March) **96**:248
Betsey Bobbet: A Drama (Holley) **99**:336
A Better Class of Person (Osborne) **153**:242-43, 245, 247-48, 250, 290, 320, 339
Better than at Home (Moricz)
See *Jobb mint otthon*
"Die Bettler" (Rilke) **195**:231
Der Bettler von Syrakus (Sudermann) **15**:436
"Betty Perrin" (Coppard) **5**:178
Betty's Formynder (Kielland) **5**:279
Betty's Guardian (Kielland)
See *Betty's Formynder*
"Between Brielle and Manasquan" (Gogarty) **15**:109
Between Heaven and Earth (Werfel) **8**:483
"Between Léda's Lips" (Ady) **11**:21
Between Life and Death (Sarraute)
See *Entre la vie et la mort*
"Between Mountains" (Bergelson) **81**:23
"Between Night and Morning" (Gibran) **9**:93
Between Our Selves (Lorde) **173**:73
"Between Ourselves" (Lorde) **173**:87
Between Paris and St. Petersburg (Hippius) **9**:169
Between Past and Future (Arendt) **193**:43, 75-6, 78, 82-3, 167, 181, 183
Between St. Dennis and St. George: A Sketch of Three Civilisations (Ford) **15**:83
Between Tears and Laughter (Lin) **149**:321
Between the Acts (Woolf) **1**:533, 538-39, 542, 544, 546; **5**:508, 510-12, 518; **20**:347; **43**:387-88, 409; **56**:361, 367, 375-76, 378, 380, 384, 387; **101**:227; **128**:328, 344, 350, 360, 363-64, 366, 369, 376, 381-82
Between the Battles (Bjoernson)
See *Mellem slagene*
Between the Lines (Tomlinson) **71**:397
"Between the Window and the Screen" (Nemerov) **124**:252
"Between Two Cities" (Agnon)
See "Ben sete 'arim"
"Between Two Cliffs" (Peretz)
See "Tzvishen Zwee Berg"
Between Two Masters (Bradford) **36**:63
"Between Two Mountains" (Peretz)
See "Tzvishen Zwee Berg"
"Between Two Prisoners" (Dickey) **151**:199, 216, 224
Between Two Worlds (Murry) **16**:338-39, 343-44, 353; **36**:403-04
Between Us Girls (Orton) **157**:344-47
Betyár (Moricz) **33**:247
Beware of Pity (Zweig)
See *Ungeduld des Herzens*
"Beware the Unhappy Dead!" (Lawrence) **93**:56, 57
"Bewitched" (Wharton) **3**:578; **129**:363-64
Bewitched Love (Arlt)
See *El amor brujo*
"The Bewitched Tailor" (Aleichem)
See "Der farkishefter shnayder"
"Beyond" (Faulkner) **170**:138
Beyond (Galsworthy) **45**:47-8, 70
"Beyond Connecticut, Beyond the Sea" (Bishop) **103**:9
Beyond Defeat (Glasgow) **2**:191
Beyond Desire (Anderson) **1**:48, 51, 55, 57, 61-2; **10**:41, 45; **123**:100
Beyond Good and Evil: Prelude to a Philosophy of the Future (Nietzsche)
See *Jenseits von gut und Böse: Vorspiel einer Philosophie der zukunft*
Beyond Human Might, II (Bjoernson)
See *Over ævne, II*
Beyond Human Power, I (Bjoernson)
See *Over ævne, I*
Beyond Human Power, II (Bjoernson)
See *Over ævne, II*
Beyond Life (Cabell) **6**:62-4, 68, 70, 73, 76-7
"The Beyond of Mr Cogito" (Herbert)
See "Zaswiaty Pana Cogito"
Beyond Our Power, I (Bjoernson)
See *Over ævne, I*
Beyond Psychology (Rank) **115**:230, 263, 265-68, 272, 275-76, 287, 325, 330
"Beyond Survival" (Levi) **109**:293
"Beyond the Bayou" (Chopin) **14**:69; **127**:154, 157
"Beyond the Black River" (Howard) **8**:130-31, 133, 136
"Beyond the Blue Septentrions" (Sharp) **39**:376
Beyond the Breakers, and Other Poems (Sterling) **20**:373-74, 386
Beyond the Desert (Rhodes) **53**:329
Beyond the Dragon's Mouth (Naipaul) **153**:227, 230, 233-35
Beyond the Dreams of Avarice (Kirk) **119**:253, 256, 266
Beyond the Farthest Star (Burroughs) **2**:78
"Beyond the Gamut" (Carman) **7**:134-35, 141-42, 146
Beyond the Gates (Phelps) **113**:344-45, 355
Beyond the Hills of Dream (Campbell) **9**:30
Beyond the Horizon (O'Neill) **1**:381, 384-85, 404; **6**:330, 334-371; **49**:266, 270
Beyond the "Isms" (Stapledon) **22**:322
Beyond the Outpost (Faust) **49**:53
"Beyond the Pale" (Kipling) **17**:207
"Beyond the Pleasure Principle" (Nemerov) **124**:151, 178, 196-97, 254
Beyond the Pleasure Principle (Freud)
See *Jenseits des Lustprinzips*
Beyond the Rocks (Glyn) **72**:126, 135
"Beyond the Screen" (Nemerov) **124**:232
Beyond the Strengh (Bjoernson)
See *Over ævne, I*
Beyond the Strength (Bjoernson)
See *Over ævne, II*
"Beyond the Sunset" (Williams) **81**:439
"Beyond the Tops of Time" (Roberts) **8**:318, 321
"Beyond the Wall" (Bierce) **44**:13, 15, 45, 49; **7**:91
Beyond the Wall (Abbey) **160**:17, 39, 41-42, 104
Beyond Thirty (Burroughs) **2**:78-9; **32**:72-3
Beyond Victory (Riggs) **56**:205
Bez dogmatu (Sienkiewicz) **3**:422-23, 426, 428, 430
"Bez iazyka" (Korolenko) **22**:176
"Bez piati minut barin" (Remizov) **27**:340, 349
Bezette stad (van Ostaijen) **33**:405-06, 412-14, 418-23
"Bezglagol'nost" (Balmont) **11**:36
Bezhin Meadow (Eisenstein) **57**:178, 190-91
The BFG (Dahl) **173**:20, 25-26, 28, 32
Bhanu Singha (Tagore)
See *Bhanusinga Thakurer Padavali*
Bhānu singha (Tagore)
See *Bhanusinga Thakurer Padavali*
Bhanusinga Thakurer Padavali (Tagore) **3**:484; **53**:340
"Bhasar Katha" (Tagore) **53**:350
Bhavani Mandir (Aurobindo) **63**:27
Bhikhārī (Devkota) **23**:48
"Bhūtlāī jhatāro" (Devkota) **23**:52
"Bi no setsumei" (Nishida) **83**:229
"Bianca" (Symons) **11**:439
Bianche e nere (Pirandello) **4**:332; **29**:291
The Bias of Communication (Innis) **77**:341-2, 346, 348, 359, 424
"El 'Biathanatos'" (Borges) **109**:54
"Bibbles" (Lawrence) **93**:33
Der Biberpelz (Hauptmann) **4**:193-94, 196
"The Bible and Literature" (Frye) **165**:258, 260
"The Bible and Progress" (Wilson) **79**:484
The Bible and the Common Reader (Chase) **124**:18, 29
La Bible d'Amiens (Proust) **7**:535
"The Bible Defense of Slavery" (Harper) **14**:260
The Biblical Way (Schoenberg)
See *Der Biblische Weg*
"A Bibliography of Thorstein Veblen" (Innis) **77**:337
"La biblioteca de Babel" (Borges) **109**:88, 128, 156-57, 161
"La biblioteca infernal" (Lugones) **15**:294
Eine Bibliothek der Weltliteratur (Hesse) **196**:259
Der Biblische Weg (Schoenberg) **75**:311, 337
"The Bibulous Business of a Matter of Taste" (Sayers) **15**:379
Bich Bozhy (Zamyatin) **8**:549, 553; **37**:429
"La Bicha" (Pardo Bazán) **189**:229
"Bicocca di San Giacomo" (Carducci) **32**:102-04
A Bicycle of Cathay (Stockton) **47**:327
The Bicycle Rider in Beverly Hills (Saroyan) **137**:168, 181
"Bicycle Story" (Engel) **137**:138
"The Bicycles and the Apex" (Oppen) **107**:303
"Bidmi yameha" (Agnon) **151**:62-63, 65-68
Biedermann und die Brandstifter: Ein Lehrstück ohne Lehre (Frisch) **121**:205, 230, 232, 236, 308
"The Bielkonsky Estate" (Pilnyak) **23**:303
"La Bievre" (Huysmans) **69**:25, 33, 35
"Bife titanik" (Andrić) **135**:17, 84, 96
Biffen's Millions (Wodehouse) **108**:371
"The Big Baboon" (Belloc) **18**:39
Big Bang (Sarduy)
See *Cocuyo*
"Big Blonde" (Parker) **143**:292-97, 314, 332, 335-38, 341-42, 350
The Big Bow Mystery (Zangwill) **16**:449
"Big Boy Blues" (Runyon) **10**:429
"Big Boy Leaves Home" (Wright) **136**:272, 315-18
"The Big Bridegroom Revolt" (Benchley) **55**:3
The Big Drum (Pinero) **32**:405, 415
"The Big Drunk Draf" (Kipling) **17**:204
"Big Fish, Little Fish" (Calvino)
See "Pesci grossi, pesci piccoli"
Big Friendly Giant (Dahl)
See *The BFG*
The Big Gold Dream (Himes) **139**:253, 255, 258, 300-301
The Big House (Bowen) **148**:28
The Big House of Inver (Somerville & Ross) **51**:332, 340-41, 344, 349, 351-54, 357, 361, 377, 386
"Big John Henry" (Walker) **129**:272, 330
"The Big Knockover" (Hammett) **187**:80, 82, 131, 133, 137, 203
The Big Knockover: Selected Stories and Short Novels (Hammett) **187**:45, 131, 133-34, 137, 171, 202-3
Big Lake (Riggs) **56**:198, 203-4, 215-16
"The Big Money" (Lardner) **3**:331
Big Money (Wodehouse) **108**:370
The Big Names (Bernhard)
See *Die Berühmten*
The Big Pond (Sturges) **48**:283, 294, 311
The Big Sleep (Chandler) **1**:168, 170-73, 175; **7**:167-68, 171-76, 178-79, 181, 183; **179**:69,

71-74, 76, 80, 82, 87-95, 97-103, 107-9, 117, 120, 124-25, 128, 132-36, 138, 143, 146-47, 149, 151, 153, 155-58, 162, 164-65, 167, 173, 175-77, 179-84, 188-91, 193-95, 202-4, 222-23, 226-30, 232
Big Sur (Kerouac) **117**:214, 248-50, 252, 265, 272
The Big Town: How I and the Mrs. Go to New York to See Life and Get Katie a Husband (Lardner) **2**:327, 338-39; **14**:305, 309-10, 317, 320
Big Toys (White) **176**:219, 225, 227
"Big Two-Hearted River" (Hemingway) **115**:174
"Big Volodya and Little Volodya" (Chekhov)
See "Volodja bolšoj i Volodja malen'kij"
"A Big-Eared Rat" (Lindsay) **17**:240
"The Bight" (Bishop) **121**:57
Bílá nemoc (Čapek) **37**:42, 53, 56-7, 59, 68; **192**:175, 202-05
"Bild der Mutter" (Heyse) **8**:113
Bild-Bonn-Boenisch (Böll) **185**:151-52, 157
Bilderbuch (Hesse) **196**:259
Das Bilderbuch meiner Jugend (Sudermann) **15**:429-32, 438
"Bildungsroman and its Significance in the History of Realism" (Bakhtin) **160**:110, 195-96
"Bilet" (Nabokov) **108**:82
"The Bill" (Malamud) **184**:241
A Bill of Rites, a Bill of Wrongs, a Bill of Goods (Morris) **107**:135, 152
"Bill the Bomber" (Service) **15**:399
Billard um halb zehn (Böll) **185**:5, 18-19, 21, 32-3, 50, 57-8, 64, 69, 78-9, 82-3, 87, 97, 99, 104-5, 109-10, 112-15, 118, 128-30, 145, 149, 153, 162
"Billbrook" (Borchert) **5**:103-04, 110
Le billet de Junius (Bourget) **12**:69
Billets de Sirius (Benda) **60**:60
"A Billiard Marker's Notes" (Tolstoy) **28**:398
Billiards at Half-Past Nine (Böll)
See *Billard um halb zehn*
Billie (Cohan) **60**:171
Die Billigesser (Bernhard) **165**:96, 116
Billy Goat (Dickey) **151**:136
"Billy Skywonkie" (Baynton) **57**:7-11, 19, 23-24
"Billy, the Dog That Made Good" (Seton) **31**:279
Bimbâshi Barûk of Egypt (Rohmer) **28**:282, 285
Bin; oder, Die Reise nach Peking (Frisch) **121**:198
"The Binding of the Beast" (Sterling) **20**:386
The Binding of the Beast, and Other War Verse (Sterling) **20**:374, 386
"The Binding of the Hair" (Yeats) **31**:417
"Binding the Dragon" (Sarton) **120**:318
"Bindur Chhēlē" (Chatterji) **13**:75
Bindur ChhēlēŌ Anyānyagalpa (Chatterji) **13**:80-1
Bing (Beckett) **145**:80, 83, 91-92, 97
"Bingo, the Story of My Dog" (Seton) **31**:270-72, 279
"Biografía de Tadeo Isidoro Cruz (1829-1874)" (Borges) **109**:98, 127
Biografie: Ein Spiel (Frisch) **121**:205-09, 227, 240
"Biographical Note" (Bachmann)
See "Biographisches"
"Biographical Resume" (Kerouac) **117**:127
"Biographical Sketch" (Cather) **152**:93
"Biographisches" (Bachmann) **192**:131
Biography: A Game (Frisch)
See *Biografie: Ein Spiel*
Biography and Bibliographies (Hergesheimer) **11**:275
"Biography and the Human Heart" (Bradford) **36**:59
Biography and the Human Heart (Bradford) **36**:56, 58-9
Biography for Beginners (Bentley) **12**:15, 25
Biography in a Somewhat Different Form (Hrabal)
See *Zivotopis trochu jinak*
"Biography in Encounters" (Schoenberg)
See "Lebensgeschichte in Begegnungen"
The Biography of a Grizzly (Seton) **31**:256, 260, 262-63
The Biography of a Silver Fox; Or, Domino Reynard of Goldur Town (Seton) **31**:261
"Biography of a Story" (Jackson) **187**:237
"Biography of a Superman" (Middleton) **56**:176
"The Biography of Blade" (Gale) **7**:284
"A Biography of Guskobudori" (Miyazawa) **76**:288-89, 294
The Biography of Manuel (Cabell) **6**:69, 72-3, 76-8
"The Biography of Matvey Rodionych Pavlichenko" (Babel)
See "Zisneopisanie Pavlicenki, Matveja Rodionyca"
"Biography of Tadeo Isidoro Cruz" (Borges)
See "Biografía de Tadeo Isidoro Cruz (1829-1874)"
"Bios and Mythos" (Campbell) **140**:11-12, 32, 82-83, 90
Bios kai politei'a tou Alexe Zormpa (Kazantzakis) **2**:315-20; **5**:259, 263, 272; **33**:144, 147-48, 153, 155-56, 158-59, 163, 165; **181**:237, 304, 308
Bipradās (Chatterji) **13**:80
"Bir kaya parcası Gibi" (Sait Faik) **23**:293
"Birahanedeki adam" (Sait Faik) **23**:294
Birāj Bau (Chatterji) **13**:80
"Birch and Paddle" (Roberts) **8**:316
"The Bird" (Gumilev)
See "Ptica"
Bird Alone (O'Faolain) **143**:230, 237-38, 255, 270
"The Bird and the Tree" (Torrence) **97**:155
"The Bird Fancier" (Benét) **28**:2
"The Bird in the Garden" (Middleton) **56**:175, 193-95
"The Bird of God and the Ignis Fatuus" (Leino)
See "Ukon lintu ja virvaliekki"
"Bird of Night" (Aleixandre)
See "Pájaro de la noche"
"The Bird of Night" (Jarrell) **177**:154-55, 158
"Bird of Silence" (Noguchi) **80**:362
"Bird of Spring" (Kunikida Doppo)
See "Haru no tori"
"The Bird of Time" (Naidu) **80**:270, 348
The Bird of Time (Naidu) **80**:349
"The Bird of Travel" (de la Mare) **4**:81; **53**:36
the bird plus three (Arp) **115**:13, 19-21
"The Bird Sanctuary" (Naidu) **80**:348
"A Bird Trilling Its Gay Heart Out" (Rosenberg) **12**:313
"The Bird Wife" (Hearn) **9**:138
"The Bird with the Coppery, Keen Claws" (Stevens) **3**:455
"Birdbrain!" (Ginsberg) **120**:18, 79-80
"The Bird-Maiden" (Gumilev) **60**:270, 275
"The Birds" (Hansen) **32**:249
"Birds" (Lawrence) **93**:98
"Birds" (Schulz)
See "Ptaki"
The Birds (Ishikawa) **15**:131
Birds and Beasts of the Greek Anthology (Douglas) **68**:7, 10, 24
Birds and Man (Hudson) **29**:159, 163
"Birds and Their Enemies" (Lucas) **73**:171
"Birds at Evening" (Pickthall) **21**:250
Birds, Beasts, and Flowers (Lawrence) **2**:367; **93**:9, 19, 20, 25, 26, 32, 33, 36, 38, 43, 55, 58, 62, 72, 74, 75, 76, 81, 84, 96, 97, 98, 99, 100, 101, 102, 103, 104, 108, 113, 122
Birds in the Air (Balmont)
See *Ptitsy v vozdukhe*
Birds in Town and Village (Hudson) **29**:163
The Bird's Nest (Jackson) **187**:235, 237-38, 241, 257, 273, 282, 295-96
The Birds of Death (Dent) **72**:37
"The Birds of Emar" (Sharp) **39**:376
"Birds of Paradise" (Davies) **5**:199
"Birds of Passage" (Dobson) **79**:17
Birds of Prey (Braddon) **111**:215, 220-21, 225, 228, 245
"Birds without Descent" (Aleixandre)
See "Pajaros sin descenso"
"Birkath 'am" (Bialik) **25**:58, 62
"Birmingham" (Walker) **129**:273
Birobidjan (Bergelson)
See *Birobidzhan Stories*
Birobidzhan Stories (Bergelson) **81**:22,31
Birth (Gale) **7**:277, 279-86
A Birth and a Christening (Mann) **168**:175, 178
"Birth Certificate" (Bosman) **49**:14-15
The Birth of a Grandfather (Sarton) **120**:203, 205-06, 219, 222, 227, 232, 242-44
The Birth of a Nation (Griffith) **68**:135-39, 153, 161-66, 168-73, 178-79, 188-91, 193-94, 196, 208, 213-15, 217, 220-23, 226-27, 230-31, 233, 235-38
The Birth of a Soul (Sharp) **39**:397
The Birth of Britain (Churchill) **113**:127-28
"The Birth of Christ" (García Lorca)
See "Nacimiento de Cristo"
The Birth of Christ (Endo) **152**:167
The Birth of God (Heidenstam) **5**:253
"Birth of Love" (Aleixandre) **113**:55
"The Birth of Methodism in England" (Halévy) **104**:128, 135-36
The Birth of the Gods: Tutankhamen in Crete (Merezhkovsky) **29**:242
"Birth of the Lily" (Palamas) **5**:386
The Birth of Tragedy (Nietzsche)
See *Die Geburt der Tragödie aus dem Geist der Musik*
"The Birth of Venus" (Field) **43**:155, 166
"Birth of Venus" (Rilke) **195**:243
"A Birthday" (Mansfield) **2**:451, 458; **39**:293, 301, 319-20; **164**:292-93, 302, 304
"A Birthday" (Muir) **87**:183, 256
"The Birthday of the Infanta" (Wilde) **41**:375, 378
"Birthday on the Acropolis" (Sarton) **120**:276, 286
Birthday Party (Milne) **6**:319; **88**:254
"The Birthplace" (James) **47**:201
Birthright (Micheaux) **76**:246, 255-56, 272
Births (Saroyan) **137**:173
"The Bisara of Pooree" (Kipling) **8**:176
Le bische (de Filippo) **127**:287
"Bishō" (Yokomitsu) **47**:399
"The Bishop" (Chekhov)
See "Arxierej"
The Bishop Murder Case (Van Dine) **23**:353-54, 359-61
"The Bishop's Beggar" (Benét) **7**:81-2
"The Bishop's Fool" (Lewis) **2**:393
The Bishop's Son (Caine) **97**:14
"Bismillah" (Graham) **19**:128
A Bit o' Love (Galsworthy) **1**:303; **45**:52, 54
"A Bit of Theology" (Hesse) **148**:179, 181; **196**:277-79, 335
"Bitch" (Dahl) **173**:15-16, 18
The Bitch (Reymont)
See *Tomek baran, suka*
Bitlis (Saroyan) **137**:173, 181, 186
Bits of Gossip (Davis) **6**:150
Bits of Paradise: 21 Uncollected Stories by F. Scott and Zelda Fitzgerald (Fitzgerald) **52**:56, 60, 63
Bitter Creek (Boyd) **115**:62
"Bitter Flower" (Tolstoy) **18**:377, 382
Bitter Lotus (Bromfield) **11**:82
Bitter Oleander (García Lorca)
See *Bodas de sangre*
"The Bitter Smell of Tulips" (Herbert) **168**:49-50, 52-54
"Bitte-Selgen" (Jensen) **41**:308
"Bixby Canyon Ocean Path Word Breeze" (Ginsberg) **120**:73

"Bjørnjegerens hjemkomst" (Bjoernson) **37**:33
Bjærg-Ejvind og hans hustru (Sigurjónsson) **27**:362-65
En blå bok (Strindberg) **8**:406-07
The Black Abbot (Wallace) **57**:402
"Black and White" (Mayakovski) **18**:258
Black and White (Naipaul) **153**:227-28, 230, 236
The Black Arab (Prishvin) **75**:215
Black Armour (Wylie) **8**:522, 527, 532, 534, 537
The Black Avons (Wallace) **57**:398
Black Banners (Strindberg)
See *Svarta Fanor*
Black Beetles in Amber (Bierce) **44**:4, 9, 13; **7**:90, 97
"Black Bill's Honeymoon" (Noyes) **7**:512
The Black, Black Witch (Dent) **72**:24
"Black Bonnet" (Lawson) **27**:134-35
"Black Boulder" (Ingamells) **35**:137
The Black Box (Oppenheim) **45**:132
Black Boy: A Record of Childhood and Youth (Wright) **136**:223-28, 233, 240, 250, 252, 258-59, 266, 275-76, 278-82, 284, 288, 291-92, 301, 314; **180**:218, 222-23, 276, 283-84, 291, 303, 309, 313
Black Bryony (Powys) **9**:360-62, 364, 369, 375
The Black Camel (Biggers) **65**:5
"The Black Cap" (Mansfield) **39**:305
The Black Christ and Other Poems (Cullen) **4**:42-3, 45-7, 50-1; **37**:136, 145-46, 154, 156-60, 162, 167-68
"The Black Christ (Hopefully Dedicated to White America)" (Cullen) **4**:43-48, 50; **37**:136-38, 144, 146, 157, 162-63
The Black City (Mikszath)
See *A fekete város*
"Black cock hunting" (Andrić)
See "Lov na tetreba"
"Black Colossus" (Howard) **8**:133, 135
"The Black Cupid" (Hearn) **9**:125
The Black Curtain (Döblin) **13**:158
Black Diamonds (Verne)
See *Les Indes Noires*
"The Black Dog" (Coppard) **5**:177
Black Domino (Buchanan) **107**:33
Black Elk Speaks: Being the Life Story of a Holy Man of the Oglala Sioux as Told to John G. Neihardt (Flaming Rainbow) (Black Elk) **33**:5, 6-12, 14-22
The Black Eye (Bridie) **3**:141
"Black Fog" (Kuprin) **5**:301
"The Black Friar" (Chekhov)
See "Cërnyji monax"
The Black Gang (Sapper) **44**:308, 312, 316-22
"The Black Girl and the Rose" (Jiménez) **183**:332
The Black Glove (Strindberg)
See *Svarta handsken*
The Black Gold (Tolstoy)
See *Émigrés*
"Black Harmonium" (Hagiwara)
See "Kuroi fūkin"
The Black Heralds (Vallejo)
See *Los heraldos negros*
"The Black Hole of Auschwitz" (Levi)
See "Buco nero di Auschwitz"
"Black Honeymoon" (Hammett) **187**:96
The Black Hood (Dixon) **163**:165
The Black Imp (Melies) **81**:148
The Black Indes (Verne)
See *Les Indes Noires*
"Black Is My Favorite Color" (Malamud) **129**:184, 192; **184**:163, 165, 237, 242-43, 245
Black Is My Truelove's Hair (Roberts) **68**:325-26, 328-30, 342, 365
"Black Jack" (Kipling) **8**:208; **17**:208
"A Black Jack Bargainer" (Henry) **19**:172, 179
Black Jack Davy (Oskison) **35**:275-79
"The Black Kiss" (Kuttner) **10**:267
"Black Land" (Babits)
See "Fekete ország"
Black Lightning (Mais) **8**:241-46, 250
Black Lines (Kandinsky) **92**:38, 105-6
"Black Lives" (Hammett) **187**:96
"Black Magdalens" (Cullen) **37**:144, 154
"Black Magic" (Bosman) **49**:13
"Black Magic" (Musil) **68**:265
Black Magic (Roberts) **23**:238
"The Black Mammy" (Johnson) **3**:241, 244; **19**:210
"The Black Man" (Esenin) **4**:115
"The Black Man" (Olesha) **136**:111
The Black Mandarin (Rohmer) **28**:282
Black Manhattan (Johnson) **3**:246
"The Black Man's Wrongs" (Bell) **43**:91
"Black Mary" (Ingamells) **35**:136
Black Mask (Chandler) **1**:171
The Black Mask (Hornung) **59**:114
The Black Maskers (Andreyev)
See *Chernyia maski*
"The Black Mate" (Conrad) **57**:84
Black Metallurgy (Fadeyev)
See *Chornaya metallurgiya*
"The Black Monk" (Chekhov)
See "Cërnyji monax"
"Black Mother Woman" (Lorde) **173**:83
"Black Mountain" (Quiroga)
See "El monte negro"
"The Black Museum" (Nemerov) **124**:179
"The Black North" (Davis) **6**:154
Black Notebook (Rutherford) **25**:350
Black on Black: Baby Sister and Selected Writings (Himes) **139**:253
Black on White (Hippius)
See *Chornoe po belomu*
Black Oxen (Atherton) **2**:15-16
Black Pawl (Williams) **89**:359
Black Pearls (Nervo)
See *Perlas negras*
"The Black Piano" (Ady) **11**:15
Black Power (Wright) **136**:240, 242, 276, 285-89, 291-93, 303, 332
"The Black Prince" (Zoshchenko) **15**:505
The Black Prince (Murdoch) **171**:206-8, 212, 214, 217-18, 221, 227, 249, 254, 258, 269, 280-81, 311, 323, 330
Black Reconstruction: An Essay toward a History of the Part Which Black Folk Played in the Attempt to Reconstruct Democracy in America, 1860-1880 (Du Bois) **169**:95, 164
Black Reconstruction in America, 1860-1880 (Du Bois)
See *Black Reconstruction: An Essay toward a History of the Part Which Black Folk Played in the Attempt to Reconstruct Democracy in America, 1860-1880*
"Black Riddle" (Hammett) **187**:96
The Black Riders, and Other Lines (Crane) **11**:125, 128-30, 157, 164; **32**:135, 139, 165
Black Rock (Connor) **31**:105-09, 111, 113-14
The Black Rock (Fletcher) **35**:99-100, 102, 105-07
"Black Sampson of Brandywine" (Dunbar) **12**:104
"The Black Sheep" (Calvino) **183**:235
"The Black Sheep" (Darrow) **81**:64
"Black Shroud" (Ginsberg) **120**:87
"The Black Silence" (Csáth) **13**:149, 154
Black Skin, White Masks (Fanon)
See *Peau noire, masques blancs*
Black Snow: A Theatrical Novel (Bulgakov)
See *Teatral'nyi roman*
"A Black Solitude" (Wakefield) **120**:345, 358
The Black Spaniel and Other Stories (Hichens) **64**:120, 121, 129
Black Spirits and White (Cram) **45**:2, 5, 12
Black Spot (Kandinsky) **92**:62, 97
"The Black Stone" (Howard) **8**:137
"Black Stone on a White Stone" (Vallejo)
See "Piedra negra sobre una piedra blanca"
"The Black Stranger" (Howard) **8**:131, 135
Black Sun (Abbey) **160**:78, 83, 92
"The Black Swan" (Jarrell) **177**:125, 131, 152, 177
"The Black Swan" (Merrill) **173**:225, 252-53
The Black Swan (Mann)
See *Die Betrogene*
The Black Swan (Sabatini) **47**:307
The Black Swan, and Other Poems (Merrill) **173**:172, 234, 253-55
"Black Swans" (Paterson) **32**:371
"Black Tambourine" (Crane) **2**:120; **80**:199
"The Black Tartars" (Saroyan) **137**:181
"The Black Tower" (Yeats) **1**:574
"Black Umbrellas" (Hecht) **101**:36
The Black Unicorn (Lorde) **173**:54, 61, 68-69, 71-73, 75, 85
Black Venus (Carter) **139**:129, 138-44
"The Black Vulture" (Sterling) **20**:375, 381-82
"Black Was the Blossom You Sighted" (Ady)
See "Fekete virágot lattál"
"The Blackamoor's Pantomime" (Benét) **28**:6
"The Blackbird" (Musil) **68**:261
"The Blackbird and the Girl" (Bosschere) **19**:54-6, 63
"A Blackbird Rhapsody" (Scott) **6**:394
"The Blackbirds" (Ledwidge) **23**:112, 123
"The Blackbird's Promise" (Bosschere) **19**:63
"The Blackbird's Whistle" (Calvino) **183**:47-48
"Blacker Than Sin" (Cobb) **77**:138
The Blacker the Berry (Thurman) **6**:445-49, 451
Blackguard (Bodenheim) **44**:59, 65, 69-72, 74
Blackie (Leino)
See *Musti*
"The Blackmailers" (Gray) **19**:141-42
"Blackmailers Don't Shoot" (Chandler) **7**:176, 182; **179**:120, 124
The Blacks: A Clown Show (Genet)
See *Les nègres: Clownerie*
"The Blacksmith's Serenade" (Lindsay) **17**:227
"Blackstudies" (Lorde) **173**:53
"Blades for France" (Howard) **8**:138
"Blades of Steel" (Fisher) **11**:205, 209, 212
"Blagaia vest'" (Tsvetaeva) **35**:411
"Blake and Wordsworth: Two Ways of the Imagination" (Nemerov) **124**:310
"Blake's Treatment of the Archetype" (Frye) **165**:165
Le Blanc aux pieds de Nègre (Arp) **115**:32
"La blanca soledad" (Lugones) **15**:289
"Blanche la sanglante" (Schwob) **20**:323
Blanche ou l'oubli (Aragon) **123**:127
Les Blancs (Hansberry) **192**:264, 274-79, 285-86, 296-98, 305, 308-11, 313-15, 320, 323, 330-31, 335, 337
"Blancura" (Aleixandre) **113**:8
Bland franska bönder (Strindberg) **8**:419
The Blanket of the Dark (Buchan) **41**:39
"Blankets" (La Guma) **140**:206, 238
"Blasán" (Darío) **4**:63
"Blasones y talegas" (Pereda) **16**:373
"Blasons des fleurs et des fruits" (Éluard) **41**:151, 156
"Blasphemous Ballad" (Talvik) **87**:319-20
"The Blast of God" (Evans) **85**:21
Blasting and Bombardiering (Lewis) **2**:391; **104**:185-86, 225, 229-31
"Blätter" (Kandinsky) **92**:67
Blätter aus dem Brotsack (Frisch) **121**:233, 287, 290
Blaubart (Frisch) **121**:224-25, 227, 229, 233, 238-41, 245, 247, 261, 263, 265
"De blaue Abend" (Ball) **104**:12
Der blaue Boll (Barlach) **84**:76, 85-6
Der blaue Engel (Zuckmayer) **191**:322, 347
"Blaue Hortensie" (Rilke) **195**:231-32
"A Blaze" (Mansfield) **2**:457; **164**:293
Blazhenstvo (Bulgakov) **16**:84, 111
Blazing of the Trail (Ince) **89**:9
Le blé en herbe (Colette) **5**:167, 172; **16**:121
Bleak Morning (Tolstoy) **18**:365, 371-72, 374, 379

Blèche (Drieu la Rochelle) **21**:21-2, 40
"Bleeding Belgium" (Verhaeren) **12**:471
"Bleeding Hears Association of American Novelists" (Nemerov) **124**:219
Die Blendung (Canetti) **157**:10, 12, 16, 18, 21-29, 31-35, 50-63, 66-67, 70-74, 76-77, 80, 82-84, 89, 95, 97, 101, 104
"Blenheim Oranges" (Thomas) **10**:450, 464, 470-71
Les blés mouvants (Verhaeren) **12**:464
"Blessed . . . Blessed" (Arnow) **196**:88, 91, 93
Blessed Edmund Campion (Guiney) **41**:219
"Blessed Spirit, Guard" (Roberts) **68**:305, 337
The Blessing of Pan (Dunsany) **59**:17, 20, 22, 26, 28
Bleter fun Mein Leben (Cahan) **71**:41, 43, 48, 52
Le bleu du ciel (Bataille) **155**:6, 8, 77, 81-84, 89, 127-28
"Blick" (Kandinsky) **92**:67
"Blick ins Chaos" (Benét) **7**:74
"Blick und Blitz" (Kandinsky) **92**:67
"The Blight" (Post) **39**:337
Blight (Gogarty) **15**:110-11, 115-16
"Blind" (Abercrombie) **141**:7, 10, 19
"Blind" (Jiménez) **183**:337
Blind (Maeterlinck)
See *Les aveugles*
"Blind Alley" (Hedāyat) **21**:88
"The Blind Bard of Chios" (Pascoli) **45**:142
"The Blind Caravan" (Campbell) **9**:32
"Blind Geronimo and His Brother" (Schnitzler)
See "Der blinde Geronimo und sein Bruder"
"The Blind Hen and the Earthworm" (Powys) **9**:377
Blind Husbands (Stroheim) **71**:329-330, 332, 339, 357-359, 364, 366
"The Blind Kittens" (Lampedusa) **13**:293
"The Blind Man" (Andrić)
See "Quien baila se consuma"
"The Blind Man" (Khodasevich) **15**:206
"The Blind Man" (Rilke)
See "Der Blinde"
"The Blind Man" (Stephens) **4**:421
Blind Man with a Pistol (Himes) **139**:244, 248-49, 253, 262-64, 268, 278-79, 284-85, 302, 322
"Blind Man's Bluff" (Wakefield) **120**:336, 345, 348, 354, 357
Blind Man's Bluff (Futrelle) **19**:95
Blind Man's Bluff (Toller)
See *Die blinde Göttin*
"The Blind Man's Song" (Rilke)
See "Das Lied des Blinden"
"The Blind Musician" (Korolenko) **22**:170
The Blind Musician (Korolenko)
See *Slepoi muzykant*
The Blind Old Indian and his Names (Sapir) **108**:268
"The Blind on the Bridge" (Babits)
See "Vakok a hídon"
"Blind Panorama of New York" (García Lorca)
See "Panorama ceigo de Nueva York"
"The Blind Ploughman" (Hall) **12**:195
"The Blind Woman" (Rilke)
See "Die Blinde"
"Der Blinde" (Rilke) **195**:299
"Die Blinde" (Rilke) **195**:181, 183
"Der blinde Geronimo und sein Bruder" (Schnitzler) **4**:396
Die blinde Göttin (Toller) **10**:482
"The Blinded Bird" (Hardy) **53**:73
"Blinden" (Heyse) **8**:113
The Blinding (Canetti)
See *Die Blendung*
"The Blinding Light" (Gumilev)
See "Oslepitel'noe"
"A Blindman's Eyebrows" (Wright) **136**:300-301
"Blindness" (Baker) **10**:27
"Blindness" (Borges) **109**:57
"Bliss" (Mansfield) **2**:446-47, 452, 454-56, 458; **8**:275-76, 280-82, 284-85, 288; **39**:303-04, 309, 319, 322-24; **164**:225, 227-33, 239, 241, 247-49, 258-62, 281, 333
Bliss (Bulgakov)
See *Blazhenstvo*
Bliss, and Other Stories (Mansfield) **2**:446-47; **8**:282, 291; **39**:312; **164**:264, 332, 340-41
"Blithe Insecurities" (McAlmon) **97**:99-100
Blix (Norris) **24**:427; **155**:260, 262, 264, 319
"Blixten" (Södergran) **31**:295
Blíženci (Nezval) **44**:239, 245
"Blockade" (Chang)
See "Fengsuo"
"Blocks" (Remizov)
See "Kubiki"
"Les blocs d'aurore s'écroulent . . ." (Arp) **115**:41
"Blom" (Söderberg) **39**:428
The Blonde Lady (Leblanc)
See *Arsène Lupin contre Herlock Sholmès*
"Blonde Mink" (Runyon) **10**:429
Blondzhnde shtern (Aleichem) **35**:306
"Blood" (Singer) **33**:386
"Blood" (Unamuno) **2**:568
Blood (Moricz)
See *Vér*
Blood and Guts in High School (Acker) **191**:5-8, 20-4, 26-30, 33-6, 45-6, 66-7, 69, 72, 92-6, 98-9, 102-04, 106, 108, 128-29
Blood and Gold (Ady)
See *Vér és arany*
Blood and Soul (Mizoguchi)
See *Chi to rei*
"Blood and the Moon" (Yeats) **11**:519; **18**:448
"Blood Feud" (Wylie) **8**:521
Blood for a Stranger (Jarrell) **177**:138, 154-55, 163, 189
"Blood from a Stone" (Oppen) **107**:262, 302-03, 335
Blood Money (Hammett) **187**:70, 75, 98
The Blood of a Poet (Cocteau)
See *Le sang d'un poète*
The Blood of the Arena (Blasco Ibáñez)
See *Sangre y arena*
Blood of the Prophets (Masters) **2**:470
"The Blood of the Redeemer" (Field) **43**:165-67
"The Blood of the Virgins" (D'Annunzio) **6**:143
"Blood of the Walsungs" (Mann)
See *Wälsungenblut*
Blood on the Trail (Faust) **49**:40
Blood Pact (Valle-Inclán) **5**:486
"Blood Pressure" (Runyon) **10**:434
"Blood Sacrifice" (Sayers) **15**:387
"Blood, Sea" (Calvino)
See "Il sangue, il mare"
"Blood Sport" (Abbey) **160**:59
"The Blood Stain" (Artsybashev) **31**:7
Blood Wedding (García Lorca)
See *Bodas de sangre*
"Blood-Burning Moon" (Toomer) **172**:255, 258, 285, 306, 314, 328, 337, 339
"The Bloodhounds of Broadway" (Runyon) **10**:425, 434
"The Blood-Red Star" (Rohan) **22**:299
"The Bloodwood Tree" (Ingamells) **35**:138
"The Bloody Chamber" (Carter) **139**:47, 111-16, 118-19, 139-40, 216, 219
The Bloody Chamber, and Other Stories (Carter) **139**:47-48, 78, 91, 110-19, 125-27, 131, 138-40, 142, 150-51, 153, 158, 160-61, 172, 175, 187, 191-93, 195-97, 204, 209-10, 216
The Bloody Jest (Aleichem)
See *Der blutiker shpas*
"Bloody Past" (Khodasevich) **15**:202
"The Bloody Son" (Swinburne) **8**:436; **36**:299
The Bloom of Life (France)
See *La vie en fleur*
"The B'loon Man" (Smith) **25**:389
"A Blossom of Barren Lands" (Rhodes) **53**:316
The Blotting Book (Benson) **27**:17
Blow, Winds! (Rainis)
See *Pūt, vējini!*
"Bludnyj syn" (Gumilev) **60**:277-8
"Blue" (Dunbar) **12**:110
Blue (Darío)
See *Azul*
The Blue and Brown Books (Wittgenstein) **59**:215, 239, 255, 268
"Blue and Green" (Woolf) **1**:534
The Blue Angel (Zuckmayer)
See *Der blaue Engel*
The Blue Bells of Scotland (Buchanan) **107**:85
The Blue Bird (Maeterlinck)
See *L'oiseau bleu*
The Blue Boll (Barlach)
See *Der blaue Boll*
The Blue Book (Zoshchenko) **15**:502, 504
Blue Boy (Giono)
See *Jean le bleu*
The Blue Calendars (Gray) **19**:157, 165
The Blue Castle (Montgomery) **51**:188; **140**:319
Blue Cat (Hagiwara)
See *Aoneko*
"The Blue Chains" (Khlebnikov)
See "Sinie okory"
"The Blue Chest of Rachel Ward" (Montgomery) **51**:178
"The Blue Chrysanthemum" (Čapek) **6**:91; **192**:224
Blue Cities (Tolstoy) **18**:360, 370, 373, 378
"The Blue Counterpane" (Tolstoy) **18**:377
"The Blue Cross" (Chesterton) **6**:108
"The Blue Cross" (Leino)
See "Sininen risti"
The Blue Dahlia (Chandler) **179**:224-25
"Blue Dave" (Harris) **2**:209
The Blue Deep (Platonov) **14**:408
"The Blue Diamond Mystery" (Freeman) **21**:61
The Blue Duchess (Bourget)
See *La duchesse bleue*
"Blue Evening" (Brooke) **2**:59
The Blue Fairy Book (Lang) **16**:263-64, 272
A Blue Grass Penelope (Harte) **1**:342
The Blue Harlequin (Baring) **8**:37
"The Blue Hotel" (Crane) **11**:128, 137, 140-41, 146-48, 156-58, 160, 162-64, 167; **17**:70-1, 75; **32**:144-45, 165, 181, 184
The Blue Hotel (Agee) **180**:69
"Blue Hydrangea" (Rilke)
See "Blaue Hortensie"
The Blue Lantern (Colette)
See *Le fanal bleu*
"The Blue Meridian" (Toomer) **172**:261, 266-67, 270-71, 277-78, 286-90, 292-95, 312-13
The Blue Meridian, and Other Poems (Toomer) **172**:278
"The Blue Monkey" (Rohmer) **28**:286
Blue Mountain (Kandinsky) **92**:34
"The Blue Noon" (Flecker) **43**:190
"The Blue Nothing" (Kuzmin) **40**:197
The Blue of Noon (Bataille)
See *Le bleu du ciel*
Blue Plate Special (Runyon) **10**:423
The Blue Princess (Bosman) **49**:21
The Blue Rider (Kandinsky) **92**:53
The Blue Scarab (Freeman)
See *Dr. Thorndyke's Case-Book*
"The Blue Sequin" (Freeman) **21**:55
Blue Sky (Sologub)
See *Nebo goluboe*
"The Blue Sleeve Garter" (Benchley) **1**:80; **55**:5
"Blue Snow Blues" (Wright) **136**:263
"Blue Suburban" (Nemerov) **124**:171, 177
"The Blue Swallows" (Nemerov) **124**:177, 179, 181-82, 186, 188-91, 193, 212-13, 220, 226-27, 252, 268, 302-3, 309, 314
The Blue Swallows (Nemerov) **124**:148-49, 151-52, 154-55, 157, 160, 162, 165, 168, 191-92, 194, 196-97, 209, 251-55
"Blue Symphony" (Fletcher) **35**:94, 100, 103
"The Blue Woman" (Donoso) **133**:80, 122
"Bluebeard" (Millay) **49**:201

Bluebeard (Frisch)
See *Blaubart*
"Blue-Black Blues" (Wright) **136**:261
"The Blue-Flag in the Bog" (Millay) **4**:306, 310; **49**:222
"Blueprint for Negro Writing" (Wright) **136**:291-92, 315-16; **180**:247
Blues: An Anthology (Handy) **97**:42, 55, 67, 69, 79-80
"The Blues Come Around" (Williams) **81**:428
Die Blume (Borchert) **5**:108
"Die Blume die ich mir am fenster hege" (George) **14**:210, 213
Das Blumenboot (Sudermann) **15**:430
"Blurry, the Explorer" (Frank) **17**:121
"Blüte" (Schwitters) **95**:298
Blütezeit der Romantik (Huch) **13**:244, 247, 253
Der blutiker shpas (Aleichem) **1**:28; **35**:320
Bo ni natta otako (Abe) **131**:11
"The Boarded Window" (Bierce) **7**:89; **44**:16, 44-6
"The Boarding House" (Joyce) **8**:170; **35**:142, 147-48, 156, 160, 163-64, 167, 194, 197; **159**:300
"The Boards of Fate" (Khlebnikov)
See "Doski sud'by"
"The Boat" (Grove) **4**:138, 142
"Boat" (Huidobro)
See "Balandro"
The Boat of Longing (Rölvaag)
See *Loengselens baat*
"The Boat of Love" (Cram) **45**:3, 12
"A Boat on the Dead Sea" (Ady) **11**:14
The Boats of the "Glen-Carrig" (Hodgson) **13**:229-35, 237
"Bobeobi" (Khlebnikov) **20**:137
"Boboli" (Campana) **20**:84
"Bob's Lane" (Thomas) **10**:463
Bocetas al temple (Pereda) **16**:367, 380
"Bochenochek" (Remizov) **27**:339
Bocksgesang (Werfel) **8**:467, 470, 473-79
Bodas de sangre (García Lorca) **1**:308, 314-16, 318; **7**:290, 293-96, 300-01; **49**:74-80, 85-9, 94, 98-101, 103-04, 109, 111, 113-14, 116-17; **181**:29, 41, 45-50, 70, 126-27, 131, 135, 191
La bodega (Blasco Ibáñez) **12**:29-30, 37-8, 42, 47, 50
Bödeln (Lagerkvist) **144**:201, 211, 214, 237-38
"Bodies of the Dead" (Bierce) **44**:45
Bodies of Work (Acker) **191**:115, 118-19
"Bodily Union" (Tagore) **3**:490
The Bodley Head Jack London (London) **9**:269
Body and Soul (Bennett) **197**:16-18, 20
Body and Soul (Micheaux) **76**:262, 272
"Body and Spirit" (Davies) **5**:204
"The Body as Expression, and Speech" (Merleau-Ponty) **156**:197, 202-3
"The Body of God" (Lawrence) **93**:74, 128
The Body Snatcher (Lewton) **76**:200, 204, 210, 217, 219, 221-22, 231
The Bodysnatcher (Onetti)
See "Just a Little One"
Le Boeuf sur le toit (Cocteau) **119**:71-3
"Una bofetada" (Quiroga) **20**:212, 215, 219-21
The Bog of Stars (O'Grady) **5**:352, 354
"Bogg of Geebung" (Lawson) **27**:119, 148, 150
The Bogie Man (Gregory) **176**:18, 20
The Bogie Men (Gregory) **1**:332, 335, 337
La bohème (Giacosa) **7**:311, 313-15
"Bohemia" (Parker) **143**:324
La Bohemia de mi tiempo (Palma) **29**:255, 258
"Bohemia Lies by the Sea" (Bachmann) **192**:54, 67
"The Bohemian Girl" (Cather) **11**:115; **31**:29; **132**:125-26, 137; **152**:76-77
The Bohemian Life of My Time (Palma)
See *La Bohemia de mi tiempo*
Bohemian Lights (Valle-Inclán)
See *Luces de bohemia*
"The Bohemians" (Gurney) **33**:87, 95, 102
"Das böhmische Dorf" (Morgenstern) **8**:308
"Böhmischer Jahrmarkt" (Morgenstern) **8**:305
"Bois de Mametz" (Manning) **25**:278
"Bois d'ébène" (Roumain) **19**:334
Boitempo (Drummond de Andrade) **139**:226, 232-33
"Bokardo" (Robinson) **5**:403
Bokutō kidan (Nagai) **51**:92, 97-8, 103-08
"Bo'l" (Jensen) **41**:308
"The Bolas" (Graham) **19**:133
"A bölcsek köve (humoristicus novella)" (Herzl) **36**:152-53
A Bold Fellow (Tsvetaeva) **7**:557
A boldog ember (Moricz) **33**:243-44, 248, 251
"Boles" (Gorky) **8**:74
"Bolivar" (Kipling) **8**:177
Boll (Barlach)
See *Der blaue Boll*
"Bol'noi" (Gumilev) **60**:269
"Bologneser Tränen" (Meyrink) **21**:231-32
"The Bolt Behind the Blue" (Parker) **143**:332
"The Bolted Door" (Wharton) **129**:362
"The Bolter" (Warung)
See "The 'Henry Porcher' Bolter"
The Bomb (Harris) **24**:258-59, 261, 263, 265, 268, 271-74, 280
"The Bomb Shop" (O'Faolain) **143**:221
La bomba increíble (Salinas) **17**:369
"Bombardment" (Lawrence) **93**:82, 83
"Bombardment" (Lowell) **8**:235
"The Bombardment" (Norris) **155**:262
"Bombers" (Jarrell) **177**:192
"Bon Bons" (Nemerov) **124**:233
"Bona and Paul" (Toomer) **172**:257, 259, 274, 285, 304, 307, 318-19, 329-30
Bonaventure (Cable)
See *Bonaventure: A Prose Pastoral of Acadian Louisiana*
Bonaventure: A Prose Pastoral of Acadian Louisiana (Cable) **4**:28
The Bond (Strindberg) **21**:348
A Bond Honoured (Osborne) **153**:242
"La bondad de la vida" (Villaurrutia) **80**:477
"Bonde" (Hamsun) **14**:240; **49**:152
"Bondefangeren" (Jensen) **41**:303
Bondefortellinger (Bjoernson) **37**:33
Bóndinn á Hrauni (Sigurjónsson) **27**:361-62, 364
The Bondman (Caine) **97**:3, 7, 9, 14, 20-22, 26
"The Bonds of Discipline" (Kipling) **8**:195, 202; **17**:207
The Bonds of Interest (Benavente)
See *Los intereses creados*
"Bones" (Hayashi)
See "Hone"
Bones (Wallace) **57**:402
Bones in London (Wallace) **57**:402
"The Bones of Louella Brown" (Petry) **112**:299
"The Bonfire" (Kunikida Doppo)
See "Takibi"
"Bonfire" (Shiga) **172**:228, 232
Bonfire (Fisher) **87**:89
The Bonfire (Gumilev)
See *The Campfire*
"Bonga-Bonga in Whitehall" (Strachey) **12**:400
Le bonheur (Sully Prudhomme) **31**:300, 302-04, 306-07
Le Bonheur fou (Giono) **124**:55-56, 107, 115
"Un bonhomme" (Sully Prudhomme) **31**:302
La Bonne Comédie (Dobson) **79**:30
La bonne souffrance (Coppee) **25**:126
Les bonnes (Genet) **128**:121, 135, 137, 145-46, 151-52, 165, 168, 187, 189-207, 242
"Les bons élèves" (Vian) **9**:532
"Bontche Schweig" (Peretz)
See "Bontsye Shvayg"
"Bontsie Silent" (Peretz)
See "Bontsye Shvayg"
"Bontsye Shvayg" (Peretz) **16**:390, 395, 399, 402, 404
"The Bonzo's Secret" (Machado de Assis)
See "O segrêdo do bonzo"
Det Bødes der for (Nexø) **43**:329
"The Book" (Schulz)
See "Księga"
A Book about Myself (Dreiser) **35**:32, 54, 56, 76; **83**:9
The Book and the Brotherhood (Murdoch) **171**:259, 261-64, 280, 285, 300-301, 304, 311, 323, 327-28
Book for Frivolous People (Cankar)
See *Knjiga za lahkomiselne ljudi*
The Book of a Naturalist (Hudson) **29**:143
The Book of American Negro Poetry (Johnson) **3**:240; **19**:205-07, 210, 220; **175**:223-25, 230-31, 250, 252
The Book of American Negro Spirituals (Johnson) **175**:181, 199-200, 203, 224, 226-28, 233-34
A Book of Americans (Benét) **7**:79
"The Book of Annandale" (Robinson) **5**:400, 418; **101**:119
A Book of Burlesques (Mencken) **13**:363, 367, 386
The Book of Carlotta (Bennett)
See *Sacred and Profane Love*
The Book of Christopher Columbus (Claudel)
See *Le livre de Christophe Columb*
The Book of Deeds (Agnon)
See *Sefer ha-Maasim*
Book of Dreams (Kerouac) **117**:192
The Book of Earth (Noyes) **7**:506-7, 509, 513
"The Book of Ephraim" (Merrill) **173**:152, 154-57, 159, 162, 168, 170, 174, 177, 183, 186-88, 201, 204, 207, 209-10, 217, 219-22, 229-30, 241, 243, 245, 248
Book of Fables (Agnon)
See *Sefer ha-Maasim*
Book of Fairy Tales (Sologub)
See *Kniga skazok*
The Book of Folly (Herzl)
See *Das Buch der Narrheit*
Book of Franza (Bachmann)
See *Der Fall Franza, Requiem für Fanny Goldmann*
Book of Gypsy Ballads (García Lorca)
See *Primer romancero gitano*
The Book of Hours (Rilke)
See *Das Stundenbuch*
"The Book of Hours of Sister Clotilde" (Lowell) **1**:378, 380
The Book of Humorous Verse (Wells) **35**:421, 426
The Book of Images (Rilke)
See *Das Buch der Bilder*
The Book of Imaginary Beings (Borges) **109**:126
The Book of Jonah (Babits)
See *Jónás Könyre*
"The Book of Kells" (Nemerov) **124**:205
"The Book of Knowledge" (Nemerov) **124**:211
The Book of Landscapes (Lugones)
See *El libro de los paisajes*
Book of Legends (Bialik)
See *Safer Ha-agadah*
The Book of Lies (Crowley) **7**:210
The Book of Masks (Gourmont)
See *Le livre des masques*
A Book of Modern Criticism (Lewisohn) **19**:289
"The Book of Monastic Life" (Rilke)
See "Das Buch vom mönchischen Leben"
The Book of Monastic Life (Rilke)
See *Das Buch vom mönchischen Leben*
The Book of Monelle (Schwob)
See *Le livre de Monelle*
The Book of My Youth (Sudermann)
See *Das Bilderbuch meiner Jugend*
Book of Orm (Buchanan) **107**:17-18, 23, 25, 39, 45, 53, 57-8, 66-7, 72
Book of Pictures (Rilke)
See *Buch der Bilder*
Book of Pierrot (Carman) **7**:139
"The Book of Pilgrimage" (Rilke)
See "Das Buch von der Pilgerschaft"
The Book of Pilgrimage (Rilke)
See *Das Buch von der Pilgerschaft*

The Book of Pity and Death (Loti)
See *Le livre de la pitié et de la mort*
A Book of Poems (Balmont)
See *Sbornik stikhotvorenii*
Book of Poems (García Lorca)
See *Libro de poemas*
"The Book of Poverty and Death" (Rilke)
See "Das Buch von der Armut und vom Tode"
The Book of Poverty and Death (Rilke)
See *Das Buch von der Armut und vom Tode*
A Book of Prefaces (Mencken) **13**:358, 362-63, 381
A Book of Reflections (Annensky) **14**:19, 23, 31
"The Book of Sand" (Borges) **109**:60
The Book of Sand (Borges) **109**:49, 77, 109, 121
The Book of Small (Carr) **32**:116-17, 121, 125, 127
Book of Songs (García Lorca)
See *Canciones*
A Book of Strife in the Form of the Diary of an Old Soul (MacDonald) **9**:292, 300-01
"The Book of Tea" (Akutagawa Ryūnosuke) **16**:21-2
The Book of the American Indian (Garland) **3**:199, 200
Book of the Bayeux Tapestry (Belloc) **7**:39
"The Book of the Grotesque" (Anderson) **1**:61, 64; **10**:45, 50; **24**:21, 23, 25, 30, 33-4, 36-8, 44, 53, 57, 59; **123**:30-1
The Book of the Hanging Gardens (Schoenberg)
See *Das Buch der hangenden Garten*
The Book of the Homeless (Wharton) **129**:348, 362
The Book of the Law (Crowley) **7**:209, 211
"The Book of the Native" (Roberts) **8**:320
The Book of the Rose (Roberts) **8**:321
The Book of the Seasons (Jensen)
See *Aarstiderne*
Book of the Virgins (D'Annunzio)
See *Il libro delle vergini*
"The Book of Time" (Leino)
See "Ajan kirja"
The Book of Tricks (Hedāyat) **21**:67
Book of Verse (Masters)
See *A Book of Verses*
A Book of Verses (Henley) **8**:96-7, 106
A Book of Verses (Masters) **2**:471; **25**:296
A Book of Verses for Children (Lucas) **73**:158
The Book of Were-Wolves (Baring-Gould) **88**:35
The Book of Wonder (Dunsany) **2**:136-37; **59**:15, 17, 20, 29
"A Book That Was Lost" (Agnon) **151**:72
A Book That Was Lost and Other Stories (Agnon) **151**:72
"Booker T. Washington and His Critics" (Wells-Barnett) **125**:331
"Booker T. Washington and the Negro" (Dixon) **163**:210
"The Booker Washington Trilogy" (Lindsay) **17**:225
"Bookkeeping" (Brodkey) **123**:196
"Book-Lover" (Service) **15**:411-12
A Booklover's Holidays in the Open (Roosevelt) **69**:186-87, 189, 266
"Bookman's Diary" (Benét) **28**:7
"The Book-Plate's Petition" (Dobson) **79**:2
"Books" (Conrad) **25**:87
"Books" (Holmes) **77**:310
Books and Characters: French and English (Strachey) **12**:392-94, 401, 405
Books and Persons (Bennett) **20**:25
"The Books' Creed" (Cotter) **28**:40
"Books for Holidays in the Open" (Roosevelt) **69**:187
The Books of Ecologues and Eulogies, of Legends and Lays, and of the Hanging Gardens (George)
See *Die Bücher der Hirten- und Preisgedichte, der Sagen und Sänge, und der Hängenden Gärten*
"Books within Books" (Beerbohm) **24**:103, 125
"Boom!" (Nemerov) **124**:156, 171, 183, 188, 318
The Boom in Spanish American Literature: A Personal History (Donoso)
See *Historia personal del 'boom'*
"Boomerang" (Ingamells) **35**:137
"Boomtown" (Wolfe) **4**:527; **13**:492
Boon (Wells) **6**:528-29, 540, 548; **12**:484
Boon Island (Roberts) **23**:236-37, 240-41
"Boorī kākī" (Premchand) **21**:296
"Boors Carousing" (Warner) **131**:317
"Bop Lyrics" (Ginsberg) **120**:74
"Bopicuá" (Graham) **19**:105, 118
"Het bordeel van Ika Loch" (van Ostaijen) **33**:409, 412
The Border Bandit (Faust) **49**:54
The Border Kid (Faust) **49**:35, 38
Borderland (Tagore)
See *Prāntik*
The Borderland (Tagore)
See *Prāntik*
"Borderlands" (Guiney) **41**:214, 221-22, 227
Les bords de la route (Verhaeren) **12**:460, 466
"Boredom" (Gorky) **8**:73
"Borges" (Borges)
See "Borges y yo"
Borges: A Reader (Borges) **109**:144
"Borges and I" (Borges)
See "Borges y yo"
"Borges and Myself" (Borges)
See "Borges y yo"
"Borges y yo" (Borges) **109**:4, 6, 43, 61, 86, 112, 128, 131, 147, 151
Borghesia (Ginzburg) **156**:39
Borgia (Field) **43**:163
Borgia (Gale) **7**:280, 284-85
Bori notesz (Radnóti) **16**:417, 420
"A Boring Story" (Chekhov)
See "A Dreary Story"
Borislav (Vazov) **25**:455
"Borisu Pil'niaku" (Pasternak) **188**:250
Børn av tiden (Hamsun) **14**:221-22, 224; **49**:129, 134, 153-54; **151**:250
Born in Exile (Gissing) **3**:225, 228, 232-33; **24**:220, 223, 231, 233, 241, 243, 245-46, 248; **47**:120, 124, 141
"Børn og kunst" (Obstfelder) **23**:185
"Born to Run" (Springsteen) **131**:3, 11
Borozdy i mezhi (Ivanov) **33**:118
"The Borrowed House" (Rinehart) **52**:282
"A Borrowed Month" (Stockton) **47**:316
Borrowed Time (Bachmann)
See *Die gestundete Zeit*
"Bors to Elayne: The Fish of Broceliande" (Williams) **1**:512
Bosambo of the River (Wallace) **57**:402
Bosanska vila (Andrić) **135**:78-79
"Das Böse im Wertsystem der Kunst" (Broch) **20**:58
Der bösen (Mann) **9**:314
Bosman at His Best (Bosman) **49**:23, 32
Bosnian Chronicle (Andrić)
See *Travnička hronika*
Bosnian Story (Andrić)
See *Travnička hronika*
"The Bosom of the Country" (O'Faolain) **143**:226
"The Bosom of the McRorys" (Somerville & Ross) **51**:335, 360, 385-6
"El bosque" (Prado) **75**:211
"The Boss Girl" (Riley) **51**:277
"Boss Gorgett" (Tarkington) **9**:466
The Boss of Taroomba (Hornung) **59**:113
"The Boss over the Board" (Lawson) **27**:139
The Bosses (Azuela)
See *Los caciques*
"The Boss's Boots" (Lawson) **27**:139
"Boston" (Robinson) **101**:156
"The Boston Athenaeum" (Lowell) **1**:372
The Bostonians (James) **2**:262, 269; **11**:242, 326-28, 337; **40**:117; **47**:177-80, 182-86, 189-91, 193, 202-04; **64**:168, 172; **171**:194-98
A Boswell of Baghdad, with Diversions (Lucas) **73**:159
"Botan no kyaku" (Nagai) **51**:88-9
"Botanical Gardens" (Masters) **25**:290
"Botanist on Alp (No. 1)" (Stevens) **45**:296, 330, 334
"Botanist on Alp (No. 2)" (Stevens) **45**:296, 334
Botany Bay (Hall and Nordhoff) **23**:63
Botchan (Natsume) **2**:490-91, 493, 496; **10**:329, 332, 344
"Both Cheeks" (Freeman) **9**:74
Both of Them (Rebreanu)
See *Amîndoi*
"Both Sides of the Medal" (Lawrence) **93**:24
Both Sides of the Street (Cobb) **77**:129
Both Your Houses (Anderson) **2**:1, 3, 8, 10; **144**:11, 17, 34, 70, 72-73
Bothwell (Swinburne) **8**:427, 431-34, 441; **36**:300, 332
"Die Botschaft" (Böll) **185**:101
"The Bottle" (Zoshchenko) **15**:506
"A Bottle of Perrier" (Wharton) **3**:578; **9**:546; **129**:364
"Bottle Party" (Collier) **127**:251, 256
"Bottom's Dream: The Likeness of Poems and Jokes" (Nemerov) **124**:270, 291, 302
"A Bottomless Grave" (Bierce) **44**:40, 45
Bottoms Up (Nathan) **18**:297
Le bouchon de cristal (Leblanc) **49**:193, 197
Le Boulanger, la boulangère, et le petit mitron (Anouilh) **195**:38
"Boulôt and Boulotte" (Chopin) **14**:58
Bound East for Cardiff (O'Neill) **1**:396; **6**:327-29, 336; **49**:269
The Boundaries of Natural Science (Steiner)
See *Grenzen der naturerkenntnis*
"The Bouquet" (Chesnutt) **5**:131-32; **39**:82
"Bouquet of Belle Scavoir" (Stevens) **45**:348
"A Bouquet of Illusions" (Saltus) **8**:349
"Bouquet of Roses in Sunlight" (Stevens) **45**:334-35
Le bourg (Bosschere) **19**:52-5
"The Bourgeois King" (Darío)
See "El rey burgués"
Bourgeois Stanzas (Bacovia) **24**:64
Le bourgeon (Feydeau) **22**:78, 88
"La bourse" (Verhaeren) **12**:467
Le Bout de la route (Giono) **124**:49
Boute (Orton)
See *Loot*
Le bouton de Rose (Zola) **6**:567
"Bouvard et Pécuchet" (Proust) **161**:173
"La bovina" (Lardner) **14**:305
"The Bowden Reunion" (Jewett) **22**:126-27
Bowen's Court (Bowen) **148**:4, 6, 48, 51-52, 67-68, 70-71, 73, 106
"The Bowl" (Fitzgerald) **6**:167, 169
"The Bowl" (de la Mare) **4**:74; **53**:27
"The Bowl of Roses" (Rilke)
See "Die Rosenschale"
"The Bowling Green" (Morley) **87**:124
"Bowls" (Lawrence) **93**:68
"The Bowmen" (Machen) **4**:279
"Box 13" (Mann) **168**:186
"The Box behind the Door" (Aldrich) **125**:20
"A Box Called the Imagination" (Herbert) **168**:56
The Box Office Murders: An Inspector French Case (Crofts) **55**:86
"Box Seat" (Toomer) **172**:256-58, 274, 284-85, 287, 299, 329-30, 338
Boxwood (Warner) **131**:310-11

"The Boy" (Davies) **5**:201
"The Boy" (Meynell) **6**:298
"A Boy" (Tozzi)
See "Un ragazzo"
Boy: A Sketch (Corelli) **51**:70
The Boy Castaways (Barrie) **164**:62
The Boy Comes Home (Milne) **6**:308
The Boy David (Barrie) **2**:49; **164**:8-9, 16-17, 25
"The Boy Errant" (Middleton) **56**:191
"The Boy from Calabogie" (Drummond) **25**:146
The Boy Grew Older (Broun) **104**:98
The Boy in the Bush (Lawrence) **2**:348
"A Boy on Horseback" (Steffens) **20**:358
Boy Scouts' Life of Lincoln (Tarbell) **40**:433
Boy Scouts of America: A Handbook (Seton) **31**:277
Boy: Tales of Childhood (Dahl) **173**:23-29
"The Boy Who Had No Jackknife" (Rölvaag) **17**:347
"The Boy Who Talked with Animals" (Dahl) **173**:17
The Boy Who Was Never More Heard Of (Kafka)
See *Der Verschollene*
"Boy with a Bible" (Borowski) **9**:20
"The Boycott on Caroline" (Glaspell) **175**:52
"The Boyg, Peer Gynt, The One Only One" (Jarrell) **177**:127
Boyhood (Tolstoy)
See *Otrochestvo*
Boyhood and Youth (Carmack)
See *Verwandlungen einer Jugend*
Boyhood and Youth (Tolstoy) **28**:378
"The Boys" (Chekhov) **96**:35
"A Boy's Discovery" (McAlmon) **97**:114, 116-17, 120, 122
"The Boys of Summer" (Thomas)
See "I See the Boys of Summer"
A Boy's Town (Howells) **7**:372; **17**:162; **41**:275
"Boys' Weekly" (Orwell) **51**:221, 247, 255; **128**:283
"Boys Will Be Brutes" (Agee) **1**:17
Boži muka (Čapek) **6**:84-5; **37**:51-2; **192**:196, 222, 225-27
"The Bracelet" (Moody) **105**:225
"The Bracelet of Garnets" (Kuprin)
See "Granatovyi braslet"
"The Bracelet of Grass" (Moody) **105**:271
Ho Brachokipos (Kazantzakis) **181**:239
Brackie the Fool (Klabund) **44**:102, 107
Bracton's Note Book (Maitland) **65**:249, 252, 276, 280, 282-83, 288
The Bradmoor Murder: Including the Remarkable Deductions of Sir Henry Marquis of Scotland Yard (Post) **39**:345
"Braekman Blome" (Lagerkvist) **144**:212
"Brahma" (Fletcher) **35**:106
"Brahms, the Progressive" (Schoenberg) **75**:296, 330
"The Brain Goes Home" (Runyon) **10**:430
The Brain of India (Aurobindo) **63**:28
"Brainstorm" (Nemerov) **124**:172, 177, 308
"The Brakeman's Daughter" (Runyon) **10**:434
"La brama" (Saba) **33**:370, 375-77
"The Branch" (Roberts) **68**:297, 336
A Branch of May (Reese) **181**:336, 338
"A Branch on the Desk" (Ishikawa) **15**:130
"A Branch Road" (Garland) **3**:190, 196, 199
Branches of Adam (Fletcher) **35**:102, 105
"Brancusi" (Fondane) **159**:241
Brand (Ibsen) **2**:222, 225-28, 232-33, 235-37, 239; **8**:141-42, 146, 148-50; **16**:154, 156, 166, 191, 193; **37**:220, 223, 225, 242, 249, 258; **52**:153, 155, 163
Der Brand im Opernhaus (Kaiser) **9**:173, 180-81, 192
Der Brand von Egliswyl (Wedekind) **7**:580, 586
Brända tomten (Strindberg) **1**:450; **21**:353; **8**:415
Bransford in Arcadia; or, The Little Eohippus (Rhodes) **53**:306, 308, 317, 321, 327-28
Bränt barn (Dagerman) **17**:88-9, 94-5
"Branzilla" (Mann) **9**:314-15
"Braseal and the Fisherman" (Yeats) **31**:385
Braselien: Ein Land der Zukunft (Zweig) **17**:458
The Brasher Doubloon (Chandler) **7**:175
"Le brasier" (Apollinaire) **3**:36, 39, 43; **51**:14-15, 17, 32, 54, 60
Brass Ankle (Heyward) **59**:103, 106
The Brass Check: A Study of American Journalism (Sinclair) **160**:264, 286-87
Brat Farrar (Tey) **14**:449-50, 452-53, 460, 462-63
"Braun" (Chambers) **129**:46
The Brave African Huntress (Tutuola) **188**:280-83, 289-90, 302, 305, 307-08
"Brave and Cruel" (Welch) **22**:456, 462
The Brave Cowboy (Abbey) **160**:4, 71, 82, 85, 92
"A Brave Girl" (Phelps) **113**:341
"The Brave Man" (Stevens) **45**:282
Brave Men (Pyle) **75**:234-35, 241-44, 249-51, 260
"The Bravest Boat" (Lowry) **6**:240-41, 254
Braving the Elements (Merrill) **173**:170, 172, 189, 197, 208-9, 211, 218, 228, 242, 252
The Bravo of London (Bramah) **72**:7-8, 13
"A Braw Day" (Graham) **19**:104
"Brawl" (García Lorca)
See "Reyerta"
"The Brazier" (Apollinaire)
See "Le brasier"
Brazil (Bishop) **121**:89-91
"Brazil, January 1, 1502" (Bishop) **121**:23, 37, 69, 90
Brazil, Land of the Future (Zweig)
See *Braselien: Ein Land der Zukunft*
A Brazilian Mystic: Being the Life and Miracles of Antonio Conselheiro (Graham) **19**:105, 111
"Breach of Promise" (Runyon) **10**:434
"Bread" (Dickey) **151**:97, 184
"Bread" (Strindberg) **21**:366
"Bread" (Tolstoy)
See "Khleb"
"Bread Alone" (Wylie) **8**:536
"Bread and Wine" (Cullen) **37**:154, 169
The Bread Mill (Bergelson) **81**:17
"The Bread of Faithful Speech—Wallace Stevens and the Voices of Imagination" (Nemerov) **124**:146
The Bread of Idleness (Masters) **2**:471
The Bread of Our Early Years (Böll)
See *Das Brot der frühen Jahre*
"Bread Upon the Waters" (Wharton) **129**:366
Break of Day (Colette)
See *La naissance du jour*
The Break of Day (Colette)
See *La naissance du jour*
"Break of Day in the Trenches" (Rosenberg) **12**:289-92, 294, 297, 302-03, 306-08, 310-12
Break of Noon (Claudel)
See *Partage de midi*
Break Through in Grey Room (Burroughs) **121**:137
"Break with the past" (Levi)
See "Rompere con il passato"
"The Breaker Boy" (Darrow) **81**:64
Breakers and Granite (Fletcher) **35**:96-8, 100-01, 105
Breakfast at Tiffany's (Capote) **164**:100, 102, 111, 115, 129, 155-57, 159-61, 168-69, 208, 218
"Breakfast in Bed" (Millay) **169**:235
Breakfast Table Chat (Guest) **95**:211
"The Breaking of the Rainbows" (Nemerov) **124**:180, 185, 253
"The Breaking Point" (Benét) **7**:69
Breaking Point (Artsybashev) **31**:6-9, 11, 13
The Breaking Point (Rinehart) **52**:288-92
"Breakthrough into the Miracle" (Brod) **115**:87
The Breasts of Tiresias (Apollinaire)
See *Les mamelles de Tirésias*
Breath (Beckett) **145**:159
The Breath (Bernhard)
See *Der Atem*
Breath: A Decision (Bernhard)
See *Der Atem*
"A Breath of Air!" (Jozsef) **22**:165
"Breath of Allah" (Rohmer) **28**:277
"The Breath of Life" (Lawrence) **93**:51
"The Breath of Night" (Jarrell) **177**:155
La Brebis Egaree (Jammes) **75**:105, 119
La brebis galante (Péret) **20**:186
Brecht on Theatre, The Development of an Aesthetic (Brecht) **169**:12-14, 17-19, 21-22, 25, 55-56, 58
"Bredon Hill" (Housman) **10**:239, 247, 251
"The Breeze Comes Filling the Valley" (Miyazawa) **76**:300
"The Breeze Kid's Big Tear-Off" (Runyon) **10**:435
"Breide Hummelsbüttel" (Liliencron) **18**:216
Brejo das Almas (Drummond de Andrade) **139**:224, 228-29
Un brelan d'excommuniés (Bloy) **22**:30
"Brember" (Thomas) **105**:318
Bræen (Jensen) **41**:290-91, 293-95
Brennendes Geheimnis (Zweig) **17**:454-55, 457
"Brentano" (Walser) **18**:419
"Brer Rabbit, You's de Cutes' of 'Em All" (Johnson) **19**:210
Bressant (Hawthorne) **25**:229-30, 232, 236, 238, 241-42, 248-52
"Bret Harte and Mr. Howells as Dramatists" (Matthews) **95**:262
"Brethren" (Bunin) **6**:44, 58-9
The Brethren (Haggard) **11**:243
Brethren (Holley)
See *Samantha among the Brethren*
"Breughel: The Triumph of Time" (Nemerov) **124**:256
Brev, 1869-1906, I: 1869-1883 (Kielland) **5**:279
Brev, 1869-1906, II: 1884-1889 (Kielland) **5**:279
Breve til en landsmand (Nexø) **43**:330
"Breviario" (Villaurrutia) **80**:516
Breviario di estetica (Croce) **37**:95-6, 107, 113-15, 118-20, 127
"Breviary" (Herbert)
See "Brewiarz"
The Breviary of Aesthetics (Croce)
See *Breviario di estetica*
"Brewiarz" (Herbert) **168**:40
"Brick" (Slesinger) **10**:446
"Brick Row" (Lovecraft) **4**:266
"The Bricklayers' Lunch Hour" (Ginsberg) **120**:128
The Bridal Canopy (Agnon)
See *Hakhnasat kalah*
The Bridal Crown (Strindberg) **1**:449, 460; **8**:415
"Bridal Pond" (Gale) **7**:285
"Bridal Portion" (Peretz) **16**:393
The Bridal Wreath (Undset) **3**:510
"The Bride" (Lawrence) **93**:17
"The Bride Comes to Yellow Sky" (Crane) **11**:127, 131, 140-41, 155-56, 158, 160, 167; **17**:71, 74, 81; **32**:181
The Bride Feast (Housman) **7**:359
A Bride from the Bush (Hornung) **59**:113
The Bride of Corinth (France)
See *Les noces Corinthiennes*
Bride of Frankenstein (Whale) **63**:339, 341-42, 351-56, 358-60, 372-73, 375-79, 386-90
The Bride of Fu Manchu (Rohmer)
See *Fu Manchu's Bride*
Bride of Love (Buchanan) **107**:33
"The Bride of the Man-House" (Dunsany) **59**:12
The Bride of the Sun (Leroux) **25**:257, 260
Bride Roses (Howells) **7**:387-88
"The Bridegroom of Cana" (Pickthall) **21**:245, 249, 256-57

"Bride's Song" (Jozsef) **22**:155
"The Bridge" (Thomas) **10**:450
The Bridge (Crane) **2**:112-15, 117-19, 121-24; **5**:185-90, 194-95; **80**:77-216
The Bridge (Nezval)
See *Most*
The Bridge (Pickthall) **21**:242, 244-45, 247
"The Bridge of Fire" (Flecker) **43**:188
The Bridge of Fire (Flecker) **43**:188-89, 194
The Bridge of Years (Sarton) **120**:204, 206, 278, 314
The Bridge on the Drina (Andrić)
See *Na Drini cuprija*
"The Bridge on the Žepa" (Andrić)
See "Most na Žepi"
"The Bridge-Builders" (Kipling) **8**:186, 194; **17**:208
"Ein Brief" (Hofmannsthal) **11**:296, 299-300, 307-10
"Brief an den Vater" (Kafka) **179**:269-71
Brief an den Vater (Kafka) **2**:300; **6**:227; **29**:213; **53**:216; **112**:39-40, 53, 70, 99-101, 104, 113-17
Brief an die Mestizen, da erbittert Klage geführt wurde gegen die Unwirtlichkeit (Brecht) **169**:43-44
"Brief an einen jungen Katholiken" (Böll) **185**:40
Brief an einen jungen Katholiken (Böll) **185**:18, 146-47
Brief an einen jungen Nichtkatholiken (Böll) **185**:146
Brief an Felice und andere korrespondenz aus der verlobungszeit (Kafka) **6**:222; **112**:88, 108, 113; **179**:314, 319
"Brief an meine Söhne" (Böll) **185**:103
Brief aus dem Harz (Roth) **33**:347
"Brief History of My Opinions" (Santayana) **40**:359
A Brief Life (Onetti)
See *La vida breve*
"Brief Seasons of Intellectual Dissipation" (Bierce) **44**:10
"A Brief Sketch of Serrano Culture" (Benedict) **60**:147, 150
"The Brief Study of Dendrophilia" (Benchley) **55**:18
Briefe (Ball) **104**:72, 75
Briefe (Liliencron) **18**:213
Briefe (Rilke) **195**:253, 269, 275-76, 307
Briefe 1902-1924 (Kafka) **179**:289-90, 322
Briefe 1906-1907 (Rilke) **195**:239
Briefe an die Schwester Hilde, 1938-1943 (Kolmar) **40**:180
"Briefe an einen Freund jenseits der Grenzen" (Böll) **185**:50
Briefe an Felice (Kafka)
See *Brief an Felice und andere korrespondenz aus der verlobungszeit*
Briefe an Sidonie Ná derny von Borutin, 1913-1936 (Kraus) **5**:292
Briefe aus dem Gefangnis (Toller) **10**:478, 491
Briefe aus Muzot (Rilke) **195**:300
Briefe Hermann Sudermanns an seine Frau (Sudermann) **15**:434
Briefe über Cézanne (Rilke) **195**:243, 286, 289, 291, 293
"Bright" (Cummings) **137**:58, 67-68
"Bright and Morning Star" (Wright) **136**:316, 318, 320-21
"Bright Bindings" (Cullen) **37**:168
Bright Cages (Morley) **87**:140
The Bright Island (Bennett) **5**:32, 46; **197**:16, 18-19
The Bright Messenger (Blackwood) **5**:77
The Bright Shawl (Hergesheimer) **11**:267, 269, 271, 276
Bright Star (Barry) **11**:56-7, 60
Bright Unity (Kandinsky) **92**:32
"Brighten's Sister-in-Law" (Lawson) **27**:126, 128, 145, 147
"The Brighter Side" (Runyon) **10**:430
The Brightest Star (Arenas)
See *Arturo, la estrella más brillante*
Brigit (Gregory)
See *The Story Brought by Brigit*
The Brimming Cup (Fisher) **87**:75
Brindelles pour allumer la foi (Jammes) **75**:119
"Brindisi funebre" (Carducci) **32**:90
Bring the Monkey (Franklin) **7**:267-68, 270
"Bringing Home the Cows" (Roberts) **8**:320
Bringing Jazz! (Bodenheim) **44**:73-4
Brinkley Manor (Wodehouse)
See *Right Ho, Jeeves*
The Brinkmanship of Galahad Threepwood (Wodehouse) **108**:335, 372
"Bristol Fashion" (Graham) **19**:109, 129
Britain and West Africa (Cary) **196**:188
Britain's Daughter (Bottomley) **107**:3-4
"Britain's Struggle for Survival: The Labour Government after Three Years" (Orwell) **128**:260
"Britannia Victrix" (Bridges) **1**:125
The British School: An Anecdotal Guide to the British Painters and Paintings in the National Gallery (Lucas) **73**:173
Broadacre City (Wright) **95**:405
Broadway Jones (Cohan) **60**:156, 158, 163-4, 166, 172
Brodie (Borges)
See *El informe de Brodie*
Brodie's Report (Borges)
See *El informe de Brodie*
"Brodjačie muzykanty" (Zabolotsky) **52**:375
Den broendende busk (Undset) **197**:295-97, 299-300, 311
"A Broken Appointment" (Hardy) **4**:164; **53**:78
"The Broken Blade" (Rohmer) **28**:286
Broken Blossoms (Griffith) **68**:149, 153, 168, 170, 172, 214, 233, 239-40
"The Broken Bowl" (Merrill) **173**:255
The Broken Commandment (Shimazaki Toson)
See *Hakai*
"Broken Field Running" (Bambara) **116**:3-5
"The Broken Gates of Death" (Yeats) **31**:418
Broken Hearts (Gilbert) **3**:218
"The Broken Home" (Merrill) **173**:152-53, 174, 212, 214-15, 218, 234, 252, 258-60
The Broken Jug (Bernhard)
See *Der zerbrochene Krug*
"The Broken Mirror" (Hedāyat)
See "Ayina-yi shikasta"
"Broken Necks" (Hecht) **101**:36
"The Broken Nest" (Tagore)
See "Nashtanir"
"The Broken Plates" (Hartmann) **73**:128
Broken Record (Campbell) **5**:122
The Broken Root (Barea)
See *La raiz rota*
"The Broken Scaffold" (di Donato) **159**:209
The Broken Share (Lewisohn) **19**:261
Broken Souls (Kazantzakis) **181**:237
"The Broken Tower" (Crane) **2**:117, 121-22, 124-26; **5**:189; **80**:142
The Broken Trio (Svevo)
See *Terzetto spezzato*
"The Broken Tryst" (Ledwidge) **23**:120
"The Broken Wheel" (Saroyan) **137**:191, 193
The Broken Wing (Naidu) **80**:271
"The Broken Wings" (Gibran) **1**:326; **9**:90, 92-3
"Broken Wings" (James) **47**:201
"A Broken World" (O'Faolain) **143**:222, 234, 253
Bröllopsbesvär (Dagerman) **17**:94, 97
"The Broncho That Would Not Be Broken" (Lindsay) **17**:226-27
"The Bronckhurst Divorce Case" (Kipling) **8**:185
Bronenosets "Potyomkin" (Eisenstein) **57**:154, 156-57, 159-69, 174-75, 178-87, 190-91, 196-98, 200-01
The Brontës: Their Lives Recorded by Their Contemporaries (Delafield) **61**:133
"Bronz Trumpets and Sea Water" (Wylie) **8**:521
"Bronze" (Merrill) **173**:230
The Bronze Collar (Faust) **49**:53
"The Bronze David of Donatello" (Jarrell) **177**:162, 211
"The Bronze Door" (Chandler) **179**:128-29
The Bronze Hand (Wells) **35**:422
"A Bronze Head" (Yeats) **18**:447; **93**:404
"The Bronze Horses" (Lowell) **8**:226, 236
"The Bronze Paper-Knife" (Hawthorne) **25**:233, 247
"The Bronze Sounding" (Gurney) **33**:88, 98
"Bronze Tablets" (Lowell) **8**:235
"Bronzovyj poèt" (Annensky) **14**:27
Brood of the Witch Queen (Rohmer) **28**:285, 295
"The Brook" (Thomas) **10**:452, 455-56
Brook Evans (Glaspell) **55**:241-42; **175**:59, 133-34, 138, 141
"The Brook in February" (Roberts) **8**:321
The Brook Kerith (Moore) **7**:478-79, 486, 488-89, 494, 497-98
"The Brooklyn Bridge" (Mayakovski) **18**:248, 258-60
"Brooklyn Bridge" (Morley) **87**:127
"Brooklyn Bridge Nocturne" (García Lorca)
See "Ciudad sin sueño"
"Brooklyn Pinafore" (Allen) **87**:60
The Broom-Squire (Baring-Gould) **88**:27
"Broomsticks" (de la Mare) **4**:78; **53**:23
Broomsticks (de la Mare) **53**:16, 22, 27
"Das Brot" (Borchert) **5**:109
Das Brot der frühen Jahre (Böll) **185**:30, 32, 50, 83, 94, 129-30, 133, 135, 139, 149, 172-73, 176, 178-79
"Brothel" (van Ostaijen) **33**:421
"A Brother" (Mann)
See "Ein Bruder"
"Brother and Sister" (Lawrence) **93**:67
"Brother Death" (Anderson) **24**:43
"Brother, Do Not Give Your Life" (Yosano)
See "Kimi Shinitamô koto nakare"
"Brother Hitler" (Mann)
See "Bruder Hitler"
Brother Juan (Unamuno)
See *El hermano Juan o el mundo es teatro*
"Brother Lucerta" (D'Annunzio)
See "Fra' Lucerta"
Brother Man (Mais) **8**:241-50
"Brother Martin" (Bernanos) **3**:127
"A Brother of the Battuti" (Symons) **11**:428
Brother of the Cheyennes (Faust)
See *Frontier Feud*
Brother Sun (Housman) **7**:359
Brother Wolf (Housman) **7**:359
Brothereaters (Kazantzakis)
See *The Fratricides*
"Brotherhood" (Baker) **10**:27
"Brotherhood" (Markham) **47**:284
The Brotherhood of Man (Roberts) **23**:240
"The Brother-in-Arms" (George)
See "Der Waffengefährte"
"Brothers" (Bunin)
See "Brethren"
"Brothers" (Johnson) **3**:241, 244
"The Brothers" (Muir) **87**:172, 174
Brothers and Sisters (Compton-Burnett) **180**:115, 122-26, 130, 140, 192, 194-95
The Brothers Ashkenazi (Singer) **33**:382-83, 386-90, 392, 396-98, 400, 402
The Brothers at Arms (Giacosa)
See *Il fratello d'armi*
Brothers on the Trail (Faust) **49**:36, 45, 56-8, 60
Brothers Three (Oskison) **35**:276, 278-79
"Brothpot" (Verga) **3**:540
"Brought Forward" (Graham) **19**:104
"Brown Boy to Brown Girl" (Cullen) **4**:45; **37**:144, 152
"The Brown Coat" (Futrelle) **19**:96
"A Brown Girl Dead" (Cullen) **4**:49; **37**:140, 152, 160
"The Brown Man's Servant" (Jacobs) **22**:107

"Brown of Calaveras" (Harte) **25**:222
Brown on Resolution (Forester) **152**:163
The Brown Owl (Ford) **15**:93
"Brown River, Smile" (Toomer) **172**:286-87, 312
"The Brownie" (Milne) **88**:244
"Brownskin Blues" (McKay) **41**:329
Bruce (Davidson) **24**:158
"Bruchstück einer Hysterie-Analyse" (Freud) **52**:115
"Brudens blege ansigt" (Obstfelder) **23**:178-79
"Ein Bruder" (Mann) **168**:155, 158
Die Brüder (Heyse) **8**:119
Der Bruder (Mann) **9**:325
Die Brüder Grimm (Zuckmayer) **191**:288, 291
"Bruder Hitler" (Mann) **14**:362; **168**:179
"Bruder Liederlich" (Liliencron) **18**:213
"Bruges and anvers" (Verhaeren) **12**:471
"Brugglesmith" (Kipling) **8**:193, 202-04
Le bruissement de la langue (Barthes) **135**:140, 142, 149, 152, 156, 159, 162, 189
"Los brujos de la tormenta primaveral" (Asturias) **184**:14
Brulard (Sarraute) **145**:306
"Brumana" (Flecker) **43**:192, 194
"Brummy Tom" (Davies) **5**:198
"Brummy Usen" (Lawson) **27**:119
"The Bruno Philosophy" (Joyce) **159**:326
Bruno's Dream (Murdoch) **171**:269-70, 273, 275, 278, 312, 329
"The Brushwood Boy" (Kipling) **8**:182; **17**:214
Brutality (Griffith) **68**:250
"The Brute" (Chekhov)
See *Medved*
"The Brute" (Moody) **105**:225, 234, 238, 255, 271-72, 275
"The Brute" (Stephens) **4**:407
The Brute (Heyward) **59**:92, 94
The Brute (Micheaux) **76**:262
Brutus Ultor (Field) **43**:153-54, 171
Os bruzundangus (Lima Barreto) **23**:167
"Bryan, Bryan, Bryan, Bryan" (Lindsay) **17**:227, 230, 235-36, 245
"Bryan of Brittany" (Flecker) **43**:192
Brynhild (Wells) **12**:515
"Buat album D. S." (Anwar) **22**:22
"Buat Gadis Rasid" (Anwar) **22**:23
"Buat Mirat" (Anwar) **22**:24
"Bubba" (Childress) **116**:36
"The Bubble of Reputation" (Bierce) **44**:45
"Bubbling Well Road" (Kipling) **8**:185
The Buccaneer (Anderson) **2**:2; **144**:8, 37, 71
The Buccaneers (Wharton) **3**:567; **9**:544, 549, 551; **129**:364
The Buccaneers and Pirates of Our Coast (Stockton) **47**:327
Buch der Bilder (Rilke) **1**:409-10; **6**:357-58; **11**:357; **19**:302; **195**:175, 180-84, 191, 195, 266, 283-84, 292, 321
Buch der Freunde (Hofmannsthal) **11**:300
Das Buch der hangenden Garten (Schoenberg) **75**:292-93, 296, 358-59
Das Buch der Narrheit (Herzl) **36**:131-32
Das buch der Sprüche und Bedenken (Schnitzler) **4**:395
Das Buch vom mönchischen Leben (Rilke) **195**:188, 216, 250-52, 256, 263-65, 268
"Das Buch vom mönchischen Leben" (Rilke) **195**:176, 327
Das Buch von den Polnischen Juden (Agnon) **151**:36
Das Buch von der Armut und vom Tode (Rilke) **6**:364; **195**:175, 178
Das Buch von der Pilgerschaft (Rilke) **6**:364; **195**:175, 177, 308-09
Die Bücher der Hirten- und Preisgedichte, der Sagen und Sänge, und der Hängenden Gärten (George) **2**:149-50; **14**:195, 200, 205-06
"Die Bucher und der Krieg" (Zweig) **17**:458
"Buchmendel" (Zweig) **17**:444
Die Büchse der Pandora (Wedekind) **7**:575-76, 578, 582
"Buck Fanshaw's Funeral" (Twain) **59**:210
The Buck in the Snow (Millay) **169**:267
The Buck in the Snow, and Other Poems (Millay) **4**:310, 313; **49**:206-07, 227
"Buckdancer's Choice" (Dickey) **151**:92-93
Buckdancer's Choice (Dickey) **151**:89-90, 92-93, 95, 98, 100, 102, 108-10, 114, 172, 202-3, 217
"The Bucket and the Rope" (Powys) **9**:377
"Buckingham Palace" (Milne) **6**:311, 313, 315; **88**:244
"The Buckled Bag" (Rinehart) **52**:303
"Buckolt's Gate" (Lawson) **27**:131
"Buco nero di Auschwitz" (Levi) **109**:313
Bucólica (Pardo Bazán) **189**:243, 260
Bucoliques (Renard) **17**:304
"Bud of the Aloe" (Mansfield) **164**:335
Buddenbrooks (Mann) **2**:412-13, 418, 420, 425, 427, 429-30, 433, 435-36, 439; **8**:252, 254-56, 258, 261, 263, 268-69, 272; **14**:326, 341, 354; **21**:163-64, 166-67, 172, 179, 183; **35**:204-73; **44**:145, 172, 187, 189, 205-6; **60**:322, 326-28, 335, 350, 363; **168**:89-90, 116, 157, 172-73, 183, 187
Buddenbrooks: Verfall einer Familie (Mann)
See *Buddenbrooks*
Buddha (Hartmann) **73**:110-111, 116, 134
Buddha (Kazantzakis) **5**:268, 271-72; **181**:235, 308, 310-11
"Buddha and Brahma" (Adams) **52**:14
"Buddha at Kamakura" (Kipling) **8**:200
"Buddy Can You Spare a Dime" (Burroughs) **121**:140
Buddy Holly: A Rock 'n' Roll Collection (Holly) **65**:153
Buddy Holly in 1958 (Holly) **65**:137
Buddy Holly Showcase (Holly) **65**:144
The Buddy Holly Story (Holly) **65**:144-47, 151
The Buddy Holly Story, Volume II (Holly) **65**:144, 147, 150
Budem kak solntse (Balmont) **11**:29-32, 34-7, 39-40, 42
"The Budget" (Bosman) **49**:10
Un buen negocio (Sánchez) **37**:314-15
"El buen sentido" (Vallejo) **56**:309-10
"La buena fama" (Valera y Alcala-Galiano) **10**:501, 508
Buenos Aires Etchings (Arlt)
See *Aguafuertes*
"Los buenos muchachos" (Pereda) **16**:372
"Los buenos tiempos" (Pardo Bazán) **189**:226-27
El buey suelto (Pereda) **16**:367-71, 374, 377, 380
Buf-e kur (Hedāyat) **21**:67-70, 73, 76-7, 79-81, 84-5
Buffonate (Papini) **22**:274, 280-81
"Bugen" (Obstfelder) **23**:178
"Buie Anajohn" (Carman) **7**:138
The Builder of Bridges (Sutro) **6**:420, 422
The Builders (Glasgow) **2**:181, 186, 188; **7**:346-47
The Builders (Housman) **7**:359
"Builders of Ruins" (Meynell) **6**:291
Building a Character (Stanislavsky) **167**:244, 247, 253, 264, 268, 276, 279, 300, 305-7, 312, 329, 339-40
"The Building of the Skyscraper" (Oppen) **107**:344
"Building Speculation" (Calvino)
See "La speculazione edilizia"
Building Speculation (Calvino) **183**:96
Building the Earth (Teilhard de Chardin) **9**:504-05
Le buisson ardent (Rolland) **23**:261, 276
"Buiyon no tsuma" (Dazai Osamu) **11**:176-77, 179, 186-88
"The Bulgarian Language" (Vazov)
See "Balgarskijat ezik"
"The Bulgarian Soldier" (Vazov)
See "Balgarskijat vojnik"
Buliao qing (Chang) **184**:125
"Bull" (Aleixandre)
See "Toro"
"The Bull" (Södergran)
See "Tjuren"
"The Bull Fight" (Jensen) **41**:292
"The Bull That Thought" (Kipling) **8**:195, 205; **17**:208
Bulldog Drummond at Bay (Sapper) **44**:316-18, 320-22
Bulldog Drummond Returns (Sapper)
See *The Return of Bulldog Drummond*
Bulldog Drummond Strikes Back (Sapper) **44**:319
Bull-Dog Drummond: The Adventures of a Demobilized Officer Who Found Peace Dull (Sapper) **44**:312-13, 316-24
"The Buller-Podington Contract" (Stockton) **47**:323
"The Bullet of the Fated Ten" (Warung) **45**:419, 422
"The Bullfinches" (Hardy) **53**:81, 86
Bullivant and the Lambs (Compton-Burnett)
See *Manservant and Maidservant*
"The Bullock" (Paterson) **32**:381
"The Bullocky" (Ingamells) **35**:137
"Bulls" (London) **9**:281
"The Bulls of the Resurrection" (Lowry) **6**:246
The Buln-Buln and the Brolga (Furphy) **25**:174, 183
The Bulpington of Bulp (Wells) **6**:548-51
"Bulto sin amor" (Aleixandre) **113**:15, 49
The Bulwark (Dreiser) **10**:178, 184, 191-92, 194, 197; **35**:34, 36, 39, 48, 54-6; **83**:97
"Bums at Sunset" (Wolfe) **13**:492
"Bums, on Waking" (Dickey) **151**:89
The Bun (Prishvin)
See *Za volshebnym kolobkom*
"Bun bast" (Hedāyat) **21**:74, 81
"A Bunch of Blues" (Handy) **97**:70
"A Bunch of Flowers" (Cankar) **105**:165
"A Bunch of Roses" (Paterson) **32**:369
"A Bunch of Violets" (Bramah) **72**:9
"Bunches" (Andrić)
See "Snopići"
Der bund der schwachen (Asch) **3**:66
Bungaku hyōron (Natsume) **10**:332, 343-44
Bungakuron (Natsume) **10**:343-44
"Bunkai yatsu atari" (Masaoka) **18**:225
"Bunner Sisters" (Wharton) **3**:564, 566, 572, 580; **129**:362
Bunner Sisters (Wharton) **129**:352
Bunt mašin (Tolstoy) **18**:360, 368-69
Bunte Beute (Liliencron) **18**:212
Das Bunte Buch (Hauptmann) **4**:200
"Bunte Weise" (Kandinsky) **92**:67
Bunter Kreis (Kandinsky) **92**:32
Buntes Leben (Kandinsky) **92**:47
"La buonissima madre" (Svevo) **35**:369
Buoyant Billions (Shaw) **3**:397
"El buque" (Lugones) **15**:285
"Buques suicidantes" (Quiroga) **20**:212
"A Burden of Easter Vigil" (Johnson) **19**:246
"The Burden of Itys" (Wilde) **8**:495; **41**:378
The Burden of Nineveh (Housman) **7**:360
The Burden of Tyre (Brennan) **17**:43, 50-1
Bureau de change (Dunsany) **2**:144
Bürger Schippel (Sternheim) **8**:367-69, 372, 375, 377-78
Die Bürger von Calais (Kaiser) **9**:171, 173-74, 180, 183, 185-87, 189
"Bürgerliche Liebe" (Brod) **115**:94
"The Burghers" (Hardy) **4**:152
The Burghers of Calais (Kaiser)
See *Die Bürger von Calais*
"Burghers of Petty Death" (Stevens) **12**:364; **45**:349-50
"The Burgher's Wife" (Austin) **25**:35
"The Burglar of Babylon" (Bishop) **121**:7, 73-4
The Burglar of the Zodiac (Benét) **28**:6, 9

"The Burglars" (Grahame) **64**:79
Burglars in Paradise (Phelps) **113**:336, 340
"Burial" (Sarton) **120**:268
"Burial at Sea" (Ady) **11**:14
"The Burial in England" (Flecker) **43**:187-88, 190, 192, 194
"The Burial of a Queen" (Noyes) **7**:510
"The Burial of the Rats" (Stoker) **8**:394
"Buried Alive" (Hedāyat)
See "Zendeh be-gur"
Buried Alive (Bennett) **5**:24, 29, 37-8, 43, 49, 51; **20**:33; **197**:17, 36-7, 39-41, 104
The Buried Candelabrum (Zweig)
See *Der Begrabene Leuchter*
"Buried Soldiers" (Vazov) **25**:453
The Buried Temple (Maeterlinck) **3**:326-27
Buried Treasure (Roberts) **68**:298-300, 308, 312, 324, 326, 365
"Burla de D. Pedro a caballo" (García Lorca) **49**:112-13
"Burla de don Pedro a caballo" (García Lorca) **181**:91
"Una burla riuscita" (Svevo) **2**:542, 545-46, 553-54
Una burla riuscita (Svevo) **2**:542, 545-46, 553-54; **35**:333, 336-37, 345, 350-51, 364
A Burlesque Biography (Twain) **59**:168
"Burlesque, I Love It" (Cummings) **137**:4
"Burma Casualty" (Lewis) **3**:289-90
Burmese Days (Orwell) **2**:502, 505, 508, 510; **6**:342, 351; **15**:298, 322; **31**:188, 191, 193, 199, 204; **51**:219, 248, 261; **128**:255-56, 261, 264-66, 268-71, 274, 285, 291, 295; **129**:225, 234, 243, 245
"The Burned Chair" (Rinehart) **52**:291
The Burned House (Strindberg)
See *Brända tomten*
"The Burned house" (Yourcenar)
See "La Maison brûlée"
"The Burning" (Trambley) **163**:292, 321, 337-40, 346
"The Burning Baby" (Thomas) **1**:466; **45**:398, 408, 411-12; **105**:296-97, 299-301, 324, 326, 329, 336-38, 348, 353
The Burning Baby (Thomas) **105**:324-25
Burning Bright: A Play in Story Form (Steinbeck) **135**:250, 265
Burning Buildings (Balmont)
See *Goriashchie zdaniia*
The Burning Bush (Undset)
See *Den broendende busk*
Burning City (Benét) **7**:74-5, 79-80
Burning City: New Poems (Benét)
See *Burning City*
Burning Daylight (London) **9**:255, 261, 266, 273, 276, 281
The Burning Glass, and Other Poems (de la Mare) **4**:79
The Burning Mountain (Fletcher) **35**:100, 102, 107, 110
"The Burning of the Temple" (Rosenberg) **12**:288, 295, 301, 310
The Burning Secret (Zweig)
See *Brennendes Geheimnis*
The Burning Spear (Galsworthy) **45**:67, 69-70
"Burning the Leaves" (Nemerov) **124**:177, 179, 249
"Burning the Letters" (Jarrell) **177**:126, 129, 170, 176-77, 193, 195
"The Burning Town" (Söderberg) **39**:437
"The Burning Wheel" (Bishop) **103**:9-10, 18
Burning Your Boats: Stories (Carter) **139**:139
"Burns" (Henley) **8**:103
"Burns: An Ode" (Swinburne) **36**:342, 345
Burnt Belly; or, The Mad Mother (Artaud)
See *Ventre brûlé; ou, la mère folle*
A Burnt Child (Dagerman)
See *Bränt barn*
The Burnt Flower-Bed (Betti)
See *L'aiuola bruciata*
"Burnt Lands" (Roberts) **8**:314
The Burnt Offering (Duncan) **60**:184, 186-8, 206, 210, 214, 217-8, 238, 249
The Burnt Ones (White) **176**:219, 228, 244
Burroughs File (Burroughs) **121**:137-38, 142, 144
"The Burrow" (Kafka)
See "Der bau"
"A Burst of Light" (Lorde) **173**:90, 95
A Burst of Light (Lorde) **173**:89, 108, 110, 118-19, 122, 141
"Bury Me In a Free Land" (Harper) **14**:256-57, 259-61, 263
"The Bus" (Jackson) **187**:283, 337-38
La busca (Baroja) **8**:48, 61
"La busca de Averroes" (Borges) **109**:37, 103, 106, 150, 152-53
"Busca en Todas las Cosas" (Gonzalez Martinez) **72**:149
Busca mi esquela y Primer amor (Garro) **153**:72
"Los buscadores de oro" (Lugones) **15**:294
Die Büschse der Pandora (Pabst) **127**:299-300, 302-5, 308-10, 312-13, 331-32, 339, 348, 351, 354, 358
"Bush Cats" (Lawson) **27**:131
"A Bush Christening" (Paterson) **32**:373
"Bush Church" (Baynton) **57**:7-12, 23
The Bush Garden (Frye) **165**:199, 204
"Bush River" (Cary) **196**:217
Bush Studies (Baynton) **57**:2, 4, 7, 9-14, 19-20, 23-28, 30, 32
"The Bush Undertaker" (Lawson) **27**:119, 129, 132, 142-43
"A Busher's Letters Home" (Lardner) **14**:301, 312
"A Bushman's Song" (Paterson) **32**:369, 373
"Bushranging and Outlawry in Australasia" (Warung) **45**:419
"Bushwackers" (Barthes) **135**:194
The Bushwhackers and Other Stories (Barthes) **135**:194
A Business Failure (Bjoernson)
See *En fallit*
"A Business Family" (McAlmon) **97**:117
The Business of Being a Woman (Tarbell) **40**:442-45
"A Business Partnership" (Svevo) **2**:545
Busman's Honeymoon: A Love Story with Detective Interruptions (Sayers) **2**:528, 530-31, 536-37; **15**:377, 379, 381, 389, 390, 394
"Buson the Haiku Poet" (Masaoka)
See "Haijin Buson"
"The Bust of the Emperor" (Roth)
See "Die Büste des Kaisers"
"Le buste de l'empereur" (Roth)
See "Die Büste des Kaisers"
"Die Büste des Kaisers" (Roth) **33**:338, 340, 351, 362
"The Busted" (Jozsef) **22**:161
"Busy" (Milne) **6**:314-15; **88**:241
"The Busy Heart" (Brooke) **7**:124
"But at the Stroke of Midnight" (Warner) **131**:323
But Life Is Alive (Hamsun)
See *Men livet lever*
"But Not Forgotten" (Parker) **143**:323
"But now we await great things" (Lagerkvist)
See "Men nu vänta vi stora ting . . ."
But, Prince, If Winter Should Come (Babits)
See *Herceg, hátha megjön a tél is*
"But the One on the Right" (Parker) **143**:331
But Tommorrow (Grieg)
See *Men imorgen*
"But 'Twas a Famous Victory" (Graham) **19**:120
But Young the World Must Be (Grieg)
See *Ung må verden ennu vaere*
"But Your Brows Are a Storm" (Lasker-Schueler) **57**:331
"Butch Minds Baby" (Runyon) **10**:432, 434
"Butcher Rogaum's Door" (Dreiser) **10**:197-200
The Butcher's Revolt (Artaud)
See *La Révolte du Boucher*
"Butō" (Nagai) **51**:99
"Butōkai" (Akutagawa Ryūnosuke) **16**:34, 36
"The Butter War in Greenfield" (Rölvaag) **17**:347
"Das butterbrotpapier" (Morgenstern) **8**:306
"Buttercup Day" (Milne) **88**:242
"Butterflies" (Kipling) **17**:209
"Butterflies" (Roberts) **8**:321
"The Butterflies Showing Off" (Lindsay) **17**:240
"Butterfly" (Bialik)
See "Ziporeth"
"The Butterfly" (Chekhov)
See "Poprygin'ia"
"Butterfly" (Lawrence) **93**:55, 75
Butterfly (Moricz)
See *Pillangó*
The Butterfly House (Freeman) **9**:74
"A Butterfly Makes" (Wright) **136**:300
The Butterfly's Evil Spell (García Lorca)
See *El maleficio de la mariposa*
Buttress (Remizov)
See *Ukrepa*
"La buveuse du sang" (Vallette) **67**:278
"buy me an ounce" (Cummings) **137**:64
Búzakalász (Moricz) **33**:238
"By a Buddha Temple" (Noguchi) **80**:361
"By a Dying Man's Pillow" (Peretz) **16**:396
"By Al Liebowitz's Pool" (Nemerov) **124**:267, 269, 293, 295, 302
"By Ana Liffey" (Stephens) **4**:419
By Candlelight (Whale) **63**:339, 386
"By Dreams I Captured" (Balmont)
See "Ia mech'toiu lovil"
By Faith Alone (Shestov)
See *Sola Fide: Tolko veroyu*
"By Force of Karma" (Hearn) **9**:130
"By Himself" (Pirandello)
See "Da sé"
"By Moonlight" (Mansfield) **39**:295
"By Myself" (Bialik)
See "Levadi"
By Night Under the Stone Bridge (Perutz)
See *Nachts unter der steinernen Brücke*
"By Oneself" (Pirandello)
See "Da sé"
"By Severn" (Gurney) **33**:87
By the Aurelian Wall, and Other Elegies (Carman) **7**:134-35, 138-39
"By the Babe Unborn" (Chesterton) **6**:101
"By the Brandy Still" (Andrić)
See "Kod kazana"
By the Century's Deathbed (Hardy) **48**:60
"By the Cold Waters, by Pentavli" (Sikelianos) **39**:418
"By the Danube" (Jozsef) **22**:163, 165
By the Earth's Corpse (Hardy) **48**:60
"By the Fire" (Ingamells) **35**:137
"By the Gateway of India, Bombay" (Lewis) **3**:290
By the Ionian Sea (Gissing) **3**:224; **47**:123, 135
By the Light of the Fires (Bergelson) **81**:16
By the Light of the Soul (Freeman) **9**:70, 73
"By the Margin of the Great Deep" (Baker) **10**:20, 26
"By the North Sea" (Swinburne) **36**:321, 334-35, 340-44, 346
"By the Old Castle of Komoro" (Shimazaki Toson)
See "Komoro naru kojo no hotri"
By the Open Sea (Strindberg) **1**:444, 460; **21**:352-53
"By the Sea" (Khodasevich) **15**:206, 209
"By the Seashore" (Scott) **6**:391
By the Shore (Carpenter) **88**:55
By the Stars (Ivanov)
See *Po zvezdam*
"By the Statue of King Charles at Charing Cross" (Johnson) **19**:243-44, 246, 253, 255

"By the Urn of P. B. Shelley" (Carducci) **32**:96, 109
"By the Waters of Babylon" (Benét) **7**:81
"By the Waters of Paradise" (Crawford) **10**:157-58
"By the Willow Spring" (Scott) **6**:385
By the Window (Andreyev) **3**:28
"By the Yellow Moonrock" (Sharp) **39**:358, 375
"By Their Fruits" (Cullen) **37**:168
"By This Ax I Rule!" (Howard) **8**:131-32
By Way of Introduction (Milne) **6**:316; **88**:230
"By Way of Preface: The Theatre as Religion" (Anderson) **144**:34
By Way of Sainte-Beuve (Proust)
See *Contre Sainte-Beuve*
"By Word of Mouth" (Kipling) **8**:186
"Bye-Products in Evolution" (Wells) **133**:259
Bygmester Solness (Ibsen) **2**:218, 220, 222-23, 226-27, 229-36, 238; **8**:142, 149
Bygone Love (Quiroga)
See *Pasado amor*
Bygones (Pinero) **32**:412
Bylow Hill (Cable) **4**:27, 31
Byl'yo (Pilnyak) **23**:199, 207
Byōshō Rokushaku (Masaoka) **18**:224
Byron and His Group (Brandes) **10**:60
"Byron in Sintra" (Andrić)
See "Bajron u Sintri"
Byron on Wordsworth (Scott) **6**:393
"Byron's World" (Henley) **8**:105
Byvshii lyudi (Gorky) **8**:73-4
The Byzantine Achievement (Byron) **67**:89
"The Byzantine Princess" (Quiroga)
See "La princesa Bizantina"
Byzantinisches Christentum (Ball) **104**:21-22, 36, 47, 76
"Byzantium" (Yeats) **1**:560, 579, 581-82; **11**:525, 529; **18**:444-45, 452-56, 458-60; **31**:403, 411; **116**:260-343
C (Baring) **8**:38, 40
C. P. Cavafy: Unpublished Prose Pieces (Cavafy)
See *K. P. Kavafes: Anekdota peza keimena*
"Ça ira" (Carducci) **32**:106-07
A Cabal of Hypocrites (Bulgakov)
See *Kabala sviatosh*
"Caballera negra" (Aleixandre) **113**:49
"El caballero de la mesa redonda" (Alas) **29**:20-1
"El Caballero de la Triste Figura" (Unamuno) **148**:240
El caballero encantado (Pérez Galdós) **27**:268
"The Caballero's Way" (Henry) **19**:185
"Los caballos de Abdera" (Lugones) **15**:293
Cabbages and Kings (Henry) **1**:347; **19**:168, 177-78, 180-82, 192-94
"The Cabbalists" (Peretz) **16**:392, 397
"Cabeza, en el recuerdo" (Aleixandre) **113**:3
"Cabinet Government in the United States" (Wilson) **79**:484, 487, 490
The Cabinet Minister (Pinero) **32**:404-06, 411-12
The Cabinet of Dr. Caligari (Wiene)
See *Das Kabinett des Dr. Caligari*
A Cabinet of Gems (MacDonald) **9**:304
"A Cabinet of Seeds Displayed" (Nemerov) **124**:227, 259, 261
Cables to Rage (Lorde) **173**:73
"Cabrinowitsch" (Werfel) **8**:472
"Caccavone" (Papini) **22**:281
Il cacciatore d'anitre (Betti) **5**:62
Cachiporra's Puppets (García Lorca)
See *Los títeres de Cachiporra*
Cachivaches y tradiciones y artículos históricas (Palma) **29**:258-59
Los caciques (Azuela) **3**:77, 79; **145**:12, 14, 17, 28
Cactus Country (Abbey) **160**:70, 78
"Cada cosa, cada cosa" (Aleixandre) **113**:8
Cada uno y su vida (Martinez Sierra and Martinez Sierra) **6**:283
"A Caddy's Diary" (Lardner) **14**:297-98, 307
"Cadgwith" (Johnson) **19**:255-56
Cádiz (Pérez Galdós) **27**:287-88
"Cadore" (Carducci) **32**:95
Cady's Life (Frank) **17**:114
Caesar and Cleopatra (Shaw) **3**:378, 395, 400; **9**:413-14, 417, 419-20; **21**:324; **45**:221, 223, 239-40
Caesar or Nothing (Baroja)
See *César o nada*
Caesar-Antichrist (Jarry)
See *César-Antéchrist*
"Caesar's Time" (Grove) **4**:144
Caetés (Ramos) **32**:421-22, 424-28, 430-31, 433-35, 437-38
"Café des exilés" (Cable) **4**:32
"Cafe Girls" (McAlmon) **97**:93
"Cage d'oiseau" (Garneau) **13**:195, 203
The Caged Eagle, and Other Poems (Sterling) **20**:386
The Caged Lion (Yonge) **48**:376
"Caged with a Wild Man" (Crane) **11**:160
Les cages flottantes (Leroux) **25**:260
Cagliostro (Huidobro) **31**:121, 123, 138, 141-43
Cagliostro Defeated (Tolstoy) **18**:373
Cahier 57 (Proust) **161**:144-49
Cahier 60 (Proust) **161**:145
Cahier 74 (Proust) **161**:144-50
Cahier d'études (Gadda) **144**:127, 131
Cahier d'un retour au pays natal (Fanon) **188**:149
Le cahier gris (Martin du Gard) **24**:394
Cahiers (Valéry) **15**:463-64
Cahiers (Weil) **23**:382-86
Les cahiers d'André Walter (Gide) **36**:92-3; **5**:215, 222-23, 243-44; **12**:142-43, 162, 168, 172, 176, 180; **177**:12, 82, 91
Cahiers de Lorient (Alain) **41**:29
Les Cahiers de Malte Laurids Brigge (Sarraute) **145**:340
Les cahiers d'un clerc (Benda) **60**:90
"Cain" (Nemerov) **124**:151, 157, 165, 240, 251, 314
Caino (Betti) **5**:62
Cain's Altar (Hansen)
See *Kains alter*
"The Cairn" (Wakefield) **120**:354
"Cairo Jag" (Douglas) **40**:56, 64-5, 70-1, 76-8, 80-1, 90, 93
"Les Caisses à fleurs" (Yourcenar) **193**:265
"Caistealna-Sithan" (Graham) **19**:104
"A Cake of Soap" (Lu Hsun)
See "Feizao"
"The Cake That Prissy Made" (Montgomery) **51**:200
"Calchas" (Chekhov)
See *Kalkhas*
"The Calcite Vein" (Drummond) **25**:146
"Caleb" (Cotter) **28**:44, 47
Caleb, the Degenerate: A Study of the Types, Customs, and Needs of the American Negro (Cotter) **28**:40-7, 50
"The Caledonian Express, or an American Abroad" (Fields) **80**:259
Calendar (Čapek) **37**:46
The Calendar (Wallace) **57**:404
A Calendar of Confederate Papers (Freeman) **11**:225, 230
The Calendar of Nature (Prishvin) **75**:219
Calendau (Mistral) **51**:121, 136-39, 148, 150, 152, 161, 163, 166
"The Calf's Head" (Bunin) **6**:56
"Caliban upon Setebos" (Quiller-Couch) **53**:290
Caliban's Guide to Letters (Belloc) **7**:31, 38; **18**:32
California: An Intimate History (Atherton) **2**:18
"A California Mining Camp" (Foote) **108**:5, 23-4
California, the Wonderful Childern in Bondage (Markham) **47**:287
The Californians (Atherton) **2**:13-15
"Caligula" (Herbert) **168**:8
Caligula (Rolland) **23**:256
"Caline" (Chopin) **14**:69; **127**:9
"The Caliph and the Cad" (Henry) **19**:173
"The Caliph, Cupid, and the Clock" (Henry) **19**:173
"The Caliph's Design" (Lewis) **2**:391; **9**:235; **104**:209
Calixto (Desnos) **22**:69
"The Call" (Blackwood) **5**:71
"The Call" (Brooke) **2**:54
"Call" (Lorde) **173**:76-77, 142
"The Call" (Mew) **8**:298
A Call (Ford) **1**:283; **15**:68-89, 93; **39**:124; **57**:216, 260, 273
"Call for Mr. Keefe!" (Lardner) **14**:303
"Call for Mr. Kenworthy!" (Benchley) **1**:81
Call It Experience: The Years of Learning How to Write (Caldwell) **117**:3, 110, 21
"Call Me Back Again" (Tagore)
See "Ebar phirao more"
"The Call of Cthulhu" (Lovecraft) **4**:267, 269, 274; **22**:211, 231, 233-34, 238
The Call of Life (Schnitzler)
See *Der Ruf des Lebens*
"The Call of Spring" (Naidu) **80**:280, 346
Call of the Blood (Faust) **49**:41-2, 47
The Call of the Blood (Hichens) **64**:124, 126-29, 131
Call of the Blood (Vallette)
See *La voix du sang*
"The Call of the Wild" (Service) **15**:404, 407
Call of the Wild (Dickey) **151**:180
The Call of the Wild (London) **9**:254-56, 258-64, 266, 269-73, 281; **15**:260-61, 267, 271, 274, 276; **39**:259-91
"A Call on the President" (Runyon) **10**:429, 436
A Call: The Tale of Two Passions (Ford) **172**:5, 10, 53, 58, 109-10, 113-15, 122-23
"The Call to Evening Prayer" (Naidu) **80**:312
"Calle" (Storni) **5**:452
"La calle de los mudos" (García Lorca) **181**:181
"Called Early" (Field) **43**:161
"Las Calles" (Borges) **109**:10
"Calles" (Villaurrutia) **80**:477
Calligrammes (Apollinaire) **3**:33, 40, 44-5; **8**:12, 16, 20-2, 27-8; **51**:3-4, 10-11, 13, 20, 24, 29-30, 32, 35, 37, 49, 54, 57, 59, 61
"Calling Jesus" (Toomer) **172**:314, 320
"The Calling of Arthur" (Williams) **1**:515
The Calling of Dan Matthews (Wright) **183**:349, 357-59, 367-68, 370, 372-73, 376-77, 380
"The Calling of Taliessin" (Williams) **1**:512; **11**:491
The Calling of the Sea (Hodgson) **13**:230-31, 237
Callirrhoë (Field) **43**:152, 154, 160-62, 171
"The Calls" (Owen) **27**:212
Calm Tension (Kandinsky) **92**:32
"Calme" (Roumain) **19**:339, 344
"Calouste Gulbenkian" (Saroyan) **137**:187
Calpurnia's Dinner Party (Baring) **8**:32
Le Calvaire (Mirbeau) **55**:280, 283, 286-90, 292-94, 301, 311-12
Calvaries (Čapek)
See *Boži muka*
"Calvary" (Evans) **85**:34
"Calvary" (Graham) **19**:102, 104, 115-16
"Calvary" (Yeats) **93**:341
Calvary (Mirbeau)
See *Le Calvaire*
Calvary (Yeats) **11**:514; **93**:341, 364, 368
"Calvary-Talk" (Bottomley) **107**:7
"Calverly's" (Robinson) **5**:402, 414; **101**:138
"La cámara de las estatuas" (Borges) **109**:42
"La camara in attesa" (Pirandello) **29**:292-93
"La cámara oscura" (Quiroga) **20**:212
El camarada pantoja (Azuela) **3**:78; **145**:11, 15
"The Cambaroora Star" (Lawson) **27**:133
"The Cambered Foot" (Post) **39**:336
The Camberley Triangle (Milne) **6**:308
A Cambric Mask (Chambers) **41**:95
"The Camel" (Nash) **109**:362

Camel-Driver Bel-Narb (Dunsany) **2**:143
"Camelias" (Beer-Hofmann) **60**:24
"Camembert or the Lucky Lover" (van Ostaijen) **33**:410
Cameos (Corelli) **51**:66
Camera Lucida: Reflections on Photography (Barthes)
See *La chambre claire: Note sur la photographie*
Camino de perfección (Baroja) **8**:54, 61-2
"La camisa de Margarita" (Palma) **29**:256
"A Camp in the Prussian Forest" (Jarrell) **177**:126, 176, 258
"Camp Nitgedaige" (Mayakovski) **18**:258
"The Camp of the Dog" (Blackwood) **5**:70, 73, 78-9
Campā (Devkota) **23**:50
Les campagnes hallucinées (Verhaeren) **12**:458, 464, 466, 469, 482-83
"The Campaign of Economy" (Zoshchenko) **15**:503-04
Campaigns and Intervals (Giraudoux)
See *Lectures pour une ombre*
"Campana" (García Lorca) **181**:201
"La campana mística" (Gonzalez Martinez) **72**:152
The Campfire (Gumilev) **60**:260, 276
"Campo" (Aleixandre) **113**:63
"Campo" (García Lorca) **181**:123
Campo de armiño (Benavente) **3**:94, 99
"Campo de Flores" (Drummond de Andrade) **139**:227
Campos de Castilla (Machado) **3**:305, 309, 313
"Camps" (Gurney) **33**:85
"Camps and Fields" (Jarrell) **177**:193
Can Grande's Castle (Lowell) **1**:273, 371-72, 375, 379; **8**:224, 226-32, 235
Can Lloyd George Do It? An Examination of the Liberal Pledge (Keynes) **64**:216, 254-55, 264
"A Can of Dutch Cleanser" (Nemerov) **124**:148
Can Prayer Be Answered? (Austin) **25**:33
Can Such Things Be? (Bierce) **1**:86, 88, 94; **7**:89; **44**:5, 10-11, 13, 44-6, 49-51
"Can the Bolsheviks Retain State Power?" (Lenin) **67**:256-57
"Can the Mirror Speak?" (Obstfelder)
See "Kan speilet tale?"
"Can War Be Done Away With" (Adams) **80**:53
"Can You Make Out Their Voices?" (Chambers) **129**:47
"La cana" (Pardo Bazán) **189**:268, 270
"Canada" (Roberts) **8**:319
Canada Speaks of Britain (Roberts) **8**:321
"Canada to England" (Pickthall) **21**:255
"Canadian Literati" (Knister) **56**:155, 157
"The Canadian Short Story" (Knister) **56**:156, 165
"Canadian Writing Today" (Engel) **137**:110
The Canadians of Old (Roberts) **8**:323
"The Canal Bank" (Stephens) **4**:419
"The Canary" (Mansfield) **2**:448; **8**:285; **39**:303-05, 323; **164**:249, 286
The Canary Murder Case (Mankiewicz) **85**:111
The "Canary" Murder Case (Van Dine) **23**:353-54, 360
The Canavans (Gregory) **1**:332, 334; **176**:11, 34, 37
"Canção Para Álbum de Moça" (Drummond de Andrade) **139**:228
The Cancer Biopathy (Reich) **57**:338-39
The Cancer Journals (Lorde) **173**:56, 89-96, 107-8, 110, 117-18, 120-22, 130
"The Cancer Match" (Dickey) **151**:101, 105, 113-14
"Canción" (Villaurrutia) **80**:477
Canción (Jiménez) **4**:224
"Canción a una muchacha muerta" (Aleixandre) **113**:13
"Canción apasionada" (Villaurrutia) **80**:477
"Canción con movimiento" (García Lorca) **181**:179
Canción de cuna (Martinez Sierra and Martinez Sierra) **6**:273, 275-76, 278, 281-84, 286-87
"Canción de despacho" (Jiménez) **183**:290
"Canción de jinete" (García Lorca) **181**:34
"Canción de la mujer astuta" (Storni) **5**:450
"Canción de taurus" (Mistral) **2**:478
"Canción de virgo" (Mistral) **2**:478
"Canción del naranjo seco" (García Lorca) **49**:121
"Canción menor" (García Lorca) **181**:119-20, 122-23
"Canción oriental" (García Lorca) **181**:119
"Canción otoñal" (García Lorca) **181**:121-22
"Canción para la luna" (García Lorca) **181**:121-22
"Cancionero apócrifo" (Machado) **3**:306, 313
Canciones (García Lorca) **1**:312, 314, 318, 322; **7**:292, 296-97; **49**:91, 119-22; **181**:25, 63-64, 66, 69, 83, 92, 177, 180, 183, 185; **197**:229
Canciónes (Jiménez) **183**:290
"Canciones de hogar" (Vallejo) **3**:531
"Las canciones de la nueva luz" (Jiménez) **183**:290, 292
"Canciones de luna" (García Lorca) **181**:181, 183
Canciones del suburbio (Baroja) **8**:51
Canciones en la noche (Huidobro) **31**:124
Canciones y cuentos del pueblo quechua (Arguedas) **147**:94
"Candelora" (Pirandello) **4**:350
Candida (Shaw) **3**:381, 384, 389, 395; **9**:413; **21**:306-07, 309, 317, 327-28, 330; **45**:210, 237-38, 243
A Candidate for Truth (Beresford) **81**:7,10-2
Candide (Hellman) **119**:167, 171, 173-74
"The Candle" (Balmont) **11**:41
"A Candle a Saint" (Stevens) **12**:379
"A Candle in a Gale Wind" (Childress) **116**:40
Candle in the Wind (Anderson) **144**:38
The Candle of Vision (Baker) **3**:9; **10**:14-15, 17, 26
"Candle-Lightin' Time" (Dunbar) **12**:106, 110
"Candlemas" (Pirandello)
See "Candelora"
"Candles for Maria" (Böll) **185**:18
"Candour in Fiction" (Hardy) **10**:218
Cane (Toomer) **172**:254-61, 263, 266-67, 271-74, 276, 282-87, 293-94, 296, 298, 300, 303-10, 312-16, 318-20, 323-25, 327-31, 334-40
"Canéfora de pesadilla" (García Lorca) **181**:169
"Cannabalism in the Cars" (Twain) **12**:425
Canne al vento (Deledda) **23**:41-2
Cannery Row (Steinbeck) **135**:252
The Cannibals (Morris) **107**:103-05
"Canning Time" (Guest) **95**:205
"Canoe" (Douglas) **40**:54-5
"A Canomante" (Machado de Assis) **10**:291
"Canon Alberic's Scrap-Book" (James) **6**:212-13
"Canonica" (Stevens) **3**:477; **45**:283
Caños y barro (Blasco Ibáñez) **12**:30, 32, 38-9, 41-6, 50-3
Cánovas (Pérez Galdós) **27**:256, 283
"Canta l'epistola" (Pirandello) **29**:282
Cantando en el pozo (Arenas) **191**:158, 200
Cantata dei giorni pari (de Filippo) **127**:285
"Cântec de razboi" (Tzara) **168**:270, 277, 322
"Cantelman's Spring-Mate" (Lewis) **2**:388-89, 392, 396; **104**:237, 243-44, 257
"The Canterville Ghost: A Hylo-Idealistic Romance" (Wilde) **8**:492; **41**:359
Canti di Castelvecchio (Pascoli) **45**:146, 148-49, 154-56
Canti orfici (Campana) **20**:82-8, 90
"A Canticle" (Percy) **84**:198
"Canticle of Mesa" (Claudel) **2**:108
The Canticle of the Wing (Rostand) **6**:381
"Cantiga de esponsais" (Machado de Assis) **10**:291
"Cantilènes" (Moréas) **18**:286
Les cantilènes (Moréas) **18**:275, 278-82, 285-88, 290
"Cantique des colonnes" (Valéry) **4**:491, 498
"Canto à la Argentina" (Darío) **4**:61-2
"Canto a la primavera" (Villaurrutia) **80**:462
Canto a la primavera (Villaurrutia) **80**:460, 487
"El canto de la angustia" (Lugones) **15**:286, 289
"Canto de la tarde y de la muerte" (Lugones) **15**:285
"Canto del amor y de la noche" (Lugones) **15**:285
"Canto del sole" (D'Annunzio) **40**:37-8
"Canto dell'ospite" (D'Annunzio) **40**:38
"Canto di marzo" (Carducci) **32**:95
El canto errante (Darío) **4**:61
Canto novo (D'Annunzio) **40**:12, 37
"The Canto of Ulysses" (Levi) **109**:300
El cantor vagabundo (Baroja) **8**:58
Cantos de vida y esperanza (Darío) **4**:56-7, 59-61, 64
"Cantos nuevos" (García Lorca) **181**:124
Cantos seculares (Lugones) **15**:290
Canute the Great (Field) **43**:154, 171
"Canzone" (Manning) **25**:277
"Canzone di Legnano" (Carducci) **32**:90
Canzones (Okigbo)
See *Poems: Four Canzones*
Le canzoni d'oltremare (D'Annunzio) **40**:11
Il canzoniere (Saba) **33**:366-69, 371, 375-77
Cap and Bells (Pirandello)
See *Il berretto a sonagli*
"The Cap and the Bells" (Yeats) **11**:527
Le Cap de Bonne-Espérance (Cocteau) **119**:106-9
"The Cap that Fits" (Dobson) **79**:27
"Capbreton" (Balmont) **11**:41
"Cape Breton" (Bishop) **121**:7-9, 21, 23, 26-7
"Cape Cod" (Santayana) **40**:340
"Cape Hatteras" (Crane) **2**:121, 126; **80**:81, 83-5, 88-9, 99, 101, 106, 110, 113, 127-8, 139-41, 144, 157, 159-62, 169, 173-4, 176-7, 186, 190, 212-3
"Cape Race" (de la Mare) **53**:35
"Cape Solitude" (Abbey) **160**:90
Capel Sion (Evans) **85**:2-3, 5, 21, 32
"La capilla aldeana" (Huidobro) **31**:124
Capillária (Karinthy) **47**:269, 272-73
"The Capital" (Rilke)
See "Das Kapitäl"
"Capital and Industrial Fluctuations" (Hayek) **109**:196
Capital Capitals (Stein) **48**:264
Capital Cities (Kahanovitsch)
See *Hoyptshtet*
"The Capital Difficulty of Prose" (Quiller-Couch) **53**:292
"The Capital Difficulty of Verse" (Quiller-Couch) **53**:292
Capital of Pain (Éluard)
See *Capitale de la douleur*
"The Capital of the Ruins" (Beckett) **145**:184-85
Capitale de la douleur (Éluard) **7**:247-48, 250, 252; **41**:150, 154
Capitalism and Schizophrenia (Deleuze)
See *Capitalisme et schizophrénie*
Capitalisme et schizophrénie (Deleuze) **116**:81-2, 84-5, 89-91, 95, 150-51
"Capitals" (Nemerov) **124**:258
"El capitán Funes" (Güiraldes) **39**:190
"La capitana" (Pardo Bazán) **189**:236
"Capitol Air" (Ginsberg) **120**:79-80
Capítulos de literatura española (Reyes) **33**:323
"La capra" (Saba) **33**:368-69, 373, 376
"Le capre ci guardano" (Calvino) **183**:237
"Caprice" (Cullen) **37**:154
"Caprice" (Naidu) **80**:314
Caprice (Firbank) **1**:227
Les Caprices du poete (Jammes) **75**:117, 119
"Capricho de Limeña" (Palma) **29**:256

Capricious Line (Kandinsky) **92**:32
"The Captain" (McCrae) **12**:211
Captain Antifer (Verne) **6**:502
A Captain at Fifteen (Verne) **6**:500
Captain Blood (Sabatini) **47**:300, 303-04, 306
Captain Brassbound's Conversion (Shaw) **3**:378; **9**:414
Captain Caution (Roberts) **23**:229-30, 232, 235-36, 239
"Captain Craig" (Robinson) **5**:404, 416-17; **101**:96, 110-12, 118-19, 123-25, 133, 197
Captain Craig and Other Poems (Robinson) **101**:97, 119, 123, 133, 136
Captain Dieppe (Hope) **83**:181
Captain Gault: Being the Exceedingly Private Log of a Sea Captain (Hodgson) **13**:231
Captain Horatio Hornblower (Forester) **152**:153
Captain Horn (Stockton)
See *The Adventures of Captain Horn*
"Captain John's Silly Adventures" (García Lorca)
See "Aventuras idiotas del capitán John"
Captain Macklin (Davis) **24**:203
"Captain Maconochie's 'Bounty for Crime'" (Warung) **45**:418
Captain Mansana (Bjoernson)
See *Kaptejn Mansana*
A Captain of Industry (Sinclair) **160**:255-56
The Captain of St. Margaret's (Molnár)
See *A gőzoszlop*
"The Captain of 'The Camel'" (Bierce) **44**:45
The Captain of the Gray-Horse Troop (Garland) **3**:192-94, 204-05
"Captain Stormfield" (Twain) **185**:329-30
"The Captains" (Gumilev)
See "Kapitany"
"The Captains" (Jewett) **22**:136
Captains Courageous (Kipling) **8**:193, 200; **17**:202-03, 208, 210-11
The Captain's Daughter (Valle-Inclán)
See *La hija del capitán*
The Captain's Death Bed and Other Essays (Woolf) **128**:324
"The Captain's Doll" (Lawrence) **2**:344; **9**:216; **16**:290
The Captain's Toll-Gate (Stockton) **47**:324
"The Captain's Vices" (Coppee) **25**:121
Un captif amoureux (Genet) **128**:131, 176-81, 233-36, 239-40, 243-49
"The Captive" (Graham) **19**:130
The Captive (Proust)
See *La prisonnière*
The Captive and the Free (Cary) **1**:141-42, 144; **29**:91, 102, 104-05, 108
"A Captive Bird" (Södergran)
See "En fången fågel"
The Captive in the Caucasus (Tolstoy) **11**:465
Captive Lion (Moricz)
See *Rab oroszlán*
"A Captive of the Khan" (Tsvetaeva)
See "Khansky polon"
A Captive Spirit: Selected Prose (Tsvetaeva) **7**:571-72; **35**:395
The Captives (Walpole) **5**:492-93, 503
"The Captivity" (Lewis) **3**:287
Capt'n Davy's Honeymoon (Caine) **97**:7
"Captured" (Heidenstam) **5**:253
"The Captured and the Freed" (Anwar)
See "Jang terampas dan jang luput"
"Captured by the Khan" (Tsvetaeva)
See "Khansky polon"
"The Captured Goddess" (Lowell) **1**:375; **8**:232-35
"Caput Tuum ut Carmelus" (Field) **43**:170
La cara de Dios (Valle-Inclán) **5**:489
"La cara de la desgracia" (Onetti) **131**:170, 296-98, 300, 302
La cara de la desgracia (Onetti) **131**:135-36
Cara de plata (Valle-Inclán) **5**:486
Caractères (Gide) **177**:46
Carapina po nebu (Khlebnikov) **20**:137, 140
"Carasoyn" (MacDonald) **9**:305; **113**:212
Caravan: The Assembled Tales of John Galsworthy (Galsworthy) **45**:69
The Caravaners (Elizabeth) **41**:122-23, 128, 130-31
"A Carberry Deer Hunt" (Seton) **31**:259
Il carcere (Pavese) **3**:338, 342-43
The Card (Bennett) **5**:26, 29, 32, 38, 42-3, 50-2; **197**:14, 27-8, 30, 102, 108, 177
The Card Game (Gumilev)
See *Igra*
The Card Regent (Bennett) **197**:10
Cardigan (Chambers) **41**:94, 101
"Cardinal Manning" (Strachey) **12**:395, 397, 416
Carducci: A Selection of His Poems (Carducci) **32**:98-9
Carducci the Man (Papini) **22**:273
"A Career" (Dunbar) **12**:117, 121
The Career of Katherine Bush (Glyn) **72**:137, 141
"Cares" (Södergran)
See "Sorger"
"The Cares of a Family Man" (Kafka) **2**:306
"A Cargo of Cat" (Bierce) **44**:45
Cargo Unknown (Dent) **72**:26
Caricatures of Twenty-Five Gentlemen (Beerbohm) **24**:98, 115
The Carillon of Love (Kuzmin) **40**:191
"Carl Hamblin" (Masters) **25**:309
Carl Rogers: Dialogues (Levi) **125**:282
Carl Van Doren (Van Doren) **18**:409
Carl XII (Strindberg) **1**:459; **8**:418
The Carlist War (Valle-Inclán)
See *La Guerra Carlista*
"Carlos among the Candles" (Stevens) **12**:356
"Carlyle" (Harris) **24**:271
"The Carlyle House" (Natsume)
See "Kārairu hakubutsukan"
"Carma" (Toomer) **172**:256, 297-98, 337
The Carmelites (Bernanos)
See *Dialogues des Carmélites*
Carnacki the Ghost-Finder (Hodgson) **13**:230, 232
"The Carnation" (Mansfield) **39**:320
"Carnaval Carioca" (Andrade) **43**:18-19
"El carnaval negro" (Lugones) **15**:294
"The Carnegie Library" (Jarrell)
See "The Carnegie Library, Juvenile Division"
"The Carnegie Library, Juvenile Division" (Jarrell) **177**:129, 152, 169
Carnet (Ramuz) **33**:310
Carnets (Saint-Exupéry) **169**:316, 346
"Carnets de notes de Mémoires d'Handrien" (Yourcenar) **193**:272, 355-56, 362, 364-65
Les Carnets du Major Thompson (Sturges) **48**:283, 291, 309
Il carnevale de Morti (Pirandello) **29**:291
Carnival (Mackenzie) **116**:184, 189, 192-93, 197, 203, 205-06, 212-14, 227, 229-30, 232-33, 239, 243, 245, 247, 251
Carnival (Molnár)
See *Farsang*
Carnival Confession (Zuckmayer)
See *Die Fastnachtsbeichte*
"Carnival in Rio" (Andrade)
See "Carnaval Carioca"
The Carnival of the Dead (Pirandello)
See *Il carnevale de Morti*
Carnival Scenes (Caragiale)
See *D'ale carnavalului*
The Carnovsky Family (Singer)
See *Di mishpokhe Karnovski*
"Caro luogo" (Saba) **33**:374
Caro Michele (Ginzburg) **156**:5, 37-8, 59, 63, 69-70, 77, 108
"El carocol del faro" (Miro) **5**:335
"Carol" (Nemerov) **124**:143, 185
"A Carol for Margaret Chester" (Coppard) **5**:177-78
Carolina Chansons (Heyward) **59**:86
Caroling Dusk: An Anthology of Verse by Negro Poets (Cullen) **4**:42; **37**:137, 151, 159, 161
Carols of an Old Codger (Service) **15**:411, 413
La Caronne et La Lyre (Yourcenar) **193**:280
The Carpathian Castle (Verne)
See *Castle of the Carpathians*
"The Carpenter's Wife: A Capriccio" (Zangwill) **16**:461
"Carrettiere" (Pascoli) **45**:155-56
"Carriego" (Borges) **109**:70
"Carrier" (Jarrell) **177**:193
"La carriola" (Pirandello) **172**:177
Carrots (Renard)
See *Poil de carotte*
"Carry On" (Wodehouse) **108**:387
Carry On, Jeeves (Wodehouse) **108**:392
"Carskaja nevesta" (Khlebnikov) **20**:139
Carson of Venus (Burroughs) **32**:59, 75
Cartagena and the Banks of the Sinú (Graham) **19**:111
De Cartago a Sagunto (Pérez Galdós) **27**:276
Cartas (Hostos) **24**:303
Cartas a Benito Pérez Galdós (Pardo Bazán) **189**:240
"Cartas al amigo" (Unamuno) **148**:311
Cartas de Mário de Andrade a Manuel Bandeira (Andrade) **43**:14-15, 26
Cartas de mujeres (Benavente) **3**:93, 98
Cartas inéditas de Miguel de Unamuno (Unamuno) **148**:287
"Carte postale à Jean Royère" (Apollinaire) **51**:35
"Cartel de ferias" (Valle-Inclán) **5**:478
Carter, and Other People (Marquis) **7**:437
"Cartes postales" (Radnóti) **16**:412, 420
Cartesian Meditations (Husserl)
See *Meditations cartesiennes*
Cartesianische Meditationen (Husserl)
See *Meditations cartesiennes*
"Cartmell Bells" (Bottomley) **107**:4
Cartones de Madrid (Reyes) **33**:316, 323
Cartoons: "The Second Childhood of John Bull" (Beerbohm) **1**:68; **24**:111
"Cāru" (Devkota) **23**:47, 49
"Un cas de conscience" (Bourget) **12**:74
La casa abandonada (Prado) **75**:201, 205-06, 211-12
"Casa al mare" (Ginzburg) **156**:14, 63, 112
Casa al mare (Ginzburg) **156**:112
Casa braccio (Crawford) **10**:140-41, 148, 150, 155
La casa de Aizgorri (Baroja) **8**:53, 60-1
"La casa de Asterión" (Borges) **109**:23, 40, 152
La casa de Bernarda Alba (García Lorca) **1**:314-16, 318-20, 324; **49**:76-80, 87-9, 98, 103, 111, 115-18; **181**:1, 9, 11, 14, 16, 21, 29, 41, 45-47, 49-50, 54, 70-71, 77, 79, 97, 132-33, 139, 191-92
Casa de campo (Donoso) **133**:45-47, 49-50, 56, 75, 80, 82, 97-101, 105-6, 108-9, 111-12, 116-17, 119-20, 124-25, 134-36, 140, 148-49, 171, 178, 187
La casa de la primavera (Martinez Sierra and Martinez Sierra) **6**:279
"La casa de Pizarro" (Palma) **29**:256
"La casa del Granella" (Pirandello) **4**:331
"La casa della mia nutrice" (Saba) **33**:369, 371, 377
Casa e campagna (Saba) **33**:369, 372-73, 376
La casa in collina (Pavese) **3**:338, 340, 344
La Casa junto al rio (Garro) **153**:24, 46, 48, 51
La casa sull'acqua (Betti) **5**:58
"Casabianca" (Bishop) **121**:42, 46-8
"Casada e viúva" (Machado de Assis) **10**:295
"La casada infiel" (García Lorca) **7**:290, 300; **49**:113; **181**:90
Casandra (Pérez Galdós) **27**:268
Casanova (Apollinaire) **8**:14-15
Casanova in Spa (Schnitzler) **4**:396-97
"Casanova's Escape from the Piombi" (Sabatini) **47**:300

Casanovas Heimfahrt (Schnitzler) **4**:401
Casanova's Homecoming (Schnitzler)
See *Casanovas Heimfahrt*
"The Cascades of the Gatineau" (Scott) **6**:394
Cascando (Beckett) **145**:136, 139-40, 178-79
The Case for African Freedom (Cary) **196**:188, 190, 193-94, 214, 217
"A Case for the Oracle" (Lawson) **27**:150
"A Case from Guidance Practice" (Adler) **61**:32
"A Case from Practice" (Chekhov)
See "Slučaj iz praktiki"
"Case History of a Pinky" (Paton) **165**:304-5
"A Case of Amnesia" (Quiroga)
See "La ausencia"
"The Case of 'Ca'line': A Kitchen Monologue" (Dunbar) **2**:128
The Case of Charles Dexter Ward (Lovecraft) **4**:266; **22**:218, 226, 228, 230, 232, 241
"A Case of Conscience" (Dowson) **4**:84, 89
"A Case of Eavesdropping" (Blackwood) **5**:75
"The Case of General Ople and Lady Camper" (Meredith) **17**:287
"A Case of Identity" (Doyle) **7**:241
The Case of Jennie Brice (Rinehart) **52**:283, 289-90, 293, 299, 301
The Case of Miss R. (Adler) **61**:34
The Case of Mr. Crump (Lewisohn) **19**:264-66, 271-72
The Case of Mrs. A. (Adler) **61**:34
The Case of Mrs. Wingate (Micheaux) **76**:239-40
"A Case of Murder" (Hagiwara)
See "Satsujin jiken"
"The Case of Oscar Brodski" (Freeman) **21**:47, 55, 60, 62
A Case of Rape (Himes)
See *Une affaire de viol*
The Case of Richard Meynell (Ward) **55**:417-21, 425
"The Case of the Antichrist's Donkey" (Hedāyat)
See "Qaziya-hi khar dajjal"
"The Case of the Masked Corporal, That Is, The Poet Resuscitated" (Apollinaire) **51**:49
"The Case of the Rock-Salt" (Hedāyat)
See "Qaziva-hi namak-i turki"
"The Case of Wagner" (Nietzsche)
See "Der Fall Wagner: Ern Muskikanten-Problem"
The Case-Book of Sherlock Holmes (Doyle) **7**:220, 238
Cashel Byron's Profession (Shaw) **3**:379, 400; **9**:414, 422; **21**:306, 327, 337
"Casi artista" (Pardo Bazán) **189**:317-21
"Casida del sueño al aire libre" (García Lorca) **49**:112
"Casidas" (García Lorca) **1**:308
The Casino Murder Case (Van Dine) **23**:360
Casino Royale (Fleming) **193**:195-99, 205, 208, 211, 216-17, 223, 232, 234, 238-41
The Cask (Crofts) **55**:82, 85-8
"A Cask of Amontillado" (Bierce) **1**:84
A Cask of Jerepigo (Bosman) **49**:5, 7, 10, 15, 19
"Caso do Vetido" (Drummond de Andrade) **139**:230
"Časovoj" (Zabolotsky) **52**:378
Caspar Hauser; oder, Die Trägheit des Herzens (Wassermann) **6**:509, 511, 514-15, 520
"Caspar Hauser Song" (Trakl) **5**:461, 467
"Les Casquetes" (Swinburne) **8**:428; **36**:342, 344
Cass Timberlane (Lewis) **13**:338-40; **23**:139; **39**:234
"Cassandra" (Nightingale) **85**:231, 233, 236-7, 239, 261-72, 293-4, 299, 302-3
"Cassandra" (Robinson) **101**:112, 138, 195
Cast the First Stone (Himes) **139**:247, 312-13, 320, 336
The Castaways (Jacobs) **22**:100, 108
I castelli Valdostani e Canoresi (Giacosa) **7**:309
Castellio gegen Calvin; oder, Ein Gewissen gegen die Gewalt (Zweig) **17**:426-27, 442, 457-58
Castilla (Unamuno) **9**:515
The Casting Away of Mrs. Lecks and Mrs. Aleshine (Stockton) **47**:312, 315, 317, 320-22, 324, 330
Casting Out the Lecherous Devil (Tolstoy) **18**:382
"Casting the Runes" (James) **6**:208, 210-13
"The Casting Vote" (Murfree) **135**:207
"The Cast-Iron Canvasser" (Paterson) **32**:380-81
"The Castle" (Gonzalez Martinez) **72**:147
"The Castle" (MacDonald) **9**:303; **113**:214
"The Castle" (Muir) **87**:167, 189
The Castle (Kafka)
See *Das Schloss*
The Castle Builders; or, The Deferred Confirmation (Yonge) **48**:366, 378, 384
Castle Corner (Cary) **1**:142, 144, 146; **29**:66-8, 71, 77-80, 82, 84-5, 87, 108-09; **196**:137, 172, 197-98, 214
"Castle Corrib" (Gogarty) **15**:103
Castle Gay (Buchan) **41**:38, 41, 45, 74
The Castle of Crossed Destinies (Calvino)
See *Il castello dei destini incrociati*
Castle of the Carpathians (Verne) **6**:502; **52**:356
"The Castle of the King" (Stoker) **144**:253
"Casual Poem about the Standing of Socialism" (Jozsef) **22**:159
"Časy" (Zamyatin) **8**:553
"The Cat" (Cullen) **37**:158, 170
The Cat (Colette)
See *La chatte*
"The Cat and Cupid" (Bennett) **5**:46
"The Cat and the Moon" (Yeats) **18**:459
The Cat and the Moon, and Certain Poems (Yeats) **11**:515
"The Cat and the Policeman" (Calvino)
See "Il gatto e il poliziotto"
"Cat Blues" (Wright) **136**:263
"The Cat in the Jacal" (Adams) **56**:11
"Cat in the Rain" (Hemingway) **115**:184
"The Cat Is on the Mat" (Aldrich) **125**:19
"The Cat Pegasus" (Lindsay) **17**:240
Cat People (Lewton) **76**:189-94, 196-97, 199-213, 218, 222-28, 230
"Catalina" (Storni) **5**:454
Catarina av Siena (Undset) **197**:300, 303, 312
"The Catch" (Coffin) **95**:17
"A Catch" (Nemerov) **124**:273
Catch-22 (Heller) **131**:16-53; **151**:298-315, 319-25, 327-32, 334-35, 339-41
Catch-22: A Dramatization (Heller) **131**:22, 42, 44
"Catching the Train" (Bennett) **5**:46
"A Catechism" (Buchanan) **107**:73
La catedrál (Blasco Ibáñez) **12**:29-30, 34-5, 37, 42, 46-8
"Caterpillars" (Benson) **27**:13, 16, 19
Catharina of Siena (Undset)
See *Catarina av Siena*
Catharine Furze (Rutherford) **25**:336, 338, 341, 344-45, 349, 355, 358-59, 361-62
The Cathedral (Huysmans)
See *La cathédrale*
"The Cathedral" (Rilke)
See "Die Kathedrale"
The Cathedral (Schwitters) **95**:344
The Cathedral (Walpole) **5**:494-96, 502-03
"The Cathedral Bell" (Wright) **136**:302
"La cathédral de Reims" (Verhaeren) **12**:471
"The Cathedral of Barcelona" (Unamuno) **2**:568
La cathédrale (Huysmans) **7**:406-11; **69**:7, 12, 14-16, 28, 37, 40-1, 43-4, 47-8, 56
La cathédrale interrompue (Rolland) **23**:269
"Catherine Carr" (Freeman) **9**:72
Catherine Parr (Baring) **8**:32
Cathleen ni Houlihan (Gregory) **176**:13, 46, 61-62, 64, 66, 81
Cathleen ni Houlihan (Yeats) **1**:553; **11**:514; **31**:420-21
The Catholic Church and Art (Cram) **45**:9, 18
"The Catholic Church at Novograd" (Babel)
See "Kostel v Novograde"
"The Catholic Novelist in the Protestant South" (O'Connor) **132**:322
"Catholic Novelists and Their Readers" (O'Connor) **132**:261, 321
Catholic Tales and Christian Songs (Sayers) **15**:395
"Catholicism in England: A Non-Scientific Survey" (Guiney) **41**:219
"Catilina összeesküvése" (Herzl) **36**:154
Catiline (Ibsen) **37**:243; **52**:155, 194
The Cat-Nappers (Wodehouse)
See *Aunts Aren't Gentlemen*
"Catnip Jack" (Scott) **6**:386, 395
"Cato Braden" (Masters) **25**:298
"Cats" (Cullen) **37**:158
"Cats" (Hagiwara)
See "Neko"
"Cats" (MacCarthy) **36**:254
The Cat's Bridge (Sudermann) **15**:418
The Cat's Claw (Giacosa)
See *La zampa del gatto*
Cat's Cradle (Baring) **8**:32, 36-7, 39-40, 43
The Cat's Eye (Freeman) **21**:55, 58-60
"The Cats of Cobblestone Street" (Benét) **28**:6, 9
"The Cats of Ulthar" (Lovecraft) **4**:266
"The Cattle" (Chang)
See "Niu"
Cattle Brands (Adams) **56**:4, 6, 19
"The Cattle Dealers" (Chekhov) **3**:152
"The Cattle on a Thousand Hills" (Adams) **56**:10, 23
The Caucasian Chalk Circle (Brecht)
See *Der kaukasische Kreidekreis*
"The Caucasian Storms Harlem" (Fisher) **11**:213
Los caudillos de 1830 (Baroja) **8**:57
Caught (Ophuls) **79**:173, 175, 238
"A causa secreta" (Machado de Assis) **10**:291, 296
Cause for Wonder (Morris) **107**:119, 124, 126-29, 132, 152, 158
"The Causeless War and Its Lessons for Us" (Bryan) **99**:133
Causes and Consequences (Chapman) **7**:187, 191, 193, 196
"Causes and Outbreak of the Great and Glorious Revolution in Revon" (Schwitters) **95**:309, 323
"A Cautionary Note on the Ghostly Tale" (Kirk) **119**:275, 279, 283, 292
Cautionary Tales for Children (Belloc) **7**:38-9, 42; **18**:28, 40, 42
Cautionary Verses (Belloc)
See *Cautionary Verses: The Collected Humorous Poems*
Cautionary Verses: The Collected Humorous Poems (Belloc) **18**:39-40
"The Cavalier" (Kuzmin)
See "Vsadnik"
The Cavalier (Cable) **4**:27-9, 31
Le Cavalier bizarre (Ghelderode) **187**:4-5
Il cavaliere inesistente (Calvino) **183**:5-6, 96, 144, 158-59, 189, 192, 197, 202-5, 212-13, 221, 224-25, 238, 240-41
"The Cavaliers" (Mikszath)
See "A gavallérok"
Cavaliers (Kandinsky) **92**:48
Cavaliers arabes (Kandinsky) **92**:49
Les Cavaliers de l'orage (Giono) **124**:55
Cavalleria Rusticana and Other Stories (Verga)
See *Vita dei campi*
Cavalleria Rusticana, and Other Tales of Sicilian Peasant Life (Verga)
See *Vita dei campi*

Cavanagh, Forest Ranger: A Romance of the Mountain West (Garland) **3**:192
"Cavanelle" (Chopin) **14**:70; **127**:22
"The Cave" (Zamyatin)
See "Peschera"
"Cave Canem" (Millay) **49**:223
The Cave Dwellers (Saroyan) **137**:154, 170, 181
The Cave Girl (Burroughs) **32**:57, 76
"The Cave of Ali Baba" (Sayers)
See "The Adventurous Exploit of the Cave of Ali Baba"
The Cave of Illusion (Sutro) **6**:418-19
Cavender's House (Robinson) **5**:406; **101**:117, 184-85
La caverna del humorismo (Baroja) **8**:63
"La caverne" (Desnos) **22**:73
Les caves du Vatican (Gide) **5**:214-15, 222-23, 229-30, 232, 235, 239; **12**:144-45, 148-49, 151-53, 160, 170-71, 177-80; **36**:87, 90, 92-4, 105, 108-112, 114, 116-18; **177**:5, 35, 73
"Los caynas" (Vallejo) **56**:308, 320-23
El cazador (Reyes) **33**:316, 322
"Los cazadores de ratas" (Quiroga) **20**:213
"Ce monde où nous mourons" (Bataille) **155**:89, 96
Cecè (Pirandello) **172**:188
Cecelia (Crawford) **10**:150
"Cecil" (Jensen) **41**:307
Cécile; ou, L'École des Pères (Anouilh) **195**:11, 14, 25
Cédulas de San Juan (Sánchez) **37**:313-14
Cegen Abend (Kandinsky) **92**:49
"The Celebrated Jumping Frog of Calaveras County" (Twain) **6**:460, 467; **161**:275
The Celebrated Jumping Frog of Calaveras County, and Other Sketches (Twain) **6**:453, 455, 475
"Celebrating the Marriage of the Crown Prince" (Masaoka) **18**:223
"The Celebration" (Dickey) **151**:90-93, 121
"A Celebration for George Sarton" (Sarton) **120**:268
Celebrities (Bernhard)
See *Die Berühmten*
Celebrities and Simple Souls (Sutro) **6**:422
The Celebrity at Home (Hunt) **53**:187, 191-92, 197-99
The Celebrity's Daughter (Hunt) **53**:186-87, 199
"Cele-Kula" (Popa) **167**:159
"Celephais" (Lovecraft) **4**:272
"Celestial Freedom" (Aleixandre) **113**:25
"Celestial Globe" (Nemerov) **124**:162, 172, 177, 180, 183, 191, 213, 253
The Celestial Omnibus (Bramah) **72**:11
Celestine: Being the Diary of a Chambermaid (Mirbeau)
See *Le journal d'une femme de chambre*
Celestino antes del alba (Arenas) **191**:135, 137-38, 145, 158-59, 162, 177, 185, 195, 200-01, 208
Celibates (Moore) **7**:484, 490-91, 493
The Celibates' Club (Zangwill) **16**:451, 455, 462
"Céline Lacoste: Souvenirs de la vie réelle" (Bourget) **12**:67
"Cell Number 6" (Williams) **89**:374, 384
"The Cellar" (Peretz) **16**:401
The Cellar (Bernhard)
See *Der Keller*
"The Cellar of Little Egypt" (Kirk) **119**:278, 280, 335
"The Cellar—1860-1863" (Bishop) **103**:12
"Celle de toujours, toute" (Éluard) **7**:247; **41**:147
"Celle Qui Fût Héaulmiette" (Stevens) **3**:472
"Cell-formations and Their Work" (Benchley) **55**:16
"Celtic" (Sharp) **39**:355, 371, 378, 395
Celtic Bones (Raabe) **45**:202
"The Celtic Gloom" (Sharp) **39**:374
Celtic Speech (Johnson) **19**:241
The Celtic Twilight (Yeats) **1**:569; **11**:511, 537-39; **31**:404, 409
"Celui qui" (Péret) **20**:185
Cement (Gladkov) **27**:88-91, 93-8, 100
"El cementerio de los soldados" (Huidobro) **31**:125
"Cementerio judío" (García Lorca) **1**:317; **197**:187, 191, 243
"Los cementerios Belgas" (Quiroga) **20**:213
"Cemeteries" (Jiménez) **183**:332
"The Cemetery at Kozin" (Babel)
See "Kladbishche v Kozine"
"The Cemetery of Souls" (Ady) **11**:14
"Cemiento en la nieve" (Villaurrutia) **80**:484
"La cena" (Reyes) **33**:322, 324
"La cena miserable" (Vallejo) **56**:288
El cencerro de cristal (Güiraldes) **39**:184, 186
Les Cenci (Artaud) **3**:49, 54-5, 61-2; **36**:11-12, 21, 29, 39
The Cenci (Artaud)
See *Les Cenci*
Cenere (Deledda) **23**:31-4, 37, 39, 41
Ceneri e faville (Carducci) **32**:106
"Censorship" (Cobb) **77**:133
"Censorship in the Saorstat" (Beckett) **145**:88
"The Censorship of Fiction" (Stoker) **8**:394; **144**:298
Cent Cinquante Marks ou la Foi, L'Espérance, la Charité (Horvath)
See *Glaube Liebe Hoffnung*
"Cent mètres" (Roumain) **19**:333, 339
Cent millions qui tombent (Feydeau) **22**:89, 93
The Centaur (Blackwood) **5**:70-1, 73-4, 77
"The Centaurs" (Kipling) **8**:193
"The Centaur's Farewell" (Benét) **28**:2
"The Centenary of Alexandre Dumas" (Swinburne) **36**:341, 345
"Centipede Sonnet" (Villa) **176**:95, 103
Cento e cento e cento e cento pagine del libro segreto di Gabriele d'Annunzio tentato di morire (D'Annunzio) **6**:145
Cento pagine di poesia (Papini) **22**:271, 280
El central (Arenas) **191**:137-38, 185-91
"El Central: A Sugar Mill" (Arenas) **191**:149
"Central Africa" (Harris) **24**:272
"Central Figure" (Wakefield) **120**:357
The Central Motion: Poems, 1968-1979 (Dickey) **151**:143, 147-48
Central Park (Benjamin) **39**:65
The Century of the Child (Key)
See *Barnets arhundrade*
"The Cephalopod" (Gladkov) **27**:91-2
"Cerameicus Tombs" (Palamas) **5**:386
"Cerements" (Balmont)
See "Savany"
"Ceremonial Ode" (Abercrombie) **141**:19
"Ceremony after a Fire Raid" (Thomas) **1**:470, 472; **8**:451; **45**:377, 379, 402; **105**:348
Ceremony in Lone Tree (Morris) **107**:111-13, 116, 199, 122, 132, 135-36, 138-39, 142-43, 147-53, 156-58, 203, 206, 208, 214, 226
La cerezas del cemenerio (Miro) **5**:339
"Cèrilo" (Carducci) **32**:91
"Čerkešenka" (Zabolotsky) **52**:377-78
"Cërnyji monax" (Chekhov) **3**:146, 149, 159; **10**:100
"Cero" (Salinas) **17**:358, 369
"Cerrada" (Aleixandre) **113**:3
"Cerrada puerta" (Aleixandre) **113**:14
Certa voz na noite ruivamente (Sá-Carneiro) **83**:411
A Certain Dr. Thorndyke (Freeman) **21**:58
The Certain Hour (Cabell) **6**:67-8
A Certain Man and the Death of His Sister (Shiga)
See *Aru otoko, sono ane no shi*
A Certain Man: His Sister's Death (Shiga)
See *Aru otoko, sono ane no shi*
A Certain Man, the Death of His Sister (Shiga)
See *Aru otoko, sono ane no shi*
A Certain Measure (Glasgow) **7**:335, 340, 348
"A Certain Morning" (Shiga)
See "Aru asa"
Certain People (Wharton) **129**:364
"Certain Phenomena of Sound" (Stevens) **12**:360
"A Certain Professor's Statement Upon Retirement" (Nishida)
See "Arv kyoju no taishoku no ji"
Certains (Huysmans) **7**:405-06; **69**:6-7, 32-3, 43
Cervantes (Frank) **81**:102
"Le Cerveau Noir de Piranèse" (Yourcenar) **193**:272, 275
"Červená povídka" (Čapek) **6**:84
Ces Plaisirs (Colette) **5**:172; **16**:118, 122-23, 129, 136
Cesar Cascabel (Verne) **6**:502
César o nada (Baroja) **8**:47, 49, 51, 57, 62
César Vallejo: Obra poética complete (Vallejo) **56**:503-4, 316
César Vallejo: The Complete Posthumous Poetry (Vallejo)
See *César Vallejo: Obra poética complete*
César-Antéchrist (Jarry) **2**:279, 281; **14**:272, 278, 282; **147**:243-44, 259, 290, 311-12, 314, 331
C'est beau (Sarraute) **145**:265-68, 316-18, 322-23
"C'est chez nous . . ." (Sarduy) **167**:220
C'est les bottes de sept lieues cette phrase: "Je me vois" (Desnos) **22**:60-1
Cetywayo and His White Neighbours (Haggard) **11**:236, 243, 253
Céu em fogo (Sá-Carneiro) **83**:399, 405
Ceux de la glèbe (Lemonnier) **22**:198, 203
"Cezanne" (Villaurrutia) **80**:477
"Cézanne's Doubt" (Merleau-Ponty) **156**:137
"Cézanne's Doubt" (Rilke) **195**:292
Chácharas de café (Ramoacn y Cajal) **93**:146
Chad Gadja: Das Pesachbuch (Agnon) **151**:36
"Chagrin" (Rosenberg) **12**:310
Chain of Circumstances (Rohan)
See *Renkanki*
The Chain of Gold (O'Grady) **5**:349, 354
The Chain of Kashchey (Prishvin)
See *Kashcheeva Tsep'*
Chained Links (Chang)
See *Lianhuantao*
"Chains" (Apollinaire)
See "Liens"
"Chains" (Dreiser) **35**:70, 73, 75
"The Chains" (Palamas) **5**:377
"Chains" (Stringer) **37**:343
Chains (Dreiser) **35**:70-1
Chains of Dew (Glaspell) **55**:247, 271, 276; **175**:74, 149
Chaitāli (Tagore) **3**:490
Chaka (Mofolo) **22**:245-46, 248-55, 257-62, 264
Chakhchygys-Taasu (Remizov) **27**:348
Challenge (Sapper) **44**:316, 319-22
"The Challenge of Our Time" (Forster) **125**:183
Challenge to Clarissa (Delafield) **61**:127
"A Challenge to Fate" (Naidu) **80**:316
The Challenge to Sirius (Kaye-Smith) **20**:96-98, 100-02, 109-10
"The Challenge to the Labyrinth" (Calvino)
See "La sfida al labirinto"
"Chaluz Castle" (Guiney) **41**:207
"Chamber" (Carter)
See "The Bloody Chamber"
Chamber Music (Joyce) **3**:255, 270; **8**:158; **16**:212, 221, 227; **35**:144, 176-77; **159**:279, 282-85
"The chamber of statues" (Borges)
See "La cámara de las estatuas"
Chambers of Imagery (Bottomley) **107**:5-6
La chambre claire: Note sur la photographie (Barthes) **135**:135, 144-45, 147, 157, 162-64, 170

Chambre d'hotel (Colette) **5**:169; **16**:129-31, 133-34
The Chameleon (Johnson)
See *The Autobiography of an Ex-Colored Man*
Chamfort erzählt seinen Tod (Frank) **81**:102
"Champagne" (Pardo Bazán) **189**:299, 317, 320-21
"Champak Blossoms" (Naidu) **80**:295
"Champion" (Lardner) **2**:329, 335, 337-38; **14**:291, 295, 305, 307, 312-14, 319-20
The Champion (Tsvetaeva)
See *Molodets*
"The Champion of the Weather" (Henry) **19**:174
"The Champion of the World" (Dahl) **173**:13
"Champs" (Giono) **124**:126
"Chance" (Hamsun) **151**:248
Chance (Conrad) **1**:196, 200, 203, 209, 217; **6**:113, 121-22; **13**:117; **25**:87; **57**:37
A Chance Acquaintance (Howells) **7**:365, 371, 375, 377, 391; **17**:176, 180, 183; **41**:234
Chance Acquaintances: Hotel Room (Colette)
See *Chambre d'hotel*
Chance Aquaintances (Colette)
See *Chambre d'hotel*
"A Chance Meeting" (Cather) **132**:137
"Chance to Work" (Gurney) **33**:106, 108
Le Chancellor: Journal du passager J.-R. Kazallon; Martin Paz (Verne) **52**:352
"The Chances" (Owen) **5**:366-67, 369, 371, 374; **27**:212, 214-15, 227, 229, 236
"Chances R" (Ginsberg) **120**:86
La chandelle verte (Jarry) **14**:281-82
Chandos (Ouida) **43**:341, 347, 350, 365-66, 375
Chandranāth (Chatterji) **13**:75, 80
Change for a Halfpenny (Lucas) **73**:168
A Change in the Cabinet (Belloc) **18**:32, 35
"The Change in the Position of Women" (Howe) **21**:111
"The Change: Kyoto-Tokyo Express" (Ginsberg) **120**:41
A Change of Air (Hope) **83**:164
"A Change of Leaders" (Norris) **155**:331
A Change of Spirit (Griffith) **68**:250
"A Change of Treatment" (Jacobs) **22**:97
"The Change of Vocabulary in the Critical Essay" (Lin) **149**:342, 344
"The Changeling" (Mew) **8**:294-95
"Changes" (Gurney) **33**:103
Changes in Bodily Form of Descendants of Immigrants (Boas) **56**:82
"Changes of Attitude and Rhetoric in Auden's Poetry" (Jarrell) **177**:187
"The Changing Beauty of Park Avenue" (Fitzgerald) **52**:58-9
Changing Concepts of Time (Innis) **77**:341, 346, 369
The Changing Light at Sandover (Merrill) **173**:162, 171, 174, 180-82, 186-87, 189-95, 201, 203, 207, 210, 217-24, 229-33, 235, 238-39, 241-44, 246-47, 249-50, 253, 256-58
"Changing the Slums" (Riis) **80**:437
"Channel Firing" (Hardy) **143**:212
"A Channel Passage" (Brooke) **2**:50, 52, 55, 60; **7**:127
"A Channel Passage" (Swinburne) **8**:428
A Channel Passage, and Other Poems (Swinburne) **8**:428
The Channel Road (Woollcott) **5**:522, 528
Chanson complète (Éluard) **7**:250; **41**:158
"Chanson de l'automne" (Gourmont) **17**:129
La chanson du carillon (Lemonnier) **22**:199
"Chanson du déserteur" (Vian) **9**:530
"La chanson du mal-aimé" (Apollinaire) **3**:33-4, 36-9, 41, 43-4; **8**:13, 16; **51**:7, 9, 13-17, 19, 21, 38, 53, 57, 59-61
"Chanson pour Sophie" (Arp) **115**:53
Chansons (Ramuz) **33**:294
Chansons de fou (Verhaeren) **12**:473
Chant de la coupe (Mistral) **51**:150
Le chant de la résurrection (Rolland) **23**:269
"Chant de l'horizon en champagne" (Apollinaire) **51**:36
"Chant d'honneur" (Apollinaire) **8**:17; **51**:36
"Le Chant du déserteur" (Tzara) **168**:321
Le chant du monde (Giono) **124**:40, 43-4, 46, 53, 60, 63-5, 69-73, 93, 96, 100-2, 124, 130-31, 135
"Chant for Dark Hours" (Parker) **143**:321
"Chant of Doom" (Brennan) **17**:46
A Chant of Doom, and Other Verses (Brennan) **17**:48
"The Chant of the Vultures" (Markham) **47**:285
"The Chant of Women" (Sharp) **39**:360
"Le chante d'amour" (Apollinaire) **51**:36
Chantecler (Rostand) **37**:283-84, 286-87, 290-91, 294, 297-98, 300, 305; **6**:377-78, 382-83
"Le chanteur de Kymé" (France) **9**:52-3, 57
Chanticleer (Rostand)
See *Chantecler*
"Chant-Pagan" (Middleton) **56**:174
"Chantre" (Apollinaire) **51**:35, 61
"The Chantry of the 'Nona'" (Belloc) **18**:41
"Chants the Epistle" (Pirandello)
See "Canta l'epistola"
"Chaos" (Benn) **3**:110
"Chaos" (Lasker-Schueler) **57**:314-15, 318-19, 326, 328, 334
Chaos (Lagerkvist)
See *Kaos*
"Chaos and Poetry" (Lawrence) **93**:111
"Chaos in Motion and Not in Motion" (Stevens) **45**:310
Ch'ao-yin chi (Su Man-shu) **24**:458, 462
"The Chapel of Wadham College" (Grieg) **10**:208
"Chapelle de la morte" (Nelligan) **14**:397
The Chaplet of Pearls; or, The White and Black Ribaumont: A Romance of French History, 1572 (Yonge) **48**:376
Chaplet of Verse (Crowley) **7**:205
"Chaplinesque" (Crane) **5**:188, 190
"A Chapter in the Philosophy of Value" (Simmel) **64**:338
Chapter the Last (Hamsun)
See *Siste kapitel*
Chapters for the Orthodox (Marquis) **7**:439, 446-47, 452
Chapters from a Life (Phelps) **113**:338, 342-43, 376, 394-97
Chapters of a Life (Phelps) **113**:363
"Chapters of a Longer Work" (Bergelson) **81**:23
Chaque fois que l'aube paraît (Daumal) **14**:96
Chār adhyāy (Tagore) **3**:495
Character Analysis (Reich)
See *Charakteranalyse*
Character and Comedy (Lucas) **73**:159, 170, 174
Character and Opinion in the United States (Santayana) **40**:362, 384, 412-13
Character Formation and the Phobias of Childhood (Reich) **57**:342
"The Character of Man" (Twain) **6**:461
"A Character Sketch" (Woolf) **43**:407
Characteristics (Mitchell) **36**:265-66, 273, 276
"The Characteristics of Japanese Poetry" (Hagiwara) **60**:294
"Characters" (Pirandello)
See "Personaggi"
Characters and Commentaries (Strachey) **12**:400
Characters and Events: Popular Essays in Social and Political Philosophy (Dewey) **95**:69
Characters of the Reformation (Belloc) **18**:45
"A Character's Tragedy" (Pirandello)
See "La tragedia di un personaggio"
Charakteranalyse (Reich) **57**:338-39, 341, 360, 384-85
"Charcoal" (Scott) **6**:398
"Charcoal Burners" (Quiroga)
See "Los fabricantes de carbón"
"The Charcoal-Burner" (Milne) **88**:260
"The Charcoal-Makers" (Quiroga)
See "Los fabricantes de carbón"
"Charenton en 1810" (Swinburne) **8**:440
"A Charge with Prince Rupert" (Higginson) **36**:171, 175
The Chariot of Elijah (Ady)
See *Az illés szekerén*
"Chariot of Fire" (Phelps) **113**:342
The Chariot of Fire (De Voto) **29**:114, 126
"The Charioteer of Delphi" (Merrill) **173**:256
Les Charitées d'Alcippe (Yourcenar) **193**:270
Charitrahīn (Chatterji) **13**:79-80, 83
"Charity" (Bowen) **148**:84
"Charity" (Gilman) **9**:97
"Charity" (Graham) **19**:119, 130
Charity (Gilbert) **3**:208, 219
The Charity Ball (Belasco) **3**:88
Charlas de café (Ramoacn y Cajal) **93**:138, 142, 146
The Charlatan (Buchanan) **107**:34, 86
"Charles" (Jackson) **187**:239
"Charles and Mary" (Morley) **87**:145
"Charles Carvlle's Eyes" (Robinson) **101**:111, 197
"Charles Dickens" (Orwell) **51**:247; **128**:283
Charles Dickens (Chesterton) **1**:178, 184; **6**:101, 109
Charles Dickens (Gissing) **3**:224; **24**:221
Charles Lamb and the Lloyds (Lucas) **73**:158, 161, 168, 173
"Charles Lamb and the Theater" (Matthews) **95**:228
Charles Lamb Day Book (Lucas) **73**:173
The Charles Men (Heidenstam)
See *Karolinerna*
Charles Sheeler: Artist in the American Tradition (Rourke) **12**:320, 322-24, 329-30, 332
"Charles Sumner" (Forten) **16**:150
Charles the First, King of England (Belloc) **18**:23
Charles XII (Strindberg)
See *Carl XII*
El charlestón (Donoso) **133**:52, 157
Charleston, 1820 (Heyward) **59**:100
Charleston and Other Stories (Donoso)
See *El charlestón*
Charley Is My Darling (Cary) **1**:142, 144, 148; **29**:68, 72-3, 79, 83, 87, 92, 101, 104, 109; **196**:140, 171, 176
"Charlie" (Chopin) **14**:62, 80-1
Charlie (Hecht) **101**:74
Charlie and the Chocolate Factory (Dahl) **173**:4-5, 9
Charlie and the Great Glass Elevator (Dahl)
See *Charlie and the Great Glass Elevator: The Further Adventures of Charlie Bucket and Willy Wonka, Chocolate-Maker Extraordinary*
Charlie and the Great Glass Elevator: The Further Adventures of Charlie Bucket and Willy Wonka, Chocolate-Maker Extraordinary (Dahl) **173**:5, 8
Charlie Chan Carries On (Biggers) **65**:2, 4, 9
"Charlie Graham" (Rhodes) **53**:315-16
"Charlie's Greek" (O'Faolain) **143**:266
"Charlotte Brontë" (Woolf) **128**:339
Charlotte Brontë (Benson) **27**:11
"Charlotte Corday" (Forten) **16**:150
Charlotte Löwensköld (Lagerloef) **4**:235; **36**:237, 238, 241
Charlotte Perkins Gilman: A Nonfiction Reader (Gilman) **117**:134-36, 139-41
The Charlotte Perkins Gilman Reader (Gilman) **117**:90, 134-36
Charlotte's Inheritance (Braddon) **111**:215, 220, 225, 228, 231, 245
"Charlotte's Quest" (Montgomery) **51**:212
"Charm Incorporated" (Wharton) **129**:364
Charmes; ou, Poèmes (Valéry) **4**:489, 491-92; **15**:445, 447, 466
"Charmides" (Wilde) **8**:495

"Charming Fellow, Anastacia" (Rhodes) **53**:321
"Charming Pact" (Morgenstern)
See "Anmutiger Vertrag"
"Charms" (Benét) **28**:5
Charms of the Earth (Sologub)
See *Ocharovaniia zemli*
"Charnel Ground" (Ginsberg) **120**:73, 109, 113
Les charniers (Lemonnier) **22**:197, 200-02
Charodjnaja chasha (Sologub) **9**:444
"Une charogne" (Bryusov) **10**:81
"Charondas" (Guiney) **41**:206
"La charrette" (Schwob) **20**:323
"Chartres" (Oppen) **107**:303
The Charwoman's Daughter (Stephens) **4**:406, 408, 411, 414-16, 418-21
The Charwoman's Shadow (Dunsany) **59**:5, 17, 21, 26
"The Chase" (Toomer) **172**:279
The Chase of the Golden Plate (Futrelle) **19**:90
"Chased Away" (Lasker-Schueler) **57**:336
The Chasm (Cahan) **71**:30
La Chasseur (Kandinsky) **92**:49
Le chasseur François (Vian) **9**:531
The Chaste Wanton (Williams) **1**:518
Chastelard (Swinburne) **8**:423, 425, 431-34, 436, 439; **36**:295, 316-17
Chasy (Remizov) **27**:332-33, 346
Le château des pauvres (Éluard) **41**:151
"Le chateau hermetique" (Vallette) **67**:319, 321
"Châteaux en Espagne" (Nelligan) **14**:392
The Châtelaine of La Trinité (Fuller) **103**:59, 61-62, 65-66, 68, 76, 83, 95, 114, 116
Chats on Bashō (Masaoka)
See *Bashō zatsudan*
"Chattanooga-Choo-Choo" (Donoso) **133**:123, 137-39, 147, 149, 151-56, 186, 189
La chatte (Colette) **5**:172; **16**:134, 136
Chaucer (Chesterton) **6**:101
Le Chaudron Infernal (Melies) **81**:122
"La chaumière incendiée" (Coppee) **25**:124
"Chava" (Aleichem) **35**:325
Chaver Nachman (Singer) **33**:383, 387, 399-401
Chayka (Chekhov) **3**:147-49, 154, 162, 164, 166, 169, 173-75; **10**:101, 103-5, 107, 109, 111, 114-15; **31**:73-78, 81-82, 86, 88-90, 93; **55**:60-64, 75; **96**:8, 14-17, 39-42, 51, 65; **163**:1-135
"Une che si salva" (Jovine) **79**:44
Cheap and Contented Labor: The Picture of a Southern Mill Town in 1929 (Lewis) **13**:334
Cheap Books and Good Books (Matthews) **95**:270
Cheap Jack Zita (Baring-Gould) **88**:23-4
"Cheap Order" (Levi)
See "L'ordine a buon mercato"
The Cheap-Eaters (Bernhard)
See *Die Billigesser*
The Cheat (Čapek)
See *Život a dílo skladatele Foltýna*
"The Cheated Child" (Montgomery) **51**:181
Cheeks on Fire (Radiguet)
See *Les joues en feu*
Cheer Up (Rinehart) **52**:283
Cheerful Yesterdays (Higginson) **36**:167, 170-72, 177, 187
A Cheery Soul (White) **176**:186, 225, 228, 259, 322
"Cheese" (Chesterton) **1**:184
"The Cheese Museum" (Calvino) **183**:48
Cheezo (Dunsany) **2**:144; **59**:3, 13, 26
"Chef de section" (Apollinaire) **3**:35
Chef's d'oeuvre (Bryusov) **10**:79, 81-2, 86, 95-6
"Chelkash" (Gorky) **8**:73
"Chelovecheskii material" (Olesha) **136**:102-3, 136, 154, 161, 163, 168, 172, 174
"Chelovek" (Mayakovski) **18**:257-58
"Chelovek predmestya" (Bagritsky) **60**:17
Le chemin de la Croix-des-Ames (Bernanos) **3**:128
"Le chemin de l'Institut" (Barrès) **47**:45
Le chemin de velours (Gourmont) **17**:127, 130, 134, 138, 142, 145, 150, 152
"La chemise" (France) **9**:57-8
"Chenille" (Dickey) **151**:97, 109, 167
"Chenxiang xue: diyi luxiang" (Chang)
See "Ashes of Descending Incense: Second Brazier"
Cher Antoine (Anouilh) **195**:40, 49
"Les chercheurs" (Sully Prudhomme) **31**:306
Chéri (Colette) **1**:190-92; **5**:163, 168, 172; **16**:115, 120, 127-29, 133, 137
Chéri-Bibi et Cecily (Leroux) **25**:260
"Cherished Tales" (Remizov)
See "Zavetnye skazki"
"Cherkes" (Korolenko) **22**:182
"Chernyi chelovek" (Olesha) **136**:182, 184
Chernyi chelovek (Olesha) **136**:74, 79, 111
Chernyia maski (Andreyev) **3**:21-3
The Cherokee Night (Riggs) **56**:201, 205, 208, 211, 214-15, 218
"Cherries" (Dazai Osamu)
See "Ōtō"
Cherry (Tarkington) **9**:460, 466
Cherry Blossom Festival (Klabund) **44**:106
The Cherry Garden (Chekhov)
See *Visňevyi sad*
The Cherry Orchard (Chekhov)
See *Visňevyi sad*
"The Cherry Robbers" (Lawrence) **93**:16, 66, 115, 121
The Cherry Stone (Olesha)
See *Vishnevaya kostochka*
"The Cherry Tree" (Coppard) **5**:180
"The Cherry Tree" (Nemerov) **124**:186, 252
"The Cherry Trees" (Thomas) **10**:467
"Cherry White" (Parker) **143**:325
"Cherrylog Road" (Dickey) **151**:89-90, 97, 104, 106, 169
"Chertykhanets" (Remizov) **27**:341
"The Cheshire Cheese" (Pilnyak)
See "Ye Olde Cheshire Cheese"
"Chesniki" (Babel) **13**:33; **171**:22, 30, 74, 83, 86-87
"Chess" (Borges) **109**:21
"Chess" (MacCarthy) **36**:254
The Chessmen of Mars (Burroughs) **32**:58
"Chesterton and Detective Fiction" (Borges) **109**:148
The Chestnut Tree (Yeats) **1**:570
"Chet McAusland of Fraternity" (Williams) **89**:399
"Chetvrdnadcati-oye dekabrya" (Hippius) **9**:161
"Chetyre epokhi razvitiya" (Tolstoy) **173**:285, 291-94, 298, 304, 314, 321
Le cheval de Troie (Nizan) **40**:308-11, 313-24
Le chevalier du passé (Dujardin) **13**:189-90
The Chevalier of Pensieri-Vani, together with Frequent Allusions to the Prorege of Arcopia (Fuller) **103**:52, 58-66, 68-70, 73, 75-76, 83, 91, 95, 107, 110-11, 115-117, 120-22
Les chevaliers de la table ronde (Cocteau) **119**:68, 99, 101-4
Les chevaux de Diomède (Gourmont) **17**:135, 137, 141, 151, 157
"Chevaux de frise" (Apollinaire) **51**:36
"Les Chevaux sauvages" (Yourcenar) **193**:265
Chevengur (Platonov) **14**:409-10, 422-24, 427, 429
Le chèvrefeuille (D'Annunzio) **6**:136-37; **40**:10-11
Cheyenne Gold (Faust) **49**:41, 47
The Cheyne Mystery (Crofts)
See *Inspector French and the Cheyne Mystery*
Chez la Muse (Jarry) **147**:244
"Chez Madame Ubu" (Jarry) **147**:263
Chi è chiù felice 'e me! (de Filippo) **127**:281, 290, 292
Chi to rei (Mizoguchi) **72**:322
"Chiang sha chi" (Su Man-shu) **24**:461
"Chiarezza" (Ginzburg) **156**:105, 107
La chiave a stella (Levi) **109**:280, 290, 316, 342
"Chicago to Salt Lake by Air" (Ginsberg) **120**:25
"Chicago: Where Now" (Wirth) **92**:359
The Chichovtsi (Vazov)
See *Cičovci*
"Chickamauga" (Bierce) **1**:87; **7**:88-9, 92; **44**:15, 24, 44-5, 47
"Chickamauga" (Wolfe) **4**:516, 520
"A Chicken or a Horse" (Adams) **56**:8
"The Chickens" (Mori Ogai)
See "Niwatori"
Chidi zhilian (Chang)
See *Naked Earth*
"The Chief Mourner of Marne" (Chesterton) **6**:100
"The Chief Operator" (Phelps) **113**:342
"The Chief Warrior" (Eastman) **55**:170
"Le chien de l'ecriture" (Drieu la Rochelle) **21**:27
"Le chien perdu" (Coppee) **25**:124
Les chiens de garde (Nizan) **40**:290, 294-95, 297-98, 314-16, 324
Les chiens de paille (Drieu la Rochelle) **21**:20, 22, 34, 37-8, 40
"La chiesa di Polenta" (Carducci) **32**:103, 105, 110
"Chijo" (Shiga) **172**:214
Chikamatsu Monogatari (Mizoguchi) **72**:293, 304, 309-10, 324, 326
"Chikumagawa no suketchi" (Shimazaki Toson) **5**:431, 439
"A Child" (Undset) **197**:290
"A Child Asleep" (Roberts) **68**:336
"A Child Asleep in Its Own Life" (Stevens) **3**:459; **45**:302
"Child at Sea" (Jiménez) **183**:334, 339
"Child by Tiger" (Wolfe) **13**:493
"The Child Dying" (Muir) **87**:190
"Child Fancies" (Naidu) **80**:289
"A Child in the Dark, and a Foreign Father" (Lawson) **27**:132, 141
"The Child in the Orchard" (Thomas) **10**:467
"Child in the Universe" (Roberts) **68**:305
Child Lovers, and Other Poems (Davies) **5**:199
Child Man (Pinero) **32**:403, 405, 411
"The Child Musician" (Dobson) **79**:11, 18-9
The Child of Allah (Gumilev)
See *Ditja Allaxa*
"Child of Destiny" (Baker) **3**:4
Child of Manhattan (Sturges) **48**:283, 285, 311, 316
The Child of Montmarte (Léautaud) **83**:194-7
A Child of Nature (Buchanan) **107**:85
A Child of Our Time (Horvath)
See *Ein Kind unserer Zeit*
The Child of Pleasure (D'Annunzio)
See *Il piacere*
Child of Storm (Haggard) **11**:242, 246, 253-55
A Child of the Century (Hecht) **101**:57-9, 61, 66, 74, 84, 90
"Child of the Infinite" (Roberts) **8**:318, 321
A Child of the Jago (Morrison) **72**:356-57, 359-62, 364-74, 376-78, 380-85, 388-89, 391-92, 395
"The Child on the Cliffs" (Thomas) **10**:452, 467
Child Pictures from Dickens (Higginson) **36**:168
"The Child World" (Riley)
See *A Child-World*
"Childbirth and Ability" (Yosano) **59**:350
The Childermass (Lewis) **2**:285, 387-91, 393-98; **9**:237, 240, 248; **104**:178, 181, 186, 201, 206, 208, 214
"Childhood" (Baker) **10**:21
"Childhood" (Devkota)
See "Bālakkāl"
"Childhood" (Ginzburg) **156**:24
"Childhood" (Gumilev)
See "Detstvo"
"Childhood" (Muir) **87**:218

"Childhood" (Nemerov) **124**:273
A Childhood (Carossa)
See *Eine Kindheit*
Childhood (Ivanov) **33**:136
Childhood (Ramos)
See *Infância*
Childhood (Sarraute)
See *Enfance*
Childhood (Tolstoy)
See *Detstvo*
"Childhood II: At Grandmother's" (Babel) **13**:32
Childhood and Adolescence (Tolstoy)
See *Detstvo*
Childhood and Other Stories (Babel)
See *Detstvo i drugie rasskazy*
Childhood and Youth (Tolstoy) **4**:445, 447; **11**:459; **17**:377
Childhood at Brindabella (Franklin) **7**:271
"Childhood: At Grandmother's" (Babel) **2**:28
Childhood. Boyhood. Youth (Tolstoy) **4**:451, 456, 473
"Childhood Cradle Songs" (García Lorca) **49**:90
"Childhood Friends" (Heidenstam) **5**:249
Childhood Is the Kingdom (Millay) **169**:292
The Childhood of Edward Thomas (Thomas) **10**:458
The Childhood of Louvers (Pasternak) **188**:226
"Childhood without Hatred" (Chang)
See "Tongnian wuji"
"A Childish Discourse" (Chang) **184**:149
"The Childless Woman" (Monroe) **12**:216
"Childlessness" (Merrill) **173**:209-12, 214, 232, 257-59
The Childlike Life of the Black Tarantula (Acker) **191**:4, 6, 8, 12, 42, 67-70, 95, 127
Children (Andrić) **135**:8
The Children (Prus)
See *Dzieci*
The Children (Wharton) **3**:561, 563; **9**:548; **129**:350, 363, 365-66
"Children and Art" (Obstfelder)
See "Børn og kunst"
"Children and Civilians" (Jarrell) **177**:195
Children Are Civilians Too (Böll) **185**:65
"Children Are the Best People" (Morris) **107**:169
Children of Abraham: The Short Stories of Scholem Asch (Asch)
See *Die kinder Abrahams: Novellen aus America*
The Children of Captain Grant (Verne)
See *Les enfants du Capitaine Grant*
"Children of Captivity" (Somerville & Ross) **51**:331
The Children of Finkenrode (Raabe)
See *Die Kinder von Finkenrode*
Children of God (Fisher) **140**:149, 151, 154-55, 182, 184-85
Children of Israel (Aleichem) **1**:29-30
"The Children of Lir" (Baker) **3**:10
"The Children of Lir" (Tynan) **3**:501, 503, 505-06
"The Children of Nineveh" (Leino) **24**:370
Children of the Age (Hamsun)
See *Børn av tiden*
Children of the Bush (Lawson) **27**:129, 131
"Children of the Dark Star" (Sharp) **39**:358
The Children of the Dream (Bettelheim) **143**:8-10
"Children of the Earth" (Roberts) **68**:348-50, 352
"The Children of the Foam" (Campbell) **9**:29
Children of the Frost (London) **9**:255, 259, 262, 264, 274
Children of the Game (Cocteau)
See *Les enfants terribles*
Children of the Ghetto: Being Pictures of a Peculiar People (Zangwill) **16**:439-42, 444-47, 449-55, 462-64, 466, 469
The Children of the King (Crawford) **10**:141, 143-44, 148-50, 158
Children of the Market Place (Masters) **2**:467-69
"Children of the Moon" (Middleton) **56**:176, 192
The Children of the Night (Robinson) **5**:401-02, 404, 410, 418; **101**:95-97, 110, 118-19, 123-24, 133, 136, 196
The Children of the Poor (Riis) **80**:435
"Children of the Time" (Lagerkvist)
See "Tiden barn"
Children of the Wind (Shiel) **8**:360
Children of the World (Heyse)
See *Kinder der welt*
"The Children of the Zodiac" (Kipling) **8**:195
The Children of To-morrow (Sharp) **39**:373, 385
"Children of Water" (Sharp) **39**:377
"Children on a Country Road" (Kafka) **179**:307
"Children on Their Birthdays" (Capote) **164**:100, 110, 112, 114, 155-61
"Children Selecting Books in a Library" (Jarrell) **177**:138-40, 157, 169, 231
The Children Sing in the Far West (Austin) **25**:34
"Children's Arms" (Jarrell) **177**:181
The Children's Crusade (Schwob)
See *La croisade des enfants*
"Children's Easter" (Papadiamantis) **29**:273
"The Children's Hour" (Benchley) **55**:13
The Children's Hour (Hellman) **119**:123, 142-43, 167, 175, 178-80, 188-90, 192-95, 214, 220, 222-25, 227, 235-36
"The Children's Hurdy Gurdy" (Guro)
See "Detskaja šarmanocka"
"The Children's Song" (Kipling) **8**:191
Children's Tales (Zoshchenko) **15**:505
"A Child's Christmas in Wales" (Thomas) **45**:398; **105**:358
"A Child's Garden of Verses" (Benchley) **1**:76
"A Child's Japan" (Sarton) **120**:264
A Child's Memories (Lagerloef) **4**:238
"The Child's Relations with Others" (Merleau-Ponty) **156**:199-200, 210, 231
A Child's Romance (Loti)
See *Le roman d'un enfant*
"Child's Song at Christmas" (Pickthall) **21**:250
A Child-World (Riley) **51**:284
"A Chilhowee Lily" (Murfree) **135**:208
"Chilterns" (Brooke) **7**:121-22
"Chimeny Sweepers" (Bishop) **121**:44-46, 48
"La chimera" (Campana) **20**:84, 90
La chimera (D'Annunzio) **6**:143
The Chimera (Pardo Bazán)
See *La quimera*
"Chimes for Yahya" (Merrill) **173**:163, 170, 228-29
"Chimes of Love" (Kuzmin)
See "Kuranty liubvi"
"The Chimney Sweep's Wife" (Söderberg)
See "Sotarfun"
Chimneysmoke (Morley) **87**:123
"China" (Donoso) **133**:42-43
China, Japan, and the U.S.A. (Dewey) **95**:68
Chinatown Family (Lin) **149**:324, 332, 337
"Chincoteague" (Pyle) **81**:381
"The Chinese" (Söderberg) **39**:437, 439
"Chinese Banalities" (Schwitters) **95**:351
"Chinese Lanterns" (Upward) **85**:391
"Chinese Laundry" (Burroughs) **121**:132
"The Chinese Nightingale" (Lindsay) **17**:227, 230
The Chinese Nightingale, and Other Poems (Lindsay) **17**:225, 227
The Chinese Parrot (Biggers) **65**:4-5, 7
"Chinese Poems" (Upward) **85**:394
"A Chinese Story" (Harris) **24**:272
"A Chinese Tale" (Bulgakov) **16**:83-5
A Chinese Torture Garden (Mirbeau)
See *Le jardin des supplices*
The Chinese Wall (Frisch)
See *Die chinesische Mauer: Eine Farce*
Chinesische Betrachtung (Hesse) **196**:324
Die chinesische Mauer: Eine Farce (Frisch) **121**:198, 221, 236, 274, 281, 303, 305
Der chinesische Mauer: Eine Farce (Frisch)
See *Die chinesische Mauer: Eine Farce*
Chinesischer Vatermord (Brecht) **169**:42
"Chink" (Seton) **31**:279
"The Chink and The Child" (Burke) **63**:127
The Chink in the Armour (Lowndes) **12**:201, 203
Chinmoku (Endo) **152**:167, 169-72, 177-78, 185, 187-88, 194, 196-99, 201-8, 212-16, 218-27, 229-30, 240
"Chinmoku no to" (Mori Ogai) **14**:387
"Chiostro verde" (Scott) **6**:394-95
"Chiote à l'esprit" (Artaud) **3**:51
The Chip and the Block (Delafield) **61**:127, 136
The Chip-Chip Gatherers (Naipaul) **153**:226, 230, 234
"Chips from an Old Philosopher" (Benchley) **1**:78
Chips Off the Old Benchley (Benchley) **55**:5
"Chiquenaude" (Roussel) **20**:227, 229, 235, 246
"Chiquita" (Harte) **25**:191
"La chirla" (Unamuno) **148**:310
Chiru yanagi mado no yūbae (Nagai)
See *Gesakusha no shi*
"Chirurgie esthétique" (Apollinaire) **51**:20
Chita (Hearn) **9**:118, 122, 128, 131-32, 135, 138-40
"Chitateli gazet" (Tsvetaeva) **35**:404
Chivalry (Cabell) **6**:63, 67, 69
Chivalry Peak (Cobb) **77**:129
Chloe Marr (Milne) **6**:318
Chłopi (Reymont) **5**:390-94, 396-98
Chō o yumemu (Hagiwara) **60**:287
"El chocolate de los jesuitas" (Palma) **29**:264
"Chocorua to Its Neighbor" (Stevens) **45**:299
Chōei (Ishikawa) **15**:124, 129
"Choice" (Gumilev)
See "Vybor"
"The Choice" (Wharton) **129**:362
The Choice of a Bride (Kuzmin)
See *Vybor nesty*
"Choice of Jello or Rice Pudding" (Cobb) **77**:134
"A Choice of Profession" (Malamud) **184**:163, 171, 237, 244, 246
"The Choice of Reuben and Gad" (Foote) **108**:34
Choix desélues (Giraudoux) **2**:164-65; **7**:318-20, 326
"Le chômage" (Zola) **6**:569
"Choosing a Mast" (Campbell) **5**:123-24
Chop at the Roots (Jozsef) **22**:155
Chopin: The Man and His Music (Huneker) **65**:157, 165, 170, 198, 205, 207
Chopin und Nietzsche (Przybyszewski) **36**:280, 286
"Chopin's Funeral March" (Stephens) **4**:420
"Chopo muerto" (García Lorca) **181**:122-23
"A Chorale" (Agee) **1**:11; **19**:23
"Choriambics" (Brooke) **2**:58-9
Chornaya metallurgiya (Fadeyev) **53**:55
Chornoe po belomu (Hippius) **9**:161
"Chortik" (Remizov) **27**:341, 347-48
Chortik (Khlebnikov) **20**:136
Chortov log i polunoshchnoe solntse (Remizov) **27**:346
Chortova kukla (Hippius) **9**:155, 158, 161-62, 169
"Chorus" (Fondane) **159**:256
"A Chorus Girl Speaks in a Dream to a Former Lover" (Bodenheim) **44**:62
"The Chorus of Slaves" (Talvik) **87**:320
Chorus of the Newly Dead (Muir) **87**:180, 194
"A Chorus of Wagner" (Moody) **105**:262
A Chosen Few (Stockton) **47**:327
The Chosen Ones (Giraudoux)
See *Choix desélues*
The Chosen People (Laski) **79**:135-6
Chosen Poems (Monroe) **12**:222

Chosen Poems: Old and New (Lorde) **173**:52, 54, 73, 77
The Chosen Valley (Foote) **108**:10-12, 36-7
"The Chosen Vessel" (Baynton) **57**:2, 5-6, 9-11, 13-16, 18-19, 23, 32
"Choses tues" (Valéry) **15**:464
"A Chouan" (Guiney) **41**:207
"Chrevo" (Zamyatin) **8**:546, 551-53
Chris Christopherson (O'Neill)
See *Anna Christie*
"Chrismus on the Plantation" (Dunbar) **12**:115
"Chrisp Street, Poplar" (Morrison) **72**:375
Christ (Hartmann) **73**:110-11, 116, 134
Christ (Kazantzakis) **33**:159, 171
Christ and Antichrist (Merezhkovsky) **29**:230-31, 233, 241
Christ and Christmas (Eddy) **71**:149
Christ and the Media (Muggeridge) **120**:168, 192
"Le Christ au cinématographe" (Jacob) **6**:199, 202
Le Christ dans la matière: Trois histoires comme Benson (Teilhard de Chardin) **9**:481, 491
"Christ in Concrete" (di Donato) **159**:189-90
Christ in Concrete (di Donato) **159**:183, 185-96, 198-99, 202-14, 216-17, 222-23, 226-30
Christ in Italy (Austin) **25**:33, 35
"Christ in Plastic" (di Donato) **159**:193, 196, 223-24, 228, 230
Christ in Rome (Sikelianos) **39**:415, 419
"Christ in the Castle" (Papadiamantis) **29**:272
"Christ in the Museum" (Pickthall) **21**:245, 250
Christ Legends (Lagerloef)
See *Kristuslegender*
The Christ of Velázquez (Unamuno)
See *El Cristo de Velázquez*
Christ; or, The Lamb and the Wild Beast (Strindberg) **8**:418
Christ Recrucified (Kazantzakis)
See *Ho Christos xanastauronetai*
Christ Stopped at Eboli (Levi)
See *Cristo si è fermato a Eboli*
"Christ, the Man" (Davies) **5**:209
"A Christã nova" (Machado de Assis) **10**:279
Christchurch (Coffin) **95**:4
"Christd in the Tirol" (Lawrence) **93**:70
"The Christening" (Milne) **88**:242
Das Christentum als Mystische Tatsache (Steiner) **13**:441, 445-46, 449-50
Christentum, Judentum und Heidentum (Brod) **115**:78, 85, 90-1, 99, 106
The Christian Captives (Bridges) **1**:124
"Christian Citizenship" (Bryan) **99**:108
"Christian Confession of Faith" (Södergran)
See "Kristen trosbekännelse"
The Christian Doctrine (Tolstoy) **11**:463; **79**:79, 335, 428
"Christian Faith and Contemporary Culture" (Sayers) **15**:389
Christian Letters to a Post-Christian World (Sayers) **15**:378
Christian Science (Twain) **12**:436
The Christian Teaching (Tolstoy)
See *The Christian Doctrine*
"Christian Trevalga" (Symons) **11**:448
Christian Wahnschaffe (Wassermann) **6**:508-11, 515-16
"Le Christianisme" (Owen) **27**:203, 212, 215-16, 236
"Christianisme et philosophie" (Merleau-Ponty) **156**:121, 123-24, 126, 129-30
Christianity and Class Struggle (Berdyaev) **67**:30
"Christianity and Literature" (Endo) **152**:167
Christianity and Morals (Westermarck) **87**:361, 395-96
"Christianity and Patriotism" (Tolstoy) **79**:429
Christianity and the Machine Age (Gill) **85**:82, 84, 87-8
Christianity as Mystical Fact and the Mysteries of Antiquity (Steiner)
See *Das Christentum als Mystische Tatsache*
Christianity, Jewry and Heathendom (Brod)
See *Christentum, Judentum und Heidentum*
The Christianity of the New Testament (von Hartmann) **96**:211, 222
Christianity's Place in History (Rozanov) **104**:382
Christians (Andreyev) **3**:26
Christians Only (Broun) **104**:80
"Christie Christison" (Graham) **19**:136
Christina Alberta's Father (Wells) **19**:452
Christinas Heimreise (Hofmannsthal) **11**:292, 296, 301
Christina's Journey Home (Hofmannsthal)
See *Christinas Heimreise*
Christine (Elizabeth) **41**:131
"The Christmas" (Muir) **87**:168
"Christmas" (Quiroga)
See "La navidad"
Christmas (Gale) **7**:283
"Christmas, 1917" (Benson) **17**:33
"Christmas and Ireland" (Johnson) **19**:230
"Christmas Antiphones" (Swinburne) **8**:437; **36**:318
"Christmas Bread" (Papadiamantis) **29**:272
"Christmas by Injunction" (Henry) **19**:178
"A Christmas Carol" (Swinburne) **8**:436; **36**:299
"A Christmas Chronicle" (Caragiale) **76**:169
"Christmas Eve" (Hardy) **143**:198
"Christmas Eve" (Obstfelder)
See "Juleaften"
"Christmas Eve" (Vallejo)
See "Nochebuena"
Christmas Eve (Brennan) **124**:3-4
Christmas Formula, and Other Stories (Benson) **17**:32
A Christmas Garland (Beerbohm) **1**:67, 69, 72; **24**:101, 104, 107, 112, 116, 119-20, 122-23, 125
"A Christmas Ghost-Story" (Hardy) **53**:100
"Christmas Guest" (Hawthorne) **25**:235
Christmas in July (Sturges) **48**:270-72, 274, 276, 283, 287-89, 301, 303, 309-10, 319, 321-22
"Christmas Is a Comin'" (Dunbar) **12**:114
Christmas Madonna (Babits)
See *Karácsonyi Madonna*
"A Christmas Memory" (Capote) **164**:112, 157
"Christmas Morning" (Nemerov) **124**:180, 253
"Christmas Morning" (Roberts) **68**:301, 336
"The Christmas of Sir Galahad" (Phelps) **113**:376
"The Christmas Offering" (Rölvaag) **17**:347
"Christmas on the Hudson" (García Lorca)
See "Navidad en el Hudson"
"Christmas on the Plantation" (Dunbar)
See "Chrismus on the Plantation"
"Christmas Pantomimes" (Benchley) **55**:3
"The Christmas Roses" (Jarrell) **177**:214-15, 224-26
"The Christmas Shadrach" (Stockton) **47**:325, 327
"A Christmas Song" (Dunbar) **12**:110
"The Christmas Star" (Pasternak) **188**:196
"A Christmas Storm" (Nemerov) **124**:269
"Christmas Story" (Mencken) **13**:387
A Christmas Story (Shepherd) **177**:315
The Christmas Tales of Flanders (Bosschere) **19**:56
"The Christmas Tree" (Fletcher) **35**:106
"The Christmas Tree at the Sventitskys" (Pasternak) **188**:261
"Christmas under Arms" (Sterling) **20**:386
"The Christmas Wreck" (Stockton) **47**:312, 320
The Christmas Wreck (Stockton) **47**:314
"Christofer Columbus" (Jensen) **41**:300
Christoph Columbus, der Don Quichote des Ozeans (Wassermann) **6**:517
Christoph Pechlin (Raabe) **45**:171, 175, 178, 200
Christophe Colomb (Ghelderode) **187**:5, 18, 22, 24
Christopher and Columbus (Elizabeth) **41**:124
Christopher Columbus (Ghelderode)
See *Christophe Colomb*
"Christopher Columbus" (Mayakovski) **18**:258
Christopher Columbus (Jensen) **41**:295, 298
"Christopher Comes Back" (Benson) **27**:19
Christos (Kazantzakis) **181**:308-10
Christos Milionis (Papadiamantis) **29**:271
Ho Christos xanastauronetai (Kazantzakis) **2**:317-20, 323; **5**:262-64, 268; **33**:145-47, 149, 159, 160, 163-64, 172; **181**:244, 252, 280, 286, 309, 328-31
Christowell (Blackmore) **27**:25, 28, 35-9, 42, 44-7
Christ's Christianity (Tolstoy) **79**:327
Christ's Emperor (Sayers) **15**:388
"Christs Procession" (Cankar) **105**:155
"Christus Natus Est" (Cullen) **37**:163
Christus-Visionen (Rilke) **195**:258-59, 261
"The Chronic Argonauts" (Wells) **133**:225, 235, 242, 259, 323-25, 338-42
The Chronicle of 1917 (Remizov) **27**:331, 334
"Chronicle of a Village" (Ginzburg)
See "Cronaca di un paese"
"A Chronicle of Changing Clothes" (Chang) **184**:152-53
Chronicle of Dawn (Sender)
See *Crónica del alba*
Chronicle of Early Youth (Sender)
See *Crónica del alba*
A Chronicle of gilded fetters (Chang)
See *Jin suo ji*
The Chronicle of Sparrow Street (Raabe)
See *Die Chronik der Sperlingsgasse*
The Chronicle of Tebaldeo Tebaldei (Swinburne) **8**:444
The Chronicle of the Town Okurov (Gorky) **8**:77
"The Chronicle of Young Satan" (Twain) **161**:242; **185**:256, 265-66, 269-73, 276, 279-81, 296-98, 307-16, 318-21, 324-25, 327-32
The Chronicles of Clovis (Saki) **3**:365, 370
The Chronicles of Count Antonio (Hope) **83**:171
Chronicles of Hell (Ghelderode)
See *Fastes d'enfer*
Chronicles of Martin Hewitt (Morrison) **72**:363
Chronicles of Pantouflia (Lang) **16**:264, 267
Chronicles of the House of Borgia (Rolfe) **12**:267, 275, 282-83
Chronicles of Wasted Time (Muggeridge) **120**:155, 157, 181, 187, 190, 192-93
Die Chronik der Sperlingsgasse (Raabe) **45**:160, 165, 169-70, 179-81, 187, 190, 201-02
Chronik von des zwanzigsten Jahrhunderts Beginn (Sternheim) **8**:368, 372
Chronique de septembre (Nizan) **40**:316
Chroniques (Giono) **124**:50, 55, 69, 73
Chroniques (Proust) **161**:124
Chroniques (Schwob) **20**:329
Chroniques d'art (Apollinaire) **51**:39
Chrpy a města (Nezval) **44**:241, 249
"Chrysanthemum" (Wen I-to) **28**:410
The Chrysanthemum and the Sword (Benedict) **60**:93-4, 97, 120, 130, 133-36, 147, 151-3
"Chrysanthemum Turning Sour" (Hagiwara) **60**:296
"Chto takoe iskusstvo?" (Tolstoy) **4**:477, 479-80; **11**:462, 469; **28**:357-58; **79**:338, 374, 379, 392-97, 421
Chto takoe iskusstvo? (Tolstoy) **173**:286
"Chto ya?" (Tolstoy) **173**:294-95
"Chu, zashumeli vdrug oblaka" (Khlebnikov) **20**:137
"Chuang shiji" (Chang) **184**:138-39, 141, 143
Chuanqi xiaoshuoji (Chang) **184**:106, 127-28, 131, 145, 147, 151
"Chudnaya" (Korolenko) **22**:179, 182
"Chudo" (Remizov) **27**:339

"The Church" (Lawrence) **93**:104
"The Church" (Muir) **87**:193
"The Church and the Fiction Writer" (O'Connor) **132**:237, 321
"Church and Theatre" (Sayers) **15**:388
"The Church at Antioch" (Kipling) **8**:207; **17**:213
Church at Murnau (Kandinsky) **92**:38
"The Church at Novograd" (Babel) See "Kostel v Novograde"
"Church Bells" (Vilakazi) See "Izinsimbi zesonto"
"Church Building" (Harper) **14**:264
Church Manual (Eddy) See *Manual of the Mother Church*
"A Church Mouse" (Freeman) **9**:75
"The Church of a Dream" (Johnson) **19**:243, 247, 255
"The Church of Polenta" (Carducci) See "La chiesa di Polenta"
"The Church of the Gospels" (Gumilev) See "Evangelicheskaja cerkov'"
"The Church Supper" (Benchley) **55**:3
"The Church with an Overshot Wheel" (Henry) **19**:176, 180, 189-90
"The Church-Builder" (Hardy) **4**:154
"The Churchyard" (Buchanan) **107**:25
"Churchyard Arabesque" (Söderberg) **39**:438
Chute de Constantinople (Giono) **124**:97
La chute de la maison Usher (Epstein) **92**:2, 10-1, 13, 16
La chute de Miss Topsy (Rod) **52**:309
"Chūtō" (Akutagawa Ryūnosuke) **16**:34
Chuzhoe nebo (Gumilev) **60**:260, 269-70, 277
Ciano's Diplomatic Diaries (Muggeridge) **120**:191
"Le Ciaromelle" (Pascoli) **45**:149
Ciascuno a suo modo (Pirandello) **4**:334-35, 338, 340, 346, 348, 352; **29**:301-03, 314-15; **172**:150, 162, 167-68, 174, 193
"Ciaula Discovers the Moon" (Pirandello) **4**:330
"Cibernetica e fantasmi (Appunti sulla narrativa come processo comtinatiorio)" (Calvino) **183**:9-10, 47, 62, 65, 67, 103, 142, 145, 152-53, 156, 194, 246
"Cicadas" (Bunin) **6**:47, 52
"The Cicadas" (Bunin) **6**:47, 52
"Cicely" (Harte) **25**:191, 200
"Cicely's Dream" (Chesnutt) **5**:132; **39**:82
"Ci-Cît, précédé de la culture Indienne" (Artaud) **3**:51
Cičovci (Vazov) **25**:454, 456
"Le ciel est un ceuf" (Arp) **115**:41
"Cielo" (Jiménez) **183**:268
"Cielo vivo" (García Lorca) **197**:207-08, 232
"Los cielos" (Aleixandre) **113**:16, 25
Los cien mil hijos de San Luis (Pérez Galdós) **27**:287
"La cifra" (Borges) **109**:6
La cifra (Borges) **109**:6, 117
"Cigánydal" (Babits) **14**:39
"Un cigare allume que Fume" (Apollinaire) See "Paysage"
"Le cigare romanesque" (Apollinaire) **51**:20
"The Cigarette Case of the Commander" (Hunt) **53**:200
"The Cigarette Packet" (Bagritsky) See "Papirosnyy korobok"
The Cigarette-Maker's Romance (Crawford) **10**:141, 143, 146-47, 151
"¡Cigarra!" (García Lorca) **181**:120, 123
"Ćilim" (Andrić) **135**:84, 96
Cimbelina en 1900 y pico (Storni) **5**:453
Cimbrernes Tog (Jensen) **41**:295, 298
The Cimbrians (Jensen) See *Cimbrernes Tog*
"Le cimetière" (Desnos) **22**:73
"Le cimetière marin" (Valéry) **4**:488, 491-92, 495; **15**:455, 458-59
"Cimio" (Ball) **104**:71, 76-77
"Cinching Up" (Foote) **108**:34-5
"Cinderella" (Jarrell) **177**:152-53
"Cinderella's Slipper" (March) **96**:261
"Cinders" (Hulme) **21**:142-43
Cinéma (Deleuze) **116**:89, 95, 97, 103
Cinéma (Desnos) **22**:63
"Cinema 33" (Fondane) **159**:240
"Cinema and the Novel: Problems of Narrative" (Calvino) **183**:107
"Cinéma frénétigue et cinéma académique" (Desnos) **22**:64
Cinema I (Deleuze) See *Cinema 1: L'image-Movement*
Cinema 1: L'image-Movement (Deleuze) **116**:67-8, 78, 80, 83-5, 165-66, 168-70
Cinema 1: The Movement-Image (Deleuze) See *Cinema 1: L'image-Movement*
Cinema 2 (Deleuze) See *Cinema 2: L'image-Temps*
Cinema 2: L'image-Temps (Deleuze) **116**:68, 78, 83, 85, 165, 169, 175
"A Cinema-Goer's Autobiography" (Calvino) **183**:234
"Cinematic" (Aleixandre) See "Cinemática"
"Cinemática" (Aleixandre) **113**:3
"Cinematograph" (Mandelstam) **2**:403
"The Cinematographic Principle and the Ideograph" (Eisenstein) **57**:165
Cinématoma (Jacob) **6**:191
Cinnamon and Angelica (Murry) **16**:332, 353-55
"Cinnamon Shops" (Schulz) **5**:422
Cinnamon Shops, and Other Stories (Schulz) See *Sklepy cynamonowe*
Les cinq cents millions de la Begúm, suivi de les revoltés de la "Bounty" (Verne) **6**:496, 500; **52**:331, 347, 350, 353
Cinq grandes odes (Claudel) **2**:104, 107-08; **10**:121, 123, 128, 130, 132-33
Cinq récits (Verhaeren) **12**:472
"Les cinq rondels du tout jeune homme" (Éluard) **41**:150
Cinq semaines en ballon (Verne) **6**:493-94, 497, 499; **52**:331, 336, 343-44, 348-49, 352
"A Cinque Port" (Davidson) **24**:164
The Cinque Ports: A Historical and Descriptive Record (Ford) **172**:7
Cinque romanzi brevi (Ginzburg) **156**:44, 63, 112
"Le cinquième poème visible" (Éluard) **41**:157
"Cîntecul lebedei" (Rebreanu) **28**:267
"The cipher" (Borges) See "La cifra"
The Cipher (Borges) See *La cifra*
Circe the Enchantress (Devkota) See *Māyāvinī Sarsī*
"A Circle in the Fire" (O'Connor) **132**:247, 257, 284, 300, 302, 305-6, 355, 357
"The Circle of Affection" (Scott) **6**:398
The Circle of Chalk (Klabund) See *Der Kreidekreis*
The Circle of Reading (Tolstoy) See *Krug chtenija*
Circles within Circles (Kandinsky) **92**:147
Les circonstances de la vie (Ramuz) **33**:295
"Circuit" (Aleixandre) See "Circuito"
"Circuit" (Dickey) **151**:175
"Circuito" (Aleixandre) **113**:7, 47
"The Circular Ruins" (Borges) See "Las ruinas circulares"
The Circular Staircase (Rinehart) **52**:279-81, 283-84, 287-90, 293-94, 299-301
The Circular Study (Green) **63**:148, 151-52, 156
"Circulo vicioso" (Machado de Assis) **10**:279-80
Circumstance (Mitchell) **36**:263, 267-68, 270, 273
"Circumstances" (Cahan) **71**:13, 26, 44, 71
"Circus" (Andrić) See "Cirkus"
"The Circus" (Saroyan) **137**:166
"The Circus Animals' Desertion" (Yeats) **1**:580; **18**:447, 458, 463; **116**:343
"Circus at Dawn" (Wolfe) **13**:468
"The Circus at Denby" (Jewett) **22**:116, 136
"The Circus Horse" (Colette) **16**:139
Circus World (Hecht) **101**:63, 80
"The Circus Wrestlers" (Kuprin) **5**:300
"La Cire verte" (Colette) **16**:121, 129, 138
"Cirkus" (Andrić) **135**:28
Cisimo (Calvino) **183**:114
"Cisma" (Drummond de Andrade) **139**:233
El cisne de Vilamorta (Pardo Bazán) **189**:205, 260
Citadelle (Saint-Exupéry) **2**:517-19, 521-23, 526; **56**:225, 235; **169**:309, 313-17, 321, 323-24, 334, 338-39, 342-46
"La cité dormante" (Schwob) **20**:323
"The Cited" (García Lorca) See "Romance del emplazado"
"Cities and Desire" (Calvino) **183**:68, 71
"Cities and Memory" (Calvino) **183**:68, 71
Cities and Men (Lewisohn) **19**:292-94
"Cities of Italy" (Baroja) See "Ciudades de Italia"
Cities of the Plain (Proust) See *Sodome et Gomorrhe*
Cities of the Red Night: A Boys' Book (Burroughs) **121**:137, 144, 166, 168-70
Citizen Kane (Mankiewicz) **85**:105-112, 115, 118-9, 121, 123-57, 163, 167, 170, 173, 176-7, 180, 182-5
"Citizen Wolie Brenner" (Bergelson) **81**:20
"Citizens of Japan, A Mourning Song" (Yosano) See "Nihon kokumin asa no uta"
"Citizenship in a Republic" (Roosevelt) **69**:181
Città del silenzio (D'Annunzio) **6**:139
La città e la casa (Ginzburg) **156**:5, 63, 65, 69-70, 108
Le città invisibili (Calvino) **183**:13, 15-16, 24-25, 27-30, 41-42, 44, 47, 51, 57, 67-70, 96, 101, 112, 144, 148, 153, 156, 158, 164, 171, 173, 194-95, 222, 230-31
La città morta (D'Annunzio) **6**:130, 134-35, 141, 144; **40**:6, 8
"La Città pensata: la misura degli spazi" (Calvino) **183**:103
"La città scritta: epigrafi e graffiti" (Calvino) **183**:101
"City" (Arenas) See "Ciudad"
"The City" (Baker) **10**:21
"The City" (Blok) **5**:91, 95
"The City" (Cavafy) **2**:94; **7**:156
"The City" (Dreiser) **35**:64
"City" (Guro) See "Gorod"
The City (Claudel) See *La ville*
The City and Man (Strauss) **141**:230, 233, 315
City and Suburb (Riddell) **40**:335
The City and the House (Ginzburg) See *La città e la casa*
The City and the Solitude (Palamas) **5**:385
"The City as Protagonist in Balzac" (Calvino) **183**:105
The City Commander of Bugul'ma (Hašek) See *Velitelem města Bugul'my*
"The City Curious" (Bosschere) **19**:59
"A City Flower" (Dobson) **79**:22
"The City Limits" (Jozsef) **22**:161
"City Midnight Junk Strains for Frank O'Hara" (Ginsberg) **120**:55, 128
"City of Builders" (van Ostaijen) **33**:409
The City of Byblos (Coleridge) **73**:8
"The City of Dreadful Night" (Hardy) **143**:76
"The City of Dreadful Night" (Kipling) **8**:185
"The City of Dreadful Night" (Stephens) **4**:407
City of Dreadful Night (Abbey) **160**:61
"The City of Dreadful Thirst" (Paterson) **32**:369
The City of Dream (Buchanan) **107**:66-7

The City of Fog (Baroja)
See *La ciudad de la niebla*
City of Illusion (Fisher) **140**:188
The City of Peril (Stringer) **37**:336
The City of Pleasure (Bennett) **5**:37
"The City of Refuge" (Fisher) **11**:205, 207, 209, 212, 214
"City of Sleep" (Kipling) **8**:186
"The City of the Dead" (Gibran) **9**:84
The City of the Discreet (Baroja)
See *La feria de los discretos*
"The City of the Gone Away" (Bierce) **44**:45
"The City of Torment" (Heym) **9**:145
"The City of Towers" (Nezval)
See "Město věží"
"The City on Mallington Moor" (Dunsany) **59**:21
"City Stillife" (van Ostaijen)
See "Stad stilleven"
"The City: Suggestions for the Investigation of Human Behavior in the Urban Environment" (Park) **73**:203
"City Trees" (Millay) **4**:306; **49**:202
Ciudad (Arenas) **191**:191
"Ciudad" (Arenas) **191**:186
"La ciudad absorta" (Gonzalez Martinez) **72**:152
"La ciudad de Espeja" (Unamuno) **148**:311
La ciudad de la niebla (Baroja) **8**:48, 52, 62
"Ciudad sin sueño" (García Lorca) **1**:308; **48**:94, 123; **181**:28; **197**:191, 217, 244, 279
"El ciudadano del olvido" (Huidobro) **31**:126
"Las ciudades" (Huidobro) **31**:125
"Ciudades de Italia" (Baroja) **8**:63
Ciuleandra (Rebreanu) **28**:271-72
"Civil Disobedience" (Arendt) **193**:43
Civil War (Bergelson) **81**:30
"Civilisation" (Bierce) **44**:14
Civilisation (Clark) **147**:127, 132
Civilization (Ince) **89**:12-3, 18
Civilization and Its Discontents (Freud)
See *Das Unbehagen in der Kultur*
"Civilization in Crisis" (Pratolini) **124**:333
Civilization: Its Cause and Cure (Carpenter) **88**:63, 71, 97, 100, 106, 121-2, 127, 132, 135, 138
Clā do jabuti (Andrade) **43**:38
"The Claim of the Living" (Woolf) **43**:407
"The Claims of the Muse" (Dobson) **79**:3
"Clair de lune" (Apollinaire) **51**:58-9
"Clair de lune intellectuel" (Nelligan) **14**:392
"Claire's Herd" (van Ostaijen) **33**:409
"Le clairière" (Desnos) **22**:73
Clairieres dans le Ciel (Jammes) **75**:113-115, 119
"Clamor" (García Lorca) **181**:201
"Clampherdown" (Kipling) **8**:177
"The Clan of No Name" (Crane) **11**:140, 167
"Clancy of the Mounted Police" (Service) **15**:404, 407
"Clancy of the Overflow" (Paterson) **32**:369-70, 374
The Clandestine Marriage (Belasco) **3**:86
The Clansman (Griffith) **68**:161, 189
The Clansman: An Historical Romance of the Ku Klux Klan (Dixon) **163**:140-50, 152-55, 160, 162-64, 170, 178, 184-85, 187, 189-90, 192, 198, 209-12, 215-18, 223, 225, 227, 229, 231, 235, 238-39, 241-48, 250-59, 265-66, 268-69, 272, 274, 277-79
Clara d'Ellebeuse ou l'Histoire d'une Ancienne Jeune Fille (Jammes) **75**:104, 115, 117-18
Clara dos anjos (Lima Barreto) **23**:164, 168
Clara Hopgood (Rutherford) **25**:336, 338, 341, 344, 346, 349, 355-58, 361-62
Clara Vaughan (Blackmore) **27**:22-3, 31, 36-8, 40, 44
"Clara's Little Escapade" (Rinehart) **52**:282
"Clarence" (Harte) **25**:213
Clarence (Tarkington) **9**:461-62, 465
"Clarity" (Ginzburg)
See "Chiarezza"
Clarivigilia primaveral (Asturias) **184**:16, 36-37
"Clark Gable's Secret Wish" (Erskine) **84**:185
Claro enigma (Drummond de Andrade) **139**:224, 226-27, 231
Clarté (Barbusse) **5**:14, 17-20
The Clash (Barea) **14**:46, 48-9, 51, 53
"Clash by Night" (Kuttner) **10**:269, 273, 275
The Clasped Skeletons (Hardy) **48**:59
"Class and Art" (Trotsky) **22**:380
"Class Poem" (Austin) **25**:34
"Classical Dreams" (Babits)
See "Klasszikus álmok"
"Classicism and Romanticism" (Carducci)
See "Classicismo e romanticismo"
Classicism and Teutonism (Heidenstam) **5**:253
"Classicismo e romanticismo" (Carducci) **32**:83, 90, 101
"Claude" (Cather) **132**:124, 128-29
Claudelle Inglish (Caldwell) **117**:21
"Claude's Aunt" (Leverson) **18**:200-01
"Claudine" (Huysmans) **69**:8, 12, 23
Claudine à l'école (Colette) **5**:166; **16**:131, 136
Claudine à Paris (Colette) **5**:166, 173
Claudine and Annie (Colette)
See *Claudine s'en va*
Claudine at School (Colette)
See *Claudine à l'école*
Claudine en ménage (Colette) **5**:166, 173; **16**:136
Claudine in Paris (Colette)
See *Claudine à Paris*
Claudine Lamour (Lemonnier) **22**:198
Claudine Married (Colette)
See *Claudine en ménage*
Claudine s'en va (Colette) **5**:166
Claudius (Kaiser) **9**:173-74
"Claudius' Diary" (Shiga)
See "Kurōdiasu no nikki"
"Claudius' Journal" (Shiga)
See "Kurōdiasu no nikki"
"Claudius's Diary" (Shiga)
See "Kurōdiasu no nikki"
"Claud's Dog" (Dahl) **173**:12
Claus Peymann kauft sich eine Hose (Bernhard) **165**:72, 74
Claus Peymann und Hermann Beil auf der Sulzwiese (Bernhard) **165**:62, 72, 74
Clavecin de Diderot (Crevel) **112**:6
Claverhouse (Tey) **14**:460-61
"Clavering" (Robinson) **101**:138
"Clay" (Gurney) **33**:97
"Clay" (Joyce) **8**:167; **35**:144, 150, 160, 164-65, 167, 184, 192, 195, 197; **159**:299, 303, 314-16
Clay Doves (Kuzmin) **40**:191-92
"Clay in the Hands of the Potter" (Bennett) **197**:133
Clayhanger (Bennett) **5**:23-6, 29-30, 32, 34, 38, 40-4, 47-8; **20**:17-21, 29, 39-40; **197**:9, 11-12, 14, 18, 20, 23, 25-6, 30, 55, 62, 75, 78-82, 94-8, 100, 108-12, 114, 116, 125-26, 130-31, 133-34, 175
The Clayhanger Family (Bennett) **5**:36, 40-1, 44; **197**:79, 82
"Cleansing and Rejuvenating" (Cankar) **105**:155
Clear Enigma (Drummond de Andrade)
See *Claro enigma*
Clear Horizon (Richardson) **3**:358
"Clearances" (Herbert) **168**:44
"A Cleared Path" (Gilman) **37**:213-14
"Clearhearing" (Musil) **68**:261
"Clearing the Title" (Merrill) **173**:230
"Clearing the Wild Land (Opus 1017)" (Miyazawa) **76**:290, 292
"La Clef de l'oeuvre de Jean Cocteau" (Cocteau) **119**:76
"Les Clefs de l'église" (Yourcenar) **193**:265
"La Clemence" (Campbell) **5**:123
The Clenched Fist (Lagerkvist)
See *Den knutna näven*
"Cleopatra" (Heyse) **8**:113, 125
Cleopatra (Giacosa) **7**:305
Cleopatra (Haggard) **11**:246
Cleopatra in Judaea (Symons) **11**:433
Clerambault, histoire d'une conscience libre pendant la guerre (Rolland) **23**:261-62
"A Clergyman" (Beerbohm) **1**:67; **24**:117, 125
A Clergyman's Daughter (Orwell) **2**:502-03, 508, 510; **6**:342, 344, 348, 351; **15**:310; **51**:227-28, 255; **128**:254-56, 264-65, 268-71, 282, 291, 295, 301, 304; **129**:223, 248
A Cleric's Journal (Obstfelder)
See *En praests dagbog*
"Clerk Maxwell's Influence on the Evolution of the Idea of Physical Reality" (Einstein) **65**:73
"Clerkenwell" (Morrison) **72**:373
"Clerks" (Lawrence) **93**:69
"The Clerks" (Robinson) **101**:103, 119, 133, 156, 198
"The Clever Cockatoo" (Bentley) **12**:15, 20
The Clever Ones (Sutro) **6**:421
The Clever Woman of the Family (Yonge) **48**:372, 374, 382, 388
Clevinger's Trial (Heller) **131**:22, 42, 46
The Clicking of Cuthbert (Wodehouse) **108**:362
Client-Centered Therapy (Levi) **125**:258, 291
The Cliff Dwellers (Fuller) **103**:57, 59, 61-62, 65-66, 68, 71-74, 84, 91-94, 102-04, 112, 117
"Cliff Klingenhagen" (Robinson) **101**:119, 198
"A Cliff out of the Future" (Khlebnikov) **20**:151
"Clifford Ridell" (Masters) **25**:299
"Cliffrose and Bayonets" (Abbey) **160**:22, 95-96
The Cliffs (Doughty) **27**:53, 59, 61-2, 65, 69-70, 84
"The Cliffside Path" (Swinburne) **36**:344-45
"Clin d'oeil" (Péret) **20**:187
"Clinamen" (Jarry) **147**:311, 313-14
"The Clinging Vine" (Robinson) **101**:111
Clinique et critique (Deleuze)
See *Critique et clinique*
"Clio" (Péguy) **10**:404
The Clio (Myers) **59**:123-5, 129, 132, 136, 150
The Clipper of the Clouds (Verne)
See *Robur le conquérant*
"Clipper Ships" (Fletcher) **35**:98, 101
"The Cloak" (Chekhov) **3**:146
A Cloak of Light (Morris) **107**:185-89, 208, 214
Les cloches de bâle (Aragon) **123**:143
"Clock" (Hagiwara) **60**:309
The Clock (Remizov)
See *Chasy*
"The Clock Has Stopped" (Hippius) **9**:157
"The Clock of the Years" (Hardy) **53**:101
The Clock Strikes One (Zuckmayer) **191**:327-28
The Clock Strikes Twelve (Wakefield) **120**:335, 343, 349, 355-59
"A Clock with No Hands" (Nemerov) **124**:213
Clock without Hands (McCullers) **155**:169, 180, 189, 209, 214
"The Clocks of Rondaine" (Stockton) **47**:329
The Clocks of Rondaine (Stockton) **47**:314
A Clockwork Orange (Kubrick) **112**:143, 145-47, 152, 172-73, 188, 204-05, 207, 213, 225, 234-36, 264
"A Clod of Earth" (Akutagawa Ryūnosuke)
See "Ikkai no tsuchi"
"A Clod of Soil" (Akutagawa Ryūnosuke)
See "Ikkai no tsuchi"
"Clodia" (Schwob) **20**:323
Cloister Lugau (Raabe)
See *Kloster Lugau*
"The Cloisters" (Borges) **109**:5
Le cloître (Verhaeren) **12**:458, 464, 469, 479-82
"Le cloître noir" (Nelligan) **14**:397
Les cloportes (Renard) **17**:302
Clorinda Walks in Heaven (Coppard) **5**:179, 181

Clorindy; or, The Origin of the Cakewalk (Dunbar) **12**:122
Close Harmony (Parker) **143**:316
"A Close Look at France" (Drieu la Rochelle)
See "Mesure de la France"
Close of the Book (Glaspell) **55**:236
"Close Ranks" (Du Bois) **169**:213
Close to the Sun Again (Callaghan) **145**:254
"The Closed Door" (Donoso)
See "La puerta cerrada"
"The Closed Door" (Scott) **6**:386, 388-89
The Closed Door (Bosschere)
See *La porte fermée*
Closely Observed Trains (Hrabal)
See *Ostře sledované vlaky*
Closely Watched Trains (Hrabal)
See *Ostře sledované vlaky*
"Closer Union" (Schreiner) **9**:400
"The Closest Attention: Gays in Cuba" (Arenas) **191**:145
Closing Time (Heller) **131**:21; **151**:319, 321-26, 340-41
"Cloth'd Now with Dark Alone" (Brennan) **17**:44
"Clothe the Naked" (Parker) **143**:297, 332, 335-36
"The Clothing of Ghosts" (Bierce) **44**:15
"Clotilde" (Apollinaire) **3**:39
"The Cloud" (Crane) **2**:121
"The Cloud" (Gurney) **33**:97
"Cloud" (Meynell) **6**:294
"Cloud" (Toomer) **172**:279
Cloud and Silver (Lucas) **73**:155
"Cloud and Sun" (Tagore)
See "Megh o Roudra"
Cloud Handkerchief (Tzara)
See *Mouchoir de nuages*
Cloud Howe (Gibbon) **4**:120-23, 125-26, 128
"A Cloud in Trousers" (Mayakovski)
See "Oblako v shtanakh"
"Cloud, Lake, Tower" (Nabokov) **108**:83
Cloud, Stone, Sun, and Vine (Sarton) **120**:263, 269, 299, 303
The Cloud That Lifted (Maeterlinck)
See *Le malheur passe*
"A Cloudburst of Light" (Tsvetaeva) **7**:570
"Clouded Skies" (Nagai)
See "Donten"
Clouded Sky (Radnóti)
See *Tajtékos ég*
"Clouds" (Brooke) **7**:124
"Clouds" (Lyotard) **103**:218
"Clouds" (Nagai)
See "Kumo"
"Clouds" (Pirandello)
See "Nuvole"
"Clouds" (Shimazaki Toson)
See "Kumo"
The Clouds (Doughty) **27**:59, 62, 65, 69-70
"Clouds above the Chapel—Wisps of Pale-Blue Air" (Tsvetaeva) **35**:394
Clouds of Witness (Sayers) **2**:531; **15**:378, 381, 389, 393
"The Clouds over Ferrara" (Herbert) **168**:48
"The Cloud's Swan-Song" (Thompson) **4**:439-40
Clouds without Water (Crowley) **7**:209
"Cloudy Days" (Shiga)
See "Kumori-bi"
"Clough" (MacCarthy) **36**:253
"The Clout and the Pan" (Powys) **9**:377
The Cloven Foot (Braddon) **111**:231
"The Cloverfields Carriage" (Stockton) **47**:313
The Clown (Böll)
See *Ansichten eines Clowns*
Le Club des menteurs (Ghelderode) **187**:5-6
The Club of Queer Trades (Chesterton) **6**:108
"The Club Secretary" (Dunsany) **59**:27
Clue: A Guide through Greek to Hebrew Scriptures (Abbott) **139**:25-26
The Clue of the New Pin (Wallace) **57**:394-95, 398, 402
Cluster of Songs (Tagore)
See *Gitāli*
"Cnards" (Aleichem) **1**:32
"The Coach" (Hunt) **53**:190, 192, 200
"The Coach House" (Chekhov) **3**:152
"Coagulum" (Meyrink) **21**:221
"Coal" (Lorde) **173**:69, 71
Coal (Lorde) **173**:54, 73
"Coal Thieves" (Molnár)
See "Szentolvajok"
A Coarsened City (Bergelson) **81**:18
"Coasa" (Rebreanu) **28**:273
"The Coast Guard's Cottage" (Wylie) **8**:533, 538
The Coast of Bohemia (Howells) **7**:376; **17**:185
"The Coast of Slaves" (Khlebnikov)
See "Nevolnichy bereq"
The Coastguard's Secret (Hichens) **64**:130-31
"A Coat" (Yeats) **11**:528; **31**:385
The Coat without Seam (Baring) **8**:36-7, 43
Coats (Gregory) **1**:332; **176**:20-21
"¿Cobardía?" (Pardo Bazán) **189**:299-301, 305-06
Cobbers (Baynton)
See *Bush Studies*
Cobb's Anatomy (Cobb) **77**:116, 127
Cobb's Bill of Fare (Cobb) **77**:127
Cobhurst (Stockton)
See *The Girl at Cobhurst*
"Cobra" (Aleixandre) **113**:14
Cobra (Sarduy) **167**:198-99, 201-4, 206, 213, 215, 217-18, 222, 224-33
"The Cobweb" (Gale) **7**:285
"The Cobweb" (Saki) **3**:363
Cobwebs from an Empty Skull (Bierce) **44**:9-10, 12; **7**:97
"Cocette" (White) **176**:159, 171
"The Cock and the Pearl" (Jacob)
See "Le coq et la perle"
Cock Robin (Barry) **11**:47, 54, 65
"The Cockatoos" (White) **176**:229, 309
Cockatoos (Franklin) **7**:264, 267-73
The Cockatoos (White) **176**:159, 219, 228-29, 247
"Cock-Crow" (Thomas) **10**:450, 455, 467
"The Cocked Hat" (Masters) **25**:288
"Cockney Corners" (Morrison) **72**:371-72, 374-75
The Cockpit (Zangwill) **16**:466
"Cockroaches" (Schulz) **51**:314-15
"Cocktail Hour" (Benchley) **55**:13
"Coconuts" (Williams) **89**:395, 398, 400
Cocuyo (Sarduy) **167**:199, 213-14, 220, 222
The Cod Fisheries: The History of an International Economy (Innis) **77**:337, 370, 398
"Coda: The Higher Keys" (Merrill)
See "The Higher Keys"
"The Code of a Gentleman" (Nash) **109**:360
Code of the Woosters (Wodehouse) **108**:339, 347, 356-58, 361-64, 378-9, 383, 385, 387, 392
"A Coed" (Khlebnikov)
See "Uchilitsa"
Coeli Enarrant (Ruskin) **63**:251
"Coeur" (Apollinaire) **8**:12, 17
Le Coeur à gaz (Tzara) **168**:240, 256, 260, 264, 293, 309-10, 312
"Coeur, couronne et miroir" (Apollinaire) **8**:12, 17-18; **51**:54
Coeur d'Alene (Foote) **108**:18, 42
Un coeur de femme (Bourget) **12**:72
"Le coeur de la matière" (Teilhard de Chardin) **9**:482
Coeur double (Schwob) **20**:319, 321, 323, 326, 329
"Coeur en bouche" (Desnos) **22**:60
Coeur fidèle (Epstein) **92**:2-3, 11
Coeur pensif ne sait où il va (Bourget) **12**:69
"Le coeur sur l'arbre" (Éluard) **41**:153
Un coeur virginal (Gourmont) **17**:130, 133, 138, 151, 153
"Les Coeurs arrachés" (Yourcenar) **193**:265
"Coffee for the Road" (La Guma) **140**:229
"The Coffee House of Surat" (Tolstoy) **11**:463
"Coffee, Meg and Ilk, Please" (Benchley) **55**:17
"The Coffin Merchant" (Middleton) **56**:174, 182, 194-95
"The Coffin on the Hill" (Welch) **22**:441, 456
La cognizione del dolore (Gadda) **144**:81, 87-92, 94, 96-97, 101, 104-5, 107, 109-10, 118, 122-23, 125-26, 134-37, 139-40, 142
the Cohan Revue (Cohan) **60**:171
Cohen, the Outcast (Adams) **56**:7
"The Coin" (Gurney) **33**:100
"Coin from Syracuse" (Gogarty) **15**:102, 104
A Coin in Nine Hands (Yourcenar)
See *Denier du rêve*
"A Coincidence at Hunton" (Wakefield) **120**:354
The Coiners (Gide)
See *Les faux-monnayeurs*
"Cokher bali" (Tagore) **3**:499
Colberg (Heyse) **8**:119
"Les colchiques" (Apollinaire) **3**:43
"The Cold Argument with Clear Thinking" (Bernhard) **165**:95
"Cold Climate" (Stein) **48**:254
"Cold, Cold Heart" (Williams) **81**:420,438,444
"Cold Fear" (Roberts) **68**:336
Cold Friday (Chambers) **129**:19, 22, 32, 43, 45, 48-50
"A Cold Greeting" (Bierce) **44**:45
"The Cold Heaven" (Yeats) **93**:341, 352, 353
"Cold Iron" (Kipling) **8**:191
A Cold June (Pinero) **32**:399
The Cold Light (Zuckmayer)
See *Das kalte Licht*
"Cold morning" (García Lorca)
See "Mañanita fría"
"A Cold Spring" (Bishop) **121**:23, 27
A Cold Spring (Bishop) **121**:3, 5, 21, 55, 102
Cold Steel (Shiel) **8**:361-62
Cold Stone Jug (Bosman) **49**:3-5, 11, 17, 19, 24, 30, 32
"Cold War" (Kuttner) **10**:269
"Cold-Blooded Creatures" (Wylie) **8**:530
"The Colder the Air" (Bishop) **121**:9, 46-9
Coldness and Cruelty (Deleuze) **116**:136, 145-46
Colette Baudoche (Barrès) **47**:38-40, 42, 51, 60, 81, 94, 99
Colibrí (Sarduy) **167**:191-92, 198-99, 213, 215, 217-18, 222
Colin (Benson) **27**:17
Colin II (Benson) **27**:17
"The Collaborators" (Hichens) **64**:131
"The Collapse of American Strategy" (Bourne) **16**:66
"Collapse of Time" (Bishop) **103**:10
"The Collar" (Davies) **5**:201
El collar de estrellas (Benavente) **3**:94, 99
"Collect for Dominion Day" (Roberts) **8**:319
"A Collect of Philosophy" (Stevens) **45**:287, 291
The Collected Dorothy Parker (Parker) **143**:280
Collected Edition of Heywood Broun (Broun) **104**:93
Collected Essays (Bishop) **103**:12, 15, 37, 41-2
Collected Essays (Woolf) **43**:407, 425
Collected Essays and Papers (Saintsbury) **31**:232, 239
The Collected Essays, Journalism and Letters of George Orwell (Orwell) **2**:512; **15**:360; **31**:190; **51**:235, 250; **129**:235, 237, 247, 254
Collected Essays on Scientific Methodology (Weber)
See *Gesammelte Aufsatze zur Wissenschaftslehre*
Collected Fictions (Borges) **109**:152
Collected Last Plays of Lorraine Hansberry (Hansberry) **192**:334
Collected Legal Papers (Holmes) **77**:217, 262
The Collected Letters (Thomas) **105**:358-59

The Collected Letters of D. H. Lawrence (Lawrence) **2**:369; **61**:212
The Collected Letters of Katherine Mansfield (Mansfield) **164**:258-59, 261, 268, 275, 338-41
Collected Letters of Thomas Hardy (Hardy) **143**:104, 152
Collected Lyrics (Millay) **49**:216
Collected Papers (Maitland) **65**:253
The Collected Papers of Charles S. Peirce (Peirce) **81**:199,204,206
The Collected Plays (Gregory) **176**:84
Collected Plays (Hellman) **119**:215, 217
Collected Plays (Shaw) **9**:425
The Collected Plays of William Butler Yeats (Yeats) **11**:513
The Collected Poems (Agee) **1**:15
Collected Poems (Arp) **115**:13-14, 16
Collected Poems (Baker) **3**:3, 6; **10**:13, 20-1
Collected Poems (Beckett) **145**:190, 202
Collected Poems (Bialik) **25**:64
Collected Poems (Bishop) **103**:3-4, 15, 31
Collected Poems (Campbell) **5**:118
The Collected Poems (Chesterton) **1**:186
The Collected Poems (Coppard) **5**:177
Collected Poems (Cummings) **137**:14, 27-28, 66
Collected Poems (Ford) **172**:5
Collected Poems (García Lorca) **181**:63-68
Collected Poems (Hardy) **4**:167; **32**:281; **143**:146, 150, 176, 196, 212
Collected Poems (Hippius) **9**:158
Collected Poems (Khodasevich)
See *Sobranie stikhov*
Collected Poems (Levi) **109**:287-88, 300
The Collected Poems (Lowell) **8**:237
Collected Poems (Merrill) **173**:251-59
Collected Poems (Meynell) **6**:299-300
Collected Poems (Millay) **49**:216; **169**:232, 239, 248, 258, 276, 300-01, 303
Collected Poems (Noyes) **7**:502, 515
Collected Poems (Oppen) **107**:265-67, 287, 302-09, 311, 319-27, 329-30, 334-35, 350, 352-53, 358-61, 365-66
Collected Poems (Robinson) **101**:97, 126, 134, 146, 184, 196
Collected Poems (Rosenberg) **12**:304, 306
Collected Poems (Scott) **6**:388
Collected Poems (Stephens) **4**:412, 416
Collected Poems (Stevens) **3**:449, 466, 472; **12**:367-68; **45**:276, 287, 299, 311, 313, 345
Collected Poems (Thomas) **10**:452-53, 459-60, 465
Collected Poems (Warner) **131**:310-11, 360
The Collected Poems (Yeats) **1**:581-82; **11**:533; **93**:340, 364, 401; **116**:260, 280, 334
Collected Poems, 1921-1951 (Muir) **2**:482, 484-85, 488; **87**:153, 161, 167
Collected Poems (1930-1993) (Sarton) **120**:299, 317
Collected Poems, 1934-1952 (Thomas) **1**:469-70, 472, 477; **8**:458-59; **10**:452-3, 459-60, 465; **45**:360, 362-63, 399, 401, 405; **105**:306, 308, 314
Collected Poems, 1943-1976 (Popa) **167**:179
Collected Poems, 1947-1980 (Ginsberg) **120**:15, 17, 22-9, 31, 34-41, 48, 53, 74-5, 78, 80-2, 87, 115, 130, 134-35, 137
Collected Poems and Plays (Tagore) **53**:347
The Collected Poems of D. H. Lawrence (Lawrence) **2**:351, 367; **9**:230; **16**:288; **93**:14, 35, 43, 44-47, 52,53,65, 65, 67-69, 97, 100, 101, 104, 115-120, 121, 123-25, 127
The Collected Poems of Edmund Gosse (Gosse) **28**:142
Collected Poems of Elinor Wylie (Wylie) **8**:530, 534
The Collected Poems of Hart Crane (Crane) **5**:188
The Collected Poems of Howard Nemerov (Nemerov) **124**:211-12, 215-17, 225, 228, 246-61, 264, 273-77, 287-89, 297-98
Collected Poems of Ivor Gurney (Gurney) **33**:94, 96-7, 105
The Collected Poems of James Agee (Agee) **180**:64-65
The Collected Poems of James Elroy Flecker (Flecker) **43**:191, 194
The Collected Poems of Jean Toomer (Toomer) **172**:316
The Collected Poems of Keith Douglas (Douglas) **40**:58, 60-1, 65, 69-72, 74-6
The Collected Poems of Mary Coleridge (Coleridge) **73**:25
The Collected Poems of Oliver St. John Gogarty (Gogarty) **15**:106-07, 113, 117
Collected Poems of Raymond Knister (Knister) **56**:154-55
The Collected Poems of Rupert Brooke (Brooke) **7**:125
The Collected Poems of Sara Teasdale (Teasdale) **4**:427
Collected Poems of W. H. Davies (Davies) **5**:201, 204, 207, 209
"The Collected Poems of Wallace Stevens" (Jarrell) **177**:176, 186
The Collected Poems of Wilfred Campbell (Campbell) **9**:31-2
The Collected Poems of Wilfred Owen (Owen) **5**:370; **27**:214
The Collected Poems of William Alexander Percy (Percy) **84**:201, 215-16, 218
Collected Poetry (Bishop) **103**:, 12
The Collected Prose (Bishop) **121**:26, 65, 67-9, 103-4
Collected Prose (Flecker) **43**:210
Collected Short Fiction (Cather)
See *Willa Cather's Collected Short Fiction, 1892-1912*
The Collected Short Prose of James Agee (Agee) **1**:16; **19**:24; **180**:56
Collected Short Stories (Benson) **17**:32
The Collected Short Stories of Edith Wharton (Wharton) **129**:364
The Collected Short Stories of Sean O'Faolain (O'Faolain) **143**:256-59
Collected Shorter Plays (Beckett) **145**:179-80, 206
Collected Sonnets (Millay) **49**:216
The Collected Stories (Babel) **2**:20
Collected Stories (Bowen)
See *The Collected Stories of Elizabeth Bowen*
Collected Stories (Mansfield) **164**:241
The Collected Stories (Thomas) **105**:357-58
The Collected Stories of Colette (Colette) **16**:125, 127, 135, 137
The Collected Stories of Elizabeth Bowen (Bowen) **148**:83-84, 116
Collected Stories of Katherine Mansfield (Mansfield)
See *Collected Stories*
The Collected Stories of M. R. James (James) **6**:211, 214-15
The Collected Stories Of Seán O'Faoláin (O'Faolain) **143**:260-64, 272
Collected Stories of William Faulkner (Faulkner) **170**:225
Collected Works (Adorno)
See *Gesammelte Schriften*
Collected Works (Couperus)
See *Verzamelde werken*
Collected Works (Dewey) **95**:173
Collected Works (Hamsun) **151**:242
Collected Works (Harte) **25**:221
Collected Works (Henley) **8**:107
Collected Works (Mann)
See *Gesammelte Werke*
Collected Works (Molnár) **20**:173
Collected Works (Nishida)
See *Nishida Kitaro zenshu*
Collected Works (O'Connor) **132**:326-27, 366
Collected Works (Przybyszewski) **36**:290
Collected Works (Sologub)
See *Sobranie sochenenii*
Collected Works (Vivekananda) **88**:365-8, 381
The Collected Works of Ambrose Bierce (Bierce) **1**:88; **7**:96; **44**:11-12, 14-15, 44-5
The Collected Works of Arthur Symons (Symons) **11**:445
The Collected Works of Isaac Rosenberg (Rosenberg) **12**:290-91, 312
Collected Works of James Joyce (Joyce) **159**:345-46
Collected Works of Konstantin Stanislavsky (Stanislavsky) **167**:251, 257, 274-75, 279-80, 328, 334, 340-41
The Collected Works of Mahatma Gandhi (Gandhi) **59**:78
The Collected Works of Northrop Frye (Frye) **165**:256, 261
Collected Works of Rosa Luxemburg (Luxemburg) **63**:162
The Collected Writings of John Maynard Keynes (Keynes) **64**:239-42, 248-53, 255, 257, 267, 281, 287-89
Collection of Fairy Tales (Dazai Osamu)
See *Otogi zōshi*
The Collection of Fallen Plums (Shimazaki Toson)
See *Rakubaishu*
Collection of Sand (Calvino)
See *Collezione di sabbia*
A Collection of Sand (Calvino)
See *Collezione di sabbia*
Collection of Short Songs on Innocent Love (Hagiwara)
See *Junjo shokyoku shu*
The Collection of Ten Thousand Leaves (Hagiwara) **60**:304
Collection of Verse: Second Book (Hippius)
See *Sobranie stikhov: Kniga vtoraya*
"The Collective Life" (Ginzburg) **156**:36, 116
Collectivist Economic Planning (Hayek) **109**:202, 241
The Collector's Whatnot (Roberts) **23**:238
"The College of Science" (Stephens) **4**:419
College of Sociology (Bataille) **155**:93
"Collège socratique" (Bataille) **155**:90
College Swing (Sturges) **48**:312
Collezione di sabbia (Calvino) **183**:50-52, 96, 101-7, 111, 216, 1237
"Colli Toscani" (Carducci) **32**:102-03
"The Collier's Wife" (Lawrence) **93**:55, 66
Colline (Giono) **124**:32-3, 41-2, 52-3, 55-6, 65, 92, 95, 98-102, 111, 126-27
La colline inspirée (Barrès) **47**:52, 60-1, 66-7, 78, 93-4
"Les collines" (Apollinaire) **3**:33; **8**:20, 28; **51**:32, 37
Collision (Schwitters)
See *Zusammenstoâ*
"Colloque sentimental" (Andrade) **43**:7
"Colloqui coi personaggi" (Pirandello) **172**:160, 166, 178, 183, 191-92
"Colloquy in a Garden" (Bishop) **103**:6
"Colloquy of the Centaurs" (Darío)
See "Coloquio de los centauros"
"Colloquy With A King-Crab" (Bishop) **103**:4, 6-7, 9
"Colloquy with a Polish Aunt" (Stevens) **45**:269
Colman and Guaire (Gregory) **1**:337
Colombe (Anouilh) **195**:5, 11, 14, 17, 25-6, 31, 36, 39, 47
Colombe blanchet (Alain-Fournier) **6**:28
"La colombe poignardée et le jet d'eau" (Apollinaire) **51**:35
Colombi e sparvieri (Deledda) **23**:35, 41
"Colomen" (Webb) **24**:473
Colonel (Buchanan) **107**:31
Colonel Carter of Cartersville (Thomas) **97**:140
"Colonel Starbottle's Client" (Harte) **25**:203

Colonel Wotherspoon, and Other Plays (Bridie) **3**:131
"The Colonel's Awakening" (Dunbar) **12**:107
The Colonel's Dream (Chesnutt) **5**:133-34, 137, 140; **39**:92, 96-100
"La Colonna Traiana raccontata" (Calvino) **183**:103
The Colony (Hansen) **32**:248, 251
"Coloquio de los centauros" (Darío) **4**:60
"Coloquio espiritual" (Huidobro) **31**:124
Color (Cullen) **4**:40-7, 49-51; **37**:135, 142-43, 151-54, 156, 159-61, 165, 167-69
"Color and Texture in Photography" (Hartmann) **73**:146
The Color Curtain (Wright) **136**:240, 242, 276, 285-90, 332
El color del verano (Arenas) **191**:158-62, 200, 217, 248-53
The Color of a Great City (Dreiser) **10**:191
The Color of Summer (Arenas)
See *El color del verano*
"The Color out of Space" (Lovecraft) **4**:269; **22**:215, 217, 228, 231, 233, 241
"The Color Sergeant" (Johnson) **19**:210
Colorado (Bromfield) **11**:83
Colorado (Thomas) **97**:126, 140
"Colorado Mountains" (Sarton) **120**:264
Colorado Springs Notes, 1899-1900 (Tesla) **88**:306, 312
"The Colorado War" (Reed) **9**:386
"The Colored Band" (Dunbar) **12**:104
"Colored Blues Singer" (Cullen) **37**:140
"The Colored Soldiers" (Dunbar) **2**:129; **12**:109, 116, 125
"Colors" (Cullen) **37**:142, 153
"Colors" (Wen I-to) **28**:409
Colors (Gourmont)
See *Couleurs*
"Colour and Line" (Babel) **13**:14; **171**:14
"Colour in Composition" (Baring-Gould) **88**:23-4
The Colour of Life, and Other Essays on Things Seen and Heard (Meynell) **6**:293, 296
"The Colour Out of Space" (Lovecraft) **4**:269; **22**:215, 217, 228, 231, 233, 241
The Colour Sense in Literature (Ellis) **14**:142
The Coloured Lands (Chesterton) **64**:42
Le colpe altrui (Deledda) **23**:42
The Columbian Ode (Monroe) **12**:216, 224
"Columbus and Amerigo Vespucci" (Reyes) **33**:318
Columbus, Don Quixote of the Seas (Wassermann)
See *Christoph Columbus, der Don Quichote des Ozeans*
"Columbus Moors to the Shore" (Petrov) **21**:154, 157
"Columbus Puts To" (Petrov)
See "Kolumb prichalivayet k beregu"
"El comadrón" (Pardo Bazán) **189**:290, 294-96
"The Combat" (Muir) **87**:159, 190, 207
Combat avec l'ange (Giraudoux) **2**:156, 163, 165; **7**:326
Combatative Life (Brod) **115**:87
"The Combe" (Thomas) **10**:463
The Combined Maze (Sinclair) **3**:437, 440-42
"Combray" (Proust) **161**:145, 163, 187-88, 190, 192, 195, 204
"Come" (Kolmar) **40**:177
"Come All Ye Brave Boys" (Ginsberg) **120**:26, 28
Come Along With Me (Jackson) **187**:236, 247-48, 283, 293, 300
"Come and Dine" (Powys) **9**:375
"Come Back Baby" (Holly) **65**:137, 141, 148
Come Back, Charleston Blue (Himes) **139**:322
Come Back to Erin (O'Faolain) **143**:230, 232, 269-70
Comé die (Beckett) **145**:99-100, 104-7, 124, 126, 150, 154, 176-81
"Come el vilano" (Aleixandre) **113**:50
Come Forth (Phelps) **113**:336
Come Hither! (de la Mare) **4**:78, 81
Come in at the Door (March) **96**:235, 237-38, 249-51, 259, 264-66
Come le foglie (Giacosa) **7**:305-06, 308, 310-11, 313-14
Come Live with Me and Be My Love (Buchanan) **107**:40-1, 87
"Come On In" (Abbey) **160**:50
"Come on in My Kitchen" (Johnson) **69**:78, 84, 92
"Come on-a my house" (Saroyan) **137**:151
"Come Out with Me" (Milne) **88**:243
Come prima, meglio di prima (Pirandello) **4**:326; **29**:283, 285, 299, 301, 318
Come si seducono le donne (Marinetti) **10**:322
Come Spring (Williams) **89**:366, 369-70, 389-90
"Come Thunder" (Okigbo) **171**:341, 357-58, 360
"Come to the Stone . . ." (Jarrell) **177**:173
Come tu mi vuoi (Pirandello) **4**:333, 338, 346, 353; **29**:298, 301, 318; **172**:162
Come Walkabout (Ingamells) **35**:124
"Come-by-Chance" (Paterson) **32**:375
Comedia sin título (García Lorca) **49**:105, 108-09; **181**:110-11
"The Comedian" (Lowry) **6**:238
"The Comedian" (Tsvetaeva) **35**:410
"The Comedian as the Letter C" (Stevens) **3**:447, 454-55, 461-62, 472-74; **12**:356-57, 373, 380-81, 383; **45**:269, 278, 289, 297, 321, 347, 352
Comedians All (Nathan) **18**:295
"La comédie de Charleroi" (Drieu la Rochelle) **21**:27-8
The Comedienne (Reymont)
See *Komediantka*
Comedies (Kuzmin)
See *Komedii*
Comedy: A Tragedy in One Act (Kazantzakis)
See *Komodia*
"The Comedy at Fountain Cottage" (Bramah) **72**:13
"A Comedy in Rubber" (Henry) **19**:173, 181
The Comedy of Alexis, Man of God (Kuzmin)
See *Komediia o Aleksee cheloveke Bozh'em*
"A Comedy of Ducks" (Lu Hsun) **3**:303
The Comedy of Eudoxia of Heliopolis (Kuzmin)
See *Komediia o Evdokii iz Geliopoliia*
A Comedy of Masks (Dowson) **4**:83-4, 89, 92
The Comedy of St. Alexis (Kuzmin)
See *Komediia o Aleksee cheloveke Bozh'em*
The Comedy of Vanity (Canetti)
See *Die Komödie der Eitelkeit*
Comedy of Vanity (Canetti)
See *Die Komödie der Eitelkeit*
"Comedy's Greatest Era" (Agee) **180**:100
El comendador Mendoza (Valera y Alcala-Galiano) **10**:497, 499, 502, 507-08
"Com'era nuovo il Nuovo Mondo" (Calvino) **183**:103
"The Comet" (Huneker) **65**:169
"The Comet" (Schulz)
See "Kometa"
"El Cometa Halley" (Arenas) **191**:210-17, 219-21
La Comète (Pinero) **32**:399
"Cometh Comet" (Bosman) **49**:7, 16
"Come-Uppance" (Williams) **89**:401
"The Comfort" (Tynan) **3**:507
"Comfort in Self-Despite" (Muir) **87**:177
"The Comfort of Criticism" (Corelli) **51**:81
Comfortless Memory (Baring) **8**:42, 43
"The Comforts of Home" (O'Connor) **132**:229, 287, 289-90
The Comic Artist (Glaspell) **55**:242, 247-50; **175**:151
"Comienza el Desfile" (Arenas) **191**:238-41, 243-46
"Coming" (Davidson) **24**:164, 186
"Coming, Aphrodite!" (Cather) **11**:92; **132**:134
"Coming Awake" (Lawrence) **93**:18
"Coming, Eden Bower!" (Cather)
See "Coming, Aphrodite!"
"Coming Home" (Abbey) **160**:58
"Coming Home" (Bowen) **148**:91
"Coming Home" (Wharton) **129**:362
"The Coming Huns" (Bryusov) **10**:87
The Coming of Cuculain (O'Grady) **5**:348, 352-53, 356
Coming of Mrs. Patrick (Crothers) **19**:73
The Coming of Peace (Hauptmann)
See *Das Friedenfest*
"The Coming of Spring" (Naidu) **80**:346
"The Coming of the Lord" (Carpenter) **88**:83
The Coming of William (Saki)
See *When William Came: A Story of London under the Hohenzollerns*
"The Coming of Winter" (Foote) **108**:34
"The Coming Poet" (Ledwidge) **23**:111
Coming Up for Air (Orwell) **2**:498, 503, 505, 510; **6**:342, 348, 352; **15**:298, 310, 322-23; **31**:190-91, 193, 204; **51**:224-25, 241, 246-49, 264, 269; **128**:257, 259, 263, 283, 286, 296; **129**:239, 241-43, 245, 248, 263
"Coming Up Oxford Street: Evening" (Hardy) **53**:117
"The Coming Victory of Democracy" (Mann) **14**:332
"Comintern" (Mayakovski) **18**:269
The Command Is Forward (Woollcott) **5**:526
"Command to the Army of Art" (Mayakovski) **4**:295
Commander Mendoza (Valera y Alcala-Galiano)
See *El comendador Mendoza*
The Commander of II Brigade (Babel) **171**:19
Comme deux gouttes d'eau (Éluard) **41**:150
Comme l'eau qui coule (Yourcenar) **193**:302, 305
Comme nous avons été (Adamov) **189**:10, 42
Comme va le ruisseau (Lemonnier) **22**:203
"Una commedia in lingua impossibile" (Svevo) **35**:363
Una commedia inedita (Svevo) **35**:353, 369
Commedie e scene (Giacosa) **7**:309
"The Commemoration" (Muir) **87**:189
"Commencement perpetual" (Garneau) **13**:203
Comment c'est (Beckett) **145**:126, 138
Comment j'ai écrit certains de mes livres (Roussel) **20**:229-32, 234, 236, 240-41, 243-44, 246-47, 250, 252-54
"Comment je vois" (Teilhard de Chardin) **9**:481
"A Comment on August 23, 1944" (Borges) **109**:23
Comment on fait un roman (Unamuno) **148**:274
"Comment on Recent Criticisms of Some Points in Moral and Logical Theory" (Dewey) **95**:173
"Comment Wang-Fô fut sauvé" (Yourcenar) **193**:283-87, 298
Commentaire pour servir à la construction pratique de la machine à explorer le temps (Jarry) **147**:242, 311, 314
A Commentary (Galsworthy) **45**:32-3
Commentary of the Shadows (D'Annunzio)
See *Notturno*
"Commentary on 'Government'" (Rohan) **22**:296
"Comments on Russia" (Innis) **77**:341
"Comments on the Art of Knowing Others and Oneself" (Alain) **41**:21
"The Commerce of Thought" (Quiller-Couch) **53**:297
"Commitment" (Adorno)
See "Engagement"
The Commmon Reader: Second Series (Woolf)
See *The Second Common Reader*
"A Commodity of Dreams" (Nemerov) **124**:230-31, 291

A Commodity of Dreams and Other Stories (Nemerov) **124**:151, 161, 230, 232-33, 318
The Commodore (Forester)
See *Commodore Hornblower*
Commodore Hornblower (Forester) **152**:133, 135, 137-38, 160-61
The Commodore's Daughter's (Lie)
See *Kommandørens døtre*
"The Common Bases of Hinduism" (Vivekananda) **88**:361
A Common Faith (Dewey) **95**:36, 145, 166
"The Common Grave" (Dickey) **151**:90, 109
The Common Law (Chambers) **41**:97, 111
The Common Law (Holmes) **77**:223, 226-7, 235-7, 241-2, 250, 262, 266, 271-2, 279, 298-300, 302, 304-6, 316-9, 323-4
"The Common Life" (Stevens) **45**:333, 348
"Common Lodging Houses" (Orwell) **128**:282
"Common Meter" (Fisher) **11**:208-11, 213
The Common Reader (Woolf) **43**:380, 388, 393-94, 396, 402, 409, 413, 416, 421, 424-25; **1**:529-30; **5**:507; **20**:392, 406; **43**:400; **101**:212; **128**:333-34, 376
The Common Reader, First Series (Woolf)
See *The Common Reader*
"The Common Round" (Mansfield) **39**:321
"A Common Saw" (Nemerov) **124**:259
Common Sense about Women (Higginson) **36**:175
The Common Women (Pirandello)
See *Le popolane*
Commonplace Book (Forster) **125**:163
Commonplace Book (Gissing) **47**:137
"A Commonplace Day" (Hardy) **53**:115
"A Commonplace Woman" (Montgomery) **51**:181
The Communicating Vases (Marinetti)
See *I vasi communicanti*
"A Communication to My Friends" (Moore) **7**:497
"Communications" (Frye) **165**:183
"Communion" (Coppard) **5**:176
"Communion" (Gurney) **33**:86
"Communism" (Du Bois) **169**:96
Communism (Laski) **79**:115
Les communistes (Aragon) **123**:143
"The Community and the Institution" (Mead) **89**:101
Community Life and Social Policy (Wirth) **92**:359
"Community Organization and Juvenile Delinquency" (Park) **73**:179
"Community Organization and the Romantic Temper" (Park) **73**:179
"Como" (Scott) **6**:394-95
Como empieza y como acaba (Echegaray) **4**:101
Como eu não possuo (Sá-Carneiro) **83**:409
"Como la mar, los besos" (Aleixandre) **113**:50
Cómo se hace una novela (Unamuno) **2**:569; **148**:233, 253, 256, 273-77, 297, 307, 309, 335, 337-42
"Como sutil neblina" (Gonzalez Martinez) **72**:148
Il compagno (Pavese) **3**:342
Compagnons de route (Rolland) **23**:273, 279
"De compaña y de hora" (Jiménez) **183**:311
Companie (Beckett) **145**:97, 114-20, 188, 202, 205
"The Companion of a Mile" (Noyes) **7**:512
A Companion to Mr. Wells's "Outline of History" (Belloc) **7**:34
A Companion Volume (McAlmon) **97**:88, 90, 115
"Companion—North-East Dug-Out" (Gurney) **33**:94
"The Companions" (Nemerov) **124**:151, 157, 162, 177-79, 252, 288, 315
Companions of Pickle (Lang) **16**:270
Company (Beckett)
See *Companie*
Company K (March) **96**:235, 237-38, 241-43, 246-47, 249-52, 254, 258-59, 263-66
"The Company of Wolves" (Carter) **139**:47, 113, 127, 131, 139, 142-43, 197, 216-17, 219
"Compasión" (Güiraldes) **39**:185, 190
"Compassion: An Ode in Celebration of the Centenart of the Royal Society for the Prevention of Cruelty to Animals" (Hardy) **72**:170
"Compensation" (Dunbar) **12**:106
"Complaint" (Gray) **19**:151, 157
"Complaint of the Dying Peasantry" (Muir) **87**:204
"Complaint of Time" (Coppard) **5**:178-79
La complainte du ridicule (Adamov) **189**:14, 31, 33-4
"The Complaints of the Mother" (Vazov) **25**:453
The Complaynt of Scotlande (Murray) **117**:286-87
The Complete Buddy Holly (Holly) **65**:144
The Complete Clerihews of E. Clerihew Bentley (Bentley) **12**:26
The Complete Dramatic Works (Beckett) **145**:179-80
The Complete Fiction of Bruno Schulz (Schulz) **51**:323
"A Complete History of Germany and Japan" (Brautigan) **133**:3
The Complete Life (Erskine) **84**:185
"The Complete Life of John Hopkins" (Henry) **19**:173
The Complete Notebooks of Henry James (James) **171**:129, 131-32, 135, 173-74
The Complete Novels (Hammett) **187**:45
Complete Plays (Orton) **157**:325-30
The Complete Plays of Yury Olesha (Olesha) **136**:74
The Complete Poems (Bishop) **121**:3, 20, 25-7, 29, 31, 64, 66-7, 88, 90, 94-5, 103-05
The Complete Poems (Hardy) **143**:158
Complete Poems (Housman) **10**:258
Complete Poems (Jarrell) **177**:145-50, 154, 157-59, 162, 164, 172, 219-31, 239, 241-42, 259
The Complete Poems, 1910-1962 (Cummings) **137**:41, 43-50, 53-65, 67-69
The Complete Poems, 1927-1979 (Bishop) **121**:98
The Complete Poems of D. H. Lawrence (Lawrence) **2**:371; **93**:115
The Complete Poems of Francis Ledwidge (Ledwidge) **23**:120-21, 123
The Complete Poems of George Santayana (Santayana) **40**:414
The Complete Poems of Keith Douglas (Douglas) **40**:79, 85, 93, 95
The Complete Poems of Marjorie Pickthall (Pickthall) **21**:256
The Complete Poems of Robert Service (Service) **15**:403, 411
Complete Poems of Saint Denys Garneau (Garneau)
See *Poésies complètes*
The Complete Poems of W. H. Davies (Davies) **5**:207
Complete Poetical Works (Buchanan) **107**:45, 65
The Complete Poetical Works of James Whitcomb Riley (Riley) **51**:297
The Complete Poetical Works of T. E. Hulme (Hulme) **21**:139-40
The Complete Poetical Works of Thomas Hardy (Hardy) **143**:185-92
The Complete Sherlock Holmes (Doyle) **7**:230
Complete Short Prose (Beckett) **145**:202
The Complete Stories (Hurston) **131**:82
Complete Stories (Hurston) **131**:82
The Complete Stories (Malamud) **184**:290
The Complete Stories (O'Connor) **132**:257, 271, 287-90, 302-7, 320, 353, 355-59
The Complete Twenty Thousand Leagues Under the Sea (Verne)
See *Vingt mille lieues sous les mers*
Complete Verse (Belloc) **18**:39
Complete Works (Aleixandre)
See *Obras completas*
Complete Works (Borges)
See *Obras completas*
Complete Works (Péguy) **10**:414
Complete Works (Reyes) **33**:322
Complete Works (Stanislavsky) **167**:306-9
The Complete Works of Algernon Charles Swinburne (Swinburne) **36**:330
The Complete Works of Kate Chopin (Chopin) **127**:124-28, 167-75, 192, 195
The Complete Works of Nathanael West (West) **1**:478
The Complete Works of the Gawain-Poet (Gardner) **195**:127
The Completion of Love (Musil)
See "Vollendung der Liebe"
Complications sentimentales (Bourget) **12**:68
Composing for the Films (Adorno)
See *Komposition für den Film*
Composition (Lewis) **104**:201
"Composition and Fate in the Short Novel" (Nemerov) **124**:146, 270
"Composition as Explanation" (Stein) **48**:242, 253
Composition as Explanation (Stein) **1**:432; **6**:403, 406; **28**:307, 324, 326, 338; **48**:243
Composition in Portraiture (Hartmann) **73**:122
Composition IV (Kandinsky) **92**:134, 136
Composition V (Kandinsky) **92**:38, 134, 136, 140
Composition VI (Kandinsky) **92**:37, 40, 62
Composition VII (Kandinsky) **92**:38
"Composition with Twelve Notes" (Schoenberg)
See "Composition with Twelve Tones"
"Composition with Twelve Tones" (Schoenberg) **75**:323, 332, 339, 360, 378, 380, 410
"Composure" (Meynell) **6**:302
"The Comprehension of Private Copper" (Kipling) **8**:200
"A Compromise" (Hesse) **148**:177
"Compromise and Keeping the Faith" (Anderson) **144**:34
The Compromise of the King of the Golden Isles (Dunsany) **59**:3, 13, 26
"Compulsion" (Zweig)
See "Der Zwang"
"The Compulsory Herculés" (Ady) **11**:15
"Compulsory Marriage" (Strindberg) **8**:407
"The Comrade" (Quiller-Couch) **53**:291
The Comrade (Pavese)
See *Il compagno*
Comrade Nahman (Singer)
See *Chaver Nachman*
"Comrade Typist" (Mayakovski) **18**:269
"Comrades" (Phelps) **113**:342
Comrades (Dixon) **163**:168, 253
Comrades (Strindberg)
See *Kamraterna*
"The Comte de Pralines" (Somerville & Ross) **51**:360
"La comtesse Esmerée" (Moréas) **18**:286
"Con el pino" (Jiménez) **4**:224
Con gli occhi chiusi (Tozzi) **31**:312, 314-20, 322-23, 326-28, 332-33
"Con la cruz del sur" (Jiménez) **183**:281
"Con la mirada homilde . . ." (Villaurrutia) **80**:480
Con la penna d'oro (Svevo) **35**:346, 353
Con los Ojos Cerrados (Arenas) **191**:196, 238-39, 241
"Con todo respeto" (Aleixandre) **113**:8, 47
"Con una alemana" (Pardo Bazán) **189**:254
Conan the Conqueror (Howard) **8**:129, 131-33, 136-37
"The Concealed Path" (Post) **39**:338

"Concentration" (Balmont)
See "Sosredotochie"
"The Concentration Camps" (Arendt) **193**:96-7
"Concepción Arenal y sus ideas acerca de la mujer" (Pardo Bazán) **189**:318
"The Concept and Tragedy of Culture" (Simmel) **64**:338
"Concept of Enlightenment" (Horkheimer) **132**:194
"The Concept of Freedom" (Arendt) **193**:67
The Concept of Love in Augustine (Arendt) **193**:140
The Concept of Nature (Whitehead) **97**:197, 220
"The Concept of Race" (Du Bois) **169**:94
"The Concept of Race as Applied to Social Culture" (Locke) **43**:238, 241
"The Concept of Scientific History" (Berlin) **105**:144
The Concept of the Guardian Spirit in North America (Benedict) **60**:149
"The Conception and Development of Poetry in Zulu" (Vilakazi) **37**:403, 409
Conception materialististe de l'Histoire (Sorel) **91**:197
"The Conception of Intrinsic Value" (Moore) **89**:182
Conceptions of the World and of Life in the Nineteenth Century (Steiner)
See *Welt- und Lebensanschauungen im 19. Jahrhundert*
Concepts and Categories: Philosophical Essays (Berlin) **105**:20-1, 50, 132
"Conceptual Exposition" (Weber) **69**:314
"Concern with Politics in Recent European Thought" (Arendt) **193**:164
Concerning a Journey to the Land of the Tarahumaras (Artaud)
See *D'un voyage au pays des Tarahumaras*
"Concerning a Woman of Sin" (Hecht) **101**:74, 77, 89
"Concerning Aesthetic Qualities" (Simmel) **64**:339
"Concerning Animal Perception" (Mead) **89**:168
"Concerning Breakfast" (Lucas) **73**:171
Concerning Children (Gilman) **9**:104; **37**:177; **117**:49, 81, 125, 140
"Concerning Environmental Values" (Ingamells) **35**:129
"Concerning Jude the Obscure" (Ellis) **14**:131
Concerning People (Čapek) **37**:46
"Concerning Poor B. B." (Brecht)
See "Of Poor B. B."
"Concerning Present-day Religion" (Nishida)
See "Genkon no shukyo ni tsuite"
"Concerning Self-Consciousness" (Nishida) **83**:323
"Concerning the Best Man" (Aldrich) **125**:19
Concerning the Eccentricities of Cardinal Pirelli (Firbank) **1**:227-29
"Concerning the most recent painting" (Arp) **115**:16
"Concerning the Philsophy of Life" (Nishida)
See "Inochi no tetsugaku"
Concerning the Spiritual in Art (Kandinsky)
See *Über das Geistige in der Kunst*
"Concerning Violence" (Fanon) **188**:111, 133
"The Concert" (Millay) **49**:208
"Le concert" (Roussel) **20**:234, 240, 245, 251
Concert (Lasker-Schueler)
See *Konzert*
"Concert at the Railroad Station" (Mandelstam)
See "Koncert na vokzale"
"The Concert in Katerinenstadt" (Babel) **171**:44
"A Concert of Giorgione" (Bottomley) **107**:2
The Conch (Hansen)
See *Kokyljen*
"Conciencia hoy azul" (Jiménez) **183**:279-80
"Conciencia plena" (Jiménez) **183**:309
"Concits an' Thin's" (Smith) **25**:389
"Conclusion to A Literary History of Canada" (Frye) **165**:180
Conclusive Evidence: A Memoir (Nabokov)
See *Speak, Memory: An Autobiography Revisited*
"Le concombre fugitif" (Mirbeau) **55**:301
Concord and Liberty (Ortega y Gasset)
See *Del imperio romano*
"Concord Church" (Masters) **25**:316
Concrete (Bernhard)
See *Beton*
Concurso (García Lorca) **181**:196
The Condemned (Dagerman)
See *Den dödsdömde*
El Condenado por Desconfiado (Garro) **153**:21
Condensed Novels, and Other Papers (Harte) **25**:188-89, 219
Condensed Novels, second series: New Burlesques (Harte) **1**:341, 344
La condition postmoderne (Lyotard) **103**:140, 144, 146, 158, 161, 166-67, 177, 179, 194, 196-98, 219-22, 226-27, 241, 260, 272-73, 275-76, 279
Conditional Culture (Ingamells) **35**:129, 132, 135
Conditioned Reflexes: An Investigation of the Physiological Activity of the Cerebral Cortex (Pavlov) **91**:102
"La condizione femminile" (Ginzburg) **156**:27, 44-45, 51, 112
"Conduct and Experience" (Dewey) **95**:150
"The Cone" (Wells) **133**:258
A Confederate General from Big Sur (Brautigan) **133**:2-4, 6-7, 10, 17-19, 23-6, 28-9
Confederate Portraits (Bradford) **36**:66
"A Conference of the Powers" (Kipling) **17**:208
"Confesión de culpa" (Unamuno) **148**:299
"A Confession" (Anderson) **144**:74
"Confession" (Blackwood) **5**:72, 80
"The Confession" (Čapek) **192**:224
"Confession" (Cullen) **37**:155
"Confession" (London) **9**:281
"A Confession" (Tolstoy)
See "Ispoved"
"Confession" (Wen I-to) **28**:418
"Confession" (Wharton) **129**:364-65
Confession (Gorky)
See *Ispoved*
The Confession (Rinehart) **52**:283, 289, 301
A Confession (Tolstoy)
See *Ispoved*
La confession de Claude (Zola) **6**:569; **41**:407
"Confession d'un enfant du siècle" (Desnos) **22**:74
"La confession d'une jeune fille" (Proust) **7**:538-39; **161**:123
"Confession nocturne" (Nelligan) **14**:400
Confession of a Modern Poet (Nervo)
See *La amada inmóvil*
The Confession of Ina Kahr (Pabst) **127**:363
"The Confession of Kai Lung" (Bramah) **72**:3
"A Confession of Unfaith" (Lovecraft) **22**:210
"The Confessional" (Wharton) **9**:541; **129**:360
"Le confessioni del vegliardo" (Svevo) **35**:345, 352
Confessioni e battaglie (Carducci) **32**:106
Confessions (Rebreanu) **28**:268
Confessions (Sorel) **91**:193
Confessions: A Study in Pathology (Symons) **11**:437, 449, 452
Confessions and Criticisms (Hawthorne) **25**:240, 248, 250
Confessions of a Barbarian: Selections from the Journal of Edward Abbey, 1951-1989 (Abbey) **160**:41-44, 50-54, 56, 58, 60-61, 75, 78, 89
Confessions of a Bohemian Tory (Kirk) **119**:253, 256, 266, 276-77, 285, 291, 346
"Confessions of a Book Reviewer" (Orwell) **51**:266
"Confessions of a 'Colyumist'" (Morley) **87**:127
"Confessions of a Dishwasher" (Orwell) **128**:255
The Confessions of a Fool (Strindberg)
See *Le plaidoyer d'un fou*
Confessions of a Hooligan (Esenin)
See *Ispoved' khuligana*
Confessions of a Mask (Mishima)
See *Kamen no kokuhaku*
Confessions of a Murderer (Roth) **33**:363
Confessions of a Twentieth-Century Pilgrim (Muggeridge) **120**:101, 104, 107
The Confessions of a Wife (Phelps) **113**:338-39
"Confessions of a Young Girl" (Proust)
See "La confession d'une jeune fille"
Confessions of a Young Man (Moore) **7**:474-75, 479-80, 482, 485-91, 495-97
The Confessions of Aleister Crowley (Crowley) **7**:207-08, 211-12
The Confessions of Arsène Lupin (Leblanc)
See *Le confidences d'Arsène Lupin*
The Confessions of Faith of a Man of Science (Haeckel)
See *Der Monismus als Band zwischen Religion und Wissenschaft*
Confessions of Felix Krull, Confidence Man (Mann)
See *Bekenntnisse des Hochstaplers Felix Krull*
Confessions of Zeno (Svevo)
See *La coscienza di Zeno*
Confianza (Salinas) **17**:357, 359-60, 363, 369-70
"Confianza en el anteojo" (Vallejo) **56**:311
"A Confidence" (Dunbar) **12**:108
Confidence Africaine (Martin du Gard) **24**:384, 386-87, 394, 397
"Confidences" (Chopin) **127**:215
Le confidences d'Arsène Lupin (Leblanc) **49**:197
"Confidência do Itabirano" (Drummond de Andrade) **139**:224, 235
A Confident Tomorrow (Matthews) **95**:253, 272
"Configuration" (Arp) **115**:22, 40-1
"Configurations of Culture in North America" (Benedict) **60**:107, 139, 147, 150-53
A confissão de Lúcio (Sá-Carneiro) **83**:399, 401, 404
"Confissões de uma viúva moça" (Machado de Assis) **10**:295
"Confiteor" (Przybyszewski) **36**:285
"The Conflagration" (Remizov)
See "Pozhar"
The Conflict (Phillips) **44**:268, 275, 278, 291
"A Conflict Ended" (Freeman) **9**:77
"The Conflict in Modern Culture" (Simmel) **64**:338, 340, 360
The Conflict in Modern Culture, and Other Essays (Simmel) **64**:338, 340
Conflicts (Zweig)
See *Verwirrung der Gefühle*
Conflits intimes (Bourget) **12**:69
"Confronto" (Drummond de Andrade) **139**:230
Confucius (Hartmann) **73**:110, 116, 134
"Confusión" (García Lorca) **49**:120-21
La confusion des races (Kandinsky) **92**:48
"The Confusion of Language in Political Thought" (Hayek) **109**:232
"Congedo" (Carducci) **32**:106, 109
"Los congelados" (Nervo) **11**:394
"Congo" (Lindsay) **17**:222, 225, 227-28, 230, 235, 237, 239, 247-48
The Congo and Other Poems (Lindsay) **17**:222, 224-25, 227, 231-32
"The Congo Love Song" (Johnson) **175**:225
"Congo-Ocean" (Roumain) **19**:347
"Congolese Patriot" (Hansberry) **192**:276
Congressional Government: A Study in American Politics (Wilson) **79**:469, 485, 499-500, 502, 519-20, 527-8, 534

"Congresso Internacional do Medo" (Drummond de Andrade) **139**:339
"Conjectural Poem" (Borges)
See "Poema conjectural"
Los conjurados (Borges) **109**:117, 119
"Conjuration" (Södergran)
See "Besvärjelsen"
The Conjure Man Dies: A Mystery Tale of Dark Harlem (Fisher) **11**:204-08, 214
The Conjure Woman (Chesnutt) **5**:129-32, 134-36, 138; **39**:70-2, 74-5, 79, 82, 101-03, 107-08
"The Conjurer's Revenge" (Chesnutt) **39**:73, 91, 94-5, 104
"The Conjuring Contest" (Dunbar) **12**:111
"The Conjuror" (Middleton) **56**:194-95
Connaissance de l'est (Claudel) **2**:103
La connaissance surnaturelle (Weil) **23**:403-04
A Connecticut Yankee in King Arthur's Court (Twain) **6**:455, 457, 460, 471, 473-74, 477, 480-82; **12**:429, 431-33, 435-36, 446, 448-49; **19**:379, 387; **36**:350-420; **48**:335-37, 339-40, 344, 354-56; **59**:168, 182, 185; **161**:223, 237, 327, 329-34; **185**:250, 281, 307, 319, 321, 324-25, 327
The Connoisseur, and Other Stories (de la Mare) **4**:78; **53**:13, 16, 27
"Connoisseur of Chaos" (Stevens) **3**:453; **45**:269
"The Conqueror" (Fisher)
See "A Good Fight and the Faith Kept"
The Conqueror: Being the True and Romantic Story of Alexander Hamilton (Atherton) **2**:15, 17-18
Conqueror of the Seas: The Story of Magellan (Zweig)
See *Magellan*
The Conquerors (Bagritsky)
See *Pobediteli*
"Conquest of Bookcases" (Rohan) **22**:296
The Conquest of Bread (Kropotkin)
See *La conquête du pain*
The Conquest of Canaan (Tarkington) **9**:455
"A Conquest of Humility" (Freeman) **9**:67
The Conquest of Mexico (Artaud)
See *La conquête du Mexique*
The Conquest of New Granada (Graham) **19**:111, 124-25
The Conquest of Rome (Huch) **13**:241
The Conquest of the Pole (Melies)
See *A La Conquete du Pole*
The Conquest of the River Plate (Graham) **19**:108, 111, 124-25
"Conquest of the Wind" (Bishop) **103**:9
The Conquest: The Story of a Negro Pioneer (Micheaux) **76**:236-42, 249-52, 263, 265, 267, 269-71
The Conquest: The Story of a Negro Pioneer by the Pioneer (Micheaux)
See *The Conquest: The Story of a Negro Pioneer*
La conquête de Plassans (Zola) **21**:416; **41**:412
La conquête des étoiles (Marinetti) **10**:316
La conquête du Mexique (Artaud) **36**:22, 39
La conquête du pain (Kropotkin) **36**:191, 199-203, 221
"La conquista" (Jiménez) **183**:291
"La conquista" (Nervo) **11**:396
Conrad der Leutnant (Spitteler) **12**:338, 342, 345-49, 351
"Conrad Is Dead" (Tomlinson) **71**:396
"Conroy's Gap" (Paterson) **32**:369, 374
La conscience malheureuse (Fondane) **159**:238
"Conscience of the Court" (Hurston) **131**:62
The Conscience of Words (Canetti)
See *Das Gewissen der Worte*
Conscience reciale (Roumain) **19**:342
"Conscientious Objector" (Millay) **169**:268
"Conscious" (Owen) **5**:367, 370; **27**:212, 217-18, 229
"Consciousness" (Jozsef) **22**:162, 164
Consciousness and the Acquisition of Language (Merleau-Ponty) **156**:183
Consciousness: Animal, Human, and Superman (Orage) **157**:245, 248, 250, 273, 275
"The Conscript" (Coppard) **5**:177
"A Conscript on Education" (Kirk) **119**:314
Conseils à un jeune poète (Jacob) **6**:194-95
"Conseils familiers à un jeune écrivain" (Gourmont) **17**:138
"Consensus and Mass Communication" (Wirth) **92**:359, 375
"The Consent" (Nemerov) **124**:209, 259
Consequences (Delafield) **61**:124-5, 127, 135
"Consequences of the Fact That It Was Not Woman Who Killed the Father" (Andreas-Salome) **56**:56
The Consequences of the Reformation (Ball)
See *Die Folgen der Reformation*
"The Conservation of Races" (Du Bois) **169**:151, 159-62, 211
Conservatism: Dream and Reality (Nisbet) **117**:342-44, 346, 348, 351, 362
"The Conservative" (Gilman) **37**:176
"A Conservative" (Hearn) **9**:130
The Conservative Constitution (Kirk) **119**:329
The Conservative Mind (Kirk) **119**:242-44, 247, 250, 253-56, 266, 270, 275-76, 286-87, 291, 297-305, 312-13, 315
The Conservative Mind from Burke to Eliot (Kirk)
See *The Conservative Mind*
The Conservative Mind from Burke to Santayana (Kirk)
See *The Conservative Mind*
Consider Her Ways (Grove) **4**:136, 138, 140
"Considerando en frío, imparcialmente" (Vallejo) **56**:318
"Considerations Concerning the Fundaments of Theoretical Physics" (Einstein) **65**:74
"Considerations on Technique" (Ortega y Gasset) **9**:340
"Considérations sur la mythologie grecque" (Gide) **177**:8786
"Considerazioni sui principi fondamentali dell' economia politica pura" (Pareto) **69**:137
"Consolazione" (Saba) **33**:372
The Consort (Duncan) **60**:209, 244, 247, 249
"The Conspiracies of the Gowries" (Lang) **16**:254
Conspiracy (Aldanov) **23**:19-20, 23
The Conspiracy (Nizan)
See *La conspiration*
"Conspiracy of Catiline" (Herzl)
See "Catilina összeesküvése"
"A Conspiracy of Silence" (Somerville & Ross) **51**:335, 385
La conspiration (Nizan) **40**:288, 294, 297, 311-12, 314-17
The Conspirators (Borges)
See *Los conjurados*
Constab Ballads (McKay) **7**:459-60, 464; **41**:319, 328, 343
"Constance Hately" (Masters) **25**:312
"Constance, Lady Willet" (Welch) **22**:462
Constance Markievicz, or the Average Revolutionary (O'Faolain) **143**:230, 235, 269
Constance Trescot (Mitchell) **36**:266-68, 272, 274
"Constancy" (Field) **43**:158, 169
The Constant Lover (Nervo) **11**:403
Constant Reader (Parker) **143**:334
A Constitution for the Socialist Commonwealth of Great Britain (Webb and Webb) **22**:402, 414, 418, 425, 429, 431
"The Constitution of a Liberal State" (Hayek) **109**:205
The Constitution of Liberty (Hayek) **109**:180, 188, 204, 213-14, 233, 241-42
"Constitutional Argument" (Anthony) **84**:21, 23
Constitutional Government in the United States (Wilson) **79**:487, 490-1, 527-9
The Constitutional History of England (Maitland) **65**:259, 267
The Construction of Christian Poetry in Old English (Gardner) **195**:112
"Constructions in Analysis" (Freud)
See "Konstruktionen in der Analyse"
Constructive Theme Writing for College Freshmen (Chase) **124**:28
"The Consul General at the Palace Ball" (Söderberg) **39**:438
"Consulta" (García Lorca) **181**:119
La consultation (Martin du Gard) **24**:394-95, 410
The Consumer's Co-Operative Movement (Webb and Webb) **22**:412
A Contaminated Family (Tolstoy) **11**:464
Contango (Hilton) **21**:92
"Conte d'amour" (Moréas) **18**:285
El contemplado (Salinas) **17**:354, 359-60, 363, 368-69
"Contemplation" (Thompson) **4**:435, 440
Contemplation (Kafka)
See *Betrachtung*
Contemplations (Kahanovitsch)
See *Gedakht*
Contemplazione della morte (D'Annunzio) **6**:145; **40**:7, 11
"Contemporaneousness" (Gumilev)
See "Sovremennost"
Contemporaries (Higginson) **36**:167, 170, 177
Contemporaries of Shakespeare (Swinburne) **8**:430
The Contemporary American Novel (Van Doren) **18**:404
Contemporary American Novelists (Van Doren) **18**:393, 405
Contemporary History (France)
See *Histoire contemporaine*
Contemporary Portraits (Harris) **24**:260, 262-63, 265, 271, 273, 277, 280
"Contemporary Russian Prose" (Zamyatin)
See "Sovremennaia russkaia proza"
Contemporary Spanish Novels (Pérez Galdós)
See *Novelas españolas contemporáneas*
"The Contemporary Unification in Experiment of the Main Aspects of Medicine, as Exemplified by Digestion" (Pavlov) **91**:150
Contending Forces: A Romance Illustrative of Negro Life North and South (Hopkins) **28**:169-71, 173-76
Content Are the Quiet Ranges (Ingamells) **35**:129
"The Contented Man" (Service) **15**:402
Contes à Ninon (Zola) **6**:568
Contes de la chaumière (Mirbeau)
See *Lettres de ma chaumière*
Les contes d'un matin (Giraudoux) **7**:324
Contes en vers et poésies diverses (Coppee) **25**:124
Contes et nouvelles (Vallette) **67**:316, 319
Contes flamands et wallons (Lemonnier) **22**:203
Contes retrouvés (Apollinaire) **51**:19
Conti sardi (Deledda) **23**:35
"The Continental Angle" (Fitzgerald) **52**:56
The Continental Op (Hammett) **187**:131-32, 134-37, 170
"Continuation of a Long Poem of these States" (Ginsberg) **120**:71
"The Continuation of the Story of a Horse" (Babel)
See "The Story of a Horse, Continued"
"Continuity" (Lovecraft) **22**:241
"Conto alexandrino" (Machado de Assis) **10**:290, 296
Contos flumineneses (Machado de Assis) **10**:295
"Contra el secreto profesional: a propósito de Pablo Abril de Vivero" (Vallejo) **56**:310, 315, 322
Contra esto y aquello (Unamuno) **9**:514; **148**:230, 236-37
Contraataque (Sender) **136**:210, 215-17, 219

Corto viaggio sentimentale e altri racconti inediti (Svevo) **2**:545; **2**:545; **35**:345, 352, 369
Čortov most (Aldanov) **23**:17, 19-20, 23
Coruisken Sonnets (Buchanan) **107**:69
"Corvée matinale" (Loti) **11**:353
"Cory" (Robinson)
See "Richard Cory"
Corydon (Gide) **5**:217, 244; **12**:143, 146, 163; **177**:102, 111
Corydon (Yourcenar) **193**:355
"Corymbus for Autumn" (Thompson) **4**:440
The Coryston Family (Ward) **55**:421
"Cosas de Don Paco" (Pereda) **16**:379
"Cosas de gansos" (Lugones) **15**:294
La coscienza di Zeno (Svevo) **2**:539-41, 543, 545-50, 552-54; **35**:331-39, 344-46, 348, 350-52, 356-57, 360, 365-66, 368-71
"Cosè il re" (Verga) **3**:543, 546
Cose leggere e vaganti (Saba) **33**:369, 373, 375
Cosíè (se vi pare) (Pirandello) **4**:325-26, 331, 334, 337, 340-41, 346-47, 353, 356; **29**:285, 297-98, 301, 315, 318-19; **172**:140, 156, 158, 160, 162
Cosima (Deledda) **23**:42
Cosmic Carols (Service) **15**:411, 413
"Cosmic Comics" (Nemerov) **124**:260
Cosmic Memory: Prehistory of Earth and Man (Steiner) **13**:447
Le cosmicomiche (Calvino) **183**:6, 8-11, 13, 38, 40-43, 46, 95-96, 112, 126, 141, 147, 158-59, 161, 163, 165, 193, 222, 227-28, 230, 237-38, 240, 243-44, 247
Cosmicomics (Calvino)
See *Le cosmicomiche*
Cosmopolis (Bourget) **12**:65
"The Cosmopolitan" (Sinclair) **3**:441; **11**:412
"Cosmopolitan Greetings" (Ginsberg) **120**:112
Cosmopolitan Greetings (Ginsberg) **120**:73-4, 109, 112
"A Cosmopolite in a Café" (Henry) **19**:200
The Cossacks (Tolstoy) **79**:324, 367, 376, 415
The Cossacks: A Tale of the Caucasus in 1852 (Tolstoy)
See *Kazaki*
The Cost (Phillips) **44**:253-54, 257, 262, 274, 276, 282-83, 285-86
"The Cost of Letters" (Bowen) **148**:47
"The Cost of Living" (Malamud) **129**:180; **184**:164, 237-40
Costado (Jiménez) **183**:327
"Costello the Proud" (Yeats) **31**:419
"A Costume Piece" (Hornung) **59**:115
"La costurera" (Pereda) **16**:380
Côte à côto (Rod) **52**:309, 323
Le côté de Guermantes (Proust) **7**:540, 545, 549; **33**:254, 257, 272; **161**:142, 149, 156, 163, 203, 205
"Le coteau" (Desnos) **22**:73
"El coto de los Carvajales" (Valle-Inclán) **5**:478
"Cotswold Ways" (Gurney) **33**:87, 91
"Cottage by the Tracks" (Wolfe) **13**:492
"The Cottagette" (Gilman) **37**:216
Cotton Comes to Harlem (Himes)
See *Retour en Afrique*
"Cotton in Your Ears" (Apollinaire) **8**:27
"Cotton Song" (Toomer) **172**:274-75, 327, 330
Couché dans le pain (Himes) **139**:253, 256, 282, 284, 321
"Could I Have Found a Better Love Than You?" (Engel) **137**:102-3
"Could We But Know" (Montgomery) **51**:209
Couleur du temps (Apollinaire) **8**:13-15, 22; **51**:10, 24
Couleurs (Gourmont) **17**:137
"Les coulisses" (Hearn) **9**:126
"The Council of Five" (Tolstoy) **18**:373, 384
The Council of Justice (Wallace) **57**:408
"A Council of State" (Dunbar) **2**:130; **12**:112, 120
"A Council of War" (Gilman) **37**:215; **117**:78
"Counsel" (Johnson) **19**:256
"Counsel of Grief" (Bishop) **103**:5
The Counsel of Literary Age (Howells) **7**:373
Counselor Ayres' Memorial (Machado de Assis)
See *Memorial de Ayres*
Count Bruga (Hecht) **101**:48, 73, 77
"Count Cagliostro" (Tolstoy) **18**:384
"Count Magnus" (James) **6**:214, 216
Count Öderland (Frisch)
See *Graf Öderland*
The Count of Charolais (Beer-Hofmann)
See *Der Graf von Charolais*
The Count of Darkness (Fitzgerald) **157**:169
"The Count of Monte Cristo" (Calvino) **183**:44, 47, 71, 194
"The Count of Saint Germain" (Lang) **16**:254
"Count Philip Königsmark and the Princess Sophia Dorothea" (Sabatini) **47**:300
Count Your Dead: They Are Alive! or, A New War in the Making (Lewis) **2**:386; **9**:234; **104**:212, 231, 237, 239-42, 299
"Counter Mood" (Cullen) **4**:46; **37**:156, 159, 162
A Counterfeit Presentment (Howells) **41**:263
The Counterfeiters (Gide)
See *Les faux-monnayeurs*
Counter-Heaven (Daumal) **14**:89
"Counterparts" (Joyce) **8**:165; **35**:141-42, 148-49, 156, 160, 164, 167, 195, 197; **159**:313
The Counter-Revolution of Science: Studies On the Abuse of Reason (Hayek) **109**:177, 206, 253, 259
Counterweights (Kandinsky) **92**:32
"Countess Cathleen" (Tynan) **3**:502
The Countess Cathleen, and Various Legends and Lyrics (Yeats) **1**:570; **11**:507, 509, 511, 513-14, 526-27; **18**:446; **31**:386, 412
"Countess Marie of the Angels" (Dowson) **4**:88
The Countess Mizzie (Schnitzler) **4**:387-89
The Countess of Albany (Lee) **5**:314-15, 319
"The Countess of Pembroke's Arcadia" (Woolf) **43**:425
Countries (Palamas) **5**:384
Countries of the Mind (Murry) **16**:341, 343, 355
"The Country Barber Shop" (Marquis) **7**:440
Country By Ways (Jewett) **1**:361, 367; **22**:129, 140-41
"The Country Churchyard" (Warner) **131**:310
The Country Cousin (Tarkington) **9**:464-65
"The Country Doctor" (Kafka)
See "Ein landarzt"
The Country Doctor (Griffith) **68**:186
A Country Doctor (Jewett) **1**:359, 364, 367-68; **22**:117-20, 123, 128, 137-38, 145-48
A Country Doctor (Kafka)
See "Ein landarzt"
A Country Doctor and Other Texts Printed in his Lifetime (Kafka)
See *Ein Landarzt*
A Country Doctor's Notebook (Bulgakov)
See *Zapiski iunogo vracha*
"Country Full of Swedes" (Caldwell) **117**:315
"Country Girls in Town" (Davis) **6**:154
"A Country House" (Sarton) **120**:264
The Country House (Galsworthy) **1**:294, 299-300; **45**:41, 44, 47, 50, 63, 66, 68-70
The Country I Come From (Lawson) **27**:121
"A Country Incident" (Sarton) **120**:269
Country Judge (Prado)
See *Un juez rural*
"A Country Letter" (Agee) **1**:17
"A Country Life" (Jarrell) **177**:127
"Country Lover" (Tynan) **3**:503
"The Country Mouse" (Bishop) **121**:76
The Country of a Thousand Years of Peace and Other Poems (Merrill) **173**:172, 207, 225, 256-57
"The Country of Har" (Carman) **7**:135, 138
"The Country of the Blind" (Wells) **6**:539, 541; **19**:425, 427, 436, 442, 425, 427, 436, 442; **133**:279
The Country of the Blind, and Other Stories (Wells) **6**:533, 538; **133**:280
The Country of the Pointed Firs (Jewett) **1**:359-65, 367-69; **22**:121, 123-27, 130-39, 142, 145, 147-49
"A Country Passion" (Callaghan) **145**:255
"A Country Pathway" (Riley) **51**:282
Country Place (Petry) **112**:290, 292, 294, 297, 302-03, 328, 356-58, 362, 368, 389, 391
"Country Sabbath" (Coppard) **5**:178
"Country Songs" (Hardy) **143**:81
Country Tales (Verga)
See *Novelle rusticane*
"The Countryman's Return" (Thomas) **105**:359
The Country's Best (Leino)
See *Maan parhaat*
The Count's Ball (Radiguet)
See *Le bal du comte d'Orgel*
"The Count's Courtship" (de la Mare) **53**:27
"The County of Mayo" (Yeats) **31**:384
"The Coup de Grâce" (Bierce) **7**:88; **44**:44-5, 48, 51
"The coup d'etat in Vladivostok" (Khlebnikov)
See "Perevorot v Vladivostoke"
Le coup de grâce (Yourcenar) **193**:256, 261, 267, 270-71, 308, 321-22, 329-31, 343
Coup d'État: The Technique of Revolution (Malaparte)
See *Le technique du coup d'état*
Le coupable (Bataille) **155**:13, 15-20, 67-69, 71, 94, 104, 110, 114, 127-28
Le coupable (Coppee) **25**:126
"Le couperet" (Larbaud) **9**:199
"A Couple of Nuts" (Fitzgerald) **52**:63-5
"Coupon" (Čapek)
See "Kupón"
"Courage" (Éluard) **41**:168
"Courage" (Lane) **177**:284
"Courage" (Percy) **84**:198
Couragemodell (Brecht) **35**:25-6
"Couronne" (Apollinaire) **8**:18
Courrier sud (Saint-Exupéry) **2**:515, 517-20, 523-26; **56**:222, 228, 230, 235; **169**:316, 321, 323-24, 335-37, 341-44, 346
Cours de linguistique générale (Saussure) **49**:302-03, 307-09, 311, 315, 318-23, 325, 327, 329-31, 333-42, 344, 346-51, 355-56, 358, 360, 364-66, 371, 374
Cours d'economie politique (Pareto) **69**:117, 130, 137-40, 150, 152, 154-56, 164-65, 167
Cours naturel (Éluard) **7**:250, 255; **41**:156, 167
La course à la mort (Rod) **52**:309-11, 315-16, 320-25
Course in General Linguistics (Saussure)
See *Cours de linguistique générale*
"The Course of a Particular" (Stevens) **45**:300; **12**:377-78
"The Course of American History" (Wilson) **79**:488
The Course of Empire (De Voto) **29**:127, 129-30
"Coursing Rabbits on the Plains" (Remington) **89**:294
"The Court Jeweler" (Remizov)
See "Pridvornyi iuvelir"
The Court of Charles IV (Pérez Galdós)
See *La corte de Carlos IV*
The Court of Miracles (Valle-Inclán)
See *La corte de los milagros: El ruedo Ibérico I*
"The Court of the Dragon" (Chambers) **41**:88, 101, 103-08
"Court Order Can't Make Races Mix" (Hurston) **131**:63, 70
"The Courtesan" (Rilke) **195**:165
"The Courtesy Call" (Dazai Osamu)
See "A Visitor"
"The Courting of Dinah Shadd" (Kipling) **8**:188, 198
"The Courting of Sister Wisby" (Jewett) **22**:148
The Courts of the Morning (Buchan) **41**:38, 41, 44, 53-6, 67
"The Courtship" (Tolstoy) **18**:377

Courtship Is Like a Battlefield (Chang)
See *Qingchang ru zhangchang*
"The Courtship of Mr. Lyon" (Carter) **139**:114
"The Courtyard of Light" (Babits)
See "A világosság udvara"
Cousin Cinderella (Duncan) **60**:177, 197, 207, 209, 226, 228, 233, 247, 249
"Cousin Larry" (Parker) **143**:331
Cousin Philip (Ward) **55**:437, 443, 446
"Couvre-feu" (Éluard) **41**:152, 161
"Covekovo zanimanje" (Popa) **167**:164
"The Covenant" (Muir) **87**:209
"Coventry Patmore's Genius" (Johnson) **19**:233
"The Coverfield Sweepstakes" (Norris) **155**:258
"A Cover's Progress" (Symons) **11**:426
"The Coves of Crail" (Sharp) **39**:389, 391, 393
"The Cow" (Esenin) **4**:113
"Cow" (García Lorca)
See "Vaca"
"The Cow" (Nash) **109**:362
"The Cow Coroner" (Adams) **56**:7
Cow in Moscow (Kandinsky) **92**:37
"The Coward" (Kipling) **8**:196
"The Coward" (Kuprin) **5**:298
"The Coward" (Premchand)
See "Kayar"
"The Coward" (Service) **15**:399
"The Coward" (Sharp) **39**:375
"A Coward" (Wharton) **3**:551, 554; **129**:360
"Cowards" (Saroyan) **137**:156
"Cowboy" (Huidobro) **31**:124, 135
The Cowboy Philosopher on Prohibition (Rogers) **8**:336; **71**:283
The Cowboy Philosopher on the Peace Conference (Rogers) **8**:336, 338-39; **71**:283
"Cowboys and Indians" (Abbey) **160**:22, 96
"Cowboys and Indians, Part II" (Abbey) **160**:96
"Cowper" (Bradford) **36**:57
Cow-Wheat (Pilnyak) **23**:201
"Cox-City" (Apollinaire) **51**:20
Crab Apples (Hansen)
See *Paradisæblerne*
"Crab Nebula" (Burroughs) **121**:132
"The Crab Trees" (Gogarty) **15**:112
"The Crack-Up" (Fitzgerald) **157**:208, 222
The Crack-Up (Fitzgerald) **1**:239, 242, 246, 250, 253; **6**:160-61, 167-68; **28**:101; **55**:220; **157**:164-65, 167, 169, 172, 203-6, 208-9
"The Cradle" (Dobson) **79**:23
"Cradle Song" (Jiménez) **183**:330
The Cradle Song (Martinez Sierra and Martinez Sierra)
See *Canción de cuna*
"The Cradles of Gold" (Yeats) **31**:418
"Cradle-Song" (Naidu) **80**:289
"Cradle-Song at Twilight" (Meynell) **6**:299
Cradock Nowell (Blackmore) **27**:29, 33, 36, 38-41, 46
Craft (Tsvetaeva)
See *Remeslo*
"A Craftsman of Bowls" (Cavafy)
See "A Craftsman of Wine Bowls"
"A Craftsman of Wine Bowls" (Cavafy) **7**:163-64
Craftsmanship (Tsvetaeva)
See *Remeslo*
"Crainquebille" (France) **9**:47
Crainquebille, and Other Profitable Tales (France)
See *L'affaire Crainquebille*
Craişortil (Rebreanu) **28**:272
"The Crane" (Khlebnikov)
See "Zhuravl"
Crane Homeland (Prishvin) **75**:215, 217-18, 221
Crane's Birthplace (Prishvin)
See *Crane Homeland*
Cranks (Tolstoy) **18**:373
Cranmer (Belloc) **18**:28, 45
"Crapy Cornelia" (James) **2**:275; **40**:140; **47**:201
"Craving for Spring" (Lawrence) **93**:109
"Crazed" (de la Mare) **53**:42
"Crazy" (Devkota)
See "Pāgal"
"The Crazy Batlen" (Peretz) **16**:389
"The Crazy Beggar-Student" (Peretz)
See "The Crazy Batlen"
"Crazy for This Democracy" (Hurston) **131**:62
"Crazy Girls Song" (Coppard) **5**:177-78
"Crazy in the Stir" (Himes) **139**:319
"Crazy Jane Talks with the Bishop" (Yeats) **31**:398
The Crazy Kill (Himes)
See *Couché dans le pain*
The Crazy Locomotive (Witkiewicz)
See *Szalona lokomotywa*
Crazy Man (Bodenheim) **44**:60, 62, 65, 70-1, 74
"Crazy Mary" (McKay) **41**:329
"Crazy Sunday" (Fitzgerald) **1**:262; **55**:191, 207
La creación pura (Huidobro)
See *Création pure*
The Cream in the Well (Riggs) **56**:201-02, 209-10, 215, 218
The Cream of the Jest (Cabell) **6**:62, 64, 68, 70-1, 74-6
The Created Legend (Sologub)
See *Tvorimaja legenda*
Creating a Role (Stanislavsky) **167**:264, 267, 276, 279, 305, 307-8, 312, 329
"Creation" (Bierce) **7**:97
"The Creation" (Johnson) **19**:207, 209, 211; **175**:225, 233, 251-54, 256
"Creation" (McAlmon) **97**:87
Creation and Recreation (Frye) **165**:165, 168-69, 193, 257
"Creation Light" (Bell) **43**:90-1
"Creation Myth on a Moebius Band" (Nemerov) **124**:192, 257, 275
"Creation of Anguish" (Nemerov) **124**:151
Création pure (Huidobro) **31**:122, 126, 133
Le création subconsciente (Gourmont) **17**:154
"Le Créationnisme" (Huidobro) **31**:130
Creations (Khlebnikov)
See *Tvorenija*
Creative America (Lewisohn) **19**:270, 273, 289
"Creative Criticism" (Woolf) **43**:404, 406
Creative Evolution (Bergson)
See *L'évolution créatrice*
The Creative Life (Lewisohn) **19**:264-65, 293-94
Creative Mythology (Campbell)
See *The Masks of God: Creative Mythology*
The Creative Will (Van Dine) **23**:350, 358
"Creative Writers and Day-Dreaming" (Freud)
See "Der Dichter und das Phantasieren"
"The Creators" (Södergran) **31**:286
The Creators (Sinclair) **3**:437-38
A Creature of the Twilight (Kirk) **119**:253, 279, 284, 292, 339, 345, 348-49
"The Creatures" (de la Mare) **4**:78; **53**:16-17, 23, 27, 29, 33
Creatures (Lawrence) **2**:349; **93**:98
"Creatures in the Dawn" (Aleixandre)
See "Criaturas de la Aurora"
Creatures of Impulse (Gilbert) **3**:219
"Credences of Summer" (Stevens) **3**:467; **45**:279-80, 299-300, 310, 312-13
"Credentials of the Painter" (Lewis) **104**:204
Creditors (Strindberg)
See *Fordringsägare*
"Credo" (Abbey) **160**:40
"Credo" (Lane) **177**:273, 275, 286
"Credo" (Robinson) **5**:413; **101**:128
"Credo" (Santos) **156**:315
Creed or Chaos? (Sayers) **15**:374, 387
"Creepy Letters" (Burroughs) **121**:144
"The Cremation of Sam McGee" (Service) **15**:403, 405-06, 410-11
"The Cremona Violin" (Lowell) **8**:224
The Creoles of Louisiana (Cable) **4**:37
"Crépuscule" (Apollinaire) **3**:33, 39
"Crepúsculo" (Storni) **5**:450
Los crepúsculos del jardín (Lugones) **15**:285, 287-88, 291
The Crescent Moon (Tagore) **53**:334, 344, 347
"Cresiente" (Gonzalez Martinez) **72**:149
"Cressy" (Harte) **25**:193, 199, 217
"Crève-coeur" (Schwob) **20**:323
"Crewe" (de la Mare) **4**:80; **53**:25, 27, 34-7
Crewe Train (Macaulay) **7**:427, 429; **44**:126
"Le cri" (Verhaeren) **12**:471
El criador de gorilas (Arlt) **29**:51
"Criaturas de la Aurora" (Aleixandre) **113**:73-5
Las criaturas saturnianas (Sender) **136**:208, 214-15
Cricket All His Life (Lucas) **73**:172
"Cricket and the Backward Look" (Lucas) **73**:174
"The Crickets" (Mistral)
See "Li grihet"
"The Crime" (Beerbohm) **24**:124-25
A Crime (Bernanos)
See *Un crime*
Un crime (Bernanos) **3**:124-5
"Crime and Why" (Dreiser) **83**:117
"The Crime at the Post Office" (Čapek) **192**:224
Un crime d'amour (Bourget) **12**:57, 72
Le crime de Sylvestre Bonnard (France) **9**:38-40, 51, 53
Crime: Its Cause and Treatment (Darrow) **81**:77
The Crime of Mr. S. Karuma (Abe)
See *S. Karuma-shi no hanzai*
The Crime of S. Karma (Abe)
See *S. Karuma-shi no hanzai*
The Crime of Sylvester Bonnard (France)
See *Le crime de Sylvestre Bonnard*
The Crime of the Congo (Doyle) **7**:221
"The Crime on Christmas Night" (Leroux) **25**:260
Crime on Goat Island (Betti)
See *Delitto all'isola delle capre*
"The Crime on the Farm" (Čapek) **192**:224
"The Crime or Impossible" (Aleixandre)
See "El crimen o imposible"
"The Crime was in Grenada" (Machado)
See "El crimen fue en Granada"
El crimen del otro (Quiroga) **20**:211
"El crimen fue en Granada" (Machado) **3**:309-10
"Crimen libre" (Pardo Bazán) **189**:270
"El crimen o imposible" (Aleixandre) **113**:5
Crimes of Passion (Orton) **158**:299, 352, 355, 357
The Criminal (Ellis) **14**:110, 114, 132
The Crimson Circle (Wallace) **57**:402
The Crimson Island (Bulgakov)
See *Bagrovyi ostrov*
"The Crimson Moon" (Sharp) **39**:382
"The Crimson Saber" (Khlebnikov)
See "Malinovaya shashka"
The Crimston Serpent (Dent) **72**:23
Crinolines (Kandinsky) **92**:34
"Crippled Phoenix" (Heller) **151**:308-10, 313, 315
Cripps the Carrier (Blackmore) **27**:31, 36, 40-1, 44-5, 47
Crisálidas (Machado de Assis) **10**:279
"The Crises of the Mind" (Valéry) **4**:503
Crises of the Republic (Arendt) **193**:43
"Crisi di civiltà" (Levi) **125**:215, 250
"Una crisis" (Storni) **5**:453
Crisis (Husserl)
See *Die Krisis der europaeischen Wissenschaften und die transzendentale Phänomenologie, Eine Einleitung in die phaenomenologische Philosophie*
"The Crisis in Culture" (Arendt) **193**:119, 123-24
The Crisis in Ireland (O'Grady) **5**:351
The Crisis in the German Social Democracy (Luxemburg) **63**:167
The Crisis of Christianity (von Hartmann) **96**:211

The Crisis of Consciousness and Henrik Ibsen (Bely) **7**:59
"The Crisis of Culture" (Simmel) **64**:360
The Crisis of European Science and Transcendental Phenomenology: An Introduction to Phenomenological Philosophy (Husserl)
See *Die Krisis der europaeischen Wissenschaften und die transzendentale Phänomenologie, Eine Einleitung in die phaenomenologische Philosophie*
The Crisis of Social-Democracy (Luxemburg)
See *Juniusbroschure*
Crisis of the European Sciences and Transcendental Phenomenology (Husserl)
See *Die Krisis der europaeischen Wissenschaften und die transzendentale Phänomenologie, Eine Einleitung in die phaenomenologische Philosophie*
Crisscross through My Life (Babits)
See *Keresztülkasul az életemen*
The Cristian (Caine) **97**:5-6, 10-11, 14, 26
Una cristiana-La preuba (Pardo Bazán) **189**:240-48, 250-51
El Cristo de la Rue Jacob (Sarduy) **167**:191-92, 199-201, 213-15, 217, 220, 223
El Cristo de Velázquez (Unamuno) **2**:562, 567-68; **9**:510, 514-15; **148**:243, 304
Cristo e santi (Papini) **22**:287
Cristo si è fermato a Eboli (Levi) **125**:194-98, 200-204, 207, 209-11, 213, 216-17, 219, 221-22, 225-26, 231, **125**:237-38, 242, 244-45, 247-51
Cristobical (García Lorca) **181**:14
"Criteria of Negro Art" (Du Bois) **169**:124
"The Criterion in Art" (Gill) **85**:53
The Critic and the Drama (Nathan) **18**:318
"The Critic as Artist" (Wilde) **1**:498; **8**:493, 502; **23**:425; **41**:376-77, 379, 381-82
The Critic as Artist (Wilde) **175**:313
The Critic in Judgment; or, Belshazzar of Barons Court (Murry) **16**:330-31, 354
"The Critic Who Gossips" (Huneker) **65**:189
"La critica" (Ginzburg) **156**:31, 46, 59
Critica (Hostos) **24**:303
Critica e arte (Carducci) **32**:93, 106
La crítica en la edad ateniense (Reyes) **33**:316, 323
La critica letteraria (Croce) **37**:94-5, 113-15, 119, 127
"Critica negativa" (Svevo) **35**:362-64
The Critical Attitude (Ford) **15**:95; **172**:97
A Critical Edition of W. B. Yeat's A Vision (Yeats) **93**:362
Critical Essays (Barthes)
See *Essais critiques*
Critical Essays (Orwell) **6**:341; **15**:333; **51**:220-22, 225, 227-28, 247; **128**:259, 298
A Critical Fable (Lowell) **8**:227, 229, 237
"Critical Languages" (Acker) **191**:101, 128
"The Critical Path" (Frye) **165**:239
The Critical Path (Frye) **165**:147, 153-58, 168, 183, 189, 191-92, 227-28, 230, 241, 256
Critical Poetry (Desnos)
See *Poésie critique*
"The Critical Process" (Mencken) **13**:395
The Critical Reception of Martin Heidegger's Existential Philosophy (Bachmann)
See *Die kritische Aufnahme der Existentialphilosophie Martin Heideggers*
Critical Studies (Ouida) **43**:370
Critical Writings of James Joyce (Joyce) **159**:326, 334
"Criticism" (Ginzburg)
See "La critica"
Criticism (MacCarthy) **36**:252, 259
Criticism and Fiction (Howells) **7**:375, 377, 388-89; **17**:161; **41**:255-56, 284
Criticism and Truth (Barthes)
See *Critique et vérité*
A Criticism of Dogmatic Theory (Tolstoy)
See *Issledovanie dogmaticheskogo bogoslavja*
"The Criticism of Fiction" (Wharton) **149**:288
"Criticism of Words" (Čapek) **37**:46
Criticisms and Portraits (Brandes)
See *Critiker og portraiter*
Un crítico incipiente (Echegaray) **4**:104-05
Critiker og portraiter (Brandes) **10**:60, 70
Critique (Ball)
See *Zur Kritik der deutschen Intelligenz*
"Critique de la poésie" (Éluard) **7**:250; **41**:151
Critique et clinique (Deleuze) **116**:86-7, 104
Critique et vérité (Barthes) **135**:114-17, 185
"Critique of Critics" (Kandinsky) **92**:18
Critique of Dogmatic Theology (Tolstoy) **11**:463; **79**:335, 399, 407, 420, 425, 460
The Critique of Dogmatic Theory (Tolstoy)
See *Issledovanie dogmaticheskogo bogoslavja*
"Critique of Force" (Benjamin)
See "Critique of Violence"
"A Critique of Monsieur Poe" (Post) **39**:347
"Critique of Poetry" (Popa) **167**:174
"Critique of Satisfaction" (Hulme) **21**:122
"The Critique of the Foundations of the Hegelian Dialectic" (Bataille) **155**:97-98, 105
The Critique of the German Intelligentsia (Ball)
See *Zur Kritik der deutschen Intelligenz*
"Critique of Violence" (Benjamin) **39**:8, 41
Critique of Words (Čapek) **192**:218
"Croce's Philosophy of History" (Collingwood) **67**:130, 155, 182-83
The croci (Tozzi) **31**:312-17, 319-21, 324, 329-30, 333-34
La crociata degli innocente (D'Annunzio) **6**:135
The Crock of Gold (Stephens) **4**:407-08, 410-21
"The Crock of Problems" (Toomer) **172**:312-13
"Crocker's Hole" (Blackmore) **27**:44
"Crocknaharna" (Ledwidge) **23**:115
"Crocodile at the Ancient Tombs" (Nemerov) **124**:313
"Crocuses in the Grass" (Gray) **19**:152
La croisade des enfants (Schwob) **20**:321-23
Cromwell (Belloc) **18**:45
Cromwell (Drinkwater)
See *Oliver Cromwell*
"Cronaca di un paese" (Ginzburg) **156**:105
Cronache di Poveri Amanti (Pratolini) **124**:337, 344-45, 347, 349-51
"Cronache fiorentine XX secolo" (Pratolini) **124**:351
Crónica del alba (Sender) **136**:208, 215
Crónica del pueblo en armas (Sender) **136**:215
The Crooked Mile (De Voto) **29**:114, 126-27
"The Crooked Stick" (Wylie) **8**:521
The Crooked Timber of Humanity: Chapters in the History of Ideas (Berlin) **105**:89, 118, 132
Crooked Trails (Remington) **89**:304
The Croquet Player (Wells) **6**:540, 553
Croquis Parisiens (Huysmans) **7**:405-06; **69**:23-5, 30, 33-4, 42, 47
"The Cross" (Gumilev)
See "Krest"
"Cross" (Huidobro)
See "Cruz"
The Cross (Obstfelder)
See *Korset*
The Cross (Undset)
See *Korset*
Cross Creek (Rawlings) **4**:364, 366-67
Cross Currents in Europe To-Day (Beard) **15**:20
"A Cross in the Forest" (Ady) **11**:15
"Cross of Gold" (Bryan) **99**:22, 85, 87, 129, 131, 149, 160
The Cross on the Mountain (Cankar)
See *Križ na gori*
Cross Roads (Čapek) **192**:225
"Cross the Wounded Galaxies" (Burroughs) **121**:126
"Cross-Currents in Modern French Literature" (Huneker) **65**:189
"The Crossing" (Nemerov) **124**:256
"Crossing Alone the Nighted Ferry" (Housman) **10**:242
"Crossing into Poland" (Babel)
See "Perechod cerez Zbruc"
"Crossing the Zbruch" (Babel)
See "Perechod cerez Zbruc"
"Crossing the Zbruck" (Babel)
See "Perechod cerez Zbruc"
Crossings (de la Mare) **53**:16, 22
"Crossroad Blues" (Johnson) **69**:82
"Crossroads Chapel" (Nezval) **44**:242
"Crossroads (July 1920)" (García Lorca)
See "Encrucijada (Julio de 1920)"
"Cross-Section" (Ingamells) **35**:121
"The Crow Becomes Discursive" (McAlmon) **97**:97
"The Crow Comes Last" (Calvino) **183**:145, 221, 223
The Crow Comes Last (Calvino) **183**:96
"Crow Moon" (Engel) **137**:113, 116
The Crowd (Lewis) **104**:201
The Crowd and the Public (Park) **73**:194-6, 198, 211
Crowds and Power (Canetti)
See *Masse und Macht*
Crowds of Lourdes (Huysmans)
See *Les foules de Lourdes*
"The Crown" (Lawrence) **2**:347, 360; **33**:199, 206
The Crown (Lawrence) **61**:211
The Crown Bride (Strindberg) **47**:369
The Crown of Life (Gissing) **3**:223, 232, 234; **24**:220, 222, 241, 243, 248-49; **47**:137
The Crown of Wild Olive (Ruskin) **20**:29; **63**:298
"The Crowning of Arthur" (Williams) **1**:515
The Crow's Nest (Day) **25**:132, 137
"The Croxley Master" (Doyle) **7**:216, 239
"Cruchette" (Schwob) **20**:323
Crucial Conversations (Sarton) **120**:256-59
Crucial Instances (Wharton) **3**:555, 561, 570; **9**:541; **129**:360; **149**:255
Crucible (Williams) **89**:400
The Crucified Woman (Mizoguchi) **72**:293
"A Crucifix" (Gray) **19**:154-55, 157
"Crucifix Corner" (Gurney) **33**:86, 93-4
"Crucifixion" (Čapek) **192**:186, 189
"Crucifixion" (García Lorca)
See "Crucifixión"
"Crucifixión" (García Lorca) **49**:94; **181**:28; **197**:187, 191, 193, 196-97, 247, 251
"The Crucifixion" (Johnson) **19**:209, 211; **175**:254, 257
Crucifixion (Cocteau) **119**:76, 78
"The Crucifixion of the Outcast" (Yeats) **31**:403, 416
"Crude Foyer" (Stevens) **45**:299, 331
Cruel Iphigenia (Reyes)
See *Ifigenia cruel*
"The Cruel Painter" (MacDonald) **113**:214
Cruelle énigme (Bourget) **12**:57-9, 67, 72
"Cruelty and Love" (Lawrence) **93**:46, 65
"The Cruise" (Merrill) **173**:225
The Cruise of the Aardvark (Nash) **109**:355
The Cruise of the Corwin (Muir) **28**:244, 259
"The Cruise of the Galleon" (Carman) **7**:134
"The Cruise of the 'Idlewild'" (Dreiser) **35**:75
The Cruise of the Jasper B. (Marquis) **7**:434-35, 437, 447
The Cruise of the "Nona" (Belloc) **7**:33, 39; **18**:42-3, 45-6
The Cruise of the "Snark" (London) **9**:271, 282-84
The Cruise of the Vanadis (Wharton) **129**:364
"'Crumbling Idols' by Hamlin Garland" (Chopin) **127**:19, 216

Crumbling Idols: Twelve Essays on Art, Dealing Chiefly with Literature, Painting, and the Drama (Garland) **3**:190-91, 193, 195, 203, 205
"The Crumbs of One Man's Year" (Thomas) **45**:399
Črumnyj Xleb (Pilnyak) **23**:212
Crusade for Justice: The Autobiography of Ida B. Wells (Wells-Barnett) **125**:306-19, 329-30
The Crusade of the Excelsior (Harte) **25**:222
The Crusade of the Innocent (D'Annunzio)
See *La crociata degli innocente*
Crusader Castles (Lawrence) **18**:159, 180-81
The Crusaders of the Cause (Valle-Inclán)
See *Los cruzados de la causa*
"Crusoe in England" (Bishop) **121**:4, 21, 28, 56, 72
Crusts (Claudel)
See *Le pain dur*
"The Crutile" (Williams) **89**:378
The Crux (Gilman) **9**:113, 115; **37**:177; **117**:152-53, 156-58
Crux: The Letters of James Dickey (Dickey) **151**:202, 220
"Cruz" (Huidobro) **31**:135
"Cruz alta" (Graham) **19**:134
"Cruzadas" (Pereda) **16**:379
Los cruzados de la causa (Valle-Inclán) **5**:486, 488
"Cry" (Artaud) **36**:4, 16
"A Cry" (MacDonald) **113**:233
Cry Baby (Hayashi)
See *Nakimushi kozō*
The Cry for Justice (London) **9**:257
Cry for Love (Osborne) **153**:251
"Cry of Seagulls" (Radnóti) **16**:418
"The Cry of the Child" (Hichens) **64**:122
Cry, the Beloved Country (Paton)
See *Cry, the Beloved Country: A Story of Comfort in Desolation*
Cry, the Beloved Country: A Story of Comfort in Desolation (Paton) **165**:265-337
"Cry to Rome: From the Chrysler Building Tower" (García Lorca)
See "Grito hacia Roma"
"The Crying of the Earth" (Symons) **11**:435
"The Crying of Water" (Symons) **11**:435
"Crying, Waiting, Hoping" (Holly) **65**:147
The Crypt of the Capuchins (Roth)
See *Die Kapuzinergruft*
A Crystal Age (Hudson) **29**:140, 145, 153-54, 160, 162
The Crystal Bell (Güiraldes)
See *El cencerro de cristal*
The Crystal Box (Walpole) **5**:498
"The Crystal Cabinet" (Lawrence) **93**:109
The Crystal Cabinet (Butts) **77**:98, 104-7, 109
"The Crystal Dreamer" (Manning) **25**:278
"The Crystal Egg" (Wells) **12**:488, 510; **19**:434
"A Crystal Forest" (Sharp) **39**:387
"The Crystal Gazer" (Futrelle) **19**:90
"The Crystal Girl" (Valéry) **4**:498
"The Crystal Palace" (Davidson) **24**:172, 189-91
The Crystal Spider (Vallette)
See *L'araignee de cristal*
The Crystal Stopper (Leblanc)
See *Le bouchon de cristal*
"Crystals" (Calvino)
See "I cristalli"
"A csendéletekből" (Babits) **14**:39
"Csillagokig" (Babits) **14**:39
Cuaderno San Martín (Borges) **109**:7, 9-11, 163
"Cuadrivio laico" (Quiroga) **20**:213
"Cuadro" (Villaurrutia) **80**:477
"Cuadro de estio: el invalido" (Prado) **75**:194, 207
Cuadros religiosos (Pardo Bazán) **189**:248
"Cuadros y angulos" (Storni) **5**:446
Cuando entonces (Onetti) **131**:250-51, 253-54, 283, 287-88
"Cuando la tarde . . ." (Villaurrutia) **80**:480
"Cuando se es pobre" (Prado) **75**:194, 207
Cuando ya no importe (Onetti) **131**:262, 284
Cuando yo era niño (Ramoacn y Cajal) **93**:146
"Cuatro" (Jiménez) **4**:214
Los cuatro jinetes del apocalipsis (Blasco Ibáñez) **12**:31-5, 37-8, 43, 45, 47, 49-50
Cuatro para Delfina (Donoso) **133**:124, 140
"Cuatro socialistas" (Pardo Bazán) **189**:235
The Cubist Painters: Aesthetic Meditations (Apollinaire)
See *Méditations esthétiques: Les peintres cubistes*
"Cuchulain Comforted" (Yeats) **1**:570; **11**:533
Cuchulain of Muirthemne: The Story of the Men of the Red Branch of Ulster (Gregory) **176**:5-6, 12, 25, 28-29
"The Cuckoo" (Thomas) **10**:467
Cuckoo Songs (Tynan) **3**:502, 504
Cuckoo's Tears (Tolstoy) **18**:382
Cuculcán, Serpeinte-Envuelta en plumas (Asturias) **184**:14, 71, 78-79, 82-83
"Čudo u Olovu" (Andrić) **135**:15, 23, 96
"The Cue" (Burke) **63**:131
"Cuento Griego—El sátiro sordo" (Darío)
See "The Deaf Satyr"
"Cuento para novios" (Quiroga) **20**:214
"Cuento primitivo" (Pardo Bazán) **189**:313
"Cuento sin razón, pero cansado" (Quiroga) **20**:211, 222
"Cuento soñata" (Pardo Bazán) **189**:227
Cuentos (Donoso) **133**:43-44
Cuentos completos (Onetti) **131**:133, 286
Cuentos completos (Pardo Bazán) **189**:291
Cuentos completos de Rubén Darío (Darío) **4**:66
Cuentos de amor (Pardo Bazán) **189**:226, 228-29
Cuentos de amor, de locura, y de muerte (Quiroga) **20**:207, 210-11, 215
Cuentos de la selva (Quiroga) **20**:213, 217, 219
Cuentos de Marineda (Pardo Bazán) **189**:234, 305
Cuentos de muerte y de sangre (Güiraldes) **39**:175-77, 186, 190
Cuentos de vacaciones (Ramoacn y Cajal) **93**:146
Cuentos, dialogos, y fantasias (Valera y Alcala-Galiano) **10**:501
Cuentos fatales (Lugones) **15**:286, 292-93, 295
Cuentos misteriosos (Nervo) **11**:394
Cuentos nuevos (Pardo Bazán) **189**:234-35
Cuentos sacro-profanos (Pardo Bazán) **189**:247
Cuentos valencianos (Blasco Ibáñez) **12**:41, 45
Los cuernos de don Friolera (Valle-Inclán) **5**:480-81, 483, 486
"Cuerpo de piedra" (Aleixandre) **113**:14
"Cuervo" (Alas) **29**:20-1
Cuesta abajo (Pardo Bazán) **189**:197-99
La cuestión palpitante (Pardo Bazán) **189**:202, 205, 222, 233-34, 254, 266, 269, 271, 273
Cuestiones estéticas (Reyes) **33**:316-17, 323
Cuestiones gongorinas (Reyes) **33**:323
"Cueva de noche" (Aleixandre) **113**:50
"Cuídate, España . . ." (Vallejo) **56**:311
"Cuilidh Mhoire" (Sharp) **39**:377
"Le cuirassé Potemkine" (Desnos) **22**:65
"La cuisine" (Verhaeren) **12**:465
La cuisine creole (Hearn) **9**:135
"Cul de sac" (Hedāyat) **21**:66
"La culpable" (Pardo Bazán) **189**:228-29
"The Culprit" (Housman) **10**:247
"The Cult of Hope" (Mencken) **13**:363
Le culte du moi (Brandon) **47**:61
"El culto de la flor" (Lugones) **15**:293
"El culto de los libros" (Borges) **109**:66
"Cultural Criticism" (Adorno)
See "Kulturkritik und Gesellschaft"
"Cultural Criticism and Society" (Adorno)
See "Kulturkritik und Gesellschaft"
The Cultural Life of Modern America (Hamsun)
See *Fra det moderne Amerikas aandsliv*
"Culture" (Erskine) **84**:183
"Culture and Apartheid in South Africa" (La Guma) **140**:233
"Culture and Democracy" (Orwell) **51**:259
Culture and Personality (Sapir) **108**:257
"Culture and Socialism" (Trotsky) **22**:380
Culture and Value (Wittgenstein)
See *Vermischte Bemerkungen*
La culture des idées (Gourmont) **17**:127, 129, 138, 143, 150, 154, 158
"Culture, Genuine and Spurious" (Sapir) **108**:252-52, 257, 270, 273-74, 276-77
"Culture Industry Reconsidered" (Adorno) **111**:54
La cuna de América (Hostos) **24**:303
"Cunner-Fishing" (Jewett) **22**:136, 140
Cuor morituro (Saba) **33**:374-77
"The Cup" (Scott) **6**:389, 393
Cup of Blizzards (Bely)
See *Kubok metelej: Chetviortiia simfoniia*
A Cup of Coffee (Sturges) **48**:311, 317
"A Cup of Cold Water" (Wharton) **3**:551, 567; **9**:546; **27**:385; **129**:360
Cup of Gold: A Life of Henry Morgan, Buccaneer, with Occasional References to History (Steinbeck) **135**:264-65
"A Cup of Leaves" (Tagore)
See "Patraput, No. 3"
The Cup of Life (Bunin) **6**:45
The Cup of Snowstorms (Bely)
See *Kubok metelej: Chetviortiia simfoniia*
"A Cup of Tea" (Mansfield) **2**:456; **8**:284; **39**:304
"A Cup of Tea" (Söderberg)
See "En kopp te"
The Cup of Water (Field) **43**:159
Cupid and Commonsense (Bennett) **5**:27; **20**:36; **197**:16-17, 20-3
El cura de Monleón (Baroja) **8**:63
"Curado" (Pardo Bazán) **189**:236
The Curate of Monleón (Baroja)
See *El cura de Monleón*
Los curdas (Sánchez) **37**:314
A Cure for Curables (Biggers) **65**:2
"Cure for Melancholy" (Herzl) **36**:141
"The Curé of Calumette" (Drummond) **25**:143-44
"The Cure of Death" (Pilnyak)
See "Smertel'noe manit"
A Cure of Souls (Sinclair) **3**:438, 442; **11**:414
La curée (Zola) **6**:565-66; **41**:412
"The Curé's Progress" (Dobson) **79**:3, 6, 19, 23
"Curfew" (Coppard) **5**:178
Curfew (Donoso)
See *La Desesperanza*
Curiosités esthétiques (Apollinaire) **3**:42
"The Curious Man Punished" (Caragiale) **76**:170
Curious Myths of the Middle Ages (Baring-Gould) **88**:8-9
"The Curious Republic of Goudour" (Twain) **48**:356
The Curious room: Plays, Film Scripts, and an Opera (Carter) **139**:150
"Curious Shifts of the Poor" (Dreiser) **35**:65
"Curly Locks" (Riley) **51**:289
"Curried Cow" (Bierce) **1**:91; **44**:45
"The Curse" (Millay) **4**:308
The Curse (Caragiale)
See *Năpastă*
The Curse at Farewell (Tagore) **3**:492
"Curse for Kings" (Lindsay) **17**:227
"The Curse of a Thousand Kisses" (Rohmer) **28**:286
"Curse of Education" (Davis) **6**:154
"The Curse of Eve" (Doyle) **7**:221
The Curse of the Beast (Andreyev) **3**:23
The Curse of the Cat People (Lewton) **76**:197-98, 202, 204-05, 210-11

"The Curse of the Fires and of the Shadows" (Yeats) **31**:415
"The Curse of the Wilderness" (Bialik) **25**:50
The Curse of the Wise Woman (Dunsany) **59**:17, 21-3, 26, 28-9
"The Cursed Pool" (Yourcenar)
See "La Mare maudite"
Lo cursi (Benavente) **3**:98
"The Curtain" (Chandler) **7**:176; **179**:73, 111-12, 124-25
"Curtain" (Kandinsky) **92**:93
"Curtain Raiser" (Nabokov) **108**:110
"The Cusser" (Remizov)
See "Chertykhanets"
Custard and Company (Nash) **109**:358-59
"The Custard Heart" (Parker) **143**:332
Custer's Last Fight (Ince) **89**:9, 17-8
"La custode" (Teilhard de Chardin) **9**:491
Custom and Myth (Lang) **16**:260
The Custom of the Country (Wharton) **3**:557-58, 560-63, 572, 574, 579; **9**:541, 544, 548, 550, 552; **27**:384, 394; **53**:361, 388, 393; **129**:346, 362; **149**:142, 146, 234, 245, 253, 259
"Cut Flowers" (Gurney) **33**:98, 100
"Cut Glass Bowl" (Fitzgerald) **1**:262
"Cut Is the Branch That Might Have Grown Full Straight" (Anderson) **144**:34
Cutie-A-Warm Mama (Hecht) **101**:72
The Cutters (Aldrich) **125**:10, 12-15, 18
Cutting It Short (Hrabal)
See *Postřižiny*
Cutting Timber (Bernhard)
See *Holzfällen: Eine Erregung*
"Cutty Sark" (Crane) **5**:186-87
"Cuvarkuca" (Popa) **167**:164
"Cvety zapozdalye" (Chekhov) **163**:79
"Cybernetics" (Nemerov) **124**:178
"Cybernetics and Ghosts" (Calvino)
See "Cibernetica e fantasmi (Appunti sulla narrativa come processo comtinatiorio)"
"The Cychic Delusion" (Wells) **19**:436
"The Cycle of a Farm Pond" (Bromfield) **11**:86
The Cycle of Quatrains (Palamas) **5**:385
"The Cyclists" (Lowell) **1**:372
"Le cygne" (Sully Prudhomme) **31**:301
"A Cynic's Apology" (Stephen) **23**:326
The Cynic's Word Book (Bierce)
See *The Devil's Dictionary*
Cyntherea (Hergesheimer) **11**:267-73, 276, 282-83, 286
The Cypress Chest (Annensky)
See *Kiparisovy larets*
"Cypresses" (Lawrence) **93**:125
Cyrano de Bergerac (Rostand) **6**:372-83; **37**:277, 279-81, 283-84, 286-88, 290-94, 296-300, 302-08
Czar Dadon (Remizov) **27**:333
The Czarina of Kazalar (Vazov)
See *Kazalarskata carica*
"The Czars" (Rilke)
See "Die Zaren"
"The Czar's Bride" (Khlebnikov)
See "Carskaja nevesta"
"Czas" (Herbert) **168**:39
"Czesniki" (Babel)
See "Chesniki"
"D. G. R." (Gosse) **28**:132
D. H. Lawrence and Maurice Magnus: A Plea for Better Manners (Douglas) **68**:23, 34
D. L. Moody: A Worker in Souls (Bradford) **36**:56, 64
Da (Bernhard)
See *Ja*
"Da Budet" (Guro) **56**:132
"Da prendersela coi giovani" (Calvino) **183**:154
"Da quando" (Saba) **33**:374
"Da sé" (Pirandello) **29**:282
"Da un colle" (Saba) **33**:369
Dachniki (Gorky) **8**:92-3
"Dada Manifesto 1918" (Tzara) **168**:224-25, 236, 251, 308, 313, 317
"Dada was no childish romp" (Arp) **115**:19
Dadakonzil (Arp) **115**:11
"Los dados eternos" (Vallejo) **3**:532
"Daedalus" (Crowley) **7**:208
"Daedalus" (Sikelianos) **39**:404, 421
Daedalus in Crete (Sikelianos) **39**:415, 419
"The Daemon Lover" (Jackson) **187**:243, 245
The Daemonic Genius of Richard Wright (Walker)
See *Richard Wright: A Daemonic Genius*
"Dag" (Obstfelder) **23**:179
Dagbok för Selma Lagerlöf (Lagerloef) **36**:235
"Den dagen" (Lagerkvist) **144**:158
"Dagen svalnar" (Södergran) **31**:284-85, 289
The Dagger in the Sky (Dent) **72**:16
Daglannet (Bjoernson) **7**:112, 114; **37**:15, 17, 19
"Dagon" (Lovecraft) **4**:266; **22**:208-09, 232
Dagsedlar (Dagerman) **17**:96
"Daguerreotype" (Moody) **105**:225, 234-35, 237, 247, 254, 260-61
"The Dahlias and the Crane" (Miyazawa) **76**:278
"Dahomey" (Lorde) **173**:85-86
"Daihakken" (Mori Ogai) **14**:384
"The Daily Globe" (Nemerov) **124**:179, 250
The Dain Curse (Hammett) **187**:45, 48-49, 51, 56-57, 60, 63, 66, 68-9, 79-80, 82-6, 88, 93, 96-100, 108, 156-59, 166, 170, 214-15
"The Dainty and the Hungray Man" (Sapir) **108**:249
Dainty Shapes and Hairy Apes (Witkiewicz)
See *Nadobnisie i koczkodany*
"Daisansha" (Kunikida Doppo) **99**:298, 303-04
Daisies and Buttercups (Riddell) **40**:335
"Daisy" (Thompson) **4**:435, 439
The Daisy Chain; or, Aspirations (Yonge) **48**:365-67, 371, 373, 375-81, 383-85, 388
Daisy Miller: A Study (James) **2**:246-47, 249, 274-75; **11**:321, 325, **24**:325; **47**:174-77, 199-200, 205; **64**:133-96
Daisy's Escape (Pinero) **32**:412
Daiyon kampyoki (Abe) **131**:11
"Dakar Doldrums" (Ginsberg) **120**:75
Dākghar (Tagore) **3**:497; **53**:334-36, 341
"Dāl-Bhāt-Dukū" (Devkota) **23**:52
D'ale carnavalului (Caragiale) **76**:162-65, 168
Dalekie i bliskie (Bryusov) **10**:78, 87
"Daleko u nama" (Popa) **167**:153-55, 176-77, 179
Daleko u nama (Popa) **167**:171
"Dali ou l'Anti-obscurantisme" (Crevel) **112**:13
Dallas Galbraith (Davis) **6**:148-52
"Dall'erta" (Saba) **33**:374
"Dall'uomo a Dio" (Papini) **22**:283
Dam 'ah wabitisāmah (Gibran) **1**:328; **9**:84-5, 88, 90-2
La Dama boba (Garro) **153**:17, 21-22, 72
Dama de corazones (Villaurrutia) **80**:465, 479
La dama errante (Baroja) **8**:48-9, 62
La dama joven (Pardo Bazán) **189**:237-38, 259-60
"Dama s sobačkoj" (Chekhov) **3**:149, 153, 155; **10**:111-13, 115; **55**:68
Damaged Souls (Bradford) **36**:51-2, 57, 59
"Damayanti to Nala in the Hour of Exile" (Naidu) **80**:316
"La dame au Tzigane" (Gourmont) **17**:126
"Dame auf einem Balkon" (Rilke) **195**:227
"La dame blanche des Hohenzollern" (Apollinaire) **51**:28
Dame Care (Sudermann)
See *Frau Sorge*
La dame de Challant (Giacosa) **7**:305, 309, 313-14
La dame de chez Maxim (Feydeau) **22**:77-9, 82, 84, 87, 91-4
"La Dame du Photographe" (Colette) **16**:128-30, 132
"Dame Edith Sitwell Reading" (Villa) **176**:96, 119-20
Die Dame in Schwarz (Herzl) **36**:132
Dame mit Facher (Kandinsky) **92**:49
La dame qui perdu son peintre (Bourget) **12**:69
"The Dame Regnant" (Scott) **6**:388, 393, 397
"Dame vor dem Spiegel" (Rilke) **195**:227
Damer's Gold (Gregory) **1**:334, 337; **176**:20, 22, 35-36, 38
Dames de volupté (Lemonnier) **22**:198, 204
"Damiens" (Huysmans) **69**:25
"Dammerung" (Lasker-Schueler) **57**:312
Dämmerung (Horkheimer) **132**:214-16
"The Damn Fool" (Chambers) **129**:45
Damn You, England (Osborne) **153**:339
"Damnation" (Lasker-Schueler) **57**:328, 334
The Damnation of Faust (Melies) **81**:139
"The Damned" (Blackwood) **5**:75-6
The Damned and the Saved (Levi) **109**:290
"The Damned Thing" (Bierce) **7**:92, **44**:13, 15, 44-6
The Damned Yard (Andrić)
See *Prokleta avlija*
Les damnés de la terre (Fanon) **188**:3, 5, 7-10, 12, 26, 32, 35, 41, 44-50, 65, 68-71, 73-4, 79, 81-2, 84-5, 91-3, 111-25, 128, 130-35, 137, 140, 146, 148, 151
"Damp Mother Earth" (Pilnyak) **23**:219
"Damp Sheets" (Wakefield) **120**:345, 348
The Damsel and the Sage (Glyn) **72**:138
A Damsel in Distress (Wodehouse) **108**:370
Dan Barry's Daughter (Faust) **49**:45, 49, 51
Dan Drew (Brecht) **169**:37
Dan Russell the Fox (Somerville & Ross) **51**:340, 359-60, 374
"Dan the Wreck" (Lawson) **27**:139-40
"Dan u Rimu" (Andrić) **135**:79
"Dana" (Baker) **3**:11; **10**:17
"Danaan Quicken Tree" (Yeats) **116**:334-36
"A Danaidák" (Babits) **14**:39
"The Danaïdes" (Babits)
See "A Danaidák"
"Les Danaïdes" (Sully Prudhomme) **31**:302, 304
Danby Croker (Freeman) **21**:56, 59
"The Dance" (Abercrombie) **141**:22
"The Dance" (Crane) **2**:112, 121; **80**:83, 88, 101, 115, 127, 132, 140, 143, 161, 166, 168, 170, 210, 212-3
"Dance" (Nagai)
See "Butō"
"Dance" (Stephens) **4**:416
Dance (Sá-Carneiro)
See *Bailado*
Dance and the Soul; Eupalinos; or, The Architect (Valéry)
See *Eupalinos; ou, L'architecte*
"The Dance at Corncob Corners" (Knister) **56**:162
Dance Lessons for Adult and Advanced Pupils (Hrabal)
See *Taneční hodiny pro starší a pokročilé*
"The Dance of Death" (Blok)
See "Danse macabre"
"Dance of Death" (García Lorca)
See "Danza de la muerte"
The Dance of Death (Strindberg)
See *Dödsdansen första delen*
Dance of Death (Stroheim)
See *La Danse de la Mort*
Dance of Herodias (Remizov)
See *Plias Irodiady*
"The Dance of Life" (Naidu) **80**:305
The Dance of Life (Ellis) **14**:108, 110-11, 113-14, 116, 123, 127
"The Dance of Love" (Cullen) **37**:168
"The Dance of the Atoms" (Balmont)
See "Pliaska atomov"
"The Dance of the Future" (Duncan) **68**:72-5
The Dance of the Future (Duncan) **68**:79
Dance of the Herons (Zuckmayer) **191**:328-29, 331
"The Dance of the Little People" (Eastman) **55**:167

"Dance of the Painted Maidens" (Okigbo) **171**:340, 345
"The Dance of the Veils" (Rohmer) **28**:286
"The Dance of the Widower-Bachelors" (Ady) **11**:15
"Dance the orange" (Rilke)
See "Tanzt die Orange"
"The Dancer" (Nagai)
See "Opera no maihime"
"Dancer" (Stephens) **4**:407, 410
"Dancer to Audience" (Dickey) **151**:152
"Dances of Death" (Blok)
See "Danse macabre"
Danchōtie nichijō (Nagai) **51**:98
"The Dancin' Party at Harrison's Cove" (Murfree) **135**:195, 197, 199-202, 204, 214, 218-19, 227
The Dancing Demon (Remizov)
See *Pliashushchii demon*
The Dancing Floor (Buchan) **41**:38, 41, 44-5, 54
"The Dancing Girl" (Apollinaire) **3**:38
"The Dancing Girl" (Mori Ogai)
See "Maihime"
The Dancing Girl (Nagai)
See *Odoriko*
Dancing Lessons for the Advanced in Age (Hrabal)
See *Taneční hodiny pro starší a pokročilé*
"The Dandelion" (Lindsay) **17**:229
"Dandelions" (Nemerov) **124**:185
"Dandies and Dandies" (Beerbohm) **24**:108-09, 116
Dandy Dick (Pinero) **32**:395-96, 404, 406, 410-12
"Dandy Jim's Conjure Scare" (Dunbar) **12**:111
"Dane's Breechin" (Somerville & Ross) **51**:335
"Danger!" (Doyle) **7**:225
Danger Lies East (Dent) **72**:27
The Danger Mark (Chambers) **41**:92, 95-6, 101
The Danger of Being a Gentleman (Laski) **79**:156
"The Danger of Writing Defiant Verse" (Parker) **143**:325
Dangerous Ages (Macaulay) **7**:425, 428-29; **44**:118, 120, 125, 132
"Dangerous Connections" (Zoshchenko) **15**:505
Dangerous Days (Rinehart) **52**:282, 288, 294-96
"Dangerous Dreams" (Södergran) **31**:284
Dangerous Game (Villaurrutia) **80**:458
"The Dangerous Guard" (Kuzmin) **40**:195
"A Dangerous Little Play" (Zoshchenko) **19**:499
The Dangerous Precaution (Kuzmin)
See *Opasnaia predostorozhnost'*
"Dangerous Walk" (Hagiwara) **60**:296
"Die Dänin" (Benn) **3**:107
Danish Weather (Hansen)
See *Dansk vejr*
Dan'l Druce, Blacksmith (Gilbert) **3**:207-08
"Dann" (Lasker-Schueler) **57**:302
"The Dan-nan-Ron" (Sharp) **39**:355, 357, 362, 373, 395
"Danny" (Jewett) **22**:116
"Danny Deever" (Kipling) **8**:188, 190-91, 201; **17**:201
"Danny Deever" (Service) **15**:401
"Danny Murphy" (Stephens) **4**:406
Danny: The Champion of the World (Dahl) **173**:25-27
Danny's Own Story (Marquis) **7**:434-35, 437, 447, 450
Dans la maison (Rolland) **23**:277-78
Dans la prière et dans la lutte (Coppee) **25**:126
"Dans l'Abri-Caverne" (Apollinaire) **51**:36
"Dans le chemin qui s'enfonce" (Alain-Fournier) **6**:28
La Danse de la Mort (Stroheim) **71**:336, 341
La Danse de Sophocle (Cocteau) **119**:59
"Danse d'oignons" (Arp) **115**:41
"La danse du poète-clown" (Roumain) **19**:344
"Danse mabraque" (Fargue) **11**:201
"Danse macabre" (Balmont) **11**:36
"Danse macabre" (Blok) **5**:85
Le danseur mondain (Bourget) **12**:69
Dansk vejr (Hansen) **32**:251
Danskere (Jensen) **41**:296
"A Dante" (Jiménez) **183**:274
"Dante" (Santayana) **40**:390
Dante (Chapman) **7**:187
Dante (Merezhkovsky) **29**:242
Dante als Dichter der Irdischen Welt (Auerbach) **43**:47, 62, 72
"Dante and the Anglo-Saxon Visionaries" (Borges) **109**:154
"Dante . . . Bruno. Vico . . . Joyce" (Beckett) **145**:78, 84-85, 110-11
"Dante in the Bowery" (Roosevelt) **69**:188, 255-56
Dante, Poet of the Secular World (Auerbach)
See *Dante als Dichter der Irdischen Welt*
"Dante Street" (Babel) **13**:26, 34
Dante vivo (Papini) **22**:281-82, 289
Danton (Belloc) **7**:31, 39-40; **18**:19, 28
Danton (Rolland) **23**:257-58, 260
Danton's Death (Tolstoy) **18**:382
"Danza de la muerte" (García Lorca) **197**:183, 200, 205, 227-28, 242, 247, 254, 258, 273, 276-77
"Daphne" (Millay) **4**:306; **169**:281
Daphne Adeane (Baring) **8**:35-6, 38-40, 42
Daphne Laureola (Bridie) **3**:132-33, 141-42
Daphne; or, Marriage à la Mode (Ward) **55**:420
"The Dappled Fawn" (March) **96**:241, 254
D'après Dürer (Yourcenar) **193**:270-71, 279
D'après Greco (Yourcenar) **193**:279
D'après Rembrandt (Yourcenar) **193**:302
Dar (Nabokov) **108**:52, 54-56, 83, 85, 93, 104, 110, 115, 118, 121, 124-26, 133-34, 141, 146, 174, 179, 195, 200, 216, 223, 226; **189**:71, 147
Dar mudrykh pchol (Sologub) **9**:439-40, 434, 436
The D'Arblay Mystery (Freeman) **21**:50, 52, 57
Darby and Joan (Baring) **8**:34, 37, 43
"Dare to be Wise" (McTaggart) **105**:197
Dare-Dare (Himes)
See *Run Man Run*
"Dare's Gift" (Glasgow) **7**:342
Dariel (Blackmore) **27**:29-30, 33, 37, 40, 44-5
"The Daring Young Man on the Flying Trapeze" (Saroyan) **137**:155-57, 168, 170, 178, 191-92, 194
The Daring Young Man on the Flying Trapeze, and Other Stories (Saroyan) **137**:143-44, 168-69, 185-86, 188-89, 191, 194
"The Dark" (Roberts) **68**:336
"The Dark Age" (Baker) **10**:26
"The Dark Angel" (Johnson) **19**:242, 244, 246-47, 253, 255
Dark As the Grave Wherein My Friend Is Laid (Lowry) **6**:214-42, 245, 251, 254
Dark Avenues, and Other Stories (Bunin)
See *Tyomnyye allei*
"Dark Band" (Levi)
See "Schiera bruna"
"Dark Blood" (Walker) **129**:298
The Dark Brain of Piranesi and Other Essays (Yourcenar) **193**:280
Dark Bridwell (Fisher) **140**:151-52, 171, 173, 175, 177, 179
The Dark Cloud (Boyd) **111**:200
Dark Encounter (Riggs) **56**:210
The Dark Face (Rozanov)
See *Temnyi lik*
The Dark Flower (Galsworthy) **1**:300; **45**:47-8, 67-70
"The Dark Forest" (Thomas) **10**:455
The Dark Forest (Walpole) **5**:496, 499, 502-03
"Dark Girl's Rhyme" (Parker) **143**:317
"Dark Heritage" (Kuttner) **10**:268
"The Dark Hills" (Robinson) **101**:192
Dark Hollow (Green) **63**:137-38
The Dark Hours (Marquis) **7**:437, 446-47, 451-52
"Dark in the Forest, Strange as Time" (Wolfe) **61**:315
"The Dark Lady of the Sonnets" (Baker) **10**:17, 22
The Dark Lady of the Sonnets (Shaw) **45**:256
Dark Laughter (Anderson) **1**:38-9, 41, 44, 48-9, 51, 53, 55, 57-8, 61-2; **10**:37-9, 41-5; **24**:44; **123**:3, 5-6, 47-8, 53, 57, 87
"A Dark Month" (Swinburne) **36**:342
"Dark Night" (Remizov)
See "Noch'temnaia"
The Dark Night (Sinclair) **11**:410, 420
A Dark Night's Passing (Shiga)
See *Anya Kōro*
Dark of the Moon (Teasdale) **4**:426-31
"The Dark One" (Leino) **24**:376-78
"Dark Ones" (Dickey) **151**:149
"The Dark Ones" (Lagerkvist)
See "Det mörka folket"
"Dark Rapture" (Baker) **10**:17
The Dark River (Hall and Nordhoff) **23**:62
"The Dark Room" (Quiroga)
See "La cámara oscura"
Dark Soil (Stringer) **37**:331, 343
The Dark Tower (Woollcott) **5**:522, 528-29
The Dark Wing (Stringer) **37**:337
"Dark Words" (Bachmann) **192**:54
"Dark World" (Kuttner) **10**:269
The Dark-Blue Star (Gumilev)
See *K sinei zvezde*
"The Darkling Thrush" (Hardy) **10**:234; **48**:60; **53**:98; **143**:157, 199
"Darkness" (Andrić) **135**:78
"Darkness" (Cobb) **77**:136, 138
"The Darkness" (Johnson) **19**:246
Darkness and Dawn (Tolstoy) **18**:360-61
Darkness and Day (Compton-Burnett) **180**:130, 132, 144, 146
"Darkness and Nathaniel" (Powys) **9**:366, 371
Darkness and the Deep (Fisher) **140**:155, 185
Darkness and the Light (Stapledon) **22**:316, 318, 322, 332-33, 337
"The Darling" (Chekhov) **3**:155, 165
The Darling of the Gods (Belasco) **3**:86-7, 90
Darwin (Bradford) **36**:55-6, 64
"Darwin among the Machines" (Butler) **33**:35, 49, 65
Darwin on the Origin of Species (Butler) **33**:49
"Darwin Superseded" (Dunsany) **59**:28
"Das" (Kandinsky) **92**:68
"Das ist der Ast in deinem Holz" (Morgenstern) **8**:305
Das ist unser Manifest (Borchert) **5**:106, 109-10
"A Dashing Fellow" (Nabokov) **108**:119
Dassai shooku haiwa (Masaoka) **18**:225, 234
"Dast-i bar qaza" (Hedāyat) **21**:75
Daugava (Rainis) **29**:392
"Daughter" (Dickey) **151**:175
"Daughter of Albion" (Chekhov) **3**:145
A Daughter of Astrea (Oppenheim) **45**:132
"The Daughter of Demeter" (Stringer) **37**:332
"A Daughter of Eve" (Harris) **24**:264
Daughter of Fu Manchu (Rohmer) **28**:280, 286, 294, 298, 300
"Daughter of Hades" (Meredith) **17**:256
The Daughter of Heaven (Loti) **11**:357
"The Daughter of Huang Chow" (Rohmer) **28**:282, 286
"A Daughter of Israel" (Bialik) **25**:50
The Daughter of Jorio (D'Annunzio)
See *La figlia di Iorio*
A Daughter of Marionis (Oppenheim) **45**:132
"The Daughter of Reb Avrom Leib" (Cahan) **71**:12, 29, 66
A Daughter of the Congo (Micheaux) **76**:247, 255
"The Daughter of the Forest" (Gibran)
See "Amām 'arsh al-jamāl"
"Daughter of the Frontier" (Fisher) **87**:101
A Daughter of the Land (Stratton-Porter) **21**:265, 267, 276

A Daughter of the Middle Border (Garland) **3**:193
A Daughter of the Morning (Gale) **7**:283, 287
Daughter of the Revolution, and Other Stories (Reed) **9**:383
A Daughter of the Snows (London) **9**:257, 262-64, 276, 281; **39**:285-86
The Daughter of the Vine (Atherton) **2**:15
The Daughter of Time (Tey) **14**:449-57, 460-63
A Daughter of Today (Duncan) **60**:207, 226, 228, 230
Daughters and Sons (Compton-Burnett) **180**:114, 122, 124, 129, 131, 134, 140, 146, 158, 161-64, 199
The Daughters of Babylon (Hichens) **64**:131
Daughters of Dawn (Carman) **7**:139
Daughters of Eve (Bradford) **36**:57
"The Daughters of the Late Colonel" (Mansfield) **2**:451, 456, 458; **8**:280, 282-83, 285; **39**:303, 305, 309-10, 318, 320-23; **164**:237-38, 323
"The Daughters of the Moon" (Calvino)
See "Le figlie della luna"
"The Daughters of the Vicar" (Lawrence) **2**:354; **33**:188
"Daughters of War" (Rosenberg) **12**:287-88, 291-93, 297, 299-301, 303, 310
"Däumerle und Bäumerle or The Future" (Herzl) **36**:142
"The Daunt Diana" (Wharton) **129**:362
"Dauntaun" (Hayashi) **27**:104, 106
"Davanti San Guido" (Carducci) **32**:95, 102, 107-08, 111
"Davanti una cattedrale" (Carducci) **32**:112
Dave (Gregory) **1**:333; **176**:34, 38
"Dave's Neckliss" (Chesnutt) **39**:98
"David" (MacDonald) **9**:304
"David and Jonathan" (Lasker-Schueler)
See "David und Jonathan"
"David B. Hill" (Phillips) **44**:277
"'David Copperfield'" (Woolf) **43**:404
David Elginbrod (MacDonald) **9**:291, 308-09; **113**:200, 213, 242, 282
"David Gaunt" (Davis) **6**:151-53
David Gray and Other Essays (Buchanan) **107**:52, 64
David Levinsky (Cahan)
See *The Rise of David Levinsky*
"David Sings before Saul" (Rilke)
See "David singt vor Saul"
"David singt vor Saul" (Rilke) **195**:228, 230
"David Strauss, the Confessor and Writer" (Nietzsche) **10**:354
"David, the Hunchback" (Hedâyat)
See "Davud-i kuzh-pusht"
David und Goliath (Kaiser) **9**:181
"David und Jonathan" (Lasker-Schueler) **57**:329, 336
"Davud-i kuzh-pusht" (Hedâyat) **21**:71
Davy Crockett (Rourke) **12**:316, 321, 323, 328-29, 331
"Dawn" (Baker) **10**:26
"Dawn" (Brooke) **2**:59
"Dawn" (García Lorca)
See "La aurora"
"Dawn" (Hagiwara) **60**:296
"Dawn" (Pasternak) **188**:190-91
"Dawn" (Pickthall) **21**:243, 252
"The Dawn" (Södergran)
See "Gryningen"
"Dawn" (Unamuno) **2**:568
"The Dawn" (Yeats) **93**:350-52
Dawn (Dreiser) **10**:174, 191, 198, 201; **18**:58; **83**:9
Dawn (Haggard) **11**:237-38, 243-44, 253
Dawn (Heijermans) **24**:293
The Dawn (Verhaeren)
See *Les aubes*
"Dawn Adventure" (Lowell) **8**:226
"Dawn after the Dance" (Hardy) **10**:232
Dawn & Decline (Horkheimer)
See *Dämmerung*
"Dawn behind Night" (Rosenberg) **12**:310
"Dawn Elegy" (Radnóti) **16**:418
The Dawn in Britain (Doughty) **27**:52-3, 58, 60-1, 63, 66-7, 69, 73-4, 84
Dawn in Lyonesse (Chase) **124**:14
"Dawn in New York" (García Lorca) **197**:185, 207, 263-64, 267
"The Dawn of Darkness" (Baker) **10**:26
The Dawn of Day (Nietzsche)
See *Die Morgenröt: Gedanken über die moralische vorurteile*
"The Dawn of Freedom" (Bell) **43**:88, 91
The Dawn of Manchukuo and Mongolia (Mizoguchi) **72**:322
"Dawn over Illion" (Aurobindo) **63**:7
"Dawn Parley" (Moody) **105**:237, 252
"Dawning" (Jiménez) **183**:341
Dawn's Left Hand (Richardson) **3**:357-58
The Dawson Pedigree (Sayers)
See *The Unnatural Death*
"Day" (Baker) **10**:26
"A Day" (Heidenstam) **5**:249
"The Day after Christmas" (Andrić)
See "Na drugi dan Božića"
"Day and night" (Arp) **115**:24
"Day and Night" (Muir) **87**:169, 297
Day and Night Stories (Blackwood) **5**:77
"The Day before the Last Day" (Muir) **2**:489; **87**:175
The Day Before Yesterday (Middleton) **56**:192, 195
"The Day Boy and the Night Girl" (MacDonald) **113**:264-70
"The Day Cools" (Södergran)
See "Dagen svalnar"
"A Day Goes By" (Pirandello) **4**:349-50
"A Day in Harmenze" (Borowski) **9**:21-2, 26
"A Day in Rome" (Andrić)
See "Dan u Rimu"
"A Day in the Dark" (Bowen) **148**:123
"A Day in the Jungle" (Jackson) **187**:248
"A Day in the Life of a Writer" (Slesinger) **10**:442, 445
A Day in the Life of Tsar Peter (Tolstoy) **18**:378
"The Day of Accusation" (Kolmar) **40**:177
"The Day of Atonement" (Korolenko) **22**:173
Day of Deliverance (Benét) **28**:12
The Day of Glory (Fisher) **87**:72
"The Day of Judgment" (Evans) **85**:27
The Day of Judgment (Dagerman) **17**:96
The Day of the Battle (Tolstoy) **18**:382
Day of the Fight (Kubrick) **112**:134-35, 262
"The Day of the Funeral" (Wharton) **129**:364
The Day of the Locust (West) **1**:478-79, 481-84, 486-92; **14**:469-70, 473-77, 479, 481-82, 485-87, 490-94; **44**:367-69, 373, 378, 389, 396, 412
"Day of the Most Holy Virgin" (Kuzmin) **40**:189
Day of the Proletariat (Toller)
See *Tag des Proletariats*
"The Day of the Rabblement" (Joyce) **52**:234
The Day of the Swallows (Trambley) **163**:292, 294-98, 303, 307-8, 310-11, 334-36, 346-47, 361, 364, 375, 377
"The Day of Victory" (Gurney) **33**:85
"A Day on the Big Branch" (Nemerov) **124**:155, 172, 185, 213, 220, 287
"Day That I Have Loved" (Brooke) **2**:58
"The Day the Dancers Came" (Santos) **156**:307-8
The Day the Dancers Came (Santos) **156**:296
"The Day the Mountains Move" (Yosano)
See "Yama no ugoku hi"
The Day the World Ended (Rohmer) **28**:282, 295
"Day to the Night" (Meynell) **6**:291
The Day Will Come (Braddon) **111**:227
"A Day with Conrad Green" (Lardner) **14**:307, 314
"A Day With Governor Arthur" (Warung) **45**:418
"Daybreak" (Dickey) **151**:175
"Daybreak" (Guiney) **41**:213
"Daybreak" (Jiménez) **183**:338-39
Daybreak (Schnitzler)
See *Spiel im Morgengrauen*
"Daydream" (Walker)
See "I Want to Write"
"Day-Dream in Macedon" (Wakefield) **120**:336, 344, 348
Dayland (Bjoernson)
See *Daglannet*
"The Daylight Is Dying" (Paterson) **32**:370
"Daylight Savings" (Parker) **143**:323
"The Day-Night Lamp" (Morgenstern) **8**:305
"Days" (Hippius) **9**:159
"The Days" (Muir) **87**:172
Days and Nights (Symons) **11**:426-28, 431, 445, 451
Days and Nights: Journal of a Deserter (Jarry)
See *Les jours et les nuits: Roman d'un déserter*
"The Days and Nights of China" (Chang)
See "Zhongguo de riye"
"Days and Years" (Davies) **5**:209
"Day's Ending" (Teasdale) **4**:426
Days in the Sun (Nexø)
See *Soldage*
"Days in White" (Bachmann) **192**:65
"The Days like Smitten Cymbals" (Lowry) **6**:238
"Days of 1896" (Cavafy) **7**:152
"Days of 1935" (Merrill) **173**:180, 209, 211, 234
"Days of 1941 and '44" (Merrill) **173**:230
"Days of 1964" (Merrill) **173**:215, 218, 221, 228
"The Days of Autumn" (Södergran)
See "Höstens dagar"
The Days of H. L. Mencken (Mencken) **13**:385
Days of Life and Death and Escape to the Moon (Saroyan) **137**:181
"Days of Piety" (Radnóti) **16**:418
The Days of the Commune (Brecht) **1**:104
Days of the Consuls (Andrić)
See *Travnička hronika*
"Days of the Dog Star" (D'Annunzio)
See "Solleone"
Days of the Turbins (Bulgakov)
See *Dni Turbinykh*
The Days of the Turbins (Bulgakov)
See *Dni Turbinykh*
The Day's Play (Milne) **6**:315; **88**:249
"A Day's Pleasure" (Garland) **3**:199
Day's Sonnets (Reyes)
See *Jornada en sonetos*
Days to Come (Hellman) **119**:164, 166-67, 170-71, 175-77, 179
Days with Walt Whitman (Carpenter) **88**:72
Days without End (O'Neill) **1**:387-88, 392, 396; **6**:332, 335-36
"A Day's Work" (Capote) **164**:142, 144
"Dayspring Mishandled" (Kipling) **8**:196, 209; **17**:211
"Dazzle" (Capote) **164**:200
"D.C." (Millay) **4**:308
Los de abajo (Azuela)
See *Los de Abajo: Novela de la revolucion mexicana*
Los de Abajo: Novela de la revolucion mexicana (Azuela) **3**:75-76, 78-82; **145**:3-6, 10-11, 14, 16-18, 21-22, 24-25, 27, 34-39, 41-42, 44-46, 48, 52-59, 61-66, 68-72
Un de baumugnes (Giono) **124**:32-5, 42-3, 46, 53, 91, 99-101, 126-27
La de Bringas (Pérez Galdós) **27**:250, 261-63, 276, 280, 282-83
"De la cité socialiste" (Péguy) **10**:413
"De la grippe" (Péguy) **10**:414
"La de la mil" (Vallejo) **3**:530, 532
"De la traduction" (Larbaud) **9**:204

"De l'érotisme considéré dans ses manifestations écrites et de point de vue de l'esprit moderne" (Desnos) **22**:57, 69
La de los tristes destinos (Pérez Galdós) **27**:276, 282
"De modo que Cervantes era manco" (Arenas) **191**:195
"De profundis" (Gurney) **33**:85
"De profundis" (Johnson) **19**:244
"De profundis" (Merezhkovsky) **29**:248
De profundis (Wilde) **1**:494, 499, 502, 509; **8**:491, 494, 498, 503; **23**:443-44; **41**:358, 361, 374, 376, 396-97
"De puro calor . . ." (Vallejo) **56**:311
De quelques avantages de l'ecrivains conservateur (Benda) **60**:74
Deacon Brodie: The Double Life (Henley) **8**:102, 107-08
"The Dead" (Brooke) **2**:56; **7**:123, 125, 129-30
"Dead" (Johnson) **19**:244, 246, 254
"The Dead" (Joyce) **3**:274; **8**:158, 165-67, 169-71; **16**:218, 232, 245; **35**:144, 151, 154, 156, 159, 161-62, 164-65, 167-69, 171, 183-84, 189, 191-92, 196-97; **52**:242, 248; **159**:268, 276-77, 285, 301, 306, 308, 312-16, 358-59
"The Dead and the Living One" (Hardy) **53**:100
"The Dead Beat" (Grove) **4**:141
"Dead Center" (Sarton) **120**:246
"The Dead Christ" (Howe) **21**:108
The Dead City (D'Annunzio)
See *La città morta*
The Dead Day (Barlach)
See *Der Tote Tag*
"A Dead Dog" (Anderson) **24**:43
"The Dead End" (Hedāyat)
See "Bun bast"
"Dead Faun" (Carman) **7**:138, 149
"The Dead Forest" (Kraus)
See "Der Tote Wald"
The Dead Girls (Ibarguengoitia)
See *Las muertas*
"A Dead Harvest" (Meynell) **6**:299
"The Dead Heroes" (Rosenberg) **12**:288
"The Dead in Melanesia" (Jarrell) **177**:127, 195
"The Dead Kings" (Ledwidge) **23**:123
"A Dead Letter" (Dobson) **79**:26
Dead Letters (Baring) **8**:32, 37, 41, 44
"The Dead Man" (Borges)
See "El muerto"
"The Dead Man" (Quiroga)
See "El hombre muerto"
"The Dead Man at Grandview Point" (Abbey) **160**:24-25, 96
"Dead Man's Dump" (Rosenberg) **12**:288, 291, 293-95, 299, 301, 303-04, 308, 310-12
Dead Man's Rock (Quiller-Couch) **53**:289
"Dead Men" (Douglas) **40**:70, 73, 76, 78, 80, 90
Dead Men (Sánchez)
See *Los muertos*
"Dead Nocturne" (Villaurrutia) **80**:483
"The Dead of the Wilderness" (Bialik) **25**:50, 52, 58, 66
"Dead Pals" (Patton) **79**:301
"The Dead Past" (Rosenberg) **12**:310
"The Dead Patriot" (Tynan) **3**:503
"Dead Roses" (White) **176**:193, 228-29
"The Dead Season" (Schulz)
See "Martwy sezon"
"The Dead Smile" (Crawford) **10**:149, 153, 157-59
"The Dead Spring" (Tynan) **3**:503
"The Dead Torero" (Campbell) **5**:120
"The Dead Traveler" (Papadiamantis) **29**:272
"The Dead II" (Brooke) **2**:61
"The Dead Village" (Robinson) **101**:197
"Dead Water" (Wen I-to) **28**:412-15, 417, 419-20
"The Dead Wingman" (Jarrell) **177**:193, 223-24, 227
"The Dead with Overcoats" (Drummond de Andrade) **139**:239
The Dead Woman in the House (Kuzmin) **40**:197
"Dead Yellow Women" (Hammett) **187**:79
Dead Yesterdays (Ginzburg)
See *Tutti i nostri ieri*
"The Dead-Beat" (Owen) **5**:369-71; **27**:206, 208, 212, 214, 217-18, 224, 229, 236
"Deadbeat Blues" (Wright) **136**:261
The Deadlined (Canetti)
See *Die Befristeten*
"Deadlock" (Kuttner) **10**:268
Deadlock (Richardson) **3**:356-57
"The Deadly Nightshade" (Balmont) **11**:41
"Deadsunday" (van Ostaijen) **33**:421
The Deaf (Bergelson) **81**:15
Deaf Ballads (Reyes)
See *Romances sordos*
"The Deaf One" (Bergelson)
See "Der Toyber"
"The Deaf Satyr" (Darío) **4**:60, 67-8
"A Deal in Cotton" (Kipling) **17**:209
Dealings with the Fairies (MacDonald) **9**:291, 304; **113**:210, 301
"Dear" (Yokomitsu)
See "Ommi"
"Dear Annie" (Freeman) **9**:74
Dear Antoine (Anouilh)
See *Cher Antoine*
Dear Brutus (Barrie) **2**:40-4, 46, 48; **164**:8
"The Dear Departed" (Saltus) **8**:346
Dear Departed (Yourcenar) **193**:320
"Dear Friends" (Robinson) **101**:142, 148, 150, 153-58, 160, 162
"Dear Friends and Gentle Hearts" (Cullen) **4**:44; **37**:166
"Dear Friends and Gentle Hearts" (Woollcott) **5**:529
Dear Michael (Ginzburg)
See *Caro Michele*
"Dear Noel Coward" (Bodenheim) **44**:74
"The Dear Page" (Sologub) **9**:436
"Dearest" (Holly) **65**:138, 149-50
Dearest Father (Kafka) **6**:223
"The Dearness of Common Things" (Gurney) **33**:99
"Death" (Aleixandre)
See "Muerte"
"Death" (Anderson) **1**:59, 65; **10**:55-56; **24**:28, 30, 34-35, 43; **123**:13, 15, 37-38, 40, 73
"Death" (Bodenheim) **44**:59, 74
"Death" (Calvino) **183**:228
"Death" (García Lorca) **197**:186, 209
"Death" (Gumilev)
See "Smert'"
"A Death" (Johnson) **19**:246
"Death" (Nabokov) **108**:52
"Death" (Nezval) **44**:238
"Death" (Svevo)
See "La morte"
"Death" (Wen I-to) **28**:409, 416
"Death" (Yeats) **31**:397
"Death and Life" (Naidu) **80**:287
"Death and Memory" (Manning) **25**:277
"Death and Nature" (Manning) **25**:277
Death and Taxes (Parker) **143**:324-26
"Death and the Child" (Crane) **11**:124-25, 127-28, 158, 160, 167
"Death and the Compass" (Borges)
See "La muerte y la brújula"
Death and the Fool (Hofmannsthal)
See *Der Tor und der Tod*
"Death at Bearwallow" (Roberts) **68**:348-51
"Death by Advertisement" (Sologub) **9**:446
"Death Cell" (Bosman) **49**:32
Death Comes for the Archbishop (Cather) **1**:154, 156-59, 161-63, 165; **11**:95-9, 107; **31**:27, 49, 54, 67; **99**:165-290; **132**:123, 125, 127, 129-31, 135-38, 141, 149, 154; **152**:8, 16, 21, 87
"Death Comes for the Yaya" (Engel) **137**:118
"Death Drag" (Faulkner) **141**:134
"Death Feast" (Khlebnikov) **20**:135
Death Has Yellow Eyes (Dent) **72**:24, 38
Death in Monte Carlo (Bromfield) **11**:83
Death in Silver (Dent) **72**:21, 23
"Death in Sinan Monastery" (Andrić)
See "Smrt u sinanovoj tekiji"
"Death in Sinan's Tekke" (Andrić)
See "Smrt u sinanovoj tekiji"
Death in the Afternoon (Hemingway) **115**:149, 163-64, 189, 194
"A Death in the Country" (Benét) **7**:82, 85
"Death in the Desert" (Agee) **1**:16
"A Death in the Desert" (Cather) **11**:92, 101; **99**:281
A Death in the Family (Agee) **1**:1, 3-10, 12-16, 18; **19**:24, 26, 28-9, 31-2, 37, 40-1, 45, 48; **180**:22-24, 27, 46-48, 52, 54-55, 57-58, 60-61, 63-65, 67, 70-71, 76-80
"A Death in the Forest" (Anderson) **123**:22-3
"Death in the Woods" (Anderson) **1**:44, 46, 54; **10**:37, 44-7, 52-3; **24**:43; **123**:18-23, 85
Death in Venice (Mann)
See *Der Tod in Venedig: Novelle*
Death into Life (Stapledon) **22**:323, 332, 337-38
Death Is a Round Black Spot (Dent) **72**:27, 38
Death Mask and Clover (Storni)
See *Mascarilla y trébol*
"Death May Be Very Gentle" (Gogarty) **15**:110
"Death of a Boy" (Rilke) **19**:308
"Death of a Bumblebee" (Wakefield) **120**:336, 344, 352
"The Death of a Dandy" (Bishop) **103**:26
"Death of a Freedom Fighter" (Borowski) **9**:21
"Death of a Frog" (Hagiwara)
See "Kaeru no shi"
"Death of a Martyr" (Akutagawa Ryūnosuke)
See "Hōkyōnin no shi"
"Death of a Poacher" (Wakefield) **120**:344, 349, 356, 358
"Death of a Psychiatrist" (Sarton) **120**:266
Death of a Scribbler (Nagai)
See *Gesakusha no shi*
"The Death of a Soldier" (Stevens) **12**:363, 367, 373
Death of a Train (Crofts) **55**:88
The Death of Agamemnon (Hauptmann) **4**:208
The Death of Agrippina (Symons) **11**:433
The Death of Ahasuerus (Lagerkvist)
See *Ahasverus död*
"The Death of Ailill" (Ledwidge) **23**:113
"The Death of Akoose" (Scott) **6**:387
"Death of an Alcoholic" (Hagiwara) **60**:292, 296
"The Death of Ankou" (Lewis) **104**:177, 284-90
"Death of Antoñito the Camborio" (García Lorca)
See "Muerte de Antoñito el Camborio"
"Death of Apollinaire" (Villa) **176**:96
"The Death of April" (Fisher) **140**:179
"Death of Archimedes" (Čapek) **192**:189
"Death of Autumn" (Millay) **49**:225
"The Death of Baron Gandara" (Čapek)
See "Smrt barona Gandary"
"The Death of Bill Graves" (Anderson) **24**:43
"The Death of Captain Waskow" (Pyle) **75**:266, 269-70, 272-73
"The Death of Children" (Saroyan) **137**:186
The Death of Cuchulain (Yeats) **1**:571; **11**:512; **116**:332
The Death of Digenis (Sikelianos) **39**:419
The Death of Doctor Faust (Ghelderode)
See *La mort du Docteur Faust*
"The Death of Dolgushov" (Babel) **2**:27
"The Death of Dolgusov" (Babel)
See "Smert' Dolgusova"
The Death of Eve (Moody) **105**:234, 238-43, 245-46, 253, 256, 260, 269, 273, 277-80, 284-85
The Death of Felicity Taverner (Butts) **77**:76-7, 83, 100, 103-8
The Death of George (Beer-Hofmann)
See *Der Tod Georgs*
"The Death of God" (Nemerov) **124**:256

The Death of Good Fortune (Williams) **1**:517; **11**:498
"The Death of Halpin Frayser" (Bierce) **7**:89, 94; **44**:6, 8, 13, 16, 33, 44-5, 49
"The Death of Halpin Frayser" (Lovecraft) **4**:267
"The Death of Hanrahan" (Yeats) **31**:419
"Death of Immortality" (Babits)
See "A halhatatlanság halála"
"The Death of Isolde" (Quiroga)
See "La muerte de Isolda"
The Death of Ivan Ilych (Tolstoy)
See *Smert Ivana Ilyicha*
"The Death of Leag, Cuchulain's Charioteer" (Ledwidge) **23**:117
"The Death of Li Po" (Wen I-to) **28**:409, 415-16
"The Death of Lincoln" (Bell) **43**:91
The Death of Marlowe (Symons) **11**:438
"The Death of Me" (Malamud) **184**:163, 237, 240-41
The Death of Mr. Baltisberger (Hrabal)
See *Automat svet*
"The Death of My Father" (Svevo) **2**:545
"The death of my mother and my new mother" (Shiga)
See "Haha no shi to atarishi haha"
"The Death of My Mother and the Memory of Socks" (Shiga)
See "Haha no shi to tabi no kioku"
"The Death of Nationalism" (O'Faolain) **143**:233
"The Death of Pan" (Dunsany) **59**:10
"The Death of Procris" (Field) **43**:166-67
"The Death of Puck" (Lee-Hamilton) **22**:191
"Death of Schillenger" (Borowski) **9**:22
The Death of Simon Fuge (Bennett) **5**:38, 42, 47, 49; **197**:29, 40, 94, 102-03, 109, 172, 177
"The Death of Smet-Smet" (Brooke) **2**:59
"The Death of the Author" (Barthes)
See "La mort de l'auteur"
"The Death of the Ball Turret Gunner" (Jarrell) **177**:126, 131, 134, 136, 176, 194, 196, 205, 243-48
"The Death of the Canary" (Quiroga)
See "La muerte del canario"
"The Death of the Communists" (Chambers) **129**:47
"The Death of the Duchess Isabella" (Lee-Hamilton) **22**:188
"The Death of the Empress of China" (Darío)
See "La muerte de la emperatriz de China"
The Death of the Father (Martin du Gard) **24**:388
The Death of the Gods (Merezhkovsky)
See *Julian the Apostate*
The Death of the Heart (Bowen) **148**:11, 17-18, 24, 29-30, 36-37, 46-48, 53-54, 82, 85, 88-90, 96, 98, 104-5
The Death of the King's Canary (Thomas) **8**:462; **105**:352
"The Death of the Lion" (Herbert) **168**:45
"Death of the Lovers" (Heym) **9**:145
"The Death of the Moth" (Woolf) **128**:320
The Death of the Moth, and Other Essays (Woolf) **12**:507; **43**:386, 388, 392, 413
"The Death of the Musician" (Peretz) **16**:406
"The Death of the Old Sea King" (Harper) **14**:256
"The Death of the Poet" (Rilke) **6**:363
"The Death of the Poet Catullus" (Ady) **11**:15
"The Death of the Slave Lewis" (Howe) **21**:107, 112
The Death of the Swan (Gonzalez Martinez)
See *La muerte de cisne*
The Death of Tintagiles (Maeterlinck)
See *La mort de Tintagiles*
The Death of Titian (Hofmannsthal)
See *Der Tod des Tizian*
The Death of Virgil (Broch)
See *Der Tod des Vergil*
"Death or the Waiting Room" (Aleixandre) **113**:41
"The Death Ring of Sneferu" (Rohmer) **28**:277, 286
"Death Shall Have No Dominion" (Thomas)
See "And Death Shall Have No Dominion"
"Death the Proud Brother" (Wolfe) **4**:526, 527; **13**:492, 494
Death to the French (Forester)
See *Rifleman Dodd*
"Death to the Poor" (Cullen) **37**:166
"Death to Van Gogh's Ear!" (Ginsberg) **120**:48, 77-8
"Death Will Arrive" (Bachmann)
See "Der Tod wird kommen"
Death Women (Bernhard)
See *Die Totenweiber*
"The Death-Child" (Sharp) **39**:389
"Deaths" (Pilnyak)
See "Smerti"
"Deaths and Entrances" (Thomas) **1**:473; **8**:458; **45**:403-04, 406
Deaths and Entrances (Thomas) **105**:306, 359
Death's Carter (Lagerloef) **36**:242
"Death's Dainty Ways" (Bradford) **36**:63
"Death's Guerdon" (Reese) **181**:347
Death's Mistake (Khlebnikov)
See *Oshibka smerti*
Death's Victory (Ishikawa) **15**:124
The Death-Trap (Saki) **3**:376
Deathwatch (Genet)
See *Haute surveillance*
La débâcle (Zola) **1**:563, 567, 587, 592, 595, 597; **21**:426; **41**:414-15, 422, 439
Les débâcles (Verhaeren) **12**:460, 462-63, 465, 469-70, 473
"Debate with the Rabbi" (Nemerov) **124**:153, 184, 298-99
The Debauched Hospodar (Apollinaire)
See *Les onze mille verges*
Debbie Go Home (Paton) **165**:295, 298
Dēbdās (Chatterji) **13**:80
"Debet och Kredit" (Strindberg) **21**:353
Debit and Credit (Strindberg)
See "Debet och Kredit"
Debits and Credits (Kipling) **8**:195
Deborah (Abercrombie) **141**:3-4, 10, 12-13
"Deborah and Deirdre as Drunk Bridesmaids Foot-Racing at Daybreak" (Dickey) **151**:152
"Deborah as Scion" (Dickey) **151**:152
"Deborah in Ancient Lingerie, in Thin Oak over Creek" (Dickey) **151**:152
"Debris of Life and Mind" (Stevens) **3**:470; **45**:350
"Debt" (Oppen) **107**:269
"The Debt" (Wharton) **129**:362
"The Debtor" (Muir) **2**:485
The Debtor (Freeman) **9**:73
"A Debussy Serenade" (Percy) **84**:198
Decadence, and Other Essays on the Culture of Ideas (Gourmont)
See *La culture des idées*
Decadence and Renewal in the Higher Education (Kirk) **119**:275, 334
The Decadent: Being the Gospel of Inaction (Cram) **45**:4, 12
"The Decadent Movement in Literature" (Symons) **11**:440
"A Decadent's Lyric" (Johnson) **19**:249
"Decálogo del perfecto cuentista" (Quiroga) **20**:216
"Decalogue of the Perfect Short Story Writer" (Quiroga)
See "Decálogo del perfecto cuentista"
"The Decapitated Chicken" (Quiroga)
See "La gallina degollada"
The Decapitated Chicken, and Other Stories (Quiroga) **20**:218, 220-21
"La decapitazione dei Capi" (Calvino) **183**:129
"Decay" (Hecht) **101**:36
The Decay of Capitalist Civilisation (Webb and Webb) **22**:403, 414, 416, 418
"The Decay of Lying" (Wilde) **1**:506; **8**:490, 493, 497, 502-03
The Decay of Lying (Wilde) **175**:317
The Decay of the Angel (Mishima)
See *Tennin Gosui*
"The Deceased" (Douglas) **40**:67
Deceit (Micheaux) **76**:245
"The Deceived" (Mann)
See *Die Betrogene*
"December" (Belloc) **18**:41
"A December Day" (Teasdale) **4**:428
"A December Day in Dixie" (Chopin) **14**:82
"December Eighth" (Dazai Osamu)
See "Jūnigatsu yōka"
"December Night" (Lawrence) **93**:18
December the Fourteenth (Merezhkovsky) **29**:231
The Decembrists (Tolstoy) **18**:382
Decennalia (Carducci) **32**:84, 86
The Deception (Canetti)
See *Die Blendung*
"The Deception of the Thrush" (Engel) **137**:108, 115-16
"Décima muerte" (Villaurrutia) **80**:460, 483-7, 489
"Décimas de nuestro amor" (Villaurrutia) **80**:464, 512
"Décimas of Our Love" (Villaurrutia) **80**:464
"Décimos" (Villaurrutia) **80**:464
"Decivilised" (Meynell) **6**:290
"Declamation and Discussion for Girls" (Anthony) **48**:15
"La Declaration d'amour acceptee" (Jammes) **75**:119
"Declaration for Literature of the Ruins" (Böll)
See "Bekenntnis zur Trümmerliteratur"
The Declaration of Independence: A Study in the History of Political Ideas (Becker) **63**:63-4, 75, 81, 99, 102, 109
"The Decline in the Efficiency of Instruments Essential in Equilibrium" (Innis) **77**:342
"Decline of The English Murder" (Orwell) **51**:249
"The Decline of the Novel" (Rourke) **12**:329
"The Decline of Utopian Ideas in the West" (Berlin) **105**:90
The Declining Years (Dazai Osamu)
See *Bannen*
La Decomposition du Marxisme (Sorel) **91**:332
"Decor" (Bacovia) **24**:70
The Decoration (Nagai)
See *Kunshō*
"Decoration Day" (Higginson) **36**:170
"Decoration Day" (Jewett) **22**:142
The Decoration of Houses (Wharton) **53**:361, 401; **129**:344, 349, 352-53, 60; **149**:232, 236, 245, 255, 258-59, 290
Decorations (Dowson) **4**:84, 90
The Decorative Art of the Indians of the North Pacific Coast (Boas) **56**:81
"The Decoy" (Blackwood) **5**:72
Dedicated (Field) **43**:156, 164
"Dedication" (Agee) **19**:23-4; **180**:64
"Dedication" (Gourmont) **17**:129
"A Dedication" (Merrill) **173**:225
"Dedication" (van Ostaijen) **33**:421-22
"Dedication Day" (Agee) **1**:16; **180**:23
"Dedication, To Ernest Dowson" (Dickey) **151**:213
Dedicatory Ode (Belloc) **7**:33
"The Deed" (Davies) **5**:209
"Deeds, Not Words" (Williams) **89**:375
The Deeds of Alexander the Great (Kuzmin) **40**:191, 194
The Deemster (Caine) **97**:3, 6, 10-11, 13-14, 20-1
"A Deep Experience" (Paton) **165**:305
Deep River (Endo)
See *Fukai kawa*

Deep Rivers (Arguedas)
See *Los ríos profundos*
Deep Sightings and Rescue Missions (Bambara) **116**:14-16
The Deep Sleep (Morris) **107**:97, 105, 111, 113, 119-20, 126, 156, 174, 188, 243
"A Deep Sleeper" (Chesnutt) **39**:95
Deep Song (García Lorca)
See *Poema del cante jondo*
Deep Song, and Other Prose (García Lorca) **7**:302
Deep South: Memory and Observation (Caldwell) **117**:3, 26-7, 34-5
"Deep Stuff" (Williams) **89**:383
"Deep Woods" (Nemerov) **124**:153-54, 312
The Deepening Stream (Fisher) **87**:84
Deephaven (Jewett) **1**:361, 363-64, 367, 369; **22**:116-17, 120-21, 123-26, 132-33, 135-38, 141, 148
"Deephaven Cronies" (Jewett) **22**:116
"Deephaven Excursions" (Jewett) **22**:116
"Deephaven Society" (Jewett) **22**:136
"The Deer Hunt" (Kunikida Doppo)
See "Shikagari"
"Deer in Mooreland" (Benét) **28**:9
"The Deer Lay Down Their Bones" (Abbey) **160**:43
Defeat (Grieg)
See *Nederlaget: Et skuespill om Pariser-komunen*
Defeat (Huch) **13**:242-43
"The Defeat of the City" (Henry) **19**:172, 181
"The Defeated Husband" (Yokomitsu)
See "Maketa Otto"
"A Defence of Common Sense" (Moore) **89**:196-8, 216-7, 244-5
"A Defence of Cosmetics" (Beerbohm)
See "The Pervasion of Rouge"
"The Defence of Democracy" (Murry) **16**:342
"The Defence of Semidvorie" (Platonov) **14**:414
The Defendant (Chesterton) **6**:101
"La defensa de la ilusión" (Lugones) **15**:294
"A Defense" (Bishop) **103**:6
The Defense (Nabokov)
See *Zashchita Luzhina*
La défense de Tartufe (Jacob) **6**:193, 197-99, 202
A Defense of Idealism: Some Questions and Conclusions (Sinclair) **11**:417-18, 420
A Defense of Indian Culture (Aurobindo) **63**:30
"Defense of P. G. Wodehouse" (Orwell) **51**:222
The Defense of Terrorism (Trotsky) **22**:364
The Defense of the Bride and Other Poems (Green) **63**:135
Defiance (Jensen)
See *Trods*
"The Definition of a University" (Frye) **165**:184
"The Definition of the Psychical" (Mead) **89**:166, 168, 171-2
"El definitivo" (Lugones) **15**:293
"Definizioni di territori: il fantastico" (Calvino) **183**:104
"Defoe" (Woolf) **56**:405
Defy the Foul Fiend (Collier) **127**:246-48, 250, 257-58, 260
"Degenerate Nero's Death" (Ady) **11**:15
Degeneration (Huysmans) **7**:407
Degeneration and Regeneration of the Nervous System (Ramoacn y Cajal)
See *Estudios sobre la degeneración del sistema nervioso*
"Degollación de los inocentes" (García Lorca) **49**:93; **181**:27; **197**:236
"Degollación del Bautista" (García Lorca) **49**:92-3; **181**:26-7; **197**:236
Degradation of Academic Dogma (Nisbet) **117**:299, 311, 344, 384, 387-88
The Degradation of the Democratic Dogma (Adams) **4**:8; **80**:13
Le degré zéro de l'écriture (Barthes) **135**:112, 127, 130, 138, 151, 157, 164-65, 184-85
"Degrees of Explanation" (Hayek) **109**:207
"La dehesa española" (Unamuno) **148**:240
"The Dehumanization of Art" (Ortega y Gasset) **9**:336, 339, 344, 348-49
"Gli dèi della città" (Calvino) **183**:103, 107
"The Deified Invalid" (Apollinaire) **51**:49
Deirdre (Baker) **3**:4-5, 12-13, 22
Deirdre (Stephens) **4**:414, 416, 418-21
Deirdre (Yeats) **1**:561; **11**:527
Deirdre of the Sorrows (Gregory) **1**:334
Deirdre of the Sorrows (Synge) **6**:426, 428-31, 434-35, 439; **37**:348, 365, 367, 382-83, 390
Deistvo o Georgii Khrabrom (Remizov) **27**:328-29, 335
"The Deith-Tide" (Sharp) **39**:354
Déjàvu (Osborne) **153**:293-97, 304, 307, 312, 314-15, 325, 333-34
"Dejection" (Douglas) **40**:63, 73
Dejemos hablar al viento (Onetti) **131**:183, 217, 283, 286-88
Dekabr' skaia noch (Nabokov) **108**:142
"Dekorative Kunst" (Hartmann) **73**:141
Del cielo y del infierno (Borges) **109**:8
"Del color de la nada" (Aleixandre) **113**:5
"Del engaño y renuncia" (Aleixandre) **113**:5
Del imperio romano (Ortega y Gasset) **9**:355
Del natural (Gamboa) **36**:75
"Del sánscrito" (Jiménez) **183**:257
"Del sentimento in arte" (Svevo) **35**:362-63
Del sentimento trágico de la vida (Unamuno)
See *Del sentimiento de la vida en los hombres y en los pueblos*
Del sentimiento de la vida en los hombres y en los pueblos (Unamuno) **2**:559-60, 565, 569; **9**:509, 512-15, 520, 522-23
Del sentimiento trágico de la vida (Unamuno) **148**:229, 231, 235, 241, 243, 245-46, 256, 276, 279-80, 282-83, 298-302, 304, 335
Del vivir (Miro) **5**:340, 342
Dela (Popa) **167**:154, 175
"Delayed Hearing" (Nemerov) **124**:232
The Delectable Duchy (Quiller-Couch) **53**:290
"Delectación morosa" (Lugones) **15**:289
Delia Blanchflower (Ward) **55**:420, 437, 441
"The Deliberation of Mr. Dunkin" (Dunbar) **12**:111
"Delicia otoñal" (Lugones) **15**:289
"Delicta carnis" (Nervo) **11**:396
The Delight of Great Books (Erskine) **84**:177
"The Delights of an Incognito" (Guiney) **41**:209
"Delincuente honrado" (Pardo Bazán) **189**:226, 228
Delirium in a Studio (Melies) **81**:122
"Delirium in Vera Cruz" (Lowry) **6**:237
Delitto all'isola delle capre (Betti) **5**:56, 66
"The Deliverance" (Harper) **14**:264
The Deliverance (Chatterji)
See *Niskrti*
Deliverance (Dickey) **151**:98, 105, 107, 110, 112, 118, 121, 126, 133, 137, 140, 149, 152, 154-56, 158-62, 173, 179-80, 184-89, 191-94, 196-97, 199, 202-4, 212, 222
The Deliverance (Glasgow) **2**:175-76, 185-86, 189, 191; **7**:333, 340
The Deliverance (Vazov) **25**:450
"The Deliverer" (Fisher) **87**:73
The Deliverer (Gregory) **1**:332, 334, 337; **176**:12, 34, 37-38
Delo Artmunovykh (Gorky) **8**:75, 77, 80, 87
"Delo korneta Elagina" (Bunin) **6**:59
"Delo smerti" (Pilnyak) **23**:213
"The Delphic Oracle upon Plotinus" (Yeats) **116**:336
The Delphic Union (Sikelianos) **39**:412
"Delta" (Walker) **129**:298, 317, 328-29
"Delta Autumn" (Faulkner) **141**:101, 113, 162-63, 165; **170**:175-76, 205, 210
The Delta Autumn (Percy) **84**:198
The Deluge (Aleichem)
See *Der mabl*
Deluge (Kandinsky) **92**:62
The Deluge (Phillips) **44**:253-54, 262, 274, 276, 283, 286, 290
The Deluge (Sienkiewicz)
See *Potop*
The Delusion (Canetti)
See *Die Blendung*
"Dem Monch" (Lasker-Schueler) **57**:298
"The Demand for Party Recognition" (Anthony) **48**:23
"The Demanding Guest" (Lagerkvist)
See "Den fordringfule gästen"
The Demesne of the Swans (Tsvetaeva)
See *Lebediny stan*
Demian (Hesse) **148**:172; **196**:250, 255, 260-67, 269-70, 274, 277-79, 323, 329-31, 335-36, 338-39
The Demi-Gods (Stephens) **4**:408-11, 415, 417-19, 421
"Demiurge" (Lawrence) **2**:368; **93**:73, 74
"Democracy" (Lawrence) **61**:231
Democracy: An American Novel (Adams) **4**:2, 9-10, 12, 14-18, 20; **52**:40
Democracy and Education: An Introduction to the Philosophy of Education (Dewey) **95**:25-6, 36, 56, 97, 106, 122
"Democracy and Efficiency" (Keynes) **64**:243
Democracy and Social Ethics (Addams) **76**:2, 13, 22, 37, 45, 70-1, 84, 108, 120
"Democracy and the Arts" (Brooke) **7**:127
"Democracy in Crisis" (Laski) **79**:87, 150, 169
"Democracy Is for the Unafraid" (Himes) **139**:325
"Democracy Is Service" (Lawrence) **93**:24
"Democracy's Temple" (Anderson) **144**:34
"The Demoiselle d'Ys" (Chambers) **41**:87-8, 94, 101, 103, 106, 110
"Les demoiselles de Suave" (Gray) **19**:144, 151
Die demoliete Literatur (Kraus) **5**:286
"Demon and Beast" (Yeats) **11**:520; **31**:407
Le demon de l'absurde (Vallette) **67**:270, 272, 276, 299, 315, 319, 321
Le démon de midi (Bourget) **12**:66, 69
"The Demon Lover" (Bowen) **148**:9, 18
The Demon Lover and Other Stories (Bowen) **148**:40, 107
Demon of Absurdity (Vallette)
See *Le demon de l'absurde*
The Demon of Progress in the Arts (Lewis) **2**:390-91
The Demon of the Absurd (Vallette)
See *Le demon de l'absurde*
Demons and Night Visions (Kubin) **23**:95
"Demons in the Stream" (Papadiamantis) **29**:272
Demos: A Story of English Socialism (Gissing) **3**:222, 227-28, 230, 232-33, 237; **24**:215, 220, 224-25, 230-31, 234-35, 243, 248; **47**:103, 141, 143
"Demos and Dionysus" (Robinson) **101**:195
"Demus" (Robinson) **101**:195
"Dengaku tōfu" (Mori Ogai) **14**:379
Denis Dent (Hornung) **59**:113
Het denkende hart van de barak: Brieven van Etty Hillesum (Hillesum) **49**:183
Denry the Audacious (Bennett)
See *The Card*
"La dent" (Vallette) **67**:319, 321
The Dentist (Fields) **80**:234-5
Denton Welch: Extracts from His Published Works (Welch) **22**:445
The Denton Welch Journals (Welch) **22**:442, 444, 446-49, 452-54, 456-60, 462
Les dents du tigre (Leblanc) **49**:195-97
"Denver Doldrum" (Ginsberg) **120**:77
Denys the Dreamer (Tynan) **3**:505
Denzil Quarrier (Gissing) **3**:232; **24**:220, 223, 238-39, 248
"Le depart" (Verhaeren) **12**:461
"Depart from me, I know thee not" (Coleridge) **73**:11
Departing (Bergelson)
See *Departure*
Departmental Ditties (Kipling) **8**:176, 193, 205

"Departure" (Anderson) **1**:152, 60; **24**:28, 34, 36, 40, 43, 54; **123**:40
"Departure" (Dickey) **151**:167
"Departure" (Jiménez) **183**:337, 340
"The Departure" (Lagerkvist)
See "Uppbrottet"
"Departure" (Lawrence) **93**:72, 75, 76
"Departure" (Liliencron) **18**:208
"Departure" (Millay) **4**:308
Departure (Bergelson) **81**:19
Departure (Sá-Carneiro)
See *Partida*
"Departure from England" (Bachmann)
See "Abschied von England"
"The Departure of Dindrane" (Williams) **1**:514
"The Departure of the Shadow" (Apollinaire) **51**:49
"The Dependencies" (Nemerov) **124**:259, 305
Le dépeupleur (Beckett) **145**:80, 82, 92, 95, 97-98
"Depression Before Spring" (Stevens) **45**:309
"The Depths" (Apollinaire)
See "Loin du pigeonnier"
"An der Landstraß im Graben" (Raabe) **45**:189
"Deracinated Encounters" (McAlmon) **97**:100
Les déracinés (Barrès) **47**:37, 44, 60, 63-4, 66, 68-9, 71-3, 79, 95, 97-9
"The Derailed Streetcar" (Gumilev)
See "Zabludivshijsja tramvaj"
Derborence (Ramuz) **33**:297-98, 300-02, 309-11
Derecho constitucional (Hostos) **24**:303
Los derechos de la salud (Sánchez) **37**:311-16, 318
"The Derelict" (Hodgson) **13**:237
"The Derelict" (Tomlinson) **71**:402
The Derelict (Hall and Nordhoff) **23**:65
"Derelict: A Tale of the Wayward Sea" (Stockton) **47**:325, 327
The Derelict Boat (Molnár)
See *Egy gazdátlan csónak története*
The Derelict of Skull Shoal (Dent) **72**:38
Derevnya (Bunin) **6**:43-7, 49-50, 53, 55
"Derev'ya" (Tsvetaeva) **35**:406
"Derido; or, the Giant's Quilt" (Stockton) **47**:331
Dérive à partir de Marx et Freud (Lyotard) **103**:153, 156-57, 197, 227
"Le dernier amour du prince Genghi" (Yourcenar) **193**:289
Le dernier des métiers (Vian) **9**:529, 534
Denier du rêve (Yourcenar) **193**:250-52, 254-55, 265, 270-71, 273, 307-08, 319-20, 322-31, 343, 365
"Dernier malheur dernière chance" (Péret) **20**:197, 202
"Le dernier poème" (Desnos) **22**:63
Dernier refuge (Rod) **52**:310, 312
"La dernière idylle" (Rod) **52**:316
"La dernière nuit" (Schwob) **20**:320
La dernière nuit de Don Juan (Rostand) **37**:305
"La dernière nuit du condamnéà mort" (Péret) **20**:201
"Les derniers jours de Pékin" (Loti) **11**:356
Derniers poèmes en vers en prose (Jacob) **6**:202
Derrière le rideau (Lemonnier) **22**:200
De derrière les fagots (Péret) **20**:196, 200
"Derring-Do" (Capote) **164**:200
Deru tjampur debu (Anwar) **22**:18-19
The Deruga Trial (Huch)
See *Der Fall Deruga*
Dervorgilla (Gregory) **1**:339; **176**:10, 34, 36-37, 40, 61
"Des chansons graves" (Arp) **115**:36
"Des Dispositifs Pulsionnels" (Lyotard) **103**:197, 219, 260
"Des Faux" (Apollinaire) **51**:58
Des fins ultimes (Weininger)
See *Über die letzten Dinge*
"Des Königs Ritt" (Raabe) **45**:188
"Des Menschen Hand" (Raabe) **45**:190
"Des Paysagistes contemporains" (Huysmans) **69**:9
Des Taches dans le Vide (Arp) **115**:28-30, 41, 46
"Des Turms Auferstehung" (Werfel) **8**:478
"Des Wanderes Heimweh in die Welt" (Werfel) **8**:477
El desalojo (Sánchez) **37**:314
Desbandada (Romero) **14**:433-35, 441, 443
"The Desborough Connections" (Harte) **25**:198
"Descartes" (Borges) **109**:5
The Descendant (Glasgow) **2**:189; **7**:332, 339, 342
"Descent into Egypt" (Blackwood) **5**:70, 74
Descent into Hell (Williams) **1**:517-21, 523-25; **11**:487, 494, 496, 499-500, 502
"The Descent of Man" (Wharton) **129**:360
The Descent of Man (Wharton) **3**:555, 571; **129**:345, 360; **149**:248, 255
The Descent of the Dove (Williams) **1**:521; **11**:485, 502
"Description of a Fight" (Kafka) **2**:301; **29**:208; **112**:83, 85-7
"Description of a Notation for the Logic of Relatives" (Peirce) **81**:197
Description of a Struggle (Kafka) **179**:311
"A Description of Himmerland" (Jensen)
See "Himmerlands Beskrivelse"
"A Description of the King" (Herbert) **168**:24
"Description without Place" (Stevens) **12**:360, 372, 377; **45**:303
"Descriptions of a Battle" (Kafka)
See "Description of a Fight"
"Descriptive Voyage from New York to Aspinwall" (Bell) **43**:91
"El descubrimiento de la circunferencia" (Lugones) **15**:293
"Desde dentro" (Jiménez) **183**:259, 290
Desde el principio hasta el fin (Baroja) **8**:63
"Desde el rincón. Una carta" (Unamuno) **148**:306
"Desde la soledad" (Unamuno) **148**:306-7
"A desejada des gentes" (Machado de Assis) **10**:291
Les désenchantées: Roman des harems turcs contemporains (Loti) **11**:360, 364-65, 367-68
"Deseo" (Villaurrutia) **80**:488
"El deseo sin nombre" (Prado) **75**:195
La desequilibrada (Echegaray) **4**:101
"Desert" (Aleixandre)
See "Desierto"
"Le désert" (Loti) **11**:355
The Desert and the Sown (Bell)
See *Syria: The Desert and the Sown*
The Desert and the Sown (Foote) **108**:12-14, 16-18
"Desert Flowers" (Douglas) **40**:73, 76-8, 81-2, 91
Desert Gold (Grey) **6**:177
"The Desert Islander" (Benson) **17**:33
Desert Islands (de la Mare) **4**:81
Desert Solitaire: A Season in the Wilderness (Abbey) **160**:3, 11-14, 16-17, 20-21, 23, 25-27, 30-32, 34-36, 38-46, 49, 53-54, 58, 70-71, 78-82, 84-85, 88, 90-98, 102
"Deserted Fortresses" (van Ostaijen) **33**:421
"The Deserted House" (Reese) **181**:338
"The Deserted Plantation" (Dunbar) **12**:108, 121
"Deserted Village" (Wen I-to) **28**:412
"Deserted Wives" (Agnon)
See "Agunot: A Tale"
"The Deserter" (Davis) **24**:203-04, 207
"The Deserter" (Oppenheim) **45**:124
The Deserter (Abercrombie) **141**:10-13
"Le déserteur" (Drieu la Rochelle) **21**:27, 30
Le désespéranto (Tzara) **168**:281
La Desesperanza (Donoso) **133**:83, 124-25, 139, 191-93, 195, 198-99
Le désespéré (Bloy) **22**:30, 37-9, 45-6, 49, 51, 53
"Désespoir du soleil" (Desnos) **22**:61
"Los desgraciados" (Vallejo) **56**:307, 311-12
La desheredada (Pérez Galdós) **27**:248, 250, 261-63, 266, 283, 285, 288
Le déshonneur des poètes (Péret) **20**:185, 191-93, 198, 202-03
"Deshora" (Vallejo) **56**:294
"Desideria" (Johnson) **19**:229
"Desiderio in novembre" (Calvino) **183**:213
"Desierto" (Aleixandre) **113**:8
"El desierto" (Quiroga) **20**:217-18
"The Design of the Novel" (Sarton) **120**:246, 248
"Desine" (Stephens) **4**:417
"Désir" (Apollinaire) **8**:28; **51**:36
The Desirable Alien (Hunt) **53**:187, 192
"Desire" (Toomer) **172**:279
"Desire" (Villaurrutia) **80**:488
The Desire and Pursuit of the Whole (Rolfe) **12**:269-71, 274, 276-78, 280, 284
"Desire in November" (Calvino)
See "Desiderio in novembre"
"The Desire named Marx" (Lyotard) **103**:229, 231
"The Desire of Nations" (Markham) **47**:278-79
The Desire of the Moth (Rhodes) **53**:307, 318-20, 324, 327
Desire to Be Loved (Ady)
See *Szeretném, ha szeretnáenek*
Desire under the Elms (O'Neill) **1**:382, 384, 387, 390-91, 393, 400, 403-04; **6**:330; **49**:237-99
"Désirée's Baby" (Chopin) **5**:147, 155-56; **14**:57, 61, 65, 76-7; **127**:92-3, 111, 165, 167, 173, 185, 206-7, 224, 226-27
Le désirs de Jean Servien (France) **9**:40
Desjataja simfonija (Aldanov) **23**:22-3, 25-8
"Desjatiminutnaja droma" (Zamyatin) **8**:553
"Desk" (Tsvetaeva)
See "Stol"
El deslinde: Prolegómenos a la teoría literaria (Reyes) **33**:317-18, 323
Las desnudas (Pardo Bazán) **189**:237
"El desnudo" (Aleixandre) **113**:14
Desolación (Mistral) **2**:475-80
"Desolate" (McKay) **7**:456
"A Desolate Shore" (Henley) **8**:110
"Desolation" (Field) **43**:160, 165
"Desolation" (Smith) **25**:380, 384-85, 393, 397
Desolation (Mistral)
See *Desolación*
Desolation Angels (Kerouac) **117**:186, 190-91, 196-204, 206, 215, 252, 265-66, 272
Desolation Is a Delicate Thing (Wylie) **8**:529
"The Desolations" (Muir) **87**:231
"Despair" (Talvik) **87**:319
Despair (Donoso)
See *La Desesperanza*
Despair (Mistral)
See *Desolación*
Despair (Nabokov)
See *Otchaianie*
"Despedida recordando un adiós" (Vallejo) **56**:307, 311
"A Desperate Case" (Premchand) **21**:294
Desperate Remedies (Hardy) **4**:147, 157-58, 160; **10**:215, 217, 225; **18**:100; **48**:71; **53**:71, 77, 84, 93; **72**:237; **143**:75-76, 83, 154, 181, 204; **153**:100, 136, 179, 191
Desperation (Donoso)
See *La Desesperanza*
"Despicable Bastard" (Endo)
See "Iya na yatsu"
"Despierto a mediodía" (Jiménez) **183**:308
The Despoiler (Ince) **89**:18
"El despojo" (Arguedas) **147**:67
The Despot of Broomsedge Cove (Murfree) **135**:223
"Despotisms" (Guiney) **41**:221
"Después de la guerra" (Aleixandre) **113**:51
"Despues de la muerte" (Aleixandre) **113**:11
"Después de pasar" (García Lorca) **181**:193, 197

El desquite (Azuela) **3**:78; **145**:6, 11, 15, 27, 30, 33
Les dessous d'une vie ou la pyramide humaine (Éluard) **41**:150
"Los desterrados" (Quiroga) **20**:212, 218
"Los destiladores de naranja" (Quiroga) **20**:212
Destillationen: Neue Gedichte (Benn) **3**:107, 109
Destined for half a lifetime (Chang)
See *Bansheng yuan*
"Destinée arbitraire" (Desnos) **22**:60
"El destino" (Pardo Bazán) **189**:236
"Destino alegre" (Salinas) **17**:363
"Destino de la carne" (Aleixandre) **113**:76-7
Destino del hombre (Aleixandre) **113**:15
"Destino trágico" (Aleixandre) **113**:49
"Destiny" (Bachmann) **192**:66
"Destiny" (Fargue) **11**:201
"Destiny at Drybone" (Wister) **21**:400
Destiny of Man (Aleixandre)
See *Destino del hombre*
The Destiny of Man (Berdyaev) **67**:27, 71
The Destiny of Russia (Berdyaev) **67**:32-33
"El destripador" (Pardo Bazán) **189**:234, 236
Un destripador de antaño (Pardo Bazán) **189**:234
La destrucción o el amor (Aleixandre) **113**:8-10, 13-15, 23, 27-30, 36-37, 41, 44, 48, 58, 67, 69-70, 72
Destruction (Marinetti) **10**:316
"Destruction de Paris" (Giono) **124**:42
"The Destruction of Jerusalem by the Babylonian Hordes" (Rosenberg) **12**:288, 295, 297, 301, 310
"The Destruction of Personality" (Gorky) **8**:87
The Destruction of Sodom (García Lorca) **49**:97
"Destruction of the Man" (Pirandello)
See "La distruzione dell'uomo"
Destruction or Love (Aleixandre)
See *La destrucción o el amor*
"Destructions" (Andrić)
See "Razaranja"
"The Destructive Character" (Benjamin)
See "Der destruktive Charakter"
"Der destruktive Charakter" (Benjamin) **39**:5, 38, 49
Destry Rides Again (Faust) **49**:35, 47, 57-9, 61
"Desvelo" (Jiménez) **183**:292
"Detachment and the Writing of History" (Becker) **63**:91, 99, 113
"Details of a Sunset" (Nabokov)
See "Katastrofa"
"A Detective Novel in Geology" (Gadda)
See "Un romanzo giallo nella geologia"
Determinism and Indeterminism in Modern Physics (Cassirer)
See *Determinismus und Indeterminismus in der Modernen Physik*
Determinismus und Indeterminismus in der Modernen Physik (Cassirer) **61**:92
Deti satany (Przybyszewski)
See *Satans Kinder*
Deti vydry (Khlebnikov) **20**:137, 139-41, 144
Détours (Crevel) **112**:21-2
Les détours du coeur (Bourget) **12**:69
"Detskaja šarmanocka" (Guro) **56**:139
"Detskaya" (Zamyatin) **8**:548
"Detstvo" (Gumilev) **60**:270, 279
Detstvo (Gorky) **8**:73-4, 77-8, 83
Detstvo (Tolstoy) **4**:444-45, 456, 459-60, 469, 473; **11**:464; **17**:377; **28**:398; **79**:324, 365, 379, 395, 415, 445
Detstvo i drugie rasskazy (Babel) **171**:7-12, 96
Detstvo nikity (Tolstoy) **18**:359, 364, 377-78
Deucalion (Ruskin) **63**:251, 254
"La deuda mutua" (Güiraldes) **39**:190
Le Deuil des primeveres (Jammes) **75**:102, 115, 118
Deuil pour deuil (Desnos) **22**:64-5, 71
"Deus noster ignis consumens" (Housman) **7**:353
"Deutsch Durch Freud" (Jarrell) **177**:152
Deutsche Charaktere und Begebenheiten (Wassermann) **6**:518
Der Deutsche Hinkemann (Toller) **10**:477, 481-82, 485, 487, 491
Der Deutsche Maskenball (Döblin) **13**:167, 175
Deutsche Menschen (Benjamin) **39**:45, 56
"Die Deutsche Revolution" (Sternheim) **8**:368, 377
Das Deutsche Schicksal (Sudermann) **15**:436
Deutscher Adel (Raabe) **45**:166, 194, 200-01
Deutscher Novellenschatz (Heyse) **8**:120, 122
"Deutsches Requiem" (Borges) **109**:152
"Deutschland" (Toller) **10**:490
"Deutschland und die Deutschen" (Mann) **44**:147, 164; **168**:158
Deux artistes lyriques (Larbaud) **9**:199
Les Deux Bourreaux (Adamov) **189**:43
Deux cavaliers de l'orage (Giono) **124**:55-56, 97, 113, 115
Les deux consciences (Lemonnier) **22**:198
Les deux femmes du bourgeois de Bruges (Barrès) **47**:70
Les deux pierrots (Rostand) **37**:286
Les deux soeurs (Bourget) **12**:69
La deuxième aventure celeste de Monsieur Antipyrine (Tzara) **168**:240, 293, 319, 322
"2e canonnier conducteur" (Apollinaire) **51**:35
"Deuxième elégie XXX" (Péguy) **10**:418
"Le deuxième livre des masques" (Gourmont) **17**:129-30, 138, 143, 147, 157-58
Dev Künstler (Rank) **115**:226, 231, 234, 243-44, 246, 249, 251, 255-56,261, 267-68, 270, 300-01, 306, 310-11, 314-15, 319, 325-30, 347
"Devant le feu" (Nelligan) **14**:392, 399
Devastation (Mistral)
See *Tala*
Devatero pohádek (Čapek) **192**:180
"The Development of a People" (Du Bois) **169**:143
The Development of Capitalism in Russia (Lenin) **67**:225
The Development of Metaphysics in Persia (Iqbal) **28**:179-80
"The Development of Morality" (Westermarck) **87**:366
"The Development of Philosophy Prior to Hume" (Nishida)
See "Hyumu izen no tetsugaku no hattatsu"
The Development of Psychoanalysis (Rank) **115**:228, 339, 341
The Development of the Drama (Matthews) **95**:246
Development of the Legend of Œdipus (Rod)
See *Le développment de la légende d'Œdipe dans l'histoire de la littérature Européene*
Le développment de la légende d'Œdipe dans l'histoire de la littérature Européene (Rod) **52**:309
Devenir! (Martin du Gard) **24**:386-87, 392-94, 396-97
"The Devil" (Stephens) **4**:417
"The Devil" (Tolstoy) **4**:482; **11**:463-64, 470-71; **17**:415; **79**:374, 387
"The Devil" (Tsvetaeva) **7**:571
The Devil (Molnár)
See *Az ördög*
The Devil (Neumann) **100**:314-15
The Devil (Papini)
See *Il diavolo*
The Devil and All (Collier) **127**:249-50
"The Devil and Daniel Webster" (Benét) **7**:81, 84-5
"The Devil and the Deep Sea" (Kipling) **8**:195
The Devil and the Statue (Melies) **81**:138
"The Devil and Tobacco" (Akutagawa Ryūnosuke)
See *Tobaku tu akuma*
The Devil and Tobacco (Akutagawa Ryūnosuke)
See *Tobaku tu akuma*
The Devil Doctor (Rohmer) **28**:277, 279, 288, 293, 298-99
"The Devil, George and Rosie" (Collier) **127**:251
"The Devil in Iron" (Howard) **8**:131, 135
The Devil in the Hills (Pavese)
See *Il diavolo sulle colline*
"The Devil in Us" (Brennan) **124**:5
The Devil Inside Him (Osborne) **153**:244, 251
The Devil Is Jones (Dent) **72**:38
"The Devil Man" (McCoy) **28**:223
"The Devil Said to Me" (Papini) **22**:284
The Devil to Pay (Heijermans)
See *Eva bonheur*
The Devil to Pay (Sayers) **2**:535; **15**:372-73, 381
"The Devil We Know" (Kuttner) **10**:269
The Devil Within (Radiguet)
See *Le diable au corps*
"Devils" (Douglas) **40**:82, 89, 92
The Devil's Advocate (Frazer) **32**:203
"The Devil's Book" (Yeats) **31**:413-14, 416
The Devil's Bridge (Aldanov)
See *Čortov most*
"The Devil's Case" (Buchanan) **107**:67
"The Devil's Church" (Machado de Assis)
See "A igreja do diabo"
The Devil's Comedy (Remizov)
See *Besovskoe deistvo*
The Devil's Dictionary (Bierce) **1**:85, 92, 94, 96; **7**:89, 92-4; **44**:2, 5, 14-16, 28, 32, 37, 39, 50
"Devil's Dirge" (Buchanan) **107**:17
The Devil's Disciple (Shaw) **3**:378, 381, 396, 398; **9**:414; **21**:306, 327; **45**:210, 212, 214
The Devil's Doll (Hippius)
See *Chortova kukla*
The Devil's General (Zuckmayer)
See *Des Teufels General*
The Devil's Lair and the Midnight Sun (Remizov)
See *Chortov log i polunoshchnoe solntse*
"The Devil's Little Plaything" (Zoshchenko) **15**:500
The Devil's Motor (Corelli) **51**:75
The Devil's Mystics (Buchanan) **107**:39
Devils of the Deep (Dent) **72**:21, 23
The Devil's Own Dear Son (Cabell) **6**:76, 78
The Devil's Passkey (Stroheim) **71**:329-330, 332, 339, 341, 358
The Devil's Playground (Dent) **72**:23
"The Devil's Sabbath" (Buchanan) **107**:66
Devil's Tor (Lindsay) **15**:225-27, 229-30, 232-34, 236-39
The Devil's Yard (Andrić)
See *Prokleta avlija*
Devjatoe termidora (Aldanov) **23**:16-17, 19-21, 23
Devochka v tsirke (Olesha) **136**:109
Le devoir et l'inquiétude (Éluard) **41**:153
"A Devon Estuary" (Tomlinson) **71**:400
Devonshire Characters and Strange Events (Baring-Gould) **88**:25
"A Devonshire Ditty" (Noyes) **7**:512-13
"The Devoted Friend" (Wilde) **41**:383
"Devotion" (Naidu) **80**:272
"Devushke" (Gumilev) **60**:280
"Devuška" (Zamyatin) **8**:551-52
Devy bog (Khlebnikov) **20**:136, 141
"The Dewpond" (Powys) **9**:366, 372
The Dharma Bums (Kerouac) **117**:185, 187, 196, 212, 225, 265-67, 269, 271-73
"Dhoya" (Yeats) **31**:413-14
Di goldgreber (Aleichem) **35**:307
"Di grasso" (Babel) **2**:28; **13**:23-4; **171**:14
Di mishpoke Mashber (Kahanovitsch) **56**:111, 116-121, 123-125, 127, 129-130
"Di ronda alla spiaggia" (Saba) **33**:372
"Di shtot fun di kleyne mentshelek" (Aleichem) **35**:306
"El día que me quieras" (Nervo) **11**:395
Diaário íntimo (Lima Barreto) **23**:156

"Diabetes" (Dickey) **151**:105, 113, 143
"Diabetes, I" (Dickey) **151**:100
Le diable au corps (Radiguet) **29**:347-50, 352-57, 361, 364, 367-73, 375-78
Le diable boiteux (Martin du Gard) **24**:395
"Diable—A Dog" (London)
See "Batard"
"Diaboliad" (Bulgakov) **16**:85
Diaboliad, and Other Stories (Bulgakov)
See *D'iavoliada*
The Diabolical Principle and the Dithyrambic Spectator (Lewis) **2**:391; **9**:239
Diabolo (Nezval) **44**:239
Diabolus Amans (Davidson) **24**:180, 186
"Diagnosis" (Wharton) **129**:364
"A Diagnosis of Death" (Bierce) **44**:45-6
"Diagnostic de l'Europe" (Yourcenar) **193**:322-23, 330
Dialectic and Alienation (Brecht) **13**:53
"A Dialectic Approach to Film Form" (Eisenstein) **57**:165, 181
Dialectic of Enlightenment (Adorno)
See *Dialektik der Aufklarung*
Dialectic of Enlightenment (Horkheimer)
See *Dialektik der Aufklärung*
Dialectical and Historical Materialism (Stalin) **92**:183
"Dialectical Dramatics" (Brecht) **13**:53
The Dialectical Imagination (Adorno)
See *La Dialectique de la raison*
"Dialectical Materialism and Psychoanalysis" (Reich) **57**:350
The Dialectical World (Nishida) **83**:343
La Dialectique de la durée (Bachelard) **128**:54
La Dialectique de la raison (Adorno) **111**:53, 64
Dialektik der Aufklarung (Adorno) **111**:4, 6, 18-20, 26, 28, 38, 42, 45-6, 50-1, 53-5, 62, 75-6, 98-100, 102-3, 106, 108, 137, 144-46, 148-51, 154-56, 161, 181-82, 184-196
Dialektik der Aufklärung (Horkheimer) **132**:180, 191, 194-97, 200, 203, 205, 208, 212, 222
"Dialektik und Verfremdung" (Brecht) **169**:20
"Die dialektische Methode" (von Hartmann) **96**:187
"Dialog" (Jozsef) **22**:161-62
"A Dialog and Words" (Güiraldes)
See "Diálogo y palabras"
Dialoghi con Leucò (Pavese) **3**:336, 340
The Dialogic Imagination (Bakhtin)
See *Voprosy literatury i estetiki*
Dialogo (Levi) **109**:302-03
"Diálogo de ls enajenados" (Aleixandre) **113**:51
"Diálogo del Amargo" (García Lorca) **7**:300; **49**:78
"Dialogo di due scrittori in crisi" (Calvino) **183**:104, 193
"Diálogo y palabras" (Güiraldes) **39**:176
Diálogos Borges-Sábato (Borges) **109**:119
Diálogos del conocimiento (Aleixandre) **113**:22, 36, 44, 50-51, 68, 70
Diálogos fantásticos (Martinez Sierra and Martinez Sierra) **6**:285
"Dialogue" (Muir) **87**:231
"Dialogue" (Sarton) **120**:303
"Dialogue at Three in the Morning" (Parker) **143**:331, 343
"Dialogue Between a Past and Present Poet" (Bodenheim) **44**:62
"A Dialogue between an Egoist and His Friend" (Ishikawa) **15**:126
"A Dialogue between Two Women" (Yosano) **59**:346
"Dialogue Between Two Writers in Crisis" (Calvino)
See "Dialogo di due scrittori in crisi"
Dialogue de l'auteur avec son ombre (Rolland) **23**:261
"A Dialogue from Plato" (Dobson) **79**:5
"A Dialogue in Purgatory" (Moody) **105**:237, 239, 254-55, 271
"A Dialogue of Self and Soul" (Yeats) **1**:571; **31**:401, 403, 409-10; **116**:329
"Dialogue of the Bitter One" (García Lorca)
See "Diálogo del Amargo"
Dialogues (Abercrombie) **141**:5
Dialogues (Deleuze) **116**:60-2, 86, 123
Dialogues à Byzance (Benda) **60**:59-60, 64, 79, 85
Dialogues de bêtes (Colette) **5**:167
Dialogues des amateurs (Gourmont) **17**:127, 138, 145-46
Dialogues des Carmélites (Bernanos) **3**:122
"Dialogues for One Voice" (Colette) **16**:128
Dialogues in Limbo (Santayana) **40**:373
"The Dialogues of Ascetic and King" (Borges) **109**:157
Dialogues of Knowledge (Aleixandre)
See *Diálogos del conocimiento*
Dialogues of the Refugees (Brecht)
See *Flüchtlingsgespräche*
"Dialogues with Characters I & II" (Pirandello)
See "Colloqui coi personaggi"
Dialogues with Leucò (Pavese)
See *Dialoghi con Leucò*
Dialogues With Mothers (Bettelheim) **143**:7
Dialstone Lane (Jacobs) **22**:108-10
Diamantes y pedernales (Arguedas) **147**:12, 94
"The Diamond as Big as the Ritz" (Fitzgerald) **1**:234, 249, 262; **14**:182; **28**:115, 120; **55**:191; **157**:142
"A Diamond Badge" (Welch) **22**:441, 456
Diamond Cuts Diamond (Chekhov) **31**:99
"Diamond Dick and the First Law of Woman" (Fitzgerald) **157**:194
"Diamond Eye" (Hrabal) **155**:150
"A Diamond Guitar" (Capote) **164**:105, 111-12, 115
Diamond Jim (Sturges) **48**:286, 291, 294-95, 311, 316, 321
The Diamond Master (Futrelle) **19**:95
The Diamond of Restlessness (Nervo) **11**:403
Diamonds and Flints (Arguedas)
See *Diamantes y pedernales*
Diamonds Are Forever (Fleming) **193**:193, 195, 198-99, 201, 206, 223, 228, 230, 240-41
Le diamont de la reine (Bourget) **12**:69
Diana of Kara-Kara (Wallace)
See *Double Dan*
Diana of the Crossways (Meredith) **17**:257, 259, 263, 265, 278, 281, 291, 297; **43**:256, 259, 290, 296, 299
"Diana Vaughan" (Gourmont) **17**:126
Diana's Hunting (Buchanan) **107**:86-7
Diaries (Orton) **157**:309, 337
Diaries (Tolstoy)
See *Dnevniki*
Diaries and Letters (Lowndes) **12**:205
The Diaries of Charlotte Perkins Gilman (Gilman) **117**:146-50, 153-164
The Diaries of Franz Kafka (Kafka)
See *Tagebücher, 1910-1923*
The Diaries of Sylvia Townsend Warner (Warner) **131**:359-60
Diario (Hostos) **24**:303
Diario de poeta y mar (Jiménez) **183**:257-65
Diario de un poeta recién casado (Jiménez) **183**:268, 276-77, 281, 286, 292, 296, 301-2, 304, 314, 318-19, 330-37, 340
Diario di guerra per l'anno 1917 (Gadda) **144**:145
Diario di Villa Rosa (Pratolini) **124**:332
Diario íntimo (Unamuno) **148**:298, 301-2, 312-16
Diario per la fidanzata (Svevo) **35**:364
Diarmuid and Grania (Moore) **7**:482, 498
Diaro Däubler (Barlach) **84**:93
Diary (Artaud)
See *Fragments d'un journal d'enfer*
Diary (Pilnyak) **23**:201
Diary Kept in 1909 (Yeats) **31**:400
The Diary of a Country Priest (Bernanos)
See *Journal d'un curé de campagne*
The Diary of a Drug Fiend (Crowley) **7**:205
Diary of a film (Cocteau) **119**:50-3, 60-2, 86, 88-9
"Diary of a Madman" (Lu Hsun)
See *Kuangren riji*
"The Diary of a Madman" (Tolstoy)
See *Zapiski sumasshedshego*
"The Diary of a Man of Fifty" (James) **47**:199-200
"The Diary of a Meshumad" (Zangwill) **16**:441
"Diary of a Mystic" (Morgenstern)
See "Tagebuch eines Mystikers"
"The Diary of a Newly-Returned Traveler" (Nagai)
See "Shinkichōsha no nikki"
Diary of a Newlywed Poet (Jiménez)
See *Diario de un poeta recién casado*
The Diary of a Pilgrimage (Jerome) **23**:83
Diary of a Provincial Lady (Delafield) **61**:127-30
"The Diary of a Successful Man" (Dowson) **4**:92
The Diary of a War Correspondent (Molnár)
See *A Haditudosito Naploja*
The Diary of a Young Girl (Frank)
See *Het achterhuis*
"Diary of Adam" (Twain) **12**:428
The Diary of Beatrice Webb (Webb and Webb) **22**:426
"The Diary of Chianine" (Bataille) **155**:89
"The Diary of Claudius" (Shiga)
See "Kurōdiasu no nikki"
The Diary of Helena Morley (Drummond de Andrade)
See *Minha Vida de Menina*
"The Diary of Mr. Poynter" (James) **6**:212
A Diary of My Times (Bernanos)
See *Les grandes cimetières sous la lune*
The Diary of Virginia Woolf (Woolf) **5**:516; **56**:384
Diatessarica (Abbott) **139**:23
D'iavoliada (Bulgakov) **2**:63; **16**:83-4
Il diavolo sulle colline (Pavese) **3**:338, 343-44
The (Diblos) Notebook (Merrill) **173**:187, 231-36, 238-39
Diccionario de la lengua española (Palma) **29**:263
Dice (Nezval) **44**:240
"Dice, Brassknuckles, and Guitar" (Fitzgerald) **6**:166
The Dice Cup (Jacob)
See *Le cornet à dés*
"La dicha" (Aleixandre) **113**:13
"Der Dichter" (Huch) **13**:251
Dichter (Walser) **18**:428
"Der Dichter und das Phantasieren" (Freud) **52**:129, 131-32
"Der Dichter und diese Zeit" (Hofmannsthal) **11**:300
"Dichtung und Energie" (Kaiser) **9**:174
"Dick Boyle's Business Card" (Harte) **25**:213
Dick Sheridan (Buchanan) **107**:34
"Dick Turpin's Ride" (Noyes) **7**:515
Der Dicke Mann im Spiegel (Werfel) **8**:478
Dickens (Zweig) **17**:429
Dickens, Dali, and Others (Orwell)
See *Critical Essays*
"The Dickensian" (Chesterton) **6**:109
Dickon (Tey) **14**:451, 459
Dicta and Contradictions (Kraus)
See *Sprüche und Widersprüche*
"The Dictaphone" (Zoshchenko) **15**:510
"Dictator of the Americas" (Kuttner) **10**:268
"Dictatorships Do Not Grow Out of Strong and Successful Governments, but Out of Weak and Helpless Ones" (Roosevelt) **93**:184
"Diction and Poetry" (Shimazaki Toson)
See "Gagen to shika"
"Dictionary Ned" (Warung) **45**:419

"Dictionary of Current Personal Names" (Rohan) **22**:297
Dictionnaire abrégé du Surréalisme (Éluard) **41**:153
"Dictum" (Cullen) **37**:169
"Did Shakespeare Write Bacon?" (Stephen) **23**:326
Der Dieb (Heym) **9**:142-43, 147-50
Diechtungen und Dokumente (Lasker-Schueler) **57**:303, 309, 329
"Died at Dawn" (García Lorca)
See "Murió al amanecer"
"Died of Starvation" (Harper) **14**:260
"Diego Rivera Discovers Painting" (Reyes) **33**:323
"Dienen" (Kolmar) **40**:178
Dienstbüchlein (Frisch) **121**:237
"Dieppe-Grey and Green" (Symons) **11**:451
"Diergaarde voor kinderen van nu" (van Ostaijen) **33**:412
Dies Indische Lilie (Sudermann) **15**:428, 438
"Dies Irae" (Grahame) **64**:65-6
"Dies Irae" (Gregory) **176**:61
"Dies irae" (Talvik) **87**:319
An diesem Dienstag (Borchert) **5**:105
Diesseits und Jenseits (Brod) **115**:85, 87, 90-2, 100
Le Dieu bleu (Cocteau) **119**:68
"Dieu d'amour" (Wharton) **129**:364
"Le Dieu nu" (Cocteau) **119**:59
"Dieu-donné" (Drummond) **25**:143
Les dieux (Alain) **41**:23-5, 30
Les dieux ont soif (France) **9**:49-50, 52-3
El 19 de marzo y el 2 de mayo (Pérez Galdós) **27**:288
"The Difference" (Glasgow) **7**:343-44
Difference and Repetition (Deleuze)
See *Différence et répétition*
Différence et répétition (Deleuze) **116**:87-8, 100, 110, 113-14, 123-24, 128-29, 131, 147, 174
Le différend (Lyotard) **103**:158, 166-67, 175-75, 190, 198-99, 201, 206, 211-12, 214, 219, 241, 260-61, 263, 275, 277
The Differend: Phrases in Dispute (Lyotard)
See *Le différend*
"Different Faces" (Agnon)
See "Panim aherot"
A Different Person (Merrill) **173**:231-32, 251-53, 255-59
"Difficult Death" (Lawrence) **93**:56, 58
Difficult Death (Crevel)
See *La Mort difficile*
The Difficult Hour (Lagerkvist)
See *Den svåra stunden*
"Difficult Idylls" (Calvino) **183**:92-93
"A Difficult Life" (Calvino) **183**:93-94
Difficult Loves (Calvino)
See *Gli amori difficili*
The Difficult Man (Hofmannsthal)
See *Der Schwierige*
"Difficult Memories" (Calvino) **183**:93, 95
The Difficult Moment (Lagerkvist)
See *Den svåra stunden*
The Difficult Ones (Frisch)
See *Die Schwierigen; oder, J'adore ce qui me brûle*
La Difficulté d'être (Cocteau) **119**:70, 74, 03
Diff'rent (O'Neill) **1**:384-85, 387, 393; **6**:324-25; **49**:264
"Dig rörde aldrig mörkret" (Lagerkvist) **144**:179
"Digging" (Thomas) **10**:463
"Digitale purpurea" (Pascoli) **45**:152, 156
"Digression On My Works" (Shiga)
See "Sosaku yodan"
"Digressions" (Barthes) **135**:159
"Digressions around a Crow" (Nemerov) **124**:291, 295
Digte (Jensen) **41**:301
Digte (Obstfelder) **23**:177, 179, 182
Digte og sange (Bjoernson) **7**:110; **37**:27
Diked (Toomer)
See *The Gallonwerps*
"Diktaren och samvetet" (Dagerman) **17**:92
Diktatur der Vernunft (Mann) **9**:329
Dikter (Heidenstam) **5**:250, 253-56
Dikter (Södergran) **31**:284, 286, 288-91
Dikter på vers och prosa (Strindberg) **8**:419
Dilecta (Ruskin) **63**:255-56
"Dilemma" (Parker) **143**:323
A Dilemma (Huysmans)
See *Un Dilemme*
"The Dilemma of Determinism" (James) **15**:182; **32**:348, 351
"The Dilemma of Diderot" (Becker) **63**:113-14, 117
"The Dilemma of Modern Socialism" (Keynes) **64**:243
The Dilemma of Our Times: An Historical Essay (Laski) **79**:130, 160, 167
"The Dilemma of Segregation" (Locke) **43**:239
"The Dilemma of Specialization" (Hayek) **109**:207-08
"Dilemma of the Negro Writer" (Himes) **139**:285
Dilemmas (Dowson) **4**:84-5, 89-90
Un Dilemme (Huysmans) **69**:29, 31
"The Dilettant" (Dobson) **79**:2
"The Dilettante" (Mann) **2**:432; **35**:251
"The Dilettante" (Wharton) **3**:555; **129**:361
"A Dill Pickle" (Mansfield) **2**:451, 458; **8**:284; **164**:239, 248, 322, 324
Dílo XXVII-XXVII-XXIX (Nezval) **44**:244
"Dimanche à Marseille" (Jacob) **6**:199
"Dimensions for a Novel" (Bishop) **121**:45-8, 50
"Dimesjid" (Anwar) **22**:24
"The Diminishing Road" (Noyes) **7**:512
"Diminuendo" (Beerbohm) **24**:115
Diminutive Dramas (Baring) **8**:32, 37, 41, 44
Dimple Hill (Richardson) **3**:356-58
"L'din vzgromozhdennykh" (Khodasevich) **15**:205
Le dindon (Feydeau) **22**:77-8, 81, 84-7, 91-3
Le dîner de têtes (Anouilh) **195**:51
"Ding Dong Bell" (de la Mare) **53**:26
Ding Dong Bell (de la Mare) **4**:75; **53**:36, 38, 42
Ding-Gedichte (Rilke) **1**:419; **195**:165, 286
Dingiswayo, Son of Jobe (Vilakazi)
See *UDingiswayo kaJobe*
Dingo (Mirbeau) **55**:281, 285
"Dining-Room Tea" (Brooke) **2**:59-60; **7**:120-21, 123-24
"A Dinner at ———" (Henry) **19**:201
Dinner at Eight (Mankiewicz) **85**:114
The Dinner of Heads (Anouilh)
See *Le dîner de têtes*
"The Dinosaurs" (Calvino)
See "I dinosauri"
"Dintele" (Rebreanu) **28**:273
The Dionysian Spirit of the Age, Consciousness: Animal, Human, Superman, An Alphabet of Economics (Orage) **157**:237
Dionysos (Couperus) **15**:46
"Dionysos in the Crib" (Sikelianos) **39**:408
Dionysus Dithyramben (Nietzsche) **10**:389
"Dionysus in Doubt" (Robinson) **101**:195
Dionysus in Doubt (Robinson) **101**:146
Dionysus in Hades (Faust) **49**:36, 45
Dios deseado y deseante: Animal de fondo con numerosos poemas ineditos (Jiménez) **183**:270, 277-82, 284, 286, 288
"Dios primero" (Jiménez) **183**:263
Dioses y hombres de huarochiri (Arguedas) **147**:44, 90, 97
"Dip in the Pool" (Dahl) **173**:11
"Dipo negoro" (Anwar) **22**:19, 24
Dir zur Feier (Rilke) **195**:258, 261
Le directeur de l'opéra (Anouilh) **195**:48
Direction (Eisenstein) **57**:154
The Direction of the March (Adamov)
See *Le sens de la marche*
"Directions for the Use of Poetry" (van Ostaijen) **33**:406
The Director of the Opera (Anouilh)
See *Le directeur de l'opéra*
"A Dirge" (Bialik) **25**:50
"Dirge" (Dickey) **151**:213
"The Dirge" (Dunbar) **12**:105
"The Dirge" (Grove) **4**:138
"Dirge" (Naidu) **80**:345
"Dirge for a Righteous Kitten" (Lindsay) **17**:228, 230
"The Dirge of the Feal" (Papadiamantis) **29**:272-74
"The Dirge of the Four Cities" (Sharp) **39**:371-72, 378
"Dirge Without Music" (Millay) **169**:229
"Der Dirigent" (Werfel) **8**:471
"The Dirigible Air-Ship" (Herzl) **36**:141-42
"Dirty Deceivers" (Himes) **139**:245
Dirty Dingus Magee (Heller) **131**:22
"Dirty Emma" (March) **96**:262, 263-64
"Dirty Negroes" (Roumain)
See "Sales-nègres"
"Dirty Work" (McCoy) **28**:223-24
"Diş ve diş ağrısınedir bilmeyen adam" (Sait Faik) **23**:294
The Disabilities of Black Folk and Their Treatment, with an Appeal to the Labour Party (Casely-Hayford) **24**:132
"Disabled" (Owen) **5**:362, 367, 371; **27**:204, 208, 212, 214, 217-18, 227, 229-30, 237
"The Disappearance of Actor Benda" (Čapek) **37**:49, 54
"The Disappearance of an Actor" (Čapek) **192**:224
"The Disappearance of Luisa Porto" (Drummond de Andrade) **139**:237
"Disappearance of Marie Severe" (Bramah) **72**:6
"The Disappearing City" (Wright) **95**:369, 400, 405, 408
The Disappearing Daily (Sinclair) **160**:313-14
"The Disappearing Duke" (Chandler) **179**:128
"A Disappointment" (Pyle) **81**:393
"A Disastrous Lot" (Remizov)
See "Bedovaia dolia"
"Discard" (Fitzgerald) **6**:167
"The Discarded Imagist" (Upward) **85**:380
"The Disciple" (Tsvetaeva)
See "Uchenik"
The Disciple (Bourget)
See *Le disciple*
Le disciple (Bourget) **12**:59-60, 65, 67-8, 70, 72, 76-7
The Disciple (MacDonald) **9**:300
"Discipline" (Lawrence) **93**:44
"Discipline in Elementary Schools" (Orage) **157**:249
"The Discipline of Poetry" (Bishop) **103**:5, 23
"El disco" (Borges) **109**:49
"Disconsolate Morning" (Roberts) **68**:337
"Discord" (O'Faolain) **143**:222
"Discord in Childhood" (Lawrence) **93**:12, 23, 45, 65, 66, 117
"The Discounters of Money" (Henry) **19**:174
"Discouragement" (Hardy) **53**:81
Discours à la nation européenne (Benda) **60**:65
Discours à l'Académie (Barrès) **47**:69
Discours de réception (Yourcenar) **193**:364
Discours du Grand Sommeil (Cocteau) **119**:107
Discours e dicho (Mistral) **51**:168
Discours/figure (Lyotard) **103**:127, 151-58, 166, 169, 219, 226, 260, 263
Discourse/Figure (Lyotard)
See *Discours/figure*
"Discourse in the Novel" (Bakhtin) **160**:109-10, 117, 122-24, 138, 206, 209, 211
The Discourse of the Great Sleep (Cocteau)
See *Discours du Grand Sommeil*

"Discourse on the Tachanka" (Babel) **13**:32; **78**:6, 48, 51, 87, 132, 138; **171**:17, 19, 22, 89
Discourse on Vietnam (Weiss)
See *Viet Nam Diskurs*
Discourses on Various Philosophical Subjects (Croce) **37**:113
"Discourses with Calypso on Music and Love" (Döblin) **13**:166
Discoursi di religione (Gentile) **96**:85, 87
"Discovered" (Dunbar) **12**:108
"The Discoverers" (Campbell) **9**:32
Discoveries (Yeats) **31**:400
"Discovery" (Södergran)
See "Upptäckt"
"The Discovery of America" (Fenollosa) **91**:2
"The Discovery of America" (Gumilev)
See "Otkrytie Ameriki"
The Discovery of Freedom (Lane) **177**:270
"The Discovery of the Future" (Wells) **6**:552; **19**:428; **133**:323
"A Discovery of Thought" (Stevens) **12**:378
Discrete Series (Oppen) **107**:251-54, 256, 258-59, 262-63, 269, 274, 282, 301-02, 306, 310, 312-14, 319-24, 326-29, 333-34, 340-41, 343-45, 347, 352, 355, 358
"Discurso por Virgilio" (Reyes) **33**:323-24
Discusión (Borges) **109**:16, 77, 84-5, 148, 156
"Discussing Legislation to be Recommended to the Extraordinary Session of the Congress" (Roosevelt) **93**:184
"Discussing the Plan for Reorganization of the Judiciary" (Roosevelt) **93**:184, 186
"Discussion" (Mencken) **13**:363
A Discussion of Human Affairs (Beard) **15**:30
"A Discussion of the Existence or Nonexistence of A Priori Knowledge" (Nishida)
See "Senten chishiki no umu o ronzu"
Discussions (Borges)
See *Discusión*
"Discussions, ou phraser après Auschwitz" (Lyotard) **103**:160, 176
"The Disease of Money-Getting" (Davis) **6**:154
The Disenchanted (Loti)
See *Les désenchantées: Roman des harems turcs contemporains*
Disengaged (James) **11**:339
Disent les imbéciles (Sarraute) **145**:277, 309-13, 320, 332-36, 344, 348
"El disfraz" (Pardo Bazán) **189**:236
"Disgraceful Persecution of a Boy" (Twain) **161**:288
"A Dish of Orts" (MacDonald) **9**:292
A Dish of Orts: Chiefly Papers on the Imagination, and on Shakespeare (MacDonald) **113**:232, 264-65, 291, 300
A Dish of Spices (Huysmans)
See *Le drageoir àèpices*
The Dishonor of Poets (Péret)
See *Le déshonneur des poètes*
Dishonored Lady (Hecht) **101**:75
"Disillusioned" (de la Mare) **53**:15-7, 27
"Disillusionment" (Mann) **2**:432; **168**:183-84, 187
"The Disinherited" (Bowen) **148**:18
"Disintegration" (Wharton) **149**:253
"The Disintegration Machine" (Doyle) **7**:226
Disjecta: Miscellaneous Writings and a Dramatic Fragment (Beckett) **145**:77-78, 85, 87-91
"The Disk" (Borges)
See "El disco"
"The Dismissal of Tyng" (Harper) **14**:260
"Disobedience" (Milne) **88**:243
Disorder and Early Sorrow (Mann) **60**:354; **168**:178
"La disparition d'honoré Subrac" (Apollinaire) **51**:20
"Dispersão" (Sá-Carneiro) **83**:397-9, 408-11, 414
Dispersion (Sá-Carneiro)
See "Dispersão"
"The Displaced Person" (O'Connor) **132**:246, 248, 258, 266, 280-81, 284, 352, 355-59, 364, 366
"The Displeasure of the Seleucid" (Cavafy) **2**:87
"The Dispute Among German Historians" (Levi) **109**:313
"Disraeli, Marx and the Search for Identity" (Berlin) **105**:37
"The Dissection" (Heym)
See "Die Sektion"
Dissemination of Tales among the Natives of North America (Boas) **56**:80
The Dissenting Opinions of Mr. Justice Holmes (Holmes) **77**:206
"Dissertation on Man" (Garvey) **41**:183
"Dissipation" (Nagai)
See "Hōtō"
"Dissociation des idées" (Gourmont) **17**:127, 141, 153
The Dissolution of Christianity and the Religion of the Future (von Hartmann)
See *Die Selbstersetzung des Christentums und die Religion der Zukunft*
Dissonanzen (Adorno) **111**:131
"Distance" (Parker) **143**:325
"The Distance of the Moon" (Calvino)
See "La distanza della luna"
"Distances" (Okigbo) **171**:338, 341-44, 346, 353-56
Distances (Bryusov) **10**:90
"Distances IV" (Okigbo) **171**:342-43
"The Distances They Keep" (Nemerov) **124**:182, 252
"Distances VI" (Okigbo) **171**:345
"Distant Country" (Sharp) **39**:359
Distant Melody (Sá-Carneiro)
See *Distante melodia*
Distant Moods in a Blue Evening (Rainis)
See *Tālas noskanas zilā vakarā*
"A Distant Thank You" (Burroughs) **121**:132
Distante melodia (Sá-Carneiro) **83**:399, 401, 413
"La distanza della luna" (Calvino) **183**:146, 161, 215, 227
"The Distillers of Oranges" (Quiroga)
See "Los destiladores de naranja"
"Distinguished Air" (McAlmon) **97**:92, 105, 123
Distinguished Air (Grim Fairy Tales) (McAlmon) **97**:91-92, 105, 107, 110, 112, 118-19
"The Distracted Preacher" (Hardy) **4**:159
Distressing Dialogues (Millay) **169**:231, 234-37, 239, 273-74, 276, 278
"Distrust Between the Sexes" (Horney) **71**:233
"La distruzione dell'uomo" (Pirandello) **4**:350
Disturbances (Bernhard)
See *Verstörung*
"A Disturbed Sabbath" (Peretz) **16**:405
"Le dit de arbes" (Gourmont) **17**:129
"Le dit d'un Chevalier" (Moréas) **18**:281
"A Ditch" (Kuprin) **5**:298
The Ditch (Remizov) **27**:334
Ditegli sempre di sì (de Filippo) **127**:293
"Ditelo coi nodi" (Calvino) **183**:105
"Die Dithmarschen" (Liliencron) **18**:217
The Dithyramb of the Rose (Sikelianos) **39**:416, 419
Dithyramber i aftonglans (Ekelund) **75**:95
Dithyrambs in Evening-Luster (Ekelund)
See *Dithyramber i aftonglans*
Ditja Allaxa (Gumilev) **60**:265-6
"Ditsvey shidukhim" (Cahan) **71**:39, 41, 86
"Ditt hufvud, Jesu böjes" (Lagerkvist) **144**:179
Ditte: Daughter of Man (Nexø)
See *Ditte menneskebarn*
Ditte: Girl Alive! (Nexø)
See *Ditte menneskebarn*
Ditte menneskebarn (Nexø) **43**:314-16, 328-30
Ditte: Towards the Stars (Nexø)
See *Ditte menneskebarn*
"Ditty of No Tone" (Riley) **51**:282
El Diván de Tamarit (García Lorca) **49**:116
Diván del Tamarit (García Lorca) **181**:63
Divan of the Tamarit (García Lorca)
See *El Diván de Tamarit*
The Diva's Ruby (Crawford) **10**:151, 155
Diverging Roads (Lane) **177**:279
Divers Vanities (Morrison) **72**:364, 379
Les diverses familles spirituelles de la France (Barrès) **47**:45
Divertissements (Gourmont) **17**:127, 129, 137
"Divided" (Baker) **10**:27
"Dividends" (O'Faolain) **143**:230
Dividends (Adams) **56**:7-8
Divinas palabras (Valle-Inclán) **5**:481, 486
"The Divine Adventure" (Sharp) **39**:355, 359
The Divine Adventure. Iona. By Sundown Shores: Studies in Spiritual History (Sharp) **39**:355, 359, 364, 373-75
"The Divine Afflatus" (Mencken) **13**:363
The Divine Archer (Nervo)
See *El arquero divino*
"The Divine Child" (Södergran)
See "Gudabarnet"
Divine Comedies (Merrill) **173**:153-55, 157, 162, 170, 174, 195, 211, 229-30, 245
La Divine Douleur (Jammes) **75**:119
The Divine Fire (Sinclair) **3**:434-35, 437-38, 440-41; **11**:408-09, 411, 413
"Divine Judgement" (Güiraldes)
See "El juicio de Dios"
Divine Justice (Bergelson) **81**:19
"The Divine Milieu" (Teilhard de Chardin)
See "Le milieu divin"
The Divine Mystery (Upward) **85**:375, 377, 379-81, 385-7, 394, 398, 403-9
"A Divine Nativity" (Bishop) **103**:7-8, 19-21
The Divine Passion (Fisher) **140**:156, 186
"The Divine Vision" (Baker) **10**:20
The Divine Vision, and Other Poems (Baker) **3**:1-4
Divine Words (Valle-Inclán)
See *Divinas palabras*
"Divinity Student" (Bosman) **49**:14
Division and Reunion, 1829-1889 (Wilson) **79**:485-6, 527
"The Division of Languages" (Barthes) **135**:159
"Divisions on a Ground" (Symons) **11**:434
Divisions on a Ground (Frye) **165**:188, 190-93, 196-97, 228
"Divorce" (Lu Hsun) **3**:302
Un divorce (Bourget) **12**:69-72
Divorce (Williams) **1**:517-18, 521
Divorce: A Domestic Tragedy of Modern France (Bourget)
See *Un divorce*
"A Divorce of Lovers" (Sarton) **120**:263, 269-70, 292, 303, 318
"Dizzy with Success" (Stalin) **92**:167
"D'javoliada" (Bulgakov)
See "Diaboliad"
"Djordje Djordjević" (Andrić) **135**:86
"Dlaczego klasycy" (Herbert) **168**:1
Dmitry Merezhkovsky (Hippius) **9**:163, 169
Dnes ještě zapadá slunce nad Atlandtidou (Nezval) **44**:242, 249
"Dnes vesna" (Remizov) **27**:341
Dnevniki (Tolstoy) **79**:415, 420
Dnevniki, 1891-1901 (Bryusov) **10**:83
Dni Turbinykh (Bulgakov) **16**:74, 76, 80-4, 86, 91, 94-5, 110; **159**:139, 162
Do Butlers Burgle Banks? (Wodehouse) **108**:370
"Do Not Go Gentle into That Good Night" (Thomas) **8**:461; **45**:362
"Do Not Let Your Pride Fall" (Södergran)
See "Låt ej din stolthet falla"
"Do Seek Their Meat from God" (Roberts) **8**:325

"Do They Think That I Do Not Know?" (Lawson) **27**:140
"Do We Need a 'Superorganic'" (Sapir) **108**:251
Do You Hear Them? (Sarraute)
See *Vous les entendez?*
"do you love me?" (Burroughs) **121**:128
"Do You Not Father Me" (Thomas) **45**:362
"Do You Use Real People in Fiction?" (Engel) **137**:110
"Doa" (Anwar) **22**:24
"Dobbin" (Noyes) **7**:515
Dobro v uchenii Tolstovo i Nietzsche: filosofia i propoved' (Shestov) **56**:263, 270, 272-73
"Doby's Gone" (Petry) **112**:300
"Doc Hill" (Masters) **25**:287
"Doc Mellhorn and the Pearly Gates" (Benét) **7**:81
"Doc Sifers" (Riley) **51**:292
"Doch Noch?" (Kandinsky) **92**:67
Le docteur Ox (Verne) **6**:500, 502
Le docteur Pascal (Zola) **1**:587, 590, 592; **6**:562-66; **41**:411, 414, 421, 424, 450-51, 453
"Doctor" (Robinson)
See "Doctor of Billiards"
The Doctor (Connor) **31**:106, 108, 111-12, 114
The Doctor (Rinehart) **52**:288, 294-96
"The Doctor and His Divorced Wife" (Agnon)
See "The Doctor's Divorce"
"The Doctor and His Divorcée" (Agnon)
See "The Doctor's Divorce"
Doctor and Patient (Mitchell) **36**:271
The Doctor and the Devils (Thomas) **8**:456-57; **105**:296, 299, 303-04, 356
"The Doctor and the Doctor's Wife" (Hemingway) **115**:179
Doctor Breen's Practice (Howells) **7**:365-66, 376-77, 392; **17**:185; **41**:234
Doctor Brodie's Report (Borges)
See *El informe de Brodie*
El doctor Centeno (Pérez Galdós) **27**:261, 267
"Doctor Chevalier's Lie" (Chopin) **14**:69
Doctor Claudius (Crawford) **10**:138, 142-44, 146, 151, 156
Doctor Faustus Lights the Lights (Stein) **1**:435-37; **48**:232, 264
Doctor Faustus: The Life of the German Composer Adrian Leverkühn as Told by a Friend (Mann)
See *Doktor Faustus: Das Leben des deutschen Tonsetzers Adrian Leverkühn, erzählt von einem Freunde*
Doctor Gion (Carossa)
See *Der Arzt Gion*
"The Doctor, His Wife, and the Clock" (Green) **63**:140, 143, 148, 153-54
The Doctor in Spite of Himself (Gregory) **176**:36, 76
Doctor Kerkhoven (Wassermann)
See *Etzel Andergast*
"Doctor of Billiards" (Robinson) **101**:150, 153, 157-60, 162
"A Doctor of Medicine" (Kipling) **17**:207
Doctor Ox (Verne)
See *Le docteur Ox*
Doctor Sax: Faust Part Three (Kerouac) **117**:248, 252, 266
Doctor Warrick's Daughters (Davis) **6**:149, 152
"Doctor Zay" (Phelps) **113**:405
Doctor Zay (Phelps) **113**:336, 339-41, 355-59, 394-95, 400-05
Dr. Zhivago (Pasternak) **188**:157-269
The Doctor's Dilemma (Shaw) **3**:381, 384, 401; **21**:316; **45**:215, 226-27, 244-45, 247, 257
"The Doctor's Divorce" (Agnon) **151**:22
"The Doctor's Duty" (Pirandello)
See "Il dovere del medico"
The Doctor's Duty (Pirandello)
See *Il dovere del medico*
The Doctor's Secret (Melies)
See *Hydrotherapie Fantastique*
"A Doctor's Visit" (Chekhov)
See "Slučaj iz praktiki"
The Doctor's Wife (Braddon) **111**:215, 221, 227, 305, 311-14
"The Doctrine of Chances" (Peirce) **81**:183
The Documents in the Case (Sayers) **2**:530-31; **15**:371, 390-92, 394
The Documents of the Birdsong (Raabe) **45**:204
Documents pour servir de canevas (Roussel) **20**:231, 234
The Dodecalogue of the Gypsy (Palamas)
See *Ho dodekálogos tou gýphtou*
Ho dodekálogos tou gýphtou (Palamas) **5**:377, 379-87
"Dodo" (Schulz) **51**:308
Dodo (Benson) **27**:2-4, 6-8, 12, 18-19
Dodo Wonders (Benson) **27**:5
Dodo's Daughter (Benson) **27**:4-5
Dödsdansen första delen (Strindberg) **1**:446, 460-62; **8**:407, 411, 417; **21**:348, 350-51, 353, 359-61, 368
Den dödsdömde (Dagerman) **17**:88-9, 94-5
Dodsworth (Lewis) **4**:252, 257, 259-60; **13**:338-40, 346, 350-52; **23**:151-52; **39**:234, 240, 254
"A Doer of the World" (Dreiser) **35**:71
"Does a Man Want Much Land?" (Tolstoy) **4**:458
"Does a Moment of Revolt Come Sometime to Every Married Man?" (Fitzgerald) **52**:58
"Does Culture Matter?" (Forster) **125**:58
"Does Political Theory Still Exist?" (Berlin) **105**:132, 144
"Does the Inertia of a Body Depend on Its Energy?" (Einstein) **65**:88
"Dog and Duck" (Machen) **4**:283
"The Dog Hervey" (Kipling) **8**:195-96
"A Dog of Flanders" (Ouida) **43**:350
A Dog of Flanders, and Other Stories (Ouida) **43**:357
"The Dog of the Man from the Bak Farm" (Jensen)
See "Bakmandens Hund"
"A Dog Sleeping on My Feet" (Dickey) **151**:90
"A Dog Waits His Dead Mistress" (Sterling) **20**:386
"A Dog without a Master" (Söderberg)
See "En herrelös hund"
"The Dogma Is the Drama" (Sayers) **15**:387
"The Dogs" (Bachmann)
See "Das Gebell"
"The Dogs" (Symons) **11**:430
The Dogs (Garro)
See *Los Perros*
The Dogs Bark: Public People and Private Places (Capote) **164**:137, 139, 142, 153, 199-204
"A Dog's Lot" (Remizov)
See "Sobach'ia dolia"
The Dogs, or The Paris Comedy (Saroyan) **137**:178
The Dogs, or The Paris Comedy and Two Other Plays: Chris Sick, or Happy New Year Anyway, Making Money and 19 Other Very Short Plays (Saroyan) **137**:178
"The Dogs' Tale" (Čapek)
See "Pohádka psí"
"A Dog's Tale" (Twain) **161**:223
"Dogwood" (Fletcher) **35**:106
Dōhyō (Miyamoto) **37**:296-70, 275
"The Doings of Raffles Haw" (Doyle) **7**:224
"Dois Dedos" (Ramos) **32**:431
Dōke no hana (Dazai Osamu) **11**:174-75, 181-82, 184
Doktor Bürger (Carossa)
See *Die Schicksale Doktor Bürgers*
Doktor Faustus (Mann)
See *Doktor Faustus: Das Leben des deutschen Tonsetzers Adrian Leverkühn, erzählt von einem Freunde*
Doktor Faustus: Das Leben des deutschen Tonsetzers Adrian Leverkühn; erzählt von einem Freunde (Mann) **2**:422-23, 427-28, 430-31, 433-36, 438, 440-43; **8**:258, 264-67, 272; **14**:356; **21**:177, 179, 205; **35**:221-22, 224, 231, 240-41, 265, 270-71; **44**:144-235; **60**:326, 329-30; **168**:90, 92-102, 114-17, 120-21, 129, 155-61, 164, 168-69, 172-73, 179-80, 187
Doktor Glas (Söderberg) **39**:429-31, 435, 438-39
"Doktor Murkes gesammeltes Schweigen" (Böll) **185**:27, 42
Doktor Murkes gesammeltes Schweigen (Böll) **185**:50, 105
Dolce far niente (Nezval) **44**:244
"The Doll" (Chesnutt) **39**:97
"The Doll" (Lowell) **8**:237
The Doll (Prus)
See *Lalka*
The Doll: A Happy Story (Hunt) **53**:186, 192
"Dollars and the Demimondaine" (Calvino) **183**:92
The Dollmaker (Arnow) **196**:14-17, 19-20, 23, 25-9, 31-4, 36-43, 49-51, 53-60, 66-9, 73-6, 78-80, 82-3, 85-98, 101, 103-04, 106-08, 111-13, 116-18, 120-23, 126, 128-29
"The Dolls" (Akutagawa Ryūnosuke) **16**:21
"The Doll's Ghost" (Crawford) **10**:158-59
"The Doll's House" (Mansfield) **2**:450-51, 454, 458; **8**:280-82, 284, 286-88; **39**:295, 303-04, 307, 319-21, 325, 329-30; **164**:249, 300, 305, 335, 340, 342
"A Doll's House" (Strindberg) **8**:407
A Doll's House (Ibsen)
See *Et dukkehjem*
"Dolly" (Larbaud) **9**:206
The Dolly Dialogues (Hope) **83**:165
"Dolor" (Gonzalez Martinez) **72**:152
"Dolor" (Mistral) **2**:478
"Dolor Oogo" (Quiller-Couch) **53**:291
"Dolores" (Swinburne) **8**:424, 427, 429, 441; **36**:305, 325, 336
Dolores (Compton-Burnett) **180**:134, 141, 168, 175, 177, 195-96
Dolorine et les ombres (Bosschere) **19**:52-3, 55, 62-6
"Doloy Shillera!" (Fadeyev) **53**:65-6
"Le dom" (Schwob) **20**:320
Dom Casmurro (Machado de Assis) **10**:280, 282-84, 286-89, 292, 297, 300-02
"Dom s mezoninom" (Chekhov) **10**:114-15
"Dom s mezoninom: Rasskaz khudozhnika" (Chekhov)
See "An Artist's Story"
The Domain of the Ndlambe People (Mqhayi)
See *Izwe lakwandlambe*
Domaine public (Desnos) **22**:62-3, 69
"Domashnie" (Guro) **56**:132
De dömdas ö (Dagerman) **17**:86-8, 92-4
A Dome of Many-Coloured Glass (Lowell) **1**:371-72, 374-75, 378; **8**:224, 234, 235
La Domenica della povera gente (Pratolini) **124**:337
The Domesday Book (Masters) **2**:461-62, 470; **25**:291, 293-94, 296-97, 299, 303, 315-16
Domesday Book and Beyond (Maitland) **65**:253, 258, 260, 264, 269, 272, 275-76, 279, 281, 284, 291
Domestic Breviary (Brecht) **1**:103
Domestic Dramas (Bourget)
See *Drames de famille*
Domestic Happiness (Tolstoy)
See *Semeinoe schaste*
Domesticities: A Little Book of Household Impressions (Lucas) **73**:162, 167, 174
Dometilo Wants To Be a Congressman (Azuela)
See *Domitilo quiere ser diputado*
"Domicilium" (Hardy) **53**:94
The Dominant City (Fletcher) **35**:89-90
"Domination of Black" (Stevens) **12**:372, 376; **45**:307
Dominations and Powers (Santayana) **40**:385

"Domine" (Pirandello) **4**:330
"Domingo" (Villaurrutia) **80**:517
"Dominica in palmis" (Johnson) **19**:253
The Dominion of Dreams (Sharp) **39**:355, 358, 364, 366, 374
"Dominique" (Drummond) **25**:157
Dominique (Marsh) **99**:356-57, 359-63
"Dominique de Gourgues" (Scott) **6**:388-89
The Domino Parlor (Riggs) **56**:215-16, 218
"El dominó verde" (Pardo Bazán) **189**:226-28
Domitilo quiere ser diputado (Azuela) **3**:77; **145**:9
Domnei (Cabell) **6**:62, 64-5, 67, 69-70, 74
"Domoj!" (Hippius) **9**:167
Domrémy (Péguy) **10**:410-11
"Domus angusta" (Meynell) **6**:294
Don Bravlio (Valera y Alcala-Galiano)
See *Pasarse de listo*
Don Camalèo (Malaparte) **52**:272-73
Don Friolera's Horns (Valle-Inclán)
See *Los cuernos de don Friolera*
"Don Giovanni Explains" (Shaw) **9**:427
Don Giovanni in Sicilia (Brancati) **12**:80-3, 85, 88, 90-1
Don Giovanni involontario (Brancati) **12**:84
Don Gonzalo González de la Gonzalera (Pereda) **16**:365, 367-68, 371, 373-74, 377-82
Don Juan (Flecker) **43**:205-06, 209
Don Juan (Lewisohn) **19**:272, 281-82
Don Juan (Sternheim) **8**:371, 381-82
Don Juan Comes Home (Horvath)
See *Don Juan kommt aus dem Krieg*
Don Juan de España (Martinez Sierra and Martinez Sierra) **6**:274, 278
Don Juan de Marana (Bennett) **5**:46; **20**:29; **197**:16, 18-20, 52
"Don Juan Explains" (Shaw) **21**:329
The Don Juan Figure (Rank)
See *Die Don Juan-Gestalt*
Don Juan in Egypt (Gumilev)
See *Don Žuan v Egipte*
Don Juan kommt aus dem Krieg (Horvath) **45**:78, 85, 102, 111
The Don Juan Legend (Rank)
See *Die Don Juan-Gestalt*
"Don Juan Manuel" (Güiraldes) **39**:190
Don Juan; oder, Die Liebe zur Geometrie (Frisch) **121**:273-74, 287
Don Juan; or, The Love of Geometry (Frisch)
See *Don Juan; oder, Die Liebe zur Geometrie*
"Don Juan to the Statue" (Nemerov) **124**:182, 302
Die Don Juan-Gestalt (Rank) **115**:221, 247, 249-51
"Don Juan—In the Russian Manner" (Chekhov) **10**:109
Don Juan's Failure (Baring) **8**:32
Don Juan's Last Night (Rostand)
See *La dernière nuit de Don Juan*
"Don Manuel le paresseux" (Giraudoux) **7**:324
Don Orsino (Crawford) **10**:143-44, 146-48, 155, 157
Don Perlimplím (García Lorca)
See *Amor de Don Perlimplín*
Don Perlimplín (García Lorca)
See *Amor de Don Perlimplín con Belisa en su jardín*
Don Quijote en Fuerteventura (Unamuno) **148**:233
"Don Quijote y Bolivar" (Unamuno) **148**:240
Don Quixote (Acker) **191**:4-7, 10-13, 15, 17-18, 40, 42, 55-62, 66-71, 92, 104-07, 109-10, 122, 128-29
"Don Quixote" (Dobson) **79**:3
Don Quixote (Pabst) **127**:361
Don Renato: An Ideal Content Historical Romance (Rolfe) **12**:275-79, 283
Don Rodriguez (Dunsany) **59**:17, 21, 29
Don Segundo Sombra (Güiraldes) **39**:174-75, 177-90, 192-95, 197
Don Tarquinio: A Kataleptic Phantasmatic Romance (Rolfe) **12**:275-79, 283
Don Žuan v Egipte (Gumilev) **60**:265-6
"Dona Benedita" (Machado de Assis) **10**:291
Doña luz (Valera y Alcala-Galiano) **10**:496-97, 505, 507-08
Dona Milagros (Pardo Bazán) **189**:243-44, 263-64, 269-70, 309-14
Doña Perfecta (Pérez Galdós) **27**:244-46, 249, 252, 254, 256-58, 263, 265-66, 273-74, 285, 288
Doña Rosita la soltera (García Lorca) **1**:314; **7**:292; **49**:76, 88; **181**:45, 51-56, 58-59, 179
Doña Rosita the Spinster; or, The Language of Flowers (García Lorca)
See *Doña Rosita la soltera*
El donador de almas (Nervo) **11**:404-05
Donal Grant (MacDonald) **113**:209, 245, 282
"Donde ni una gota de tristeza es pecado" (Aleixandre) **113**:8
De donde son los cantantes (Sarduy) **2**:974, 976, 978-80, 983, 985, 987-89; **167**:185, 198-99, 203, 206, 209-11, 218, 221, 230
Donde van a morir los elefantes (Donoso) **133**:205
"Dónde y cómo el diablo perdió el poncho" (Palma) **29**:258, 262
Done in the Open (Remington) **89**:301
"The Donkey" (Chesterton) **6**:101
The Donkey Prince (Carter) **139**:125-28
"Donna" (Saba) **33**:370
"La donna è mobile" (Güiraldes) **39**:190
"Donna genovese" (Campana) **20**:83
"Donnaia trava" (Balmont) **11**:39
Les données immédiates de la conscience (Bergson) **32**:8, 12, 20, 27, 31, 40, 44, 51
The Donnellan Lectures (Dunsany) **59**:18
Donner à voir (Éluard) **7**:250, 253-54; **41**:163
"The Don't Care Negro" (Cotter) **28**:42
Don't Go Away Mad (Saroyan) **137**:149
"Don't Grow Old" (Ginsberg) **120**:35, 55
"Don't Look Now" (Kuttner) **10**:269, 274
"Don't Send Your Son to College" (Lane) **177**:286
"Don't They Make You Sad" (Wright) **136**:301
"Don't Try to Account for Anything" (Shepherd) **177**:296
"Donten" (Nagai) **51**:88
"Doof" (Schwitters) **95**:344
"Doom and She" (Hardy) **53**:81, 86
"Doom Ferry" (Quiller-Couch) **53**:291
The Doom of Youth (Lewis) **2**:391; **104**:164, 226-27, 231, 237, 239
"A Doom on the Sun" (Thomas) **105**:353
"The Doom That Came to Sarnath" (Lovecraft) **22**:219, 232
"The Doomdorf Mystery" (Post) **39**:338, 340-41, 344
Doomsday (Talvik)
See "Kohtupaev"
The Doomswoman (Atherton) **2**:12
The Door (Rinehart) **52**:288-91, 300-01
"The Door in the Wall" (Wells) **6**:541
The Door of Dread (Stringer) **37**:336
The Door with Seven Locks (Wallace) **57**:397-98
The Doorman (Arenas)
See *El portero*
A Doorway in Fairyland (Housman) **7**:355
Dope (Rohmer) **28**:282, 293, 295, 301
Dopelleben: Zwei Selbstdarstellungen (Benn) **3**:110
Dopo il divorzio (Deledda) **23**:38-9, 43-4
Dopo la vittoria (Gentile) **96**:144-45
"Dopo una passeggiata" (Saba) **33**:373
Der Doppelgänger (Rank) **115**:263, 284, 336
"Dopper and Papist" (Bosman) **49**:32
La doppia notte dei tigli (Levi) **125**:204-7, 210-11
"Dora versus Rose" (Dobson) **79**:26
El Dorado (Torrence) **97**:143-44, 146-48, 156-57, 159, 164
"El dorador" (Lugones) **15**:289
"Dora's Gingerbread" (Montgomery) **51**:199
"Der Dorfdadaist" (Ball) **104**:17
"Dorfgeschichte" (Walser) **18**:419
Dorian Gray (Wilde)
See *The Picture of Dorian Gray*
"La dormeuse" (Valéry) **15**:463
Dormez! Je le veux! (Feydeau) **22**:87
"Los dormidos" (Aleixandre) **113**:33
Dormir, dormir dans les pierres (Péret) **20**:201
"The Dormouse and the Doctor" (Milne) **88**:240
"Doroga" (Babel) **2**:25, 28; **13**:34; **171**:9-11
"Dorothy" (Dobson) **79**:5, 8
Dorothy and the Wizard in Oz (Baum) **7**:13, 20, 25, 27; **132**:36, 49, 52, 75, 79, 84-89, 98
"Dorothy Grumpet, Graduate Lady" (Heyward) **59**:93
The Dorrington Deed-box (Morrison) **72**:364
"The Dorsetshire Labourer" (Hardy) **143**:156, 178, 206
Los dos augures (Reyes) **33**:324
Dos crímenes (Ibarguengoitia) **148**:216, 218-19
Dos fanatismos (Echegaray) **4**:105
Dos groyse gevins (Aleichem) **35**:320
"¡Dos Hermanas!" (Jiménez) **183**:335
Dos madres (Unamuno) **2**:570; **9**:515; **148**:257
"Dos muchachas" (García Lorca) **181**:196, 199
"Dos poemas y un comentario" (Aleixandre) **113**:66
"Los dos reyes y los dos laberintos" (Borges) **109**:40
"Dos rivales" (Nervo) **11**:394
"Dos Shtraiml" (Peretz) **16**:390
"Dos tepl" (Aleichem) **35**:315, 319
"Dos teppel" (Aleichem)
See "Dos tepl"
"Dos vidas" (Aleixandre) **113**:37
"Doski sud'by" (Khlebnikov) **20**:144
Dostigaev and Others (Gorky) **8**:89
Dostoevski i Nietzsche: Filosofiia Tragedii (Shestov) **56**:263-64, 270-74
"Dostoevskii bez dostoevshchiny" (Nabokov) **108**:133, 223
Dostoevsky (Berdyaev) **67**:29
Dostoevsky and Nietzsche: The Philosophy of Tragedy (Shestov)
See *Dostoevski i Nietzsche: Filosofiia Tragedii*
"Dostoevsky without Dostoevskianism" (Nabokov)
See "Dostoevskii bez dostoevshchiny"
Dostojewskij: Tragödie-Mythos-Mystik (Ivanov) **33**:131-32
Dot and Tot in Merryland (Baum) **7**:13; **132**:92
"A Dot on the Map" (Sait Faik)
See "Haritada bir nokta"
A Dot on the Map: Selected Short Stories and Poems (Sait Faik) **23**:298
"Două loturi" (Caragiale) **76**:156, 159, 176
The Double (Rank)
See *Der Doppelgänger*
"Double Absence" (Muir) **87**:169
"A Double Buggy at Lahey's Creek" (Lawson) **27**:121, 128, 131, 145
Double Dan (Wallace) **57**:398
"The Double Fifth" (Lu Hsun) **3**:301
The Double Game (Baring) **8**:41
Double Harness (Hope) **83**:170
Double Indemnity (Chandler) **179**:97, 224
Double Life (Rinehart) **52**:281
The Double Life of Mr. Alfred Burton (Oppenheim) **45**:127
"Double Poem of Lake Eden" (García Lorca)
See "Poema doble del lago Eden"
"The Double Standard" (Harper) **14**:257, 260-61, 263-64
A Double Story (MacDonald) **113**:213
The Double Traitor (Oppenheim) **45**:134, 137
La double vie de Théophraste Longuet (Leroux) **25**:260
The Double Vision (Frye) **165**:193, 208, 210, 214, 224, 249

"The Double Vision of Michael Robartes" (Yeats) **11**:528; **93**:341, 368, 369
A Double-Barrelled Detective Story (Twain) **12**:436
"A Double-Dyed Deceiver" (Henry) **19**:190
La doublure (Roussel) **20**:228-30, 234-35, 240, 242, 245, 253-54
"Doubt No More That Oberon" (Millay) **4**:306
"Doubting Makar" (Platonov)
See "Usomnivshiisia Makar"
"Doubts" (Bosschere)
See "Doutes"
"Doudou" (Babel) **171**:7
Doughty Deeds (Graham) **19**:112
"Doute" (Zola) **21**:456
"Doutes" (Bosschere) **19**:54, 57-9, 63
Les XII filles d'Edmond Grasset (Bloy) **22**:46
"The Dove in Spring" (Stevens) **45**:309-10
"The Dove in the Belly" (Stevens) **45**:306, 309-10
The Dove in the Eagle's Nest (Yonge) **48**:376
"The Dove of Thought" (Heidenstam) **5**:250
"Dove That Swims in Its Own Blood" (Lasker-Schueler) **57**:330
A Doveglion Book of Philippine Poetry (Villa) **176**:95, 103
The Dover Road (Milne) **6**:306-09
"Il dovere del medico" (Pirandello) **29**:282, 317, 319
Doves and Sparrowhawks (Deledda)
See *Colombi e sparvieri*
"The Doves Nest" (Mansfield) **8**:280, 282; **39**:303
The Doves' Nest, and Other Stories (Mansfield) **2**:447
Down and Out in Paris and London (Orwell) **2**:498, 504-05, 508-10; **6**:341-42, 351-52; **15**:322, 333, 359-60; **31**:180, 188; **51**:227-28, 236, 250, 252, 254, 261-62; **128**:254-56, 259, 261-63, 265, 268, 271, 274, 280, 282, 295, 311; **129**:228, 234, 238
"Down at the Dump" (White) **176**:159-60, 191, 228
"Down by the Carib Sea" (Johnson) **19**:210
"Down by the Riverside" (Wright) **136**:317-18
Down Hill (Sánchez)
See *Barranca abajo*
"Down Home" (Montgomery) **51**:210
"Down Pens" (Saki) **3**:372
"Down the Long Coasts" (Hodgson) **13**:230
"Down the Ravine" (Murfree) **135**:217, 227
"Down the River" (Abbey) **160**:15, 24, 26, 93, 97, 102
"Down the River" (Buchanan) **107**:25
Down the River (Abbey) **160**:39, 52, 54, 59
"Down the River with Henry Thoreau" (Abbey) **160**:42, 52
"Down the Waterway of Sunset Drove to Shore a Ship of Gold" (Housman) **10**:242
Down There (Huysmans)
See *Là-bas*
"Down to the Capital" (Riley) **51**:284
Down Under Donovan (Wallace) **57**:397
Down Went McGinty (Sturges)
See *The Great McGinty*
Downfall (Mizoguchi) **72**:313, 316-17, 319
"The Downfall of Abner Joyce" (Fuller) **103**:69, 74, 85
The Downfall of Canada (D'Annunzio) **6**:131
"The Downfall of Mulligan's" (Paterson) **32**:380
Downfall of Osen (Mizoguchi) **72**:321
Downstream (Asch)
See *The Return*
Downstream (Huysmans)
See *À vau-l'eau*
"Doznanie" (Kuprin) **5**:303-04
"Dr. Arnold" (Strachey) **12**:395
"Dr. Booker T. Washington to the National Negro Business League" (Cotter) **28**:43, 46
Dr. Brodie's Report (Borges)
See *El informe de Brodie*
Dr. Bürger (Carossa)
See *Die Schicksale Doktor Bürgers*
"Dr. Burney's Evening Party" (Woolf) **43**:394
Dr. Clinksales (Adams) **56**:9
Dr. Cupid (Buchanan) **107**:32
"Dr. Gowdy and the Squash" (Fuller) **103**:70, 74
"Dr. Hachiya's Hiroshima Diary" (Canetti) **157**:69
Dr. Harmer's Holidays (Pinero) **32**:403-05
"Dr. Johnson's Writings" (Stephen) **23**:305
"Dr. Mejzlík's Case" (Čapek)
See "Případ dra Mejzlíka"
Dr. Montessori's Own Handbook: A Manual for Teachers and Parents (Montessori) **103**:289
Dr. Murke's Collection of Silence (Böll)
See *Doktor Murkes gesammeltes Schweigen*
Dr. No (Fleming) **193**:196, 198-99, 203, 210, 213, 215, 223, 228, 239, 241-42
Dr. North and His Friends (Mitchell) **36**:265-67, 271, 273, 276
Dr. Ox's Experiment (Verne)
See *Le docteur Ox*
"Dr. Pechal's Theory" (Hawthorne) **25**:247
Dr. Rung (Sigurjónsson) **27**:361, 364
"Dr. Scudder's Clinical Lecture" (Masters) **25**:290
Dr. Sevier (Cable) **4**:25-7, 29-31, 35-6
Dr. Strangelove; or, How I Learned to Stop Worrying and Love the Bomb (Kubrick) **112**:125, 127-33, 153, 172, 187-88, 201, 213-14, 225, 233, 236, 258, 262-63, 265, 267, 269, 273
Dr. Thorndyke's Case-Book (Freeman) **21**:58, 61
Dr. Thorndyke's Cases (Freeman)
See *John Thorndyke's Cases*
"Drab Rambles" (Bonner) **179**:42, 56, 58, 60
Dracula (Murnau)
See *Nosferatu, eine Symphonie des Grauens*
Dracula (Stoker) **8**:384-400, 402; **144**:246-364
"Dracula's Guest" (Stoker) **144**:320
Dracula's Guest, and Other Weird Stories (Stoker) **144**:295
"The Draft Convention for Financial Assistance by the League of Nations" (Keynes) **64**:245
"A Draft on the Bank of Spain" (Mitchell) **36**:264
The Draft Program of the Communist International (Trotsky) **22**:365
Le drageoir àépices (Huysmans) **7**:404, 410, 415; **69**:7, 23, 48, 56
"The Dragon" (Akutagawa Ryūnosuke) **16**:27
"The Dragon" (Zamyatin) **37**:424, 431
The Dragon (Gregory) **1**:334; **176**:38-40
The Dragon (Shiel) **8**:362
The Dragon (Zamyatin) **37**:423-24
The Dragon and the Dove (Bridie) **3**:137
"The Dragon and the Poet" (Miyazawa) **76**:280, 291
The Dragon Murder Case (Van Dine) **23**:355, 360
"The Dragonfly" (Nemerov) **124**:177, 185
La dragonne (Jarry) **14**:280; **147**:261, 267-68, 275-76, 278-81
"The Drained Cup" (Lawrence) **93**:46, 69
Drake (Noyes) **7**:502-03, 507-08, 512-15
"Drama" (Nemerov) **124**:182, 184
The Drama and the Stage (Lewisohn) **19**:279, 293
"Drama at the Crossroads" (Wen I-to) **28**:421
"Drama Cleansing and Pressing" (Benchley) **55**:3
El Drama de los hijas de Loth (García Lorca) **49**:109
A Drama from the Days of the Last Kings (Zuckmayer) **191**:329-30
A Drama in Muslin (Moore) **7**:473, 477, 482, 484, 486-87, 489-90, 499
The Drama of Kings (Buchanan) **107**:25, 40-8, 58, 67, 70-2, 83
The Drama of Love and Death (Carpenter) **88**:109, 120
"Drama of the Doctor's Window" (Dobson) **79**:5
"A Drama of Youth" (Middleton) **56**:175-76, 182
"The Dramatic Actor and Reality" (Simmel) **64**:339
"The Dramatic Funeral" (Coppee) **25**:121
Dramatic Opinions and Essays (Shaw) **21**:319
"The Dramatic Outlook in America" (Matthews) **95**:228, 262
Dramatic Sonnets, Poems, and Ballads: Selections from the Poems of Eugene Lee-Hamilton (Lee-Hamilton) **22**:190
Dramatis Personae (Yeats) **31**:390
Dramatische Dichtungen in drei Sprachen (Beckett) **145**:180
Dramatische Historie (Werfel) **8**:479
Dramatische Legende (Werfel) **8**:479
Dramatist in America (Anderson) **144**:35-36
"The Dramatization of Novels" (Matthews) **95**:228
Un drame dans le monde (Bourget) **12**:69
Die Dramen (Barlach) **84**:73
Drames de famille (Bourget) **12**:68
The Dram-Shop (Zola) **1**:594
Der Dräumling (Raabe) **45**:175, 177, 179, 189, 192, 200
The Dräumling Swamp (Raabe)
See *Der Dräumling*
Draussen vor der Tür (Borchert) **5**:103-04, 106-10
Draw the Fires (Toller)
See *Feuer aus den Kesseln*
The Drawback (Baring) **8**:32
"Drawing" (Oppen) **107**:326
"Drawing Lessons" (Nemerov) **124**:217, 300
"Drawing of Roses and Violets" (Field) **43**:166
Drawings (Kahanovitsch)
See *Tseykhenungen*
The Drawings of Bruno Schulz (Schulz) **51**:323
"Dray Wara Yow Dee" (Kipling) **17**:208
Drayman Henschel (Hauptmann) **4**:197
"The Dread of Height" (Thompson) **4**:435
"The Dread Skeleton" (Remizov)
See "Ligostai strashnyi"
"The Dread Voyage" (Campbell) **9**:29-30
The Dread Voyage, and Other Poems (Campbell) **9**:29-33
"Dreaded Hell" (Onetti)
See "El infierno tan temido"
"The Dreadful Dragon of Hay Hill" (Beerbohm) **1**:68; **24**:111
The Dreadful Night (Williams) **89**:360
"A Dream" (Benson) **17**:32
"The Dream" (Bishop) **103**:3-4
"The Dream" (Henry) **19**:170
"Dream" (Riley) **51**:300
"Dream" (Sarton) **120**:305, 318
The Dream (Bennett) **5**:46
A Dream (Nervo) **11**:403
The Dream (Wells) **6**:553
A Dream and a Forgetting (Hawthorne) **25**:249
"Dream and Madness" (Trakl)
See "Traum und Umnachtung"
Dream and Reality (Berdyaev) **67**:71-2
"A Dream Come True" (Montgomery) **51**:181
"A Dream Come True" (Onetti)
See "Un sueño realizado"
Dream Days (Grahame) **64**:54, 59, 63-6, 78-9, 81-2, 87-8, 91-5, 110; **136**:23-27
The Dream Detective (Rohmer) **28**:282, 285
"The Dream Fiancée" (Chekhov) **31**:96
"A Dream Forgotten" (Csáth) **13**:149
A Dream Fulfilled, and Other Stories (Onetti)
See *Un sueño realizado y otros cuentos*
"Dream Kitsch" (Benjamin) **39**:10

"Dream Land" (Sharp) **39**:381
"A Dream Lies Dead" (Parker) **143**:324
The Dream Life of Balso Snell (West) **1**:479, 481-83, 485-90, 492; **14**:468, 470-72, 476-79, 481-82, 485-89; **44**:367, 369, 373, 375, 386, 389-90, 396, 400, 404, 410
"Dream Love" (Baker) **10**:28
"Dream Nocturne" (Villaurrutia) **80**:482
The Dream of a Spring Morning (D'Annunzio)
See *Sogno d'un mattino di primavera*
The Dream of a Woman (Gourmont)
See *Le song d'une femme*
The Dream of an Autumn Sunset (D'Annunzio)
See *Il sogno d'un tramonto d'autunno*
"The Dream of an Hour" (Chopin)
See "The Story of an Hour"
"A Dream of Armageddon" (Wells) **19**:437
"A Dream of Artemis" (Ledwidge) **23**:109, 111, 122-23
"The Dream of Beg Karčic" (Andrić)
See "San bega Karčića"
"The Dream of Children" (Baker) **10**:21, 27
"The Dream of Eternity" (Söderberg) **39**:436-37, 439
Dream of Fair to Middling Women (Beckett) **145**:77, 108-13
"A Dream of Fear" (Sterling) **20**:378
"The Dream of Flying Comes of Age" (Nemerov) **124**:182
"A Dream of Italy" (Masters) **2**:471
"A Dream of Kites" (Hearn) **9**:134
"Dream of November" (Gosse) **28**:143
"A Dream of Old Vienna" (Merrill) **173**:257
"A Dream of Prayer" (Schreiner) **9**:400
"The Dream of the Flesh of Iron" (Lockridge) **111**:332-33, 349
"The Dream of the Higher Magic" (Hofmannsthal) **11**:294
"The Dream of the World without Death" (Buchanan) **107**:39
"A Dream of Two Dimensions" (Rutherford) **25**:355
"A Dream of Youth" (Johnson) **19**:253
"A Dream on the Train / . . . No, in my Berth" (Jiménez) **183**:337
"Dream on the Wave" (Papadiamantis) **29**:270, 272
The Dream Physician (Martyn) **131**:102, 107, 110, 125
Dream Play (Kraus)
See *Traumstück*
The Dream Play (Pirandello) **29**:303
The Dream Play (Strindberg)
See *Ett drömspel*
"Dream River" (Pickthall) **21**:256
"Dream Sequence" (Agee) **180**:24
Dream Street (Griffith) **68**:169, 173-76, 219
Dream Theater (Kraus)
See *Traumtheater*
"Dream Traces" (Hesse) **196**:272-73
"A Dream within a Dream" (Phelps) **113**:401
The dream-captain's log (Arp)
See *Logbuch des Traumkapitä*
"A Dreamer" (Baynton) **57**:4, 9-11, 20-23, 32
"The Dreamer" (Papadiamantis) **29**:272-73
"The Dreamer" (Tolstoy)
See "Aggei Korovin"
The Dreamer (Reymont) **5**:390, 393
A Dreamer in Portugal (Dixon) **163**:174
Dreamers (Hamsun)
See *Svaermere*
The Dreamers (Kuzmin)
See *Mechtateli*
Dreamers of the Ghetto (Zangwill) **16**:443-45, 447, 452
A Dreamer's Tales (Dunsany) **2**:136; **59**:4, 17, 20, 25, 28-9
"Dreaming and Waking under the Grabić" (Andrić)
See "San i java pod Grabićem"
Dreaming of Babylon: A Private Eye Novel, 1942 (Brautigan) **133**:32-33
Dreaming of Butterflies (Hagiwara)
See *Chō o yumemu*
The Dreaming of the Bones (Yeats) **1**:571; **11**:515
"Dreamless City" (García Lorca) **197**:184
The Dream-Quest of the Unknown Kadath (Lovecraft) **4**:266, 272; **22**:213, 220
"Dreams" (Chesterton) **64**:42
"Dreams" (Jarrell) **177**:155
Dreams (Remizov) **27**:334
Dreams (Schreiner) **9**:393-96, 400, 402, 404-05
"Dreams about Clothes" (Merrill) **173**:197, 209
Dreams and Dust (Marquis) **7**:434-35, 437, 446-47
Dreams and Experiences (Andrić)
See *Šta sanjam i šta mi se dogada*
Dreams and Fates (Yourcenar)
See *Les Songes et les sorts*
Dreams and Gibes (Sapir) **108**:247, 249-50, 268
Dreams and Projects (Arp) **115**:29, 32
"The Dreams in the Witch-House" (Lovecraft) **4**:267-68; **22**:209, 219, 224, 238
"Dreams Nascent" (Lawrence) **93**:44
Dreams of a Bad Death (Donoso)
See *Sueños de la mala muerte*
"The Dreams of a Prophet" (Dunsany) **59**:18
"The Dreams of Chang" (Bunin) **6**:45
"The Dreams of Debs" (London) **15**:270-71
"Dreams of Movie Stardom" (Frank) **17**:114, 121
"Dreams of the Sea" (Davies) **5**:199
"Dreams of To-day and Yesterday" (Naidu) **80**:281
"Dreams Old" (Lawrence) **93**:44
"Dreams within Dreams" (Sharp) **39**:380
"Dream-Song" (Middleton) **56**:175
"Dreamtigers" (Borges)
See "El hacedor"
Dreamtigers (Borges)
See *El hacedor*
"The Dreamt-Of Place" (Muir) **87**:307
Dreamy Bourgeoisie (Drieu la Rochelle) **21**:39
"A Dreary Story" (Chekhov) **3**:101, 147-48, 152, 159; **10**:100, 107-08, 115; **55**:65; **96**:15; **163**:43, 78, 109, 133
"Dreary Windblown Yellow Meads" (Hartmann) **73**:118
"Dregs" (Vallejo)
See "Heces"
Dregs (Hecht) **101**:36-7, 44, 49, 73
Drei Abhandlungen zur Sexualtheorie (Freud) **52**:115, 119
Drei Einakter (Kaiser) **9**:179-80
Drei Frauen (Musil) **12**:240, 246, 251-53, 261; **68**:288
"Drei Matones" (Peretz) **16**:402
Drei Reden (Sudermann) **15**:431
"Dreizehn Jahre später" (Böll) **185**:50
Die drei Reiherfedern (Sudermann) **15**:418-20, 430, 433-34, 438
Die drei Sprünge des Wang-lun (Döblin) **13**:158, 160, 162, 166-67, 173-74, 180
"Die Drei Stufen der Ethik" (Sudermann) **15**:433
Drei Wege zum See (Bachmann)
See *Simultan*
"Drei Wege zum See" (Bachmann) **192**:32-33, 36, 78, 81-83, 87-88
Die Dreigroschenoper (Brecht) **1**:100, 106-09, 114, 122; **6**:36-7; **35**:9, 11-12; **169**:51-56, 61
Die Dreigroschenoper (Pabst) **127**:301, 304, 327-28, 330-32, 334, 339, 348, 354, 359-60, 362
Dreiklang (Klabund) **44**:111
Dreimals Sieben Lieder des Pierrot Lunaire (Schoenberg) **75**:290, 292-93, 298, 300, 302, 323, 326, 328, 332, 344-48, 351, 361, 363, 372, 406
Dreiser Looks at Russia (Dreiser) **10**:183
Das dreißigste Jahr (Bachmann) **192**:9-10, 12, 25, 44, 70, 137
"Das dreißigste Jahr" (Bachmann) **192**:10-11, 137
"Drenched in Light" (Hurston) **131**:71
"A Dresden Lady in Dixie" (Chopin) **14**:82
"The Dress" (Thomas) **105**:296, 318-320, 327, 333-34, 337-38
"The Dressing Room" (Herzl) **36**:141
"Drewniana kostka" (Herbert) **168**:14
"Dreyfus in Kasrilevke" (Aleichem) **35**:306, 322, 324
The Dreyfus Revolution (Sorel)
See *Revolution Dreyfusienne*
"Die Drie dunklen Könige" (Borchert) **5**:105, 109
"Dried Marjoram" (Lowell) **1**:371; **8**:225
"Drieka and the Moon" (Bosman) **49**:19
The Drift Fence (Grey) **6**:187
The Drift of Pinions (Pickthall) **21**:241, 244, 246, 251, 255-57
"Drifted Back" (Lawson) **27**:125, 148, 150
"Drifting" (Quiroga)
See "A la deriva"
"Drifting Apart" (Lawson) **27**:132, 145
Drifting Away from Marx and Freud (Lyotard)
See *Dérive à partir de Marx et Freud*
The Drifting Clouds (Futabatei)
See *Ukigumo*
"Drifting Down Lost Creek" (Murfree) **135**:201, 203-4, 212-13, 218, 220-21, 227, 231
"A Driftwood Fire" (Higginson) **36**:167-68
"Drikkevise" (Obstfelder) **23**:177
"Drink" (Anderson) **1**:59; **10**:56; **24**:33-4, 45
"Drinking Dirge" (Belloc) **7**:33
"Drinking From a Helmet" (Dickey) **151**:89, 105
The Drinking Gourd (Hansberry) **192**:265, 267, 269, 272-73, 285-86, 289-90, 296-98, 314-20, 323, 334-36
"The Driver" (Dickey) **151**:199
"The Driver" (Merrill) **173**:239
"The Driver" (Peretz) **16**:389
"Drizzle" (Söderberg) **39**:437-38
"A Drizzling Easter Morning" (Hardy) **53**:90-1
Le Droit de rever (Bachelard) **128**:55, 73
Drôle de voyage (Drieu la Rochelle) **21**:18-19, 22, 33-4
Ett drömspel (Strindberg) **1**:446, 449-51, 454, 459-61, 463; **8**:407, 412, 414-16; **21**:350, 353-54, 359; **47**:339, 354, 362, 369, 372-75
Dronning Tamara (Hamsun) **14**:221, 224, 244; **49**:127
A Drop of Ink (Masaoka) **18**:225-28, 233
"A Drop of Rain and a Speck of Dust" (Sologub)
See "Kaplja i pylinka"
Drops from the Forest (Prishvin)
See *Lesnaia kapel*
Drops of Blood (Sologub) **9**:436-38
"Drops of Dew" (Rohan)
See "Tsuyu dandan"
"Drought" (Reese) **181**:345
"Drought" (Tomlinson) **71**:400
"Drought" (Tynan) **3**:505
"Drouth" (Austin) **25**:35
"Drovers" (Grove) **4**:141
"The Drover's Wife" (Lawson) **27**:121, 128-30, 141-43, 148-50, 152
The Drowned and the Saved (Levi)
See *I sommersi e i salvati*
"The Drowned Man" (Brennan) **124**:5
"The Drowning Poet" (Merrill) **173**:253
Drowning with Others (Dickey) **151**:90, 99-100, 102, 104-5, 171, 202-3
"The Drowsy Day" (Dunbar) **12**:105
"Droyb" (Bergelson) **80**:30,32-3
"The Drug Store" (Fields) **80**:262
Drugi pokój (Herbert) **168**:29-32, 34, 36, 39
"Drugomu" (Annensky) **14**:27
"The Drug-Shop; or, Endymion in Edmonstown" (Benét) **7**:78

"Druhá loupeznická pohádka" (Čapek) **192**:180
The Druid Circle (Van Druten) **2**:574-75
"Druidic Rimes" (Nemerov) **124**:257
"The Drum Goes Dead" (Aldrich) **125**:15
The Drum Goes Dead (Aldrich) **125**:10
"Drummer Hodge" (Hardy) **53**:77; **143**:156, 168, 170, 187
"Drums" (Bosschere) **19**:63
Drums (Boyd) **115**:62-4, 66-8, 70-3
Drums in the Night (Brecht)
See *Trommeln in der nacht*
The Drums of Fu Manchu (Rohmer) **28**:280, 294-95, 300
"The Drums of the Fore and Aft" (Kipling) **8**:182; **17**:204
"Drunk" (Kahanovitsch)
See "Shiker"
"Drunkard" (Baker) **47**:20
"The Drunkard" (Tagore)
See "Matal"
The Drunkard (Bishop) **121**:72
"The Drunkard's Child" (Harper) **14**:260
The Drunkard's Reformation (Griffith) **68**:186, 214-15
"The Drunken Sailor" (Cary) **29**:65; **196**:172, 219
Drunken Sun (Gladkov) **27**:91
The Dry Heart (Ginzburg)
See *E stato cosí*
The Dry Little Thorn (Tey) **14**:451, 459
"Dry Loaf" (Stevens) **45**:283
"The Dry Millenium" (Mencken) **13**:363
"Dry September" (Faulkner) **141**:101, 173-74; **170**:127, 185-86, 189
Dry Valley (Bunin)
See *Sukhodol*
Dryden (Saintsbury) **31**:214
Dryss (Nexø) **43**:329
Du côté de chez Swann (Proust) **7**:519, 521-22, 540, 543-45, 549, 551; **13**:401-02, 404, 406, 410, 421-23; **33**:254, 256, 261-62, 271-72, 274; **161**:123, 129, 138, 162-63, 179, 206
"Du coton dans les oreilles" (Apollinaire) **51**:34, 37
"Du fond de la forêt" (Péret) **20**:198
Du haut en bas (Pabst) **127**:361
"Du Lehnest Wider eine silberweide" (George) **14**:201
"Du muet au parlant: Grandeur et décadence du cinéma" (Fondane) **159**:240
Du poétique (Benda) **60**:65-8
Du sang, de la volupté, et de la mort (Brandon) **47**:54-9, 77
"Du som aldrig gått ut ur dit trädgårdsland" (Södergran) **31**:288
"Du store Eros" (Södergran) **31**:295
Du style d'ideés (Benda) **60**:65, 68-70
"Duality" (Baker) **10**:28
DuBarry (Belasco) **3**:85, 90
Dubin's Lives (Malamud) **129**:76, 117-24, 126-28, 137, 189, 193, 197, 205-9; **184**:222, 224, 227-28, 232, 234-35, 253, 265-66, 268-69, 277, 299, 301
"Dubious Battle in California" (Steinbeck) **135**:339
"Dublin Men" (Stephens) **4**:419
"Dublin Revisited I" (Gogarty) **15**:120
"Dublin Revisited II" (Gogarty) **15**:120
Dubliners (Joyce) **3**:252-54, 259, 266-70, 273-75, 277, 282; **8**:158, 165-67, 169-71; **16**:202, 212, 218-21, 230, 232-33, 237, 240, 244; **35**:139-203; **52**:207, 226, 237, 242; **159**:266-69, 275-77, 279, 297-98, 301, 303-16, 358-61, 363
"The Dublin-Galway Train" (Gogarty) **15**:109
"The Duchess at Prayer" (Wharton) **9**:541; **27**:382; **129**:360
"The Duchess of Newcastle" (Woolf) **43**:394; **128**:333
The Duchess of Padua (Wilde) **1**:496; **8**:494; **41**:354, 376; **175**:281, 312
The Duchess of Wrexe (Walpole) **5**:492, 499, 503
La duchesse bleue (Bourget) **12**:65
La duchesse des Folies-Bergère (Feydeau) **22**:92, 94
"Duck" (Popa) **167**:153
"A Duck for Dinner" (Stevens) **45**:269
Duck Soup (Mankiewicz) **85**:112, 149, 155
La duda (Echegaray) **4**:101
"Dudh-ka dam" (Premchand) **21**:292, 294
Dudley and Gilderoy (Blackwood) **5**:77
"Due democrazie" (Gentile) **96**:145
"I due mondani" (Brancati) **12**:82
"Due Notice" (Abbey) **160**:78
"Due Notice to the FBI" (De Voto) **29**:131
"Duèl" (Chekhov) **3**:160-61, 164; **10**:107-08, 113-14; **163**:103
"The Duel" (Chekhov)
See "Duèl"
"The Duel" (Kuprin) **5**:299-300
"Duel in the Snow" (Shepherd) **177**:293
Duel of Angels (Giraudoux)
See *Pour lucrèce*
Das Duell (Weiss) **152**:286-87, 289
"Duende" (Trambley) **163**:287, 320-21, 331-32
Los duendes de la camarilla (Pérez Galdós) **27**:276
A Duet, with an Occasional Chorus (Doyle) **7**:240
Duineser Elegien (Rilke) **1**:409, 411, 414, 416-22, 424; **6**:358-61, 363, 365, 367-9; **19**:305, 310, 314, 316; **195**:163-66, 168-69, 178-79, 197, 200-02, 244-46, 251, 256, 265, 269, 276, 307, 310-11, 313, 316, 320, 323, 328, 330, 333, 338-40
Duino Elegies (Rilke)
See *Duineser Elegien*
Duke Herring (Bodenheim) **44**:73-4
"The Duke in His Domain" (Capote) **164**:137, 142, 150, 199-200
The Duke of Gandia (Swinburne) **8**:434, 444
"Duke of Onions and Duke of Garlic" (Bialik) **25**:53
Et dukkehjem (Ibsen) **2**:223-26, 228-30, 233, 235, 237, 240-41; **8**:143, 146-48, 150-53; **16**:154, 156, 169, 175, 187, 189; **37**:219-64; **52**:143, 155, 158, 162, 184, 191
El dulce daño (Storni) **5**:444, 447-48, 451
Dulce dueño (Pardo Bazán) **189**:209, 229, 243, 248, 251, 322-27
"Dulce Et Decorum Est" (Owen) **5**:362, 366-67, 370-71; **27**:208, 210, 212-13, 217-18, 221, 226, 228-30, 236
"The Dulham Ladies" (Jewett) **22**:125, 127, 147
"A Dull Story" (Chekhov)
See "A Dreary Story"
Duma pro Opanasa (Bagritsky) **60**:15-6
"The Dumb Girl" (Peretz) **16**:396
The Dumb Gods Speak (Oppenheim) **45**:133, 136-37
"The Dumb Man" (Anderson) **1**:42
"The Dumb Witness" (Chesnutt) **39**:103
"Dumitru and Sigrid" (Cahan) **71**:12, 28
The Dummy (Mankiewicz) **85**:111
"The Dummy That Lived" (Baum) **132**:30
D'un diable qui prêcha merveilles (Ghelderode) **187**:5
"D'un monstre à Lyon ou l'envie" (Apollinaire) **51**:20
D'un Ordre condsidére comme une anarchie (Cocteau) **119**:110
D'un pays lointain (Gourmont) **17**:136
D'un voyage au pays des Tarahumaras (Artaud) **3**:51, 54; **36**:6
"Duna" (Pickthall) **21**:252, 256
"The Dune" (Wakefield) **120**:354, 357
"Dunes on the March" (Bishop) **103**:21
The Dungeon (Micheaux) **76**:246
"Der Dunkle" (Benn) **3**:107
"A Dunnet Sheperdess" (Jewett) **22**:135
"The Dunwich Horror" (Lovecraft) **4**:267-68, 270; **22**:213, 233, 235-36, 238, 241
Duo (Colette) **16**:120
"El dúo de la tos" (Alas) **29**:20
"Duoshao hen" (Chang) **184**:138-39, 143
Duoshao hen (Chang) **184**:125-26
"The Duplicity of Hargraves" (Henry) **19**:172, 174
Le dur désir de durer (Éluard) **41**:151
A Durable Fire (Sarton) **120**:260-61, 266, 268-69, 271-73, 286, 304-05
"Durasa" (Tagore) **53**:353
"Duration" (Wharton) **129**:364
"Durbuddhi" (Tagore) **3**:498-99
"Der durchgesetzte Baum" (Morgenstern) **8**:306
"Duriesdyke" (Swinburne) **8**:439-40
"During a Solar Eclipse" (Nemerov) **124**:268
"During Music" (Sharp) **39**:388
During the Absence of Lanciotto (D'Annunzio)
See *Nell' assenza di Lanciotto*
During the Rains (Nagai)
See *Tsuyu no atosaki*
"During the Springtime Inundation" (Bjoernson) **7**:102
"During Warm Days" (Singer) **33**:386
"During Wind and Rain" (Hardy) **4**:164; **53**:114; **143**:156, 186, 189
The Dusantes: A Sequel to "The Casting Away of Mrs. Lecks and Mrs. Aleshine" (Stockton) **47**:315, 318, 321
"Dusk" (Baker) **10**:13, 26-7
"Dusk" (Coppard) **5**:179
"Dusk" (Saki) **3**:365, 371
"Dusk before Fireworks" (Parker) **143**:283
Dusk in the Garden (Lugones)
See *Los crepúsculos del jardín*
Dusk of Dawn (Du Bois) **169**:82, 85-86, 94-97, 124, 146, 154, 192, 209, 212
Dusk of Dawn: An Essay toward an Autobiography of a Race Concept (Du Bois)
See *Dusk of Dawn*
"The Dusk of Horses" (Dickey) **151**:89, 105
"Dusky Ruth" (Coppard) **5**:175-76, 180
"Dust" (Baker) **10**:19
"Dust" (Brooke) **2**:54, 59; **7**:121, 124
"Dust" (Fisher) **11**:213
Dust (Hawthorne) **25**:237, 241, 249
"Dust My Broom" (Johnson) **69**:77, 79, 82
Dust of Death (Dent) **72**:21-22
The Dust of Suns (Roussel)
See *La poussière de soleils*
Dust Tracks on a Road (Hurston) **121**:319, 344; **131**:58-59, 68, 70, 72, 77, 88
The Dust Which Is God (Benét) **28**:10, 12
"The Dusty Wind" (Platonov) **14**:410
"Dusza Pana Cogito" (Herbert) **168**:21
"The Dutch Cheese" (de la Mare) **53**:22
A Dutch Drama (van Schendel)
See *Een Hollandsch drama*
"Dutch Graves in Bucks County" (Stevens) **3**:448
"Dutch Interior" (Sarton) **120**:263
A Dutch Tragedy (van Schendel)
See *Een Hollandsch drama*
Duty and Anguish (Éluard)
See *Le devoir et l'inquiétude*
Duvet d'ange (Vallette) **67**:328
Dva pastukha i nimfa v khizhine (Kuzmin) **40**:201-03
"Dvadcat' vosem' tysjač pečatnyx znakov" (Pilnyak) **23**:212
Dvádtsat' shesti i odná (Gorky) **8**:72, 74, 77, 81, 89
"2-g noiabria" (Khodasevich) **15**:211-12
Dvärgen (Lagerkvist) **144**:189, 201, 211, 214, 222, 224, 235, 239-40
Dvenadsat (Blok) **5**:83-5, 88, 92-3, 95, 98
Dvenadtsat stulyev (Petrov) **21**:151, 153-54, 157-59
"Dvoe" (Tsvetaeva) **7**:566, 568
Dvoe (Nabokov) **108**:145

"Dvorianskoe semeistvo" (Tolstoy) **173**:347, 350
"The Dwarf" (Stevens) **45**:281
The Dwarf (Lagerkvist)
See *Dvärgen*
Dwarf Bamboo (Nagai)
See *Okamezasa*
"The Dweller in the Tomb" (Kuttner) **10**:267
"The Dweller of the Threshold" (Harte) **1**:342
The Dweller on the Threshold (Hichens) **64**:121, 127, 129
Dwellers in the Hills (Post) **39**:339, 343, 347-48
"Dwie krople" (Herbert) **168**:43
Dyadya Vanya (Chekhov) **3**:149, 154, 156-58, 162, 166, 170-75; **10**:103, 109, 111-12, 114-16; **31**:76, 78-9, 81-2, 84, 86, 92-3, 96, 101-02; **55**:60-2, 74; **96**:15-16, 24, 34-37, 39, 51, 53-54; **163**:16, 101, 104, 116, 118, 134
"Dygdens lön" (Strindberg) **8**:419
"Dying" (Schnitzler)
See "Sterben"
"The Dying Bondman" (Harper) **14**:257, 259
A Dying Colonialism (Fanon)
See *L'An V de la révolution algérienne*
The Dying God (Frazer) **32**:222
"The Dying House" (Higginson) **36**:180
"The Dying of Francis Donne" (Dowson) **4**:85, 88, 93-4
"A Dying Poet" (Anderson) **24**:43
"Dying Race" (Bosman) **49**:13
"The Dying Soldier" (Rosenberg) **12**:287, 312
"A Dynamic Theory of History" (Adams) **4**:18; **52**:47
Dynamics of Prejudice (Bettelheim) **143**:7
Dynamo (O'Neill) **1**:386-88, 398; **6**:329, 335; **49**:252
The Dynasts: A Drama of the Napoleonic Wars (Hardy) **4**:157-58, 163-64, 167, 170-72, 174; **10**:217, 227, 229; **32**:280-82, 307; **48**:59-60; **53**:71, 75-6, 80, 84-5, 88, 91, 93, 96, 113, 115; **72**:168, 256, 265; **143**:74-77, 79, 103-5, 143, 174, 176, 184, 187, 194, 196, 205-6, 215; **153**:102, 105, 129
Dynevor Terrace; or, The Clue of Life (Yonge) **48**:364-66, 374-75, 388
Dyre rein (Lie) **5**:331
Dyrendal (Bojer) **64**:19, 21, 23
Dyrenes Forvandling (Jensen) **41**:294
Dzhan (Platonov) **14**:406-07, 411-12, 417-18, 424, 429
Dzieci (Prus) **48**:166, 168, 180
"Džigit" (Andrić) **135**:85
"D-Zug" (Benn) **3**:109
E domani lunedi (Pirandello) **29**:292, 294
"E due" (Pirandello) **29**:294
"E. St. V. M." (Millay) **169**:247, 282-83
E stato cosí (Ginzburg) **156**:16-20, 59, 64, 105, 112
Each in His Own Way (Pirandello)
See *Ciascuno a suo modo*
Each in His Role (Pirandello)
See *Il giuoco delle parti*
Each of Us His Own Part (Pirandello)
See *Il giuoco delle parti*
"Each Thing, Each Thing" (Aleixandre)
See "Cada cosa, cada cosa"
"The Eagle" (Gumilev)
See "Orë"
The Eagle and His Mate (Tolstoy) **18**:383
"The Eagle and the Mole" (Wylie) **8**:521-22, 527, 533, 535
The Eagle Has Two Heads (Cocteau)
See *L'aigle à deux têtes*
"The Eagle Hunt" (Apollinaire) **51**:49
"Eagle of Tiberius" (Lee-Hamilton) **22**:191
"The Eagle Speaks" (Scott) **6**:394
"The Eagle That Is Forgotten" (Lindsay) **17**:224, 226, 230, 235-36
"The Eagles" (Aleixandre)
See "Las águilas"
"Eagles" (Dickey) **151**:175
The Eagle's Heart (Garland) **3**:194
"The Eagle's Mile" (Dickey) **151**:175
The Eagle's Mile (Dickey) **151**:174-76, 178, 199
The Eagle's Nest (Ruskin) **63**:242, 247
"Eagle's Shadow" (Davidson) **24**:194
The Eaglet (Rostand)
See *L'aiglon*
Earl Birber of Bjälbo (Strindberg) **8**:417
Earl Lavender (Davidson) **24**:169, 177, 192
Early Afternoon (Nagai)
See *Hirusugi*
"Early American Music" (Rourke) **12**:318, 330
Early Autumn (Bromfield) **11**:74-5, 85, 87
Early Bardic Literature of Ireland (O'Grady) **5**:353
"Early Beliefs" (Keynes) **64**:207-8
"Early Dawn" (Södergran)
See "Tidig gryning"
Early Frost (Rilke) **6**:369
The Early Goebbels Diaries 1925-1926 (Goebbels) **68**:92
The Early History of Jacob Stahl (Beresford) **81**:7,12
"The Early History of Malice Aforethought" (Maitland) **65**:282
"Early in the Morning" (Holly) **65**:139, 153
The Early Life and Adventures of Sylvia Scarlett (Mackenzie) **116**:156-87, 189, 194, 196-97, 201, 206, 208, 210-12, 214, 227, 230, 250-55
The Early Life of Abraham Lincoln (Tarbell) **40**:433
The Early Life of Mark Rutherford (Rutherford) **25**:359, 362-63
The Early Life of Thomas Hardy (Hardy) **143**:87
"Early Noon" (Bachmann) **192**:63-64, 67
"The Early Novels of Virginia Woolf" (Forster) **125**:162-63
"The Early Novels of Wilkie Collins" (de la Mare) **4**:81
Early One Morning (de la Mare) **4**:78, 81
Early Remininsces, 1834-1864 (Baring-Gould) **88**:15, 17, 34-5
"Early Sorrow" (Mann)
See *Disorder and Early Sorrow*
"Early Spring" (Guro)
See "Rannyaya vesna"
"Early Spring" (Kandinsky) **92**:75
"Early Success" (Fitzgerald) **157**:208
"An Early Train" (Morley) **87**:127
"Early Twentieth Century Literature" (Saintsbury) **31**:241
The Early Worm (Benchley) **1**:81; **55**:7
Earnest (Wilde)
See *The Importance of Being Earnest*
The Earnest Atheist (Muggeridge) **120**:191
"Ears in the Turrets Hear" (Thomas) **8**:459; **45**:364
"The Earth" (Hippius) **9**:159
The Earth (Bryusov) **10**:87
"The Earth" (Pasternak) **188**:190-92, 196-97
"Earth" (Toomer) **172**:273
Earth and Her Birds (Noyes) **7**:508
Earth and Moon (García Lorca)
See *Tierra y luna*
Earth Apples (Abbey) **160**:86
"The Earth Breath" (Baker) **10**:27
The Earth Breath, and Other Poems (Baker) **3**:3-4; **10**:12-13, 19, 26-8
"Earth Deities" (Carman) **7**:139
Earth Erect (Popa)
See *Uspravna zemlja*
"Earth, Fire, and Water" (Sharp) **39**:377
"The Earth Gives All and Takes All" (Evans) **85**:31
The Earth Gives All and Takes All (Evans) **85**:23, 31
The Earth Gods (Gibran) **1**:327; **9**:88-9, 91-2, 94
The Earth Horizon (Austin) **25**:29, 38
The Earth Is Waiting (Bosman) **49**:16
"Earth Love" (Davies) **5**:202
Earth Pain (Singer) **33**:385
"Earth to Earth" (Davidson) **24**:164
"The Earth Was Transformed into an Ash-Heap" (Södergran)
See "Jorden blev förvandlad till en askhög"
Earth Woes (Singer)
See *Earth Pain*
Earthen Pitchers (Davis) **6**:152, 154-55
"Earthgod and the Fox" (Miyazawa) **76**:277, 302
Earthly Paradise (Colette) **5**:173; **16**:115-16
"Earthquake" (Runyon) **10**:432
"The Earthquake Disaster" (Yokomitsu)
See "Shin Sai"
"Earth's Complines" (Roberts) **8**:318
Earth's Enigmas (Roberts) **8**:318, 325
Earth's Enigmas: A Book of Animal and Nature Life (Roberts)
See *Earth's Enigmas*
"Earth's Last Citadel" (Kuttner) **10**:269
Earth's Voices. Transcripts from Nature. Sospitra, and Other Poems (Sharp) **39**:361, 379, 381, 387
Earthy Delights, Unearthly Adornments: American Writers as Image Makers (Morris) **107**:184, 187-89
Earwitness: Fifty Characters (Canetti)
See *Der Ohrenzeuge: Fünfzig Charaktere*
East and West: The Discovery of America, and Other Poems (Fenollosa) **91**:2
The East End of Europe (Upward) **85**:380, 400-2
The East I Know (Claudel)
See *Connaissance de l'est*
East of Eden (Singer)
See *Chaver Nachman*
East of Eden (Steinbeck) **135**:285-86, 317, 321, 349
East of Mansion House (Burke) **63**:127
East River (Asch)
See *1st River*
East Wind (Lowell) **8**:228, 231-32, 237
The East Wind of Love (Mackenzie) **116**:215, 232, 239-40, 242-43
"An East-End Curate" (Hardy) **53**:117
"Easter" (Toomer) **172**:261-63, 265
"Easter" (Vilakazi) **37**:410
Easter (Strindberg)
See *Påsk*
"Easter 1916" (Yeats) **11**:522, 541; **18**:446; **31**:401, 420-22; **93**:346, 389, 404
"Easter Bells" (Hansen)
See "Paaskeklokken"
"An Easter Candle" (Caragiale)
See "O facile de Paste"
"The Easter Cantor" (Papadiamantis) **29**:272
"The Easter Egg" (Saki) **3**:366, 372-73
"Easter Eve" (Carman) **7**:139
"Easter in the Country" (Papadiamantis) **29**:273
"Easter Midnight Mass" (Welch) **22**:459
"An Easter Night" (Korolenko) **22**:169
The Easter of the Greeks (Sikelianos) **39**:404, 418
"Easter Sunday" (Ginsberg) **120**:127
"Easter Week" (Pasternak) **188**:182-83
"Eastern Front" (Trakl) **5**:461
The Eastern Front (Churchill) **113**:105
"The Eastern Mystery" (Bramah) **72**:6
"Eastern United States" (Jiménez) **183**:331, 333
Eastward (Couperus)
See *Oostwaarts*
"Eastward into Eden" (Williams) **89**:375
"Eastward to Eden" (Williams)
See "Eastward into Eden"
The Easy Chair (De Voto) **29**:131
"Easy Lessons in Law" (Darrow) **81**:74
Easy Living (Sturges) **48**:286-88, 290-91, 294, 301, 309, 312, 321
"The Eater of Souls" (Kuttner) **10**:267
"The Eathen" (Kipling) **8**:193
"Eating Crow" (Harris) **24**:267
Eating Together (Hellman) **119**:132

L'eau courante (Rod) **52**:309, 312, 316
L'Eau et les Reves: Essai sur l'imagination de la matière (Bachelard) **128**:5, 9, 32-3, 35-8, 40, 46, 55, 57-8, 62, 64-9, 74, 77
L'eau profonde (Bourget) **12**:69
"The Eavesdropper" (Carman) **7**:146
"Ebar phirao more" (Tagore) **3**:496
"Ébauche d'un serpent" (Valéry) **15**:458-59, 464
"Ebb and Flow" (Dunsany) **2**:136
"Ebbri Canti" (Saba) **33**:374
"Ebb-Tide" (Pickthall) **21**:252
"Ecce homo" (Papini) **22**:281
"Ecce homo" (Unamuno) **2**:568
Ecce homo (Nietzsche) **55**:323, 326-27, 332, 351, 354, 358-59, 364; **10**:389
Ecce Puella (Sharp) **39**:361
"The Eccentric Miss X" (Williams) **89**:384
"The Eccentricities of Reformers" (Higginson) **36**:167
"Eccentrics" (Tolstoy) **18**:377
The Eccentrics (Gorky) **8**:92
L'echange (Claudel) **2**:101; **10**:128, 134
L'echéance (Bourget) **12**:68
"Échelon" (Apollinaire) **51**:34, 36
"Echi mondani" (Svevo) **35**:362
"Echo" (Popa) **167**:175, 177
"The Echo" (Stringer) **37**:343
"Echoes" (Baker) **10**:27
"Echoes" (Henley) **8**:108
Echoes from Vagabondia (Carman) **7**:139, 143
"Echoes of the Jazz Age" (Fitzgerald) **6**:169; **157**:146, 215, 219
The Echoing Green (Baker) **119**:32
Echo's Bones and Other Precipitates (Beckett) **145**:79
Die echten Sedemunds (Barlach) **84**:73, 83, 88
"The Eclipse" (Korolenko) **22**:170
Eclipse of Reason (Horkheimer) **132**:212
"Eclogue of the Downs" (Davidson) **24**:186
Eclogues (Radnóti) **16**:410, 417, 419-21
"Eco" (García Lorca) **181**:181
"Eco" (Villaurrutia) **80**:478
"Eco-Defense" (Abbey) **160**:39, 54, 103
L'Ecole buissoniere (Jammes) **75**:119-20
L'ecole des bouffons (Ghelderode) **187**:4, 10, 40
L'école des femmes (Gide) **5**:229, 243; **12**:145, 147, 159; **177**:102
L'école des indifférents (Giraudoux) **2**:165-66; **7**:324
"Ecologue" (Ginsberg) **120**:87, 129-30
"Ecologues of These States 1969-1971" (Ginsberg) **120**:129
The Economic Basis of Politics (Beard) **15**:18-19, 25, 30, 33
The Economic Consequences of Mr. Churchill (Keynes) **64**:236, 249, 258-9
The Economic Consequences of the Peace (Keynes) **64**:209, 212-13, 218-19, 236, 240, 242, 247, 249, 260, 264-65, 293-94
"Economic Evolution" (Graham) **19**:121
An Economic Interpretation of the Constitution of the United States (Beard) **15**:17-18, 25, 29, 31-2, 34
"Economic Nationalism" (Innis) **77**:337-8
"Economic Notes on Free Trade II. A Revenue Tariff and the Cost of Living" (Keynes) **64**:244
Economic Origins of Jeffersonian Democracy (Beard) **15**:18, 29, 31-2
Economic Planning in Soviet Russia (Hayek) **109**:202
"Economic Problems of Socialism in the U.S.S.R." (Stalin) **92**:166, 169-70, 183, 185-6
"Economics" (Bishop) **121**:28
"Economics and Knowledge" (Hayek) **109**:206, 243
"Economics as a Philosophical Science" (Collingwood) **67**:156
Economics for Helen (Belloc) **7**:39
Économie libidinale (Lyotard) **103**:127-29, 131, 34, 146, 151, 157, 168, 180, 197, 199, 214, 219, 228-29, 260, 263, 276
"Economies" (Bishop) **121**:28
Economy and Society: An Outline of Interpretive Sociology (Weber)
See *Wirtschaft und Gesellschaft*
"Economy Program" (Zoshchenko) **15**:499
L'écornifleur (Renard) **17**:302-03, 308, 316
"Ecos de asmodeo" (Valle-Inclán) **5**:478
Ecos del alma (Huidobro) **31**:124, 132
"L'ecrevisse" (Apollinaire) **3**:42
Ecrire en dansant (Sarduy) **167**:221
Ecrits de guerre (Saint-Exupéry) **169**:321, 324, 330, 332-34
Écrits du temps de la guerre, 1916-1919 (Teilhard de Chardin) **9**:494
Ecrits pour le cinéma (Fondane) **159**:239-41, 243-44, 246
Ecrits sur l'art (Éluard) **41**:149, 152
"The Ecstasies of Dialectic" (Nemerov) **124**:143
"Ecstasy" (Huysmans) **7**:415; **69**:23
"Ecstasy" (Naidu) **80**:276, 294
Ecstasy (Couperus)
See *Extase*
"Ecuatorial" (Huidobro) **31**:135
L'écume des jours (Vian) **9**:529-34, 536-37
"Eddie" (Schulz) **51**:315
"Edel" (Bourget) **12**:73-4, 76
Eden (Saltus) **8**:346
L'edera (Deledda) **23**:33-4, 36, 41
Edgar Allan Poe (Ewers) **12**:133-34
Edgar Allen Poe (Griffith) **68**:235
The Edge of Darkness (Chase) **124**:25
"Edge of Love" (Aleixandre)
See "Filo del amor"
Edgewater People (Freeman) **9**:74
Edifices anciens (Bosschere) **19**:61
An Edinburgh Eleven (Barrie) **164**:61
"Edison" (Nezval) **44**:239-40, 243, 245
Edith Bonham (Foote) **108**:4, 17-18
"Editha's Christmas Burglar" (Benchley) **55**:3
Edith's Letters (Södergran) **31**:287
The Editor (Bjoernson)
See *Redaktøren*
Editor Lynge (Hamsun) **2**:204; **14**:221, 237; **49**:127; **151**:232
"Editors" (Middleton) **56**:179
"The Editor's Easy Chair" (Woollcott) **5**:529
"An Editor's Progress" (Orage) **157**:246
Edmund Burke: A Genius Reconsidered (Kirk) **119**:255
"Edmund Gosse" (Woolf) **43**:406
Edo and Enam (Agnon) **151**:41-44
"La educación del hombre y de la mujer" (Pardo Bazán) **189**:317
Educated Evans (Wallace) **57**:403, 404
The Educated Imagination (Frye) **165**:147, 149, 151-52, 163, 188, 201, 206, 227, 240, 261
"Educating the Sexes Together" (Anthony) **84**:15
The Education (Cahan) **71**:85
Education (Thorndike) **107**:418
"Education after Auschwitz" (Adorno)
See "Erziehung nach Auschwitz"
Education and Living (Bourne) **16**:54, 58
Education and Scoiology (Durkheim) **55**:140
"The Education of a Storyteller" (Bambara) **116**:15
"Education of a Stuffed Shirt" (Machado de Assis) **10**:288
"The Education of Audrey" (Mansfield) **39**:318-19
The Education of Children (Adler) **61**:31-3
The Education of Harriet Hatfield (Sarton) **120**:312, 315-16
The Education of Henry Adams (Adams) **4**:5-7, 10-14, 16-21; **52**:1-49
The Education of Henry Adams: A Study in Twentieth-Century Multiplicity (Adams)
See *The Education of Henry Adams*
"Education of the People" (Lawrence) **61**:213, 215
The Education of Uncle Paul (Blackwood) **5**:69-70
"Education without Books" (Eastman) **55**:164
Educational Psychology (Thorndike) **107**:370, 378, 383, 386-87, 409, 417-18, 420
Educational Psychology: Briefer Course (Thorndike) **107**:410
"Edward the Conqueror" (Dahl) **173**:14
Een Hollandsch drama (van Schendel) **56**:238-39
Een lent van vaerzen (Couperus) **15**:45
"Effects of Analogy" (Stevens) **12**:380, 386; **45**:328, 331
The Efficiency Expert (Burroughs) **32**:58
Effie Hetherington (Buchanan) **107**:86-7
"Effigies" (Muir) **87**:169
"Effigy of a Nun" (Teasdale) **4**:427
"Efforts of Affection" (Bishop) **121**:65
"The Eftest Way" (Williams) **89**:371, 395
"L'égalité des sexes" (Éluard) **41**:160
"The Egg" (Saroyan) **137**:181
"The Eggs of the Silver Moon" (Chambers) **41**:114
"The Eggs Speak Up" (Arendt) **193**:47
Égi és földi szerelem (Molnár) **20**:166, 168, 175
Egil's Saga (Eddison) **15**:59
Egipetskaya marka (Mandelstam) **2**:400, 408; **6**:260-61, 264
"Eglantina" (Freeman) **9**:73
Eglantine (Giraudoux) **2**:163, 165; **7**:320, 326
"Egle" (Carducci) **32**:91
"L'Eglise habillee de Feuilles" (Jammes) **75**:102, 107, 111, 119
"Eglogue à Francine" (Moréas) **18**:281
The Ego and the Id (Freud)
See *Das Ich und das Es*
"Ego Confessions" (Ginsberg) **120**:38-9, 53
"Ego Dominus Tuus" (Yeats) **11**:520, 522, 528; **31**:389, 408-09; **93**:339
"The Ego Machine" (Kuttner) **10**:269
"Ego veličestvo" (Pilnyak) **23**:211
"Egoism" (Keynes) **64**:295
"Egoism in Religion" (Andreas-Salome) **56**:46
The Egoist (Hecht) **101**:31, 39, 48, 70, 73
Egoist (Natsume) **2**:494
Gli egoist (Tozzi) **31**:315, 324, 333
The Egoist: A Comedy in Narrative (Meredith) **17**:255-56, 259-61, 265-67, 269, 272-73, 277-78, 281-82, 284, 286-89, 291, 296-97; **43**:250-306
"L'Egoista" (Gadda) **144**:93
Egoists (Tozzi)
See *Gli egoist*
Egoists: A Book of Supermen (Huneker) **65**:163, 167, 170, 179, 184-5, 188, 217
"Egolatria" (Papini) **22**:281
"Egoriy" (Esenin) **4**:116
Egotism in German Philosophy (Santayana) **40**:415
"Egotists" (O'Faolain) **143**:222
"Egy filozófus halálára" (Babits) **14**:39
Egy gazdátlan csónak története (Molnár) **20**:164, 174-75
"Egy lázadó pap" (Herzl) **36**:153
"Egy olasc reformátor" (Herzl) **36**:153
"Egypt" (Douglas) **40**:68, 89
The Egyptian Nights (Bryusov) **10**:88
"Egyptian Sorcery" (Blackwood) **5**:72
The Egyptian Stamp (Mandelstam)
See *Egipetskaya marka*
Egyszer jóllakni (Moricz) **33**:248
Eh Joe (Beckett) **145**:138, 151
Die Ehe (Döblin) **13**:158
"Die eheringe" (Morgenstern) **8**:305
Az éhes város (Molnár) **20**:164, 174-75
Die Ehre (Sudermann) **15**:417, 419-20, 421-22, 424, 426-27, 430, 433, 438
Eichmann in Jerusalem (Arendt) **193**:43, 87-8, 95, 99-100, 126-27, 163
Eidola (Manning) **25**:265, 276-78

"Eidsvoll and Norge" (Grieg) **10**:206
"Eiendomligheter i Obstfelder's Digtning" (Obstfelder) **23**:180
Eight Day World (Toomer) **172**:265
The Eight Hours Day (Webb and Webb) **22**:412
Eight Hundred Leagues on the Amazon (Verne) **6**:502
813 (Mizoguchi) **72**:322
Eight Men (Wright) **136**:227, 240, 276
Eight Stanzas to Sri Arunachala (Ramana Maharshi)
See *Arunacala-astakam*
Eight Stories (Lie) **5**:325
Eight Strokes of the Clock (Leblanc)
See *Les huit coups de l'horloge*
Eight Verses on Arunachala (Ramana Maharshi)
See *Arunacala-astakam*
"The Eighteen-Carat Kid" (Wodehouse) **108**:371
The Eighteen-Carat Kid and Other Stories (Wodehouse) **108**:373
"1889" (Jacob) **6**:198
"1889-1916" (Jacob) **6**:191
"1887" (Housman) **10**:248-49, 257
"1886" (Benn) **3**:110
"MDCCCIII" (Hearn) **9**:137
18 Poems (Thomas) **1**:471, 473; **8**:456, 458, 459; **45**:399, 404; **105**:297, 305-06
The Eighteen Seconds (Artaud) **36**:34-5, 37-8, 40
"1870-1871" (Gosse) **28**:138
"1867" (Jacob) **6**:198
Eighteen Springs (Chang)
See *Shiba chun*
"18 West 11th Street" (Merrill) **173**:182
18 wierszy (Herbert) **168**:38
"Eighteenth-Century Vignette" (Dobson) **79**:12
"Eighth Air Force" (Jarrell) **177**:126, 129, 149, 172, 176, 191-94, 245, 248
The Eighth Compartment of the Inferno (Peretz) **16**:392
"The Eighth Deadly Sin" (Huneker) **65**:156, 169, 197
"Eighth Eclogue" (Radnóti) **16**:412, 420
"The Eighth Elegy" (Rilke) **1**:413; **195**:165
The Eighth Sin (Morley) **87**:124
Eighty: An Autobiography (Lin) **149**:342
Eighty Years and More (1815-1897): Reminiscences of Elizabeth Cady Stanton (Stanton) **73**:243, 258, 264-65, 268
Het Eiland in de Zuidzee (van Schendel) **56**:241
Eimi (Cummings) **137**:34
Ein- und Zusprüche (Böll) **185**:104, 127
Einander (Werfel) **8**:475-78
Einar Elkær (Jensen) **41**:296, 303
Der Einbruch der Sexualmoral (Reich) **57**:347
Einfach kompliziert (Bernhard) **165**:72, 75, 96
"Eingang" (Rilke) **195**:283-85, 292
"Eingeengt" (Benn) **3**:107
"Das Einhorn" (Kolmar) **40**:178
"Einige Psychische Folgen des Anatomischen Geschlechtsunterschieds" (Freud) **52**:109
"Einiges" (Kandinsky) **92**:68
Einkehr (Morgenstern) **8**:304, 310
"Einladung" (Nietzsche) **55**:388-89
Einleitung (Husserl)
See *Die Krisis der europaeischen Wissenschaften und die transzendentale Phänomenologie, Eine Einleitung in die phaenomenologische Philosophie*
Einleitung in die Moralwissenschaft (Simmel) **64**:338, 354
Einmischung erwünscht (Böll) **185**:97
Einsame (Kandinsky) **92**:49
Einsame Menschen (Hauptmann) **4**:192-93, 197, 203
Der einsame Weg (Schnitzler) **4**:387-89, 391
Die Einsamen (Brod) **115**:93
"Einsanes Haus am Hussendeich" (Liliencron) **18**:206
"Einstein and the Crisis of Reason" (Merleau-Ponty) **156**:167
"Einstein Freud & Jack" (Nemerov) **124**:260, 290
Einstein: Philosopher-Scientist (Einstein)
See *Albert Einstein: Philosopher-Scientist*
Einund Zusprüche (Böll) **185**:97, 100-104
Either of One or of No One (Pirandello)
See *O di uno o di nessuno*
"Either/Or" (Luxemburg) **63**:220
Either Someone's or No-One's (Pirandello)
See *O di uno o di nessuno*
"Ek sundarī veśyāprati" (Devkota) **23**:48
Ekatmapanchakam (Ramana Maharshi) **84**:262
"Ekjan Lok" (Tagore) **53**:342
"Ekskurzija" (Andrić) **135**:89
Eksotiske Noveller (Jensen) **41**:294
"El ha-zipor" (Bialik) **25**:51, 62
"Ela" (Zamyatin) **8**:553-54; **37**:430
"An Elaborate Elopement" (Jacobs) **22**:106
"The Elagin Affair" (Bunin)
See "Delo korneta Elagina"
"Elaine" (Knister) **56**:156, 163
"Elaine" (Millay) **4**:316
Elämän koreus (Leino) **24**:371
"Die Elbe" (Borchert) **5**:105
Elder Conklin, and Other Stories (Harris) **24**:253-55, 258, 264-65, 267, 269, 271
"Elder Gods" (Lovecraft) **4**:272
"The Elder Knight" (Sayers) **15**:370
"The Elder Sister" (Hedāyat)
See "Abji khanum"
"The Elder Sister" (Pascoli) **45**:145
"The Elder Sister" (Tagore) **3**:485
Elders and Betters (Compton-Burnett) **180**:114, 124-25, 131, 144, 146-47, 178
The Eldest Son (Galsworthy) **1**:303; **45**:52, 54
"Eldorado" (Hellman) **119**:167, 174
Eleanor (Ward) **55**:412, 417-18, 420, 422, 426
"Eleanora Duse" (Villa) **176**:96
The Elect Lady (MacDonald) **9**:292
"Elected Silence: Three Sonnets" (Morley) **87**:145
"Electioneerin' on Big Injun Mounting" (Murfree) **135**:201-5, 219, 227
Electra (Giraudoux)
See *Electre*
Electra (Hofmannsthal)
See *Elektra*
Electre (Giraudoux) **2**:158, 160-63, 167, 172, 174; **7**:320-22, 329
Elèctre ou la chute des masques (Yourcenar) **193**:270, 343
Electric Function of Sexuality and Anxiety (Reich) **57**:342
"The Electric Slide Boogie" (Lorde) **173**:143
"Electricity" (Hippius) **9**:158
"Electronic Revolution" (Burroughs) **121**:138-39
"Elegant Appetite" (Hagiwara) **60**:287, 297
"An Elegant Escape" (Stein) **48**:234
"Elegía" (García Lorca) **181**:51, 185
"Elegía" (Lugones) **15**:285
"Elegia de abril" (Andrade) **43**:13
"Elegia del Monte Spluga" (Carducci) **32**:111
"Elegia Fortinbrasa" (Herbert) **168**:8, 39, 47
Elegia na odejscie (Herbert) **168**:40, 45, 47, 56
Elegías (Jiménez) **183**:289
"Elegie" (Lasker-Schueler) **57**:334
"Elegie des poetischen Ichs" (Werfel) **8**:478
Elegie renane (Pirandello) **29**:310
Elegie romane (D'Annunzio) **6**:136
Elegier (Ekelund) **75**:95
Elegies (Ekelund)
See *Elegier*
Elegies (Jammes) **75**:111
Elegies (Jiménez)
See *Elejías*
Elegies and Laments (Radnóti) **16**:418
the elegies to Sophie (Arp) **115**:23
"Elegy" (Jammes) **75**:108, 111
"Elegy" (Jozsef) **22**:161-62, 164
"Elegy" (Merrill) **173**:225
"Elegy" (Millay) **4**:306
"Elegy" (Swinburne) **36**:343-44
"Elegy Che Guevara" (Ginsberg) **120**:23
"Elegy for a Nature Poet" (Nemerov) **124**:178-79, 249-50, 282, 317
"Elegy for Alto" (Okigbo) **171**:341, 360-61
"Elegy for an 88 Gunner" (Douglas) **40**:55, 71
"Elegy for an Enemy" (Benét) **7**:69
An Elegy for Departure (Herbert)
See *Elegia na odejscie*
"Elegy for Louise Bogan" (Sarton) **120**:266
"Elegy for Slit-Drum" (Okigbo) **171**:341, 346, 355, 359-61
Elegy for the Departure (Herbert)
See *Elegia na odejscie*
"Elegy for the Departure of Pen, Ink, and Lamp" (Herbert) **168**:40, 57
"The Elegy of Fortinbras" (Herbert)
See "Elegia Fortinbrasa"
"Elegy, of Icon, Nailless" (Radnóti) **16**:418
"Elegy of the Wind" (Okigbo) **171**:355-60
"Elegy on the Death of a Hobo" (Radnóti) **16**:418
"Elegy on the Death of the Archpoet" (Gogarty) **15**:109
"Elegy on the Last Judgment" (Fletcher) **35**:106
"Elegy on the Russian Revolution" (Fletcher) **35**:106
"Elegy to Mount Spluga" (Carducci)
See "Elegia del Monte Spluga"
Elejías (Jiménez) **4**:213
Elektra (Hauptmann) **4**:208
Elektra (Hofmannsthal) **11**:292-94, 296, 303
"The Element of Ethics, with a View to an Appreciation of Kant's Moral Philosophy" (Moore) **89**:226
The Element of Lavishness: Letters of William Maxwell and Sylvia Townsend Warner, 1938-1978 (Warner) **131**:363
"Elemental" (Lawrence) **93**:55
"Elementals" (Blackwood) **5**:71
The Elementary Formes of the Religious Life: A Study in Religious Sociology (Durkheim)
See *Les Formes élémentaires de la vie religieuse: le système totémique en Australie*
"The Elementary Scene" (Jarrell) **177**:219
Elemente einer phänomenologischen Aufklärung der Erkenntnis (Husserl)
See *Untersuchungen zur Phänomenologie und Theorie der Erkenntnis*
Elementi di scienza politica (Mosca) **75**:124, 126, 130-33, 137-38, 140, 149-50, 153-57, 160, 162-65, 167-68, 171-72, 180, 184, 186
"Elementos de preceptiva" (Borges) **109**:165-66
Elements (Mosca)
See *Elementi di scienza politica*
"The Elements and Culture" (Blok) **5**:95
"Éléments de Pataphysique" (Jarry) **147**:264
Eléments d'une doctrine radicale (Alain) **41**:13
Elements of a Phenomenological Enlightenment of Knowledge (Husserl)
See *Untersuchungen zur Phänomenologie und Theorie der Erkenntnis*
The Elements of Drawing (Ruskin) **63**:243
"Elements of Haiku" (Masaoka) **18**:233
Elements of Mathematics (Peirce) **81**:198
Elements of Political Science (Mosca)
See *Elementi di scienza politica*
The Elements of Psychology (Thorndike) **107**:370, 378, 400, 417
"Elements of Rhetoric" (Borges) **109**:147-48
The Elements of Style (Strunk) **92**:347-56
"The Elements of the Novel" (Futabatei)
See "Shōsetsu sōron"
"Elephant" (Lawrence) **93**:125
"Elephant and Colosseum" (Lowry) **6**:240, 250; **40**:261
"The Elephant Is Slow to Mate" (Lawrence) **93**:82
Élet és irodalem (Babits) **14**:41

Életem regénye (Moricz) **33**:239, 244, 248
Eleuthéria (Beckett) **145**:82
Elevación (Nervo) **11**:394, 399-401
Elevation (Nervo)
See *Elevación*
The Elevator (Howells) **7**:387-88
Eleven Stanzas to Sri Arunachala (Ramana Maharshi)
See *Arunakala-padigam*
Eleven Verse Plays (Anderson) **144**:35
Eleven Verses on Aruncala (Ramana Maharshi)
See *Arunakala-padigam*
Eleven Years (Undset)
See *Elleve aar*
"The Elf Child" (Markham) **47**:279
"Elfin Skates" (Lee-Hamilton) **22**:191
"The Elf-Queen's Wand" (Södergran)
See "Alvdrottningens spira"
"Elia" (Bottomley) **107**:5
Elias Portolu (Deledda) **23**:36, 41-2
"Elijah Browning" (Masters) **25**:299
"Elin" (Lagerkvist) **144**:216
Eline Vere (Couperus) **15**:43, 45-6
The Elinor Glyn System of Writing (Glyn) **72**:140
Eliot and His Age: T. S. Eliot's Moral Imagination in the Twentieth Century (Kirk) **119**:251, 255, 259, 265-66, 275, 297, 304
Elisabeth II (Bernhard) **165**:71, 96, 109
The Elixir of Life (Hedāyat)
See *Ab-i zindigi*
"Eliza Harris" (Harper) **14**:262
"Elizabeth" (Jackson) **187**:241, 243
Elizabeth and Essex: A Tragic History (Strachey) **12**:397-99, 403-05, 407, 409-12, 414-15, 418-19, 421
Elizabeth and Her German Garden (Elizabeth) **41**:117-18, 121-22, 124, 127, 129-31, 138-39
"Elizabeth and the Golden City" (Engel) **137**:119
"Elizabeth Charlotte" (Heyse) **8**:114
"Elizabeth Stock's One Story" (Chopin) **14**:68; **127**:124, 126-27, 206, 210-12
Elizabeth the Queen (Anderson) **2**:1-4, 7, 9; **144**:7, 10, 13, 17, 34, 36-37, 70-73
Elizabeth Visits America (Glyn) **72**:127, 137-38, 142
"The Elizabethan Clergy" (Baring-Gould) **88**:22
Elizabethan Commentary (Belloc) **18**:26
"The Elizabethan Lumber Room" (Woolf) **43**:400
"Elizabeth's Thanksgiving Dinner" (Montgomery) **51**:200
Elle est là (Sarraute) **145**:265-67, 311-12, 314, 316, 318, 320, 323
"Ellen Chesser's Dream of Italy" (Roberts) **68**:337
"Ellen West—and Loneliness" (Levi) **125**:296
Elletra (D'Annunzio) **6**:136
Elleve aar (Undset) **3**:523-24
"Ellice Quentin" (Hawthorne) **25**:235
"Ello es el lugar . . ." (Vallejo) **56**:311, 315
Ellos (Nervo) **11**:394
"Ellos y yo" (Villaurrutia) **80**:499
"Elly" (Faulkner) **170**:185, 189
Elmer (Faulkner) **141**:40-42
Elmer Gantry (Lewis) **4**:248-51, 254-55, 257, 259, 261; **13**:332-33, 335, 338, 344, 346-47, 351-52; **23**:136, 139; **39**:224, 234, 246-47, 254
Elmer the Great (Lardner) **14**:294
The Elm-Tree on the Mall (France)
See *L'orme du mail*
Èloge de la philosophie (Merleau-Ponty) **156**:121-22, 124-27, 129, 183
"Eloge des Plēïades" (Cocteau) **119**:58-9
"Elogio da vaidade" (Machado de Assis) **10**:291
"Elogio de la sombra" (Borges) **109**:57
Elogio de la sombra (Borges) **109**:8
"Elogio e compianto dell'Inghilterra" (Ginzburg) **156**:97-98
"The Elopement" (Hardy) **72**:216
"An Eloquence of Grief" (Crane) **11**:163
Elsa of the Fir (Raabe)
See *Else von der Tanne*
Else (Kielland) **5**:275-76
Else von der Tanne (Raabe) **45**:182, 199, 201-02
"Elses Bryllup" (Jensen) **41**:306
Else's Wedding (Jensen)
See "Elses Bryllup"
"Elsie" (McAlmon) **97**:87
Elsie (Kielland)
See *Else*
"Elsie and the Child" (Bennett) **197**:71
Elsie and the Child, and Other Stories (Bennett) **5**:32, 46; **197**:20
"Elskovshvisken" (Obstfelder) **23**:187
Eltham House (Ward) **55**:421-22, 424, 437, 444
"An Elucidation" (Stein) **48**:242
Elusive Isabel (Futrelle) **19**:95
"Elysium" (Lawrence) **33**:181
Elza pilóta vagy a tökéletes társadalom (Babits) **14**:40, 42
"Elza Ramsey" (Masters) **25**:297
"Emaliol'" (Remizov) **27**:340-41
The Emancipated (Gissing) **3**:235; **24**:220, 233, 235; **47**:139
The Emancipated Women (Prus)
See *Emancypantki*
"Emancipation" (Bell) **43**:88
"Emancipation: A Life Fable" (Chopin) **14**:62; **127**:112
"The Emancipation of Irish Writers" (O'Faolain) **143**:229, 239
The Emancipation of Massachusetts; The Dream and the Reality (Adams) **80**:5, 8, 10-1, 15, 26, 36, 46, 50-1, 58, 60, 65-6
The Emancipationists (Prus)
See *Emancypantki*
Emancypantki (Prus) **48**:159-60, 163-64, 169, 175, 179
"The Embarkation" (Bottomley) **107**:6
"Embarkation Sonnets" (Merrill) **173**:253
"L'embarquement" (Field) **43**:166
"L'embarquement pour Cythére" (Field) **43**:166-67
"The Embarrassed Eliminators" (Lucas) **73**:174
Embarrassments (James) **2**:272
"Les embaumeuses" (Schwob) **20**:323
"Embers" (Güiraldes)
See "Al rescoldo"
"Embers" (Vallejo)
See "Ascuas"
Embers (Beckett) **145**:134
Embers (Rebreanu)
See *Jar*
Embezzled Heaven (Werfel) **8**:470
"The Emblem" (Muir) **87**:168, 210
"The Emblematics of Meaning" (Bely) **7**:59
"Emblème" (Moréas) **18**:288
Emblems of Love (Abercrombie) **141**:3, 8, 10
"Embryos" (Rozanov) **104**:347
"Emče organa" (Tsvetaeva) **7**:560
Emelina (Darío) **4**:65
"Emelyan and the Empty Drum" (Tolstoy)
See "The Empty Drum"
Emen hetan (Sender) **136**:208, 213-15
"The Emerald" (Merrill) **173**:258
The Emerald City of Oz (Baum) **7**:21-2, 24, 27; **132**:44, 46, 49, 52, 56, 73, 88, 91-93, 95, 99-100
"Emergency Exit" (Coppard) **5**:181
"The Emergency Mistress" (Stockton) **47**:329
"Emerson" (Chapman) **7**:187-88
Emerson Among the Eccentrics (Baker) **119**:33-34
Emerson, and Other Essays (Chapman) **7**:185-87, 190, 193
"Emerson Sixty Years After" (Chapman) **7**:185
"Emeryt" (Schulz) **51**:309
"The Emigrant" (Jensen) **41**:308
"L'emigrant de Landor Road" (Apollinaire) **51**:60
The Emigrants (Bojer)
See *Vor egen stamme*
L'émigré (Bourget) **12**:69-72
Émigrés (Tolstoy) **18**:360, 373-74, 378
Émile Durkheim (Nisbet) **117**:354
Emile Verhaeren (Zweig) **17**:423
"Emile Zola and His Novels" (Nagai)
See "Emiru Zoru to sono shōsetsu"
"Emile Zola et L'assomoir" (Huysmans) **69**:10
"Emile Zola's 'Lourdes" (Chopin) **127**:215
Emily (Montgomery) **140**:319
"Emily Brosseau" (Masters) **25**:298
Emily Climbs (Montgomery) **51**:185-88; **140**:329
Emily of New Moon (Montgomery) **51**:185-86, 188-90, 194, 216; **140**:320, 330, 332
"Emily Sparks" (Masters) **25**:287
Emily's Quest (Montgomery) **51**:185, 188-89
Eminent Victorians: Cardinal Manning, Florence Nightingale, Dr. Arnold, General Gordon (Strachey) **12**:391-93, 395-403, 410-11, 413-15, 417-21
"Emiru Zoru to sono shōsetsu" (Nagai) **51**:87
"Emlé-kezés egy nyáréjszakára" (Ady) **11**:18
"Emma" (Lyotard) **103**:260-63, 265-67
"Emma Zunz" (Borges) **109**:87
Emmanuel Burden (Belloc) **7**:31-2, 41; **18**:25, 32, 34-5
"Emmett Burns" (Masters) **25**:297
"Emotional Monologue" (Bodenheim) **44**:62
O empalhador de passarinho (Andrade) **43**:13-15
"Empédocle" (Schwob) **20**:323
Empédocle (Rolland) **23**:256
"Emperor" (Herbert) **168**:24
Emperor and Galilean (Ibsen)
See *Kejser og Galilaeer*
The Emperor Constantine (Sayers) **15**:382, 387
Emperor Fu Manchu (Rohmer) **28**:279, 281, 294-95, 300
The Emperor Jones (O'Neill) **1**:384-85, 390, 394, 403-04, 406; **6**:324-25, 327-29; **49**:247, 269-70, 286
The Emperor Julian (Ibsen) **8**:150
The Emperor of America (Rohmer) **28**:281
"The Emperor of Ice-Cream" (Stevens) **3**:462, 475; **12**:363-64, 367, 376; **45**:299, 304, 307-08, 310, 344
The Emperor of Portugallia (Lagerloef) **36**:242, 246, 248
"The Emperor's Dream" (Gogarty) **15**:101
"The Emperor's Dream" (Herbert) **168**:24
"The Emperor's New Sonnet" (Villa) **176**:101, 103-4
"The Emperor's Rhyme" (Milne) **6**:314
The Emperor's Tomb (Roth)
See *Die Kapuzinergruft*
Empire and Communications (Innis) **77**:337, 341, 346, 359, 400, 424
"The Empire Builders" (Rinehart) **52**:282
The Empire Builders (Vian)
See *Les bâtisseurs d'empire; ou, Le schmürz*
L'empire des signes (Barthes) **135**:116, 130-33, 135, 147, 159, 166-73, 184
"Empire in India and Elsewhere" (Carpenter) **88**:128
Empire of Signs (Barthes)
See *L'empire des signes*
"The Empire of the Ants" (Wells) **19**:429, 442; **133**:231-32
Empire of the Senseless (Acker) **191**:3-6, 8-9, 17, 40, 42, 51, 58, 66-71, 78-81, 83-7, 92, 102-04, 106-11, 114, 122, 129
"The Empire Speaks of Britain" (Roberts) **8**:318
Empiricism and Subjectivity (Deleuze)
See *Empirisme et subjectivité*
Empirisme et subjectivité (Deleuze) **116**:129-28
The Empress Yang Kwei Fei (Mizoguchi)
See *Yokihi*

"Empty" (Anwar)
See "Hampa"
"The Empty Chair" (Hall and Nordhoff) **23**:59
"Empty Cinema" (van Ostaijen) **33**:421
"An Empty Cup" (Holly) **65**:143
"Empty Drawing Room" (Borges)
See "Sala vacía"
"The Empty Drum" (Tolstoy) **4**:469
The Empty Fortress: Infantile Autism and the Birth of the Self (Bettelheim) **143**:11
Empty Hands (Stringer) **37**:336-37
"The Empty House" (Blackwood) **5**:75
"The Empty House" (Doyle) **7**:223
"The Empty House" (Fletcher) **35**:96
The Empty House (Phelps) **113**:342
The Empty House, and Other Ghosts (Blackwood) **5**:77
Empty Mirror (Ginsberg) **120**:76-7, 94
"The Empty Shoes" (Arenas) **191**:145
"The Empty Sleeve" (Blackwood) **5**:72
The Empyrean Path (Nabokov)
See *Gornii put*
En allemagne (Lemonnier) **22**:200
"En amoroso llenar" (Jiménez) **183**:311
En attendant Godot (Beckett) **145**:82, 104, 124-29, 134-35, 142-44, 159, 161, 178-79
"En derrota" (Azuela) **145**:21
"En Dieu" (Jammes) **75**:119
"En el agua dormida" (Villaurrutia) **80**:477
"En el alba" (Aleixandre) **113**:4, 73
"En el bosque de las toronjas de luna (Poema extatico)" (García Lorca) **181**:65
"En el día americano" (Reyes) **33**:323
"En el fondo del pozo" (Aleixandre) **113**:7, 47
"En el instituto y en la universidad" (García Lorca) **181**:182
"En el jardín de las toronjas de luna" (García Lorca) **181**:65
En el otro costado (Jiménez) **183**:326
"En el presidio" (Pardo Bazán) **189**:270
En el puño de la espada (Echegaray) **4**:105
En etrange pays dans mon pays lui-même (Aragon) **123**:119
En familia (Sánchez) **37**:311-15, 317-18
"En favor del trabajo de la mujer" (Pardo Bazán) **189**:317
"En februarimorgon" (Ekelund) **75**:94
En Fiacre (Adamov) **189**:14
"En Hollande" (Huysmans) **69**:9
Az én kortársaim (Mikszath) **31**:169
En la luna (Huidobro) **31**:138
"En la muerte de José de Ciria y Escalante" (García Lorca) **181**:67
"En la noche" (Quiroga) **20**:216-17
"En la plaza" (Aleixandre) **113**:21-22, 34
"En la vidal poeta: el amor y la poesía" (Aleixandre) **113**:67
"En Málaga" (García Lorca) **181**:186
En ménage (Huysmans) **7**:405-06, 410; **69**:26-30, 47, 52-3, 55
En moder (Nexø) **43**:329
"En Pierre d'Air" (Arp) **115**:31
En pilgrimsgang (Bojer) **64**:22
En qué piensas? (Villaurrutia) **80**:471, 474
En rade (Huysmans) **7**:405-06, 413; **69**:8, 11, 25, 30-1, 39, 52-3, 56, 68-70
"En regardant au fond des crevasses" (Barrès) **47**:60
"En regardant un cyclotron" (Teilhard de Chardin) **9**:482
En route (Huysmans) **7**:405-11; **69**:13, 15, 17-18, 22-3, 30, 37-9, 43, 46, 52, 56, 71
"En torno a Galileo" (Ortega y Gasset) **9**:343-44
En torno al casticismo (Unamuno) **2**:559; **9**:508, 514; **148**:241-45, 287, 337-38
En torno al estudio de la religión griega (Reyes) **33**:323
En tranvía (Pardo Bazán) **189**:234, 237
En un vasto dominio (Aleixandre) **113**:21-22, 33-34, 36, 44, 50, 70
En voz baja (Nervo) **11**:393, 400, 403
"The Enameller" (Huysmans) **69**:23
"El encaje roto" (Pardo Bazán) **189**:227, 299
El encaje roto y otros cuentos (Pardo Bazán) **189**:313
El encanto, tendajón mixto (Garro) **153**:9, 13-18, 71-72
The Enchanted (Giraudoux)
See *Intermezzo*
Enchanted Aisles (Woollcott) **5**:527
The Enchanted April (Elizabeth) **41**:124-25, 129, 132, 137
"The Enchanted Bluff" (Cather) **99**:173, 208, 266
The Enchanted Cottage (Mankiewicz) **85**:149
The Enchanted Cottage (Pinero) **32**:400, 415
The Enchanted Cup (Sologub)
See *Charodjnaja chasha*
"The Enchanted House" (Musil) **12**:252
The Enchanted House (Musil)
See *Die Versuchung der Stillen Veronika*
The Enchanted Island of Yew (Baum) **7**:14; **132**:80
"The Enchanted Kiss" (Henry) **19**:173, 180
"The Enchanted Knight" (Muir) **87**:167
"The Enchanted Organ" (Woolf) **43**:402
The Enchanted Pimp (Callaghan) **145**:254
"An Enchanted Place" (Middleton) **56**:195
An Enchanted Sea (Martyn) **131**:101-2, 104-6, 124
"The Enchanted Tailor" (Aleichem) **35**:323
The Enchanted Trousers (Gogarty) **15**:116-17
Enchanted Valleys (Sharp) **39**:372
The Enchanted Woods (Lee) **5**:310, 313
"The Enchanter" (Tsvetaeva) **35**:408, 411-12
The Enchanter (Nabokov)
See *Volshebnik*
"Enchanter's Handmaiden" (Wylie) **8**:536
L'Enchanteur Alcofrisbas (Melies) **81**:22
L'enchanteur pourrissant (Apollinaire) **3**:38-9, 42; **8**:20; **51**:2, 9, 19, 28
Enchantment: Five and Dime (Garro)
See *El encanto, tendajón mixto*
Enchantment, General Store (Garro)
See *El encanto, tendajón mixto*
"Encher Tempo" (Machado de Assis) **10**:285
"Encina" (García Lorca) **181**:124
"Encirclement" (Lewis) **3**:289
"The Enclosure" (Dickey) **151**:104
"L'enclume des forces" (Artaud) **36**:20
Encontres Avec Shestov (Fondane) **159**:239
Encore: A Journal of the 80th Year (Sarton) **120**:319
"An Encounter" (Joyce) **8**:170; **16**:240; **35**:142, 144, 146, 156-58, 162-63, 165, 167, 190, 192, 197-99; **159**:276, 299, 310-11, 313-14, 316
"An Encounter" (Khodasevich) **15**:208, 212
"Encounter" (Pasternak) **188**:187-88, 190
"An Encounter by Mortstone Pond" (Kirk) **119**:282, 292, 335, 342
"Encounter in April" (Sarton) **120**:269, 271
Encounter in April (Sarton) **120**:260, 271-72, 299
"Encounter in the Cage Country" (Dickey) **151**:212
"Encounter with a God" (Douglas) **40**:66-7, 73
"An Encounter with a Pickpocket" (Guiney) **41**:209
"Encounter with a Skull" (Rohan)
See "Taidokuro"
"An Encounter with the Law" (Nemerov) **124**:231
Encounters and Diversions (Lucas) **73**:159, 170
"Encrucijada (Julio de 1920)" (García Lorca) **181**:63-64, 194-96
"Encuentro" (García Lorca) **181**:198
Encyclopaedia of the Theatre (Nathan) **18**:316, 322
"The End" (Borges)
See "El fin"
"The End" (Ginsberg) **120**:9
"The End" (Herbert)
See "Koniec"
"The End" (Owen) **27**:203, 227
The End (Tagore)
See *Parisesh*
The End and the Beginning (Rainis)
See *Gals un sākums*
End of a Mission (Böll)
See *Ende einer Dienstfahrt*
The End of a Primitive (Himes)
See *The Primitive*
The End of All Men (Ramuz)
See *Présence de la mort*
"End of Another Home Holiday" (Lawrence) **93**:49, 55, 66, 116, 117
"The End of Atlantis" (Khlebnikov)
See "Gibel Atlantidy"
"The End of Christy Tucker" (Caldwell) **117**:8
The End of Democracy (Cram) **45**:7, 9-10, 19-21
The End of Everything (Bergelson) **81**:17,19
"The End of General Gordon" (Strachey) **12**:396, 417, 420
The End of Her Honeymoon (Lowndes) **12**:201
"The End of Jealousy" (Proust)
See "La fin de la jalousie"
The End of Laissez-faire (Keynes) **64**:208, 214, 217, 219, 264
"The End of March" (Bishop) **121**:33, 36-7
The End of Me Old Cigar (Osborne) **153**:323
The End of Our Time (Berdyaev) **67**:26
"The End of Summer School" (Nemerov) **124**:186
End of the Chapter (Galsworthy) **45**:47
"End of the Chase" (Adams) **56**:8
"The End of the Day" (Scott) **6**:388
"The End of the Duel" (Borges) **109**:143
"The End of the Episode" (Hardy) **53**:111
The End of the House of Alard (Kaye-Smith) **20**:100-04, 106, 109-11, 113-14, 116
"The End of the Line" (Jarrell) **177**:175, 178, 215, 220-21
"The End of the Nineteenth Century" (Matthews) **95**:263
"The End of the Old Folks' Home" (Babel) **13**:34; **171**:8
"The End of the Opera" (Nemerov) **124**:290, 292-93, 299
"The End of the Passage" (Kipling)
See "At the End of the Passage"
The End of the Primitive (Himes)
See *The Primitive*
"The End of the Rainbow" (Jarrell) **177**:152, 158-59, 162, 170, 172-73, 175, 177, 215-16, 218, 226
"The End of the River" (Thomas) **105**:318
"The End of the Road" (Belloc) **7**:43
"The End of the Road" (Bromfield) **11**:83
"The End of the Road" (Post) **39**:336
"The End of the Tether" (Conrad) **13**:100; **25**:111; **57**:84
"The End of the Trail" (Carman) **7**:133
"The End of the World" (Bottomley) **107**:4
The End of the World (Abercrombie) **141**:5, 8, 10-13, 19, 21-22
The End of the World through Black Magic (Kraus)
See *Untergang der Welt durch die Schwarze Magic*
"The End, the Beginning" (Lawrence) **93**:51
"Das Ende der Welt" (Walser) **18**:421-22
"Das Ende des Siegers" (George) **14**:206
Ende einer Dienstfahrt (Böll) **185**:10, 34, 36, 41, 43, 51, 97-98, 100-101, 107, 143, 153
"Endegeeste" (Nemerov) **124**:192
Endgame (Beckett)
See *Fin de partie*
Endgame (Orton) **157**:294
"An Ending" (Nemerov) **124**:261
"Endless Anxiety" (Lawrence) **93**:45
"End-of-October Hexameters" (Radnóti) **16**:419
"En-Dor" (Kipling) **8**:201
Endor (Nemerov) **124**:151, 157, 165, 248, 251
L'Endroit et l'envers (Cocteau) **119**:106

"Endurance and the Profession" (Lyotard) **103**:167
"The Enduring Chill" (O'Connor) **132**:229, 231, 237, 246, 283, 288-90, 320, 345-46, 358
"Endymion" (Austin) **25**:34
Endymion (Heidenstam) **5**:250, 253
Ene (Obstfelder) **23**:179
"Enemies" (Bergelson) **81**:19
"The Enemies" (Thomas) **8**:455; **45**:409; **105**:300, 324, 326-27, 329, 332-33, 338, 355
Enemies (Artsybashev) **31**:9
The Enemies (Gorky) **8**:92
Enemies of the Permanent Things: Observations of Abnormality in Literature and Politics (Kirk) **119**:253-54, 256, 261, 266, 284, 287
"Enemies of the Republic" (Steffens) **20**:338
The Enemies of Women (Blasco Ibáñez)
See *Los enemigos de la mujer*
"The Enemies to Each Other" (Kipling) **8**:195; **17**:207
"The Enemies United" (Thomas) **105**:333
Los enemigos de la mujer (Blasco Ibáñez) **12**:35, 37, 43
The Enemy from Eden (Dickey) **151**:162
An Enemy of the Church (Leino)
See *Kirkon vihollinen*
An Enemy of the People (Ibsen)
See *En folkefiende*
The Enemy of the Stars (Lewis) **2**:389, 391, 396; **9**:243-45, 249-50; **104**:156-57, 168-69, 171-73, 181, 232, 279-80, 288, 298
Enemy Salvoes (Lewis) **104**:274-76
"Enereida" (Vallejo) **3**:531
L'énergie spirituelle (Bergson) **32**:27, 45
"Energumen Capitalism" (Lyotard) **103**:197
Enfance (Sarraute) **145**:268, 276-79, 294-306, 325-26, 329-30, 341, 345, 347, 349-50, 353, 364-65
Les enfances Pascal (Barrès) **47**:67
"L'enfant de la balle" (Coppee) **25**:120
"L'enfant du Crapaud" (Lemonnier) **22**:198
"L'enfant malade" (Colette) **5**:170; **16**:129
Enfantines (Larbaud) **9**:196, 198-201, 204, 206-07
"Enfants" (Garneau) **13**:195
Les enfants du Capitaine Grant (Verne) **6**:500; **52**:352
Les enfants humiliés: Journal, 1939-1940 (Bernanos) **3**:128
Les enfants terribles (Cocteau) **119**:40-2, 63, 69, 82-3, 87, 104-8, 110-11
L'enfer (Barbusse) **5**:14-17
"Enfidaville" (Douglas) **40**:76-7, 88-9
"The Enfranchised Reviewer" (Lucas) **73**:171
Engaged (Gilbert) **3**:208, 210, 218
"Engagement" (Adorno) **111**:177, 184-87
L'Engagement rationaliste (Bachelard) **128**:52-4
"Engeki kairyō ronja no kenten ni odoroku" (Mori Ōgai) **14**:381
"Der Engel im Walde" (Kolmar) **40**:178
Der Engel schwieg (Böll) **185**:146-47
Der Engel vom westlichen Fenster (Meyrink) **21**:218, 220, 231
"Engine Driver's Wife" (Platonov) **14**:414
Engine Fight Talk (Lewis)
See *One-Way Song*
"The Engineer" (Kornbluth) **8**:216
"The Engineer" (Milne) **88**:260
Engineer Garins Hyperboloid (Tolstoy) **18**:360, 370, 373
The Engineers and the Price System (Veblen) **31**:353, 362, 366
"England" (Campbell) **9**:31
England (Kazantzakis) **33**:164
England: A Dying Oligarchy (Bromfield) **11**:82
"England, All Hail" (Redcam) **25**:330
England and the English (Ford) **39**:124
"England and Yesterday" (Guiney) **41**:208-09
"England, Arise! A Socialist Marching Song" (Carpenter) **88**:77, 106
"England Day by Day" (Dobson) **79**:12
England in 1815 (Halévy)
See *Histoire du peuple anglais au xlxe siècle. iv. Le milieu du siècle, 1841-52*
"England Your England" (Orwell) **2**:498, 502; **51**:266; **128**:284
England Your England (Orwell) **51**:227
England's Pleasant Land (Forster) **125**:168
England's Antiphon (MacDonald) **9**:288; **113**:291
England's Effort (Ward) **55**:437, 440-42, 445
"England's Ideal" (Carpenter) **88**:63, 98
England's Ideal and Other Papers on Social Subjects (Carpenter) **88**:98
"Engle Ferry" (Rhodes) **53**:316
Der Englische Sender (Kaiser) **9**:181
The English, Are They Human? (Lewis) **2**:392
English at the North Pole (Verne) **6**:501
English Farming and Why I Turned It Up (Bramah) **72**:7-8
"The English Festival of Spoken Poetry" (Thomas) **105**:320
"The English Flag" (Kipling) **8**:177
English Folk-Songs for Schools (Baring-Gould) **88**:21
"An English Garden in Austria" (Jarrell) **177**:127, 196
An English Girl (Ford) **15**:88; **39**:136
"The English Huswife's Gossip" (Buchanan) **107**:15
English Law and the Renaissance (Maitland) **65**:265, 287
English Leaves (Lucas) **73**:174
English Lessons for English People (Abbott) **139**:12, 25, 36, 39
English Literature and Society in the Eighteenth Century (Stephen) **23**:308, 317, 322-24, 329, 336, 339, 345
"English Literature in Our Universities" (Quiller-Couch) **53**:292
English Local Government from the Revolution to the Municipal Corporations Act (Webb and Webb) **22**:399, 412, 416
English Men of Letters (James) **2**:262
English Men of Letters (Stephen) **23**:314
"English Men of Letters and Newspapers and Magazines" (Natsume) **10**:331
The English Novel (Ford) **15**:95; **39**:147
The English Novel (Saintsbury) **31**:242-44
The English Novel: From the Earliest Days to the Death of Joseph Conrad (Ford) **172**:100
"The English People" (Orwell) **128**:284
The English People (Orwell) **31**:190; **51**:260; **128**:259, 284
The English Poetic Mind (Williams) **11**:502
English Poets' Ideas of Nature (Natsume) **10**:331
English Poor Law History (Webb and Webb) **22**:415
"The English Revolution" (Orwell) **128**:284
English Rhetoric and Composition (Fisher) **87**:72
"The English Ritual" (Orwell) **128**:287
The English Rose (Buchanan) **107**:33, 87
"An English Saint" (Harris) **24**:267
"English Summer" (Chandler) **179**:128-29
English Tales (Pilnyak) **23**:198
"English Thornton" (Masters) **25**:305
The English Utilitarians (Stephen) **23**:323-24, 328
An Englishwoman's Love Letters (Housman) **7**:353
The Engravings of Eric Gill (Gill) **85**:101
"The Enigma" (Scott) **6**:394
The Enigmatic Man (Hamsun)
See *The Enigmatic One*
The Enigmatic One (Hamsun) **49**:131, 136, 155
Enjoying Life (Barbellion) **24**:75, 77, 80, 84-5
"The Enjoyment of Gloom" (Day) **25**:131
"Enlighten Your Child" (Jozsef) **22**:157, 165
"Enlightenment of Love" (Rohan) **22**:301
"The Enlightment of Modern Japan" (Natsume)
See "Watakushi no kojinshugi"
"Enna Blake" (Mansfield) **164**:263
L'ennemie des lois (Barrès) **47**:44, 63, 78, 90
Ennemonde (Giono) **124**:115
"L'ennui de vivre" (Bryusov) **10**:93
Enoch Arden (Griffith)
See *After Many Years*
"Enoch Soames" (Beerbohm) **1**:67-8, 71; **24**:102, 107, 118-19
Enone au clair visage, etc. (Moréas) **18**:279, 281, 287-88
The Enormous Crocodile (Dahl) **173**:28
The Enormous Room (Cummings) **137**:10-11, 26-27, 53
Enough (Beckett)
See *Assez*
Enough Rope (Parker) **143**:312, 317, 320-22
Une enquête aux pays du Levant (Barrès) **47**:67
"The Enquiry" (Kuprin)
See "Doznanie"
An Enquiry Concerning the Principles of Natural Knowledge (Whitehead) **97**:197, 199-200
L'enracinement (Weil) **23**:370-71, 375-76, 378, 380-81, 385, 399, 402-03, 405
Enrico IV (Pirandello) **4**:329, 331-40, 347, 349-51, 353, 356-57; **29**:285-86, 298, 302, 304-05, 311, 313, 318-19; **172**:134, 156, 174, 178
Ensayos . . . (Prado) **75**:205-06
Ensayos (Unamuno) **9**:514
Ensayos didactos (Hostos) **24**:304
"The Ensign Streameth Red, Killed" (Redcam) **25**:330
"Die Entdeckung Dantes in der Romantik" (Auerbach) **43**:62
"Entering Scott's Night" (Dickey) **151**:209
Entering the War (Calvino)
See *L'entrada en guerra*
"Enterrar y callar" (Éluard) **7**:251
Enterrement (Kandinsky) **92**:50
The Entertainer (Osborne) **153**:242, 251, 307, 312-13, 320
Entertaining Mr. Sloane (Orton) **157**:289-97, 299-301, 308, 311, 313-14, 316-17, 322-24, 329-32, 336-38, 340, 345, 347-51, 355-57
The Entertainment (Delafield) **61**:133
Entertainments (Devkota)
See *Manoranjan*
"Die Entfaltung der Seele durch Lebenskunst" (Key) **65**:238-41
Entfernung von der Truppe (Böll) **185**:36, 43, 51-3 99, 128-29, 139, 159
Der entfesselte Wotan (Toller) **10**:482
"Die Entfremdung" (Werfel) **8**:477
L'Enthousiasme (Lyotard) **103**:198
Enthralled (Saltus) **8**:346
"Enthusiasm for Hats" (Nemerov) **124**:186
An Enthusiast (Somerville & Ross) **51**:338, 340, 344, 353
"An Entire Life" (Pilnyak)
See "Tselaya zhizn"
"Entpersönlichung" (Huch) **13**:243, 245, 247, 253
Entr'actes in the Ravine (Kuzmin) **40**:197
L'entrada en guerra (Calvino) **183**:95-96, 189, 237
"Entrance" (Rilke)
See "Eingang"
L'entrave (Colette) **1**:192; **5**:167-68; **16**:136, 138
"Entre dos oscuridades un relámpago" (Aleixandre) **113**:34
"Entre el zolor y el placer" (Vallejo) **56**:287
Entre la vie et la mort (Sarraute) **145**:262, 288, 310, 339-41, 345, 352-53, 357, 359-61
Entre naranjos (Blasco Ibáñez) **12**:30, 36, 38

"Entre O Ser E As Coisas" (Drummond de Andrade) **139**:228
"Entre santos" (Machado de Assis) **10**:291
Entretiens (Léautaud) **83**:199, 206-7
Entretiens au bord de la mer (Alain) **41**:30
Entretiens avec Roger Stéphane (Cocteau) **119**:87
Entretiens chez le sculpteur (Alain) **41**:30
Les Entretiens d'Ostende (Ghelderode) **187**:5, 9, 13
"Entrevue" (Jacob) **6**:193
The Entry into War (Calvino)
See *L'entrada en guerra*
Entscheidung vor Morgengrauen (Zuckmayer) **191**:305
Die Entstehung des Doktor Faustus (Mann) **44**:153, 174, 180, 188-90, 192, 210; **168**:99
"Enttäuschung" (Mann) **35**:259
Entwicklung (Benn) **3**:112
Entwicklungsziele der Psychoanalyse (Rank) **115**:247
"Enueg I" (Beckett) **145**:79
"Enueg II" (Beckett) **145**:79, 112
L'envers du décor (Bourget) **12**:69
"Envoi" (Lewis) **2**:397
"L'envoi" (Wilde) **41**:367
Envoi à la France (D'Annunzio) **6**:145
"The Envoy of Mr Cogito" (Herbert)
See "Przestanie"
Envy (Olesha)
See *Zavist'*
Envy and Other Works (Olesha) **136**:137
"Enya of the Dark Eyes" (Sharp) **39**:372, 377
"Enzio's Kingdom" (Percy) **84**:199, 213, 215-7, 220
Enzio's Kingdom and Other Poems (Percy) **84**:197-8, 201, 213, 228
"The Eolian Harp" (Leino)
See "Tuulikannel"
Épaisseurs (Fargue) **11**:200
"Epaphroditos" (Herzl) **36**:141-42
"L'épave" (Coppee) **25**:120, 126
Les épaves (Sully Prudhomme) **31**:302
Eperdument (Verhaeren) **12**:462
"Ephraim" (Merrill)
See "The Book of Ephraim"
"Epic and Lyric in Contemporary Russia" (Tsvetaeva) **7**:570
"Epic and Novel" (Bakhtin) **160**:134, 206
Epic of the Forgotten (Vazov)
See *Epopeya na zabravenite*
Epic Voices (Valle-Inclán)
See *Voces de gesta*
"The Epick of San Georgio" (Rolfe) **12**:266
L'epidémie (Mirbeau) **55**:284
Epifanskie shlyuzy (Platonov) **14**:404, 407, 409, 417, 423, 427
Epifany Locks (Platonov)
See *Epifanskie shlyuzy*
Epigrafe (Saba) **33**:366
"Epigrafía callejera" (Baroja) **8**:63
"Epigrama para Emilio Moura" (Drummond de Andrade) **139**:229
"Epigramas de Boston" (Villaurrutia) **80**:489
Epilog burzy (Herbert) **168**:39
L'epilogo (Pirandello) **172**:188
"Epilogue" (Cullen) **37**:159
"Epilogue" (Henley) **8**:110
"Epilogue" (Lawrence) **93**:45
"The Epilogue" (Masters) **2**:473; **25**:298-99, 303, 313, 315-16
"Epilogue" (Strauss) **141**:294
Epilogue (Halévy)
See *Verla démocratie sociale et vers la guerre*
Epilogue (Martin du Gard) **24**:383, 388, 397-98
The Epilogue (Pirandello)
See *L'epilogo*
"Epilogue by Roger Bantock" (Wakefield) **120**:355
"Epilogue I: Pension Seguin" (Mansfield) **164**:339
Epilogue of a Storm (Herbert)
See *Epilog burzy*
"The Epilogue of the Lyricist" (Babits)
See "A lírikus epilógja"
"Epilogue to Betrayal" (Santos) **156**:314
"Epilogue to Eighteenth Century Vignettes" (Dobson) **79**:18
"Epilogue to Fleet Street Eclogues" (Davidson) **24**:186
"An Epilogue to Love" (Symons) **11**:434
Epilogues (Gourmont) **17**:125-27, 130, 136, 138
Epiphanies (Joyce) **16**:232; **159**:279, 281-82, 285, 306
Episcopo and Company (D'Annunzio)
See *Giovanni Episcopo*
"Episode" (Khodasevich) **15**:204, 208, 212
"An Episode at the Dentist's" (Fields) **80**:258
Épisode de la vie d'un auteur (Anouilh) **195**:38, 48
"An Episode in a Lodging House" (Blackwood) **5**:73
Episode in Palmetto (Caldwell) **117**:20, 22
"An Episode in the Life of Ezekial Whitmore" (Arnow) **196**:91
"An Episode of Cathedral History" (James) **6**:215
"An Episode of Lawn Tennis" (Fields) **80**:259
Episode of the Wandering Knife (Rinehart) **52**:288, 302-03
"An Episode on the Links" (Fields) **80**:258
"Episodes and Visions" (Abbey) **160**:16
Episodes before Thirty (Blackwood) **5**:75, 77
Episodes in the Life of a Seeker (Korolenko) **20**:171
Episodios nacionales (Pérez Galdós) **27**:244, 246-49, 252, 256-59, 275-77, 282-83, 286-88
Epistel (Brecht) **169**:43-44
"Epistle Dedicatory" (Shaw) **3**:388
"An Epistle from Corinth" (Percy) **84**:196
"Epistle to Passers-By" (Vallejo) **3**:526
"Epistle to the Olympians" (Nash) **109**:364
"Epistle to the Pinzons" (Reyes) **33**:318
Epistolario (García Lorca) **181**:90
Epístolas y poemas (Darío) **4**:58-9
"Epitafio ideal" (Jiménez) **183**:271
Epitafios (Sarduy) **167**:199, 204-5
"Epitaph" (Abercrombie) **141**:23
"Epitaph" (Hardy) **143**:151
"The Epitaph" (Lagerloef) **36**:239
"Epitaph" (Levi) **109**:287
Epitaph (Dreiser) **10**:196
"Epitaph for a Sailor Buried Alive" (Roberts) **8**:315
"An Epitaph (For Amy Lowell)" (Cullen) **37**:164
Epitaph for George Dillon (Osborne) **153**:242, 244, 251, 313, 322
"Epitaph for the Race of Man" (Millay) **169**:250, 252, 255
Epitaph for the Race of Man (Millay) **4**:312, 314, 316; **49**:210, 219; **169**:268
"Epitaph on a Pessimist" (Hardy) **143**:155
"Epitaph on a Philosopher the Reports of Whose Death Have Been Grossly Minimized" (Nemerov) **124**:274
"Epitaph on an Army of Mercenaries" (Housman) **10**:245, 256-57
"Epitaph on John Keats" (Davies) **5**:203
"Epitaph on the Politician Himself" (Belloc) **18**:41
"Epitaphio do Mexico" (Machado de Assis) **10**:279
"Epitaphs" (Villaurrutia) **80**:463, 489, 515
"Epitaphs of the War" (Kipling) **8**:191, 196
"Epithalamion" (Cummings) **137**:41
"Epithalamium" (Agee) **180**:65
"Epithalamium" (Bishop) **103**:6
"Epithalamium" (Gosse) **28**:132
"The Epithalamium" (Housman) **1**:353
"Epithalamium" (Middleton) **56**:173
"Epître" (Moréas) **18**:281
Epochs of Chinese and Japanese Art: An Outline of East Asiatic Design (Fenollosa) **91**:3
Epopeya na zabravenite (Vazov) **25**:453, 455-56, 459
"L'epouse fidèle" (Moréas) **18**:286
Les épreuves (Sully Prudhomme) **31**:300, 302, 304, 306-07
"The Equality of the Sexes" (Éluard)
See "L'égalité des sexes"
L'equarrissage pour tous (Vian) **9**:530-32, 537
"Equations of a Villanelle" (Nemerov) **124**:215, 221, 258
"Equilibrium" (Bridie) **3**:139
El equipaje del rey José (Pérez Galdós) **27**:287
"L'equitable balance" (Moréas) **18**:288
"L'équivoque de la culture" (Bataille) **155**:90
"er nimnt zwei vögel ab" (Arp) **115**:11
Er soll dein Herr sein (Heyse) **8**:121
"The Era of Tyrannies" (Halévy) **104**:117
The Era of Tyrannies: Essays on Socialism and War (Halévy)
See *L'Ere des tyrannies: Etudes sur le socialisme et la guerre*
"Era un aire suave" (Darío) **4**:58
"Erasmus" (Robinson) **101**:119, 124
Erasmus of Rotterdam (Zweig)
See *Triumph und Tragik des Erasmus von Rotterdam*
"Erdbeeren" (Roth) **33**:363
"Erde" (Kandinsky) **92**:66
Erdély (Moricz) **33**:234, 238, 242, 247-48
Erdgeist: Earth Spirit (Wedekind) **7**:575, 579-80, 582
Die Erdmordung einer Butterblume (Döblin) **13**:158, 166
L'Ere des tyrannies: Etudes sur le socialisme et la guerre (Halévy) **104**:119-20
L'Ere du soupçon (Sarraute)
See *L'ere du soupçon: Essais sur le roman*
L'ere du soupçon: Essais sur le roman (Sarraute) **145**:269, 315, 344
"Ere Sleep Comes Down to Soothe the Weary Eyes" (Dunbar) **12**:106, 108, 121-22
Erechtheus (Swinburne) **8**:426-27, 441; **36**:300, 313, 324, 332
Ereignis (Kandinsky) **92**:49
Ereignisse (Bernhard) **165**:37, 94
Erema (Blackmore) **27**:38, 42
"Eremita a Parigi" (Calvino) **183**:105
Erewhon; or, Over the Range (Butler) **1**:133-38; **33**:26, 28, 35, 38, 41-2, 44, 46, 49, 51-60, 64, 66-7, 69-76
Erewhon Revisited Twenty Years Later (Butler) **1**:134-35, 137; **33**:28, 38-9, 57-60, 66, 68, 70, 73-6
"Erfahrung" (Rilke) **195**:330
Erfahrung und Urteil (Husserl) **100**:34, 39-40, 59-60, 70-72, 97
Erfolg: Drei jahre Geschichte einer Provinz (Feuchtwanger) **3**:178-83, 186-88
Éri phyle et Sylves nouvelles (Moréas) **18**:278, 281-82, 284, 288
Eric Brighteyes (Haggard) **11**:245-46
Erik Dorn (Hecht) **101**:31, 35-6, 38-41, 44-5, 47, 55-61, 70-1, 86
Erik XIV (Strindberg) **1**:449; **8**:517
Erindringer (Nexø) **43**:329, 333
Erindringer: Et lille kræ (Nexø)
See *Erindringer*
Erindringer: For Lud og koldt vand (Nexø)
See *Erindringer*
Erindringer: Under aaben himmel (Nexø)
See *Erindringer*
Erindringer: Vejs ende (Nexø)
See *Erindringer*
"Erinna" (Teasdale) **4**:424
Erinnerungen von Ludolf Ursleu dem Jüngeren (Huch) **13**:240-41, 243-45, 247, 251, 253
"Erkaufte Mutter" (Broch) **20**:52
"Erkenntnis" (Borchert) **5**:105

Das Erlebnis des Marschalls vom Bassompierre (Hofmannsthal) **11**:302-04
"The Erl-King" (Carter) **139**:116-17, 204, 209-10
Erma bifronte (Pirandello) **4**:332; **29**:282, 291, 308
The Ermine (Anouilh)
See *L'Hermine*
"L'ermite" (Apollinaire) **3**:38, 43; **51**:14, 59-60
Die Ermittlung (Weiss)
See *Die Ermittlung: Oratorium in Elf Gesëngen*
Die Ermittlung: Oratorium in Elf Gesëngen (Weiss) **152**:264, 267, 270, 285, 296-300, 304-5, 307-12, 315-16, 318-24
Ermyntrude and Esmeralda (Strachey) **12**:413
Ernest Hemingway: A Life Story (Baker) **119**:11, 13, 15, 18, 20-21, 27
Ernest Hemingway: Selected Letters, 1917-1961 (Baker) **119**:22, 24, 27-30
Ernest Pontifex; or, The Way of All Flesh (Butler)
See *The Way of All Flesh*
Ernesto (Saba) **33**:378
Ein ernstes Leben (Mann) **9**:326-27
"Ero sicut Deus" (Brennan) **17**:56
"Die Eroberung" (Benn) **3**:109
L'eroe (D'Annunzio) **6**:133
"Eröltelt menet" (Radnóti) **16**:412
"Eros" (Lasker-Schueler) **57**:328
Eros (Ivanov) **33**:123
Eros (Verga) **3**:539, 542
Eros and Psyche (Bridges) **1**:129, 132
"Eros and the Poet" (Kraus) **5**:289
"Eros con bastón" (García Lorca) **181**:184, 186-87
Eros e Priapo (Gadda) **144**:81, 93, 110, 122
"Eros hemlighet" (Södergran) **31**:289, 295
"Eros Makes the World Anew" (Södergran)
See "Eros skapar världen ny"
"Eros' Secret" (Södergran)
See "Eros hemlighet"
"Eros skapar världen ny" (Södergran) **31**:295
"Eros tempel" (Södergran) **31**:295
"Eros Turannos" (Robinson) **5**:405, 407, 418-19; **101**:98-103, 109, 113, 127, 129-30, 133-35, 164, 170-72, 180, 191-93
"Eros-Hero" (Papadiamantis) **29**:273
"Erotic" (Lorde)
See "The Uses of the Erotic, The Erotic as Power"
Eroticism (Bataille)
See *L'érotisme*
L'érotisme (Bataille) **155**:9, 11, 28, 32, 34-35, 37-45, 62-64, 77-78, 81-82, 85, 90, 93, 109
The Erpingham Camp (Orton) **157**:295, 301-3, 308, 316, 324, 329, 332, 336-38, 340, 357, 360
"Erpresste Versöhnung" (Adorno) **111**:29
"Um erradio" (Machado de Assis) **11**:291
"The Errand Imperious" (Markham) **47**:291
"Error de cálculo" (Salinas) **17**:358
"The Error of William Van Broom" (Post) **39**:338
Erste Gedichte (Rilke) **195**:258
Der Erwählte (Mann) **2**:431; **21**:179; **35**:242; **44**:171; **168**:98, 156
Erwartung (Schoenberg) **75**:301-02, 312, 320, 323, 326-28, 331, 340, 358, 363, 371-73, 379
Erzahlungen (Bernhard) **165**:96
Erzählungen (Kafka) **179**:254
"Erziehung nach Auschwitz" (Adorno) **111**:51, 188
Es geschah am 20 Juli (Pabst) **127**:363
"Es ist ein eigen Ding" (Raabe) **45**:190
Es ist Genug (Kaiser) **9**:193
Es lebe das Leben! (Sudermann) **15**:418-20, 426-27, 433, 438
"Es verdad" (García Lorca) **181**:179-80
Es War (Sudermann) **15**:423-24, 430, 438
"Es wird etwar geschehen" (Böll) **185**:27
"Esa capacidad para soñar" (Arenas) **191**:216, 218
"Esa órbita abierta" (Jiménez) **183**:281, 308
Esa sangre (Azuela) **3**:76; **145**:25
"Esarhaddon, King of Assyria" (Tolstoy) **4**:469
"Esattezza" (Calvino) **183**:102, 106
"Esbozo" (Azuela) **145**:21
Esbozos y rasguños (Pereda) **16**:372
"The Escalade" (Andrade) **43**:7
La escalinata de un trono (Echegaray) **4**:102
El escándalo (Pardo Bazán) **189**:256-57
Escapade (Mankiewicz) **85**:164
"The Escapade of the Rev. Joshua Geer" (Scott) **6**:398
"An Escape" (Abercrombie) **141**:4, 8
"The Escape" (Dickey) **151**:97, 109
"The Escape" (Gurney) **33**:95, 99, 103
"The Escape" (Mansfield) **8**:284-85; **164**:241
"Escape" (Wylie) **8**:521, 533
"The Escape of Mr. Trimm" (Cobb) **77**:120, 123-4, 127, 133, 136-7
Escape on Venus (Burroughs) **32**:59
The Escaped Cock (Lawrence)
See *The Man Who Died*
"Escapism" (Cather) **99**:216, 281; **132**:137, 143
"El escarabajo" (Aleixandre) **113**:14
"L'escaut" (Verhaeren) **12**:468
Escenas montañesas (Pereda) **16**:363-65, 367, 373, 379-82
Esch; or, Anarchy, 1903 (Broch) **20**:46-7, 63, 73
"Eschatological Forebodings of Mr. Cogito" (Herbert)
See "Przeczucia eschatologiczne Pana Cogito"
"Eschyle et Aristophane" (Schwob) **20**:327
L'esclusa (Pirandello) **4**:332, 353
"Los escoleros" (Arguedas) **147**:8
A escrava que não é Isaura (Andrade) **43**:10-13, 18
Escrito sobre un cuerpo (Sarduy) **2**:974, 980; **167**:199
"El escritor argentino y la tradición" (Borges) **109**:13, 41, 71, 93-4, 154, 163
"Escritor fracasado" (Arlt) **29**:45
Escritos de juventud (Pereda) **16**:379
"La escritura del Dios" (Borges) **109**:29
"El escuerzo" (Lugones) **15**:293
Escurial (Ghelderode) **187**:4-5, 19, 40
"Eseldorf" (Twain) **185**:243-44, 258, 290-92, 306
La esfera (Sender) **136**:208
La esfinge (Unamuno) **148**:267, 269-70
Esir (Khlebnikov) **20**:136
"Esistono cattolici" (Papini) **22**:281
"Eskadronnyi Trunov" (Babel) **2**:22; **13**:32; **171**:9-10, 14, 19, 23, 34-35, 39, 71, 75, 78, 84, 86
"Èskadronnyj Trunov" (Babel)
See "Eskadronnyi Trunov"
"Eskaqua Cove" (Murfree) **135**:229
"Esli" (Hippius) **9**:166
Esoteric Essences of Chinese-English Poetry (Su Man-shu) **24**:458
Espaces (Fargue) **11**:194-95
"Les espaces du sommeil" (Desnos) **22**:60
"Espacio" (Aleixandre) **113**:19
"Espacio" (Jiménez) **4**:219, 224; **183**:286, 290, 320-24, 326-28
Espacio (Jiménez) **183**:289, 291, 294, 303-4
"Espacio (3 estrofas)" (Jiménez) **183**:320, 322, 324, 326-28
"Espacio (fragmento primero de la segunda estrofa)" (Jiménez) **183**:326
Espadas como labios (Aleixandre) **113**:4, 6-8, 10, 23, 27, 40, 44-46, 67, 70, 72, 79, 81
The Espalier (Warner) **131**:310
"España, aparta de mí este cáliz" (Vallejo) **56**:301-02, 305
España, aparta de mí este cáliz (Vallejo) **3**:527, 533-34, 536; **56**:291-92, 299, 304-5, 312, 316
"España. Sin día" (Jiménez) **183**:272
"Especially When the October Wind" (Thomas) **8**:450, 456; **45**:361, 363
"El espejo de agua" (Huidobro) **31**:123, 125, 144
El espejo de la muerte (Unamuno) **9**:513; **148**:256
El espejo de Lida Sal (Asturias) **184**:17
"El espejo de los enigmas" (Borges) **109**:55-6
"El espejo negro" (Lugones) **15**:293
"Los espejos" (Borges) **109**:150
"La Esperanza" (Prado) **75**:211
Esperanza nuestra (Martinez Sierra and Martinez Sierra) **6**:274, 280-81
"Espergesia" (Vallejo) **3**:532; **56**:289
"Esperteza" (Drummond de Andrade) **139**:228
"El espíritu castellano" (Unamuno) **148**:245
La esposa del vengador (Echegaray) **4**:99
"Esposizioni-Esplorazioni" (Calvino) **183**:50
"L'Esprit contre la Raison" (Crevel) **112**:13
"Esprit de Corps in Elementary Schools" (Orage) **157**:249
"L'esprit et l'eau" (Claudel) **2**:104, 107; **10**:132-33
"Un Esprit non prévenu" (Gide) **177**:98
"L'esprit nouveau et les poètes" (Apollinaire) **8**:14; **51**:14, 28, 32, 37, 43, 45
Esqueçer Para Lembrar (Drummond de Andrade) **139**:230
Esquisse (Kandinsky) **92**:48
Esquisse Biographique sur Don Bosco (Huysmans) **69**:43
"Esquisses en plein air" (Garneau) **13**:199, 203
Essai de critique indirecte (Cocteau) **119**:111
Essai d'un discours cohérent sur les rapports de dieu et du monde (Benda) **60**:48, 64, 79
Essai sur la connaissance approchée (Bachelard) **128**:53-4, 88-90
Essai sur la mystique et l'action de l'Inde vivante (Rolland) **23**:26
"Essai sur le roman sentimental et le roman naturalist" (Rostand) **37**:295
"Essais" (Léautaud) **83**:199
Essais (Hostos) **24**:303
Essais critiques (Barthes) **135**:117, 156
Essais de psychologie contemporaine (Bourget) **12**:57-8, 65, 67, 74, 76
Essais et Mémoires (Yourcenar) **193**:351
"Essay" (Cocteau) **119**:92-3
"The Essay as Form" (Adorno) **111**:190
Essay in Autobiography (Pasternak) **188**:202
"An Essay in Criticism" (Woolf) **43**:414
"An Essay in Equality" (Stringer) **37**:335
An Essay on Comedy and the Uses of the Comic Spirit (Meredith) **17**:266-67, 286-88; **43**:261, 275, 278, 280-81, 292, 301-03
"An Essay on Imagination" (Cary) **196**:164
"Essay on Limitation" (Ortega y Gasset) **9**:334
Essay on Man (Cassirer) **61**:48-51, 53, 57, 59, 61, 66-7, 70-1, 73-4, 77, 88-9, 95, 99, 106, 108, 110-11, 115, 118
An Essay on Metaphysics (Collingwood) **67**:102, 104, 106, 134, 136, 138-39, 142, 146, 151, 182, 189, 191, 195
An Essay on Philosophical Method (Collingwood) **67**:104-6, 134, 139, 148, 151, 156, 173, 177, 182-86, 189, 194
Essay on the Art of Writing (Ellis) **14**:142
"An Essay on the Chinese Written Character as a Medium for Poetry" (Fenollosa) **91**:7, 15
"Essay on the Objective of Plastic Art" (Lewis) **104**:204
An Essay on the Restoration of Property (Belloc) **7**:39
Essay on the Situation of Poetry (Tzara) **168**:274
Essays (Mann) **168**:161
Essays (Prado)
See *Ensayos . . .*
Essays (Yeats) **1**:555; **18**:443

Essays and Introductions (Yeats) **93**:402-05
Essays and Soliloquies (Unamuno) **148**:230, 235
Essays by James Huneker (Huneker) **65**:199
Essays in Biography (Keynes) **64**:201, 203, 206, 208, 246
Essays in Experimental Logic (Dewey) **95**:28
Essays in Literary Criticism (Santayana) **40**:394
Essays in Little (Lang) **16**:256
"Essays in Old French Poems" (Dobson) **79**:18
Essays in Our Changing Order (Veblen) **31**:362
Essays in Persuasion (Keynes) **64**:203-4, 207, 245
Essays in Radical Empiricism (James) **15**:187; **32**:340
Essays in the Philosophy of Art (Collingwood) **67**:124
Essays in Verse (Sinclair) **11**:407-08
Essays in Zen Buddhism (Suzuki) **109**:375-81, 383, 390
Essays of a Catholic (Belloc) **18**:45
Essays Old and New (Burke) **63**:125
Essays on Architecture and Poetry (Prado)
See *Ensayos . . .*
Essays on Freethinking and Plainspeaking (Stephen) **23**:302, 310, 313
Essays on Literature and Society (Muir) **87**:183
Essays on Practical Politics (Roosevelt) **69**:178
Essays on the Gita (Aurobindo) **63**:30-2, 34-6
Essays, Speeches, and Public Letters by William Faulkner (Faulkner) **170**:211, 216, 240
Essays upon the Fine Arts (Sully Prudhomme) **31**:307
"The Essence of National Economic Productivity" (Weber) **69**:320
"The Essence of the Aesthetic" (Croce) **37**:93
"The Essence of the Hindu" (Vivekananda) **88**:379
"The Essence of Tragedy" (Anderson) **2**:6, 10; **144**:35, 42, 45, 48
The Essence of Tragedy and other Footnotes (Anderson) **144**:71
Die Essenholer (Böll) **185**:5
The Essential Kropotkin (Kropotkin) **36**:221
The Essential Peirce (Peirce) **81**:329
The Essential Robinson (Robinson) **101**:192
Essentials (Toomer) **172**:286, 293, 313
"Essentials of Spontaneous Prose" (Kerouac) **117**:190-91, 205, 220, 226
"Esta noche, noche buena" (Güiraldes) **39**:176
"Una estación de amor" (Quiroga) **20**:211-12
La estación total (Jiménez) **4**:214, 216; **183**:256-61, 263-65, 271, 279, 286, 290-92
La estafeta romántica (Pérez Galdós) **27**:254
"The Estaminet" (Gurney) **33**:112
"El estampido de la vacuidad" (Sarduy) **167**:220
"La estancia vieja" (Güiraldes) **39**:176
"Estancias nocturnas" (Villaurrutia) **80**:463
El estanque de los lotos (Nervo) **11**:396, 399, 401
Estas ruinas que ves (Ibarguengoitia) **148**:216
"Estas trovas" (Huidobro) **31**:124
The Estate of Poetry (Muir) **87**:204
"Estatua" (Villaurrutia) **80**:489
"Estaunie" (Čapek) **37**:52
Este Domingo (Donoso) **133**:39, 54-55, 82, 122, 147-50, 152, 177, 186-88, 192
"Estefanía" (Quiroga) **20**:213
"Ester Primavera" (Arlt) **29**:45-7, 55, 59
Estetica come scienza dell' espressione e linguistica generale (Croce) **37**:80, 93-6, 105, 108-10, 113-19, 121-27, 129, 131
Estética y ética estética (Jiménez) **183**:303
"Esther" (Lasker-Schueler) **57**:336
"Esther" (Obstfelder) **23**:178
"Esther" (Toomer) **172**:258
Esther (Adams) **4**:9-10, 12, 15, 17, 20; **52**:40
"Esther Kahn" (Symons) **11**:448
Esther Waters (Moore) **7**:474-78, 480-87, 489-90, 495, 499-500
"The Esthetic Significance of the Motion Picture" (Hartmann) **73**:132
"Esthetic Theories: Art as Expression" (Jarrell) **177**:221
"The Esthetic Value of Cubism" (Hartmann) **73**:148
Esthetic Verities (Hartmann) **73**:117, 119
Esthetics and Evolution (Jensen)
See *Æsteik og Udvikling*
"Esthetics, Criticism, and Life" (Bodenheim) **44**:74
Esthétique de la langue française (Gourmont) **17**:126-27, 129, 138, 145-46
Esthétique du mal (Stevens) **3**:455-56, 462, 478; **12**:364, 384; **45**:298, 300, 302-04, 345
"Estino de la carne" (Aleixandre) **113**:76
Estío (Jiménez) **4**:216; **183**:257-62, 314-15, 319
Esto perpetua (Belloc) **7**:31; **18**:28
"Estoy midiéndome con dios" (Jiménez) **183**:277-80
A estranha morte do Professor Antena (Sá-Carneiro) **83**:403-5
La Estrella de Sevilla (Garro) **153**:21
"La estrella venida" (Jiménez) **183**:263
"Estudio preliminar" (Darío) **4**:66
"Estudios sobre el amor" (Ortega y Gasset) **9**:344
Estudios sobre la degeneración del sistema nervioso (Ramoacn y Cajal) **93**:137, 142
Et folketog (Bojer) **64**:5-6, 8-12, 19, 22, 24
"Et main tenant que c'est la pluie" (Alain-Fournier) **6**:28
"Et Møde" (Jensen) **41**:303
Et nunc manet in te, suivi de journal intime (Gide) **12**:173-74
Et on tuera tous les affreux (Vian) **9**:531-32
"Et voilà" (van Ostaijen) **33**:413
Etant donnés (Tzara) **168**:231
L'étape (Bourget) **12**:69-72
Etapper: Ny raekke (Undset) **3**:520; **197**:311, 315-17
Etat civil (Drieu la Rochelle) **21**:17, 20, 32
"Etched in Moonlight" (Stephens) **4**:417
L'été, 1914 (Martin du Gard) **24**:381-82, 385, 388, 390, 392, 394, 396-98, 408
"Étendards" (Apollinaire) **51**:35
"The Eternal" (Gumilev)
See "Vechnoe"
The Eternal Act of Creation (Frye) **165**:191, 238
"The Eternal Adam" (Verne)
See "L'Eternel Adam"
"Eternal Blue Skies back of the Clouds" (Babits)
See "Órókkék ég a felhők mőgőtt"
The Eternal Bourgeois (Horvath)
See *Der ewige Spießer*
"Eternal Calendar of the Mother Tongue" (Andrić) **135**:42
The Eternal City (Caine) **97**:3, 7, 10, 14-15
Eternal Companions (Merezhkovsky) **29**:230, 249
"Eternal Death" (Noguchi) **80**:363
"The Eternal Duel" (Huneker) **65**:196
"The Eternal Fugitive" (Hecht) **101**:36
The Eternal Lover (Burroughs) **32**:57, 79
The Eternal Masculine (Sudermann) **15**:420
"Eternal Nocturne" (Villaurrutia) **80**:486
The Eternal Road (Werfel)
See *Der Weg der Verheissung*
Eternal Slave (Bergelson) **81**:16
The Eternal Smile and Other Stories (Lagerkvist)
See *Det eviga leendet*
The Eternal Strife (Bojer)
See *Den evige krig*
"Eternal Struggle and Honeymoon" (Ady) **11**:20
"Eternal Treasure" (Gurney) **33**:85
"Eternal Truth of Idols" (Bryusov) **10**:80, 88, 91
"The Eternal Wedding" (Abercrombie) **141**:8
"L'Eternel Adam" (Verne) **6**:497, 501; **52**:331, 350, 360-61
"L'éternel féminin" (Teilhard de Chardin) **9**:493
Eternidades (Jiménez) **4**:215; **183**:256-63, 268, 270-71, 273-74, 285, 290, 296, 301-2
"Eterno" (Jiménez) **183**:259-60
Ethan Frome (Wharton) **3**:556-58, 560-61, 563, 566, 568-70, 572, 578-80; **9**:541-43, 551-54; **27**:381-417; **53**:361, 387; **129**:345-46, 362, 365; **149**:255
Ether and Me (Rogers) **8**:336
"Ethical Fragments" (Croce) **37**:106
"Ethical Principles Underlying Education" (Dewey) **95**:66
Ethical Relativity (Westermarck) **87**:329, 338, 355, 372,-77, 379, 393-94
Ethics (Stanislavsky) **167**:248
"Ethics in Relations to Conduct" (Keynes) **64**:288, 290, 292
"The Ethics of Culture" (Locke) **43**:239, 241
"The Ethics of Democracy" (Dewey) **95**:63
"The Ethics of Elfland" (Chesterton) **1**:185; **6**:109
"The Ethics of Greene" (Nishida) **83**:235
"The Ethics of Living Jim Crow" (Wright) **136**:276, 316, 320
"The Ethics of Pig" (Henry) **19**:184
"The Ethics of Plagiarism" (Matthews) **95**:226
"The Ethics of Terminology" (Peirce) **81**:199
"The Ethics of the Detective Story—from Raffles to Miss Blandish" (Orwell) **128**:287
The Ethics of the Dust (Ruskin) **20**:282; **63**:206, 255, 293-94, 312-13, 315, 333-35
Ethics: Origin and Development (Kropotkin) **36**:194, 204, 221
"Ethik" (Broch) **20**:56
"Ethiopia" (Harper) **14**:260
Ethiopia Unbound (Casely-Hayford) **24**:131-39
L'étoile au front (Roussel) **20**:227-28, 234, 242-43, 246
L'etoile de bois (Schwob) **20**:323
L'etoile vesper (Colette) **5**:169-70
L'etonnante aventure de la mission Barsac (Verne) **6**:495, 497; **52**:347, 350, 352, 356
"L'Etranger" (Proust) **161**:174
"L'étranger" (Sully Prudhomme) **31**:306
"Être et vivre" (Jarry) **147**:314
Etruscan Places (Lawrence) **2**:368; **48**:121, 149; **93**:56, 76
"Etterskrift" (Undset) **197**:306
"Etude" (La Guma) **140**:234
Etudes (Bachelard) **128**:53
Études et portraits (Bourget) **12**:65, 74-5
Etudie 1 (Kandinsky) **92**:49
Etudie 2 (Kandinsky) **92**:49
L'étui de nacre (France) **9**:40
Etzel Andergast (Wassermann) **6**:511-12, 519-20
"Euclid" (Millay) **4**:308
Eudoxia (Kuzmin)
See *Komediia o Evdokii iz Geliopoliia*
Eugene Onegin (Nabokov) **189**:75
Eugenics, and Other Evils (Chesterton) **6**:97, 110
"Eulogy of Aphrodite" (Tsvetaeva)
See "Khvala Afrodite"
Eupalinos; ou, L'architecte (Valéry) **4**:494-95, 497; **15**:445
Euphorion (Lee) **5**:310, 314
"Euphrasia" (Graham) **19**:137
Europa (Kaiser) **9**:173, 179
Europa (Sternheim) **8**:368, 381
"Europa and the Bull" (Gogarty) **15**:106, 110, 113
"Europa and the Bull" (Torrence) **97**:158
Az Europai irodalom története (Babits) **14**:41-2
Europe after 8:15 (Van Dine) **23**:357
"Europe! Europe!" (Ginsberg) **120**:9
Europe Unite (Churchill) **113**:104
"The European" (Hesse) **148**:172
The European (James) **2**:255, 275; **40**:122-23, 150; **47**:205; **64**:157
"European Diagnosis" (Yourcenar)
See "Diagnostic de l'Europe"

European Literature in the Nineteenth Century (Croce)
See *Poesia e non poesia: Note sulla letteratura euròpa del secolo decimonono*
European Night (Khodasevich)
See *Evropeyskaya noch'*
Europe's Morning After (Roberts) **23**:238
Eurydice (Anouilh) **195**:10-11, 17, 20-21, 38-9, 42, 48, 54-7, 64
Eurythmie als sichtbare sprache (Steiner) **13**:459
Eurythmy as Visible Speech (Steiner)
See *Eurythmie als sichtbare sprache*
Euvres complètes (Sarraute) **145**:341-42
Éva (Molnár) **20**:164
Eva (Verga) **3**:539, 547
Eva bonheur (Heijermans) **24**:288-89, 292
Eva Trout; or, Changing Scenes (Bowen) **148**:22-24, 36-37, 45-47, 66-67, 69-70, 73-76, 78, 82-83, 89-90, 94-101, 103, 113-23, 126, 129-33
Evan Harrington; or, He Would Be a Gentleman (Meredith) **17**:261, 266, 276, 284; **43**:259, 280
"Evangelicheskaja cerkov'" (Gumilev) **60**:280
"The Evangelistic Beasts" (Lawrence) **93**:98
Évangiles (Zola) **6**:562, 564
Evaristo Carriego (Borges) **109**:7, 53, 70, 131, 156, 159, 164
La evasión hacia el fondo (Aleixandre) **113**:4
Evasion toward the Deep (Aleixandre)
See *La evasión hacia el fondo*
"The Eve" (Bunin) **6**:56
"Eve" (Obstfelder) **23**:188-89
"Eve" (Stephens) **4**:407
Eve (Baring-Gould) **88**:12, 26-7
Eve (Péguy) **10**:403-04, 409, 418-19
"Eve Blossom" (Schwitters)
See "An Anna Blume"
Eve of Retirement (Bernhard)
See *Vor dem Ruhestand*
"The Eve of Revolution" (Swinburne) **8**:445
The Eve of St. Mark (Anderson) **2**:11; **144**:7, 38
The Eve of the Revolution: A Chronicle of the Breach with England (Becker) **63**:64-65, 80, 99, 103
"Evelina's Garden" (Freeman) **9**:63-4
"Eveline" (Joyce) **8**:166, 170; **35**:144, 147, 159, 163, 166-67, 190, 197; **159**:275-76, 361
Evelyn Innes (Moore) **7**:478, 483, 484, 485, 486, 491, 494, 499
"Evelyn Ray" (Lowell) **8**:227, 232
Evelyn's Husband (Chesnutt) **5**:140
"Evening" (Babel)
See "Vecer"
"Evening" (Devkota) **23**:47
"Evening" (García Lorca)
See "Tarde"
"Evening" (Gray) **19**:145
"Evening" (Gumilev) **60**:269
"Evening" (Lagerkvist)
See "Kväll"
"Evening" (Lasker-Schueler) **57**:331
Evening Album (Tsvetaeva)
See *Vecherny albom*
"Evening at Ravello" (Scott) **6**:394
"Evening Clouds" (Ledwidge) **23**:116
Evening Dress (Howells) **7**:387
Evening Glow (Hamsun)
See *Aftenrøde*
"Evening Hymn" (Roberts) **68**:305-6, 338
"Evening in England" (Ledwidge) **23**:121
"Evening in February" (Ledwidge) **23**:111
"Evening in Skåne" (Rilke)
See "Abend in Skåne"
"Evening in the Garden" (Radnóti) **16**:419
"Evening in the MacDonnells" (Ingamells) **35**:137
"Evening in the Mountain" (Anwar)
See "Malam di pegunungan"
"The Evening Land" (Lawrence) **93**:98, 101
Evening Land (Lagerkvist)
See *Aftonland*
"Evening Music" (Sarton) **120**:272
"Evening on the Broads" (Swinburne) **36**:320-21, 340, 344-45
"An Evening on the Riviera" (McAlmon) **97**:89, 121
"Evening Primrose" (Collier) **127**:251
"The Evening Primrose" (Parker) **143**:325
"Evening Promenade" (Södergran)
See "Aftonvandring"
"Evening Song" (Carducci)
See "Serenata"
Evening Songs (Tagore)
See *Sandhya sangit*
"Evening Walk in France" (Sarton) **120**:263
"An Evening with Mrs. Hawthorne" (Higginson) **36**:167
"Evening without Angels" (Stevens) **45**:269, 282
"Evening: Woman, Child on Her Back" (Radnóti) **16**:418
The Event (Nabokov) **108**:52-56
"L'eventail" (Čapek) **6**:84
"L'eventail" (Sully Prudhomme) **31**:306
"Éventail des saveurs" (Apollinaire) **51**:34-5
"Eventide" (Bryusov) **10**:88
Events (Bernhard)
See *Ereignisse*
Events and Embroideries (Lucas) **73**:159
Evered (Williams) **89**:359-60, 364, 394
Everest (Brancati) **12**:84
"The Evergreen" (Nemerov) **124**:305
The Everlasting Man (Chesterton) **6**:102, 109
"The Everlasting Sorrow: A Japanese Noh Play" (Noguchi) **80**:387
The Everlasting Struggle (Bojer)
See *Folk ved sjøen*
Evermore sorrow (Chang)
See *Duoshao hen*
"Everness" (Borges) **109**:28
"Every Day" (Bachmann)
See "Alle Tage"
"Every Lover" (Cullen) **37**:158, 170
Everybody's Autobiography (Stein) **1**:429-30; **6**:412; **28**:313-14, 326; **48**:211, 213-14, 216, 218, 220, 222, 240
"Everyday" (Holly) **65**:138-40, 142, 145, 153
Everyday (Crothers) **19**:75
Everyday Life (Rilke) **6**:370
Everyman (Hofmannsthal)
See *Jedermann*
"Everyman His Own Historian" (Becker) **63**:67, 69-70, 77, 91, 100, 103, 109, 112, 114
Everyman His Own Historian (Becker) **63**:65, 69, 72-4, 89, 98-9, 101, 102
Everyman's Genius (Austin) **25**:28, 33
"Everything" (Jiménez) **183**:334-35, 337-40
"Everything and Nothing" (Borges) **109**:92, 97
"Everything That Rises Must Converge" (O'Connor) **132**:229, 232, 246, 284, 287-90, 320, 358
Everything That Rises Must Converge (O'Connor) **132**:366
Everything's Jake (Marquis) **7**:451
"Everywhere there are Moths" (Yokomitsu)
See "Ga wa Dokonidemo Iru"
"Eve's Diary" (Twain) **6**:477; **12**:431
"Eve's Dream" (Frank) **17**:121
The Eves of Spain (Reyes)
See *Las vísperas de España*
Eve's Ransom (Gissing) **3**:223, 227, 230, 232-33; **24**:239
The Evidence for the Resurrection of Jesus Christ (Butler) **33**:70
Det eviga leendet (Lagerkvist) **144**:210
Den evige krig (Bojer) **64**:5-7, 9-11, 13, 22
"Evil Allures, but Good Endures" (Tolstoy) **11**:463
"Evil Days" (Pasternak) **188**:190-91, 196
The Evil Doers of Good (Benavente)
See *Los malhechores del bien*
"The Evil Eye" (Pavese) **3**:340
"The Evil Eye" (Svevo)
See "Il malocchio"
"Evil in Platonism and Sadism" (Bataille) **155**:93, 111
The Evil Kettle (Dunsany) **59**:14, 22
Evil Powers (Lie)
See *Onde magter*
Evil Sagas (Lagerkvist)
See *Onda sagor*
Evil Spells (Balmont) **11**:37
The Evil Spirit (Tolstoy) **18**:382
Evil Tales (Lagerkvist)
See *Onda sagor*
The Evil That Men Do (Shiel) **8**:361-62
"Evil Wind in the Chaotic World" (Rohan) **22**:298
"The Evil World-Soul" (Lawrence) **93**:73
Evoe (Huch) **13**:241
L'évolution créatrice (Bergson) **32**:6-7, 9-10, 20, 27, 30, 34, 38, 51-2
Evolution of an Intellectual (Murry) **16**:342
"The Evolution of Copyright" (Matthews) **95**:256
The Evolution of Man (Haeckel)
See *Anthropogenie oder Entwickelungsgeschichte des Menschens*
"Evolution of Modesty" (Ellis) **14**:130
"The Evolution of Mystery" (Maeterlinck) **3**:326
"The Evolution of the Cow-Puncher" (Wister) **21**:400-01, 406
"The Evolution of the Human Intellect" (Thorndike) **107**:370-71
Evolution, Old and New (Butler) **1**:133; **33**:29, 42, 44, 49, 52
L'Evolution pédagogique en France (Durkheim) **55**:134, 144
"Evolutionary Love" (Peirce) **81**:273,358,361
Evropeyskaya noch' (Khodasevich) **15**:201-02, 205, 209-10, 212, 214
Der ewige Spießer (Horvath) **45**:76, 83-4, 86, 97, 99, 102
"Ex cathedra" (Machado de Assis) **10**:291
Ex Libris Carissimis (Morley) **87**:146
"Ex ore infantium" (Thompson) **4**:436
Ex Ponto (Andrić) **135**:8, 14-15, 33, 53, 87-88, 91
"Ex Tenebris" (Kirk) **119**:278, 280
Ex Voto (Butler) **33**:29
"Exactitude" (Calvino) **183**:67, 125, 142, 145, 192
"Examen de la obra de Herbert Quain" (Borges) **109**:161
"The Examination" (Pirandello) **4**:342
"Examination of a Popular Virtue" (Mencken) **13**:363
An Examination of Dogmatic Theology (Tolstoy)
See *Issledovanie dogmaticheskogo bogoslavja*
An Examination of the Charges of Apostasy against Wordsworth (Rutherford) **25**:346
"Examination of the Hero in a Time of War" (Stevens) **12**:383; **45**:269, 290
"An Examination of the Work of Herbert Quain" (Borges)
See "Examen de la obra de Herbert Quain"
Examples of the Architecture of Venice (Ruskin) **63**:262-63
"El excelentísimo señor" (Pereda) **16**:367
Except the Lord (Cary) **29**:70, 76, 93, 97-9; **196**:137, 158, 164, 166, 168-69, 172, 175, 177-78
"Exceptions and Rules" (Nemerov) **124**:319
"Excerpts from a Diary" (Pilnyak) **23**:216
Excerpts from the Intimate Notes of Fellow Traveler Sand (Olesha) **136**:63
Exchange (Claudel)
See *L'echange*
"Exchanges" (Dickey) **151**:126, 147, 152
"Exchanging Hats" (Bishop) **121**:34

"Ex—Ci-Devant" (Tsvetaeva) **35**:394
"Excluded Middle" (Masters) **25**:290
Ex-Colored Man (Johnson)
See *The Autobiography of an Ex-Colored Man*
"The Ex-Communists" (De Voto) **29**:131
"The Excursion" (Andrić)
See "Ekskurzija"
"Excursion Train" (Lawrence) **93**:50, 67
"Excursus I: Odysseus or Myth and Enlightenment" (Horkheimer) **132**:196
"The Executioner" (Ball)
See "Der Henker"
"The Executioner's Beautiful Daughter" (Carter) **139**:186-87
"The Executive" (Nemerov) **124**:234
Exégèse des lieux communs (Bloy) **22**:30, 48
Exemple de Cézanne (Ramuz) **33**:301
"Exercice" (Apollinaire) **8**:22; **51**:10, 37
Exercice d'un enterré vif (Benda) **60**:62-3, 65, 69
"Exeunt omnes" (Mencken) **13**:363
"Exil" (Bachmann) **192**:54, 66
Exil (Feuchtwanger) **3**:178, 181-83, 188
"Exile" (Bachmann)
See "Exil"
"Exile" (Nabokov) **108**:147
"The Exile" (Rosenberg) **12**:311
"The Exile" (Sharp) **39**:371
"The Exile" (Tynan) **3**:504
The Exile (Micheaux) **76**:247, 253, 273
"Exiled" (Millay) **4**:306
"Exiled Prisoner" (Wen I-to) **28**:410
L'éxilee (Coppee) **25**:126
"The Exiles" (Davis) **24**:205
"The Exiles" (Quiroga)
See "Los desterrados"
Exiles (Joyce) **3**:262, 278; **8**:169; **16**:212, 232, 237, 240; **35**:141, 151; **52**:207; **159**:279-81,285-89
"The Exile's Tear" (Bialik) **25**:50
"Existe un mutilado" (Vallejo) **56**:310
"Existences" (Jammes) **75**:115, 117-18
"Existential Graphs" (Peirce) **81**:187
Existential Monday and the Sunday of History (Fondane)
See *Le Lundi existentiel et le dimanche de l'histoire*
Existentialists and Mystics: Writings on Philosophy and Literature (Murdoch) **171**:324
Exit (Wright) **183**:349
Exit, an Illusion (Bonner) **179**:7, 19, 30, 51
Exit Laughing (Cobb) **77**:131
"The Exit of Anse Dugmore" (Cobb) **77**:136, 138
"Exit the Professor" (Kuttner) **10**:269
"Exkurs uber den Adel" (Simmel) **64**:322
L'Exode: Super Flumina Babylonis (Fondane) **159**:254-56, 258
"Les exodes" (Verhaeren) **12**:471
"Exodo" (Arenas) **191**:186, 193
"Exodus" (Arenas)
See "Exodo"
"Exodus" (Fondane) **159**:258
"Exodus" (Oppen) **107**:267, 311
Exodus (Fondane)
See *L'Exode: Super Flumina Babylonis*
The Exodus and Wayside Flowers (Nervo) **11**:402
Exotic Japanese Stories: The Beautiful and the Grotesque (Akutagawa Ryūnosuke) **16**:21
Exotic Tales (Jensen)
See *Eksotiske Noveller*
Exotics (MacDonald) **9**:292
Exotics and Retrospectives (Hearn) **9**:132
"Expanses" (Dickey) **151**:176
The Expectant Guest (Lagerkvist)
See "Den fordringfule gästen"
"Expedition to the Dardanelles" (Drieu la Rochelle) **21**:26
"The Expelled" (Beckett)
See "L'Expulsé"
Expensive Halo (Tey) **14**:448, 460-61
Ex-People (Gorky)
See *Byvshii lyudi*
"Experience" (Gosse) **28**:132
"Experience" (Rilke) **195**:329
Experience (MacCarthy) **36**:253
"Experience and Fiction" (Jackson) **187**:236, 294
Experience and Judgement (Husserl)
See *Erfahrung und Urteil*
Experience and Nature (Dewey) **95**:30, 34-6, 38, 45-7
"Une expérience fondamentale" (Daumal) **14**:88, 91
"Experience in the West" (Bishop) **103**:18
L'expérience intérieure (Bataille) **155**:3, 6, 9, 12, 14-17, 27, 36, 67-68, 71, 87, 89-96, 98-99, 102, 104-7, 110, 112-14, 119-21, 124, 127, 129-30, 135-39, 141
Experiences Facing Death (Austin) **25**:33
La experiencia literaria (Reyes) **33**:317, 319
Experiment in Autobiography (Wells)
See *Experiment in Autobiography: Discoveries and Conclusions of a Very Ordinary Brain*
Experiment in Autobiography: Discoveries and Conclusions of a Very Ordinary Brain (Wells) **6**:552; **12**:502, 509; **133**:238, 259, 310, 321, 335
"An Experiment in Economy" (Davis) **24**:200
"An Experiment in Luxury" (Crane) **11**:165
"An Experiment in Misery" (Crane) **11**:128, 131, 142, 159, 167; **17**:65-6, 68-9; **32**:164-65, 167
"The Experiment of Professor Rouss" (Čapek) **37**:48-9; **192**:223
"Experimental Dream" (Tzara) **168**:275
Experimente (Brod) **115**:93-4
"Experiments" (Brooke) **2**:51
Experiments (Douglas) **68**:3-5, 10, 33
"Experiments in Comparative Psychology" (Thorndike) **107**:398
"Experiments with Alternating Currents of Very High Frequency and Their Application to Methods of Artificial Illumination" (Tesla) **88**:287
"The Expert Detective" (Post) **39**:344
"Expert Dope" (Benchley) **55**:19
"Expiation" (Benson) **27**:17
"Expiation" (Scott) **6**:398
"The Expiation" (Tagore) **3**:483
"Expiation" (Wharton) **129**:364
The Expiation (Griffith) **68**:186
Expiation (Oppenheim) **45**:131-32
"Explained" (Milne) **6**:314; **88**:243
"Explanation" (Pasternak) **188**:183-84, 193-94
"An Explanation of Beauty" (Nishida)
See "Bi no setsumei"
Expletives Deleted (Carter) **139**:100-101, 191-93, 200
Les expliots d'un jeune Don Juan (Apollinaire) **51**:28
The Exploding Lake (Dent) **72**:27, 38
The Exploit (Nabokov)
See *Podvig*
"The Exploit of Choolah, the Chicksaw" (Murfree) **135**:195
Exploits and Opinions of Doctor Faustroll, Pataphysician (Jarry)
See *Gestes et opinions du Dr. Faustroll, pataphysicien, roman néo-scientifique*
The Exploits of Arsène Lupin (Leblanc)
See *Arsène Lupin, gentleman-cambrioleur*
The Exploits of Brigadier Gerard (Doyle) **7**:239
The Exploits of Captain O'Hagan (Rohmer) **28**:285, 295
The Exploits of Danby Croker (Freeman) **21**:57
The Exploits of the Great Aleksander (Kuzmin)
See *The Deeds of Alexander the Great*
Explorations (McAlmon) **97**:86
Explorations (Yeats) **93**:364, 366, 372, 373, 404
The Explorers (Kornbluth) **8**:216
Explorers (van Schendel)
See *Avonturiers*
"La explosión" (Aleixandre) **113**:50
"The Explosion" (Aleixandre)
See "La explosión"
"Exposition coloniale" (Jacob) **6**:191
An Exposition of the Gospels (Tolstoy) **11**:463
"Exposure" (Owen) **5**:360, 364-65, 372; **27**:199, 206, 208, 212-13, 226, 231-32
"Exprés" (Huidobro) **31**:125, 135
"Express Train" (Kraus)
See "Schnellzug"
Expressing Willie (Crothers) **19**:75, 78, 80
"Expression" (Rosenberg) **12**:296-97
"Expression, Etc." (Hulme) **21**:138
Expression in America (Lewisohn) **19**:267-68, 270, 273, 275, 278-81, 283, 289-95
Expression in the Fine Arts (Sully Prudhomme) **31**:299
"L'expression personnelle" (Zola) **6**:561
"Expressionism" (Rosenberg) **12**:310
Expressionism in Philosophy: Spinoza (Deleuze)
See *Spinoza et le problème de l'expression*
"Expressionisme in Vlaanderen" (van Ostaijen) **33**:411
"Expropriation" (Kropotkin) **36**:205
"L'Expulsé" (Beckett) **145**:82
"L'extase" (Huysmans) **7**:404
Extase (Couperus) **15**:45
"Extension to Francis Thompson" (Douglas) **40**:87
The Extent of My Hope (Borges)
See *El tamaño de mi esperanza*
"Extermination of Tyrants" (Nabokov)
See "Istreblinie tiranov"
Exterminator! (Burroughs)
See *The Exterminator*
The Exterminator (Burroughs) **121**:124
"External and Internal Relations" (Moore) **89**:241
Extinction (Bernhard)
See *Auslöschung*
"The Extinction of Man" (Wells) **19**:429; **133**:244
"The Extra Man" (Grove) **4**:141
"Extract from Memoirs" (Nemerov) **124**:255
"Extract from Work in Progress" (McAlmon) **97**:100
"Extracts from Addresses to the Academy of Fine Ideas" (Stevens) **3**:478; **12**:367
Extracts from Captain Stormfield's Visit to Heaven (Twain) **6**:460-61, 477; **12**:429, 432, 436; **48**:356; **59**:210
"Extracts from Eve's Diary" (Twain) **6**:477
Extramundana (Spitteler) **12**:338, 348
"An Extraordinary Adventure Which Befell Vladimir Mayakovsky in a Summer Cottage" (Mayakovski) **4**:295; **18**:245, 261
Extraordinary Illusions (Melies)
See *Illusions funambulesques*
"Extraordinary Little Cough" (Thomas) **8**:456, 463; **105**:303, 321-22, 345-46, 357
Extraordinary Women: Theme and Variations (Mackenzie) **116**:230-31, 246, 254
"Extreme Unction" (Field) **43**:160
"Extremely Interesting Preface" (Andrade)
See "Prefácio interessantíssimo"
Extremes Meet (Mackenzie) **116**:250
"Extricating Young Gussie" (Wodehouse) **108**:391, 394
"Eyan kirja" (Leino) **24**:370
"Eya's Book" (Leino)
See "Eyan kirja"
"Eye" (Storni)
See "Ojo"
The Eye (Nabokov)
See *Sogliadatai*

"Eye and Mind" (Merleau-Ponty) **156**:137, 212, 224, 270, 282
Eye and Mind (Merleau-Ponty) **156**:186
An Eye for an Eye (Darrow) **81**:64,74,76-7
"The Eye of Allah" (Kipling) **8**:195, 205, 207; **17**:207
The Eye of Osiris (Freeman) **21**:44, 48, 52, 56
The Eye of Siva (Rohmer) **28**:282
"The Eye of the Fire" (Dickey) **151**:215, 221
"The Eye of the Needle" (Pickthall) **21**:245-46
The Eye of the Storm (White) **176**:142-43, 145-46, 148, 166, 181-82, 184-85, 190, 192, 194-96, 199-202, 218-19, 235, 239-40, 242, 244-45, 248, 250, 284, 306-9, 322, 328
"Eye to Eye: Black Women, Hatred and Anger" (Lorde) **173**:54
"The Eye-Beaters" (Dickey) **151**:98, 100-102, 105, 110, 113-14, 116-17, 144-45, 172
The Eye-Beaters, Blood, Victory, Madness, Buckhead, and Mercy (Dickey) **151**:98-103, 108, 113-14, 116, 118, 121, 143-44, 162, 170
"The Eyes" (Wharton) **3**:572, 577; **9**:546-47; **27**:408; **129**:362, 364
"The Eyes" (Zamyatin) **37**:431
"Eyes, and Ears, and Walking" (Lowell) **8**:236
"Eyes for the Blind" (Fisher) **87**:74
"The Eyes of Fu Manchu" (Rohmer) **28**:301
The Eyes of Love (Bojer) **64**:21, 23
The Eyes of Max Carrados (Bramah) **72**:5, 7-8
Eyes of My Soul (Palamas) **5**:379-80, 382, 386-87
"Eyes of Pride" (Dowson) **4**:88-9, 92
"The Eyes of the Blind" (Fisher)
See "Eyes for the Blind"
The Eyes of the Buried (Asturias)
See *Los ojos de los enterrados*
The Eyes of the Earth (Prishvin) **75**:218
"The Eyes of the Panther" (Bierce) **44**:12, 44-5
The Eyes of the World (Wright) **183**:346, 349-52, 359, 372, 374, 376, 379, 382
"Eyes to Wonder" (Bachmann)
See "Ihr glücklichen Augen"
Eyes Wide Shut (Kubrick) **112**:262-73, 277-86
"Eyesore" (Tagore)
See "Cokher bali"
"Eye-Witness" (Torrence) **97**:152-53, 155
The Eyewitness (Belloc) **7**:39; **18**:27, 45
Eyiptos (Kazantzakis) **181**:211
"Ezekiel" (Fisher) **11**:213
"Ezekiel Learns" (Fisher) **11**:213
"Ezinkomponi" (Vilakazi) **37**:404, 409-10
Faber; oder, Die verlorenen Jahre (Wassermann) **6**:510, 513
Faber; or, The Lost Years (Wassermann)
See *Faber; oder, Die verlorenen Jahre*
Fabian Essays in Socialism (Wallas) **91**:365, 374, 376
Fabian und Sebastian (Raabe) **45**:166, 200-01
"Fabla Salvaje" (Vallejo) **56**:284, 287, 308
"Fable" (García Lorca)
See "Fábula"
A Fable (Faulkner) **141**:33-34, 56-60, 62, 114; **170**:115, 128, 185, 221, 239-40
"The Fable About a Nail" (Herbert) **168**:56
"Fable and Ring-Game of the Three Friends" (García Lorca)
See "Fábula y rueda de los tres amigos"
"Fable and Round of the Three Friends" (García Lorca)
See "Fábula y rueda de los tres amigos"
"A Fable of Moderns" (Dunsany) **59**:28
"A Fable of the War" (Nemerov) **124**:153
Fabled Shore (Macaulay) **44**:124, 132
"The Fables" (Dobson) **79**:20
Fables (La Fontaine)
See *Les fourmis*
Fables (Powys) **9**:366, 370, 374, 377
Fables and Fairy Tales (Tolstoy) **4**:469
"Fables and Stories" (Calvino) **183**:234
Fables for Grown-Up Children (Zamyatin)
See *Tales for Adult Children*
Fables for Parents (Fisher) **87**:105
Fables of Identity (Frye) **165**:156, 173, 190, 229
Fables of Jean De La Fontaine (Marsh) **99**:355-56, 363
"Fables of the Moscow Subway" (Nemerov) **124**:144, 152
"Fabliau of Florida" (Stevens) **45**:297
El fabricante de fantasmas (Arlt) **29**:43-4
"Los fabricantes de carbón" (Quiroga) **20**:212, 215-18
"Fábula" (García Lorca) **49**:91; **181**:25
"Fábula que no duele" (Aleixandre) **113**:5
"Fábula y rueda de los tres amigos" (García Lorca) **1**:317; **49**:82, 121; **197**:183, 237, 242, 273
Fábula y signo (Salinas) **17**:357, 363-65, 368
FAC (George Orwell: Nineteen Eighty-Four: The Facsimile of the Extant Manuscript) (Orwell) **129**:226-27
Un faccioso más y algunos frailes menos (Pérez Galdós) **27**:276, 286
"The Face" (Benson) **27**:13, 16-17
"The Face" (Jarrell) **177**:140, 175, 207, 214
"The Face" (de la Mare) **53**:35
"The Face" (Manning) **25**:265, 279
"Face" (Toomer) **172**:256, 273-75, 327
Face, and Other Stories (Mais) **8**:245
"The Face and the Image" (Agnon)
See "Ha-panim la-panim"
Face au drapeau (Verne) **52**:350
"The Face in the Picture" (Tynan) **3**:506
"The Face in the Stream" (Carman) **7**:135
The Face of a Nation (Wolfe) **13**:479
The Face of Another (Abe)
See *Tanin no kao*
The Face of Misfortune (Onetti)
See *La cara de la desgracia*
"The Face of Peace" (Éluard) **41**:149
The Face of the Earth (Tomlinson) **71**:400
"The Face of the War" (Wolfe) **13**:492
The Face of the World (Bojer)
See *Verdens ansigt*
La face sombre du Christ (Rozanov) **104**:344, 353
Facelia (Prishvin) **75**:217, 224
"Faces" (Stringer) **37**:343
Faces (Andrić)
See *Lica*
"Faces in the Street" (Lawson) **27**:122, 132-33, 135-36, 140
"Faces Seen Once" (Dickey) **151**:90
Facile (Éluard) **7**:250; **41**:150
"Facing East: A Story of a Great Adventure in Turkey" (Dixon) **163**:173
Facing the Music (Upward) **85**:380
Die Fackel (Kraus) **5**:285-88, 290-92
Die Fackel im Ohr (Canetti)
See *Die Fackel im Ohr: Lebensgeschichte 1921-1931*
Die Fackel im Ohr: Lebensgeschichte 1921-1931 (Canetti) **157**:19-24, 37-38, 59, 62-63, 68, 77-78, 83, 97, 104-5, 109
"Fact and Idea" (Brennan) **17**:47
"A Fact and Some Fictions" (Toomer) **172**:304
"Fact and the Mystic" (Guiney) **41**:207
"The Fact of Blackness" (Fanon) **188**:96
"The Factory" (Dreiser) **35**:65
"The Factory Chicken" (Calvino) **183**:93
"Factory District: Night" (Jozsef) **22**:161
The Factory of the Absolute (Čapek)
See *Továrna na absolutno*
The Factory of Youth (Tolstoy) **18**:382
"The Facts" (Lardner) **14**:305
"Facts concerning the Late Arthur Jermyn and His Family" (Lovecraft) **4**:272; **22**:211, 231
"The Facts Concerning the Recent Carnival of Crime in Connecticut" (Twain) **6**:462; **19**:386, 393; **36**:403-04; **48**:352; **185**:234
Facts for Socialism (Webb and Webb) **22**:412
"Facture baroque" (van Ostaijen) **33**:419
La faculté de juger (Lyotard) **103**:176
"Facundo" (Güiraldes) **39**:190
"Faded Pictures" (Moody) **105**:235, 254
"A Fading of the Sun" (Stevens) **12**:382-83; **45**:275
"The Fading Rose" (Hardy) **143**:157
Fadren (Strindberg) **1**:443-44, 448, 450-51, 453-54, 461-62; **8**:405-07, 409, 411-13, 419-20; **21**:344, 348-49, 356-58, 361-63, 367-69; **47**:338, 341-42, 344-47, 349-51, 355, 358, 360-62, 368-69, 372-76
"Faenza" (Campana) **20**:85
Faery Lands of the South Seas (Hall and Nordhoff) **23**:57, 65-6
"Fafaia" (Brooke) **2**:61
Die Fähigkeit zu trauern (Böll) **185**:99-100, 102-04, 120, 156-57
Fahrten (Zweig) **17**:457
"Failing Sight" (Bosman) **49**:16
"Failure" (Arnow) **196**:91
"Failure" (Brooke) **2**:59
"Failure" (Fletcher) **35**:89
"The Failure" (Wetherald) **81**:409
"The Failure of David Berry" (Jewett) **22**:129
"The Failure of Hope & Wandel" (Bierce) **44**:45
"La Faim" (Huysmans) **69**:24
"Faint in Summer Haze" (Wright) **136**:301
Faint Perfume (Gale) **7**:280, 283-85
"Faint Trails" (Glaspell) **175**:149
"Fair Day" (Jewett) **22**:147
"Fair Dublin" (O'Faolain) **143**:240
The Fair Haven (Butler) **1**:134; **33**:29, 36, 41-2, 49, 55-9
"The Fair Lady" (Blok) **5**:94
The Fair Lavinia, and Others (Freeman) **9**:73
Fair Margaret (Crawford) **10**:146, 151, 155
The Fair Prosperina (Devkota)
See *Sundarī Projerpinā*
Fair Rosamund (Field) **43**:154
Faire-Part, Les Vocalises de Bacher Selim (Cocteau) **119**:57
"The Fairer Hope, a Brighter Morn" (Harper) **14**:260
"Fairfax Hunter" (Fisher) **87**:112
The Fairground Booth (Blok) **5**:99, 100
The Fair-Haired Lady (Leblanc)
See *Arsène Lupin contre Herlock Sholmès*
A Fairly Honourable Defeat (Murdoch) **171**:209, 223, 229, 243, 245, 266, 282, 299-300, 307, 311-13, 323, 325-26
Fair-Weather Geta (Nagai)
See *Hiyori Geta*
Fairy and Folk Tales of the Irish Peasantry (Yeats) **11**:537, 539
The Fairy Chessman (Kuttner) **10**:265, 269, 274, 276
The Fairy Child (Heyse)
See *Das Feenkind*
"The Fairy Curate" (Gilbert) **3**:212-13
"The Fairy Foster-mother" (Buchanan) **107**:15
"The Fairy Foster-Mother" (Tynan) **3**:504
"A Fairy Funeral" (Scott) **6**:387
Fairy Garden (Moricz)
See *Tündérkert*
"Fairy Godmothers" (Lee-Hamilton) **22**:191
"The Fairy Goldsmith" (Wylie) **8**:521-22
"The Fairy Isle of Janjira" (Naidu) **80**:306
"The Fairy Land" (Lindsay) **17**:241
"A Fairy Tale" (Dobson) **79**:3
"A Fairy Tale" (Lowell) **8**:235
"Fairy Tale" (Pasternak) **188**:186-87, 194-95
Fairy Tales (Dazai Osamu)
See *Otogi zōshi*
Fairy Tales (MacDonald) **113**:266-67, 269-70
Fairy Tales (Sologub) **9**:447-49
Fairy Tales of Melpomene (Chekhov) **163**:39
The Fairy, the Bassoon and the Stage-Hand (Kuzmin)
See *Feia, fagot i mashinist*
Fairyland (Mikszath)
See *Tündérvilág*

Fairyland (Moricz)
See *Tündérkert*
Fairyland: Or, the Kingdom of the Fairies (Melies) **81**:122,146,148
The Fairylogue and Radio-Plays (Baum) **132**:87, 93
The Fairy's Dilemma (Gilbert) **3**:209
"Fairy-Tale" (Bodenheim) **44**:74
"Fairytales" (Arp) **115**:15
Fairy-Tales (Čapek) **6**:85
Faites vos jeux (Tzara) **168**:228-30, 269, 273
"Faith" (Fletcher) **35**:108
"Faith" (Graham) **19**:112, 119, 131
"Faith" (Rutherford) **25**:341
"Faith and a Doubting World" (Cardozo) **65**:41
Faith and Political Philosophy: The Correspondence between Leo Strauss and Eric Voeglin, 1934-1964 (Strauss) **141**:273
"Faith and Reason" (Collingwood) **67**:133
Faith and Reason (Collingwood) **67**:132
"The Faith Cure Man" (Dunbar) **12**:120
The Faith Healer (Moody) **105**:224, 226, 233, 242, 245-46, 251, 253-54, 259, 269
"Faith, Hope, and Charity" (Cobb) **77**:141-2
Faith, Hope, and Charity (Cobb) **77**:134
Faith, Hope, and Charity (Horvath)
See *Glaube Liebe Hoffnung*
"The Faith of Men" (London) **9**:262
Faith, Reason and Civilization (Laski) **79**:130, 145, 160
Faithful Are the Wounds (Sarton) **120**:199-200, 203, 205-06, 209, 242-43, 246, 278, 306-07, 310
The Faithful Wife (Tagore)
See *Satī*
The Faithful Wife (Undset)
See *Den trofaste hustru*
"The Faithless Bride" (García Lorca)
See "La casada infiel"
"The Faithless Wife" (García Lorca)
See "La casada infiel"
Fake Aesthetic Treatise (Fondane)
See *Faux traité d'esthétique*
"Fake Shepherds" (Shepherd) **177**:317
"Fakes" (Apollinaire)
See "Des Faux"
A fáklya (Moricz) **33**:233, 237, 244, 246-47, 249
The Falconer of God (Benét) **28**:6, 9, 12
Falcons of France: A Tale of Youth and the Air (Hall and Nordhoff) **23**:58, 65, 67
"Falk" (Conrad) **13**:102; **57**:60-61, 77
"The Fall" (Muir) **2**:486; **87**:167
The Fall (Sá-Carneiro)
See *A queda*
"The Fall Again" (Nemerov) **124**:185, 249
Der Fall Deruga (Huch) **13**:243, 252
Der Fall Franza, Requiem für Fanny Goldmann (Bachmann) **192**:25, 40, 44, 50-51, 69, 78, 83, 86, 127-28, 150, 154, 159, 163
Der Fall Maurizius (Wassermann) **6**:511, 517-19
The Fall of a Nation (Dixon) **163**:171
The Fall of America: Poems of These States 1965-1971 (Ginsberg) **120**:9, 35, 41, 57, 59, 71-3, 80, 86, 121, 129
"The Fall of Babbulkund" (Dunsany) **2**:136; **59**:9
"The Fall of King Chris" (Oskison) **35**:280-81
The Fall of Mussolini: His Own Story, by Benito Mussolini (Mussolini)
See *Il tempo del bastone e della carota*
"The Fall of the House of Usher" (Bierce) **1**:84
The Fall of the House of Usher (Epstein)
See *La chute de la maison Usher*
The Fall of the King (Jensen)
See *Kongens Fald*
"The Fall River Axe Murders" (Carter) **139**:90-91, 96, 139-44, 146, 207
"Der Fall Wagner: Ern Muskikanten-Problem" (Nietzsche) **10**:391, 393
"Fallen" (Mann)
See "Gefallen"
"Fallen" (Rilke) **195**:220
The Fallen (Gladkov)
See *Izgoi*
"The Fallen Angel" (Lasker-Schueler)
See "Der gefallene Engel"
The Fallen Angel (Mofolo) **22**:253
Fallen Leaves (Rozanov)
See *Opavshie list'ia*
Fallen Leaves: Basketful One (Rozanov)
See *Opavshie list'ia. Korob pervyj*
Fallen Leaves: Basketful Two (Rozanov)
See *Opavshie list'ia. Korob vtoroj*
"Fallen Moon" (Aleixandre) **113**:23-25, 27
"A Fallen Yew" (Thompson) **4**:440
"Falling" (Dickey) **151**:100-101, 109-10, 115, 166, 192, 199, 204, 212
Falling (Dickey) **151**:108
"Falling Asleep in America" (Ginsberg) **120**:127
"A Falling Petal" (Wright) **136**:301
"Falling Rocks, Narrowing Road, Cul-de-sac, Stop" (O'Faolain) **143**:227, 238
The Falling Star's Path (Yosano) **59**:327
En fallit (Bjoernson) **7**:104, 107, 111, 113; **37**:11, 18-20, 29-30
"Fallmerayer the Stationmaster" (Roth)
See "Stationschef Fallmerayer"
"The Fallow Deer at the Lonely House" (Hardy) **143**:157
Der falsche Nero (Feuchtwanger) **3**:187
"False and True" (Riley) **51**:303
"The False Coupon" (Tolstoy) **11**:464
False Dawn (Wharton) **3**:559; **9**:550; **53**:383; **129**:350, 363
False Dawn (The 'Forties) (Wharton)
See *False Dawn*
"The False Heart" (Belloc) **18**:41
False Justice (Hagiwara)
See *Kyomō no seigi*
False Notes (Pirandello)
See *Fuori di chiave*
"False Prophet" (Wylie) **8**:536
The False Sound of the Lute (Natsume)
See *Koto no sorane*
False Witness (Caragiale)
See *Năpastă*
"False Youth, Autumn, Clothes of the Age" (Dickey) **151**:125, 147
"False Youth: Two Seasons" (Dickey) **151**:124, 201
"The Falsehood of Truth" (Daumal) **14**:88
"Falseta" (García Lorca) **181**:200
"Fame" (Mew) **8**:294, 298
Fame and the Poet (Dunsany) **59**:3, 13, 26, 29
La famiglia Manzoni (Ginzburg) **156**:39, 63, 69, 108, 114-16
La familia de León Roch (Pérez Galdós) **27**:244, 246, 249, 252, 255-58, 274
"A Familiar Epistle" (Dobson) **79**:2
"The Familiar Faces" (Warner) **131**:315
Die Familie Grossglück (Asch) **3**:66
Familjen paa Gilje (Lie) **5**:323-24, 330
"Une famille d'arbes" (Renard) **17**:302
"The Family" (Pavese) **3**:340
The Family (Sánchez)
See *En familia*
The Family (Shimazaki Toson)
See *Ie*
A Family and a Fortune (Compton-Burnett) **180**:122, 124, 127, 129, 132, 134, 143, 148-50, 152, 156, 158, 164-66
The Family at Gilje (Lie)
See *Familjen paa Gilje*
"A Family Feud" (Dunbar) **2**:131; **12**:106-07
"The Family Ford" (Fields) **80**:258
"The Family Friend" (Rinehart) **52**:282
Family Happiness (Tolstoy)
See *Semeinoe schaste*
Family Life (Sánchez)
See *En familia*
"Family Life in America" (Benchley) **1**:81; **55**:17
The Family Man (Galsworthy) **45**:52
The Family Mashber (Middleton)
See *Di mishpoke Mashber*
"A Family of Gentlefolk" (Tolstoy)
See "Dvorianskoe semeistvo"
"The Family of Koiwai" (Miyamoto)
See "Koiwaike no ikka"
"Family Portrait" (Andrić)
See "Porodična slika"
"Family Portrait" (Drummond de Andrade) **139**:237
"Family Portraits" (Hardy) **53**:100
The Family Question in Russia (Rozanov)
See *Semeinyi Vopros v Rossii*
Family Sayings (Ginzburg)
See *Lessico famigliare*
"Family Walls" (Brennan) **124**:4-6
"Family Week at Oracle Ranch" (Merrill) **173**:230
A Family without a Name (Verne) **6**:495-96, 501
"The Famine" (Eastman) **55**:167, 170
Famira kifared (Annensky) **14**:17-18, 21-3, 28
The Famous Box Trick (Melies)
See *Illusions fantasmagorique*
"The Famous Gilson Bequest" (Bierce) **44**:44-5
Famous Imposters (Stoker) **8**:394
Famous Men (Agee)
See *Let Us Now Praise Famous Men*
The Famous Ones (Bernhard)
See *Die Berühmten*
"The Fan" (Čapek)
See "L'eventail"
Fan (Hudson) **29**:160
Le fanal bleu (Colette) **1**:192; **5**:169-70; **16**:118, 131
The Fanatics (Dunbar) **12**:112
Fancies and Goodnights (Collier) **11**:183-85; **127**:250
Fancies versus Fads (Chesterton) **6**:109
Fanciulle (Saba) **33**:373
"Fancy and Fact" (Pyle) **81**:393
"A Fancy from Fontenelle" (Dobson) **79**:3
Fancy's Following (Coleridge) **73**:2, 4-6, 10
"Fancy's Fool" (Montgomery) **51**:181
Fancy's Guerdon (Coleridge) **73**:2, 10, 25
"Fanfare, Coda and Finale" (Walker) **129**:320
"En fången fågel" (Södergran) **31**:289
Fangen som sang (Bojer) **64**:20, 22-23
"Fanny" (Quiroga) **20**:213
Fanny and the Servant Problem (Jerome) **23**:88
Fanny Essler (Grove) **4**:142, 144
Fanny's First Play (Shaw) **21**:324
Fanny's Khasonim (Cahan) **71**:43, 44
"Fantasi" (Obstfelder) **23**:177
"Fantasia" (Scott) **6**:387
"Fantasia" (Zangwill) **16**:461
Fantasia of the Unconscious (Lawrence) **2**:346-48; **9**:215-16; **16**:284, 293-94, 306; **61**:296, 212, 215, 234, 264; **93**:18, 29, 64, 84, 116
"Fantasie printaniere" (Norris) **24**:447
"Fantasies" (Mori Ogai) **14**:371
"Un fantasma" (Gonzalez Martinez) **72**:150, 152
"El fantasma" (Pardo Bazán) **189**:228
Fantastic Dialogues (Martinez Sierra and Martinez Sierra)
See *Diálogos fantásticos*
Fantastic Fables (Bierce) **1**:87-8, 94; **7**:89; **44**:13, 50
"The Fantastic Imagination" (MacDonald) **113**:220, 246, 259, 264, 295-96, 298, 300
The Fantastic Island (Dent) **72**:23
A Fantastic Tale (Tolstoy) **18**:378, 382
The Fantasticks (Rostand) **37**:280
Fantastics, and Other Fancies (Hearn) **9**:125-26, 134-37
Fantazius Mallare (Hecht) **101**:31, 35, 39, 42, 44, 47, 61, 70-1, 85

Les fantoches (Roumain) **19**:331-32, 338, 340-43, 345
Le fantôme (Gourmont) **17**:138, 153, 155
La fantôme de l'opéra (Leroux) **25**:256, 258, 260
"Un fantóme de nuées" (Apollinaire) **3**:33; **51**:31-2, 55-6
Fantôme d'Orient (Loti) **11**:356
Far and Near Ones (Bryusov)
See *Dalekie i bliskie*
"The Far and the Near" (Wolfe) **4**:519
"Far Away" (Pirandello)
See "Lontano"
Far Away and Long Ago (Hudson) **29**:142-43, 145-46, 156-57, 159, 161-62
"Far Away, Far Away" (Babits)
See "Messze . . . Messze"
"Far Away the Rachel-Jane" (Lindsay) **17**:227
Far End (Sinclair) **11**:411, 419
"Far, Far Away" (Santos) **156**:310
Far from the Madding Crowd (Hardy) **4**:147-49, 153, 155-56, 158, 160, 168, 175, 177; **10**:217, 226, 229; **18**:87, 92, 111; **32**:268, 274; **48**:40, 51-3, 71, 73, 79, 84; **53**:84, 97; **72**:159, 220-21, 241; **143**:69, 76-77, 80, 94, 106, 110, 113, 115, 123, 135, 154, 166, 170, 196, 206-8; **153**:94-220
Far Future Calling (Stapledon) **22**:327, 333
"Far in a Western Brookland" (Housman) **10**:247, 252
Far in the Forest (Mitchell) **36**:272
"The Far Islands" (Buchan) **41**:73
"Far Known to Sea and Shore" (Housman) **10**:247
"Far och jag" (Lagerkvist) **144**:200, 212
Far Off Things (Machen) **4**:278, 280, 285
"Fârâbî's Plato" (Strauss) **141**:334-36, 338-41
"Faraghaol" (Sharp) **39**:375
Faraon (Prus) **48**:159-60, 164-66, 169-71, 179
The Far-Away Bride (Benson)
See *Tobit Transplanted*
The Faraway Princess (Rostand)
See *La princesse lointaine*
Farben (Schoenberg) **75**:300
La Farce des ténébreux (Ghelderode) **187**:4
"Le fard des Argonautes" (Desnos) **22**:64
"Farda" (Hedāyat) **21**:75
"Farewell" (Ekelund)
See "Afsked"
"Farewell" (Ivanov) **33**:138
"Farewell" (Naidu) **80**:293
"Farewell, Go with God" (Unamuno) **9**:523
Farewell, Miss Julie Logan (Barrie) **164**:8, 14-16, 29, 37
"The Farewell Murder" (Hammett) **187**:79, 165
Farewell, My Friend (Tagore)
See *Śesher kavitā*
Farewell My Heart (Molnár) **20**:164
Farewell, My Lovely (Chandler) **1**:172, 175-76; **7**:167-68, 172-75, 179; **179**:81-82, 87, 89, 91, 97-99, 101-3, 111, 116, 126, 128, 132-33, 136-38, 142, 144-45, 147-49, 155, 157-59, 162-64, 168, 170-71, 180-82, 188, 191, 193, 195, 199-201, 204, 222-23, 226-28, 230
"The Farewell of Paracelsus to Aprile" (Crowley) **7**:208
"Farewell Performance" (Merrill) **173**:224, 230
"Farewell Performance" (Wakefield) **120**:352
Farewell, Summer (Santmyer) **133**:214, 218-19
"Farewell to All Those!" (Wakefield) **120**:350
A Farewell to Arms (Hecht) **101**:63
A Farewell to Arms (Hemingway) **115**:122-219
Farewell to Autumn (Witkiewicz)
See *Pożegnanie jesieni*
"Farewell to Florida" (Stevens) **12**:367; **45**:269, 275-76, 282, 345-47, 349
"Farewell to Many Cities" (Bishop) **103**:9
Farewell to Maria (Borowski)
See *Pożegnanie z Maria*
Farewell to Mary (Borowski)
See *Pożegnanie z Maria*
Farewell to Poesy, and Other Poems (Davies) **5**:199-200
"Farewell to the City" (Herbert) **168**:43-44
Farewell to the Sea (Arenas)
See *Otra vez el mar*
Farewell to the Theatre (Granville-Barker) **2**:195-96
"Farewell without a Guitar" (Stevens) **45**:345
Farewells (Onetti)
See *Los adioses*
Farfetched Fables (Shaw) **3**:397; **9**:425
"Färgernas längtan" (Södergran) **31**:289
Farinet (Ramuz) **33**:308-09
"Farish Street" (Walker)
See *My Farish Street Green*
A farkas (Molnár) **20**:159-60, 166, 169
"Der farkishefter shnayder" (Aleichem) **35**:306
"Et farlig frieri" (Bjoernson) **37**:33
The Farm (Bromfield) **11**:77-8, 85-9
The Farm (Tozzi)
See *Il podere*
Farmacia di turno (de Filippo) **127**:285-87
"Farmer" (Hamsun)
See "Bonde"
"Farmer" (Shimazaki Toson)
See "Nōfu"
"Farmer Finch" (Jewett) **22**:146
Farmer Giles of Ham (Tolkien) **137**:351
Farmer of the Clouds and Poetry until Now (Drummond de Andrade)
See *Fazendeiro do ar & poesia até agora*
Farmer on Kõrboja (Tammsaare)
See *Kõrboja peremees*
"Farmers" (Dickey) **151**:174
"The Farmer's Bride" (Mew) **8**:294, 296-300
A Farmer's Year (Haggard) **11**:241, 245
Farmington (Darrow) **81**:37-8,64,72
Farm-Rhymes (Riley)
See *Riley Farm-Rhymes*
Farn mabul (Asch) **3**:67-9
"Faro en la noche" (Storni) **5**:446
Farsa de la enamorada del rey (Valle-Inclán) **5**:483
Farsang (Molnár) **20**:166, 170
The Fascinating Mr. Vanderveldt (Sutro) **6**:420-21
Fascinating Mrs. Francis (Griffith) **68**:244-45, 249
"Fascism and Democracy" (Bennett) **128**:284
Fascist Socialism (Drieu la Rochelle) **21**:35-7
The Fashionable Adventures of Joshua Craig (Phillips) **44**:258, 262, 265, 275, 277-78, 286
Fashions for Men (Molnár)
See *Úri divat*
Fast and Loose (Sturges) **48**:283, 311
Fast and Loose (Wharton) **129**:352, 364; **149**:226, 256
"The Fast Girl" (McAlmon) **97**:101, 120
Fastes d'enfer (Ghelderode) **187**:8-11, 13-14, 19, 21-6
Die Fastnachtsbeichte (Zuckmayer) **191**:328
Fat and Blood (Mitchell) **36**:265
"The Fat Man" (Schwob) **20**:329
"Fata morgana" (Balmont) **11**:36
Fata Morgana (Remizov)
See *Mara*
"The Fatal Cipher" (Futrelle) **19**:96
The Fatal Conceit (Hayek) **109**:226
"The Fatal Eggs" (Bulgakov)
See "Rokovye iaitsa"
The Fatal Force (Crowley) **7**:208
The Fatal Glass of Beer (Fields) **80**:234
"Fatal Interview" (Millay) **169**:255
Fatal Interview (Millay) **4**:311, 313, 315; **49**:206, 208-10, 213, 219-20, 224, 228, 232; **169**:231, 242, 248, 290
The Fatal Three (Braddon) **111**:227
A Fatal Wedding (García Lorca)
See *Bodas de sangre*
Fatalitas! (Leroux) **25**:260
"La fatalité" (Sully Prudhomme) **31**:302
"Fate" (Ledwidge) **23**:116
Fate (Rohan)
See *Unmei*
"Fate and Character" (Benjamin) **39**:41
"Fate and the Artist" (Middleton) **56**:175, 194-95
"Fate o' Women" (Rilke)
See "Frauenschicksal"
"The Fate of a Voice" (Foote) **108**:17
"The Fate of Faustina" (Hornung) **59**:112
"The Fate of Humphrey Snell" (Gissing) **24**:226
"The Fate of King Feargus" (Tynan) **3**:503
"The Fate of Mrs. Lucier" (Knister) **56**:156, 163
The Fate of the Jury: An Epilogue to Domesday Book (Masters) **2**:471; **25**:299, 303, 315-16
The Fateful Game of Love (Čapek) **6**:84; **37**:50-1, 53; **192**:194
Fateful Journey (Döblin)
See *Schicksalreise*
"The Fates" (Owen) **5**:374
"Fate's Purse" (Kirk) **119**:281, 335
"The Father" (Babel)
See "Otets"
"The Father" (Bjoernson) **7**:112
"Father" (Guest) **95**:205
"The Father" (Smith) **25**:385, 393, 399
Father (Elizabeth) **41**:130, 132
The Father (Strindberg)
See *Fadren*
Father Abraham (Faulkner) **141**:38
"Father against Mother" (Machado de Assis)
See "Pai contra mãe"
A Father and His Fate (Compton-Burnett) **180**:180, 187
"Father and I" (Lagerkvist)
See "Far och jag"
"Father and Son" (Sait Faik)
See "Baba oğul"
Father and Son: A Study of Two Temperaments (Gosse) **28**:140-41, 146, 148, 150, 155-61, 163-66
Father Anthony (Buchanan) **107**:86-7
"Father Archangel of Scotland" (Graham) **19**:101
Father Brown: Selected Stories (Chesterton) **64**:36
"Father Garasse" (Swinburne) **8**:439
Father Goose, His Book (Baum) **132**:75, 103
"A Father in Sion" (Evans) **85**:19-20
Father of the Blues (Handy) **97**:66, 68, 79, 81-2
"Father, on His Unsonment" (Villa) **176**:93
"Father Riley's Horse" (Paterson) **32**:369, 373
Father Sergius (Tolstoy)
See *Otetz Sergii*
"Father, Son" (Csáth) **13**:151, 153-54
"Father versus Mother" (Machado de Assis)
See "Pai contra mãe"
"Fatherlands" (Palamas) **5**:383
Fathers and Children (Berlin) **105**:7, 9
"Fathers and Sons" (Dickey) **151**:90
"Father's Last Escape" (Schulz)
See "Ostatnia ucieczka ojca"
The Father's Tragedy, William Rufus, and Loyalty or Love (Field) **43**:154, 162-62, 171
Fatseliia (Prishvin)
See *Facelia*
Fattige skjaebner (Undset) **3**:522; **197**:300
Faulkner in the University (Faulkner) **141**:38, 93, 195
"Les faulx visaiger" (Schwob) **20**:323
"The Faun" (Sterling) **20**:372, 374
"The Faun" (Tolstoy) **18**:377
"Fauns at Noon" (Symons) **11**:426
"The Faun's Punishment" (Field) **43**:166
Faust (Murnau) **53**:240, 252-54, 262-63, 274-75, 278-80
"Faustina, ein Gespräch über die Liebe" (Wassermann) **6**:514
"Faustina; or, Rock Roses" (Bishop) **121**:7, 89

Faustina Strozzi (Lie) **5**:324
"Faustine" (Swinburne) **8**:425, 442; **36**:311
"Faustus and Helen (II)" (Crane) **5**:191; **80**:199
La faute de l'Abbé Mouret (Zola) **1**:587, 589, 597; **6**:564-65, 567, 569; **21**:416, 421, 425; **41**:412, 451
La faute de Madame Charvet (Lemonnier) **22**:198, 203
"Les faux saulniers" (Schwob) **20**:323
Faux traité d'esthétique (Fondane) **159**:238-41, 246-47, 250-51, 254-55
Les faux-monnayeurs (Gide) **5**:213-16, 222-23, 227-30, 234-37, 239, 241-42, 244; **12**:144-51, 153-55, 157-60, 167, 170-72; **36**:85-123; **177**:10, 35, 46, 73, 102
Faville del maglio (D'Annunzio) **40**:7, 12
La favola del figlio cambiato (Pirandello) **29**:319-20
Favola di natale (Betti) **5**:62
"The Favorite" (Apollinaire) **51**:49
"The Fawn" (Millay) **49**:208
Fayvel's Mayses (Bergelson) **81**:30
Fayvel's Tales (Bergelson)
See *Fayvel's Mayses*
Fazendeiro do ar & poesia até agora (Drummond de Andrade) **139**:224
Fazio (Belasco) **3**:86
"The FB Eye Blues" (Wright) **136**:262-63
F. D. R.: His Personal Letters (Roosevelt) **93**:181
"Fear" (Frank) **17**:114
"Fear" (Millay) **169**:266-68
"Fear" (Pirandello) **4**:349-50
"Fear" (Symons) **11**:446
"Fear" (Zweig)
See "Angst"
Fear (Wells) **6**:533
"Fear and Death" (Kraus)
See "Todesfurcht"
Fear and Desire (Kubrick) **112**:127, 188, 262, 280
Fear and Misery of the Third Reich (Brecht)
See *Furcht und Elend des dritten Reiches*
"The Fear Deep in My Blood" (Lasker-Schueler) **57**:328, 334
"The Fear for Thee, My Country" (Markham) **47**:285
"Fear Is Vanishing, Confidence Is Growing, Faith Is Being Renewed in the Democratic Form of Government" (Roosevelt) **93**:184
"Fear Nocturne" (Villaurrutia) **80**:480
Fear of Freedom (Levi) **125**:200
The Fear of the Dead in Primitive Religions (Frazer) **32**:203, 234
"Fear on the Trail" (Calvino)
See "Paura sul sentiero"
"The Fear That Walks by Noonday" (Fisher) **87**:97, 108
A Fearful Joy (Cary) **1**:143; **29**:65-8, 71, 73, 79-80, 84-5, 87, 92, 95-6, 103-04; **196**:172
A Fearful Responsibility, and Other Stories (Howells) **7**:377; **17**:176, 179
Fearful Symmetry: A Study of William Blake (Frye) **165**:140-41, 154, 164-65, 167, 179, 189-90, 192, 224-25, 228-29, 235, 238, 249, 258, 261
"The Feast" (Beerbohm) **24**:121-22
"The Feast" (Gogarty) **15**:114
"The Feast" (Naidu) **80**:273
"Feast Day in Santa Maria Mayor" (Graham) **19**:105
A Feast for Boris (Bernhard)
See *Eine Fest für Boris*
The Feast of Bacchus (Bridges) **1**:124
The Feast of Ortolans (Anderson) **2**:7
"A Feast of Snails" (Baring-Gould) **88**:22
Feasts of Fear and Agony (van Ostaijen)
See *De feesten van angst en pijn*
Feasts of Fear and Pain (van Ostaijen)
See *De feesten van angst en pijn*
"Feather" (Pirandello)
See "Piuma"
The Feather of the Dawn (Naidu) **80**:289, 315
"The Feather Pillow" (Quiroga)
See "El almohadón de pluma"
Feather Woman of the Jungle (Tutuola) **188**:289-90, 292, 302, 307
Feathers (Orton) **157**:292
February (Bagritsky)
See *Fevral*
"February Days" (Sarton) **120**:268
Fécondité (Zola) **1**:587, 589; **21**:428; **41**:421, 450
Federigo, or, The Power of Love (Nemerov) **124**:144, 151, 155, 159-61, 239-41, 243, 274, 291, 295
Fedor (Brancati) **12**:84
"Fedora" (Chopin) **14**:69; **127**:23
Fedra (D'Annunzio) **6**:137, 142; **40**:9-11
Fedra (Tsvetaeva) **35**:393; **7**:565, 568
Fedra (Unamuno) **9**:516; **148**:267, 269-70
"Le fée amoureuse" (Zola) **6**:569
"Feed My Lambs" (O'Faolain) **143**:238
"Feed My Sheep" (Eddy) **71**:132
Das Feenkind (Heyse) **8**:114, 119
De feesten van angst en pijn (van Ostaijen) **33**:405-06, 412-14, 418
Feia, fagot i mashinist (Kuzmin) **40**:201
Feindbild und Frieden (Böll) **185**:157-59, 163
"Feine Pelzmoden" (Schwitters) **95**:351
Feinye skazki (Balmont) **11**:36, 39
Feirtag (Kandinsky) **92**:49
"Feizao" (Lu Hsun) **3**:300-01, 303
"Fekete ország" (Babits) **14**:39
A fekete város (Mikszath) **31**:168, 170-71, 173-74
"Fekete virágot lattál" (Ady) **11**:18, 20
Der Feldzug nach Sizilien (Heym) **9**:145-46
"La felicidad escrita" (Borges) **109**:86
"La felicidad imminente" (Salinas) **17**:368
"Felicita" (Saba) **33**:370
Felicitá dell'infelice (Papini) **22**:287
"The Felicitious Reminiscences of Scourger James" (Warung) **45**:423
Felipe Angeles (Garro) **153**:71-72, 87
"Félise" (Swinburne) **8**:437; **36**:298
"Felix" (Aleixandre) **113**:34-5
Felix: Three Years of a Life (Hichens) **64**:122, 126-31
Fell the Tree-Trunks (Jozsef) **22**:164
Felling (Mistral)
See *Tala*
"Felling a Tree" (Gurney) **33**:97, 103
Fellow Captains (Fisher) **87**:72
"The Fellow that Goes Alone" (Grahame) **136**:28
A Fellowe and His Wife (Sharp) **39**:365, 372-73, 375
"Fellowship" (Field) **43**:156, 177
"The Fellowship of Caiaphas" (Marquis) **7**:448
The Fellowship of the Ring (Tolkien) **137**:238, 258-61, 296-301, 310, 317, 319-20, 358-60
"The Felons of our Land" (Gregory) **176**:67
"Female Emancipation" (Heyse)
See "Frauenemancipation"
"The Female God" (Rosenberg) **12**:299-300, 307, 309
The Female of the Species (Griffith) **68**:250
The Female of the Species (Sapper) **44**:308, 316, 319-22
Femeninas (Valle-Inclán) **5**:485
"The Feminine" (Hippius)
See "Zhenskoe"
Feminine Beauty (Clark) **147**:126
"The Feminine Condition" (Ginzburg)
See "La condizione femminile"
"Femininity" (Freud)
See "Die Weiblichkeit"
"Feminism and Social Progress" (Gilman) **117**:134, 137-38, 155-56, 167, 171
Feminism, Feminity, and the Spanish Spirit (Martinez Sierra and Martinez Sierra) **6**:274
Feminism in Spain (Martinez Sierra and Martinez Sierra) **6**:277
"Feminismus" (Benn) **3**:112
"Feminista" (Pardo Bazán) **189**:299
La femme assise (Apollinaire) **3**:42; **8**:12, 16; **51**:3, 21, 28
La femme cachée (Colette) **5**:169
La femme d'Henri Vanneau (Rod) **52**:309
La Femme du boulanger (Giono) **124**:49, 74-75
Une femme è sa fenêtre (Drieu la Rochelle) **21**:33
La femme pauvre (Bloy) **22**:30-3, 38-9, 45-6, 50-1, 53
"Une femme qui passe" (Campana) **20**:83
"Les femmes" (Apollinaire) **3**:37-8
"Femte natten" (Strindberg) **8**:419-20
"Le fen et l'eau" (Rod) **52**:316
"Fen River" (Lovecraft) **22**:213
"Fence Wire" (Dickey) **151**:106
"Fences" (Remizov) **27**:334
"Les fenêtres" (Apollinaire) **3**:44; **51**:29-31
"Fengsuo" (Chang) **184**:128-29, 133, 138
"Fenimore Cooper's Literary Offenses" (Twain) **6**:477; **161**:225, 273-74
Fennel (Jerome) **23**:82
Fenomenal'naia amerikanka (Kuzmin) **40**:201
"Un fenómeno inexplicable" (Lugones) **15**:293
"Die Fensterrose" (Rilke) **1**:410
Fenwick's Career (Ward) **55**:422, 424
"Feodaly a rezidentsiya" (Korolenko) **22**:182
"Fergus and the Druid" (Yeats) **11**:512; **18**:461; **31**:415
Feria d'agosto (Pavese) **3**:336
La feria de los discretos (Baroja) **8**:61
Fermina Márquez (Larbaud) **9**:196, 198, 202, 204, 206-07
"Fern" (Toomer) **172**:256, 258, 285, 298, 328, 337
"Fern Hill" (Thomas) **1**:470-71, 473, 475; **8**:460-61; **45**:362, 364, 379, 398, 407-08, 412; **105**:351, 353, 359
"Fernando and Elvira" (Gilbert) **3**:213
"The Fernery" (Crane) **2**:119
Fernhurst (Stein) **28**:339-40; **48**:264
The Ferrari in the Bedroom (Shepherd) **177**:296-97, 299, 315, 319
"The Ferreira Millions" (Bosman) **49**:10
"Ferroviaria" (Güiraldes) **39**:176
"The Ferry of Unfulfillment" (Henry) **19**:173
Ferrying Across (Tagore)
See *Kheya*
Fervor de Buenos Aires (Borges) **109**:7, 9-11, 163
Fervor of Buenos Aires (Borges)
See *Fervor de Buenos Aires*
"Fessler's Bees" (Riley) **51**:282, 284
Eine Fest für Boris (Bernhard) **165**:17, 96-97, 108, 122-23, 126, 132
Ein Fest für Boris (Bernhard)
See *Eine Fest für Boris*
"A Festa do Mangue" (Drummond de Andrade) **139**:230
"Festal Slaughter" (Csáth) **13**:148-49, 155
Le Festin de Balthazar (Fondane) **159**:248-50
"Festina lente" (Hamsun) **14**:240, 242
"The Festival" (Lovecraft) **22**:219
"The Festival of Memory" (Naidu) **80**:307
"The Festival of Serpents" (Naidu) **80**:294
The Festival of Steel (Arlt)
See *La fiesta del hierro*
"The Festival of the Sea" (Naidu) **80**:316
"Festnacht und Frühgang" (Liliencron) **18**:206, 215
"The Fête" (Mew) **8**:294, 298, 301
La Fête automobile (Jarry) **147**:278
"A Fête Champêtre" (Field) **43**:165-67
Fetes des moutons (Kandinsky) **92**:50
"The Fetish Character of Music and the Regression of Listening" (Adorno)

111:108, 134, 140
Le feu (Barbusse) **5**:11-14, 17-20
Le feu follet (Drieu la Rochelle) **21**:19, 21-4, 33, 40
Feu la mère de madame (Feydeau) **22**:79, 91, 95
"Feudal" (Liliencron) **18**:209
Feuer aus den Kesseln (Toller) **10**:480, 485, 489, 492
"Feuille d'Album" (Mansfield) **164**:247, 249
Feuilles dans le Vent (Jammes) **75**:115, 119
Feux (Yourcenar) **193**:262-64, 322, 333, 335, 337, 355, 365
Feux croisés (Kazantzakis) **181**:237
"Fever" (Lasker-Schueler) **57**:328
"A Fever" (Merrill) **173**:183, 228
Fever (Talvik)
See *Palavik*
Die Fever-Kantate (Toller) **10**:489-90
Fevral (Bagritsky) **60**:16-7, 20
A Few Figs from Thistles (Millay) **4**:306-10, 313-17; **49**:202-03, 205, 216, 220, 223-24, 226, 228; **169**:231, 245, 248, 274, 294
"A Few Hours in Singapore" (Nagai)
See "Shingapōru no sūjikan"
"A Few Notes on Two of My Books" (Acker) **191**:38-43, 65, 81-2, 85, 92, 98, 129
"A Few Opinions" (Caragiale) **76**:166, 170, 173-75
"A Few Reflections on Amateur and Artistic Photography" (Hartmann) **73**:128, 146
"A Few Words about War and Peace" (Tolstoy) **28**:376, 383
"Fey Joan" (Noyes) **7**:515
Fiabe italiene (Calvino) **183**:94, 96-97, 149, 157, 220-21, 224-25
La fiaccola sotto il moggio (D'Annunzio) **6**:137, 142; **40**:9, 11
"Fiametta" (Bishop) **103**:3-4
"Le fiamme in fiamme" (Calvino) **183**:106
"Les fiançailles" (Apollinaire) **3**:36, 39, 43-4; **51**:9, 54, 57, 59-61
Les fiançailles (Maeterlinck) **3**:323
Les fiancés de Loches (Feydeau) **22**:77
"Fiat" (Guro)
See "Da Budet"
Die Fibel: Auswahl erste Verse (George) **14**:204
Ficciones, 1935-1944 (Borges) **109**:50, 55, 58, 61, 66, 76, 84, 87, 151, 158, 161
"Fiction" (Nemerov) **124**:210
Fiction (Bernhard)
See *Prosa*
"Fiction: A Young Bank Officer" (Shiga)
See "Shosetsu: Wakai ginkoin"
"Fiction: Hayao's Younger Sister" (Shiga)
See "Shosetsu: Hayao no imoto"
"Fiction: On the Way to Abashiri" (Shiga)
See "Abashiri made"
"The Fiction Writer and his Country" (O'Connor) **132**:274, 296, 319
Fictions (Borges)
See *Ficciones, 1935-1944*
"The Fiddle" (Riley) **51**:276
"The Fiddle and the Slipper" (Lee-Hamilton) **22**:192
Fiddle O'Dreams (Morrison) **72**:383
"A Fiddle the Sphinx Forgot" (Nemerov) **124**:277
"Fiddler Jones" (Masters) **25**:297
"Fidelity" (Lawrence) **93**:53, 113
Fidelity (Glaspell) **55**:241, 244-46; **175**:59, 61-64, 66-67, 135
Fidessa (Couperus) **15**:46
"Das Fieber" (Meyrink) **21**:227
"Das Fieberspital" (Heym) **9**:142
"The Field" (Dickey) **151**:104
"A Field Hospital" (Jarrell) **177**:195
"The Field of Honor" (Williams) **89**:386, 393
"The Field of Kulikovo" (Blok) **5**:85
"The Field of Mustard" (Coppard) **5**:180
"The Field of the Potter" (Muir) **87**:180
The Field of Vision (Morris) **107**:94-5, 97, 199, 101-06, 108-09, 111, 113, 115, 118, 124-26, 128, 131-32, 135-39, 142, 147-50, 152, 154-57, 185, 188, 196-97, 203, 206-08, 211, 223, 226, 229, 235-37, 241, 243
"Fielding" (Henley) **8**:103
Fields and Woods (Vazov) **25**:450
Fields, Factories and Workshops (Kropotkin) **36**:197, 200-02, 207, 221
Fields of Castile (Machado)
See *Campos de Castilla*
Fields of Victory (Ward) **55**:437, 443
"The Fiend" (Dickey) **151**:110, 172, 180, 200, 204
The Fiend's Delight (Bierce) **44**:11-12, 29, 34
"Fientliga stjärnor" (Södergran) **31**:294
"Las fieras" (Arlt) **29**:45-7, 59
The Fierce Dispute (Santmyer) **133**:214, 216, 218-19
The Fiery Angel (Bryusov)
See *Ognennyi angel*
The Fiery Dawn (Coleridge) **73**:23
The Fiery Menace (Dent) **72**:24
"Fiesta" (Jiménez) **183**:261
Fiesta (Hemingway)
See *The Sun Also Rises*
La fiesta del hierro (Arlt) **29**:44
"Fièvre" (Garneau) **13**:195
"Fifteen from Company K" (March) **96**:241, 254
"XV (O, Seeded Grass)" (Fletcher) **35**:93
Fifteen Sonnets of Petrarch (Higginson) **36**:179
"The Fifteenth of April" (Scott) **6**:393
The Fifth Column (Hemingway) **115**:143
"Fifth Eclogue" (Radnóti) **16**:420
"Fifth Elegy" (Rilke) **1**:412, 420
"The Fifth International" (Mayakovski) **4**:292; **18**:270
"The Fifth of December" (Ivanov) **33**:138
"The Fifth of May" (Ivanov) **33**:138
"The Fifth of October" (Heym)
See "Der Fünfte Oktober"
The Fifth Plague (Remizov)
See *Pjataja jazva*
The Fifth Queen: And How She Came to Court (Ford) **1**:282-83, 288, 291; **15**:85-86, 92, 94; **57**:215, 273; **172**:4-6, 8, 10, 21, 24
Fifth Queen Crowned (Ford) **57**:232, 260; **172**:4, 6, 9, 11, 25-26
The Fifth Queen Trilogy (Ford) **172**:10, 21, 53, 94, 96, 118
"Fifth Roman Sonnet" (Ivanov) **33**:138
The Fifth Seal (Aldanov)
See *Načalo konca*
"The Fifth Wheel" (Henry) **19**:172
"Fifty Faggots" (Thomas) **10**:463
"Fifty Grand" (Hemingway) **115**:143
"Fifty Grand" (Lardner) **2**:329
Fifty Miles from Boston (Cohan) **60**:170
Fifty Poems (Cummings) **137**:29
50 Poems (Cummings)
See *Fifty Poems*
Fifty Poems in Classical Japanese (Miyazawa) **76**:293
"Fifty Years" (Johnson) **3**:239
"Fifty Years After" (Heidenstam) **5**:255
Fifty Years, and Other Poems (Johnson) **3**:239, 241, 243, 245; **19**:209-11
"Fifty Years of American Poetry" (Jarrell) **177**:179, 183, 188-89
Fifty-One Tales (Dunsany) **2**:136-37, 140-41; **59**:2-3, 17, 27
Figaro Gets Divorced (Horvath)
See *Figaro läßt sich scheiden*
Figaro läßt sich scheiden (Horvath) **45**:78, 82, 101, 111
"The Fight" (Thomas) **8**:456, 463; **45**:395-96; **105**:302, 321, 345-46
"The Fight between Jappe and Do Escobar" (Mann) **8**:261
The Fight for Life (Steinbeck) **135**:344
"The Fight for the Crowd" (Monroe) **12**:216
"Fight! O My Young Men" (Lawrence) **93**:68
"Fight with the Great One" (Ady)
See "Harc a nagyúrral"
Fight Your Own War (Saroyan) **137**:155
"Fighters" (Lasker-Schueler)
See "Streiter"
Fightin' Fool (Faust) **49**:35
The Fighting Chance (Chambers) **41**:92, 95-6, 101
Fighting France, from Dunkerque to Belfort (Wharton) **129**:348, 362
"Fighting, Growing and Making" (Gilman) **117**:100
The Fighting Littles (Tarkington) **9**:469
The Fighting Man of Mars (Burroughs) **2**:82
The Fighting Years (Sinclair) **160**:307, 314, 332
La figlia di Iorio (D'Annunzio) **6**:131, 141; **40**:11, 13, 15, 29
"Le figlie della luna" (Calvino) **183**:101, 215
"Figs" (Lawrence) **93**:43, 98, 100
"Figura" (Auerbach) **43**:47-8, 55, 78-9, 84
"Figuraciones" (Jiménez) **183**:257
Figuras de la pasion del Señor (Miro) **5**:335-37
"The Figure in the Carpet" (James) **2**:262
The Figure in the Carpet (James) **47**:195, 208
"The Figure in the Scene" (Hardy) **143**:156, 189-91
"The Figure of Arthur" (Williams) **1**:519
The Figure of Beatrice: A Study in Dante (Williams) **1**:512, 519; **11**:496, 502
"The Figure of the Youth as Virile Poet" (Stevens) **12**:362; **45**:346, 349
"The Figure of Venus in 'Spring" (Field) **43**:165-66
"Figures" (Hofmannsthal) **11**:294
Figures et choses qui passaient (Loti) **11**:356
Figures of Earth (Cabell) **6**:64-5, 69, 71, 75
Figures of the Passion of Our Lord (Miro)
See *Figuras de la pasion del Señor*
"Figures of Thought" (Nemerov) **124**:260
Figures of Thought: Speculations on the Meaning of Poetry and Other Essays (Nemerov) **124**:214-15, 217, 224, 228, 316
"Figury sna" (Zabolotsky) **52**:376
Un fil à la patte (Feydeau) **22**:77, 86, 93
"Filboid Studge, The Story of a Mouse that Helped" (Saki) **3**:365
"Filial Sentiments of a Parricide" (Proust) **161**:126-27
Filibuth (Jacob) **6**:191
The Filigree Ball (Green) **63**:140-41
"The Filipino and the Drunkard" (Saroyan) **137**:194
"Filippo's Wife" (Bishop) **103**:26
"Le fille de Lilith" (France) **9**:40, 57
La fille du policeman (Swinburne) **8**:438-41, 443
"Filling Station" (Bishop) **121**:42
"Film" (Babits)
See "Mozgófénykép"
Film (Beckett) **145**:97
Film Form: Essays in Film Theory (Eisenstein) **57**:161
"Film Language" (Eisenstein) **57**:166, 181
The Film Sense (Eisenstein) **57**:159, 161, 194, 197, 199-200
"A Film that you will never see" (Anouilh) **195**:54
"Films" (Benét) **28**:6
"Filo del amor" (Aleixandre) **113**:16, 24, 28
"Filomania" (Papini) **22**:281
Filosofia della practica, economica ed etica (Croce) **37**:80, 82, 93-4, 114, 123-24
La filosofia dell'arte (Gentile) **96**:110, 114, 120-21, 124-25
"Filosofia e letteratura" (Calvino) **183**:104
Filosofia e letterature (Papini) **22**:287
Filosoficamente (de Filippo) **127**:287, 289
"Filosoficheskie zamechaniia na rechi Zh.Zh. Russo" (Tolstoy) **173**:328

Filumena Marturano (de Filippo) **127**:270-71, 280, 284, 292
Fimiamy (Sologub) **9**:444
"El fin" (Borges) **109**:88
"Fin" (Huidobro) **31**:124
La fin de Antonia (Dujardin) **13**:189-91
La fin de Babylone (Apollinaire) **51**:20, 28
La fin de Chéri (Colette) **5**:163, 168-69; **16**:117, 120, 133, 137
"Fin de fête" (Mew) **8**:297-98
"La fin de la jalousie" (Proust) **7**:538-39; **161**:124
La fin de l'éternel (Benda) **60**:76
"La fin de Marko Kraliévitch" (Yourcenar) **193**:283, 296-97, 299
Fin de partie (Beckett) **145**:76, 94-95, 124-26, 128, 134, 142-44, 148, 150, 157-60, 162, 164-65, 167, 178, 180
"Fin de race" (Graham) **19**:116
Fin de Siecle (Morley) **87**:138
El fin de una raza (Pereda) **16**:364-65
La fin des bourgeois (Lemonnier) **22**:198, 202-03
La fin du monde antique (Sorel) **91**:193, 197, 213, 233, 301, 321-2, 329
Le Fin du Potomak (Cocteau) **119**:76-8
"La fin d'une guerre" (Drieu la Rochelle) **21**:27-9
"Une Fin et un Commencement" (Adamov) **189**:17-18
"Final" (Aleixandre) **113**:4
Final Causes (Sully Prudhomme) **31**:309
The Final Count (Sapper) **44**:314, 316, 318-19, 321-22
Final Edition (Benson) **27**:12-13
The Final Entries 1945: Diaries of Joseph Goebbels (Goebbels) **68**:106, 109-10
"Final Fire" (Aleixandre) **113**:23-4
Final Journal (Arguedas) **147**:77
"The Final Lesson" (Stringer) **37**:342
"Final Performance" (Merrill) **173**:227
"Final Soliloquy of the Interior Paramour" (Stevens) **12**:364, 387; **45**:311-12, 345, 348, 350
"Final Song" (George) **14**:215
"Finalities" (Bodenheim) **44**:59
"'Finality' in Freeport" (Glaspell) **55**:245
"The Finances of the Gods" (Kipling) **8**:185, 204
The Financier (Dreiser) **10**:164-65, 167-69, 173, 175-80, 182-87; **18**:53-5, 57, 60-1, 63-6, 68-72; **35**:51-2, 62-3, 65; **83**:90
Financiers (Leino)
See *Pankkiherroja*
"Financing Finnegan" (Fitzgerald) **6**:172
"The Find" (Ledwidge) **23**:116
"Find meat on bones" (Thomas) **105**:333
"The Finding of the Princess" (Grahame) **64**:55, 62, 78-9
"The Finding of Zach" (Dunbar) **12**:108, 120
Der Findling (Barlach) **84**:74, 76, 144
"The Fine" (Belloc) **18**:41
A Fine and Private Place (Callaghan) **145**:254-55
"A Fine Beginning" (Thomas) **105**:303, 356
"Fine Feathers" (Coppard) **5**:180
"Fine Fiddle" (Chopin) **5**:145
"Fine Furniture" (Dreiser) **10**:193; **35**:72, 74
Fine Furniture (Dreiser) **35**:71
A Fine Gentleman (Tynan) **3**:505
The Fine Prospect (Horvath)
See *Zur schönen Aussicht*
"A Fine Son" (Dahl)
See "Genesis and Catastrophe"
"A Fine Summer Evening" (Jozsef) **22**:164
"Fine Weather on the Digentia" (Buchanan) **107**:14
"Fine Work with Pitch and Copper" (Ginsberg) **120**:128
The Finer Grain (James) **2**:246, 258
Finest Short Stories of Seán O'Faoláin (O'Faolain) **143**:224
"Finger Man" (Chandler) **7**:172; **179**:121, 162, 165-66
"The Finger of Mrs. Knox" (Somerville & Ross) **51**:360
"A Finger on the Pulse" (Baring-Gould) **88**:22
"Fingerposts to Religion" (Alexander) **77**:29, 56
"The Fingers" (Remizov) **27**:352-53
Finis (Millay) **169**:262
Finis terrae (Epstein) **92**:2-3, 11, 13
"The Finish of Patsy Barnes" (Dunbar) **12**:120
Finished (Haggard) **11**:246, 254-55
Finita comoedia (Rolland) **23**:269
"Finlandia" (Guro) **56**:134, 139
"Finlandia" (Saroyan) **137**:181
Finn and His Companions (O'Grady) **5**:348, 352, 355-56
Finnegans Wake (Joyce) **3**:255, 259-63, 268-77, 280-82; **8**:160-62, 167, 169-70, 172; **16**:208, 227-28, 233, 237, 241; **35**:156-57, 163, 170, 176-77; **52**:197-257; **159**:279-80, 283-84, 287, 291, 325-28, 330-33, 337, 340
Les fins de l'homme (Lyotard) **103**:160, 176, 200
"Fior di Memoria" (Sharp) **39**:391
Fiorenza (Mann) **14**:341, 350, 354; **60**:330; **168**:109, 111, 173
"The Fir Woods" (Roberts) **8**:314
"Firdausi in Exile" (Gosse) **28**:132, 140
"Fire!" (Jozsef) **22**:160
"Fire" (Toomer) **172**:273-74
Fire (Jensen)
See *Det tabte Land*
"Fire and Cloud" (Wright) **136**:277, 315-16, 318-20; **180**:298
Fire and Ice (Dent) **72**:27
Fire and Ice (Jensen) **41**:291, 297-98
Fire and Night (Rainis)
See *Uguns un nakts*
"Fire and Sleet and Candlelight" (Wylie) **8**:521
"The Fire and the Hearth" (Faulkner) **141**:103, 160, 163-64
The Fire and the Sun: Why Plato Banished the Artists (Murdoch) **171**:208, 234, 252, 279, 286-87, 308
"A Fire at Tranter Sweattey's" (Hardy) **4**:152
The Fire Bird (Porter) **21**:267
The Fire Bringer (Moody) **105**:225, 228, 231-32, 234, 238-44, 249, 255, 258, 260, 263, 267-69, 273, 275-77, 279-80, 283-84
"The Fire Builders" (Wetherald) **81**:413
"Fire by Night" (Fisher) **11**:209, 212-13
The Fire Goddess (Rohmer) **28**:281, 286
The Fire in the Flint (White) **15**:473-75, 480-81, 483-86
"Fire in the Heavens" (Brennan) **17**:43
Fire in the Olive Grove (Deledda)
See *L'incendio nell' oliveto*
Fire in the Opera House (Kaiser)
See *Der Brand im Opernhaus*
"The Fire in the Wood" (Welch) **22**:446, 456
"Fire Lookout" (Abbey) **160**:15, 59
The Fire of Egliswyl (Wedekind)
See *Der Brand von Egliswyl*
The Fire of Things (Remizov)
See *Ogon' veshchei*
Fire on the Mountain (Abbey) **160**:3-5, 58, 82-83, 85
The Fire Screen (Merrill) **173**:228
Fire Sermon (Morris) **107**:133, 142, 151-53, 148, 203, 224
"Fire Song" (Rhodes) **53**:316
"The Fire Stone" (Miyazawa) **76**:278
The Firebird (Balmont)
See *Zhar-ptitsa*
"The Firebombing" (Dickey) **151**:90, 95, 100, 106-8, 139-40, 149, 172, 200, 212, 221
The Firebugs: A Learning Play without a Lesson (Frisch)
See *Biedermann und die Brandstifter: Ein Lehrstück ohne Lehre*
The Fire-Cantata (Toller)
See *Die Fever-Kantate*
Fireflies (Naipaul) **153**:225-26, 228, 230, 232, 234
"Firelight in Sunlight" (Nemerov) **124**:177, 252, 254
"The Firemen's Ball" (Lindsay) **17**:222, 224-25, 227
"Firenze" (Campana) **20**:85
"Firenze" (Saba) **33**:374
"Firenze libera!" (Levi) **125**:219, 228
Fires (Yourcenar)
See *Feux*
"The Fires of God" (Drinkwater) **57**:142
The Fires of St. Dominic (Zamyatin)
See *Ogni svyatogo Dominika*
Fireside and Sunshine (Lucas) **73**:159, 162, 174
"Fireside Chat Opening Third War Loan Drive" (Roosevelt) **93**:184
Fire-Tongue (Rohmer) **28**:282
"The Fire-Weed" (Wetherald) **81**:411
"Fireworks" (Lowell) **8**:230
"Fireworks" (Nagai)
See "Hanabi"
The Fireworks (Leino)
See *Ilotulitus*
Fireworks: Nine Profane Pieces (Carter) **139**:47, 99, 130-31, 185, 187-88
Fir-Flower Tablets (Lowell) **8**:226, 229, 237
The Firing Line (Chambers) **41**:92, 95, 101
The Firm Desire to Endure (Éluard) **7**:260-61
"First" (March) **96**:252
"The First American" (Toomer) **172**:271, 278, 287, 290, 312-13
First and Last Things: A Confession of Faith . . . and a Rule of Life (Wells) **6**:529; **12**:490; **19**:436
"First anniversary" (García Lorca)
See "Primer aniversario"
The First Battle (Bryan) **99**:5, 11, 14, 34
The First Celestial Adventure of Monsieur Antipyrine (Tzara)
See *La prèmiere aventure celeste de Monsieur Antipyrine*
"The First Chapter of Spring" (Wen I-to) **28**:414-15
The First Christmas at the 4D Ranch (Adams) **56**:7
The First Cities (Lorde) **173**:73, 77
The First Common Reader (Woolf)
See *The Common Reader*
"The First Day" (Nemerov) **124**:177-79, 181, 217, 254
"The First Day of an Immigrant" (Grove) **4**:142
"The First Day of Spring" (Knister) **56**:156, 163
"The First Day of Spring" (Wright) **136**:300-301
The First day of Spring: Stories and Other Prose (Knister) **56**:164
"First Death in Nova Scotia" (Bishop) **121**:17, 19, 24, 42
"The First Deer Dance" (Miyazawa) **76**:278, 285
"The First Dime" (March) **96**:265
"First Elegy" (Rilke) **1**:412, 419-20
The First Encounter (Bely)
See *Pervoe svidanie*
"A First Family of Tasajara" (Harte) **25**:223
"First Fig" (Millay) **49**:216
First Flight (Anderson) **144**:5, 8, 37, 71
"First Fruit" (Rosenberg) **12**:299
"The First Game" (Lardner) **14**:300-01
The First Gentleman of America (Cabell) **6**:76-7
"The First Idea Is Not Our Own" (Stevens) **3**:448
"First in the North" (Muir) **87**:208
"First in the World" (Éluard) **41**:147
First Journal (Arguedas) **147**:76
The First Lady Chatterley (Lawrence) **9**:228; **48**:110-12, 119, 138, 146-47, 149

"First Love" (Babel)
See "Pervaya lyubov"
"First Love" (Pavese)
See "Primo amore"
First Love (Beckett)
See *Premier amour*
First Love, and Other Stories (Beckett)
See *Premier amour*
The First Man (O'Neill) **1**:384; **6**:325; **49**:252
"First Manifesto of the Theatre of Cruelty" (Artaud) **36**:11, 28
The First Meetings (Bely)
See *Pervoe svidanie*
The First Men in the Moon (Wells) **6**:524, 533, 539, 542, 544-45, 547, 554; **12**:487-88, 505-06, 510-11, 515; **19**:423, 426, 428-29, 434, 436, 438-39, 441-42, 446-47, 449-50; **133**:238, 244, 246, 257, 299, 302, 304, 323
"The First Morning" (Abbey) **160**:21, 94
"First Morning" (Lawrence) **93**:48
"First New Suit Out of the Army" (Shepherd) **177**:316
"First Night in the Churchyard" (Heidenstam) **5**:249
"The First of Spring" (Thomas) **10**:458
First Person Singular (Benét) **28**:10
First Plays (Milne) **6**:306
"The First Ploughing" (Roberts) **8**:321
"First Poem" (Gurney) **33**:84
First Poems (García Lorca)
See *Primeras canciones*
First Poems (Merrill) **173**:186, 207, 225, 234, 238, 254-57
First Poems (Muir) **87**:152-53
"The First Poet" (London) **39**:270
"The First Point of Aries" (Nemerov) **124**:177, 249
"The First Rain" (Sikelianos) **39**:421
"The First Ride" (Arnow) **196**:88, 92
The First Rescue Party (Čapek) **6**:86; **37**:52, 54, 57, 60
"The First Seven Years" (Malamud) **129**:109, 180, 190-93, 195, 197, 199, 201; **184**:226, 285-86
"First Shaves" (Shepherd) **177**:316
"The First Sheaf" (Wakefield) **120**:342, 358
"First Snow" (Nemerov) **124**:210, 217, 259
"The First Snow" (Scott) **6**:393
"The First Snowfall" (Montgomery) **51**:210-11
First Songs (García Lorca)
See *Primeras canciones*
"The First Spring Rain" (Ekelund)
See "Det forsta varregnet"
The First Step (Tolstoy) **79**:413, 430
"The First Surveyor" (Paterson) **32**:376
The First Symphony (Bely)
See *Severnaia simfoniia: Pervia geroicheskaia*
The First Terrorists (Tolstoy) **18**:378
"The First Time After" (Fisher) **87**:74
"First Time In" (Gurney) **33**:93, 102
The First Trilogy (Cary) **1**:142
A First View of English Literature (Moody) **105**:268
"First Wedding Night" (Pirandello)
See "Prima notte"
First Whisper of "The Wind in the Willows" (Grahame) **64**:88; **136**:17-18, 23, 26
A First Year in Canterbury Settlement, with Other Essays (Butler) **33**:41, 70
"Fisches Nachtgesang" (Morgenstern) **8**:305, 308
"The Fish" (Bishop) **121**:6, 9
"The Fish" (Brooke) **2**:51, 60; **7**:120-21, 124
"Fish" (Lawrence) **9**:229; **33**:221; **93**:15, 33, 81, 102, 122
A Fish Dinner in Memison (Eddison) **15**:53-4, 56-7, 60, 62
"Fisher lassies" (Montgomery) **51**:203
"A Fisher of Men" (Freeman)
See "The Blue Diamond Mystery"
"A Fisher of Men" (Galsworthy) **45**:32
"The Fisher of Men" (Sharp) **39**:362, 376
"The Fisher of Men" (Zamyatin)
See "Lovets chelovekov"
"Fisher of Men" (Zamyatin)
See "Lovets chelovekov"
The Fisher-Maiden (Bjoernson) **7**:105-07; **37**:3, 5-6, 17
"The Fisherman" (Yeats) **18**:446
"The Fisherman and His Soul" (Wilde) **1**:503; **41**:381-82
Fisherman of the Seine (Zweig) **17**:458
"Fishhead" (Cobb) **77**:119-20, 136-7, 141-2
"A Fishing Story" (Wakefield) **120**:356, 359
"Fishmonger's Fiddle" (Coppard) **5**:180
"A Fish-Scale Sunrise" (Stevens) **45**:331
"A Fist Fight for Armenia" (Saroyan) **137**:191
A Fistful of Fig Newtons (Shepherd) **177**:303, 315
"A Fit of Madness" (Harris) **24**:272
"A Fit of the Blues" (Gorky) **8**:85
"The Fitting" (Millay) **49**:219, 228; **169**:272, 295
The Fitzgerald Reader (Fitzgerald) **1**:264
Five and Dime (Garro)
See *El encanto, tendajón mixto*
"Five British Water Colours" (Warner) **131**:313
"Five Bulls" (Gumilev)
See "Pjat'bykov"
"Five Carols for Christmastide" (Guiney) **41**:217
The Five Cornered Square (Himes)
See *For Love of Imabelle*
"5/derbies-with-men-in-them smoke Helmar" (Cummings) **137**:42
Five Early Works (Lagerkvist) **144**:236, 238, 240
Five Fingers (Nezval) **44**:240
"Five Flights Up" (Bishop) **121**:29
Five Great Odes (Claudel)
See *Cinq grandes odes*
"Five Grotesque Pieces" (Stevens) **45**:348
Five Hymns to Arunacala (Ramana Maharshi)
See *Arunacala-pancakam*
"5. Jahrhundert" (Benn)
See "V. Jahrhundert"
The Five Jars (James) **6**:207
"Five Loaves of Bread" (Čapek) **37**:44
"Five Men" (Herbert) **168**:26-27
Five Men and Pompey (Benét) **7**:78
Five Men and Pompey: A Series of Dramatic Portraits (Benét)
See *Five Men and Pompey*
"Five Men at Random" (Mencken) **13**:365
Five Minutes beyond the City (Nezval)
See *Pět minut za městem*
Five Modern Nō Plays (Mishima)
See *Kindai nogakushu*
Five O'Clock Tea (Howells) **7**:387
"Five Old Favorites" (Merrill) **173**:257
"The Five Orange Pips" (Doyle) **7**:216
Five Orchestral Pieces (Schoenberg) **75**:292
Five Plays (Dunsany) **59**:17, 26
The Five Red Herrings (Sayers) **15**:371, 393
Five Senses (Jarry) **147**:331
Five Short Novels (Ginzburg)
See *Cinque romanzi brevi*
Five Signs of God's Decay (Mishima)
See *Tennin Gosui*
Five Tales (Galsworthy) **1**:294; **45**:49
Five Verses on Arunacala (Ramana Maharshi)
See *Arunacala-pancaratnam*
Five Verses on the One Self (Ramana Maharshi)
See *Ekatmapanchakam*
Five Verses on the Self (Ramana Maharshi)
See *Ekatmapanchakam*
"Five Vignettes" (Toomer) **172**:273
Five Weeks in a Balloon (Verne)
See *Cinq semaines en ballon*
"The Five White Mice" (Crane) **11**:140, 155, 160, 164
Five Women (Musil) **12**:252
"Five Years of It" (Benét) **28**:7
"Five-Foot Lambs" (Gumilev) **60**:271
"Five-pound Notes" (Bosman) **49**:13
"The Five-Storied Pagoda" (Rohan)
See "Gojū no tō"
The Five-Syllables and the Pathetic Whispers (Palamas) **5**:385
"The Fixation of Belief" (Peirce) **81**:177-8,180,183,187,292,355
The Fixer (Malamud) **129**:61, 67, 69, 84, 96-8, 104, 106, 108, 110, 112-17, 120, 124-26, 136-37, 139, 141-42, 167, 179, 184, 187, 189, 193, 195, 197; **184**:171, 173-74, 176-78, 180, 182, 184, 189, 221, 223-25, 244, 252, 258-59, 266, 276, 285, 287-88, 291, 311, 315, 318, 323
Fizzles (Beckett)
See *Foirades*
Fjalla-Eyvindur (Sigurjónsson)
See *Bjærg-Ejvind og hans hustru*
"Le flacon" (Bryusov) **10**:81
"The Flag" (Howe) **21**:113
The Flag (Grieg)
See *Flagget*
A Flag is Born (Hecht) **101**:62
Det flager i byen og på havnen (Bjoernson) **7**:107-08, 114, 117
Flagget (Grieg) **10**:209
Flags in the Dust (Faulkner)
See *Sartoris*
Les flamandes (Verhaeren) **12**:458, 460, 462-63, 465-66, 468, 470-71, 473
Les flambeaux noirs (Verhaeren) **12**:460, 462-63, 465-66, 469-70
"The Flame" (Quiroga)
See "La llama"
Flame and Shadow (Teasdale) **4**:425, 427-28, 430
"The Flame of a Candle" (Nemerov) **124**:253
The Flame of Life (D'Annunzio)
See *Il fuoco*
"Flame on the Wind" (Sharp) **39**:371
"Flame-Heart" (McKay) **7**:456-57; **41**:344
"Flames" (Babits)
See "Tüzek"
The Flames (Stapledon) **22**:323, 336-38
Flames: A London Phantasy (Hichens) **64**:119, 121, 126-28, 131
"Flames Flicker" (Radnóti) **16**:419
The Flamethrowers (Arlt)
See *Los lanzallamas*
Flametti oder vom Dandysmus der Armen (Ball) **104**:19-21, 31, 59
The Flaming Circle (Sologub)
See *Plamennyi krug*
The Flaming Sword (Dixon) **163**:156, 169-70, 229-36
The Flaming Terrapin (Campbell) **5**:115-19, 123, 125-26
"Die Flamingos" (Rilke) **195**:236-40
La Flamme d'une chandelle (Bachelard) **128**:11, 46, 55, 63, 68-70, 77-8
"Flammonde" (Robinson) **5**:403, 408; **101**:98, 134
The Flamp, the Ameliorator, and the Schoolboy's Apprentice (Lucas) **73**:158
"Flanagan and His Short Filibustering Adventure" (Crane) **11**:125, 160
"Le flâneur des deux rives" (Apollinaire) **51**:19
"The Flapper" (Parker) **143**:337
Flappers and Philosophers (Fitzgerald) **6**:161; **157**:182
A Flash in the Pan (Upward) **85**:380
A Flash of Light: The Way of Man (Griffith) **68**:244, 246-47, 249
"The Flashlight" (Scott) **6**:398
Flatland: A Romance of Many Dimensions (Abbott) **139**:1-42
Flaubert (Mann) **9**:327
"Flavia and Her Artists" (Cather) **11**:92, 100-01
"Flavian: A Clerical Portrait" (Guiney) **41**:220
"The Flaw in Paganism" (Parker) **143**:325

"The Flaw in the Crystal" (Sinclair) **11**:420-21
Flaws in the Glass: A Self-Portrait (White) **176**:200-201, 204, 206, 218, 225, 240, 243, 264-65, 269, 280, 286-87, 296, 298, 308, 310, 330
The Fleas; or, The Dance of Pain (Wedekind)
See *Die Flöhe; oder, Der Schmerzentanz*
Fledermäuse (Meyrink) **21**:232
The Fledgling (Hall and Nordhoff) **23**:56, 71
Fleet Street, and Other Poems (Davidson) **24**:172, 191-92
Fleet Street Eclogues (Davidson) **24**:159, 162, 164, 175-76
Fleeting Moments (Tagore)
See *Kshanikā*
Fleeting Thoughts (Tagore)
See *Kshanikā*
"A Fleeting Wonder" (Davies) **5**:203
"Fleisch" (Benn) **3**:112
Fleischhacker (Brecht) **169**:53
"Fleming's Hallucination" (Bierce) **44**:13
"Flesh and the Mirror" (Carter) **139**:99, 188
"The Fleshly School of Poetry" (Buchanan) **107**:53-5, 61, 65, 78
The Fleshy School of Poetry and Other Phenomena of the Day (Buchanan) **107**:55, 58, 61
"Fletcher McGee" (Masters) **25**:298, 308, 313
"Fleur de cing pierres" (Schwob) **20**:320, 323
"La fleur de Napoléon" (Péret) **20**:201-02
"Fleurs de jadis" (Gourmont) **17**:129
Fleurs d'ennui (Loti) **11**:353, 368
Fleurs d'exil (Loti) **11**:356
"Flick" (Lewis) **3**:288
"Der Fliegende Holländer" (Heym) **9**:142
Die Fliegenpein (Canetti) **157**:69, 96
"Flies" (Quiroga)
See "Las moscas"
The Flies (Azuela)
See *Las moscas*
"Flight" (Brooke) **2**:60
"Flight" (Lasker-Schueler)
See "Weltflucht"
"The Flight" (Roberts) **8**:319
"The Flight" (Scott) **6**:386
"The Flight" (Teasdale) **4**:426
Flight (Bulgakov)
See *Beg*
Flight (White) **15**:475-76, 480, 483-86
"Flight at Sunrise" (McCoy) **28**:226
The Flight from the Enchanter (Murdoch) **171**:221-24, 226, 311, 318, 323, 329
"Flight from the Land" (Caldwell) **117**:13
"Flight from the World" (Lasker-Schueler)
See "Weltflucht"
"The Flight from Womanhood" (Horney) **71**:230, 232, 235
"Flight into Blackness" (Naipaul) **153**:228-29, 231
Flight into Darkness (Schnitzler)
See *Flucht in die Finsternis*
"The Flight of Betsey Lane" (Jewett) **1**:361; **22**:147
A Flight of Cranes (Tagore)
See *Balākā*
"Flight of Love" (Lasker-Schueler) **57**:329
A Flight of Swans (Tagore)
See *Balākā*
"The Flight of the Culdees" (Sharp) **39**:376
The Flight of the Eagle (O'Grady) **5**:348-49, 352, 354
The Flight of the Marseillaise (Rostand) **6**:381
The Flight of the Queen (Dunsany) **59**:13, 26
The Flight of the Shadow (MacDonald) **9**:292
The Flight of the Wild Gander: Explorations in the Mythological Dimension (Campbell) **140**:32, 97, 134
"The Flight of the Wild Geese" (Tynan) **3**:503
Flight out of Time (Ball) **104**:39, 71, 75-76
Flight to Arras (Saint-Exupéry)
See *Pilote de guerre*
Flight without End (Roth)
See *Die Fluchte ohne Ende*
Flightpoint (Weiss)
See *Fluchtpunkt*
Flights (Artaud) **36**:37
Flighty Phyllis (Freeman) **21**:54, 56
The Flint Anchor (Warner) **131**:309, 320, 324
"Flint and Fire" (Fisher) **87**:73
"The Flint Eye" (Merrill) **173**:254
The Flirt (Tarkington) **9**:460, 467, 473
The Flirt and the Flapper (Glyn) **72**:142
Flirtation (Schnitzler)
See *Liebelei*
A Floating City (Verne)
See *Une Ville flottante*
Floating Cloud (Hayashi)
See *Ukigumo*
The Floating Clouds (Futabatei)
See *Ukigumo*
The Floating Island (Verne)
See *L'Ile à hélice*
"The Floating Prince" (Stockton) **47**:328-30
The Floating Prince, and Other Fairy Tales (Stockton) **47**:319, 328, 331
The Flock (Austin) **25**:17, 23-8, 31, 33, 36, 40
A Flock of Poor Folk (Miyamoto)
See *Mazushiki hitobito no mure*
"A Flock of Sheep" (Scott) **6**:385
Die Flöhe; oder, Der Schmerzentanz (Wedekind) **7**:584
"Flöjten" (Lagerkvist) **144**:221-22
"The Flood" (Fadeyev) **53**:51, 58
"The Flood" (Nagai)
See "Kōzui"
The Flood (Barlach)
See *Die Sündflut*
The Flood (Zamyatin)
See *Navodnenie*
Flor de mayo (Blasco Ibáñez) **12**:30, 35, 41, 43-5, 47, 49
Flor de santidad (Valle-Inclán) **5**:472, 475-76, 485, 489
"Flor que vuelve" (Jiménez) **183**:290, 292
"La flor seca" (Pardo Bazán) **189**:290, 296-97
"Flóra" (Jozsef) **22**:165
Flora (Bennett) **197**:16-18
Flora MacDonald (Sharp) **39**:374
Florence (Childress) **116**:25-6, 51-2
The Florentine Dagger (Hecht) **101**:31, 70-2, 77
"Florentine Pilgrim" (Service) **15**:413
A Florentine Tragedy (Wilde) **23**:411
Flores de cardo (Prado) **75**:207, 210
Flores de escarcha (Martinez Sierra and Martinez Sierra) **6**:285
"Florida" (Bishop) **121**:4
Florida: A Guide to the Southernmost State (Hurston) **131**:59
Florida Loafing (Roberts) **23**:238
"Floridian Reveries" (Hearn) **9**:133, 135
"Flos florum" (Symons) **11**:451
"Flos mercatorum" (Noyes) **7**:512
"flotsam and fetsam" (Cummings) **137**:54
"The Flow of Evening" (Bryusov) **10**:88
"Flower Arrangements" (Nemerov) **124**:258
"Flower Basket" (Nagai)
See "Hanakago"
The Flower beneath the Foot (Firbank) **1**:227, 229, 232
"Flower Days" (Walser) **18**:437
"The Flower Gatherer" (Thomas) **10**:458
"The Flower Girl" (Radiguet) **29**:357
"A Flower Given to my Daughter" (Joyce) **159**:284
A Flower in the Shade (Nagai)
See *Hikage no hana*
The Flower o' the Vine (Sharp) **39**:361
The Flower of Buffoonery (Dazai Osamu)
See *Dōke no hana*
"The Flower of Coleridge" (Borges) **109**:149
"Flower of Death: The Kiss" (Ady) **11**:20-1
The Flower of Hell (Nagai)
See *Jogoku no hana*
"Flower of Karma" (Miyazawa) **76**:284, 291
"The Flower of Mending" (Lindsay) **17**:229
"A Flower of Mullein" (Reese) **181**:345
"The Flower of Old Japan" (Noyes) **7**:502, 512
Flower of Sanctity (Valle-Inclán)
See *Flor de santidad*
The Flower of the Chapdelaines (Cable) **4**:31
"A Flower on the Ground" (Platonov) **14**:420
"The Flower That Never Fades" (Robinson) **101**:188
"A Flower-Arranging Summer" (Sarton) **120**:269
"The Flowerboxes" (Yourcenar)
See "Les Caisses à fleurs"
"The Flower-Fed Buffaloes" (Lindsay) **17**:235
Flowering Cherry (Bolt) **175**:8-10, 15-16
"The Flowering Dream: Notes on Writing" (McCullers) **155**:182, 193
Flowering of the Cumberland (Arnow) **196**:29, 34, 38, 95, 98-100
"The Flowering of the Strange Orchid" (Wells) **19**:429, 442; **133**:244
"The Flowering Past" (Lowry) **6**:238
Flowering Reeds (Campbell) **5**:120, 123-24
Flowering Wilderness (Galsworthy) **45**:42-4, 47, 50
"The Flowering Year" (Naidu) **80**:315
"Flowers" (Lawrence) **93**:98, 101
"Flowers and Poetry" (de la Mare) **4**:81
"Flowers Do Not Live at My Place" (Gumilev)
See "U menja ne zhivut cvety"
"Flowers of Night" (Hippius) **9**:157
Flowers of Passion (Moore) **7**:487, 489-91
"The Flower's Tragedy" (Hardy) **53**:117
Flowing with Mountains and Rivers (Santoka)
See *Sangyo suigyo*
"Der fluch der Erkenntnis" (Mann) **2**:412
"Die Flucht" (Carossa) **48**:25
Die Flucht aus der Zeit (Ball) **104**:3, 5, 10, 13, 15, 22, 24-25, 33, 36, 46-47
Flucht in die Finsternis (Schnitzler) **4**:393
Die Flucht nach Venedig (Kaiser) **9**:173, 181-82
Die Flucht zu Gott (Zweig) **17**:453
Die Fluchte ohne Ende (Roth) **33**:329, 333, 335, 347-55, 362-63
Flüchtlingsgespräche (Brecht) **13**:62-3
Fluchtpunkt (Weiss) **152**:246-48, 251-53, 285-86, 288, 293-95, 300, 309
"Fluctuat nec mergitur" (Vian) **9**:537
"The Fluctuating Woodlot" (Williams) **89**:374
Das Flug auf der Zeit (Ball) **104**:49
The Flurried Years (Hunt) **53**:191-93, 196
Flush (Woolf) **1**:546; **56**:410
"Flush of Gold" (London) **9**:277
"The Flute" (Lagerkvist)
See "Flöjten"
"La flute" (Schwob) **20**:322
A Flute for Mice (Remizov)
See *Myshkina dudochka*
"The Flute-Player of Brindaban" (Naidu) **80**:287
"Flutter-Duck" (Zangwill)
See "Flutter-duck, A Ghetto Grotesque"
"Flutter-duck, A Ghetto Grotesque" (Zangwill) **16**:442
"The Fly" (Mansfield) **2**:451; **8**:281-82, 291; **39**:303-05, 318, 324; **164**:240, 305
"The Fly" (Yokomitsu)
See "Hae"
The Fly (Zamyatin) **37**:433
Fly by Night (Jarrell) **177**:157-59
Flying Colours (Forester) **152**:132-33, 135, 137-38, 163
The Flying Fifty-Fifty (Wallace) **57**:397
"Flying Fish" (Carman) **7**:138
"The Flying Fish" (Gray) **19**:147, 157, 165
"The Flying Fish" (Lawrence) **2**:359; **48**:121
Flying Fool (Wallace) **57**:402
"The Flying Gang" (Paterson) **32**:376

The Flying Inn (Chesterton) **1**:178; **6**:98-9, 103-04; **64**:35
The Flying Islands of the Night: A Fantastic Drama in Verse (Riley) **51**:283, 285, 292
The Flying King of Kurio (Benét) **28**:10
Flying Padre (Kubrick) **112**:127, 135
Flying Squad (Wallace) **57**:402
"Flypaper" (Hammett) **187**:78, 203
"Flypaper" (Musil) **68**:260
"Foam" (Seton) **31**:279
The Fobidden Epic (Spitteler) **12**:340
"Fog" (Reese) **181**:344
"Fog Envelopes the Animals" (Dickey) **151**:104, 171
"Fog Horns" (Gogarty) **15**:108
"Fog Patterns" (Hecht) **101**:38, 47
Foggerty's Fairy (Gilbert) **3**:210
Foggy Harbor (Mizoguchi) **72**:322
"The Fog's Density" (Wright) **136**:301
"Foi et bonne foi" (Merleau-Ponty) **156**:121-22, 128-30
Foirades (Beckett) **145**:97
La Foire d'empoigne (Anouilh) **195**:30, 34, 36
La foire sur la place (Rolland) **23**:261, 268, 277, 282
"Fokstrot" (Zabolotsky) **52**:375, 377
"Folck stora coh sma" (Lagerkvist) **144**:187
The Folding Screens (Genet)
See *Les paravents*
Die Folgen der Reformation (Ball) **104**:22, 36, 46-47, 57
Foliage (Davies) **5**:199-200
"Folies-Bergere" (Huysmans) **69**:25
Folk som sjöng och andra essayer (Bengtsson) **48**:12
Folk ved sjøen (Bojer) **64**:23
"Folke filbyter" (Heidenstam) **5**:252, 255
En folkefiende (Ibsen) **2**:219, 222-26, 237; **8**:148-49, 151-52; **16**:154-56, 166, 171, 173, 177, 181, 186, 190-91; **37**:224-25, 239, 241, 243; **52**:141-95
Folk-Lore in the Old Testament (Frazer) **32**:202-03, 223, 234
Folks from Dixie (Dunbar) **2**:130; **12**:106-09, 119-20, 122
"Folksong" (Rilke)
See "Volksweise"
Folk-Tales of the Russian People (Remizov) **27**:331, 334
Folkungasagan (Strindberg) **1**:449, 460; **8**:415, 417-18
Folkungaträdet (Heidenstam) **5**:252-53, 255-56
La folle de Chaillot (Giraudoux) **2**:159, 161-63, 168-70; **7**:322-23, 329
Folle Farine (Ouida) **43**:338, 347, 349-50
"The Followers" (Thomas) **105**:351
Following the Color Line (Baker) **47**:4, 15-17, 31-2
Following the Equator (Twain) **6**:455-56, 458; **12**:432; **59**:168; **161**:265, 267; **185**:251
"The Folly of Anti-Semitism" (Orage) **157**:282
"The Folly of Being Comforted" (Yeats) **18**:446
The Folly of Eustace and Other Stories (Hichens) **64**:126, 128, 131
Foma Gordeyev (Gorky) **8**:68-70, 72, 75, 77, 81, 83, 85-7, 89
"Fonari" (Guro) **56**:147
Fond de cantine (Drieu la Rochelle) **21**:27
Fond de l'eau (Jacob) **6**:193, 202
"La fontaine de jouvence" (Sully Prudhomme) **31**:302
"Fontainebleau" (Teasdale) **4**:427
La fontana de oro (Pérez Galdós) **27**:252, 256-57, 265, 282, 288
The Fonts of Doña Blanca (Garro)
See *Los pilares de doña Blanca*
Food (Hayashi)
See *Meshi*
The Food of the Gods, and How It Came to Earth (Wells) **6**:524-25, 534, 539-40, 544; **12**:514; **19**:426-27, 437-38, 440; **133**:299, 302
"The Fool" (Dixon) **163**:166
"The Fool" (Service) **15**:401
The Fool and the Madman (Bernhard)
See *Der Ignorant und der Wahnsinnige*
The Fool in Christ, Emanuel Quint (Hauptmann)
See *Der Narr in Christo, Emanuel Quint*
"Fool o' the Moon" (Lowell) **8**:227, 233, 235, 237
The Fool of the World, and Other Poems (Symons) **11**:434-35, 446
"The Foolish Heart" (Cullen) **37**:136, 165
Foolish Notion (Barry) **11**:62, 65
"Foolish Passion" (Shiga)
See "Chijo"
The Foolish Virgin (Dixon) **163**:171-72
Foolish Wives (Stroheim) **71**:328-332, 334-336, 339-340, 357-359, 361-362, 364, 366, 377
"Fool-Proof" (Éluard) **41**:149
"The Fool's Adventure" (Abercrombie) **141**:7
"A Fool's Errand" (Montgomery) **51**:181
Fool's Gold (Fletcher) **35**:89-90
"A Fool's Life" (Akutagawa Ryūnosuke)
See "Aru ahō no isshō"
Fools of Fate (Griffith) **68**:245
"Fool's Paradise" (Holly) **65**:149
"The Fool's Prayer" (Vilakazi)
See "Umkhuleko wesiphoxo"
The Fool's Progress (Abbey) **160**:56, 59-62, 78-79, 82-83, 88
Fools Say (Sarraute)
See *Disent les imbéciles*
"The Foot of Tucksport" (Coffin) **95**:2
Footfalls (Beckett) **145**:124, 126, 129, 134, 156
"Footing Up a Total" (Lowell) **8**:231
"A Foot-Note to a Famous Lyric" (Guiney) **41**:207
"Footnote to Howl" (Ginsberg) **120**:41-2, 49, 52, 94, 116, 125, 137
"A Footnote to the War Books" (Tomlinson) **71**:406
Footnote to Youth: Tales of the Philippines and Others (Villa) **176**:93, 114-15
"The Footprint" (Čapek)
See "Slépej"
Footprints (Reyes) **33**:322
"Footsloggers" (Ford) **15**:72
Footsteps of Fate (Couperus)
See *Noodlot*
"Footstool" (Herbert) **168**:14
"For a Commemoration on the Death of Arnold Böcklin" (Hofmannsthal) **11**:294
"For a Daughter's Wedding" (Morley) **87**:145
"For a Dead Lady" (Robinson) **5**:418; **101**:99-100, 105, 113, 117, 138
"For a Fatalist" (Cullen) **37**:146
"For a Lady I Know" (Cullen) **37**:148, 153, 160
"For a Lady Who Must Write Verse" (Parker) **143**:324
"For a Lovely Lady" (Cullen) **4**:40
"For a Marriage in Spring" (Carducci) **32**:102
"For a Mouthy Woman" (Cullen) **4**:44
For a Nameless Tomb (Onetti)
See *Para una tumba sin nombre*
"For a Poet" (Cullen) **37**:154
"For a Sad Lady" (Parker) **143**:321
"For a Skeptic" (Cullen) **37**:146
"For a Time and Place" (Dickey) **151**:170
"For a Virgin" (Cullen) **37**:147, 153
For a Wife's Honor (Griffith) **68**:249
"For Adolf Eichmann" (Levi) **109**:287
"For Adults Only" (Rilke) **195**:339
"For All We Have and Are" (Kipling) **8**:201
"For an Atheist" (Cullen) **37**:153
"For an Emigrant" (Jarrell) **177**:214, 251
"For an Evolutionist and His Opponent" (Cullen) **37**:164
"For Andy Goodman—Michael Schwerner—and James Chaney (Three Civil Rights Workers Murdered in Mississippi on June 21, 1964)" (Walker) **129**:273, 305
"For Ann Scott-Moncrieff (1914-1943)" (Muir) **87**:167
"For Auld Lang Syne" (Lawson) **27**:119
For Authors Only, and Other Gloomy Essays (Roberts) **23**:240
"For Balmont" (Tsvetaeva) **7**:571
"For Better" (Evans) **85**:25, 27-8
"For Bread" (Sienkiewicz) **3**:425
"For City Spring" (Benét) **7**:75
"For C. W. B." (Bishop) **121**:50-1
"For D. S.'s Album" (Anwar)
See "Buat album D. S."
"For Daughters of Magdalen" (Cullen) **37**:154
"For de Faldne" (Nexø) **43**:315
For Ever (Vilakazi)
See *Noma nini*
For Farish Street (Walker)
See *My Farish Street Green*
"For Hazel Hall, American Poet" (Cullen) **37**:164
"For He Had Great Possessions" (Middleton) **56**:174
"For Herself or Another" (Bryusov) **10**:78
For His Son (Griffith) **68**:250
"For John Keats, Apostle of Beauty" (Cullen) **37**:143
"For Laurie" (Sarton) **120**:245, 247
"For Life I Had Never Cared Greatly" (Hardy) **143**:151
For Love of Gold (Griffith) **68**:150, 185
For Love of Imabelle (Himes) **139**:244-45, 248, 250, 252-56, 264, 270, 282, 285, 300-02, 304, 311, 320, 336
"For Love of the Hills" (Glaspell) **175**:53-54
"For Marcel Janko" (Tzara) **168**:314
"For Me" (Péguy)
See "Pour moi"
"For Mercedes in Her Flight" (García Lorca) **181**:See"A Mercedes en su vuelo"
"For Mirat" (Anwar)
See "Buat Mirat"
"For Miss Gadis Rasid" (Anwar)
See "Buat Gadis Rasid"
"For My Birthday" (Jozsef) **22**:165
"For My Grandmother" (Cullen) **37**:153
"For My Grandmother" (Shiga)
See "Sobo no tame ni"
"For My People" (Walker) **129**:269, 271, 293-94, 297, 305, 313-15, 317-20, 322-23, 325, 328
For My People (Walker) **129**:269-72, 276, 287, 297-98, 305, 311, 315-17, 319-23, 327-28, 330-32, 334-35
"For Paul Laurence Dunbar" (Cullen) **37**:153
"For R. C. B." (Parker) **143**:323
"For Radicals" (Bourne) **16**:60-1
"For Robert Bhain Campbell" (Dickey) **151**:171
"For Rosalind on Her Seventy-fifth Birthday" (Sarton) **120**:266
For the Beauty of an Idea: Prelude (Sharp) **39**:378, 394
"For the Blood Is the Life" (Crawford) **10**:149, 158-59
For the Crown (Coppee)
See *Pour la couronne*
"For the Death of Lombardi" (Dickey) **151**:126-27, 147
"For the Eye Altered Alters All" (Nemerov) **124**:206
"For the Faith" (Fuller) **103**:86
For the Flag (Verne)
See *Face au drapeau*
For the Guitar (Borges)
See *Para las seis cuerdas*
"For the Heroes Are Dipped in Scarlet" (Lawrence) **93**:59, 62, 73-75
For the Homeless (Sologub)
See *Rodine*
"For the Honour of the Gods" (Dunsany) **59**:19
"For the Last Wolverine" (Dickey) **151**:111

"For the Marriage of Faustus and Helen" (Crane) **2**:111, 119-21, 123-24; **5**:188, 190; **80**:96
"For the Running of the New York City Marathon" (Dickey) **151**:170
"For the Russian Land" (Remizov)
See "Za Russkuiu zemliu"
"For the Sea" (Tsvetaeva) **7**:566
For the six strings (Borges)
See *Para las seis cuerdas*
For Thee the Best (Aldanov)
See *Mogila voina*
For to end yet again and Other Fizzles (Beckett)
See *Foirades*
"For Tomorrow" (Glaspell) **175**:52
For Tonight (Onetti)
See *Para esta noche*
"For 'Under the Volcano'" (Lowry) **6**:237
"For Walter Allen, '53" (Cary) **196**:158
"For Whom Do You Write?" (Benda) **60**:89
For Whom the Bell Tolls (Hemingway) **115**:143, 146, 157, 162
"For Winter, For Summer" (Millay) **169**:235
For You Departed (Paton)
See *Kontakion for You Departed*
For Your Eyes Only (Fleming) **193**:195, 198-99, 208, 223
"For'ard" (Lawson) **27**:139
Forays and Rebuttals (De Voto) **29**:117, 119
Forbidden Colors (Mishima)
See *Kinjiki*
Forbidden Fruit (Pérez Galdós)
See *Lo prohibido*
Force (Barbusse) **5**:18
"La Force des faibles" (Lyotard) **103**:160
"Force Majeure" (Levi) **109**:302
The Force of Habit (Bernhard)
See *Die Macht der Gewohnheit*
"The Force That through the Green Fuse Drives the Flower" (Thomas) **45**:361-62, 365, 376, 383, 387, 409-10; **105**:354
"Forced March" (Radnóti) **16**:411, 420
"Forces du passé" (Yourcenar) **193**:330
Les forces tumultueuses (Verhaeren) **12**:459-60, 464
The Forcing House (Zangwill) **16**:466
The Ford (Austin) **25**:25-6, 33, 35
Ford Madox Brown: A Record of His Life and Work (Ford) **172**:6
"Den fordringfule gästen" (Lagerkvist) **144**:210
Fordringsägare (Strindberg) **8**:419
Den fordringsfulla gästen (Lagerkvist) **144**:222
"Forecast" (Lawrence) **93**:45, 67
A Foregone Conclusion (Howells) **7**:364-65, 371, 391-92; **17**:162, 180, 191
Foreign Affairs (O'Faolain) **143**:227
Foreign Exchange (Tarkington) **9**:464
Foreign Skies (Gumilev)
See *Chuzhoe nebo*
Foreign Students (Endo)
See *Ryugaku*
Foreign Studies (Endo)
See *Ryugaku*
"The Foreigner" (Jewett) **22**:135, 148-49
The Foreigner (Connor) **31**:105-08, 114, 116
Forel razbyvaet lyod (Kuzmin) **40**:197, 199-200, 202-03, 209, 215-16
The Forerunner (Gibran) **9**:89-92
The Foreshore of England; or, Under the Red Ensign (Tomlinson) **71**:389, 391, 397
"The Forest" (Gumilev) **60**:270
"The Forest" (Walser) **18**:434, 436
"Forest Born" (Pickthall) **21**:253
"Forest Darkness" (Södergran)
See "Skogsdunkel"
Forest Drip-Drop (Prishvin)
See *Lesnaia kapel*
Forest Flower (Devkota)
See *Van kusum*
A Forest in Flower (Mishima)
See *Hanazakari no mori*
The Forest in Full Bloom (Mishima)
See *Hanazakari no mori*
The Forest in Full Flower (Mishima)
See *Hanazakari no mori*
"The Forest Lake" (Södergran)
See "Skogs sjön"
Forest Leaves (Harper) **14**:255
"The Forest Maiden" (Khlebnikov)
See "Lesnaja deva"
Forest Murmurs (Heidenstam) **5**:253
Forest Notes (Lee-Hamilton) **22**:194
"The Forest of Night" (Brennan) **17**:38-9, 41-3, 45, 48, 50, 52-4
Forest of the Hanged (Rebreanu)
See *Padurea spînzuratilor*
"The Forest of Wild Thyme" (Noyes) **7**:512-13
"The Forest on the Superhighway" (Calvino) **183**:227
"The Forest Path to the Spring" (Lowry) **6**:239-41, 245, 247, 254-55
"The Forest Road" (Mew) **8**:298
The Forest Whispers (Korolenko) **22**:169
"La foresta e gli dèi" (Calvino) **183**:102-3
"Forever" (Balmont)
See "Navek"
"Forevermore" (Agnon)
See "Ad Olam"
"Foreward!" (Abbey) **160**:17
"Foreword" (Merrill) **173**:180
"A Foreword to Krazy" (Cummings) **137**:6
"The Forge" (Gray) **19**:157
The Forge (Barea) **14**:44-5, 48-9, 51, 53
The Forge (Hall) **12**:195
A Forge in the Forest (Roberts) **8**:323
The Forged Note: A Romance of the Darker Races (Micheaux) **76**:237-39, 250, 252, 263
"The Forgers" (Scott) **6**:397
"Forget Her" (Wen I-to) **28**:414, 420
The Forging of a Rebel (Barea)
See *La forja de un rebelde*
"Forgive Us Our Righteousness" (Kaye-Smith) **20**:107
Forgive Us Our Virtues (Fisher) **140**:182
"Forgiveness" (Baker) **3**:2
"Forgotten Books" (Lucas) **73**:174
"The Forgotten Grave" (Dobson) **79**:23
The Forgotten Island (Hall) **12**:195
"The Forgotten Man" (Lane) **177**:276
"The Forgotten Man" (Patton) **79**:305
The Forgotten One, and Other True Tales of the South Seas (Hall and Nordhoff) **23**:66
"Forgotten People" (Ingamells) **35**:138
Forgotten People (Ingamells) **35**:124, 129, 134
"Forgotten the Red Leaves" (Douglas) **40**:67, 70
The Forgotten Village (Steinbeck) **135**:344
La forja de un rebelde (Barea) **14**:46-8, 51-2
Forjando el porvenir Americano (Hostos) **24**:303
The Fork River Space Project (Morris) **107**:158, 226-27
"Forlorn Beauty" (Ingamells) **35**:137
"Form" (Aleixandre)
See "Forma"
"Form and Content in Art" (Collingwood) **67**:126-27
"Form Destructionist-Sculptor" (McAlmon) **97**:86
"The Form of Poetry" (Wen I-to) **28**:413, 420
"The Form of Space" (Calvino)
See "La forma dello spazio"
"Form without Love" (Aleixandre) **113**:24, 27-28
"Forma" (Aleixandre) **113**:3
"Forma" (Borges)
See "La forma de la espada"
"Forma Christi" (Teilhard de Chardin) **9**:493
"La forma de la espada" (Borges) **109**:14, 87-8
"La forma dell'albero" (Calvino) **183**:106
"La forma dello spazio" (Calvino) **183**:145
"La forma que me queda" (Jiménez) **183**:260, 311
"La forma y no el infinito" (Aleixandre) **113**:5
Formación de una cultura nacional indoamericana (Arguedas) **147**:81
The Formal and Transcendental Logic (Husserl)
See "Formale und transzendentale Logik"
Formal Defect (Levi)
See *Vizio di forma*
"The Formal Lovers" (Merrill) **173**:253-55
"Formale und transzendentale Logik" (Husserl) **100**:9, 15-16, 28, 40, 71, 123-25, 154
Formale und transzendentale Logik (Husserl)
See "Formale und transzendentale Logik"
Formal'nyi metod v literaturovedenii: Kriticheskoe vvedenie v sociologicheskuju poètiku (Bakhtin) **160**:157
"Formas sobre el mar" (Aleixandre) **113**:8
La Formation de l'esprit scientifique (Bachelard) **128**:5, 20, 23, 25, 47, 49-50, 53
La Formation du Radicalisme Philosophique en Angleterre (Halévy) **104**:108, 110-11, 137
Les Formes élémentaires de la vie religieuse: le système totémique en Australie (Durkheim) **55**:91, 93, 98, 102, 104, 111, 118-19, 121, 140, 143-44, 154
"La formica Argentina" (Calvino) **183**:94, 118, 121, 190-91, 208, 229, 238
"Forms of Death" (Merrill) **173**:254-55
"Forms of Love" (Oppen) **107**:258
"Forms of the Implicit Love of God" (Weil) **23**:371
"Forms of the Rock in a Night-Hymn" (Stevens) **45**:317
"Forms on the Sea" (Aleixandre)
See "Formas sobre el mar"
Forró mezok (Moricz) **33**:242
Fors Clavigera: Letters to the Workmen and Labourers of Great Britain (Ruskin) **20**:265, 272, 280, 285-88, 305; **63**:238, 255-57, 261, 268, 270, 273, 203, 2 331, 333-35
"The Forsaken" (Lowell) **1**:375; **8**:235
"The Forsaken" (Scott) **6**:387-88, 390, 393, 395, 397
"A Forsaken Garden" (Swinburne) **36**:318-19, 334, 337, 345
"Forschungen eines hundes" (Kafka) **2**:297, 306; **6**:226; **29**:214; **47**:245
Forse che sì forse che no (D'Annunzio) **6**:133-34, 137, 144-45; **40**:5, 7, 11
"Forse un giorno diranno" (Saba) **33**:373
"Det forsta varregnet" (Ekelund) **75**:92-93
The Forsyte Chronicles (Galsworthy) **1**:305
The Forsyte Saga (Galsworthy) **1**:296-98, 300, 302, 305-06; **45**:46-7, 58-62, 67-9
"Forsythe and Forsythe" (Gilman) **37**:213; **117**:77-8
Fort Sumter (Heyward) **59**:108
Den fortabte generation (Nexø) **43**:330
Fortaellingen om Viga-Ljot og Vigdis (Undset) **3**:518, 524-25; **197**:311
Fortoellinger om Kong Arthur og Ridderne av det Runde Bord (Undset) **197**:325
"Forth went the candid man" (Crane) **11**:130
"A Forthcoming Book" (Adams) **56**:8
"The Fortified House" (Heidenstam) **5**:253
"Fortissimo" (Lasker-Schueler) **57**:329, 336
Fortitude (Walpole) **5**:497, 499, 501, 503
"The Fortress" (Remizov)
See "Krepost"
The Fortress (Walpole) **5**:500
"The Fortress Unvanquishable Save for Sacnoth" (Dunsany) **59**:8, 21
"Fortschritt" (Rilke) **195**:182
Fortuna (Kielland) **5**:279
"Fortunate Love" (Gosse) **28**:131, 151
"Fortunatus Nimium" (Bridges) **1**:126
"Fortune and the Fifth Card" (Fisher) **87**:72

La fortune des Rougon (Zola) **6**:562-63; **21**:421; **41**:411
"Fortune from America" (Papadiamantis) **29**:272-73
The Fortune Hunter (Phillips) **44**:262, 274
"The Fortune Teller" (Post) **39**:336
Fortunes (Desnos) **22**:69
Fortune's Fool (Hawthorne) **25**:241, 249
Fortune's Fool (Sabatini) **47**:303
The Fortunes of Richard Mahony (Richardson) **4**:371-74, 376, 380-83
"Fortune-Telling" (Tsvetaeva)
See "Gadan'e"
The Forty Days of Musa Dagh (Werfel)
See *Die vierzig Tage des Musa Dagh*
The 47 Ronin (Mizoguchi)
See *Genroku Chushingura*
"Forty Singing Seamen" (Noyes) **7**:510-11
Forty Verses on Existence (Ramana Maharshi)
See *Ulladu Narpadu*
Forty Verses on Reality (Ramana Maharshi)
See *Ulladu Narpadu*
Forty-five Minutes from Broadway (Cohan) **60**:156, 163-4, 166-70, 172
XLI Poems (Cummings) **137**:27, 34, 41, 45, 50
Forty-Two Poems (Flecker) **43**:194
"A Forty-Year-Old Man" (Endo)
See "Yonjussai no otoko"
The Forum Exhibition of Modern American Painters, March Thirteenth to March Twenty-Fifth, 1916 (Van Dine) **23**:358
"Förvandling" (Södergran) **31**:293
"Forward" (Abbey) **160**:39
"Forward! Forward!" (Carducci)
See "Avanti! Avanti!"
"Forward Observation Post" (Lewis) **3**:289
The Fossil (Sternheim)
See *Das Fossil*
Das Fossil (Sternheim) **8**:378
"Fossils" (Stephens) **4**:407
"Foster the Light" (Thomas) **45**:365
"Foster-Sister" (Coppee) **25**:121
Fotosnimki (Prishvin) **75**:225
"Le fou" (Nelligan) **14**:392
Foucault (Deleuze) **116**:84-5
"La foule" (Verhaeren) **12**:469
Les foules de Lourdes (Huysmans) **7**:411; **69**:26, 44-6
"Foundation" (Arenas)
See "Fundación"
"The Foundation" (Balmont)
See "Osnova"
"The Foundation of the General Theory of Relativity" (Einstein) **65**:92, 97
The Foundations (Galsworthy) **1**:295
Foundations of a Philosophy of Right (Gentile) **96**:134-36
The Foundations of Indian Culture (Aurobindo) **63**:30, 34, 36
Foundations of Leninism (Stalin) **92**:183
The Foundations of Sovereignty (Laski) **79**:75-6, 104
"Foundations, Universities, and Research" (Laski) **79**:91
"The Founders" (Gumilev)
See "Osnovateli"
"The Founding and Manifesto of Futurism" (Marinetti)
See "Manifeste du futurisme"
"The Founding of the Company" (Williams) **1**:513
The Foundling (Barlach)
See *Der Findling*
Foundling Mick (Verne) **6**:501
"The Fount of Tears" (Dunbar) **12**:104
"The Fountain" (Moody) **105**:234, 237
The Fountain (O'Neill) **1**:382, 384; **6**:336; **49**:241, 266, 270, 292
"The Fountain Maiden" (Hearn) **9**:138
The Fountain of Blood (Artaud)
See *Le jet de sang*
"Fountain of Castelvecchio" (Pascoli) **45**:141
"The Fountain of God" (Hearn) **9**:134
"The Fountain of Shadowy Beauty" (Baker) **10**:27
The Fountain of Youth (Lee-Hamilton) **22**:188-89, 191-93
The Fountain Pit (Platonov)
See *Kotlovan*
Fountains in the Sand (Douglas) **68**:5, 16, 39, 43-4
"The Four Ages" (Nemerov) **124**:260, 282-83, 286
Four and Twenty Minds (Papini) **22**:276
"Four buttons two holes four brooms" (Arp) **115**:22
Four Canzones (Okigbo)
See *Poems: Four Canzones*
Four Chapters (Tagore)
See *Chār adhyāy*
"Four Colloquies" (Guiney) **41**:207
Four Day's Wonder (Milne) **6**:318
The Four Devils (Murnau) **53**:239-40, 275
Four Essays on Liberty (Berlin) **105**:6, 8, 11, 16-17, 20, 71-4, 76, 82, 109, 132, 134
"Four Eyes" (Wakefield) **120**:343, 350
Four Faultless Felons (Chesterton) **6**:104-05, 108
Four for Delfina (Donoso)
See *Cuatro para Delfina*
"Four Forms of Scepticism" (Mead) **89**:195
"The Four Friends" (Milne) **6**:315
The Four Gospels Harmonised and Translated (Tolstoy)
See *Soedinenie I perevod chetyrex evangelij*
The Four Horsemen of the Apocalypse (Blasco Ibáñez)
See *Los cuatro jinetes del apocalipsis*
The Four Just Men (Wallace) **57**:397, 402-3, 408-9
The Four Just Men of Cordova (Wallace) **57**:402
"The Four Lost Men" (Wolfe) **13**:492
"The Four Meetings" (James) **2**:247; **64**:157
The Four Men (Belloc) **7**:33; **18**:21, 30-3, 44-5
The Four Million (Henry) **1**:346-48
Four Mystery Plays (Steiner) **13**:438, 444
"Four Nude Studies" (D'Annunzio) **6**:143
"The Four Periods of Development" (Tolstoy)
See "Chetyre epokhi razvitiya"
Four Phases of Love (Heyse)
See *Novellen*
Four Pieces (Schoenberg) **75**:311
Four Plays (White) **176**:186, 189, 226
Four Plays for Dancers (Yeats) **93**:341
"Four Poems" (Muir) **87**:260
"Four Poems for Children" (Noyes) **7**:515
Four Poetic Plays (Drinkwater) **57**:139
"Four Portraits" (Bulgakov) **16**:85
The Four Roads (Kaye-Smith)
See *Little England*
Four Saints in Three Acts (Stein) **1**:429-30, 432-33; **6**:411-12; **28**:313, 333; **48**:208-10, 230-33, 248, 264
Four Short Plays (Abercrombie) **141**:10, 12
"Four Sides to a House" (Lowell) **8**:230-31
"The Four Sons of Eve" (Blasco Ibáñez) **12**:39
The Four Troublesome Heads (Melies)
See *L'homme de tetes*
Four Verse Plays (Anderson) **144**:35
The Four Winds of Love (Mackenzie) **116**:228, 232, 239, 241, 244-46, 254
Four Years: 1887-1891 (Yeats) **31**:399
Four-and-Twenty Blackbirds (Thomas) **10**:458
"Four-and-Twenty Hours in a Woman's Life" (Zweig)
See "Vierundzwanzig Stunden aus dem Leben einer Frau"
"Fourfold Hackword" (Mayakovski) **18**:269
Les fourmis (Vian) **9**:531-32
"A Four-Point Program for Jewry" (Schoenberg) **75**:408
Four-Square (Fisher) **87**:105
"XIV" (Sarduy) **167**:220
Le fourteen Juillet (Rolland) **23**:257-58, 260
The Fourteen Lines (Palamas) **5**:385
Fourteen Prayers (Jammes)
See *Quatorze Prieres*
Fourteen Red Huts (Platonov) **14**:423, 425
Fourteen Years After (Bromfield) **11**:82
"The Fourteenth of December" (Hippius)
See "Chetvrdnadcati-oye dekabrya"
"Fourth Eclogue" (Radnóti) **16**:414, 420
"Fourth Elegy" (Rilke) **1**:412
"IV Internatsional" (Mayakovski) **18**:257
The Fourth Magus (Graham) **19**:115
"The Fourth of July" (Nemerov) **124**:288
"The Fourth of November" (Ivanov) **33**:138
The Fourth Symphony (Bely)
See *Kubok metelej: Chetviortiia simfoniia*
"The Fox" (Lawrence) **2**:362-63; **9**:216; **48**:117
"The Fox" (Nagai)
See "Kitsune"
The Fox and the Hedgehog (Berlin)
See *The Hedgehog and the Fox*
"The Fox Hunt" (Roberts) **68**:304
"Foxes and Graves" (Coffin) **95**:16
Foxglove Manor (Buchanan) **107**:61, 86-7
Le foyer (Mirbeau) **55**:281, 283, 301
"Fra Angelico at Fiesole" (Tynan) **3**:503
"Fra Celeste" (Huch) **13**:249-50
Fra Celeste und andere Erzählungen (Huch) **13**:252
Fra det moderne Amerikas aandsliv (Hamsun) **14**:221, 237-39, 246-47, 250; **151**:231, 241-44, 248, 273
"Fra det ubevidste Sjaeleliv" (Hamsun) **14**:251; **49**:132; **151**:247-48, 254
"Fra det unbevidste sjæleliv" (Hamsun) **49**:167
"Fra Giacomo" (Buchanan) **107**:25
"Fra Lippi and Me" (Arnow) **196**:80, 88, 90
"Fra' Lucerta" (D'Annunzio) **40**:38
Fråan fjärdingen och svartbächen (Strindberg) **8**:408-09
Los fracasados (Azuela) **3**:77; **145**:8, 14, 17, 22-25
"Fragment" (Borges)
See "Fragmento"
"A Fragment" (Lewis) **3**:290
"Fragment" (Robinson) **101**:117
"Fragment" (Södergran) **31**:288, 292
"Fragment 1956" (Ginsberg) **120**:109-11
"Fragment av en stämning" (Södergran) **31**:293
"Fragment d'une confession" (Roumain) **19**:339, 344
"Fragment eines Weitbildes" (Kubin) **23**:100
"Fragment from Verses to Akhmatova" (Tsvetaeva) **35**:386
"The Fragment: Names II" (Ginsberg) **120**:37
"Fragment of a Greek Tragedy" (Housman) **10**:259
"Fragment of a Life" (Hamsun) **151**:239
"A Fragment of a Life Story" (Welch) **22**:440-41
"Fragment of a Mood" (Södergran)
See "Fragment av en stämning"
"Fragment of an Analysis of a Case of Hysteria" (Freud)
See "Bruchstück einer Hysterie-Analyse"
"Fragment of an Ode to Canada" (Scott) **6**:386, 388, 394
"A Fragment of Life" (Machen) **4**:280
"A Fragment of Velestino" (Crane) **11**:159
"Fragmente aus verlorenen Tagen" (Rilke) **195**:266
Fragmente: Neue Gedichte (Benn) **3**:107
"Fragmento" (Borges) **109**:14
"Fragmento de una carta" (Pereda) **16**:379
"Fragmento Tercero" (Jiménez) **183**:294
"Fragments" (Genet) **128**:158
"Fragments" (Hecht) **101**:36
"Fragments" (O'Neill) **6**:337
Fragments (Glyn) **72**:140
Fragments (Wittgenstein)
See *Zettel*

"Fragments de comédie italienne" (Proust) **161**:172
"Fragments du narcisse" (Valéry) **4**:492, 496, 499; **15**:458
Fragments d'un discours amoureux (Barthes) **135**:129, 142-45, 147, 159, 165-66, 188-89
Fragments d'un journal d'enfer (Artaud) **36**:5
Fragments d'un paradis (Giono) **124**:108, 113
Fragments . . . et autres texts (Genet) **128**:208
"Fragments from lost days" (Rilke)
See "Fragmente aus verlorenen Tagen"
"Fragments from the Song of the Sun" (Palamas) **5**:383
Fragments of a Diary in Hell (Artaud)
See *Fragments d'un journal d'enfer*
Fragments of the Lost Journals of Piero di Cosimo (Sharp) **39**:361, 374
Fragments of the Magic Mirror (Undset)
See *Splinten av trollspeilet*
"Fragments out of the Deluge" (Okigbo) **171**:340, 352, 354
Fragola e panna (Ginzburg) **156**:63
"Fragoletta" (Swinburne) **36**:297
"A Frameup" (Lardner) **2**:331; **14**:291, 307
Framtidens skugga (Södergran) **31**:285-87, 294
Frana allo scalo nord (Betti) **5**:56, 58, 62, 66-7
La France (Sully Prudhomme) **31**:302
"France Aims to Lead the World in the Air" (Mitchell) **81**:168
"France and England: The Future of Their Intellectual Relations" (Gosse)
See "France et l'angleterre: l'avenir de leurs relations intellectuelles"
La France byzantine (Benda) **60**:59, 62-3, 65, 69
"France et Allemagne" (Verhaeren) **12**:471
"France et l'angleterre: l'avenir de leurs relations intellectuelles" (Gosse) **28**:151
Frances Waldeaux (Davis) **6**:149, 152
"Francesca" (Carpenter) **88**:119
"Francesca" (Lugones) **15**:286
Francesca da Rimini (Crawford) **10**:144-45, 156
Francesca da Rimini (D'Annunzio) **6**:132, 142; **40**:7, 9-10, 29
The Franchise Affair (Tey) **14**:449-50, 452-54, 461-64
"Francie's Fingers" (Wylie) **8**:536
Francis (Klabund) **44**:106
Francis Bacon (Deleuze) **116**:100, 102
Francis of Assisi (Merezhkovsky) **29**:242
"Franciscan Adventures" (Lewis) **104**:200
François de Voltaire (Brandes) **10**:71
"Francois Rabelais in the History of Realism" (Bakhtin) **160**:110
"Françoise" (Tolstoy) **11**:463
"Frank Confessions of a Publisher's Reader" (Morley) **87**:148
Frank Harris on Bernard Shaw (Harris) **24**:266, 272
"Frank Wedekind" (Huneker) **65**:199
Frankenstein (Whale) **63**:339-45, 347-51, 355-56, 358-61, 364-65, 371-73, 375, 377, 380-84
Frankfurter Vorlesungen (Böll) **185**:45, 138-39, 142-43, 153, 160, 164
Frankie Kerek (Moricz)
See *Kerek Ferkó*
Den Franske aesthetik i vore dage (Brandes) **10**:60, 70, 74
"Franz Kafka" (Muir) **87**:183
Franz Kafka: Eine Biographie (Brod) **115**:78, 80, 82, 84
Franz Kafka's Glauben und Lehre (Brod) **115**:84, 87
Franz Liszt (Huneker) **65**:165, 170
"Franz Liszt's Work and Being" (Schoenberg) **75**:339
Franz Müllers Drahtfrühling (Schwitters) **95**:323, 325-6, 330
The Franza Case (Bachmann)
See *Der Fall Franza, Requiem für Fanny Goldmann*
Franziska (Wedekind) **7**:585, 590
"Una frase sulla Mandragola" (Svevo) **35**:363
Fraternity (Galsworthy) **1**:301; **45**:30, 32, 38-9, 44-5, 47-8, 50, 64, 66-7
"Fraternity Village" (Williams) **89**:390
The Fratricides (Kazantzakis) **33**:150, 155, 166
Frau Beate und ihr Sohn (Schnitzler) **4**:396-97
"Frau Blahas Magd" (Rilke) **195**:175
"Frau Brechenmacher Attends a Wedding" (Mansfield) **8**:282; **39**:297, 301, 318; **164**:269, 291-93, 325
"Die Frau des Richters" (Schnitzler) **4**:403
Die Frau des Steffen Tromholt (Sudermann) **15**:433-34, 437
Die Frau, die nicht enttäuscht (Brod) **115**:84, 97-8, 109
"Frau Fischer" (Mansfield) **39**:298; **164**:293, 325
"Die Frau im Fenster" (Hofmannsthal) **11**:292, 303
Die Frau Ohne Schatten (Hofmannsthal) **11**:301-03
Frau Sorge (Sudermann) **15**:417-18, 423-24, 427-28, 430, 432-33, 438
Die Frau und die Tiere (Kolmar) **40**:174-75
Frauds Exposed; or, How the People Are Deceived and Robbed, and Youth Corrupted (Comstock) **13**:95-7
Frauen vor Flußlandschaft (Böll) **185**:94, 104-07, 119-26, 128-30, 151-52, 154, 158-59, 161, 163-64, 180, 184-85
"Frauenemancipation" (Heyse) **8**:114, 121
Das Frauenopfer (Kaiser) **9**:173, 180-81, 192
"Frauenschicksal" (Rilke) **6**:357
Fraülein Else (Schnitzler) **4**:393, 396, 398
Fräulein Schmidt and Mr. Anstruther (Elizabeth) **41**:122-23, 132, 136
"Fraülein Schwartz" (Hall) **12**:188
The Freaks (Pinero) **32**:405
Freckles (Porter) **21**:260, 262-64, 271, 276-77
"Freckles M'Grath" (Glaspell) **175**:94
The Fred Allen Show (Allen) **87**:17, 36, 46-7
Fred Allen's Letters (Allen) **87**:16
Fred and Madge (Orton) **157**:344-46
Freddy's Book (Gardner) **195**:131, 138, 141-42
Frederick and the Grand Coaltion (Mann)
See *Friedrich und die grosse Koalition*
Frederick and the Great Coalition (Mann)
See *Friedrich und die grosse Koalition*
"Frederick Douglass" (Dunbar) **12**:109, 124
"Frederick Jackson Turner" (Becker) **63**:65, 73
Den fredlöse (Strindberg) **1**:452; **21**:345
"Free" (Dreiser) **10**:180-81, 197; **35**:56, 69, 71, 74-5
Free Air (Lewis) **4**:248, 251, 256, 259; **13**:338, 351; **23**:139-41
Free, and Other Stories (Dreiser) **35**:71
"Free Fantasia on Japanese Themes" (Lowell) **8**:234
The Free Fishers (Buchan) **41**:39
"Free Florence!" (Levi)
See "Firenze libera!"
"Free Joe and the Rest of the World" (Harris) **2**:209-11
Free Land (Lane) **177**:266-67, 270-71, 273-80, 286-87
Free Men (Gladkov) **27**:93
Free Opinions Freely Expressed on Certain Phases of Modern Social Life and Conduct (Corelli) **51**:66, 73, 82-3
"Free Passage" (Tsvetaeva) **35**:414
"The Free Press" (Belloc) **18**:21
"A Free Press" (Benchley) **55**:26
"Free Speech: The Cowboy and His Cow" (Abbey) **160**:58
"Free Topic" (Walser) **18**:427
"Free Will" (Pavese) **3**:340
"Free Will and Its Moral Significance" (Westermarck) **87**:358
"Freedom" (Markham) **47**:285
Freedom and Culture (Dewey) **95**:56-7, 69, 71
Freedom and Responsiblitity in the American Way of Life (Becker) **63**:74-6, 118
Freedom and the Spirit (Berdyaev) **67**:22-5, 27-9
Freedom and the Tragic Life (Ivanov)
See *Dostojewskij: Tragödie-Mythos-Mystik*
"Freedom and Wilderness, Wilderness and Freedom" (Abbey) **160**:37
Freedom or Death (Kazantzakis)
See *Ho kapetan Michales*
"Freedom, Power, and Values in Our Present Crisis" (Wirth) **92**:378
"Freedom's a Hard-Bought Thing" (Benét) **7**:81
The Freelands (Galsworthy) **45**:45, 47-9, 67
The Freethinker (Strindberg) **1**:452
"A Freeze-Out" (Fitzgerald) **6**:167
Het fregatschip Johanna Maria (van Schendel) **56**:237-43
"Frei Simão" (Machado de Assis) **10**:295
Freie Wissenschaft und freie Lehre (Haeckel) **83**:142, 147
Freiheit und Form (Cassirer) **61**:113
Freiwild (Schnitzler) **4**:388, 390
Der Fremde (Weiss) **152**:284-87, 289, 295
Der Fremde Stadt (Kandinsky) **92**:49
Den fremsynte (Lie) **5**:323-24, 326, 330-32
French Aesthetics at the Present Day (Brandes)
See *Den Franske aesthetik i vore dage*
French Dramatists of the Nineteenth Century (Matthews) **95**:225, 232, 246
"French for Americans" (Benchley) **55**:3
French Leave (Somerville & Ross) **51**:344
French Leave (Wodehouse) **108**:372
French Leaves (Lucas) **73**:173
"French Mons" (Heidenstam) **5**:253
"The French Prisoner of War" (Hedāyat)
See "Asir-i faransaui"
French Stories (Nagai)
See *Furansu monogatari*
The French They Are a Funny Race (Sturges)
See *Les Carnets du Major Thompson*
French Ways and Their Meaning (Wharton) **53**:388; **129**:362
La frente pensativa (Jiménez) **183**:268
Frenzied Fiction (Leacock) **2**:379
Frenzied Fricassee (Hecht) **101**:73
Frescoes: Dramatic Sketches (Ouida) **43**:371
"Fresh Fields" (Gogarty) **15**:109, 114
"Fresh Well Water" (Platonov) **14**:414
"The Freshest Boy" (Fitzgerald) **14**:189
Freshwater (Woolf) **1**:550
Freud and Man's Soul (Bettelheim) **143**:11
"Freud and the Future" (Mann)
See "Freud und die Zukunft"
The Freud Journal of Lou Andreas-Salomé (Andreas-Salome) **56**:35, 42-43, 56-57
"Freud to Paul: The Stages of Auden's Ideology" (Jarrell) **177**:187
"Freud und die Zukunft" (Mann) **2**:428; **44**:196-97, 202, 219-20, 224; **168**:157
Freuden and Tage (Proust) **161**:173
Freuden und Tage (Proust)
See *Les plaisirs et les jours*
"Freudian Fiction" (Woolf) **43**:408
Die freudlose Gasse (Pabst) **127**:305, 330, 342, 345-46, 351, 355-56, 358, 360, 375
"Freud's Position in the History of Modern Thought" (Mann) **21**:170
"Freundschaft und Liebe" (Lasker-Schueler) **57**:299, 332
"Freya of the Seven Isles" (Conrad) **1**:203; **57**:84, 100
Frida (Hamsun) **151**:231
"Frida; or the Lover's Leap" (Blackmore) **27**:44
"Friday the Thirteenth" (Ginsberg) **120**:78
Friday's Business (Baring) **8**:34, 36, 43
Das Friedenfest (Hauptmann) **4**:192, 196
Friedli der Kolderi (Spitteler) **12**:338, 348
"The Friedmans' Annie" (Slesinger) **10**:441-42

Friedrich Nietzsche (Brandes) **11**:62
Friedrich Nietzsche in seinen Werken (Andreas-Salome) **56**:37, 39, 55
Friedrich Nietzsche: The Dionysian Spirit of the Age (Orage) **157**:245, 248, 250, 274
Friedrich und Anna (Kaiser) **9**:173, 179-81
Friedrich und die grosse Koalition (Mann) **2**:436; **168**:174-75
"The Friend" (Dickey) **151**:90
"A Friend" (Johnson) **19**:243-44, 256
"The Friend" (Milne) **88**:242, 244
A Friend in Power (Baker) **119**:9-10
Friend Manso (Pérez Galdós)
See *El amigo Manso*
"The Friend of Her Youth" (Somerville & Ross) **51**:360, 383
"The Friend of Paul" (Manning) **25**:265, 269, 279
"A Friend of the Family" (Kipling) **8**:196, 204
"The Friend of the Fourth Decade" (Merrill) **173**:228
"Friend to Man" (Kornbluth) **8**:216-17
"Friendless Blues" (Handy) **97**:40
"Friendly Brook" (Kipling) **8**:194, 201, 209
The Friendly Enemy (Van Doren) **18**:404
"The Friendly Foe" (Coleridge) **73**:8
The Friendly Road (Baker) **47**:19, 22, 24, 27
The Friendly Town: A Little Book for the Urbane (Lucas) **73**:158, 165, 170, 173
"Friends" (Caragiale) **76**:165
"Friends" (Johnson) **19**:255-56
"Friends" (Obstfelder) **23**:187-88
Friends (Abe)
See *Tomodachi, enemoto takekai*
Friends and Relations (Bowen) **148**:17, 20, 37, 42, 48, 83, 85-86, 88, 90, 96-98, 107
"Friends Beyond" (Hardy) **4**:152; **143**:156, 169
The Friends for Nation (Phelps) **113**:395
"Friends of Tamás Esze" (Ady) **11**:21
"Friends of the People of Faery" (Yeats) **11**:539
"A Friend's Song for Simoisius" (Guiney) **41**:205, 218
"Friends That Fail Not" (Johnson) **19**:257
"Friends—With a Difference" (Coleridge) **73**:25
Friendship (Ouida) **43**:343, 348, 350-52, 354, 357, 364-65, 367, 370, 376
"Friendship and Love" (Lasker-Schueler)
See "Freundschaft und Liebe"
The Friendship of Art (Carman) **7**:139, 143
Friendship Village (Gale) **7**:277, 281-82, 286
Friendship Village Love Stories (Gale) **7**:281-82, 287
"Friendship's Garland" (Butts) **77**:106
Fries der Lauschenden (Barlach) **84**:95
"A Frieze" (Bishop) **103**:4, 6
The Frigate Johanna Maria (van Schendel)
See *Het fregatschip Johanna Maria*
"Fright" (Storni)
See "Miedo"
"Fright in the Dining Room" (García Lorca)
See "Susto en el comedor"
The Frightened Wife and Other Murder Stories (Rinehart) **52**:289-91, 304
A Fringe of Leaves (White) **176**:161-66, 181-85, 188, 191-97, 219, 230-32, 234-35, 237-40, 244-45, 247, 249, 284, 306-7, 309
"El frío" (Aleixandre) **113**:13
"Friso" (Darío) **4**:58, 64
"Frisson d'hiver" (Nelligan) **14**:398
Frithof Saga (Bjoernson) **7**:100
Fritz Kochers Aufsätze (Walser) **18**:416, 422-23, 428
Fritz Schwigerling (Wedekind) **7**:584
Fritzchen in Morituri (Sudermann) **15**:420, 427
The Frivolous Prince (Cocteau)
See *Le Prince Frivole*
"Fro" (Platonov) **14**:410-11, 413, 419, 425
Fro, and Other Stories (Platonov) **14**:423-24
"The Frog Killer" (Vallette)
See "Le tueur de grenouilles"
"Frogs" (Hearn) **9**:129
"Frohe Tage. London Symphony" (Schwitters) **95**:315
Der fröhliche Weinberg (Horvath) **45**:77
Der fröhliche Weinberg (Zuckmayer) **191**:289, 296, 301-02
Die Fröhliche Wissenschaft (Nietzsche) **10**:388-89, 393-94; **55**:323, 328, 336, 355, 359, 364, 367, 370, 387-92
"Le Froid et le Cruel" (Deleuze) **116**:135
"Froim grach" (Babel) **13**:34; **171**:50, 57-58, 97, 107-10
Fröken Julie (Strindberg) **1**:444-48, 450-51, 453-55, 457, 460-63; **8**:406-07, 411-13, 419; **21**:344, 348, 350, 362-64, 367-68; **47**:334-84
From 1905 (Kahanovitsch)
See *Fun finftn yor*
"From a Berlin Street" (Khodasevich) **15**:209
"From a Cotton Field" (Wright) **136**:302
"From a Dying People" (Ingamells) **35**:121-22
"From a Green Hilltop" (Wright) **136**:302
"From a Kentucky Standpoint" (Cotter)
See "On Hearing James W. Riley Read (From a Kentucky Standpoint)"
"From a Land of Grass without Mirrors" (Burroughs) **121**:132
From a Land Where Other People Live (Lorde) **173**:73
"From a Letter from Lesbia" (Parker) **143**:325
"From a London Balcony" (Bramah) **72**:9
"From a Lost Anthology" (Pickthall) **21**:246
"From a Play" (Lewis) **3**:287
"From a Stormy Night" (Rilke)
See "Aus einer Sturmnacht"
"From a Surgeon's Diary" (Freeman) **21**:54-5
From a Swedish Homestead (Lagerloef) **36**:238, 242
"From a Tenement" (Wright) **136**:302
"From A to Z" (Glaspell) **175**:54, 56, 96
"From a Train Window" (Millay) **49**:208
"From a Train-Window" (Sarton) **120**:266
"From a View to a Kill" (Fleming) **193**:193, 237
"From Absolutism to Experimentalism" (Dewey) **95**:138, 141
From Activity to the Seeing (Nishida)
See *Hataraku mono miru mono e*
From Adam's Peak to Elephanta: Sketches in Ceylon and India (Carpenter) **88**:66, 92-6, 102, 120-1, 126-8, 135-6
"From Afar" (Lasker-Schueler) **57**:332
"From All Our Journeys" (Sarton) **120**:302
"From Altar to Chimney-piece" (Butts) **77**:76, 106
From Altar to Chimney-Piece (Butts) **77**:75
From an Old House (Hergesheimer) **11**:277, 283
From Bed to Worse (Benchley) **55**:18
"From Beyond" (Lovecraft) **22**:241
"From Boston to New York" (Jiménez) **183**:333
From Col di Tenda to Blocksberg (Heidenstam) **5**:250, 254
"From Cosmos to Cosmogenesis" (Teilhard de Chardin) **9**:482
From Cuba with a Song (Sarduy)
See *De donde son los cantantes*
From Death to Morning (Wolfe) **4**:519, 526-27; **13**:491-92, 495
"From Disaster" (Oppen) **107**:257
"From drawings in Kokoschka's sketch-book" (Arp) **115**:16-18, 20
"From Each according to His Ability" (Henry) **19**:174
"From Far, from Eve and Morning" (Housman) **10**:239
"From France" (Rosenberg) **12**:297
"From Hope and Fear Set Free" (Berlin) **105**:45-6
From India: Sketches of an Indian Journey (Hesse) **196**:328
From Island to Island (Weiss)
See *Von Insel zu Insel*
From London to Ladysmith (Churchill) **113**:148, 160
"From Loves's First Fever to Her Plague" (Thomas) **45**:361, 378
"From Man to God" (Papini) **22**:269
From Man to Man (Schreiner) **9**:396-400, 402-03, 405
From Marlowe to Shaw (Ellis) **14**:127
"From Materials on the Ethnography of the Sysol and Vechegda Zyrians: the National Deities (According to Contemporary Beliefs)" (Kandinsky) **92**:117
"From Mauss to Claude Lévi-Strauss" (Merleau-Ponty)
See "De Mauss à Lévi-Strauss"
"From Morelia to Mexico City on Horseback" (Foote) **108**:27-8
From Morn to Midnight (Kaiser)
See *Von Morgens bis Mitternachts*
"From Morning into Morning" (Merrill) **173**:234
"From My Diary" (Khodasevich) **15**:206
"From My Diary, July, 1914" (Owen) **5**:369, 374
From My Experience: The Pleasures and Miseries of Life on a Farm (Bromfield) **11**:84
"From My Little Corner" (Yosano)
See "Hitosumi-yori"
From My Treasures (Kahanovitsch)
See *Fun meine giter*
"From Mythology" (Herbert) **168**:27
From Nine to Nine (Perutz)
See *Zwischen neuen und neuen*
From October to Brest-Litovsk (Trotsky) **22**:364
From Oriental Motifs (Rozanov) **104**:314
"From Outer Darkness" (Wakefield) **120**:357
From Paris (Yosano)
See *Parii yori*
"From Paul Verlaine" (Symons) **11**:427
From Rousseau to Proust (Ellis) **14**:119, 127, 142
From Russia, With Love (Fleming) **193**:198-200, 203-04, 207-08, 211, 213-15, 217, 223, 229, 231, 236-37, 239-42
From Shakespeare to Pope (Gosse) **28**:133, 137
From the Acting to the Seeing (Nishida)
See *Hataraku mono miru mono e*
"From the Ashes" (Chang)
See "Jingyu lu"
"From the Beast to the God" (Andreas-Salome) **56**:46
From the Beginning to the End (Baroja)
See *Desde el principio hasta el fin*
"From the Beyond" (Asch) **3**:69
From the Book of Myths (Carman) **7**:137-38
From the Book of the Myths (Carman)
See *From the Book of Myths*
From the Book of the Valentines (Carman)
See *From the Book of Valentines*
From the Book of Valentines (Carman) **7**:137, 139
"From the Bridge" (Marquis) **7**:434
"From the Cabby's Seat" (Henry) **19**:173
"From the Cherry Tree" (Wright) **136**:302
"From the Cupola" (Merrill) **173**:164, 166, 180, 183, 259
"From the Dark Tower" (Cullen) **4**:45; **37**:149, 155, 159
"From the Desert of the Poet's Life" (Babits)
See "A költőéletének pusztájáról"
"From the Desk of the Laureate: For Immediate Release" (Nemerov) **124**:181
"From the Diary of a New York Lady" (Parker) **143**:287-90, 342
"From the Diary of Silas Flannery" (Calvino) **183**:145
From the Earth to the Moon (Verne)
See *De la Terre à la Lune*
From the Eastern Sea (Noguchi) **80**:360, 367, 377

From the Fair (Aleichem)
See *Funem yarid*
From the Fifth Year (Kahanovitsch)
See *Fun finftn yor*
From the First Nine: Poems 1947-1976 (Merrill) **173**:174, 253
"From the Flowers of Disgust" (Radnóti) **16**:419
From the Four Winds (Galsworthy) **45**:46
From the Green Book of Bards (Carman) **7**:138
From the Green Book of the Bards (Carman)
See *From the Green Book of Bards*
"From the Hand of a Child" (Markham) **47**:278
From the Heart of Europe (Matthiessen) **100**:164-66, 192, 203, 207, 209, 213, 218, 232, 234, 238-41, 258
From the Hills of Dream: Mountain Songs and Island Runes (Sharp) **39**:354, 359, 372, 381-82, 387, 391-93
"From the History of God" (Andreas-Salome) **56**:47
From the Home Country (Nezval)
See *Z domoviny*
From the Homeland (Nezval)
See *Z domoviny*
From the Hymns and Wraths (Palamas) **5**:380
"From the Idle Papers of a Confused Contemporary" (Hansen) **32**:253
From the Kaiserhof to the Reich Chancellery (Goebbels) **68**:86-8, 128-9
"From the Kingdom of Necessity" (Jarrell) **177**:244
"From the Letters of the Young Girl Claire Valmont to Rosalie Toutelle Meyer" (Kuzmin) **40**:194
"From the Meadows—The Abbey" (Gurney) **33**:86, 97
"From the Memoirs of a Poznan Tutor" (Sienkiewicz) **3**:430
"From the Month of the Sahara" (Graham) **19**:104
"From the Mouse's Point of View" (Dunsany) **59**:23
"From the Night of Forebeing" (Thompson) **4**:435, 440
From the Other Side (Fuller) **103**:59, 61, 63, 65, 86
"From the Prehistory of Novelistic discourse" (Bakhtin) **160**:206
"From the Rainy Dark" (Wright) **136**:301
"From the Same" (Belloc) **18**:41
"From the Sea" (Teasdale) **4**:428
"From the Seacoast" (Tsvetaeva)
See "S morya"
"From the Secret Notebook of Fellow-Traveler Sand" (Olesha)
See "Koe-chto iz sekretnykh zapisei poputchika Zanda"
From the Sick-Bed (Tagore)
See *Rogsajyae*
"From the Sun" (Balmont) **11**:42
"From the Terrace" (Calvino) **183**:47, 143
"From the Tideless Sea" (Hodgson) **13**:237
"From the Unconscious Life of the Mind" (Hamsun)
See "Fra det ubevidste Sjaeleliv"
"From the Vasty Deep" (Wakefield) **120**:352
"From the Wreck" (Paterson) **32**:373
"From Time" (Dickey) **151**:174
"From Top to Bottom Clarity" (Tzara) **168**:275
"From Trollope's Journal" (Bishop) **121**:42, 80
"From Women's Letters" (Kuprin) **5**:301
"From Work to Text" (Barthes) **135**:159
From Working Things to Seeing Things (Nishida)
See *Hataraku mono miru mono e*
"From Yasukichi's Notebooks" (Akutagawa Ryūnosuke)
See "Yasukichi no techōkara"
"From Yumi-chō: Poems to Eat" (Ishikawa) **15**:129
A Fronded Isle and Other Essays (Lucas) **73**:174
Frondes Aggrestes (Ruskin) **63**:251
"Fronleichnamsprozession" (Heym) **9**:142-43
"A Front" (Jarrell) **177**:126, 129, 193-94, 223, 227
The Front Page (Hecht) **101**:62-4, 72, 77, 80, 83, 87
"Front the Ages with a Smile" (Masters) **2**:461
"The Front Wave" (Gilman) **9**:102
Frontier Feud (Faust) **49**:41-2, 47
"The Frontier Guards" (Wakefield) **120**:343, 357
Frost (Bernhard) **165**:10-11, 17-22, 36, 38, 50-52, 54-55, 79, 97, 106, 108, 111, 122
The Frost (Leino)
See *Halla*
"Frost Flowers" (Lawrence) **93**:53, 55
Frost Flowers (Martinez Sierra and Martinez Sierra)
See *Flores de escarcha*
"The Frost Giant's Daughter" (Howard) **8**:131, 134-35
"Frost Rides Alone" (McCoy) **28**:225
"Frost Song" (Pickthall) **21**:247
"A Frosty Morning" (Davidson) **24**:164
"A Froward Child" (de la Mare) **4**:78; **53**:25, 27, 35
"The Frozen City" (Nemerov) **124**:151
Fru Hjelde (Undset) **3**:512, 522
Fru Inger til Østraat (Ibsen) **8**:146; **37**:231
Fru Marta Oulie (Undset) **3**:511-12, 516-17, 522; **197**:299, 301, 306, 311
Fru Waage (Undset) **3**:512
"Fruchtland" (Rilke) **1**:420
"Fruchtlos" (Kolmar) **40**:178
Fruen fra havet (Ibsen) **2**:222-23, 227, 229, 233; **8**:148; **16**:166, 168; **37**:223, 225; **52**:144
Die Frühen Kränze (Zweig) **17**:424
"Früher Apollo" (Rilke) **1**:410
Früher dachte ich (Brecht) **169**:43-44
"Früheste Erlebnisse" (Spitteler) **12**:351
"Frühling" (Kandinsky) **92**:67
"Fruhling" (Lasker-Schueler) **57**:299
"Frühling der Seele" (Trakl) **5**:457
Frühlings Erwachen (Wedekind) **7**:574, 577, 580-81, 584, 586, 590-91
"Frühlingstänzerin" (Ball) **104**:12
"Fruit of the Flower" (Cullen) **37**:135
The Fruit of the Tree (Wharton) **3**:558, 562, 571, 579-80; **9**:548, 552; **27**:384-85; **53**:403; **129**:361; **149**:142, 146-47, 255, 266
The Fruitful Vine (Hichens) **64**:121, 125-27, 129
Fruit-Gathering (Tagore) **3**:481; **53**:338-40, 347
"Fruits" (Lawrence) **93**:98, 101
Les fruits d'or (Sarraute) **145**:274, 309, 331-32, 357, 360-61
The Fruits of Culture (Tolstoy) **4**:453; **11**:466
The Fruits of the Earth (Gide)
See *Les nourritures terrestres*
Fruits of the Earth (Gide)
See *Les nourritures terrestres*
Fruits of the Earth (Grove) **4**:134, 136, 138, 140
Früling in der Schweiz (Huch) **13**:247
"Frustration" (Parker) **143**:323
Frye Street and Environs: The Collected Works of Marita Bonner (Bonner) **179**:17, 27, 31
Fu Manchu's Bride (Rohmer) **28**:280, 300
Il fu Mattia Pascal (Pirandello) **172**:160, 188
Fūchisō (Miyamoto) **37**:268-75
"Fuda-no-Tsuji" (Endo) **152**:202
"La fuente" (Aleixandre) **113**:3
"Fuente Oculta" (Gonzalez Martinez) **72**:146
De Fuerteventura a París (Unamuno) **148**:256
Las fuerzas extrañas (Lugones) **15**:286, 292-93, 295
"Fuga a caballo" (Aleixandre) **113**:5
La fuga in Egitto (Deledda) **23**:33
"Fugaku hyakkei" (Dazai Osamu) **11**:175-76, 184
La fuggitiva (Betti) **5**:66
The Fugitive (Betti)
See *La fuggitiva*
The Fugitive (Galsworthy) **1**:293-95, 303; **45**:52, 54
The Fugitive (Proust)
See *Albertine Disparue*
Fugitive (Tagore)
See *Palātakā*
The Fugitive from Utopia (Herbert) **168**:65
Fugitive Life (Ady)
See *A menekülaio élet*
"Fugitives" (Moore) **7**:492
Fugitive's Return (Glaspell) **55**:241-42; **175**:59, 114, 133, 135-38, 141
"The Fugitive's Wife" (Harper) **14**:258-59, 262
"Fugue" (Nemerov) **124**:259
"Fugue" (O'Faolain) **143**:221, 224, 257-60
"A Fugue in Time" (Abbey) **160**:57
"Fühler und Vorhang" (Liliencron) **18**:214
Führmann Henschel (Hauptmann) **4**:194-95
Führung und Geleit (Carossa) **48**:20-1, 27
"La fuite de l'enfance" (Nelligan) **14**:398
"La fuite de temps" (Nelligan) **14**:398
"Fuji" (Lowell) **8**:230
"Fuji at Sunrise" (Fenollosa) **91**:3
"Fukagawa no uta" (Nagai) **51**:88-9, 104
Fukai kawa (Endo) **152**:213, 229, 234, 240
"Fulano" (Machado de Assis) **10**:291
"Fulfillment" (Dreiser) **35**:73-5
"Fulgentius's Exposition Vergiliana Continentia and the Plan of Beowulf: Another Approach to the Poem's Style and Structure" (Gardner) **195**:127
"Fulguración del as" (Aleixandre) **113**:5
Full Circle (Collier) **127**:244-45, 250-51
"Full Circles" (Wharton) **129**:362
"Full Employment" (Levi) **109**:292
Full Metal Jacket (Kubrick) **112**:187-89, 196-204, 209-11, 224-25, 234, 251, 259, 263, 272, 279
The Full Moon (Gregory) **1**:332, 337-38; **176**:20-21, 34
A Full Moon in March (Yeats) **1**:566, 571
"A Full Professor" (Nemerov) **124**:273
"The Fullness of Life" (Wharton) **129**:352, 360
"The Fulness of Time" (Stephens) **4**:409
"Fumes" (Pirandello)
See "Il fumo"
"Fumizukai" (Mori Ogai) **14**:369, 378-79
"Il fumo" (Pirandello) **4**:327
"Fumo" (Saba) **33**:374
Fun finftn yor (Kahanovitsch) **56**:116-17, 119, 120
Fun meine giter (Kahanovitsch) **56**:118, 120
Le Funambule (Genet) **128**:181-82
"The Function of Metaphysics in Civilization" (Collingwood) **67**:190-91
"The Function of Poetry in the Drama" (Abercrombie) **141**:14
The Function of Reason (Whitehead) **97**:281
The Function of the Orgasm (Reich)
See *Die Funktion Des Orgasmus*
"Fundación" (Arenas) **191**:186
"Fundación mítica de Buenos Aires" (Borges) **109**:11
"A Fundamental Experiment" (Daumal)
See "Une expérience fondamentale"
Fundamental Questions of Sociology (Simmel)
See *Grundfragen der Soziologie*
The Fundamentals of Learning (Thorndike) **107**:379
Funem yarid (Aleichem) **35**:319
"A Funeral" (Lucas) **73**:172
"The Funeral" (March) **96**:261
"The Funeral" (Williams) **81**:434
"Funeral Earth" (Bosman) **49**:19-21, 23
Funeral Games (Orton) **157**:294-96, 299, 305, 324, 326, 329, 352, 356-57, 360
Funeral Lieder (Jarry) **147**:331
"Funeral of the Alpine Guide" (Carducci) **32**:101
"The Funeral of Youth" (Brooke) **2**:54; **7**:121,

"Funeral Oration for Leo Reins" (Schwitters)
See "Rede am Grabe Leo Reins"
"The Funeral Procession" (Ishikawa) **15**:130
Funeral Rites (Genet)
See *Pompes funèbres*
"A Funeral Toast" (Carducci)
See "Brindisi funebre"
"Funere mersit acerbo" (Carducci) **32**:101
"Funes" (Borges)
See "Funes el memorioso"
"Funes el memorioso" (Borges) **109**:37-8, 40-1, 72-3, 76, 127
"Funes, His Memory" (Borges)
See "Funes el memorioso"
"Funes the Memorious" (Borges)
See "Funes el memorioso"
"Fünf Gesänge August, 1914" (Rilke) **1**:412
Funf Orchesterstucke (Schoenberg) **75**:410
"Der Fünfte Oktober" (Heym) **9**:142, 147-48
"Fungi from Yuggoth" (Lovecraft) **4**:266; **22**:213, 241
"Funk" (Service) **15**:401
Die Funktion Des Orgasmus (Reich) **57**:338-39, 341, 349, 356-58, 360
"Funny Darkies" (Stockton) **47**:325
"The Funny Little Fellow" (Riley) **51**:289
"Funzione spirituale" (Pratolini) **124**:332
"Fuori alla certosa di Bologna" (Carducci) **32**:111
Fuori di chiave (Pirandello) **29**:308, 310
"The Fur Coat" (O'Faolain) **143**:235
"The Fur Coat" (Söderberg)
See "Pälsen"
"The Fur Coat" (Stephens) **4**:417
The Fur Country; or, Seventy Degrees North Latitude (Verne)
See *Le pays des fourrures*
"The Fur Hat" (Peretz)
See "Dos Shtraiml"
The Fur Trade in Canada: An Introduction to Canadian Economic History (Innis) **77**:337, 370, 374-5, 384, 391, 398-9
"Fur und Wider den Jazz" (Adorno) **111**:132, 134, 144
Furansu monogatari (Nagai) **51**:87, 98-9, 101-02
"The Fur-Cap" (Peretz)
See "Dos Shtraiml"
Furcht und Elend des dritten Reiches (Brecht) **1**:99, 108; **6**:36; **35**:3; **169**:4
"Furibondo" (Campana) **20**:83
"Die Furie" (Heyse) **8**:116
"The Furies" (Masters) **25**:289
"The Furies" (Sarton) **120**:293-4
"Furit aestus" (D'Annunzio) **40**:43-5
The Furnace (Macaulay) **7**:426
"Furnes" (Rilke) **195**:23
"The Furnished Room" (Henry) **19**:172, 181, 185, 189-90
Furrows and Boundaries (Ivanov)
See *Borozdy i mezhi*
Fürsorgliche Belagerung (Böll) **185**:94-5, 97-101, 105-06, 128-31, 153
Fürstin Russalka (Wedekind) **7**:574-75, 586
Further Confessions of Zeno (Svevo) **2**:554; **35**:356-57, 359-61
"The Further Determination of the Absolute" (McTaggart) **105**:197
Further Diary of a Provincial Lady (Delafield) **61**:128
Further Experiences of an Irish R.M. (Somerville & Ross) **51**:335, 342, 354, 358, 362
Further Foolishness: Sketches and Satires on the Follies of the Day (Leacock) **2**:379
Further Impressions of Africa (Roussel)
See *Nouvelles impressions d'Afrique*
Further Reminiscneces, 1864-1894 (Baring-Gould) **88**:34-5
"Furto in una pasticceria" (Calvino) **183**:92, 224
Furusato (Mizoguchi) **72**:313, 315
"The Fury" (Heyse)
See "Die Furie"
Fury Never Leaves Us (Evans) **85**:43
"Fury of Sneezing" (Schwitters) **95**:327
"Fūryūbutsu" (Rohan) **22**:294, 298-99, 304
"Fushigi ga kagami" (Mori Ogai) **14**:379
"Futatabi geki oronjite yo no hyōka ni kotau" (Mori Ogai) **14**:381
Futatsu no niwa (Miyamoto) **37**:267, 269-70
"Futbol" (Zabolotsky) **52**:378
The Futile Life of Pito Pérez (Romero)
See *La vida inútil de Pito Pérez*
"Futility" (Owen) **5**:362, 370, 372-73; **27**:212, 217-18, 226, 230-33
"Futility" (White) **176**:126
"The Futility of Energy" (McAlmon) **97**:87
"The Future" (Fletcher) **35**:106, 108
The Future in America: A Search after Realities (Wells) **12**:509-10; **133**:323
The Future of an Illusion (Freud) **52**:120-21, 125, 134, 136
A Future of Ice (Miyazawa) **76**:298
The Future of Man (Teilhard de Chardin)
See *L'avenir de l'homme*
"The Future of Our Culture" (Simmel) **64**:360
The Future of Painting (Van Dine) **23**:358
The Future of the American Negro (Washington) **10**:515
"The Future of the English Language" (Matthews) **95**:271
"The Future of the Novel" (James) **47**:152; **171**:146
The Future of University Hall (Ward) **55**:433
The Future Poetry (Aurobindo) **63**:10, 30-1, 34, 36
"Future Religion" (Lawrence) **93**:73, 75-78
"Future Rome" (Merezhkovsky) **29**:246
"The Future Union of East and WEst" (Fenollosa) **91**:2
"Future War" (Nezval) **44**:249
"!Futurian!" (Khlebnikov) **20**:150-51
"Futurist Anti-Tradition" (Apollinaire)
See "L'anti-tradition futuriste"
"Futurist Political Programme" (Marinetti) **10**:325
"The Futurist Synthetic Theatre" (Marinetti) **10**:318-19
"Futuros" (Salinas) **17**:369-70
"Fuzzy-Wuzzy" (Kipling) **8**:201
Fyodor Dostoevsky: A Critical Study (Murry) **16**:329-30, 343, 354
G F Watts (Chesterton) **6**:101
G. K.'s Weekly (Chesterton) **1**:188
"Ga wa Dokonidemo Iru" (Yokomitsu) **47**:388
Gaa paa! (Lie) **5**:324, 330
"The Gable Window" (Montgomery) **51**:204, 208-09
Gabriel Conroy (Harte) **1**:342; **25**:191-92, 199, 224
"Gabriel Péri" (Éluard) **41**:161, 168
Gabriel Samara, Peacemaker (Oppenheim) **45**:133, 137
Gabriel Schillings Flucht (Hauptmann) **4**:196
Gabriel Tolliver: A Story of Reconstruction (Harris) **2**:211
"Gabriele d'Annunzio I" (Hofmannsthal) **11**:307
"Gabriele d'Annunzio II" (Hofmannsthal) **11**:307
"Gabriel-Ernest" (Saki) **3**:370
"Gadan'e" (Tsvetaeva) **35**:402, 404
"Gadji beri bimba" (Ball) **104**:13-16, 45
The Gadsbys (Kipling)
See *The Story of the Gadsbys*
"Gagen to shika" (Shimazaki Toson) **5**:434
"Gail" (Schulz) **51**:316
Gaily, Gaily (Hecht) **101**:57, 59, 65, 74
Galahad at Blandings (Wodehouse)
See *The Brinkmanship of Galahad Threepwood*
Galahad: Enough of His Life to Explain His Reputation (Erskine) **84**:159-67
"Galamb a kalitkában" (Mikszath) **31**:167, 171
"I galantuomini" (Verga) **3**:546
The Galanty Show (Summers) **16**:434-35
"Galar Dúithche" (Moore) **7**:492
Las galas del difunto (Valle-Inclán) **5**:480
La Galère (Genet) **128**:159
"Galeria póstuma" (Machado de Assis) **10**:291, 294
Galgenlieder (Morgenstern) **8**:304-10
"La galilée" (Loti) **11**:355-56
Galilei in Captivity (Brod)
See *Galilei in Gefangenschaft*
Galilei in Gefangenschaft (Brod) **115**:84, 87-8
Galileo (Brecht)
See *Leben des Galilei*
Gallantry (Cabell) **6**:63, 67, 72, 74
"Gallegher" (Davis) **24**:199, 201, 203-06
A Gallery of Children (Milne) **6**:317
A Gallery of Women (Dreiser) **18**:62-8
"The Galley-Slave" (Kipling) **17**:206
Gallimaufry (Wakefield) **120**:333, 348, 355
"La gallina degollada" (Quiroga) **20**:212, 214, 219, 222
Gallions Reach (Tomlinson) **71**:391, 394, 397-398, 400, 403-405
Gallipoli Memories. (Mackenzie) **116**:250
The Gallonwerps (Toomer) **172**:265, 286, 292-93
"Galloping Foxley" (Dahl) **173**:10
"The Gallows" (Thomas) **10**:452, 464
Gallows Songs (Morgenstern)
See *Galgenlieder*
"The Gallowsmith" (Cobb) **77**:136, 139
Gallybird (Kaye-Smith) **20**:109
Galpa Guccha (Tagore) **53**:352
Gals un sākums (Rainis) **29**:380, 391-92
The Gambler (Betti)
See *Il giocatore*
"The Gambler, the Nun, and the Radio" (Hemingway) **115**:143
"Gambling" (Devkota) **23**:50
"Gambrinous" (Kuprin) **5**:301
The Game (London) **9**:253-54, 261, 265, 277
"A Game at Salzburg" (Jarrell) **177**:125, 129, 196, 216-17
"A Game in Hell" (Khlebnikov)
See "Igra v adu"
Game of Chess (Giacosa)
See *Il partita a scacchi*
A Game of Chess (Leino)
See *Shakkipeli*
The Game of Life (Hamsun)
See *Livets spil*
"Gamecock" (Dickey) **151**:90, 97
Games Authors Play (Calvino) **183**:39
The Games of Night (Dagerman)
See *Nattens lekar*
"Gamesters All" (Heyward) **59**:95, 104
"Det gamla huset" (Södergran) **31**:288
Det gamla och det nya (Strindberg) **8**:408
"Gammelyn, the Dressmaker" (Housman) **7**:361
Gan (Mori Ogai) **14**:374-75, 380-81, 384-85
The Gandavyuha Sutra (Suzuki) **109**:387
Gāndharir āvedan (Tagore) **3**:485
Gandle Follows His Nose (Broun) **104**:98
"Gandytown" (Kornbluth) **8**:217
The Gang (Gladkov)
See *Vataga*
"Gang zum Schützengraben" (Toller) **10**:490
"Gang zur Ruhestellung" (Toller) **10**:490
"The Gangrened People" (Ingamells) **35**:131, 138
"Ganhardine" (Manning) **25**:265
Das Gänsemännchen (Wassermann) **6**:508-09, 517
Le gant rouge (Rostand) **6**:377
The Gaol Gate (Gregory) **1**:334, 336-37; **176**:4, 12, 14, 18-19, 23, 36, 40, 43, 69-72, 81
"A Gap" (Caragiale)
See "O lacună"
The Gap in the Curtain (Buchan) **41**:38, 41, 44
"Gapa guzhva" (Babel) **13**:35
"Gaps" (Lyotard) **103**:218-19

The Garbage Wind (Platonov)
See *Musornyi veter*
"Garchooka the Cockatoo" (Ingamells) **35**:137
"The Garden" (Borges)
See "El jardín de senderos que se bifurcan"
"The Garden" (Gurney) **33**:95
"Garden" (Tynan) **3**:503
"Garden Abstract" (Crane) **2**:117
"Garden by Moonlight" (Lowell) **8**:231
"Garden Chidings" (Guiney) **41**:207
"A Garden Idyll" (Dobson) **79**:30
"The Garden Lodge" (Cather) **11**:100-01
The Garden Murder Case (Van Dine) **23**:355, 360-61
The Garden Next Door (Donoso)
See *El jardín de al lado*
The Garden of Allah (Hichens) **64**:119-21, 123-29, 131
"A Garden of Babies" (Gilman) **117**:76-8
"The Garden of Childhood" (Sarton) **120**:268
"The Garden of Cymodoce" (Swinburne) **36**:339
The Garden of Eden (Faust) **49**:45
The Garden of Eden (Hemingway) **115**:216
The Garden of Epicurus (France)
See *Le jardin d'Épicure*
"The Garden of Gethsemane" (Pasternak) **188**:190-91, 196-97, 225
The Garden of Krakonoš (Čapek)
See *Krakonošova zahrada*
Garden of Love (Kandinsky)
See *Improvisation 27*
"Garden of Nightingales" (Blok)
See "The Nightingale Garden"
"The Garden of Proserpine" (Swinburne) **36**:305, 337
The Garden of Survival (Blackwood) **5**:71
"The Garden of the Forking Paths" (Borges)
See "El jardín de senderos que se bifurcan"
The Garden of the Prophet (Gibran) **1**:326; **9**:92
"The Garden Party" (Mansfield) **2**:449, 454; **8**:278, 280-81, 283-84, 291; **39**:295, 298, 303-05, 309-10, 316, 326; **164**:239, 247, 297-98, 300, 305, 307, 315, 332, 340, 342
The Garden Party, and Other Stories (Mansfield) **2**:445-47; **8**:282; **164**:244
"The Garden Seat" (Hardy) **53**:114
"A Garden Story" (Jewett) **22**:147
"The Garden Vigil" (Naidu) **80**:348
"The Gardener" (Kipling) **8**:195, 201, 208-09; **17**:207, 211, 213-14
"The Gardener" (Kolmar) **40**:175
The Gardener (Tagore) **53**:344, 347
"The Gardener's Boy" (Pickthall) **21**:245, 250
The Gardener's Year (Čapek) **192**:233
Gardens of France (Gonzalez Martinez)
See *Jardines de Francia*
"Gardens of the Sea" (Sterling) **20**:373
Gardens of This World (Fuller) **103**:70, 83, 90, 116
"Gare" (Huidobro) **31**:134-35
"Gare de l'est" (Ady) **11**:15
Gargoyles (Bernhard)
See *Verstörung*
Gargoyles (Hecht) **101**:31, 35-6, 39-42, 44, 47-8, 70-1
"Garīb" (Devkota) **23**:48
The Garin Death Ray (Tolstoy) **18**:384-85
Garland of Songs (Tagore)
See *Gitimālya*
"Garm, a Hostage" (Kipling) **8**:196
"Garrakeen" (Ingamells) **35**:137
The Garroters (Howells) **7**:367, 387
"Der Garten" (Heym) **9**:142
"Garten in Sommer" (Kolmar) **40**:178
"Die Gärten schliessen" (George) **14**:204
"The Garter" (Parker) **143**:284-85, 331
Garth (Hawthorne) **25**:236, 238-39, 241-42, 249-52
Der Gärtner von Toulouse (Kaiser) **9**:181, 192
"Garuda o la cigüeña blanca" (Valera y Alcala-Galiano) **10**:504-05, 508
The Gary Schools (Bourne) **16**:54, 58
"Gas from a Burner" (Joyce) **159**:279
Gas II (Kaiser) **9**:184-85, 189, 191
"The Gas Inspector" (Rohmer) **28**:293
"Gasnut rozovye kraski" (Bryusov) **10**:82
"Gaspar, Melchior, Balthasar" (Thomas) **105**:335
"Gaspar Ruiz" (Conrad) **57**:87
"Gaspard de la nuit" (Donoso) **133**:76, 80, 123, 147, 149, 151, 153-54, 156, 192
The Gaspards of Pine Croft (Connor) **31**:105-06
"I gaspiri" (Lardner) **14**:305-07
Gäst hos verkligheten (Lagerkvist) **144**:164, 200-201, 210, 212
"The Gate" (Muir) **2**:484; **87**:167, 216
The Gate (Natsume)
See *Mon*
"The Gate of Delight" (Naidu) **80**:287
The Gate of Smaragdus (Bottomley) **107**:6
"The Gate of the Hundred Sorrows" (Kipling) **8**:176, 185
Gated notebook (Levi)
See *Quaderno a cancelli*
The Gates Ajar (Phelps) **113**:334-35, 343-46, 355, 363, 368, 394, 396
The Gates Between (Phelps) **113**:338, 345-46, 355
"Gates of Damascus" (Flecker) **43**:188, 192
The Gates of Doom (Sabatini) **47**:303
"The Gates of Dreamland" (Baker) **3**:3
"The Gates of Paradise" (Sayers) **15**:370
Gates of the Dream (Aleixandre) **113**:47
The Gates of Wrath (Bennett) **5**:37, 45; **20**:18
"The Gateway of the Monster" (Hodgson) **13**:236
Gathered Leaves from the Prose of Mary Coleridge (Coleridge) **73**:7-9
Gathering Evidence: A Memoir (Bernhard) **165**:92-93, 96
The Gathering Storm (Churchill) **113**:100-03, 162, 185
"La gatita de Mari-Ramos que halaga con la cola y araña con las manos" (Palma) **29**:256
Gats (Kaiser) **9**:174
The Gaucho War (Lugones)
See *La guerra gaucha*
The Gaudy Empire (Neumann) **100**:316-17
Gaudy Life (Leino)
See *Elämän koreus*
Gaudy Night (Sayers) **2**:528-32, 536; **15**:370-72, 379-82, 387, 390-94
Gauguin und Van Gogh (Sternheim) **8**:379-81
A Gauntlet (Bjoernson)
See *En hanske*
"A gavallérok" (Mikszath) **31**:167, 172-73
"Gave Proof through the Night" (Burroughs) **121**:132
The Gaverocks: A Tale of the Cornish Coast (Baring-Gould) **88**:12-4, 24
"Gavin O'Leary" (Collier) **127**:259
"Gavon's Eve" (Benson) **27**:17, 19
"A Gay Adventure" (Zoshchenko)
See "A Gay Little Episode"
The Gay Crusader (Connor) **31**:113-14
The Gay Genius: The Life and Times of Su Tungpo (Lin) **149**:323, 345
Gay Hunter (Gibbon) **4**:129-30
"A Gay Little Episode" (Zoshchenko) **15**:499
The Gay Lord Quex (Pinero) **32**:389, 393, 398, 412, 414
The Gay Science (Nietzsche)
See *Die Fröhliche Wissenschaft*
Gays under the Cuban Revolution (Arenas) **191**:177
"Gaze on Me" (Gogarty) **15**:101
"Gazella Dorcas" (Rilke) **195**:296, 299-300
"Die Gazelle" (Rilke) **195**:230, 296-300
"Gazetnoe obyavlenie" (Guro) **56**:133
Gde moi dom? (Balmont) **11**:38
Gdziekolwiek ziemia (Borowski) **9**:22
Gea's Easter (Pirandello)
See *Pasqua di Gea*
"Das Gebell" (Bachmann) **192**:78, 82-83
"Gebet" (Heym) **9**:152
"Gebet" (Lasker-Schueler) **57**:298, 303
"Das Gebet" (Lasker-Schueler) **57**:298
"Die Gebete" (Rilke) **195**:175-76, 181
Die Gebete (Rilke) **195**:263
"Gebrauchsanweisung" (Horvath) **45**:95, 105-06, 109-110
Gebrauchslyrik (Brecht) **1**:103
"Gebruiksaanwijzing der lyriek" (van Ostaijen) **33**:417
"Geburt" (Trakl) **5**:456
Die Geburt der Tragödie aus dem Geist der Musik (Nietzsche) **10**:353-54, 359, 366-67, 372, 378, 385, 393-94, 396-98; **18**:340, 342, 344-46, 351; **55**:341, 360, 362
Die Geburt der Venus (Heyse) **8**:119
"The Gecko's Belly" (Calvino) **183**:46, 50
Gedakht (Kahanovitsch) **56**:109-10, 120
"Gedali" (Babel) **2**:22, 31; **13**:22-3, 32; **171**:10, 21, 34, 38, 44, 74, 76, 82-84
Gedanken im Kriege (Mann) **14**:338; **60**:352; **168**:174
Gedanken un motiven (Kahanovitsch) **56**:117
Gedenkrede auf Wolfgang Amadé Mozart (Beer-Hofmann) **60**:36
"Gedicht 25" (Schwitters) **95**:296, 326
Gedichte (Huch) **13**:253
Gedichte (Walser) **18**:425
Gedichte, 1902-1943 (Lasker-Schueler) **57**:297
Gedichte aus den Jahren, 1908-1945 (Werfel) **8**:471
Gedichte der Gefangenen (Toller) **10**:489, 491
Gedlöcke (Raabe) **45**:192
"Geese" (Aleichem)
See "Genz"
"The Geese" (Sarton) **120**:273
The Geese of Bützow (Raabe) **45**:193, 203
"Gefallen" (Mann) **35**:259; **44**:153-54, **168**:184, 186
"Der gefallene Engel" (Lasker-Schueler) **57**:317, 328
"Gefangener reicht dem Tod die Hand" (Toller) **10**:491
"Gefangener und Tod" (Toller) **10**:491
"Gefsimanskaja noe" (Shestov) **56**:278
"Gehazi" (Kipling) **8**:191; **17**:196
Das Geheimherz der Uhr: Aufzeichnungen 1973-1985 (Canetti) **157**:37, 62, 96-99, 101
Geheimnisse des reifen Lebens (Carossa) **48**:20-3, 27-8, 30
Geheimnisse einer Seele (Pabst) **127**:312, 337-40, 342-43, 354, 356-58, 362, 374-77, 379-82
"Geheimopfer" (George) **14**:201
Die Geheimwissenschaft im Umriss (Steiner) **13**:446
"Gehemnisse" (Carossa) **48**:21, 25
Gehen (Bernhard) **165**:79
"Der Gehenkte" (George) **14**:200
"Das Gehirn" (Meyrink) **21**:221
Gehirne (Benn) **3**:109
Der Gehülfe (Walser) **18**:417, 424-25, 428, 431
Geijutsu to dotoku (Nishida) **83**:229
Geisha in Rivalry (Nagai)
See *Udekurabe*
Der Geist der Antike (Kaiser) **9**:174, 179
"Geist und Tat: Franzosen, 1780-1930" (Mann) **9**:327
"Gekept" (Kahanovitsch) **56**:111, 113-14
"Das Geländer" (Arp) **115**:37
Der Gelbe Klang (Kandinsky) **92**:27, 48, 83, 140
"Das Gemeine" (Dazai Osamu) **11**:182, 184
"Gemini" (Kipling) **8**:185
"Gemini" (Radnóti) **16**:415
Gemini (Collier) **127**:240
"Gemini, Gemino" (Engel) **137**:102, 104

"Gen Oji" (Kunikida Doppo) **99**:299, 302-05, 307
"Gendai Nihon no kaika" (Natsume) **10**:347
Gendan (Rohan) **22**:307
"Le Genderme incompris" (Cocteau) **119**:57
The Genealogy of Morals (Nietzsche)
See *Zur genealogie der Moral*
"Gen'ei no tate" (Natsume) **10**:344
"De generaal" (van Ostaijen) **33**:417
"The General" (Akutagawa Ryūnosuke)
See "Shōgun"
The General (Forester) **152**:140, 144-46, 163
"General Aims and Theories" (Crane) **5**:188; **80**:125, 183
General Besserley's Puzzle Box (Oppenheim) **45**:132
General Besserley's Second Puzzle Box (Oppenheim) **45**:132
General Economic History (Weber) **69**:324, 355, 380
General Impressions (Delafield) **61**:135
A General Introduction to Psychoanalysis (Freud)
See *Vorlesungen zur Einführung in die Psychoanalyse*
"General Joubert" (Kipling) **8**:200
The General Line (Eisenstein)
See *Staroi i novoie*
The General Morphology of Organisms (Haeckel)
See *Generalle Morphologie der Organismen*
"General Sociology" (Weber) **69**:314
General Sociology (Pareto)
See *Trattato di sociologia generale*
"General Son Ba-yu and Three Physicians" (Miyazawa) **76**:293
"The General Theory of Employment" (Keynes) **64**:202, 232
The General Theory of Employment, Interest and Money (Keynes) **64**:199-205, 209-14, 221-30, 235-36, 238-39, 241, 245-46, 248-50, 253-56, 258-60, 263, 265-67, 271-72, 280-87, 293, 296-99, 301, 303, 304
General Theory of Mind as Pure Act (Gentile)
See *Teoria generale dello Spirito come puro atto*
The General Theory of Relativity (Einstein) **65**:111
General Theory of the Neuroses (Freud) **52**:134
General Theory of the Spirit as Pure Act (Gentile)
See *Teoria generale dello Spirito come puro atto*
"General William Booth Enters into Heaven" (Lindsay) **17**:222-24, 227, 230, 235, 237, 247-48
General William Booth Enters into Heaven, and Other Poems (Lindsay) **17**:222-23, 227
Generalle Morphologie der Organismen (Haeckel) **83**:126, 138, 145-7, 149-52
"The General's Bluff" (Wister) **21**:399
The General's Ring (Lagerloef)
See *Löwensköldska ringen*
The General's Tea Party (Vian)
See *Le goûter des généraux*
"Generous Wine" (Svevo)
See "Vino generoso"
La Genèse (Zola) **21**:456
"Die Genesende" (Rilke) **195**:227, 231
Genesi e struttura della societa (Gentile) **96**:120, 130, 136, 144-45
"Genesis" (Chang)
See "Chuang shiji"
"Genesis" (Lasker-Schueler) **57**:336
"Genesis" (Swinburne) **8**:437-38; **36**:318
"Genesis and Catastrophe" (Dahl) **173**:14
Genesis and Structure of Society (Gentile)
See *Genesi e struttura della societa*
"The Genesis of Cement" (Gladkov) **27**:97
"The Genesis of Self and Social Control" (Mead) **89**:79
"Genet, Mailer and the New Paternalism" (Hansberry) **192**:336
"Genevieve" (Lorde)
See "Memorial II"
Geneviéve (Gide) **12**:147, 159
Genevra's Money (Lucas) **73**:156-57, 159, 162
Gengangere (Ibsen) **2**:218, 220, 223-26, 228-29, 232, 235, 239-40; **8**:142, 144, 148-51; **16**:162, 171-72, 175, 177, 187, 189-90, 193; **37**:223, 225, 232, 242-43; **52**:142-44, 146, 155, 157, 162, 164, 166, 179-80, 183-84, 186-88, 191, 193
"The Genial Epoch" (Schulz)
See "The Age of Genius"
"Das Genie" (Walser) **18**:421
Le génie latin (France) **9**:51
Genio y figura (Valera y Alcala-Galiano) **10**:500-01, 505-08
"The Genital and the Neurotic Character" (Reich) **57**:342
The "Genius" (Dreiser) **10**:165-66, 168-69, 173, 176, 178-79, 182, 184-86, 191, 193, 195, 198, 201; **18**:53, 61-3; **35**:39, 52, 57, 73-4; **83**:3-4, 54
Genius (Lagerkvist) **144**:164
Genius and the Mobocracy (Wright) **95**:394
Genius Loci (Lee) **5**:312-13
"The Genius of Japanese Civilization" (Hearn) **9**:130
"Genkon no shukyo ni tsuite" (Nishida) **83**:230
Gennariniello (de Filippo) **127**:291
"Le genou fendu" (Péret) **20**:196
"Genova" (Campana) **20**:84, 86-7
"Genre" (Obstfelder) **23**:177-78
The Genres of Discourse (Bakhtin) **160**:111
Genroku Chushingura (Mizoguchi) **72**:313, 315, 323, 325
A Gent from Bear Creek (Howard) **8**:137
La gente allegra (Pirandello) **172**:188
Gente conocida (Benavente) **3**:93, 96, 98
"The Genteel Artist" (Chandler) **7**:182
The Genteel Tradition at Bay (Santayana) **40**:362
Gentein Aspromonte (Alvaro) **60**:2, 4-6, 8-12
"The Gentle Breeze Fills the Valley" (Miyazawa) **76**:289
"A Gentle Dying" (Kornbluth) **8**:216
The Gentle Grafter (Henry) **19**:170, 178-79, 190, 200
Gentle Jack (Bolt) **175**:8, 11-12, 16, 18-19
The Gentle Joseph (Kuzmin)
See *Nezhnyi Iosif*
Gentle Julia (Tarkington) **9**:461
"The Gentle Lena" (Stein) **6**:408; **28**:334; **48**:225-27
"The Gentle Savage" (Quiller-Couch) **53**:291
"A Gentleman" (Thomas) **10**:463
A Gentleman Condemned to Death (Feydeau)
See *Un monsieur qui est condamnéà mort*
The Gentleman from Indiana (Tarkington) **9**:452-60, 462-63, 466, 475
"The Gentleman from San Francisco" (Bunin) **6**:43-5, 52-4, 56
The Gentleman from San Francisco, and Other Stories (Bunin)
See *Gospodin iz San-Frantsisko*
"The Gentleman from Shallot" (Bishop)
See "The Gentleman of Shallot"
The Gentleman in Grey (Mackenzie) **116**:205
"A Gentleman of Athens" (Bradford) **36**:56
"A Gentleman of Bayou Têche" (Chopin) **14**:68; **127**:122, 218
"A Gentleman of Fifty Soliloquizes" (Marquis) **7**:440
"The Gentleman of Shallot" (Bishop) **121**:46-9, 72
"A Gentleman of the Old School" (Dobson) **79**:5, 26
"A Gentleman Sharper and Steelman Sharper" (Lawson) **27**:131
"Gentleman, the King!" (Runyon) **10**:425, 432
The Gentleman's Way of Having Fun (Moricz)
See *Úri muri*
Gentlemen at Gyang Gyang (Franklin) **7**:264, 267-71, 273
Gentlemen Make Merry (Moricz)
See *Úri muri*
"Gentlemen of the Press" (Wolfe) **4**:516
Gentlemen Prefer Blondes (Mankiewicz) **85**:111
Gentlemen's Relish (Morley) **87**:140
Gentles, Attend (Morley) **87**:148
The Gentlest Art: A Choice of Letters by Entertaining Hands (Lucas) **73**:168, 173
"The Gentlest Lady" (Parker) **143**:323
Gentry Roistering (Moricz)
See *Úri muri*
The Genuine Sedemunds (Barlach)
See *Die echten Sedemunds*
"The Genuine Tabard" (Bentley) **12**:15
"Genz" (Aleichem) **35**:319
"Geoffroy and Garcinde" (Heyse) **8**:114, 121
Geografi og kærlighed (Bjoernson) **7**:112, 114; **37**:15, 17, 19-21, 29
The Geographical History of America; or, The Relation of Human Nature to the Human Mind (Stein) **1**:433-35, 437, 441; **28**:316, 327-28, 330-32, 334-35, 339-40; **48**:212-17, 236, 248
Geography and Love (Bjoernson)
See *Geografi og kærlighed*
Geography and Plays (Stein) **1**:428; **6**:403, 406; **28**:313; **48**:216, 251
"Geography and Some Explorers" (Conrad) **43**:101
Geography III (Bishop) **121**:3-4, 6-7, 10, 19, 21, 56, 91, 102, 104-5
The Geography of Witchcraft (Summers) **16**:425, 429-30, 432
"Geography on the Jew's Harp" (Coppard) **5**:178
La geôle (Bourget) **12**:69
"Geological Madrigal" (Harte) **25**:190
"The Geological Spieler" (Lawson) **27**:128, 130, 132
"Geologie" (van Ostaijen) **33**:416, 418-19
"Geology" (van Ostaijen)
See "Geologie"
"Geometric and Mechanical Splendour and Numerical Sensitivity" (Marinetti) **10**:325
"Georg Trakl" (Lasker-Schueler) **57**:336
"George" (Adorno) **111**:176
"George" (Tsvetaeva)
See "Georgii"
"George Ancelys" (Bourget) **12**:73
The George and the Crown (Kaye-Smith) **20**:103
George Bernard Shaw: His Plays (Mencken) **13**:357, 386
"George Bowring" (Blackmore) **27**:44
George Chapman (Swinburne) **36**:310
"George Chapman—The Iliad" (Gurney) **33**:97
George Eliot (Stephen) **23**:340-41
George Geith of Fen Court (Riddell) **40**:331, 334-35
George Helm (Phillips) **44**:276, 278, 287
"George Lucy's Grandchild" (Rutherford) **25**:346
George MacDonald: An Anthology (MacDonald) **9**:293
"George Thurston" (Bierce) **44**:45
George Washington (Freeman) **11**:223, 225
George Washington (Wilson) **79**:486, 527
George Washington, Jr. (Cohan) **60**:157, 164, 166, 168, 170
George Washington, Vol. I: Young Washington (Freeman) **11**:223
George Washington, Vol. II: Young Washington (Freeman) **11**:223
George Washington, Vol. III: Planter and Patriot (Freeman) **11**:224
George Washington, Vol. IV: Leader of the Revolution (Freeman) **11**:224

George-Lieder (Schoenberg) **75**:327
George's Mother (Crane) **11**:123-27, 131, 137, 147-50, 160, 162, 165, 167; **17**:68-9; **32**:158-59, 163-65
Georgia Boy (Caldwell) **117**:16, 17
"Georgia Dusk" (Toomer) **172**:274-75, 325-28, 330
The Georgiad (Campbell) **5**:118, 120, 123
Georgian Poetry (Marsh) **99**:354, 363, 366
"Georgia's Ruling" (Henry) **19**:179, 183
Georgie May (Bodenheim) **44**:71-3
"Georgii" (Tsvetaeva) **7**:567; **35**:392, 411
"Georgine Sand Miner" (Masters) **2**:464
Les Georgiques Chretiennes (Jammes) **75**:102, 107, 114, 119
"Georgy Porgy" (Dahl) **173**:14-15
"Gerächt" (Mann) **35**:259
"Geraldine and Jane" (Woolf) **43**:394
"The Geranium" (O'Connor) **132**:363
"Geraniums" (Roberts) **8**:316
"Gerard Manley Hopkins" (Bishop) **121**:48, 50
Der gerettete Alkibiades (Kaiser) **9**:173, 179, 182-83, 185, 190
Das Gerettete Bürgertum (Sternheim) **8**:377
Das Gerettete Venedig (Hofmannsthal) **11**:293, 303
Die gerettete Zunge: Geschichte einer Jugend (Canetti) **157**:19-23, 36-37, 68, 70, 77, 97, 100, 104-10
Der Gerichstag (Werfel) **8**:475, 479
"German" (Mann) **168**:162-63
"German Address: An Appeal to Reasons" (Mann) **168**:178
German Diary (Goebbels) **68**:112-13
A German Fairytale in Four Acts (Zuckmayer) **191**:322
German Garden (Elizabeth)
See *Elizabeth and Her German Garden*
German History (Huch) **13**:247
The German Masquerade Ball (Döblin)
See *Der Deutsche Maskenball*
German Men (Benjamin)
See *Deutsche Menschen*
German Nobility (Raabe)
See *Deutscher Adel*
German Pension (Mansfield)
See *In a German Pension*
German Philosophy and Politics (Dewey) **95**:69
The German Phoenix (Sinclair) **160**:321
"The German Refugee" (Malamud) **129**:109, 159, 165, 193; **184**:165, 237, 243-44, 281, 285, 287, 290-91, 293-96
"Germans at Meat" (Mansfield) **39**:297, 300; **164**:270, 290, 324-25
"Germany and the Germans" (Mann)
See "Deutschland und die Deutschen"
"Germany's Air Traffic Leads the World" (Mitchell) **81**:168
"Germinal" (Baker) **10**:17, 21
Germinal (Zola) **1**:587-90, 593-96; **6**:561-64, 566-70; **21**:421, 423-26, 429-32, 434, 437-42, 452-60; **41**:414-15, 421-22, 425-26, 437-49, 451-54
Gerona (Pérez Galdós) **27**:256, 276, 287
Gertrud (Söderberg) **39**:428
Gesakusha no shi (Nagai) **51**:102-03
Gesammelte Aufsätze zur romanischen Philologie (Auerbach) **43**:60
Gesammelte Aufsatze zur Wissenschaftslehre (Weber) **69**:314, 383
Gesammelte Briefe (Hesse) **148**:162, 164; **196**:335
Gesammelte Gedichte (Ball) **104**:77
Gesammelte Gedichte (Bernhard) **165**:95
Gesammelte Gedichte (Carossa) **48**:25
Gesammelte Gedichte (Lasker-Schueler) **57**:304, 333
Gesammelte Gedichte 1 (Arp) **115**:3-6, 34, 52-5
Gesammelte Schriften (Adorno) **111**:144, 148, 151, 156
Gesammelte Schriften (Hesse) **148**:150; **196**:255, 270, 318, 335
Gesammelte Schriften (Huch) **13**:253
Gesammelte Werke (Brecht) **169**:37-40, 42-44, 57-58, 63
Gesammelte Werke (Huch) **13**:253
Gesammelte Werke (Lasker-Schueler) **57**:329
Gesammelte Werke (Luxemburg)
See *Collected Works of Rosa Luxemburg*
Gesammelte Werke (Mann) **8**:263; **168**:171
Gesammelte Werke (Zuckmayer) **191**:301
Gesammelte Werke in zeitlicher Folge (Frisch) **121**:192, 211, 232, 240
Die Gesammelten Gedichte (Hofmannsthal) **11**:293, 308
Die gesammelten Gedichte (Zweig) **17**:424
Das Gesamtwerk (Borchert) **5**:105, 109
"Ein Gesang der Toten vor neuem Leben" (Werfel) **8**:478-79
"Gesang des Abgeschiedenen" (Trakl) **5**:457
Der Gesang im Feuerofen (Zuckmayer) **191**:279-80, 282-85, 298, 306
"Gesang ist Dasein" (Rilke) **195**:211
Gesang vom Kindchen (Mann) **14**:325, 355-56
Gesang vom lusitanischen Popanz (Weiss) **152**:311
"Gesang Zur Sonne" (Carossa) **48**:21
"Gesänge" (Benn) **3**:110
Ein Geschäft mit Träumen (Bachmann) **192**:144, 147
Die Geschichte der jungen Rendte Fuchs (Wassermann) **6**:510
Geschichte einer Jugend (Carossa) **48**:34
Die Geschichte von der 1002. Nacht (Roth) **33**:352-55
Geschichten (Walser) **18**:421
Geschichten aus dem Wiener Wald (Horvath) **45**:77, 79-81, 83, 87, 89-90, 92-3, 96-100, 102, 107-10, 112-16, 118
Die Geschichten Jaakobs (Mann) **8**:271
Geschichten vom Fräulein Pollinger (Horvath) **45**:91, 93, 108
"Geschichten vom Lieben Gott" (Rilke) **195**:285, 289
Geschichten vom Lieben Gott (Rilke) **195**:175-78, 186
Die Geschichten von Garibaldi (Huch) **13**:253
Geschichtsphilosophische Thesen (Benjamin) **39**:3, 5, 19, 26, 36, 52-4, 61
Geschlecht und Charakter. Eine prinzipielle Untersuchung (Weininger) **84**:288, 290, 293, 301-6, 308, 310, 313, 320, 325, 327, 332, 342, 346, 351-3, 355, 358-61, 369, 371-4, 376-7, 379-81, 383-8, 390-2
Geschwister (Sudermann) **15**:429
Die Geschwister Oppermann (Feuchtwanger) **3**:178, 180-81, 183
Die Geschwister Tanner (Walser) **18**:416-17, 423-24, 428, 431
Die Geschwister von Neapel (Werfel) **8**:470, 477, 480-81
"Das Gesetz" (Mann) **168**:157
Gesichte (Lasker-Schueler) **57**:331
"Gespräch" (Benn) **3**:113
Ein Gespräch (Werfel) **8**:479
"Gespräch über den Dächern" (Borchert) **5**:104
"Gesshützwache" (Toller) **10**:490
"Gestalt at Sixty" (Sarton) **120**:236, 272-73, 304-05
Gestalten und gedanken (Brandes) **11**:68
Gestern (Hofmannsthal) **11**:291, 306, 309
Gestes et opinions du Docteur Faustroll, pataphysicien, roman néo-scientifique (Jarry) **147**:242-43, 259, 264, 266, 268-72, 296-97, 303, 305-8, 311, 313, 330
Gestes et opinions du Dr. Faustroll, pataphysicien, roman néo-scientifique (Jarry) **2**:283; **14**:274, 276, 278-79, 281-82, 285, 287
Der gestohlene Mond (Barlach) **84**:63, 71, 100-1
Die gestundete Zeit (Bachmann) **192**:9, 13, 53-54, 63, 108
Gestos (Sarduy) **167**:198-99, 221-22
Gestures (Sarduy)
See *Gestos*
"Gestures of Death" (Merrill) **173**:254
Get Away Old Man (Saroyan) **137**:170
"Gethsemane, 1914-18" (Kipling) **8**:196, 200
"Getrennter Liebender Gebet zu einander" (Morgenstern) **8**:310
Get-Rich-Quick Wallingford (Cohan) **60**:156-9, 166, 172
"Getting a Job" (Williams) **89**:363, 382
Getting a Polish (Tarkington) **9**:464
"Getting Americanized" (Fuller) **103**:107
Getting Married (Shaw) **3**:393, 403; **9**:428; **45**:210
The Getting of Wisdom (Richardson) **4**:371, 373, 375-76, 379-80
Getting Too-Loose (March) **96**:237
Getting Toulouse (March) **96**:240
Das Gewissen der Worte (Canetti) **157**:62-63, 69; **157**:75, 82-83, 90, 96
"Das Gewitter" (Trakl) **5**:464
"Gewölke gleich" (Heym) **9**:142-43
Dos gezang fun tol (Asch) **3**:68, 72
Gezang un gebet (Kahanovitsch) **56**:117
"Ghanashyam" (Naidu) **80**:343
Ghare-Bāire (Tagore) **3**:484-85, 491, 494, 497, 499, **53**:334
"The Ghât" (Tagore) **3**:483
"Ghater Katha" (Tagore) **53**:353
"Ghedali" (Babel)
See "Gedali"
Ghetto (Heijermans) **24**:287-88, 291-96, 300
The Ghetto (Wirth) **92**:359, 387-8, 390
Ghetto Comedies (Zangwill) **16**:445, 455-58, 467
Ghetto Tragedies (Zangwill) **16**:441-42, 447, 455
"A Ghetto Wedding" (Cahan) **71**:11, 26, 66, 68, 71
The Ghost (Bennett) **5**:45; **20**:28; **197**:20, 104
"A Ghost, A Real Ghost" (Jarrell) **177**:140
"The Ghost at Massingham Mansions" (Bramah) **72**:6
"The Ghost Children of Tacoma" (Brautigan) **133**:3
The Ghost Girl (Saltus) **8**:347-48
"Ghost Hunt" (Wakefield) **120**:350
The Ghost Kings (Haggard) **11**:243
"A Ghost May Come" (Ginsberg) **120**:77
"The Ghost of the Helen of Troy" (Heyward)
See "Gamesters All"
"The Ghost of the Valley" (Dunsany) **59**:25
The Ghost Pirates (Hodgson) **13**:229-30, 232-33, 236-37
"The Ghost Ship" (Middleton) **56**:174-76, 182, 184, 195-96
The Ghost Ship (Lewton) **76**:197-99, 205, 210, 220
The Ghost Ship, and Other Stories (Middleton) **56**:173-74, 176, 192, 194
The Ghost Sonata (Strindberg)
See *Spöksonaten*
"A Ghost Speaks" (Marquis) **7**:436
Ghost Stories (Wakefield) **120**:349, 356-57
Ghost Stories of an Antiquary (James) **6**:205, 210, 216
"A Ghost Story" (Jarrell) **177**:155
"Ghost Town" (Prado)
See "El pueblo muerto"
"The Ghost Wife" (Eastman) **55**:172
"Ghostkeeper" (Lowry) **6**:254; **40**:261, 268
A Ghostly Company (Wakefield) **120**:349, 356-57
"The Ghostly Kiss" (Hearn) **9**:136
The Ghostly Tales of Henry James (James) **24**:352
"Ghosts" (Cullen) **4**:43; **37**:146, 148, 157, 168
"Ghosts" (Lawrence) **93**:98
Ghosts (Ibsen)
See *Gengangere*
Ghosts (Wharton) **129**:364
"Ghosts as Cocoons" (Stevens) **45**:309

"Ghosts at Chaldon Herring" (Warner) **131**:311
"Ghosts at #9" (Burroughs) **121**:142
"Ghosts Dancing" (Graham) **19**:121
"Ghosts in My Tower" (Stockton) **47**:327
"Ghosts of a Lunatic Asylum" (Benét) **7**:79
"The Ghosts of the Buffaloes" (Lindsay) **17**:226
"Ghosts of the Great White Way" (Runyon) **10**:429
"The Ghosts on the Roof" (Chambers) **129**:45
Ghosts on the Roof: Selected Journalism of Whittaker Chambers, 1931-59 (Chambers) **129**:41, 46-7,
"Ghoul's Wharf" (Bishop) **103**:2
"La giachetta di cuoio" (Pavese) **3**:340
Giacomo Joyce (Joyce) **159**:279-81, 284-85
"Giambattista Vico, Discoverer of Esthetic Science" (Croce)
See "Giambattista Vico scorpitore della scienza estetica"
"Giambattista Vico scorpitore della scienza estetica" (Croce) **37**:122
"Giambattista Vico und die Idee der Philologie" (Auerbach) **43**:62-3
Giambi ed epodi (Carducci) **32**:90-1, 97, 100-01, 107-08
The Giant, and Other Stories (Molnár)
See *Az orias es Egyeb Elbeszelesek*
Giant Buddy Holly (Holly) **65**:144, 150
Giant of Mars (Burroughs) **2**:81
"Giant Snail" (Bishop) **121**:6, 63
"Giant Toad" (Bishop) **121**:6, 63, 65
"The Giant Wistaria" (Gilman) **117**:93
"The Giant's Heart" (MacDonald) **113**:212
Giants in the Earth: A Saga of the Prairie (Rölvaag) **17**:321-27, 330, 332-47
"La giara" (Pirandello) **29**:300
"Giardino autunnale" (Campana) **20**:88
"Gib'at hahol" (Agnon)
See "Gib'ath ha-hol"
"Gib'ath ha-hol" (Agnon) **151**:22
"Gibberish" (Coleridge) **73**:21
"Gibel Atlantidy" (Khlebnikov) **20**:130-31, 139, 144
Gideon Planish (Lewis) **13**:339, 343, 350; **39**:249
Gideon's Band (Cable) **4**:27, 31
"Gier" (Bachmann) **192**:78, 83
"A Gift" (Lowell) **1**:372; **8**:230
"The Gift" (Naidu) **80**:315
"The Gift" (Sinclair) **3**:441
The Gift (Nabokov)
See *Dar*
A Gift from the Grave (Wharton) **149**:141
"The Gift of God" (Robinson) **5**:418; **101**:99, 103-04, 134
"The Gift of Harun Al-Rashid" (Yeats) **11**:520; **31**:407; **93**:353
"The Gift of India" (Naidu) **80**:296
"The Gift of the Emperor" (Hornung) **59**:120
"The Gift of the Magi" (Henry) **19**:170, 172
"Gift of the Muses" (Mansfield) **164**:337
The Gift of the Wise Bees (Sologub)
See *Dar mudrykh pchol*
Giftas (Strindberg)
See *Spöksonaten*
"The Gifted" (Beer-Hofmann)
See "Die Beschenkten"
"Gifts" (Stringer) **37**:341
"The Gifts Demanded" (Fletcher) **35**:107
Gifts of Fortune: With Some Hints to Those about to Travel (Tomlinson) **71**:386, 390-391, 395, 400
"Gifts of Oblivion" (Fisher)
See "A Sleep and a Forgetting"
I giganta della montagna (Pirandello) **29**:319-20; **172**:150, 161-62, 164, 193
Gigi (Colette) **5**:169; **16**:115, 128, 137
Le Gigot, sa vie et son oeuvre (Péret) **20**:184, 197
"Gila Bend" (Dickey) **151**:175
Gilda (Hecht) **101**:76, 89
The Gilded Age (Twain) **6**:457, 462, 467, 476; **12**:430, 432, 437; **19**:355, 359; **36**:358, 407, 409; **48**:335; **161**:225, 289, 321
The Gilded Chair (Post) **39**:339, 347
"The Gilded Six-Bits" (Hurston) **131**:72
Giles Corey, Yeoman (Freeman) **9**:63
Gilles (Drieu la Rochelle) **21**:21-2, 30, 34, 36, 40
Gilles de Raíz (Huidobro) **31**:123
Gilles und Jeanne (Kaiser) **9**:173
Gillets Hemlighet, the Secret of the Guild (Strindberg) **8**:406
"Gilui we-chisui be-lashon" (Bialik) **25**:61, 65
"Gimnazye" (Aleichem) **1**:32; **35**:303
"Gin and Goldenrod" (Lowry) **6**:240
"Gina from the Chinatown" (Burke) **63**:130
"Gīne Gīt" (Devkota) **23**:49
The Gingerbread Rabbit (Jarrell) **177**:155
Gingertown (McKay) **7**:457, 461; **41**:318, 328-30, 336, 342
Der gingganz (Morgenstern) **8**:307
"Ginkgoes in Fall" (Nemerov) **124**:259
Ginseng (Prishvin)
See *Zhen'-shen': koren' zhizni*
"Giochi senza fine" (Calvino) **183**:159-60
"La Gioconda" (Field) **43**:166-67
La Gioconda (D'Annunzio) **6**:129-30; **40**:6-8, 10
"Giolittismo ideale" (Levi) **125**:233
Gion Festival Music (Mizoguchi) **72**:313-14, 324-25
Gion no Shimai (Mizoguchi) **72**:314, 316, 319, 324, 328, 335
"Giordano Bruno giudicato da Arturo Schopenhauer" (Svevo) **35**:362
"Giorgio Ohnet" (Svevo) **35**:363
Giornale di guerra e di prigionia (Gadda) **144**:96, 124-25, 144
"Giornata" (Calvino) **183**:161
La giornata d'uno scrutatore (Calvino) **183**:96, 118-20, 122-23, 187, 192-95, 208, 213, 229, 238, 243-45
"Un giorno, Adamo" (Calvino) **183**:159
Giovani (Tozzi) **31**:314
Giovanni Episcopo (D'Annunzio) **6**:127, 133, 144; **40**:4
"Giovanni Moroni" (Apollinaire) **51**:48
"Gipsy" (Lawrence) **93**:12
Gipsy Ballads (Lorca)
See *Primer romancero gitano*
"The Giraffe" (Gumilev) **60**:264
Girard (Bradford) **36**:62
"Girdab" (Hedāyat) **21**:71
"Girgenti" (Percy) **84**:199
"Girl" (Kolmar) **40**:175
The Girl and Her Trust (Griffith) **68**:250
"The Girl and the Habit" (Henry) **19**:173
The Girl at Cobhurst (Stockton) **47**:318, 324-25, 327
"A Girl at Twilight" (Roberts) **68**:337
"Girl Child" (Benét) **7**:75
Girl Crazy (Mankiewicz) **85**:147
A Girl Detective (Wallace) **57**:399
"The Girl Dreams That She Is Giselle" (Jarrell) **177**:152
"Girl Drowned in a Well" (García Lorca) **197**:208
The Girl From Chicago (Micheaux) **76**:273
"The Girl from Down-Town" (Glaspell) **175**:52
The Girl from Farris's (Burroughs) **32**:58
"The Girl from Galt" (Engel) **137**:107
The Girl from Hollywood (Burroughs) **32**:58
The Girl from Maxim's (Feydeau)
See *La dame de chez Maxim*
The Girl from the Big Horn Country (Chase) **124**:27
The Girl from the Marsh Croft (Lagerloef) **36**:238
"Girl Held Without Bail" (Walker) **129**:306
The Girl I Left Behind (Endo) **152**:229, 234, 239
The Girl I Left behind Me (Belasco) **3**:86, 90
"A Girl in a Library" (Jarrell) **177**:131-32, 140, 143, 155, 169, 172, 176, 178-79, 207, 216, 218, 254
"Girl in a Nightgown" (Stevens) **12**:360
The Girl in Blue (Wodehouse) **108**:371
"The Girl in the Pink Hat" (Gilman) **9**:113
"The Girl of My Dreams" (Malamud) **129**:68, 74; **184**:265-66, 269
The Girl of the Golden West (Belasco) **3**:86-7, 90-1
A Girl of the Limberlust (Porter) **21**:261-63, 265, 267, 271-72, 275-76
"Girl on My Mind" (Holly) **65**:148
The Girl That Water the Sweetbasil and the Inquisitive Prince (García Lorca) **181**:82
"The Girl, the Horse, and the Hounds" (Adams) **56**:8
"The Girl the Prince Liked" (Fitzgerald) **52**:59-61
"Girl to Soldier on Leave" (Rosenberg) **12**:288, 293, 299, 312
The Girl Who Stayed at Home (Griffith) **68**:169-70
"The Girl Who Went to Ailey" (Stringer) **37**:329
"A Girl with Ambition" (Callaghan) **145**:255
"The Girl With Talent" (Fitzgerald) **52**:59, 61-2
"The Girl with the Silver Eyes" (Hammett) **187**:78, 82, 85, 132
Girls and Boys (Pinero) **32**:412
"Girls and the Land" (Gilman) **37**:216
"Girl's Letter" (Meynell) **6**:299
"A Girl's Thought" (Rosenberg) **12**:311
"Girolamo Savonarola" (Herzl) **36**:154
The Girondin (Belloc) **18**:27
"Giselheer dem Knaben" (Lasker-Schueler) **57**:320, 331
"Giselheer dem Tiger" (Lasker-Schueler) **57**:320
Gitabitan (Tagore) **53**:337-38
Gitāli (Tagore) **3**:491; **53**:338
"La gitana" (Crowley) **7**:206
"Gitanette" (Colette) **16**:139
Gitanjali (Tagore) **3**:481, 484, 491; **53**:333-35, 341-45, 347
Gitimālya (Tagore) **3**:491; **53**:341
"Le giton" (Apollinaire) **51**:20
Giudizio universale (Papini) **22**:286
"Give" (Frank) **17**:114
"Give Me Liberty" (Lane) **177**:275, 286
"Give My Regards to Broadway" (Cohan) **60**:162-3, 165, 167, 172
The Giver of Souls (Nervo) **11**:403
The Givers (Freeman) **9**:73
"Giving a Son to the Sea" (Dickey) **151**:101
Giving and Receiving: Essays and Fantasies (Lucas) **73**:159, 162, 170
La glace à trois faces (Epstein) **92**:2
The Glacier (Jensen)
See *Bræen*
"The Glacier Meadows" (Muir) **28**:257
En glad gut (Bjoernson) **7**:101-02, 105-08, 110, 112-13, 117; **37**:3, 5-6, 17, 22-24
Gladiator-at-Law (Kornbluth) **8**:213, 215, 218
"Gladiators" (La Guma) **140**:204-5, 236-37, 262
"Gladius Dei" (Mann) **2**:429, 432; **14**:350; **168**:173
"Glahn's Death" (Hamsun) **49**:137-45, 162-63, 167
Le glaive et le bandeau (Rod) **52**:325
"Glamorgan" (Thomas) **10**:459
"The Glamour of the Snow" (Blackwood) **5**:74
"Glans en verval van een politiek man" (van Ostaijen) **33**:412
Das Glasperlenspiel (Hesse) **148**:137-87; **196**:250, 254, 258, 266, 269, 274, 276, 278, 295, 305, 330, 333
The Glass Bead Game (Hesse)
See *Das Glasperlenspiel*
"Glass Blower of Venice" (Malamud) **129**:82-3; **184**:185-86, 188, 202
The Glass Cape (Nezval)
See *Skleněný havelok*

"Glass Dialectic" (Nemerov) **124**:313
The Glass Havelock (Nezval)
See *Skleněný havelok*
The Glass Key (Hammett) **187**:45, 49, 51, 56, 58, 60, 77, 79, 81, 90-5, 101, 103, 106-07, 110, 133, 138-39, 141, 145-47, 149-52, 213
The Glass Mender and Other Stories (Baring) **8**:42
"A Glass of Beer" (Stephens) **4**:416, 421
"A Glass of Water" (Sarton) **120**:304
"The Glass of Water" (Stevens) **45**:283
"A Glass of Wine" (La Guma) **140**:204-5, 208, 220, 235
The Glass Slipper (Molnár)
See *Az üvegcipő*
The Glass Wall (Delafield) **61**:133-4
"The Glass Window" (Ishikawa) **15**:126
The Glassy Sea (Engel) **137**:117, 119, 123-26, 128-30, 132-33
"Der glaube" (Morgenstern) **8**:306
Glaube Liebe Hoffnung (Horvath) **45**:77, 81, 83, 92, 97-100, 110-12, 115-17
"Glauco" (Saba) **33**:372
"Glaza" (Bryusov) **10**:82
"The Gleaner" (Papadiamantis) **29**:272-73
"Gleaning" (Jarrell) **177**:177-78
"Gleba" (Vallejo) **56**:311, 316
"Glenasmole" (Gogarty) **15**:108
Glengarry School Days (Connor) **31**:106-07, 111, 116
The Glimpse (Bennett) **197**:40-2, 52, 104
"A Glimpse" (Wharton) **129**:346
The Glimpse (Bennett) **5**:36, 38, 43, 46; **20**:28
A Glimpse of America (Stoker) **144**:285-86, 288, 307
"A Glimpse of Tendencies" (Hearn) **9**:130
"Glimpses of New England" (Forten) **16**:147
The Glimpses of the Moon (Wharton) **3**:561, 573, 580; **9**:542-43; **129**:350, 363
Glimpses of Unfamiliar Japan (Hearn) **9**:119, 125, 128-30
Glinda of Oz (Baum) **7**:22, 24-5, 27; **132**:12, 16, 81, 101-3
"Glinyanyy dom v̇ uyezdnom sadu" (Platonov) **14**:413, 422
"Glissez, M'Sieu Kellee, Glissez" (Williams) **89**:374, 384
The Glittering Gate (Dunsany) **2**:138-39, 143-45; **59**:5-7, 20, 26
"Glocke" (Kandinsky) **92**:67
"Glockenklang" (Raabe) **45**:189
Glockenlieder (Spitteler) **12**:348
Glocken-und Gras-lieder (Spitteler) **12**:350
"The Gloom" (Johnson) **19**:246
La gloria (D'Annunzio) **6**:137; **40**:9
Gloria (Pérez Galdós) **27**:244, 246, 249, 252, 254-58, 266, 271-74
"Gloria tropical" (Quiroga) **20**:214, 216-17
"Gloriana Dying" (Warner) **131**:311
"The Gloriosa Lily" (Naidu) **80**:315
"The Glorious Survivors" (Coppard) **5**:177
Glory (Nabokov) **108**:108-11, 179
"Glory in the Daytime" (Parker) **143**:314, 332
"The Glory of Grey" (Chesterton) **1**:184
"Glory of Hueless Skies" (Rosenberg) **12**:310
The Glory of the Conquered (Glaspell) **55**:241-43, 246
The Glory of the Conquered: The Story of a Great Love (Glaspell) **175**:52, 54-55, 57-59
"The Glory of the Day Was in Her Face" (Johnson) **3**:241
The Glory of the Nightingales (Robinson) **5**:406, 411; **101**:184-85, 189
"The Glory of Venice" (Chambers) **129**:48
"The Glory That Was Sion's" (Evans) **85**:15
"Glottalized continuants in Navaho" (Sapir) **108**:257
"Gloucester Harbor" (Guiney) **41**:203, 206
"Gloucester Moors" (Moody) **105**:224, 234, 237-38, 240, 246, 252-55, 259, 267
A Glove (Bjoernson)
See *En hanske*
Glück im Winkel (Sudermann) **15**:430
Das Glück von Rothenburg (Heyse) **8**:121
Die gluckliche Hand (Schoenberg) **75**:298, 300, 302, 312, 320-22, 332, 345-46, 363, 369, 371, 410
"Gnomes" (Nemerov) **124**:182
Gnomes and Occasions (Nemerov) **124**:187, 189, 192, 195, 197, 255-57, 277, 304
"Go Down Death" (Johnson) **3**:243; **19**:211; **175**:254, 256
"Go Down, Moses" (Faulkner) **141**:160, 163-64
Go Down, Moses and Other Stories (Faulkner) **141**:39, 58-59, 100-1, 103-5, 112-13, 115, 156-60, 163-65, 169, 172-74, 176; **170**:112, 134, 162, 166, 171-72, 175, 177-78, 183-85, 195-96, 209, 211, 213, 215-16, 223, 230, 242, 244
"Go East, Young Man" (Lewis) **4**:257
"Go, Man, Go!" (Jarrell) **177**:239
The Goal Attained (Bernhard)
See *Am Ziel*
"The Goat" (Saba)
See "La capra"
A Goat for Azazel (Fisher) **140**:157, 186
"The Goat Paths" (Stephens) **4**:416
Goat Song (Werfel)
See *Bocksgesang*
"Goatherd at Luncheon" (Calvino)
See "Pranzo con un pastore"
La gobernadora (Benavente) **3**:97-8, 100
The Goblet of Blizzards (Bely)
See *Kubok metelej: Chetviortiia simfoniia*
"The Goblin Laugh" (Markham) **47**:279
Goblins and Pagodas (Fletcher) **35**:94, 97, 102, 105, 113-14
"God" (Jozsef) **22**:160
"God" (Powys) **9**:369
"God" (Rosenberg) **12**:292, 295, 299, 306
"The God Abandons Antony" (Cavafy) **2**:94-7; **7**:164
"God: An Introduction to the Science of Metabiology" (Murry) **16**:335, 352, 355
A God and His Gifts (Compton-Burnett) **180**:122-24, 132, 142-43, 145-46, 186
"God and Magog" (Marquis) **7**:440
God and Mammon (Davidson) **24**:176, 182
God and My Father (Day) **25**:132, 134, 137
God and the Groceryman (Wright) **183**:349, 359, 377, 382
God and the Man (Buchanan) **107**:31, 60, 64, 83
God and Woman (Bojer)
See *Dyrendal*
God Desired and Desiring (Jiménez)
See *Dios deseado y deseante: Animal de fondo con numerosos poemas ineditos*
"God Evolving" (Buchanan) **107**:71
"The God Forsakes Anthony" (Cavafy)
See "The God Abandons Antony"
"God Forsakes Antony" (Cavafy)
See "The God Abandons Antony"
"God Hear" (Lasker-Schueler)
See "Gott hor"
"God ikh zhizni" (Pilnyak) **23**:203, 211
"The God in the Bowl" (Howard) **8**:131, 134, 136
The God in the Car (Hope) **83**:165
"God Is Good. It Is a Beautiful Night" (Stevens) **3**:460; **12**:387
God Knows (Heller) **131**:21; **151**:310, 320
"God Made Blind" (Rosenberg) **12**:286, 295-96, 299, 309
"God of Battles" (Patton) **79**:299-300
"The God of His Fathers" (London) **9**:273
The God of His Fathers (London) **9**:263, 273-74
The God of Quiet (Drinkwater) **57**:128, 145
"The God of the City" (Heym)
See "Der Gott der Stadt"
"The God of the Gongs" (Chesterton) **6**:100
The God of the Living (Deledda)
See *Il dio dei viventi*
"God of the South Sea" (Wen I-to) **28**:410-11
The God of Vengeance (Asch)
See *Der got fun nekomeh*
God or Caesar? (Fisher) **140**:185
God Owns Everything (Pirandello)
See *Padron Dio*
"God Rest Ye, Merry Gentlemen" (Crane) **11**:134, 161
"God Save the King" (Flecker) **43**:192
"God Sees the Truth but Waits" (Tolstoy) **11**:463, 465; **79**:394, 421
"God Send the Regicide" (Lindsay) **17**:226
"God the Invisible King" (Wells) **6**:529
God the Known and God the Unknown (Butler) **1**:134; **33**:50, 56
The God within Him (Hichens) **64**:131
Godan (Premchand) **21**:285-87, 291, 293-97
"God-creation" (Andreas-Salome) **56**:45
"God-Darkness" (Unamuno) **2**:568
"Goddess in the Wood" (Brooke) **2**:59
Goddess of Fire (Burroughs) **32**:59
The Goddess of Sagebrush Gulch (Griffith) **68**:168
"God-Forgotten" (Hardy) **53**:86
"The God-Forgotten Election" (Lawson) **27**:139
Godfrida (Davidson) **24**:180-81
"The Godhead as Lynx" (Sarton) **120**:293
"Godliness" (Anderson) **1**:59; **10**:51, 55; **24**:21, 28, 33-4, 38, 45, 56; **123**:12-13, 75-5, 85
"The God-Maker, Man" (Marquis) **7**:446
"Godoleva" (D'Annunzio) **6**:143
"Godolphin Horne Who Was Cursed with the Sin of Pride and Became a Boot-Black" (Belloc) **7**:42; **18**:40
"Gods" (Cullen) **4**:46; **37**:146, 159, 161-62
The Gods (Alain)
See *Les dieux*
Gods and Fighting Men: The Story of the Tuatha de Danaan and of the Fianna of Ireland (Gregory) **176**:5-6, 12, 28, 43-44
"The Gods and God" (Endo)
See "Kamigami to kami to"
The Gods and Mr. Perrin (Walpole)
See *Mr. Perrin and Mr. Traill*
The Gods Are Athirst (France)
See *Les dieux ont soif*
"The Gods Are Coming" (Södergran)
See "Gudarna komma"
"The Gods Are Here" (Toomer) **172**:277
The Gods Arrive (Wharton) **3**:573; **9**:549, 551; **149**:226
"God's Battle-Ground" (Service) **15**:412
"God's Bird" (Tynan) **3**:502
"God's Chastisement Is This Curse" (Bialik) **25**:50
God's Counterpoint (Beresford) **81**:8
God's Country and My People (Morris) **107**:203, 215, 219, 221-22, 243
"God's Creature" (Hippius) **9**:158-59
The Gods Die, Man Lives On (Babits)
See *Az Istenek halnak, az ember él*
"God's Fool" (Rinehart) **52**:282
"God's Funeral" (Hardy) **53**:88
God's Good Man (Corelli) **51**:68, 76
God's Grace (Malamud) **129**:189, 193; **184**:222, 225-26, 241, 248-60, 277, 285, 287-89, 299-300, 302, 309, 314
God's Images (Dickey) **151**:152, 162-63, 165-67
God's Little Acre (Caldwell) **117**:3, 5, 8-9, 18-20, 22-3
"God's Little Traveling Salesman" (Lagerkvist) **144**:240
"God's Lonely Man" (Wolfe) **4**:521
"God's Mercy" (Malamud) **184**:252
"The Gods of Germany" (Zangwill) **16**:461
The Gods of Mars (Burroughs) **2**:77, 80; **32**:57-8, 66, 68-9
"The Gods of Pegana" (Dunsany) **59**:2

The Gods of Pegana (Dunsany) **2**:136, 141; **59**:7, 17-21, 25, 28-9
Gods of the Lightning (Anderson) **2**:1-3; **144**:3-6, 10, 17, 20, 37, 52, 57-62, 71
The Gods of the Mountain (Dunsany) **2**:137, 139, 142-45; **59**:3, 5-6, 9-10, 12, 14
"Gods of the North" (Howard)
See "The Frost Giant's Daughter"
"Gods of War" (Baker) **10**:21
God's Pauper (Kazantzakis) **181**:276, 278
"God's Remembrance" (Ledwidge) **23**:116
Gods, Saints, and Men (Lee-Hamilton) **22**:186, 188-89
"The God's Script" (Borges)
See "La escritura del Dios"
"God's Skallywags" (Service) **15**:413
God's Stepchildren (Micheaux) **76**:246-47, 254-56, 267-69
"God's Thought" (Lagerkvist)
See *Gudstanken*
God's Tree (Bunin) **6**:45
God's Trombones: Seven Negro Sermons in Verse (Johnson) **3**:240-41, 243, 245; **19**:206-7, 209, 211, 217, 220; **175**:167, 225, 249-56, 258
"God's Truce" (Lagerloef) **36**:240
"God's World" (Millay) **4**:307, 316; **49**:208; **169**:226
The God-Seeker (Lewis) **4**:260; **13**:339
"Godt år fór Norge" (Grieg) **10**:206, 208
"Godwin" (Murry) **16**:341
The Goebbels Diaries 1942-1943 (Goebbels) **68**:87
"Goethe" (Murry) **16**:341
Goethe (Croce) **37**:127
Goethe (Simmel) **64**:338
"Goethe and the Eighteenth Century" (Cassirer)
See *Freiheit und Form*
"Goethe and Tolstoi" (Mann) **14**:357; **21**:168, 170, 190; **44**:165; **168**:117
"Goethe and Tolstoy" (Mann)
See "Goethe and Tolstoi"
Goethe and Tolstoy (Mann) **168**:91
Goethe as Representative of the Bourgeois Age (Mann) **35**:253
Goethe et Beethoven (Rolland) **23**:269
Goethe's "Elective Affinities" (Benjamin)
See *Goethes "Wahlverwandtschaften"*
"Goethes Lezte Nacht in Italien" (George) **2**:150
Goethes "Wahlverwandtschaften" (Benjamin) **39**:3-4, 11-12, 21, 35, 44, 47-8, 59
Gog (Papini) **22**:278-79, 281, 288, 291
Gog and MacGog (Bridie) **3**:134
Gogo no eiko (Mishima) **161**:28-29, 51
Gógol and the Devil (Merezhkovsky) **29**:231
"Goin' Back" (Dunbar) **12**:115
"The Going" (Hardy) **53**:93; **143**:147, 157
Going Abroad (Macaulay) **7**:430; **44**:127
"Going Away" (Hagiwara)
See "Ryojō"
"Going Away" (Nemerov) **124**:177
"The Going Away of Liza" (Chopin) **14**:69
"Going Blind" (Lawson) **27**:125
"Going Critical" (Bambara) **116**:15
"Going for the Milk" (Webb) **24**:473
"Going Home" (Dickey) **151**:114
"Going Home" (Service) **15**:401
Going Home (Callaghan) **145**:232
Going Home (Dazai Osamu)
See *Kikyōrai*
"Going Home (Burlington Route)" (Cather) **132**:131
Going Native (Gogarty) **15**:105, 119
"Going to Headquarters" (Calvino) **183**:221, 223-24
"Going to Norway" (Dahl) **173**:28
Going to Pieces (Woollcott) **5**:527, 529
"Going to Shrewsbury" (Jewett) **22**:147
"Going to the Bakery" (Bishop) **121**:90, 92
"Going West" (Austin) **25**:34
"Gojaste Dezh" (Hedāyat) **21**:76
"Gojiingahara no katakiuchi" (Mori Ogai) **14**:380, 384
"Gojū no tō" (Rohan) **22**:295, 297-98, 300-02, 305
"Gokhale" (Naidu) **80**:314
"The Gold" (Freeman) **9**:72-3
Gold (O'Neill) **1**:385; **6**:327; **49**:252
Gold and Iron (Hergesheimer) **11**:263, 266
"The Gold Axe" (Leroux) **25**:260
"Gold Brocade" (Balmont)
See "Zolotaia parcha"
Gold Coast Land Tenure and the Forest Bill (Casely-Hayford) **24**:132
Gold Coast Native Institutions (Casely-Hayford) **24**:132-35, 137
The Gold Diggers (Aleichem)
See *Di goldgreber*
"The Gold Fish" (Graham) **19**:110, 136
Gold, Frankincense and Myrrh (Cram) **45**:22
Gold in Azure (Bely)
See *Zoloto v lazuri*
A Gold Mine (Matthews) **95**:243
"The Gold Mines" (Vilakazi)
See "Ezinkomponi"
The Gold of Fairnilee (Lang) **16**:264-66
The Gold of the Tigers: Selected Later Poems (Borges)
See *El oro de los tigres*
Gold Rushes and Mining Camps of the Early American West (Fisher) **140**:164, 180-82
"The Gold Standard: An Historical Study" (Adams) **80**:53
"The Golddigger" (Jensen)
See "Guldgraveren"
The Golden Age (Grahame) **64**:54-6, 61-6, 78, 80-2, 87-8, 91-98, 103, 108, 110; **136**:9, 13, 23-27
The Golden Apple (Gregory) **1**:334; **176**:37-39
Golden Apples (Rawlings) **4**:360-61, 365
The Golden Arrow (Webb) **24**:464-69, 471, 473-74, 482-84
The Golden Bird and Other Tales from Grimm (Jarrell) **177**:153
"The Golden Boat" (Tagore)
See "Sonar tari"
The Golden Boat (Tagore)
See *Sonar tari*
The Golden Book of Springfield (Lindsay) **17**:223, 230, 237, 240, 243, 246
"The Golden Bough" (Bishop) **103**:19
"Golden Bough" (Wylie) **8**:530
The Golden Bough (Frazer) **32**:193, 195, 197-98, 200-07, 209-13, 215-16, 219-39, 241-44
The Golden Bowl (James) **2**:246-49, 254, 256, 258, 263-64, 271-74; **11**:321, 326, 332-34, 337, 342, 346; **24**:342, 345; **40**:132-33, 147, 169; **47**:150, 158,161-62, 164, 166-68, 170-71, 173-75, 177, 185-87, 189, 191-95, 201, 207-08; **171**:127, 180
"The Golden Cangue" (Chang)
See "Jinsuo ji"
The Golden Cangue (Chang)
See *Jin suo ji*
"The Golden Cassia" (Naidu) **80**:280
The Golden Chain (Peretz)
See *Di goldené keyt*
The Golden Country (Endo) **152**:177, 213-15
The Golden Doom (Dunsany) **2**:137, 139-40; **59**:6, 9-10, 14
Golden Dragon City (Dunsany) **59**:26, 28
"The Golden Drugget" (Beerbohm) **1**:72; **24**:103
Golden Eye (Fleming) **193**:235
Golden Fleece (Benét) **28**:8, 12
The Golden Fleece (Phillips) **44**:253, 257, 262, 273, 276
"Golden Florins" (Morley) **87**:148
"The Golden Fly" (Zola) **6**:563
The Golden Fruits (Sarraute)
See *Les fruits d'or*
"The Golden Head" (Flecker) **43**:188
"The Golden Honeymoon" (Lardner) **2**:329, 335; **14**:291, 293, 296-98, 306, 309
"The Golden Horseshoe" (Hammett) **187**:64, 84, 134, 136-39, 165, 167
"The Golden Journey" (Moody) **105**:224
"The Golden Journey to Samarkand" (Flecker) **43**:190, 198-99
The Golden Journey to Samarkand (Flecker) **43**:186, 188, 194-96, 210, 214-15
"The Golden Key" (MacDonald) **9**:294, 298-99, 301, 305-07; **113**:199, 211-12, 214, 221, 234, 266-67, 270, 278-80, 286, 289-90, 293-97, 300-02
The Golden Key (MacDonald) **113**:214, 216, 259, 263, 265
The Golden Key; or, The Adventures of Buratino (Tolstoy) **18**:377
The Golden Keys (Lee) **5**:313
Golden Knight (Faust) **49**:36
"Golden Land" (Faulkner) **170**:138
"Golden Leaves" (Faulkner) **170**:128
Golden Morning (Devkota)
See *Sunko bihāna*
Golden Mud (Moricz)
See *Sárarany*
The Golden Peril (Dent) **72**:21
The Golden Pomp: A Procession of English Lyrics from Surrey to Shirley (Quiller-Couch) **53**:291
The Golden Pool (Freeman) **21**:54, 56-7
The Golden Road (Montgomery) **51**:199-200, 213
The Golden Rooms (Fisher) **140**:156, 185
"Golden Rowan of Menalowan" (Carman) **7**:135, 144
The Golden Scarecrow (Walpole) **5**:498, 503
The Golden Scorpion (Rohmer) **28**:282, 292, 301
"Golden Shoes" (Peretz) **16**:398
The Golden Six (Anderson) **144**:36, 39
The Golden Slipper and Other Problems for Violet Strange (Green) **63**:141, 153-54, 156
The Golden Steed (Rainis)
See *Zelta zirgs*
"Golden Stockings" (Gogarty) **15**:103, 109, 112
The Golden Threshold (Naidu) **80**:271, 278
The Golden Vase (Lewisohn) **19**:273, 278
The Golden Vulture (Dent) **72**:36
"The Golden Wand" (Tagore)
See "Sonar Kathi"
"The Golden Whales of California" (Lindsay) **17**:227, 229, 236
Di goldené keyt (Peretz) **16**:396-97, 400
Der goldene segel (Kandinsky)
See *Einsame*
Der goldene Spiegel (Wassermann) **6**:509, 518
Goldfinger (Fleming) **193**:194-95, 198-99, 201, 203, 205-06, 214, 223, 225-26, 228, 234, 236-37, 239, 241-44
"Goldfish" (Chandler) **179**:124
"Goldfish" (Nemerov) **124**:250
Goldmachergeschichten (Meyrink) **21**:231
"The Golem" (Borges) **109**:18-19, 151
Der Golem (Meyrink) **21**:217-20, 230-32, 235, 237-38
The Golem (Meyrink)
See *Der Golem*
The Golf Specialist (Fields) **80**:235-6
Una golondrina (Storni) **5**:454
"Golondrinas" (Storni) **5**:453
Goly god (Pilnyak) **23**:196-202, 204-05, 207-08, 210-12, 214-23
A Gólyakalifa (Babits) **14**:40, 42
Gombo zhebes (Hearn) **9**:135
"Gomborskii les" (Zabolotsky) **52**:367
"Gomez" (Kornbluth) **8**:216
"Gompers and Cobb" (Cobb) **77**:132
"Les Goncourts" (Gray) **19**:160
Gondla (Gumilev) **60**:265-6, 268, 275
"Gondola Song" (Nietzsche)
See "Venice"

Gondolat és írás (Babits) **14**:41
The Gondoliers; or, The King of Barataria (Gilbert) **3**:213-15, 217-18
"Gone" (Coleridge) **73**:25
"Gone, Gone Again" (Thomas)
See "Blenheim Oranges"
Gone to Earth (Webb) **24**:465-67, 469-70, 472, 474, 476, 479, 482-84
Gone with the Wind (Mitchell) **11**:371-91; **170**:1-103
"Goneril, Lear's Daughter" (Čapek) **37**:44
La gonfle (Martin du Gard) **24**:394, 404
"Gongyu shenghuo jiqu" (Chang) **184**:123
"Gongs of Violence" (Burroughs) **121**:127
"Good!" (Mayakovski) **18**:266, 268
The Good and Faithful Servant (Orton) **157**:294-96, 303, 305, 324, 329-30
"The Good Anna" (Stein) **6**:408; **28**:334; **48**:225-26
The Good Apprentice (Murdoch) **171**:206, 221, 259, 285, 301, 304, 308-9, 312, 323
Good As Gold (Heller) **131**:21; **151**:294, 296, 320
"Good Bad Books" (Orwell) **51**:247-48, 267; **128**:288
A Good Bargain (Dunsany) **59**:13, 26
"The Good Blonde" (Kerouac) **117**:255
Good Company: A Rally of Men (Lucas) **73**:158, 170, 173
"A Good Conscience" (Kielland) **5**:276
"Good Country People" (O'Connor) **132**:229-30, 237, 246, 257, 260-61, 287-89, 300, 302, 304-6, 317, 320, 329, 345, 347-48, 355
"The Good Cow" (Platonov)
See "Korova"
The Good Day (Raabe) **45**:201
"A Good Deed" (Herzl) **36**:141
The Good Earth (Slesinger) **10**:446
A Good Enough Parent: A Book on Child Rearing (Bettelheim) **143**:11-12
The Good Fairy (Molnár) **20**:167, 169, 171
The Good Fairy (Sturges) **48**:285, 294, 311
The Good Fellow (Mankiewicz) **85**:109
"A Good Fight and the Faith Kept" (Fisher) **87**:74
"Good Fortune" (Nexø)
See "Lykken"
"Good Friday Night" (Moody) **105**:235, 237-38, 240, 245, 255, 266, 275
"A Good Game Is Over Quickly" (Calvino) **183**:92
The Good Glory (Pereda) **16**:365
The Good God of Manhattan (Bachmann)
See *Der gute Gott von Manhattan*
The Good Hope (Heijermans)
See *Op hoop van zegen*
The Good in the Teachings of Tolstoy and Nietzsche: Philosophy and Preaching (Shestov)
See *Dobro v uchenii Tolstovo i Nietzsche: filosofia i propoved'*
The Good Life (Abbey) **160**:60-61
"The Good Little Girl" (Milne) **6**:314; **88**:243
"Good Luck" (Gogarty) **15**:100, 103, 109
"Good Luck" (Jewett) **22**:117
Good Luck! (Heijermans) **24**:292
"Good Man, Bad Woman" (Stevens) **45**:344-45
"The Good Man in Hell" (Muir) **87**:167
"A Good Man Is Hard to Find" (O'Connor) **132**:229-30, 232-36, 238, 247-48, 257, 259, 263-64, 267, 269, 280-81, 283-84, 289-90, 297-99, 329, 333, 355
A Good Man Is Hard to Find and Other Stories (O'Connor) **132**:331, 366
A Good Man's Love (Delafield)
See *Thank Heaven Fasting*
Good Men and True (Rhodes) **53**:306-07, 311, 317, 321, 324, 326-27
"Good News" (van Ostaijen) **33**:422
Good News (Abbey) **160**:3-4, 15, 45, 80, 85
Good Old Anna (Lowndes) **12**:202
The Good Palóc People (Mikszath)
See *A jó Palócok*
"A Good Prince" (Beerbohm) **24**:109
"Good Reading" (Caragiale) **76**:174
"The Good Rich Man" (Chesterton) **6**:98
The Good Soldier: A Tale of Passion (Ford) **1**:276-80, 282-90; **15**:70, 74, 78-80, 85-90, 92-4; **39**:112-71; **57**:214, 228, 230, 233-35, 239, 243, 247, 253, 256, 260-61, 266, 273, 278-79, 282, 287-89; **172**:4-5, 7, 10-11, 17, 29-30, 36-37, 41, 43, 46-53, 55, 66-68, 70-73, 76, 86-91, 93-94, 96-97, 101-5, 109, 111, 114-15, 118, 122-23, 125
The Good Soldier Schweik (Hašek)
See *Osudy dobrého vojáka Švejka za světoné války*
"Good Tidings" (Tsvetaeva)
See "Blagaia vest'"
The Good Time (Barlach)
See *Die gute Zeit*
"The Good Town" (Muir) **2**:482; **87**:159, 190
A Good Woman (Bennett) **197**:18
A Good Woman (Bromfield) **11**:77, 85, 87
The Good Woman of Setzuan (Brecht)
See *Der gute Mensch von Sezuan*
"Good Year for Norway" (Grieg)
See "Godt år fór Norge"
"Good-By, Jim" (Riley) **51**:285
"Goodbye" (Lewis) **3**:286
Goodbye (Chandler)
See *The Long Good-bye*
Goodbye (Dazai Osamu) **11**:177, 188
"Goodbye! / Dreaming on the Train" (Jiménez) **183**:341
"Good-Bye, Flo" (Cohan) **60**:167
"Goodbye Mother" (Arenas) **191**:193
Good-Bye, Mr. Chips (Hilton) **21**:93-8
Goodbye, Stranger (Benson) **17**:21, 24, 28, 30-1
Goodbye to Western Culture (Douglas) **68**:2-4, 9
A Goodbye—A Handkerchief (Nezval) **44**:240, 244
The Goodbyes (Onetti)
See *Los adioses*
"The Goodly Creatures" (Kornbluth) **8**:216-17
A Goodly Fellowship (Chase) **124**:13-14, 27
A Goodly Heritage (Chase) **124**:13-14
"A Goodly Life" (Bunin) **6**:45
"Good-night, Babette!" (Dobson) **79**:23, 27
"The Goophered Grapevine" (Chesnutt) **5**:135; **39**:70, 72, 84, 95-6, 101, 104
"Goose" (Babel)
See "Moi pervyi gus"
"The Goose Fish" (Nemerov) **124**:147, 153, 160, 180, 291
"The Goose Girl" (Millay) **4**:316
"Goose Island" (Walker) **129**:285
Goose Island (Walker) **129**:333
The Goose Man (Wassermann)
See *Das Gänsemännchen*
"Gooseberries" (Chekhov)
See "Kryžovnik"
Goose-Quill Papers (Guiney) **41**:209-10
Gopa (Valera y Alcala-Galiano) **10**:505
Gorā (Tagore) **3**:494-95, 499
Görbe tükör (Karinthy) **47**:269
"Gore" (Chekhov) **3**:152
Gore i smekh (Khlebnikov) **20**:137
"The Gorge of the Churel's" (Wakefield) **120**:345, 351
"Gorgeous Dream" (Jozsef) **22**:163
"La Gorgue" (Gurney) **33**:102
Goriashchie zdaniia (Balmont) **11**:30-2, 34-6, 39, 42
Gorila (Rebreanu) **28**:272
The Gorilla (Rebreanu)
See *Gorila*
Gorilla, My Love (Bambara) **116**:13-15
Gornii put (Nabokov) **108**:142, 144
"Gorod" (Bryusov)
See "V stenax"
"Gorod" (Guro) **56**:134, 142, 147, 149
"Gorodu" (Bryusov) **10**:83
The Goslings (Beresford) **81**:6
"Go-Slow Strike" (Bosman) **49**:13
"The Gospel according to Mark" (Borges) **109**:72
"The Gospel of Atheism" (Besant) **9**:17-18
"Gospel of Beauty" (Lindsay) **17**:240
"The Gospel of Being" (Balmont) **11**:34
The Gospels (di Donato) **159**:202-3
The Gospels in Brief (Tolstoy) **79**:335, 400
Gospels of Anarchy (Lee) **5**:312, 315-16
Gospodin iz San-Frantsisko (Bunin) **6**:43-5, 47
"Gospodjicd" (Andrić) **135**:17, 84, 90, 97
Gospozha Lenis (Khlebnikov) **20**:136, 150
Gossips (Chang)
See *Liuyan*
Gösta Berling's saga (Lagerloef) **4**:229, 231-32, 234-42; **36**:229-30, 232-34, 238-39, 241-44, 246-48
"Gosudarevyyamshchiki" (Korolenko) **22**:182
Der got fun nekomeh (Asch) **3**:65-6, 68, 71
La gota de sangre (Pardo Bazán) **189**:268-70
"Gotami" (Bunin) **6**:58
The Gothic Bibliography (Summers) **16**:429, 433
"Gothic Novel" (Merrill) **173**:232
The Gothic Quest (Cram) **45**:18-19
The Gothic Quest: A History of the Gothic Novel (Summers) **16**:429-30, 433
The Gothic Renaissance (Jensen)
See *Den gotiske Renaissance*
The Gothic Revival (Clark) **147**:114, 121
Den gotiske Renaissance (Jensen) **41**:300-01, 308-09
"Der Gott der Stadt" (Heym) **9**:147
"Der Gott des Morgens" (Ball) **104**:6
"Gott hor" (Lasker-Schueler) **57**:334
Gott und Gottheiten der Arier (Otto) **85**:319
"Gottes Auge" (Borchert) **5**:109
"Gottfried Benn" (Lasker-Schueler) **57**:320
Gottfried Keller (Huch) **13**:253
Die Göttinnen (Mann) **9**:316, 322-23, 325-27
Die götzendämmerung; oder, Wie man mit dem Hammer philosophiert (Nietzsche) **10**:356, 378, 393; **18**:352; **55**:367, 374, 376
"Le gousset" (Huysmans) **7**:406
Le goûter des généraux (Vian) **9**:530, 534, 537-38
"Goutou-Goupatou" (Papadiamantis) **29**:272
Gouverneurs de la rosée (Roumain) **19**:331-33, 335, 338, 345, 347-48
The Governess (Hunt) **53**:191
"Government in Relation to Business" (Wilson) **73**:300; **79**:487
The Governor's Son (Cohan) **60**:162, 164, 166, 169-70
"The Governor's Vrouw" (Erskine) **84**:168
Goya; oder, Der arge Weg der Erkenntnis (Feuchtwanger) **3**:182-83
A gőzoszlop (Molnár) **20**:164, 173
"Graabølle" (Jensen) **41**:308
Grab and Grace; or, It's the Second Step (Williams) **1**:517; **11**:499
"Das grab des Hunds" (Morgenstern) **8**:306
Grab it while you can (Anouilh)
See *La Foire d'empoigne*
"Gracchus the Huntsman" (Kafka)
See "Der jäger Gracchus"
"Grace" (Joyce) **8**:167, 170; **35**:151, 153-54, 160-61, 164, 167, 190-91, 197; **159**:276, 300, 310
"Grace" (Mistral)
See "La gracia"
Grace in Christianity and Hinduism (Otto)
See *India's Religion of Grace and Christianity*
"Grace of the Way" (Thompson) **4**:438, 440
"The Graceful Giraffe Cannot Become a Monkey" (p'Bitek) **149**:16, 19
"La gracia" (Mistral) **2**:478
The Gracie Allen Murder Case (Van Dine) **23**:360

"Grading, a study in semantics" (Sapir) **108**:257
"Graf Mark und die Prinzessin von Nassau-Usingen" (Huch) **13**:249
Graf Öderland (Frisch) **121**:201
Der Graf von Charolais (Beer-Hofmann) **60**:27, 32
Der Graf von Ratzburg (Barlach) **84**:98-9, 146
"Graffiti 12th Cubicle Men's Room Syracuse Airport" (Ginsberg) **120**:37
"Gráfico de la Petenera" (García Lorca) **181**:200-201
The Grafting (Pirandello)
See *L'innesto*
Le grain de la voix: Entretiens 1962-1980 (Barthes) **135**:146, 148, 150-51, 153, 156, 158-59, 161
Grain of Dust (Phillips) **44**:262, 268, 294
A Grain of Mustard Seed (Sarton) **120**:260-61, 267, 304
"A Grain of Sand" (Harper) **14**:259
The Grain of the Voice: Interviews, 1962-1980 (Barthes)
See *Le grain de la voix: Entretiens 1962-1980*
"Grains and Issues" (Tzara) **168**:275
Grains and Issues (Tzara) **168**:276-77
"Grain's Way" (Khodasevich) **15**:211, 213
"Gramigna's Lover" (Verga)
See "L'amante di Gramigna"
"Gramigna's Mistress" (Verga)
See "L'amante di Gramigna"
A Grammar of Politics (Laski) **79**:85, 104-6, 132, 144-6, 159, 163, 166, 168
"The Grammar School" (van Schendel) **56**:240
"A Grammarian" (Stein) **48**:233
"The grammarian and his language" (Sapir) **108**:273, 279-80, 283
"Grammar—Wireless Imagination—Free Words" (Marinetti) **10**:324
Grammata, Volume I (Palamas) **5**:379
"The Gramophone" (Bosman) **49**:6, 9
The Gramophone (Mackenzie) **116**:228
El gran Galeoto (Echegaray) **4**:97, 99, 102-05
"La gran metropolis" (Darío) **4**:62
El gran torbellino del mundo (Baroja) **8**:57
"Granada, Paradise Closed to Many" (García Lorca) **197**:210
"Granada y 1850" (García Lorca) **181**:187
"Granatovyi braslet" (Kuprin) **5**:298, 300-01, 304, 307
The Grand Alliance (Churchill) **113**:104
The Grand Babylon Hotel (Bennett) **5**:23, 37, 43; **20**:26; **197**:28, 104, 109
The Grand Duke; or, The Statutory Duel (Gilbert) **3**:218
Le grand écart (Cocteau) **119**:81-2
"Grand Hymn of Thanksgiving" (Brecht) **1**:114
Le grand jeu (Péret) **20**:183, 185, 187, 196
"The Grand Jury" (Galsworthy) **45**:33
Le Grand Macabre (Ghelderode) **187**:5
Le grand meaulnes (Alain-Fournier) **6**:12-19, 22-8
"The Grand Old Flag" (Cohan)
See *It's a Grand Old Flag*
"La grand peur des bien-pensants, Edouard Drumont" (Bernanos) **3**:127
"Grand River Marshes" (Masters) **25**:298
"Le grand Sadique à tout casser" (Arp) **115**:32
Le Grand Saigneur (Vallette) **67**:283
"Le grand Saint Nicholas" (France) **9**:57
The Grand Slam (Andreyev) **3**:28
Le grand troupeau (Giono) **124**:43, 68-9, 95, 124
The Grandchildren of the Ghetto (Zangwill) **16**:447, 463
La grande beuverie (Daumal) **14**:89, 92-5
"La grande epoque" (Larbaud) **9**:206
La grande épreuve des démacraties (Benda) **60**:54, 57, 81
La grande et la petite manœuvre (Adamov) **189**:7-8, 13, 19, 30, 39, 42, 52, 56-7
La grande guerre du Sondrebund (Ramuz) **33**:294
La Grande Magia (de Filippo) **127**:265-67, 269-73, 281, 289, 295
"La grande monade" (Teilhard de Chardin) **9**:492
"La grande mouche la moustache et la petite mandoline" (Arp) **115**:41
El Grande Oriente (Pérez Galdós) **27**:257, 287
"La grande ourse" (Sully Prudhomme) **31**:304
La grande peur dans la montagne (Ramuz) **33**:296, 303-05, 308-10
"La Grande Signorina" (Ginzburg) **156**:43
A grande sombra (Sá-Carneiro) **83**:401, 405
Les grandes cimetières sous la lune (Bernanos) **3**:116-17, 127-28
Les grandes époques créatrices (Rolland) **23**:268-69
Les Grandeurs libres (Giono) **124**:97
"The Grandfather" (Nabokov) **108**:52
The Grandfather (Pérez Galdós)
See *El abuelo*
"The Grandfather and the Grandson" (Kahanovitsch) **56**:119
"Grandfather's Three Lives" (Day) **25**:131
"Grandfather-Soldier" (Platonov) **14**:419
The Grandissimes (Cable) **4**:24-37
"Grandma's Jewelbox" (Prus)
See "Szkatulka babki"
"Grandmither, Think Not I Forget" (Cather) **11**:93
Grandmother's Trinket Box (Kuzmin) **40**:197
"Grandparents" (Bishop) **121**:19
"Grand-Pré" (Carman)
See "Low Tide on Grand Pré"
Les grands chemins (Giono) **124**:76-7; 114;
"Les grands jours du poète" (Desnos) **22**:61
Les grands moments du 19e siècle français (Ramuz) **33**:306
"The Grandstand Passion Play of Delbert and the Bumpus Hounds" (Shepherd) **177**:305
"Grandview Point" (Abbey) **160**:43
"Granella's House" (Pirandello)
See "La casa del Granella"
Grangecolman (Martyn) **131**:101, 106
Grania (Gregory) **1**:332, 334-36; **176**:6, 10-11, 18, 34, 37, 39, 43-44, 47, 61-62, 64, 69-72, 81-86
Granite and Rainbow (Woolf) **43**:420
"Granny Magone" (Bierce) **7**:92
Granny Maumee (Torrence) **97**:148-52, 157, 159-61
Granny Maumee, The Rider of Dreams, Simon the Cyrenian: Plays for a Negro Theater (Torrence) **97**:157-58, 163
"Granny's Hut" (Platonov) **14**:420
"Granos de trigo" (Palma) **29**:256
Granville de Vigne (Ouida) **43**:347-48, 364, 366, 369
"Grape Gatherers of Sodom" (Vallette)
See "Les vendanges de Sodome"
"Grape Juice" (Miyazawa) **76**:280
"Grapes" (Knister) **56**:155, 163
"Grapes" (Lawrence) **93**:98, 100, 122
The Grapes of Wrath (Steinbeck) **135**:240-364
Grass (Pilnyak)
See *Byl'yo*
Grass and Tree Stupa (Santoka)
See *Somokuto*
Grass Figures (Hecht) **101**:38
The Grass Harp (Capote) **164**:100, 111-12, 115, 146, 155-57, 159, 168, 176
"The Grass in Lohina" (Mikszath)
See "A Lohinai fú"
Grass on the Wayside (Natsume)
See *Michikusa*
"The Grasscutter" (Devkota) **23**:47
Grass-grown (Pilnyak)
See *Byl'yo*
"The Grasshopper" (Chekhov)
See "Poprygin'ia"
Grasshoppers (Dazai Osamu)
See *Kirigirisu*
Grata compañía (Reyes) **33**:323
Gratia plena (Nervo) **11**:401
"Gratitude" (Akutagawa Ryūnosuke) **16**:22
"Das Grauen" (Trakl) **5**:462
De grauwe vogels (van Schendel) **56**:238-239
"Grave" (Ivanov) **33**:138
The Grave (Palamas)
See *Ho táfus*
Grave Inscriptions (Nezval) **44**:239
"The Grave of Shaka" (Vilakazi)
See "Phezu kwethuna likaShaka"
"The Grave of the Dog" (Eastman) **55**:171
"The Grave of the Horseman" (Graham) **19**:129
"The Gravedigger" (Carman) **7**:138, 142
"The Grave-Digger" (Gibran) **9**:91
"Graven Image" (Bosman) **49**:5, 7
"A Gravestone" (Anwar)
See "Nisan"
"The Graveyard by the Sea" (Valéry)
See "Le cimetière marin"
"The Graveyard of Dead Creeds" (Hardy) **53**:101
The Graveyard of Dreams (Benavente) **3**:94
The Graveyard Rats (Kuttner) **10**:267, 272
"Gravis Dulcis Immutabilis" (Flecker) **43**:188
Gravity and Grace (Weil)
See *La pesanteur et la grâce*
"Gravy Planet" (Kornbluth) **8**:216
"A Gray and Dusty Daylight" (Brennan) **17**:43
Gray Birds (van Schendel)
See *De grauwe vogels*
"Gray Days" (Colette) **16**:139
"The Gray Man" (Jewett) **22**:141
"Gray Stones and Gray Pigeons" (Stevens) **45**:275
"The Gray Wolf's Ha'nt" (Chesnutt) **5**:130, 132; **39**:73-4, 95, 104
Graybeal's Guest (Adams) **56**:9
The Great Accident (Williams) **89**:360, 363, 386, 393
The Great Adventure (Bennett) **5**:27, 43-4; **197**:16-17, 23, 40
"The Great Adventure of Max Breuck" (Lowell) **8**:231
"The Great Adventure: Present-Day Studies in American Nationalism" (Roosevelt) **69**:186
"The Great American Desert" (Abbey) **160**:41
"The Great American Novel" (Wharton) **9**:549; **53**:388
"The Great American Novelist" (Norris) **155**:340-41
"The Great and Little Weavers" (Roberts) **8**:321
"Great Aryan Myth" (Belloc) **18**:25
"The Great Aspiration" (Pascoli) **45**:142
"The Great Auk" (Cobb) **77**:129, 137-8
"The Great Auto Mystery" (Futrelle) **19**:89
The Great Betrayal (Benda)
See *La trahison des clercs*
The Great Beyond (Quiroga)
See *Más allá*
"The Great Breath" (Baker) **3**:4; **10**:20, 26
The Great Broxopp (Milne) **6**:308-09
The Great Buddy Holly (Holly) **65**:144
"The Great Cats' Tale" (Čapek)
See "Velká kocicí pohádka"
"The Great Circus of the Holy Ghost" (van Ostaijen) **33**:422
The Great Clock (Nezval) **44**:241
The Great Code: The Bible and Literature (Frye) **165**:147-49, 152-54, 156, 161-62, 165, 173-74, 188, 193, 198-201, 208-13, 215-16, 227-30, 233-35, 241, 243, 249-50, 254, 258-59
Great Contemporaries (Churchill) **113**:105, 115, 137, 147, 149, 161, 187
The Great Creative Periods (Rolland)
See *Les grandes époques créatrices*
"The Great Dark" (Twain) **185**:327, 329-30
Great Days (Harris) **24**:265, 272, 280

The Great Detective Stories (Van Dine) **23**:360
"A Great Discovery" (Mori Ogai)
See "Daihakken"
The Great Divide (Moody) **105**:222, 224, 232-33, 236, 242, 245-46, 252, 254-55, 259, 268-69, 279
"The Great Doctors' Tale" (Čapek)
See "Velká pohádka doktorská"
Great Expectations (Acker) **191**:12, 32, 36-40, 42-3, 54-62, 66-7, 72, 92, 110, 126, 128-29
The Great Fight (Drummond) **25**:146
The Great French Revolution: 1789-1793 (Kropotkin) **36**:192-93, 197
Great Fugue (Kandinsky) **92**:35
The Great Galeoto (Echegaray)
See *El gran Galeoto*
The Great Garrick (Whale) **63**:339, 378
The Great Gatsby (Fitzgerald) **1**:237-48, 250-56, 258-74; **6**:160-66, 168-70, 173; **14**:147-89; **28**:90, 92, 10 4, 108, 110, 115, 120; **55**:191, 193-99, 201-02, 206-07, 209-11, 214-18, 22 0, 222, 225-29; **157**:112-235
The Great German War (Huch) **13**:241
The Great God Brown (Anderson) **144**:18
The Great God Brown (O'Neill) **1**:384, 395-96, 402, 404, 406; **6**:326-27, 329-31, 335; **49**:252, 257, 285-86, 291, 294
"The Great God Pan" (Machen) **4**:277-79, 284
The Great God Pan and the Inmost Light (Machen) **4**:285
The Great God Success (Phillips) **44**:253, 257, 262, 268, 273, 276-78, 282, 287, 295, 298, 301
"The Great Good Place" (James) **2**:246, 262; **171**:173
"The Great Grey Plain" (Lawson) **27**:140
The Great Highway (Strindberg)
See *Stora landsvägen*
"The Great Homecoming" (Sikelianos) **39**:410, 413-14, 419, 421
The Great Hunger (Bojer)
See *Den store hunger*
The Great Impersonation (Oppenheim) **45**:127-29, 131-32, 135
"The Great Interrogation" (London) **9**:264, 273
"The Great Keinplatz Experiment" (Doyle) **7**:238
"The Great Lament of My Obscurity One" (Tzara) **168**:273
"Great Landscape Near Vienna" (Bachmann) **192**:64
"Great Lesson from a Great Man" (Zweig) **17**:458
"The Great Lover" (Brooke) **2**:55-6, 58, 61; **7**:121, 123-26, 130
"The Great Man" (Middleton) **56**:174-76
A Great Man (Bennett) **5**:43, 50-1; **20**:18; **197**:22, 30, 108
The Great McGinty (Sturges) **48**:272-74, 276-77, 282-83, 287-88, 291, 301, 303-04, 309, 311, 313, 317, 319-22
The Great Meadow (Roberts) **68**:295-96, 298-99, 307-9, 312-13, 316-17, 321, 324, 326, 328, 330, 332, 335, 339-42, 360, 363
The Great Men and A Practical Novelist (Davidson) **24**:194
"Great Men and Their Environment" (James) **32**:347
The Great Miss Driver (Hope) **83**:167
The Great Mistake (Rinehart) **52**:287, 299-300, 302
The Great Mistake (Villaurrutia) **80**:458
The Great Moment (Glyn) **72**:129-30, 133-35, 137, 140
The Great Moment (Sturges) **48**:273, 276, 283-85, 291-92, 295-96, 301, 303, 309, 313, 315-17
"A great moon-meeting" (Arp) **115**:24
"The Great Mouse Plot" (Dahl) **173**:28
Great Oaks (Williams) **89**:378, 396-7
The Great O'Neill, A Biography of Hugh O'Neill, Earl of Tyrone, 1550-1616 (O'Faolain) **143**:230, 269
"The Great Police Tale" (Čapek)
See "Velká policejní pohádka"
Great Possessions (Baker) **47**:25, 27
The Great Prince (Moricz) **33**:250
The Great Prince Shan (Oppenheim) **45**:127
"Great Race" (Lovecraft) **4**:269
"The Great Refusal" (Fisher) **87**:72
The Great Rehearsal (Van Doren) **18**:410
The Great Remedy (Marinetti) **10**:320
"The Great Return" (Carman) **7**:149
The Great Return (Machen) **4**:280, 284-85
"The Great River" (Fletcher) **35**:96
The Great Secret (Oppenheim) **45**:123-24, 128
"The Great Silence" (Zweig) **17**:431
The Great Society: A Psychological Analysis (Wallas) **91**:354, 357, 359-61, 365, 369-70, 372, 379-80, 383, 390-1, 394, 402
"The Great Society, Mark X" (Nemerov) **124**:182-83
The Great South Land (Ingamells) **35**:123-24, 138
"The Great Statue" (Stevens) **3**:448
"The Great Statues" (Bishop) **103**:21
The Great Stone of Sardis (Stockton) **47**:317, 322, 325, 327
A Great Success (Ward) **55**:438
"The Great Switcheroo" (Dahl) **173**:16, 18
The Great Thousand Years (Cram) **45**:19, 21
Great Trade Route (Ford) **15**:75-6, 87, 89; **172**:7
"The Great Transparencies" (Sarton) **120**:266
"Great Types of Modern Business—Politics" (Steffens) **20**:362
"Great Uncle McCarthy" (Somerville & Ross) **51**:356, 360, 380, 385
The Great Valley (Masters) **25**:289, 296, 315
"The Great Visions" (Palamas) **5**:377
"The Great Wall of China" (Kafka) **2**:303
The Great Wall of China, and Other Pieces (Kafka)
See *Beim Bau der Chinesischen Mauer*
The Great Wall of China: Stories and Reflections (Kafka)
See *Beim Bau der Chinesischen Mauer*
The Great War Syndicate (Stockton) **47**:313, 314, 317, 321-22, 325, 328, 331
The Great Well (Sutro) **6**:421-22
The Great White Wall (Benét) **28**:3, 6, 9
"The Great Worm" (Gray) **19**:156-57
Great Writers (Woodberry) **73**:368, 377
"The Greater Chopin" (Huneker) **65**:199
The Greater Inclination (Wharton) **3**:551, 555, 566, 570; **9**:540; **129**:344-45, 353-54, 360; **149**:255
"Greater Love" (Owen) **5**:358, 360, 363-64, 366-68, 374; **27**:201-03, 206, 208-09, 212, 217, 222, 225, 235-36
"Greater Than Love" (Evans) **85**:24
The Greater Trumps (Williams) **1**:523, 525; **11**:487, 493, 500
"The Greatest Drama Ever Staged" (Sayers) **15**:378, 387
"The Greatest of Australia's Dead" (Warung) **45**:419
The Greatest Question (Griffith) **68**:170
The Grecians (Flecker) **43**:193, 206, 209, 213-14, 217
Le Greco ou le secrét de Tolède (Barrès) **47**:55-6, 58-9, 81
Greece in My Life (Mackenzie) **116**:227
"Greed" (Bachmann)
See "Gier"
Greed (Stroheim) **71**:331-332, 334-335, 339-343, 347-350, 357, 359-365, 367-368, 374-375, 377
"The Greek Dance" (Millay) **169**:236
"Greek Easter" (Papadiamantis) **29**:273
Greek Genius, and Other Essays (Chapman) **7**:188, 198
"The Greek Goddess" (Higginson) **36**:182
"Greek Letters" (Grieg) **10**:208
Greek Memories (Mackenzie) **116**:228, 239, 247-48, 250
The Greek Passion (Kazantzakis)
See *Ho Christos xanastauronetai*
"Greek Tragedy" (Lardner) **14**:319
The Greek Vase (Baring) **8**:32
"The Greeks Are Coming!" (Lawrence) **93**:62, 71, 73, 75, 78
"Green" (Butts) **77**:106
"Green" (Lawrence) **93**:125
Green Alps (Crowley) **7**:208, 211
Green Apple Harvest (Kaye-Smith) **20**:101-03, 109-10, 114, 118
The Green Archer (Wallace) **57**:398, 402
Green Arras (Housman) **7**:352-53
"Green Atom Number Five" (Donoso)
See "Atomo verde número cinco"
"The Green Automobile" (Ginsberg) **120**:46, 48, 134-37
The Green Bay Tree (Bromfield) **11**:71-5, 77, 81-2, 85, 87
Green Bays: Verses and Parodies (Quiller-Couch) **53**:289-90
The Green Bicycle Case (Wakefield) **120**:349
"Green Blades of Spears" (Miyazawa) **76**:293
The Green Book of the Bards (Carman)
See *From the Green Book of Bards*
The Green Bough: A Tale of the Resurrection (Austin) **25**:35
"The Green Bowl" (Jewett) **22**:147
The Green Carnation (Hichens) **64**:119-21, 126-28, 130-31
"Green Centuries" (Bishop) **103**:6, 18
The Green Cloister (Scott) **6**:388, 394-95
The Green Cockatoo (Schnitzler)
See *Der Grüne Kakadu*
"The Green Corridor!" (Heidenstam) **5**:251
The Green Death (Dent) **72**:23
"The Green Door" (Henry) **19**:173, 175
The Green Elephant (Baring) **8**:40
"The Green Eye" (Merrill) **173**:234
The Green Eye of Goona (Morrison) **72**:364
The Green Eyes of Bst (Rohmer) **28**:285
The Green Face (Meyrink)
See *Das Grüne Gesicht*
The Green Fairy Book (Lang) **16**:267, 272
Green Fields and Running Brooks (Riley) **51**:273
Green Fire: A Romance (Sharp) **39**:373-74
"Green Flute" (Hagiwara)
See "Midoriiro no fue"
"The Green Fly and the Yellow Squirrel" (Mikszath)
See "A zóld légy és a sárga mókus"
Green Fruit (Bishop) **103**:4, 15, 26, 45, 47
A Green Garden: Kissing Words (Balmont)
See *Zelënyi vertograd: Slova potseluinye*
Green Ginger (Morrison) **72**:364
"The Green Gnome" (Buchanan) **107**:15
"Green Grow the Grasses" (McAlmon) **97**:96, 120, 122
Green Grow the Lilacs (Riggs) **56**:200-03, 205-08, 211, 215-17
Green Hell (Whale) **63**:339
The Green Helmet (Yeats) **18**:442
The Green Helmet, and Other Poems (Yeats) **1**:558, 561; **11**:527-28; **18**:442; **31**:385, 389, 399
The Green Hills of Africa (Hemingway) **115**:189
The Green Hussar (Molnár)
See *A zöld huszár*
The Green Knight (Murdoch) **171**:242-47, 259-61, 266, 268, 285, 298, 302-4, 308-9, 323, 328-29
Green Mansions (Hudson) **29**:137-38, 142, 145-47, 149, 151-54, 159-60, 164
The Green Master (Dent) **72**:38
The Green Meadow (Bely) **7**:59
"The Green Mirror" (Woolf) **43**:407-08
The Green Mirror (Walpole) **5**:503
The Green Mouse (Chambers) **41**:95
The Green Overcoat (Belloc) **7**:38

"The Green Parrakeet" (Lowell) **8**:235, 237
The Green Pope (Asturias)
See *El papa verde*
The Green Ray (Verne)
See *Le Rayon-vert suivi de Dix Heures en chasse*
The Green Ring (Hippius)
See *Zelyonoye kol'tso*
"Green Roads" (Thomas) **10**:464, 470-71
"The Green Room" (de la Mare) **4**:78; **53**:16, 21, 37
"Green Sealing Wax" (Colette)
See "La Cire verte"
"Green Slates" (Hardy) **53**:117
The Green Stick (Muggeridge) **120**:156-57, 182-83, 185, 192
The Green Stockings (Abe) **131**:13-14
"Green Symphony" (Fletcher) **35**:94
"Green Thoughts Are" (Rosenberg) **12**:312
"Green Wood" (Pavese) **3**:335
"A Greendown of the Sun" (Jozsef) **22**:163
The Greene Murder Case (Van Dine) **23**:353-54, 359-61
"The Greenest Continent" (Stevens) **45**:269, 271
"The Greenhand Rouseabout" (Lawson) **27**:139
"Greenleaf" (O'Connor) **132**:229-30, 238, 247, 284, 289-90, 316-17, 329, 345, 349
Greenmantle (Buchan) **41**:36-8, 41-2, 53-5, 64, 66-7, 81-3
The Greenwood Hat (Barrie) **164**:14
"The Greeting" (Akutagawa Ryūnosuke) **16**:24
"A Greeting" (Dobson) **79**:23
"Greetings to the Optimist" (Darío)
See "Salutación del optimista"
The Greetings to the Sunborn Woman (Palamas) **5**:383
Greifenstein (Crawford) **10**:140, 143-44, 148-49
"Les grenades" (Valéry) **15**:468
"Grenadier" (Housman) **10**:257
Grendel (Gardner) **195**:78-159
Grenzen der naturerkenntnis (Steiner) **13**:463
Gretchen (Gilbert) **3**:208
Gretchen's Tochter (Pascoli) **45**:148-49
"La grève des électeurs" (Mirbeau) **55**:291-92
La grève des forgerons (Coppee) **25**:119, 124, 126
"A Grey Day" (Moody) **105**:220, 237, 271
"The Grey Eros" (Baker) **10**:19
Grey Face (Rohmer) **28**:278, 285, 295
Grey Granite (Gibbon) **4**:120-23, 125-26, 128-30
"The Grey Mornings" (Tynan) **3**:504
"The Grey Rock" (Yeats) **31**:385
"Grey Rocks and Greyer Sea" (Roberts) **8**:320
"A Grey Sleeve" (Crane) **11**:158, 166
The Grey Stocking (Baring) **8**:31, 40
Grey Weather: Moorland Tales of My Own People (Buchan) **41**:34, 72
The Grey Wig: Stories and Novelettes (Zangwill) **16**:455
"The Grey Wolf" (MacDonald) **113**:214
Grhadāha (Chatterji) **13**:75, 78, 80-1, 83
"Gribiche" (Colette) **16**:127, 129
"Gridale" (Bosschere) **19**:54, 57-8, 63
"Griechische Dramen" (Kaiser) **9**:179
Griechischer Frühling (Hauptmann) **4**:198
"Grief" (Hodgson) **13**:235
"A Grief Ago" (Thomas) **45**:362-63, 376-80
Grief and Laughter (Khlebnikov)
See *Gore i smekh*
"Le grief de l'homme noir" (Roumain) **19**:346
"Grief of Others" (Davies) **5**:201-02
"Grief Thief of Time" (Thomas) **105**:322
"Grifel' naja oda" (Mandelstam) **2**:403, 409; **6**:260
"Griffey the Cooper" (Masters) **25**:309
The Griffin and the Minor Canon (Stockton) **47**:318, 322, 328-32
"Griggby's Station" (Riley) **51**:292, 300
"Grigia" (Musil) **12**:242, 251-52; **68**:264, 278
The Grim Smile of the Five Towns (Bennett) **5**:42, 46; **20**:17; **197**:13, 102, 106
"Grimace d'artiste" (Södergran) **31**:287, 291
"The Grimoire" (Summers) **16**:434
The Grimoire, and Other Supernatural Stories (Summers) **16**:434
La gringa (Sánchez) **37**:311-15, 317
"The Grip of the Law" (Cobb) **77**:137
"Griselda" (Hippius) **9**:158
Griselda (Hauptmann) **4**:195
"El grito" (García Lorca) **181**:193-94, 197
"Grito hacia Roma" (García Lorca) **49**:82-3; **197**:188, 191, 193, 195-97, 200, 213, 221, 233, 237, 242-43, 251, 256, 258, 274-75, 277
De Grizje Vogels (van Schendel)
See *De grauwe vogels*
"Grizzly Papers V" (Bierce) **44**:32
"Grjaduščie gunny" (Bryusov) **10**:93
Das grobe Wagnis (Brod) **115**:101, 108, 115-17
"The Grocery Store" (Malamud) **184**:282
"Grodek" (Trakl) **5**:461, 464
Der Grosse Krieg in Deutschland (Huch) **13**:244, 247, 251
"Das grosse Lalula" (Morgenstern) **8**:304
Der Grosse Traum (Hauptmann) **4**:205-07
Der Grosse Wurstl (Schnitzler) **4**:396, 402-03
"Grotesque" (Lasker-Schueler) **57**:330
"Grotesque" (Manning) **25**:265, 279
Grotesque Tragedies (Baroja)
See *Las tragedias grotescas*
"Grotesques" (Morgenstern) **8**:304
Grotesques and Fantasies (Zangwill)
See *The King of Schnorrers: Grotesques and Fantasies*
La grotte (Anouilh) **195**:24, 27, 36, 49
The Grotto (Anouilh)
See *La grotte*
The Grotto of Humor (Baroja)
See *La caverna del humorismo*
"The Ground" (Nemerov) **124**:258
"The Ground God and the Fox" (Miyazawa)
See "Earthgod and the Fox"
"Grounds of Validity of the Laws of Logic: Further Consequences of Four Incapacities" (Peirce) **81**:194,287
The Groundswell (Foote) **108**:4, 17
A Group of Noble Dames (Hardy) **72**:237; **143**:72
"A Group of Statuary" (Thomas) **10**:458
"Group of Three Persons" (Hagiwara) **60**:294
Group Portrait with Lady (Böll)
See *Gruppenbild mit Dame*
"Group Psychology and the Analysis of the Ego" (Freud) **52**:112
"Grove" (García Lorca) **181**:83
"The Grove" (Muir) **2**:486; **87**:167, 212
The Grove (Kuzmin)
See *Lesok*
"A Grove and Thoughts" (Miyazawa) **76**:282
"The Grove of Ashtaroth" (Buchan) **41**:34
"Growing a Ghost" (Nemerov) **124**:252
"Growing Gray" (Dobson) **79**:32
"Growing Old" (Ledwidge) **23**:111
"Growing Out of Shadow" (Walker) **129**:285-86
Growing Pains (Carr) **32**:118, 121-29
"Growing Up" (Milne) **88**:244
"Grown-up" (Millay) **49**:224
Growth (Tarkington) **9**:468, 473
"Growth a Nightmare" (Santos) **156**:315
"Growth and Combat" (Gilman) **117**:167, 170-171, 174-75
The Growth of a Soul (Strindberg) **21**:352
Growth of Indian Mythologies (Boas) **56**:80
"The Growth of 'Lorraine'" (Robinson) **101**:119, 192
The Growth of Love (Bridges) **1**:124
The Growth of Philosophic Radicalism (Halévy)
See *La Formation du Radicalisme Philosophique en Angleterre*
The Growth of the Law (Cardozo) **65**:22, 29, 32, 34-5, 39, 41
Growth of the Soil (Hamsun)
See *Markens grøde*
"The Growtown 'Bugle'" (Jewett) **22**:146
Gruach (Bottomley) **107**:3-4
Gruach and Britain's Daughter (Bottomley) **107**:3-4
"Grub Street Recessional" (Morley) **87**:143
Grundfragen der Soziologie (Simmel) **64**:318, 326, 334
"Der Gründliche" (Nietzsche) **55**:390-91
Grundlinien einer Erkenntnistheorie der Goetheschen Weltanschauung (Steiner) **13**:455
"Grundmotivet i Obstfelder's Digtning" (Obstfelder) **23**:180
Grundproblem der Erkenntisstheorie (von Hartmann) **96**:198, 203
Grundriss der Axiologie (von Hartmann) **96**:229
Grundzüge einer Genetischen Psychologie (Rank) **115**:347-48
Das Grüne Gesicht (Meyrink) **21**:218, 220, 230-31
Der Grüne Kakadu (Schnitzler) **4**:392-93, 402-03
"Der grüne König" (Ball) **104**:17
Gruppenbild mit Dame (Böll) **185**:42, 44, 51, 58-60, 63-5, 67-71, 73, 99-101, 119, 127-28, 130, 138-43, 148, 150, 153, 179, 184
"La gruta de las maravillas" (Palma) **29**:256
La gruta del silencio (Huidobro) **31**:122, 124, 132
"Gryningen" (Södergran) **31**:292
"The Gualichu Tree" (Graham) **19**:103
Guard over the Quarantined Ship (Papadiamantis) **29**:271-72
"El guardabosque comediante" (Quiroga) **20**:211
"Guardando il mare" (Pirandello) **29**:310
"The Guardian" (de la Mare) **53**:35, 37
"Guardian Angels" (Johnson) **19**:255
"Guardian of the Law" (Fisher) **11**:212, 213
The Guardian of the Threshold (Steiner)
See *Der Hüter der Schwelle*
Guardians of the Treasure (Sapper) **44**:316
The Guards Came Through (Doyle) **7**:227
The Guardsman (Molnár)
See *A testőr*
Gubijinso (Natsume) **2**:493-96; **10**:329, 345
"Gudabarnet" (Södergran) **31**:291, 293
"Gudarna komma" (Södergran) **31**:292
"Gudstanken" (Lagerkvist) **144**:217-18
Gudstanken (Lagerkvist) **144**:220
"Guduzhe" (Lu Hsun) **3**:295
"The Guelder Roses" (Lawrence) **93**:116
"Güele" (Güiraldes) **39**:176
"Guenevere" (Teasdale) **4**:424
"Guerdon" (Naidu) **80**:275
La guérison des maladies (Ramuz) **33**:295
The Guermantes Way (Proust)
See *Le côté de Guermantes*
Guermantes' Way (Proust)
See *Le côté de Guermantes*
"Guernica" (Éluard) **41**:164, 166-67
La Guerra Carlista (Valle-Inclán) **5**:474, 486
Guerra e fede (Gentile) **96**:144
Guerra en España (Jiménez) **183**:303
La guerra gaucha (Lugones) **15**:291-92
La guerre dans le haut-pays (Ramuz) **33**:310
La guerre de Troie n'aura pas lieu (Giraudoux) **2**:157-61, 163, 165, 172, 174; **7**:322, 327
"The Guess" (Muir) **2**:486
"A Guess at the Riddle" (Peirce) **81**:285
"Guess I'll Have to Telegraph My Baby" (Cohan) **60**:163, 169
"A Guest at Home" (Jewett) **22**:145-46
"A Guest at the Spa" (Hesse) **148**:181
A Guest for the Night (Agnon)
See *Ore'ah natah lalun*
The Guest of Quesnay (Tarkington) **9**:455, 460

Guest of Reality (Lagerkvist)
See *Gäst hos verkligheten*
"The Guest of the Peonies" (Nagai)
See "Botan no kyaku"
"The Guests of Mrs. Timms" (Jewett) **22**:147
"The Guests of Phineus" (Benét) **28**:3
"Le guetteur, Mélancolique" (Apollinaire) **51**:13
Guidance and Companionship (Carossa)
See *Führung und Geleit*
A Guide for the Bedeviled (Hecht) **101**:74
"Guide to The Charterhouse of Parma for the Use of New Readers" (Calvino) **183**:103
Guide to the New World: A Handbook of Constructive World Revolution (Wells) **6**:533
Guide to the Principal Pictures in the Academy (Ruskin) **63**:251
Guide to the Ruins (Nemerov) **124**:143, 151-53, 171
A Guide to the Varieties and Rarity of English Regal Copper Coins,Charles II-Victoria, 1671-1860 (Bramah) **72**:7-8
Guidepost (Miyamoto)
See *Dōhyō*
Guiding the Child (Adler) **61**:31-2
"Guignol" (Jarry) **2**:281, 284-85
"Guihua zheng: axiao bei qiṳ" (Chang) **184**:138-39
"El guijarro" (Prado) **75**:211
Guilderoy (Ouida) **43**:366
"Guilt" (Lasker-Schueler) **57**:328
"Guilt by Distinction" (De Voto) **29**:131
The Guiltless (Broch)
See *Die Schuldlosen*
The Guilty (Bataille)
See *Le coupable*
"The Guilty Shall Be Found Out and Punished" (Nemerov) **124**:231
The Guinea Pig (Sturges) **48**:310, 317
"Guinée" (Roumain) **19**:337, 344, 347
"Guinevere" (Gosse) **28**:131
"Guinevere" (Phelps) **113**:389
La guirlande des dunes (Verhaeren) **12**:465
"Guistino d'Arienzo" (Jovine) **79**:44
"Guitar or Moon" (Aleixandre)
See "Guitarra o luna"
"La guitarra" (García Lorca) **181**:195
"Guitarra o luna" (Aleixandre) **113**:16, 25
"Gujerat" (Naidu) **80**:340
"Guldgraveren" (Jensen) **41**:307
Gulf Coast Stories (Caldwell) **117**:21
"The Gull" (Balmont) **11**:34
Gullible's Travels, Etc. (Lardner) **2**:327, 332, 338-39; **14**:304, 313, 316
"The Gulls" (Nemerov) **124**:153
"Gulmore the Boss" (Harris) **24**:254
"Gul-Mulla" (Khlebnikov) **20**:127
"Gul-Mullah's Trumpet" (Khlebnikov)
See "Truba Gul-Mully"
"Gum" (Toomer) **172**:273
Gumtops (Ingamells) **35**:122, 128-31, 134
The Gun (Forester) **152**:162
"Gun Crazy" (Allison) **153**:3
The Gun Runner (Stringer) **37**:336
"Gunga Din" (Kipling) **8**:201; **17**:201, 203
Gunhild (Fisher) **87**:79
Gunman's Gold (Faust) **49**:57-60
Gunnar's Daughter (Undset)
See *Fortaellingen om Viga-Ljot og Vigdis*
"Gunner" (Jarrell) **177**:176
Gunner Cade (Kornbluth) **8**:216
"The Guns" (Manning) **25**:279
Guns and the Cross (Endo)
See *Ju to jujika*
"Guns as Keys: And the Great Gate Swings" (Lowell) **8**:226, 228, 236
"Guns at Cyrano's" (Chandler) **179**:123, 200
The Gunsaulus Mystery (Micheaux) **76**:246, 262, 272
"Gunsho ni watare" (Kunikida Doppo) **99**:294
"Gunvald og Emma" (Undset) **197**:302
"Guptadhan" (Tagore) **53**:354
Gurrelieder (Schoenberg) **75**:291-93, 296, 341, 345-47, 372, 394
"Guru Om" (Ginsberg) **120**:72
"Gusev" (Chekhov) **3**:153
Gusla (Vazov) **25**:456
Gustav (Spitteler) **12**:338, 348-50
Gustav III (Strindberg) **8**:418
Gustave Vasa (Strindberg) **1**:449; **8**:517
Der gute Gott von Manhattan (Bachmann) **192**:5, 9, 53, 127, 129
Der gute Mensch von Sezuan (Brecht) **1**:100-1, 104-5, 113, 116-17; **6**:36-37; **35**:9, 18; **169**:10
"Der Gute Ruf" (Sudermann) **15**:433
"Gute Stunde" (Raabe) **45**:191
Die gute Zeit (Barlach) **84**:98, 132
Gutmanns Reisen (Raabe) **45**:167, 172, 175, 178, 200-01
Gutmann's Travels (Raabe)
See *Gutmanns Reisen*
Gutta Percha Willie (MacDonald) **9**:292
"The Gutting of Couffignal" (Hammett) **187**:48, 79, 82, 85, 134, 137, 139, 203
"Guxiang" (Lu Hsun) **3**:295, 298, 302-3
Guy and Pauline (Mackenzie)
See *Plashers Mead*
"Guy de Maupassant" (Babel) **2**:28; **13**:18, 34; **171**:8, 14, 102
Guy Domville (James) **2**:261; **11**:318-19; **47**:165
"Guyon" (Sinclair) **11**:407
Guys and Dolls (Runyon) **10**:422-23
"Gwynedd" (Johnson) **19**:242, 244
Gyakkō (Dazai Osamu) **11**:175
"Gyerekkor" (Radnóti) **16**:412
Gyilkosok (Karinthy) **47**:269
Gymnadenia (Undset) **3**:519, 523; **197**:295-97, 299-300, 303, 311
"Gymnasium" (Aleichem)
See "Gimnazye"
"Gymnastics" (Higginson) **36**:175
"Gyofukuki" (Dazai Osamu) **11**:173, 182, 186
"Gyogenski" (Mori Ogai) **14**:380
"The Gypsy" (Thomas) **10**:463
Gypsy (Anderson) **2**:2; **144**:10, 71
Gypsy Balladeer (García Lorca)
See *Primer romancero gitano*
Gypsy Ballads (García Lorca)
See *Primer romancero gitano*
"The Gypsy Christ" (Sharp) **39**:374-75
The Gypsy Girl (Papadiamantis) **29**:271
"The Gypsy Nun" (García Lorca)
See "La monja gitana"
"Gypsy Song" (Babits)
See "Cigánydal"
"The Gyres" (Yeats) **18**:447; **93**:344, 404
"Gyroscope" (Nemerov) **124**:259, 273
Gyubal Wahazar (Witkiewicz) **8**:510-12
"Gyūniko to jagaimo" (Kunikida Doppo) **99**:304
"Gyūniku to Bareishō" (Kunikida Doppo) **99**:298, 302-03
H. G. Wells: Early Writings in Science and Science Fiction (Wells) **133**:260-65
H.M.S. Pinafore; or, The Lass That Loved a Sailor (Gilbert) **3**:209-10, 214-15, 217-18
Ha (Dazai Osamu) **11**:174, 177, 181-82
Ha! Ha! Among the Trumpets: Poems in Transit (Lewis) **3**:284, 286-87, 289-91
Ha llegado el momento (Villaurrutia) **80**:467
Há uma gôta de sangue em cada poema (Andrade) **43**:7
"Habakuk Jephson's Statement" (Doyle) **7**:234, 238
Habilitation (Weber) **69**:316
The Habit of Being: Letters of Flannery O'Connor (O'Connor) **132**:229-30, 237-44, 260, 275-76, 282, 286, 296, 300, 309, 315-16, 322-23, 328-29, 332, 337, 366
"The Habitant" (Drummond) **25**:141, 144, 146-47, 153
The Habitant, and Other French-Canadian Poems (Drummond) **25**:141-43, 148, 151, 155-56
"Les habitants du continent des chas sans aiguilles" (Arp) **115**:39
"The Habitant's Jubilee Ode" (Drummond) **25**:154
"An Habitation Enforced" (Kipling) **8**:194
The HAC in Africa (Childers) **65**:53
"El hacedor" (Borges) **109**:6, 43, 92, 99
El hacedor (Borges) **109**:8, 21, 33, 97-8, 108, 146, 152
El hacedor, Epílogo (Borges) **109**:99
Hachi no ko (Santoka) **72**:404
"Hachnisini tahath kenafech" (Bialik) **25**:48, 63
"Hacia el amor sin destino" (Aleixandre) **113**:5
"Hacia el azul" (Aleixandre) **113**:6
"Hackman's Night" (Knister) **56**:162, 165
"Had I a Golden Pound" (Ledwidge) **23**:112, 116
"Hadda Be Playing on the Jukebox" (Ginsberg) **120**:36, 79
A Haditudosito Naploja (Molnár) **20**:164
El Hadj (Gide) **177**:35
Hadji Akhiel (Vazov) **25**:450
Hadji Murád (Tolstoy)
See "Khadzi murat"
Hadji Murad (Tolstoy)
See "Khadzi murat"
"Hadji Murat" (Fadeyev) **53**:58
"Hadjii murád" (Tolstoy)
See "Khadzi murat"
"Hadleyburg" (Twain)
See "The Man That Corrupted Hadleyburg"
"Hadom ve'Khiseh" (Agnon) **151**:36
Hadrian (Heyse) **8**:115, 119
Hadrian the Seventh (Rolfe) **12**:266-68, 270, 273-74, 277-80, 282-83
"Haduvig im Kreuzgang" (Huch) **13**:249-50
"Hae" (Yokomitsu) **47**:387, 394
Haendel (Rolland) **23**:280
Haermaendene på Helgeland (Ibsen) **2**:227; **8**:146, 149
"Ha-eynayim ha-re 'eboth" (Bialik) **25**:63
Hafvets stjarna (Ekelund) **75**:95
"A hágár oltára" (Ady) **11**:21
"Hagar und Ismael" (Lasker-Schueler) **57**:316
"The Haggis of Private McPhee" (Service) **15**:399
"Hagomoro" (Noguchi) **80**:400
"Haha naru mono" (Endo) **152**:200, 203-4, 216
"Haha no shi to atarashii haha" (Shiga)
See "Haha no shi to atarishi haha"
"Haha no shi to atarishi haha" (Shiga) **172**:202
"Haha no shi to tabi no kioku" (Shiga) **172**:202
"Der Hahn von Quakenbrück" (Huch) **13**:252
"Haidebilder" (Liliencron) **18**:206, 213
Der Haidegänger und andere Gedichte (Liliencron) **18**:214
"Haijin Buson" (Masaoka) **18**:235
"Haiku on Excrement" (Masaoka) **18**:230-31
"Haiku Wastebasket" (Masaoka) **18**:229
Haikyo no naka (Mizoguchi) **72**:322
"Hail and Farewell" (Coleridge) **73**:12
"Hail and Farewell" (Gurney) **33**:86
Hail and Farewell: Ave (Moore) **7**:476-80, 482-83, 486, 495-98
Hail the Conquering Hero (Sturges) **48**:269, 272-73, 275-77, 279, 283, 289, 291-92, 294-95, 301-09, 314, 316, 319-23
"Hail Wind!" (Vilakazi)
See "We moya!"
"Le haine emporte tout" (Barrès) **47**:55, 57
"Haircut" (Lardner) **2**:335; **14**:299, 302, 307, 309, 312-13, 317
"A Haircut in Toulouse" (March) **96**:263
The Haircutting (Hrabal)
See *Postřižiny*
The Hairy Ape (O'Neill) **1**:382, 384-85, 394, 400, 402, 404, 406; **6**:324-25, 327, 330; **49**:238, 252, 259-60, 270, 282
The Hairy Arm (Wallace) **57**:395

"Hairy Gertz and the Forty-Seven Crappies" (Shepherd) **177**:294, 297
"Hairy Hearts" (Arp) **115**:22
"Haïta the Shepherd" (Bierce) **7**:88; **44**:12, 44-5
"Haiti" (Capote) **164**:200
Hakai (Shimazaki Toson) **5**:432-35, 440-41
Hakhnasat kalah (Agnon) **151**:52
Hakobune sakura maru (Abe) **131**:2
"Hakon of Thule" (Buchanan) **107**:25
"Halakah and Aggadah" (Bialik) **25**:60
Halálfiai (Babits) **14**:40, 42
"Halalf" (Huidobro) **31**:134
Halalí (Huidobro)
See *Hallali*
Halb Mähr, halb mehr (Raabe) **45**:188
"Halberdier of the Little Rheinschloss" (Henry) **19**:140
"The Halcyon Birds" (Benét) **28**:2
Halcyone (Glyn) **72**:137
"Haldernablou" (Jarry) **14**:273, 287
Haldernablou (Jarry) **147**:242, 290, 312, 329-31
"Half a Dozen Handkerchieves" (Undset)
See "Et halvt dusin lommetørklaer"
Half a Minute's Silence, and Other Stories (Baring) **8**:42
"Half as Much" (Williams) **81**:426
"A Half Day" (Mori Ogai)
See "Hannichi"
"Half Free and Fighting On" (Steffens) **20**:363
"The 'Half Moon'" (Ford) **172**:7, 11
"Half Pint Flask" (Heyward) **59**:92-3, 100-01, 105
Half-a-Hero (Hope) **83**:171
"Half-Crown Bob" (Warung) **45**:419
Half-Crown Bob and Tales of the Rivertime (Warung) **45**:418-19
The Half-Hearted (Buchan) **41**:41-4, 46
"Halfway Down" (Milne) **6**:314; **88**:242
Halfway to Silence (Sarton) **120**:224, 228, 247, 260, 269, 271, 273, 296, 305
"A halhatatlanság halála" (Babits) **14**:38
"A hall lovai" (Ady) **11**:13, 18
"Hall Marked" (Galsworthy) **45**:33
"Hall of the Missing Footsteps" (Huneker) **65**:169, 196
Halla (Leino) **24**:368, 370
Hallali (Huidobro) **31**:122, 125, 137, 141
"El hallazgo de la belleza" (Lugones) **15**:294
"Hallazgo de la vida" (Vallejo) **56**:287
"Hallelujah" (Abbey) **160**:12
"Halley's Comet" (Arenas)
See "El Cometa Halley"
"Hallowel's Pretty Sister" (Jewett) **22**:146
Hallucinated City (Andrade)
See *Paulicea desvairada*
Hallucinations (Arenas)
See *El mundo alucinante*
Halma (Pérez Galdós) **27**:250, 257
A Halottak élén (Ady) **11**:17-18, 23, 25
"La halte des heures" (Éluard) **41**:157
Halte Hulde (Bjoernson) **7**:100-01, 103, 112, 116; **37**:8-9, 23, 29, 30-1
"A Halting Sonnet" (Gray) **19**:151
"Et halvt dusin lommetørklaer" (Undset) **197**:290, 301
The Ham Funeral (White) **176**:129, 179, 189, 196, 225-27, 257-59, 263-65
The Hambledon Men (Lucas) **73**:158, 172
"Hamburger Binge" (Shepherd) **177**:316
The Hamlet (Faulkner) **141**:39, 58, 61, 75-76, 78, 82, 84, 114, 202-4, 207, 211-12; **170**:127-29, 134, 166, 177, 184, 244-45
"Hamlet" (Pasternak) **188**:182, 190, 192, 195-96, 209
Hamlet Had an Uncle (Cabell) **6**:76-7
Hamlet; oder, Die lange Nacht nimmt ein Ende (Döblin) **13**:175-78
Hamlet; or, The Long Night Comes to an End (Döblin)
See *Hamlet; oder, Die lange Nacht nimmt ein Ende*
"Hamlet, Prince of Denmark" (Čapek) **192**:186-87
"The Hammam Name" (Flecker) **43**:190
"The Hammerless Gun" (Pascoli) **45**:155
"Hampa" (Anwar) **22**:24
The Hampdenshire Wonder (Beresford) **81**:3-5,13
Hampshire Days (Hudson) **29**:136, 138, 147, 151
"Han no hanza" (Shiga) **172**:207-8, 213-14, 229
"Han no hanzai" (Shiga)
See "Han no hanza"
Han som fick leva om sitt liv (Lagerkvist)
See *Han som fik leva om sitt liv*
Han som fik leva om sitt liv (Lagerkvist) **144**:158, 162, 211
"Hana" (Akutagawa Ryūnosuke) **16**:17, 20, 27, 34-5
"Hanabi" (Nagai) **51**:103
"Ha'nacker Mill" (Belloc) **7**:32; **18**:28
"Hanakago" (Nagai) **51**:89
Ha-navi (Asch) **3**:73
Hanazakari no mori (Mishima) **161**:27
"Hanazono no Shisô" (Yokomitsu) **47**:388, 396-97
Hanba domowa (Herbert) **168**:38
"The Hand" (Douglas) **40**:86-7, 91-2
"The Hand" (Dreiser) **35**:74-6
"The Hand" (Service) **15**:413
Hand and Ring (Green) **63**:140, 148, 150-52, 155
The Hand and the Glove (Machado de Assis)
See *A mão e a luva*
"The Hand Car" (Akutagawa Ryūnosuke)
See "Torokko"
"The Hand of Destiny" (Forester) **152**:129
The Hand of Ethelberta (Hardy) **4**:148-49; **10**:215, 217, 226; **18**:86, 100; **53**:110; **143**:82, 129, 174-75, 180, 204, 206; **153**:119, 150
The Hand of Fu Manchu (Rohmer)
See *The Si-Fan Mysteries*
The Hand of Peril (Stringer) **37**:336
The Hand of the Mandarin Quong (Rohmer) **28**:286
The Hand of the Potter (Dreiser) **10**:171
Handbook of American Indian Languages (Boas) **56**:81
A Handbook to the 37 1/2 Foot Motor Boats of the 200 Class (Lawrence) **18**:179
"Handcarved Coffins: A Nonfiction Account of an American Crime" (Capote) **164**:122-23, 134, 138, 142, 150-54, 202-4
A Handful of Lavender (Reese) **181**:336, 338, 346
A Handful of Sand (Ishikawa)
See *Ichiaku no suna*
"The Handicapped—By One of Them" (Bourne) **16**:68-9
"The Handkerchief" (Akutagawa Ryūnosuke)
See "Hankechi"
Handkerchief of Clouds (Tzara)
See *Mouchoir de nuages*
The Handling of Words (Lee) **5**:317-18
"Hands" (Anderson) **1**:42, 49, 59, 64; **10**:41, 44-5, 50; **24**:20-1, 24, 28-9, 33-4, 37-8, 44-5, 58; **123**:71-2, 78-9, 105
"The Hands" (Bonner) **179**:41
"Hands" (Childress) **116**:37
"Hands Across the Void" (Kuttner) **10**:268
Hands Around (Schnitzler)
See *Reigen*
"The Hands of Ethiopia" (Du Bois) **169**:137
"The Hands of God" (Lawrence) **93**:72, 125
The Hands of Orlac1 (Wiene)
See *Orlacs Hände*
"Handsome Harry" (Howe) **21**:107
"The Handsome Lady" (Coppard) **5**:177
A Handy Guide for Beggars (Lindsay) **17**:241
"A Handy Guy like Sande" (Runyon) **10**:437
Hang On to Love (Riggs)
See *The Domino Parlor*
"Die Hängenden Gärten" (George) **2**:149; **14**:202, 205-06
"A Hanging" (Orwell) **31**:194; **51**:250-52, 255, 261; **128**:254-55, 262-63, 274-75, 282; **129**:234
"The Hanging Gardens" (George)
See "Die Hängenden Gärten"
The Hanging Gardens (Schoenberg)
See *Das Buch der hangenden Garten*
"Hanging in Heaven" (Hagiwara)
See "Tenjō Ishi"
"The Hangman" (Ball)
See "Der Henker"
The Hangman (Lagerkvist)
See *Bödeln*
Hangman's Holiday (Sayers) **15**:379
"Hangman's Oak" (Millay) **49**:210; **169**:267
Hangover House (Rohmer) **28**:284, 296
"Hangover Reflections" (Talvik) **87**:319
Hangsaman (Jackson) **187**:238, 241-42, 257, 271, 281-83, 295, 297, 299
"Hania" (Sienkiewicz) **3**:426
"Hankechi" (Akutagawa Ryūnosuke) **16**:22, 31
"Hank's Woman" (Wister) **21**:382, 391, 393-95, 398
"Hannah Thomburn" (Lawson) **27**:140
"Hannibal" (Twain) **185**:250, 258
Hannibal Lecter, My Father (Acker) **191**:109, 126
"Hannichi" (Mori Ogai) **14**:384
"Hannukah Money" (Aleichem)
See "Khanike-gelt"
Hanrahan's Oath (Gregory) **1**:333; **176**:20
Hans Alienus (Heidenstam) **5**:250, 253-54
"Hans Benzmann" (Rilke) **195**:292
"Han's Crime" (Shiga)
See "Han no hanza"
Hans Holbein the Younger: A Critical Monograph (Ford) **172**:6
Hans Lange (Heyse) **8**:119
"Han-shan and Shihte" (Mori Ogai)
See "Kanzan jittoku"
En hanske (Bjoernson) **7**:111, 114; **37**:14, 17, 19, 29
"La hanul lui Mînjoală" (Caragiale) **76**:157, 159
"Hap" (Hardy) **53**:103, 117
"Ha-panim la-panim" (Agnon) **151**:3
Ha-panim la-panim (Agnon) **151**:3
Happe-Chair (Lemonnier) **22**:198, 200, 202
"Happiness" (Chekhov) **31**:96
"Happiness" (Jiménez) **183**:330
"Happiness" (Owen) **27**:207, 235-36
"Happiness" (Zoshchenko) **15**:491
Happiness in a Corner (Sudermann) **15**:420
The Happiness of the Family (Dazai Osamu)
See *Katei no kōfuku*
The Happy Age (Undset)
See *Den lykkelige alder*
"Happy and Unhappy Theologians" (Yeats) **11**:539
"The Happy Autumn Fields" (Bowen) **148**:16-18, 20
The Happy Boy (Bjoernson)
See *En glad gut*
"The Happy Children" (Machen) **4**:284
"Happy Clouds" (Aleixandre)
See "Nube feliz"
Happy Days (Beckett) **145**:99, 102, 104, 125-28, 146, 157, 161-62, 170-75, 177
Happy Days, 1880-1892 (Mencken) **13**:378, 385, 387-88, 395, 397
Happy Dispatches (Paterson) **32**:381-82
The Happy End (Hergesheimer) **11**:263, 266
The Happy End (Williams) **89**:365
Happy Ending: The Collected Lyrics of Louise Imogen Guiney (Guiney) **41**:212, 214-15, 219, 229
"Happy Endings" (Hall and Nordhoff) **23**:64
Happy Ever After (Wakefield) **120**:348
"Happy Family" (Lu Hsun) **3**:301
"The Happy Fatalist" (Scott) **6**:389, 393

"Happy Home" (Khodasevich)
See "A Happy Little House"
The Happy Hypocrite (Beerbohm) **1**:68, 70, 74; **24**:98, 100, 110-11, 126-27
"Happy Jack" (March) **96**:260
"Happy Life" (Davies) **5**:199
"The Happy Life" (Webb) **24**:473
"The Happy Little Cripple" (Riley) **51**:292-93
"A Happy Little House" (Khodasevich) **15**:197, 206, 208, 210-11
A Happy Man (Moricz)
See *A boldog ember*
"Happy Marriage" (Cary) **196**:207
Happy People (Pirandello)
See *La gente allegra*
"The Happy Prince" (Wilde) **1**:503; **8**:492; **41**:389
The Happy Prince, and Other Tales (Wilde) **1**:504; **41**:376
The Happy Return (Forester)
See *Beat to Quarters*
"The Happy Townland" (Yeats) **11**:527
Happy Valley (White) **176**:126-29, 133, 145, 171-77, 183, 186, 191-92, 199, 219, 243, 308
The Happy-Go-Lucky Morgans (Thomas) **10**:451, 458
"Har gaat og higet" (Obstfelder) **23**:177
"Här sitter jag" (Lagerkvist) **144**:222
Haratch (Saroyan) **137**:175
"A Harbinger" (Chopin) **127**:9
"The Harbinger" (Henry) **19**:173
"Harbor Dawn" (Crane) **80**:83, 127, 136, 140, 166, 209
"The Harbor-Master" (Chambers) **41**:102
"The Harbour" (Belloc) **18**:40
"The Harbour Bridge" (Hardy) **143**:150
"Harboured" (Graham) **19**:112
"Harc a nagyúrral" (Ady) **11**:15, 18
"A Hard Death" (Sarton) **120**:279
"Hard, from Hand to Mouth" (Caragiale) **76**:181
"Hard Labor" (Ginsberg) **120**:112
Hard Labor (Pavese)
See *Lavorare stanca*
Hard Lines (Nash) **109**:357, 366
A Hard Woman (Hunt) **53**:186, 191, 197
"The Hare Ivanych" (Remizov) **27**:352-53
"La Hareng saur" (Huysmans) **69**:7, 23, 25
"Haritada bir nokta" (Sait Faik) **23**:293
"Hark, From the Tomb!" (Cobb) **77**:116, 134
"Harlem" (Benét) **28**:8
"Harlem" (Dunbar) **2**:128
Harlem (Thurman) **6**:445-46, 448-49, 451
"The Harlem Dancer" (McKay) **7**:455, 457, 462
Harlem: Negro Metropolis (McKay) **7**:470-71; **41**:328, 330, 335
"Harlem Shadows" (McKay) **7**:457, 462
Harlem Shadows (McKay) **7**:457, 462, 467; **41**:316, 328, 336, 343
"Harlem Wine" (Cullen) **37**:150-51
"The Harlot's House" (Wilde) **8**:492; **41**:397
Harmer John (Walpole) **5**:496
"Harmon Whitney" (Masters) **25**:309
"Harmonics" (Moody) **105**:225, 237, 271
Harmonielehre (Schoenberg) **75**:296, 316, 319, 329, 358
Harmonium (Stevens) **3**:444, 448, 453, 455, 458-62, 466-69, 476-77; **12**:355-56, 363-64, 366-67, 370, 376, 382, 384-85; **45**:268-69, 273-75, 277, 280-82, 295, 297-99, 317-18, 332, 338, 346, 349, 351-52
"Harmony" (García Lorca)
See "Armonia"
"Harmony" (Lardner) **2**:334, 337; **14**:319-20
"The Harmony of Virtue" (Aurobindo) **63**:29, 35-6
"Harnack and the Apostolic Creed" (Andreas-Salome) **56**:45
"The 'Harnt' That Walks Chilhowee" (Murfree) **135**:196, 199, 202, 205, 219, 223, 227
"Harold Arnett" (Masters) **25**:309
"Harold's Super Service" (Shepherd) **177**:299
"Harp" (Hardy) **10**:234
"The Harp Song of the Dane Women" (Kipling) **8**:191, 208
Harper of Heaven (Service)
See *Harper of Heaven: A Record of Radiant Living*
Harper of Heaven: A Record of Radiant Living (Service) **15**:411
"The Harping of Cravetheen" (Sharp) **39**:372, 377
"The Harp-Weaver" (Millay)
See "The Ballad of the Harp-Weaver"
The Harp-Weaver, and Other Poems (Millay) **4**:309-10, 316; **49**:208, 213-15, 218, 220-21, 232; **169**:239, 301
"Harriet Waage" (Undset) **3**:522
"Harrigan" (Cohan) **60**:163
"Harry Carey Goodhue" (Masters) **25**:312
"Harry the Actor" (Bramah) **72**:13
"Harsh World That Lashest Me" (Cullen) **4**:45, 50; **37**:144-45, 160, 165
Hartmann, Düring, and Lange (Vaihinger) **71**:420
"Hartrott and Hitler" (Zweig) **17**:458
Haru (Shimazaki Toson) **5**:431-32, 435-36
"Haru no tori" (Kunikida Doppo) **99**:302-06
Haru no yuki (Mishima) **161**:3-4, 30-31, 51, 55, 73
"Haru to Shura" (Miyazawa) **76**:291, 299
Haru to shura (Miyazawa) **76**:279-83, 287, 293, 297, 299
"Haru wa Basha ni Notte" (Yokomitsu) **47**:388, 396
"Harvard Indifference" (Broun) **104**:83
Harvard Memorial Biographies (Higginson) **36**:167, 170-71
"Harvest" (p'Bitek)
See "They Sowed and Watered"
"The Harvest" (Scott) **6**:385, 393
Harvest (Giono)
See *Regain*
The Harvest (Grove) **4**:133
Harvest (Ward) **55**:444, 446
"The Harvest Gypsies" (Steinbeck) **135**:339
"Harvest Hymn" (Naidu) **80**:303
The Harvest Moon (Thomas) **97**:139
"The Harvest of Diamonds" (Coffin) **95**:11
"The Harvest of the Sea" (McCrae) **12**:210
"Harvest Slumber Song" (Campbell) **9**:30
"Harvest Song" (Toomer) **172**:257-58, 274, 276, 295, 330
The Harvester (Porter) **21**:261-62, 264, 271-72, 276
The Harvesters (Pavese)
See *Paesi tuoi*
The Harvesters (Symons) **11**:433
"A Harvesting" (Grahame) **136**:13
"The Harvests" (Mistral)
See "Les moissons"
"The Harvests of Sodom" (Vallette)
See "Les vendanges de Sodome"
"Has Anybody Seen Miss Dora Dean?" (Petry) **112**:298-301, 328, 331
"Has She Forgotten?" (Riley) **51**:303
"Has the Christian Religion Done Ought for Woman?" (Stanton) **73**:259
"Has Your Soul Sipped" (Owen) **5**:369; **27**:218
Hashire merosu (Dazai Osamu) **11**:176, 183-84
"Hashish" (Quiroga) **20**:211
"The Hashish Man" (Dunsany) **2**:136; **59**:20
Hasidism (Peretz) **16**:397
Hassan (Flecker) **43**:195-202, 205, 207-10, 217
Die hässliche Herzogin (Feuchtwanger) **3**:178-79, 182, 186
Hast du was, dann bist du was (Böll) **185**:158
"Hasta el día en que vuelva" (Vallejo) **3**:533
"Hasten My Dream" (Santos) **156**:314-15
Hastenbeck (Raabe) **45**:165-66, 171-72, 179, 182, 185, 187, 201
"Hastió" (Machado) **3**:307
A Hasty Bunch (McAlmon) **97**:87-89, 99, 113-15, 117-18, 121
"The Hat" (Bennett) **5**:46
"The Hat and the Post" (Powys) **9**:378
Hat holdas rózsakert (Babits) **14**:40
Hataraku mono miru mono e (Nishida) **83**:235, 237, 251, 254, 278, 282, 290, 311, 313
"Hateful Kuma Eats His Lunch" (Miyazawa) **76**:302
"The Hateful Word" (Welch) **22**:456
"The Haters" (Coffin) **95**:16
"Hatred of Metaphor and Simile" (Bodenheim) **44**:61
A hattyú (Molnár) **20**:160-62, 166, 170-71, 178
"Haughty Error" (Popa) **167**:154
"Haunted" (Lowell) **8**:234
The Haunted (O'Neill) **1**:388; **6**:331
The Haunted Bookshop (Morley) **87**:118, 121, 124, 127, 129, 140, 146-8
Haunted Castle (Murnau)
See *Schloß Vogelöd*
The Haunted Chair (Leroux) **25**:260
"The Haunted Chamber" (Chopin) **5**:153; **14**:62; **127**:127
"The Haunted Island" (Blackwood) **5**:80
Haunted Lady (Rinehart) **52**:302
The Haunted Mirror (Roberts) **68**:324, 326
"The Haunted Oak" (Dunbar) **2**:131; **12**:104, 124, 126-27
Haunted Ocean (Dent) **72**:23
"The Haunted Ones" (Quiroga)
See "Los perseguidos"
"The Haunted Palace" (Roberts) **68**:306, 325, 348, 351
"The Haunted Valley" (Bierce) **1**:91; **44**:45
The Haunted Woman (Lindsay) **15**:221, 225-28, 230-34, 237
The Haunted Woods (Lee) **5**:312
"The Haunter" (Hardy) **53**:101
"The Haunter of the Dark" (Lovecraft) **4**:274; **22**:221, 228, 241
The Haunting of Hill House (Jackson) **187**:235-38, 241, 259, 267-68, 284, 288, 296-97, 299, 337-38
"The Haunting of Low Fennel" (Rohmer) **28**:286
Hauntings (Lee) **5**:320
"Das Haupt des heiligen Johannes auf der Schüssel" (Liliencron) **18**:214
Der Hauptmann von Köpenick (Zuckmayer) **191**:284-85, 289, 296, 303, 305, 324, 335-37, 348
"Haupt-Städtisches Journal" (Böll) **185**:40
Das Haus am Meer (Zweig) **17**:452
Das Haus des Alchimisten (Meyrink) **21**:231-32
Haus ohne Hüter (Böll) **185**:5, 50, 83, 129-30, 182-83
"Hausfriedensbruch" (Böll) **185**:129
Hausfriedensbruch (Böll) **185**:129-30
Die Hauspostille (Brecht) **1**:97-98, 114, 118; **169**:19, 37, 42
Hauspotille (Brecht)
See *Die Hauspostille*
Haute solitude (Fargue) **11**:200-01
Haute surveillance (Genet) **128**:134-35, 145, 150-52, 154, 159, 163, 201
Havana (di Donato) **159**:196
"Havasu" (Abbey) **160**:24, 31, 40, 43, 82
Have Come, Am Here (Villa) **176**:103, 107, 112, 114-19
Have His Carcase (Sayers) **15**:389
Have You Anything to Declare? (Baring) **8**:37, 42, 44
"Have You Ever Been Lonely" (Holly) **65**:150
"Have You Ever Made a Just Man?" (Crane) **11**:130
"Have You Seen This Movie?" (Ginsberg) **120**:79
"A Haven" (Swinburne) **36**:344
"The Hawk" (Yeats) **93**:341, 364
The Hawkline Monster: A Gothic Western (Brautigan) **133**:30

Hawthorne (James) **11**:321
Hawthorne and His Circle (Hawthorne) **25**:240
Hawthorne and Lavender (Henley) **8**:108-09
"Hay and Hell and Booligal" (Paterson) **32**:369
"Hay más" (Aleixandre) **113**:14
"Hay un lugar que yo me sé" (Vallejo) **56**:308
Hayduke Lives (Abbey) **160**:6-7, 12, 14, 17, 27-28, 32, 34-36, 80, 82, 85, 92
"Haymaking" (Thomas) **10**:461, 464
"Hayvanca gülen adam" (Sait Faik) **23**:294
"Haz de tus pies" (Storni) **5**:449
A Hazard of New Fortunes (Howells) **7**:368, 372, 376, 378, 384-85, 390, 393, 395, 397-400; **17**:178, 186-88; **41**:269
"He" (Fondane) **159**:255
"He" (Lovecraft) **22**:218
"He" (Nemerov) **124**:258
"He Abjures Love" (Hardy) **10**:221
"He Also Serves" (Henry) **19**:175
"He and I" (Ginzburg)
See "Lui e io"
"He and She" (Peretz) **16**:389
He and She (Crothers) **19**:74-7, 79, 84
He asálleute zoé (Palamas) **5**:377, 379-80, 383-85
He Came Down from Heaven (Williams) **1**:512, 518-19; **11**:485, 497, 502
He Chews to Run (Rogers) **71**:326
"He Cometh and He Passeth By" (Wakefield) **120**:336, 345-46, 349, 356-57
"He Hoes" (Coffin) **95**:15
"He Is White" (Hippius) **9**:163
"He Knew Lincoln" (Tarbell) **40**:433
"He Never Expected Much" (Hardy) **53**:117; **143**:151
He phlogéra tou basilá (Palamas) **15**:379-82, 384-85, 387-88
He phonissa (Papadiamantis) **29**:268, 270-72, 275-77
"He Prefers Her Earthly" (Hardy) **143**:189
"He Remembered" (Chekhov) **96**:35
"He Resolves To Say No More" (Hardy) **143**:192
"He Revisits His First School" (Hardy) **53**:114
"he sang his didn't he danced his did" (Cummings) **137**:56
"He Seen It in the Stars" (Himes) **139**:324
He Sent Forth a Raven (Roberts) **68**:300, 311-13, 324-25, 335, 338, 360, 364-65
"He Sings the Epistle" (Pirandello)
See "Canta l'epistola"
He, the One Who Gets Slapped (Andreyev)
See *Tot, kto poluchaet poshchechiny*
"He, to Her" (Hardy) **53**:94
"He Understood" (Chekhov) **96**:33
"He who finds a horseshoe" (Mandelstam)
See "Nashedshij podkovu"
"He who found a Horseshoe" (Mandelstam)
See "Nashedshij podkovu"
He Who Lived His Life Over Again (Lagerkvist)
See *Han som fik leva om sitt liv*
He Who Must Die (Kazantzakis) **5**:263-64
He Who Says No (Brecht) **1**:104
He Who Says Yes (Brecht) **1**:104
"Head and Bottle" (Thomas) **10**:467
"Head and Shoulders" (Fitzgerald) **6**:160
"The Head and the Bottle" (Sait Faik) **23**:298
"The Head at the Prow" (Tzara) **168**:228
Head in Green Bronze, and Other Stories (Walpole) **5**:504
"Head, in My Memory" (Aleixandre)
See "Cabeza, en el recuerdo"
"The Head of the District" (Kipling) **8**:185, 197, 208; **17**:205
"The Head of the Family" (Chekhov) **3**:149
The Head of the Firm (Riddell) **40**:335
"The Head of Wisdom" (Jarrell) **177**:162
Head to Toe (Orton) **157**:294, 296, 305, 307, 330, 354
"Head Up Like a Deer's" (Coffin) **95**:15
"Head-Deep in Strange Sounds: Free-Flight Improvisations from the un-English" (Dickey) **151**:147
Head-Deep in Strange Sounds: Free-Flight Improvisations from the unEnglish (Dickey) **151**:162, 171, 174
"The Head-Hunter" (Henry) **19**:184
"The Headless Hawk" (Capote) **164**:99-103, 109-10, 112, 158, 199
The Headless Men (Dent) **72**:21, 23
"The Headless Mummies" (Rohmer) **28**:282
Heads (Bernhard)
See *Köpfe*
"Heads and Bellies" (Yokomitsu)
See "Atama Narabi ni Hara"
The Headswoman (Grahame) **136**:11, 18-19
"Heady Wine" (Svevo)
See "Vino generoso"
"The Heal-All" (Roberts) **8**:318
"Healing" (Lawrence) **93**:57, 58
"Healing and Psychics" (Zoshchenko) **15**:512
"Health" (Thomas) **10**:463
A Health Book for the Tailoring Trade (Adler) **61**:23
"The Health Card" (Childress) **116**:36
"The Health of Our Girls" (Higginson) **36**:175
"The Heap of Rags" (Davies) **5**:203
A Heap o'Livin (Guest) **95**:205, 208, 220
"Hear O Israel" (Peretz) **16**:396
Hear Us O Lord from Heaven Thy Dwelling Place (Lowry) **6**:237, 240-41, 248, 250, 254-55
"Hear Yaroslavna" (Tsvetaeva) **35**:394
"Hear Yaroslavna, Mourning Her Loved One" (Tsvetaeva) **35**:394
Hearken to the Evidence (Wakefield) **120**:334, 349, 355-56
Hearken unto the Voice (Werfel) **8**:470
"The Hearse-Horse" (Carman) **7**:139, 142
"Hearst Headline Blues" (Wright) **136**:262
The Heart (Mann) **9**:315
Heart (Natsume) **2**:495; **10**:334
"Heart, Crown and Mirror" (Apollinaire)
See "Coeur, couronne et miroir"
The Heart Is a Lonely Hunter (McCullers) **155**:167-255
The Heart of a Dog (Bulgakov)
See *Sobach'e serdtse*
The Heart of a Goof (Wodehouse) **108**:362
"The Heart of a Mother" (Tynan) **3**:502
The Heart of a Peacock (Carr) **32**:118
Heart of Darkness (Conrad) **1**:200, 202, 205, 207, 210, 212, 217-18, 220-22; **6**:119-20, 122-24; **13**:99-142; **25**:85-6, 89, 110-11; **43**:133, 135, 137-38, 144-45; **57**:42, 53-54, 61, 66, 85, 87, 100, 103, 108-10, 112, 115, 118, 120
The Heart of England (Thomas) **10**:449, 466
Heart of Europe (Cram) **45**:10, 18, 20
"Heart of God" (Lindsay) **17**:234
The Heart of Happy Hollow (Dunbar) **12**:107-09, 119-20
Heart of Man and Other Papers (Woodberry) **73**:361, 365-68, 371, 378
The Heart of Maryland, and Other Plays (Belasco) **3**:84-5, 90
The Heart of Paddy Whack (Crothers) **19**:74, 77
The Heart of Penelope (Lowndes) **12**:201
The Heart of Princess Osra (Hope) **83**:172
The Heart of Rome (Crawford) **10**:150
"The Heart of Sourdough" (Service) **15**:404
"The Heart of Spring" (Yeats) **31**:414-17, 419
The Heart of the Ancient Wood (Roberts) **8**:318, 323-24
"Heart of the Blues" (Handy) **97**:51
"The Heart of the Quartz Pebble" (Popa) **167**:179
"The Heart of the Swamp" (Marquis) **7**:448
The Heart of the West (Henry) **1**:348, **19**:181, 191
"The Heart Sutra" (Chang)
See "Xinjing"
The Heart That Knows (Roberts) **8**:324
"Heartache" (Chekhov)
See "Toska"
"Heartbeat" (Holly) **65**:137-38, 140-43, 152
Heartbreak House (Shaw) **3**:385-86, 390-93, 397-98, 402, 404, 406-07; **9**:421-22
"Hearts and Crosses" (Henry) **19**:190
"Heart's Blood" (Gladkov) **27**:91-2
"Heart's Desire" (Stringer) **37**:335
"Heart's Desmesne" (Gray) **19**:148, 157
The Heart's Highway (Freeman) **9**:72
Heart's Kindred (Gale) **7**:283
"Hearts More Transparent Than a Vessel" (Khlebnikov)
See "Serdtsa, prozrachney, chem sosud"
Hearts of the World (Griffith) **68**:138, 170, 233
"Heart's Wild-Flower" (Moody) **105**:237, 250, 254, 265, 271
Heartsease; or, The Clue of Life (Yonge) **48**:374-75, 388
The Heartsnatcher (Vian)
See *L'arrache-coeur*
"Heat in the City" (Roberts) **8**:321
"The Heat of Noon" (Abbey) **160**:22, 49
The Heat of the Day (Bowen) **148**:4, 6, 8, 17, 29-30, 36-38, 40-41, 45, 47-54, 57-60, 62-64, 79-80, 82, 87-89, 96, 103, 105-7, 114-19, 123, 126-29, 131-33
"The Heat of the Sun" (O'Faolain) **143**:226-27
The Heat of the Sun: Stories and Tales (O'Faolain) **143**:226, 230
"Heathen Chinee" (Harte)
See "Plain Language from Truthful James"
Heathen Days, 1890-1936 (Mencken) **13**:385, 387, 397
Heather and Snow (MacDonald) **113**:197
The Heather Field (Martyn) **131**:98-104, 106-15, 124
The Heat's On (Himes)
See *Ne nous énervons pas*
"Heaven" (Anwar)
See "Sorga"
"Heaven" (Brooke) **2**:55; **7**:122, 124, 129
"Heaven Alive" (García Lorca) **197**:185
"Heaven Has Changed" (Himes) **139**:324
"The Heaven of Animals" (Dickey) **151**:95, 99, 104, 172
Heaven—And Earth (Murry) **16**:341-42, 351, 356-57
Heavenly and Earthly Love (Molnár)
See *Égi és földi szerelem*
"The Heavenly Choir" (Hecht) **101**:87
The Heavenly City of the Eighteenth-Century Philosophers (Becker) **63**:60, 63-6, 72, 81-2, 84-5, 87-93, 95, 97-8, 100-101, 107, 109, 111, 113-14, 117
The Heavenly Ladder (Mackenzie) **116**:214-16, 231
The Heavenly Path (Nabokov)
See *Gornii put*
Heavenly Words (Hippius)
See *Nebesnye slova*
Heaven's Secret (Lagerkvist)
See *Himlens hemlighet*
Heavensgate (Okigbo) **171**:344-45, 349, 354, 356
Heavensgate III (Okigbo) **171**:354, 356
Heavenwards (Horvath)
See *Himmelwärts*
The Heavy Lyre (Khodasevich) **15**:200, 202, 204, 206, 208, 210, 212-14
Heavy Weather (Wodehouse) **108**:384
Das Hebraeland (Lasker-Schueler) **57**:300, 303, 319-325
Hebraische Balladen (Lasker-Schueler) **57**:298, 304, 316, 332, 333
Hebrew Ballads (Lasker-Schueler)
See *Hebraische Balladen*
"The Hebrew Father's Prayer" (Campbell) **9**:31-2

"Hebrews in Summer Hotels—How They Are Treated—A Strange but Strictly True Illustration" (Cahan) **71**:85
"Hecate" (Manning) **25**:277
"Heces" (Vallejo) **3**:531
Hector Servadac: Travels and Adventures Through the Solar System (Verne)
See *Hector Servadac: Voyages et aventures à travers le monde solaire*
Hector Servadac: Voyages et aventures à travers le monde solaire (Verne) **6**:500, 502-03; **52**:336, 352
"He'd Come Back" (Lawson) **27**:148
Hedda Gabler (Ibsen) **2**:220, 223, 226-27, 229-35, 237-38, 241; **8**:142, 144, 148-49, 151; **16**:187; **52**:159
"Heddon's Month" (Johnson) **19**:244
"Hedebonden" (Jensen) **41**:308
The Hedge and the Horse (Belloc) **18**:25
"Hedge Island, a Retrospect and a Prophecy" (Lowell) **8**:236
"Hedge Life" (Dickey) **151**:97
Hedged In (Phelps) **113**:340
"The Hedgehog and the Fox" (Berlin) **105**:132, 145
The Hedgehog and the Fox (Berlin) **105**:3, 5, 8, 19, 71-2, 74
"Hedger" (Gurney) **33**:104
"The Heel of Achilles" (Wodehouse) **108**:371
The Heel of Achilles (Delafield) **61**:127
"Heels and Head" (Stephens) **4**:412, 417
"Hegel, Mary, Freud" (Jozsef) **22**:157
"Hegel's Conception of Nature" (Alexander) **77**:58
"Hegeso sírja" (Babits) **14**:38
"The Hegira" (Graham) **19**:110, 131
Hegira, a Hatchment (Graham) **19**:111
Heibon (Futabatei) **44**:90, 100
Der Heidegänger (Liliencron) **18**:212
Heidegger and "the Jews" (Lyotard)
See *Heidegger et "les juifs"*
"Heidegger at Eighty" (Arendt) **193**:155
Heidegger et "les juifs" (Lyotard) **103**:199, 202-04, 249-52, 254, 260, 263, 267, 269-70
"A Heifer without Blemish" (Evans) **85**:22
"The Height of Land" (Scott) **6**:386, 389-90, 394-96
Das Heilige (Otto) **85**:311-2, 314-5, 317-323, 328, 329, 332, 334-5, 337-42, 344-5, 349, 354, 358, 361, 365-6, 370-1
Die heilige Johanna der Schlachthöfe (Brecht) **1**:99, 101, 112-13; **6**:34-7; **13**:52
Die heilige Johanna der Schlachtöfe (Brecht) **169**:4
"Die heiligen drei Könige" (Rilke) **195**:181
Die Heilung durch den Geist: Franz Anton Mesmer, Mary Baker Eddy, Sigmund Freud (Zweig) **17**:426
Heimat (Sudermann) **15**:417, 419-20, 422, 424-28, 433, 438
"Die Heimat der Toten" (Heym) **9**:146
"Heimlich zur Nacht" (Lasker-Schueler) **57**:307
"Heimliche Landschaft" (Carossa) **48**:21, 24
"Un heimlicher Teich" (Liliencron) **18**:214
Heinrich Böll Werke: Essayistische Schriften und Reden (Böll) **185**:93-7, 101, 103-04, 119, 151-55, 157-58, 160, 163, 166, 176
Heinrich Böll Werke: Hoerspiele, Theaterstuecke, Drehbuecher, Gedichte (Böll) **185**:95
Heinrich Böll Werke: Interviews (Böll) **185**:94-7, 100, 103-04, 119, 123, 127, 152-55, 157
Heinrich Böll Werke: Romane und Erzählungen (Böll) **185**:159-64, 173-78
Heinrich Heine Artist in Revolt (Brod) **115**:98
"Heir and Serf" (Marquis) **7**:436
The Heir of Linne (Buchanan) **107**:84-5
The Heir of Redclffe (Yonge) **48**:364-65, 371, 374, 376-81, 383-88
"The Heir of the McHulishes" (Harte) **25**:213
"The Heiress and the Architect" (Hardy) **4**:152
"An Heiress from Red Horse" (Bierce) **7**:88; **44**:44
"An Heiress of Red Dog" (Harte) **25**:193
Heirs and Assigns (Cabell) **6**:76-8
"Heirs of Time" (Higginson) **36**:179
"Der heisse Soldat" (Meyrink) **21**:220, 225
"Der Heizer" (Kafka) **2**:223; **13**:284; **179**:242, 252, 266, 284, 289-90, 297-98, 302-3, 312, 315-16, 323, 325
Hekher fun der erd (Kahanovitsch) **56**:117
"Helas!" (Wilde) **175**:276
Helbeck of Bannisdale (Ward) **55**:411-12, 416-18, 421-22, 431, 441
Held in Bondage (Ouida)
See *Granville de Vigne*
Heldenplatz (Bernhard) **165**:11-12, 64-67, 69, 71, 79, 88-89, 96
"Helen" (Hellman) **119**:121-22
"Helen, After Illium" (Stringer) **37**:332
Helen of Memphis (Bromfield) **11**:84
Helen of the Old House (Wright) **183**:349, 377, 381
"Helen of Troy" (Masters) **25**:288
"Helen of Troy" (Teasdale) **4**:424
Helen of Troy (Lang) **16**:250-51, 256, 258
Helen of Troy, and Other Poems (Teasdale) **4**:424, 426, 428-29
"Helen, the Nonexistent Woman" (Andrić)
See "Jelena, žena koje nema"
Helen Vardon's Confession (Freeman) **21**:52, 59
Helen with the High Hand (Bennett) **5**:29; **197**:13, 28, 30
"Helena" (Čapek) **6**:84
Helena (Machado de Assis) **10**:282, 292, 298
Helena's Path (Hope) **83**:167
Hélène de sparte (Verhaeren) **12**:464, 479-82
"Helen's Babies" (Orwell) **51**:249
Helen's Husband (Verga)
See *Il marito di Elena*
"Helgi of Lithend" (Manning) **25**:275
"Helian" (Trakl) **5**:461, 463-64, 466
Heliga Birgittas pilgrimsfärd (Heidenstam) **5**:250, 253, 255
Det heliga landet (Lagerkvist) **144**:165, 174, 204-5, 207, 212, 215, 217, 222, 224, 235, 240, 242
Héliogabale; ou, L'anarchiste couronné (Artaud) **3**:54, 62
Helkavirsiä (Leino) **24**:367-71, 373-78
Hell Below (Dent) **72**:24
Hell Flowers (Nagai)
See *Jogoku no hana*
Hell Has No Limits (Donoso)
See *El lugar sin límites*
"A Hell of a Mess in Rome" (Chekhov) **163**:38
"The Hell Screen" (Akutagawa Ryūnosuke)
See "Jigokuhen"
"Hell So Feared" (Onetti)
See "El infierno tan temido"
The Hell We Dread (Onetti)
See *El infierno tan temido y otros cuentos*
Hellenic Religion of the Suffering God (Ivanov) **33**:123
"Hellhound on My Trail" (Johnson) **69**:77
Hellman Collection (Hellman) **119**:190-92
Hello Broadway (Cohan) **60**:166, 168, 171-2
Hello, I'm Erica Jong (Acker) **191**:6, 126
Hello Out There (Saroyan) **137**:168, 181, 201-2, 205-7
Hello Out There (Whale) **63**:378
Hello, Sister! (Stroheim)
See *Walking Down Broadway*
"Hello Stranger" (Capote) **164**:138
"Hell's Stepsons" (McCoy) **28**:223
Helmets (Dickey) **151**:90, 100, 102, 105-6, 202-3
Héloïse and Abélard (Moore) **7**:479, 483, 486, 494, 497-99
"Héloïse et Abélard" (Artaud) **36**:4
"Helpless Revolt" (Sapir) **108**:249
The Helpmate (Sinclair) **3**:434, 440; **11**:408-09, 411-12
"Hembygden" (Lagerkvist) **144**:212
"Ein Hemd aus grüner Seide" (Böll) **185**:101
Hemingway: The Writer as Artist (Baker) **119**:2-3,
"Den hemliga liljan" (Ekelund) **75**:95
"Hemmelig ve" (Hamsun) **14**:248
"The Hemp" (Benét) **7**:69, 78
Hempfield (Baker) **47**:23, 27-30
Hemsöborna (Strindberg) **1**:460; **8**:409-11, 419
"The Hen" (Dunsany) **59**:3
"Hendecasyllabics" (Swinburne) **36**:299
"Hendecasyllables" (Moore) **7**:487
"Der Henker" (Ball) **104**:7-11, 15-16, 58, 71-73, 75-76
Der Henker von Brescia (Ball) **104**:25
"Henley's Criticism" (Woolf) **43**:401
"Henri Hayden, homme-peintre" (Beckett) **145**:91
Henriette (Coppee) **25**:121
"Henry" (Bunin) **6**:51
"Henry A. Harper" (Campbell) **9**:32
"Henry Adams Once More" (Becker) **63**:117
Henry and Cato (Murdoch) **171**:206, 212, 243, 260, 307, 323
Henry Brocken (de la Mare) **4**:77
Henry Dunbar (Braddon) **111**:215, 229-31
Henry for Hugh (Ford) **15**:87, 89-90; **172**:52-54, 57-60
Henry Gross and His Dowsing Rod (Roberts) **23**:240
"Henry I to the Sea, 1120" (Lee-Hamilton) **22**:194
Henry IV (Pirandello)
See *Enrico IV*
Henry James: A Critical Study (Ford) **39**:116, 119; **172**:7, 98
"Henry James, Jr." (Howells) **17**:167
Henry James Letters (James) **171**:177
Henry James: The Major Phase (Matthiessen) **100**:160, 182-84, 186, 201-03, 205, 238, 242, 276, 282
Henry, King of France (Mann)
See *Die Vollendung des königs Henri Quatre*
"The 'Henry Porcher' Bolter" (Warung) **45**:421-26
"Henry Tripp" (Masters) **25**:298
"The Hens" (Roberts) **68**:297, 336
"Hens and Hounds and Hants and Wars" (Coffin) **95**:12
"Hephæstus" (Stringer) **37**:331-32
Hephzibah Guinness (Mitchell) **36**:264
Heptalogia (Swinburne) **36**:312
"Her Arms" (Tagore) **3**:490
"Her Bush Sweetheart" (Baynton) **57**:10
"Her Eyes" (Bialik) **25**:50
"Her Eyes" (Robinson) **5**:400
"Her Eyes Say Yes, Her Lips Say No" (Symons) **11**:435
"Her Fabled Mouth" (Rosenberg) **12**:311
"Her Father" (Hardy) **53**:100
Her Father's Daughter (Porter) **21**:266-67, 277
"Her First Appearance" (Davis) **24**:205
"Her First Ball" (Mansfield) **2**:458; **8**:283-84; **39**:295, 298, 303, 322; **164**:247-48, 266266
"Her Housekeeper" (Gilman) **37**:213, 216; **117**:77
Her Husband's Affairs (Hecht) **101**:78
Her Infinite Variety: A Feminine Portrait Gallery (Lucas) **73**:173
"Her Letters" (Chopin) **14**:70; **127**:206, 209-10, 212
"Her Lips Are Copper Wire" (Toomer) **172**:258, 273
"Her Lover" (Gorky)
See "Boles"
"Her Majesty the Dust" (Bryusov) **10**:88
"Her Memories" (Gilman) **117**:77
Her Mountain Lover (Garland) **3**:192-93
"Her Music" (Belloc) **18**:40

Her Only Way (Bradford) **36**:63
"Her Pretty Golden Hair" (Montgomery) **140**:321
Her Privates We (Manning) **25**:266-75
Her Serene Highness (Phillips) **44**:262, 273, 277
"Her Son" (Wharton) **129**:364
Her Son's Wife (Fisher) **87**:75
"Her Table Spread" (Bowen) **148**:23
"Her Virginia Mammy" (Chesnutt) **39**:80, 97, 99
"Hera die Braut" (Spitteler) **12**:350
Heracles (Couperus) **15**:46
Heraclitus (Aurobindo) **63**:30
"Heraldic: Deborah and Horse in Morning Forest" (Dickey) **151**:152
Los heraldos negros (Vallejo) **3**:526-27, 530-32, 534; **56**:288-89, 292-99, 301, 303-04
"Heraldry" (Muir) **87**:209
Herb O'Grace: Poems in War-Time (Tynan) **3**:506-07
L'herbe rouge (Vian) **9**:529, 532, 537
"Herberge zur Heimat" (Zuckmayer) **191**:305
Herbert Engelmann (Zuckmayer) **191**:276, 284-86, 290, 293
Herbs and Apples (Santmyer) **133**:214, 216, 219
"Herbst" (Lasker-Schueler) **57**:300, 305
"Der Herbst des Einsamen" (Trakl) **5**:456
Herbstfeuer (Huch) **13**:251
"Herbsttag" (Rilke) **195**:252-53
Herceg, hátha megjön a tél is (Babits) **14**:39
"Herd Instinct and its Bearing on the Psychology of Civilized Man" (Trotter) **97**:172, 183
"Herder and the Enlightenment" (Berlin) **105**:125
"The Herder of Storm Mountain" (Murfree) **135**:209
"Here" (Éluard) **7**:260
Here and Beyond (Wharton) **129**:363
Here Are Ladies (Stephens) **4**:410, 417, 420-21
Here Come the Clowns (Barry) **11**:59-65, 67
"Here Comes the Bride" (Millay) **169**:235
Here Comes, There Goes, You Know Who (Saroyan) **137**:179, 181, 186
"Here I sit" (Lagerkvist)
See "Här sitter jag"
"Here, If Forlorn" (Gurney) **33**:98
"Here in the Corner of the Field" (Warner) **131**:311
"Here in this Spring" (Thomas) **45**:377
Here Is Your War (Pyle) **75**:228-29, 234, 236, 241, 244, 249-50, 258-59, 261
Here Lies: The Collected Stories of Dorothy Parker (Parker) **143**:287, 343
Here Today and Gone Tomorrow (Bromfield) **11**:78, 82
"Here We Are" (Parker) **143**:287-90, 332
"Hereditary Memories" (Hearn) **9**:134
"Heredity" (Graham) **19**:129
"Herefords in the Wilderness" (Grove) **4**:142
Here-Lies (Artaud) **3**:58
"Here's to the Mice!" (Lindsay) **17**:226
"L'Hérésiarque" (Apollinaire) **3**:40; **51**:20
L'hérésiarque et cie (Apollinaire) **3**:39-40; **8**:12, 16; **51**:2, 7, 19-20, 28, 47, 49
"Heresy" (Akutagawa Ryūnosuke) **16**:27
The Heretic of Soana (Hauptmann)
See *Der Ketzer von Soana*
"De heretico comburendo" (Graham) **19**:101
Heretics (Chesterton) **1**:178; **6**:101, 106
"Los heridos" (Arenas) **191**:138
"Heriot's Ford" (Kipling) **8**:200
"Heritage" (Cullen) **4**:40-1, 43-6, 48-53; **37**:139-42, 144-45, 148, 150-53, 158-59, 161-62
A Heritage and Its History (Compton-Burnett) **180**:124, 144-47
"The Heritage of Dedlow Marsh" (Harte) **25**:223
The Heritage of Hatcher Ide (Tarkington) **9**:469, 473
The Heritage of Quincas Borba (Machado de Assis)
See *Quincas Borba*
The Heritage of the Desert (Grey) **6**:176-77, 181-83, 185
The Heritage of the Kurts (Bjoernson)
See *Det flager i byen og på havnen*
Les héritiers Rabourdin (Zola) **6**:566-67
Herland (Gilman) **9**:108-10, 115; **37**:177, 183, 185, 187-88, 200-05; **117**:49, 54-5, 58-63, 65, 69, 75-6, 78, 80-6, 109, 111, 113, 115, 122-24, 126-31, 136-39, 141, 151, 166-71, 173-77
L'Herluberlu (Anouilh) **195**:30
"La hermana agua" (Nervo) **11**:395, 398, 400, 402-03
"Hermann Cohen, 1842-1918" (Cassirer) **61**:120
Hermann Hesse, His Life and Work (Ball)
See *Hermann Hesse, sein Leben und sein Werke*
Hermann Hesse, sein Leben und sein Werke (Ball) **104**:36
Hermann Lauscher (Hesse) **196**:274-75
"El hermano de Atahualpa" (Palma) **29**:256
El hermano Juan (Unamuno) **148**:257
El hermano Juan o el mundo es teatro (Unamuno) **9**:516-17, 521
"Hermaphroditus" (Swinburne) **8**:442; **36**:294, 297-98, 315, 320, 323
"Hermes" (Schwob) **20**:320
Hermes, Dog and Star (Herbert)
See *Hermes, pies i gwiazda*
Hermes, pies i gwiazda (Herbert) **168**:38, 42
"The Hermetic Chateau" (Vallette)
See "Le chateau hermetique"
L'Hermine (Anouilh) **195**:10, 12, 16-17, 24, 26, 31, 38, 50, 54-6
"Hermine von Preuschen" (Rilke) **195**:292
Hermione and Her Little Group of Serious Thinkers (Marquis) **7**:437, 443, 445-46, 451
"The Hermit" (Apollinaire)
See "L'ermite"
"The Hermit" (Gorky) **8**:76
"The Hermit and the Wild Woman" (Wharton) **129**:361
The Hermit and the Wild Woman (Wharton) **129**:361
The Hermit and the Wild Woman and Other Stories (Wharton)
See *The Hermit and the Wild Woman*
"The Hermit Thrush" (Foote) **108**:35-6
"The Hermitage at the Center" (Stevens) **45**:306, 310
"Hermosa entre las hermosas" (Palma) **29**:262
Hernando de Soto (Graham) **19**:111, 123, 125
The Herne's Egg (Yeats) **31**:407
The Hero (D'Annunzio)
See *L'eroe*
A Hero Ain't Nothin but a Sandwich (Childress) **116**:30-1
The Hero and the Nymph (Aurobindo) **63**:4
"A Hero Closes a War" (Griggs) **77**:192, 194
"The Hero of Currie Road" (Paton) **165**:298
"The Hero of Redclay" (Lawson) **27**:126, 131, 150-51
The Hero of Santa Maria (Hecht) **101**:37, 43, 73
"A Hero of Tomato Can" (Norris) **155**:311
Hero Tales from American History (Roosevelt) **69**:177, 188, 206
The Hero with a Thousand Faces (Campbell) **140**:5-7, 11-12, 15, 26, 29-31, 43, 47, 52-53, 65, 67, 69-70, 75, 78-86, 91, 94, 108, 112, 117, 123, 130-35, 137, 139
"Hero with Girl and Gorgon" (Nemerov) **124**:209
Herod and Mariamne (Lagerkvist)
See *Mariamne*
Herod and Marianne (Lagerkvist)
See *Mariamne*
"The Heroes" (Baker) **10**:20
The Heroes (Verhaeren)
See *Les héros*
Heroes and Villains (Carter) **139**:46, 86, 159-60, 162, 165-70, 193, 195, 204
Heroes' Square (Bernhard)
See *Heldenplatz*
"Heroic Love" (Baker) **10**:28
"Heroic Poem in Praise of Wine" (Belloc) **18**:28, 42
"Heroics" (Wylie) **8**:536
Heroines and Villains (Carter) **139**:194
Heroines of Fiction (Howells) **41**:277
"The Herons" (Kolmar) **40**:177
"The Herons" (Ledwidge) **23**:118, 120
"Der Heros" (Hauptmann) **4**:201
Les héros (Verhaeren) **12**:465, 468
The Hero's Journey (Campbell) **140**:101-3, 107, 111, 116
Herr Arne's Hoard (Lagerloef)
See *Arne's Treasure*
Herr Bengts Hustru (Strindberg) **8**:406; **47**:364
Herr Puntila and His Servant Matti (Brecht)
See *Herr Puntila und sein Knecht Matti*
Herr Puntila und sein Knecht Matti (Brecht) **1**:100, 104, 107, 109; **6**:37-8; **35**:22; **169**:7
Herr über Leben und Tod (Zuckmayer) **191**:289, 325
Herr und Hund (Mann) **168**:175
"En herrelös hund" (Söderberg) **39**:428, 436, 437
"The Herring" (Huysmans)
See "La Hareng saur"
"The Herring Weir" (Roberts) **8**:314
Herself Surprised (Cary) **1**:140-41, 143-45, 148; **29**:64, 67-9, 71, 73, 77, 80, 84, 88, 91-2, 101; **196**:142, 157, 161, 175, 177, 203, 223
"Hershel Toker" (Bergelson) **81**:20
"Hertha" (Swinburne) **8**:426, 429, 437-38; **36**:318
Herzgewachse (Schoenberg) **75**:290, 292
"Hesitant Ode" (Radnóti) **16**:416, 420
"The Hesitating Veteran" (Bierce) **44**:22
"Hesitation Blues" (Handy) **97**:69
Hesper (Garland) **3**:192
"Hesperia" (Swinburne) **36**:332, 339
"Hesperides" (Torrence) **97**:152
Hesperides (Torrence) **97**:151-53, 155, 157-58, 165
"Hester Dominy" (Powys) **9**:362, 364, 369, 375
Hester's Mystery (Pinero) **32**:412
Hetty Wesley (Quiller-Couch) **53**:296
"Hetzjagd" (Liliencron) **18**:209-10, 212
Heu-Heu; or, The Monster (Haggard) **11**:250
L'heure de la noce (Bloy) **22**:43
Les heures (Verhaeren) **12**:470, 473
"Les heures claires" (Verhaeren) **12**:464, 467
"Les heures d'aprés-midi" (Verhaeren) **12**:464, 467, 471
"Les heures du soir" (Verhaeren) **12**:464, 467
"Les heures mornes" (Verhaeren) **12**:461
Le hevre sexuelle (Vallette) **67**:268, 306
"He-Who-Intones-the-Epistle" (Pirandello)
See "Canta l'epistola"
"Hey, Good Lookin" (Williams) **81**:423
"Hey, Rub-a-Dub-Dub!" (Dreiser) **10**:194
Hey Rub-a-Dub-Dub: A Book of the Mystery and Wonder and Terror of Life (Dreiser) **10**:190, 194, 196; **18**:54, 58, 60; **35**:48; **83**:55, 85
"The Heyday of the Blood" (Fisher) **87**:73
"Hiball" (McKay) **41**:342
"Hibon naru Bonjin" (Kunikida Doppo) **99**:294, 303
"Hiccups" (Mori Ogai)
See "Kitsugyaku"
Hidalla; oder, Sein und haben (Wedekind) **7**:575-76
The Hidden Force (Couperus)
See *De stille kracht*

"Hidden Gardens" (Capote) **164**:142
"A Hidden Life" (MacDonald) **9**:304; **113**:200
A Hidden Life, and Other Poems (MacDonald) **9**:291, 300
The Hidden Paths (Gonzalez Martinez)
See *Los senderos ocultos*
"The Hidden Pool" (Sterling) **20**:380
"Hidden Riches" (Tagore)
See "Guptadhan"
"Hidden Spring" (Gonzalez Martinez)
See "Fuente Oculta"
The Hidden Woman (Colette) **16**:118
"Hide & Seek" (Nemerov) **124**:257, 273
Hide and Seek (Morley) **87**:120
"The Hiding of Black Bill" (Henry) **19**:182
"The Hiding-Away of Blessed Angus" (Tynan) **3**:504
La hiedra (Villaurrutia) **80**:468
"Hierarchie" (van Ostaijen) **33**:412
"La hierba milagrosa" (Pardo Bazán) **189**:234-35
Hièroglyphes (Gourmont) **17**:127
"Hieroglyphics" (Machen) **4**:281-83
"Hierzulande" (Böll) **185**:188-94, 196
Higan sugi made (Natsume) **10**:330
"Higginson's Dream" (Graham) **19**:129
"The Higgler" (Coppard) **5**:180-81
"The High Cost of Prejudice" (Locke) **43**:238-39, 241
"High Fashion Furs" (Schwitters)
See "Feine Pelzmoden"
The High Hand (Futrelle) **19**:95
"The High Hills" (Gurney) **33**:93-4, 99, 103
"High Noon at Midsummer on the Campagna" (Sharp) **39**:391
The High Place (Cabell) **7**:68, 72, 75, 77
"High Stepper" (Bonner) **179**:41, 43, 58
"High Talk" (Yeats) **93**:351
"High Tea at Mckeown's" (Somerville & Ross) **51**:335
"High Tide at Malahide" (Gogarty) **15**:108
High Tor (Anderson) **2**:4, 6, 8, 10-11; **144**:7, 10-13, 17, 19, 34-35, 37, 63-68, 70, 72-73, 77-78
High Trumps (Couperus)
See *Hooge troeven*
The High Window (Chandler) **1**:172; **7**:168, 173-74, 180; **179**:80, 89, 97-98, 100-103, 128, 157-59, 180-82, 188-91, 194-95, 203-4, 223, 227, 229-30, 233
"High Yaller" (Fisher) **11**:206, 208-09, 212, 214
"The Higher Abdication" (Henry) **19**:189-90
"Higher Education" (Vilakazi)
See "Imfundo ephakeme"
"The Higher Keys" (Merrill) **173**:230, 241
The Higher Learning in America (Veblen) **31**:343, 346-47, 349, 353, 362, 366, 372-74, 376
"The Higher Pragmatism" (Henry) **19**:181
Higher than the Earth (Kahanovitsch)
See *Hekher fun der erd*
"The Highly-Prized Pajamas" (McAlmon) **97**:100, 121
"The High-School Lawn" (Hardy) **143**:150
"A High-Toned Old Christian Woman" (Stevens) **3**:446; **45**:344
"A Highway Pimpernel" (Davidson) **24**:164
"The Highwayman" (Dunsany) **59**:20
"The Highwayman" (Noyes) **7**:511-15
Highways and Byways in Sussex (Lucas) **73**:157, 162, 170, 173
Hiihtajan virsia (Leino) **24**:368
"Hija de la mar" (Aleixandre) **113**:14
La hija del capitán (Valle-Inclán) **5**:481, 486
"El hijo" (Quiroga) **20**:214, 219, 221
El hijo de carne yel hijo de hierro (Echegaray) **4**:101
El hijo de Don Juan (Echegaray) **4**:96-7, 100-02, 105
El hijo santo (Miro) **5**:338
"El hijo y la madre" (Arenas) **191**:136, 208
"Hijos de los compos" (Aleixandre) **113**:75-6
Hikage no hana (Nagai) **51**:86, 97
"Hilary Maltby and Stephen Braxton" (Beerbohm) **1**:67, 71; **24**:102
Hilda Lessways (Bennett) **5**:25-6, 29, 34, 40-2, 47; **20**:21; **197**:26-7, 31, 78-82, 94, 96
Hilda Lessways Wants (Bennett) **197**:20
"Hildebrand" (Campbell) **9**:30
"Das hilflose Europa; oder, Reise vom Hundertsteinins Tausendste" (Musil) **12**:258
"The Hill" (Brooke) **2**:55; **7**:121
"The Hill" (Faulkner) **170**:138
"The Hill" (Masters) **25**:298, 307, 313
"The Hill" (Muir) **87**:254
The Hill of Dreams (Machen) **4**:277-83, 286
The Hill of Lies (Mann)
See *Ein ernstes Leben*
"The Hill of Sand" (Agnon)
See "Gib'ath ha-hol"
"The Hill of St. Sebastien" (Drummond) **25**:151
The Hill of Vision (Stephens) **4**:406-08, 410, 419-20
"Hill One Hundred: Outline for an Unwritten Novel" (Lewis) **2**:399
"The Hill Tarn" (Sharp) **39**:368
"Hillbilly Philosophy" (Fletcher) **35**:106, 111
"Hillcrest" (Robinson) **5**:407-08; **101**:113-14, 130, 134, 193
"Hills" (Kandinsky) **92**:72
"The Hills" (MacDonald) **9**:303
"The Hills" (Oppen) **107**:330-31
Hills and the Sea (Belloc) **18**:28, 45
The Hills Beyond (Wolfe) **4**:515-16, 520, 525; **13**:486, 495
"Hills Like White Elephants" (Hemingway) **115**:184
The Hills Were Joyful Together (Mais) **8**:240-50
Hillsboro People (Fisher) **87**:72
"The Hillsboro Shepherd" (Fisher) **87**:73
"Hillsboro's Good Luck" (Fisher) **87**:73
"Hill-Side Tree" (Bodenheim) **44**:58
"The Hill-Wind" (Sharp) **39**:361-62, 374
"The Hilton's Holiday" (Jewett) **1**:361
Him (Cummings) **137**:17, 22, 24, 34, 47, 50-52
"Him with His Tail in His Mouth" (Lawrence) **61**:219
"Himalya" (Fenollosa) **91**:3
Himlens hemlighet (Lagerkvist) **144**:210, 214
Himmelwärts (Horvath) **45**:78, 101, 111
Himmerland People (Jensen) **41**:306, 309
Himmerland Stories: Third Collection (Jensen) **41**:306
"Himmerlands Beskrivelse" (Jensen) **41**:308
Himmerlandshistorier (Jensen) **41**:294, 296
Himmlische und irdische Liebe (Heyse) **8**:121
"Himno a la luna" (Lugones) **15**:289
"Himno a los voluntarios de la República" (Vallejo) **3**:533; **56**:312-13
"Himnusz Iriszhez" (Babits) **14**:39
Hin und Her (Horvath) **45**:78, 101, 111
A Hind in Richmond Park (Hudson) **29**:144, 164
Hind Swarajo; or, Indian Home Rule (Gandhi) **59**:38-9, 46, 54, 71
The Hindered Hand (Griggs) **77**:146, 148-9, 167-71, 176-7
The Hindoo Dagger (Griffith) **68**:250
Hindu Mysticism: Six Lectures on the Development of Indian Mysticism (Dasgupta) **81**:91-3
"Hingabe" (Lasker-Schueler) **57**:299
The Hinge of Fate (Churchill) **113**:104-05, 118
Hinkemann (Toller)
See *Der Deutsche Hinkemann*
"Hinter Baumen berg ich mich" (Lasker-Schueler) **57**:310
"Hinter Smichov" (Rilke) **195**:259
Hints for Home Teaching (Abbott) **139**:18
"Hints for Those about to Travel" (Tomlinson) **71**:395, 401
Hints on Writing and Speech Making (Higginson) **36**:170
Hiob (Roth) **33**:329-30, 350, 362-63
"Hiouen-Thrang" (Hearn) **9**:126
Hippolytus (Howe) **21**:109
"The Hippopotamus" (Nash) **109**:365
Hips and Haws (Coppard) **5**:177
"Hiraki-bumi" (Yosano) **59**:333
Hired Guns (Faust) **49**:44
"The Hired Man on Horseback" (Rhodes) **53**:307, 316, 328
"Hiroshige" (Noguchi) **80**:368
Hiroshige (Noguchi) **80**:368
"Hirten-und Preisgedichte" (George) **2**:149
"Hirusugi" (Nagai) **51**:99
Hirusugi (Nagai) **51**:105
"His Ally" (Benét) **28**:5
"His America" (Glaspell) **175**:97
"His Bad Angel" (Davis) **24**:202
"His Bargain" (Yeats) **116**:261
"His Blood" (Lasker-Schueler) **57**:329
"His Chance in Life" (Kipling) **8**:185
"His Christmas Miracle" (Murfree) **135**:207
"His Country, After All" (Lawson) **27**:121
"His 'Day in Court'" (Murfree) **135**:206
"His Father's Mate" (Lawson) **27**:129
"His Father's Son" (Wharton) **129**:362
His Father's Son (Matthews) **95**:253, 272-7
His Fellow Men (Dunsany) **59**:17, 20, 27
"His First Love" (Reese) **181**:347
"His French Mademoiselle" (Merrill) **173**:175
His Girl Friday (Hecht) **101**:62
His Honour, and a Lady (Duncan) **60**:194-5, 207, 209, 211, 213-5, 217-8
His Hour (Glyn) **72**:128-29, 137, 139
His House in Order (Pinero) **32**:395-96, 398, 400, 405, 414
"His Immortality" (Hardy) **10**:234
"His Last Bow: The War Service of Sherlock Holmes" (Doyle) **7**:231, 238
His Majesty (Granville-Barker) **2**:197
"His Majesty Kneeb Piter Komandor" (Pilnyak) **23**:220
"His Majesty the King of France" (Milne) **6**:314
His Majesty's Embassy (Baring) **8**:40-1
"His Masterpiece" (Paterson) **32**:380
His Monkey Wife or Married to a Chimp (Cohen) **127**:239-41, 243, 245, 247-48, 250-52, 256-58
"His Mother" (Gilman) **117**:155
"His New Mittens" (Crane) **11**:128
His Own People (Tarkington) **9**:460
"His Pa's Romance" (Riley) **51**:292
"His People" (Graham) **19**:115, 129
"His Phoenix" (Yeats) **93**:349, 350
"His Private Honour" (Kipling) **8**:193, 198, 204
His Proper Self (Benavente) **3**:94
His Religion and Hers: A Study of the Faith of Our Fathers and the Work of Our Mothers (Gilman) **9**:102-03; **37**:177; **117**:49, 125, 127, 140
"His Return" (Graham) **19**:129, 131
His Royal Happiness (Duncan) **60**:233, 244, 249
His Sainted Grandmother (Dunsany) **59**:23
"His Son, in His Arms, in Light, Aloft" (Brodkey) **123**:194, 200, 202-3, 214
"His Unquiet Ghost" (Murfree) **135**:208
His Vanished Star (Murfree) **135**:207, 223
"His Visitor" (Hardy) **53**:101
"His Wedded Wife" (Kipling) **8**:202
His Widow's Husband (Benavente) **3**:93
"His Wife" (Phelps) **113**:338
"His Wife's Deceased Sister" (Stockton) **47**:312, 317, 320
"Hish" (Dunsany) **2**:145
"Hi-shosetsu: Sobo" (Shiga)
See "Aru asa"
Histoire comique (France) **9**:43-4, 47, 53
L'histoire comique de Keizer Karel (Ghelderode) **187**:40
Histoire contemporaine (France) **9**:42, 48-9
L'Histoire d'Auguste (Yourcenar) **193**:270

"L'Histoire de l'érotisme" (Bataille) **155**:32, 39, 42-44
Histoire de l'oeil (Bataille) **155**:11, 77-81, 84-85
Histoire de mes pensées (Alain) **41**:7, 10, 26, 28, 30
Histoire de rats (Bataille) **155**:106
Histoire di Soldat (Schoenberg) **75**:326
Histoire du peuple anglais au xlxe siècle. iv. Le milieu du siècle, 1841-52 (Halévy) **104**:106-10, 111-12, 116, 118-20, 122, 125-27
"Histoire d'une famille vertueuse, d'une hotte et d'un calcul" (Apollinaire) **51**:20
Histoire naturelle (Péret) **20**:197, 202
Histoires magiques (Gourmont) **17**:136-37, 151
Histoires naturelles (Renard) **17**:303-04, 308, 310-11
Histology of the Nervous System (Ramoacn y Cajal) **93**:137, 142
Historia amoris (Saltus) **8**:345, 347, 352, 356
"Historia como sistema" (Ortega y Gasset) **9**:341-42
"La historia de Don Sandalio" (Unamuno) **2**:558
Historia de la eternidad (Borges) **109**:36, 47-8, 50, 61, 75, 77, 117, 152, 154, 156
Historia de la noche (Borges) **109**:7
"Historia de los dos que soñaron" (Borges) **109**:42
Historia de Roca (Lugones) **15**:291
Historia de Sarmiento (Lugones) **15**:291
Historia de un amor turbio (Quiroga) **20**:207, 209, 211
"Historia de una excomunión" (Palma) **29**:262
Historia del corazón (Aleixandre) **113**:21, 28, 31, 33-34, 37, 49-50, 67, 69-70, 72, 75
"Historia del guerrero y de la cautiva" (Borges) **109**:98
Historia personal del 'boom' (Donoso) **133**:81, 157, 159-60, 203-4
Historia universal de la infamia (Borges) **109**:7, 70-1, 97
"Los historiadores" (Ibarguengoitia) **148**:203
Histórias de meia-noite (Machado de Assis) **10**:295
Histórias incompletas (Ramos) **32**:427
Historias romanticas (Machado de Assis) **10**:285
"The Historic Basis of Socialism" (Webb and Webb) **22**:412
"The Historic Home of Grout" (Vilakazi) **37**:410
A Historic Portrait (Nezval)
See *Historický obraz*
The Historical Atlas of World Mythology (Campbell) **140**:2-5, 11, 85, 119, 134
A Historical Drama of the Present (Zuckmayer) **191**:327
"Historical Fiction" (Sabatini) **47**:306
"Historical Inevitability" (Berlin) **105**:4, 7, 17, 132, 144-45
An Historical Manual of English Prosody (Saintsbury) **31**:239
Historical Materialism and the Economics of Karl Marx (Croce) **37**:121, 123
Historical Mysteries (Lang) **16**:254
The Historical Nights' Entertainment (Sabatini) **47**:300, 303
"The Historical Theories of Professor Loria" (Croce)
See "La teorie storiche del professor Loria"
Historical-Philosophical Fragment (Benjamin)
See *Geschichtsphilosophische Thesen*
"Historicity of Things" (Alexander) **77**:58
Historický obraz (Nezval) **44**:245
"Historie des Jason" (Giono) **124**:55
"Historie dirigenta Kaliny" (Čapek) **192**:179
Die Historie von König David (Beer-Hofmann) **60**:36
"Historieläraren" (Söderberg) **39**:428, 437
Historietter (Söderberg) **39**:438
"History" (Lawrence) **93**:18
"History as a System" (Ortega y Gasset)
See "Historia como sistema"
"History as Literature" (Roosevelt) **69**:186, 202, 205, 265, 268
History as Literature and Other Essays (Roosevelt) **69**:188-89
History, Its Theory and Practice (Croce)
See *Teoria e storia della storiografia*
History of a Character (Stanislavsky) **167**:295
"The History of a Dedication" (Tsvetaeva) **7**:571
"The History of a Jackaroo in Five Letters" (Paterson) **32**:380
"History of a Literary Movement" (Nemerov) **124**:152, 184
"History of a Literary Radical" (Bourne) **16**:46-7
The History of a Literary Radical, and Other Essays (Bourne) **16**:48, 54
History of a Man Reforged (Zoshchenko) **15**:504
A History of American Art (Hartmann) **73**:117, 122, 133-34, 140-46
"A History of Angels" (Borges) **109**:17
History of Anthony Waring (Sinclair) **11**:411
"A History of Chemistry" (Peirce) **81**:235,328
"The History of Conductor Kalina" (Čapek)
See "Historie dirigenta Kaliny"
A History of Criticism and Literary Taste in Europe (Saintsbury) **31**:221-22, 225-27, 233-34, 236-38, 246, 248-49
The History of David Grieve (Ward) **55**:406, 409-13, 421, 425, 432
A History of Elizabethan Literature (Saintsbury) **31**:232
History of England (Belloc) **7**:39
History of England in the Nineteenth Century (Halévy)
See *Histoire du peuple anglais au xlxe siècle. iv. Le milieu du siècle, 1841-52*
The History of English Law Before the Time of Edward I (Maitland) **65**:262-64, 270-72, 274, 276, 279, 282, 284, 292
History of English Literature (Lang) **16**:258
A History of English Literature (Moody) **105**:236, 252, 254, 267-68
A History of English Prose Rhythm (Saintsbury) **31**:221-22, 224, 231, 235-36, 239-40
A History of English Prosody (Saintsbury) **31**:221, 228, 235-36, 238-39
The History of English Thought in the Eighteenth Century (Stephen) **23**:306, 316, 318-19, 321-23, 326-29, 338, 342
A History of Eternity (Borges)
See *Historia de la eternidad*
The History of European Literature (Babits)
See *Az Europai irodalom története*
History of German Aesthetics since Kant (von Hartmann) **96**:222
The History of Human Marriage (Westermarck) **87**:325, 334, 337-38, 340, 342-43, 356, 360, 390
A History of Indian Philosophy (Dasgupta) **81**:88,90,93-5,97,99
History of Infamy (Borges)
See *Historia universal de la infamia*
History of Ireland: Critical and Philosophical (O'Grady) **5**:349, 351, 354-55
The History of Ireland: Cuculain and His Contemporaries (O'Grady) **5**:350, 353-54
History of Ireland: The Heroic Period (O'Grady) **5**:347-48, 350, 352-54, 357
History of Italian Philosophy (Gentile) **96**:83
The History of Mr. Polly (Wells) **6**:536-37, 539, 543, 545, 547-48, 553; **12**:506-07; **19**:428, 440, 452; **133**:228
The History of My Contemporary (Korolenko)
See *Istoria moego sovremennika*
A History of Myself (Dreiser) **18**:51
A History of Nineteenth Century Literature, 1780-1895 (Saintsbury) **31**:222, 245
"History of Our Own Times" (Ford) **172**:7
"The History of Photogen and Nycteris" (MacDonald) **9**:305; **113**:212
History of Political Philosophy (Strauss) **141**:223
History of Roca (Lugones)
See *Historia de Roca*
History of Sarmiento (Lugones)
See *Historia de Sarmiento*
History of Scotland from the Roman Occupation (Lang) **16**:270
"History of Six Empty Houses" (Nezval) **44**:240
A History of the American People (Wilson) **79**:486, 500, 527
A History of the Borgias (Rolfe)
See *Chronicles of the House of Borgia*
The History of the Civil War in the U.S.S.R. (Stalin) **92**:157
"A History of the Echoes of a Name" (Borges) **109**:157
History of the English People in the Nineteenth Century (Halévy)
See *Histoire du peuple anglais au xlxe siècle. iv. Le milieu du siècle, 1841-52*
A History of the English-Speaking Peoples (Churchill) **113**:115, 127, 130, 132-33, 137, 143, 145-46, 152-53, 162, 184
A History of the French Novel (Saintsbury) **31**:232, 235-36, 241-42
The History of the Heart (Aleixandre)
See *Historia del corazón*
The History of the Idea of Progress (Nisbet) **117**:331, 334-37, 340-41, 344, 359
The History of the Knight d'Alessio (Kuzmin)
See *Istorya rytsaria d'Alessio*
History of the Moral Ideas (Westermarck) **87**:328
History of the Naval War of 1812 (Roosevelt) **69**:176, 182, 185, 197, 224, 240-42, 250-51, 276
A History of the Night (Borges)
See *Historia de la noche*
History of the Realm of Naples (Croce) **37**:100
The History of the Russian Revolution to Brest-Litovsk (Trotsky)
See *Istoriya Russkoi Revolyutsii*
History of the Second World War (Churchill) **113**:133, 143
The History of the Standard Oil Company (Tarbell) **40**:422-24, 426-27, 430-31, 433, 436-39, 441
History of the United States of America during the Administrations of Thomas Jefferson and James Madison (Adams) **4**:2, 4, 6, 9, 13, 16-17, 20-1; **52**:4, 13-14, 18-19, 31
"History of the Warrior and the Captive" (Borges)
See "Historia del guerrero y de la cautiva"
The History of Trade Unionism (Webb and Webb) **22**:412, 417-18, 429-30
The History of Witchcraft and Demonology (Summers) **16**:423-24, 428-31
History of Woman Suffrage (Anthony) **84**:5, 9, 17, 26, 33
History of Woman Suffrage (Stanton) **73**:242, 245, 262, 264, 271-72, 274
A History of Wood Engraving (Woodberry) **73**:377
"History Subsumed under the General Concept of Art" (Croce) **37**:101
"The History Teacher" (Söderberg)
See "Historieläraren"
Histrionics (Bernhard)
See *Der Theatermacher*
Hit the Line Hard (Rhodes) **53**:307, 317
"The Hitchhiker" (Dahl) **173**:17
"Hitching Bertha to the Sled" (Knister) **56**:161
"Hitler" (Lewis) **2**:392; **9**:241, 248
Hitler (Lewis) **104**:191-98, 201, 211-12, 214, 231-32, 237-42, 245-46, 280-81
"Hitler, According to Speer" (Canetti) **157**:69

The Hitler Cult (Lewis) **104**:154, 192-94, 198, 212-14, 225, 232, 241-42
Hitohabune (Shimazaki Toson) **5**:439
"Hitosumi yori" (Yosano) **59**:345, 347
"Hittite siyata and Gen. 14:3" (Sapir) **108**:257
"Hiver à boire" (Huidobro) **31**:125
"Hiver sentimental" (Nelligan) **14**:398
"Un Hivernage dans les glaces" (Verne) **52**:349
Hiyori Geta (Nagai) **51**:95
Hjärtats sånger (Lagerkvist) **144**:211
Hjulet (Jensen) **41**:291, 294, 296, 301-03
Hlapec Jernej in njegova pravica (Cankar) **105**:152-55,
"The Hoardings" (Fletcher) **35**:89
"The Hoax" (Svevo)
See "Una burla riuscita"
The Hoax (Svevo)
See *Una burla riuscita*
"The Hoax of Success" (Saroyan) **137**:182
Hobbes (Stephen) **23**:340
The Hobbit; or, There and Back Again (Tolkien) **137**:225, 233-34, 247, 253, 467, 272, 287-90, 296, 298-99, 301-2, 316-17, 326, 329, 337, 339, 341, 343, 351, 355, 358-60
The Hobby Horse (Pinero) **32**:395, 398, 404, 412-13
"Hoboe" (Kandinsky) **92**:67
"Hoboes That Pass in the Night" (London) **9**:281
Hobohemia (Lewis) **23**:127
Die Hochzeit (Canetti) **157**:21, 25, 38-40, 62, 67, 77, 82-85, 104
"Der Hochzeit der Sobeïde" (Hofmannsthal) **11**:292, 303
Hochzeit des Figaro (Horvath) **45**:78
"Die Hochzeit des Theseus" (Spitteler) **12**:339
Hochzeiten im Hause (Hrabal) **155**:159, 165
"Hochzeitsvorbereitungen auf dem Lande" (Kafka) **47**:233; **179**:272, 307
Hochzeitsvorbereitungen auf dem Lande und andere Prosa aus dem Nachlas (Kafka) **179**:259, 263
"Hod Putt" (Masters) **25**:298
"Hodel" (Aleichem) **1**:32; **35**:314
"Hodocasca" (Popa) **167**:158
"Hodos Chameliontis" (Yeats) **116**:273
Hodos Chameliontos (Yeats) **11**:521; **31**:394
Hofmeyr (Paton) **165**:295, 298
Un hogar sólido (Garro) **153**:9, 17-18, 71-72
The Hogarth Essays (Woolf) **1**:530
Das hohe Lied (Sudermann) **15**:423-25, 427-28, 430, 437-38
"Hohensalzburg: Fantastic Variations on a Theme of Romantic Character" (Jarrell) **177**:152, 155, 159, 196, 208
"Hojas de trabajo" (Unamuno) **148**:306
"Hojas de yedra" (Unamuno) **148**:310
Hōjō Katei (Mori Ogai) **14**:376, 378-79
Hōjō no umi (Mishima) **161**:3, 6, 8, 30, 51-53, 56, 66-68, 92
"Hōkyōnin no shi" (Akutagawa Ryūnosuke) **16**:35
"Hold, Hard, These Ancient Minutes in the Cuckoo's Mouth" (Thomas) **8**:459; **45**:362
"Holderlin's Journey" (Muir) **87**:201, 260-65
"Holding Her Down" (London) **9**:281
"Holding the Mirror up to Nature" (Nemerov) **124**:155, 172, 179, 181, 196, 203, 226, 280
"The Holdout" (Lardner) **14**:320
"The Hole in the Mahogany Panel" (Post) **39**:336
The Hole in the Wall (Morrison) **72**:359-60, 363, 365, 369-71, 373, 377, 379, 384-85, 395
"A Holiday" (Grahame) **64**:59-60, 62, 78, 88
A Holiday (Andreyev) **3**:20, 28
Holiday (Barry) **11**:48-56, 60-6, 68
Holiday, and Other Poems (Davidson) **24**:172, 175, 191
"Holiday at Hampton Court" (Davidson) **24**:191
"Holiday in Reality" (Stevens) **12**:361; **45**:335
"A Holiday in the South" (Andrić)
See "Letovanje na jugu"
"Holiday Memory" (Thomas) **45**:399; **105**:320, 356
Hölle Weg Erde (Kaiser) **9**:173-75, 180-81, 191-92
"Hollow Harbour" (van Ostaijen) **33**:421-22
"The Hollow Nut" (Colette) **16**:128
"The Hollow Temple" (Hammett) **187**:96
"The Hollow Wood" (Thomas) **10**:457
"Holly Hop" (Holly) **65**:150
Holly in the Hills (Holly) **65**:149
"The Holly Wreath" (March) **96**:241, 249, 262
"Hollywood on the Moon" (Kuttner) **10**:267
"The Holm Oak" (Ivanov) **33**:137
"Holmesiana; or, About Detective Stories" (Čapek) **37**:47; **192**:223
Holmes-Pollock Letters (Holmes) **77**:217
Holnapp reggel (Karinthy) **47**:269, 273
"Holstius" (White) **176**:178
"The Holy Caravan" (Ady) **11**:15
The Holy City (Lagerloef)
See *Jerusalem 2: I det heliga landet*
Holy Europe (Adamov)
See *Sainte Europe*
The Holy Flower (Haggard) **11**:246, 254
"The Holy Island" (Somerville & Ross) **51**:357, 362, 381, 384
The Holy Land (Lagerkvist)
See *Det heliga landet*
"The Holy Man" (Akutagawa Ryūnosuke) **16**:27
Holy Memorial Cards (Yourcenar)
See *Souvenirs pieux*
"Holy Morning" (Roberts) **68**:348, 352
"Holy Mountain" (Mayakovski) **18**:270
"The Holy Night" (Čapek) **192**:186
"Holy Night" (Remizov)
See "Sviatoi vecher"
Holy Orders: The Tragedy of a Quiet Life (Corelli) **51**:66, 75-76
"Holy Saturday" (Carducci)
See "Sabato Santo"
The Holy Sinner (Mann)
See *Der Erwählte*
"The Holy Six" (Thomas) **45**:391, 409; **105**:296-97, 300-01, 325-27, 329, 332-33, 338
"Holy Spring" (Thomas) **8**:460
The Holy Spring (Raabe) **45**:200
"Holy Stove" (Gilman) **9**:96
"A Holy Terror" (Bierce) **7**:88; **44**:12, 44-5
The Holy Terror (Wells) **6**:550, 553; **12**:504; **19**:437
The Holy Terrors (Cocteau)
See *Les enfants terribles*
"The Holy Time" (Stephens) **4**:412
A Holy Tradition of Working: Passages from the Writings of Eric Gill (Gill) **85**:101
The Holy War (Tynan) **3**:506
"Holy Well" (Coffin) **95**:16
"Das Holz für morgen" (Borchert) **5**:105-06, 109
Holzfällen: Eine Erregung (Bernhard) **165**:12, 17, 77, 79, 83-86, 96-98, 102, 111
"Homage a Goya" (Huysmans) **69**:30
"The Homage of Death" (Field) **43**:160
Homage to Catalonia (Orwell) **2**:499, 503, 507, 510; **6**:349-53; **15**:322-23, 330, 333, 343, 355, 359-60, 362; **31**:179, 190, 192; **51**:219, 228, 252, 254, 256, 261; **128**:257, 262-63, 267-69, 274, 276-77, 281, 283, 295-96, 307-08; **129**:228, 245
"Homage to Flanders" (Sarton) **120**:301
"Homage to Hemingway" (Bishop) **103**:12, 16
"Homage to James Bond" (Ibarguengoitia)
See "Homenaje a James Bond"
"Homage to Lope de Vega" (García Lorca)
See "Homenaje a Lope de Vega"
"El hombre a quien Ie dolía el pensamiento" (Nervo) **11**:394
"El Hombre de la esquina rosada" (Borges) **109**:70-72, 153
Hombre de tierra (Aleixandre) **113**:4
"El hombre del árbol" (Lugones) **15**:293
el hombre del buho. Misterio de una vocación (Gonzalez Martinez) **72**:154
"El hombre en el umbral" (Borges) **109**:40-2
"Hombre en la orilla" (Salinas) **17**:357
"El hombre muerto" (Quiroga) **20**:210, 212, 214-15, 217-23
El hombre negro (Echegaray) **4**:102
"Un hombre pasa" (Vallejo) **56**:311
"Hombre pequeñito" (Storni) **5**:445
El hombre y la gente (Ortega y Gasset) **9**:356
El hombrecito (Benavente) **3**:98
"Hombres de las orillas" (Borges)
See "El Hombre de la esquina rosada"
Hombres de maíz (Asturias) **184**:9-12, 14-16, 21, 24-26, 31, 33, 36-37, 39-45, 62-71, 73, 75-77, 85-88
Los hombres de pro (Pereda) **16**:363, 365, 368, 371, 373, 377
Hombres e ideas (Hostos) **24**:303
"Hombres pelearon" (Borges) **109**:72
"Home" (Dunbar) **2**:128
"Home" (Heidenstam) **5**:249, 255
"Home" (Jackson) **187**:236
"Home" (Ledwidge) **23**:116
"Home" (Percy) **84**:202
"Home" (Thomas) **10**:460
"Home and State" (Lagerloef) **36**:245
The Home and the World (Tagore)
See *Ghare-Bāire*
Home Country (Pyle) **75**:233
"Home Creatures" (Guro)
See "Domashnie"
Home Fires in France (Fisher) **87**:72
A Home for the Heart (Bettelheim) **143**:10
"Home for the Holidays" (Nemerov) **124**:284, 288
"Home from a walk" (Garcíá Lorca)
See "Vuelta de paseo"
"Home in the Pyrenees" (Rostand) **6**:381
The Home: Its Work and Influence (Gilman) **37**:182, 187, 198; **117**:49, 125, 127, 140
The Home Place (Morris) **107**:94, 96, 98, 105, 114, 142-44, 145-47, 156, 159, 165-67, 174-75, 177, 179, 181-83, 208, 215-19, 221, 225, 242-43
Home Rhymes (Guest) **95**:208, 211
"Home Sickness" (Moore)
See "Galar Dúithche"
"Home, Sweet Home" (Benson) **27**:17
Home, Sweet Home (Griffith) **68**:217, 248
Home, Sweet Home (Riddell) **40**:334-35
"Home There's No Returning" (Kuttner) **10**:269-70
"Home Thoughts from Abroad" (Lewis) **3**:290
Home to Harlem (McKay) **7**:455-58, 464-69; **41**:317-18, 320-22, 325, 328-29, 334-40
"Homecoming" (Arnow) **196**:92-3
"Homecoming" (Bosman) **49**:17
"Homecoming" (Platonov) **14**:410-12, 414-15, 420
The Homecoming (Hecht) **101**:73
The Homecoming (O'Neill) **1**:387-88; **6**:331
The Homecoming (Orton) **157**:331
The Home-Coming and Other Stories (Aldrich) **125**:10, 18
The Homecoming Game (Nemerov) **124**:151, 159-61, 241, 243, 291
"The Homecoming of Beorhtnoth Beorthelm's Son" (Tolkien) **137**:284
"The Home-Coming of 'Rastus Smith" (Dunbar) **2**:133
"The Homecoming of the Sheep" (Ledwidge) **23**:116-18, 120
"Homeland" (Ivanov) **33**:138
"Homeland" (Lagerkvist)
See "Hembygden"
"Homeless" (Cankar) **105**:164
"Homeless Russia" (Esenin) **4**:113
The Home-Maker (Fisher) **87**:78, 84
"Homenaje" (Nervo) **11**:395

"Homenaje a James Bond" (Ibarguengoitia) **148**:218
"Homenaje a Lope de Vega" (García Lorca) **181**:185
"Homer" (Carducci) **32**:86
"Homer Again" (Carducci) **32**:86
"Homer Marsh Dwells in His House of Planks" (Bosschere)
See "Homère Mare"
"Homère Mare" (Bosschere) **19**:53-4, 57-8, 63-4
Homero en Cuernavaca (Reyes) **33**:317
"The Homesick Woman" (Papadiamantis) **29**:270
"Homesickness" (Bishop) **121**:55
"Homesickness" (Tsvetaeva) **7**:565; **35**:397
"Homesickness in the Land of Sunlight" (Ady) **11**:14
The Homesteader (Micheaux) **76**:237-41, 243-45, 249-54, 263, 265-66, 269, 271-72
"Home-Thoughts" (McKay) **41**:344
"Hometown" (Lu Hsun)
See "Guxiang"
Hometown (Dazai Osamu)
See *Kokyō*
Hometown (Mizoguchi)
See *Furusato*
"Homeward!" (Mayakovski) **4**:292; **18**:258, 260
Homeward: Songs by the Way (Baker) **3**:3-6, 9-10; **10**:12, 18, 26-8
"Homework" (Ginsberg) **120**:39
"Homilía por la cultura" (Reyes) **33**:323
"Homily" (Herbert) **168**:47
Homing with the Birds (Porter) **21**:265-66, 278
"Hommage à Jack B. Yeats" (Beckett) **145**:91
L'homme à cheval (Drieu la Rochelle) **21**:22, 34, 40
L'homme a la tete de caoutchouc (Melies) **81**:123
L'homme approximatif (Tzara) **168**:231, 273, 316, 321, 323
L'homme couvert de femmes (Drieu la Rochelle) **21**:18-19, 32-3
Un homme d'affaires (Bourget) **12**:68
L'homme de chair et l'homme reflet (Jacob) **6**:191
L'homme de cristal (Jacob) **6**:202
"L'homme de quarante ans" (Bosschere) **19**:59
L'homme de tetes (Melies) **81**:138
"L'homme double" (Schwob) **20**:323
L'homme en amour (Lemonnier) **22**:198, 202
"L'homme et la coquille" (Valéry) **15**:468
"L'homme et l'adversité" (Merleau-Ponty) **156**:121
L'homme et l'enfant (Adamov) **189**:15, 20-1, 24-5, 27-8, 31, 47, 57-9
"L'homme gras" (Schwob) **20**:323
"L'homme la femme" (Arp) **115**:41
Un homme libre (Barrès) **47**:35-6, 46-7, 49-50, 61-2, 73, 76, 78, 85-91, 93, 95, 97
Un homme obscure (Yourcenar) **193**:302, 305, 357
"L'homme qui a aimé les Néréides" (Yourcenar) **193**:283, 289-94
L'Homme transcendental (Merleau-Ponty) **156**:174
"L'homme voilé" (Schwob) **20**:321, 323
Homo Faber: A Report (Frisch)
See *Homo faber: Ein Bericht*
Homo faber: Ein Bericht (Frisch) **121**:186-90, 193, 201-02, 213-16, 226, 231, 234, 246, 260, 278, 280-82, 285, 287-93, 295, 298-300, 302
Homo Sapiens (Przybyszewski) **36**:280-82, 284, 290
"Homo sum" (Sully Prudhomme) **31**:302
"Homogenic Love" (Carpenter) **88**:90-1
Homogenic Love and Its Place in a Free Society (Carpenter) **88**:97
Honba (Mishima) **161**:3-4, 31, 51, 53-56, 58, 68
"La honda inquietud única" (Unamuno) **148**:299
"Hone" (Hayashi) **27**:104
Honest People (Deledda)
See *Anime oneste*
"An Honest Woman" (Gilman) **9**:113; **117**:100, 102, 116, 119, 123
"Honesty of Purpose" (Callaghan) **145**:253
Honey (Mankiewicz) **85**:114
Honey from beyond the Pale (Prishvin) **75**:220
Honey in the Hive: Judith Matlack, 1898-1982 (Sarton) **120**:267
"Honeybunch" (Tolstoy) **18**:377, 382
Honeybuzzard (Carter)
See *Shadow Dance*
Honeycomb (Richardson) **3**:345-47, 356, 358
"A Honeycombe" (Stephens) **4**:416
Honeyflow (Williams) **89**:367, 371, 398
The Honeyman Festival (Engel) **137**:115, 117, 123
"Honeymoon" (Lawrence) **93**:67
"Honeymoon" (Mansfield) **8**:284; **39**:304; **164**:322-23
The Honeymoon (Bennett) **197**:16-18, 20
The Honeymooners (Cohan) **60**:170
Honey-Paw (Leino)
See *Mesikammen*
The Honeysuckle (D'Annunzio)
See *Le chèvrefeuille*
"Hong meigui yü bai meigui" (Chang) **184**:109, 115-19, 127, 138
L'honneur du nom (Bourget) **12**:69
"Honor" (Faulkner) **141**:134; **170**:236
Honor (Sudermann)
See *Die Ehre*
"Honor Bright" (Millay) **169**:237
The Honor of Thieves (Griffith) **68**:248
"The Honorary Member" (Dunsany) **59**:28
The Honour of the Name (Green) **63**:149
"The Honours of War" (Kipling) **17**:209
Hooge troeven (Couperus) **15**:46
"The Hooligan" (Esenin) **4**:117
Hoopla! Such Is Life! (Toller)
See *Hoppla, wir Leben!*
A Hoosier Holiday (Dreiser) **10**:169; **35**:55-6, 72
"Hop Plant" (Pasternak) **188**:185
Hop Signor! (Ghelderode) **187**:4, 6, 10-11, 24, 26-7, 29
"Hope" (Jarrell) **177**:145-46, 148, 155, 206
"Hope" (Prado)
See "La Esperanza"
Hope (Graham) **19**:119
"Hope Abandoned" (Davies) **5**:199
"Hope against Hope" (Benson) **17**:32
Hope against Hope, and Other Stories (Benson) **17**:32
"Hope for the Unattainable" (Tagore)
See "Durasa"
"The Hope of My Heart" (McCrae) **12**:210
"The Hope of Pessimism" (Gissing) **24**:247-48
"The Hope of the Poor Destitute" (Bialik) **25**:49
The Hope That Is Ours (Martinez Sierra and Martinez Sierra)
See *Esperanza nuestra*
Hopelessly (Storni)
See *Irremediablemente*
Hopelessness (Donoso)
See *La Desesperanza*
Hopes and Fears; or, Scenes from the life of a Spinster (Yonge) **48**:365-67, 372, 381-82, 387-88
"Hop-Picking" (Orwell) **128**:255, 268, 282
"Hoppity" (Milne) **88**:250
Hoppla, wir Leben! (Toller) **10**:477, 480, 482, 484-85, 488
"Hora" (Jiménez) **183**:263
La hora inútil (Gonzalez Martinez) **72**:148
"Horace the Haymow" (Knister) **56**:163
"Horace to Leuconoë" (Robinson) **5**:400
Horacker (Raabe) **45**:160, 166, 169-70, 172, 174, 176-79, 201
Horae solitariae (Thomas) **10**:449
Horas de sol (Martinez Sierra and Martinez Sierra) **6**:279, 285
Las horas doradas (Lugones) **15**:286, 288
Las horas solitarias (Baroja) **8**:63
The Horatians and the Curiatians (Brecht) **6**:37
La horda (Blasco Ibáñez) **12**:29-30, 34-5, 38, 40, 42, 47
Hordubal (Čapek) **6**:86-8; **37**:50, 54, 59-60; **192**:175-76, 223
Horedströmninger i det nittende aahundredes literatur (Brandes) **10**:61-2, 65-74
Höret die Stimme (Werfel) **8**:479-80, 482
Horizon carré (Huidobro) **31**:124-26, 130, 137
El horizonte económico en los albores de Grecia (Reyes) **33**:323
Horn of My Love (p'Bitek) **149**:51, 55, 58, 67, 71, 92, 114-15, 120
The Horn of Wanza (Raabe)
See *Das Horn von Wanza*
Das Horn von Wanza (Raabe) **45**:164-67, 176-79, 194, 202
"Hornblower and His Majesty" (Forester) **152**:133
Hornblower and the Atropos (Forester) **152**:129, 131, 135, 138-39, 141
Hornblower and the Crisis (Forester)
See *Hornblower during the Crisis*
Hornblower and the Hotspur (Forester) **152**:130, 139-40, 160
The Hornblower Companion (Forester) **152**:134-35, 162
Hornblower during the Crisis (Forester) **152**:130-1, 135, 139
Hornblower in the West Indies (Forester)
See *Admiral Hornblower in the West Indies*
"Hornblower's Charitable Offering" (Forester) **152**:132
"Hornblower's Temptation" (Forester) **152**:130
"El horno viejo" (Arguedas) **147**:108
Hōrōki (Hayashi) **27**:103, 105-06
The Horoscope of Man (Upward) **85**:390
"The Horror at Red Hook" (Lovecraft) **22**:221-24
"The Horror from the Mound" (Howard) **8**:128
"The Horror Horn" (Benson) **27**:9, 13, 16
The Horror Horn, and Other Stories: The Best Horror Stories of E. F. Benson (Benson) **27**:13
"The Horror of the Heights" (Doyle) **7**:224-25
"The Horse Dealer" (Jensen)
See "Prangeren"
"The Horse Fair at Opdorp" (Verhaeren) **12**:472
Horse Feathers (Mankiewicz) **85**:112, 149, 155
The Horse of Diomedes (Gourmont)
See *Le pèlerin du silence*
"The Horse of the Invisible" (Hodgson) **13**:236
"The Horse of the Plains" (Remington) **89**:299, 304
"The Horse, the Lamb, and the Rabbit" (Mikszath)
See "A ló, báránya és a nyúl"
"The Horse Thief" (Benét) **28**:5-6, 8
"The Horse-Dealer's Daughter" (Lawrence) **2**:362; **33**:202
"A Horseman in the Sky" (Bierce) **1**:88; **7**:88-9; **44**:6, 12, 44-7
The Horseman on the Roof (Giono)
See *Le hussard sur le toit*
"The Horseman's Song" (García Lorca)
See "Canción de jinete"
"Horsemanship" (Andrić)
See "Džigit"
Horsemen of the Apocalypse (Kandinsky) **92**:62
"Horses" (Muir) **2**:489; **87**:174
"The Horses" (Stephens) **4**:421
Horses and Men (Anderson) **1**:44, 46; **10**:36, 45; **123**:85, 96, 98
"The Horse's Ha" (Thomas) **105**:301, 328-29
The Horse's Mouth (Cary) **1**:140-41, 143-49; **29**:64-5, 67-73, 76-8, 80-1, 84, 88-9, 91-2,

101, 103, 109; **196**:139, 141, 144, 148, 153-54, 156-57, 174-75, 177, 180-82, 186-87, 193, 202, 218
"The Horses of Death" (Ady)
See "A hall lovai"
The Horses of the Conquest (Graham) **19**:109, 124
"Horses of the Plains" (Remington)
See "The Horse of the Plains"
"Horses on the Camargue" (Campbell) **5**:123
"A Horse's Tale" (Twain) **161**:223
"Horseshoes" (Lardner) **14**:291, 317, 319
"Horses—One Dash" (Crane) **11**:140, 154-55, 160, 162, 164
"The Horsethieves" (Kuprin) **5**:298, 300
"Horsie" (Parker) **143**:314-15, 332
Les hors-nature (Vallette) **67**:280, 303, 324-27
Horst Wessel (Ewers) **12**:139
Hortense a dit: "Je m'en fous!" (Feydeau) **22**:82, 88
Hortense Said: "I Don't Give a Damn!" (Feydeau)
See *Hortense a dit: "Je m'en fous!"*
Die Hose (Sternheim) **8**:367-69, 371-72, 374-75, 379
"Hoshi" (Kunikida Doppo) **99**:302, 304
"Hospital Barge at Cérisy" (Owen) **5**:374; **27**:212, 226
"Hospital Outlines" (Henley)
See "In Hospital"
"The Hospital Visit" (Dickey) **151**:204
"The Hospital Window" (Dickey) **151**:121, 203
The Hospital Window (Ishikawa) **15**:129
"Hospitality" (Capote) **164**:200
"Höst" (Södergran) **31**:288
The Hostage (Claudel)
See *L'otage*
Hostages of Life (Sologub) **9**:434
"Höstens dagar" (Södergran) **31**:286, 288
Hostess to Death (Wakefield) **120**:355
"The Hostile Sea" (Kuzmin)
See "Vrazhdebnoe more"
"Hostile Stars" (Södergran)
See "Fientliga stjärnor"
Hostile Valley (Williams) **89**:394, 399
"The Hosting of the Sidhe" (Yeats) **31**:407
"Hosts and Guests" (Beerbohm) **1**:67; **24**:103
A Hot Country (Naipaul) **153**:228, 230, 234-35
Hot Day, Hot Night (Himes)
See *Blind Man with a Pistol*
"Hot Potatoes" (Bennett) **5**:46
"The Hot Summer" (Remizov)
See "Zharkoe leto"
"Hot Tamale Alley" (Cohan) **60**:169
"Hôtel" (Apollinaire) **51**:61
"The Hotel" (Monroe) **12**:216-17
The Hotel (Bowen) **148**:40, 79, 82, 84-85, 88
"Hotel at Alpena, Michigan" (Masters) **25**:300
"Hôtel de l'Univers et de Portugal" (Merrill) **173**:172, 256
L'Hôtel du Libre-Echange (Feydeau) **22**:77-80, 89, 91
Hotel Haywire (Sturges) **48**:286, 291, 312
The Hotel in Amsterdam (Osborne) **153**:242, 321-22
Hotel Paradiso (Feydeau)
See *L'Hôtel du Libre-Echange*
"Hotel Room in Chartres" (Lowry) **6**:254
Hotel Savoy (Roth) **33**:333-34, 346-47, 362-63
Hotel Universe (Barry) **11**:49-50, 52-7, 59-61, 64-8
"Die Hoteltreppe" (Werfel) **8**:477
"Hot-Foot Hannibal" (Chesnutt) **39**:71, 95-6, 107
"Hōtō" (Nagai) **51**:98-9
"The Hottest Coon in Dixie" (Dunbar) **12**:122
"The Hound" (Lovecraft) **4**:270, 272
"Hound of Heaven" (Thompson) **4**:434-38, 440-41
The Hound of the Baskervilles (Doyle) **7**:220, 230, 236, 238
"The Hounds of Fate" (Saki) **3**:366-70, 372
"The Hour and the Man" (Rhodes) **53**:315
"The Hour before Dawn" (Yeats) **31**:407
The Hour of God (Aurobindo) **63**:27
"The Hour of Magic" (Davies) **5**:201
Hour of Smiles (Allen) **87**:24
The Hour of the Dragon (Howard)
See *Conan the Conqueror*
"The Hour of the King" (Baker) **10**:28
"The Hour of Victory" (Hippius) **9**:159
"Hourglass" (Merrill) **173**:177, 255
The Hour-Glass (Yeats) **11**:513; **31**:408-09, 411
"Hourglass II" (Merrill) **173**:162, 177
"The Hours" (Bishop) **103**:28, 50
"Hours in a Library" (Woolf) **43**:409, 415, 426
Hours in a Library (Stephen) **23**:301-02, 306, 309, 312-14, 317, 329, 337, 341, 346
"The House" (Agee) **180**:22
"The House" (di Donato) **159**:196
"The House" (Douglas) **40**:75-6
"The House" (de la Mare) **53**:36, 38
"The House among the Laurels" (Hodgson) **13**:236
"House and Home" (Tynan) **3**:502-03
A House and Its Head (Compton-Burnett) **180**:114, 123-25, 129, 131, 134-37, 143, 145, 186-87, 200, 203
"House and Man" (Thomas) **10**:463
"The House at Old Pimen" (Tsvetaeva) **7**:571
The House at Pooh Corner (Milne) **6**:318, 320-22; **88**:229, 231-2, 234, 237, 286-61
The House Behind the Cedars (Chesnutt) **5**:133-34; **39**:75-6, 78-9, 84-5, 88-9, 92, 96-7, 99
The House Behind the Cedars (Micheaux) **76**:262, 269
The House by the Medlar-Tree (Verga)
See *I malavoglia*
The House by the Sea: A Journal (Sarton) **120**:231-32, 240, 247, 319-20, 326-28
"The House by the Side of the Road" (Fields) **80**:262
The House by the Stable (Williams) **1**:517-18; **11**:499
"House City I" (van Ostaijen) **33**:422
House Divided (Williams) **89**:365, 402
House for a Mistress (Nagai)
See *Mekake taku*
"House Guest" (Bishop) **121**:90
The House in a Secluded Place (Andrić)
See *Kuča na osami*
The House in a Secluded Space (Andrić)
See *Kuča na osami*
The House in Demetrius Road (Beresford) **81**:9,11,13
The House in Dormer Forest (Webb) **24**:465, 467, 469, 473-74, 476-78, 484
The House in Haarlem (van Schendel)
See *Een Hollandsch drama*
The House in Paris (Bowen) **148**:17-18, 20, 37, 79, 82, 87, 89, 96, 98, 103-4, 108
A House in the Country (Donoso)
See *Casa de campo*
A House in the Middle of the Highway (Popa)
See *Kuća nasred druma*
A House in the Uplands (Caldwell) **117**:19
"The House in the Wood" (Jarrell) **177**:134-36, 209-10
"The House in the Wood" (Manning) **25**:278
"The House in Turk Street" (Hammett) **187**:78, 134-36, 139, 166, 169
The House of a Hundred Lights: A Psalm of Experience after Reading a Souplet of Bidpai (Torrence) **97**:143, 145, 146, 151, 153, 156-57, 164
The House of All Sorts (Carr) **32**:117, 125-26
"The House of Asterión" (Borges)
See "La casa de Asterión"
The House of Atreus (Hauptmann) **4**:208
"The House of Beauty" (Sharp) **39**:372
The House of Bernarda Alba (García Lorca)
See *La casa de Bernarda Alba*
House of Cards (Babits)
See *Kártyavár*
A House of Children (Cary) **1**:144; **29**:66-8, 79-80, 83-4, 87, 92, 103-04, 109; **196**:136, 140, 175
"The House of Clocks" (Green) **63**:143
The House of Coalport, 1750-1950 (Mackenzie) **116**:228
The House of Cobwebs, and Other Stories (Gissing) **3**:228; **24**:220
The House of Danger (Wallace) **57**:402
"The House of Darkness" (Hedāyat) **21**:81
A House of Darkness (Griffith) **68**:215
"The House of Euripides" (Manning) **25**:265, 269
"The House of Fahy" (Somerville & Ross) **51**:382
House of Flowers (Capote) **164**:100, 114
"The House of Idiedaily" (Carman)
See "In the House of Idiedaily"
"House of Life; Inclusiveness" (Moody) **105**:225
The House of Liliecrona (Lagerloef)
See *Liljecronas hem*
The House of Many Mirrors (Hunt) **53**:186, 192
The House of Martha (Stockton) **47**:325
The House of Mirth (Wharton) **3**:551-54, 558, 560, 562, 565-66, 571-76, 579-80; **9**:542, 545-46, 548, 550-52; **27**:384, 394; **53**:361, 391, 393; **129**:345-49, 351, 361, 364-65; **149**:141-56, 158-60, 162-71, 173-4, 176-7, 182, 185, 190-3, 195-6, 198, 200-03, 205-9, 217, 219-20, 224-6, 229-32, 234, 238-9, 241, 244-63, 265-6, 272, 275-6, 280-3, 287, 289, 293, 296-300, 302-4
The House of Mourning (Werfel) **8**:471
"The House of Offence" (Austin) **25**:26
"The House of Orchids" (Sterling) **20**:372
The House of Orchids, and Other Poems (Sterling) **20**:372-74, 378, 385-86
"The House of Pale Women" (Yourcenar)
See "La Maison des femmes pâles"
A House of Pomegranates (Wilde) **41**:376
The House of Souls (Machen) **4**:277
"The House of Sounds" (Shiel) **8**:359, 361
"The House of Stene" (Grove) **4**:138
The House of Sun-Goes-Down (De Voto) **29**:126
The House of the Aizgorri (Baroja)
See *La casa de Aizgorri*
"The House of the Dead" (Apollinaire)
See "La maison des mortes"
The House of the Four Winds (Buchan) **41**:38, 41, 44-6, 74
"The House of the Fox" (Villaurrutia) **80**:459
The House of the Octopus (Williams) **1**:517; **11**:498-99
"The House of the Titans" (Baker) **3**:6-7, 11
The House of the Titans, and Other Poems (Baker) **10**:17, 22
The House of the Trees and Other Poems (Wetherald) **81**:408,413
The House of the Whispering Pines (Green) **63**:140, 152
The House of Usna (Sharp) **39**:360, 370-72, 377-78, 380
The House of Women (Bromfield) **11**:75-6
The House on Its Own (Andrić)
See *Kuča na osami*
"The House on the Beach" (Meredith) **17**:287
The House on the Borderland, and Other Novels (Hodgson) **13**:229-33, 235-36
"A House on the Heights" (Capote) **164**:201-2
"The House on the Hill" (Robinson) **5**:400, 414; **101**:197
The House on the Hill (Pavese)
See *La casa in collina*
The House on the Water (Betti)
See *La casa sull'acqua*
"The House Party" (Butts) **77**:75, 81
"The House Surgeon" (Kipling) **8**:195
"The House that Jack Built" (Allen) **87**:62
"The House to the Man" (Fletcher) **35**:112
"The House Was Quiet and the World Was Calm" (Stevens) **3**:454; **12**:361

"A House with a History" (Hardy) **143**:169
"The House with a Mezzanine" (Chekhov)
See "Dom s mezoninom"
"The House with a Mezzanine: An Artist's Story" (Chekhov)
See "An Artist's Story"
"The House with an Attic" (Chekhov)
See "Dom s mezoninom"
The House with Closed Shutters (Griffith) **68**:186
"The House with the Brick-Kiln" (Benson) **27**:19
The House with the Echo (Powys) **9**:366
The House with the Green Shutters (Brown) **28**:13-38
"The House with the Maisonette" (Chekhov)
See "Dom s mezoninom"
"The House with the Mezzanine" (Chekhov)
See "Dom s mezoninom"
The House Without a Key (Biggers) **65**:3-5, 8-9, 13
"A House without Love Is not a Home" (Williams) **81**:435
"Household Adjustment" (Addams) **76**:2
"Household Art" (Dobson) **79**:3
Household Bread (Renard)
See *Le pain de ménage*
"The Houseless Dead" (Lawrence) **93**:58
Housemates (Beresford) **81**:6
"The Houses of the Outskirts" (Herbert) **168**:44
"The Housewife" (Galsworthy) **45**:33
"Housework Gives Me the Crazies" (Engel) **137**:108, 110
"How a Little Girl Danced" (Lindsay) **17**:229
How About Europe? (Douglas) **68**:9, 38, 43-4
"How Annandale Went Out" (Robinson) **5**:402; **101**:100
"How Are You Sanitary?" (Harte) **25**:189
"How Bateese Came Home" (Drummond) **25**:142, 145, 153
"How Beastly the Bourgeois Is" (Lawrence) **93**:128
"How 'Bigger' Was Born" (Wright) **136**:230, 245, 250, 277, 308-9, 316, 329-30; **180**:218, 235, 242, 245, 262, 265, 272, 286, 299-300, 320-21
How Britain Is Striding forward in the Air (Mitchell) **81**:168
"How Can You Refuse Him now" (Williams) **81**:434-5
"How Could This Rose Die?" (Wright) **136**:301
"How Dasdy Came Through" (Chesnutt) **39**:99
"How Do Concepts Arise from Precepts?" (Dewey) **95**:96
How Far the Promised Land? (White) **15**:481-82
"How Fârâbî Read Plato's Laws" (Strauss) **141**:334, 336, 338, 340
"How Fear Departed from the Long Gallery" (Benson) **27**:19
"How Gilbert Died" (Paterson) **32**:369
"How He Captured Saragossa" (Doyle) **7**:233
"How He Did It, and Oh!—Where Were Hitler's Pagan Gods?" (Wright) **136**:261
How He Lied to Her Husband (Shaw) **3**:393, 400; **9**:414
"How Hefty Burke Got Even" (Davis) **24**:201
"How I Became a Poet" (Lorde) **173**:39-40, 60, 63, 83, 92
"How I Became an Author" (Bengtsson) **48**:12
"How I Began to Write" (McCullers) **155**:244
"How I Knew When the Right Man Came Along" (Aldrich) **125**:70
"How I Learned About Psychoanalysis" (Bettelheim) **143**:11
"How I Left the Navy" (Warner) **131**:308
"How I Shot a Policeman" (Paterson) **32**:380
"How I Went to the Mines" (Harte) **25**:219
"How I Wrote Certain of My Books" (Roussel) **20**:239, 251-52
How I Wrote Certain of My Books (Roussel)
See *Comment j'ai écrit certains de mes livres*
"How I Wrote Jubilee" (Walker) **129**:285-86
How I Wrote Jubilee (Walker) **129**:269, 312, 316, 321
"How I Wrote my First Books" (Holley) **99**:314, 341
How It Is (Beckett)
See *Comment c'est*
"How It Strikes a Contemporary" (Woolf) **43**:415-16; **128**:334
"How It Was" (Abbey) **160**:41
"How It Was Done in Odessa" (Babel)
See "Kak eto delalos v Odesse"
How Italy Is Mobilizing a Sky Army (Mitchell) **81**:168
"How John Quit the Farm" (Riley) **51**:301
"How Labor Is Organized" (Baker) **47**:7
"How Lin McLean Went East" (Wister) **21**:390, 394, 398, 406
"How Love Came to Professor Guildea" (Hichens) **64**:122
"How Lucy Backslid" (Dunbar) **12**:122
"How Mandy Went Rowing with the 'Cap'n'" (Foote) **108**:6
"How Much Hatred" (Chang)
See "Duoshao hen"
"How Much Land Does a Man Need?" (Tolstoy) **79**:437
"How Muster-Master Stoneman Earned His Breakfast" (Warung) **45**:421, 425-26
"How Naked, How without a Wall" (Millay) **49**:227
How New Will the Better World Be? (Becker) **63**:64, 72, 74-5, 84, 118
"How Old Timofei Died Singing" (Rilke)
See "Wie der alte Timofei singend starb"
"How Order No. 6 Went Through" (Remington) **89**:307
"How Oswald Dined with God" (Markham) **47**:285
"How Pearl Button Was Kidnapped" (Mansfield) **2**:454; **39**:308, 319; **164**:342
"How Plash-Goo Came to the Land of None's Desire" (Dunsany) **59**:9
"How Poe Wrote the Raven" (Hartmann) **73**:119-20
How Right You Are, Jeeves (Wodehouse) **108**:336
"How Russia Seeks to Dominate the Air" (Mitchell) **81**:168
"How Samson Bore Away the Gates of Gaza" (Lindsay) **17**:230
"How Santa Claus Came to Simpson's Bar" (Harte) **25**:193, 201, 222
"How Schleiermacher Rediscovered Religion" (Otto) **85**:315
"How Seamus Commara Met the Banshee" (Benchley) **55**:18
"How 7 Went Mad" (Stoker) **144**:253-55, 261
"How Shall I Word It?" (Beerbohm) **24**:102
"How Shall My Animal" (Thomas) **45**:377, 399
"How She Came By Her Name" (Bambara) **116**:14-15
"How Should One Read a Book?" (Woolf) **43**:383, 403, 407, 409-11
"How Steelman Told His Story" (Lawson) **27**:121, 130
"How Sweet to Be a Cloud" (Milne) **88**:254
"How the Brigadier Slew the Fox" (Doyle) **7**:233
"How the Brigadier Triumphed in England" (Doyle) **7**:233
How the Circus Came to Tea (Blackwood) **5**:77
"How the Favourite Beat Us" (Paterson) **32**:373
"How the Great Guest Came" (Markham) **47**:285
"How the Mead-Slave Was Set Free" (Moody) **105**:237
How the Old Woman Got Home (Shiel) **8**:360
How the Other Half Lives (Riis) **80**:416, 418-20, 422-23, 425-28, 433, 435-37, 440, 443
"How the Poor Die" (Orwell) **51**:228, 256, 261-62; **128**:259
"How the Pump Stopped at the Morning Watch" (Foote) **108**:2, 17, 36
"How the 'Real World' at Last Became a Myth" (Bataille) **155**:98
How the Revolution Armed Itself (Trotsky)
See *Kak voorzhalas Revolyutsiya*
"How the Spark was Nearly Extinguished" (Lenin) **67**:219
How They Do It (Čapek) **37**:46
"How They Took the Town of Lungtungpen" (Kipling) **8**:176
"How Things Were Done in Odessa" (Babel)
See "Kak eto delalos v Odesse"
"How to Avoid a Slump" (Keynes) **64**:244
"How to be a Poet" (Thomas) **105**:352
"How to Be Happy Though Good" (Millay) **169**:237-38
How to Beat the Boer: A Conversation in Hades (Harris) **24**:266
"How to Become a Pillar of the Establishment" (Machado de Assis)
See "Teoria do medalhão"
How to Become an Author (Bennett) **5**:46; **197**:20-1
"How to Begin at the Top and Work Down" (Cobb) **77**:125
"How to Catch Unicorns" (Benét) **28**:6
How to Compose Tanka (Yosano) **59**:323-6
"How to Kill" (Douglas) **40**:70, 76, 78, 90-2
How to Live on Twenty-Four Hours a Day (Bennett) **197**:30, 73, 108
"How to Make a March/Spectacle" (Ginsberg) **120**:14
"How to Make Our Ideas Clear" (Peirce) **81**:183,187,205,216,241,292
How to Make the Best of Life (Bennett) **5**:49; **197**:9, 11
How to Obtain Knowledge of Higher Worlds (Steiner) **13**:445
How to Pay for the War: A Radical Plan for the Chancellor of the Exchequer (Keynes) **64**:221, 246, 251, 269, 285
How to Read the Gospels (Tolstoy) **79**:335
How to Seduce Women (Marinetti)
See *Come si seducono le donne*
"How to Serve the Cow" (Gandhi) **59**:52
"How to Succeed in Life" (Warner) **131**:323
"How to Watch Football" (Benchley) **55**:3
How to Write (Stein) **1**:427, 435, 441; **6**:415; **28**:330, 340; **48**:250, 253, 255
"How to Write a Great Play" (Saroyan) **137**:179
"How to Write a Novel" (Nagai)
See "Shôsetsu sakuhô"
"How to Write a Short Story" (O'Faolain) **143**:227, 264, 273
How to Write Clearly (Abbott) **139**:25
"How to Write Poetry" (Hagiwara) **60**:299
How to Write Short Stories—With Samples (Lardner) **2**:325; **14**:303, 306-07
"How Tom Snored" (Barbellion) **24**:79
How Treachery Came to Russia" (Rilke)
See "Wie der Verrat nach Rußland kam"
How We Elect Our Presidents (Rogers) **71**:325
"How we love to keep on listening" (Arp) **115**:25
How We Think (Dewey) **95**:27, 132
"Howard Lamson" (Masters) **2**:464
A Howard Nemerov Reader (Nemerov) **124**:286, 289-91, 294-96
Howard Pyle's Book of Pirates (Pyle) **81**:404-6
Howards End (Forster) **125**:73-192
Howdy, Honey, Howdy (Dunbar) **12**:124
"Howdy, Neighbor!" (Benchley) **55**:17
"Howells Discussed at Avon-by-the-Sea" (Crane) **11**:159
"Howells James" (Fuller) **103**:76, 116

"Howl" (Ginsberg) **120**:4, 9-12, 14-15, 18, 21-28, 30, 33, 35, 37, 41-3, 45, 48-52, 54-5, 68-9, 71-4, 76-8, 86, 88-96, 198-100, 102-06, 108-10, 113-21, 125, 136-37
Howl, and Other Poems (Ginsberg) **120**:11, 69, 76-7, 85, 89, 98-9, 101, 105, 112, 115, 136-37
"Howl for Carl Solomon" (Ginsberg) **120**:136
Howl II (Ginsberg) **120**:10
Howling at the Moon (Hagiwara)
See *Tsuki ni hoeru*
"Howling Dog" (Hagiwara) **60**:300-02
Höxter und Corvey (Raabe) **45**:192, 196, 200
Hoyptshtet (Kahanovitsch) **56**:118
"Hr. Jesper" (Jensen) **41**:308
The Hraun Farm (Sigurjónsson)
See *Bóndinn á Hrauni*
"Hua diao" (Chang) **184**:138-39, 141
"Huai-chiu" (Lu Hsun)
See "Huaijiu"
"Huaijiu" (Lu Hsun) **3**:299, 302-03
Hubert's Arthur (Rolfe) **12**:271, 276-79
"Huddie Ledbetter, Famous Negro Folk Artist, Sings the Songs of Scottsboro and His People" (Wright) **136**:260
Hudson River Bracketed (Wharton) **3**:562-63, 573; **9**:549, 551; **129**:363; **149**:234
Huellas (Reyes) **33**:316
"La huerta" (Arguedas) **147**:108
The Huge Season (Morris) **107**:93-5, 97, 100-01, 113, 122, 128, 155, 157-58, 235-38, 241, 244
"Hügel" (Kandinsky) **92**:67
Der Hügel ruft: Ein kleiner Roman (Brod) **115**:110
Hugh Sutherland's Pansies (Buchanan) **107**:16
Hugh Wynne, Free Quaker (Mitchell) **36**:262-63, 267, 272, 274-76
"Hughey's Dog" (Paterson) **32**:381
Hughie (O'Neill) **6**:336
"Hughley Steeple" (Housman) **10**:247
Hugo (Bennett) **5**:37, 43; **197**:30
Hugo von Hoffmansthal and His Time: The European Imagination (Broch) **20**:77-8
"Huguenin's Wife" (Shiel) **8**:363
Les huit coups de l'horloge (Leblanc) **49**:196-97
Huite jours chez M. Renan (Barrès) **47**:75, 78
The Human Age (Lewis) **2**:391, 394-95; **9**:239-40, 242, 246-48; **104**:181, 278
Human, All Too Human: A Book for Free Spirits (Nietzsche)
See *Menschliches, Allzumenschliches: Ein Buch für freie Geister*
Human Being (Morley) **87**:128, 146
"Human Being Means Brotherhood" (Toomer) **172**:303
"Human Burning" (Aleixandre) **113**:26
The Human Chord (Blackwood) **5**:71, 73-4, 77
The Human Comedy (Saroyan) **137**:153-55, 168, 170, 184, 188
The Human Condition (Arendt) **193**:30, 42-3, 47-8, 52-3, 55, 62, 64, 75, 79, 86, 96, 99, 111, 119, 121, 124, 159, 168, 170
"The Human Condition" (Nemerov) **124**:179, 182, 227, 253
The Human Cycle (Aurobindo) **63**:18, 30, 32, 34, 36, 51, 54, 56
"Human Document" (Zola) **6**:561
The Human Drift (London) **9**:267
"Human Evolution, An Artificial Process" (Wells) **133**:263, 265
The Human Fly (Melies) **81**:147
"The Human Fold" (Muir) **87**:167
"Human Grief" (Trakl)
See "Menschliche Trauer"
"Human Happiness Is Sensuous" (Lin) **149**:341
The Human Inheritance. The New Hope. Motherhood (Sharp) **39**:361, 379-80, 387
The Human Interest: A Study in Incompatibilities (Hunt) **53**:191
"Human Lost" (Dazai Osamu) **11**:178, 184, 191; **22**:184, 191
The Human Machine (Bennett) **197**:9
Human Nature (Wharton) **129**:364
Human Nature and Conduct (Dewey) **95**:36, 60, 137
"Human Nature and Human History" (Collingwood) **67**:155, 185
Human Nature and the Social Order (Thorndike) **107**:380, 405, 419-21
"Human Nature Can Change" (Horney)
See "The Flight from Womanhood"
The Human Nature Club (Thorndike) **107**:415, 419-20
Human Nature in Politics (Wallas) **91**:354-5, 357-60, 362-3, 365, 368-70, 374-6, 378-9, 390-4, 402, 404
Human Odds and Ends (Gissing) **3**:228
Human Poems (Vallejo)
See *Poemas humanos, 1923-1938*
The Human Province (Canetti)
See *Die Provinz des Menschen: Aufzeichnungen, 1942-1972*
"Human Relationships" (Ginzburg) **156**:46
Human Shows, Far Phantasies, Songs, and Trifles (Hardy) **53**:117; **143**:148, 192, 213
"Human Studies" (Nishida)
See "Ningengaku"
"The Human Thing" (O'Faolain) **143**:255
"Human Things" (Nemerov) **124**:157, 249
Human Toll (Baynton) **57**:3-6, 11-12, 19, 23, 25-26, 28, 30-37
"Human Voice" (Aleixandre)
See "Humana voz"
Human Work (Gilman) **9**:105; **37**:176; **117**:125, 140
"Humana voz" (Aleixandre) **113**:13
Humanism and Terror (Merleau-Ponty)
See *Humanisme et terreur*
"Humanism and the Present" (Mandelstam) **6**:268
"Humanism and the Religious Attitude" (Hulme) **21**:132, 138
"Humanisme et hermetisme chez Thomas Mann" (Yourcenar) **193**:277
Humanisme et terreur (Merleau-Ponty) **156**:134, 185, 189, 213-14
"Humanistic quietism" (Beckett) **145**:87
"The Humanistic Tradition of Afro-American Literature" (Walker) **129**:289
"Humanitad" (Wilde) **8**:495
"Humanity I Love You" (Cummings) **137**:53
"Humano ardor" (Aleixandre) **113**:15, 49
"Humayun to Zobeida" (Naidu) **80**:285
A Humble Romance, and Other Stories (Freeman) **9**:60, 62-3, 65, 67, 74, 76
Les humbles (Coppee) **25**:119-21, 124-26
Humbug: A Study in Education (Delafield) **61**:127
"L'hume qui tue les femmes" (Lemonnier) **22**:198
"Hume's Law of Causation" (Nishida)
See "Hyumu no ingaho"
La humilde verdad (Martinez Sierra and Martinez Sierra) **6**:279
"Humiliation" (Blok) **5**:85
The Humiliation of the Father (Claudel)
See *Le père humiliè*
"Humility" (Acker) **191**:65, 67, 107
"Humility" (Service) **15**:412
El humo dormido (Miro) **5**:335, 341, 345
Humor and Humanity: An Introduction to the Study of Humor (Leacock) **2**:378
"Humor and Irony" (Mann) **44**:220
"Humoresque" (Hecht) **101**:36
The Humours of the Court (Bridges) **1**:124
"Humpty Dumpty" (Kuttner) **10**:266, 271
Humpty Dumpty (Hecht) **101**:48, 57-8, 60, 73
Humulus le muet (Anouilh) **195**:40
"The Hunchback in the Park" (Thomas) **45**:399; **105**:297, 348
"Die Hundeblume" (Borchert) **5**:104
"Hunden" (Obstfelder) **23**:179
The Hundred Sonnets of Robert David (Nezval) **44**:241
"The Hundred Tales" (Mori Ogai)
See "Hyakumonogatari"
A Hundred Years of Trent Bridge (Lucas) **73**:174
Hundreds and Thousands: The Journals of Emily Carr (Carr) **32**:119-21, 123-25, 128-29
Hundreds . . . of Pages of the Secret Book of Gabriele d'Annunzio Tempted by Death (D'Annunzio)
See *Cento e cento e cento e cento pagine del libro segreto di Gabriele d'Annunzio tentato di morire*
The Hundredth Man (Stockton) **47**:315, 318, 321
"Hundstage" (Lasker-Schueler) **57**:317
"Huneker" (Mencken) **13**:365
"Hunger" (Cullen) **37**:155
"The Hunger" (Huysmans)
See "La Faim"
"Hunger" (Stephens) **4**:417, 421
Hunger (Hamsun)
See *Sult*
"Hunger and Thirst" (Bishop) **103**:5
The Hunger Pastor (Raabe)
See *Der Hungerpastor*
"A Hunger-Artist" (Kafka)
See "Ein Hungerkünstler"
"The Hunger-Artist" (Kafka)
See "Ein Hungerkünstler"
The Hungerers (Saroyan) **137**:202
"Ein Hungerkünstler" (Kafka) **29**:214; **47**:216; **112**:107, 115; **179**:275-76
Der Hungerpastor (Raabe) **45**:160-62, 164, 169-70, 174, 177-81, 187, 191-98, 200
The Hungry City (Molnár)
See *Az éhes város*
"Hungry Eyes" (Bialik)
See "Ha-eynayim ha-re 'eboth"
The Hungry Heart (Phillips) **44**:256, 258-59, 262, 265, 275, 277-79, 281
"The Hungry Man Was Fed" (Davis) **24**:200
"The Hungry Stones" (Tagore)
See "Kshudhita Pashan"
"The Hunt after Happiness" (Prishvin) **75**:215-16
"A Hunt in the Black Forest" (Jarrell) **177**:134, 145, 147
The Hunted (O'Neill) **1**:387, 388; **6**:331
"The Hunter" (Arnow) **196**:88-90
The Hunter (Reyes)
See *El cazador*
"The Hunter Gracchus" (Kafka)
See "Der jäger Gracchus"
The Hunter Usa Gali (Khlebnikov)
See *Okhotnik Usa-Gali*
Hunter's Horn (Arnow) **196**:4-7, 9, 12-13, 17, 23-9, 32, 34-9, 42-3, 47, 49, 60, 62, 64-7, 76-7, 80, 89-93, 96, 101-02, 116
"Hunting Civil War Relics at Nimblewill Creek" (Dickey) **151**:98, 170
"Hunting Horns" (Apollinaire) **3**:39
The Hunting Party (Bernhard)
See *Die Jagdgesellschaft*
"Hunting the King" (Lee-Hamilton) **22**:187, 189
The Hunting Trips of a Ranchman (Roosevelt) **69**:175, 177, 187, 251, 277-78
Huntingtower (Buchan) **41**:38, 41, 46, 49, 74-5
Huntsman, What Quarry? (Millay) **49**:219-20, 222-23, 233
The Huntsmen are Up in America (Bishop) **103**:32-3
The Hurdy-Gurdy (Guro)
See *Sharmanka*
L'Hurluberlu ou le réactionnarire amoureux (Anouilh) **195**:25, 27, 36, 38
Hurrah for My Owner (Valle-Inclán)
See *Viva mi dueño: El ruedo Ibérico II*
"Hurrah for Thunder" (Okigbo) **171**:346, 358-59, 361

"The Hurricane" (Crane) **5**:186, 189
The Hurricane (Hall and Nordhoff) **23**:62, 66
"Hurry Kane" (Lardner) **14**:307, 314, 317, 319-20
A Husband (Svevo)
See *Un marito*
The Husband in Love with His Wife (Giacosa)
See *Il marito amante della moglie*
The Husband's Story (Phillips) **44**:256-60, 262, 265-66, 268, 275-79, 281
Husfrue (Undset) **197**:326, 333-35
"Hush hareah" (Agnon) **151**:26, 56, 81, 84
Hushove (Vazov) **25**:453
The Hussar on the Roof (Giono)
See *Le hussard sur le toit*
Le hussard sur le toit (Giono) **124**:37, 50-1, 53-6, 83-5, 87-8, 97, 101, 105, 116
Der Hüter der Schwelle (Steiner) **13**:438, 443, 457, 459
"The Huxter" (Thomas) **10**:463
"Hvepsen" (Obstfelder) **23**:177, 182
"Hverrestens-Ajes" (Jensen) **41**:308
Hyacinth Halvey (Gregory) **1**:334-35, 337; **176**:13-15, 17, 20-21, 31-32, 40, 62
Hyakuchū jisshu (Masaoka) **18**:221, 226
"Hyakumonogatari" (Mori Ogai) **14**:379, 385
"The Hyborian Age" (Howard) **8**:136
"Hyde Park at Night, before the War" (Lawrence) **93**:69
"Hydrangea" (Nagai)
See "Ajisai"
"Hydro Poles on a Moonlight Night" (Miyazawa) **76**:293
Hydrotherapie Fantastique (Melies) **81**:122
"Hyenas" (Kolmar) **40**:177
"Hygeia at the Solito" (Henry) **19**:191
"Hylas" (Middleton) **56**:184
"Hymn" (Ginsberg) **120**:8
"A Hymn at Night" (Coffin) **95**:4
"Hymn for a Spring Festival" (Howe) **21**:113
"Hymn from a Watermelon Pavilion" (Stevens) **12**:376
"Hymn in Contemplation of Sudden Death" (Sayers) **15**:370
"The Hymn of Abdul Hamid" (Davidson) **24**:164, 186
"Hymn of Breaking Strain" (Kipling) **8**:201
"A Hymn of Form" (Bottomley) **107**:7
"A Hymn of Imagination" (Bottomley) **107**:7
"Hymn of Man" (Swinburne) **8**:426, 437; **36**:318
"Hymn of the Great Return" (Sikelianos)
See "The Great Homecoming"
"A Hymn of Touch" (Bottomley) **107**:7
"Hymn to Artemis Orthia" (Sikelianos) **39**:421
Hymn to Athena (Palamas) **5**:379, 382, 386
"Hymn to Beauty" (Merezhkovsky) **29**:246
"Hymn to Indra, Lord of Rain" (Naidu) **80**:316, 343
"A Hymn to Iris" (Babits)
See "Himnusz Iriszhez"
"Hymn to Life" (Palamas) **5**:386
"Hymn to Priapus" (Lawrence) **9**:213; **93**:16, 18, 88-93
"Hymn to Proserpine" (Swinburne) **8**:435, 441; **36**:295, 313, 317, 322, 327-29, 337
Hymn to Satan (Carducci)
See *Inno a Satana*
Hymn to the Mother (Aurobindo) **63**:6
"Hymn to the Scholar" (Mayakovski) **4**:292
"Hymn to the Sun" (Fletcher) **35**:89
"Hymn to the Valiant" (Palamas) **5**:380
"Hymne" (Heym) **9**:142
Hymnen (George) **2**:149-50; **14**:196, 203-04, 210-12
"Hymns in a Man's Life" (Lawrence) **93**:124
"Hymns—Ancient and Padded" (Baring-Gould) **88**:22
"Hymnus" (Kandinsky) **92**:67
"Hyōhakusha no uta" (Hagiwara) **60**:315
Hyōtō (Hagiwara) **60**:295, 298-9, 315-6
"Hyperion" (Crane) **2**:115
Hyperthvleana (Gogarty) **15**:113-14
"The Hypnotised Township" (Lawson) **27**:132
"The Hypnotist" (Bierce) **44**:45
L'hystérique (Lemonnier) **22**:198, 200, 202
"Hyumu izen no tetsugaku no hattatsu" (Nishida) **83**:223, 235
"Hyumu no ingaho" (Nishida) **83**:223, 235
"I" (Bryusov) **10**:87
"I" (Leino)
See "Minä"
"I" (Mayakovski) **18**:245-46
"I" (Södergran)
See "Jag"
I (Mayakovski)
See *Ya*
I Am a Camera (Van Druten) **2**:575-76
I Am a Cat (Natsume)
See *Wagahai wa neko de aru*
"I Am a Victim of Telephone" (Ginsberg) **120**:22
"I Am Destiny" (Aleixandre) **113**:53
"I Am Going to Speak of Hope" (Vallejo)
See "Voy a hablar de la esperanza"
"I Am I" (Toomer) **172**:315
"I Am in Love with Life" (Redcam) **25**:331
"I Am Paying Rent" (Wright) **136**:301
"I Am Sad" (Lasker-Schueler) **57**:335
"I am the One" (Hardy) **143**:155
"I Am the Way" (Meynell) **6**:303
"I Am the Woman" (Moody) **105**:234, 239, 242, 260, 273
"I Am Writer" (Stephens) **4**:420
"I Am Your Sister" (Lorde) **173**:118
"I and E" (Khlebnikov)
See "I i E"
I and I (Lasker-Schueler)
See *Ich und Ich*
I and the World (Morgenstern)
See *Ich und die Welt*
I and the World of Objects (Berdyaev)
See *Solitude and Society*
"I and Thou" (Nishida)
See "Watakushi to nanji"
"I Arise Enfeebled from My Bed" (Khodasevich) **15**:209
"I Asked of God" (Montgomery) **51**:209
"I baffi bianchi" (Ginzburg) **156**:54
"I bambini" (Ginzburg) **156**:13-15
"I Bear Witness" (Mayakovski) **18**:258
"I beatniks e il 'sistema'" (Calvino) **183**:101
"I Been North and East" (Wright) **136**:262
"I Beg You Come Back & Be Cheerful" (Ginsberg) **120**:36, 39-40
"I, being born a woman and distressed" (Millay) **49**:232
"I Believe" (Austin) **25**:36
"I Believe in My Sister" (Södergran)
See "Ja tror på min syster"
"I Believe, Sang the Guns" (Khlebnikov) **20**:129
"I Built Myself a House of Glass" (Thomas) **10**:464
"I bygden er det uro" (Bjoernson) **7**:117
"I Cannot Be Silent" (Tolstoy) **11**:463; **79**:412, 430
"I Cannot Know" (Radnóti)
See "Nem tudhatom"
"I Cannot Tell in the Dark" (Tsvetaeva) **35**:394
"I Can't Breathe" (Lardner) **2**:335; **14**:307, 311
"I Can't Help It if I'm Still in Love with You" (Williams) **81**:423,445
"i carry your heart with me / i carry it in" (Cummings) **137**:55
"I Choose April" (Bjoernson) **7**:110
"I Climbed into the Tousled Hayloft" (Mandelstam) **2**:409
"I cristalli" (Calvino) **183**:62, 66, 145, 228
I de dage: Fortoelling om Norske nykommere i Amerika (Rölvaag) **17**:320, 337
I de dage: Riket grundlaegges (Rölvaag) **17**:320, 337
"I Didn't Get Over" (Fitzgerald) **6**:172
"I dinosauri" (Calvino) **183**:227
"I Do, I Will, I Have" (Nash) **109**:354
"I do not know if the sea is, today" (Jiménez)
See "No sé si el mar es, hoy"
"I Do Not Know the Dances of White People" (p'Bitek) **149**:131
"I Do Not Regret Writing in Quechua" (Arguedas) **147**:30
"I Don't Care if Tomorrow never Comes" (Williams) **81**:428
I Don't Cheat on My Husband (Feydeau)
See *Je ne trompe pas mon mari*
I Dream a World (Walker) **129**:291
"I Dreamed My Genesis" (Thomas) **8**:454, 458; **45**:361-62
I Dreamt I Was a Nymphomaniac: Imagining (Acker) **191**:42, 67-8, 125
I due cavrioli (Pascoli) **45**:148
"I due farciulli" (Pascoli) **45**:151
"I Endeavor to Entertain the Seasick Man" (Twain) **161**:241
"I Fellowed Sleep" (Thomas) **45**:361
"I figli poltroni" (Calvino) **183**:92, 187
"I Find the Real American Tragedy" (Dreiser) **83**:82-8
I Follow Saint Patrick (Gogarty) **15**:105, 118
"I francobolli degli stati d'animo" (Calvino) **183**:104
I giganti della montagna (Pirandello)
See *I giganta della montagna*
I giovani del Po (Calvino) **183**:188, 237-38
"I Go to Church" (Childress) **116**:36
"I Got the Blues" (Handy) **97**:54
"I Guess I Was Just a Fool" (Holly) **65**:149
"I Guess It Doesn't Matter Anymore" (Holly) **65**:145-46, 150-51
"I Had Scarcely Fallen Asleep" (Fletcher) **35**:106
"I Had to Tramp through Solar Systems" (Södergran)
See "Till fots fick jag gå genom solsystemen"
I Hate Actors (Hecht) **101**:74
"I Hate America" (Ginsberg) **120**:77
"I Have a Rendezvous with Life" (Cullen) **4**:41
"I Have a Thing to Tell You" (Wolfe) **13**:493
"I Have Been Taught" (Muir) **87**:241
"I Have Been through the Gates" (Mew) **8**:296-97, 299-300
"I Have Believed That I Prefer to Live" (Wylie) **8**:530
"I Have Embraced You" (Toller)
See "Ich habe euch umarmt"
"I Have Every Right to Speak Where There May Be a Clear Issue Between Candidates for a Democratic Nomination Involving Principles, or a Clear Misuse of My Own Name" (Roosevelt) **93**:184
"I Have Longed to Move Away" (Thomas) **45**:362
"I Have Loved Hours at Sea" (Teasdale) **4**:428
I Have Neither Father, Nor Mother (Jozsef) **22**:164
I Have This to Say (Hunt)
See *The Flurried Years*
"I Hear a Rumbling" (Walker) **129**:314
"I Hear an Army" (Joyce)
See "XXXVI"
"I Heard Immanuel Singing" (Lindsay) **17**:225
"I i E" (Khlebnikov) **20**:131, 139
"I, in My Intricate Image" (Thomas) **8**:454, 459; **45**:362, 382, 405
I Juliet (Rolland) **23**:252
"I Kiss Miss-Kisses" (Ady) **11**:14
I Knew a Phoenix: Sketches for an Autobiography (Sarton) **120**:218, 230, 280-82
"I Know" (Lasker-Schueler)
See "Ich weiss"
"I Know I Am but Summer to Your Heart" (Millay) **49**:215
"I Know Who I Love" (Jackson) **187**:248, 281

"I Laid My Mother Away" (Williams) **81**:423
"I Lay Love on my Knee" (Ginsberg) **120**:26
I Left My Grandfather's House: An Account of His First Walking Tour (Welch) **22**:458, 460
"I Lie Somewhere by the Side of the Road" (Lasker-Schueler) **57**:335
"I Like Americans" (Millay) **169**:237
"i like my body when it is with your" (Cummings) **137**:21, 55
"I Liked Workin' at That Place" (Childress) **116**:36
"I Live in the Heart of the Young" (Ady)
See "Ifjú szivekben élek"
"I Live on Your Visits" (Parker) **143**:331
"I livelli della realtà letteratura" (Calvino) **183**:102, 107, 164
I livelli della realtà letteratura (Calvino) **183**:164
"I Look into My Glass" (Hardy) **4**:152; **53**:111, 114
"I Looked Up From My Writing" (Hardy) **143**:188-89, 192
"I Love" (Mayakovski) **4**:299; **18**:241
"I Love Life" (Sigurjónsson) **27**:364
"I Love My Bonny Bride" (Roberts) **68**:348, 350-51
"I Love You" (Éluard) **7**:261
"I Loved" (Saba)
See "Amai"
"I. M.: Margaritae Soroi" (Henley) **8**:110
"I Make This in a Warring Absence" (Thomas) **45**:362, 399, 405
I Married you for Fun (Ginzburg)
See *Ti ho sposato per allegria*
"I Mavromantilou" (Papadiamantis) **29**:272
"I Met Me Ould Love" (Stringer) **37**:334
"I mille giardini" (Calvino) **183**:106
"I Napoleon" (Herzl) **36**:154
"I Never Ast No Favours" (Kornbluth) **8**:217
"I Never Saw That Land Before" (Thomas) **10**:467
"I nostri figli" (Ginzburg) **156**:105-8
"I Once Had" (Saba)
See "Avevo"
"I Only Am Escaped Alone to Tell Thee" (Nemerov) **124**:153-4, 180, 216, 275
"I Pharmakolytria" (Papadiamantis) **29**:272
I Played, I Danced (Rainis)
See *Spēlēju, dancoju*
I Pose (Benson) **17**:17, 19, 20, 22, 24, 26-8, 30
I racconti (Calvino) **183**:4, 91-98, 162, 190-91, 208-11, 213-15, 223, 237
"I rapporti umani" (Ginzburg) **156**:96-97, 100
"I Recognised the Voice" (Wakefield) **120**:356
"I Remember" (Pasternak) **188**:179
I Remember! I Remember! (O'Faolain) **143**:225, 230, 260
I Remember Mama (Van Druten) **2**:573
"I rose up as my custom is" (Hardy) **53**:101
I Salute You, Free Latvia! (Rainis)
See *Sveika, brīvā Latvija!*
"I Saw a Tree" (Södergran)
See "Jag såg ett träd"
"I Saw the Light" (Williams) **81**:423-4,441
I Saw Three Ships (Quiller-Couch) **53**:296
"I See" (Obstfelder)
See "Jeg ser"
"I See America Dancing" (Duncan) **68**:75
"I See Phantoms of Hatred and of the Heart's Fullness and of the Coming Emptiness" (Yeats) **11**:535
"I See the Boys of Summer" (Thomas) **45**:361, 386-87; **105**:301, 347
"I Sekuin" (Burroughs) **121**:126
I Served the King of England (Hrabal)
See *Obsluhoval jsem anglického krále*
"I Shall Never See You Again" (Masters) **25**:298
I Should Have Stayed Home (McCoy) **28**:211-13, 222, 232, 237
"I Sing of Olaf Glad and Big" (Cummings) **137**:49, 54
"I Sit in My Room" (Toomer) **172**:278
i: Six Nonlectures (Cummings) **137**:14, 17, 29-31, 62
"I snova" (Bryusov) **10**:81
I sommersi e i salvati (Levi) **109**:280-1, 283-5, 287, 290, 299, 302, 309, 311-13, 315-16, 318, 322, 329, 332-4, 338, 340-1, 345, 347, 349-50
"I Still Live" (Éluard) **7**:262
"I Take Great Pleasure in Presenting" (Cummings) **137**:17
"i thank You God for most this amazing" (Cummings) **137**:56
I Thought About the Golden Times (Hrabal)
See *Ich dachte an die goldenen Zeiten*
"I Thought I Stood" (Schreiner) **9**:394
"I to My Perils" (Housman) **10**:247, 258
"I, Too, Have Lived in Arcadia": A Record of Love and of Childhood (Lowndes) **12**:204
"I Tried to Be a Communist" (Wright) **136**:277
I Æventyrland (Hamsun) **49**:128
I Waited on the King of England (Hrabal)
See *Obsluhoval jsem anglického krále*
"I Walked the Boulevard" (Cummings) **137**:42
I Walked with a Zombie (Lewton) **76**:192, 194-98, 200, 202, 204-05, 210, 218, 230
"I Want to Know Why" (Anderson) **1**:42, 46, 50, 54, 58, 61; **10**:33; **123**:23
"I Want to Be Raped Every Night. Story of a Rich Woman" (Acker) **191**:84
"I Want to Write" (Walker) **129**:275, 288, 314
"I Wanted to Come to Broadway" (Cohan) **60**:169
I Was a German (Toller)
See *Eine jugend in Deutschland*
"I Was Born in Virginia" (Cohan) **60**:168
"I Was Washing Outside in the Darkness" (Mandelstam) **2**:409
"I Went to the Movie of Life" (Ginsberg) **120**:112
I Will Not Rest (Rolland)
See *Quinze ans de combat, 1919-1934*
"I Will Not Serve" (Huidobro)
See "Non serviam"
I Will Not Weep (Esenin) **4**:115
"I Will Put Chaos into Fourteen Lines" (Millay) **49**:226; **169**:293, 296
"I Wish I Could See a Woman of Carthago" (Leino)
See "Tahtoisin nähdä mä Kartagon naisen"
"I Wish I Was a Poet" (Childress) **116**:37
"I Wonder" (Montgomery) **51**:204
"I Wonder How Long" (Wright) **136**:300
I Would Be Private (Macaulay) **44**:123
"I Would Like a Bell" (Wright) **136**:300
"I Would Like to Describe" (Herbert) **168**:16
I Wouldn't Have Missed It: Selected Poems of Ogden Nash (Nash) **109**:356-57, 360
I Wrote The Uprising (Rebreanu) **28**:270
"Ia izyskannost' Russkoi medlitel'noi rechi" (Balmont) **11**:42
"Ia mech'toiu lovil" (Balmont) **11**:35
"Ia ne ishchu garmonii v prirode" (Zabolotsky) **52**:380
Ia Orana Maria (Jarry) **147**:331
"Ia smotriu v proshloe" (Olesha) **136**:102, 108, 136, 154, 161, 163, 174, 182
"Ia tol'ko devochka" (Tsvetaeva) **35**:389
Iaiá Garcia (Machado de Assis)
See *Yayá Garcia*
Iambics and Epodes (Carducci)
See *Giambi ed epodi*
Íamboi kai anápaestoi (Palamas) **5**:379, 380, 382, 384, 387
Iambs and Anapaests (Palamas)
See *Íamboi kai anápaestoi*
Ian Hamilton's March (Churchill) **113**:148, 160
Iaponia-Kina (Kazantzakis) **181**:236-40, 325
Iasen' (Balmont) **11**:38, 40, 42
Iberian Ring (Valle-Inclán)
See *El ruedo Ibérico*
"Ibn Hakkan" (Borges)
See "Abencaján el Bojarí, muerto en su laberinto"
"Ibn Hakkan al-Bokhari, Dead in His Labryinth" (Borges)
See "Abencaján el Bojarí, muerto en su laberinto"
"I—Brasil" (Sharp) **39**:371
"Ibsen et les critiques Français" (Gourmont) **17**:126
"Ibsen Is Dead" (Ady) **11**:24
"Ibsen the Playwright" (Matthews) **95**:246
Ice (Jensen)
See *Bræen*
Ice in the Bedroom (Wodehouse) **108**:333
The Ice Land (Hagiwara)
See *Hyōtō*
"The Ice Palace" (Fitzgerald) **1**:262; **6**:169
"The Ice Skin" (Dickey) **151**:89
"The Iceberg" (Roberts) **8**:321, 326-27
The Iceburg, and Other Poems (Roberts) **8**:318, 321
"The Icehouse in Summer" (Nemerov) **124**:172, 310-11
An Iceland Fisherman (Loti)
See *Pêcheur d'Islande*
The Iceman Cometh (O'Neill) **1**:389-90, 392, 398-402, 405-06; **6**:332, 336; **49**:247, 249, 252, 260
"Ich bin der Traum" (Arp) **115**:55
Ich dachte an die goldenen Zeiten (Hrabal) **155**:165
"Ich habe euch umarmt" (Toller) **11**:490
"Ich liebe dich" (Lasker-Schueler) **57**:305
"Ich liege wo am wegrand" (Lasker-Schueler) **57**:313-14
"Ich raume auf" (Lasker-Schueler) **57**:314
Ich raume' auf! Meine Anklage gegen meine Verleger (Lasker-Schueler) **57**:321
"Ich saume liebentlang" (Lasker-Schueler) **57**:300
"Ich schlafe in der Nacht" (Lasker-Schueler) **57**:318
"Ich schreibe fuer Leser" (Frisch) **121**:201
"Ich sterbe" (Sarraute) **145**:338-42
Das Ich über der Natur (Döblin) **13**:174
Das Ich und das Es (Freud) **52**:91
Ich und die Welt (Morgenstern) **8**:309
Ich und Du (Morgenstern) **8**:306, 311
Ich und Ich (Lasker-Schueler) **57**:294
"Ich weiß im Wald ein kleines Haus" (Raabe) **45**:190
"Ich weiss" (Lasker-Schueler) **57**:328
"Ich werde gegangen" (Schwitters) **95**:296
Ichiaku no suna (Ishikawa) **15**:123, 125, 127
Ichiya (Natsume) **10**:329
Ici et maintenant (Adamov) **189**:30, 36, 39, 47, 50, 55-7
Iconoclasts: A Book of Dramatists (Huneker) **65**:157-59, 163, 165, 167, 170, 179, 185, 188, 217
I'd Rather Be Right (Cohan) **60**:161
"Ida" (Bunin) **6**:45
Ida Elisabeth (Undset) **3**:519, 521, 523; **197**:296, 299, 301
Idaho, A Guide in Word and Picture (Fisher) **140**:182
The Idaho Encyclopedia (Fisher) **140**:182
Idaho Lore (Fisher) **140**:182
Idalia (Ouida) **43**:338, 341-42, 344, 353, 357, 370, 375
"Idea" (Aleixandre) **113**:3, 62, 64
"Idea" (Nemerov) **124**:182, 192, 251
La idea de principio en Leibniz y la evolución de la teoría deductiva (Ortega y Gasset) **9**:355
"Idea de teatro" (Ortega y Gasset) **9**:355
"The Idea of a Pure Logic" (Husserl) **100**:39
"The Idea of a University" (Nemerov) **124**:233, 291
"The Idea of Fate in Ancient Tragedy" (Brandes) **11**:70

Idea of Great Poetry (Abercrombie) **141**:10
The Idea of History (Collingwood) **67**:93, 107-8, 124, 127-28, 138-39, 146, 151, 153, 156, 182, 184-92
The Idea of National Interest (Beard) **15**:23
The Idea of Nature (Collingwood) **67**:139, 142, 144, 151, 182, 184-85
"The Idea of Order at Key West" (Stevens) **3**:455; **12**:376; **45**:269, 275, 277-78, 282, 290, 297, 306, 326, 328, 334, 348
"The Idea of Perfection" (Murdoch) **171**:237
The Idea of Phenomenology (Husserl) **100**:121
"The Idea of Preexistence" (Hearn) **9**:119, 130
The Idea of Principle in Leibniz and the Evolution of Deductive Theory (Ortega y Gasset)
See *La idea de principio en Leibniz y la evolución de la teoría deductiva*
The Idea of Progress (Nisbet) **117**:385
The Idea of the Holy (Otto)
See *Das Heilige*
"The Idea of the Theater" (Ortega y Gasset)
See "Idea de teatro"
"The Idea of Value" (Alexander) **77**:62-4
"Ideal" (Flecker) **43**:206
"The Ideal" (Sterling) **20**:383
"L'ideal" (Sully Prudhomme) **31**:301
"An Ideal Craftsman" (de la Mare) **4**:78; **53**:21, 27, 42
"An Ideal Family" (Mansfield) **39**:304; **164**:240
The Ideal Giant (Lewis) **2**:386; **104**:257
"Ideal Giolittism" (Levi)
See "Giolittismo ideale"
An Ideal Husband (Wilde) **1**:497-98, 504, 506, 508; **8**:489, 494; **23**:411-12, 415, 420, 435, 438, 445; **41**:397; **175**:264-325
The Ideal of Human Unity (Aurobindo) **63**:30-2, 36, 51, 54
The Ideal of the Karmayogin (Aurobindo) **63**:28
Ideal Passion (Woodberry) **73**:364
"Idealism" (Gourmont) **17**:149
"Idealism and Materialism" (Lovecraft) **22**:210
Idéalisme (Gourmont) **17**:156
"Ideals and Doubts" (Holmes) **77**:262
Ideas (Husserl)
See *Jarbuch fuer Philosophie un Phaenomenologische Forschung*
"Ideas and Ideals as Sources of Power in the Modern World" (Wirth) **92**:375
Ideas and Opinions (Einstein) **65**:133
Ideas concerning Pure Phenomenology (Husserl)
See *Ideen I*
Ideas I (Husserl)
See *Ideen I*
Ideas II (Husserl)
See *Phaenomenologie Untersuchungen zur Konstitution*
Ideas III (Husserl)
See *Die Phaenomenologie und die Fundamente de Wissenschaften*
"Ideas of a Flower Garden" (Yokomitsu)
See "Hanazono no Shisô"
Ideas of Good and Evil (Yeats) **1**:576; **31**:385; **116**:263
Ideas of Order (Stevens) **3**:477; **12**:376, 382-83; **45**:268-69, 274-76, 282, 346, 352-53
"Ideas of the New Rural Society" (Baker) **10**:24
"Ideas sobre la novela" (Ortega y Gasset) **9**:344-46
"Ideas y creencias" (Ortega y Gasset) **9**:338
"Idee der Phänomenologie" (Husserl)
See *Ideen I*
Idée Fixe (Valéry)
See *L'idée fixe*
L'idée fixe (Valéry) **4**:494
Idee und Gestalt (Cassirer) **61**:52
Ideen (Husserl)
See *Jarbuch fuer Philosophie un Phaenomenologische Forschung*
Ideen I (Husserl) **100**:10, 49, 80, 89-90, 97, 119-20, 123, 154-55
Ideen II (Husserl)
See *Phaenomenologie Untersuchungen zur Konstitution*
Ideen III (Husserl)
See *Die Phaenomenologie und die Fundamente de Wissenschaften*
Ideen zu einer reinen Phaenomenologie und phaenomenologischen Philosophie (Husserl) **100**:10, 19, 25, 45, 59
Les idées du jour (Gourmont) **17**:138
Les idées et les âges (Alain) **41**:3, 28, 30
"Idéis de canário" (Machado de Assis) **10**:290-91
"Identités" (Éluard) **41**:156
La ideocracia (Unamuno) **148**:236
"Ideological Aspects of Social Disorganization" (Wirth) **92**:378
Ideologie and Utopie (Mannheim) **65**:295, 301-02, 307-08, 312, 319, 321-22, 333, 338
"Ideology and Terror" (Arendt) **193**:46
Ideology and Utopia (Mannheim)
See *Ideologie and Utopie*
"The Ides of March" (Cavafy) **2**:88
"The Ides of March" (Hornung) **59**:112, 114, 119-21
"Un idilio" (Quiroga) **20**:213
"Idilio muerto" (Vallejo) **56**:294
"Idillio maremmano" (Carducci) **32**:96, 102-03, 110-11
"The Idiom of the Argentines" (Borges)
See *El idioma de los Argentinos*
"Idiom of the Hero" (Stevens) **45**:283
El idioma de los Argentinos (Borges) **109**:65, 78, 86, 148, 156
"The Idiot" (Crane) **5**:189
"An Idiot" (Riley) **51**:292
"The Idiot Martinec" (Cankar) **105**:161-62
"L'idiote aux cloches" (Nelligan) **14**:392
Idiot's Delight (Sherwood) **3**:410-14, 416
"Idiots First" (Malamud) **129**:66, 69, 74, 158-60, 163-64, 193; **184**:198, 224, 226, 237-38, 261, 278, 280-81
Idiots First (Malamud) **129**:64, 66, 109-10, 113-14; **184**:158, 163-65, 184, 221, 237-46
Idle Days in Patagonia (Hudson) **29**:135, 138-40, 143, 145, 156-58, 162
"Idle Days on the Yann" (Dunsany) **59**:20-21
"An Idle Fellow" (Chopin) **14**:69
The Idle Thoughts of an Idle Fellow (Jerome) **23**:77, 80, 86-7, 90
"Idleness" (Tozzi)
See "Ozio"
"Ido ve'Enam" (Agnon) **151**:36
"The Idolator" (Williams) **89**:399
Idolatry (Hawthorne) **25**:230, 232-33, 238, 241-42, 248, 250-52
Les idoles (Rolland) **23**:262
"Idols" (Rolland) **23**:254-55
"An Idyl" (Quiroga)
See "Un idilio"
"Idyl of a French Snuffbox" (Hearn) **9**:125, 134, 136
"The Idyl of Melool Woodpile" (Warung) **45**:419
"The Idyl of Red Gulch" (Harte) **1**:343; **25**:191
"Idyl of the Anchorite" (Lee-Hamilton) **22**:186
"Idyll" (Hofmannsthal) **11**:294
"An Idyll of Dandaloo" (Paterson) **32**:372, 377
"The Idyll of the Carp" (Dobson) **79**:27
"Idyll of the Maremma" (Carducci)
See "Idillio maremmano"
An Idyll of the Shops (Hecht) **101**:73
"Une idylle pendant le siège" (Coppee) **25**:126
Une idylle tragique (Bourget) **12**:72
"An Idyllic Home" (Peretz) **16**:405-06
Idyls and Legends of Inverburn (Buchanan) **107**:14, 63, 78
Ie (Shimazaki Toson) **5**:431-38, 441
"Ieli the Herd Boy" (Verga)
See "Jeli il pastore"
Iesu no shogai (Endo) **152**:178-79, 184, 186, 191-92, 209, 213, 224
"If" (Kipling) **8**:186
"If" (Pirandello)
See "Se . . ."
If (Dunsany) **2**:144; **59**:12-3, 17, 26
"If at Your Window" (Hichens) **64**:130
"If Dead Indeed" (Cavafy) **2**:91
"If Everything Happens That Can't Be Done" (Cummings) **137**:55
If Five Years Pass (García Lorca)
See *Así que pasen cinco años*
If He Hollers Let Him Go (Himes) **139**:245, 265-68, 280, 286-88, 290-95, 312-13, 320, 323, 325-27, 333-35
"If I Could Know" (Muir) **87**:231
"If I Could Live My Life Over Again" (Lane) **177**:282
If I Forget Thee, Jerusalem (Faulkner) **170**:115, 131, 144
If I Had Money (Tarkington) **9**:464
"If I had Possession over Judgement Day" (Johnson) **69**:76
"if i have made, my lady, intricate" (Cummings) **137**:55
If I May (Milne) **6**:316
"If I Should Ever by Chance" (Thomas) **10**:452, 455
"If I Were a Man" (Gilman) **9**:113, 115
"If I Were Four-and-Twenty" (Yeats) **93**:366
"If I Were King" (Milne) **88**:241
If I Were King (Sturges) **48**:285, 291, 295, 312, 316
"If I Were Rothschild" (Aleichem)
See "Ven ikh bin Roytshild"
"If I Were Tickled by the Rub of Love" (Thomas) **45**:361, 383
If I Were You (Wodehouse) **108**:373
If It Die (Gide)
See *Si le grain ne meurt*
"If It Were Only Yesterday" (Rinehart) **52**:291
"If It Weren't for the Honeysuckle . . ." (Trambley) **163**:288, 292, 300-301, 310, 312, 318-19, 346, 375
"If It's Ever Spring Again" (Hardy) **53**:81
"If Love Be Staunch" (Cullen) **37**:170
"If Love Should Faint" (Gosse) **28**:151
"If My Head Hurt a Hair's Foot" (Thomas) **45**:365, 377, 379
"If Not Higher" (Peretz) **16**:406
If Not Now, When? (Levi)
See *Se non ora, quando?*
If on a Winter's Night a Traveler (Calvino)
See *Se una notte d'inverno un viaggiatore*
"If Only" (Bishop) **103**:14, 18, 33
"If only—1867-1900" (Bishop) **103**:13
If Shakespeare Lived Today (Dunsany) **59**:3, 13, 26
"If So the Man You Are" (Lewis) **2**:397-98; **104**:174
"If Some Day" (Chopin) **5**:153
If Summer Were to Return (Adamov)
See *Si l'été revenait*
If the Sun Didn't Rise Again (Ramuz)
See *Si le soleil ne revenait pas*
"If the Vicious Spiral of Inflation Ever Gets Under Way, the Whole Economic System Will Stagger" (Roosevelt) **93**:184
If the War Goes On . . . Reflections on War and Politics (Hesse) **148**:171-72, 176
If This Be a Man (Levi)
See *Se questo è un uomo*
If This Is a Man (Levi)
See *Se questo è un uomo*
"If Thou Would'st Know the Source" (Bialik) **25**:48
"if (touched by love's own secret) we, like homing" (Cummings) **137**:55
"If Truth in Hearts That Perish" (Housman) **10**:249, 251
"If Washington Should Come to Life" (Cohan) **60**:168
"If We Must Die" (McKay) **7**:457, 461, 463, 467-68; **41**:318-19, 345

"If You Are on Fire and I Am Fire" (Rosenberg) **12**:311
"If You Should Go" (Cullen) **37**:145, 154, 167
"If You Want to Get Along with Me" (Childress) **116**:36
"If You Were Called Nelson" (Arenas) See "Si te llamaras Nelson"
"If You Were Dead" (Naidu) **80**:288
"If You Would Know" (Bialik) **25**:50
"If You'll Be a Baby to Me" (Williams) **81**:434,438
If You're Only Human (Biggers) **65**:2
"Ifigenia" (De La Parra) **185**:216
Ifigenia: Diario de una señorita que escribió porque se fastidiaba (De La Parra) **185**:203, 208-16, 218, 220-22
Ifigenia cruel (Reyes) **33**:316-17, 320-22
"Ifjú szivekben élek" (Ady) **11**:17
"Iglesia abandonada" (García Lorca) **197**:191-97, 251-52
"Ignat" (Bunin) **6**:45
"Ignoble Martyr" (Davis) **6**:154
The Ignoramus and the Madman (Bernhard) See *Der Ignorant und der Wahnsinnige*
Der Ignorant und der Wahnsinnige (Bernhard) **165**:41, 96, 123, 126-27
"The Ignu" (Ginsberg) **120**:36
Igra (Gumilev) **60**:264
"Igra stvaranja sveta" (Popa) **167**:164
"Igra v adu" (Khlebnikov) **20**:131
"Igre" (Popa) **167**:154-55, 177
"A igreja do diabo" (Machado de Assis) **10**:290-91
"Igual-Desigual" (Drummond de Andrade) **139**:231
Így írtok ti (Karinthy) **47**:268, 271, 273
"Ihalempi" (Leino) **24**:376
Ihicus; or, The Adventures of Nevzorov (Tolstoy) **18**:370, 373, 378
"Ihr dummen kleinen Tage" (Arp) **115**:26
"Ihr glücklichen Augen" (Bachmann) **192**:81
"Ihr Worte" (Bachmann) **192**:53, 67
"Ijul'skaja groza" (Platonov) **14**:425
"Ika Loch's Brothel" (van Ostaijen) See "Het bordeel van Ika Loch"
"Ikkai no tsuchi" (Akutagawa Ryūnosuke) **16**:20
Ikrek hava: Napló a gyerekkorról (Radnóti) **16**:412
"Iku-Turso" (Leino) **24**:368, 370
"Ikyō no koi" (Nagai) **51**:98-9
"Il borgo" (Saba) **33**:370, 376-77
"Il bove" (Carducci) **32**:87, 91, 95, 101
"Il bove" (Pascoli) **45**:152
"Il buon vecchio e la bella fanciulla" (Svevo) **2**:545
"Il canto dell' amore" (Carducci) **32**:108
"Il castello dei destini incrociati" (Calvino) **183**:175, 228
Il castello dei destini incrociati (Calvino) **183**:10, 15-16, 26, 38, 41-42, 47, 55-61, 91, 96-97, 112, 124-25, 129-31, 135, 153-54, 159-60, 163-64, 171, 174-75, 177, 189, 194, 201, 214, 228
"Il ciocco" (Pascoli) **45**:143, 149, 152
"Il ciuchino" (Tozzi) **31**:325
"Il compagno dei taglialegna" (Pascoli) **45**:154
"Il comune rustico" (Carducci) **32**:111
"Il contadino e l'orologio" (Levi) **125**:234
Il conte rosso (Giacosa) **7**:305, 308-09, 313
Il Contratto (de Filippo) **127**:276
Il crepuscolo dei filosofi (Papini) **22**:268-69, 280-81, 283
"Il croce e la croce" (Papini) **22**:280
"Il crollo del tempo" (Calvino) **183**:102
Il delirio (D'Annunzio) **6**:144
"Il demonio tentato" (Papini) **22**:280
Il diavolo (Papini) **22**:284, 286, 289, 291
"Il dilettantismo" (Svevo) **35**:363
Il diluvio (Betti) **5**:61
Il dio dei viventi (Deledda) **23**:40
Il diritti dell' anima (Giacosa) **7**:308, 311, 313
Il dovere del medico (Pirandello) **172**:188
"Il était une boulangère" (Péret) **20**:199, 201
"Il fanciullino" (Pascoli) **45**:150, 155
Il ferro (D'Annunzio) See *Le chèvrefeuille*
"Il figlio dell'uomo" (Ginzburg) **156**:45, 97, 105, 107-8
Il filo (Giacosa) **7**:310
"Il focolare" (Pascoli) **45**:143
Il fratello d'armi (Giacosa) **7**:305-07, 309, 313
Il fuoco (D'Annunzio) **6**:129, 133-34, 140-41, 144; **40**:5, 18, 29, 46-51
Il futuro ha un cuore antico (Levi) **125**:207, 209-11
"Il gatto e il poliziotto" (Calvino) **183**:187, 214
Il gattopardo (Lampedusa) **13**:291-305, 307, 311-16, 318-21
"Il gelsomino notturno" (Pascoli) **45**:154, 156
Il giocatore (Betti) **5**:54, 60, 65
"Il giorno dei morti" (Pascoli) **45**:143
Il giuoco delle parti (Pirandello) **29**:283, 301; **172**:134, 138, 158, 160, 162-63, 172, 174, 190-92
"Il guidatore notturno" (Calvino) **183**:191
Il guidizio universale (Papini) **22**:286
Il ladro in casa (Svevo) **35**:370
Il lampo (Pascoli) **45**:154
"Il libro" (Pascoli) **45**:147, 149, 156
Il libro ascetico dell Giovane Italia (D'Annunzio) **6**:145
Il libro ascetico della Giovane Italia (D'Annunzio) **40**:19
Il libro delle vergini (D'Annunzio) **6**:133, 137
"'Il libro di Don Chisciotte' di E. Scarfoglio" (Svevo) **35**:362-63
"Il maiale e l'archeologo" (Calvino) **183**:103
"Il malocchio" (Svevo) **35**:369
"Il mare dell'oggettività" (Calvino) **183**:44, 94, 100-101, 194, 241-43
"Il maresciallo" (Ginzburg) **156**:14
Il marito amante della moglie (Giacosa) **7**:307, 309, 313
Il marito di Elena (Verga) **3**:548
"Il mendico" (Saba) **33**:373
Il Metodo della Pedagogia Scientifica applicato all' educazione infantile nelle Case dei Bambini (Montessori) **103**:289-90, 293, 302, 316
"Il midollo del leone" (Calvino) **183**:5, 44, 94, 101, 103, 114, 117-18, 158, 162, 164, 187, 193, 238, 241
"Il mihrab" (Calvino) **183**:105
Il mio fiume (Papini) **22**:280
"Il mio mestiere" (Ginzburg) **156**:97-98
"Il mio ozio" (Svevo) **2**:541; **35**:345, 352
"Il mistero" (Verga) **3**:546
Il Monumento (de Filippo) **127**:275
"Il monumento storico" (Jovine) **79**:44
"Il museo dei mostri di cera" (Calvino) **183**:101, 105
Il nibbio (Pirandello) **172**:188
"Il nome il naso" (Calvino) **183**:232-33
"Il nonno" (Deledda) **23**:35
Il nostro padrone (Deledda) **23**:35-6
"Il novantanovesimo albero" (Calvino) **183**:103
"Il nunzio" (Pascoli) **45**:156
Il paese delle vacanze (Betti) **5**:62
Il paese di Pulcinella (de Filippo) **127**:271, 274
Il Paradosso (Calvino) **183**:5, 7
Il partita a scacchi (Giacosa) **7**:305-09, 313
Il pastore sepolto (Jovine) **79**:44, 59, 61
"Il patrimonio dei draghi" (Calvino) **183**:105
"Il penseroso" (Yeats) **18**:447
Il piccolo Berto (Saba) **33**:370
Il pitota cieco (Papini) **22**:274, 280-81
Il più forte (Giacosa) **7**:306, 308, 311
"Il plebiscito" (Carducci) **32**:90
"Il pleut" (Apollinaire) **51**:33-4
Il pleut des coups durs (Himes) **139**:253, 255-58, 281-82, 300-302, 305, 321
Il podere (Tozzi) **31**:314-17, 319-24, 328-29, 333-34
Il Ponte (Calvino) **183**:96
"Il pubblico" (Svevo) **35**:363-64
Il quartetto tactile (Marinetti) **10**:320
Il quartiere (Pratolini) **124**:339, 343
"Il Quod Visum Placet" (Gill) **85**:53
"Il racoconto come operazione logica o come mito" (Calvino) **183**:246
"Il rapporto con la luna" (Calvino) **183**:104
"Il reverendo" (Verga) **3**:543, 546
"Il ritorno" (Campana) **20**:83
"Il ritorno del figlio" (Deledda) **23**:35
Il Ritorno del Giullare (Pascoli) **45**:146, 148
Il romanzo (Calvino) **183**:122
"Il romanzo come spettacolo" (Calvino) **183**:104
"Il sangue, il mare" (Calvino) **183**:228
Il secreto dell' uomo solitario (Deledda) **23**:40-1
Il sentiero dei nidi di ragno (Calvino) **183**:6, 37, 39-41, 72-73, 75-76, 78-81, 83-87, 96-97, 112, 145, 152, 187-88, 195, 198, 200, 208, 220-21, 223, 227, 232, 235-39, 244
"Il sesto giorno" (Levi) **49**:6; **109**:292-93, 297-98
"Il signor Nella e Napoleone" (Svevo) **35**:362
"Il sogno" (Dowson) **4**:85
Il sogno d'un tramonto d'autunno (D'Annunzio) **6**:137; **40**:8
"Il sonno di Odisseo" (Pascoli) **45**:142, 154
Il tamburo di fuoco (Marinetti) **10**:317
"Il teatro di varietà" (Marinetti) **10**:317-19
"Il tempio di legno" (Calvino) **183**:107
Il tempo del bastone e della carota (Mussolini) **96**:281-82
"Il traforo" (Ginzburg) **156**:103-5, 107-8
Il tragico quotidiano (Papini) **22**:274, 280-81
"Il transito" (Pascoli) **45**:142
Il trionfo d'amore (Giacosa) **7**:305-07, 309, 313
Il trionfo della morte (D'Annunzio) **6**:128, 131, 133, 138, 140-41, 143-44; **40**:3-4, 13, 28-9, 39-40
Il vecchio con gli stivali (Brancati) **12**:83, 85-7, 93
Il vecchio della montagna (Deledda) **23**:36, 38, 40
Il vecchio e i fonciulli (Deledda) **23**:40
Il vecchione (Svevo) **35**:336-38, 345, 349, 352, 354
Il vento notturno (Betti) **5**:56
"Il Versificatore" (Levi) **109**:293, 295
"Il vetro rotto" (Saba) **33**:374
Il viale degli dei (Papini) **22**:281
"Il viandante nella mappa" (Calvino) **183**:103
"Il vischio" (Pascoli) **45**:155
"Il vulture del sole" (D'Annunzio) **40**:43
"Il y a" (Apollinaire) **3**:45; **51**:20, 36
Ile (O'Neill) **1**:396
L'Ile à hélice (Verne) **52**:331, 350, 359
"Ile de la liberté" (Schwob) **20**:323
L'Île de pingouins (France) **9**:45, 49-51, 53
L'Ile du Diable: Pièce Secrète en 3 ans et plusieurs Tableaux (Jarry) **147**:277
L'ile mystérieuse (Verne) **6**:491, 499-500, 503; **52**:330, 343-44, 350
L'Île Vierge (Lemonnier) **22**:199, 203
"Ilia Isaakovich and Margarita Prokofievna" (Babel) **13**:32
"The Ilicet" (Carman) **7**:136
"Ilicet" (Swinburne) **36**:305, 323
"Ilímite" (Jiménez) **183**:291
Ilja Muromietis (Rainis) **29**:386, 393
"Ilks" (Zamyatin) **8**:553
"I'll Be Waiting" (Chandler) **179**:128
"Ill Fortune" (Andrić) See "Napast"
"I'll never Get out of this World Alive" (Williams) **81**:419,424
"Ill Omens" (Akutagawa Ryūnosuke) See "Kyō"
Ill Seen Ill Said (Beckett) See *Mal vu mal dit*

I'll Stand by You: Selected letters of Sylvia Townsend Warner and Valentine Ackland (Warner) **131**:366
Az illés szekerén (Ady) **11**:13, 17, 21-2, 25
An Ill-Fated Love (Quiroga)
See *Historia de un amor turbio*
"The Illinois State Mews" (Lindsay) **17**:241
"The Illinois Village" (Lindsay) **17**:240
Illion: An Epic in Quantitative Hexametres (Aurobindo) **63**:36
"An Illiterate but Interesting Woman" (McAlmon) **97**:88
The Illiterate Digest (Rogers) **8**:332, 336
Illness (Klabund) **44**:105
"The Illness of Signor Lambert" (Doyle) **7**:216
"Illuminating Episodes in the Lives of Hon. General Poynyard and His Bride" (Wylie) **8**:528
Illuminations (Benjamin) **39**:16
"Illusion" (Baker) **10**:28
"Illusion" (Sterling) **20**:379
"Illusion in Religion" (Abbott) **139**:32
"The Illusion of Historic Time" (Meynell) **6**:294
"The Illusion of the Third World" (Naipaul) **153**:229
Les Illusions du progres (Sorel) **91**:188, 193, 198, 200, 219, 224-5, 227, 295, 316, 332
Illusions fantasmagorique (Melies) **81**:138
Illusions funambulesques (Melies) **81**:138
The Illusions of Progress (Sorel)
See *Les Illusions du progres*
Illusive Village (Martinez Sierra and Martinez Sierra)
See *Aldea ilusoria*
"Illusory Psychology" (Dewey) **95**:94
"Illustrations of the Logic of Science" (Peirce) **81**:195,300,303
"Illustrations of the Poetic as a Sense" (Stevens) **3**:477
"Illustratori, attori e traduttori" (Pirandello) **172**:188
"Illustrators, Actors, and Translators" (Pirandello)
See "Illustratori, attori e traduttori"
"L'illustre estinto" (Pirandello) **29**:282
"The Illustrious Deceased" (Pirandello)
See "L'illustre estinto"
The Illustrious Prince (Oppenheim) **45**:136
Ilotulitus (Leino) **24**:372
"A Ilusão do Migrante" (Drummond de Andrade) **139**:240
Las ilusiones del Doctor Faustino (Valera y Alcala-Galiano) **10**:500, 502, 505-08
Ilya of Murom (Rainis)
See *Ilja Muromietis*
"I'm a Fool" (Anderson) **1**:42, 46, 50, 58; **10**:36, 43, 45; **123**:96, 107
"I'm a Yankee Doodle Dandy" (Cohan) **60**:172
Im alten Eisen (Raabe) **45**:166, 171, 174, 177-79, 196, 200-03
"Im Anfang" (Lasker-Schueler) **57**:303-4, 316,334
"Im Armenhaus" (Bernhard) **165**:55
"I'm Changin' All Those Changes" (Holly) **65**:148
Im dickicht der städte (Brecht) **1**:108, 112, 119; **6**:35; **169**:37, 41
"Im Gewitter der Rosen" (Bachmann) **192**:53-54
"I'm Gonna Love You Too" (Holly) **65**:138, 140, 153
"I'm Gonna Set My Foot Down" (Holly) **65**:148
Im Grafenschloss (Heyse) **8**:121
"Im Hoffnungslosen" (Arp) **115**:8-9
Im Kampf um Gott (Andreas-Salome) **56**:28, 40, 42, 48
"Im Lande der Rujuks" (Böll) **185**:27
"Im Mai, im Mai Schrie der Kuckuck" (Borchert) **5**:105, 108-09
I'm Not Stiller (Frisch)
See *Stiller*
Im Paradiese (Heyse) **8**:115, 119
I'm Putting Things in Order! (Lasker-Schueler)
See *Ich raume' auf! Meine Anklage gegen meine Verleger*
Im Schlaraffenland (Mann) **9**:319, 323, 326-29
"Im Schnee, im sauberen Schnee" (Borchert) **5**:105
"I'm so Lonesome I Could Cry" (Williams) **81**:422,426,438,444
"I'm Still Not Patriarch" (Mandelstam) **2**:409
"I'm Sure She Said Six-Thirty" (Nash) **109**:354
"I'm the Last Poet of the Village" (Esenin) **4**:117
"I'm to Marry a Nobleman" (Cohan) **60**:171
"Im Wald" (Kandinsky) **92**:69
Im Zwielicht (Sudermann) **15**:429, 432
"The Image" (Warner) **131**:310
The Image (Gregory) **176**:13, 18, 34-35, 44
The Image, and Other Plays (Gregory) **1**:333-36
The Image and the Law (Nemerov) **124**:150-53, 171, 206, 211, 225, 261, 268, 287, 297, 313
"An Image from a Past Life" (Yeats) **93**:390, 391
"The Image in the Mirror" (Sayers) **15**:379
The Image in the Sand (Benson) **27**:17
"The Image Maker" (Merrill) **173**:230
"The Image of Hell" (Arendt) **193**:75, 77, 79
Image of Josephine (Tarkington) **9**:469
"The Image of Misfortune" (Onetti)
See "La cara de la desgracia"
The Image of Misfortune (Onetti)
See *La cara de la desgracia*
The Image of the City, and Other Essays (Williams) **11**:497
"Image of the Engine" (Oppen) **107**:335
"The Image of the Lost Soul" (Saki) **3**:371
"Image on the Heart" (Fitzgerald) **6**:167
L'Image-mouvement (Deleuze)
See *Cinema 1:l'image-Movement*
The Image-Movement (Deleuze)
See *Cinema 1:l'image-Movement*
"Imagen española de la muerte" (Vallejo) **56**:302
La imagen poética de don Luis de Góngora (García Lorca) **181**:96, 192, 198
"Images" (Muir) **87**:237-38
"Images I" (Muir) **87**:279
Images in a Mirror (Undset) **197**:295, 298
Images of Good and Evil (Symons) **11**:431-32, 435, 446
The Image-Time (Deleuze)
See *Cinema 2 l'image-Temps*
"Imaginación, inspiración, evasión" (García Lorca) **49**:90, 93, 109; **181**:26; **197**:223, 230
An Imaginary Character Named Saroyan (Saroyan) **137**:147
"The Imaginary Iceberg" (Bishop) **121**:9, 23, 50
Imaginary Letters (Butts) **77**:83, 103-4
Imaginary Life (Ginzburg)
See *Vita immaginaria*
"Imaginary Ministers" (Mikszath)
See "Képzeletbeli miniszterek"
Imaginary Prisons (Yourcenar) **193**:272
Imaginary Sonnets (Lee-Hamilton) **22**:188-89, 191, 193-94
Imaginary Woman (Tagore)
See *Mānasī*
"Imagination" (Arendt) **193**:182
"Imagination" (Coleridge) **73**:11
Imagination (MacDonald) **9**:292
The Imagination, and Other Essays (MacDonald) **9**:288
"Imagination as Value" (Stevens) **45**:291
Imagination Dead Imagine (Beckett)
See *Imagination morte imaginez*
"Imagination, Inspiration, Evasion" (García Lorca)
See "Imaginación, inspiración, evasión"
"The Imagination: Its Function and Culture" (MacDonald) **113**:232, 258, 298
Imagination morte imaginez (Beckett) **145**:80, 92, 96-97
Imaginations and Reveries (Baker) **10**:17
An Imaginative Man (Hichens) **64**:122, 126-28, 131
"Imagine a Man in a Box" (Wakefield) **120**:333
Imagine a Man in a Box (Wakefield) **120**:333, 348, 355, 357, 359
"Imagined America—How a Young Russian Pictured It" (Cahan) **71**:85
Imago (Spitteler) **12**:335, 339, 341-42, 348-49, 351-53
"The Imam Bara" (Naidu) **80**:342
Iman (Sender) **136**:209
"Imatran tarina" (Leino) **24**:369
"Imenie Belokonskoe" (Pilnyak) **23**:211, 213
"Imfundo ephakeme" (Vilakazi) **37**:403
"Imifula yomhlaba" (Vilakazi) **37**:404
Imihobe nemibongo yokufundwa ezikolweni (Mqhayi) **25**:324
"Imitación" (Sarduy) **167**:205
La imitación de Cristo (Pardo Bazán) **189**:220
"Imitation" (Dobson)
See "Ballade of Imitation"
"Imitation" (Gurney) **33**:97
Imitation of Life (Sturges) **48**:286, 294
"The Immaculate Devil" (Gladkov) **27**:92
L'immaculée conception (Éluard) **41**:152
"Immagini del viaggio e della montagna" (Campana) **20**:84
Immanuel Kant (Bernhard) **165**:96, 108, 130, 133
"Les Immatériaux" (Lyotard) **103**:172-73, 235-40
Immaturity (Shaw) **3**:400-01; **9**:422; **21**:329
"The Immediate Present" (Morris) **107**:104
The Immigrant Press and Its Control (Park) **73**:185
Immigrant Saint: The Life of Mother Cabrini (di Donato) **159**:183, 189, 195-96, 202, 207
The Immigrant Woman (Papadiamantis) **29**:271, 273
"Los Immigrantes" (Quiroga) **20**:212, 216-17
"Immigrants" (Quiroga)
See "Los Immigrantes"
The Immigrant's Daughter (Sánchez)
See *La gringa*
"Immigration Blues" (Santos) **156**:326
"Immoral" (Acker) **191**:109
The Immoralist (Gide)
See *L'immoraliste*
L'immoraliste (Gide) **36**:86, 93, 103, 110; **117**:1-121
L'Immoraliste (Yourcenar) **193**:355
"The Immortal" (Borges)
See "El inmortal"
"The Immortal" (Pickthall) **21**:250, 252
"An Immortal" (Sharp)
See "The Unborn Child"
"Immortal Bird" (Wakefield) **120**:345, 352
"The Immortal Free Spirit of Man" (Kazantzakis) **33**:163
The Immortal Hour (Sharp) **39**:370, 377, 379-80
The Immortal Husband (Merrill) **173**:174
Immortal Longings (Williams) **89**:395
"Immortal Man" (Döblin)
See "Der unsterbliche Mensch"
The Immortal Moment: The Story of Kitty Tailleur (Sinclair) **11**:409
"Immortality" (Kaye-Smith) **20**:108
"Immortality in the Plays and Sonnets of Shakespeare" (Anderson) **144**:70
"The Immortals" (Parker) **143**:320
"The Immortals" (Rhodes) **53**:316
"The Immortals" (Rosenberg) **12**:294, 302, 312
"L'immortel" (Svevo) **35**:363
Immortelle maladie (Péret) **20**:201
"Immutable" (Naidu) **80**:315
"Imogayu" (Akutagawa Ryūnosuke) **16**:35
El Imparcial (Pardo Bazán) **189**:300

Impatient Maiden (Whale) **63**:339, 383
"The Impenitent Thief" (Graham) **19**:112
"Impenitentia ultima" (Dowson) **4**:87
An Imperative Duty (Howells) **7**:370; **17**:185
An Imperative Play (Howells) **7**:393
"The Impercipient" (Hardy) **143**:157, 160, 186
"An Impercipient at a Cathedral Service" (Hardy) **32**:281
"An Imperfect Conflagration" (Bierce) **44**:40, 45
An Imperfect Mother (Beresford) **81**:8
"Imperial Delhi" (Naidu) **80**:295
"An Imperial Elegy" (Owen) **27**:211
Imperial Germany and the Industrial Revolution (Veblen) **31**:342, 346, 362
"The Imperial Kailyard" (Graham) **19**:121-22
Imperial Orgy (Saltus) **8**:355
The Imperial Palace (Bennett) **5**:38; **197**:30-1, 36, 41-2, 62-3, 65-6
"Imperial Panorama" (Benjamin) **39**:39
Imperial Peking: Seven Centuries of China (Lin) **149**:331
Imperial Purple (Saltus) **8**:344, 346-50, 352, 354-55
"Imperial Sentiment in Canada" (Duncan) **60**:215, 239
Imperialism (Arendt) **193**:134
Imperialism: The Highest Stage of Capitalism (Lenin) **67**:225-26
The Imperialist (Duncan) **60**:175-7, 180-1, 183, 195, 197-8, 201-3, 207-11, 215-9, 222-4, 233-4, 238-9, 241-2, 244-5, 247, 249
Imperium in Imperio (Griggs) **77**:146, 150-5, 162, 164, 166, 168-71, 175, 182-6, 190-1
L'impero in provincia (Jovine) **79**:44, 65
"Impi ja pajarin poika" (Leino) **24**:368, 377
Impious Tales (Zamyatin)
See *Nechestivye rasskazy*
"Implacable" (Nervo) **11**:398-99
"The Implacable Aphrodite" (Millay) **169**:278
"Implosion" (Calvino)
See "L'implosione"
"L'implosione" (Calvino) **183**:98
"Impophoma yeVictoria" (Vilakazi) **37**:402
The Importance of Being Earnest (Wilde) **1**:495, 498-500, 503-09; **8**:494, 498, 500; **23**:406-52; **41**:388; **175**:272, 275, 279, 287, 291, 298, 310, 313-14, 317
"The Importance of Being Oscar" (Leverson) **18**:201
"The Importance of Individuals" (James) **32**:333
The Importance of Living (Lin) **149**:314-15, 326-27, 341
"The Importance of Loafing" (Lin) **149**:341
"Importancia histórica y artística del primitivo canto andaluz llamado 'cante jondo'" (García Lorca) **181**:190; **197**:275
"Important People" (Milne) **6**:314
"Important—Einstein's Universe" (Rhodes) **53**:315-16
"The Imported Bridegroom" (Cahan) **71**:12, 16-19, 27, 42, 64, 67-68, 71
The Imported Bridegroom and Other Tales of the New York Ghetto (Cahan) **71**:9, 13, 21, 26, 28-29, 39, 86
The Imposition of Sexual Morality (Reich) **57**:350
L'impossible (Bataille) **155**:114-15
The Impossible (Howells) **7**:387-88
"The Impossible Fact" (Morgenstern) **8**:305
An Impossible Voyage (Melies) **81**:147
"A Impossível Communhão" (Drummond de Andrade) **139**:230
Los impostores joviales (Baroja) **8**:63
L'imposture (Bernanos) **3**:118, 120, 122-5
"Impoverished" (Bergelson)
See *Yordim*
"Impresiones de un estudiante" (Azuela) **145**:21
Impresiónes y Paisajes (García Lorca) **49**:119; **181**:119, 166-73, 192, 195
Impresiones y recuerdos (Gamboa) **36**:71-2
"Impression II" (Cummings) **137**:42
Impression III (Concert) (Kandinsky) **92**:37
Impression of Russia (Brandes)
See *Intryk fra Rusland*
"Impressionas of Wolf Baiting" (Chekhov)
See "Na volchey sadke"
Impression-Moscow (Kandinsky) **92**:140
Impressions (Sully Prudhomme) **31**:307
Impressions and Comments (Ellis) **14**:106-07, 110, 112-14, 116, 123, 127
Impressions and Landscapes (García Lorca)
See *Impresiónes y Paisajes*
Impressions and Opinions (Moore) **7**:474, 490-91
Impressions d'Afrique (Roussel) **20**:226-31, 234-35, 237-39, 241-44, 246-47, 249, 251
"Impressions de route en automobile" (Proust) **161**:154, 160-65
"Impressions IX" (Cummings) **137**:42
"The Impressions of a Cousin" (James) **47**:200
Impressions of Africa (Roussel)
See *Impressions d'Afrique*
"Impressions of Europe, 1913-1914" (Bourne) **16**:46, 52
Impressions of Italy (Bourget)
See *Sensations d'Italie*
Impressions of Japanese Architecture and the Allied Arts (Cram) **45**:9, 14, 18
Impressions of Poland (Brandes) **10**:60-1
"Impressions of Prague" (Muir) **87**:296
Impressions of Soviet Russia (Dewey) **95**:69
"Impressions II" (Cummings) **137**:42
"Imprint for Rio Grande" (Toomer) **172**:278
"L'Imprompto d'Alice" (Cocteau) **119**:57
"Impromptu" (Scott) **6**:394
"L'Impromptu de Bouffes-Parisiens" (Cocteau) **119**:57
"Improving the Lives of the Rich" (Day) **25**:131
Improvisation 6 (Kandinsky) **92**:78
Improvisation 7 (Kandinsky) **92**:62, 73, 76
Improvisation 8 (Kandinsky) **92**:73
Improvisation 20 (Kandinsky) **92**:73
Improvisation 22 (Kandinsky) **92**:73, 140
Improvisation 25 (Kandinsky) **92**:73
Improvisation 27 (Kandinsky) **92**:62, 73
Improvisation 28a (Kandinsky) **92**:73, 97
Improvisation 30 (Kandinsky) **92**:73
"Improvisation on an Old Song" (Scott) **6**:389
"Improvisation on the Sickness of America" (Andrade)
See "Improviso do mal da América"
Improvisation without Title (Kandinsky) **92**:38
"Improviso do mal da América" (Andrade) **43**:17, 23
"Impudence" (Davies) **5**:201
"The Impudent Lady's Maid" (Williams) **89**:383
"An Impulse" (Guro)
See "Poryv"
"Impulsive Dialogue" (Bodenheim) **44**:60, 62
"The Impure Tragedians and the Leprous Playwrights" (Chekhov) **163**:38
"In a Backwater" (Graham) **19**:105
In a Backwoods Town (Bergelson) **81**:30
"In a Bar's Doorway" (Wright) **136**:301
"In a Carnival Night" (Asch) **3**:67
"In a Castle" (Lowell) **1**:375; **8**:235
"In a Cemetery" (Aleixandre) **113**:23
"In a Closed Bowl" (Guro)
See "V zakrytoi chashe"
"In a Closed Chalice" (Guro)
See "V zakrytoi chashe"
"In a Concentrated Thought a Sudden Noise Startles" (Rosenberg) **12**:299-300
"In a Dark Hour" (Bjoernson) **37**:27
"In a Distant Valley" (Balmont) **11**:41
"In a Eweleaze near Weatherbury" (Hardy) **4**:152; **143**:172, 186
"In a Far Country" (London) **9**:263, 267-68, 273; **15**:257-58, 276
"In a Former Resort after Many Years" (Hardy) **143**:160
In a Garden (Barry) **11**:47, 49-50, 52-5, 59-60, 64, 66
In a German Pension (Mansfield) **2**:447-48, 451; **8**:281, 283, 285; **39**:293, 297-98, 300, 318, 327; **164**:268-70, 288-89, 293-94, 324-27, 272271
"In a German Tramp" (Graham) **19**:109, 112
"In a Gothic Cathedral" (Carducci)
See "In una Chiesa Gotica"
"In a Gothic Church" (Carducci)
See "In una Chiesa Gotica"
"In a Grove" (Akutagawa Ryūnosuke)
See "Yabu no naka"
"In a Latticed Balcony" (Naidu) **80**:346
In a Low Voice (Nervo)
See *En voz baja*
"In a Monastery Garden" (Pickthall) **21**:245, 250
"In a Music Hall" (Davidson) **24**:188
In a Music Hall, and Other Poems (Davidson) **24**:160-62
"In a network of lines that intersect" (Calvino) **183**:131
"In a Restless Hour" (Radnóti) **16**:419, 420
"In a Room in 1936" (Bishop) **121**:48
"In a Rosary" (Swinburne) **36**:345
In a Sanctuary (Pirandello) **29**:297
"In a Strange City" (Baker) **10**:21
"In a Time of Dearth" (Lowell) **8**:236
"In a Time of Flowers" (Naidu) **80**:346
"In a Township of Asia Minor" (Cavafy) **7**:154
In a Valley of this Restless Mind (Muggeridge) **120**:147, 185
In a Vast Dominion (Aleixandre)
See *En un vasto dominio*
In a Vision (Peretz) **16**:396-97
"In a Wet Season" (Lawson) **27**:119
In a Winter City (Ouida) **43**:339, 348
"In a Wood" (Hardy) **53**:81
"In a Workingman's Rooming House" (Anderson) **1**:38
"In After Days" (Dobson) **79**:20
In an Age of Iron (Nexø) **43**:334
"In an Auction Room" (Morley) **87**:124
"In an Iris Meadow" (Carman) **7**:137
"In an Underground Prison" (Bryusov) **10**:80
"In and Out of Old Nachitoches" (Chopin) **14**:61, 82; **127**:167
"In Another Country" (Hemingway) **115**:180, 194
"In Another Country-2" (Hemingway) **115**:194
"In April Once" (Percy) **84**:199, 228
In April Once (Percy) **84**:196
"In Bad Company" (Korolenko) **22**:170, 183
In Bad With Sinbad (Stringer) **37**:336
"In Barracks" (Ledwidge) **23**:118
In Black and White (Kipling) **8**:185, 188
"In Borrowed Plumes" (Jacobs) **22**:105
In Boundlessness (Balmont)
See *V bezbrezhnosti*
"In Business" (Morrison) **72**:362
"In Camp" (Andrić)
See "In the Camp"
"In Camp" (Ledwidge) **23**:118
In Candidum (Ekelund) **75**:95
"In Captivity" (Remizov)
See "V plenu"
"In Cell No. 115" (Andrić)
See "U ćeliji br. 115"
In Chancery (Galsworthy) **1**:293-94; **45**:46, 69
In Chancery (Pinero) **32**:409, 412
"In Church" (Bottomley) **107**:6
"In Church" (Montgomery) **51**:210
In Cold Blood: A True Account of a Multiple Murder and Its Consequences (Capote) **164**:105, 113, 116-18, 122-23, 129-32, 134-35, 137-40, 143, 145-46, 148, 150-53, 162, 165, 167-71, 173, 176-89, 201, 208
"In Collaboration" (Wakefield) **120**:343, 355, 357
In Colonial Times (Freeman) **9**:72
"In Conclusion" (Benchley) **55**:21
"In Connerama" (Baker) **3**:3
"In Country Heaven" (Thomas) **105**:351-52

"In Country Sleep" (Thomas) **8**:461; **45**:362, 409; **105**:315, 337, 355
"In Dark New England Days" (Jewett) **22**:129
"In Darkness and Confusion" (Petry) **112**:299, 301, 304, 331
"In Death Valley" (Markham) **47**:278
In Death's Foreranks (Ady) **11**:22
"In Deep Deference" (Wright) **136**:302
"In Defence of Comrade Zilliacus" (Orwell) **129**:247
"In Defence of English Cooking" (Orwell) **128**:288; **129**:235
"In Defence of the Bush" (Paterson) **32**:369-70
"In Defence of the Novel" (Orwell) **128**:282
"In Defence of the Novel, I" (Orwell) **128**:282
"In Defence of the Novel, II" (Orwell) **128**:282
"In Defense of Harriet Shelley" (Twain) **12**:431, 438
"In Defense of Myself" (Caldwell) **117**:3
"In Defense of Pat Garrett" (Rhodes) **53**:314-15, 324
"In Defense of the Redneck" (Abbey) **160**:59
In Defense of Women (Mencken) **13**:383
"In der Certosa" (Rilke) **195**:181
In der Höhe (Bernhard) **165**:94-95
"In der Strafkolonie" (Kafka) **2**:293, 304, 306; **6**:222-23, 226; **13**:280, 284; **29**:170-71, 213-14; **47**:222; **53**:202-236; **112**:43, 75, 92; **179**:303, 305
In Distances Drawn Apart (Balmont)
See *V razdvinutoi dali*
In Divers Tones (Roberts) **8**:313, 316-17, 319-20, 325, 327
"In Dreams throughout the Night" (Chopin) **5**:153
In Dubious Battle (Steinbeck) **135**:264, 271, 273, 286, 316, 332, 343, 353
"In Due Season" (McCrae) **12**:211
"In Dull Devonshire" (Powys) **9**:366, 369
"In Duty, Bound" (Gilman) **117**:148
"In England" (Johnson) **19**:254
"In Excelsis" (Lowell) **8**:234, 237
"In Exile" (Foote) **108**:6-8, 39-41, 43
In Fairyland (Vazov) **25**:453
In Fairy-Tale Land (Hamsun)
See *I Æventyrland*
"In Flanders Fields" (McCrae) **12**:208-11
In Flanders Fields, and Other Poems (McCrae) **12**:208
"In Florida" (Forten) **16**:150
"In freien viereck mit den Gelben Steinen" (George) **14**:213
"In Front of a Cathedral" (Carducci)
See "Davanti una cattedrale"
"In Front of Prince Silence" (Ady)
See "Jó csöndherceg előtt"
In Full Voice (Mayakovski) **18**:244
"In Galleries" (Jarrell) **177**:162, 229-30
In God We Trust, All Others Pay Cash (Shepherd) **177**:292-95, 298, 300, 304, 310, 315, 319
In God's Land (Nexø)
See *Midt i en jærntid*
In God's Way (Bjoernson)
See *På Guds veje*
"In Gokhale's Garden" (Naidu) **80**:340
"In Good Earth" (Powys) **9**:374
"In Green Ways" (Stephens) **4**:412, 416
"In Grenada" (Scott) **6**:394
"In Half Delight of Shy Delight" (Rosenberg) **12**:313
In Harbor (Huysmans)
See *En rade*
"In Haying Time" (Montgomery) **51**:204
"In His Image" (Bryan) **99**:16, 134
In His Image (Futabatei)
See *Sono omokage*
In His Own Image (Rolfe) **12**:266-68, 274, 282-83
"In His Twenty-Fifth Year" (Cavafy) **7**:152
"In Holy Week" (Pasternak) **188**:193, 195-96
In Honour's Name (Kuprin)
See *Poedinok*
In hora mortis (Bernhard) **165**:95
"In Horatium" (Babits) **14**:39
"In horis aæternum" (Aurobindo) **63**:9
"In Hospital" (Henley) **8**:97, 106-07, 109-10
"In Houses" (Balmont) **11**:30
In Job's Balances (Shestov)
See *Na vesakh Iova*
"In Just Spring" (Cummings) **137**:9, 13, 41, 56
"In Kashmir" (Sarton) **120**:265
"In Kropfsberg Keep" (Cram) **45**:5
"In Lace and Whalebone" (Dickey) **151**:152
"In le Havre" (Lowry) **6**:254
"In Leinster" (Guiney) **41**:207
"In Letters of Fire" (Leroux) **25**:260
"In Love for Long" (Muir) **87**:189, 256
"In Malaga" (García Lorca)
See "En Málaga"
"In Man's Memory" (Tzara) **168**:322-23
In Maremma (Ouida) **43**:342, 347, 352, 356, 366-67, 375-76
"In memoria di Roland Barthes" (Calvino) **183**:105
"In Memoriam" (Grove) **4**:138
"In Memoriam" (Léautaud) **83**:199, 207
"In Memoriam" (Reese) **181**:344
In Memoriam (Léautaud) **83**:186, 190, 197, 204
"In memoriam Herman van den Reeck" (van Ostaijen) **33**:413
In Memoriam to Identity (Acker) **191**:65, 67, 70, 126
"In Memorium" (de la Mare) **4**:81
"In Memory" (Johnson) **19**:244, 256
"In Memory of Ann Jones" (Thomas)
See "After the Funeral: In Memory of Anne Jones"
"In Memory of Annensky" (Gumilev) **60**:269
"In Memory of Col. Charles Young" (Cullen) **37**:154
"In Memory of Eva Gore-Booth and Con Markiewicz" (Yeats) **31**:420
"In Memory of Katherine Mansfield" (Murry) **16**:352
"In Memory of L. H. W." (Fisher) **87**:73
"In Memory of Major Robert Gregory" (Yeats) **1**:566; **11**:525; **31**:422
"In Memory of My Father" (Agee) **180**:24
"In Memory of the Actor, Mitlerwurzer" (Hofmannsthal) **11**:294
"In Merioneth" (Johnson) **19**:239
"In Michigan" (Masters) **25**:289
In Mizzoura (Thomas) **97**:126-27, 134-36, 140
In Montibus Sanctis (Ruskin) **63**:251
In Morocco (Wharton) **129**:349, 363
"In Mount Holly" (Fletcher) **35**:106
In Mr. Knox's Country (Somerville & Ross) **51**:335, 340, 342, 345, 348, 354, 359-60, 362
"In My Craft or Sullen Art" (Thomas) **45**:360, 363
In My End Is My Beginning (Baring) **8**:42-3
"In My Estates" (Kahanovitsch) **56**:125
"In Nature There Is Neither Right Nor Left Nor Wrong" (Jarrell) **177**:218
"In New New England" (Fisher) **87**:73
"In New York" (Percy) **84**:199
"In Nine Sleep Valley" (Merrill) **173**:228
"In Notre Dame" (Roberts) **8**:314
"In November" (Scott) **6**:393
"In Nunhead Cemetery" (Mew) **8**:297, 301
"In Odessa" (Babel) **2**:36
In Old Plantation Days (Dunbar) **12**:107, 109, 111, 119-20, 122
In Orbit (Morris) **107**:122-24, 155, 158, 165-68, 181-84, 214
In Order to Live on This Earth (Éluard)
See *Pour vivre ici*
In Orpheus' Footsteps (Radnóti) **16**:419
In Our Time (Hemingway) **115**:131, 133-35, 142-43, 175, 179
In Our Town (Runyon) **10**:436
In Paradise (Heyse)
See *Im Paradiese*
"In Paris" (Bunin) **6**:56
In Person (Cather) **99**:281
"In Petrovsky Park" (Khodasevich) **15**:212
In Phanta's Schloss (Morgenstern) **8**:305, 307, 309
"In Planting Time" (Montgomery) **51**:208
In Polish oif der Kay (Peretz) **16**:400
"In Praise of Aphrodite" (Tsvetaeva)
See "Khvala Afrodite"
"In Praise of Darkness" (Borges)
See "Elogio de la sombra"
In Praise of Darkness (Borges)
See *Elogio de la sombra*
"In Praise of Gulmohur Blossoms" (Naidu) **80**:293
"In Praise of Henna" (Naidu) **80**:291, 344
"In Praise of Leisure" (Čapek) **37**:46
"In Praise of Newspapers" (Čapek) **37**:47; **192**:227, 232
In Praise of Philosophy (Merleau-Ponty)
See *Èloge de la philosophie*
"In Praise of Walking" (Stephen) **23**:345
"In principis" (Claudel) **10**:123
"In Prison" (Bishop) **121**:50, 67
"In Prison" (Remizov)
See "V sekretnoi"
In Pursuit of the Grey Soul (Dickey) **151**:162
"In Quest of the Dingue" (Chambers) **41**:102
"In Romney Marsh" (Davidson) **24**:164, 176, 182
In Russian and French Prisons (Kropotkin) **36**:208
"In Sabine" (Chopin) **5**:145; **14**:58, 70; **127**:167, 171-72, 176
"In Salutation to My Father's Spirit" (Naidu) **80**:272, 314
"In Salutation to the Eternal Peace" (Naidu) **80**:310
"In schönen Frülingstagen" (Raabe) **45**:188
In Search of Bisco (Caldwell) **117**:25-7
In Search of Lost Time (Proust)
See *À la recherche du temps perdu*
In Search of Myself (Grove) **4**:135, 138-39
"In Search of Socks" (Mayakovski) **18**:269
In Search of the Supreme (Gandhi) **59**:60, 62
In Search of the Unknown (Chambers) **41**:95, 100, 102, 113-14
In Search of Wagner (Adorno) **111**:53, 134
"In Search of Yage" (Ginsberg) **120**:135
"In Shadow" (Crane) **2**:119
"In Shadow" (Jewett) **22**:116, 126, 140
In shturm (Aleichem)
See *Der mabl*
"In Society" (Ginsberg) **120**:31, 74
"In Spite of Death" (Cullen) **4**:46; **37**:155, 159, 162, 164
In Spring (Obstfelder)
See *Om Våren*
"In Springtime" (Andreyev) **3**:20
"In St. Valentine's Church" (Babel)
See "U sviatogo Valenta"
In Such Days (Bryusov) **10**:90
"In Tenebris (I)" (Hardy) **53**:103; **143**:212
"In Tenebris II" (Hardy) **10**:224; **53**:102, 109; **143**:155
"In Texas" (Sarton) **120**:301
"In the Abyss" (Pirandello) **4**:350
"In the Abyss" (Wells) **12**:511; **19**:435, 441
"In the Afternoon" (Roberts) **8**:314, 316
In the Arena (Tarkington) **9**:456, 460, 466
"In the Art Gallery" (Stringer) **37**:328
"In the Avu Observatory" (Wells) **19**:429
"In the Backwoods" (Zamyatin)
See *Na kulichkakh*
"In the Baggage Room at Greyhound" (Ginsberg) **120**:129
"In the Bar at Night" (Hagiwara) **60**:291
"In the Basement" (Babel) **2**:28; **13**:20, 35; **171**:14, 94
"In the Basement" (Peretz) **16**:405

"In the Bay" (Swinburne) **8**:426-27; **36**:332
"In the Bazars of Hyderabad" (Naidu) **80**:346
"In the Beginning" (Bishop) **103**:26
"In the Beginning" (Lasker-Schueler) **57**:334
"In the Beginning" (Levi) **109**:301
"In the Beginning" (Thomas) **8**:458; **45**:361, 387
In the Beginning (Douglas) **68**:3, 6, 9, 17, 29, 32-3, 43
"In the Beyond" (Hippius) **9**:157
In the Black Square (Kandinsky) **92**:32
"In the Blood" (Calvino)
See "La stessa cosa del sangue"
"In the Cage" (Masters) **2**:461
"In the Camp" (Andrić) **135**:10, 95
"In the Carquinez Woods" (Harte) **25**:212
"In the Carthusian Monastery" (Rilke)
See "In der Certosa"
"In the Caucasus" (Tolstoy) **18**:378
"In the Change of Years" (Leverson) **18**:200-01
"In the Cities" (Lawrence) **93**:73
"In the City of Execution" (Bialik)
See "Be 'ir ha-haregah"
"In the City of Slaughter" (Bialik) **25**:50, 59, 65
In the Clouds (Murfree) **135**:223, 225, 229-30
In the Cold (Bernhard)
See *Die Kälte: Eine Isolation*
"In the College" (Bosschere) **19**:59, 63
"In the Confidence of a Story-Writer" (Chopin) **127**:126
"In the Cornfield" (Bialik) **25**:50
"In the Country Churchyard: To the Memory of My Father" (Scott) **6**:385, 393
"In the Crowd" (Sologub) **9**:446
"In the Crowd at Goodwood" (Thomas) **10**:459
"In the Dark" (Kuprin)
See "V potmakh"
"In the Dark" (Lawrence) **61**:182; **93**:55
In the Darkest Night; or, The Surrealist Bluff (Artaud)
See *À la grande nuit; ou, le bluff surréaliste*
"In the Darkness" (Jensen) **41**:306-07
In the Days of the Comet (Wells) **6**:539, 548; **12**:490; **19**:425-26, 440, 450-53
In the Days of the Messiah (Aleichem)
See *Moshiekhs tsaytn*
"In the Days When the World Was Wide" (Lawson) **27**:132, 140
In the Days When the World Was Wide, and Other Verses (Lawson) **27**:136
"In the Dead Town" (Peretz) **16**:390
"In the Deep of the Forest" (Kuprin) **5**:298
In the Desert and Wilderness (Sienkiewicz)
See *W pustyni i puszczy*
"In the Direction of the Beginning" (Thomas) **105**:299-300, 325-26, 328
"In the Dordogne" (Bishop) **103**:5
"In the Droving Days" (Paterson) **32**:370
"In the Dusk" (Ledwidge) **23**:120, 122
"In the Ear of a Girl" (García Lorca)
See "Al oído de una muchacha"
"In the Flower of Age" (Colette) **16**:135
"In the Fog" (Davis) **24**:205
In the Fog (Andreyev) **3**:26
In the Fog of the Season's End (La Guma) **140**:196, 201-2, 205-6, 210, 213-17, 227-28, 234, 249, 253, 256-57, 260, 262, 266-73
In the Footsteps of the Lincolns (Tarbell) **40**:433, 436
"In the Forest" (de la Mare) **53**:34
"In the Forest" (Naidu) **80**:294
"In the Forest of the Lunar Grapefruits (A Static Poem)" (García Lorca)
See "En el bosque de las toronjas de luna (Poema extatico)"
In the Frame of Don Cristóbal (García Lorca)
See *Retablillo de Don Cristóbal*
"In the Gallery" (Kafka)
See "Auf der Galerie"
In the Gallery (Kafka) **47**:233
"In the Garden of the Lunar Grapefruits" (García Lorca)
See "En el jardín de las toronjas de luna"
In the Gates of the North (O'Grady) **5**:352-53, 356
"In the Glass of Fashion" (Nemerov) **124**:280
"In the Gold Mines" (Vilakazi)
See "Ezinkomponi"
"In the Granary" (Warung) **45**:418
"In the Gray Cabins of New England" (Davis) **6**:154
In the Great Steep's Garden (Roberts) **68**:326
In the Green Tree (Lewis) **3**:288
In the Grip of Life (Hamsun)
See *Livet ivold*
"In the Guest House" (Andrić) **135**:13
In the Hands of God (Babits)
See *Isten kezében*
In the Heart of the Rhodope (Vazov) **25**:450, 452
"In the hopeless" (Arp) **115**:22-3
"In the House of Dreams" (Scott) **6**:385, 393, 397
"In the House of Idiedaily" (Carman) **7**:133
"In the Interests of the Brethren" (Kipling) **8**:196, 201
"In the Isle of Dogs" (Davidson) **24**:164, 183, 192
In the Jungle of Cities (Brecht)
See *Im dickicht der städte*
In the Land of Cockaigne (Mann)
See *Im Schlaraffenland*
In the Land of the Unfrightened Birds (Prishvin)
See *V Kraiu Nepugannykh Ptits*
"In the Land of Time" (Dunsany) **2**:136
In the Land of Youth (Stephens) **4**:414, 418, 420-21
"In the Landau" (Chekhov) **163**:77-78
"In the Laundry Room" (Childress) **116**:37
In the Making (White) **176**:310
"In the Manner of Verlaine" (Ekelund)
See "Verlaine stamning"
"In the Marble Quarry" (Dickey) **151**:172, 202
"In the Market-Place" (Nemerov) **124**:280
"In the Meadow" (Parker) **143**:325
"In the Mediterranean" (Ledwidge) **23**:115-16
"In the Mermaid Cafeteria" (Morley) **87**:142
"In the Middle of the Night" (Quiroga) **20**:221
"In the Middle of the Road" (Drummond de Andrade) **139**:223
"In the Midst of Life" (Cullen) **37**:165
In the Midst of Life (Bierce)
See *Tales of Soldiers and Civilians*
"In the Midst of the Large City" (Morgenstern)
See "Inmitten der grossen Stadt"
"In the Mist" (Pascoli) **45**:142
"In the Month of Athyr" (Cavafy) **2**:87
"In the Morning" (Dunbar) **12**:124
In the Morning of Time (Roberts) **8**:318, 323-25
In the Mountain Gorge (Bergelson) **81**:16
In the Mountains (Elizabeth) **41**:131, 136
In the Name of Time (Field) **43**:175
"In the Night" (Quiroga)
See "En la noche"
"In the Night" (Roberts) **68**:336
"In the Night" (Tagore)
See "Nisithe"
"In the Night Watches" (Roberts) **8**:326
"In the Old Theatre at Fiesole" (Hardy) **143**:169
In the Outer Skerries (Strindberg) **8**:410; **47**:335
In the Palace of the King: A Love Story of Old Madrid (Crawford) **10**:148, 151, 156
"In the Park" (Guro)
See "V parke"
"In the Pavilion" (Rinehart) **52**:282
"In the Penal Colony" (Kafka)
See "In der Strafkolonie"
"In The Plaza" (Aleixandre)
See "En la plaza"
"In the Pocket" (Dickey) **151**:98
"In the Prime of Her Life" (Agnon)
See "Bidmi yameha"
In the Quarter (Chambers) **41**:87-90, 94, 114
"In the Ravine" (Chekhov)
See "V ovrage"
"In the Redbrush" (Williams) **89**:374, 384
"In the River" (Chekhov)
See "V ovrage"
In the Roar of the Sea (Baring-Gould) **88**:24
In the Ruins (Mizoguchi)
See *Haikyo no naka*
"In the Rukh" (Kipling) **17**:202
"In the Same Boat" (Kipling) **8**:191
In the Saxon Park (Prus) **48**:156
"In the School and in the University" (García Lorca)
See "En el instituto y en la universidad"
In the Seven Woods (Yeats) **1**:558; **11**:527
"In the Seventh Shop" (Cahan) **71**:87
In the Shadow (Bennett) **197**:72
In the Shadow of the Glen (Synge) **6**:425-26, 428-29, 431-33, 439-42; **37**:348, 351, 362-63, 367, 377-79, 382-83, 386, 388-89
"In the Shadows" (Ledwidge) **23**:116
"In the Sierra Madre with the Punchers" (Remington) **89**:301
"In the Silent Forest" (Wright) **136**:299-300
In the Snare (Sabatini) **47**:300, 303
"In the South" (Walker) **129**:324
"In the Sphere of the Holy" (Otto) **85**:335
"In the Springtime" (Cankar) **105**:164
"In the Square" (Aleixandre)
See "En la plaza"
"In the Square" (Bowen) **148**:53
"In the Steppe" (Gorky)
See "V Stepi"
"In the Storm of Roses" (Bachmann)
See "Im Gewitter der Rosen"
In the 'Stranger People's' Country (Murfree) **135**:223
"In the Street of Beautiful Children" (Burke) **63**:125
"In the Streets of Cyprus" (Burke) **63**:125
"In the Streets of Rich Men" (Burke) **63**:125
"In the Swamp" (Talvik) **87**:319
In the Swamp (Brecht)
See *Im dickicht der städte*
"In the Sweatshop" (Cahan) **71**:88
In the Sweet Dry and Dry (Morley) **87**:120
"In the Tarumensian Woods" (Graham) **19**:101
"In the Tavernas" (Cavafy) **2**:98
In the Teeth of Evidence (Sayers) **15**:373, 379
In The Tennessee Mountains (Murfree) **135**:195-202, 205, 211-13, 216, 218-20, 223, 227-29, 231
"In the Time of Prince Charley" (London) **9**:273
"In the Trenches" (Rosenberg) **12**:312
"In the Trenches" (Vazov)
See "V okopa"
"In the Tube" (Benson) **27**:17
"In the Tules" (Harte) **25**:222
"In the Tunnel" (Harte) **25**:191
"In the Twilight" (Andrić) **135**:78
"In the Twilight of the Gods" (Talvik) **87**:319
"In the Two Lights" (Stephens) **4**:417
"In the Underworld" (Rosenberg) **12**:299, 311
"In the Valley" (Noguchi) **80**:364
"In the Valley of the Sorceress" (Rohmer) **28**:286
In the Vanguard of the Dead (Ady)
See *A Halottak élén*
"In the Vast House" (Welch) **22**:462
"In the Vernacular" (Jarrell) **177**:185
In the Victory Wreath (Raabe) **45**:202
"In the Village" (Bishop) **121**:3, 15, 26, 36, 55
In the Village of Viger (Scott) **6**:386
"In the Waiting Room" (Bishop) **121**:7, 10, 12, 15, 19, 25, 31, 34-7, 56, 61, 78, 84, 91-2, 95, 99
"In the Waiting Room" (Drummond de Andrade) **139**:238
In the Wake of King James (O'Grady) **5**:352

"In the Ward: The Sacred Wood" (Jarrell) **177**:125, 127, 129, 176
"In the White Giant's Thigh" (Thomas) **1**:469, 473; **8**:461; **45**:362
"In the Wild" (Hedāyat)
See "Zir-i buta"
"In the Wilde Awe and Wisdom of the Night" (Roberts) **8**:318, 320-21
In the Wilderness (Undset) **197**:321
"In the Wineshop" (Lu Hsun)
See "Zai jiulou shang"
"In the Winter Dusk" (Wright) **136**:302
"In the Withaak's Shade" (Bosman) **49**:7, 19
"In the Womb" (Baker) **10**:27
"In the wood" (Arp) **115**:14-15
"In the Woods" (Akutagawa Ryūnosuke) **16**:28-31
"In the Woods" (Shimazaki Toson) **5**:439
"In the World" (Olesha) **136**:102
In the World of the Obscure and the Uncertain (Rozanov)
See *V mire neiasnogo i nereshennogo*
In the World of the Unclear and the Unresolved (Rozanov)
See *V mire neiasnogo i nereshennogo*
In the Wrong Paradise (Lang) **16**:256
"In the Year 2889" (Verne) **52**:350
In the Year of Jubilee (Gissing) **3**:222, 227, 231-32, 234; **24**:220, 230-31, 238-39, 243-44, 248
In the Zone (O'Neill) **6**:329
In This Our Life (Glasgow) **2**:178, 183-85, 191; **7**:336-37, 341-42
In This Our World (Gilman) **9**:96-7, 100, 102; **37**:176; **117**:125, 144
"In This Rented Room" (Wright) **136**:301
"In This Way, Kissing" (Stein) **48**:235
"In Those Days" (Kunikida Doppo)
See "Ano jibun"
"In Time Like Air" (Sarton) **120**:263
In Time Like Air (Sarton) **120**:206, 267-68, 302-03, 318
In Time of Peace (Boyd) **111**:202-05
"In Time of Revolt" (Brooke) **2**:59
"In Time of 'The Breaking of Nations'" (Hardy) **72**:168; **143**:15, 188, 212
"In Town" (Dobson) **79**:36
In Tragic Life (Fisher) **140**:147, 149, 151-55, 165, 168, 182, 184
"In Transport" (Remizov)
See "Po etapu"
"In Trust" (Wharton) **3**:554; **129**:361
"In Two Houses" (Gilman) **117**:164-65
"In Two Moods" (Korolenko) **22**:170
"In Ulster" (Guiney) **41**:207
"In una Chiesa Gotica" (Carducci) **32**:88, 96
"In una rete di linee che s'allacciano" (Calvino) **183**:155
"In Vain" (Anwar)
See "Sia-Sia"
"In Valleys Green and Still" (Housman) **10**:247-48
In vino veritas (Blok) **5**:84
"In War" (Rosenberg) **12**:291, 294-95, 297, 303, 312
In War Time (Mitchell) **36**:262, 264-67
In Watermelon Sugar (Brautigan) **133**:3-7, 10, 20-21, 28-29
"In Which Pooh Invents a New Game and Eeyore Joins In" (Milne) **6**:321
In Wicklow and West Kerry (Synge) **6**:432, 439; **37**:356
"In Winter" (Scott) **6**:394
In Youth Is Pleasure (Welch) **22**:438-42, 446, 451-58, 461
In Zeno's World (Nemerov) **124**:268
"Ina mia" (Anwar) **22**:24
Inadmissible Evidence (Osborne) **153**:242, 291, 313, 321
"The Inarticulate" (Lyotard) **103**:266
"Inasmuch Mission" (Jiménez) **183**:330
"Inaugural Lecture, Collège de France" (Barthes)
See *Leçon inaugurale faite le vendredi 7 janvier 1977*
Inaugural Lesson at the College de France (Barthes)
See *Leçon inaugurale faite le vendredi 7 janvier 1977*
"In-Between Ladies" (McAlmon) **97**:101
L'incalco (Tozzi) **31**:332-34
"Incantation by Laughter" (Khlebnikov)
See "Zaklyatie smekhom"
"Incarnate Devil" (Thomas) **45**:372, 379, 383, 400; **105**:337
"The Incarnate One" (Muir) **87**:190, 213
L'incendie (Rod) **52**:312
"L'incendie terrestre" (Schwob) **20**:323
L'incendio nell' oliveto (Deledda) **23**:37, 42
Incense (Sologub)
See *Fimiamy*
"Incense Ashes: The First Offering" (Chang)
See "Ashes of Descending Incense: First Brazier"
"Incense Ashes: The Second Offering" (Chang)
See "Ashes of Descending Incense: Second Brazier"
"The Incense Bearers" (Gurney) **33**:104
"The Incest Drama and Its Complications" (Rank) **115**:297
Incest Theme in Literature and Legend: The Fundamentals of a Psychology of Literary Creation (Rank)
See *Das Inzest-Motiv in Dichtung und Sage: Grundzüge einer Psychologie des dichterischen*
"Incident" (Cullen) **4**:49; **37**:140, 142, 145-46, 149, 153, 160
The Incident at Sakai, and Other Stories (Mori Ogai) **14**:375
"The Incident in Basseynaya Street" (Tolstoy) **18**:378
"An Incident in Practice" (Chekhov)
See "Slučaj iz praktiki"
"Incident on a Lake" (Collier) **127**:251
"An Incident on the Volga" (Zoshchenko) **15**:499, 506
Incidental Numbers (Wylie) **8**:527
"Incidents" (Barthes) **135**:162, 174, 182
Incidents (Barthes) **135**:162, 174-78, 180, 183, 188
"The Incineration of Dictionary Ned" (Warung) **45**:419
"El incivil maestro de ceremonias Kotsuké no Suké" (Borges) **109**:40
Inclinations (Firbank) **1**:227, 229
"Include Me Out" (Service) **15**:412
"Incognita" (Dobson) **79**:26
La incógnita (Pérez Galdós) **27**:263
"Incolor" (Villaurrutia) **80**:477
"The Incomparable Beauty of Modern Dress" (Beerbohm) **24**:108
The Incomparable Max (Beerbohm) **1**:74
Incomplete Stories (Ramos)
See *Histórias incompletas*
"L'inconsolable" (Roussel) **20**:228, 230, 240, 245
Incredible Adventures (Blackwood) **5**:70, 73, 75, 77
The Incredible Adventures of Dennis Dorgan (Howard) **8**:132
The Incredible Borgias (Klabund) **44**:104
The Incredulity of Father Brown (Chesterton) **6**:102
"Incurable" (Heyse)
See "Unheibar!"
"Incurable" (Johnson) **19**:246
"The Incurable" (Zangwill) **16**:441
L'Inde, sans les Anglais (Loti) **11**:361
"Indeed Green is Magnificent" (Santos) **156**:315
"The Indefinite Huntress" (McAlmon) **97**:95-96, 123
The Indefinite Huntress and Other Stories (McAlmon) **97**:89, 94, 118
"Independence" (Milne) **6**:314; **88**:243
The Independence of Triangles (Witkiewicz) **8**:510
"The Independent Candidate: A Story of Today" (Howells) **7**:391
"An Independent Thinker" (Freeman) **9**:76
"Independent Thomas" (Lindsay) **17**:241
Les Indes Noires (Verne) **6**:500; **52**:350, 357
"India, China and Ourselves" (Carpenter) **88**:128
The India Rubber Men (Wallace) **57**:402
"India, the Holy Land" (Vivekananda) **88**:381
Indian Boyhood (Eastman) **55**:161-62, 167-70, 173-74, 177-78, 180-87
"Indian Camp" (Hemingway) **115**:166, 174, 179
Indian Course of Life (Hesse)
See *Indischer Lebenslauf*
Indian Currency and Finance (Keynes) **64**:217, 218, 240, 252
"Indian Dancers" (Naidu) **80**:291
"Indian Day" (Lewis) **3**:290
The Indian Fighter (Hecht) **101**:80
"The Indian Gipsy" (Naidu) **80**:293
The Indian Giver (Howells) **7**:387
Indian Heroes and Great Chieftains (Eastman) **55**:163, 165, 172-73, 176
Indian Idealism (Dasgupta) **81**:97
"The Indian Lily" (Sudermann)
See "Die Indische Lilie"
The Indian Lily, and Other Stories (Sudermann)
See *Dies Indische Lilie*
"An Indian Love Song" (Naidu) **80**:276, 291
"An Indian Love Song from the North" (Naidu)
See "A Love Song from the North"
Indian Massacre (Ince) **89**:9
Indian Scout Talks: A Guide Book for Boy Scouts and Campfire Girls (Eastman) **55**:164, 166, 173
"Indian Summer" (Knister) **56**:164
"Indian Summer" (Kunikida Doppo)
See "Koharu"
"Indian Summer" (Remizov) **27**:352
"Indian Summer" (Stringer) **37**:327
Indian Summer (Howells) **7**:367, 372, 381-82, 392; **17**:178, 183; **41**:256, 263, 269, 286
"Indian Summer" (Pasternak) **188**:184-85
Indian Summer (Thomas) **97**:140
"Indian Summer: Ah Hsiao's Autumnal Lament" (Chang)
See "Guihua zheng: axiao bei qiu"
"The Indian Summer of a Forsyte" (Galsworthy) **1**:298; **45**:46, 58
"The Indian Summer of Dry Valley Johnson" (Henry) **19**:178
"The Indian to His Love" (Yeats) **18**:462; **116**:334, 336
The Indian Today: The Past and Future of the First American (Eastman) **55**:169, 173, 178
"The Indian upon God" (Yeats) **18**:462
"Indian Weavers" (Naidu) **80**:275
"Indiana" (Crane) **2**:112; **80**:83, 88, 128, 136, 140, 166, 182, 201-4, 212
"Indians and an Englishman" (Lawrence) **61**:233
India's Religion of Grace and Christianity (Otto) **85**:314, 319
An Indication of the Cause (Bernhard) **165**:60
Indícious de ouro (Sá-Carneiro) **83**:411-3
"The Indictment" (Dazai Osamu) **11**:183-84
"Indifference" (Hippius) **9**:159
"L'indifférent" (Field) **43**:165-66
"Indigenous Social Ills" (p'Bitek) **149**:110
"The Indigent Harlequin" (Guro)
See "Nishchii Arlekin"
"Indignation: An Ode" (Abercrombie) **141**:4, 19
"The Indigo Bird" (Wetherald) **81**:410

"The Indigo Glass in the Grass" (Stevens) **45**:283, 297
"Indirect" (Jarry) **147**:331
"Indirect Language and the Voices of Silence" (Merleau-Ponty) **156**:199, 202, 204-5
"Die Indische Lilie" (Sudermann) **15**:428, 430
Indische Reisebilder (Haeckel) **83**:146-7
Indische Reisebriefe (Haeckel) **83**:147
Indischer Lebenslauf (Hesse) **148**:153-54, 160-66; **196**:308, 370
"An Indiscreet Journey" (Mansfield) **8**:282; **39**:320
The Indiscretion of the Duchess (Hope) **83**:165
"Indiscretions of Archie" (Wodehouse) **108**:370
"Indiscriminate Attacks on the Literary World" (Masaoka)
See "Bunkai yatsu atari"
"Individual and Mass Behavior in Extreme Situations" (Bettelheim) **143**:3, 5, 29, 33, 38-39, 44
"Individual Art" (Södergran) **31**:287
"Individual Powers" (Bryan) **99**:5, 34
Individual Psychology in the School (Adler)
See *Individualpsychologie in der Schule*
Individualism and Economic Order (Hayek) **109**:202, 214
"The Individualism of Value" (McTaggart) **105**:197
Individualism, Old and New (Dewey) **95**:36
Individualism: True and False (Hayek) **109**:181, 230
"Un individualista" (Svevo) **35**:363
Individualpsychologie in der Schule (Adler) **61**:11
L'indocile (Rod) **52**:312
"Indo-European prevocalic s in Macedonian" (Sapir) **108**:257
"The Indo-European Words for 'tear'" (Sapir) **108**:257
"Inductions" (Agee) **180**:10
"El indulto" (Pardo Bazán) **189**:236, 290-91
Industrial Democracy (Webb and Webb) **22**:412, 429-30
The Industrial Revolution (Beard) **5**:17, 34, 37
"Industrialism" (Anderson) **10**:48
"Industrialism and Cultural Values" (Innis) **77**:341, 369
"The Indy 500" (Shepherd) **177**:299
Inediti (Campana) **20**:82-4, 87
"Inefable ausencia" (Lugones) **15**:292
"Inevitability" (Jiménez) **183**:259
The Inevitable (Couperus) **15**:45
"The Inevitable Hour" (Pickthall) **21**:253
"L'infaillibilité" (Apollinaire) **51**:20
Infamy (Borges)
See *Historia universal de la infamia*
Infância (Ramos) **32**:419, 424, 428, 431, 435-36, 438-40
"Infancy" (Drummond de Andrade) **139**:237-38
The Infant Prodigy (Mann)
See *Das Wunderkind*
"Infanta Marina" (Stevens) **3**:449; **45**:348
"The Infanta's Ribbon" (Bishop) **103**:3
"The Infantry Officer" (Drieu la Rochelle) **21**:26
Infants of the Spring (Thurman) **6**:447-51
An Infected Family (Tolstoy) **79**:382
"Inferior Religions" (Lewis) **9**:234; **104**:153, 299
Inferior Religions (Lewis) **104**:288-89
Inferiorità (Svevo) **2**:552-53; **35**:352-53
Inferiority (Svevo)
See *Inferiorità*
The Infernal Desire Machines of Doctor Hoffman (Carter) **139**:99, 119, 162, 170, 192, 204
The Infernal Grove (Muggeridge) **120**:192
The Infernal Machine (Cocteau)
See *La machine infernale*
"Das infernalische Abendmahl" (Heym) **9**:142
Inferno (Barbusse)
See *L'enfer*
Inferno (Strindberg) **8**:406-07, 411; **21**:351-52, 367; **47**:373
"El infierno tan temido" (Onetti) **131**:133, 135, 146, 153
El infierno tan temido y otros cuentos (Onetti) **131**:133
"Los ínfimos" (Lugones) **15**:288
"The Infinite Lawn" (Calvino) **183**:140, 143
"Influencia de las mujeres en la formación del alma americana" (De La Parra) **185**:211
"The Influence of Art in Religion" (Carpenter) **88**:61
"The Influence of France on English Poetry" (Gosse) **28**:151
The Influence of Women—And Its Cure (Erskine) **84**:184
"The Informal Execution of Soupbone Pew" (Runyon) **10**:428, 435
El informe de Brodie (Borges) **109**:67, 70, 84, 126, 130
The Informed Heart: Autonomy in a Mass Age (Bettelheim) **143**:3, 6-7, 10-11, 29, 31, 33-34, 36, 38-41, 59-60
Ingen går fri (Dagerman) **17**:89, 96
L'ingénue libertine (Colette) **5**:171
"An Ingènue of the Sierra" (Harte) **25**:213
"Ingerid Sletten" (Bjoernson) **7**:117
"The Inglorius End" (Zoshchenko) **15**:505
"The Ingrate" (Dunbar) **2**:128, 131; **12**:120
"Ingredient X" (Wakefield) **120**:350, 357-58
"An Inhabitant of Carcosa" (Bierce) **44**:44-5; **7**:88
"An Inhabitant of the Soil" (Jensen)
See "En Beboer af Jorden"
"The Inhabitants" (Morris) **107**:96, 174-75
The Inhabitants (Morris) **107**:104-05, 114, 142-43, 145, 147, 174, 178, 202, 205, 214, 216, 219-22, 242-43
Inhale and Exhale (Saroyan) **137**:145, 187, 193, 197
"Inheritance" (Baker) **10**:18, 26
Inheritance (Braddon) **111**:229
The Inheritor (Benson) **27**:17
"The Inheritors" (Conrad) **13**:101
The Inheritors (Ford)
See *The Inheritors: An Extravagant Story*
Inheritors (Glaspell) **55**:234-42, 247-49, 260-61, 267, 271, 273-76; **175**:62, 74, 108, 112-13, 146, 150, 153, 157
The Inheritors: An Extravagant Story (Ford) **15**:67-8, 72-3, 90-1, 93; **57**:273; **172**:7-8, 11
The Inhuman (Lyotard) **103**:260, 263-64, 266-68
"Inhuman World" (Aleixandre) **113**:25-26
"The Inhumanity of Western Dress" (Lin) **149**:341
"Iniciação Amorosa" (Drummond de Andrade) **139**:229
"Inimigo" (Drummond de Andrade) **139**:230
The Inimitable Jeeves (Wodehouse) **108**:363, 392
"Initial Postulate" (Bataille) **155**:93, 109-10
Initials Only (Green) **63**:147, 152
"The Initiation" (Crowley) **7**:208
"Initiation" (Okigbo) **171**:354
Initiation and Its Results: A Sequel to "The Way of Initiation" (Steiner) **13**:435
"The Initiation of Pine Tree Jack" (Warung) **45**:418
"Initium" (García Lorca) **49**:119, 122; **181**:65
"Inkelekele yakwaXhoza" (Vilakazi) **37**:407
Inkondlo kaZulu (Vilakazi) **37**:397-98, 401-02, 407
"Inland" (Millay) **4**:306
"Inmitten der grossen Stadt" (Morgenstern) **8**:309
"El inmortal" (Borges) **109**:38-9, 52, 92-6, 98-100, 155
"The Inmost Light" (Machen) **4**:279
"Inn at Kyoto" (Sarton) **120**:265
"Inn of Castile" (García Lorca)
See "Méson de Castilla"
"The Inn of Gentle Death" (Verhaeren) **12**:472
"The Inn of Terror" (Leroux) **25**:260
The Inn of Tranquillity: Studies and Essays (Galsworthy) **45**:32-4, 36, 51, 54
An Inn on the Harbor (Betti)
See *Un albergo sul porto*
"Innanzi, innanzi!" (Carducci) **32**:90
The Inner Experience (Bataille)
See *L'expérience intérieure*
The Inner Gardens (Nervo)
See *Los jardines interiores*
Inner Ice Age (Abe)
See *Daiyon kampyoki*
Inner Landscape (Sarton) **120**:269070, 299-300, 318
The Inner Reaches of Outer Space: Metaphor as Myth and as Religion (Campbell) **140**:4, 35, 94, 113, 134, 138
The Inner Room (Merrill) **173**:224, 230
"The Inner Temple" (Coffin) **95**:17
The Innermost Man (Platonov)
See *Sokrovennyi chelovek*
Die Innerste (Raabe) **45**:165
L'innesto (Pirandello) **29**:285
"The Innkeeper's Handkerchiefs" (Coppard) **5**:178
Inno a Satana (Carducci) **32**:84, 92, 97-9, 105, 108
"Innocence" (Brodkey) **123**:194, 196-97, 200, 203-4, 209, 212, 214, 225, 237
"Innocence" (Lane) **177**:277
"L'innocence et l'expérience" (Péguy) **10**:416
The Innocence of Father Brown (Chesterton) **6**:102
"The Innocence of Layamon" (Borges) **109**:157
Innocencies (Tynan) **3**:507
Innocent Birds (Powys) **9**:365, 367, 370, 373-74, 376
Innocent: Her Fancy and His Fact (Corelli) **51**:75
"Innocent Man" (Knister) **56**:162
"The Innocent One" (Mann)
See "Die Unschuldige"
"Innocent Song" (Jozsef) **22**:155
The Innocent Village (Romero)
See *El pueblo inocente*
L'innocente (D'Annunzio) **6**:127-28, 133, 135, 138; **40**:4, 17-18, 28-9
The Innocents (Broch) **20**:60, 67
The Innocents (Lewis) **4**:251, 256, 259
The Innocents Abroad (Twain) **161**:244-45, 270
The Innocents Abroad; or, The New Pilgrim's Progress (Twain) **6**:453-59, 475; **12**:424, 426, 430-31, 436-37; **19**:358, 363; **36**:352, 355, 358, 361, 371-72, 379, 382; **48**:330-32, 334; **59**:210; **185**:250, 289
L'innommable (Beckett) **145**:83, 87, 197-201
"Innumerable Friend" (Sarton) **120**:199
"Inochi no tetsugaku" (Nishida) **83**:329
"Inochi o Kezuru" (Yosano) **59**:337
Inoniya (Esenin) **4**:109-10, 112
"Inqomfi" (Vilakazi) **37**:397, 402, 407
"The Inquest" (Davies) **5**:199
La inquietud del rosal (Storni) **5**:444, 447, 453
"Inquietude" (Sully Prudhomme) **31**:302
Las inquietudes de Shanti Andía (Baroja) **8**:49, 54, 62
"Inquirendo" (Guiney) **41**:208
Inqutries and Opinions (Matthews) **95**:233, 266
Inquiries concerning the Phenomenology and Theory of Knowledge (Husserl)
See *Untersuchungen zur Phänomenologie und Theorie der Erkenntnis*
The Inquiry (Betti)
See *Ispezione*
An Inquiry into the Good (Nishida)
See *Zen no kenkyu*
Inquisiciones (Borges) **109**:9, 88, 146, 154, 156, 161
Inquistions (Borges)
See *Inquisiciones*

Insatiablilty (Witkiewicz)
See *Nienasycenie*
"Inscripción en cualquier sepulcro" (Borges) **109**:14
"Inscription for a Mirror in a Deserted Dwelling" (Benét) **28**:12
"The Insect" (Ball)
See "Das Insekt"
The Insect Comedy (Čapek)
See *Ze života hmyzu*
Insect Life (Čapek)
See *Ze života hmyzu*
The Insect Play (Čapek)
See *Ze života hmyzu*
Insect Story (Čapek)
See *Ze života hmyzu*
Insects (Čapek)
See *Ze života hmyzu*
Insegnamenti sociali della economia contemporanea (Sorel) **91**:296-301, 303, 305
"Das Insekt" (Ball) **104**:9, 71, 74
"Insensibility" (Owen) **5**:366; **27**:201, 208, 212, 217-18, 226-27, 229, 237
L'inserzione (Ginzburg) **156**:2-6, 83
Inside Benchley (Benchley) **55**:16-17
Inside Germany (Sinclair) **160**:325
"An Inside Outside Complex" (O'Faolain) **143**:227
The Inside Story of the Harding Tragedy (Dixon) **163**:173
Inside the Lines (Biggers) **65**:2
Inside the Onion (Nemerov) **124**:304
"Inside the River" (Dickey) **151**:203
"Inside the Whale" (Orwell) **6**:353; **15**:324, 333, 342, 348; **51**:221, 224-25, 235, 241, 257, 263-64, 268; **128**:283
Inside the Whale, and Other Essays (Orwell) **51**:228; **128**:257, 259, 263, 283, 286, 296; **129**:235
The Insidious Dr. Fu Manchu (Rohmer)
See *The Mystery of Dr. Fu Manchu*
"An Insincere Wish Addressed to a Beggar" (Coleridge) **73**:26
Insolación (Pardo Bazán) **189**:222-24, 240, 243-45, 250-51, 261-62, 272-73, 275-81, 283-86
"La insolación" (Quiroga) **20**:215, 218, 221
Insolación (Alas) **29**:7
"The Insoluble Problem" (Chesterton) **6**:100
"The Insolvent Bank" (Premchand)
See "Bank ka diwala"
"Insomnia" (Bishop) **121**:72
"Insomnia" (Davidson) **24**:164
"Insomnia" (Lardner) **14**:307
"Insomnia" (Thomas) **10**:459
Insomnia (Tsvetaeva) **7**:563
"Insomnia I" (Nemerov) **124**:268
"Insomnie" (Roumain) **19**:334, 339
"Insônia" (Ramos) **32**:431
"L'insonnia in una notte d'estate" (Saba) **33**:373
"Inspection" (Caragiale) **76**:159
"Inspection" (Owen) **5**:367; **27**:206, 208, 211-12, 217-18, 224, 229-30
Inspector French and the Cheyne Mystery (Crofts) **55**:83, 85-6, 88
Inspector French and the Starvel Tragedy (Crofts) **55**:82-3, 86, 88
"Inspector French's Greatest Case" (Crofts) **55**:83, 86-8
The Inspector General (Caragiale) **76**:163
"Inspector General with a Kicking Out" (Bulgakov) **16**:84
"Inspector General with an Ejection" (Bulgakov)
See "Inspector General with a Kicking Out"
"Inspiration" (Andrade) **43**:9
"The Inspiration" (Post) **39**:344
"The Inspiration of Mr. Budd" (Sayers) **15**:379
The Inspiration of Poetry (Woodberry) **73**:377
"Inspired Goose" (Gladkov) **27**:91-2
"Inspired People" (Platonov) **14**:414
Instant de recueillement (Loti) **11**:356
"Instantanées" (Schwob) **20**:323
"Instantaneous Photographs" (Norris) **155**:261
"Instead of Faith" (Lagerkvist)
See "I stäallet för tro"
"Instinct" (Lasker-Schueler) **57**:328-29
The Instinct of Workmanship (Veblen) **31**:342, 346, 350-51, 353, 355, 362
"The Instinctive Reactions of Young Chicks" (Thorndike) **107**:370
The Instincts of the Herd in Peace and War (Trotter) **97**:176, 180, 183, 185, 187, 190, 192
Instruction in Thirty Verses (Ramana Maharshi)
See *Upadesa Saram*
"Instructions for Use" (Horvath)
See "Gebrauchsanweisung"
Instructions païennes (Lyotard) **103**:159-65, 168
"The insulting master of etiquette Kotsuké no Suké" (Borges)
See "El incivil maestro de ceremonias Kotsuké no Suké"
The Insurance (Weiss)
See *Die Versicherung*
Insurekcja (Reymont) **5**:398
Insurgent Mexico (Reed) **9**:381, 383, 385-91
The Insurrection (Reymont)
See *Insurekcja*
Insurrections (Stephens) **4**:406-09, 411, 415, 419, 421
"Intaba kandoda" (Mqhayi) **25**:322
"Integra" (Aleixandre) **113**:4
"Integrity" (Erskine) **84**:183
"Inteligencia" (Jiménez) **4**:214
"Intelijencia, dame" (Jiménez) **183**:290
"Intellect and Art" (Mann) **168**:173
Intellect and Ideas in Action: Selected Correspondence of Zinaida Hippius (Hippius) **9**:169
"The Intellectual in America" (Jarrell) **177**:190
"The Intellectual Mutt and Jeff" (Knister) **56**:153
"Intellectuals" (Barthes) **135**:170, 173
"Intellectuals are Target" (Cobb) **77**:132
"An Intelligent Woman's Guide to Socialism" (Shaw) **3**:392
"The Intelligentsia and the People" (Blok) **5**:95
The Intelligentsia's Spiritual Crisis (Berdyaev)
See *Solitude and Society*
The Intemperate Professor (Kirk) **119**:253
"Intensidad y altura" (Vallejo) **56**:316
Intentions (Wilde) **1**:496, 504; **8**:493, 497
Inter Arma (Gosse) **28**:151
Inter Ice Age 4 (Abe)
See *Daiyon kampyoki*
"The Intercepter" (Muir) **87**:178
"Intercessions by Denis Devlin" (Beckett) **145**:88
The Intercessor, and Other Stories (Sinclair) **11**:412
Los intereses creados (Benavente) **3**:96-7, 99, 101
"Interest as Related to Training of the Will" (Dewey) **95**:59
Interieur (Kandinsky) **92**:50
Intérieur (Maeterlinck) **3**:322, 327
"Interim" (Millay) **4**:306-07, 313; **49**:201, 207
Interim (Richardson) **3**:356-58
"Interior" (Bishop) **103**:26
"Interior" (García Lorca) **181**:187
"Interior" (Villaurrutia) **80**:477
Interior (Maeterlinck)
See *Intérieur*
"The Interior of the Rose" (Rilke)
See "Das Rosen-Innere"
"Interiors" (Nemerov) **124**:252-53
"Interlocutors" (Ginzburg) **156**:73
"The Interlopers" (Saki) **3**:374
"An Interlude" (Bishop) **103**:4, 26
"Interlude" (Bodenheim) **44**:59
"Interlude" (García Lorca) **49**:80
"The Interlude" (Pickthall) **21**:254
"Interlude: On Jargon" (Quiller-Couch) **53**:301
Interludes and Poems (Abercrombie) **141**:3-4, 10, 18-20
"Intermède" (Fondane) **159**:256
"The Intermediate Sex" (Carpenter) **88**:91-2
The Intermediate Sex (Carpenter) **88**:72, 75, 99, 122, 145
Intermediate Types among Primitive Folk (Carpenter) **88**:72, 92, 123
Intermedios (Baroja) **8**:63
Intermezzi (Baroja)
See *Intermedios*
"Intermezzo" (van Ostaijen) **33**:412
"Intermezzo" (Zangwill) **16**:461
Intermezzo (Giraudoux) **2**:157-59, 167-68, 173; **7**:321-22, 326-29
Intermezzo (Schnitzler)
See *Zwischenspiel*
Intermezzo di rime (D'Annunzio) **6**:136, 143; **40**:38
"An International Affair" (Wodehouse) **108**:371
"An International Episode" (James) **11**:321; **40**:150, 162; **64**:157
The International Jew: The World's Foremost Problem (Ford) **73**:59, 71, 93-7, 99-106
"The International Jew: The World's Problem" (Ford) **73**:96
"International Prejudices" (Stephen) **23**:326
"Interplanetary Man" (Stapledon) **22**:336
Una interpretación de la historia universal, en torno a Toynbee (Ortega y Gasset) **9**:350-51
"Interpretation" (Nietzsche) **55**:388
The Interpretation of Dreams (Freud)
See *Die Traumdeutung*
An Interpretation of Genesis (Powys) **9**:363, 373
An Interpretation of Universal History (Ortega y Gasset)
See *Una interpretación de la historia universal, en torno a Toynbee*
Interpretations of Literature (Hearn) **9**:123
Interpretations of Poetry and Religion (Santayana) **40**:339, 351, 394, 397, 400, 412
"The Interpreters" (Swinburne) **36**:347
The Interpreters (Baker) **3**:5; **10**:12, 17, 19, 22-3, 25-6
"The Interrogation" (Muir) **87**:205
Interrogation (Drieu la Rochelle) **21**:17, 32, 40
"An Interrupted Fox Hunt" (Adams) **56**:8
An Interrupted Life: The Diaries of Etty Hillesum, 1941-1943 (Hillesum)
See *Het verstoorde leven: Dagboek van Etty Hillesum, 1941-1943*
"Interruptions to School at Home" (Arnow) **196**:88
"Interval for Metaphysics" (Weinberg) **131**:307
"An Interview" (Colette) **16**:139
"Interview" (Parker) **143**:322
"An Interview with Iris Murdoch" (Murdoch) **171**:311
Interviews imaginaires (Gide) **36**:99
"Interviews with Characters" (Pirandello)
See "Colloqui coi personaggi"
"Intés az őrzőkhöz" (Ady) **11**:18
Intimate Journals (Benjamin) **39**:47
Intimate Notebooks (Nathan) **18**:314
Intimate Relations (Cocteau)
See *Les parents terribles*
The Intimate Strangers (Tarkington) **9**:465
"An Intimate Talk with the People of the United States on Banking" (Roosevelt) **93**:183, 185
Intimate Things (Čapek) **37**:46
"Intimates" (Lawrence) **93**:53
Intimations of Eve (Fisher) **140**:156, 186
Intimité (Adamov) **189**:14, 31-4
Les intimités (Coppee) **25**:119, 122
"Into a Contemporary's Passport" (Radnóti) **16**:419

"Into a Line" (Hippius) **9**:158-59
"Into Her Lying Down Head" (Thomas) **45**:378
"Into Outer Darkness" (Wakefield) **120**:342, 349, 357-58
"Into the Depths" (Ford) **172**:93
Into the Stone and Other Poems (Dickey) **151**:100, 102-4, 108, 202
"Into Thirty Centuries Born" (Muir) **87**:231
Intolerance (Griffith) **68**:137-38, 140, 152-53, 156-57, 166-68, 170-73, 182, 184, 187-96, 198, 200-1, 203-12, 214, 217, 220-33, 235, 239-43
"The Intoxicated" (Jackson) **187**:292
"Intoxication" (Pasternak) **188**:185
"Intoxication" (Premchand) **21**:294
L'intreuse (Maeterlinck) **3**:317, 320, 322, 331-32
"Intrigue" (Crane) **11**:130
Introducción a la literatura inglesa (Borges) **109**:53
"The Introducers" (Wharton) **27**:414
Introducing Irony (Bodenheim) **44**:57, 59, 64, 68
"Introduction" (Abbey) **160**:97
"Introduction" (Agee) **180**:99, 106
"Introduction" (Apollinaire) **51**:22-3
"Introduction" (Frye) **165**:196
"Introduction" (Merleau-Ponty) **156**:198-201, 203
"Introduction à la méthode de Léonard de Vinci" (Valéry) **4**:489-90, 495; **15**:461, 463
L'Introduction a l'Economie Moderne (Sorel) **91**:205, 209, 332
"Introduction à une étude du politique selon Kant" (Lyotard) **103**:164, 167
Introduction au "Livre de Ruth" (Claudel) **2**:104
Introduction aux études de philologie romane (Auerbach) **43**:56-7
"Introduction on the American Negro in Art" (Heyward) **50**:101
An Introduction to English Literature (Borges)
See *Introducción a la literatura inglesa*
Introduction to Mathematics (Whitehead) **97**:197
Introduction to Metaphysics (Bergson) **32**:27, 44-5
Introduction to Moral Philosopy (Simmel)
See *Einleitung in die Moralwissenschaft*
Introduction to Our Epoch (Jensen)
See *Introduktion till vor Tidsalder*
"Introduction to Poïetics" (Valéry) **15**:451
An Introduction to Rembrandt (Clark) **147**:126
Introduction to Sally (Elizabeth) **41**:125
An Introduction to the English Historians (Beard) **15**:17
"An Introduction to The Heritage of Henry Adams" (Adams) **80**:16, 24, 70
"Introduction to the Method of Leonardo da Vinci" (Valéry)
See "Introduction à la méthode de Léonard de Vinci"
Introduction to the Philosophy of Moral (Simmel)
See *Einleitung in die Moralwissenschaft*
Introduction to the Science of Sociology (Park) **73**:181, 183, 186, 189, 193-96, 212-13
Introduction to the Sociology of Music (Adorno) **111**:51, 53, 85, 132
"Introduction to the Structural Analysis of Narrative" (Barthes) **135**:128
An Introduction to the Study of American Literature (Matthews) **95**:252, 256-8
An Introduction to the Study of Browning (Symons) **11**:426, 450
Introduction to the Study of Romance Philology (Auerbach)
See *Introduction aux études de philologie romane*
An Introduction to the Theory of Mental and Social Measurements (Thorndike) **107**:378, 410
The Introduction to the Theory of Pure Form in the Theatre (Witkiewicz) **8**:511
"Introduction to these Paintings" (Lawrence) **93**:64
An Introduction to Zen Buddhism (Suzuki) **109**:387-88
"Introductory Essay on Coleridge" (Swinburne) **36**:309
"Introductory Lecture" (Housman) **10**:253, 255
Introductory Lectures on Psychoanalysis (Freud)
See *Vorlesungen zur Einführung in die Psychoanalyse*
"Introductory Note to The Castle" (Muir) **87**:180
Introductory Notes on Lying-In Institutions (Nightingale) **85**:242
Introduktion till vor Tidsalder (Jensen) **41**:294
"Introno a una fossa vuota" (Calvino) **183**:16
"The Intruder" (Borges)
See "La intrusa"
"An Intruder" (Sarton) **120**:263
The Intruder (Blasco Ibáñez)
See *El intruso*
The Intruder (Borges)
See *La intrusa*
The Intruder (D'Annunzio)
See *L'innocente*
The Intruder (Maeterlinck)
See *L'intreuse*
Intruder in the Dust (Faulkner) **141**:57-59, 62, 167-69, 171-73; **170**:109, 115, 129, 183, 185, 208-11, 229-30, 238-40, 244
"La intrusa" (Borges) **109**:84, 86
La intrusa (Borges) **109**:86
"The Intrusion of the Personal" (Glaspell) **175**:52
The Intrusions of Peggy (Hope) **83**:169
El intruso (Blasco Ibáñez) **12**:29-30, 42-3, 47
Intryk fra Rusland (Brandes) **10**:59-61
Intuition and Reflection in Self-Consciousness (Nishida)
See *Jikaku ni okeru chokkan to hansei*
L'Intuition de l'instant (Bachelard) **128**:45, 54, 75-7
"L'intuition philosophique" (Bergson) **32**:24
Les intuitions pré-Chrétiennes (Weil) **23**:378, 392
"L'intuizione pura e il carattere lirico dell' arte" (Croce) **37**:95-6, 114-15
"Intus" (Gonzalez Martinez) **72**:149
"Intus" (Sully Prudhomme) **31**:302
"Invaders" (Douglas) **40**:80-1, 88
"The Invaders" (Milne) **88**:241
"The Invalid" (Gumilev)
See "Bol'noi"
L'Invasion (Adamov) **189**:6-7, 11, 17-19, 23, 42
The Invasion of Compulsory Sex Morality (Reich) **57**:350
"The Invasion of the Church of the Holy Ghost" (Kirk) **119**:282, 331, 335-36, 340, 343-44
Invasion of the Sea (Verne)
See *La'Invasion de la mer*
"The Invasion of the Starlings" (Calvino) **183**:143
L'invitation au château (Anouilh) **195**:4, 10, 13-14, 16, 18, 24-5, 35, 38, 47, 50
Invitation to a Beheading (Nabokov) **189**:89, 93, 99, 117
L'invendable (Bloy) **22**:45
"Inventar la verdad" (Villaurrutia) **80**:488
"Invention and Imagination" (Matthews) **95**:234
Inventions, Researches, and Writings of Nikola Tesla (Tesla) **88**:287
"Inverno in Abruzzo" (Ginzburg) **156**:16, 91, 97-98, 105
The Investigation (Weiss)
See *Die Ermittlung: Oratorium in Elf Gesëngen*
An Investigation of Dogmatic Theology (Tolstoy)
See *Issledovanie dogmaticheskogo bogoslavja*
"Investigations of a Dog" (Kafka)
See "Forschungen eines hundes"
Investigations on Hegel (Croce) **37**:113
"Investments Abroad" (Keynes) **64**:244
"Invictus" (Henley) **8**:97, 104, 106-08
"Invierno en la batalla de Tervel" (Vallejo) **3**:536
"Invincible" (Naidu) **80**:313
"INVISIBLE" (Villa) **176**:108
The Invisible (Lagerkvist)
See *Den osynlige*
"Invisible Ancient Enemy of Mine" (Rosenberg) **12**:299
Invisible Cities (Calvino)
See *Le città invisibili*
The Invisible Event (Beresford) **81**:7,10-2
The Invisible Knight (Calvino)
See *Il cavaliere inesistente*
Invisible Landscapes (Masters) **25**:300, 316
Invisible Links (Lagerloef) **4**:235; **36**:238-39, 241
The Invisible Man (Wells) **6**:523, 534, 539, 542-45, 547; **12**:487-88, 506; **19**:421, 424-25, 435, 438-39, 441, 446; **133**:224, 258, 284, 329
The Invisible Man (Whale) **63**:338-42, 360, 384-87
The Invisible One (Lagerkvist)
See *Den osynlige*
The Invisible Voices (Shiel) **8**:363
Invitación a la muerte (Villaurrutia) **80**:458, 464, 468, 471, 474, 480, 495-6
"An Invitation" (Field) **43**:154
"Invitation" (Nietzsche)
See "Einladung"
Invitation to a Beheading (Nabokov)
See *Priglashenie na kazn*
"Invitation to a Voyage" (Gumilev)
See "Priglashenie v puteshestvie"
"Invitation to a Young but Learned Friend" (Flecker) **43**:188
Invitation to Death (Villaurrutia)
See *Invitación a la muerte*
"Invocation" (Benét) **7**:71, 73, 82, 85
"Invocation" (Bierce) **7**:88, 90-1, 97; **44**:13
"Invocation" (Coleridge) **73**:12-13
"Invocation" (Naidu) **80**:308
"Invocation and Promise" (Heidenstam) **5**:250
"Invocation de la momie" (Artaud) **36**:17-18
"Invocation of the Mummy" (Artaud)
See "Invocation de la momie"
"Invocation to Kali" (Sarton) **120**:261, 295-96, 304-05, 318
"The Invocation to Kali 3: The Concentration Camps" (Sarton) **120**:296
"Invocation to Spring" (Masters) **2**:471
Invocation to the Great Bear (Bachmann)
See *Anrufung des Grossen Bären*
"Invocation to the Moon" (Lawrence) **93**:55, 58-60
Involuntary Homicide (Abe) **131**:12-14
"Invulnerable" (Benét) **28**:5
Inward Ho! (Morley) **87**:125
Das Inzest-Motiv in Dichtung und Sage: Grundzüge einer Psychologie des dichterischen (Rank) **115**:247, 297, 299-307
I-nzuzo (Mqhayi) **25**:320, 325-27
Io, l'erede (de Filippo) **127**:296
Iola Leroy; or, Shadows Uplifted (Harper) **14**:255, 257-58, 263
Iolanthe; or, The Peer and the Peri (Gilbert) **3**:214-15, 218-19
Iolaus: An Anthology of Friendship (Carpenter) **88**:72, 75, 109

Iole (Chambers) **41**:95
Iom-Kipour (Korolenko) **22**:169
Ion (Rebreanu) **28**:267-68, 270-73
"Iona" (Sharp) **39**:375
"Ionitch" (Chekhov)
See "Ionyc"
"Ionyc" (Chekhov) **3**:153, 166; **10**:111, 115
Iorio's Daughter (D'Annunzio)
See *La figlia di Iorio*
"Iov i Magdalina" (Remizov) **27**:355
The Ipané (Graham) **19**:108-09, 112, 121
Iphigenia, the Diary of a Young Lady Who Wrote Because She was Bored (De La Parra)
See *Ifigenia: Diario de una señorita que escribió porque se fastidiaba*
Iphigénie (Moréas) **18**:280, 284, 288
Iphigenie in Aulis (Hauptmann) **4**:208-09
"Ipissimus" (Lee-Hamilton) **22**:189, 194
"Ippansha no jiko gentei" (Nishida) **83**:251
"Ippongi Plain" (Miyazawa) **76**:285
"La ira cuando no existe" (Aleixandre) **113**:5
"Iram dhāt al-'imād" (Gibran) **9**:89
Le ire di Giuliano (Svevo) **35**:370
"Ire When It Exists Not" (Aleixandre)
See "La ira cuando no existe"
"Ireland" (Johnson) **19**:229-31
Ireland (Baker) **10**:22
"Ireland and the Hour" (O'Grady) **5**:351
"Ireland Long Ago" (Tynan) **3**:505
Ireland, with Other Poems (Johnson) **19**:229-30, 232, 241, 244
"Ireland's Dead" (Johnson) **19**:230, 246
"Irene" (Middleton) **56**:174, 181, 184
Irene innocente (Betti) **5**:63
Irene the Innocent (Betti)
See *Irene innocente*
"Iris" (Hesse) **196**:269-70
Iris (Pinero) **32**:390-91, 393-94, 397, 400-01, 404-05, 414
"Iris Murdoch, Informally" (Murdoch) **171**:287
Irische Tagebuch (Böll) **185**:20, 50
The Irish (O'Faolain) **143**:230, 232, 239
"An Irish Airman Foresees His Death" (Yeats) **1**:566; **31**:422
"The Irish Cliffs of Moher" (Stevens) **45**:312
An Irish Cousin (Somerville & Ross) **51**:328, 337-38, 343, 348, 361, 366, 372, 378
"An Irish Face" (Baker) **3**:3; **10**:21
Irish Fairy Tales (Stephens) **4**:414, 418-21
Irish Folk-History Plays, first series: Kincora. Grania. Dervorgilla (Gregory) **1**:332, 334
Irish Folk-History Plays, second series: The Canavans. The White Cockade. The Deliverer (Gregory) **1**:334
Irish Impressions (Chesterton) **1**:178
Irish Journal (Böll)
See *Irische Tagebuch*
An Irish Journey (O'Faolain) **143**:230
Irish Memories (Somerville & Ross) **51**:340, 360
Irish Poems (Stringer) **37**:340
The Irish R.M. (Somerville & Ross) **51**:332, 334, 337-49, 351, 353-60, 362, 374, 376, 378-80
The Irish R.M. and His Experiences (Somerville & Ross) **51**:383
Irodalmi problé mák (Babits) **14**:41
Iron and Man (Lagerkvist)
See *Järn och människor*
Iron and Men (Lagerkvist)
See *Järn och människor*
Iron and Smoke (Kaye-Smith) **20**:114
"The Iron Characters" (Nemerov) **124**:157, 159, 179, 273, 277, 314
The iron coin (Borges)
See *La moneda de hierro*
"Iron Curtain Speech" (Churchill) **113**:163, 174
The Iron Dish (Riggs) **56**:199-200, 205
"The Iron Fan" (Huneker) **65**:198
Iron Garden (Popa) **167**:172, 174, 178-80
The Iron Heel (London) **9**:254, 260-63, 265, 270, 272, 278-79; **15**:260-61, 269, 271-72, 276
"Iron Horse" (Ginsberg) **120**:129-30
"The Iron Horse" (Riley) **51**:277
"The Iron Mask" (Lang) **16**:254
"Iron Mills" (Davis)
See "Life in the Iron Mills"
The Ironing Board (Morley) **87**:138
"Irony" (Lowell) **8**:233-34
The Irony of Life: The Polanetzki Family (Sienkiewicz)
See *Rodzina połanieckich*
Irradiations—Sand and Spray (Fletcher) **35**:91-2, 94, 96-7, 100-01, 104-05, 107, 113-15
Irralie's Bushranger (Hornung) **59**:113
"Irrande moln" (Södergran) **31**:288
"The Irrational Element in Poetry" (Stevens) **45**:282
The Irrational Knot (Shaw) **3**:379-80, 401; **9**:422
"Der Irre" (Heym) **9**:142-43, 148-51
Irremediablemente (Storni) **5**:444, 447-48, 451
"The Irriating Ditch" (Foote) **108**:34
is 5 (Cummings) **137**:4, 34, 47, 49-50
"Is America Too Hospitable?" (Gilman) **117**:136-38, 163
"Is England Decadent?" (Middleton) **56**:192
"Is it a comedy? Is it a tragedy?" (Bernhard)
See "Ist es eine Trogödie? Ist es eine Komödie?"
"Is It a Crime for a United States Citizen to Vote?" (Anthony) **84**:54
"Is It All for Nothing?" (Davis) **6**:154
"Is Knowledge Possible?" (Dewey) **95**:31
"Is Life Worth Living?" (James) **32**:335, 348-49
"Is My Team Ploughing" (Housman) **10**:247
"Is Shakespeare Dead?" (Twain) **161**:243-45; **185**:239
"Is the Republican Party Breaking Up?" (Baker) **47**:13
"Is the Theatre Literature?" (Caragiale) **76**:173
"Is the Ux Extinct?" (Chambers) **41**:102
"Is Woman's Suffrage a Failure?" (Tarbell) **40**:444
"Isa" (Anwar) **22**:24
"Isaac and Archibald" (Robinson) **5**:401, 404, 413, 418; **101**:100, 111-13, 119, 130, 133, 140-41, 192-93
"Isaac and Rebecca" (Harris) **24**:264
Isaac Babel: The Lonely Years, 1925-1939 (Babel) **171**:6
Isabel Clarendon (Gissing) **3**:230, 236-37; **24**:220
Isabelle (Gide) **5**:214-15, 222; **12**:145, 148, 159, 177; **36**:110; **177**:9, 31
Isadora Speaks (Duncan) **68**:55
"Isaiah" (Crowley) **7**:208
"Isaiah Beethoven" (Masters) **25**:298-99
"Isanalwana" (McCrae) **12**:211
Isanatori (Rohan) **22**:295, 299, 302
"Isandlwana" (Mqhayi) **25**:322
Isaotta Guttadauro ed altre poesie (D'Annunzio) **6**:136, 143
"I'se Jes' er Little Nigger" (Cotter) **28**:42
"Iseult of Brittany" (Parker) **143**:325
"Ishiki no mondai" (Nishida) **83**:242
"Ishthar's Lament for Tammuz" (Okigbo) **171**:345
"Isidoro Acevedo" (Borges) **109**:11
Isidro (Austin) **25**:33, 38
"Isis and Osiris" (Musil)
See "Isis und Osiris"
"Isis und Osiris" (Musil) **12**:250; **68**:271
Iskander (Couperus) **15**:45
"Iskusstvo pri svete sovesti" (Tsvetaeva) **7**:562
La isla desierta (Arlt) **29**:54
"The Island" (Coffin) **95**:14
"Island" (Jackson) **187**:238
"The Island" (Milne) **6**:314; **88**:244
"The Island" (Muir) **2**:483
"An Island" (Robinson) **5**:402
Island and Sea (Babits)
See *Sziget és tenger*
The Island of Dr. Moreau (Wells) **6**:534-35, 538, 540-43, 545, 547, 554-55; **12**:488, 506, 511-12; **19**:420-21, 424, 428-31, 433-36, 438-39, 441-42, 444-50; **133**:224, 227, 230, 238, 257, 261, 263-64, 284
The Island of Fu Manchu (Rohmer) **28**:280, 294, 300
The Island of Sheep (Buchan) **41**:38, 41, 53-8, 67
"The Island of Statues" (Yeats) **11**:517; **116**:334
"The Island of the Blest" (Gosse) **28**:132
The Island of the Innocent (Fisher) **140**:157, 186
The Island Pharisees (Galsworthy) **1**:296-97, 299, 304; **45**:39-41, 46, 48, 67, 69
"An Island Tale" (Muir) **87**:239
Island Tales (London)
See *On the Makaloa Mat*
The Island Within (Lewisohn) **19**:271-72, 277-78, 281-82, 288-89
"The Islanders" (Kipling) **8**:180; **17**:212
Islanders (Zamyatin)
See *Ostrovityane*
The Islanders (Zamyatin)
See *Ostrovityane*
"Isle Iranim" (Fletcher) **35**:106
The Isle of Lies (Shiel) **8**:362, 364
Isle of the Dead (Lewton) **76**:200, 202, 210, 212-13, 215-16, 227, 231, 233
Isle of Thorns (Kaye-Smith) **20**:94, 97, 102, 109, 113
The Isles of Gold (Mistral)
See *Lis isclo d'or*
Isma (Sarraute) **145**:265, 267, 312, 316-17, 322-23
Isn't Life Wonderful? (Griffith) **68**:153, 169-70, 178
"Isn't Today the Day?" (Saroyan) **137**:156
L'isola meravigliosa (Betti) **5**:61
"The Isolate" (Lu Hsun) **3**:303
"Isolde's Mother" (Huneker) **65**:169
Ispania (Kazantzakis) **33**:166; **181**:325
Ispezione (Betti) **5**:54-5
"Ispoved" (Tolstoy) **4**:450, 475-76, 480, 482; **11**:458, 460-63, 465, 469, 474; **79**:322, 324, 327, 333, 335, 338, 350, 363-4, 374, 384, 386, 411, 417, 424-6, 428, 431-3, 435-6, 442-7, 452-3, 455, 460-2
Ispoved (Gorky) **8**:76-7, 81-2, 86-7
Ispoved (Tolstoy) **173**:294
Ispoved' khuligana (Esenin) **4**:109, 111, 117
Israel (Lewisohn) **19**:272
Issledovanie dogmaticheskogo bogoslavja (Tolstoy) **11**:463; **79**:335, 431
"An Issue of Life" (Nemerov) **124**:273-74
"Issues of Pragmaticism" (Peirce) **81**:200
"Das ist die Jungfrau im Wald" (Raabe) **45**:190
"Das ist die Zeit" (Ball) **104**:6, 16
"Ist es eine Trogödie? Ist es eine Komödie?" (Bernhard) **165**:37, 122
Ist River (Asch) **3**:69, 72
Az Isten háta mögött (Moricz) **33**:237, 242, 244, 247, 249
Isten kezében (Babits) **14**:39
Az Istenek halnak, az ember él (Babits) **14**:40
"The Isthmus of Karelia" (Leino)
See "Karjalan kannas"
Istoki (Aldanov) **23**:22-4
Istoria moego sovremennika (Korolenko) **22**:173, 175-76, 178, 183-84
"Istoriia moei golubiatni" (Babel) **2**:28; **13**:26; **171**:7, 9-10, 94, 98-99
"Istoriia odnoi loshadi" (Babel) **13**:35; **171**:7, 18, 23, 73, 80, 84
Istoriya Russkoi Revolyutsii (Trotsky) **22**:353, 355, 357, 361, 364-69, 381-82, 386-87, 389-91
"Istoriya veherashnego dnya" (Tolstoy) **173**:294

Istorya rytsaria d'Alessio (Kuzmin) **40**:198-99, 201-02
"Istreblinie tiranov" (Nabokov) **108**:55
"Isusov grekh" (Babel) **171**:7
"It" and Other Stories (Glyn) **72**:140, 142
It Can't Be Serious (Pirandello)
See *Ma non è una cosa seria*
It Can't Happen Here (Lewis) **4**:250, 255, 258, 261; **13**:350; **39**:232, 249
"It Couldn't Be Done" (Guest) **95**:208
It Depends What You Mean: An Improvisation for the Glockenspiel (Bridie) **3**:141
"It Feels Good as It Is" (Stevens) **3**:448
It Happened in Florida (Cabell) **6**:76-7
"It Happened That" (Hedāyat)
See "Dast-i bar qaza"
It Is Enough (Kaiser)
See *Es ist Genug*
"It Is Everywhere" (Toomer) **172**:278
It Is I (Bryusov) **10**:95
"It Is near Toussaints" (Gurney) **33**:110-12
"It Is No Longer Possible" (Aleixandre) **113**:25-6
It is Not Enough (Aleixandre) **113**:42
"It Is Parallels That Are Deadly" (Dreiser)
See "Tabloid Tragedy"
"It is Prettiest When Dusk Comes" (Lagerkvist)
See "Det är vackrast när det skymmer"
It Is So (Pirandello) **172**:150
It Is So, If You Think So (Pirandello)
See *Cosíè (se vi pare)*
"It Is the Sinners' Dust-Tongued Bell" (Thomas) **8**:459
"It is True" (García Lorca)
See "Es verdad"
"It Is Winter" (Gurney) **33**:112
It Isn't This Time of Year at All! An Unpremeditated Autobiography (Gogarty) **15**:106, 120
"It May Not Always Be So: And I Say" (Cummings) **137**:54
"It Must Be Abstract" (Stevens) **45**:285, 298, 340
"It Must Be the Milk" (Nash) **109**:363-64
It Must Be Your Tonsils (Roberts) **23**:240
"It Must Change" (Stevens) **45**:298
"It Must Give Pain" (Stevens) **45**:298
"It Must Give Pleasure" (Stevens) **45**:298, 341, 351
It Needs to Be Said (Grove) **4**:134, 136-40
"It Seems a Lie" (Villaurrutia) **80**:458
It Seems To Me (Broun) **104**:82
"It Takes a Heap o'Livin't make a House a Home" (Guest) **95**:211
It Takes All Kinds (Bromfield) **11**:82
"It Walks by Night" (Kuttner) **10**:267
"It Was a Gentle Breeze" (Darío)
See "Era un aire suave"
"It Was a Soft Air" (Darío)
See "Era un aire suave"
"It Was Summer" (Jozsef) **22**:160
It Was the Nightingale (Ford) **57**:210, 236-37, 242-43, 273, 275, 279-80, 282, 286; **172**:7, 71-72, 122
L'Italia e Libia (Mosca) **75**:172
Italian Backgrounds (Wharton) **3**:552; **129**:361; **149**:255
Italian Fables (Calvino)
See *Fiabe italiene*
Italian Fantasies (Zangwill) **16**:445, 451, 461
Italian Folktales (Calvino)
See *Fiabe italiene*
The Italian Girl (Murdoch) **171**:221, 225-27, 279, 305
Italian Hours (James) **47**:208
Italian Journeys (Howells) **7**:377
Italian Night (Horvath)
See *Italienische Nacht*
Italian Novellas (Merezhkovsky) **29**:230
"Italian Painter" (Radnóti) **16**:418
"The Italian Queen" (Quiroga)
See "La reina Italiana"
"An Italian Reformer" (Herzl)
See "Egy olasc reformátor"
"Italian Sunshine" (Babel)
See "Solntse Italii"
Italian Villas and Their Gardens (Wharton) **3**:552; **129**:345, 360; **149**:255
"L'italiano, una lingua tra le altre lingue" (Calvino) **183**:102, 142
Italienische Nacht (Horvath) **45**:76-7, 81, 89, 91, 94, 96-9, 104, 107, 113-16
"Italija" (Vazov) **25**:458
"Italy's Sun" (Babel)
See "Solntse Italii"
"Itching Heels" (Dunbar) **12**:110
"Iterumne" (Roberts) **8**:319
"Ithaca" (Cavafy) **2**:88, 94-5; **7**:153, 155, 163
"Ithaca" (Joyce) **3**:280
"Ithaka" (Cavafy)
See "Ithaca"
Ithaka (Benn) **3**:109, 114
"L'itinéraire" (Drieu la Rochelle) **21**:32
It's a Free Country (Williams) **89**:390
It's a Gift (Fields) **80**:228, 231
It's a Grand Old Flag (Cohan) **60**:160, 163, 165, 168, 170, 173
It's a Great Life (Rinehart) **52**:282
It's a Wonderful World (Mankiewicz) **85**:163
"It's All Very Complicated" (McAlmon) **97**:100
It's Beautiful (Sarraute)
See *C'est beau*
It's Hard to Be a Jew (Aleichem)
See *Shver tsu zayn a yid*
It's in the Bag (Allen) **87**:55
"it's just like a coffin's / inside when you die" (Cummings) **137**:42
"It's Not I Who Shouts" (Jozsef) **22**:164
"It's Raining" (Apollinaire)
See "Il pleut"
"It's So Easy" (Holly) **65**:153
It's Too Late Now (Milne) **88**:253
"Its Walls Were as of Jasper" (Grahame) **64**:79, 94
Ityala lamawele (Mqhayi) **25**:321, 323-24, 326-27
"Itylus" (Swinburne) **36**:327, 329
"Iunomu poetu" (Bryusov) **10**:95
Iunost' (Tolstoy)
See *Yunost*
Ivalyo (Vazov) **25**:455
Ivan Aleksandar (Vazov) **25**:457
Ivan Groznyi (Eisenstein) **57**:157-61, 164, 166-67, 179, 191-92, 197, 199-201
Ivan Groznyi: Boyarskii Zagovor (Eisenstein) **57**:157, 159-60, 168, 198
"Ivan Ivanivich and the Devil" (Hippius) **9**:163
"Ivan Lande" (Artsybashev) **31**:4-5, 8, 10
Ivan Moscow (Pilnyak) **23**:212
Ivan Sudarev's Stories (Tolstoy) **18**:379
"Ivan the Fool" (Tolstoy) **4**:469
Ivan the Terrible (Tolstoy) **18**:361-63, 375, 383
Ivan the Terrible, Part I (Eisenstein)
See *Ivan Groznyi*
Ivan the Terrible, Part II: The Boyars' Plot (Eisenstein)
See *Ivan Groznyi: Boyarskii Zagovor*
Ivan Vasil'evich (Bulgakov) **16**:95-6
Ivanov (Chekhov) **55**:64, 66; **96**:15; **163**:16-17, 38, 74, 100-104, 107, 110, 112, 128
"The Ivanov Family" (Platonov)
See "Homecoming"
"Ivanovy" (Zabolotsky) **52**:371, 375
"The Ivans" (Babel)
See "Ivany"
"Ivany" (Babel) **171**:24, 36-37, 46, 72, 78-79, 87
Ivory Apes and Peacocks (Huneker) **65**:161, 165, 170, 185, 193, 198, 203, 205-06, 218
The Ivory Child (Haggard) **11**:246, 250-51, 254-55
The Ivory Door (Milne) **6**:319; **88**:253
The Ivory Tower (James) **2**:251, 256-58, 260, 275; **47**:165
"The Ivory Woman" (Andrić)
See "Žena iz slonove kosti"
"L'ivresse" (Verhaeren) **12**:469
Ivy (Deledda)
See *L'edera*
The Ivy (Villaurrutia) **80**:458
"Ivy Day in the Committee Room" (Joyce) **8**:158, 166; **35**:142, 144, 151, 156, 160, 164-65, 167, 190, 196-97; **159**:300
"Ivy Gripped the Steps" (Bowen) **148**:20-21, 89, 116, 123
"Iya na yatsu" (Endo) **152**:202
"Iz ada izvedënnye" (Bryusov) **10**:81
"Iz zapisok kniazia D. Nekhliudova. Liutsern" (Tolstoy) **28**:367; **173**:280
Izawa Ranken (Mori Ogai) **14**:376, 378
Izbrannoe (Olesha) **136**:135, 151
Izbrannye proizvedeniaa v shesti tomakh (Eisenstein) **57**:190, 197
Izgoi (Gladkov) **27**:90
"Izinsimbi zesonto" (Vilakazi) **37**:404, 410
"Izlet" (Andrić) **135**:89
"Izmedu igara" (Popa) **167**:155
"Izmena" (Babel) **171**:40, 73, 86-87
Iznanka poèzii (Annensky) **14**:24
Izobretenie Val'sa (Nabokov) **108**:52, 55-56
Izwe lakwandlambe (Mqhayi) **25**:326
J. Poindexter, Colored (Cobb) **77**:117-18, 127
Ja (Bernhard) **165**:79, 96, 100, 116
"Ja, hvordan?" (Nexø) **43**:331
"Ja tror på min syster" (Södergran) **31**:293
"Ja, vi elsker dette landet" (Bjoernson) **7**:110
Jaákobs Traum (Beer-Hofmann) **60**:28, 30-1, 33, 35-7
Jaana Rönty (Leino) **24**:372
Jacaranda in the Night (Bosman) **49**:3, 12, 24, 30
"J'accuse" (Zola) **1**:591
"Jack Dunn of Nevertire" (Lawson) **27**:134
The Jack Kerouac Collection (Kerouac) **117**:220
Jack Liverpool (London) **9**:259
"The Jack Rabbit Drive" (McAlmon) **97**:98, 120, 122
"Jack Rose" (Bodenheim) **44**:59
Jack the Fisherman (Phelps) **113**:336
"Jack the Giant Killer" (Roberts) **68**:306
The Jackdar (Gregory) **1**:334
The Jackdaw (Gregory) **176**:13-14, 16-17, 19, 21, 34, 40
The Jacket (London) **15**:260-61
"Jackie" (Smith) **25**:390
"The Jack-Rabbit" (Stevens) **12**:367
Jackson's Dilemma (Murdoch) **171**:305-13, 324, 330
Jacob (Kielland) **5**:277
"Jacob and the Indians" (Benét) **7**:81
"Jacob and the Other" (Onetti)
See "Jacob y el otro"
Jacob Stahl (Beresford) **81**:2,6,10,12
The Jacob Street Mystery (Freeman) **21**:58-9
"Jacob y el otro" (Onetti) **131**:133, 162, 195, 254-56, 258-60
Les Jacobites (Coppee) **25**:127
Jacob's Dream (Beer-Hofmann)
See *Jaákobs Traum*
Jacob's Ladder (Housman) **7**:360
Jacob's Ladder (Schoenberg)
See *Jakobsleiter*
Jacob's Room (Woolf) **1**:527-29, 531-33, 536, 538-39, 542-43, 545; **5**:508, 516; **20**:397, 409, 425, 428-29; **43**:420; **56**:359-60; **101**:297; **128**:327, 333-34, 337-38, 341, 344-45, 349, 357, 363-65, 371-72, 379-80, 384, 385-86
"Jacques de la Cloche" (Lang) **16**:254
"Jacques l'égoïste" (Giraudoux) **3**:324
"The Jade Elegy" (Fletcher) **35**:106
"Jag" (Södergran) **31**:288
"Jag såg ett träd" (Södergran) **31**:289
Die Jagd nach Liebe (Mann) **9**:323, 325-27

Die Jagdgesellschaft (Bernhard) **165**:41-43, 46, 96, 121, 124-28
"Der jäger Gracchus" (Kafka) **47**:235
"El jahad" (Graham) **19**:129
"Jahr" (George) **14**:210
Das Jahr der Schönen Täuschungen (Carossa) **48**:28-30, 34
Der Jahr der Seele (George) **2**:149, 151; **14**:196, 200-02, 204, 206, 209-12, 215-16
"Jailbird" (Gale) **7**:285
Jakob von Gunten (Walser) **18**:415, 417-18, 420-21, 424-25, 428-29, 431-34
Jakobsleiter (Schoenberg) **75**:303, 311-12, 315, 323, 337, 347, 349-52, 361, 363, 366, 369, 398, 401, 411
"Jaldaboath" (Benét) **28**:8
"The Jamaica Funeral" (Freneau) **120**:269, 271
"Jamaica Marches On" (Redcam) **25**:330
"Jamaican Rose" (Rohmer) **28**:286
"Jambalaya" (Williams) **81**:423,444
"James and Maggie" (Lawson) **27**:132
James and the Giant Peach (Dahl) **173**:20-21, 26
James Burnham and the Managerial Revolution (Orwell) **31**:190
The James Dickey Reader (Dickey) **151**:203
The James Family: A Group Biography (Matthiessen) **100**:238
"James James" (Milne) **6**:313
"James Pethel" (Beerbohm) **24**:100-01
James Shore's Daughter (Benét) **3**:80-1
"James Thomson" (Noyes) **7**:506
"Jamestown" (Jarrell) **177**:162, 172, 228
"Jamiol" (Sienkiewicz) **3**:430
Jan Compagnie (van Schendel) **56**:237-43
"Jan in Mourning" (Nezval) **44**:240
"Jane" (Rinehart) **52**:282
"Jane Austen" (Woolf) **128**:334
Jane Field (Freeman) **9**:63, 68-9
Jane Mecom (Van Doren) **18**:410
"Jane Mollet's Box" (Powys) **9**:372
Jane of Lantern Hill (Montgomery) **140**:331, 334
Jane Oglander (Lowndes) **12**:200
"The Janeites" (Kipling) **8**:195-96
Jane's Career (De Lisser) **12**:95-100
"Jang terampas dan jang luput" (Anwar) **22**:24
Janika (Csáth) **13**:147
"Janko the Musician" (Sienkiewicz) **3**:425-27
Janmadinay (Tagore)
See *Janmadine*
Janmadine (Tagore) **3**:488; **53**:343
"Janmadine, No. 5" (Tagore) **3**:489
"January, 1939" (Thomas) **8**:459; **45**:365
"January Thaw" (Cobb) **77**:140
"Jap Miller" (Riley) **51**:292
Japan: An Attempt at Interpretation (Hearn) **9**:123, 126, 128-32
Japan and American (Noguchi) **80**:377
Japan-China (Kazantzakis)
See *Iaponia-Kina*
Japanese Art (Hartmann) **73**:117, 122
"Japanese Erotica" (Carter) **139**:188
Japanese Fairy Tales (Hearn) **9**:128
"The Japanese Hokku Poetry" (Noguchi) **80**:388
Japanese Hokkus (Noguchi) **80**:388
The Japanese Letters of Lafcadio Hearn (Hearn) **9**:123
"The Japanese Noh Play" (Noguchi) **80**:396
"Japanese Prints" (Sarton) **120**:265, 304
Japanese Prints (Fletcher) **35**:95, 105, 115
"Japonerías del estío" (Huidobro) **31**:124
Japoneries d'automne (Loti) **11**:361
"The Jar" (Pirandello)
See "La giara"
Jar (Rebreanu) **28**:271-72
Jarbuch fuer Philosophie un Phaenomenologische Forschung (Husserl) **100**:10, 29-30, 33, 38-40, 49, 75, 77-78, 125, 134, 146-47
"El jardín" (Borges)
See "El jardín de senderos que se bifurcan"
"Jardín" (Villaurrutia) **80**:477
"Le jardin d'Antan" (Nelligan) **14**:392
El jardín de al lado (Donoso) **133**:56, 86-92, 129-34, 157-60, 178, 186, 189, 200, 203, 205
Le Jardin de Bérénice (Barrès) **47**:35-6, 41, 49-50, 60, 97-8
"El jardín de senderos que se bifurcan" (Borges) **109**:37-8, 40, 59, 76, 107-09, 112, 127
Le jardin d'Épicure (France) **9**:42
Le Jardin des chimères (Yourcenar) **193**:354
Le jardin des rochers (Kazantzakis) **2**:317; **5**:270; **33**:150; **181**:236-40
Le jardin des supplices (Mirbeau) **55**:281-86, 288, 295, 301, 303-04, 310, 313
"Jardin Exotique" (White) **176**:177, 179
"Jardin sentimental" (Nelligan) **14**:398-99
Un jardin sur l'Oronte (Barrès) **47**:60-1, 66-7, 75
Jardines de Francia (Gonzalez Martinez) **72**:148
"Jardines dolientes" (Jiménez) **183**:269
Los jardines interiores (Nervo) **11**:400, 402
Jardines lejanos (Jiménez) **4**:213, 223; **183**:269, 289, 298
The Jargon of Authenticity (Adorno) **111**:53, 73
"Járkálj csak, halálraitélt!" (Radnóti) **16**:411
Järn och människor (Lagerkvist) **144**:224
"Jasbo Brown" (Heyward) **59**:95
Jasbo Brown (Heyward) **59**:106
"Jashūmon" (Akutagawa Ryūnosuke) **16**:18
Jaskinia filozofow (Herbert) **168**:39
The Jasmine Farm (Elizabeth) **41**:129, 132
"Jasmine Tea" (Chang)
See "Moli xiangpian"
"Jason" (Field) **43**:156
"Jason and Medea" (Lewis) **3**:287
Jason Edwards, an Average Man (Garland) **3**:192
"Jasper's Song" (Pickthall) **21**:245
Játék a kastélyban (Molnár) **20**:161, 166, 170, 178
"Jaufré Rudel" (Carducci) **32**:90, 101
"La jaula de pájaro" (Valle-Inclán) **5**:478
Jaunais spēks (Rainis) **29**:392
Jaune bleu blanc (Larbaud) **9**:199, 208
Java Head (Hergesheimer) **11**:261-65, 269, 271, 276, 281, 283, 285-86
"Javanese Dancers" (Symons) **11**:445, 451
Javid-namah (Iqbal) **28**:182, 191, 204
"Jay Walkers" (Wakefield) **120**:350
Jayhawker (Lewis) **4**:257
Jāzeps un vina brāli (Rainis) **29**:380-81, 386, 393
"Jazz" (Adorno)
See "Abschied vom Jazz"
The Jazz Age (Fitzgerald) **157**:202
Je . . . Ils (Adamov) **189**:15
Je ne mange pas de ce pain-là (Péret) **20**:195, 198, 202
"Je ne parle pas français" (Mansfield) **2**:448, 453; **8**:280-82, 285-86, 291-92; **39**:293, 303, 313; **164**:241-44, 264, 281-82, 284-85, 287, 319
Je ne suis pas Français (Adamov) **189**:14, 31-4
Je ne trompe pas mon mari (Feydeau) **22**:79, 83
Je sublime (Péret) **20**:184-85, 187, 196, 202
"Jea" (Proust) **161**:161
The Jealous Wife (Belasco) **3**:86
"Jealousy" (Brooke) **2**:59; **7**:122
"Jealousy" (Dreiser)
See "The Shadow"
"Jealousy" (Lasker-Schueler) **57**:328
Jealousy (Artsybashev) **31**:9, 11
Jean Arp: Collected French Writings (Arp) **115**:38
Jean Barois (Martin du Gard) **24**:382-83, 385-87, 390-95, 398, 402-04, 412
"Jean Cocteau" (Stein) **6**:403; **48**:254-55
"De Jean Coste" (Péguy) **10**:408
"Jean de Noarrieu" (Jammes) **75**:109, 112, 117-18
"Jean Desprez" (Service) **15**:401
Jean Huguenot (Benét) **7**:80
"JEAN LAFITTE, The Baratarian" (Walker) **129**:277
Jean le bleu (Giono) **124**:37, 39-40, 43, 49, 60, 68, 90, 97, 100-1, 103, 106-7, 110-16, 124
Jean Maquenem (Bourget)
See *Le retour*
Jean Santeuil (Proust) **7**:528, 533-34, 536, 539; **13**:415-18, 420-21, 429; **33**:262, 271
Jean Shepherd's America (Shepherd) **177**:298, 304, 311, 314
Jean-Christophe (Rolland) **23**:249-53, 256, 259-63, 270-71, 276-79, 282-85
Jean-Luc persécuté (Ramuz) **33**:294-95, 302, 306
Jeanne d'Arc (Melies) **81**:146
Jeanne d'Arc (Péguy) **10**:407-08, 410
La "Jeanne d'Arc" de M. Anatole France (Lang)
See *The Maid of France*
"Jeanne de Courtisols" (Bourget) **12**:73
Jeanne de Piennes (Rolland) **23**:256
Jeanne of the Marshes (Oppenheim) **45**:135
"Jeanne: Relapse et sainte" (Bernanos) **3**:127
Jedermann (Hofmannsthal) **11**:295-8, 301, 303
Jeeves and the Feudal Spirit (Wodehouse) **108**:335, 386
"Jeeves and the Impending Doom" (Wodehouse) **108**:335-6
Jeeves and the Tie That Binds (Wodehouse) **108**:335, 370
Jeeves in the Offing (Wodehouse)
See *How Right You Are, Jeeves*
Jeeves Omnibus (Wodehouse) **108**:391, 394
"Jeeves Takes Charge" (Wodehouse) **108**:378-79
"Jeff Brigg's Love Story" (Harte) **1**:342
"Jefferson Howard" (Masters) **25**:312
Jefta und Seine Tochter (Feuchtwanger) **3**:182-83, 186
"Jeg ser" (Obstfelder) **23**:177, 180, 189
"Jelena, the Woman Who Does not Exist" (Andrić)
See "Jelena, žena koje nema"
"Jelena, the Woman Who Was Not" (Andrić)
See "Jelena, žena koje nema"
"Jelena, žena koje nema" (Andrić) **135**:15, 23, 52-53, 89-92
"Jeli il pastore" (Verga) **3**:547
"Jeli, the Shepard" (Verga)
See "Jeli il pastore"
Jen Sheng: The Root of Life (Prishvin)
See *Zhen'-shen': koren' zhizni*
"Jener" (Benn) **3**:107
Jennie Gerhardt (Dreiser) **10**:163-65, 167, 173, 177, 181-82, 186-87, 198-200; **18**:53, 63-6; **35**:35-7, 40-1, 43, 46-8, 65, 74; **83**:3, 36, 54
Jennifer Lorn (Wylie) **8**:523-25, 527-28, 530-31, 537-38
Jenny (Undset) **3**:510, 512, 516-18, 521-22; **197**:294-95, 299, 301, 307, 311
"Jens" (Jensen) **41**:307
Jenseits des Lustprinzips (Freud) **52**:101, 109, 132, 134
Jenseits von gut und Böse: Vorspiel einer Philosophie der zukunft (Nietzsche) **10**:355, 360, 362, 385-86, 388-90, 393; **18**:342, 351; **55**:333, 337, 368, 374, 376
Jeptha and His Daughter (Feuchtwanger)
See *Jefta und Seine Tochter*
Jeremy (Walpole) **5**:498
Jeremy and Hamlet (Walpole) **5**:498
Jeremy at Crale (Walpole) **5**:498
Jericho: The South Beheld (Dickey) **151**:152, 162-67
"Jerome" (Jarrell) **177**:162-64, 167, 170, 173
Jerome, a Poor Man (Freeman) **9**:61, 63, 69-72, 74
"Jerry Bundler" (Jacobs) **22**:99

Jerry of the Islands (London) **9**:267
"Jerusalem" (Douglas) **40**:76
"Jerusalem" (Lasker-Schueler) **57**:300, 333
"Jérusalem" (Loti) **11**:355-56, 362
Jerusalem (Lagerloef)
See *Jerusalem 1: I Dalarne*
Jerusalem 1: I Dalarne (Lagerloef) **4**:229-32, 234-35, 238-39, 241; **36**:230-31, 238-41, 243-48
Jerusalem 2: I det heliga landet (Lagerloef) **36**:230-31, 238-39, 241, 243
"Jerusalem and Athens: Some Preliminary Reflections" (Strauss) **141**:237, 266-67, 273, 289
Jerusalem: I det heliga landet (Lagerloef) **4**:231
The Jervaise Comedy (Beresford) **81**:11
"Jeshurun Waxed Fat" (Williams) **89**:372
Jess (Haggard) **11**:239
"Jesse James: American Myth" (Benét) **28**:11
The Jest (Cabell) **6**:61
The Jester (Gregory) **1**:337; **176**:34, 39
"The Jesters" (Marquis) **7**:434
"The Jesters of the Lord" (Manning) **25**:265, 269
Jests of Death and Life (Pirandello)
See *Beffe della morte e della vita*
"A Jesuit" (Graham) **19**:101, 136
"Jesus" (Anwar)
See "Isa"
Jésus (Barbusse) **5**:14, 18
Jesus Came Again (Fisher) **140**:157, 186
Jesus: Man of Genius (Murry) **16**:355
Jesus Rediscovered (Muggeridge) **120**:155, 162, 164, 172
"Jesus the Jew" (Andreas-Salome) **56**:30, 31, 44-46
Jesus: The Man Who Lives (Muggeridge) **120**:164065, 187, 192
Jesus, the Son of Man (Gibran) **1**:326; **9**:82, 86, 91-2, 94
Jesus the Unknown (Merezhkovsky) **29**:242
"Jesus und der Aser-Weg" (Werfel) **8**:477
"The Jesuve" (Bataille) **155**:65
Le jet de sang (Artaud) **3**:53, 61; **36**:20-4, 30, 32-3
"Jet d'eau" (Apollinaire) **8**:12
"Jeter le Gant aux Vents" (Arp) **115**:32
"Jets of Water" (García Lorca)
See "Surtidores"
"Jetsam" (Dunsany) **59**:19
"Jetsam" (Moody) **105**:224, 260, 263
"La Jeune Belgique" (Sharp) **39**:365
Le jeune Européen (Drieu la Rochelle) **21**:17-18
La jeune fille neu (Jammes) **75**:115, 118
La jeune fille Violaine (Claudel) **2**:106; **10**:128
La Jeune Née (Genet) **128**:129
La jeune parque (Valéry) **4**:487-91, 495, 501; **15**:447-49, 455, 458-64
"Jeunes filles" (Sully Prudhomme) **31**:299
La jeunesse d'un clerc (Benda) **60**:62, 71
"The Jew" (Rosenberg) **12**:292, 295, 307
"Jew and a Half" (Babel) **171**:9
"The Jew and Trans-National America" (Bourne)
See "Trans-National America"
The Jew as Pariah (Arendt) **193**:77, 153
"The Jew as Pariah: A Hidden Tradition" (Arendt) **193**:78
A Jew in Love (Hecht) **101**:63, 87, 90
The Jew of Rome (Feuchtwanger)
See *Die Söhne*
"The Jewbird" (Malamud) **129**:69; **184**:163, 167, 199, 237, 241-42, 253, 260-61, 278, 280, 310
The Jewel of Seven Stars (Stoker) **8**:385-86, 394, 399; **144**:273, 279
The Jeweled Casket and the Two Urashima (Mori Ogai)
See *Tamakushige futari Urashima*
"The Jeweller's Shop in Wartime" (Howe) **21**:113
"Jewels of Gwahlur" (Howard) **8**:133
"The Jewess" (Kuprin) **5**:301
"Jewish Cemetery" (García Lorca)
See "Cementerio judío"
"Jewish History in the United States" (Ford) **73**:60, 62
Jewish Influences in American Life (Ford) **73**:93
"Jewish Massacres and the Revolutionary Movement in Russia" (Cahan) **71**:30
"The Jewish Refugee" (Malamud)
See "The German Refugee"
The Jewish State: An Attempt at a Modern Solution of the Jewish Question (Herzl)
See *Der Judenstaat, Versuch einer modernen Lösung der Judenfrage*
"The Jewish Trinity" (Zangwill) **16**:447
The Jewish Widow (Kaiser)
See *Die Jüdische Witwe*
"The Jewish Woman" (Kolmar) **40**:175, 178
"The Jews" (Markham) **47**:285
The Jews (Belloc) **18**:36, 42, 45, 47
The Jews, Are They Human? (Lewis) **2**:392; **104**:225, 232, 241, 245, 247
"Jews at Haifa" (Jarrell) **177**:251
The Jews of Zindorf (Wassermann)
See *Die Juden von Zirndorf*
"Jezebel" (Crowley) **7**:208
Jézabel (Anouilh) **195**:6, 12, 16-17, 24, 26
"Jigokuhen" (Akutagawa Ryūnosuke) **16**:18, 27, 32-3, 35
"Jiisan baasan" (Mori Ogai) **14**:378, 380
Jikaku ni okeru chokkan to hansei (Nishida) **83**:226, 250, 290
Jill the Reckless (Wodehouse) **108**:370, 372
The Jilt (Griffith) **68**:245
"Jim" (Harte) **25**:191
"Jim" (Riley) **51**:292
"Jim and Arabel's Sister" (Masters) **25**:288
Jim Dandy: Fat Man in a Famine (Saroyan) **137**:170, 178
Jim Maitland (Sapper) **44**:309, 317
"Jim Smiley and His Jumping Frog" (Twain)
See "The Celebrated Jumping Frog of Calaveras County"
Jimbo (Blackwood) **5**:69-70, 73
"The Jimmyjohn Boss" (Wister) **21**:377, 383, 385
The Jimmyjohn Boss, and Other Stories (Wister) **21**:377, 391, 405
Jim's Book: A Collection of Poems and Short Stories (Merrill) **173**:172, 237
"Jimsella" (Dunbar) **12**:106, 108-09, 120, 122, 124
Jin suo ji (Chang) **184**:103, 135-36, 140-41, 152
"A Jingle or Drowsy Chime" (Brennan) **17**:50
"Jingles and Croons" (Johnson) **3**:243-44
Jingling in the Wind (Roberts) **68**:298, 300, 324, 360, 362
"Jingo, Counter Jingo and Us" (Locke) **43**:240, 243
"Jingyu lu" (Chang) **184**:133, 150, 153
"Jinny" (Harte) **25**:223
Jinny the Carrier (Zangwill) **16**:449, 462, 464
"Jinshin no giwaku" (Nishida) **83**:231
"Jinsuo ji" (Chang) **184**:138-40
J'irai cracher sur vos tombes (Vian) **9**:528, 536
Jiu San (Dent) **72**:25-26
"Jivanmukta" (Aurobindo) **63**:9
"Jivitra O Mrita" (Tagore) **53**:354
"Jó csöndherceg előtt" (Ady) **11**:15, 17
A jó Palócok (Mikszath) **31**:170
Joan and Peter: The Story of an Education (Wells) **6**:527-28, 532; **12**:495, 507
"Joan Miró" (Éluard) **41**:149
"Joan of Arc" (Tynan) **3**:502-03
Joan of Arc (Belloc) **7**:39
Joan of Arc (Merezhkovsky) **29**:242
Joan of Arc (Péguy)
See *Jeanne d'Arc*
Joan of Lorraine (Anderson) **2**:9, 11; **144**:7, 17, 33-35, 39, 71
"Joanna and Ulysses" (Sarton) **120**:197, 210-12, 244
Joanna Godden (Kaye-Smith) **20**:99, 103, 109-11, 113-18
Joanne (Engel) **137**:123
The Job (Burroughs) **121**:137-39, 141-44
The Job (Lewis) **4**:248, 251, 256-57, 259; **13**:343, 350; **23**:132; **39**:217, 234, 241
"Job and Magdalene" (Remizov)
See "Iov i Magdalina"
Job le pauvre (Bosschere) **19**:60, 62-5
Job: The Story of a Simple Man (Roth)
See *Hiob*
Jobb mint otthon (Moricz) **33**:242-43
"Jobs in the Sky" (Slesinger) **10**:441, 445-46
Jocelyn (Galsworthy) **45**:46
Joe (Molnár)
See *Jozsi*
Joe Fleischhacker (Brecht) **169**:37
"Joe Hunter" (Fisher) **140**:165
"Joe Louis Blues" (Wright) **136**:261-63
"Joe Turner Blues" (Handy) **97**:41-42
Joe Wilson and His Mates (Lawson) **27**:121, 126, 129, 131-32, 152
"Joe Wilson's Courtship" (Lawson) **27**:121, 126-28, 131, 143-45, 147, 152
"Joey" (Tomlinson) **71**:395
"Jofroi de la Maussan" (Giono) **124**:126
"The Jogo Blues" (Handy) **97**:54, 68-69
Jogoku no hana (Nagai) **51**:87, 91
Johan Wilhelm (Leino) **24**:371
The Johanna Maria (van Schendel)
See *Het fregatschip Johanna Maria*
"Johannes" (Spitteler) **12**:339
Johannes (Sudermann) **15**:418, 420, 422, 424, 436
"An Johannes Molzahn" (Schwitters) **95**:301
Johannes Reuchlin and His Struggle (Brod) **115**:99
Johannisfeuer (Sudermann) **15**:420, 427, 431
John (Barry) **11**:46-8, 50, 66
"John Anderson" (Douglas) **40**:91
John Andross (Davis) **6**:149, 151-52, 154
"John Archer's Nose" (Fisher) **11**:214
John Barleycorn (London) **9**:257-59, 266, 268-70; **15**:261; **39**:288
"John Bartine's Watch" (Bierce) **44**:45
John Bodewin's Testimony (Foote) **108**:17, 34, 39-40, 42-3
"John Bottom" (Khodasevich) **15**:206
"John Brown" (Lindsay) **17**:226, 230
"John Brown" (Robinson) **5**:407; **101**:117, 130
John Brown (Sinclair) **160**:300, 302
"John Brown's Body" (Benét) **7**:73, 77-8
John Bull (Shaw) **3**:384
John Bull's Other Island (Shaw) **9**:412; **21**:327, 338; **45**:247
John Bunyan (Rutherford) **25**:341, 346
John Burnet of Barns (Buchan) **41**:34
"John Carter" (Agee) **1**:15
John Carter of Mars (Burroughs) **2**:81
John Christopher (Rolland)
See *Jean-Christophe*
"John Cobbler" (de la Mare) **53**:23
The John Collier Reader (Collier) **127**:251-52, 258
John Company (van Schendel)
See *Jan Compagnie*
"John Crowe Ransom: Tennesseean" (Stevens) **45**:327
"John Davidson: Realist" (Flecker) **43**:210
John Dawn (Coffin) **95**:5, 8
"John Delavoy" (James) **40**:133
"John Donne's Satue" (Bishop) **103**:4
John Dough and the Cherub (Baum) **7**:19-21; **132**:82, 87, 103
John Ermine of the Yellowstone (Remington) **89**:300-2,304, 307-8, 310-12
"John Evereldown" (Robinson) **5**:401, 403, 416; **101**:111, 198
John Gabriel Borkman (Ibsen) **2**:220, 229, 234, 236-37; **8**:148-49; **37**:241, 258; **52**:142

John Gayther's Garden (Stockton) **47**:320, 324, 326
John Glayde's Honour (Sutro) **6**:422
"John Henry Blues" (Handy) **97**:40
John Herring (Baring-Gould) **88**:24, 26-7
"John Keats" (Sikelianos) **39**:418
John Knox and the Reformation (Lang) **16**:270
John Knox: Portrait of a Calvinist (Muir) **87**:195
"John L. Sullivan, the Strong Boy of Boston" (Lindsay) **17**:227
"John Lamar" (Davis) **6**:151-53
John Macnab (Buchan) **41**:38, 41, 44-5, 47, 49, 51
John March, Southerner (Cable) **4**:25-7, 31, 34-5
John Marchmont's Legacy (Braddon) **111**:215-16, 224
John Meade's Woman (Mankiewicz) **85**:117
John Mistletoe (Morley) **87**:128
"John Mortonson's Funeral" (Bierce) **7**:91; **44**:13, 45, 50
"John Norton" (Moore) **7**:490
John Pierpoint Morgan (Sternheim) **8**:375
John Randolph (Adams) **4**:16-17
John Randolph of Roanoke (Kirk) **119**:242, 254, 262, 266, 276, 297, 302, 304
"John Ransom's Poetry" (Jarrell) **177**:199
"John Redding Goes to Sea" (Hurston) **131**:70-71, 93
John Sherman (Yeats) **31**:415; **116**:334
John Sherwood, Ironmaster (Mitchell) **36**:274
"John Silence" (Blackwood) **5**:69
John Silence, Physician Extraordinary (Blackwood) **5**:69-70, 73-5, 77-8
John Smith—Also Pocahontas (Fletcher) **35**:106, 110
John Stuart Mill and Harriet Taylor (Hayek) **109**:205-06
John the Baptist (Sudermann)
See *Johannes*
"John the Untalented and Helen the Wise" (Platonov) **14**:420
John the Weeper (Bunin) **6**:45
John Thomas and Lady Jane (Lawrence) **9**:228; **48**:124, 127-29, 135, 139, 147
John Thorndyke's Cases (Freeman) **21**:44, 48, 51
John Webster and the Elizabethan Drama (Brooke) **2**:56, 59; **7**:123
"John Wesley's Place in History" (Wilson) **79**:489
"John Who Lost a Fortune by Throwing Stones" (Belloc) **7**:42
"Johnnie Courteau" (Drummond) **25**:151, 154
Johnnie Courteau, and Other Poems (Drummond) **25**:142-43, 156
Johnny (Csáth)
See *Janika*
"Johnny Appleseed" (Lindsay) **17**:229, 236, 240
Johnny Bear (Seton) **31**:259
"Johnny Pye and the Fool-Killer" (Benét) **7**:81, 84-5
"Johnsonham, Jr." (Dunbar) **2**:133
"La joie" (Verhaeren) **12**:469
La joie (Bernanos) **3**:118, 120-22, 124-25
Joie dans le ceil (Ramuz)
See *Terre du ciel*
Le joie de vivre (Zola) **41**:413, 451, 453
"La 'Joie de vivre' di Emile Zola" (Svevo) **35**:363
"Join Me in the Countryside" (Tzara)
See "Viens a la campagne avec moi"
Jókai Mór élete és kora (Mikszath) **31**:169, 171
The Joke and Its Relation to the Unconscious (Freud)
See *Der Wit und seine Beziehung zum Unbewussten*
"The Joker" (Brennan) **124**:7
"The 'Jola'" (Zamyatin) **8**:558
"La jolie rousse" (Apollinaire) **8**:13-14, 20, 28; **51**:10, 37, 61-2
"The Jolly Company" (Brooke) **2**:59; **7**:121
"The Jolly Corner" (James) **2**:262, 275; **11**:345
"The Jolly Dead March" (Lawson) **27**:139
A Jolly Fellowship (Stockton) **47**:316
"A Jolly Surprise for Henry" (Wakefield) **120**:354
"Jonah" (Jarrell) **177**:127, 152, 156
Jonah and the Whale (Bridie) **3**:136
Jonah's Gourd Vine (Hurston) **121**:341, 343, 347, 351-52, 354-56; **131**:57-59, 72-74, 76, 78, 83, 85-86, 90, 94, 96
"Jonan" (Kunikida Doppo) **99**:299, 303-04
Jónás Könyre (Babits) **14**:40, 42
Jonatans rejse (Hansen) **32**:248, 251, 256, 260
"Jonathan" (Heym) **9**:142, 148
"Jonathan and David" (Phelps) **113**:342
Jonathan Fisher: Maine Parson (Chase) **124**:20
Jonathan Swift (Murry) **16**:346, 357
"Jonathan Swift Somers" (Masters) **25**:314
Jonathan Troy (Abbey) **160**:56, 59-61
Jonathan's Journey (Hansen)
See *Jonatans rejse*
"Jones's Alley" (Lawson) **27**:130
"Jones's Karma" (Sinclair) **11**:421
"Joney" (Riley) **51**:292
"Le jongleur de Notre Dame" (France) **9**:47, 53
La jongleuse (Vallette) **67**:272, 281, 286, 292-302, 335-37
"Jordan's End" (Glasgow) **7**:342-44
"Jorden blev förvandlad till en askhög" (Södergran) **31**:285, 293
Jorges Luis Borges: Prosa Completa (Borges) **109**:77
Jørgine (Jensen) **41**:306, 308
Jornada en sonetos (Reyes) **33**:321
"Jornada régia" (Valle-Inclán) **5**:478
"El jorobadito" (Arlt) **29**:45-7
"A jóság dala" (Babits) **14**:39
José (Drummond de Andrade) **139**:230
José Antonio Paez (Graham) **19**:111
Joseph and His Brothers (Mann)
See *Joseph und seine Brüder*
Joseph and His Brothers (Rainis)
See *Jāzeps un vina brāli*
"Joseph and Mary" (Flecker) **43**:194
"Joseph Conrad" (Woolf) **43**:406
Joseph Conrad: A Personal Remembrance (Ford) **15**:73; **39**:120; **172**:12, 17, 53
Joseph der Ernährer (Mann) **2**:418, 421; **8**:271-72; **44**:146; **168**:170
Joseph Fouché (Zweig) **17**:427, 429, 445
Joseph Furphy (Franklin) **7**:268
Joseph in Ägypten (Mann)
See *Joseph und seine Brüder*
"A Joseph in Egypt" (Csáth) **13**:146, 149
Joseph in Egypt (Mann)
See *Joseph und seine Brüder*
Joseph Kerkhovens dritte Existenz (Wassermann) **6**:512, 518-19
Joseph Schur (Bergelson) **81**:30
Joseph the Provider (Mann)
See *Joseph der Ernährer*
Joseph und seine Brüder (Mann) **2**:418, 425, 433, 435; **8**:254, 257, 267-68, 271-72; **14**:331; **35**:217, 222; **44**:62-3, 165, 172, 174, 185, 188, 197, 202; **168**:113, 121-24, 126-29, 155, 170, 178
"Josephine, die Sängerin oder Das Volk der Mäuse" (Kafka) **2**:303, 305; **13**:276
"Josephine Encounters a Siren" (Aldrich) **125**:19
"Josephine the Chanteuse" (Kafka)
See "Josephine, die Sängerin oder Das Volk der Mäuse"
"Josephine, the Mouse" (Kafka)
See "Josephine, die Sängerin oder Das Volk der Mäuse"
"Josephine the Singer, or the Mouse Folk" (Kafka)
See "Josephine, die Sängerin oder Das Volk der Mäuse"
"Josephine the Songstress" (Kafka)
See "Josephine, die Sängerin oder Das Volk der Mäuse"
"Joseph's House" (Evans) **85**:28-9
Joseph's Sweetheart (Buchanan) **107**:31-32
Josephus (Feuchtwanger)
See *Der jüdische Krieg*
"Joshi no tettei shita bokuritsu" (Yosano) **59**:348
Joshua Craig (Phillips)
See *The Fashionable Adventures of Joshua Craig*
Joshua Haggard's Daughter (Braddon) **111**:248
Josiah Allen on the Woman Question (Holley) **99**:330
Josiah Allen's Wife as a P.A. and P.I.: Samantha at the Centennial (Holley) **99**:323, 336
"Jossel Bers and Jossel Schmaies" (Peretz) **16**:389
"Josua Qualen" (Liliencron) **18**:217
Les joues en feu (Radiguet) **29**:347, 349, 352, 355
Jounal (Cocteau) **119**:104
"Un jour" (Jammes) **75**:113, 117-18, 120
Jour de fete (Kandinsky) **92**:48
The Journal (Bennett) **197**:18, 20, 22, 25, 37-43, 65, 104, 107, 111, 125-28, 134, 172
Journal (Garneau) **13**:196-204
Journal, 1889-1939 (Gide) **5**:230, 234; **12**:164, 177; **177**:25-26, 28, 30, 51
Journal, 1912-1935 (Larbaud) **9**:200
"Journal 1920-1921" (Hesse) **196**:330-31
Journal, 1942-1949 (Gide) **5**:230, 234; **12**:164, 177
Journal à rebours (Colette) **5**:169
"Le journal de la Chambre" (Barrès) **47**:53
Le Journal d'En Route (Huysmans) **69**:15
Le journal des faux-monnayeurs (Gide) **5**:214; **12**:145, 149-50, 153-56, 158-59; **36**:86-7, 89-90, 95, 97-9, 101, 107, 110, 113, 116, 120
Journal du voleur (Genet) **128**:129, 131, 133, 158-59, 164, 198, 234
Journal d'un curé de campagne (Bernanos) **3**:118-20, 122-6, 128
"Journal d'un délicat" (Drieu la Rochelle) **21**:40
Journal d'un homme trompé (Drieu la Rochelle) **21**:40
Journal d'un inconnu (Cocteau) **119**:86-7
"Journal d'une apparition" (Desnos) **22**:62
Le journal d'une femme de chambre (Mirbeau) **55**:281-82, 285, 287-88, 295, 298-99, 310, 312-13
Journal intime (Loti) **11**:367
Journal intime (Sully Prudhomme) **31**:307-09
Journal litteraire (Léautaud) **83**:185-6, 190, 193, 195, 197, 206-7, 209
"Journal Night Thoughts" (Ginsberg) **120**:26
Journal of a Clerk (Tozzi)
See *Ricordi di un impiegato*
The Journal of a Disappointed Man (Barbellion) **24**:74-9, 81-92
Journal of a Novel (Steinbeck) **135**:284
Journal of a Solitude (Sarton) **120**:216-18, 228, 231, 233, 236-39, 247, 278-82, 284-85, 287, 289, 319-21, 326-27
Journal of a Vagabond (Hayashi)
See *Hōrōki*
The Journal of Arthur Stirling (Sinclair) **160**:276
The Journal of Charlotte L. Forten: A Free Negro in the Slave Era (Forten) **16**:145-48
The Journal of Gamaliel Bradford, 1883-1932 (Bradford) **36**:55-8, 69
"Journal of Henry Luxulyan" (Symons) **11**:436, 449
The Journal of Jules Renard (Renard) **17**:305-15, 317
Journal of Katherine Mansfield (Mansfield) **39**:325; **164**:250-51, 253, 257, 259, 261, 267, 275, 286

The Journal of My Other Self (Rilke) **19**:300-01, 305, 325
The Journal of Saint-Demy Garneau (Garneau)
See *Journal*
Journal of the Counterfeiters (Gide)
See *Le journal des faux-monnayeurs*
Journal of the Fictive Life (Nemerov) **124**:150-51, 153-54, 158, 160-62, 165, 168-70, 173-74, 244-45, 249, 251, 255, 258, 283, 291, 302-3
"Journalism for Women" (Bennett) **5**:46
Journals: Early Fifties, Early Sixties (Ginsberg) **120**:50
The Journals of André Gide, 1889-1939 (Gide) **5**:217, 219, 230, 234; **12**:157-59, 165; **36**:97, 107
The Journals of Arnold Bennett (Bennett) **5**:50-1
The Journals of Denton Welch (Welch)
See *The Denton Welch Journals*
Une journée parlementaire (Barrès) **47**:55
"Journées de lecture" (Proust) **7**:535-36
"The Journey" (Babel)
See "Doroga"
"The Journey" (Lewis) **3**:289
"Journey" (Millay) **4**:306
"A Journey" (Wharton) **3**:551, 555; **129**:360
Journey (Gilman) **117**:149
"The Journey Back" (Muir) **87**:167
Journey Continued (Paton) **165**:295, 298
"Journey Day" (Fletcher) **35**:107
The Journey Home (Abbey) **160**:3, 14, 20, 37-38, 41, 45-46, 50-51, 54, 56, 59, 69-70, 75, 83, 85, 88
Journey into Christmas and Other Stories (Aldrich) **125**:4, 10
"The Journey of Alija Djerzelez" (Andrić)
See "Put Alije Djerzeleza"
The Journey of Sir John Fairfax in Turkey and Other Remarkable Countries (Kuzmin) **40**:194
"The Journey of the King" (Dunsany) **59**:18
The Journey of the Soul (Dunsany) **59**:23
A Journey Round My Skull (Karinthy)
See *Utazás a koponyám körül*
"Journey to an Unknown Destination" (Tagore)
See "Niruddesh yatra"
A Journey to Faremido (Karinthy)
See *Utazás Faremidóba*
"The Journey to Hanford" (Saroyan) **137**:165
Journey to Jerusalem (Anderson) **2**:11; **144**:10, 34
Journey to Nowhere: A New World Tragedy (Naipaul)
See *Black and White*
A Journey to the Center of the Earth (Verne)
See *Voyage au centre de la terre*
Journey to the East (Hesse)
See *Die Morgenlandfahrt*
The Journey to the East (Hesse)
See *Die Morgenlandfahrt*
A Journey to the Moon (Verne)
See *Le Voyage dans la Lune*
Journey to the Morea (Kazantzakis) **5**:267-68
"Journey Toward America" (Sarton) **120**:263
"Journey toward Poetry" (Sarton) **120**:291
Journeying (Kazantzakis) **181**:324-26
"The Journeyman Baker" (Huysmans) **69**:25
Journeys and Places (Muir) **87**:180
Journey's End (Whale) **63**:339-41, 345, 378-80
Jours effeuillés: Poémes, essais, souvenirs, 1920-1965 (Arp) **115**:29-32, 34-6, 39-40, 45-50, 53, 55-6
Les jours et les nuits: Roman d'un déserter (Jarry) **14**:274, 278-82, 286-87; **147**:240, 262-63, 276-77, 296-99, 302-6, 309
The Jovial Imposters (Baroja)
See *Los impostores joviales*
"Joy" (Stephens) **4**:417
Joy (Bernanos)
See *La joie*
"Joy and Pleasure" (Rohan) **22**:296
"Joy in Russia" (Bely) **7**:50
"Joy in the House" (Wharton) **129**:364
Joy in the Morning (Wodehouse) **108**:335-6, 385, 388
Joy in the Sky (Ramuz)
See *Terre du ciel*
"The Joy of Apartment Living" (Chang)
See "Gongyu shenghuo jiqu"
"The Joy of Being Poor" (Service) **15**:402
The Joy of Life: An Anthology of Lyrics Drawn Chiefly from the Works of Living Poets (Lucas) **73**:158, 173
"The Joy of Little Things" (Service) **15**:402
The Joy of Living (Sudermann)
See *Es lebe das Leben!*
The Joy of Living (Wharton) **149**:158
"The Joy of the Spring Time" (Naidu) **80**:294
Joyce Cary: Selected Essays (Cary) **196**:196, 201
The Joyful Wisdom (Nietzsche)
See *Die Fröhliche Wissenschaft*
The Joyous Season (Barry) **11**:55-7, 60, 64-5, 67
"The Joys of the Road" (Carman) **7**:133
Joyū nana (Nagai) **51**:87
"Joyū nana kōgai" (Nagai) **51**:87
Joyzelle (Maeterlinck) **3**:323
Jozsi (Molnár) **20**:166
Ju lin Wai Shih (Liu) **15**:246
Ju to jujika (Endo) **152**:200
"Juan Darién" (Quiroga) **20**:213, 220, 222
"Juan Fiel" (Jiménez) **183**:291
Juan Martín el Empecinado (Pérez Galdós) **27**:256, 287
Juana (Kaiser) **9**:173, 179
Juana de Ashaje (Nervo) **11**:403
"Juanita" (Chopin) **127**:22-3
Juanita la larga (Valera y Alcala-Galiano) **10**:500-01, 507-09
"Jubal the Selfless" (Strindberg) **21**:367
"Jubilate" (Hardy) **53**:100
Jubilean (Mayakovski) **18**:244
Jubilee (Walker) **129**:269, 273, 277, 282-90, 298, 305, 307-12, 314-16, 318-21, 330
"Jubilee Year" (Mayakovski) **18**:258
"Jubilo" (Williams) **89**:386, 393, 401, 403
Jud Süss (Feuchtwanger) **3**:178-81, 186-87
"Judas" (Heym) **9**:142
"Judas and Jesus" (Ady) **11**:20
Les Judas de Jésus (Barbusse) **5**:18
Der Judas des Leonardo (Perutz) **60**:370
"Judas Iscariot" (Cullen) **37**:146, 154
Judas Iscariot and Others (Andreyev) **3**:25-6
"The Judas Tree" (Welch) **22**:441, 456
Judd Rankin's Daughter (Glaspell) **175**:59, 69
Jude the Obscure (Hardy) **4**:150, 153-54, 159-60, 165, 172, 176-77; **10**:217-23, 227-31; **18**:117; **32**:270, 274-81, 309-10; **48**:40, 46, 63-5, 67, 69, 71, 79; **53**:71, 74, 81, 83, 92, 96, 99, 102-03; **72**:157-289; **143**:73, 76, 79, 87-88, 108-9, 111, 125, 129-31, 134-37, 139-40, 143, 154-55, 166, 170, 174, 177-78, 195-96, 204, 213; **153**:103-4, 116, 122, 128
Juden auf Wanderschaft (Roth) **33**:336
Die Juden von Zirndorf (Wassermann) **6**:509-10, 513-14
Das Judengrab (Huch) **13**:248
Der Judenstaat, Versuch einer modernen Lösung der Judenfrage (Herzl) **36**:128-31, 135-38, 141-49, 155-58, 160
Judge for Yourself (Allen) **87**:11
Judge Priest Turns Detective (Cobb) **77**:134
Judge Sári (Moricz)
See *Sári bíró*
"The Judgement" (Kafka)
See "Das Urteil"
Judgement at Chelmsford (Williams) **1**:518; **11**:498
"The Judgement Day" (Johnson) **19**:207, 209; **175**:251-52, 254, 257
"Judgement Day" (O'Connor) **132**:229-32, 244, 271-73, 276
"The Judgement of Eve" (Sinclair) **3**:434, 440; **11**:408, 411
"The Judgement of God" (Remizov)
See "Sud Bozhii"
"Judges" (Evans) **85**:26-7
"The Judge's House" (Stoker) **8**:394
"The Judge's Wife" (Schnitzler)
See "Die Frau des Richters"
"The Judgment Day" (Johnson) **175**:251-52, 254, 257
"Judgment Day" (Korolenko) **22**:170
"Judgment Hour" (Adams) **56**:7-8
"Judgment Night" (Kuttner) **10**:276
"The Judgment of Dungara" (Kipling) **8**:185; **17**:205-06
"A Judgment of Paris" (Dunbar) **12**:120
"Judicieux dans le différend" (Lyotard) **103**:176
Jüdinnen (Brod) **115**:107-8, 115
Der jüdische Krieg (Feuchtwanger) **3**:178, 181, 183-85, 187
Die Jüdische Witwe (Kaiser) **9**:171, 173, 175, 179-81, 183, 185, 190
Judith (Bennett) **5**:32, 46; **197**:16, 18
Judith (Giraudoux) **2**:158, 161, 163, 165, 167, 172, 174; **7**:321-23, 328
Judith of Bethulia (Griffith) **68**:185, 213, 215-16, 218-21
Judith Paris (Walpole) **5**:500, 502
"Judy's Service of Gold Plate" (Norris) **24**:447
Juego peligroso (Villaurrutia) **80**:471, 475
Juego y teoría del duende (García Lorca) **181**:190
"Juegos" (García Lorca) **181**:178, 181, 183-84
Un juez rural (Prado) **75**:192-95, 204-05, 207-08, 210-11
"Jug blagoslovennyj" (Kuprin) **5**:303
"Jug of Silver" (Capote) **164**:100, 109-12, 115, 146
"A Jug of Syrup" (Bierce) **44**:6, 45
"Jugend" (Kraus) **5**:285
Die Jugend des königs Henri Quatre (Mann) **9**:317, 326
Eine jugend in Deutschland (Toller) **10**:478
Jugend ohne Gott (Horvath) **45**:75, 79, 83-7, 93-4, 103-04, 120
"Jugend und Theater" (Zuckmayer) **191**:288, 290-91
"Jugendschriften" (Nietzsche) **55**:389
"Jugendschutz" (Böll) **185**:50
The Juggler (Murfree) **135**:223
The Juggler (Vallette)
See *La jongleuse*
El juguete rabioso (Arlt) **29**:42, 45, 51-5
Juhana herttuan ja Catharina Jagellonican lauluja (Leino) **24**:371
"Juichigatsu mikka gogo no koto" (Shiga) **172**:202
"El juicio de Dios" (Güiraldes) **39**:176
"Le juif latin" (Apollinaire) **51**:20
La Juive (Crowley) **7**:211
"Juleaften" (Obstfelder) **23**:182, 188-89
"Julia" (Hellman) **119**:123-26, 130, 151-53, 189, 193-95
Julia Bride (James) **2**:275
"Julian at Eleusis" (Johnson) **19**:245
"Julian at Nicodemia" (Cavafy) **7**:158
Julian the Apostate (Merezhkovsky) **29**:225-27, 229-31, 233, 241, 247-48
Julie de Carneilhan (Colette) **5**:172
Juliette au pays des hommes (Giraudoux) **2**:165; **7**:325
Juliette in the Land of Men (Giraudoux)
See *Juliette au pays des hommes*
Julius Le Vallon (Blackwood) **5**:71-2, 77
"July" (Dobson) **79**:31, 36
"July Storm" (Platonov) **14**:413
"Jumalien keinu" (Leino) **24**:377
Jumbo (Hecht) **101**:63
"The Junction, on a Warm Afternoon" (Nemerov) **124**:182
"June" (Riley) **51**:300
"June in Paradise" (Alexandre) **113**:55

June Moon (Lardner) **2**:339; **14**:294, 307, 313
"June Rains" (Nezval) **44**:241
"A June Song" (Stringer) **37**:328
"June Sunset" (Naidu) **80**:272, 280, 295
Der junge David (Beer-Hofmann) **60**:27-8, 30, 33
Der Junge Joseph (Mann) **2**:418; **8**:271-72
Der junge Medardus (Schnitzler) **4**:386, 389
Jungenderrinnerungen und Bekenntnisse (Heyse) **8**:120, 122-23
Die Jungfern vom Bischofsberg (Hauptmann) **4**:196
Die Jungfrau auf dem Dach (Zuckmayer) **191**:305
"Jungfruns död" (Södergran) **31**:291
"The Jungle" (Bowen) **148**:83-84, 91
"The Jungle" (Lewis) **3**:286-87, 290
The Jungle (Sinclair) **160**:223-98
"The Jungle and the Sea" (Aleixandre) **113**:41
The Jungle Books (Kipling) **8**:178, 186, 196-97, 200-01, 205, 208; **17**:202, 203
Jungle Tales of Tarzan (Burroughs) **32**:62, 75
"Das jüngste Gericht" (Rilke) **195**:181
Der jüngste Tag (Horvath) **45**:78, 102, 112
"Jūnigatsu yōka" (Dazai Osamu) **11**:176
The Junius Pamphlet (Luxemburg)
See *Juniusbroschure*
Juniusbroschure (Luxemburg) **63**:165, 176, 202, 227
Junjo shokyoku shu (Hagiwara) **60**:315
"Junk in the Basement" (Shepherd) **177**:316
"Junk Mail" (Ginsberg) **120**:36
Junkie: The Confessions of an Unredeemed Drug Addict (Burroughs) **121**:118-19, 123-24, 174-82
Junky (Burroughs)
See *Junkie: The Confessions of an Unredeemed Drug Addict*
"Juno's Lover" (Khlebnikov)
See "Lyubovnik yunony"
"Junsui Shōsetsu Ron" (Yokomitsu) **47**:394
Junta cádaveres (Onetti) **131**:133, 146, 149, 151-53, 157, 162-63, 215-16, 218-19, 245-46, 248-49, 286
Junta de sombras (Reyes) **33**:323
Junta, the Body Snatcher (Onetti)
See *Junta cádaveres*
"Jupiter Doke, Brigadier-General" (Bierce) **44**:44-5
Jupiter poveržennyi (Bryusov) **10**:85
Jupiter's Thunderbolts (Melies) **81**:122
"Jure" (Cankar) **105**:158
Jürg Reinhart (Frisch) **121**:211
Jurgen (Cabell) **6**:62-3, 65-75, 77
Jurie Steyn's Post Office (Bosman) **49**:8, 13-14, 17
"Jurisprudence" (Cardozo) **65**:35, 37, 39
"A Jury of Her Peers" (Glaspell) **55**:250-51, 254-55, 262-64, 266; **175**:59, 61, 69, 117, 124-25, 127-32, 134, 138
"Jus primae noctis" (van Ostaijen) **33**:407
"Just a Good Man" (Runyon) **10**:429
"Just a Little One" (Parker) **143**:331
Just a Little Simple (Childress) **116**:50-1, 53-4
Just Ask For George (Callaghan) **145**:232
"Just Before Dawn" (Fields) **80**:255, 259
"Just Checking Your Summer Recordings" (Burroughs) **121**:139
Just Gaming (Lyotard)
See *Au juste*
Just Glad Things (Guest) **95**:211
"Just like Little Dogs" (Thomas) **8**:463; **45**:392; **105**:302, 341, 345-46
"A Just Man in Sodom" (Evans) **85**:34
"The Just of Droom Avista" (Kuttner) **10**:267
Just So Stories (Kipling) **8**:194-95, 200
Just the Other Day (Collier) **127**:241, 243
The Just Vengeance (Sayers) **15**:382, 387-88
Just Yesterday (Agnon) **151**:45, 52
"La justa proporción de las cosas" (Quiroga) **20**:211
"Justice" (Bryan) **99**:6, 34
"A Justice" (Faulkner) **170**:110, 138
Justice (Bromfield) **11**:81
Justice (Galsworthy) **1**:301, 303, 305; **45**:30-2, 48, 51-5
La justice (Sully Prudhomme) **31**:300, 302, 304, 306-07
Justice and Smile (Dazai Osamu)
See *Seigi to bishō*
"Justice Denied in Massachusetts" (Millay) **169**:265-68, 296
Justice Denied in Massachusetts (Millay) **4**:316, 321
"Justice in Parentheses" (Babel)
See "Spravidlivost' v skobkakh"
"Justice in Quotation Marks" (Babel)
See "Spravidlivost' v skobkakh"
The Justice of the Duke (Sabatini) **47**:303
"¿Justicia?" (Pardo Bazán) **189**:226-27
Le justicier (Bourget) **12**:69
"Justo José" (Güiraldes) **39**:190
Juudit (Tammsaare) **27**:373, 377-79
"Juvenilia" (Nietzsche)
See "Jugendschriften"
Juvenilia (Carducci) **32**:86, 99-100, 108
Juvenilia (Lee) **5**:311, 315
Juvenilia (Tsvetaeva)
See *Yunosheskie stikhi*
"Juvenile Protection" (Böll)
See "Jugendschutz"
"Juventud" (Aleixandre) **113**:3
Juventud (Pardo Bazán) **189**:199
Juventud, egolatría (Baroja) **8**:63
"Južnoslavjanska solidarnost" (Vazov) **25**:455
"Juzovskij zavod" (Kuprin) **5**:302
"K" (Khlebnikov) **20**:149-50
"K" (Rinehart) **52**:281, 283, 288, 295
"K bol'šoj medvedice" (Bryusov) **10**:82
"K filosofii postupka" (Bakhtin) **160**:143-45, 148, 152-53, 155-60, 186-87, 207, 215
K. P. Kavafes: Anekdota peza keimena (Cavafy) **7**:162
"K samomu sobe" (Bryusov) **10**:96
"K sčastlivym" (Bryusov) **10**:93
K sinei zvezde (Gumilev) **60**:260, 262, 273, 275
K zvezdam (Andreyev) **3**:19-20
Ka (Khlebnikov) **20**:127, 136, 141-43
"Ka no yō ni" (Mori Ogai) **14**:379-80
"Kaa's Hunting" (Kipling) **8**:205
"Kabala práctica" (Lugones) **15**:293
Kabala sviatosh (Bulgakov) **2**:65; **16**:76, 96-7; **159**:5, 8, 132, 138-39, 163
"Kabar dari laut" (Anwar) **22**:22
Das Kabinett des Dr. Caligari (Wiene) **56**:326-55
"Kabnis" (Toomer) **172**:258-60, 274, 285, 287, 296-300, 303, 314, 318-20, 330-31, 335, 339
"Kaddish" (Ginsberg) **120**:4, 10, 12, 15, 25, 31-2, 48, 50, 54, 56, 71, 74-5, 77, 82-7, 89, 95, 105, 108-10, 114-21, 128
Kaddish, and Other Poems (Ginsberg) **120**:22, 82, 85
"Kaeru no shi" (Hagiwara) **60**:311
"Kaeru yo" (Hagiwara) **60**:313
Kafan (Premchand) **21**:293
"Der Kaffee ist undefinierbar" (Borchert) **5**:108-09
"Käfig" (Kandinsky) **92**:67
"The Kafir Drum" (Bosman) **49**:4, 29
Kafka (Deleuze)
See *Kafka: Pour une littérature mineure*
Kafka als Wegweisende Gestalt (Brod) **115**:87
"Kafka and His Precursors" (Borges)
See "Los precursores de Kafka"
Kafka: Pour une littérature mineure (Deleuze) **116**:77-8, 86-7
Kafka: Toward a Minor Literature (Deleuze)
See *Kafka: Pour une littérature mineure*
"Kafka y sus precursores" (Borges)
See "Los precursores de Kafka"
Kafka's Other Trial (Canetti)
See *Der andere Prozeß*
A Kafū Anthology (Nagai)
See *Kafū shū*
Kafū shū (Nagai) **51**:101
"Kageboshi" (Endo) **152**:208, 240
Kai Lung Beneath the Mulberry Tree (Bramah) **72**:7, 9, 11
The Kai Lung Omnibus (Bramah) **72**:7
Kai Lung Unrolls His Mat (Bramah) **72**:7, 9-11
Kai Lung's Golden Hours (Bramah) **72**:4, 7, 9-10
"Kaijin" (Mori Ogai) **14**:383
"Kaika no satsujin" (Akutagawa Ryūnosuke) **16**:36
Kains alter (Hansen) **32**:251
Kairokō (Natsume) **10**:329, 344
The Kaiser and English Relations (Benson) **27**:10
"Der Kaiser und die Hexe" (Hofmannsthal) **11**:292
Das Kaiserreich (Mann) **9**:319-20, 325, 327
"Kak delat' stikhi?" (Mayakovski) **18**:243
"Kak eto delalos v Odesse" (Babel) **13**:34; **171**:7-11, 50-53, 56-57, 78, 97-101, 103, 105-7
"Kak tsarstvo belogo snega" (Bryusov) **10**:96
"Kak vo logočke" (Khlebnikov) **20**:147
Kak voorzhalas Revolyutsiya (Trotsky) **22**:364
Kakekomi uttae (Dazai Osamu) **11**:176
Kaki (Hayashi) **27**:105
Kaki no ha (Santoka) **72**:414, 418
"Kako" (Shiga) **172**:202, 214
"Kakspaari ja üksainus" (Tammsaare) **27**:369, 373
"Kalechina-Malechina" (Remizov) **27**:351
"Kaleva" (Leino) **24**:376
"Kâli décapitée" (Yourcenar) **193**:295
"Kali the Mother" (Naidu) **80**:316
Kalkhas (Chekhov) **96**:60
Das Kalkwerk (Bernhard) **165**:11, 30, 33-35, 79, 97, 99, 101-2, 108, 116-17, 130
Kallmunz (Kandinsky) **92**:49
"The Kallyope Yell" (Lindsay) **17**:230, 237, 244
"Kalnā kāpējs" (Rainis) **29**:380
Die Kälte (Bernhard)
See *Die Kälte: Eine Isolation*
Die Kälte: Eine Isolation (Bernhard) **165**:11-12
Das kalte Licht (Zuckmayer) **191**:284-86, 288-89, 298, 305-06, 327
Kamakura (Noguchi) **80**:380
"Kamen'" (Gumilev) **60**:279
Kamen' (Mandelstam) **2**:401, 403, 406-09; **6**:257, 259, 262, 265-66
Kamen (Mori Ogai) **14**:371-72, 383
Kamen no kokuhaku (Mishima) **161**:7-8, 11, 13-14, 16-17, 29, 32-37, 41-42, 46-51, 59-60, 62-65, 95, 99, 101, 108-17, 119
"Kamennaya baba" (Khlebnikov) **20**:132
Kamera Obskura (Nabokov) **108**:60, 62-3, 65, 73, 83-147, 171, 179; **189**:14
Kameradschaft (Pabst) **127**:338, 348, 354-55, 359-60, 368-72
"Kami no tsuru" (Dazai Osamu) **11**:178
Kamienny swiat (Borowski) **9**:22-5
"Kamigami no bisho" (Endo) **152**:196
"Kamigami to kami to" (Endo) **152**:167-68, 170, 239
Kaminingyo haru no sayaki (Mizoguchi) **72**:322
"Kamisori" (Shiga) **172**:203
"Kamizelka" (Prus) **48**:161, 172, 176
Der Kammersänger (Wedekind) **7**:585
Kammersymphonie (Schoenberg) **75**:292
Kämpande ande (Lagerkvist) **144**:213
Der Kampf um den Entwickelungs—Gedanken (Haeckel) **83**:147
"Der Kampf um Rom" (Huch) **13**:253
Kamraterna (Strindberg) **1**:447-48, 453; **8**:406; **47**:364
"Kamyk" (Herbert) **168**:16
"Kan speilet tale?" (Obstfelder) **23**:177, 187
"The Kanaka Surf" (London) **9**:267
"Kanashi Tsukio" (Hagiwara) **60**:292

Kanashiki gangu (Ishikawa) **15**:125-27, 132
Kanashimi no Daika (Yokomitsu) **47**:394-95
Kanga Creek: An Australian Idyll (Ellis) **14**:113, 127
Kangaroo (Lawrence) **2**:371; **9**:217; **33**:184, 202, 205; **48**:102, 117; **93**:33, 58, 97
Kangaroo Notebook (Abe) **131**:14-15
Kangastuksia (Leino) **24**:368-69
"Kangokusho no ura" (Nagai) **51**:88, 101
"Kanhaya" (Naidu) **80**:316
"Kankaku-Katsudô" (Yokomitsu) **47**:387, 390
"Kankal" (Tagore) **53**:354
"Kanraku" (Nagai) **51**:88, 100-01
Kanraku (Nagai) **51**:88, 101-02
"Kansas" (Becker) **63**:63-4, 113
"Kant. Ostatnie dni" (Herbert) **168**:39
"Kant. The Last Days" (Herbert)
See "Kant. Ostatnie dni"
Kantisch-Friessche Religionsphilosophie (Otto) **85**:315, 339
"Kanto rinrigaku" (Nishida) **83**:220, 235
"Kant's Ethics" (Nishida)
See "Kanto rinrigaku"
"Kant's Philosophy and the Enlightenment" (Horkheimer) **132**:209
"Kanzan jittoku" (Mori Ogai) **14**:384
Kanzlist Krahler (Kaiser) **9**:173-74, 191
Kaos (Lagerkvist) **144**:182, 210, 230
"Kapetan Elia" (Kazantzakis) **33**:155
Ho kapetan Michales (Kazantzakis) **2**:318-20; **5**:260, 262-63, 268; **33**:146-48, 150, 155, 163-64; **181**:281-82, 285, 288-89, 291, 329
"Das Kapitäl" (Rilke) **195**:231
"Kapitany" (Gumilev) **60**:278
"Kaplja i pylinka" (Sologub) **9**:448
Kappa (Akutagawa Ryūnosuke) **16**:18, 28, 36
Kaptejn Mansana (Bjoernson) **7**:104, 116
"Kapuanska dolina" (Vazov) **25**:458
Kaputt (Malaparte) **52**:264, 266-68, 271-75
Die Kapuzinergruft (Roth) **33**:338-40, 352-54, 363
Karácsonyi Madonna (Babits) **14**:40
"Kārairu hakubutsukan" (Natsume) **10**:344
"Karanje Village" (Lewis) **3**:289-90
"Karawane" (Ball) **104**:13-15, 18
"Der Kardinal Napellus" (Meyrink) **21**:232
"Kardinal' nye voprosy" (Olesha) **136**:183
"Karel Čapek about Himself" (Čapek) **192**:234
"Karen" (Kielland) **5**:278
"Karenoshō" (Akutagawa Ryūnosuke) **16**:23, 34
Kari o komal (Tagore) **3**:490
"Karintha" (Toomer) **172**:255-56, 274, 283, 285, 310, 327-28, 335
"Karjalan kannas" (Leino) **24**:371
Karjalan kuningas (Leino) **24**:372
Karl den XII:s levnad (Bengtsson) **48**:2, 5-6, 8-12
"Karl Jaspers: Citizen of the World" (Arendt) **193**:39
"Karl Kraus: The School of Resistance" (Canetti) **157**:63
Karl Ludwig's Window (Saki) **3**:376
Karl Marx (Berlin) **105**:2, 6
"Karl Marx: Das Kapital" (Hesse) **148**:181
"Kärlek" (Södergran) **31**:284, 290
Karleken och Aktenskapet (Key) **65**:242
"Karl-Yankel" (Babel) **13**:34; **171**:11
"Karma" (Lasker-Schueler) **57**:329, 330
Karmabhumi (Premchand) **21**:283-86
Karolinerna (Heidenstam) **5**:250-56
"Karos, the God" (Upward) **85**:387
Kártyavár (Babits) **14**:40, 42
Kashcheeva Tsep' (Prishvin) **75**:214-17, 220-21
"Kashima no onna" (Nagai) **51**:96
Kasimir und Karoline (Horvath) **45**:77, 81, 83, 88-90, 96-100, 106, 108-10, 112-16
Kāśīnāth (Chatterji) **13**:80
"Kaspar Hauser" (Lang) **16**:254
"kaspar is dead" (Arp)
See "kaspar ist tot"
"kaspar ist tot" (Arp) **115**:5-8, 10, 20-1, 28, 34
"Kasrilevker Srayfes" (Aleichem) **35**:315
"Kasrilevker Tramvay" (Aleichem) **35**:315
"Kassandra Prophesies" (Bottomley) **107**:5
Die Kassette (Sternheim) **8**:370, 374, 378-79
"Katánghy levelei" (Mikszath) **31**:169
"Katánghy's Letters" (Mikszath)
See "Katánghy levelei"
Katarina av Siena (Undset)
See *Catarina av Siena*
"Katarynka" (Prus) **48**:156, 161, 176
"Katastrofa" (Nabokov) **108**:210
Kate Bonnet (Stockton) **47**:322-23, 325
A Kate Chopin Miscellany (Chopin) **127**:126-28, 192
Kate Fennigate (Tarkington) **9**:469
Katei no kōfuku (Dazai Osamu) **11**:176
Katharina Knie (Zuckmayer) **191**:296, 321
Katharine Lauderdale (Crawford) **10**:146, 148-50, 153, 155
"Die Kathedrale" (Rilke) **195**:231
Katherine Christian (Walpole) **5**:502
Katherine Mansfield, and Other Literary Studies (Murry) **16**:341, 356-57
The Katherine Mansfield Notebooks (Mansfield) **164**:339-40
Katherine Mansfield: Short Stories (Mansfield) **39**:310
Katherine Mansfield's Letters to John Middleton Murry, 1913-22 (Mansfield) **164**:280
"Kathleen" (Morley) **87**:120, 124
Kathy Goes to Haiti (Acker) **191**:45-7, 49, 71-2, 129
"Katisje's Patchwork Dress" (Smith) **25**:390
"Katorikku sakka no mondai" (Endo) **152**:232
"Katzen und Pfauen" (Ball) **104**:13-14, 18
Der Katzensteg (Sudermann) **15**:423-24, 427, 430, 433, 437-38
Der kaukasische Kreidekreis (Brecht) **1**:100-01, 104-05, 107-09, 113, 116-18; **6**:32, 37; **35**:5, 18
"Kawagiri" (Kunikida Doppo) **99**:293, 299, 302-04
"Kaw-Liga" (Williams) **81**:419,423
Kayakalp (Premchand) **21**:283-84, 286
"Kayar" (Premchand) **21**:289, 291, 294
Kazaki (Tolstoy) **173**:280, 295
Kazalarskata carica (Vazov) **25**:453, 455, 457
Kazan (Endo) **152**:176-77, 190, 198, 213, 215, 237
"Kazennaia dacha" (Remizov) **27**:340
Kdo jsem (Hrabal) **155**:155
"Keats" (Stringer) **37**:342
Keats and Shakespeare: A Study of Keats' Poetic Life from 1816 to 1820 (Murry) **16**:334, 350, 355
"Keen" (Millay) **49**:215
"Keep a Pluggin' Away" (Dunbar) **12**:110
"Keep Going Down That Road, Mate!" (Calvino)
See "Va' cosí che vi bene"
"Keep Innocency" (de la Mare) **4**:73
Keep the Aspidistra Flying (Orwell) **2**:502-05, 509-11; **6**:342, 348, 350-52; **31**:191, 199; **51**:241, 247, 249, 254, 265;66; **128**:255-56, 262, 264-65,267-69, 271, 276-77, 291, 294-95, 298, 204; **129**:225, 239, 242, 245, 248
The Keeper of the Bees (Porter) **21**:274, 276
"A Keeper of the Doors" (Evans) **85**:21,26
Keeper of the Keys (Biggers) **65**:4, 8, 16
"Keeping His Promise" (Blackwood) **5**:79
"Keeping Informed in D.C." (Nemerov) **124**:162, 171
Keeping Up Appearances (Macaulay) **7**:430; **44**:122, 125
"Keesh, the Son of Keesh" (London) **9**:274
"Die Kegelbahn" (Borchert) **5**:109
"Keine Delikatessen" (Bachmann) **192**:53, 67
Keith Douglas: A Prose Miscellany (Douglas) **40**:94
Kejser og Galilaeer (Ibsen) **8**:149-50, 155; **16**:189
"Kelev Meshuga" (Agnon) **151**:36
Der Keller (Bernhard) **165**:57-58, 60, 106
"The Kelpie Riders" (Carman) **7**:135, 138
The Kempton-Wace Letters (London) **9**:264-65; **39**:262
"Ken" (Mew) **8**:295
"The Kenju Wood" (Miyazawa) **76**:277
The Kennel Murder Case (Van Dine) **23**:360
"Las kenningar" (Borges) **109**:14
"Kenny" (Bromfield) **11**:83
"Kensaku no tsuioku" (Shiga) **172**:215
"Kensaku's Reminiscences" (Shiga)
See "Kensaku no tsuioku"
Kensington Rhymes (Mackenzie) **116**:206
The Kentons (Howells) **7**:372-73, 375; **17**:185
The Kentucky Trace (Arnow) **196**:29, 38-9, 95, 98-102
"Kenya's Kikuyu: A Peaceful People Wage Struggle Against the British" (Hansberry) **192**:278
"Kepada kawan" (Anwar) **22**:23
"Kepada pluki's Affandi" (Anwar) **22**:22, 25
Le képi (Colette) **16**:121, 129
The Képi (Colette)
See *Le képi*
"Kept-the-Faith" (Bryan) **99**:84
"Képzeletbeli miniszterek" (Mikszath) **31**:173
"The Kerchief" (Quiller-Couch) **53**:292
Kerek Ferkó (Moricz) **33**:238
Keresztülkasul az életemen (Babits) **14**:41
"Kerfol" (Wharton) **9**:547; **129**:362, 364-65
Kerikil tadjam dan jang terampas dan jang putus (Anwar) **22**:18
Kerkhoven's Third Existence (Wassermann)
See *Joseph Kerkhovens dritte Existenz*
"La Kermesse de Rubens" (Huysmans) **69**:8
The Kernel and the Husk (Abbott) **139**:11-15, 26, 32-34, 40
"Kerry" (Pickthall) **21**:252
"Kerry's Kid" (Rohmer) **28**:282
"Kesabaran" (Anwar) **22**:24
"Keskiyön kuoro" (Leino) **24**:371
A két koldusdiák (Mikszath) **31**:168
Két választás Magyarországon (Mikszath) **31**:172-73
"Ketchup Making Saturday" (Arnow) **196**:91, 93
"Kettle Song" (Gurney) **33**:98
Der Ketzer von Soana (Hauptmann) **4**:198, 204
"Kew Gardens" (Woolf) **56**:359; **128**:371
Kew Gardens (Woolf) **20**:397; **128**:327
"The Key" (Malamud) **129**:74
"The Key" (Millay) **169**:234
The Key (Aldanov)
See *Ključ*
Key Largo (Anderson) **2**:5-7, 10; **144**:5, 10, 18, 20-24, 36, 38, 51-53, 56
"Key of Mysteries" (Bryusov) **10**:87
"The Key of the Field" (Powys) **9**:366
"The Key to Grief" (Chambers) **41**:102
"Key to Health" (Gandhi) **59**:51
"Key West: An Island Sheaf" (Crane) **2**:117, 121; **5**:189; **80**:139
Key-Escape-Cave (Aldanov) **23**:24
"The Keys of the Church" (Yourcenar)
See "Les Clefs de l'église"
The Keys of the Kingdom (Strindberg) **1**:448
Keys to Heaven (Strindberg) **8**:413
"The Keys to the Gate" (Frye) **165**:165
"Khadzhi-Tarkhan" (Khlebnikov) **20**:131
"Khadzi murat" (Tolstoy) **4**:482-83; **11**:463-64, 469
"Khalani maZulu" (Vilakazi) **37**:402, 407
Khaled: A Tale of Arabia (Crawford) **10**:143-44, 146, 148, 151, 157-58
"Khanike-gelt" (Aleichem) **35**:312, 319
"Khansky polon" (Tsvetaeva) **35**:403-04, 411
"Khat" (Dreiser) **35**:71
Kheya (Tagore) **53**:341
"Khleb" (Tolstoy) **18**:363, 372, 374-75
Kholstomér (Tolstoy) **11**:464

Khorovod vremën: Vseglasnost' (Balmont) **11**:37
Khozyain i rabotnik (Tolstoy) **4**:476, 483; **11**:463, 469, 471; **79**:374, 446
"Khvala Afrodite" (Tsvetaeva) **7**:560; **35**:411
Ki kérdezett? (Karinthy) **47**:269
Ki látott engem? (Ady) **11**:18, 23
"Kicking Off the Combined Federal Campaign, October 11, 1988" (Nemerov) **124**:305
"The Kicking Twelfth" (Crane) **11**:140
"Kicks" (Nemerov) **124**:227
"Kiddie-Kar Travel" (Benchley) **55**:3, 13, 17
The Kidnap Murder Case (Van Dine) **23**:360
"Kidnappers" (Yeats) **11**:538
"The Kidnapping" (Shiga)
See "Ko o nusumu hanashi"
"Kienast" (Walser) **18**:437
Kievskie tipy (Kuprin) **5**:302, 304
Kif (Tey) **14**:460-61
Kiiroi hito (Endo) **152**:167, 176, 198, 214-15, 234, 237, 239
"Kikai" (Yokomitsu) **47**:391, 393, 397-98
Kikyōrai (Dazai Osamu) **11**:191
"Kildharn's Oak" (Hawthorne) **25**:235
"The Kilikov Trial or a Life for a Life" (Agnon) **151**:73, 77-79
"Killed at Resaca" (Bierce) **44**:8, 12, 44-5, 47
"Killer in the Rain" (Chandler) **7**:176, 183; **179**:73, 121-23, 125
Killer in the Rain (Chandler) **179**:122, 124-26, 128, 158
"The Killers" (Hemingway) **115**:143
Killer's Kiss (Kubrick) **112**:134, 188, 235, 262, 266
"Killing" (Söderberg) **39**:437
The Killing (Kubrick) **112**:127, 134, 188, 225, 262, 267, 269, 282
"Killing His Bear" (Crane) **11**:163
"The Killing of Julius Caesar" (Twain) **12**:425
"The Killing of Julius Caesar 'Localized'" (Twain) **161**:241, 248
Kilmeny of the Orchard (Montgomery) **140**:319
"Kilns" (Gurney) **33**:87
The Kiltartan History Book (Gregory) **176**:43, 50
The Kiltartan Poetry Book: Prose Translations from the Irish (Gregory) **176**:43
The Kiltartan Wonder Book (Gregory) **176**:50, 52
Kim (Kipling) **8**:180, 185-86, 188, 192, 197, 199, 201, 204-06, 208; **17**:208, 209, 211-13
"Kimi Shinitamô koto nakare" (Yosano) **59**:331-4, 336-9
"Kimmo's Revenge" (Leino) **24**:376
"Kimono" (Merrill) **173**:210
"Kimura Sakae-kun no omoide" (Nishida) **83**:215
"Kin to Sorrow" (Millay) **49**:201
Kincaid's Battery (Cable) **4**:27, 29, 31
Kincora (Gregory) **1**:334; **176**:9, 11, 37, 39, 81-84
"Das Kind" (Beer-Hofmann) **60**:24-6
"Kind and Gentle Moonlight" (Andrić) **135**:78
"The Kind Ghosts" (Owen) **5**:363, 371-72, 374
"A Kind of Story" (Walser) **18**:432
Ein Kind unserer Zeit (Horvath) **45**:75, 78-9, 83, 85-8, 93, 102-04, 113-15
Kindai nogakushu (Mishima) **161**:51
Die kinder Abrahams: Novellen aus America (Asch) **3**:69
Kinder Brauchen Märchen (Bettelheim) **143**:10
Kinder der welt (Heyse) **8**:155-17, 119
"Der Kinder Sünde, der Väter Fluch" (Heyse) **8**:113
Die Kinder von Finkenrode (Raabe) **45**:171, 182, 200, 203
Eine Kindheit (Carossa) **48**:16-20, 27, 29-30, 34
"Kindliness" (Brooke) **2**:54
Kindness in a Corner (Powys) **9**:366-67
The Kindred of the Wild (Roberts) **8**:315
The Kindred of the Wild: A Book of Animal Life (Roberts)
See *The Kindred of the Wild*
Kinds of Love (Sarton) **120**:199, 212-14, 219-20, 222, 227, 231-35, 237, 239, 242, 278, 305-06, 309-10
The Kinds of Poetry (Erskine) **84**:160
"Kinds of Rationalism" (Hayek) **109**:204, 207
Kindui nogaku shu (Mishima)
See *Kindai nogakushu*
"The King" (Babel)
See "Korol'"
"The King" (Grieg)
See "Kongen"
"The King" (Kipling) **17**:197
The King (Bjoernson)
See *Kongen*
The King (Lagerkvist)
See *Konungen*
King Alfred and the Neat-Herd (Baring) **8**:32
A King and a Few Dukes (Chambers) **41**:88
The King and the Queen (Sender)
See *El rey y la reina*
King Argimenes and the Unknown Warrior (Dunsany) **2**:137, 139, 142-43; **59**:6-7, 9-10
King Arthur (Pyle)
See *The Story of King Arthur and His Knights*
"King Arthur's Men Have Come Again" (Lindsay) **17**:242
"King Christmas" (Lee-Hamilton) **22**:191
King Coal (Sinclair) **160**:234
"King Cophetua's Queen" (Tynan) **3**:503
"King David" (Benét) **7**:78-9
"King David in His Tomb" (Bialik) **25**:66
"King Devil's Bargain" (Arnow) **196**:91, 93
King Duffus and Other Poems (Warner) **131**:310-11
"King Essarhadon" (Tolstoy) **11**:463
"King George the Fourth" (Beerbohm) **24**:109
King Haber (Neumann) **100**:315
King Hunger (Andreyev) **3**:20-1, 26
The King in the Golden Mask, and Other Writings (Schwob)
See *Le roi au masque d'or, et autres nouvelles*
The King in the Square (Blok)
See *Korol na ploshchadi*
"The King in Yellow" (Chandler) **179**:127-29
The King in Yellow (Chambers) **41**:87-90, 94, 101-02, 104, 107-08, 113-14
King Jasper (Robinson) **101**:105, 107, 128, 134, 184-85, 188
King John of Jingalo (Housman) **7**:353
"King John's Christmas" (Milne) **6**:314
King Kull (Howard) **8**:136
"King Lear" (Swinburne) **36**:309
King Lear's Wife (Bottomley) **107**:3-5
King Leopold's Soliloquy (Twain) **6**:477; **12**:436
"A King Listening" (Calvino)
See "Un re in ascolto"
The King Maiden (Tsvetaeva)
See *Tsar-devitsa*
King Maximilian (Remizov) **27**:335
King Midas: A Romance (Sinclair)
See *Springtime and Harvest: A Romance*
King Nicolo; or, Such is Life; Such is Life (Wedekind)
See *König Nicolo; oder, So ist das Leben*
The King of Alsander (Flecker) **43**:193, 210, 216-17
The King of Elfland's Daughter (Dunsany) **59**:4-5, 17, 21-2, 25
The King of Folly Island and Other People (Jewett) **22**:145, 147-48
"The King of Harlem" (Undset)
See "El rey de Harlem"
The King of Karelia (Leino)
See *Karjalan kuningas*
"The King of Mamozekel" (Roberts) **8**:323
King of May (Ginsberg) **120**:41
The King of Schnorrers: Grotesques and Fantasies (Zangwill) **16**:442, 444-45, 447-49, 455-57, 462-64, 467
The King of Spain (Bodenheim) **44**:71
King of the Ants (Herbert) **168**:40-41
King of the Beggars, a Life of Daniel O'Connell (O'Faolain) **143**:222, 230, 232-33, 269, 272
"The King of the Cats" (Benét) **7**:81
King of the Delta Blues Singers (Johnson) **69**:94
King of the Delta Blues Singers: Volume II (Johnson) **69**:94
The King of the Golden Isles (Dunsany) **59**:13
The King of the Great Clock Tower (Yeats) **11**:514; **116**:331-32
"The King of the World" (Coppard) **5**:175-76
"The King of Ys" (Carman) **7**:138
King, Queen, Knave (Nabokov)
See *Korol, dama, valet*
"King Solomon" (Remizov)
See "Tsar' Solomon"
"King Solomon and the Queen of Sheba" (Lindsay) **17**:225
King Solomon's Mines (Haggard) **11**:237-38, 241-47, 249-52, 254, 256-57
King Sverre (Bjoernson)
See *Kong Sverre*
"The King That Was Not" (Dunsany) **59**:18
The King Was in His Counting House (Cabell) **6**:76-7
The King with Two Faces (Coleridge) **73**:7, 10, 12, 22-3, 27
"The Kingbird" (Seton) **31**:267
The Kingdom Come (George)
See *Das Neue Reich*
"Kingdom County Come" (Mosher) **131**:309, 312, 317, 322, 332, 340, 346, 360, 365
"The Kingdom of All-Souls" (Woodberry) **73**:363
The Kingdom of All-Souls, and Two Other Poems (Woodberry) **73**:363
"The Kingdom of Cards" (Tagore) **3**:485
The Kingdom of God (Martinez Sierra and Martinez Sierra)
See *El reino de Dios*
The Kingdom of God and the Son of Man (Otto) **85**:320
"The Kingdom of Heaven Is within Us" (Tolstoy) **11**:463; **79**:336-7, 412, 427
The Kingdom of the Blind (Oppenheim) **45**:134-35
The Kingdom of the Fairies (Melies)
See *Fairyland: Or, the Kingdom of the Fairies*
"The Kingfisher" (Davies) **5**:203
"The Kings" (Guiney) **41**:204, 207-08, 221-22
"Kings" (Quiroga)
See "Reyes"
Kings and the Moon (Stephens) **4**:416-17, 420
Kings before the Flood (Arp) **115**:23
The King's Breakfast (Milne) **6**:309; **88**:241
"The King's Daughter" (Swinburne) **36**:299
"The King's Favor" (Crane) **11**:167
The King's Flute (Palamas)
See *He phlogéra tou basilá*
The King's Henchman (Millay) **4**:310-14, 318
The King's Indian (Gardner) **195**:105
"The King's Messenger" (Crawford) **10**:158
The King's Minion (Sabatini) **47**:306
The King's Mirror (Hope) **83**:170
Kings of England: A History for Young Children (Yonge) **48**:369
"Kings of the Night" (Howard) **8**:137
King's Stork (Babits)
See *A Gólyakalifa*
The King's Threshold (Yeats) **31**:386
Kingsblood Royal (Lewis) **4**:260; **13**:338-40, 343, 350; **39**:247, 250
Kinjiki (Mishima) **161**:29-30, 51
"A Kink in Space-Time" (Wakefield) **120**:336, 351

Kinkakuji (Mishima) **161**:9, 27-29, 51-53, 77-78, 80, 83-84, 107-8, 112-13
"Kinofilosofiia" (Olesha) **136**:183
"Kinosaki nite" (Shiga) **172**:202, 232
"Kinsey Keene" (Masters) **25**:312
The Kinsey Report (Kinsey) **91**:42
"Kinship" (Roberts) **8**:318, 326
The Kinship of Nature (Carman) **7**:139, 143
Kiparisovy larets (Annensky) **14**:17-20
Kipling, Auden & Co.: Essays and Reviews (Jarrell) **177**:183, 185, 187, 190, 220-22, 231, 241, 245-47
Kipps: The Story of a Simple Soul (Wells) **6**:525-26, 536-37, 539-40, 543, 545, 547-48, 553; **12**:495, 506, 509; **19**:428, 440; **133**:228
"Kir lanulea" (Caragiale) **76**:156, 159, 170-71
"Das kirchlein" (Morgenstern) **8**:305
Kirigirisu (Dazai Osamu) **11**:176
Kirkon vihollinen (Leino) **24**:372
"Kirmak-i-Shab Taab" (Iqbal) **28**:198
"Kirsten's Last Journey" (Jensen)
See "Kirstens sidste Rejse"
"Kirstens sidste Rejse" (Jensen) **41**:307
"A kis csizmák" (Mikszath) **31**:167
Kis hármaskönyu (Molnár) **20**:173-74
"The Kiss" (Babel)
See "Potselui"
"The Kiss" (Chekhov)
See "Poceluj"
"The Kiss" (Chesnutt) **39**:97
"A Kiss" (Dobson) **79**:32, 37
"The Kiss" (Söderberg) **39**:438
"A Kiss and Good-Bye" (Hichens) **64**:130
"Kiss Ass" (Ginsberg) **120**:25
The Kiss before the Mirror (Whale) **63**:339 341, 384
A Kiss for Cinderella (Barrie) **2**:43
Kiss, Kiss (Dahl) **173**:10, 13-15
Kiss of Death (Hecht) **101**:75
"The Kiss of Moses" (Peretz) **16**:395
"The Kiss of the Unborn" (Sologub) **9**:447
The Kiss of the Unborn, and Other Stories (Sologub) **9**:445
Kiss Tomorrow Good-Bye (McCoy) **28**:210, 212-13, 222, 233-37
"Kisses in the Train" (Lawrence) **93**:17, 70
"Kissless Living in Kisses" (Ady) **11**:20
Kit and Kitty (Blackmore) **27**:28-9, 35-7, 39, 43, 45
Kit Brandon (Anderson) **1**:42, 55, 57; **10**:43
Kit O'Brien (Masters) **2**:467-69
Kitajskaja povest' (Pilnyak) **23**:212
"The Kitchen" (O'Faolain) **143**:263, 265, 267
Kitchen Fugue (Kaye-Smith) **20**:112
"A Kitchen Knife" (Warner) **131**:322
Kitchener's Mob: The Adventures of an American in Kitchener's Army (Hall and Nordhoff) **23**:55
The Kite (Pirandello)
See *Il nibbio*
"The Kith of the Elf-Folk" (Dunsany) **59**:20
"Kitsugyaku" (Mori Ogai) **14**:384
"Kitsune" (Hearn) **9**:129
"Kitsune" (Nagai) **51**:88
"Kitty" (Frank) **17**:109
Kitty Alone: A Story of Three Fires (Baring-Gould) **88**:26-7
Kitty Foyle (Morley) **87**:126, 132, 134, 137-8, 140, 147
"Kitty Kemble" (Buchanan) **107**:79
Kitty's Choice; or, Berrytown (Davis) **6**:152
Kivesjärvelaiset (Leino) **24**:368-69
Kivilágos kivirradtig (Moricz) **33**:237, 244, 247, 250
Kjaerlighedens komedie (Ibsen) **2**:227; **8**:146; **37**:242, 258; **52**:153, 156, 192-93
Kjoere Dea (Undset) **197**:305
"Kladbishche v Kozine" (Babel) **171**:10, 46, 72-74, 84, 89
"Klage" (Trakl) **5**:464
"Klage um Jonathan" (Rilke) **195**:228
"Klage-Wijsa" (Lagerkvist) **144**:186-87
Klange (Kandinsky) **92**:66-9, 71-2, 91-2
"Klare morgen og vaate kveld" (Rölvaag) **17**:347
"Klasszikus álmok" (Babits) **14**:39
Klawitter (Kaiser) **9**:181
Klee Wyck (Carr) **32**:116-17, 121, 124-25, 130
"Der Kleiderschrank" (Mann) **14**:347
"Klein Sterbelied" (Lasker-Schueler) **57**:320
"Klein und Wagner" (Hesse) **148**:170
"Kleine Aster" (Benn) **3**:112
"Kleine Ballade" (Liliencron) **18**:213
"Die Kleine Berlinerrin" (Walser) **18**:419
"Kleine Fabel" (Kafka) **47**:242
"Kleine Geschichte" (Morgenstern) **8**:309
Der kleine Herr Friedemann (Mann) **2**:431; **35**:209-10, 213, 251; **60**:340
Das Kleine Mahagonny (Brecht) **169**:52
"Kleine Reise hach Brasilien" (Zweig) **17**:457
Die kleine Stadt (Mann) **9**:314-15, 322, 324-25, 327-29
Kleine Stucke fur Kammerorchester (Schoenberg) **75**:410
Klein und Wagner (Hesse) **196**:269, 273, 276, 307-09, 323-24, 326
"Das kleine Welttheater" (Hofmannsthal) **11**:292
De kleine zielen (Couperus) **15**:44-7
Kleines Organon für das Theatre (Brecht) **1**:106; **13**:45, 59, 65; **35**:8; **169**:12-13, 18, 26, 58
"Kleist in Thun" (Walser) **18**:437
Klesh (Dunsany) **2**:143
Kleyne mentshelekh mit kleyne hasoges (Aleichem) **35**:305
"Klingsor" (Hesse) **196**:273
"Klingsor's Last Summer" (Hesse)
See "Klingsors letzter Sommer"
Klingsor's Last Summer (Hesse)
See *Klingsors letzter Sommer*
"Klingsors letzter Sommer" (Hesse) **196**:260, 269, 273
Klingsors letzter Sommer (Hesse) **196**:255-57, 307-09, 323-26, 333
Ključ (Aldanov) **23**:24
De kloge jomfruer (Undset) **3**:517, 522
"De kloke jomfruer" (Rölvaag) **17**:347
De kloke jomfruer (Undset) **197**:302
"Klondike" (Robinson) **101**:115
Klop (Mayakovski) **4**:292, 299, 302; **18**:243, 246, 248, 254, 262-63
Kloster Lugau (Raabe) **45**:165-66, 172, 198, 201
Klusā grāmata (Rainis) **29**:392
Kmoryu-okeanu (Remizov) **27**:334, 338
"Der Knabe Herakles" (Hauptmann) **4**:201
"The Knack of Politics" (Güiraldes)
See "La Politiquería"
The Knacker's ABC (Vian)
See *L'equarrissage pour tous*
The Knave of Bergen (Zuckmayer)
See *Der Schelm von Bergen*
Knave of Hearts (Symons) **11**:434, 439
"Kneeb Piter Komandor" (Pilnyak) **23**:211
"Knee-Deep in June" (Ritchie) **51**:286
"The Knees of the Gods" (Hornung)
See "The Ides of March"
Knickerbocker Holiday (Anderson) **2**:8; **144**:3-4, 11, 17-22, 24, 38, 52, 72
Knick-Knacks and Traditions and Historical Articles (Palma)
See *Cachivaches y tradiciones y artículos históricas*
"Knie" (Morgenstern) **8**:305
"The Knife" (Douglas) **40**:76, 86
"The Knife That Killed Po Hancy" (Stockton) **47**:324, 327
"The Knife Thrower" (Böll)
See "Der Mann mit den Messern"
Kniga skazok (Sologub) **9**:447
"Knight" (Rilke)
See "Ritter"
"The Knight, Death, and the Devil" (Jarrell) **177**:162, 167
"The Knight Errant" (Guiney) **41**:205, 221, 227
Knight of Black Art (Melies) **81**:123
The Knight of the Maypole (Davidson) **24**:182
"The Knight Whose Armour Didn't Squeak" (Milne) **88**:241
Knight without Armour (Hilton) **21**:92
"Knight-Errant" (Burke) **63**:131
"Knight-in-Armour" (Milne) **88**:260
Knight's Gambit (Faulkner) **141**:62
The Knights of the Round Table (Cocteau)
See *Les chevaliers de la table ronde*
Kniha apokryfů (Čapek) **37**:44; **192**:183-87, 189, 191
Knives from Syria (Riggs) **56**:203, 207
Knjiga za lahkomiselne ljudi (Cankar) **105**:161
"The Knock at the Manor Gate" (Kafka) **29**:186
"Knock! Knock! Who's There?" (Wakefield) **120**:356-57
"Knock Wood" (Millay) **169**:236
"Knocked Up" (Lawson) **27**:140
Knocking on the Door (Paton) **165**:298
Knockout (Sapper) **44**:316, 319-22
Knockout (Sternheim) **8**:375
"The Knot-Hole" (Fisher) **87**:105
"Knotting" (Grahame) **64**:62
"Know Deeply, Deeper than Love" (Lawrence) **93**:54
"Know Deeply, Know Thyself More Deeply" (Lawrence) **93**:53, 55
"Knowledge" (Coleridge) **73**:12
"Knowledge" (Lasker-Schueler) **57**:329-30
"Knowledge" (Nemerov) **124**:195, 256
"Knowledge and the Relativity of Feeling" (Dewey) **95**:58
"Knowledge as Idealization" (Dewey) **95**:94
"Knowledge Dethroned" (Nisbet) **117**:316
"The Knowledge Experience Again" (Dewey) **95**:152
Knox om pax (Crowley) **7**:206
"Knoxville: Summer of 1915" (Agee) **180**:22, 24, 47-49, 77, 79
Knulp (Hesse) **196**:250
Knut der Herr (Liliencron) **18**:213, 216
Knut the Lord (Liliencron)
See *Knut der Herr*
Den knutna näven (Lagerkvist) **144**:189, 211, 214, 220, 223
"Ko o nusumu hanashi" (Shiga) **172**:202
Kōcha no ato (Nagai) **51**:89
Kochel (Kandinsky) **92**:49
"Kod kazana" (Andrić) **135**:14, 85, 94
"Kod lekara" (Andrić) **135**:89
"Koe-chto iz sekretnykh zapisei poputchika Zanda" (Olesha) **136**:58, 162
Kōfu (Natsume) **10**:329
"Kôgao no shi" (Yosano) **59**:334-7, 339
"Kogda opuskaetsja štora" (Bryusov) **10**:92
"Kogda sižu odin i v komnate temno" (Bryusov) **10**:92
"Koharu" (Kunikida Doppo) **99**:296
"Kohtupaev" (Talvik) **87**:319, 321
"Koi wo koi suru hito" (Hagiwara) **60**:313
"Koide shidō" (Hagiwara) **60**:315
"Koiteki chokkan" (Nishida) **83**:330
"Koiwai Farm" (Miyazawa) **76**:300
"Koiwaike no ikka" (Miyamoto) **37**:267-68
Kōjin (Natsume) **2**:491-92; **10**:329, 331-32, 334, 336-38, 345
Kokoro (Hearn) **9**:123, 128-30
Kokoro (Natsume) **2**:491-93; **10**:330-32, 336-37, 346
Kokyljen (Hansen) **32**:250
Kokyō (Dazai Osamu) **11**:191
Kol Nidre (Schoenberg) **75**:311, 317, 347
Kolchan (Gumilev) **60**:260, 262, 269-71, 282
Kolesno vremeni (Kuprin) **5**:304
Kollege Crampton (Hauptmann) **4**:194
"Kolniyatsch" (Beerbohm) **24**:102
Kolportage (Kaiser) **9**:181
"A költőéletének pusztájáról" (Babits) **14**:39

"Kolumb prichalivayet k beregu" (Petrov) **21**:157
"Kolymen-Gorod" (Pilnyak) **23**:211
"Kolyvushka" (Babel) **13**:35
"Komboloi" (Merrill) **173**:173
De komedianten (Couperus) **15**:47
Komediantka (Reymont) **5**:390, 392-93, 395-96
Komedii (Kuzmin) **40**:202
Komediia o Aleksee cheloveke Bozh'em (Kuzmin) **40**:190, 202-03
Komediia o Evdokii iz Geliopoliia (Kuzmin) **40**:200, 202
"Kometa" (Schulz) **5**:420, 422, 424, 429; **51**:311, 316
"Komm in den totgesagten Park und Schau" (George) **2**:150
"Komm l'atrébate" (France) **9**:57
Kommandørens døtre (Lie) **5**:325-26, 329, 331
Kommentierte Ausgabe (Rilke) **195**:310
Komodia (Kazantzakis) **181**:210, 304-6, 313
Komödianten (Pabst) **127**:315-17, 320-25, 354, 359, 362-63
Komödie (Bernhard) **165**:36
Die Komödie der Eitelkeit (Canetti) **157**:37-42, 62, 67, 77, 82-85
"Komoro naru kojo no hotri" (Shimazaki Toson) **5**:439
Komposition für den Film (Adorno) **111**:17-18, 20-6
"Komsorg" (Olesha) **136**:155
"Komu skazaten'ki" (Khlebnikov) **20**:147
Konarmiia (Babel) **2**:20-3, 25-32, 34-5, 37; **13**:15-18, 20-30, 32-40; **171**:3-4, 10-11, 13-14, 16-26, 29-31, 35, 37-41, 43-48, 58, 60, 62-63, 70-90, 92, 96, 104
"Kon'bled" (Bryusov) **10**:83, 91
"Koncert na vokzale" (Mandelstam) **6**:267
Konerne ved vandposten (Hamsun) **2**:206; **14**:224, 237, 250-51; **49**:130, 135, 145, 159, 161; **151**:234
"Die Konfirmanden" (Rilke) **195**:181
Kong Eystejn (Bjoernson) **37**:29
Kong Sverre (Bjoernson) **7**:110, 113, 116; **37**:18, 29
"Kongen" (Grieg) **10**:208
Kongen (Bjoernson) **7**:104, 111-12, 115-16; **37**:11, 19-20, 29-32
Kongens Fald (Jensen) **41**:293-94, 296, 306, 309-13
Kongs emnerne (Ibsen) **2**:227; **8**:149; **52**:186
"Koniec" (Herbert) **168**:39
König Hahnrei (Kaiser) **9**:171, 173, 179, 181
König Nicolo; oder, So ist das Leben (Wedekind) **7**:585
Könige und Baueren (Liliencron) **18**:213
Königliche Hoheit (Mann) **2**:429; **8**:253-54; **14**:354, 356; **35**:243; **60**:333; **168**:173
"Königseid!" (Raabe) **45**:188
"Konkin" (Babel) **171**:78
"Konkrete Kunst" (Arp) **115**:6
"A könnytelenek könnyei" (Babits) **14**:39
"Konrad Myrdton" (Fisher) **140**:165
"Das Konservative Denken" (Maitland) **65**:310
Konstantin Strobel (Kaiser) **9**:174
"Konstruktion der Historischen Wirklichkeit" (Broch) **20**:57
"Konstruktionen in der Analyse" (Freud) **52**:137
Kontakion for You Departed (Paton) **165**:295, 298
Konungen (Lagerkvist) **144**:241
"Konzert" (Toller) **10**:490
Konzert (Lasker-Schueler) **57**:332, 334
"Kopai" (Tagore) **53**:342
Der Kopf (Mann) **9**:319-20, 323, 325-26, 328-29
Köpfe (Bernhard) **165**:122
"En kopp te" (Söderberg) **39**:428
"Kopyto inzhenera" (Bulgakov) **159**:101
Kora (Popa) **167**:152, 154, 156, 164, 171, 176, 178-79
Die Koralle (Kaiser) **9**:172-74, 184, 189-90
Kõrboja peremees (Tammsaare) **27**:372-73
"Kore" (Manning) **25**:277
"Korf's Clock" (Morgenstern) **8**:305
"Die korfsche Uhr" (Morgenstern) **8**:306
Kormchie zvezdy (Ivanov) **33**:117
"Das kornfeld" (Morgenstern) **8**:310
Korni japonskogo solnca (Pilnyak) **23**:212
"Korochun" (Remizov) **27**:352
"Korol'" (Babel) **2**:33, 36; **13**:14; **171**:8-9, 11-13, 50-53, 55-56, 92, 96, 101-2, 104, 106-7
Korol, dama, valet (Nabokov) **108**:60, 62-63, 67-68, 74, 90, 112-19, 147, 179, 201
Korol na ploshchadi (Blok) **5**:99
"Korova" (Platonov) **14**:419, 425-26
Korrektur (Bernhard) **165**:2, 23-24, 27-29, 79, 96, 98, 111, 114-16, 118-19
Korset (Obstfelder) **23**:177-78, 181-82, 187, 190-91
Korset (Undset) **3**:510; **197**:325, 327-28, 336
"Kosa" (Andrić) **135**:84
"Kosovo polje" (Popa) **167**:159
"Kost kosti" (Popa) **167**:154-55
"Kostel v Novograde" (Babel) **2**:23, 27; **171**:8, 11, 22-26, 31-33, 44, 74, 82-83, 86-87
Koster (Gumilev) **60**:268, 270
Koster dorozhnyi (Sologub) **9**:444
"Kostroma" (Remizov) **27**:352
"Kot Bot" (Guro) **56**:138
"Kot Kotofeich" (Remizov) **27**:352
"Kot Vat" (Guro) **56**:138
Kotik Letaev (Bely) **7**:47-9, 52, 55-6, 61, 66
Kotlovan (Platonov) **14**:410, 415-16, 421-24, 429
Koto no sorane (Natsume) **10**:329
"Kouta" (Leino) **24**:368-69, 373, 376
"The Kozin Cemetery" (Babel)
See "Kladbishche v Kozine"
"The Kozino Cemetery" (Babel)
See "Kladbishche v Kozine"
"Közui" (Nagai) **51**:87
"Hét kracjár" (Moricz) **33**:234, 241, 245, 248-49
"Krag, the Kootenay Ram" (Seton) **31**:259, 261, 269, 271, 278-79
"Die Krähen fliegen abends nach Hause" (Borchert) **5**:104
Krakatit (Čapek) **6**:83, 85, 91, 93-4; **37**:46, 49-50, 52-4, 56-7, 59, 61, 68, 72; **192**:175, 196, 202
Krakonošova zahrada (Čapek) **37**:51; **192**:235
"Kral Majales" (Ginsberg) **120**:4, 17-18, 23
Kranichtanz (Zuckmayer) **191**:306
Kransen (Undset) **197**:327-29, 333-35
Krapp's Last Tape (Beckett) **145**:82, 99-101, 124-25, 129-30, 149-51, 155, 177, 179, 206
"Krasnaja bavarija" (Zabolotsky) **52**:367-68, 375, 378-79
Krasnoe derevo (Pilnyak) **23**:213, 217
Krasnyi smelch (Andreyev) **3**:16, 18, 23, 27
"Krasota sily" (Olesha) **136**:184
Krauklītis (Rainis) **29**:393
"Krawang-Bekasi" (Anwar) **22**:24
"Kreide und Russ" (Kandinsky) **92**:68
Der Kreidekreis (Klabund) **44**:103, 106, 109
"Kreisrichter" (Heyse) **8**:113
Kreitserova sonata (Tolstoy) **4**:449-50, 453, 457, 463, 468-69, 476, 480-83; **11**:463, 469-70, 478; **17**:415; **28**:394-95, 397, 401; **44**:353; **79**:334, 337, 347, 370, 374, 387, 411, 412, 419, 447
"Krepost" (Remizov) **27**:340, 347, 349
"Krest" (Gumilev) **60**:279
Krestovye sestry (Remizov) **27**:330-31, 333, 342, 347
The Kreutzer Sonata (Tolstoy)
See *Kreitserova sonata*
"Der Kreuzgang" (Raabe) **45**:190
Kreuzweg (Zuckmayer) **191**:300
Křídla (Nezval) **44**:249
"Der Krieg" (Heym) **9**:145, 147, 152
Krieg und Frieden (Hesse) **196**:238
Kriegsnovellen (Liliencron) **18**:213, 216
Krilya (Kuzmin) **40**:191, 195-200, 202-06, 215
Kringen (Hansen) **32**:251
"Krishna" (Baker) **10**:20
Die Krisis der europaeischen Wissenschaften und die transzendentale Phänomenologie, Eine Einleitung in die phaenomenologische Philosophie (Husserl) **100**:10, 42-43, 60, 69, 71, 111-12, 114, 119, 121, 129, 132, 135, 147, 151
"Kristen trosbekännelse" (Södergran) **31**:289
Kristin Lavransdatter (Undset) **3**:512-19, 521, 524; **197**:289-92, 304-05, 312-13, 324, 326-33, 335-36
Kristina (Strindberg) **8**:418
Kristuslegender (Lagerloef) **4**:232; **36**:230
Krisztus vagy Barabas (Karinthy) **47**:269
Kritik (Ball)
See *Zur Kritik der deutschen Intelligenz*
Die kritische Aufnahme der Existentialphilosophie Martin Heideggers (Bachmann) **192**:53, 63, 130
Kritische Grudlegung des Transcendentalen Realismus (von Hartmann) **96**:198
Križ na gori (Cankar) **105**:161
"Krjaži" (Zamyatin) **8**:552
Eine Krone für Zion (Kraus) **5**:286
Kronika z konce století (Nezval) **44**:244
Kroniki tugodniowe (Prus) **48**:176
Krug chtenija (Tolstoy) **44**:330
"Krysolov" (Tsvetaeva) **7**:556, 558, 561-62; **35**:374-77, 398, 414-15
"Kryžovnik" (Chekhov) **3**:168
Krzyżacy (Sienkiewicz) **3**:422, 424-27, 429
Kshanikā (Tagore) **3**:490; **53**:338, 340-42, 350-51
"Kshudhita Pashan" (Tagore) **3**:483, 485; **53**:356-58
"Księga" (Schulz) **5**:424; **51**:309, 315-16
"Kto sozdan iz kamnia, kto sozdan iz gliny" (Tsvetaeva) **35**:391
"K'uang-jen jih-chi" (Lu Hsun)
See *Kuangren riji*
Kuangren riji (Lu Hsun) **3**:295, 297-98, 300-01, 303
"Kubiki" (Remizov) **27**:339, 341
Kubok metelej: Chetviortiia simfoniia (Bely) **7**:46, 50, 57-8
Kuča na osami (Andrić) **135**:25, 29, 44, 52-53, 58
Kuća nasred druma (Popa) **167**:164, 172
"Kuda idet Angliya?" (Trotsky) **22**:352
"Kudzu" (Dickey) **151**:199
Kuhle Wampe (Brecht) **13**:63; **169**:66, 68
"Kukkha. Rozanovy pis'ma" (Remizov) **27**:334, 350
Különös házasság (Mikszath) **31**:170-72, 174
Der Kulterer (Bernhard) **165**:79
"Eine Kulturfrage" (Musil) **12**:236
"Kulturkritik und Gesellschaft" (Adorno) **111**:50, 144, 175-76, 182-85, 187-88
"Kumo" (Nagai) **51**:99
"Kumo" (Shimazaki Toson) **5**:439
"Kumori-bi" (Shiga) **172**:202
"Kung I-chi" (Lu Hsun) **3**:295, 301, 303
"Kunigundula-configuration" (Arp) **115**:22
Kunjinī (Devkota) **23**:50
Kunshō (Nagai) **51**:98
Die kunst der rezitation und deklamation (Steiner) **13**:442
Der Künstler (Rank) **115**:226, 231, 234, 243-44, 246, 249, 251, 255-56, 261, 267-68, 300-01, 306, 310-11, 314-15, 319, 325-30, 347
"De Künstler und die Zietkrankheit" (Ball) **104**:36
Das Kunstwerk im Zeitalter seiner technischen Reproduzierbarkeit (Benjamin) **39**:8, 19, 24, 27, 30-1, 51, 54
"Der Kuntsenmakher" (Peretz) **16**:402
"Kuny" (Zamyatin) **8**:553
"Kupón" (Čapek) **37**:49
"Kuranty liubvi" (Kuzmin) **40**:216
Kurent (Cankar) **105**:162-63

"Kuresaare vanad" (Tammsaare) **27**:369
Kuriyama daizen (Mori Ogai) **14**:378
"Kurōdiasu no nikki" (Shiga) **172**:207, 229
"Kuroi fūkin" (Hagiwara) **60**:314
Kuruc (Ady) **11**:22
Kurymushka (Prishvin) **75**:214, 216
"Kusamakura" (Shimazaki Toson) **5**:434
Kusamakura (Natsume) **2**:491, 494-95; **10**:329, 332, 341-45
"Kusum" (Premchand) **21**:289-90
"Kval" (Obstfelder) **23**:177
"Kväll" (Lagerkvist) **144**:217
Kvinnororelsen (Key) **65**:226, 234, 237-38
Kwaidan (Hearn) **9**:123, 125, 131
Kwakiutl Culture as Reflected in Mythology (Boas) **56**:81
"Kyō" (Akutagawa Ryūnosuke) **16**:36
"Kyoko" (Sarton) **120**:264
Kyomō no seigi (Hagiwara) **60**:294
L. N. Tolstoy and His Epoch (Lenin) **67**:208
"A la ciencia" (Gonzalez Martinez) **72**:149
A La Conquete du Pole (Melies) **81**:122,140
De la division du travail social:étude sur l'organisation des sociétés supérieures (Durkheim) **55**:91, 100-04, 106-09, 115, 120, 126, 128, 130-33, 142-43, 146-47
"A la muerta" (Aleixandre) **113**:13
"L. A. Nocturne: Los Angeles" (Villaurrutia) **80**:519
"'La protectora' y 'La libertadora'" (Palma) **29**:263
De la Terre à la Lune (Verne) **52**:330, 345, 347, 349, 355
De la traduction (Larbaud)
See *Sous l'invocation de St. Jérôme*
Lábadozó szél (Radnóti) **16**:418-19
Là-bas (Huysmans) **7**:406-10, 413, 415; **69**:10-13, 17-18, 21-22, 29, 31, 37, 39, 44-5, 47, 53-6
Laberinto (Jiménez) **4**:212, 216; **183**:301
El laberinto de las sirenas (Baroja) **8**:63
"Labirynt nad morzem" (Herbert) **168**:52
"Lablon'ka" (Remizov) **27**:339
"Labor" (Bryan) **99**:5, 34
"Labor and the Angel" (Scott) **6**:393, 397
Une laborantine (Bourget) **12**:69
Le laboratoire central (Jacob) **6**:191-92, 197-98, 202
"Laboratory Poem" (Merrill) **173**:225
Laboremus (Bjoernson) **7**:112, 114; **37**:19, 22, 29
Laborers in the Vineyard (Papini)
See *Gli operai della vigna*
Labor's Poem (Martinez Sierra and Martinez Sierra)
See *El poema del trabajo*
"The Labour of Night" (Brennan) **17**:39, 41, 54, 56, 60
"Labrie's Wife" (Scott) **6**:398
"Labyrinth" (Borges) **109**:8
"The Labyrinth" (Muir) **2**:482; **87**:264, 266-67
Labyrinth (Jiménez)
See *Laberinto*
The Labyrinth (Muir) **87**:159, 167, 220-25
"The Labyrinth by the Sea" (Herbert)
See "Labirynt nad morzem"
The Labyrinth by the Sea (Herbert) **168**:73
The Labyrinth of the Sirens (Baroja)
See *El laberinto de las sirenas*
The Labyrinth of the World (Yourcenar)
See *Le Labyrinthe du Monde*
Le Labyrinthe du Monde (Yourcenar) **193**:257, 262, 266, 280, 302
Labyrinths (Borges)
See *Labyrinths: Selected Stories, and Other Writings*
"The Labyrinths of the Detective Story and Chesterton" (Borges) **109**:157
Labyrinths: Selected Stories, and Other Writings (Borges) **109**:18, 47, 49, 51-2, 76
Labyrinths, with Path of Thunder (Okigbo) **171**:338-41, 344-46, 348-57, 360-61
"The Lacework Kid" (Runyon) **10**:432
Lachende Wahrheiten (Spitteler) **12**:339
"Der Lacher" (Böll) **185**:27
"Lachrymae Christi" (Crane) **2**:117, 120-21; **5**:188-91
"The Lacking Sense" (Hardy) **53**:81, 86
"Lacustrine" (Bacovia) **24**:69
"The Lad" (Tsvetaeva) **7**:567
The Lad and the Lion (Burroughs) **2**:79
Laddie (Porter) **21**:261-62, 266, 271-74
"The Ladies" (Kipling) **8**:201
Ladies and Gentlemen (Belloc) **7**:42; **18**:40
Ladies and Gentlemen (Cabell) **6**:68, 76
Ladies and Gentlemen (Cobb) **77**:133
Ladies and Gentlemen in Victorian Fiction (Delafield) **61**:132
"Ladies and Gentlemen, into the Gas Please" (Borowski)
See "This Way for the Gas, Ladies and Gentlemen"
Ladies Letter Writer (Benavente)
See *Cartas de mujeres*
The Ladies' Man (Drieu la Rochelle)
See *L'homme couvert de femmes*
"The Ladies of St. James's" (Dobson) **79**:5, 23, 26
Ladies of the Corridor (Parker) **143**:316
"The Ladies of the Lake" (Chambers) **41**:114
Ladies Whose Bright Eyes (Ford) **15**:76, 78, 87, 89, 93; **39**:128; **39**:128; **172**:6-7, 57
"Ladies Wild" (Benchley) **55**:13
"Ladomir" (Khlebnikov) **20**:126-27, 129, 132-33, 139, 143
Ladro di galline (Jovine) **79**:44, 61, 65
"The Lady" (Andrić)
See "Gospodjicd"
"A Lady" (Lowell) **1**:375; **8**:235
The Lady Aristocrat (Zoshchenko) **15**:491
"Lady at Her Mirror" (Rilke)
See "Dame vor dem Spiegel"
Lady Audley's Secret (Braddon) **111**:210, 212-18, 220-22, 225, 227, 231-32, 238-40, 242-43, 246, 248-49, 251-52, 256, 262-63, 268-73, 277-78, 280-81, 283, 286-87, 290-93, 296-98, 300-01, 305-08, 310-11
Lady Baltimore (Wister) **21**:376-79, 384, 404-05
"Lady Barbarina Lemon" (James) **64**:157
"Lady Bates" (Jarrell) **177**:129, 155, 159, 172, 224
Lady Bountiful (Pinero) **32**:398, 403-04, 413
Lady Charing Is Cross (Tey) **14**:459
Lady Chatterley's Lover (Lawrence) **2**:345-46, 348, 350-51, 353-54, 356, 364-67, 370-72; **9**:217-19, 227-29; **16**:284-85, 312; **33**:188, 193-96, 203, 206-07; **48**:90-150; **61**:186, 192, 197, 210; **93**:14, 43, 62, 84, 97, 127
Lady Clare (Buchanan) **107**:31
Lady Connie (Ward) **55**:421, 426, 437-38, 446
The Lady Eve (Sturges) **48**:270, 274, 281, 283, 287-88, 290-92, 294-96, 301, 303-04, 309, 312-13, 316, 318-19, 321
"Lady Evelyn" (Gray) **19**:151
"Lady Ferry" (Jewett) **22**:118, 149
"A Lady from Red Horse" (Bierce) **44**:45
The Lady from the Sea (Ibsen)
See *Fruen fra havet*
Lady Gladys (Buchanan) **107**:87
Lady Gregory's Journal (Gregory) **1**:334
"Lady Hester Stanhope" (Strachey) **12**:392
"The Lady in Fetters" (Sologub) **9**:436
"The Lady in Hosea" (Sharp) **39**:375
"The Lady in the Lake" (Chandler) **179**:127-29
The Lady in the Lake (Chandler) **1**:172, 175-76; **7**:173, 175, 180; **179**:87, 98-99, 101, 103, 127-28, 144, 147-49, 153, 155-58, 162, 180-83, 188, 191, 198-99, 203-4, 223, 226, 228, 230
Lady Inger of Østraat (Ibsen)
See *Fru Inger til Østraat*
Lady Kilpatrick (Buchanan) **107**:85-6
"Lady Letitia's Lilliput Hand" (Buchanan) **107**:50
"Lady Lucifer" (O'Faolain) **143**:222
"Lady Macbeth's Daughter" (Warner) **131**:311, 313
"A Lady of Bayou St. John" (Chopin) **14**:70; **127**:20-2, 172-74, 187-88
The Lady of Challant (Giacosa)
See *La dame de Challant*
"The Lady of Giorgione" (Bottomley) **107**:2
A Lady of Rome (Crawford) **10**:150, 155
"The Lady of Shallot" (Phelps) **113**:376, 388-89
The Lady of the "Aroostook" (Howells) **7**:364, 371, 376-77, 392; **17**:176, 178; **41**:234, 266
The Lady of the Hillside (Coleridge) **73**:8
"The Lady of the House of Love" (Carter) **139**:48, 116, 142, 146, 187
"The Lady of the Lake" (Malamud) **129**:74-5, 97, 106, 190, 192; **184**:171-72, 197, 244, 269, 280, 290-96
"The Lady of the Lattice" (Rohmer) **28**:277
The Lady of the Shroud (Stoker) **8**:387, 394, 399; **144**:273, 279, 295, 305
"Lady on a Balcony" (Rilke)
See "Dame auf einem Balkon"
The Lady on Her Balcony (Garro)
See *La Señora en su balcón*
The Lady on the Drawing Room Floor (Coleridge) **73**:23
"The Lady, or the Tiger?" (Stockton) **47**:312, 316, 319, 322-24, 327-28, 330-31
The Lady, or the Tiger? and Other Stories (Stockton) **47**:314, 320
A Lady Quite Lost (Stringer) **37**:336
Lady Rose's Daughter (Ward) **55**:412, 415, 422, 424-25
"Lady S. S." (Sarduy) **167**:222
Lady Windermere's Fan (Wilde) **1**:495, 497, 502-04, 506, 508; **8**:494; **23**:409, 411-12, 420, 427-28, 435; **175**:267, 271-72, 274-75, 283, 287, 290, 313
"Lady with a Falcon" (Sarton) **120**:267
"Lady with a Lamp" (Parker) **143**:343
"Lady with a Little Dog" (Chekhov)
See "Dama s sobačkoj"
"The Lady with the Dog" (Chekhov)
See "Dama s sobačkoj"
"The Lady With the Pet Dog" (Chekhov)
See "Dama s sobačkoj"
"The Ladybird" (Lawrence) **9**:216
"The Lady's Maid" (Mansfield) **2**:448; **8**:282, 285-86; **39**:303, 320
"The Lady's Maid's Bell" (Wharton) **3**:578; **129**:360, 364
The Lady's Mile (Braddon) **111**:232, 236, 311, 314
"The Lady's Reward" (Parker) **143**:326
A Lady's Virtue (Crothers) **19**:75
"Lae Souci" (Drummond) **25**:143
"Laeta" (Ivanov) **33**:138
Lafcadio's Adventures (Gide)
See *Les caves du Vatican*
Lagar (Mistral) **2**:479
"El lagarto viejo" (García Lorca) **181**:122
De l'age divin a l'age ingrat (Jammes) **75**:119
De låghåriga merovingerna och andra essayer (Bengtsson) **48**:6, 12
"Lago biasa" (Anwar) **22**:19
The Lagoon's Regrets (Palamas) **5**:379
"Una lágrima en mayo" (Salinas) **17**:363
Lagrimas de cera (Machado de Assis) **10**:279
"Lágrimas de Xerxes" (Machado de Assis) **10**:290-91
"Lagu siul" (Anwar) **22**:19
Là-haut (Rod) **52**:309, 311, 315
La'Invasion de la mer (Verne) **6**:502
The Lair of the White Worm (Stoker) **8**:386, 395, 399, 402; **144**:279, 301
"Le lait de la mort" (Yourcenar) **193**:287, 289, 294, 296-97, 342-44

Lak tar miyo kinyero wi lobo (p'Bitek) **149**:51, 90-94, 108, 115-16
"The Lake" (Hecht) **101**:38
The Lake (Moore) **7**:476, 478, 481-84, 486
"Lake Boats" (Masters) **25**:298
"The Lake Isle of Innisfree" (Yeats) **1**:553-54, 579; **11**:508, 512; **18**:442, 445; **116**:333-34, 336
"The Lake Laughed" (Ady) **11**:15
Lake Lyrics (Campbell) **9**:29-30
"The Lake of Gaube" (Swinburne) **36**:324, 340-41, 346-47
"Lake Powell" (Abbey) **160**:16
Lakes of Autumn (Kuzmin)
See *Osennie ozera*
"Lakes of Värmland" (Dickey) **151**:174
"Lakshmi, the Lotus-Born" (Naidu) **80**:316
"Lal of Kilrudden" (Carman) **7**:138
Lalazar (Remizov) **27**:348
Lalek (Herbert) **168**:39
Lalka (Prus) **48**:157-59, 162-64, 167-75, 177-81
Lalli (Leino) **24**:371
"The Lama" (Nash) **109**:360
"Lamb to Slaughter" (Dahl) **173**:11
"Un lambeau de Patrie" (Verhaeren) **12**:471
Lambkin's Remains (Belloc) **7**:31, 38; **18**:27, 32
"The Lame Boy and the Fairy" (Lindsay) **17**:227
"The Lame Shall Enter First" (O'Connor) **132**:229, 237, 246, 257, 259, 277, 281, 283, 286-87, 289, 320
The Lame Squire (Tolstoy) **18**:359, 373, 377
Lame-Hulda (Bjoernson)
See *Halte Hulde*
"Lament" (Cullen) **37**:168
"Lament" (Millay) **4**:306, 308
"Lament" (Remizov)
See "Placha"
"Lament" (Thomas) **8**:461; **45**:379, 388, 402; **105**:352
"Lament" (Trakl)
See "Klage"
Lament for Ignacio Sánchez Mejías (García Lorca)
See *Llanto por Ignacio Sánchez Mejías*
"Lament for Jonathan" (Rilke)
See "Klage um Jonathan"
"A Lament for My Disappointed Love" (Lu Hsun) **3**:297
Lament for the Death of a Bullfighter (García Lorca)
See *Llanto por Ignacio Sánchez Mejías*
Lament for the Death of a Bullfighter, and Other Poems (García Lorca)
See *Llanto por Ignacio Sánchez Mejías*
The Lament for the Ruin of Russia (Remizov) **27**:331, 333, 335, 347, 349
"Lament of the Drums" (Okigbo) **171**:345, 353
"Lament of the Flutes" (Okigbo) **171**:339
"Lament of the Lavender Mist" (Okigbo) **171**:339-41, 346
"Lament of the Masks" (Okigbo) **171**:340, 354-55
"Lament of the Silent Sisters" (Okigbo)
See "Silences: Lament of the Silent Sisters"
"Lamentación de la Muerte" (García Lorca) **181**:197
"Lamentación de primavera" (Villaurrutia) **80**:477
"Lamentations" (Evans) **85**:48
Laments for the Living (Parker) **143**:287
Das Lamm des Armen (Zweig) **17**:453
"Lammas" (Davidson) **24**:163, 175, 180, 186, 188-89
"Lamorack and the Queen Morgause of Orkney" (Williams) **1**:512
"Lamorna Cove" (Davies) **5**:201
The Lamp and the Bell (Millay) **4**:311-12; **169**:233
"A Lamp in a Window" (Capote)
See "A Lamp in the Window"
"A Lamp in the Window" (Capote) **164**:200
The Lamp of Marvels: Spiritual Exercises (Valle-Inclán)
See *La lampara maravillosa: Ejer cicios espirituales*
"The Lamp of Poor Souls" (Pickthall) **21**:245, 250-51
The Lamp of Poor Souls, and Other Poems (Pickthall) **21**:241, 244-45, 255-56
"The Lamp of Psyche" (Wharton) **129**:352, 360
"The Lamp That Was Kept Alight" (Lu Hsun) **3**:302
La lampara maravillosa: Ejer cicios espirituales (Valle-Inclán) **5**:475, 477-79, 485
La Lampe d'Alladin (Cocteau) **119**:57
La lampe de psyché (Schwob) **20**:323
"The Lanawn Shee" (Ledwidge) **23**:123
"Lance Jack" (Lewis) **3**:288
Lancelot (Robinson) **5**:404-06, 408-09, 417; **101**:95, 113, 115, 130, 134, 188
"Lancer" (Housman) **10**:257
Lanceurs de graines (Giono) **124**:49
"The Land" (Kipling) **8**:191
"Land" (Lewis) **4**:257
The Land (Gibbon) **4**:126
"The Land beyond the Blow" (Bierce) **44**:8, 14, 50
"The Land Ironclads" (Wells) **19**:438
"The Land Is Cleared" (Fletcher) **35**:107
The Land of Always-Night (Dent) **72**:22
"The Land of Biscay" (Housman) **10**:247
The Land of Fear (Dent) **72**:21, 23
The Land of Heart's Desire (Yeats) **11**:509, 511, 526; **31**:386, 412
The Land of Journeys' Ending (Austin) **25**:23-4, 26-8, 31-3, 36, 38, 40-1
The Land of Little Rain (Austin) **25**:17, 23, 25-6, 28, 30-1, 33, 36, 38-9, 41-4
The Land of Long JuJu (Dent) **72**:22
Land of Lorne (Buchanan) **107**:53
"The Land of Rascals" (Esenin) **4**:109
The Land of Silence and Other Poems (Sarton) **120**:203, 302
The Land of Terror (Burroughs) **2**:81; **32**:58
The Land of Terror (Dent) **72**:17, 37
"The Land of the Dead" (Heym)
See "Die Heimat der Toten"
"The Land of the Giants" (Benét) **28**:6
The Land of the Mist (Doyle) **7**:225, 235
The Land of the Sun (Austin) **25**:31
"The Land Surveyor" (Zamyatin)
See "Zemlemer"
"The Land That Is Not" (Södergran) **31**:285
The Land That Is Not (Södergran)
See *Landet som icke är*
The Land That Time Forgot (Burroughs) **2**:78-9; **32**:58, 72-3
"The Land Within" (Webb) **24**:473
"Ein landarzt" (Kafka) **2**:306; **13**:284
Ein Landarzt (Kafka) **179**:289, 319, 324
"Lande's Death" (Artsybashev)
See "Ivan Lande"
Landet som icke är (Södergran) **31**:285-87
"The Landing Steps' Tale" (Tagore)
See "Ghater Katha"
"The Landlady" (Dahl) **173**:13-14
"The Landless Farmer" (Jewett) **22**:117
The Landlord at Lion's Head (Howells) **7**:393, 400; **17**:162, 165, 178, 184; **41**:286
"Landlord for a Generation" (Dazai Osamu) **11**:180-81, 183
A Landlord's Morning (Tolstoy) **4**:474; **11**:459; **28**:367; **79**:445
Landmarks (Lucas) **73**:159
Landmarks in French Literature (Strachey) **12**:390, 394, 401, 413-14
Landmarks in Russian Literature (Baring) **8**:31, 43
A Landowner's Morning (Tolstoy)
See *Utro pomeshchika*
L'Eau vive (Giono) **124**:98, 101-4
L'Orologio (Levi) **125**:198-202, 206-11, 224, 226-32, 234
Landru, the French Bluebeard (Wakefield) **120**:355
The Land's End (Hudson) **29**:138, 151
"Landscape" (Herbert) **168**:43
"The Landscape" (Masters) **25**:298
"Landscape" (Parker) **143**:323
Landscape and Figure Composition (Hartmann) **73**:122, 149
"The Landscape Chamber" (Jewett) **22**:148
"Landscape: How to Make It" (Drummond de Andrade) **139**:240
"Landscape I" (Andrade) **43**:7
"The Landscape Inspector" (Miyazawa) **76**:300
Landscape into Art (Clark) **147**:115-16
"Landscape of a Dead Love" (Storni)
See "Paisaje del amor muerto"
"Landscape of the Urinating Multitudes (Battery Place Nocturne)" (García Lorca)
See "Paisaje de la multitud que orina"
"Landscape of the Vomiting Multitudes (Coney Island Dusk)" (García Lorca)
See "Paisaje de la multitud que vomita"
Landscape Painting (Clark) **147**:118
"Landscape with Boat" (Stevens) **12**:360; **45**:278, 334
Landscape with Church (Kandinsky) **92**:147
"Landscape with Figures" (Nemerov) **124**:184-85, 253
"Landscape with Figures I" (Douglas) **40**:82, 89-91
"Landscape with Figures II" (Douglas) **40**:71, 83, 89-91, 93
"Landscape with Figures III" (Douglas) **40**:83, 89-91
"Landscape with Two Tombs and an Assyrian Hound" (García Lorca) **197**:186
"A Landscape-Painter" (James) **47**:199
Landscapes and Portraits (Colette)
See *Paysages et portraits*
"Landschaft" (Trakl) **5**:460
Landslide (Betti)
See *Frana allo scalo nord*
Landstrykere (Hamsun) **2**:202-03; **14**:225-28, 241, 246-47; **49**:130, 134, 144, 146; **151**:234, 255, 261
"The Land-Surveyor" (Zamyatin)
See "Zemlemer"
"The Lane That Ran East and West" (Blackwood) **5**:72
Langage cuit (Desnos) **22**:59-60, 72
"Le Langage des Fleurs" (Bataille) **155**:141
"Le langage indirect et les voix du silence" (Merleau-Ponty) **156**:124, 129
Die Lange Lange Strasse lang (Borchert) **5**:108
Den lange Rejse (Jensen) **41**:291-99, 302
De l'Angelus de l'Aube a l'Angelus de soir (Jammes) **75**:107, 113-15, 117
Die langen Wege (Zuckmayer) **191**:288-89, 291, 297
Langour (Storni)
See *Languidez*
"Langston Hughes" (Roumain) **19**:334
"Längtan heter min arvedel" (Lagerkvist) **144**:194
Language (Kraus)
See *Die Sprache*
Language (Sapir) **108**:247, 252, 257-58, 261-62, 266, 269, 282
"Language and Culture" (Mandelstam) **6**:264, 268
Language and Myth (Cassirer)
See *Sprach und Mythos: Ein Beitrag zum Problem der Göttemamen*
"The Language of Flowers or Stars" (Radiguet) **29**:357
"A Language of New York" (Oppen) **107**:256, 264, 304
"The Language of the Argentines" (Borges)
See *El idioma de los Argentinos*
"The Language of the Body" (Acker) **191**:56

"The Language of Trees" (Renard) **17**:311
"Lánguidamente su licor" (Vallejo) **56**:310
Languidez (Storni) **5**:444, 447-48, 451-52
The Lankavatara Sutra (Suzuki) **109**:376, 383, 387
A Lantern in Her Hand (Aldrich) **125**:2, 6-12, 14, 16-18
"Lantern Slides" (Nabokov) **108**:110
A Lantern to See By (Riggs) **56**:203-05, 215-16
"Lanterns" (Guro)
See "Fonari"
Lanterns on the Levee: Reflections of a Planter's Son (Percy) **84**:200-1, 204-16, 218, 222-3, 226-30, 233, 238-41
"L'antilingua" (Calvino) **183**:102, 142
Los lanzallamas (Arlt) **29**:38, 41-2, 45, 47-54, 57-8
Lao Ts'an yu-chi (Liu) **15**:246-52
Laodameia (Babits) **14**:41
Laodamia (Annensky) **14**:17, 22
Laodice and Danaë (Bottomley) **107**:3
A Laodicean; or, The Castle of the De Stancys (Hardy) **4**:149, 159; **10**:217, 227; **18**:100; **48**:38; **143**:73, 83, 175, 181, 204
A Laodicoean (Hardy) **153**:98
"Lapis Lazuli" (Yeats) **18**:459-60, 463, 459-60, 463; **31**:408; **116**:343-44
"A Lapse of Judgment" (Tagore)
See "Durbuddhi"
"Lapsed Crisis" (Knister) **56**:155
The Lar (Raabe)
See *Der Lar*
Der Lar (Raabe) **45**:166, 200-01
"Larch Barden" (Gale) **7**:284
"Larches" (Gurney) **33**:103
"L'archipelago dei luoghi immaginari" (Calvino) **183**:104
The Larder of the Sun (Prishvin) **75**:219
The Lardners and the Laurelwoods (Kaye-Smith) **20**:113, 116
Larenopfer (Rilke) **6**:358; **195**:258, 263, 266
"Large Bad Picture" (Bishop) **121**:75
"Large Red Man Reading" (Stevens) **12**:360; **45**:300
"Largely an Oral History of My Mother" (Brodkey) **123**:197, 225, 236
A Larger History of the United States (Higginson) **36**:166
"The Larger Life" (Bryan) **99**:108
"The Larger Success" (Johnson) **175**:234
"Larghetto" (Coleridge) **73**:25
Largo lamento (Salinas) **17**:359
The Lark (Anouilh)
See *L'alouette*
"The Lark" (Service) **15**:401
"The Lark" (Vilakazi)
See "Inqomfi"
"Larks" (Tynan) **3**:505
Les larmes d'Éros (Bataille) **155**:77, 92, 94, 97, 109, 114
Larramee's Ranch (Faust) **49**:56-8, 60
"Le larron" (Apollinaire) **3**:36, 43; **51**:48
"The Lascar's Walking-Stick" (Tomlinson) **71**:383
"Lass Drowned in a Well" (García Lorca) **197**:186
"The Last Aboriginal" (Sharp) **39**:388
"The Last Act" (Dahl) **173**:16-18
The Last Address (Lowry)
See *Lunar Caustic*
Last and First Men: A Story of the Near and Far Future (Stapledon) **22**:311-12, 315-25, 327-28, 333-34, 336-38, 342-45
The Last and the First (Compton-Burnett) **180**:141, 146
The Last Assembly Ball (Foote) **108**:12, 17, 34
"The Last Asset" (Wharton) **3**:554; **9**:547; **129**:361
"The Last Ballad" (Davidson) **24**:164
The Last Ballad, and Other Poems (Davidson) **24**:163, 191-92
The Last Barrier (Roberts) **8**:322, 326
The Last Book of Wonder (Dunsany) **59**:17, 20-1, 29
"The Last Bus" (Agnon)
See "Ha'Autobus ha'Aharon"
"The Last Centaur" (Heyse)
See "Der Letzte Centaur"
The Last Chapter (Hamsun)
See *Siste kapitel*
Last Chapter (Pyle) **75**:250-52
"The Last Circle" (Hippius)
See "Posledny krug"
"The Last Confessional" (Drinkwater) **57**:124
"The Last Day" (Benchley) **55**:3, 17
"The Last Day" (Wen I-to) **28**:417, 420
"The Last Day of Shraft" (Somerville & Ross) **51**:358, 383
"The Last Days" (Sterling) **20**:375
The Last Days of Mankind (Kraus)
See *Die letzten Tage der Menschheit*
"The Last Days of Pekin" (Loti)
See "Les derniers jours de Pékin"
The Last Days of Shylock (Lewisohn) **19**:271, 273, 278
The Last Days—Pushkin (Bulgakov)
See *Posledniye dni*
"The Last Debut" (Kuprin)
See "Poslednii deb i st"
Last Diaries (Tolstoy) **44**:343
A Last Diary (Barbellion) **24**:78-9, 81, 83-6, 88-9, 91
The Last Diet of the Republic (Reymont) **5**:397
The Last Ditch (Hunt) **53**:186-87, 192
"The Last Dream of Bwona Khubla" (Dunsany) **59**:21
"Last Ear" (Coffin) **95**:14
"The Last Encounter" (Forester) **152**:129, 135, 139-40
The Last Epiphany (Aleixandre)
See *Nacimiento último*
"The Last Epos; or, Novel for Maids" (Čapek) **37**:47
Last Essays (Conrad) **43**:101
Last Essays (Croce)
See *Ultima saggi*
Last Essays (Mann) **168**:160, 167, 171
"The Last Fair Deal Gone Down" (Johnson) **69**:84
"The Last Faith" (Buchanan) **107**:71
"The Last Fantasy of James Achanna" (Sharp) **39**:366
"Last Farewell" (Miyazawa) **76**:279
"The Last Faun" (Guiney) **41**:207
"The Last First Night" (Leverson) **18**:200, 202
"The Last Flight of Father" (Schulz)
See "Ostatnia ucieczka ojca"
"The Last Frontier" (Fletcher) **35**:106
"The Last Furrow" (Markham) **47**:279
"The Last Generation" (Flecker) **43**:193, 212-13
"The Last Gleeman" (Yeats) **11**:539
"The Last Godchild" (Papadiamantis) **29**:273
"The Last God's Dream" (Kirk) **119**:280, 335, 339, 343, 349
The Last Harvest (Tagore)
See *Chaitāli*
"The Last Hermit of Warkworth" (Coleridge) **73**:4
The Last Human Being (Lagerkvist)
See *Sista mänskan*
The Last Inspection (Lewis) **3**:285-88
The Last Joy (Hamsun)
See *Den sidste glaede: Skildringer*
"The Last Judgment" (Čapek)
See "Poslední soud"
"Last Judgment" (Fletcher) **35**:109
"The Last Judgment" (Rilke)
See "Das jüngste Gericht"
Last Judgment (Kandinsky) **92**:62
The Last Judgment (Kraus)
See *Weltgericht*
"The Last Laugh" (Owen) **27**:212, 217, 223
The Last Laugh (Murnau)
See *Der letzte Mann*
"The Last Leaf" (Henry) **19**:172, 192, 196
"The Last L'Envoi" (Rhodes) **53**:316
Last Letters to a Friend (Macaulay) **44**:132
"Last Looks at the Lilacs" (Stevens) **3**:445, 452; **45**:348
Last Love Poems of Paul Eluard (Éluard) **7**:261-62
The Last Man (Lagerkvist)
See *Sista mänskan*
The Last Man (Murnau)
See *Der letzte Mann*
The Last Man in Europe (Orwell) **129**:235
"The Last Meeting" (March) **96**:252
"The Last Meeting of Two Old Friends" (Wakefield) **120**:352
Last Men in London (Stapledon) **22**:317, 320, 322, 327, 333-34, 338
"Last Message" (Bryan) **99**:129
"Last Message" (Mitchell) **81**:164
The Last Miracle (Shiel) **8**:359, 361-62
"The Last Mohican" (Malamud) **129**:63, 67-8, 76, 78-80, 83, 106, 108, 116, 125, 151-52, 154, 190, 192; **184**:159, 164, 166-67, 185-86, 189, 199, 203, 306
"The Last Monster" (Sterling) **20**:386
"The Last Music" (Johnson) **19**:232
"Last Night" (Cram) **45**:3
"Last Night" (Holly) **65**:143
The Last Night (Bagritsky)
See *Poslednyaya noch*
"The Last Night in the Old Home" (Bowen) **148**:23
"The Last Night in the Old House" (Bowen)
See "The Last Night in the Old Home"
The Last Night of Don Juan (Rostand)
See *La dernière nuit de Don Juan*
Last Octave (Tagore)
See *Shesh saptak*
The Last of Chéri (Colette)
See *La fin de Chéri*
The Last of Mankind (Lagerkvist)
See *Sista mänskan*
"Last of Summer" (Stringer) **37**:340
"The Last of the Belles" (Fitzgerald) **1**:255; **6**:170
The Last of the Knights (Strindberg) **8**:417
"The Last of the Legions" (Benét) **7**:81
"The Last of the Light Brigade" (Kipling) **8**:208
The Last of the Plainsmen (Grey) **6**:176, 181
"The Last of the Udege Tribe" (Fadeyev)
See *Posledniy iz Udege*
The Last of the Vikings (Bojer)
See *Den siste viking*
"The Last Oracle" (Swinburne) **8**:427
The Last Orphic Dithyramb (Sikelianos)
See *The Dithyramb of the Rose*
"Last Poems" (Tagore)
See "Śesh lekhā"
Last Poems (Housman) **1**:353-56, 358; **10**:240-41, 251
Last Poems (Lawrence) **93**:20, 26, 35, 55-58, 61, 62, 70-78, 83, 97, 103, 104, 113, 124
Last Poems (Thomas) **10**:451, 455
Last Poems (Warner) **131**:311
"Last Poems: I" (Housman) **10**:255
"Last Poems: IV" (Housman) **10**:255
"Last Poems: XVI" (Housman) **10**:255
"Last Poems: XX—The Night Is Freezing Fast" (Housman) **10**:251-52, 262
"Last Poems: XXV" (Housman) **10**:251
"Last Poems: XXVI" (Housman) **10**:251
"Last Poems: XXVII" (Housman) **10**:251
"Last Poems: XXX" (Housman) **10**:251-52
"Last Poems: XL" (Housman) **1**:356
Last Poems and Plays (Yeats) **1**:561, 563, 580; **18**:443, 445, 447, 463; **31**:398, 403, 421
The Last Poems of Elinor Wylie (Wylie) **8**:534
"The Last Portage" (Drummond) **25**:143-45, 157
The Last Post (Ford) **1**:280, 282, 284; **15**:74, 78, 81, 88; **39**:136; **57**:204-90; **172**:29, 34, 36, 38, 48, 57, 72-73, 75, 77, 81, 83-85

The Last Puritan (Santayana) **40**:364-66, 385, 388, 390, 394, 408, 414
"The Last Question" (Parker) **143**:323
"The Last Ray" (Korolenko) **22**:171
The Last Refuge (Fuller) **103**:59, 62-65, 69, 83, 88, 108, 116
The Last Revolution (Dunsany) **59**:17, 24, 27
"The Last Ride" (Campbell) **9**:29, 31
The Last Robin (Wetherald) **81**:413
The Last Romantics (Baroja)
See *Los últimos románticos*
"The Last Rose" (Davidson) **24**:164
The Last September (Bowen) **148**:3, 18-20, 37, 40, 42, 47, 52, 79, 81, 88-89, 104, 107, 123
The Last Septet (Tagore)
See *Shesh saptak*
"The Last Serenade" (Middleton) **56**:184
The Last Sheaf (Thomas) **10**:458
A Last Sheaf (Welch) **22**:441, 445, 456-59
The Last Ships (Ady)
See *Az utolsó hajók*
Last Songs (Ledwidge) **23**:110, 112, 120, 122
"Last Spring They Came Over" (Callaghan) **145**:253, 255
"The Last Supper" (Bryusov) **10**:88
"The Last Supper" (Service) **15**:412
"The Last Supper" (Sharp) **39**:362, 370, 376
"The Last Tea" (Parker) **143**:331-32
The Last Temptation of Chirst (Kazantzakis)
See *Ho teleutaios peirasmos*
The Last Temptation of Christ (Kazantzakis)
See *Ho teleutaios peirasmos*
The Last Thirty Days of Christ (Hartmann) **73**:111, 117
"The Last to Leave" (Wakefield) **120**:354
"The Last Trip In" (Foote) **108**:34
"The Last Trolley" (Gumilev) **60**:261
The Last Tycoon (Fitzgerald) **1**:239-41, 243-45, 247-48, 250, 253-54, 259, 261, 263-64, 266, 270, 272; **6**:162, 167; **28**:104; **55**:191-203, 206-11, 213-29, 231; **157**:164-66, 169-72, 186, 216, 221-22
"The Last Voyage" (Williams) **1**:514
The Last Voyage (Smith) **25**:388
"The Last War" (Muir) **2**:489; **87**:159, 175, 231
"The Last War of the Republic" (Sinclair) **160**:327
The Last Will of an Eccentric (Verne)
See *Le Testament d'un excentrique*
"The Last Word" (Bialik) **25**:60
"A Last Word" (Sarton) **120**:263
"Last Words" (Crane) **11**:128
Last Words on Evolution: A Popular Restrospect and Summary (Haeckel) **83**:131
"Last Words to Miriam" (Lawrence) **93**:43, 45, 64, 70
Last Writings (Nishida) **83**:334
"The Last Years" (Davies) **5**:209
"Last Year's Song" (Andrić) **135**:78
"A Lasting Visage" (Stevens) **3**:448
"Låt ej din stolthet falla" (Södergran) **31**:290
"Late at Night" (Mansfield) **39**:303
"Late Autumn" (Hagiwara) **60**:287
"Late Autumn" (Shiga)
See "Banshu"
"Late Autumn" (Wen I-to) **28**:410
"Late Butterflies" (Nemerov) **124**:256
"Late Chrysanthemum" (Hayashi)
See "Bangiku"
"Late Edition" (La Guma) **140**:237-38
"A Late Encounter with the Enemy" (O'Connor) **132**:246-47, 355-56
Late Harvest (Douglas) **68**:8, 10-11, 29, 32-3, 36
"A Late Lark Twitters" (Henley) **8**:108
"Late, Late Show" (Nemerov) **124**:210
Late Lyrics and Earlier with Many Other Verses (Hardy) **53**:91, 94, 100, 113, 115, 117; **143**:151, 192, 212
The Late Mattia Pascal (Pirandello)
See *Il fu Mattia Pascal*
"The Late Mr. Wells" (Mencken) **13**:384
The Late Mrs. Null (Stockton) **47**:313, 315, 318, 321, 324
"Late Night" (Jiménez) **183**:333
Late Notebooks (Frye) **165**:256-58, 260-61
Late Repentance (Giacosa)
See *La tardi ravveduta*
Late Settings (Merrill) **173**:230
"Late Summer" (Nemerov) **124**:210, 261
"Late Sunday Morning" (Agee) **180**:5, 33, 36
"The Late Swallow" (Muir) **87**:229
"Late-Blooming Flowers" (Chekhov)
See "Cvety zapozdalye"
Later Collected Verse (Service) **15**:413
The Later D. H. Lawrence (Lawrence) **2**:356
Later Days (Davies) **5**:206-07
Later Lyrics (Howe) **21**:113
Later Poems (Carman) **7**:137, 143, 147
Later Poems (Yeats) **1**:553
The Later Poetry of Charlotte Perkins Gilman (Gilman) **117**:144
"The Later Poetry of W. B. Yeats" (Sharp)
See "The Shadowy Waters"
Later Soliloquies (Santayana) **40**:345
Later Works (Wright) **136**:288-89
Later Years (Einstein)
See *Out of His Later Years*
"The Latest Freed Man" (Stevens) **12**:362; **45**:269, 283, 336
Le latin mystique (Gourmont) **17**:126-27, 129-31, 135, 138, 144, 152, 157
Latitudes (Muir) **2**:481; **87**:163
"Lattenzun mit Zwischen raum" (Morgenstern) **8**:305
Latter-Day Psalms (Stapledon) **22**:322
"Latteria" (Saba) **33**:374
"De l'attitude critique devant la poésie" (Daumal) **14**:98
Laudi del cielo, del mare, della terra e degli eroi (D'Annunzio) **6**:136, 139, 144; 40;20, 40-1
Laudin und die Seinen (Wassermann) **6**:513, 517-18
"The Laugh in the Desert" (Prado)
See "La risa en el desierto"
Laugh It Off If You Can (Chekhov) **31**:99
The Laugh of Death (Dent) **72**:21, 23
Laughing Anne (Conrad) **1**:199
"The Laughing Funeral" (McAlmon) **97**:122
"Laughing Gas" (Ginsberg) **120**:77
Laughing Gas (Dreiser) **18**:59, 61
Laughing Gas (Wodehouse) **108**:369-70, 372-73
The Laughing Lady (Sutro) **6**:421-22
The Laughing Matter (Saroyan) **137**:154, 156-57, 159
The Laughing Woman (Tey) **14**:451, 458-59
"The Laughing-Mill" (Hawthorne) **25**:235
"Laughter" (Beerbohm) **1**:75; **24**:115
"Laughter" (Hecht) **101**:36
Laughter (Bergson)
See *Le rire*
Laughter (Mankiewicz) **85**:112
"Laughter and Tears" (Ady) **11**:20
"Laughter in Ireland" (Gregory) **176**:42, 67, 82
Laughter in the Dark (Nabokov)
See *Kamera Obskura*
Laughter, Not for a Cage (Franklin) **7**:268
"The Laughter of Peterkin" (Sharp) **39**:376
The Laughter of Peterkin (Sharp) **39**:359
"The Laughter of Scathach" (Sharp) **39**:376
"Laughter of the Dead" (Kuttner) **10**:267
"The Laughter of the English" (Marquis) **7**:436
"Laughter of the Gods" (Merezhkovsky) **29**:246
The Laughter of the Gods (Dunsany) **59**:3, 6, 11-12
"Laulu suuresta tammesta" (Leino) **24**:368
"Launcelot and Elaine" (Masters)
See "The Ballad of Launcelot and Elaine"
"Launcelot and the Four Queens" (Roberts) **8**:313, 319, 328-29
"The Laundry Song" (Wen I-to) **28**:410
Launzi (Molnár) **20**:167-69
Laura Ruthven's Widowhood (Davidson) **24**:193
Laurence Albani (Bourget) **12**:69
"Laurencis" (Lasker-Schueler) **57**:304
Les lauriers sont coupés (Dujardin) **13**:183-86, 188-89
"Laus Veneris" (Swinburne) **8**:430; **36**:298, 312-13, 318, 320, 329, 332-33, 337
Laus Veneris, and Other Poems and Ballads (Swinburne)
See *Poems and Ballads*
Laus vitae (D'Annunzio) **40**:42, 45
"Lausanne: In Gibbon's Old Churchyard" (Hardy) **53**:100
"Lauter Diamant" (Lasker-Schueler) **57**:298
Lautréamont (Bachelard) **128**:67, 90, 92
"Lavandare" (Pascoli) **45**:154-56
"Laventie" (Gurney) **33**:112
Lavorare stanca (Pavese) **3**:334-35, 339-40
"L'Avventura di un automobilista" (Calvino) **183**:191
"L'Avventura di un bandito" (Calvino) **183**:191
"L'Avventura di una bagnante" (Calvino) **183**:213
"L'Avventura di una moglie" (Calvino) **183**:214
"L'Avventura di uno sciatore" (Calvino) **183**:191
"The Law" (Muir) **87**:178
Law and Authority (Kropotkin) **36**:223
"Law and Literature" (Cardozo) **65**:46
Law and Literature and Other Essays and Addresses (Cardozo) **65**:41
"Law in Science and Science in Law" (Holmes) **77**:287, 321
"Law Lane" (Jewett) **22**:125
Law, Legislation, Liberty (Hayek) **109**:214, 231, 233, 241, 258
"The Law of Causation in Hume" (Nishida)
See "Hyumu no ingaho"
The Law of Civilization and Decay: An Essay on History (Adams) **80**:3, 5, 11-2, 14-7, 26-7, 30-3, 35-7, 41, 43-4, 46-8, 53, 55, 64-9, 71
"The Law of Life" (London) **9**:273-74
The Law of Parallels in the History of Religions (Otto) **85**:320
"The Law of Real Property" (Maitland) **65**:274
The Law of the Four Just Men (Wallace) **57**:402
"The Law of the Jungle" (Kipling) **17**:212
The Law of the Savage (Artsybashev) **31**:10-11
"The Law of the Yukon" (Service) **15**:402, 404
"The Law of Value and Automony" (Otto)
See "Wertgesetz und Autonomie"
A Law unto Herself (Davis) **6**:152
Lawd Today (Wright) **136**:233-40, 250, 259, 276
Lawino (p'Bitek)
See *Wer pa Lawino*
Lawrence of Arabia (Bolt) **175**:26
"Laws and Hypotheses of Behavior" (Thorndike) **107**:370
"The Laws of God, the Laws of Man" (Housman) **10**:247
The Lawsuit of the Twins (Mqhayi)
See *Ityala lamawele*
A Laxative for Baby (Feydeau)
See *On purge bébé*
"Lay" (Sayers) **15**:370
The Lay Anthony (Hergesheimer) **11**:260, 263-65, 274, 279, 284-85
"The Lay Cuadrivium" (Quiroga)
See "Cuadrivio laico"
Lay of Opanas (Bagritsky)
See *Duma pro Opanasa*
"A Layman's View of an Art Exhibition" (Roosevelt) **69**:266
"A Layman's Views on Scientific Nomenclature" (Roosevelt) **69**:177
Lazare (Zola) **41**:450
Lazarillo de Tormes (Arenas) **191**:258
Lazarillo de Tormes (Mann) **2**:424
Lazarine (Bourget) **12**:69
"Lazaro" (Prado) **75**:191-92

"Lazarus" (Robinson) **101**:111
Lazarus (Andreyev) **3**:18, 23
Lazarus (Pirandello)
See *Lazzaro*
Lazarus Laughed (O'Neill) **1**:383, 386, 388, 398, 402; **6**:329, 331, 335; **49**:283, 286
"The Lazarus of Empire" (Campbell) **9**:31
"Laziness" (Ginzburg)
See "Pigrizia"
"The Lazo" (Graham) **19**:133
"Lazurnye beregа" (Kuprin) **5**:303
Lazurnye gory (Sologub) **9**:443
"The Lazy Sons" (Calvino)
See "I figli poltroni"
"Lazybones" (Grove) **4**:141
"Lazybones" (Williams) **89**:371
Lazzaro (Pirandello) **29**:318-20
Lead (Bacovia) **24**:64
"The Leaden-Eyed" (Lindsay) **17**:230, 235, 244
"A Leader" (Baker) **10**:28
"The Leader of the People" (Steinbeck) **135**:271
"The Leaders of the Crowd" (Yeats) **93**:346, 389, 402
"The Leader's Return" (Tsvetaeva)
See "Vozrashchenie vozhdia"
"Leaf by Niggle" (Tolkien) **137**:236, 321, 327, 329
"A Leaf Chases Wind" (Wright) **136**:299
"A Leaf from the Devil's Jest Book" (Markham) **47**:279
A Leaf in the Storm: A Novel of War-Swept China (Lin) **149**:319
"Leafless April" (Wetherald) **81**:408
"The League of Old Men" (London) **9**:264
The League of the Weak (Asch)
See *Der bund der schwachen*
The League of Youth (Ibsen)
See *De unges forbund*
"A Lean and Hungry Look" (Nemerov) **124**:280
"The Lean Year" (Roberts) **68**:338
"The Leaning Tower" (Woolf) **43**:395, 399, 425
"The Leap" (Dickey) **151**:199
"Lear, Tolstoy, and The Fool" (Orwell) **51**:248, 260
"Learnin'" (Fisher)
See "The South Lingers On"
"Learning About Water" (Sarton) **120**:304
Learning, and Other Essays (Chapman) **7**:196
"Learning By Doing" (Nemerov) **124**:182, 185, 252
"Learning the Game" (Holly) **65**:147, 151
"Learning the Trees" (Nemerov) **124**:220
"Learning to Be Dead" (Calvino) **183**:144
"The Least of These" (Quiller-Couch) **53**:291
"Leastrygonians" (Kuprin) **5**:297
"The Leather Jacket" (Pavese)
See "La giachetta di cuoio"
"A Leather Worker" (Güiraldes)
See "Trenzador"
The Leatherwood God (Howells) **7**:370, 391, 393; **17**:178, 184
"Leave" (Jarrell) **177**:194
Leave Her to Heaven (Williams) **89**:364, 366, 372, 390, 402
Leave It to Psmith (Wodehouse) **108**:341, 386-87
The Leavenworth Case: A Lawyer's Story (Green) **63**:134-41, 143-44, 146-52, 157
"Leaves" (Manning) **25**:265
"Leaves" (Scott) **6**:395
"Leaves" (Tynan) **3**:504
Leaves (Dazai Osamu)
See *Ha*
Leaves and Fruit (Gosse) **28**:147
"Leaves from a Young Person's Notebook" (Welch) **22**:456
Leaves from Iris' Wreath (Babits)
See *Levelek Irisz koszorújából*
Leaves from My Life (Cahan)
See *Bleter fun Mein Leben*
Leaves from the Diary of an Impressionist (Hearn) **9**:133, 135
The Leaves of the Tree (Sarton) **120**:302
The Leavetaking (Weiss)
See *Abschied von den Eltern: Erzählung*
"Leaving the Doctor" (Wright) **136**:301
Leaving the Hermitage (Rohan)
See *Shutsuro*
Lebedinaia pesnia (Chekhov) **31**:80
Lebediny stan (Tsvetaeva) **7**:559-61, 565; **35**:394-95, 402-04, 409-11, 416
Leben des Galilei (Brecht) **1**:100, 105, 107-10, 113; **6**:33, 37-8; **13**:42-70; **35**:3, 18-19; **169**:57-63
"Das Leben des Grafen Federigo Confalonieri" (Huch) **13**:253
Das Leben des Horace A. W. Tabor (Zuckmayer) **191**:306
Leben Eduards des Zweiten (Brecht) **169**:41
Leben mit einer Göttin (Brod) **115**:78
Leben und Lieder (Rilke) **195**:258
"Leben und Lüge" (Liliencron) **18**:210, 213, 216
Lebensabriss (Mann) **2**:416; **14**:356
Lebensanschauung: Vier metaphysische Kapitel (Simmel) **64**:338, 351
"Lebensgeschichte in Begegnungen" (Schoenberg) **75**:349
"Lebensläufe" (Hesse) **148**:158-60, 162-63, 166
Lebensrückblick: Grundriß einiger Lebenser innerungen (Andreas-Salome) **56**:26, 54
"Lebensweisheitspielerei" (Stevens) **45**:315, 349
Die Lebenswunder (Haeckel) **83**:127, 138, 142, 147
Lecciones de derecho constitucional (Hostos) **24**:304
Une leçon de morale (Éluard) **41**:151
"Une Leçon de théâtre: Le numéro Barbette" (Cocteau) **119**:91-3
Leçon inaugurale faite le vendredi 7 janvier 1977 (Barthes) **135**:123, 143
Leçons de la guerre (Bourget) **12**:69
Leçons de sociologie: Physique des moeurs et du droit (Durkheim) **55**:135
"Lecture: A Poet in New York" (García Lorca) **197**:229-31, 234
"Lecture on Ethics" (Wittgenstein) **59**:271, 305-6
"A Lecture on Modern Poetry" (Hulme) **21**:144, 147
"Lectures" (Claudel) **10**:123
Lectures and Conversations on Aesthetics, Psychology, and Religious Belifes (Wittgenstein) **59**:250
Lectures d'enfance (Lyotard) **103**:260, 263, 267, 269
Lectures from Childhood (Lyotard)
See *Lectures d'enfance*
Lectures from Colombo to Almora (Vivekananda) **88**:381
Lectures in America (Stein) **1**:441; **6**:415; **28**:315; **48**:212, 214, 216, 233, 236, 252, 255
Lectures on Conditioned Reflexes (Pavlov) **91**:123
Lectures on Ethics (Wittgenstein) **59**:266
Lectures on Kant's Political Philosophy (Arendt) **193**:124-25, 182-83
Lectures on Literature (Nabokov) **108**:104, 108
"Lectures on Religious Belief" (Wittgenstein) **59**:307
Lectures on Russian Literature (Nabokov) **108**:108, 116, 122, 133, 171, 222, 225-26
Lectures on the Consciousness of Inner Time (Husserl)
See *Vorlesungen zur Phänomenologie des innern Zeitbewusstseins*
Lectures on the Phenomenology of Time-Consciousness (Husserl)
See *Vorlesungen zur Phänomenologie des innern Zeitbewusstseins*
Lectures on the Work of the Main Digestive Glands (Pavlov)
See *The Work of the Digestive Glands*
Lectures on Three Hundred Tanka (Yosano) **59**:324
Lectures on Time-Consciousness (Husserl)
See *Vorlesungen zur Phänomenologie des innern Zeitbewusstseins*
Lectures pour une ombre (Giraudoux) **2**:163; **7**:317
"Leda" (Gray) **19**:158
Léda (Jarry) **147**:236-38
"Leda and the Swan" (Gogarty) **15**:104-07, 110, 113
"Leda and the Swan" (Yeats) **1**:572; **11**:519, 532; **31**:397, 420; **93**:390-92, 402
La Leda senza cigno (D'Annunzio) **40**:7, 11
Leda without Swan (D'Annunzio)
See *La Leda senza cigno*
The Led-Horse Claim: A Romance of the Mining Camp (Foote) **108**:8-10, 17, 34-5, 39-40, 42-3
"Ledjanaja tjur'ma" (Annensky) **14**:29
"Ledoxod" (Pilnyak) **23**:212
Lee (Drinkwater)
See *Robert E. Lee*
Lee: A Dramatic Poem (Masters) **25**:295
Lee and the Ladies (Freeman) **11**:232
The Lee Shore (Macaulay) **7**:421, 428; **44**:120
Lee the American (Bradford) **36**:47, 53-4, 65-8
"Leech Gatherer" (Thompson) **4**:439
Lee's Dispatches (Freeman) **11**:225
Lee's Lieutenants: A Study in Command (Freeman) **11**:221-22, 224-26, 228-29
"Leetle Bateese" (Drummond) **25**:151-52, 157
"Leffingwell" (Robinson) **101**:111
"Left" (Runyon) **10**:437
"The Left Bank" (Huysmans) **69**:23
"Left Behind" (Howe) **21**:113
"The Left Leg" (Powys) **9**:370, 376
"Left March" (Mayakovski) **18**:247
"Left Wings and the C3 Mind" (Lewis) **104**:232
Left Wings Over Europe: or, How to Make a War About Nothing (Lewis) **104**:212, 231, 237, 239-42
"Legacies" (Wetherald) **81**:411
"Legend" (Crane) **2**:119-20; **5**:190
"Legend" (Grove) **4**:144
"Legend" (Olesha) **136**:161-62, 164-69, 171-73
"The Legend" (Wharton) **129**:362, 365
"The Legend of Florus" (Korolenko) **22**:172
The Legend of Leonara (Barrie) **2**:41
"The Legend of Mirth" (Kipling) **17**:196
"A Legend of Old Egypt" (Prus)
See "Z legend dawnego Egiptu"
"A Legend of Porcelain" (Lowell) **1**:371, 373; **8**:226, 230
"The Legend of Red Hair" (Fisher) **140**:152
"The Legend of Saamstadt" (Harte) **25**:212, 225
"The Legend of St Francis of Assisi" (Andrić) **135**:39
"Legend of the Christmas Rose" (Lagerloef) **36**:240
The Legend of the Conquering Jew (Zangwill) **16**:448
"A Legend of the Dawn" (Dunsany) **2**:136; **59**:25
The Legend of the Great Inquisitor (Rozanov)
See *Legenda o Velikon inkvizitore*
"The Legend of the Little Fay" (Buchanan) **107**:15
Legend of the Lost (Hecht) **101**:80
"The Legend of the Stepmother" (Buchanan) **107**:15
"The Legend of the Telegraph" (Herzl) **36**:142
"The Legend of the Three and the Four" (Bialik)
See "Agadat sheloshah ve'arba'ah"
"Legenda o Lauri i Petrarki" (Andrić) **135**:52-53
Legenda o Velikon inkvizitore (Rozanov) **104**:307, 309, 313, 330, 382
"Legendary" (Talvik) **87**:319-20

La legénde d'Antonia (Dujardin) **13**:189-91
"La legende du boeuf sur le toit" (Cocteau) **119**:76
Legende eines Lebens (Zweig) **17**:452-53
Die Legende vom heiligen Trinker (Roth) **33**:339, 341-42, 344
"Legende von Vincent und Paul" (Sternheim) **8**:379-80
Legendem om Babel (Bengtsson) **48**:5, 12
Legends (Chang)
See *Chuanqi xiaoshuoji*
Legends (Lowell) **1**:371, 373, 375; **8**:224-27, 230, 237
Legends (Strindberg) **8**:411
"Legends and Lays" (George)
See "Sagen und Sänge"
Legends in September (Hansen) **32**:260
Legends of Tsarevets (Vazov) **25**:454
"Leggerezza" (Calvino) **183**:101, 106, 163
"A Legionary of Life" (Redcam) **25**:330
The Legitimate Wife (Villaurrutia) **80**:458
"Legkedvesebb könyveim" (Mikszath) **31**:174
Légy jó mindhalálig (Moricz) **33**:237, 240, 242-44, 247, 249
Lehrstücken (Brecht) **1**:98, 116
"Leibniz's New Essays concerning the Human Understanding" (Dewey) **95**:95
"Leichen in Priesterwald" (Toller) **10**:490
"Das Leid und diese last" (George) **14**:211
Das Leid von Bernadette (Werfel) **8**:469-70, 472-73, 476-77, 480
Das Leilende Weib (Sternheim) **8**:378
"Leili" (Naidu) **80**:271
Leimonarium (Remizov)
See *Limonar: Lug dukhovnyi*
"Leipzig" (Hardy) **4**:152
Leith Sands, and Other Short Plays (Tey) **14**:459
Leka med elden (Strindberg) **1**:463; **8**:413
"The Lemnian" (Buchan) **41**:34
"The Lemon" (Thomas) **105**:297, 325-27, 329
"The Lemon Orchard" (La Guma) **140**:206, 208, 239
Lemon Verbena and Other Essays (Lucas) **73**:174
De l'emploi du génitif absolu en sanscrit (Saussure) **49**:339
Lemuel Barker (Howells) **7**:366-67
"Lemury" (Balmont) **11**:36
Lena and the Geese (Griffith) **68**:233
"L'enciclopedia d'un visionario" (Calvino) **183**:104
"Length of Days—To the Early Dead in Battle" (Meynell) **6**:302
"The Lengthening Shadow of Lee" (Freeman) **11**:230
"La lengua" (Quiroga) **20**:210
Leninism (Stalin) **92**:158, 219, 223, 227
"Leninism or Marxism?" (Luxemburg) **63**:204, 221
"Lenoch ka" (Kuprin) **5**:306
Léocadia (Anouilh) **195**:13, 15, 18, 26, 50-1, 54-6, 68
"El león" (Quiroga) **20**:213
Leonarda (Bjoernson) **7**:104-05, 111, 114; **37**:11, 17, 19, 29
Leonardo da Vinci (Lucas) **73**:164
"Leonardo da Vinci and a Memory of His Childhood" (Freud) **52**:130
Leonardo's Judas (Perutz)
See *Der Judas des Leonardo*
Léonie est en avance (Feydeau) **22**:79
Leonora (Bennett) **5**:24, 26, 38, 40-1, 47; **20**:26; 15, 31, 49, 106, 117-18, 176
The Leopard (Lampedusa)
See *Il gattopardo*
"The Leopard Lady" (Sayers) **15**:373
The Leopard Man (Lewton) **76**:192, 195-96, 203-04, 209-10, 230-31
The Leopard's Spots: A Romance of the White Man's Burden (Dixon) **163**:138, 140, 144, 149-51, 153-55, 158-62, 164, 168, 170, 178-82, 184-85, 187-90, 192-98, 202, 209-18, 223, 227, 229, 231-32, 239-43, 245-48, 252-53, 255-57, 265-72, 275-77
"Lepanto" (Chesterton) **1**:178, 180, 186; **6**:98, 109
"Lepbenslauf des heiligen Wonnebald Púuck" (Huch) **13**:249, 252
"The Leper" (Swinburne) **8**:430, 436, 442; **36**:299, 314, 318
"A Leper" (Warner) **131**:311
Leper Colony (Arenas)
See *Leprosorio*
The Lepers (Housman) **7**:359
"La lèpre" (Apollinaire) **51**:21
Leprosorio (Arenas) **191**:186, 190, 193-94
"The Leprous White Giant in the Landscape" (Tzara) **168**:265
"Les" (Gumilev) **60**:281
Lesbia Brandon (Swinburne) **8**:437-43, 445; **36**:317
"Lese Majesty of the Law" (Williams) **89**:375
Lesebuch fur Städtebewohner (Brecht) **169**:37-39, 43, 45
"Der Lesende" (Rilke) **195**:183
"Der Leser" (Rilke) **195**:298
Leshy (Chekhov) **3**:156-57, 161-62, 164-65; **10**:109; **31**:78, 81, 101-02; **96**:15, 34-36; **163**:16, 63, 74, 102, 118, 128, 134
"Leslie Stephen" (Woolf) **43**:409, 424; **128**:319
Leslie Stephen (MacCarthy) **36**:259
Leslie Stephen (Maitland) **65**:276
Lesnaia kapel (Prishvin) **75**:219, 224
"Lesnaja deva" (Khlebnikov) **20**:131, 139
"Lesnaya toska" (Khlebnikov) **20**:126, 132
Lesok (Kuzmin) **40**:202
"Less" (Jiménez) **183**:336
"Less Than Daintily" (Stephens) **4**:417
"The Lesser Children: A Threnody at the Hunting Season" (Torrence) **97**:143-44, 152, 164-68
The Lesser Evil (Griffith) **68**:186
Lessico famigliare (Ginzburg) **156**:3, 15, 31, 33, 40-42, 45-47, 50, 65, 68-69, 72, 74-75, 87-95, 104, 108-9, 112, 114-15
Lessness (Beckett)
See *Sans*
"Lesson" (Cullen) **37**:167
"The Lesson" (Scott) **6**:389, 393
"Lesson for Americans" (Du Bois) **169**:212
"A Lesson from the Aquarium" (Dreiser) **35**:65
"The Lesson of Balzac" (James) **47**:154
"The Lesson of Landscape" (Meynell) **6**:294
"The Lesson of the Master" (James) **2**:247, 254, 259; **11**:321; **40**:133
The Lesson of the Master (James) **47**:195, 206, 208
Lesson of Things (Drummond de Andrade)
See *Lição de coisas*
The Lessons of October (Trotsky)
See *1917 Uroki Oktyabrya*
"Lestnica" (Bryusov) **10**:92
"Lestnitsa" (Tsvetaeva)
See "Poèma lestnitsy"
"Let It Be Forgotten" (Teasdale) **4**:425
"Let Me at the Enemy—An George Brown" (Himes) **139**:323
"Let Me Feel Your Pulse" (Henry) **19**:170
Let Me Lie (Cabell) **6**:73, 78
"Let me say beginning I don't believe in Soul" (Ginsberg) **120**:39
"Let My People Go" (Johnson) **19**:209
"Let No Charitable Hope" (Wylie) **8**:530, 536
"Let race alone" (Sapir) **108**:279
Let the Hurricane Roar (Lane) **177**:266-67, 271-75, 278, 284-87
Let Us Be Gay (Crothers) **19**:79-80, 82
"Let Us Die Young" (Heidenstam) **5**:249
"Let us eat shadows" (Aleixandre) **113**:57
"Let Us Follow Him" (Sienkiewicz) **3**:426, 430
"Let Us Forget" (Riley) **51**:303
"Let Us Now Praise Famous Men" (Agee) **1**:3-7, 9-12, 14, 16-19; **19**:18-19, 24-6, 28-9, 33-7, 39-43, 45-8
Let Us Now Praise Famous Men (Agee) **180**:3, 8, 11-23, 25-26, 28, 30-33, 36, 39-43, 45, 55-60, 76-77, 82-92, 100-103, 106-7
"Let Us Talk, Let Us Laugh" (Lawrence) **93**:68
"Leto" (Zabolotsky) **52**:375
"Letovanje na jugu" (Andrić) **135**:53, 89
Letras de la Neuva España (Reyes) **33**:317, 319, 323
Let's Be Like the Sun (Balmont)
See *Budem kak solntse*
Let's Be the Victors (Yosano)
See *Yucrshocrsha to nare*
"Let's Have Some Rotten Eggs! Review No. 1" (Mayakovski) **18**:269
"Let's Play King" (Lewis) **4**:257
"A Letter" (Babel)
See "Pis'mo"
"Letter" (Malamud) **184**:281
"The Letter" (Chekhov)
See "Pis'mo"
"The Letter" (Malamud) **129**:162; **184**:280
"The Letter" (Muir) **87**:169
"Letter" (Orwell) **129**:248
"The Letter" (Owen) **5**:369, 371; **27**:212, 229, 236
"The Letter" (Wharton) **129**:361
"Letter 24 July 1946" (Merrill) **173**:253
"Letter 28 Sept. 1946" (Merrill) **173**:253
"Letter Addressed to Miss Mary Robinson" (Lee-Hamilton) **22**:188
"A Letter from 1920" (Andrić)
See "Pismo iz 1920 godine"
"Letter from a Girl to Her Own Old Age" (Meynell) **6**:291, 295, 300, 302
Letter from an Unknown Woman (Ophuls) **79**:173, 175, 180-2, 185-6, 189, 193, 197, 199-201, 204, 207, 212, 215, 219-20, 223-6, 228-32, 244, 248, 258-64, 266
Letter from an Unknown Woman (Zweig) **17**:429, 454-55
"Letter from Chicago for Virginia Woolf" (Sarton) **120**:266, 318
"A Letter from John Keats to Fanny Brawne" (Percy) **84**:198
"A Letter from Lesbos" (Carman) **7**:137, 149
"Letter from Lezama" (Sarduy) **167**:200
"Letter from Paris to Comrade Kostrov on the Nature of Love" (Mayakovski) **4**:299; **18**:246, 248, 262
"Letter from the Year 1920" (Andrić)
See "Pismo iz 1920 godine"
"Letter from Tomi" (Babits)
See "Level Tomiból"
"A Letter Home" (Bennett) **197**:77
A Letter of Introduction (Howells) **7**:387
"The Letter of the Lord Chandos" (Hofmannsthal)
See "Ein Brief"
"Letter on Lautréamont" (Artaud) **36**:5
"A Letter That Was Not Written" (Beerbohm) **24**:103, 123
"A Letter to a Dyspeptic" (Higginson) **36**:175
Letter to a Hostage (Saint-Exupéry)
See *Lettre à un otage*
"Letter to a Northern Editor" (Faulkner) **170**:239
Letter to a Priest (Weil)
See *Lettre à un religieux*
"Letter to a Psychiatrist" (Sarton) **120**:304
Letter to a Young Catholic (Böll)
See *Brief an einen jungen Katholiken*
"A Letter to a Young Contributor" (Higginson) **36**:176-77
"Letter to a Young Critic" (Morris) **107**:188
A Letter to a Young Poet (Woolf) **43**:388, 391
A Letter to American Teachers of History (Adams) **4**:8, 17-18; **52**:14, 41-2
"Letter to Hamish Hamilton, April 22, 1949" (Chandler) **179**:142

"Letter to Hamish Hamilton, September 19, 1951" (Chandler) **179**:210
"Letter to Hamish Hamilton, September 28, 1950" (Chandler) **179**:142
"Letter to Hardwick Moseley, April 23, 1949" (Chandler) **179**:142
Letter to His Father (Kafka)
See *Brief an den Vater*
"Letter to His Wife" (Radnóti) **16**:411, 420
Letter to Jackie (Anderson) **144**:39
"Letter to James Sandoe, October 17, 1948" (Chandler) **179**:141
"Letter to James Sandoe, September 14, 1949" (Chandler) **179**:144
"A Letter to James Stephens" (Sarton) **120**:300
"Letter to John Houseman, November 10, 1950" (Chandler) **179**:203
"Letter to Marie von Thurn und Taxis" (Rilke) **195**:323
"Letter to Mark Schorer" (Cary) **196**:155
"A Letter to My Aunt" (Thomas) **105**:358
"A Letter to My Fellow Countrymen" (Osborne) **153**:248
"Letter to the English Institute" (Frye) **165**:227
"A Letter to the Leaders of the Negro Race" (Faulkner) **170**:239
"Letter to V—" (Wylie) **8**:536
"Letter to Withold Hulewicz" (Rilke) **195**:327
"Lettera ad un amico pianista studente al Conservatorio di . . ." (Saba) **33**:372
La letteratura americana e altri saggi (Calvino) **183**:5
Lettere algi vomini di Papa Celestino VI (Papini) **22**:290
"The Letters" (Wharton) **3**:553; **129**:362
Letters (Bennett) **197**:125, 127-28, 154
Letters (Chandler)
See *Selected Letters of Raymond Chandler*
Letters (Fitzgerald) **157**:164-65, 169, 187, 189, 218
Letters (Hardy) **72**:261
Letters (Harte) **1**:344
Letters (Joyce) **159**:301, 303, 305, 310
Letters (Lewis) **104**:228-29, 231, 245
Letters (Muir) **28**:250
Letters (Norris) **155**:337-39
Letters (Warner) **131**:310, 312, 314
Letters (White)
See *Patrick White: Letters*
Letters (Yeats) **93**:368, 399, 400; **116**:306
"Letters à Angèle" (Gide) **177**:27, 100
Letters about Cézanne (Rilke)
See *Briefe über Cézanne*
Letters and Diaries (Coleridge) **73**:10
Letters and Drawings of Bruno Schulz: with Selected Prose (Schulz) **51**:323
The Letters and Journals of Katherine Mansfield: A Selection (Mansfield) **164**:268, 275
Letters and Religion (Chapman) **7**:188, 191
Letters from 74 Rue Taitbout (Saroyan) **137**:171, 187
Letters from America (Brooke) **2**:52; **7**:122, 129
Letters from America (Rölvaag) **17**:335, 338
Letters from Bohemia (Hecht) **101**:74
Letters from China and Japan (Dewey) **95**:68
Letters from Colette (Colette) **5**:173; **16**:116
Letters from England (Čapek)
See *Anglické listy*
Letters from Italy (Čapek) **6**:85
Letters from Julia (Stead) **48**:193
"Letters from Maine" (Sarton) **120**:245
Letters from Maine: New Poems (Sarton) **120**:245, 260, 267, 272, 292
Letters from Prison: Including Poems and a New Version of "The Swallow-Book" (Toller)
See *Briefe aus dem Gefangnis*
"Letters from the Caucasus" (Stalin) **92**:226
"Letters from the Earth" (Twain) **6**:485; **185**:297, 302, 328-30
Letters from the Earth (Twain) **185**:289
Letters From Westerbork (Hillesum)
See *Het denkende hart van de barak: Brieven van Etty Hillesum*
Letters Home (Howells) **41**:256
Letters I (Joyce) **159**:275, 283-84
"Letters in the Wind" (Dazai Osamu) **11**:187
The Letters of A. E. Housman (Housman) **1**:358
Letters of a Self-Made Diplomat to His President (Rogers) **8**:332, 336
"Letters of Advice" (Dobson) **79**:26
The Letters of Ambrose Bierce (Bierce) **44**:10
The Letters of Edith Wharton (Wharton) **129**:364
Letters of Edna St. Vincent Millay (Millay) **169**:232-34, 239
Letters of Ford Madox Ford (Ford) **172**:59
The Letters of Frederic Willia Maitland (Maitland) **65**:276
Letters of Gertrude Bell (Bell) **67**:13
Letters of Heinrich and Thomas Mann, 1900-1949 (Mann) **168**:118, 120, 168
The Letters of Henry James (James) **171**:194
The Letters of J. M. Barrie (Barrie) **164**:14
The Letters of J. R. R. Tolkien (Tolkien) **137**:261-62, 264, 266, 268, 270, 284, 297, 300, 338, 355
The Letters of James Agee to Father Flye (Agee) **1**:6; **19**:48
Letters of James Agee to Father James Flye (Agee) **180**:46, 82, 84
Letters of James Huneker (Huneker) **65**:198
The Letters of James Joyce (Joyce) **52**:244, 247-49
The Letters of John Middleton Murry to Katherine Mansfield (Murry) **16**:358
The Letters of Katherine Mansfield (Mansfield) **8**:281; **164**:250, 252-53, 262, 274, 332, 339
The Letters of Lincoln Steffens (Steffens) **20**:339-41, 344
The Letters of Olive Schreiner, 1876-1920 (Schreiner) **9**:395
The Letters of Oscar Wilde (Wilde) **41**:372; **175**:290
"Letters of Silvia and Aurelia" (Leverson) **18**:200
Letters of Sri Aurobindo, second series (Aurobindo) **63**:33
The Letters of Thomas Mann (Mann) **44**:220, 224
The Letters of Thomas Wolfe (Wolfe) **61**:313-15
Letters of Vachel Lindsay (Lindsay) **17**:246
The Letters of Virginia Woolf (Woolf) **5**:517-18; **43**:421
The Letters of Virginia Woolf, Vol. VI, 1936-1941 (Woolf) **5**:517
Letters of Wallace Stevens (Stevens) **45**:272, 285-87, 289-91, 341, 352
Letters on the Christian Religion (von Hartmann) **96**:222
Letters on Yoga (Aurobindo) **63**:48
Letters to a Friend (Macaulay) **44**:132, 134
"Letters to a Friend across the Border" (Böll)
See "Briefe an einen Freund jenseits der Grenzen"
Letters to a Tanka Poet (Masaoka) **18**:225-26
Letters to a Tanka Poet, No. 13 (Masaoka) **18**:226
Letters to a Writer (Zoshchenko) **15**:501
"Letters to Contemporaries" (Goebbels) **68**:98
Letters to Dead Authors (Lang) **16**:254, 256
Letters to Felice (Kafka)
See *Brief an Felice und andere korrespondenz aus der verlobungszeit*
Letters to Friends (Kafka) **112**:116, 122
Letters to Garnett (Conrad) **43**:133
Letters to Harriet (Moody) **105**:286
"Letters to John Cornstalk" (Lawson) **27**:132
Letters to Lady Welby (Peirce) **81**:206
"Letters to Rachel Blau De Plessis" (Oppen) **107**:352
Letters to the Amazon (Gourmont)
See *Lettres à l'amazone*
Letters to the Sphinx from Oscar Wilde, with Reminiscences of the Author (Leverson) **18**:200-01
Letters to the Women of Spain (Martinez Sierra and Martinez Sierra) **6**:274, 277
Letters to Vernon Watkins (Thomas) **105**:358-59
"Un letto di passaggio" (Calvino) **183**:92
"Un letto di passagio" (Calvino) **183**:191
"Lettre à Bernard Grasset" (Ramuz) **33**:299, 301
"Lettre à ceux qui m'accusent" (Rolland) **23**:262
"Lettre à la jeunesse" (Zola) **6**:560
Lettre à un otage (Saint-Exupéry) **2**:520-22; **56**:222, 227; **169**:321, 330
Lettre à un religieux (Weil) **23**:382, 391, 403-04
"Lettre au Général X" (Saint-Exupéry) **169**:316, 322, 324
"Lettre autobiographique" (Bourget) **12**:67, 76
Lettre aux Anglais (Bernanos) **3**:128
Lettre aux paysans sur la pauvreté et la paix (Giono) **124**:46, 95
"Lettre d'un mobile breton" (Coppee) **25**:124
"Lettre-Océan" (Apollinaire) **8**:28; **51**:33-4, 55
Lettres à Jacques Doucet (Jacob) **6**:194
Lettres a Jean Marais (Cocteau) **119**:79
Lettres à l'amazone (Gourmont) **17**:137, 141, 150
Lettres à l'amie inventée (Saint-Exupéry) **169**:317
Lettres a ma mere (Léautaud) **83**:205
Lettres à Roger Blin (Genet) **128**:130
Lettres à sa fiancée (Bloy) **22**:46
Lettres à Sergio Solmi sur la philosophie de Kant (Alain) **41**:11
Lettres à ses pairs (Colette) **16**:116
Lettres à sixtine (Gourmont) **17**:138
Lettres de la vagabonde (Colette) **16**:116
Lettres de ma chaumière (Mirbeau) **55**:280, 286
Lettres de Rodez (Artaud) **36**:5
Lettres d'un satyre (Gourmont) **17**:137, 153
"Lettres d'un Soldat" (Stevens) **45**:297
Letty (Pinero) **32**:391, 393, 397, 399, 405, 414
"Letzer Abend im Jahr" (Lasker-Schueler) **57**:300, 312, 320
Der Letzte Akt (Pabst) **127**:354, 363-64
"Der Letzte Centaur" (Heyse) **8**:114, 116, 121
"Letzte Fernsicht" (Morgenstern) **8**:305
Der letzte Mann (Murnau) **53**:238-41, 250-54, 274
Das letzte Recht (Raabe) **45**:182
Der letzte Sommer (Huch) **13**:248
Die letzten Tage der Menschheit (Kraus) **5**:282-85, 289-90, 292-94
"Leukothea" (Douglas) **40**:63
Leurs figures (Barrès) **47**:42, 55, 60, 62, 64, 76, 79, 81, 93, 99-100
"Die Leute von Seldwyla" (Huch) **13**:250
Leutnant Gustl (Schnitzler) **4**:385, 393, 396, 398, 400
"Lev" (Zamyatin) **8**:553
"Lev Tolstoy and Culture" (Ivanov) **33**:130
"La leva" (Pereda) **16**:363-64, 379-80
"Levadi" (Bialik) **25**:63
"Levél a Hitveshez" (Radnóti) **16**:412
"Level Tomiból" (Babits) **14**:39
Levelek Irisz koszorújából (Babits) **14**:38
"The Levelled Churchyared" (Hardy) **53**:100
"Levels of Cultural Identity" (Frye) **165**:191
"Levels of Reality in Literature" (Calvino) **183**:147, 221
Levia gravia (Carducci) **32**:86, 91, 102, 108
Levinsky (Cahan)
See *The Rise of David Levinsky*
"Levski" (Vazov) **25**:456
"Lewis Carroll" (de la Mare) **4**:81
"Lewis Thomas, Montaigne and Human Happiness" (Nemerov) **124**:319
"Lex Talionis" (Kirk) **119**:281, 285, 340, 343
"La ley natural" (Lugones) **15**:294
Leyenda (Jiménez) **183**:285-86, 289-91, 293-94, 321, 327

"Leyenda de la Tatuana" (Asturias) **184**:14
"Leyenda de un héroe hueco" (Jiménez) **183**:289
"Leyenda del cadejo" (Asturias) **184**:14
"Leyenda del lugar florido" (Asturias) **184**:14
"Leyenda del volcan" (Asturias) **184**:14
"Leyenda policial" (Borges) **109**:164
Leyendas de Guatemala (Asturias) **184**:9, 11, 13, 15-16, 36, 71, 79
"Leyendas del antiguo Oriente" (Valera y Alcala-Galiano) **10**:504
Lezioni americane (Calvino) **183**:101-2, 105-6, 124, 127, 217
"Lezioni su Stendhal" (Lampedusa) **13**:314-16, 318-19
"Li grihet" (Mistral) **51**:139
"Li meissoun" (Mistral)
See "Les moissons"
"Liaison" (Lawrence) **93**:43
"Lianhuan tao" (Chang) **184**:138
Lianhuantao (Chang) **184**:148
"The Liar" (James) **24**:327; **47**:199-200
The Liar (Hansen)
See *Løgneren*
"Liars" (O'Faolain) **143**:233
"Libellus de Generatione" (Collingwood) **67**:183
Liber Aleph: The Book of Wisdom or Folly (Crowley) **7**:210
Liberalism Ancient and Modern (Strauss) **141**:231, 233, 336, 340
"Liberalism and Industry" (Keynes) **64**:243
"Liberalism and Labour" (Keynes) **64**:219-20, 245
Liberalism and Social Action (Dewey) **95**:36, 69
"Liberalism—a Way Station" (Becker) **63**:72
Liberation (Sá-Carneiro)
See *O resgate*
"The Liberation of the Other Three" (Warung) **45**:420
"I liberi cristiani" (Papini) **22**:281
"Libertad" (Aleixandre) **113**:8
"Liberté" (Éluard) **7**:257, **41**:151, 161, 168
La liberté ou l'amour! (Desnos) **22**:57-8, 66-7, 69, 71-2, 74
"La liberté pour quoi faire" (Bernanos) **3**:121
"Liberty" (Crane) **80**:159
"Liberty" (Éluard)
See "Liberté"
Liberty (Bennett) **5**:46
"Liberty for All" (Khlebnikov) **20**:135
"Liberty Hall" (Lardner) **14**:312
Liberty in the Modern State (Laski) **79**:90, 93, 105, 126, 144
Liberty Jones (Barry) **11**:60, 62-5
Libidinal Economy (Lyotard)
See *Économie libidinale*
"The Library of Babel" (Borges)
See "La biblioteca de Babel"
A Library of World Literature (Hesse)
See *Eine Bibliothek der Weltliteratur*
"Libri, riviste, giornali" (Pratolini) **124**:335
El libro de arena (Borges) **109**:81, 86
El libro de la fuerza, de la bondad y del ensueño (Gonzalez Martinez) **72**:148, 150
El libro de los paisajes (Lugones) **15**:286, 288, 291
Libro de poemas (García Lorca) **1**:308, 318; **7**:296-98; **49**:119-20; **181**:63, 66-67, 118-24, 185; **197**:191, 202
El libro fiel (Lugones) **15**:286, 288
El libro talonario (Echegaray) **4**:101, 105
Libros de poesía (Jiménez) **183**:268, 270-71, 279, 285, 289-93
Librussa (Sternheim) **8**:368
"Lica" (Andrić) **135**:25
Lica (Andrić) **135**:88
Lição de coisas (Drummond de Andrade) **139**:232
"Licciu papa" (Verga) **3**:543
"Lice" (Akutagawa Ryūnosuke) **16**:27
Licenza (D'Annunzio) **40**:7
"A Lickpenny Lover" (Henry) **19**:180, 193
"Lída" (Čapek) **37**:51
Lida Sal's Mirror (Asturias)
See *El espejo de Lida Sal*
"L'idéal de M. Gindre" (Rod) **52**:316
Lidice (Mann) **9**:326
The Lie (Andreyev) **3**:18
A Lie (Nervo) **11**:403
"The Lie of the Land" (Lee) **5**:313
"Lie Thee Down, Oddity!" (Powys) **9**:372
"Liebe blue grave Nacht" (Borchert) **5**:109
Die Liebe der Jeanne Ney (Pabst) **127**:304, 330, 346, 354-55, 358, 362
Liebelei (Ophuls) **79**:173, 175-6, 184, 187, 198, 215-6, 234-9, 243, 271
Liebelei (Schnitzler) **4**:385-88, 390-97
"Eine Liebesgeschichte" (Zuckmayer) **191**:324
"Ein Liebeslied" (Lasker-Schueler) **57**:299-300, 326, 328, 330, 335-36
"Liebestod" (Parker) **143**:323
Der Liebestrank (Wedekind) **7**:584
"Das Lied" (George) **2**:148, 154; **14**:203
"Lied" (Kandinsky) **92**:67
"Ein Lied" (Lasker-Schueler) **57**:301, 336
"Ein Lied an Gott" (Lasker-Schueler) **57**:303
"Das Lied des Blinden" (Rilke) **195**:183
"Das Lied des Gesalbten" (Lasker-Schueler) **57**:302, 307
"Das Lied des Spielprinzen" (Lasker-Schueler) **57**:304, 320
"Das Lied Meines Lebens" (Lasker-Schueler) **57**:313, 336
"Das lied vom blonden Korken" (Morgenstern) **8**:306
"Das Lied von der Gerechtigkeit" (Rilke) **195**:215-16
"lied voor mezelf" (van Ostaijen) **33**:419
"Lieder" (George) **2**:151, 154
"Lieder der Gefangenen" (Toller) **10**:490, 491
"Lieder der Völker" (Raabe) **45**:189
Lieder des Pierrot lunaire (Schoenberg)
See *Dreimals Sieben Lieder des Pierrot Lunaire*
"Lieder von Traum und Tod" (George) **2**:154
"Liens" (Apollinaire) **51**:29, 32, 37, 61-2
"Les liens spirituels de la France et de l'Espagne" (Barrès) **47**:55
"Lieschen" (Herzl) **36**:143
Lieutenant Bones (Wallace) **57**:402
"Le lieutenant des Tirailleurs" (Drieu la Rochelle) **21**:27, 30
Lieutenant Gustl (Schnitzler)
See *Leutnant Gustl*
Lieutenant Hornblower (Forester) **152**:130, 138, 141
"Lieutenant-Captain Rybnikov" (Kuprin) **5**:298-99
Le lieutenant-colonel de Maumort (Martin du Gard) **24**:398, 412
The Lieutenant's Lady (Aldrich) **125**:9
The Lieutenant's Last Fight (Ince) **89**:9
"Life" (Aleixandre) **113**:5, 41, 47
"Life" (Anwar)
See "Penghidupan"
"Life" (Davies) **5**:209
"Life" (Dunbar) **2**:129, **12**:106
"Life" (Hecht) **101**:36
"Life" (Lawrence) **61**:231; **93**:45
"Life" (Mistral)
See "Vida"
"Life" (Naidu) **80**:316
"Life" (Södergran)
See "Livet"
"Life" (Stringer) **37**:339
Life (Bojer)
See *Liv*
Life (Hardy) **153**:110-11, 114, 139
A Life (Morris) **107**:132-33, 142, 152-54, 156, 158, 203, 224
A Life (Svevo)
See *Una vita*
Life along the Wabash (Saroyan) **137**:154
Life Among the Abandoned Farmers (Cobb) **77**:127
Life Among the Savages (Jackson) **187**:235, 247, 259-62, 273, 281, 297-98, 308, 331-32, 334, 339
"The Life and Adventures of Matthew Pavlichenko" (Babel)
See "Zisneopisanie Pavlicenki, Matveja Rodionyca"
The Life and Adventures of Santa Claus (Baum) **7**:13; **132**:80, 82, 86, 103-4
The Life and Death of Harriet Frean (Sinclair) **3**:437-38, 442; **11**:410-12, 414, 422
The Life and Death of the Mayor of Casterbridge: A Story of a Man of Character (Hardy)
See *The Mayor of Casterbridge: The Life and Death of a Man of Character*
Life and Gabriella (Glasgow) **2**:181, 185; **7**:343, 345
Life and Habit (Butler) **1**:133, 135; **33**:27, 29, 35, 44, 49, 52, 55, 64, 66-7
"Life and I" (Wharton) **149**:253
Life and I: An Autobiography of Humanity (Bradford) **36**:53-4, 57, 64
Life and Language in the Old Testament (Chase) **124**:29
Life and Letters (Conrad) **43**:132, 136
The Life and Letters of Charles Lamb (Lucas) **73**:158, 161-63, 173
The Life and Letters of Lafcadio Hearn (Hearn) **9**:122, 124
"Life and Lie" (Liliencron)
See "Leben und Lüge"
Life and Literature (Babits)
See *Élet és irodalem*
Life and Myself (Papini)
See *Il tragico quotidiano*
"The Life and Opinions of Moses Hess" (Berlin) **105**:22
"Life and the Novelist" (Woolf) **20**:419
The Life and Times of Chaucer (Gardner) **195**:105
The Life and Times of Mór Jókai (Mikszath)
See *Jókai Mór élete és kora*
The Life and Work of Composer Foltýn (Čapek)
See *Život a dílo skladatele Foltýna*
The Life and Work of Jesus (Otto) **85**:322
The Life and Works of Thomas Hardy (Hardy) **53**:99, 110, 112, 115; **143**:152-56, 159, 174, 197
"Life/Art" (Wharton) **149**:250
"Life, Art, and America" (Dreiser) **83**:55
"Life as Revealed by Fiction" (Bosman) **49**:11
"The Life Beyond" (Brooke) **2**:59
The Life Brew (Zuckmayer)
See *Der Seelenbräu*
The Life Convict (Lie) **5**:329
"Life Cycle of Common Man" (Nemerov) **124**:156, 171, 179, 297
A Life Disturbed (Hillesum)
See *Het verstoorde leven: Dagboek van Etty Hillesum, 1941-1943*
The Life Divine (Aurobindo) **63**:13-17, 24, 30-7, 40-4, 56
"Life Everlastin'" (Freeman) **9**:61, 76
The Life Everlasting: A Reality of Romance (Corelli) **51**:68, 70
"The Life Heavens" (Aurobindo) **63**:9
The Life I Gave Thee (Pirandello)
See *La vita che ti diedi*
The Life I Gave You (Pirandello)
See *La vita che ti diedi*
Life Immutable (Palamas)
See *He asálleute zoé*
Life in the Fields (Verga)
See *Vita dei campi*
"Life in the Iron Mills" (Davis) **6**:150-57
"Life Is a Dream" (Unamuno) **2**:568

"Life Is Better Than Death" (Malamud) **184**:164, 237, 244-46
"Life Is Motion" (Stevens) **12**:379
Life Is My Song (Fletcher) **35**:101, 104-07
"A Life Lesson" (Riley) **51**:289, 298
Life Lines (Key)
See *Lifslinjer*
"The Life of a Certain Idiot" (Akutagawa Ryūnosuke)
See "Aru ahō no isshō"
The Life of Abraham Lincoln (Tarbell) **40**:427, 433
The Life of Albert Gallatin (Adams) **4**:2, 16-18, 20-1
Life of Arseniev (Bunin) **6**:46
"The Life of Birds" (Higginson) **36**:175, 186
Life of Bishop Patteson (Yonge) **48**:377
The Life of Cesar Borgia of Grance (Sabatini) **47**:303
The Life of Charles XII, King of Sweden 1697-1781 (Bengtsson)
See *Karl den XII:s levnad*
Life of Don Quixote and Sancho (Unamuno)
See *Vida de Don Quijote y Sancho*
The Life of Don Quixote and Sancho, according to Miguel de Cervantes Saavedra (Unamuno)
See *Vida de Don Quixote y Sancho, según Miguel de Cervantes Saavedra, explicada y comentada por Miguel de Unamuno*
The Life of Edward II, King of England (Brecht) **6**:35-6
The Life of Francis Place (Wallas) **91**:352, 355, 396, 402
The Life of Galileo (Brecht)
See *Leben des Galilei*
The Life of George Cabot Lodge (Adams) **4**:14, 19
The Life of Governeur Morris (Roosevelt) **69**:176, 197, 200, 254
The Life of Henry Fawcett (Stephen) **23**:340
The Life of Horace A. W. Tabor (Zuckmayer) **191**:329, 331
"The Life of Irony" (Bourne) **16**:60
A Life of Jesus (Endo)
See *Iesu no shogai*
Life of Jesus (Papini)
See *Storia di Cristo*
The Life of Joan of Arc (France)
See *Vie de Jeanne d'Arc*
Life of Johan Picus, Earl of Mirandula (More) **11**:183-85
Life of John Coleridge Patteson, Missionary Bishop of the Melanesian Islands (Yonge)
See *Life of Bishop Patteson*
The Life of Klim Samgin (Gorky) **8**:75, 87-8
"Life of Ma Parker" (Mansfield) **2**:448, 451; **8**:282, 285-87; **39**:303, 305, 309, 311; **164**:237, 248, 339
The Life of Man (Andreyev)
See *Zhizń chelovieka*
Life of Marlborough (Churchill) **113**:127-28
The Life of Mary Baker G. Eddy and the History of Christian Science (Cather) **132**:132
The Life of Matvey Kozhemyakin (Gorky) **8**:75, 86-7
The Life of Monsieur de Molière (Bulgakov)
See *Zhizn gospodina de Mol'era*
The Life of Nancy (Jewett) **22**:140
The Life of Oharu (Mizoguchi)
See *Saikaku Ichidai Onna*
"The Life of Pavlichenko" (Babel)
See "Zisneopisanie Pavlicenki, Matveja Rodionyca"
The Life of Philip Henry Gosse F.R.S. (Gosse) **28**:156-57, 164
The Life of Pico della Mirandula (More)
See *Life of Johan Picus, Earl of Mirandula*
Life of Picus (More)
See *Life of Johan Picus, Earl of Mirandula*
The Life of Reason; or, The Phases of Human Progress (Santayana) **40**:343-44, 346, 350, 366, 373, 376, 382-83, 388, 401-06, 414, 416
Life of Scott (Buchan)
See *Sir Walter Scott*
The Life of Sir James Fitzjames Stephen (Stephen) **23**:340
"The Life of Tadeo Isidoro Cruz" (Borges)
See "Biografía de Tadeo Isidoro Cruz (1829-1874)"
"The Life of the Bee" (Maeterlinck)
See "La viè des abeilles"
The Life of the Insects (Čapek)
See *Ze života hmyzu*
"The Life of the Magi" (Henry) **19**:184, 190-91, 199-201
The Life of the Mind (Arendt) **193**:30-1, 33, 36, 41, 62, 86, 95, 100-02, 119, 157-58, 160
The Life of Thomas Hardy (Hardy) **143**:104, 129, 132-33
Life of Thomas Hart Benton (Roosevelt) **69**:176, 197-98, 200-01, 253-54
Life of Vasily Fiveysky (Andreyev) **3**:23
"The Life of Vergie Winters" (Bromfield) **11**:82, 86
Life of W. W. Story (James) **11**:321
Life of William Congreve (Gosse) **28**:144-45
"Life on a Battleship" (Stevens) **45**:290
Life on the Mississippi (Twain) **6**:455, 458, 468, 473-74; **12**:429-30; **19**:353, 355, 358-59, 363, 377-78, 382-83, 386; **36**:355, 366, 369, 371, 373, 384, 409; **48**:336-37; **59**:196, 205, 210-11; **161**:233, 237, 271-72, 274, 289, 295, 338; **185**:256
"The Life on the Table" (Stringer) **37**:343
"Life Story Briefly Told" (Hesse) **148**:181
"The Life Story of Pavlichenko" (Babel)
See "Zisneopisanie Pavlicenki, Matveja Rodionyca"
"A Life Term" (Riley) **51**:282
Life with a Goddess (Brod)
See *Leben mit einer Göttin*
Life with Father (Day) **25**:134-37
Life with Mother (Day) **25**:135
The Life Worth Living (Dixon) **163**:174
"The Life You Save May Be Your Own" (O'Connor) **132**:258, 283, 310-11, 313-14
"The Lifeguard" (Dickey) **151**:97-99
Life-Histories of Northern Animals: An Account of the Mammals of Manitoba (Seton) **31**:254-56, 262, 267, 271
Life—Literature—Yoga: New Letters with Questions (Aurobindo) **63**:33
"Life's a Funny Proposition After All" (Cohan) **60**:167
A Life's Assize (Riddell) **40**:334
Life's Handicap (Kipling) **8**:184; **17**:202
Life's Little Ironies (Hardy) **53**:75; **72**:237; **143**:72
"Life's Meaning" (Tolstoy) **79**:427
A Life's Morning (Gissing) **3**:222, 225-26, 230, 232, 234, 237; **24**:220, 222, 230, 233
"Life's Tragedy" (Dunbar) **12**:104, 124
Life-Terms (Canetti)
See *Die Befristeten*
"Liffey Bridge" (Gogarty) **15**:108
"Lifne'aron ha-sefarim" (Bialik) **25**:64
Lifslinjer (Key) **65**:226-27
"Lift Every Voice and Sing" (Johnson) **3**:241; **175**:167, 186, 201-2, 205
"Lift Thy Head" (Bjoernson) **7**:110
Lifted Masks (Glaspell) **55**:241-42; **175**:52, 93, 96, 98
"Der ligger et land" (Bjoernson) **7**:110
"Lighea" (Lampedusa) **13**:296-97, 302
"Light" (Aleixandre)
See "Luz"
"Light" (Gray) **19**:156
Light and Airy Things (Saba)
See *Cose leggere e vaganti*
Light and Darkness (Natsume)
See *Meian*
Light and Serious Verse (Cardùcci)
See *Levia gravia*
Light and Twilight (Thomas) **10**:451
Light and Wandering Things (Saba)
See *Cose leggere e vaganti*
"Light Becomes Where No Sun Shines" (Thomas)
See "Light Breaks Where No Sun Shines"
The Light Beyond (Oppenheim) **45**:131
Light Beyond the Darkness (Harper) **14**:263
"Light Breaks Where No Sun Shines" (Thomas) **8**:450, 458; **45**:361, 365
"A Light Breath" (Bunin)
See "Light Breathing"
"Light Breathing" (Bunin) **6**:57
A Light for Fools (Ginzburg)
See *Tutti i nostri ieri*
"Light! For the Stars Are Pale" (Johnson) **19**:246
The Light from the East (Carpenter) **88**:123
Light in August (Faulkner) **141**:30-36, 39, 42, 49, 57, 101, 117-19, 121-22, 124-26, 169, 172-74, 176-80, 183-84, 186, 192, 195, 197-200; **170**:112, 116-20, 123, 125-28, 131, 141, 144, 146, 160-61, 163-64, 183, 185, 189, 191-202, 209, 212, 215, 224, 234, 244
"Light in Dark Places" (Bonner) **179**:22
"A Light in France" (Runyon) **10**:432
"The Light in Mother's Eyes" (Montgomery) **51**:210
A Light in the Window (Rinehart) **52**:296
"Light Lady" (Cullen) **37**:164
"A Light Left On" (Sarton) **120**:266, 318
"The Light o' the Moon" (Lindsay) **17**:224
Light of Love (Schnitzler)
See *Liebelei*
"The light of the South-West" (Barthes)
See "La lumière du Sud-Ouest"
The Light of the Star (Garland) **3**:192
The Light of Western Stars (Grey) **6**:177, 179, 182
Light on a Dark Horse (Campbell) **5**:120-21
"The Light Princess" (MacDonald) **9**:291, 304-06; **113**:201, 210-12, 214-15, 220-21, 266, 269, 297-300, 313-14, 316, 325-27
The Light Princess (MacDonald) **113**:232
Light Shining through Darkness (Tolstoy) **11**:466; **79**:408
The Light that Came (Griffith) **68**:247
The Light That Failed (Kipling) **8**:180, 187, 199; **17**:198, 210
"Light Transcendent" (Remizov)
See "Svet nerukotvorennyi"
The Light under the Bushel (D'Annunzio)
See *La fiaccola sotto il moggio*
Light Woman (Gale) **7**:284
"Light Woven into Wavespray" (McAlmon) **97**:116, 121
"A Lighted Cigar That Is Smoking" (Apollinaire)
See "Paysage"
The Lighted Way (Oppenheim) **45**:125, 132
Light-Fingered Gentry (Phillips) **44**:254, 262, 264, 268, 274, 277-78, 283, 286
The Lighthouse (Oppen) **107**:288
The Lighthouse (Woolf)
See *To the Lighthouse*
Lighthouse (Woolf)
See *To the Lighthouse*
"The Lighthouse Keeper of Aspinwall" (Sienkiewicz) **3**:425, 430
"Lightness" (Calvino) **183**:146, 217
"Lightning" (Lawrence) **93**:12, 80
The Lightning of August (Ibarguengoitia)
See *Los relámpagos de agosto*
"Lightning Storm on Fuji" (Nemerov) **124**:284
Lights in Sicily (Pirandello)
See *Lumíe di Sicilia*
Lights in the Valley (Bodenheim) **44**:65, 73

Lights of Bohemia (Valle-Inclán)
See *Luces de bohemia*
"The Lights of Cobb and Co." (Lawson) **27**:134
The Lights of Home (Buchanan) **107**:33
"The Lights of Leith" (Buchanan) **107**:60
Lights on Yoga (Aurobindo) **63**:33
"Lights Out" (Thomas) **10**:451, 455, 464
Lights Out (Gale) **7**:284
The Light-Shadowed (Sikelianos)
See *Alafroiskiotos*
"Ligostai strashnyi" (Remizov) **27**:355
"Like a Bad Dream" (Böll) **185**:18
"Like a bit of Rock Cliff" (Sait Faik)
See "Bir kaya parcası Gibi"
"Like a Bull" (Radnóti) **16**:419
"Like a snake" (Aleixandre) **113**:53
"Like a Winding Sheet" (Petry) **112**:300, 346-53
"Like a Wolf on the Fold" (Rinehart) **52**:282, 291
Like and Unlike (Braddon) **111**:231
"Like Brother and Sister" (Gonzalez Martinez) **72**:145
"Like Decorations in a Nigger Cemetery" (Stevens) **12**:372, 381; **45**:283, 285, 330
"Like Hebredian" (Gurney) **33**:88
Like One of the Family: Conversations from a Domestic's Life (Childress) **116**:34, 36-7, 51
"Like the Touch of Rain" (Thomas) **10**:454
"The Likely and the Unlikely" (Bernhard)
See "Wahrscheinliches, Unwahrscheinliches"
A Likely Story (Howells) **7**:387
"Li'l Gal" (Dunbar) **12**:124, 126
"Li'l Liza Jane" (Toomer) **172**:257
Lilac Blossom (Raabe) **45**:191
"The Lilac Tree" (Mansfield) **164**:261
"Lilacs" (Chopin) **14**:70; **127**:113
"Lilacs" (Lowell) **8**:227, 229-30, 234, 237
"Lilacs and Hummingbirds" (Scott) **6**:394-95
"Lilacs for First Love" (Knister) **56**:163
"Lili Lalauna" (Andrić) **135**:53
Lilian (Bennett) **197**:30
Liliane und Paul (Mann) **9**:327
"Lilie der Aue" (George) **14**:206
Liliecrona's Home (Lagerloef)
See *Liljecronas hem*
Liliom (Molnár) **20**:158-61, 165, 167, 170, 173, 178
Lilít e altri racconti (Levi) **109**:305, 315-16, 318-19
"Lilith" (Brennan) **17**:39-41, 43-4, 47, 50, 54, 57-60
"Lilith" (Rod) **52**:316
Lilith (Gourmont) **17**:127, 130-31, 133, 137
Lilith (MacDonald) **9**:292-95, 298-300, 302, 304, 306-07, 311; **113**:197-200, 202, 204-09, 211, 214, 217-251, 228-30, 234-36, 238-43, 253, 255, 259, 268, 281, 283, 285-86, 289-91, 298
Lilith (Sterling) **20**:376, 378, 380
"Lilith, and Other Stories" (Levi)
See *Lilít e altri racconti*
Liljecronas hem (Lagerloef) **36**:237, 242, 246, 248
"Lille Ahasverus" (Jensen) **41**:303
Lille Eyolf (Ibsen) **2**:222, 234; **8**:149; **16**:166
"Lillgubben" (Södergran) **31**:287, 291
Lilli (Reymont) **5**:390
Lillian (Bennett) **5**:32; **20**:26
"Lillian Morris" (Sienkiewicz) **3**:430
"Lillian's Business Adventure" (Montgomery) **51**:200
Liluli (Rolland) **23**:260-61
A Lily among Thorns (Martinez Sierra and Martinez Sierra)
See *Lirio entre espinas*
"The Lily of St. Leonards" (Lawson) **27**:140
"The Lily of St. Pierre" (Runyon) **10**:424-25, 432
"Limbo" (Lee) **5**:319
Limbo, and Other Essays (Lee) **5**:313
The Lime Works (Bernhard)
See *Das Kalkwerk*
Limehouse Nights (Burke) **63**:121, 123-24, 127-29, 131
"Limehouse Rhapsody" (Rohmer) **28**:286
"Limestone and Water" (Gogarty) **15**:109
The Limestone Tree (Hergesheimer) **11**:274
"Liminary" (Brennan) **17**:43
The Limit (Leverson) **18**:188-91, 193-94, 199
"Limitations of Medicine" (Dowson) **4**:93
"Les Limited de l'art" (Gide) **177**:49
"Limites" (Borges) **109**:150
"Limits" (Borges)
See "Limites"
"Limits" (Nemerov) **124**:277
Limits (Okigbo) **171**:340
Limits and Rewards (Kipling) **8**:196
"Limits II" (Okigbo) **171**:356
"Limits of Political Economy" (Dewey) **95**:140
"Limits VIII" (Okigbo) **171**:340
"Limits X" (Okigbo) **171**:340, 346
Limonar: Lug dukhovnyi (Remizov) **27**:334, 346, 350-51, 354-56
Limping Hulda (Bjoernson)
See *Halte Hulde*
"Lin McLean" (Wister) **21**:385
"Lin McLean's Honey-Moon" (Wister) **21**:406
"A Lina" (Saba) **33**:372
Linamenti (Croce) **37**:95
Un linceul n'a pas de poches (McCoy)
See *No Pockets in a Shroud*
"Lincoln" (Bell) **43**:88
"Lincoln" (Dunbar) **12**:104
"Lincoln" (Fletcher) **35**:96, 100, 105-06
Lincoln (Drinkwater)
See *Abraham Lincoln*
Lincoln, and Other Poems (Markham) **47**:287
Lincoln Steffens Speaking (Steffens) **20**:339, 360
Lincoln, the Man (Masters) **2**:466-67, 470
"Lincoln, the Man of the People" (Markham) **47**:281, 286, 292
Linda Condon (Hergesheimer) **11**:262-64, 266, 269, 271, 273, 286
"The Lindby Marksman" (Jensen)
See "Lindby-Skytten"
"Lindby-Skytten" (Jensen) **41**:307
"Line and Color" (Babel)
See "Colour and Line"
"The Line of Least Resistance" (Rhodes) **53**:327
The Line of Love (Cabell) **7**:67
"The Line Which Found Its Fisherman" (Sait Faik)
See "Balikcisini bulan olta"
"Lineage" (Walker) **129**:298, 317, 322, 331-32
"The Lineage of English Literature" (Quiller-Couch) **53**:292
"Líneas que pude haber perdido o escrito hacia 1922" (Borges) **109**:12
The Linen-Measurer (Tolstoy) **4**:458
"Lines" (Harper) **14**:260
"The Lines" (Jarrell) **177**:195
"Lines" (Noguchi) **80**:363
"Lines & Circularities" (Nemerov) **124**:255-56
"Lines and Squares" (Milne) **88**:252
"Lines in Memory of Edmund Morris" (Scott) **6**:387, 394
Lines Long and Short (Fuller) **103**:59, 61, 63, 65, 75, 85, 90, 106-07
Lines of Life (Key)
See *Lifslinjer*
Lines of White on a Sullen Sea (Griffith) **68**:247
"Lines of Winter Rain" (Wright) **136**:302
"Lines on a Monument" (Scott) **6**:389
"Lines on the Death of Dr. P. P. Quimby, Who Healed with the Truth hat Christ Taught in Contradistinction to All Isms" (Eddy) **71**:105
"Lines on the Death of Edward John Trelawny" (Swinburne) **36**:347
"Lines on Various Fly-Leaves" (Guiney) **41**:209
"Lines to a Don" (Belloc) **18**:41
"Lines to a Well Known Tune" (Palamas) **5**:385
"Lines to an Old-Fashioned Icon" (Vazov) **25**:453
"Lines Written in an Album" (Rosenberg) **12**:310
"Lines Written in Dejection" (Yeats) **31**:389
"Lines Written on a Sleepless Night" (Annensky) **14**:20
"Lingard and the Stars" (Robinson) **101**:111
Lingéres légères (Éluard) **41**:151
"Lingering Love" (Chang)
See "Liu qing"
Linit Bath Club Revue (Allen) **87**:37, 52
"The Link" (George)
See "Die Spange"
The Link (Strindberg) **1**:445-46, 448; **8**:407
"Linked Rings" (Chang) **184**:104-5
"Links" (Apollinaire)
See "Liens"
Links (Heijermans) **24**:292
"Lintel" (Jarry) **147**:332
A l'intérieur de la vie (Éluard) **41**:157
"De l'inutilité du théâtre au théâtre" (Jarry) **2**:278, 281; **14**:272; **147**:247
Liolà (Pirandello) **4**:325, 340-42, 353, 356-57; **29**:301, 320
"Łiompa" (Olesha) **136**:77, 103-9, 152, 154, 165
"The Lion" (Quiroga)
See "El león"
"Lion & Honeycomb" (Nemerov) **124**:155, 157-58, 180-82, 226, 250
The Lion and the Fox: The Role of the Hero in the Plays of Shakespeare (Lewis) **2**:391, 399; **9**:241; **104**:173, 186, 201, 210-13, 276-81
"The Lion and the Lamb" (Wylie) **8**:536
The Lion and the Rose (Sarton) **120**:203, 261, 262, 268-69, 272-73, 300-02, 304
"The Lion and the Unicorn" (Kuttner) **10**:274
The Lion and the Unicorn: Socialism and the English Genius (Orwell) **2**:498; **15**:342; **31**:190; **51**:227; **128**:258-59, 267, 274, 284, 296; **129**:223, 244
"The Lion for Real" (Ginsberg) **120**:48
Lion in the Garden (Faulkner) **141**:38, 93, 170
"Lion of St. Mark" (Lawrence) **93**:20
"Lions in Sweden" (Stevens) **45**:269-70, 282
"The Lion's Marrow" (Calvino)
See "Il midollo del leone"
The Lion's Share (Bennett) **20**:24; **197**:28
The Lion's Skin (Sabatini) **47**:303
"Lipa nasred srca" (Popa) **167**:157
Lipikā (Tagore) **3**:491-92, 497
"Lipschitz" (Stein) **48**:254
Liricheskie dramy (Blok) **5**:99-100
"A lírikus epilógja" (Babits) **14**:39
Lirio entre espinas (Martinez Sierra and Martinez Sierra) **6**:275, 278, 287
El lirismo (Pardo Bazán) **189**:240
Lirismos (Gonzalez Martinez) **72**:147-48, 155
Lis isclo d'or (Mistral) **51**:136, 139, 145, 148, 150, 166
Lis Oulivado (Mistral) **51**:152, 166
"Lisette and Eileen" (Robinson) **101**:111
"Lisheen Races, Second-Hand" (Somerville & Ross) **51**:331, 343, 350, 357-8, 360, 381, 383
"Lispet, Lispett & Vaine" (de la Mare) **53**:17
"Lispeth" (Kipling) **8**:205, 207
"A List of Assets" (Olesha)
See "Spisok blagodeyany"
"A List of Benefits" (Olesha)
See "Spisok blagodeyany"
"(listen)" (Cummings) **137**:11-12, 13-15
"Listen" (Mayakovski) **4**:294
"Listen for the Music" (Childress) **116**:37
Listen, Little Man! (Reich) **57**:338-39
"Listen, Lord—A Prayer" (Johnson) **19**:211; **175**:255
"Listen to Me" (Holly) **65**:138-43

"The Listener" (Blackwood) **5**:73, 79-80
The Listener (Bromfield) **11**:82
The Listener, and Other Stories (Blackwood) **5**:77
"The Listeners" (de la Mare) **53**:28
The Listeners, and Other Poems (de la Mare) **4**:74
Listener's Lure: An Oblique Narration (Lucas) **73**:158, 172-73
"Listening to Foxhounds" (Dickey) **151**:90, 167
Listrigony (Kuprin) **5**:302-03
Listy z podróży do Ameryki (Sienkiewicz) **3**:427
"Le lit la table" (Éluard) **7**:251
"Litanies de la rose" (Gourmont) **17**:129
"A Litany" (Swinburne) **36**:299
"Litany for Dictatorships" (Benét) **7**:74
"A Litany for Survival" (Lorde) **173**:61
A Litany for Survival (Lorde) **173**:107-8, 110-11, 141, 144
"The Litany of the Dark People" (Cullen) **4**:43, 46; **37**:155, 159, 162
"The Litany of the Heroes" (Lindsay) **17**:229
Litauische Geschichten (Sudermann) **15**:438-39
Literal Madness (Acker) **191**:57
Literarische Gleichnisse (Spitteler) **12**:338, 348, 350
Das literarische Werk (Schwitters) **95**:315, 329
"Literary and Mechanical Models" (Frye) **165**:181
Literary Art and Pictorial Art (Lagerkvist)
See *Ordkonst och bildkonst*
"Literary Booms" (MacCarthy) **36**:252
"The Literary Character of the Guide for the Perplexed" (Strauss) **141**:336
Literary Criticism (Natsume)
See *Bungaku hyōron*
Literary Criticism (Norris) **155**:340
Literary Diary (Prishvin) **75**:218
Literary Diary, 1889-1907 (Hippius)
See *Literaturny dnevnik, 1889-1907*
The Literary Discipline (Erskine) **84**:157
"Literary Drama" (Symons) **11**:454
Literary Essays (Roosevelt) **69**:255
Literary Essays (Woodberry) **73**:365
Literary Essays and Memoirs (Khodasevich) **15**:208
Literary Exiles (Rozanov) **104**:318
The Literary Fallacy (De Voto) **29**:122, 125, 127, 131
"The Literary Fop" (Chandler) **7**:172
Literary Friends and Acquaintance (Howells) **17**:162
Literary Geography (Sharp) **39**:387
Literary Language and Its Public in Late Latin Antiquity and in the Middle Ages (Auerbach)
See *Literatursprache und Publikum in der lateinischen Spätantike und im Mittelalter*
Literary Lapses (Leacock) **2**:378, 382
Literary Memoirs of the Nineteenth Century (Woodberry) **73**:365
"The Literary merit of Our Latter-Day Drama" (Matthews) **95**:234, 244
Literary Notebooks (Hardy) **143**:153-54
The Literary Notes of Thomas Hardy (Hardy) **143**:159
Literary Problems (Babits)
See *Irodalmi problé mák*
"Literary Psychology" (Santayana) **40**:394
Literator (Babits) **14**:41
Literatur; oder, Man wird doch da sehn (Kraus) **5**:286
Literatur und Lüge (Kraus) **5**:285
"Literature" (Calvino) **183**:64
"Literature" (Nemerov) **124**:307
Literature and Evil (Bataille)
See *La littérature et le mal*
Literature and Lie (Kraus)
See *Literatur und Lüge*
"Literature and Life" (La Guma) **140**:240
Literature and Life (Howells) **7**:373
Literature and Life (Peretz) **16**:390
Literature and Revolution (Trotsky)
See *Lituratura i revolyutsiya*
"Literature and Society" (Bergelson) **81**:30
Literature and the Irish Language (Moore) **7**:476
"Literature and the Left" (Orwell) **128**:286
Literature and the Nation (Tolstoy) **18**:377
Literature at Nurse; or, Circulating Morals (Moore) **7**:477, 490-91
Literature in My Time (Mackenzie) **116**:227, 233
"Literature in the East" (Norris) **155**:339
"Literature in the New Century" (Matthews) **95**:234, 266
The Literature Machine (Calvino)
See *Una pietra sopra: Discorsi di letteratura e societa*
Literature of Northern Europe (Gosse) **28**:144-45
The Literature of the French Emigrés (Brandes) **10**:60
"The Literature of the Negro in the United States" (Wright) **136**:259
Literature; or, We'll See About That (Kraus)
See *Literatur; oder, Man wird doch da sehn*
"The Literature Teacher" (Chekhov)
See "Učitel' Slovesnosti"
Literaturny dnevnik, 1889-1907 (Hippius) **9**:161
"Literaturnym prokuroram" (Tsvetaeva) **7**:559
Literatursprache und Publikum in der lateinischen Spätantike und im Mittelalter (Auerbach) **43**:54-7, 59, 63, 68, 72
Lithuania (Brooke) **2**:60; **7**:128
"Un litigio original" (Palma) **29**:262
The Littel Ottleys (Leverson) **18**:197, 202
Litteratörer och militärer (Bengtsson) **48**:6, 12
"Littérature" (Valéry) **15**:458
La littérature et le mal (Bataille) **155**:9, 34, 59-62, 91
"Littérature et poésie" (Jacob) **6**:191
"Little Ai" (Chang)
See "Xiao ai"
The Little Aircraft (Nemerov) **124**:268
Little Apple (Perutz)
See *Wohin rollst du, Äpfelchen . . .*
"The Little Apple Tree" (Remizov)
See "Yablonka"
"Little Baby" (Holly) **65**:138, 147
"The Little Barrel" (Remizov)
See "Bochenochek"
"The Little Bear" (Remizov) **27**:352
"The Little Beauty That I Was Allowed" (Wylie) **8**:530
"Little Big Horn Medicine" (Wister) **21**:399
"The Little Bird" (Remizov)
See "Ptichka"
"The Little Bird Melancholy" (Morgenstern)
See "Vöglein Schwermut"
"The Little Birds Who Won't Sing" (Chesterton) **6**:109
"The Little Black Bag" (Kornbluth) **8**:217, 221
"The Little Black Book" (McCoy) **28**:224
"The Little Black Hen" (Milne) **88**:242
"Little Blue Eyes and Golden Hair" (Campbell) **9**:30
"Little Blue-Ribbons" (Dobson) **79**:3
"The Little Boots" (Mikszath)
See "A kis csizmák"
"The Little Box" (Popa) **167**:172, 178-79
The Little Box (Popa) **167**:174
Little Boy Blue (Asturias)
See *El Alhajadito*
"A Little Boy in the Morning" (Ledwidge) **23**:111, 118, 120, 122
A Little Boy Lost (Hudson) **29**:163
"Little Boy Stanton" (García Lorca)
See "El niño Stanton"
"Little Brothers of the Ground" (Markham) **47**:278
"Little Brown Baby" (Dunbar) **12**:110, 122, 124
"The Little Cars" (Jarrell) **177**:239
"A Little Child Shall Lead Them" (Harper) **14**:257
Little Children (Saroyan) **137**:169, 186
"A Little Cloud" (Joyce) **8**:171; **35**:145, 149, 156, 164, 167, 194, 197; **159**:298, 311, 314, 316, 358-59, 361
"The Little Cock" (Remizov)
See "Petushok"
The Little Comedy, and Other Stories (Schnitzler) **4**:403
"Little Daylight" (MacDonald) **113**:266, 269, 324-28
"The Little Devil" (Remizov)
See "Chortik"
The Little Devil (Khlebnikov)
See *Chortik*
"The Little Donkey" (Tozzi)
See "Il ciuchino"
The Little Dream (Galsworthy) **1**:303; **45**:34, 51
"A Little Duck Bathes" (Radnóti) **16**:418
The Little Duke; or, Richard the Fearless (Yonge) **48**:376-77
"Little Elegy" (Wylie) **8**:530-31
"The Little Elephant" (Remizov)
See "Slonenok"
The Little Elephant Is Dead (Abe) **131**:12
"Little Emma" (Csáth) **13**:151, 154-55
Little England (Kaye-Smith) **20**:96-8, 101-03, 109, 114-15
A Little English Gallery (Guiney) **41**:208-09
The Little Eohippus (Rhodes)
See *Bransford in Arcadia; or, The Little Eohippus*
Little Essays (Santayana) **40**:350, 414
Little Essays of Love and Virtue (Ellis) **14**:124, 141
Little Eyolf (Ibsen)
See *Lille Eyolf*
"Little Fable" (Kafka)
See "Kleine Fabel"
"The Little Fan" (Pirandello)
See "Il ventaglino"
"The Little Fauns to Proserpine" (Pickthall) **21**:243
A Little Flutter (Bramah) **72**:7
"Little Foxes" (Kipling) **8**:202-04
The Little Foxes (Hellman) **119**:123, 132, 134-36, 138-43, 164-68, 170-75, 177-78, 183-87, 215, 227-36
"A Little Free Mulatto" (Chopin) **14**:61, 82; **127**:167
"Little French Mary" (Jewett) **22**:137
Little Friend, Little Friend (Jarrell) **177**:138, 176, 194
"The Little General" (Muir) **87**:189
"The Little Girl" (Mansfield) **2**:454; **39**:293, 301-03, 329; **164**:251
The Little Girl, and Other Stories (Mansfield) **2**:447
"Little Girls" (Undset) **197**:290
The Little Girls (Bowen) **148**:17, 20-24, 36-37, 43, 45, 66-68, 70-75, 82-83, 94, 103, 108, 110-11, 113-17, 119-20, 123, 126-27, 131-33
The Little Golden Calf (Petrov)
See *Zolotoi telenuk*
"The Little Governess" (Mansfield) **2**:458; **8**:276, 282; **39**:298-302, 304; **164**:252, 307, 339
"Little Haly" (Riley) **51**:282
Little Hearts (Pickthall) **21**:242, 244-45, 247, 250, 257
Little Henrietta (Reese) **181**:339
"Little Herr Friedemann" (Mann) **168**:186
Little Herr Friedemann and Other Stories (Mann)
See *Der kleine Herr Friedemann*
"The Little Hill" (Millay) **4**:316; **49**:207, 222
"The Little Hours" (Parker) **143**:282-83, 285, 331, 335
"The Little House" (Jackson) **187**:283

"The Little House Next Door" (Aldrich) **125**:7, 20
The Little Hunchback (Arlt)
See "El jorobadito"
"The Little Hut" (Pirandello) **4**:349
"Little Ivory Figures Pulled with a String" (Lowell) **8**:234
Little Johnny Jones (Cohan) **60**:157, 159, 162, 164, 166-71
A Little Journey (Crothers) **19**:74, 77
"A Little Kansas Leaven" (Fisher) **87**:74
The Little Karoo (Smith) **25**:376-79, 381-82, 384, 386-87, 389, 392-93, 397, 402
"The Little King" (Nabokov) **108**:83
The Little Knight (Sienkiewicz) **3**:427
"Little Lac Grenier" (Drummond) **25**:150, 157
The Little Lady of the Big House (London) **9**:257-58, 267, 280
"Little Lamb, Get Lost" (Carter) **139**:205
A Little Less Than Gods (Ford) **15**:78, 89; **172**:7, 53, 58
"A Little Letter" (Bialik) **25**:58
Little Libby: the Adventures of Liberation Chabalala (La Guma) **140**:261-62
"Little Lizzy" (Mann) **2**:429
"The Little Maid at the Door" (Freeman) **9**:64, 72
"Little Man" (Storni)
See "Hombre pequeñito"
The Little Man, and Other Stories (Galsworthy) **45**:32-3
The Little Manx Nation (Caine) **97**:6
Little Mary (Barrie) **2**:43; **164**:63, 69
The Little Master (Natsume)
See *Botchan*
"The Little Milliner" (Scott) **6**:398
The Little Millionaire (Cohan) **60**:166, 168, 171
The Little Minister (Barrie) **2**:42-3, 47; **164**:6, 14
Little Miss Marker (Runyon) **10**:423
"The Little Mistress" (Coppard) **5**:181
"The Little Monk" (Remizov) **27**:351, 355
"The Little More" (Dickey) **151**:176
Little Nelly Kelly (Cohan) **60**:159, 165
"Little Next Door" (Rhodes) **53**:316
"The Little Ninny" (McAlmon) **97**:120
Little Novels of Sicily (Verga)
See *Novelle rusticane*
"Little O'Grady and the Grindstone" (Fuller) **103**:74
"The Little Old Lady in Lavender Silk" (Parker) **143**:325
"Little Old Man" (Södergran)
See "Lillgubben"
"Little Old Scaffold" (Wister) **21**:385
A Little Organum for the Theater (Brecht)
See *Kleines Organon für das Theatre*
Little Orphan (Moricz)
See *Árvácska*
"Little Orphant Annie" (Riley) **51**:286, 292, 297
"The Little People" (Howard) **8**:137
"The Little People" (Rhodes) **53**:316
Little People with Little Minds (Aleichem)
See *Kleyne mentshelekh mit kleyne hasoges*
Little Pierre (France)
See *Le petit Pierre*
"De Little Pikaninny's Gone to Sleep" (Johnson) **3**:243
"The Little Pin" (Oppen) **107**:354
Little Plays (Sutro) **6**:421
Little Plays of St. Francis (Housman) **7**:354, 356, 359-61
"A Little Poem" (Jarrell) **177**:138
"The Little Portress" (Mew) **8**:299-300
"The Little Pot" (Aleichem)
See "Dos tepl"
"Little Priest of the Bogs" (Blok) **5**:84
The Little Prince (Saint-Exupéry)
See *Le petit prince*
"Little Rain" (Roberts) **68**:302, 336
"A Little Ramble" (Walser) **18**:437
The Little Raven (Rainis)
See *Krauklītis*
"Little Recipes from Modern Magic" (Apollinaire) **51**:49
"The Little Red Kitten" (Hearn) **9**:135
"The Little Red Mouth" (Douglas) **40**:94
"The Little Regiment" (Crane) **11**:167
The Little Regiment, and Other Episodes of the American Civil War (Crane) **17**:73
The Little Round Loaf (Prishvin)
See *Za volshebnym kolobkom*
"A Little Sermon on Success" (Benchley) **55**:15
"Little Sheik" (McKay) **41**:329
The Little Sister (Chandler) **1**:173; **7**:168, 174, 180; **179**:88, 91, 97-101, 103, 108-10, 113, 116, 119, 143-45, 148, 155-56, 158, 160, 180-81, 183-84, 191, 195, 198-201, 203-5, 209, 215, 217-22, 226, 229-30, 233
"The Little Sister of the Prophet" (Pickthall) **21**:248, 256-57
"The Little Soldier" (Platonov) **14**:420
"Little Soldiers" (Nezval) **44**:249
"A Little Song" (Scott) **6**:385
"Little Sonnet to Little Friends" (Cullen) **37**:165
Little Stories for Big Men (Peretz) **16**:390
"The Little Story" (Bierce) **44**:45
"Little Story" (Morgenstern)
See "Kleine Geschichte"
The Little Tales of Smethers, and Other Stories (Dunsany) **59**:17, 27-8
"A Little Talk about Literature" (Corelli) **51**:81
"The Little Theater of the World; or, The Fortunate Ones" (Hofmannsthal)
See "Das kleine Welttheater"
"Little Things" (Stephens) **4**:416
Little Things (Ellis) **14**:106
Little Tich (Rohmer) **28**:293, 295
Little Tiger (Hope) **83**:181
"The Little Tike" (Williams) **89**:383
"Little Tin Gods on Wheels" (Hartmann) **73**:131
"Little Tobrah" (Kipling) **17**:207
A Little Tour in France (James) **47**:182
The Little Town Where Time Stood Still (Hrabal)
See *Mestecko, kde se zastavil cas*
A Little Trilogy (Gladkov) **27**:91-2
"Little Viennese Waltz" (García Lorca) **197**:217
The Little Virtues (Ginzburg)
See *Le piccole virtù*
Little Waif (Moricz)
See *Árvácska*
"Little Warhorse" (Seton) **31**:280
"A Little While" (Teasdale) **4**:429
The Little White Bird (Barrie) **2**:48; **164**:6-8, 28, 62, 66, 80
"The Little Wife" (March) **96**:237-38, 249, 252, 259, 265
The Little Wife, and Other Stories (March) **96**:235, 237, 254
"Little Words" (Parker) **143**:325
The Little World (Benson) **17**:21, 23, 34
"The Little World Left Behind" (Lawson) **27**:121
"Littoral Zone" (Hagiwara) **60**:308
Lituratura i revolyutsiya (Trotsky) **22**:364-65, 379-81, 387-88
Liturgiia krasoty (Balmont) **11**:36, 39
The Liturgy of Beauty (Balmont)
See *Liturgiia krasoty*
"Liu qing" (Chang) **184**:124, 138-39, 141
"Liubka the Cossack" (Babel) **171**:9, 11, 104, 107-8
"Liubor" (Bryusov) **10**:95-6
"Liubov" (Olesha) **136**:102, 130, 132, 136, 154-56
Liubov (Olesha) **136**:63, 67, 154, 185
Liudi lunnogo sveta (Rozanov) **104**:314, 398
Liuyan (Chang) **184**:137, 145-46, 148-49, 151
"Liv" (Obstfelder) **23**:177, 179, 182, 190-91
Liv (Bojer) **64**:18, 23
Live and Let Die (Fleming) **193**:195, 198-99, 206, 215, 223, 232, 238
The Lively Lady (Roberts) **23**:229, 232-33, 235-36, 239
"Liverpool Street" (Davidson) **24**:191
The Lives and Times of Archy and Mehitabel (Marquis) **7**:440-43, 446-47
Lives of Game Animals (Seton) **31**:262, 268
"The Lives of Gulls and Children" (Nemerov) **124**:152-53
Lives of the British Saints (Baring-Gould) **88**:21
Lives of the Hunted: A True Account of the Doings of Five Quadrupeds and Three Birds (Seton) **31**:270, 272, 275
Lives of the Saints (Baring-Gould) **88**:21, 36
"Livet" (Södergran) **31**:290
Livet ivold (Hamsun) **2**:202, 204; **14**:221, 224-45; **49**:127
Livets spil (Hamsun) **2**:202; **14**:221, 243-4; **49**:127
Living Alone (Benson) **17**:17-20, 22, 24, 27-9
"Living and Dead" (Tagore)
See "Jivitra O Mrita"
The Living and the Dead (White) **176**:126-31, 134, 143, 153, 173-77, 179, 182-83, 192, 199, 219, 226, 244
The Living City (Wright) **95**:400, 402, 408
The Living Corpse (Tolstoy)
See *Zhivoy trup*
The Living Daylights (Fleming) **193**:235
The Living Dead (Burroughs) **32**:59
"Living Earth" (Toomer) **172**:277-78
Living Faces (Hippius)
See *Zhivye litsa*
The Living Fire Menace (Dent) **72**:20
The Living Is Easy (West) **108**:306-09, 311, 313-16, 321, 324, 326-28
The Living Mask (Pirandello)
See *Enrico IV*
Living My Life (Goldman) **13**:217, 222, 224
The Living Novel (Morris) **107**:103
The Living of Charlotte Perkins Gilman (Gilman) **37**:191, 198, 200; **117**:42, 53, 67-8, 70, 92-3, 95-6, 124-26, 136, 138-40, 145, 148-49, 162-64, 167, 171, 177
"Living on Other Planets" (Stapledon) **22**:335
"Living or Dead?" (Tagore) **3**:485
Living Portraits (Hippius)
See *Zhivye litsa*
"Living Sky" (García Lorca)
See "Cielo vivo"
"Living There" (Dickey) **151**:101
The Living Thoughts of Thoreau (Dreiser) **83**:14
Living Together (Huysmans)
See *En ménage*
Living Together (Sutro) **6**:422
The Living Torch (Baker) **3**:8; **10**:17
"Living Waves" (Ruskin) **63**:320, 322
"A Living Word about a Living Man" (Tsvetaeva) **7**:571
Le Livre blanc (Cocteau) **119**:58, 87, 93, 110
Le livre de Christophe Columb (Claudel) **10**:34
Le livre de la pitié et de la mort (Loti) **11**:356
Le livre de mon ami (France) **9**:38, 40, 47, 51
Le livre de Monelle (Schwob) **20**:322-25, 328-29
Le Livre de Saint Joseph (Jammes) **75**:119
Le livre des masques (Gourmont) **17**:126-28, 130, 133, 137-38, 143, 145, 147, 157-58
Le livre ouvert, 1938-1940 (Éluard) **7**:248, 250, 257; **41**:156-57, 159-60
"Les livres" (Verhaeren) **12**:469
Les livres des litanies (Gourmont) **17**:137
Les Livres des quatrains (Jammes) **75**:119
Livsslaven (Lie) **5**:323-24
"Liz" (Buchanan) **107**:25
"A Liz Town Humorist" (Riley) **51**:284, 292
"Lizards" (D'Annunzio)
See "Lucertole"
"Lizerunt in the Mean Streets" (Morrison) **72**:353, 356-57, 362, 386-87, 390
Lizzie Borden: A Study in Conjecture (Lowndes) **12**:203

"Lizzie's Tiger" (Carter) **139**:139, 143, 145-46, 206-8
"Ljubav belutka" (Popa) **167**:155
"Ljubav u kasabi" (Andrić) **135**:93-94
La llaga (Gamboa) **36**:71, 73, 77
"Llagas de amor" (García Lorca) **181**:68
"La llama" (Quiroga) **20**:213
El llamado del mundo (Prado) **75**:211
Llana of Gathol (Burroughs) **2**:81; **32**:60
"Llanto por Ignacio Sánchez Mejías" (Machado) **3**:310
Llanto por Ignacio Sánchez Mejías (García Lorca) **1**:308-09, 312-14, 317, 323; **7**:290, 299; **49**:87, 94, 111, 113, 116; **181**:29
Llareggub Hill (Thomas) **105**:304
Llaregyb, a Piece for Radio Perhaps (Thomas) **45**:367; **105**:304
"La lluvia de fuego" (Lugones) **15**:293
"A ló, bárányka és a nyúl" (Mikszath) **31**:167
"A lo que salga" (Unamuno) **148**:308, 310
Lo, the Poor Indian (Adams) **56**:8
"The Loaded Dog" (Lawson) **27**:128, 131-32
"The Loading" (Knister) **56**:155
"The Loafing Negro" (Cotter) **28**:42
"The Loan" (Malamud) **129**:74, 109, 190; **184**:226
"Lob" (Thomas) **10**:452, 454, 460, 463-65
"Lobo, King of the Currumpaw" (Seton) **31**:259, 262, 266, 271-73
Lobo, Rag, and Vixen (Seton) **31**:271
"Lobsters" (Nemerov) **124**:253
La loca de la casa (Pérez Galdós) **27**:247, 255, 268
The Local Authority (de Filippo) **127**:281
Local Color (Capote) **164**:150, 199, 201
"Local Colour" (Bosman) **49**:12
"Local Objects" (Stevens) **45**:309
"Loch Torridon" (Swinburne) **36**:347-8
The Lock (Tolstoy) **18**:377
"The Lock Keeper" (Gurney) **33**:82, 87-8, 95, 99
"The Locked Box" (Marquis) **7**:437
"Locked Doors" (Rinehart) **52**:302
The Locket (Masters) **2**:471
"The Locket that was Baked" (Montgomery) **51**:200
"Lockhart's Criticism" (Woolf) **43**:414
Lock-Out (Vallejo) **56**:312
El loco dios (Echegaray) **4**:100-03
"Locomotive 38, the Ojibway" (Saroyan) **137**:163
Locrine (Swinburne) **8**:432, 434
Locus solus (Roussel) **20**:226-28, 230, 234, 236-37, 239, 241-42, 246-50, 254
"Lodeinikov" (Zabolotsky) **52**:365
"Lodge Faith and Works, 5837" (Kipling) **8**:196
"The Lodger" (Carman) **7**:135
The Lodger (Lowndes) **12**:201-05
"The Lodging House" (McAlmon) **97**:91, 107, 123
"The Lodging House Fire" (Davies) **5**:198, 200
Lodsen og hans hustru (Lie) **5**:323-24, 326, 330-31
Loengselens baat (Rölvaag) **17**:332-33, 338-40, 345
Loftur the Magician (Sigurjónsson)
See *Løgneren*
The Log from the Sea of Cortez (Steinbeck)
See *Sea of Cortez: A Leisurely Journal of Travel and Research*
The Log of a Cowboy (Adams) **56**:2-8, 10-6, 19-21, 23-4
"Log of a Voyage, 1935" (Tomlinson) **71**:400-402
Logbook of the Coiners (Gide)
See *Le journal des faux-monnayeurs*
Logbuch des Traumkapitä (Arp) **115**:5, 13, 12, 26-7, 34, 37
Logic (Gentile)
See *Sistema di logica*
Logic as the Science of the Pure Concept (Croce)
See *Logica come scienzo del concetto puro*
"Logic of Judgements of Practice" (Dewey) **95**:152
"The Logic of Mathematics in Relation to Education" (Peirce) **81**:198
"The Logic of Place and the Religious World-View" (Nishida)
See "Bashoteki ronri to shuyoteki sekaikan"
"The Logic of Science" (Peirce) **81**:193,237
The Logic of Sense (Deleuze)
See *Logique du Sens*
The Logic of the Humanities (Cassirer)
See *Zur Logik der Kulturwissenschaften: Fünf Studien*
"The Logic of the Place of Nothingness and the Religious Worldview" (Nishida)
See "Bashoteki ronri to shuyoteki sekaikan"
"The Logic of the Universe" (Peirce) **81**:274
Logic: The Theory of Inquiry (Dewey) **95**:27, 181, 185
Logica come scienzo del concetto puro (Croce) **37**:80, 88, 93-5, 122-24
Logical Investigations (Husserl)
See *Logische Untersuchungen*
Logical Survey (Husserl)
See *Logische Untersuchungen*
Logique du Sens (Deleuze) **116**:79-80, 82, 85, 87, 99, 104, 110, 113, 116, 122, 147
Logische Untersuchungen (Husserl) **100**:9-11, 18, 29-32, 34, 37-40, 44-45, 47-49, 52, 56-57, 77, 92, 101, 103, 121-22, 124, 145-47, 154
Løgneren (Hansen) **32**:249-54, 257, 264
Løgneren (Sigurjónsson) **27**:364-65
"Logos" (Bialik) **25**:50
"Logutka" (Tolstoy) **18**:377
The Lohengrin Legend (Rank)
See *Die Lohengrinsage*
Die Lohengrinsage (Rank) **115**:247, 301
"A Lohinai fú" (Mikszath) **31**:167
La Loi de la Civilisation et de la Decadence (Adams)
See *The Law of Civilization and Decay: An Essay on History*
"Loin du pigeonnier" (Apollinaire) **51**:34-5
"Les lois" (Verhaeren) **12**:469
Loiterer's Harvest (Lucas) **73**:159, 162, 170
Loitering (Natsume) **2**:454
"Loka" (Chopin) **14**:70; **127**:23
"Lokator poddasza" (Prus) **48**:176
"Lokmanya Tilak" (Naidu) **80**:340
"La Lola" (García Lorca) **181**:196
Lola, la comedianta (García Lorca) **181**:78, 83, 86
Lola Montes (Ophuls) **79**:175-6, 186-7, 193, 212-3, 227, 235, 244, 247
"Lolita" (Parker) **143**:285
Lolita (Kubrick) **112**:165-66, 188, 225, 236, 262-63, 267, 273, 280
Lolita (Nabokov) **108**:49, 52, 59-60, 63, 65-66, 68-69, 74, 77, 82-86, 90, 92, 94, 101-03, 115, 121-28, 135, 143, 147, 153-60, 167-68, 173, 175, 177, 180-85, 200-10, 216, 225, 228-35; **189**:76, 89, 115, 140, 144, 154, 164, 174, 178-79
Lolita: A Screenplay (Nabokov) **108**:178
Lolly Willowes, or The Loving Huntsman (Warner) **131**:310, 314, 316-17, 320, 324, 340, 346, 349-50, 352, 358-60
La Loma del Angel (Arenas) **191**:215
"London" (Aleichem) **35**:308-10
"London" (Grieg) **10**:206
"London" (Jarrell) **177**:147
"London at Night" (Fletcher) **35**:89
"London Excursion" (Fletcher) **35**:94, 103, 114
"London Hospital" (Morrison) **72**:375
"A London Idyl" (Buchanan) **107**:15
London Lamps (Burke) **63**:124
London Lavender (Lucas) **73**:162
"London Letter" (Orwell) **128**:284-85
London Life (Bennett) **197**:16, 19-20
A London Life (James) **47**:207
"London Miniatures" (Thomas) **10**:459
London Nights (Symons) **11**:427-29, 431-32, 439, 445-46, 450-51
London Poems (Buchanan) **107**:24, 52, 57, 63-4
The London Programme (Webb and Webb) **22**:412
London River (Tomlinson) **71**:383-384, 386, 389, 391, 400
The London Spy (Burke) **63**:125, 127
London Street Games (Douglas) **68**:10-11, 16
London Tower (Natsume)
See *Rondon tō*
London Town (Morrison)
See *To London Town*
London Types (Henley) **8**:106
"London Voluntaries" (Henley) **9**:97-8, 106, 109-10
The Londoners: An Absurdity (Hichens) **64**:119, 121, 128-29, 131
"Londres" (Verhaeren) **12**:466
"The Lone Charge of William B. Perkins" (Crane) **11**:161
"A Lone Star" (Bialik) **25**:50
The Lone Star Ranger (Grey) **6**:178, 183, 187-88
"Lone Swan" (Wen I-to) **28**:410
The Lone Swan (Su Man-shu) **24**:458-60
The Lonedale Operator (Griffith) **68**:168
The Loneliest Mountain, and Other Poems (Davies) **5**:209
"Loneliness" (Anderson) **1**:59; **24**:25, 34, 37-8, 49, 51, 59; **123**:12, 78-80
"Loneliness" (Iqbal) **28**:186
"Loneliness" (Schulz) **5**:429; **51**:311
Loneliness (Andreyev) **3**:18
"The Loneliness of the City" (Dreiser) **35**:64
"A Lonely Character" (Hagiwara)
See "Sabishii jinkaku"
"Lonely City" (van Ostaijen) **33**:421
Lonely Crusade (Himes) **139**:244, 247, 265, 267-69, 280, 312-13, 320, 323, 325, 327-28
"The Lonely God" (Stephens) **4**:409, 420
"The Lonely Hunter" (Sharp) **39**:394
The Lonely Lady of Dulwich (Baring) **8**:36, 42
Lonely Lives (Hauptmann)
See *Einsame Menschen*
"The Lonely Man" (Jarrell) **177**:226
Lonely O'Malley (Stringer) **37**:335
"The Lonely Star" (Hergesheimer) **11**:278-79
The Lonely Villa (Griffith) **68**:150, 168, 199, 241
The Lonely Way (Schnitzler)
See *Der einsame Weg*
"The Loner" (Lu Hsun)
See "Guduzhe"
"Lonesome" (Dunbar) **2**:128
"Lonesome Ben" (Chesnutt) **39**:95, 98
"Lonesome Tears" (Holly) **65**:149
Lonesome Traveler (Kerouac) **117**:212, 254, 265-66, 271
The Lonesome West (Riggs) **56**:204, 215, 217
"Long Ago" (Dunbar) **12**:115
Long Ago (Field) **43**:154-55, 159-60, 163-64, 169, 171, 178-79
"Long Ago: A Reminiscence" (White) **176**:171
The Long Arm (Oppenheim) **45**:131
Long before Forty (Forester) **152**:158
"Long Black Song" (Wright) **136**:318
Long Day's Journey into Night (O'Neill) **1**:395, 398-407; **6**:333-37; **49**:245-46, 249, 252, 287, 295
Long Distance Wireless Photography (Melies) **81**:140
The Long Dream (Wright) **136**:225, 240, 264, 276; **180**:222
"The Long Exile" (Tolstoy)
See "God Sees the Truth but Waits"
A Long Gay Book (Stein) **1**:428; **28**:313, 315, 328, 331-32, 338; **48**:264

"Long Gone Lonesome Blues" (Williams) **81**:423,428,444
The Long Good-bye (Chandler) **179**:79-83, 87, 91, 97-98, 100-103, 109-20, 130, 132, 135-36, 138, 140-41, 144, 146-51, 155-57, 159, 162-64, 166, 173, 176-78, 180-81, 184-85, 187-88, 191-95, 200, 202, 205-6, 210, 222-23, 228-30, 232-34
The Long Goodbye (Chandler) **1**:170, 172-76; **7**:168-70, 174-75, 181-82
"The Long Hill" (Teasdale) **4**:425
Long Hunt (Boyd) **115**:62
"Long John Nelson and Sweetie Pie" (Walker) **129**:271-72
The Long Journey (Jensen)
See *Den lange Rejse*
Long Live the King! (Rinehart) **52**:283
Long, Long Ago (Woollcott) **5**:527, 529
"The Long Night" (Bambara) **116**:4-5
"The Long Porter's Tale" (Dunsany) **59**:21
"The Long Race" (Robinson) **5**:412
The Long Road (Gray) **19**:143, 147, 158, 165
The Long Road of Woman's Memory (Addams) **76**:15
"The Long Run" (Wharton) **9**:547; 362; **149**:245
The Long Ships (Bengtsson)
See *Röde Orm, sjöfarare i västerled*
The Long Ships: A Saga of the Viking Age (Bengtsson)
See *Röde Orm, sjöfarare i västerled*
The Long Steps (Tammsaare)
See *Pikad sammud*
The Long Valley (Steinbeck) **135**:289, 321
The Long Voyage Home (O'Neill) **3**:330
A Long Way From Home (McKay) **7**:470-71; **41**:325, 328, 335, 343, 345
"A Long Way Round to Nirvana" (Santayana) **40**:389
"Long Wolf" (Graham) **19**:131
The Longest Journey (Forster) **125**:24, 80, 114
"The Long-haired Merovingians" (Bengtsson) **48**:4
Longing (Ishikawa)
See *Akogare*
"Longing for Colors" (Södergran)
See "Färgernas längtan"
"Long-Legged Fly" (Yeats) **11**:532
Une longue réflexion amoureuse (Éluard) **41**:151
The Long-Winded Lady (Brennan) **124**:2
"Lontano" (Pirandello) **29**:310
"The Look" (Pardo Bazán)
See "La mirada"
Look at America: New England (Chase) **124**:19-20
"Look at Me" (Holly) **65**:138, 141
Look at the Harlequins! (Nabokov) **108**:77, 79-80, 117, 122, 133, 178, 185, 200, 226; **189**:180
Look Back in Anger (Osborne) **153**:239, 242, 244-45, 248-49, 251-56, 258-60, 262-63, 265, 268, 270, 281, 284, 286-95, 297-304, 306-7, 313, 319-20, 325, 327, 333-36, 338-41
Look Back on Happiness (Hamsun)
See *Den sidste glaede: Skildringer*
Look Homeward, Angel (Wolfe) **4**:506-07, 509-11, 513-14, 516, 521-27, 530-31, 535-36, 538; **13**:467, 469-70, 472, 474-76, 479, 482, 484, 486-90, 493-95; **29**:394-434; **61**:280-81, 283-16, 289-92, 299, 301, 310, 315-16, 318
"A Look into the Gulf" (Markham) **47**:278
"Look Me Up" (Millay) **169**:237
A Look Round Literature (Buchanan) **107**:61
"Look Up There!" (Wakefield) **120**:336, 345, 347, 354
Look! We Have Come Through! (Lawrence) **2**:367; **9**:213; **16**:310; **33**:181; **48**:121; **61**:181; **93**:3, 6, 7, 9, 11, 14, 18, 19, 24, 43, 47, 54, 72, 79, 88, 89, 97, 98, 102, 108, 115, 121, 122
"Looking Across the Fields and Watching the Birds Fly" (Stevens) **45**:312-13
Looking at Pictures (Clark) **147**:120-21
"Looking at the Sea" (Pirandello)
See "Guardando il mare"
Looking Back (Douglas) **68**:9-11, 13, 16, 26, 35-6, 44-6
"Looking Back Eight Years" (Fitzgerald) **52**:58
"Looking Back on The Spanish War" (Orwell) **51**:224, 226, 237, 255, 269
"Looking Back to the Past" (Lu Hsun) **3**:301
Looking Beyond (Lin) **149**:327, 347
"Looking Down on the White Heads of My Contemporaries" (Howe) **21**:110
"Looking for Camp" (Foote) **108**:34-5
"Looking for the Buckhead Boys" (Dickey) **151**:100-101, 114, 144
"The Looking Glass" (de la Mare) **53**:36
"The Looking Glass" (Machado de Assis)
See "O espelho"
"The Looking Glass" (Wharton) **129**:364
The Looking Glass (March) **96**:235, 237-38, 250-51, 259, 264, 266
"Looking There" (Gurney) **33**:97-8
"The Loom" (Masters) **25**:298
The Loom of Destiny (Stringer) **37**:334-35
The Loom of Dreams (Symons) **11**:431, 435
The Loom of Years (Noyes) **7**:502
"Looney, the Mutt" (Marquis) **7**:437
"The Loon's Cry" (Nemerov) **124**:193-94, 196, 206, 220, 282, 284, 287, 295
"The Loop" (Masters) **25**:288-89
Loot (Orton) **157**:291-93, 295-97, 308-9, 311, 314-16, 322, 324, 326-32, 336-38, 340, 345-46, 350-57, 359-60
Loot of the Cities (Bennett) **197**:28
Lorca: El poeta y su pueblo (Barea) **14**:47
"Lorca inédito" (García Lorca) **181**:90
Lorca: The Poet and His People (Barea)
See *Lorca: El poeta y su pueblo*
Lorca's Theatre (García Lorca) **1**:309
"The Lord" (Muir) **87**:168
The Lord (Sá-Carneiro)
See *O Lord*
Lord Adrian (Dunsany) **59**:17, 22-23, 26
Lord Alistair's Rebellion (Upward) **85**:380
"Lord Arthur Savile's Crime: A Study of Duty" (Wilde) **8**:492; **23**:435-36; **41**:359-60, 362, 397; **275**:283
"Lord Bajron" (Pilnyak) **23**:213
Lord Chumley (Belasco) **3**:88
"Lord Douglas" (Lawson) **27**:147
"Lord Finchley" (Belloc) **7**:42
"The Lord Fish" (de la Mare) **53**:28
"The Lord Gives" (Ady)
See "Ad az isten"
Lord Halewyn (Ghelderode)
See *Sire Halewyn*
Lord Hornblower (Forester) **152**:129, 133, 138, 161
"The Lord in the Air" (Dickey) **151**:113
Lord Jim (Conrad) **1**:196, 200-01, 203, 205, 208-09, 212, 218-19, 221-22; **6**:113-17, 119, 122-23; **13**:117; **25**:89, 103, 111; **43**:94-150; **57**:39, 42-3, 58, 66, 69, 80, 94, 115
The Lord of Fontenelle (Harte) **25**:212
The Lord of Labraz (Baroja)
See *El mayorazgo de Labraz*
"The Lord of Life" (Lucas) **73**:171, 174
The Lord of Misrule (Noyes) **7**:503, 507
"Lord of My Heart's Elation" (Carman) **7**:147
The Lord of the Harvest (Housman) **7**:359
Lord of the Hollow Dark (Kirk) **119**:281-84, 291-92, 334, 339, 341-42, 347
"Lord of the Jackals" (Rohmer) **28**:277, 286
"Lord of the Lions" (Kuttner) **10**:267
The Lord of the Rings (Tolkien) **137**:209-362
The Lord of the Sea (Shiel) **8**:358-59, 361, 363-64
Lord Ormont and His Aminta (Meredith) **17**:269, 290-94; **43**:290, 296
The Lord Peter Omnibus (Sayers) **15**:377
Lord Peter Views the Body (Sayers) **2**:531; **15**:370, 379
Lord Raingo (Bennett) **5**:32-3, 36, 38, 40, 42; **197**:31, 36, 41-2, 49, 52-4, 104, 109
"Lord Ronald's Wife" (Buchanan) **107**:15
"Lord Winton's Adventure" (Post) **39**:343
Lords and Commons (Pinero) **32**:398, 412
"The Lord's Arrival" (Ady) **11**:15
"The Lord's Bread" (Leino)
See "Luojan leipa"
The Lords of the Ghostland (Saltus) **8**:344-45, 347-48, 353, 356
"Lord's Prayer" (Lawrence) **93**:63
"The Lord's Prayer in B" (Huneker) **65**:196
Lorenz Scheibenhart (Raabe) **45**:189
"Lorenzo Givstiniani's Mother" (Meynell) **6**:295
Lorna Doone (Blackmore) **27**:23, 25-6, 28, 30-3, 36-8, 40-7
Lorraine (Chambers) **41**:88, 91
Lorraine Hansberry: The Collected Last Plays (Hansberry) **192**:290
Das Los des Ossian Balvesen (Kaiser) **9**:181
Losango cáqui (Andrade) **43**:14
Lose with a Smile (Lardner) **2**:329, 338; **14**:307
The Loser (Bernhard)
See *Der Untergeher*
"Losing the Marbles" (Merrill) **173**:230
"Loss in the West" (Bishop) **103**:18
"Losses" (Jarrell) **177**:127, 152, 176, 192, 194, 219, 247
Losses (Jarrell) **177**:138
"Lost" (Paterson) **32**:369
"Lost Anchors" (Robinson) **5**:407
"Lost at C" (Shepherd) **177**:299-300
"The Lost Blend" (Henry) **1**:349; **19**:180
Lost Borders (Austin) **25**:23, 26, 31, 36, 40
"The Lost Boy" (Wolfe) **4**:516, 521; **13**:477, 493
"The Lost Castle" (Sayers) **15**:370
"The Lost Centaur" (Grahame) **64**:81
"The Lost Child" (Benét) **7**:75
"The Lost Children" (Jarrell) **177**:177, 207, 218
"Lost City" (Bosman) **49**:17
"Lost Corner" (Fletcher) **35**:110
"The Lost Dancer" (Toomer) **172**:277
"The Lost Decade" (Fitzgerald) **6**:162, 172
Lost Diaries (Baring) **8**:32, 37, 41, 44
"The Lost Dryad" (Carman) **7**:138, 149
Lost Ecstacy (Rinehart) **52**:288
Lost Edition (Sinclair) **160**:295
"The Lost Elixir" (Dobson) **79**:3
Lost Face (London) **9**:266
"The Lost Galleon" (Harte) **25**:189
The Lost Galleon, and Other Tales (Harte) **25**:189
"The Lost Ghost" (Freeman) **9**:72
The Lost Giant (Dent) **72**:25-26
The Lost Girl (Lawrence) **2**:346, 348, 371; **9**:213-14, 216, 221, 227; **16**:286; 48;104, 108, 121; **93**:97
"Lost Hearts" (James) **6**:213, 215-16
"Lost Heir and Happy Families" (Engel) **137**:119
The Lost Honor of Katharina Blum (Böll)
See *Die verlorene Ehre der Katharina Blum*
Lost Horizon (Hilton) **21**:92-5, 97-100, 102
"The Lost Horseman" (Ady) **11**:13
"The Lost House Key" (van Ostaijen)
See "De verloren huissleutel"
Lost in the Stars (Anderson) **144**:4-5, 18, 20, 22-23, 36, 39, 52
"Lost in Translation" (Merrill) **173**:153, 155, 161-63, 166, 170, 174-77, 182-83, 189, 195-96, 198-204, 211, 237
"The Lost Jewels" (Tagore)
See "Manihara"
Lost Labor's Love (Anderson) **144**:70
"The Lost Lady" (Post) **39**:336
A Lost Lady (Cather) **1**:152-54, 158, 162-63; **11**:95-9, 101-03, 111; **31**:30, 47-8, 59; **99**:167, 201, 207, 209, 228, 274-78;

132:127, 134, 137-39, 141, 147, 154; **152**:10, 16, 21, 27, 53, 77
A Lost Lady of Old Years (Buchan) **41**:34
"Lost Lake" (Kirk) **119**:277, 279, 334
The Lost Land (Jensen)
See *Det tabte Land*
A Lost Leader (Oppenheim) **45**:132
Lost Lectures: or, The Fruits of Experience (Baring) **8**:34, 44
"The Lost Legion" (Kipling) **17**:204
A Lost Letter (Caragiale)
See *O scrisoare pierdută*
"A Lost Lover" (Jewett) **22**:118, 133, 137, 145-46
Lost Man's Lane: A Second Episode in the Life of Amelia Butterworth (Green) **63**:148, 152, 154, 156
Lost Morning (Heyward) **59**:103, 106
"Lost Mr. Blake" (Gilbert) **3**:213
The Lost Oasis (Dent) **72**:22
"Lost on Dress Parade" (Henry) **19**:173
Lost on Du Corrig (O'Grady) **5**:349, 354
Lost on Venus (Burroughs) **32**:59, 75
"The Lost Ones" (Ledwidge) **23**:116, 120
The Lost Ones (Beckett)
See *Le dépeupleur*
"The Lost Orchard" (Pickthall) **21**:254
Lost Paradise (Coffin) **95**:22
"The Lost Phoebe" (Dreiser) **10**:181; **35**:69, 71-2, 74-6
The Lost Princess (MacDonald) **9**:292, 294, 300-02; **113**:213, 259
The Lost Princess of Oz (Baum) **7**:22-3, 25; **132**:95-97
"The Lost Race" (Howard) **8**:137
"The Lost Radium" (Futrelle) **19**:96
The Lost Silk Hat (Dunsany) **2**:140; **59**:6, 10, 26, 29
The Lost Soul (MacDonald) **9**:291
"The Lost Stick" (Lucas) **73**:170
"A Lost Story" (Norris) **24**:449; **155**:340
Lost Tales (Tolkien) **137**:345
"The Lost Thrill" (Riley) **51**:303
"The Lost Track" (de la Mare) **4**:78; **53**:15, 17
"The Lost Tram" (Gumilev)
See "Zabludivshijsja tramvaj"
The Lost Valley, and Other Stories (Blackwood) **5**:77
The Lost Valley of Iskander (Howard) **8**:136
The Lost Viol (Shiel) **8**:361-62
"The Lost Wine" (Valéry)
See "Le vin perdu"
Lost without Trace (Kafka)
See *Der Verschollene*
Lost Wolf (Faust) **49**:53
"Lost Women" (Gilman) **117**:100, 102-03 107, 116, 119-20, 123
"The Lost World" (Jarrell) **177**:129, 132-34, 136, 143, 145, 158, 172-74, 176-77, 179-82, 191, 201, 204-5, 207, 211
The Lost World (Doyle) **7**:224-25, 239
The Lost World (Jarrell) **177**:130, 137, 140, 144, 155, 162, 165, 173, 175-77, 179-80, 193, 212, 218, 238
"Lost Years" (Lee-Hamilton) **22**:190
The Lost Zoo (A Rhyme for the Young, but Not Too Young) (Cullen) **4**:44; **37**:138, 159
"Lot Later" (Nemerov) **124**:147, 249, 273
"Lot No. 249" (Doyle) **7**:238
"La lotería en Babilonia" (Borges) **109**:40, 88
"Lothaw" (Harte) **1**:342; **25**:192
"Lot's Wife" (Nemerov) **124**:151, 171
Lotta fino all'alba (Betti) **5**:59-60, 65
Lotte in Weimar (Mann) **2**:431; **8**:255, 271; **21**:177; **35**:240, 257; **44**:145, 172; **60**:329; **168**:155, 167
"Lotterisvensken" (Nexø) **43**:329
The Lottery (Aleichem)
See *Dos groyse gevins*
"The Lottery" (Jackson) **187**:235, 237-39, 242, 247, 255, 257, 259, 264-65, 267-68, 279, 287, 296-98, 322, 329
The Lottery; or, The Adventures of James Harris (Jackson) **187**:297, 322-23
"The Lottery in Babylon" (Borges)
See "La lotería en Babilonia"
"The Lottery of Babylon" (Borges)
See "La lotería en Babilonia"
"The Lotus" (Naidu) **80**:287, 294
The Lotus Pond (Nervo) **11**:403
"Lou cant dou soulèu" (Mistral) **51**:139
"Lou parangoun" (Mistral) **51**:166
Lou pouèma dóu Rose (Mistral) **51**:141, 148, 152, 163, 166
"Lou prègo-diéu" (Mistral) **51**:140
"Lou saume de la penitènci" (Mistral) **51**:140
Lou tresor dóu Felibrige (Mistral) **51**:148, 152
"Louie" (Hardy) **143**:150
"Louis Aragon ou le Paysan de Paris" (Fondane) **159**:246
Louis de Gonzague (Péguy) **10**:411, 414
"Louisa" (Freeman) **9**:65
"Louisa, Please Come Home" (Jackson) **187**:283
Louise de la Vallière, and Other Poems (Tynan) **3**:501-04, 506
"Loukatut" (Leino) **24**:371
Les loups (Rolland) **23**:257-58, 260, 281
Lourdes (Zola) **1**:588; **6**:564; **21**:426; **41**:422, 438
"Louse Hunting" (Rosenberg) **12**:287, 289, 292, 297, 302, 306-07, 310
"Lov na tetreba" (Andrić) **135**:84
"Love?" (Arnow) **196**:88, 92
"Love" (Baker) **10**:28
"Love" (Bodenheim) **44**:64
"Love" (Brooke) **7**:122
"Love" (Dreiser)
See *Chains*
"Love" (Hagiwara)
See "Airen"
"Love" (Jiménez) **183**:330
"Love" (de la Mare) **4**:81
"Love" (Nemerov) **124**:302
"Love" (Sarton) **120**:271
"Love" (Södergran)
See "Kärlek"
Love (Carter) **139**:53-54, 194-95
Love (Elizabeth) **41**:125, 127, 137
Love Affair: a Venetian Journal (Morris) **107**:200
Love among the Artists (Shaw) **3**:379-81, 394, 401; **9**:422-23; **21**:323; **45**:209
Love among the Cannibals (Morris) **107**:104-05, 118, 124, 130, 132, 157
Love Among the Chickens (Wodehouse) **108**:375
"Love among the Haystacks" (Lawrence) **16**:309; **33**:206
"Love among the Thinkers" (Benchley) **1**:81
"Love and Death" (Naidu) **80**:287
"Love and Death" (Papini)
See "Amore e morte"
Love and Death (Aurobindo) **63**:4, 36
Love and Death in a Hot Country (Naipaul)
See *A Hot Country*
Love and Ethics (Key) **65**:229
Love and Geography (Bjoernson)
See *Geografi og kærlighed*
"Love and Hate for Poetry" (Miyazawa) **76**:295
"Love and Honour" (Belloc) **18**:40
Love and Life in Norway (Bjoernson)
See *Synnøve Solbakken*
Love and Lore (Saltus) **8**:346-47, 354
"Love and Lust" (Rosenberg) **12**:309
Love and Marriage (Key) **65**:225, 227, 229, 237-38
Love and Mr. Lewisham (Wells) **6**:536, 540-41, 548; **12**:487-88; **19**:450
"Love and the Price of Grain" (Strindberg) **21**:366
Love and the Soul Maker (Austin) **25**:23, 35
Love at Arms (Sabatini) **47**:303
"Love at Sea" (Jiménez) **183**:331
Love at Second Sight (Leverson) **18**:194, 196, 199, 202-03
"Love at the USO" (Shepherd) **177**:316
Love Before Breakfast (Sturges) **48**:312
"The Love Boat" (Fitzgerald) **6**:166
"Love Bodhisattva" (Rohan)
See "Fūryūbutsu"
"Love by the Highway" (Roberts) **68**:348, 351
"Love Came Back at Fall of Dew" (Reese) **181**:347
"Love Comfortless" (Tynan) **3**:506
The Love Complex (Dixon) **163**:171-72
Love Conquers All (Benchley) **1**:76-7, 81
"Love Declared" (Thompson) **4**:440
Love Eternal (Haggard) **11**:256
Love, Freedom, and Society (Murry) **16**:344, 357
The Love Game (Schnitzler)
See *Liebelei*
Love Goes Visiting (Jarry)
See *L'amour en visites*
Love Has No Resurrection, and Other Stories (Delafield) **61**:133
Love, Here is My Hat and Other Short Romances (Saroyan) **137**:186, 194
"Love in a Cottage Is Best" (Dunbar) **12**:122
"Love in a Fallen City" (Chang)
See "Qing cheng zhi lian"
"Love in a Foreign Land" (Nagai)
See "Ikyō no koi"
Love in Dian's Lap (Thompson) **4**:435
"Love in Harvest" (Roberts) **68**:304, 337
"Love in the Asylum" (Thomas) **105**:348
"Love in the Casbah" (Andrić)
See "Ljubav u kasabi"
"Love in the Kasaba" (Andrić)
See "Ljubav u kasabi"
"Love in the Snow" (Papadiamantis) **29**:270, 273
"Love in the Valley" (Meredith) **17**:253, 256, 277, 283
"Love in Vain" (Johnson) **69**:82
"Love in Youth" (Harris) **24**:263
Love Insurance (Biggers) **65**:4
Love Is a Golden Book (Tolstoy) **18**:382
Love Is More Powerful than Death (Rainis)
See *Mīla stiprāka par nāvi*
"Love is More Thicker than Forget" (Cummings) **137**:55
Love Is Not Enough: The Treatment of Emotionally Disturbed Children (Bettelheim) **143**:7
"Love Is Not Relief" (Aleixandre) **113**:41
"Love Is Stronger Than Death" (Merezhkovsky) **29**:249
"Love Lament" (Radnóti) **16**:419
"Love Letter" (Ginsberg) **120**:134
"Love Letter" (Sait Faik)
See "Sevgiliye mektup"
"Love Letters Made Easy" (Lardner) **14**:312
"Love Lies Sleeping" (Bishop) **121**:48, 50, 71
"A Love Match" (Warner) **131**:309, 315, 317, 322
The Love Match (Bennett) **197**:16-18, 20
Love Me Forever (Buchanan) **107**:85
"The Love Nest" (Lardner) **2**:337; **14**:293, 299, 307, 313
The Love Nest (Sherwood) **3**:418
The Love Nest, and Other Stories (Lardner) **14**:307
"Love Newborn" (Roberts) **68**:337
"Love of All" (Babits)
See "Mindenek szerelme"
The Love of Annunziata (di Donato) **159**:218, 220-23, 227-28, 230
"The Love of Antelope" (Eastman) **55**:171, 174
Love of Brothers (Tynan) **3**:506
The Love of Don Perlimplín and Belisa in the Garden (García Lorca)
See *Amor de Don Perlimplín*

The Love of Don Perlimplín for Belisa in His Garden (García Lorca)
See *Amor de Don Perlimplín con Belisa en su jardín*
The Love of Landry (Dunbar) **2**:129; **12**:107, 112, 118-19, 122-23
"Love of Life" (London) **15**:262
Love of Life, and Other Stories (London) **9**:262, 266
Love of One's Neighbor (Andreyev)
See *Lyubov k blizhnemu*
The Love of Parson Lord, and Other Stories (Freeman) **9**:68, 72
The Love of Sumako the Actress (Mizoguchi) **72**:315, 324
The Love of the Last Tycoon: A Western (Fitzgerald) **157**:223, 229-30
"The Love of the Saints" (Lee) **5**:315
Love of the World (Ramuz)
See *L'amour du monde*
"Love Omnipotent" (Naidu) **80**:308
"Love Omnipresent" (Naidu) **80**:353
"Love on the Bon-Dieu" (Chopin) **14**:58; **127**:207
"Love on the Farm" (Lawrence) **93**:12, 46, 49, 65, 128
"Love or Eugenics" (Fitzgerald) **157**:187
"Love Poem in the Forest" (Radnóti) **16**:419
"Love Poem on a Theme by Whitman" (Ginsberg) **120**:26
"Love Poem on Istenhegy" (Radnóti) **16**:419
Love Poems (Davies) **5**:204
Love Poems, and Others (Lawrence) **2**:343; **93**:2, 3, 22, 43, 45, 46, 70
"The Love Potion" (Bosman) **49**:7
"Love Replied" (Ginsberg) **120**:26
"Love Song" (Wylie) **8**:530
"A Love Song from the North" (Naidu) **80**:291, 315
Love Songs (Teasdale) **4**:425-26, 428, 430-31
Love Sonnets of a Cave Man, and Other Verses (Marquis) **7**:446
Love Stories (Rinehart) **52**:281-82
"A Love Story" (Zuckmayer)
See "Eine Liebesgeschichte"
"Love Suffered" (Aleixandre) **113**:41
"The Love That Felled a City" (Chang) **184**:103, 106, 109
Love, the Fiddler (Osbourne) **93**:132
"Love Thy Neighbor" (Bjoernson) **7**:110
Love Thy Neighbor (Allen) **87**:40, 55, 62
"The Love Tree" (Cullen) **37**:155, 160, 169
"Love Which Is Brother to Death" (Hearn) **9**:134
"Love Whispers" (Obstfelder)
See "Elskovshvisken"
Love without Love (Pirandello)
See *Amori senza amore*
The Loved and the Lost (Callaghan) **145**:222-23, 248, 254
"Loved I Not Honor More" (Rhodes) **53**:310-11
"A Love-letter" (Dobson) **79**:8
"Loveliest of Trees" (Housman) **10**:250-51, 259
"Loveliness" (Phelps) **113**:339
The Lovely Ambition (Chase) **124**:25
"The Lovely Lady" (Lawrence) **16**:290
The Lovely Lady (Austin) **25**:33
"The Lovely Leave" (Parker) **143**:314, 331-32, 334-35, 340
"Lovely Linda" (Carter) **139**:194
"The Lovely Myfanwy" (de la Mare) **53**:22
"A Lovely Woman" (Davies) **5**:199
Love—Or a Name (Hawthorne) **25**:241
"Love-o'-Women" (Kipling) **8**:188, 200
"The Love-Philtre of Ikey Schoenstein" (Henry) **19**:190, 200
"A Lover" (Coppard) **5**:179
"The Lover" (Kolmar) **40**:175
The Lover (Martinez Sierra and Martinez Sierra) **6**:279
"Lover Loquitur" (Guiney) **41**:206
"The Lover of Love" (Hagiwara)
See "Koi wo koi suru hito"
"The Lovers" (Calvino)
See "Gli amanti"
"Lovers" (Field) **43**:169
"Lovers" (Popa) **167**:179
"The Lovers" (Roberts) **68**:304, 337
Lovers (Popa) **167**:174
Lovers are Never Losers (Giono)
See *Un de baumugnes*
Lover's Breast Knot (Tynan) **3**:502, 506
A Lover's Discourse: Fragments (Barthes)
See *Fragments d'un discours amoureux*
"Lovers Embracing" (Fletcher) **35**:95
Lover's Gift (Tagore) **53**:347
Lovers of Louisiana (Cable) **4**:25-6, 29
"The Lovers of Orelay" (Moore) **7**:478, 487, 493
"Lovers of the Lake" (O'Faolain) **143**:224, 253, 266
Lovers' Saint Ruth's, and Three Other Tales (Guiney) **41**:209
"The Lover's Song" (Yeats) **31**:398
"Love's Apotheosis" (Dunbar) **12**:122
Love's Blindness (Glyn) **72**:139
Love's Comedy (Ibsen)
See *Kjaerlighedens komedie*
"Love's Coming" (Davies) **5**:201
Love's Coming of Age (Carpenter) **88**:66, 72, 92, 98, 127-8, 132, 142
Love's Cross-Currents: A Year's Letters (Swinburne) **8**:438-39, 441-43, 445
Love's Cruel Enigma (Bourget)
See *Cruelle énigme*
Love's Dance of Death (Przybyszewski) **36**:289
"love's function is to fabricate unknowingness" (Cummings) **137**:55
"Love's Hero-World" (Markham) **47**:285
"Love's House" (Manning) **25**:278
"Love's Last Leave" (Hunt) **53**:200
"Love's Made a Fool of You" (Holly) **65**:137-38, 141, 144, 148, 152-53
"Love's Morning Star" (Garvey) **41**:198
"Love's Mortality" (Middleton) **56**:191
"The Loves of Lady Purple" (Carter)
See "The Loves of the Lady Purple"
The Loves of Pelleas and Etarre (Gale) **7**:277, 281-82
"The Loves of the Age of Stone" (Gray) **19**:156
"The Loves of the Lady Purple" (Carter) **139**:47, 188
Love's Old Sweet Song (Saroyan) **137**:155, 196-98, 201, 203-7
"Love's Phases" (Dunbar) **12**:122
Love's Pilgrim (Beresford) **81**:10
Love's Pilgrimage (Sinclair) **160**:277
"Love's Remorse" (Muir) **87**:190
Love's Shadow (Leverson) **18**:187-89, 194, 196, 202
"Love's Tangle" (Cotter) **28**:43
"Love's Way" (Cullen) **37**:167
"Love's Young Dream" (O'Faolain) **143**:262, 264
"Lovesick Blues" (Williams) **81**:420,422,436
"A Lovesong" (Lasker-Schueler)
See "Ein Liebeslied"
"Lovets chelovekov" (Zamyatin) **8**:542, 544, 548, 552, 558-60; **37**:419, 428, 431
Love—What I Think of It (Glyn)
See *The Philosophy of Love*
"The Loving Youth and the Scornful Maid" (Pyle) **81**:391
"Low Tide" (Carman)
See "Low Tide on Grand Pré"
"Low Tide" (Huysmans) **69**:25
"Low Tide" (Millay) **4**:306; **49**:226
"Low Tide at Grand Pré" (Carman)
See "Low Tide on Grand Pré"
"Low Tide on Grand Pré" (Carman) **7**:141, 146
Löwensköldska ringen (Lagerloef) **4**:235
The Lower Depths (Gorky)
See *Na dne*
The Loyal 47 Ronin (Mizoguchi)
See *Genroku Chushingura*
"The Loyal Minister of Art" (Wen I-to) **28**:408, 415
Loyalties (Galsworthy) **1**:294-95, 303; **45**:45, 51-2
"Lübeck als geistige Lebensform" (Mann) **60**:363
"La luce negli occhi" (Calvino) **183**:103, 107
"Lucerne" (Tolstoy)
See "Iz zapisok kniazia D. Nekhliudova. Liutsern"
"Lucertole" (D'Annunzio) **40**:37
Luces de bohemia (Valle-Inclán) **5**:476-77, 480-83, 486
"Lucha eterna" (Gonzalez Martinez) **72**:148
La lucha por la vida (Baroja) **8**:52, 55, 61-2
Lucia in London (Benson) **27**:9, 14
"Lucía Martínez" (García Lorca) **181**:184
Lucian, Plato, and Greek Morals (Chapman) **7**:189, 193
"Luciana" (Ramos) **32**:431
Lucia's Progress (Benson) **27**:9
Lucidor (Hofmannsthal) **11**:302
La luciérnaga (Azuela) **3**:75-6, 78, 80, 82-3; **145**:11, 15, 18-19, 27-28, 30-33
"Lucifer" (Lawrence) **93**:104, 113
Lucifer (Santayana) **40**:372, 400
"Lucila Strindberg" (Quiroga) **20**:213
Lucinda (Hope) **83**:170
Lucio's Confession (Sá-Carneiro)
See *A confissão de Lúcio*
"The Luck of Roaring Camp" (Harte) **25**:189, 194, 197-98, 203-04, 207-08, 210, 212-14, 221-23
The Luck of Roaring Camp, and Other Sketches (Harte) **25**:189, 197, 203-04, 207, 214-15
The Luck of the Bodkins (Wodehouse) **108**:362, 366-67
The Luck of the Strong (Hodgson) **13**:237
The Luck of the Vails (Benson) **27**:17-18
Luck of the Year: Essays, Fantasies, and Stories (Lucas) **73**:159
Luck, or Cunning, as the Main Means of Organic Modifications? (Butler) **1**:133; **33**:27, 29, 42, 50, 52-3
"The Luck Piece" (Cobb) **77**:141-2
Lucky Kristoffer (Hansen)
See *Lykkelige Kristoffer*
Lucky Larribee (Faust) **49**:38
The Lucky One (Milne) **6**:306, 308
Lucky Pear (Strindberg)
See *Lycko-Pers resa*
Lucky Peter's Travels (Strindberg)
See *Lycko-Pers resa*
"Lucky's Grove" (Wakefield) **120**:3490, 358-59
"Lucrère" (Schwob) **20**:323
"Lucubratio Ebria" (Butler) **33**:35, 49, 65
"Lucy" (de la Mare) **4**:78; **53**:27
Lucy Brandon (Buchanan) **107**:31
Lucy Church, Amiably (Stein) **1**:430; **28**:315, 322, 324, 332-33; **48**:237
Lucy Gayheart (Cather) **1**:154-55, 158, 163; **11**:99, 107-09, 113-15; **99**:211; **132**:136-37, 143, 148; **152**:53
Les ludions (Fargue) **11**:199-200
"Ludovitje" (Smith) **25**:380, 384-85
"Luella Miller" (Freeman) **9**:72
"Lueurs des Tirs" (Apollinaire) **51**:36
"The Luftbad" (Mansfield) **39**:324; **164**:324
El Lugar del hombre (Sender) **136**:208
El lugar sin límites (Donoso) **133**:39, 51, 53-55, 71, 82-83, 122, 147-49, 157, 186, 188
"Lugares. I" (Villaurrutia) **80**:478
"Lui e io" (Ginzburg) **156**:32, 97, 107, 111-12
"Lui et elle" (Lawrence) **9**:230
"Luis de Camões" (Campbell) **5**:124
"Luis de Torres" (Ingamells) **35**:137
"Luis G. Urbina" (Reyes) **33**:318
Luisa (Giacosa) **7**:305, 310, 313
"Luischen" (Mann) **168**:185

"Luke Havergal" (Robinson) **5**:418; **101**:123, 129, 133, 135, 164, 172-74, 193-94, 198
"Luke the Poor" (Chekhov) **96**:34
"The Lull" (Saki) **3**:372
"Lullaby" (Dunbar) **12**:106
"A Lullaby" (Jarrell) **177**:193
"Lullaby" (Jozsef) **22**:165
"Lullaby" (Middleton) **56**:190
Lullaby (Jarry) **147**:331
"Lulú" (Valera y Alcala-Galiano) **10**:504
Lulu (Carter) **139**:150-51, 158
Lulu (Wedekind) **7**:576, 578, 582, 590
"Lulu Gay" (Stevens) **45**:344
"Lulu Morose" (Stevens) **45**:344
"Il lume dell'altra casa" (Pirandello) **29**:292-93
Lumíe di Sicilia (Pirandello) **4**:325; **29**:297, 317; **172**:188
"La lumière du Sud-Ouest" (Barthes) **135**:162, 174
Luminous Depths (Čapek)
See *Zářivé hlubiny*
"Luna" (Hippius) **9**:161
La luna (Jiménez) **183**:289, 332
Luna benamor (Blasco Ibáñez) **12**:43
"La luna come un fungo" (Calvino) **183**:215
"La Luna corre dietro alla luna" (Calvino) **183**:103
Luna de enfrente (Borges) **109**:7, 9-12, 163
"Luna de los amores" (Lugones) **15**:289
"Luna di pomeriggio" (Calvino) **183**:216
"Luna e GNAC" (Calvino) **183**:211, 226
La luna e i falo (Pavese) **3**:336-38, 342-44
"La luna es una ausencia" (Aleixandre) **113**:14
"La luna roja" (Arlt) **29**:44
"Luna y panorama de los insectos" (García Lorca) **197**:187, 211-12, 244-45, 264, 277
Lunar Caustic (Lowry) **6**:240-1, 254; **40**:274
"Lunaria" (Ekelund) **75**:95
Lunario sentimental (Lugones) **15**:287, 292
The Lunatic Republic (Mackenzie) **116**:234, 237
Lunatic Villas (Engel) **137**:117, 123-24, 133, 138
"Lunching at the Ritzmore" (Himes) **139**:323
Le Lundi existentiel et le dimanche de l'histoire (Fondane) **159**:258
"Lundi rue Christine" (Apollinaire) **3**:44; **51**:30-1, 55
Lundy's Lane, and Other Poems (Scott) **6**:386, 388, 394
"La lune de pluie" (Colette) **16**:128, 130-33
Lungo Viaggio di Natale (Pratolini) **124**:337
Lūnī (Devkota) **23**:50
Lunnye muravyi (Hippius) **9**:161, 163
"Luojan leipa" (Leino) **24**:368, 376
La lupa. In portinaio. Cavalleria Rusticana. Drammi (Verga) **3**:539, 545, 547
"The Lure" (Ledwidge) **23**:116, 121
"Lure of Souls" (Rohmer) **28**:277
"The Lurking Fear" (Lovecraft) **4**:268, 271; **22**:220
"Lusisti Satis" (Grahame) **64**:63
"The Lusitania" (Rosenberg) **12**:301
"Lust" (Brooke) **2**:55, 60
"Lust" (Hecht) **101**:36
"Luste" (Valéry) **4**:498
"The Lute Song" (Naidu) **80**:334
Luther (Huch) **13**:247
Luther (Osborne) **153**:242, 251, 270-71, 275, 280, 302, 307, 310-11, 313, 320
"Luther on Sweet Auburn" (Bambara) **116**:15
Luthers Glaube: Briefe an einan Freud (Huch) **13**:253
Le luthier de Crémone (Coppee) **25**:119, 127
De l'utilite du pragmatisme (Sorel) **91**:194, 307
"Lutsiferi laulud" (Talvik) **87**:319-20, 322
"La lutte contre la multitude" (Teilhard de Chardin) **9**:492
"La lutte contre les evidences" (Shestov) **56**:277
"Luvius' Transformations" (Herbert) **168**:43
"Lux in tenebris" (Tynan) **3**:505
"Lux in tenebris lucet" (Sienkiewicz) **3**:430
De Luxe (Bromfield) **11**:78, 82
Le luxe des autre (Bourget) **12**:67
"Luz" (Aleixandre) **113**:13, 55, 73
"Luz lunar" (Prado) **75**:194, 208
"Luz para Ciegos" (Asturias) **184**:59
"Luz tú" (Jiménez) **183**:292
"La lycanthropia" (Lugones) **15**:293
Den lyckliges väg (Lagerkvist) **144**:211, 218-19, 229-30
Lycko-Pers resa (Strindberg) **1**:460; **8**:407, 412; **47**:369
Lydia Bailey (Roberts) **23**:234, 240
"Lydia und Mäxchen" (Döblin) **13**:166
"Lyft dig pa blodiga vingar" (Lagerkvist) **144**:182-86
"Lying Awake" (Hardy) **143**:157
"Lying in the Grass" (Gosse) **28**:132, 142
Lying Lips (Micheaux) **76**:270
Den lykkelige alder (Undset) **197**:289, 299-301, 305, 307
Lykkelige Kristoffer (Hansen) **32**:248, 251, 256-60
"Lykken" (Nexø) **43**:333
"Lyn Dyer's Dream" (Rhodes) **53**:316
"The Lynching" (McKay) **7**:461
"The Lynching of Jube Benson" (Dunbar) **2**:131; **12**:108-09, 120
"The Lynching of Nigger Jeff" (Dreiser)
See "Nigger Jeff"
"Lynching, Our National Crime" (Wells-Barnett) **125**:332
"Lynn Fontanne" (Parker) **143**:336
"The Lynn of Dreams" (Sharp) **39**:374
"Lyra Elegantiarum" (Dobson) **79**:9
"The Lyre Degenerate" (Campbell) **9**:33
"The Lyric Beasts" (Dickey) **151**:152
Lyric Life (Sikelianos) **39**:417, 420
"A Lyric of the Dawn" (Markham) **47**:278-79
Lyrical Dramas (Blok)
See *Liricheskie dramy*
The Lyrical Poems of Hugo von Hofmannsthal (Hofmannsthal) **11**:294
"Lyrics" (Roberts) **8**:320-21
Lyrics and Sonnets (Wetherald) **81**:409,413
"Lyrics for Households of Two or More" (Morley) **87**:142
Lyrics of a Lowbrow (Service) **15**:411
Lyrics of Love and Laughter (Dunbar) **2**:131; **12**:109, 124
"Lyrics of Love and Sorrow" (Dunbar) **12**:104
Lyrics of Lowly Life (Dunbar) **12**:106, 108-09, 121-22
Lyrics of Sunshine and Shadow (Dunbar) **12**:109, 124
Lyrics of the Hearthside (Dunbar) **12**:109, 122, 124
"Lyrisme militaire" (Jarry) **147**:277
Le lys rouge (France) **9**:41-2, 47, 53
Lysbeth (Haggard) **11**:243, 246
"Lysergic Acid" (Ginsberg) **120**:12, 77
Lyubasha's Tragedy (Gladkov) **27**:91-3
Lyubov k blizhnemu (Andreyev) **3**:22
"Lyubovnik yunony" (Khlebnikov) **20**:130
Lyudi (Zoshchenko) **15**:507-08
"M Antitête" (Tzara) **168**:228
"M. de Charlus pendant la guerre" (Proust) **161**:142-44, 149, 151
M. le Cure d'Ozeron (Jammes) **75**:119
M. le Modéré (Adamov) **189**:15, 34, 59
M. Lecoq (Green) **63**:149
M. M. Bakhtin: Sobranie sochinenii (Bakhtin) **160**:197-98
Ma Cinderella (Wright) **183**:359
"Ma conversion" (Claudel) **10**:130
Ma Fille Bernadette (Jammes) **75**:114, 116-17, 119
Ma non è una cosa seria (Pirandello) **29**:282, 301, 318
"M.AA l'Antiphilosphe" (Tzara) **168**:228, 240
Maaliskuun lauluja (Leino) **24**:373
"Ma'ame Pélagie" (Chopin) **14**:61; **127**:20, 167
Maan parhaat (Leino) **24**:372
"Maata" (Mansfield) **164**:250
Der mabl (Aleichem) **35**:306
"Maboroshi" (Kunikida Doppo) **99**:303-04
Maboroshi no tate (Natsume) **10**:329
MAC (Beckett) **145**:79
Macaire (Henley) **8**:98-100, 102, 107-08
"Mac-American" (Reed) **9**:383
"La macchina spasmodica" (Calvino) **183**:102
MacDonough's Wife (Gregory) **1**:332-33, 336-37
The Macedonian (Butts) **77**:96
"Macedonian Sonnets" (Vazov)
See "Makedonski soneti"
Der Mäcen (Liliencron) **18**:210, 212, 216
"MacGreevy on Yeats" (Beckett) **145**:88
The MacHaggis (Jerome) **23**:82
"The Machine" (Yokomitsu)
See "Kikai"
The Machine (Heijermans) **24**:293
La machine àécrire (Cocteau) **119**:70
"La machine à parler" (Schwob) **20**:323
"The Machine Gun" (Jarrell) **177**:214
La machine infernale (Cocteau) **119**:39, 45, 47, 49, 76, 81-2, 87, 108
"Machine Politics in New York City" (Roosevelt) **69**:177
"Machine Shop Blues" (Wright) **136**:262
The Machine to Kill (Leroux) **25**:258
"Machine-Age Romance" (McAlmon) **97**:121
Machines and Wolves (Pilnyak)
See *Mashiny i volki*
Les Machines célibataires (Jarry) **147**:245
The Machine-Wreckers (Toller)
See *Die Maschinenstürmer*
"El macho cabrío" (García Lorca) **181**:122
Die Macht der Gewohnheit (Bernhard) **165**:71, 96-97, 108, 124-25, 131
Macht und Mensch (Mann) **9**:329
"Macon Prairie" (Cather) **152**:73
"Macon Prairie (Nebraska)" (Cather) **132**:131
"Macquarie Harbour" (Ingamells) **35**:127
"Macquarie's Mate" (Lawson) **27**:119, 129, 132
The Macropulos Case (Čapek)
See *Věc Makropulos*
Macunaíma: O herói sem nenhum caráter (Andrade) **43**:16-19, 22-41, 43-4
Mad (Symons) **11**:437
"Mad Dog" (Agnon)
See "Kelev Meshuga"
Mad Grandeur (Gogarty) **15**:119
"The Mad Idler" (Peretz)
See "Der meshugener batlen"
The Mad Professor (Sudermann)
See *Der tolle Professor*
"The Mad Scene" (Merrill) **173**:209-10, 218
"The Mad Talmudist" (Peretz)
See "Der meshugener batlen"
A Mad Tour (Riddell) **40**:334
Mad Wednesday (Sturges)
See *The Sin of Harold Diddlebock*
Madam Sapphira (Saltus) **8**:346
"Madame a Tort!" (Millay) **169**:237, 277-78, 280
Madame Adonis (Vallette) **67**:299, 303, 310-11, 315
Madame 'Alaviya (Hedāyat)
See *Alaviyeh Khanom*
Madame Butterfly (Belasco) **3**:85, 87-8, 90
Madame Butterfly (Giacosa) **7**:311, 313-15
"Madame Celestin's Divorce" (Chopin) **14**:57
Madame Chrysanthême (Loti) **11**:353-54, 356, 361, 366-67
Madame de . . . (Anouilh) **195**:38
Madame de . . . (Ophuls) **79**:174, 176, 180-82, 187-90, 192-5, 197-8, 216, 235, 237, 244, 247
Madame de Lydone, assassin (Vallette) **67**:284
"Madame de Mauves" (James) **2**:246, 248; **40**:151
Madame de Sade (Mishima)
See *Sado koshaku fujin*
Madame de Treymes (Wharton) **3**:554, 558, 562, 567; **9**:548; **53**:362; **129**:361

Madame Death (Vallette)
See *Madame la Mort*
"Madame Déliceuse" (Cable) **4**:32
Madame Delphine (Cable) **4**:24, 47
Madame d'Ora (Jensen) **41**:291, 294, 296, 300, 303
Madame Dorthea (Undset) **3**:521, 524; **197**:303
"Madame Edwarda" (Bataille) **155**:77-79, 81-82, 84-85
Madame Edwarda (Bataille) **155**:129
"Madame Houdin" (Warner) **131**:308
"Madame La Fleurie" (Stevens) **12**:364-65; **45**:311, 349
"Madame La Gimp" (Runyon) **10**:432
Madame la Mort (Vallette) **67**:270, 275
Madame Lupar (Lemonnier) **22**:198
"Madame Martel's Christmas Eve" (Chopin) **14**:70
Madame Roland (Tarbell) **40**:427
Madame Salome (Raabe) **45**:192, 196
"Madame Waage" (Undset) **197**:289
Madame Yuki (Mizoguchi)
See *Yuki Fujin Ezu*
Mademoiselle Jaïre (Ghelderode) **187**:4, 6, 14, 24-7
A Madcap Prince (Buchanan) **107**:30
Madcaps (Kuzmin)
See *Venetian Madcaps*
"Mädchen am Ofen" (Raabe) **45**:189
"Das Mädchen von Dobrowlany" (Carossa) **48**:24
"Das Mädchen von Treppi" (Heyse) **8**:113, 119, 121
Die Mädchenfeinde (Spitteler) **12**:338, 347-51
"Made in U.S.A." (Morris) **107**:155, 157, 160
"Madeleine" (Alain-Fournier) **6**:19
"Madeleine" (Hedāyat)
See "Madlin"
Madeleine Férat (Zola) **6**:561-62, 567
"Madeleine in Church" (Mew) **8**:294-98, 301
Madelon (Freeman) **9**:63-4, 69, 71
"Mademoiselle" (Dowson) **4**:87
Mademoiselle Annette (Rod) **52**:309, 311, 316, 323
Mademoiselle Coeur-Briśe (West)
See *Miss Lonelyhearts*
Mademoiselle Fifi (Lewton) **76**:203, 210
"Mademoiselle Joan" (Davis) **6**:152
"Mademoiselle O" (Nabokov) **108**:104, 116, 147
"Mademoiselle's Campaigns" (Higginson) **36**:171, 175
Madero: Biografía novelada (Azuela) **3**:76
Madge o' the Pool (Sharp) **39**:375
La madia (D'Annunzio) **6**:137
"Madlin" (Hedāyat) **21**:72
"The Madman" (Gibran) **9**:82
"The Madman" (Heym)
See "Der Irre"
The Madman and the Nun, and Other Plays (Witkiewicz) **8**:506-08, 513-15
The Madman Divine (Echegaray)
See *El loco dios*
The Madman, His Parables and Poems (Gibran) **1**:325-26; **9**:85, 89-91
Madman or Saint (Echegaray)
See *Ó locura ó santidad*
A Madman's Defense (Strindberg)
See *Le plaidoyer d'un fou*
"Madman's Song" (Wylie) **8**:521
"Madness" (Dickey) **151**:98, 113, 166
"Madness" (Kolmar) **40**:177
"Madness" (Premchand)
See "Unmad"
"The Madness of Bald Eagle" (Eastman) **55**:170, 174
"The Madness of John" (Gibran) **1**:327
"The Madness of King Goll" (Yeats) **11**:512; **18**:461-62
"The Madness of Much Power" (Phillips) **44**:277
"The Madonna" (Merrill) **173**:237
Madonna and Child (Anderson) **144**:72
La madonna dei filosofi (Gadda) **144**:122, 124-25, 129-30
"Madonna Naturo" (Sharp) **39**:388
"Madonna of the Evening Flowers" (Lowell) **8**:227, 231
"The Madonna of the Future" (James) **2**:246-47
"The Madonna of the Purple Dots" (Aldrich) **125**:19
"A Madonna of the Streets" (Service) **15**:401
"A Madonna of the Trenches" (Kipling) **8**:194-96, 200
"Madonna with Two Angels" (Scott) **6**:394
The Madras House (Granville-Barker) **2**:192, 194-97, 199-200
"La madre" (Carducci) **32**:96
"La madre" (Ginzburg) **156**:14, 16, 19, 51-53, 56-60, 63
"Le madre" (Svevo) **35**:336, 345
La madre (Deledda) **23**:32-4, 37, 39, 41-2
"Madre gallega" (Pardo Bazán) **189**:236
Madre Isla (Hostos) **24**:303
"Madre, Madre" (Aleixandre) **113**:8
"Madre mia" (Hodgson) **13**:235
La madre naturaleza (Pardo Bazán) **189**:198, 205-08, 222, 224, 229, 234, 244-47, 251, 260-61, 275, 277, 299
"Madrid" (Roumain) **19**:346
Madrid Moscú (Sender) **136**:209-10
"A Madrigal" (Dobson) **79**:3
"Madrigal" (García Lorca) **181**:119
"Madrigal" (Jiménez) **183**:335, 340
Madrigal (Martinez Sierra and Martinez Sierra) **6**:277
"Madrigal Lúgubre" (Drummond de Andrade) **139**:229
"Madrigal sombrío" (Villaurrutia) **80**:488
"Madrugada" (García Lorca) **181**:199
The Madwoman of Chaillot (Giraudoux)
See *La folle de Chaillot*
"Maecenas" (Santos) **156**:314
The Maecenas (Liliencron)
See *Der Mäcen*
A Maelstrom (Lie)
See *En malstrom*
"Maelzel's Chessplayer" (Bierce) **44**:16
"The Maenad" (Ivanov) **33**:127
"Maestria" (Nemerov) **124**:155, 157, 181
Maeve (Martyn) **131**:98, 101-2, 104-6, 111-12, 114-15, 124
Mafarka il futurista (Marinetti) **10**:315, 324
"Mafeking Road" (Bosman) **49**:19-21, 31
Mafeking Road (Bosman) **49**:2-3, 5-9, 11-12, 17-20
"A Magazine of the '60s" (Benét) **28**:7
Magda (Sudermann)
See *Heimat*
"The Magdalen" (Field) **43**:166
"Magdalene" (Pasternak) **188**:188, 190
"Magdalene I" (Pasternak) **188**:190, 222
"Magdalene II" (Pasternak) **188**:189-90, 224
"Magdalina" (Tsvetaeva) **35**:393
Magdolna é egyeb elbeszélések (Molnár) **20**:174
Magellan (Zweig) **17**:427, 429, 442, 457
Maggie: A Girl of the Streets (Crane) **11**:121-23, 125-26, 128-29, 131, 134-35, 137, 140-41, 144, 147-50, 152-53, 157-58, 160-62, 164-67; **17**:65, 68-9, 73, 80; **32**:133, 139, 158, 163-66, 168
Maggie Cassidy (Kerouac) **117**:248, 254-57, 259, 261, 264, 266
"Magi" (Henry)
See "The Gift of the Magi"
"The Magi" (Yeats) **18**:446; **31**:385; **93**:341, 342
"Magias parciales del Quijote" (Borges) **109**:40
"Magic" (Johnson) **19**:256
"Magic" (Yeats) **1**:582
"The Magic Arrows" (Eastman) **55**:172
"The Magic Barrel" (Malamud) **129**:61, 66, 69, 71, 74, 106, 193; **184**:159, 171, 175, 266, 268-73, 275, 278, 280, 285-87, 289, 310
The Magic Barrel (Malamud) **129**:64, 71, 73, 84, 108-9, 112, 114, 169, 180, 197, 206; **184**:158-59, 164, 167, 184, 221, 237
"The Magic Casket" (Freeman) **21**:58
The Magic Chair (Karinthy) **47**:271
"The Magic Egg" (Stockton) **47**:325, 327
"The Magic Eye of Leo Strauss" (Berlin) **105**:132
"The Magic Flute" (Carman) **7**:149
"The Magic Flute" (Hrabal) **155**:150, 165
"The Magic House" (Scott) **6**:385, 389, 397
The Magic House, and Other Poems (Scott) **6**:385-86, 388-89, 391, 393-96
The Magic Lantern (Melies) **81**:140
The Magic Lantern (Tsvetaeva)
See *Volshebny fonar*
The Magic Mountain (Mann)
See *Der Zauberberg*
The Magic of Oz (Baum) **7**:25; **132**:12, 100-101
The Magic of Shirley Jackson (Jackson) **187**:248-50
"The Magic of Spring" (Naidu) **80**:346
"The Magic Origin of Moorish Designs" (Westermarck) **87**:334
"The Magic Pill" (Pyle) **81**:381,389
"Magic Psalm" (Ginsberg) **120**:9, 25
The Magic Realm of Love (Brod) **115**:98
"The Magic Ring" (Grahame) **64**:79
The Magic Ring (Platonov) **14**:420
Magic: The Flesh and Blood of Poetry (Péret)
See *La parole est è péret*
The Magic Toyshop (Carter) **139**:45, 78-82, 84, 86, 119, 159-63, 165-70, 184, 192, 196-97, 214-16, 219
"The Magic Veimeer" (Huneker) **65**:161
The Magic Word: Studies in the Nature of Poetry (Lewisohn) **19**:294-95
The Magical Monarch of Mo and His People (Baum) **7**:14; **132**:82
"The Magician" (Peretz)
See "Der Kuntsenmakher"
The Magician (Frank)
See *Der Magier*
The Magician (Nabokov)
See *Volshebnik*
"The Magician Dies" (Csáth) **13**:147
"The Magician's Daughter" (Stockton) **47**:328-29
"The Magician's Garden" (Csáth) **13**:148, 152
The Magician's Garden, and Other Stories (Csáth) **13**:150-51, 155
Magick in Theory and Practice (Crowley) **7**:210-13
La Magie en Poitou: Gilles De Rais (Huysmans) **69**:40
Magie rouge (Ghelderode) **187**:4, 14-16, 26-7
Der Magier (Frank) **81**:102
Magische Trilogie (Werfel) **8**:479
Magister Ludi (Hesse)
See *Das Glasperlenspiel*
The Magistrate (Pinero) **32**:393, 396, 398, 400, 406, 408-09, 411-12
Magna (Gale) **7**:285
"Magnetism" (Fitzgerald) **55**:206
"Magnets" (Cullen) **37**:158
Magnhild (Bjoernson) **7**:104, 116; **37**:11
"Magnificat" (Claudel) **2**:108; **10**:133
"Magnificat" (Symons) **11**:429
The Magnificent Ambersons (Tarkington) **9**:454, 456-57, 459-61, 463, 467, 472, 474
The Magnificent Spinster (Sarton) **120**:245-47, 280-81, 283-84
"Magnitudes" (Nemerov) **124**:301
"Magnolia" (Fletcher) **35**:111
Magpie's Tales (Tolstoy) **18**:358
A magunk szerelme (Ady) **11**:18, 23, 25
The Magus of the North (Berlin) **105**:112-13, 116
"A magyar költő" (Herzl) **36**:150
"The Magyar Poet" (Herzl)
See "A magyar költő"

"Mahabharata" (Tagore) **3**:497
Mahadevbhaini Diary (Gandhi) **59**:73
"Mahamaya" (Tagore) **53**:353
Mahārānā Pratāp (Devkota) **23**:51
Maharashi's Gospel (Ramana Maharshi) **84**:257
The Mahatna (Tolstoy) **18**:383
Mahēś (Chatterji) **13**:78-9, 81
Mahogany (Pilnyak)
See *Krasnoe derevo*
"The Mahratta Ghats" (Lewis) **3**:287, 289-90
Mahua (Tagore) **3**:493
Mai devi domandarmi (Ginzburg) **156**:32, 73, 111-12, 116
Maia (D'Annunzio) **6**:136, 138
"Maiakovskomu" (Tsvetaeva) **35**:416
"The Maid" (Papadiamantis) **29**:272-73
The Maid (Heijermans)
See *De meid*
"The Maid and the Son of the Boyar" (Leino)
See "Impi ja pajarin poika"
The Maid at Arms (Chambers) **41**:94
Maid in Waiting (Galsworthy) **45**:47, 49, 63
"Maid Most Dear" (Rhodes) **53**:328
The Maid of France (Lang) **16**:258-59, 271-72
"The Maid of Saint Phillippe" (Chopin) **14**:70
The Maid of Sker (Blackmore) **27**:28, 31, 36-41
"Maiden Form" (Ingamells) **35**:121
The Maiden Tribute of Modern Babylon (Stead) **48**:186, 189-91, 193-96, 198, 200
Maiden Voyage (Welch) **22**:435-47, 452, 454-58, 460-61
"The Maiden with the Dreamy Eyes" (Johnson) **175**:225
"Maidens and Heroes" (Musil) **68**:263
"The Maiden's Death" (Södergran)
See "Jungfruns död"
The Maidens' God (Khlebnikov)
See *Devy bog*
The Maidens of the Rocks (D'Annunzio)
See *Le vergini delle rocce*
The Maiden's Progress: A Novel in Dialogue (Hunt) **53**:186-87, 191, 197
The Maids (Genet)
See *Les bonnes*
The Maids of Paradise (Chambers) **41**:91
"The Maid's Shoes" (Malamud) **184**:164, 237, 245-46
"Maidstone Comfort" (Gilman) **37**:216; **117**:77
"Maihime" (Mori Ogai) **14**:369, 372-73, 378-81, 384-85
"Maihime" (Nagai)
See "Opera no maihime"
"Mail Call" (Jarrell) **177**:193
"Mailied" (George) **2**:150
"Mailman Bring Me No More Blues" (Holly) **65**:138-41
"The Main Deep" (Stephens) **4**:417
The Main Line (Belasco) **3**:88
The Main Literary Currents in the Nineteenth Century (Brandes)
See *Horedströmninger i det nittende aahundredes literatur*
La main passe (Feydeau) **22**:78, 92-3
Main Street (Anderson) **1**:36
Main Street: The Story of Carol Kennicott (Lewis) **4**:246-55, 257, 259-60; **13**:326-30, 332-33, 335-40, 343-53; **23**:125-54; **39**:203-06, 208, 210, 214, 216-17, 219-21, 223, 232, 234-35, 239-47, 249-54
Mainā (Devkota) **23**:51
Maine Ballads (Coffin) **95**:4
Mainly on the Air (Beerbohm) **1**:68
"Mains" (Garneau) **13**:196
The Mainsprings of Russia (Baring) **8**:43
"Maintaining Freedom of the Seas" (Roosevelt) **93**:188
"The Maintenance of Capital" (Hayek) **109**:200
Main-Travelled Roads (Garland) **3**:190-94, 196-97, 199, 201-02
Mainz Thriller about Schinderhannes (Zuckmayer)
See *Mainzer Moritat vom Schinderhannes*
Mainzer Moritat vom Schinderhannes (Zuckmayer) **191**:296, 319-21
Mais n'te promène donc pas toute nue! (Feydeau) **22**:77, 79
Maisa Jons (Lie) **5**:325
"La maison" (Desnos) **22**:73
La Maison à vapeur: Voyage à travers l'Inde septentrionale (Verne) **52**:350
"La Maison brûlée" (Yourcenar) **193**:265
La maison dans la forêt (Alain-Fournier) **6**:28
La maison de Claudine (Colette) **1**:191; **5**:164-66, 169; **16**:118, 128
"La Maison des femmes pâles" (Yourcenar) **193**:265
"La maison des mortes" (Apollinaire) **3**:38; **51**:28, 60
"La maison fermée" (Claudel) **2**:108; **10**:133
La maison mystérieuse (Jacob) **6**:193
Maître du monde (Verne) **6**:497, 501; **52**:347, 350, 353-54
"Maître Zacharius:" (Verne) **52**:349, 361
"La maîtresse maternelle" (Moore) **7**:487
Maitreya (Sarduy) **167**:190, 198-99, 201-4, 206, 213, 215-18, 222
La maîtrise du monde et le règne de Dieu (Teilhard de Chardin) **9**:491
"Die Maiwiese" (Huch) **13**:248-50
La maja desnuda (Blasco Ibáñez) **12**:29-30, 35-6, 50
Majesteit (Couperus) **15**:43-4, 46
Majesty (Couperus)
See *Majesteit*
"Lo májico esencial nombrado" (Jiménez) **183**:278
The Major (Connor) **31**:105-06, 114-16
Major Barbara (Shaw) **3**:384, 392, 397-98, 406-07; **45**:243, 249
Major Problems of Philosophy (Simmel) **64**:338
Majors and Minors (Dunbar) **2**:127-28, 130; **12**:103, 108, 121-22, 125, 127
"The Major's Tale" (Bierce) **44**:45
"Majstor senki" (Popa) **167**:158
"Majutah" (Fisher)
See "The South Lingers On"
"Maka" (Remizov) **27**:339
"Makapan's Caves" (Bosman) **49**:3, 6, 9-10, 19, 29
"Makar Chudra" (Gorky) **8**:73
"Makar's Dream" (Korolenko)
See "Son Makara"
Make Believe (Milne) **6**:309
"Make Big Money at Home! Write Poems in Spare Time!!" (Nemerov) **124**:181, 183, 277
Make Bright the Arrows (Millay) **4**:317; **169**:290
"Make of Your Voice a Dawn" (Bodenheim) **44**:64
Make Way for Lucia (Benson) **27**:14
"Make with the Shape" (Himes) **139**:323
"Make-Believe" (Williams) **89**:398
"Makedonski soneti" (Vazov) **25**:456
"The Maker" (Borges)
See "El hacedor"
The Maker (Borges)
See *El hacedor*
A Maker of History (Oppenheim) **45**:127-128, 133
"The Maker of Moons" (Chambers) **41**:102, 107
The Maker of Moons (Chambers) **41**:88, 90, 94, 100, 104, 106-08, 114
"The Makers" (Nemerov) **124**:260, 269, 302
Makers of Literature (Woodberry) **73**:367
The Makers of Miracles (Housman) **7**:356
"Maketa Otto" (Yokomitsu) **47**:395
Making (White)
See *In the Making*
"Making a Change" (Gilman) **9**:113; **37**:213-14
"Making a Man of Rayburn" (Heyward)
See "The Winning Loser"
The Making of a Bigot (Macaulay) **7**:421, 426-27; **44**:132
"The Making of a Red" (Benchley) **55**:2
"The Making of a Writer: Condemned to Write about Real Things" (Merrill) **173**:259
The Making of Americans: Being a History of a Family's Progress (Stein) **1**:427-31, 433-34, 438, 440, 442; **6**:404, 406-07, 409-11, 414-15; **28**:312-13, 315, 318-20, 327-28, 331-33, 335-36, 338-41; **48**:211, 233, 242, 246, 248, 253, 264
The Making of Americans: The Hersland Family (Stein)
See *The Making of Americans: Being a History of a Family's Progress*
The Making of an American (Riis) **80**:435
The Making of Doctor Faustus (Mann)
See *Die Entstehung des Doktor Faustus*
The Making of Modern Society (Nisbet) **117**:304
The Making of Personality (Carman) **7**:136, 139
The Making of Religion (Lang) **16**:260
"The Making of the Magic Mountain" (Mann) **21**:197; **168**:195
"The Making of Thieves in New York" (Riis) **80**:440
"The Making of Viola" (Thompson) **4**:435-36
"Making Pictures" (Lawrence) **48**:122
"The Makin's" (Bonner) **179**:13, 21, 53, 59
Makov tsvet (Hippius) **9**:161, 167, 169
The Makropoulos Affair (Čapek)
See *Věc Makropulos*
The Makropoulos Secret (Čapek)
See *Věc Makropulos*
"Makt" (Södergran) **31**:294
"Le mal de siècle" (Kazantzakis) **5**:272
Le Mal des fantômes (Fondane) **159**:248-49
"Mal du Départ" (Sarton) **120**:271
Mal giocondo (Pirandello) **29**:309-10
Mal vu mal dit (Beckett) **145**:87, 97, 121
"De mala bebida" (Güiraldes) **39**:190
Mala hierba (Baroja) **8**:48, 61
Mala yerba (Azuela) **3**:75, 77; **145**:3, 6, 9, 14, 17, 24-26
Mala Yerba: Novela de costumbres nacionales (Azuela)
See *Mala yerba*
Malabar Farm (Bromfield) **11**:83-4, 89
The Malakand Field Force (Churchill)
See *The Story of the Malakand Field Force*
"Malam di pegunungan" (Anwar) **22**:23
"Malaria" (Verga) **3**:543, 546
I malavoglia (Pirandello) **29**:320
I malavoglia (Verga) **3**:538, 541, 543-46, 548
Malay Waters (Tomlinson) **71**:400
Malbone (Higginson) **36**:168-71, 184, 186
"Mal'čik iz trall" (Pilnyak) **23**:213
Malcolm (MacDonald) **9**:292
"Malcolm X" (Walker) **129**:306
La maldición (Azuela) **3**:76
Un mâle (Lemonnier) **22**:197-98, 200-02
"The Male Coquette" (Davidson) **24**:186
"Male Diary" (Radnóti) **16**:418
"A Male Magdalene" (Holley) **99**:323
Maledetti toscani (Malaparte) **52**:273, 276
"La maledizione di Pudelaggio" (Lardner) **14**:305
El maleficio de la mariposa (García Lorca) **1**:318; **7**:291, 300; **49**:106-07; **181**:67, 78-79, 82-83, 86, 96-97, 100; **197**:278
"Malenka Manon" (Saroyan) **137**:181
"Der Maler" (Walser) **18**:428
"Malfuta, o della fondazione di un villaggio" (Jovine) **79**:44
Los malhechores del bien (Benavente) **3**:94, 96-7
Le malheur passe (Maeterlinck) **3**:323
"Les malheurs d'un dollar" (Péret) **20**:185, 201
La malhora (Azuela) **3**:76, 78; **145**:6, 11, 15, 27-33
Malign Fiesta (Lewis) **2**:390-91, 393, 398
Malina (Bachmann) **192**:13-15, 17, 19-20, 22-25, 35-36, 41-42, 44-47, 49-51, 53, 55-57,

60-61, 69-71, 74, 76, 78, 83, 88, 94-99, 101-2, 127, 133, 144, 146-48, 150-65
Mālini (Tagore) **3**:492
"Malinovaya shashka" (Khlebnikov) **20**:136
"Mallard's Vacation" (Gale) **7**:284
Mallare (Hecht)
See *Fantazius Mallare*
Mallarmé entre Nosotros (Reyes) **33**:317
Mallarmè et l'idée de décadence (Gourmont) **17**:151
"Mallarmé's Blumen" (Ball) **104**:54
"Mallarmé's Flowers" (Ball)
See "Mallarmé's Blumen"
Malone Dies (Beckett)
See *Malone meurt*
Malone meurt (Beckett) **145**:197-9
"Malos agüeros" (Valle-Inclán) **5**:478
"Malourène" (Apollinaire) **51**:61
La malquerida (Benavente) **3**:93, 97, 101
En malstrom (Lie) **5**:325
The Maltese Falcon (Hammett) **187**:45, 49, 51-4, 56, 60-1, 66, 68-9, 79-91, 93-4, 101-04, 106-08, 110, 112, 114, 117, 131, 137, 153, 155-56, 158-59, 167, 169-70, 181-83, 185-86, 190-91, 194, 196, 204-7, 212, 214-16
The Maltese Parrot (Allen) **87**:61
"Malva" (Gorky) **8**:68, 73
"Mama" (Jozsef) **22**:164
Mamá (Martinez Sierra and Martinez Sierra) **6**:277, 280
Mama Blanca's Souvenirs (De La Parra)
See *Las memorias de Mamá Blanca*
"Mama, Rimma, and Alla" (Babel) **13**:32
"Mamai" (Zamyatin) **8**:544-47, 552, 555-56; **37**:424, 431
Mamba's Daughters (Heyward) **59**:86-94, 101, 103, 105-06
Les mamelles de Tirésias (Apollinaire) **8**:13-15, 19-25, 27; **51**:10, 19, 21-8
"Mamina" (Vilakazi) **37**:409
"Mamma" (Lardner) **2**:338
"A mamma" (Saba) **33**:369, 372
Mammon and His Message (Davidson) **24**:174-75, 184-85
"Mammon and the Archer" (Henry) **19**:172
"Mamouche" (Chopin) **5**:142
"Man" (Mayakovski) **4**:291, 293; **18**:241, 246-47, 250-51, 261, 265-67, 270
"A Man" (Roberts) **68**:305, 337
"A Man" (Tagore)
See "Ekjan Lok"
Man (Ivanov) **33**:127
The Man (Stoker) **8**:394; **144**:277, 279
"The Man against the Sky" (Robinson) **5**:406-07, 410, 415; **101**:113, 117, 134-35, 148, 166-67, 169, 173-74, 193
The Man against the Sky (Robinson) **101**:97, 110, 133-34
"A Man and a Woman" (Stringer) **37**:328
"Man and Bat" (Lawrence) **9**:230; **93**:55, 102
Man and Boy (Morris) **107**:91-2, 96-7, 105, 111, 118-19, 124, 152, 158
"Man and Crisis" (Ortega y Gasset)
See "En torno a Galileo"
"Man and Death" (Orage) **157**:275
"Man and Dog" (Thomas) **10**:463
"Man and His Brother" (Muir) **87**:197
A Man and His Older Sister's Death (Shiga)
See *Aru otoko, sono ane no shi*
Man and His Works (Thorndike) **107**:371, 376
Man and Maid (Glyn) **72**:139
Man and People (Ortega y Gasset)
See *El hombre y la gente*
Man and Society in an Age of Reconstruction (Mannheim)
See *Mensch und Gesellschaft im Zeitalter des Umbaus*
"A Man and Some Others" (Crane) **11**:128, 154, 160, 164, 167
Man and Superman (Shaw)
See *Man and Superman: A Comedy and a Philosophy*
Man and Superman: A Comedy and a Philosophy (Shaw) **3**:378-79, 386, 388, 390, 392, 396-98, 400-01; **9**:416-17, 425-29; **21**:300-41; **45**:210, 214-15, 217, 240-41, 243, 245, 259
The Man and the Moment (Glyn) **72**:140-41
"The Man and the Shadow" (Buchanan) **107**:19
"The Man and the Snake" (Bierce) **44**:12, 44-5, 48; **7**:88-9
The Man and the Woman (Buchanan) **107**:85
"Man and Woman" (Eddy) **71**:170-171
Man and Woman: A Study of Human Secondary Sexual Characters (Ellis) **14**:102, 105, 110-12, 114, 123, 132
"The Man at the Next Table" (Chambers) **41**:104
Man, Beast, and Virtue (Pirandello)
See *L'uomo, la bestia, e la virtù*
The Man Born to Be King: A Play-Cycle on the Life of Our Lord and Savior, Jesus Christ, Written for Broadcasting (Sayers) **2**:531; **15**:376, 382, 384-88
Man Burnt to Ashes (Bryusov) **10**:87
"A Man Called Spade" (Hammett) **187**:70
A Man Called White (White) **15**:479, 485-86
"Man Carrying Thing" (Stevens) **12**:360
A Man Could Stand Up (Ford) **1**:280, 284; **15**:73-4, 78, 80-1; **57**:204-290; **172**:29, 72-73, 75, 77-83
Man Covered with Women (Drieu la Rochelle) **21**:38-9
A Man Divided (Stapledon) **22**:316-17, 323
"Man Doesn't Exist" (Aleixandre) **113**:26-7
The Man Farthest Down (Park) **73**:200
"A Man for a Father" (Coffin) **95**:2
A Man for All Seasons (Bolt) **175**:4, 7-16, 18-28, 31-32, 34, 37-38, 46
Man Freed (Lagerkvist) **144**:165
"The Man from Athabaska" (Service) **15**:401
The Man from Glengarry (Connor) **31**:105-07, 116-17
The Man from Home (Tarkington) **9**:464-65
"The Man from Ironbark" (Paterson) **32**:372-73
"The Man from Kilsheelan" (Coppard) **5**:176
"The Man from Snowy River" (Paterson) **32**:369, 372-74, 378
The Man from Snowy River, and Other Verses (Paterson) **32**:378
The Man from the Norlands (Buchan)
See *The Island of Sheep*
A Man from the North (Bennett) **5**:22-3, 38, 40; **197**:72-4, 76-7, 94, 97-100, 111, 126-27, 172-77
"Man from the South" (Dahl) **173**:11
The Man from the U.S.S.R (Nabokov) **108**:52
"A Man Greatly Gifted" (Sayers) **15**:370
"The Man Higher Up" (Henry) **19**:184
The Man I Love (Mankiewicz) **85**:111
The Man in Gray (Dixon) **163**:166
The Man in the Case (Phelps) **113**:339-41
"The Man in the Crow's Nest" (Hulme) **21**:137
"Man in the Drawer" (Malamud) **184**:222, 281, 283
Man in the Holocene (Frisch)
See *Der Mensch erscheint im Holozän*
The Man in the Iron Mask (Whale) **63**:339, 378
The Man in the Lower Ten (Rinehart) **52**:281, 284, 288-90, 299, 303-04
"Man in the Moon" (Baring-Gould) **88**:7
"The Man in the Pub" (Sait Faik)
See "Birahanedeki adam"
The Man in the Queue (Tey) **14**:448, 451, 454, 460-61, 464
The Man in the Tree (La Guma) **140**:260
"Man Intolerant" (Roberts) **68**:304-5, 338
Man is Man (Brecht)
See *Mann ist Mann*
"Man Is More than Homo Species" (Lawrence) **93**:38
Man Is Strong (Alvaro)
See *L'uomo è forte*
The Man Jesus (Austin) **25**:21, 23, 31, 33, 35
"A Man Meets a Woman in the Street" (Jarrell) **177**:150, 158, 172, 174, 176, 228-29, 231
"The Man of Color and the White Woman" (Fanon) **188**:3
Man of a Hundred Faces (Leroux) **25**:260
The Man of Bronze (Dent) **72**:17, 19, 33, 37, 39
The Man of Destiny (Shaw) **9**:413
A Man of Devon (Collected Works of John Galsworthy) (Galsworthy) **45**:32, 46
Man of Earth (Aleixandre)
See *Hombre de tierra*
"The Man of Flesh and Blood" (Glaspell) **175**:95, 97
"A Man of Forty" (Bosschere) **19**:63
"A Man of Ideas" (Anderson) **1**:55; **24**:24, 30, 35; **123**:14, 63, 65, 67, 76
The Man of Last Resort; or, the Clients of Randolph Mason (Post) **39**:337, 339-40
"A Man of Leisure" (Gissing) **24**:248
A Man of Mark (Hope) **83**:169
A Man of Means (Wodehouse) **108**:376
"A Man of Plot" (Williams) **89**:394
The Man of Promise (Van Dine) **23**:348-50, 358
The Man of Property (Galsworthy) **1**:292-94, 297-99, 301-02, 305; **45**:26, 32-3, 38, 40-4, 46, 48, 57, 59, 61, 63-4, 69-70
"Man of the Earth" (Roberts) **68**:337
"The Man of the House" (Tynan) **3**:502
"A Man of the Outskirts" (Bagritsky)
See "Chelovek predmestya"
The Man of the World (Lewis) **104**:159, 162, 186, 188, 201
"The Man of the Year Million" (Wells) **12**:510; **19**:424-25, 434; **133**:244, 246, 324
"The Man of Tyre" (Lawrence) **93**:55, 60-62, 72, 74, 76
The Man on Horseback (Drieu la Rochelle)
See *L'homme à cheval*
"A Man on the Beach" (Harte) **25**:223
"The Man on the Bench" (Dreiser) **35**:65
"The Man on the Dump" (Stevens) **3**:462; **45**:283
The Man on the Flying Trapeze (Fields) **80**:240
"The Man on the Ground" (Howard) **8**:128
"The Man on the Moor" (Sharp) **39**:377
"Man on the Pink Corner" (Borges)
See "El Hombre de la esquina rosada"
"The Man on the Stairs" (Summers) **16**:434
"The Man on the Threshold" (Borges)
See "El hombre en el umbral"
"The Man out of the Nose" (Bierce) **44**:45
The Man Outside (Borchert)
See *Draussen vor der Tür*
"The Man Overboard" (Bierce) **44**:45
"Man Overboard!" (Crawford) **10**:157-59
Man Possessed (Benét) **28**:8-9, 12
The Man Shakespeare and His Tragic Life Story (Harris) **24**:259, 261-62, 264, 270-71, 277, 279
Man sollte nicht zu kritisch sein (Brecht) **169**:43-44
"Man Sometimes Helps" (Coffin) **95**:16
Man Songs (Villa) **176**:114
"The Man That Came to Buy Apples" (Somerville & Ross) **51**:384
"The Man That Corrupted Hadleyburg" (Twain) **6**:462, 469, 477; **12**:427-28, 432, 436; **19**:393; **59**:181-82; **185**:250
The Man That Corrupted Hadleyburg, and Other Stories and Essays (Twain) **12**:436
"Man, the Sky, and the Elephant" (Calvino) **183**:104
"Man the Ungrown" (Carpenter) **88**:87
"The Man to the Angel" (Baker) **10**:21
"The Man under the Stone" (Markham) **47**:278
Der man vun Notzeres (Asch) **3**:67-70
The Man Who Ate the Phoenix (Dunsany) **59**:17, 27-8

"The Man Who Became a Woman" (Anderson) **1**:44, 46; **10**:45; **123**:96, 98
The Man Who Came Back from the Dead (Leroux) **25**:260
The Man Who Caught the Weather (Aldrich) **125**:18
"The Man Who Could Work Miracles: A Pantoum in Prose" (Wells) **12**:488
"The Man Who Couldn't Sleep" (Čapek)
See "Muž, který nemohl spát"
The Man Who Couldn't Sleep (Stringer) **37**:336
The Man Who Diasppeared (Kafka)
See *Der Verschollene*
The Man Who Died (Lawrence) **2**:356-57, 360, 367, 371-72; **16**:284, 322; **33**:206; **48**:121, 125; **61**:269; **93**:57, 97-8, 103-4
The Man Who Died Twice (Robinson) **5**:406
"The Man Who Discovered the Use of a Chair" (Noyes) **7**:515
"The Man Who Doesn't Know What a Tooth or a Toothache Is" (Sait Faik)
See "Diş ve diş ağrısınedir bilmeyen adam"
"The Man Who Dreamed of Fairyland" (Yeats) **1**:578; **11**:508
"The Man Who Fell in Love With the Cooperative Stores" (Benson) **17**:32
"The Man Who Forgot" (Lawson) **27**:130
The Man Who Had Everything (Bromfield) **11**:85
"The Man Who Invented Sin" (O'Faolain) **143**:222, 236-37
The Man Who Invented Sin (O'Faolain)
See *Teresa, and Other Stories*
"The Man Who Killed" (Stringer) **37**:341
"The Man Who Killed His Passionate Self" (Hedāyat) **21**:80
The Man Who Knew Coolidge: Being the Soul of Lowell Schmaltz, Constructive and Nordic Citizen (Lewis) **4**:251, 254-55; **13**:332-33, 338; **39**:215, 240
"The Man Who Knew Gods" (Day) **25**:131
"The Man Who Knew How" (Sayers) **15**:379
The Man Who Knew Too Much (Chesterton) **1**:181; **6**:103-04, 108
"The Man Who Liked Dogs" (Chandler) **179**:124, 127, 168
The Man Who Lived His Life Over (Lagerkvist)
See *Han som fik leva om sitt liv*
The Man Who Lived His Life Over Again (Lagerkvist)
See *Han som fik leva om sitt liv*
"The Man Who Lived Underground" (Wright) **136**:225, 252, 255, 263, 291; **180**:222
"A Man Who Loves Love" (Hagiwara)
See "Koi wo koi suru hito"
The Man Who Made Friends with Himself (Morley) **87**:138-9, 144-5
The Man Who Missed the Bus (Benson) **17**:32
The Man Who Owns Broadway (Cohan) **60**:157, 164, 166, 172
"The Man Who Played upon the Leaf" (Blackwood) **5**:72
The Man Who Shook the Earth (Dent) **72**:19
The Man Who (Thought He) Looked Like Robert Taylor (Santos) **156**:317, 326-31, 333-34, 335336
The Man Who Turned into a Stick (Abe)
See *Bo ni natta otako*
"The Man Who Was" (Kipling) **8**:182, 195, 199
"The Man Who Was Away" (Paterson) **32**:372
The Man Who Was Given His Life to Live Again (Lagerkvist)
See *Han som fik leva om sitt liv*
The Man Who Was Lost Sight Of (Kafka)
See *Der Verschollene*
The Man Who Was There (Morris) **107**:95, 144, 156, 174-76, 208, 212, 236, 243
The Man Who Was Thursday (Chesterton) **1**:178, 180, 184, 187; **6**:99, 102, 105-08; **64**:27-52
The Man Who Went Away (Wright) **183**:359
"The Man Who Went Too Far" (Benson) **27**:17
"The Man Who Would Be King" (Kipling) **8**:182-83, 198, 204, 207; **17**:205, 208
"The Man Whom the Trees Loved" (Blackwood) **5**:71, 75
"The Man Whose Pharynx Was Bad" (Stevens) **3**:447
A Man with a Heart (Sutro) **6**:422
"A Man with a View" (Woolf) **43**:408
Man with the Axe (Jarry) **147**:331
The Man with the Black Feather (Leroux) **25**:256, 260
"The Man with the Blue Guitar" (Stevens) **3**:448, 461, 468, 474-75, 477; **12**:374, 381-82, 384; **45**:269-70, 276-77, 282-83, 285, 292-95, 297-98, 316, 322, 324-25, 327, 334, 346, 350
The Man with the Blue Guitar, and Other Poems (Stevens) **12**:376, 382-83
The Man with the Coat (Callaghan) **145**:212
"The Man with the Copper Fingers" (Sayers) **15**:379
"The Man with the Flower in His Mouth" (Pirandello) **4**:349-50
The Man With the Golden Gun (Fleming) **193**:197-98, 212, 226, 232, 235-37, 240-41
"The Man with the Heart in the Highlands" (Saroyan) **137**:155-56, 169
"The Man with the Hoe" (Markham) **47**:275-76, 279-82, 285-86, 288-90, 292, 294-95
The Man with the Hoe, and Other Poems (Markham) **47**:278, 287
"The Man with the Idiot Smile" (Sait Faik)
See "Hayvanca gülen adam"
"The Man with the Package" (Borowski) **9**:22
The Man with the Rubber Head (Melies)
See *L'homme a la tete de caoutchouc*
"The Man with the Shaven Skull" (Rohmer) **28**:282
"The Man with the Tortoise" (Carman) **7**:143
"The Man with the Twisted Lip" (Doyle) **7**:231, 241
"The Man with the Watches" (Doyle) **7**:238
The Man with Two Left Feet and Other Stories (Wodehouse) **108**:391
"A Man with Two Lives" (Bierce) **44**:45
"The Man without a Soul" (Burroughs)
See *The Mucker*
"The Man without a Temperament" (Mansfield) **2**:453; **8**:276, 282; **39**:293, 303-04; **164**:339
"A Man Without Character" (Musil) **68**:261
The Man without Qualities (Musil)
See *Der Mann ohne Eigenschaften*
"Manacled" (Crane) **11**:129
Manalive (Chesterton) **1**:178, 184, 187; **6**:103-04, 108; **64**:35
"Mañana" (García Lorca) **181**:120-21
"Mañana" (Huidobro) **31**:124
"Mañana no viviré" (Aleixandre) **113**:12
"Mañanita fría" (García Lorca) **181**:182
Manao Tùpapaù (Jarry) **147**:331
"Manas" (Döblin) **13**:162
Mānasī (Tagore) **3**:484-85, 490; **53**:350
"Manasiya" (Popa) **167**:158
Manassas: A Novel of the War (Sinclair) **160**:226, 242, 247-48, 260, 277
"La Mancha" (Jiménez) **183**:334
"A Manchester Poem" (MacDonald) **9**:301
"Mandala" (Merrill) **173**:219
Mandala (White)
See *The Solid Mandala*
"Mandalay" (Kipling) **8**:178, 201
"Mandarin Oranges" (Akutagawa Ryūnosuke) **16**:31
"Mandarin's Jade" (Chandler) **7**:176; **179**:126, 128, 168, 170
Mandelstam: The Complete Critical Prose and Letters (Mandelstam) **6**:269
"The Mandolin" (Lee-Hamilton) **22**:192
"The Mandolin, the Carnation and the Bamboo" (Apollinaire)
See "La mandoline, l'oeillet et le bambou"
"La mandoline, l'oeillet et le bambou" (Apollinaire) **51**:33
"Mandy, Won't You Let Me Be Your Beau" (Johnson) **175**:225
"Månens hemlighet" (Södergran) **31**:285-86, 291
Mangalsutra (Premchand) **21**:299
Mangan (Dazai Osamu) **11**:176
"The Mangel-Bury" (Gurney) **33**:98, 103
"Mangham" (Dickey) **151**:97, 114
"Mangolds" (Warner) **131**:311
Mangue (Drummond de Andrade) **139**:231
"Manhattan" (Anderson) **10**:49
"Manhattan" (Fletcher) **35**:100
"Manhattan May Day Midnight" (Ginsberg) **120**:87
"Manhattan Sketches" (Kerouac) **117**:213
The Manhood of Humanity (Korzybski) **61**:140-2, 159, 169
"The Man-Hunter" (Zamyatin) **8**:543
"Manifest li héraire de l'ecole Symboliste" (Moréas) **18**:275
"Manifeste de Monsieur Antipyrine" (Tzara) **168**:225, 228, 247, 304, 313-14, 320
"Manifeste du futurisme" (Marinetti) **10**:318, 324-5
"Manifeste en langage clair" (Artaud) **36**:4
"Manifeste millimètre infini" (Arp) **115**:29
"Manifeste pour un théâtre avorté" (Artaud) **36**:25-6
Manifestes (Huidobro) **31**:123, 126
"Manifesto" (Ginsberg) **120**:39
"Manifesto" (Lawrence) **2**:367; **33**:181-83; **93**:4, 53, 54, 107, 109, 128
"Manifesto" (Thomas)
See "Poetic Manifesto"
"Manifesto for an Aborted Theatre" (Artaud)
See "Manifeste pour un théâtre avorté"
"A Manifesto to Both Officials and Commoners" (Su Man-shu) **24**:455
"Manihara" (Tagore) **53**:356-7
"Mankind" (Ingamells) **35**:131
Mankind in the Making (Wells) **6**:525, 536-37, 552; **12**:489
"The Manly Art" (Runyon) **10**:429
"The Man-Made World" (Gilman) **9**:104
The Man-Made World; or, Our Androcentric Culture (Gilman) **9**:104; **117**:49, 68-70 75, 99, 103, 109, 125-26, 151-53, 145, 167, 174
"The Man-Moth" (Bishop) **121**:20, 48, 90
"Der Mann auf der Flasche" (Meyrink) **21**:222-23, 232
Mann ist Mann (Brecht) **1**:107, 109, 112, 119-20; **6**:34, 36; **13**:48; **169**:33, 41, 52-53
Der Mann mit dem goldenen Arm (Zuckmayer) **191**:305
"Der Mann mit den Messern" (Böll) **185**:50
Der Mann Moses und die monotheistische Religion (Freud) **52**:92-4, 120, 133
Der Mann ohne Eigenschaften (Musil) **12**:230-39, 241-43, 246-48, 250-62; **68**:260-61, 263-67, 269-75, 277-90
Le mannequin d'osier (France) **9**:42
"The Manner of Men" (Kipling) **17**:208, 213
Mannerhouse (Wolfe) **4**:521; **13**:483-84
"Manners" (Bishop) **121**:19, 41-3, 83
"Manners" (Bowen) **148**:29
Människor (Lagerkvist) **144**:210, 213, 219, 224
"La mano" (Aleixandre) **113**:34
"Mano entregada" (Aleixandre) **113**:69
Manon Lescaut (Nezval) **44**:241
Manon Lescaut (Sternheim) **8**:378
"The Manor Farm" (Thomas) **10**:452, 454, 457, 460, 463
Manoranjan (Devkota) **23**:52
"Las manos" (Prado) **75**:191
Manosque des Plateaux (Giono) **124**:32
A Man's a Man (Brecht)
See *Mann ist Mann*

"A Man's Death" (Palamas)
See "Thánatos tou palikariú"
Man's Genesis (Griffith) **68**:169
"Man's glory" (Ginsberg) **120**:37
A Man's House (Drinkwater) **57**:149
"A Man's Job" (Heyward) **59**:93
"Man's Place in Nature" (Teilhard de Chardin)
See "La place de l'homme dans la nature"
"Man's Prospects" (Stapledon) **22**:336
A Man's Shadow (Buchanan) **107**:32
"The Man's Story" (Anderson) **123**:48
A Man's Woman (Norris) **24**:423, 425, 448-49; **155**:263, 319, 331, 333
A Man's World (Crothers) **19**:70-1, 73-9, 81, 83
Manservant and Maidservant (Compton-Burnett) **180**:115, 123, 127-29, 131, 141-42, 146, 164
The Mansion (Faulkner) **141**:62; **170**:128-29, 184, 244-45
"Mansion on the Hill" (Williams) **81**:419,430
Mansoul; or, The Riddle of the World (Doughty) **27**:56-60, 65, 69-70
The Man-Stealers (Shiel) **8**:361-62
The Mantle of Elijah (Zangwill) **16**:445, 462-64
"The Mantle of Whistler" (Parker) **143**:331
"The Man-Trap" (Sapper) **44**:307
Mantrap (Lewis) **4**:256; **13**:335, 338, 351
"Mantsin laulu" (Leino) **24**:369, 376
A Manual of Piety (Brecht)
See *Die Hauspostille*
Manual of the Mother Church (Eddy) **71**:98, 114, 120, 144-145, 151-154, 156
"Manual of the Perfect Short Story Writer" (Quiroga) **20**:219
The Manual of Zen Buddhism (Suzuki) **109**:387
Manuale d'economie politique (Pareto)
See *Manuale di economie politica*
Manuale di economie politica (Pareto) **69**:99, 113, 130
Manucure (Sá-Carneiro) **83**:413
"Manuel" (George) **14**:209
"Manuel Comnenus" (Cavafy) **2**:87
Manuel de l'Anti-chrétien (Bataille) **155**:95-96, 98
Manuel of Political Economy (Pareto)
See *Manuale di economie politica*
"Manuelzinho" (Bishop) **121**:7, 69
"Manus animam pinxit" (Thompson) **4**:440
A Manuscript Found under a Bed (Tolstoy) **18**:360, 378
The Manuscripts of Howards End (Forster) **125**:64-67
The Manxman (Caine) **97**:3, 10, 14-16, 26
"Many Are Called" (Robinson) **5**:407; **101**:136
Many Cargoes (Jacobs) **22**:97, 99-100, 102, 104-05
Many Cities (Belloc) **7**:36
The Many Colored Coat (Callaghan) **145**:222, 237, 254
Many Dimensions (Williams) **11**:487, 493, 496, 500
Many, Many Women (Stein) **1**:428; **48**:264
Many Marriages (Anderson) **1**:35-6, 39, 44-5, 48, 53, 55, 57; **10**:34-8, 41-4; **24**:46; **123**:3-5, 50, 57, 59, 87
Many Minds (Van Doren) **18**:393-95, 405
"Many Soldiers" (Masters) **25**:309, 314
"Many Swans" (Lowell) **1**:371, 373; **8**:226, 230
Many Thousands Gone (Bishop) **103**:12-14, 16-7, 24-5, 33, 47
"Many Thousands Gone—1864" (Bishop) **103**:13, 45
Many Voices (Villa) **176**:114
"Many Waters" (Bunin)
See "Vody mnogie"
"Las manzanas verdes" (Lugones) **15**:292
The Manzoni Family (Ginzburg)
See *La famiglia Manzoni*
A mão e a luva (Machado de Assis) **10**:293, 297-99
"Mãos dadas" (Drummond de Andrade) **139**:235
"The Map" (Bishop) **121**:8-9, 25, 50, 54, 58
"The Map of Love" (Thomas) **105**:297, 300, 325-26, 329, 332, 338, 349, 354
The Map of Love (Thomas) **1**:472-73; **8**:455-56, 458-60; **45**:360, 373, 399, 408, 411, 413; **105**:325, 336, 353, 357
"The Maple" (Roberts) **8**:319
Mapp and Lucia (Benson) **27**:9
"The Mappined Life" (Saki) **3**:369, 373
The Maquerader (Cankar)
See *Kurent*
"Maquillage" (Symons) **11**:427
"El mar" (Jiménez) **4**:226
"Mar" (Jiménez) **183**:277, 281, 334, 338
"Mar" (Villaurrutia) **80**:489
"Mar en la tierra" (Aleixandre) **113**:13, 42, 48
"El mar no es una hoja de papel" (Aleixandre) **113**:5
"Mar y aurora" (Aleixandre) **113**:3, 46
"Mar y noche" (Aleixandre) **113**:4, 46
"Mara" (Bunin) **6**:52
Mara (Remizov) **27**:331, 334, 348
"Mara milosnica" (Andrić) **135**:11, 14, 90, 94-96
"Mara the Concubine" (Andrić)
See "Mara milosnica"
"The Maracot Deep" (Doyle) **7**:226
"Marasya Poisoned Herself" (Mayakovski) **18**:269
Marat/Sade (Weiss) **152**:264, 268-70, 298
Marathon (Heym) **9**:147
Mårbacka (Lagerloef) **4**:238, 241; **36**:234-35, 237, 239, 242
The Marble Faun (Faulkner) **170**:236
Marbleface (Faust) **49**:56-7, 59-60
Marcel Proust et Jacques Rivière: Correspondence, 1914-1922 (Proust) **33**:279
Marcel Proust et les signes (Deleuze) **116**:101
Marcel Proust: Selected Letters, 1880-1903 (Proust) **13**:428, 430
Marcela: A Mexican Love Story (Azuela)
See *Mala yerba*
Marcella (Ward) **55**:406-08, 410-13, 420-21, 424, 437, 441
"March" (Gurney) **33**:87
"The March" (Kuprin)
See "Pokhod"
"March" (Pasternak) **188**:182, 193
"March for the Red Dead" (Chambers) **129**:46
"March in New England" (Sarton) **120**:268
"The March of Death" (Santos) **156**:314
The March of Literature from Confucius' Day to Our Own (Ford) **15**:87, 93; **172**:5, 7
"The March of Progress" (Chesnutt) **5**:140
"March of the Red International" (Nezval) **44**:250
"The March of Trivia" (Allen) **87**:28, 54
March to Quebec: Journals of the Members of Arnold's Expedition (Roberts) **23**:236, 239
Marcha triunfal (Darío) **4**:56, 59
"La marchande des journaux" (Coppee) **25**:120
La marchanta (Azuela) **3**:76
"Marche funèbre" (Genet) **128**:134
"The Märchen" (Jarrell) **177**:134, 155, 169, 205
Das Märchen (Schnitzler) **4**:388
Das Märchen der 672. Nacht, und andere Erzahlungen (Hofmannsthal) **11**:302-03
"Marching" (Rosenberg) **12**:288, 297, 302
Marching in Mexico (Patton) **79**:303
Marching Men (Anderson) **1**:35, 38, 40, 44, 48, 55-7; **10**:32-3, 36-7, 42, 44, 50; **24**:30; **123**:47-8, 102, 104, 106, 114
"The Marching Morons" (Kornbluth) **8**:219-21
Marching On (Boyd) **115**:59, 62, 68-73
"Marching Song" (Toller)
See "Marschlied"
"Marching to Zion" (Coppard) **5**:175
The Marchioness of Loria (Donoso)
See *La misteriosa desaparición de la Marquesita de Loria*
The Marchioness Rosalinda (Valle-Inclán)
See *La marquesa Rosalinda*
"Marcia notturna" (Saba) **33**:372
Marco Millions (O'Neill) **1**:385; **6**:329, 331-32; **49**:260
"Marcovaldo at the Supermarket" (Calvino) **183**:226
Marcovaldo, or The Seasons in the City (Calvino)
See *Marcovaldo ovvero le stagioni in città*
Marcovaldo ovvero le stagioni in città (Calvino) **183**:95-96, 160, 192, 195, 222, 226-27, 238, 247
"Marcus Curtius" (Gogarty) **15**:101
Mardi Gras (Kandinsky) **92**:48
"La Mare maudite" (Yourcenar) **193**:265
Mare nostrum (Blasco Ibáñez) **12**:31-2, 35, 38, 43, 50
"Mare Ships" (Esenin) **4**:115-16
"Maremma Idyl" (Carducci)
See "Idillio maremmano"
"Mares árticos" (Huidobro) **31**:136
Marevo (Balmont) **11**:38
"Margaret Fuller Slack" (Masters) **25**:314
Margaret Ogilvy (Barrie) **2**:47; **164**:22, 24, 38-39
"Margery" (Sinclair) **11**:407
"Margery of the Fens" (Symons) **11**:426
Margherita Spoletina (Heyse) **8**:119
"Margot" (Söderberg) **39**:427
Margret Howth: A Story of To-Day (Davis) **6**:147, 150-53, 155
"I mari del sud" (Pavese) **3**:339, 341
Maria (Asch) **3**:68-70, 72
Maria (Babel)
See *Mariia*
"María Abascal" (Palma) **29**:262
"Maria Cora" (Machado de Assis) **10**:296
María Luisa (Azuela) **3**:75, 77; **145**:8, 14, 17, 21-22, 28
"Maria Moroni" (Heyse) **8**:114
Maria Stuart (Zweig) **17**:429, 442, 457
Maria Stuart i Skotland (Bjoernson) **7**:100, 103, 109, 111, 113-14, 116; **37**:8, 18, 29
"Mariä Verkündigung" (Rilke) **195**:220
"Maria Vetsera" (Khlebnikov)
See "Mariya Vechora"
"Maria Who Made Faces and a Deplorable Marriage" (Belloc) **18**:39
"Maria-Fly" (de la Mare) **53**:16, 23, 27
Le Mariage Basque (Jammes) **75**:119
Le mariage de Barillon (Feydeau) **22**:89
Le mariage de Loti (Loti) **11**:351, 353-54, 356, 359-61, 365-67
Mariamne (Lagerkvist) **144**:168, 170-72, 212, 215, 242
"Marian Drury" (Carman) **7**:135, 139, 146
Marian Engel Archive (Engel) **137**:107-10
Marian Pineda (García Lorca)
See *Mariana Pineda*
"Mariana" (Machado de Assis) **10**:291, 296
Mariana (Echegaray) **4**:96, 98, 101, 103
Mariana Pineda (García Lorca) **1**:320; **7**:291-93, 296, 300; **49**:72, 75-6, 85, 105, 107, 109, 111; **181**:3-5, 9-10, 85-86, 96-105, 107-8
Marianela (Pérez Galdós) **27**:244, 249-50, 256
"Marianna Alcoforando" (Teasdale) **4**:424
Marianna Sirca (Deledda) **23**:36-7, 39
Marianne Thornton, 1797-1887: A Domestic Biography (Forster) **125**:183
Maria's Adventure (Svevo)
See *L'avventura di Maria*
"Marico Revisited" (Bosman) **49**:7, 9
"Marie" (Apollinaire) **3**:37, 39; **51**:9, 21
Marie (Haggard) **11**:243, 246, 255
Marie Antoinette (Belloc) **7**:39
Marie la misérable (Ghelderode) **187**:5
"Marie Vaux of the Painted Lips" (Service) **15**:412
"Marie von Nazareth" (Lasker-Schueler) **57**:308, 326

"An Mariechen" (Khodasevich) **15**:209
Marie-Magdeleine (Maeterlinck) **3**:323, 331
Les mariés de la Tour Eiffel (Cocteau) **119**:71-3, 99-104
Marietta: A Maid of Venice (Crawford) **10**:148, 151
"Marigolds and Mules" (Arnow) **196**:88-9
The Marihuana Pipe (Valle-Inclán)
See *La pipa de kif*
Mariia (Babel) **2**:23-4; **13**:30-1
"Marijuana Notation" (Ginsberg) **120**:77
"Marinera" (Huidobro) **31**:125
"Marino" (Huidobro) **31**:125, 144
"Un marino" (Pereda) **16**:380
Marino Faliero (Swinburne) **8**:432-33
Mario and the Magician (Mann)
See *Mario und der Zauberer: Ein tragisches Rieseerlebnis*
Mario und der Zauberer: Ein tragisches Rieseerlebnis (Mann) **44**:145, 173, 206; **60**:354
"Marion" (Heyse) **8**:113, 119, 121
Marion Darche (Crawford) **10**:143-44, 146, 150
The Marionette (Muir) **2**:486; **87**:194
Marionettes (Faulkner) **141**:93
"¿Una mariposa?" (Lugones) **15**:292
"Mariposa" (Millay) **4**:315
Mariquita y Antonio (Valera y Alcala-Galiano) **10**:506, 508
"The Marital Garland of a Hundred and Eight Verses to Sri Arunacha la" (Ramana Maharshi)
See "Arunacala-aksara-mana-malai"
Un marito (Svevo) **35**:353, 370
"Mariya Vechora" (Khlebnikov) **20**:130, 139
"Marizibill" (Apollinaire) **3**:36; **51**:53, 55-6
"Marjatan poika" (Leino) **24**:371
"The Mark" (Coffin) **95**:14
"Mark of the Monkey" (Rohmer) **28**:286
"The Mark on the Shutter" (MacCarthy) **36**:256
"The Mark on the Wall" (Woolf) **56**:381; **128**:371
The Mark on the Wall (Woolf) **1**:527; **56**:359; **128**:332
Mark Only (Powys) **9**:360-62, 365, 369, 375-76
Mark Rutherford's Deliverance (Rutherford) **25**:335, 340, 342-43, 345, 350-51, 355-56, 360-64
"Mark Twain and His Recent Works" (Stockton) **47**:326
Mark Twain at Work (De Voto) **29**:121
Mark Twain-Howells Letters (Twain) **161**:252
Mark Twain's America (De Voto) **29**:115-16, 118, 121, 124, 127, 130-31
Mark Twain's Autobiography (Twain) **6**:460; **12**:437-38; **19**:385; **36**:373, 382; **59**:211
Mark Twain's Mysterious Stranger Manuscripts (Twain) **185**:258, 269, 309, 318
"The Marked Tree" (Chesnutt) **39**:99, 103
Markens grøde (Hamsun) **2**:202, 204-08; **14**:221-22, 224-26, 228-31, 235, 237, 240-41, 243, 248; **49**:129-30, 134-35, 145, 151-55; **151**:232, 234, 261
"Marker's Hobbies" (Williams) **89**:383
"The Market" (Babits)
See "A Vásár"
"The Market" (Nezval)
See "Tržnice"
"Market Day" (Webb) **24**:472
Market Place in Tunis (Kandinsky) **92**:34
"Market Square" (Milne) **88**:243
Markiza dezes (Khlebnikov) **20**:136
"Marklake Witches" (Kipling) **17**:207
Marksizm i filosofia iazyka: Osnovnye problemy sociologicheskogo metoda v nauke o jazyke (Bakhtin) **160**:109, 135
Marlborough: His Life and Times (Churchill) **113**:93, 96-99, 106, 112-13, 142
Marlowe (Chandler) **7**:175
"Marlowe Takes on the Syndicate" (Chandler) **179**:129
"Marmalade" (O'Faolain) **143**:264
"The Marmozet" (Belloc) **18**:39
The Marne (Wharton) **3**:572; **129**:349, 362
"The Maroons of Jamaica" (Higginson) **36**:176
"The Maroons of Surinam" (Higginson) **36**:176
Der Marques de Bolibar (Perutz) **60**:367-68, 370
El marqués de Lumbría (Unamuno) **9**:511, 515
La marquesa Rosalinda (Valle-Inclán) **5**:472-73, 486
The Marquis de Bolibar (Perutz)
See *Der Marques de Bolibar*
The Marquis of Keith (Wedekind)
See *Der Marquis von Keith*
The Marquis of Lossie (MacDonald) **9**:292, 308
"The Marquis of Lumbria" (Unamuno) **148**:238
The Marquis of Montrose (Buchan) **41**:60
Der Marquis von Keith (Wedekind) **7**:580, 582, 585, 590
"Une Marquise" (Dobson) **79**:5, 22
La Marquise de Sade (Vallette) **67**:268-69, 274, 292, 295, 297, 299, 303, 324-26, 335-36
Marquise Desaix (Khlebnikov)
See *Markiza dezes*
"Marrakech" (Orwell) **6**:345; **51**:256; **128**:283
"Marriage" (Carpenter) **88**:72
"Marriage" (Drummond) **25**:146
Marriage (Döblin)
See *Die Ehe*
Marriage (Wells) **6**:525-26, 529, 531, 539; **12**:495-96, 508
"Marriage à la mode" (Mansfield) **8**:282-85; **39**:303-04; **164**:248, 320, 333, 339
Marriage by Capture (Buchanan) **107**:87
Marriage by Capture (Stringer) **37**:336
"A Marriage by Proxy" (Cahan) **71**:28, 68
Marriage Ceremonies in Morocco (Westermarck) **87**:334
"Le marriage d'André Salmon" (Apollinaire)
See "Poème lu au mariage d'André Salmon"
The Marriage Feast (Lagerkvist) **144**:238, 240, 243
Marriage Is No Joke (Bridie) **3**:131
Marriage Lines (Nash) **109**:354
"Marriage Made Easy" (Lardner) **14**:312
"The Marriage of a Geologist" (Carducci) **32**:102
"Marriage of Bacchus and Ariadne" (Field) **43**:165-66
"The Marriage of Phaedra" (Cather) **11**:100
The Marriage of William Ashe (Ward) **55**:414-15, 420-22, 424-25, 437, 441
"The Marriage Plate" (Ouida) **43**:376
The Marriage Proposal (Chekhov)
See *Predlozhenie*
"Marriage—For One" (Dreiser) **10**:181; **35**:71-4
"Married" (Dreiser) **35**:56, 72-3
Married (Strindberg)
See *Spöksonaten*
Married II (Strindberg) **47**:366
Married Life (Lie)
See *Et samliv*
The Married Lover (Colette)
See *Duo*
"A Married Man's Story" (Mansfield) **2**:451; **8**:281-82, 292; **39**:303; **164**:281, 285, 287, 302-4, 323
"The Marring of Malyn" (Carman) **7**:135
The Marrow of Tradition (Chesnutt) **5**:133-34, 138-40; **39**:69, 76-7, 79, 82, 84, 87-8, 92, 94, 96-9
"The Marry Month of May" (Henry) **19**:180
The Marrying of Ann Leete (Granville-Barker) **2**:193-97
Mars Child (Kornbluth) **8**:216
Mars His Idiot (Tomlinson) **71**:398, 406
"Mars Jeems's Nightmare" (Chesnutt) **39**:94-6, 99, 105-06
Mars; or, The Truth about War (Alain)
See *Mars ou la guerre jugée*
Mars ou la guerre jugée (Alain) **41**:2-3, 5, 10, 16, 25
Der Marsch nach Hause (Raabe) **45**:182, 190
"Marschlied" (Toller) **10**:480, 490
The Marsden Case (Ford) **15**:88, 93; **39**:148; **172**:70-71, 118-26
Marseille (Kandinsky) **92**:49-50
"Marseilles Express Train" (Norris) **155**:259
"Marsh Fire" (Grove) **4**:142
A Marsh Island (Jewett) **1**:359, 367, 369; **22**:135, 138
"Marsh Rosemary" (Jewett) **22**:125, 129, 133, 146
"The Marshal President" (Goebbels) **68**:99
"Marshall's Mate" (Lawson) **27**:140
"The Marshland" (Akutagawa Ryūnosuke) **16**:27
Marshlands (Gide)
See *Paludes*
"De marsj van de hete zomer" (van Ostaijen) **33**:418
"Marstube" (Kornbluth) **8**:215
"Marsyas" (Carman) **7**:149
"Marsyas" (Masters) **25**:289
"Marsyas" (Roberts) **8**:320
Marsyas, or on the Margin of Literature (Čapek) **6**:85; **37**:46-7
Marta Gruni (Sánchez) **37**:314
"Marta Riquelme" (Hudson) **29**:141, 155-56
Martereau (Sarraute) **145**:265, 274, 364
Martes de carnaval (Valle-Inclán) **5**:486
"Martha" (Thomas) **105**:337
Martha (Stockton)
See *The House of Martha*
"Martha and Mary" (Čapek) **37**:44; **192**:189
Marthe (Huysmans) **7**:404, 407, 410; **69**:7-9, 23, 26, 43
Marthe and the Madam (Bosschere)
See *Marthe et l'enragé*
Marthe et l'enragé (Bosschere) **19**:59, 61, 63-6
Marthe, histoire d'une fille (Huysmans)
See *Marthe*
Martin Birck's Youth (Söderberg) **39**:426-28, 439
Martin Eden (London) **9**:255, 257, 260, 263, 265, 268-70, 273, 275-77; **15**:255-56, 260-61, 271-72, 277
Martin Hewitt, Investigator (Morrison) **72**:363, 370
Martin Luther (Moore) **7**:486-87
"Martin Luther on Celibacy and Marriage" (Brandes) **10**:61
Martin Paz (Verne) **6**:490
"Martina" (Pardo Bazán) **189**:227
"Martina sull'albero" (Jovine) **79**:44
"Martinique Sketches" (Hearn) **9**:133
"Martin's Close" (James) **6**:206, 212-13
"Martirio de Santa Olalla" (García Lorca) **49**:92, 112; **181**:27
"Martwy sezon" (Schulz) **5**:423; **51**:307-08, 315
"The Martyr" (Akutagawa Ryūnosuke)
See "Hōkyōnin no shi"
"The Martyr" (Södergran)
See "Martyren"
"The Martyr of Alabama" (Harper) **14**:260, 263
The Martyr of Alabama, and Other Poems (Harper) **14**:263
The Martyrdom of Madeline (Buchanan) **107**:61, 64, 83-4
"Martyrdom of Saint Eulalia" (García Lorca)
See "Martirio de Santa Olalla"
The Martyrdom of Saint Sebastian (D'Annunzio)
See *Le martyre de Saint-Sébastien*
Le martyre de Saint-Sébastien (D'Annunzio) **6**:136-37; **40**:10-11
"Martyren" (Södergran) **31**:292, 294
The Martyr's Idyl, and Shorter Poems (Guiney) **41**:207-08, 214
"Maruja" (Harte) **25**:213, 223
"The Marvel" (Douglas) **40**:75-6, 87, 92
"A Marvellous Decade" (Berlin) **105**:8-9
A Marvellous Decade (Berlin) **105**:7

The Marvellous Shoemaker's Wife (García Lorca)
See *La zapatera prodigiosa*
The Marvelous Arithmetics of Distance: Poems 1987-1992 (Lorde) **173**:138, 140
The Marvelous Land of Oz (Baum) **7**:14, 20-3, 25, 27; **132**:12-14, 16, 30, 36, 49, 51, 75, 77, 80-81, 83-89, 91, 99
The Marvelous Life of Joseph Balzamo, The Count Cagliostro (Kuzmin) **40**:194
"Marx" (Murry) **16**:341
Marxism and Linguistics (Stalin) **92**:183, 321, 323, 326
"Marxism and Philosophy" (Merleau-Ponty) **156**:136
Marxism and the National and Colonial Question (Stalin) **92**:154
"Marxism and the National Question" (Stalin)
See "The National Question and Social Democracy"
"Marxism Is a Weapon, a Method of Firearm Quality—So Use This Method Knowledgeably!" (Mayakovski) **18**:269
"Mary" (Cohan) **60**:159
"Mary" (Mansfield) **39**:293
Mary (Asch)
See *Maria*
Mary (Braddon) **111**:215
Mary (Nabokov)
See *Mashen'ka*
"Mary and Gabriel" (Brooke) **7**:122
"Mary and Martha" (Jewett) **22**:147
Mary and the Bramble (Abercrombie) **141**:3, 10, 20
"Mary and Veronica" (Ady) **11**:20
Mary Anerley (Blackmore) **27**:28, 36-8, 42, 47
"Mary at the Feet of Christ" (Harper) **14**:260
Mary Baker Eddy (Toller)
See *Mary Baker Eddy; oder, Wunder in Amerika*
Mary Baker Eddy (Zweig) **17**:442
Mary Baker Eddy; oder, Wunder in Amerika (Toller) **10**:483
"Mary Button's Principles" (Gilman) **37**:213
Mary Christmas (Chase) **124**:22
"The 'Mary Gloster'" (Kipling) **8**:191
Mary Magdalen (Saltus) **8**:343, 346, 348-49, 352
Mary Magdalene (Maeterlinck)
See *Marie-Magdeleine*
"Mary Magdalene" (Pasternak) **188**:196
Mary, Mary (Stephens)
See *The Charwoman's Daughter*
"Mary of Egypt" (Remizov) **27**:355
Mary of Magdala (Heyse) **8**:118-19
"Mary of Nazareth" (Lasker-Schueler)
See "Marie von Nazareth"
Mary of Scotland (Anderson) **2**:4-6, 8; **144**:7, 11, 17, 70-73
Mary Oliver (Sinclair) **3**:434-35, 437-38, 440-42; **11**:411, 413-17, 419-20, 422
Mary Peters (Chase) **124**:13-14, 16, 21, 23-25
"Mary Postgate" (Kipling) **8**:195; **17**:213
Mary Rose (Barrie) **2**:43-4, 49; **164**:8-9, 16, 18, 22, 26-27, 29-33, 35
"Mary Shepherdess" (Pickthall) **21**:243, 245, 250
"Mary Smith" (Tarkington) **9**:467
Mary Stuart (Drinkwater) **57**:125-26, 130-31, 133, 138, 141-44
Mary Stuart (Swinburne) **8**:432-33
Mary Stuart in Scotland (Bjoernson)
See *Maria Stuart i Skotland*
Mary, the Queen of Scots (Zweig)
See *Maria Stuart*
Mary the Third (Crothers) **19**:75, 77, 80-1, 84
"Mary Tired" (Pickthall) **21**:245, 250
"Mary's a Grand Old Name" (Cohan) **60**:168, 170, 172
Mary's Neck (Tarkington) **9**:469
"Mary's Son" (Leino)
See "Marjatan poika"
Mary's Tuesday (Kuzmin)
See *Vtornik Meri*
Marzio's Crucifix (Crawford) **10**:139-41, 143-44, 146, 148, 150, 152
"Märztag" (Liliencron) **18**:213
"Más allá" (Pardo Bazán) **189**:226, 228
Más allá (Quiroga) **20**:213-14
"El más bello amor" (Aleixandre) **113**:7, 47
"Más que lento" (Villaurrutia) **80**:477
"Más sociabilidad!" (Unamuno) **148**:240
Masaroa (Mofolo) **22**:248
"Máscaras" (Güiraldes) **39**:176, 185
Mascarilla y trébol (Storni) **5**:445, 447, 449-50, 452
"La maschera dimenticata" (Pirandello) **4**:351
Maschere nude (Pirandello) **29**:282, 295, 300, 308, 315, 318-20; **172**:189
Die Maschinenstürmer (Toller) **10**:475, 477, 479, 481, 483, 487, 491-93
"Masculine Literature" (Gilman) **117**:49-50, 53
"El masgad" (Graham) **19**:105
The Mashber Family (Kahanovitsch)
See *Di mishpoke Mashber*
Mashen'ka (Nabokov) **108**:60, 83, 104-111, 113, 118-129, 221-22
Mashiny i volki (Pilnyak) **23**:199-201, 212, 214-17, 219
"Masjid-i-Qurtuba" (Iqbal) **28**:199
"The Mask" (Chambers) **41**:101, 103-6, 108, 110, 114
"The Mask" (Chekhov) **55**:65
The Mask (Mori Ogai)
See *Kamen*
Mask and Clover (Storni)
See *Mascarilla y trébol*
The Mask of Fu Manchu (Rohmer) **28**:280, 286, 300
"The masked dyer of Merv" (Borges)
See "El tintorero enmascarado Hákim de Merv"
"The Masked Face" (Hardy) **53**:89, 91
Die Masken Erwin Reiners (Wassermann) **6**:509-10
"Maskers" (van Ostaijen) **33**:418
"Masks" (Güiraldes)
See "Máscaras"
"The Masks" (Hedāyat)
See "Suratak-ha"
Masks (Bely) **7**:49, 52
Masks (Leino)
See *Naamioita*
The Masks of God (Campbell) **140**:11-12, 22, 25, 28, 30, 32, 45, 51, 78, 80, 87, 89, 94, 96, 112, 123, 132-34
The Masks of God: Creative Mythology (Campbell) **140**:34, 40-41, 51-52, 54, 80, 83, 86, 89, 96-97, 99-101, 103-4, 132, 134, 136, 138
The Masks of God: Occidental Mythology (Campbell) **140**:94-96, 100-102, 118, 132
The Masks of God: Oriental Mythology (Campbell) **140**:85, 87-89, 132
The Masks of God: Primitive Mythology (Campbell) **140**:30, 119, 132, 139
"Maslacak" (Popa) **167**:155
The Masque of Judgment (Moody) **105**:218, 220, 225, 227, 230-32, 234, 238-45, 251, 253-54, 256, 259-60, 263, 266-67, 269, 274-84
The Masque of Kings (Anderson) **2**:6-8; **144**:10, 17, 34, 37-38, 71, 73
The Masque of Pedagogues (Anderson) **144**:70
"The Masque of Queen Bersabe" (Swinburne) **8**:445; **36**:299
The Masque of Snow (Blok)
See *Snezhnye maski*
"The Masque of the Magi" (Flecker) **43**:194
"The Masque of the Months" (Dobson) **79**:19, 23
"The Masquer in the Street" (Quiller-Couch) **53**:291
The Masquerade (Micheaux) **76**:248
The Masquerade of Souls (Lagerkvist)
See *Själarnas maskerad*
Masques Ostendais (Ghelderode) **187**:5
"Mass" (Heym)
See "Die Messe"
"Mass at Dawn" (Campbell) **5**:122-23
"Mass for the Imprisoned" (Herbert) **168**:45
The Mass Psychology of Fascism (Reich) **57**:338-39, 344, 350, 360, 369, 380-81
The Mass Strike, The Political Party, and the Trade Unions (Luxemburg) **63**:184, 186, 214
The Massacre (Fadeyev)
See *Razgrom*
"Massacre of the Innocents" (García Lorca)
See "Degollación de los Inocentes"
The Massarenes (Ouida) **43**:361-62, 369, 372
Masse Mensch (Toller) **10**:474-77, 479-81, 483, 485, 487-89, 491-92
Masse und Macht (Canetti) **157**:12, 20-21, 44, 46, 48, 50, 52-55, 59, 62-63, 65-66, 69, 71, 73-82, 85-86, 90, 95-101, 104, 109
Masse und Publikum (Park)
See *The Crowd and the Public*
"The Massed, Angered Forces of Common Humanity Are on the March" (Roosevelt) **93**:184
Massenpsychologie: Schriften aus dem Nachlass (Broch) **20**:68-70
Massenstreik, Partei und Gewerkschaft (Luxemburg)
See *The Mass Strike, The Political Party, and the Trade Unions*
"The Masses" (Jozsef) **22**:161-62
Masses and Men (Toller)
See *Masse Mensch*
Die Massnahme (Brecht) **1**:104, 109, 121; **6**:33, 36; **13**:57; **35**:20; **169**:17, 34, 68-69, 71
"Master" (Carter) **139**:185
"The Master" (Robinson) **5**:411
The Master (Brod)
See *Die Meister*
The Master (Zangwill) **16**:441-43, 445, 461-64
Master and Dog (Mann)
See *Herr und Hund*
"Master and Guest" (Coleridge) **73**:4, 11, 21
Master and Man (Tolstoy)
See *Khozyain i rabotnik*
The Master and Margarita (Bulgakov)
See *Master i Margarita*
"The Master at a Mediterranean Port" (Nemerov) **124**:205
Master Author (Raabe)
See *Meister Autor*
The Master Builder (Ibsen)
See *Bygmester Solness*
Master Builders (Zweig)
See *Baumeister der Welt*
"Master Hynek Ráb of Kufstejn" (Čapek) **192**:189
Master i Margarita (Bulgakov) **2**:64-7, 69-71, 73; **16**:77-9, 81-7, 89-91, 93, 99, 100, 104-05, 107-11; **159**:1-180
"Master Kao" (Lu Hsun) **3**:301
The Master Key: An Electrical Fairy Tale (Baum) **132**:80
The Master Mason's House (Grove)
See *Maurermeister Ihles Haus*
The Master Mind of Mars (Burroughs) **32**:58, 63
"Master Misery" (Capote) **164**:99-100, 103-4, 106, 109, 112, 115, 156, 199
"A Master of Cobwebs" (Huneker) **65**:156
A Master of Craft (Jacobs) **22**:108-10
The Master of Hestviken (Undset) **3**:514, 516, 519, 521, 524; **197**:291-93, 318-23
"The Master of Hollow Grange" (Rohmer) **28**:286
The Master of Man (Caine) **97**:8, 10-11, 15
The Master of Mrs. Chilvers (Jerome) **23**:88
"The Master of Mystery" (London) **9**:274

The Master of the Day of Judgment (Perutz)
See *Der Meister des Jüngsten Tages*
The Master of the House (Hall) **12**:188, 190, 196
"The Master of the Isles" (Carman) **7**:135
The Master of the Magicians (Phelps) **113**:336
The Master of the Mill (Grove) **4**:136, 138-40, 145
The Master of the Mine (Buchanan) **107**:87
Master of the Revels (Marquis) **7**:451
"Master of the Scud" (Carman) **7**:138, 144
Master of the World (Verne)
See *Maître du monde*
Mäster Olof (Strindberg) **1**:452; **8**:406, 408, 412, 417, 419
Master over Life and Death (Zuckmayer)
See *Herr über Leben und Tod*
"The Master Poisoner" (Bodenheim) **44**:74
The Master Poisoner (Hecht) **101**:37, 73
The Master Rogue (Phillips) **44**:262, 273-74, 277
"Master Zacharias" (Verne)
See "Maître Zacharius:"
The Master-Christian: A Question of the Time (Corelli) **51**:66, 68, 75
A Masterpiece of Diplomacy (Howells) **7**:388
Masterpieces of Tanka on Love (Hagiwara) **60**:303
Masters of the Dew (Roumain)
See *Gouverneurs de la rosée*
"Mastro-don Gesualdo" (Svevo) **35**:363
Mastro-Don Gesualdo (Verga) **3**:543-44, 548-49
Mat' (Gorky) **8**:72, 75-7, 81, 84-6, 88, 90-1
Mat' syra zemlya (Pilnyak) **23**:202, 212-13
"The Matador of the Five Towns" (Bennett) **5**:42, 46; **20**:33, 35; **197**:29, 40
"Matal" (Tagore) **53**:351
"A Match" (Swinburne) **36**:315
The Mate (Schnitzler) **4**:387
"The Mate of Susie Oaks" (Williams) **89**:384, 392, 400
"The Mate of the Daylight" (Jewett) **22**:117
The Mate of the Daylight, and Friends Ashore (Jewett) **1**:367; **22**:137
Matelot (Loti) **11**:364, 366-67
"Le matelot d'Amsterdam" (Apollinaire) **51**:20
Maten al león (Ibarguengoitia) **148**:189-90, 192-93, 217-18
Mater Dei (Sikelianos)
See *The Mother of God*
"Materia" (Aleixandre) **113**:4
"The Material and the Models" (Weiss) **152**:311
"Materialism" (Bataille) **155**:111
"Materialism" (Södergran) **31**:285
Materialism and Empirio-Criticism (Lenin) **67**:200, 202-3, 223, 245
"Materialism and Metaphysics" (Horkheimer) **132**:213
"Materialism and Morality" (Horkheimer) **132**:200, 213, 216, 2215
Le Matérialisme rationnel (Bachelard) **128**:52, 54
"The Materialist Today" (Lovecraft) **22**:210
The Materials (Oppen) **107**:255, 257, 262-63, 282, 286-87, 302-04, 310-11, 328-30, 334, 354-55
Materials for a Novel (Pilnyak) **23**:204-08, 214
Materials for a Theory of the Proletariat (Sorel)
See *Materiaux d'une theorie du proletariat*
"The Materials for English Legal History" (Maitland) **65**:281
Materiaux d'une theorie du proletariat (Sorel) **91**:184, 201, 332
"Maternity" (Tynan) **3**:503
"Mateship" (Lawson) **27**:132
"Mateship in Shakespeare's Rome" (Lawson) **27**:132
Mathias Sandorf (Verne) **6**:502
Matière et mémoire (Bergson) **32**:20, 27, 38, 42, 44, 48
Matilda (Dahl) **173**:20, 26, 28
Le matin (Rolland) **23**:261
Matinée (Proust) **161**:146-48
"Matinees" (Merrill) **173**:176, 233, 256
"Matinees-Wednesday and Saturdays" (Benchley) **55**:13
The Mating Season (Wodehouse) **108**:375, 379, 384, 386
Matka (Čapek) **192**:175, 204-5
Matka (Witkiewicz) **8**:507, 512-13, 515
"Matri delectissimae" (Henley) **8**:102, 108-09
"Matricide" (Csáth) **13**:146, 149, 151, 153, 155
"A Matron's Summer" (Pasternak) **188**:185
Matt: A Story of a Caravan (Buchanan) **107**:87
Matter and Memory (Bergson)
See *Matière et mémoire*
A Matter of Honour (Dunsany) **59**:28
"A Matter of Interest" (Chambers) **41**:113-14
"The Matter of Manner" (Bierce) **44**:31
A Matter of Millions (Green) **63**:148, 151
"A Matter of Prejudice" (Chopin) **127**:229
"A Matter of Principle" (Chesnutt) **5**:131-32; **39**:70, 80, 90-1, 93, 100
"A Matter of Taste" (La Guma) **140**:205, 207
"Matthew Arnold's New Poems" (Swinburne) **8**:440; **36**:314
Matthew Porter (Bradford) **36**:63
Matthias at the Door (Robinson) **5**:411, 415; **101**:105, 108, 184-85
"Mattie and Her Sweetman" (McKay) **41**:329
"Mattinata" (Carducci) **32**:90
"Die Mauer" (Borchert) **5**:109
"Maulša's Granddaughter" (Khlebnikov)
See "Vnučka Maluši"
"Maundy Thursday" (Owen) **27**:216
Maunu tavast (Leino) **24**:372
"Maupassant" (Babel)
See "Guy de Maupassant"
Maurermeister Ihles Haus (Grove) **4**:142-44
Maurice (Forster) **125**:146, 165
Maurice Guest (Richardson) **4**:370-73, 375-81
The Maurizius Case (Wassermann)
See *Der Fall Maurizius*
The Mausoleum Book (Stephen) **23**:342-43
"De Mauss à Lévi-Strauss" (Merleau-Ponty) **156**:183, 192
Les mauvais bergers (Mirbeau) **55**:281, 283
Un mauvais rêve (Bernanos) **3**:121, 124
"Max Brod's Book on Kafka" (Benjamin) **39**:16
"Max Bruns, Lenz" (Rilke) **195**:288
Max Carrados (Bramah) **72**:5, 8, 13
Max Carrados Mysteries (Bramah) **72**:8
Max in Verse: Rhymes and Parodies (Beerbohm) **1**:71-2
"Max Liebermann and Some Phases of Modern German Art" (Huneker) **65**:161
Maximilian (Masters) **25**:296
"Maximus" (Lawrence) **93**:72, 74
Max's Nineties: Drawings, 1892-1899 (Beerbohm) **1**:74
Maxwell Drewitt (Riddell) **40**:334-35
"May" (Ledwidge) **23**:117
"May 17, 1940" (Grieg) **10**:208
"May 23" (Thomas) **10**:463
"May Day" (Fitzgerald) **1**:241; **6**:169-71; **55**:191
"May Day" (Teasdale) **4**:429
"The May Day Dancing" (Nemerov) **124**:155, 273
"May Day Eve" (Blackwood) **5**:81
"May Day Sermon" (Dickey) **151**:105, 109, 115, 152, 166, 169, 172, 212
"May Days" (Ginsberg) **120**:74, 112
"may i feel said he" (Cummings) **137**:55
"May I Feel Said He (I'll Squeal Said She)" (Cummings)
See "may i feel said he"
"May Janet" (Swinburne) **36**:299
"may my heart always be open to little" (Cummings) **137**:56
"May Walk" (Sarton) **120**:268
"Maya" (Mann) **168**:173
"Maya" (Sharp) **39**:374
"The Mayan Caper" (Burroughs) **121**:126-27
Māyāvinī Sarsī (Devkota) **23**:51
Maybe: A Story (Hellman) **119**:120-21, 128, 130
"Maybe Baby" (Holly) **65**:145
"Maybe Love" (Ginsberg) **120**:35
"Mayday" (Davidson) **24**:163
Mayday (Faulkner) **141**:96
De Mayerling a Sarajevo (Ophuls) **79**:173
"The Mayfield Miracle" (Heyward) **59**:93
The Mayflower (Blasco Ibáñez)
See *Flor de mayo*
The Mayor of Casterbridge (Hardy)
See *The Mayor of Casterbridge: The Life and Death of a Man of Character*
The Mayor of Casterbridge: The Life and Death of a Man of Character (Hardy) **4**:149, 153, 157, 159, 174-75, 177; **10**:217, 220-21, 227; **18**:100, 102; **32**:265-327; **48**:38, 40, 59, 63-4, 67, 69; **72**:209-10, 237; **143**:71-72, 76-77, 82, 86-87, 92-94, 112-14, 119, 123, 142, 169, 196, 207; **153**:106, 117, 119, 129-31, 194, 196, 212
"La mayorazga de Bouzas" (Pardo Bazán) **189**:236
El mayorazgo de Labraz (Baroja) **8**:60-1
"A mayse mit a nozir un mit a tsigele" (Kahanovitsch) **56**:109
Mayselakh in ferzn (Kahanovitsch) **56**:117
Mayses far yidishe kinder (Aleichem) **35**:305
"The Maysville Minstrel" (Lardner) **2**:337; **14**:307
Maytime (Heijermans) **24**:292
"Mazeppa" (Campbell) **5**:123
Mazushiki hitobito no mure (Miyamoto) **37**:266
"McAndrew's Hymn" (Kipling) **8**:191; **17**:197
"McCluskey's Nell" (Service) **15**:412
"McDermott" (Marquis) **7**:437
McDonough's Wife (Gregory) **176**:20, 23-24
"McEwen of the Shining Slave Makers" (Dreiser) **10**:197, 199-200; **35**:71, 75
"McKane's Falls" (Merrill) **173**:170
McLeod's Folly (Bromfield) **11**:82
McTeague (Norris) **24**:416-18, 420, 422-28, 432-35, 440-41, 444-48; **155**:259-61, 263-65, 269, 277-78, 280, 288, 292-99, 303, 305, 307, 311, 314, 335-41
"Me" (Anwar)
See "Aku"
Me and My Bike (Thomas) **105**:347
"Me and the Devil" (Johnson) **69**:82, 86
"Me and the Devil Blues" (Johnson)
See "Me and the Devil"
Me eum esse (Bryusov) **10**:81, 84, 86, 95-6
"Me viene, haydías, un gana uberrima, política" (Vallejo) **56**:307
Mea (Bryusov) **10**:90
"Meadowlarks" (Teasdale) **4**:429
The Meaning and the Task of a Modern University (Otto) **85**:323
"The Meaning of Art" (Bely) **7**:60
"The Meaning of Causality" (McTaggart) **105**:197
The Meaning of Creative Work (Berdyaev)
See *The Meaning of Creativity*
The Meaning of Creativeness (Berdyaev)
See *The Meaning of Creativity*
The Meaning of Creativity (Berdyaev) **67**:24, 26, 30, 32-3, 73-4, 80
"The Meaning of 'Ethical Neutrality' in Sociology and Economics" (Weber) **69**:318, 320
The Meaning of History (Berdyaev) **67**:26, 30, 32-3
The Meaning of Holy Writ (Huch) **13**:247
"The Meaning of Insurgency" (Baker) **47**:14
"The Meaning of Life" (Adler) **61**:34
The Meaning of Relativity (Einstein) **65**:91, 105
"The Meaning of R.U.R." (Čapek) **192**:236
The Meaning of the Creative Act (Berdyaev)
See *The Meaning of Creativity*
The Meaning of Truth (James) **32**:340, 357

"The Means Massacre" (Coffin) **95**:2
The Means to Prosperity (Keynes) **64**:210
"Meantime" (Fondane) **159**:255-56
"Measles" (Kuprin) **5**:301
Measure of Justice (Bergelson)
See *Midas Hadin*
"The Measure of Poetry" (Nemerov) **124**:210, 300
The Measured Passion (Drummond de Andrade)
See *A Paixão Medida*
The Measurement of Intelligence (Thorndike) **107**:379, 410, 424
The Measurement of Variable Quantities (Boas) **56**:82
Measurements of Twins (Thorndike) **107**:400, 406
The Measures Taken (Brecht)
See *Die Massnahme*
"Meat and Potatoes" (Kunikida Doppo)
See "Gyūniku to Bareishō"
"La mécanique d'Ixion" (Jarry) **147**:314
La meccanica (Gadda) **144**:101-2
"The Mechanic" (Zoshchenko) **15**:499
"The Mechanical Optimist" (Stevens) **3**:448
Mechanics (Gadda)
See *La meccanica*
"The Mechanism of Social Consciousness" (Mead) **89**:168, 170-1
Mechtateli (Kuzmin) **40**:195, 199
"Mechtildes, die goede meid" (van Ostaijen) **33**:412
"La medaglie" (Pirandello) **4**:330
"Medallions" (Jozsef) **22**:160, 164
"The Meddler" (Williams) **89**:398
"Medea" (Bryusov) **10**:88
"Medea" (Cullen)
See "The Medea: A New Version"
"The Medea: A New Version" (Cullen) **4**:51; **37**:138, 170
The Medea, and Some Poems (Cullen) **4**:43, 47, 49, 51; **37**:138, 145, 156-60, 163, 166, 169
"Medea da Carpi" (Lee) **5**:320
Médée (Anouilh) **195**:13-14, 20-1, 26, 39, 42
"Las medias rojas" (Pardo Bazán) **189**:237
"Medicine" (Lu Hsun)
See "Yao"
"Medicine and Colonialism" (Fanon) **188**:73
"The Medicine Man" (Gissing) **24**:248
The Medicine Man (Hichens) **64**:131
"Médieuses" (Éluard) **41**:159
Médieuses (Éluard) **41**:150, 159
"Mediocre Men and Superior Individuals" (Rohan) **22**:296
Mediocrity (Futabatei)
See *Heibon*
"Meditación" (García Lorca) **181**:168
Meditacion de Europa (Ortega y Gasset) **9**:356
Meditaciones del Quixote (Ortega y Gasset) **9**:341, 345, 347-48, 354
"Meditation" (Radnóti) **16**:418
"Meditation at Perugia" (Scott) **6**:386, 389, 394
"Meditation Celestial and Terrestrial" (Stevens) **3**:463
"A Meditation in Time of War" (Yeats) **93**:389, 402
Meditation on Europe (Ortega y Gasset)
See *Meditacion de Europa*
"Meditation under Stars" (Meredith) **17**:277
"Meditationen zur Metaphysik" (Adorno) **111**:177, 189-90
Méditations (Bryusov) **10**:92
Meditations (Kafka)
See *Betrachtung*
Meditations (Nietzsche) **10**:393
Meditations cartesiennes (Husserl) **100**:40, 71, 90, 97-98, 120, 122-24
Méditations esthétiques: Les peintres cubistes (Apollinaire) **3**:42; **8**:14-15, 19, 28; **51**:9, 14, 30, 38, 45, 49
"Meditations in a Cemetery" (Bodenheim) **44**:59
"Meditations in Time of Civil War" (Yeats) **11**:518, 533-36; **18**:442, 459; **31**:401, 420-22; **93**:341, 364, 401
Meditations of a Non-Political Man (Mann)
See *Betrachtungen eines Unpolitischen*
"Meditations of Mr Cogito on Redemption" (Herbert) **168**:19
"Meditations on metaphysics" (Adorno)
See "Meditationen zur Metaphysik"
"Meditations on Quixote" (Ortega y Gasset)
See *Meditaciones del Quixote*
Meditazione milanese (Gadda) **144**:95-96, 101, 107, 113, 115, 117-18, 124, 127, 132-33, 138-41, 144-49
Mediterranee (Saba) **33**:366, 368-70, 374
"Medlars and Sorb-Apples" (Lawrence) **93**:26, 80, 96, 98-100
"Medley" (Naidu) **80**:348
"The Medusa" (Merrill) **173**:225, 253-55
"Medusa" (Percy) **84**:203
Medved (Chekhov) **31**:80
The Meeker Ritual (Hergesheimer) **11**:267
Meerfahrt mit Don Quijote (Mann) **168**:156
"A Meeting" (Graham) **19**:115, 130-31
"The Meeting" (Kornbluth) **8**:220
"A Meeting" (Markham) **47**:279
"Meeting" (Pasternak) **188**:194
"Meeting" (Pirandello)
See "Convegno"
"The Meeting" (Roberts) **68**:306
The Meeting (Reymont)
See *Spotkanie*
"Meeting a Moscow Acquaintance in the Detachment" (Tolstoy) **4**:474
"Meeting among the Mountains" (Lawrence) **9**:221; **93**:54
Meeting at Night (Bridie) **3**:141
"The Meeting at the Mixed Club" (Apollinaire) **51**:49
"Meeting Mother" (Csáth) **13**:149, 153
"A Meeting South" (Anderson) **123**:50
A Meeting with Despair (Hardy) **48**:60
"Meeting-House Hill" (Lowell) **1**:380; **8**:227, 229-30, 237
Meetings with Remarkable Men (Gurdjieff) **71**:187, 190, 193-194, 197-198, 201
"Meetings With Russian Writers in 1945" (Berlin) **105**:52
"Meg Blane" (Buchanan) **107**:16, 25
Még egyszer (Ady) **11**:19
Még mindig így írtok ti (Karinthy) **47**:268
"Megh o Roudra" (Tagore) **3**:485
"Megillath ha-'esh" (Bialik) **25**:49-50, 54, 56, 59-60, 64-6
Mehalah: A Story of the Salt Marshes (Baring-Gould) **88**:12, 14-5, 20, 23-8, 30, 32-6
Meian (Natsume) **2**:493-95; **10**:332-36, 338, 346
De meid (Heijermans) **24**:287-88
Le meilleur choix de poèmes est celui que l'on fait pour soi (Éluard) **41**:152
"Mein blaues Klavier" (Lasker-Schueler) **57**:298, 327, 336
Mein blaues Klavier (Lasker-Schueler) **57**:297, 299, 305-6, 322, 324, 327, 334
"Mein bleicher Bruder" (Borchert) **5**:109
"Mein Drama" (Lasker-Schueler) **57**:311, 326, 329
"Mein Glaube" (Hesse) **148**:180; **196**:265, 277, 285, 312, 318, 328-29
Mein Glaube (Hesse) **148**:164, 171-72, 176, 179-81
"Mein Herz ruht mude" (Lasker-Schueler) **57**:302
Mein Kampf (Hitler) **53**:120-83
Mein Lebensgang (Steiner) **13**:446
Mein Name sei Gantenbein (Frisch) **121**:187-88, 197-98, 200-02, 205, 213, 226-29, 233, 238, 242, 245-46, 265, 275-76, 281
Mein neuer Vetter (Zuckmayer) **191**:305
"Mein Schaffen und mein Werk" (Spitteler) **12**:352
"Mein stilles Lied" (Lasker-Schueler) **57**:305, 311-13, 319, 324, 330, 335-36
"Mein Tanzlied " (Lasker-Schueler) **57**:313
"Mein Volk" (Lasker-Schueler) **57**:298, 322-25, 332-33
Mein Weg als Deutscher und Jude (Wassermann) **6**:517
"Mein Weltenstuck" (Bernhard) **165**:94
"Meine Andacht" (Lasker-Schueler) **57**:297, 299
"Meine Ortschaft" (Weiss) **152**:297
"Mein trauriges Gesicht" (Böll) **185**:26, 32, 129
"Mein Vogel" (Bachmann) **192**:5, 8-9
Meine Wunder (Lasker-Schueler) **57**:309, 327, 330-31
Meine Zeit (Mann) **168**:170
"Meiosi" (Calvino) **183**:10, 228
"Meiosis" (Calvino)
See "Meiosi"
Die Meister (Brod) **115**:87-8, 99
Meister Autor (Raabe) **45**:166, 176, 179, 203
Der Meister des Jüngsten Tages (Perutz) **60**:368-69
"Meister Leonhard" (Meyrink) **21**:232
Mējdidi (Chatterji) **13**:80
Los Mejores cuentos de Donoso (Donoso)
See *Cuentos*
Mekake taku (Nagai) **51**:105
Melancholie (Morgenstern) **8**:304-05, 310
"Melancholy" (Bely) **7**:50
"Melancholy" (Thomas) **10**:455, 462
Melancholy (Leino)
See *Melankolia*
"Melancolía" (Lugones) **15**:285
Melancolía (Jiménez) **183**:300-301
"Mélancolie du cinéma" (Desnos) **22**:65
"Mélancolique villégiature de Mme. de Breyves" (Proust) **7**:538; **161**:172-74
"Melanctha—Each One as She May" (Stein) **1**:427, 430, 433, 437, 440; **6**:405, 408, 410, 413; **28**:306, 311-12, 324, 336; **48**:225-29, 245, 253, 255, 263
Melankolia (Leino) **24**:372
Melannippe the Philosopher (Annensky) **14**:17, 21
Meleager (Heyse) **8**:115
"La mélinite: Moulin Rouge" (Symons) **11**:445
Mélissa (Kazantzakis) **5**:268
Melkii bes (Sologub) **9**:433-38, 441-42, 444-45, 449
Mellem slagene (Bjoernson) **7**:100, 102, 106, 112-13, 116; **37**:8, 23, 29
"Mellstock" (Hardy) **143**:154
"Meloči" (Guro) **56**:139
Melodier i skymning (Ekelund) **75**:94-95
Melodies in Twilight (Ekelund)
See *Melodier i skymning*
"Melodies of the Day" (Peretz) **16**:396
The Melodramatists (Nemerov) **124**:151, 158-60, 234, 237-40, 243, 291
Le Melomane (Melies) **81**:123,138
Le Melomaniac (Melies)
See *Le Melomane*
Melomaniacs (Huneker) **65**:156-58, 169-70, 195, 216
"The Melting Pot" (Gilman) **117**:167
The Melting Pot (Zangwill) **16**:445, 452, 466-69
"The Melting Pot Begins to Smell" (Fuller) **103**:102, 107-08
Melting Snow (Nagai)
See *Yukige*
"Melusine" (Moréas) **18**:286
"Melymbrosia: An Early Version of The Voyage Out" (Woolf) **128**:331, 339
A Member of the Third House (Garland) **3**:192
The Member of the Wedding (McCullers) **155**:175, 180, 183, 187-89, 209-10, 213-14, 216, 235, 241
Members of the Family (Wister) **21**:377-78, 405

"Memento" (Morgenstern) **8**:310
"Memnon" (Roberts) **8**:313, 328-30
Memoir (Yokomitsu)
See *Oboegaki*
Memoir of Prosper Mérimée (Guiney) **41**:209
Mémoire sur le sytème primitif des voyelles dans les langues indo-européennes (Saussure) **49**:303-05, 332-34, 339, 341
"Mémoires de Benjamin Péret" (Péret) **20**:191
Mémoires de Dirk Raspe (Drieu la Rochelle) **21**:30, 35, 37-9
"Mémoires de l'espion" (Jacob) **6**:191
Les Mémoires d'Hadrien (Yourcenar) **193**:250, 256, 265, 270-72, 274, 280, 306-17, 320-21, 347, 353-58, 360, 363
"Mémoires d'un poèms" (Valéry) **15**:465
"Memoirs" (Tolstoy)
See "Vospominaniya"
Memoirs (Anderson) **1**:51, 61; **10**:42, 44; **24**:27, 29, 54
Memoirs (Bryan) **99**:34-35
Memoirs (Yeats) **116**:306
"The Memoirs of a Billiard-marker" (Tolstoy) **173**:269
The Memoirs of a Billiard-Marker (Tolstoy) **4**:445; **11**:464
Memoirs of a Confirmed Bachelor (Pardo Bazán)
See *Memorias de un solterón*
Memoirs of a Disciple of St. Paul (Abbott) **139**:26
Memoirs of a Madman (Tolstoy)
See *Zapiski sumasshedshego*
Memoirs of a Man of Action (Baroja)
See *Las memorias de un hombre de acción*
Memoirs of a Midget (de la Mare) **4**:71-4, 77-8, 80; **53**:27-8, 35
Memoirs of a Napoleonic Officer (Barrès)
See *Les souvenirs d'un officier de la grande armée*
Memoirs of a Native (Romero)
See *Apuntes de un lugareño*
Memoirs of a Revolutionist (Kropotkin) **36**:190-91, 208, 225
Memoirs of a Young Rakehell (Apollinaire) **8**:25
"Memoirs of an Octogenarian" (Lin) **149**:342
Memoirs of Dirk Raspe (Drieu la Rochelle)
See *Mémoires de Dirk Raspe*
The Memoirs of God (Papini)
See *Le memorie d'Iddio*
Memoirs of Hadrian (Yourcenar)
See *Les Mémoires d'Hadrien*
Memoirs of Many in One (White) **176**:296, 298, 330
Memoirs of Marau Taaroa, Last Queen of Tahiti (Adams) **4**:11, 18
The Memoirs of Martynov (Hippius) **9**:163
Memoirs of Mistral (Mistral)
See *Mes origines*
Memoirs of My Dead Life (Moore) **7**:478, 480, 493, 496-97, 499
"Memoirs of My Dreamed Life" (Yourcenar) **193**:266
Memoirs of Sarah Bernhardt (Bernhardt)
See *My Double Life: Memoirs of Sarah Bernhardt*
The Memoirs of Sherlock Holmes (Doyle) **7**:216, 220, 238
"Memoirs of the Kalda Railroad" (Kafka) **112**:38
Memoirs of World War I: From Start to Finish of Our Greatest War (Mitchell) **81**:161-2
Memorable Body (Éluard) **7**:260-61
Memoranda de Parliamento (Maitland) **65**:282
"Memoranda for a Sonnet Sequence" (Morley) **87**:123
"Memorandum" (Ingamells) **35**:131
"Memorandum" (Lyotard) **103**:276
Memorandum (Bataille) **155**:113
"Memorandum Book" (Levi) **109**:287
"Memorandum by the Treasury on the Indemnity Payable by the Enemy Powers for Reparation and Other Claims" (Keynes) **64**:242
"Memorandum Confided by a Yucca to a Passion-Vine" (Lowell) **1**:371, 373, 375
"Memoria" (Aleixandre) **113**:4
La memoria del mondo (Calvino) **183**:93, 95-96, 101, 215
Memorial de Ayres (Machado de Assis) **10**:285, 292, 295
"Memorial I" (Lorde) **173**:77
"Memorial II" (Lorde) **173**:77-78
"A Memorial of Marxism: For Pierre Souyri" (Lyotard) **103**:201, 218
"Memorial Service" (Mencken) **13**:365
"Memorial Verse" (Naidu) **80**:340
Memorias de España 1937 (Garro) **153**:72
Las memorias de Mamá Blanca (De La Parra) **185**:203-06, 209
"Memorias de novelas" (Ibarguengoitia) **148**:217
Memorias de un cortesano de 1815 (Pérez Galdós) **27**:287
Las memorias de un hombre de acción (Baroja) **8**:49, 53, 63
Memorias de un solterón (Pardo Bazán) **189**:241-43, 257, 262-65, 267, 299-300
Memórias do cárcere (Ramos) **32**:428-29, 434-37
Memórias pósthumas de Braz Cubas (Machado de Assis) **10**:280-89, 292, 294, 299-300, 303-07
"Le memorie dei fratelli Goncourt" (Svevo) **35**:363
Le memorie d'Iddio (Papini) **22**:280-81
"Memories" (Galsworthy) **45**:33
"Memories" (Holly) **65**:149
"Memories" (Matthews) **95**:253-4
Memories (MacCarthy) **36**:254
Memories and Notes (Hope) **83**:174
"Memories of a Battle" (Calvino) **183**:234
"Memories of a Working Women's Guild" (Woolf) **128**:349
"Memories of Christmas" (Thomas) **45**:399; **105**:356
"Memories of Eastern United States, Written in Spain" (Jiménez) **183**:331
Memories of Home (La Guma) **140**:274
"Memories of Kimura Sakae" (Nishida)
See "Kimura Sakae-kun no omoide"
"Memories of Mariposa" (Sienkiewicz) **3**:430
"Memories of My Grandmother" (Wright) **136**:259, 261, 263-64
Memories of My Life (Bernhardt) **75**:9
"Memories of Shiko" (Nishida)
See "Shiko no omide"
"Memories of Yamamoto Chosui" (Nishida)
See "Yamamoto Chosui-kun no omoide"
"Memories Roused by a Roman Theatre" (Patton) **79**:304
"Memory" (Aleixandre)
See "Memoria"
"Memory" (Benét) **7**:75, 79
"A Memory" (Brooke) **2**:53
"Memory" (Coleridge) **73**:25
"Memory" (Devkota)
See "Samjhanā"
"Memory" (Gumilev) **60**:264, 270-3
"Memory" (Gurney) **33**:94
"A Memory" (Pascoli) **45**:145
Memory Hold-the-Door (Buchan) **41**:59, 63, 66, 77-8, 81, 84
"The Memory of a Summer Night" (Ady)
See "Emlé-kezés egy nyáréjszakára"
The Memory of Certain Persons (Erskine) **84**:168, 171-2, 174
"Memory of Hills" (Ingamells) **35**:127, 131
Memory of Hills (Ingamells) **35**:121, 129, 137
"A Memory of June" (McKay) **7**:468
"The Memory of Martha" (Dunbar) **12**:112
"A Memory of My Friend" (Nemerov) **124**:255
"A Memory of the Players in a Mirror at Midnight" (Joyce) **3**:255; **159**:279, 284
Memory of the World (Calvino)
See *La memoria del mondo*
"Memory of Yamashina" (Shiga)
See "Yamashina no kioku"
"The Memphis Blues" (Handy) **97**:38-45, 50-51, 55-56, 59, 62-63, 67-70
The Memphis Diary of Ida B. Wells: An Intimate Portrait of the Activist as a Young Woman (Wells-Barnett) **125**:333-34
Memsahib (Duncan)
See *The Simple Adventures of a Memsahib*
"Men" (Toomer) **172**:277
Men against the Sea (Hall and Nordhoff) **23**:60-3, 66, 69-70
Men and Ideas: Essays (Wallas) **91**:356
"Men and Wheat" (Torrence) **97**:158
Men and Wives (Compton-Burnett) **180**:114-15, 122, 125, 127, 129, 131, 142, 192, 194-95, 197
Men and Women (Belasco) **3**:88
"Men Fought" (Borges)
See "Hombres pelearon"
"Men I'm Not Married To" (Parker) **143**:281
Men imorgen (Grieg) **10**:206, 209
"Men Improve with the Years" (Yeats) **1**:566
Men in Dark Times (Arendt) **193**:43, 77, 157, 160
"Men in New Mexico" (Lawrence) **93**:103
"The Men in the Storm" (Crane) **11**:131, 167; **17**:65-6, 68-9
Men Like Gods (Wells) **6**:539-40, 548, 553; **19**:428, 437, 439, 441, 452-53, 428, 437, 439, 441, 452-53
Men livet lever (Hamsun) **49**:130
"Men Made Out of Words" (Stevens) **45**:343
"Men nu vänta vi stora ting . . ." (Lagerkvist) **144**:222
"Men of Aquino" (Johnson) **19**:243
"Men of Assisi" (Johnson) **19**:243
"The Men of Forty Mile" (London) **9**:268
Men of Corn (Asturias)
See *Hombres de maíz*
Men of the Deep Waters (Hodgson) **13**:237
"The Men Who Made Australia" (Lawson) **27**:136
"The Men Who Made the Money Trust" (Phillips) **44**:277
"Men Who March Away" (Hardy) **143**:188
"The Men who Pushed the Forest Down" (Coffin) **95**:2
"Men with Broken Hearts" (Williams) **81**:434
"Men with Goats Thrashing" (Lowry) **6**:238
"Men with Pasts" (Gorky) **8**:71
Men without Art (Lewis) **2**:385, 390-94, 399; **9**:239, 243, 249; **104**:165, 172, 178, 188-89, 202, 254-58, 296
Men without Merry (Döblin)
See *Pardon wird nicht gegeben*
Men without Women (Hemingway) **115**:133-34, 180
Men, Women, and Ghosts (Lowell) **1**:372; **8**:226, 228, 235
Men, Women, and Guns (Sapper) **44**:306
Men, Women and Places (Undset)
See *Selvportretter og landskapsbilleder*
"The Menace of Darwinism" (Bryan) **99**:150
"The Menace of Love" (Naidu) **80**:287
Le ménage du Pasteur Naudié (Rod) **52**:310, 315
"The Menagerie" (Moody) **105**:234, 240, 259, 271-72
Menagerie (Khlebnikov) **20**:142-43
Menahem Mendel, the Dreamer (Aleichem) **1**:29-30; **35**:306-08, 310, 327
"Menalcas" (Agee) **19**:42
A Mencken Chrestomathy (Mencken) **13**:395-96
"Mendacity" (Coppard) **5**:178
"Mendel Breines" (Peretz) **16**:399
Le mendiant ingrat (Bloy) **22**:45, 50
Mendicant Rhymes (Housman) **7**:353
"Los mendigos políticos" (Asturias) **184**:14
Mendizábal (Pérez Galdós) **27**:283

A menekülaio élet (Ady) **11**:18, 23
"Menelaus and Helen" (Brooke) **2**:54, 59; **7**:122, 125
Le meneur de louves (Vallette) **67**:283, 299
Menino antigo (Drummond de Andrade) **139**:230-31
"Den menneskelige natur" (Grieg) **10**:208
"Menos" (Jiménez) **183**:263
"Menoschen und Schickesale aus dem Risorgimento" (Huch) **13**:253
"Mensaje" (Aleixandre) **113**:20
Der Mensch erscheint im Holozän (Frisch) **121**:213, 228-29, 233, 235-37, 241, 247, 274
Mensch und Gesellschaft im Zeitalter des Umbaus (Mannheim) **65**:303, 314, 333
Mensch Wanderer (Morgenstern) **8**:305-06, 310
Menschenkenntnis (Adler) **61**:8, 11, 28, 32-3
"Menschliche Trauer" (Trakl) **5**:461
Menschliches, Allzumenschliches: Ein Buch für freie Geister (Nietzsche) **10**:355, 357, 362, 367, 372, 387-89, 393; **18**:342-43
"Menses" (Millay) **49**:222
Menší růžová zahrada (Nezval) **44**:239, 245
Le mensonge (Sarraute) **145**:265, 267, 314, 316-17, 320, 321321
Mensonges (Bourget) **12**:59, 67, 72-3
"Los mensú" (Quiroga) **20**:212, 214-15, 219
La menta del bambino (Montessori) **103**:317, 319-20, 324
"Mental Cases" (Owen) **5**:362, 367, 370-72; **27**:202, 208, 212, 214-15, 217, 227, 229-30
Mental Efficiency: And other Hints to Men and Women (Bennett) **5**:39; **197**:108
Mental Healers (Zweig)
See *Die Heilung durch den Geist: Franz Anton Mesmer, Mary Baker Eddy, Sigmund Freud*
"The Mental Life of the Monkeys" (Thorndike) **107**:370
"A Mental Suggestion" (Chopin) **14**:70
"La menuda floración" (Jiménez) **183**:270
"A Mephistophelian" (Hearn) **9**:136
"Le meraviglie della cronaca nera" (Calvino) **183**:103
"A Mercedes en su vuelo" (García Lorca) **181**:67
"The Merchantman and the Market-Haunters" (Davidson) **24**:164
"Merchants from Cathay" (Benét) **28**:3, 5
Merchants of Disaster (Dent) **72**:20-21
The Merchants of Nations (Papadiamantis) **29**:271
"The Merchant's Wife" (Lewis) **3**:287
Mercier and Camier (Beckett)
See *Mercier et Camier*
Mercier et Camier (Beckett) **145**:76, 79, 81-83
"Mercy" (Dickey) **151**:143
The Mercy of Allah (Belloc) **7**:38, 40; **18**:45
"The 'Mercy' of God" (Dreiser) **35**:71, 74
A Mere Accident (Moore) **7**:473, 484-86, 489-90
Mere Man (Thomas) **97**:139
"Mère Pochette" (Jewett) **22**:137
"Merely Mary Ann" (Zangwill) **16**:465
Les Mères (Genet)
See *Les paravents*
"Mergui Isles" (Kolmar) **40**:179
"Meriggio" (D'Annunzio) **40**:43-5
"The Merino Sheep" (Paterson) **32**:381
"A Meritorious Villainous Baker_Man" (Lindsay) **17**:240
"Merknut znaki zodiaka" (Zabolotsky) **52**:366
"Merkwaardige aanval" (van Ostaijen) **33**:412, 418
"Merle" (Renard) **17**:311
"Le merle et la jeune fille" (Bosschere) **19**:59
Merlette (Gourmont) **17**:127-28
"Merlin" (Muir) **87**:188
Merlin (Heyse) **8**:117-19
Merlin: A Poem (Robinson) **5**:403; **101**:95, 111, 113, 115-16, 130, 134, 188-89, 192
"Merlin et la vieille femme" (Apollinaire) **3**:34, 43
The Mermaid (Melies) **81**:123
Merope (D'Annunzio) **6**:136
The Merovingians (Liliencron) **18**:208
"Die Merowinger" (Liliencron) **18**:216
The Merry Adventures of Robin Hood of Great Renown in Nottinghamshire (Pyle) **81**:385, 391, 394-400
"Merry Folk" (Sudermann) **15**:428
The Merry Frolics of Satan (Melies) **81**:122
"The Merry Guide" (Housman) **10**:247, 252
"The Merry Maid" (Millay) **4**:307
"The Merry Policeman" (Stephens) **4**:417
The Merry Vineyard (Zuckmayer) **191**:319, 321-22
The Merry Widow (Stroheim) **71**:329-332, 336-340, 357, 361-362, 366
The Merry Wives of Westminster (Lowndes) **12**:205
"The Merry-Go-Round" (Buchanan) **107**:67
Merry-Go-Round (Schnitzler)
See *Reigen*
Merry-Go-Round (Stroheim) **71**:330-332, 339, 374
"Mersa" (Douglas) **40**:74, 76
"Mertvecy osveščennye gazom" (Bryusov) **10**:82
"Merveilles de la guerre" (Apollinaire) **8**:17, 28-9; **51**:36
Mes apprentissages (Colette) **5**:171; **16**:118, 129, 133
Mes cahiers (Barrès) **47**:48, 51, 56, 61, 63, 65, 67-8, 76, 92, 98
Mes haines (Zola) **6**:567; **41**:407
Mes origines (Mistral) **51**:142-46
Mes Statues (Ghelderode) **187**:7
Mescal: A New Artificial Paradise (Ellis) **14**:112
"Mescaline" (Ginsberg) **120**:48, 77
Meshi (Hayashi) **27**:107
"Der meshugener batlen" (Peretz) **16**:401
"Der meshulekh" (Peretz) **16**:389-90, 399
Mesikammen (Leino) **24**:372
"The Mesmeric Mountain" (Crane) **11**:148
"Méson de Castilla" (García Lorca) **181**:170
"Mesopotamia, 1917" (Kipling) **8**:200
"A Mess of Pork" (Arnow) **196**:88-9
"A Mess of Pottage" (Dunbar) **2**:30; **12**:111
"Message" (Aleixandre)
See "Mensaje"
"A Message from the Deep Sea" (Freeman) **21**:59
Message in the Bottle (Karinthy) **47**:271
The Message of Kafka (Hedāyat)
See *Piyam-e Kafka*
"The Message of St. John" (Baker) **10**:28
The Message of the East (Iqbal)
See *Payam-i mashriq*
The Message to the Planet (Murdoch) **171**:242, 259, 261, 265, 268, 285, 323, 327
"Message to Young Writers" (Tolstoy) **18**:372
"Messages" (Dickey) **151**:114, 143
Messalina of the Suburbs (Delafield) **61**:127
"Messalina Prepares a Festival" (Bishop) **103**:26
Messaline (Jarry) **147**:227-30, 266-68, 290, 309, 312-14
"Messaline au Cirque" (Swinburne) **8**:440
"Die Messe" (Heym) **9**:142, 144-45
La messe là-bas (Claudel) **10**:123
"La messe sur le monde" (Teilhard de Chardin) **9**:481-82
"The Messenger" (Chambers) **41**:88, 102
"The Messenger" (Lovecraft) **4**:266
"The Messenger" (Peretz)
See "Der meshulekh"
The Messiah (Merezhkovsky) **29**:242
"Messidor" (Swinburne) **36**:318
Messingkauf Dialogues (Brecht) **35**:20
"Messrs Turkes and Talbot" (Wakefield) **120**:356
"Messze . . . Messze" (Babits) **14**:39
Mestecko, kde se zastavil cas (Hrabal) **155**:151-54, 158, 160
Il mestiere di vivere: Diario, 1935-1950 (Pavese) **3**:340
"Město věží" (Nezval) **44**:246
"Mesu ni tsuite" (Dazai Osamu) **11**:175
"Mesure de la France" (Drieu la Rochelle) **21**:18, 27, 32
Metafizyka dwuglowego dielecia (Witkiewicz) **8**:512, 514
"Metamorphoses" (Kolmar) **40**:176
"Metamorphoses: according to Steinberg" (Nemerov) **124**:183, 250
"Metamorphoses of M" (Bishop) **103**:5, 16
"Metamorphosis" (Agnon)
See "Panim aherot"
"Metamorphosis" (Dazai Osamu)
See "Gyofukuki"
"The Metamorphosis" (Dobson) **79**:27, 30
"Metamorphosis" (Stevens) **45**:281
Metamórphosis (Gamboa) **36**:74-6
The Metamorphosis (Kafka)
See *Die verwandlung*
"Metamorphosis of Capitalism" (Drieu la Rochelle) **21**:36-7
"La metamúsica" (Lugones) **15**:293
"The Metaphor" (Borges) **109**:24
"Metaphor as Degeneration" (Stevens) **3**:473; **12**:364
"Metaphor as Pure Adventure" (Dickey) **151**:135
"The Metaphor Depot" (Olesha) **136**:157
"The Metaphor Shop" (Olesha) **136**:157
"Metaphors of a Magnifico" (Stevens) **12**:360
"The Metaphysical Automobile" (Nemerov) **124**:260-61
"Metaphysical Criticism" (Endo) **152**:167
"The Metaphysical Garden" (Sarton) **120**:269
"The Metaphysical in Man" (Merleau-Ponty) **156**:213
Metaphysics as a Guide to Morals (Murdoch) **171**:222, 230-40, 242, 244, 258, 260-61, 270, 281, 284
Metaphysics of a Two-Headed Calf (Witkiewicz)
See *Metafizyka dwuglowego dielecia*
"Metaphysics of Being" (Artaud) **36**:17
"Metaphysics of Youth" (Benjamin) **39**:3
"La métaphysique dans l'homme" (Merleau-Ponty) **156**:121, 123-27
"Metel'" (Pilnyak) **23**:196
"Metel'" (Tolstoy) **4**:445
Metello (Pratolini) **124**:324-27, 329, 337, 350
"Metempsicosis" (Lugones) **15**:285
"The Meteor" (Bradford) **36**:63
Meteor (Čapek)
See *Provětroň*
"The Meteorite" (Jarrell) **177**:228
"Method and Metaphysics" (Collingwood) **67**:184
"Method of Composition with Twelve Tones Related Only to One Another" (Schoenberg)
See "Composition with Twelve Tones"
Méthode de méditation (Bataille) **155**:10, 89-90, 98, 112, 127
"The Methodist Spirit: A Tribute" (Riis) **80**:439
"Eine Methodologische Novelle" (Broch) **20**:55
"Methods in Social Anthropology" (Westermarck) **87**:335
"The Methods of Ethnology" (Boas) **56**:98
"Methods of Montage" (Eisenstein) **57**:181
"Methods of Science" (Peirce) **81**:291
Methods of Social Study (Webb and Webb) **22**:415, 424
Métiers divins (Bosschere) **19**:52-5, 63-4
"El metro de doce" (Nervo) **11**:400
"The Metropolis and Mental Life" (Simmel) **64**:360, 362
"Metropolitan Melancholy" (Stevens) **45**:347
Metropolitan Symphony (Mizoguchi) **72**:322
"Les Metteurs en Scène" (Wharton) **129**:361

"Mettus Curtius" (Field) **43**:165-66
"Les meules qui brûlent" (Verhaeren) **12**:467
"Le meunier" (Verhaeren) **12**:466-67
"The Mexican" (London) **9**:262; **15**:262
The Mexican Bandits (White) **176**:225
"Mexican Interval" (McAlmon) **97**:94, 96-97, 121
"Mexican Quarter" (Fletcher) **35**:105, 107
"Mexico" (Mayakovski) **18**:259
Mexico City Blues (Kerouac) **117**:215, 218, 222
Mexico in a Nutshell, and Other Essays (Reyes) **33**:322
"Mexico's Epitaph" (Machado de Assis)
See "Epitaphio do Mexico"
The Mezentian Gate (Eddison) **15**:53-5, 57, 60, 62
"Mezzogiorno alpino" (Carducci) **32**:91, 103, 112
"The Mezzotint" (James) **6**:212
Mezzotint (Mackenzie) **116**:237
Mezzotints in Modern Music (Huneker) **65**:157, 165, 170, 177, 188, 199, 215
"Mgnovenija" (Bryusov) **10**:81
Mhendu (Devkota) **23**:50
M'hijo el dotor (Sánchez) **37**:311-17
Mhudi: An Epic of South African Native Life a Hundred Years Ago (Plaatje) **73**:220-39
"Mi amante el mar" (Arenas) **191**:196
Mi caballo, mi perro y mi rifle (Romero) **14**:434, 444
Mi diario (Gamboa) **36**:71-2
De mi país (Unamuno) **148**:243
"Mi religión" (Unamuno) **2**:560; **9**:513; **148**:298
Mi religión y otros ensayos (Unamuno) **9**:514
"Mi suicidio" (Pardo Bazán) **189**:226-27, 299, 305
"De mi tierra" (Azuela) **145**:21
"Mi triste ansia" (Jiménez) **4**:214
"Mi verso" (Nervo) **11**:400
"Mi voz" (Aleixandre) **113**:7
"A mia moglie" (Saba) **33**:373, 377
Miau (Pérez Galdós) **27**:248, 250, 257, 263
Micah Clarke (Doyle) **7**:217, 220, 224, 226-27, 234, 239
"Michael" (Baker) **10**:17, 21, 25
Michael (Goebbels) **68**:88, 91, 103-04, 108, 111-13, 115-16, 118-20, 125
Michael and Mary (Milne) **88**:247
"Michael Angelo" (Lawrence) **93**:45
Michael Angelo (Shaw) **3**:381
"Michael Angelo's Sonnets" (Chapman) **7**:185
Michael, Brother of Jerry (London) **9**:267
"Michael Clancy, the Great Dhoul, and Death" (Yeats) **31**:416, 418
Michael Kramer (Hauptmann) **4**:194-95, 197
Michael O'Halloran (Porter) **21**:271, 274, 276
Michael Robartes and the Dancer (Yeats) **1**:559; **11**:522, 528; **31**:421; **93**:339, 340, 344, 362, 389, 391, 398
Michael Strogoff, the Courier of the Czar (Verne)
See *Michel Strogoff, Moscow-Irkowtsk*
"Michael Trevanion" (Rutherford) **25**:361
Michael Unger (Huch)
See *Vita somnium breve*
"Michaelmas" (Davidson) **24**:163, 186, 193
"Michałko" (Prus) **48**:162, 172, 177
Michel Strogoff, Moscou-Irkoutsk (Verne)
See *Michel Strogoff, Moscow-Irkowtsk*
Michel Strogoff, Moscow-Irkowtsk (Verne) **6**:502
Michel Strogoff; or, The Courier of the Czar (Verne)
See *Michel Strogoff, Moscow-Irkowtsk*
Michel-Ange (Rolland) **23**:282
Michelangelo (Brandes) **11**:66
Michelangelo (Papini)
See *Vita di Michelangelo*
Michelangelo's Nose (Ball)
See *Die Nase des Michelangelo*
"A mi-chemin" (Péret) **20**:196-97
"Michigan Avenue" (Hecht) **101**:38
"A Michigan Soldier's Diary, 1863" (Kirk) **119**:314
Michikusa (Natsume) **2**:492-93; **10**:338, 346
"Miching Mallecho" (Williams) **89**:393
"The Microbe" (Belloc) **18**:39
Mid-American Chants (Anderson) **1**:36, 46-7, 50, 56-7, 61; **10**:37, 41, 45, 47-50; **123**:8, 48, 111-12, 114-15
"Mid-American Prayer" (Anderson) **10**:47; **123**:113-14
Midaregami (Yosano) **59**:323, 326, 332, 341-5
Midas Hadin (Bergelson) **81**:31
Mid-Channel (Lewisohn) **19**:269, 271-73, 277, 281, 287-88, 290
Mid-Channel (Pinero) **32**:395, 397-98, 400-02, 405, 410, 414-15
"En middag" (Kielland) **5**:275
"Midday in the Alps" (Carducci)
See "Mezzogiorno alpino"
"Middle Age Phrases for a Historical Study" (Twain) **48**:357
"The Middle Ages" (Chambers) **129**:48
"The Middle Ages" (Gumilev) **60**:271
"The Middle Drawer" (Wakefield) **120**:350
"Middle Ground" (Faulkner) **170**:138
The Middle Kingdom (Morley) **87**:140
"The Middle of the World" (Lawrence) **61**:227; **93**:59, 124
The Middle Parts of Fortune (Manning)
See *Her Privates We*
The Middle Span (Santayana) **40**:385
"The Middle Toe of the Right Foot" (Bierce) **7**:88; **44**:15, 44-5, 49
The Middle Years (James) **11**:321; **24**:314
"Middle-Aged" (Bennett) **5**:46
Middle-Class Illusions (Drieu la Rochelle)
See *Rêveuse bourgeoisie*
"Middleton's Peter" (Lawson) **27**:131
"Middleton's Rouseabout" (Lawson) **27**:140
"Midget Car" (Fields) **80**:259
The Midlander (Tarkington) **9**:458, 460, 467-68, 474
"Mid-Night" (Howe) **21**:106
"Midnight" (Villaurrutia) **80**:477
"Midnight Dance" (Nagai)
See "Butō"
"Midnight in India" (Lewis) **3**:290
"Midnight in Moscow" (Mandelstam) **2**:409
"Midnight in Russia" (Steffens) **20**:355
"Midnight Mass" (Machado de Assis) **10**:288, 306
"Midnight Rendezvous" (Rohmer) **28**:286
"The Midnight Service" (Bialik) **25**:50
"Midnight Shift" (Holly) **65**:151
Midnight Sketches (Crane) **11**:134, 163
"Midnight Snack" (Merrill) **173**:257
"The Midnight Song" (Leino)
See "Keskiyön kuoro"
The Midnight Sun (Remizov)
See *Polunoshchnoe solntse*
"Midoriiro no fue" (Hagiwara) **60**:291
Midsommardröm i fattighuset (Lagerkvist) **144**:211
"Midsommerfesten" (Hansen) **32**:249, 251
"Midsummer Customs in Morocco" (Westermarck) **87**:334
"Midsummer Day" (Davidson) **24**:163
Midsummer Dream in the Workhouse (Lagerkvist)
See *Midsommardröm i fattighuset*
"The Midsummer Feast" (Hansen)
See "Midsommerfesten"
"Midsummer Frost" (Rosenberg) **12**:311-12
"A Midsummer Holiday" (Swinburne) **36**:321
"Midsummer in the Forest" (Liliencron) **18**:206
"Midsummer Night Madness" (O'Faolain) **143**:221, 231, 257, 259-60
Midsummer Night Madness, and Other Stories (O'Faolain) **143**:221, 227, 256, 268, 273
"A Midsummer Night's Dream" (Hartmann) **73**:119
Midsummer Night's Dream in the Workhouse (Lagerkvist)
See *Midsommardröm i fattighuset*
"Midsummer Passion" (Caldwell) **117**:3
"Midsummer Sport" (Heidenstam) **5**:251
"A Midsummer Trip to the Tropics" (Hearn) **9**:133
Midt i en jærntid (Nexø) **43**:330
"Midwestern Drugstores and Drive-Ins" (Shepherd) **177**:316
Midwinter (Buchan) **41**:39
"Midwinter Night's Dream" (Coppard) **5**:179
"Miedo" (Storni) **5**:452
"El miedo a la muerte" (Nervo) **11**:395
"I miei amici" (Papini) **22**:280
Míg új a szerelem (Moricz) **33**:243-44
"Might, Majesty, and Dominion" (Graham) **19**:122, 136
Mightier Than the Sword (Ford)
See *Portraits from Life: Memories and Criticisms*
The Mighty and Their Fall (Compton-Burnett) **180**:124, 127-28, 143, 145, 147
The Mighty Atom (Corelli) **51**:66, 68, 82
"The Mighty Hundred Years" (Markham) **47**:284
"The Migraine Workers" (Petry) **112**:299, 301
"Migration from Curses' City" (Ady) **11**:14
"Mihan-Parast" (Hedāyat) **21**:74
Mihatenu yume (Nagai) **51**:105
Mik (Gumilev) **60**:262
The Mikado; or, The Town of Titipu (Gilbert) **3**:215, 217-19
"Mikan" (Akutagawa Ryūnosuke) **16**:20
"Mike" (Thomas) **10**:459
Mike: A Public School Story (Wodehouse) **108**:341, 364, 393-95
Mike Fletcher (Moore) **7**:484-86, 489-90
Mikhalaki (Vazov) **25**:450
Mikkai (Abe) **131**:11
Miklós Radnóti: The Complete Poetry (Radnóti) **16**:421
"Mikusha Nalymov" (Tolstoy) **18**:367, 377
"Mila and Prelac" (Andrić) **135**:14, 90, 93
Mīla stiprāka par nāvi (Rainis) **29**:393
Un milagro en Egipto (Echegaray) **4**:101
"El milagro secreto" (Borges) **109**:76, 112
The Milan Grill Room: Further Adventures of Louis, the Manager, and Major Lyson, the Raconteur (Oppenheim) **45**:131
Milanese Meditation (Gadda)
See *Meditazione milanese*
"Mildred Lawson" (Moore) **7**:484-85
Mileposts I (Tsvetaeva)
See *Vyorsty I*
Mileposts II (Tsvetaeva)
See *Vyorsty II*
Milestones (Bennett) **5**:44, 46; **197**:14, 16-17, 19, 22-3, 172
"Le milieu divin" (Teilhard de Chardin) **9**:481, 483-84, 486, 488-89, 492, 494-95
"Le milieu mystique" (Teilhard de Chardin) **9**:492, 500
"Militarism and Theology" (Strachey) **12**:400
The Military Tales (Tolstoy) **4**:445; **173**:269
Military Tricks (Valle-Inclán)
See *Baza de espadas: El ruedo Ibérico III*
"The Milkmaid's Song" (Pyle) **81**:390
"Milkweed" (Stringer) **37**:343
"The Mill" (Robinson) **5**:406, 413; **101**:159, 192, 197
"The Mill at Naul" (Gogarty) **15**:110
"The Mill Pond" (Thomas) **10**:450
Mille plateaux (Deleuze) **116**:59, 61-3, 80-5, 87, 90, 92-7, 99, 103, 123, 151, 159, 174
"The Miller" (Smith) **25**:377, 382, 386, 397
The Miller of Old Church (Glasgow) **2**:180; **7**:333, 340
"The Miller of Ostend" (Post) **39**:339
"Millet" (Lagerkvist) **144**:197
"Millie" (Mansfield) **2**:451; **39**:301, 319; **164**:340-42

Million Dollar Legs (Mankiewicz) **85**:112, 155-6
"The Millionaire" (Artsybashev) **31**:7
The Millionaire (Micheaux) **76**:266
The Millionaire of Yesterday (Oppenheim) **45**:132
"A Millionaire's Girl" (Fitzgerald) **52**:59-62
The Millionairess (Shaw) **3**:393; **45**:220
"Millions" (Aleichem)
See "Milyonen"
"The Mill-Water" (Thomas) **10**:452
Milly and Olly (Ward) **55**:409
"Milton" (Muir) **87**:156, 168, 172
Milton (Belloc) **18**:33, 45
Milton (Macaulay) **7**:423
Milton's Paradise Lost: Screenplay for Cinema of the Mind (Collier) **127**:252-53, 262
"Milyonen" (Aleichem) **35**:306, 308, 310-11
Mimes (Schwob) **20**:320, 322-23
Mimesis: Dargestellte Wirklichkeit in der abendländischen Literatur (Auerbach) **43**:47-51, 53-9, 62-8, 70-3, 75-85
Mimesis: The Representation of Reality in Western Literature (Auerbach)
See *Mimesis: Dargestellte Wirklichkeit in der abendländischen Literatur*
"Mimi" (Bennett) **5**:46
Mimma Bella: In Memory of a Little Life (Lee-Hamilton) **22**:192-93
Mimoletnoe (Rozanov) **104**:348, 397, 399, 401
"Mimosa" (Leverson) **18**:200-01
"Mimsy Were the Borogoves" (Kuttner) **10**:268, 272-74
"Min gud" (Lagerkvist) **144**:217-18, 239
"Min hembygd" (Lagerkvist) **144**:222
"Min lyra" (Södergran) **31**:292
"Min själ" (Södergran) **31**:290
"Min Svanesang" (Nexø) **43**:315
"Mina" (Aleixandre) **113**:12
"Minä" (Leino) **24**:370
Minawa-shû (Mori Ogai) **14**:369
Mince Pie (Morley) **87**:120
"The Mind" (Nemerov) **124**:258
"The Mind" (Tagore)
See *Mānasī*
The Mind and Society (Pareto)
See *Trattato di sociologia generale*
"Mind and the Symbol" (Mead) **89**:101
Mind at the End of Its Tether (Wells) **6**:548, 553; **12**:507; **133**:246, 284
"Mind Breaths" (Ginsberg) **120**:109, 111, 121
Mind Breaths: Poems, 1972-1977 (Ginsberg) **120**:26, 111, 121
Mind Energy (Bergson)
See *L'énergie spirituelle*
"The Mind of Fu Manchu" (Rohmer) **28**:292, 301
The Mind of J. G. Reeder (Wallace) **57**:402
The Mind of Light (Aurobindo) **63**:20
The Mind of Primitive Man (Boas) **56**:63, 74, 79, 92, 94
"The Mind of the Maker" (Sayers) **2**:534; **15**:374, 376, 383, 390, 395
"Mind Over Motor" (Rinehart) **52**:280
Mind, Self, and Society (Mead) **89**:50, 64, 71-2, 75, 100, 102, 104, 106-7, 147, 158-9, 161-3, 165, 172
"The Mind Speaks" (Davies) **5**:209
The "Mind the Paint" Girl (Pinero) **32**:393, 405, 413, 415
"Mind versus Mill-Stream" (Howe) **21**:107
"Mind Your Own Business" (Williams) **81**:423,429
"Mindenek szerelme" (Babits) **14**:39
A minden-titkok verseiből (Ady) **11**:18, 23
"The Mind-Reader" (Herzl) **36**:140, 143
The Mind's Creation (Tagore)
See *Mānasī*
"Mind's Eye Trouble" (Benchley) **55**:7, 8
"The Mind's Own Place" (Oppen) **107**:357
"The Mindworm" (Kornbluth) **8**:216
"Mine" (Aleixandre)
See "Mina"
"The Mine at Falun" (Hofmannsthal)
See "Das Bergwerk zu Falun"
"Mine Enemy's Dog" (Williams) **89**:371
"Mine Field" (Calvino) **183**:95
"Mine Host" (McCrae) **12**:208, 211
Mine the Harvest (Millay) **49**:215, 222-23, 226, 232; **169**:251
The Mine with the Iron Door (Wright) **183**:349
Mine-Haha (Wedekind) **7**:586
"Los mineros salieron de la mina . . ." (Vallejo) **56**:311, 316
"Miners" (Owen) **5**:361, 363, 366, 369, 374; **27**:201, 212, 227
"Minerva's Owl" (Innis) **77**:337
"Minetta Lane, New York" (Crane) **11**:142
Minetti: Portrait of the Artist as an Old Man (Bernhard)
See *Minetti: Porträt des Künstlers als alter Mann*
Minetti: Porträt des Künstlers als alter Mann (Bernhard) **165**:129-32
"Ming Tseuen and the Emergency" (Bramah) **72**:9
"A Mingled Yarn" (Tomlinson) **71**:403
A Mingled Yarn: Autobiographical Sketches (Tomlinson) **71**:400, 403
"Mingo: A Sketch of Life in Middle Georgia" (Harris) **2**:209
"Mîngol'ă's Inn" (Caragiale)
See "La hanul lui Mînjoală"
Minha Vida de Menina (Drummond de Andrade) **139**:237
"The Miniature" (Foote) **108**:20
Miniaturen (Brandes) **11**:68
Miniatures of French History (Belloc) **7**:40
Minima Moralia (Adorno) **111**:9, 11-13, 49-50, 53, 120-24, 127, 144, 146-49, 151, 160-69, 176, 182, 186
"The Minister and the Elfin" (Buchanan) **107**:15
"The Minister's Books" (Benét) **7**:81
The Minister's Charge; or, The Apprenticeship of Lemuel Barker (Howells) **7**:370, 372, 376, 393, 395, 397, 399; **17**:185; **41**:256, 268-69, 286
"The Minister's Oath" (Hawthorne) **25**:247-48
"Ministry" (Santos) **156**:315
The Ministry of Art (Cram) **45**:13, 21
"Miniver Cheevy" (Robinson) **5**:418; **101**:98, 112-13, 128, 138, 198
"A Mink of One's Own" (Capote) **164**:99-102, 106
Minna and Jim (Walker) **129**:275
Minna and Myself (Bodenheim) **44**:56, 58, 64, 68
"Minor Litany" (Benét) **7**:79
The Minor Pleasures of Life (Macaulay) **44**:126
Minor Poets of the Caroline Period (Saintsbury) **31**:236
Minorities (Lawrence) **18**:177
Minority Report: H. L. Mencken's Notebooks (Mencken) **13**:385, 388
"Minsk" (Ramos) **32**:431
The Mint (Lawrence) **18**:135-38, 142-43, 145-49, 155-56, 160-61, 163-66, 171, 174, 177-82
"Mint Julep Night" (Morley) **87**:141
The Minus Sign (Drummond de Andrade) **139**:232
"Minuta" (Tsvetaeva) **7**:560
Minute Logic (Peirce) **81**:199,372
Minute Particulars (Bishop) **103**:2, 4-5, 9, 18-19, 21
"Minutely Hurt" (Cullen) **37**:156
Les minutes de sable mémorial (Jarry) **2**:279, 281, 284; **14**:272-73, 276, 281; **147**:242, 259, 264, 276, 296, 330-32
Minutes to Go (Burroughs) **121**:124
"The Minx" (Leverson) **18**:199
Mío Cid Campeador (Huidobro) **31**:121, 123, 131, 138-41, 143
"Mio marito" (Ginzburg) **156**:14, 59
"Mirabeau Bridge" (Apollinaire)
See "Le pont Mirabeau"
Mirabell: Books of Number (Merrill) **173**:152, 154, 156-59, 188-90, 194, 201, 220, 222, 241, 249
"The Miracle" (Beresford) **81**:6
"Miracle" (Pasternak) **188**:190-91, 196
"The Miracle" (Remizov)
See "Chudo"
"The Miracle" (Rinehart) **52**:282
"Miracle" (Wen I-to) **28**:413
The Miracle (Thorndike) **107**:408
"The Miracle at Olovo" (Andrić)
See "Čudo u Olovu"
Miracle de la rose (Genet) **128**:130, 133-35, 158-59, 213
"A Miracle Demanded" (Cullen) **37**:156
"Miracle des trois dames" (Alain-Fournier) **6**:19, 28
"A Miracle for Breakfast" (Bishop) **121**:49-51, 70-2, 75, 88
"The Miracle in Olovo" (Andrić)
See "Čudo u Olovu"
Miracle in the Rain (Hecht) **101**:80
The Miracle Man (Cohan) **60**:162
"A Miracle of Bethlehem" (Flecker) **43**:192
"The Miracle of Danrossane" (Heller) **151**:308-10, 313, 315
"Miracle of Eighteen" (di Donato) **159**:188
The Miracle of Morgan's Creek (Sturges) **48**:268, 272, 275-76, 279, 283, 285, 288, 291-92, 295, 301-09, 313-14, 316, 321, 323
"The Miracle of Purun Bhagat" (Kipling) **8**:208; **17**:212
"The Miracle of Saint Jubanus" (Kipling) **8**:196, 200, 202
Miracle of the Bells (Hecht) **101**:80
"The Miracle of the Boy Linus" (Sologub) **9**:436
Miracle of the Rose (Genet)
See *Miracle de la rose*
"The Miracle of the Stigmata" (Harris) **24**:267-68, 273
Miracle Plays: Our Lord's Coming and Childhood (Tynan) **3**:502, 504
"The Miracle Worker" (Peretz) **16**:398
Miracles (Alain-Fournier) **6**:19, 28
"Miracles and Dreams" (Cummings) **137**:7
The Miracles of Antichrist (Lagerloef)
See *Antikrists mirakler*
The Miracles of Our Lord (MacDonald) **9**:288
Miraculous Bird (Nervo)
See *Pájaro milaroso*
"La mirada" (Pardo Bazán) **189**:305
"La mirada extendida" (Aleixandre) **113**:33
"Mirada final" (Aleixandre) **113**:50
"La mirada infantil" (Aleixandre) **113**:34
"Mirage" (Carman) **7**:143
"Mirage" (Graham) **19**:136
"The Mirage" (Tolstoy) **18**:378
Mirage (Balmont)
See *Marevo*
Mirage (Masters) **2**:468-69; **25**:293-94
The Mirage of Social Justice (Hayek) **109**:214
Mirages (Graham) **19**:129, 136
"Miragoane" (Roumain) **19**:344-45
"Mirahuano" (Graham) **19**:129, 136
"Miramar" (Carducci) **32**:103-05
"Miranda's Supper" (Wylie) **8**:531
Mirandolina (Gregory) **176**:36, 44
"Mircath" (Sharp) **39**:376
Mirèio (Mistral) **51**:112, 121-22, 124, 135-39, 142-43, 147-51, 152-58, 160-61, 163, 166-72
Mirele (Bergelson) **81**:15
Mirely ou le petit trou pas cher (Apollinaire) **51**:18
"Miriam" (Capote) **164**:99-103, 109-10, 112, 115, 142
Miriam's Schooling (Rutherford) **25**:341, 345, 355-56, 361-62

"Mirlo fiel" (Jiménez) **183**:279
"Miroir" (Apollinaire) **8**:18
"Le miroir d'un moment" (Éluard) **41**:154
"Mirovoe koltso" (Balmont) **11**:36
"The Mirror" (Machado de Assis)
See "O espelho"
"The Mirror" (Merrill) **173**:186, 225
"The Mirror" (Nemerov) **124**:196
"The Mirror" (Rosenberg) **12**:311
"The Mirror in the Front Hall" (Cavafy) **7**:163
The Mirror Maker (Levi)
See *Terza pagina: Racconti e Saggi*
The Mirror of a Mage (Huidobro)
See *Cagliostro*
The Mirror of Kong Ho (Bramah) **72**:5, 7, 9-11
"The Mirror Of Madmen" (Chesterton) **64**:41
The Mirror of Maids (Kuzmin)
See *Zerkalo dev*
"The Mirror of St. John" (Palamas) **5**:386
"The Mirror of the Enigmas" (Borges) **109**:18, 24
The Mirror of the Past (Beerbohm) **24**:115, 118-19
The Mirror of the Sea (Conrad) **25**:74; **43**:102; **57**:39, 71
"Mirror Suite" (García Lorca)
See "La suite de los espejos"
"Mirrors" (Borges)
See "Los espejos"
Mirrors (Hippius)
See *Zerkala*
Mirrors and Windows (Nemerov) **124**:151, 155-56, 164, 192-93, 196, 203, 206, 212-13, 249, 282, 284-85
"The Mirrors of the Lord" (MacDonald) **113**:266
"The Mirrors of Tuzun Thune" (Howard) **8**:136-37
Mirskonca (Khlebnikov) **20**:135-36, 142, 150
Mis filosofías (Nervo) **11**:394
"Misa de primavera" (Lugones) **15**:294
Misalliance (Shaw) **3**:387, 393; **9**:428
"The Misanthrope" (Lu Hsun)
See "Guduzhe"
"Misbehavior" (Söderberg)
See "Oskicket"
"Miscellanea Ethica" (Keynes) **64**:290-92
Miscellaneous Essays (von Hartmann) **96**:209
Miscellaneous Notes (Yosano)
See *Zakkicho*
Miscellaneous Papers (Machado de Assis)
See *Papéis avulsos*
Miscellaneous Poems (Harper)
See *Poems on Miscellaneous Subjects*
Miscellaneous Writings (Eddy) **71**:95, 99
Miscellanies (Wilde) **41**:367
Mischief (Williams) **89**:394
The Mischief-Maker (Oppenheim) **45**:128
"A Misdeal" (Somerville & Ross) **51**:385
"Mise-en-Scène for a Parricide" (Carter) **139**:140
"A Miserable Man" (Shiga)
See "Aware no otoko"
Misericordia (Pérez Galdós) **27**:248-50, 267, 283
"Misery" (Chekhov)
See "Toska"
Mishima ou La Vision du Vide (Yourcenar) **193**:280
Mishima Yukio zenshu (Mishima) **161**:107, 109-12
"Mishka" (Gray) **19**:148-50, 152, 157
Di mishpokhe Karnovski (Singer) **33**:387, 393-94, 396, 401-02
Misinforming a Nation (Van Dine) **23**:358
La misión de la universidad (Ortega y Gasset) **9**:344
"The Mislabeled Menagerie" (Sapir) **108**:249
"Miss Anstruther's Letters" (Macaulay) **44**:124
"Miss Becky's Pilgrimage" (Jewett) **22**:147
"Miss Betty" (Stoker) **8**:394
Miss Bishop (Aldrich) **125**:4, 9-12, 14-17
Miss Bretherton (Ward) **55**:405, 409
"Miss Brill" (Mansfield) **2**:458; **8**:282-86; **39**:296, 303-04, 321, 324; **164**:236, 244, 247, 307, 320
Miss Brown (Lee) **5**:309, 311, 314-15, 318
Miss Brown of the X.Y.O. (Oppenheim) **45**:133, 135
"Miss Christian Jean" (Graham) **19**:137
"Miss Cow Falls Victim to Mr. Rabbit" (Harris) **2**:213
"Miss Cynthie" (Fisher) **11**:205-06, 208, 210, 212, 214
"Miss Daisy" (March) **96**:259
"Miss Dora Dean" (Petry)
See "Has Anybody Seen Miss Dora Dean?"
"Miss Dorothy Phillips, mi esposa" (Quiroga) **20**:207, 214
"Miss Dorothy Phillips, My Wife" (Quiroga)
See "Miss Dorothy Phillips, mi esposa"
"Miss Duveen" (de la Mare) **4**:78; **53**:27, 41
"Miss Ella" (Fitzgerald) **52**:62-5
"Miss Furr and Miss Skeene" (Stein) **48**:252-53, 255
Miss Gascoyne (Riddell) **40**:334
Miss Hobbs (Jerome) **23**:83
Miss Jairus (Ghelderode)
See *Mademoiselle Jaïre*
"Miss Jemima" (de la Mare) **4**:78; **53**:16, 22
Miss Julie (Strindberg)
See *Fröken Julie*
"Miss Kate-Marie" (Roberts) **68**:336
"Miss Knight" (McAlmon) **97**:91, 106, 123
Miss Knight and Others (McAlmon) **97**:123
Miss Lonelyhearts (West) **1**:478-79, 481-91, 493; **14**:468, 470-76, 479, 481-90, 492; **44**:365-419
Miss Lulu Bett (Gale) **7**:277-87
Miss Mapp (Benson) **27**:9
"Miss Mary Pask" (Wharton) **3**:577; **129**:363-64
"Miss McEnders" (Chopin) **14**:61, 68, 81
Miss Mehaffy (Bromfield) **11**:82
"Miss Miller" (de la Mare) **53**:27
"Miss Mix" (Harte) **1**:342
"Miss Muriel" (Petry) **112**:297-301, 328, 331
Miss Muriel, and Other Stories (Petry) **112**:297-99, 301, 328, 356
"Miss Ogilvy Finds Herself" (Hall) **12**:188
Miss Oyu, the Madonna (Mizoguchi)
See *Oyusama*
"Miss Padma" (Premchand) **21**:289-90
Miss Peck's Promotion (Jewett) **1**:360
Miss Pickthorn and Mr. Hare (Sarton) **120**:210-11, 309
Miss Pinkerton (Rinehart) **52**:301-02
Miss Pym Disposes (Tey) **14**:449, 452-53, 462, 464
Miss Richard's Boy (Holley) **99**:326
"Miss T" (de la Mare) **4**:74
"Miss Tempy's Watcher's" (Jewett) **22**:125, 137, 147, 149
Miss Tomboy (Buchanan) **107**:33
"Miss Witherwell's Mistake" (Chopin) **14**:68; **127**:124-25, 211, 215
Miss Z, the Dark Young Lady (Carter) **139**:125-28
Missbrukad Kvinnokraft och Naturenliga arbetsomraden for kvinnor (Key) **65**:242, 244
"Missing" (de la Mare) **53**:14-5, 17-8, 21, 27, 34, 37
Missing (Ward) **55**:437, 441-43, 446
"The Missing All" (Bishop) **103**:15, 18
"The Missing Idol" (Hecht) **101**:87
"The Missing Necklace" (Futrelle) **19**:96
"Missing Page Thirteen" (Green) **63**:143
The Missing Person (Kafka)
See *Der Verschollene*
"The Mission of Jane" (Wharton) **129**:360-61, 365
"The Mission of the Trees" (Scott) **6**:386, 390, 393, 397
Mission of the University (Ortega y Gasset)
See *La misión de la universidad*
"The Missionary" (Bosman) **49**:23
"Missis Flinders" (Slesinger) **10**:441, 444-45
Mississippi (Kaiser) **9**:181
Mist (Unamuno)
See *Niebla*
"Mist on Meadows" (Gurney) **33**:88
"Mist on the Meadow" (March) **96**:259
"A Mistake" (Prus)
See "Omyłka"
Mister Antonio (Tarkington) **9**:464-65
Mister Bow Wow (Hedāyat)
See *Vagh vagh sahab*
Mister Johnson (Cary) **1**:144, 146, 148; **29**:67-8, 70, 72, 77-8, 80, 82-5, 92, 97, 101-02, 104-05, 107; **196**:155, 175-76, 188-89, 192-94, 213-16, 218-21, 226, 230-31
Mister Witt en el Cantón (Sender) **136**:209
Misteria-Buff (Mayakovski) **4**:291-92, 295-98, 301-03; **18**:241-43, 247, 253-54, 271
"Misterio de la muerta del toro" (Aleixandre) **113**:51
Misterio de una vocación (Gonzalez Martinez) **72**:154
Misterios de la vida diaria (Ibarguengoitia) **148**:225
La misteriosa desaparición de la Marquesita de Loria (Donoso) **133**:56, 74-75, 80, 124, 136-37, 139-40, 155, 171-76, 178
"Mist-Green Oats" (Knister) **56**:155, 158, 160-61, 165
"De mística y humanismo" (Unamuno) **148**:245
Místicas (Nervo) **11**:398, 400, 403
The Mistress (Betti)
See *La padrona*
Mistress Branican (Verne) **6**:501; **52**:359
"The Mistress' Home" (Nagai)
See "Shōtaku"
Mistress of a Foeigner (Mizoguchi) **72**:325
The Mistress of Atlantis (Pabst) **127**:360, 362
"Mistress of Death" (Howard) **8**:138
The Mistress of Husaby (Undset) **3**:510
Mistress of Mistresses (Eddison) **15**:52-5, 57, 59-60, 62
Mistress of the House (Martinez Sierra and Martinez Sierra)
See *El ama de la casa*
"The Mistress of Vision" (Thompson) **4**:435, 438
"Misty Night" (Nagai)
See "Oboroyo"
"La misura della bellezza" (Levi) **109**:295, 297
Misused Womanpower (Key)
See *Missbrukad Kvinnokraft och Naturenliga arbetsomraden for kvinnor*
Mit dem Kopf durch die Wand (Horvath) **45**:101, 111
Mit dem linken Ellenbogen (Liliencron) **18**:216
"Mit der Pinasse" (Liliencron) **18**:215
"Mit leichter Brise segeln" (Broch) **20**:52
Mitch Miller (Masters) **2**:461-62, 467-69, 471-72; **25**:291, 293-94, 315-16
"Mitchell on Matrimony" (Lawson) **27**:128, 131, 150-52
"Mitchell on the 'Sex,' and Other 'Problems'" (Lawson) **27**:150, 152
Mithraic Emblems (Campbell) **5**:117-18, 120, 123
Mitina lyubov' (Bunin) **6**:45-6, 51
"Mito" (Pavese) **3**:339
Mitos, leyendas y cuentos peruanos (Arguedas) **147**:94
"Mitosis" (Calvino) **183**:228
Mitre Court (Riddell) **40**:333
Mitrofan i Dormidolski (Vazov) **25**:450
Mitsou (Colette) **1**:191; **16**:129
Die Mittagsgöttin (Werfel) **8**:476-77, 479
Mitya's Love (Bunin)
See *Mitina lyubov'*
"Mityzacja rzeczywistości" (Schulz) **5**:423; **51**:308

Mixed Brands (Adams) **56**:8
Mixed Relations (Jacobs) **22**:101
Mixed Vintages: A Blend of Essays Old and New (Lucas) **73**:170
"M'Liss: An Idyl of Red Mountain" (Harte) **25**:192, 197, 199, 217-18
"MM. Burke et Hare, assassins" (Schwob) **20**:323
"Mme. de Sévigné" (Woolf) **43**:402
"Mnemagoghi" (Levi) **109**:293, 298
"The Mnemogogues" (Levi) **109**:292
"Moabit" (Borchert) **5**:109
"Moanin' the Blues" (Williams) **81**:428
The Mob (Blasco Ibáñez)
See *La horda*
The Mob (Galsworthy) **1**:303; **45**:52
Mob Rule in New Orleans: Robert Charles and His Fight to the Death (Wells-Barnett) **125**:333
"Mobled King" (Beerbohm) **24**:102
"The Mock Wife" (Hardy) **143**:150
Mockery Gap (Powys) **9**:365-66, 376
"The Mocking-Bird" (Bierce) **7**:89; **44**:12, 44-5
Mod dagningen: Skildringer fra Rusland (Nexø) **43**:317, 330
"The Model" (Malamud) **184**:264-69
"A Model Millionaire: A Note of Admiration" (Wilde) **8**:492; **41**:359
"Models" (Nemerov) **124**:304
Models for Beginners in Composition (Schoenberg) **75**:319
"Models of Our Present" (Acker) **191**:3-4, 57, 62, 105
Moder Lea (Bojer) **64**:5, 7, 10, 12-13, 22
"Moderatucoli" (Carducci) **32**:106-07
"The Modern Actor" (Gray) **19**:151
Modern American Prose (Van Doren) **18**:405
Modern American Sculpture (Hartmann) **73**:134
"Modern Art and Its Philosophy" (Hulme) **21**:131, 147
The Modern Century: The Whidden Lectures 1967 (Frye) **165**:180, 182, 195-96, 199, 201-3, 205, 242
"Modern Children" (Aleichem) **1**:31
A Modern Comedy (Galsworthy) **1**:302; **45**:46-7, 70
Modern Democracy (Becker) **63**:64, 66
The Modern Drama (Lewisohn) **19**:273
Modern Education (Rank) **115**:234, 265
"The Modern Essay" (Woolf) **43**:409
"Modern Fairy Tales" (Baum) **132**:19
"Modern Fiction" (Woolf) **20**:397, 419, 430; **43**:384, 390, 406, 415-16; **101**:318; **128**:332, 334-35, 363
A Modern Hero (Bromfield) **11**:77, 85, 88
A Modern Hero (Pabst) **127**:354, 360-61
Modern History: The Rise of a Democratic, Scientific, and Industrialized Civilization (Becker) **63**:80, 109
Modern Icelandic Plays (Sigurjónsson) **27**:362
"A Modern Idyll" (Harris) **24**:254, 280
A Modern Instance (Howells) **7**:364-66, 372, 375-77, 380-82, 384, 392, 395-97; **17**:162, 178, 180-82, 185, 189, 191; **41**:233-34, 247, 252, 262-63, 265-66, 270, 275, 277
"A Modern King Lear" (Addams) **76**:94
"Modern Love" (Meredith) **17**:253
Modern Love, and Poems of the English Roadside, with Poems and Ballads (Meredith) **17**:253-54, 261, 272, 282-83, 285, 289, 291; **43**:277
A Modern Lover (Moore) **7**:473, 477, 484-86, 489, 496
"The Modern Magic" (Chesterton) **1**:182
"The Modern Man and Nature" (Fuller) **103**:112
"Modern Moses, or 'My Policy' Man" (Bell) **43**:89, 91, 93
"The Modern Mother" (Meynell) **6**:300
"The Modern Novel" (Knister) **56**:153
"Modern Novels" (Orage) **157**:252, 283
"Modern Novels" (Woolf) **128**:332, 334
Modern Painters: Their Superiority in the Art of Landscape Painting to the Ancient Masters (Ruskin) **20**:258-59, 261, 265-66, 271-72, 277, 280-82, 294-97, 299-300, 303-04, 308; **63**:238-40, 244, 251, 253-58, 262-63, 268-72, 275, 278, 284, 291-92, 303-9, 312, 316-18, 321-22, 330;
"Modern Painting" (Apollinaire) **51**:41
Modern Painting (Moore) **7**:482, 491
Modern Painting (Van Dine) **23**:357
"Modern Philosopher" (Heyward) **59**:95
"A Modern Poem" (Moore) **7**:487
"A Modern Poet" (Nemerov) **124**:181, 288
"Modern Poetry" (Crane) **80**:86
"Modern Poetry" (Rilke)
See "Moderne Lyrik"
Modern Psalm (Schoenberg) **75**:311, 347-48
Modern Psychology (von Hartmann)
See *Die moderne Psychologie*
"Modern Russian Art Movements" (Rilke) **195**:216
Modern Science: A Criticism (Carpenter) **88**:127
Modern Science and Anarchism (Kropotkin) **36**:211
"The Modern Scrooge" (Chesterton) **6**:109
"The Modern Soul" (Mansfield) **2**:456; **39**:298-300; **164**:269, 291, 293
"The Modern Speaks" (Stringer) **37**:341-42
Modern teater: Synpunkter och angrepp (Lagerkvist) **144**:158-60, 214, 236, 238
Modern Theatre: Points of View and Attack (Lagerkvist)
See *Modern teater: Synpunkter och angrepp*
"The Modern Theme" (Ortega y Gasset)
See "El tema de nuestro tiempo"
A Modern Theory of Ethics: A Study of the Relations of Ethics and Psychology (Stapledon) **22**:309, 314, 322
The Modern Traveller (Belloc) **7**:31, 38, 42; **18**:39-40
A Modern Utopia (Wells) **6**:524-25, 536, 553; **12**:514; **19**:437-38, 451-53; **133**:251, 284, 326-27, 335
The Modern Woman (Martinez Sierra and Martinez Sierra) **6**:274
The Modern Writer (Anderson) **24**:36; **123**:11
"The Modern Young Man as Critic" (Buchanan) **107**:64
Moderne geister (Brandes) **11**:68
Det moderne gjennembruds maend (Brandes) **10**:74
"Moderne Lyrik" (Rilke) **195**:257, 259-60, 288-89
Die moderne Psychologie (von Hartmann) **96**:221
"Moderskärlek" (Lagerkvist) **144**:216
Modes of Thought (Whitehead) **97**:282, 298
Moeti oa bochabela (Mofolo) **22**:246-49, 253, 257-58
Moetsukita chizu (Abe) **131**:3, 11, 15
"Moeurs littéraires" (Jacob) **6**:191
Mogila voina (Aldanov) **23**:18-19, 23
Mogreb-el-Acksa (Graham) **19**:101-02, 112, 114-15, 134
"Moguer" (Jiménez) **183**:335
Mohammed (Hartmann) **73**:110, 116, 134
"Moi pervyi gonovar" (Babel) **13**:27; **171**:12, 94
"Moi pervyi gus" (Babel) **2**:22; **13**:22, 33; **171**:7, 10, 18-19, 21, 24-26, 40, 46, 60, 62-68, 70, 77, 79, 82, 84, 87
"Moi predki" (Kuzmin) **40**:198
Moi universitety (Gorky) **8**:74, 77
Moi współcześni (Przybyszewski) **36**:288
"Moia zhizn" (Esenin) **4**:116
Moine (Kandinsky) **92**:49
Les moines (Verhaeren) **12**:458, 460, 462-63, 465-66, 468, 473
"Moines en défilade" (Nelligan) **14**:393, 397
"Les moissons" (Mistral) **51**:135, 145, 147, 163, 171
"Moj Puškin" (Tsvetaeva) **7**:562, 571
"Mojave" (Capote) **164**:99, 105-6
Mojo: A Black Love Story (Childress) **116**:29
"Moli xiangpian" (Chang) **184**:106, 109-10, 138-39, 141-42
Molière: His Life and Works (Matthews) **95**:246
"El molino" (Miro) **5**:335
"Molitva" (Tsvetaeva) **35**:402, 407-08
"Molitva vucjem pastiru" (Popa) **167**:161
"Molla's Heart Attack" (Rölvaag) **17**:347
"La molle luna" (Calvino) **183**:215, 228
Mollentrave on Women (Sutro) **6**:419
Molloy (Beckett) **145**:93-95, 118, 185, 188, 197-202, 204
"Molly Trefusis" (Dobson) **79**:2
"Moloch" (Kuprin) **5**:298, 304-06
Molodaya gvardiya (Fadeyev) **53**:54-5
Molodets (Tsvetaeva) **7**:556, 562; **7**:556-57, 562, 566; **35**:375, 379, 402, 410, 413-15
"Molteplicità" (Calvino) **183**:102, 107
"Mom Bi: Her Friends and Enemies" (Harris) **2**:211
"A Moment" (Coleridge) **73**:3, 11-12
"The Moment" (Korolenko) **22**:172
"Moment" (Nemerov) **124**:177, 213, 248
The Moment (Bryusov) **10**:90
Moment (Sá-Carneiro)
See *Apice*
The Moment After (Buchanan) **107**:86
The Moment and Other Essays (Woolf) **43**:388, 394
"The Moment Has Come" (Villaurrutia) **80**:458
Moment in Peking: A Novel of Contemporary Chinese Life (Lin) **149**:316-17, 319
Moments of Being (Woolf) **5**:517; **101**:276-77; **128**:320-23, 325, 343, 352, 369, 374
Moments of Reprieve (Levi)
See *Lilít e altri racconti*
"Moments of Thunder" (Santos) **156**:315
Moments of Vision and Miscellaneous Verses (Hardy) **143**:151, 175, 186-89
Momentum catastrophicum (Baroja) **8**:63
Mon (Natsume) **2**:491-93; **10**:329, 331, 339, 341, 345, 347-48
"Mon âme" (Roussel) **20**:228, 230, 234-35, 240, 244-45
"Mon amie" (Bourne) **16**:47
Mon cher petit: lettres à Lucien Daudet (Proust) **161**:170
Mon corps et moi (Crevel) **112**:12, 22-3, 26
"Mon Dieu m'a dit" (Gray) **19**:155
Mon Faust (Valéry) **4**:496-97; **15**:450, 461
Mon frère Yves (Loti) **11**:353-54, 359, 361-62, 364, 366
"Mon plus secret conseil" (Larbaud) **9**:198-202, 207
"Monad and Multitude" (Gosse) **28**:142
The Monarch of Dreams (Higginson) **36**:186
Monarch, the Big Bear of Tallac (Seton) **31**:261, 279
Monarchy (Belloc) **18**:44
Mondaufgang (Kandinsky) **92**:49
"Monday or Tuesday" (Woolf) **101**:300
Monday or Tuesday (Woolf) **1**:528, 531, 534, 537; **20**:409
"Le monde du souvenir et du rêve" (Arp) **115**:51
Le monde hallucinant (Arenas)
See *El mundo alucinante*
"Le monde s'arme" (Verhaeren) **12**:471
Der Mondreigen von Schlaraffs (Huch) **13**:247-49
Mondsand (Arp) **115**:5, 23-7, 33, 35
"Mondtreffen" (Arp) **115**:34-5
La moneda de hierro (Borges) **109**:28
Moneda falsa (Sánchez) **37**:311
"Monet" (Nemerov) **124**:269
"The Monetary Policy of the United States Since the Crisus of 1920" (Hayek) **109**:196
Monetary Reform (Keynes)
See *A Tract on Monetary Reform*
Monetary Theory and the Trade Cycle (Hayek) **109**:196

"Money" (Čapek) **37**:51
"Money" (Jarrell) **177**:172
"Money" (Nemerov) **124**:162, 182, 253, 274
"Money" (Tolstoy) **79**:333
Money & Morals (Gill) **85**:77, 80
Money and Other Stories (Čapek)
See *Trapné provídky*
"Money for Hanukka" (Aleichem)
See "Khanike-gelt"
Money in the Bank (Wodehouse) **108**:342
"Money-Changers in Literature" (Orage) **157**:252, 283
The Money-Spinner (Pinero) **32**:388, 399, 412-13
"Mongan's Frenzy" (Stephens) **4**:414
"The Mongols" (Roosevelt) **69**:264
"Monisch" (Peretz) **16**:389, 391, 400, 403
"Monism as the Bond Between Religion and Science" (Haeckel) **83**:136, 146
Der Monismus als Band zwischen Religion und Wissenschaft (Haeckel) **83**:135, 147
"La monja de la llave" (Palma) **29**:262
"La monja gitana" (García Lorca) **49**:113, 119; **181**:91-92
"The Monk" (Papadiamantis) **29**:272
The Monk and the Hangman's Daughter (Bierce) **1**:84, 89; **7**:90; **44**:9, 13, 29-31, 39
"The Monk Erasmus" (Zamyatin) **37**:430
"Monk Lewis" (Lovecraft) **4**:269
Monk of Fife (Lang) **16**:252, 265
Monk Vendt (Hamsun)
See *Munken Vendt*
"Monk Wakes an Echo" (Shiel) **8**:363
"The Monkey" (Khodasevich) **15**:205, 208, 211-12
"The Monkey and the Microscope" (Buchanan) **107**:57
Monkey Business (Hecht) **101**:62, 78, 80
Monkey Business (Mankiewicz) **85**:112, 149, 155
"The Monkey Island" (Dazai Osamu)
See "Sarugashima"
The Monkey Wrench Gang (Abbey) **160**:3-5, 10, 14, 16, 31-37, 58, 74, 80, 82-83, 85, 96, 102-3
"The Monkey-Masked Clown" (Dazai Osamu)
See "Sarumen kanja"
"The Monkey's Cousin" (Stephens) **4**:417
"The Monkey's Paw" (Jacobs) **22**:99, 103, 106-07, 109-10, 112
The Monkey's Wrench (Levi)
See *La chiave a stella*
Monks Are Monks (Nathan) **18**:310-11, 316
"The Monk's Walk" (Dunbar) **12**:106
Monna Vanna (Maeterlinck) **3**:323, 325, 327-29, 331
"Le monocle de mon oncle" (Stevens) **3**:448-49, 451, 455-56; **12**:357, 364, 367, 373-74; **45**:281, 299, 304, 309, 328, 338, 340
Monodromos (Engel) **137**:107, 110, 116-19, 125, 130, 132, 138
Monograph on the Medusa (Haeckel) **83**:145
Monograph on the Radiolaria (Haeckel) **83**:137
"Ein Monolog des Fürsten Myschkin zu der Ballettpantomime 'Der Idiot'" (Bachmann) **192**:5, 15
Le monologue intérieur: Son apparition, ses origines, sa place dans l'oeuvre de James Joyce et dans le roman contemporain (Dujardin) **13**:184, 186-87, 189
"Monologue of a Mother" (Lawrence) **93**:22
Monologues (Middleton) **56**:179, 192, 195
"Monologul lui Balthazar" (Fondane) **159**:249
"Monotonía" (Jiménez) **4**:225
"Monotony" (Jiménez) **183**:336
"Mons angelorum" (Pickthall) **21**:249
"Mons univers" (Teilhard de Chardin) **9**:493
Un monsieur (Graham) **19**:111, 114
Monsieur Beaucaire (Tarkington) **9**:453-55, 459-60, 465-66
"Monsieur Brzekowski" (Arp) **115**:45-6
Monsieur chasse! (Feydeau) **22**:77-8, 83, 91
"Monsieur de Grignan" (Warner) **131**:311
Monsieur Goes Hunting! (Feydeau)
See *Monsieur chasse!*
"Monsieur Henri": A Foot-Note to French History (Guiney) **41**:207-08
Monsieur Jonquelle, Prefect of Police of Paris (Post) **39**:343-45
Monsieur Ouine (Bernanos) **3**:120, 122, 124-26
Un monsieur qui est condamnéà mort (Feydeau) **22**:88
"Monsieur Teste" (Valéry) **4**:488, 502; **15**:450
Monsieur Venus (Vallette) **67**:269, 272-74, 279, 285-92, 295-99, 303, 315, 318, 324-26, 330-31, 335
Monsieur Vernet (Renard) **17**:316
The Monster (Crane) **11**:165, 167; **17**:76-8, 81; **32**:165
The Monster (Saltus) **8**:347, 351
The Monster, and Other Stories (Crane) **11**:136, 140-41
The Monster Men (Burroughs) **32**:57
"The Monster of Mr. Cogito" (Herbert)
See "Potwór Pana Cogito"
Monsterrat (Hellman) **119**:215
The Monsters and the Critics, and Other Essays (Tolkien) **137**:333, 340, 349, 351
"Monstre d'été" (Arp) **115**:41
Monstre gai (Lewis) **2**:390, 393, 398; **9**:246; **104**:178
"The Monstrous Little Voice" (Williams) **89**:375
"Monstrous Regiment" (Wakefield) **120**:351
"Monsunen" (Jensen) **41**:303
Le mont analogue (Daumal) **14**:87, 89-94, 96-8
Mont Saint Michel and Chartres: A Study in Thirteenth Century Unity (Adams) **4**:4-6, 8, 11-12, 15, 18, 20-1; **52**:2, 4, 7, 9, 13, 15, 27-8, 35, 40, 46-7
"Montage of Attractions" (Eisenstein) **57**:197
La montagne ensorcelée (Roumain) **19**:331-33, 343, 345
"Montaigne" (Murry) **16**:341
"Montaigne" (Woolf) **56**:408; **128**:334
"Montale's Rock" (Calvino) **183**:106
La montálvez (Pereda) **16**:368, 370, 372, 378
"La montaña" (Nervo) **11**:396
Montana Rides! (Faust) **49**:57-8
"Las montañas del oro" (Lugones) **15**:285
Montauk (Frisch) **121**:187, 197-202, 227-29, 233, 236, 241, 245-47, 260, 265, 274-75
"Monte Cristo" (Calvino)
See "The Count of Monte Cristo"
"A Monte Flat Pastoral" (Harte) **25**:217
"El monte negro" (Quiroga) **20**:212
Montes de Oca (Pérez Galdós) **27**:257
"Montes the Matador" (Harris) **24**:261, 263-64, 267-68
Montes the Matador, and Other Stories (Harris) **24**:258, 271
La montespan (Rolland) **23**:257
The Montessori Method (Montessori)
See *Il Metodo della Pedagogia Scientifica applicato all' educazione infantile nelle Case dei Bambini*
A Montessori Mother (Fisher) **87**:72
"A Month After" (Murry) **16**:352
"The Monthly Wage Earners" (Quiroga)
See "Los mensú"
"Montrachet-le-Jardin" (Stevens) **45**:269, 295
Montrose (Buchan) **41**:59-63
"Montserrat" (Symons) **11**:435
"The Monument" (Bishop) **121**:3, 9, 25, 48-9, 56, 58, 88
"The Monument" (Coffin) **95**:15
"The Monument Maker" (Hardy) **53**:101
"Monument to a Hero" (Bosman) **49**:17
Monuments à Lécher (Arp) **115**:32
"Mood" (Cullen) **4**:45; **37**:149, 160, 162
Mood Indigo (Vian)
See *L'écume des jours*
"Moods" (Fletcher) **35**:96
Moods (Joyce) **159**:282
Moods, Cadenced and Declaimed (Dreiser) **10**:190, 196; **18**:51-2
Moods, Songs and Doggerels (Galsworthy) **45**:34
"Moon" (Artaud) **3**:52
"The Moon" (Hippius)
See "Luna"
"The Moon" (Jiménez)
See *La luna*
"The Moon" (Thomas) **10**:459
"Moon" (Unamuno) **2**:568
Moon across the Way (Borges)
See *Luna de enfrente*
"Moon and Gnac" (Calvino)
See "Luna e GNAC"
"The Moon and GNAC" (Calvino)
See "Luna e GNAC"
"Moon and Panorama of the Insects" (García Lorca)
See "Luna y panorama de los insectos"
"The Moon and Shiseishin" (Hagiwara) **60**:297
The Moon and the Bonfires (Pavese)
See *La luna e i falo*
The Moon Ants (Hippius)
See *Lunnye muravyi*
"Moon Dial" (Carman) **7**:134-35
The Moon Endureth (Buchan) **41**:34-5, 37, 41, 73
A Moon for the Misbegotten (O'Neill) **1**:393, 398, 401-02, 405-06; **6**:336; **49**:247, 282
"The Moon in Letters" (Bierce) **44**:15
"Moon in the Afternoon" (Calvino)
See "Luna di pomeriggio"
"Moon Is an Absence" (Aleixandre)
See "La luna es una ausencia"
The Moon is Red (Rohmer) **28**:284
"The Moon like a Mushroom" (Calvino)
See "La luna come un fungo"
The Moon Maid (Burroughs) **2**:78-9, 81; **32**:58, 72-3
"Moon Night" (Noguchi) **80**:363
Moon of Madness (Rohmer) **28**:283-84
The Moon of Much Gladness, Related by Kai Lung (Bramah) **72**:7, 9-11
"The Moon of Skulls" (Howard) **8**:130
The Moon of the Caribbees (O'Neill) **6**:330
"mOOn Over tOwns mOOn" (Cummings) **137**:63
"A moon turned in on itself" (Arp) **115**:24
"The Moon under Water" (Orwell) **128**:288
"moon-angels surround the great rose" (Arp) **115**:25
Moonbeams from the Larger Lunacy (Leacock) **2**:379
Moon-Calf (Lewis) **23**:148
"The Moon-Child" (Sharp) **39**:355, 392-93
"Moondreams" (Holly) **65**:147
"Moonlight" (Apollinaire)
See "Clair de lune"
"Moonlight" (Prado)
See "Luz lunar"
The Moonlight (Cary) **29**:67-8, 71-2, 74-5, 80, 84-7, 92, 104; **196**:195-200, 203, 207-08
"Moonlight on the Snow" (Crane) **17**:71, 74
Moonlight People (Rozanov)
See *Liudi lunnogo sveta*
"Moonlit Night" (Hagiwara) **60**:296-7
"The Moonlit Road" (Bierce) **44**:13, 44-5, 49
"The Moon-Moth" (Moody) **105**:237-38, 246, 267, 271-72
Moonraker (Fleming) **193**:198-99, 201-02, 206, 214, 229-30, 234, 237-38, 242-43
"Moonrise from Iona" (Sharp) **39**:388
Moons of Grandeur (Benét) **28**:7
"Moon's Revenge" (Carducci)
See "Vendette della luna"
Moonsand (Arp)
See *Mondsand*
Moonshine and Clover (Housman) **7**:355
"Moonshine Lake" (Bulgakov) **16**:85
"The Moonshiners of Hoho-Hehee Falls" (Murfree) **135**:207-8, 223

"Moorawathimeering" (Ingamells) **35**:134, 136
"The Moorland Peasant" (Jensen)
See "Hedebonden"
The Moors and the Fens (Riddell) **40**:335
"The Moose" (Bishop) **121**:6, 9, 21, 25-8, 40, 43, 81
"Moose in the Morning" (Sarton) **120**:305
"Mōpasan no sekizō o hai-su" (Nagai) **51**:99
"The Mopper-Up" (McCoy) **28**:226
"Mora Montravers" (James) **40**:140; **47**:201
A Moral Alphabet (Belloc) **7**:38-9, 42; **18**:39
"The Moral Content of the Christian Doctrine of Life after Death" (Westermarck) **87**:361
"Moral Eduction" (Montessori) **103**:286
"The Moral Element in Literature" (Stephen) **23**:333
"Moral Emotion" (Westermarck) **87**:361
"La moral en el arte" (Valera y Alcala-Galiano) **10**:499
"The Moral Fibrature" (Andrade) **43**:7
"The Moral Obligation to Be Intelligent" (Erskine) **84**:163
The Moral Obligation to Be Intelligent (Erskine) **84**:157, 175
Moral Order and Progress (Alexander) **77**:30, 49, 61-5
"The Moral Philosopher and the Moral Life" (James) **32**:349; **171**:180
"Moral Philosophy and the Moral Life" (James) **32**:349
Moral Social (Hostos) **24**:303-04, 306-09, 311
"Moral Theory and Practice" (Dewey) **95**:96
"La morale du cinéma" (Desnos) **22**:65
"La morale du malheur: La Peste" (Bataille) **155**:92
"Moralità . . . fanfullarda" (Carducci) **32**:107
"La moralité" (Zola) **6**:561
Morality and Criminality (Kraus)
See *Sittlichkeit und Kriminalität*
"Morality and the Novel" (Lawrence) **48**:132
The Morality of Women (Key) **65**:237
"Morals and Civilization" (Wells) **133**:263
"Morals, Not Art or Literature" (Comstock) **13**:92
Morals of the City of Pests (Molnár)
See *Pesti Erkolcsok*
Moran of the Lady Letty (Norris) **24**:418, 427; **155**:259, 319, 330-33, 335, 337-38, 342
Morass of Souls (Drummond de Andrade)
See *Brejo das Almas*
"Moravia" (Ginzburg) **156**:110
"Morbidezza" (Symons) **11**:427
"Der Mord lügt" (Borchert) **5**:109
"Mordecai and Cocking" (Coppard) **5**:177
"Mordmaschine 43" (Schwitters) **95**:320
"Mordred" (Campbell) **9**:30
More (Beerbohm) **1**:66-7; **24**:98, 115-16
"A More Ancient Mariner" (Carman) **7**:142
More Beasts—For Worse Children (Belloc) **7**:42; **18**:39
More Books on the Table (Gosse) **28**:152
More Collected Verse (Service) **15**:413
"More Democracy or Less? An Inquiry" (Dreiser) **10**:194-95
More Essays of Love and Virtue (Ellis) **14**:114
More Guys and Dolls (Runyon) **10**:429
More Joy in Heaven (Callaghan) **145**:223, 254
More Limehouse Nights (Burke)
See *Whispering Windows*
"More Obituaries" (Saroyan) **137**:173
"More of Qfwfq" (Calvino) **183**:227
"More of Such Trunovs" (Babel) **171**:86
More Pages from a Journal (Rutherford) **25**:348
More Pansies (Lawrence) **93**:52, 53, 59, 104, 117
More Peers (Belloc) **7**:38, 42; **18**:28, 40
More People (Masters) **25**:316
More Poems (Housman) **10**:241-42, 245, 252, 255
More Pricks than Kicks (Beckett) **145**:202
"More Songs for Meller" (Benchley) **55**:13, 17
More Spook Stories (Benson) **27**:19
More Stately Mansions (O'Neill) **1**:400, 405
More Tales of the Uneasy (Hunt) **53**:197, 200
"More Than a Fool's Song" (Cullen) **4**:43, 50
"More Than Just a House" (Fitzgerald) **6**:167
More Women than Men (Compton-Burnett) **180**:114, 125-27, 129, 131, 158, 161-64, 166, 191-97
Morgan Bible (Evans) **85**:30
Morgante the Lesser: His Notorious Life and Wonderful Deeds (Martyn) **131**:102, 111, 113
"Morgen" (Toller) **10**:490
"Morgenfahrt" (Morgenstern) **8**:309
Die Morgenlandfahrt (Hesse) **148**:141, 170-74, 184; **196**:266, 277, 307, 339
Die Morgenröt: Gedanken über die moralische vorurteile (Nietzsche) **10**:355, 367, 393; **18**:339, 342, 351
"Morgiana Dances" (Benét) **28**:5
Morgonen (Lagerkvist) **144**:212
"Morgonrodnan mig skall väcka" (Lagerkvist) **144**:186
"Die Morgue" (Heym) **9**:142, 144, 146
Morgue und andere Gedichte (Benn) **3**:104, 106, 112
"El moribundo" (Aleixandre) **113**:49
Morir en junio y con la lengua afuera (Arenas) **191**:186, 190-93
"Morir es solo / mirar adentro" (Jiménez) **183**:290
Morir por no despertar (Echegaray) **4**:101
Morituri (Sudermann) **15**:420, 437
"Moriturus" (Millay) **49**:226
"Det mörka folket" (Lagerkvist) **144**:220, 222
"Mormon Lilies" (Muir) **28**:250
"Morning" (Baker) **10**:12
"Morning" (Mayakovski) **18**:246
"Morning" (Talvik) **87**:320
"Morning" (Toller)
See "Morgen"
Morning (Campbell) **9**:32
The Morning (Lagerkvist)
See *Morgonen*
"Morning After" (Morley) **87**:145
"The Morning after the Ball" (Tolstoy)
See "After the Ball"
"Morning and Evening" (Carman) **7**:137
Morning Face (Porter) **21**:277
"The Morning Glory" (Suzuki) **109**:399
"A Morning in February" (Ekelund)
See "En februarimorgon"
"Morning in the Northwest" (Stringer) **37**:341
The Morning Is Near Us (Glaspell) **175**:59, 62, 138
"The Morning of a Landed Proprietor" (Tolstoy)
See *A Landlord's Morning*
"The Morning of Acmeism" (Mandelstam) **6**:264
"Morning Ride" (Morgenstern)
See "Morgenfahrt"
"Morning Sea" (Cavafy) **7**:163
The Morning Season (Wodehouse) **108**:385
"Morning Shadows" (Artsybashev) **31**:7
"Morning Song" (Carducci)
See "Mattinata"
Morning Songs (Tagore)
See *Prabhat sangit*
"Morning Spirits" (Bialik) **25**:58
"Morning Twilight" (Johnson) **19**:246
"A Morning Walk" (Chopin) **14**:69
"The Morning Walk" (Milne) **88**:242
"Morning Watch" (Foote) **108**:18
The Morning Watch (Agee) **1**:1, 4-5, 16, 18; **19**:19, 24, 29, 36-7, 39, 41; **180**:22-23, 25, 63, 65, 67, 70-72, 74, 76
"Morning Window" (Guro) **56**:142
"The Morning-Glory (A Dramatic Fragment)" (Noguchi) **80**:396
"Mornings in a New House" (Merrill) **173**:228, 254
Mornings in Florence (Ruskin) **20**:283, 287, 301; **63**:297
Mornings in Mexico (Lawrence) **2**:344, 351, 356-57; **93**:14
"Morocco" (Loti)
See "Au Maroc"
Morocco the Most Holy (Graham)
See *Mogreb-el-Acksa*
"Moroz" (Korolenko) **22**:181-82
"Morphine" (Bulgakov) **16**:91
Morriña (Pardo Bazán) **189**:240, 244, 261-62
"Morris" (Murry) **16**:341
"Mors" (Carducci) **32**:84
La morsa (Pirandello) **29**:317
Morsamor (Valera y Alcala-Galiano) **10**:504-05, 507-08
"Morshchinka" (Remizov) **27**:352
Morskoe svechenie (Balmont) **11**:38
"Le Mort" (Bataille) **155**:77, 79, 84
Le mort (Lemonnier) **22**:198, 200, 202-03
A mort (Vallette) **67**:298, 327
La Mort conduit l'attelage (Yourcenar) **193**:270-71, 302
La mort du Docteur Faust (Ghelderode) **187**:18, 23, 30, 32, 34-5
Mort d'un personnage (Giono) **124**:50, 84, 105-7, 110-11, 113, 115
"La mort d'Antinous" (Vallette) **67**:277
"La mort de Baldassare Silvande" (Proust) **7**:538; **161**:173-74
"La mort de Balzac" (Mirbeau) **55**:309-13
"La mort de l'auteur" (Barthes) **135**:159
La mort de Tintagiles (Maeterlinck) **3**:320-21, 332
"Le mort de Venise" (Barrès) **47**:65
La Mort difficile (Crevel) **112**:6, 12, 20-1
"La mort d'odjigh" (Schwob) **20**:322-23
"La Mort du Poete" (Jammes) **75**:113, 120
Mortadello; or, The Angel of Venice (Crowley) **7**:206
"Mortal Combat" (Coleridge) **73**:14
"Mortal Enemy" (Parker) **143**:323
"Una morte" (Svevo)
See "La morte"
"La morte" (Svevo) **2**:542
"La morte" (Verhaeren) **12**:466
La morte del cervo (D'Annunzio) **40**:14
Morten hin røde (Nexø) **43**:329-30, 332, 334
Morten in Red (Nexø)
See *Morten hin røde*
The Mortgaged Heart (McCullers) **155**:244, 247-48
Mortgaged Time (Bachmann)
See *Die gestundete Zeit*
"I morti amici" (Saba) **33**:374
"The Mortis" (Vallette)
See "Le mortis"
"Le mortis" (Vallette) **67**:278, 316-19
Mortomley's Estate (Riddell) **40**:334-35
Mosada (Yeats) **11**:506
"Las moscas" (Quiroga) **20**:214
Las moscas (Azuela) **3**:77, 79; **145**:9-10, 14, 17, 27-28, 30
"Mosche cocchiere" (Carducci) **32**:107
Moscow (Asch) **3**:67-8
Moscow (Bely) **7**:49
The Moscow Eccentric (Bely) **7**:52
Moscow Is Threatened by the Enemy (Tolstoy) **18**:379
Moscow Lady (Kandinsky) **92**:147
Moscow under the Blow (Bely) **7**:52
"Moses" (Muir) **87**:268
"Moses" (Nemerov) **124**:284
Moses (Carpenter) **88**:62
Moses (Hartmann) **73**:116
Moses: A Play (Rosenberg) **12**:287-89, 291-92, 295, 297-301, 304-11, 313
Moses: A Story of the Nile (Harper) **14**:255, 257, 259-64
"Moses and Joshua" (Lasker-Schueler) **57**:332, 336

Moses and Monotheism (Freud)
See *Der Mann Moses und die monotheistische Religion*
Moses in Red: The Revolt of Israel as a Typical Revolution (Steffens) **20**:343, 346, 349, 355-57
Moses, Man of the Mountain (Hurston) **121**:319, 335; **131**:57, 60-61, 67, 70, 74, 76, 79, 85, 95
Moses; or, From the Wilderness to the Promised Land (Strindberg) **8**:418
Moses und Aron (Schoenberg) **75**:302-03, 305-06, 309-315, 333-37, 347-48, 350-51, 365, 371, 394-404, 409, 411
Moshiekhs tsaytn (Aleichem) **35**:306
"The Mosi Fair" (Caragiale) **76**:169
"Mōsō" (Mori Ogai) **14**:379-80
"Mosque of the Caliph" (Dobson) **79**:18
Mosquee (Kandinsky) **92**:49
"Mosquito" (Lawrence) **93**:33, 55, 101
Mosquitoes (Faulkner) **141**:30, 33, 39, 41-42; **170**:115, 128, 171, 226
Most (Nezval) **44**:238, 245, 250
"A Most Extraordinary Case" (James) **40**:115
The Most General Ideals of Life (Prus)
See *Najogólniejsze ideały zyciowe*
"Most na Žepi" (Andrić) **135**:16, 20, 41, 79, 87
The Most of Malcolm Muggeridge (Muggeridge) **120**:151-54
"Most Primitive Emotion" (Hagiwara) **60**:297
"Mosza azul" (Machado de Assis) **10**:279
"Mot betalming" (Strindberg) **47**:366
The Mote and the Beam (Plaatje) **73**:220
"The Mote in the Middle Distance" (Beerbohm) **24**:116-17, 120-21
"Motetts of William Byrd" (Gurney) **33**:98
"The Moth That God Made Blind" (Crane) **5**:194-95
Moth-Eaten Clothing (Palma)
See *Ropa apolillada*
"Mother" (Anderson) **1**:59; **10**:33; **24**:24, 31, 33, 35, 58
"The Mother" (Campbell) **9**:29-31
The Mother (Čapek)
See *Matka*
"A Mother" (Galsworthy) **45**:32
"Mother" (Guest) **95**:205
"Mother" (Herbert) **168**:44
"A Mother" (Joyce) **35**:144, 151, 153, 164, 167, 196-97; **159**:300, 304
"A Mother" (Kolmar) **40**:175, 177
"Mother" (Lasker-Schueler)
See "Mutter"
"The Mother" (Manning) **25**:278
"Mother" (Platonov) **14**:420
"Mother" (Reese) **181**:344
"The Mother" (Svevo)
See "Le madre"
The Mother (Asch)
See *Di muter*
The Mother (Aurobindo) **63**:33
The Mother (Brecht)
See *Die Mutter*
The Mother (Čapek) **37**:53, 57
Mother (Witkiewicz)
See *Matka*
"Mother Africa" (Petry) **112**:299-301
"Mother and Daughter" (Lawrence) **2**:363; **16**:290
"Mother and Music" (Tsvetaeva) **7**:571
Mother and Son (Compton-Burnett) **180**:115, 122-23, 130-31, 144
The Mother and the Father (Howells) **7**:388
The Mother and the Law (Griffith) **68**:166, 188, 190
Mother Courage and Her Children (Brecht)
See *Mutter Courage und ihre Kinder*
Mother Earth, and Other Stories (Pilnyak)
See *Mat' syra zemlya*
Mother Goose in Prose (Baum) **7**:13; **132**:55
"The Mother Hive" (Kipling) **17**:209
"A Mother in Egypt" (Pickthall) **21**:243, 245, 251
Mother India (Aurobindo) **63**:7
"Mother is Gone" (Williams) **81**:434
"Mother Love" (Lagerkvist)
See "Moderskärlek"
"Mother Love" (Palma)
See "Amor de madre"
Mother Mary (Mann)
See *Mutter Marie*
Mother Mason (Aldrich) **125**:10, 18
"Mother, Mother" (Aleixandre)
See "Madre, Madre"
"The Mother Mourns" (Hardy) **53**:86, 117
Mother Nature (Pardo Bazán)
See *La madre naturaleza*
"Mother Night" (Johnson) **3**:241
"The Mother of Dante" (Sikelianos) **39**:418
The Mother of God (Sikelianos) **39**:407, 414, 418, 420
The Mother of Us All (Stein) **28**:341; **48**:231-32, 248, 257
"Mother, Said the Child" (Jarrell) **177**:155
"Mother to a Baby" (Coleridge) **73**:11
"Mother to Child" (Gilman) **9**:100
"Mother to Dinner" (Slesinger) **10**:441-42, 444-45
"The Mother Tongue" (Warner) **131**:319
"Motherhood" (Anderson) **1**:42
"Motherhood" (Sharp) **39**:379, 388
The Mothering Heart (Griffith) **68**:247
Motherland (Tolstoy) **18**:379
Motherliness and Education for Motherhood (Key) **65**:234
Motherlove (Strindberg) **21**:348
The Mother-of-Pearl Box (France)
See *L'étui de nacre*
"The Mothers" (Bishop) **103**:71
"Mothers" (Endo)
See "Haha naru mono"
"Mothers" (Gilman) **9**:97
"The Mothers" (Kraus)
See "Die Mütter"
The Mothers (Fisher) **140**:188
Mothers and Children (Fisher) **87**:72
"A Mother's Counsel" (Lucas) **73**:171
"Mother's Dash for Liberty" (Aldrich) **125**:20
"Mother's Death and the New Mother" (Shiga)
See "Haha no shi to atarishi haha"
Mother's Marvel (Evans) **85**:12
"Mothers of Immigrants—Unofficial Function of the Barge Office Matron" (Cahan) **71**:85
"The Mother's Portrait" (Heyse)
See "Bild der Mutter"
The Mother's Recompense (Wharton) **3**:567; **9**:548, 550-51; **129**:350, 363; **149**:253
"A Mother's Tale" (Agee) **1**:16
Mothers to Men (Gale) **7**:282
"The Mother's Tragedy" (Crowley) **7**:204
"A Mother's Vision" (Peretz) **16**:397
Moths (Machado de Assis)
See *Phalenas*
Moths (Ouida) **43**:351-52, 354, 356, 364, 366, 369, 373
Moths of the Limberlost (Stratton-Porter) **21**:261-2
"The Moth-Signal" (Hardy) **48**:60; **53**:100
Mothwise (Hamsun)
See *Svaermere*
Motifs (Lagerkvist)
See *Motiv*
"Motion and Rest" (Toomer) **172**:279
The Motion Menace (Dent) **72**:21
Motiv (Lagerkvist) **144**:164, 210
"The Motive for Metaphor" (Stevens) **12**:360; **45**:299
"Los motivos de la conducta" (Reyes) **33**:323
"Motivos de mar" (Storni) **5**:450
"Motke Arbel and His Romance" (Cahan) **71**:37, 39, 85
Motke ganev (Asch) **3**:65-6, 68, 71
Motl Peysi dem khazns (Aleichem) **1**:23, 29-30; **35**:307, 319
Motl, the Son of Peysi the Cantor (Aleichem)
See *Motl Peysi dem khazns*
A Motley (Galsworthy) **45**:32-3
Motley, and Other Poems (de la Mare) **4**:74-5, 79
"The Motor: 1905" (Guiney) **41**:221
A Motor-Flight through France (Wharton) **1219**:345, 361
Mottel ben Peisi, the Cantor (Aleichem)
See *Motl Peysi dem khazns*
Mottke the Vagabond (Asch)
See *Motke ganev*
"Motus Motus" (Arp) **115**:31
Mouchette (Bernanos)
See *Nouvelle histoire de Mouchette*
Mouchoir de nuages (Tzara) **168**:241, 256-61
"Moufflou" (Ouida) **43**:357
"Le moulin" (Verhaeren) **12**:466
Le Moulin de Pologne (Giono) **124**:50, 54, 57-58, 60, 78-82, 113, 115
"The Mound" (Lovecraft) **22**:238
Mount Analogue (Daumal)
See *Le mont analogue*
"Mount Derision" (Stephens) **4**:420
"Mount Ida" (Noyes) **7**:502
Mount Music (Somerville & Ross) **51**:340, 344, 352-54, 358, 378
The Mountain (Bernhard)
See *Der Berg*
Mountain Blood (Hergesheimer) **11**:263-65, 279, 285-86
"The Mountain Chapel" (Thomas) **10**:452, 463
"The Mountain Christ" (Crowley) **7**:208
"A Mountain Gateway" (Carman) **7**:143
The Mountain Giants (Pirandello)
See *I giganta della montagna*
"Mountain Lion" (Lawrence) **9**:230; **93**:128
The Mountain Lovers (Sharp) **39**:355, 358-59, 365, 367-68, 373-74, 378-79, 396
Mountain Man (Fisher) **140**:159, 182, 188-89
Mountain Meadow (Buchan)
See *Sick Heart River*
The Mountain Monster (Dent) **72**:19, 21-22
The Mountain of Light (Couperus)
See *De berg van licht*
"The Mountain of the Signs" (Artaud) **36**:30
Mountain Path (Arnow) **196**:4, 9, 11, 29, 31-2, 37-8, 49, 60-4, 66, 75-6, 79, 91, 96, 118
The Mountain Railway (Horvath)
See *Die Bergbahn*
The Mountain School-Teacher (Post) **39**:343, 347
"The Mountain Sweep Stakes" (Fields) **80**:259-60
"The Mountain Tent" (Dickey) **151**:199
Mountain Time (De Voto) **29**:126
"The Mountain Tomb" (Yeats) **31**:411
Mountain Torrents (Giacosa)
See *Aquazzoni in montagna*
"Mountain Victory" (Faulkner) **170**:185, 189
"The Mountain Whippoorwill" (Benét) **7**:78
"The Mountaineer" (Rainis)
See "Kalnā kāpējs"
"The Mountains" (Muir) **87**:188
The Mountains (Wolfe) **13**:483
The Mountains of California (Muir) **28**:240, 242, 245, 247, 254, 256-59, 262
Mountains, Sea, and Giants (Döblin)
See *Berge, Meere, und Giganten*
The Mountebanks (Gilbert) **3**:219
Mourir de ne pas mourir (Éluard) **7**:247; **41**:150, 154, 160
"The Mourners" (Malamud) **129**:69, 112, 166-70, 172, 193; **184**:166
"The Mourner's Bench" (Masters) **25**:299
"Mournin' for Religion" (Masters) **25**:299
Mourning Becomes Electra (O'Neill) **1**:385-88, 391-93, 395, 397-98, 400-01, 403-05; **6**:327, 329, 331, 334; **49**:247, 249, 252, 255, 257, 269, 285-86, 295

Mourning Becomes Mrs. Spendlove, and Other Portraits Grave and Gay (Gogarty) **15**:120
"Mourning City" (van Ostaijen) **33**:422
"The Mourning Dove" (Foote) **108**:35-6
Mourning for the Dead (Esenin) **4**:116
"Mourning the Death of the Empress Dowager" (Masaoka) **18**:232
"Mourning to Do" (Sarton) **120**:267
"The Mouse" (Coppard) **5**:176
"The Mouse" (Saki) **3**:365
"Mouse: A Sad Story" (Engel) **137**:114
"Mouse and Cat" (Bennett) **5**:46
"The Mouse and the Woman" (Thomas) **45**:372-73, 390; **105**:297-301, 320, 324, 326-27, 347, 357
The Mouses Trap (Howells) **7**:387
"The Mouse-Trap" (Slesinger) **10**:446
"Moustaches" (Devkota) **23**:50
Le moutardier du pape (Jarry) **14**:273
"Un Mouton à quatre Tiges" (Arp) **115**:31
The Move (Garro)
See *La Mudanza*
"Move It on Over" (Williams) **81**:419,423
The Movement (Hansberry) **192**:280
"Movement Is Life" (Duncan) **68**:70
"The Movement of Fish" (Dickey) **151**:104
The Movement-Image (Deleuze)
See *Cinema 1:l'image-Movement*
Movements of Thought in the Nineteenth Century (Mead) **89**:52, 70-1
"The Movers" (Howells) **7**:363
"Moving" (Jarrell) **177**:127, 224
"The Moving Finger" (Wharton) **129**:360
Moving Forward (Ford) **73**:32
"Moving Landscape With Falling Rain" (Bishop) **103**:9
"Moving Landscape With Rain" (Bishop) **103**:3
"The Moving Picture Crew" (McAlmon) **97**:89
Moving the Mountain (Gilman) **9**:108-10, 115; **117**:49-50, 75-6, 82, 124-31
"Mowing" (Roberts) **8**:327
"Moxon's Master" (Bierce) **44**:6, 13, 15, 16, 45-6
"Moya Zhizn" (Tolstoy) **173**:294
Moya zhizn'v iskusstve (Stanislavsky) **167**:240, 247, 251-52, 259-61, 263-64, 266-68, 271-72, 277, 280, 288-89, 294, 300-303, 305, 308, 329, 332, 334, 337-40, 348
"Mozart, 1935" (Stevens) **45**:296
"Mozgófénykép" (Babits) **14**:39
Mqhayi of the Mountain of Beauty (Mqhayi)
See *U-Mqhayi Wase-Ntab'ozuko*
Mr. and Mrs. Daventry (Harris) **24**:255, 257-58, 269
"Mr and Mrs Dove" (Mansfield) **8**:282, 284; **39**:304, 322; **164**:240
"Mr. and Mrs. Elliot" (Hemingway) **115**:184
"Mr. and Mrs. Fix-It" (Lardner) **14**:307, 312
Mr. and Mrs. Nevill Tyson (Sinclair) **3**:437; **11**:408-09
Mr. Antiphilos, Satyr (Gourmont)
See *Lettres d'un satyre*
Mr. Apollo (Ford)
See *Mr. Apollo: A Just Possible Story*
Mr. Apollo: A Just Possible Story (Ford) **15**:87, 89-90, 93; **172**:57
"Mr Ash's Studio" (Wakefield) **120**:356
Mr. Belloc Objects to 'The Outline of History' (Wells) **12**:498
"Mr. Bellows the Monkey and the Turtle" (Wakefield) **120**:333
Mr. Bennett and Mrs. Brown (Woolf) **1**:527, 536; **20**:393, 403; **43**:386, 388-89, 400; **101**:295
Mr. Blettsworthy on Rampole Island (Wells) **6**:532, 553
"Mr. Bliss" (Tolkien) **137**:242
Mr. Bolfry (Bridie) **3**:131-32, 137, 139
"Mr. Bosphorus and the Muses" (Ford) **57**:277
Mr. Bosphorus and the Muses (Ford) **172**:57
"Mr. Brinks' Day Off" (Crane) **11**:165
Mr. Britling Sees It Through (Wells) **6**:528, 532, 548; **12**:501, 506-07
"Mr. Burnshaw and the Statue" (Stevens) **45**:276
"Mr. Charles" (Schulz) **5**:422
Mr. Clutterbuck's Election (Belloc) **18**:27, 32, 35
Mr. Cogito (Herbert)
See *Pan Cogito*
Mr Cogito (Herbert)
See *Pan Cogito*
"Mr Cogito: Actual Position of His Soul" (Herbert)
See "Pan Cogito: Aktualna pozycja duszy"
"Mr. Cogito and the Imagination" (Herbert) **168**:12, 21
"Mr Cogito and the Pearl" (Herbert) **168**:19
"Mr. Cogito Considers the Difference between the Human Voice and the Voice of Nature" (Herbert)
See "Pan Cogito rozwaza róznice miedzy glosem ludzkim a glosem przyrody"
"Mr Cogito Looks at His Face in the Mirror" (Herbert) **168**:8, 71
"Mr Cogito Meditates on Suffering" (Herbert) **168**:8, 19
"Mr. Cogito on the Need for Precision" (Herbert) **168**:11
"Mr. Cogito on Upright Attitudes" (Herbert)
See "Pan Cogito o postawie wyprostowanej"
"Mr. Cogito Reads the Newspaper" (Herbert) **168**:19
"Mr Cogito Tells about the Temptations of Spinoza" (Herbert) **168**:46
"Mr Cogito Thinks of Returning to the City Where He Was Born" (Herbert) **168**:18
"Mr Cogito—Notes from the Dead House" (Herbert) **168**:44
"Mr. Cogito's Soul" (Herbert)
See "Dusza Pana Cogito"
"Mr. Cogito-The Return" (Herbert)
See "Pan Cogito-Powrót"
"Mr. Cornelius Johnson, Office Seeker" (Dunbar) **12**:120
"Mr. Costyve Duditch" (Toomer) **172**:261, 263-65
"Mr. Crump" (Handy)
See "The Memphis Blues"
"Mr. Dallas Larabee, Sinner" (Millay) **169**:274-75
Mr. Dickens Goes to the Play (Woollcott) **5**:520
Mr. Dooley in Peace and War (Dunne) **28**:53-4, 56, 66, 70
Mr. Dooley in the Hearts of His Countrymen (Dunne) **28**:53, 56
Mr. Dooley Says (Dunne) **28**:55, 82
"Mr. Durant" (Parker) **143**:314, 343
Mr. Faithful (Dunsany) **59**:17, 22-4, 26
Mr. Fleight (Ford) **15**:89, 93; **172**:10, 111, 118-19
"Mr. Flood's Party" (Robinson) **5**:411; **101**:111, 133, 138-39, 179, 193
Mr. Fortune's Maggot (Warner) **131**:312, 314, 316-18, 320, 325, 361, 363, 365
"Mr. Frisbie" (Lardner) **14**:307
Mr. George Jean Nathan Presents (Nathan) **18**:296
Mr. Gillie (Bridie) **3**:135-36, 142
Mr. Grex of Monte Carlo (Oppenheim) **45**:131
Mr. Hodge and Mr. Hazard (Wylie) **8**:524, 527, 529-30, 532, 538
"Mr Howells as a Critic" (Matthews) **95**:265
Mr. Huffam (Walpole) **5**:504
"Mr. Humphreys and His Inheritance" (James) **6**:212, 216
Mr. Incoul's Misadventure (Saltus) **8**:342, 345-46, 348, 350, 352, 355
Mr. Ingleside (Lucas) **73**:159, 162, 173
Mr. Isaacs: A Tale of Modern India (Crawford) **10**:138-39, 141-44, 146, 148-49, 151, 155, 157-58
"Mr. J. M. Keynes Examines Mr. Lloyd George's Pledge" (Keynes) **64**:243
"Mr. Jack Hamlin's Mediation" (Harte) **135**:147, 165
"Mr. Jones" (Wharton) **3**:578; **9**:547; **129**:364
Mr. Jorkens Remembers Africa (Dunsany) **59**:27-8
"Mr. Judd and His Snail, A Sorry Tale" (Nash) **109**:356
Mr. Justice Raffles (Hornung) **59**:114
"Mr. Kempe" (de la Mare) **4**:80; **53**:13-5, 17, 26-7, 36
"Mr. Keynes's Lecture" (Keynes) **64**:246
"Mr. Keynes's Plan. Control of Boom and Slump" (Keynes) **64**:246
"Mr. Lightfoot in the Green Isle" (Coppard) **5**:180
"Mr. Lyon" (Carter)
See "The Courtship of Mr. Lyon"
"Mr. Mandragon, the Millionaire" (Chesterton) **6**:109
"Mr. Marshall's Doppelganger" (Wells) **133**:262
"Mr. Masthead, Journalist" (Bierce) **44**:45
"Mr. Maximilian Morningdew's Advice" (Hawthorne) **25**:247
Mr. Meeson's Will (Haggard) **11**:240
Mr. Midshipman Hornblower (Forester) **152**:129-30, 138, 140-41, 159
Mr. Mirakel (Oppenheim) **45**:131-33, 137
Mr. Moderate (Adamov)
See *M. le Modéré*
"Mr. Mori" (Akutagawa Ryūnosuke) **16**:27
"Mr. Palmer's Party" (Slesinger) **10**:445
Mr. Palomar (Calvino)
See *Palomar*
"Mr. Palomar in the Garden" (Calvino) **183**:42
"Mr. Pamirs the Scholar Takes a Walk" (Miyazawa) **76**:300
"Mr. Peebles' Heart" (Gilman) **9**:113, 115
"Mr. Pennybaker at Church" (Roberts) **68**:336
Mr. Perrin and Mr. Traill (Walpole) **5**:496, 502-03
"Mr. Pim and the Holy Crumb" (Powys) **9**:378
Mr. Pim Passes By (Milne) **6**:308, 310, 318; **88**:249
Mr. Polton Explains (Freeman) **21**:62
"Mr. Ponting's Alibi" (Freeman) **21**:58
Mr. Pottermack's Oversight (Freeman) **21**:53, 59, 62
Mr. President (Asturias)
See *El señor presidente*
Mr. Price (Witkiewicz) **8**:512
Mr. Prohack (Bennett) **5**:29, 37, 43, 50-1; **197**:13, 16-17, 19-20, 27
Mr. Puntila and His Man Matti (Brecht)
See *Herr Puntila und sein Knecht Matti*
"Mr. Reginald Peacock's Day" (Mansfield) **39**:301, 304; **164**:235-36, 302, 304-5
"Mr. Rockefeller's Prayer" (Gilman) **9**:96
Mr. Skeffington (Elizabeth) **41**:131-32
"Mr. Smellingscheck" (Lawson) **27**:121
Mr. Standfast (Buchan) **41**:38, 41-2, 48, 50, 54, 57-8, 64, 66-7, 73, 77, 80
"Mr. Swiddler's Flip-Flap" (Bierce) **44**:45
"Mr. Symons' Essays" (Woolf) **43**:403
Mr. Tasker's Gods (Powys) **9**:364-65, 369, 373, 376
"Mr. Tolman" (Stockton) **47**:327
"Mr Tritas on the Roofs" (Thomas) **105**:336
Mr. Waddington of Wyck (Sinclair) **3**:435; **11**:411, 414
"Mr. Wells and the New History" (Becker) **63**:116
Mr. Weston's Good Wine (Powys) **9**:362, 364-67, 370-71, 373-76, 378
"Mr. Winkelburg" (Hecht) **101**:42
Mr. Witt's Widow (Hope) **83**:171
"Mračnoj pavilikoj" (Bryusov) **10**:82
"Mrs. Alfred Uruguay" (Stevens) **45**:289
"Mrs. Amworth" (Benson) **27**:13, 17, 19
"Mrs. Andrews' Control" (Benson) **27**:19

"Mrs. Bathurst" (Kipling) **8**:192, 195, 200, 209; **17**:207
"Mrs. Beazley's Deeds" (Gilman) **117**:100, 102, 116, 118-20, 123
"Mrs. Bixby and the Colonel's Coat" (Dahl) **173**:14
"Mrs. Blaha's maid" (Rilke)
See "Frau Blahas Magd"
"Mrs. Bonny" (Jewett) **22**:116
"Mrs. Carrington and Mrs. Crane" (Parker) **143**:331
Mrs. Cliff's Yacht (Stockton) **47**:317-18, 321, 325
Mrs. Dalloway (Woolf) **1**:527-33, 535-39, 541-42, 544-45; **5**:506-10, 515-16; **20**:390-432; **43**:397-98, 408; **56**:358, 367, 371, 374; **101**:212, 238, 294; **128**:318, 324, 326-27, 334, 336, 338, 341, 343-44, 348, 357-58, 362-65, 371, 376, 379-80, 382, 384
Mrs. Dalloway's Party (Woolf) **20**:421
Mrs. Dukes' Million (Lewis) **104**:181, 278, 299
"Mrs. Fairfax" (Rutherford) **25**:346
Mrs. Farrell (Howells) **17**:184
Mrs. Fiske: Her Views on Actors, Acting, and the Problems of Production (Woollcott) **5**:520
"Mrs. Frola and Her Son-in-Law, Mr. Ponza" (Pirandello)
See "La Signora Frola e il signor Ponza, suo genero"
Mrs. Gailey (Kaye-Smith) **20**:113, 116
Mrs. Gainsborough's Diamonds (Hawthorne) **25**:235, 238, 241
"Mrs. Hannah" (Peretz) **16**:405
"Mrs. Hines' Money" (Gilman) **117**:77-8
Mrs. Hjelde (Undset)
See *Fru Hjelde*
"Mrs. Laneham" (Knister) **56**:155
Mrs. Leffingwell's Boots (Thomas) **97**:134-36, 139
Mrs. Lenine (Khlebnikov)
See *Gospozha Lenis*
"Mrs. Mandrill" (Nemerov) **124**:157, 171, 248
"Mrs. Manstey's View" (Wharton) **129**:352, 360
Mrs. Marta Oulie (Undset)
See *Fru Marta Oulie*
Mrs. Mason Protests (Hope) **83**:167
"Mrs. Merrill's Duties" (Gilman) **37**:213
"Mrs. Mobry's Reason" (Chopin) **127**:18, 20, 23, 112, 206, 208
"Mrs. Packletide's Tiger" (Saki) **3**:365
Mrs. Parkington (Bromfield) **11**:86
"Mrs. Paulatim" (Calvino) **183**:93, 95
"Mrs. Powers' Duty" (Gilman) **37**:213
Mrs. Reynolds (Stein) **28**:332, 334-36; **48**:249, 264
"Mrs. Ripley's Trip" (Garland) **3**:190
Mrs. Stevens Hears the Mermaids Singing (Sarton) **120**:197, 210, 212, 215, 217-21, 223, 231, 246, 248, 276-84, 286-89, 294, 306-07, 309-10, 314
"Mrs. Suffrin's Smelling-Bottle" (Hawthorne) **25**:247
"Mrs. Van Bartan" (Post) **39**:337
Mrs. Warren's Profession (Shaw) **3**:384, 405; **9**:412, 414; **21**:306-07, 333, 337-38; **45**:243
"M'sieu Smit" (Drummond) **25**:142
"Mt. Pisgah's Christmas Possum" (Dunbar) **2**:133; **12**:111
"Mtasipol" (Fondane) **159**:240, 242, 244, 246
Mu no jikakuteki gentei (Nishida) **83**:251, 362
"Mučeniki nauki" (Zamyatin) **8**:553
Much Ado about Me (Allen) **87**:50, 57
Much Obliged, Jeeves (Wodehouse)
See *Jeeves and the Tie That Binds*
The Mucker (Burroughs) **2**:78-9, 81; **32**:57-8
Mud Flats (Platonov) **14**:406-07
"A Mud Hen" (Lindsay) **17**:240
"The Mud Turtle" (Nemerov) **124**:148, 213, 252, 286, 302
La Mudanza (Garro) **153**:17, 19-20, 72
"Muddy Mind" (Shiga)
See "Nigotta atama"
"Mudo de noche" (Aleixandre) **113**:8
"Mudrost'" (Zoshchenko) **15**:511
"Muere en el mar el ave que volvó de buque" (Unamuno) **9**:510
Las muertas (Ibarguengoitia) **148**:197, 200-01, 216-19
"La muerte" (Aleixandre) **113**:14
"Muerte" (Aleixandre) **113**:7
"Muerte" (García Lorca) **197**:261
"Muerte de Antoñito el Camborio" (García Lorca) **7**:300; **49**:82, 113
La muerte de cisne (Gonzalez Martinez) **72**:148, 150
"La muerte de Isolda" (Quiroga) **20**:211
"La muerte de la emperatriz de China" (Darío) **4**:68
"La muerte de la señorita Clementina" (Lugones) **15**:293
"La muerte de los hermanos Arango" (Arguedas) **147**:93
"La muerte del canario" (Quiroga) **20**:211
"La muerte del poeta" (Huidobro) **31**:124
"Muerte en el frío" (Villaurrutia) **80**:484
"La muerte es una madre nuestra antigua" (Jiménez) **183**:290
"La muerte o antesala de consulta" (Aleixandre) **113**:5
"La muerte y la brújula" (Borges) **109**:16-17, 27, 87-8, 109-10, 112, 148, 159
La muerte y la niña (Onetti) **131**:162, 164-72
"El muerto" (Borges) **109**:32-4, 87, 159
"Muerto de amor" (García Lorca) **49**:119; **181**:91-92, 95
"Muerto y resucitado" (Nervo) **11**:394
Los muertos (Sánchez) **37**:311-12, 314-16, 318
Los muertos mandan (Blasco Ibáñez) **12**:30, 35, 43, 50
Mufti (Sapper) **44**:311-12, 323
"Mugging" (Ginsberg) **120**:88, 111-12
"Muime Chriosd" (Sharp) **39**:376
"La muiron" (France) **9**:57
"La mujer" (Jiménez) **183**:290
La mujer (Ramoacn y Cajal) **93**:146
"La mujer del César" (Pereda) **16**:367
La mujer del héroe (Martinez Sierra and Martinez Sierra) **6**:278
"La mujer desnuda" (Jiménez) **183**:302-3
La mujer desnuda (1918-1923) (Jiménez) **183**:302
La mujer domada (Azuela) **3**:76
"La mujer española" (Pardo Bazán) **189**:304, 316-17
La mujer legítima (Villaurrutia) **80**:466
Muktadhārā (Tagore) **3**:492
La mulata de Córdoba (Villaurrutia) **80**:459
Mulata de tal (Asturias) **184**:16, 36-39, 71, 85, 88-89
"The Mulatto Woman of Cordoba" (Villaurrutia) **80**:459
The Mulatto Woman of Cordoba (Villaurrutia) **80**:459
"The Mulberry Tree" (Bowen) **148**:20
The Mulberry Tree: Writings of Elizabeth Bowen (Bowen) **148**:81-82
Muldskud (Nexø) **43**:329
Mule Bone: A Comedy of Negro Life (Hurston) **121**:352; **131**:82, 94
Mules and Men (Hurston) **121**:333, 341, 343, 347, 351, 356; **131**:62, 65, 72, 74-76, 78-79, 83, 85-86, 91
"The Mullenville Mystery" (Hawthorne) **25**:247
La multiple splendeur (Verhaeren) **12**:459-60, 464
"Multiplicity" (Calvino) **183**:68, 148
"Mumbo" (Herzl) **36**:141
A Mummer's Wife (Moore) **7**:474, 478, 480-82, 484-86, 488-90, 498
"Mummia" (Brooke) **2**:59
Munā Madan (Devkota) **23**:48-9, 51
"El mundo" (Pardo Bazán) **189**:236, 317-19, 321
Mundo a solas (Aleixandre) **113**:15, 23-29, 43, 46, 49
El mundo alucinante (Arenas) **191**:135-38, 144-45, 147, 150, 215, 255-57, 259-66
"El mundo de siete pozos" (Storni) **5**:445-47, 449-52;
El mundo es ansí (Baroja) **9**:49, 62
"El mundo está bien hecho" (Aleixandre) **113**:6
"Mundo Grande" (Drummond de Andrade) **139**:229
"Mundo inhumano" (Aleixandre) **113**:16
"Mundo poético" (Aleixandre) **113**:61
El mundo visto a los ochenta años (Ramoacn y Cajal) **93**:146
Mundos (Benson) **17**:23, 25-6
"Muñecas" (Aleixandre) **113**:8, 147
Munera pulveris (Ruskin) **20**:265, 282, 291, 304; **63**:242-46, 253, 267-68, 281, 298;
"The Municipal Gallery Revisited" (Yeats) **18**:463; **31**:423
"A Municipal Report" (Henry) **19**:172, 176, 183, 188-91, 198-201
Munken Vendt (Hamsun) **14**:221-24, 241, 244; **49**:127-28
Le Mur du Pacifique (Lyotard) **103**:160
"La muralla y los libros" (Borges) **109**:44, 87
"Murder" (Bennett) **5**:46
"The Murder" (Chekhov) **3**:160
"Murder" (Csáth) **13**:149
"Murder" (García Lorca) **197**:184
"Murder" (Kolmar) **40**:177
Murder at Monte Carlo (Oppenheim) **45**:131
The Murder Book of Mr. J. G. Reeder (Wallace)
See *The Mind of J. G. Reeder*
"A Murder during the Age of Enlightenment" (Akutagawa Ryūnosuke)
See "Kaika no satsujin"
Murder Mirage (Dent) **72**:22
Murder Must Advertise (Sayers) **2**:530-31; **15**:371, 379, 382, 387, 393-94
Murder, My Sweet (Chandler) **7**:175
Murder of a Buttercup (Döblin)
See *Die Erdmordung einer Butterblume*
"The Murder of Amy Robsart" (Sabatini) **47**:300
The Murder of Delicia (Corelli) **51**:66, 81
The Murder of Lidice (Millay) **169**:282, 290
"The Murder of the Innocents" (Higginson) **36**:174
"Murder on Belpoggio Street" (Svevo)
See *L'assassinio di via Belpoggio*
Murder or Suicide? (Fisher) **140**:150
"The Murderer" (Kuprin) **5**:297, 301
The Murderess (Papadiamantis)
See *He phonissa*
"The Murderous Attack" (Čapek) **37**:54
"Murgh-i ruh" (Hedāyat) **21**:75
Murillo (Rilke) **6**:369
"Murió al amanecer" (García Lorca) **181**:181
"Murka" (Remizov) **27**:339
"Murke's Collected Silences" (Böll) **185**:16
"The Murmuring Forest" (Korolenko) **22**:172
Muro antártico (Vallejo) **56**:309
Murphy (Beckett) **145**:78, 82, 90, 114, 142-43, 147, 184, 199
"Musa consolatrix" (Machado de Assis) **10**:279
Les musardises (Rostand) **6**:381; **37**:282-84, 286, 289-90
Musashi Myamoto (Mizoguchi) **72**:315
"Musashino" (Kunikida Doppo) **99**:295, 302, 304
Musashino (Kunikida Doppo) **99**:298-99
"The Muse as Medusa" (Sarton) **120**:273, 294
"The Muse of Brotherhood" (Markham) **47**:284
"The Muse of the Incommunicable" (Sterling) **20**:386
"Le muse qui est la grâce" (Claudel) **2**:108; **10**:133

"The Muse's Interest" (Nemerov) **124**:179, 182, 291
"Museaux-éponges" (Arp) **115**:42
"Les muses" (Claudel) **10**:132
The Muses Are Heard: An Account of the Porgy and Bess Tour to Leningrad (Capote) **164**:116-17, 130, 142, 144, 150, 201
"The Muse's Tragedy" (Wharton) **3**:553, 555; **9**:540, 547; **129**:360
"Museum Feet" (Benchley) **55**:13
"The Museum of Cheats" (Warner) **131**:321
The Museum of Cheats: Stories (Warner) **131**:320-21, 364
"The Musgrave Ritual" (Doyle) **7**:227
"Mushrooms in the City" (Calvino)
See "Funghi in città"
"Music" (Gibran) **9**:90
"Music" (de la Mare) **58**:38
"Music" (Sterling) **20**:379, 384
Music (Molnár)
See *Muzsika*
Music and Its Lovers (Lee) **5**:316
The Music and Life of Carl Michael Bellman (Zuckmayer)
See *Ulla Winblad oder Musik und Leben des Carl Michael Bellman*
"Music and Nietzsche" (Mann) **44**:174
Music for Chameleons (Capote) **164**:116-17, 123, 134, 138-39, 144-46, 151, 153-54, 199-204
"Music For One" (Santos) **156**:315
"Music in a Snowy Street" (Hardy) **143**:169
"Music in Venice" (Symons) **11**:437
"The Music Maker" (Bosman) **49**:18-19
"The Music of Erich Zann" (Lovecraft) **4**:266, 270; **22**:209, 221
"The Music of Landscape and the Fate of Montage Counterpoint at a New Stage" (Eisenstein) **57**:199-200
"The Music of the Future" (Huneker) **65**:215
Music of the Wild, with Reproductions of the Performers, Their Instruments, and Festival Halls (Porter) **21**:262
"Music of Tomorrow" (Mencken) **13**:363
"The Music on the Hill" (Saki) **3**:365, 368-70
"Music on Water" (Ledwidge) **23**:117, 122
"The Musical Box" (Hardy) **53**:101
"The Musical Club Concert" (Benchley) **55**:3
A Musical Companion (Erskine) **84**:184
"The Musical Foundations of Verse" (Sapir) **108**:252
"Musical Life" (Lee) **5**:310
"Musical Moon" (Cohan) **60**:168
"Musical Qualities in Basho's Haiku" (Hagiwara) **60**:306
A Musical Tour Through Eighteenth-Century Europe (Rolland)
See *Voyage musical à travers l'Europe du XVIII siècle*
A Musical Tour Through the Land of the Past (Rolland)
See *Voyage musical aux pays du passé*
Music-Hall (van Ostaijen) **33**:405, 411, 422
Music-Hall Sidelights (Colette) **16**:129
"The Musician" (Remizov)
See "Muzykant"
"The Musician of Saint Merry" (Apollinaire)
See "Le musicien de Saint-Merry"
"The Musicians" (Csáth) **13**:148
Musicians of the Past (Rolland)
See *Musiciens d'autrefois*
Musicians of Today (Rolland)
See *Musiciens d'aujourd'hui*
"Le musicien de Saint-Merry" (Apollinaire) **3**:44-5; **8**:25-6, 28; **51**:6, 31-2, 35
Musiciens d'aujourd'hui (Rolland) **23**:267
Musiciens d'autrefois (Rolland) **23**:267
Musik (Wedekind) **7**:582
"Die Musik kommt" (Liliencron) **18**:207, 213-15
The Musketeers of Pig Alley (Griffith) **68**:168, 197
Musornyi veter (Platonov) **14**:404-05, 407, 414, 418
"Must One Recognize the Existence of Natural Law, and If So, in What Sense?" (Westermarck) **87**:366
"Must We Occupy Ourselves with an Examination of the Ideal of a Future System?" (Kropotkin) **36**:204
"Mustafa the Hungarian" (Andrić) **135**:10
Musti (Leino) **24**:372
"Mutabile Semper" (Grahame) **64**:88
"Mutability" (Brooke) **2**:58
Mutant (Kuttner) **10**:266
"The Mute" (Peretz) **16**:405
The Mute (McCullers) **155**:169-70, 179, 192, 207, 222, 225
Di muter (Asch) **3**:69, 72
Der Mutige Seefahrer (Kaiser) **9**:181
"Mutilation" (Lawrence) **93**:55
The Mutiny (Van Doren) **18**:410
Mutiny in January (Van Doren) **18**:410
The Mutiny of the Elsinore (London) **9**:257, 259, 267
Mutiny on the Bounty (Hall and Nordhoff) **23**:59-60, 62-3, 66-71
"Die Mütter" (Kraus) **5**:290
"Mutter" (Lasker-Schueler) **57**:307, 318
Die Mutter (Brecht) **6**:33, 36-7; **13**:63, 65; **35**:3; **169**:4, 17, 20, 64-71
Eine Mutter (Kolmar) **40**:184
Mutter Courage und ihre Kinder (Brecht) **1**:99-100, 104-05, 107-09, 113, 117, 119-20; **6**:37-8; **13**:64-5; **35**:1-29; **169**:4-5, 7-11, 28-29
Mutter Marie (Mann) **9**:315, 326
"Den Müttern" (Toller) **10**:490
Mutual Aid: A Factor of Evolution (Kropotkin) **36**:192-95, 197, 200-03, 221
"The Mutual Influence of Theology and Philosophy" (Strauss) **141**:273
"Muž, který nemohl spát" (Čapek) **37**:54
"The Muzhik" (Gumilev) **60**:276
"The Muzhiks" (Chekhov) **10**:112
"Muziki" (Chekhov) **3**:168; **10**:100, 117
Muzsika (Molnár) **20**:164, 173-74
"Muzykant" (Remizov) **27**:340
"The M'Villin" (Rohmer) **28**:286
My (Zamyatin) **8**:542-43, 545-50, 552-55, 557-58; **37**:417-19, 422-25, 427-30, 432-34, 436-44, 446-47
My African Journey (Churchill) **113**:155
"My Ancestors" (Kuzmin)
See "Moi predki"
My Ántonia (Cather) **1**:151, 153, 156-59, 162-63, 165, 167; **11**:92-8, 102, 104-07, 112, 114; **31**:24-69; **99**:204, 207-09, 211, 213, 228-31, 241, 265, 267-68, 274-75, 281, 285; **132**:123-27, 129-31, 133-34, 137-39, 141, 143, 147-49, 154; **152**:8, 10, 16, 20-21, 25, 27-30, 50, 55-56, 61, 77, 85, 93, 97, 105-6, 108-9
My Apprencticeships (Colette)
See *Mes apprentissages*
My Apprenticeship (Gorky) **8**:77
My Apprenticeship (Webb and Webb) **22**:414-15, 419, 423
My Apprenticeships (Colette)
See *Mes apprentissages*
"My Army, O, My Army!" (Lawson) **27**:122, 133
My Autobiography (Cather) **132**:132
"My Banker" (Rhodes) **53**:316
My Battle (Hitler)
See *Mein Kampf*
"My Bay'nit" (Service) **15**:399
"My Beautiful Mother" (Lasker-Schueler) **57**:333
My Belief (Hesse)
See *Mein Glaube*
"My Belongings" (Endo)
See "Watakushi no mono"
My Best Poems (Aleixandre) **113**:23
"My Big Brother" (Premchand) **21**:287
My Birds (Davies) **5**:206
"My Birthday" (Gibran) **9**:85
"My Blue Piano" (Lasker-Schueler)
See "Mein blaues Klavier"
My Blue Piano (Lasker-Schueler)
See *Mein blaues Klavier*
"My Blush" (Lasker-Schueler) **57**:328
"My Boy Jack" (Kipling) **8**:200
My Brilliant Career (Franklin) **7**:264, 266-74
"My Brother and I" (Naipaul) **153**:226
"My Brother Paul" (Dreiser) **10**:181; **35**:71
My Brother Yves (Loti)
See *Mon frère Yves*
My Career Goes Bung (Franklin) **7**:267-68, 270-74
"My Castle on the Nile" (Johnson) **175**:225
My Childhood (Gorky)
See *Detstvo*
"My Cicely" (Hardy) **4**:152; **53**:117
"My Closet Companions" (Bengtsson) **48**:13
"My Coffin Steed" (Ady) **11**:14
My Confessional: Questions of Our Day (Ellis) **14**:116-17, 127
My Contemporaries (Mikszath)
See *Az én kortársaim*
My Country and My People (Lin) **149**:310-13, 315-16, 321-22, 346
"My Country, Right or Left" (Orwell) **15**:355; **128**:284
"My Country Tish of Thee" (Rinehart) **52**:281
"My Countrymen" (Gibran) **1**:328
"My Cousin Dickran, The Orator" (Saroyan) **137**:166
"My Cousin Dikran, the Orator" (Saroyan)
See "My Cousin Dickran, The Orator"
My Creator (Dreiser) **10**:197
"My Creed" (Campbell) **9**:32
"My Creed" (Guest) **95**:205
"My Daughter the Junkie on a Train" (Lorde)
See "To My Daughter the Junkie on a Train"
My Days and Dreams (Carpenter) **88**:62, 65-6, 70, 90, 117-9, 126
My Dear Miss Aldrich (Mankiewicz) **85**:163
"My Dear One Is Ill" (Radnóti) **16**:418
My Death My Life by Pier Paolo Pasolini (Acker) **191**:6, 57, 67-8, 129
"My Decrepit Barn" (Wright) **136**:301
"My Descendants" (Yeats) **11**:534-35
"My Discovery of America" (Mayakovski) **4**:292
My Disillusionment in Russia (Goldman) **13**:215
My Double Life: Memoirs of Sarah Bernhardt (Bernhardt) **75**:12, 39, 41
"My Drama" (Lasker-Schueler)
See "Mein Drama"
My Dream World (Kubin) **23**:95
"My Early Beliefs" (Keynes) **64**:245, 289, 295
My Early Life (Churchill) **113**:118, 148
"My Efforts" (Walser) **18**:427
My Evolution (Schoenberg) **75**:338-39
My Family! (de Filippo) **127**:280-81
My Farish Street Green (Walker) **129**:276, 316, 318
"My Father" (Bialik)
See "Avi"
"My Father" (Runyon) **10**:435
"My Father He Was a Fisherman" (Pickthall) **21**:252
"My Father Joins the Fire Brigade" (Schulz) **51**:316
My Father: The Rev. William Stead (Stead) **48**:199
"My Fathers Came from Kentucky" (Lindsay) **17**:227
"My Father's Grave" (Masaoka) **18**:232
My Faust (Valéry)
See *Mon Faust*

"My Favorite Books" (Mikszath)
See "Legkedvesebb könyveim"
"My Favorite Murder" (Bierce) **1**:88; **7**:88-9, **44**:14, 29, 32-3, 40, 44-5, 51
"My Fellow-Traveller" (Gorky) **8**:73
My Few Last Words (Baring-Gould) **88**:23
"My First Article" (Frank) **17**:108, 114
"My First Fee" (Babel)
See "Moi pervyi gonovar"
"My First Goose" (Babel)
See "Moi pervyi gus"
"My First Honorarium" (Babel)
See "Pervy gonorar"
"My First Impression of Paris" (Yosano) **59**:346-7
"My First Novels (There Were Two)" (Cather) **132**:130, 132, 137, 140, 152; **152**:32, 76, 79
My First Play (Gregory) **176**:13
My First Summer in the Sierra (Muir) **28**:243, 245, 247-48, 259, 264
"My Flag" (Cohan) **60**:169
My Flight from Siberia (Trotsky) **22**:364
My Four Weeks in France (Lardner) **14**:290
My Friend, Julia Lathrop (Addams) **76**:70
"My Friend Meurtrier" (Coppee) **25**:121
"My Friend of the Left" (Goebbels) **68**:98
"My Friends" (Service) **15**:404
My Friend's Book (France)
See *Le livre de mon ami*
My Garden (Davies) **5**:206
"My God" (Lagerkvist)
See "Min gud"
"My Grandmother's Leg" (Williams) **89**:402
"My Grandmother's Love Letters" (Crane) **2**:119-20; **5**:188; **80**:200
My Haiku (Masaoka)
See *Wa ga haiku*
My Hates (Zola)
See *Mes haines*
"My Heart" (Roberts) **68**:336
My Heart and My Flesh (Roberts) **68**:297-300, 309-10, 313, 326, 329, 335, 339, 342, 360-64
My Heart's in the Highlands (Saroyan) **137**:144, 152, 155-56, 161, 168-69, 182, 196-97, 200-206
"My Hero Bares His Nerves" (Thomas) **45**:380
My Holy Satan (Fisher) **140**:158, 173, 186
"My Home Town" (Lagerkvist)
See "Min hembygd"
"My Hope" (Södergran) **31**:286
My Host the World (Santayana) **40**:385
"My House" (Yeats) **11**:534-35
"My Husband" (Ginzburg)
See "Mio marito"
"My Husband's Tongue Is Bitter" (p'Bitek) **149**:16
"My inheritance is called yearning" (Lagerkvist)
See "Längtan heter min arvedel"
My Ireland (Dunsany) **59**:15-6
My Island Home (Hall and Nordhoff) **23**:66
"My Job as a Father" (Guest) **95**:209
My Kid the Doctor (Sánchez)
See *M'hijo el dotor*
My Lady (Wallace) **57**:398
"My Lady Brandon and the Widow Jim" (Jewett) **22**:136
"My Lady Comes" (Davies) **5**:201
"My Lady Loves Her Will" (Dunsany) **59**:11
My Lady's Garter (Futrelle) **19**:90, 95
"My Lady's Lips Are Like de Honey" (Johnson) **19**:210
My Larger Education: Being Chapters from My Experience (Washington) **10**:525
"My Last Duchess" (Herbert) **168**:8
"My Library" (Service) **15**:412
"My Life" (Chekhov) **3**:152, 155-56, 160; **10**:108, 111, 114; **55**:65
"My Life" (Esenin)
See "Moia zhizn"
"My Life" (Tolstoy)
See "Moya Zhizn"
My Life (Duncan) **68**:49, 51, 57-8, 75, 78
My Life (Ellis) **14**:120, 123-24, 127-29
My Life (Trotsky) **22**:389
My Life and Loves (Harris) **24**:263, 271-73, 275-80
My Life and Times (Jerome) **23**:83, 86
My Life and Times (Mackenzie) **116**:227, 229-30, 234, 239
My Life and Work (Ford) **73**:101
My Life as a Teacher (Erskine) **84**:185
My Life as German and Jew (Wassermann)
See *Mein Weg als Deutscher und Jude*
My Life in Architecture (Cram) **45**:12-13, 18, 21
"My Life in Literature" (Erskine) **84**:185
My Life in Music (Erskine) **84**:168
My Life in the Bush of Ghosts (Tutuola) **188**:274, 279-80, 282-83, 286, 288-89, 292, 303, 305, 307-08, 321
My Life of Absurdity (Himes) **139**:251-56, 258, 262, 269-75, 280-81, 283-84, 300, 302-4, 313, 321
"My Life with R. H. Macy" (Jackson) **187**:235
"My Light with Yours" (Masters) **25**:298
"My Literary Experience—To the Beginning Author" (Fadeyev) **53**:58
My Literary Passions (Howells) **7**:398
My Little Chickadee (Fields) **80**:222, 231, 241, 245
"My Little Girl" (Holly) **65**:144
My Lives and How I Lost Them (Cullen) **4**:51; **37**:159
My Lord Duke (Hornung) **59**:113
"My Lord the Elephant" (Kipling) **8**:197
"My Lost City" (Fitzgerald) **6**:172; **157**:208
"my love" (Cummings) **137**:54
My Love and My Heart (de Filippo) **127**:280
My Love Burns (Mizoguchi)
See *My Love Has Been Burning*
My Love Has Been Burning (Mizoguchi) **72**:315, 324
"My Love Is Gone into the East" (Moody) **105**:237, 252
"My Lover the Sea" (Arenas)
See "Mi amante el mar"
"My Love's on a Faraway Island" (Anwar)
See "Tjintaku djauh dipulau"
"My Lyre" (Södergran)
See "Min lyra"
My Man Jeeves (Wodehouse) **108**:391-92
My Mark Twain (Howells) **7**:370
"My Mate" (Service) **15**:399
My Miracles (Lasker-Schueler)
See *Meine Wunder*
My Mortal Enemy (Cather) **1**:154; **11**:95, 97-8, 101-02; **99**:201, 209, 220, 252-53, 274-76, 281; **132**:135, 138, 141, 148; **152**:21, 53
"My Most Memorable Christmas in America" (Santos) **156**:307-8
"My most. My most. O my lost!" (Villa) **176**:94
"My Mother" (Jozsef) **22**:164
"My Mother" (Ledwidge) **23**:109
My Mother: Demonology (Acker) **191**:43, 47-50, 65, 67-8, 70, 102, 104, 107, 128
My Mother, My Father, and Me (Hellman) **119**:144, 167, 171, 173
"My Mother Won the War" (Warner) **131**:308
"My Mother's Death and the Coming of My New Mother" (Shiga)
See "Haha no shi to atarishi haha"
My Mother's House (Colette)
See *La maison de Claudine*
"My Muse" (Böll) **185**:182
My Name is Aram (Saroyan) **137**:163, 167, 169, 181, 183, 194, 201
My Name Is Saroyan (Saroyan) **137**:170, 191
My Neighbours (Evans) **85**:5,24
"My Night" (Riley) **51**:302
"My Ninety Acres" (Bromfield) **11**:86
"My Old Home" (Lu Hsun)
See "Guxiang"
"My Old Man" (Hemingway) **115**:143
"My Old Man" (Lardner) **2**:329
My Old Man (Hemingway) **115**:131, 174
My Old Man (Runyon) **10**:430, 435-36
My Opinions and Betsy Bobbet's (Holley) **99**:309-14, 318-19, 324, 326-27, 331, 334-35, 341, 343-45
"My Origins" (Bagritsky)
See "Proiskhozhdeniye"
"My Outdoor Study" (Higginson) **36**:175
My Own Fairy Book (Lang) **16**:264, 272
"My Own Gold" (Jiménez) **183**:338-40
My Own Story (Pankhurst) **100**:323, 325
"My Pal" (Service) **15**:412
"My Past" (Shiga)
See "Kako"
"My Path" (Esenin) **4**:115
"My Pedagogic Creed" (Dewey) **95**:66
"My People" (Lasker-Schueler)
See "Mein Volk"
My People (Evans) **85**:2-3, 5, 10, 12, 15, 17, 19, 29, 32, 36-7, 43-50
"My People, My People" (Hurston) **131**:68
"My Platonic Sweetheart" (Twain) **185**:321
My Poetic (Palamas) **5**:385
"My Poetry" (Bialik) **25**:65
"My Poetry" (Noguchi) **80**:362
My Political Confession (Horkheimer) **132**:175
"My Potplants" (Mansfield) **164**:268
"My prishli" (Gumilev) **60**:280
"My Pushkin" (Tsvetaeva)
See "Moj Puškin"
"My Quiet Song" (Lasker-Schueler)
See "Mein stilles Lied"
"My Readers" (Gumilev) **60**:263-4
"My Religion" (Unamuno)
See "Mi religión"
My Religion (Tolstoy)
See "V chiom moya vera"
"My Religious History" (Cary) **196**:218
My Remarkable Uncle, and Other Sketches (Leacock) **2**:378
My Reminiscences (Tagore) **53**:339
My Road (Tolstoy) **18**:371
"My Roomy" (Lardner) **2**:338; **14**:305, 318-20
"My Roses" (Nietzsche) **55**:390
"My Sad Self" (Ginsberg) **120**:39-40, 111, 128
"My School Days Are Over" (Fields) **80**:259
"My Side of the Matter" (Capote) **164**:108-10, 112
My Sister, Life (Pasternak) **188**:239
"My Sisters, O My Sisters" (Sarton) **120**:236, 261, 272-73, 289, 301, 318
"My Sixty-First Poem on the Moon" (Lindsay) **17**:241
My Son the Doctor (Sánchez)
See *M'hijo el dotor*
"My Son the Murderer" (Malamud) **129**:161-62, 165; **184**:280-81
"My Song" (Brooke) **2**:58
"My Songs" (Yosano)
See "Waga Uta"
"My Soul" (Roussel)
See "Mon âme"
"My Soul" (Södergran)
See "Min själ"
"My Spirit Sore From Marching" (Millay) **169**:268
"My Standpoint" (Mori Ogai)
See "Yo ga tachiba"
My Star Predominant (Knister) **56**:158-59, 165
My Story (Caine) **97**:2, 4-5, 12-13
My Story (Rinehart) **52**:300
My Struggle (Hitler)
See *Mein Kampf*
"My Subconscious" (Benchley) **55**:17
"My Suicide" (Pardo Bazán)
See "Mi suicidio"
"My Sunday at Home" (Kipling) **8**:192, 202, 204; **17**:207

"My Table" (Yeats) **11**:534-35; **18**:459
My Talks with Dean Spanley (Dunsany) **59**:22, 24, 26, 29
My Ten Years in a Quandary, and How They Grew (Benchley) **1**:77; **55**:5-6, 14, 18
"My Thanks to Freud" (Andreas-Salome) **56**:29
My Theory of Soul Atoms (Hartmann) **73**:111, 119
"My Translataphone" (Stockton) **47**:325, 328
"My Travelling Companion" (Gorky)
See "My Fellow-Traveller"
"My Uncle Daniel" (Cummings) **137**:9
My Uncle Dudley (Morris) **107**:90, 103-04, 123, 132-33, 151, 155, 202-03, 216
My Uncle Oswald (Dahl) **173**:10, 18-19
"My Universe" (Noguchi) **80**:379
My Universities (Gorky)
See *Moi universitety*
"My v tsentre goroda" (Olesha) **136**:158
"My Views on Anarchism" (Dagerman) **17**:93
"My Views on Chastity and Sutteeism" (Lu Hsun) **3**:296
"My Views on Religion" (Kerouac) **117**:270
"My Vocation" (Ginzburg) **156**:18, 32, 44, 73, 92
"My Voice" (Aleixandre)
See "Mi voz"
My Wayward Pardner; or, My Trials with Josiah, America, the Widow Bump, and Etcetery (Holley) **99**:309
My Wife Ethel (Runyon) **10**:436-37
My Wonder (Lasker-Schueler)
See *Meine Wunder*
"My Words Will Be There" (Lorde) **173**:142
"My Work on the Novel Cement" (Gladkov) **27**:93
My Year in a Log Cabin (Howells) **41**:253
"My Youngsters Don't Worry Me" (Guest) **95**:211
My Youth in Vienna (Schnitzler) **4**:401-02
"Mylo Jones's Wife" (Riley) **51**:300-01
Myricae (Pascoli) **45**:146, 148, 153-54, 156
Mys guron (Kuprin) **5**:303
Myself Bettina (Crothers) **19**:73
Myself When Young (Richardson) **4**:374-75
Myshkina dudochka (Remizov) **27**:349
Mysl (Andreyev) **3**:17
Le Mystère d'Alceste (Yourcenar) **193**:270, 283, 333
Le mystère de la chambre jaune (Leroux) **25**:255-58, 260
La mystère de la charité de Jeanne d'Arc (Péguy) **10**:404-05, 408-09, 412-13, 416
Le mystère des saints innocents (Péguy) **10**:405, 409, 412
Le mystère en pleine lumière (Barrès) **47**:67-8
Le Mystère laïc (Cocteau) **119**:105, 109
Mystères de Marseille (Zola) **6**:567
Mysterier (Hamsun) **2**:202-04, 206-08; **14**:221, 227-28, 235, 237, 245, 247-48; **49**:127, 131-35, 138, 142, 145-46, 153-55, 157, 159, 161-63, 167; **151**:231, 234, 238, 250-61
Mysteries (Hamsun)
See *Mysterier*
Mysteries Lyrical and Dramatic (Crowley) **7**:208
"Mysteriet" (Södergran) **31**:285, 294
"The Mysterious Case of My Friend Browne" (Hawthorne) **25**:246
"The Mysterious Chamber" (Twain) **6**:462
Mysterious Depths (Pabst) **127**:354
"The Mysterious Destruction of Mr. Ipple" (Bennett) **5**:46
The Mysterious Disappearance of the Young Marchioness of Loria (Donoso)
See *La misteriosa desaparición de la Marquesita de Loria*
"Mysterious Disappearances" (Bierce) **44**:14, 45
The Mysterious Island (Verne)
See *L'ile mystérieuse*
"The Mysterious Lily" (Ekelund)
See "Den hemliga liljan"
The Mysterious Mr. Sabin (Oppenheim) **45**:128, 132-35, 137
"The Mysterious Rabbit" (Remizov)
See "Tainstvennyi zaichik"
Mysterious Stories (Nervo)
See *Místicas*
"The Mysterious Stranger" (Twain)
See "No. 44, The Mysterious Stranger"
The Mysterious Stranger (Twain) **6**:460, 466, 486; **12**:432, 434, 436-37, 442, 449; **19**:387; **36**:361, 363-64, 378, 392, 399, 411; **48**:344; **59**:168, 170; **161**:223; **185**:226-338
"The 'Mysterious Stranger' Defense" (Post) **39**:344
Mysterious Stranger Manuscripts (Twain) **161**:236, 242
"Mysterium der Liebe" (Carossa) **48**:25
"Mystery" (Baker) **10**:26
"The Mystery" (Dunbar) **12**:105
"The Mystery" (Södergran)
See "Mysteriet"
"Mystery" (Sterling) **20**:380
Mystery and Manners: Occasional Prose (O'Connor) **132**:256, 258-59, 270-71, 273-76, 296-97, 319, 321-22, 324-26, 330-31
Mystery at Geneva (Macaulay) **7**:427; **44**:119, 125
The Mystery at the Blue Villa (Post) **39**:339, 343
The Mystery in Palace Gardens (Riddell) **40**:334-35
"A Mystery in the Lager" (Levi) **109**:320
"The Mystery of a Derelict" (Hodgson) **13**:237
The Mystery of Alcestis (Yourcenar)
See *Le Mystère d'Alceste*
The Mystery of Angelina Frood (Freeman) **21**:58-9, 62
The Mystery of Choice (Chambers) **41**:88, 90, 94, 102, 106, 113-14
"The Mystery of Dave Regan" (Lawson) **27**:131
The Mystery of Dr. Fu Manchu (Rohmer) **28**:276-77, 279-80, 288, 290, 293-94, 296, 298-99, 301
"A Mystery of Heroism" (Crane) **11**:163
"The Mystery of Hoo Marsh" (Freeman) **21**:57
"The Mystery of Justice" (Maeterlinck) **3**:326
Mystery of Mary Stuart (Lang) **16**:270
The Mystery of the Charity of Joan of Arc (Péguy)
See *La mystère de la charité de Jeanne d'Arc*
"The Mystery of the Four Husbands" (Leroux) **25**:260
The Mystery of the Hasty Arrow (Green) **63**:148, 150, 152-53
The Mystery of the Holy Innocents (Péguy)
See *Le mystère des saints innocents*
"The Mystery of the Paneled Room" (Rohmer) **28**:283
"The Mystery of the Poisoned Dish of Mushrooms" (Bramah) **72**:6
The Mystery of the Sea (Stoker) **144**:277
The Mystery of the Yellow Room (Leroux)
See *Le mystère de la chambre jaune*
The Mystery of Thirty-One New Inn (Freeman) **21**:43-5, 50-3, 56
"The Mystery of Witch-Face Mountain" (Murfree) **135**:209
Mystery on Happy Bones (Dent) **72**:31
"A Mystery Play" (Scott) **6**:395
"Mystery Story" (Nemerov) **124**:256
Mystery under the Sea (Dent) **72**:19
Mystery-Bouffe (Mayakovski)
See *Misteria-Buff*
"Mystic" (Lawrence) **93**:26
"Mystic and Cavalier" (Johnson) **19**:244-45
"Mystic Garden and Middling Beast" (Stevens) **45**:270
Mystic Trees (Field) **43**:155-56, 160-61, 169
"The Mystic Turned Radical" (Bourne) **16**:60
"The Mystical Milieu" (Teilhard de Chardin)
See "Le milieu mystique"
"Mysticism" (McTaggart) **105**:197
Mysticism at the Dawn of the Modern Age (Steiner)
See *Die Mystik im Aufgange des neuzeitlichen Geisteslebens und ihr Vehältnis zu modernen Weltschauung*
Mysticism East and West (Otto) **85**:314, 319, 324, 327
Mysticism in Relation to the Modern World-Conception (Steiner) **13**:445
"Le Mysticisme" (Bataille) **155**:93, 106-7, 114
"Le mysticisme bien tempéré" (Gourmont) **17**:126
Mystics of the Renaissance and Their Relation to Modern Thought (Steiner) **13**:436
"The Mystic's Prayer" (Sharp) **39**:394
Die Mystik im Aufgange des neuzeitlichen Geisteslebens und ihr Vehältnis zu modernen Weltschauung (Steiner) **13**:441, 448
"Myten om människorna" (Lagerkvist) **144**:200-201, 207, 214-15
"Myten som Kunstform" (Jensen) **41**:309
"The Myth" (Muir) **87**:167, 276
"Myth" (Pavese)
See "Mito"
Myth and Metaphor: Selected Essays, 1974-1980 (Frye) **165**:161-62, 188-89, 191-92, 197, 224, 226, 237, 256, 260
"Myth & Ritual" (Nemerov) **124**:304
"Myth in the Narrative" (Calvino) **183**:129
"Myth of America" (Crane) **80**:85
"The Myth of Mankind" (Lagerkvist)
See "Myten om människorna"
A Myth of Shakespeare (Williams) **1**:518
The Myth of the Birth of the Hero (Rank)
See *Der Mythus von der Geburt des Heldens*
Myth of the Blaze (Oppen) **107**:306, 335
The Myth of the State (Cassirer) **61**:62, 65-6, 69-70, 110, 112, 114, 117, 119
Myth, Ritual, and Religion (Lang) **16**:260-61
"Myth Today" (Barthes) **135**:133
The Mythic Image (Campbell) **140**:11-12, 22-24, 82, 113, 135
"The Mythical Journey" (Muir) **87**:208
Mythical Thought (Cassirer)
See *Philosophie der symbolischen Formen*
"Die mythische Erbschaft der Dichtung" (Broch) **20**:69
"Mythogenesis" (Campbell) **140**:32
Mythologies (Barthes) **135**:112, 114-15, 117, 119, 127-29, 132-33, 136, 151, 163-65, 169, 177, 182, 184
Mythologies (Yeats) **31**:418
"The Mythologization of Reality" (Schulz)
See "Mityzacja rzeczywistości"
Mythology and Folk-Tales of the North American Indians (Boas) **56**:81
"Mythos" (van Ostaijen) **33**:418-19
Myths to Live By (Campbell) **140**:52, 54, 75, 80-81, 87, 90, 101, 134-37
"Mythus und Religion in Wundts Völkerpsychologie" (Otto) **85**:314
Der Mythus von der Geburt des Heldens (Rank) **115**:246, 262, 301, 306, 335
"Na arca" (Machado de Assis) **10**:291
Na bolshoi doroge (Chekhov) **31**:80
"Na civiluku" (Popa) **167**:152, 154
Na dne (Gorky) **8**:70-1, 78-9, 81, 88, 92
Na Drini cuprija (Andrić) **135**:4, 7-8, 14-16, 33, 43, 46, 52, 77, 79-81, 83, 86-87, 89, 93, 97
Na drogach duszy (Przybyszewski) **36**:290
"Na drugi dan Božića" (Andrić) **135**:84, 86, 89
"Na Kamennyx otrogax Pierii" (Mandelstam) **6**:267
"Na kraju" (Popa) **167**:155
"Na krasnom kone" (Tsvetaeva) **7**:560-62, 568; **35**:386, 390-91, 404, 410-11, 415-16

Na kulichkakh (Zamyatin) **8**:546, 551, 557-58; **37**:427, 430-31
"Na mesecini" (Popa) **167**:155
"Na plotakh" (Gorky) **8**:68, 80, 85
"Na pocetku" (Popa) **167**:155
Na polu chwały (Sienkiewicz) **3**:427
"Na rynke" (Zabolotsky) **52**:371, 375, 377-78
"Na střes nom sude" (Shestov) **56**:277
"Na suncu" (Popa) **167**:155
"Na večernem asfal'te" (Bryusov) **10**:92
Na vesakh Iova (Shestov) **56**:248, 258, 276-80
"Na volchey sadke" (Chekhov) **96**:33
"Na zare tumannoy yunosti" (Platonov) **14**:422, 425
Naamioita (Leino) **24**:371
"Nabeg" (Tolstoy) **4**:445, 474; **11**:464; **79**:445; **173**:280
Nabokov's Dozen (Nabokov) **108**:207
The Nabokov-Wilson Letters (Nabokov) **108**:123
"Naboth's Vineyard" (Benson) **27**:17
"Naboth's Vineyard" (Post) **39**:339
Naboth's Vineyard (Somerville & Ross) **51**:329, 338, 343, 351, 360-61, 370-72
Načalo konca (Aldanov) **23**:17, 22-3
"Nach dem Ball" (Liliencron) **18**:208
"Nach der Lese" (George) **14**:210
"Nach einem Flug" (Frisch) **121**:290
Nachala i kontsy (Shestov) **56**:248, 260
"Nachal'nik konzapasa" (Babel) **2**:27; **13**:21; **171**:21, 38, 73
"Nachgelassene Gedichte" (Borchert) **5**:109
Nachla (Weiss) **152**:297
Nachlass (Merleau-Ponty) **156**:174
Nachlass (Schoenberg) **75**:331-33
Nachlaß-Bibliothek (Böll) **185**:165
"Nachmittag" (George) **14**:210
"Ein Nachmittag" (Heym) **9**:149
"Die Nacht" (Heym) **9**:142
"Die Nacht" (Trakl) **5**:457
Die Nacht (Kandinsky) **92**:38
"Die Nacht, die Nacht ist still und mild" (Raabe) **45**:188
Nachtasyl (Gorky) **8**:71
"Nächte" (Schwitters) **95**:296
"Nächte" (Toller) **10**:491
Die Nachte der Tino von Baghdad (Lasker-Schueler) **57**:327
"Nachtergebung" (Trakl) **5**:457
Nachträge aus Hampstead (Canetti) **157**:96
Nachts (Kraus) **5**:291
"Nachts schlafen die Ratten doch" (Borchert) **5**:109
Nachts unter der steinernen Brücke (Perutz) **60**:370
"Naciemto Última" (Aleixandre) **113**:47
"Nacimiento de Cristo" (García Lorca) **49**:94; **181**:28; **197**:185, 191, 193, 195-97, 251, 264-68
Nacimiento último (Aleixandre) **113**:7, 19, 47, 49
"Nad ovragom" (Pilnyak) **23**:211, 213
Nada menos que todo un hombre (Unamuno) **2**:564; **9**:511, 515, 517-19; **148**:317, 319-20
Nada the Lily (Haggard) **11**:241, 246, 257
"Nadadora sumergida" (García Lorca) **197**:229
"La nadería de la personalidad" (Borges) **109**:14, 85-6, 88, 147, 150
"Nadie" (Aleixandre) **113**:16, 26-7
Nadobnisie i koczkodany (Witkiewicz) **8**:513
Nagelaten gedichten (van Ostaijen) **33**:414, 416, 418
"Die Nähe" (Morgenstern) **8**:306-07
Naissance de l'Odyssée (Giono) **124**:41-2, 69, 90-1, 96, 99-100, 102, 119-22
La naissance du jour (Colette) **5**:164-66; **16**:125, 129, 133
"La Naissance du Poete" (Jammes) **75**:113
"Naive Song to the Wife" (Radnóti) **16**:416
Naivedya (Tagore) **3**:491; **53**:341
"The Naivete of Verdi" (Berlin) **105**:139
Najogólniejsze ideały zyciowe (Prus) **48**:166
Naked (Pirandello)
See *Vestire gli ignudi*
Naked Author (di Donato) **159**:186-89, 196, 205
The Naked Beast at Heaven's Gate (Bataille)
See *Madame Edwarda*
Naked Earth (Chang) **184**:106
"The Naked Infinity" (Jiménez) **183**:288
Naked Life (Pirandello)
See *La vita nuda*
Naked Lunch (Burroughs) **121**:113-27, 131, 133-35, 147, 154-61, 173-74, 181
Naked Masks (Pirandello)
See *Maschere nude*
"Naked Nude" (Malamud) **129**:80, 82, 151-52; **184**:164, 171, 185-88, 200-201, 237, 243
Naked on Roller Skates (Bodenheim) **44**:72-4
The Naked Streets (Pratolini)
See *Il quartiere*
"A Naked Town" (Herbert) **168**:45
The Naked Year (Pilnyak)
See *Goly god*
"Nakhes fun kinder" (Aleichem) **35**:307
"Nakhutore" (Bunin) **6**:58
Nakimushi kozō (Hayashi) **27**:105
"Nam Bok the Unveracious" (London) **9**:254, 274
"The Name" (Pavese) **3**:340
"The name acquired from the names" (Jiménez)
See "El nombre conseguido de los nombres"
"The Name and Nature of Poetry" (Housman) **1**:356; **10**:243, 245, 258-59
"A Name in the Plaza" (Hearn) **9**:133
"The Name on the Stone" (Hearn) **9**:134
"The Name, the Nose" (Calvino)
See "Il nome il naso"
"The Name-Day" (Saki) **3**:374
"The Name-Day Party" (Chekhov) **3**:152, 169; **10**:107
"Nameless" (Obstfelder)
See "Navnløs"
"Nameless and Immortal" (Heidenstam) **5**:249
"The Nameless City" (Lovecraft) **22**:226, 232
"The Nameless Quest" (Crowley) **7**:204
The Nameless Thing (Post) **39**:347
A Nameless Tomb (Onetti)
See *Para una tumba sin nombre*
"The Nameless Wish" (Prado)
See "El deseo sin nombre"
"Names in a Tree" (Coffin) **95**:16
"Names—Especially Women's" (Gilman) **117**:120
"Namiki" (Shimazaki Toson) **5**:432
Nan Yar? (Ramana Maharshi) **84**:260
Nana (Zola) **1**:585, 587-88, 590, 596; **6**:563, 569; **21**:415-17, 428-29, 434-35, 449; **41**:414-15; 436, 439, 442-44, 447-49
"Nana del caballo grande" (García Lorca) **49**:114
"Las nanas infantiles" (García Lorca) **181**:118-19
"Nancy" (Wylie) **8**:521, 536
"Nancy Hanks" (Monroe) **12**:216
"The Nancy's Pride" (Carman) **7**:135
Naniwa Elegy (Mizoguchi)
See *Naniwa Hika*
Naniwa Hika (Mizoguchi) **72**:304-05, 314-15, 320, 325, 328
"Nanon" (Roussel) **20**:227
Não (Sá-Carneiro) **83**:405, 411
"The Nap" (de la Mare) **53**:17, 27, 33
A nap árnyéka (Moricz) **33**:243
"Napast" (Andrić) **135**:85
Năpastă (Caragiale) **76**:155, 157-59
"Napoleon" (Sternheim) **8**:368
Napoleon (Merezhkovsky) **29**:242
Napoleón en Chamartín (Pérez Galdós) **27**:287
Napoleon Fallen (Buchanan) **107**:53
The Napoleon of Notting Hill (Chesterton) **1**:178, 184, 187; **6**:102-05, 109; **64**:34-5, 38
"Napoleon Shave-Tail" (Wister) **21**:386
Napoli Millioniaria (de Filippo) **127**:267, 271-72, 276, 278, 280-81, 292-93
Når den ny vin blomstrer (Bjoernson) **37**:14, 19, 29
Når vi døde vågner (Ibsen) **2**:219, 222, 226-27, 229, 233-34, 236-37, 239; **8**:149, 152, 154-55; **16**:168
"Narcisse parle" (Valéry) **15**:450
"Narcissism" (Stevens) **45**:286
"Narcissism as Double Directionality" (Andreas-Salome) **56**:56
"Narcissus" (Carpenter) **88**:62
"Narcissus" (Flecker) **43**:188
Narcissus (Gide)
See *Le Traité du Narcisse*
Narcissus and Goldmund (Hesse)
See *Narziss und Goldmund*
"Narcissus Bay" (Welch) **22**:441, 456, 462
"The Narcissus Cantata" (Valéry) **4**:496-97
"Narcissus Speaks" (Valéry)
See "Narcisse parle"
Nārīr Mūlya (Chatterji) **13**:80-1
"Narky" (Rohmer) **28**:286, 296
"Narodnyj dom" (Zabolotsky) **52**:378
"Narodnyj dom II" (Zabolotsky) **52**:379
Der Narr in Christo, Emanuel Quint (Hauptmann) **4**:197-99, 201, 204
Narraciones (García Lorca) **7**:297
Narration (Stein) **1**:427; **48**:214, 221
"The Narrative" (Oppen) **107**:264
"A Narrative" (Oppen) **107**:260, 304, 324, 366
"Narrative Art and Magic" (Borges)
See "El arte narrativo y la magia"
The Narrative of Arthur Gordon Pym (Verne) **6**:501
Narrenweisheit; oder, Tod und Verkiarung des Jean-Jacques Rousseau (Feuchtwanger) **3**:182-83, 186
"The Narrow Door" (Mew) **8**:294, 296
"A Narrow Escape" (Merrill) **173**:232
The Narrow Place (Muir) **87**:167
The Narrows (Petry) **112**:295, 302-09, 311, 315, 328, 331, 356, 367-68, 370, 372, 389-92, 394-95
Narziss und Goldmund (Hesse) **196**:250, 298, 305
"Nascent" (Lawrence) **93**:44
"Nascer de Novo" (Drummond de Andrade) **139**:230
Die Nase des Michelangelo (Ball) **104**:4, 21, 25
"Nashedshij podkovu" (Mandelstam) **2**:405, 409; **6**:260-61, 266
"Nashtanir" (Tagore) **3**:499
"Nastoyashchee" (Khlebnikov) **20**:133, 144
"Nastuplenie" (Gumilev) **60**:282-4
"Nasturtiums" (Naidu) **80**:334
Natale in Casa Cupiello (de Filippo) **127**:267, 270, 280, 291, 293
"Natalie" (Bunin) **6**:56-7
Natalie Mann (Toomer) **172**:258, 282-85, 308-11
"Natasha" (Olesha) **136**:155, 182
Natasqua (Davis) **6**:152
Nathaniel Hawthorne and His Wife (Hawthorne) **25**:240
"Die Nation als Ideal und Wirklichkeit" (Musil) **12**:258
"The National Being" (Baker) **10**:15
The National Being: Some Thoughts on an Irish Polity (Baker) **10**:22-3
"National Bulletin" (Bryan) **99**:147
National Episodes (Pérez Galdós)
See *Episodios nacionales*
"National Legislative Program" (Bryan) **99**:147
"The National Letters" (Mencken) **13**:362, 364, 393-94
"The National Policy" (Drummond) **25**:142, 153
"National Polity" (Nishida) **83**:333
"The National Question and Autonomy" (Luxemburg) **63**:202, 225

"The National Question and Social Democracy" (Stalin) **92**:183
"National Self-sufficiency" (Keynes) **64**:221, 244
The National Value of Art (Aurobindo) **63**:28-9
"National Winter Garden" (Crane) **5**:195; **80**:115
"Die Nationale Kurzwelle" (Roth) **33**:336
"Nationale Musik" (Schoenberg) **75**:333
"Nationalism: Past Neglect and Present Power" (Berlin) **105**:22, 38
The Nationalization of Health (Ellis) **14**:110, 116
The Nationalizing of Business, 1878-1898 (Tarbell) **40**:428-29, 438
"National-Mindedness and International-Mindedness" (Mead) **89**:104
"Native Country" (Tolstoy) **18**:377
"Native Dada" (Lardner) **2**:339
Native Labour in South Africa (Plaatje) **73**:221
"The Native Land" (Bachmann) **192**:65
"The Native Land" (Blok) **5**:94-5
"Native Land" (Heidenstam) **5**:249
The Native Land of the Cranes (Prishvin)
See *Crane Homeland*
Native Life in South Africa (Plaatje) **73**:221, 225-27, 231, 234
"Native of Winby" (Jewett) **22**:122, 136
"Native Poetry of New Spain" (Reyes) **33**:318
Native Son (Wright) **136**:223, 226, 229-36, 238, 241-45, 247-53, 259, 261-62, 266-67, 272, 274-78, 284, 304-10, 312-13, 316, 318, 323-30, 336; **180**:210-330
Natsuksa (Shimazaki Toson) **5**:439
"Natten" (Obstfelder) **23**:177
Nattens lekar (Dagerman) **17**:88-94
"Nätter" (Strindberg) **8**:419
"Nätternas" (Strindberg) **8**:419
"Natura e storia nel romanzo" (Calvino) **183**:94, 101, 103
The Natural (Malamud) **129**:60, 64, 66, 68, 71-5, 84-5, 87-8, 95-6, 116-18, 120-21, 129-30, 133, 135, 137-38, 142, 175, 182-83, 187, 192, 195, 210-11, 213, 216, 218; **184**:159, 161-62, 170-72, 174, 177, 180-82, 184, 188-89, 191, 197-99, 221, 223-25, 236, 244, 265-66, 268, 277, 300-301
Natural History (Renard)
See *Histoires naturelles*
The Natural History of Creation (Haeckel)
See *Natürliche Schöpfungs-geschichte*
"A Natural History of the Dead" (Hemingway) **115**:189
The Natural History of the Ten Commandments (Seton) **31**:272, 276
"Natural Law" (Holmes) **77**:243
"A Natural Obstacle" (Strindberg) **8**:407
Natural Right and History (Strauss) **141**:230, 233, 235, 253, 256, 264-65, 278, 280, 291, 294, 297-99, 302-3, 307, 327, 330-31
"Natural Science and Historical Science" (Nishida)
See "Shizenkagaku to rekishigaku"
"Natural Selection in Literature" (Adams) **80**:12
"Natural Selection in Morals" (Alexander) **77**:66
Natural Stories (Levi)
See *Storie naturali*
"Natural Theology" (Lang) **16**:256
"Naturaleza" (Mistral) **2**:478
Naturalism and Religion (Otto)
See *Naturalistische und religiöse Weltansicht*
Naturalism in England (Brandes) **11**:62, 72
El naturalismo (Pardo Bazán) **189**:227
"The Naturalist at Law" (Freeman) **21**:58
The Naturalist in La Plata (Hudson) **29**:134, 139-40, 144, 154
A Naturalist of Souls (Bradford) **36**:53, 56, 65
Naturalistische und religiöse Weltansicht (Otto) **85**:315
"Nature" (Mistral)
See "Naturaleza"
Nature (Rozanov) **104**:338
"The Nature and Aim of Fiction" (O'Connor) **132**:325
"The Nature and Aims of a Philosophy of History" (Collingwood) **67**:120, 156
"The Nature and Reality of Objects of Perception" (Moore) **89**:241
"The Nature and Tragedy of Culture" (Simmel)
See "On the Concept and Tragedy of Culture"
Nature in Downland (Hudson) **29**:136, 146-47, 161
"Nature in the Raw" (Adams) **56**:8, 22
"The Nature of a Crime" (Ford) **15**:91
The Nature of a Crime (Ford) **172**:64-66, 68
The Nature of Existence (McTaggart) **105**:168, 175, 181, 188-89, 197, 201
"The Nature of Gothic" (Ruskin) **63**:290
"The Nature of Man" (Grieg)
See "Den menneskelige natur"
The Nature of Peace and the Terms of Its Perpetuation (Veblen) **31**:342-43, 346, 357-58, 362
The Nature of the Judicial Process (Cardozo) **65**:21-2, 29, 32, 35, 39, 41, 43-5
"The Nature of the Task" (Nemerov) **124**:233-34
Nature Poems, and Others (Davies) **5**:199-200, 207, 209
"Nature Theater" (Trakl)
See "Naturtheater"
"Nature's Place in Canadian Culture" (Lewis) **2**:399
"Nature's Questioning" (Hardy) **53**:81; **143**:184-88, 200
Natürliche Schöpfungs-geschichte (Haeckel) **83**:126, 131, 138, 147
"Naturtheater" (Trakl) **5**:462
"Náufragas" (Pardo Bazán) **189**:235-36, 317, 319, 321
Le naufrage (Coppee) **25**:126
Les naufragés du "Jonathan" (Verne) **6**:497
The Naulahka (Kipling) **8**:185; **17**:203, 205
La nausée (Vian) **9**:536
"Navacerrada, abril" (Salinas) **17**:364
Navajātak (Tagore) **3**:488-89; **53**:336
The Naval War of 1812 (Roosevelt)
See *History of the Naval War of 1812*
La nave (D'Annunzio) **6**:137, 141-42; **40**:9, 11-12, 19
"Navek" (Balmont) **11**:40
"The Navel" (Remizov)
See "Pupochek"
The Navel (Anouilh)
See *Le nombril*
"La navidad" (Quiroga) **20**:213
Navidad (Martinez Sierra and Martinez Sierra) **6**:282, 287-88
"Navidad en el Hudson" (García Lorca) **197**:184, 191-93, 196-97, 205, 226-27, 251, 258, 264-69, 283
"Le navire" (Verhaeren) **12**:475
"Navnløs" (Obstfelder) **23**:175, 177
Navodnenie (Zamyatin) **8**:544-45, 548, 553-54, 558; **37**:424, 431
"Naya vivah" (Premchand) **21**:292-93
The Nazarene (Asch)
See *Der man vun Notzeres*
Nazareth (Housman) **7**:359
Nazarín (Pérez Galdós) **27**:250, 283
Nb Notizbücher (Weiss) **152**:295, 297, 299
"Ne me tangito" (Mew) **8**:299
Ne nous énervons pas (Himes) **139**:253, 259-61, 283, 300, 302, 321-22
"Ne pas manger de raisin sans le laver" (Péret) **20**:201
"Ne sam borec" (Vazov) **25**:455
"Ne za mnoj" (Hippius) **9**:167
"Neanderthal" (Masters) **25**:290
"Neap-tide" (Swinburne) **36**:340, 344
"Near a Church" (Agee) **180**:5, 33, 36
The Near and the Far (Myers) **59**:123-4, 126, 128-34, 136, 143, 150
"Near Lanivet, 1872" (Hardy) **53**:79
"Near the Old People's Home" (Nemerov) **124**:258
"A Near View of the Sierra" (Muir) **28**:258
"Near White" (Cullen) **37**:152
"Near-White" (McKay) **41**:329
"Die Nebel" (Carossa) **48**:24
Nebeneinander (Kaiser) **9**:174-75, 181, 191
"Nebeski prsten" (Popa) **167**:157-58
Nebesnye slova (Hippius) **9**:162-63
Nebesye verblyuzhata (Guro) **56**:133, 135, 146
Nebo goluboe (Sologub) **9**:444
"Nebraskans' Bitter Fight for Life" (Crane) **11**:159
"Nebulosa thulé" (Lugones) **15**:285
The Necessary Angel: Essays on Reality and the Imagination (Stevens) **3**:456; **12**:386; **45**:279-80, 285-90, 296, 298, 331, 337, 339, 347, 353
"The Necessary Knocking on the Door" (Petry) **112**:299-300
Les nécessités de la vie et les conséquences des rêves (Éluard) **7**:253, 256; **41**:153
The Necessity of Belief (Gill) **85**:54, 56, 68, 75, 80-2
"The Necessity of Communism" (Murry) **16**:338, 348-49
Nechestivye rasskazy (Zamyatin) **37**:432
"Neck" (Dahl) **173**:12
The Necklace of Stars (Benavente)
See *El collar de estrellas*
Necrophilia (Crowley) **7**:211
"Nedda" (Verga) **3**:541, 546-47
Nedda (Jovine) **79**:46
Nederlaget: Et skuespill om Pariser-komunen (Grieg) **10**:207, 209
"Ned's Psalm of Life for the Negro" (Cotter) **28**:42
"Need: A Chorale for Black Women's Voices" (Lorde) **173**:50
"The Need for a Recovery of Philosophy" (Dewey) **95**:34
"The Need for Fear" (Levi) **109**:286
"A Need for Gardens" (Brautigan) **133**:3
The Need for Roots (Weil)
See *L'enracinement*
Needle's Eye (Oppen)
See *Seascape: Needle's Eye*
"Needs Must" (Strindberg) **21**:367
Der Neffe des Herren Bezenval (Spitteler) **12**:349, 351
"Nég Créol" (Chopin) **5**:145; **14**:61, 82; **127**:167
"Negation" (Stevens) **45**:297
Negative Dialectics (Adorno)
See *Negative Dialektik*
Negative Dialektik (Adorno) **111**:6, 9, 52-3, 94-5, 98, 100, 158, 177, 180, 182, 187-91, 196
"Negative Gravity" (Stockton)
See "A Tale of Negative Gravity"
"Negative Information" (Douglas) **40**:90
"A Neglected Argument for the Reality of God" (Peirce) **81**:172,199,247,259,274,349-50,354-6
"Negotium Perambulans" (Benson) **27**:9, 13, 16, 19
Les nègres: Clownerie (Genet) **128**:108-09, 111, 113-14, 131-32, 136-38, 140, 143, 145-46, 153, 155, 166-76, 195
The Negro (Du Bois) **169**:160
Negro Americans, What Now? (Johnson) **175**:205
"The Negro and Hegel" (Fanon) **188**:30
The Negro and His Music (Locke) **43**:245-46
"The Negro and Language" (Fanon) **188**:3, 80
"The Negro and Psychopathology" (Fanon) **188**:55-6, 81

"The Negro and the New Deal" (Du Bois) **169**:95
"Negro Contributions to America" (Locke) **43**:235
"The Negro Emergent" (Toomer) **172**:318, 320
"The Negro Group" (Locke) **43**:239, 241
The Negro in America (Locke) **43**:235, 239
"The Negro in the Low-Country" (Heyward) **59**:88
"Negro Love Song" (Cotter) **28**:42
"A Negro Love Song" (Dunbar) **12**:122, 124, 126
"Negro Martyrs Are Needed" (Himes) **139**:324
Negro Poems (Tzara) **168**:289
"The Negro Question" (Bryan) **99**:117
The Negro Question (Cable) **4**:30-1
"Negro songs" (Tzara) **168**:305
Negro Tales (Cotter) **28**:47
"The Negro Woman" (Cotter) **28**:42
"The Negro Writer and His Roots" (Hansberry) **192**:318
"A Negro Writer to His Critics" (McKay) **41**:336
The Negroes in America (McKay) **41**:331-32, 335
"The Negro's Contribution to American Culture" (Locke) **43**:239
"The Negro's Educational Creed" (Cotter) **28**:43
"The Negro's Ten Commandments" (Cotter) **28**:44
"The Negro's Tragedy" (McKay) **41**:318
"La neige" (Verhaeren) **12**:466
"Neighbor Rosicky" (Cather) **152**:89
Neighborhood Stories (Gale) **7**:281, 283
"Neighbors" (Chekhov) **163**:78, 109, 130-31
"The Neighbor's Landmark" (Jewett) **22**:124, 140
"Neighbour Rosicky" (Cather) **11**:98; **132**:136
Neighbours (Gale) **7**:283
"The Neighbour's Children" (Webb) **24**:473
"Neistovye rěci" (Shestov) **56**:278
Neizdannaja proza (Bryusov) **10**:85
"Neko" (Hagiwara) **60**:309, 313
"Neko no shigai" (Hagiwara) **60**:300-1, 315
"Nekrasivaya devochka" (Zabolotsky) **52**:367
"Nel regno della pietra" (Deledda) **23**:41
"Nell" (Buchanan) **107**:25
"Nell' annuale della fondazione di Roma" (Carducci) **32**:106
Nell' assenza di Lanciotto (D'Annunzio) **6**:133
"Nella sera della domenica di Pasqua" (Saba) **33**:369, 372
Nell'Anno Mille e schemi di altri drammi (Pascoli) **45**:146-49
"Nelly Trim" (Warner) **131**:311
"Nelse Hatton's Revenge" (Dunbar) **12**:109, 111
"Nelse Hatton's Vengeance" (Dunbar)
See "Nelse Hatton's Revenge"
"Nelson Redline" (Hammett) **187**:89
"Nelson's Year" (Noyes) **7**:513
Nem mondhatom El Senkinek (Karinthy) **47**:268
"Nem tudhatom" (Radnóti) **16**:410, 416
"Nemesis" (Lawrence) **93**:24
Némésis (Bourget) **12**:69
Nemesis (Thomas) **97**:138, 140
"The Nemesis of Fire" (Blackwood) **5**:71, 73-4, 78
The Nemesis of Mediocrity (Cram) **45**:16, 21
Nemiri (Andrić) **135**:87-88
"Nemirna godina" (Andrić) **135**:86
"Neobkhodimost" (Korolenko) **22**:175
Neologismos y americanismos (Palma) **29**:260
Nepālī Śākuntala (Devkota) **23**:48, 50-2
Nepocin-polje (Popa) **167**:156, 171
"Neputevyj" (Zamyatin) **8**:552
"Nerina" (Heyse) **8**:121
"Neroždënnaja povest" (Pilnyak) **23**:212
Nerto (Mistral) **51**:131-32, 136-39, 142, 148, 152, 156
"Nerval, le nyctalope" (Daumal) **14**:96
"Nervazón de angustia" (Vallejo) **56**:294
The Nerve Meter (Artaud)
See *Le pèse-nerfs*
Nervometer (Artaud)
See *Le pèse-nerfs*
"Nervous" (Walser) **18**:437
"A Nervous Breakdown" (Chekhov)
See "Pripadok"
The Nervous Character (Adler)
See *Über den nervösen Charakter*
"Nervous Gust of Anguish" (Vallejo)
See "Nervazón de angustia"
"The Nervous People" (Zoshchenko) **15**:504
"Nervus Erotis" (Lasker-Schueler) **57**:302, 328
Neshomeh yesere (Cahan) **71**:42-43
"Nest Feathers" (Fitzgerald)
See "Head and Shoulders"
"A Nest of Hepaticas" (Scott) **6**:393, 397
A Nest of Simple Folk (O'Faolain) **143**:230, 269
"A Nest of Singing Birds" (de la Mare) **53**:26
"Nestus Gurley" (Jarrell) **177**:152, 173
"A Net to Snare the Moonlight" (Lindsay) **17**:224
"Net vozrata" (Hippius) **9**:161
The Nether World (Gissing) **3**:222-25, 227-29, 231-36; **24**:220-21, 230, 233, 240, 242-43, 248; **47**:103, 114, 134
Netherwood (White) **176**:225, 261
Nets (Kuzmin)
See *Seti*
Nets to Catch the Wind (Wylie) **8**:521-22, 527, 532, 534, 537
Nettles (Lawrence) **93**:20
"Der neue Advokat" (Kafka) **53**:225
Neue Gedichte (Huch) **13**:253
Neue Gedichte (Rilke) **1**:409-11, 415-16, 418-20, 422; **6**:358-59, 364, 368; **19**:303-07; **195**:163, 165, 183, 193, 195, 202, 226-31, 233-34, 236, 243-45, 250, 257, 264, 266, 285-88, 292-96, 298-99, 303-04, 315-16, 320, 328, 331
"Der Neue Heilige" (Huch) **13**:249
Neue Novellen (Heyse) **8**:113
Neue politische und literarische Schriften (Böll) **185**:58
Das Neue Reich (George) **2**:148-49, 152, 154; **14**:194, 196, 202-04, 207, 212
"Neue Romantik" (Mann) **9**:331
Der Neuen Gedichte Anderer Teil (Rilke) **1**:419
"Neumestnye rifmy" (Hippius) **9**:164
Neurosis and Human Growth (Horney) **71**:227, 235, 239, 245, 251, 257, 261, 265, 267, 269
The Neurotic Constitution (Adler)
See *Über den nervösen Charakter*
The Neurotic Personality of Our Time (Horney) **71**:220, 226, 257-262
"The Neurotic's Conception of the World" (Adler) **61**:15
"Neutral Tones" (Hardy) **4**:152, 164; **10**:233; **18**:113; **53**:76, 116-17
Neuyomny Buben (Remizov) **27**:331, 333, 342
"Nevada Gas" (Chandler) **7**:183; **179**:122-23, 125, 128, 174
"Nevada's Dead Towns" (Muir) **28**:250
"Nevasta" (Rebreanu) **28**:273
"Der Neve Roman von d'Annunzio" (Hofmannsthal) **11**:307
"Never About You" (Herbert) **168**:74
"Never Been so Lonesome" (Williams) **81**:428
Never Despair (Reymont)
See *Nil desperandum*
Never Ending Love (Chang)
See *Buliao qing*
Never Fail Blake (Stringer)
See *The Shadow*
Never Give a Sucker an Even Break (Fields) **80**:226, 232, 244
Never Must You Ask Me (Ginzburg)
See *Mai devi domandarmi*
Never No More (O'Faolain) **143**:272
Never Say Never Again (Fleming) **193**:235
"Never Say Die" (Marquis) **7**:437
Never Say Die (Sturges) **48**:312
"Never to Dream of Spiders" (Lorde) **173**:140-41
"Nevesta" (Chekhov) **3**:160-61, 166; **10**:108; **31**:88; **55**:66; **163**:13
"Nevicata" (Carducci) **32**:102
Nevicata (Pascoli) **45**:154
"Nevol'nich'ja" (Gumilev) **60**:278
"Nevolnichy bereq" (Khlebnikov) **20**:133
The New Abelard (Buchanan) **107**:86-7
"The New Accelerator" (Wells) **12**:488, 511; **19**:434, 437
"The New Administration" (Post) **39**:343
"The New Advocate" (Kafka)
See "Der neue Advokat"
The New American Credo (Nathan) **18**:316
New and Selected Essays (Nemerov) **124**:269, 319
New and Selected Poems (Nemerov) **124**:150-51, 155-57, 170-72, 174, 195, 205-6, 245, 248
The New Art of Projecting Concentrated Non-Dispersive Energy through the Natural Media (Tesla) **88**:332
"The New Baby in Our Home" (Guest) **95**:211
"A New Ballad of Tannhäuser" (Davidson) **24**:163, 175
New Ballads (Davidson) **24**:163, 165, 176
"The New Beginning" (Abbey) **160**:35
"The New Biography" (Woolf) **20**:423; **43**:401; **56**:381
New Blood (Thomas) **97**:140
"The New Boots" (Hardy) **53**:117
The New Born (Tagore)
See *Navajātak*
"The New Boy" (Middleton) **56**:175-76, 182
"New Bridge" (Gogarty) **15**:108
New Cautionary Tales (Belloc) **7**:42; **18**:40
The New Colony (Pirandello)
See *La nuova colonia*
New Comedies (Gregory) **176**:20-21, 33
New Comedies: The Bogie Men. The Full Moon. Coats. Damer's Gold. MacDonough's Wife (Gregory) **1**:332
The New Cook (Ince) **89**:9
New Cosmopolis (Huneker) **65**:168, 170
"A New Counterblast" (Higginson) **36**:175
"The New Country House" (Chekhov)
See "Novaja doca"
"The New Dacha" (Chekhov)
See "Novaja doca"
"The New Dawn" (Middleton) **56**:174
"A New Defense of Poetry" (Woodberry) **73**:362, 378
The New Deliverance (Witkiewicz)
See *Nowe wyzwolenie*
A New Dictionary of Quotations (Mencken) **13**:387
"New Dresses" (Mansfield) **39**:329; **164**:251
"The New Dynasty" (Twain) **36**:387
New Earth (Hamsun) **14**:221-22
"New Elements" (Peirce) **81**:199
New Elements of Geometry Based on Benjamin Peirce's Work & Teachings (Peirce) **81**:198
The New Elements of Mathematics by Charles S. Peirce (Peirce) **81**:206
The New Empire (Adams) **80**:12, 38, 46, 64
"The New Endymion" (Gosse) **28**:139
"New England" (Robinson) **101**:111, 138, 143-48, 150-54, 156
"New England Fallen" (Lovecraft) **4**:265
A New England Nun, and Other Stories (Freeman) **9**:60, 63, 65, 67, 70, 74
"New England Victorian Episodes" (McAlmon) **97**:101
"The New Englander" (Anderson) **1**:36
A New English Dictionary on Historical Principles (Murray) **117**:276-77, 280, 282-83, 287-88

New Evidence in Regard to the Instability of Human Types (Boas) **56**:82
New Faces of 1962 (Shepherd) **177**:311
The New Flag (Fuller) **103**:69, 85, 106
The New Freedom (Wilson) **79**:487
New Fruits of the Earth (Gide) **12**:166
"The New Gentry" (Baring-Gould) **88**:22
"New Georgia" (Jarrell) **177**:127, 195
The New Ghetto (Herzl) **36**:133-34, 136
"The New Ghost" (Jarrell) **177**:177
"The New God: A Miracle" (Abercrombie) **141**:6, 10, 19-20
The New Golden Bough (Frazer) **32**:207, 216, 234
New Ground (Hamsun)
See *Ny jord*
New Grub Street (Gissing) **3**:222-25, 227-29, 231-36; **24**:215-16, 220, 222-24, 227-28, 230-31, 233-37, 243-45, 247; **47**:102-12, 114, 116, 120-25, 127, 129-31, 133-39, 141-44
The New Hamlet (Dazai Osamu)
See *Shin Hamuretto*
New Harlequinade (Baroja)
See *Nuevo tablado de Arlequín*
"New Heaven and Earth" (Lawrence) **2**:350; **33**:181-82; **93**:4, 19, 109
New Himmerland Stories (Jensen) **41**:306, 308
"The New Hope" (Sharp) **39**:380
New Hope for Britain (Stapledon) **22**:314, 322
The New Humpty Dumpty (Ford) **15**:93; **172**:10
The New Idealism (Sinclair) **11**:418
"A New Kind of Prayer" (Childress) **116**:34
"New Koide Road" (Hagiwara)
See "Koide shidō"
New Lamps for Old (Aurobindo) **63**:26
The New Land (Vazov)
See *Nova zemya*
New Leaf Mills (Howells) **7**:370; **17**:176, 178, 184
The New Leviathan (Collingwood) **67**:124, 136-39, 142, 151-53, 156-57, 165, 167, 184, 195
New Liberties for Old (Becker) **63**:64, 72-3
New Life (Hrabal)
See *Vita Nuova*
A New Life (Malamud) **129**:60, 64, 67, 70-2, 74-5, 114, 116-20, 122, 124, 142-45, 147-48, 183-84, 189, 193, 197; **184**:158-60, 162, 164-65, 168-73, 175, 177, 179-80, 184, 189, 198, 203-4, 206, 214, 218, 221-24, 226, 236, 259, 276, 299, 301
A New Life (Shimazaki Toson)
See *Shinsei*
The New Literary Criticism (Lin) **149**:343, 346
"New Love" (Middleton) **56**:189
"The New Love" (Parker) **143**:317
The New Machiavelli (Wells) **6**:525-26, 529, 537, 539, 552; **12**:492
"The New Marriage" (Premchand)
See "Naya vivah"
"The New Medusa" (Lee-Hamilton) **22**:187-88
The New Medusa, and Other Poems (Lee-Hamilton) **22**:186-89, 192-93
"A New Melody" (Peretz) **16**:397
The New Middle Ages (Berdyaev) **67**:30, 32-4
The New Minnesinger (Field) **43**:155-56, 164, 170, 178, 182
"The New Mirror" (Petry) **112**:297, 299, 328, 331
"The New Mistress" (Housman) **10**:251-52
New Moon (Radnóti)
See *Újhold*
"The New Nationalism" (Roosevelt) **69**:246-48
The New Negro (Locke) **43**:222-25, 229-30, 235, 242
"The New Note in Southern Literature" (Heyward) **59**:89
The New Old Nick of Hell's Bottom (Tammsaare)
See *Põrgupõhja uus Vanapagan*
"The New Painting" (Apollinaire) **51**:41
"The New Parishioner" (Jewett) **22**:117
A New Pattern for a Tired World (Bromfield) **11**:84
New People (Hippius)
See *Novye lyudi*
"New Pinions" (Stephens) **4**:420
"New Plays for Old" (Benchley) **55**:18, 22
New Poems (Bridges) **1**:132
New Poems (Davies) **5**:198-200, 208-09
New Poems (Heidenstam)
See *Nya dikter*
New Poems (Lawrence) **93**:6, 22, 28, 29, 43, 47, 67, 113
New Poems (Rilke)
See *Neue Gedichte*
New Poems (Thomas) **1**:466
New Poems (Thompson) **4**:434-35, 438
New Poems (Tynan) **3**:504
"New Poems and Adaptations" (Villa) **176**:105
New Poems: Eighty Songs at Eighty (Markham) **47**:292
"The New Poet" (Gurney) **33**:95, 98
"The New Poetry and Mr. A. E. Housman's Shropshire Lad" (Flecker) **43**:211
New Political and Literary Writings (Böll)
See *Neue politische und literarische Schriften*
"The New Psychology" (Dewey) **95**:58, 95, 98-9
"The New Railway" (Liliencron) **18**:207
"A New Refutation of Time" (Borges)
See "Nueva refutación del tiempo"
The New Revelation (Doyle) **7**:225
The New Revelations of Being (Artaud)
See *Les nouvelles révélations de l'être*
New Rhymes (Carducci)
See *Rime nuove*
"The New Romanticism" (Orage) **157**:249
The New Rome (Buchanan) **107**:23
The New Russia (Singer) **33**:386
"New Salem Hill" (Masters) **25**:302, 316
"The New Situation" (Anthony) **84**:21
"A New Song of Spring Gardens" (Dobson) **79**:2
The New Spirit (Ellis) **14**:102, 106, 108, 110, 114, 122-23, 131-35, 142
"The New Spirit and the Poets" (Apollinaire)
See "L'esprit nouveau et les poètes"
The New Spoon River (Masters) **2**:463, 472-73; **25**:294, 296-97, 299, 311, 313, 316
New Stories (Bergelson) **81**:23
New Strength (Rainis)
See *Jaunais spēks*
The New Suit (de Filippo) **127**:295
The New System (Bjoernson)
See *Det ny system*
"A New System of Alternating Current Motors and Transformers" (Tesla) **88**:268, 282, 296
The New Temple (Bojer)
See *Det nye tempel*
A New Testament (Anderson) **1**:35, 37, 56; **10**:45, 47; **24**:43; **123**:8-9
"The New Theatre and the Old" (Pirandello) **172**:156
"A New Theme" (Baker) **3**:2; **10**:21
"New Thoughts of Pascal or Thoughts of Hell" (Arenas) **191**:252
"New Traits of the New American" (Davis) **6**:154
"The New Trinity" (Markham) **47**:292
"New Verse" (Mandelstam) **6**:265
New Verse (Merezhkovsky) **29**:248
New Verses (Ady)
See *Új versek*
"The New Villa" (Chekhov)
See "Novaja doca"
New Ways in Psychoanalysis (Horney) **71**:208, 210, 219-220, 222, 224
New Wessex Edition (Hardy) **143**:104
"New Wine" (Fuller) **103**:108
"New Women" (Cary) **196**:207-09, 214
A New Wonderland (Baum) **132**:103
The New Word (Upward) **85**:376-7, 379-80, 385-7, 394, 399-400, 403-8
"New Words" (Orwell) **129**:249
"A New World" (Baker) **10**:27
The New World (Churchill) **113**:130
The New World (Jensen)
See *Den ny Verden*
The New World (Masters) **2**:470; **25**:300-01, 315
The New World and the New Book (Higginson) **36**:177
New World Lyrics and Ballads (Scott) **6**:386, 388, 390, 393, 395, 397
New Writings by Swinburne (Swinburne) **8**:439
"The New Year" (Remizov)
See "Novyi god"
"The New Year" (Thomas) **10**:454
"New Year Presents" (Palamas) **5**:386
"New Year's Bells" (Dreiser)
See "When the Old Century Was New"
"New Year's Chimes" (Thompson) **4**:438
"New Year's Day" (Davidson) **24**:162
"New Year's Day" (Wharton) **9**:550; **129**:350, 363
"New Year's Eve" (Gurney) **33**:93
"New Year's Eve" (Lawrence) **93**:18
"A New Year's Eve" (Swinburne) **36**:347
"New Year's Eve, 1913" (Bottomley) **107**:5
"New Year's Greetings" (Tsvetaeva)
See "Novogodnee"
"The New Year's Sacrifice" (Lu Hsun)
See "Zhufu"
"New York" (Baker) **10**:21
"New York as a Historic Town" (Matthews) **95**:257
"New York as a Literary Center" (Norris) **155**:338
"New York by Campfire Light" (Henry) **19**:174
"New York City" (Bodenheim) **44**:69
"New York City 1970" (Lorde) **173**:52
"New York City in 1979" (Acker) **191**:128
"The New York Gold Conspiracy" (Adams) **4**:18
"New York Harbor" (McAlmon) **97**:120, 122
The New York Hat (Griffith) **68**:226
New York Head Shop and Museum (Lorde) **173**:52-53, 73
"New York Lady" (Parker)
See "From the Diary of a New York Lady"
"New York Letter" (Matthews) **95**:269
New York Madness (Bodenheim) **44**:73
New York Nocturnes (Roberts) **8**:321
New York Nocturnes (Stringer) **37**:340
"New York: Office and Denunciation" (García Lorca)
See "Nueva York: Oficina y denuncia"
New York Quartet (Wharton)
See *Old New York*
"New York Sleepwalking" (McAlmon) **97**:100
"New York to Detroit" (Parker) **143**:286, 331
"A New Yorker a Hundred Years Hence" (Morley) **87**:128
"The New Zealander" (Mansfield) **164**:269
New Zrinyiad (Mikszath)
See *Uj Zrinyiász*
"Newcomer" (Okigbo) **171**:350
The Newer Ideals of Peace (Addams) **76**:7, 12, 22-3, 37, 84-5, 108
"Newer Shades and Shadows" (Mikszath)
See "Ujabb fény és árnyképek"
"A New-Fashioned Flavoring" (Montgomery) **51**:199-200
The Newly-Married Couple (Bjoernson)
See *De nygifte*
"Newman's Littlemore: A Few Addenda" (Guiney) **41**:220
"Newport and Rome" (Howe) **21**:106
"News" (Coleridge) **73**:12
"The News" (Vazov) **25**:454
"The News and the Weather" (Stevens) **45**:272, 281

"News for the Delphic Oracle" (Yeats) **1**:573; **31**:411; **116**:261, 313, 335
"News from the Sea" (Anwar)
See "Kabar dari laut"
News from Venus (Herzl) **36**:131, 140
"News Item" (Parker) **143**:320
"News of Paris—Fifteen Years Ago" (Fitzgerald) **6**:172
News of the Sun (Ingamells) **35**:129
"A Newspaper Ad" (Guro)
See "Gazetnoe obyavlenie"
Newspaper Days (Dreiser) **10**:191; **35**:60-1, 63, 67
Newspaper Days, 1899-1906 (Mencken) **13**:385, 387-88, 397
"The Newspaper in Economic Development" (Innis) **77**:337
"A Newspaper Puff" (Pyle) **81**:393
"Newspaper Readers" (Tsvetaeva)
See "Chitateli gazet"
"Newton" (García Lorca) **181**:65
"New-Year Glad Rags" (Bosman) **49**:13
"The Next Book" (Bowen) **148**:47
"Next Day" (Jarrell) **177**:140, 172, 176-77, 199-201, 207, 211, 219, 222-24, 226, 231-32
The Next Religion (Zangwill) **16**:445, 451
The Next Room of the Dream (Nemerov) **124**:145, 151, 155, 157-58, 160, 165, 170, 185, 192, 204, 248-49, 251, 289, 297, 301, 303
Next Time We Love (Sturges) **48**:286, 294, 312
"Next to of Course God America I" (Cummings) **137**:53
"Next to Reading Matter" (Henry) **19**:172
"The Next War" (Owen) **5**:368; **27**:212, 227
"Nezdeshnii vecher" (Tsvetaeva) **35**:384-85
Nezhnyi Iosif (Kuzmin) **40**:190, 195, 197, 199
"Nezhuzhashchie" (Balmont) **11**:41
Neznakomka (Blok) **5**:84, 86, 92, 94, 99
"Nezrelost'" (Zabolotsky) **52**:376
"Ngoba . . . sewuthi" (Vilakazi) **37**:404
Ni dnia bez strochki (Olesha) **136**:59-61, 66, 69, 75-77, 101, 107-10, 112-13, 124, 135, 148, 152-54, 157-58, 181
"Ni la leve zozobra" (Villaurrutia) **80**:477, 516
"Niani" (Machado de Assis) **10**:279
"Nianqing de shihou" (Chang) **184**:138
"Nice" (Jacob) **6**:199
The Nice and the Good (Murdoch) **171**:224, 284, 309, 311-12, 329
"A Nice Cup of Tea" (Orwell) **128**:288; **129**:235
"De Nice Leetle Canadienne" (Drummond) **25**:142
"Nice Old Lady" (Lane) **177**:268
"The Nice Old Man and the Pretty Girl" (Svevo)
See "La novella del buon vecchio e della bella fanciulla"
The Nice Old Man and the Pretty Girl and Other Stories (Svevo)
See *La novella del buon vecchio e della bella fanciulla e altri scritti*
"A Nice Old-Fashioned Romance with Love Lyrics and Everything" (Saroyan) **137**:166
Nice People (Crothers) **19**:74-5, 77, 80
Nichiren shōnin tsuji zeppō (Mori Ogai) **14**:382
Nichirin (Yokomitsu) **47**:394-95
Nicholas (Khlebnikov)
See *Nikolay*
Nicholas Crabbe; or, The One and the Many (Rolfe) **12**:273-75, 278-80
Nicht der Mörder, der Ermordete ist schuldig (Werfel) **8**:477, 479, 481-82
"Nicht nur zur Weihnachtszeit" (Böll) **185**:26, 105
"Nick the Saint" (Remizov)
See "Nikola Ugodnik"
Nickel Mountain (Gardner) **195**:104-05
"Nicodemus" (Nemerov) **124**:144
"Nicodemus" (Robinson) **5**:417
Nicodemus (Robinson) **101**:105
"Nicotine Alley" (Allen) **87**:60
"Le nid brisé" (Sully Prudhomme) **31**:308
El nida ajeno (Benavente) **3**:98
Nie wieder Friede (Toller) **10**:480, 484
Niebla (Unamuno) **2**:558-59, 561-62, 564-67, 571; **9**:511, 513, 515-19; **148**:231, 235, 252-53, 256-57, 261, 273, 287, 307, 309, 337, 340-42
Nieblas (Palma) **29**:255
Nienasycenie (Witkiewicz) **8**:507, 516-18
"El nieto del Cid" (Pardo Bazán) **189**:236
Nietzsche (Andreas-Salome)
See *Friedrich Nietzsche in seinen Werken*
Nietzsche and Philosophy (Deleuze)
See *Nietzsche et la philosophie*
"Nietzsche contra Wagner: Aktenstücke eines Psychologen" (Nietzsche) **10**:372
Nietzsche et la philosophie (Deleuze) **116**:69-73, 75, 123, 154-56
"Nietzsche et Thomas Mann" (Bataille) **155**:107-8
Nietzsche in Basel (Ball) **104**:41-43, 45
"Nietzsche in Basel: A Polemic" (Ball) **104**:57
Nietzsche in Outline and Aphorism (Orage) **157**:245, 248, 250
"Nietzscheism and Realism" (Lovecraft) **22**:210
"Nietzsches Philosophie in Lichte unserer Erfahrung: Vortag" (Mann) **44**:165; **168**:99
"Nietzsche's Philosophy in the Light of Our Experience" (Mann)
See "Nietzsches Philosophie in Lichte unserer Erfahrung: Vortag"
"Nigger Jeff" (Dreiser) **10**:181, 197, 199-200; **35**:60, 70-1, 75
"Nigger Lover" (McKay) **41**:329
The Nigger of the "Narcissus" (Conrad) **1**:201-02, 213, 218, 221; **6**:112, 118-19; **13**:117-19, 136, 141; **25**:111; **43**:112, 114, 129, 133, 135-36, 144; **57**:40, 43, 66
"Niggers" (Graham) **19**:108-09, 112, 120-22
"Night" (Aleixandre)
See "La noche"
"Night" (Baker) **10**:26
"Night" (Bosschere) **19**:54
"Night" (Bunin) **6**:59
"Night" (Esenin) **4**:114
"Night" (Mayakovski) **18**:246
"Night" (Montgomery) **51**:204
"Night" (Rosenberg) **12**:313
"Night" (Scott) **6**:394
"Night" (Symons) **11**:435
Night (Dickey) **151**:159-60
"Night and Day" (Rosenberg) **12**:294-95
Night and Day (Woolf) **1**:527-29, 531-32, 536, 542; **5**:510; **20**:397-98, 409, 423; **56**:371; **128**:319-22, 328, 334, 341, 344, 348, 350, 352-54, 357, 360-61, 363-65, 367, 380-82, 384-85
"Night and Morning" (Dunsany) **2**:136
"Night and Storm" (Roberts) **68**:337
"Night and the Pines" (Scott) **6**:391, 393-94
"Night and Wind" (Symons) **11**:426
A Night at an Inn (Dunsany) **2**:137, 140, 142-44; **59**:3, 5, 10, 14
The Night before Christmas (Howells) **7**:387-88
"The Night before the Night before Christmas" (Jarrell) **177**:125, 148, 159, 170-72, 177, 204-5, 211, 216-18, 224, 226
"Night before the Soviets" (Khlebnikov)
See "Nochyu pered sovetomi"
"Night Bird" (Dickey) **151**:175
"Night Calls" (Ivanov) **33**:138
"The Night Came Slowly" (Chopin) **127**:22-3
"The Night Cometh" (McCrae) **12**:209, 211
The Night Cometh (Bourget)
See *Le sens de la mort*
Night Dances (Sologub)
See *Nochnyi plyaski*
"The Night Driver" (Calvino)
See "Il guidatore notturno"
"Night Flight" (Bachmann) **192**:65
Night Flight (Saint-Exupéry)
See *Vol de nuit*
The Night Flower (Faust) **49**:36
The Night Horseman (Faust) **49**:44, 46-7, 49-51
Night Hurdling (Dickey) **151**:203
"Night Hymns on Lake Nipigon" (Scott) **6**:393
"A Night in a Trench" (Khlebnikov)
See "Noch v okope"
"A Night in Acadie" (Chopin) **127**:190, 207, 221
A Night in Acadie (Chopin) **5**:142, 144-46, 157; **14**:57-8, 60; **127**:121, 186, 212
Night in Bombay (Bromfield) **11**:79, 86
"A Night in Cordoba" (Scott) **6**:398
"Night in Huntington" (Jiménez) **183**:330, 333
"A Night in June" (Scott) **6**:391, 393-94
"A Night in March" (Scott) **6**:393
"A Night in New Arabia" (Henry) **19**:175
"A Night in New Jersey" (Himes) **139**:246-47
"Night in Persia" (Khlebnikov) **20**:150
"Night in State Street" (Monroe) **12**:216
A Night in the Luxembourg (Gourmont)
See *Une nuit au Luxembourg*
"A Night in the Oak Grove" (Miyazawa) **76**:280
"Night in the Old Home" (Hardy) **53**:100
"Night in the Pastures" (Montgomery) **51**:208
"Night in the Slums" (Jozsef) **22**:155, 164
"A Night in the Winter's Month of Pus" (Premchand)
See "Pus-ki-rat"
Night Is Darkest (Bernanos)
See *Un mauvais rêve*
"The Night Is Freezing Fast" (Housman)
See "Last Poems: XX—The Night Is Freezing Fast"
"The Night Journey" (Brooke) **2**:58
"Night Journey" (Noyes) **7**:515
The Night Land (Hodgson) **13**:230-35, 237
"Night Lodgings" (Kuprin) **5**:298
"Night Message" (Rhodes) **53**:317
"The Night of Acacias" (Nezval)
See "Noc akátů"
"Night of Creation" (Beresford) **81**:6
The Night of Loveless Nights (Desnos) **22**:61, 67
"The Night of Martyrdom" (Naidu) **80**:341
"A Night of New Roses" (Himes) **139**:326
"The Night of Numbers" (Calvino) **183**:92-93
"A Night of Questionings" (Hardy) **53**:101
A Night of Serious Drinking (Daumal)
See *La grande beuverie*
"Night of the Great Season" (Schulz)
See "Noc wielkiego sezonu"
"The Night of Varamin" (Hedāyat)
See "Shab-ha-yi Varamin"
Night on Bald Mountain (White) **176**:189, 225-26, 261
"Night on Hungerford Bridge" (Middleton) **56**:184
"A Night on the Galactic Railway" (Miyazawa) **76**:281
"Night Operations Coastal Command RAF" (Nemerov) **124**:306
Night over Taos (Anderson) **2**:1, 3; **144**:4, 10, 17, 37, 39-46, 71
"The Night People vs. Creeping Meatballism" (Shepherd) **177**:314
"Night Piece" (Coppard) **5**:178
"A Night Poem" (Welch) **22**:458
The Night Refuge (Gorky)
See *Nachtasyl*
"The Night Search" (Khlebnikov)
See "Nochnoi obysk"
"Night Songs" (Lawrence) **93**:69
Night Tales of Shimbashi (Nagai)
See *Shimbashi yawa*
The Night the Prowler (White) **176**:159-60, 196, 227, 229, 244, 319, 321
"Night Train" (Hagiwara)
See "Yogisha"
"The Night Violet" (Blok) **5**:91
"Night Visions" (Tolstoy) **18**:377
"The Night Visitor" (Bennett) **5**:46

The Night Visitor and Other Stories (Bennett) **197**:20
"Night Wanderers" (Davies) **5**:204
"The Night Wind" (Apollinaire) **3**:38
Night Wind (Betti)
See *Il vento notturno*
"A Night with Lions" (Jarrell) **177**:180-81
"The Night-Blooming Jasmine" (Lorde) **173**:143
"The Night-Born" (London) **9**:266; **15**:261-62
"The Night-Doings at 'Deadman's'" (Bierce) **44**:45, 49; **7**:98
"Nightfall" (Crowley) **7**:208
"Nightfall" (Vilakazi)
See "Ukuhlwa"
"Nightfall in the City of Hyderabad" (Naidu) **80**:290
"The Nighthawk" (Miyazawa) **76**:302
"The Nighthawk Star" (Miyazawa) **76**:278
"The Nightingale Garden" (Blok) **5**:85, 92
"The Nightingale of Keats" (Borges) **109**:47
The Nightingale of Wittenberg (Strindberg)
See *Nüktergalen i Wittenberg*
"Nightingales" (Bridges) **1**:129
Nightingales (Robinson)
See *The Glory of the Nightingales*
"Nightmare" (Toller)
See "Alp"
The Nightmare (Forester) **152**:141
"Nightmare Blues" (Wright) **136**:263
The Nightmare Has Triplets (Cabell) **6**:76-7
"A Nightmare of Odors" (Jiménez) **183**:330, 332-33
"Nightmare of Peace" (Muir) **87**:175
"Nightmare Town" (Hammett) **187**:75
"Nightmares" (Borges) **109**:57
"Nightpiece" (Joyce) **16**:227; **159**:279, 284
"Nights" (Toller)
See "Nächte"
Nights and Days (Bryusov)
See *Nochi i dni*
Nights and Days (Merrill) **173**:152-53, 195, 212-15, 218, 227-28, 242, 252, 258-59
Nights at the Circus (Carter) **139**:46-49, 51-53, 57-58, 60-61, 63-67, 69, 74-76, 91, 99, 101, 115, 118-19, 197, 199-200, 217, 219
Nights in Town (Burke) **63**:123, 125-27
The Nights of Phemius (Palamas) **5**:385
"The Nights of the UNPA" (Calvino)
See "Le notti dell'UNPA"
Nights with Uncle Remus: Myths and Legends of the Old Plantation (Harris) **2**:211, 212
"Nightsong" (Trakl) **5**:468
"Nightsong of Lord Culverin on the Drawbridge of Castle Querulous" (Morley) **87**:145
"The Night-Washers" (Carman) **7**:142
"Nigotta atama" (Shiga) **172**:202-3, 207-8
"Nihilism" (Johnson) **19**:243
"Nihon bunka no mondai" (Nishida) **83**:242
"Nihon kokumin asa no uta" (Yosano) **59**:335-7
Nihonbashi (Mizoguchi) **72**:321
Nihyakutōka (Natsume) **10**:329
"Nijudai ichimen" (Shiga) **172**:202
Nikiphóros Phokás (Kazantzakis) **33**:171
Nikita's Childhood (Tolstoy)
See *Detstvo nikity*
"Nikola Ugodnik" (Remizov) **27**:355
Nikolay (Khlebnikov) **20**:127, 136, 150
Nikon Stavokolemy (Prishvin) **75**:215
Nil desperandum (Reymont) **5**:397-98
Nils Holgerssons underbara resa genom Sverige (Lagerloef) **4**:232, 234, 238; **36**:238, 241-46
"the / nimble / heat" (Cummings) **137**:42
"Nimrod" (Schulz) **5**:421-22
"Nina" (Artsybashev) **31**:7
"Niña ahogada en el pozo" (García Lorca) **197**:282
"La niña mártir" (Pardo Bazán) **189**:235
"Nine Brasenose Worthies" (Buchan) **41**:59
The Nine Days' Queen (Buchanan) **107**:31
"Nine Lives" (Merrill) **173**:230
"Nine O'Clock To-Morrow" (Bennett) **5**:46
Nine Plays by Eugene O'Neill (O'Neill) **49**:249
"Nine Prisoners" (March) **96**:241, 244, 248, 252, 254
Nine Stories (Nabokov) **108**:82
The Nine Tailors: Changes Rung on an Old Theme in Two Short Touches and Two Full Peals (Sayers) **2**:530-31, 535; **15**:371, 378, 381-84, 387, 389-90, 393
Nine Tales (Čapek)
See *Devatero pohádek*
"Niñeez" (Aleixandre) **113**:3
The Nineteen (Fadeyev)
See *Razgrom*
1918 (Tolstoy) **18**:359, 365, 371-72, 374, 379
1984 (Orwell)
See *Nineteen Eighty-Four*
Nineteen Eighty-Four (Orwell) **2**:498, 500-01, 504-06, 508-12; **6**:340-42, 344-45, 348, 350-51, 353-54; **15**:296-367; **31**:179-80, 182, 187-89, 191-93, 195, 197-98, 200, 202, 208; **51**:235, 259, 264-65; **51**:223-29, 240, 243, 248-49, 252; **128**:254-55, 258-60, 264-74, 278-79, 285-87, 289, 293, 297-98, 307-11; **129**:223-65
"1915" (Apollinaire) **51**:35
"1943" (Anwar) **22**:21-2
"1945: The Death of the Gods" (Jarrell) **177**:195, 239
"1914" (Jarrell) **177**:192
"1914" (Owen) **5**:371
1914, and Other Poems (Brooke) **2**:55-6, 58, 61; **7**:120-21, 125, 127, 129
"1900" (Jacob) **6**:198
"Nineteen Hundred and Nineteen" (Yeats) **11**:534-36; **18**:454; **31**:401, 408; **93**:364, 399, 400
"Nineteen Miscellaneous Poems Written during My Sojourn in Japan, No. 2" (Su Man-shu) **24**:457
"Nineteen Miscellaneous Poems Written during My Sojourn in Japan, No. 3" (Su Man-shu) **24**:457
"1908" (Brennan) **17**:56
1905 (Trotsky) **22**:361, 386-87
"1905-1908" (Brooke) **2**:51
"1909" (Apollinaire) **51**:59-60
1917 Uroki Oktyabrya (Trotsky) **22**:364-65
"1969" (Hardy) **53**:110-11
"1910" (García Lorca) **197**:183, 201, 238, 240, 252, 280
"1910 (Intermedio)" (García Lorca) **197**:216, 231
"1910 (Intermission)" (García Lorca)
See " **197**:1910 (Intermedio)"
1913 (Sternheim) **8**:368, 372, 378
1930 Diary (Yeats) **18**:454
"Nineteen Thirty-One" (Rhodes) **53**:316
"1930's" (Oppen) **107**:921
1921-1925 (Mandelstam) **2**:408; **6**:265
"1928 Story" (Agee) **19**:33; **180**:22-23
The Nineteenth Century: An Utopian Retrospect (Ellis) **14**:111, 114, 134
"Ninety-Eight" (Johnson) **19**:230
95 Poems (Cummings) **137**:15, 26, 32
99 Fables (March) **96**:258
"90 North" (Jarrell) **177**:170, 172, 174, 176-77, 214, 220, 222, 224, 228, 232
"La ninfa" (Darío) **4**:60, 67
Ninfeas (Jiménez) **4**:216
Ningen shikkaku (Dazai Osamu) **11**:172-75, 177, 179, 185-88, 191
"Ningengaku" (Nishida) **83**:326
"Nino Diablo" (Hudson) **29**:155
"De niño yo canté como vosotros" (García Lorca) **181**:121
"Ninon de l'Enclos, on Her Last Birthday" (Parker) **143**:325
Ninth Avenue (Bodenheim) **44**:70, 74
"Ninth Elegy" (Rilke) **1**:413, 415, 420
The Ninth Thermidor (Aldanov)
See *Devjatoe termidora*
"The Ninth Wave" (Sharp) **39**:362
The Ninth Wave (Van Doren) **18**:396-97
"Niobe" (Palamas) **5**:386
Niobe (Rolland) **23**:256
"Nipona" (Huidobro) **31**:124
Nirjharer svapnabhanga (Tagore) **3**:496; **53**:339-40
"Niruddesh yatra" (Tagore) **53**:340
"Nirvana" (Aurobindo) **63**:9
"Nisan" (Anwar) **22**:18
"Nishchii Arlekin" (Guro) **56**:133-34
Nishida Kitaro zenshu (Nishida) **83**:234, 323
Nishida's Complete Works (Nishida)
See *Nishida Kitaro zenshu*
"Nisithe" (Tagore) **53**:355, 357
Niskrti (Chatterji) **13**:73, 80-1
"Nisshin kokumin no shinwa" (Yosano) **59**:337
"Niu" (Chang) **184**:138-39
"Niwatori" (Hagiwara) **60**:309, 313
"Niwatori" (Mori Ogai) **14**:384
"Niwatori" (Shimazaki Toson) **5**:439
"Die Nixe" (Liliencron) **18**:214
"N'Jawk" (Flecker) **43**:213
Nje nempela (Vilakazi) **37**:405
"¡No!" (Jiménez) **183**:334, 336
"No. 44, The Mysterious Stranger" (Twain) **59**:182, 186; **161**:242; **185**:256, 258-59, 265-66, 269-70, 272, 274, 276-81, 289, 292-93, 296-98, 308-22, 324-25, 327-30, 332
No and Yes (Eddy) **71**:165
"No basta" (Aleixandre) **113**:48
"No Bigger Than a Man's Hand" (Millay) **169**:235235
No Boundaries (Kuttner) **10**:269
"No busques no" (Aleixandre) **113**:11
"No Coward's Song" (Flecker) **43**:191, 199
"No Crime in the Mountains" (Chandler) **7**:173; **179**:129
"No Delicacies" (Bachmann)
See "Keine Delikatessen"
"No Door" (Wolfe) **4**:527; **13**:492, 495
No Enemy (Ford) **15**:87-9, 92-3; **57**:282
No Enemy: A Tale of Reconstruction (Ford) **172**:120
"No existe el hombre" (Aleixandre) **113**:15, 46
"No Gumption" (Knister) **56**:161
No Laughing Matter (Heller) **131**:21; **151**:320, 322
"No Lilies for Lisette" (Service) **15**:412
No Longer Human (Dazai Osamu)
See *Ningen shikkaku*
No Love Lost: A Romance of Travel (Howells) **7**:370, 391
"No Man's Land" (Davidson) **24**:186
No Man's Land (Onetti)
See *Tierra de nadie*
No Man's Land (Sapper) **44**:307
"No Mean City" (Rhodes) **53**:311
"No More Masterpieces" (Artaud) **3**:49
"No More of This Trapped Gazing" (Muir) **87**:260
No More Parades (Ford) **1**:280-82, 284; **15**:73-4, 78, 80-2; **39**:140-41; **57**:204-90; **172**:32, 71-72, 74-76, 78-83, 85
No More Peace! (Toller)
See *Nie wieder Friede*
"No More the Senator" (Bishop) **103**:26
No Name (Onetti)
See *Para una tumba sin nombre*
"No, No Food Shall I Find Today" (Khodasevich) **15**:209
No Nudes Is Good Nudes (Wodehouse) **108**:372
No One Knows How It Happens (Pirandello) **4**:339
No Painted Plumage (Powys)
See *Fables*
"No Place for a Woman" (Lawson) **27**:121, 152
No Pockets in a Shroud (McCoy) **28**:211-12, 221-23, 237
No Poems (Benchley) **55**:6-7, 18

"No Possom, No Sop, No Taters" (Stevens) **3**:448; **45**:299
"No sé si el mar es, hoy" (Jiménez) **183**:318
"No Second Troy" (Yeats) **11**:528; **18**:446; **31**:385, 401; **93**:348-49
"No Sinecure" (Hornung) **59**:42
"No Still Path" (Lowry) **6**:238
No Swank (Anderson) **24**:43
"No te achicopales Cacama" (Ibarguengoitia) **148**:203
No Thanks (Cummings) **137**:37
"No title" (Cummings) **137**:47
No Villain Need Be (Fisher) **140**:155, 165, 169, 182, 185
No Way (Ginzburg)
See *Caro Michele*
"No Woman Born" (Kuttner) **10**:269
Noa Noa (Agee) **180**:69
"A No-Account Creole" (Chopin) **127**:167-68, 172, 190-91, 207
Noah an' Jonah an' Cap'n John Smith (Marquis) **7**:437, 439
"Noah Built the Ark" (Johnson) **3**:245; **19**:209; **175**:254-55, 257
The Nobility of Labor (Liliencron) **18**:208
"The Noble Rider and the Sound of Words" (Stevens) **12**:372, 386; **45**:274, 283, 296, 325, 338, 341
"The noblewoman" (Arp) **115**:19, 22
"Nobody" (Aleixandre)
See "Nadie"
"Nobody Knows" (Anderson) **24**:20, 24, 30, 33-4, 51, 54; **123**:13, 33, 105
"Nobody yet knows who I am" (Villa)
See "Poem 3"
"Nobody's Lookin' but de Owl and de Moon" (Johnson) **19**:210; **175**:225
Nobody's Man (Oppenheim) **45**:130
Nobuko (Miyamoto) **37**:266-69, 272, 274-75
"Noc akátů" (Nezval) **44**:247
"Noc wielkiego sezonu" (Schulz) **5**:422; **51**:308, 314, 324
Les noces Corinthiennes (France) **9**:40
"Les noces d'ary" (Schwob) **20**:319
"Noces d'or" (Rod) **52**:316
"Noch v okope" (Khlebnikov) **20**:132, 137
"Noch' yu" (Korolenko) **22**:176
"La noche" (Aleixandre) **113**:14
"Noche" (García Lorca) **181**:193, 199
"Noche" (Villaurrutia) **80**:477-8
Noche (Sender) **136**:209
La noche del sábado (Benavente) **3**:97, 99
"Noche incial" (Aleixandre) **113**:3
"Noche sinfónica" (Aleixandre) **113**:11, 42
"Noche terrible" (Arlt) **29**:45-7
"Nochebuena" (Vallejo) **3**:532; **56**:293
Nochi i dni (Bryusov) **10**:78, 84
"Nochnoi obysk" (Khlebnikov) **20**:127, 133, 137, 144-45
Nochnyi plyaski (Sologub) **9**:439-40
"Noch'temnaia" (Remizov) **27**:353
"Nochyu pered sovetomi" (Khlebnikov) **20**:126-27, 133, 144-45
"Nocturna en que nada se oye" (Villaurrutia) **80**:463, 484
"Nocturnal Beacon" (Storni)
See "Faro en la noche"
"Nocturnal Turnings" (Capote) **164**:154, 204
"Nocturne" (Burke) **63**:126
"Nocturne" (Coppard) **5**:177
"Nocturne" (Cullen) **37**:164, 168
"Nocturne" (La Guma) **140**:203, 208, 220
"Nocturne" (Hecht) **101**:36
"Nocturne" (Jiménez) **183**:334, 336, 338-40
"Nocturne" (Lowry) **6**:238
"Nocturne" (Middleton) **56**:173
"Nocturne" (Mistral)
See "Nocturno"
"Nocturne" (Obstfelder) **23**:182, 188
"Nocturne" (Södergran) **31**:288
"Nocturne" (Symons) **11**:427
Nocturne (D'Annunzio)
See *Notturno*
"Nocturne: Death Speaks" (Villaurrutia) **80**:479, 519
"Nocturne: Dream" (Villaurrutia) **80**:519
"Nocturne from Nowhere" (Chandler) **179**:207
"Nocturne: Imprisoned" (Villaurrutia) **80**:519
"Nocturne in Outline" (García Lorca)
See "Nocturno esquemático"
"Nocturne in Which Nothing is Heard" (Villaurrutia) **80**:463, 484, 519
"Nocturne of the Void" (García Lorca)
See "Nocturno del hueco"
"A Nocturne of Trysting" (Roberts) **8**:321
"Nocturno" (Anwar) **22**:22
"Nocturno" (García Lorca) **181**:124
"Nocturno" (Güiraldes) **39**:185, 190
"Nocturno" (Jiménez) **4**:226
"Nocturno" (Mistral) **2**:479
"Nocturno" (Villaurrutia) **80**:481
"Nocturno amor" (Villaurrutia) **80**:481
"Nocturno de la alcoba" (Villaurrutia) **80**:482
"Nocturno de la estatua" (Villaurrutia) **80**:463, 482
"Nocturno de los ángeles" (Villaurrutia) **80**:506
"Nocturno de los avisos" (Salinas) **17**:358
"Nocturno del hueco" (García Lorca) **49**:94; **181**:28
"Nocturno en que habla la muerte" (Villaurrutia) **80**:479
"Nocturno esquemático" (García Lorca) **181**:66
"Nocturno eterno" (Villaurrutia) **80**:481
"Nocturno grito" (Villaurrutia) **80**:463
"Nocturno mar" (Villaurrutia) **80**:481
"Nocturno solo" (Villaurrutia) **80**:480
"Nocturnos" (Villaurrutia) **80**:463
Nocturnos (Villaurrutia) **80**:463, 480
"Nod" (de la Mare) **53**:28
"The Nodder" (Wodehouse) **108**:369
Noé (Giono) **124**:111-13, 138-39
"Nōfu" (Shimazaki Toson) **5**:439
Noh, or Accomplishment: A Study of the Classical Stage of Japan (Fenollosa) **91**:5
Noir et blanc no. 1 (Kandinsky) **92**:50
Noir et blanc no. 2 (Kandinsky) **92**:50
Noir et blanc no. 3 (Kandinsky) **92**:50
Noir et blanc no. 4 (Kandinsky) **92**:50
The Noise of Time (Mandelstam)
See *Shum vremeni*
The Noises of the Town (Remizov) **27**:331, 334
The Noises That Weren't There (Williams) **11**:495
Noizement-les-Vierges (Martin du Gard) **24**:396
"Nojabr" (Annensky) **14**:26
Nokh Alemen (Bergelson) **81**:24,30
Noli me tangere (Kaiser) **9**:174
"Nollekans" (Jarrell) **177**:127, 162
Noma nini (Vilakazi) **37**:401
"The Nomads of Beauty" (Ivanov) **33**:123
"No-Man's-Land" (Buchan) **41**:37, 73
"El nombre conseguido de los nombres" (Jiménez) **183**:319
"Les nombres" (Verhaeren) **12**:469
Le nombril (Anouilh) **195**:48-9
"Nomenclature of Deserted Things" (van Ostaijen) **33**:421
"Nómina de huesos" (Vallejo) **56**:287
"Non blandula illa" (Gogarty) **15**:101
"Non darò piú fiato alle trombe" (Calvino) **183**:103
"Non dolet" (Gogarty) **15**:100, 103, 111
"Non dolet" (Swinburne) **36**:318
"Non Omnis Moriar" (Stringer) **37**:341
Non possumus (Benda) **60**:67-9
Non Sequitur (Coleridge) **73**:4, 6, 24
"Non serviam" (Huidobro) **31**:126, 134, 137
Non si sa come (Pirandello) **4**:339; **29**:301
"Non sum qualis eram bonae sub regno Cynarae" (Dowson) **4**:85-6; **4**:86, 88, 91
Non ti pago (de Filippo) **127**:280-81, 289, 295
"Non voglio esser più quel che sono" (Papini) **22**:280
Non-Combatants (Macaulay) **7**:421-22, 426
None but the Brave (Schnitzler)
See *Leutnant Gustl*
"None Have Seen the House of the Lord" (Rosenberg) **12**:308
"None of That" (Lawrence) **93**:21
"Nonentity" (Lawrence) **93**:48, 49
The Nonexistent Knight (Calvino)
See *Il cavaliere inesistente*
"Nonfiction: Grandmother" (Shiga)
See "Aru asa"
Nonindifferent Nature (Eisenstein) **57**:196-200, 202
A Nonsense Anthology (Wells) **35**:420
Nonsense Novels (Leacock) **2**:377-79
"Nonsense Poetry" (Orwell) **51**:247-48
Noodlot (Couperus) **15**:42-3, 45
"Noon" (Khodasevich) **15**:204, 208, 212
"Noon Street Nemesis" (Chandler) **179**:124
Noored hinged (Tammsaare) **27**:370, 373
Nootka texts (Sapir) **108**:257
"Nor Iron Bars" (Powys) **9**:366
"Nora" (Toomer) **172**:314
Nora (Ibsen)
See *Et dukkehjem*
"Nora Criona" (Stephens) **4**:406, 416
"Nora on the Pavement" (Symons) **11**:445
Norge i vare hjerter (Grieg) **10**:207-09
Norma Ashe (Glaspell) **175**:51, 141
"Norma y paraíso de los negros" (García Lorca) **49**:122
"Normal Madness" (Santayana) **40**:373
"Normaltive und psychologische Ethik" (Westermarck) **87**:364
The Norman Church (Milne) **6**:319
Norne-Gæst (Jensen) **41**:295
Norse Tales and Sketches (Kielland) **5**:278
Norte y Sur (Reyes) **33**:323
"The North" (Zamyatin) **8**:544, 555-56; **37**:424, 427, 431
North Against South (Verne) **6**:501
North America, Continent of Conjecture (McAlmon) **97**:93-94, 110-11
"North and South" (McKay) **41**:318-19
North & South (Bishop) **121**:3, 6, 21, 31, 33, 43-4, 55, 69, 102
"North Carolina Blues" (Villaurrutia) **80**:484
North Coast and Other Poems (Buchanan) **107**:16, 63
"A North Dakota Surveying Party" (McAlmon) **97**:88
"The North Family" (Fisher) **140**:165
"North Haven" (Bishop) **121**:22
"North Labrador" (Crane) **2**:119; **80**:114
North of South: An African Journey (Naipaul) **153**:222, 227, 230-31, 234
"The North Pole" (Nabokov) **108**:52
"The North Sea" (Benjamin) **39**:57-8
"The North Shore Watch" (Woodberry) **73**:363, 369
The North Shore Watch (Woodberry) **73**:367
The North Wall (Davidson) **24**:193
The North Wind of Love (Mackenzie) **116**:239-40, 242
Northern Heroic (Bely)
See *Severnaia simfoniia: Pervia geroicheskaia*
A Northern Night (Sharp) **39**:374, 397
"Northern Pines" (Stringer) **37**:341
"A Northern Suburb" (Davidson) **24**:164, 186, 191
Northern Symphony (Bely)
See *Severnaia simfoniia: Pervia geroicheskaia*
"A Northern Vigil" (Carman) **7**:146
A Northern Voice for the Dissolution of the Union (Stockton) **47**:331
"Northerners Can Be So Smug" (Childress) **116**:34
Northrop Frye in Conversation (Frye) **165**:189, 227

Northrop Frye on Culture and Literature (Frye) **165**:141-42, 148, 150-51, 189
Northrop Frye on Religion (Frye) **165**:258-61
Northrop Frye's Student Essays, 1932-1938 (Frye) **165**:229
Northwest Passage (Roberts) **23**:230, 232-36, 239-44
Norway in Our Hearts (Grieg)
See *Norge i vare hjerter*
"Norwegian Mountains" (Gumilev) **60**:271
Nos actes nous suivent (Bourget) **12**:69
"The Nose" (Akutagawa Ryūnosuke)
See "Hana"
"A Nose" (de la Mare) **53**:23
Nosferatu, A Symphony of Horror (Murnau)
See *Nosferatu, eine Symphonie des Grauens*
Nosferatu, eine Symphonie des Grauens (Murnau) **53**:240, 250, 253-55, 257-60, 262, 265, 271-72, 274-75, 278-86
Nosotros los maestro (Arguedas) **147**:80
"Nostalgia" (Jiménez)
See "Nostaljia"
Nostalgia (Deledda)
See *Nostalgie*
Nostalgia de la muerte (Villaurrutia) **80**:460, 464, 476, 478-80, 484, 486-7, 489, 501, 505-6, 516
"Nostalgia de la nieve" (Villaurrutia) **80**:484
"Nostalgia for the Particular" (Murdoch) **171**:239
"Nostalgias" (Villaurrutia) **80**:480
"Nostalgias imperiales" (Vallejo) **3**:531, 535
Nostalgie (Deledda) **23**:34
"La nostalgie du front" (Teilhard de Chardin) **9**:481, 492
"Nostaljia" (Jiménez) **4**:225
I nostri antenati (Calvino) **183**:4-5, 8-9, 94-96, 113, 119, 157-59, 162-63, 188-89, 237-39, 245
I nostri sogni (Betti) **5**:61-2
Nostromo (Conrad) **1**:196, 200-03, 205-06, 209-11, 215-16, 218, 221; **6**:118-123; **13**:114, 117; **25**:70-116; **43**:116; **57**:83
"Not All Is Lost" (Zoshchenko) **15**:515
Not Alone Lost (McAlmon) **97**:93, 97, 118
"Not Because They Shuttered Up and Closed the Bakers'" (Tsvetaeva) **35**:394
Not by Strange Gods (Roberts) **68**:325-26, 348
"Not Counting Niggers" (Orwell) **128**:277, 283
Not Dying (Saroyan) **137**:156, 168, 170, 173
"Not Fade Away" (Holly) **65**:137, 144, 146, 151-52
"Not for a Nation" (Millay) **169**:296
Not Honour More (Cary) **1**:148; **29**:76, 79, 93, 97-8; **196**:158, 162, 166-69, 175, 177-79
Not I (Beckett) **145**:83, 134-35, 137, 149-51, 153-56, 159, 179
"Not Ideas about the Thing but the Thing Itself" (Stevens) **3**:472, 478; **12**:387; **45**:302, 317
"The Not Impossible Him" (Millay)
See "To the Not Impossible Him"
"Not Listening to Music" (Forster) **125**:32
Not Long Ago (Vazov) **25**:450
"Not Memory, Nor Magic" (Radnóti) **16**:420
Not on the Screen (Fuller) **103**:70, 90
"Not Only I" (Hardy) **53**:101; **143**:192
Not Peace but a Sword (Merezhkovsky) **29**:231
"Not Quite Cricket" (Wakefield) **120**:349, 357
"Not Sacco and Vanzetti" (Cullen) **37**:158
"Not Sixteen" (Anderson) **123**:53-4, 56
Not So Deep as a Well (Parker) **143**:326
"Not So Far as the Forest" (Millay) **49**:228
"Not So—The Chronicler Lies, Saying Igor Returned Home" (Tsvetaeva) **35**:394
Not That I Would Boast (Beerbohm) **1**:68
Not That It Matters (Milne) **6**:316
Not the Murderer (Werfel)
See *Nicht der Mörder, der Ermordete ist schuldig*
Not This August (Kornbluth) **8**:214, 216, 221
"Not to Be Realized" (Stevens) **3**:448
"Not to Strike Back" (Jozsef) **22**:160
Not under Forty (Cather) **1**:156; **132**:130, 137, 143, 152
"Not With Libations" (Millay) **49**:234-35
"Not Worthy of a Wentforth" (March) **96**:260
"Nota 1960" (Calvino) **183**:198-201, 203-4
"Nota sobre Walt Whitman" (Borges) **109**:85
Notabilities (Bernhard)
See *Die Berühmten*
"A Notable Collection of Relics for Oxford" (Guiney) **41**:220
"Notas" (Borges) **109**:77
"Notas sobre la inteligencia Americana" (Reyes) **33**:318, 325
"Notas sobre 'Martín Fierro' y el gaucho" (Güiraldes) **39**:189
"Note" (Ginzburg) **156**:74
"Note" (Villa) **176**:99-101
"Note conjointe sur Monsieur Descartes et la philosophie Cartésienne" (Péguy) **10**:415
Note et digression (Valéry) **4**:494
"Note for the Bourgeois" (Tzara) **168**:238-39
"A Note on Dante Rossetti" (Buchanan) **107**:61
"A Note on Folklore" (Rourke) **12**:323
"Note on Moonlight" (Stevens) **45**:314
"A Note on Paul Bourget" (Ellis) **14**:132-33
"Note on Realism" (Anderson) **24**:50; **123**:8
"Note on the Psychology of Fishes" (Thorndike) **107**:370
"Note on the Theory of the Economy of Research" (Peirce) **81**:352
"Note on Two Songs: 'Follow the Drinking Gourd' and 'Steal Away'" (Hansberry) **192**:272
"Note sul linguaggio politico" (Calvino) **183**:102
"Note sur Monsieur Bergson et la philosophie Bergsonienne" (Péguy) **10**:415, 419
"Note to Fan-jen" (Su Man-shu) **24**:457
Notebook (Anderson) **1**:56; **10**:38
Notebook (Merrill)
See *The (Diblos) Notebook*
Notebook (Twain) **185**:297-99
Notebooks (Andrić)
See *Sveske*
Notebooks (Chekhov) **10**:112
Notebooks (Fitzgerald) **157**:167
Notebooks (Frye) **165**:228-29, 233-38, 241, 243-44, 258
Notebooks (James) **64**:157
Notebooks (Twain) **36**:416-17
Notebooks (Valéry) **4**:499
Notebooks (Weiss) **152**:276, 279
Notebooks, 1914-1916 (Wittgenstein) **59**:258, 265-6, 298
The Notebooks of André Walter (Gide)
See *Les cahiers d'André Walter*
The Notebooks of F. Scott Fitzgerald (Fitzgerald) **6**:167-68
The Notebooks of Henry James (James) **24**:343; **40**:167, 169; **47**:165, 171, 202
The Notebooks of Malte Laurids Brigge (Rilke)
See *Die Aufzeichnungen des Malte Laurids Brigge*
Note-Books of Samuel Butler (Butler) **1**:137; **33**:30, 41-2, 50, 53, 58-9
The Notebooks of Simone Weil (Weil)
See *Cahiers*
The Noted Sword (Mizoguchi) **72**:315
Noten zur Literature (Adorno) **111**:53, 56, 180, 184-86, 190
Notes (Korolenko) **22**:173
"Notes for a Young Writer" (Jackson) **187**:237, 292-93
"Notes for 1946" (Anwar)
See "Tjatetan th. 1946"
"Notes for Howl and Other Poems" (Ginsberg) **120**:12, 136
"Notes for the Aloe" (Mansfield) **164**:253
"Notes for The Horse's Mouth" (Cary) **196**:180, 182, 185
Notes for Understanding Our Century (Drieu la Rochelle)
See *Notes pour comprendre le siècle*
Notes from a Diary (Gorky) **8**:74
"Notes from a Lady at a Dinner Party" (Malamud) **184**:222
Notes from Hampstead (Canetti)
See *Nachträge aus Hampstead*
"Notes from India" (Sarton) **120**:265
"Notes from Outside Sources" (Fenollosa) **91**:23
"Notes from the Front Line" (Carter) **139**:45, 48, 56, 78, 84, 206
Notes from the Underground: The Whittaker Chambers-Ralph de Toledano Letters, 1949-1960 (Chambers) **129**:50-51
"Notes générales sur la marche de l'œuvre" (Zola) **41**:451
"Notes in a Brittany Convent" (Mew) **8**:300
"Notes made in 1970-71" (Bakhtin) **160**:216
Notes of a Camp-Follower on the Western Front (Hornung) **59**:113
"Notes of a Cavalryman" (Gumilev)
See "Zapisky kavalerista"
"Notes of a Madman" (Tolstoy)
See "Zapiski sumashshedshego"
Notes of a Madman (Tolstoy)
See *Zapiski sumasshedshego*
Notes of a Publicist under Sentence of Death (Korolenko)
See *Present Customs*
Notes of a Son and Brother (James) **11**:321
"Notes of a Writer" (Olesha) **136**:153
The Notes of a Young Doctor (Bulgakov)
See *Zapiski iunogo vracha*
"Notes of the Week" (Orage) **157**:246
"Notes of Transliteration" (Nabokov) **108**:115
Notes on a Cellar-Book (Saintsbury) **31**:249
"Notes on Albert Durer" (Holmes) **77**:309, 311
"Notes on Apartment Life" (Chang) **184**:150
"Notes on an Elizabethan Play" (Woolf) **43**:405
Notes on Child Study (Thorndike) **107**:378, 416, 420
"Notes on D. H. Lawrence" (Woolf) **43**:397, 421
Notes on Democracy (Mencken) **13**:369, 387-88
Notes on Hospitals (Nightingale) **85**:200
"Notes on Language and Style" (Hulme) **21**:140, 147-48
Notes on Life and Letters (Conrad) **1**:196
Notes on Literature (Adorno)
See *Noten zur Literature*
"Notes on Logic" (Wittgenstein) **59**:292
Notes on matters Affecting the Health, Efficiency, and Hospital Administration of the British Army (Nightingale) **85**:235, 241, 278
"Notes on Nationalism" (Garneau) **13**:203
"Notes on Nationalism" (Orwell) **128**:287, 297; **129**:228
Notes on Novelists, with Some Other Notes (James) **2**:248
Notes on Nursing (Nightingale) **85**:215, 240-1, 254, 256-7, 259, 273
Notes on Poems and Reviews (Swinburne) **36**:305, 307, 310, 329
"Notes on Poetry" (Tzara) **168**:323
"Notes on Pre-Columbian Art" (Péret) **20**:198-200
Notes on Prosody? (Oppen) **107**:316
Notes on Prosody (Nabokov) **189**:72
Notes on Religion (Chapman) **7**:188, 191
Notes on Some Pictures of 1868 (Swinburne) **36**:305
"Notes on the Article of N. I. Bukharin 'On the Theory of the Imperialistic State'" (Lenin) **67**:230
"Notes on the Construction of Sheepfolds" (Ruskin) **63**:260, 261, 264
"Notes on the Cuffs" (Bulgakov) **16**:85
"Notes on the Decline of Courage" (Dickey) **151**:164

"Notes on the Decline of Outrage" (Dickey) **151**:94, 141
"Notes on the Designs of the Old Masters in Florence" (Swinburne) **8**:441
Notes on the District of Menteith (Graham) **19**:112
"Notes on the Documentary Theater" (Weiss) **152**:319, 321
"Notes on the Greatness and Decadence of Europe" (Valéry) **4**:493
"Notes on the Novel" (MacCarthy) **36**:252
"Notes on the Novel" (Ortega y Gasset) **9**:339
"Notes on the Petty Bourgeois Mentality" (Gorky) **8**:87
"Notes on the Text of Shelley" (Swinburne) **36**:320
Notes on the Turner Collection (Ruskin) **63**:257
"Notes on Writing Weird Fiction" (Lovecraft) **22**:231
Notes pour comprendre le siècle (Drieu la Rochelle) **21**:31, 34-5, 39
Notes sur André Gide (Martin du Gard) **24**:394, 396
Notes sur des oasis et sur Alger (Jammes) **75**:117
"Notes sur la crucifixion" (Cocteau) **119**:76
"Notes sur le Salon de 1877: portraits et natures mortes" (Huysmans) **69**:6
"Notes to Account of My First Wound" (Holmes) **77**:310
"Notes to Be Left in a Cornerstone" (Benét) **7**:80
Notes To Literature (Adorno)
See *Noten zur Literature*
"Notes toward a Metaphysic" (Collingwood) **67**:184-85
Notes toward a Supreme Fiction (Stevens) **3**:448, 453, 455-56, 460, 462, 468, 472-74, 477-78; **12**:360-61, 368, 374, 377-79, 385, 387; **45**:269-70, 278, 283-85, 290, 294, 298-300, 319, 323, 325, 327-28, 336, 338-39, 342-44, 347, 349, 351
"Notes Toward a Theory of Painting" (Lewis) **104**:211
"Nothin' to Say" (Riley) **51**:282, 284, 300
"Nothin' to Say, My Daughter" (Riley) **51**:284
"Nothing and Something" (Harper) **14**:257, 260
"Nothing at All" (Stephens) **4**:408
"Nothing but Gingerbread Left" (Kuttner) **10**:268
"Nothing Endures" (Cullen) **37**:136, 147, 165
"nothing false and possible is love" (Cummings) **137**:55
"Nothing Happens in Brooklyn" (Runyon) **10**:429, 436
Nothing Here Not but the Recordings (Burroughs) **121**:137
"Nothing Less than a Man" (Unamuno) **148**:239
"Nothing New" (Bonner) **179**:8-11, 13, 21, 33-36, 40, 53-54, 57
Nothing Sacred (Carter) **139**:168, 188-89, 200
Nothing Sacred (Hecht) **101**:61, 63, 73
Nothing So Strange (Hilton) **21**:98-9
Nothing to Pay (Evans) **85**:5, 12, 30
"Nothing will yield" (Nemerov) **124**:157
"Nothingness!" (Jiménez) **183**:336
"The Nothingness of Personality" (Borges)
See "La nadería de la personalidad"
"Noticia de los Kenningar" (Borges) **109**:165
Notícias Amorosas (Drummond de Andrade) **139**:226
"La notion de dépense" (Bataille) **155**:10, 32, 41, 95, 111
"The Notion of Expenditure" (Bataille)
See "La notion de dépense"
"Notizen zur Situation des Dramas" (Zuckmayer) **191**:288, 2391
Notorious (Hecht) **101**:75-7
The Notorious Elinor Lee (Micheaux) **76**:248
The Notorious Mrs. Ebbsmith (Pinero) **32**:387, 389-91, 393-96, 398, 401, 403, 405, 409, 411-12, 414
Notre Dame (Mandelstam) **6**:259
Notre dame des fleurs (Genet) **128**:110, 115-23, 130-32, 134-35, 161, 179-80, 183-84, 194, 216, 218-29
"Notre-Dame-des-Hirondelles" (Yourcenar) **193**:283, 292-95, 297
"Notre jeunesse" (Péguy) **10**:404, 408, 411, 415
"Notre patrie" (Péguy) **10**:408, 411, 414
"Notre petit continent" (Arp) **115**:39
"Notre vie" (Éluard) **41**:161
"Notre-Dame" (Mayakovski) **18**:258
"The Not-Returning" (Gurney) **33**:97-8, 104
"Notruf" (Sudermann) **15**:433
"La notte" (Campana) **20**:84-6
"Notte d'estate" (Saba) **33**:374
"Le notti dell'UNPA" (Calvino) **183**:96, 189
"Nottingham Hunt" (Cram) **45**:4, 11-12
I notturni (Campana) **20**:85
Notturno (D'Annunzio) **6**:134, 145; **40**:7-8, 12
"Notturno teppista" (Campana) **20**:83, 88
"Noubousse" (Apollinaire) **51**:61
Noughts and Crosses (Quiller-Couch) **53**:290
Nouka-Dubi (Tagore) **3**:499
Les nourritures terrestres (Gide) **5**:214, 218, 227, 229, 233-34, 244; **12**:143, 146-47, 150, 153, 166, 168, 171-72, 176-77, 180-81; **36**:94, 97, 106, 122; **177**:4, 7, 12-16, 25-26, 31, 34, 48, 78, 81, 84, 93, 99, 115
Les nourritures terrestres (Larbaud) **9**:205
Nous autres (Barbusse) **5**:13
Nous autres (Zamyatin)
See *My*
Nous autres Français (Bernanos) **3**:127
"Nous sommes" (Éluard) **41**:147, 158
"Nouveau sermon nègre" (Roumain) **19**:334, 337, 346-47
"Un nouveau thèologien" (Péguy) **10**:415
Nouveaux contes à ninon (Zola) **1**:585; **6**:568
Nouveaux essais de psychologie contemporaine (Bourget) **12**:65, 74
Les nouveaux pastels (Bourget) **12**:68
Le Nouvel Esprit scientifique (Bachelard) **128**:17, 44-5, 49, 53-5, 89
Nouvelle critique ou nouvelle imposture (Barthes) **135**:185
Le nouvelle della Pescara (D'Annunzio)
See *San Pantaleone*
La nouvelle Eurydice (Yourcenar) **193**:265, 271, 321
Nouvelle histoire de Mouchette (Bernanos) **3**:119, 123, 125
La nouvelle journée (Rolland) **23**:261
Une nouvelle manière en peinture (Zola) **41**:436
Nouvelles et morceaux (Ramuz) **33**:295
Nouvelles et textes pour rien (Beckett)
See *Textes pour rien*
Nouvelles impressions d'Afrique (Roussel) **20**:228, 230-31, 234-35, 240, 246-47, 253
Les Nouvelles orientales (Yourcenar) **193**:283-85, 292-94, 296-97, 299, 342, 344
Nouvelles pages de critique et le doctrine (Bourget) **12**:74
Les nouvelles révélations de l'être (Artaud) **3**:54, 60; **36**:6
"A nova Califórnia" (Lima Barreto) **23**:169-72
Nova Express (Burroughs) **121**:116, 123-25, 130-33, 137, 140, 142-43, 147
Nova zemya (Vazov) **25**:455, 457
"Novaia dacha" (Chekhov)
See "Novaja doca"
"Novaja doca" (Chekhov) **3**:159
Novale (Tozzi) **31**:319, 321-22
"The Novel" (Bierce) **44**:16, 30, 43
"The Novel" (Grove) **4**:134
"The Novel" (Lawrence) **33**:188
"The Novel" (Mencken) **13**:365
"The Novel as Social Criticism" (Petry) **112**:389, 394
"The Novel Démeublé" (Cather) **99**:213; **132**:128-29, 137, 141, 152
Novel for a Young Man (Klabund) **44**:105-06
A Novel Fragment (Welch) **22**:458
A Novel I Have Loved (Endo)
See *Watashi no aishita shosetsu*
Novel Notes (Jerome) **23**:83
A Novel of Thank You (Stein) **28**:332-33; **48**:264
"The Novel of the Black Seal" (Machen) **4**:279, 284
"The Novel of the White Powder" (Machen) **4**:280, 284
"The Novel with a 'Purpose'" (Norris) **24**:432
La novela de Don Sandalio (Unamuno) **148**:257, 306-11
La novela de don Sandalio, jugador de ajedrez (Unamuno)
See "La historia de Don Sandalio"
La novela del amigo de mi suegro (Unamuno) **148**:311
"La novela novelesca" (Pardo Bazán) **189**:229
"La novela y la expresión literaria" (Arguedas) **147**:8, 68, 84
Novelas de la primera época (Pérez Galdós) **27**:276
Novelas españolas contemporáneas (Pérez Galdós) **27**:247-49, 257, 259-60, 276
Novelas y cuentos completos (Vallejo) **56**:308
"Novelist and Believer" (O'Connor) **132**:326
"The Novelist as Social Critic" (Petry) **112**:389, 394
El novelista y su ambiente (Azuela) **145**:27-28
"Novelist's Allegory" (Galsworthy) **45**:33
A Novelist's Tour 'round the World (Blasco Ibáñez)
See *La vuelta al mundo de un novelista*
"La novella del buon vecchio e della bella fanciulla" (Svevo) **35**:333, 335-37, 343, 349, 351-52, 365
La novella del buon vecchio e della bella fanciulla e altri scritti (Svevo) **2**:541
Novella seconda (Gadda) **144**:131, 140
Novelle per un anno (Pirandello) **4**:327, 329; **29**:301; **172**:174
Novelle rusticane (Verga) **3**:543, 546, 548
Novelle valdostane (Giacosa) **7**:305
Novellen (Beer-Hofmann) **60**:24
Novellen (Heyse) **8**:113
Novelletter (Kielland) **5**:275-76, 279
The Novels and Tales of Henry James (James) **40**:145
The Novels of Dashiell Hammett (Hammett) **187**:45
"The Novels of E. M. Forster" (Woolf) **43**:405
The Novels of Swinburne (Swinburne) **36**:314
"The Novels of Thomas Hardy" (Woolf) **43**:404
"The Novel—What It Is" (Crawford) **10**:144, 148, 152
"Novel-Writing and Novel-Reading" (Howells) **7**:389
"November" (Davidson) **24**:191
"November 8" (Hippius) **9**:159
November, 1918 (Döblin) **13**:171, 175
"November Blue" (Meynell) **6**:299
"November by the Sea" (Lawrence) **93**:83
"November Cotton Flower" (Toomer) **172**:256, 274, 315-16, 327-28
"November Day" (Rilke)
See "Der Novembertag"
"November Eves" (Flecker) **43**:190, 199
November Hurricane (Hrabal) **155**:149-50
"The November Muse" (Sarton) **120**:272
"November Ode" (Merrill) **173**:216-17
"November Third" (Miyazawa) **76**:280, 298, 300-302
"Der Novembertag" (Rilke) **195**:258, 266
"Novembre" (Pascoli) **45**:154, 156
"La novia de Corinto" (Nervo) **11**:394
"La novia fiel" (Pardo Bazán) **189**:229, 290, 293-94
"La novia imposible" (Lugones) **15**:286, 289, 292
"La novia robada" (Onetti) **131**:218
La novia robada (Onetti) **131**:262
"Novissima polemica" (Carducci) **32**:107
"Novodevichy Monastery" (Ivanov) **33**:139

"Novogodnee" (Tsvetaeva) **35**:396-99
"The Novograd Church" (Babel)
See "Kostel v Novograde"
Novye lyudi (Hippius) **9**:160
"Novyi god" (Remizov) **27**:340, 349
"Novyj byt" (Zabolotsky) **52**:375
"Now" (Thomas) **8**:454
"Now and in the Hour of Our Death" (Rilke) **6**:369
"Now and Then" (Lardner) **2**:337
Now and Then: From Coney Island to Here (Heller) **131**:21; **151**:339-41
Now He Gives Up (Hansen)
See *Nu opgiver han*
"Now I Become Myself" (Sarton) **120**:318
"Now I Lay Me" (Hemingway) **115**:175, 180, 194
"Now It Is Spring" (Remizov)
See "Dnes vesna"
"Now Little by Little We Depart" (Esenin) **4**:115
"Now That April's Here" (Callaghan) **145**:226-27
"Now That I Am Awake" (Bryusov) **10**:81
"Now That Your Eyes Are Shut" (Wylie) **8**:528, 533-34
"Now the Day Is Over" (Baring-Gould) **88**:15
Now They Sing Again (Frisch)
See *Nun singen sie wieder*
Now They've Started Singing Again (Frisch)
See *Nun singen sie wieder*
Now We Are Six (Milne) **6**:309, 317; **88**:229
"Now We Know" (Mais) **8**:245, 247
"Now We're One" (Holly) **65**:147
Now With His Love (Bishop) **103**:2-5, 16-8
"Nowadays" (Dunsany) **59**:18
Nowaki (Natsume) **2**:491; **10**:345
Nowe wyzwolenie (Witkiewicz) **8**:513
Nowhere at Home: Letters from Exile of Emma Goldman and Alexander Berkman (Goldman) **13**:223
"Les noyades" (Swinburne) **8**:442
"Noyau de comète" (Péret) **20**:190
"N.S.A. Dope Calypso" (Ginsberg) **120**:113
"Nu" (García Lorca) **181**:185
"Nu löser solen sitt blonda har" (Lagerkvist) **144**:182, 185-87, 210
Nu opgiver han (Hansen) **32**:251, 260
"Nu Vaagner alle smaa vover" (Obstfelder) **23**:177
"Nu vänder mor sitt bibelblad" (Lagerkvist) **144**:178
"Nuances of a Theme by Williams" (Stevens) **45**:285, 297
"Nube feliz" (Aleixandre) **113**:14
"Las nubes" (Nervo) **11**:394
Nubes del estío (Pereda) **16**:379
"Nude!" (Jiménez) **183**:337
The Nude: A Study of Ideal Art (Clark) **147**:127-29
Nude and Costume (Mishima)
See *Ratai to Isho*
Nude in Mink (Rohmer) **28**:281
"Nuestra juventud" (Baroja) **8**:63
"Nuestras imposibilidades" (Borges) **109**:84, 87, 139, 157
"Nuestro amor" (Villaurrutia) **80**:487
Nuestro padre San Daniel (Miro) **5**:335, 337-40
"Nuestro primer cigarro" (Quiroga) **20**:211
Nuestros hijos (Sánchez) **37**:312-15, 318
Nueva burguesía (Azuela) **3**:78; **145**:12, 16, 18
La nueva cuestion palpitante (Pardo Bazán) **189**:234
"Nueva refutación del tiempo" (Borges) **109**:51, 76, 99, 112, 120, 122, 145, 156
"Nueva York: Oficina y denuncia" (García Lorca) **49**:81-2, 120
Nuevas canciones (Machado) **3**:305
"Los nueve monstruos" (Vallejo) **3**:531, 533; **56**:290, 306, 312
Nuevo tablado de Arlequín (Baroja) **8**:63
Nugget (Moricz)
See *Sárarany*
Nuggets and Dust Panned Out in California (Bierce) **44**:11, 34
Une nuit au Luxembourg (Gourmont) **17**:130, 133, 135, 137-40, 144, 146, 151-52, 154
"La nuit blanche" (Kipling) **8**:191
"Nuit blanche" (Lowell) **8**:237
"Nuit dans le port" (Larbaud) **9**:205
"La nuit d'Avril, 1915" (Apollinaire) **8**:28
"Nuit Rhénane" (Apollinaire) **51**:53
"Nuits partagées" (Éluard) **41**:149, 155, 158
Nüktergalen i Wittenberg (Strindberg) **8**:418
"Nullo" (Toomer) **172**:274-75, 287
Numa e ninfa (Lima Barreto) **23**:167-68
"Numa Ridge" (Abbey) **160**:15
Number One (Anouilh)
See *Le nombril*
"No. 2, The Pines" (Beerbohm) **1**:67; **24**:103, 123
Number 6 (Kandinsky)
See *Improvisation 6*
"No. 13: The Elpit-Rabkommun Building" (Bulgakov) **16**:83-4
Number 25 (Kandinsky)
See *Improvisation 25*
No. 26 Jayne Street (Austin) **25**:25-6, 30, 33, 35
Number 28a (Kandinsky)
See *Improvisation 28a*
No. Fifty-Five (Bromfield) **11**:82
A Number of People (Marsh) **99**:362, 365
"Number Three on the Docket" (Lowell) **8**:230
The Numbered (Canetti)
See *Die Befristeten*
"Numbers in the Dark" (Calvino) **183**:235
Numbers in the Dark and Other Stories (Calvino) **183**:221, 223, 234
Numquid et tu (Gide) **12**:144, 152
"Nun ist die Welt dein Haus . . ." (Raabe) **45**:190
Nun singen sie wieder (Frisch) **121**:218-23
"Nunc Dimittis" (Dahl) **173**:12
Nuns and Soldiers (Murdoch) **171**:206, 224, 262, 282-83, 307, 326-27
The Nun's Curse (Riddell) **40**:334-35
"Nuns of the Perpetual Adoration" (Dowson) **4**:85, 88
Nuori nainen (Leino) **24**:372
"Nuori Nietzsche" (Leino) **24**:371
La nuova colonia (Pirandello) **4**:345; **29**:301, 318-20
Nuove odi barbare (Carducci) **32**:87
Nuove poesie (Carducci) **32**:83, 107
Nuove Rime (Carducci)
See *Rime nuove*
Nuovi argomenti (Calvino) **183**:96
Nuovi versi alla Lina (Saba) **33**:373
The Nuptial Flight (Masters) **2**:467-69; **25**:293
Nuptial Song (Valle-Inclán) **5**:485
"Nuralkamar" (Lugones) **15**:293
"The Nürnberg Stove" (Ouida) **43**:350
"The Nurse" (Williams) **89**:396
"The Nurse or Attendant" (Machado de Assis)
See "O infemeiro"
"The Nursery" (Meynell) **6**:298
"The Nursery" (Zamyatin)
See "Detskaya"
"Nursery Chairs" (Milne) **88**:242
"A Nursery Tale" (Nabokov) **108**:205-11
Nursery Tales (Dazai Osamu) **11**:186
"Nurse's Story" (Wakefield) **120**:353
"Nurse's Tale" (Wakefield) **120**:354
"Nursing the Sick" (Nightingale) **85**:258
"Nutmeg Burley" (Williams) **89**:402
Nuts and Wine (Wodehouse) **108**:376
La nuvola di smog (Calvino) **183**:93-94, 118, 190-91, 193, 208, 210, 229, 238
"Nuvole" (Pirandello) **29**:310
Ny jord (Hamsun) **2**:204; **14**:220, 222-23, 226-27, 240; **49**:133-35, 153, 155, 162, 167-68; **151**:232, 234, 240
Det ny system (Bjoernson) **7**:104, 113; **37**:19
Den ny Verden (Jensen) **41**:290, 300-01, 303
Nya dikter (Heidenstam) **5**:253-55
Det nye tempel (Bojer) **64**:23
De nygifte (Bjoernson) **37**:18, 23, 29
"The Nymph" (Darío)
See "La ninfa"
"Nympholepsy" (Faulkner) **141**:94-96
"A Nympholept" (Swinburne) **8**:428, 445; **36**:321, 340-42, 347
Nymphs of the Valley (Gibran)
See *'Ar' is al-muruj*
A nyugtalanság völgye (Babits) **14**:39
"O alienista" (Machado de Assis) **10**:290-91
"O Amor bate na Aorta" (Drummond de Andrade) **139**:228
"O Basileus Klaudios" (Cavafy) **7**:162
"O Black and Unknown Bards" (Johnson) **3**:241; **19**:210, 216; **175**:233-34
"O Carib Isle!" (Crane) **5**:189; **80**:127
"O caso de vara" (Machado de Assis) **10**:285, 298
"O Cat with Gray Eyes" (Wright) **136**:301
"O Child of Uranus" (Carpenter) **88**:145
"O chizhe, kotoryi lgal, i o diatle liubitele istiny" (Gorky) **8**:73
"O cônego" (Machado de Assis) **10**:291
"O Cover Your Pale Legs" (Bryusov) **10**:96
"O, Deine Hande" (Lasker-Schueler) **57**:320
O di uno o di nessuno (Pirandello) **29**:299
"O dicionário" (Machado de Assis) **10**:291
"O Didn't He Ramble" (Johnson) **175**:225, 232
"O espelho" (Machado de Assis) **10**:290, 293, 296
"O facile de Paste" (Caragiale) **76**:157-59, 170
O fixador dos instantes (Sá-Carneiro) **83**:401
"O Florida, Venereal Soil" (Stevens) **12**:367
"O Germanii" (Tsvetaeva) **35**:388
"O Gott" (Lasker-Schueler) **57**:304
"O Graves" (Palamas) **5**:386
O homem dos sonhos (Sá-Carneiro) **83**:404
"O ich mocht aus der Welt" (Lasker-Schueler) **57**:305
O incesto (Sá-Carneiro) **83**:401
"O infemeiro" (Machado de Assis) **10**:280, 291
"O It's Nice to Get Up In, the slipshod mucous kiss / of her riant belly's fooling bore" (Cummings) **137**:45
"O kuu" (Natsume) **10**:338
"O lacună" (Caragiale) **76**:156
"O Let Not Virtue Seek" (Bishop) **103**:7, 19
"O Light, Resplendence, Sun-Eyed Morning!" (Radnóti) **16**:418
"O Literature, Revolution and Entropy" (Zamyatin)
See "O literature, revolyutsii i entropii"
"O literature, revolyutsii i entropii" (Zamyatin) **8**:556-57; **37**:429, 441, 444, 446-47
Ó locura ó santidad (Echegaray) **4**:97, 100-04, 106
O Lord (Sá-Carneiro) **83**:400
"O, Love's But a Dance" (Dobson) **49**:37
"O Make Me a Mask" (Thomas) **45**:400
"O malých poměrech" (Čapek) **37**:59
"O matuška, gde ty" (Bryusov) **10**:81
"O Mensch! Gib acht!" (Nietzsche) **10**:389
"O mina solbrandsfärgade toppar" (Södergran) **31**:285
"O Miracle of Fishes! The Long Dead Bite!" (Thomas) **45**:365
"O My Peaks Tinged with the Sun's Fire" (Södergran)
See "O mina solbrandsfärgade toppar"
"O net, ne stan" (Annensky) **14**:32
O noapte furtunoasă (Caragiale) **76**:155, 161-62, 164, 168, 177-78, 180
"O nową sztukę" (Przybyszewski) **36**:290
"O Peace of Ancient Prisons" (Radnóti) **16**:419
"O Pioneers" (Bishop) **103**:18
O Pioneers! (Cather) **1**:150-51, 153, 156-59, 162-65, 167; **11**:92, 94-8, 102, 104, 107, 110-13; **31**:24-5, 27-9, 33, 35, 37, 47, 59,

62; **99**:183, 207-08, 245, 257, 267-68, 281; **132**:123, 126, 129-32, 137, 140, 146-47, 152; **152**:1-126
"O poesia poesia" (Campana) **20**:83
O poezii (Mandelstam) **2**:410; **6**:265
O ponimanii (Rozanov) **104**:313, 344, 350, 382
"o pr / gress" (Cummings) **137**:67
"O relógio do hospital" (Ramos) **32**:431
"O reparatie" (Caragiale) **76**:156
O resgate (Sá-Carneiro) **83**:399
"O Russet Witch!" (Fitzgerald) **132**:136-37, 142
O scrisoare pierdută (Caragiale) **76**:155-56, 158-60, 162-65, 182, 184
"O segrêdo de Augusta" (Machado de Assis) **10**:295
"O segrêdo do bonzo" (Machado de Assis) **10**:290-91
"O Solitary of the Austere Sky" (Roberts) **8**:318
"O Thou That Achest" (Brennan) **17**:53
O věcech obecných čili ZOON POLITIKON (Čapek) **37**:59
Oaha (Wedekind) **7**:576
"An Oak" (Fletcher) **35**:95
Oak and Ivy (Dunbar) **2**:128; **12**:106, 108, 121-23, 127
"Oak and Olive" (Flecker) **43**:189, 192, 205
"Oak Leaves" (Austin) **25**:34
"Oak Leaves Are Hands" (Stevens) **12**:362; **45**:290
The Oakdale Affair (Burroughs) **32**:58
"The Oaks" (Herbert) **168**:57
"Oath by Laughter" (Khlebnikov) **20**:128
"The Oath by the Styx" (Sikelianos) **39**:408
The Oath of Allegiance (Phelps) **113**:342
Obakasan (Endo) **152**:167, 171, 177, 189, 191, 213, 216, 234, 239
Obasute (Dazai Osamu) **11**:175
"Obelisk" (Balmont) **11**:40
"The Oberiu Manifesto" (Zabolotsky) **52**:379
Oberland (Richardson) **3**:349, 352, 357-58
Oberlins drei Stufen und Sturreganz (Wassermann) **6**:510, 513
Oberlin's Three Stages (Wassermann) See *Oberlins drei Stufen und Sturreganz*
"Obervogelsang" (Schwitters) **95**:315
"Obeschaite!" (Guro) **56**:133
El obispo leproso (Miro) **5**:335, 338-41
"Los obispos del ajedrez" (Unamuno) **148**:308-9
Obiter Scripta (Santayana) **40**:366, 369, 406, 408
Obituaries (Saroyan) **137**:168, 171, 173
"The Objective Method in Aesthetics with a View to Creative Art" (Čapek) **192**:226, 235
"The Objective of International Price Stability Rejoinder to Hayek" (Keynes) **64**:259
"'Objectivity' in Social Science and Social Policy" (Weber) **69**:317-18, 382
"Oblako v shtanakh" (Mayakovski) **4**:291, 293-94, 297-98, 301; **18**:241-42, 245-48, 250-51, 255, 257, 261-62, 265-67, 270
L'oblat (Huysmans) **7**:406, 409-11; **69**:15, 43-5
The Oblate (Huysmans) See *L'oblat*
"The Oblation" (Swinburne) **36**:318
"Oblegči nam stradanija, Bože!" (Bryusov) **10**:93
Das obligate Rezitativ (Schoenberg) **75**:300
The Oblique Plane (Reyes) See *El plano oblicuo*
Obliteration (Bernhard) See *Auslöschung*
"Oblivion" (Sterling) **20**:373
"Oblivion's Sea" (Dunsany) **59**:27
Oboegaki (Yokomitsu) **47**:386
"Oboroyo" (Nagai) **51**:89
"Oborvanec" (Gumilev) **60**:279
"La Obra" (Jiménez) **183**:259, 262, 290, 296
Obra (Jiménez) **183**:256, 289-94
Obra completa (Drummond de Andrade) **139**:225
Obra en marcha de J. R. J. (Jiménez) **183**:270-71
Obra escogida (De La Parra) **185**:221
Obra: Narrativa, ensayos, cartas (De La Parra) **185**:211
Obra poética (Jiménez) **183**:270
Obra poetica, 1923-1964 (Borges) **109**:61, 78
"Obra y Sol" (Jiménez) **183**:290
Obras (Ibarguengoitia) **148**:202-3
Obras completas (Aleixandre) **113**:23, 58, 69
Obras completas (Azuela) **145**:21
Obras completas (Borges) **109**:28, 32, 54-6, 75, 77-8, 84-5, 92-6, 140, 151, 155-57
Obras Completas (García Lorca) **49**:89; **181**:44-50, 67, 90-93, 118, 122, 137-47
Obras completas (Huidobro) **31**:127
Obras completas (Miro) **5**:343
Obras completas (Nervo) **11**:399
Obras completas (Pardo Bazán) **189**:197, 199, 222, 227, 230, 235, 241, 259, 266-67, 269-70
Obras completas (Pereda) **16**:380
Obras completas (Unamuno) **148**:253-54, 258-59, 313, 337
Obras completas de Mário de Andrade (Andrade) **43**:13
Obras completas de Mário de Sá-Carneiro (Sá-Carneiro) **83**:409
"El obrero" (Storni) **5**:452
The O'Brien Girl (Cohan) **60**:165
Obručenie daši (Bryusov) **10**:86
The Obscene Bird of Night (Donoso) See *El obsceno pájaro de la noche*
El obsceno pájaro de la noche (Donoso) **133**:39-42, 45-46, 49-58, 60-62, 64-67, 69, 71, 75, 78, 80, 82, 100, 118, 122-23, 127, 129-30, 132, 135, 140, 146-51, 154-55, 157, 159, 161-62, 164, 166, 168-71, 185-89, 192
L'obscur à Paris (Bosschere) **19**:66-8
The Obscurantists (Tolstoy) **18**:382
Obscure Destinies (Cather) **1**:154; **11**:95, 98, 107-08
"The Obscurity of the Poet" (Jarrell) **177**:154, 157, 222, 238, 240, 242
"Obsequies of the Dead" (McAlmon) **97**:87
"An Observation" (Sarton) **120**:267, 295
"Observation Post: Forward Area" (Lewis) **3**:290
Observations (Capote) **164**:199
"Observe How Miyanoshita Cracked in Two" (Millay) **4**:316
The Obsession (Tolstoy) **18**:378
Obsessions (Nemerov) **124**:231
Obshchestvo pochetnykh zvonarey (Zamyatin) **8**:558; **37**:419
Obsluhoval jsem anglického krále (Hrabal) **155**:145, 147-48, 151, 153, 158, 161, 163
Obstinate (Kandinsky) **92**:32
L'Obvie et l'obtus (Barthes) **135**:137, 139-41, 161
"The Obvious Secret" (Ivanov) **33**:138
Obyčejnýživot (Čapek) **37**:50, 54, 57, 59-60; **192**:176, 185, 223, 230
"Occasional Licenses" (Somerville & Ross) **51**:384
"An Occasional Poem" (Jozsef) **22**:162
"Occasional Poems, No. 1" (Su Man-shu) **24**:456
"Occasional Poems, No. 4" (Su Man-shu) **24**:457
"Gli occhiali" (Pirandello) **29**:310
Occidentaes (Machado de Assis) **10**:279
Occidental Mythology (Campbell) See *The Masks of God: Occidental Mythology*
Occult Happenings (Mann) See *Okkulte Erlebnisse*
Occupe-toi d'Amélie (Feydeau) **22**:77, 79, 81, 84, 87, 94-5
Occupied City (van Ostaijen) See *Bezette stad*
"An Occurrence at Brownville" (Bierce) **44**:44-5
"An Occurrence at Owl Creek Bridge" (Bierce) **1**:84, 87, 95; **7**:88, 92, 95; **44**:6, 12, 29, 32-3, 44-5, 47, 50-1
"An Occurrence Up a Side Street" (Cobb) **77**:119, 133, 136, 140-1
"The Occurrences" (Oppen) **107**:266, 335, 359-60
"Ocean" (Callaghan) **145**:253
"The Ocean and Japanese Literature" (Rohan) **22**:302
"Océan de terre" (Apollinaire) **8**:29; **51**:37
"The Ocean Liner" (Monroe) **12**:216
"The Ocean of Sex" (Carpenter) **88**:107
"Ocean of the Full Moon" (Devkota) See "Pūrnimāko jaladhi"
"Ocean Oneness" (Aurobindo) **63**:8
"Ocean Sunsets" (Sterling) **20**:386
"The Ocean to Cynthia" (Nemerov) **124**:232, 291
"Ocean-Letter" (Apollinaire) See "Lettre-Océan"
Ocharovaniia zemli (Sologub) **9**:444
Ocher (Storni) See *Ocre*
Ochre (Storni) See *Ocre*
Ocol (p'Bitek) See *Song of Ocol*
Ocre (Storni) **5**:444, 447, 448, 450, 452
Octave Four (Mackenzie) See *My Life and Times*
"Octaves" (Robinson) **101**:99, 119, 123, 193
"October" (Dunbar) **12**:106, 121
"October" (Lorde) **173**:142
"October" (Percy) **84**:198
"October" (Thomas) **10**:453-55
"October, Afternoon" (Radnóti) **16**:419
October, and Other Poems (Bridges) **1**:124
October Ferry to Gabriola (Lowry) **6**:244-47, 250-51, 254; **40**:260-61
"October Island" (March) **96**:259
October Island (March) **96**:238, 251, 259, 264, 267
October Journey (Walker) **129**:273, 276, 305, 316, 318
October Light (Gardner) **195**:105, 150
"October Night" (Jensen) See "Oktobernat"
"October on the Neva" (Khlebnikov) See "Oktyabr na neve"
"An October Ride" (Jewett) **22**:140
October: Ten Days that Shook the World (Eisenstein) See *Oktyabre*
"October Tragedy" (Bishop) **103**:5-6
The Octopus (Norris) **24**:417-18, 420-32, 435-40, 442, 444, 449-52; **155**:258-60, 263-66, 269-70, 311, 317-19, 322, 331, 333-34, 338-41
"The Octopush" (Crane) **11**:159
"Óda a bűnhöz" (Babits) **14**:39
"Oda a los ganados y las mieses" (Lugones) **51**:289-90
"Oda a Salvador Dali" (García Lorca) **1**:314
"Óda a szépségről" (Babits) **14**:39
"Oda a Walt Whitman" (García Lorca) **1**:308
Uma oda de anacreonte (Machado de Assis) **10**:279
Odas seculares (Lugones) **15**:286, 288, 291
Odd Craft (Jacobs) **22**:102
Odd John: A Story between Jest and Earnest (Stapledon) **22**:311, 322-23, 325-31, 334, 337-38, 344
"The Odd Slipper" (Calvino) **183**:143
The Odd Women (Gissing) **3**:232-33; **24**:216-17, 230-31, 233-34, 239, 247; **47**:117, 139
"Odds Bodkins" (Lardner) **14**:308
"Ode" (Apollinaire) **8**:21
"Ode" (Bishop) **103**:6
"Ode" (Gray) **19**:158

"Ode" (Jozsef) **22**:162, 164
Ode aux poètes catalans (Mistral) **51**:150, 168
"Ode for the Keats Centenary" (Scott) **6**:386-88, 394
"An Ode in Time of Hesitation" (Moody) **105**:221-22, 224, 234, 237-38, 240, 253, 255, 260, 266-68, 272, 275
"Ode: My Twenty-Fourth Year" (Ginsberg) **120**:76
"Ode No Cinqüentenário do Poeta Brasileiro" (Drummond de Andrade) **139**:229
"Ode of the Virgin Mary" (Sikelianos) **39**:404
"Ode on a White Porcelain Vase" (Shimazaki Toson) **5**:431
"Ode on Melancholy" (Cullen) **4**:53
"Ode on Melancholy" (Owen) **27**:210
"Ode on the Coronation" (Carman) **7**:137
"Ode on the Coronation of Edward VII" (Davidson) **24**:187
"Ode on the Death of the Prince Imperial" (Carducci) **32**:103-04
"Ode on the Insurrection in Candia" (Swinburne) **36**:308
"Ode secrète" (Valéry) **4**:491
"Ode to a Beggar Girl" (Moore) **7**:487
"Ode to a Dead Body" (Moore) **7**:487
"Ode to Alexander II" (Vazov) **25**:453
"Ode to Austrian Socialists" (Benét) **7**:74
"An Ode to Beauty" (Babits)
See "Óda a szépségről"
"An Ode to Drowsihood" (Roberts) **8**:313-14, 319
"Ode to Ethiopia" (Dunbar) **12**:105, 109, 121, 125
"Ode to Fame" (Masters) **25**:296
"Ode to Ferrara" (Carducci) **32**:102, 104
"Ode to H. H. the Nizam of Hyderabad" (Naidu) **80**:314
"Ode to India" (Naidu) **80**:334
Ode to Napoleon (Schoenberg) **75**:302, 317-18, 347-48
"Ode to Psyche" (Crane) **2**:123
"Ode to Psyche" (Rilke) **195**:244
"Ode to Rhyme" (Carducci)
See "Alla rima"
"Ode to Rome" (Carducci)
See "Roma"
"Ode to Salvador Dali" (García Lorca)
See "Oda a Salvador Dali"
"Ode to Silence" (Millay) **4**:306, 310, 316
"An Ode to Sin" (Babits)
See "Óda a bűnhöz"
"Ode to the Bourgeois Gentleman" (Andrade) **43**:7
Ode to the Catalans (Mistral)
See *Ode aux poètes catalans*
"Ode to the Mediterranean" (Santayana) **40**:340
"Ode to the Setting Sun" (Thompson) **4**:435
"Ode to the Spirit of Auguste Comte" (Buchanan) **107**:71
"Ode to the Springs of Clitumnus" (Carducci)
See "Alle fonti del Clitumno"
"Ode to Walt Whitman" (Benét) **7**:74
"Ode to Walt Whitman" (García Lorca)
See "Oda a Walt Whitman"
Ode to Walt Whitman (García Lorca) **181**:160
"Oderzhimy" (Gumilev) **60**:279
Odes of Horace (Marsh) **99**:355, 363
Odes to the Sacrament (García Lorca) **1**:314
"Odessa" (Babel)
See "Kak eto delalos v Odesse"
The Odessa Stories (Babel)
See *Odesskie rasskazy*
The Odessa Tales (Babel)
See *Odesskie rasskazy*
Odesskie rasskazy (Babel) **171**:15, 50-51, 54, 56-58, 61, 92-93, 96, 104
Das Odfeld (Raabe) **45**:164, 169, 172, 177, 179, 182-83, 185, 198
Odi barbare (Carducci) **32**:84-7, 91-2, 97, 99, 101-02, 108-09
Odi navali (D'Annunzio) **6**:136
"Odin" (Zamyatin) **8**:551-52
The Odin Field (Raabe)
See *Das Odfeld*
Ödipus und die Sphinx (Hofmannsthal) **11**:292
Odna lyubov' (Sologub) **9**:444
Odnoetazhnaya Amerika (Petrov) **21**:152, 154-58
Odoriko (Nagai) **51**:98
"The Odor-Organ" (Morgenstern) **8**:305
"The Odour of Chrysanthemums" (Lawrence) **9**:220
Odyseia (Kazantzakis) **2**:312-14, 317-23; **5**:261-64, 267-68, 272; **33**:148, 152-53, 155, 163, 166, 168, 170, 173-74; **181**:208-12, 215, 217-19, 221-22, 224-28, 295, 303, 313, 316-17, 325
Odysseus (Kazantzakis) **33**:171
"The Odyssey" (Lewis) **3**:287
The Odyssey: A Modern Sequel (Kazantzakis)
See *Odyseia*
Odyssey of a Friend (Chambers) **129**:8, 10-11, 19, 43
"The Odyssey of 'Erbert 'Iggins" (Service) **15**:399
"An Odyssey of the North" (London) **9**:274; **15**:257, 262
"The Odysseys Within the Odyssey" (Calvino) **183**:102
Oedipe (Gide) **5**:232; **36**:99; **177**:86
Oedipe-Roi, pied gonflés (Cocteau) **119**:77
"Oedipus" (Muir) **2**:482; **87**:167
Oedipus and the Sphinx (Hofmannsthal)
See *Ödipus und die Sphinx*
Oedipus tyrannos (Giraudoux) **2**:167
"Oeillet" (Apollinaire) **8**:12
L'oeuvre (Zola) **1**:589; **6**:566, 569; **41**:413-14, 422, 424, 435, 442
L'Oeuvre au noir (Yourcenar) **193**:250-51, 256, 265, 270-75, 279-80, 302, 306, 320-21, 347, 351-52, 364
Oeuvres complètes (Apollinaire) **51**:19-20
Oeuvres complètes (Artaud) **36**:31
Œuvres (Barrès) **47**:93
Oeuvres complètes (Barthes) **135**:184-85
Oeuvres complètes (Bataille) **155**:4, 7-8, 118
Oeuvres complètes (Bourget) **12**:69-70
Oeuvres complètes (Genet) **128**:179
Œuvres complètes (Jarry) **147**:242-45, 305-7, 310-13, 315
Oeuvres complètes (Tzara) **168**:269, 271, 273, 275-77, 317, 321-23
Oeuvres complètes d'André (Gide) **177**:14, 25-28, 34, 39, 46, 48-50, 61, 73, 100
Oeuvres completes de Vilfredo Pareto (Pareto) **69**:155
Oeuvres, vol. I (Sully Prudhomme) **31**:301
"Of a Land, a River and Lakes" (Bachmann) **192**:65
"Of a Woman, Dead Young: (J. H., 1905-1930)" (Parker) **143**:325
Of a World That Is No More (Singer) **33**:387, 402
"Of Alexander Crummell" (Du Bois) **169**:115, 208
Of All Things (Benchley) **1**:81; **55**:2, 6
"Of Being Numerous" (Oppen) **107**:257, 259-60, 264, 304, 317, 322, 330, 335, 358-60, 366
Of Being Numerous (Oppen) **107**:255-56, 258, 260, 263-64, 304, 306, 311, 316, 323, 328, 349, 352
"Of Cruelty" (Gurney) **33**:88
"Of Demetrius Soter, 162-150 B.C." (Cavafy) **7**:157
Of Fear and Freedom (Levi)
See *Paura della libertà*
"Of Ghosts and Goblins" (Hearn) **9**:129
"Of Grief" (Sarton) **120**:268
"Of Hartford in a Purple Light" (Stevens) **45**:281
"Of History" (Valéry) **4**:493
"Of Hours" (Oppen) **107**:291, 294, 296, 306, 356
Of Kings and the Crown (Huch)
See *Von den Königen und der Krone*
"Of Kings' Treasuries" (Ruskin) **63**:313
"Of Mere Being" (Stevens) **45**:287
Of Mice and Men (Steinbeck) **135**:264, 289-90, 321, 343, 349
"Of Modern Poetry" (Stevens) **3**:459; **45**:269, 277-78, 296, 302, 325, 349-50
"Of Mollusks" (Sarton) **120**:271
"Of Mr. Booker T. Washington and Others" (Du Bois) **169**:110, 187, 208
"Of Mutability" (Hofmannsthal) **11**:294
Of My Possessions (Kahanovitsch)
See *Fun meine giter*
Of Old Proteus (Raabe) **45**:201
Of One Blood, or The Hidden Self (Hopkins) **28**:175-76
"Of Our Spiritual Strivings" (Du Bois) **169**:81, 94, 103, 106-7, 120, 129, 137-38, 141-42, 182, 202
"Of Poor B. B." (Brecht) **1**:103, 115
"Of Protest" (Abbey) **160**:103
"Of Queens' Gardens" (Ruskin) **63**:291-94, 312-15
"Of Sensuous Activity" (Yokomitsu)
See "Kankaku-Katsudô"
"Of Souls" (Hearn) **9**:129
Of the Almighty, and Others (Rilke)
See *Vom liebe Gott und Andres*
"Of the Best Stories" (Lucas) **73**:171
Of the Categories (Alexander)
See *Space, Time, and Deity*
"Of the Color of Nothingness" (Aleixandre)
See "Del color de la nada"
"Of the Coming of John" (Du Bois) **169**:89, 105, 125, 127-28, 184-85, 190, 204
"Of the Dawn of Freedom" (Du Bois) **169**:110, 120, 140, 184
"Of the Faith of the Fathers" (Du Bois) **169**:89, 104, 120, 140, 149-50
Of the Fifth Year (Kahanovitsch)
See *Fun finftn yor*
"Of the Futility of the 'Theatrical' in the Theater" (Jarry)
See "De l'inutilité du théâtre au théâtre"
"Of the Golden Age" (Guiney) **41**:207
"Una of the Hill Country" (Barthes) **135**:209
"Of the Meaning of Progress" (Du Bois) **169**:103, 132, 192
Of the Mind (Tagore)
See *Mānasī*
"Of the Muse" (Sarton) **120**:245, 297
"Of the Passing of the First-Born" (Du Bois) **169**:89, 105, 141, 153-61, 192
"Of the Sons of Master and Man" (Du Bois) **169**:100, 109, 121, 167
"Of the Sorrow Songs" (Du Bois) **169**:80-81, 83-84, 87-88, 91, 93-94, 120, 127, 135, 137, 139-41, 144, 149, 154, 190, 203
"Of the Surface of Things" (Stevens) **45**:297
"Of the Training of Black Men" (Du Bois) **169**:100, 109, 167, 185, 190, 200
"Of the Wings of Atalanta" (Du Bois)
See "Of the Wings of Atlanta"
"Of the Wings of Atlanta" (Du Bois) **169**:104, 110, 190
Of This (Mayakovski) **18**:243-44, 248
Of Time and the River (Wolfe) **4**:507-08, 511-16, 518-21, 523, 525, 527-28, 531-32, 536-39; **13**:467-68, 470, 472-75, 479, 490, 492, 494-96; **29**:405, 409, 412; **61**:280-319
"Of Troy" (Herbert) **168**:44
Of Us Now Living: A Novel of Australia (Ingamells) **35**:124
"Of Women" (Dazai Osamu)
See "Mesu ni tsuite"
"Of Women's Novels" (Matthews) **95**:276
"Ofermod" (Tolkien) **137**:284
Off Broadway (Anderson) **144**:7, 34, 48, 71
Off Limits (Adamov) **189**:15, 59

Off on a Comet! (Verne)
See *Hector Servadac: Voyages et aventures à travers le monde solaire*
"Off Pelorus" (Roberts) **8**:316
"Off Riviere du Loup" (Scott) **6**:388
"Off Shore" (Swinburne) **36**:346
Off the Arm (Marquis) **7**:446
"Off the Cherry Tree" (Wright) **136**:299
"Off the Sand Road" (Kirk) **119**:278
"Off the Turnpike" (Lowell) **8**:230
"Off to the Country" (Fields) **80**:258, 260
Off-Color Sauce (Palma)
See *Tradiciones en salsa verde*
"Offen" (Kandinsky) **92**:66
"The Offended Man" (Čapek) **37**:51
"The Offensive" (Douglas) **40**:87
"The Offensive 2" (Douglas) **40**:83
"Öffentilichkeit als Partner" (Frisch) **121**:201, 233
"The Offering of Plebs" (Bosschere)
See "L'offre de plebs"
An Offering of Swans, and Other Poems (Gogarty) **15**:100-01, 103, 114
"L'offre de plebs" (Bosschere) **19**:52, 54-5, 58-9, 63-4
Offret (Strindberg) **8**:408
"Off-Shore" (Tomlinson) **71**:400
"Ofilire" (Rebreanu) **28**:273
"Ofort" (Zabolotsky) **52**:377-78
Oft in der Nacht träume ich (Brecht) **169**:40
"L'oganisation matrimoniale australienne" (Durkheim) **55**:91
Ognennyi angel (Bryusov) **10**:79-81, 83-5, 87, 90-1, 96
Ognennyi kon' (Gladkov) **27**:89-90
Ognennyi stolp (Gumilev) **60**:260, 262, 268-73, 276
Ogni svyatogo Dominika (Zamyatin) **8**:543, 546-47, 558; **37**:429, 432
Ogniem i mieczem (Sienkiewicz) **3**:422-24, 426-27, 429-30
"Ognjena vucica" (Popa) **167**:161
Ogon' veshchei (Remizov) **27**:349
"Ogon'ki" (Korolenko) **22**:180
"Ograda" (Hippius) **9**:156
"Oh Boy!" (Holly) **65**:143, 145, 148
"Oh death shall find me" (Brooke) **7**:124
"Oh, for a Little While Be Kind" (Cullen) **4**:40; **37**:153, 167-68
"Oh Happy Eyes" (Bachmann)
See "Ihr glücklichen Augen"
"Oh, He's Charming" (Parker) **143**:331
"Oh l'anima vivente" (Campana) **20**:83
"Oh, Little Town of Houffalice" (Patton) **79**:307
"Oh, Love! Oh, Fire!" (Somerville & Ross) **51**:335, 357, 384
"Oh, Madam . . ." (Bowen) **148**:53
"Oh My Homeland, You Are Like Health" (Cankar) **105**:163
"Oh No, It Is Not Your Figure" (Annensky)
See "O net, ne stan"
"Oh, See How Thick the Gold Cup Flowers" (Housman) **10**:249
"Oh To Be in 'Bartlett' Now that April's Here" (Morley) **87**:146
"Oh Whistle and I'll Come to You, My Lad" (James) **6**:206, 209, 211-13, 215
"Oh, Who Is That Young Sinner with the Handcuffs on His Wrist?" (Housman) **10**:245
"Oh, You Wonderful Girl" (Cohan) **60**:168
"O'Halloran's Luck" (Benét) **7**:75, 81
Oharu (Mizoguchi)
See *Saikaku Ichidai Onna*
Ohio Impromptu (Beckett) **145**:133-41, 150, 152, 155-56
The Ohio Lady (Tarkington) **9**:464
Ohio Pastorals (Dunbar) **12**:132
Ohio Town (Santmyer) **133**:210, 214, 216, 219
Ein ohne Männer (Horvath) **45**:78, 80, 82, 112
"Ohola greska" (Popa) **167**:153, 156
"Ohrensausen" (Meyrink) **21**:223
Der Ohrenzeuge: Fünfzig Charaktere (Canetti) **157**:63
"L'oie bleue" (Vian) **9**:532
The Oil Islands (Feuchtwanger)
See *Die Petroleuminseln*
"Oil of Dog" (Bierce) **1**:88; **44**:29, 32-3, 40, 45, 51
"Un oiseau a fienté sur mon veston salaud" (Péret) **20**:184
L'oiseau bleu (Maeterlinck) **3**:322, 324, 329, 331
"Un oiseau chante" (Apollinaire) **3**:35; **51**:36
"Oisin" (Yeats) **93**:347
"O-Jii-San" (Pickthall) **21**:246
"Ojo" (Storni) **5**:452
"Los ojos" (García Lorca) **49**:120
"Los ojos de la reina" (Lugones) **15**:286
Los ojos de los enterrados (Asturias) **184**:16, 45-46, 48-49, 87-88
Okamezasa (Nagai) **51**:86, 94-5
Okay: An American Novel (Pilnyak) **23**:208-09
"Oke of Okehurst" (Lee) **5**:320
Okhotnik Usa-Gali (Khlebnikov) **20**:127, 136, 150
Okhrannaia gramota (Pasternak) **188**:251-52
"Okitsu yagoemon no isho" (Mori Ogai) **14**:378, 380
Okkulte Erlebnisse (Mann) **44**:162
"Oktobernat" (Jensen) **41**:306
Oktobertag (Kaiser) **9**:180-81, 186
"Oktyabr na neve" (Khlebnikov) **20**:136, 150
Oktyabre (Eisenstein) **57**:152-53, 161, 163, 165-70, 172-73, 175, 178, 186-87, 189-91, 196
Okubo dayori (Nagai) **51**:104
"Okume" (Shimazaki Toson) **5**:439
Ola Hansson (Przybyszewski) **36**:286
"Olaf and His Girlfriend" (Petry) **112**:300-01
Olav Audunssøn i Hestviken (Undset) **3**:513; **197**:324, 336
The Old Adam (Bennett)
See *The Regent*
"Old Age" (Akutagawa Ryūnosuke)
See "Rōnen"
"Old Age" (Bodenheim) **44**:59
Old Age and Youth (Deledda)
See *Il vecchio e i fonciulli*
"The Old Age of Queen Maeve" (Yeats) **11**:512
"The Old Age Pensioner" (Schulz)
See "Emeryt"
"Old Ancestor Envy" (Ady) **11**:15
The Old and the New (Eisenstein)
See *Staroi i novoie*
The Old and the New (Strindberg)
See *Det gamla och det nya*
"The Old and the New Masters" (Jarrell) **177**:156, 162, 164, 167, 240-41
The Old and the Young (Pirandello)
See *I vecchi e i giovani*
"Old Aunt Peggy" (Chopin) **127**:167
"Old Autumn" (Davies) **5**:203
"Old 'Barge' Bill" (Davies) **5**:198
"Old Battleship" (Flecker) **43**:189
"The Old Beauty" (Cather) **11**:109; **132**:137
The Old Beauty and Others (Cather) **1**:155, 160; **11**:107; **132**:137
"The Old Bell-Ringer" (Korolenko) **22**:169-70
Old Blastus of Bandicoot (Franklin) **7**:267-68, 270, 274
Old Burnside (Arnow) **196**:29, 95
Old Bush Songs (Paterson) **32**:374
"The Old Cabin" (Dunbar) **12**:114
Old Calabria (Douglas) **68**:3, 5, 7, 9-11, 16, 25, 27, 39, 43-5
Old Cambridge (Higginson) **36**:170
"Old Chartist" (Meredith) **17**:254
"Old Christmas" (Lovecraft) **4**:265; **22**:241
Old Clothing (Palma)
See *Ropa vieja*
"The Old Comedies" (Matthews) **95**:228
The Old Country (Aleichem) **1**:22; **35**:313
"Old Country Advice to the American Traveler" (Saroyan) **137**:165
Old Creole Days (Cable) **4**:24, 26-7, 29-33
The Old Dark House (Whale) **63**:340-42, 351, 355-58, 360, 379, 383-84, 388
"Old Dibs" (Osbourne) **93**:132
"The Old Disorder in Europe" (Becker) **63**:116
The Old Dog Barks Backwards (Nash) **109**:356-57, 366
"The Old Doll's House" (Runyon) **10**:434
"Old Earth" (Johnson) **3**:243
"Old Engine .007" (Kipling) **17**:209
Old English (Galsworthy) **1**:303; **45**:52
"The Old Farm" (Masters) **25**:316
"The Old Flag Never Touched the Ground" (Johnson) **175**:225
Old Fogy (Huneker) **65**:165-67, 188, 205
The Old Folk of the Centuries (Dunsany) **59**:17, 22-3, 26
"Old Folks" (Mikszath)
See "Az öregek"
"Old Folks Christmas" (Lardner) **14**:314
"The Old Folks of Mäetaguse" (Tammsaare)
See "Kuresaare vanad"
"The Old Fool in the Wood" (Noyes) **7**:515
"An Old Friend" (Riley) **51**:294
Old Friends (Lang) **16**:256
Old Friends and New (Jewett) **1**:359, 361, 367; **22**:118
"The Old Front Gate" (Dunbar) **12**:104
"Old Furniture" (Hardy) **53**:106; **143**:108, 169
"Old Garbo" (Thomas) **8**:456, 463; **45**:393-94, 396, 398; **105**:302, 321, 344, 346
"The Old Garden" (Stringer) **37**:328
"Old Garfield's Heart" (Howard) **8**:128
"Old Gen" (Kunikida Doppo)
See "Gen Oji"
"The Old Gestures" (Knister) **56**:155
"The Old Gods" (Muir) **87**:167, 203
"Old Gongh" (Gray) **19**:156
Old Heidelberg (Stroheim) **71**:338
Old Home Town (Lane) **177**:266-70, 272, 282
"The Old Horse" (Tolstoy)
See "Staraya loshad"
"The Old Horse Player" (Runyon) **10**:429, 437
"The Old House" (Södergran)
See "Det gamla huset"
The Old House in the Country (Reese) **181**:339
Old House of Fear (Kirk) **119**:253, 277-79, 283-84, 291, 302, 345-48
"An Old Hungarian Portrait" (Babits)
See "Régi magyar arckép"
Old Indian Days (Eastman) **55**:163, 167-72, 174
Old Iron (Raabe)
See *Im alten Eisen*
"Old Japanese Songs" (Hearn) **9**:129
"The Old Jimmy Woodser" (Lawson) **27**:134
Old Junk (Tomlinson) **71**:383, 386, 400-402
"Old King Cole" (Robinson) **101**:111
The Old King's Tale (Dunsany) **59**:14
The Old Ladies (Walpole) **5**:496-97, 501
"The Old Lady Counts Her Injuries" (Slesinger) **10**:445
"Old Lady Pingree" (Freeman) **9**:74
The Old Lady Shows Her Medals (Barrie) **2**:41
Old Lady Thirty-One (Crothers) **19**:71-2, 77
"The Old Lag" (Freeman) **21**:44, 51, 54, 59
Old Lamps for New (Lucas) **73**:170
"Old Lovers at a Ballet" (Sarton) **120**:318
"Old Loving-Kindness" (Williams) **89**:396
"The Old Lutheran Bells at Home" (Stevens) **3**:472
"The Old Maid" (Gumilev)
See "Staraja deva"
"Old Maid" (Lane) **177**:267-68
"The Old Maid" (Wharton) **129**:350, 363
The Old Maid (The 'Fifties) (Wharton) **9**:550; **129**:365
The Old Maids' Club (Zangwill) **16**:444, 462
An Old Maid's Paradise (Phelps) **113**:336
"The Old Malign" (Ady)
See "Az ős kaján"
"Old Man" (Bodenheim) **44**:62

"Old Man" (Faulkner) **141**:49-50, 53-55, 117-18, 121, 124
"The Old Man" (Slesinger) **10**:446
"Old Man" (Thomas) **10**:454, 463, 465
"The Old Man and the Old Woman" (Platonov) **14**:419
The Old Man and the Sea (Hemingway) **115**:163
"An Old Man Asleep" (Stevens) **45**:302
Old Man in New World (Stapledon) **22**:322, 332-33
"Old Man Murtrie" (Marquis) **7**:437
The Old Man of the Mountain (Deledda) See *Il vecchio della montagna*
"The Old Man of the Sea" (Brennan) **124**:5
"The Old Man with a Wen" (Dazai Osamu) **11**:186
"Old Mandarin" (Morley) **87**:146
"Old Man's Beard" (Wakefield) **120**:343
Old Man's Beard: Fifteen Disturbing Tales (Wakefield) **120**:347, 353-54, 357
"An Old Man's Confessions" (Svevo) See "Le confessioni del vegliardo"
"The Old Man's Wife" (Slesinger) **10**:446
"Old Martinmas Eve" (Gurney) **33**:94, 103
"The Old Masters" (Herbert) **168**:73; **168**:23
Old Masters (Bernhard) See *Alte Meister*
"The Old Men of the Twilight" (Yeats) **31**:417
"Old Miss" (Handy) **97**:44
"The 'Old Mole'" (Bataille) **155**:97, 110-11
"The Old Mole" (Luxemburg) **63**:220
"Old Mrs. Crosley" (Gilman) **37**:215
"Old Mrs. Harris" (Cather) **11**:98, 107-08; **132**:121, 136, 138
"The Old Neighborhood" (Dreiser) **35**:71, 74-6
Old Nests (Raabe) See *Alte Nester*
Old New York (Wharton) **3**:558-59, 574, 580; **9**:550-51; **129**:363; **149**:245
Old Offenders and a Few Old Scores (Hornung) **59**:113
The Old, Old Man (Svevo) See *Il vecchione*
"Old, Old, Old, Old Andrew Jackson" (Lindsay) **17**:236
"Old Olives at Bordighera" (Scott) **6**:394
"An Old Pain" (Ledwidge) **23**:119
"Old Pardon, the Son of Reprieve" (Paterson) **32**:373-74, 376
"Old Paul and Old Tim" (Gilbert) **3**:212
"The Old People" (Faulkner) **141**:103, 113; **170**:162, 166
Old People and the Things That Pass (Couperus) See *Van oude menschen de dingen de voorbigaan*
"Old Pipes and the Dryad" (Stockton) **47**:323, 327, 329
"Old Pourquoi" (Moody) **105**:237, 246, 267, 272
"An Old Priest Is My Mother's Uncle" (Babits) See "Anyám nagybátyja réji pap"
"The Old Prometheus" (Herbert) See "Stary Prometeusz"
"The Old Ranch" (Güiraldes) See "La estancia vieja"
"The Old Ringer" (Korolenko) See "The Old Bell-Ringer"
"Old Rogaum and His Theresa" (Dreiser) **35**:72
Old Rosa (Arenas) **191**:226
Old Secret (Gladkov) See *Staraya sekretnaya*
"Old Sedan Chair" (Dobson) **79**:2, 18
"The Old Servant" (Sienkiewicz) **3**:426
Old Shellover (de la Mare) **4**:82
"The Old Shepherd's Prayer" (Mew) **8**:299-300
"The Old Ships" (Flecker) **43**:191, 193-94, 198-99
The Old Soak (Marquis) **7**:440, 446-47, 450-51
The Old Soak's History of the World, with Occasional Glances at Baycliff, L.I., and Paris, France (Marquis) **7**:437, 446, 450
"An Old Song" (Thomas) **10**:452, 463
"Old Sorority Sister" (March) **96**:248
"The Old South" (Fletcher) **35**:98
"Old Spring" (Lasker-Schueler) **57**:328-29, 336
Old Square No. 4 (Babel) See *Staraja ploščad', 4*
"Old Step-Mother Nature" (Benchley) **55**:6
"The Old Stone Cross" (Yeats) **31**:411
"An Old Story" (Cullen) **37**:165, 168
"An Old Story" (Robinson) **5**:400; **101**:197
"An Old Sweetheart of Mine" (Riley) **51**:291, 297, 302
"The Old Swimmin' Hole" (Riley) **51**:276-78
The Old Swimmin' Hole, and 'Leven More Poems (Riley) **51**:277
Old Tales (Bojer) **64**:16
"Old Tar" (Mansfield) **39**:319
"The Old Telegraph Station, Strangways" (Ingamells) **35**:137
Old Testament Plays (Housman) **7**:358
"Old Thought" (Gurney) **33**:103
"The Old Tibetan Carpet" (Lasker-Schueler) See "Der alte Tibetteppich"
"An Old Time Christmas" (Dunbar) **12**:120
"Old Times on the Mississippi" (Twain) **6**:466, 471; **19**:358, 384-85
The Old Town (Riis) **80**:434
"Old Trails" (Robinson) **101**:102-03, 134
"Old Trees" (Gosse) **28**:132
"The Old Vicarage, Grantchester" (Brooke) **2**:54-6, 58, 60-1; **7**:121, 123-27, 129
"The Old Warship Ablaze" (Flecker) **43**:191
"Old Water" (Gilman) **117**:100, 102-3
The Old Wives' Fairy Tale Book (Carter) **139**:140
Old Wives for New (Phillips) **44**:255-57, 260, 262, 265-66, 268, 275-78
"Old Wives' Tale" (Benchley) **55**:11
The Old Wives' Tale (Bennett) **5**:22-4, 26-30, 32-6, 38, 40-4, 47-50; **20**:17-20, 24, 26-7, 29-30, 32-5, 39-40; **197**:4, 7, 9, 11-12, 15, 18, 20, 25-6, 29-32, 35, 37-8, 41, 49, 54-5, 62, 72-73, 78, 82-9, 92, 94-5, 103-04, 107-09, 111, 114, 144-45, 152, 160-62, 164-65, 167-69
"The Old Woman" (Bosschere) **19**:54, 63
"An Old Woman" (Webb) **24**:466, 473
"The Old Woman and the Statue" (Stevens) **45**:276, 282, 348
The Old Woman Izergil (Gorky) **8**:73
"The Old Woman of Iron" (Platonov) **14**:413, 420
The Old Woman of the Movies, and Other Stories (Blasco Ibáñez) **12**:39
"The Old Woman Remembers" (Gregory) **176**:42
The Old Woman Remembers, and Other Irish Poems (Stringer) **37**:333
Old World Traits Transplanted (Park) **73**:211
"The Oldest Drama" (McCrae) **12**:211
"The Oldest Profession in the World" (Gilman) **117**:152, 159
The Oldest Story in the World (Saroyan) **137**:156
"Old-Fashioned Roses" (Riley) **51**:300-01
Old-Fashioned Roses (Riley) **51**:285
Old-Fashioned Tales (Gale) **7**:284
The Old-Fashioned Way (Fields) **80**:223
Old-New Land (Herzl) See *Altneuland*
The Oldster (Svevo) See *Il vecchione*
"The Old-Time Religion" (Bryan) **99**:153
Oldtown Days (Higginson) **36**:171
Old-World Idylls (Dobson) **79**:21, 38
"Ole Stormoen" (Bjoernson) **37**:33
"Ole Underwood" (Mansfield) **39**:301, 319; **164**:340-42
Olesya (Kuprin) **5**:301
"Olga" (Gumilev) **60**:272
"Olive and Camilla" (Coppard) **5**:181
Oliver Cromwell (Buchan) **41**:39, 51, 59, 62-3
Oliver Cromwell (Drinkwater) **57**:127-28, 130-31, 141-42
Oliver Cromwell (Roosevelt) **69**:243, 254
"Oliver Goldsmith" (Woolf) **43**:401
Oliver Goldsmith (Thomas) **97**:134
Oliver Wiswell (Roberts) **23**:235-36, 240, 243-44
Olivier (Coppee) **25**:120, 126
Olli suurpää (Leino) **24**:372
"Ollie McGee" (Masters) **25**:308
Olton, Tides, Loyalties (Drinkwater) **57**:148
"Olujaci" (Andrić) **135**:84, 95
"El olvido" (Aleixandre) **113**:36
Olya (Remizov) **27**:348-49
"Olympia" (Molnár) **20**:166
"The Olympian" (Dickey) **151**:170, 176
"The Olympians" (Abercrombie) **141**:18
"The Olympians" (Grahame) **64**:56
"Om" (Baker) **3**:4; **10**:21
"Om Modern drama och modern theater" (Strindberg) **47**:336, 362
Om Våren (Obstfelder) **23**:192
Omaenimo tsumi ga aru (Abe) **131**:11
L'ombilic des limbes (Artaud) **3**:51-2; **36**:16, 21, 25, 29, 32-3, 57
"L'ombre" (France) **9**:57
Ombre de mon amour (Apollinaire) **8**:14; **51**:8, 10, 13
L'ombre s'étend sur la montagne (Rod) **52**:309-10, 312
"El Ombú" (Hudson) **29**:155-56
"Omega" (García Lorca) **197**:211
Omens of the Earth (Tsvetaeva) **35**:410
Omer Pasha Latas (Andrić) **135**:96
"An Ominous Babe" (Crane) **11**:128
"Omkring sedelighetsballet" (Undset) **197**:302
"Ommi" (Yokomitsu) **47**:394
"Omnia Vincit Amor" (Morley) **87**:140
Omoidasu (Natsume) **10**:330
Omoide (Dazai Osamu) **11**:174-75, 178, 186
"Omyłka" (Prus) **48**:181-84
"On a Bayonet" (Wright) **136**:300
"On a Book Entitled Lolita" (Nabokov) **108**:121, 123-24; **189**:144, 186
"On a Certain Critic" (Lowell) **8**:237
"On a Country Road" (Swinburne) **36**:345
"On a Dead Child" (Middleton) **56**:174, 190
"On a Dead Hostess" (Belloc) **7**:33
"On a décidé de faire la nuit" (Garneau) **13**:195
"On a Door Knocker" (Rosenberg) **12**:311
"On a Fan that Belonged to the Marquise de Pompadour" (Dobson) **79**:6, 36
On a Field of Azure (Remizov) See *V pole blakitnom*
"On a Forgotten Kind of Writing" (Strauss) **141**:341
"On a Great Election" (Belloc) **18**:28
"On a Great Name" (Belloc) **7**:43
"On a Grecian Colonnade in a Park" (Lovecraft) **4**:266
"On a Lost Manuscript" (Belloc) **18**:25
"On a Midsummer Eve" (Hardy) **53**:111
"On a Mountain" (Bierce) **44**:30
"On a New England Village Seen by Moonlight" (Lovecraft) **4**:266; **22**:241
"On a New List of Categories" (Peirce) **81**:185,195,240
"On a Path in the Field" (Shimazaki Toson) **5**:439
"On a Picture" (Gray) **19**:148, 150, 153-54, 156-57
"On a Picture of a Black Centaur by Edmund Dulac" (Yeats) **31**:407
"On a Political Prisoner" (Yeats) **31**:421; **93**:389
"On a Red Steed" (Tsvetaeva) See "Na krasnom kone"
"On a Return from Egypt" (Douglas) **40**:60, 62, 68, 91
"On a Side Track" (Foote) **108**:35

"On a Singing Girl" (Wylie) **8**:536
"On a Small Scale" (Čapek)
See "O malých pomĕrech"
"On a Soldier Fallen in the Philippines" (Moody) **105**:221, 224, 237, 240, 255, 260, 267
"On a Sudden Departure" (Coleridge) **73**:27
"On a Two-Hundredth Birthday" (Gurney) **33**:97
"On a Wedding Anniversary" (Thomas) **45**:402
"On Account of a Hat" (Aleichem) **35**:323
On achève bien les chevaux (McCoy)
See *They Shoot Horses, Don't They?*
"On Acrocorinth" (Sikelianos) **39**:420
"On Amaryllis, a Tortoyse" (Pickthall) **21**:256
On an Antique Littoral (Percy) **84**:203
"On an Autumn Night, I Think of My Friends" (Sarduy) **167**:200
"On an Invitation to Visit the United States" (Hardy) **143**:109, 161, 169
"On Approaching Forty" (Mankiewicz) **85**:116
"On Art and Artists" (Acker) **191**:127
"On Babies" (Jerome) **23**:87
"On Bad Terms with the World" (Andrić) **135**:21
On Baile's Strand (Gregory) **1**:336
On Baile's Strand (Yeats) **1**:561; **11**:512, 514, 527; **31**:408, 412; **93**:342, 364
"On Beautiful Clarity" (Kuzmin) **40**:192, 216
On Becoming a Person (Levi) **125**:262
"On Behalf of Some Irishmen Not Followers of Tradition" (Baker) **3**:9; **10**:13, 18, 21
"On Being a Member of the Jury for a Poetry Prize" (Nemerov) **124**:274
"On Being an American" (Mencken) **13**:365
"On Being Female, Black, and Free" (Walker) **129**:274, 311
On Being Female, Black and Free: Essays by Margaret Walker 1932-1992 (Walker) **129**:316
"On Being Hard Up" (Jerome) **23**:87
"On Being Human" (Wilson) **79**:502
"On Being Idle" (Jerome) **23**:87
"On Being Ill" (Woolf) **43**:394; **101**:260
"On Being in a Hurry" (Morley) **87**:127
"On Being in Love" (Jerome) **23**:87
"On Being in the Blues" (Jerome) **23**:87
"On Being Religious" (Lawrence) **93**:45
"On Being Shy" (Jerome) **23**:87
"On Being Told That Her Second Husband Has Taken His First Lover" (Slesinger) **10**:445
"On Being Young—A Woman—and Colored" (Bonner) **179**:16, 27, 30
"On Believing and Not Believing in God" (Ginzburg) **156**:34-35, 46
"On belyj" (Hippius) **9**:167
On Birthdays (Tagore)
See *Janmadine*
"On Blackwell Pier" (Morrison) **72**:372
"On Cape LeForce" (Montgomery) **51**:203, 209
"On Cats and Dogs" (Jerome) **23**:87
"On Certain Wits: who amused themselves over the simplicity of Barnett Newman's paintings shown at Bennington College in May of 1958" (Nemerov) **124**:182
On Certainty (Wittgenstein) **59**:239, 242, 244-9, 261, 275-6, 279
"On Cheating the Fiddler" (Parker) **143**:323
"On Chesterton" (Borges) **109**:17
"On Christianity" (Riis) **80**:443
"On Clerk Maxwell's Influence" (Einstein)
See "Clerk Maxwell's Influence on the Evolution of the Idea of Physical Reality"
"On Contemporary Poetry" (Khlebnikov) **20**:149
On Dark Ground (Raabe) **45**:200
"On Death. An Essay" (Lagerkvist) **144**:164
"On Dialectical and Historical Materialism" (Stalin) **92**:184, 186
"On dirait Qu'une ligne" (Lyotard) **103**:169
"On Drama" (Orage) **157**:283
"On Dress and Deportment" (Jerome) **23**:87
"On Duty by the Cannon" (Toller)
See "Gesshützwache"
"On Dying Considered as a Dramatic Situation" (Guiney) **41**:209
On Earth and in Hell (Bernhard)
See *Auf der Erde und in der Holle*
"On Eating and Drinking" (Jerome) **23**:87
On Education (Frye) **165**:169
"On Embarkation" (Lewis) **3**:287
"On Environmental Values" (Ingamells) **35**:128
"On Fairy Stories" (Tolkien) **137**:235-36, 243, 250, 254, 262, 265-66, 284-85, 349, 351, 355-56, 361
"On Filling an Inkwell" (Morley) **87**:127
"On Finding Things" (Lucas) **73**:160
On Forgotten Paths (Rölvaag) **17**:336
"On Foscombe Hill" (Gurney) **33**:97
"On Furnished Apartments" (Jerome) **23**:87
"On Getting On in the World" (Jerome) **23**:87
"On Getting Out of Vietnam" (Nemerov) **124**:257
"On Going" (Cullen) **37**:164, 168
On Gray (Kandinsky) **92**:35
"On Great Men" (Rohan) **22**:301
"On Greenhow Hill" (Kipling) **17**:204, 208
"On Hearing James W. Riley Read (From a Kentucky Standpoint)" (Cotter) **28**:43
"On Heaven" (Ford) **15**:69, 72
On Heaven, and Poems Written on Active Service (Ford) **15**:70-1
On Her Majesty's Secret Service (Fleming) **193**:198-201, 203, 213, 224, 239, 241
"On Herodias' Frenzy" (Remizov) **27**:354
On Himself (Aurobindo) **63**:50
On Humor (Pirandello)
See *L'umorismo*
"On Impressionism" (Ford) **57**:261; **172**:48
"On Inns" (Belloc) **18**:25
"On Insanity" (Tolstoy) **79**:370
"On Interpreting Haiku" (Hagiwara) **60**:304
"On Intoxication" (Mishima) **161**:12
"On Invisible Government" (Ginzburg) **156**:25
"On Irony" (Belloc) **18**:32
"On Jazz" (Adorno)
See "Abschied vom Jazz"
On Job's Balances (Shestov)
See *Na vesakh Iova*
"On Juhu Sands" (Naidu) **80**:313
"On Lac Sainte Irénée" (Pickthall) **21**:255
"On Language" (Shimazaki Toson) **5**:432
"On Language as Such and on the Language of Men" (Benjamin) **39**:40
On Learning to Read: The Child's Fascination with Meaning (Bettelheim) **143**:11
"On Leaving School" (Douglas) **40**:59
"On Leaving Winchester" (Guiney) **41**:208, 216
"On Leprechauns" (Wolfe) **4**:520
On Life (Tolstoy) **44**:328-29; **79**:337, 410-1, 413, 427
"On Literary Criticism" (Bierce) **44**:16
"On Literary Technique" (Valéry) **4**:495
"On Literature" (Lin) **149**:345
On Literature (Natsume) **10**:331-32
"On Little Joys" (Hesse) **148**:180
"On Loneliness at Twenty-Three" (Wolfe) **4**:516
"On Looking at a Copy of Alice Meynell's Poems Given to Me Years Ago by a Friend" (Lowell) **1**:379; **8**:231, 238
"On Love" (Orage) **157**:245
"On Love" (Ortega y Gasset)
See "Estudios sobre el amor"
"On Lullabies" (García Lorca) **7**:302
"On Lying" (Belloc) **18**:25
"On Lying in Bed" (Chesterton) **1**:184
"On Lyric Poetry and Society" (Adorno) **111**:184-85
"On Making Values Explicit" (Wirth) **92**:372
On Many Roads (Morgenstern)
See *Auf vielen Wegen*
"On Memory" (Jerome) **23**:87
"On Metaphor" (Nemerov) **124**:270, 287, 296, 299
"On modern Drama and Modern Theatre" (Strindberg)
See "Om Modern drama och modern theater"
On Moral Courage (Mackenzie) **116**:226
On Moral Fiction (Gardner) **195**:109, 119, 121, 150, 153-54
"On Music" (Chang) **184**:147
"On My Friendly Critics" (Santayana) **40**:346
"On My Own Tentatives" (Buchanan) **107**:52, 64
"On My Return" (Bialik) **25**:50
"On My Songs" (Owen) **27**:210
On My Way (Arp)
See *Jours effeuillés: Poémes, essais, souvenirs, 1920-1965*
"On My Way Out I Passed over You and the Verrazano Bridge" (Lorde) **173**:78
"On Mystic Realism" (Buchanan) **107**:44, 72
"On Narcissism: An Introduction" (Freud)
See "Zur Einführung des Narzissmus"
"On National Culture" (Fanon) **188**:68-9, 74, 112, 119
"On Neal's Ashes" (Ginsberg) **120**:77
"On New Poetry" (Lowell) **1**:377
On Nietzsche (Bataille) **155**:15-16, 20, 88, 92-93, 96, 99-102, 108, 114
"On no work of words" (Thomas) **105**:322
"On Nocturanal and Diurnal Realities" (Tzara) **168**:275
"On Not Knowing Greek" (Woolf) **43**:405; **101**:204
"On Obscure Writing" (Levi) **109**:288
"On Official Duty" (Chekhov) **3**:152
On Overgrown Paths (Hamsun)
See *Paa gjengrodde stier*
"On Painting the Portrait of a Harpsichord Player, Poem 2" (Su Man-shu) **24**:457
On Party Organization and Party Literature (Lenin) **67**:205
"On Philosophy and Its Study" (Westermarck) **87**:364
"On Physical Reality" (Einstein) **65**:132
"On Pisgah Height" (Bialik) **25**:50
On Poems of Walt Whitman: A Representative Egalitarian Writer (Natsume) **10**:331
"On Poetry" (Davidson) **24**:175
"On Poetry" (Khlebnikov) **20**:151
"On Point of View in the Arts" (Ortega y Gasset) **9**:349
On Political Things; or, Zoon Politicon (Čapek)
See *O věcech obecných čili ZOON POLITIKON*
"On Ponus Ridge" (Carman) **7**:139
"On Popular Music" (Adorno) **111**:85, 150
"On Preparing to Read Kipling" (Jarrell) **177**:185
On purge bébé (Feydeau) **22**:77, 79, 82
"On Purpose" (Sudermann) **15**:428
"On Quantity" (Peirce) **81**:198
On Racine (Barthes)
See *Sur Racine*
"On Reading" (Barthes) **135**:157, 159
"On Reading Aloud" (Lucas) **73**:171, 174
"On Receiving News of the War" (Rosenberg) **12**:295, 301
"On Rein's Critique of the Monist Theory of the Mind" (Westermarck) **87**:358
"On Re-Reading Novels" (Woolf) **43**:410-11, 426
"On Rest" (Belloc) **18**:25
"On Rest" (Gurney) **33**:80, 112
On Revolution (Arendt) **193**:9, 43, 46, 48-9, 52-3, 56, 62, 64, 67, 73, 104, 106, 110, 123, 136
"On Rhythm" (Hagiwara) **60**:305
"On Running after One's Hat" (Chesterton) **6**:109
"On Sacramental Things" (Belloc) **7**:38

"On Saying Little at Great Length" (Benchley) **55**:13
"On Seeing a Piece of Our Artillery Brought into Action" (Owen) **27**:212
"On Sitting in Chairs" (Lin) **149**:341
"On Slaughter" (Bialik)
See "'Al ha-shehitah"
On Social Differentiation: Sociological and Psychological Investigations (Simmel)
See *Uber soziale Differenzierung*
"On Some Current Conceptions of the Term 'Self'" (Dewey) **95**:96
"On Some Motifs of Baudelaire" (Benjamin)
See "Über einige Motive bei Baudelaire"
"On Some Questions of the History of Bolshevism" (Stalin) **92**:280
"On sonne" (Péret) **20**:196-97
On Strange Soil (Singer) **33**:386
"On Subject Matter and War Poetry" (Fletcher) **35**:112-13
"On Synthesism" (Zamyatin) **8**:558
"On Teaching One's Grandmother How to Suck Eggs" (Guiney) **41**:209-10
"On the 101st Mile" (Bergelson) **81**:19
"On the Afternoon of the Third of November" (Shiga)
See "Juichigatsu mikka gogo no koto"
"On the Algebra of Logic" (Peirce) **81**:197
"On the Altar" (Bonner) **179**:36
"On the Anniversary of the Founding of Rome" (Carducci)
See "Nell' annuale della fondazione di Roma"
"On the Apotheosis of the Romantic Will" (Berlin) **105**:91
On the Art of Writing (Quiller-Couch) **53**:292, 296
"On the Asylum Road" (Mew) **8**:296, 298
"On the Bank of the Rup-Narain" (Tagore) **53**:347
"On the Bank of the Tone" (Shimazaki Toson) **5**:439
"On the Banks of the Tisza" (Ady)
See "A Tisza-Parton"
"On the Bearing of Esthetics and Ethics upon Logic" (Peirce) **81**:291
On the Boiler (Yeats) **31**:407-08, 412
"On the Boy Scout Movement" (Riis) **80**:437
"On the Brighton Road" (Middleton) **56**:182, 184
"On the Building of Springfield" (Lindsay) **17**:240
"On the Butchery" (Bialik) **25**:50
"On the carpet of leaves illuminated by the moon" (Calvino)
See "Sul tappeto di foglie illuminate dalla luna"
"On the Causes of the Color of the Water in the Rhine and Facts and Considerations on the Strata of Mont Blanc" (Ruskin) **63**:238, 255
"On the Causes of the Present Decline and the New Currents of Contemporary Russian Literature" (Merezhkovsky) **29**:236, 246
"On the City Wall" (Kipling) **8**:176; **17**:208
"On the Cliffs" (Swinburne) **36**:324, 339, 341
"On the Clothes Rack" (Popa) **167**:152
On the Coast of the Dead Sea (Endo) **152**:167, 172
"On the Concept and Tragedy of Culture" (Simmel) **64**:339, 341, 360, 362
"On the Concept of History" (Peirce) **81**:362,364
On the Concept of History (Benjamin) **39**:10
"On the Contradictions of Marxism" (Weil) **23**:400
"On the Coosawattee" (Dickey) **151**:199
"On the Creek" (Roberts) **8**:316-17
"On the Cult of Books" (Borges) **109**:17
On the Cultural Life of Modern America (Hamsun)
See *Fra det moderne Amerikas aandsliv*
On the Darwinian Hypothesis of Sexual Selection (Douglas) **68**:43
"On the Death of a Metaphysician" (Santayana) **40**:341
"On the Death of Claude Debussy" (Scott) **6**:387, 389
"On the Death of Francis Thompson" (Noyes) **7**:503
"On the Death of José de Ciria y Escalante" (García Lorca)
See "En la muerte de José de Ciria y Escalante"
"On the Death of the Actor, Hermann Miller" (Hofmannsthal) **11**:294
"On the Definition of Logic" (Peirce) **81**:203
"On the Departure Platform" (Hardy) **53**:117
"On the Divide" (Cather) **152**:68
On the Division of Labor in Society (Durkheim)
See *De la division du travail social:étude sur l'organisation des sociétés supérieures*
"On the Downs" (Swinburne) **36**:318
"On the Economic Significance of Culture" (Innis) **77**:340
"On the Edge" (Fisher) **87**:73
On the Edge (de la Mare) **4**:78; **53**:23, 27, 35, 39
"On the Electrodynamics of Moving Bodies" (Einstein) **65**:86, 95, 106
"On the Epistemology of Social Science" (Simmel) **64**:352
"On the Farm" (Bunin)
See "Nakhutore"
"On the Fetish-Character in Music and the Regression of Listening" (Adorno)
See "The Fetish Character of Music and the Regression of Listening"
On the Field of Glory (Sienkiewicz)
See *Na polu chwały*
"On the French Spoken by those Who Do Not Speak French" (Matthews) **95**:227
"On the Future of Poetry" (Dobson) **79**:32
"On the Gate" (Kipling) **8**:196
"On the Genesis of the Castration Complex in Women" (Horney) **71**:231
"On the German Republic" (Mann)
See "Von deutscher Republik"
"On the Ghost in 'Macbeth'" (Natsume) **10**:332
"On the Gravestone of a Spanish Peasant" (Jozsef) **22**:163
"On the Great Wall" (Kipling) **8**:194
"On the Gulf Shore" (Montgomery) **51**:209
On the Herpetology of the Grand Duchy of Baden (Douglas) **68**:38, 43
On the High Road (Chekhov)
See *Na bolshoi doroge*
"On the Highway" (Chekhov)
See *Na bolshoi doroge*
"On the Hill" (Roberts) **68**:303
"On the Himalayas' Staircase" (Södergran)
See "På Himalayas trappor"
"On the Holy Trinity" (Gray) **19**:157
"On the House" (Jackson) **187**:245
"On the Interpretation of Genesis" (Strauss) **141**:259
"On the Intersection of Social Circles" (Simmel) **64**:317
"On the Island of Khalka" (Tolstoy) **18**:378
"On the Labor of Death" (Morgenstern)
See "Vom Tagewerk des Todes"
On the Last Things (Weininger)
See *Über die letzten Dinge*
"On the Logic of Drawing History from Ancient Documents, Especially from Testimonies" (Peirce) **81**:198,352
"On the Logical Conception of Mind" (Peirce) **81**:203
"On the Loneliness of Priests" (Guiney) **41**:220
"On the Makaloa Mat" (London) **9**:267
On the Makaloa Mat (London) **9**:258
"On the Marriage of a Virgin" (Thomas) **45**:402
"On the Massacre" (Bialik) **25**:49
"On the Massacre of the Christians in Bulgaria" (Wilde) **8**:487
"On the Materialistic Conception of History" (Croce)
See "Sulla concezione materialistica della storia"
"On the Measure of Poetry" (Nemerov) **124**:270
"On the Method for an Ethnographically-Based Society . . ." (Westermarck) **87**:364
"On the Method of Theoretical Physics" (Einstein) **65**:68, 95, 100
"On the Mimetic Faculty" (Benjamin) **39**:40
On the Mountain (Bernhard)
See *In der Höhe*
"On the Mountainside" (Roberts) **68**:348-51
"On the Mutual Relations of Physiology and Medicine in Questions of Digestion" (Pavlov) **91**:150
"On the Nature of Poetry" (Douglas) **40**:60, 80
"On the Nature of the Word" (Mandelstam) **6**:270
"On the Nature of Totalitarianism" (Arendt) **193**:181
"On the Need for a Wilderness to Get Lost In" (Abbey) **160**:37
"On the New Arts; or, The Risk in Artistic Production" (Strindberg) **1**:463
"On the Novel 'Aylwin'" (Natsume) **10**:332
"On the Occasion of National Mourning" (Nemerov) **124**:291
"On the One-Directionality of Time and Its Ethical Significance" (Weininger) **84**:328
"On the Origin of Christianity" (Andreas-Salome) **56**:46
On the Other Side of the Latch (Duncan) **60**:197
"On the Outskirts of the City" (Jozsef) **22**:164
"On the Phenomenology of Language" (Merleau-Ponty) **156**:197, 199, 201-4
"On the Platform" (Nemerov) **124**:162, 179, 181
"On the Plaza" (Carman) **7**:143
"On the Pond's Green Scum" (Wright) **136**:300
"On the Porch" (Agee) **1**:17; **180**:14, 35, 40, 103
"On the Porch: 2" (Agee) **180**:18, 102-4
"On the Prairie" (Hamsun) **14**:242
"On the Psychology of Money" (Simmel) **64**:352
"On the Pure Novel" (Yokomitsu)
See "Junsui Shōsetsu Ron"
"On the Question of Form" (Kandinsky)
See "Über die Formfrage"
On the Racecourse (Gregory) **1**:338
"On the Rafts" (Gorky)
See "Na plotakh"
"On the Railway Platform" (Jarrell) **177**:138
"On the Reefs" (Talvik) **87**:319
"On the Relation Between Art and Society" (Adorno) **111**:90
"On the Religious Affect" (Andreas-Salome) **56**:47
"On the Republic" (Mann) **44**:165
"On the Resemblances between Science and Religion" (Nemerov) **124**:218
"On the Restoration of Idealism" (Cram) **45**:14
"On the River" (Andreyev) **3**:20
"On the River" (Dunbar) **12**:121
"On the River" (Moody) **105**:225
"On the Road" (Akutagawa Ryūnosuke) **16**:27
"On the Road" (Korolenko) **22**:169
On the Road (Kerouac) **117**:184-96, 203-04, 706-09, 211-12, 219, 222, 224-76, 228-29, 238, 241, 244, 248-50, 252, 255, 262, 265-67, 269, 271, 273
"On the Road Home" (Stevens) **3**:452, 471; **12**:362; **45**:269, 283
"On the Road to the Sea" (Mew) **8**:296
On the Rocks (Shaw) **3**:399
On the Scrap-Iron (Raabe)
See *Im alten Eisen*
"On the Sense of Responsibility" (Otto) **85**:322

On the Sick-Bed (Tagore)
See *Rogsajyae*
"On the Significance of Militant Materialism" (Lenin) **67**:203
"On the Soul" (Hesse) **196**:277
"On the Soul that Suffered from Being its Body" (Vallejo)
See "El alma que sufrió de ser su cuerpo"
"On the South Coast" (Noyes) **7**:513
"On the South Coast" (Swinburne) **36**:342, 344
On the Spiritual in Art (Kandinsky)
See *Über das Geistige in der Kunst*
On the Spot (Wallace) **57**:399, 401-2, 404
"On the Spur" (Graham) **19**:129
"On the Square" (Aleixandre)
See "En la plaza"
On the Stage—and Off: The Brief Career of a Would-Be Actor (Jerome) **23**:79, 86-7, 90
"On the Stairs" (Cavafy) **2**:98
"On the Stairs" (Morrison) **72**:353, 376
On the Stairs (Fuller) **103**:60-63, 65, 74, 86-89, 114
"On the Streetcar" (Kafka) **179**:307
"On the Structure of Things" (Eisenstein) **57**:196-97
"On the Surgical Method of Incestigation of the Secretory Phenomena of the Stomach" (Pavlov) **91**:150
"On the Tears of the Great" (Belloc) **18**:25
On the Theory of Governments and Parliamentary Government: Historical and Social Studies (Mosca)
See *Sulla teorica dei governi e sul governo parlamentare*
"On the Third Dimension in Art" (Simmel) **64**:339
"On the Threshold of His Greatness, the Poet Comes Down with a Sore Throat" (Nemerov) **124**:182, 275-76
"On the Tower" (Teasdale) **4**:424
On the Track and Over the Sliprails (Lawson) **27**:121, 126, 129-30, 150, 152
"On the Trail" (Carman) **7**:141
"On the Trapeze" (Nezval) **44**:241
"On the Truth and Lie in Extra-moral Sense" (Nietzsche)
See "Über Warheit und Lüge im aussermoralischen Sinn"
"On the Use and Disadvantage of History for Life" (Nietzsche) **10**:354
On the Variety of Lines of Descent Represented in a Population (Boas) **56**:82
"On the Waterfront" (Benét) **28**:9
"On the Waves" (Brodkey) **123**:194-95
"On the Way to Abashiri" (Shiga)
See "Abashiri made"
"On the Way to Golconda" (Naidu)
See "At Twilight: On the Way to Golconda"
"On the Way to Kew" (Henley) **8**:102
"On the Way to Rest Quarters" (Toller)
See "Gang zur Ruhestellung"
"On the Way to the Mission" (Scott) **6**:388, 393, 395, 397
"On the Way to the Trenches" (Toller)
See "Gang zum Schützengraben"
"On the Weather" (Jerome) **23**:87
On the White Stone (France) **9**:48
"On the Wide Heath" (Millay) **49**:209, 222, 227
On the Wisdom of America (Lin) **149**:325
On These I Stand: An Anthology of the Best Poems of Countee Cullen (Cullen) **4**:43-4, 51; **37**:140, 143, 145, 150, 163
"On Tour" (Hamsun) **151**:239, 245
"On Trades" (Peretz) **16**:389
"On Trained Nursing for the Sick Poor" (Nightingale) **85**:258
"On Translation" (Belloc) **18**:25
"On Troy" (Gogarty) **15**:113
"On Turning 70" (Paton) **165**:312
"On Two Ministers of State" (Belloc) **18**:42
On Tyranny: An Interpretation of Xenophon's Hiero (Strauss) **141**:230, 233
On Ultimate Things (Weininger)
See *Über die letzten Dinge*
On Understanding (Rozanov)
See *O ponimanii*
"On Unknown People" (Belloc) **7**:40
"On Value-Judgements" (Frye) **165**:158
"On Vanity and Vanities" (Jerome) **23**:87
On Viol and Flute (Gosse) **28**:131, 139, 143, 151
On Violence (Arendt) **193**:169, 172
"On Violence" (Arendt) **193**:48, 62
"On Virtue" (Mann) **168**:189
"On Wenlock Edge" (Housman) **10**:247
"'On with the Dance!' A Review" (Bierce) **44**:45
"On Woman" (Chang) **184**:126
"On Writing" (Bowen) **148**:47, 49, 52-53
On Writing (Cather) **1**:156; **132**:137; **152**:78
On Writing: Critical Studies on Writing as an Art (Cather)
See *On Writing*
On Yoga I: The Synthesis of Yoga (Aurobindo) **63**:20, 32-6
De Oñate a la Granja (Pérez Galdós) **27**:276
"Onbeduidende polka" (van Ostaijen) **33**:418
"Onbewuste avond" (van Ostaijen) **33**:419
"Once Aboard the Whaler" (Williams) **89**:384
Once Again (Ady)
See *Még egyszer*
Once Again (Tagore)
See *Punascha*
"Once at the Angelus" (Dobson) **79**:27
Once Five Years Pass (García Lorca)
See *Así que pasen cinco años*
Once in a Blue Moon (Hecht) **101**:63
"Once in the Night" (Tolstoy) **18**:368
Once in the Saddle (Rhodes) **53**:319, 328-29
"Once More" (Galsworthy) **45**:32
"Once More At Chartres" (Sarton) **120**:304
"Once More on the Structure of Things" (Eisenstein) **57**:196, 199
Once on a Time (Milne) **6**:318; **88**:228
Once There Lived (Andreyev) **3**:26
Once upon a Time (Crothers) **19**:74
Onda sagor (Lagerkvist) **144**:210, 214
Onde magter (Lie) **5**:325
Ondine (Giraudoux) **2**:158-59, 161, 168, 173-74; **7**:321-23, 328-29
"One Afternoon" (Riley) **51**:282
"One and Many" (Howe) **21**:113
"One Art" (Bishop) **121**:54, 56, 59, 75, 78, 85, 92
One Art: Letters (Bishop) **121**:54, 60, 80-2, 85, 87-9, 103
"One Block from Fifth Avenue" (Cobb) **77**:136
"One Boaster" (Lindsay) **17**:240
"One Boy's Story" (Bonner) **179**:31, 33, 36, 38, 41
One Brown Girl and . . . (Redcam) **25**:331-32
One Christmas (Capote) **164**:199
"One Dash—Horses" (Crane)
See "Horses—One Dash"
"One Day" (Yosano) **59**:325
One Day (Douglas) **68**:41
One Day (Morris) **107**:155, 158-59, 169
One Day and Another (Lucas) **73**:154, 159, 170, 174
"One Day I Told My Love" (Cullen) **37**:170
"One Day in the Afternoon of the World" (Saroyan) **137**:148
One Day More (Conrad) **1**:195-96, 199
"One Day We Play a Game" (Cullen) **37**:169
"One Evening" (Apollinaire) **3**:37, 39
One Exciting Night (Griffith) **68**:137-39
"One Foot in Eden" (Muir) **2**:483; **87**:215
One Foot in Eden (Muir) **87**:161, 168, 170, 172, 174, 193-94, 208, 235, 237, 256, 285
"One Forever Alien" (Nemerov) **124**:183-84
"One Generation" (Bodenheim) **44**:65
One Handful of Sand (Ishikawa)
See *Ichiaku no suna*
"One Hundred and Three" (Lawson) **27**:140
"$106,000 Blood Money" (Hammett) **187**:82, 203
"150,000,000" (Mayakovski) **4**:290-91, 295, 297; **18**:242-43, 246-47, 262-63, 268
152 proverbes mis au goût du jour (Éluard) **41**:153
One Hundred Poems in Classical Japanese (Miyazawa) **76**:287, 293
One Hundred Thousand (Tolstoy) **18**:382
"125th Street and Abomey" (Lorde) **173**:85
"One Hundred Views of Mount Fuji" (Dazai Osamu)
See "Fugaku hyakkei"
"One in a Darkness" (Coffin) **95**:16
"The One in Rags" (Gumilev)
See "Oborvanec"
"1 January 1924" (Mandelstam) **2**:409
"One Kind of Officer" (Bierce) **44**:45
One Life at a Time Please (Abbey) **160**:39, 43, 45-46, 54-55, 58-59, 72
"The One Lost" (Rosenberg) **12**:299, 309
One Love (Sologub)
See *Odna lyubov'*
One Man in His Time (Glasgow) **2**:181; **7**:346
"One Man's Fortune" (Dunbar) **2**:128, 133; **12**:108, 120, 123
"One Moment in Eternity" (Nemerov) **124**:257
One More River (Galsworthy)
See *Over the River*
One More River (Whale) **63**:339-42, 358, 378, 387
"One More Way to Die" (Himes) **139**:324
One Morning (Shiga) **172**:223, 232
"One Night" (Roberts) **8**:319
"One Night" (Verhaeren) **12**:472
One Night (Natsume)
See *Ichiya*
"One Night in New Jersey" (Himes) **139**:244
"One Night in Turin" (O'Faolain) **143**:225
One, None, and a Hundred Thousand (Pirandello)
See *Uno, nessuno e centomila*
"One of Cleopatra's Nights" (Dunsany) **59**:10
One of Cleopatra's Nights (Hearn) **9**:127
One of Life's Slaves (Lie)
See *Livsslaven*
One of My Sons (Green) **63**:148, 152
One of Our Conquerors (Meredith) **17**:265, 269, 276, 286, 296-97; **43**:277, 290-91, 296, 299
One of Ours (Cather) **1**:151-52, 154, 156, 158; **11**:93, 101, 103; **31**:27, 59; **99**:204, 209, 274; **132**:118, 121, 124, 127, 129-31, 133-34, 140-43, 148, 150, 154; **152**:10, 27
"One of the Girls in Our Party" (Wolfe) **4**:519
"One of the Missing" (Bierce) **44**:44-5, 47-8
"One of the Shepherds" (Montgomery) **51**:209
"One of the Three Is Still Alive" (Calvino) **183**:95
"One of Their Gods" (Cavafy) **7**:154, 157
"One of Those Impossible Americans" (Glaspell) **175**:93, 96, 98
"One of Twins" (Bierce) **44**:13, 45-6
"One Officer, One Man" (Bierce) **44**:44-5
"One Perfect Rose" (Parker) **143**:322
"One Person" (Wylie) **8**:529-30, 532, 534-36, 538
"The One Pill Box" (Hearn) **9**:125, 136
One Springtime (Raabe)
See *A Springtide*
"One Summer Evening" (Carpenter) **88**:118
"One Summer Night" (Bierce) **44**:45, 50-1
"I (The Spattering of the Rain)" (Fletcher) **35**:93
"The One Thing" (Knister) **56**:153, 155-56, 163
One Thing Leading to Another, and Other Stories (Warner) **131**:319
One Third Off (Cobb) **77**:127
1001 Afternoons in Chicago (Hecht) **101**:31, 35, 38-9, 42, 47-8, 53, 70
1x1 (Cummings) **137**:29
One Touch of Venus (Nash) **109**:360
"One Trip Abroad" (Fitzgerald) **6**:169, 171
"One True Love" (Bonner) **179**:23, 58

"One Warm Saturday" (Thomas) **8**:456, 462-63; **45**:396-97; **105**:303, 322-24, 341, 343, 346, 355, 357
"One Way" (Nemerov) **124**:168, 177, 254
One Way Street (Engel)
See *Monodromos*
One Way to Heaven (Cullen) **4**:49, 51; **37**:136, 157, 171-72
"The One Who Has Lost" (Gumilev)
See "Oderzhimy"
One Who Vanished (Kafka)
See *Der Verschollene*
"The One Who Was Different" (Jarrell) **177**:133, 222
The One Woman (Dixon) **163**:140, 151, 167-69, 211
"One Word" (Benn)
See "Ein Wort"
One-Horse Farm (Coffin) **95**:22
Onesimus (Abbott) **139**:26
One-Smoke Stories (Austin) **25**:31, 36
One-Storied America (Petrov)
See *Odnoetazhnaya Amerika*
One-Way Song (Lewis) **2**:397-98; **9**:241
One-Way Street (Benjamin) **39**:8, 10-11, 39, 44-5, 47-8, 53, 56, 58, 63
"An ongeleygter bris" (Aleichem) **35**:306
De Ongelv kkige (Couperus) **15**:47
"The Onion" (Schwitters)
See "Die Zweibel"
"Onirocritique" (Apollinaire) **8**:20; **51**:19
Onkel Moses (Asch) **3**:66, 68-9, 71-2
"Only a Boche" (Service) **15**:399
"Only a Jockey" (Paterson) **32**:369
"Only a Nigger" (Twain) **6**:473
"Only a Subaltern" (Kipling) **8**:198; **17**:208
The Only Jealousy of Emer (Yeats) **11**:514; **31**:412
Only love (Balmont)
See *Tol'ko liubov*
"An Only Son" (Jewett) **22**:125
"Only the Dead Know Brooklyn" (Wolfe) **4**:519; **13**:484, 495
"Only the Master Shall Praise" (Oskison) **35**:280-81
"Only the Polished Skeleton" (Cullen) **4**:44; **37**:164-65
"Only the Sea Has Come" (Jozsef) **22**:160
The Only Thing (Glyn) **72**:139
"The Only Way" (Montgomery) **51**:209
Only Yesterday (Agnon)
See *Temol shilshom*
Onna no kettō (Dazai Osamu) **11**:176, 186
"Onnagata" (Mishima) **161**:100
"The Onondaga Madonna" (Scott) **6**:393
Ønsket (Sigurjónsson) **27**:362, 364-65
"Ontogénie" (Jarry) **147**:329
"An Ontological Idealism" (McTaggart) **105**:197
"Onward, Christian Soldiers" (Baring-Gould) **88**:15, 19-20
Onze chapîtres sur Platon (Alain) **41**:3
Les onze mille verges (Apollinaire) **3**:38; **8**:25; **51**:18, 20, 28
Onze peintres vus par Arp (Arp) **115**:45
Oostwaarts (Couperus) **15**:47
Op hoop van zegen (Heijermans) **24**:284-86, 288-89, 292, 296-300
Op. I (Sayers) **15**:370, 395
"Op in My 'Ansom" (Cohan) **60**:167
O. P.: Orden público (Sender) **136**:209
"Der Opal" (Meyrink) **21**:221-22, 231
"Opalčenite na Šipka" (Vazov) **25**:456
Opasnaia predostorozhnost' (Kuzmin) **40**:201-03
Opavshie list'ia (Rozanov) **104**:304, 318, 345, 351, 353-54, 356-57, 361, 384, 386-89, 392-94, 396-98
Opavshie list'ia. Korob pervyj (Rozanov) **104**:355
Opavshie list'ia. Korob vtoroj (Rozanov) **104**:317, 355
"The Open Boat" (Crane) **11**:125, 127, 136, 139-41, 146, 148, 158, 160, 162-64, 167; **17**:65-7, 78, 82; **32**:150, 165
The Open Boat, and Other Tales of Adventure (Crane) **11**:125, 127-29, 137
Open Confession to a Man from a Woman (Corelli) **51**:68, 83
"The Open Conspiracy" (Wells) **12**:502; **19**:453, 453; **133**:236
The Open Door at Home: A Trial Philosophy of National Interest (Beard) **15**:22-4
"Open Letter" (Yosano)
See "Hiraki-bumi"
An Open Letter to a Non-Pacifist (Macaulay) **44**:123
"Open Letter to Jacques Rivière" (Tzara) **168**:228
"An Open Letter to Lincoln Steffens" (Sinclair) **160**:286
"Open Letter to Mary Daly" (Lorde) **173**:86
An Open Letter to the Intimate Theatre (Strindberg) **47**:340
"An Open Letter to the Moon" (Guiney) **41**:210
Open Letter to the Waka Poets (Masaoka)
See *Utayomi ni atauru sho*
Open Letters (Strindberg) **1**:460
An Open Life (Campbell) **140**:93, 97, 112
The Open Mind (Bernanos)
See *Monsieur Ouine*
The Open Road: A Little Book for Wayfarers (Lucas) **73**:158, 165, 168, 170, 173
The Open Sea (Masters) **25**:296-98, 315
"The Open Secret" (Carpenter) **88**:53, 56
"Open the Door, Richard!" (Dagerman) **17**:93
"Open, Time" (Guiney) **41**:205
Open Water (Stringer) **37**:330, 339-43
"The Open Window" (Saki) **3**:365, 373
An Open-Eyed Conspiracy (Howells) **17**:184
"An Opening for Novelists" (Norris) **155**:337-38
The Opening of the Eyes (Stapledon) **22**:317-18, 322
"Opera" (Remizov) **27**:340, 349
L'opéra au dix-septième siècle (Rolland) **23**:267
L'opéra au dix-septième siècle en Italie (Rolland) **23**:267
"Opera Dancer" (Nagai)
See "Opera no maihime"
Opera in Italy in the Seventeenth Century (Rolland)
See *L'opéra au dix-septième siècle en Italie*
"Opera no maihime" (Nagai) **51**:99
Gli operai della vigna (Papini) **22**:281, 288
"The Operation" (Hunt) **53**:190
The Operation (Henley) **8**:97
Opere (Levi) **109**:338-39, 342
"Das Opfer" (Kolmar) **40**:178
"Das Opfer" (Werfel) **8**:477
Opgang (Bergelson) **81**:30
"Ophelia" (Heym) **9**:143, 145-47
Ophis kai krinos (Kazantzakis) **5**:272; **181**:239, 285, 305
"An Opinion Concerning a Proposed National Park Site" (Miyazawa) **76**:300
Opinion or Insight? (Schoenberg) **75**:342
"Una opinión sobre la mujer" (Pardo Bazán) **189**:317
Opinions (Holley)
See *My Opinions and Betsy Bobbet's*
Les opinions de Jérome Coignard (France) **9**:41-2
"Opium" (Csáth) **13**:147, 150, 152
Opium (Cocteau) **119**:38, 58, 81, 105, 107
Opium, and Other Stories (Csáth)
See *The Magician's Garden, and Other Stories*
"The Opium Smoker" (Symons) **11**:439
Opium Smokers (Reymont) **5**:392
"Oppel and the Elephant" (Miyazawa) **76**:289
The Oppermanns (Feuchtwanger)
See *Die Geschwister Oppermann*
"Opportunity" (Guest) **95**:205
"Opsednuta vedrina" (Popa) **167**:152, 154, 176-77, 179
The Optimist (Delafield) **61**:125-6
"The Optimist's Salutation" (Darío)
See "Salutación del optimista"
"Opus 728" (Miyazawa) **76**:293
"Opus 739" (Miyazawa) **76**:296
"Opus 1063" (Miyazawa) **76**:284, 290, 296
"Opus 1087" (Miyazawa) **76**:291
Opus Posthumous (Stevens) **3**:459, 467; **45**:274, 278-79, 283, 286-87, 289, 291-92, 317, 336, 345
Opus 7 (Warner) **131**:310-11, 363
L'or des mers (Epstein) **92**:11
"Or Ever the Knightly Years Were Gone" (Henley) **8**:102
"L'ora di Barga" (Pascoli) **45**:156
Ora et labora (Heijermans) **24**:286, 292, 296, 298-300
"Oracion al despertar" (Prado) **75**:202
"La oración del ateo" (Unamuno) **148**:298
"The Oracle" (Coppard) **5**:179
"The Oracle" (Paterson) **32**:381
"Oracles" (Apollinaire) **8**:22; **51**:34
Orage as Critic (Orage) **157**:257, 279
Oraisons mauvaises (Gourmont) **17**:138
"The Oral and Written Literature of the Nguni" (Vilakazi) **37**:405
"Oral Literature and Its Social Background among the Acoli and Lang'o" (p'Bitek) **149**:120
Oral Tradition (Sikelianos)
See "Agraphon"
"Orang berdua" (Anwar) **22**:18
"The Orange Grove" (Lewis) **3**:288-89, 292
"L'orangeade" (Apollinaire) **51**:20
"The Orange-Distillers" (Quiroga)
See "Los destiladores de naranja"
"Oranges" (Merrill) **173**:254
"Oranthe" (Proust) **161**:173
"An Oration" (Douglas) **40**:72, 88
Oration on the Downfall of the Russian Land (Remizov)
See *The Lament for the Ruin of Russia*
The Orator (Wallace) **57**:402
"Orazio Cima" (Svevo) **35**:369
Orbs of Pearl (Sologub)
See *Zhemchuzhnye zvetila*
"The Orchard" (Bosschere) **19**:54, 56, 63
"The Orchard in Moonlight" (Scott) **6**:394
The Orchard of Tears (Rohmer) **28**:277, 283, 293-94, 296
"Orchard Row" (White) **176**:170
"The Orchard Wind-Break" (Foote) **108**:34
"The Orchards" (Thomas) **6**:455; **45**:375, 398; **105**:297-301, 324-27, 329, 336-38, 357
"An Orchestral Violin" (Dowson) **4**:92
L'Orchestre (Anouilh) **195**:25, 35, 38, 40
"The Orchid" (Lindsay) **17**:240
"Orchideen" (Meyrink) **21**:218
Orchideëon (Couperus) **15**:45
Orchids (Couperus)
See *Orchideëon*
"Ordalii" (Balmont) **11**:40
"The Ordeal" (Davidson) **24**:163
The Ordeal (Murfree) **135**:224
Ordeal (Tolstoy) **18**:359, 364-66, 377-81
"The Ordeal at Mt. Hope" (Dunbar) **12**:107, 109, 120
"Ordeal by Beauty" (Cram) **45**:9
The Ordeal of Richard Feverel: A History of Father and Son (Meredith) **17**:256, 260-62, 265-66, 269, 273, 275-77, 279-81, 283-86, 289-90, 297; **43**:251-52, 255-56, 258-59
"Order and Disorder of Love" (Éluard) **7**:260
"Order of the Black Cross" (p'Bitek) **149**:89, 94
"Order on the Cheap" (Levi)
See "L'ordine a buon mercato"
"The Order Squamata" (Calvino) **183**:143
"An Ordinary Evening in New Haven"

(Stevens) **3**:455, 470, 477; **12**:362, 365, 373-74, 378-79; **45**:285, 300, 311, 337
"The Ordinary Hairpins" (Bentley) **12**:15
An Ordinary Life (Čapek)
See *Obyčejnýživot*
"An Ordinary Man" (Tolstoy) **18**:370
"An Ordinary Song" (Anwar)
See "Lago biasa"
"Ordinary Women" (Stevens) **12**:357, 366
L'ordination (Benda) **60**:65, 73
"L'ordine a buon mercato" (Levi) **109**:293, 295-97, 299
Ordkonst och bildkonst (Lagerkvist) **144**:159, 164, 191, 209-10, 214, 217, 219, 222-25, 236
Az ördög (Molnár) **20**:156-59, 165, 167, 170, 172, 178
"Orë" (Gumilev) **60**:278
Ore paniche (D'Annunzio) **40**:8
"Ore que dessus ma tête" (Moréas) **18**:288
Ore'ah natah lalun (Agnon) **151**:52, 70-1
"Az öregek" (Mikszath) **31**:167
"La oreja" (Aleixandre) **113**:35
Oreste (Anouilh) **195**:20, 67, 71-4
"Orestes at Tauris" (Jarrell) **177**:145
"Orfano" (Pascoli) **45**:156
"Orfeo" (Merrill) **173**:238
"The Organ and the Vitriol" (Artaud) **3**:52
"Organ Grinder" (Artaud) **3**:52
"Organ-Grinder" (Prus)
See "Katarynka"
Organic Architecture (Wright) **95**:376
"Organism, Community, and Environment" (Mead) **89**:101
"The Organist from Ponikla" (Sienkiewicz) **3**:430
The Organization of Thought (Whitehead) **97**:197
"Organizational Questions of the Russian Social Democracy" (Luxemburg)
See "Leninism or Marxism?"
"Organized Guilt and Universal Responsibility" (Arendt) **193**:164
"The Organizer's Wife" (Bambara) **116**:3-4
"Orgie" (Lasker-Schueler) **57**:328
"The Orginality of Machiavelli" (Berlin) **105**:8, 89
"Orgy" (Lasker-Schueler)
See "Orgie"
Az orias es Egyeb Elbeszelesek (Molnár) **20**:164
Orient and Occident (Bely) **7**:51
"The Orient Express" (Jarrell) **177**:129, 196, 230
"Orient Ode" (Thompson) **4**:435, 438
Oriental Motifs (Rozanov) **104**:306
Oriental Mythology (Campbell)
See *The Masks of God: Oriental Mythology*
"Orientation of Hope" (Locke) **43**:225
The Origin and Development of Moral Ideas (Westermarck) **87**:325, 334, 336, 338, 342, 354, 358-59, 362-66, 370, 372-74, 384-85, 393-94, 397
Origin and Development of Religious Belief (Baring-Gould) **88**:32
Origin of a Species (Morris) **107**:155
The Origin of German Tragic Drama (Benjamin)
See *Ursprung des deutschen Trauerspiels*
"The Origin of Marriage" (Westermarck) **87**:334, 356
The Origin of Russian Communism (Berdyaev) **67**:60
"The Origin of the Birds" (Calvino)
See "L'origine degli Uccelli"
The Origin of Truth (Merleau-Ponty)
See *L'Origine de la vérité*
"The Original Follies" (Fitzgerald) **52**:59-60
"The Original Place" (Muir) **87**:307
"The Original-Intent Controversy" (Kirk) **119**:318
The Originality of Machiavelli (Berlin) **105**:22
L'Origine de la vérité (Merleau-Ponty) **156**:174, 176, 178, 184
"L'origine degli Uccelli" (Calvino) **183**:10, 228
Origines de l'opèra Allemand (Rolland) **23**:267
Les origines du théatre lyrique (Rolland) **23**:266
"Origins" (Arendt) **193**:80
The Origins and the Development of the Incest Taboo (Durkheim)
See "L'oganisation matrimoniale australienne"
Origins of a Master Craftsman (Platonov)
See *Proiskhozhdenie mastera*
The Origins of German Opera (Rolland)
See *Origines de l'opèra Allemand*
The Origins of Opera (Rolland)
See *Les origines du théatre lyrique*
The Origins of the Modern Lyric Theater: History of the Opera in Europe Before Lully and Scarlatti (Rolland) **23**:256
The Origins of Totalitarianism (Arendt) **193**:4, 6, 42-4, 46, 52, 61, 75-7, 79-84, 91, 95, 97-9, 102, 120-21, 124, 132, 134, 145, 147, 163, 166-67, 176-82
"Orilla" (Salinas) **17**:359
"Orion" (Roberts) **8**:313-14, 318-20, 328-30
Orion, and Other Poems (Roberts) **8**:313, 316, 319-20, 325, 328-30
The Orissers (Myers) **59**:123-26, 129-30, 132, 136, 150, 152-3
"Orjade Koor" (Talvik) **87**:322
"Orjan poika" (Leino) **24**:369-70, 376
"Orkan" (Obstfelder) **23**:177, 186, 188-89
Orlacs Hände (Wiene) **56**:338
Orlando (Woolf) **1**:530-31, 533, 538-39, 544, 546, 550; **5**:516; **20**:428-29; **43**:382, 387, 409, 417; **56**:358-412; **101**:207, 225, 227; **128**:333, 341, 344, 355, 358-60, 362, 366, 377, 382
Orlando Furioso di Ludovico Ariosto raccontato da Italo Calvino (Calvino) **183**:241
Orlóff and His Wife (Gorky) **8**:71
Orm og tyr (Hansen) **32**:250-51, 257, 260-61
"Orm the Celt" (Buchanan) **107**:17
L'orme du mail (France) **9**:42, 48, 51
Ormen (Dagerman) **17**:85, 88, 92-4
Ornifle (Anouilh) **195**:30, 33, 36, 38-40
El oro de los tigres (Borges) **109**:117
"Oro mío" (Jiménez) **4**:226
"Órókkék ég a felhők mőgőtt" (Babits) **14**:40
Oros son triunfos (Pereda) **16**:372
"Orovilca" (Arguedas) **147**:13
The Orphan Angel (Wylie) **8**:524, 527-30, 532, 534, 537-38
Orphan Island (Macaulay) **7**:427, 429; **44**:118-20, 125, 133
"Orphanhood" (Bialik) **25**:66
Orphans (Rilke) **6**:370
Orphans in Gethsemane: A Novel of the Past in the Present (Fisher) **140**:154, 157-58, 160, 182, 185-86, 190
Orphans of the Storm (Griffith) **68**:137, 149, 169-70, 176-77, 206, 214, 239
Orphée (Cocteau) **119**:39-40, 45-9, 57-8, 70, 74, 81-2, 87
"Orpheus" (Ball) **104**:54
"Orpheus" (Rilke) **1**:418
Orpheus (Cocteau)
See *Orphée*
Orpheus (Crowley) **7**:208-09
"Orpheus and Eurydice" (Bryusov) **10**:80, 88
"Orpheus and Eurydice" (Noyes) **7**:505
"Orpheus and Oisin" (Sharp) **39**:377
"Orpheus. Eurydice. Hermes" (Rilke) **195**:228, 243-44, 321, 329
Orpheus in Mayfair and Other Stories and Sketches (Baring) **8**:42
Orphic (Sikelianos) **39**:419
"Orphic Scenario" (Nemerov) **124**:283-86
Orphic Songs (Campana)
See *Canti orfici*
Orsino (Rolland) **23**:256
Ein Ort für Zufälle (Bachmann) **192**:141
"Orta or the One Dancing" (Stein) **48**:235
Orthodoxy (Chesterton) **6**:102, 106, 109; **64**:31-2, 34
The Orton Diaries (Orton) **157**:307, 309, 331
The O'Ruddy (Crane) **11**:137, 143, 162, 166-67
"Orxidei i mimozy" (Bryusov) **10**:82
"Az ős kaján" (Ady) **11**:16
Osaka Elegy (Mizoguchi)
See *Naniwa Hika*
"Osan" (Dazai Osamu) **11**:187
"Osatičani" (Andrić) **135**:21, 60
Osatićans (Andrić)
See "Osatičani"
"Osayo" (Shimazaki Toson) **5**:439
"Osborne's Revenge" (James) **47**:199
Oscar Wilde: An Idler's Impressions (Saltus) **8**:348
Oscar Wilde: His Life and Confessions (Harris) **24**:262, 268-69, 271
"Oscar Wilde: The Poet of Salomé" (Joyce) **159**:345
Osennie ozera (Kuzmin) **40**:189, 191, 215-16
Osennii son (Guro) **56**:133, 147
Oshibka smerti (Khlebnikov) **20**:136
"Oskicket" (Söderberg) **39**:428
"Oslepitel'noe" (Gumilev) **60**:279-80
"Osnova" (Balmont) **11**:41
"Osnovateli" (Gumilev) **60**:279
"Ossi di seppia" (Saba) **33**:374
Ost (Dent) **72**:73
"Ostatnia ucieczka ojca" (Schulz) **5**:423, 427-28; **51**:309-10, 315
"Die Oste" (Morgenstern) **8**:305, 310
"Osterhas" (Raabe) **45**:188
"An Ostracised Race in Ferment" (Baker) **47**:13
Ostře sledované vlaky (Hrabal) **155**:148, 151, 153, 158, 160, 163-64
"Ostros nocturnos" (Villaurrutia) **80**:480
Ostrovityane (Zamyatin) **8**:542-45, 548, 552, 558; **37**:417, 419-20, 422-23, 427-31
Osudy dobrého vojáka Švejka za světoné války (Hašek) **4**:181-90
"Oswald Spengler and the Theory of Historical Cycles" (Collingwood) **67**:182-83
Den osynlige (Lagerkvist) **144**:211
Őszi utazás (Molnár) **20**:175, 177
L'otage (Claudel) **2**:99, 101, 105-06; **10**:120-21, 128
Otchaianie (Nabokov) **108**:52, 60, 63-67, 69-70, 83, 91-92, 133-34, 163-65, 167-68, 171, 219, 222-23, 225-26; **189**:78, 80, 96, 174
"Oterma and Katerma" (Leino) **24**:376
"Otets" (Babel) **171**:7-11, 50-51, 53-54
Otetz Sergii (Tolstoy) **4**:476, 480, 482; **11**:464, 471, 473; **17**:415; **79**:387
Othello Returns (Kazantzakis) **181**:254-56
"The Other" (Borges)
See "El otro, el mismo"
"The Other" (Thomas) **10**:451, 459, 462-63
"The Other Death" (Borges)
See "La otra muerte"
"The Other Fellow" (Guest) **95**:205
"The Other Frost" (Jarrell) **177**:186
The Other Girls (Holley) **99**:316
"The Other Gods" (Lovecraft) **4**:273
The Other Half: A Self Portrait (Clark) **147**:126
"The other, himself" (Borges)
See "El otro, el mismo"
"The Other House" (James) **47**:206
The Other House (James) **24**:343
Other Inquisitions, 1937-1952 (Borges)
See *Otras inquisiciónes, 1937-1952*
"The Other Oedipus" (Muir) **87**:172
"The Other One" (Borges)
See "El otro, el mismo"
The Other One (Colette)
See *La seconde*
"Other People's Books" (Lucas) **73**:171
Other People's Lives (Milne) **88**:246
Other People's Point of View (Pirandello)
See *La ragione degli altri*

Other People's Trades (Levi)
See *L'altrui mestiere*
Other Provinces (Van Doren) **18**:395-96, 405
The Other Room (Herbert)
See *Drugi pokój*
Other Shores (Nabokov) **108**:83
"The Other Side" (Lardner) **2**:329
The Other Side (Kubin)
See *Die andere Seite*
"The Other Side of a Mirror" (Coleridge) **73**:11
"The Other Side of Paradise" (Fitzgerald) **157**:169
The Other Son (Pirandello)
See *L'altro figlio*
The other, the same (Borges)
See *El otro, el mismo*
"The Other Tiger" (Borges)
See "El otro tigre"
"The Other Two" (Wharton) **3**:555; **9**:546-47; **129**:360, 365; **149**:245, 280, 282
Other Voices, Other Rooms (Capote) **164**:100, 105-6, 108, 111-12, 115, 129, 136, 142, 150, 167-68, 190-93, 195-97, 199, 201, 205-14, 216-18
"The Other Whitman" (Borges)
See "El otro Whitman"
"The Other Wing" (Blackwood) **5**:79
"The Other Woman" (Anderson) **1**:42
"The Other Woman" (Davis) **24**:199
"Other's" (Lyotard) **103**:274, 277, 279
"Others I Am Not the First" (Housman) **10**:247
Others Who Returned (Wakefield)
See *Old Man's Beard: Fifteen Disturbing Tales*
"An Otherworldly Evening" (Tsvetaeva)
See "Nezdeshnii vecher"
Othmar (Ouida) **43**:352-54, 358
"Otkrytie Ameriki" (Gumilev) **60**:282
"L'otmika" (Apollinaire) **51**:20
"Ōtō" (Dazai Osamu) **11**:171, 174
Otogi zōshi (Dazai Osamu) **11**:174, 176-77
"Otomi no teiso" (Akutagawa Ryūnosuke) **16**:20
"Otomi's Virginity" (Akutagawa Ryūnosuke)
See "Otomi no teiso"
"Otoño regular" (Huidobro)
See *Automne régulier*
"La otra muerte" (Borges) **109**:76, 108
Otra vez el mar (Arenas) **191**:145, 158-59, 162, 181, 200, 206
Otras inquisiciónes, 1937-1952 (Borges) **109**:16, 18, 21-4, 47, 50-1, 66, 74, 78, 84-5, 156, 161
Otravlennaja tunika (Gumilev) **60**:265-6, 275
"Otravlennyj" (Gumilev) **60**:279
"El otro" (Borges)
See "El otro, el mismo"
El otro (Unamuno) **9**:516; **148**:267, 271-72
"Otro clima" (Machado) **3**:311
"El otro, el mismo" (Borges) **109**:77, 81, 86
El otro, el mismo (Borges) **109**:12, 14, 28, 119, 150
"El otro tigre" (Borges) **109**:8
"El otro Whitman" (Borges) **109**:85
Otrochestvo (Tolstoy) **4**:444-45, 459-60, 473; **11**:464; **17**:374; **79**:379-80, 413, 449; **173**:265-354
"Otrok" (Tsvetaeva) **35**:404-05
"Otshel'nik" (Balmont) **11**:40
Ōtsu junkichi (Shiga) **172**:200, 202-8, 214
The Otter's Children (Khlebnikov)
See *Deti vydry*
Ottilie (Lee) **5**:310, 314, 319
"Où es-tu" (Péret) **20**:188
"Ouedéme a calentar la tinta . . ." (Vallejo) **56**:311
"Ought Women to Learn the Alphabet?" (Higginson) **36**:170-71, 175, 178-79
"Ouija" (Patton) **79**:305-6
"Ou-pa Carel's" (Smith) **25**:389
Our Air Force (Mitchell) **81**:157
"Our All-American Almanac and Prophetic Messenger" (Millay) **169**:237-38
Our Ancestors (Calvino)
See *I nostri antenati*
"Our Androcentric Culture" (Gilman) **37**:201
"Our Book of Changes" (Nemerov) **124**:226
"Our Bourgeois Literature" (Sinclair) **160**:225, 282-83, 285
"Our Bourgeois Literature: The Reason and the Remedy" (Sinclair)
See "Our Bourgeois Literature"
"Our Brains and What Ails Them" (Gilman) **117**:100
Our Brains and What Ails Them (Gilman) **117**:125
"Our Canal" (Monroe) **12**:216
"Our Children" (Ginzburg)
See "I nostri figli"
Our Children (Sánchez)
See *Nuestros hijos*
"Our Country" (Howe) **21**:113
"Our Cultural Humility" (Bourne) **16**:46
Our Daily Bread (Grove) **4**:134, 136, 138, 140, 142
Our Dead Behind Us (Lorde) **173**:54, 73, 75
"Our Duty to Dependent Races" (Harper) **14**:263
Our English Cousins (Davis) **24**:202, 208
"Our Eunuch Dreams" (Thomas) **45**:361, 366, 372, 377; **105**:334
Our Father San Daniel (Miro)
See *Nuestro padre San Daniel*
"Our Fearful Innocence" (O'Faolain) **143**:227
"Our First Cigar" (Quiroga)
See "Nuestro primer cigarro"
"Our Foundation" (Khlebnikov) **20**:147
Our Friend the Charlatan (Gissing) **3**:233; **24**:228, 235; **47**:141
Our Gang and He (Ishikawa) **15**:129
"Our Garden" (Anwar)
See "Taman"
Our Great Experiment in Democracy: A History of the United States (Becker)
See *The United States: An Experiment in Democracy*
"Our Greatest Want" (Harper) **14**:264
"Our Hero" (Service) **15**:399
"Our Hired Girl" (Riley) **51**:292
"Our Impossibilities" (Borges)
See "Nuestras imposibilidades"
"Our Inabilities" (Borges)
See "Nuestras imposibilidades"
"Our Inadequacies" (Borges)
See "Nuestras imposibilidades"
Our Inner Conflicts (Horney) **71**:226, 234, 257, 261-262
Our Irish Theatre: A Chapter in Autobiography (Gregory) **176**:10, 13, 18
"Our Lady" (Coleridge) **73**:13
Our Lady of Lies (Bourget)
See *Mensonges*
Our Lady of Poverty (Housman) **7**:359
"Our Lady of Sparta" (Sikelianos) **39**:407
Our Lady of the Flowers (Genet)
See *Notre dame des fleurs*
Our Lady of the Snows (Callaghan) **145**:254
"Our-Lady-of-the-Swallows" (Yourcenar)
See "Notre-Dame-des-Hirondelles"
"Our Lady of Twilight" (Noyes) **7**:512
"Our Lady's Exile" (Tynan) **3**:504
"Our Landlady" (Baum) **132**:27, 80
"Our Latent Loyalty" (Duncan) **60**:211
"Our Learned Fellow-Townsman" (Gissing) **24**:248
Our Life and Letters (France)
See *La vie littéraire*
"Our Lord and St. Peter" (Lagerloef) **36**:240
Our Lord God's Chancellory (Raabe) **45**:200
"Our Love" (Villaurrutia) **80**:488
"Our Man, Our Worry and Concern" (Döblin)
See "Unsere Sorge, der Mensch"
"Our March" (Mayakovski) **18**:247-48
"Our Martyred Soldiers" (Dunbar) **12**:121
Our Military Chaos (Sinclair) **160**:324, 358
"Our Mother Pocahontas" (Lindsay) **17**:236
"Our Motherland" (Péguy)
See "Notre patrie"
Our Mr. Wrenn: The Romantic Adventures of a Gentle Man (Lewis) **4**:246, 248, 251-52, 256, 259; **13**:325, 351; **39**:229, 234, 241
Our National Parks (Muir) **28**:245, 247, 259
"Our Need" (Walker) **129**:334
"Our Neighbors, the Ancients" (Roosevelt) **69**:268
"Our New Horse" (Paterson) **32**:376
Our New Prosperity (Baker) **47**:5-6
"Our Orders" (Howe) **21**:113
"Our Own Have Nots" (Orwell) **15**:353
"Our Own Movie Queen" (Fitzgerald) **52**:57-60, 64
Our Own People (Bojer)
See *Vor egen stamme*
Our Partnership (Webb and Webb) **22**:415, 421, 424, 426
Our Power and Our Glory (Grieg)
See *Våar aere og vår makt*
"Our Prophet's Criticism of Contemporary Arabian Poetry" (Iqbal) **28**:188
"Our Shameless Past" (Benét) **28**:7
Our Slovak Kinfolk (Mikszath)
See *A tót atyafiak*
Our Social Heritage (Wallas) **91**:359, 361, 365, 370, 372, 390, 394, 402, 404
"Our Story" (Stockton) **47**:312, 319, 323, 327
"Our Unpopular Novelists" (Norris) **155**:336
Our Women (Bennett) **5**:32
Our Writers (Papini)
See *Scittori nostri*
"Our Youth" (Baroja)
See "Nuestra juventud"
"Ourland" (Gilman)
See "With Her in Ourland"
Ourland (Gilman)
See *With Her in Ourland*
L'ours (Kandinsky) **92**:50
L'ours et la lune (Claudel) **10**:123-24
Ourselves (Crothers) **19**:74-5, 77
"Ourselves and Our Buildings" (Khlebnikov) **20**:150-51
"Ourselves and the Future" (Stapledon) **22**:338
"Out Back" (Lawson) **27**:133, 140
"Out in the Dark" (Thomas) **10**:452, 455-57, 464, 471
"Out o' doors" (Montgomery) **51**:209
"Out of Boredom" (Gorky)
See "Boredom"
"Out of Darkness" (La Guma) **140**:204-5, 235-36
Out of Dust (Riggs) **56**:215, 218
Out of His Later Years (Einstein) **65**:123, 131-34
Out of India (Hesse)
See *Aus Indien*
Out of Mulberry Street (Riis) **80**:435
"Out of Nowhere into Nothing" (Anderson) **1**:35; **10**:33-4; **24**:46
"Out of Pompeii" (Campbell) **9**:32
"Out of Reach of the Baby" (Millay) **169**:236
Out of Soundings (Tomlinson) **71**:394
"Out of the Deep" (de la Mare) **4**:78; **53**:16, 18-9, 27, 38
Out of the Earth (Bromfield) **11**:84
Out of the East (Hearn) **9**:128-30
"Out of the Night That Covers Me" (Henley) **8**:102
Out of the Question (Howells) **7**:370, 387
"Out of the Rose" (Yeats) **31**:415
Out of the Sea (Marquis) **7**:451
"Out of the Sighs" (Thomas) **45**:362, 383
"Out of the Storm" (Hodgson) **13**:236
"Out of the Strong, Sweetness" (Nabokov) **108**:143
Out of the World and in It (Bergelson) **81**:19
"Out of the Wrack I Rise" (Wakefield) **120**:352

"Out to Old Aunt Mary's" (Riley) **51**:292
"The Outage" (Nemerov) **124**:234
An Outback Marriage (Paterson) **32**:382
"The Outcast" (Benson) **27**:16
"Outcast" (McKay) **7**:462
"The Outcast" (Peretz) **16**:399
The Outcast (Lagerloef) **36**:238, 241-42
The Outcast (Pirandello)
See *L'esclusa*
The Outcast (Vazov) **25**:450
An Outcast of the Islands (Conrad) **1**:203, 221; **6**:118-19; **13**:113; **25**:84, 111; **43**:95, 115, 133
"The Outcasts of Poker Flat" (Harte) **1**:340, 344; **25**:192-93, 197-98, 200, 211-12, 214, 222-23
"The Outcasts of Poker Flat" (Norris) **155**:311
"An Outdoor Litany" (Guiney) **41**:214
"The Outer World" (Ford) **172**:93
"Out-foxed" (Adams) **56**:8
"The Outgoing of the Tide" (Buchan) **41**:73
"The Outing" (Andrić)
See "No basta"
Outland (Austin) **25**:33-4
"The Outlaw" (Čapek) **37**:53
The Outlaw (Moricz)
See *Betyár*
The Outlaw (Strindberg)
See *Den fredlöse*
The Outlaw (Weiss)
See *Der Vogelfreie*
The Outlaw of Torn (Burroughs) **32**:58
The Outlet (Adams) **56**:2, 4, 6, 22
"An Outline Classification of the Sciences" (Peirce) **81**:199
"Outline of a Philosophy of History" (Collingwood) **67**:183
"Outline of Great Books" (Erskine) **84**:178
The Outline of History (Wells) **6**:529-30, 537, 540, 551-53; **12**:497-99, 501, 504, 506, 514, 516-17; **133**:325
An Outline of Humor (Wells) **35**:426
An Outline of Occult Science (Steiner)
See *Die Geheimwissenschaft im Umriss*
An Outline of Russian Literature (Baring) **8**:41, 43
An Outline of Sanity (Chesterton) **6**:110
"An Outline of the Actress Nana" (Nagai)
See "Joyū nana kōgai"
"Outlines (II: Dr. Bentley)" (Woolf) **43**:402
Outlines in Local Color (Matthews) **95**:272
Outlines of a Critical Theory of Ethics (Dewey) **95**:59, 64, 97
Outlines of a Philosophy of Art (Collingwood) **67**:124-27, 139, 181
Outlines of Mahayana Buddhism (Suzuki) **109**:369-70, 382
"The Outlook for Intelligence" (Valéry) **4**:503
"The Outlook for Literature" (Roberts) **8**:327
The Outpost (Prus)
See *Placówka*
The Outpost of Progress (Conrad) **1**:202
Outre-mer (Bourget) **12**:61, 64, 75
The Outside (Glaspell) **55**:233, 236, 247, 249, 257, 259, 269; **175**:62, 69, 107, 111-12, 147-48
"Outside Eden" (Muir) **87**:161, 172, 307
Outside Looking In (Anderson) **2**:2; **144**:3-4, 8
"Outside of Wedlock" (Stevens) **45**:348
"Outside the Charterhouse of Bologna" (Carducci)
See "Fuori alla certosa di Bologna"
"The Outsider" (Lovecraft) **4**:266-68, 270-71; **22**:211
The Outsider (Wright) **136**:240, 250-51, 270, 276, 278, 285, 288; **180**:222, 276
"An Outsider Sees the Depressed Areas" (Orwell) **128**:256
Outsiders (Chambers) **41**:91, 95
"Outsitters" (Mayakovski) **4**:289
"Outward Bound" (Dobson) **79**:30
"Over 2,000 Illustrations and a Complete Concordance" (Bishop) **121**:3, 24-5
Over Bemerton's: An Easy-Going Chronicle (Lucas) **73**:159, 162, 170, 173, 175
"Over de höje fjelde" (Bjoernson) **7**:101, 110, 118
"Over Glistening Gravel" (Lasker-Schueler)
See "Uber glitzernden Kies"
Over Here (Guest) **95**:211
"Over Insurance" (Collier) **127**:261
"Over My Cell" (Toller)
See "Über meiner Zelle"
"Over on the T'other Mounting" (Murfree) **135**:196, 201-5, 209, 219, 227
Over Prairie Trails (Grove) **4**:133, 136-37, 140-41
Over Seventy (Wodehouse)
See *America, I Like You*
"Over Sir John's Hill" (Thomas) **1**:473; **8**:461; **45**:362-64, 377; **105**:351
"Over St. John's Hill" (Thomas)
See "Over Sir John's Hill"
"Over the Grave of Shaka" (Vilakazi)
See "Phezu kwethuna likaShaka"
"Over the Hills" (Coleridge) **73**:13
"Over the Hills" (Thomas) **10**:455, 465
"Over the Lofty Mountains" (Bjoernson)
See "Over de höje fjelde"
"Over the Ravine" (Pilnyak)
See "Nad ovragom"
Over the River (Galsworthy) **45**:47, 49, 66
"Over There" (Cohan) **60**:161, 165-6, 171, 173
Over ævne, I (Bjoernson) **7**:111, 114-16; **37**:11-12, 15, 19-21, 29-32, 35
Over ævne, II (Bjoernson) **7**:112, 115-16; **37**:19-22, 29-30
"Overconfidence" (Pyle) **81**:393
"Overdue Pilgrimage to Nova Scotia" (Merrill) **173**:230
"The Overflow" (Fadeyev)
See "The Flood"
"Overflowing Heavens" (Rilke)
See "Überfließende Himmel verschwendeter Sterne"
"The Overgrown Pasture" (Lowell) **1**:372; **8**:235
"Overheard Fragment of a Dialogue" (Leverson) **18**:199
"Overjoyed When Meeting" (Chang)
See "Xiangjian huan"
Overlooked (Baring) **8**:32, 36, 40, 42
Overshadowed (Griggs) **77**:146-7, 176-81
"An Oversight of Steelman's" (Lawson) **27**:121
"Oversoul" (Baker) **10**:20
"Overtones" (Percy) **84**:202
Overtones: A Book of Temperaments (Huneker) **65**:157, 159, 170
"Ovid among the Goths" (Bradford) **36**:56
"Ovid and Universal Contiguity" (Calvino) **183**:102
"Ovtsy" (Nabokov) **108**:143
Owarishi michi no shirube ni (Abe) **131**:11
"Owatari Bridge" (Hagiwara)
See "Ōwatari-bashi"
"Ōwatari-bashi" (Hagiwara) **60**:315
"Owen Ahern and His Dancers" (Yeats) **31**:403
Owen Glen (Williams) **89**:389, 402
"Oweneen the Sprat" (Somerville & Ross) **51**:357, 381-2
"The Owl" (Thomas) **10**:460
"The Owl in the Sarcophagus" (Stevens) **12**:364; **45**:295, 300
"The Owl King" (Dickey) **151**:98, 104-5, 114
The Owl King (Dickey) **151**:162
"The Owl's Bedtime Story" (Jarrell) **177**:159
Owl's Clover (Stevens) **3**:464, 472, 477; **45**:269, 276-77, 282-83, 285, 288
Owl's Pentecost (Raabe) **45**:201
Own Your Own Home (Lardner) **2**:332, 338-39; **14**:304
"The Ox" (Carducci)
See "Il bove"
"The Ox" (Gray) **19**:157
"Ox Wagons on Trek" (Bosman) **49**:20
"The Oxen" (Hardy) **53**:88-9, 91; **143**:78, 198
Oxford (Thomas) **10**:449, 458
The Oxford Book of English Verse (Quiller-Couch) **53**:300
The Oxford English Dictionary (Murray) **117**:785-86
"Oxford Nights" (Johnson) **19**:243, 248
Oxford Sermons (Abbott) **139**:33
Oxford University and the Cooperative Movement (Baker) **10**:22
"The Oxford Voice" (Lawrence) **93**:128
"Az Oxigén" (Herzl) **36**:152
"The Ox-Pull at the Fair" (Coffin) **95**:17
Oxtime (Drummond de Andrade)
See *Boitempo*
"The Oxygen" (Herzl)
See "Az Oxigén"
"Oye a tu masa" (Vallejo) **56**:286-87, 311
Oyf vos badarfn yidn a land (Aleichem) **35**:306
The Oyster (Hayashi)
See *Kaki*
Oyuki the Virgin (Mizoguchi)
See *Oyuki Ugetsu*
Oyuki Ugetsu (Mizoguchi) **72**:316, 325
Oyusama (Mizoguchi) **72**:315, 325, 336, 339
"Ozème's Holiday" (Chopin) **14**:70; **127**:167
"Ozio" (Tozzi) **31**:325
Ozma of Oz (Baum) **7**:13, 21, 23, 25, 27; **132**:13, 15-16, 36, 49, 51, 68, 77, 80-86, 88-89, 91, 93
"Ozymandias II" (Nemerov) **124**:220, 275
"P. C., X, 36" (Beerbohm) **24**:105
På Guds veje (Bjoernson) **7**:105, 107-08, 114, 117
"På Himalayas trappor" (Södergran) **31**:293
På Storhove (Bjoernson) **7**:112; **37**:17, 19, 22, 29
Paa gjengrodde stier (Hamsun) **14**:247-8; **49**:128; **151**:233
Paa glemte veie (Rölvaag) **17**:344, 347
"Paa Memphis Station" (Jensen) **41**:304, 306
"Paaskeklokken" (Hansen) **32**:249, 251
Paavo Kontio, lakitieteen tohtori (Leino) **24**:372
Paavo Kontio, LL.D. (Leino)
See *Paavo Kontio, lakitieteen tohtori*
"Păcat" (Caragiale) **76**:157-59, 170
"The Pace of Youth" (Crane) **11**:128, 142, 158
The Pace That Kills (Saltus) **8**:346
Pachín González (Pereda) **16**:379
"Pacific Radio Fire" (Brautigan) **133**:18
Pacific Wall (Lyotard)
See *Le Mur du Pacifique*
"The Pacifist" (Post) **39**:339
"The Pacifist" (Williams) **89**:385
"The Pacing Mustang" (Seton) **31**:280
A Packet for Ezra Pound (Yeats) **11**:520; **93**:372
Pacsirtaszó (Moricz) **33**:238
"Pacto primero" (Jiménez) **4**:214
El Padre Agustin Rivera (Azuela) **145**:14
"Padre Ignazio" (Wister) **21**:386
"Un padre nuestro" (Nervo) **11**:400
"Los padres de un santo" (Pardo Bazán) **189**:236
Padron Dio (Pirandello) **29**:310
La padrona (Betti) **5**:55, 58
Padurea spînzuratilor (Rebreanu) **28**:267, 272
Paese di mare (Ginzburg) **156**:63
"Paese infido" (Calvino) **183**:209
Paesi tuoi (Pavese) **3**:340, 342-44
"Pāgal" (Devkota) **23**:48, 52
"Pagan Marjorie" (Noyes) **7**:515
Pagan Papers (Grahame) **64**:63, 72, 80-1, 91, 94, 97; **136**:22
Pagan Poems (Moore) **7**:487-91
"Pagan Prayer" (Cullen) **4**:40, 43, 46; **37**:146, 152-53, 159, 161
The Pagan Review (Sharp) **39**:367, 372, 391, 397
"Pagan Salute" (Radnóti) **16**:418
Pagan Salute (Radnóti)
See *Pogány köszöntő*

Pagan Spain (Wright) **136**:240, 276, 285, 332, 336
Une page d'amour (Zola) **1**:587; **6**:563, 569; **41**:413
"Une page du folklore breton" (Roussel) **20**:227
"Page from a Tale" (Stevens) **3**:450, 472
"Page from the Koran" (Merrill) **173**:230
The Pageant of Georgy the Bold (Remizov)
See *Deistvo o Georgii Khrabrom*
A Pageant of Life (Bradford) **36**:62
"Pageant of Siena" (Lee-Hamilton) **22**:187
Pages choisies (Roussel) **20**:241
Pages de critique et le doctrine (Bourget) **12**:74
Pages from a Journal (Rutherford) **25**:340-41, 344, 346, 352, 361
"Page's Road Song" (Percy) **84**:199
Página dum suicida (Sá-Carneiro) **83**:405
Páginas escogidas (Arguedas) **147**:75-76
Páginas escogidas (Baroja) **8**:57
Páginas escojidas (Jiménez) **183**:296, 301, 319
"Páginas íntimas" (Azuela) **145**:21
Páginas intimas (Hostos) **24**:303
Pagine sparse (Croce) **37**:113
Las pagodas ocultas (Huidobro) **31**:124, 132-33
"Pagodes souterraines" (Loti) **11**:353
"The Pahty" (Dunbar) **12**:108, 121-22
"Pai contra mãe" (Machado de Assis) **10**:293
"Pain" (Baker) **10**:21
"Pain" (Gurney) **33**:94, 105
"The Pain" (Smith) **25**:376, 380-82, 384-85, 387, 393-94, 398
"Pain" (Teasdale) **4**:428
"The Pain Continuum" (Brodkey) **123**:236
Le pain de ménage (Renard) **17**:316
Le pain dur (Claudel) **2**:106; **10**:129
The Pain Is Great (Jozsef) **22**:165
"A Painful Case" (Joyce) **8**:166; **16**:232; **35**:144, 147, 149, 151, 153, 161, 164, 167, 191, 195-97; **159**:275-77, 299, 312, 314, 316, 361
Painful Stories (Čapek)
See *Trapné provídky*
Painful Tales (Čapek)
See *Trapné povídky*
The Painted Lady (Griffith) **68**:226, 244, 247-51
The Painted Veil (Huneker) **65**:170, 185-87, 195-97, 205, 209-11, 213, 219
"The Painter Dreaming in the Scholar's House" (Nemerov) **124**:255, 257, 304, 306, 309
The Painter's Eye (James) **171**:139
"A Painter's Holiday" (Carman) **7**:143
The Painters of Japan (Morrison) **72**:384
"Painting a Mountain Stream" (Nemerov) **124**:155, 170, 200, 206, 226, 309-10
Painting with Troika (Kandinsky) **92**:147
"The Paintspreader" (Musil) **68**:261
"Painuva päivä" (Leino) **24**:371
A Pair of Blue Eyes (Hardy) **4**:148-49, 156, 158-59; **10**:217, 225, 227; **18**:92; **32**:268; **48**:38, 71, 74; **53**:95, 110-12; **72**:162; **143**:129-32, 137-38, 180, 204; **153**:98, 100, 106, 110-12, 115, 150, 153, 187-88, 190-91
"A Pair of Silk Stockings" (Chopin) **127**:112
"País de ensueño" (Gonzalez Martinez) **72**:149
"Paisaje" (García Lorca) **181**:193
"Paisaje" (Huidobro) **31**:124
"Paisaje de la multitud que orina" (García Lorca) **49**:80; **197**:184, 206, 243, 255, 274, 279
"Paisaje de la multitud que vomita" (García Lorca) **49**:80, 121; **197**:184, 194, 218, 224, 239-42, 247, 255, 263, 267, 274, 279
"Paisaje del amor muerto" (Storni) **5**:445
"Paisajes" (Lugones) **15**:289
La Paix du Dimanche (Osborne)
See *Look Back in Anger*
"La paix et le salut" (Larbaud) **9**:206
"A Paixão Medida" (Drummond de Andrade) **139**:231
A Paixão Medida (Drummond de Andrade) **139**:226, 230-32
"Pajarita de papel" (García Lorca) **181**:120-22, 124
"El pájaro azul" (Lugones) **15**:295
"Pájaro de la noche" (Aleixandre) **113**:3
Pájaro milaroso (Nervo) **11**:394
"El pájaro verde" (Valera y Alcala-Galiano) **10**:504, 508
Pájaros de la playa (Sarduy) **167**:195, 199-200, 214-15, 217
Los pajaros errantes (Prado) **75**:191, 195, 202, 206, 211-12
"Pajaros sin descenso" (Aleixandre) **113**:15, 25, 27
A Pál utcai fiúk (Molnár) **20**:161-64, 174, 176, 178
"La palabra" (Aleixandre) **113**:7
"Palabra" (Villaurrutia) **80**:488
La palabra del viento (Gonzalez Martinez) **72**:148, 150
"Palabras" (Aleixandre) **113**:8
"Palace" (Apollinaire)
See "Palais"
"The Palace of Pan" (Swinburne) **36**:343
The Palace of Sadness (Martinez Sierra and Martinez Sierra)
See *El palacío triste*
"The Palace of the Sun" (Darío)
See "El palacio del sol"
The Palace of the White Skunks (Arenas)
See *Le palais des trés blanches mouffettes*
The Palace of Truth (Gilbert) **3**:208-09, 212
Palace Plays (Housman) **7**:357
Palace Scenes: More Plays of Queen Victoria (Housman) **7**:358
"El palacio del sol" (Darío) **4**:67
El palacío triste (Martinez Sierra and Martinez Sierra) **6**:277
"Palais" (Apollinaire) **51**:58-9, 61
Das Palais Bourbon, Bilder aus dem französischen Parlamentsleben (Herzl) **36**:134, 140
Le Palais des 1001 Nuits (Melies) **81**:121-2
Le palais des trés blanches mouffettes (Arenas) **191**:135-43, 145, 158-59, 162, 185, 196, 200
"Le palais du Tonnerre" (Apollinaire) **8**:28
"The Palanquin-Bearers" (Naidu) **80**:273
Palas et Chéri-Bibi (Leroux) **25**:260
"Palata No. 6" (Chekhov) **3**:159, 165-66, 168; **10**:100, 107-8, 117; **163**:130
Palātakā (Tagore) **3**:491-92
"Palau" (Benn) **3**:107, 109
Palavik (Talvik) **87**:317, 319, 321
The Pale Ape, and Other Pulses (Shiel) **8**:363
"Pale Fire" (Nabokov) **108**:182-83, 218; **189**:64-6, 70-1, 79-82, 84-6, 90-3, 95, 101, 117-20, 122, 125-29, 131, 146-47, 164, 166, 171, 181-83, 186-87
Pale Fire (Nabokov) **108**:59, 63, 66, 69-71, 77, 85-6, 89-90, 108, 118, 154, 161, 163-66, 168, 178, 182-83, 185-88, 199-203, 205, 216, 224; **189**:62-190
"Pale Horse" (Bryusov) **10**:91
"A Pale Winter Moon" (Wright) **136**:300
Paleface: The Philosophy of the "Melting Pot" (Lewis) **2**:391; **104**:163-64, 201, 226, 231, 233-34, 236-37, 239, 242, 246
Palicio (Bridges) **1**:124
"The palimpsest" (Morley) **87**:126
"Palimpsesto" (Darío) **4**:58
"Pâline" (Apollinaire) **51**:61
"Palingenesis" (Gosse) **28**:142
"Palinoidia" (Ivanov) **33**:140
"Pallas" (Benn) **3**:112
Pallī-Samāj (Chatterji) **13**:78-9, 81
The Palm Beach Story (Sturges) **48**:270-71, 275, 280, 283, 287-88, 290-92, 294-96, 299, 301, 303, 304-05, 309, 316, 318, 324
"The Palm Tree" (Palamas) **5**:383-84, 387
The Palm-Wine Drinkard and His Dead Palm-Wine Tapster in the Deads' Town (Tutuola) **188**:272-74, 276-79, 281-82, 285-90, 292, 295-99, 301-03, 305-07, 310-11, 318, 321
Palma Kunkel (Morgenstern) **8**:307
La palma rota (Miro) **5**:337
"Palmas y guitarras" (Vallejo) **56**:286-87
"Palmetto and the Pine" (Bryan) **99**:5, 35
Palmetto Country (Caldwell) **117**:16
Palmström (Morgenstern) **8**:304-05, 307, 310
Palmy Days (Thomas) **97**:138, 140
Palmyre Veulard (Rod) **52**:309
"La paloma negra" (Pardo Bazán) **189**:235
Palomar (Calvino) **183**:25-26, 38, 41-45, 47, 51-53, 57, 96, 101, 110-12, 140, 143-44, 147-48, 153-54, 177-79, 194-95, 216, 220, 231-32
"Palomides before His Christening" (Williams) **1**:514
"Palomnik" (Gumilev) **60**:269, 280
"Palomnik" (Nabokov)
See "The Aurelian"
"Pälsen" (Söderberg) **39**:428, 437, 439
"Paltān" (Devkota) **23**:52
"The Paltry Nude Starts on a Spring Voyage" (Stevens) **12**:356-7, 376; **45**:297, 307
Paludes (Gide) **36**:108-09; **5**:215, 223; **12**:143, 167-71, 178; **177**:34-35, 67
"Pampas" (Graham) **19**:101
"Pampassange" (Obstfelder) **23**:177, 188
"Pan" (Buchanan) **107**:14, 67
"Pan" (Huneker) **65**:196
"Pan" (Ledwidge) **23**:112
"Pan" (Schulz) **5**:421-22; **51**:308
"Pan" (Sikelianos) **39**:418
Pan (Hamsun)
See *Pan, af løitnant Thomas Glahns papirer*
Pan, af løitnant Thomas Glahns papirer (Hamsun) **2**:202; **14**:221, 224, 226-28, 235, 237, 242-43, 247-48; **49**:127-28, 131, 133, 137-45, 147-50, 153, 159, 162, 164, 166-68; **151**:232, 234, 250, 253, 255, 257
"Pan Apolek" (Babel) **2**:22-3, 27-8, 32; **13**:20; **171**:7, 10, 12, 22, 26, 37, 46, 82
Pan Cogito (Herbert) **168**:7-10, 18-20
"Pan Cogito: Aktualna pozycja duszy" (Herbert) **168**:40
"Pan Cogito o postawie wyprostowanej" (Herbert) **168**:10
"Pan Cogito rozwaza róznice miedzy glosem ludzkim a glosem przyrody" (Herbert) **168**:18
"Pan Cogito-Powrót" (Herbert) **168**:21
"Pan in America" (Lawrence) **61**:239
"Pan in the Catskills" (Carman) **7**:143, 150
"Pan Karol" (Schulz)
See "Pan"
Pan Michael (Sienkiewicz)
See *Pan Wołodyjowski*
"El pan nuestro" (Vallejo) **56**:288
"Pan the Fallen" (Campbell) **9**:33
Pan Trilogy (Giono) **124**:90-91, 99, 115
Pan Wołodyjowski (Sienkiewicz) **3**:422-25, 427-29
"La panchina" (Calvino) **183**:211, 214
Pandit Maśī (Chatterji) **13**:80
"Pandora" (James) **64**:157-58, 187
Pandora Lifts the Lid (Marquis) **7**:437
Pandora Lifts the Lid (Morley) **87**:124-5
Pandora no hako (Dazai Osamu) **11**:179, 188
Pandora's Box (Dazai Osamu)
See *Pandora no hako*
Pandora's Box (Wedekind)
See *Die Büchse der Pandora*
"Pandora's Song" (Moody) **105**:272-72
"Pane nero" (Verga) **3**:546
"Panico" (D'Annunzio) **40**:38, 41, 45
"Panie, / wiem ie dni moje sa policzone" (Herbert) **168**:40
"Panim aherot" (Agnon) **151**:22
Pankkiherroja (Leino) **24**:372

Pankraz erwacht (Zuckmayer) **191**:300-02, 306-07, 329, 331
"Panorama" (Andrić) **135**:22, 24, 28, 44, 68, 89
"Panorama ceigo de Nueva York" (García Lorca) **1**:308; **197**:185, 206-07, 209, 241, 256
Panorama de la religión griega (Reyes) **33**:323
"Pan-pipes" (Chekhov) **163**:130
Panpipes (Sologub)
See *Svirel'*
Pan's Garden (Blackwood) **5**:70-1, 77
Pansies (Lawrence) **2**:372; **48**:112; **93**:20, 25-27, 34, 53, 68-70, 72, 83
Pantagleize (Ghelderode) **187**:6, 8, 19, 22-3
Pantagruel (Jarry) **14**:273; **147**:268
Pantaloon (Barrie) **164**:7, 66
"Pantaloon in Black" (Faulkner) **141**:101-5, 159-60, 175-76; **170**:127-28, 166
"Panteismo" (Carducci) **32**:90, 101
"Panthea" (Wilde) **8**:495
Pantheism (Carducci)
See "Panteismo"
"Pantheism and Theism" (Higginson) **36**:170
"Der Panther" (Rilke) **195**:228, 266
"The Panther of Jolton's Ridge" (Murfree) **135**:195, 197
"Panthera" (Hardy) **4**:173
"La panthere" (Vallette) **67**:276
Pantomima (Nezval) **44**:238, 245
Pantomime (Nezval)
See *Pantomima*
"Pantomime and the Poetic Drama" (Symons) **11**:454
"The Pantomime Man" (Middleton) **56**:191
The Pantomime Man (Middleton) **56**:190, 192
"Pantomina" (Lugones)
See "El pierrot"
"Paolo" (Zola) **21**:456
Paolo il caldo (Brancati) **12**:80-1, 83, 86, 88-91
Paolo Paoli (Adamov) **189**:12-15, 19-20, 22, 24-5, 27-30, 32, 36, 39, 49-50, 53, 59
"Paolo Uccello's Battle Horses" (Bishop) **103**:3
"Paolo Ucello" (Pascoli) **45**:147
El papa del mar (Blasco Ibáñez) **12**:47-8
Papa La Fleur (Gale) **7**:284
Papá o el diario de Alicia Mir (Huidobro) **31**:123
El papa verde (Asturias) **184**:16, 45-46, 48, 87-88
Papa You're Crazy (Saroyan) **137**:181
Papéis avulsos (Machado de Assis) **10**:295
Papeletas lexicográficas (Palma) **29**:255, 260
"The Paper Crane" (Dazai Osamu)
See "Kami no tsuru"
Paper Doll's Whisper of Spring (Mizoguchi)
See *Kaminingyo haru no sayaki*
"Paper Fishes" (Lowell) **8**:230
Paper Lives (Mackenzie) **116**:237
"Paper Pills" (Anderson) **1**:59, 64-5; **10**:32-3, 50, 55; **24**:24, 30, 33-4, 45, 57; **123**:13, 38, 72
The Paper Rose Sacrilege (Valle-Inclán) **5**:486
"Papers" (Aleichem) **35**:308, 310
Papers on Acting (Matthews) **95**:243
Papers on Playmaking (Matthews) **95**:243
La papesse du diable (Desnos) **22**:57
La Papesse Jeanne (Jarry) **147**:290
"The Papineau Gun" (Drummond) **25**:142, 147
"Papirosnyy korobok" (Bagritsky) **60**:16-7
Paprika (Stroheim) **71**:332-334, 339
Par ce demi-clair matin (Péguy) **10**:409, 411
Par la fenêtre (Feydeau) **22**:82, 89-90
Par la révolution, la paix (Rolland) **23**:273
Par la taille (Jarry) **14**:273; **147**:265
Para esta noche (Onetti) **131**:133-34, 136, 158, 162-63, 202-3, 214, 216-18
Para la voz (Sarduy) **167**:199
Para las seis cuerdas (Borges) **109**:119
"Para que no cantes" (Valle-Inclán) **5**:478
"Para un libro" (Gonzalez Martinez) **72**:154
Para una tumba sin nombre (Onetti) **131**:133, 135-36, 140, 152-53, 155, 162-63, 170, 191-92, 194-95, 197, 201, 203-4, 213-14, 238, 252-53
"The Parable of the Doorkeeper" (Kafka) **2**:307
"The Parable of the Old Man and the Young" (Owen) **27**:205-06, 208, 211-12, 226
Parables (Fletcher) **35**:105
Parables (MacDonald) **9**:302
Parables and Paradoxes (Kafka) **29**:219
"Parábola de huésped sin nombre" (Gonzalez Martinez) **72**:152
"Parábola de los viajeros" (Gonzalez Martinez) **72**:152
"Parábola del sol, del viento y de la luna" (Gonzalez Martinez) **72**:152
Parabolas (Kuzmin) **40**:191, 197
Parábolas y otros poemas (Gonzalez Martinez) **72**:148, 150-52
Paracelsus (Pabst) **127**:339, 354, 362
Paracelsus (Schnitzler) **4**:393
Parade (Cocteau) **119**:41, 67, 71-4, 100-1
"A Parade of the Pyatigorsk Autumns" (Khlebnikov)
See "Shestvie oseney pyatigorska"
Parade's End (Ford) **1**:280, 282, 284-90; **15**:81-4, 86, 93-4; **39**:124, 137, 143, 165; **57**:204-90; **172**:6-7, 11, 28-30, 32-42, 48, 52, 58, 71-73, 76-77, 81, 83, 85-86, 95-96, 105, 109, 118, 123-26
Las Parades oyen (Garro) **153**:21
The Paradine Case (Hecht) **101**:75
Paradisæblerne (Hansen) **32**:251
Paradise (Kandinsky) **92**:62
Paradise Found (Upward) **85**:380
"Paradiset" (Lagerkvist) **144**:200-201, 207
"Parado en una piedra" (Vallejo) **56**:285
"Paradoks" (Korolenko) **22**:176
"A Paradox" (Korolenko) **22**:170
The Paradoxes of Legal Science (Cardozo) **65**:32-3, 44
The Paradoxes of Mr. Pond (Chesterton) **1**:181; **6**:104-05, 108; **64**:35
"Paragon and Paradise of the Blacks" (García Lorca)
See "Norma y paraíso de los negros"
"El paraíso de buen tono" (Lugones) **15**:294
"Un paraíso terrenal" (Unamuno) **148**:306
Paralipomena (Jarry) **147**:330
"Les Paralipomènes d'Ubu" (Jarry) **147**:259
"Paralipomènes d'Ubu" (Jarry) **2**:272
"The Paralle" (Bishop) **103**:4
"Paraphrase" (Crane) **2**:120
"Parasitism and Civilized Vice" (Gilman) **117**:151, 159
Les paravents (Genet) **128**:131-33, 135-36, 138, 145-46, 151, 155-56, 177, 187, 189, 240
Le parc d'Achtyrka (Kandinsky) **92**:49
Parched Lives (Ramos)
See *Vidas sêcas*
"The Pardah Nashin" (Naidu) **80**:292
"Pardon" (Howe) **21**:113
"Le Pardon" (Rod) **52**:316
Pardon wird nicht gegeben (Döblin) **13**:166, 171, 175
"The Pardoner's Tale" (Merrill) **173**:162
Parece mentira (Villaurrutia) **80**:466
"Un parecido" (Pardo Bazán) **189**:228
"Parentage" (Meynell) **6**:295, 300
"Parenticide" (Bierce) **1**:96
Parents and Children (Compton-Burnett) **180**:114, 126-27, 130, 134, 142-43, 178, 188
Les parents terribles (Cocteau) **119**:60, 82
La parfum de la dame en noir (Leroux) **25**:255-58
Pargiters (Woolf) **56**:410; **128**:376
Parii yori (Yosano) **59**:346
Parinīta (Chatterji) **13**:80
Paris (Zola) **1**:592, 597, 426; **6**:562-66; **41**:421-22
"Paris, 7 a.m." (Bishop) **121**:48, 71
"Paris, abril, modelo" (Salinas) **17**:365
Paris Bound (Barry) **11**:48-52, 54, 56, 64-7
"Paris, Capital of the Nineteenth Century" (Benjamin) **39**:10, 24, 27, 43, 48, 59
Paris clair-obscur (Bosschere) **19**:66-8
Paris de ma fenêtre (Colette) **5**:169
Paris France (Stein) **1**:433, 442; **28**:313; **48**:250-51, 253-55
Paris Gazette (Feuchtwanger)
See *Exil*
"The Paris Gown" (Trambley) **163**:287, 289, 300, 310, 312-13, 318-19, 324-25, 327, 330-32, 346, 375
Paris Nights (Bennett) **20**:24; **197**:40-2, 63, 65
"Paris, October, 1936" (Vallejo) **3**:527
"The Paris of the Second Empire in Baudelaire" (Benjamin) **39**:49
Paris Peasant (Aragon)
See *Le paysan de Paris*
Parisesh (Tagore) **53**:336, 342
"Parisian evenings" (Barthes)
See "Soirées de Paris"
"A Parisian Idyll" (Moore) **7**:487
Parisian Sketches (Huysmans)
See *Croquis Parisiens*
La Parisina (D'Annunzio) **40**:10-11
Park: A Fantastic Story (Gray) **19**:143-44, 146-47, 156, 158-59, 162-65
"The Park Bench" (Calvino)
See "La panchina"
"Park-Bench Vacation" (Calvino) **183**:226
"Parker Adderson, Philosopher" (Bierce) **44**:12, 44-5
"Parker's Back" (O'Connor) **132**:229-32, 242, 244, 256, 266-67, 271-74, 276, 328, 333
Parler seul (Tzara) **168**:280
"Parliament and Government in a Reconstructed Germany" (Weber) **69**:344
Parliamentary Government in England (Laski) **79**:145
"Parliamentary Regime in Italy" (Pareto) **69**:151
The Parlor Car (Howells) **7**:387; **17**:185
"Parmi les noirs" (Roussel) **20**:241
Parmiles cendres (Verhaeren) **12**:472
Parnassus on Wheels (Morley) **87**:117, 121, 124, 127, 129, 140, 146-8
"Parnell" (Johnson) **19**:230, 244
"Parnell and His Island" (Moore) **7**:477
"Parochial Theme" (Stevens) **45**:283
La Parodie (Adamov) **189**:5-6, 9, 11, 13-14, 19, 21, 41-2, 49, 56-7
A Parody Anthology (Wells) **35**:420
"Le parolacce" (Calvino) **183**:102
Parole (Saba) **33**:366, 370-71, 374
Parole e sangue (Papini) **22**:280-81
La parole est è péret (Péret) **20**:190-92, 198, 200-01
Le parole sono pietre (Levi) **125**:203-4, 211, 223
"Paroles des rochers" (Desnos) **22**:62
Paroles d'un révolté (Kropotkin) **36**:221
"The Parricide" (Howe) **21**:113
"The Parrot" (Merrill) **173**:255
"A Parrot" (Sarton) **120**:263
"The Parrot Fish" (Merrill) **173**:257
"Parson Ford's Confessional" (Warung) **45**:418
"Parsondes" (Valera y Alcala-Galiano) **10**:501, 504-05, 508
"The Parson's Cows" (Söderberg) **39**:437-38
"Parson's Pleasure" (Dahl) **173**:13
Parsons' Pleasure (Morley) **87**:122
The Parson's Progress (Mackenzie) **116**:207-08, 213, 215-16, 231
La part maudite (Bataille) **155**:3-4, 7, 10, 54, 61, 112
A Part of Myself (Zuckmayer)
See *Als wär's ein Stück von mir*
"Part of the Vigil" (Merrill) **173**:209-10
Partage de midi (Claudel) **2**:99-101, 105-08; **10**:127, 129, 132-34
"Parted" (Dunbar) **12**:110, 114
"Partial Comfort" (Parker) **143**:323

"Partial Enchantments of the Quixote" (Borges)
See "Magias parciales del Quijote"
"Partial Magic in the Quixote" (Borges)
See "Magias parciales del Quijote"
"A Partial Solution to the Labour Problem" (Taylor)
See "A Piece-Rate System, Being a Step Toward a Partial Solution of the Labor Problem"
"Partida" (Aleixandre) **113**:7
Partida (Sá-Carneiro) **83**:397-9, 401, 409
"La partie de plaisir" (Alain-Fournier) **6**:19
"Parting" (Baker) **10**:27
"Parting" (Kolmar)
See "Abschied"
"Parting" (Lasker-Schueler)
See "Abschied"
"Parting" (Pasternak) **188**:187, 190, 194
"Parting" (Thomas) **10**:463
Parting (Tsvetaeva) **7**:557
Parting Friends (Howells) **7**:387
"Parting Gift" (Wylie) **8**:533
"A Parting Hymn" (Forten) **16**:147, 150
Partiti e sindacati nella crisi del regime parlamentare (Mosca) **75**:169
"Partly from the Greek" (Belloc) **18**:41
"The Partners" (Chesnutt) **39**:98
Partners (Buchanan) **107**:32
"Partners in Silence" (Engel) **137**:14
The Partridge (Hansen)
See *Aferhønen*
"The Partridge Festival" (O'Connor) **132**:229
Parts of a World (Stevens) **3**:452, 457, 477; **12**:360, 376, 382-83; **45**:269, 283, 297, 332
"The Party" (Chekhov)
See "The Name-Day Party"
"The Party" (Dunbar)
See "The Pahty"
"A Party" (Welch) **22**:458
"The Party at Jack's" (Wolfe) **4**:527; **13**:495
The Party Dress (Hergesheimer) **11**:274, 276
A Party for Boris (Bernhard)
See *Eine Fest für Boris*
"Party on Shipboard" (Oppen) **107**:322, 324, 352, 359
Party Organization and Party Literature (Lenin)
See *On Party Organization and Party Literature*
The Party System of the House of Commons (Belloc) **18**:44
"Les pas" (Valéry) **15**:460
Pas suivi de quatre esquisses (Beckett) **145**:129
El pasado (Baroja) **8**:49
Pasado amor (Quiroga) **20**:208, 214
Pasado inmediato, y otros ensayos (Reyes) **33**:323
El pasajero: claves líricas (Valle-Inclán) **5**:476-77
Pasando y pasando (Huidobro) **31**:137
Pasarse de listo (Valera y Alcala-Galiano) **10**:507-08
Pascal's Mill (Williams) **89**:394
"Pascal's Sphere" (Borges) **109**:18
Pascarèl (Ouida) **43**:342, 345, 366, 374-76
The Pascarella Family (Werfel)
See *Die Geschwister von Neapel*
Pascua florida (Martinez Sierra and Martinez Sierra) **6**:279
Pascual Aguilera (Nervo) **11**:403-04
Pascual Lópex (Pardo Bazán) **189**:243
Pasenow; or, Romanticism (Broch) **20**:46-7, 62-3, 73
"Paseo" (Donoso) **133**:147-49, 177
"El paseo de Buster Keaton" (García Lorca) **197**:278
"El paseo de los amigos" (Huidobro) **31**:132
"Paseo matinal" (Lugones) **15**:289
"Pasha Tumanov" (Artsybashev) **31**:10
"The Pasha's Concubine" (Andrić)
See "Mara milosnica"
"La pasión" (Quiroga) **20**:213
Pasión de la tierra (Aleixandre) **113**:4-5, 20, 23, 30-32, 36, 41, 43-50, 58, 67-68, 70, 72, 79
Påsk (Strindberg) **1**:449, 459-60; **8**:407, 415; **47**:372
"Paso" (García Lorca) **181**:192
El Paso del Norte (Azuela) **145**:14
Pasó por Aquí (Rhodes) **53**:311-13, 319, 321, 324-27
"Los pasos" (Ibarguengoitia) **148**:203-4
Los pasos de López (Ibarguengoitia) **148**:216
"Los pasos lejanos" (Vallejo) **3**:531; **56**:288
Pasqua di Gea (Pirandello) **29**:310
Pasquala Ivanovitch (Loti) **11**:353
"The Pass" (Csáth) **13**:146, 154
"Passage" (Crane) **2**:115, 120; **5**:190
"Passage" (Drinkwater) **57**:149
"The Passage" (Okigbo) **171**:344-45
Passage de Carmencita (Loti) **11**:356
Passage de sultan (Loti) **11**:356
Passage d'enfant (Loti) **11**:356
Passage du poète (Ramuz) **33**:295
"A Passage in the Life of Mr. John Oakhurst" (Harte) **1**:341
A Passage in the Night (Asch) **3**:72
A Passage to India (Forster) **125**:24, 30-1, 64, 70, 72, 91, 98-9, 107, 110-11, 114, 116-17, 154, 162-63, 165-66
Le passant (Coppee) **25**:119, 122, 124, 126-27
"Le passant de Prague" (Apollinaire) **3**:38; **51**:20, 29
Le passé défini (Cocteau) **119**:57, 59, 71, 79
Passengers of Destiny (Aragon)
See *Les voyageurs de l'impériale*
"Passer mortuus est" (Millay) **4**:306; **169**:296
Passer Mortuus Est (Millay) **49**:217
"The Passerby of Prague" (Apollinaire)
See "Le passant de Prague"
"Passeri a sera" (Pascoli) **45**:152
"Passeur" (Chambers) **41**:88
Passing Along (Huidobro)
See *Pasando y pasando*
Passing By (Baring) **8**:35, 40-3
"Passing by Kamata" (Su Man-shu) **24**:456
"Passing by San Guido" (Carducci)
See "Davanti San Guido"
"The Passing Freight" (Dreiser) **18**:51
Passing Judgements (Nathan) **18**:322
"The Passing of Caoilte" (Ledwidge) **23**:117
"The Passing of Danny Deever" (Kipling) **17**:197
"Passing of Edward" (Middleton) **56**:175
"A Passing of Faith" (Bottomley) **107**:6
"The Passing of Grandison" (Chesnutt) **39**:70, 81, 91, 93
"The Passing of Peg-Leg" (Adams) **56**:13
"Passing of Père Pierre" (McCrae) **12**:209, 211
"The Passing of Political Economy" (Innis) **77**:339
"The Passing of Summer" (Noguchi) **80**:364
The Passing of the Third Floor Back, and Other Stories (Jerome) **23**:78, 82-3, 87-90
"The Passing Show" (Bierce) **7**:90
"Passing Visit to Helen" (Lawrence) **93**:17, 69
A Passing World (Lowndes) **12**:205
Passings and Greetings (Palamas) **5**:385
"The Passion Considered as an Uphill Bicycle Race" (Jarry) **14**:274
"La passion de Notre Dame" (Péguy) **10**:416
The Passion Flower (Benavente)
See *La malquerida*
Passion Flowers (Howe) **21**:106-07, 109, 111
"The Passion for Perpetuation" (Barbellion) **24**:79
A Passion in Rome (Callaghan) **145**:222
"Passion of Brother Hilarion" (Sharp) **39**:362
"The Passion of Jesus" (Quiroga)
See "La pasión"
The Passion of New Eve (Carter) **139**:55-57, 78, 80, 86, 115, 154, 168, 170, 195-96, 200, 204
"The Passion of Pablo Picasso" (Bishop) **103**:3
Passion of the Earth (Aleixandre)
See *Pasión de la tierra*
The Passionate Elopement (Mackenzie) **116**:192, 194, 197, 203, 205, 208, 212-13, 227, 229, 247, 251
The Passionate Friends (Wells) **6**:526, 528, 539; **12**:493
"A Passionate Pilgrim" (James) **2**:246-47
The Passionate Puritan (Mander) **31**:148-50, 153, 158, 160
"The Passionate Student to His Junior Bursar" (Morley) **87**:141
The Passionate Year (Hilton) **21**:91-2
"Passions and Ancient Days" (Cavafy) **7**:162
Passions Spin the Plot (Fisher) **140**:147, 155, 165, 168, 182, 184
"The Past" (Glasgow) **7**:342
"The Past" (Lu Hsun)
See "Huaijiu"
"Past and Present" (Naidu) **80**:293
"Past Carin'" (Lawson) **27**:134, 140
"Past Days" (Swinburne) **36**:342, 344-5
"Past Noon" (Nagai)
See "Hirusugi"
The Past Recaptured (Proust)
See *Le temps retrouvé*
"Past the Panes" (Sterling) **20**:386
"Pastel" (Symons) **11**:427
Pastels (Bourget) **12**:68
Le pasteur pauvre (Rod) **52**:325
"Pastiche a la Villon" (Talvik)
See "Blasphemous Ballad"
Pastiches et mélanges (Proust) **7**:535; **161**:126
"The Pastons and Chaucer" (Woolf) **43**:402; **56**:380
"The Pastor Caballero" (Stevens) **3**:449
Pastor Hall (Toller) **10**:481, 483
Pastor Naudier's Young Wife (Rod)
See *Le ménage du Pasteur Naudié*
Pastor Sang (Bjoernson)
See *Over ævne, I*
"Pastoral" (Millay) **4**:306
"The Pastoral Loves of Daphnis and Chloe" (Moore) **7**:498
"A Pastoral Nun" (Stevens) **12**:362
"A Pastoral of Giorgione" (Bottomley) **107**:2
The Pastoral Symphony (Gide)
See *La Symphonie pastorale*
"Pastorale" (Crane) **2**:119
Pastorale (Kandinsky) **92**:34
Pastorales (Jiménez) **4**:213, 216, 223-24
Los pastores (Martinez Sierra and Martinez Sierra) **6**:274-75, 278, 284, 287
Pastors and Masters (Compton-Burnett) **180**:115, 122, 124-26, 132, 134, 141, 143, 168-73, 195-96
"The Pastor's Daughter" (Smith) **25**:379, 385, 399
The Pastor's Wife (Elizabeth) **41**:119, 122-24, 132, 134, 136-37
"Pastramă trufanda" (Caragiale) **76**:159, 170
Pastures and Other Poems (Reese) **181**:337, 339
The Pastures of Heaven (Steinbeck) **135**:285, 290
"Las pataguas" (Prado) **75**:211
"Pataphysics and the Revelation of Laughter" (Daumal) **14**:86
"Pataphysique" (Jarry) **147**:314
"Patch Quilt" (Bonner) **179**:37
Patches of Sunlight (Dunsany) **59**:17
"Patchwork" (Moore) **7**:492
The Patchwork Girl of Oz (Baum) **7**:21, 25, 28; **132**:12-13, 98, 101
The Patent (Pirandello)
See *La patente*
Patent 119 (Tolstoy) **18**:383
La patente (Pirandello) **29**:297, 317-18
Le pater (Coppee) **25**:119, 127
"Paternity" (Benét) **28**:5
"Paterson" (Ginsberg) **120**:9, 11, 48, 67, 77-8

"The Path" (Thomas) **10**:454, 459, 463
"The Path in the Woods" (Wright) **136**:300
The Path of the Conquistadors (Gumilev)
See *Put' konkvistadorov*
The Path of the Happy Man (Lagerkvist)
See *Den lyckliges väg*
The Path of the King (Buchan) **41**:37-8
"The Path of the Law" (Holmes) **77**:232, 235-6, 252, 287, 321, 329
Path of Thunder (Okigbo)
See *Labyrinths, with Path of Thunder*
Path of Velvet (Gourmont) **17**:134
The Path to Home (Guest) **95**:208
The Path to Rome (Belloc) **7**:32, 34, 39-41; **18**:28, 30-1, 33, 44-6
The Path to the Nest of Spiders (Calvino)
See *Il sentiero dei nidi di ragno*
Pathēr dābrmī (Chatterji) **13**:77-8, 81-3
"Pathos" (Eisenstein) **57**:199
The Pathos of Distance (Huneker) **65**:164-65, 170, 185, 218
"Paths" (Andrić)
See "Staze"
Paths and Crossroads (Bryusov) **10**:77, 87
The Paths and the Roads of Poetry (Éluard)
See *Les sentiers et les routes de la poésie*
"Paths Leading Away from Judaism" (Peretz) **16**:405
Paths of Glory (Kubrick) **112**:127, 131, 188, 201, 205-07, 213, 215, 225, 234, 262, 267, 269, 272
"Patience" (Anwar)
See "Kesabaran"
"Patience" (Lowell) **8**:233
"Patience" (Merrill) **173**:175
"La Patience de Pénélope" (Cocteau) **119**:57
Patience; or, Bunthorne's Bride (Gilbert) **3**:209, 211, 214-16, 219
Patience Sparhawk and Her Times (Atherton) **2**:12-14
"Patraput, No. 3" (Tagore) **3**:489
"Patria" (Pascoli) **45**:156
Patria (Tey) **14**:459
"The Patriarch" (Colette) **16**:118, 120
"Patriarch Papinianus" (Söderberg) **39**:437-38
"Patriarchal Poetry" (Stein) **28**:340; **48**:238, 248-49
"Patricia, Edith, and Arnold" (Thomas) **8**:456, 463; **45**:396; **105**:302, 345
The Patrician (Galsworthy) **1**:300; **45**:45, 47, 49-50, 66-7, 70
Patrick White: Letters (White) **176**:323
"La patrie aux soldats morts" (Verhaeren) **12**:471
Patrins, to Which Is Added an Inquirendo into the Wit & Other Good Parts of His Late Majesty King Charles the Second (Guiney) **41**:209-11, 219
"The Patriot" (O'Faolain) **143**:221, 259-60
The Patriot (Neumann) **100**:313
A Patriot For Me (Osborne) **153**:242, 251, 270, 307, 310-11, 320, 341
The Patrioteer (Mann)
See *Der Untertan*
"Patriotism" (Mishima) **161**:7, 12, 50, 86-87, 92
Patriotism (Mishima) **161**:51, 57
"Patriotism and Government" (Tolstoy) **79**:429
"Patriotism Incorporated" (van Ostaijen)
See "De trust de vaderlandsliefde"
"Patriots and Revolutionaries" (Orwell) **128**:284
The Patrol of the Sun Dance Trail (Connor) **31**:105-06
"The Patron and the Crocus" (Woolf) **43**:415
"A Patron of Art" (Davis) **24**:200
The Pattern of Life (Adler) **61**:18, 31-2
"The Pattern that Gulls Weave" (March) **96**:252, 265
"Patterns" (Lowell) **1**:379; **8**:224, 229-31, 235
Patterns of Culture (Benedict) **60**:94, 97, 100-4, 107-11, 116-17, 122-28, 130-31, 133-41, 143-48, 150-53
The Patton Papers (1885-1940) (Patton) **79**:286-7
"Paudeen" (Yeats) **93**:352-53
Paul I (Merezhkovsky) **29**:231
Paul among the Jews (Werfel)
See *Paulus unter den Juden*
"Paul and Virginia" (Csáth) **13**:148
"Paul Blecker" (Davis) **6**:151
Paul, Envoy Extraordinary (Muggeridge) **120**:190
Paul et Virginie, Opéra Comique en Zactes (Cocteau) **119**:57, 66, 76
Paul Faber (MacDonald) **9**:292
"Paul Farlotte" (Scott) **6**:398
Paul Gauguin (Fletcher) **35**:110
Paul Kelver (Jerome) **23**:78, 81, 83, 86, 89-90
Paul Lange and Tora Parsberg (Bjoernson)
See *Paul Lange og Tora Parsberg*
Paul Lange og Tora Parsberg (Bjoernson) **37**:19, 28-9, 31-3
Paul les oiseaux (Artaud) **36**:32-3
Paul Patoff (Crawford) **10**:143-44, 151, 155
"Paul Revere" (Benchley) **55**:3
Paul Schippel, Esq. (Sternheim)
See *Bürger Schippel*
The Paul Street Boys (Molnár)
See *A Pál utcai fiúk*
Paul the Bird-Like (Artaud)
See *Paul les oiseaux*
Paula, ein Fragment (Beer-Hofmann) **60**:36-9
Paul-Augustine (Merezhkovsky) **29**:242
Paulicea desvairada (Andrade) **43**:5, 7, 8-13, 16-20
Pauline, and Other Poems (Stringer) **37**:327, 330
"Pauline Barrett" (Masters) **2**:474
"Pauline Gueble" (Tolstoy) **18**:382
"Paul's Case" (Cather) **11**:92, 101; **132**:132, 148
Paulus (Asch) **3**:68-70
Paulus unter den Juden (Werfel) **8**:473, 479
"Pauper" (Devkota)
See "Garīb"
Pauper, Brawler, and Slanderer (Tutuola) **188**:302-03, 306-08
"Paupières mûres" (Fondane) **159**:240, 242-46
"Paura della libertà" (Levi) **125**:225
Paura della libertà (Levi) **125**:197, 206-7, 209-10, 213-17, 219, 222, **125**:223-24, 226-27, 229-30, 233-35, 245, 247-50
La Paura Numero Uno (de Filippo) **127**:265-67, 270, 279
"Paura sul sentiero" (Calvino) **183**:208
Pause (Carr) **32**:123, 125-28
Pause (Rohmer) **28**:293
Pauvre Bitos (Anouilh) **195**:26, 30-1, 33-6, 38-9, 47-8, 50-1, 60
"Le pauvre chemisier" (Larbaud) **9**:200
Le pauvre de Monsieur Pascal (Barrès) **47**:67
Pávatollak (Babits) **14**:41
Pavements and Pastures (Burke) **63**:127
"Pavese: Essere e fare" (Calvino) **183**:94
"Pavliček's Crown" (Cankar) **105**:164
"Pavlichenko" (Babel)
See "Zisneopisanie Pavlicenki, Matveja Rodionyca"
"Pavlovna in London" (Flecker) **43**:189
"Pavlovo Sketches" (Korolenko) **22**:170
The Pawns Count (Oppenheim) **45**:134-36
"Pax Christi" (Johnson) **19**:243
"Pay Color" (Burroughs) **121**:132
"Pay the Criers" (Trambley) **163**:287, 315, 320-21, 375
Payam-i mashriq (Iqbal) **28**:182, 196-97
"The Payment" (Strindberg) **8**:81, 85 **21**:367
Payment Deferred (Forester) **152**:162
Le pays des fourrures (Verne) **6**:490, 500
"Paysage" (Apollinaire) **51**:33-4
"Paysage fauve" (Nelligan) **14**:396, 398
"Paysage II" (Garneau) **13**:195
Paysages et portraits (Colette) **16**:131
"Paysages spirituels" (Gourmont) **17**:129
Le paysan de Paris (Aragon) **123**:119, 131-32, 139, 147-8, 150-7
"Les paysans" (Verhaeren) **12**:468
Paz en la guerra (Unamuno) **2**:558, 561, 564; **9**:513, 515-16; **148**:241, 243, 250, 255-57, 287-94
"La paz, la avispa, el taco, las vertients" (Vallejo) **56**:287
Los pazos de Ulloa (Pardo Bazán) **189**:198, 205, 209, 213-14, 218-20, 222-24, 230-31, 233-34, 242, 244-45, 247, 254, 257, 260, 262, 275, 299
"Peace" (Brooke) **7**:125, 128-30
"Peace" (Gibran) **9**:85
"Peace" (Ivanov) **33**:138
"Peace" (Lawrence) **93**:98, 101
"Peace" (Yeats) **93**:349
Peace and Bread in Time of War (Addams) **76**:6-8, 34, 46
Peace in Friendship Village (Gale) **7**:277, 281, 283
"Peace in Our Time" (Nemerov) **124**:143
Peace in War (Unamuno)
See *Paz en la guerra*
Peace like a River (Fisher) **140**:157, 186
"The Peace Maker" (Eastman) **55**:171
The Peace of the Augustans (Saintsbury) **31**:224, 240-41
Peace with Honour (Milne) **88**:253
"The Peaceful Tree" (Jiménez) **183**:332
"Peacefulness" (Radnóti) **16**:418
"The Peacemaker" (Noyes) **7**:513
"Peach" (Lawrence) **93**:55, 98-100
"The Peaches" (Thomas) **8**:455, 463; **45**:393, 397; **105**:302, 320, 341, 344, 346, 348, 355, 357
"Peaches, Peaches" (Knister) **56**:163-64
"The Peacock" (Merrill) **173**:255
Peacock Feathers (Babits)
See *Pávatollak*
Peacock Pie (de la Mare) **4**:71, 74; **53**:28
"The Peacock's Vision" (Tagore) **3**:488
"Pear-Blossom" (Lawrence) **93**:119
"The Pearl" (Naidu) **80**:272
A Pearl at the Bottom (Hrabal)
See *Perlička na dně*
The Pearl Cannon (Hedāyat)
See *Tup-i murvari*
"The Pearl Diver" (Benét) **28**:6
The Pearl Lagoon (Hall and Nordhoff) **23**:58, 65, 71
Pearl Maiden (Haggard) **11**:243
Pearl of the Deep (Hrabal)
See *Perlička na dně*
"Pearl Oyster" (Levi) **109**:301
"The Pearl-Handled Cane" (Hippius) **9**:163
"Pearls" (Singer) **33**:386
Pearls (Gumilev)
See *Zhemchuga*
Pearls and Other Stories (Singer) **33**:385
"Pearls Are a Nuisance" (Chandler) **179**:128
"The Peasant" (Devkota) **23**:47
"The peasant and the watch" (Levi)
See "Il contadino e l'orologio"
The Peasant from Paris (Aragon)
See *Le paysan de Paris*
The Peasant from Taunus and Other Stories (Zuckmayer)
See *Der Bauer aus dem Taunus und andere Geschichten*
"The Peasant Yagafar" (Platonov) **14**:420
"The Peasants" (Chekhov)
See "Muziki"
"The Peasants" (Lewis) **3**:289
The Peasants (Reymont)
See *Chłopi*
"The Peasant's Confession" (Hardy) **4**:152
La peau (Malaparte) **52**:267-75
Peau noire, masques blancs (Fanon) **188**:3, 8, 12, 21, 27, 30-1, 33-5, 37-8, 41, 43-8, 50,

55-61, 68, 78-83, 85, 89-94, 96, 99, 103, 110-12, 114, 121-24, 128, 130-32, 136-37, 140-41, 146-52
"Pebble" (Herbert)
See "Kamyk"
"The Pebble" (Prado)
See "El guijarro"
"El pecado original" (Alas) **29**:20, 22
Una peccatrice (Verga) **3**:540-41, 547
"Pécheresse" (Mew) **8**:299
"Péchés d'artistes " (Benda) **60**:60
Pêcheur d'Islande (Loti) **11**:353-54, 358, 360-62, 364, 366-67
"Pecksniffiana" (Stevens) **45**:283
"La pecorella smarrità" (Pascoli) **45**:154
"The Peculiar Demesne of Archvicar Gerontion" (Kirk) **119**:281, 283, 339-41
Pedagogia (Gentile)
See *Sommario di pedagogia*
Pedagogical Anthropology (Montessori) **103**:284-85
Peder Victorious: A Tale of the Pioneers Twenty Years Later (Rölvaag) **17**:323-24, 326-27, 329, 332-34, 337, 345-46
"The Pedigree" (Hardy) **143**:160
"The Pedlar" (Mew) **8**:297
"The Pedlar" (Scott) **6**:398
"The Pedlar's Song" (Gurney) **33**:87
Uma pedra no meio do caminho: Biografia de um poema (Drummond de Andrade) **139**:224
Pedro de Valdivia, Conqueror of Chile (Graham) **19**:106, 111, 123-25
Pedro Moreno, el Insurgente (Azuela) **145**:14
Pedro Sánchez (Pereda) **16**:365, 367-68, 370-71, 374, 378-79, 382
"A Peep into the Past" (Beerbohm) **24**:108
Peer Gynt (Ibsen) **2**:225-28, 231-33, 235-36, 238-39; **8**:141-42, 146, 148-50, 155; **16**:154, 169, 171, 193; **37**:223, 225, 239, 242, 252, 256-58; **52**:146, 153, 163
"Peers" (Toomer) **172**:277-78
Peers (Belloc) **7**:38
"A Peg on Which to Hang" (Wakefield) **120**:357
"Pegasus at the Plow" (Rhodes) **53**:316
"The Pegging-Out of Overseer Franke" (Warung) **45**:418, 420
"Peggy Sue" (Holly) **65**:138-44
"Peggy Sue Got Married" (Holly) **65**:147
Les peintres cubistes (Apollinaire)
See *Méditations esthétiques: Les peintres cubistes*
"Peintres de l'empêchement" (Beckett) **145**:88-89
"La peinture des van Velde ou le monde et le pantalon" (Beckett) **145**:88
"Pekarnja" (Zabolotsky) **52**:375, 378
"Peking Street Scene" (Lu Hsun) **3**:302
"Un pelado" (Graham) **19**:109, 129
"Pelagea" (Coppard) **5**:178
"Pelang" (Drummond) **25**:142
Le pèlerin du silence (Gourmont) **17**:127, 137
Le pèlerin passioné (Moréas) **18**:275-76, 278-79, 281-83, 285-88, 290
"Les pèlerins piémontais" (Apollinaire) **51**:21, 29
"The Pelican" (Merrill) **173**:255
"The Pelican" (Wharton) **3**:551, 555, 571; **9**:540-41; **129**:360
The Pelican (Strindberg)
See *Pelikanen*
A Pelican at Blandings (Wodehouse)
See *No Nudes Is Good Nudes*
The Pelicans (Delafield) **61**:124, 127
Pelikanen (Strindberg) **1**:456; **8**:415
"Pelino Viera's Confession" (Hudson) **29**:156
La pelle (Malaparte)
See *La peau*
Pelle: Apprenticeship (Nexø)
See *Pelle erobreren*
Pelle: Boyhood (Nexø)
See *Pelle erobreren*
Pelle: Daybreak (Nexø)
See *Pelle erobreren*
Pelle erobreren (Nexø) **43**:309-18, 320, 322-23, 327-33
Pelle the Conqueror (Nexø)
See *Pelle erobreren*
Pelle: The Great Struggle (Nexø)
See *Pelle erobreren*
Pelleas und Melisande (Schoenberg) **75**:298, 331
"Pellegrinaggio" (D'Annunzio) **40**:37
Pellucidar (Burroughs) **2**:81; **32**:58, 77
"Pema mlade istine" (Popa) **167**:157
Pembroke (Freeman) **9**:61, 63-5, 69-71, 74
Pemmican (Fisher) **140**:149, 188
"The Pen" (London) **9**:281; **39**:279-80
Pen and Ink (Matthews) **95**:225
"The Pen in the First Person" (Calvino)
See "La penna in prima persona"
The Pen of My Aunt (Tey) **14**:459
"Pen, Pencil, and Poison" (Wilde) **8**:493; **41**:359
Pen, Pencil and Poison (Wilde) **175**:314
Peña Labra (Jiménez) **183**:322-24
"Penalosa" (Rhodes) **53**:307, 315-16
"Penance" (McCrae) **12**:210
Peñas arriba (Pereda) **16**:367, 369, 373, 378-79, 381-84
"The Pencil" (Chandler) **179**:82, 129, 143, 185
"The Pencil Seller" (Service) **15**:402
Pendant la guerre (Gourmont) **17**:153
Pendant l'orage (Gourmont) **17**:138
"A Pen-Drawing of Leda" (Field) **43**:166, 168
"The Penduline Tit" (Remizov)
See "Remez-pervaia ptashka"
"The Pendulum" (Henry) **19**:173, 180
"Pene" (Balmont) **11**:40
Penek (Bergelson) **81**:20
"Penelope" (Buchanan) **107**:14
"Penelope" (Parker) **28**:362
Penelope Brandling (Lee) **5**:315
"Penelope in Doubt" (Muir) **87**:302-03
"Penerimaan" (Anwar) **22**:16
"The Penetrative Powers of the Price System" (Innis) **77**:339
"Penghidupan" (Anwar) **22**:18
Penguin Island (France)
See *L'Île de pingouins*
"Peniel" (Campbell) **9**:32
Le pénitencier (Martin du Gard) **24**:394
"The Penitent" (Millay) **4**:306-07; **169**:231-32, 234
The Penitent (di Donato) **159**:184-85, 189, 196, 202, 206-7
"Penitent Art" (Santayana) **40**:388, 394
Les pénitents en maillots roses (Jacob) **6**:198-99, 201-02
"La penna in prima persona" (Calvino) **183**:29-30, 102-3
"The Pennant Pursuit" (Lardner) **14**:300-01
"Pennsylvania Station" (Faulkner) **170**:128
A Penny Saved Is Impossible (Nash) **109**:359
The Pennycomequicks (Baring-Gould) **88**:12-4
"Penobscot" (Oppen) **107**:308-09
Penrod (Tarkington) **9**:453, 455, 459, 467, 470, 472, 474
Penrod and Sam (Tarkington) **9**:455, 459, 471
The Penrose Mystery (Freeman) **21**:59, 61
Pensaci, Giacomino! (Pirandello) **4**:326; **29**:282, 285, 297, 301
Pensamiento de los jardines (Gonzalez Martinez) **72**:148
Pensamientos escogidos (Ramoacn y Cajal) **93**:146
"La pensée" (Sully Prudhomme) **31**:308
"La pensée est une et indivisible" (Péret) **20**:189-90, 192-93
"La Pensée mise en plis" (Deleuze) **116**:83
Pensees des jardins (Jammes) **75**:119-20
"Pensez" (Éluard) **7**:251
Pension (Mansfield) **164**:239
"I pensionati della memoria" (Pirandello) **29**:293
"The Pensioner" (Ingamells) **35**:138
"The Pensioners of Memory" (Pirandello)
See "I pensionati della memoria"
"Der pensionierte Salonsozialist" (Bernhard) **165**:86
"Pensions for Poets" (Middleton) **56**:192
Pensive Flamdes (Arp) **115**:13, 23-7
Pensive flames (Arp) **115**:13, 23-7
"The Pensive Prisoner" (Flecker) **43**:190, 194
"Pentheus" (Flecker) **43**:213
Pentimento: A Book of Portraits (Hellman) **119**:119-21, 123-25, 142, 147-48, 151-53, 175, 177, 193, 199, 201, 217, 227, 232
"La penúltima versión de la realidad" (Borges) **109**:11, 77
Penultimate Words (Shestov)
See *Nachala i kontsy*
"Penumbra" (Lowell) **8**:234
"El peón" (Quiroga) **20**:212
"People" (Benét) **28**:6
"People" (Toomer) **172**:277-78
"The People" (Yeats) **31**:407; **93**:350
The People (Glaspell) **55**:236; **175**:107, 110, 112
People (Lagerkvist)
See *Människor*
"A People and Destiny" (Gibran) **9**:85
"People as Pictures" (Carter) **139**:168
People by the Sea (Bojer)
See *Vor egen stamme*
The People from the Forest (Raabe) **45**:192, 199-200
"The People from Veletovci" (Andrić)
See "Velevtovci"
"The People in the Black Circle" (Howard) **8**:133, 135-36
"People Marching" (Borowski) **9**:21
The People of Hemsö (Strindberg)
See *Hemsöborna*
"The People of Osatica" (Andrić)
See "Osatičani"
"People of the Abyss" (Morrison) **72**:383
The People of the Abyss (London) **9**:257, 265, 270, 272; **15**:260
The People of the Mist (Haggard) **11**:243, 251
"People of Unrest" (Walker) **129**:298
"People To Talk To" (Ginzburg) **156**:30, 46
"The People v. Abe Lathan, Colored" (Caldwell) **117**:8
The People with Light Coming Out of Them (Saroyan) **137**:184
People You Didn't Expect to Meet (Allen) **87**:51, 53
"People's Blessing" (Bialik)
See "Birkath 'am"
"A People's Constitution" (Bryan) **99**:147
The People's Rose (Drummond de Andrade)
See *A Rosa do povo*
"A People's Theatre" (Yeats) **93**:364, 366
Pepel' (Bely) **7**:46, 50
Pepita Jiménez (Valera y Alcala-Galiano) **10**:495-502, 506-08
"Pepita's Wedding" (Heidenstam) **5**:253-54
Pepper & Salt; Or, Seasoning for Young Folk (Pyle) **81**:392
"Pequena história da república" (Ramos) **32**:434
"Pequeño responso a un héroe de la República" (Vallejo) **56**:313
Per Amica Silentia Lunæ (Yeats) **11**:522; **31**:388, 404, 411; **93**:338, 339, 341
"Per chi si scrive (Lo scaffale ipotetico)" (Calvino) **183**:107-8, 193, 195
"Per Fourier III" (Calvino) **183**:101
"Per Giuseppe Monti e Gaetano Tognetti" (Carducci) **32**:99
"Per iter tenebricosum" (Gogarty) **15**:112
Per la più grande Italia (D'Annunzio) **6**:145
"Per le nozze di mia figlia" (Carducci) **32**:102
Per le vie (Verga) **3**:543
"Per un critico" (Svevo) **35**:362-63
"Per un saggio" (Pratolini) **124**:349

La perception du changement (Bergson) **32**:17, 24
"Perceptional Activities" (Yokomitsu)
See "Kankaku-Katsudô"
The Perch and the Goldfishes (Leino)
See *Ahven ja kultakalat*
"Perchatki" (Remizov) **27**:339
"Perdjurit djaga malam" (Anwar) **22**:23
"The Perdu" (Roberts) **8**:318
"Le Père François" (Lewis) **104**:200
Le père humiliè (Claudel) **2**:105-06; **10**:123-24
"Père Lalemant" (Pickthall) **21**:242, 245, 250, 256
"Perechod cerez Zbruc" (Babel) **2**:22, 26, 29-30; **13**:38; **171**:4, 7-9, 19, 21, 23, 25, 30-31, 36, 40, 48, 70, 72, 74, 79, 81-82, 87
"Pered vesnoi" (Guro) **56**:132, 142-43
Pered voskhodom solntsa (Zoshchenko) **15**:496-97, 502, 505-06, 511-14
La peregrinación de Bayoán (Hostos) **24**:303-04, 306
Peregrinations (Lyotard) **103**:218-20
"Peregrine" (Wylie) **8**:531, 533, 536
"Perekopsky entuziazm" (Mayakovski) **18**:258
"Perennial" (Adorno)
See "Perennial Fashion"
Perennial (Gogarty) **15**:105
"Perennial Fashion" (Adorno) **111**:134-36, 139
"Peresvet" (Balmont) **11**:40
Pereulochki (Tsvetaeva) **7**:557; **35**:410-12
"Perevorot v Vladivostoke" (Khlebnikov) **20**:133
"Perexod cerez Zbruc" (Babel)
See "Perechod cerez Zbruc"
"Perfect Grief" (Symons) **11**:446
"The Perfect Husband" (Nash) **109**:362
"The Perfect Setting" (Warner) **131**:309
The Perfect Wagnerite (Shaw) **3**:380
"The Perfect Widow" (Lucas) **73**:171
The Perfecting of a Love (Musil)
See "Vollendung der Liebe"
"Perfection" (Gogarty) **15**:103
"A Perfectly Free Association" (Jarrell) **177**:227
"Perfecto Luna" (Garro) **153**:40, 43-44
Perfervid; or, The Career of Ninian Jamieson (Davidson) **24**:159-60, 168-69, 176-77, 192-93
Perfidy (Hecht) **101**:80, 90-1
"The Performance" (Dickey) **151**:97, 104, 106, 124, 168, 199, 212, 215-16
"Perfume" (Gosse) **28**:132
The Perfume of Eros (Saltus) **8**:347
The Perfume of the Lady in Black (Leroux)
See *La parfum de la dame en noir*
Perfumed Death (D'Annunzio)
See *La pisanelle ou la mort parfumée*
"Perg Jasper" (Fisher) **140**:165
"Perhaps: A Dirge" (Wen I-to) **28**:417, 420
Perhindérion (Jarry) **147**:275
Pericolosamente (de Filippo) **127**:287
Peril (Osbourne) **93**:132
The Peril and Preservation of the Home (Riis) **80**:435
Peril in the North (Dent) **72**:27
"The Perilous Road" (Lindsay) **17**:248
The Periodic Table (Levi)
See *Il sistema periodico*
"The Perishing of the Pendragons" (Chesterton) **1**:186
"La perla rosa" (Pardo Bazán) **189**:226-27
Perlas negras (Nervo) **11**:398, 400, 402
Les perles mortes (Mirbeau) **55**:303
"Perlhuhn" (Morgenstern) **8**:305
Perlička na dně (Hrabal) **155**:165
Perlimplín (García Lorca)
See *Amor de Don Perlimplín*
"Perlite English Boy" (Smith) **25**:390
Perlycross (Blackmore) **27**:27-9, 31, 33, 37-9, 43-7
"Perman taru" (Leino) **24**:369
The Permanent Horizon (Lewisohn) **19**:274
"Permanent Human Values" (Campbell) **140**:49, 133, 138
"Permanent Wave" (Wharton) **129**:364
"The Permissionaire" (Fisher) **87**:73
Permit Me Voyage (Agee) **1**:2, 4, 9-10, 13-15; **19**:17, 23-4, 40; **180**:63-65
"Pero" (García Lorca) **181**:199
Perpetual Light (Benét) **28**:7
The Perplexed Husband (Sutro) **6**:420
"Perplext" (Naidu) **80**:315
El Perro del hortelano (Garro) **153**:21
"El perro rabioso" (Quiroga) **20**:210
Perronik the Fool (Moore) **7**:498
"Le perroquet" (Nelligan) **14**:392
Los Perros (Garro) **153**:17, 19-20, 72
"Perry Chumly's Eclipse" (Bierce) **44**:45
"Persecution" (Andrić) **135**:19, 60
"Persecution and the Art of Writing" (Strauss) **141**:336
Persecution and the Art of Writing (Strauss) **141**:233-34, 249, 316, 334-36, 339-41
"Los perseguidos" (Quiroga) **20**:218, 210-11, 220-21
"Persetudjuan dengan Bung Karno" (Anwar) **22**:20, 23, 26
"Perseus" (Heyse) **8**:116
Perseus the Deliverer (Aurobindo) **63**:4-5
"A Persian Long Song" (Naidu) **80**:344
"A Persian Lute Song" (Naidu) **80**:344
"Persian Miniature" (Gumilev) **60**:272
A Persian Pearl, and Other Essays (Darrow) **81**:74
Persian Pictures (Bell)
See *Safar Nameh. Persian Pictures. A Book of travel*
Persimmon Leaves (Santoka)
See *Kaki no ha*
"The Person in Question" (Gray) **19**:145, 156, 160-62, 165
A Person of Some Importance (Osbourne) **93**:132
"Personae" (Ford) **172**:93
"Personaggi" (Pirandello) **172**:176-77, 191-92
A Personal Anthology (Borges)
See *Antologia personal*
Personal Anthology (Borges)
See *Antologia personal*
Personal Enemy (Osborne) **153**:244, 251
A Personal History of the "Boom" (Donoso)
See *Historia personal del 'boom'*
Personal Impressions (Berlin) **105**:50-2, 71
"Personal Letter" (March) **96**:252, 254-55, 258, 264-65
"Personal Liberty" (Rhodes) **53**:316
A Personal Library (Borges)
See *Antologia personal*
Personal Pleasures (Macaulay) **44**:126
Personal Recollections of Joan of Arc (Twain) **6**:455, 457, 460, 466, 471-72, 486; **12**:431-32, 436, 438; **48**:342-43; **185**:235, 237, 269, 271, 290, 307, 317-21
A Personal Record (Conrad) **1**:206; **13**:105; **25**:98; **43**:102, 136, 138, 144; **57**:39, 110
Personal Reminiscences of Henry Irving (Stoker) **144**:286
"A Personal View of Science" (Valéry) **15**:460
Personal Writings (Hardy) **143**:154, 156, 159
"Personalities" (Woolf) **43**:401
"Personality" (McTaggart) **105**:197
"Personality and the Buddha" (Borges) **109**:157
Personally Conducted (Stockton) **47**:329
Persons and Places: The Background of My Life (Santayana) **40**:396, 412, 414-15
"Perspectiva" (García Lorca) **181**:65
"Perspectives Are Precipices" (Bishop) **103**:3-4, 7-8, 17, 21
Perspectives on Life: Four Chapters in Metaphysics (Simmel)
See *Lebensanschauung: Vier metaphysische Kapitel*
"Peru: The Landscape Game" (Merrill) **173**:170
Pervaja simfonija (Bely) **7**:58
"The Pervasion of Rouge" (Beerbohm) **24**:96, 116, 119
"Pervaya lyubov" (Babel) **2**:28; **13**:22-23, 34; **171**:8, 11, 94, 98-99
Perverted Tales (Norris) **155**:311
"Pervigilium" (Flecker) **43**:186
"Pervoe maia" (Olesha) **136**:182
Pervoe svidanie (Bely) **7**:47, 66
"Pervy gonorar" (Babel) **13**:26
"Pervyye studencheskiye gody" (Korolenko) **22**:177
"La pesadilla" (Gonzalez Martinez) **72**:152
La pesanteur et la grâce (Weil) **23**:367
"Los pescadores de vigas" (Quiroga) **20**:216
"Peschera" (Zamyatin) **8**:543-46, 552, 555-56; **37**:424-27, 431
"Pesci grossi, pesci piccoli" (Calvino) **183**:213
Le pèse-nerfs (Artaud) **3**:51, 56-7; **36**:5
"Pesma Cele-Kule" (Popa) **167**:159
"Pesn miryazya" (Khlebnikov) **20**:136
"Pesni goroda" (Guro) **56**:132, 144
Pesni mstitelia (Balmont) **11**:32, 37, 42
"Pesnia" (Babel) **2**:28; **171**:21-22, 24-26, 79, 85, 87
"Pesnia starika razboinika" (Esenin) **4**:116
"Pesnikove lestvice" (Popa) **167**:164
"Pesnja" (Hippius) **9**:164
Pesnya sudby (Blok) **5**:99-100
"Pessimism in Literature" (Forster) **125**:126
"The Pessimist of Plato Road" (Gissing) **24**:247
"La peste" (Schwob) **20**:323
Pesti Erkolcsok (Molnár) **20**:164
Pět minut za městem (Nezval) **44**:249
Pete (Caine) **97**:14
"Peter" (Cather) **132**:129, 137; **152**:68
Peter and Alexis (Merezhkovsky) **29**:226-27, 229-31, 233, 241
"Peter and John" (Wylie) **8**:538
"Peter and Paul" (Wylie) **8**:531
"Peter and the Wolf" (Carter) **139**:78-79, 86, 129-33
Peter and Wendy (Barrie) **2**:48; **164**:53, 70, 73
"Peter Anderson and Co." (Lawson) **27**:133
Peter Ashley (Heyward) **59**:103, 109-10
Peter Camenzind (Hesse) **196**:250, 339
Peter Goes to Town (Bernhard) **165**:16
The Peter Hille Book (Lasker-Schueler)
See *Das Peter Hille Buch*
Das Peter Hille Buch (Lasker-Schueler) **57**:327
"Peter Ibbetson" (Jewett) **22**:121
Peter Pan; or, The Boy Who Would Not Grow Up (Barrie) **2**:39, 43-44, 46, 48-49; **164**:6-8, 11-13, 18-22, 25, 32-33, 36-39, 41, 45, 53-58, 61-65, 67-70, 73, 80, 87-88, 90-94
"Peter Quince at the Clavier" (Stevens) **3**:448, 452, 455, 461, 465; **12**:356, 365, 376; **45**:281, 291, 322, 347
"Peter Rugg the Bostonian" (Guiney) **41**:207
"Peter Schroeder" (Harte) **25**:224
Peter Stuyvesant (Matthews) **95**:243-4
Peter the Czar (Klabund) **44**:102, 104
Peter the First (Tolstoy) **18**:359-64, 370-71, 373-75, 379, 383
Peter the Great (Tolstoy) **18**:361
"Peter Waydelin" (Symons) **11**:448
Peterburg (Bely) **7**:47-9, 51-5, 62-5
Peter's Day (Tolstoy) **18**:371, 375
"Petersburg" (Khodasevich) **15**:206
Petersburg (Asch) **3**:67-8
Petersburg Diary (Hippius) **9**:155
"Petersburg Stanzas" (Mandelstam) **2**:403
Le Petit (Bataille) **155**:93
Le Petit Ami (Léautaud) **83**:186, 188-91, 193, 195-9, 202-7, 209-11
"La petit auto" (Apollinaire) **3**:42; **51**:21, 35-6
Le petit bonhomme (France) **9**:38
Le petit homme de Dieu (Lemonnier) **22**:199
Le petit Pierre (France) **9**:46
Le petit prince (Saint-Exupéry) **2**:517, 519, 521-23; **56**:221-35; **169**:309, 312, 315, 321, 327-35, 342

"Petit, the Poet" (Masters) **2**:466; **25**:304, 313
"Petite mise en perspective de la décadence et de quelques combats minoritaires ày mener" (Lyotard) **103**:161, 165
La Petite Molière (Anouilh) **195**:25
Les petites villes à pignons (Verhaeren) **12**:465
"Petitie" (Caragiale) **76**:156
De petits faits vrais (Bourget) **12**:69
Petits spectacles (Vian) **9**:537
The Petrified Forest (Sherwood) **3**:410-14, 418
"Petrográd" (Hippius) **9**:155
"Petrol Shortage" (Muir) **2**:489; **87**:241
Die Petroleuminseln (Feuchtwanger) **3**:181
"Pétrone" (Schwob) **20**:323
The Petty Demon (Sologub)
See *Melkii bes*
"Petunias—That's for Remembrance" (Fisher) **87**:73
"Petushok" (Remizov) **27**:334, 339-41
"Un Peu d'Amour" (Chambers) **41**:113-14
"La Peur Chez L'Amour" (Jarry) **147**:263
The Peyote Dance (Artaud) **36**:29-30
"The Peyote Rite" (Artaud)
See "Le rite du peyotl"
Pferdewechsel (Kaiser) **9**:181, 192
Pfister's Mill (Raabe)
See *Pfisters Mühle*
Pfisters Mühle (Raabe) **45**:166-67, 170, 172, 174, 176-77, 196
"Die Pflanzen des Dr. Cinderella" (Meyrink) **21**:222
Die Pforte der Einweihung (Steiner) **13**:438, 442-43, 446, 456-58
Die Phaenomenologie und die Fundamente de Wissenschaften (Husserl) **100**:112, 119
Phaenomenologie Untersuchungen zur Konstitution (Husserl) **100**:80-88, 99
"Phaethon" (Campbell) **9**:32
Phalenas (Machado de Assis) **10**:279
Phālgunī (Tagore) **3**:486, 491
Le phanérogame (Jacob) **6**:191
Phänomenolgoie des sittlichen Bewusstseins (von Hartmann) **96**:206
Phantastes: A Faerie Romance (MacDonald) **9**:291-92, 294-95, 297-99, 301-04, 306-08, 310-11; **113**:197-99, 201-03, 206-07, 210, 214-17, 221-25, 227, 230, 233-43, 247, 249, 264, 268, 272, 281, 285-86, 289-90, 297, 305, 311-13
"Phantasy" (Sharp) **39**:354
The Phantom (de la Mare) **4**:79
Phantom (Murnau) **53**:252, 262
The Phantom City (Dent) **72**:23
"The Phantom Fleet" (Noyes) **7**:502
"Phantom Gold" (Dreiser) **35**:71, 74
"The Phantom Horsewoman" (Hardy) **53**:111
The Phantom Journal and Other Essays and Diversions (Lucas) **73**:174
"A Phantom Lover" (Lee) **5**:320
The Phantom Lover (Kaiser)
See *Oktobertag*
"The Phantom Motor" (Futrelle) **19**:90, 96
"A Phantom of Clouds" (Apollinaire)
See "Un fantóme de nuées"
"The Phantom of the Open Hearth" (Shepherd) **177**:298-99
Phantom of the Open Hearth (Shepherd) **177**:304
The Phantom of the Opera (Leroux)
See *La fantôme de l'opéra*
"The Phantom Rickshaw" (Kipling) **8**:176, 199
The Phantom Rival (Molnár) **20**:167, 169
The Phantom Shield (Natsume)
See *Maboroshi no tate*
Phantom Wires (Stringer) **37**:336
"Phantoms" (Kunikida Doppo)
See "Maboroshi"
Phantoms (Andreyev) **3**:26
"The Phantoms of the Foot-Bridge" (Murfree) **135**:208-9
Pharais: A Romance of the Isles (Sharp) **39**:355, 359-62, 365-68, 373-75, 378-79, 387, 394, 396
The Pharao (Prus)
See *Faraon*
"Pharao und Joseph" (Lasker-Schueler) **57**:329-30, 336
"Pharaoh" (Kielland) **5**:275-76
The Pharaoh and the Priests (Prus)
See *Faraon*
"Pharaoh and the Sergeant" (Kipling) **8**:193
"La Pharmacienne" (Fisher) **87**:74
The Pharmacist (Fields) **80**:235-6
"The Pharmacist's Wife" (Giraudoux) **7**:324
Pharoah (Prus)
See *Faraon*
Phases of an Inferior Planet (Glasgow) **2**:189; **7**:339
"Phases of Fiction" (Woolf) **1**:531; **43**:405-06, 421, 425, 427
"Phases of State Legislation" (Roosevelt) **69**:177
"The Phases of the Moon" (Yeats) **11**:528; **31**:406; **93**:358
"Phædra" (Swinburne) **8**:431; **36**:298-99, 322
Le phénix (Éluard) **7**:260-61; **41**:151-52, 158
The Phenomenal American Girl (Kuzmin)
See *Fenomenal'naia amerikanka*
Le phénomène humain (Teilhard de Chardin) **9**:477, 479-80, 483, 485-89, 495-96, 498, 500
La Phénoménologie (Lyotard) **103**:152, 226
La Phénoménologie de la perception (Merleau-Ponty) **156**:121-24, 126-27, 133-34, 143, 157-59, 162, 164, 174-75, 178-79, 183-84, 197-98, 200-202, 204-5, 208-11, 216, 218, 221, 225-34, 242-43, 247-48, 258, 260, 271, 273-75, 280, 287, 291, 269262, 272265
"Phenomenology" (Husserl) **100**:121
"Phenomenology and Anthropology" (Husserl) **100**:134
Phenomenology and the Foundations of the Sciences (Husserl)
See *Die Phaenomenologie und die Fundamente de Wissenschaften*
The Phenomenology of Internal Time-Consciousness (Husserl)
See *Vorlesungen zur Phänomenologie des innern Zeitbewusstseins*
Phenomenology of Linguistic Form (Cassirer)
See *Philosophie der symbolischen Formen*
The Phenomenology of Perception (Merleau-Ponty)
See *La Phénoménologie de la perception*
The Phenomenon of Man (Teilhard de Chardin)
See *Le phénomène humain*
"Phezu kwethuna likaShaka" (Vilakazi) **37**:407
The Philadelphia Negro (Du Bois) **169**:91, 155, 212
The Philadelphia Story (Barry) **11**:60-1, 65, 67-8
"Philai Te Kou Philai" (Oppen) **107**:361
The Philanderer (Shaw) **3**:380; **9**:412-14; **21**:311, 323, 327, 329
"The Philanthropist and the Peaceful Life" (Fisher) **87**:72
"Philanthropy from the Point of View of Ethics" (Mead) **89**:38
"Philhellene" (Cavafy) **2**:97
"Philip Marlowe's Last Case" (Chandler) **179**:129
Philippe II (Verhaeren) **12**:464, 479-82
"Philiströsität, Realismus, Idealismus der Kunst" (Broch) **20**:55-6
"Phillipa's Foxhunt" (Somerville & Ross) **51**:335
Philochristus: Memoirs of a Disciple of the Lord (Abbott) **139**:26, 29
Philoctète (Fondane) **159**:248-51
Philoctéte (Gide) **5**:232; **12**:144; **177**:105
Philoctetes (Fondane)
See *Philoctète*
"Philologie der Weltliteratur" (Auerbach) **43**:63, 71
Philomythus: an Antidote against Credulity (Abbott) **139**:31-34, 36, 38-40
"The Philopena" (Stockton) **47**:329
"Phil-O-Rum Juneau" (Drummond) **25**:151
Philosophenbuch (Nietzsche) **8**:346
"The Philosopher" (Anderson) **1**:59; **24**:32, 35, 45, 49; **123**:13, 85
"The Philosopher and His Shadow" (Merleau-Ponty) **156**:210, 291
Philosopher or Dog? (Machado de Assis)
See *Quincas Borba*
"Philosopher That Failed" (Lucas) **73**:159
"Philosophers and Philodoxers" (Kirk) **119**:258
The Philosopher's Den (Herbert)
See *Jaskinia filozofow*
"The Philosopher's Progress" (Crowley) **7**:208
The Philosopher's Pupil (Murdoch) **171**:263, 266, 285, 299-300, 323, 327, 330-31
The Philosopher's Stone (Artaud) **36**:35
"The Philosophers' Stone (Humorous Short Story)" (Herzl)
See "A bölcsek köve (humoristicus novella)"
"The Philosophes" (Becker) **63**:116
Les philosophes célèbres (Merleau-Ponty) **156**:121, 129-30
"The Philosophical Basis of Ethics" (Mead) **89**:47
"Philosophical Conceptions and Practical Results" (James) **32**:357, 359
Philosophical Essays (Nishida) **83**:252
"The Philosophical Foundations of Mathematics" (Nishida)
See "Sugako no tetsugakuteki kisozuke"
The Philosophical Grammar (Wittgenstein)
See *Philosophiche Grammatik*
Philosophical Investigations (Wittgenstein)
See *Philosophische Bemerkungen*
Philosophical Notebooks (Lenin) **67**:210
"Philosophical Reflections on the Speeches of J.-J. Rousseau" (Tolstoy)
See "Filosoficheskie zamechaniia na rechi Zh.Zh. Russo"
Philosophical Remarks (Wittgenstein)
See *Philosophische Bemerkungen*
Philosophical Studies (McTaggart) **105**:196
Philosophical Studies (Moore) **89**:182, 185, 204-6, 240-2
Philosophical Tales (Herzl) **36**:140, 142
Philosophiche Grammatik (Wittgenstein) **59**:239-40, 242, 298, 305
"Philosophie als strenge Wissenschaft" (Husserl) **100**:10, 121, 123, 145-47, 149
Philosophie der Arithmetik (Husserl) **100**:2, 9, 11, 36-39
Die Philosophie der Aufklärung (Cassirer) **61**:67
Die Philosophie der Freiheit (Steiner) **13**:438-40, 443, 446, 449
Philosophie der Neuen Musik (Adorno) **111**:9, 18-19, 24, 42, 46, 49, 53-4, 164
Philosophie der symbolischen Formen (Cassirer) **61**:38, 48-9, 59, 74, 77-9, 81-91, 94-5, 97-9, 107-9, 115
Die Philosophie des Als Ob (Vaihinger) **71**:409, 412, 421, 424
Philosophie des Geldes (Simmel) **64**:318-20, 324, 327, 330, 338, 352, 357, 359-61
Die Philosophie des Unbewussten (von Hartmann) **96**:150, 153-54, 187, 203, 206-07, 215, 218-19, 224-31
La Philosophie du non (Bachman) **128**:89
Philosophie und Gesetz (Strauss) **141**:233, 236, 238, 286, 335
"Philosophies" (Stringer) **37**:341

Philosophische Bemerkungen (Wittgenstein) **59**:214, 216, 222-29, 234, 236, 238-44, 246, 254-55, 259-61, 264, 267-68, 27286-87, 289, 293-94, 297, 300, 305, 308-10
Philosophische Kultur (Simmel) **64**:320
"Philosophy" (Dunbar) **12**:104
"Philosophy" (Nemerov) **124**:256
"Philosophy" (Parker) **143**:321
"Philosophy and Art" (Brennan) **17**:47, 55
Philosophy and Law (Strauss)
See *Philosophie und Gesetz*
"Philosophy and Literature" (Calvino) **183**:195
Philosophy and Living (Stapledon) **22**:322
Philosophy and Non-Philosophy Since Hegel (Merleau-Ponty) **156**:182-83, 185, 191
The Philosophy and Opinions of Marcus Garvey; or, Africa for the Africans (Garvey) **41**:187, 190-91, 194, 199
"Philosophy and Politics" (Arendt) **193**:122, 124-25, 158
"Philosophy as a Rigorous Science" (Husserl)
See "Philosophie als strenge Wissenschaft"
Philosophy as Rigorous Science (Husserl)
See "Philosophie als strenge Wissenschaft"
"Philosophy as Strict Science" (Husserl)
See "Philosophie als strenge Wissenschaft"
Philosophy Four (Wister) **21**:377-78, 380, 384
Philosophy in State Examinations (Vaihinger) **71**:416
"Philosophy in the Light of Contemporary Events" (Mann) **44**:220
Philosophy of Arithmetic (Husserl)
See *Philosophie der Arithmetik*
Philosophy of Art (Gentile)
See *La filosofia dell'arte*
The Philosophy of "As If" (Vaihinger)
See *Die Philosophie des Als Ob*
The Philosophy of Conflict, and Other Essays in War-Time (Ellis) **14**:112
The Philosophy of Disenchantment (Saltus) **8**:342, 345, 348-49, 351-53, 355
Philosophy of Freedom (Berdyaev) **67**:27, 78
The Philosophy of Friedrich Nietzsche (Mencken) **13**:386, 389
The Philosophy of G. E. Moore (Moore) **89**:195
The Philosophy of History (Collingwood) **67**:134
Philosophy of Inequality (Berdyaev) **67**:30, 32
The Philosophy of Love (Glyn) **72**:138, 142
Philosophy of Modern Music (Adorno)
See *Philosophie der Neuen Musik*
The Philosophy of Money (Simmel)
See *Philosophie des Geldes*
Philosophy of New Music (Adorno)
See *Philosophie der Neuen Musik*
Philosophy of Practice (Croce)
See *Filosofia della practica, economica ed etica*
"A Philosophy of Progress" (Collingwood) **67**:182-83, 192
"The Philosophy of Relative Existences" (Stockton) **47**:327
The Philosophy of Religion (Otto)
See *Kantisch-Friessche Religionsphilosophie*
The Philosophy of Spiritual Activity (Steiner)
See *Die Philosophie der Freiheit*
The Philosophy of Symbolic Forms (Cassirer)
See *Philosophie der symbolischen Formen*
The Philosophy of the Act (Mead) **89**:52, 62-6, 70-2, 74, 78, 91-2, 160-2
"The Philosophy of the Astonished" (Oppen) **107**:335-36, 339
Philosophy of the Beautiful (von Hartmann) **96**:222
The Philosophy of the Enlightenment (Cassirer)
See *Die Philosophie der Aufklärung*
The Philosophy of the Marquise (Lowndes) **12**:200
Philosophy of the Practical: Economic and Ethic (Croce)
See *Filosofia della practica, económica ed etica*
Philosophy of the Present (Mead) **89**:52, 64, 72, 78, 81, 90, 165
"The Philosophy of the Short Story" (Matthews) **95**:226, 228
Philosophy of the Spirit (Croce) **37**:80-1, 93-4, 97-8, 121-23
The Philosophy of the Unconscious (von Hartmann)
See *Die Philosophie des Unbewussten*
Philosophy, Poetry, History (Croce) **37**:127
"Phoenix" (Lawrence) **93**:71, 77, 78, 114, 128
"Phoenix" (Nemerov) **124**:172
"The Phoenix" (Strindberg) **21**:366
Phoenix (Abercrombie) **141**:10-16
The Phoenix (Éluard)
See *Le phénix*
Phoenix (Lawrence) **48**:112, 121, 132, 140, 147; **61**:253, 269; **93**:43
"The Phoenix Again" (Sarton) **120**:260, 305
Phoenix II (Lawrence) **48**:136, 141, 146; **61**:269
"The Phoenix on the Sword" (Howard) **8**:131-33, 135
"Phonograph Blues" (Johnson) **69**:80
Phonographe (Jarry) **147**:245-46, 331
"Phonographs" (Villaurrutia) **80**:477-8
"The Photograph" (Bradford) **36**:63
"The Photographer's Wife" (Colette)
See "La Dame du Photographe"
"A Photographic Enquête" (Hartmann) **73**:130
"Photographs" (Morris) **107**:225
Photographs and Words (Morris) **107**:174, 207
"Photography and Reality" (Morris) **107**:176
"Phrases and Philosophies for the Use of the Young" (Wilde) **23**:425
Phroso (Hope) **83**:165
"Phyllida" (Marquis) **7**:436
"Physic" (de la Mare) **53**:27
"Physical Courage" (Higginson) **36**:175
The Physical Phenomena of Mysticism (Summers) **16**:433
"The Physical Thing" (Mead) **89**:90
"The Physician as Educator" (Adler) **61**:23
"The Physician's Duty" (Pirandello)
See "Il dovere del medico"
"Physics and Reality" (Einstein)
See "Physik and Realitat"
"Physics of Poetry" (Éluard)
See "Physique de la poésie"
Physics of Poetry (Éluard)
See *Physique de la poésie*
"Physik and Realitat" (Einstein) **65**:92, 94, 97, 101
"Physiological Surgery of the Digestive Canal" (Pavlov) **91**:150
Physiologie de l'amour moderne (Bourget) **12**:67, 74
The Physiology of Love (Gourmont)
See *Physique de l'amour*
"Physique de la poésie" (Éluard) **7**:254; **41**:149
Physique de la poésie (Éluard) **41**:164
Physique de l'amour (Gourmont) **17**:128, 130, 133, 135, 137, 142, 146, 152, 153
Il piacere (D'Annunzio) **6**:128, 131, 133, 137, 140, 143-44; **40**:4, 15-20, 26-31
Il piacere dell'onestà (Pirandello) **4**:335, 340; **29**:285, 296-97, 318
I piaceri (Brancati) **12**:87-9
"Piano" (Lawrence) **93**:17, 67, 117, 127
"The Piano" (Williams) **89**:371
"Piano Practice" (Rilke)
See "Übung am Klavier"
"Pianto antico" (Carducci) **32**:101
"P'ianyi rytsar'" (Nabokov) **108**:144
Piave (Brancati) **12**:84
La piave (D'Annunzio) **40**:10
"Piazza" (Campana) **20**:85
Pic (Kerouac) **117**:187-88, 229
Pícaro (Hall and Nordhoff) **23**:57, 65
"Piccadilly Circus at Night" (Lawrence) **93**:23
"Le piccole virtù" (Ginzburg) **156**:97
Le piccole virtù (Ginzburg) **156**:3, 5, 68, 73, 96, 107, 109, 111
"Picking Mushrooms" (Bishop) **121**:50
Pickle the Spy; or, The Incognito of Prince Charles (Lang) **16**:252, 269-70
"Pickman's Model" (Lovecraft) **4**:266, 269-70; **22**:221, 223-24
"Pick-Up on Noon Street" (Chandler) **7**:176; **179**:124
Pickup on Noon Street (Chandler) **179**:123
"A Picnic among the Ruins" (Howe) **21**:107
"Pictor's Transformations" (Hesse) **196**:262, 269-70, 278
"A Picture" (Nemerov) **124**:180, 316
The Picture (Tolstoy) **18**:377
Picture Book (Hesse)
See *Bilderbuch*
"The Picture in the Fire-place Bedroom" (Foote) **108**:17
"The Picture in the House" (Lovecraft) **4**:266, 271; **22**:223, 225-26, 241
"A Picture in the Snow" (Welch) **22**:456
The Picture of Dorian Gray (Wilde) **1**:496-98, 500-04, 507-08; **8**:488-92, 494, 496, 499-500, 503; **23**:420, 435-37; **41**:347-403; **175**:275-76
"A Picture of Flowers and Birds: July" (Miyazawa) **76**:293
"The Picture of Gysbert Jonker" (Bosman) **49**:19-20
"The Picture of Lenin" (Gladkov) **27**:95
A Picture of Madame Yuki (Mizoguchi)
See *Yuki Fujin Ezu*
The Picture Palace (Muggeridge) **120**:178-80, 190
Picture This (Heller) **131**:21; **151**:321-22, 326
Picture with a Circle (Kandinsky) **92**:135
"Pictures" (London) **9**:281
"Pictures" (Mansfield) **2**:451; **8**:284, 286; **39**:304, 321, 324; **164**:236-37, 239, 339
"Pictures" (Woolf) **43**:394
"Pictures and Conversations" (Bowen) **148**:20
Pictures and Conversations (Bowen) **148**:20, 67-68, 71, 73-74
Pictures and Songs (Tagore) **3**:490
Pictures from an Institution (Jarrell) **177**:169, 172, 190, 230
"Pictures from Life's other Side" (Williams) **81**:424
"Pictures in the Fire" (Collier) **127**:259
"Pictures in the Smoke" (Parker) **143**:322
Pictures of a Provincial Journey (Peretz) **16**:389
Pictures of Fidelman: An Exhibition (Malamud) **129**:61-2, 66, 73, 76, 83, 106, 117, 149, 185, 187; **184**:184-86, 189, 199, 202-3, 221, 223, 248, 304-9
"Pictures of the Artist" (Malamud) **129**:82, 153, 187; **184**:186, 188, 201-2
"Pictures of the Far West" (Foote) **108**:34-5
"Pictures of the Floating World" (Miyazawa) **76**:302
Pictures of the Floating World (Lowell) **1**:373-74; **8**:228, 234
Picturesque Showcase (Baroja)
See *Vitrina pintoresca*
"A Picturesque Transformation" (Hawthorne) **25**:247
Pièce-concert (Anouilh) **195**:38, 40
"A Piece of Chalk" (Chesterton) **1**:184; **6**:109
"A Piece of Coffee" (Stein) **48**:252
"A Piece of My World" (Bernhard)
See "Mein Weltenstuck"
"A Piece of Red Calico" (Stockton) **47**:313, 327
"A Piece of Steak" (London) **15**:262
"The Piece That Got Me Fired" (Broun) **104**:83
"A Piece-Rate System, Being a Step Toward a Partial Solution of the Labor Problem" (Taylor) **76**:339, 355, 372, 374-75, 378, 382, 399

Pièces baroques (Anouilh) **195**:50
Pièces brillantes (Anouilh) **195**:24, 50
Pièces costumées (Anouilh) **195**:27, 50
Pièces grinçantes (Anouilh) **195**:26, 50
Pièces noires (Anouilh) **195**:38, 50, 56
Pieces of Hate (Broun) **104**:98
Pièces roses (Anouilh) **195**:38, 50, 56
Pièces secrètes (Anouilh) **195**:50
"The Pied Piper" (Tsvetaeva)
See "Krysolov"
The Pied Piper (Zuckmayer)
See *Der Rattenfänger*
Pied Piper of Hamelin (Buchanan) **107**:34
The Pied Piper of Hamelin (Raabe) **45**:194
"Piedmont" (Carducci)
See "Piemonte"
La piedra angular (Pardo Bazán) **189**:242, 244, 247, 250
"Piedra negra sobre una piedra blanca" (Vallejo) **56**:304
Piedra y cielo (Jiménez) **4**:218; **183**:256-64, 274, 290
"Las piedras" (Arenas) **191**:217
Les Pieds dans le plat (Crevel) **112**:6, 12, 21-2
"les pieds du matin" (Arp) **115**:41
"Le piege a revenant" (Vallette) **67**:277
"Piemonte" (Carducci) **32**:90, 95, 103, 105
Pieno impiego (Levi) **109**:295
Piensa mal . . . ¿y acertarás? (Echegaray) **4**:100
Piero della Francesca (Clark) **147**:119-20
"La pierre de l'univers aux cheveux de sandwiches" (Arp) **115**:41
Pierre et Luce (Rolland) **23**:262
"Pierre Menard, Author of the Quixote" (Borges)
See "Pierre Menard, autor del Quixote"
"Pierre Menard, autor del Quixote" (Borges) **109**:24, 73, 81, 100, 127, 138, 145, 161
"Pierre Reverdy" (Fondane) **159**:247
"Les pierres domestiques" (Arp) **115**:41
"El pierrot" (Lugones) **15**:289
Pierrot lunaire (Schoenberg)
See *Dreimals Sieben Lieder des Pierrot Lunaire*
The Pierrot of the Minute (Dowson) **4**:91
"A Pietá" (Field) **43**:166-67
"Pieta" (Liliencron) **18**:205
"Pieter Marinus" (Pickthall) **21**:250, 252
"Le piéton de Paris" (Fargue) **11**:201
Una pietra sopra (Calvino)
See *Una pietra sopra: Discorsi di letteratura e societa*
Una pietra sopra: Discorsi di letteratura e societa (Calvino) **183**:44, 49-50, 97, 100-7, 117, 141-42, 145, 147, 152, 157, 162, 164, 170-71, 187, 192-95, 213, 220-22, 236
Pietro Ghisleri (Crawford) **10**:141, 143-44, 148, 150, 155
"Piffingcap" (Coppard) **5**:175
"Pig" (Dahl) **173**:13
"Pig" (Popa) **167**:154
"Pig Hoo-o-o-o-ey!" (Wodehouse) **108**:373
The Pigeon (Galsworthy) **1**:295; **45**:36, 52
"Pigeon in a Cage" (Mikszath)
See "Galamb a kalitkában"
"Pigeons" (Bagritsky) **60**:16
"The Pigeons of St. Marks" (Service) **15**:413
"Piger" (Obstfelder) **23**:177
"Piggy Bank" (Kuttner) **10**:268
"Pigrizia" (Ginzburg) **156**:111
"Pig's Eye View of Literature" (Parker) **143**:323, 330, 335
Pikad sammud (Tammsaare) **27**:370, 373
"Un pilar soportando consuelos . . ." (Vallejo) **56**:307
Los pilares de doña Blanca (Garro) **153**:9, 71
"The Pilaster" (Roberts) **68**:303
"Pilate's Creed" (Čapek) **192**:185, 189
"Pilatus" (Heym) **9**:142-43
Pilgerfahrten (George) **2**:149-50; **14**:196, 203-04, 212
"Pil'gram" (Nabokov)
See "The Aurelian"
"Pilgrim" (Devkota)
See "Yātrī"
"The Pilgrim" (Gumilev)
See "Palomnik"
"The Pilgrim" (Lowry) **6**:237
"The Pilgrim" (Naidu) **80**:272
Pilgrim at Sea (Lagerkvist)
See *Pilgrim på havet*
The Pilgrim of the East (Mofolo)
See *Moeti oa bochabela*
Pilgrim of the Sea (Lagerkvist)
See *Pilgrim på havet*
"A Pilgrim on the Gila" (Wister) **21**:385, 399
Pilgrim på havet (Lagerkvist) **144**:153, 204, 212, 215, 222, 235, 240-41
"Pilgrim Sons" (Fuller) **103**:106
"Pilgrimage" (D'Annunzio)
See "Pellegrinaggio"
"The Pilgrimage" (Remizov) **27**:352
"Pilgrimage" (Stevens) **12**:387
"Pilgrimage" (Trambley) **163**:320
A Pilgrimage (Bojer)
See *En pilgrimsgang*
The Pilgrimage (Noguchi) **80**:361, 381-2
Pilgrimage (Richardson) **3**:347-50, 352-61
The Pilgrimage of Bayoán (Hostos)
See *La peregrinación de Bayoán*
The Pilgrimage of Eternity (Iqbal)
See *Javid-namah*
Pilgrimage to Jasna Gora (Reymont) **5**:390
Pilgrimages (George)
See *Pilgerfahrten*
Pilgrimen (Lagerkvist) **144**:215
"The Pilgrims" (McCrae) **12**:211
Pilgrims in a Foreign Land (Evans) **85**:9-10, 31
"The Pilgrim's Packets" (Stockton) **47**:326-27
"Pilgrims to Mecca" (Foote) **108**:17
Pilgrim's Way (Buchan)
See *Memory Hold-the-Door*
"Pilipino Old Timers" (Santos) **156**:334
Pillangó (Moricz) **33**:243
The Pillar of Fire (Gumilev)
See *Ognennyi stolp*
"Pillar of Salt" (Jackson) **187**:248, 336-37
"The Pillar of Words" (Hergesheimer) **11**:278
"The Pillars of Sion" (Evans) **85**:26
The Pillars of Society (Ibsen)
See *Samfundets støtter*
Pillars of the Community (Ibsen)
See *Samfundets støtter*
The Pillars of the House; or, Under Wode, Under Rode (Yonge) **48**:375-78
"Pillow of Grass" (Shimazaki Toson)
See "Kusamakura"
The Pilot and His Wife (Lie)
See *Lodsen og hans hustru*
Pilot Elza; or, The Perfect Society (Babits)
See *Elza pilóta vagy a tökéletes társadalom*
"A Pilot from the Carrier" (Jarrell) **177**:192, 204-5, 210, 223
Pilot Stars (Ivanov)
See *Kormchie zvezdy*
Pilote de guerre (Saint-Exupéry) **2**:517-23, 526; **56**:221, 229-30, 232; **169**:314, 316, 320, 323-24, 326, 328, 336-37
"Le pilote et les puissances naturelles" (Saint-Exupéry) **169**:318
Los pilotos de altura (Baroja) **8**:57
"Pilots, Man Your Planes" (Jarrell) **177**:192
Le Pilul du Diable (Melies) **82**:120,122
"A Pimp's Revenge" (Malamud) **129**:80, 152, 186, 188; **184**:185-86, 188, 201
"Piña" (Pardo Bazán) **189**:299
"Pinched" (London) **9**:281; **39**:279
Pindare (Yourcenar) **193**:321
"Pine" (Dickey) **151**:98
"The Pine Trees and the Sky" (Brooke) **2**:59; **7**:122
Ping (Beckett)
See *Bing*
Le ping-pong (Adamov) **189**:10-15, 19-25, 30, 32, 36, 41, 43, 49, 58-9
"The Pink Corner Man" (Borges)
See "El Hombre de la esquina rosada"
"Pink Dog" (Bishop) **121**:23, 70, 74-5, 94-5
"Pink Melon Joy" (Stein) **48**:254
"The Pink Sphinx" (Engel) **137**:117-18
Pinktoes (Himes) **139**:245, 252, 322, 336
"El pino de la corona" (Jiménez) **4**:224
"Pio bove" (Levi) **109**:287
"Piomingo Cove" (Murfree) **135**:229
"The Pioneers" (Fletcher) **35**:110
Pioneers on Parade (Franklin) **7**:267-68
La pipa de kif (Valle-Inclán) **5**:476-77, 486
"Pipacsok a buzában" (Mikszath) **31**:167
"The Pipe" (Akutagawa Ryūnosuke) **16**:17
"The Pipe" (Chekhov) **55**:63
Pipe All Hands (Tomlinson) **71**:397
The Pipe of Kiff (Valle-Inclán)
See *La pipa de kif*
Pipefuls (Morley) **87**:120
"The Piper" (Montgomery) **51**:210-11
"The Piper of Arll" (Scott) **6**:385-89, 393-96, 399
"Piper, Play!" (Davidson) **24**:164
Pipers and a Dancer (Benson) **17**:22-4, 29-30
"The Piper's Son" (Kuttner) **10**:274
Pipes O' Pan at Zekesbury (Riley) **51**:285
"The Pipes of Pan" (Carman) **7**:149
"The Pipes of Pan" (Roberts) **8**:314
The Pipes of Pan (Carman) **7**:138, 142, 149-50
"Il pipistrello" (Pirandello) **29**:284
Pipistrello, and Other Stories (Ouida) **43**:376
"Pippo Spano" (Mann) **9**:315
"The Pirate Way" (Montgomery) **51**:206
"Pirates" (Benson) **27**:19
The Pirates of Penzance; or, The Slave of Duty (Gilbert) **3**:208-10, 216, 218-19
Pirates of Venus (Burroughs) **2**:81; **32**:59, 75
Pirate's Purchase (Williams) **89**:378, 398
"A piros harangok" (Mikszath) **31**:167
The Pisan Woman (D'Annunzio)
See *La pisanelle ou la mort parfumée*
La pisanelle ou la mort parfumée (D'Annunzio) **6**:136-37, 142; **40**:10-11
"Pisces" (Agnon) **151**:72
Pisma (Sienkiewicz) **3**:421
"Pis'mo" (Babel) **2**:27; **13**:14, 21, 33; **171**:13, 19-21, 24, 26, 73-74, 78, 84-86
"Pis'mo" (Chekhov) **55**:63
"Pismo iz 1920 godine" (Andrić) **135**:18
"Pit" (Norris) **155**:322
The Pit (Norris) **24**:418, 421-28, 432, 444, 449-52; **155**:258, 265, 269-70, 315-23, 340-41
The Pit (Onetti)
See *El pozo*
Pitcairn's Island (Hall and Nordhoff) **23**:60-2, 66, 69-71
"The Pitfalls of National Consciousness" (Fanon) **188**:68-9, 119
The Pit-Prop Syndicate (Crofts) **55**:83, 86
Pitseng (Mofolo) **22**:246, 248-50, 253, 257
"Pittsburgh" (Dreiser) **35**:65
"Pity" (Baker) **10**:19, 21, 26
"Pity" (Davies) **5**:202
"Pity Me" (Wylie) **8**:536
"Pity Me Not" (Millay) **49**:215
"The Pity of the Leaves" (Robinson) **5**:418; **101**:111, 117, 129
"Pity the Deep in Love" (Cullen) **37**:155, 168
"pity this busy monster, manunkind" (Cummings) **137**:4
Più che l'amore (D'Annunzio) **6**:137, 139; **40**:9, 11
"Piuma" (Pirandello) **29**:284
"Piuma al vento" (Lugones) **15**:292
Piyam-e Kafka (Hedāyat) **21**:76
Pjataja jazva (Remizov) **27**:330-31, 334, 336, 342, 344-45, 347
"Pjat'bykov" (Gumilev) **60**:278

Place Called Estherville (Caldwell) **117**:20-1
A Place Calling Itself Rome (Osborne) **153**:311
La place de l'étoile: Antipoème (Desnos) **22**:72
"La place de l'homme dans la nature" (Teilhard de Chardin) **9**:489
The Place Hunters (Martyn) **131**:101, 105
"A Place in Venice" (Bennett) **5**:46
"The Place Is Different Now" (Malamud) **129**:180
A Place of Chance (Bachmann)
See *Ein Ort für Zufälle*
The Place of Dead Roads (Burroughs) **121**:137, 144
"The Place of Menger's Grundsatze in the History of Economic Thought" (Hayek) **109**:231
"The Place of Pain" (Shiel) **8**:363
"Place of Refuge" (Brecht) **6**:39
The Place of Science in Modern Civilization (Veblen) **31**:362
"The Place of Storms" (Hodgson) **13**:230
"The Place of the Gods" (Benét)
See "By the Waters of Babylon"
The Place of the Lion (Williams) **1**:524; **11**:486-87, 494, 496, 500, 502
A Place without Boundaries (Donoso)
See *El lugar sin límites*
Place Your Bets (Tzara)
See *Faites vos jeux*
"Places" (Hardy) **53**:97
"Places" (Teasdale) **4**:425
"Places of My Infancy" (Lampedusa) **13**:293
Places Where I Have Done Time (Saroyan) **137**:146
"Placha" (Remizov) **27**:338
"A Placid Man's Epitaph" (Hardy) **143**:151
Placówka (Prus) **48**:157, 162, 166-67, 172-73, 177, 181
"Plague of Florence" (Lee-Hamilton) **22**:186
"The Plaid Dress" (Millay) **49**:223; **169**:295
Le plaidoyer d'un fou (Strindberg) **1**:448, 462; **8**:406-08; **21**:335; **47**:350, 364
"The Plain" (Obstfelder)
See "Sletten"
"Plain Fishing" (Stockton) **47**:326
"Plain Language from Truthful James" (Harte) **25**:191, 200, 217
"The Plain Man" (Galsworthy) **45**:33
The Plain Man and His Wife (Bennett) **5**:28
Plain Tales (Kipling)
See *Plain Tales from the Hills*
Plain Tales from the Hills (Kipling) **8**:175-76, 184-85, 187, 202, 205; **17**:202-03, 207-08
"Plain-chant" (Cocteau) **119**:106
Les plaines (Verhaeren) **12**:465
Plains Song: For Female Voices (Morris) **107**:158, 160, 169-73, 190-93, 195, 205-06, 214, 223, 225-27, 230, 232
"Plaint" (Remizov) **27**:352, 354-55
"A Plaint to Man" (Hardy) **53**:88
Plainte contre inconnu (Drieu la Rochelle) **21**:18
Le Plaisir (Ophuls) **79**:174, 208-11, 227
Le plaisir de rompre (Renard) **17**:316
Le plaisir du texte (Barthes) **135**:118-25, 138, 141-2, 146-59, 167, 184
Les plaisirs et les jours (Proust) **7**:518, 534, 538-39; **13**:412, 415-16, 423; **33**:262; **161**:123, 170-74, 177
Plamennyi krug (Sologub) **9**:443
Plan B (Himes) **139**:248, 268, 311-14
Plan of War (Lewis) **104**:201
"Plan or Perish" (Laski) **79**:153
"Plane" (Nemerov) **124**:260
"Planes of Personality" (Lowell) **8**:236
Planet News: 1961-1967 (Ginsberg) **120**:3, 23, 35, 41, 71, 86
"The Planet on the Table" (Stevens) **3**:472; **12**:365, 368; **45**:281, 349
The Planetarium (Sarraute)
See *Le planétarium*
Le planétarium (Sarraute) **145**:263, 265, 282-84, 345-46, 348, 351, 357, 361, 363, 365
"Planeterna" (Södergran) **31**:294
"The Planets" (Södergran)
See "Planeterna"
"Plangôn et Bacchis" (Schwob) **20**:323
El plano oblicuo (Reyes) **33**:316, 322
"Plans for Work" (Agee) **180**:45
Plant Dreaming Deep (Sarton) **120**:218, 230, 232-37, 278, 285, 320
"The Planted Heel" (Quiller-Couch) **53**:291
"The Planter of Malata" (Conrad) **57**:87
"Planting Bulbs" (Tynan) **3**:503
"Planting the Poplar" (Guiney) **41**:218, 229
"The Plaque" (Ishikawa) **15**:130
Plashers Mead (Mackenzie) **116**:184, 193-95, 197-98, 203, 206, 209, 212, 214-15, 227, 230, 251-52
"Platen, Tristan, and Don Quixote" (Mann) **8**:255
Platero and I (Jiménez)
See *Platero y Yo*
Platero and I: An Andalusion Elegy (Jiménez)
See *Platero y Yo*
Platero y Yo (Jiménez) **183**:264, 276-77, 282, 320, 322
Platkops Children (Smith) **25**:389-90
"Plato" (Holmes) **77**:311
"Plato in London" (Johnson) **19**:252-53
"plato told" (Cummings) **137**:69
"Platonic Love in Some Italian Poets" (Santayana) **40**:390
"Platonic Narrative" (Bodenheim) **44**:74
Platonism and the Spiritual Life (Santayana) **40**:361
Platonov (Chekhov) **3**:163; **31**:99-101
"The Plattner Story" (Wells) **6**:545; **12**:488; **133**:256
Plavaiushchie-puteshestvuiushchie (Kuzmin) **40**:194, 216
"The Play" (Mori Ogai)
See "Asobi"
A Play (Stein) **48**:264
"Play and Earnest" (Pyle) **81**:394
"Play Ball" (Malamud) **184**:160
"A Play for Puppets" (Chambers) **129**:45
The Play of Everyman (Hofmannsthal)
See *Jedermann*
Play of the Death of the Rich Man (Hofmannsthal)
See *Jedermann*
The Play of the Eyes (Canetti)
See *Das Augenspiel: Lebensgeschichte 1931-1937*
"Play on an Execution Block" (Olesha) **136**:74
Play Things (Saroyan) **137**:178
A Play without a Title (Chekhov)
See *Platonov*
Play without a Title (García Lorca)
See *Comedia sin título*
"Playa ignorante" (Aleixandre) **113**:8
Playback (Chandler) **1**:173; **7**:181-82; **179**:81, 91, 109, 113, 115, 143, 191, 194, 207-9, 225, 227, 229-30, 234
The Playboy of the Western World (Synge) **6**:425-32, 434-42; **37**:344-95
The Played-Out Man (Papini)
See *Un uomo finito*
"Player on Pan's Pipes" (Yeats) **31**:408
"The Player Piano" (Jarrell) **177**:149, 155, 174, 176, 178, 222
The Player Queen (Yeats) **1**:571; **31**:408
"The Players" (Matthews) **95**:228
The Playground of Europe (Stephen) **23**:326
"Playgrounds for City Schools" (Riis) **80**:440
"A Play-House in the Waste" (Moore)
See "San n-Diothramh Dubh"
The Playhouse of Pepys (Summers) **16**:427, 431
"Playing Cards Drawing" (Lindsay) **17**:241
"Playing I-Spy, Red Light, the Marriage Trick" (Merrill) **173**:238
"Playing Skittles" (Nemerov) **124**:259, 273
"Playing the Game" (Bolt) **175**:26
"Playing the Inventions" (Nemerov) **124**:260, 273
Playing with Fire (Strindberg)
See *Leka med elden*
Playing with Love (Schnitzler)
See *Liebelei*
Plays (Davidson) **24**:159
Plays, Acting, and Music (Symons) **11**:429, 442
Plays Baroque (Anouilh)
See *Pièces baroques*
Plays Black (Anouilh)
See *Pièces noires*
Plays Bright (Anouilh)
See *Pièces brillantes*
Plays by Philip Barry (Barry) **11**:47
Plays for a Negro Theater (Torrence)
See *Granny Maumee, The Rider of Dreams, Simon the Cyrenian: Plays for a Negro Theater*
Plays for Dancers (Yeats) **1**:557, 561
Plays for Earth and Air (Dunsany) **59**:17, 24, 26, 28
Plays for Puritans (Shaw) **21**:302
Plays Grating (Anouilh)
See *Pièces grinçantes*
Plays Hidden (Anouilh)
See *Pièces secrètes*
Plays of Gods and Men (Dunsany) **2**:137; **59**:17, 26, 29
Plays of Near and Far (Dunsany) **59**:12, 26
Plays of the Natural and the Supernatural (Dreiser) **18**:59; **83**:6
Plays One (Osborne) **153**:339
Plays Pink (Anouilh)
See *Pièces roses*
Plays Pleasant (Shaw)
See *Plays: Pleasant and Unpleasant*
Plays: Pleasant and Unpleasant (Shaw) **3**:383; **9**:413; **45**:250
The Play's the Thing (Molnár)
See *Játék a kastélyban*
Plays Unpleasant (Shaw)
See *Plays: Pleasant and Unpleasant*
Playwrights on Playmaking (Matthews) **95**:240
"The Plea" (Glaspell) **175**:95
"Plea" (Guest) **95**:206
A Plea for Better Manners (Douglas)
See *D. H. Lawrence and Maurice Magnus: A Plea for Better Manners*
"A Plea for Culture" (Higginson) **36**:170
"A Plea for Farce" (Matthews) **95**:228
"A Plea for Good Taste and Common Sense" (Hartmann) **73**:148
Plea for Liberty: Letters to the English, the Americans, the Europeans (Bernanos)
See *Lettre aux Anglais*
"A Plea for Romantic Fiction" (Norris) **24**:449; **155**:339-40
"The Plea for Shorter Novels" (Fuller) **103**:74, 86, 88
"A Plea for Straight Photography" (Hartmann) **73**:128, 147
A Plea for Time (Innis) **77**:342
Pleas of the Crown for the County of Gloucester, 1221 (Maitland) **65**:249, 260, 265, 274
"A Pleasant Evening" (Chambers) **41**:88, 102
The Pleasant Memoirs of the Marquís de Bradomín (Valle-Inclán)
See *Sonatas: Memoirs of the Marquis de Bradomin*
Pleasant Valley (Bromfield) **11**:83-4
"Please, Master" (Ginsberg) **120**:17, 25, 27-8, 73, 87, 90
"Pleasure" (Nagai)
See "Kanraku"
Pleasure (Nagai)
See *Kanraku*
"Pleasure from One's Children" (Aleichem)
See "Nakhes fun kinder"

The Pleasure of Honesty (Pirandello)
See *Il piacere dell'onestà*
Pleasure of Honor (Pirandello)
See *Il piacere dell'onestà*
The Pleasure of Parting (Renard)
See *Le plaisir de rompre*
Pleasure of Ruins (Macaulay) **44**:124, 126, 129
The Pleasure of the Text (Barthes)
See *Le plaisir du texte*
Pleasure Trove (Lucas) **73**:170
Pleasures and Days (Proust)
See *Les plaisirs et les jours*
Pleasures and Days, and Other Writings (Proust)
See *Les plaisirs et les jours*
"The Pleasures and Pains of Ireland" (O'Faolain) **143**:230
Pleasures and Regrets (Proust)
See *Les plaisirs et les jours*
Pleasures and Speculations (de la Mare) **4**:81
"Plebiscitum" (Carducci)
See "Il plebiscito"
"Plegaria" (Villaurrutia) **80**:516
"La Plegaría de la Noche en la Selva" (Gonzalez Martinez) **72**:145
"Plenitud" (Aleixandre) **113**:13
"Plenitud" (Jiménez) **183**:257
Plenitud (Nervo) **11**:399-401, 403
Plenitude (Nervo)
See *Plenitud*
"Plennyj dux" (Tsvetaeva) **7**:562
"Plentitud del amor" (Aleixandre) **113**:75-6
"Plentitude" (Aleixandre)
See "Plenitud"
Pleureuses (Barbusse) **5**:14, 16, 20
Le Pli (Deleuze) **116**:85
Plias Irodiady (Remizov) **27**:348
Pliashushchii demon (Remizov) **27**:349
"Pliaska atomov" (Balmont) **11**:36
"The Pliocene Skull" (Harte) **25**:189
The Plot That Thickened (Wodehouse) **108**:366-67
The plotters (Borges)
See *Los conjurados*
"Ploughing on Sunday" (Stevens) **3**:472; **45**:282
"The Ploughman" (White) **176**:125
The Ploughman and Other Poems (White) **176**:125, 171
Ploughman of the Moon: An Adventure into Memory (Service) **15**:411
The Ploughman's Progress (Kaye-Smith) **20**:113
"The Plowman" (Knister) **56**:155, 164
"Plowman Without a Plow" (Coffin) **95**:18
Pluck and Luck (Benchley) **1**:77
"La pluie" (Verhaeren) **12**:466
Plum Pie (Wodehouse) **108**:334
Plum Pudding (Morley) **87**:124
"The Plum Tree by the House" (Gogarty) **15**:101, 104
The Plumed Serpent (Lawrence) **2**:346, 355-57, 359, 371; **33**:216; **48**:102, 104, 110, 115-17, 120-22, 125, 131, 133; **93**:21, 50, 96, 97, 103, 104
"Plummets to Circumstance" (Lowell) **8**:236
The Plum-Tree (Phillips) **44**:253-54, 262, 274, 276, 278, 282-83, 285-86
"A Plunge into Real Estate" (Calvino)
See "La speculazione edilizia"
A Plunge into Real Estate (Calvino) **183**:94, 190-91
"Pluralism and Ideological Peace" (Locke) **43**:228
A Pluralistic Universe (James) **15**:157, 162, 171, 175; **32**:337, 339, 350
"Plus de sang" (Coppee) **25**:124
Le plus jeune (Éluard) **7**:245
The Plutocrat (Tarkington) **9**:461, 463, 468, 473
Plutonian Ode: Poems, 1977-1980 (Ginsberg) **120**:35
Pnin (Nabokov) **108**:81, 83, 86, 118-19, 143-44, 173, 178, 181-82, 185, 201, 216; **189**:83, 145, 174
"Po etapu" (Remizov) **27**:347
Po karnizam (Remizov) **27**:348
Po nebu polunochi (Platonov) **14**:405, 414
"Po' Sandy" (Chesnutt) **5**:130, 134, 136-37; **39**:104-05
Po zvezdam (Ivanov) **33**:118, 127
"P'oasis" (Desnos) **22**:59
Pobeda smerti (Sologub) **9**:434, 439-40
Pobediteli (Bagritsky) **60**:16
La pobra gente (Sánchez) **37**:314
Pobrecito Juan (Martinez Sierra and Martinez Sierra) **6**:277-78
"Poceluj" (Chekhov) **10**:100
Pocket Philosophies (Bennett) **5**:31
Pocket Stories (Čapek)
See *Tales from Two Pockets*
"The Pocket-book Game" (Childress) **116**:36
"The Pocket-Hunter's Story" (Austin) **25**:26
"Pockets" (Nemerov) **124**:210
Pod igoto (Vazov) **25**:449-51, 453-59
Pod severnym nebom (Balmont) **11**:32, 35, 42
"Pod zemljom" (Popa) **167**:155
"Poder" (Schwob) **20**:319-20
El poder de la impotencia (Echegaray) **4**:101
"Poderío de la noche" (Aleixandre) **113**:49
"Podivuhodny kouzelnik" (Nezval) **44**:238-39, 250
"Podolie" (Apollinaire) **51**:61
"Podrazavanje sunca" (Popa) **167**:157
Podstrizhennymi glazami (Remizov) **27**:349, 356, 358-59
Podvig (Nabokov) **108**:52
"Poe and His Polish Contemporary" (Huneker) **65**:196
Poedinok (Kuprin) **5**:296-98, 304-06
"Poem" (Bishop) **121**:75, 81-2
"Poem" (Forten) **16**:150
"Poem" (Gray) **19**:145, 150-51, 153, 157
"Poem 3" (Villa) **176**:99, 101
"Poem 5" (Jiménez) **183**:274
"Poem 14" (Villa) **176**:102
"Poem 15" (Villa) **176**:98
"Poem 17" (Villa) **176**:99
"Poem 19" (Villa) **176**:101
"Poem 30" (Villa) **176**:97
"Poem 31" (Villa) **176**:98
"Poem 32" (Villa) **176**:97
"Poem 35" (Villa) **176**:97
"Poem 37" (Villa) **176**:97
"Poem 40" (Villa) **176**:97
"Poem 41" (Villa) **176**:97
"Poem 44" (Villa) **176**:101
"Poem 45" (Villa) **176**:101
"Poem 46" (Villa) **176**:101
"Poem 55" (Villa) **176**:99
"Poem 63" (Villa) **176**:101
"Poem 72" (Jiménez) **183**:274
"Poem 76" (Villa) **176**:102
"Poem 81" (Jiménez) **183**:274
"Poem 90" (Villa) **176**:101
"Poem 100" (Villa) **176**:101
"Poem 106" (Villa) **176**:96
"Poem 107" (Villa) **176**:99
"Poem 110" (Villa) **176**:99
"Poem 115" (Villa) **176**:102
"Poem 125" (Villa) **176**:99
"Poem 127" (Villa) **176**:97
"Poem 150" (Villa) **176**:99
"Poem 154" (Villa) **176**:101
"Poem 155" (Villa) **176**:101
"Poem 156" (Villa) **176**:97
"Poem 157" (Villa) **176**:97
"Poem 158" (Villa) **176**:97
"Poem 211" (Villa) **176**:98
"Poem 214" (Villa) **176**:98
"The Poem as Icon" (Stevens) **45**:316
A Poem Entitled "The Day and the War": Delivered on January 1, 1864, at Platt's Hall at the Celebration of the First Anniversary of President Lincoln's Emancipation Proclamation (Bell) **43**:93
A Poem Entitled "The Triumph of Liberty": Delivered April 7, 1870 at Detroit Opera House, on the Occasion of the Fifteenth Amendment to the Constitution of the United States (Bell) **43**:90-92
A Poem for Farish Street (Walker)
See *My Farish Street Green*
"A Poem for Max Nordau" (Robinson) **5**:400
"Poem in C" (Toomer) **172**:274
"Poem in October" (Thomas) **1**:470-71, 473; **8**:460-61; **45**:362-363, 365, 372, 377, 399, 404-05; **105**:351
"Poem of Autumn" (Darío)
See "Poema de otoño"
The Poem of David (Hecht) **101**:73
A Poem of Gardens (D'Annunzio)
See *Poema pardisiaco*
"A Poem of God's Mercy" (Lowry) **6**:237
"Poem of Love" (Aleixandre)
See "Poema de amor"
"Poem of Love" (García Lorca) **197**:187
"Poem of Seven Faces" (Drummond de Andrade) **139**:225
Poem of the Cante Jondo (García Lorca)
See *Poema del cante jondo*
The Poem of the Deep Song (García Lorca)
See *Poema del cante jondo*
Poem of the Deep Song (García Lorca)
See *Poema del cante jondo*
"Poem of the End" (Tsvetaeva)
See "Poèma kontsa"
"Poem of the Gifts" (Borges)
See "Poema de los dones"
"Poem of the Hill" (Tsvetaeva)
See "Poèma gory"
"Poem of the Mountain" (Tsvetaeva)
See "Poèma gory"
The Poem of the Rhone (Mistral)
See *Lou pouèma dóu Rose*
"Poem of the Staircase" (Tsvetaeva)
See "Poèma lestnitsy"
"Poem of These States" (Ginsberg) **120**:129
"A Poem on America" (Ginsberg) **120**:35
"Poem on His Birthday" (Thomas) **1**:473; **8**:461; **45**:362, 402; **105**:322, 351
"Poem, or Beauty Hurts Mr. Vinal" (Cummings) **137**:48
"The Poem That Took the Place of a Mountain" (Stevens) **3**:473
"Poem to Be Read and Sung" (Vallejo)
See "Poema para ser leído y cantado"
"Poem to David" (Buchanan) **107**:16
"Poem With Rhythms" (Stevens) **45**:269
"Poem Written at Morning" (Stevens) **45**:332
"Poema conjectural" (Borges) **109**:4, 129
"Poema de amor" (Aleixandre) **113**:7
"Poema de la saeta" (García Lorca) **181**:199
"Poema de la siguiriya gitana" (García Lorca) **181**:192
"Poema de la soléa" (García Lorca) **181**:192-93
"Poema de los dones" (Borges) **109**:150
"Poema de otoño" (Darío) **4**:62
"Poema de un día" (Machado) **3**:306-07
Poema del cante jondo (García Lorca) **1**:309, 312, 317, 321-22; **7**:299-300; **49**:72, 89-91, 116; **181**:24, 63-64, 93, 179-80, 188-200; **197**:208, 232, 272-73, 277, 283
El poema del trabajo (Martinez Sierra and Martinez Sierra) **6**:285-86
"Poema doble del lago Eden" (García Lorca) **49**:120; **197**:185, 207, 217, 232, 252, 257, 281
"Poèma gory" (Tsvetaeva) **7**:557-58, 561, 565-67; **35**:412-13
"Poèma kontsa" (Tsvetaeva) **35**:374, 381, 398, 405, 411-13, 415; **7**:556-58, 561, 564-66
"Poèma lestnitsy" (Tsvetaeva) **35**:415
"El poema para mi hija" (Huidobro) **31**:124
"Poema para ser leído y cantado" (Vallejo) **56**:300

Poema pardisiaco (D'Annunzio) **6**:136
Poemas (Drummond de Andrade) **139**:225
Poemas (Nervo) **11**:400, 402
Poemas árticos (Huidobro) **31**:125, 132-33, 137, 144
Poemas de amor (Storni) **5**:450-52
Poemas de la consumación (Aleixandre) **113**:22, 36-37, 50, 68, 70
"Poemas de las madres" (Mistral) **2**:476
Poemas humanos, 1923-1938 (Vallejo) **3**:526-27, 529-31, 533, 535-36; **56**:284-88, 290, 292, 296, 299, 300-01, 304, 311-12, 315-16, 318, 320-21
Poemas místico (Güiraldes) **39**:186
Poemas solariegos (Lugones) **15**:291
Poemas solitarios (Güiraldes) **39**:186
Poemas sueltos (García Lorca) **49**:119, 123
"Poème" (Jacob) **6**:191
"Le poème à Florence" (Desnos) **22**:61
"Poème lu au mariage d'André Salmon" (Apollinaire) **8**:16, 20; **51**:61
"Poème mondain" (Tzara) **168**:322
Poèmes (Cocteau) **119**:75
Poèmes (Éluard) **41**:153
Poèmes d'avant Dada (Tzara) **168**:269, 321
Poèmes d'un riche amateur (Larbaud) **9**:197, 200, 205
Poèmes légendaires de Flandre et de Brabant (Verhaeren) **12**:472
Les Poemes Mesures (Jammes) **75**:115
Poèmes politiques (Éluard) **41**:151, 162
Poèmes pour la paix (Éluard) **41**:150, 153-54
"Poèmes pour Raymond Radiguet" (Cocteau) **119**:57
Poèmes sans prénoms (Arp) **115**:30, 33, 41, 53
"Poèmes, suivis de pour la musique" (Fargue) **11**:194, 195, 199, 200
Poemetti (Pascoli) **45**:146, 156
Poemi conviviali (Pascoli) **45**:146, 149, 153
Poems (Balmont) **11**:37
Poems (Brooke) **2**:50-1; **7**:120-21
Poems (Dickey) **151**:184
Poems (Drinkwater) **57**:142
Poems (García Lorca)
See *Libro de poemas*
Poems (Gray) **19**:158, 164
Poems (Harper) **14**:255, 259, 262-63
Poems (Harte) **25**:190
Poems (Heidenstam)
See *Dikter*
Poems (Henley) **8**:109-10
Poems (Holley) **99**:326
Poems (Johnson) **19**:228-29, 232
Poems (Kraus)
See *Worte in Versen*
Poems (de la Mare) **4**:74, 78
Poems (MacDonald) **9**:291, 300, 304
Poems (Mackenzie) **116**:192
Poems (Manning) **25**:275-78
Poems (Meynell) **6**:291-92, 294
Poems (Moody) **105**:218, 222, 250, 267
Poems (Morley) **87**:144
Poems (Naidu)
See *The Sceptered Flute: Songs of India*
Poems (Nervo)
See *Poemas*
Poems (Owen) **5**:359; **27**:199, 206
Poems (Roberts) **8**:321
Poems (Rosenberg) **12**:296
Poems (Södergran)
See *Dikter*
Poems (Swinburne) **36**:325
Poems (Symons) **11**:439
Poems (Tagore) **3**:481
Poems (Thomas) **10**:450, 455
Poems (Thompson) **4**:435
Poems (Torrence) **97**:155, 157-58
Poems (Unamuno)
See *Poesías*
Poems (Vazov) **25**:453
Poems (Wilde) **8**:487, 492
Poems (Yeats) **11**:508, 511
Poems, 1913 (Brennan) **17**:39-41, 43-4, 48-50, 52-6, 59
Poems, 1912-1924 (O'Neill) **6**:337
Poems, 1913-1956 (Brecht) **1**:122
Poems, 1917-1918 (Murry) **16**:354
Poems, 1923-1954 (Cummings) **137**:19, 21, 29-30, 37, 46
Poems, 1957-1967 (Dickey) **151**:93, 96-100, 108, 110, 118, 121, 133, 199-200
"Poems about America" (Mayakovski) **18**:258
Poems about Moscow (Tsvetaeva) **7**:563; **35**:385
Poems All Over the Place, Mostly '70s (Ginsberg) **120**:77
Poems and Ballads (Quiller-Couch) **53**:290-91
Poems and Ballads (Swinburne) **8**:423-24, 427, 429, 431, 434, 436-39, 442, 446; **36**:294-95, 297-98, 300-01, 306-08, 310, 312, 314, 317-19, 321-22, 324-25, 327-30, 341, 343
Poems and Ballads, Second Series (Swinburne) **8**:426
Poems and Ballads, Third Series (Swinburne) **8**:428
The Poems and Dramas (Sharp) **39**:372
Poems & Dynasts (Hardy) **143**:215
Poems and Lyrics of the Joy of Earth (Meredith) **17**:256
The Poems and Plays of William Vaughn Moody (Moody) **105**:234, 254
Poems and Portraits (Marquis) **7**:435, 437, 447
Poems and Problems (Nabokov) **108**:219
Poems and Songs (Bjoernson)
See *Digte og sange*
Poems and Songs (Middleton) **56**:173-75, 191
Poems and The Spring of Joy (Webb) **24**:472
Poems and Transcripts (Lee-Hamilton) **22**:186, 188-89, 192
Poems and Translations (Synge) **6**:435
Poems before Dada (Tzara)
See *Poèmes d'avant Dada*
Poems by an Unknown (Abe)
See *Poems of an Unknown Poet*
Poems by Ivor Gurney (Gurney) **33**:86-8
"Poems for an Unhumble One" (Villa) **176**:98
"Poems for Basuki Resobowo" (Anwar)
See "Sadjak buat Basuki Resobowo"
Poems for Men (Runyon) **10**:437
Poems: Four Canzones (Okigbo) **171**:338-39, 341, 350, 354-55
Poems from France (Mew) **8**:301
Poems from the Book of Hours (Rilke)
See *Das Stundenbuch*
"Poems from the Chinese" (Lewis) **3**:287
Poems from the Divan of Hafiz (Bell) **67**:13
Poems from the Norwegian of Sigbjørn Obstfelder (Obstfelder) **23**:188
Poems Here at Home (Riley) **51**:280-81, 285
Poems in Prose (Przybyszewski) **36**:282
Poems, Letters, and Memories of Philip Sidney Nairn (Eddison) **15**:59
"Poems of 1912-13" (Hardy) **53**:92-5, 99, 101, 105, 111; **143**:147, 150, 189-90; **143**:196-97
Poems of a Multimillionaire (Larbaud)
See *A. O. Barnabooth, ses oeuvres complètes, c'est-à-dire: Un conte, ses poèmes, et son journal intime*
Poems of Adoration (Field) **43**:155, 160, 169
The Poems of Alice Meynell (Meynell) **6**:301
Poems of American Patriotism (Matthews) **95**:257
Poems of an Unknown Poet (Abe) **131**:10
Poems of Conformity (Williams) **1**:516-17, 521; **11**:483
Poems of Consummation (Aleixandre)
See *Poemas de la consumación*
"The Poems of Dante Gabriel Rossetti" (Swinburne) **36**:311
The Poems of Duncan Campbell Scott (Scott) **6**:385
The Poems of Ernest Dowson (Dowson) **4**:85
The Poems of General George S. Patton, Jr. (Patton) **79**:307
"Poems of Krishna" (Naidu) **80**:342
The Poems of Lascelles Abercrombie (Abercrombie) **141**:18-20, 22-23
"The Poems of Our Climate" (Stevens) **45**:283
Poems of Patriotism (Guest) **95**:206
Poems of People (Masters) **25**:300, 316
The Poems of St. John of the Cross (Campbell)
See *San Juan de la Cruz*
Poems of the Night (Nezval)
See *Básně noci*
Poems of the Past and Present (Hall) **12**:195
Poems of the Past and Present (Hardy) **4**:154; **53**:71, 86, 102; **143**:187, 196
"Poems of the War" (Howe) **21**:113
Poems of Thirty Years (Bottomley) **107**:5
Poems of Two Friends (Howells) **7**:363, 391
The Poems of Wilfred Owen (Owen) **5**:361
Poems on Children (Thompson) **4**:435-36
Poems on Miscellaneous Subjects (Harper) **14**:255-8, 262
Poems, Scots and English (Buchan) **41**:72
Poems to Akhmatova (Tsvetaeva)
See "Stikhi K Akhmatovoi"
Poems to Blok (Tsvetaeva)
See *Stikhi K Blok*
"Poems to Bohemia" (Tsvetaeva)
See "Stikhi k Chekhii"
"Poems to Eat" (Ishikawa) **15**:125, 131
"Poems without Titles, No. 6" (Su Man-shu) **24**:457
"Poe's Helen" (Woolf) **43**:402
"La poesia" (Pascoli) **45**:156
"Poesía" (Villaurrutia) **80**:478-9
La poesia (Croce) **37**:95, 97, 107, 110, 113, 126-27, 131
La poesía (Huidobro) **31**:133
Poesía (Jiménez) **4**:221; **183**:259, 290, 292, 294
Poesia até agora (Drummond de Andrade) **139**:224
Poesia completa e prosa (Drummond de Andrade) **139**:225
La poesia di Dante (Croce) **37**:127
Poesia e non poesia: Note sulla letteratura euròpa del secolo decimonono (Croce) **37**:92, 127, 131
Poesía española (Jiménez) **183**:320
La Poesía hermética de Juan Ramón Jiménez (Jiménez) **183**:281
Poesía superrealista (Aleixandre) **113**:27, 44
Poesía y prosa (Huidobro) **31**:126
Poesias (Drummond de Andrade) **139**:224
Poesías (Unamuno) **2**:562-63, 568; **9**:510; **148**:256, 304
Poesías (Valera y Alcala-Galiano) **10**:499-500
Poesías completas (Machado) **3**:313-14
Poesías últimas escojidas (Jiménez) **183**:302-4
Poesie (Carducci) **32**:85
Poésie critique (Desnos) **22**:63
Poesie dell'adoloscenza e giovanili (Saba) **33**:372
"La poésie doit avoir pour but la vérité pratique" (Éluard) **41**:162
Poésie et pensée abstraite (Valéry) **15**:468
Poésie et vérité (Éluard) **7**:249; **41**:162
"Poésie ininterrompue" (Éluard) **7**:245-46, 248-52, 257, 260; **41**:151, 153
Poésie involontaire et poésie intentionelle (Éluard) **41**:151-52
Poesie scritte durante la guerra (Saba) **33**:369, 373
Poésies complètes (Garneau) **13**:197, 204
Les poésies d'André Walter (Gide) **12**:176
"Poesies diverses" (Jammes) **75**:119
"Poesy" (Sterling) **20**:383
"The Poet" (Aleixandre)
See "El poeta"
"The Poet" (Čapek) **192**:223
"The Poet" (Chekhov) **3**:168
"The Poet" (Cullen) **37**:155
"The Poet" (Dunbar) **12**:124
"The Poet" (Esenin) **4**:116
"Poet" (Khlebnikov) **20**:132

"The Poet" (Markham) **47**:282
"The Poet" (Muir) **87**:231
"The Poet and Criticism" (Tsvetaeva) **35**:406
"The Poet and His Book" (Millay) **4**:306; **49**:213; **169**:291
"The Poet and His Song" (Dunbar) **12**:105-06, 121
"The Poet and the Critics" (Dobson) **79**:3
The Poet and the Donkey (Sarton) **120**:210, 212, 309
The Poet and the Lunatics (Chesterton) **1**:181; **6**:104, 108; **64**:35
The Poet and the Moorish Woman (Roussel) **20**:228
"The Poet and the Peasant" (Henry) **19**:195-96
"The Poet and This Time" (Hofmannsthal) **11**:311-12
"The Poet and Time" (Tsvetaeva)
See "Poèt i vremja"
"Poet Andrew" (Buchanan) **107**:15, 25
"The Poet as Eagle Scout" (Nemerov) **124**:256
The Poet Assassinated (Apollinaire)
See *Le poète assassiné*
"The Poet at Forty" (Nemerov) **124**:179, 248
"The Poet from Baalbeck" (Gibran) **9**:87
"Poèt i vremja" (Tsvetaeva) **7**:562, 570; **35**:400, 410
"The Poet III" (Rosenberg) **12**:299-300
Poet in New York (García Lorca)
See *Poeta en Nueva York*
"Poet in Residence" (Sarton) **120**:300-1
"Poet in Residence—Carbondale, Illinois" (Sarton) **120**:263-64
"Poèt o kritike" (Tsvetaeva) **7**:562, 570; **35**:410, 413
"A Poet on Criticism" (Tsvetaeva)
See "Poèt o kritike"
"The Poet, or Seer" (Buchanan) **107**:64
The Poet Passes (Ramuz)
See *Passage du poète*
"The Poet Speaks with His Beloved on the Telephone" (García Lorca)
See "El poeta pide a su amor que le escriba"
"The Poet to Death" (Naidu) **80**:316
"The Poet to His Beloved" (Vallejo)
See "El poeta a su amada"
"The Poet to His Childhood" (Meynell) **6**:291
"The Poet Turns on Himself" (Dickey) **151**:132, 142, 145
"El poeta" (Aleixandre) **113**:49
"El poeta à las musas" (Darío) **4**:59
"El poeta a su amada" (Vallejo) **56**:294
Poeta en Nueva York (García Lorca) **1**:308, 312, 314, 317-19, 322-23; **7**:297-99; **49**:77, 80-3, 85, 87-8, 93-5, 111, 119-22; **181**:28, 41, 171, 180; **197**:180-285
"El poeta pide a su amor que le escriba" (García Lorca) **181**:68
"El poeta se acuerda de su vida" (Aleixandre) **113**:50
"Poeta y palabra" (Jiménez) **183**:271, 290
"Los Poetas celestes" (Aleixandre) **113**:35
Le poète assassiné (Apollinaire) **3**:32-3, 38, 42; **8**:12, 14, 16, 19, 21; **51**:3, 5, 19-21, 29, 47-8
Le Poete et l'oiseau (Jammes) **75**:118
"Le Poete et sa Femme" (Jammes) **75**:104, 113, 119-20
Le Poete Rustique (Jammes) **75**:119-20
Les poetès (Aragon) **123**:130-42
Poetes d'aujourd'hui (1800-1900) (Léautaud) **83**:185
Poetic Art (Claudel)
See *Art poétique*
The Poetic Bus-Driver (Erskine) **84**:160
A Poetic Equation: Conversations between Nikki Giovanni and Margaret Walker (Walker) **129**:316, 333
"Poetic Evidence" (Éluard) **41**:144
"The Poetic Image of Don Luis de Góngora" (García Lorca) **7**:302; **49**:90; **197**:232
"Poetic Images" (Kunikida Doppo)
See "Shisō"
"Poetic Manifesto" (Thomas) **45**:402; **105**:302
Poetic Meditations (Garvey) **41**:198
Poetic Remains of the Swallow's Mausoleum (Su Man-shu) **24**:457
Poetic Studies (Phelps) **113**:336
Poetical Remains (Dickey) **151**:213
Poetical Works (Johnson) **19**:245
Poetical Works (Lang) **16**:258
The Poetical Works of James Madison Bell (Bell) **43**:90-1, 93
The Poetical Works of Rupert Brooke (Brooke) **7**:123
The Poetical Works of William Henry Drummond (Drummond) **25**:146
Poetics (Artaud) **3**:51
The Poetics of Reverie (Bachelard)
See *La Poétique de la réverie*
The Poetics of Space (Bachelard)
See *La Poétique de l'espace*
La Poétique de la réverie (Bachelard) **128**:11, 18, 23-4, 29-31, 39-41, 48, 55, 58, 62-6, 68-70, 75, 92, 95-100
La Poétique de l'espace (Bachelard) **128**:6, 10, 20, 23-5, 27-9, 32-4, 39-41, 46-9, 55-6, 58, 63-70, 91-2, 95-7, 99-101, 104
"Poetry" (Villaurrutia) **80**:478-9
Poetry: An Introduction to the Criticism and to the History of Poetry and Literature (Croce)
See *La poesia*
"Poetry and Design in William Blake" (Frye) **165**:165
Poetry and Fiction (Nemerov) **124**:145, 147, 151, 164, 168, 173, 175, 180, 202-6
"Poetry and Grammar" (Stein) **28**:322-23, 330; **48**:236
"Poetry and History" (Nemerov) **124**:317
"Poetry and Meaning" (Nemerov) **124**:270, 294
"Poetry and Painting" (Bishop) **103**:3, 6, 8
"Poetry and Painting" (Nemerov) **124**:215
"Poetry and Patriotism in Ireland" (Johnson) **19**:233, 241, 254
Poetry and Poets (Lowell) **8**:237
"Poetry and Prose" (Hagiwara) **60**:299
Poetry and the Age (Jarrell) **177**:143, 154, 172, 179, 183-84, 186-87, 190, 221-22, 239-40, 242, 245-46, 248
"Poetry and the Novel" (Yokomitsu) **47**:391
"Poetry and the Tradition" (Yeats) **31**:404
"Poetry and Verse" (Bierce) **44**:33
"Poetry as Witchcraft" (Balmont) **11**:31
Poetry at Present (Williams) **11**:497
"Poetry Black, Poetry White" (Daumal) **14**:91
"Poetry in Prose" (de la Mare) **4**:81
"Poetry in the Theater" (Anderson) **144**:34-35
"Poetry Is a Destructive Force" (Stevens) **3**:470; **45**:283
"Poetry is Not a Luxury" (Lorde) **173**:41, 54-55, 62-63, 86
The Poetry of Architecture (Ruskin) **20**:298; **63**:243, 253-54, 258, 274-80, 282
"The Poetry of Barbarism" (Santayana) **40**:388
"The Poetry of Blake" (Strachey) **12**:392, 395
"The Poetry of Catalogues" (Lucas) **73**:174
The Poetry of Life (Carman) **7**:139
"The Poetry of Nature" (Roberts) **8**:327
The Poetry of Search and the Poetry of Statement, and Other Posthumous Essays on Literature, Religion, and Language (Sayers) **2**:533
"Poetry of the Present" (Lawrence) **48**:140; **93**:52
"The Poetry of Wallace Stevens" (Nemerov) **124**:190
Poetry Package (Morley) **87**:144
"Poetry, Prose, and Oratory: Value of This Triple Distinction for Literary Criticism" (Croce) **37**:110
Poetry until Now (Drummond de Andrade)
See *Poesia até agora*
"Poetry, Violence" (Ginsberg) **120**:136
"The Poets" (Douglas) **40**:86
Poets (Aragon)
See *Les poetès*
"The Poet's Allegory" (Middleton) **56**:175, 187
"Poets and Critics" (Middleton) **56**:192
Poets and Dreamers (Gregory) **176**:10, 36, 50, 55, 62
"Poets and the Rain" (Sarton) **120**:290
Poets and Their Art (Monroe) **12**:218
"The Poet's Chart" (Guiney) **41**:207-08
The Poets' Corner (Beerbohm) **24**:98, 115, 119
"Poets, Critics, and Readers" (Jarrell) **177**:182
"The Poet's Death Is His Life" (Gibran) **9**:84
"A Poet's Holiday" (Middleton) **56**:190
"Poets in This War" (Douglas) **40**:81-2, 88, 95
A Poet's Life: Seventy Years in a Changing World (Monroe) **12**:221
"The Poet's Love Song" (Naidu) **80**:315
The Poet's Mission (Hagiwara) **60**:309-10
Poets of Modern France (Lewisohn) **19**:293
Poets on Poetry (Nemerov) **124**:200, 202, 204
A Poet's Pilgrimage (Davies) **5**:206-07
The Poet's Reconstruction (Herbert)
See *Rekonstruckcja poetry*
"The Poets Share" (Caragiale) **76**:169
"The Poet's Thought" (Montgomery) **51**:207
"The Poets, Tomorrow . . ." (Gonzalez Martinez) **72**:147
"A Poet's Wife" (Meynell) **6**:303
"Poètu" (Annensky) **14**:27
"Poètu" (Bryusov) **10**:87-90, 92, 96-7
"Poety" (Tsvetaeva) **35**:393
"Poezd zhizni" (Tsvetaeva) **35**:392
Pogány köszöntő (Radnóti) **16**:413-14, 418
"Poggfred" (Liliencron) **18**:206, 211-12, 215-16
Pogrom (Werfel) **8**:482
"Pohádka post'ácká" (Čapek) **192**:180
"Pohádka psí" (Čapek) **192**:180
"Pohádka ptací" (Čapek) **192**:179
"Pohádka vodnická" (Čapek) **192**:180
"Pohvala vucjem pastiru" (Popa) **167**:161
Le Poids du ciel (Giono) **124**:45, 95-96
Poil de carotte (Renard) **17**:302-04, 306-08, 312-13, 316
Point and Line to Plane: A Contribution to the Analysis of the Pictorial Elements (Kandinsky)
See *Punkt und Linie zur Fläche*
"A Point at Issue!" (Chopin) **127**:19
Un point c'est tout (Péret) **20**:188, 202
"A Point in Morals" (Glasgow) **7**:343-44
"Point of Honour" (Meynell) **6**:290
"The Point of View" (James) **2**:247
The Point of View for My Work as an Author (Hansen) **32**:252
"A Point to Be Remembered by Very Eminent Men" (Beerbohm) **24**:103
Pointed Firs (Jewett)
See *The Country of the Pointed Firs*
Pointed Roofs (Richardson) **3**:345-46, 350-52, 355-58
Pointing the Way (Griggs) **77**:146, 149-51
"Poison" (Dahl) **173**:11
"Poison" (Mansfield) **2**:448; **8**:284; **164**:320-21, 323
Poison (Kielland) **5**:279
The Poison Belt (Doyle) **7**:225, 239-40
"The Poisoned Man" (Dickey) **151**:172
"The Poisoned One" (Gumilev)
See "Otravlennyj"
"The Poisoned Pastries" (Donoso) **133**:80, 122
The Poisoned Tunic (Gumilev)
See *Otravlennaja tunika*
"The Poisoners" (Hearn) **9**:127
"Poisson" (Éluard) **7**:250
"Poisson d'Avril" (Somerville & Ross) **51**:358, 378, 382-83
Pokahontas (Liliencron) **18**:208, 216
"Poker-Talk" (Matthews) **95**:227
"Pokhod" (Kuprin) **5**:304
"Poklonjenje hromome vuku" (Popa) **167**:160
"Pokrovennaia" (Remizov) **27**:341

"Poland" (Machado de Assis)
See "Polonia"
"The Polano Plaza" (Miyazawa) **76**:290
The Polar Treasure (Dent) **72**:23
Poldekin (Tarkington) **9**:465
The Pole Jump (Lewis) **104**:210-11
"Polemic: Industrial Tourism and the National Parks" (Abbey) **160**:16, 22, 83, 95
"Polemical Introduction" (Frye) **165**:143, 145, 147, 180
Polemiche religiose (Papini) **22**:281, 286
"Une polémique sur les moeurs Grecques" (Gourmont) **17**:126
"Poles" (Stephens) **4**:420
Police!!! (Chambers) **41**:102, 113-14
"A Police Petruchio" (Williams) **89**:374, 384
Policeman Bluejay (Baum) **132**:80
"The Policeman's Prophecy" (Dunsany) **59**:28
"The Policy of the Closed Door" (Somerville & Ross) **51**:358
"Polikarp" (Cankar) **105**:157
Polikushka (Tolstoy) **4**:445, 450, 458, 474; **11**:464; **79**:334
Polite Farces for the Drawing Room (Bennett) **5**:27; **197**:16-17
"Politeness" (Milne) **88**:242
Política poética (Jiménez) **183**:284, 286
Political and Economic Writings (Orage) **157**:246
"Political Beggars" (Asturias)
See "Los mendigos políticos"
Political Economy and the Modern State (Innis) **77**:346
The Political Economy of Art (Ruskin) **63**:243-45, 249, 251
Political Fairy Tales (Sologub)
See *Političeskie skazčki*
The Political Ideal of the Rule of Law (Hayek) **109**:204
"Political Ideas in the Twentieth Century" (Berlin) **105**:132
The Political Order of a Free Society (Hayek) **109**:214
Political Parties: A Sociological Study of the Oligarchial Tendencies of Modern Democracy (Michels)
See *Zur Soziologie des Parteiwesens in der modernen Demokratie*
"Political Philosophy and the Crisis of our Time" (Strauss) **141**:239
The Political Philosophy of Hobbes (Strauss) **141**:233, 291
The Political Principles of Robert A. Taft (Kirk) **119**:275
The Political Prisoner (Pavese)
See *Il carcere*
"Political Reform" (Addams) **76**:2
Political Theories of the Middle Age (Maitland) **65**:250, 253, 278
"Political Thought in Islam" (Iqbal) **28**:203
Političeskie skazčki (Sologub) **9**:436, 447-48
"a politician is an arse upon" (Cummings) **137**:54
"Politicians (Opus 1053)" (Miyazawa) **76**:283, 289
Politics (Acker) **191**:8, 92, 127
"Politics and the English Language" (Orwell) **15**:307, 348; **51**:240, 252, 257, 259-61, 264-65, 268-69; **128**:259, 263, 268, 288, 297; **129**:228, 257
"Politics as a Vocation" (Weber) **69**:294, 345
"Politics for Craftsmen" (Orage) **157**:249
"The Politics of Artistic Expression" (Lewis) **104**:289
The Politics of "King Lear" (Muir) **87**:167
The Politics of Prudence (Kirk) **119**:288
The Politics of Waste (Adamov)
See *La politique des restes*
"Politics vs. Literature: An Examination of Gulliver's Travels" (Orwell) **15**:348; **51**:242, 259; **128**:270, 289; **129**:235
"Politik" (Mann) **21**:185
"Politik in Österreich" (Musil) **12**:259
La politique des restes (Adamov) **189**:15, 59
"La Politiquería" (Güiraldes) **39**:176
Politiques de la Philosophie (Lyotard) **103**:161
Politische Novelle (Frank) **81**:102
"Polly" (Chopin) **127**:10
Polly Oliver (Coppard) **5**:181
Polnoe sobranie sochinenii (Tolstoy) **173**:345-47
Les polonais (Jarry) **14**:272
"Polonia" (Machado de Assis) **10**:279
"Polonius Passing Through a Stage" (Nemerov) **124**:183, 250, 273, 283-84
"Poltarnees, Beholder of Ocean" (Dunsany) **59**:26
"Poltava" (Heidenstam) **5**:251
Polunoshchnoe solntse (Remizov) **27**:338
"Los polvos de la condesa" (Palma) **29**:256
Polya i gori (Vazov) **25**:456
"Polydore" (Chopin) **5**:142; **14**:70
"Polyn" (Pilnyak) **23**:203, 211, 213
"Polypheme's Passion" (Buchanan) **107**:14
"Pomegranate" (Lawrence) **93**:98-101
"Pomegranate Flower" (Rohmer) **28**:277, 286
"Pomegranate Seed" (Wharton) **3**:577; **9**:547; **129**:364
"The Pomegranate Trees" (Saroyan) **137**:155, 166, 168
"Pomegranates" (Valéry)
See "Les grenades"
"Un pomeriggio Adamo" (Calvino) **183**:92
Pomes All Sizes (Kerouac) **117**:271
Pomes Penyeach (Joyce) **3**:255; **16**:227-28; **159**:279, 282, 284
Pomme d'anis ou l'Histoire d'une jeune fille infirme (Jammes) **75**:105, 115, 118-19
The Pomp of Mr. Pomfret (Tey) **14**:459
"pompe à mots" (Arp) **115**:50
"Pompe Funebre" (Chambers) **41**:88
"Pompeii" (Lowry)
See "Present Estate of Pompeii"
Pompeji, Komödie eines Erdbebens (Horvath) **45**:78, 82, 101, 112
Pompes funèbres (Genet) **128**:131-32, 134, 185, 188, 197-99, 201, 207-13, 221-23
The Pomps of Satan (Saltus) **8**:347, 355
"The Pond" (Millay) **169**:295
"The Pond" (Nemerov) **124**:153, 185, 213, 263
The Pond (Bromfield) **11**:83
The Pond (Remizov)
See *Prud*
Pongo and the Bull (Belloc) **18**:35
"Ponocno sunce" (Popa) **167**:157
The Ponson Case (Crofts) **55**:85-6
"Le pont des soupirs" (Péret) **20**:201
"Pont du Carrousel" (Rilke) **195**:184
"Le pont Mirabeau" (Apollinaire) **3**:33-4, 36-7, 39, 41; **51**:7, 9, 14, 29
Pontifex, Son and Thorndyke (Freeman) **21**:53, 59
Pony Tracks (Remington) **89**:294-5, 304, 306
"Poocim vukova" (Popa) **167**:164
"Poodle" (Lardner) **2**:338
The Poodle Springs Story (Chandler) **1**:172; **7**:182; **179**:81-82, 91, 114, 129, 143, 159, 162, 185, 193-94, 225
"The Pool" (Bialik) **25**:58-9
"The Pool" (Manning) **25**:278
"The Pool in the Desert" (Duncan) **60**:209
The Pool in the Desert (Duncan) **60**:193, 209
The Pool of Memory: Memoirs (Oppenheim) **45**:131
"The Pool of the Black One" (Howard) **8**:133, 135-36
The Pool of Vishnu (Myers) **59**:133-4, 137, 139, 144, 150, 156-7
"Pool Shootin' Roy" (Runyon) **10**:437
"The Poor" (Simmel) **64**:336
"The Poor and Burning Arab" (Saroyan) **137**:155
Poor Bitos (Anouilh)
See *Pauvre Bitos*
Poor Blue Beard (Villaurrutia) **80**:458
"The Poor Boy" (Peretz) **16**:401
"Poor Butterfly" (Carter) **139**:185
Poor Cicero (Brod) **115**:88
The Poor Cousin (Barlach)
See *Der arme Vetter*
"A Poor Defenceless Widow" (Grove) **4**:141
"A Poor Devil" (Tolstoy) **79**:326
Poor Folk (Moricz)
See *Szegény emberek*
Poor Fortunes (Undset)
See *Fattige skjaebner*
"Poor Girl" (Benét) **28**:9
"Poor Harlequin" (Guro)
See "Nishchii Arlekin"
Poor Mamma! (Housman) **7**:357
"The Poor Man" (Coppard) **5**:177, 180
The Poor Man (Benson) **17**:20, 22, 24, 26, 29, 31
The Poor Man and the Lady (Hardy) **10**:225; **14**:176; **143**:76
The Poor Man of God (Kazantzakis) **5**:262-63; **33**:147-49
"Poor Marty" (Cather) **132**:121, 131
"A Poor Mexican" (Graham)
See "Un pelado"
"Poor Miss Tox" (Dobson) **79**:3
"Poor Pierrot" (Masters) **25**:298
"Poor Poll" (Bridges) **1**:132
"The Poor Relation" (Robinson) **101**:130, 133-34, 193
Poor Relations (Mackenzie) **116**:190-91, 194-95, 197-98, 203, 206, 212
"Poor Rhymes" (Khodasevich) **15**:206
"Poor Richard" (James) **171**:126
"Poor Romeo!" (Beerbohm) **24**:110
"Poor Saint" (Papadiamantis) **29**:272
"Poor Salieri" (Eisenstein) **57**:196
Poor Tom (Muir) **2**:486; **87**:194
Poor White (Anderson) **1**:35-6, 39, 44, 48, 54-7, 61; **10**:32-3, 36, 38-44, 48, 50; **24**:44; **123**:3-4, 26-7, 57-8, 60-2, 91, 108-9
A Poor Wise Man (Rinehart) **52**:283, 288
"Poor Working Girl" (Fitzgerald) **52**:59-60
The Poorhouse (Gregory) **1**:336; **176**:18
"Pope as a Moralist" (Stephen) **23**:328
The Pope of the Sea (Blasco Ibáñez)
See *El papa del mar*
Le popolane (Pirandello) **172**:188
"Poppies among the Wheat" (Mikszath)
See "Pipacsok a buzában"
"Poppies of the Red Year (A Symphony in Scarlet)" (Fletcher) **35**:94
"Poppy" (Radnóti) **16**:419
"The Poppy" (Thompson) **4**:435-36
The Poppy (Mizoguchi) **72**:315
"Poprygin'ia" (Chekhov) **3**:161; **10**:100; **163**:107, 128
Popular Allegories (Villaurrutia) **80**:458
"Popular Front in the Street" (Bataille) **155**:89, 106, 111
A Popular History of Witchcraft (Summers) **16**:430
The Popular Theater (Nathan) **18**:296
"Popularising Science" (Wells) **19**:446
Popularity (Cohan) **60**:157
Por que se ama (Benavente) **3**:94
Por tierras de Portugal y de España (Unamuno) **9**:514; **148**:231
"Por último" (Aleixandre) **113**:8
Le porche du mystère de la deuxieme vertu (Péguy) **10**:405, 409, 412
The Porcupine (Robinson) **5**:403; **101**:185
Põrgupõhja uus Vanapagan (Tammsaare) **27**:372, 374-76
Porgy (Heyward) **59**:84-6, 88, 90-101, 103-06
Porgy and Bess (Heyward) **59**:92, 100, 104-05
"pornographisches i-gedicht" (Schwitters) **95**:315
"Pornography and Obscenity" (Lawrence) **33**:208

"Pornography in the service of women" (Carter) **139**:171
"Porodična slika" (Andrić) **135**:84, 96
"Port" (Jiménez) **183**:333, 336
"Port of Call: Brazil" (Lewis) **3**:290
"Port of Embarkation" (Jarrell) **177**:195
Port of Seven Seas (Sturges) **48**:285, 291, 312
Port of Seven Seas (Whale) **63**:339
La porta sbagliata (Ginzburg) **156**:4, 63, 83
The Portable Dorothy Parker (Parker) **143**:284, 287
The Portable Faulkner (Faulkner) **141**:117, 168; **170**:106, 147, 151, 181, 222, 225, 235-37
"The Portable Phonograph" (McAlmon) **97**:98
The Portable Woollcott (Woollcott) **5**:525
The Portal of Initiation (Steiner)
See *Die Pforte der Einweihung*
La porte étroite (Gide) **5**:213-16, 218, 222-23, 227-29, 237-39, 243, 245-46; **12**:144, 147-49, 151-53, 157-62, 164, 167-68, 171, 173-74, 177-79; **36**:86, 93, 100, 102, 122; **177**:31, 36, 46, 102
La porte fermée (Bosschere) **19**:52-5, 57-9, 62-5
The Portent: A Story of the Inner Vision of the Highlanders, Commonly Called the Second Sight (MacDonald) **9**:291-92; **113**:209, 213-14, 236, 281-82, 313
"Portepeefähnrich Schadius" (Liliencron) **18**:216
El portero (Arenas) **191**:144-45, 150-52, 175-79, 190
"Les portes de l'opium" (Schwob) **20**:321
"Les porteuses" (Hearn) **9**:138
"Pórtico" (Darío) **4**:56
The Portico of the Mystery of the Second Virtue (Péguy)
See *Le porche du mystère de la deuxieme vertu*
The Portion of Labor (Freeman) **9**:67, 70, 72
Les portiques (Larbaud) **9**:205
"Portrait" (Alain-Fournier) **6**:28
"Portrait" (Aleixandre)
See "Retrato"
"The Portrait" (Chekhov) **3**:146
"The Portrait" (Davies) **5**:202
"A Portrait" (Field) **43**:166
"Portrait" (Garneau) **13**:195
"Portrait" (Millay) **49**:222
"A Portrait" (Parker) **143**:321
"Portrait" (Percy) **84**:198
"The Portrait" (Thomas) **105**:355
"The Portrait" (Tolstoy) **18**:377
"Portrait" (Villaurrutia) **80**:477
"The Portrait" (Wharton) **3**:551; **9**:540; **129**:360
The Portrait (Ford) **172**:7
Portrait d'un inconnu (Sarraute) **145**:263-66, 274, 321, 339-40, 357-60, 364-65
"Portrait in Georgia" (Toomer) **172**:274-75, 314-15, 327, 340
"Portrait of a Baby" (Benét) **7**:69
Portrait of a Dictator, F. S. Lopez (Graham) **19**:111
"Portrait of a Friend" (Ginzburg)
See "Ritratto di un amico"
The Portrait of a Generation, Including the Revolving Mirror (McAlmon) **97**:92-94, 118
"Portrait of a Lady" (Day) **25**:131
The Portrait of a Lady (James) **2**:246, 255-56, 259, 262, 264-66, 269; **11**:326, 328, 331-32, 335, 337, 342; **40**:97-172; **47**:161, 167, 171-74, 177-78, 185-86, 188, 190, 201, 208; **64**:171-73, 179; **171**:130, 158, 196
"Portrait of a Lover" (Cullen) **37**:155, 168
Portrait of a Man Unknown (Sarraute)
See *Portrait d'un inconnu*
Portrait of a Man with Red Hair (Walpole) **5**:497
"Portrait of a Mathematician" (Morley) **87**:146
Portrait of a Paladin (Huidobro)
See *Mío Cid Campeador*
"Portrait of a Philosopher" (Fisher) **87**:73
"The Portrait of a Saint" (Bradford) **36**:56
"Portrait of a Writer" (Ginzburg) **156**:32, 46
Portrait of America: Letters (Sienkiewicz)
See *Listy z podróży do Ameryki*
Portrait of an American (Coffin) **95**:20
Portrait of an Artist, as an Old Man (Heller) **131**:21
"A Portrait of Bascom Hawke" (Wolfe) **4**:526-27; **13**:493; **61**:313, 319
"A Portrait of Carl Van Vechten" (Stein) **48**:210
"Portrait of Eliane at Fourteen" (Larbaud) **9**:198
"Portrait of Herwarth Walden" (Schwitters) **95**:342
Portrait of Mabel Dodge at the Villa Curonia (Stein) **28**:306; **48**:241
Portrait of Madame Yuki (Mizoguchi)
See *Yuki Fujin Ezu*
The Portrait of Mr. W. H. (Wilde) **8**:493-94, 499; **41**:359, 371, 375-77, 381, 389, 398
"Portrait of Mrs. C: Aetatis suae 75" (Bishop) **103**:27-8
"Portrait of One Person as by Georgia O'Keeffe" (Sarton) **120**:272
"Portrait of Rudolf Blümner" (Schwitters) **95**:342-3
"Portrait of the Artist" (Parker) **143**:322
"Portrait of the Artist as a Prematurely Old Man" (Nash) **109**:364
Portrait of the Artist as a Young Dog (Thomas) **1**:471-73; **8**:455-56, 462-63; **45**:389, 391-93, 395-96, 398, 408, 412; **105**:301, 303, 311, 315, 318, 320, 322-23, 325, 340, 343-45, 348-50, 355, 357-58
A Portrait of the Artist as a Young Man (Joyce) **3**:252, 254, 256, 262, 267-79, 282; **8**:161-63, 171; **16**:201-46; **35**:143-44, 156-57, 161-63, 165-66, 169-70, 176, 194; **52**:206-07, 212, 224-26, 235, 237-39, 242; **159**:267-75, 279, 282, 305, 307-10, 313-14, 335-46, 350, 352-54, 358, 361-62
Portrait of the Artist, as an Old Man (Heller) **151**:340-41
"Portrait of Three Conspirators" (Nemerov) **124**:281
Le Portrait surnaturel de Dorian Gray (Cocteau) **119**:57-8, 60
"Portrait with Background" (Gogarty) **15**:109
"Portraits" (Gurney) **33**:98
Portraits and Jewels of Mary Stuart (Lang) **16**:270
Portraits and Prayers (Stein) **48**:209, 249, 254
"Portraits and Repitition" (Stein) **48**:249
Portraits de famille (Alain) **41**:30
Portraits from Life: Memories and Criticisms (Ford) **1**:288; **15**:76; **39**:165
Portraits I (MacCarthy) **36**:251-53
Portraits in Miniature, and Other Essays (Strachey) **12**:399-400, 404
Portraits of American Women (Bradford) **36**:67
"Portraits of the Artist" (Malamud) **184**:307-9
Portraits of the Confederacy (Bradford) **36**:46
Portraits of Women (Bradford) **36**:52, 66, 68
Portraits with a Name (Aleixandre)
See *Retratos con nombre*
Portraits-souvenir (Cocteau) **119**:66, 82, 107, 111
Die Portugiesin (Musil) **12**:242, 246, 251-52
The Portuguese Lady (Musil)
See *Die Portugiesin*
"El porvenir" (Darío) **4**:59
"Poryv" (Guro) **56**:133
Posedlost (Nezval) **44**:244
"Poseidon" (Dunsany) **59**:28
"Posesión" (Aleixandre) **113**:4
"Posición de América" (Reyes) **33**:318-19, 325
"The Position of America" (Reyes)
See "Posición de América"
The Position of America, and Other Essays (Reyes) **33**:318
"The Position of Judaism" (Zangwill) **16**:462
"The Position of Psychology" (Wells) **133**:316
"Position of the Flesh" (Artaud)
See "Positions de la chair"
"Positions de la chair" (Artaud) **36**:4, 17
"Positions et propositions" (Claudel) **10**:130
"Positions of the Union on Essential Points" (Bataille) **155**:111
"The Positive Critique of the Materialist Conception of History" (Weber) **69**:308
The Positivist Dispute in German Sociology (Adorno) **111**:53
"Posle boia" (Babel) **2**:22; **171**:10, 19, 23, 79, 87
"Posle boja" (Babel)
See "Posle boia"
"Posle igre" (Popa) **167**:155
"Posle koncerta" (Annensky) **14**:27
"Posle pocetka" (Popa) **167**:155
Posle Rossii (Tsvetaeva) **7**:557, 560-61; **35**:388, 391-94, 400, 404, 406, 415-16
Poslednaya liubov' (Zabolotsky) **52**:374
"Poslední soud" (Čapek) **37**:49; **192**:224, 227
Poslednie stikhi, 1914-1918 (Hippius) **9**:154
Poslednie stranicy iz dnevnika ženščing (Bryusov) **10**:84
"Poslednii deb i st" (Kuprin) **5**:303
Posledniy iz Udege (Fadeyev) **53**:46, 51-55
Posledniye dni (Bulgakov) **2**:65; **16**:97, 110
"Posledny krug" (Hippius) **9**:159, 163, 165
Poslednyaya noch (Bagritsky) **60**:16-7
Posolon (Remizov) **27**:334, 338, 346, 350-52, 354-56
Le possédé (Lemonnier) **22**:198, 202
The Possessed (Ewers)
See *Die Besessenen*
"The Possession" (Warner) **131**:311
Possession (Bromfield) **11**:72-5, 85, 87
Possession: A Peep-Show in Paradise (Housman) **7**:354-55
"Possession for Year and Day" (Maitland) **65**:282
"Possessions" (Crane) **2**:117, 120-21; **5**:188, 191
"The Possibility of Evil" (Jackson) **187**:245
"The Possibility of Philosophy" (Merleau-Ponty) **156**:186
A Possible Triad on Black Notes (Bonner) **179**:12, 53
"Posson Jone'" (Cable) **4**:32
"Post Impressions II" (Cummings) **137**:42
"The Post Office" (Hearn) **9**:126
The Post Office (Tagore)
See *Dākghar*
Post-Adolescence: A Selection of Short Fiction (McAlmon) **97**:89-91, 100, 102, 115, 118-20, 122
"Post-Bellum—Pre-Harlem" (Chesnutt) **39**:94
"Postcard from Adam Zagajewski" (Herbert) **168**:45, 47
"A Postcard from the Volcano" (Stevens) **45**:282
Postcard Poems (Nezval) **44**:239
"Postcards" (Radnóti) **16**:414, 420
"Post-Graduate" (Parker) **143**:323
Posthumous Papers of a Living Author (Musil) **68**:260-63, 265
Posthumous Poems (Annensky) **14**:19-20
Posthumous Reminiscences of Braz Cubas (Machado de Assis)
See *Memórias pósthumas de Braz Cubas*
Post-Liminium (Johnson) **19**:233-34, 236, 238, 241, 254-55
"The Postmen's Tale" (Čapek)
See "Pohádka post'ácká"
The Postmodern Condition (Lyotard)
See *La condition postmoderne*
The Postmoderne Explained to Children (Lyotard)
See *Le Postmoderne expliqué aux enfants*
Le Postmoderne expliqué aux enfants (Lyotard) **103**:224
"Postmodernism" (Acker) **191**:102
"Postponement" (Hardy) **72**:238-39
Postřižiny (Hrabal) **155**:151-54, 158

Postscript to Adventure (Connor) **31**:109-11
Postscripts (Tagore)
See *Punascha*
"Postwar Stories" (Calvino) **183**:224
"The Pot" (Aleichem)
See "Dos tepl"
The Pot of Broth (Gregory) **176**:13
"The Pot of Fire" (Malamud) **184**:160
"Potato Diggers" (Coffin) **95**:17
"The Potato Harvest" (Roberts) **8**:314, 316, 327
"Potato Picking" (McAlmon) **97**:98, 120, 122
"The Potatoes' Dance" (Lindsay) **17**:225, 239
Potatoes in the Field and Garden Culture (Prishvin) **75**:214
"The Pot-Boiler" (Wharton) **129**:361
Pot-bouille (Zola) **1**:589; **6**:559, 563-65, 570; **21**:421; **41**:412, 415
"Potega smaku" (Herbert) **168**:10, 65
The Pot-Maker (Bonner) **179**:7, 19, 30, 51
Le Potomak (Cocteau) **119**:77, 83, 105-8, 110
Potop (Sienkiewicz) **3**:422-24, 427-29
"Potowatomis Datter" (Jensen) **41**:303-04
"Potselui" (Babel) **2**:29; **13**:26; **171**:70, 74, 76, 88
"The Potteries: A Sketch" (Bennett) **197**:128
Potterism (Macaulay) **7**:422, 425-30; **44**:116-18, 122, 125, 132-33
"Potwór Pana Cogito" (Herbert) **168**:21, 25-26
"Potyra" (Machado de Assis) **10**:279
"Pour Avigdor Arikha" (Beckett) **145**:91
Pour en finir avec le jugement de dieu (Artaud) **3**:58
Pour finir encour et Autres Foirades (Beckett)
See *Foirades*
Pour la couronne (Coppee) **25**:125-28
Pour la révolution africaine (Fanon) **188**:12, 79, 81, 91, 111, 115, 118, 120-21, 123
Pour Lénine (Sorel) **91**:293
Pour lucrèce (Giraudoux) **2**:159, 172-73
"Pour Milo" (Schwob) **20**:319
"Pour moi" (Péguy) **10**:414
"Pour Prende Congé" (Parker) **143**:323
Pour saluer Melville (Giono) **124**:41, 84, 87, 97, 115
Pour un herbier (Colette) **5**:169
Pour un oui ou pour un non (Sarraute) **145**:265, 267, 287-88, 292-93, 316, 318, 320, 323
"Pour un rêve de jour" (Desnos) **22**:61
Pour une nouvelle culture (Nizan) **40**:325
"Pour vivre ici" (Éluard) **41**:152, 169
Pour vivre ici (Éluard) **41**:154
Pourquoi je ne suis pas feministe (Vallette) **67**:303, 309
La poussière de soleils (Roussel) **20**:226-28, 231, 234-35, 242-43, 246
Pouvoir tout dire (Éluard) **7**:255; **41**:152
"poux fardés" (Arp) **115**:40
"Poverty" (Lagerkvist)
See "Armod"
"Poverty" (Zoshchenko) **15**:506
"The Poverty Programs" (Nemerov) **124**:257
"Poverty's Lot" (Wetherald) **81**:409
Povest' nepogašennoj luny (Pilnyak) **23**:202, 212
"Povest nepogašhennoy luny" (Pilnyak) **23**:203, 217, 219
Povest' o dvukh zveriakh: Ikhnelat (Remizov) **27**:349
"Povest o Petre i Fevronii" (Remizov) **27**:349
Povídky z, druhé kapsy (Čapek) **192**:180, 223
Povídky z, jedné kapsy (Čapek) **192**:223
"Povratak u Beograd" (Popa) **167**:158
"Powassan's Drum" (Scott) **6**:387, 390
The Powder of Sympathy (Morley) **87**:123
"Powder, Rouge and Lip-stick" (Millay) **169**:235, 276
"Power" (Crowley) **7**:208
"Power" (Södergran)
See "Makt"
Power (Feuchtwanger)
See *Jud Süss*
Power (Gladkov) **27**:91
Power (Stringer) **37**:337
"Power and Light" (Dickey) **151**:100, 121, 199, 201
The Power and the Glory (Sturges) **48**:273-74, 276, 283-85, 290-96, 311, 316, 320-21
"The Power behind the Throne" (Phillips) **44**:277
Power in Men (Cary) **29**:65; **196**:140, 142-43, 164, 168, 178
"The Power of a Curse" (Premchand) **21**:287
The Power of a Lie (Bojer)
See *Troens magt*
The Power of Creative Work Is Inexhaustible (Tolstoy) **18**:379
Power of Darkness (Tolstoy) **4**:453-54; **11**:466, 469; **79**:374
The Power of Faith (Bojer)
See *Troens magt*
The Power of Myth (Campbell) **140**:28, 33, 36, 43, 45, 48-49, 60, 62, 75, 79, 83, 89-91, 94, 97-99, 101-3, 106-8, 110-11, 113, 138-39
"The Power of Taste" (Herbert)
See "Potega smaku"
The Power of the Dead (Maeterlinck)
See *La puissance des morts*
The Power of the Keys (Shestov)
See *Vlast' klyuchei: Potestas clavium*
"The Power of the Pen" (Corelli) **51**:81, 83
"Power Song" (Jozsef) **22**:160
"Power to the People" (Nemerov) **124**:256-57, 277
"Power-feeling and Machine-age Art" (Lewis) **104**:210
The Power-House (Buchan) **41**:38, 40-1, 53, 65, 67-8, 70-1
"Powhatan's Daughter" (Crane) **2**:124; **5**:186; **80**:81, 83
"Powrót prokonsula" (Herbert) **168**:8, 24-25
Pożegnanie jesieni (Witkiewicz) **8**:507
Pożegnanie z Maria (Borowski) **9**:21-3
"Poželtevšij berezovy list, kaplja, i nižnee nebo" (Sologub) **9**:448
"Pozëmka" (Pilnyak) **23**:211
"Pozhar" (Remizov) **27**:338, 341, 348
"Poznámka k Franzi Kafkovi" (Muir)
See "Franz Kafka"
El pozo (Onetti) **131**:132-34, 136, 139-40, 142-47, 153, 155, 157-59, 162, 178, 194, 214-17, 226-28, 245-46, 261, 265, 268-69, 283-84, 286-87, 293
pppppp (Schwitters) **95**:350
Prabhat sangit (Tagore) **3**:490; **53**:339-40
"Prachka" (Khlebnikov) **20**:133
Practical Agitation (Chapman) **7**:187-88, 191, 193, 196
Practical Deductions (Nightingale) **85**:242
A Practical Novelist (Davidson) **24**:159-60
The Practice and Theory of Individual Psychology (Adler)
See *Praxis und Theorie der Individualpsychologie*
"The Practice of Joy before Death" (Bataille) **155**:96, 104, 107-8
"The Practiced Hand" (March) **96**:251, 259
"Praeludium" (Henley) **8**:109
En praests dagbog (Obstfelder) **23**:176, 178-84, 186, 189, 191-93
Praeterita (Ruskin) **20**:281-82, 285, 290, 301; **63**:254-56, 269-72, 291, 298-6, 318, 321-22
Der Prager Kreis (Brod) **115**:92
Pragmatism (Čapek) Pragmatismus cili filosofie praktického zivota
Pragmatism (Papini)
See *Pragmatismo*
Pragmatism: A New Name for Some Old Ways of Thinking (James) **15**:148, 162-63, 177, 187; **32**:337, 340, 351, 357, 359
Pragmatism as a Principle and Method of Right Thinking (Peirce) **81**:290,291
Pragmatismo (Papini) **22**:271, 283, 287
Pragmatismus cili filosofie praktického zivota (Čapek) **192**:189, 215
"The Pragmatist Account of Truth and Its Misunderstanders" (James) **32**:357
The Prague Pedestrian (Nezval)
See *Pražský chodec*
Prague Stories (Rilke) **195**:180
"Prague, When You Are in Danger" (Nezval) **44**:249
"Prague with Fingers of Rain" (Nezval)
See "Praha s prsty deště"
Prague with Fingers of Rain (Nezval)
See *Praha s prsty deště*
"Praha s prsty deště" (Nezval) **44**:248
Praha s prsty deště (Nezval) **44**:241, 245-46, 249
"The Prairie Battlements" (Lindsay) **17**:226
The Prairie Child (Stringer) **37**:338
"Prairie Dawn" (Cather) **132**:131
"The Prairie Farmer" (Rhodes) **53**:316
Prairie Folks (Garland) **3**:192-93, 196
The Prairie Mother (Stringer) **37**:338
Prairie Songs: Being Chants Rhymed and Unrhymed of the Level Lands of the Great West (Garland) **3**:197
"Prairie Spring" (Cather) **132**:131; **152**:4, 7, 13, 34, 36, 76, 79
The Prairie Wife (Stringer) **37**:336-38
Praise (Agee)
See *Let Us Now Praise Famous Men*
"Praise for an Urn" (Crane) **2**:117, 120; **5**:188-89
"Praise of Dionysus" (Gosse) **28**:139
"Praise of Her Own Beauty" (Naidu) **80**:317
"Praise of Learning" (Brecht) **169**:68
Praises of the Sky, of the Sea, of the Earth, and of Heroes (D'Annunzio)
See *Laudi del cielo, del mare, della terra e degli eroi*
Prakovszky, a siket kovács (Mikszath) **31**:167
Prakovszky, the Deaf Smithy (Mikszath)
See *Prakovszky, a siket kovács*
Pramithas (Devkota)
See *Prometheus*
Prancing Nigger (Firbank) **1**:229-30
"Prangeren" (Jensen) **41**:308
Prāntik (Tagore) **3**:487, 489; **53**:343
"Pranzo con un pastore" (Calvino) **183**:187
Pranzo con un pastore (Calvino) **183**:4, 6
"Prapamjat'" (Gumilev) **60**:272, 276, 280
"Das Präparat" (Meyrink) **21**:221, 225, 232
Der Präsident (Bernhard) **165**:96
Der Präsident (Kaiser) **9**:174, 181
"Pravda večnaja kumirov" (Bryusov) **10**:81, 91
Praxis und Theorie der Individualpsychologie (Adler) **61**:2-3, 18
Pray and Work (Heijermans)
See *Ora et labora*
"Prayer" (Anwar)
See "Doa"
"The Prayer" (Hunt) **53**:190
"Prayer" (Jammes) **75**:110
"A Prayer" (Joyce) **3**:255
"Prayer" (Lasker-Schueler) **57**:332, 334-36
"Prayer" (Lawrence) **93**:59
"A Prayer" (Montgomery) **51**:209
"A Prayer" (Pickthall) **21**:243
"Prayer" (Service) **15**:412
"Prayer" (Toomer) **172**:257, 274-75
"A Prayer" (Tsvetaeva)
See "Molitva"
The Prayer (Coppee)
See *Le pater*
"Prayer for a New Mother" (Parker) **143**:325-26
"Prayer for a Prayer" (Parker) **143**:325-26
"A Prayer for My Daughter" (Yeats) **1**:556; **11**:523, 531; **31**:389, 421-22; **93**:340, 363, 389, 392, 401; **116**:343
"A Prayer for My Son" (Yeats) **1**:580; **116**:264
"A Prayer for Old Age" (Yeats) **116**:305, 338
"The Prayer of Islam" (Naidu) **80**:341
"The Prayer of the Flowers" (Dunsany) **59**:27
"The Prayer of Women" (Sharp) **39**:354, 373, 398

"Prayer on Waking" (Prado)
See "Oracion al despertar"
"Prayer to the Virgin of Chartres" (Adams) **4**:15
"A Prayer—For These" (Thomas) **10**:464
"The Prayers" (Rilke)
See "Die Gebete"
The Praying Man (Santos) **156**:317, 319
"Pražký chodec" (Nezval) **44**:246
Pražský chodec (Nezval) **44**:249
"Pre igre" (Popa) **167**:154-55
"Preacher's Legend" (Capote) **164**:100, 107-8
"The Precept of Silence" (Johnson) **19**:244, 246
"Preciosa and the Wind" (García Lorca)
See "Preciosa y el aire"
"Preciosa y el aire" (García Lorca) **7**:290; **49**:91, 97; **181**:47; **197**:224
"Precious and the Wind" (García Lorca) **181**:25
Precious Bane (Webb) **24**:466-68, 471-73, 475-80, 483-84
The Precious Stones of the Bible (Ellis) **14**:127
"Precise Intersection Points" (Burroughs) **121**:143
Précision (1930-1937) (Benda) **60**:88-9
Précisions (Giono) **124**:46, 95
The Preconceptions of Economic Science (Veblen) **31**:351
Precursores (Azuela) **145**:14
"Los precursores de Kafka" (Borges) **109**:13, 76, 95
"Pred kraj" (Popa) **167**:155
"A Predecessor of Perseus" (Nemerov) **124**:170, 203, 249
"Predeli" (Popa) **167**:154, 175
"Predestined Half a Lifetime" (Chang)
See "Bansheng yuan"
"A Predicament" (Callaghan) **145**:255
"The Predicate in Moral Judgements" (Westermarck) **87**:363
"Prediction" (Himes) **139**:285
"Predimiento de Antoñito el Camborio" (García Lorca) **181**:27
Predlozhenie (Chekhov) **31**:80
"Preface" (Fondane) **159**:256
"Preface" (Pirandello) **172**:156, 158, 161-62
"Préface à la vie d'un bureaucrate" (Roumain) **19**:339-41, 343, 345
"Preface on Bosses" (Shaw) **3**:393
Preface to a Life (Gale) **7**:282-83, 285
"Preface to a Novel" (Lowry) **40**:225
"Preface to Preludes and Symphonies" (Fletcher) **35**:100, 104
"Preface to the Scientific Romances" (Wells) **133**:294
"Préface-Collage, ou menu déchiré en velle vue" (Arp) **115**:47
Prefaces (James) **2**:268
Prefaces (Marquis) **7**:437, 440
Prefaces to Shakespeare (Granville-Barker) **2**:195, 198
"Prefácio interessantíssimo" (Andrade) **43**:2, 7, 10-11, 17-19
"Prefatory Essay" (Cary) **196**:197-98
"The Prefectural Engineer's Statement Regarding Clouds" (Miyazawa) **76**:300-01
"Pregunta" (García Lorca) **181**:65
"Le pregunté al poetia . . ." (Villaurrutia) **80**:515
Prejudices (Mencken) **13**:361, 379, 381, 386-87, 393-94
Prejudices: A Philosophical Dictionary (Nisbet) **117**:334, 344, 352-53, 358-9, 305
Prejudices, first series (Mencken) **13**:360
Prejudices, second series (Mencken) **13**:362
Prejudices, third series (Mencken) **13**:365, 395
Prekrasayia sabinianki (Andreyev) **3**:22
"Prelude" (Baker) **10**:26, 28
"Prelude" (Benét) **7**:73
"Prelude" (Mansfield) **2**:446, 450-58; **8**:275, 277, 280-82, 287, 291-93; **39**:293-95, 298, 301-04, 306-07, 314, 318-19, 321-22, 324-26, 329; **164**:241, 247-51, 253-55, 265-66, 268, 270-75, 283, 297, 301, 309, 326-28, 332-37, 339-40
"Prélude" (Mirbeau) **55**:292
"Prelude" (Pirandello) **29**:310
"Prelude" (Service) **15**:409
"A Prelude and a Song" (Stephens) **4**:406, 409-10, 419-20
"Prélude de Pan" (Giono) **124**:42, 93, 100
Prelude to Adventure (Walpole) **5**:503
"A Prelude to Life" (Symons) **11**:436, 447-49
"Prelude to Objects" (Stevens) **45**:283
Prelude to Waking (Franklin) **7**:264-70
Preludes (Meynell) **6**:290, 292, 298-99
Preludio e canzonette (Saba) **33**:370, 373
Preludio e fughe (Saba) **33**:366, 370, 374
Preludios (Gonzalez Martinez) **72**:147-48, 154
Premashram (Premchand) **21**:284-85, 297
"The Premature Senility of Film" (Artaud) **36**:39
"Pre-Memory" (Gumilev)
See "Prapamjat'"
Premier amour (Beckett) **145**:83, 202-05
The Premier and the Painter (Zangwill) **16**:444, 462, 464
"Le Premier Pas" (Hornung)
See "The Ides of March"
"Premier Plan" (Nezval) **44**:239
Première anthologie vivante de la poésie du passé (Éluard) **41**:152
La prèmiere aventure celeste de Monsieur Antipyrine (Tzara) **168**:240, 257, 273, 287, 292-93
"Première du monde" (Éluard) **7**:247, 259
Les premières armes du Symbolisme (Moréas) **18**:285
Premières vues anciennes (Éluard) **41**:152
"Premise" (Levi) **109**:301
"Prem-ki holi" (Premchand) **21**:293
"Prendimiento de Antoñito el Camborio" (García Lorca) **49**:92, 112-13
"The Preposterous Motive" (Glaspell) **175**:96-97
"Pre-Raphaelitism" (Ruskin) **63**:262, 310
Presagios (Salinas) **17**:357, 359, 361, 363-66
The Presbyterian Child (Hergesheimer) **11**:283
Préséances (Genet)
See *Haute surveillance*
"Presence" (Roberts) **8**:321
Présence de la mort (Ramuz) **33**:295, 297-98, 300
"A Present" (Andreyev) **3**:20
"The Present" (Khlebnikov)
See "Nastoyashchee"
"Present, Afterwards" (Aleixandre)
See "Presente, después"
"The Present Age" (Harper) **14**:259, 263
The Present Age from 1914 (Muir) **87**:163
The Present Age: Progress and Anarchy in Modern America (Nisbet) **117**:344-48, 366, 379
The Present and the Past (Compton-Burnett) **180**:114-15, 127-29, 132
"Present at a Hanging" (Bierce) **44**:45
"Present at the End" (Wakefield) **120**:354, 357
"The Present Condition of Jamaica and Jamaicans" (Redcam) **25**:331
Present Customs (Korolenko) **22**:173
"The Present Dilemma in Philosophy" (James) **15**:181
"Present Estate of Pompeii" (Lowry) **6**:240
"A Present from Clonmacnois" (O'Faolain) **143**:273
"The Present Meeting of East and WEst" (Fenollosa) **91**:2
"The Present Need of a Philosophy" (Collingwood) **67**:193
"The Present Position of Minority Groups in the United States" (Wirth) **92**:377
"The Present Situation of Social Philosophy and the Tasks of an Institute for Social Research" (Horkheimer) **132**:162
"The Present State of the Age of Repression" (Ishikawa) **15**:129
"Presentación" (Arenas) **191**:258
Présentation Critique de Constantin Cavafy (Yourcenar) **193**:270
Présentation Critique d'Hortense Flexner (Yourcenar) **193**:280
Présentation de Pan (Giono) **124**:32
Présentation de Sacher-Masoch (Deleuze) **116**:86, 104
"Presente, después" (Aleixandre) **113**:50
"Presentimento" (Villaurrutia) **80**:477
Presenting Moonshine (Collier) **127**:249-50
Preserving Mr. Panmure (Pinero) **32**:411-12
The President (Asturias)
See *El señor presidente*
The President (Bernhard)
See *Der Präsident*
President (Molnár) **20**:171
President Fu Manchu (Rohmer) **28**:280, 300
"The President Reports on the Home Front" (Roosevelt) **93**:184
"President Roosevelt Is Magificently Right" (Keynes) **64**:210
Press On (Lie)
See *Gaa paa!*
Prester John (Buchan) **41**:34-6, 38, 41, 44, 49
"The Pretence of Knowledge" (Hayek) **109**:233
"Pretend an Interest" (Burroughs) **121**:126
The Pretender: A Story of the Latin Quarter (Service) **15**:398
The Pretenders (Ibsen)
See *Kongs emnerne*
"Pretending" (Beerbohm) **24**:116, 126
"The Pretext" (Wharton) **129**:361
Prétexte: Roland Barthes (Barthes) **135**:156-58
De Pretore Vincenzo (de Filippo) **127**:283
"Le prêtre" (Teilhard de Chardin) **9**:493
"A Pretty Girl in the West" (Foote) **108**:34
The Pretty Lady (Bennett) **5**:38, 42, 44, 47, 48; **20**:22-4, 27-8; **197**:31
"Pretty Poll" (de la Mare) **53**:14-5, 17
"The Pretty Redhead" (Apollinaire)
See "La jolie rousse"
"Pretty Sights and Good Feelin's" (Childress) **116**:37
"Pretty Words" (Wylie) **8**:530, 536
La Preuba (Pardo Bazán)
See *Una cristiana-La preuba*
Preussische Wappen (Kolmar) **40**:184
"Prevalent Design" (Lewis) **104**:210
"The Prevention of Literature" (Orwell) **6**:344; **15**:309; **31**:181; **51**:243, 259, 266; **128**:259, 288, 297; **129**:223, 228
A Previous Engagement (Howells) **7**:387
"Pri dverjav" (Pilnyak) **23**:211
"Pri soli" (Saba) **33**:373
"Priblizheniia" (Balmont) **11**:36
"Priča" (Andrić) **135**:29
"Priča o vezirovom slonu" (Andrić) **135**:24, 89
"The Price for Civilization Must Be Paid in Hard Work and Sorrow and Blood" (Roosevelt) **93**:184
"The Price of a Soul" (Bryan) **99**:52
"The Price of Admiralty" (Lowndes) **12**:201
"The Price of Leadership" (Murry) **16**:342
The Price of Love (Bennett) **5**:26, 36, 50; **197**:30
"The Price of Milk" (Premchand)
See "Dudh-ka dam"
"The Price of Realism" (Symons) **11**:454
"The Price of the Harness" (Crane) **11**:134, 161
The Price of Unhappiness (Yokomitsu)
See *Kanashimi no Daika*
The Price She Paid (Phillips) **44**:262, 268, 275
"The Price Was High" (Fitzgerald) **6**:167
The Price Was High: The Last Uncollected Stories of F. Scott Fitzgerald (Fitzgerald) **157**:194
"Prices and Production" (Hayek) **109**:240

Prices and Production (Hayek) **109**:171, 196
"Prickly Pear" (García Lorca) **197**:208
"Pridah" (Bialik) **25**:53, 59
Pride (Gladkov) **27**:91
The Pride of Bear Creek (Howard) **8**:137
A Pride of Sonnets (Morley) **87**:145
"The Pride of the Cities" (Henry) **19**:174
Pride of the Yankees (Mankiewicz) **85**:147, 158, 163
"Pridvornyi iuvelir" (Remizov) **27**:341-42, 349
"La prière" (Sully Prudhomme) **31**:306
"Prière du soir" (Nelligan) **14**:399
"Prière impromptue 3" (van Ostaijen) **33**:413
"Priere pour Aller au Paradis avec les Anes" (Jammes) **75**:114
"Prière pour nous autres charnels" (Péguy) **10**:405-06
"Priest of the Temple of Serapis" (Cavafy) **2**:89
"The Priestly Prerogative" (London) **9**:273-74
"Priezd v derevnju" (Guro) **56**:136-37, 145
I prigioni (Saba) **33**:373, 375
Prigionieri (Marinetti) **10**:317
Priglashenie na kazn (Nabokov) **108**:51, 55, 65, 83-84, 116, 119, 134, 189-91, 194-96, 200-01, 216, 223-24
"Priglashenie v puteshestvie" (Gumilev) **60**:279
Prikliuchenie (Tsvetaeva) **7**:568; **35**:390, 394, 410
"Prikliucheniia obez'iany" (Zoshchenko)
See "Adventures of a Monkey"
Prilis hlucná samota (Hrabal) **155**:148-50, 153, 158, 161, 163
Prim (Pérez Galdós) **27**:282
Prima del Ballo (Svevo) **35**:369
The Prima Donna (Crawford) **10**:151, 155
"Prima notte" (Pirandello) **29**:282, 292
"The Primacy of Perception" (Merleau-Ponty) **156**:135, 162, 253
The Primacy of Perception (Merleau-Ponty) **156**:137
"The Primacy of the Abstract" (Hayek) **109**:208
"Primal Memories" (Gumilev)
See "Prapamjat'"
"Primal Sonata" (Schwitters)
See "Ursonate"
"Primal Sound" (Rilke) **1**:423
The Primate of the Rose (Shiel) **8**:364
"Primavera" (Carducci) **32**:103
"La primavera" (Jiménez) **4**:225
"Primavera" (Saba) **33**:374
"Primavera de agosto" (Prado) **75**:211
"Primavera en la tierra" (Aleixandre) **113**:33, 73-4
Primavera en otoño (Martinez Sierra and Martinez Sierra) **6**:277-78
"Primavere elleniche" (Carducci) **32**:86, 91, 96, 101, 108, 110
"Prime" (Lowell) **8**:227, 234
"Prime Salted" (Caragiale)
See "Pastramă trufanda"
The Primer (Tolstoy)
See *Azbuka*
"Primer amor" (Pardo Bazán) **189**:227
"Primer aniversario" (García Lorca) **181**:183
"Primer Class" (Bishop) **121**:26
A Primer of French Literature (Saintsbury) **31**:228
"A Primer of the Daily Round" (Nemerov) **124**:182, 274-75
Primer romancero gitano (García Lorca) **1**:309-10, 313-15, 317-20; **7**:291-93, 297-300; **49**:69, 77-8, 80, 82, 85, 89, 92, 95-9, 111-13, 116, 119; **181**:25, 27, 63, 80, 90-91; 182, 191, 197-98, 216, 220-21, 223-24, 228-29, 235-36, 238, 252, 272-74, 277-78, 281-82
"Primera invitación a los amigos" (Huidobro) **31**:133
Primeras canciones (García Lorca) **1**:312; **49**:91; **181**:26, 64, 93
Las primeras letras de Leopoldo Lugones (Lugones) **15**:294
Primeras poesias (Jiménez) **183**:298
Primeros libros de poesía (Jiménez) **183**:289-90
Primeros poemas (Villaurrutia) **80**:499
Primi poemetti (Pascoli) **45**:149
The Primitive (Himes) **139**:244, 247-50, 252-53, 312, 320
Primitive (Oppen) **107**:294-95, 306, 334, 337, 355-56
Primitive Art (Boas) **56**:63, 68-69, 98
"A Primitive Like an Orb" (Stevens) **3**:454, 478; **12**:387; **45**:292, 295-96, 300, 347
Primitive Mythology (Campbell)
See *The Masks of God: Primitive Mythology*
"Primo amore" (Pavese) **3**:340
Primo vere (D'Annunzio) **6**:133, 136; **40**:13, 36-7
"The Primrose Dance: Tivoli" (Symons) **11**:445
"The Prince" (Jarrell) **177**:145-46, 177
"Prince Alberic and the Snake Lady" (Lee) **5**:319
The Prince and Betty (Wodehouse) **108**:369, 371, 373
The Prince and the Pauper (Twain) **6**:455, 457, 462, 466, 471, 476, 480; **12**:431, 436; **36**:352, 369, 379-80, 402,409; **48**:327-37, 339-52, 355-61; **59**:168, 170, 172, 182, 203; **161**:217, 236, 242; **185**:307, 319
Prince Charles Edward Stuart (Lang) **16**:270
"Prince Charlie's Weather-Vane" (Lee-Hamilton) **22**:192
Prince Deukalion (Moody) **105**:232
Le Prince Frivole (Cocteau) **119**:59, 84
"Prince Hassak's Match" (Stockton) **47**:328-29, 331
Prince Jali (Myers) **59**:123, 127-28, 131, 134, 136, 150, 154
"The Prince of Peace" (Bryan) **99**:14, 17, 22, 31, 43-44, 52, 86, 150
A Prince of Sinners (Oppenheim) **45**:132
A Prince of the Captivity (Buchan) **41**:41-2, 44-5, 54, 58, 67, 80
"The Prince of the Fairies" (Davidson) **24**:164
The Prince of the Hundred Soups (Lee) **5**:311, 314, 319
The Prince of the Mountains (Rebreanu)
See *Craişortil*
Prince Prigio (Lang) **16**:264-66, 268
Prince Reuveni (Bergelson) **81**:23
Prince Ricardo of Pantouflia: Being the Adventures of Prince Prigio's Son (Lang) **16**:264-66, 268
"The Prince Who Was a Thief" (Dreiser) **35**:71
Prince Zaleski (Shiel) **8**:358-61
La princesa Bebé (Benavente) **3**:97, 99-100
"La princesa Bizantina" (Quiroga) **20**:211
"A Princess" (Graham) **19**:104, 131
"Princess" (MacDonald) **113**:289
The Princess Aline (Davis) **24**:200, 202-03
The Princess and Curdie (MacDonald) **9**:290, 294, 298, 300, 302, 305-06, 311; **113**:200, 202, 205, 212, 214, 245-47, 249-52, 259-61, 268, 279, 285-86, 288, 290-91, 302, 305
The Princess and the Butterfly (Pinero) **32**:389, 398, 405, 413, 415
The Princess and the Goblin (MacDonald) **9**:289-90, 292, 294-95, 298-300, 305-06; **113**:200, 212, 214-15, 245-47, 249-52, 259, 261-62, 266, 268-69, 279-80, 283, 286, 288, 290, 297, 301-02, 305, 328
The Princess Casamassima (James) **2**:255, 269-70; **11**:325, 327-29, 336-38, 342; **24**:343; **47**:158-59, 177, 180, 183-85, 205, 208; **171**:155
The Princess Far-Away (Rostand)
See *La princesse lointaine*
Princess Fish (Raabe)
See *Prinzessin Fisch*
Princess Ida; or, Castle Adamant: A Respectable Operatic Per-version of Tennyson's "Princess" (Gilbert) **3**:214, 216-17
The Princess Maleine (Maeterlinck)
See *La princesse Maleine*
"Princess Mymra" (Remizov)
See "Tsarevna Mymra"
Princess Napraxine (Ouida) **43**:352-54, 358, 366-67
The Princess Nobody (Lang) **16**:264
"The Princess of All Lands" (Kirk) **119**:283, 285, 340, 343
The Princess of All Lands (Kirk) **119**:280, 283-84, 291-92, 334, 337-38
"A Princess of Egypt" (Marquis) **7**:448
"The Princess of Kingdom Gone" (Coppard) **5**:175
A Princess of Mars (Burroughs) **2**:77, 80; **32**:56-8, 63-9
"The Princess of the Golden Isles" (Saltus) **8**:346
"The Princess of the Sun" (Saltus) **8**:346
The Princess Priscilla's Fortnight (Elizabeth) **41**:122-23
Princess Russalka (Wedekind)
See *Fürstin Russalka*
The Princess Who Liked Cherry Pie (Tey) **14**:459
The Princess Yang (Mizoguchi)
See *Yokihi*
The Princess Yang Kwei Fei (Mizoguchi)
See *Yokihi*
The Princess Zoubaroff (Firbank) **1**:227
La princesse des tenebres (Vallette) **67**:302-6
La princesse lointaine (Rostand) **6**:372-78, 380; **37**:283, 286-88, 290-91, 293, 295-99, 303-04
La princesse Maleine (Maeterlinck) **3**:317, 319, 325
La princesse Phénissa (Gourmont) **17**:130-31
"Princeton" (Fitzgerald) **157**:84
"Princeton for the Nation's Service" (Wilson) **79**:529
Principia Ethica (Moore) **89**:176, 181, 204-5, 209, 213-5, 217, 225-6, 240, 251-2, 254, 269, 277-9
Principia Mathematica (Whitehead) **97**:196-97, 210, 238, 290
Principio (Sá-Carneiro) **83**:405
"Los principios de moral" (Lugones) **15**:292
The Principle of Relativity (Einstein) **65**:91, 97-8
The Principle of Relativity (Whitehead) **97**:197
"The Principles of a Liberal Social Order" (Hayek) **109**:205
The Principles of Art (Collingwood) **67**:97, 124-25, 127, 138-41, 151, 156, 171-73, 175, 178, 180-81, 194
The Principles of Nationalities (Zangwill) **16**:461
The Principles of Poetry (Hagiwara)
See *Shi no genri*
The Principles of Psychology (James) **15**:139, 142, 178-80, 183-86, 188, 190, 192; **32**:332, 334, 338-40, 343, 347, 350-51, 359-63
"Principles of Research" (Einstein) **65**:73
The Principles of Scientific Management (Taylor) **76**:337, 350, 359, 361, 379, 382, 384, 386, 394-95, 406, 409-12, 419, 421-23, 427
The Principles of Teaching (Thorndike) **107**:417-18, 420
"Prinkin' Leddie" (Wylie) **8**:521
The Print of My Remembrance (Thomas) **97**:140
"Print Shop" (Twain) **185**:243-44, 258, 266, 306
"Printemps" (Éluard) **41**:158
Printemps (Kandinsky) **92**:50
Le printemps 71 (Adamov) **189**:15, 20, 31, 37-9, 49-54, 59
"Printemps et cinématographe mêlés" (Jacob) **6**:198-99
"Printemps: Journal d'un convalescent" (Zola) **21**:456
Prinzen aus Genieland (Herzl) **36**:132

Prinzessin Fisch (Raabe) **45**:167, 176-77, 179, 196, 199
"Případ dra Mejzlíka" (Čapek) **37**:49
"Případ Selvinuv" (Čapek) **37**:49
"Pripadok" (Chekhov) **3**:159; **10**:107
"Priscilla" (Calvino) **183**:63-64, 66, 69, 227
"Prishchepa" (Babel) **2**:27; **13**:21; **171**:30, 73, 75, 89
"Prism" (Merrill) **173**:257
Le prisme (Sully Prudhomme) **31**:306
Prismen (Adorno) **111**:49-50, 53, 160, 175, 182-83
Prisms (Adorno)
See *Prismen*
"Prison Bound" (Bonner) **179**:32, 42
"Prison Mass" (Himes) **139**:326
Prison Memoirs (Ramos)
See *Memórias do cárcere*
"A Prisoner" (Baker) **3**:9
"The Prisoner" (Douglas) **40**:63-5, 85, 89
"Prisoner" (Parker) **143**:326
Prisoner (p'Bitek)
See *Song of Prisoner*
"Prisoner and Death" (Toller)
See "Gefangener und Tod"
"Prisoner at a Desk" (Sarton) **120**:318
Prisoner in Fairyland: The Book That "Uncle Paul" Wrote (Blackwood) **5**:70-1
Prisoner of Grace (Cary) **1**:140, 147-48; **29**:68-9, 73, 76-8, 92, 96-9, 107, 109; **196**:18, 138, 159, 162, 164-67, 169, 175, 177-79, 203
The Prisoner of Love (Genet)
See *Un captif amoureux*
"The Prisoner of the Caucasus" (Tolstoy) **79**:394, 421
"Prisoner of the Sands" (Saint-Exupéry) **2**:516
The Prisoner of Zenda (Hope) **83**:164-6, 169-71, 173-8, 181-2
"A Prisoner Shakes Hands with Death" (Toller)
See "Gefangener reicht dem Tod die Hand"
The Prisoner Who Sang (Bojer)
See *Fangen som sang*
Prisoners (Molnár)
See *Rabock*
The Prisoners of Hartling (Beresford) **81**:9
"The Prisoners of the Pitcher-Plant" (Roberts) **8**:323
The Prisoners' Poems (Toller)
See *Gedichte der Gefangenen*
"The Prisoners' Songs" (Toller)
See "Lieder der Gefangenen"
La prisonnière (Proust) **7**:549; **33**:258, 272-73, 287; **161**:125, 127, 131, 163, 200
"Les Prisons imaginaires" (Yourcenar) **193**:270
Prisons, Politics and Punishments (Carpenter) **88**:72
"Privacy as a Subject of Photography" (Morris) **107**:175, 189
"A Private" (Thomas) **10**:463
"Private Eye" (Kuttner) **10**:276
"The Private Eye" (Nemerov) **124**:251
"A Private History of a Campaign That Failed" (Twain) **6**:466; **19**:385-86; **161**:276
Private Inquiry (Upward) **85**:380
"Private Jones" (Lewis) **3**:285, 288
The Private Life of an Eminent Politician (Rod)
See *La vie privée de Michel Teissier*
The Private Life of Helen of Troy (Erskine) **84**:158-9, 161-7, 183
Private Lives of Chinese Scholars (Liu)
See *Ju lin Wai Shih*
A Private Mythology (Sarton) **120**:260, 265-67, 269, 303-04
"A Private Mythology-I" (Sarton) **120**:260
"A Private Mythology-II" (Sarton) **120**:260
The Private Papers of Henry Ryecroft (Gissing) **3**:224-26, 230, 232-33, 236-37; **24**:218, 222, 226-27, 230, 249; **47**:123, 137-38
"Private Properties" (Carpenter) **88**:98
Private Theatricals (Howells) **7**:383; **17**:189
The Private Tutor (Bradford) **36**:63
Private View (de la Mare) **4**:81
The Privateer (Tey) **14**:450, 460
"The Private's Story" (Crane) **11**:166
Privy Seal: His Last Venture (Ford) **172**:4, 9, 25
"The Prize" (Muir) **87**:176
"Pro aris" (Rolland) **23**:255
Pro aris et focis (Davis) **6**:154
Pro Domo (Zuckmayer) **191**:280, 283, 288-89
Pro domo et mundo (Kraus) **5**:291
"Pro domo suo" (Bryusov) **10**:81
"Pro eto" (Mayakovski) **18**:257-58
"Pro patria" (Drummond) **25**:145
Pro patria (Sender)
See *Iman*
"Pro rege nostro" (Henley) **8**:106
Das Problem des Homosexualitat (Adler) **61**:11
A Problem in Greek Ethics (Carpenter) **88**:143
"The Problem of Cell Thirteen" (Futrelle) **19**:91-3, 95-7
The Problem of Cell Thirteen (Futrelle)
See *The Thinking Machine*
"Problem of Consciousness" (Nishida)
See "Ishiki no mondai"
"The problem of content, material, and form in verbal art" (Bakhtin) **160**:214
The Problem of Homosexuality (Adler)
See *Das Problem des Homosexualitat*
"The Problem of Increasing Human Energy" (Tesla) **88**:287, 317
"The Problem of Japenese Culture" (Nishida)
See "Nihon bunka no mondai"
Problem of Knowledge (Cassirer) **61**:63
"A Problem of Life" (Bjoernson) **7**:103
"The Problem of Man" (Haeckel) **83**:154
"The Problem of Minority Groups" (Wirth) **92**:372
"The Problem of Old Harjo" (Oskison) **35**:280-81
"The Problem of Our Laws" (Kafka)
See "Zur Frage unserer Gesetze"
The Problem of Rebirth (Aurobindo) **63**:21
"The Problem of Sociology" (Simmel) **64**:354, 359
The Problem of Sovereignty (Laski) **79**:76-7, 104
"The Problem of Space, Ether, and the Field of Physics" (Einstein) **65**:70
The Problem of Style (Murry) **16**:347, 348, 351, 355, 358
"The Problem of the Stolen Rubens" (Futrelle) **19**:96
"The Problem of Unemployment" (Keynes) **64**:244
El problema religioso en Méjico (Sender) **136**:209
Probleme der Lyrik (Benn) **3**:111
Probleme der Seschichtsphilosophie (Simmel) **64**:312, 314, 338, 354, 357
Probleme der Sozialphilosphie (Michels) **88**:150
Le problème du style (Gourmont) **17**:126-27, 130, 138, 142-43, 148, 150, 155
"Probleme, Probleme" (Bachmann) **192**:78, 80-82
Problemi di estetica e contributi all storia dell' estetica italiana (Croce) **37**:115-16, 119, 124
Problems in Social Philosophy (Michels)
See *Probleme der Sozialphilosphie*
"The Problems of Catholic Writers" (Endo) **152**:167
Problems of Dostoevsky's Art (Bakhtin)
See *Problemy poetiki Dostoevskogo*
Problems of Dostoevsky's Poetics (Bakhtin)
See *Problemy poetiki Dostoevskogo*
"The Problems of Islam" (Andreas-Salome) **56**:46
Problems of Leninism (Stalin)
See *Leninism*
"The Problems of Marriage" (Horney) **71**:233-235
"Problems of Minority Groups in the United States" (Wirth) **92**:377
Problems of Neurosis: A Book of Case Histories (Adler) **61**:32
Problems of Russian Religious Consciousness (Berdyaev) **67**:24
Problems of Staple Production in Canada (Innis) **77**:337
"The Problems of Surrealism" (Bataille) **155**:94, 113-14
Problems of the Philosophy of History (Simmel)
See *Probleme der Seschichtsphilosophie*
"Problems, Problems" (Bachmann)
See "Probleme, Probleme"
Problemy poetiki Dostoevskogo (Bakhtin) **160**:121, 129-30, 132-33, 135, 139, 183, 196, 198
"Probuzhdenie" (Babel) **2**:28; **13**:26, 35; **171**:78, 94
"Proč nejsem komunistou" (Čapek) **37**:59; **192**:189, 213, 235
Le Proces de Gilles de Rais (Bataille) **155**:92, 95, 109
"Procès de l'inspiration" (Cocteau) **119**:76
Le proces de Socrate (Sorel) **91**:193, 205, 209, 213-4, 233, 291, 295, 321, 329
"Procesión" (García Lorca) **181**:199
Process and Reality (Whitehead) **97**:211, 214, 219-20, 237-38, 241-42, 271, 279-82,284-85, 287-88, 296-98, 300-02, 346, 348, 356
"A Process in the Weather of the Heart" (Thomas) **45**:361
The Process of Real Freedom (Cary) **29**:65
"Procession of the Flowers" (Higginson) **36**:175
A Procession of the People (Bojer)
See *Et folketog*
"Processional" (Merrill) **173**:183
Processions (Gibran) **9**:90-1
"Procházky" (Nezval) **44**:247
"Prochožij" (Zabolotsky) **52**:378
Le procuateur de Judée (France) **9**:47-8, 52-4
The Procurator of Judea (France)
See *Le procuateur de Judée*
The Prodigal (Foote) **108**:12
The Prodigal Parents (Lewis) **4**:251; **13**:350; **23**:136
"The Prodigal Son" (Bishop) **121**:21-2, 72-4
"The Prodigal Son" (Gumilev)
See "Bludnyj syn"
"The Prodigal Son" (Johnson) **19**:220; **175**:256
"The Prodigal Son" (White) **176**:196, 218, 243, 250, 310
The Prodigal Son (Caine) **97**:3, 7
"Prodigals" (Dobson) **79**:8
"Proditoriamente" (Svevo) **2**:541; **35**:345
"Product" (Oppen) **107**:308
"Proem" (Buchanan) **107**:44
"Proem" (Jozsef) **22**:160
"Proem" (Miyazawa) **76**:281
"Proem: To Brooklyn Bridge" (Crane) **5**:187-88; **80**:81, 83, 87, 93, 97, 103, 126, 139-40, 143-4, 157, 162, 172, 176, 187
Proemio (D'Annunzio) **40**:11
Profane Proses (Darío)
See *Prosas profanas, y otros poemas*
Le professeur Taranne (Adamov) **189**:8-10, 13, 24, 27, 41-2, 46-8, 57-8
"The Professional Instinct" (Glasgow) **7**:343
"Professional Youth" (Parker) **143**:282
"Professions for Women" (Woolf) **56**:410; **128**:354
The Professor (Kielland)
See *Professoren*
"The Professor and the Mermaid" (Lampedusa) **13**:293, 295
Professor Bernhardi (Schnitzler) **4**:387-88, 390, 397-98, 401
"Professor Bingo's Snuff" (Chandler) **179**:129

"The Professor Goes in for Sweetness and Light" (Parker) **143**:298-99, 301, 303
"Professor Pownall's Oversight" (Wakefield) **120**:336, 345, 347
Professor Unrat (Mann) **9**:322-25, 327, 329, 331
Professoren (Kielland) **5**:279
The Professor's House (Cather) **1**:153-54, 156-58, 163; **11**:95, 97-9, 102, 107, 109, 111; **31**:26-7, 48-9, 54; **99**:219-20, 241, 245, 252-53, 268, 274-75, 281; **132**:123, 125-26, 134, 137-38, 141, 148-49, 154; **152**:8, 16, 42, 68
"Professors in War-Time" (Sapir) **108**:249
"The Professor's Sister" (Hawthorne) **25**:249
"The Profile" (Cather) **132**:123, 129
"Profit" (Platonov) **14**:409
"Profit from My Experience" (Zweig) **17**:458
"The Profitable Reading of Fiction" (Hardy) **48**:51; **143**:77
Profits, Interest, and Investment (Hayek) **109**:200
The Profligate (Pinero) **32**:387-89, 393, 397-401, 412-13
The profound rose (Borges)
See *La rosa profunda*
"De profundis" (García Lorca) **181**:192
De Profundis (Przybyszewski) **36**:290
"Un progetto di pubblico" (Calvino) **183**:103
A Program for Conservatives (Kirk) **119**:253, 255-56, 261, 266, 275
"Program of the Coming Philosophy" (Benjamin) **39**:4
"Progress" (Graham) **19**:104, 116, 129, 135
"Progress" (Rilke)
See "Fortschritt"
Progress and Power (Becker) **63**:81-2, 92, 99, 114-15
"The Progress of Poesy" (Hardy) **143**:154
"The Progress of the Gold Coast Native" (Casely-Hayford) **24**:132
"Progress or Return?" (Strauss) **141**:264, 268
"Progress Reached Our Valley" (Arnow) **196**:95
"The Progressive" (Vazov) **25**:454
Lo prohibido (Pérez Galdós) **27**:250, 252, 257, 285
"La prohibition de l'inceste et ses origines" (Durkheim) **55**:91
La proie et l'ombre (Roumain) **19**:331, 338-43, 345
Proiskhozhdenie mastera (Platonov) **14**:409, 423
"Proiskhozhdeniye" (Bagritsky) **60**:17
"Project of Novel" (James) **171**:129, 132, 159, 173
"Projection" (Nemerov) **124**:155, 178-79, 186, 254
Prokleta avlija (Andrić) **135**:7, 10, 25, 29, 31-33, 35-37, 39-41, 43, 51-54, 74, 77, 92
Prolegomena (Jarry) **147**:330
"Prolegomena to an Apology for Pragmatism" (Peirce) **81**:199-200
Prolegomena zur reinen Logik (Husserl) **100**:9, 39
"The Proletarian at the Trap Drum" (Saroyan) **137**:181
"Prolog" (Bryusov)
See "Gasnut rozovye kraski"
"Prolog" (Herbert) **168**:43
"Prolog for a Monument to Goldoni" (Giacosa) **7**:309
"Prolog zum Hörspiel" (Weiss) **152**:285
Prologal Act (Jarry) **147**:332
"Prólogo" (García Lorca) **181**:122
"Prólogo" (Jiménez) **183**:322-28
"Prólogo" (Unamuno) **148**:257, 307
"Prólogo y notas previas a Mis poemas mejores" (Aleixandre) **113**:66, 69
"Prologue" (Henley) **8**:110
"Prologue" (Herbert)
See "Prolog"
"Prologue" (Mann) **168**:190
"Prologue" (Thomas)
See "Author's Prologue"
"Prologue to a Life" (West) **108**:307, 310
"Prologue to a Saga" (Parker) **143**:324-25
"Prologue to an Adventure" (Thomas) **45**:412; **105**:297, 299, 329, 335, 351
A Prologue to "King Lear," Marshall, and The Violet (Molnár)
See *Szinház: Előjáték Lear Királyhoz, Marshall, Az ibolya*
The Prologue to Life (Sikelianos) **39**:404, 418
"Prologue to Lyrical Life" (Sikelianos) **39**:412-13, 416-18
"Prologue to the Radio Play" (Weiss)
See "Prolog zum Hörspiel"
"Prologue to Women in Love" (Lawrence) **93**:68
Prologues and Addresses-of-Mourning (Hofmannsthal) **11**:294
"The Prologues and Epilogues" (Dobson) **79**:20
"Prologues to What Is Possible" (Stevens) **3**:450; **45**:280, 312, 315
"Prolongación de paisaje" (Jiménez) **183**:258, 330
"Prolongation of the Landscape" (Jiménez)
See "Prolongación de paisaje"
Proluky (Hrabal) **155**:159, 165
"Promenade" (Proust) **161**:172
Promenade à cheval (Kandinsky) **92**:48
Promenade gracieuse (Kandinsky) **92**:50
Promenades littéraires (Gourmont) **17**:127, 130, 136, 138, 145-46, 148-50, 158
Promenades of an Impressionists (Huneker) **65**:170, 188, 217
Promenades philosophiques (Gourmont) **17**:127, 130, 136
"La promesse du merle" (Bosschere) **19**:58-9
Le Prométhée mal enchaîné (Gide) **5**:215, 235; **12**:171-72, 178; **36**:108-9; **177**:34, 46
"Prometheus" (Muir) **87**:230
Prometheus (Devkota) **23**:48, 50-2
Prometheus and Epimetheus (Spitteler)
See *Prometheus und Epimetheus*
Prometheus der Dulder (Spitteler) **12**:340, 349-50
Prometheus Illbound (Gide)
See *Le Prométhée mal enchaîné*
Prometheus Misbound (Gide)
See *Le Prométhée mal enchaîné*
"Prometheus' Punishment" (Čapek) **37**:45; **192**:185
Prometheus the Firegiver (Bridges) **1**:124, 130, 132
"Prometheus Unbound" (Yeats) **93**:342
Prometheus und Epimetheus (Spitteler) **12**:335-39, 342, 347-50, 352
Promethidenlos (Hauptmann) **4**:205
Die Prominenten (Bernhard)
See *Die Berühmten*
"Promise" (Baker) **3**:6
"Promise!" (Guro)
See "Obeschaite!"
"The Promise" (Toomer) **172**:279-80
"Promise and Fulfillment" (Dunbar) **12**:106
The Promise of Air (Blackwood) **5**:72
"The Promised Land" (Fisher) **11**:210, 212, 214
The Promised Land (Reymont)
See *Ziemia obiecana*
"The Promisers" (Owen) **5**:374
"Promotion" (Guest) **95**:207
"Un pronóstico cumplido" (Palma) **29**:262
Pronounced Rose (Kandinsky) **92**:36
"Proof of an External World" (Moore) **89**:195, 244
"Proof of the Pudding" (Henry) **19**:183
"Proof Positive" (Čapek) **37**:49
"Proofs of Holy Writ" (Kipling) **8**:205
Propeller Island (Verne)
See *L'Ile à hélice*
A Proper Impropriety (Thomas) **97**:139
"Property Under Socialism" (Wallas) **91**:374, 376
"The Prophet" (Bosman) **49**:19-23, 29
"The Prophet" (Lawrence) **93**:44
"Prophet" (Pickthall) **21**:254
The Prophet (Asch)
See *Ha-navi*
The Prophet (Gibran) **1**:325-29; **9**:82-7, 89-94
"The Prophet and the Country" (Kipling) **8**:202
"The Prophet Lost in the Hills at Evening" (Belloc) **18**:41
The Prophet of Berkeley Square: A Tragic Extravaganza (Hichens) **64**:128
A Prophet of Joy (Bradford) **36**:62-3
The Prophet of the Great Smoky Mountains (Murfree) **135**:216-17, 219, 222-23, 225, 227, 229-31, 233, 236-37
The Prophet of the Russian Revolution (Merezhkovsky) **29**:231
The Prophet Unarmed (Trotsky) **22**:376
"Propheta gentium" (Johnson) **19**:243
"Prophetic Soul" (Parker) **143**:317, 321
"Prophets, Ancient and Modern" (Housman) **7**:359
"Prophets for a New Day" (Walker) **129**:274, 306
Prophets for a New Day (Walker) **129**:273-74, 276, 291, 305, 318
"Die Prophezeiung an Alexander" (Werfel) **8**:478
La propia estimación (Benavente) **3**:94
"Propos confus" (Anouilh) **195**:53
Les propos d'Alain (Alain) **41**:3
A propos de l'Assommoir (Rod) **52**:309
Propos de littérature (Alain) **41**:27
"Propos déplaisants" (Anouilh) **195**:53
Propos d'exil (Loti) **11**:353
"A Propos of Lady Chatterley's Lover" (Lawrence) **48**:55, 102, 108, 112, 122, 130, 132, 149
"Propos sans suite" (Roumain) **19**:340, 345
Propos sur le bonheur (Alain) **41**:3, 21-2, 29
Propos sur le christianisme (Alain) **41**:3
Propos sur l'éducation (Alain) **41**:9, 29
"The Proposal" (Chekhov)
See *Predlozhenie*
"Propositions" (Bataille) **155**:88
"Propositions Applicable to Themselves" (McTaggart) **105**:197
"Prorok" (Olesha) **136**:155
Die Prosa (Barlach) **84**:116
Prosa (Bernhard) **165**:122
"Prosa fetida" (Campana) **20**:83
Prosa II (Hofmannsthal) **11**:308
Prosas profanas, y otros poemas (Darío) **4**:57-63, 65
Prosas profanos, and Other Poems (Darío)
See *Prosas profanas, y otros poemas*
"Proščanie" (Zabolotsky) **52**:367
Prose (Agee)
See *The Collected Short Prose of James Agee*
"Prose and Anticombinatorics" (Calvino) **183**:65
"Prose and Rhyme" (Dobson)
See "Ballade of Prose and Rhyme"
La Prose du monde (Merleau-Ponty) **156**:120, 174, 176, 178-80, 184-85, 209-10
The Prose of Christopher Brennan (Brennan) **17**:46
"Prose of Departure" (Merrill) **173**:230
The Prose of Osip Mandelstam: The Noise of Time. Theodosia. The Egyptian Stamp (Mandelstam) **6**:259
The Prose of Rupert Brooke (Brooke) **7**:126
The Prose of the World (Merleau-Ponty)
See *La Prose du monde*
Prose Papers (Drinkwater) **57**:139, 142
"The Prose Poem of Roast Meat" (Huysmans) **69**:25
"Prosëlki" (Pilnyak) **23**:211
"Prosélyte à prix fixe" (Tzara) **168**:322
Proserpina (Ruskin) **20**:312-15; **63**:251, 254
Proserpine (Gide) **177**:107

Proses moroses (Gourmont) **17**:127
"A Prospect of the Sea" (Thomas) **45**:390, 409, 412-13; **105**:297, 299, 301, 320, 325-29, 338, 353
A Prospect of the Sea and Other Stories and Prose Writings (Thomas) **105**:318-20, 322, 325, 348-49, 352-53
"The Prospector" (Service) **15**:404
The Prospector (Connor) **31**:106-11, 114, 116
A Prospectus on Reasoning (Peirce) **81**:291
"Prosperity" (Coleridge) **73**:9
"The Prosperity of England. Mr. Keynes's Reassuring Picture" (Keynes) **64**:244
"The Protected" (Remizov)
See "Pokrovennaia"
"Protect-Your-Men" (Williams) **89**:396
Protée (Claudel) **10**:123, 127
"A Protégée of Jack Hamlin's" (Harte) **25**:203
"Protégeons l'armée" (Jarry) **147**:277
Protesilaj umeršij (Bryusov) **10**:84
"Protest" (Cullen) **37**:164
The Protestant Ethic and the Spirit of Capitalism (Weber)
See *Die protestantische Ethik und der "Geist" des Kaptialismus*
"The Protestant Reformation" (Chambers) **129**:48
Die protestantische Ethik und der "Geist" des Kaptialismus (Weber) **69**:293, 318, 324-25, 327-28, 333-35, 355-57, 365, 378
"Protestations" (Stringer) **37**:329
"Proteus" (Buchanan) **107**:14
"Protiv verkhoglyadstva" (Fadeyev) **53**:58, 63, 65
"Protocols" (Jarrell) **177**:147, 177, 195, 222, 258
Protractatus (Wittgenstein) **59**:289
Proud Destiny (Feuchtwanger)
See *Waffen für Amerika*
"Proud Error" (Popa) **167**:153
"The Proud Farmer" (Lindsay) **17**:240
"The Proud Heart" (Cullen) **37**:165
The Proud Sheriff (Rhodes) **53**:317, 319, 327, 330
"Proud Songsters" (Hardy) **10**:225; **143**:144-45
"Proust" (Merrill) **173**:257
Proust (Beckett) **145**:84-88, 114, 151
Proust and Signs (Deleuze)
See *Marcel Proust et les signes*
"Proust in pieces" (Beckett) **145**:87
Provence (Ford) **15**:87; **57**:283
Provence (Giono) **124**:106
"A Provence Rose" (Ouida) **43**:350
Proverbs in Porcelain (Dobson) **79**:8, 11, 22, 27, 36-7
Provětroň (Čapek) **6**:86-8, 91; **37**:50, 54, 59-60; **192**:176, 185, 22
"Providence" (Lovecraft) **4**:266
"A Providential Intimation" (Bierce) **44**:45
"A Providential Match" (Cahan) **71**:12, 24-26, 37, 39-40, 68, 71, 86-88
"The Provider" (Guiney) **41**:209
The Province of the Human (Canetti)
See *Die Provinz des Menschen: Aufzeichnungen, 1942-1972*
"A Provincial Capital of Mexico" (Foote) **108**:26
The Provincial Lady in War-Time (Delafield) **61**:129-31, 136
A Provincial Tale (Zamyatin)
See *Uezdnoe*
Provinciales (Giraudoux) **2**:159, 163; **7**:324-25
The Provincials (Zamyatin)
See *Uezdnoe*
Die Provinz des Menschen: Aufzeichnungen, 1942-1972 (Canetti) **157**:37, 59, 62, 77, 80, 86-87, 96-98
"Provoda" (Tsvetaeva) **35**:399-400, 404
La próxima (Huidobro) **31**:123, 138
Proza (Tsvetaeva) **35**:383
Der Prozess (Kafka) **2**:290, 294-96, 300, 303, 306-07; **6**:219-20, 224-28; **13**:261, 263, 275; **29**:167-222; **47**:211-12, 222-24, 226, 244-47, 255, 257-58, 262; **53**:203, 205, 232; 112; **179**:240, 242-44, 247-51, 253-58, 267, 272, 275, 286, 289-90, 292, 296, 300-303, 311, 314, 322-23, 325, 327-28
Der Prozess (Pabst) **127**:354, 363
"Die Prozession" (Werfel) **8**:476
Prud (Remizov) **27**:333, 338, 341, 346, 349
The Prude's Progress (Jerome) **23**:77
Die Prüfung der Seele (Steiner) **13**:438, 443, 457
Prunella (Housman) **7**:353
"Pruning the Orchard" (Sarton) **120**:269, 305
"The Prussian Officer" (Lawrence) **9**:220
The Prussian Officer, and Other Stories (Lawrence) **2**:343, 354
"Przeczucia eschatologiczne Pana Cogito" (Herbert) **168**:27
"Przestanie" (Herbert) **168**:10, 25-26, 40, 48
"Przygoda Stasia" (Prus) **48**:156, 162, 182
"Przyszto do glowy, Stanelo w glowie" (Herbert) **168**:40
"Psalm" (Bachmann) **192**:19
"A Psalm" (Bulgakov) **16**:85
"Psalm" (Ginsberg) **120**:8
"Psalm" (Ivanov) **33**:138-39
"Psalm" (Oppen) **107**:256, 263, 304, 348
"Psalm" (Trakl) **5**:462-63
"Psalm I" (Ginsberg) **120**:77
"Psalm for Man's Voice" (Babits)
See "Zsoltár férfihangra"
"Psalm III" (Ginsberg) **120**:8, 12
"Psalm IV" (Ginsberg) **120**:35
"Psalm of Life" (Forten) **16**:150
A Psalm of Montreal (Butler) **33**:59
The Psalmody of Persia (Iqbal)
See *Zabur-i ajam*
Psalms and Songs (Lowry) **6**:254
The Psalms for the Common Reader (Chase) **124**:29
"Psalms of Rapture" (Radnóti) **16**:418
"Psalmul leprului" (Fondane) **159**:248
"The Pseudo-Believer" (Lewis) **104**:188
Psicología de Don Quijote y el quijotismo (Ramoacn y Cajal) **93**:146
Psikheya (Tsvetaeva) **35**:410
"Psikhologiia tvorchestva" (Zamyatin) **37**:429
Psmith, Journalist (Wodehouse) **108**:341, 352-53
La Psychanalyse du feu (Bachelard) **128**:3, 5, 17, 20-34, 36, 40, 44, 46-7, 58, 62-6, 68-70, 78, 80, 90, 92
"Psychanalyse et peinture" (Lyotard) **103**:229
"Psyche" (Hippius) **9**:155, 158
Psyche (Couperus) **15**:46
Psyche (De Lisser) **12**:95
Psyche (Tsvetaeva)
See *Psikheya*
"Psyche and the Pskyscraper" (Henry) **1**:352; **19**:179
"Psyche's Lament" (Chopin) **127**:28
Psyche's Task: A Discourse Concerning the Influence of Superstition on the Growth of Institutions (Frazer) **32**:203, 206, 229
"The Psychiatrist" (Machado de Assis) **10**:289, 306
"A Psychical Invasion" (Blackwood) **5**:73, 78
"The Psychical Mallards" (Benson) **27**:19
"Psychical Research" (Brooke) **7**:124
"The Psychical Secretion of the Salivary Glands (Complex Nervous Phenomena in the Work of the Salivary Glands)" (Pavlov) **91**:150
Psychoanalysis and the Unconscious (Lawrence) **2**:347, 359; **9**:215-16; **16**:292; **61**:207, 215, 221-3, 225; **93**:18, 84, 110
"Psycho-Analysis in Relation to Sex" (Ellis) **14**:112
Psychoanalysis of Fire (Bachelard)
See *La Psychanalyse du feu*
"The Psychoanalyzed Girl" (McAlmon) **97**:114, 116, 118, 120
"The Psychogenesis of a Case of Homosexuality in a Woman" (Freud)
See "Über die Psychogenese eines Falles von Weiblicher Homosexualität"
"Psychological and Ethnological Studies on Music" (Simmel)
See "Psychologische und Ethnologische Studien uber Musik"
"Psychological Peculiarities of the Prophets" (Weber) **69**:331
"Psychological reality of the phoneme" (Sapir) **108**:257
"A Psychological Shipwreck" (Bierce) **44**:45
"The Psychological Structure of Fascism" (Bataille) **155**:93, 106
"Psychological Studies of Elementary Logic" (Husserl) **100**:38
"Psychological Types in the Cultures of the Southwest" (Benedict) **60**:107, 139, 147, 150-51
"Psychologie nouvelle" (Gourmont) **17**:138
"Psychologische und Ethnologische Studien uber Musik" (Simmel) **64**:332, 339-40
"Psychology" (Mansfield) **2**:458; **8**:275, 280; **39**:293; **164**:229, 247-48, 322
Psychology (Dewey) **95**:58, 131
Psychology and the Soul (Rank)
See *Seelenglaube und Psychologie*
"Psychology as Philosophic Method" (Dewey) **95**:95
The Psychology of Arithmetic (Thorndike) **107**:378
"The Psychology of Belief" (James) **32**:362
"The Psychology of Creativity" (Zamyatin)
See "Psikhologiia tvorchestva"
The Psychology of Culture (Sapir) **108**:285-86
"The Psychology of Descartes" (Thorndike) **107**:394
"The Psychology of Kant" (Dewey) **95**:58
"The Psychology of Myth" (Campbell) **140**:139
The Psychology of Social Development (Aurobindo)
See *The Human Cycle*
"The Psychology of the Half-Educated Man" (Thorndike) **107**:409
The Psychology of Wants, Interests, and Attitudes (Thorndike) **107**:379
"El psychón" (Lugones) **15**:293
"Psychopathic Characters on the Stage" (Freud) **52**:131
"The Psychophant" (Levi) **109**:292
"Psychopompos" (Lovecraft) **4**:265-66
"Psykologisk Literatur" (Hamsun) **49**:147
"Ptaki" (Schulz) **5**:423-24; **51**:308, 314-15
"Ptica" (Gumilev) **60**:279
"Ptichka" (Remizov) **27**:339
Ptitsy v vozdukhe (Balmont) **11**:37
"The Pub with No Beer" (Paterson) **32**:377
The Public (García Lorca)
See *El público*
The Public and Its Problems (Dewey) **95**:34, 134-5
"The Public as Art Critic" (Flecker) **43**:210-11
"The Public as Partner" (Frisch)
See "Öffentilichkeit als Partner"
Public Order (Sender)
See *O. P.: Orden público*
The Public Papers and Addresses of Franklin D. Roosevelt (Roosevelt) **93**:170, 176, 178, 180, 183, 184
The Public Papers of Woodrow Wilson (Wilson) **79**:484, 491, 496
"Public Recreation and Social Morality" (Addams) **76**:37
The Public Rose (Éluard)
See *La rose publique*
El público (García Lorca) **49**:88, 105, 117; **181**:29-31, 33-34, 41, 67, 79-81, 84, 152-53, 155-61; **197**:190, 232, 274, 280, 282
La puce à l'oreille (Feydeau) **22**:78, 93

La puchera (Pereda) **16**:363-65, 372-73, 378
Puck (Ouida) **43**:347, 354, 364, 371, 375
"Puck of Pook's Hill" (Kipling) **8**:187
Pudd'nhead Wilson (Twain)
See *The Tragedy of Pudd'nhead Wilson*
"Pueblo" (García Lorca) **181**:195-96
"Pueblo" (Villaurrutia) **80**:477
El pueblo inocente (Romero) **14**:432-34, 441-43
"El pueblo muerto" (Prado) **75**:194, 208-09, 211
Puella (Dickey) **151**:151-52, 167, 171, 173, 199
"Puella Mea" (Cummings) **137**:41
"La puerta" (Gonzalez Martinez) **72**:150
"La puerta cerrada" (Donoso) **133**:43
Pugacev (Esenin) **4**:109-10, 112
"The Pug-Nosed Fox" (Somerville & Ross) **51**:336, 348, 358
La puissance des morts (Maeterlinck) **3**:323
"Le puissance spirituelle de la matière" (Teilhard de Chardin) **9**:482
Le puits de Maule (Fondane) **159**:248
Le puits de Sainte Claire (France) **9**:40, 42
Pull Devil, Pull Baker (Benson) **17**:22, 25-6, 32
"Pull My Daisy" (Ginsberg) **120**:67, 88
"Pullman Sleeper" (Fields) **80**:258
"La pulperia" (Graham) **19**:133
"The Pulpit" (Roberts) **68**:336
Pulpit and Press (Eddy) **71**:96
The Pulse of Life (Lowndes) **12**:201
"Pulvis et umbra" (Carman) **7**:133, 141, 149
"Puñal" (García Lorca) **181**:194-95
"El puñal" (Lugones) **15**:286
Punascha (Tagore) **53**:336, 342-3
Punch and Judy and Other Essays (Baring) **8**:44
Punch, Brothers, Punch, and Other Sketches (Twain) **6**:476
Punch Vodka (Aldanov)
See *Punševaja vodka*
"Puncovaja krov'" (Kuprin) **5**:303
"Pundari" (Hearn) **9**:138
"Punishment" (Tagore)
See "Shasti"
"The Punishment of Prometheus" (Čapek)
See "Prometheus' Punishment"
"The Punishment of the Faithless Knight" (Calvino)
See "Storia dell'ingrato punito"
Punishments (Kafka) **112**:98, 122
Punkt und Linie zur Fläche (Kandinsky) **92**:25-6, 81-2, 87, 108
Punševaja vodka (Aldanov) **23**:23, 27-8
A puntes un lugareño (Romero) **14**:434, 441-43
Puntila (Brecht)
See *Herr Puntila und sein Knecht Matti*
"Puntjak" (Anwar) **22**:23
"The Pupil" (James) **24**:350; **47**:199-200, 206; **64**:165
"Pupochek" (Remizov) **27**:339
Puppet (Prus)
See *Lalka*
"The Puppet behind the Curtain" (Hedāyat)
See "Arusak-i pust-i parda"
Puppet Play (Jarry) **147**:331
The Puppet Show (Blok)
See *Balaganchik*
The Puppet Show of Memory (Baring) **8**:34, 36-7
The Puppet-Booth (Fuller) **103**:63, 65, 85, 88
"Le pur concept" (Moréas) **18**:280, 286
Le pur et l'impur (Colette)
See *Ces Plaisirs*
Purabi (Tagore) **3**:493
"Purakurichi" (Rohan) **22**:299
"Puratonikku rabu" (Shiga) **172**:202
The Purchase of the North Pole (Verne)
See *Sans dessus dessous*
The Pure and Impure (Colette)
See *Ces Plaisirs*
"Pure as the Driven Snow, or As Ye Snow So Shall Ye Sweep" (Allen) **87**:65
The Pure Evil (Dent) **72**:22
Pure Gold (Moricz)
See *Sárarany*
Pure Gold (Rölvaag)
See *To tullinger: Et billede fra ida*
"The Pure Good of Theory" (Stevens) **45**:285, 299
The Pure in Heart (Werfel)
See *Barbara; oder, Die Frömmigkeit*
"Pure Letters" (Ford) **172**:94
The Pure Theory of Capital (Hayek) **109**:196, 200-01, 208
"The Pure Theory of Money. A Reply to Dr. Hayek" (Keynes) **64**:303
"The Purgation of Christianity" (Murry) **16**:342
Purgatory (Yeats) **1**:571; **31**:412
"The purist" (Nash) **109**:357
"The Puritan" (Sarton) **120**:266
"Puritanism as a Literary Force" (Mencken) **13**:358, 383
"Pūrnimāko jaladhi" (Devkota) **23**:48-9
Purple and Fine Women (Saltus) **8**:346, 349
"Purple Anemones" (Lawrence) **93**:94
The Purple Cloud (Shiel) **8**:359-60, 362, 364
"The Purple Emperor" (Chambers) **41**:102, 113-14
The Purple Flower (Bonner) **179**:3, 6-8, 10-11, 13, 19, 30, 51-52
"Purple Grackles" (Lowell) **8**:227, 234, 237
The Purple Land (Hudson) **29**:138-40, 142, 146-49, 155
The Purple Murder Case (Van Dine) **23**:355
"The Purpose of Philosophy" (Berlin) **105**:132
"Purposely Ungrammatical Lovesong" (Parker) **143**:325
"The Purse of Aholibah" (Huneker) **65**:197
A Purse of Coppers (O'Faolain) **143**:222, 227, 273
"The Pursued" (Quiroga)
See "Los perseguidos"
"Pursuit from Under" (Dickey) **151**:90, 97, 109
"The Pursuit of Beauty" (Woolf) **43**:408
"The Pursuit of Diarmid and Grainne" (Tynan) **3**:503
"The Pursuit of the Ideal" (Berlin) **105**:89
Purumūla (Mori Ogai) **14**:382
"Purun Bhagat" (Kipling)
See "The Miracle of Purun Bhagat"
"Der purzelbaum" (Morgenstern) **8**:306
"Pushkin" (Zoshchenko) **15**:499
"Pushkin and Pugachev" (Tsvetaeva) **7**:572; **35**:414
"Pushkin and Scriabin" (Mandelstam) **6**:270
"Pus-ki-rat" (Premchand) **21**:292
"Puss-in-Boots" (Carter) **139**:47, 204, 209
Pussy, King of the Pirates (Acker) **191**:44-5, 47, 49-51, 70, 92, 102, 104, 113-16, 118-23, 129
Pustur svet (Vazov) **25**:453
"Put Alije Djerzeleza" (Andrić) **135**:8, 53, 79, 87, 92
"Put Down Two and Carry One" (Somerville & Ross) **51**:335
Put' konkvistadorov (Gumilev) **60**:260, 262, 267-70, 278
Put out of the Way (Davis) **6**:154
"Put' v Brody" (Babel) **2**:27; **171**:12, 14, 19, 24-26, 30, 37, 74-75, 78, 82-83, 85
Pūt, vējini! (Rainis) **29**:386, 393
"Puti i pereput ya" (Bryusov) **10**:83
The Putrescent Enchanter (Apollinaire)
See *L'enchanteur pourrissant*
"Putting a Town on the Map" (McAlmon) **97**:88
"Putting Literature Into the Drama" (Matthews) **95**:244
"Putting Out the Light" (Wright) **136**:302
"The Puzzle" (Nemerov) **124**:256, 273
"Puzzle" (Villaurrutia) **80**:477
The Puzzle Lock (Freeman) **21**:58
"The Puzzler" (Kipling) **8**:202
"Puzzo di cristianucci" (Papini) **22**:281
"Pygmalion" (Herzl) **36**:141
"Pygmalion" (Meynell) **6**:291
Pygmalion (Kaiser) **9**:177-78, 181, 192
Pygmalion (Shaw)
See *Pygmalion: A Romance in Five Acts*
Pygmalion: A Romance in Five Acts (Shaw) **3**:384, 399-400, 402, 406; **45**:207-65
"Pygmalion and Galatea" (Stringer) **37**:328
Pygmalion and Galatea (Gilbert) **3**:210
"Pygmalion the Sculptor" (Buchanan) **107**:14
Pyhä kevät (Leino) **24**:368
"Pyhät on pihlajat pihalla" (Leino) **24**:373
Pylon (Faulkner) **141**:113-14, 128-36; **170**:115, 128, 233
"Pyotr and Fevroniya" (Remizov)
See "Povest o Petre i Fevronii"
Pyramid petticoat (Arp) **115**:21
La pyramide humaine (Éluard) **7**:250
Pyramidenrock (Arp) **115**:3,5
The Pyre (Gumilev)
See *Koster*
"La pythie" (Valéry) **4**:491, 499; **15**:458
"The Python" (Nash) **109**:366
"Pytka" (Bryusov) **10**:81
"Qafan" (Premchand) **21**:296
"Qaziva-hi namak-i turki" (Hedāyat) **21**:75
"Qaziya-hi khar dajjal" (Hedāyat) **21**:75
Q.E.D. (Stein)
See *Things As They Are*
"Qing cheng zhi lian" (Chang) **184**:126, 128-30, 132-33, 138-39
Qingchang ru zhangchang (Chang) **184**:126
"The Quade Sense of Humor" (Heyward) **59**:92-3
Quaderni di Serafino Gubbio operatore (Pirandello)
See *Si gira*
Quaderno a cancelli (Levi) **125**:222
"Quaerendo Invenietis" (Nemerov) **124**:197, 256, 277
"Quaestio de Centauris" (Levi) **109**:293-94
"Quai d'Orléans" (Bishop) **121**:6, 61
"Quaker Hill" (Crane) **5**:186; **80**:82-4, 89, 106, 143, 147, 171-2, 186, 191, 201, 203
The Quality of Hurt (Himes) **139**:251, 269-76, 309, 311, 313, 319, 323, 328
"The Quality of Mercy" (Oskison) **35**:280
The Quality of Mercy (Howells) **7**:376, 378-79, 385, 397; **17**:178, 184
Quality Street (Barrie) **2**:43, 48; **164**:7, 63
Quand j'etais jeune (Vallette) **67**:308
Quand'ero matto (Pirandello) **29**:291
Quando si è qualcuno (Pirandello) **4**:345-46; **29**:298
"Quanto scommettiamo" (Calvino) **183**:160
"Quantum of Solace" (Fleming) **193**:208
"The Quarry" (Moody) **105**:222, 237-38, 240, 260, 272
"The Quarry" (Nemerov) **124**:153, 172
"Le quart d'une vie" (Péret) **20**:195-96
"Quartet for Prosperous Love Children" (Nash) **109**:358
Quase (Sá-Carneiro) **83**:399, 406
Quasi un racconto (Saba) **33**:374
"Les quat' saisons" (Fargue) **11**:201
Quatorze Prieres (Jammes) **75**:110-11, 114, 118
Quatrains of the Philosopher Omar Khayyam (Hedāyat) **21**:82
Quatre heures à Chatila (Genet) **128**:233
"Les quatre journées de Jean Gourdon" (Zola) **6**:569
Quatre-vingt-un chapîtres sur l'esprit et les passions (Alain) **41**:3
Qué es el budismo (Borges) **109**:35
Qué es filosofía? (Ortega y Gasset) **9**:354
"Que font les olives" (Péret) **20**:184
Que ma joie demeure (Giono) **124**:35, 37, 40, 43-6, 53, 56, 63, 65-6, 70-3, 92-3, 95-7, 99-104, 115, 124, 130
"Qué me da . . . ?" (Vallejo) **3**:533; **56**:311
"Lo que pudo no ser" (Huidobro) **31**:133
Que sais-je? (Sully Prudhomme) **31**:307
"Que se ve ser" (Jiménez) **183**:281-82, 310
Que Viva Mexico! (Eisenstein) **57**:190

"Que vlo-ve?" (Apollinaire) **51**:21, 28
A queda (Sá-Carneiro) **83**:399
The Queen and the Rebels (Betti)
See *La regina e gli insorti*
"The Queen and the Slave" (Stringer) **37**:328
Queen Christina (Strindberg)
See *Kristina*
"Queen Elizabeth's Day" (Davidson) **24**:163
Queen Kelly (Stroheim) **71**:330, 333, 340, 357, 361-365
Queen Lucia (Benson) **27**:4, 9-10
The Queen Mother and Rosamond (Swinburne) **8**:423, 432-33, 436
"Queen of Hearts" (Holly) **65**:145
Queen of Hearts (Villaurrutia) **80**:479
The Queen of Rapa Nui (Prado)
See *La reina de Rapa Nui*
Queen of Scots (Tey) **14**:451, 458-59
The Queen of the Air (Ruskin) **20**:291-92, 313; **63**:243, 307, 310, 312, 315, 320
"Queen of the Ballroom" (Holly) **65**:149
"Queen of the Black Coast" (Howard) **8**:133, 135
Queen Ortruda (Sologub) **9**:436-38
The Queen Pédauque (France)
See *La rôtisserie de la reine Pédauque*
"The Queen Remembered" (Warner) **131**:308
Queen Sheba's Ring (Haggard) **11**:241, 246, 250
Queen Tamara (Hamsun)
See *Dronning Tamara*
The Queen versus Billy (Osbourne) **93**:132
Queen Victoria (Strachey) **12**:392-93, 395-98, 400, 403-04, 406-07, 409, 412-15, 417, 419, 421
"Queen Victoria's Jubilee" (Twain) **12**:438
Queen Zixi of Ix (Baum) **7**:13, 21; **132**:80, 103-4
"Queens" (Synge) **6**:435
The Queen's Comedy: A Homeric Fragment (Bridie) **3**:134-35, 137-40
The Queen's Enemies (Dunsany) **2**:140, 143; **59**:6, 10-12, 14, 21
The Queen's Husband (Sherwood) **3**:416, 418
"The Queen's Museum" (Stockton) **47**:329
"Queens of Beauty" (Sharp) **39**:377
The Queens of Kungahälla (Lagerloef) **36**:233
The Queen's Progress: Palace Plays, second series (Housman) **7**:357
"The Queen's Rival" (Naidu) **80**:293
"The Queen's Servant" (Williams) **1**:514
"The Queen's Song" (Flecker) **43**:188, 193
The Queen's Treasure (Freeman) **21**:56
"The Queen's Twin" (Jewett) **22**:124, 130, 135, 142
"Queer" (Anderson) **24**:24, 35-7, 45, 53, 59; **123**:78, 80, 85
Queer (Burroughs) **121**:174, 178-82
"The Queer Feet" (Chesterton) **6**:100
"Queer Visitors from the Marvelous Land of Oz" (Baum) **132**:80, 83
Quei figuri di trent'anni fa (de Filippo) **127**:287
Quelques hommes (Jammes) **75**:119
"Quelques notes autour de lb millimètres" (Cocteau) **119**:76
Quelques témoignages (Bourget) **12**:74
Quer Durch (Toller) **10**:477-78
Quer pasticciaccio brutto de via Merulana (Gadda) **144**:81-85, 95-99, 101-2, 107, 117, 122-23, 128-29, 131-32, 134, 138-40, 142
"La quercia caduta" (Pascoli) **45**:156
Querelle de Brest (Genet) **128**:134-35, 154, 158-61, 170, 201, 225
"La querelle de l'existentialisme" (Merleau-Ponty) **156**:123
Querelle of Brest (Genet)
See *Querelle de Brest*
"Quero Me Casar" (Drummond de Andrade) **139**:229
Querschnitte (Böll) **185**:151
"The Quest" (Crowley) **7**:208
"The Quest" (Naidu) **80**:343
The Quest (Baroja)
See *La busca*
"Quest and Cycle in Finnegans Wake" (Frye) **165**:229
The Quest for Certainty (Dewey) **95**:30, 41, 133
The Quest for Community (Nisbet) **117**:291-93, 301, 310, 342, 348-51, 353, 366-69, 378, 304, 386
"The Quest for Sorrow" (Leverson) **18**:202
The Quest for Winter Sunshine (Oppenheim) **45**:131
"The Quest of Silence" (Brennan) **17**:38, 41, 54
"The Quest of the Queen's Tears" (Dunsany) **59**:20
The Quest of the Sacred Slipper (Rohmer) **28**:282-83
The Quest of the Spider (Dent) **72**:17
"Quest of the Star Stone" (Kuttner) **10**:267
Questa sera si recita a soggetto (Pirandello) **4**:336, 348, 352; **29**:298, 306, 320; **172**:150, 167-68, 193
Qu'est-ce que la philosophie? (Deleuze) **116**:87, 102-04, 108, 128-29, 131
"Qu'est-ce qui se passe" (Apollinaire) **8**:22
"Qu'est-ce qu'on peut pour" (Garneau) **13**:195
Questi Fantasmi (de Filippo) **127**:266-67, 271-73, 281, 289-90, 295
"Question" (García Lorca)
See "Pregunta"
"Question" (Grove) **4**:144
"The Question" (Howe) **21**:113
"Question" (Tagore) **3**:488
"The Question of High Wages" (Keynes) **64**:246
A Question of Memory (Field) **43**:172-73, 176
"The Question of Nationality and Autonomy" (Luxemburg)
See "The National Question and Autonomy"
"Questioni sul realismo" (Pratolini) **124**:326
"Questions" (Nemerov) **124**:257
"Questions Are Remarks" (Stevens) **45**:302
"Questions Concerning Certain Faulties of Man" (Peirce) **81**:194,286
Questions de poésie (Valéry) **15**:468
"Questions de théâtre" (Jarry) **2**:285; **14**:271-72, 277
"The Questions of the Human Heart" (Nishida)
See "Jinshin no giwaku"
"Questions of Travel" (Bishop) **121**:3-4, 23
Questions of Travel (Bishop) **121**:3, 6-7, 19, 21, 26, 42, 55, 80, 102
"Qui est-ce" (Péret) **20**:200
Qui n'a pas son Minotaure? (Yourcenar) **193**:256, 267, 283-84, 333
"Qui Renovat Juventutem Meam" (Field) **43**:160
"Quia imperfectum" (Beerbohm) **1**:73
The Quick and the Dead (Bradford) **36**:56-7, 64
"The Quick-Lunch Counter" (Benét) **28**:6
"Quickness" (Calvino) **183**:145, 148
"The Quicksand" (Wharton) **129**:361
"Quidnunc the Poet and Mr. Gigadibs" (Nemerov) **124**:218
"Quien baila se consuma" (Aleixandre) **113**:51
"Quiero pisar" (Aleixandre) **113**:14
"Quiero saber" (Aleixandre) **113**:12
"Quiet" (Coppard) **5**:179
Quiet Cities (Hergesheimer) **11**:275
"Quiet Fireshine" (Gurney) **33**:98
The Quiet Guard (Kuzmin)
See *Tikhii strazh*
Quiet Harmony (Kandinsky) **92**:32
"The Quiet House" (Mew) **8**:294, 298
"The Quiet Light" (Field) **43**:156
"Quiet Lines, Head Bowed" (Radnóti) **16**:418
"Quiet Mogens" (Jensen)
See "Den stille Mogens"
Quiet Please (Cabell) **6**:78
"Quiet Rain" (Nagai)
See "Ame Shōshō"
A Quiet Road (Reese) **181**:338, 347
The Quiet Sentinel (Kuzmin)
See *Tikhii strazh*
"The Quiet Woman" (Coppard) **5**:176
"Quietly" (Pirandello) **4**:354
"A Quilt Pattern" (Jarrell) **177**:125, 128-29, 147-48, 196, 205-8
"The Quiltmaker" (Carter) **139**:206-8
La quimera (Pardo Bazán) **189**:193-94, 197, 209, 229, 243, 248, 251, 254, 257
"Quimera lunar" (Lugones) **15**:289
Quincas Borba (Machado de Assis) **10**:281-83, 287, 292
"Quince" (Radnóti) **16**:419
Quince presencias (Reyes) **33**:324
"De Quincey's Autobiography" (Woolf) **43**:404
"The Quincunx" (de la Mare) **53**:37
Quinten metsys (Bosschere) **19**:61
The Quintessence of Ibsenism (Shaw) **3**:380; **9**:414; **45**:12-13
Quinze ans de combat, 1919-1934 (Rolland) **23**:273-74
Quisante (Hope) **83**:166
"Quisque sous manes" (Johnson) **19**:256
"Quite Early One Morning" (Thomas) **45**:366; **105**:304
Quite Early One Morning (Thomas) **45**:409; **105**:296, 320
"Quite Forsaken" (Lawrence) **93**:19
The Quiver (Gumilev)
See *Kolchan*
Quo Vadis (Sienkiewicz) **3**:422-27, 429, 431
Quoi? l'éternité (Yourcenar) **193**:280, 302-03, 343
R. E. Lee (Freeman) **11**:218-20, 222-26, 228-29, 231-33
R. U. R. (Čapek) **6**:81-4, 88-90, 92, 94; **37**:40-3, 46, 52-3, 56-9, 61-2, 64-5, 67-9, 72; **192**:175, 191, 195-97, 199, 202, 208-9, 214-16, 219-20, 225, 228
Rab oroszlán (Moricz) **33**:243
Rabagas (Caragiale) **76**:163
"The Rabbi" (Babel) **2**:30; **13**:32, 38; **171**:8, 10, 26, 38, 44-45, 48, 82-83, 88
"Rabbi Eliezer's Christmas" (Cahan) **71**:11, 28
Rabbi Esra (Wedekind) **7**:586
"La rabbiata" (Heyse)
See "L'arrabiata"
"The Rabbi's Son" (Babel) **2**:22, 23, 27, 29; **13**:20, 32, 38; **171**:4-5, 11, 14, 38, 44, 79, 88
"The Rabbit" (Millay) **49**:227
"A Rabbit as King of the Ghosts" (Stevens) **3**:450; **12**:362
"The Rabbit-Pen" (Anderson) **123**:48
"The Rabbits" (Milne) **88**:249
"The Rabbit's Revenge" (Dazai Osamu) **11**:186
Rabble in Arms (Roberts) **23**:229-30, 232-33, 235-36, 238-39, 241-44
Rabelais and Folk Culture of the Middle Ages and Renaissance (Bakhtin) **160**:183
Rabelais and His World (Bakhtin) **160**:110-11, 135, 169, 174, 177, 180-81, 184, 213, 218
"Die Raben" (Trakl) **5**:456
The Rabid Toy (Arlt)
See *El juguete rabioso*
Rabock (Molnár) **20**:164
Rabota aktera nad soboi (Stanislavsky) **167**:271, 326
Racconti (Lampedusa) **13**:293, 295, 301
I racconti: accoppiamenti giudiziosi (Gadda) **144**:130
Racconto italiano di ignoto del novecento (Gadda) **144**:96, 113, 122-24, 127-31, 133-34, 140, 144-46, 148
"The Race" (Nemerov) **124**:177, 183, 185
Race and Democratic Society (Boas) **56**:94
"The Race at Left Bower" (Bierce) **44**:45
The Race for Wealth (Riddell) **40**:329, 331, 335
Race, Language, and Culture (Boas) **56**:63, 66, 105, 106

"Race Prejudice and the Negro Artist" (Johnson) **175**:250-51
"Race Pride" (Gilman) **117**:164
"The Race Welcomes Dr. W. E. B. Du Bois as Its Leader" (Cotter) **28**:43
The Races of Mankind (Benedict) **60**:119
Rachel rechtet mit Gott (Zweig) **17**:440, 457
Rachel Strives with God (Zweig)
See *Rachel rechtet mit Gott*
"Racial Decadence" (Roosevelt) **69**:268
"Racism and Culture" (Fanon) **188**:111
"Radi" (Borchert) **5**:105, 109
"Radiance" (Bialik) **25**:58
Radiances (Hippius)
See *Siyaniya*
"Radiant Fatherhood" (Steffens) **20**:357
The Radiant Road (Wetherald) **81**:408,413
"Radicals for Democracy" (Böll) **185**:56
"The Radio of the Future" (Khlebnikov) **20**:150-51
Rafael Narizokh Becomes a Socialist (Cahan)
See *Rafoel naarizokh iz gevorn a sotsialist*
The Raffle (Dunsany) **59**:23, 28
Raffles (Hornung) **59**:112, 114
Raffles (Orwell) **128**:287
"Raffles and Miss Blandish" (Orwell) **15**:332, 362; **51**:222, 239, 248; **128**:287
Rafoel naarizokh iz gevorn a sotsialist (Cahan) **71**:38-39, 41, 85-86
"The Raft" (Cary) **196**:217
"The Raft" (Lee-Hamilton) **22**:186-89
"The Raft-Builders" (Dunsany) **59**:27
"Rafuiala" (Rebreanu) **28**:273
"Un ragazzo" (Tozzi) **31**:325
"Ragazzo al buio" (Jovine) **79**:44
The Rage for the Lost Penny (Jarrell) **177**:137-38, 213-14
A Rage in Harlem (Himes)
See *For Love of Imabelle*
Ragged Lady (Howells) **17**:185
"The Ragged Stocking" (Harper) **14**:260
"The Raggedy Man" (Riley) **51**:286, 288, 292
"Raggylug, the Story of a Cottontail" (Seton) **31**:259, 262-63, 270-73, 276-77
La ragione degli altri (Pirandello) **29**:284, 299, 303, 318
Ragotte (Renard) **17**:304
Rahel Varnhagen: The Life of a Jewish Woman (Arendt) **193**:140-47, 153-54
Las raíces (Pardo Bazán) **189**:199
"The Raid" (Bulgakov) **16**:85
"The Raid" (Tolstoy)
See "Nabeg"
"Raider of the Spaceways" (Kuttner) **10**:267
"Raiders' Dawn" (Lewis) **3**:289
Raiders' Dawn, and Other Poems (Lewis) **3**:286-87, 289-91
The Raids of the Cimbri (Jensen)
See *Cimbrernes Tog*
"Räikkö Räähkä" (Leino) **24**:369-70, 376
"Räikkö the Wretch" (Leino)
See "Räikkö Räähkä"
"Rail and Raid" (Davidson) **24**:191
"The Railings" (Arp) **115**:27-8
"Railroad" (Csáth) **13**:154
The Railroad and the Churchyard (Bjoernson) **7**:103; **37**:23
"The Railroad Earth" (Kerouac) **117**:266
"Railroad Yards (Long Island City)" (Chambers) **129**:46
"Railroads and the Popular Unrest" (Baker) **47**:13
The Railway Timetable of the Heart (Tzara) **168**:274
Railways as Public Agents: A Study in Sovereignty (Adams) **80**:13
"Raimundo" (Drummond de Andrade) **139**:225
"Rain" (Gumilev) **60**:269
"The Rain" (Meynell) **6**:295
"Rain" (Obstfelder)
See "Regn"
"Rain" (Thomas) **10**:459, 467
Rain (Anderson) **144**:72
"The Rain Guitar" (Dickey) **151**:127, 147
"The Rain Gutter" (Dickey) **151**:126
Rain of Scorpions and Other Writings (Trambley) **163**:287, 291-94, 299-300, 305, 307, 310, 314, 320, 322, 324, 330, 346, 375-79
"Rain on a Grave" (Hardy) **143**:189
"Rain or Hail" (Cummings) **137**:55
"Rain Patter" (Percy) **84**:198
The Rainbow (Lawrence) **2**:350-51, 353, 357-61, 366, 369, 371-73; **9**:212-13, 215-16, 219, 222, 226-27; **16**:295, 300, 306, 312-13, 317-18, 322; **33**:178, 182, 188, 193, 196-97, 199-200, 202, 204, 206-09, 211, 214-15, 217, 224, 226, 228; **48**:99-101, 104, 113-14, 117, **48**:121, 125, 130, 132, 134, 142; **61**:180-277
The Rainbow Trail (Grey) **6**:183
Rainbow Valley (Montgomery) **51**:212-13, 215; **140**:278, 331, 333-34
"Raining in My Heart" (Holly) **65**:146
The Rains Came: A Novel of Modern India (Bromfield) **11**:82-3, 86
"Rainshower" (Miyazawa) **76**:294
Raintree County (Lockridge) **111**:317-74
"A Rainy Day in April" (Ledwidge) **23**:121
"The Rainy Moon" (Colette)
See "La lune de pluie"
"A Rainy Morning" (Wetherald) **81**:409
"Rainy Season: Sub-Tropics" (Bishop) **121**:6, 61-4, 67-8
"raise the shade / will youse dearie" (Cummings) **137**:42
A Raisin in the Sun (Hansberry) **192**:242-46, 248, 252, 259-60, 262-65, 271, 275-76, 280-86, 290-91, 293-94, 296-302, 305-9, 314-15, 318-20, 322-24, 326-27, 330, 335-36, 2150
Raising Demons (Jackson) **187**:235, 247, 259, 262-63, 273, 281, 294-95, 297-98, 308, 331-32, 334-35, 339
La raiz rota (Barea) **14**:48
Raja Yoga (Vivekananda) **88**:351, 381
Rajah Amar (Myers) **59**:134, 150
The Rajah's Sapphire (Shiel) **8**:361
"A Rajput Love Song" (Naidu) **80**:292
The "Rake" (Dreiser) **83**:83-5
The Rake's Progress (Wharton) **3**:552
"Raksha Bandham" (Naidu) **80**:295
"The Rakshasas" (Aurobindo) **63**:8
Raktakarabī (Tagore) **3**:486
Rakubaishu (Shimazaki Toson) **5**:439
Rakudai bôzu no rirekisho (Endo) **152**:193
Ralentir travaux (Éluard) **41**:152
The Rally (D'Annunzio)
See *La ricossa*
"Ralph Waldo Emerson" (Higginson) **36**:167
The Ralstons (Crawford) **10**:146, 148-50, 153, 155
"Rama's Reformation" (Chatterji)
See "Ramer sumati"
"Ramblin' Man" (Williams) **81**:443
"Rambling Round Evelyn" (Woolf) **43**:394
"The Rambling Sailor" (Mew) **8**:298
"Ramer sumati" (Chatterji) **13**:75, 80-1
"Rameses II" (Lindsay) **17**:227
"Ramplonería" (Unamuno) **148**:308
Ramsey Milholland (Tarkington) **9**:455
Ramuntcho (Loti) **11**:356, 361, 364, 366-67
Ramuz-i-bekhudi (Iqbal) **28**:182-84, 201
Ranald Bannerman's Boyhood (MacDonald) **9**:292
Ranch Life and the Hunting Trail (Roosevelt) **69**:175, 206, 251-52, 277-79
The Ranch on the Beaver (Adams) **56**:7
Rancor (Riggs) **56**:204, 208, 215, 217
Randall and the River of Time (Forester) **152**:141, 143-44, 146
Randall Jarrell's Letters: An Autobiographical and Literary Selection (Jarrell) **177**:191, 193-94, 222, 224, 228-29, 237
Randolph of Roanoke (Kirk)
See *John Randolph of Roanoke*
Random Harvest (Hilton) **21**:97-8
A Random Itinerary (Davidson) **24**:159-60
Rangabhumi (Premchand) **21**:282, 285-87, 296-97
"The Range in the Desert" (Jarrell) **177**:194
"Rank and File" (Noyes) **7**:503
"Rannyaya vesna" (Guro) **56**:132, 136
The Ransom of John Ringgold (Adams) **56**:22
"Die Rantzow und die Pogwisch" (Liliencron) **18**:213, 216
"The Rantzows and Pogwisch's" (Liliencron)
See "Die Rantzow und die Pogwisch"
"The Rape of Progress" (Nisbet) **117**:335
"Rapidità" (Calvino) **183**:106
"El rápido Paris-Orán" (Miro) **5**:337
"Rapids at Night" (Scott) **6**:393, 395, 397
"Rapisardiana" (Carducci) **32**:107
"Raport z oblezonego miasta" (Herbert) **168**:47-48
Raport z oblezonego miasta (Herbert)
See *Raport z oblezonego miasta i inne wiersze*
Raport z oblezonego miasta i inne wiersze (Herbert) **168**:13, 21, 39, 76-79, 81-83
"Le rappel" (Vian) **9**:533-35
Le rapport d'Uriel (Benda) **60**:71, 73
"Rapto" (Drummond de Andrade) **139**:228
Raquel, the Jewess of Toledo (Feuchtwanger)
See *Spanische Ballade*
"El raquero" (Pereda) **16**:364, 380
Rarahu; or, The Marriage of Loti (Loti)
See *Le mariage de Loti*
"The Rarity of the God-Fearing Man" (Kirk) **119**:298
"Los raros" (Darío) **4**:62
"Die Raschhoffs" (Sudermann) **15**:433
Rascoala (Rebreanu) **28**:269-71, 273
The Rash Act (Ford) **15**:79, 87, 89-90; **172**:52-54, 57-61, 123
"Rashōmon" (Akutagawa Ryūnosuke) **16**:17, 24, 32-4
Rashomon, and Other Stories (Akutagawa Ryūnosuke) **16**:19
"Raskol" (Popa) **167**:156-57
"Rasplësnutoe vremja" (Pilnyak) **23**:212
Rasplyosnutoye vremya (Pilnyak)
See "Rasplësnutoe vremja"
Rasputin; or, The Conspiracy of the Empress (Tolstoy) **18**:373, 382
"Rasskaz o samom glavnom" (Zamyatin) **8**:545, 547-48, 553-54; **37**:424, 429, 431
"Rasskaz o tom, kak odin Russkii grazhdanin poekhal v Evropu omalazhivat'sya" (Zoshchenko) **15**:510
Rasskazy (Babel) **13**:13
Rasskazy (Remizov) **27**:346
El Rastro (Garro) **153**:37, 72
"The Rat" (Robinson) **101**:158
Rat and Devil: Journal Letters of F. O. Matthiessen and Russell Cheney (Matthiessen) **100**:209-10, 212, 215-16, 239-40, 249-58, 261, 285-86
"Rat Hunters" (Quiroga)
See "Los cazadores de ratas"
Ratai to Isho (Mishima) **161**:83
"The Ratcatcher" (Tsvetaeva)
See "Krysolov"
"The Ratcatcher's Daughter" (Housman) **7**:355, 360-61
"The Rate of Change in Species" (Wells) **133**:262, 324
"The Rathskeller and the Rose" (Henry) **19**:182
"A Rational Anthem" (Bierce) **44**:5, 40
The Rational Hind (Williams) **89**:394-5
Le Rationalisme appliqué (Bachelard) **128**:55
"Rationality, Activity and Faith" (James) **32**:348
"Rats" (James) **6**:216
"Rats" (Lawson) **27**:119
"The Rats" (Trakl) **5**:466

The Rats (Hauptmann)
See *Die Ratten*
"The Rats in the Walls" (Lovecraft) **4**:266, 270; **22**:215
Die Rätsel der Philosophie (Steiner) **13**:440-41
"Die Ratten" (Trakl) **5**:456
Die Ratten (Hauptmann) **4**:196, 204
Der Rattenfänger (Zuckmayer) **191**:331-33
"Rattle-Snake Mountain Fable I" (Bodenheim) **44**:74
Raucho: Momentos de una juventud contemporánea (Güiraldes) **39**:175, 177-78, 182-83, 186, 190
Rāvan-Jatāyu-Yuddha (Devkota) **23**:48
"Rave On" (Holly) **65**:137-39, 142, 148, 153
Raven's Brood (Benson) **27**:17, 19
"The Ravines" (Tolstoy) **18**:367-68
Raw Material (Fisher) **87**:77
Raymond Chandler Speaking (Chandler) **1**:170; **7**:169; **179**:86, 90-91, 194-95
Le Rayon-vert suivi de Dix Heures en chasse (Verne) **52**:352
"Razaranja" (Andrić) **135**:84
"Razglednica I" (Radnóti) **16**:412
"Razglednica II" (Radnóti) **16**:412
"Razglednica IV" (Radnóti) **16**:412
Razglednicák (Radnóti) **16**:410-12, 420
"Razgovor o Dante" (Mandelstam) **2**:404, 409-10; **6**:265, 268, 270
"Razgovor v foie kinematografa" (Olesha) **136**:183, 185
"Razgovori sa Gojom" (Andrić) **135**:41, 52-53, 89
Razgrom (Fadeyev) **53**:45-8, 51-5, 57-63, 68
"Razin's Boat" (Khlebnikov)
See "Ustrug Razina"
"Razluka" (Tsvetaeva) **35**:407, 411
"Razmirica" (Popa) **167**:156
Razón de amor (Salinas) **17**:357, 359-63, 365, 367-69
La razón de la sinrazón (Pérez Galdós) **27**:268
"The Razor" (Shiga)
See "Kamisori"
Razskaz o semi povieshennykh (Andreyev) **3**:17-18, 23, 26-7
Razzle Dazzle (Saroyan) **137**:202
"Re dei Bastoni" (Calvino) **183**:153
"Un re in ascolto" (Calvino) **183**:217, 232
"Reaction" (Manning) **25**:278
"The Reader" (Rilke)
See "Der Lesende"; "Der Leser"
Reader (Gilman)
See *The Charlotte Perkins Gilman Reader*
Reader (Lyotard) **103**:277
"Readers and Writers" (Orage) **157**:243, 246, 251, 253-55, 283-84
Readers and Writers (Orage) **157**:243, 246, 253
A Reader's Guide to the Short Stories of Willa Cather (Cather) **132**:137
A Reader's History of American Literature (Higginson) **36**:178
"Reading" (Woolf) **43**:409
"Reading a Wave" (Calvino) **183**:45-46, 143
"Reading in Wartime" (Muir) **87**:167
"Reading, its pleasures and advantages" (Murray) **117**:287
"Reading the Signs, Empowering the Eye" (Bambara) **116**:14
Reading the World (Frye) **165**:189-91
Reading, Writing, and Remembering (Lucas) **73**:166
Readings from the Bible (Chase) **124**:29
Readings of Poetry (Croce) **37**:113
"Ready Teddy" (Holly) **65**:138-39, 141
"Re-Agents" (Ford) **172**:92
Real and Imaginary Portraits (Reyes)
See *Retratos reales e imaginarios*
The Real Charlotte (Somerville & Ross) **51**:329-33, 338-41, 343-44, 346-54, 357, 359-63, 365, 372, 374, 376-77, 379, 386-89, 391-92
The Real Cool Killers (Himes)
See *Il pleut des coups durs*
The Real Dope (Lardner) **2**:332; **14**:303-04
The Real Life of Sebastian Knight (Nabokov) **108**:52, 85, 93, 96, 98, 110, 115, 176, 178-80, 191, 194-95, 216, 220, 223-24; **189**:77, 174
The Real Motive (Fisher) **87**:72
"Real News" (Benchley) **55**:19
"The Real Romance" (Hawthorne) **25**:246-47
The Real Situation in Russia (Trotsky) **22**:365
"The Real Thing" (Wolfe) **4**:516
"The Real Things of Life" (Rogers) **71**:297-99
Real Utopias (Strindberg) **21**:348-49
The Real Woman (Hichens) **64**:131
"La realidad" (Aleixandre) **113**:34
"La realidad" (Quiroga) **20**:213
Realidad: novela en cinco jornadas (Pérez Galdós) **27**:250, 263, 267-68
La realidad y el delirio (Echegaray) **4**:104
"Realism" (Cahan) **71**:24, 83
"Realism in Prose Fiction" (Sapir) **108**:250, 295
"Realism in Religion" (Andreas-Salome)
See "Der Realismus in der Religion"
"Realism in the Modern Spanish Novel" (Barea) **14**:49
"Der Realismus in der Religion" (Andreas-Salome) **56**:36, 44, 45
"The Realists" (Yeats) **31**:385
"Realities" (Nemerov) **124**:249-50
Realities of Yesterday and Today (Tozzi)
See *Realtà diieri e di oggi*
"Reality" (Quiroga)
See "La realidad"
"The Reality Effect" (Barthes) **135**:159
"The Reality of Dream" (Pirandello)
See "La realtà del sogno"
Reality Sandwiches (Ginsberg) **120**:111
The Realm of Essence (Santayana) **40**:368, 380
The Realm of Matter (Santayana) **40**:368, 371
"The Realm of Resemblance" (Stevens) **12**:361
The Realm of Spirit (Santayana) **40**:380, 382
The Realm of the Spirit and the Realm of Caesar (Berdyaev) **67**:60
"The Realm of the Ultimate Pole" (Davidson) **24**:194
"The Realm of the Unreal" (Bierce) **44**:45-6
Realms of Being (Santayana) **40**:368, 376, 380, 382-83, 406-07, 416
"La realtà del sogno" (Pirandello) **29**:284
Realtà diieri e di oggi (Tozzi) **31**:318
"Reap It as You Sow It" (Bonner) **179**:45-46, 53, 58-59
"Reapers" (Toomer) **172**:256, 274, 287, 316, 327
"Reaping" (Lowell) **8**:230
Reason and Beauty in the Poetic Mind (Williams) **11**:484, 502
"Reason and Religion" (Tolstoy) **79**:428
Reason in Art (Santayana) **40**:344, 366
Reason in Common Sense (Santayana) **40**:403
Reason in Religion (Santayana) **40**:350
Reason in Science (Santayana) **40**:380
Reason in Society (Santayana) **40**:344, 383
The Reason of Others (Pirandello)
See *La ragione degli altri*
The Reason Why (Glyn) **72**:137
The Reason Why the Colored American Is Not in the World's Columbian Exposition—The Afro-American's Contribution to Columbian Literature (Wells-Barnett) **125**:329, 333
"The Reasons for Writing a Book" (Bataille) **155**:113-14
The Reawakening (Levi)
See *La tregua*
"Reb Jossel" (Peretz) **16**:389
Reb Shloyme nogid (Asch) **3**:71
"The Rebbe" (Babel)
See "The Rabbi"
"The Rebbe's Son" (Babel)
See "The Rabbi's Son"
"The Rebel" (Belloc) **18**:41
"The Rebel" (Middleton) **56**:173
"The Rebel" (Stephens) **4**:407
La rebelion de las masas (Ortega y Gasset) **2**:337, 341, 343-44, 350-51
Rebellion (Drinkwater) **57**:139, 142, 144
Die Rebellion (Roth) **33**:333-35, 340, 346, 350-51
Rebellion in the Backlands (Cunha)
See *Os sertões*
"A Rebellious Priest" (Herzl)
See "Egy lázadó pap"
The Rebels (Neumann) **100**:314-15
"Rebels of the Moon" (Huneker) **65**:169
"Rebirth" (Bergelson) **81**:20
"Rebirth" (Kipling) **8**:200
"Rebirth" (Muir) **87**:197
The Rebirth of Classical Political Rationalism (Strauss) **141**:259
"Rebuilding the International" (Luxemburg) **63**:220
Recapture (Sturges) **48**:310, 316-17
"Recast" (Trambley) **163**:321
"The Receipt" (Čapek) **192**:224
"Recent Irish poetry" (Beckett) **145**:88
"Recent Italian Comedy" (Howells) **17**:179
"Recent Minor Poetry" (Higginson) **36**:183
"Recent Theories of Consciousness" (Vaihinger) **71**:416, 419
"Recessional" (Kipling) **8**:179, 191, 193, 201; **17**:198
"Recessional" (Masters) **25**:298
"Recessional" (Roberts) **8**:318
Rechts und Links (Roth) **33**:335-36, 363
Rechtssoziologie (Weber) **69**:339, 342, 347-48
La rechute (Bourget) **12**:69
"Reci" (Andrić) **135**:20, 59-61
"Recieved Payment" (Williams) **89**:375, 383
"Reciprocity" (Drinkwater) **57**:124
"Récit secret" (Drieu la Rochelle) **21**:35
Recitativ (Babits) **14**:39
"Recitative" (Crane) **2**:120-21
Recitative (Babits)
See *Recitativ*
Recitative (Merrill) **173**:219, 231, 239, 247, 254-55, 257-58
Récits et elegies (Coppee) **25**:126
Reckless (Riggs) **56**:204, 206
The Reckless Moment (Ophuls) **79**:173, 239-43, 253-5, 257-8
"The Reckoning" (Wharton) **9**:547; **129**:361
The Reckoning (Chambers) **41**:94
A Reckoning (Sarton) **120**:227-29, 231, 240, 243, 247, 285
The Reckoning (Schnitzler)
See *Liebelei*
Reclaiming a Partrimony (Kirk) **119**:266
"A Recluse" (de la Mare) **53**:16, 21-3, 25, 27, 34, 36, 39-41
The Recluse (Hedāyat)
See *Buf-e kur*
"Recognition" (Rhodes) **53**:316
"La Recoleta" (Borges) **109**:10
"A Recollection" (Bishop) **103**:4, 16, 26
Recollections (Dazai Osamu)
See *Omoide*
Recollections (Gorky) **8**:74
Recollections (Tolstoy) **44**:339, 342
Recollections and Reflections (Bettelheim) **143**:2
Recollections of Andreev (Gorky) **8**:74
Recollections of Ludolf Ursleu the Younger (Huch)
See *Erinnerungen von Ludolf Ursleu dem Jüngeren*
Recollections of My Life (Ramoacn y Cajal) **93**:151
Recollections of Rossetti (Caine) **97**:13
Recollections of Things to Come (Garro)
See *Los Recuerdos del porvenir*

Recollections of Tolstoy (Gorky) **8**:74
Recommencements (Bourget) **12**:68
"Recompense" (Gurney) **33**:85
"Recompense" (Percy) **84**:200
"Reconciliation" (Baker) **3**:2; **10**:17
"Reconciliation" (Lasker-Schueler) **57**:331, 336
"The Reconciliation" (Montgomery) **51**:180
Reconciliation (Shiga)
See *Wakai*
"Reconciliation under Duress" (Adorno) **111**:151
Reconquista (Gamboa) **36**:71-3, 77
"Reconstruction" (Anthony) **84**:22
"Reconstruction in Europe. An Introduction" (Keynes) **64**:243
Reconstruction in Philosophy (Dewey) **95**:32, 68
"Recontre au bord du lac" (Proust) **161**:174
"La recontre au cercle mixte" (Apollinaire) **51**:20
"The Record" (Čapek)
See "Rekord"
"Record" (Sharp) **39**:372
"Record at Oak Hill" (Roberts) **68**:348, 350
Record of an Honest Man (Kunikida Doppo)
See *Azamuzakaru no ki*
A Record of Childhood and Youth (Wright) **136**:227
Recordações do escrivão Isaías caminha (Lima Barreto) **23**:156-57, 159-60, 163, 166-69
Recovered texts (Borges)
See *Textos recobrados*
Recovering: A Journal, 1978-1979 (Sarton) **120**:227, 231, 285, 319, 326-28
"The Recovery" (Chopin) **14**:69
"The Recovery" (Wharton) **9**:541; **129**:360
Recovery (Tagore)
See *Ārogya*
"Recovery of Family Life" (Davis) **6**:154
The Re-creation of Brian Kent (Wright) **183**:349
"The Recruit" (Housman) **10**:250
"Recruiting" (Nabokov) **108**:216-18
The Rector (Crothers) **19**:73
The Rector of Wyck (Sinclair) **11**:414
"Recuerdo" (Millay) **49**:209
Recuerdos de España (Palma) **29**:260
Recuerdos de mi vida (Ramoacn y Cajal) **93**:138, 141, 142, 146
Recuerdos de niñez y mocedad (Unamuno) **148**:243, 252, 338
Los Recuerdos del porvenir (Garro) **153**:2-3, 5-7, 17, 23, 27-28, 30-33, 56, 61-65, 67-68, 71-72, 86-89, 91
"The Recurrence" (Muir) **2**:485; **87**:167, 210
Recusant Poets (Guiney) **41**:217, 221, 223-24
The Red and the Green (Murdoch) **171**:221, 225, 227-28, 307
"Red Autumn in Valvins" (Brennan) **17**:54
The Red Badge of Courage: An Episode of the American Civil War (Crane) **11**:121, 124-27, 129, 131-41, 143-51, 153, 157-67; **17**:65-6, 71-5, 78-9, 81-3; **32**:132-90
"Red Bean" (Wen I-to) **28**:411
"The Red Bells" (Mikszath)
See "A piros harangok"
"The Red Blanket" (Miyazawa) **76**:278
"Red Bredbury's End" (Symons) **11**:426, 428, 451
"The Red Candle" (Wen I-to) **28**:414
Red Candle (Wen I-to) **28**:408-11, 419-20
Red Cavalry (Babel)
See *Konarmiia*
"Red Clay Blues" (Wright) **136**:262
"Red Cloud" (Herbert) **168**:44
The Red Count (Giacosa)
See *Il conte rosso*
"The Red Cow Group" (Morrison) **72**:353
"Red Crown" (Bulgakov) **159**:153
Red Dawn (Baroja)
See *Aurora roja*
"Red Dog Clarion" (Harte) **25**:191
The Red Drops (Obstfelder)
See *De røde dråber*
"The Red Drummer" (Coffin) **95**:16
Red Eve (Haggard) **11**:243, 246
The Red Fairy Book (Lang) **16**:263-64, 272
"Red Feathers" (Wakefield) **120**:357-58
"Red Geranium and Godly Mignonette" (Lawrence) **93**:74
Red Hair (Glyn) **72**:142
"Red Hand" (Reed) **9**:388
"The Red Hand" (Wakefield) **120**:353-54
"Red Handed" (Cobb) **77**:127
"Red Hanrahan's Curse" (Yeats) **31**:416-17
Red Harvest (Hammett) **187**:45, 47-8, 51, 54-6, 60, 68-70, 72-6, 79-80, 83-4, 86, 90-1, 96, 98-102, 106-08, 110, 112, 114-15, 117, 121-22, 124-25, 127-29, 136-37, 158, 164-67, 169-72, 174-77, 180-81, 203-04, 213, 215, 218-29
The Red House Mystery (Milne) **6**:311, 318
Red Hugh's Captivity (O'Grady) **5**:351-52, 354
Red Hunters and the Animal People (Eastman) **55**:163, 167-70, 172-73, 175
The Red Lamp (Rinehart) **52**:292, 301, 303-04
The Red Laugh (Andreyev)
See *Krasnyi smelch*
"Red Leaves" (Faulkner) **170**:110, 127-28, 138
Red Likker (Cobb) **77**:129, 134
The Red Lily (France)
See *Le lys rouge*
"The Red Lodge" (Wakefield) **120**:332, 334, 344-46, 357
Red Magic (Ghelderode)
See *Magie rouge*
Red Men and White (Wister) **21**:373, 377, 390, 396, 399-400, 405
The Red Mill (Molnár)
See *A vörös malom*
"The Red Mist" (Rohmer) **28**:282
"The Red Moon" (Arlt)
See "La luna roja"
"Red Nails" (Howard) **8**:128, 133-34, 136
Red Oleanders (Tagore)
See *Raktakarabī*
Red Orm (Bengtsson)
See *Röde Orm, sjöfarare i västerled*
Red Oval (Kandinsky) **92**:35
The Red Pony (Steinbeck) **135**:316
The Red Poppy (Hippius)
See *Makov tsvet*
Red Poppy (Natsume)
See *Gubijinso*
The Red Poppy (Sologub)
See *Alyi mak*
The Red Priest (Lewis) **2**:393
The Red Republic (Chambers) **41**:88, 91, 101
"The Red Retreat" (Service) **15**:401
"The Red Room" (Wells) **19**:446-48
The Red Room (Strindberg)
See *Röda Rummet*
"Red Rose and White Rose" (Chang)
See "Hong meigui yü bai meigui"
Red Shadows (Howard) **8**:130, 137
Red Sky in the Morning (Coffin) **95**:5-7, 9
"Red Slippers" (Lowell) **8**:230
The Red Snow (Dent) **72**:18, 21
Red Spider (Baring-Gould) **88**:25-7, 30-2
The Red Spider (Dent) **72**:38
"Red Story" (Čapek)
See "Červená povídka"
The Red Tapeworm (Mackenzie) **116**:234-35, 237-38
The Red Terrors (Dent) **72**:23
The Red Thumb Mark (Freeman) **21**:43-4, 50-2, 54-7, 62
"The Red Time" (Lagerkvist)
See "Den röda tiden"
The Red Triangle (Morrison) **72**:364
"Red Wind" (Chandler) **179**:114, 126, 128
"The Red Wind" (Johnson) **19**:230, 244
"Red Wings: Concerning Richard Prince's 'Spiritual America'" (Acker) **191**:118
"Red Wolf" (Lawrence) **93**:103
Red Wolf (Carman) **7**:138, 140
Redaktøren (Bjoernson) **7**:104, 106, 111-13; **37**:11, 18-19, 30
Redatr Lynge (Hamsun) **49**:162, 167-68
"Rede am Grabe Leo Reins" (Schwitters) **95**:345
"Die Rede Gabriele d'Annunzios" (Hofmannsthal) **11**:307
"Rede uber Lyrik und Gesellschaft" (Adorno) **111**:30, 176
"Redemption" (Evans) **85**:38
"La redenzione degli oggetti" (Calvino) **183**:101, 107
"Redeployment" (Nemerov) **124**:150, 153, 184
"The Red-haired Man's Wife" (Gregory) **176**:14
"The Red-Haired Man's Wife" (Stephens) **4**:407, 419
"The Red-Headed League" (Doyle)
See "The Adventure of the Red-Headed League"
"The Rediscovery of the Unique" (Wells) **6**:538; **19**:436, 436; **133**:268, 270, 278, 292
"The Red-Lipped Guest" (Sologub) **9**:447
"Redoble fúnebre a los escombros de durango" (Vallejo) **56**:291
Redoute (Kandinsky) **92**:50
"Redruff" (Seton) **31**:266, 270-71, 273, 277
Reed Anthony, Cowman (Adams) **56**:3-4, 6, 10, 22-3
"The Reed Flute" (Chekhov)
See "Svirel'"
"The Reed Pipe" (Chekhov)
See "Svirel'"
"The Reed-Player" (Scott) **6**:393, 397
Reeds and Mud (Blasco Ibáñez)
See *Caños y barro*
Reeds in the Wind (Deledda)
See *Canne al vento*
"Reedy River" (Lawson) **27**:140
The Reef (Wharton) **3**:555-56, 567, 572, 576; **9**:541, 552-54; **27**:384-85; **53**:362; **129**:346, 362; **149**:168
Reencuentro de personajes (Garro) **153**:51-52, 54-55
Re-Enter Dr. Fu Manchu (Rohmer) **28**:280, 295, 300-01
"Referred to the Author" (Morley) **87**:123, 143
"The Refiner's Gold" (Harper) **14**:260
"The Reflecting Well" (Södergran)
See "Den speglande brunnen"
"A Reflection" (Chopin) **127**:128
"Reflection" (Nemerov) **124**:212
"Reflection in Oval Mirror, the Home Place, 1947" (Morris) **107**:214
"Reflection in Sleepy Eye" (Ginsberg) **120**:71
"Reflection on Ice-Breaking" (Nash) **109**:360, 363-64
"Reflections" (Čapek) **192**:226
"Reflections" (Carter) **139**:188
"Reflections" (Lowell) **8**:233-34
"Reflections" (Toomer) **172**:265
Reflections (Villaurrutia)
See *Reflejos*
"Reflections at Lake Louise" (Ginsberg) **120**:35
Reflections in a Golden Eye (McCullers) **155**:179-80, 184, 186-87, 189, 209
"Reflections of a Gothic Mind" (Kirk) **119**:276
Reflections of a Nonpolitical Man (Mann)
See *Betrachtungen eines Unpolitischen*
Reflections of a Non-Political Man (Mann)
See *Betrachtungen eines Unpolitischen*
The Reflections of Ambrosine (Glyn) **72**:127
"Reflections of an Earth-Being" (Toomer) **172**:280, 304
"Reflections on Communication and Culture" (Park) **73**:198
"Reflections on Gandhi" (Orwell) **51**:258; **128**:260, 290
Reflections on Photography (Barthes) **135**:147
"Reflections on Poetry" (Desnos)
See "Réflexions sur la poésie"

"Reflections on the Composition of Memoirs of Hadrian" (Yourcenar) **193**:314-15, 354, 364
Reflections on the Death of a Porcupine, and Other Essays (Lawrence) **2**:357; **9**:219; **61**:219
"Reflections on the Pure Theory of Money of Mr. J. M. Keynes" (Hayek) **109**:196
"Reflections on the Race Riots" (Toomer) **172**:336
Reflections on the Revolution of Our Time (Laski) **79**:160
Reflections on the World Today (Valéry) See *Regards sur le monde actuel*
Reflections on Violence (Sorel) See *Reflexions sur la violence*
"Reflections on Wallace Stevens" (Jarrell) **177**:186
Reflejos (Villaurrutia) **80**:460, 476
"Reflex Action and Theism" (James) **32**:347-48
"The Reflex Arc Concept of Psychology" (Dewey) **95**:59
"Reflexion of a Novelist" (Nemerov) **124**:260
Reflexions on Poetry and Poetics (Nemerov) **124**:167, 205, 290, 317
"Réflexions sur la poésie" (Desnos) **22**:64, 69
Reflexions sur la violence (Sorel) **91**:173, 176-8, 183-4, 188, 190, 193, 195, 199, 204-5, 209-10, 213-4, 219, 225, 233, 257, 263, 267, 272-4, 277, 291-3, 295-6, 301, 303, 305, 307-8, 311, 322, 332, 336, 344
"Réflexions sur le spectacle" (Fondane) **159**:241
"The Reflex-Man of Whinnymuir Close" (Kirk) **119**:282-83, 292, 335
The Reform of Education (Gentile) See *Riforma della dialettica*
"Reform or Revolution?" (Luxemburg) **63**:219, 220
Reforma Gentile (Gentile) **96**:135
"The Reformer" (Dreiser) **10**:194
"Refranero limeño" (Palma) **29**:262
"Refuge" (Baker) **3**:4
"The Refuge of the Derelicts" (Twain) **185**:327
"The Refugee" (Fisher) **87**:74
"The Refugees" (Jarrell) **177**:251, 253-58
"The Refugees" (Muir) **87**:267
"The Refugees" (Wharton) **129**:364
The Refugees (Doyle) **7**:220, 224
"The Refugees Born for a Land Unknown" (Muir) **87**:241
Refus d'obéissance (Giono) **124**:43, 95
"A Refusal to Mourn" (Thomas) See "A Refusal to Mourn the Death, by Fire, of a Child in London"
"A Refusal to Mourn the Death, by Fire, of a Child in London" (Thomas) **1**:470, 472; **45**:360, 362-63, 365, 376, 408; **105**:336, 348
"The Refutation of Idealism" (Moore) **89**:185, 216, 240, 251, 269, 273
Regain (Giono) **124**:32, 39, 42, 53, 63, 91-2, 96, 99-100, 121, 126
"Regarding an American Village" (Bodenheim) **44**:69
Regards et jeux dans l'espace (Garneau) **13**:194-95, 198-201, 204
Regards sur le monde actuel (Valéry) **4**:493
Regeneration (Haggard) **11**:241
Regeneration (Svevo) See *Rigenerazione*
"The Regeneration of Lord Ernie" (Blackwood) **5**:70
Der Regenmacher (Hesse) **148**:160, 162-66
"Die Regennacht" (Raabe) **45**:188-89
The Regent (Bennett) **5**:29, 37, 43, 51; **197**:20, 22, 28, 30, 172-74, 177
The Regent (Strindberg) **8**:417
La Regenta (Alas) **29**:2-12, 14-22, 26-34
"Régi magyar arckép" (Babits) **14**:39
La regina e gli insorti (Betti) **5**:54-7, 62, 66
Regina landa (Azuela) **3**:78; **145**:12
Regina; or, The Sins of the Fathers; Regine (Sudermann) See *Der Katzensteg*
Reginald (Saki) **3**:369, 374
Reginald in Russia, and Other Stories (Saki) **3**:369
"The Region November" (Stevens) **12**:378
The Region of the Summer Stars (Williams) **1**:515-16, 519; **11**:489-91
"The Regional Writer" (O'Connor) **132**:324, 363
The Register (Howells) **7**:387
"Registro" (Azuela) **145**:21
Les règles de la méthode sociologique (Durkheim) **55**:91, 101-02, 105, 113-14, 116, 127, 134, 141
Reglos y consejos (Ramoacn y Cajal) **93**:142, 146
"Regn" (Obstfelder) **23**:186, 189
Le règne de l'esprit malin (Ramuz) **33**:293-96
"Règnes" (Éluard) **41**:160
"Regreso al sur" (Onetti) **131**:193, 195
"El regreso de Anaconda" (Quiroga) **20**:212-14
"Regret" (Chopin) **5**:153; **14**:61-2, 69; **127**:194
"Regret" (Patton) **79**:299
"Regret Not Me" (Hardy) **53**:101; **143**:157
"Regrets" (Santoka) **72**:411
"Les Regrets, rêveries couleur du temps" (Proust) **161**:172
Regrets sans repentir (Himes) **139**:251
The Regularity of the Reliquary (Jarry) **147**:331-32
A Regulator of the Century (Benda) See *Un régulier dans le siécle*
Un régulier dans le siécle (Benda) **60**:63, 71
"Das Reh" (Raabe) **45**:191
The Rehearsal (Baring) **8**:32
Rehearsal (Morley) **87**:125
Das Reich Gottes in Böhmen (Werfel) **8**:473, 479
Reigen (Schnitzler) **4**:386, 388, 390-91, 394, 398-400
The Reign of Gilt (Phillips) **44**:253, 261-62, 273-74, 287, 290, 299
The Reign of the Evil One (Ramuz) See *Le règne de l'esprit malin*
La reina de Rapa Nui (Prado) **75**:194-95, 197, 203, 211
"La reina Italiana" (Quiroga) **20**:213
"La reina maga" (Prado) **75**:194, 208
"Reincarnation" (Dickey) **151**:90, 172
"Reincarnation" (Graham) **19**:112
"Reincarnation" (Sterling) **20**:384
"Reincarnation I" (Dickey) **151**:96, 110
"Reincarnation II" (Dickey) **151**:110, 116, 180, 199
Reincarnations (Stephens) **4**:415, 420-21
La Reine des Pommes (Himes) See *For Love of Imabelle*
El reino de Dios (Martinez Sierra and Martinez Sierra) **6**:274-75, 278-79, 281-82, 284, 287
La rèino Jano (Mistral) **51**:148, 152
Reise des Humors und des Beobachtungsgeistes (Barlach) **84**:100
Die Reise nach dem Glück (Heyse) **8**:121
Der Reisepass (Frank) **81**:102-5
Reishō (Nagai) **51**:88-9, 92
Reitendes Paar (Kandinsky) **92**:49
Reiter (Cheveaux arabes) (Kandinsky) **92**:50
Reiter in deutscher Nacht (Ewers) **12**:136
Reitergeschichte (Hofmannsthal) **11**:302-05
The Reivers (Faulkner) **141**:33, 101; **170**:128-29
"A Reiver's Neck-Verse" (Swinburne) **8**:427
Reja Sil'vija (Bryusov) **10**:78, 85-6
"The Rejected Manuscript" (Phelps) **113**:342
"A Rejoinder" (Keynes) **64**:303
Rejouer le politique (Lyotard) **103**:164
Rejse på Island (Hansen) **32**:251
"The Rejuvenation of Major Rathborn" (London) **9**:273
Reka igrayet (Korolenko) **22**:174
"Reka Potudan" (Platonov) **14**:413, 418, 420
"Rekishi" (Nishida) **83**:328-30
"Rekishi sono mama to rekishibanare" (Mori Ogai) **14**:381
Rekonstruckcja poetry (Herbert) **168**:39
"Rekord" (Čapek) **37**:48; **192**:224
Rektor Kleist (Kaiser) **9**:173-74, 179, 182
Los relámpagos de agosto (Ibarguengoitia) **148**:196-97, 216, 224
"The relation of American Indian linguistics to general linguistics" (Sapir) **108**:257
"The Relation of Art and Life" (James) **2**:252
"A Relation of Art and Life" (Nemerov) **124**:178-79, 253, 306
"The Relation of Art and the Artist" (James) **2**:252
"The Relation of Currency Inflation to Prices" (Keynes) **64**:241
"The Relation of the Poet to Day-Dreaming" (Freud) See "Der Dichter und das Phantasieren"
"The Relation of Time to Eternity" (McTaggart) **105**:197
Relations (Kandinsky) **92**:83
"Relations and Connectives in Pure Experience" (Nishida) **83**:307
"The Relations between Poetry and Painting" (Stevens) **3**:457; **45**:296, 298, 330, 333
"The Relations of Theory to Practice in Education" (Dewey) **95**:101
"The Relationship of Thought and Its Subject-Matter" (Dewey) **95**:28
"The Relationship to the Text" (Schoenberg) See "Das Verhaltnis zum Text"
Relatives (Moricz) See *Rokonok*
"Relativity for Ladies" (Rhodes) **53**:316
"Relax Is All" (Slesinger) **10**:441-42
"Release" (Lawrence) **93**:17
"The Relenting of Sardinac" (Dunsany) **59**:20
"A Relic" (Beerbohm) **24**:102, 117
"The Relic" (Belloc) **7**:40
"Relics" (Swinburne) **8**:441
"Relieving Guard" (Harte) **25**:190
Religiia i kul'tura (Rozanov) **104**:307, 309, 347
Religio Journalistici (Morley) **87**:125
"Religion" (Andrade) **43**:7
"Religion" (Zola) **21**:456
Religion and Civilization (Rozanov) See *Religiia i kul'tura*
"Religion and Culture" (Andreas-Salome) **56**:46, 48
Religion and Culture (Rozanov) See *Religiia i kul'tura*
Religion and Individual Psychology (Adler) See *Religion und Individualpsychologie*
Religion and Literature (Endo) See *Shukyo to bungaku*
"Religion and Morality" (Tolstoy) **79**:428
Religion and Philosophy (Collingwood) **67**:119, 139, 148-49, 155
"Religion and Politics" (Arendt) **193**:165
"Religion and the Theatre" (Betti) **5**:60
Religion in the Making (Whitehead) **97**:197-98, 219-20, 237, 247, 308
"Religion not the Crying Need of India" (Vivekananda) **88**:379
The Religion of Man (Tagore) **53**:335
"The Religion of Slaves" (Iqbal) **28**:182
Religion of the Central Luo (p'Bitek) **149**:68, 108, 120, 122-23
Religion of the Spirit (von Hartmann) **96**:212
Religion und Individualpsychologie (Adler) **61**:28
"La religione sta de sè" (Papini) **22**:281, 286
Religious Consciousness (von Hartmann) **96**:212
Religious Essays (Otto) **85**:314
"The Religious Work of Vladimir Solov'yov" (Ivanov) **33**:131
Le réliquaire (Coppee) **25**:119, 122

Réliquas de casa velha (Machado de Assis) **10**:285
"Reloj" (Aleixandre) **113**:4
"The Reluctant Dragon" (Grahame) **136**:10-11, 26
The Reluctant Dragon (Grahame) **64**:55, 58, 64
"Reluctant Foreword" (Bodenheim) **44**:58
The Reluctant Tragedian (Chekhov)
See *Tragik ponevole*
"The Reluctant Voyagers" (Crane) **32**:180
"El remanso" (Güiraldes) **39**:185, 190
"The Remarkable Case of Davidson's Eyes" (Wells) **12**:510; **19**:434, 434
"The Remarkable Hero" (Chandler) **7**:172
"The Remarkable Wreck of the Thomas Hyke" (Stockton) **47**:312, 314, 318, 320, 327
"Remarks of a Dramatist" (Olesha) **136**:111
"Remarks on Bertrand Russell's Theory of Knowledge" (Einstein) **65**:92
Remarks on Colour (Wittgenstein) **59**:239, 296
"Remarks on Frazer's The Golden Bough" (Wittgenstein) **59**:307
"Remarks on Poetry" (Valéry) **15**:452
"Remarks on the Article of N. I. Bukharin 'The Imperialistic Robber State'" (Lenin) **67**:231
"Remarks on the Crisis Character of Modern Society" (Arendt) **193**:54
Remarks on the Foundations of Mathematics (Wittgenstein) **59**:267, 310-11
"Remarks on the Predicates of Moral Judgements" (Westermarck) **87**:363
"Remarks on the Present State of Meteorological Science" (Ruskin) **63**:282
"Remarks on the Psychological Appeal of Totalitarianism" (Bettelheim) **143**:33
"Remarks to the Back of a Pew" (Benét) **28**:2, 5
"The Rembrandt" (Wharton) **3**:571; **9**:541; **129**:360
Rembrandt (Simmel) **64**:338
Rembrandt and the Italian Renaissance (Clark) **147**:121
"Rembrandt to Rembrandt" (Robinson) **5**:407, 409, 411, 413, 417; **101**:130, 192
"Rembrandt's Hat" (Malamud) **129**:192
Rembrandt's Hat (Malamud) **129**:62, 64, 73; **184**:221-23, 309
"Rembrandt's Old Woman Cutting Her Nails" (Oppen) **107**:350
"The Remedy: Geography" (Pirandello)
See "Rimedio: La geografia"
Remember Last Night (Whale) **63**:339
Remember the Night (Sturges) **48**:286, 291, 295, 312, 316
"Remembering Chrysanthemum" (Wen I-to) **28**:417
"Remembering My Father" (Herbert) **168**:21, 44
"Remembering Poem" (Radnóti) **16**:415
"A Remembrance" (Carman) **7**:137
"Remembrance" (Esenin)
See "Vospominanie"
"A Remembrance" (Meynell) **6**:292, 294
Remembrance of Things Past (Proust)
See *À la recherche du temps perdu*
"Remembrance of Things to Come" (Péret) **20**:198
"Remembrances" (Dazai Osamu) **11**:181
"Remembrances" (Moréas) **18**:280-81, 285
"Remembrances of the Past" (Lu Hsun)
See "Huaijiu"
Remeslo (Tsvetaeva) **7**:557-58, 560-61, 566; **35**:381, 386, 390-92, 394, 404, 406, 410-12, 416
"Remez-pervaia ptashka" (Remizov) **27**:353, 355
"Reminder" (Lawrence) **93**:64
"A Reminder to the Watchers" (Ady)
See "Intés az őrzőkhöz"
"A Reminiscence" (Conrad)
See "Falk"
"Reminiscences" (Bosman) **49**:7
"Reminiscences" (Kandinsky)
See "Rückblicke"
"Reminiscences" (Tolstoy)
See "Vospominaniya"
"Reminiscences" (Woolf) **128**:331
Reminiscences (Conrad) **25**:76
Reminiscences (Foote) **108**:7, 10
Reminiscences (Gorky) **8**:82
Reminiscences (Howe) **21**:110, 114
"Reminiscences of Childhood" (Thomas) **45**:399; **105**:348, 350, 356
"Reminiscences of My Primary School Days" (Hagiwara) **60**:294
"Reminiscences of Yeats" (Gogarty) **15**:120
"Reminiscing" (Holly) **65**:137-38, 141
Reminiscing (Holly) **65**:147-48, 150
"Remnants" (Bergelson)
See "Droyb"
"Remordimiento" (Borges)
See "Remordimiento por cualquier defunción"
"Remordimiento por cualquier defunción" (Borges) **109**:11
"The Remount Officer" (Babel)
See "Nachal'nik konzapasa"
Remous (Yourcenar) **193**:256, 302, 305
"Remue-Ménage" (Arp) **115**:49
"Renaissance" (Gosse) **28**:131
"The Renaissance at Charleroi" (Henry) **19**:200
Renaissance Fancies and Studies (Lee) **5**:315
The Renaissance in India (Aurobindo) **63**:30
The Renaissance of Motherhood (Key) **65**:235, 237, 242
"Renan" (MacCarthy) **36**:253
"Renascence" (Heidenstam) **5**:254
"Renascence" (Lawrence) **93**:48
"Renascence" (Millay) **4**:306-10, 313-14, 316, 318-19; **49**:200-03, 207-8, 210, 213-14, 216, 231; **169**:226, 231, 241, 245, 268, 290, 292-94, 300
Renascence, and Other Poems (Millay) **4**:306-07, 322; **49**:200-01, 230; **169**:245, 290
Rencontres avec Léon Shestov (Fondane) **159**:258
"The Rendezvous" (Colette) **16**:126
"Le rendezvous" (Sully Prudhomme) **31**:300-01
Le rendez-vous de Senlis (Anouilh) **195**:4, 6, 14, 17-18, 38-9, 54-6
Rendre à César (Yourcenar) **193**:270, 323
René Auberjonois (Ramuz) **33**:311-12
Renée (Zola) **6**:567
"The Renegade" (Jackson) **187**:236, 335-36
"The Renegade" (Osbourne) **93**:132
"Renegades of the Rio" (McCoy) **28**:223
"Renewal" (Roberts) **8**:318
"Renewal of Strength" (Harper) **14**:260
"The Renewal of Youth" (Baker) **3**:4-5
Renkanki (Rohan) **22**:307
"Renouncement" (Meynell) **6**:292, 300, 302-03
"Renunciation" (Bodenheim) **44**:65
"Renunciation" (Parker) **143**:321
"The Renunicant" (Balmont)
See "Samorazvenchannyi"
"Renzo's Fist" (Levi) **109**:286
"The Repairer of Reputations" (Chambers) **41**:101, 103-09, 114
"Repayment in Gratitude" (Akutagawa Ryūnosuke) **16**:31
"Repeated Theme" (Huysmans) **69**:23
Repel (Dent) **72**:21
"Repercussions of the Mind" (Papadiamantis) **29**:272
"A Repertory Theatre" (Graham) **19**:137
La répétition; ou, l'amour puni (Anouilh) **195**:6, 14, 26, 38
Répétitions (Éluard) **41**:150
"Repetitions of a Young Captain" (Stevens) **12**:383; **45**:285, 299
Replenishing Jessica (Bodenheim) **44**:70, 73-4
"Replies to an Enquiry" (Thomas) **45**:372, 375
"Replies to the Objections" (Marinetti) **10**:324
"Répliques au Révérénd Père Foisset" (Roumain) **19**:342
"The Reply" (Ginsberg) **120**:9
"The Reply of a Physiologist to Psychologists" (Pavlov) **91**:84
"Reply to A. C. H." (Bodenheim) **44**:74
"Reply to Criticisms" (Einstein) **65**:126
"Reply to Dr. Aginsky" (Benedict) **60**:143
"A Reply to Eric Voegelin's Review of *The Origins of Totalitarianism* " (Arendt) **193**:75, 82, 177-78
"A Reply to My Critics" (Moore) **89**:201, 204-6, 208, 244-5
Reply to the Synod's Edict of Excommunication (Tolstoy) **79**:429, 439
"Réponse à Jean-Paul Sartre" (Bataille) **155**:87
"Report from Paradise" (Herbert) **168**:17, 27
"Report from the Besieged City" (Herbert)
See "Raport z oblezonego miasta"
Report from the Besieged City (Herbert)
See *Raport z oblezonego miasta i inne wiersze*
Report from the Besieged City and Other Poems (Herbert)
See *Raport z oblezonego miasta i inne wiersze*
"Report on Knowledge" (Lyotard) **103**:169, 227
Report on the State of Mind of the Nation (Böll)
See *Berichte zur Gesinnungslage der Nation*
"A Report to an Academy" (Kafka)
See "Ein Beriht für eine Akademie"
Report to Greco (Kazantzakis)
See *Anaphora ston Gkreko*
"The Reporter Who Made Himself King" (Davis) **24**:203
"The Reportorial Dance Marathon" (Benchley) **55**:19
"Repose of Rivers" (Crane) **2**:120; **80**:182
"Re-présentation de Masoch" (Deleuze) **116**:86
Représentations individuelles et représentations collectives (Durkheim) **55**:100, 117
Representative Irish Tales (Yeats) **11**:537-38
"The Reprimand" (Bishop) **121**:47, 50
"The Reproach of a Goddess" (Stringer) **37**:328
The Reprobate (James) **11**:339-40
The Reproducible Work of Art (Benjamin)
See *Das Kunstwerk im Zeitalter seiner technischen Reproduzierbarkeit*
"Reproof" (Sapir) **108**:249
"Reptiles" (Lawrence) **93**:98, 102
The Republic: Conversations on Fundamentals (Beard) **15**:25, 33
The Republic of Letters in America: The Correspondence of John Peale Bishop & Allen Tate (Bishop) **103**:48
"The Republic of the Southern Cross" (Bryusov)
See "Respublika juznogo kresta"
The Republic of the Southern Cross, and Other Stories (Bryusov) **10**:78, 87
A Reputed Changeling; or, Three Seventh Years Two Centuries Ago (Yonge) **48**:377
"Requesting Cooperation in the Taking of the Unemployment Census" (Roosevelt) **93**:184
"Requiem" (Gurney) **33**:107
Requiem (Rilke) **195**:247-49, 267
"Requiem aeternam dona eis" (Pirandello) **4**:330
"Requiém del espadón" (Valle-Inclán) **5**:478
Requiem den gemordeten Brüdern (Toller) **10**:489-90
"Requiem for a Friend" (Rilke) **195**:243-44, 246
Requiem for a Nun (Faulkner) **141**:62, 101, 175; **170**:177, 183, 210, 215-16
"Requiem for a Twentieth-Century Outlaw: In Memoriam Charles, 'Pretty Boy' Floyd" (Fletcher) **35**:102

Requiem for the Murdered Brothers (Toller)
See *Requiem den gemordeten Brüdern*
Requiem für einen Freund (Borchert) **5**:108
Requiem für Fanny Goldmann (Bachmann)
See *Der Fall Franza, Requiem für Fanny Goldmann*
"Requiem Mass" (Roth) **33**:354
"Requiem of Karl von Kalckreuth" (Rilke) **6**:358
"Requiescam" (Cullen) **37**:160, 165
"Requital" (Howe) **21**:113
Rereading Frye: The Published and Unpublished Works (Frye) **165**:236
Resa a discrezione (Giacosa) **7**:307, 310, 313
"Resaca" (Aleixandre) **113**:7
"The Rescue" (Field) **43**:165-66
The Rescue (Conrad) **1**:203, 214, 218; **6**:121
The Rescue of Broken Arrow (Faust) **49**:38
The Research Magnificent (Wells) **6**:528; **12**:508
"The Residence at Whitminster" (James) **6**:212-13
"Resident of the State" (Platonov) **14**:424
Residential Quarter (Aragon)
See *Les beaux quartiers*
"The Residue under the Will" (Adams) **56**:8
"Resignation" (Lasker-Schueler) **57**:319
The Resistible Ascension of Arturo Ui (Brecht)
See *Der aufhaltsame Augstieg des Arturo Ui*
The Resistible Rise of Arturo Ui (Brecht)
See *Der aufhaltsame aifstieg des Arturo Ui*
"Resolve" (Södergran) **31**:287
"Resort" (Oppen) **107**:263
"The Resources of San Miniato al Tedesco" (Carducci)
See "Le risorse di San Miniato al Tedesco"
"Respectability" (Anderson) **1**:59; **24**:34, 45, 49, 57; **123**:14, 63, 69, 77
"A Respectable Woman" (Chopin) **14**:70, 72; **127**:9, 23, 113, 128, 187-89, 191
"The Respite" (Colette) **16**:135
El resplandor de la hoguera (Valle-Inclán) **5**:486
"Résponses" (Barthes) **135**:148
"Responsibilities" (Matthiessen)
See "The Responsibilities of the Critic"
Responsibilities, and Other Poems (Yeats) **1**:566; **11**:528; **18**:442, 446; **31**:389, 420
"The Responsibilities of the Critic" (Matthiessen) **100**:163, 196, 211, 227, 232, 239, 284, 288, 290, 293-94
Responsibilities of the Critic: Essays and Reviews (Matthiessen) **100**:161-62, 209, 211-12, 229, 232
The Responsibilities of the Novelist (Norris) **155**:316, 318-20
The Responsibility of Forms (Barthes)
See *L'Obvie et l'obtus*
"Respublika juznogo kresta" (Bryusov) **10**:78, 81, 83-4
"Ressurection" (Bishop) **103**:16
Ressurreição (Machado de Assis) **10**:282, 287, 297-301, 304-05
"Rest" (Symons) **11**:433, 435
Rest beyond the Peaks (Bernhard)
See *Über allen Gipfeln ist Ruh: ein deutscher Dichtertag um 1980*
"Restatement on Xenophon's Hiero" (Strauss) **141**:339, 341
"The Restaurant of Many Orders" (Miyazawa) **76**:289
The Restaurant of Many Orders (Miyazawa) **76**:283
Restless Guests (Raabe)
See *Unruhige Gäste*
The Restlessness of Shanti Andía (Baroja)
See *Las inquietudes de Shanti Andía*
The Restoration (Griffith) **68**:250
The Restoration Theatre (Summers) **16**:427, 431
"El resucitador y el resucitado" (Nervo) **11**:395
"Resuélvame este caso" (Ibarguengoitia) **148**:218
"The Results of Human Action but Not of Human Design" (Hayek) **109**:207
"Résumé" (Parker) **143**:324
Resume (Pareto) **69**:137
"A Resumed Identity" (Bierce) **44**:13, 45
"Resurgam" (Carman) **7**:139
"Resurgam" (Gonzalez Martinez) **72**:148
"Resurgam" (Pickthall) **21**:257
"Resurrection" (Lawrence) **61**:269
The Resurrection (Gardner) **195**:88, 104-05, 126, 150
Resurrection (Machado de Assis)
See *Ressurreição*
Resurrection (Tolstoy)
See *Voskresenie*
The Resurrection (Yeats) **1**:568; **31**:403, 408; **93**:342; **116**:335
"Resurrection Mystery" (Södergran)
See "Uppståndelsemysterium"
"The Resurrection of Jesus" (Harper) **14**:260
The Resurrection of Jesus (Endo) **152**:167
The Resurrection of Jimber-Jaw (Burroughs) **2**:79
The Resurrection of the Gods (Merezhkovsky)
See *The Romance of Leonardo da Vinci*
"The Resurrection of the Negro" (Garvey) **41**:184
Retablillo de Don Cristóbal (García Lorca) **9**:292; **49**:107-08
Retablo de la avaricia, la lujuria, y la muerte (Valle-Inclán) **5**:483
Retaliation (Blok)
See *Vozmezdie*
A Retelling of the Tales from the Provinces (Dazai Osamu) **11**:183-85
"The Reticence of Lady Anne" (Saki) **3**:365
"La rétine des vertébrés" (Ramoacn y Cajal) **93**:137
"The Retired Man" (Schulz)
See "Emeryt"
"Retirement" (Levi)
See "Trattamento di quiescenza"
"Retirement Fund" (Levi) **109**:299
"Retorno" (Gonzalez Martinez) **72**:152
Retouches à mon retour de l'U.R.S.S. (Gide) **12**:152
Le retour (Bourget) **12**:67
Le retour d'Alsace (Giraudoux) **7**:317
Le Retour de l'Enfant prodigue (Gide) **12**:144; **177**:46
Retour de l'U.R.S.S. (Gide) **12**:152
Retour en Afrique (Himes) **139**:245, 248, 252-53, 255, 260-62, 281, 283-85, 314-19, 322
"La Retraite de M. Bougran" (Huysmans) **69**:55
La retraite sentimentale (Colette) **1**:192
"Retrato" (Aleixandre) **113**:3, 63-64
Retratos con nombre (Aleixandre) **113**:22, 70
Retratos reales e imaginarios (Reyes) **33**:316, 322
"Retread" (Bromfield) **11**:83
"The Retreat" (van Ostaijen)
See "De aftocht"
Retreat from Love (Colette) **16**:120
"Retribution" (Blok) **5**:88-90, 94
"Retribution" (Harper) **14**:260, 263
"Retribution" (Zoshchenko) **15**:505
Retribution (Blok)
See *Vozmezdie*
"A Retrieved Reformation" (Henry) **19**:172-3, 200
"Retrospect" (Brooke) **2**:53, 61; **7**:124-25
"Retrospection" (Quiller-Couch) **53**:289
Retrospection and Introspection (Eddy) **71**:91, 129-130, 132-135
Les Retrouvailles (Adamov) **189**:10, 19, 43
"The Return" (Bishop) **103**:4, 8, 17
"The Return" (Conrad) **13**:101, 113
"Return" (Gumilev)
See "Vozvrashchenie"
"The Return" (Kipling) **8**:201
"The Return" (de la Mare) **53**:28
"Return" (Lawrence) **93**:17
"Return" (Liliencron) **18**:208
"The Return" (Millay) **169**:268
"The Return" (Muir) **2**:485; **87**:157
"The Return" (Noyes) **7**:512
"The Return" (Oppen) **107**:263
"The Return" (Palamas) **5**:383-84
"The Return" (Sikelianos)
See "The Great Homecoming"
The Return (Asch) **3**:71
The Return (Bely)
See *Vozvrat: Tretiia simfoniia*
The Return (de la Mare) **4**:71, 73-5, 77; **53**:36-8
Return from Cormoral (Dent) **72**:22, 38
Return from the U.S.S.R. (Gide)
See *Retour de l'U.R.S.S.*
Return Home (Esenin) **4**:110
"Return Journey" (Thomas) **105**:356
"The Return of a Private" (Garland) **3**:190
"The Return of Alcibiade" (Chopin) **127**:20
"The Return of Anaconda" (Quiroga)
See "El regreso de Anaconda"
"The Return of Aphrodite" (Sarton) **120**:291
The Return of Buck Gavin (Wolfe) **13**:482
The Return of Bulldog Drummond (Sapper) **44**:316, 318, 320-22
The Return of Chorb (Nabokov)
See *Vozvrashchenie Chorba*
The Return of Don Quixote (Chesterton) **6**:103-05, 109
The Return of Dr. Fu Manchu (Rohmer)
See *The Devil Doctor*
The Return of Jeeves (Wodehouse) **108**:372, 381, 388
The Return of Kai Lung (Bramah)
See *The Moon of Much Gladness, Related by Kai Lung*
"The Return of Odysseus" (Muir) **87**:304
The Return of Olga from America (Svevo) **35**:369
The Return of Peter Grimm (Belasco) **3**:87, 90-1
"Return of Returns" (Lawrence) **93**:55
"The Return of Rhoda" (Glaspell) **175**:53-54
The Return of Sherlock Holmes (Doyle) **7**:220, 238
Return of Sumuru (Rohmer) **28**:281
The Return of Tarzan (Burroughs) **2**:79-80; **32**:57, 60, 62, 79
"The Return of the Chiff-Chaff" (Hudson) **29**:142, 161
The Return of the King (Tolkien) **137**:238, 259-60, 268-69, 272, 298-99, 302, 317, 325, 358-61
"The Return of the Nances" (Knister) **56**:155
The Return of the Native (Carossa) **48**:37
The Return of the Native (Hardy) **4**:147-49, 153-55, 158, 162-63, 166, 174-75; **10**:216, 226-28; **18**:92, 97, 100, 102, 111, 116; **32**:274-75, 277, 280-81, 288, 300, 306, 312, 317, 323; **48**:36-89; **53**:83-4; **72**:159, 162, 178, 195, 211, 268, 276, 279; **143**:71-72, 76, 78-80, 82, 86-88, 91, 93-94, 96, 98-101, 109, 118-19, 124, 169, 206-7; **153**:100-101, 104, 119, 1
"The Return of the Native to the Indiana Mill Town" (Shepherd) **177**:293
"The Return of the Proconsul" (Herbert)
See "Powrót prokonsula"
"The Return of the Prodigal" (Wolfe) **4**:516
The Return of the Prodigal (Gide)
See *Le Retour de l'Enfant prodigue*
"Return of the Sea" (Bishop) **103**:21
"The Return of the Smiling Wimpy Doll" (Shepherd) **177**:295, 309
"Return of the Swallows" (Gosse) **28**:138
The Return of Ulysses (Bridges) **1**:123-24, 132
"Return the Bridewealth" (p'Bitek) **149**:89, 93-94
Return to Abyssinia (White) **176**:225
"Return to Connecticut" (Bishop) **103**:9

Return to Japan (Hagiwara) **60**:294
The Return to Pellucidar (Burroughs) **32**:58
Return to Yesterday (Ford)
See *Return to Yesterday: Reminiscences 1894-1914*
Return to Yesterday: Reminiscences 1894-1914 (Ford) **1**:276; **15**:93; **172**:7, 58, 92-96, 119
"Returning North of Vortex" (Ginsberg) **120**:72, 80
Returning to Emotion (Bodenheim) **44**:71
"Returning to My Parents' Home" (Hagiwara) **60**:298
Returning Wave (Prus) **48**:157
"Returning, We Hear The Larks" (Rosenberg) **12**:306
"Returning We Hear the Larks" (Rosenberg) **12**:291, 294, 305, 307-08, 310-12
"Reuben Bright" (Robinson) **101**:111, 119, 132-33, 137-38, 193
Rëubeni, Fürst der Juden (Brod) **115**:78, 84, 88, 97, 99
Rëubeni, Prince of Jews (Brod)
See *Rëubeni, Fürst der Juden*
Reunião (Drummond de Andrade) **139**:225
"Reunion" (Lardner) **14**:307
"Reunion" (Robinson) **5**:412
Reunion in Vienna (Sherwood) **3**:411-12, 415-16, 418
The Rev. Annabel Lee (Buchanan) **107**:86
Le Rêve (Pardo Bazán) **189**:237
"Rêve" (Proust) **161**:174
La rêve (Zola) **1**:587, 589; **6**:564-65; **41**:412, 451
"Rêve d'artiste" (Nelligan) **14**:392, 397
"Rêve de Watteau" (Nelligan) **14**:396
"Rêve d'une nuit d'hôpital" (Nelligan) **14**:395
"Rêve fantasque" (Nelligan) **14**:394
"Le Reveil de l'ame francaise, le Mystere de la Charite de Jeanne de'Arc" (Sorel) **91**:241
"The Reveille" (Harte) **25**:190
"Reveillé" (Housman) **10**:250
"Reveille" (Levi) **109**:300
"Revelation" (Herbert) **168**:43
"La révélation" (Jacob) **6**:193
"The Revelation" (Montgomery) **51**:209
"Revelation" (O'Connor) **132**:229-32, 241-42, 244, 248, 280, 287-89, 300, 302-5, 320, 357, 359, 363
"Revelation and Concealment in Language" (Bialik)
See "Gilui we-chisui be-lashon"
"Revelation and Decline" (Trakl) **5**:465, 468
"Revelations" (Mansfield) **8**:284-85; **39**:304; **164**:240-41
The Revelations of Death (Shestov) **56**:250
The Revellers (Housman) **7**:359
"A Revenant" (de la Mare) **4**:78; **53**:27, 36
"The Revenant" (Woodberry) **73**:373
"Revenants des enfants" (Manning) **25**:277
"Revenge" (Lasker-Schueler) **57**:328, 334
"A Revenge" (Symons) **11**:426
Revenge (De Lisser) **12**:95, 99
The Revenge for Love (Lewis) **2**:386-89, 391-92, 394, 399; **9**:245-46, 248, 250; **104**:148-49, 151, 214-19, 295
"Revenge Is Sour" (Orwell) **51**:254, 256
"The Revenge of the Adolphus" (Crane) **11**:161
Revenge of the Lawn: Stories, 1962-1970 (Brautigan) **133**:2-3
The Revengers' Comedies (Orton) **157**:358
"The Rev. E. Kirk" (Davidson) **24**:186
"Reverie of Poor Susan" (Moody) **105**:237
"Reverie on the Fifteenth of August" (Papadiamantis) **29**:270, 272
Reveries over Childhood and Youth (Yeats) **11**:517; **93**:338
"The Reverse Side of Poetry" (Annensky) **14**:24
Rêveuse bourgeoisie (Drieu la Rochelle) **21**:20, 22, 33-4, 40
"Review" (Adorno) **111**:139
"A Review and Criticism of Spencer's Data of Ethics" (Thorndike) **107**:396
"Review of the Benson Murder Case" (Hammett) **187**:46
"Review of the Progress of the War—Fireside Chat Opening Fifth War Loan Drive" (Roosevelt) **93**:184
Reviewing (Woolf) **43**:407, 413, 415
Reviews and Critical Papers (Johnson) **19**:239
"Revision as Creation" (Sarton) **120**:262
A Revision of the Treaty: Being a Sequel to "The Economic Consequences of the Peace" (Keynes) **64**:245
Revisions (Bernhard)
See *Korrektur*
"Revival" (Fisher)
See "The South Lingers On"
"The Revolt" (Stringer) **37**:342
"Revolt and Submission" (Shestov) **56**:250
Revolt in Aspromonte (Alvaro)
See *Gentein Aspromonte*
Revolt in the Desert (Lawrence) **18**:129-31, 134, 139-40, 142, 156, 168, 170, 175
"The Revolt of Capital" (Day) **25**:131, 137
"The Revolt of Modern Democracy against Standards of Duty" (Adams) **80**:13
"The Revolt of 'Mother'" (Freeman) **9**:61-2, 64-6, 74, 78-9
The Revolt of the Angels (France)
See *La révolte des anges*
The Revolt of the Birds (Post) **39**:347
The Revolt of the Butcher (Artaud)
See *La Révolte du Boucher*
"A Revolt of the Gods" (Bierce) **44**:40, 45
"The Revolt of the Home Gods" (Dunsany) **59**:18
The Revolt of the Machines (Tolstoy)
See *Bunt mašin*
The Revolt of the Masses (Ortega y Gasset)
See *La rebelion de las masas*
"The Revolt of the Oyster" (Marquis) **7**:437
"The Revolt of the Philistines" (Middleton) **56**:192
Revolt on Slope 3018 (Horvath)
See *Revolte auf Côte 3018*
La révolte (Rolland) **23**:261, 268, 277
Revolte auf Côte 3018 (Horvath) **45**:80, 92, 96, 106
La révolte des anges (France) **9**:45, 47, 49, 52-3
La Révolte du Boucher (Artaud) **36**:38
Revolting Rhymes (Dahl) **173**:29
La revolución de julio (Pérez Galdós) **27**:283
La revolución y la novela en Rusia (Pardo Bazán) **189**:249-50, 269
"Revolution" (Du Bois) **169**:95
"Revolution" (Nezval) **44**:250
Revolution (Beresford) **81**:8
Revolution, and Other Essays (London) **9**:265
"The Revolution Betrayed" (Trotsky) **22**:360, 365, 369, 373-74, 376-78, 389
Revolution Dreyfusienne (Sorel) **91**:188, 334
"Revolution in Revon" (Schwitters)
See "Causes and Outbreak of the Great and Glorious Revolution in Revon"
The Revolution in Tanner's Lane (Rutherford) **25**:337-38, 341-42, 344-46, 349, 353, 355, 358, 360-61
"The Revolution of the Women" (Cary) **196**:205
"The Revolutionary" (Lawrence) **93**:98, 101
"A Revolutionary Relic" (Dobson) **79**:3, 17-8
"Revolutionary Socialist Organization" (Luxemburg)
See "Leninism or Marxism?"
Revolutionary Tales (Artsybashev) **31**:6-7
"The Revolutionist's Handbook" (Shaw) **3**:388-89, 397
"The Revolutionists Stop for Orangeade" (Stevens) **3**:446, 463
Revolving Lights (Richardson) **3**:356-58
"Revolyutsiya" (Mayakovski) **18**:256
"Revues" (Ford) **172**:96
"Revulsion" (Nagai)
See "Akkan"
"The Reward" (Post) **39**:336, 344
Reward (Mqhayi)
See *I-nzuzo*
"The Reward of Virtue" (Strindberg) **21**:365-66
Rewards and Fairies (Kipling) **8**:194, 200
Rewards of Wonder (Gurney) **33**:94, 96-7, 102
"Rex Doloris" (Sayers) **15**:395
"El rey burgués" (Darío) **4**:60, 66-7
"El rey de Harlem" (García Lorca) **1**:317
El Rey mago (Garro) **153**:71-72
El rey y la reina (Sender) **136**:208
"Reyerta" (García Lorca) **49**:71, 74, 90, 112
"Reyes" (Quiroga) **20**:213
"Reynaldo" (Proust) **161**:173
Rez (Popa) **167**:172-74, 178
Rezánov (Atherton) **2**:15
R.F.C. H.Q. (Baring) **8**:40
R. G. Collingwood: Essays in the Philosophy of History (Collingwood) **67**:182
"A Rhapsodist at Lord's" (Lucas) **73**:171, 174
"A Rhapsody" (Zangwill) **16**:461
"A Rhapsody on Irish Themes" (Jarrell) **177**:172
Rhea Silvia (Bryusov)
See *Reja Sil'vija*
"Der Rhein" (Böll) **185**:181, 184
Rhineland Elegies (Pirandello)
See *Elegie renane*
"Rhineland Night" (Apollinaire)
See "Nuit Rhénane"
"Rhobert" (Toomer) **172**:292
Rhoda Fleming: A Story (Meredith) **17**:258-59, 261, 265, 275, 279-80; **43**:259
"Rhodos" (Gumilev) **60**:280
"Rhoecus Seeks for His Soul" (March) **96**:248
"The Rhondda" (Lewis) **3**:287
"A Rhyme for All Zionists" (Lindsay) **17**:227
"Rhyme for My Tomb" (Service) **15**:412
"A Rhymed Letter" (Leino)
See "Runokirje"
"Rhymed Life of St. Patrick" (Tynan) **3**:504
"A Rhymer's Epilogue" (Stringer) **37**:334
Rhymes (Jiménez)
See *Rimas*
Rhymes à la mode (Lang) **16**:261
"Rhymes and Rhythms" (Henley) **8**:96-7, 110
Rhymes and Rhythms (Carducci)
See *Rime e ritmi*
Rhymes For My Rags (Service) **15**:411, 413
Rhymes of a Rebel (Service) **15**:411
Rhymes of a Red Cross Man (Service) **15**:399-402, 406, 413
Rhymes of a Rolling Stone (Service) **15**:399, 413
Rhymes of a Roughneck (Service) **15**:411-13
Rhymes of Childhood (Riley) **51**:285
Rhymes of the Firing Line (Runyon) **10**:437
Rhymes to Be Traded for Bread (Lindsay) **17**:223, 239, 248
"Rhyming on the Counterattack" (Levi) **109**:301
Rhyming Poems (Lawrence) **93**:64, 66-68
"Rhythm" (Lardner) **14**:307
"Rhythm" (Shiga)
See "Rizumu"
"Rhythm in Tanka" (Hagiwara) **60**:306
The Rhythm of Life, and Other Essays (Meynell) **6**:290, 292-93, 295-96
The Ribbon (Feydeau)
See *Le ruban*
"Ribereñas" (García Lorca) **181**:184
Rice and a Carriage (Blasco Ibáñez)
See *Arroz y tartana*
Rice Bowl (Santoka)
See *Hachi no ko*
"Rice-Farming Episode" (Miyazawa) **76**:289
"Rice Pudding" (Milne) **6**:314
The Rice-Sprout Song (Chang)
See *Yangge*
La ricera delle radici (Levi) **109**:342
"La ricerca di una morale" (Calvino) **183**:164

Riceyman Steps (Bennett) **5**:29, 32, 35-6, 38, 40, 42-3; **20**:25, 27, 40-1; **197**:9, 12, 15, 20, 23, 31-5, 49, 52, 54-5, 57-8, 60-1, 67-71, 97, 109, 160, 168-69
"The Rich Boy" (Fitzgerald) **1**:241, 255, 261-62; **6**:169-70; **14**:173, 175; **157**:142
The Rich Man (van Schendel)
See *De Rijke Man*
A Rich Man's Daughter (Riddell) **40**:335
Rich Relatives (Mackenzie) **116**:198, 203, 206, 212, 231-32
Richard Cable (Baring-Gould) **88**:12
"Richard Cory" (Robinson) **5**:403, 406, 408, 416-18; **101**:98, 111, 119, 128, 136, 150, 153, 157, 159-62, 197-98
Richard Jefferies (Thomas) **10**:451
Richard of Bordeaux (Tey) **14**:449, 451, 453, 458-60
Richard Savage (Barrie) **164**:16
Richard Strauss und Hugo von Hofmannsthal: Breifwechsel (Hofmannsthal) **11**:311
"Richard Wagner in Bayreuth" (Nietzsche) **10**:354, 359, 387
Richard Wright: A Daemonic Genius (Walker) **129**:275, 283-84, 290, 316, 319
Richard Wright: Early Works (Wright) **136**:276
Richard Wright Reader (Wright) **180**:287
Richelieu (Belloc) **18**:28
The Richer, the Poorer (West) **108**:328
"Riches" (Schnitzler) **4**:403
"Riches in Custody" (Tagore)
See "Sampatti-Samarpan"
The Riches of the Great Khan (Blasco Ibáñez)
See *Las riquezas del Gran Kan*
Ricordi di un impiegato (Tozzi) **31**:317-24, 326, 332-33
La ricossa (D'Annunzio) **40**:21
"The Riddle" (de la Mare) **4**:78; **53**:27, 36
The Riddle, and Other Stories (de la Mare) **4**:73, 78; **53**:13, 16, 27, 36, 38
"The Riddle of the Rocks" (Murfree) **135**:206
The Riddle of the Sands (Childers) **65**:50-2, 54-61
The Riddle of the Universe (Haeckel) **83**:127, 131, 142, 152, 160
"The Riddle Solved" (Tagore) **3**:485
Riddles of Philosophy (Steiner)
See *Die Rätsel der Philosophie*
"The Ride" (Woodberry) **73**:371, 374
"The Ride Back" (Moody) **105**:237, 240
Ride the Pink Horse (Hecht) **101**:75
A Ride through Kansas (Higginson) **36**:172
"A Ride through Spain" (Capote) **164**:137
"The Ride to the Lady" (Moody) **105**:237
The Rider of Dreams (Torrence) **97**:148, 152, 157, 160-62
Rider of the Night (Ewers)
See *Reiter in deutscher Nacht*
Riders in the Chariot (White) **176**:128, 130, 132-33, 135-36, 138-39, 143-44, 147-48, 153-54, 156, 158, 162-64, 166-70, 181, 183-94, 196, 199, 219, 242-44, 246-47, 249, 251, 269, 274, 276, 278, 281, 284, 286-89, 301, 303, 306-10, 312, 315-17, 322
Riders of the Purple Sage (Grey) **6**:176-80, 182-84, 187-88
Riders to the Sea (Synge) **6**:425-32, 435, 439-42; **37**:348, 351, 353-55, 365, 378-79, 383, 390
"Rides of an Adjutant" (Liliencron)
See "Adjutantentrite"
"Ridin' the Bus" (Childress) **116**:34
"Riding Down from Bangor" (Orwell) **51**:249; **128**:289
"Riding in Mist" (Galsworthy) **45**:33
"The Riding of Ninemileburn" (Buchan) **41**:73
"Riduzioni drammatiche" (Svevo) **35**:363-64
Rienzi (Giacosa) **7**:305
"Riez Bailleul—'Riez Bailleul in Blue Tea-Time'" (Gurney) **33**:100
Rifleman Dodd (Forester) **152**:162
Riforma della dialettica (Gentile) **96**:83
Rīgas ragana (Rainis) **29**:393
Rigby's Romance (Furphy) **25**:173-74, 177, 182-83
Rigenerazione (Svevo) **35**:346, 352, 354
Right and Left (Roth)
See *Rechts und Links*
"Right and Might" (Johnson) **19**:230
"Right and Wrong Political Uses of Literature" (Calvino)
See "Usi politici giusti e sbagliati della letteratura"
"The Right Eye of the Commander" (Harte) **25**:222
"Right Here at Home" (Riley) **51**:281
Right Ho, Jeeves (Wodehouse) **108**:335-36, 363, 374-75, 378, 386, 392
"The Right of Way" (Davis) **24**:202
The Right to Heresy: Castellio against Calvin (Zweig)
See *Castellio gegen Calvin; oder, Ein Gewissen gegen die Gewalt*
"The Right to Work" (Baker) **47**:8
Right You Are! (If You Think So) (Pirandello)
See *Cosíè (se vi pare)*
Right You Are, If You Think You Are (Pirandello)
See *Cosíè (se vi pare)*
"Righteous Anger" (Stephens)
See "A Glass of Beer"
"A Righteous Faith for a Just and Durable Peace" (Dulles) **72**:79
The Rights of Health (Sánchez)
See *Los derechos de la salud*
Rights of the Soul (Giacosa)
See *Il diritti dell' anima*
"The Rights of Youth" (Woolf) **43**:408
De Rijke Man (van Schendel) **56**:239
Riley Farm-Rhymes (Riley) **51**:300-01
Rilke-Salome riefwechsel (Rilke) **195**:284
Rilla of Ingleside (Montgomery) **51**:211; **140**:278, 331-32, 334-35
Rimas (Jiménez) **4**:223-24; **183**:267, 289
Rimbaud le voyou (Fondane) **159**:239, 341
Rime e ritmi (Carducci) **32**:101-02, 105, 108-09
Rime nuove (Carducci) **32**:86, 91, 101, 106, 108-09
"Rimedio: La geografia" (Pirandello) **29**:284
"Rimorsi" (Papini) **22**:280
"Riña" (Aleixandre) **113**:3
"The Ring" (Gumilev) **60**:270
"The Ring" (Muir) **87**:167
"The Ring" (Warung)
See "The Secret Society of the Ring"
Ein Ring (Heyse) **8**:121
The Ring and the Book (Shaw) **3**:384
The Ring and the Book (Tagore) **3**:491
"The Ring and the Castle" (Lowell) **1**:371, 373; **8**:225, 230
"The Ring Cycle" (Merrill) **173**:230
Ring for Nancy: A Sheer Comedy (Ford) **15**:79
The Ring Is Closed (Hamsun)
See *Ringen sluttet*
The Ring Lardner Reader (Lardner) **14**:302
The Ring of the Löwenskölds (Lagerloef) **4**:239; **36**:241-42, 248
"The Ring of Thoth" (Doyle) **7**:238
"A Ring of Worlds" (Balmont)
See "Mirovoe koltso"
Ring Round the Moon (Anouilh)
See *L'Invitation au château*
Ringen sluttet (Hamsun) **14**:232, 241-42; **49**:130-31, 136, 145, 161
"Der Ringende" (Toller) **10**:490
"Der Ringer" (George) **14**:201
The Ringer (Wallace) **57**:398-99, 402
"Ringsend" (Gogarty)
See "Aphorism"
"Ringtail" (Fisher) **11**:209, 212
Rinkitink in Oz (Baum) **7**:21-2, 25, 27; **132**:13, 98
"Río" (Aleixandre) **113**:8
"El río" (Aleixandre) **113**:76
Rio Grande (Adams) **56**:9
Rio Grande (Thomas) **97**:140
"Rio Grande's Last Race" (Paterson) **32**:369, 374
"Río-Mar-Desierto" (Jiménez) **183**:293
Los ríos profundos (Arguedas) **147**:3, 6, 8-9, 12, 23, 27, 76-77, 84-87, 93-94, 96, 99, 101, 107-8
De ríos que se van (Jiménez) **183**:924
"The Riot at Amalfi" (Herzl) **36**:141
Rip Tide (Benét) **28**:4, 8, 10
"Ripe Figs" (Chopin) **14**:82-3; **127**:121
The Ripening Seed (Colette)
See *Le blé en herbe*
Rip-off Red, Girl Detective (Acker) **191**:127
"Ripulitura difficile" (Papini) **22**:281
Las riquezas del Gran Kan (Blasco Ibáñez) **12**:43
Le rire (Bergson) **32**:20, 27
"Le rire dans l'armée" (Jarry) **147**:277
"La risa en el desierto" (Prado) **75**:194, 208-09, 211
The Rise and Fall of Free Speech in America (Griffith) **68**:138, 189, 213, 222-23
The Rise and Fall of the City Mahogonny (Brecht)
See *Aufstieg und Fall der Stadt Mahagonny*
The Rise and Fall of the City of Mahagonny (Brecht)
See *Aufstieg und Fall der Stadt Mahagonny*
"Rise, Ebony Moon" (Ady) **11**:15
The Rise of American Civilization (Beard) **15**:21-2, 30-2, 37
The Rise of Arturo Ui (Brecht)
See *Der aufhaltsame Augstieg des Arturo Ui*
The Rise of David Levinsky (Cahan) **71**:2, 5-7, 9-11, 13, 15-16, 18-21, 23-24, 29, 33, 36-37, 40, 44-45, 47-48, 54-57, 62-63, 67-68, 70-72, 79-80, 83, 86-88
The Rise of European Liberalism (Laski) **79**:161
The Rise of Silas Lapham (Howells) **7**:364-66, 370, 372, 375-76, 378, 381-86, 392, 395, 397, 399; **17**:167-72, 178, 182, 185-87; **41**:231-87
"The Rise of Silas Needham" (Howells) **41**:267
The Rise of the Russian Empire (Saki) **3**:362, 373
"The Rise of the Short Story" (Harte) **25**:201, 219
"The Rise of the Tide" (Guiney) **41**:207
"The Rise of Theatricals" (Rourke) **12**:318, 322, 330
"The Risen Lord" (Lawrence) **48**:121; **61**:269
Risifi's Daughter: A Drama (Green) **63**:135
"Risico" (Fleming) **193**:199
Das Risiko des Schreibens (Böll) **185**:154
The Rising of the Court (Lawson) **27**:129, 132
The Rising of the Moon (Gregory) **1**:334-38; **176**:12, 14-16, 19, 23, 36, 39-41
"The Rising of the Storm" (Dunbar) **12**:108
Rising of the Tide: The Story of Sabinsport (Tarbell) **40**:428, 441, 443
"The Rising Sun" (Jarrell) **177**:155
The Rising Sun (Heijermans) **24**:290, 292-93
A Rising Wind: A Report of the Negro Soldier in the European Theater of War (White) **15**:478-79
"Le risorse di San Miniato al Tedesco" (Carducci) **32**:111
"Risposta a Benedetto" (Papini) **22**:281
"Ristimine" (Talvik) **87**:321
"Rita's Marriage" (Bosman) **49**:11
"Le rite du peyotl" (Artaud) **36**:5-7, 29
Rite of Saturn (Crowley) **7**:212
Rites of Eleusis (Crowley) **7**:211-13
"Ritornello" (Huysmans) **69**:23
"Ritratto di un amico" (Ginzburg) **156**:33-34, 50, 97-98, 109
"Der Ritter" (Rilke) **195**:191, 321
Ritter, Dene, Voss (Bernhard) **165**:74, 96
"Der Ritter der sich verschlief" (George) **14**:205

"Ritual" (Benét) **28**:2
Ritual and Belief in Morocco (Westermarck) **87**:334
"Ritual for Birth and Naming" (Torrence) **97**:158
"Ritual for the Body's Passing" (Torrence) **97**:158
"Rituals for the Events of Life" (Torrence) **97**:152
Ritzy (Glyn) **72**:141
Rivage (Jacob) **6**:193, 202
"The Rival Beauties" (Jacobs) **22**:106
"The Rival Celestial" (Benét) **28**:3
The Rival Monster (Mackenzie) **116**:234
"A Rival of Fallopius" (Lee-Hamilton) **22**:188
"The Rival Singers" (Guiney) **41**:206
Rivalen (Zuckmayer) **191**:322
Rivalry (Nagai)
See *Udekurabe*
"The Rivals" (Colette) **16**:135
"The Rivals" (Johnson) **19**:210
Rivals (Zuckmayer)
See *Rivalen*
"River" (Aleixandre)
See "Río"
"The River" (Crane) **5**:187, 190; **80**:83, 103, 127, 140, 142, 146-7, 166, 170, 210
"The River" (O'Connor) **132**:238, 256, 260, 263, 265, 283, 286-89, 331-37, 339, 342
"The River at Play" (Korolenko) **22**:170
"River Driftwood" (Jewett) **22**:120
"River Dwellers" (García Lorca)
See "Ribereñas"
"River Mist" (Kunikida Doppo)
See "Kawagiri"
River Mist and Other Stories (Kunikida Doppo) **99**:293, 304
"The River of Life" (Kuprin) **5**:298-99
"The River of Rivers in Connecticut" (Stevens) **3**:472
"The River Potudan" (Platonov)
See "Reka Potudan"
"River Roses" (Lawrence) **93**:93
The River Sumida (Nagai)
See *Sumidagawa*
"River Thieves" (Quiroga)
See "Los pescadores de vigas"
"The River Town" (Scott) **6**:393
The River War: An Historic Account of the Reconquest of the Soudan (Churchill) **113**:111, 118, 147-48, 162
"The Riverman" (Bishop) **121**:6, 23
"The Rivers of the World" (Vilakazi)
See "Imifula yomhlaba"
Rivers to the Sea (Teasdale) **4**:424-25, 428-29
The Rivet in Grandfather's Neck (Cabell) **6**:67, 70, 74
"Riviera" (Bishop) **103**:3, 9
"Riviera Stories" (Calvino) **183**:224
"Rizpah, the Daughter of Ai" (Harper) **14**:260
"Rizumu" (Shiga) **172**:201
"The Road" (Babel)
See "Doroga"
"The Road" (Muir) **87**:174, 188
The Road (London) **9**:272, 280; **15**:260-61, 272; **39**:279-80
"Road and Rail" (Davidson) **24**:172
"The Road at My Door" (Yeats) **11**:535-36
The Road Away from Revolution (Wilson) **79**:489
The Road Back (Whale) **63**:339-40, 383-84
"Road Discontinued" (Williams) **89**:369, 372, 402
The Road Goes Ever On (Tolkien) **137**:347-48
"The Road Home" (Parker) **143**:331-32
The Road Hymn for the Start (Moody) **105**:224, 235, 237, 240, 251, 260, 266, 278
"The Road Is Empty" (Wright) **136**:301
The Road Leads On (Hamsun)
See *Men livet lever*
"The Road of Ali Djerzelez" (Andrić)
See "Put Alije Djerzeleza"
"The Road of Casualty" (Williams) **89**:376, 378
"The Road of Excess" (Frye) **165**:257
The Road of the Happy Man (Lagerkvist)
See *Den lyckliges väg*
Road Sign (Miyamoto)
See *Dōhyō*
The Road Sign at the End of the Road (Abe)
See *Owarishi michi no shirube ni*
The Road Sign at the End of the Street (Abe)
See *Owarishi michi no shirube ni*
The Road Through the Wall (Jackson) **187**:237-38, 273, 281, 322, 333-35, 338-39
"The Road to Avignon" (Lowell) **1**:372
"The Road to Brody" (Babel)
See "Put' v Brody"
The Road to Calvary (Tolstoy) **18**:357, 366, 370-77
"The Road to Elysium and Hades" (Södergran)
See "Vägen till Elysium och Hades"
"The Road to Emmaus" (Ivanov) **33**:127
"The Road to England" (Higginson) **36**:167
The Road to France (Verne) **6**:501
"The Road to Gundagai" (Paterson) **32**:376
The Road to Mandalay (Mankiewicz) **85**:109
The Road to Oxiana (Byron) **67**:85-86, 88-89
The Road to Oz (Baum) **7**:21, 24-8; **132**:13-15, 49, 52, 81, 84, 87-93, 98-100
The Road to Rome (Sherwood) **3**:410-12, 414-17
"The Road to San Giovanni" (Calvino) **183**:233
The Road to Serfdom (Hayek) **109**:176-77, 186, 194, 204, 214, 237-41, 244, 271-77
The Road to the City (Ginzburg)
See *La strada che va in città*
The Road to the Open (Schnitzler)
See *Der Weg ins Freie*
The Road to the Temple (Glaspell) **55**:242-43, 267; **175**:74, 107, 135-41
The Road to Wigan Pier (Orwell) **2**:502, 505-11; **6**:350-52; **15**:322, 325, 333, 355, 358-60; **31**:188; **51**:219, 227, 236, 248, 250, 252-57, 261-62; **128**:256-57, 262-63, 265-69, 274,-76, 281, 287, 295-96; **129**:228, 234, 237, 244-45
The Road to Within (Hesse)
See *Der Weg nach Innen*
The Road to Yesterday (Montgomery) **51**:180-81
"The Road under the Snow" (Yourcenar)
See "La Route sous la neige"
"Road-Kids and Gay Cats" (London) **9**:281
"Roads" (Thomas) **10**:452, 464, 469
"Roads of Destiny" (Henry) **1**:347; **19**:180, 200
Roadside (Riggs) **56**:200, 203-7, 215-17
A Roadside Harp (Guiney) **41**:204-05, 207-08, 210, 213-14
Roadside Meetings (Garland) **3**:197
Roancero gitano (García Lorca) **197**:274
"The Roaring Days" (Lawson) **27**:133, 137-38
"La roba" (Verga) **3**:546
The Robber (Čapek) **6**:83; **192**:194-95
"The Robber Girl" (Kolmar) **40**:175
"The Robbers" (Akutagawa Ryūnosuke) **16**:22-3
"Robbie's Statue" (Lawson) **27**:139
"Robecq Again" (Gurney) **33**:86, 112
"Robert" (Toomer)
See "Rhobert"
Robert (Gide) **5**:243; **12**:145, 147, 159
"Robert Aghion" (Hesse) **196**:258, 328
Robert Browning (Chesterton) **1**:178; **6**:101
Robert E. Lee (Drinkwater) **57**:127-30, 133, 141-42, 146, 148
Robert E. Lee: An Interpretation (Wilson) **79**:488
Robert Elsmere (Ward) **55**:396-97, 399, 401-02, 404-07, 409-10, 412-13, 417-18, 421-23, 425-36
Robert Emmet: A Survey of His Rebellion and of His Romance (Guiney) **41**:218, 220
Robert Falconer (MacDonald) **9**:290, 292, 295-96, 309-10; **113**:198
"Robert Fulton Tanner" (Masters) **25**:308, 314
"Robert Gould Shaw" (Dunbar) **12**:106
Robert Johnson: The Complete Recordings (Johnson) **69**:94
Robert Louis Stevenson (Chesterton) **6**:101
"Robert Malthus. Centenary Allocution" (Keynes) **64**:246
Robert Peckham (Baring) **8**:33, 36, 42-3
"Robert the Bruce" (Muir) **87**:210
Robespierre (Belloc) **7**:31, 39
Robin Hood (Pyle)
See *The Merry Adventures of Robin Hood of Great Renown in Nottinghamshire*
"The Robing of the King" (Baker) **3**:4
"The Robin's Vesper" (Pyle) **81**:390
"Robinson Crusoe" (Unamuno) **148**:307
"Robinson Crusoe" (Woolf) **43**:400, 405, 426
La robla (Pereda) **16**:373
Robur le conquérant (Verne) **6**:495, 497, 501-02; **52**:346, 350, 353
Robur the Conqueror (Verne)
See *Robur le conquérant*
"Robustezza!" (Davies) **5**:199
"Le roc" (Verhaeren) **12**:469
Les roches blanches (Rod) **52**:310
"The Rock" (Jackson) **187**:236
The Rock (Stevens) **3**:449, 453, 474, 478; **12**:368, 370, 383; **45**:302, 316-18
"Rock and Hawk" (Abbey) **160**:40
The Rock and the River (Connor) **31**:114-15, 117
"Rock Around with Ollie Vee" (Holly) **65**:148
The Rock Garden (Kazantzakis)
See *Le jardin des rochers*
Rock Sinister (Dent) **72**:27
Rock Wagram (Saroyan) **137**:152, 156-58, 160, 186, 188
Rockaby (Beckett) **145**:137
"Rock-a-Bye Rock" (Holly) **65**:148
"The Rocket" (Tolstoy) **18**:377, 382
The Rocket (Pinero) **32**:409
"The Rocket of 1955" (Kornbluth) **8**:216
Rockets Galore (Mackenzie) **116**:234
The Rocking Horse (Morley) **87**:120, 124
"Rocks" (Abbey) **160**:22, 95
The Rocky Road to Dublin (Stephens) **4**:415, 419
"The Rod of Justice" (Machado de Assis)
See "O caso de vara"
Röda Rummet (Strindberg) **1**:460; **8**:408-11, 419; **21**:349, 353
"Den röda tiden" (Lagerkvist) **144**:217
De røde dråber (Obstfelder) **23**:178-79, 192
Röde Orm, hemma i österled (Bengtsson)
See *Röde Orm, sjöfarare i västerled*
Röde Orm, sjöfarare i västerled (Bengtsson) **48**:3-7, 9-10, 12-13
"Roderich von der Leine" (Raabe) **45**:190
Roderick Hudson (James) **2**:246, 255, 262; **11**:317-18, 325, 328; **40**:108-09, 115-16, 134; **47**:205-06
Rodin in Rime (Crowley)
See *Chaplet of Verse*
Rodine (Sologub) **9**:443
"Rodney" (Cotter) **28**:44
Rodney Stone (Doyle) **7**:216-17, 220, 239
"Rodomontade" (Stevens) **45**:286
Rodopio (Sá-Carneiro) **83**:401
Rodzina połanieckich (Sienkiewicz) **3**:422-23, 425-26, 428-30
"Roger Clay's Proposal" (Merrill) **173**:188
Roger Fry (Woolf) **43**:417; **56**:380; **101**:297-98; **128**:351, 373
Roggen und Weizen (Liliencron) **18**:213
Rogsajyae (Tagore) **3**:488-89; **53**:343
Rogue Herries (Walpole) **5**:499-500
The Rogueries of Scapin (Gregory) **176**:36
"Rogues in the House" (Howard) **8**:133, 135
The Rogue's March (Hornung) **59**:113
"Roi au masque d'or" (Schwob) **20**:323
Le roi au masque d'or, et autres nouvelles (Schwob) **20**:321, 323, 326, 329
"Le roi boit" (France) **9**:57

Le roi bombance (Marinetti) **10**:310, 316
Le roi Candaule (Gide) **5**:213, 215; **12**:144; **177**:105, 107
Le roi de Béotie (Jacob) **6**:191
Un roi sans divertissement (Giono) **124**:50, 54-6, 106, 11, 113, 115-16, 136-39
Rok 1794 (Reymont) **5**:390, 392-93, 395, 397, 399
Rokonok (Moricz) **33**:247, 250
"Rokovye iaitsa" (Bulgakov) **2**:64; **16**:73, 79-80, 83-5, 92-3, 100-03, 109-11
Roland Barthes by Roland Barthes (Barthes) See *Roland Barthes par Roland Barthes*
Roland Barthes par lui-même (Barthes) See *Roland Barthes par Roland Barthes*
Roland Barthes par Roland Barthes (Barthes) **135**:127-29, 131, 133, 135, 137-38, 141-42, 147-48, 150-52, 154-57, 159, 162-63, 166, 168, 173-74, 185-88
Roland Blake (Mitchell) **36**:265-68, 271
"The Role of Aggression in Civilization: Some Thoughts and Objections Regarding Freud's Death Instinct and Drive for Destruction" (Horney) See "The Problems of Marriage"
"The Role of the Australian Citizen in a Nuclear War" (White) **176**:227
"Roles and Salt" (Millay) **169**:235
Rolf in the Woods (Seton) **31**:263-64
Roll River (Boyd) **115**:59-62
"Roll Up at Talbragar" (Lawson) **27**:132, 134
The Roll-Call (Bennett) **20**:22, 24; **197**:20, 40
"The Roll-Call on the Reef" (Quiller-Couch) **53**:303
Rolling Down the Lea (Gogarty) **15**:120
"The Rolling English Road" (Chesterton) **6**:98
"Rolling, Rolling" (Toomer) **172**:278
"A Rolling Stone" (Chekhov) **31**:96
"Roma" (Carducci) **32**:91, 103-04
"Romagna" (Pascoli) **45**:155
Roman Bartholow (Robinson) **5**:413; **101**:105, 108
Roman Canon Law in the Church of England (Maitland) **65**:251, 259, 266
Le roman comique d'un musicien au XVII siécle (Rolland) **23**:267
Le roman de l'énergie nationale (Barrès) **47**:42-3
Le Roman de Lievre (Jammes) **75**:104-05, 115, 117-18
Roman der Stiftsdame (Heyse) **8**:119
Roman Diary (Ivanov) **33**:140
"Roman Diary of 1944" (Ivanov) **33**:138
Le roman d'un enfant (Loti) **11**:362, 367
Le roman d'un Spahi (Loti) **11**:352-55, 353, 359-60, 365-66
Le roman éxperimental (Zola) **1**:595; **6**:560, 566; **41**:444, 449, 451
"Roman Fever" (Wharton) **3**:571; **129**:364-65
The Roman Gravemounds (Hardy) **48**:59
"Roman Holiday" (Kuttner) **10**:268
Roman Holiday (Hecht) **101**:78-80
Roman Holidays (Howells) **7**:373
Roman Law and the British Empire (Innis) **77**:342
"Le roman réaliste et la roman piétiste" (Bourget) **12**:67
"The Roman Road" (Grahame) **64**:55, 66, 95
"A Roman Round-Robin" (Dobson) **79**:3, 31
A Roman Singer (Crawford) **10**:143-44, 146-48, 150
Roman Sonnets (Ivanov) **33**:136, 138
"Romance" (Artaud) **3**:52
"Romance" (Orwell) **128**:254
"Romance" (Valera y Alcala-Galiano) **10**:504
Romance (Ford) **1**:283, 288; **15**:70, 73, 90-1, 93; **57**:282; **172**:11-19
"Romance against Romanticism" (Matthews) **95**:265
"Romance and Realism" (Ouida) **43**:371
"Romance and Reality" (Kielland) **5**:275-76
"Romance and Sally Byrd" (Glasgow) **7**:343
"Romance and the Modern Stage" (Dunsany) **59**:19, 24
"A Romance at Sea" (McAlmon) **97**:101
"Romance at the Baillie Galleries" (Rosenberg) **12**:294
"Romance de la Guardia Civil Española" (García Lorca) **7**:290, 297; **49**:69, 71, 97, 119; **181**:90
"Romance de la luna, luna" (García Lorca) **197**:238
"Romance de la pena negra" (García Lorca) **49**:96-7, 113-14
Romance de lobos (Valle-Inclán) **5**:472-74, 486
"Romance del emplazado" (García Lorca) **49**:90, 112-13
"Romance du vin" (Nelligan) **14**:391, 393, 400
"Romance for a Demoiselle Lying in the Grass" (Stevens) **45**:347
"A Romance in Oil" (Adams) **56**:8
"Romance in the Roaring Forties" (Runyon) **10**:423-24
Romance Island (Gale) **7**:277, 281-82
"The Romance of a Busy Broker" (Henry) **19**:173, 190
The Romance of a Plain Man (Glasgow) **2**:176, 180; **7**:333, 340, 348-50
The Romance of a Queen (Glyn) See *Three Weeks*
The Romance of a Spahi (Loti) See *Le roman d'un Spahi*
"The Romance of Digestion" (Benchley) **55**:13, 16
The Romance of Leonardo da Vinci (Merezhkovsky) **29**:226, 228-31, 233-34, 241, 249
The Romance of Sorcery (Rohmer) **28**:285
"The Romance of Sunrise Rock" (Murfree) **135**:201-4, 219, 227
"The Romance of the Bill" (Phelps) **113**:342
"The Romance of the First Radical" (Lang) **16**:265
"Romance of the Spanish Civil Guard" (García Lorca) See "Romance de la Guardia Civil Española"
The Romance of the Swag (Lawson) **27**:131
A Romance of Two Worlds (Corelli) **51**:66-7, 72, 79, 82-3
"Romance sonámbulo" (García Lorca) **7**:300; **49**:72, 78, 96, 113; **181**:90-91
Romancero (Lugones) **15**:286
Romancero del Destierro (Unamuno) **148**:234, 256
"Romancero gitano" (Machado) **3**:310
Romancero gitano (García Lorca) See *Primer romancero gitano*
The Romancers (Rostand) See *Les romanesques*
Romancers del Río Seco (Lugones) **15**:291
Romances (Chang) See *Chuanqi xiaoshuoji*
Romances, canciones, y poesias (Valera y Alcala-Galiano) **10**:500
Romances de Coral Gables (Jiménez) **4**:225
Romances gitanos (Jiménez) **4**:214
"Romances históricos" (García Lorca) **7**:290
Romances of the Río Seco (Lugones) See *Romancers del Río Seco*
Romances sordos (Reyes) **33**:321
Les romanesques (Rostand) **6**:375-78, 383; **37**:280, 282, 286-87, 291, 295, 298-99, 303
"The Romanian Letters and Arts in the Second Half of the 19th Century" (Caragiale) **76**:168
"The Romanian Nation" (Caragiale) **76**:169
Romans, récits et soties (Gide) **177**:99-101
The Romantic (Sinclair) **3**:435; **11**:413
Romantic Adventure (Glyn) **72**:132
"The Romantic Adventures of a Milkmaid" (Hardy) **4**:172; **10**:217; **153**:103
The Romantic Age (Milne) **6**:308
Romantic Ballads and Poems of Phantasy (Sharp) **39**:352, 371-72, 378-79, 381, 388
The Romantic Comedians (Glasgow) **2**:182-84, 186, 189-90; **7**:337, 341, 343, 346-47
Romantic Comedies (Molnár) **20**:171-72
A Romantic Farce (Davidson) **24**:182
Romantic Flowers (Gumilev) See *Romanticheskie tsvety*
"Romantic Ireland's Dead and Gone" (Yeats) **31**:385
The Romantic Movement in English Poetry (Symons) **11**:434, 447
The Romantic Rebellion (Clark) **147**:122-23
The Romantic School in France (Brandes) See *Den romantiske skole i Frankrig*
The Romantic School in Germany (Brandes) See *Den romantiske skole i Tydskland*
Romantic Times (Nabokov) See *Glory*
Romantic Young Lady (Martinez Sierra and Martinez Sierra) See *Sueño de una noche de agosto*
Romanticheskie tsvety (Gumilev) **60**:260, 262, 269
"Romanticism and Classicism" (Hulme) **21**:131-32, 136, 140, 147
"Romanticism in Spanish Poetry" (Vallejo) **56**:295
The Romanticists (Merezhkovsky) **29**:231
Romantics (Rostand) See *Les romanesques*
Die Romantik (Huch) **13**:245, 254
Romantisches Drama (Werfel) **8**:479
Den romantiske skole i Frankrig (Brandes) **11**:62, 72
Den romantiske skole i Tydskland (Brandes) **10**:60, 62, 72
"Romantisme" (Cocteau) **119**:76
Roman-Tsarevich (Hippius) **9**:155, 161-62, 169
Romany (Bulgakov) **159**:11-12, 14, 16-17, 42
The Romany Stain (Morley) **87**:125
I romanzi della rosa (D'Annunzio) **6**:137-38
Romanzi e racconti (Calvino) **183**:187-88, 208, 212, 237-41, 244
"Un romanzo dentro un quadro" (Calvino) **183**:103
"Un romanzo giallo nella geologia" (Gadda) **144**:81
"Rome" (Howe) **21**:106
Rome (Zola) **41**:421-22; **1**:587, 589; **6**:564; **41**:421-22
"Rome on the Palatine" (Hardy) **143**:169
"Romeo and Juliet" (Čapek) **37**:45
Romeo and Juliet (Cocteau) See *Roméo et Juliette*
Roméo et Jeannette (Anouilh) **195**:7-8, 10, 12-13, 17, 39
Roméo et Juliette (Cocteau) **119**:57
El romero alucinado (Gonzalez Martinez) **72**:148, 150
"Das römische Bad" (Sudermann) **15**:432
Römisches Reich deutscher Nation (Huch) **13**:253
"Rompere con il passato" (Levi) **125**:218
Ronald Standish (Sapper) **44**:317
"Ronda de la vida riendo" (Huidobro) **31**:126
La Ronde (Ophuls) **79**:173-4, 176, 180, 192, 215-6, 227, 234, 238, 271-3
La Ronde (Schnitzler) See *Reigen*
Die Rondköpfe und die Spitzköpfe (Brecht) **1**:104; **6**:31, 37
Rondon tō (Natsume) **10**:328-29, 344
"Rōnen" (Akutagawa Ryūnosuke) **16**:33
"Le rongeur maudit" (Bosschere) **19**:67
The Roofing Feast (Strindberg) **1**:460
"The Roofs of Marseilles" (Nezval) **44**:240, 243
"The Rooinek" (Bosman) **49**:4-6, 9, 20-1, 29
Room 13 (Wallace) **57**:402
Room Forty-Five (Howells) **7**:387
"The Room in the Tower" (Benson) **27**:13, 16

A Room of One's Own (Woolf) **1**:530, 534, 544; **20**:394, 394; **43**:395-97, 402, 423; **56**:371, 376, 386, 390-391; **101**:204, 307, 326; **128**:318, 341, 345, 361
A Room with a View (Forster) **125**:24-5, 30-1, 58-9, 80-1, 114
"Roosevelt" (Lindsay) **17**:236
Roosevelt and Hopkins, an Intimate History (Sherwood) **3**:419
Roosevelt: The Story of a Friendship (Wister) **21**:380, 385
"Rooster" (Hagiwara)
See "Niwatori"
"The Roosters" (Bishop) **121**:4, 6, 9, 31-3, 36-7, 40, 43-4, 51, 71-2, 75, 80, 88-90, 98
The Root and the Flower (Myers) **59**:131, 134-7, 142, 147, 150, 152-3, 155-7
The Root of Evil (Dixon) **163**:168
The Root of Life—Ginseng (Prishvin)
See *Zhen'-shen': koren' zhizni*
"Root-Light; or, The Lawyer's Daughter" (Dickey) **151**:125, 147, 173
Roots (Haley)
See *Roots: The Saga of an American Family*
"The Roots of American Culture" (Rourke) **12**:318, 322, 330-31
The Roots of American Culture, and Other Essays (Rourke) **12**:318, 322-23, 329-32
The Roots of American Order (Kirk) **119**:266, 275, 297, 320-21
Roots: The Saga of an American Family (Haley) **147**:136-224
Ropa apolillada (Palma) **29**:258
Ropa vieja (Palma) **29**:258-59
The Rope (O'Neill) **6**:336; **49**:252, 260, 264
Rope and Faggot: A Biography of Judge Lynch (White) **15**:476-78, 480
"The Rope's End" (Nemerov) **124**:148, 159, 186, 191-92
Rory and Bran (Dunsany) **59**:22, 24, 26
Rosa (Hamrick) **49**:128-29, 133-34, 141, 144, 153, 159
"Rosa Alchemica" (Yeats) **31**:414; **93**:339; **116**:336
"La rosa de oro" (Valle-Inclán) **5**:478
A Rosa do povo (Drummond de Andrade) **139**:224, 226, 232-33
Rosa i krest (Blok) **5**:85, 97-8, 100
"Rosa íntima" (Jiménez) **183**:260
Rosa Luxemburg Speaks (Luxemburg) **63**:201
Rosa mundi (Crowley) **7**:206
La rosa profunda (Borges) **109**:8
"La rosa y la espina" (Lugones) **15**:293
"Rosa y serpiente" (Aleixandre) **113**:5
Le Rosaire au soleil (Jammes) **75**:119
Rosamond, Queen of the Lombards (Swinburne) **8**:433-34, 436
"Rosamund Grief" (Bottomley) **107**:6
Rosamunde Floris (Kaiser) **9**:176, 180-81, 185, 192
Rosario de sonetos líricos (Unamuno) **2**:562; **9**:510, 514; **148**:256
"A Rosary" (Davidson) **24**:179
Rosary of Lyric Sonnets (Unamuno)
See *Rosario de sonetos líricos*
"Rosas del calvario" (Lugones) **15**:285
Rosaura (Güiraldes) **39**:175-77, 182, 186, 190
"Roscoe Purkapile" (Masters) **25**:304
"Die Rose" (Rilke) **195**:305
"Rose" (Unamuno) **2**:568
"The Rose" (Yeats) **93**:346
Die Rose (Walser) **18**:421-22
The Rose (Yeats) **1**:558, 569; **18**:442; **31**:394
"Rose and Serpent" (Aleixandre)
See "Rosa y serpiente"
The Rose and the Cross (Blok)
See *Rosa i krest*
"The Rose and the Rock" (Stringer) **37**:328
Rose Bernd (Hauptmann) **4**:195, 197
Rose Briar (Tarkington) **9**:465
"La rose de Hildesheim ou les trésors des rois mages" (Apollinaire) **3**:38; **51**:20
Rose Deeprose (Kaye-Smith) **20**:111
"The 'Rose Delima'" (Drummond) **25**:151
"A Rose for Emily" (Faulkner) **170**:225
"The Rose Garden" (James) **6**:210
The Rose Garden (Brennan) **124**:7
"The Rose of Dixie" (Henry) **19**:174
Rose of Dutcher's Coolly (Garland) **3**:192-94, 198
"A Rose of Glenbogie" (Harte) **25**:199, 213
"The Rose of Hildesheim" (Apollinaire)
See "La rose de Hildesheim ou les trésors des rois mages"
"The Rose of Hope" (Scott) **6**:398
The Rose of Life (Braddon) **111**:215
"The Rose of Shadows" (Yeats) **31**:416
The Rose of the Rancho (Belasco) **3**:85, 90
"The Rose of the World" (Yeats) **1**:558, 574
"The Rose of Tuolumne" (Harte) **25**:191, 200
A Rose of Yesterday (Crawford) **10**:150
"Rose Pink" (Gale) **7**:277
La rose publique (Éluard) **7**:248, 250, 256; **41**:150
"The Rose Tree" (Yeats) **31**:421; **93**:389
"Roseamond" (Apollinaire)
See "Rosemonde"
The Rose-Bearer (Hofmannsthal)
See *Der Rosenkavalier*
Rosedale (Wharton) **149**:160
"Rose-Leaves" (Dobson) **79**:32, 35
"Rosemary" (Millay) **4**:306
"Rosemary of Remembrance" (Aldrich) **125**:6-7, 9-10, 14-16, 19
"Rosemonde" (Apollinaire) **51**:58-9, 61
"Rosen" (Obstfelder) **23**:179
Rosen (Sudermann) **15**:430
Rosen der Einöde (Bernhard) **165**:122
"Rosenaltaret" (Södergran) **31**:292
Rosenda (Romero) **14**:434-35
"Das Rosen-Innere" (Rilke) **195**:304
Der Rosenkavalier (Hofmannsthal) **11**:296, 301, 311
"Die Rosenschale" (Rilke) **195**:243-44, 250-51, 303, 305, 308
"Roser" (Obstfelder) **23**:190
"Roses" (Obstfelder)
See "Roser"
"Roses" (Sarton) **120**:268
"Roses" (Södergran) **31**:294
Les Roses (Rilke) **195**:190, 305
"Roses Can Wound" (Abercrombie) **141**:19
Roses for Bettina (Pabst) **127**:363
Roses of Loneliness (Bernhard)
See *Rosen der Einöde*
"The Rosicrucian" (Crowley) **7**:204, 208
Rosmersholm (Ibsen) **2**:223-25, 227, 229-32, 235, 241-42; **8**:144, 148, 151; **16**:158, 162, 166-68, 173, 177, 187, 193; **37**:223, 225; **52**:143-44
Rossetti and His Circle (Beerbohm) **1**:68; **24**:104, 115, 119
Roßhalde (Hesse) **196**:323, 335, 338
"Rosso malpelo" (Verga) **3**:539, 548
Rossum's Universal Robots (Čapek)
See *R. U. R.*
"Rostro final" (Aleixandre) **113**:36
The Rosy Shorelines (Papadiamantis) **29**:270-72
"Rosy-Checked Death" (Yosano)
See "Kôgao no shi"
"Rothenberger's Wedding" (Graham) **19**:136
La rôtisserie de la reine Pédauque (France) **9**:41-2, 51, 53, 55
"Rotting Clam" (Hagiwara) **60**:296
Rotting Hill (Lewis) **2**:391, 393; **9**:242
Rouen (Péguy) **10**:410-11
"Rouge et bleue" (Tsvetaeva) **35**:389, 407
Rouge of the North (Chang)
See *Jin suo ji*
"Rouge ou noire" (Sully Prudhomme) **31**:302
Rough for Theatre II (Beckett) **145**:142
Rough Justice (Braddon) **111**:228-31
The Rough Rider, and Other Poems (Carman) **7**:139, 143
The Rough Riders (Roosevelt) **69**:203, 243, 257
Rough-Hewn (Fisher) **87**:77
Roughing It (Twain) **6**:455, 457-58, 471, 476; **12**:426, 430, 435, 437, 452; **36**:355, 358, 371, 379; **48**:344, 358; **161**:217, 270
Les Rougon-Macquart (Zola) **1**:585-88, 594; **6**:559-61, 563-65, 567-70; **21**:421
Les rouilles encagées (Péret) **20**:186
A Roumanian Diary (Carossa)
See *Tagebuch im Kriege*
Round about the Congress (Horvath)
See *Rund um den Kongreß*
The Round Dance (Schnitzler)
See *Reigen*
A Round Dance of the Times: All Voices (Balmont)
See *Khorovod vremën: Vseglasnost'*
Round Heads and Peakheads (Brecht)
See *Die Rundköpf und die Spitzköpf*
The Round Heads and the Pointed Heads (Brecht)
See *Die Rondköpfe und die Spitzköpfe*
"A Round of Visits" (James) **2**:275
"Round River Rendezvous: The Rio Grande" (Abbey) **160**:75
"Round the Lake" (Papadiamantis) **29**:270
Round the Moon (Verne)
See *Autour de la lune*
Round the Red Lamp (Doyle)
See *Round the Red Lamp: Being Facts and Fancies of Medical Life*
Round the Red Lamp: Being Facts and Fancies of Medical Life (Doyle) **7**:216, 219
Round the World in Eighty Days (Verne)
See *Le tour du monde en quatre-vingt jours*
Round Up (Lardner) **2**:327, 333-34; **14**:297-98, 307
"The Roundel" (Swinburne) **8**:439-40; **36**:315
The Roundheads and the Peakheads (Brecht)
See *Die Rondköpfe und die Spitzköpfe*
"Rounding the Cape" (Campbell) **5**:117
Roundsman Of The Lord (Broun) **104**:98
"Rousseau" (Murry) **16**:341
Rousseau, Kant, Goethe: Two Essays (Cassirer) **61**:68
The Rout (Fadeyev)
See *Razgrom*
"The Rout of the White Hussars" (Kipling) **8**:202
"Route" (Oppen) **107**:260, 264, 352-53, 360, 365
"The Route of the North" (Chang)
See "Yuan nu"
"La Route sous la neige" (Yourcenar) **193**:265
"Route Two" (Nemerov) **124**:259
"Rouwstad" (van Ostaijen) **33**:418
"The Rover" (Pickthall) **21**:252
The Rover (Conrad) **1**:209, 218; **6**:114; **25**:111
Rovigo (Herbert) **168**:47
The Roving Critic (Van Doren) **18**:391-92, 405
Roving East and Roving West (Lucas) **73**:157
"A Row of Horse Stalls" (Knister) **56**:156, 161
"The Rowan Tree Fire" (Esenin) **4**:115
"Roy Rene" (Cram) **45**:3
The Royal Americans (Foote) **108**:15-17
Royal Blossom; or, Trisevyene (Palamas)
See *Trisévgene*
"A Royal Command" (Somerville & Ross) **51**:335
Royal Dream (Heijermans) **24**:293
The Royal Family of Broadway (Mankiewicz) **85**:114, 164
The Royal Game (Zweig)
See *Schachnovelle*
Royal Highness (Mann)
See *Königliche Hoheit*
"Royal Jelly" (Dahl) **173**:14
"Royal Palm" (Crane) **5**:189

"The Royal Tombs of Golconda" (Naidu) **80**:314
The Royal Vagabond (Cohan) **60**:171
"Royalist Songs" (Cram) **45**:12
"Rozanov's Letters" (Remizov)
See "Kukkha. Rozanovy pis'ma"
"Rozhanitsa" (Remizov) **27**:353-54
"Rozhdestvenskaia zvezda" (Pasternak) **188**:190, 230, 250
Rózsa Sándor a lovát ugratja (Moricz) **33**:243, 247, 251
Rózsa Sándor összevonja a szemöldökét (Moricz) **33**:243, 247, 251
Rrose Sélavy (Desnos) **22**:58-60
"Rubáiyát of Doc Sifers" (Riley) **51**:292
Le ruban (Feydeau) **22**:77, 83, 92
"The Rubber Check" (Fitzgerald) **6**:167
"El rubí" (Darío) **4**:60
The Rubicon (Benson) **27**:3, 8
"Rubka lesa" (Tolstoy) **4**:445, 474; **11**:461, 464; **173**:280
Rubruk v mongolii (Zabolotsky) **52**:373
Ruch der Hirten (George) **14**:196
Rückblick (Liliencron) **18**:208, 215
"Rückblicke" (Kandinsky) **92**:37, 81
Die rückkehr vom Hades (Mann) **9**:320
Rudder Grange (Stockton) **47**:316, 319, 322
Ruddigore; or, The Witch's Curse (Gilbert) **3**:213, 216
Rude Assignment (Lewis) **2**:391; **9**:242-43; **104**:157, 171-72, 177, 180, 209, 214, 225-27, 230, 240, 242, 274, 276, 282
"A Rude Awakening" (Chopin) **14**:70
"Rude Noises in Company K" (Shepherd) **177**:316
Rudimental Divine Science (Eddy) **71**:92
"Rudyard Kipling" (Orwell) **128**:282, 285
Rue (Housman) **7**:353
"Rue Barrée" (Chambers) **41**:88, 94
"The rue de la Chine" (Huysmans) **69**:25
"Rue des Nations" (Cankar) **105**:161
El ruedo Ibérico (Valle-Inclán) **5**:485, 487-89
Der Ruf des Lebens (Schnitzler) **4**:386, 389
"Le ruffian" (Moréas) **18**:286
The Ruffian on the Stair (Orton) **157**:292, 294-96, 300, 302, 308, 316, 329, 342, 355-56, 60
"The Rug" (Andrić)
See "Ćilim"
"Rugg" (Söderberg) **39**:437, 439
The Rugged Path (Sherwood) **3**:416, 418-19
"The Rugged Way" (Dunbar) **12**:104
"Ruin" (García Lorca)
See "Ruina"
"Ruina" (García Lorca) **49**:94; **181**:28
"Las ruinas circulares" (Borges) **109**:8, 18-20, 52, 58, 60, 119, 128, 143, 152
Ruine (Kandinsky) **92**:50
La ruine du monde antique (Sorel)
See *La fin du monde antique*
Ruined Abbeys of Great Britain (Cram) **45**:9
"The Ruined Maid" (Hardy) **4**:154
The Ruined Map (Abe)
See *Moetsukita chizu*
"Ruines" (Nelligan) **14**:392
"Ruins" (Bergelson) **81**:19
"Ruins" (García Lorca) **197**:186, 210-11
"The Ruins" (Tomlinson) **71**:381
"Ruit hora" (Carducci) **32**:87
"Rule by Machines" (Čapek) **37**:70; **192**:230
"The Rule of Phase Applied to History" (Adams) **4**:17-18; **52**:27, 41
"The Rulers" (Patton) **79**:302
Rulers of Kings (Atherton) **2**:14
The Rulers of the Mediterranean (Davis) **24**:201
Rules and Counsels for the Scientific Investigator (Ramoacn y Cajal)
See *Reglos y consejos*
Rules and Order (Hayek) **109**:214-15
"The Rules of Existential Graphs" (Peirce) **81**:199
"Rules of Illative Transformation" (Peirce) **81**:187
The Rules of Sociological Method (Durkheim)
See *Les règles de la méthode sociologique*
Rules of the Game (Pirandello)
See *Il giuoco delle parti*
"Rules, Perception and Intelligibility" (Hayek) **109**:207-08
The Ruling Class (Mosca)
See *Elementi di scienza politica*
The Ruling Passion (Riddell) **40**:335
Rum Island (van Schendel)
See *Rumeiland*
Rumbin Galleries (Tarkington) **9**:469
The Rumbledump (Raabe)
See *Der Schüdderump*
Rumeiland (van Schendel) **56**:241
"Rumori" (Brancati) **12**:86
Run Man Run (Himes) **139**:53, 258, 265, 281
Run, Melos! (Dazai Osamu)
See *Hashire merosu*
Run, Sheep, Run (Bodenheim) **44**:73-4
"Runagate Niggers" (March) **96**:235, 265
The Runagates Club (Buchan) **41**:41, 44
The Runaway, and Other Stories (Tagore)
See *Palātakā*
Runaway Horses (Mishima)
See *Honba*
Rund um den Kongreß (Horvath) **45**:76, 81, 100-02, 104-06
Die Rundköpf und die Spitzköpf (Brecht) **169**:4, 12
Rundt Kap det Gode Haab: Vers fra sjøen (Grieg) **10**:205, 207-08
"A Rune Found in the Starlight" (Buchanan) **107**:17
"The Rune of Age" (Sharp) **39**:398
"The Rune of the Passion of Women" (Sharp) **39**:398
"Runes" (Nemerov) **124**:150, 156, 170, 172, 174-75, 182-83, 185-87, 195, 203, 205, 208, 216-17, 226, 245-46, 248-49, 285, 291, 314
Runes of Women (Sharp) **39**:397-98
"Runes on Weland's Sword" (Kipling) **8**:191
"The Runnable Stag" (Davidson) **24**:178, 182
The Runner (Connor) **31**:114-17
"The Running Away of Chester" (Montgomery) **51**:212; **140**:334
"Running for Office" (Cohan) **60**:169-71
"Runokirje" (Leino) **24**:371
"Run-Out Harbor" (Coffin) **95**:15
Runyon First and Last (Runyon) **10**:428, 435
"Rupert Brooke" (Verhaeren) **12**:471
"Rupert Brooke and the Intellectual Imagination" (de la Mare) **4**:81
Rupert of Hentzau (Hope) **83**:170
"Ruptura sin palabras" (Salinas) **17**:365
The Rural Community (Baker) **10**:22
"Rural Enchantment" (Khlebnikov)
See "Selskaya ocharovannost"
Rural England (Haggard) **11**:245
A Rural Judge (Prado)
See *Un juez rural*
"The Rural Pan" (Grahame) **64**:77-8
"Rus'" (Zamyatin) **8**:553; **37**:427
"Rusia" (Bunin) **6**:57
Rusia en 1931. Reflexiones al pie del Kremlin (Vallejo) **56**:219-92, 299
"Rusija" (Vazov) **25**:455
Ruskin Family Letters (Ruskin) **63**:320
Ruskin's Letters from Venice: 1851-52 (Ruskin) **63**:262
Ruskin's Philosophy (Collingwood) **67**:125, 127
Russell Cheney, 1881-1945, A Record of His Work (Matthiessen) **100**:258
"Russell Kincaid" (Masters) **25**:299
Russet Mantle (Riggs) **56**:201, 209, 216
"Russia" (Balmont) **11**:41
"Russia" (Vazov)
See "Rusija"
Russia: A Chronicle of Three Journeys in the Aftermath of the Revolution (Kazantzakis)
See *Te eida set Rousia*
"Russia and 1848" (Berlin) **105**:17
Russia in the Whirlwind (Remizov)
See *Vzvikhrennaia Rus*
Russia in Writ (Remizov) **27**:333-34
Russia Laughs (Zoshchenko) **15**:491
"Russian Art" (Rilke)
See "Russische Kunst"
The Russian Character (Tolstoy) **18**:379
Russian Diary (Barlach)
See *Russisches Tagebuch*
The Russian Nile (Rozanov) **104**:384
The Russian People (Baring) **8**:43
"The Russian Point of View" (Woolf) **43**:415, 422; **128**:334
"The Russian Realists and Southern Literature" (McCullers) **155**:200
"The Russian Religious Idea" (Berdyaev) **67**:24
The Russian Revolution (Luxemburg) **63**:202, 215, 221, 228
"A Russian Tale" (Herbert) **168**:24
Russian Thinkers (Berlin) **105**:16, 20-1, 50, 71
"The Russian Tragedy" (Luxemburg) **63**:220
"Russian Writers, Censors, and Readers" (Nabokov) **189**:149
"Russians" (Douglas) **40**:90-1
"Russische Kunst" (Rilke) **195**:175, 216, 263
Russisches Tagebuch (Barlach) **84**:93
"The Rustic Commune" (Carducci)
See "Il comune rustico"
"Rustic Country" (Hall) **12**:195
"A Rustic Eclogue" (White) **176**:170
"Rustic Friendship" (Khlebnikov)
See "Selskaya druzhba"
The Rustle of Language (Barthes)
See *Le bruissement de la langue*
"Rusya" (Bunin)
See "Rusia"
"Ruth and Delilah" (Ady) **11**:20
"Ruth and Naomi" (Harper) **14**:260
"The Rutherford Shows" (Williams) **89**:374
Rutland (Lie) **5**:324, 330
"Ru'ya'" (Gibran) **9**:88
"Rye Road" (Ford) **172**:94
"Ryojō" (Hagiwara) **60**:311
Les rythmes souverains (Verhaeren) **12**:459-60, 464, 475
"Ryton Firs" (Abercrombie) **141**:22
Ryugaku (Endo) **152**:175-76, 194, 198, 237
"The Rzav Hills" (Andrić) **135**:15-16
S. Karuma-shi no hanzai (Abe) **131**:11
"S morya" (Tsvetaeva) **35**:411
"S ognenoi past'iu" (Remizov) **27**:348
"S P" (Apollinaire) **51**:34
"S.S. Atlas" (Graham) **19**:109
S.S. Glencairn (O'Neill) **6**:329; **49**:238
S/Z (Barthes) **135**:112, 115-16, 128, 131-32, 141, 147-48, 153, 159, 164, 168, 170, 186
"Sábado" (Storni) **5**:451
"Sabala Fairy Tale" (Sienkiewicz) **3**:430
Sabatai Zewi (Wassermann) **6**:513
Sabato, Demenica e Lunedi (de Filippo) **127**:280
"Sabato Santo" (Carducci) **32**:102
Sabbatai zewi (Asch) **3**:66-7
"The Sabbath Breaker" (Zangwill) **16**:441
"Sabina" (Quiller-Couch) **53**:291
The Sabine Women (Andreyev)
See *Prekrasayia sabinianki*
Die Sabinerrinnen (Heyse) **8**:119
"Un sabio" (Pereda) **16**:367
"Sabishii jinkaku" (Hagiwara) **60**:314
El sabor de la tierruca (Pereda) **16**:362-63, 367, 374, 378, 381-82
"Šabos-naxmu" (Babel) **2**:32
"Sac au dos" (Huysmans) **7**:405; **69**:24
"Sacco and Vanzetti" (Broun) **104**:83
"Sack of Prato" (Lee-Hamilton) **22**:186, 188
"Sacrament" (Cullen) **37**:154, 169

The Sacrament as Manifestation of the Holy (Otto) **85**:323
"Le sacre coeur" (Mew) **8**:296, 299
Sacred and Profane Love (Bennett) **5**:32, 38, 41, 43-4; **20**:28; **197**:11, 16-17, 22, 31, 36-9, 42, 106
The Sacred and Profane Love Machine (Murdoch) **171**:210, 254, 280, 329-30
Sacred & Secular &c. (Gill) **85**:79, 90-1
"Sacred Are the Mountain Ashes in the Yard" (Leino)
See "Pyhät on pihlajat pihalla"
Sacred Blood (Hippius)
See *Svyataya krov*
"The Sacred Conspiracy" (Bataille) **155**:111
"Sacred Emily" (Stein) **48**:237
"The Sacred Factory" (Toomer) **172**:265, 286, 290, 292-93
Sacred Families; Three Novellas (Donoso)
See *Tres novelitas burguesas*
The Sacred Fount (James) **2**:258, 261, 270; **11**:320, 348; **24**:345, 358; **40**:133, 141, 148; **47**:195-99
"Sacred Love" (Kuprin) **5**:298
The Sacred Pipe: Black Elk's Account of the Seven Rites of the Oglala Sioux (Black Elk) **33**:4, 8-9
"Sacred, Voluptuous Hollows Deep" (Rosenberg) **12**:311
"The Sacred Way" (Sikelianos) **39**:406, 410, 419, 421
Las sacrificadas (Quiroga) **20**:212
"Sacrifice" (Hansen) **32**:249
"The Sacrifice" (Kolmar)
See "Das Opfer"
"Sacrifice" (Manning) **25**:278
"The Sacrifice" (Remizov)
See "Zhertva"
Sacrifice (Benavente)
See *Sacrificios*
Sacrifice (Tagore)
See *Vāsarjan*
Le sacrifice impérial (Jacob) **6**:193, 202
"The Sacrifice of Love" (Premchand)
See "Prem-ki holi"
"The Sacrifice of the Maidens" (Roberts) **68**:324, 348-49, 351
"A Sacrifice unto Sion" (Evans) **85**:37
The Sacrificed (Quiroga)
See *Las sacrificadas*
"A Sacrificed Author" (Nemerov) **124**:274
"Sacrifices" (Bataille) **155**:94
"Sacrificial Mutilation and the Severed Ear of Vincent Van Gogh" (Bataille) **155**:65
Sacrificios (Benavente) **3**:98
La Sacrifiée (Rod) **52**:310, 314-15
Sacrilege (Valle-Inclán) **5**:486
Sad Airs (Jiménez)
See *Arias tristes*
Sad as She Is (Onetti)
See *Tan triste como ella*
The Sad End of Policarpo Quaresma (Lima Barreto)
See *Triste fim de Policarpo Quaresma*
The Sad Geraniums (Borchert)
See *Die Traurigen Geranien, und andere Geschichten aus dem Nachlass*
"Sad Green" (Weinberg) **131**:311
"A Sad Heart at the Supermarket" (Jarrell) **177**:172, 177, 231-32, 239-40
A Sad Heart at the Supermarket (Jarrell) **177**:153, 179, 183, 185, 190, 223, 231-32, 239
"Sad Moonlit Night" (Hagiwara)
See "Kanashi Tsukio"
"The Sad Mother" (Tynan) **3**:504
"The Sad Queen" (Sharp) **39**:376, 378
"A Sad Story" (Chekhov) **3**:112
"Sad Strains of a Gay Waltz" (Stevens) **45**:269, 275, 296
Sad Toys (Ishikawa)
See *Kanashiki gangu*
Sadakichi Hartmann: Critical Modenist: Collected Art Writings (Hartmann) **73**:110
"The Saddest Man" (Marquis) **7**:437
The Saddest Story (Ford)
See *The Good Soldier: A Tale of Passion*
Sade, Fourier, Loyola (Barthes) **135**:116, 133, 138, 142, 147, 149, 156, 158-59
The Sadeian Woman: An Exercise in Cultural History (Carter) **139**:45-46, 49, 64, 66, 78-80, 82, 113-15, 131, 134, 143, 146, 150, 153, 170-73, 176-79, 184, 193, 200, 204, 211, 214-15
"Sadgati" (Premchand) **21**:298
"Sadjak buat Basuki Resobowo" (Anwar) **22**:23
Sado koshaku fujin (Mishima) **161**:92-3
Sadok sudei (Guro) **56**:132
"Saeta" (García Lorca) **181**:199
Safar Nameh. Persian Pictures. A Book of travel (Bell) **67**:13, 16
Safe Conduct (Pasternak)
See *Okhrannaia gramota*
"Safe Conduct" (Pasternak) **188**:196
Safer Ha-agadah (Bialik) **25**:53, 60
"Safety" (Brooke) **7**:129
"Safety Second" (Benchley) **55**:14
"The Saga of Perma" (Leino)
See "Perman taru"
Saga of Saints (Undset) **197**:311-16
The Saga of the Folkungs (Strindberg)
See *Folkungasagan*
"A Saga of the Seas" (Grahame) **64**:87
"Saga y Agar" (Pardo Bazán) **189**:228
Sagas of Vaster Britain (Campbell) **9**:32
"The Sage" (Robinson) **101**:119
"Sagen und Sänge" (George) **2**:149; **14**:201, 205-06
La sagesse et la destinée (Maeterlinck) **3**:318, 325-26, 329
Saggi (Calvino) **183**:187, 193-95, 236, 242-43, 245
Saggi di critica del Marxismo (Sorel) **91**:332
"Saggio sullo Hegel" (Croce) **37**:84
"A Saghalinian" (Korolenko) **22**:170
"Saghan tamisráprati" (Devkota) **23**:48
"Sag-i vilgard" (Hedāyat) **21**:74
Sagittario (Ginzburg) **156**:59, 71, 112
Sagittarius (Ginzburg)
See *Sagittario*
Sagor (Strindberg) **47**:369
Sagra del Signore della nave (Pirandello) **29**:317, 320
"Sahaj Path" (Tagore) **3**:496
"The Sahara" (Loti)
See "Le désert"
"The Sahara of Bozart" (Mencken) **13**:363
"Sahashi jingorō" (Mori Ogai) **14**:376
"A Sahibs' War" (Kipling) **8**:200; **17**:207
"Said the Young-Young Man to the Old-Old Man" (Stephens) **4**:408, 420
"Saigo no ikku" (Mori Ogai) **14**:380
Saikaku Ichidai Onna (Mizoguchi) **72**:293, 306-07, 310, 313, 319-20, 323, 336, 339, 342-43, 346, 348-51
"Sail" (Dent) **72**:28-30
"The Sail of Ulysses" (Stevens) **45**:313-14, 327, 329
"Sailing after Lunch" (Stevens) **3**:462; **45**:269, 275, 282
"Sailing of the Swallow" (Swinburne) **8**:426-27
"Sailing to America" (Roberts) **68**:306
"Sailing to Byzantium" (Yeats) **1**:567-69, 579, 581-82; **11**:520, 529, 533; **18**:445-47, 449, 451-54, 456, 458-60, 462-63; **31**:398, 402-03, 410, 423; **93**:344; **116**:259-343
"Saillant" (Apollinaire) **51**:34
"Sailor" (Davies) **5**:198
Sailor Thieves (Dunsany) **2**:143
The Sailor Who Fell from Grace with the Sea (Mishima)
See *Gogo no eiko*
"A Sailor's Song" (Dunbar) **12**:105
"The Sailor's Sweetheart" (Scott) **6**:394
Sails and Mirage, and Other Poems (Sterling) **20**:386
"Saint" (Merrill) **173**:256
"A Saint about to Fall" (Thomas) **8**:450; **45**:399
A Saint, and Others (Bourget)
See *Pastels*
"The Saint and the Goblin" (Saki) **3**:371
Saint Augustine (Papini)
See *San't Agostino*
"Saint Catherine of Siena" (Meynell) **6**:295, 300
"Saint Deseret" (Masters) **2**:461
Saint Emmanuel the Good, Martyr (Unamuno)
See *San Manuel Bueno, mártir*
"Saint Francis and Lady Clare" (Masters) **25**:298
Saint George and the Dragon (Heidenstam) **5**:253
"Saint Georges" (Verhaeren) **12**:466
Saint Helena: Little Island (Aldanov)
See *Svjataja Elena: Malen' kij ostrov*
Saint Jan of the Stockyards (Brecht)
See *Die heilige Johanna der Schlachtöfe*
"Saint Jerome in the Desert" (Field) **43**:167
Saint Joan (Shaw) **3**:389, 394-95, 398, 402, 406; **9**:416-17; **45**:238
"Saint Julien l'hospitalier" (Schwob) **20**:323
"Saint Katherine of Alexandria" (Field) **43**:165-66
"Saint Margaret's Island" (Ady) **11**:15
Saint Matorel (Jacob) **6**:191
Saint Olaf (Bojer) **64**:22
"Le saint satyre" (France) **9**:52-3
"Saint Sebastian" (Field) **43**:165-67
"Saint Sebastian" (Gray) **19**:154, 157
Sainte Lydwine de Schiedam (Huysmans) **7**:408, 411; **69**:7, 16, 40-1, 43, 46, 69
Sainte Europe (Adamov) **189**:15, 59
"Sainte-Nitouche" (Robinson) **5**:400
Saint-Louis (Rolland) **23**:256-57
"The Saints" (Bishop) **103**:5, 7-8, 19, 21
"Saints and Lodgers" (Davies) **5**:200
Saints and Revolutionaries (Stapledon) **22**:315, 322
Saints and Sinners (Bradford) **36**:68-9
Saints and Strangers (Carter)
See *Black Venus*
"Saints and Their Bodies" (Higginson) **36**:171, 174-75
Les saints du paradis (Gourmont) **17**:129
Saints in Sussex (Kaye-Smith) **20**:101, 107-08
Saint's Progress (Galsworthy) **1**:300; **45**:47-8, 64
"The Saint's Story" (Buchanan) **107**:16
Saison en astrologie (Fargue) **11**:201
"Les saisons" (Apollinaire) **3**:34; **51**:36
Saisons choisies (Huidobro) **31**:122-23
"Les saisons de l'horloge de la fraise des animaux veloutés et du" (Arp) **115**:30
"Les Saisons leurs Astérisques et leurs Pions" (Arp) **115**:30
"Saji" (Shiga) **172**:214
"Sakai jiken" (Mori Ogai) **14**:380
"Sakazuki" (Mori Ogai) **14**:369-70
"Lo Sakhmod" (Peretz) **16**:393-94
The Sal Hepatica Review (Allen) **87**:37
"Sala vacía" (Borges) **109**:10
The Salad Bowl Review (Allen) **87**:37
"Salamanca" (Unamuno) **2**:568
"The Salamander" (Heyse)
See "Der Salamander"
"Der Salamander" (Heyse) **8**:114, 116
"Sale of St Thomas" (Abercrombie) **141**:6
The Sale of St Thomas (Abercrombie) **141**:3, 10, 21-22
"Salem Campground" (Fletcher) **35**:107
"The Salem Horror" (Kuttner) **10**:267
"a salesman is an it that stinks Excuse" (Cummings) **137**:54
Salesman of the Sun (Vallette)
See *Le vendeur du soleil*
"Sales-nègres" (Roumain) **19**:334, 338, 346-47

"La Salle à manager" (Jammes) **75**:119
Sällskap för en eremit (Bengtsson) **48**:6, 12
Sally (Elizabeth)
See *Introduction to Sally*
Salmo (Unamuno) **148**:230
"Salmos" (Unamuno) **148**:304
"Salome" (Apollinaire) **8**:16
"Salomé" (Huidobro) **31**:124
Salomé (Wilde) **1**:494, 497-98, 503-04, 506, 508; **8**:494, 500; **23**:411, 435-37, 450; **41**:377; **175**:310, 312
"Salome's Dancing-lesson" (Parker) **143**:325
"Salón" (Aleixandre) **113**:8
Salon de Bruxelles (Lemonnier) **22**:201
Salon de Paris (Lemonnier) **22**:201
"Salonique" (Apollinaire) **51**:61
"Salt" (Babel)
See "Sol"
"Salt" (Roberts) **8**:316
"Salt and Sincerity" (Norris) **155**:338-40
The Salt Eaters (Bambara) **116**:6-7, 9-12, 14-15
"The Salt Garden" (Nemerov) **124**:150, 153, 203
The Salt Garden (Nemerov) **124**:151-56, 171, 188, 194, 203, 205, 208, 213, 219, 247
"Salt Lick" (Sarton) **120**:305
"The Salt Marsh" (Dickey) **151**:169
"Saltbush Bill" (Paterson) **32**:373
"Salted Meat and Cucumber" (Dagerman) **17**:93
Salted with Fire (MacDonald) **9**:292; **113**:197
Salthaven (Jacobs) **22**:99, 108
Saltimbank (Heijermans) **24**:292
"Saltimbanques" (Apollinaire) **3**:33, 36
"Les Saltimbanques" (Lewis) **104**:285
Saltwater Farm (Coffin) **95**:3
Le salut par les Juifs (Bloy) **22**:32-3, 39
"Salutación angélica" (Vallejo) **56**:301, 311
"Salutación del optimista" (Darío) **4**:61
"Salutaris hostia" (Pickthall) **21**:245
Salutary Lesson (Griffith) **68**:247
"Salutation" (Baker) **10**:21
Salutation paysanne (Ramuz) **33**:297
"Salutatory" (Howe) **21**:112
Salute to Adventurers (Buchan) **41**:38
Salute to Bazarada, and Other Stories (Rohmer) **28**:282, 286
The Salvaging of Civilization: The Probable Future of Mankind (Wells) **6**:553
"El salvaje" (Quiroga) **20**:212-14
Salvation (Asch)
See *Der tehillim yid*
"Salvation by Starvation" (Graham) **19**:121
"Salvation Gap" (Wister) **21**:373
"The Salvation of a Forsyte" (Galsworthy) **45**:32
"The Salvation of Nature" (Davidson) **24**:194
Salvation through the Jews (Bloy)
See *Le salut par les Juifs*
Salvatores Dei (Kazantzakis) **2**:313-14, 319; **33**:150, 165-66, 170, 172-73
Salvatores Dei: Asketike (Kazantzakis) **181**:208-14, 216, 219, 228, 235-37, 239, 244, 258-62, 276-78, 280, 288, 313-18, 324
Salwàre (Zuckmayer) **191**:280, 325
Sam Ego's House (Saroyan) **137**:150, 191
Sam the Highest Jumper of Them All (Saroyan) **137**:151, 181
Samantha among the Brethren (Holley) **99**:322, 326, 335, 345
Samantha among the Colored Folks (Holley) **99**:322
Samantha at Saratoga (Holley) **99**:320, 326, 345
Samantha at the Centennial (Holley)
See *Josiah Allen's Wife as a P.A. and P.I.: Samantha at the Centennial*
Samantha at the St. Louis Exposition (Holley) **99**:337, 345
Samantha at the World's Fair (Holley) **99**:318, 323
Samantha on the Race Problem (Holley) **99**:326, 344
Samantha on the Woman Question (Holley) **99**:309, 313, 334
Samantha Rastles (Holley) **99**:344
Samantha vs. Josiah (Holley) **99**:345
La Samaritaine (Rostand) **6**:374, 377-78, 380; **37**:283, 286, 291-92, 296, 299-300, 303
Samfundets støtter (Ibsen) **2**:224-27, 235; **8**:143, 146, 148, 150-51; **16**:154-56, 169, 172, 175; **37**:225, 232-33, 241-43, 249, 257-58, 260; **52**:142, 144-45, 163, 191
"Samhallsmoderlighet" (Key) **65**:243
"Samjhanā" (Devkota) **23**:49
Et samliv (Lie) **5**:325
"Samooborona" (Zangwill) **16**:447
"Samorazvenchannyi" (Balmont) **11**:40
"Samos" (Merrill) **173**:190
"Sampatti-Samarpan" (Tagore) **53**:354
"Samson" (Péret) **20**:183
Sämtliche Werke (Rilke) **195**:175, 215-16, 227, 257-67, 282-85, 288-92, 294, 296, 298-99, 303
Samuel (London) **9**:257
"Samuel Butler et Al." (Masters) **25**:290
Samuel Drummond (Boyd) **111**:200
Samuel Johnson (Stephen) **23**:307, 340
Samuel, the King-Maker (Housman) **7**:360
Samum (Strindberg) **8**:419
The Samurai (Endo) **152**:167, 171, 179-80, 182, 188, 192-93, 196, 199, 201-2, 205, 207-9, 212-13, 217, 221, 224-27, 229, 235, 240
"San Antonio" (Güiraldes) **39**:176
"San bega Karčića" (Andrić) **135**:89
San Cristóbal de la Habana (Hergesheimer) **11**:266, 271, 283
"San Francisco" (Austin) **25**:35
San Francisco Blues (Kerouac) **117**:213
San Francisco de Asís (Pardo Bazán) **189**:247-49
"San Francisco Falling" (Markham) **47**:286
"A San Francisco Journal" (Abbey) **160**:76
San Gabriel de Valdivias (Azuela) **145**:11, 18
San Gabriel de Valdivias, communidad indígena (Azuela) **3**:78
"The San Gabriel Mountains" (Muir) **28**:250
"San Giorgio in casa Brocchi" (Gadda) **144**:130
San Gloria (Redcam) **25**:330
"San i java pod Grabićem" (Andrić) **135**:89
"San Jose" (Graham) **19**:135
San Juan de la Cruz (Campbell) **5**:124
San Manuel Bueno, mártir (Unamuno) **2**:561; **9**:515-19, 523, 525-26; **148**:241, 246, 257, 279-83, 285, 287, 297, 307, 326
San Martín Copybook (Borges)
See *Cuaderno San Martín*
San Martin Notebook (Borges)
See *Cuaderno San Martín*
"San n-Diothramh Dubh" (Moore) **7**:494
San Pantaleone (D'Annunzio) **6**:131-33, 137, 143; **6**:131-33, 137, 143; **40**:8
"San Rafael (Córdoba)" (García Lorca) **181**:91
"San Sebastian" (Hardy) **4**:152
"San Vigilio" (Heyse) **8**:125
Sanatorium pod klepsydra (Schulz) **5**:426-29; **51**:307, 309, 311, 313, 315-17, 323-24
"Sanatorium under the Sign of the Hourglass" (Schulz) **51**:317-19, 325
Sanatorium under the Sign of the Hourglass (Schulz)
See *Sanatorium pod klepsydra*
Sanatorium under the Water Clock (Schulz)
See *Sanatorium pod klepsydra*
Sancho's Master (Gregory) **1**:333-34
"Sancta syluarum" (Johnson) **19**:244
The Sanctification of the Name (Asch) **3**:72
The Sanctified Church (Hurston) **131**:70
The Sanctity of Evil (Bataille) **155**:108
"Sanctity Will Out" (Bernanos)
See "Jeanne: Relapse et sainte"
"Sanctuaries" (Bottomley) **107**:5
"The Sanctuary" (Benson) **27**:16
"Sanctuary" (Douglas) **40**:80-1
"Sanctuary" (Dreiser) **35**:71-2, 75
"Sanctuary" (Guiney) **41**:218, 221-22, 225
"The Sanctuary" (Naidu) **80**:288, 335
"The Sanctuary" (Nemerov) **124**:153-54, 172, 180, 182, 185-86, 194, 200
"Sanctuary" (Parker) **143**:325
Sanctuary (Faulkner) **141**:42, 138-45, 191-92; **170**:109, 115, 128-29, 131, 172, 181, 233, 236-37, 241, 244-46
Sanctuary (Wharton) **27**:384; **129**:345, 360; **149**:248, 255
Sand and Foam: A Book of Aphorisms (Gibran) **1**:326; **9**:89
"Sand Castles" (Brautigan) **133**:3
"The Sand Hill" (Agnon)
See "Gib'ath ha-hol"
"Sand-between-the-Toes" (Milne) **6**:316; **88**:241
The Sandcastle (Murdoch) **171**:221, 224, 324
Sanders of the River (Wallace) **57**:397-98, 402-3
"The Sandhill Crane" (Austin) **25**:34
Sandhya sangit (Tagore) **3**:485, 490; **53**:339
Sándor Rózsa Frowns (Moricz)
See *Rózsa Sándor összevonja a szemöldökét*
Sándor Rózsa Jumps His Horse (Moricz)
See *Rózsa Sándor a lovát ugratja*
Sándor Rózsa Puckers His Brow (Moricz)
See *Rózsa Sándor összevonja a szemöldökét*
Sándor Rózsa Spurs His Horse (Moricz)
See *Rózsa Sándor a lovát ugratja*
Sandover (Merrill)
See *The Changing Light at Sandover*
"Sandpiper" (Bishop) **121**:6, 42
Sandra Belloni (Meredith) **43**:279, 288, 293; **17**:256, 269, 279, 286, 288, 290, 296-97
"Sandridge" (Masters) **25**:316
"The Sandshore in September" (Montgomery) **51**:209
"The Sandwich Islands" (Twain) **12**:439
"Sandy the Christ" (Babel)
See "Sashka Khristos"
"Sandymount" (Gogarty) **15**:103
Sanetomo, the Minister of the Right (Dazai Osamu)
See *Udaijin Sanetomo*
"Le sang coule aux Antilles sous domination française" (Fanon) **188**:148
Le sang du pauvre (Bloy) **22**:39
Le sang d'un poète (Cocteau) **119**:38-40, 42-3, 45-7, 49, 61, 69, 74, 82, 87, 89, 93, 105, 111
Le sang et les roses (Lemonnier) **22**:199
"Der Sänger" (Huch) **13**:248
Sängerin, Die Nacht (Kandinsky) **92**:49
La Sanglante Ironie (Vallette) **67**:271, 275
"Sangre real" (Lugones) **15**:294
Sangre y arena (Blasco Ibáñez) **12**:29-30, 33-5, 37, 43, 45, 47, 50
Sangsu (Williams) **89**:375
Sangyo suigyo (Santoka) **72**:414, 418
"Sanies I" (Beckett) **145**:202
Sanin (Artsybashev) **31**:2-9, 11, 15-16, 19-21
Sanine (Artsybashev)
See *Sanin*
The Sanity of Art (Shaw) **21**:319
Sankt Hans fest (Kielland) **5**:279
Sankt Thomas (Raabe) **45**:182
Sans (Beckett) **145**:78, 92
"Sans âge" (Éluard) **7**:255
Sans dessus dessous (Verne) **52**:331, 355, 357-58, 360
"Sans tomates pas d'artichauts" (Péret) **20**:184
Sanshirō (Natsume) **2**:491, 496; **10**:329, 339, 345
"Sanshō dayū" (Mori Ogai) **14**:378, 380-81, 384
Sansho Dayu (Mizoguchi) **72**:293, 296-98, 300-03, 315, 320, 324, 326, 328, 336-38
Sansho the Bailiff (Mizoguchi)
See *Sansho Dayu*
San't Agostino (Papini) **22**:281, 287
Sant' Ilario (Crawford) **10**:143-44, 147-48, 155
"A 'Sant' Imagine" (Field) **43**:167

Santa (Gamboa) **36**:71, 74-7
"Santa Claus" (Nemerov) **124**:303
Santa Claus in Summer (Mackenzie) **116**:232
"Santa Claus in the Bush" (Paterson) **32**:373
Santa Cruz (Frisch) **121**:198, 218
"The Santa Fe Trail" (Lindsay) **17**:222, 224, 227, 230, 248
Santa Go Home: A Case History for Parents (Nash) **109**:355
Santa Juana de Castilla (Pérez Galdós) **27**:274
Santa Lucia (Austin) **25**:33
"Santa Lucía y San Lázaro" (García Lorca) **49**:93; **181**:27
"Santa Susanna" (Howe) **21**:108
Santa Teresa, reina (Pardo Bazán) **189**:248
"Santander: Antaño y hogaño" (Pereda) **16**:380
"Santarém" (Bishop) **121**:36-7, 56
"Santelices" (Donoso) **133**:43-44, 149
"Santiago" (García Lorca) **181**:120
"Santo Domingo Corn Dance" (Riggs) **56**:200
"Santoral" (Vallejo) **56**:315
"Santorin" (Flecker) **43**:191
"Santorini: Stopping the Leak" (Merrill) **173**:230
São Bernardo (Ramos) **32**:419-35, 438
"The Sapling" (Coppard) **5**:178-79
"A Sapphic Dream" (Moore) **7**:487
"Sapphics" (Swinburne) **36**:299, 328
Sapphira and the Slave Girl (Cather) **1**:155-56, 158; **11**:107, 109, 116-17; **99**:211, 220; **132**:116, 120, 129, 137-38, 143, 147; **152**:51
"Sappho" (Moore) **7**:487
"Sappho" (Muir) **87**:267
"Sappho" (Roberts) **8**:328, 330
"Sappho" (Stringer) **37**:332
"Sappho" (Teasdale) **4**:424, 428
Sappho in Leucadia (Stringer) **37**:332, 342
Sappho in Levkas and Other Poems (Percy) **84**:198, 228
Sappho: One Hundred Lyrics (Carman) **7**:137, 139
"Sappho, or Suicide" (Yourcenar)
See "Sappho ou le suicide"
"Sappho ou le suicide" (Yourcenar) **193**:264, 321
"Sappho's Tomb" (Stringer) **37**:329, 342
"Sara Coleridge" (Woolf) **43**:402
"Sarabande" (Nemerov) **124**:185
"The Saracen's Head" (Chesterton) **6**:98
Saracinesca (Crawford) **10**:139-40, 143-44, 146-48, 155, 157
Sāradotsab (Tagore) **3**:486
Sarah Bastard's Notebooks (Engel) **137**:109, 112, 118-19, 123
Sarah Bernhardt (Baring) **8**:33
"Sarah Byng Who Could Not Read and Was Tossed into a Thorny Hedge by a Bull" (Belloc) **7**:42
"Sarah Dewitt" (Masters) **25**:297
"Sarah Gwynn" (Moore) **7**:491
"Sarah Holzmann" (Herzl) **36**:141
Sarah Orne Jewett (Matthiessen) **100**:167, 218-21, 238, 241, 258
Sarah Orne Jewett Letters (Jewett) **22**:146-47
Sarah Simple (Milne) **88**:253
"Sarajevo" (Nemerov) **124**:182, 215-16, 255
Sárarany (Moricz) **33**:236, 241-42, 246-47, 249
"Sarastro" (Werfel) **8**:478
The Sardonic Arm (Bodenheim) **44**:57, 64, 69
Sári bíró (Moricz) **33**:238
Saroyan's Fables (Saroyan) **137**:183
Sartoris (Faulkner) **141**:38-45, 49, 57, 187-8, 190; **170**:107, 128-29, 162-63, 171-72, 176
Sartre: Romantic Rationalist (Murdoch) **171**:231-32, 237, 239, 242, 286, 308
"Sarugashima" (Dazai Osamu) **11**:181
"Sarumen kanja" (Dazai Osamu) **11**:178
"Sarvodaya" (Gandhi) **59**:55
"Sarzano" (Campana) **20**:85
"Sasha" (Kuprin) **5**:297
"Sashka Khristos" (Babel) **171**:9, 11, 21, 23, 47-48, 87, 89
"Sashka the Christ" (Babel)
See "Sashka Khristos"
"Sashok" (Prishvin) **75**:214
Sata ja yksi laulua (Leino) **24**:368
"Satan Mekatrig" (Zangwill) **16**:441
"Satan, the Major and the Court Chaplain" (Söderberg) **39**:438
Satan the Waster (Lee) **5**:312, 316
"A Satana" (Carducci)
See *Inno a Satana*
Satan's Invisible World Displayed; or, Despairing of Democracy: A Study of Greater New York (Stead) **48**:188
Satans Kinder (Przybyszewski) **36**:290
"Sather Gate Illumination" (Ginsberg) **120**:136
Satī (Tagore) **3**:492
The Satin Slipper (Claudel)
See *Le soulier de satin*
Satire and Fiction (Lewis) **2**:385; **104**:188, 207, 246
A Satire Anthology (Wells) **35**:420
"A Satire of the Sea" (Post) **39**:336
"Satires of Circumstance" (Hardy) **53**:80
Satires of Circumstance (Hardy) **53**:71, 75, 84; **143**:147, 175, 188, 214
Sátiro o el poder de las palabras (Huidobro) **31**:123
Satori in Paris (Kerouac) **117**:213-15, 252
"Satsujin jiken" (Hagiwara) **60**:312
"Saturday" (Storni)
See "Sábado"
"Saturday Evening" (Csáth) **13**:149
"Saturday Evening in Jerusalem" (Douglas) **40**:76
"Saturday Night at the Crossroads" (Grove) **4**:141-42
"Saturday Night: Horses Going to Pasture" (Fletcher) **35**:90
"Saturday's Child" (Cullen) **4**:49; **37**:135, 152, 163
Saturday's Child (Hall) **12**:190
Saturday's Children (Anderson) **2**:2; **144**:8-10, 71
"The Satyr" (Buchanan) **107**:14
"Sauce for the Gander" (Rinehart) **52**:282
Saül (Gide) **5**:232; **12**:172; **177**:30, 105-6, 108
Saunterer's Rewards (Lucas) **73**:174
La sauvage (Anouilh) **195**:4, 6, 8, 10, 12, 16, 30, 36, 38-40, 48, 54-6
Savage Holiday (Wright) **136**:240-41, 250, 276; **180**:284, 315
Savage Pellucidar (Burroughs) **2**:81; **32**:58, 69
A Savant's Vendetta (Freeman)
See *The Uttermost Farthing*
"Savany" (Balmont) **11**:40
Save Me the Waltz (Foulkes) **52**:51-6, 63-5, 70-1, 73-7
"Save Yourself, Whoever Can!" (Čapek) **192**:190
Saved (Howells) **7**:387-88; **17**:178
"Saved by Faith" (Harper) **14**:260
Saverìo el cruel (Arlt) **29**:43-4, 54
"Savin izvor" (Popa) **167**:158
"Saving and Spending" (Keynes) **64**:244
The Saving Salt (Adams) **56**:9
"Saving the Day" (Griggs) **77**:194
The Saviors of God (Kazantzakis)
See *Salvatores Dei*
The Saviors of God: Spiritual Exercises (Kazantzakis)
See *Salvatores Dei: Asketike*
"Saviourgate" (Kirk) **119**:281, 283, 338-39
Savitri: A Legend and a Symbol (Aurobindo) **63**:25, 30, 35-6, 38, 47-9, 55
Sāvitrī-Satyavān (Devkota) **23**:48-9
"Savonarola" (Heym) **9**:142-43
The Savour of Life (Bennett) **197**:22
The Savoy of London (Mackenzie) **116**:228
Savrola (Churchill) **113**:154
Savva (Andreyev) **3**:19-20, 26
"Sawdust and Sin" (Grahame) **64**:65-6
Sawdust and Sixguns (Faust) **49**:38-9
"Saxon Epitaph" (Pickthall) **21**:256
Saxon Studies (Hawthorne) **25**:234, 239-40
Say, Is This the U.S.A. (Caldwell) **117**:13
"Say It Softly" (Lasker-Schueler) **57**:331-32
Say It with Oil—A Few Remarks about Wives (Lardner) **14**:291, 311-12
"Say, Lad, Have You Things to Do" (Housman) **10**:247
"Say Now Shibboleth" (Rhodes) **53**:314
"Say 'Shibboleth'—A Dialogue between a Sentimental Citizen and an Advertising Expert" (Millay) **169**:234
"Say Then that Life Is Grim" (McAlmon) **97**:97
Sayings (Upward) **85**:389
"Sayonara" (Hearn) **9**:129
"Sbírka známek" (Čapek) **37**:54
Sbornik stikhotvorenii (Balmont) **11**:35, 39
Scala di Giacobbe (Papini) **22**:281
"The Scales of the Eyes" (Nemerov) **124**:147-78, 153, 156, 171, 204, 216-17, 245, 290
The Scallop and the Clergyman (Artaud)
See *La Coquille et le Clergyman*
Scalpel (McCoy) **28**:210, 212-13, 222, 237
Scamandro (Pirandello) **172**:188
"Scandal" (Cather) **11**:92
Scandal (Endo)
See *Sukyandaru*
The Scandal and Credulities of John Aubrey (Collier) **127**:247
"A Scandal in Bohemia" (Doyle) **7**:216, 231, 241
Scandale de la vérité (Bernanos) **3**:127
"The Scandinavian Destiny" (Borges) **109**:157
The Scapegoat (Caine) **97**:7, 14, 21, 26
The Scarab Murder Case (Van Dine) **23**:355, 360
Scaramouch in Naxos (Davidson) **24**:159, 169, 184
Scaramouche (Sabatini)
See *Scaramouche: A Romance of the French Revolution*
Scaramouche: A Romance of the French Revolution (Sabatini) **47**:301-7
"Scarcely Disfigured" (Éluard)
See "A peine défigurée"
"The Scarecrow" (Roberts) **68**:348, 350
The Scarecrow of Oz (Baum) **7**:25, 27; **132**:13, 16, 53, 97
Scarface (Hecht) **101**:61-3, 88
The Scarlet Car (Davis) **24**:208
"The Scarlet Citadel" (Howard) **8**:133, 135
The Scarlet Plague (London) **9**:258, 267
A Scarlet Sword (Hippius)
See *Aly mech*
"The Scarlet Thread" (Futrelle) **19**:96
"Le scarpe rotte" (Ginzburg) **156**:97
"The Scarred Girl" (Dickey) **151**:89
"The Scatter Skies Unsown" (Jozsef) **22**:161
"Scatterbrain, madman, soarer" (Guro)
See "Vetrogon, sumasbrod, letatel"
Scattered and Dispersed (Aleichem)
See *Tsezeyt un tseshpreyt*
A Scattering of Salts (Merrill) **173**:230
Scattering of the Seed (Khodasevich) **15**:202
"The Scavenger" (Hecht) **101**:36
Scences of the Seige of Sebastopol (Tolstoy)
See *Sebastopol Sketches*
Scéne (Kandinsky) **92**:50
"A Scene at Lake Manitou" (Scott) **6**:394
"Scene Mounting of the Future" (Norris) **155**:337
Scenes and Characters; or, Eighteen Months at Beechcroft (Yonge) **48**:375
Scenes and Portraits (Manning) **25**:264, 268-69, 276
Scènes de la vie cosmopolite (Rod) **52**:316
Scènes et doctrines du nationalisme (Barrès) **47**:65, 70, 81
Scenes from the Drama of European Literature (Auerbach) **43**:59
Scenes from the Life of Cleopatra (Butts) **77**:96
Scenes from the Mesozoic (Day) **25**:133, 137

"Scenes of Childhood" (Merrill) **173**:257-58
Scenes of Childhood (Warner) **131**:306-8, 310, 319-20, 322
"Scent of Apples" (Santos) **156**:307-8, 324
"Scent of Irises" (Lawrence) **93**:43
"Scent of the Rose" (Palamas) **5**:385
"Scented Leaves from a Chinese Jar" (Upward) **85**:391
The Sceptered Flute: Songs of India (Naidu) **80**:276, 333
Scepticism and Animal Faith (Santayana) **40**:345, 352, 367, 381, 406, 409
"The Scepticism of the Instrument" (Wells) **19**:436; **133**:262
"The Sceptics" (Carman) **7**:142
Schachnovelle (Zweig) **17**:440-44, 446-48, 454-55, 457-58
Die schallmühle (Morgenstern) **8**:305
"The Schartz-Metterklume Method" (Saki) **3**:373
Der Schatten des Körpers des Kutchers (Weiss) **152**:249-54, 261-63, 291, 295
Der Schatten des Körpers des Kutschers (Weiss) **152**:287-9
Der Schatz (Pabst) **127**:354, 356
"Der Schauende" (Rilke) **195**:183, 266-67
"Schaukelstuhl" (Morgenstern) **8**:304
"Schauspielerin" (Mann) **9**:315-16
"The Scheldt" (Verhaeren)
See "L'escaut"
Der Schelm von Bergen (Zuckmayer) **191**:284, 289, 296-97, 324
"Schema der Massenkultur" (Adorno) **111**:39
"Schematic Plan of Studies and Work of the Institute of Art Culture" (Kandinsky) **92**:26
"Scherzo" (Södergran) **31**:287
"Schicksal" (Morgenstern) **8**:306
"Schicksal und Wille" (Schnitzler) **4**:395
Die Schicksale Doktor Bürgers (Carossa) **48**:20, 22, 27-9
Schicksalreise (Döblin) **13**:163-64
"Schiera bruna" (Levi) **109**:289
"Das Schiff" (Heym) **9**:148
"Schiff 'Erde'" (Morgenstern) **8**:306
"Schillerpreis-Rede" (Frisch) **121**:232
Schimmen van Schoonheid (Couperus) **15**:47
"Das Schlachtschiff Téméraire" (Liliencron) **18**:215
"Der Schlaf" (Trakl) **5**:457
"Schlaflied fur Miriam" (Beer-Hofmann) **60**:25, 32, 36
Die Schlafwandler (Broch) **20**:46-50, 54, 57-8, 62-6, 68, 70-3, 75, 77
"Schlangen-Beschwörung" (Rilke) **195**:315-17
Der Schleier der Beatrice (Schnitzler) **4**:386, 388-89, 393
Schloß Vogelöd (Murnau) **53**:262
Das Schloss (Kafka) **2**:289-91, 294-96, 298, 301, 306-08, 310; **6**:219-20, 225-27; **13**:261; **29**:171, 177, 179, 209, 214; **47**:211-13, 217, 220, 222-24, 226-29, 235-42, 245-50, 255-62; 112; **179**:240, 242-44, 247, 249-50, 252, 255-57, 260, 267, 271-72, 285-86, 292, 297, 300-302, 311, 314, 322-23
Schloss Nornepygge (Brod) **115**:77, 87, 90, 93-4, 106-7
Ein Schluck Erde (Böll) **185**:101
Schluck und Jau (Hauptmann) **4**:194
Schmetterlinge (Spitteler) **12**:335, 338, 348, 350
"Schmetterlingsgedanken" (Liliencron) **18**:216
Die Schmetterlingsschlacht (Sudermann) **15**:420, 426
"Schneethlehem" (Arp) **115**:3-5
"Schneethlehem 1" (Arp) **115**:4
"Schneethlehem 2" (Arp) **115**:4-5
"Schneethlehem 3" (Arp) **115**:3
"Schneethlehem 4" (Arp) **115**:5
Der Schnellmaler; oder, Kunst und Mammon (Wedekind) **7**:583
"Schnellzug" (Kraus) **5**:285
"Schnurrmilch" (Arp) **115**:6
Scholar Gipsies (Buchan) **41**:34
"The Scholars" (Yeats) **31**:417
The Scholar's Italian Book (Flecker) **43**:193, 213-14
The School and Society (Dewey) **95**:60
"The School as Social Center" (Dewey) **95**:66
"School Days" (Lasker-Schueler) **57**:330
School for Buffoons (Ghelderode)
See *L'ecole des bouffons*
The School for Rogues (Baroja)
See *La feria de los discretos*
School for the Indifferent (Giraudoux)
See *L'école des indifférents*
"The School for Witches" (Thomas) **1**:466; **45**:391; **105**:297, 300-01, 329
The School for Wives (Gide)
See *L'école des femmes*
"School Girls" (Baring-Gould) **88**:22
"The School of Babylon" (Sarton) **120**:262
"A School Story" (James) **6**:206
"The Schoolboy's Tragedy" (Davidson) **24**:193
"Schoolfellows" (Stephens) **4**:417
"Schoolhouse Hill" (Twain) **185**:269-70, 292, 307, 310, 312-16, 318-20, 322, 325, 327, 329-32
"The Schooling of Richard Orr" (Coffin) **95**:2
"The Schoolmaster" (Smith) **25**:386, 389, 395, 399
"The Schoolmaster's Dissipation" (Oskison) **35**:280-81
"The Schoolmistress" (Chekhov) **3**:152
The Schoolmistress (Pinero) **32**:396, 398, 406, 409-12
"The Schoolroom of Poets" (Benét) **28**:6
"Schopenhauer als Erzieher" (Nietzsche) **10**:354-55, 360-61, 366-67
"Schopenhauer as Educator" (Bataille) **155**:98
"Schopenhauer as Educator" (Nietzsche)
See "Schopenhauer als Erzieher"
"Schöpsoglobin" (Meyrink) **21**:225
"Das schreibende Ich" (Bachmann) **192**:155
Schriften (Benjamin) **39**:3
Ein Schritt nach Gomorrha (Bachmann) **192**:127
"Ein Schritt nach Gomorrha" (Bachmann) **192**:12, 25-26, 31, 40-42, 69-70, 95, 135-38
"Schubert" (Gurney) **33**:87
Der Schüdderump (Raabe) **45**:160, 163-66, 169, 174, 176, 178, 192, 194, 199-201
Die Schuldlosen (Broch) **20**:51-5, 64-5, 69
Das Schwalbenbuch (Toller) **10**:478, 483, 489-91
"Schwalbensiziliane" (Liliencron) **18**:214
Die schwärmer (Musil) **12**:232, 234, 242-45, 252, 261-62
"Schwarze Visionen II" (Heym) **9**:143
Schweiger (Werfel) **8**:466, 473
Die schweigsame Frau (Zweig) **17**:453
Schweik in the Second World War (Brecht) **1**:104
"Der Schweinhüter" (Bernhard) **165**:16, 94
Schwere Stunde (Mann) **168**:167
Die Schwestern (Wassermann) **6**:509
Die Schwestern und der Fremde (Frank) **81**:102
Der Schwierige (Hofmannsthal) **11**:296, 298, 300-01, 304
Die Schwierigen; oder, J'adore ce qui me brûle (Frisch) **121**:212, 287
"Schwierigkeiten mit der Brüderlichkeit" (Böll) **185**:130
Lo Scialo (Pratolini) **124**:324-27, 337
"Science" (Grove) **4**:133
"Science and Fiction" (Stapledon) **22**:336
Science and Health with Key to the Scriptures (Eddy) **71**:91, 93-99, 103, 106-107, 109, 111-114, 116, 126, 133, 135, 138-139, 142, 151, 153, 158, 165, 167-168
"Science and Literature" (Stapledon) **22**:334-36
"Science and Religion" (Mead) **89**:106
Science and Sanity (Korzybski) **61**:142, 144-5, 148-9, 151, 159, 162-3, 165, 167-73
"Science and Stories" (Nemerov) **124**:305
Science and the Modern World (Whitehead) **97**:197-99, 206, 211, 220, 240, 282, 317-22, 324-31
"Science as a Vocation" (Weber) **69**:302, 318, 339-41
"The Science of Criticism" (James) **47**:152
The Science of Ethics (Stephen) **23**:308, 312, 323, 328-29, 337
The Science of Life: A Summary of Contemporary Knowledge about Life and Its Possibilities (Wells) **6**:536
The Science of Living (Adler) **61**:32
"Science with a Human Face" (Abbey) **160**:95
A Scientific Book of Synonyms in the English Language (Peirce) **81**:205
"Scientific Experiences of a European Scholar in America" (Adorno) **111**:151, 160
Scientific Management (Taylor)
See *The Principles of Scientific Management*
"Scientific Method and Moral Sciences" (Mead) **89**:47, 110
Scientific Pedagogy as Applied to Child Education in the Children's House (Montessori)
See *Il Metodo della Pedagogia Scientifica applicato all' educazione infantile nelle Case dei Bambini*
Scientific Romances (Wells) **133**:230, 319, 340
Scientism and the Study of Society (Hayek) **109**:206, 214
"Scientists and Tramps" (Agee) **180**:23
"Sciroco" (Campana) **20**:85
Scittori nostri (Papini) **22**:274
"The Scope of Fiction" (Dreiser) **35**:68-9
"The Scorched Face" (Hammett) **187**:137, 203
"The Scorn of Women" (London) **9**:277
"The Scorpion of Friar Gomez" (Palma)
See "El alacrán de Fray Gómez"
"Scotland, 1941" (Muir) **2**:488; **87**:205
"Scots of the Riverina" (Lawson) **27**:132
A Scots Quair (Gibbon) **4**:121-24, 126-27, 130
Scott and Scotland: The Predicament of the Scottish Writer (Muir) **87**:163
"Scottish Eclogue" (Buchanan) **107**:16
Scottish Stories (Graham) **19**:104
"Scottsboro, Too, Is Worth Its Song (A Poem to American Poets)" (Cullen) **37**:150, 158, 160
The Scoundrel (Hecht) **101**:61
Scoundrel Time (Hellman) **119**:116, 119-20, 123-24, 129-30, 156, 161, 197-98, 200-3, 205-11, 213-17, 236
The Scourge of God (Zamyatin)
See *Bich Bozhy*
"Scrammy 'And" (Baynton) **57**:5,6,9-11, 23, 31
"A Scrap and a Sketch" (Chopin) **127**:22
Scrap Book (Saintsbury) **31**:226, 230
"Scream toward Rome" (García Lorca)
See "Grito hacia Roma"
The Screaming Man (Dent) **72**:26-27
"The Screaming Skull" (Crawford) **10**:153-54, 157-59
"The Screech Owl" (Wetherald) **81**:410
The Screens (Gannon)
See *Les paravents*
The Screens (Genet)
See *Les paravents*
Screw Island (Verne)
See *L'Ile à hélice*
"The Scribbling Mania" (Hall and Nordhoff) **23**:64
Scripts for the Pageant (Merrill) **173**:152, 156, 158-60, 177, 182, 188, 191, 202, 221-22, 224, 241, 244-46
The Scripture of the Golden Eternity (Kerouac) **117**:186
Scritti vari e postumi (Gadda) **144**:140
"Scrittori che disegnano" (Calvino) **183**:105
"The Scroll of Fire" (Bialik)
See "Megillath ha-'esh"
"Scrub" (Millay) **49**:225

Un scrupule (Bourget) **12**:68
"A Scullion's Diary" (Orwell) **128**:262
"The Sculptor's Funeral" (Cather) **11**:92, 101-02; **99**:266; **132**:132; **152**:16
La sculpture anversoise (Bosschere) **19**:61
"Le sculture e i nomadi" (Calvino) **183**:101, 106
"Scut Farkas and the Murderous Mariah" (Shepherd) **177**:306
"The Scythe" (Andrić)
See "Kosa"
"The Scythe" (Rebreanu)
See "Coasa"
"Scythe of Love" (Aleixandre) **113**:53
"The Scythians" (Blok)
See "Skify"
"Scythians?" (Zamyatin) **8**:555; **37**:441
"Se . . ." (Pirandello) **29**:284
Se non ora, quando? (Levi) **109**:297, 305, 313, 316
"Se querían" (Aleixandre) **113**:14
Se questo è un uomo (Levi) **109**:281-83, 285-86, 290-92, 299-300, 302-03, 305-06, 309-13, 315-21, 324-26, 329-33, 338-40, 342, 351
"Se una notte d'inverno un narratore" (Calvino) **183**:130
Se una notte d'inverno un viaggiatore (Calvino) **183**:11, 13, 15-17, 21, 38-39, 41-42, 55, 57, 66-67, 97, 124, 130-31, 134-36, 145, 147, 153, 155-57, 159, 163-64, 170, 187, 194-95, 214, 220, 222, 228, 230-32
se vi pare (Pirandello)
See *Cosîè (se vi pare)*
"Se voir" (Beckett) **145**:91
"The Sea" (Jiménez)
See "Mar"
"The Sea" (Lawrence) **93**:4
"The Sea" (Nezval) **44**:241
"The sea" (Paz)
See "El mar"
"The Sea and Its Shore" (Bishop) **121**:49-50
"Sea and Night" (Aleixandre)
See "Mar y noche"
The Sea and Poison (Endo)
See *Umi to dokuyaku*
Sea and Sardinia (Lawrence) **93**:86
The Sea and the Jungle (Tomlinson) **71**:380, 382-383, 385-388, 391, 393, 397, 400-401, 404-405
"The Sea Bird" (Douglas) **40**:71
"The Sea Birds Are Still Alive" (Bambara) **116**:4-5
The Sea Birds Are Still Alive: Collected Stories (Bambara) **116**:2, 4-5, 14-15
"The Sea Borders" (Gurney) **33**:97, 101
The Sea Bride (Williams) **89**:360, 363, 375, 385
"The Sea by the Wood" (Scott) **6**:393, 397
"Sea Constables" (Kipling) **8**:195
"A Sea Cycle" (Hall) **12**:194
"The Sea Fit" (Blackwood) **5**:75
Sea Gleams (Balmont)
See *Morskoe svechenie*
"Sea gulls" (Montgomery) **51**:209
The Sea in Being (Hemingway)
See *The Old Man and the Sea*
"The Sea is Not a Sheet of Paper" (Aleixandre)
See "El mar no es una hoja de papel"
The Sea Lady (Wells) **6**:532-33; **12**:487; **19**:426, 426; **133**:257
"Sea Love" (Mew) **8**:296-97, 300
The Sea Mystery: An Inspector French Detective Story (Crofts) **55**:83, 86
"Sea Nocturne" (Villaurrutia) **80**:481
Sea of Cortez: A Leisurely Journal of Travel and Research (Steinbeck) **135**:300, 309, 313, 317, 337, 344, 349
The Sea of Fertility (Mishima)
See *Hōjō no umi*
The Sea of Fertility: A Cycle of Novels (Mishima)
See *Hōjō no umi*
"The Sea of Objectivity" (Calvino)
See "Il mare dell'oggettività"
Sea of San Juan: A Contemplation (Salinas)
See *El contemplado*
"The Sea Raiders" (Wells) **12**:511; **19**:429, 435, 442, 429, 435, 442; **133**:231, 244, 246
"The Sea Song" (Montgomery) **51**:209
"The Sea Spirit" (Kolmar) **40**:175
"Sea Surface Full of Clouds" (Stevens) **3**:467; **12**:360, 366, 376, 380; **45**:281-82, 285-86, 311, 332, 338, 340
The Sea, the Sea (Murdoch) **171**:206, 210, 243-45, 248, 250, 252-53, 268, 280, 284, 286-91, 311-12, 323, 330
The Sea Tower (Walpole) **5**:501
Sea Vd. breve (Villaurrutia) **80**:467
Sea Voyage with Don Quixote (Mann)
See *Meerfahrt mit Don Quijote*
Sea Wife (Anderson) **2**:1
The Sea Wolf (London) **9**:253-57, 260-61, 264, 273, 276, 281; **15**:262, 264-65, 267-69, 271-72; **39**:262, 271, 288
"Sea-Blue and Blood-Red" (Lowell) **1**:378; **8**:226, 236
The Seaboard Parish (MacDonald) **9**:292
"The Seafarer" (Dickey) **151**:174
"The Sea-Farmer" (London) **9**:257
The Seagull (Chekhov)
See *Chayka*
"Seagulls" (Dazai Osamu) **11**:186
"Sea-Gulls at Fresh Pond" (Higginson) **36**:179
"The Sea-Gull's Song" (Pyle) **81**:389
The Sea-Hawk (Sabatini) **47**:303, 305-06
"Sealed" (Benét) **28**:7
"A Sealed House" (Garneau) **13**:204
"Sealed off" (Chang)
See "Fengsuo"
Sealed Orders (Phelps) **113**:376
"A Sealed Pod" (Bonner) **179**:8, 13-14, 35-36, 53-54, 59
"The Sea-Madness" (Sharp) **39**:375, 396
"A Seamark, a Threnody for Robert Louis Stevenson" (Carman) **7**:138
"The Seamstress" (Colette) **16**:128
"A Seaport on the Pacific" (Foote) **108**:6, 24
"The Search" (Guiney) **41**:207
A Search for America (Grove) **4**:135-36, 139-40
Search the Sky (Kornbluth) **8**:215
"The Searcher of the End House" (Hodgson) **13**:236
The Searching Wind (Hellman) **119**:134, 143, 164-66, 175, 177, 179-80, 214, 236
"Sears" (Dickey) **151**:172
"Sears Roebuck" (Jarrell) **177**:172
"Seas of Loneliness" (Noguchi) **80**:379
"Seascape" (Bishop) **121**:28
"Seascape" (Éluard) **7**:261
Seascape: Needle's Eye (Oppen) **107**:287, 291, 294-95, 306, 334, 359
"Sea-Shell Murmurs" (Lee-Hamilton) **22**:189
"Seaside" (Brooke) **2**:58
The Season at Sarsaparilla (White) **176**:127, 183, 225-27, 260
"A Season of Love" (Quiroga)
See "Una estación de amor"
Seasoned Timber (Fisher) **87**:89
"Seasoning" (Lorde) **173**:139-40
The Seasons of Love (Kuzmin) **40**:190
"The Sea-Swallows" (Swinburne) **8**:436; **36**:299
"Sea-Things" (Ingamells) **35**:128
"Seaton's Aunt" (de la Mare) **4**:75, 80; **53**:18-9, 21, 27, 29, 33, 35-7, 40-1
Seaward Lackland (Symons) **11**:450
"The Seaweed and the Cuckoo-Clock" (Powys) **9**:374
"Seaweed from Mars" (Bodenheim) **44**:60, 68, 74
"Sebastian Cabot" (Campbell) **9**:31
Sebastian im Traum (Trakl) **5**:548
Sebastian Strome (Hawthorne) **25**:236, 238, 240-42, 247, 249
Sébastien Roch (Mirbeau) **55**:279-81, 283-84, 289, 292-95
"Sebast'jan" (Bryusov) **10**:92
"Sebastopol in December, in May, and in August" (Tolstoy) **79**:325
Sebastopol Sketches (Tolstoy) **79**:334, 392, 445
"Secession" (Kandinsky) **92**:18
Sechs Essays (Arendt) **193**:157
Sechs kleine Geschicten (Walser) **18**:429
Sechuana Proverbs and their European Equivalents (Plaatje) **73**:221-23
Sechuana Reader in International Phonetics (Plaatje) **73**:221-22, 230
"Second Air Force" (Jarrell) **177**:126, 141, 194
"Second Anniversary" (García Lorca)
See "Segundo aniversario"
Second April (Millay) **4**:306-07, 309, 314, 317; **49**:201, 205, 207-08, 222, 232-33; **169**:274, 300
"The Second Bandits' Tale" (Čapek)
See "Druhá loupeznická pohádka"
A Second Book (Mandelstam)
See *Vtoraya kniga*
The Second Book of American Negro Spirituals (Johnson) **175**:199-200, 204-5, 232
A Second Book of Reflections (Annensky) **14**:19, 24
"Second Canzonette" (Gumilev) **60**:279
"The Second Choice" (Dreiser) **35**:56, 72, 75
"The Second Coming" (Moody) **105**:238, 245, 267, 275, 287
"The Second Coming" (Yeats) **1**:572; **11**:518, 523, 525, 530-32, 540, 556; **18**:447; **31**:399, 407-08, 420-21; **93**:337-408
The Second Common Reader (Woolf) **5**:507; **43**:380, 387-88, 409, 421, 425
"Second Eclogue" (Radnóti) **16**:419-20
"Second Elegy" (Rilke)
See "Second Song"
"Second Fig" (Millay) **49**:216
"The Second Generation" (Crane) **11**:161
The Second Generation (Phillips) **44**:255-57, 262-65, 274, 276, 278, 289-91, 299
The Second Jungle Book (Kipling) **8**:178, 196, 200-01, 205-06, 208
"The Second Missouri Compromise" (Wister) **21**:373, 399
The Second Mrs. Tanqueray (Pinero) **32**:386-90, 392-93, 395-401, 403, 405, 409, 411-15
"Second Night" (Bennett) **5**:46
"The Second of November" (Khodasevich)
See "2-g noiabria"
"Second Oldest Story" (Parker) **143**:323
Second Overture (Anderson) **2**:7
"Second Political Manifesto" (Marinetti) **10**:325
The Second Post: A Companion to The Gentlest Art (Lucas) **73**:168, 173
"The Second Rape of the West" (Abbey) **160**:14
"Second Song" (Rilke) **1**:412-3, 419-20
"Second Spring" (Lorde) **173**:73, 77
"The Second Spring" (Sarton) **120**:302
Second String (Hope) **83**:181
Second String Quartet (Schoenberg) **75**:379
The Second Symphony (Bely)
See *Vtoraia simfoniia: Dramaticheskaia*
Second Thoughts on James Burnham (Orwell) **31**:183; **128**:289
"Second Thoughts on the Abstract Gardens of Japan" (Sarton) **120**:261, 304
Second Threshold (Barry) **11**:58, 60, 63-5, 67-8
The Second Twenty Years at Hull-House (Addams) **76**:101-03
The Second World War 1939-45 (Churchill) **113**:100, 103-06, 110, 112, 115-16, 118-231, 149, 162, 184
"The Second-Best Bed" (Nemerov) **124**:183, 280
"Second-Class Gods" (Herzl) **36**:132
La seconde (Colette) **5**:170; **16**:120

La seconde vie de Michel Teissier (Rod) **52**:310, 313
La Seconde Vie, ou Macaber (Jarry) **147**:329
"The Secret" (Baker) **10**:27
"The Secret" (Naidu) **80**:335
"The Secret" (Rinehart) **52**:302-03
The Secret Agent (Conrad) **1**:199, 201-02, 207, 212, 218-19, 221; **6**:118-24; **13**:117; **25**:84, 86, 89, 111; **43**:113; **57**:39
Secret Agent Number One (Faust) **49**:36
"Secret Agent X-9" (Hammett) **187**:77
The Secret, and Other Stories (Milne) **6**:319
The Secret Annex (Frank)
See *Het achterhuis*
The Secret Battalion (Laski) **79**:145
"The Secret Cause" (Machado de Assis)
See "A causa secreta"
The Secret City (Walpole) **5**:496, 499, 503
Le Secret de Wilhelm Storitz (Verne) **52**:356, 359
"The Secret Garden" (Saint-Exupéry) **2**:521
The Secret Glory (Machen) **4**:277, 280
The Secret Heart of the Clock: Notes, Aphorisms, Fragments, 1973-1985 (Canetti)
See *Das Geheimherz der Uhr: Aufzeichnungen 1973-1985*
The Secret History of the American Revolution (Van Doren) **18**:408-10
"Secret Journal, and Other Writings" (Drieu la Rochelle)
See "Récit secret"
"Secret Landscape" (Carossa)
See "Heimliche Landschaft"
The Secret Life (Granville-Barker) **2**:195, 197
"The Secret Miracle" (Borges)
See "El milagro secreto"
"The Secret of a Train" (Chesterton) **6**:109
The Secret of Childhood (Montessori) **103**:301
"Secret of Dunstan's Tower" (Bramah) **72**:6
"The Secret of Far Eastern Painting" (Fletcher) **35**:114
"The Secret of Father Brown" (Chesterton) **1**:189
The Secret of Heaven (Lagerkvist)
See *Himlens hemlighet*
"The Secret of Kralitz" (Kuttner) **10**:267
"The Secret of Macarger's Gulch" (Bierce) **44**:13, 44-5
"The Secret of the Flying Saucer" (Rohmer)
See "The Mind of Fu Manchu"
"The Secret of the Growing Gold" (Stoker) **8**:394
The Secret of the League (Bramah)
See *What Might Have Been: The Story of a Social War*
"The Secret of the Moon" (Södergran)
See "Månens hemlighet"
The Secret of the Night (Leroux) **25**:260
"The Secret of the Ruins" (Rohmer) **28**:283
The Secret of the Solitary Man (Deledda)
See *Il secreto dell' uomo solitario*
The Secret of the Three (Merezhkovsky) **29**:242-43
The Secret of the Veda (Aurobindo) **63**:30-1, 34, 36
The Secret of the West (Merezhkovsky) **29**:242
"The Secret of the Zoo Exposed" (Cummings) **137**:18
The Secret of William Storitz (Verne)
See *Le Secret de Wilhelm Storitz*
"The Secret of Writing Fables. The Sense of Smell" (Agnon)
See "Hush hareah"
Secret Places of the Heart (Wells) **6**:553; **133**:262
The Secret Power: A Romance of the Time (Corelli) **51**:75, 77-8
Le secret professional (Cocteau) **119**:44, 107
Secret Rendezvous (Abe)
See *Mikkai*
The Secret Rivers (Macaulay) **7**:422
"The Secret Room" (Trambley) **163**:288-89, 320
"The Secret Rose" (Yeats) **18**:446
"The Secret Sharer" (Conrad) **1**:203, 219, 221-22; **6**:120-22; **13**:103-04, 112, 118; **43**:100-01, 104, 107; **57**:38-122
"A Secret Society" (Nemerov) **124**:159, 232, 318
"The Secret Society of the Ring" (Warung) **45**:417, 421-22, 425-26
"Secret Suffering" (Hamsun)
See "Hemmelig ve"
Secret World (Kubin) **23**:95
"Secret Worship" (Blackwood) **5**:70, 73, 78-9
"Secreta Silvarum" (Brennan) **17**:39
"Secretly at Night" (Lasker-Schueler) **57**:331
"El secreto de Don Juan" (Lugones) **15**:292
Secrets of the Courts of Europe (Upward) **85**:380
Secrets of the Earth (Prishvin) **75**:218
The Secrets of the Heart (Gibran) **1**:327-28; **9**:83
The Secrets of the Self (Iqbal)
See *Asrar-i khudi*
"The Sect of the Phoenix" (Borges)
See "La secta del Fénix"
"La secta del Fénix" (Borges) **109**:17, 58-9, 84, 87
"Sectionalism Is Dead" (Bryan) **99**:120
Secular Passion (Toller)
See *Weltliche Passion*
The Secular Scripture (Frye) **165**:154, 228, 236, 257
Secular Songs (Lugones)
See *Cantos seculares*
"The Secularization of the Sacred" (Campbell) **140**:97, 132, 138
Secum sola (Bourget) **12**:67
"The Sedative" (Williams) **89**:399
Sedemunds (Barlach)
See *Die echten Sedemunds*
"Ein See" (Benn) **3**:111
"See Through X-Ray Eyes" (Shepherd) **177**:316
"See Where Capella with Her Golden Kids" (Millay) **4**:316
Seed of Adam (Williams) **1**:517; **11**:498
"The Seed of Faith" (Wharton) **129**:363
The Seed of McCoy (London) **9**:262-63
"Seed Time" (Sapper) **44**:307
Seedtime on the Cumberland (Arnow) **196**:29, 34, 38, 95
"Seeds" (Anderson) **1**:42; **123**:48
"Seed-time and Harvest" (Bosman) **49**:10, 19
"Seeing" (Éluard) **41**:149
"Seeing Gender" (Acker) **191**:107, 116
"Seeing People Off" (Beerbohm) **24**:116
"Seeing Things" (Nemerov) **124**:260
Seeing Things at Night (Broun) **104**:98
"Seeing, We See Not" (Bourne) **16**:62
"Seeing with the Streets" (Chang) **184**:151-52
"Seek Not, O Maid" (Dobson) **79**:37
"The Seeker" (Yeats) **31**:407, 415
Seeland (Walser) **18**:419
"Seele im Raum" (Jarrell) **177**:129, 138, 140-43, 170, 172-73, 177, 180, 196, 229-31
Der Seelen Erwachen (Steiner) **13**:438, 443, 457, 459
Der Seelenbräu (Zuckmayer) **191**:304, 325
Seelenglaube und Psychologie (Rank) **115**:249, 263-66, 275, 300
"Seelenlärm" (Broch) **20**:52
Seen and Unseen or, Monologues of a Homeless Snail (Noguchi) **80**:360
"Seen from a Hilltop" (Wright) **136**:302
"Seen from Afar" (Levi) **109**:292
"Seepferdchen und Flugfische" (Ball) **104**:13-15
"The Seer" (Baker) **10**:27
"See-Saw" (Mansfield) **39**:303
See-Saw (Biggers) **65**:2
Seespeck (Barlach) **84**:62-6, 75, 94, 100-1, 116
"Sefer HaMa'asim" (Agnon) **151**:36
Sefer ha-Maasim (Agnon) **151**:3, 34, 56
Segelfoss by (Hamsun) **2**:205; **14**:222, 226-27; **49**:129, 152-54; **151**:234
Segelfoss Town (Hamsun)
See *Segelfoss by*
"Los seghidores" (Graham) **19**:103-04, 133
"Un segno nello spazio" (Calvino) **183**:11-12, 40
La segretaria (Ginzburg) **156**:63
Segunda antología poética (Jiménez) **183**:296, 298, 300-302
La segunda casaca (Pérez Galdós) **27**:276, 287
"Segundo aniversario" (García Lorca) **181**:181
Seguro azar (Salinas) **17**:359, 363-64
"Seh qatreh khun" (Hedāyat) **21**:71-2, 76, 80
"Sehen" (Kandinsky) **92**:68
"Sehnsucht" (Kolmar) **40**:178
Sei fenblasen (Huch) **13**:247, 252
Sei personaggi in cerca d'autore (Pirandello) **4**:326-27, 329-30, 336, 338, 349-50, 352-53, 356; **29**:283-86, 291, 295-96, 298-300, 302, 304-08, 311, 313, 316, 318-20; **172**:131-95
Sei poesie della vecchiaia (Saba) **33**:370
Seid nett zu Mr. Sloane (Orton)
See *Entertaining Mr. Sloane*
Seigi to bishō (Dazai Osamu) **11**:178
"Seigneur berbère" (Saint-Exupéry) **169**:314
Seine Hoheit (Herzl) **36**:132
"Seine k. und k. apostolische Majestät" (Roth) **33**:336
"Las seis cuerdas" (García Lorca) **181**:195
Seis relatos para don Isidro Parodi (Borges) **109**:138
Seis relatos porteños (Güiraldes) **39**:175-76
"Sekai no jiko doitsu to renzoku" (Nishida) **83**:330
"Die Sektion" (Heym) **9**:149
"Selbstanzeige des Essaybuches 'Versuch uber Wagner'" (Adorno) **111**:43
Die Selbstersetzung des Christentums und die Religion der Zukunft (von Hartmann) **96**:206, 210
Ein Selbsterzähltes Leben (Barlach) **84**:92, 105
"Selbstgespräch" (Werfel) **8**:478
Seleced writings (Sapir) **108**:259
Select Conversations with an Uncle Now Extinct, and Two Other Reminiscences (Wells) **12**:487
Select Passages from the Works of Bracton and Azo (Maitland) **65**:275
Selected Articles (Hurston) **131**:70
Selected Criticism, 1916-1957 (Murry) **16**:345
Selected Essays (Belloc) **7**:39; **18**:25
Selected Essays (Cary) **196**:154-55
Selected Essays (Maitland) **65**:253, 257
Selected Essays (Murry) **16**:356
Selected Essays, 1934-1943 (Weil) **23**:395-96
Selected Essays and Critical Writings of A. R. Orage (Orage) **157**:240, 246, 254
Selected Journalism (Duncan) **60**:211-2, 216
The Selected Journals of L. M. Montgomery (Montgomery) **140**:302-3, 307-8, 310-11, 329
Selected Letters (García Lorca) **197**:229-30
Selected Letters (Nabokov) **189**:179
Selected Letters (Oppen) **107**:333, 341, 366
Selected Letters (Thomas) **105**:358
Selected Letters (Wolfe) **13**:482
Selected Letters of E. E. Cummings (Cummings) **137**:58, 60, 69
Selected Letters of George Edward Woodberry (Woodberry) **73**:370
Selected Letters of James Joyce (Joyce) **159**:334, 336
Selected Letters of Malcolm Lowry (Lowry) **6**:249
Selected Letters of Raymond Chandler (Chandler) **179**:119, 121, 124, 131, 136, 138-39, 146, 157, 159, 167, 188, 191-94, 222, 234
Selected Letters of William Faulkner (Faulkner) **141**:138, 170; **170**:225-26

Selected Literary Criticism (James) **171**:196
Selected Non-Fictions (Borges) **109**:152, 154
Selected Pages (Roussel) **20**:239
Selected Poems (Baker) **10**:17
Selected Poems (Bishop) **103**:2-4, 8-9, 19, 21, 48
Selected Poems (Bodenheim) **44**:68, 73
Selected Poems (Borges) **109**:129, 131, 151-52
Selected Poems (Brecht) **169**:63
Selected Poems (Campbell) **5**:122
The Selected Poems (Dickey) **151**:199, 203
Selected Poems (Douglas) **40**:58, 71, 85
Selected Poems (Gogarty) **15**:102, 104
Selected Poems (Herbert)
See *Wybór wierszy*
Selected Poems (Jarrell) **177**:125-27, 130, 138, 140, 195-96, 210, 218, 222, 244
Selected Poems (Lowry) **6**:237
Selected Poems (Masters) **25**:316
Selected Poems (McKay) **41**:318-19, 344
Selected Poems (Merrill) **173**:162, 232, 234
Selected Poems (Millay) **169**:246, 292-93, 298
Selected Poems (Nash) **109**:360
Selected Poems (Percy) **84**:201, 228
The Selected Poems (Reese) **181**:336, 339, 347-48
Selected Poems (Robinson) **101**:66
Selected Poems (Sterling) **20**:374
Selected Poems, 1923-1967 (Borges) **109**:18-19, 21, 126
Selected Poems 1947-1995 (Ginsberg) **120**:85-6, 88, 97
Selected Poems and New (Villa) **176**:93-95, 103-7, 112, 114, 118-19
Selected Poems (Fletcher) (Fletcher) **35**:105
Selected Poems (Ingamells) (Ingamells) **35**:127, 129
The Selected Poems of Bliss Carman (Carman) **7**:147
Selected Poems of Byron (Su Man-shu) **24**:458, 461
The Selected Poems of Marjorie Pickthall (Pickthall) **21**:258
Selected Poems of May Sarton (Sarton) **120**:223-29, 260, 266
Selected Poems of Vachel Lindsay (Lindsay) **17**:239
Selected Poems of William Vaughn Moody (Moody) **105**:259
Selected Poetry and Critical Prose (Roberts) **8**:326
Selected Short Stories of Lewis Sinclair (Lewis) **4**:257
Selected Stories (Coppard) **5**:181
Selected Stories (Mansfield) **164**:341-42
Selected Stories (Peretz) **16**:402
Selected Stories (Seton) **31**:277-78
Selected Stories (Villa) **176**:93
Selected Stories of Sylvia Townsend Warner (Warner) **131**:322
Selected Tales (Morrison) **72**:383
Selected Works of Alfred Jarry (Jarry) **14**:273-74
The Selected Works of Henry Lawson (Lawson) **27**:135
Selected Works of Ida B. Wells-Barnett (Wells-Barnett) **125**:329, 332-33
Selected Writings (Berlin) **105**:50
Selected Writings (Gregory) **176**:61-65, 67
Selected Writings of Benjamin Nathan Cardozo (Cardozo) **65**:32-3, 44
Selected Writings of Gertrude Stein (Stein) **48**:249, 251
Selected Writings of Guillaume Apollinaire (Apollinaire) **51**:39
Selected Writings of Juan Ramon Jimenez (Jiménez)
See *Antolojía poética (1898-1953)*
The Selected Writings of Lafcadio Hearn (Hearn) **9**:131
"Selections from 'Ripples in the Pool' and Other Writings" (Onetti) **131**:283
Selections from the Correspondence of Theodore Roosevelt and Henry Cabot Lodge (Roosevelt) **69**:197
"The Selector's Daughter" (Lawson) **27**:131, 150
"The Self and The Other" (Borges)
See "El otro, el mismo"
The Self and the Other (Borges)
See *El otro, el mismo*
"The Self as Agent" (Dickey) **151**:135
"Self Criticism" (Cullen) **37**:156, 159
"Self Defense" (Zangwill)
See "Samooborona"
"Self Denial" (MacDonald) **113**:222
"Self Examination" (Griggs) **77**:192-3
The Self over Nature (Döblin)
See *Das Ich über der Natur*
"Self Portrait" (Wylie) **8**:522
"Self Realization as the Moral Ideal" (Dewey) **95**:96
Self Sacrifice (Howells) **7**:387
Self-Analysis (Horney) **71**:210, 217, 222, 231, 260-61, 263
The Self-Aware Determination of Radical Negativity (Nishida)
See *Mu no jikakuteki gentei*
Self-Condemned (Lewis) **2**:390-91, 393-96, 398-99; **9**:240, 246, 248, 250; **104**:189-91, 219, 232
"The Self-Conscious Determination of Nothingness" (Nishida)
See *Mu no jikakuteki gentei*
"The Self-Determination of the Universal" (Nishida)
See "Ippansha no jiko gentei"
"Self-Discipline" (Baker) **10**:26
Self-enquiry (Ramana Maharshi)
See *Vicara-sangraham*
"Self-Epitaph" (Arenas)
See "Autoepitafio"
"Self-Haunted Girl" (Roberts) **68**:304
"Self-Image" (Santoka) **72**:410
Self-Interviews (Dickey) **151**:98-99, 101, 104-5, 110, 131-34, 158-59, 162, 164, 184, 215, 217
"The Selfish Giant" (Wilde) **8**:492
"The Selfishness of Amelia Lamkin" (Freeman) **9**:74
Self-Knowledge (Berdyaev) **67**:82
"Self-Love, Other-Love, and Dialectic" (Nishida) **83**:329
"The Self-Made Man" (Kunikida Doppo)
See "Hibon naru Bonjin"
"Self-Portrait" (Evans) **85**:25
"Self-Portrait" (Lewis) **39**:215
"Self-Portrait in Tyvek Windbreaker" (Merrill) **173**:230
"Self-Ridicule" (Santoka) **72**:410
"Self-Righteousness" (Wetherald) **81**:410
Self's the Man (Davidson) **24**:180-82, 184
A Self-Told Life (Barlach)
See *Ein Selbsterzähltes Leben*
"The Self-Unconscious" (Hardy) **53**:110
"The Self-Unseeing" (Hardy) **4**:164; **10**:234
"Selina's Parable" (de la Mare) **53**:16-7
"The Selons-Rose" (Bosman) **49**:8
"Selskaya druzhba" (Khlebnikov) **20**:131
"Selskaya ocharovannost" (Khlebnikov) **20**:131
"La selva y el mar" (Aleixandre) **113**:11, 48
"The Selvin Case" (Čapek)
See "Případ Selvinuv"
Selvportretter og landskapsbilleder (Undset) **197**:312
"Sem' besov" (Remizov) **27**:340
Sem' zemnyx soblaznov (Bryusov) **10**:86
"La semaine pâle" (Péret) **20**:184
La Semana de colores (Garro) **153**:74
"Semangat" (Anwar) **22**:25
A Semantic Count of English Words (Thorndike) **107**:381
Semeinoe schaste (Tolstoy) **4**:445, 451, 457, 474, 481-82; **11**:464, 469-70; **17**:412; **79**:374, 387, 389; **173**:280
Semeinyi Vopros v Rossii (Rozanov) **104**:310, 313
"Semi" (Hearn) **9**:129
The Semiotic Challenge (Barthes)
See *L'Aventure sémiologique*
"Semiramis" (Valéry) **4**:496-97
"The Semi-Sentimental Dragon" (Zangwill) **16**:465
Semite (Oppen) **107**:288
Las señales furtivas (Gonzalez Martinez) **72**:148, 151
Senator North (Atherton) **2**:14-15
"Senator Upjohn" (March) **96**:264
"Sence You Went Away" (Johnson) **19**:210
"Sencillez" (Jiménez) **183**:258
"Send Round the Hat" (Lawson) **27**:131
La senda dolorosa (Baroja) **8**:57
Sendas perdidas (Azuela) **3**:76; **145**:18
Sender Blank (Aleichem) **1**:28; **35**:320
El sendero (Güiraldes) **39**:186
Los senderos ocultos (Gonzalez Martinez) **72**:145, 147-49, 151
"The Sending of Dara Da" (Kipling) **8**:185
"Sendja di pelabuhan ketjil" (Anwar) **22**:22
"The Send-Off" (Owen) **5**:370; **27**:208, 212, 217, 224, 230, 232-33
"Séneca en las orillas" (Borges) **109**:165
"Sengiyakholma" (Vilakazi) **37**:410-13
"Sengiyokholwa-ke" (Vilakazi) **37**:410-13
"A senhora do Galvão" (Machado de Assis) **10**:291
Senilità (Svevo) **2**:540-43, 545-50; **35**:332-38, 342-46, 348-49, 351, 354-56, 365-69
"Senility" (Anderson) **1**:36
Señjuti (Tagore) **3**:487, 489
"Senna Hoy" (Lasker-Schueler) **57**:329
"S'ennuyer" (Péret) **20**:196
El Señor Presidente (Asturias) **184**:4-5, 8-11, 14-15, 17-19, 21-22, 25, 33-34, 36, 42, 45, 47, 50-51, 54-57, 59, 61, 85-87, 89-91, 95-96
Señora Ama (Benavente) **3**:93, 100
Señora Carrar's Rifles (Brecht) **6**:36
La Señora en su balcón (Garro) **153**:17, 19-20, 72-73, 75, 78
"La señorita Leona" (Quiroga) **20**:213
Le sens de la marche (Adamov) **189**:8-9, 27, 42-3
Le sens de la mort (Bourget) **12**:66, 69
Le sens de la vie (Rod) **52**:310, 313, 315, 317, 321-25
Sens et non-sens (Merleau-Ponty) **156**:120, 134, 136, 138-39, 213
"La sensation artistique" (Verhaeren) **12**:477, 479
"Sensations and Images" (Alexander) **77**:49
Sensations de nouvelle-France (Bourget) **12**:75
Sensations d'Italie (Bourget) **12**:75
Sense and Nonsense (Merleau-Ponty)
See *Sens et non-sens*
The Sense of Beauty (Santayana) **40**:376, 392, 400, 414
A Sense of Detachment (Osborne) **153**:242, 323
"The Sense of Smell" (Agnon)
See "Hush hareah"
The Sense of the Past (James) **2**:251, 258; **47**:165
Sense of the World (Drummond de Andrade)
See *Sentimento do mundo*
"The Sensible Thing" (Fitzgerald) **14**:182
"The Sensitive Plant" (Meynell) **6**:291
The Sensory Order (Hayek) **109**:206
"Sensual Ecstasy" (Lasker-Schueler) **57**:328, 329
La sensualidad pervertida (Baroja) **8**:51, 55, 61, 63
The Sensualists (Hecht) **101**:74
"Senten chishiki no umu o ronzu" (Nishida) **83**:226

Sentences (Nemerov) **124**:265, 267, 269, 273, 277
Sentences and Paragraphs (Davidson) **24**:179
Les sentiers et les routes de la poésie (Éluard) **41**:152, 161
"Sentiment" (Parker) **143**:331, 342-43
"The Sentiment of Rationality" (James) **32**:340, 348, 351
"A Sentimental Cellar" (Saintsbury) **31**:230
"Sentimental Education" (Brodkey) **123**:209
Sentimental Novellas (Zoshchenko) **15**:490, 504
"A Sentimental Rebellion" (Huneker) **65**:197
"A Sentimental Romance" (Kuprin) **5**:301
"Sentimental Salon" (Millay) **169**:233
Sentimental Tommy: The Story of His Boyhood (Barrie) **2**:45, 47-48; **164**:5, 67-68, 80, 82
The Sentimental Traveller (Lee) **5**:312-13
Sentimentale Erinnerungen (Brecht) **169**:43
Sentimento do mundo (Drummond de Andrade) **139**:224, 228-29, 231-32
Les sentiments de Critias (Benda) **60**:60
"Sentiments filiaux d'un parricide" (Proust) **7**:538
"The Sentry" (Lewis) **3**:290
"The Sentry" (Owen) **27**:203, 212, 217
"A Sentry at Night" (Anwar)
See "Perdjurit djaga malam"
"Senza colori" (Calvino) **183**:12-13
"Senza Fine" (Scott) **6**:394
"The Separated East" (Fenollosa) **91**:2
"The Separated Lovers Pray to Each Other" (Morgenstern)
See "Getrennter Liebender Gebet zu einander"
"The Separated West" (Fenollosa) **91**:2
"Separation" (Bialik)
See "Pridah"
"Separation" (Tsvetaeva)
See "Razluka"
Separation (Tsvetaeva) **35**:415-16
La séparation des races (Ramuz) **33**:295
Separation of Races (Ramuz)
See *La séparation des races*
"Les sept epées" (Apollinaire) **51**:19, 59
"Les sept femmes de la Barbe-Bleue" (France) **9**:57
Les sept femmes de la Barbe-Bleue, et autres contes merveilleux (France) **9**:53, 57-8
Sept manifestes dada (Tzara) **168**:228, 274, 288-91, 293, 318, 320
"Les Sept poémes d'amour en guerre" (Éluard) **7**:251
Les sept princesses (Maeterlinck) **3**:317, 326, 332
"September" (Belloc) **18**:41
"September" (Ledwidge) **23**:112
"September 1913" (Yeats) **31**:420-21; **93**:346
The September Lyre (Södergran)
See *Septemberlyran*
"September Mist" (Hansen)
See "Septembertaagen"
Septemberlyran (Södergran) **31**:283-88, 290-93
"Septembertaagen" (Hansen) **32**:249, 251
"Sepulcro judío" (García Lorca) **197**:221
"Sepulcros de Burgos" (García Lorca) **181**:119
"El sepulturero" (Miro) **5**:345-46
"Sequel to Experience and Thought" (Nishida)
See "Zoku keiken to shisaku"
"A Sequel to the 'Cadian Ball" (Chopin) **14**:64
"Sequel to the Pied Piper of Hamelin" (Cotter) **28**:40, 43
"Sequelula to The Dynasts" (Beerbohm) **24**:112
"Sequence" (Wylie) **8**:531
The Sequence (Glyn) **72**:131
"Ser de esperanza y lluvia" (Aleixandre) **113**:5, 46
"Ser súbito" (Jiménez) **183**:257
"La sera del dí di festa" (Calvino) **183**:211
Serafino Gubbio, Cameraman (Pirandello) **4**:343
The Seraglio (Merrill) **173**:174, 186, 231-35, 237-38, 241
Seraph on the Suwanee (Hurston) **131**:58, 60, 62, 69, 72-74, 77, 80, 85, 91-92, 95
The Seraphic Visions (Housman) **7**:359
"Serdtsa, prozrachney, chem sosud" (Khlebnikov) **20**:144
"Serebrianye lozhki" (Remizov) **27**:340, 349
Serena Cruz (Ginzburg) **156**:70
La serena disperazione (Saba) **33**:369, 373
"Serenade" (Carducci)
See "Serenata"
"Serenade" (Davidson) **24**:164
"Serenade" (Gurney) **33**:94-5
Serenade (Schoenberg) **75**:290-91
"Sérénade triste" (Nelligan) **14**:392
"Serenata" (Carducci) **32**:90
"Serenata" (García Lorca) **181**:185
The Serene Blockhead (Petrov) **21**:153
Serenidad (Nervo) **11**:394, 399-401, 403
"A sereníssima República" (Machado de Assis) **10**:290-91
"Serenity" (Coffin) **95**:4
Serenity (Nervo)
See *Serenidad*
"The Serf" (Campbell) **5**:120, 124, 126
Sergeant Michael Cassidy (Sapper) **44**:317
"The Sergeant's Private Madhouse" (Crane) **11**:161
"The Sergeant's Weddin'" (Kipling) **8**:178
"Sergeiu Efron-Durnovo" (Tsvetaeva) **7**:567
Série blême (Vian) **9**:531
"A Series of Tricks" (Chang)
See "Lianhuan tao"
The Serious Game (Söderberg)
See *Den allvarsamma leken*
A Serious Thing (Gogarty) **15**:116-17
"Le serment de John Glover" (Roussel) **20**:254
"Sermón sobre la muerte" (Vallejo) **3**:533; **56**:311, 320
Sermons (MacDonald) **113**:266-68, 270
The Sermons of a Buddhist Abbot (Suzuki) **109**:387
"Le serpent" (Valéry)
See "Ébauche d'un serpent"
The Serpent (Sologub)
See *Zmii*
Serpent and Bull (Hansen)
See *Orm og tyr*
Serpent and Lily (Kazantzakis)
See *Ophis kai krinos*
Le serpent d'etoiles (Giono) **124**:32, 44, 68-9, 96, 98-101, 124
Serpent Eyes (Sologub)
See *Zmeinye ochi*
"The Serpent in Literature" (Hudson) **29**:163
The Serpent in the Wilderness (Masters) **25**:316
"The Serpent Trains" (Khlebnikov)
See "Zmei poezda"
"The Serpent's Crown" (Guiney) **41**:207
"The Serpents of Paradise" (Abbey) **160**:13, 22, 26, 95
Serres chaudes (Maeterlinck) **3**:319, 324-25, 329
Os sertões (Cunha) **24**:141-54
"The Servant" (Levi) **109**:292
"A Servant of the People" (Premchand) **21**:294
A servant of the Public (Hope) **83**:167
The Servants and the Snow (Murdoch) **171**:227
Service with a Smile (Wodehouse) **108**:335
"La serviette des poétes" (Apollinaire) **51**:20
The Servile State (Belloc) **7**:38-40; **18**:26, 28, 33, 44-7
"Servitude" (Gurney) **33**:105
Śēs praśna (Chatterji) **13**:78-9, 81-3
"Sesame" (García Lorca) **181**:64
Sesame and Lilies (Ruskin) **20**:263, 291-92; **63**:243, 245, 247-48, 251, 253, 291-95, 298, 312-14, 330, 3
Sésame et les lys (Proust) **7**:534
"Śesh lekhā" (Tagore) **3**:489; **53**:343
Śesher kavitā (Tagore) **3**:495
"The Session of the Poets" (Buchanan) **107**:51
"Sestina" (Bishop) **121**:19, 41-3
Sestry (Bryusov) **10**:83
Set in Authority (Duncan) **60**:184-7, 209-10
Set My People Free (Heyward)
See *Charleston, 1820*
"Set of Country Songs" (Hardy) **143**:150
A Set of Six (Conrad) **1**:196
"Séta bölcső-helyem körül" (Ady) **11**:18
Sete canções de declínio (Sá-Carneiro) **83**:401, 413-4
Seti (Kuzmin) **40**:189, 191, 196-200, 215-16
"Setiembre" (Vallejo) **3**:531
"The Setting of Antares" (Sterling) **20**:386
"The Setting Sun" (Leino)
See "Painuva päivä"
The Setting Sun (Dazai Osamu)
See *Shayō*
Settlers of the Marsh (Grove) **4**:132-34, 136, 140, 142
"Settling Accounts" (Rebreanu)
See "Rafuiala"
"Settling on the Land" (Lawson) **27**:128, 130
Une seule pensée (Éluard) **7**:249
Seva sadan (Premchand) **21**:286, 296
Sevastopol (Tolstoy)
See *Tales of Sevastopol*
"Sevastopol in August, 1855" (Tolstoy) **4**:474; **11**:464
"Sevastopol in December 1854" (Tolstoy) **4**:474; **11**:464
"Sevastopol in May, 1855" (Tolstoy) **4**:474; **11**:464
"Sevastopol' v avguste 1855 goda" (Tolstoy) **173**:280, 302-3
"Sevastopol' v mae" (Tolstoy) **173**:280, 302-3
"Sevdalija's love" (Andrić)
See "Sevdalijina ljubav"
"Sevdalijina ljubav" (Andrić) **135**:85
The Seven Ages of Woman (Mackenzie) **116**:204-05
"The Seven Candles of Blessing" (Peretz) **16**:390
"Seven Centuries of China" (Lin)
See *Imperial Peking: Seven Centuries of China*
"Seven Conjectural Readings" (Warner) **131**:311, 313
Seven Dada Manifestos and Lampisteries (Tzara)
See *Sept manifestes dada*
Seven Days (Rinehart) **52**:283
Seven Days in Which the World Was Robbed (Tolstoy) **18**:360, 373
"The Seven Days of Mourning" (Bialik)
See "Shivah"
The Seven Deadly Sins (Brecht)
See *Die sieben Todsünden der Kleinburger*
The Seven Deadly Sins of the Petit-Bourgeois (Brecht) **169**:47
"Seven Demons" (Remizov)
See "Sem' besov"
"Seven Farthings" (Moricz)
See "Hét kracjár"
"VII (Flickering of Incessant Rain)" (Fletcher) **35**:93
Seven for a Secret (Webb) **24**:465, 467-69, 472, 474-77, 480-81, 484
Seven Keys to Baldpate (Biggers) **65**:2, 4, 9
Seven Keys to Baldpate (Cohan) **60**:158-59, 162, 166
The Seven Lamps of Architecture (Ruskin) **20**:260-61, 268, 270, 282, 297, 299-300, 302; **63**:238, 243, 251, 253, 256-57, 262-63, 265, 270, 318, 320, 323, 326-27;
The Seven Madmen (Arlt)
See *Los siete locos*
Seven Men (Beerbohm) **1**:67-8, 72, 74; **24**:101, 103, 107, 111, 114-18
Seven Modern Comedies (Dunsany) **59**:17, 23, 26, 28-9
Seven Nights (Borges) **109**:57
The Seven of Hearts (Leblanc)
See *Arsène Lupin, gentleman-cambrioleur*

"Seven Pennies" (Moricz)
See "Hét kracjár"
Seven Pillars of Peace (Stapledon) **22**:332
The Seven Pillars of Wisdom (Lawrence) **18**:128-30, 132-43, 145-48, 150-82
"The Seven Policemen" (Bennett) **5**:46
The Seven Princesses (Maeterlinck)
See *Les sept princesses*
Seven Red Sundays (Sender)
See *Siete domingos rojos*
"The Seven Sages" (Yeats) **31**:403
"Seven Seals" (Lawrence) **93**:17
The Seven Seas (Kipling) **8**:178
Seven Short Plays (Gregory) **176**:14-15, 18-20
Seven Sins (Rohmer) **28**:282, 293-94
Seven Sleepers of Ephesus (Coleridge) **73**:5-7, 12, 22
"The Seven Swords" (Apollinaire)
See "Les sept epées"
"Seven Things" (Carman) **7**:133
"Seven Types of Ambiguity" (Jackson) **187**:245
The Seven Who Were Hanged (Andreyev)
See *Razskaz o semi povieshennykh*
Seven Winters (Bowen) **148**:4-5, 68
"The Seven Wives of Bluebeard" (France)
See "Les sept femmes de la Barbe-Bleue"
The Seven Wives of Bluebeard, and Other Marvellous Tales (France)
See *Les sept femmes de la Barbe-Bleue, et autres contes merveilleux*
"Seven Years of Plenty" (Peretz)
See "Zibn Gite Yor"
The Seven-League Crutches (Jarrell) **177**:132, 139, 162, 176, 194, 196, 217-18, 229
"Seven-Sided Poem" (Drummond de Andrade) **139**:240
Seventeen (Tarkington) **9**:453-55, 457, 461, 467, 473
"The Seventeenth Hole at Duncaster" (Wakefield) **120**:336, 344, 347, 350
Seventeenth-Century Opera (Rolland)
See *L'opéra au dix-septième siècle*
"The Seventh Angel" (Herbert) **168**:27, 71
The Seventh Commandment (Heijermans)
See *Het zevende gebod*
The Seventh Day (Lasker-Schueler)
See *Der siebente Tag*
"The Seventh Dream" (Pickthall) **21**:254
"Seventh Eclogue" (Radnóti) **16**:410, 412, 420-21
"Seventh Elegy" (Rilke) **1**:412-13, 415, 420
The Seventh Man (Faust) **49**:44, 46, 49, 51
"The Seventh Pawn" (Benét) **28**:6
The Seventh Ring (George)
See *Der Siebente Ring*
The Seventh Sense (Roberts) **23**:240
"The Seventh Stair" (Millay) **169**:233, 280
"Seventh Street" (Toomer) **172**:256, 292, 329, 335-36
The Seventh Victim (Lewton) **76**:204-05, 210
Seventy Poems from the Underworld (Nezval) **44**:241
"Seventy Thousand Assyrians" (Saroyan) **137**:157-58, 168, 185-88, 191-92
Seventy Years: Being the Autobiography of Lady Gregory (Gregory) **176**:41-42, 47
73 Poems (Cummings) **137**:11, 13-14
"Sever" (Zamyatin) **8**:552-53
Several Perceptions (Carter) **139**:194
A Severed Head (Murdoch) **171**:221, 223-27, 247, 279, 318, 320, 323, 329
Severn and Somme (Gurney) **33**:81-2, 85-6, 90, 92, 94-6, 101, 105-10, 112
Severnaia simfoniia: Pervia geroicheskaia (Bely) **7**:57
Severo Torelli (Coppee) **25**:127
"Sevgiliye mektup" (Sait Faik) **23**:294, 298
"Sevilla" (García Lorca) **181**:199
Sewanee (Percy) **84**:205
"The Sewing of the Wedding Gown" (Peretz) **16**:388-89, 391
Sex and Character: A Fundamental Investigation (Weininger)
See *Geschlecht und Charakter. Eine prinzipielle Untersuchung*
Sex and the Single Girl (Heller) **131**:22
"Sex Love" (Carpenter) **88**:72
"Sex, Religion, and Business" (Day) **25**:137
"The Sexes" (Parker) **143**:331-32
Sex-Pol: Essays 1929-1934 (Reich) **57**:350, 387
"Sexto" (Güiraldes) **39**:176
El sexto (Arguedas) **147**:12-14, 78, 93, 107
Sexual Behavior in the Human Female (Kinsey) **91**:58, 68
Sexual Behavior in the Human Male (Kinsey) **91**:41, 44, 46, 68-70
Sexual Ethics (Michels) **88**:150
The Sexual Hour (Vallette)
See *Le hevre sexuelle*
Sexual Maturity, Abstinence and Conjugal Morality (Reich) **57**:350
The Sexual Revolution (Reich) **57**:338-39, 349-50, 356, 360
The Sexual Struggle of Youth (Reich) **57**:348, 350, 354
"La sfida al labirinto" (Calvino) **183**:44, 94, 101, 134, 164, 193-94, 241, 243-44
La sfida al labirinto (Calvino) **183**:242
"S.G.L.L." (Hedāyat) **21**:81
"Lo sguardo dell'archeologo" (Calvino) **183**:104
"Shabbes nakhamu" (Babel) **13**:33
Shabbethai zebi (Asch)
See *Sabbatai zewi*
"The 'Shabbles-Goy'" (Peretz) **16**:402
"Shab-ha-yi Varamin" (Hedāyat) **21**:71
"Shabos nahamu" (Babel)
See "Shabbes nakhamu"
"Shack Dye" (Masters) **25**:309
The Shackle (Colette)
See *L'entrave*
Shade and Light (Hedāyat) **21**:67
Shade from a Palm (Gumilev) **60**:263
"The Shade of Helen" (Lang) **16**:251
The Shade of the Sun (Moricz)
See *A nap árnyéka*
"The Shades of Spring" (Lawrence) **2**:354
"The Shadow" (Dreiser) **10**:181; **35**:71-4
The Shadow (Stringer) **37**:336-37
"The Shadow Builder" (Stoker) **144**:279
Shadow Dance (Carter) **139**:53, 163, 166, 184, 193-94, 199
"The Shadow Figure" (Endo) **152**:214
The Shadow Flies (Macaulay) **7**:427; **44**:122-23, 125, 127-28
"The Shadow Kingdom" (Howard) **8**:132
"The Shadow Line" (Conrad) **6**:121; **13**:112; **57**:40, 42-43, 60, 77, 82-83, 101
Shadow of a Bird (Ishikawa)
See *Chōei*
The Shadow of a Crime (Caine) **97**:10, 13
The Shadow of a Dream (Howells) **7**:393, 399
Shadow of a Man (Sarton) **120**:201, 203, 209, 227, 243
Shadow of Fu Manchu (Rohmer) **28**:278-80, 284, 295, 300-01
"The Shadow of Lilith" (Brennan) **17**:54, 56
Shadow of Paradise (Aleixandre)
See *Sombra del paraíso*
The Shadow of the Cathedral (Blasco Ibáñez)
See *La catedrál*
The Shadow of the Coachman's Body (Weiss)
See *Der Schatten des Körpers des Kutschers*
"The Shadow of the Cross" (McCrae) **12**:210
"The Shadow of the Future" (Södergran) **31**:283, 294
Shadow of the Future (Södergran)
See *Framtidens skugga*
The Shadow of the Glen (Synge)
See *In the Shadow of the Glen*
The Shadow of the Sun (Moricz) **33**:250
The Shadow of the Sword (Buchanan) **107**:31, 83
The Shadow of the Tower (Babits)
See *A torony arnyéka*
The Shadow of the Wolf (Freeman) **21**:56
The Shadow on the Dial, and Other Essays (Bierce) **1**:91; **44**:14, 17, 39
"The Shadow on the Stone" (Hardy) **143**:189
The Shadow on the Wall (Coleridge) **73**:23
"The Shadow out of Time" (Lovecraft) **4**:267-69; **22**:215, 225-26, 230, 239
"The Shadow over Innsmouth" (Lovecraft) **22**:241
"The Shadow Side" (Nemerov) **124**:305
"A Shadow, Silent as a Cloud" (O'Faolain) **143**:225
Shadow Verses (Bradford) **36**:62
"Shadowed Souls" (Sharp) **39**:388
"Shadows" (Endo)
See "Kageboshi"
"Shadows" (Lawrence) **93**:77
"Shadows" (Quiller-Couch) **53**:291
Shadows (Lawrence) **2**:368; **93**:55-57
"Shadows from the Big Woods" (Abbey) **160**:59
"Shadows in the Moonlight" (Howard) **8**:133, 135
"Shadows in Zamboula" (Howard) **8**:133, 136
Shadows of Beauty (Couperus)
See *Schimmen van Schoonheid*
Shadows of Ecstasy (Williams) **1**:525; **11**:487-88, 493, 496-97, 500
Shadows on the Rock (Cather) **1**:154, 156-57, 159, 163-65; **11**:95-6, 98-9, 107; **99**:172, 175, 183, 211, 256, 281, 284-85; **132**:127, 129-31, 136-38, 142, 154
"The Shadows on the Wall" (Freeman) **9**:72
Shadowy Dawn (Verhaeren) **12**:469
The Shadowy Third, and Other Stories (Glasgow) **7**:342-43
"The Shadowy Waters" (Sharp) **39**:378, 397
The Shadowy Waters (Yeats) **1**:557, 560-61, 571; **11**:512, 526-27, 529; **31**:386, 410; **116**:329-30, 334-36
"Shadrack O'Leary" (Robinson) **101**:112
"Shady Groves Two Images" (Agee) **180**:102
"Shaheen" (Iqbal) **28**:198
"Shaka, Son of Senzangakhona" (Vilakazi)
See "UShaka kaSenzangakhona"
"The Shakers" (Rourke) **12**:318, 330
Shakes versus Shav (Shaw) **3**:397
"Shakespeare" (Murry) **16**:341
Shakespeare As a Playwright (Matthews) **95**:246
"Shakespeare Explained" (Benchley) **55**:8
Shakespeare in Art (Hartmann) **73**:117, 122
"The Shakespeare Memorial" (Chesterton) **1**:186
"Shakespeare, Moliere, and Modern English Comedy" (Matthews) **95**:228
"Shakespeare the Man" (Stephen) **23**:313
A Shakespearean Grammar (Abbott) **139**:19, 25-26
"Shakespeare's Final Period" (Strachey) **12**:392
"Shakespeare's The Tempest" (Frye) **165**:239
Shakespeare's Workmanship (Quiller-Couch) **53**:294
Shaking a Leg (Carter) **139**:100-102, 105
Shakkipeli (Leino) **24**:372
"Shall God Be Said to Thump the Clouds" (Thomas) **45**:364, 379
Shall I Slay My Brother Boer? (Stead) **48**:194
"Shall Not Perish" (Faulkner) **170**:138
Shall We Join the Ladies? (Barrie) **164**:29
"Shall We Join the League?" (Dewey) **95**:68
"Shallow Philosophy in Deep Places" (Mayakovski) **18**:258
Shallow Soil (Hamsun)
See *Ny jord*
"Shaman i Venera" (Khlebnikov) **20**:126, 131, 134
"The Shame of Minneapolis" (Steffens) **20**:335-37, 342, 345
The Shame of Motley (Sabatini) **47**:303

The Shame of the Cities (Steffens) **20**:333, 339, 341-42, 345, 351-52, 360-65
"A Shameful Affair" (Chopin) **14**:61, 69-70, 72; **127**:7, 10, 31-2, 220
"The Shamelessness of St. Louis" (Steffens) **20**:335
"The Shamraken Homeward Bounder" (Hodgson) **13**:235, 237
"The Shamrock and the Palm" (Henry) **19**:172
Shamrocks (Tynan) **3**:501-04
Shandygaff (Morley) **87**:117, 148
Shanghai (Yokomitsu)
See *Shanhai*
Shanghai Drama (Pabst) **127**:354, 359, 361-63
Shanghaied (Norris) **155**:338
Shanhai (Yokomitsu) **47**:396-97
"Shantung, Or the Empire of China Is Crumbling Down" (Lindsay) **17**:227
"The Shanty-Keeper's Wife" (Lawson) **27**:121
Shanwalla (Gregory) **1**:333; **176**:38
"The Shape of Fear" (Williams) **89**:398
The Shape of Terror (Dent) **72**:25, 38
"The Shape of the Sword" (Borges)
See "La forma de la espada"
"The Shape of Things" (Capote) **164**:100, 106
The Shape of Things to Come (Wells) **19**:437, 439, 441
Shapes of Clay (Bierce) **7**:97; **44**:2, 4, 11, 13
Shapes That Pass (Hawthorne) **25**:240
"Shared Nights" (Éluard)
See "Nuits partagées"
"Sharer" (Conrad)
See "The Secret Sharer"
"The Shark's Parlor" (Dickey) **151**:145, 172
Sharmanka (Guro) **56**:132-36, 138-39, 141-43, 146-48
Sharp Gravel (Anwar)
See *Kerikil tadjam dan jang terampas dan jang putus*
Sharp-calm Pink (Kandinsky) **92**:32
"Sharper Than a Ferret's Tooth" (Somerville & Ross) **51**:358
Sharps and Flats (Tagore)
See *Kari o komal*
"Shasti" (Tagore) **3**:498-99
"Shatrang-ké-khilāri" (Premchand) **21**:296
The Shaving of Shagpat: An Arabian Entertainment (Meredith) **17**:259, 262; **43**:278, 280
Shawm (Pirandello)
See *Zampogna*
Shayō (Dazai Osamu) **11**:172-73, 176-77, 179-80, 184-89
She (Haggard) **11**:238, 241, 243-49, 251, 255-57
She (Peretz) **16**:396
She and Allan (Haggard) **11**:255-56
"She Being Brand-New" (Cummings) **137**:55-56
"She dwelt among untrodden ways" (Hardy) **53**:94
"She Goat" (Lawrence) **93**:33
"She Is Overheard Singing" (Millay) **4**:306-07
"She Looks Back" (Lawrence) **93**:54
"She of All Time, All" (Éluard)
See "Celle de toujours, toute"
"She Said as Well to Me" (Lawrence) **33**:182; **93**:14, 52, 54, 55
"She Shall Be Called Woman" (Sarton) **120**:272-73, 294, 299, 301
"She, to Him" (Hardy) **53**:94
"She Was a Sinner" (Mew) **8**:299
"She Was Rosa" (Platonov) **14**:414
"She Was the Spring" (Coffin) **95**:17
"She Weeps over Rahoon" (Joyce) **159**:279
She Who Sleeps (Rohmer) **28**:283-84
A Sheaf of Verses (Hall) **12**:195
Sheaf of Wheat (Moricz)
See *Búzakalász*
The Shearer's Colt (Paterson) **32**:382
"The Sheath" (Wen I-to) **28**:409
"The Sheaves" (Robinson) **5**:407; **101**:145, 199-200
"Sheba's Love-Pearls" (Rohmer) **28**:286
The She-Dragoon (Jarry)
See *La dragonne*
"Sheener" (Williams) **89**:386
"Sheep" (Nabokov)
See "Ovtsy"
"The Sheep" (Saki) **3**:369
"The Sheep Child" (Dickey) **151**:97, 145, 166, 200, 212
The Sheepfold (Housman) **7**:353, 355
"Sheeps and Lambs" (Tynan) **3**:505
"A Shell" (Manning) **25**:265, 279
"Shell" (Sarton) **120**:245
"The Shell" (Stephens) **4**:407
"The Shell above the City" (van Ostaijen) **33**:421
The Shell and the Clergyman (Artaud)
See *La Coquille et le Clergyman*
"Shell in Rock" (Roberts) **68**:336
"Shelley" (Murry) **16**:341
"Shelley" (Santayana) **40**:390
"Shells" (Nemerov) **124**:181, 186
The Sheltered Life (Glasgow) **2**:177-78, 183-86, 189-90; **7**:341-43, 345-47
"Shemà" (Levi) **109**:287, 300
"Shepherd Bound for Mountain Pass" (Aleixandre) **113**:22
"The Shepherd Boy" (Pickthall) **21**:245, 250-51
"Shepherd, Lead Us" (Fisher)
See "The South Lingers On"
The Shepherd of the Hills (Wright) **183**:349, 355-56, 358, 360-67, 370, 372, 378-81
"A Shepherd-Boy" (Field) **43**:165-67
"The Shepherdess" (Meynell) **6**:302
Shepherds in Sackcloth (Kaye-Smith) **20**:114
"The Shepherd's Interval" (Roberts) **68**:348-50
A Shepherd's Life (Hudson) **29**:138, 140-41, 149-51
Shepherd's Pie (Shepherd) **177**:304, 311
Sheridan: Military Narrative (Hergesheimer) **11**:275
"The Sheridans" (Mansfield) **39**:295
"The Sheriff of Gullmore" (Post) **39**:337
"The Sheriff's Children" (Chesnutt) **5**:130-31; **39**:82-3, 99
"The Sheriff's Posse" (Foote) **108**:34
"Sherwood" (Noyes) **7**:502, 512
The Sherwood Anderson Reader (Anderson) **24**:43; **123**:54
Sherwood Anderson's Memoirs (Anderson) **123**:21-2, 52, 56
Shesh saptak (Tagore) **53**:336
"Shesto chuvstvo" (Gumilev) **60**:272, 274, 279
Shestov Anthology (Shestov) **56**:276
"Shestvie oseney pyatigorska" (Khlebnikov) **20**:137
"Sheumas, a Memory" (Sharp) **39**:375
"Shevu'at Emunim" (Agnon) **151**:36
The Shewing-Up of Blanco Posnet (Shaw) **3**:381; **21**:337
The She-Wolf and Other Stories (Verga)
See *La lupa. In portinaio. Cavalleria Rusticana. Drammi*
Shi no genri (Hagiwara) **60**:294-6
Shiba chun (Chang) **184**:106
Shibue chūsai (Mori Ogai) **14**:376, 378-79
"A Shield of Phantom" (Natsume)
See "Gen'ei no tate"
The Shifting of the Fire (Ford) **15**:67
Shiga Naoya shu (Shiga) **172**:202
Shiga Naoya zenshu (Shiga) **172**:200-204, 207, 209, 214-15, 217
"Shikagari" (Kunikida Doppo) **99**:302-03
"Shiker" (Kahanovitsch) **56**:111, 113, 115
"Shiko no omide" (Nishida) **83**:218
A Shilling for Candles (Tey) **14**:451, 461, 463
Shimbashi yawa (Nagai) **51**:89, 104
Shin Hamuretto (Dazai Osamu) **11**:176, 179, 183-84, 186
Shin Heike Monogatari (Mizoguchi) **72**:296, 302
"Shin Sai" (Yokomitsu) **47**:386
Shine and Dark (Joyce) **159**:282
"Shingapōru no sūjikan" (Nagai) **51**:99
The Shining (Kubrick) **112**:134, 137, 152-54, 158, 168-69, 172-74, 176-81, 183, 186, 188-89, 203, 212-19, 225, 233, 240-41, 245, 247-51, 259, 262-64, 274-77, 279-80, 282
Shining Deeps (Čapek)
See *Zářivé hlubiny*
Shining Ferry (Quiller-Couch) **53**:296
"The Shining Pyramid" (Machen) **4**:284
"The Shining Slave Makers" (Dreiser)
See "McEwen of the Shining Slave Makers"
"Shinkichōsha no nikki" (Nagai) **51**:88
Shinkobunrin (Kunikida Doppo) **99**:294
Shinsei (Shimazaki Toson) **5**:432, 435-37
Shinyū Kōkan (Dazai Osamu) **11**:177
"The Ship" (Heym)
See "Das Schiff"
"The Ship" (Hodgson) **13**:230
The Ship (D'Annunzio)
See *La nave*
The Ship (Jensen)
See *Skibet*
"Ship from Thames" (Ingamells) **35**:127
"A Ship Full of Crabs" (Calvino)
See "Un bastimento carico di granchi"
"The Ship of Death" (Lawrence) **48**:121; **61**:239; **93**:14, 51, 55, 56, 58, 71-77, 98, 113, 127, 128
The Ship of Death, and Other Poems (Lawrence) **2**:368; **93**:22
Ship of the Line (Forester) **152**:132, 135, 137
The Ship Sails On (Grieg)
See *Skibet gaar videre*
"The Ship That Found Herself" (Kipling) **8**:193; **17**:209
"Ships and Sealing-Wax" (Millay) **169**:236
Ship's log (Arp) **115**:13, 15
"The Ships of St. John" (Carman) **7**:135
"Ships That Pass in the Night" (Dunbar) **12**:105-06
"A Shipwreckollection" (Bierce) **44**:45
The Shipyard (Onetti)
See *El astillero*
Shira (Agnon) **151**:52-54
Shiroi hito (Endo) **152**:167, 170, 176, 198, 213-14, 229-30, 234, 237, 239
"The Shirt" (France) **9**:47
"Shishiphush" (Borchert) **5**:103, 108
"Shisō" (Kunikida Doppo) **99**:302, 304
"Shit on the Spirit" (Artaud)
See "Chiote à l'esprit"
"Shit to the Spirit" (Artaud)
See "Chiote à l'esprit"
"Shiv and the Grasshopper" (Kipling) **17**:196
"Shivah" (Bialik) **25**:53
"Shizenkagaku to rekishigaku" (Nishida) **83**:241
Shizuka (Mori Ogai) **14**:383
"The Shock" (Kuttner) **10**:269
Shocks (Blackwood) **5**:77
The Shoemakers (Witkiewicz)
See *Szewcy*
The Shoemaker's Prodigious Wife (García Lorca)
See *La zapatera prodigiosa*
"The Shoes of Happiness" (Markham) **47**:285
The Shoes of Happiness and Other Poems (Markham) **47**:287
"Shōgun" (Akutagawa Ryūnosuke) **16**:18
Shokoku-banashi (Dazai Osamu) **11**:176-77
"Shōnen no Hiai" (Kunikida Doppo) **99**:295
"Shoon of the Dark" (Hodgson) **13**:235
Shoot (Pirandello)
See *Si gira*
Shoot! The Notebooks of Serafino Gubbio, Cinematographer Operator (Pirandello)
See *Si gira*
Shoot the Works (Broun) **104**:98

"Shooting an Elephant" (Orwell) **6**:344; **15**:333; **31**:194; **51**:250, 256, 261-62; **128**:254, 263, 274-75, 282
Shooting an Elephant, and Other Essays (Orwell) **51**:227, 250; **129**:234
"The Shooting of Dan McGrew" (Service) **15**:402, 404-05, 410-11
"The Shooting of Shinroe" (Somerville & Ross) **51**:383
The Shooting Party (Chekhov) **3**:159
"The Shooting Range" (Brodkey) **123**:195-96
"Shop Girl" (Bodenheim) **44**:69
"A Shop in St. Louis, Missouri" (March) **96**:260
Shop Management (Taylor) **76**:340, 342-45, 356, 360-61, 406, 413, 418
"Shopkeepers at War" (Orwell) **128**:284
"Shoplifting" (Shepherd) **177**:316
"The Shore House" (Jewett) **22**:116
"A Short History of England" (March) **96**:265
Short History of England (Chesterton) **6**:102
A Short History of English Literature (Saintsbury) **31**:218, 236, 238
A Short History of French Literature (Saintsbury) **31**:228
Short History of Scotland (Lang) **16**:270
A Short Life (Onetti)
See *La vida breve*
Short Organum (Brecht)
See *Kleines Organon für das Theatre*
"A Short Sentimental Journey" (Svevo)
See *Corto viaggio sentimentale e altri racconti inediti*
Short Songs of Pure Feelings (Hagiwara)
See *Junjo shokyoku shu*
Short Stories (Merrill) **173**:232
Short Stories (Pirandello) **4**:341
Short Stories for a Morning (Giraudoux)
See *Les contes d'un matin*
Short Stories in Prose and Verse (Lawson) **27**:129-30, 133
Short stories of Eileen Chang (Chang)
See *Zhang Ailing duanpian xiaoshuoji*
The Short Stories of Katherine Mansfield (Mansfield) **164**:225-27, 269, 271, 273-74
"The Short Story" (Bierce) **44**:25, 43
The Short Story (O'Faolain) **143**:223, 252, 265, 273
Short Takes (Runyon) **10**:425, 430, 432, 436
Short Tales (Bunin) **6**:56-7
"A Short Trip Home" (Fitzgerald) **1**:255
A Short View of Russia (Keynes) **64**:219
"Shortening Their Lives" (Yosano)
See "Inochi o Kezuru"
Shorter Novels and Stories (White)
See *The Cockatoos*
Shorter Poems (Bridges) **1**:131
The Shorter Tales (Conrad) **57**:80
"Shosetsu: Abashiri made" (Shiga)
See "Abashiri made"
"Shosetsu: Hayao no imoto" (Shiga) **172**:201
"Shôsetsu sakuhô" (Nagai) **51**:107
"Shōsetsu sōron" (Futabatei) **44**:78-80, 91-2
"Shosetsu: Wakai ginkoin" (Shiga) **172**:201
"Shōtaku" (Nagai) **51**:89
"Should the Negro Be Encouraged to Seek Cultural Equality?" (Locke) **43**:236
"Should Women Use Violence" (Gilman) **117**:175
The Shoulders of Atlas (Freeman) **9**:70-1
Shouts and Murmurs (Woollcott) **5**:521, 527
"The Show" (Owen) **5**:359, 365, 370-71, 373-74; **27**:200-01, 208-09, 212, 226-27
"'Show Mr. and Mrs. F. to Number—'" (Fitzgerald) **52**:56
The Show Piece (Tarkington) **9**:469, 474
Showboat (Whale) **63**:339, 342, 378
Showcase (Holly) **65**:148-50
A Shower of Summer Days (Sarton) **120**:203, 206
The Show-Off (Mankiewicz) **85**:114
"The Shrine of St. Edward the Confessor" (Guiney) **41**:220
A Shropshire Lad (Housman) **1**:353-56, 358; **10**:239, 241, 245-46, 249, 252-55, 259-61
"A Shropshire Lad: XI" (Housman) **10**:249
"A Shropshire Lad: XV" (Housman) **10**:249
"A Shropshire Lad: XXX" (Housman) **10**:252
"A Shropshire Lad: XXXI" (Housman) **10**:252
"A Shropshire Lad: XLI" (Housman) **10**:255
"A Shropshire Lad: XLII" (Housman) **10**:247, 249, 252
"A Shropshire Lad: L" (Housman) **10**:252
"A Shropshire Lad: LV" (Housman) **10**:252
"A Shropshire Lad: LX" (Housman) **10**:252
"A Shropshire Lad: LXI" (Housman) **10**:252
"The Shroud" (Millay) **49**:201
"The Shroud of Color" (Cullen) **4**:38-41, 45, 49-50, 53; **37**:135, 142, 144, 146, 152, 159-60, 164
Shrove Tuesday (Valle-Inclán)
See *Martes de carnaval*
"Shtreiml" (Peretz) **16**:392
"Shugaku-In, Imperial Villa" (Sarton) **120**:265
"Shukuhai" (Nagai) **51**:88, 101-02
Shukyo to bungaku (Endo) **152**:176
"Shulamite" (Lasker-Schueler)
See "Sulamith"
"Shule, Shule, Shule, Agrah!" (Sharp) **39**:392
Shum vremeni (Mandelstam) **6**:260-61, 264
"Les shumit" (Korolenko) **22**:176
"The Shunned House" (Lovecraft) **4**:266; **22**:241
"Shun'ya" (Hagiwara) **60**:313
"Shut a Final Door" (Capote) **164**:99-100, 102-3, 109, 112, 115
"Shut-In" (Pickthall) **21**:250
Shutsuro (Rohan) **22**:303, 306
"Shūzan zu" (Akutagawa Ryūnosuke) **16**:20, 27, 33
Shver tsu zayn a yid (Aleichem) **35**:320
Die shwarze Galeere (Raabe) **45**:182
"Shylock" (Svevo) **35**:363
"Shyness" (Jerome) **23**:77
"Si dorme come cani" (Calvino) **183**:92
Si gira (Pirandello) **29**:301; **172**:160, 162, 168
Si le grain ne meurt (Gide) **36**:107; **5**:219, 243-44; **12**:146, 148, 174; **177**:51, 102
Si le grain ne meurt (Yourcenar) **193**:355
Si le soleil ne revenait pas (Ramuz) **33**:302
Si l'été revenait (Adamov) **189**:15, 59-60
"Si mis manos pudieran deshojar" (García Lorca) **181**:119
"Si te llamaras Nelson" (Arenas) **191**:196
"Siamo noi hegeliani?" (Croce) **37**:123
"Siao sin" (Papini) **22**:281
"Sia-Sia" (Anwar) **22**:19
"The Siberian Carriers" (Korolenko) **22**:170
"Sibyl" (Baker) **10**:17
The Sibyl (Lagerkvist)
See *Sibyllan*
The Sibyl (Sikelianos) **39**:405, 408, 415, 419
Sibyllan (Lagerkvist) **144**:155, 189, 203-4, 207, 211, 215, 235, 237, 240-41
"Eine Sibylle" (Rilke) **195**:294
"Sic Transit" (McCrae) **12**:211
"Sicilian Actors" (Symons) **11**:453
"Sicilian Cyclamens" (Lawrence) **93**:14, 55, 58, 122-24
"Sicilian Limes" (Pirandello) **4**:354
Sicilian Limes (Pirandello)
See *Lumíe di Sicilia*
The Sicily Campaign (Heym)
See *Der Feldzug nach Sizilien*
"The Sick Child" (Colette)
See "L'enfant malade"
"A Sick Child" (Jarrell) **177**:127, 143, 152, 172
"Sick 'Em" (Lardner) **14**:320
Sick Heart River (Buchan) **41**:40-1, 43, 45, 47, 50, 53, 57-8, 73
"The Sick Man" (Stringer) **37**:328
"The Sick Man and the Birds" (Dobson) **79**:11
"The Sick Nought" (Jarrell) **177**:178, 194, 223, 225, 232
Sick Russia (Merezhkovsky) **29**:231
"The Sickness of the Age" (Kazantzakis)
See "Le mal de siècle"
"Sick-Nursing and Health-Nursing" (Nightingale) **85**:258
Siddhartha: An Indic Poem (Hesse)
See *Siddhartha, eine indische Dichtung*
Siddhartha, eine indische Dichtung (Hesse) **148**:159, 172; **196**:233-344
Sidestreets (Tsvetaeva)
See *Pereulochki*
Sidney Yorke's Friend (Bennett) **197**:30
Sido (Colette) **5**:164-66; **16**:118, 135
Den sidste glaede: Skildringer (Hamsun) **14**:223, 231-32; **49**:128-29, 155
"Sie lächelt" (Sudermann) **15**:432
Sieben Jahre: Chronik der Gedanken und Vorgange (Mann) **9**:329
"Sieben schizophrene Sonette" (Ball) **104**:16
Die sieben Todsünden der Kleinburger (Brecht) **6**:30
Der Siebente Ring (George) **2**:147-49, 154, 250-52; **14**:202, 204-06, 210, 212, 214
Der siebente Tag (Lasker-Schueler) **57**:329-30
"Sieg des Sommers" (George) **14**:211
Siege (Millay) **49**:217
Le siége de l'air (Arp) **115**:30, 39-40, 42, 53
Le siège de Montoue (Rolland) **23**:256
The Siege of Beszterce (Mikszath)
See *Beszterce ostroma*
"The Siege of London" (James) **40**:162; **64**:157-58
"Siegesfest" (Liliencron) **18**:214
"Siegfried" (Jarrell) **177**:149, 170, 172, 192-93
Siegfried (Giraudoux) **2**:157-58, 160, 165, 167-68; **7**:320-22, 327-28
Siegfried et le Limousin (Giraudoux) **2**:163, 165; **7**:317, 325, 327
Siegfried von Kleist (Giraudoux)
See *Siegfried et le Limousin*
"Siempre" (Aleixandre) **113**:8
Siempre en ridículo (Echegaray) **4**:101
"Siena" (Swinburne) **8**:429; **36**:318
Het sienjaal (van Ostaijen) **33**:405, 411-15, 419
La siepe (Pascoli) **45**:154
"Sierpe de amor" (Aleixandre) **113**:33, 49
Siesta (Hamsun) **14**:248
"Siesta in Xbalba and Return to the States" (Ginsberg) **120**:35
"La sieste" (Desnos) **22**:73
Siete conversaciones con Jorge Luis Borges (Borges) **109**:119
El 7 de julio (Pérez Galdós) **27**:257
Siete domingos rojos (Sender) **136**:209
Los siete locos (Arlt) **29**:38-42, 45-7, 50-4, 57-8
Los siete sobre Deva (Reyes) **33**:324
"Sieur George" (Cable) **4**:28, 32
The Si-Fan Mysteries (Rohmer) **28**:277, 279, 286-87, 293, 298-99
"Sigh No More" (Lawrence) **93**:52
"Sight" (Parker) **143**:326
Sight and Song (Field) **43**:152-55, 164-68
Sight Unseen (Rinehart) **52**:289, 292, 301, 303
"Sightseers" (Nemerov) **124**:196
"Sign" (Apollinaire)
See "Signe"
"The Sign" (Manning) **25**:265
"The Sign" (Masters) **2**:465; **25**:298
"The Sign" (Zamyatin) **37**:430
The Sign in Sidney Brustein's Window (Hansberry) **192**:245-46, 248, 250, 252, 254-57, 259-60, 263-65, 286, 296-98, 322, 324-25, 337
"A Sign in Space" (Calvino)
See "Un segno nello spazio"
The Sign of Four (Doyle) **7**:215-16, 220, 231, 234-37
"Sign of Space" (Calvino)
See "Un segno nello spazio"
"The Sign of the Golden Shoe" (Noyes) **7**:512
The Sign of the Prophet Jonah (Bridie)
See *Jonah and the Whale*

Signa (Ouida) **43**:342, 345, 347, 349-50, 364, 366-67
"Den signade dag" (Lagerkvist) **144**:185-86
The Signal (van Ostaijen)
See *Het sienjaal*
Signal Driver (White) **176**:219, 225, 227
"Signe" (Apollinaire) **51**:57, 61
Signes (Merleau-Ponty) **156**:129, 134-36, 144, 183, 191-92, 198, 210, 274-76
Les signes parmi nous (Ramuz) **33**:295
"Significance" (Rosenberg) **12**:311
"The Significance of the Blues" (Handy) **97**:61
"Significations" (Jacob) **6**:194
"Signing the Pledge" (Harper) **14**:260
Signora Ava (Jovine) **79**:43, 45-6, 50, 58-9, 61-2, 65
La Signora di tutti (Ophuls) **79**:197, 237-8, 243-5, 247-52
"La Signora Frola e il signor Ponza, suo genero" (Pirandello) **172**:162
"The Sign-Post" (Thomas) **10**:454, 463
Signs (Merleau-Ponty)
See *Signes*
"Signs along the Road" (Andrić)
See "Znakovi pored puta"
"Signs and Tokens" (Hardy) **4**:170
Signs and Wonders (Beresford) **81**:6,9
Signs by the Roadside (Andrić)
See "Znakovi pored puta"
Signs of Earth (Tsvetaeva)
See *Zemnye primety*
"Signs of the Times" (Dunbar) **12**:108
"Siguiriya gitana" (García Lorca) **49**:89
Sigurd Jerusalem-Farer (Bjoernson) **37**:23
Sigurd Jorsalfar (Bjoernson) **37**:29
Sigurd Slembe (Bjoernson) **7**:100, 103, 105-06, 109, 111, 113, 116; **37**:18-20, 23, 29-32
Sigurd the Bastard (Bjoernson)
See *Sigurd Slembe*
Sigurd the Crusader (Bjoernson) **37**:10
"Sigurd the Proud" (Lagerloef) **36**:240
Sigurd's Return (Bjoernson) **37**:9
Sigurd's Second Flight (Bjoernson) **37**:9
Sik-Sik, l'artefice magico (de Filippo) **127**:288-90
Silanus, the Christian (Abbott) **139**:26
Silas Crockett (Chase) **124**:12, 16, 23-5
"Silas Jackson" (Dunbar) **2**:128; **12**:120
Silberne Saiten (Zweig) **17**:424
"The Silence" (Fletcher) **35**:109
"Silence" (Freeman) **9**:64
"Silence" (Ginzburg) **156**:49, 88
"Silence" (Jiménez)
See "¡Silencio!"
"Silence" (Lawrence) **93**:17, 57, 125
"Silence" (Maeterlinck) **3**:318
"Silence" (Masters) **2**:464; **25**:298, 315
"Le silence" (Verhaeren) **12**:466
Silence (Endo)
See *Chinmoku*
Silence (Ginzburg) **156**:20
Le silence (Rod) **52**:310, 314
The Silence (Sarraute)
See *Le silence*
Le silence (Sarraute) **145**:264-65, 267-68, 287, 309, 316, 320-22
Silence, and Other Stories (Andreyev) **3**:18, 26
Silence, and Other Stories (Freeman) **9**:63, 71-2
"Silence, Exile & Death" (Chambers) **129**:48
Silence Farm (Sharp) **39**:372-74, 378, 387
The Silence Now (Sarton) **120**:260
"The Silence of Love" (Naidu) **80**:307
"The Silence of the Valley" (O'Faolain) **143**:223, 235, 238, 252-53
The Silencer (Murdoch) **171**:222
Silences (Okigbo) **171**:341, 344, 352-54
"Silences: Lament of the Silent Sisters" (Okigbo) **171**:345, 352-53, 362, 365
"El Silencio" (García Lorca) **181**:197
"¡Silencio!" (Jiménez) **183**:314-19, 330
"Silencio" (Lugones) **15**:289
Silencio de muerte (Echegaray) **4**:101
"Silent Bees" (Balmont)
See "Nezhuzhashchie"
"Silent Bontche" (Peretz)
See "Bontsye Shvayg"
"The Silent Eaters" (Garland) **3**:199
"The Silent Land" (Chambers) **41**:88, 107
"The Silent Lover" (Middleton) **56**:183
The Silent Mr. Palomar (Calvino)
See *Palomar*
"The Silent One" (Gurney) **33**:88, 93, 102, 104
The Silent Partner (Phelps) **113**:347-49, 352-53, 355, 368-73, 400
"Silent Partners" (Engel) **137**:115
"Silent Samuel" (Dunbar) **12**:120
"Silent Sisters" (Okigbo)
See "Silences: Lament of the Silent Sisters"
The Silent South, Together with the Freedman's Case in Equity and the Convict Lease System (Cable) **4**:30-1
Silent System (Matthews) **95**:243
A Silent Witness (Freeman) **21**:48, 57
The Silent Witness (Post) **39**:345
Siléntér (Gonzalez Martinez) **72**:147, 149, 155
"Silentium" (Mandelstam) **2**:403
"Silenzio" (Ginzburg) **156**:96, 99-100
"A Silhouette" (Graham) **19**:129, 133
"Silhouette of a Serpent" (Valéry)
See "Ébauche d'un serpent"
Silhouettes (Symons) **11**:426-28, 431-32, 445-46, 450-51
Silhouettes of American Life (Davis) **6**:151-52, 154
"Silk o' the Kine" (Sharp) **39**:372-73, 377
The Silmarillion (Tolkien) **137**:233, 246, 249, 253-55, 257-58, 262, 271-72, 275, 300
"Silver" (de la Mare) **53**:28
The Silver Box (Galsworthy) **1**:293, 300, 303; **45**:31, 33, 41-3, 45-6, 50-3, 55
"The Silver Crown" (Malamud) **184**:222, 237, 278, 280, 285, 287-88, 310, 312-13
"A Silver Cup" (Cather) **132**:131
The Silver Domino; or, Side Whispers, Social and Literary (Corelli) **51**:73
The Silver Dove (Bely) **7**:48-51, 54
"Silver Filigree" (Wylie) **8**:531, 533
The Silver Fox (Somerville & Ross) **51**:330, 340, 345, 359, 372, 378
"The Silver Key" (Lovecraft) **4**:266-67
The Silver Mask (Walpole) **5**:502
"The Silver Pageant" (Crane) **11**:142
The Silver Poppy (Stringer) **37**:335, 337
"Silver Smoke of Dreams" (Burroughs) **121**:140, 142
The Silver Spoon (Galsworthy) **1**:298; **45**:46-7, 70
"Silver Spoons" (Remizov)
See "Serebrianye lozhki"
The Silver Stair (Williams) **1**:517, 521
The Silver Stallion (Cabell) **6**:68, 71, 75-6
"The Silver Swanne" (Dowell) **129**:66-7, 69, 74, 159-61, 165
The Silver Thorn (Walpole) **5**:504
Silverpoints (Gray) **19**:141-44, 147-48, 150-58, 160, 162
Silversködarna (Bengtsson) **48**:6, 12
"Silverspot" (Seton) **31**:270-71, 273
Silvertip's Roundup (Faust) **49**:46-7
"Silvia" (Marquis) **7**:434
Silvia im Stern (Hofmannsthal) **11**:306
"Silvina y Montt" (Quiroga) **20**:207
"Simaetha" (Manning) **25**:265
Simbi and the Satyr of the Dark Jungle (Tutuola) **188**:275-76, 281, 283, 289-90, 304-05, 307-08
Simfonija (1-aga) (Bely)
See *Severnaia simfoniia: Pervia geroicheskaia*
Simfonija (2-aja) (Bely)
See *Vtoraia simfoniia: Dramaticheskaia*
"Simian Civilization" (Bosman) **49**:15
"Similiar Cases" (Gilman) **9**:96-7, 102; **37**:176; **117**:145
Simo hurtta (Leino) **24**:372
"Simome, poème champêtre" (Gourmont) **17**:129-30
"Simon Bolívar Liberator" (Andrić) **135**:39
"Simón Carvajal" (Borges) **109**:8
Simon Dale (Hope) **83**:165
Simon le pathétique (Giraudoux) **2**:166; **7**:320, 324-25
"Simon Legree" (Lindsay) **17**:225-26, 235, 241
"Simon Mage" (Apollinaire) **51**:20-1
Simon the Cyrenian (Torrence) **97**:149, 151-52, 160-62
"Simon the Cyrenian Speaks" (Cullen) **37**:143-44, 146, 154
Simon the Sensitive (Giraudoux)
See *Simon le pathétique*
"Simon Wheeler, Detective" (Twain) **161**:236, 311
Simone (Feuchtwanger) **3**:182
Simone (Gourmont) **17**:137, 142
Simonsen (Undset) **3**:522
"The Simoom" (Quiroga)
See "El simún"
Simoon (Strindberg) **1**:448
Simpatías y diferencias (Reyes) **33**:316, 322
The Simple Adventures of a Memsahib (Duncan) **60**:184, 187, 193-6, 207, 209, 212-4, 218, 244, 247, 249-56
"The Simple Art of Murder" (Chandler) **7**:171, 176-77; **179**:79, 87, 105, 131-32, 187, 192, 201-3, 206-7, 209, 222
The Simple Art of Murder (Chandler) **179**:128, 188
The Simple Case of Susan (Futrelle) **19**:95
The Simple Life Limited (Ford) **15**:93; **172**:118
"The Simple Lifers" (Rinehart) **52**:281
"The Simple Purposes and the Solid Foundation of Our Recovery Program" (Roosevelt) **93**:184
"Simple Simon" (Coppard) **5**:176
"Simple Story" (Agnon)
See "Sippur pasut"
"The Simple Truth" (Cullen) **37**:157, 170
"Simples" (Joyce) **3**:256; **159**:284
The Simpleton of the Unexpected Isles (Shaw) **3**:393
"Simplification of Life" (Carpenter) **88**:98
"Simplify Me When I'm Dead" (Douglas) **40**:68, 72, 91
Simply Complicated (Bernhard)
See *Einfach kompliziert*
"Simson" (Heym) **9**:142
La simulación (Sarduy) **167**:188-92, 199, 210, 227
"The Simulators" (Chekhov) **3**:151
Simultan (Bachmann) **192**:24-25, 32, 44, 66, 76, 78, 83, 140
"Simultan" (Bachmann) **192**:78, 83, 87, 116-19, 122-25
Simultaneità (Marinetti) **10**:319
"Simultanéités" (Apollinaire) **3**:35; **51**:36
Simultaneity (Marinetti)
See *Simultaneità*
Simultaneous (Bachmann)
See *Simultan*
"El simún" (Quiroga) **20**:214, 216-17
"The Simurgh and the Eagle" (Borges) **109**:154
"Sin" (Caragiale)
See "Păcat"
"The Sin" (Jozsef) **22**:161
Sin amor (Azuela) **3**:77; **145**:9, 14, 17, 25-26
Sin and Original Guilt (Otto) **85**:314
"Sin luz" (Aleixandre) **113**:12
The Sin of Harold Diddlebock (Sturges) **48**:282-283, 285, 289, 291, 309, 313
"The Sin of Jesus" (Babel)
See "Isusov grekh"
"Sin Razón, pero cansado" (Quiroga)
See "Cuento sin razón, pero cansado"
"Since 1619" (Walker) **129**:297-98, 327
"Since Then" (Lawson) **27**:140
"Sincerities" (Benét) **28**:2

Sinclair Lewis (Van Doren) **18**:398
"The Sin-Eater" (Sharp) **39**:362, 373, 396
The Sin-Eater, and Other Tales (Sharp) **39**:354-55, 364, 373, 379, 395
"Sinews of Peace" (Churchill) **113**:164, 174-77, 179-80
"Sinfire" (Hawthorne) **25**:240
"Sinfonía en gris mayor" (Darío) **4**:58
"Sing the Baby to Sleep, Marietta" (McAlmon) **97**:115
"Sing the Epistle" (Pirandello)
See "Canta l'epistola"
"The Singer" (Benn) **3**:114
"The Singer Sings before a Child of Princes" (Rilke) **195**:165
"The Singers in a Cloud" (Torrence) **97**:152, 155
"Singing" (Balmont)
See "Pene"
"The Singing Angels of the Nativity" (Martyn) **131**:124
The Singing Bone (Freeman) **21**:44, 48, 50-2, 56, 58
"Singing Children" (Pickthall) **21**:245
Singing from the Well (Arenas)
See *Celestino antes del alba*
Singing Guns (Faust) **49**:35, 45, 47, 56-7, 60-1
"The Singing Lesson" (Mansfield) **8**:280; **39**:303; **164**:235, 307
"A Singing Lesson" (Swinburne) **36**:343
"Singing on My Way to Yodoe" (Su Man-shu) **24**:456
The Singing Sands (Tey) **14**:452
"The Singing Skyscrapers" (Benét) **28**:6
"The Singing Spirit" (Eastman) **55**:167
The Single Hound (Sarton) **120**:227, 231, 233, 243, 277-78, 315
"Singolare avventura di Francesco Maria" (Brancati) **12**:86
Singolare viaggio di avventura (Brancati) **12**:84-5
A Singular Life (Phelps) **113**:340
"Sinie okory" (Khlebnikov) **20**:133
"Sininen risti" (Leino) **24**:368, 370, 376
Sinister Madonna (Rohmer) **28**:281
The Sinister Man (Wallace) **57**:396, 402
The Sinister Ray (Dent) **72**:36
Sinister Street (Mackenzie) **116**:183-84, 192-94, 196-99, 201, 204, 206-10, 212, 214-15, 224, 227-34, 239, 241, 247, 251-53
"Sink" (Trakl) **5**:468
"The Sink of Iniquity" (Frank) **17**:121
Sinking and Swimming (Nagai)
See *Ukishizumi*
Der Sinn des Lebens (Adler) **61**:18, 28
Sinnende Flammer (Arp) **115**:34-5
"Sinnenrausch" (Lasker-Schueler) **57**:302
"The Sinner" (Asch) **3**:67
"The Sinner" (Kolmar) **40**:177
"The Sinner" (Smith) **25**:377, 379, 387, 393, 399
The Sinner (Singer)
See *Yoshe Kalb*
"Sinners" (Lawrence) **93**:55
Sinners in Paradise (Whale) **63**:339
Sino al contine (Deledda) **23**:35, 39
"The Sins of Prince Saradine" (Chesterton) **1**:186; **6**:100
The Sins of Séverac Bablon (Rohmer) **28**:281-83
"The Sins of the Children, the Curse of the Fathers" (Heyse)
See "Der Kinder Sünde, der Väter Fluch"
The Sins of the Father (Dixon) **163**:172, 187, 190-92, 197-98, 211-12, 217-18, 240, 243-48, 253
The Sins of the Fathers (Cram) **45**:20, 22
"Le sionisme" (Gourmont) **17**:126
"Sioux Mythology" (Eastman) **55**:162
Sippur pashut (Agnon) **151**:45, 51-2
"Sippur pasut" (Agnon) **151**:22
Sippur pasut (Agnon)
See *Sippur pashut*
Sir Bengt's Wife (Strindberg)
See *Herr Bengts Hustru*
"Sir C. Frazer e la magia" (Papini) **22**:281
"Sir Galahad" (Masters) **25**:298
Sir George Tressady (Ward) **55**:410, 421-22, 424
Sir Gibbie (MacDonald) **9**:292, 294, 309
"Sir Jesper" (Jensen)
See "Hr. Jesper"
Sir John Magill's Last Journey: An Inspector French Case (Crofts) **55**:82-3, 86
"Sir Lancelot" (Campbell) **9**:29-31
Sir Nigel (Doyle) **7**:221, 238-39
"Sir Oswald Mosley's Manifesto" (Keynes) **64**:244
Sir Quixote of the Moors (Buchan) **41**:33
Sir Walter Raleigh (Buchan) **41**:59
Sir Walter Scott (Buchan) **41**:45, 59-63
Sirah (Agnon) **151**:22
"Siramour" (Desnos) **22**:67-8, 72
Sire Halewyn (Ghelderode) **187**:4, 24, 26-7
"The Siren" (Buchanan) **107**:14
Siren Land (Douglas) **68**:3, 5, 10, 29, 39, 43-5
"Siren Limits" (Okigbo) **171**:351
"Siren Limits II" (Okigbo) **171**:351
"Siren Limits III" (Okigbo) **171**:351
La sirena negra (Pardo Bazán) **189**:209-10, 213, 229, 234, 243, 248-49, 251
"Sirène-Anémone" (Desnos) **22**:72
The Sirens Wake (Dunsany) **59**:18
Sirius: A Fantasy of Love and Discord (Stapledon) **22**:316, 322-23, 326, 329-30, 337-38, 344
"Sirota odsutnost" (Popa) **167**:158
"Sis' Becky's Pickaninny" (Chesnutt) **5**:130; **39**:72, 94-5, 99, 106
Sis Marigold (Bennett) **197**:125, 127, 135
Sis Tellwright (Bennett) **197**:125, 127
"Sishutirtha" (Tagore) **3**:489
"The Siskin Who Lied and the Truth-Loving Woodpecker" (Gorky)
See "O chizhe, kotoryi lgal, i o diatle liubitele istiny"
Sista mänskan (Lagerkvist) **144**:158, 210, 214
Siste kapitel (Hamsun) **14**:228, 241; **49**:155
Den siste viking (Bojer) **64**:16-19, 21-25
"Sistema" (Calvino) **183**:101
Sistema di logica (Gentile) **96**:118, 123
Il sistema periodico (Levi) **109**:281, 290, 296, 301, 304-07, 313, 319-20, 340-42
Sister Béatrice (Maeterlinck)
See *Soeur Béatrice*
Sister Carrie (Dreiser) **10**:163-65, 169, 171, 173-74, 176-77, 181-82, 184-85, 187, 191-92, 199-200; **18**:54, 59, 63-4; **35**:37-41, 48-50, 54-9, 62-3, 65, 74; **83**:3-4, 15, 19, 36, 41, 54, 98
"Sister Helen" (Kipling) **8**:188
"Sister Mary of the Plague" (Lee-Hamilton) **22**:188-89, 194
"Sister Mary van der Deck" (Lee-Hamilton) **22**:192
"Sister, My Sister" (Södergran)
See "Syster, min syster"
"The Sister of Compassion" (Sharp) **39**:361-62
"The Sister of Percivale" (Williams) **1**:512
"The Sister of the Baroness" (Mansfield) **39**:301; **164**:293
Sister Outsider: Essays and Speeches (Lorde) **173**:39-41, 43-44, 54, 89
Sister Songs (Thompson) **4**:435-36, 440
Sister Teresa (Moore) **7**:482, 484-86, 491, 494, 498
"Sister Water" (Nervo)
See "La hermana agua"
"The Sister-in-Law" (D'Annunzio) **6**:144
"Sisters" (Bergelson) **81**:19
"The Sisters" (Campbell) **5**:117
"The Sisters" (Joyce) **8**:166, 169-70; **35**:142, 144-46, 156-57, 159, 161-63, 166-67, 169, 190-92, 197; **159**:275-77, 298-99, 302-6, 308, 310-11, 314-16
"The Sisters" (Lowell) **1**:379; **8**:227, 235, 237
"The Sisters" (Smith) **25**:379, 399
The Sisters (Conrad) **13**:113
The Sisters (Tolstoy) **18**:365, 374, 379-80
The Sisters: A Tragedy (Swinburne) **8**:434, 444; **36**:343
"Sisters in Arms" (Lorde) **173**:75-76, 82
Sisters of the Cross (Remizov)
See *Krestovye sestry*
Sisters of the Gion (Mizoguchi)
See *Gion no Shimai*
"The Sisters, the Lightnings" (Khlebnikov)
See "Syostry-molnii"
"The Sisters Three and the Kilmaree" (Stockton) **47**:330
"Sit and Stand and Kill and Die" (Jozsef) **22**:160, 164
Sitting Bull. Ein Indianer-Roman (Zuckmayer) **191**:301-02
Sitting On The World (Broun) **104**:98
Das sittliche Bewusstsein (von Hartmann) **96**:228-29
Sittlichkeit und Kriminalität (Kraus) **5**:285, 290
"La situation des bonnes au Mexique" (Jacob) **6**:191
"The Situation Does Not Change" (Nemerov) **124**:225
"Sivriada geceleri" (Sait Faik) **23**:293, 298
"Sivriada Nights" (Sait Faik)
See "Sivriada geceleri"
"S. I. W." (Owen) **5**:367, 371; **27**:206, 212, 217-19, 222-23, 225, 229
"Siwash" (London) **9**:277
"Six Boys in the Sun" (Coffin) **95**:17
Six Characters in Search of an Author (Pirandello)
See *Sei personaggi in cerca d'autore*
"Six Discordant Songs" (Stevens) **45**:281
"Six février" (Péret) **20**:195
Six French Poets (Lowell) **1**:372, 377; **8**:228-29, 235
"The Six Handkerchiefs" (Undset)
See "Et halvt dusin lommetørklaer"
La 628-E-8 (Mirbeau) **55**:281, 287, 301, 309-11, 313
Six Lectures on the Reconstruction of Religious Thought in Islam (Iqbal) **28**:190, 195, 197, 204
Six Memos for the Next Millennium (Calvino) **183**:62, 64, 67-71, 110-12, 124, 127, 132, 141-46, 148, 163, 171, 174, 179, 220, 222
"Six More Miles to the Graveyard" (Williams) **81**:419
"Six Nuns" (Mayakovski) **18**:258
"Six O'Clock in Princes Street" (Owen) **5**:374; **27**:226
The Six of Calais (Shaw) **3**:393
"The Six Pillars of Peace" (Dulles) **72**:79-80
Six Stories (Güiraldes)
See *Seis relatos porteños*
Six stories by Don Isidro Parodi (Borges)
See *Seis relatos para don Isidro Parodi*
"Six Years After" (Mansfield) **39**:305; **164**:300-301
Six-Acre Rose Garden (Babits)
See *Hat holdas rózsakert*
"Sixes and Sevens" (Bosman) **49**:11
A Sixfoot Sickbed (Masaoka) **18**:227-28
"Sixpence" (Mansfield) **2**:454
1601; or, Conversation as It Was by the Fireside in the Time of the Tudors (Twain) **6**:476; **12**:436; **48**:349, 357, 360; **161**:240, 242-43
"Sixteen and the Unknown Soldier" (March) **96**:241, 254
"Sixteen Dead Men" (Yeats) **93**:389
Sixteen Self Sketches (Shaw) **45**:215
"The Sixth" (Güiraldes)
See "Sexto"
The Sixth (Arguedas)
See *El sexto*
The Sixth Beatitude (Hall) **12**:188-89

Sixth Commandment (Buchanan) **107**:34
"The Sixth Day" (Levi)
See "Il sesto giorno"
The Sixth Day (Levi)
See "Il sesto giorno"
The Sixth Day and Other Tales (Levi) **109**:292-93, 299
"Sixth Eclogue" (Radnóti) **16**:412, 414
"Sixth Elegy" (Rilke) **1**:413
"The Sixth of August" (Ivanov) **33**:138
"Sixth Sense" (Gumilev)
See "Shesto chuvstvo"
"The Sixth Sense" (Söderberg) **39**:438
The Sixth Sense (Nervo) **11**:403
Sixtine: Roman de la vie cérébrale (Gourmont) **17**:127-29, 133, 137, 144, 147, 151, 156
"Sixty and Six; or, A Fountain of Youth" (Higginson) **36**:179
Sixty Seconds (Bodenheim) **44**:71-2
Siyaniya (Hippius) **9**:162-63, 167
Själarnas maskerad (Lagerkvist) **144**:201, 213, 215
"The Skaters" (Fletcher) **35**:94, 115
Skazanie (Nabokov) **108**:133
"Skazaniye o flore" (Korolenko) **22**:175
"Skazka" (Nabokov) **108**:205-6, 208, 210
"Skazka o kamennom veke" (Khlebnikov) **20**:126
Skeeters Kirby (Masters) **2**:467-69; **25**:293
"The Skeleton" (Tagore)
See "Kankal"
A Skeleton Key to Finnegans Wake (Campbell) **140**:4, 30, 34-35, 66-67, 75-80, 85-86, 91, 129
Skeleton Men (Burroughs) **2**:81
"Sketch" (Bennett) **197**:129
"Sketch for a New Weltanschauung" (Hulme) **21**:121
"The Sketch in Indian Ink" (Söderberg) **39**:436-37
"A Sketch of Individual Development" (MacDonald) **9**:305; **113**:212, 320, 323
A Sketch of My Life (Mann) **60**:357, 360-61, 363
"A Sketch of the Past" (Woolf) **128**:369, 372
Sketchbook, 1946-1949 (Frisch)
See *Tagebuch, 1946-1949*
Sketchbook, 1966-1971 (Frisch)
See *Tagebuch, 1966-1971*
Sketches and Moments (Caragiale) **76**:165
Sketches and Outlines (Pereda) **16**:364
Sketches from Life (Carpenter) **88**:119, 126
Sketches from Marlborough (Benson) **27**:5, 7
Sketches in Charcoal (Sienkiewicz) **3**:425-26, 430
Sketches New and Old (Borg) **48**:349
"Sketches of a Life of Action" (Warung) **45**:419
Sketches of a Provincial Journey (Peretz) **16**:403-05
Sketches of a Siberian Tourist (Korolenko) **22**:170, 172
Sketches of Southern Life (Harper) **14**:255, 257-64
Sketches Old and New (Twain) **59**:168
Skibet (Jensen) **41**:290-91, 295
Skibet gaar videre (Grieg) **10**:205, 207-08, 210-13
"The Skies" (Aleixandre)
See "Los cielos"
"Skify" (Blok) **5**:85, 88, 94, 98
"The Skilled Man" (Sarton) **120**:305
"Skin" (Dahl) **173**:12
The Skin (Malaparte)
See *La peau*
The Skin Game (Galsworthy) **1**:295, 303, 305; **45**:45, 51-2
Skin Trade (Thomas)
See *Adventures in the Skin Trade, and Other Stories*
The Skinners (Marquis) **7**:451
"the skinny voice" (Cummings) **137**:42
Skipper Worse (Kielland) **5**:276-79
"The Skipper's Wooing" (Jacobs) **22**:107
The Skipper's Wooing. The Brown Man's Servant (Jacobs) **22**:102
"Skitaniia" (Bryusov) **10**:95-6
Skleněný havelok (Nezval) **44**:240, 245, 249
Sklepy cynamonowe (Schulz) **5**:420-27, 429; **51**:307-08, 310-14, 316-17, 319-25
"Skogs sjön" (Södergran) **31**:288
"Skogsdunkel" (Södergran) **31**:288
Skovviser (Obstfelder) **23**:177-79
Skuggan av-mart (Dagerman) **17**:89, 95
"The Skull and the Orchid" (Levi) **109**:286
Skull Face (Rohmer) **28**:282
"The Skull in the Desert" (Campbell) **5**:124
"Skull-Face" (Howard) **8**:132
"Skvorez" (Zabolotsky) **52**:367
"Sky" (Jiménez) **183**:336
The Sky Ablaze (Sá-Carneiro)
See *Céu em fogo*
The Sky and the Forest (Forester) **152**:141-44, 146
Sky Blue (Bataille)
See *Le bleu du ciel*
Sky Blue (Kandinsky) **92**:83
Sky in Flames (Sá-Carneiro)
See *Céu em fogo*
Sky Island (Baum) **7**:20
The Sky Pilot (Connor) **31**:105-06, 108-09, 111-13, 116
The Sky Pilot in No Man's Land (Connor) **31**:105-06, 113-14
"The Sky Warrior" (Eastman) **55**:167
Sky with Clouds (Radnóti)
See *Tajtékos ég*
"Skyberia" (Kirk) **119**:278, 285
Sky-Blue Depths (Platonov) **14**:417
Skygger (Nexø) **43**:329
Skylines and Horizons (Heyward) **59**:86
"Skyloyiannis" (Palamas) **5**:386
"Skymning" (Södergran) **31**:290
"Skyscape" (Hagiwara) **60**:297
"A Skyscraper in Cross-Section" (Mayakovski) **18**:259
Sladek der schwartze Reichswehrmann (Horvath) **45**:76, 80, 93-4, 99, 101-02, 106
Sladek, the Soldier of the Army (Horvath)
See *Sladek der schwartze Reichswehrmann*
Slain by the Doones (Blackmore) **27**:43
"A Slap in the Face" (Quiroga)
See "Una bofetada"
"A Slap in the Public's Face" (Mayakovski) **18**:261
"The Slate Ode" (Mandelstam)
See "Grifel' naja oda"
"Slava tolpe" (Bryusov) **10**:83
The Slave (Hichens) **64**:119, 121-122
"The Slave Auction" (Harper) **14**:258-62
"The Slave Mother" (Harper) **14**:258-59, 261
"The Slave Mother I" (Harper) **14**:262
"The Slave Mother II" (Harper) **14**:263
"The Slave of God" (Benson) **17**:18
"Slave Quarters" (Dickey) **151**:95, 110, 121, 170, 200
The Slave-Girl Who Is Not Isaura (Andrade)
See *A escrava que não é Isaura*
"The Slave-Girl's Prayer" (Forten) **16**:147, 150
"The Slave's Appeal" (Stanton) **73**:270, 272-73, 275
Slaves of Society (Upward) **85**:380
The Slaves of the Fish Men (Burroughs) **32**:59
"Slaves of the Lamp" (Kipling) **17**:208
"The Slave's Song" (Gumilev)
See "Nevol'nich'ja"
The Slayer of Souls (Chambers) **41**:102, 114
"Sled Burial, Dream Ceremony" (Dickey) **151**:90, 170
"Sleep" (Cullen) **37**:166
"Sleep" (Pickthall) **21**:245, 250
"Sleep" (Riley) **51**:302
"Sleep" (Rosenberg) **12**:309
Sleep (Chandler)
See *The Big Sleep*
"A Sleep and a Forgetting" (Fisher) **87**:74
"Sleep and Walking" (Lawrence) **93**:56
"The Sleep Child" (Dickey) **151**:95
"Sleep Hath Composed the Anguish of My Brain" (Santayana) **40**:400
Sleep! I Command You! (Feydeau)
See *Dormez! Je le veux!*
"Sleep, My Pretty, My Dear" (Roberts) **68**:337
"The Sleep of Odysseus" (Pascoli)
See "Il sonno di Odisseo"
"The Sleep Worker" (Hardy) **53**:81, 86; **143**:200
"Sleeping Beauty" (Nemerov) **124**:177, 180, 310
Sleeping Beauty (Heijermans) **24**:293
"The Sleeping Beauty in the Fridge" (Levi) **109**:299
"The Sleeping Beauty: Variation of the Prince" (Jarrell) **177**:125, 129, 152
"The Sleeping Boys of Warwickshire" (de la Mare) **53**:22
A Sleeping Car (Howells) **7**:387
A Sleeping Clergyman (Bridie) **3**:132-33, 136-38
Sleeping Fires (Gissing) **24**:235, 248
"Sleeping like Dogs" (Calvino)
See "Si dorme come cani"
"Sleeping on the Ceiling" (Bishop) **121**:71
"Sleeping Out on Easter" (Dickey) **151**:103, 199
"The Sleeping Porch" (Fields) **80**:258
"Sleeping Venus" (Field) **43**:165-67
"Sleepless City" (García Lorca)
See "Ciudad sin sueño"
"Sleeplessness" (Andrić) **135**:42
"Sleepwalker Ballad" (García Lorca)
See "Romance sonámbulo"
The Sleepwalkers (Broch)
See *Die Schlafwandler*
"Sleet" (Dagerman) **17**:93
"Slepac" (Andrić) **135**:53-54
"Slépej" (Čapek) **192**:181
"Slepo sunce" (Popa) **167**:157
Slepoi muzykant (Korolenko) **22**:168-70, 172, 174, 176
"Sletten" (Obstfelder) **23**:178-80, 182, 190-91
The Sleuth of St. James's Square (Post) **39**:336, 343-45
"Slim Scott" (Fisher) **140**:165
"A Slip of the Leash" (Freeman) **9**:75-6
"Slipper Satin" (La Guma) **140**:205, 219, 235
"The Slippers of the Goddess of Beauty" (Lowell) **8**:227, 232-33
"The Sliprails and the Spur" (Lawson) **27**:123, 125, 134, 140
"Slip-Shoe Lovey" (Masters) **25**:297
"Slith" (Dunsany) **2**:146
"The Slithering Shadow" (Howard) **8**:133, 135
Slivnitsa (Vazov) **25**:450
Slobberdom, Sneerdom and Boredom (Hecht) **101**:33
"Slobbus Americanus in the Cultural Vanguard" (Shepherd) **177**:299, 302
"Slonenok" (Remizov) **27**:339
"The Slot Machine" (Saroyan) **137**:197
"Slova ljubvi i tepla" (Guro) **56**:138-39
"Slove predostavljaetsja tovarišču Čuryginu" (Zamyatin) **8**:553
"Slovene Culture" (Cankar)
See "Slovene People and Slovene Culture"
"Slovene Culture, War and the Working Class" (Cankar) **105**:155
"Slovene People and Slovene Culture" (Cankar) **105**:154-55
"Slovo" (Nabokov) **108**:140
Slow Attack (Lewis) **104**:201
The Slow Coach (Lucas) **73**:158, 163
Slow Vision (Bodenheim) **44**:73-4
"Slučaj iz praktiki" (Chekhov) **3**:149, 159-60; **163**:130, 134
"Sluchai iz praktiki" (Chekhov)
See "Slučaj iz praktiki"

"The Sluggards" (Jensen)
See "Syvsoverne"
"The Slum Cat" (Seton) **31**:279-80
"A slumber did my spirit steal" (Hardy) **53**:94
"Slumber Songs" (McCrae) **12**:210
"Slushy" (Cobb) **77**:133
Smaastykker (Bjoernson) **37**:35
The Small Bachelor (Wodehouse) **108**:369-72, 380
A Small Book of Tales (Agnon) **151**:73
"A Small Boy And Others" (Riley) **51**:287
A Small Boy and Others (James) **171**:123, 139
A Small Boy, and Others (James) **2**:247; **11**:321, 345
"Small Brook" (Wen I-to) **28**:417
"The Small Duke" (Giraudoux) **7**:324
"Small Heart" (Herbert) **168**:48, 56
"The Small Hours" (Parker) **143**:320
"A Small, Infinite Poem" (García Lorca) **197**:200, 213
"The Small Lady" (O'Faolain) **143**:236
Small Leaf-Boat (Shimazaki Toson)
See *Hitohabune*
"Small Moment" (Nemerov) **124**:149, 179-80, 254, 282
Small Organon (Brecht)
See *Kleines Organon für das Theatre*
The Small Room (Sarton) **120**:197-99, 206, 208, 210, 219-21, 247, 278-79, 315
Small Souls (Couperus)
See *De kleine zielen*
The Small Town (Mann)
See *Die kleine Stadt*
A Small Town Man (Austin)
See *The Man Jesus*
Small Town Tyrant (Mann)
See *Professor Unrat*
"Small Viennese Waltz" (García Lorca) **197**:189
The Smaller Rose Garden (Nezval)
See *Menší růžová zahrada*
"Smart-Aleck Kill" (Chandler) **7**:176, 182; **179**:121, 124, 201
"The Smell of Homes" (Shepherd) **177**:316
"Smelling the Wind" (Lorde) **173**:140
"Smert'" (Gumilev) **60**:279
"Smert Dolgushova" (Babel)
See "The Death of Dolgushov"
"Smert' Dolgusova" (Babel) **171**:9-10, 21, 23, 25, 37, 45, 72-73, 81, 85
Smert Ivana Ilyicha (Tolstoy) **4**:450-51, 458, 463, 468, 472, 476, 479-80, 483; **11**:463, 469, 471, 476-78; **44**:325-64; **79**:326, 334, 374-5, 434, 437-9, 460-2
Smert' Zanda (Olesha) **136**:111
"Smertel'noe manit" (Pilnyak) **23**:211, 213
"Smerti" (Pilnyak) **23**:210
"The Smile" (Merrill) **183**:257-58
"Smile" (Yokomitsu)
See "Bishō"
"A Smile of Fortune" (Conrad) **57**:84, 100
"The Smile of Winter" (Carter) **139**:188
"Smile, Smile, Smile" (Owen) **5**:366; **27**:203, 206, 212, 215, 221-22, 224, 229-30
"Smiles" (Davies) **5**:203
Smiling Charlie (Faust) **49**:39
"The Smiling Wimpy Doll" (Shepherd) **177**:310
Smire (Cabell) **6**:76-7
Smirt (Cabell) **6**:76-7
Smith (Cabell) **6**:76-7
Smith (Davidson) **24**:171, 180, 184
Smith Is Dead (Dent) **72**:35
"Smithy" (Verhaeren) **12**:468
"Smog" (Calvino) **183**:92, 94, 161, 229
Smog (Calvino)
See *La nuvola di smog*
"Smoke" (Reese) **181**:340
Smoke and Ashes (Sologub) **9**:436-37
"Smoke and Earth" (Aleixandre) **113**:23, 25
The Smoking Car (Howells) **7**:387-88
Smoky Day's Wigwam Evenings (Eastman)
See *Wigwam Evenings: Sioux Folktales Retold*
"Smolensk Marketplace" (Khodasevich) **15**:208
"La Smorfia" (di Donato) **159**:188
"Smrt barona Gandary" (Čapek) **37**:49; **192**:224
"Smrt in pogreb Jakoba Nesreče" (Cankar) **105**:157
"Smrt suncevog oca" (Popa) **167**:157
"Smrt u sinanovoj tekiji" (Andrić) **135**:12, 86, 91, 93
Smug Citizens (Gorky) **8**:92
Smugglers of Lost Soul's Rock (Gardner) **195**:150
"Smyook i struny" (Annensky) **14**:27
"Snaekoll's Saga" (Graham) **19**:109
"The Snake" (Andrić)
See "Zmija"
"The Snake" (Crane) **11**:157
"The Snake" (Himes) **139**:246-47, 325
"Snake" (Lawrence) **9**:223, 230; **93**:55, 61, 81-84, 86, 87, 102, 128
"Snake-Charming" (Rilke)
See "Schlangen-Beschwörung"
"Snake Doctor" (Cobb) **77**:136, 140
"The Snake Kite" (Remizov)
See "Zmei"
Snake Train (Khlebnikov) **20**:142
"Snakebite" (Dickey) **151**:103
"The Snake-Charmer" (Naidu) **80**:291
The Snake's Pass (Stoker) **8**:384
"Snakeskin and Stone" (Douglas) **40**:76, 89
"Snap" (Seton) **31**:280
"Snap-Dragon" (Lawrence) **93**:8, 65; **93**:8, 65
"The Snare" (Stephens) **4**:412
Sne (Kielland) **5**:279
"Sne talmide hakamim sehayu be'irenu" (Agnon) **151**:21, 23
The Sneer (Nagai)
See *Reishō*
"Sneezles" (Milne) **6**:314
"Sneg" (Annensky) **14**:32
"Snega" (Pilnyak) **23**:203, 211
Snezhimochka (Khlebnikov) **20**:136
"Snezhinka" (Balmont) **11**:36
Snezhnye maski (Blok) **5**:84-5, 93
"Sngeovye runy" (Balmont) **11**:40
"SNO" (Cummings) **137**:43, 61-63
The Snob (Sternheim)
See *Der Snob*
Der Snob (Sternheim) **8**:368, 371-72, 375-76
Snooty Baronet (Lewis) **2**:386, 389, 392; **9**:245; **104**:181, 214, 293
"Snopići" (Andrić) **135**:85
"Snow" (Annensky)
See "Sneg"
"Snow" (Artaud) **3**:52
"Snow" (Davidson) **24**:189
"Snow" (Higginson) **36**:175-76, 186
"Snow" (Thomas) **10**:452, 457, 467
Snow (Kielland)
See *Sne*
"The Snow Child" (Carter) **139**:116, 139
"The Snow Fairy" (McKay) **41**:344
"Snow in the Suburbs" (Hardy) **53**:81, 117
"The Snow Leopard" (Jarrell) **177**:127
Snow Maiden (Khlebnikov)
See *Snezhimochka*
"The Snow Man" (Stevens) **12**:377, 385; **45**:287, 293, 297, 299, 304, 306-07, 310, 340
The Snow Mask (Blok)
See *Snezhnye maski*
"Snow on a Southern State" (Dickey) **151**:170
"Snow on Kurakake" (Miyazawa) **76**:288
"Snow Runes" (Balmont)
See "Sngeovye runy"
"The Snow Storm" (Tolstoy) **173**:269
The Snow Storm (Tolstoy)
See "Metel"
"Snow Thickets" (Dickey) **151**:176
"Snow Wind" (Pilnyak) **23**:220
"Snowdrifts" (Tsvetaeva)
See "Sugroby"
"Snowfall" (Carducci)
See "Nevicata"
"Snowflake" (Balmont)
See "Snezhinka"
"Snowflakes" (Nemerov) **124**:256
"The Snows" (Pilnyak)
See "Snega"
"The Snows of Kilimanjaro" (Hemingway) **115**:143
"The Snowstorm" (Pilnyak)
See "Metel"
The Snowstorm (Tolstoy)
See "Metel"
"A Snowstorm in the Alps" (March) **96**:265
"Snowthlehem" (Arp) **115**:21
"Snowy Mountains and Riviera" (Ady) **11**:20
"A Snowy Night on West Forty-Ninth Street" (Brennan) **124**:3, 7
"Snoya more" (Gumilev) **60**:282
"Snt. George" (Beerbohm) **24**:105
"So It Is" (Hippius)
See "Tak est"
"So lange ist es her" (Lasker-Schueler) **57**:307
"So Long, Big Bill Broonzy" (Wright) **136**:259, 264
"So Long, Mary" (Cohan) **60**:163, 168, 170, 172
"So Much the Worse for Boston" (Lindsay) **17**:230
"So Pack Your Ermines" (Burroughs) **121**:131
"So Softly Smiling" (Himes) **139**:244, 323
So the Wind Won't Blow It All Away (Brautigan) **133**:33
"So Various" (Hardy) **143**:191-92
"So We Grew Together" (Masters) **25**:288
So Well Remembered (Hilton) **21**:98
"So-and-So Reclining on Her Couch" (Stevens) **45**:347
"Soap" (Lu Hsun)
See "Feizao"
Sobach'e serdtse (Bulgakov) **2**:65; **16**:84-5, 91-2, 100-03, 109, 111; **159**:166
"Sobach'ia dolia" (Remizov) **27**:353
"Sobo no tame ni" (Shiga) **172**:202-3
Sobranie sochenenii (Sologub) **9**:443-44, 447
Sobranie stikhov (Khodasevich) **15**:205, 208-09, 212-13
Sobranie stikhov (Kuzmin) **40**:216
Sobranie stikhov. Kniga III (Sologub) **9**:443
Sobranie stikhov. Kniga IV (Sologub) **9**:443
Sobranie stikhov: Kniga vtoraya (Hippius) **9**:161
"Sobre el ajedrez" (Unamuno) **148**:308
"Sobre el fulanismo" (Unamuno) **148**:240
"Sobre el marasmo actual de España" (Unamuno) **148**:245
"Sobre Oscar Wilde" (Borges) **109**:84
"Sobre tu pecho unas letras" (Aleixandre) **113**:5
Sobytie (Nabokov) **108**:54
Sochineniia (Remizov) **27**:350-52, 354-56
The Social Bond (Nisbet) **117**:302, 315 334
Social Change and History (Nisbet) **117**:294, 296, 290 302, 312
"Social Consciousness and the Consciousness of Meaning" (Mead) **89**:170
Social Credit and the Labour Party: An Appeal (Muir) **87**:163
Social Decay and Regeneration (Freeman) **21**:45-6, 57
A Social Departure: How Orthodocia and I Went Round the World by Ourselves (Duncan) **60**:178, 184, 206-7, 212-3, 245, 249
Social Differentiation (Simmel) **64**:338
Social Ethics (Hostos)
See *Moral Social*
"Social Evolution" (Roosevelt) **69**:255
Social Foundations of Contemporary Economics (Sorel)
See *Insegnamenti sociali della economia contemporanea*

Social Interest: A Challenge to Mankind (Adler)
See *Der Sinn des Lebens*
Social Judgment (Wallas) **91**:357-9, 363, 372, 375, 381
"Social Justice" (Leacock) **2**:377-78
Social Justice, Socialism and Democracy (Hayek) **109**:275
"The Social Life of the Newt" (Benchley) **55**:7, 16
The Social Philosophers: Conflict and Crisis in Western Thought (Nisbet) **117**:302, 313, 315, 386
"Social Planning and Human Nature" (Park) **73**:198
"The Social Problem" (Kazantzakis) **181**:224
"Social Psychology as Conterpart of Physiological Psychology" (Mead) **89**:169
"The Social Psychology of the World Religions" (Weber) **69**:331
"Social Purity" (Anthony) **84**:11-2, 23
"Social Realities versus Police Court Fictions" (Dewey) **95**:71
Social Reform or Revolution? (Luxemburg) **63**:186, 187
"Social Science and Social Responsibility" (Reyes) **33**:318
"Social Science Techniques and the Study of Concentration Camps" (Arendt) **193**:78-9
The Social Secretary (Phillips) **44**:253-54, 262, 274, 277, 284
"The Social Self" (Mead) **89**:171
The Social Significance of the Modern Drama (Goldman) **13**:221
"Socialism" (Weber) **69**:383
Socialism and Saint-Simon (Durkheim)
See *Le socialisme*
"Socialism for Millionaires" (Shaw) **3**:388
Socialism in England (Webb and Webb) **22**:412
Le socialisme (Durkheim) **55**:145
"The Socialist Calculation: Competitive 'Solution'" (Hayek) **109**:202
"The Socialist Calculation: Nature and History of the Problem" (Hayek) **109**:202
"The Socialist Calculation: State of the Debate" (Hayek) **109**:202
"Socialist Psychology" (Gilman) **117**:134, 139
"Socialists" (Jozsef) **22**:160
Society Butterfly (Buchanan) **107**:34
The Society for the Redemption of the Abandoned Women in St. Peter's Parish's (Kielland) **5**:277
The Society of Honorary Bell Ringers (Zamyatin)
See *Obshchestvo pochetnykh zvonarey*
"Sociological Aesthetics" (Simmel) **64**:338-39, 341, 359
"Sociological Applications of the Psychology of the Herd Instinct" (Trotter) **97**:183
"The Sociological Methods of William Graham Sumner, and of William I. Thomas and Florian Znaniecki" (Park) **73**:184
The Sociological Tradition (Nisbet) **117**:296, 302, 310, 342
Sociology As an Art Form (Nisbet) **117**:329
Sociology: Investigation into the Forms of Association (Simmel) **64**:308-9, 317, 338, 352, 354, 356
"The Sociology of Social Entertainment" (Simmel) **64**:326
"Sociology of Socialibility" (Simmel) **64**:336
Socrates and Aristophanes (Strauss) **141**:228, 230, 233
Socrates; or, Hellas (Strindberg) **8**:418
Sodom and Gomorrah (Giraudoux)
See *Sodome et Gomorrhe*
Sodom and Gomorrah (Kazantzakis) **181**:207
Sodom and Gomorrah (Proust)
See *Sodome et Gomorrhe*
Sodome et Gomorrhe (Giraudoux) **2**:159, 165, 167, 172-73
Sodome et Gomorrhe (Proust) **7**:527, 540, 546-47, 549; **33**:254, 271; **161**:134, 143, 162
Sodoms Ende (Sudermann) **15**:417, 419, 423-24, 427, 433
Soedinenie I perevod chetyrex evangelij (Tolstoy) **79**:335, 431, 460
Soeur Béatrice (Maeterlinck) **3**:323, 332
La soeur de la reine (Swinburne) **8**:438, 440, 443, 445
Les soeurs vatard (Huysmans) **7**:403, 405, 407, 410; **69**:23-4
The Soft Machine (Burroughs) **121**:120-23, 125-28, 130, 136-37, 140, 175
"The Soft Moon" (Calvino)
See "La molle luna"
The Soft Side (James) **2**:272
"A Soft Summer Night" (Jozsef) **22**:160, 162
"The Soft Touch of Grass" (Pirandello) **4**:342
Sogliadatai (Nabokov) **108**:52, 60, 134, 142, 216, 218-19, 222-24; **189**:78-9, 96
"Sogni di Natale" (Svevo) **35**:362
"Sogni d'oro di Michele" (Jovine) **79**:44
Sogno d'un mattino di primavera (D'Annunzio) **40**:8
"La soguilla de Caronte" (Valle-Inclán) **5**:478
"Der Sohn" (Schnitzler) **4**:403
Söhne (Benn) **3**:104, 106
Die Söhne (Feuchtwanger) **3**:181
"Un soir" (Apollinaire) **51**:59
"Le soir" (Sully Prudhomme) **31**:306
"Un soir" (Verhaeren) **12**:461
"Soir d'hiver" (Nelligan) **14**:398-401
"La soirée avec M. Teste" (Valéry) **15**:463
"Soirées de Paris" (Barthes) **135**:162, 174-83, 187-88
Les soirs (Verhaeren) **12**:460, 463, 465
"Soirs d'automne" (Nelligan) **14**:392
"Soirs hypochondriaques" (Nelligan) **14**:398
"Soissons" (Douglas) **40**:81
"Soissons 1940" (Douglas) **40**:81, 88
"Sojourn in the Desert" (Bishop) **103**:21
The Sojourner (Rawlings) **4**:364-65, 367
"Sokolinets" (Korolenko) **22**:178-79, 181-82
Sokrovennyi chelovek (Platonov) **14**:427
"Sol" (Babel) **2**:27; **13**:14; **171**:17, 19, 21-22, 25, 40, 72-73, 75, 85-86
Sol de la tarde (Martinez Sierra and Martinez Sierra) **6**:274, 279
"Sol e amore" (Carducci) **32**:87, 108
Un sol que nace y un sol que muere (Echegaray) **4**:101
"El sol victorioso" (Aleixandre) **113**:15, 25
Sola Fide: Tolko veroyu (Shestov) **56**:264
"Solace of Men" (Gurney) **33**:81
The Solar Airplane (Artaud) **36**:37
"Sold Down the River" (Bosman) **49**:3
Soldage (Nexø) **43**:329
Der Soldat Tanaka (Kaiser) **9**:176, 181
"The Soldier" (Brooke) **2**:61; **7**:125, 127-30
"The Soldier" (Dahl) **173**:10
"The Soldier and the Girl" (Hansen) **32**:249
"Soldier, Soldier" (Kipling) **8**:178
"Soldier: Twentieth Century" (Rosenberg) **12**:288, 293, 306, 312
"Soldier Vote of '64" (Aldrich) **125**:21
"The Soldier Walks under the Trees of the University" (Jarrell) **177**:221
"Soldier-Folk" (Bierce) **44**:45
"Soldiers" (Bierce) **7**:89
"Soldiers" (Jarrell) **177**:195
"A Soldier's Burial" (Patton) **79**:301, 308, 312
"Soldier's Dream" (Owen) **27**:206, 211-12, 214
The Soldier's Faith (Holmes) **77**:259-60, 314
"Soldier's Home" (Hemingway) **115**:189
Soldiers of Fortune (Davis) **24**:203, 207
"Soldiers of the Republic" (Parker) **143**:331-32, 343
Soldiers' Pay (Faulkner) **141**:30, 39, 41-44, 61; **170**:115, 128, 131, 226, 233
"Soldier's Religion" (Patton) **79**:299
Soldiers Three (Kipling) **8**:175-76, 184, 208; **17**:204, 209-10
"La soléa" (García Lorca)
See "Poema de la soléa"
"Soledad" (Gonzalez Martinez) **72**:149
"Soledad" (Unamuno) **148**:307-8, 310-11
"Soledad" (Villaurrutia) **80**:467
Soledad (Unamuno) **148**:254
La soledad sonora (Jiménez) **4**:213, 224
Soledades, galerías, y otros poemas (Machado) **3**:306-09
Soledades: Poesías (Machado) **3**:306-09, 311-13
"Soleil couchant" (Manning) **25**:278
"Soleil route usée" (Péret) **20**:196-97
Le soleil se couche (Ghelderode) **187**:5, 40
A Solid Home (Garro)
See *Un hogar sólido*
The Solid Mandala (White) **176**:126-27, 130, 132-39, 143, 145, 148, 182, 186-88, 190, 192-93, 195, 199-202, 208, 214, 219, 247-48, 301, 306-7, 309, 314, 323
"Ein solider Artikel" (Schwitters) **95**:322
"Soliloque au fond de la salle obscure" (Anouilh) **195**:53
Soliloquies in England (Santayana) **40**:344-46, 355-56, 376
"Soliloquies of a Hermit" (Powys)
See "The Soliloquy of a Hermit"
Soliloquios y conversaciones (Unamuno) **9**:514
"Soliloquy" (Ledwidge) **23**:112
"The Soliloquy of a Hermit" (Powys) **9**:359-61, 367-68, 376
"Solipsism & Solecism" (Nemerov) **124**:189, 257
"Le solitair" (Valéry) **15**:450
"Solitaire" (Aleixandre)
See "El solitario"
"Solitaire" (Lowell) **8**:230, 234
Solitaña (Unamuno) **148**:291
Solitaria (Rozanov)
See *Uedinennoe*
"El solitario" (Aleixandre) **113**:5
"The Solitary" (Lu Hsun) **3**:297
Solitary Hours (Baroja)
See *Las horas solitarias*
Solitary Jottings (Rozanov) **104**:380, 384-85
The Solitary Summer (Elizabeth) **41**:117-18, 122, 128, 130
"The Solitary Woodsmen" (Roberts) **8**:317, 321
"Solitude" (Gonzalez Martinez)
See "Soledad"
"Solitude" (Kuprin) **5**:298
"Solitude" (Milne) **6**:314
"Solitude" (Naidu) **80**:294
"A Solitude" (Swinburne) **36**:346
"Solitude" (Villaurrutia) **80**:477
Solitude and Society (Berdyaev) **67**:23, 30, 78
"Solitude de la Pitié" (Giono) **124**:126-27
Solitude de la pitié (Giono) **124**:42, 74-75, 93, 100-101, 112, 124
"Solitude in the City (Symphony in Black and Gold)" (Fletcher) **35**:94
"The Solitude of Self" (Stanton) **73**:245-46, 249, 256
Les solitudes (Garneau) **13**:200-01, 204
Solitudes (Machado)
See *Soledades: Poesías*
Les solitudes (Sully Prudhomme) **31**:304, 307
Solitudes, Galleries, and Other Poems (Machado)
See *Soledades, galerías, y otros poemas*
"Solitudine" (Deledda) **23**:35
"Solleone" (D'Annunzio) **40**:37
Sollers, écrivain (Barthes) **135**:139, 156
"Solnce duxa" (Gumilev) **60**:279, 282-3
"Solntse Italii" (Babel) **2**:32; **171**:8-9, 21-23, 33, 40, 46, 61, 73, 78, 85, 87
"Solo" (Saba) **33**:374
Solo: An American Dreamer in Europe, 1933-34 (Morris) **107**:186-87, 208
"Sólo morir de día" (Aleixandre) **113**:14, 49
"Solo on the Drums" (Petry) **112**:300-01

"Solomon and the Witch" (Yeats) **31**:406; **93**:390
"Solomon's Parents" (Bottomley) **107**:5
"Solon" (Pascoli) **45**:148
"Solon in Lydia" (Herzl) **36**:140-41
Solos de Clarín (Alas) **29**:7
"La soltera en misa" (García Lorca) **181**:185-86
"El solterón" (Lugones) **15**:285, 289
El Solterón (Villaurrutia) **80**:471
"Solus Rex" (Nabokov) **108**:144
"Solution" (Dreiser) **35**:72, 75
Somber Lives (Baroja)
See *Vidas sombrías*
"La sombra" (Aleixandre) **113**:51
"La sombra de mi alma" (García Lorca) **181**:121
La sombra del padre (Martinez Sierra and Martinez Sierra) **6**:281
Sombra del paraíso (Aleixandre) **113**:2, 15-16, 20, 23, 27-29, 33, 42, 48-49, 56, 58, 67-68, 70, 72-77
"Sombra final" (Aleixandre) **113**:50
Sombras de sueño (Unamuno) **148**:254
"Sombre Figuration" (Stevens) **12**:360, 362
"Sombrero, abrigo, guantes" (Vallejo) **56**:311
"El sombrero del señor cura" (Alas) **29**:17
Sombrero Fallout: A Japanese Novel (Brautigan) **133**:31-32
"El sombrerón" (Asturias) **184**:14
Some American People (Caldwell) **117**:24
"Some Applications of the Mimete" (Levi)
See "Alcune applicazioni del Mimete"
Some Aspects of Modern Poetry (Noyes) **7**:505
"Some Aspects of Our National Character" (Dreiser) **10**:194
"Some Aspects of the Influence of Social Problems and Ideas upon the Study and Writing of History" (Becker) **63**:67, 99
Some Cambridge Poets (Noyes) **7**:505
Some Champions (Lardner) **14**:303
Some Chinese Ghosts (Hearn) **9**:118, 122, 131, 135
"Some Comments on Privacy" (Bettelheim) **143**:54
"Some Consequences of Four Incapacities" (Peirce) **81**:176,194,286
"Some Day" (Fuller) **103**:116
"Some Day" (Lawson) **27**:148, 150, 152
"Some Disadvantages of Genius" (Bierce) **44**:16
Some Do Not (Ford) **1**:281, 284, 288; **15**:73-4, 78, 80-2; **57**:204-90; **172**:33-34, 36-37, 70-83, 122
Some Dogmas of Religion (McTaggart) **105**:173-74
Some Early Impressions (Stephen) **23**:316
Some Everyday Folk and Dawn (Franklin) **7**:267-68, 270, 273
Some Experiences of an Irish R.M. (Somerville & Ross) **51**:327-31, 340, 342, 345, 354-55, 361-62, 380
"Some Experiments on Animal Intelligence" (Thorndike) **107**:398
"Some Explanations" (Alexander) **77**:49
"Some Features of the Law" (Bierce) **44**:14
"Some Foreign Forms of Verse" (Dobson) **79**:36
"Some Friends from Pascagoula" (Stevens) **45**:281-82
Some Friends of Walt Whitman: A Study of Sex in Psychology (Carpenter) **88**:72
"Some Generalities That Still Glitter" (Becker) **63**:72
"Some Haunted Houses" (Bierce) **44**:14, 45
Some Irish Yesterdays (Somerville & Ross) **51**:331, 333-4
"Some Jewish Types of Personality" (Wirth) **92**:372
"Some Ladies and Jurgen" (Cabell) **6**:61
Some Ladies in Haste (Chambers) **41**:90, 95
Some Letters of William Vaughn Moody (Moody) **105**:247, 263-64
"Some Like Them Cold" (Lardner) **2**:335, 339; **14**:291, 293-94, 296, 299, 306-07, 312-13
Some Like Them Short (March) **96**:235, 250, 254, 257
Some Limericks (Douglas) **68**:40
"Some Lines from Whitman" (Jarrell) **177**:139
"Some Love" (Ginsberg) **120**:56
Some Main Problems in Philosophy (Moore) **89**:245
Some Merry Adventures of Robin Hood of Great Renown in Nottinghamshire (Pyle)
See *The Merry Adventures of Robin Hood of Great Renown in Nottinghamshire*
"Some Musings on the Nature of History" (Arnow) **196**:95
Some Newspapers and Newspapermen (Sinclair) **160**:304-5, 313-14
"Some Niggers" (Brooke) **2**:60
"Some Notes on Miss L." (West) **44**:371, 380-82, 385, 409
"Some Notes on Salvdor Deli" (Orwell)
See "Benefit of Clergy: Some Notes on Salvador Dali"
"Some Notes on Violence" (West) **44**:386
Some Old Portraits (Tarkington) **9**:469
Some Personalities (Upward) **85**:380, 386
"Some Platitudes Concerning the Drama" (Galsworthy) **45**:33-4, 36, 51, 54
Some Poetry (Drummond de Andrade)
See *Alguma poesia*
"Some Psychical Consequences of the Anatomical Distinction between the Sexes" (Freud)
See "Einige Psychische Folgen des Anatomischen Geschlechtsunterschieds"
"Some Questions of Moral Philosophy" (Arendt) **193**:100
"Some Rabbits and a Cat" (Lu Hsun) **3**:303
"Some Rambling Notes of an Idle Excursion" (Twain) **48**:349
Some Religious Elements in English Literature (Macaulay) **44**:122, 126
"Some San Francisco Poems" (Oppen) **107**:265
"Some Scattering Remarks of Bub" (Riley) **51**:292
Some Sweet Day (Riggs) **56**:215, 219
"Some Thoughts about Ancestor-Worship" (Hearn) **9**:130
"Some Thoughts on the Common Toad" (Orwell) **51**:257; **128**:289
Some United States (Cobb) **77**:129
Some Winchester Letters of Lionel Johnson (Johnson) **19**:250-51
"Some Words about War and Peace" (Tolstoy)
See "A Few Words about War and Peace"
"Somebody Must Die" (McCoy) **28**:226-27
"Somehow I'd Like to Thank Them" (Childress) **116**:36
Someone Else's Faults (Deledda)
See *Le colpe altrui*
Someone Like You (Dahl) **173**:10-13, 15
"Someone Puts a Pineapple Together" (Stevens) **45**:287
Something about Eve (Cabell) **6**:61, 68, 72, 75-6
"Something Black" (Hammett) **187**:98
Something Childish, and Other Stories (Mansfield)
See *The Little Girl, and Other Stories*
"Something Childish but Very Natural" (Mansfield) **2**:458; **8**:282; **164**:247-48
Something Childish but Very Natural (Mansfield) **39**:318
"Something Defeasible" (Beerbohm) **24**:123
"Something Exquisite" (Wharton) **129**:352
Something Fishy (Wodehouse) **108**:372
Something Fresh (Wodehouse) **108**:341, 372, 383, 387
Something Happened (Heller) **131**:21; **151**:310, 319-21, 326, 339
"The Something in a Colored Man" (Himes) **139**:324
Something of Myself (Kipling) **8**:187, 202, 205
"Something Tapped" (Hardy) **53**:101
"Somewhere" (Nemerov) **124**:157, 177-8, 251
Somewhere in France (Zuckmayer) **191**:329
Sommario di pedagogia (Gentile) **96**:85, 122, 139
La somme athéologique (Bataille) **155**:13, 15-17, 67, 94, 104, 111, 119, 122, 124, 126-30, 135-37
Ein sommer (Morgenstern) **8**:309
"Ein Sommer in Österreich" (Zuckmayer) **191**:325
"Einen Sommer lang" (Liliencron) **18**:215
Eine Sommerschlacht (Liliencron) **18**:212
"Somnambulent Ballad" (García Lorca)
See "Romance sonámbulo"
"Somnambulist Ballad" (García Lorca)
See "Romance sonámbulo"
Sömngångarnätter på vakna dagar (Strindberg) **8**:418-19
Somokuto (Santoka) **72**:418
Somov, and Others (Gorky) **8**:89
"The Son" (Herzl) **36**:141
"The Son" (Quiroga)
See "El hijo"
"The Son" (Schnitzler)
See "Der Sohn"
"Son" (Service) **15**:399
"The Son" (Torrence) **97**:152-53, 155
"Son and Mother" (Blok) **5**:86
A Son at the Front (Wharton) **3**:559, 563, 567; **9**:548; **27**:384; **129**:363
The Son Avenger (Undset) **197**:321-22
"Son de negros en Cuba" (García Lorca) **7**:298; **197**:283
Son excellence Eugène Rougon (Zola) **6**:562, 565; **41**:411
"Son Makara" (Korolenko) **22**:169-71, 173, 175, 178, 180-81
The Son of a Servant (Strindberg)
See *Tränstekvinnans son*
"The Son of a Slave" (Leino)
See "Orjan poika"
"The Son of Allan" (Sharp) **39**:361, 372, 375, 379
The Son of Don Juan (Echegaray)
See *El hijo de Don Juan*
A Son of Hagar (Caine) **97**:13
A Son of His Father (Wright) **183**:349
"The Son of Lancelot" (Williams) **1**:514
"The Son of Man" (Ginzburg)
See "Il figlio dell'uomo"
The Son of Royal Langbrith (Howells) **17**:178
A Son of Satan (Micheaux) **76**:246, 265
The Son of Tarzan (Burroughs) **2**:82; **32**:79-80
"A Son of the Gods" (Bierce) **7**:89; **44**:12, 21, 44-5, 47
A Son of the Middle Border (Garland) **3**:191-93, 197-99
"The Son of the Spirit" (Gumilev)
See "Solnce duxa"
"The Son of the Wolf" (London) **9**:268, 273
The Son of Virgil Timár (Babits)
See *Timár Virgil fia*
Son of Woman: The Story of D. H. Lawrence (Murry) **16**:338, 356
"The Son, the Cave, and the Burning Bush" (Dickey) **151**:135
"Soñando" (Jiménez) **4**:226
"Sonar Kathi" (Tagore) **53**:337
"Sonar tari" (Tagore) **53**:340
Sonar tari (Tagore) **3**:490; **53**:340-1
Sonata de estío: Memorias del marqués de Bradomín (Valle-Inclán) **5**:472, 475-76, 482, 484-85
Sonata de invierno: Memorias del marqués de Bradomín (Valle-Inclán) **5**:472, 475-76, 482, 484-86
Sonata de otoño: Memorias del marqués de Bradomín (Valle-Inclán) **5**:472, 474-76, 482, 484-85
Sonata de primavera: Memorias del marqués de Bradomín (Valle-Inclán) **5**:472, 474-76, 482, 484-85
"The Sonata of Errors" (Söderberg) **39**:438

Sonatas: Memoirs of the Marquis de Bradomin (Valle-Inclán) **5**:472, 485, 489
"Sonate mit Urlauten" (Schwitters)
See "Ursonate"
"Sonatina" (Darío) **4**:58
The Son-Daughter (Belasco) **3**:87
"Soneto a Carmela Condón, agradeciéndole unas muñecas" (García Lorca) **181**:67
"Soneto de la esperanza" (Villaurrutia) **80**:464, 487
"Soneto de la granada" (Villaurrutia) **80**:487
"Soneto de la guirnalda de rosas" (García Lorca) **181**:67
"Soneto del temor a Dios" (Villaurrutia) **80**:489, 510
Soñetos de la muerte (Mistral) **2**:476
Sonetos del Amor oscuro (García Lorca)
See *Sonnets of Love Forbidden*
Sonetos espirituales (Jiménez) **4**:216
Die Sonette an Orpheus (Rilke) **1**:414, 416-19, 422-24; **6**:365, 369; **195**:163-64, 195, 200-03, 205-12, 219, 245-46, 254, 269-81, 305-08, 310-13, 320, 323, 327-28, 330, 332
"Sonetto di primavera" (Saba) **33**:372
Sonety solntsa, mëda, i luny (Balmont) **11**:38, 40-2
"The Song" (Babel)
See "Pesnia"
"Song" (Baker) **10**:27
"A Song" (Borowski) **9**:23
"Song" (Douglas) **40**:75
"A Song" (Holley) **99**:335
"Song" (Lowell) **8**:235
"Song" (Muir) **87**:190
"A Song" (Riley) **51**:289
"A Song" (Scott) **6**:394
"Song about a Dog" (Esenin) **4**:113
The Song about the Great Campaign (Esenin) **4**:113
"The Song against Grocers" (Chesterton) **6**:109
"The Song against Songs" (Chesterton) **6**:98
The Song and Dance Man (Cohan) **60**:159, 166, 173
Song and Its Fountains (Baker) **10**:16-17, 19
Song and Prayer (Kahanovitsch)
See *Gezang un gebet*
"The Song before Sailing" (Carman) **7**:134
The Song Book of Quong Lee (Burke) **63**:127
The Song Celestial (Ramana Maharshi) **84**:262
Le song d'une femme (Gourmont) **17**:129
"Song for a Hypothetical Age" (Muir) **87**:304
"Song for a Viola d'Amore" (Lowell) **8**:234
"A Song for Harps" (March) **96**:234
"A Song for Rosemarie" (Villa) **176**:107
"Song for the First of August" (Bell) **43**:92
"A Song from Shiraz" (Naidu) **80**:341
"The Song from the Cloud" (Södergran)
See "Visan från molnet"
"Song in Chaos" (O'Neill) **6**:337
"Song in Spite of Myself" (Cullen) **37**:160, 170
"A Song in Spring" (Naidu) **80**:294
"Song in the Meadow" (Roberts) **68**:305
Song in the Meadow (Roberts) **68**:301, 303, 306, 326, 335-37
"Song in the Mouth" (Roberts) **68**:305
"A Song in Time of Order" (Swinburne) **8**:436-37
"Song in Time of Revolution" (Swinburne) **8**:437; **36**:295, 299
"Song is Existence" (Rilke)
See "Gesang ist Dasein"
"Song Made Flesh" (Markham) **47**:283
"A Song No Gentleman Would Sing to Any Lady" (Cullen) **37**:170
"Song: Not There" (Jarrell) **177**:127
Song of a Hometown (Mizoguchi)
See *Furusato*
"The Song of Justice" (Rilke)
See "Das Lied von der Gerechtigkeit"
"Song of a Man Who Has Come Through" (Lawrence) **9**:225; **61**:232; **93**:24, 112, 121, 125
"Song of a Night" (Fletcher) **35**:89
"Song of a Second April" (Millay) **4**:306
"Song of a Train" (Davidson) **24**:164
"The Song of Allan" (Sharp) **39**:354
"Song of April" (Pascoli) **45**:141
The Song of Bernadette (Werfel)
See *Das Leid von Bernadette*
"Song of Cedric the Silent" (Anderson) **10**:48
"Song of Comfort" (McCrae) **12**:210
"The Song of Death" (Sudermann) **15**:428
"A Song of Degrees" (Nemerov) **124**:144
"A Song of England" (Noyes) **7**:502
The Song of Fate (Blok)
See *Pesnya sudby*
"The Song of Fukagawa" (Nagai)
See "Fukagawa no uta"
"The Song of Goodness" (Babits)
See "A jóság dala"
"The Song of Growth" (Roberts) **8**:318
"A Song of Harvest" (Rhodes) **53**:316
"Song of Industrial America" (Anderson) **10**:48; **123**:8, 45, 113-14
"Song of Innocence" (Jozsef) **22**:160
The Song of Labor (Martinez Sierra and Martinez Sierra) **6**:273
Song of Lawino (p'Bitek)
See *Wer pa Lawino*
Song of Lawino: A Lament (p'Bitek)
See *Wer pa Lawino*
"Song of Legnano" (Carducci)
See "Canzone di Legnano"
"The Song of Love" (Carducci)
See "Il canto dell' amore"
Song of Malaya (p'Bitek) **149**:3, 22, 24, 31-32, 36, 38, 49, 52, 54, 57-59, 89, 91, 97, 112-13
"The Song of Mantsi" (Leino)
See "Mantsin laulu"
"Song of March" (Pascoli) **45**:140
Song of Modern Shepherds (Radnóti) **16**:418
"A Song of Morning" (Roberts) **8**:319
Song of Ocol (p'Bitek) **149**:3-4, 6-7, 9, 12-14, 16, 18-20, 22, 24, 27, 31, 35, 38, 41, 49, 54-55, 58, 60-61, 80-83, 87-89, 91, 96, 109, 112-13, 119-20, 122, 125, 128, 131-34
"Song of Pain and Beauty" (Gurney) **33**:81
"The Song of Pan" (Carman) **7**:149
"A Song of Peace" (Nezval)
See "Zpěv miru"
"Song of Praise" (Cullen) **4**:40, 50; **37**:144, 147, 167
"A Song of Praise (For One Who Praised His Lady's Being Fair)" (Cullen) **37**:141, 167
"The Song of Princess Zeb-un-nissa and Muslim Religion" (Naidu) **80**:292, 341
Song of Prisoner (p'Bitek) **149**:3, 16, 19-23, 27-28, 31, 36, 38, 41, 45-46, 48, 52, 54-56, 58-59, 61, 64-65, 94-97, 100, 110, 112
"The Song of Quoodle" (Chesterton) **6**:98
"The Song of Radha the Milkmaid" (Naidu) **80**:275
The Song of Roland (Sayers) **15**:377
"The Song of Shadows" (de la Mare) **4**:82
"A Song of Sherwood" (Noyes) **7**:55
"Song of Soldier" (p'Bitek) **149**:89, 94
"A Song of Sour Grapes" (Cullen) **37**:168
"A Song of Speed" (Henley) **8**:106, 109
"The Song of St. Anne" (Tynan) **3**:505
"Song of Stephen the Westerner" (Anderson) **10**:48-9; **123**:45, 112
"Song of Summer" (Dunbar) **12**:104, 110
"Song of Summons" (Tagore)
See "Ahabansangit"
"Song of Taurus" (Mistral)
See "Canción de taurus"
"Song of the Artesian Water" (Paterson) **32**:373
"Song of the Bacchanal" (Merezhkovsky) **29**:248
"The Song of the Bayonet" (Patton) **79**:308
"Song of the Black Man Who Went to Town" (Radnóti) **16**:419
"The Song of the Bodies" (Riggs) **56**:200
Song of the Camp (Mizoguchi) **72**:325
"The Song of the Caravan" (Leino) **24**:370
The Song of the Cardinal (Porter) **21**:262-64
"Song of the Columns" (Valéry)
See "Cantique des colonnes"
"The Song of the Darling River" (Lawson) **27**:134
"Song of the Departing Day" (García Lorca) **181**:82
"The Song of the Derelict" (McCrae) **12**:210
"The Song of the Deserted Shepherdess" (Pyle) **81**:391
"The Song of the Deserter" (Tzara)
See "Le Chant du déserteur"
"The Song of the Dove" (Roberts) **68**:337
"A Song of the English" (Kipling) **8**:178
The Song of the Fiery Furnace (Zuckmayer) **191**:327
"Song of the Flogged Gypsy" (García Lorca) **49**:72
"Song of the Forest" (Okigbo) **171**:338-39, 346
"A Song of the Four Seasons" (Dobson) **79**:5
"The Song of the Fur-Seal" (Buchanan) **107**:45, 70
"Song of the Guest" (D'Annunzio)
See "Canto dell'ospite"
"Song of the Hours" (Thompson) **4**:438
"The Song of the Ill-beloved" (Apollinaire)
See "La chanson du mal-aimé"
"A Song of the Khyber Pass" (Naidu) **80**:295
"The Song of the King's Minstrel" (Middleton) **56**:173
The Song of the Lark (Cather) **1**:153, 156-57, 161, 163-65; **11**:93-6, 111, 114; **31**:24-5, 27-30, 57, 59, 62; **99**:172, 175, 208, 268; **132**:121, 123, 125, 127, 129-30, 133, 136-41, 148-50; **152**:16, 20-21, 27, 53, 93, 97
Song of the Lark (Moricz)
See *Pacsirtaszó*
"Song of the Little Square" (García Lorca)
See "Ballada de la Placeta"
The Song of the Love and Death of Cornet Christopher Rilke (Rilke) **1**:418; **6**:364
Song of the Lusitanian Bogey (Weiss)
See *Gesang vom lusitanischen Popanz*
Song of the Lusitanian Bogeyman (Weiss)
See *Gesang vom lusitanischen Popanz*
"Song of the Mad Prince" (de la Mare) **4**:71, 74, 82
"Song of the Middle World" (Anderson) **10**:50; **123**:112
"The Song of the Militant Romance" (Lewis) **2**:397
"Song of the Moderns" (Fletcher) **35**:109
"Song of the Mother of the Bitter One" (García Lorca) **7**:300
"The Song of the Mouth-Organ" (Service) **15**:401
"Song of the Norwegion Legion" (Grieg) **10**:207
"The Song of the Old Robber" (Esenin)
See "Pesnia starika razboinika"
"A Song of the Peaceful One" (Khlebnikov)
See "Pesn miryazya"
"The Song of the Poorly Beloved" (Apollinaire)
See "La chanson du mal-aimé"
"The Song of the Poppies" (Symons) **11**:439
"Song of the Rejected Lover" (Cullen) **37**:168
"Song of the Seedlings" (Gray) **19**:145, 152
"Song of the Sirens" (Crawford) **10**:158
"Song of the Soldiers' Wives and Sweethearts" (Hardy) **143**:188
"Song of the Son" (Toomer) **172**:256, 274-75, 323-27, 330-31, 340
"Song of the Soul" (Manning) **25**:277
"The Song of the Street" (Ady) **11**:21
"Song of the Sun" (D'Annunzio)
See "Canto del sole"
"Song of the Sun" (Mistral)
See "Lou cant dou soulèu"
"The Song of the Sword" (Henley) **8**:97, 101, 109-10

"The Song of the Sword" (Sharp) **39**:376-77
The Song of the Sword, and Other Verses (Henley) **8**:97, 106, 110
"The Song of the Turds of Langres" (Patton) **79**:298, 304
"Song of the Unicorn" (Williams) **1**:512
The Song of the Valley (Asch)
See *Dos gezang fun tol*
The Song of the Whip (Faust) **49**:47
"The Song of the Whippoorwill" (Pyle) **81**:390
Song of the Whore (p'Bitek)
See *Song of Malaya*
"Song of the Woman" (p'Bitek) **149**:81
The Song of the World (Giono)
See *Le chant du monde*
"Song of Virgo" (Mistral)
See "Canción de virgo"
"The Song of Wandering Aengus" (Yeats) **11**:526, 529
"A Song of Winter Weather" (Service) **15**:401
"Song of Women" (Masters) **25**:298
Song Offerings (Tagore)
See *Gitanjali*
"The Song Sparrow's Nest" (Wetherald) **81**:410
Song to Spring (Villaurrutia) **80**:476
Song to Spring and Other Poems (Villaurrutia)
See *Canto a la primavera*
"Song to the Divine Mother" (Markham) **47**:278-79
"Song to the man of the people, Charlie Chaplin" (Drummond de Andrade) **139**:233
Song-Collection (Tagore)
See *Gitabitan*
"Un songe" (Sully Prudhomme) **31**:302
Songe d'Eleuthère (Benda) **60**:64
Les songes et les sorts (Yourcenar) **193**:262, 264-65, 337
"Song-Flower and Poppy" (Moody) **105**:237, 239-40, 242, 246, 255, 279
"Song—'Only the Wanderer'" (Gurney) **33**:94, 96, 101
Songs (García Lorca)
See *Canciones*
Songs (p'Bitek) **149**:22, 38, 49, 95, 105, 108-9, 134
Songs and Satires (Masters) **2**:461; **25**:288-89, 315
Songs and Sonnets (Masters) **25**:296
Songs and Sonnets, second series (Masters) **25**:283
Songs and Tales of the Quechua People (Arguedas)
See *Canciones y cuentos del pueblo quechua*
Songs at the Start (Guiney) **41**:203, 206, 210, 212, 216
Songs before Sunrise (Swinburne) **8**:426, 437-38; **36**:300, 308, 317-18, 324, 332
"Songs for a Colored Singer" (Bishop) **121**:89
Songs for a Little House (Morley) **87**:117
Songs for My Supper (Service) **15**:411, 413
"Songs for the People" (Harper) **14**:260-62
Songs from a Northern Garden (Carman) **7**:139, 137
"Songs from an Island" (Bachmann) **192**:66
"Songs from the Church-Tower" (Heidenstam) **5**:249
Songs from Vagabondia (Carman) **7**:133, 135, 137-38, 142, 145
"The Songs I Had" (Gurney) **33**:95, 103
"Songs in Flight" (Bachmann) **192**:68
Songs of a Sun-Lover (Service) **15**:411-13
Songs of Action (Doyle) **7**:227
Songs of Africa (Paton) **165**:316
Songs of Alexandria (Kuzmin)
See *Alexandryskie pesni*
Songs of an Avenger (Balmont)
See *Pesni mstitelia*
Songs of Bhanusingh Thakur (Tagore)
See *Bhanusinga Thakurer Padavali*
Songs of Castelvecchio (Pascoli)
See *Canti di Castelvecchio*
Songs of Childhood (de la Mare) **4**:74, 78
"Songs of Corruption" (Buchanan) **107**:19
Songs of Duke John and Catharina Jagellonica (Leino)
See *Juhana herttuan ja Catharina Jagellonican lauluja*
"Songs of Education" (Chesterton) **6**:98, 109
"The Songs of Heaven" (Buchanan) **107**:17
Songs of Jamaica (McKay) **7**:456, 459-60, 463-64; **41**:319, 328, 335, 343
Songs of Joy (Davies) **5**:199-200
Songs of Joy and Lullabies (Mqhayi)
See *Imihobe nemibongo yokufundwa ezikolweni*
Songs of Khayyam (Hedāyat) **21**:82-3
Songs of Life and Hope (Darío)
See *Cantos de vida y esperanza*
"Songs of Lucifer" (Talvik)
See "Lutsiferi laulud"
Songs of March (Leino)
See *Maaliskuun lauluja*
Songs of My Country (Palamas) **5**:379-80, 382, 386-88
Songs of Myrtilla (Aurobindo) **63**:36
Songs of Overseas (D'Annunzio)
See *Le canzoni d'oltremare*
"Songs of Pampas" (Obstfelder)
See "Pampassange"
Songs of Peace (Ledwidge) **23**:109-13, 120, 122
"Songs of Poverty and Death" (Rilke) **195**:339
"Songs of Radha" (Naidu) **80**:315
Songs of the Bat (Lucas) **73**:157, 172
"Songs of the City" (Guro)
See "Pesni goroda"
"The Songs of the Civil War" (Matthews) **95**:227
Songs of the Common Day, and Ave: An Ode for the Shelley Centenary (Roberts) **8**:314, 317, 319-21, 327
Songs of the Fields (Ledwidge) **23**:108, 110-11, 113-14, 120-23
Songs of the Heart (Lagerkvist)
See *Hjärtats sånger*
"Songs of the Lake" (Palamas) **5**:386
"Songs of the Prague People" (Čapek) **37**:47
Songs of the Road (Doyle) **7**:227
Songs of the Sea (Aurobindo) **63**:8
Songs of the Sea Children (Carman) **7**:138-39, 144, 147
Songs of the Silent World (Phelps) **113**:336
Songs of the Spirit (Crowley) **7**:208
Songs of Three Counties, and Other Poems (Hall) **12**:195
Songs of Two Nations (Swinburne) **36**:318, 324
Songs of Victory I (Sikelianos) **39**:418-19
Songs of Victory II (Sikelianos) **39**:419
"Songs of war" (Tzara)
See "Cântec de razboi"
Songs of Youth (Van Dine) **23**:357
Songs of Ziklag (Upward) **85**:380
"Songs out of Sorrow" (Teasdale) **4**:430
Songspiel Mahagonny (Brecht) **169**:52, 54-56
"Sonia" (Harris) **24**:268, 274
"Sonido de la guerra" (Aleixandre) **113**:51
"Sonidos" (García Lorca) **181**:172
"Sonnenschein" (Raabe) **45**:189
"Sonnenunterrgang" (Ball) **104**:74
"Sonnet V" (Santayana) **40**:341
"Sonnet VI" (Wylie) **8**:534
"Sonnet VII" (Santayana) **40**:395
"Sonnet XIV" (Wylie) **8**:534
"Sonnet XVIII" (Wylie) **8**:534
"Sonnet XIX" (Santayana) **40**:398
"Sonnet XXIII" (Santayana) **40**:400
"Sonnet XXX" (Santayana) **40**:400
"Sonnet Dialogue" (Cullen) **37**:166
"Sonnet I" (Millay) **169**:259-60
"Sonnet: I Know Now How a Man Whose Blood Is Hot" (Cullen) **37**:169-70
"Sonnet II" (Agee) **180**:64
"Sonnet II" (Millay) **169**:258-59
"Sonnet III" (Millay) **169**:258-59
"Sonnet in Polka Dots" (Villa) **176**:103
"Sonnet IV" (Agee) **180**:64, 69
"Sonnet IV" (Millay) **169**:256, 259
"Sonnet IX" (Agee) **180**:64
"Sonnet IX" (Millay) **169**:242, 256-58, 261
"Sonnet L" (Millay) **169**:242
"Sonnet of Jack" (Roberts) **68**:304
"Sonnet of the Garland of Roses" (García Lorca)
See "Soneto de la guirnalda de rosas"
"Sonnet on an Alpine Night" (Parker) **143**:325
"Sonnet—September 1922" (Gurney) **33**:97-8, 104
"Sonnet: Some for a Little While Do Love, And Some for Long" (Cullen) **37**:158
"Sonnet: These Are No Wind-Blown Rumours, Soft Say-Sos" (Cullen) **37**:166
"Sonnet To a Child" (Owen) **5**:374
"Sonnet to an Ox" (Carducci)
See "Il bove"
"Sonnet to Carmela Condón, Thanking Her for Some Dolls" (García Lorca)
See "Soneto a Carmela Condón, agradeciéndole unas muñecas"
"Sonnet to Elinor Wylie" (Bodenheim) **44**:71
"Sonnet to J. S. Bach's Memory" (Gurney) **33**:97
"Sonnet to Virgil" (Carducci) **32**:86, 91
"Sonnet V" (Millay) **169**:258-59
"Sonnet VI" (Millay) **169**:259
"Sonnet VII" (Millay) **169**:258-60
"Sonnet VIII" (Millay) **169**:255-56, 261
"Sonnet X" (Millay) **169**:242, 256-57, 261
"Sonnet XI" (Millay) **169**:258, 260-62
"Sonnet XII" (Millay) **169**:256-57, 261
"Sonnet XIII" (Millay) **169**:256, 258, 260-62
"Sonnet XIV" (Agee) **180**:64-65
"Sonnet XIV" (Millay) **169**:256, 258, 262
"Sonnet XL" (Millay) **169**:242
"Sonnet XV" (Millay) **169**:257
"Sonnet XVI" (Millay) **169**:257-58, 262
"Sonnet XVII" (Agee) **180**:65
"Sonnet XVII" (Millay) **169**:257-58, 262
"Sonnet XVII" (Woodberry) **73**:365
"Sonnet XXII" (Agee) **180**:65
"Sonnet XXIII" (Agee) **180**:65
"Sonnet XXIV" (Agee) **180**:65
"Sonnet XXV" (Agee) **180**:65
"Sonnet XXX" (Millay) **169**:242
"Sonnet XXXIV" (Millay) **169**:242
"Sonnets" (Agee) **180**:64-65
Sonnets (Santayana) **40**:352
Sonnets: 1889-1927 (Robinson) **101**:146
Sonnets and Verse (Belloc) **18**:28, 41-2
"Sonnets by the Night Sea" (Sterling) **20**:386
Sonnets cisalpins (D'Annunzio) **6**:136, 142
"Sonnets from an Ungrafted Tree" (Millay) **4**:310; **49**:213-14, 218-21, 224, 228-29; **169**:242, 249-53, 257-58, 295, 301
"Sonnets IV-VI" (Millay) **169**:259
"Sonnets I-XI" (Millay) **169**:242
"Sonnets IX-X" (Millay) **169**:243
Sonnets of Death (Mistral)
See *Soñetos de la muerte*
"Sonnets of Life and Fate" (Lee-Hamilton) **22**:191
Sonnets of Love Forbidden (García Lorca) **181**:63
Sonnets of the Sun, Honey, and the Moon: A Songof Worlds (Balmont)
See *Sonety solntsa, mëda, i luny*
"Sonnets of the Twelve Months" (Belloc) **18**:40
Sonnets of the Wingless Hours (Lee-Hamilton) **22**:190-94
"Sonnets on the Sea's Voice" (Sterling) **20**:386
Sonnets to a Red-Haired Lady (By a Gentleman with a Blue Beard), and Famous Love Affairs (Marquis) **7**:437, 439-40, 446, 448

Sonnets to an Imaginary Madonna (Fisher) **140**:165, 180
Sonnets to Craig (Sterling) **20**:379
Sonnets to Duse, and Other Poems (Teasdale) **4**:423, 428-29, 431
"Sonnets to My Wife" (Bodenheim) **44**:60
Sonnets to Orpheus (Rilke)
See *Die Sonette an Orpheus*
"Sonnets VIII-X" (Millay) **169**:260
"Sonnets XIV-XVII" (Millay) **169**:262
"Sonnets XI-XIII" (Millay) **169**:243
"Sonnets XXXIV-LII" (Millay) **169**:242
Sono omokage (Futabatei) **44**:90, 100
Sons (Kafka) **112**:98, 122
Sons and Lovers (Lawrence) **2**:343-44, 346, 348, 354-56, 359-60; **9**:212, 216, 222-27; **16**:274-326; **33**:179, 200-01, 204, 209, 224, 226-27; **48**:100-01, 116, 121, 123, 141; **61**:188, 197-99, 203, 209-10, 212-13, 23, 236, 248, 250
The Sons of Death (Babits)
See *Halálfiai*
"Sons of Erin" (Bell) **43**:91
"The Sons of Martha" (Kipling) **8**:187
Sons of the Puritans (Marquis) **7**:446-47, 450
Sooner or Later: The Story of the Ingenious Ingenue (Hunt) **53**:187-90, 197-98
"The Sootherer" (Stephens) **4**:408
The Soothsayer (Heidenstam) **5**:253
Sophia (Buchanan) **107**:31
Sophie poems (Arp) **115**:5, 23
"Sophistication" (Anderson) **1**:52, 60; **24**:24, 28, 30-1, 34-5, 38, 46, 52, 54; **123**:31, 40
Sophy of Kravonia (Hope) **83**:170
"Sor Aparición" (Pardo Bazán) **189**:226-27, 229, 299
"Sor Candida and the Bird" (Graham) **19**:129
Sor Juana and Other Plays (Trambley) **163**:304, 346, 375, 377
Sora utsu nami (Rohan) **22**:302, 306
The Sorcerer (Gilbert) **3**:214
"The Sorcerer's Eye" (Nemerov) **124**:160, 231
"The Sorcerer's Apprentice" (Bataille) **155**:111
The Sorcerer's Apprentice (Ewers)
See *Der Zauberlehrling*
The Sorceress of Castille (Asch) **3**:67
Sorekara (Natsume) **2**:491, 493-94; **10**:329, 331-32, 339, 345
Søren Kierkegaard (Brandes) **10**:70
"Sorga" (Anwar) **22**:23
"Sorger" (Södergran) **31**:290
Die Sorina (Kaiser) **9**:171, 173
"Sorpresa" (García Lorca) **181**:193, 197
"Sorrento Photographs" (Khodasevich) **15**:206, 209-10
"Sorrow" (Chekhov)
See "Gore"
"Sorrow" (Hecht) **101**:36
"Sorrow" (Mistral)
See "Dolor"
"Sorrow" (Muir) **87**:177
"Sorrow Home" (Walker) **129**:281, 328-29
"The Sorrow of Findebar" (Ledwidge) **23**:109
"The Sorrow of Search" (Dunsany) **59**:19
"The Sorrow of the Individual" (Leino)
See "Yksilön murhe"
"A Sorrowful Guest" (Jewett) **22**:118
"Sorrowful Moonlit Night" (Hagiwara)
See "Kanashi Tsukio"
"The Sorrows of a Young Man" (Kunikida Doppo)
See "Shōnen no Hiai"
The Sorrows of Bulgaria (Vazov) **25**:450
Sorrows of Satan (Griffith) **68**:153
Sorrows of Satan; or The Strange Experience of One Geoffrey Tempest, Millionare (Corelli) **51**:66-8, 70, 83
The Sorrows of the Lagoons (Palamas) **5**:385
"The Sorrows of Thomas Wolfe" (Bishop) **103**:12, 49
"Sorry, the Line Is Busy" (Parker) **143**:332
"A Sorshoz" (Babits) **14**:39
De sorte fugle (Nexø) **43**:329
Sortie de l'acteur (Ghelderode) **187**:4-7
"Sorties" (Carter) **139**:200
Sorties (Dickey) **151**:102-3, 132-35, 162, 165, 203
"Den sortklaedte" (Obstfelder) **23**:177
"Sorworth Place" (Kirk) **119**:279-80, 335, 338, 341, 343
"Sosaku yodan" (Shiga) **172**:201, 215
Sospiri di Roma (Sharp) **39**:364, 372, 379, 381, 389-91, 393, 395, 397
"Sospitra" (Sharp) **39**:379
"Sosredotochie" (Balmont) **11**:40
Sota valosta (Leino) **24**:368-69
"Sotarfun" (Söderberg) **39**:428, 437, 439
Sotileza (Pereda) **16**:362-66, 370, 375-79, 381-82
"Sotto il sole giaguaro" (Calvino) **183**:216, 233
Sotto il sole giaguaro (Calvino) **183**:105, 131, 166, 195, 216
Souffles (Genet) **128**:129
"A Soul" (Jarrell) **177**:152, 157, 196
"The Soul" (Khodasevich) **15**:213
"Soul and Body" (Abercrombie) **141**:8
"Soul and Body" (Gumilev) **60**:270
The Soul Enchanted (Rolland) **23**:264
The Soul of a Bishop: A Novel (With Just a Little Love in It) about Conscience and Religion and the Real Troubles of Life (Wells) **6**:528; **12**:507
"The Soul of a Policeman" (Middleton) **56**:174-75
The Soul of an Indian (Eastman) **55**:161-64, 168-69, 172-73, 175, 178
The Soul of Flowers (Ewers) **12**:133
The Soul of France: Visits to Invaded Districts (Barrès)
See *L'ame française et la guerre*
"Soul of Life" (Trakl) **5**:466
The Soul of Lilith (Corelli) **51**:66, 72
"The Soul of Man" (Manning) **25**:277
"The Soul of Man under Socialism" (Wilde) **23**:436, 444, 447
The Soul of Man under Socialism (Wilde) **175**:302-4, 306, 310
The Soul of Melicent (Cabell)
See *Domnei*
The Soul of Osiris (Crowley) **7**:203-04
"The Soul of Sacred Poetry" (Johnson) **19**:233-34
The Soul of Samuel Pepys (Bradford) **36**:52, 55-6, 61, 67-8
The Soul of Spain (Ellis) **14**:111-12, 122-23, 127
"The Soul of the City Receives the Gift of the Holy Spirit" (Lindsay) **17**:225
"Soul of the Criminal" (Adler) **61**:15
The Soul of the Indian (Eastman)
See *The Soul of an Indian*
"Soul under Water" (Aleixandre) **113**:41
"The Soul-Bird" (Hedāyat)
See "Murgh-i ruh"
Le soulier de satin (Claudel) **2**:99-101, 104-05, 107-08; **10**:124, 128-30, 134-35
The Soul's Awakening (Steiner)
See *Der Seelen Erwachen*
"Souls Belated" (Wharton) **9**:546-47; **129**:360
"Soul's Destroyer" (Davies) **5**:200
The Soul's Destroyer, and Other Poems (Davies) **5**:197-98, 200, 208
Soul's Diary (MacDonald) **9**:292
"The Soul's Exile" (Sterling) **20**:384
The Souls of Black Folk (Du Bois) **169**:77-217
"The Souls of the Slain" (Hardy) **53**:100, 112; **143**:169
Souls of Violet (Jiménez)
See *Almas de violeta*
"The Soul's Prayer" (Naidu) **80**:310
The Soul's Probation (Steiner)
See *Die Prüfung der Seele*
Souls That Pass (Nervo) **11**:403
"Sound" (Gray) **19**:156-57
"The Sound and the Fury" (Benchley) **55**:19
The Sound and the Fury (Faulkner) **141**:38-43, 45, 49, 57, 59, 63-65, 68-70, 72-73, 92-95, 97, 101, 111, 114-15, 139, 142, 173, 188-90; **170**:112, 127-29, 140, 147-57, 160-63, 165, 168, 171-75, 178, 183, 212, 219-20, 222-24, 226, 228, 234, 236-37, 244
"The Sound Machine" (Dahl) **173**:12
"Sound of Blacks in Cuba" (García Lorca)
See "Son de negros en Cuba"
"The Sound of the Hammer" (Dazai Osamu) **11**:179
Sound of Trumpets (Kandinsky) **92**:62
The Sound of Waves (Mishima) **161**:51
"Sound Patterns of Language" (Sapir) **108**:257, 259, 271
"Sound Piece" (Burroughs) **121**:141
"Sound Poem" (Toomer) **172**:274, 316
"Soundings" (Nemerov) **124**:298
Sounds (Kandinsky)
See *Klange*
"Sounds Out of Sorrow" (Masters) **25**:298
"La source" (Roussel) **20**:234, 240, 245
"The Source" (Thomas) **10**:468
La source grecque (Weil) **23**:392
"Sourcedes films" (Cocteau) **119**:76
The Sources (Aldanov)
See *Istoki*
Sources (Jammes) **75**:115
The Sources of a Science of Education (Dewey) **95**:69
"Le sourire de Marko" (Yourcenar) **193**:285-92, 294, 296
Sourires pincés (Renard) **17**:312
Sous bénéfice d'inventaire (Yourcenar) **193**:266-67
Sous la lampe (Fargue) **11**:194, 201
Sous le soleil de Satan (Bernanos) **3**:118-19, 121, 123-6
"Sous les ponts de Paris" (van Ostaijen) **33**:422
Sous l'œil des barbares (Barrès) **47**:35, 49, 62, 76, 86, 88-90, 95-6
Sous l'invocation de St. Jérôme (Larbaud) **9**:204
"The South" (Borges)
See "Le Sud"
"The South" (Gumilev) **60**:280
The South (Borges)
See *Le Sud*
South Africa and Her People (Paton) **165**:313
South African Tragedy (Paton) **165**:298
South American Jungle Tales (Quiroga)
See *Cuentos de la selva*
"The South and Tradition" (Bishop) **103**:17, 50
"The South Country" (Belloc) **7**:32; **18**:41
"The South Lingers On" (Fisher) **11**:205-06, 208, 210, 212, 214
South Moon Under (Rawlings) **4**:359-63, 365, 367-68
South of Rio Grande (Faust) **49**:55, 57, 60
"South of the Slot" (London) **9**:269; **15**:270-71
The South Pole Terror (Dent) **72**:22
South Sea Island (van Schendel)
See *Het Eiland in de Zuidzee*
South Sea Tales (London) **9**:281
"South Slavic Solidarity" (Vazov)
See "Južnoslavjanska solidarnost"
South Star (Fletcher) **35**:100, 102, 106, 110-12
South to Cadiz (Tomlinson) **71**:404
The South to Posterity: An Introduction to the Writing of Confederate History (Freeman) **11**:220-21, 226
"The South Wind" (Blackwood) **5**:80
"The South Wind" (Dunsany) **2**:136
South Wind (Douglas) **68**:2-3, 5-9, 11-3, 17-21, 23-7, 35, 38-9, 43-7
The South Wind of Love (Mackenzie) **116**:239-43, 245
"Southern Cross" (Crane) **80**:84
"The Southern Girl" (Fitzgerald) **52**:59, 61
Southern Horizons (Dixon) **163**:192, 194-98

Southern Horrors: Lynch Law in All Its Phases (Wells-Barnett) **125**:302, 312, 329, 333, 337, 342
Southern Light (Dickey) **151**:167-68
Southern Mail (Saint-Exupéry)
See *Courrier sud*
Southern Paiute language (Sapir) **108**:259
"Southern Pines" (Bishop) **103**:4, 10
"Southern Song" (Walker) **129**:281
The Southerner (Dixon) **163**:166
Southwest (Bagritsky)
See *Yugozapad*
"The Southwest Chamber" (Freeman) **9**:72
"Souveniers de basoche" (Léautaud) **83**:207
"Le souvenir determinant" (Daumal) **14**:91
"A Souvenir of Japan" (Carter) **139**:185, 188
"Souvenirs" (Apollinaire) **8**:29
"Souvenirs" (Zola) **6**:568
Souvenirs (Alain) **41**:26
Souvenirs de la cour d'Assises (Gide) **12**:145
Souvenirs d'un enterré vif (Benda) **60**:73
Les souvenirs d'un officier de la grande armée (Barrès) **47**:55
"Souvenirs of an Egoist" (Dowson) **4**:89
Souvenirs pieux (Yourcenar) **193**:257, 266-68, 280, 302, 343, 346
Souvenirs sur Albert Samain (Jarry) **147**:264, 268
La Souverainité (Bataille) **155**:8, 48, 57, 92, 110
Sovereignty (Bataille)
See *La Souverainité*
The Sovereignty of Good over Other Concepts (Murdoch) **171**:208, 231, 234, 236-37
"Sovershenstvo" (Nabokov) **108**:144
Soviet Communism: A New Civilisation? (Webb and Webb) **22**:407, 415, 418, 431
"Soviet Russia" (Esenin) **4**:112, 115
"Sovremennaia russkaia proza" (Zamyatin) **37**:429
"Sovremennost" (Gumilev) **60**:279
"The Sower" (Markham) **47**:281
"The Sower" (Roberts) **8**:314, 316
"Sower of Stars" (Gonzalez Martinez) **72**:146
"The Sowing" (Teasdale) **4**:425
Sowing the Storm (Rainis)
See *Vētras sēja*
"Soy animal de fondo" (Jiménez) **183**:256, 262-64, 293, 311
"Soy el destino" (Aleixandre) **113**:13, 49
"¿Soy yo . . . ?" (Jiménez) **183**:289
Soziologie (Simmel) **64**:313, 318-320, 323, 330, 336, 350
Space (Aleixandre)
See *Ambito*
The Space Merchants (Kornbluth) **8**:212-16, 218
Space, Time, and Deity (Alexander) **77**:6, 12, 23-4, 30-6, 40, 49-53, 60
"The Spacious Days of Roosevelt" (Lindsay) **17**:227
"La spada e le foglie" (Calvino) **183**:106
La spagna nella vita italiana durante la rinascenza (Croce) **37**:101
Spain (Kazantzakis)
See *Ispania*
Spain, Let This Cup Pass from Me (Vallejo)
See *España, aparta de mí este cáliz*
"Spain, Remove This Chalice from Me" (Vallejo)
See "España, aparta de mí este cáliz"
"Spain, Take This Cup from Me" (Vallejo)
See "España, aparta de mí este cáliz"
Spain, Take This Cup from Me (Vallejo)
See *España, aparta de mí este cáliz*
"The Spalpeen" (Stephens) **4**:420
Spaltung (Benn) **3**:107
"Die Spange" (George) **14**:195, 203
"Spangled Men" (Mencken) **13**:365
Spanien (Nexø) **43**:329
Spanische Ballade (Feuchtwanger) **3**:182, 186
Spanish Bayonet (Benét) **7**:75, 80-1
"Spanish Blood" (Chandler) **7**:176; **179**:122-23, 125, 127
"Spanish Dancer" (Rilke) **195**:244
"Spanish Gin" (Himes) **139**:246
"Spanish Image of Death" (Vallejo)
See "Imagen española de la muerte"
"The Spanish Needle" (McKay) **41**:344
"The Spare Quilt" (Bishop) **103**:4-5, 10
"The Spark" (Cullen) **37**:170
The Spark (Wharton) **3**:558; **9**:550; **129**:350, 363
The Spark (The 'Sixties) (Wharton)
See *The Spark*
Sparks from a Flint: Odd Rhymes for Odd Times (Lucas) **73**:172
Sparks from the Anvil (D'Annunzio)
See *Faville del maglio*
"The Sparrow in the Zoo" (Nemerov) **124**:182
"Sparrows" (Nemerov) **124**:267
"The Sparrow's Fall" (Harper) **14**:260
Spartacus (Gibbon) **4**:123, 126
Spartacus (Kubrick) **112**:188, 205, 207, 220-25, 234, 262, 267, 269, 277
Spartacus Letters (Luxemburg)
See *Spartakus*
Spartakus (Luxemburg) **63**:164-65, 188
Spartakus-Briefe (Luxemburg)
See *Spartakus*
"Spät" (Benn) **3**:107
Die Spät bezahlte Schuld (Zweig) **17**:458
"Der Spaziergang" (Walser) **18**:422
Speak, Memory: An Autobiography Revisited (Nabokov) **108**:60, 82-83, 88-89, 104, 109-110, 116, 119, 126, 128-132, 137-38, 154, 158, 161, 165-67, 177-79, 185, 216, 221, 224; **189**:76, 91, 93, 95-96, 117, 130-31, 148-49, 182
"A Speaker from London" (Warner) **131**:321
"Speakin o' Christmas" (Dunbar) **2**:128; **12**:115
Speaking (Chandler)
See *Raymond Chandler Speaking*
Speaking for Themselves (Churchill) **113**:187
Speaking of Operations— (Cobb) **77**:116, 122, 124, 134
"Speaking of Poetry" (Bishop) **103**:4-7, 9, 17, 34, 43
"Speaking of Women" (Chang) **184**:148-49
"Speaking Silence" (Nemerov) **124**:215
Special Delivery (Cabell) **6**:76
The Special Messenger (Chambers) **41**:95
"Special Pastrami" (Caragiale)
See "Pastramă trufanda"
The Special Theory of Relativity (Einstein) **65**:111
Specially Selected (Lucas) **73**:162
"The Specific Problems of Compulsion Neurosis in the Light of Psychoanalysis" (Horney)
See *Self-Analysis*
The Specimen Case (Bramah) **72**:7-9
"Specimen Day" (Wells) **133**:315
"Specimen Jones" (Wister) **21**:383, 386, 399
"The Speckled Band" (Doyle)
See "The Adventure of the Speckled Band"
"Spectacles" (Pirandello)
See "Gli occhiali"
"Spectators" (McAlmon) **97**:88
Specter of the Rose (Hecht) **101**:77
"The Spectral Mortgage" (Stockton) **47**:324
"The Spectre of the Real" (Hardy) **143**:134
"Spectres that Grieve" (Hardy) **53**:100
Speculation and Revelation: The Religious Philosophy of Vladimir Solovyov, and Other Essays (Shestov)
See *Umozreniie i otkroveniie: Religioznaya filosofia Vladimira Solovyova i drugiie stat'i*
"The Speculation of the Building Constructors" (Calvino)
See "La speculazione edilizia"
"Speculation Turning to Itself" (Nemerov) **124**:218, 313
Speculations (Hulme) **21**:117, 124-26, 138-39, 143-44, 146
Spéculations (Héliogabale à travers les ages) (Jarry) **147**:228
"Speculations upon the Human Mind in 1915" (Trotter) **97**:172, 176
"Speculazione" (Calvino) **183**:161
"La speculazione edilizia" (Calvino) **183**:93
La speculazione edilizia (Calvino) **183**:4-5, 118, 190, 238
Speculum Mentis (Collingwood) **67**:117-21, 123-24, 127-28, 130, 138-41, 146, 148-51, 155-56, 181, 183-84, 193
"The Speech" (Dunsany) **59**:28
"Speech at Sioux Falls, S.D." (Roosevelt) **69**:247
"The Speech at Soli" (Oppen) **107**:290
"Speech to the First Congress of Soviet Writers" (Olesha) **136**:137
"Speeches" (Naidu) **80**:334
Speeches (Aurobindo) **63**:29, 34
Speeches (Holmes) **77**:217
"Speechless" (Lorde) **173**:141
Speed the Plough (Butts) **77**:80
Speedy (Faust) **49**:57-8
"Den speglande brunnen" (Södergran) **31**:285, 289
Spēlēju, dancoju (Rainis) **29**:393
A Spell before Winter (Nemerov) **124**:170, 217, 227, 249, 292, 298
Spell Land (Kaye-Smith) **20**:94, 98, 109, 113-14
The Spell of the Butterfly (García Lorca)
See *El maleficio de la mariposa*
"The Spell of the Yukon" (Service) **15**:399, 404, 406
"Spellbound" (Gissing) **24**:248
Spellbound (Hecht) **101**:72, 75, 89
"The Spellin' Bee" (Dunbar) **2**:128; **12**:108
"Spells and Incantations" (Owen) **27**:217
"The Spendthrift" (Grove) **4**:141
"Speranza" (Pilnyak) **23**:212
The Sphere (Sender)
See *La esfera*
"The Sphere of Pascal" (Borges)
See "Pascal's Sphere"
Sphinx (Lindsay) **15**:219, 225-28, 230-34
Le Sphinx des glaces (Verne) **52**:359
The Sphinx of the Ice-fields (Verne)
See *Le Sphinx des glaces*
"The Sphinx without a Secret: An Etching" (Wilde) **8**:492, 495-96; **41**:359
"The Sphynx Apple" (Henry) **19**:178
La spiaggia (Pavese) **3**:337-38, 343
"Spicewood" (Reese) **181**:343
Spicewood (Reese) **181**:339, 347
Spicilège (Schwob) **20**:321, 323
The Spider (Ewers)
See *Die Spinne*
"The Spider, the Slug, and the Raccoon" (Miyazawa) **76**:277, 289
"The Spider's Secret" (Levi) **109**:363
Der Spiegel (Kandinsky) **92**:38
Spiegelmensch (Werfel) **8**:472-73, 476-79
Spiel im Morgengrauen (Schnitzler) **4**:393, 396
Spiel vom Sterben des reichen Mannes (Hofmannsthal)
See *Jedermann*
"The Spike" (Orwell) **51**:250; **128**:255, 262-63, 281
Spikenard (Housman) **7**:352-53
Spilled Time (Pilnyak) **23**:202
"Spilling the Spanish Beans" (Orwell) **128**:283
"Spilling the Spanish Beans, I" (Orwell) **128**:283
"Spilling the Spanish Beans, II" (Orwell) **128**:283
"Spinach" (Benson) **27**:17
"The Spine-Flute" (Mayakovski) **4**:293; **18**:247
"The Spinks" (Marquis) **7**:436
Die Spinne (Ewers) **12**:136-37, 139
Das Spinnennetz (Roth) **33**:333-35, 344
"Spinning the Crystal Ball" (Dickey) **151**:135

"Spinoza" (Borges) **109**:27-8, 30
Spinoza (Alain) **41**:3
Spinoza et le problème de l'expression (Deleuze) **116**:82
Spinoza's Critique of Religion (Strauss) **141**:233, 290-91
The Spinster (Andrić) **135**:68, 73
"The Spiral Road" (Huneker) **65**:156, 195-96, 198
"Spirit" (Anwar)
See "Semangat"
"'Spirit' and 'Life' in Contemporary Philosophy" (Cassirer) **61**:118
Spirit and Reality (Berdyaev) **67**:29
A Spirit in Prison (Hichens) **64**:124, 126-29
Spirit Level (Morley) **87**:137, 144
"The Spirit of '76" (Becker) **63**:117
"The Spirit of Beauty" (Sterling) **20**:384
"The Spirit of Christ's Teaching" (Tolstoy) **79**:323
"Spirit of Humanity" (Buchanan) **107**:20
The Spirit of Japanese Art (Noguchi) **80**:368
The Spirit of Japanese Poetry (Noguchi) **80**:367
"The Spirit of Mahongui" (Remington) **89**:306
The Spirit of Modern German Literature (Lewisohn) **19**:290, 292-93
"Spirit of Place" (Hall and Nordhoff) **23**:64
The Spirit of Rome (Lee) **5**:312-13
The Spirit of the Border (Grey) **6**:180
The Spirit of the People (Ford) **39**:115-16, 141
The Spirit of the People: An Analysis of the English Mind (Ford) **172**:7-8
"The Spirit of Touchstone" (Noyes) **7**:506
The Spirit of Youth and the City Streets (Addams) **76**:17, 33-5, 37, 39, 84
"A Spirit Rises" (Warner) **131**:319
A Spirit Rises: Shaort Stories (Warner) **131**:317
Lo spirito come atto pure (Gentile)
See *Teoria generale dello Spirito come puro atto*
Spirits of the Corn and of the Wild (Frazer) **32**:211
"Spirits Rebellious" (Gibran)
See "Al-arwāh al-mutamarridah"
"Spirits Summoned West" (Lawrence) **93**:103
Spiritual Adventures (Symons) **11**:434, 436, 442, 444, 447-51
Spiritual Exercises (Kazantzakis) **2**:322-23
"Spiritual Isolation" (Rosenberg) **12**:299
Spiritual Poems (Gray) **19**:142, 144-45, 154-57
Spiritual Sonnets (Jiménez)
See *Sonetos espirituales*
Spiritual Tales (Sharp) **39**:362
"The Spiritual Unrest" (Baker) **47**:13
"Spiritual Verses" (Kuzmin) **40**:189
"A Spiritual Woman" (Lawrence) **93**:43, 46
A Spiritualist Photographer (Melies) **81**:140
Spiritus Mundi (Frye) **165**:150-51, 157-59, 188-90, 228-29, 257
"Spisak" (Popa) **167**:153-55, 177
Spisok blagodeianii (Olesha)
See "Spisok blagodeyany"
"Spisok blagodeyany" (Olesha) **136**:63, 65-66, 74-75, 78, 111-12
"Spleen" (Garneau) **13**:195
"Spleen pour rire" (van Ostaijen) **33**:417-18
The Splendid Idle Forties: Stories of Old California (Atherton) **2**:14, 18
The Splendid Spur (Quiller-Couch) **53**:296
Splendid's (Genet) **128**:189, 199-201
Splendor (Williams) **89**:365, 377, 396
Splendors of Hell (Ghelderode)
See *Fastes d'enfer*
The Splendor of the Bonfire (Valle-Inclán)
See *El resplandor de la hoguera*
Splinten av troldspeilet (Undset) **3**:517, 522; **197**:299, 301, 308
The Splinter of the Magic Mirror (Undset)
See *Splinten av troldspeilet*
The Splinter of the Troll Mirror (Undset)
See *Splinten av troldspeilet*
A Spoil of Office: A Story of the Modern West (Garland) **3**:191-92, 200-02
"The Spoilers of the Land" (Papadiamantis) **29**:271
The Spoils of Poynton (James) **2**:247, 270; **11**:345-46; **40**:120, 149, 169; **47**:185-86, 188, 191, 195, 207; **171**:180
"Spoken Action" (Pirandello)
See "L'azione parlata"
"Spoken To" (Gilman) **117**:116-20, 123
Spöksonaten (Strindberg) **1**:445, 447, 449-51, 456-57, 460-61; **8**:406-07, 411-12, 415, 419; **21**:348-49,352-53, 365-67; 368-69; **47**:339, 369, 372
The Sponger (Renard)
See *L'écornifleur*
"Sponono" (Paton) **165**:298
"Spontaneity: Its Strength and Weakness" (Fanon) **188**:69, 111
Spook (Tolstoy) **18**:359
The Spook Sonata (Strindberg)
See *Spöksonaten*
Spook Stories (Benson) **27**:17, 19
The Spoon River Anthology (Masters) **2**:460-68, 470, 472-74; **25**:283-91, 293-96, 298-316
"The Spooniad" (Masters) **2**:463, 473; **25**:287, 298-99, 303, 313, 315-16
Sporedno nebo (Popa) **167**:156, 158, 161, 163, 172, 174, 177-78, 180
"Sporenwache" (George) **14**:201, 205
"Sporgendosi dalla costa scoscesa" (Calvino) **183**:155
Sport Fairy-tales (Horvath)
See *Sportmärchen*
"The Sport Model" (Fields) **80**:259
The Sport of the Gods (Dunbar) **2**:128-30, 132; **12**:107-09, 112-14, 118, 120-21, 123-24, 128-30
Sportmärchen (Horvath) **45**:102
Spotkanie (Reymont) **5**:393
Sprach und Mythos: Ein Beitrag zum Problem der Götternamen (Cassirer) **61**:46-7, 49, 77-78, 85-8, 98, 107
Sprach Zarathustra: Ein Buch für Alle und Keinen (Nietzsche) **10**:361-62, 373-79, 383-86, 388-89, 391-93; **18**:339, 342, 350; **55**:316-21, 323-24, 326-31, 333, 335-36, 340, 347, 356, 359-60, 378-79, 381, 384, 386, 390
Die Sprache (Kraus) **5**:285, 289
"Die Sprache als Hort der Freiheit" (Böll) **185**:37, 42
Die Sprache als Hort der Freiheit (Böll) **185**:149, 152, 160, 165
"Sprachliche Beiträge zur Erklärung der Scienza nuovavon G. B. Vico" (Auerbach) **43**:62
"Spravidlivost' v skobkakh" (Babel) **171**:50-51, 53, 97, 102, 107
Spreading the News (Gregory) **1**:335-36, 338; **176**:13-14, 17, 19, 21, 23, 31-35, 40, 62-63, 74-77, 80, 83
Sprechstimme (Schoenberg) **75**:292
"The Sprig of Holly" (Stockton) **47**:329
"Spring" (Arp) **115**:14-15
"Spring" (Devkota) **23**:47
"Spring" (Esenin) **4**:114
"Spring" (Field) **43**:166-67
"Spring" (Fletcher) **35**:108
"Spring" (Guiney) **41**:203
"Spring" (Lasker-Schueler) **57**:329, 336
"Spring" (Millay) **49**:225; **169**:300
"Spring" (Naidu) **80**:295
"Spring" (Obstfelder)
See "Vår"
"The Spring" (Roussel)
See "La source"
"Spring" (Schulz)
See "Wiosna"
Spring (Reymont) **5**:392
Spring (Shimazaki Toson)
See *Haru*
The Spring (Undset)
See *Vaaren*
Spring '71 (Adamov)
See *Le printemps* **189**:*71*
"Spring, 1938" (Brecht) **6**:39
"Spring and Asura" (Miyazawa)
See "Haru to Shura"
Spring and Asura (Miyazawa)
See *Haru to shura*
"The Spring and the Fall" (Millay) **49**:215
"Spring Birds" (Kunikida Doppo)
See "Haru no tori"
Spring Breeze (Ekelund)
See *Varbis*
Spring Came on Forever (Aldrich) **125**:8, 12
"Spring Comes to Murray Hill" (Nash) **109**:360
Spring Dance (Barry) **11**:56
"Spring Dawn Is Glinting" (Wright) **136**:300
"Spring Day" (Lowell) **8**:230
"A Spring Day at Ihatove School of Agriculture" (Miyazawa) **76**:283
"A Spring Day in New Jersey" (Jiménez) **183**:332
Spring Days (Moore) **7**:484, 489
"Spring Fever" (Collier) **127**:261
Spring Fever (Wodehouse) **108**:369, 372
"Spring Floods" (Pasternak) **188**:193
"Spring Garland" (Kuzmin) **40**:189
Spring in Autumn (Martinez Sierra and Martinez Sierra)
See *Primavera en otoño*
"Spring in Dublin" (Gogarty) **15**:113
"Spring in Fialta" (Nabokov)
See "Vesna v Fial'te"
"Spring in Hellas" (Carducci)
See "Primavere elleniche"
"Spring in Kashmir" (Naidu) **80**:315
"Spring in New Hampshire" (McKay) **7**:457; **41**:344
Spring in New Hampshire, and Other Poems (McKay) **41**:344
"Spring in the Garden" (Millay) **49**:210
"Spring in the Trenches" (Guest) **95**:205
"Spring is like a perhaps hand" (Cummings) **137**:56
"Spring Light" (Wen I-to) **28**:420
"The Spring Lingers On" (Wright) **136**:302
"Spring Morning" (Milne) **6**:314-15; **88**:243
"Spring Mystery" (Södergran)
See "Vårmysterium"
"Spring Night" (Hagiwara)
See "Shun'ya"
"Spring Night" (Teasdale) **4**:429
The Spring of Joy (Webb) **24**:473
A Spring of Verse (Couperus)
See *Een lent van vaerzen*
"Spring Offensive" (Owen) **5**:370, 372-73; **27**:201, 203, 206, 209, 212-13, 222, 227, 231-32, 238-39
"Spring on Mattagami" (Scott) **6**:386, 390, 392, 397, 399
"Spring Phantoms" (Hearn) **9**:134
"Spring Pictures" (Mansfield) **39**:303
"Spring Poem" (Radnóti) **16**:418
"Spring Reminiscence" (Cullen) **37**:154
"Spring Riding in a Carriage" (Yokomitsu)
See "Haru wa Basha ni Notte"
"Spring: Rouen, May 1917" (Gurney) **33**:110, 112
Spring Snow (Mishima)
See *Haru no yuki*
"A Spring Snowstorm in Wastdale" (Crowley) **7**:208
"The Spring Sprout Song" (Chang)
See "Yangge"
"Spring Song" (Anderson) **10**:49-50; **123**:112-13
"Spring Song" (Carman) **7**:145
"Spring Song" (Davidson) **24**:164, 176
"Spring Song" (Sarton) **120**:268-69
Spring Song, and Other Stories (Cary) **1**:146
"Spring Song in the City" (Buchanan) **107**:25

"Spring Sorrow" (Lasker-Schueler) **57**:334
"Spring Thaw" (Pasternak) **188**:183-84, 187
Spring Trifles (Remizov)
See *Vesennee porosh'e*
"Spring will fall without opening" (Jiménez) **183**:341
"Springer Mountain" (Dickey) **151**:89
"The Springfield Fox" (Seton) **31**:263, 266, 270-71, 273, 279
"Springfield Town Is Butterfly Town" (Lindsay) **17**:240
Springfield Town Is Butterfly Town, and Other Poems for Children (Lindsay) **17**:240
Springhaven (Blackmore) **27**:25-6, 28-9, 34, 37, 39-40, 42-3, 45-6
Spring's Awakening (Wedekind)
See *Frühlings Erwachen*
The Springs of Affection (Brennan) **124**:5-6
"The Springs of the Clitumnus" (Carducci)
See "Alle fonti del Clitumno"
"Spring-Shock" (Dickey) **151**:176
A Springtide (Raabe) **45**:174, 191, 199
"Springtime" (Gale) **7**:285
Springtime (Undset)
See *Vaaren*
Springtime and Harvest (Sinclair)
See *Springtime and Harvest: A Romance*
Springtime and Harvest: A Romance (Sinclair) **160**:294
Sprüche und Widersprüche (Kraus) **5**:291
"Spunk" (Hurston) **131**:72
"Spur" (Yeats) **116**:280
The Spurt of Blood (Artaud)
See *Le jet de sang*
"Sputnice" (Annensky) **14**:33
"The Spy" (Nemerov) **124**:260
The Spy (Gorky) **8**:72
Spy to Paris (Van Doren) **18**:409-10
The Spy Who Loved Me (Fleming) **193**:198, 212, 223, 231, 240-41
"Squadron Commander Trunov" (Babel)
See "Eskadronnyi Trunov"
Square Horizon (Huidobro)
See *Horizon carré*
The Square Root of Wonderful (McCullers) **155**:180
"Squares and Angles" (Storni)
See "Cuadros y angulos"
"Squaring the Circle" (Henry) **19**:181-82
"The Squatter" (Roberts) **8**:321
"Squatter's Children" (Bishop) **121**:7
"The Squaw" (Stoker) **8**:394
The Squeaker (Wallace) **57**:402
"Squeaker's Mate" (Baynton) **57**:3-4, 6, 9-11, 23-25, 32
"The Squealer" (Williams) **89**:374, 392
The Squealer (Wallace)
See *The Squeaker*
"Le squelette" (Schwob) **20**:319, 321, 323
"Squinancy-Wort" (Carpenter) **88**:52
The Squire (Pinero) **32**:398-99, 412-13
"The Squire at Vauxhall" (Dobson) **79**:2
"Squire Hawkins's Story" (Riley) **51**:284
The Squirrel Cage (Fisher) **87**:72
The Squirrel Inn (Stockton) **47**:329
"Squirrles Have Bright Eyes" (Collier) **127**:261
"Sredni Vashtar" (Saki) **3**:365, 368-69, 373
Sri Aurobindo Birth Centenary Library (Aurobindo) **63**:52-6
Śrīkānta (Chatterji) **13**:73-80
St. Abe and His Seven Wives (Buchanan) **107**:84
St. Andrews (Lang) **16**:269
"St. Armorer's Church from the Outside" (Stevens) **3**:472
"St. Barbara" (Chesterton) **6**:98
St. Bernard (Ramos)
See *São Bernardo*
"St. Catherine's Eve" (Lowndes) **12**:201
"St. Columba and the River" (Dreiser) **35**:70-1, 75
"St. Dorothy" (Swinburne) **36**:299
"St. Expeditus" (Morgenstern) **8**:306
St. Francis and Others (Ellis) **14**:108
St. Francis of Assisi (Chesterton) **6**:102-03; **64**:42
"St. Francis to the Birds" (Percy) **84**:199
"St. Frideswide's Day in Oxford" (Guiney) **41**:220
St. George and St. Michael (MacDonald) **9**:292
"St. George's Day" (Davidson) **24**:163
"A St. Helena Lullaby" (Kipling) **8**:200
St. Ives (Quiller-Couch) **53**:296
"St. Jacques, Dieppe" (White) **176**:171
St. Joan of the Stockyards (Brecht)
See *Die heilige Johanna der Schlachthöfe*
"St. John and the Back-Ache" (Stevens) **12**:365
"St. John Fires" (Remizov) **27**:351
The St. Johns (Cabell) **6**:76, 78
St. John's Festival (Kielland)
See *Sankt Hans fest*
St. John's Fire (Sudermann)
See *Johannisfeuer*
"St. Kentigern" (Harte) **25**:212
"St. Louis Blues" (Handy) **97**:38, 40-42, 44-46, 54, 60-61, 78-81
St. Mark's Rest (Ruskin) **20**:287; **63**:251, 256
St. Martin's Pageant (Housman) **7**:359
St. Martin's Summer (Sabatini) **47**:303
"St. Matthew" (Lawrence) **93**:129
St. Mawr (Lawrence) **2**:356-57, 361-63, 373-74; **9**:219; **33**:203; **48**:121, 125, 142
St. Nicholas's Parables (Remizov)
See *Zvenigorod oklikannyi: Nikoliny pritchi*
St. Pantaleone (D'Annunzio)
See *San Pantaleone*
"St. Patrick and the Pedants" (Yeats)
See "The Old Men of the Twilight"
"St. Peter Relates an Incident of the Resurrection Day" (Johnson) **3**:241, 245; **19**:209, 211
St. Peter Relates an Incident: Selected Poems (Johnson) **3**:245
"St. Peter's Day" (Chekhov) **96**:32-33, 37
St. Peter's Umbrella (Mikszath)
See *Szent Péter esernyöje*
"St. Petersburg" (Hippius) **9**:156, 161
St. Petersburg (Bely)
See *Peterburg*
"St. Petersburg" (Twain) **185**:307
St. Petri-Schnee (Perutz) **60**:369-71
"St. Swithin's Day" (Davidson) **24**:162
St. Thomas Aquinas (Chesterton) **6**:103
"St. Valentine's Eve" (Davidson) **24**:162, 186
"St. Yves' Poor" (Pickthall) **21**:245-46, 250, 254
Šta sanjam i šta mi se dogada (Andrić) **135**:53
"I stäallet för tro" (Lagerkvist) **144**:210
"Stabat nuda Aestas" (D'Annunzio) **40**:43
Stachka (Eisenstein) **57**:156-57, 161, 163, 166, 178, 190-91, 196
"Stacked Ice-Floes" (Khodasevich)
See "L'din vzgromozhdennykh"
"De stad der opbouwers" (van Ostaijen) **33**:417
"Stad stilleven" (van Ostaijen) **33**:418, 421
"De stade en stade" (Fargue) **11**:194
"Stadion v Odesse" (Olesha) **136**:158
"Die Stadt" (Hesse) **148**:150
"Die Stadt" (Heym) **9**:151
"Die Stadt" (Kolmar) **40**:178
"Die Stadt der Mittellosen" (Brod) **115**:94
"Stadt, Stadt: Mutter zwischen Himmel und Erde" (Borchert) **5**:104
"Städtbilder" (Benjamin) **39**:63
The Staff Room (Tey) **14**:459
"Stafford's Cabin" (Robinson) **101**:111
"The Stage Tavern" (Jewett) **22**:146
Stage-Land: Curious Habits and Customs of Its Inhabitants (Jerome) **23**:80, 83, 86-7, 90
The Stages of the Mind (Jensen)
See *Aandens Stadier*
Stages on the Road (Undset)
See *Etapper: Ny raekke*
"The Stagnant Pool" (Peretz) **16**:390
Stained Glass Elegies (Endo) **152**:213-14
"Staircase" (Tsvetaeva)
See "Poèma lestnitsy"
The Staircase (Abercrombie) **141**:10-17
"The Staircase at the Heart's Delight" (Green) **63**:147-48
Staische Gedichte (Benn) **3**:107, 109
"Staley Fleming's Hallucination" (Bierce) **44**:45, 49
Stalin: An Appraisal of the Man and His Influence (Trotsky) **22**:361, 365-66, 369
Stalin's Letters to Molotov (Stalin) **92**:331
Stalky and Co. (Kipling) **8**:182-84, 186-88, 198, 200, 202, 208; **17**:204, 210-11
"The Stalled Ox and the Dish of Herbs" (Bialik) **25**:53
"The Stalls of Barchester Cathedral" (James) **6**:210, 212-13
"Stal'naja cikada" (Annensky) **14**:33
Stamboul Quest (Mankiewicz) **85**:163
"Stammelverse" (Liliencron) **18**:210
"Stamp Collection" (Čapek)
See "Sbírka známek"
Les stances (Moréas) **18**:280-90
Stances et poèmes (Sully Prudhomme) **31**:299, 301, 306-07
"Standards and Paradise of the Blacks" (García Lorca)
See "Norma y paraíso de los negros"
"Standards of Beauty" (Levi)
See "La misura della bellezza"
"Standort des Erzahlers im zeitgenossischen Roman" (Adorno) **111**:42
Stanislavsky on the Art of the Stage (Stanislavsky) **167**:248, 338
Stanislavsky's Legacy (Stanislavsky) **167**:305
Stanzas in Meditation (Stein) **1**:441-42; **48**:219, 249, 255
"Stanzas Written on Battersea Bridge during a South-Westerly Gale" (Belloc) **18**:41
"Star" (Huidobro)
See "Astro"
"The Star" (Masters) **25**:298
"The Star" (Morgenstern)
See "Der stern"
"The Star" (Roberts) **68**:297, 336
"The Star" (Södergran) **31**:287
"The Star" (Wells) **12**:502, 511; **19**:421, 429, 437
"Star Across the Tracks" (Aldrich) **125**:4
"Star and Candle" (Hawthorne) **25**:247
"The Star in the Valley" (Murfree) **135**:200-4, 219, 227
A Star Is Born (Parker) **143**:281
Star Maker (Stapledon) **22**:312, 318, 320-25, 328, 331, 334-35, 337, 343-45
"The Star of Australasia" (Lawson) **27**:125, 133
"The Star of Love" (Bunin) **6**:52
"The Star of Percivale" (Williams) **1**:512
The Star of Satan (Bernanos)
See *Sous le soleil de Satan*
The Star of the Covenant (George)
See *Der Stern des Bundes*
"Star of the Nativity" (Pasternak)
See "Rozhdestvenskaia zvezda"
The Star of the Sea (Ekelund)
See *Hafvets stjarna*
Star of the Unborn (Werfel)
See *Stern der Ungeborenen*
The Star on the Brow (Roussel)
See *L'étoile au front*
The Star Rover (London) **9**:267, 272; **15**:260
Star Spangled Virgin (Heyward) **59**:103
"Star Teachers" (Baker) **10**:27
"Staraja deva" (Gumilev) **60**:279
Staraja ploščad', 4 (Babel) **2**:35
"Staraja šarmanda" (Annensky) **14**:27
"Staraya aktrisa" (Zabolotsky) **52**:367
"Staraya loshad" (Tolstoy) **173**:294
Staraya sekretnaya (Gladkov) **27**:90
Star-Begotten (Wells) **6**:553; **12**:513-15
Starbrace (Kaye-Smith) **20**:94, 97, 101

"The Star-Crossed Romance of Josephine Cosnowski" (Shepherd) **177**:308
"Starers" (Davies) **5**:203
"The Stare's Nest by My Window" (Yeats) **11**:535-36
"Staring" (Drummond de Andrade)
See "Cisma"
"Stark Major" (Crane) **2**:120
The Stark Munro Letters (Doyle) **7**:217, 219, 240
"Starka hyacinter" (Södergran) **31**:291
Den Starkare (Strindberg) **1**:445-46, 448; **8**:407, 413, 419
"The Starling" (Ford) **15**:70
"Starling and Dore" (Ady) **11**:20
"Starlings on the Roof" (Hardy) **143**:198
Staroi i novoie (Eisenstein) **57**:163, 166, 170-73, 175-76, 178, 186, 190-91, 196-98
Starry Adventure (Austin) **25**:33-4
Starry Harness (Benét) **28**:8-9
"The Starry Meadow" (Leino)
See "Tähtitarha"
"The Stars" (Esenin) **4**:116
"The Stars" (Kunikida Doppo)
See "Hoshi"
"The Stars" (Remizov)
See "Zvezdy"
The Stars (Bernhard)
See *Die Berühmten*
"The Stars Abound" (Södergran)
See "Stjärnorna vimla"
The Stars Bow Down (Tey) **14**:458-59
"Stars in Their Courses" (Kipling) **8**:196
"A Start in Life" (Dreiser) **35**:69, 72-3
"Starvation under the Orange Trees" (Steinbeck) **135**:338, 343
Starved Rock (Masters) **25**:296, 315
The Starvel Tragedy (Crofts)
See *Inspector French and the Starvel Tragedy*
"The Starveling" (Colette) **16**:127
The Star-Wagon (Anderson) **2**:8, 11; **144**:11, 18-19
"Stary Prometeusz" (Herbert) **168**:20
"Staryj syr" (Pilnyak) **23**:212
"Stasio's Adventure" (Prus)
See "Przygoda Stasia"
"The State" (Jarrell) **177**:146, 173, 177
The State (Wilson) **79**:500, 503
The State and Revolution (Lenin) **67**:222, 225-26, 228-33, 250-55, 257-59
The State in Theory and Practice (Laski) **79**:87
"The State: Its Historic Role" (Kropotkin) **36**:204
"The State of Economic Science in Canada" (Innis) **77**:338
"The State of Funk" (Lawrence) **93**:64
"The State of Grace" (Brodkey) **123**:214, 219
State of Revolution (Bolt) **175**:25-26, 28-30
The State vs. Elinor Norton (Rinehart) **52**:290-92
"Statement for the English Memorial Service for Robert Lowell" (Bishop) **121**:16
"A Statement of My Impressions Upon Reading Yamamoto Annosuke's Study Entitled 'Religion and Reason'" (Nishida)
See "Yamamoto Annosuke-kun no 'Shukyo to risei' to iu rombun o yomite shokan o nobu"
"Statement of Political Principles" (Dulles) **72**:79
"The Statement of Randolph Carter" (Lovecraft) **4**:266, 268
States of Grace (Barry) **11**:67-8
"The Statesman's Holiday" (Yeats) **11**:529
Static Poems (Benn)
See *Staische Gedichte*
The Station (Byron) **67**:88
"Station Baranovich" (Aleichem) **35**:327
"The Stationary Journey" (Muir) **87**:254
"The Stations" (Morgenstern) **8**:305
"Stationschef Fallmerayer" (Roth) **33**:351, 362
"The Statue" (Belloc) **7**:33; **18**:28
The Statue (Bennett) **197**:31
"The Statue at the World's End" (Stevens)
See "Mr. Burnshaw and the Statue"
"The Statue in the Garden" (Lowell) **1**:373; **8**:225
"The Statue of Old Andrew Jackson" (Lindsay) **17**:240
"The Statue of Shadow" (Bishop) **103**:4, 8, 21
"The Statues" (Bishop) **103**:21
"The Statues" (Yeats) **18**:447; **93**:369
"The Statues in the Public Gardens" (Nemerov) **124**:180
"The Statute of Limitations" (Dowson) **4**:89
Statutory Authorities for Special Purposes (Webb and Webb) **22**:413
"Stay, O Stay" (Coppard) **5**:178-79
Staying with Relations (Macaulay) **7**:430; **44**:125-26, 133
"Staze" (Andrić) **135**:88
"Stealthily" (Svevo)
See "Proditoriamente"
The Steam House, or, a Trip Across Northern India (Verne)
See *La Maison à vapeur: Voyage à travers l'Inde septentrionale*
"Steam Tactics" (Kipling) **8**:202
"The Steampillar" (Molnár) **20**:173
"Stecak" (Popa) **167**:164
Steed of Flame (Gladkov)
See *Ognennyi kon'*
Steel (Hergesheimer) **11**:267
Steel and Iron (Singer) **33**:386, 398, 400
"The Steel Cat" (Collier) **127**:261
"The Steel Cicada" (Annensky)
See "Stal'naja cikada"
"The Steel Worker" (Stringer) **37**:343
"Steelman's Pupil" (Lawson) **27**:130, 149
"The Steep Road" (Hesse) **196**:278
Steeplejack (Huneker) **65**:170-72, 178, 183-84, 186, 189, 205, 209, 211, 219-20
Æsteik og Udvikling (Jensen) **41**:295
"Steinerner Gast" (Broch) **20**:52, 54
"The Stellar Fright" (Gumilev) **60**:264, 270
"Stellungskrieg" (Toller) **10**:490
"The Stem of Grass" (Hagiwara) **60**:296
"A Stem of Lilies" (Miyazawa) **76**:278
"Stempenu" (Aleichem) **1**:28
Stene i strømmen (Grieg) **10**:205, 207-08
"Stenographer" (Bodenheim) **44**:69
"The Step" (Benson) **27**:19
"Step" (Chekhov) **3**:153, 159, 165; **10**:55-68; **96**:33-34; **163**:77
"A Step Away from Them" (Ginsberg) **120**:128
The Step on the Stair; or, You Are the Man (Green) **63**:153-54
"The Stepdaughter" (Platonov) **14**:420
Stephan Rott, oder das Jahr der Entscheidung (Brod) **115**:85, 89
Stephania, a Trialogue (Field) **43**:172
Stephanos (Bryusov) **10**:79-81, 86-8
"Stephen Crane's Own Story" (Crane) **11**:160
Stephen Escott (Lewisohn) **19**:273, 278
Stephen Hero (Joyce) **3**:268, 270, 274-75, 278-79; **16**:208, 212, 214-16, 224-25, 228, 236-37, 239-40, 245; **35**:167; **52**:218, 223-24; **159**:266-75, 277, 281, 306-8, 310, 313, 350-52, 355-56, 358
The Stepmother (Milne) **6**:308
"The Steppe" (Chekhov)
See "Step"
Steppenfahrt (Barlach) **48**:96
Steppenwolf (Hesse)
See *Der Steppenwolf*
Der Steppenwolf (Hesse) **148**:148, 163, 170, 172-73; **196**:250, 266-67, 269, 277, 297-98, 305, 342-43
"Steps" (Morgenstern) **8**:304
"The Steps of the Commander" (Blok) **5**:85
Stepsons of Light (Rhodes) **53**:314, 316, 318, 326, 327
"Das Sterbelied" (Sudermann) **15**:430, 438
"Sterben" (Schnitzler) **4**:385, 393, 398, 401, 403-4
"Der stern" (Morgenstern) **8**:309
Stern der Ungeborenen (Werfel) **8**:471, 476-78, 480, 482-84
Der Stern des Bundes (George) **2**:148, 152; **14**:196, 202, 204-05, 207, 211-12, 214
"Sterne" (Woolf) **43**:401, 404
Sternstunden der Menschheit (Zweig) **17**:457-58
"La stessa cosa del sangue" (Calvino) **183**:187
"Steve Scaevola" (Williams) **89**:376, 385, 393
"Stevenson Twenty-Five Years After" (Knister) **56**:153
Stickeen (Muir) **28**:259, 264
"Die Stickerin von Traviso" (Heyse) **8**:114, 121
Stickfuls (Cobb) **77**:117-18
Stiff Upper Lip, Jeeves (Wodehouse) **108**:363
"Stikhi K Akhmatovoi" (Tsvetaeva) **35**:384-85
Stikhi K Blok (Tsvetaeva) **7**:557, 563; **35**:382-84, 401-02
"Stikhi k Chekhii" (Tsvetaeva) **35**:416
Stikhi. Kniga I (Sologub) **9**:443
Stikhi. Kniga II (Sologub) **9**:443
Stikhi o prekrasnoi dame (Blok) **5**:83-5, 90-1, 94
Stikhi o rossii (Blok) **5**:84, 92
Stikhotvoreniya (Zabolotsky) **52**:365-66
"The Stile" (Thomas) **10**:459
"Still Homer" (Carducci) **32**:86
"Still Life" (Babits)
See "A csendéletekből"
"Still Life" (Lowell) **8**:231, 238
"Still Life" (Malamud) **129**:78, 80, 82; **184**:185-88, 200, 237, 307, 309
Still Life (Murry) **16**:354-55
"Still Life: Carrots" (Bishop) **103**:3
Still Life with a Bridle: Essays and Apocryphas (Herbert) **168**:7, 49-54, 73
"Still Life with Herrings. S. Soutine" (Malamud) **184**:308
"The Still of the Year" (Guiney) **41**:214
"Still Questing" (Nisbet) **117**:384
Still Songs (Annensky)
See *Tikhie pesni*
Still Waters (Thomas) **97**:138, 140
"Stille der Natur" (Raabe) **45**:189
De stille kracht (Couperus) **15**:45-8
"Den stille Mogens" (Jensen) **41**:307
"Die Stille Mühle" (Sudermann) **15**:429
Stiller (Frisch) **121**:197-99, 202, 212-13, 225, 229, 231-32, 236, 241-46, 260, 265, 275-76, 278, 282
"Stilleven" (van Ostaijen) **33**:418
"Stillness" (Flecker) **43**:187, 190, 194, 199
Stillness and Shadows (Gardner) **195**:154
"The Stillness of the Frost" (Roberts) **8**:327
"Die Stimme hinter dem Vorhang" (Benn) **3**:107
"Die Stimmen" (Rilke) **195**:181, 183
"Stimmen im Strome" (George) **14**:205
Die Stimmen von Marrakesch: Aufzeichnungen nach einer Reise (Canetti) **157**:63, 69, 89-94, 101
Der Stimmenimitator (Bernhard) **165**:36, 96, 102, 106-7
"The Sting" (P'u Sung-ling)
See *English Men of Letters*
The Sting of Death (Sologub) **9**:436
Stingaree (Hornung) **59**:113
"Stirrup Cup" (Percy) **84**:203
"Stjärnorna vimla" (Södergran) **31**:294
"Stockholm" (Gumilev) **60**:271-2
Stockton's Stories (Stockton) **47**:312
"A Stoic" (Galsworthy) **1**:294
The Stoic (Dreiser) **10**:179-80, 182, 184, 192, 197; **18**:54, 60-1, 64, 71; **35**:39, 62; **83**:97
"The Stoker" (Kafka)
See "Der Heizer"
"Stol" (Tsvetaeva) **35**:406
"Stolbovaya doroga proletarskoy literatury" (Fadeyev) **53**:64-5
Stolbtsy (Zabolotsky) **52**:365, 367-68, 372-79

"The Stolen Bacillus" (Wells) **19**:441-42; **133**:294
"Stolen Bonds" (Fields) **80**:258
"The Stolen Bride" (Onetti)
See "La novia robada"
The Stolen Bride (Onetti)
See *La novia robada*
"The Stolen Cactus" (Čapek)
See "Ukradený kaktus"
"The Stolen Child" (Yeats) **11**:512; **116**:334
"The Stolen Document 139/VII Sect. C" (Čapek) **192**:223
"The Stolen Life" (Post) **39**:343
"Stolen Lumber" (Jozsef) **22**:162
"Stone" (Gumilev)
See "Kamen'"
Stone (Mandelstam)
See *Kamen'*
A Stone, A Leaf, A Door (Wolfe) **4**:518; **13**:479
"The Stone and Mr. Thomas" (Powys) **9**:372
The Stone Angel (Tsvetaeva) **35**:411
A Stone Country (La Guma) **140**:196, 200-202, 204-6, 210, 212, 221, 225-28, 233-34, 249, 254, 260, 262-63, 272-73
"The Stone Garden" (Sarton) **120**:304
A Stone in the Middle of the Road: Biography of a Poem (Drummond de Andrade)
See *Uma pedra no meio do caminho: Biografia de um poema*
"The Stone Ship" (Hodgson) **13**:237
"A Stone Woman" (Khlebnikov)
See "Kamennaya baba"
Stones in the Stream (Grieg)
See *Stene i strømmen*
The Stones of Venice I (Ruskin) **20**:260, 265, 280, 282, 292-93, 297-302, 305-06, 308; **63**:238-39, 243-44, 248, 251, 254, 256-65, 269-70, 276-, 309-10, 319-20;
The Stones of Venice II (Ruskin) **20**:298
The Stoneware Monkey (Freeman) **21**:53, 57, 59
"Stool" (Herbert) **168**:14
"The Stoop of Rhenish" (Davidson) **24**:164
"Stop Breakin' Down" (Johnson) **69**:79
Stopfkuchen (Raabe) **45**:166-70, 173, 176-79, 181, 204
Stops of Various Quills (Howells) **7**:367
Stora landsvägen (Strindberg) **1**:449, 463; **8**:416; **21**:350, 369
Den store hunger (Bojer) **64**:1-3, 10, 16, 18, 23
The Storeroom of the Sun (Prishvin) **75**:218
Storia delle dottrine politiche (Mosca) **75**:162
"Storia dell'indeciso" (Calvino) **183**:124
"Storia dell'ingrato punito" (Calvino) **183**:214
Storia di Cristo (Papini) **22**:273, 277-79, 281-82, 287, 289-91
Storia di un anno (Mussolini) **96**:282
"Storia di una capinera" (Verga) **3**:541, 544
Storia e cronistoria del "Canzoniere" (Saba) **33**:371, 375-77
"Una storia italiana" (Pratolini) **124**:324-28, 350
La storia ridotta sotti il concetto generale dell' arte (Croce) **37**:121-22, 124
Storie naturali (Levi) **109**:292-93, 295-97
"Stories" (Jarrell) **177**:169, 172
"Stories" (Peretz) **16**:394
Stories (Bernhard)
See *Erzahlungen*
Stories (Fitzgerald) **157**:189
Stories (Vallette)
See *Contes et nouvelles*
Stories about the Fairy (Balmont)
See *Feinye skazki*
Stories and Pictures (Peretz) **16**:390
Stories and Satires by Sholom Aleichem (Aleichem) **1**:26
Stories and Texts for Nothing (Beckett)
See *Textes pour rien*
Stories, Dreams, and Allegories (Schreiner) **9**:400
Stories, Fables, and Other Diversions (Nemerov) **124**:230, 233-34, 295
Stories for a Year (Pirandello)
See *Novelle per un anno*
Stories for Every Day in the Year (Pirandello)
See *Novelle per un anno*
Stories for Jewish Children (Aleichem)
See *Mayses far yidishe kinder*
Stories from One Pocket (Čapek)
See *Povídky z, jedné kapsy*
Stories from the Bible (de la Mare) **4**:78
Stories from the Other Pocket (Čapek)
See *Povídky z, druhé kapsy*
Stories from Triumph Lane (Huch)
See *Aus der Triumphgasse: Lebensskizzen*
Stories in an Almost Classical Mode (Brodkey) **123**:195, 202, 204-6, 212, 214-15, 223, 225, 236
Stories of Astonishing Adventures of American Boys and Girls with the Fairies of Their Native Land (Baum) **7**:14, 16
The Stories of Bernard Malamud (Malamud) **184**:264
Stories of Death and Blood (Güiraldes)
See *Cuentos de muerte y de sangre*
The Stories of Denton Welch (Welch) **22**:462
The Stories of Ernest Dowson (Dowson) **4**:89
The Stories of F. Scott Fitzgerald (Fitzgerald) **6**:162
Stories of God (Rilke) **1**:418; **6**:366; **19**:307; **195**:215-16
The Stories of Katherine Mansfield (Mansfield) **164**:254, 259-61, 264-66, 282, 341
"Stories of Love and Loneliness" (Calvino) **183**:224
Stories of Love, Madness, and Death (Quiroga)
See *Cuentos de amor, de locura, y de muerte*
Stories of Michael Robartes and His Friends (Yeats) **93**:340
Stories of Red Hanrahan (Yeats) **116**:340
The Stories of Seán O'Faoláin (O'Faolain)
See *Finest Short Stories of Seán O'Faoláin*
Stories of Sinebriukhov (Zoshchenko)
See *The Tales by Nazar Ilyich Sinebriukhov*
Stories of Three Decades (Mann)
See *Fiorenza*
"Stories Told by an Artist in New York" (Crane) **11**:142
Stories Toto Told Me (Rolfe) **12**:272, 274, 283
"The Storm" (Chopin) **5**:153, 158; **14**:62, 64-5, 69, 80-2; **127**:9-10, 79, 128, 211-12
"The Storm" (Crowley) **7**:208
"Storm" (Hodgson) **13**:230
"Storm" (Rilke)
See "Sturm"
"The Storm" (Södergran)
See "Stormen"
Storm (Babits)
See *Vihar*
The Storm (Drinkwater) **57**:28, 139, 147
"The Storm Cloud of the Nineteenth Century" (Ruskin) **63**:301
"The Storm Cone" (Kipling) **8**:191
Storm Days (Bergelson) **81**:19
"Storm Ending" (Toomer) **172**:258, 273
"A Storm of Angels" (Sarton) **120**:293
"Storm of Love" (Aleixandre) **113**:24
"Storm on the Heath" (Coppard) **5**:179
Storm Operation (Anderson) **144**:39, 42
Stormbeaten (Buchanan) **107**:31, 83
Storm-Brother Socrates (Sudermann)
See *Der Sturmgeselle Sokrates*
"Stormen" (Södergran) **31**:288, 291, 295
"Storming John" (Williams) **89**:385
A Stormy Night (Caragiale)
See *O noapte furtunoasă*
Stormy Waters (Buchanan) **107**:87
Stormy Weather (Strindberg) **8**:415
Le stornello (Pascoli) **45**:154
"Storona nenašinskaja" (Pilnyak) **23**:212
"The Story" (Andrić)
See "Priča"
"A Story" (Andrić)
See "Priča"
"A Story" (Jarrell) **177**:172, 174, 176-77, 213-14
"A Story" (Thomas) **8**:455; **105**:356
A Story about Death (Aldanov) **23**:23
"A Story about How a Certain Russian Citizen Went to Europe to Get Young" (Zoshchenko)
See "Rasskaz o tom, kak odin Russkii grazhdanin poekhal v Evropu omalazhivat'sya"
"Story about Kubac" (Reed) **9**:389
"The Story about the Anteater" (Benét) **7**:75
"A Story about the Most Important Thing" (Zamyatin)
See "Rasskaz o samom glavnom"
"A Story About the Rich" (Bergelson) **81**:20
"The Story about What Matters Most" (Zamyatin)
See "Rasskaz o samom glavnom"
The Story and the Fable: An Autobiography (Muir) **2**:483, 489; **87**:154, 170, 181, 201, 242-44, 247-50, 271-74, 281, 284, 286-89, 294-96, 299-300
"The Story behind A Lantern in Her Hand" (Aldrich) **125**:11
The Story Brought by Brigit (Gregory) **1**:334; **176**:34, 38, 40, 69, 72
"Story Coldly Told" (Benson) **17**:33
Story Collection (Tagore)
See *Galpa Guccha*
"A Story for the Betrothed" (Quiroga)
See "Cuento para novios"
Story from Chikamatsu (Mizoguchi)
See *Chikamatsu Monogatari*
"The Story Germ" (Aldrich) **125**:4, 11
The Story Girl (Montgomery) **51**:177-78, 199, 213; **140**:291, 319
"A Story in an Almost Classical Mode" (Brodkey) **123**:197
"The Story of a Book" (Middleton) **56**:174, 176
"The Story of a Conscience" (Bierce) **44**:44-5
"The Story of a Disappearance and an Appearance" (James) **6**:212-13, 216
"Story of a Farmer" (Day) **25**:131
"Story of a Few Plain Women" (Davis) **6**:154
The Story of a Great Love (Glaspell)
See *The Glory of the Conquered: The Story of a Great Love*
"The Story of a Horse" (Babel)
See "Istoriia odnoi loshadi"
"The Story of a Horse, Continued" (Babel) **171**:20, 72-73, 84
"The Story of a Little Gray Rabbit" (Seton)
See "Raggylug, the Story of a Cottontail"
"The Story of a Mouse" (Babel)
See "Istoriia moei golubiatni"
The Story of a New Zealand River (Mander) **31**:147-48, 150-53, 155-60, 162-63
The Story of a Novel (Wolfe) **4**:509, 519, 526-28; **13**:479, 491, 495-96; **61**:295, 309, 312, 314
The Story of a Novel: The Genesis of Doctor Faustus (Mann)
See *Die Entstehung des Doktor Faustus*
"The Story of a Piebald Horse" (Hudson) **29**:154
The Story of a Play (Howells) **7**:376; **17**:184-85
"The Story of a Poker Steer" (Adams) **56**:5
The Story of a Troubled Courtship (Quiroga)
See *Historia de un amor turbio*
The Story of a Wonder Man: Being the Autobiography of Ring Lardner (Lardner) **2**:328, 333; **14**:307
"The Story of Aibhric" (Tynan) **3**:503-04
The Story of American Literature (Lewisohn)
See *Expression in America*
The Story of an African Farm (Schreiner) **9**:393-405, 407
"The Story of an Hour" (Chopin) **14**:60, 70; **127**:128, 233, 236

"The Story of an Unknown Man" (Chekhov) **163**:79
"The Story of an Unknown Person" (Chekhov) **3**:152
"The Story of Arkansas" (Fletcher) **35**:106, 110-12
The Story of Avis (Phelps) **113**:335, 338-40, 352, 355-56, 358, 360-61, 363-66, 379, 383, 385-87, 394-99, 401-06
The Story of Bessie Costrell (Ward) **55**:411, 413, 422
The Story of Dorothy Stanfield (Micheaux) **76**:240, 269
"The Story of Ginger Cubes" (Morley) **87**:123
The Story of Gösta Berling (Lagerloef)
See *Gösta Berling's saga*
"The Story of Hair" (Lu Hsun) **3**:301, 303
"A Story of Halland" (Lagerloef) **36**:242
"The Story of Howling Wolf" (Garland) **3**:200
The Story of Ireland (O'Faolain) **143**:230, 236, 265
The Story of Ireland (O'Grady) **5**:354
The Story of Ivy (Lowndes) **12**:203
"The Story of Jees Uck" (London) **9**:277
The Story of Jurgis: A Sequel to The Jungle (Sinclair) **160**:250
The Story of King Arthur and His Knights (Pyle) **81**:385,398,400-3
"A Story of Land and Sea" (Dunsany) **2**:137; **59**:21
"The Story of Mahlon" (Caldwell) **117**:21
"The Story of Mimi-Nashi-Hōïchi" (Hearn) **9**:131
"The Story of Muhammad Din" (Kipling) **8**:185, 207; **17**:207
Story of My Childhood (Gladkov) **27**:93
"The Story of My Dovecot" (Babel)
See "Istoriia moei golubiatni"
The Story of My Life (Darrow) **81**:64
The Story of My Life (Moricz)
See *Életem regénye*
The Story of My Life (Steiner)
See *Mein Lebensgang*
The Story of My Life and Work (Washington) **10**:533, 538, 541-43
The Story of New York (Roosevelt) **69**:176
Story of O (Engel) **137**:133
"The Story of Pumpkin Pie" (Montgomery) **51**:200
The Story of Sonny Sahib (Duncan) **60**:193, 207
"The Story of St. Vespaluus" (Saki) **3**:372
"A Story of Stories" (Dreiser) **35**:70, 74
The Story of the 1002nd Night (Roth)
See *Die Geschichte von der 1002. Nacht*
"The Story of the Alcázar" (Foote) **108**:8, 17
"The Story of the Bad Little Boy that Didn't Come to Grief" (Twain) **36**:401; **59**:161-2
A Story of the Days to Come (Wells) **12**:488; **19**:428-31, 437
"Story of the Dress" (Drummond de Andrade) **139**:237
"The Story of the Dry Leaves" (Remington) **89**:301
Story of the Eye (Bataille)
See *Histoire de l'oeil*
"The Story of the First Lighthouse, or How Pincus Quagmire Brought Home the Beacon" (Allen) **87**:65
The Story of the Gadsbys (Kipling) **8**:176
"The Story of the Good Little Boy Who Didn't Prosper" (Twain) **59**:161
The Story of the Heart (Aleixandre)
See *Historia del corazón*
The Story of the Last Chrysanthemums (Mizoguchi)
See *Zangiku Monogatari*
The Story of the Late Chrysanthemums (Mizoguchi)
See *Zangiku Monogatari*
"The Story of the Little Bighorn: Told from the Indian Standpoint by One of Their Race" (Eastman) **55**:163
"The Story of the Lost Special" (Doyle) **7**:216, 238
The Story of the Malakand Field Force (Churchill) **113**:111, 142-43, 147
"The Story of the Nice Old Man" (Svevo)
See "La novella del buon vecchio e della bella fanciulla"
"The Story of the Oracle" (Lawson) **27**:150
"The Story of the Satraps" (Cabell) **6**:67
"The Story of the St. Bartholomew" (Sabatini) **47**:300
"A Story of the Stone Age" (Wells) **12**:488
"The Story of the Tenson" (Cabell) **6**:67
"Story of the Vizier's Elephant" (Andrić)
See "Priča o vezirovom slonu"
"Story of the Warrior and the Captive" (Borges)
See "Historia del guerrero y de la cautiva"
The Story of Wan and the Remarkable Shrub, and The Story of Ching-Kwei and the Destinies (Bramah) **72**:9
"Story of Yesterday" (Tolstoy)
See "Istoriya veherashnego dnya"
The Story of Yone Noguchi Told by Himself (Noguchi) **80**:368
"The Story of Yonosuke" (Akutagawa Ryūnosuke)
See "Yonosuke no hanashi"
"The Story of Yung Chang, Narrated by Kai Lung, in the Open Space Before the Tea-Shop of Celestial Principles, at Wu Whei" (Bramah) **72**:11
A Story Teller's Story (Anderson) **1**:38-9, 50, 54, 62; **10**:34-6, 38, 41-2; **24**:44, 50; **123**:6-7, 21, 50, 87, 108-9, 114
"Story Tellin' Time" (Childress) **116**:36
"A Story without a Title" (Chekhov)
See "An Anonymous Story"
"Story without Cause, but Weary" (Quiroga)
See "Cuento sin razón, pero cansado"
"The Storyteller" (Benjamin) **39**:25, 53
A Story-Teller's Holiday (Moore) **7**:482, 492-94, 497-98
A Storyteller's Pack (Stockton) **47**:326
"De Stove Pipe Hole" (Drummond) **25**:142
"The Stove That Wasn't Real" (Söderberg) **39**:438
La strada che va in città (Ginzburg) **156**:15, 17, 38, 42, 44, 59, 63-64, 74, 105, 112
"La strada di San Giovanni" (Calvino) **183**:129
La strada di San Giovanni (Calvino) **183**:5
Stradella (Crawford) **10**:148
"Strafe" (Gurney) **33**:86
Straight is the Gate (Gide)
See *La porte étroite*
"A Straight Talk" (Beerbohm) **24**:105
Strait Is the Gate (Gide)
See *La porte étroite*
Straits of Love and Hate (Mizoguchi) **72**:314, 324-25
"The Stranded Ship" (Roberts) **8**:321
Strandkinder (Sudermann) **15**:427
"The Strange Adventures of the King's Head" (Baum) **7**:14
The Strange Attraction (Mander) **31**:150, 153, 162
"The Strange Burial of Sue" (McKay) **41**:329-30
The Strange Case of Annie Spragg (Bromfield) **11**:76-7, 81, 85, 87
"Strange Comfort Afforded by the Profession" (Lowry) **6**:239-41, 254
The Strange Countess (Wallace) **57**:401
A Strange Disappearance (Green) **63**:136, 148, 151
"The Strange Elizabethans" (Woolf) **43**:425
Strange Fish (Dent) **72**:26
"The Strange Friend" (Hawthorne) **25**:247, 249
Strange Fugitive (Callaghan) **145**:240-43, 245, 254
Strange Glory (Myers) **59**:131-2, 137, 141-2, 150
"Strange Hells" (Gurney) **33**:87, 92, 98, 100
"The Strange High House in the Mist" (Lovecraft) **4**:266, 272
Strange Holiness (Coffin) **95**:3, 19
"The Strange House (Max Gate, A.D. 2000)" (Hardy) **53**:114
Strange Interlude (O'Neill) **1**:383, 385-86, 389, 392, 395-97, 399-401, 403, 406; **6**:327-29, 331, 335; **49**:255, 272, 295
Strange Journey (Drieu la Rochelle)
See *Drôle de voyage*
"The Strange Land" (Lagerkvist) **144**:223, 238
A Strange Marriage (Mikszath)
See *Különös házasság*
"Strange Meeting" (Owen) **5**:358-62, 364-68, 370, 372-75; **27**:201-04, 208-12, 214, 222-23, 226-28, 231-32, 238
"Strange Metamorphosis of Poets" (Nemerov) **124**:258
"The Strange Return" (Muir) **87**:232
"The Strange Ride of Morrowbie Jukes" (Kipling) **8**:176, 183, 207
The Strange Schemes of Randolph Mason (Post) **39**:337, 339-40, 343, 345
"Strange Service" (Gurney) **33**:101, 105
"A Strange Song" (Wylie) **8**:538
"Strange Tree" (Roberts) **68**:336
Strange True Stories of Louisiana (Cable) **4**:31
Strange Victory (Teasdale) **4**:427-31
The Strange Woman (Williams) **89**:361, 367-8, 380, 389, 402
Strange World (Braddon) **111**:227, 229
"The Stranger" (Bierce) **44**:45
"The Stranger" (Coffin) **95**:18
"A Stranger" (Johnson) **19**:256
"The Stranger" (Mansfield) **8**:280, 282, 284; **39**:303-04; **164**:295, 297, 301, 311, 315-16, 339
"A Stranger" (Undset) **3**:516
The Stranger (Blok)
See *Neznakomka*
The Stranger (Faust) **49**:39
The Stranger (Weiss)
See *Der Fremde*
Strangers (Cankar)
See *Tujci*
"Strangers and Pilgrims" (de la Mare) **53**:26-7, 38
Strangers and Pilgrims (Braddon) **111**:215
Strangers and Wayfarers (Jewett) **22**:129
"Strasbourg-configuration" (Arp) **115**:22
"Die Strasse" (Broch) **20**:57
Strathmore (Ouida) **43**:347-48, 350, 353, 371, 375
A Stratified Democracy (Webb and Webb) **22**:430-31
"Strato in Plaster" (Merrill) **173**:169
"Stravinsky's Three Pieces "Grotesques", for String Quartet" (Lowell) **8**:230
The Straw (O'Neill) **1**:384-85, 402; **49**:248, 252
Straw Dogs (Drieu la Rochelle)
See *Les chiens de paille*
"The Straw Man" (Post) **39**:338-39
"The Strawberry Shrub" (Millay) **169**:251
Straws and Prayer-Books (Cabell) **6**:76
"The Strawstack" (Knister) **56**:155, 162-63
Stray Leaves from Strange Literature (Hearn) **9**:118, 122, 131, 134, 137-38
"Stray Notes While Lying on My Back" (Masaoka) **18**:225, 227-28
"Strayed Crab" (Bishop) **121**:6, 63
Strayers from Sheol (Wakefield) **120**:342, 344, 350, 352, 355
"The Stream of Life" (Kuprin) **5**:297
Streamlines (Morley) **87**:138
"The Streams" (Coppard) **5**:179
"Streams of Water in the South" (Buchan) **41**:72-3
"The Stream's Song" (Abercrombie) **141**:23
Streber (Dagerman) **17**:88-9, 95
"The Street" (Guro)
See "Ulitsa"

"The Street" (Lovecraft) **4**:272
"The Street" (Mayakovski) **18**:246
"A Street" (Morrison) **72**:361, 372-73, 386
"The Street" (Stephens) **4**:410
"Street" (Storni)
See "Calle"
The Street (Petry) **112**:290, 292, 297, 302-05, 311, 313-15, 317-19, 322-23, 325-28, 331-33, 339-44, 356, 359, 367-68, 371-72, 374-89, 391-92
"The Street Called Crooked" (Cullen) **37**:167
"Street Cries" (Naidu) **80**:276, 316
"Street Demonstration" (Walker) **129**:306
"Street Lamps" (Galsworthy) **45**:34
"The Street of Crocodiles" (Schulz) **51**:308
The Street of Crocodiles (Schulz)
See *Sklepy cynamonowe*
"The Street of Our Lady of the Fields" (Chambers) **41**:94
"The Street of the Dumb" (García Lorca)
See "La calle de los mudos"
"The Street of the First Shell" (Chambers) **41**:88, 94
"The Street of the Four Winds" (Chambers) **41**:88, 94, 104
The Street of the Seven Stars (Rinehart) **52**:283-84, 295
"Street off Sunset" (Jarrell) **177**:146, 176, 180-81
"Street Signs" (Baroja)
See "Epigrafía callejera"
"The Streetcar Gone Astray" (Gumilev)
See "Zabludivshijsja tramvaj"
"Streetcorner Man" (Borges)
See "El Hombre de la esquina rosada"
"Streets" (Borges)
See "Las Calles"
Streitbares Leben (Brod) **115**:92
"Streiter" (Lasker-Schueler) **57**:330, 334
"The Strength of Fields" (Dickey) **151**:147, 170
The Strength of Fields (Dickey) **151**:125, 127, 143, 147
"The Strength of Gideon" (Dunbar) **2**:128; **12**:123
The Strength of Gideon and Other Stories (Dunbar) **2**:130; **12**:107-09, 111, 119-20, 122-23
"The Strength of God" (Anderson) **1**:59; **24**:17, 21, 24-5, 34, 39, 47, 52, 58; **123**:83-5, 104
"The Strength of the Strong" (London) **15**:270-71
The Strenuous Life (Roosevelt) **69**:181, 191
"Strictly Business" (Himes) **139**:247
Strictly Dishonorable (Sturges) **48**:283-84, 290, 310-12, 316-17
Strife (Galsworthy) **1**:301-03, 305; **45**:30-1, 33, 41, 51-3, 55
Strike (Eisenstein)
See *Stachka*
The Strike at Arlingford (Moore) **7**:476, 498
"Striken" (Jozsef) **22**:161
A String of Light (Herbert)
See *Struna swiala*
"The Strip" (Adams) **56**:6
"The Striver" (Toller)
See "Der Ringende"
"Strogii iunosha" (Olesha) **136**:155
Strogii iunosha (Olesha) **136**:63, 66, 74, 79, 107, 111, 113, 181, 183-88, 190
"A Stroke of Good Fortune" (O'Connor) **132**:229, 356
Stroke of Luck (Bennett) **197**:20
The Strolling Saint (Sabatini) **47**:303
Stroncature (Papini) **22**:288
The Strong Box (Sternheim)
See *Die Kassette*
"A Strong Ending" (Bergelson) **81**:19
Strong Hearts (Cable) **4**:31
"Strong Hyacinths" (Södergran)
See "Starka hyacinter"
"Strong Meat" (Sayers) **15**:387
Strong Opinions (Nabokov) **108**:65, 87-89, 104, 160-61, 167, 199-201, 224-25, 230; **189**:144, 148, 179, 183
Strong Poison (Sayers) **2**:531, 536; **15**:371, 377, 379-80, 390-92, 394
"The Strong Thing" (Gurney) **33**:86
Strong Wind (Asturias)
See *Viento fuerte*
The Stronger (Giacosa)
See *Il più forte*
The Stronger (Strindberg)
See *Den Starkare*
Structural Functions of Harmony (Schoenberg) **75**:296
"Structural Units" (Hartmann) **73**:149
La Structure du comportement (Merleau-Ponty) **156**:133, 158, 185, 191, 216, 257, 262-63, 265
"La structure fine des centres nerveux" (Ramoacn y Cajal) **93**:141, 148-49, 163
"The Structure of Neurosis" (Adler) **61**:34
"The Structure of the Epic Work" (Döblin) **13**:167
The Structure of the Novel (Muir) **2**:483; **87**:163
"The Structures and Connections of Nerve Cells" (Ramoacn y Cajal)
See "La structure fine des centres nerveux"
The Struggle (Griffith) **68**:153, 168-70
The Struggle for Berlin (Goebbels) **68**:88, 92
A Struggle for Fame (Riddell) **40**:331-32
The Struggle for God (Andreas-Salome)
See *Im Kampf um Gott*
The Struggle for Life (Baroja)
See *La lucha por la vida*
The Struggle for Self-Government (Steffens) **20**:335, 345, 352, 361
The Struggle for the Spanish Soul (Barea) **14**:45
"The Struggle Staggers Us" (Walker) **129**:307, 323, 334
Struggle till Dawn (Betti)
See *Lotta fino all'alba*
Struggle with the Angel (Giraudoux)
See *Combat avec l'ange*
Struggling for God (Andreas-Salome)
See *Im Kampf um Gott*
Struggling Spirit (Lagerkvist)
See *Kämpande ande*
The Strumpet Sea (Williams) **89**:389
Struna swiala (Herbert) **168**:38, 42
"Les stryges" (Schwob) **20**:320
"The Stubborn One" (Balmont)
See "Upriamets"
The Stubborn Structure (Frye) **165**:144, 146, 149, 154, 156, 158, 228
"Ein Stück aus dem Fernen Westen" (Zuckmayer) **191**:300
Ein Stückchen Theologie (Hesse) **148**:164
"The Student" (Chekhov) **3**:168; **10**:115
Student Comrades (Dazai Osamu) **11**:181
"Student Dies in 100 Yard Dash" (Nemerov) **124**:277
"Student Life" (Benjamin) **39**:57
"Student of Divinity" (Bosman)
See "Divinity Student"
"The Student's Room" (Rostand) **6**:381
Studie über die Minderwertigkeit von Organen (Adler) **61**:5, 14, 17, 23
Studies in a Dying Colonialism (Fanon) **188**:139
Studies in Black and White (Kipling) **8**:176
Studies in Classic American Literature (Lawrence) **2**:344, 348-49, 351, 373; **9**:217; **93**:113
"Studies in Extravagance" (Galsworthy) **45**:33
Studies in Hegelian Cosmology (McTaggart) **105**:173-74, 197, 201
Studies in Life and Letters (Woodberry) **73**:377
Studies in Literature (Quiller-Couch) **53**:293, 296, 298
Studies in Logical Theory (Dewey) **95**:27-9, 43
Studies in Love and Terror (Lowndes) **12**:201
Studies in Philosophy, Politics, and Economics (Hayek) **109**:202, 206-07, 214
Studies in Platonic Political Philosophy (Strauss) **141**:289
Studies in Prose and Verse (Symons) **11**:441
Studies in Seven Arts (Symons) **11**:442
Studies in the Lankavatara Sutra (Suzuki) **109**:387
Studies in the Psychology of Sex (Ellis) **14**:105-06, 110, 112-118, 120, 123, 127, 129, 132, 140
Studies in the Psychology of Sex, Vol. I: The Evolution of Modesty, the Phenomena of Sexual Periodity, Auto-Erotism (Ellis) **14**:102-03, 122, 125, 136-37
Studies in the Psychology of Sex, Vol. II: Sexual Inversion (Ellis) **14**:122, 125-26, 135-36, 142-43
Studies in the Psychology of Sex, Vol. III: The Analysis of the Sexual Impulse, Love, and Pain, the Sexual Impulse in Women (Ellis) **14**:125
Studies in the Psychology of Sex, Vol. IV: Sexual Selection in Man; Touch, Smell, Hearing, Vision (Ellis) **14**:125, 136-37
Studies in the Psychology of Sex, Vol. V: The Mechanism of Detumescence, the Psychic State of Pregnancy (Ellis) **14**:126, 131
Studies in the Psychology of Sex, Vol. VI: Sex in Relation to Society (Ellis) **14**:126, 138, 141
Studies in the Psychology of Sex, Vol. VII: Eonism, and Other Supplementary Studies (Ellis) **14**:126-27
Studies in the Sierra (Muir) **28**:249, 252
Studies in Wives (Lowndes) **12**:200-01
Studies in Zen (Suzuki) **109**:375
Studies of a Biographer (Stephen) **23**:306-07, 312-13, 317, 329, 338, 340-41, 346
Studies of a Litterateur (Woodberry) **73**:365
Studies of the Eighteenth Century in Italy (Lee) **5**:309, 313-14, 319
Studies of the Stage (Matthews) **95**:225, 228, 246
Studies, Specimens &c. (Hardy) **143**:157
Studium przedmiotu (Herbert) **168**:38, 47, 62
Study Abroad (Endo)
See *Ryugaku*
Study for Painting with White Form (Kandinsky) **92**:38
"A Study in Professional Frustration" (Benchley) **1**:79
A Study in Scarlet (Doyle) **7**:216, 219-20, 228, 231, 233-38
A Study in Temperament (Firbank) **1**:230
A Study of British Genius (Ellis) **14**:111, 114, 116
"Study of Death" (Sikelianos) **39**:419
Study of English Romanticism (Frye) **165**:235, 243, 260
The Study of Ethics: A Syllabus (Dewey) **95**:59, 94
"The Study of Fiction" (Matthews) **95**:251, 264
"The Study of Geography" (Boas) **56**:66, 94, 99, 105
"Study of Images II" (Stevens) **12**:383
Study of Organ Inferiority and Its Psychical Compensation (Adler)
See *Studie über die Minderwertigkeit von Organen*
"Study of Politics" (Laski) **79**:91
The Study of Public Administration (Wilson) **79**:517, 519-20, 522
"A Study of Romeo" (Chapman) **7**:185
Study of Shakespeare (Swinburne) **8**:441
A Study of the Good (Nishida)
See *Zen no kenkyu*
The Study of the Object (Herbert)
See *Studium przedmiotu*
Study of the Object (Herbert)
See *Studium przedmiotu*
"A Study of Thomas Hardy" (Lawrence) **93**:107, 111

Study of Thomas Hardy (Lawrence) **16**:302, 305; **48**:117; **61**:218-9, 234, 254
"Study of Two Pears" (Stevens) **12**:360; **45**:283, 334
Stufen (Morgenstern) **8**:310, 311
Stufen der Menschwerdung (Hesse) **148**:164
Stuffcake (Raabe)
See *Stopfkuchen*
"Stumble between Two Stars" (Vallejo)
See "Traspié entre dos estrellas"
"Stumm" (Schwitters) **95**:320
Der stumme Prophet (Roth) **33**:334-35, 337
Das Stundenbuch (Rilke) **1**:409-10, 416, 418, 422; **6**:357-59, 361, 364-66; **19**:303, 305, 307-09; **195**:175, 178-81, 183-84, 186, 252, 263, 282-84, 292, 320, 326, 339
"Stundenhexe" (Barlach) **48**:124
The Stupid Swede (Heidenstam) **5**:251-52
"Sturm" (Rilke) **195**:182-83
Sturm im Wasserglas (Frank) **81**:102
Der Sturmgeselle Sokrates (Sudermann) **15**:421-23, 427
"Style" (Nemerov) **124**:155, 310
"Style" (Quiller-Couch) **53**:293
Style and Idea: Selected Writings of Arnold Schoenberg (Schoenberg) **75**:296, 323-24, 378, 393
"Le Style Eléphant contre le Style Bidet" (Arp) **115**:29
Stylistic Aspects of Primitive Culture (Boas) **56**:80
The Stylus (Hartmann) **73**:149
Styrbiorn the Strong (Eddison) **15**:52, 59
"Styx" (Heym) **9**:146
Styx (Lasker-Schueler) **57**:297, 302-3, 326, 328-30, 336
"Su majestad la lengua española" (Unamuno) **148**:324
"Su sitio fiel" (Jiménez) **183**:259, 290, 292
Su único hijo (Alas) **29**:2-3, 13-14, 16-17
"Sub ilice" (Gogarty) **15**:109
"Subhā" (Tagore) **3**:485
"Subject and Treatment" (Hartmann) **73**:148
A Subject of Scandal and Concern (Osborne) **153**:270, 307, 310-12, 320, 324
"A Subject of Sea Change" (Bishop) **103**:3, 22, 28
"Subjective Culture" (Simmel) **64**:360
"The Subjective Necessity for Social Settlements" (Addams) **76**:53, 92, 96
Sublimated Sensuality (Baroja)
See *La sensualidad pervertida*
"Sublimation" (Percy) **84**:213
"The Sublime and the Beautiful Revisited" (Murdoch) **171**:237-39, 315
Lo sublime en lo vulgar (Echegaray) **4**:101
"Le Sublime et l'avant-garde" (Lyotard) **103**:264
"Sublunary" (Murry) **16**:354
"Submarine" (Benson) **17**:33
"The Submarine Bed" (Bishop) **103**:4-5
The Submarine Mystery (Dent) **72**:20
"Submerged Swimmer" (García Lorca) **197**:230
"A Sub-Note of Interrogation: What Will Be Our Religion in 1999?" (Nightingale) **85**:295, 300
"Subsidiary Notes as to the Introducation of Female Nursing into Military Hospitals" (Nightingale) **85**:254
"The Substance" (Herbert) **168**:46
Substance and Function (Cassirer)
See *Substanzbegriff und Funktionsbegriff*
The Substance of Gothic: Six Lectures on the Development of Architecture from Charlemagne to Henry the VIII (Cram) **45**:20-1
Substanzbegriff und Funktionsbegriff (Cassirer) **61**:30, 73-4, 76, 80, 107-8
"The Substitute" (Coppee) **25**:121
"A Substitute for the Alps" (Stephen) **23**:326
The Subterraneans (Kerouac) **117**:183-85, 212, 216, 218-22, 229, 232-34, 238, 241-44, 248, 251-52, 254, 256, 259, 263-64, 267
Subtle Secret (Ivanov) **33**:136-37
"Suburb" (Borges)
See "Arrabal"
"The Suburb" (Heym)
See "Die Vorstadt"
"Suburban" (Güiraldes)
See "Arrabalera"
"Suburban Prophecy" (Nemerov) **124**:180, 182
Suburban Sketches (Howells) **7**:377, 391
"Subway poem" (Schwitters) **95**:351-2
Le succès et l'idée de beauté (Gourmont) **17**:152
"Success" (Brooke) **2**:59
"Success" (Graham) **19**:104, 109, 112, 116, 120, 135
Success (Feuchtwanger)
See *Erfolg: Drei jahre Geschichte einer Provinz*
Success (Milne) **6**:307, 310
"The Successful Author" (Dobson) **79**:3
"Succession" (Nemerov) **124**:163
Successors of Mary the First (Phelps) **113**:337-38
"Succubus" (Crowley) **7**:208
"Such a Pretty Little Picture" (Parker) **143**:314-15, 331
Such as They Are: Poems (Higginson) **36**:180
"Such Is Life" (Pirandello) **4**:342
Such Is Life (Furphy) **25**:161-67, 169-79, 181-84
Such Is My Beloved (Callaghan) **145**:210, 214, 216-18, 248-49, 254
"Such Men Are Dangerous" (Glyn) **72**:142
"Such, Such Were the Joys" (Orwell) **51**:261-62; **129**:223, 246
Such, Such Were the Joys (Orwell) **2**:504; **6**:350-51, 354; **15**:307-08, 331, 361-62; **31**:186; **51**:223, 225-26; **128**:254, 260, 290
"Le Sud" (Borges) **109**:112
Le Sud (Borges) **109**:7
"Sud Bozhii" (Remizov) **27**:341, 347-48
"The Sudden Walk" (Kafka) **112**:38; **179**:307
"Sudny den" (Korolenko) **22**:176
"Sueño" (Villaurrutia) **80**:477
Sueño de una noche de agosto (Martinez Sierra and Martinez Sierra) **6**:278, 281
"Un sueño realizado" (Onetti) **131**:264, 283-84, 288
Un sueño realizado y otros cuentos (Onetti) **131**:133
Sueños de la mala muerte (Donoso) **133**:82
"Los sueños dialogados" (Machado) **3**:311
La suerte (Pardo Bazán) **189**:198
"The Sufferings and Greatness of Richard Wagner" (Mann) **60**:359; **168**:117
"Sufferings of a Small Person" (Harte) **25**:218
"The Sufficient Place" (Muir) **87**:210, 367
"Sugako no tetsugakuteki kisozuke" (Nishida) **83**:215, 252-4
"The Sugawn Chair" (O'Faolain) **143**:260, 263
"Suggested by the Cover of a Volume of Keats's Poems" (Lowell) **1**:372
"Suggestion" (Leverson) **18**:202
"Eine Suggestion" (Meyrink) **21**:221
"A Suggestion on the Negro Problem" (Gilman) **117**:135-36, 138, 163, 172
Suggestions for Thought to Searchers after Religious Truth (Nightingale) **85**:216, 220, 234-7, 240, 253, 268-9, 272, 278-88, 303
Suggestions on a System of Nursing for Hospitals in India (Nightingale) **85**:258
"Suggestions toward a Theory of the Philosophical Disciplines" (Mead) **89**:166
Suggestiosn on the Subject of Providing, Training, and Organizing Nurses for the Sick Poor in Workhouse Infirmaries (Nightingale) **85**:258
"Suginohara shina" (Mori Ogai) **14**:378, 380
"Sugroby" (Tsvetaeva) **35**:411
El suicida (Reyes) **33**:322-23
"Suicide" (Lasker-Schueler) **57**:328
"The Suicide" (Millay) **4**:306
Suicide (Aldanov) **23**:23-4
The Suicide (Reyes)
See *El suicida*
Suicide: A Study in Sociology (Durkheim)
See *Le suicide: étude de sociologie*
"Suicide and the State" (Middleton) **56**:179
"Suicide Chant" (Cullen) **4**:45; **37**:160, 165-66
Le suicide: étude de sociologie (Durkheim) **55**:91, 100-01, 106-07, 109, 115, 120, 136, 142, 150, 158
"Suicide in Alexandria" (García Lorca)
See "Suicidio en Alejandría"
"The Suicide's Burial" (Gilman) **117**:148
"Suicidio" (Aleixandre) **113**:8
"Suicidio en Alejandría" (García Lorca) **49**:122; **197**:230, 236
"Suicidio hacia arriba" (Salinas) **17**:362-63
Suineser Elegien (Rilke) **195**:327
Suisaigaka (Shimazaki Toson) **5**:431
The Suit of Armor (Heijermans) **24**:293
"The Suitable Surroundings" (Bierce) **7**:98; **44**:44-5
"Suite de los espejos" (García Lorca) **49**:119-20
"La suite de los espejos" (García Lorca) **181**:65
"Suite del insomnio" (Villaurrutia) **80**:477-8
Suite familière (Fargue) **11**:194, 200
Suites (García Lorca) **181**:63-65, 69
"Sui-tsan chi" (Su Man-shu) **24**:458, 460
"Un sujeto ilógico" (Lugones) **15**:293
Sukhodol (Bunin) **6**:45-6, 50-1, 55
"Sukienka balowa" (Prus) **48**:176
Sukyandaru (Endo) **152**:167, 170-71, 185, 189, 191, 193, 199, 202, 213, 217, 234, 240
"Sul far del giorno" (Calvino) **183**:12
"Sul tappeto di foglie illuminate dalla luna" (Calvino) **183**:16-17, 21
"Sul tavolo" (Saba) **33**:374
Sulamif (Kuprin) **5**:297, 304
"Sulamith" (Lasker-Schueler) **57**:303, 326
Sulamith (Kuprin)
See *Sulamif*
"Sulla concezione materialistica della storia" (Croce) **37**:120
Sulla teorica dei governi e sul governo parlamentare (Mosca) **75**:130, 132, 137-38, 150, 153-54, 160, 162-63, 165, 170-71, 180-81, 184
"Sulle montagne" (Campana) **20**:83
The Sullivan County Sketches of Stephen Crane (Crane) **11**:140, 159, 163-64; **17**:68; **32**:158-59, 163-65
Sullivan's Travel (Sturges) **48**:270-75, 279, 283-85, 287-88, 290-91, 294-303, 309, 313, 315-17, 319-20, 322-23
Sulocanā (Devkota) **23**:48-51
Sult (Hamsun) **2**:202-08; **14**:221-22, 232-33, 235-39, 242-43, 246-48, 251; **49**:127-28, 131-33,135, 137, 141, 145, 147, 153, 155-59, 161-63, 168; **151**:228-91
"Sum in Addition" (March) **96**:252
"Sumaššedšij" (Bryusov) **10**:93
"Sumerki" (Khodasevich) **15**:207
Sumerki dukha (Hippius) **9**:161
The Sumida River (Nagai)
See *Sumidagawa*
"Sumidagawa" (Nagai) **51**:89
Sumidagawa (Nagai) **51**:86, 88, 92-3, 104
Summaries and Perspectives (Trotsky) **22**:364
"Summary" (Sarton) **120**:300
Summary of Educational Theory (Gentile)
See *Sommario di pedagogia*
"Summer" (McAlmon) **97**:87-88, 99
"Summer" (Moore) **7**:487
"The Summer" (Trakl) **5**:461
Summer (Gorky) **8**:81-2
A Summer (Morgenstern)
See *Ein sommer*
Summer (Wharton) **3**:563-64, 572, 578, 580; **27**:383-84; **129**:345, 348, 362; **149**:168, 248

Summer, 1914 (Martin du Gard)
See *L'été, 1914*
"Summer Afternoon" (Milne) **88**:241
"Summer Airs" (Tynan) **3**:505
The Summer Cloud: Prose Poems (Noguchi) **80**:361
"Summer Evening: New York Subway Station" (Bodenheim) **44**:59, 74
Summer Folk (Gorky)
See *Dachniki*
Summer Grass (Shimazaki Toson)
See *Natsuksa*
"A Summer Holiday in the South" (Andrić) **135**:23, 44
"A Summer House at Public Expense" (Remizov)
See "Kazennaia dacha"
"A Summer in Austria" (Zuckmayer)
See "Ein Sommer in Österreich"
Summer in the Country—Not a Farce but a Tragedy (Chekhov)
See *Tragik ponevole*
"A Summer in the South" (Andrić)
See "A Summer Holiday in the South"
"Summer in the Town" (Pasternak) **188**:192
"Summer is Ended" (Roberts) **68**:304-35, 337
Summer Islands (Douglas) **68**:18
Summer Lightning (Wodehouse) **108**:378, 382, 387, 389
Summer Moonshine (Wodehouse) **108**:371-72
"A Summer Night" (Baker) **10**:18
"Summer Night" (Bowen) **148**:16
"Summer Night Piece" (Lowell) **8**:227
"The Summer of the Beautiful White Horse" (Saroyan) **137**:163-65
"Summer on the Coast of Normandy" (Moore) **7**:487
"Summer Past" (Gray) **19**:148, 151-52
"The Summer People" (Jackson) **187**:236, 247
"The Summer People" (Merrill) **173**:174, 228
"Summer Picture: The Cripple" (Prado)
See "Cuadro de estio: el invalido"
"A Summer Picture: The Invalid" (Prado)
See "Cuadro de estio: el invalido"
"Summer Rain" (Davidson) **24**:164
"Summer School of Philosophy" (Higginson) **36**:167
"Summer Season" (Khodasevich) **15**:209
"Summer Song" (Bialik) **25**:50
"A Summer Storm" (Scott) **6**:385, 393
Summer Storm, and Other Stories (Pavese) **3**:340
"Summer Will" (Burroughs) **121**:140
Summer Will Show (Warner) **131**:308, 316-18, 320, 323-26, 330-33, 335, 340, 342-43, 345-46, 362
"Summer Woods" (Naidu) **80**:306, 347
"Summer-Eros" (Papadiamantis) **29**:272-73
"Summer's Elegy" (Nemerov) **124**:186, 292
Summertime and Other Stories (Donoso)
See *Veraneo y otros cuentos*
"Summit and Decline" (Bataille) **155**:99, 102
"Summum Bonum" (Guiney) **41**:207, 221
Sump'n Like Wings (Riggs) **56**:203-4, 215-16
Sumuru (Rohmer) **28**:281
"Sun" (Dickey) **151**:97
"Sun" (Lawrence) **2**:356-57; **48**:121, 140; **93**:97
"The Sun" (Mayakovski) **18**:258
"The Sun" (Meynell) **6**:294, 296
"The Sun" (Trakl) **5**:461
The Sun Also Rises (Hemingway) **115**:123-24, 130, 134-35, 138, 143, 151, 156-57, 178-79, 184, 207
"Sun and Love" (Carducci)
See "Sol e amore"
"Sun and Moon" (Mansfield) **8**:275, 282; **39**:304; **164**:231, 233, 239, 249-50, 263-64, 266, 295, 297
Sun and Steel (Mishima)
See *Taiyo to tetsu*
"The Sun and the Rain" (Wolfe) **13**:492
The Sun Field (Broun) **104**:98
Sun Hunting (Roberts) **23**:238
The Sun in Heaven (Yokomitsu)
See *Nichirin*
The Sun in Splendour (Burke) **63**:127, 129-30
"Sun in the Stateroom" (Jiménez) **183**:334, 336-37
"The Sun Is Loosening her Light Blond Hair" (Lagerkvist)
See "Nu löser solen sitt blonda har"
"The Sun Is Setting" (Cankar) **105**:164
"Sun of Italy" (Babel)
See "Solntse Italii"
The Sun Virgin (Dixon) **163**:172
Suna no onna (Abe) **131**:3-7, 9-12, 14-15
Sundarī Projerpinā (Devkota) **23**:51
"Sunday" (Nemerov) **124**:179, 299
"Sunday" (Villaurrutia) **80**:477
"Sunday, 4 a.m." (Bishop) **121**:42
"Sunday at the End of Summer" (Nemerov) **124**:180, 185
"Sunday Morning" (Stevens) **3**:447-49, 451, 454-56, 459, 462, 468, 472, 474; **12**:362, 364, 367, 373, 376-77; **45**:269, 276-77, 281, 287, 299, 303, 306, 323, 328, 332, 340, 347
"Sunday Morning Apples" (Crane) **2**:119
"A Sunday Morning Tragedy" (Hardy) **143**:212
"Sunday: Outskirts of Knoxville, Tenn." (Agee) **180**:47
The Sundered Future (Canetti) **157**:69
"Sunderland" (Nemerov) **124**:284
"The Sundew" (Swinburne) **8**:441; **36**:296, 332
Die Sündflut (Barlach) **84**:68-72, 76
"The Sundial" (Dobson) **79**:23
The Sundial (Jackson) **187**:237-38, 241, 244, 257, 270, 273, 282-83, 299, 301-03, 305, 307-10
"Sundown Blues" (Handy) **97**:40, 82
Sundown Leflare (Remington) **89**:300, 303, 306-8, 311-12
"Sunflower and Poppy" (Moody) **105**:225
"Sunflower Sutra" (Ginsberg) **120**:88
Sun-Freedom (Ingamells) **35**:129, 134, 136
"The Sunglasses" (Nemerov) **124**:172
"Sunk" (Andrić) **135**:78
"Sunk" (Benchley) **55**:3
The Sunken Bell (Hauptmann)
See *Die versunkene Glocke*
"The Sunken Crown" (Robinson) **101**:158
Sunko bihāna (Devkota) **23**:52
"The Sunlanders" (London) **9**:274
The Sunlight Dialogues (Gardner) **195**:88, 94, 104-05
"The Sunlight Lay Across My Bed" (Schreiner) **9**:394, 396, 405
The Sunlight Sonata (Bridie) **3**:132, 135, 139
Sunny Hill (Bjoernson)
See *Synnøve Solbakken*
Sunny Hours (Martinez Sierra and Martinez Sierra)
See *Horas de sol*
Sunrise: A Story of Two Humans (Murnau) **53**:239-42, 243, 245-49, 254-55, 261-67, 269-70, 274-76, 278-81
"The Sunrise Side" (Williams) **89**:370
"The Sun's Farewell" (Leino)
See "Auringon hyvästijättö"
"Sunset" (Babel)
See "Zakat"
"Sunset" (Davidson) **24**:164
"Sunset" (Lovecraft) **4**:266
"Sunset" (Reese) **181**:346
"Sunset" (Talvik) **87**:320
Sunset (Babel)
See *Zakat*
"Sunset at Fòssoli" (Levi) **109**:300
Sunset Glow (Hamsun) **14**:221
Sunset Gun (Parker) **143**:320, 322-24
Sunset Land (Rhodes) **53**:310
"Sunset of Old Tales" (Sharp) **39**:377
"Sunset on the Spire" (Wylie) **8**:536
Sunset Song (Gibbon) **4**:120-23, 125-30
"Sunshine" (Lindsay) **17**:226
"Sunshine Rhymes" (Wen I-to) **28**:410-11
Sunshine Sketches of a Little Town (Leacock) **2**:378, 380-81
"The Sunstroke" (Bunin) **6**:45, 52, 55
Sunstroke (Pardo Bazán)
See "La insolación"
"Sun-Stroke" (Quiroga)
See "La insolación"
"Sunstroke" (Quiroga)
See "La insolación"
"Sunto di alcuni capitoli di un nuovo trattato di economia pura" (Pareto) **69**:137
Sunwise (Remizov)
See *Posolon*
"Super Flumina Babylonis" (Swinburne) **36**:318
Supercheria (Alas) **29**:22-3, 25-6
"Superfluous Advice" (Parker) **143**:323
"Superiority and Subordination" (Simmel) **64**:328, 355
The Supermale (Jarry)
See *Le surmâle, roman moderne*
"The Superman" (Orage) **157**:281
"A Supermarket in California" (Ginsberg) **120**:48, 54, 99
Supernatural Horror in Literature (Lovecraft) **4**:265-66, 269, 271-72; **22**:213-17, 223, 225
The Supernatural Omnibus (Summers) **16**:426, 434
"Supernatural Songs" (Yeats) **93**:400, 404
Supernatural Tales (Rohan)
See *Gendan*
"Super-Nature Versus Super-Real" (Lewis) **104**:172
Superseded (Sinclair) **3**:442; **11**:408-09
"La supersticiosa ética del lector" (Borges) **109**:148
Superstition Corner (Kaye-Smith) **20**:109
"The Superstition of Necessity" (Dewey) **95**:97
"Superstitions and Folk-lore of the South" (Chesnutt) **39**:70
"The Supper" (Reyes)
See "La cena"
"A Supper by Proxy" (Dunbar) **2**:133
Supplément au voyage au pays des Tarahumaras (Artaud) **36**:5-7
Supplement to the Voyage to the Land of the Tarahumaras (Artaud)
See *Supplément au voyage au pays des Tarahumaras*
"Supplementary Note" (Simmel) **64**:355
"Supplementary Section" (Bakhtin) **160**:152, 157
Les suppliants (Barbusse) **5**:14, 17, 20
"Suppliants parallèles" (Péguy) **10**:408, 411, 414
"Supplication" (Naidu) **80**:308
"Suppose an Eyes" (Stein) **28**:306
The Supposed Meaning of Our Monarchy (Rozanov) **104**:345
Suppressed Desires (Glaspell) **55**:234, 236, 241-42, 247, 266, 271; **175**:62
The Suppression of the African Slave-Trade to the United States of America, 1638-1870 (Du Bois) **169**:138, 212
The Supramental Manifestation upon Earth (Aurobindo) **63**:33
Suprema ley (Gamboa) **36**:71, 73-5, 77-9, 82
"Supremacy" (Robinson) **101**:158
"The Supreme Leaders" (Matthews) **95**:234
"The Supreme Sin" (Huneker) **65**:187, 197
"Sur" (Barthes) **135**:168, 170
"El Sur" (Borges) **109**:87-8
"Sur la hierarchie intellectuelle" (Gourmont) **17**:138
"Sur la mort" (Sully Prudhomme) **31**:302
"Sur la phénoménologie du langage" (Merleau-Ponty) **156**:122, 125
Sur la Pierre Blanche (France) **9**:44
"Sur la théorie" (Lyotard) **103**:153
Sur la Toscane (Bourget) **12**:75
"Sur le chemin de guinée" (Roumain) **19**:334

"Sur le passage d'un panier à salade" (Péret) **20**:201
"Sur le totémisme" (Durkheim) **55**:91
"Sur les dents" (Schwob) **20**:323
"Sur les prophéties" (Apollinaire) **51**:31-2
Sur Nietzsche (Bataille) **155**:127
Sur Racine (Barthes) **135**:143, 185
"Sur un vieux tableau" (Sully Prudhomme) **31**:302
"Suratak-ha" (Hedāyat) **21**:71-2
The Sure Hand of God (Caldwell) **117**:19
"The Sure Thing" (Williams) **89**:384
"Surely the People Are Grass" (Bialik) **25**:50
"The Surface Area of God" (Jarry) **14**:284
"The Surgeon" (Csáth) **13**:147, 152
"Surgery for the Novel—or a Bomb" (Lawrence) **48**:147
"The Surly Sullen Bell" (Kirk) **119**:335
The Surly Sullen Bell: Ten Stories and Sketches, Uncanny or Uncomfortable, With a Note on the Ghostly Tale (Kirk) **119**:253, 275, 277-78, 280-81, 291, 334
Le Surmâle (Jarry) **147**:227-28, 230-31, 240, 242, 244-46, 266-68, 270, 277, 280, 289-91, 296, 305
Le surmâle, roman moderne (Jarry) **14**:273-74, 278-82, 285-87
"A Surplus Woman" (Gilman) **37**:215
"Surprise" (Parker) **143**:323
"A Surprise Answer to Prayer" (Griggs) **77**:193-4
"The Surprise Head" (Tzara) **168**:228
"Surprise Item" (Wakefield) **120**:354
The Surprising Experiences of Mr. Shuttlebury Cobb (Freeman) **21**:56, 58
"Surrealism" (Benjamin) **39**:42
Surrealism and the postwar period (Tzara)
See *Le surréalisme et l'après-guerre*
"Le Surréalisme et l'après guerre" (Tzara) **168**:282
Le surréalisme et l'après-guerre (Tzara) **168**:272
Surrealismus v ČSR (Nezval) **44**:245
Surrealist Poetry (Aleixandre)
See *Poesía superrealista*
"The Surrealist Religion" (Bataille) **155**:88, 92
"Les Surréalistes et la Révolution" (Fondane) **159**:247
"Surrender" (Anderson) **24**:31, 34; **123**:33, 35, 75, 105
"The Surrender" (Stringer) **37**:343
Surrender (Hansen) **32**:248
Surrender at Discretion (Giacosa)
See *Resa a discrezione*
"Surrounded by Poets and Thinkers" (Musil) **68**:261
"Surtidores" (García Lorca) **181**:187
"Surview" (Hardy) **143**:192
Survival in Auschwitz: The Nazi Assault on Humanity (Levi)
See *Se questo è un uomo*
"The Survival of the Fittest" (Gilman) **9**:96
Survivals and New Arrivals (Belloc) **18**:45
"Surviving" (Bettelheim) **143**:34
Surviving, and Other Essays (Bettelheim) **143**:10, 29, 40
Surviving the Holocaust (Bettelheim)
See *Surviving, and Other Essays*
"The Survivor" (Canetti) **157**:66
"The Survivor" (Levi) **109**:287
"The Survivor among Graves" (Jarrell) **177**:195
A Survivor from Warsaw (Schoenberg) **75**:302, 311, 347, 404-11
The Survivors of the Chancellor (Verne)
See *Le Chancellor: Journal du passager J.-R. Kazallon; Martin Paz*
The Survivors of the "Jonathan" (Verne)
See *Les naufragés du "Jonathan"*
Susan and God (Crothers) **19**:76, 78-81
"Susan Ann and Immortality" (Hulme) **21**:139
"Susan Hemp" (Fisher) **140**:165
Susan Lenox: Her Fall and Rise (Phillips) **44**:271-72, 275-77, 280-81, 288-89, 291, 294, 300-02
Susan Proudleigh (De Lisser) **12**:95-7, 99
Susan Spray (Kaye-Smith) **20**:108, 116-17
Susana (Baroja) **8**:64
"Susanna" (Kolmar) **40**:185-86
"Susannah" (Mansfield) **2**:454
Susannah and the Elders, and Other Plays (Bridie) **3**:138
The Suspect in Poetry (Dickey) **151**:103, 105, 108, 131-32, 134, 200
"Suspense" (Lawrence) **93**:66
Suspense (Conrad) **1**:217
"Suspense of Love" (Merrill) **173**:253
Suspicious Characters (Sayers)
See *The Five Red Herrings*
Sussex Gorse (Kaye-Smith) **20**:93-4, 101-03, 109-10, 114-16, 118
"Susto en el comedor" (García Lorca) **181**:184
"Susy" (Harte) **25**:213
"Sutra of the heart" (Chang)
See "Xinjing"
"Suttee" (Naidu) **80**:294
"Suum cuique" (Pereda) **16**:363, 380
"Svad'ba" (Zabolotsky) **52**:375, 377-78
Svadba (Chekhov) **31**:80
"Svadbe" (Popa) **167**:155
Svaermere (Hamsun) **2**:202; **14**:223, **49**:133-34, 153
Den svåra stunden (Lagerkvist) **144**:214
Svarta Fanor (Strindberg) **1**:460; **8**:410; **47**:345
Svarta handsken (Strindberg) **1**:456; **8**:415
Svatby v domě (Hrabal) **155**:159, 165
Sveika, brīvā Latvija! (Rainis) **29**:392
Svendborg Poems (Brecht) **6**:40
Svenskarna och deras hövdingar (Heidenstam) **5**:252, 257
Sveske (Andrić) **135**:88
"Svet nerukotvorennyi" (Remizov) **27**:339
"Sveti Sava na svome izvoru" (Popa) **167**:159
Svetoslav terter (Vazov) **25**:457
"Sviatoi vecher" (Remizov) **27**:340, 349
"Svirel'" (Chekhov) **96**:34-36
Svirel' (Sologub) **9**:444
"Svivajutsja blednye teni" (Bryusov) **10**:92
Svjataja Elena: Malen' kij ostrov (Aldanov) **23**:16, 19, 21
"Svjatogor Mound" (Khlebnikov) **20**:147
"Svoeiu sobstvennoi rukoi" (Olesha) **136**:183
Svyataya krov (Hippius) **9**:168
"The Swain" (Tsvetaeva) **7**:557, 566
The Swallow-Book (Toller)
See *Das Schwalbenbuch*
"Swallows" (Pickthall) **21**:243
"Swallows" (Storni)
See "Golondrinas"
"Swallows balls" (Arp) **115**:20
"The Swamp" (Kuprin) **5**:298
"The Swan" (Balmont) **11**:34
"The Swan" (Dahl) **173**:17
"The Swan" (Gray) **19**:158
"Swan" (Lawrence) **93**:55
Swan (Merrill)
See *The Black Swan, and Other Poems*
The Swan (Molnár)
See *A hattyú*
A Swan and Her Friends (Lucas) **73**:153
"The Swan Song" (Rebreanu)
See "Cîntecul lebedei"
Swan Song (Chekhov)
See *Lebedinaia pesnia*
Swan Song (Galsworthy) **1**:297-98; **45**:46-7, 64-5
Swann's Way (Proust)
See *Du côté de chez Swann*
The Swans' Encampment (Tsvetaeva)
See *Lebediny stan*
Swanson (Lagerkvist) **144**:242
Sward Grass (Remizov)
See *Trava-Murava*
"The Swaying Form: A Problem in Poetry" (Nemerov) **124**:168, 173, 270, 285, 291, 312
"A Sweat-Shop Romance" (Cahan) **71**:13, 26, 39, 67, 71, 87-88
"Sweden" (Heidenstam) **5**:249
"Swedenborg, Mediums, and the Desolate Places" (Yeats) **31**:409
"Swedes" (Thomas) **10**:455, 463
The Swedes and Their Chieftains (Heidenstam)
See *Svenskarna och deras hövdingar*
Sweeney in the Trees (Saroyan) **137**:181
"The Sweeper of Ways" (Nemerov) **124**:253
"Sweet Boy, Give me Yr Ass" (Ginsberg) **120**:26
The Sweet Cheat Gone (Proust)
See *Albertine Disparue*
Sweet Cicely (Holley) **99**:321, 326, 344-45
The Sweet Harm (Storni)
See *El dulce daño*
"Sweet Home Chicago" (Johnson) **69**:77, 79
Sweet Kitty Bellairs (Belasco) **3**:90
Sweet Lavender (Pinero) **32**:389, 393, 399, 404, 412
Sweet Nancy (Buchanan) **107**:34
"sweet spring is your" (Cummings) **137**:55
"Sweet Tongue" (Tagore) **3**:483
"Sweet Town" (Bambara) **116**:13-14
"Sweet Youth" (Davies) **5**:199
"The Sweetness of a Man's Friend" (Rutherford) **25**:356
Swift (Stephen) **23**:340
Swift: A Biography (Van Doren) **18**:398, 409
"Swift's Epitaph" (Yeats) **116**:336
"The Swimease" (Wakefield) **120**:333
"The Swimmer of Nemi" (Sharp) **39**:390-91
"The Swimmers" (Fitzgerald) **157**:167
"The Swimmers" (Sterling) **20**:374
The Swimming Pool (Rinehart) **52**:290, 300, 303
"Swinburne at 'The Pines'" (Lucas) **73**:169
"The Swineherd" (Bernhard)
See "Der Schweinhüter"
Swing! (Micheaux) **76**:273
"Swing Low, Sweet Chariot" (Roberts) **68**:348, 350
"The Swing of the Pendulum" (Mansfield) **2**:457; **8**:282; **164**:293
Swirling Currents (Hayashi)
See *Uzushio*
Swiss Family Manhattan (Morley) **87**:146
Swiss Tales (Strindberg) **1**:444
Switch Bitch (Dahl) **173**:10, 15-19
The Switchback (Bridie) **3**:136, 140-42
"Switzerland Is a Nation without a Utopia" (Frisch) **121**:232
"Swollen Fortunes" (Phillips) **44**:277
Sword Blades and Poppy Seed (Lowell) **1**:370-72, 375, 379; **8**:223-24, 228, 232-33, 235
"The Sword Box" (Wen I-to) **28**:417
The Sword Does Not Jest: The Heroic Life of King Charles XII of Sweden (Bengtsson)
See *Karl den XII:s levnad*
The Sword of England (Noyes) **7**:503
The Sword of Imagination (Kirk) **119**:301, 303, 312-13, 315-17, 324, 329, 332, 337, 343
The Sword of Song (Crowley) **7**:204-05
"The Sword of the Sun" (Calvino) **183**:45-46, 48
The Sword of Welleran, and Other Stories (Dunsany) **2**:136; **59**:17, 20-1, 29
"Sword Woman" (Howard) **8**:138
"The Swords" (Wakefield) **120**:351
Swords and Plowshares (Drinkwater) **57**:148
Swords and Roses (Hergesheimer) **11**:273-75, 278-79
Swords Like Lips (Aleixandre)
See *Espadas como labios*
Swords of Shahrazar (Howard) **8**:136
"Swords of the Red Brotherhood" (Howard) **8**:131

"A Sybil" (Rilke)
See "Eine Sibylle"
Sydney Royal (Franklin) **7**:268
"Syllabus of Certain Topics of Logic" (Peirce) **81**:199
"Le sylphe" (Valéry) **4**:498
"The Sylvan Sadness" (Khlebnikov)
See "Lesnaya toska"
"Sylvanie" (Proust) **161**:173
Sylvia (Mackenzie)
See *The Early Life and Adventures of Sylvia Scarlett*
Sylvia and David: The Townsend Warner/Garnett Letters (Warner) **131**:360
Sylvia and Michael: The Later Adventures of Sylvia Scarlett (Mackenzie) **116**:188-89, 194, 201-02, 206, 209-10, 212, 252-53, 255
Sylvia Scarlett (Mackenzie)
See *The Early Life and Adventures of Sylvia Scarlett*
"Symbiosis and Socialization" (Park) **73**:198-99
Symbol of the Unconquered (Micheaux) **76**:262, 264, 270
"The Symbol Seduces" (Baker) **10**:21, 27
"The Symbol without Meaning" (Campbell) **140**:34
Symbolic Wounds: Puberty Rites and the Envious Male (Bettelheim) **143**:7, 16-18, 24
"Symbolism" (Baker) **10**:27
Symbolism (Bely) **7**:59
Symbolism in Nineteenth-Century Literature (Brennan) **17**:49
Symbolism: Its Meaning and Effect (Whitehead) **97**:298
"The Symbolism of Poetry" (Yeats) **11**:526; **116**:263
The Symbolist Movement in Literature (Symons) **11**:435, 440-42, 444, 447, 450, 452-53
Symbols (Merezhkovsky) **29**:230, 246
"Symbols in Literature" (Wylie) **8**:531, 537
Sympathies and Differences (Reyes)
See *Simpatías y diferencias*
"Sympathy" (Dunbar) **12**:117
"Symphonic Night" (Aleixandre)
See "Noche sinfónica"
La Symphonie pastorale (Gide) **36**:96, 100; **5**:214, 222-23, 227, 229, 240-41; **12**:145, 147, 149, 153, 157-60, 164, 177; **177**:31, 45, 49, 58-59
Symphonies (Bely) **7**:48-51
"A Symphony in Yellow" (Wilde) **8**:492
Sympósion (Kazantzakis) **181**:211
Symptoms of Being Thirty-Five (Lardner) **14**:306
"Syn rabbi" (Babel)
See "The Rabbi's Son"
"Synchronization of Senses" (Eisenstein) **57**:181
The Syndic (Kornbluth) **8**:212, 214, 216, 220
Syner (Ekelund) **75**:92
Synnøve Solbakken (Bjoernson) **7**:100-02, 105-10, 112-13, 117-18; **37**:7-8, 17, 22-3
"Synnöve's Song" (Bjoernson) **7**:110
Synopsis of Paley's Horae Paulinae (Murray) **117**:285
"Synov'ja i pasynki vremeni" (Shestov) **56**:278
The Synthesis of Yoga (Aurobindo)
See *On Yoga I: The Synthesis of Yoga*
Synthetic Men of Mars (Burroughs) **2**:81; **32**:57
"The Synthetic Theatre" (Marinetti) **10**:319
"Syostry-molnii" (Khlebnikov) **20**:137
"Syphilis" (Mayakovski) **18**:258
"The Syracusan Women" (Theocritus)
See *Across the Smiling Meadow and Other Stories*
"Syria I" (Douglas) **40**:56
"Syria II" (Douglas) **40**:89-90
Syria: The Desert and the Sown (Bell) **67**:2, 4, 5, 13, 16-17
"Syrinx" (Carman) **7**:149
"Syrinx" (Merrill) **173**:228
Syrlin (Ouida) **43**:364, 366-67
Les syrtes (Moréas) **18**:275, 278-82, 285-88, 290
"The System" (Čapek) **37**:60
A System of National Education (Aurobindo) **63**:28, 30-1
"The System of the Self-Conscious Universal" (Nishida)
See "Ippansha no jiko gentei"
Systematische Phylogenie (Haeckel) **83**:126
Système des beaux-arts (Alain) **41**:3, 6, 24, 28, 30
Le systeme historique de Renan (Sorel) **91**:260-2, 329
Le système Ribadier (Feydeau) **22**:77
Les systemes sociolistes (Pareto) **69**:112, 127, 130-31, 141, 152, 163, 165-67
"Syster, min syster" (Södergran) **31**:293
"Syvsoverne" (Jensen) **41**:307-08
Szalona lokomotywa (Witkiewicz) **8**:515-16
Szegény emberek (Moricz) **33**:246
A szelistyei asszonyok (Mikszath) **31**:172
Szent Péter esernyöje (Mikszath) **31**:165, 168-72
"Szentolvajok" (Molnár) **20**:164
Szeretném, ha szeretnáenek (Ady) **11**:18, 21, 23
Szewcy (Witkiewicz) **8**:510, 513
Sziget és tenger (Babits) **14**:40
Szinhaz (Karinthy) **47**:268
Szinház: Előjáték Lear Királyhoz, Marshall, Az ibolya (Molnár) **20**:161-62, 171
"Szkatulka babki" (Prus) **48**:181
"Le T.A.T. chez la femme musulmane: sociologie de la perception et de l'imagination" (Fanon) **188**:82
"t zero" (Calvino)
See "Ti con zero"
t Zero (Calvino)
See *Ti con zero*
"The Table" (Drummond de Andrade) **139**:237, 240
"Table" (Kandinsky) **92**:93
"La table la chaise" (Arp) **115**:41
A Table near the Band (Milne) **6**:319
"Table of Contents" (Caragiale)
See "The Mosi Fair"
"Tableau" (Cullen) **37**:152
"Tableau at Twilight" (Nash) **109**:360
The Tables of Destiny (Khlebnikov) **20**:150-51
"The Tables of the Law" (Mann)
See "Das Gesetz"
"The Tables of the Law" (Yeats) **31**:411; **116**:336
"The Tablets of the Law" (Hurston) **131**:70
Les tablettes d'eloi (Renard) **17**:303
"Tabloid Editions" (Benchley) **1**:81
"Tabloid Tragedy" (Dreiser) **35**:74
Tábor (Zuckmayer) **191**:307
Det tabte Land (Jensen) **41**:294-95
Tabu (Murnau) **53**:238-40, 251, 254-55, 274
Tabula Rasa (Sternheim) **8**:368, 372-73, 378
Tacámbaro (Romero) **14**:433
"Taches dans le vide—1936" (Arp) **115**:29
Un taciturne (Martin du Gard) **24**:384, 387, 394, 396, 404
"Tacloban" (Dickey) **151**:215
The Tactile Quartet (Marinetti)
See *Il quartetto tactile*
"Tactilism" (Marinetti) **10**:320
"Tacuara-Mansión" (Quiroga) **20**:212
Taffy (Evans) **85**:4-5, 29-30
"Taffy at Home" (Evans) **85**:13
Ho táfus (Palamas) **5**:379, 382-83
Der Tag (Barrie) **2**:41
"Der Tag der grossen Klage" (Kolmar) **40**:184-85
Der Tag des jungen Arztes (Carossa) **48**:30-2, 34
Tag des Proletariats (Toller) **10**:489-90
Der Tag wird Kommen (Feuchtwanger) **3**:181, 184
Tagaduința lui Petru (Fondane) **159**:248
Die Tage des Königs (Frank) **81**:102
Tagebuch (Brecht) **169**:43-44
Tagebuch, 1946-1949 (Frisch) **121**:193, 205, 229, 231-33, 237, 239-40, 246-47, 266, 269-70, 273, 275-76, 281-82, 288-89, 292, 302-10
Tagebuch, 1966-1971 (Frisch) **121**:229, 231, 233, 235-37, 246, 275
Tagebuch Einer Verlorenen (Pabst) **127**:299, 304, 309, 313, 355, 358-59, 363
"Tagebuch eines Mystikers" (Morgenstern) **8**:310
Tagebuch im Kriege (Carossa) **48**:15-16, 19-20, 22, 27-9
Tagebücher, 1910-1923 (Kafka) **2**:307; **6**:323; **29**:186, 189; **112**:38, 52, 83-4, 87, 91, 97; **179**:249, 251-52, 258, 261, 289, 326
Die Tagebucher von Joseph Goebbels: Samtliche Fragmente (Goebbels) **68**:128
"Die tagnachtlampe" (Morgenstern) **8**:305
"Tagore's Last Poems" (Tagore)
See "Śesh lekhā"
"Tähtitarha" (Leino) **24**:371
"Tahtoisin nähdä mä Kartagon naisen" (Leino) **24**:369
"Taidokuro" (Rohan) **22**:295, 299, 301, 305
Tailleur pour dames (Feydeau) **22**:90
"Tailors' Dummies" (Schulz)
See "Traktat o manekinach"
"Tainstvennyi zaichik" (Remizov) **27**:339
The Taira Clan (Mizoguchi) **72**:293
T'ai-Shang Kan-Ying P'ien (Suzuki) **109**:387
Taiyo to tetsu (Mishima) **161**:15-18, 20, 59-60, 62-63, 65-66, 80, 99, 101, 112
"Tajmahal" (Tagore) **53**:335
Tajtékos ég (Radnóti) **16**:419
"Tak est" (Hippius) **9**:162
"Tak zhizn idet" (Guro) **56**:132, 141-43, 148-49
"Take" (Hagiwara) **60**:312
"Take a Walk" (Lardner) **14**:320
"Take It or Leave It" (Bataille) **155**:89
"Take Me under Your Wing" (Bialik)
See "Hachnisini tahath kenafech"
"Take Pity" (Malamud) **129**:109, 165, 192; **184**:167, 198, 243, 282
"Take the Witness!" (Benchley) **55**:10, 18
"Take These Chains from My Heart" (Williams) **81**:437
"Take Your Time" (Holly) **65**:137-38, 141, 147
Taken at the Flood (Braddon) **111**:231, 245, 248
Takeoff (Kornbluth) **8**:212, 216
Taki no Shiraito (Mizoguchi) **72**:304, 313-17, 319, 323
"Takibi" (Kunikida Doppo) **99**:302-04
"Taking His Chance" (Lawson) **27**:134, 140
"Taking The Blue Ribbon at the County Fair" (Murfree) **135**:197, 207, 220
"Taking the Veil" (Mansfield) **39**:303
Takino Shiraito, the Water Magician (Mizoguchi)
See *Taki no Shiraito*
Taksidévondas (Kazantzakis) **181**:211
"Takyr" (Platonov) **14**:418
De tal palo, tal astilla (Pereda) **16**:365, 367-69, 374, 377, 381-82
Tala (Mistral) **2**:477-79
"Talab-i amurzish" (Hedāyat) **21**:71
Talalkozas egy fiatalemberrel (Karinthy) **47**:269
Tālas noskanas zilā vakarā (Rainis) **29**:392
"A Tale" (Caragiale) **76**:169
"A Tale" (Orage) **157**:282
"Tale" (Santos) **156**:310
"The Tale Died" (Ady) **11**:15
"A Tale for Dien Tamaela" (Anwar)
See "Tjerita buat Dien Tamaela"
A Tale No One Asked For (Nagai)
See *Towazugatari*
"Tale of a Broken Hairpin" (Su Man-shu)
See "Sui-tsan chi"

"A Tale of a Clown and a Mouse and Der Nister Himself" (Kahanovitsch) **56**:115
Tale of a District (Zamyatin)
See *Uezdnoe*
"A Tale of a Hermit and a Goat" (Kahanovitsch)
See "A mayse mit a nozir un mit a tsigele"
A Tale of a Lonely Parish (Crawford) **10**:144, 151, 153
The Tale of a Manor (Lagerloef) **36**:244, 248
"Tale of a Pony" (Harte) **25**:190
Tale of a Town (Martyn) **131**:100, 104-8, 126
"The Tale of an Empty House" (Benson) **27**:17, 19
"Tale of Crimson Silk" (Su Man-shu)
See "Chiang sha chi"
"The Tale of Imatra" (Leino)
See "Imatran tarina"
"A Tale of London" (Dunsany) **59**:21
"A Tale of Mere Chance" (Crane) **11**:128
"A Tale of Negative Gravity" (Stockton) **47**:313, 315, 320, 323, 327
A Tale of Passion (Ford)
See *The Good Soldier: A Tale of Passion*
A Tale of Poor Lovers (Pratolini)
See *Cronache di Poveri Amanti*
"A Tale of the Airly Days" (Riley) **51**:278, 300-01
"A Tale of the Equator" (Dunsany) **59**:21
"The Tale of the Good Old Man and the Beautiful Girl" (Svevo)
See "La novella del buon vecchio e della bella fanciulla"
"The Tale of the Missing Leg" (Čapek) **192**:224
"The Tale of the Moon and Sun" (Balmont) **11**:40
"The Tale of the Most Essential" (Zamyatin)
See "Rasskaz o samom glavnom"
"The Tale of the Peasant Siman" (Andrić) **135**:16-17
"Tale of the Stone Age" (Khlebnikov)
See "Skazka o kamennom veke"
"Tale of the Tiger Tree" (Lindsay) **17**:226
"Tale of the two dreamers" (Borges)
See "Historia de los dos que soñaron"
"The Tale of the Unextinguished Moon" (Pilnyak)
See "Povest nepogašhennoy luny"
The Tale of the Unextinguished Moon, and Other Stories (Pilnyak)
See *Povest' nepogašennoj luny*
"The Tale of the Vizier's Elephant" (Andrić)
See "Priča o vezirovom slonu"
Tale of Two Animals: Ikhnelat (Remizov)
See *Povest' o dvukh zveriakh: Ikhnelat*
"A Tale of Two Young People" (Cankar) **105**:163
Tale of Valor (Fisher) **140**:150, 162-63, 168, 188
"Tale (or Sage) of the Pogrom" (Bialik) **25**:50
"The Talent Thou Gavest" (Evans) **85**:34
"The Talented Dragon" (Söderberg) **39**:437-38
"The Talented Tenth" (Du Bois) **169**:80, 87-88, 90, 95, 106
"Tales" (Saroyan) **137**:179
Tales (Gurdjieff)
See *Beelzebub's Tales to His Grandson*
Tales (Kuprin) **5**:300
Tales (Lawrence) **61**:193
Tales (Remizov)
See *Rasskazy*
Tales and Texts for Nothing (Beckett)
See *Textes pour rien*
The Tales by Nazar Ilyich Sinebriukhov (Zoshchenko) **15**:501
Tales for Adult Children (Zamyatin) **8**:543; **37**:432
"Tales for Men Only" (Orage) **157**:246, 251, 282
Tales from a Greek Island (Papadiamantis) **29**:277
Tales from a Rolltop Desk (Morley) **87**:123
Tales from a Troubled Land (Paton) **165**:295, 298
Tales from Himmerland (Jensen)
See *Himmerlandshistorier*
Tales from One Pocket (Čapek)
See *Povídky z, jedné kapsy*
Tales from the House Behind (Frank) **17**:114
Tales from the Margin (Grove) **4**:141
Tales from the Other Pocket (Čapek)
See *Povídky z, druhé kapsy*
Tales from the Secret Annex (Frank) **17**:121
Tales from the Telling House (Blackmore) **27**:43
Tales from the Vienna Streets (Saroyan) **137**:172-73, 178-81
Tales from the Vienna Woods (Horvath)
See *Geschichten aus dem Wiener Wald*
Tales from Tolstoy (Tolstoy) **4**:452
Tales from Two Pockets (Čapek) **37**:47-9, 54-7, 70; **192**:175, 225, 227
Tales in Verse (Kahanovitsch)
See *Mayselakh in ferzn*
Tales of a Fairy Court (Lang) **16**:265
Tales of a Siberian Tourist (Korolenko) **22**:169
Tales of Alchemists (Meyrink)
See *Goldmachergeschichten*
Tales of America (Nagai)
See *Amerika monogatari*
Tales of Australian Early Days (Warung)
See *Tales of the Early Days*
Tales of Childhood (Dahl)
See *Boy: Tales of Childhood*
Tales of Chinatown (Rohmer) **28**:282, 286, 301
Tales of Country Life (Zamyatin)
See *Uezdnoe*
Tales of East and West (Rohmer) **28**:286, 301
Tales of France (Nagai)
See *Furansu monogatari*
Tales of Ghosts and Men (Wharton)
See *Tales of Men and Ghosts*
The Tales of Jacob (Mann)
See *Die Geschichten Jaakobs*
Tales of Mean Streets (Morrison) **72**:353-54, 359, 361-63, 366, 371-72, 375, 377, 383, 386-87, 390-91, 395
Tales of Men and Ghosts (Wharton) **3**:571, 577-78; **129**:362
Tales of Moonlight and Rain (Mizoguchi)
See *Ugetsu Monogatari*
Tales of My Native Town (D'Annunzio)
See *San Pantaleone*
"Tales of New England" (Jewett) **22**:133
Tales of Odessa (Babel)
See *Odesskie rasskazy*
Tales of Our Time (Benét) **7**:75
Tales of Secret Egypt (Rohmer) **28**:276-77, 286
Tales of Sevastopol (Tolstoy) **4**:469; **28**:359, 381
Tales of Soldiers and Civilians (Bierce) **1**:84, 86-9, 94; **7**:88-9; **44**:7, 10-13, 17, 39, 43-6, 49-50
Tales of Space and Time (Wells) **133**:323
Tales of the Convict System (Warung) **45**:417, 419-20
Tales of the Early Days (Warung) **45**:416-17, 419-20
Tales of the Five Towns (Bennett) **5**:42, 46
Tales of the Isle of Death (Norfolk Island) (Warung) **45**:418-19
Tales of the Jazz Age (Fitzgerald) **1**:236; **6**:161; **157**:182
Tales of the Long Bow (Chesterton) **6**:103-04, 108
Tales of the Mermaid Tavern (Noyes) **7**:502-03, 508, 511-12, 515
Tales of the Monkey King Asyka (Remizov) **27**:334
"Tales of the Moon" (Peretz) **16**:396
Tales of the Moonlight and Rain (Ueda Akinari)
See *Ugetsu Monogatari*
Tales of the Old Regime and the Bullet of the Fated Ten (Warung) **45**:417, 419, 422
Tales of the Pale and Silvery Moon after the Rain (Mizoguchi)
See *Ugetsu Monogatari*
Tales of the Provinces (Dazai Osamu)
See *Shokoku-banashi*
Tales of the Russian People (Remizov)
See *Folk-Tales of the Russian People*
Tales of the Uneasy (Hunt) **53**:186-87, 190, 192, 197, 200
Tales of Three Hemispheres (Dunsany) **59**:17, 20-1, 28-9
"Tales of Three Nations" (Beerbohm) **24**:105
Tales of Three Planets (Burroughs) **2**:81
Tales of Trail and Town (Harte) **25**:194
Tales of Troy and Greece (Lang) **16**:264
Tales of Two Countries (Kielland) **5**:275, 277
Tales of Two People (Hope) **83**:181
Tales of War (Dunsany) **59**:17
Tales of Whilomville (Crane)
See *Whilomville Stories*
Tales of Wonder (Dunsany) **2**:136-37
"Tales of Zashiki Bokko" (Miyazawa) **76**:293
Tales You Won't Believe (Porter) **21**:278
"Taliessin in the School of the Poets" (Williams) **1**:512
Taliessin through Logres (Williams) **1**:512, 515-16, 518-19; **11**:489-92, 497
Talifer (Robinson) **5**:406; **101**:105-06, 109, 185
"A Talisman" (Guiney) **41**:216
The Talk of New York (Cohan) **60**:170
The Talk of the Town (Cohan) **60**:166
"Talk on poetry and society" (Adorno)
See "Rede uber Lyrik und Gesellschaft"
The Talkers (Chambers) **41**:102
"Talking (and Singing) of the Nordic Man" (Belloc) **18**:25
Talking Bronco (Campbell) **5**:123
"Talking Horse" (Malamud) **129**:159; **184**:253, 310
Talking Horse (Malamud) **184**:296, 323
"The Talking Memories" (Apollinaire) **51**:49
The Talking Trees and Other Stories (O'Faolain) **143**:226, 263
Talks on Haiku from the Otter's Den (Masaoka)
See *Dassai shooku haiwa*
Talks on Tanka (Yosano) **59**:323-4, 326, 329
Talks to Teachers (James) **32**:358-59
Talks with an Irish Farmer (Baker) **10**:22
"The Tall Men" (Faulkner) **170**:138
"Tall Nettles" (Thomas) **10**:467
"A Tall Woman" (Hulme) **21**:139
The Talley Method (Anderson) **144**:34
The Tallons (March) **96**:235, 237-38, 248, 250-51, 259, 263-64, 266
"The Talmudic Student" (Bialik) **25**:50
"The Talmud-Student" (Bialik) **25**:57-8
"Talu and Fred" (Allen) **87**:39
Talvi-yö (Leino) **24**:368, 370
"Tam" (Huidobro) **31**:124
Tamakushige futari Urashima (Mori Ogai) **14**:371-72, 382
"Taman" (Anwar) **22**:20, 24
El tamaño de mi esperanza (Borges) **109**:17, 78, 84, 156
"Tamara" (Nabokov) **108**:110
Tamarisk Town (Kaye-Smith) **20**:95, 97, 101-02, 109, 114, 116, 118
"También tenemos el Ministerio de la Muerte" (Arenas) **191**:195
"Tambours" (Bosschere) **19**:59
Tamer of the Wild (Faust) **49**:38-9
"The Taming of Nips Blaas" (Williams) **89**:383
"The Taming of the Nightmare" (Chesterton) **6**:108
"Tammyshanty" (Phelps) **113**:342
Tampico (Hergesheimer) **11**:271-73
"Tan triste como ella" (Onetti) **131**:183-85, 187-89, 219, 236-44, 284-85
Tan triste como ella (Onetti) **131**:135, 139-47
Tanar of Pellucidar (Burroughs) **2**:81; **32**:58
Tanár úr kérem! (Karinthy) **47**:269

Tancrède (Fargue) **11**:194, 199-200
"Tandaradei" (Ford) **15**:70
"Tandy" (Anderson) **24**:24, 33-4, 58-9; **123**:30-1, 103
Taneční hodiny pro starší a pokročilé (Hrabal) **155**:160, 165
"The Tangerines" (Akutagawa Ryūnosuke)
See "Mikan"
"Tangier" (Capote) **164**:200
"Tangier" (Sarduy) **167**:201
Tangled Hair (Yosano)
See *Midaregami*
Tangled in Stars (Wetherald) **81**:408,413
A Tangled Web (Montgomery) **51**:194, 199, 201; **140**:319
"The Tangled Wood" (Khlebnikov) **20**:150
"El tango" (Borges) **109**:88
"El tango Argentino" (Graham) **19**:105, 112, 129
"Tanil" (Coppard) **5**:176
Tanin no kao (Abe) **131**:12-14
"Tanist" (Stephens) **4**:415
Tanker i en skorsten (Hansen) **32**:251
Tannhäuser (Crowley) **7**:208
"Tantalus, Fill Your Cup" (Södergran) **31**:287
"Tante Cat'rinette" (Chopin) **127**:167
Tanto tienes, tanto vales (Pereda) **16**:372
"Tantramar Revisited" (Roberts) **8**:314, 316-17, 320-21, 325-26
"The Tan-Yard Cremation" (Hearn) **9**:127
"Tanzt die Orange" (Rilke) **195**:274
"Tao: A Selection of the Sayings of Lao-Tzu" (Hesse) **196**:332
Tao Te Ching (Suzuki) **109**:387
"Taoping" (Flecker) **43**:217
"Taormina" (Roberts) **8**:321
"Taormina" (Woodberry) **73**:361
Taos Pueblo (Austin) **25**:38
"Tápé, Old Evening" (Radnóti) **16**:418
"La tapera" (Graham) **19**:104
Tapestries (Jarry) **147**:331
"The Tapestry" (Nemerov) **124**:257
The Tapestry of Life, the Songs of Dream and Death (George)
See *Der Teppich des Lebens und die Lieder von Traum und Tod, mit einem Vorspiel*
"Tapestry Weaving, A Ballad Song of Mary" (Roberts) **68**:304
Le tapin (Bourget) **12**:69
La tapisserie de Notre Dame (Péguy) **10**:405
La tapisserie de Sainte Geneviève et Jeanne d'Arc (Péguy) **10**:405
Taps at Reveille (Fitzgerald) **6**:162
Taquisara (Crawford) **10**:141, 147, 150, 155
Tar: A Midwest Childhood (Anderson) **1**:38-9, 41, 45-6, 56; **10**:38, 43; **24**:44-5, 50-1; **123**:3, 7, 87
"Tar and Feathers" (Paterson) **32**:376
Tarabas: Ein Gast auf dieser Erd (Roth) **33**:329-30
Les Tarahumaras (Artaud)
See *D'un voyage au pays des Tarahumaras*
"Tarantella" (Belloc) **7**:33; **18**:41
Tararira (Fondane) **159**:241, 247
Taratuta (Donoso) **133**:157, 159-60
"Tarde" (García Lorca) **181**:180
"Tarde" (Villaurrutia) **80**:476
"Una tarde de domingo" (Arlt) **29**:46
"Tarde de Maio" (Drummond de Andrade) **139**:228
"Tardes de aquellos años" (Gonzalez Martinez) **72**:152
La tardi ravveduta (Giacosa) **7**:307, 310, 313
"A Tardy Thanksgiving" (Freeman) **9**:76
"The Target" (Gurney) **33**:86
The Tariff in Our Times (Tarbell) **40**:439, 443
"The Tarn of Sacrifice" (Blackwood) **5**:72
Tärningkast (Bengtsson) **48**:5, 12
"Tarōbō" (Rohan) **22**:306
Tarocchi (Calvino) **183**:127
"Tarpeia" (Guiney) **41**:204, 207, 227, 229
Tarquinius superbus (Leino) **24**:372
Tarr (Lewis) **2**:385-89, 391, 395, 397-98; **9**:235, 237, 241-45, 247-50; **104**:172, 175-76, 180-81, 199, 204, 228-29, 241, 243-45, 247, 250, 254-55, 260-62, 264-72, 293, 297, 299
"Tartar Captivity" (Sienkiewicz) **3**:426, 430
"Tartary" (de la Mare) **4**:74
Tartüff (Murnau) **53**:240, 254, 257, 274
Tartuffe (Murnau)
See *Tartüff*
Tarzan and the Ant Men (Burroughs) **2**:81; **32**:56, 62, 74-6
Tarzan and the Castaways (Burroughs) **32**:80
Tarzan and "The Foreign Legion" (Burroughs) **2**:79; **32**:70, 80
Tarzan and the Golden Lion (Burroughs) **2**:79
Tarzan and the Jewels of Opar (Burroughs) **32**:72
Tarzan and the Leopard Men (Burroughs) **32**:62
Tarzan and the Lion Man (Burroughs) **32**:59
Tarzan and the Lost Empire (Burroughs) **2**:79; **32**:59
Tarzan at the Earth's Core (Burroughs) **2**:79, 81; **32**:56-8, 80
Tarzan, Lord of the Jungle (Burroughs) **32**:56, 62
Tarzan of the Apes (Burroughs) **2**:75-7, 79-80, 83-4; **32**:57-8, 60-2, 64, 78-80
Tarzan the Invincible (Burroughs) **32**:57, 62
Tarzan the Magnificent (Burroughs) **32**:62
Tarzan the Terrible (Burroughs) **2**:79; **32**:62, 80
Tarzan the Untamed (Burroughs) **2**:79; **32**:80
Tarzan Triumphant (Burroughs) **32**:62, 80
Tarzan's Quest (Burroughs) **32**:62
The Task of Social Hygiene (Ellis) **14**:104-05, 112, 114, 116, 122
"The Task of the Translator" (Benjamin) **39**:5, 15-16
Tasker Jevons: The Real Story (Sinclair) **3**:434, 437-38; **11**:411, 413-14
"Tasker Norcross" (Robinson) **5**:412
"Tasks of the Proletariat in Our Revolution" (Lenin) **67**:257
Tasso oder Kunst des Justes Milieu (Sternheim) **8**:368
"Tasso to Leonora" (Sterling) **20**:371, 378
"Taste" (Dahl) **173**:11
"Taste" (Erskine) **84**:183
"The Taste" (Oppen) **107**:265
"The Taste of the Age" (Jarrell) **177**:239
"Der Täter" (George) **14**:200
Tatiana Repina (Chekhov) **163**:128
"Tattoo Marks and Nails" (La Guma) **140**:206, 208, 238-39
"The Tattooed Woman" (Engel) **137**:103
The Tattooed Woman (Engel) **137**:100, 102, 105
"Taurine Provence" (Campbell) **5**:120, 122
"The Tavern" (Cather) **11**:93
"Tavern" (Millay) **49**:201; **169**:225-26
The Tavern (Cohan) **60**:162, 166, 173
The Tavern Knight (Sabatini) **47**:303
Tavern Moscow (Esenin) **4**:116
"The Tavern of Crossed Destinies" (Calvino)
See "La taverna dei destini incrociati"
"The Tavern of Despair" (Marquis) **7**:434
"La taverna dei destini incrociati" (Calvino) **183**:175, 214, 228
"The Tawe News" (Thomas) **105**:346
"The Taxi" (Lowell) **1**:375; **8**:233, 235
"Taxidea Americana" (Lardner) **14**:307
Taxideuontas: Iaponia Kina (Kazantzakis)
See *Iaponia-Kina*
"Tchériapin" (Rohmer) **28**:286
"Te Deum Laudamus" (Rhodes) **53**:316
Te eida set Rousia (Kazantzakis) **181**:315, 325-26
"Tea" (Stevens) **45**:320, 335
Tea with Dr. Borsig (Böll)
See *Zum Tee bei Dr. Borsig*
"The Teacher" (Anderson) **24**:22, 35, 53, 56, 59; **123**:83-5, 104
"Teacher" (Walker) **129**:271
"The Teacher of Literature" (Chekhov)
See "Učitel' Slovesnosti"
"Teacher Tomioka" (Kunikida Doppo)
See "Tomioka Sensei"
"The Teaching of Economic History in Canada" (Innis) **77**:338
"The Teaching of Hasidism" (Peretz) **16**:392
The Teaching of Political Economy in the Soviet Union (Stalin) **92**:167
"Teaching the Humanities Today" (Frye) **165**:228
"The Teams" (Lawson) **27**:140
"The Teapot" (Remizov) **27**:331, 334
A Tear and a Smile (Gibran)
See *Dam 'ah wabitisāmah*
"A Tear for Cressid" (Wylie) **8**:530
"Teardrops Fall Like Rain" (Holly) **65**:144
"Tears" (Ginsberg) **120**:12
"Tears" (Reese) **181**:344
"Tears" (Thomas) **10**:452-53, 463, 469
"Tears and Laughter" (Gibran)
See *Dam 'ah wabitisāmah*
The Tears of Eros (Bataille)
See *Les larmes d'Éros*
"The Tears of Rain" (Wen I-to) **28**:414
"The Tears of the Tearless" (Babits)
See "A könnytelenek könnyei"
"Teatr odnoy volya" (Sologub) **9**:439
Teatral'nyi roman (Bulgakov) **2**:65; **16**:76-7, 84, 90, 110-11; **159**:4-6, 8, 135, 165
Teatro (Ginzburg) **156**:30
Teatro (Pardo Bazán) **189**:197, 199
Teatro de ensueño (Martinez Sierra and Martinez Sierra) **6**:273, 277-79, 286
"A Technical Error" (Henry) **19**:183
"The Technical Manifesto of Literature" (Marinetti) **10**:324-25
Technik der Psychoanalyse (Rank) **115**:229, 233
"Technique" (Saintsbury) **31**:226
Le technique du coup d'état (Malaparte) **52**:262-63, 267, 273-74
"The Technique of Interpretation and of Resistance Analysis" (Reich) **57**:341
Technique of Psychoanalysis (Rank)
See *Technik der Psychoanalyse*
"The Technique of Psychoanalytic Therapy" (Horney) **71**:230
Technique of the Coup d'Etat (Malaparte)
See *Le technique du coup d'état*
The Technique of the Mystery Story (Wells) **35**:421-23, 426
"The Technique of the New Poetry" (Marinetti) **10**:325
"Technologies" (Oppen) **107**:309
"Technology and Public Opinion in the United States" (Innis) **77**:406
"Tecla and the Little Men" (Hudson) **29**:156
The Tedious Story (Chekhov) **3**:147-48
"A Tedious Tale" (Chekhov)
See "A Dreary Story"
Teenagers (Moricz) **33**:249
The Teeth of the Tiger (Leblanc)
See *Les dents du tigre*
Der tehillim yid (Asch) **3**:68-9, 72-3
Teja (Gregory) **176**:36
Teja (Sudermann) **15**:420, 422, 430
"Tel Aviv" (Douglas) **40**:91
"Tel qu'en songe" (Nervo) **11**:396
"The Telegram" (Čapek) **37**:57
"The Telegram" (Hunt) **53**:190
"Telegrams" (Caragiale) **76**:169, 171
"Telemachus, Friend" (Henry) **19**:189
"Telemachus Remembers" (Muir) **87**:157
"Teleological Logic" (Peirce) **81**:193
"The Telephone" (Belloc) **18**:28, 49
"A Telephone Call" (Parker) **143**:285, 287, 289-90, 314-15, 331-35, 340
"Telesforo Altamira" (Güiraldes) **39**:176
Ho teleutaios peirasmos (Kazantzakis) **2**:317-18, 320-21, 323; **5**:261-64, 267-68; **33**:145-

46, 148-49, 153, 159, 160, 164, 167; **181**:243-45, 248-52, 256, 267, 272, 276, 286, 314, 328-31
"Television Is a Baby Crawling Toward That Death Chamber" (Ginsberg) **120**:38, 41, 79
"A téli Magyarország" (Ady) **11**:17, 21
"Tell e How" (Holly) **65**:152
"Tell Me, Dusky Maiden" (Johnson) **175**:225
"Tell Me Now" (Gogarty) **15**:101, 114
Tell My Horse (Hurston) **121**:319, 351; **131**:67, 70, 74-76, 79, 85
Tell My Horse: Voodoo and Life in Haiti and Jamaica (Hurston)
See *Tell My Horse*
"The Teller of Tales" (Benjamin)
See "The Storyteller"
"Telling a Short Story" (Wharton) **9**:546
"Telling Mrs. Baker" (Lawson) **27**:121, 128, 131, 147
"Telo gektora" (Bryusov) **10**:85
"Tema" (Salinas) **17**:369
"El tema de nuestro tiempo" (Ortega y Gasset) **9**:338, 349
"El Tema del traidor y del héroe" (Borges) **109**:120-21, 123-25
Temas Cubanos (Hostos) **24**:303
Temas Sudamericanos (Hostos) **24**:303
Temblor de cielo (Huidobro) **31**:122-23, 133
Temnyi lik (Rozanov) **104**:314, 316
Temol shilshom (Agnon) **151**:22, 36, 70
Temol silsom (Agnon)
See *Temol shilshom*
"The Temperance Crusade and Woman's Rights" (Twain) **12**:438-39
"The Temperance Lecture" (Fields) **80**:254
"The Temperate Zone" (Wharton) **129**:363
Tempered Pink (Kandinsky)
See *Sharp-calm Pink*
"Tempest" (Obstfelder)
See "Orkan"
Tempest (Stroheim) **71**:340
"Tempesta solare" (Calvino) **183**:145
La tempestaire (Epstein) **92**:2
The Tempests (Gibran) **9**:90-1, 93
"The Templar" (Leino)
See "Tempppeliherra"
"The Temple" (Hammett) **187**:98
"The Temple" (Lovecraft) **22**:209, 219
"The Temple: A Pilgrimage of Love" (Naidu) **80**:287
Temple Bar (Buchanan) **107**:50
The Temple of Dawn (Mishima)
See *Akatsuki no tera*
"The Temple of Eros" (Södergran)
See "Eros tempel"
"Temple of Fame" (Davis) **6**:154
"The Temple of Janus" (Swinburne) **8**:445
The Temple of the Golden Pavilion (Mishima)
See *Kinkakuji*
"A Temple of the Holy Ghost" (O'Connor) **132**:232, 238-40, 244, 271-74, 276, 362
The Temple of the Holy Ghost (Crowley) **7**:208
Temple Tower (Sapper) **44**:316, 318-19, 321-22
"Templer" (George) **2**:150; **14**:210
"Tempo di valse" (Mencken) **13**:363
"Tempora" (Caragiale) **76**:181
"Temporal Power": A Study in Supremacy (Corelli) **51**:66, 68, 71
"The Temporary the All" (Hardy) **143**:158, 160, 195
"Tempppeliherra" (Leino) **24**:369
"Le temps dans l'art" (Jarry) **147**:227
Le temps déborde (Éluard) **7**:260-61; **41**:151, 153, 161
"Temps Perdu" (Parker) **143**:326
Le temps retrouvé (Proust) **7**:527, 529-30, 545, 549, 551-53; **13**:406, 410, 414, 419, 421, 424-26; **33**:256-57, 261, 271-72; **161**:131, 133, 135, 142-44, 149, 151, 154, 192, 195, 200, 204
Le temps viendra (Rolland) **23**:257, 282
"Temptation" (Čapek) **192**:226
"Temptation" (Dunbar) **12**:122
"The Temptation" (Moore) **7**:487
Temptation (Micheaux) **76**:247, 255
The Temptation of Quiet Veronica (Musil)
See *Die Versuchung der Stillen Veronika*
"The Temptation of Saint Anthony" (Ball)
See "Versuchung des heiligen Antonius"
The Temptation of the Silent Veronika (Musil)
See *Die Versuchung der Stillen Veronika*
"The Tempted Devil" (Papini) **22**:284
The Tempter (Broch) **20**:67
The Temptress (Blasco Ibáñez)
See *La tierra de tudos*
Ten Creeks Run (Franklin) **7**:264, 266-67, 269-73
Ten Days That Shook the World (Reed) **9**:382, 384, 386-91
Ten Ladies in One Umbrella (Melies) **81**:145
Ten Minute Stories (Blackwood) **5**:77
Ten Minutes to Live (Micheaux) **76**:258-63
"Ten' nosozdannyz sozdanij" (Bryusov) **10**:82
Ten Poems from a Hundred (Masaoka)
See *Hyakuchū jisshu*
"The Ten Righteous" (Čapek) **192**:189
Ten Stories (Hemingway) **115**:131
Ten Tales (Bierce) **44**:14
"10,000 People Killed" (Fields) **80**:259
"The Ten Worst Books" (Benét) **28**:7
A Ten Year's War: An Account of the Battle with the Slum in New York (Riis) **80**:419
"A Tenancy" (Merrill) **173**:185, 257-58
"The Tenant" (Riis) **80**:441
"A Tenant in a Garret" (Prus)
See "Lokator poddasza"
Tenants (James) **11**:338
The Tenants (Malamud) **129**:62-3, 65-6, 69, 73-6, 84, 96-7, 104, 112, 114, 117-21, 124, 126, 142, 154, 164, 184-88, 192; **184**:221, 224, 258, 260, 277
Tendencies in Modern American Poetry (Lowell) **1**:377; **8**:228, 236
"The Tendency of History" (Adams) **4**:17-19
"The Tender Achilles" (Kipling) **17**:209
Tender Buttons: Objects, Food, Rooms (Stein) **1**:428, 430-31, 434-37, 441-42; **6**:404-06, 410-11, 413, 415-16; **28**:306, 311, 313, 315, 318, 320, 322, 325, 328-32, 336-42; **48**:211, 213, 216, 236-39, 247-49, 252, 254-55, 264
"Tender, Caressing Hands" (Ady) **11**:15
Tender Is the Night (Fitzgerald) **1**:238, 241-42, 244-45, 247-48, 250, 252, 254, 258-59, 261, 263-64, 266-67, 269-71; **6**:160, 162, 165, 169, 171; **14**:174, 178; **28**:87-125; **55**:191, 193, 196-99, 201, 207, 209-10, 213-17, 220, 225-29; **157**:162, 164, 166, 168-70, 172, 186, 198, 204, 213, 215, 222-23, 227
Tender Is the Night (Lowry) **6**:250
Tender Joseph (Kuzmin)
See *Nezhnyi Iosif*
"The Tender Shoot" (Colette)
See "Le tendron"
Tenderenda der Phantast (Ball) **104**:13, 15-19, 36, 59, 72
Tenderenda the Fantast (Ball)
See *Tenderenda der Phantast*
Tenderenda the Visionary (Ball)
See *Tenderenda der Phantast*
Les tenderesses premières (Verhaeren) **12**:465
The Tenderfoot (Faust) **49**:56, 58-9
Tenderness (Mistral)
See *Ternura*
Tendre comme le souvenir (Apollinaire) **51**:8, 10, 13
La tendre ennemie (Ophuls) **79**:238
"Le tendron" (Colette) **5**:170, 173; **16**:120-21, 129, 138
Les ténèbres (Desnos) **22**:60-2, 72-3
"Tenebris Interlucentum" (Flecker) **43**:188, 194, 199
"Tengo un miedo terrible . . ." (Vallejo) **56**:311
"Teni" (Korolenko) **22**:175
"Tenjō Ishi" (Hagiwara) **60**:295, 311
"The Tennessee Hero" (Harper) **14**:259, 263
"Tennessee's Partner" (Harte) **1**:340-41; **25**:189, 191, 197, 199, 201, 205, 214, 216, 222
Tennin Gosui (Mishima) **161**:3, 5, 31, 51, 54, 56, 93-94
"Tennis" (Mandelstam) **2**:403
"Tennis Date with First Love" (Shepherd) **177**:316
"Tennyson" (de la Mare) **4**:81
The Tenor (Wedekind)
See *Der Kammersänger*
Tension (Delafield) **61**:127
The Tent (Gumilev) **60**:260, 262
"The Tentacle Head" (Tzara) **168**:228
Tentation (Bourget) **12**:67
La tentative amoureuse (Gide) **5**:244; **12**:159, 176
Tenterhooks (Leverson) **18**:194, 202
"The Tenth Clew" (Hammett) **187**:70, 86, 133
"Tenth Elegy" (Rilke) **1**:413; **6**:361
"The Tenth Muse of America" (Reyes) **33**:318
The Tenth Symphony (Aldanov)
See *Desjataja simfonija*
The Tents of the Arabs (Dunsany) **2**:140, 142-43; **59**:3, 6, 11, 14
The Tents of Trouble (Runyon) **10**:437
"Los teólogos" (Borges) **109**:18, 55-6, 88
Teoria dello Spirito (Gentile)
See *Teoria generale dello Spirito come puro atto*
"Teoria do medalhão" (Machado de Assis) **10**:290, 293
Teoria e storia della storiografia (Croce) **37**:86, 123-24
Teoria generale dello Spirito come puro atto (Gentile) **96**:85, 90, 96, 100-01, 134
"Teoría y juego del duende" (García Lorca) **49**:83, 91, 109, 116
Teorica dei governi e governo parlamentare (Mosca)
See *Sulla teorica dei governi e sul governo parlamentare*
Le teorie del conte Alberto (Svevo) **35**:370
"La teorie storiche del professor Loria" (Croce) **37**:120
Teper' kogda ja prosnulsja (Bryusov) **10**:83
Der Teppich des Lebens und die Lieder von Traum und Tod, mit einem Vorspiel (George) **2**:151, 154; **14**:199, 202, 204-06, 212
Tercera antolojía poética (Jiménez) **183**:269
Tercets (Pirandello)
See *Terzetti*
"Teresa" (O'Faolain) **143**:253
Teresa, and Other Stories (O'Faolain) **143**:222, 238
Teresa of Watling Street (Bennett) **197**:30-1
Teresa: Rimas de un poeta desconocido presentadas y presentado por Miguel de Unamuno (Unamuno) **9**:514; **148**:256-57
Termina el desfile (Arenas) **191**:135-39
"Terminal Days at Beverly Farms" (Bishop) **121**:19
Terminations. The Death of the Lion. The Coxon Fund. The Middle Years. The Altar of the Dead (James) **2**:272
"Un término" (Aleixandre) **113**:36
"Los términos" (Aleixandre) **113**:34
Ternura (Mistral) **2**:478, 480
"Terra Incognita" (Lawrence) **93**:25
"Terra incognita" (Nabokov) **108**:55, 144
"Terra Incognita: Into the Maze" (Abbey) **160**:31, 97
Terra vergine (D'Annunzio) **6**:133, 144; **40**:38
Le terrain bouchaballe (Jacob) **6**:191
"Terraplane Blues" (Johnson) **69**:94
"A Terre" (Owen) **5**:364, 371; **27**:206, 210, 212, 214, 217-18, 220, 223, 227
La terre (Zola) **1**:585, 590, 592-94, 596-97; **6**:561, 563-64, 566-69; **21**:441, 458; **41**:414-15, 438, 451

Le terre del Sacromento (Jovine) **79**:43, 45-6, 49-50, 58-62, 68, 73
Terre des hommes (Saint-Exupéry) **2**:516-17, 521, 526; **56**:221, 223, 228; **169**:316, 318-22, 324-26, 328-29, 331, 333, 337-38, 341
Terre du ciel (Ramuz) **33**:295
"La terre est bleue comme une orange . . ." (Éluard) **41**:169
La terre et les morts (Barrès) **47**:53
La Terre et les Reveries de la Volonté: Essai sur l'imagination des forces (Bachelard) **128**:10, 20, 23, 27-8, 32-7, 39-40, 47, 63-5, 67-70
La Terre et les reveries du repos (Bachelard) **128**:10, 33, 36, 38, 55, 63, 66-70
"La terre future" (Schwob) **20**:323
"Terremoto" (Vallejo) **56**:306-07
Terres maudites (Blasco Ibáñez)
See *La barraca*
"A Terrible Day Tomorrow" (Parker) **143**:331
"A Terrible Tale" (Leroux) **25**:260
The Terrible Turkish Executioner (Melies) **81**:122,151
"The Terrible World" (Blok) **5**:92, 95
"The Territory Ahead" (Morris) **107**:103-05
The Territory Ahead (Morris) **107**:112, 119, 128, 130-31, 133, 142, 146-48, 150, 154, 165, 168, 170, 173, 181, 184, 190, 196, 223-24, 236, 240-44
"Terrones y pergaminos" (Pereda) **16**:372-73
"Terror" (Anderson) **24**:34; **123**:35
The Terror (Machen) **4**:277, 284
The Terror (Wallace) **57**:402
Terror and the Lonely Widow (Dent) **72**:19, 27
El terror de 1824 (Pérez Galdós) **27**:287
Terror Keep (Wallace) **57**:406
"The Terror of Blue John Gap" (Doyle) **7**:224-25
Terror of Light (Williams) **11**:499
Terror of the Navy (Dent) **72**:22
Terror Wears No Shoes (Dent) **72**:27, 38
Tersites (Zweig) **17**:433, 451-52
Tertia vigilia (Bryusov) **10**:79, 82, 86, 95-6
Terza pagina: Racconti e Saggi (Levi) **109**:301, 303, 320, 342
Terzetti (Pirandello) **29**:291-92
Terzetto spezzato (Svevo) **35**:352-53, 369-70
Tesi fondamentali di un Estetica come scienza dell' espressione e linguistica generale (Croce) **37**:114-15, 117-19, 122-23
"El tesoro" (Pardo Bazán) **189**:235
El tesoro de Gastón (Pardo Bazán) **189**:247
Tess of the D'Urbervilles: A Pure Woman Faithfully Presented (Hardy) **4**:152-53, 159-61, 170-71, 174, 176-77; **10**:215-17, 220, 225, 227-29; **18**:79-81, 84-9, 94-100, 102-04, 108, 110-11, 114, 116, 120-24; **32**:270, 275-76, 278-81, 287-89, 309-10, 321; **48**:40, 46, 49, 56, 59, 73-4, 79; **53**:71, 81, 83, 102; **72**:160, 180, 195, 220, 226, 237, 243, 252, 255, 279; **143**:72-3, 75-8, 81-2, 86-8, 107-8, 111, 124,
Tessa (Larbaud) **9**:203
"La tessitrice" (Pascoli) **45**:156
"The Test" (Kafka) **29**:186
The Test (Sully Prudhomme)
See *Les épreuves*
"The Test of Heroes" (Zoshchenko) **15**:499
"Testament" (Musil)
See "Vermächtnis"
Le testament (Bourget) **12**:69
Le Testament de l'auteur (Jammes) **75**:117
Le testament d'Eugène Delacroix (Barrès) **47**:67
Le testament d'Orphée (Cocteau) **119**:39, 41, 45-6, 40-9, 71, 83, 87
Le testament du Père Leleu (Martin du Gard) **24**:382, 394, 404
Le Testament d'un excentrique (Verne) **52**:358
The Testament of a Man Forbid (Davidson) **24**:165-66, 174
The Testament of a Prime Minister (Davidson) **24**:174, 187
The Testament of a Vivisector (Davidson) **24**:165-66, 174, 187, 189
The Testament of an Empire-Builder (Davidson) **24**:174, 187, 190
The Testament of Beauty (Bridges) **1**:127-30, 132
The Testament of John Davidson (Davidson) **24**:167-68, 173, 187
"Testament of Man" (Fisher) **140**:149, 151, 154-59, 167-68, 170, 182, 185, 188
The Testament of Orpheus (Cocteau)
See *Le testament d'Orphée*
"The Testament of Symbolism" (Ivanov) **33**:130
Le testament poétique (Sully Prudhomme) **31**:303, 307
Un testigo perenne y delatado (Sarduy) **167**:199
I testimoni della passione (Papini) **22**:287
"El testimonio de Juan Peña" (Reyes) **33**:322, 324
Testimonios sobre Mariana (Garro) **153**:46, 48, 51, 54, 72, 81, 84
"The Testimony of Juan Peña" (Reyes)
See "El testimonio de Juan Peña"
"The Testimony of the Suns" (Sterling) **20**:370, 372-73, 377, 380, 382-86
The Testimony of the Suns, and Other Poems (Sterling) **20**:368, 373-74, 383-84
The Testing of Diana Mallory (Ward) **55**:413-14, 416, 425, 430
A testőr (Molnár) **20**:159, 161-62, 165, 170-71, 178
"Tête à Tête" (Tzara) **168**:228
Tête de méduse (Vian) **9**:531
Tête d'or (Claudel) **2**:100-01, 103-06, 108-09; **10**:127, 131
"Tete-jaune" (Scott) **6**:399
"Les Têtes de carton du carnaval de Nice" (Roussel) **20**:228, 230, 240
"Tetrazzini" (MacCarthy) **36**:253
"Teufelei I" (Huch) **13**:248-49
"Teufelei II" (Huch) **13**:249
Teufeleien (Huch) **13**:247
Des Teufels General (Zuckmayer) **191**:280-82, 284-86, 289, 294, 297, 304-05, 311-12, 316-17, 322, 324, 327, 329, 331, 339-40, 343, 345-48, 351-52
Das Teufels-Weib (Herzl) **36**:132
Das Teuflische (Barlach) **84**:74
Teutonic Knights (Sienkiewicz)
See *Krzyżacy*
The Tevye Stories, and Others (Aleichem) **1**:29, 31
Tevye the Dairyman (Aleichem) **1**:21, 29-30; **35**:306
"Tewkesbury" (Gurney) **33**:87, 111
The Texaco Star Theater (Allen) **87**:28, 37
A Texas Matchmaker (Adams) **56**:2, 4-7, 15, 24
A Texas Titan: The Story of Sam Houston (Oskison) **35**:276
"Text-Books of Fiction" (Matthews) **95**:263
Textes de grande jeunesse ou textes-genèse (Roussel) **20**:240
Textes pour rien (Beckett) **145**:183-4, 193, 201
Textos recobrados (Borges) **109**:157
Texts for Nothing (Beckett)
See *Textes pour rien*
Textura del sistema nervioso del hombre y de los vertebrados (Ramoacn y Cajal) **93**:137, 142, 145
Thaïs (France) **9**:39-40, 42, 47-8, 51-3, 55-7
"Thakur-ka-kua" (Premchand) **21**:292
"The Thakur's Well" (Premchand)
See "Thakur-ka-kua"
"Thalassius" (Swinburne) **36**:316, 320, 324, 339, 341
"Thamar y Amnón" (García Lorca) **197**:238
"Thalerò" (Sikelianos) **39**:418, 421
"Thallusa" (Pascoli) **45**:146
"The Thames Embankment" (Davidson) **24**:189, 192
"Thammuz" (Moody) **105**:237
Thamyras the Cythara Player (Annensky)
See *Famira kifared*
"Thánatos tou palikariú" (Palamas) **5**:385
Thank Heaven Fasting (Delafield) **61**:126-7, 130, 133
Thank You, Jeeves (Wodehouse) **108**:335, 344-5, 347-8, 350, 388, 392
Thankful Blossom (Harte) **1**:342; **25**:212
The Thanksgiving Visitor (Capote) **164**:100, 111-14, 199
That Affair Next Door (Green) **63**:136, 148, 151, 154, 156-57, 160
That Awful Mess on Via Merulana (Gadda)
See *Quer pasticciaccio brutto de via Merulana*
"That Awful Night" (Rinehart) **52**:281
"That Blessed Hope" (Harper) **14**:260
"That Bright Chimeric Beast" (Cullen) **4**:43; **37**:156
"That Brute Simmons" (Morrison) **72**:362
"That Day That Was That Day" (Lowell) **8**:237
"That Day You Came" (Reese) **181**:347
"That Dieth Not" (Wakefield) **120**:343
"That Evening Sun" (Faulkner) **141**:174
"That Evening Sun Go Down" (Faulkner) **170**:127-28, 138, 147, 236-37
"That Good May Come" (Wharton) **129**:352, 360
"That Makes It Tough" (Holly) **65**:147
"That Old-Fashioned Cakewalk" (Cohan) **60**:161
"That Old-Time Place" (Galsworthy) **45**:33
"That Pretty Girl in the Army" (Lawson) **27**:147-48
That Printer of Udell's (Wright) **183**:346, 349, 363, 372-73, 377
"That Share of Glory" (Kornbluth) **8**:217
That Summer in Paris: Memories of Tangled Friendships with Hemingway, Fitzgerald, and Some Others (Callaghan) **145**:220-28, 232-37, 239, 248, 250-52, 254
"That There Dog o' Mine" (Lawson) **27**:125, 132
That Time (Beckett) **145**:126, 129, 134-35, 156, 159
That Winter Night, or, Love's Victory (Buchanan) **107**:83
That Worthless Fellow Platonov (Chekhov)
See *Platonov*
"That'll Be the Day" (Holly) **65**:138, 143, 145, 150-51
"That's What They Say" (Holly) **65**:147, 151
"Thaw" (Thomas) **10**:450, 466
"Le thé de ma tante Michael" (Lemonnier) **22**:204
"'The Literature of the West': A Reply to W. R. Lighton" (Norris) **155**:311-12
""The Marital Garland of Letters for Arunacala"" (Ramana Maharshi)
See "Arunacala-aksara-mana-malai"
"Theater" (Toomer) **172**:257-58, 274, 284, 329, 335
"The Theater and Cruelty" (Artaud)
See "Le Théâtre et la Cruauté"
The Theater and Its Double (Artaud)
See *Le théâtre et son double*
"Theater for Pleasure or Theater for Instruction" (Brecht) **169**:19, 26
"Theater of Metaphors" (Olesha) **136**:157
"Theater ohne Illusion" (Frisch) **121**:198
Der Theatermacher (Bernhard) **165**:3-5, 7-8, 63, 71, 75, 96, 98, 105, 107, 130-31, 133-35
Théâtre (Adamov) **189**:17, 21, 23, 26, 47, 59
Théâtre (Gide) **177**:106
Theatre (Molnár) **20**:171
Théâtre I (Yourcenar) **193**:280
Théâtre II (Yourcenar) **193**:280
"Théâtre Alfred Jarry, première année" (Artaud) **36**:25
The Theatre Book of the Year (Nathan) **18**:317
Théâtre complet (Feydeau) **22**:87

Théâtre de la révolution (Rolland) **23**:257, 260, 262
Le Theatre de Maurice Boissard (Léautaud) **83**:207
Le théâtre du peuple (Rolland) **23**:257-58, 260
"Le Théâtre et la Cruauté" (Artaud) **36**:11, 28
Le théâtre et son double (Artaud) **3**:50, 54-5, 60; **36**:2, 6, 8-9, 12-13, 15-16, 29, 33, 36, 39
Théâtre inédit (Vian) **9**:531
Le théâtre Italien (Apollinaire) **8**:14
Théâtre Mirlitonesque (Jarry) **147**:265
Theatre of Dreams (Martinez Sierra and Martinez Sierra)
See *Teatro de ensueño*
"The Theatre of One Will" (Sologub)
See "Teatr odnoy volya"
The Theatre of the Moment (Nathan) **18**:322
The Theatre, the Drama, the Girls (Nathan) **18**:300
A Theatrical Novel (Bulgakov)
See *Teatral'nyi roman*
Theatrical Prologue to King David (Beer-Hofmann)
See *Vorspiel auf dem Theater zu "Köanig David"*
"Theatrical Recollections" (Caragiale) **76**:170
Theatricals, second series: The Album. The Reprobate (James) **11**:339-40
Theatricals: Two Comedies; Tenants. Disengaged (James) **11**:328
Theatro: Tragodies (Kazantzakis) **181**:304
The Theatrocrat (Davidson) **24**:166, 172, 184, 187
"The,bright,Centipede" (Villa)
See "Centipede Sonnet"
"The-Child-Who-Was-Tired" (Mansfield) **2**:451; **39**:295, 298, 301, 304; **164**:237, 269, 288, 292-93
"Thee and You" (Mitchell) **36**:264
"Thee Have I Sought, Divine Humility" (Coleridge) **73**:11
Theft (London) **9**:265
"Theft in a Pastry Shop" (Calvino)
See "Furto in una pasticceria"
Their Blood is Strong (Steinbeck) **135**:339
Their Days Are Numbered (Canetti)
See *Die Befristeten*
Their Eyes Were Watching God (Hurston) **121**:312-57; **131**:57-59, 66, 68, 70-76, 78-79, 81-85, 88-91, 94
Their Fathers' God (Rölvaag) **17**:325-27, 329-30, 333-34, 343, 346
Their Finest Hour (Churchill) **113**:100, 104, 118, 183
Their Hearts (Hunt) **53**:186-90, 192, 197, 199-200
"Their House of Dreams" (Aldrich) **125**:20
"Their Lawful Occasions" (Kipling) **8**:202; **17**:208
Their Lives (Hunt) **53**:186-88, 192, 197, 199-200
Their Lives and Letters (Cabell) **6**:76
Their Morals and Ours (Trotsky) **22**:358
"Their Quiet Lives" (Warner) **131**:322
Their Silver Wedding Journey (Howells) **17**:184
Their Wedding Journey (Howells) **7**:363, 365, 371-72, 377, 384-85, 391; **17**:172-75, 180, 183; **41**:234, 263
Their Yesterdays (Wright) **183**:346, 349, 379, 381
"Theism and Atheism" (Horkheimer) **132**:217
Thekla, ein Gedicht in neun Gesängen (Heyse) **8**:119
Thelma: A Norwegian Princess (Corelli) **51**:66-7
"Them, Crying" (Dickey) **151**:90, 109, 169
"Them Old Moth-Eaten Lovyers" (Murfree) **135**:210
"Thema und Variation" (Bachmann) **192**:14
Theme (Mann) **168**:170
"The Theme of Our Time" (Ortega y Gasset) **9**:344
"The Theme of the Traitor and the Hero" (Borges)
See "El Tema del traidor y del héroe"
"Theme with Variations" (Agee) **9**:24
Themes from the Lectures (Merleau-Ponty) **156**:183
"Then" (Lasker-Schueler) **57**:336
"Then and Now" (McCrae) **12**:210
"Then Came the Poor" (Bishop) **121**:44-6, 48, 87-8, 91
"Then There Is Only One Thing Left" (Borchert) **5**:103
"Then Was My Neophyte" (Thomas) **8**:450, 459
Théodat (Gourmont) **17**:130-31
Theodora (Bojer) **64**:22
Theodore Dreiser (Matthiessen) **100**:181, 184-86, 238, 241, 262
Theodore Roosevelt: An Autobiography (Roosevelt) **69**:187, 257, 266, 279
"Theodore Roosevelt As a Man of Letters" (Matthews) **95**:258
Theodore Roosevelt, the Citizen (Riis) **80**:435
Theodosia (Mandelstam) **6**:264
"Theodotos" (Cavafy) **7**:158
"The Theologians" (Borges)
See "Los teólogos"
"Theologico-Political Fragment" (Benjamin) **39**:41
Theologumena (Werfel) **8**:482-83
Théorie de la Religion (Bataille) **155**:53
Theorie der Erkenntnis (Husserl)
See *Untersuchungen zur Phänomenologie und Theorie der Erkenntnis*
La Théorie Platonicienne des Sciences (Halévy) **104**:110
"The Theory and Art of the 'Duende'" (García Lorca)
See "Teoría y juego del duende"
"Theory and Game of the Goblin" (García Lorca)
See "Teoría y juego del duende"
Theory and History of Historiography (Croce)
See *Teoria e storia della storiografia*
"The Theory and Play of the Duende" (García Lorca)
See "Teoría y juego del duende"
"Theory and practice of the Goblin" (García Lorca)
See "Teoría y juego del duende"
"Theory and Reality" (Norris) **155**:336
Theory of Aesthetic (Croce) **37**:80
"Theory of Anarchy" (Abbey) **160**:45, 72
"A Theory of Beauty" (Keynes) **64**:290
The Theory of Business Enterprise (Veblen) **31**:341-43, 346, 350-51, 353, 355-56, 358, 362, 377
"The Theory of Complex Phenomena" (Hayek) **109**:207
"The Theory of Historical Cycles" (Collingwood) **67**:182-83, 187, 189-90
A Theory of Literature (Natsume)
See *Bungakuron*
The Theory of Mind as Pure act (Gentile)
See *Teoria generale dello Spirito come puro atto*
"Theory of Rocketry" (Kornbluth) **8**:217
Theory of Social and Economic Organization (Weber)
See *Wirtschaft und Gesellschaft*
The Theory of Social Revolutions (Adams) **80**:4-5, 12, 21-2, 28, 30, 43, 46, 59
"The Theory of the Comic" (Brandes) **11**:70
The Theory of the Leisure Class (Veblen) **31**:338-39, 341, 346-49, 351-53, 355-56, 371-77
"A Theory of the Novel" (Futabatei)
See "Shōsetsu sōron"
"The Theory of the Text" (Barthes) **135**:152, 159
"The Theory of Torts" (Holmes) **77**:319, 321
Theosophie (Steiner) **14**:441, 445
Theosophy: An Introduction to the Supersensible Knowledge of the World and the Destiny of Man (Steiner)
See *Theosophie*
"There" (Nemerov) **124**:260
There and Back (MacDonald) **9**:292; **113**:283
There Are Crimes and Crimes (Strindberg) **1**:447, 460; **8**:414-15; **21**:353
"There Are No Gods" (Lawrence) **93**:53, 54
There Are Signs among Us (Ramuz)
See *Les signes parmi nous*
"There Can Be No Appeasement with Ruthlessness, We Must Be the Great Arsenal of Democracy" (Roosevelt) **93**:184
"There Can Be No One Among Us—No One Faction—Powerful Enough to Interupt the Forward March of Our People to Victory" (Roosevelt) **93**:184
"There Fate Is Hell" (March) **96**:248
There Is a Drop of Blood in Every Poem (Andrade)
See *Há uma gôta de sangue em cada poema*
There Is No More Firmament (Artaud) **3**:61
"There Is No Return" (Hippius)
See "Net vozrata"
"There is Strength in the Soil" (Stringer) **37**:343
"There Lies a Land" (Bjoernson)
See "Der ligger et land"
"There Must Be Words" (Cullen) **37**:147, 168
There Once Was a King (Peretz) **16**:395
There Shall Be No Night (Sherwood) **3**:414, 416, 418-19
"There Was" (Andreyev) **3**:20
"There was a Queen" (Faulkner) **170**:128
There Was a Rustle of Black Silk Stockings (McAlmon) **97**:118
"There Was a Saviour" (Thomas) **45**:372
"There Was One" (Parker) **143**:323
"There were a hundred" (Levī) **109**:287
"There Were Ninety-and-Nine" (Davis) **24**:199
"There Were Three" (Bonner) **179**:8, 12-14, 53, 57, 59
There Were Two Pirates (Cabell) **6**:76, 78
"There Will Come Soft Rains" (Teasdale) **4**:428
"Therefore, Adieu" (Cullen) **37**:168
"There's a Long, Long Trial a-Winding" (Kirk) **119**:280-81, 284-85, 291-92, 331-32, 335-38, 343
There's Always Another Windmill (Nash) **109**:355
There's Not a Bathing Suit in Russia, and Other Bare Facts (Rogers) **8**:332, 336
"There's Nothing Here" (Muir) **2**:487; **87**:193
"There's Wisdom in Women" (Brooke) **7**:122
Thérèse Raquin (Zola) **1**:593; **6**:561-64, 567-68; **41**:406-07, 415, 436-37
"These Clever Women" (Lawrence) **93**:23, 43, 46
"These Images Remain" (Sarton) **120**:291
These Lynnekers (Beresford) **81**:4-5
These Many Years: Recollections of a New Yorker (Matthews) **95**:272
These Restless Hands (Cabell) **6**:68, 76
These Twain (Bennett) **5**:28, 34, 42-3; **197**:15, 20, 26, 42, 78-81, 96, 109, 175-76
"These Words Also" (Nemerov) **124**:180, 251, 304
Thésée (Gide) **36**:100; **5**:218; **12**:167, 180-81; **177**:35, 46, 78, 87
Theses on the Philosophy of History (Benjamin)
See *Geschichtsphilosophische Thesen*
Theseus (Gide)
See *Thésée*
Theseus (Tsvetaeva) **7**:557, 565; **35**:378
"Theseus and Hippolyta" (Manning) **25**:275
"Theseus to Ariadne" (Bryusov) **10**:80
Thespis (Gilbert) **3**:218
"They" (Kipling) **8**:195, 201-02; **17**:212

They and I (Jerome) **23**:89-90
"They Are Alike" (Hippius) **9**:163
"They Are Not Missed" (Toomer) **172**:279-80
"They Call It Cricket" (Osborne) **153**:248, 255, 322
"They Came" (Lewis) **3**:285, 288
"They Can Only Hang You Once" (Hammett) **187**:169
They Don't Mean Any Harm (Milne) **88**:246
"They Grind Exceedingly Small" (Williams) **89**:386, 393
"They Have Taken My Lord" (Bryan) **99**:150
They Just Had to Get Married (Sturges) **48**:311
They Return at Evening: A Book of Ghost Stories (Wakefield) **120**:332-33, 342, 346, 353, 356-57
"They Say" (Jozsef) **22**:162
"They Say the Sea Is Loveless" (Lawrence) **93**:56, 60, 72
They Shall Inherit the Earth (Callaghan) **145**:254
They Shoot Horses, Don't They? (McCoy) **28**:209-18, 221-22, 227-33, 235, 237
"They Sowed and Watered" (p'Bitek) **149**:80-81, 83, 87, 89
They Stoop to Folly (Glasgow) **2**:182-84, 186, 190; **7**:333, 337, 341, 346-47
"They That Sow in Sorrow Shall Reap" (Agee) **1**:16
They That Walk in Darkness (Zangwill) **16**:445, 464, 467
"They Think They Know Joyce" (Gogarty) **15**:120
"They Wait on the Wharf in Black" (Lawson) **27**:121, 129, 131
They Went (Douglas) **68**:6-7, 14, 17, 25-9, 43, 46
They Went to Portugal (Macaulay) **44**:124
They Were Defeated (Macaulay)
See *The Shadow Flies*
They're Singing Again Now (Frisch)
See *Nun singen sie wieder*
Les Thibault (Martin du Gard) **24**:381-84, 386-88, 390, 393-401, 403-08, 411
"The Thief" (Apollinaire) **3**:37-8
"The Thief" (de la Mare) **53**:17
The Thief (Heym)
See *Der Dieb*
A Thief in the Night: The Last Chronicles of Raffles (Hornung) **59**:112, 114
The Thief's Journal (Genet)
See *Journal du voleur*
Thieves' Carnival (Anouilh)
See *Le Bal des voleurs*
"Thimble, Thimble" (Henry) **19**:172, 174
"Thin Cities" (Calvino) **183**:71
Thin Ice (Mackenzie) **116**:217-20, 231, 245, 254
"Thin Lips and False Teeth" (Lawson) **27**:149
The Thin Man (Hammett) **187**:45, 47-9, 51, 56-60, 77, 80-2, 133, 138-41, 155, 166-67, 205, 207, 214
"A Thin Waterfall" (Wright) **136**:299-300
The Thing (Chesterton) **1**:180
The Thing (from Another Planet) (Hecht) **101**:62, 78
"The Thing I Am" (Borges) **109**:7
"The Thing Imagined" (Wolfe) **4**:516
"The Thing in the Hall" (Benson) **27**:16, 19
"The Thing in the Weeds" (Hodgson) **13**:237
"The Thing Invisible" (Hodgson) **13**:236
"The Thing on the Roof" (Howard) **8**:133
"A Thing or Two" (Kandinsky) **92**:92
"Things" (Lewis) **4**:257
"Things" (Pilnyak) **23**:220
Things As They Are (Stein) **1**:433; **6**:410, 412-13; **28**:319-20, 327, 330, 338; **48**:226-28, 242, 264
"Things in Exact Proportion" (Quiroga)
See "La justa proporción de las cosas"
Things Most Frequently Encountered in Novels, Stories, and Other Such Things (Chekhov) **96**:77
Things Near and Far (Machen) **4**:278, 285
Things New and Old (Beerbohm) **24**:105
"Things of August" (Stevens) **12**:365, 383; **45**:281, 350
"Things Seen and Heard" (Vazov) **25**:453
"Things that Have Interested Me" (Bennett) **5**:46; **197**:20, 22
The Things We Are (Murry) **16**:334, 355
"Things Which Stimulate Memories" (Levi)
See "Mnemagoghi"
"Think It Over" (Holly) **65**:153
Think It Over, Giacomino! (Pirandello)
See *Pensaci, Giacomino!*
"Think No More, Lad: Laugh, Be Jolly" (Housman) **10**:247
Think of It, Giacomino! (Pirandello)
See *Pensaci, Giacomino!*
"Think of Nothing but the Day" (Symons) **11**:435
"The Thinker" (Anderson) **1**:56; **24**:35, 37, 54; **123**:15, 40, 78, 85, 105
The Thinker (Aldanov) **23**:21, 23
"Thinking and Moral Considerations" (Arendt) **193**:31, 87-8, 119, 124
"Thinking and Politics" (Arendt) **193**:119
Thinking (Arendt) **193**:30, 32-3, 36, 87, 157-58, 160
"Thinking Long" (Gogarty) **15**:109
The Thinking Machine (Futrelle) **19**:88-95
The Thinking Machine on the Case (Futrelle) **19**:90-1
"Thinking Makes It So" (Glasgow) **7**:343
"Thinking of a Relation between the Images of Metaphors" (Stevens) **45**:309-10
"The Thinking of the Body" (Yeats) **31**:400
"Thinking of the Lost World" (Jarrell) **177**:136, 141, 145, 154, 170, 173-74, 210, 218-19, 226
"Third Art" (Miyazawa) **76**:296
The "Third Book" Notebooks of Northrop Frye (Frye) **165**:256
The Third Book of Criticism (Jarrell) **177**:183, 186, 188, 190, 221
The Third Capital (Pilnyak)
See *Tretya stolitsa*
"The Third Coach" (Wakefield) **120**:332, 357
The Third Commandment (Hecht) **101**:61
"Third Eclogue" (Radnóti) **16**:420
"The Third Elegy" (Rilke) **1**:412; **195**:164
"The Third Eye" (Chambers) **41**:113
"The Third Eye" (Kuttner) **10**:274
The Third Generation (Himes) **139**:312-13
"The Third Ingredient" (Henry) **19**:190-91
"The Third Kingdom" (Huneker) **65**:158
The Third Life of Per Smevik (Rölvaag)
See *Amerika-breve fra P. A. Smevik til hans for og bror i Norge*
The Third Metropolis (Pilnyak)
See *Tretya stolitsa*
The Third Mind (Burroughs) **121**:124, 138, 142-43
"The Third of February" (Ivanov) **33**:138
"Third Party" (Kunikida Doppo)
See "Daisansha"
The Third Round (Sapper) **44**:316, 319-22
"The Third Shadow" (Wakefield) **120**:350
"The Third Son" (Platonov) **14**:408, 410-11, 413-14, 419
"Third Surrealist Manifesto" (Desnos)
See "Troisième manifeste"
The Third Symphony (Bely)
See *Vozvrat: Tretiia simfoniia*
The Third Violet (Crane) **11**:125, 131, 142-43, 162, 165-67
"The Third-and-a-Half Estate" (Benchley) **55**:19
"A Third-Class Carriage" (Thomas) **10**:459
"Thirst" (Andrić)
See "Zedj"
Thirst and Other One-Act Plays (O'Neill) **6**:329
Thirst for Love (Mishima)
See *Ai no Kawaki*
"Thirteen" (Thomas) **105**:320
"Thirteen O'Clock" (Kornbluth) **8**:216
Thirteen Poems (White) **176**:170
Thirteen Stories (Graham) **19**:104, 109, 112, 115, 133
The Thirteen Travellers (Walpole) **5**:493
"Thirteen Ways of Looking at a Blackbird" (Stevens) **3**:451, 475; **12**:365, 373, 376; **45**:285, 287, 322, 327-28, 338
"Thirteen Ways of Looking at a Skylark" (Nemerov) **124**:214
"Thirteen Years Later" (Böll)
See "Dreizehn Jahre später"
"The Thirteenth Labour" (D'Annunzio) **6**:143
The Thirties (Muggeridge) **120**:149-50, 185, 191
"Thirty Bob a Week" (Davidson) **24**:160, 178, 182-83, 188, 190-91
Thirty Day Princess (Sturges) **48**:285, 311
39 East (Crothers) **19**:74-5, 77
"XXXI" (Woodberry) **73**:365
Thirty Tales and Sketches by R. B. Cunninghame Graham (Graham) **19**:130
30,000 on the Hoof (Grey) **6**:184-85
Thirty Years Later (Micheaux) **76**:265
The Thirty-Nine Steps (Buchan) **41**:35-8, 41, 53-4, 56, 64-5, 68-71, 73, 78-80
"XXXVI" (Joyce) **159**:279
"The $30,000 Bequest" (Twain) **12**:432
The 32 (Artaud) **36**:37-8, 40
This Above All (Shiel) **8**:363
"This Africa to Come" (Fanon) **188**:122
"This Bread I Break" (Thomas) **8**:459; **45**:409
This Business of Living: Diary, 1935-1950 (Pavese)
See *Il mestiere di vivere: Diario, 1935-1950*
"This Christmas Eve" (Güiraldes)
See "Esta noche, noche buena"
"This Critic" (Bishop) **103**:4
"This Dim and Ptolemaic Man" (Bishop) **103**:4, 7
"This England" (Thomas) **10**:459
"This Flower" (Mansfield) **8**:285; **39**:304
"This Form of Life Needs Sex" (Ginsberg) **120**:25, 35
"This Horrible Case" (Burroughs) **121**:132
This in Which (Oppen) **107**:255-58, 263-65, 282, 303-04, 324, 328, 334
"This Indolence of Mine" (Svevo)
See "Il mio ozio"
"This is about Death" (Ginsberg) **120**:39
"This Is My Century" (Walker) **129**:321
This Is My Century: New and Collected Poems by Margaret Walker (Walker) **129**:276, 314, 316, 318, 323
"This Is My Country" (Coffin) **95**:21
"This Is No Case of Petty Right or Wrong" (Thomas) **10**:452, 456, 469
"This Is the Dress, Aider" (Stein) **48**:239
This Is the End (Benson) **17**:17-20, 22, 24, 27-9
This Is the Hour (Feuchtwanger)
See *Goya; oder, Der arge Weg der Erkenntnis*
"This Is the Track" (Owen) **5**:374
"'This Is the Voice of Algeria'" (Fanon) **188**:73, 97, 99
"This King Business" (Hammett) **187**:77, 88, 203
This Knot of Life (Shiel) **8**:361-62
"This Majestic Lie" (Crane) **11**:161
This Monstrous Regiment of Women (Ford) **57**:282; **172**:94
"This Night" (Davies) **5**:199
This Other World: Projections in the Haiku Manner (Wright) **136**:290-92, 299-303
"This Present Sadness Is Not Eased" (Esenin) **4**:115
This Shall Be (Tolstoy) **18**:383
This Side of Paradise (Fitzgerald) **1**:233-34, 236-37, 241-42, 244-45, 247-50, 254, 256-

59, 261, 264-65, 268-71; **6**:159-61, 168; **14**:148-49, 183; **28**:87, 89, 92, 110-11; **55**:191, 205; **157**:122, 131, 147, 182-84, 186-88, 190-91, 193-94, 198, 208-9
This Simian World (Day) **25**:130, 132, 136
"This Solitude of Cataracts" (Stevens) **3**:473
This Strange Adventure (Rinehart) **52**:296
This Sunday (Donoso)
See *Este Domingo*
"This Tenement Room" (Wright) **136**:301
"This, That, and the Other" (Nemerov) **124**:151, 178, 184, 194, 254
"This Thing Called They" (Woollcott) **5**:529
This Very Earth (Caldwell) **117**:20
"This Way for the Gas, Ladies and Gentlemen" (Borowski) **9**:21-2, 24-5
This Way for the Gas, Ladies and Gentlemen, and Other Short Stories (Borowski)
See *Kamienny swiat*
This Way to Heaven (Evans) **85**:12, 30
This Woman (di Donato) **159**:186, 189, 191, 195, 222-23, 226-30
"This World in Which We Die" (Bataille)
See "Ce monde où nous mourons"
Thistle Flowers (Prado)
See *Flores de cardo*
"Thithyphuth" (Borchert)
See "Shishiphush"
"Thomas Bernhard: Ein Versuch" (Bachmann) **192**:154
Thomas Cranmer of Canterbury (Williams) **1**:517; **11**:498, 501-02
Thomas Hardy from Serial to Novel (Chase) **124**:10-11
"Thomas Hardy's Novels" (Ellis) **14**:101
Thomas Hardy's Personal Notebooks (Hardy) **72**:261
"Thomas i Spanggaarden" (Jensen) **41**:307
"Thomas King" (Coffin) **95**:15
Thomas l'imposteur (Cocteau) **119**:80, 82, 106-7
Thomas Love Peacock (Van Doren) **18**:388
"Thomas McDonagh" (Ledwidge) **23**:111, 116-17
"Thomas of the Spang Farm" (Jensen)
See "Thomas i Spanggaarden"
Thomas Ross (Lie) **5**:324, 326, 332
Thomas the Imposter (Cocteau)
See *Thomas l'imposteur*
"Thomas Trevelyn" (Masters) **25**:298
Thomas Wendt (Feuchtwanger) **3**:181, 188
Thomas Wingfold, Curate (MacDonald) **9**:288, 292; **113**:225
Thomas-Thomas-Ancil-Thomas (Coffin) **95**:5, 8-9
The Thompson Travel Agency (Verne)
See *L'Agence Thompson and Co.*
Thoreau's Living Thoughts (Dreiser) **18**:52
The Thorn Bush (Hansen)
See *Tornebusken*
"A Thorn Forever in the Breast" (Cullen) **37**:146, 156
Thorndike Arithmetics (Thorndike) **107**:418
"The Thorough Who Get to the Bottom of Things" (Nietzsche)
See "Der Gründliche"
Those Cursed Tuscans (Malaparte)
See *Maledetti toscani*
"Those Days" (Akutagawa Ryūnosuke) **16**:27
Those Days (Bentley) **12**:18-19, 23-4
Those Delightful Americans (Duncan) **60**:177, 208, 213, 218, 226, 232
"Those Extraordinary Twins" (Twain) **6**:461, 462; **12**:432; **59**:169
"Those Images" (Yeats) **116**:305
"Those Names" (Paterson) **32**:375
"Those Spared—Will Die, Those Fallen—Rise from Under" (Tsvetaeva) **35**:394
"Those That Come Back" (Marquis) **7**:436
Those Times and These (Cobb) **77**:116
"Those Unforgettable People" (Kunikida Doppo)
See "Wasure-enu Hitobito"
Those Were the Days (Milne) **6**:316
"Those Who Die in Mussolini's Prisons" (Rolland) **23**:286
Those Who Do Not Forget (Rainis)
See *Tie, kas neaizmirst*
"Those Who Fought For the Achaean League" (Cavafy) **7**:160
"Those Who Live in the Storm" (Yeats) **31**:416
"Thou Art" (Ivanov) **33**:131-32
"Thou Famished Grave, I Will Not Fill Thee Yet" (Millay) **49**:231
"Thou Hast Done Well" (Redcam) **25**:330
"Thou Mighty Eros" (Södergran)
See "Du store Eros"
"Thou My Country" (Liliencron) **18**:208
"Thou Shall Not Covet" (Peretz)
See "Lo Sakhmod"
Thou Shalt Not Covet (Bromfield) **11**:83
"Thou Shalt Not Kill" (Tolstoy) **79**:430
"Though" (Nemerov) **124**:182, 254
Though Life Us Do Part (Phelps) **113**:340-42
"A Thought" (Milne) **88**:242
The Thought (Andreyev) **3**:18, 26
Thought and Letter (Babits)
See *Gondolat és írás*
"Thought and the Violin" (Peretz) **16**:397
"Thought for a Sunshiny morning" (Parker) **143**:323
"Thought Is One and Indivisible" (Péret)
See "La pensée est une et indivisible"
"The Thought of Trees" (Nemerov) **124**:259, 300
"A Thought Revolved" (Stevens) **12**:384; **45**:269, 344, 347, 350
"Thought the Paraclete" (Aurobindo) **63**:36
"The Thought-Reader" (Herzl) **36**:131
"Thoughts" (Nemerov) **124**:192
Thoughts and Adventures (Churchill) **113**:114
Thoughts and Aphorisms (Aurobindo) **63**:35
Thoughts and Glimpses (Aurobindo) **63**:35-6
Thoughts and Motives (Kahanovitsch)
See *Gedanken un motiven*
"Thoughts at the Trysting Stile" (Ledwidge) **23**:120
"Thoughts fer the Discuraged Farmer" (Riley) **51**:283
"Thoughts in a Zoo" (Cullen) **37**:165
"Thoughts in Loneliness" (Heidenstam) **5**:249-50, 253-56
"Thoughts in Solitude" (Heidenstam)
See "Thoughts in Loneliness"
"Thoughts in War" (Mann)
See *Gedanken im Kriege*
Thoughts Inside a Chimney (Hansen)
See *Tanker i en skorsten*
"Thoughts of Ph-a" (Hardy) **4**:152
"Thoughts of Phena" (Hardy) **53**:77; **143**:150
"Thoughts on a Breath" (Ginsberg) **120**:79
"Thoughts on Cider" (Morley) **87**:127
"Thoughts on Criticism" (Stephen) **23**:339
"Thoughts on First Passing the Hundredth Page of Finnegans Wake" (Nemerov) **124**:218
"Thoughts on Lessing" (Arendt) **193**:123
Thoughts on Machiavelli (Strauss) **141**:224-27, 233, 256
"Thoughts on Morals" (Harris) **24**:271, 280
"Thoughts on Poetry" (Ivanov) **33**:137
Thoughts on South Africa (Schreiner) **9**:400
"Thoughts on the American Mind" (Reyes)
See "Notas sobre la inteligencia Americana"
"Thoughts on the Late War" (Riley) **51**:292
"Thoughts on the Right Use of School Studies with a view of the Love of God" (Weil) **23**:376
"Thoughts on the Shape of the Human Body" (Brooke) **7**:124
Thoughts on the War (Mann)
See *Gedanken im Kriege*
Thoughts without Words (Day) **25**:133, 137
The Thousand and One Churches (Bell) **67**:17-18
"The Thousand and Second Night" (Merrill) **173**:153-54, 167, 176, 195-96, 218, 227, 259
"A Thousand Deaths" (London) **9**:273
A Thousand Plateaus (Deleuze)
See *Mille plateaux*
A Thousand Years with God (Dagerman)
See *Tusen är hos Gud*
The Thousand-Headed Man (Dent) **72**:39
A Thousand-Mile Walk to the Gulf (Muir) **28**:259, 264
The Thread (Giacosa)
See *Il filo*
Thread of Scarlet (Williams) **89**:389
"A Thread without a Knot" (Fisher) **87**:73
"Threatened City" (van Ostaijen)
See "Bedreigde stad"
"The Threatened Man" (Borges)
See "The Threatened One"
"Threatened Oedipus" (Musil) **68**:261
"The Threatened One" (Borges) **109**:109, 117
"Three" (Čapek) **6**:84
The Three (Guro)
See *Troe*
Three (Hellman)
See *Pentimento: A Book of Portraits*
Three (Singer) **33**:385
"Three Academic Pieces" (Stevens) **3**:454; **12**:361, 372, 376, 380; **45**:287, 296
Three Actors (Ghelderode)
See *Trois acteurs*
"Three Acts of Music" (Fitzgerald) **6**:167
Three against the World (Kaye-Smith) **20**:94, 102
"Three and One Are One" (Bierce) **7**:92; **44**:45
"Three and Thirty Years" (Jensen)
See "Tre og tredive Aar"
Three Antiques (Jarry) **147**:331
The Three Arrows (Murdoch) **171**:227
"The Three Bills" (Jarrell) **177**:178
The Three Black Pennys (Hergesheimer) **11**:260, 262-64, 269, 271-72, 274, 276, 278-81, 283, 285-86
"Three Blind Mice" (Kuttner) **10**:274
The Three Brides (Yonge) **48**:372, 374-75, 378
The Three Brothers (Muir) **2**:486; **87**:163, 194
"Three Bushes" (Yeats) **116**:341
Three by Flannery O'Connor (O'Connor) **132**:256-58
Three by Tey: Miss Pym Disposes. The Franchise Affair. Brat Farrar (Tey) **14**:452-53
"Three Calls" (Peretz) **16**:397
"The Three Cheers Boys" (Runyon) **10**:429
Three Circles of Light (di Donato) **159**:183, 186-89, 195-96, 202-5, 221-23, 227-30
Three Cities: A Trilogy (Asch)
See *Farn mabul*
"Three Colors" (Balmont)
See "Tri tsveta"
"The Three Conspirators" (Nemerov) **124**:282
Three Contributions to the Sexual Theory (Freud)
See *Drei Abhandlungen zur Sexualtheorie*
Three Couples (Kielland)
See *Tre par*
The Three Couriers (Mackenzie) **116**:250
Three Crosses (Tozzi)
See *The croci*
"Three Deaths" (Chekhov) **3**:153
"Three Deaths" (Tolstoy)
See "Tri smerti"
Three Deaths (Tolstoy)
See *Tri smerti*
The Three Devils (Dent) **72**:24
Three dialogues with Georges Duthuit (Beckett) **145**:88-91
"Three Disagreeable Girls" (Huneker) **65**:207
"Three Dreams in a Desert" (Schreiner) **9**:394

"Three Drops of Blood" (Hedāyat)
See "Seh qatreh khun"
Three Drops of Blood (Hedāyat) **21**:67
"Three Elucidations of the Ricardo Effect" (Hayek) **109**:207
"Three Episodes in the Life of a Brave Man" (Bierce) **44**:45
Three Essays on Sexuality (Freud)
See *Drei Abhandlungen zur Sexualtheorie*
Three Essays on the Theory of Sexuality (Freud)
See *Drei Abhandlungen zur Sexualtheorie*
Three Exemplary Novels (Unamuno)
See *Tres novelas ejemplares y un prólogo*
Three Exemplary Novels and a Prologue (Unamuno)
See *Tres novelas ejemplares y un prólogo*
The Three Fat Men (Olesha)
See *Tri tolstiaku*
The Three Fates (Crawford) **10**:141, 144, 146-50
"Three Fortunes" (Pyle) **81**:392
"The Three Friends" (de la Mare) **4**:78; **53**:27, 36
"The Three Friends" (Verhaeren) **12**:472
"Three Generations of the Same" (McAlmon) **97**:88-89
"Three Gifts" (Peretz)
See "Drei Matones"
"Three Girls" (McAlmon) **97**:114
Three Go Back (Gibbon) **4**:129-30
Three Guineas (Woolf) **1**:544; **20**:420; **43**:396-97; **56**:371, 377, 391, 405; **101**:204, 314, 324, 326; **128**:318, 337-38, 341, 345, 347, 355, 360-61, 366, 373-75
The Three Heron's Feathers (Sudermann)
See *Die drei Reiherfedern*
"The Three Holy Kings" (Rilke)
See "Die heiligen drei Könige"
The Three Hostages (Buchan) **41**:38, 41-2, 44, 46, 52, 55-8, 67-8, 71, 79-82
"Three Hours between Planes" (Fitzgerald) **6**:172
300 millones (Arlt)
See *Trescientos millones*
365 of Henry Ford's Sayings (Ford)
See *365 Sayings of Henry Ford*
365 Sayings of Henry Ford (Ford) **73**:70
"Three Imagist Poets" (Fletcher) **35**:113
The Three Impostors (Machen) **4**:276-77, 279
"Three in a Thousand" (Williams) **89**:384
Three in One (Molnár)
See *Kis hármaskönyu*
The Three Just Men (Wallace) **57**:397-98, 402, 408
"The Three Kisses" (Quiroga)
See "Los tres besos"
"The Three Lamps" (Thomas) **105**:346
The Three Leaps of Wanglun (Döblin)
See *Die drei Sprünge des Wang-lun*
"Three Letters and a Foot" (Quiroga)
See "Tres cartas y un pie"
"Three Little Heads" (Aleichem) **35**:324
"Three Little Songs" (Hofmannsthal) **11**:294
Three Lives (Stein) **1**:426-28, 430, 433-34, 440-41; **6**:404-05, 407-10, 412, 414-15; **28**:306, 309, 311-12, 318-20, 322, 324, 328, 331, 334, 336-39; **48**:211, 220, 224-27, 230, 240-42, 246-48, 250, 252, 257, 261, 264
"The Three Marvels of Hy" (Sharp) **39**:376, 393
Three Men in a Boat—To Say Nothing of the Dog (Jerome) **23**:76-8, 80-5, 86-7, 90-1
Three Men on the Bummel (Jerome) **23**:81
Three Men on Wheels (Jerome)
See *Three Men on the Bummel*
"Three Miraculous Soldiers" (Crane) **11**:167
"The Three Mirrors" (Muir) **87**:265
"The Three Mulla-Mulgars" (de la Mare) **4**:77; **53**:28, 41-2
Three Novels (Čapek) **192**:226
Three Novels (Beckett) **145**:200, 202
The Three Novels of Roger Mais (Mais) **8**:241
The Three Oak Mystery (Wallace) **57**:406-7
"Three O'Clock" (Torrence) **97**:152
"Three O'Clock in the Afternoon" (Babel) **13**:32
The Three of Us (Crothers) **19**:70, 73, 82
"Three Old Men" (Tolstoy) **4**:458
"Three Partners" (Harte) **25**:199
Three Paths to the Lake (Bachmann)
See *Simultan*
"Three Paths to the Lake" (Bachmann)
See "Drei Wege zum See"
Three Pens (Raabe) **45**:194, 202
Three Philosophical Poets (Santayana) **40**:352, 393-94, 415
Three Pieces of Pianoforte (Schoenberg) **75**:292
"Three Pirates of Penzance" (Rinehart) **52**:281
"The Three Plastic Virtues" (Apollinaire) **51**:39, 42
Three Plays (Abe) **131**:13-14
Three Plays (Kuzmin) **40**:201
Three Plays (Saroyan) **137**:202
Three Plays (Williams) **11**:489
Three Plays for Puritans (Shaw) **3**:378; **9**:414; **21**:334; **45**:212
Three Poems (Reyes)
See *Tres poemas*
Three Poems of War (Claudel)
See *Trois poèmes de guerre*
"The Three Portraits" (Lang) **16**:270
"Three Portraits With Shading" (García Lorca)
See "Tres retratos con sombra"
Three Primitives (Huysmans) **7**:412
"Three Questions" (Blok) **5**:95
"Three Questions" (Tolstoy) **11**:463
Three Rolls of the King's Court, 1194-1195 (Maitland) **65**:249
"Three Rounds" (Morrison) **72**:353
The Three Royal Monkeys (de la Mare)
See "The Three Mulla-Mulgars"
"Three Rubles" (Bunin) **6**:52; **63**:266-68, 273-74;
"The Three Seamstresses" (Peretz) **16**:406
Three Sickles (Remizov)
See *Tri serpa*
"The Three Sisters" (Khlebnikov)
See "Tri sestry"
The Three Sisters (Chekhov)
See *Tri Sestry*
The Three Sisters (Sinclair) **3**:434-35, 438-40, 442; **11**:411, 413
Three Sisters: A Drama in Four Acts (Chekhov)
See *Tri Sestry*
"Three Songs" (Crane) **5**:186; **80**:82-3, 89, 103, 126, 139, 166, 182, 189
"Three Sonnets on Oblivion" (Sterling) **20**:379, 386
"The Three Sons of Noah and the History of Mediterranean Civilization" (Weil) **23**:391
"The Three Strangers" (Hardy) **4**:159
"Three Studies on the Subject of Realism" (Herbert) **168**:24
"The Three Taverns" (Robinson) **5**:407, 409, 417; **101**:130
The Three Taverns (Robinson) **101**:105, 110, 134
The Three Temptations (Williams) **11**:499
"Three Things" (Yeats) **1**:572
"3,000 Years Among the Microbes" (Twain) **185**:327, 329
Three Times Dead or the Secret of the Heath (Braddon) **111**:214
Three Times Seven Songs of Pierrot Lunaire (Schoenberg)
See *Dreimals Sieben Lieder des Pierrot Lunaire*
Three Tragedies of Federico García Lorca (García Lorca) **181**:44-50
Three Travellers Watch a Sunrise (Stevens) **3**:465; **12**:356, 363
"Three Vagabonds of Trinidad" (Harte) **25**:213, 217, 222
"Three Versions of Judas" (Borges)
See "Tres versiones de Judas"
"The Three Voices" (Service) **15**:404
Three Ways Home (Kaye-Smith) **20**:116
Three Weeks (Glyn) **72**:127, 130, 136, 142
The Three Wild Men (Dent) **72**:27
"Three Wise Men of the East Side" (Cobb) **77**:136, 141-2
"Three Women" (Cather)
See "Old Mrs. Harris"
"Three Women" (Hammett) **187**:86
Three Women (Musil)
See *Drei Frauen*
Three Worlds (Van Doren) **18**:401-04
"Three Years" (Chekhov)
See "Tri goda"
"The Three-Brood Hen" (Remizov) **27**:351, 353
"The Threefold Place" (Muir) **87**:307
The Threefold Social Order (Steiner) **13**:446
The Threepenny Opera (Brecht)
See *Die Dreigroschenoper*
Three's a Crowd (Biggers) **65**:2
"The Three-Ten" (Ford) **15**:70
"Threnody" (Parker) **143**:321
"Threnody" (Swinburne) **36**:342
"Threnody for a Brown Girl" (Cullen) **37**:155, 165
"Threnody on a Starry Night" (Lewis) **3**:287
"Threnos" (Brennan) **17**:59
"Threshing Machine" (Meynell) **6**:299
Thrice Noble-One (Palamas) **5**:379
Thrifty Stock and Other Stories (Williams) **89**:360, 366-7, 369, 379
Thrilling Cities (Fleming) **193**:215
"Thro' Bogac Ban" (Ledwidge) **23**:112, 123
"Throat Microphone Experiments" (Burroughs) **121**:141
Thrond (Bjoernson) **7**:105-06; **37**:33-6
"Through a Glass, Darkly" (Patton) **79**:305-6
Through Darkened Vales (Griffith) **68**:247
"Through Galicia" (Tolstoy) **18**:378
Through Glacier Park (Rinehart) **52**:283
Through Nature to Christ (Abbott) **139**:11, 13-14, 26, 32, 37
Through the Brazilian Wilderness and Papers on Natural History (Roosevelt) **69**:239, 267
Through the Breakers (Griffith) **68**:245
Through the Eye of the Needle (Howells) **7**:377-78, 380
"Through the Fanlight" (Babel)
See "V shchelochku"
"Through the Fire" (Kipling) **8**:185
Through the Forests, through the Fields (Pabst) **127**:354, 359, 364
"Through the Gates of the Silver Key" (Lovecraft) **4**:266, 272; **22**:209-10, 216, 218, 238
Through the Magic Door (Doyle) **7**:221
"Through the Panama" (Lowry) **6**:240-41, 250
Through the Torii (Noguchi) **80**:383
"Through the Vortex of a Cyclone" (Hodgson) **13**:235-36
"Through the Walls" (Levi) **109**:301-02
Through the Wheat (Boyd) **111**:199-206
Through the Window (Feydeau)
See *Par la fenêtre*
"Through These Pale Cold Days" (Rosenberg) **12**:295, 301, 306
"Through Volyn" (Tolstoy) **18**:378
"Thrown Away" (Kipling) **8**:198
"The Thrown-Up Stone" (Ady) **11**:15
"Thunder Can Break" (Okigbo)
See "Come Thunder"
"Thunder in the Dawn" (Kuttner) **10**:267, 271
Thunder Mixed with Dust (Anwar)
See *Deru tjampur debu*
Thunder Moon (Faust) **49**:40-41
Thunder on the Left (Morley) **87**:124
"Thunder Storm" (Wylie) **8**:534
Thunderball (Fleming) **193**:198, 200-01, 206, 224, 228, 238, 242

The Thunderbolt (Pinero) **32**:393, 397-98, 400, 402-03, 405, 414-15
"The Thunderstorm" (Trakl)
See "Das Gewitter"
The Thunderstorm (Strindberg) **21**:353
"Thunderstorm in the Ozarks" (Fletcher) **35**:106
"Thursday" (Millay) **4**:307, 310; **49**:203
"Thursday" (Parker) **143**:318
Thursday (Chesterton)
See *The Man Who Was Thursday*
"Thus I Refute Beelzy" (Collier) **127**:249, 261
"Thus I Reply to René Dubos" (Abbey) **160**:54
"Thus Life Goes" (Guro)
See "Tak zhizn idet"
Thus Spake Zarathustra: A Book for All and None (Nietzsche)
See *Sprach Zarathustra: Ein Buch für Alle und Keinen*
Thus to Revisit: Some Reminiscences of Ford Madox Hueffer (Ford) **1**:275; **15**:79; **39**:142
Thuvia, Maid of Mars (Burroughs) **32**:58
Thy Servant Dog (Kipling) **8**:196
Thy Soul Shall Bear Witness (Lagerloef) **36**:244
Thyrza (Gissing) **3**:222, 227, 229-33; **24**:220, 233, 243, 248
"Ti con zero" (Calvino) **183**:10, 227-28, 230
Ti con zero (Calvino) **183**:8-11, 13, 15, 62-63, 71, 96, 145, 159, 191, 193-94, 216, 227
Ti ho sposato per allegria (Ginzburg) **156**:4, 63, 67, 70, 83
"A ti, viva" (Aleixandre) **113**:12, 69
La tía Tula (Unamuno) **2**:564; **9**:513, 515, 517; **148**:256, 339
"Tiare Tahiti" (Brooke) **2**:54, 56, 61; **7**:124-25, 129
"Tibet sur Seine" (Sarduy) **167**:220
"Tibulliana" (Carducci) **32**:106
"The Ticket" (Nabokov)
See "Bilet"
The Ticket That Exploded (Burroughs) **121**:116, 119-21, 123, 125, 128-30, 137-41
Tickless Time (Glaspell) **55**:234-36
The Tide of Fortune (Zweig)
See *Sternstunden der Menschheit*
"The Tide of Sorrow" (Baker) **10**:28
The Tide of Time (Masters) **2**:468-70
Tidemarks: Some Records of a Journey (Tomlinson) **71**:383-384, 386, 391-393, 397, 400-1, 405-6
"Tiden barn" (Lagerkvist) **144**:217
"Tides" (Roberts) **8**:327
"Tidig gryning" (Södergran) **31**:288
"Tidings" (Bialik) **25**:50
The Tidings Brought to Mary (Claudel)
See *L'annonce faite à Marie*
The Tidings Brought to Mary (Giraudoux)
See *L'annonce faite à Marie*
"Tidings from Ôkubo" (Nagai)
See *Okubo dayori*
"Tidogolain" (Moréas) **18**:286
"The Tie" (Kipling) **8**:196
Tie, kas neaizmirst (Rainis) **29**:392
Tiempo (Jiménez) **183**:321
"Tiempo de espera" (Huidobro) **31**:126
"The T'ien-an Gate" (Wen I-to) **28**:412
Tierra de nadie (Onetti) **131**:133-34, 136, 151-53, 155-56, 159-63, 183, 203, 216, 262, 289-92, 295-96
Tierra de promisión (Rivera) **35**:289, 291-92
La tierra de tudos (Blasco Ibáñez) **12**:36
Tierra y luna (García Lorca) **197**:229
"The Tiger and the Deer" (Aurobindo) **63**:8
The Tiger and the Horse (Bolt) **175**:8, 10, 12, 15-17
Tiger at the Gates (Giraudoux)
See *La guerre de Troie n'aura pas lieu*
Tiger Joy (Benét) **7**:78
"The Tiger's Bride" (Carter) **139**:47, 113-14, 145, 216-17, 219
"The tigers of Annam" (Borges)
See "Los tigres del Annam"
"The Tiger-Skin" (Hunt) **53**:190, 192
Tigre reale (Verga) **3**:539
Tigres azules (Borges) **109**:8
"Los tigres del Annam" (Borges) **109**:40, 43
"Las tijeras" (Unamuno) **148**:307-8
Tikhie pesni (Annensky) **14**:16, 18, 20
Tikhii strazh (Kuzmin) **40**:195, 199
Tik-Tok of Oz (Baum) **7**:21, 24, 27; **132**:12, 15-16, 50, 53, 97, 100
Til Daybreak (Moricz)
See *Kivilágos kivirradtig*
"Til dig" (Obstfelder) **23**:179
"Tilbury Town" (Robinson) **101**:112
"Tilghman's Ride from Yorktown to Philadelphia" (Pyle) **81**:390
Till Damaskus (Strindberg) **1**:448-49, 454, 456, 459-60, 463; **8**:411-14, 416; **21**:350, 365; **47**:373
"Till Eros" (Södergran) **31**:290
Till Eulenspiegel (Hauptmann) **4**:202, 205-07
"Till fots fick jag gå genom solsystemen" (Södergran) **31**:285
"Till hafvet" (Ekelund) **75**:95
"Tilly" (Joyce) **16**:228; **159**:279
Tilting at Windmills (Horvath)
See *Mit dem Kopf durch die Wand*
Timár Virgil fia (Babits) **14**:40
Timberlane (Lewis) **13**:350
"Time" (Herbert)
See "Czas"
"Time" (Lawrence) **93**:45
"Time" (Leino)
See "Aika"
"Time" (Merrill) **173**:237
"Time" (Riley) **51**:304
"Time and Beauty" (Symons) **11**:446
"Time and Eternity" (Morgenstern) **8**:304
Time and Free Will: An Essay on the Immediate Data of Consciousness (Bergson)
See *Les données immédiates de la conscience*
"Time and J. W. Dunne" (Borges) **109**:51, 77
"Time and Leigh Brothers" (March) **96**:261
"Time and Tear" (Sterling) **20**:386
Time and the Gods (Dunsany) **2**:136; **59**:7, 17-9, 29
Time and the Hunter (Calvino)
See *Ti con zero*
"Time and the Soldier" (Gurney) **33**:86, 101
Time and Tide (Ruskin) **20**:307
Time and Time Again (Hilton) **21**:99
Time and Western Man (Lewis) **2**:391, 393, 395; **9**:235-37, 239-41, 247-48; **104**:159-66, 181, 186-87, 201-02, 257-58, 274-76, 280, 286, 288, 295
"Time Does Not Bring Relief" (Millay) **49**:201
"Time Eating" (Douglas) **40**:64, 73, 86, 89, 91
A Time for Judas (Callaghan) **145**:254
"Time for Rich Silence" (Sarton) **120**:271
"Time Held in Time's Despite" (Muir) **87**:256
Time Importuned (Warner) **131**:310
A Time in Rome (Bowen) **148**:17, 20
"Time Is Fleeting" (Carducci)
See "Ruit hora"
"Time Locker" (Kuttner) **10**:268-69
The Time Machine (Wells) **6**:523, 533-34, 538, 541-45, 547-48, 554-55; **12**:487-88, 501, 506, 508-11; **19**:420, 424, 428-31, 434, 436-39, 441-42, 446-50, 452; **133**:223-344
Time of Crisis (Baroja)
See *Momentum catastrophicum*
The Time of Man (Roberts) **68**:293-94, 296, 298-99, 303, 308-9, 317, 321-27, 330, 333, 335, 338-43, 346-49, 352-53, 360-61, 363
Time of Peace (Williams) **89**:361, 389
"The Time of Roses" (Naidu) **80**:272, 316
The Time of the Angels (Murdoch) **171**:221, 225, 228-29, 245, 279, 323, 330
Time of the Butcherbird (La Guma) **140**:210, 218, 221, 228-29, 252-58, 260-62, 272-73
"The Time of Their Lives" (O'Faolain) **143**:226
The Time of Your Life (Saroyan) **137**:144, 147, 152-56, 168-69, 181-83, 186, 190, 194, 196, 201-6
Time Overflows (Éluard)
See *Le temps déborde*
"Time Passes" (Woolf) **1**:538, 540
Time Perspective in Aboriginal American Culture (Sapir) **108**:246-47, 252-53, 257, 261-63, 285
Time Pieces (Morris) **107**:235-36, 242-44
Time Present (Osborne) **153**:239, 242, 260
Time Regained (Proust)
See *Le temps retrouvé*
"Time Signal" (Nezval) **44**:240-41
Time Terror (Dent) **72**:24
Time: The Present (Slesinger) **10**:441, 445
Time Trap (Kuttner) **10**:268
The Time-Image (Deleuze)
See *Cinema 2 l'image-Temps*
The Times (Pinero) **32**:405, 412
"Time's Acre" (Lowell) **8**:231
Times Alone (Machado)
See *Soledades: Poesías*
"Times Have Changed" (Williams) **89**:402
Times Have Changed (Bromfield) **11**:82
The Times History of the War in South Africa (Childers) **65**:55
Time's Laughingstocks and Other Verses (Hardy) **53**:71, 75, 84, 117; **143**:147
"Times of Day" (Grove) **4**:144
"The Times Unsettled Are" (Slesinger) **10**:441
"The Times Worsen" (Jarrell) **177**:238
Timid and Cruel Verses (Palamas) **5**:385
"Timid Lover" (Cullen) **37**:155
"Tin Can" (Bonner) **179**:10, 13, 21, 23, 45, 53, 56-57, 59
The Tin Woodman of Oz (Baum) **7**:25; **132**:51, 97-101
"La tinaja bonita" (Wister) **21**:373, 399
Ting-a-ling Tales (Stockton) **47**:316, 328
Tinker's Leave (Baring) **8**:43
The Tinker's Wedding (Synge) **6**:427, 429-30, 432-34, 439, 441-42; **37**:348-50, 363, 377-78, 383, 386
"Tinko Ghānsiyā Gīt" (Devkota) **23**:49
"El tintorero enmascarado Hákim de Merv" (Borges) **109**:40, 42, 55
Tiny Carteret (Sapper) **44**:316, 320
Tiny Luttrell (Hornung) **59**:113
"A Tiny Wrinkle" (Remizov)
See "Morshchinka"
Tipos trashumantes (Pereda) **16**:367-68, 380
Tipos y paisajes (Pereda) **16**:373, 380
Tirano banderas (Valle-Inclán) **5**:476, 484, 487-89
"Tire Chain Bridge" (Brautigan) **133**:10-12
"The Tiredness of Rosabel" (Mansfield) **2**:453; **8**:284; **39**:301; **164**:321
"Tiresias" (Swinburne) **36**:318
"Tiresome Story" (Chekhov) **3**:152
"A Tiresomesome Story" (Chekhov)
See "A Dreary Story"
"Tirzey Potter" (Masters) **2**:465; **25**:300
Tis Folly to Be Wise; or, Death and Transfiguration of Jean-Jacques Rousseau (Feuchtwanger)
See *Narrenweisheit; oder, Tod und Verkiarung des Jean-Jacques Rousseau*
Tis Good! (Mayakovski) **18**:243
"Tisch" (Kandinsky) **92**:66
Tish (Rinehart) **52**:282
Tishina (Balmont) **11**:42
"Tish's Spy" (Rinehart) **52**:281
"A Tisza-Parton" (Ady) **11**:15, 20
The Titan (Dreiser) **10**:165-69, 173, 176-77, 180, 182-86; **18**:54-7, 60-1, 63-4, 67, 71-2; **35**:59, 62; **83**:90
Titanic (Fondane) **159**:254
"The Titanic Bar" (Andrić)
See "Bife titanik"
The Titans (Doughty) **27**:59, 65, 69
"Tite Poulette" (Cable) **4**:32

Los títeres de Cachiporra (García Lorca) **7**:292; **49**:106-08
"The Tithe of the Lord" (Dreiser) **35**:74
The Title (Bennett) **5**:43; **197**:14, 16-18, 22
"Tito" (Seton) **31**:279-80
Tittle-Tattle (Hedāyat)
See *Vilinq ari*
Tituba of Salem Village (Petry) **112**:362-67
"Tjatetan th. 1946" (Anwar) **22**:18, 22, 25
"Tjerita buat Dien Tamaela" (Anwar) **22**:18, 24, 26
"Tjintaku djauh dipulau" (Anwar) **22**:22
"Tjodolf" (Undset) **3**:523
"Tjuren" (Södergran) **31**:288, 291
"Tlön, Uqbar, Orbis Tertius" (Borges) **109**:27, 51-2, 76, 87, 158
"To a Beautiful Prostitute" (Devkota)
See "Ek sundarī veśyāprati"
"To a Belgian Friend" (Johnson) **19**:256
To a Blue Star (Gumilev)
See *K sinei zvezde*
"To a Bridegroom" (Hardy) **72**:238
"To a Brown Boy" (Cullen) **4**:40; **37**:147, 152, 168
"To a Brown Girl" (Cullen) **4**:40; **37**:146, 152, 167
"To a Buddha Seated on a Lotus" (Naidu) **80**:274
"To a Cat" (Swinburne) **36**:347
"To a Certain Nation" (Chesterton) **1**:182
"To a Child" (Morley) **87**:142
"To a Child" (Vazov) **25**:454
"To a Child Dancing on the Shore" (Yeats) **31**:385
"To a Child in Death" (Mew) **8**:297
"To a Cock" (Gogarty) **15**:114
"To a Comrade in Arms" (Lewis) **3**:287
"To a Dark Cloudy Night" (Devkota)
See "Saghan tamisráprati"
"To a Dog's Memory" (Guiney) **41**:205, 221
"To a Drawing by Marc Chagall" (Schwitters) **95**:342
"To A. E. Going to America" (Gogarty) **15**:106, 109
"To a Friend" (Anwar)
See "Kepada kawan"
"To a Friend" (Gogarty) **15**:101
"To a Friend" (Nemerov) **124**:153
"To a Friend" (Yeats) **18**:446
"To a Gentleman Who Wanted to See the First Drafts" (Lowell) **8**:231
To a God Unknown (Steinbeck) **135**:273, 290, 301, 317, 321, 357
"To a Golden-Haired Girl in a Louisiana Town" (Lindsay) **17**:241
"To a Lady at the Piano—Mrs. R—n" (Chopin) **127**:201
"To a Linnet in a Cage" (Ledwidge) **23**:118, 120
"To a Nude Walking" (Radiguet) **29**:357
"To a Passionist" (Johnson) **19**:243, 253
"To a Person Sitting in Darkness" (Twain) **6**:477; **12**:449
"To a Poetaster" (Radnóti) **16**:419
"To a Post-Office Inkwell" (Morley) **87**:124
"To a Scholar in the Stacks" (Nemerov) **124**:197, 254, 311-12
"To a Seamew" (Swinburne) **36**:342, 347
"To a Spanish Friend" (Johnson) **19**:256
"To a Stone by the Wayside" (Gonzalez Martinez) **72**:146
"To a Tree" (Bishop) **121**:21
"To a Wealthy Man" (Yeats) **31**:420; **93**:351
"To a Woman Companion" (Annensky)
See "Sputnice"
"To Aden" (Endo) **152**:167, 170
"To Akhmatova" (Tsvetaeva) **35**:386
"To Alia" (Tsvetaeva)
See "Ale"
"To All Prisoners" (Toller)
See "An alle Gegangen"
"To America" (Johnson) **19**:210
"To an Athlete Dying Young" (Housman) **1**:357; **10**:247, 250
"To an Honest Friend" (Sarton) **120**:318
"To an Ideal" (Guiney) **41**:221-23
"To an Isle in the Water" (Yeats) **116**:334, 336
"To An Old Enemy" (Buchanan) **107**:60
"To an Old Nurse" (Sterling) **20**:386
"To an Old Philosopher in Rome" (Stevens) **3**:449; **12**:368; **45**:274, 314, 325, 329
"To an Orphan Child" (Hardy) **53**:81
"To an Unknown Poet" (Cullen) **37**:156
"To an Unknown Poet" (Noguchi) **80**:380
"To an Unknown Priest" (Guiney) **41**:220
To and Fro (Horvath)
See *Hin und Her*
"To Ann Scott-Moncrieff (1914-1943)" (Muir)
See "For Ann Scott-Moncrieff (1914-1943)"
"To Antiochus of Epiphanes" (Cavafy) **7**:157
"To Aphrodite, with a Talisman" (Wylie) **8**:536
"To Augustus John" (Gogarty) **15**:114
"To Balmont" (Tsvetaeva) **35**:394
To Be a Pilgrim (Cary) **1**:143-45; **29**:64, 66-9, 71-3, 75, 79-80, 88, 90-2, 96, 105, 109; **196**:175, 177, 203, 207, 215, 222-23
To Be and To Live (Jarry) **147**:332
"To Be Carved on a Stone at Thoor Ballylee" (Yeats) **93**:389
"To Be Dead" (Jarrell) **177**:215
"To Be Filed for Reference" (Kipling) **8**:185
"To Be in Truth" (Bjoernson) **37**:28
To Be Young, Gifted, and Black (Hansberry) **192**:245, 276, 290, 305, 314, 319, 325-26, 329
"To Blok" (Tsvetaeva) **35**:394
"To Boris Pil'niak" (Pasternak)
See "Borisu Pil'niaku"
"To Brander Matthews" (Dobson) **79**:30
"To Build a Fire" (London) **9**:267, 269-70, 273; **15**:262
"To C. M." (Middleton) **56**:173
"To Campions" (Lawrence) **93**:116
"To Carl Sandburg" (Lowell) **8**:227, 230
"To Catch a Thief" (Hornung) **59**:112
"To Certain Critics" (Cullen) **4**:46; **37**:157, 159
"To Certain Friends" (Johnson) **19**:256
"To Ch'en Tu-hsiu As I Pass by Wakamatsu-cho in a State of Emotion" (Su Man-shu) **24**:456
"To C. H. P." (Morley) **87**:143
"To Claudia Homonoea" (Wylie) **8**:536
"To Clio Muse of History" (Nemerov) **124**:249, 286, 291, 301, 303-4
To Clothe the Naked (Pirandello)
See *Vestire gli ignudi*
"To Come So Far" (Warner) **131**:320
To C. T (Oppen) **107**:282, 284
"To D——, Dead by Her Own Hand" (Nemerov) **124**:273, 290, 304
To Damascus (Strindberg)
See *Till Damaskus*
To Damascus III (Strindberg) **1**:463; **8**:410
"To Dante Gabriel Rossetti" (Buchanan) **107**:60
"To David, about His Education" (Nemerov) **124**:178, 251
"To David in Heaven" (Buchanan) **107**:13
"To Desmond MacCarthy: Aet. 22" (MacCarthy) **36**:258
To Die in June, Gasping for Air (Arenas)
See *Morir en junio y con la lengua afuera*
"To Dog" (Bierce) **7**:97
"To Dorothy Wellesley" (Yeats) **31**:410
To Dream of A Butterfly (Hagiwara)
See *Chō o yumemu*
"To E. C." (Field) **43**:182
"To E. M. G." (Gray) **19**:142
To Eat One's Fill (Moricz)
See *Egyszer jóllakni*
"To Edmund CLerihew Bentley" (Chesterton) **64**:45
"To Edward Thomas" (Lewis) **3**:287, 290-91
"To Eilish of the Fair Hair" (Ledwidge) **23**:116
"To Endymion" (Cullen) **4**:43, 53; **37**:155, 164
"To Eros" (Owen) **27**:225
"To Eros" (Södergran)
See "Till Eros"
"To Fate" (Babits)
See "A Sorshoz"
To Find Oneself (Pirandello)
See *Trovarsi*
"To France" (Cullen) **37**:150, 156, 158
"To Franz Kafka" (Muir) **87**:168
"To Giuseppe Garibaldi" (Carducci) **32**:90
"To Gloucestershire" (Gurney) **33**:94
"To God" (Gurney) **33**:94, 98, 100
"To God" (Lasker-Schueler) **57**:334
"To Gurdjieff Dying" (Toomer) **172**:279
"To H. M.: On Reading His Poems" (Nemerov) **124**:181
"To Hamish Hamilton" (Chandler)
See "Letter to Hamish Hamilton, September 19, 1951"
To Have and Have Not (Hemingway) **115**:143, 145-46
To Have Done with the Judgement of God (Artaud)
See *Pour en finir avec le jugement de dieu*
"To Helen" (Bishop) **103**:5
"To Her" (Morley) **87**:140
To Him that Hath (Connor) **31**:105-06, 114, 116
"To His Love" (Gurney) **33**:88, 96
"To Houghton: Thanksgiving 1902" (Gilman) **117**:150
"To Imagination" (Sterling) **20**:383
"To India" (Naidu) **80**:289
"To Ireland in the Coming Times" (Yeats) **11**:512; **31**:416
"To Irene" (Middleton) **56**:189
"To Ironfounders and Others" (Bottomley) **107**:4
"To John Houşeman" (Chandler)
See "Letter to John Houseman, November 10, 1950"
To John Keats (Lowell) **1**:377, 380; **8**:225-27, 231
"To John Keats, Poet: At Spring Time" (Cullen) **4**:40; **37**:154, 164
"To Kentucky" (Cotter) **28**:46
"To Kill Time" (Gorky) **8**:74
To Leeward (Crawford) **10**:138, 140-41, 143-44, 150
"To Leo XIII" (Johnson) **19**:255
To Let (Galsworthy) **1**:294; **45**:41, 46, 61, 69
"To Lettice, My Sister" (Lawrence) **93**:67
"To Literary Prosecutors" (Tsvetaeva)
See "Literaturnym prokuroram"
To Live as We Wish (Aldanov)
See *Živi kak chočeš*
To London Town (Morrison) **72**:365, 369, 371-73, 388, 395
"To Long Island First" (Gurney) **33**:95, 98
"To Louise" (Dunbar) **12**:106
"To Louise Michael" (Markham) **47**:278
"To Love" (Aleixandre) **113**:24, 26
"To Love" (Naidu) **80**:344
To Love and Be Wise (Tey) **14**:449-50, 452, 461, 463-64
"To Lovers of Earth: Fair Warning" (Cullen) **4**:50; **37**:155, 165
"To Lu Chi" (Nemerov) **124**:155, 181, 200
"To Lucrezia" (Percy) **84**:213
"To Marc Chagall" (Éluard) **7**:260, 262
"To Marcus Aurelius" (Herbert) **168**:23, 78
"To Mary on Earth" (Buchanan) **107**:13
"To Mayakovsky" (Tsvetaeva)
See "Maiakovskomu"
"To Me Dead" (Carpenter) **88**:118
To Meet the Seven Deadly Sins (Bridie) **3**:139
"To Melisande" (Middleton) **56**:184
"To Milton" (Wilde) **8**:487
"To Miranda, in the Stadium" (Jiménez) **183**:330
"To Monica Thought Dying" (Thompson) **4**:435

"To Morfydd" (Johnson) **19**:228, 232, 244, 255-56
"To Morfydd Dead" (Johnson) **19**:256
"To Mother, with Love, Some Thoughts About Books on Mother's Day" (Rinehart) **52**:288
"To Music" (Rilke)
See "An die Musik"
"To My Best Friend" (Ledwidge) **23**:109
"To My Body—A Thanksgiving" (Kaye-Smith) **20**:107
"To My Child" (Lasker-Schueler)
See "An mein Kind"
"To My Children" (Naidu) **80**:290
"To My Daughter the Junkie on a Train" (Lorde) **173**:52
"To My Dear Sweet Heart" (Gilman) **117**:149
"To My Fairer Brethren" (Cullen) **4**:40, 49
"To My Fairy Fancies" (Naidu) **80**:291
"To My God-Child" (Thompson) **4**:435
"To My Mother" (Reese) **181**:344
"To My Old Friend, William Leachman" (Riley) **51**:283
"To My pal Bocephus" (Williams) **81**:443
To My Sons (Wright) **183**:372-75, 377, 381-82
"To My Students" (Miyazawa) **76**:289
"To Myself" (Bryusov)
See "K samomu sobe"
"To Myself the Beloved Are These Lines Dedicated by the Author" (Mayakovski) **4**:294
"To Natasha" (Remizov) **27**:351
"To Next Summer" (Pirandello) **29**:309
To novelletter (Obstfelder) **23**:179
"To One Consecrated" (Baker) **10**:26
"To One Dead" (Bodenheim) **44**:59
"To One Dead" (Ledwidge) **23**:116
"To One I Love" (Drinkwater) **57**:124
"To One Not There" (Cullen) **37**:158
"To One Unknown and Gone" (Coppard) **5**:179
"To One Who Bids Me Sing" (Dobson) **79**:32
"To One Who Comes Now and Then" (Ledwidge) **23**:112
"To One Who Died Young" (Trakl)
See "An einen Frühverstorbenen"
"To One Who Said Me Nay" (Cullen) **37**:154, 167
"To One Who Would Not Spare Himself" (Guiney) **41**:220
"To Our Dead" (Bodenheim) **44**:64
"To Petronius Arbiter" (Gogarty) **15**:109
"To Phœbus Apollo" (Carducci) **32**:88
"To Poetry" (Carducci)
See "Alla rima"
". . . To Reclaim the African Past" (Hansberry) **192**:276
"To Rilke" (Lewis) **3**:289-90
"To Roosevelt" (Darío)
See "A Roosevelt"
"To Rosemary" (Benét) **7**:79
"To Sai" (Manning) **25**:265, 278
To Save Her Soul (Griffith) **68**:244-46, 249
To See Ourselves: A Domestic Comedy (Delafield) **61**:126, 133-4
"To Serge Efron-Durnovo" (Tsvetaeva)
See "Sergeiu Efron-Durnovo"
"To Sergy Senin" (Mayakovski) **18**:243, 266, 269, 271
"To Some I Have Talked with by the Fire" (Yeats) **11**:512
"To Stanislaus" (Joyce) **159**:359
"To Stephen George" (Rilke)
See "An Stephen George"
To Tell Everything (Éluard)
See *Tout dire*
"To the Artists of the World" (Khlebnikov) **20**:151
"To the Babylonians" (Nemerov) **124**:158, 238
"To the Barbarian" (Lasker-Schueler) **57**:336
"To the Bird" (Bialik)
See "El ha-zipor"
"To the Bitter Sweet-Heart: A Dream" (Owen) **27**:207
"To the Bleeding Hearts Association of American Novelists" (Nemerov) **124**:158, 238
"To the Boy Elis" (Trakl)
See "An den Knaben Elis"
"To the Butterflies" (Dickey) **151**:175
"To the Canadian Mothers" (Scott) **6**:389
"To the Children of the Sea" (George) **2**:148
"To the Citizen" (Kraus)
See "An den Bürger"
"To the City" (Bryusov) **10**:88
"To the Cricket" (Markham) **47**:278
"To the Cross of Savoy" (Carducci)
See "Alla croce di Savoia"
"To the Cruel One" (Gumilev)
See "Zhestokoj"
"To the Dawn" (Carducci)
See "All'Aurora"
"To the Dead Cardinal of Westminster" (Thompson) **4**:435
"To the Dead of '98" (Johnson) **19**:230
"To the Fixed Stars" (Gogarty) **15**:109
"To the Flowers from Italy in Winter" (Hardy) **53**:109
"To the Fountain of Youth" (Hearn) **9**:133
"To the German Language" (Mandelstam) **6**:263
"To the Girl" (Gumilev)
See "Devushke"
"To the God of Pain" (Naidu) **80**:294
"To the Governor and Legislature of Massachusetts" (Nemerov) **124**:162, 182
"To the Harvest" (Kahanovitsch)
See "Tsum shnit"
"To the Hell's Angels" (Ginsberg) **120**:14
"To the Heroes of the Battle of the Warsaw Ghetto" (Einstein) **65**:122
"To the Heroic Soul" (Scott) **6**:389
"To the Immortal Memory of Charles Baudelaire" (Fletcher) **35**:89
To the Last Man (Grey) **6**:185, 188
"To the Legend" (Bialik) **25**:53
"To the Liffey with the Swans" (Gogarty) **15**:103, 109, 114
To the Lighthouse (Woolf) **1**:529-33, 535-36, 538-44, 546-50; **5**:507-12, 517; **20**:396-97, 405, 408, 411, 423, 428-29, 431; **43**:395, 398, 408; **56**:358-59, 361, 371, 374, 376, 379, 387, 405, 407-08; **101**:204-352; **128**:318-20, 322-25, 327, 329, 336, 339-40, 344, 350, 358, 361-67, 369-70, 376, 378-85
"To the Maids, Not to Walk in the Wind" (Gogarty) **15**:101
"To the Man on Trail" (London) **9**:268; **15**:257, 260
"To the Masters of the Normal School" (Hostos) **24**:307
"To the Memory of Cecil Spring-Rice" (Noyes) **7**:513
"To the Memory of Joseph S. Cotter Jr." (Cotter) **28**:43
"To the Mistral" (Nietzsche) **10**:389
"To the Mothers" (Toller)
See "Den Müttern"
"To the Mountain" (Kahanovitsch)
See "Tsum barg"
"To the Muse" (Lee-Hamilton) **22**:188
"To the New Men" (Davidson) **24**:164
"To the New Women" (Davidson) **24**:164
"To the New World" (Jarrell)
See "For an Emigrant"
"To the Niké of Paionios" (Moody) **105**:262
To the North (Bowen) **148**:11, 18, 20, 24, 37, 85, 88, 104-5
"To the Not Impossible Him" (Millay) **4**:307, 310; **49**:224
To the Ocean Sea (Remizov)
See *Kmoryu-okeanu*
"To the One of Fictive Music" (Stevens) **3**:445; **12**:376, 386; **45**:268, 345, 348
"To the Painter Affandi" (Anwar)
See "Kepada pluki's Affandi"
"To the Planetarium" (Benjamin) **39**:45
"To the Poet" (Bryusov)
See "Poètu"
"To the Poet before Battle" (Gurney) **33**:101-02
"To the Poet Who Happens to Be Black and the Black Poet Who Happens to Be a Woman" (Lorde) **173**:142
"To the Poets: To Make Much of Life" (Oppen) **107**:306
"To the Prussians of England" (Gurney) **33**:112
"To the Rear" (March) **96**:260
"To the Roaring Wind" (Stevens) **3**:445
"To the Rose upon the Rood of Time" (Yeats) **11**:512
"To the Rural Poor" (Lenin) **67**:232
"To the Saints" (Johnson) **19**:243, 246
"To the Sea" (Ekelund)
See "Till hafvet"
"To the Sea" (Teasdale) **4**:428
"To the Sister" (Trakl) **5**:465
"To the South" (Dunbar)
See "To the South: On Its New Slavery"
"To the South: On Its New Slavery" (Dunbar) **2**:131; **12**:117, 124
"To the Spirit of Auguste Comte" (Buchanan) **107**:44
"To the Spirit of Song" (Roberts) **8**:319
"To the Stars" (Babits)
See "Csillagokig"
To the Stars (Andreyev)
See *K zvezdam*
"To the Street Piano" (Davidson) **24**:160, 188
"To the Sun" (Bialik) **25**:49
To the Sun? (Verne)
See *Hector Servadac: Voyages et aventures à travers le monde solaire*
"To the Three for Whom the Book" (Cullen) **37**:156
"To the Tree" (Stephens) **4**:416
"To the Union Savers of Cleveland" (Harper) **14**:260
"To the United States Senate" (Lindsay) **17**:224
"To the Unknown God" (Hardy) **143**:201
"To the Unknown God" (Nietzsche) **10**:389; **55**:328
"To the White Fiends" (McKay) **7**:461; **41**:324, 345
To the White Sea (Dickey) **151**:173, 180, 203, 212, 215, 217-18, 220, 223
"To the Wife of a Sick Friend" (Millay) **49**:210
"To the World" (Webb) **24**:472
"To the Writers" (Toller)
See "An die Dichter"
"To This Lost Heart Be Kind" (Housman) **10**:251
"To Those Without Pity" (Millay) **169**:250, 267
"To Train a Writer" (Bierce) **44**:4, 16, 43
To tullinger: Et billede fra ida (Rölvaag) **17**:333, 344-45
"To Venus in the Ashmolean" (Morley) **87**:141
To verdener: Tanker og Indtryk fra en Ruslandsrejse (Nexø) **43**:330
"To Victor Hugo" (Swinburne) **36**:298
"To W. L. G. on Reading His 'Chosen Queen'" (Forten) **16**:149-50
"To What Red Hell" (Himes) **139**:247, 270
"To Winchester" (Johnson) **19**:228
"To Workers in the Field of Verse and Prose, Who Will Spend This Summer on a Collective Farm" (Mayakovski) **18**:269
"To You Who Read My Book" (Cullen) **37**:152, 154
"To Young America" (Markham) **47**:284
"Toad" (Csáth) **13**:149, 151
Toad of Toad Hall (Milne) **88**:229
"Toada do Amor" (Drummond de Andrade) **139**:228
"Toadstools Are Poison" (Bishop) **103**:30
"A Toast" (Patton) **79**:298

"Toasts" (Nagai)
See "Shukuhai"
"Toasts and Memories" (Gurney) **33**:112
"Tobacco" (Gurney) **33**:87
"Tobacco and the Devil" (Akutagawa Ryūnosuke)
See *Tobaku tu akuma*
Tobacco Road (Caldwell) **117**:2-3, 5, 7-9, 17-19, 22-3, 32-39
Tobaku tu akuma (Akutagawa Ryūnosuke) **16**:17, 25
"The To-Be-Forgotten" (Hardy) **53**:100
"Tobe's Tribulations" (Chesnutt) **39**:98
Tobias and the Angel (Bridie) **3**:133, 136-37, 141
"Tobias Holt, Bachelor" (Fuller) **103**:75
"Tobias Mindernickel" (Mann) **35**:209
Tobit Transplanted (Benson) **17**:23-6, 30, 32
"Tobold" (Walser) **18**:419
"La toccatina" (Pirandello) **4**:328
Die Tochter (Frank) **81**:102
The Tocsin (Andreyev) **3**:23, 26
The Tocsin of Revolt (Matthews) **95**:237
Der Tod aus Tradition (Horvath) **45**:92
"Tod den Toten" (Brod) **115**:93
Tod den Toten: Novellen des Indifferenten (Brod) **115**:93
Der Tod des Tizian (Hofmannsthal) **11**:291, 293, 309
Der Tod des Vergil (Broch) **20**:50-5, 58-9, 64-7, 70-1, 77
Der Tod Georgs (Beer-Hofmann) **60**:26, 31-2, 34, 36-8
"Den Tod hab ich geschen" (Raabe) **45**:188
"Tod in Ähren" (Liliencron) **18**:213-14
Der Tod in Venedig: Novelle (Mann) **2**:412, 420, 423, 429, 432-33, 436-39; **8**:253-55, 261-64, 269-70, 272; **14**:322-66; **21**:166-67, 202, 204-07; **35**:222, 239; **44**:146, 163, 170, 174, 181, 184, 207, 223; **60**:330, 332, 354-57; **168**:116, 122, 132-35, 137, 140, 142-43, 156-57, 160, 174, 180, 187, 209-10, 213, 215-17
Der Tod wird komen (Bachmann) **192**:145-47
"Der Tod wird kommen" (Bachmann) **192**:164-65
Toda raba (Kazantzakis) **2**:317-18; **5**:269; **181**:208, 211
"Todas las nubes arden" (Jiménez) **183**:280-82
Todas las sangres (Arguedas) **147**:8-10, 12-13, 23, 45, 76, 81, 93, 95-96, 99-100, 108
"Today" (Walker) **129**:298, 317, 325-27
"Today" (Wright) **136**:263
"Today Is Not the Day" (Lorde) **173**:108, 139, 144
Today the Sun Still Sets over Atlantis (Nezval)
See *Dnes ještě zapadá slunce nad Atlandtidou*
"To-day, this Insect" (Thomas) **45**:383-86
Tõde ja õigus (Tammsaare) **27**:371-74
"Todesfurcht" (Kraus) **5**:285
"Todo" (Jiménez) **4**:226
"Todo lo que pudo ser, aunque haya sido" (Arenas) **191**:195
Todo más daro, y otros poemas (Salinas) **17**:357-59, 363, 365, 368-69
"Tod's Amendment" (Kipling) **8**:187
"Together" (Anwar)
See "Orang berdua"
Together (Douglas) **68**:3, 9, 10, 37, 40-1, 43
"Toho in the Days of His Youth" (Nishida)
See "Wakakarishi hi no Toho"
Toilers of the Hills (Fisher) **140**:151-54, 166, 170, 175, 177, 179, 181-83
"The Token" (Sinclair) **11**:421
"Tokyo" (Hayashi)
See "Dauntaun"
Tokyo hakkei (Dazai Osamu) **11**:175, 191
"Tokyo Pastoral" (Carter) **139**:188
The Tokyo-Montana Express (Brautigan) **133**:10, 31-33
Tol'able David (Hergesheimer) **11**:266
Told after Supper (Jerome) **23**:83
Told Again (de la Mare) **4**:78
Told by an Idiot (Macaulay) **7**:423-25, 429; **44**:117-19, 121, 123, 125-26, 132-33
"Toldi Miklós" (Herzl) **36**:151
The Tolkien Reader (Tolkien) **137**:243
Tol'ko liubov (Balmont) **11**:31, 36-7, 39
The Toll of the Great Church Bell (Sologub)
See *Velikii blagovest*
Der tolle Professor (Sudermann) **15**:433, 436
"A Tolling Church Bell" (Wright) **136**:302
Tolstoi as Man and Artist (Merezhkovsky) **29**:227, 230-31, 240
Tolstóy and Dostoyévsky (Merezhkovsky)
See *Tolstoi as Man and Artist*
"Tolstoy and Enlightenment" (Berlin) **105**:19
Tolstoy and the Struggle of the Proletariat (Lenin) **67**:208
Tolstoy as a Mirror of the Russian Revolution (Lenin) **67**:207
Tom Cobb; or, Fortune's Toy (Gilbert) **3**:208
"Tom O'Roughley" (Yeats) **93**:350, 351, 352
Tom Paulding (Matthews) **95**:270
Tom Sawyer: A Drama (Twain) **161**:288
Tom Sawyer Abroad (Twain) **6**:474, 477, 486; **12**:432, 439; **19**:414; **48**:346; **161**:262; **185**:236, 290, 307
Tom Sawyer, Detective (Twain) **6**:477; **12**:432; **48**:335, 344, 349, 351, 356, 359, 361; **161**:232; **185**:307
"The Tomb" (Lovecraft) **4**:265; **22**:218
The Tomb (Palamas) **5**:380, 384, 387
"The Tomb of Hegeso" (Babits)
See "Hegeso sírja"
"The Tomb of His Ancestors" (Kipling) **8**:198; **17**:208
Le Tombeau de Jean de la Fontaine (Jammes) **75**:119
"Tombs of the Hetaerae" (Rilke) **195**:243
"The Tombstone Told When She Died" (Thomas) **45**:377
"Tombstones in the Starlight" (Parker) **143**:325
Tomek baran, suka (Reymont) **5**:393
"Tomioka Sensei" (Kunikida Doppo) **99**:295
"Tomlinson" (Kipling) **17**:196
Tommaso D'Amalfi (de Filippo) **127**:283
Tommy and Co. (Jerome) **23**:89-90
Tommy and Grizel (Barrie) **2**:45, 48; **164**:5-6, 66, 82-86
"Tommy, the Unsentimental" (Cather) **152**:92
Tommy Upmore (Blackmore) **27**:38
"Tommy's Burglar" (Henry) **19**:175, 201
Tomodachi, enemoto takekai (Abe) **131**:11, 13
"To-Morrow" (Hedāyat)
See "Farda"
"Tomorrow" (Zamyatin)
See "Zavtra"
Tomorrow (Toller)
See *Vormorgen*
Tomorrow and Tomorrow (Barry) **11**:51, 53-5, 59, 63-4, 67
Tomorrow and Tomorrow (Kuttner) **10**:265, 269, 273-74, 276
Tomorrow and Yesterday (Böll)
See *Haus ohne Hüter*
"Tomorrow Is My Birthday" (Masters) **2**:461
Tom's A-Cold (Collier) **127**:243-44, 248
"Tom's Husband" (Jewett) **22**:146
"The Tomte of Toreby" (Lagerloef) **36**:240
"Tonelli's Marriage" (Howells) **17**:179
"Tong Raa" (p'Bitek) **149**:67
"Tongnian wuji" (Chang) **184**:138
The Tongue Set Free: Remembrance of a European Childhood (Canetti)
See *Die gerettete Zunge: Geschichte einer Jugend*
"The Tongue-Cut Sparrow" (Dazai Osamu) **11**:186
"Tongueless" (Korolenko) **22**:173
Tongues of Conscience (Hichens) **64**:121
Tongues of Fires (Blackwood) **5**:77
"Tongue-Tied" (Cullen) **37**:156
Tonight We Improvise (Pirandello)
See *Questa sera si recita a soggetto*
"Tonio Kröger" (Mann) **168**:157
Tonio Kröger (Mann) **35**:214, 217, 228, 230, 242
Tonka (Musil) **12**:242, 246, 251-53
"Tonkoj, no častoju setkoj" (Bryusov) **10**:92
Tono-Bungay (Wells) **6**:526, 528-29, 532, 535-37, 539-41, 545-46, 548, 552-53; **12**:500-01, 506, 508; **19**:428, 440, 446, 450-52; **133**:228, 257
"Tonya" (Petrov) **21**:154, 156-57
"Too Dear" (Tolstoy) **11**:463
Too Late the Phalarope (Paton) **165**:275, 289, 292, 295, 297-98, 330-31
Too Loose in Toulouse (March) **96**:248
Too Loud a Solitude (Hrabal)
See *Prilis hlucná samota*
"Too many people" (Saroyan) **137**:151
Too Much Money (Zangwill) **16**:455
Too True to Be Good (Shaw) **3**:393, 404; **9**:426; **45**:210
"Toohey's Party" (Baynton) **57**:11
"Tookh Steh's Mistake" (Oskison) **35**:280-81
"The Tooth" (Jackson) **187**:243-44, 247-48, 250
"The Tooth" (Rebreanu)
See "Dintele"
"The Tooth" (Vallette)
See "La dent"
"A Tooth for Paul Revere" (Benét) **7**:81
"The Tooth, the Whole Tooth, and Nothing But the Tooth" (Benchley) **55**:17
The Top Hat (de Filippo) **127**:289-90
"The Top of the Heap" (Saltus) **8**:350
Topaze (Hecht) **101**:78
"Topical Logic and a Religious World View" (Nishida)
See "Bashoteki ronri to shuyoteki sekaikan"
Topsy Turvy (Verne)
See *Sans dessus dessous*
Der Tor und der Tod (Hofmannsthal) **11**:293, 300, 310
"The Torch" (Rhodes) **53**:323
The Torch (Kraus)
See *Die Fackel*
The Torch (Moricz)
See *A fáklya*
The Torch and Other Lectures and Addresses (Woodberry) **73**:365, 367-68, 377
The Torch in My Ear (Canetti)
See *Die Fackel im Ohr: Lebensgeschichte 1921-1931*
The Torch-Bearers (Noyes) **7**:504, 506-9, 513, 515
"Tordenkalven" (Jensen) **41**:307
"Toreador" (Bennett) **5**:46
"Tormenta" (Huidobro) **31**:124
"Tormenting" (Andrić) **135**:95
Tormento (Pérez Galdós) **27**:250, 261-62, 283
"Tormento del amor" (Aleixandre) **113**:16, 57
Tornebusken (Hansen) **32**:249, 251, 257
"Torn-out Hearts" (Yourcenar)
See "Les Coeurs arrachés"
"Toro" (Aleixandre) **113**:7
"Torokko" (Akutagawa Ryūnosuke) **16**:36
A torony arnyéka (Babits) **14**:40
"Torpedo to Revolutionize Warfare" (Tesla) **88**:287
Torquemada and the Spanish Inquisition (Sabatini) **47**:300, 303
Torre de Eiffel (Huidobro)
See *Tour Eiffel*
"The Torrent" (Robinson) **101**:197, 199
The Torrent (Blasco Ibáñez)
See *Entre naranjos*
The Torrent and the Night Before (Robinson) **5**:400, 416; **101**:118-19, 123, 132-33, 136, 194, 196
Torrid Meadows (Moricz)
See *Forró mezok*
"Torso" (Andrić) **135**:10, 28, 31-32, 96

Tortilla Flat (Steinbeck) **135**:250, 264, 321, 344
"Tortoise Family Connections" (Lawrence) **9**:230; **93**:33
"Tortoise Gallantry" (Lawrence) **9**:230
"The Tortoise in Eternity" (Wylie) **8**:521, 533
"Tortoise Shout" (Lawrence) **93**:14, 102, 108
Tortoises (Lawrence) **93**:13, 72
"Torture as a fundamental necessity of the colonial world" (Fanon) **188**:140
Torture Garden (Mirbeau)
See *Le jardin des supplices*
"The Tortures of Week-End Visiting" (Benchley) **55**:10
The Tory Lover (Jewett) **1**:359-60, 364, 369; **22**:122, 128-29, 138, 143-45
"A Tory Philosophy" (Hulme) **21**:139, 142
Toryism and the Tory Democracy (O'Grady) **5**:349, 351
Torzhestvo zemledeliia (Zabolotsky) **52**:379-85
"Torzhestvo zemledeliya" (Zabolotsky) **52**:365
Tosca (Giacosa) **7**:311, 313-15
"Toshi-sho no mondai" (Yosano) **59**:337
"Toshishun" (Akutagawa Ryūnosuke) **16**:32-3
"Toska" (Chekhov) **3**:152
"Toska mimolet-nosti" (Annensky) **14**:32
"Toska sinevy" (Annensky) **14**:26
A tót atyafiak (Mikszath) **31**:170
Tot, kto poluchaet poshchechiny (Andreyev) **3**:23, 27-8, 30-1
"Tot Stof" (Bosman)
See "Unto Dust"
Total (Huidobro) **31**:126
"Total amor" (Aleixandre) **113**:14, 42
"The Total Library" (Borges) **109**:157
Total Song (Éluard)
See *Chanson complète*
La totalita dell' arte (Croce) **37**:95
Der Tote Tag (Barlach) **84**:82, 142
"Der Tote Wald" (Kraus) **5**:285
"Totem" (Coffin) **95**:16
Totem and Taboo: Resemblances between the Psychic Lives of Savages and Neurotics (Freud)
See *Totem und Tabu: Über einige Übereinstimmungen im Seelenleben der Wilden und der Neurotiker*
Totem und Tabu: Über einige Übereinstimmungen im Seelenleben der Wilden und der Neurotiker (Freud) **52**:83-4, 120, 123, 126, 134
Totemism (Frazer) **32**:238
Totemism and Exogamy (Frazer) **32**:202-03, 205, 212-14, 221
"Totem-tants" (Agnon) **151**:35
"Totenklage" (Ball) **104**:13-15
Totenmesse (Przybyszewski) **36**:290
Die Totenweiber (Bernhard) **165**:122
"Touch" (Lawrence) **93**:53
"Touch at a Distance" (Apollinaire)
See "Le toucher à distance"
"A Touch of Autumn in the Air" (O'Faolain) **143**:225, 235, 261, 264-65
The Touch of Nutmeg (Collier) **127**:250
"A Touch of Realism" (Saki) **3**:372
A Touch of the Poet (O'Neill) **1**:398, 402, 405; **6**:335-36
"Le toucher à distance" (Apollinaire) **3**:38; **51**:20
"Touches" (Lyotard) **103**:218
"The Touchstone" (Freeman) **21**:60
The Touchstone (Wharton) **27**:384; **129**:360; **149**:255
Touchstone (Williams) **89**:396
"A Tough Tussle" (Bierce) **7**:88; **44**:12, 15, 21, 44-5, 47-8
Toulemonde (Morley) **87**:125
The Tour: A Story of Ancient Egypt (Couperus)
See *Antiek toerisme*
La tour d'amour (Vallette) **67**:271, 280-81, 299, 308, 310
Le tour du monde en quatre-vingt jours (Verne) **6**:491-92, 501; **52**:330, 350, 358
Tour Eiffel (Huidobro) **31**:125, 137, 141
"Tour Y-Ten" (Lardner) **14**:307
"Tourist" (Service) **15**:413
"Tourist's Eye" (Oppen) **107**:263, 310
"The Tournament in A.D. 1870" (Twain) **36**:369
Tous contre tous (Adamov) **189**:9, 19, 42, 49
"Tous et tant d'autres qui" (Péret) **20**:185
Toussaint (Hansberry) **192**:336
"La Toussaint" (Manning) **25**:277
"Toussaints" (Gurney) **33**:112
De tout (Huysmans) **7**:408; **69**:6, 12, 39, 42-3, 47
Tout à coup (Huidobro) **31**:132
"Tout dire" (Éluard) **41**:157
Tout dire (Éluard) **41**:157
"Tout ou rien" (Roberts) **8**:314
"Tout passe" (Manning) **25**:278
De tout temps a jamais (Jammes) **75**:116
Tout Ubu (Jarry) **147**:234, 252-53
A toute épreuve (Éluard) **7**:250, 256; **41**:150, 156
Toute la Flandre (Verhaeren) **12**:464-65, 468, 471
Toute license sauf contre l'amour (Barrès) **47**:41
Toute une jeunesse (Coppee) **25**:122, 126
Továrna na absolutno (Čapek) **6**:83, 85-6, 93; **37**:42, 46, 52-3, 55, 57, 59, 61-2, 67-9, 72-3; **192**:175, 199, 233
Toward a Critique of the German Mentality (Ball)
See *Zur Kritik der deutschen Intelligenz*
"Toward a History of Symbolism" (Bryusov) **10**:94, 96
Toward a Philosophy of the Act (Bakhtin)
See "K filosofii postupka"
"Toward a Reworking of the Dostoevsky Book" (Bakhtin) **160**:130
"Toward a Synthesis" (Murry) **16**:355
"Toward a Theory of Creativity" (Levi) **125**:292
"Toward an Enduring Peace" (Bourne) **16**:53
"Toward An Ethics of the Theatre" (Stanislavsky) **167**:248
Toward Damscus (Strindberg)
See *Till Damaskus*
Toward Dawn (Nexø) **43**:317
"Toward European Unity" (Orwell) **128**:290; **129**:223
Toward the African Revolution (Fanon)
See *Pour la révolution africaine*
Toward the Gulf (Masters) **25**:290, 296, 315
Toward the Light (Wittgenstein)
See *Akarumie*
"Toward the New World" (Fuller) **103**:102, 107-08
Toward the Radical Center (Čapek) **192**:227
"Toward the Sea" (Jiménez) **183**:331
"Towards a Philosophy of Religion with the Concept of Pre-established Harmony as Guide" (Nishida)
See "Yotei chowa o tebiki to shite shukyo tetsugaku e"
"Towards Break of Day" (Yeats) **93**:389, 390
"Towards Democracy" (Carpenter) **88**:45, 47, 51-2, 61, 63-4, 66-9, 71, 76, 82-3, 97, 106-7, 119, 136, 142, 145-6
Towards Industrial Freedom (Carpenter) **88**:72
"Towards Socialism" (Orage) **157**:246, 249-50
Towards the Goal (Ward) **55**:437, 440, 442
Towards the Great Peace (Cram) **45**:19-21
Towards the Mountain (Paton) **165**:291, 295, 298, 305
"Towards the Religious Philosophy through Pre-established Harmony" (Nishida)
See "Yotei chowa o tebiki to shite shukyo tetsugaku e"
"Towards the Source" (Brennan) **17**:37, 39-41, 44, 46, 50, 52-6
Towazugatari (Nagai) **51**:98
"The Tower" (Gurney) **33**:85-6
"The Tower" (Jarrell) **177**:221
"The Tower" (Muir) **87**:241
"The Tower" (Rilke)
See "Der Turm"
"The Tower" (Yeats) **116**:280, 306, 308-09, 337-41
The Tower (Hofmannsthal)
See *Der Turm*
The Tower (Weiss)
See *Der Turm*
The Tower (Yeats) **1**:555, 559, 570, 579-80; **11**:517, 522, 528, 534; **18**:442, 445-47, 452, 456-57; **31**:389, 394, 401; **116**:280-81, 306, 314, 337
A Tower in Italy (Abercrombie) **141**:12-13
The Tower of Babel (Canetti)
See *Die Blendung*
The Tower of Love (Vallette)
See *La tour d'amour*
The Tower of Mirrors (Lee) **5**:312-13
"The Tower of Monterrey" (Unamuno) **2**:568
"The Tower of Silence" (Mori Ogai)
See "Chinmoku no to"
"The Tower of the Elephant" (Howard) **8**:133-35
The Towers of Trebizond (Macaulay) **7**:427-28, 430-32; **44**:121-22, 124-27, 131-35, 137-41
"The Town" (Saba)
See "Il borgo"
A Town (Asch) **3**:67, 70-1
The Town (Faulkner) **141**:49; **170**:128-29, 184, 215
Town and Gown (Strindberg)
See *Fråan fjärdingen och svartbächen*
The Town and the City (Kerouac) **117**:187, 189-91, 193-94, 203-04, 209-10, 248, 266
"The Town Betrayed" (Muir) **87**:307
The Town down the River (Robinson) **5**:402, 404; **101**:97, 110, 133
"The Town Dump" (Nemerov) **124**:153, 155, 158, 216, 280-81
"Town Hall News" (Allen) **87**:28, 63
"The Town of Gradov" (Platonov) **14**:417
"The Town of the Little People" (Aleichem)
See "Di shtot fun di kleyne mentshelek"
"The Town Poor" (Jewett) **22**:147
The Town Traveller (Gissing) **3**:227, 230
The Town Was Mad (Thomas) **105**:304
"The Town Week" (Lucas) **73**:172
"Townshend" (Gurney) **33**:96
Township and Borough (Maitland) **65**:254, 276, 280, 284, 287
"Der Toyber" (Bergelson) **81**:16-8,30
Toys in the Attic (Hellman) **119**:123, 134-5, 140, 142, 144-45, 165-67, 235
"Toys of 1900" (Herzl) **36**:143
The Toys of Peace, and Other Papers (Saki) **3**:370
Tra donne solo (Pavese) **3**:338, 342-43
El trabajo gustoso (Jiménez) **183**:284
Los trabajos y los dias (Reyes) **33**:323
The Trace (Garro)
See *El Rastro*
A Tracer of Lost Persons (Chambers) **41**:95, 102, 114
Traces of Gold (Sá-Carneiro)
See *Indícious de ouro*
"Traces of Love" (Chang)
See "Liu qing"
The Track (Barea) **14**:48, 51, 53
"Track-Workers" (Bodenheim) **44**:59
A Tract on Monetary Reform (Keynes) **64**:203-4, 209-10, 213, 218-19, 227, 252-54, 260, 263, 266, 297-98, 301, 303
"A Tractate Middoth" (James) **6**:206, 212
Tractatus logico-philosophicus (Wittgenstein) **59**:214-6, 222-6, 234-9, 241, 243, 256, 264-72, 274, 292-9, 303-6, 309-10, 314-6
Tracy's Tiger (Saroyan) **137**:146, 156, 168
"The Trades" (Jarrell) **177**:194
"Trädet i skogen" (Södergran) **31**:293
"La tradición eterna" (Unamuno) **148**:244

Tradiciones (Palma)
See *Tradiciones peruanas*
Tradiciones en salsa verde (Palma) **29**:259
Tradiciones peruanas (Palma) **29**:255-59, 261-67
"Tradition" (Nemerov) **124**:231
"Tradition and Industrialization" (Wright) **136**:286
Tradition and Revolt (Nisbet) **117**:344, 353
"Tradition and the Modern Age" (Arendt) **193**:167
Tradition of Freedom (Bernanos) **3**:128
"Traditional and Critical Theory" (Horkheimer) **132**:212
"Traditions for a Negro Literature" (Rourke) **12**:322
"Los traductores de las 1001 noches" (Borges) **109**:36, 128
"Tradurre Kafka" (Levi) **109**:302, 339
"Traeet" (Obstfelder) **23**:179
Trafalgar (Pérez Galdós) **27**:248-49, 256, 286-88
"Traffic" (Ruskin) **63**:290
"Traffic in Sheets" (Gurney) **33**:103
Traffics and Discoveries (Kipling) **8**:200
"Tragédia" (Moricz) **33**:245, 248
"La tragedia di un personaggio" (Pirandello) **29**:284; **172**:160, 166, 176-78, 180, 191-92
A Tragedian in Spite of Himself (Chekhov)
See *Tragik ponevole*
Las tragedias grotescas (Baroja) **8**:61
La Tragédie de Faust (Ghelderode) **187**:32
Les tragédies de la foi (Rolland) **23**:256, 260
Tragedies of Faith (Rolland)
See *Les tragédies de la foi*
Tragediya o Iude printse Iskariotskom (Remizov) **27**:328-29, 335, 345
"Tragedy" (Baker) **10**:27
"Tragedy" (Mayakovski) **4**:292
"Tragedy" (Moricz)
See "Tragédia"
"The Tragedy at Brookbend Cottage" (Bramah) **72**:13
"The Tragedy at Three Corners" (Dunbar)
See "The Tragedy at Three Forks"
"The Tragedy at Three Forks" (Dunbar) **12**:108-09
"A Tragedy in Little" (Middleton) **56**:175, 193
"The Tragedy of a Character" (Pirandello)
See "La tragedia di un personaggio"
"The Tragedy of a Fashionable Wedding in Ten Farces" (Millay) **169**:235
Tragedy of an Elderly Gentleman (Shaw) **3**:393
The Tragedy of Errors (Villaurrutia) **80**:480
The Tragedy of Judas, Prince of Iscariot (Remizov)
See *Tragediya o Iude printse Iskariotskom*
"The Tragedy of Man" (Campbell) **9**:33
"The Tragedy of Pete" (Cotter) **28**:43
The Tragedy of Pudd'nhead Wilson (Twain) **6**:455-56, 461-62, 465, 474-75, 477; **12**:432, 439-40, 449-51; **19**:364, 372; **36**:361, 363, 373, 386; **48**:344; **59**:169; **161**:251, 330; **185**:278, 299, 327
The Tragedy of the Caesars (Baring-Gould) **88**:35
"The Tragedy of the Seigniory" (Scott) **6**:398
The Tragedy of White Injustice (Garvey) **41**:185, 198
Tragic America (Dreiser) **10**:183, 195
The Tragic Comedians: A Study in a Well-Known Story (Meredith) **17**:262, 278, 286-88; **43**:282-84
"Tragic Destiny" (Aleixandre) **113**:20
Tragic Ground (Caldwell) **117**:17-19
The Tragic Mary (Field) **43**:153-54, 172
The Tragic Muse (James) **2**:250, 254, 263, 269-70; **11**:337, 342; **40**:115, 154; **47**:177-78, 183, 185, 207
The Tragic Muse (Wharton) **3**:561
"Tragic Philosophy" (Santayana) **40**:388, 390, 394
A Tragic Role (Chekhov)
See *Tragik ponevole*
Tragic Romances (Sharp) **39**:362
The Tragic Sense of Life (Unamuno)
See *Del sentimiento trágico de la vida*
The Tragic Sense of Life in Men and Peoples (Unamuno)
See *Del sentimiento de la vida en los hombres y en los pueblos*
Tragicomedia de don Cristóbal y la señá Rosita (García Lorca) **181**:78, 84-86
Tragik ponevole (Chekhov) **31**:80
"Les Tragiques" (Yourcenar) **193**:270
"Tragisches Liebesmahl" (Liliencron) **18**:215
"Tragovi hromoga vuka" (Popa) **167**:162
La trahison (Lewis) **2**:391
La trahison des clercs (Benda) **60**:41, 44, 47-8, 57, 60-2, 72, 75-6, 84-91
"The Trail among the Ardise Hills" (Carman) **7**:144
The Trail Driver (Grey) **6**:187
Trail of an Artist-Naturalist (Seton) **31**:267, 269
The Trail of Fu Manchu (Rohmer) **28**:280, 289-90, 292, 300
The Trail of Ninety-Eight: A Northland Romance (Service) **15**:406-07, 412
The Trail of the Hawk: A Comedy of the Seriousness of Life (Lewis) **4**:248, 251, 253, 259; **13**:325; **23**:132; **39**:234
The Trail of the Sandhill Stag (Seton) **31**:261, 279
"The Trail to the Tropics" (McCoy) **28**:224
"The Trailer for Room No. 8" (Davis) **24**:205
Trailin' (Faust) **49**:46-7, 55, 60
"The Train and the City" (Wolfe) **13**:491-92, 494
Le train bleu (Cocteau) **119**:67
"Train de guerre" (Apollinaire) **51**:20
"Train Going" (Saroyan) **137**:181
"Le train numero 081" (Schwob) **20**:321, 323
"Train of Sick Soldiers" (Marinetti) **10**:314
"The Train That Goes to Ireland" (Tynan) **3**:504
"A Train Trip" (Güiraldes)
See "Ferroviaria"
The Train Was on Time (Böll)
See *Der Zug war pünktlich*
"The Train Whistled" (Pirandello)
See "Il treno ha fischiato"
The Training of a Zen Monk (Suzuki)
See *The Training of the Zen Buddhist Monk*
"The Training of Nurses" (Nightingale) **85**:258
The Training of the Zen Buddhist Monk (Suzuki) **109**:388, 398
"Trains" (Caragiale) **76**:165
"Trains" (Hall and Nordhoff) **23**:64
Traite (Pareto)
See *Trattato di sociologia generale*
Le Traité du Narcisse (Gide) **12**:143, 168, 176-77, 180; **177**:35
Traité du style (Aragon) **123**:119
"Traitement thyroïdien" (Apollinaire) **51**:20
The Traitor (Dixon) **163**:144, 154, 164-65, 178, 222-27
"Traitorously" (Svevo)
See "Proditoriamente"
"Traitors of Art" (Middleton) **56**:192
"El traje de fantasmas" (Arlt) **29**:45-8
"Trak Trak Trak" (Burroughs) **121**:127
"Trakat von der ausgestorbenen Welt" (Weiss) **152**:281-84
"Traktat o manekinach" (Schulz) **5**:424, 428-29; **51**:309, 311, 314, 316, 319-20
Tramonto (D'Annunzio) **6**:142
"The Tramp" (Baynton)
See "The Chosen Vessel"
A Tramp Abroad (Twain) **6**:455, 458, 460, 476; **12**:426, 431; **36**:369-70; **48**:330, 332, 342, 350, 357, 360
"The Tramp Transfigured" (Noyes)
See "The Tramp Transfigured: An Episode in the Life of a Corn-Flower Millionaire"
"The Tramp Transfigured: An Episode in the Life of a Corn-Flower Millionaire" (Noyes) **7**:503
"The Tramper's Grave" (Pickthall) **21**:252
The Tramping Methodist (Kaye-Smith) **20**:93-4, 97, 101, 109-10
"The Tramping Woman" (Tynan) **3**:505
The Trampling of the Lilies (Sabatini) **47**:303
Tramps (Hamsun)
See *Landstrykere*
"The Trance" (Abercrombie) **141**:7
A Transaction of Hearts (Saltus) **8**:349-50
"Transactions" (Orage) **157**:275
Transatlantic (Toomer) **172**:265, 286, 293
"A Transatlantic Interview, 1946" (Stein) **48**:224-25, 241, 252
"A Transcontinental Episode, Or, Metamorphoses at Muggins' Misery: A Co-Operative Novel by Bret James and Henry Harte" (Fuller) **103**:116
"The Transfer" (Blackwood) **5**:78-9
"The Transferred Ghost" (Stockton) **47**:323-24, 327
"The Transfiguration" (Muir) **2**:487; **87**:170, 172, 230
Transfiguration (Esenin) **4**:112
Transfiguration (Toller)
See *Die Wandlung*
"Transfigured Bird" (Merrill) **173**:256
Transfigured Night (Schoenberg)
See *Verklarte Nacht*
"Transformation" (Aurobindo) **63**:9
"Transformation" (Södergran)
See "Förvandling"
"La transformation de l'idée de Dieu" (Rod) **52**:324
"The Transformation of Evil" (Trakl) **5**:468
"The Transformation of Silence into Language and Action" (Lorde) **173**:66, 83, 136, 139
The Transformation of the Animals (Jensen)
See *Dyrenes Forvandling*
"Transformations" (Hardy) **10**:234; **143**:169
Transformations of Myth Through Time (Campbell) **140**:45, 113, 134
Transience (Rozanov)
See *Mimoletnoe*
"Transient Barracks" (Jarrell) **177**:192, 225-28
The Transient Guest (Saltus) **8**:346
"Transients in Arcadia" (Henry) **19**:173
"Transit Bed" (Calvino)
See "Un letto di passaggio"
Transition: Essays on Contemporary Literature (Muir) **2**:48; **87**:163
"Translating" (Heller) **151**:308
"Translating Kafka" (Levi)
See "Tradurre Kafka"
Translation: An Elizabethan Art (Matthiessen) **100**:188, 218-21, 238
Translations from the Chinese (Morley) **87**:124, 128
Translations from the Poetry of Rainer Maria Rilke (Rilke) **195**:163
"The Translators of the 1001 Nights" (Borges)
See "Los traductores de las 1001 noches"
"Transluscence" (Balmont)
See "Peresvet"
"Transmigración" (Nervo) **11**:398
"The Transmutation" (Muir) **87**:256
"The Transmutation of Ling" (Bramah) **72**:3, 9
"Trans-National America" (Bourne) **16**:55, 67
"La transparencia, dios, la transparencia" (Jiménez) **183**:293, 307
"Transparencies on Film" (Adorno) **111**:39, 54
Transparent Things (Nabokov) **108**:60, 77-80, 147, 178, 185, 216, 219-20
"Transplanting a Texan" (Adams) **56**:8
"The Transport" (Manning) **25**:265
Transport to Summer (Stevens) **3**:448, 454; **12**:361, 376, 383; **45**:274, 298-99

The Transposed Heads: A Legend of India (Mann)
See *Die vertauschten Köpfe: Eine indische Legende*
Tränstekvinnans son (Strindberg) **1**:452; **8**:407, 411, 419; **21**:350, 365; **47**:358
Transylvania (Moricz)
See *Erdély*
"Tranvías" (Villaurrutia) **80**:478
"The Trap" (Lindsay) **17**:224
"The Trap" (Pirandello)
See "La trappola"
"The Trap" (Zoshchenko) **15**:510-11
The Trap (Richardson) **3**:356-57
A Trap for Judges (Guro)
See *Sadok sudei*
Trapné provídky (Čapek) **6**:84; **37**:46, 51; **192**:178, 222, 225-26
"La trappola" (Pirandello) **4**:328, 351; **29**:282
"Traps for the Unwary" (Bourne) **16**:41
Traps for the Young (Comstock) **13**:95-7
Traps for Unbelievers (Butts) **77**:90, 94, 96-7, 106
"Traspié entre dos estrellas" (Vallejo) **3**:527, 531
Tratado de cocotologia (Unamuno) **148**:252
Tratado de moral (Hostos) **24**:304, 306
Tratado de sociología (Hostos) **24**:303-04, 306
"Trattamento di quiescenza" (Levi) **109**:293, 295, 297
Trattato della Divina Provvidenza (Catherine)
See "Tarde"
Trattato di sociologia generale (Pareto) **69**:98-9, 101, 108-10, 113, 125-35, 141-44, 148-50, 152, 157, 162, 167
"Traum und Umnachtung" (Trakl) **5**:456, 464-65, 468
"Ein Traum von grosser Magie" (Hofmannsthal) **11**:299
Das Trauma der Geburt (Rank) **115**:228, 231, 233-34, 247-48, 250, 252, 254, 261-62, 274, 281, 284-85, 287, 299-301, 310-11, 321, 325-27, 333, 336-40, 343-45, 347, 350
The Trauma of Birth (Rank)
See *Das Trauma der Geburt*
Die Traumdeutung (Freud) **52**:81, 90, 93, 110-13, 115, 127, 131
Traumgekrönt (Rilke) **6**:358; **195**:258
Traumstück (Kraus) **5**:286
Traumtheater (Kraus) **5**:286
"Traurige Tänze" (George) **14**:206, 210
Die Traurigen Geranien, und andere Geschichten aus dem Nachlass (Borchert) **5**:105-06, 112
"Trauriges Wiegenlied" (Raabe) **45**:189
Travail (Zola) **6**:560, 563; **21**:426, 456; **41**:421
Le travail du peintre (Éluard) **7**:246
"Le Travail du Rêve ne Pense Pas" (Lyotard) **103**:154
"The Travail of Passion" (Yeats) **1**:580
Trava-Murava (Remizov) **27**:334, 348
"Travel" (Millay) **4**:306
"The Traveler" (Apollinaire)
See "Le voyageur"
A Traveler at Forty (Dreiser) **10**:164, 201; **18**:51-2
A Traveler from Altruria (Howells) **7**:368, 376-79, 386, 393, 399-400; **41**:261, 269
The Traveler Without Luggage (Anouilh)
See *Le voyageur sans bagage*
Travelers on Land and Sea (Kuzmin)
See *Plavaiushchie-puteshestvuiushchie*
"Traveling in Peace" (Benchley) **55**:17
"Traveling Riverside Blues" (Johnson) **69**:76
"The Traveling Woman" (Kolmar) **40**:175
A Traveller in Little Things (Hudson) **29**:142, 145, 160
The Traveller to the East (Mofolo)
See *Moeti oa bochabela*
Traveller's Luck: Essays and Fantasies (Lucas) **73**:174
"Travelling in the Family" (Drummond de Andrade) **139**:236, 239
The Travelling Man (Gregory) **1**:336; **176**:14, 18, 34, 38-40
"The Travelling Post Office" (Paterson) **32**:369, 373, 376, 378
"Travelogue" (Lardner) **14**:307
"Travelogue" (Parker) **143**:331
Travels and Life in Ashanti and Jaman (Freeman) **21**:45, 61
Travels in Alaska (Muir) **28**:244, 246, 259, 264
Travels in Arabia Deserta (Doughty) **27**:50-2, 54, 56, 58-63, 65, 67-9, 71, 73-5, 78-85
Travels in Humanity (Platonov) **14**:410
Travels in Iceland (Hansen)
See *Rejse på Island*
Travels in Philadelphia (Morley) **87**:120
The Travels of Lao Ts'an (Liu)
See *Lao Ts'an yu-chi*
The Travels of Marrakesh (Canetti)
See *Die Stimmen von Marrakesch: Aufzeichnungen nach einer Reise*
Travels with Mr. Brown (Twain) **36**:382
Das Traverhaus (Werfel) **8**:471
"A travers l'Europe" (Apollinaire) **51**:32
Travnička hronika (Andrić) **135**:14-15, 33, 43, 50, 52, 63, 67, 77, 79, 86, 93, 96, 98
Travnik Chronicle (Andrić)
See *Travnička hronika*
Trayectoria de Goethe (Reyes) **33**:323
"Tre og tredive Aar" (Jensen) **41**:307
Tre par (Kielland) **5**:279
"Tre vie" (Saba) **33**:370
Treacherous Ground (Bojer)
See *Vort rige*
"Treacherous Village" (Calvino)
See "Paese infido"
"Treacherously" (Svevo)
See "Proditoriamente"
Tread Softly (Muggeridge) **120**:186
"Treading the Grape" (Field) **43**:166
"Treading the Press" (Field) **43**:166
Treading the Winepress (Connor) **31**:114-15
Treadmill to Oblivion (Allen) **87**:14, 16, 22, 50, 57
"Treason" (Babel)
See "Izmena"
"Treason" (Stephens) **4**:420
The Treason and Death of Benedict Arnold (Chapman) **7**:191
"A Treason of Nature" (Roberts) **8**:315
The Treason of the Intellectuals (Benda)
See *La trahison des clercs*
The Treason of the Senate (Phillips) **44**:262, 273, 278-79, 281, 290-91, 294, 296, 299-300
"The Treasure" (Brooke) **2**:61
"Treasure" (Peretz) **16**:398
The Treasure (Lagerloef)
See *Arne's Treasure*
The Treasure House of Martin Hews (Oppenheim) **45**:130
"Treasure of Abbot Thomas" (James) **6**:206, 212
"The Treasure of Far Island" (Cather) **152**:67-68
The Treasure of Heaven: A Romance of Riches (Corelli) **51**:66, 69, 75-6
The Treasure of the Humble (Maeterlinck)
See *Le trésor des humbles*
The Treasure of the Lake (Haggard) **11**:254-55
"The Treasure of Tranicos" (Howard) **8**:131, 135
"The Treasurer's Report" (Benchley) **55**:15-17
The Treasurer's Report (Benchley)
See *The Treasurer's Report, and Other Aspects of Community Singing*
The Treasurer's Report, and Other Aspects of Community Singing (Benchley) **1**:79, 81; **55**:14, 18
"The Treasures of Life" (Herzl) **36**:142
The Treasures of the Earth (Tolstoy) **18**:358
A Treasury of Ben Hecht (Hecht) **101**:57
"Treasury of the Blues" (Handy) **97**:42
Treat 'Em Rough: Letters from Jack the Kaiser Killer (Lardner) **2**:332; **14**:303-04
Treatise (Keynes)
See *A Treatise on Money*
"Treatise about the Died-Out World" (Weiss)
See "Trakat von der ausgestorbenen Welt"
"Treatise of the Steppenwolf" (Hesse) **196**:298
Treatise on General Sociology (Pareto)
See *Trattato di sociologia generale*
A Treatise on Money (Keynes) **64**:210, 220-21, 226-27, 229, 249-50, 253-60, 263-65, 284, 297-99, 301-4
Treatise on Morals (Hostos)
See *Tratado de moral*
A Treatise on Probability (Keynes) **64**:227-28, 230-31, 233, 235, 249, 288, 291, 204-95
Treatise on Right and Wrong (Mencken) **13**:377, 383, 387-88
Treatise on Sociology (Hostos)
See *Tratado de sociología*
Treatise on Style (Aragon)
See *Traité du style*
"Treatise on Tailors' Dummies" (Schulz)
See "Traktat o manekinach"
Treatise on the Gods (Mencken) **13**:377, 383, 387-88
Treatise on Universal Algebra (Whitehead) **97**:196-97, 210
"The Treaty with China" (Twain) **161**:235
"Tredje natten" (Strindberg) **8**:419
"The Tree" (Aleixandre)
See "El árbol"
"The Tree" (Bishop) **103**:5, 8, 20
"The Tree" (de la Mare) **4**:78; **53**:16, 23, 25, 27, 30
"The Tree" (Thomas) **45**:408-10; **105**:296-7, 302, 322, 327-31, 333-34, 337-38, 353-54
The Tree (Garro)
See *El Árbol*
"A Tree. A Rock. A Cloud." (McCullers) **155**:180
Tree and Leaf (Tolkien) **137**:356-58, 361
Tree Drippings (Prishvin)
See *Lesnaia kapel*
A Tree Grows in Brooklyn (Slesinger) **10**:445-46
"The Tree in the Forest" (Södergran)
See "Trädet i skogen"
The Tree of Heaven (Chambers) **41**:90, 95, 102, 114
The Tree of Heaven (Sinclair) **3**:434-35, 439, 442; **11**:411, 413
"The Tree of Knowledge" (Evans) **85**:26
"The Tree of Knowledge" (Gray) **19**:157
"The Tree of Knowledge" (James) **47**:201
The Tree of Knowledge (Baroja)
See *El árbol de la ciencia*
The Tree of Life (Fletcher) **35**:97-8, 114-15
The Tree of Man (White) **176**:128, 139, 143-46, 148, 163-64, 180-95, 199, 243, 247-48, 301, 306-7, 309
"A Tree of Night" (Capote) **164**:99-101, 106-8, 110, 112, 142, 199
A Tree of Night, and Other Stories (Capote) **164**:142, 146, 150
The Tree of the Folkungs (Heidenstam)
See *Folkungaträdet*
"Trees" (Lawrence) **93**:98, 101
"Trees" (Lowell) **8**:236
"Trees" (Nemerov) **124**:187
"The Trees" (Trambley) **163**:287, 289, 291-93, 300, 308, 310-11, 313, 315-16, 319
"Trees" (Tsvetaeva)
See "Derev'ya"
"Trees and Cattle" (Dickey) **151**:104
"Trees in the Garden" (Lawrence) **93**:117, 118, 119
La tregua (Levi) **109**:290, 292-93, 300, 302, 310, 312-13, 316, 350-52
Trelawney of the "Wells" (Pinero) **32**:389, 398-400, 409, 412, 414-15

Tremasteren "fremtiden"; eller, Liv nordpaa (Lie) **5**:323-24, 326, 330
"The Trembling of the Veil" (Yeats) **93**:366
The Trembling of the Veil (Murry) **16**:343
The Trembling of the Veil (Yeats) **1**:554; **116**:319
Tremendous Trifles (Chesterton) **1**:178; **6**:109
Tren en ondas (Reyes) **33**:323
"Trench Poems" (Rosenberg) **12**:290, 293-95, 303, 306-08
"The Trenches" (Manning) **25**:265, 279
Trenck, Roman eines Günstlings (Frank) **81**:102
"The Trend of Economic Thinking" (Hayek) **109**:232
Trending into Maine (Roberts) **23**:232, 240
"Il treno ha fischiato" (Pirandello) **29**:284
Trent Intervenes (Bentley) **12**:15, 20
Trent's Last Case (Bentley) **12**:12-18, 20-4
Trent's Own Case (Bentley) **12**:14-15, 20
Trent-six Femmes, La Divine Douleur (Jammes) **75**:119
"Trenzador" (Güiraldes) **39**:176
"Trepov on the Dissecting Table" (Csáth) **13**:153
"Los tres besos" (Quiroga) **20**:213
"Tres cartas y un pie" (Quiroga) **20**:214
"Las tres cosas del romero" (Gonzalez Martinez) **72**:151
Tres novelas ejemplares y un prólogo (Unamuno) **2**:567; **10**:511, 513, 515; **148**:235-39, 257
Tres novelitas burguesas (Donoso) **133**:52-53, 56, 123-24, 137, 150-51, 154, 156, 189
Tres poemas (Reyes) **33**:321
"Las tres presencias" (Jiménez) **183**:303
Las tres presencias desnudas (Jiménez) **183**:294
"Tres retratos con sombra" (García Lorca) **181**:66
Los tres tesoros (Reyes) **33**:324
"Três tesouros perdidos" (Machado de Assis) **10**:291
"Tres versiones de Judas" (Borges) **109**:23, 51, 54-6
Trescientos millones (Arlt) **29**:42-4, 54
Le trésor (Coppee) **25**:127
Le trésor des humbles (Maeterlinck) **3**:318, 327, 329
"Trespass and Negligence" (Holmes) **77**:319
The Trespasser (Lawrence) **2**:343, 359; **9**:222-24; **16**:309; **93**:3, 17
"Tretii syn" (Platonov) **14**:425
Tret'ja straža (Bryusov) **10**:82
Tretya stolitsa (Pilnyak) **23**:198, 201, 211, 214, 216-17
"Treud-nan-Ron" (Sharp) **39**:377
Treue: Ein Judisches Sammelsschrift (Agnon) **151**:36
"Tri dnja" (Zamyatin) **8**:552
"Tri goda" (Chekhov) **3**:152, 159; **10**:108, 113; **31**:78
Tri serpa (Remizov) **27**:348
"Tri sestry" (Khlebnikov) **20**:126, 132-33
Tri Sestry (Chekhov) **55**:31, 60-3, 73-4; **96**:2-81; **163**:10-11, 17, 19, 68, 77, 101, 103-4, 115-16, 128, 133-34
"Tri smerti" (Tolstoy) **173**:280
Tri smerti (Tolstoy) **11**:464, 471; **44**:329, 332; **79**:407
Tri tolstiaka (Olesha)
See *Tri tolstiaku*
Tri tolstiaku (Olesha) **136**:63, 74, 79, 154, 181, 194
"Tri tsveta" (Balmont) **11**:36
"The Triad" (Sharp) **39**:375
The Trial (Kafka)
See *Der Prozess*
Trial Balance: The Collected Short Stories (March) **96**:237, 251-52, 254, 258
Trial by Jury (Gilbert) **3**:212, 214-15, 217-18
Trial by Lynching (McKay) **41**:331
The Trial: More Links of the Daisy Chain (Yonge) **48**:372, 376-77, 383, 388
Trial of Gilles de Rais (Bataille)
See *Le Proces de Gilles de Rais*
The Trial of Lucullus (Brecht)
See *Das verhör des Lukullus*
Trial of Strength (Nagai)
See *Udekurabe*
"The Trial of the Dead Cleopatra in Her Beautiful and Wonderful Tomb" (Lindsay) **17**:235
"The Trial Sermon on Bull-Skin" (Dunbar) **2**:133, **12**:111
Trials, and Other Tribulations (Runyon) **10**:436
The Trials of a Respectable Family (Azuela)
See *Las tribulaciones de una familia decente*
"The Trials of Mrs. Morpher" (Harte) **25**:218
A Triangle (Baring) **8**:36, 40, 43
"Triangles of Life" (Lawson) **27**:132
Triangles of Life, and Other Stories (Lawson) **27**:129, 132
Las tribulaciones de una familia decente (Azuela) **3**:75, 78-80; **145**:10, 15, 18, 27-28
The Tribulations of a Chinaman in China (Verne) **6**:500
Le tribun (Bourget) **12**:69, 75
La Tribuna (Pardo Bazán) **189**:254-57, 259-60, 262, 264, 266
"Tribute" (Ingamells) **35**:130
"The Trick of Change" (Coppard) **5**:179
"Tricolour" (Service) **15**:401
Tricotrin (Ouida) **43**:348-49, 366
Tric-trac du ciel (Artaud) **3**:52; **36**:32
"The Tricycle of the Future" (Stockton) **47**:328, 330
"Trieb" (Lasker-Schueler) **57**:302
Der Triebhafte Charakter (Reich) **57**:341
"Trieste" (Saba) **33**:377
"The Triflers" (Leverson) **18**:200
"Trifles" (Guro)
See "Meloči"
Trifles (Glaspell) **55**:233-34, 236-37, 241-42, 247-50, 255-59, 262-65, 267-70, 272, 276; **175**:59, 61, 69-72, 74-75, 77-81, 98, 100, 107-13, 117, 124, 126, 130, 144-45, 147-48, 151, 153, 156-59
"Trifles from the Parliament" (Mikszath)
See "Apróságok a házból"
"Trifles of Life" (Shiga)
See "Saji"
"A Trifling Incident" (Lu Hsun) **3**:303
Trilce (Vallejo) **3**:526-30, 532-33, 535-36; **56**:288-92, 295-300, 304, 308-10, 313-15
"Trilce I" (Vallejo) **3**:527-29
"Trilce II" (Vallejo) **3**:530
"Trilce III" (Vallejo) **56**:289, 298
Trilce V (Vallejo) **56**:298-99, 309
"Trilce VI" (Vallejo) **3**:350; **56**:298
"Trilce VIII" (Vallejo) **56**:308
Trilce X (Vallejo) **56**:309
Trilce XIII (Vallejo) **56**:309
"Trilce XIV" (Vallejo) **56**:298
"Trilce XVII" (Vallejo) **56**:290, 298
"Trilce XX" (Vallejo) **56**:290
"Trilce XXI" (Vallejo) **3**:530
"Trilce XXII" (Vallejo) **3**:532
"Trilce XXIII" (Vallejo) **56**:315
"Trilce XXV" (Vallejo) **3**:529; **56**:299
"Trilce XXVII" (Vallejo) **3**:529
"Trilce XXXIII" (Vallejo) **3**:532
"Trilce XXXVI" (Vallejo) **56**:290
"Trilce XL" (Vallejo) **56**:308
"Trilce XLI" (Vallejo) **3**:532
"Trilce XLV" (Vallejo) **3**:529
"Trilce XLVII" (Vallejo) **3**:529
Trilce XLVII (Vallejo) **56**:308
"Trilce LIII" (Vallejo) **56**:297
"Trilce lv" (Vallejo) **56**:290, 295, 297
"Trilce lvi" (Vallejo) **56**:298
"Trilce lvii" (Vallejo) **56**:298
"Trilce lix" (Vallejo) **56**:296
"Trilce LX" (Vallejo) **56**:308
"Trilce LXI" (Vallejo) **56**:298
"Trilce LXV" (Vallejo) **56**:315
Trilce LXVII (Vallejo) **56**:308
"Trilce LXVII" (Vallejo) **56**:310
"Trilce LXIX" (Vallejo) **3**:529
"Trilce LXXI" (Vallejo) **3**:532; **56**:309
Trilce LXXV (Vallejo) **56**:297, 308
"Trilce LXXVI" (Vallejo) **56**:310
Trilogie de Pan (Giono) **124**:69
Trilogy (Sienkiewicz) **3**:427-31
The Trimmed Lamp (Henry) **1**:345-47
"La trinchera" (Huidobro) **31**:125
Trini (Trambley) **163**:351-52, 359-60, 375
"Trinity of Crime" (Bishop) **103**:5, 8
"Trinket's Colt" (Somerville & Ross) **51**:385
A Trio (Gorky)
See *Troe*
"Trio em lá menor" (Machado de Assis) **10**:290
Le triomphe de la raison (Rolland) **23**:257-58, 260
Triomphe de la vie (Giono) **124**:93, 96-97
Le Triomphe de la Vie (Jammes) **75**:115, 117-18
A Trip in a Balloon (Verne)
See *Cinq semaines en ballon*
Trip to Havana (Arenas)
See *Viaje a la Habana*
A Trip to the Moon (Melies) **81**:122,144,146-8
A Trip to the Moon (Verne)
See *Le Voyage dans la Lune*
Trip to the Village of Crime (Sender)
See *Viaje a la aldea del crimen*
Triptych: Three Scenic Panels (Frisch)
See *Triptychon*
Triptychon (Frisch) **121**:191, 218-23, 233, 241, 245, 247, 306
Trisévgene (Palamas) **5**:384-85
"Tristan" (Mann) **168**:157, 186
Tristan (Mann)
See *Tristan: Sechs Novellen*
"Tristan da Cunha" (Campbell) **5**:123-24
Tristan: Sechs Novellen (Mann) **2**:429, 439; **8**:261-62; **14**:323, 349, 358-59; **21**:166; **44**:145; **60**:335, 337, 354, 358, 362-63
Tristan und Isolde (von Hartmann) **96**:206, 214
Tristana (Pérez Galdós) **27**:250
Triste fim de Policarpo Quaresma (Lima Barreto) **23**:160-61, 163-64, 166, 168-72
Tristessa (Kerouac) **117**:254, 256, 259, 262-64
"La tristesse" (Pickthall) **21**:246
"La tristesse de Cornélius Berg" (Yourcenar) **193**:283, 297-99
"Tristesse d'un étoile" (Apollinaire) **51**:10, 37
Tristesses (Jammes) **75**:119
"Tristeza no Céu" (Drummond de Andrade) **139**:230
Tristi amori (Giacosa) **7**:305-06, 308-15
Tristia (Mandelstam)
See *Vtoraya kniga*
"Tristram" (Manning) **25**:277
Tristram (Robinson) **5**:405-06, 408, 414; **101**:98, 109-11, 113-14, 127, 184-85, 188, 191-92
"Tristram and Iseult" (Swinburne) **8**:426
Tristram of Lyonesse (Swinburne) **8**:430, 441; **36**:301, 315-16, 319, 321, 324, 345
"Tristram's Journey" (Muir) **87**:167
Tritte (Beckett) **145**:124, 129
The Triumph and Passing of Cuculain (O'Grady) **5**:353, 356
Triumph and Tragedy (Churchill) **113**:119-20, 183-84
The Triumph of Agriculture (Zabolotsky)
See *Torzhestvo zemledeliia*
"Triumph of Bacchus and Ariadne" (Field) **43**:165
"The Triumph of Death" (Wakefield) **120**:343, 345
The Triumph of Death (D'Annunzio)
See *Il trionfo della morte*
The Triumph of Death (Ramuz)
See *Présence de la mort*

The Triumph of Death (Sologub)
See *Pobeda smerti*
"Triumph of Existing" (Södergran) **31**:291
The Triumph of Liberty (Bell)
See *A Poem Entitled "The Triumph of Liberty": Delivered April 7, 1870 at Detroit Opera House, on the Occasion of the Fifteenth Amendment to the Constitution of the United States*
The Triumph of Love (Giacosa)
See *Il trionfo d'amore*
The Triumph of Mammon (Davidson) **24**:183-84, 194
"The Triumph of Night" (Wharton) **3**:577; **129**:362, 364
The Triumph of the Egg: A Book of Impressions from American Life in Tales and Poems (Anderson) **1**:35-6, 39, 42, 44, 46; **10**:33, 36, 41, 45; **24**:17
"The Triumph of Time" (Swinburne) **8**:429-30, 437, 446; **36**:305, 312-13, 318-19, 322, 338-39
Triumph over Pain (Sturges)
See *The Great Moment*
Triumph und Tragik des Erasmus von Rotterdam (Zweig) **17**:426-27, 431, 438, 440-42, 445-46, 448, 457-58
"Triumphs of the Free" (Bell) **43**:91
"El triunfo de procopio" (Azuela) **3**:76
"Triunfo del amor" (Aleixandre) **113**:13, 55
Trivial Breath (Wylie) **8**:526, 529, 532, 534, 538
Trixy (Phelps) **113**:339-40
Trods (Jensen) **41**:292
Troe (Gorky) **8**:70, 77, 81, 86
Troe (Guro) **56**:132, 134, 138-39
Troens magt (Bojer) **64**:2, 4, 13, 15, 18-20, 22-24
Die Troerinnen (Werfel) **8**:473, 477
"Trofast" (Kielland) **5**:278
Den trofaste hustru (Undset) **3**:519, 521, 523; **197**:301-02
"Troglodyte" (Kolmar) **40**:176
Troika (Kandinsky) **92**:147
Trois acteurs (Ghelderode) **187**:4, 24
Les trois amoureuses (Rolland) **23**:257
Les trois crimes d'Arsène Lupin (Leblanc) **49**:197
Les trois cœurs (Rod) **52**:307-08, 310, 317-21, 324-25
"Les trois dames de la Kasbah, conte Oriental" (Loti) **11**:353
Les trois Don Juan (Apollinaire) **51**:20, 28
Trois Eglises et Trois Primitifs (Huysmans) **69**:7, 47
"Trois etoiles" (Desnos) **22**:61
"Les trois gabelous" (Schwob) **20**:319
Trois idoles romantiques (Benda) **60**:79
Trois poèmes de guerre (Claudel) **2**:122
Trois Primitifs (Huysmans) **69**:12, 44
Trois Scenarii—Ciné poèmes (Fondane) **159**:239-40, 242, 245-47
Trois stations de psychothérapie (Barrès) **47**:51, 98
Les trois Villes (Zola) **1**:597
"Troisième manifeste" (Desnos) **22**:68
The Trojan Horse (Morley) **87**:147
"A Trojan Slave" (Muir)
See "Troy II"
"Trojans" (Cavafy) **2**:88
"Trojsky Bridge" (Nezval)
See "Trojský most"
"Trojský most" (Nezval) **44**:247
Trold (Lie) **5**:325
The Troll Garden (Cather) **11**:92-3, 100, 114; **99**:207, 266; **132**:123, 129, 132, 134, 140
Trolls (Lie) **5**:329-30
Le trombe d'Eustachio (Brancati) **12**:85
Trommeln in der nacht (Brecht) **6**:35-6
Trompette (Kandinsky) **92**:49
"The Troop Ship" (Rosenberg) **12**:289, 297, 312
"Trooper Jim Tasman" (Baynton) **57**:11, 25
Trooper Peter Halket of Mashonaland (Schreiner) **9**:395-99, 404-05
"The Troopship" (Johnson) **19**:244
Une trop bruyante solitude (Hrabal)
See *Prilis hlucná samota*
"Tropic of Cuba" (di Donato) **159**:196
"Tropical Disturbance" (Dent) **72**:30
"Tropical Glory" (Quiroga)
See "Gloria tropical"
"A Tropical Intermezzo" (Hearn) **9**:133
Tropical Winter (Hergesheimer) **11**:277
"The Tropics" (Mayakovski) **18**:258
"The Tropics in New York" (McKay) **41**:344
Tropismes (Sarraute) **145**:264-65, 269-71, 274, 277, 287-88, 320, 351, 356-57, 364
Tropisms (Sarraute)
See *Tropismes*
Trotsky in Exile (Weiss)
See *Trotzki im Exil*
"Trotsky's Rationalism" (Merleau-Ponty) **156**:185
Trotzki im Exil (Weiss) **152**:267-8
Trouble in July (Caldwell) **117**:23
Trouble in Mind (Childress) **116**:25-8, 30-1, 38-40, 54
"Trouble in Time" (Kornbluth) **8**:215
"Trouble Is My Business" (Chandler) **179**:128, 168
Trouble is My Business (Chandler) **179**:153, 188, 205
"Trouble on Lost Mountain" (Harris) **2**:209
The Trouble with Tigers (Saroyan) **137**:182, 186
Troubled Waters (Betti)
See *Acque turbate*
"The Troubles of a Carpet Fancier" (Čapek) **37**:48
Troupers of the Gold Coast; or, The Rise of Lotta Crabtree (Rourke) **12**:319, 321, 324, 329, 331
"The Trout" (O'Faolain) **143**:253
The Trout Breaks the Ice (Kuzmin)
See *Forel razbyvaet lyod*
Trout Fishing in America (Brautigan) **133**:3-6, 10, 12-14, 16, 19, 28, 31-33
"The Trout Stream" (Welch) **22**:456
Trovarsi (Pirandello) **29**:298, 306, 318
"Troy" (Muir)
See "Troy I"
"Troy I" (Muir) **87**:159
"Troy II" (Muir) **87**:207
"Truant" (McKay) **41**:329, 342
Truants from Life: The Rehabilitation of Emotionally Disturbed Children (Bettelheim) **143**:7
"Truba Gul-Mully" (Khlebnikov) **20**:127, 133
The Truce: A Survivor's Journey Home from Auschwitz (Levi)
See *La tregua*
"The Truce of the Bear" (Kipling) **8**:191
"The Truce of the Mohawks" (Coffin) **95**:2
"The Truck" (Akutagawa Ryūnosuke)
See "Torokko"
"Truck-Garden-Market Day" (Millay) **49**:222
"True Aesthetic Laws of Form" (Steiner) **13**:452
"True Americanism" (Roosevelt) **69**:177
"The True Duty of Critics" (Matthews) **95**:228
"The True Fin de Siècle" (Rozanov) **104**:347
"The True Function and Value of Criticism: With Some Remarks on the Importance of Doing Nothing" (Wilde) **8**:497
The True Heart (Warner) **131**:320, 325, 363
True Heart Susie (Griffith) **68**:169-70, 175-77, 214, 217, 229, 249
A True Hero (Howells) **7**:387-88
True Love (Bromfield) **11**:83
"True Love at Last" (Lawrence) **93**:53
"True Love Ways" (Holly) **65**:144, 147, 151-53
"true lovers in each happening of their hearts" (Cummings) **137**:55
"True Marriage" (Tynan) **3**:503
"The True Negro" (Cotter) **28**:42
"True Romance" (Kipling) **17**:197
The True Sedemunds (Barlach)
See *Die echten Sedemunds*
"The True Story" (Thomas) **105**:318, 331, 337
"A True Story" (Thomas)
See "The True Story"
A True Story and the Recent Carnival of Crime (Twain) **48**:360
"The True Story of Ah Q" (Lu Hsun) **3**:295
"The True Story of Guenever" (Phelps) **113**:376
"A True Story Repeated Word for Word as I Heard It" (Twain) **161**:251-52
"The True Theory of the Preface" (Matthews) **95**:226
True Tilda (Quiller-Couch) **53**:296
The True Traveller (Davies) **5**:206-07
"The True Woman" (Phelps) **113**:389
"True, yes, yes" (Jiménez)
See "Verdad, sí, sí"
True-Hearted Susie (Griffith)
See *True Heart Susie*
"Trule kobile" (Popa) **167**:155
"Truly" (Bachmann) **192**:67
Truly, Indeed (Vilakazi)
See *Nje nempela*
"The Trumpet" (de la Mare) **53**:26-7, 35-6
"The Trumpet" (Thomas) **10**:452, 464
The Trumpet Call (Buchanan) **107**:33
Trumpet of Jubilee (Lewisohn) **19**:278
"The Trumpet of the Martians" (Khlebnikov) **20**:151
The Trumpet Shall Sound (Tomlinson) **71**:400
"The Trumpeters" (Coppard) **5**:176
The Trumpet-Major (Hardy) **4**:148-49, 158-59; **10**:227; **143**:112, 204-6
Trumpets of Jubilee: Henry Ward Beecher, Harriet Beecher Stowe, Lyman Beecher, Horace Greeley, P. T. Barnum (Rourke) **12**:316, 319, 321, 323-24, 329, 331-32
"Trunov" (Babel)
See "Eskadronnyi Trunov"
Trust and Trial (Bjoernson)
See *Synnøve Solbakken*
"De trust de vaderlandsliefde" (van Ostaijen) **33**:409-10, 412
"The Trust Property" (Tagore) **3**:485
"The Trustfulness of Polly" (Dunbar) **2**:128; **12**:120, 124
"The Trusting Heart" (Parker) **143**:323
The Trusty Knaves (Rhodes) **53**:307, 309, 319, 322-23, 329
"Truth" (Baker) **10**:18
"Truth" (Harper) **14**:259, 261
"The Truth" (Jarrell) **177**:176, 195, 222, 225-26
"Truth" (Nemerov) **124**:182, 310
The Truth (Glyn) **72**:139
Truth (Svevo)
See *La verità*
The Truth about an Author (Bennett) **5**:46; **197**:22, 37, 41, 72
The Truth about Blayds (Milne) **6**:307, 310
The Truth about Ireland (Upward) **85**:380
The Truth About the West African Land Question (Casely-Hayford) **24**:132
The Truth about Tristrem Varick (Saltus) **8**:345-46, 348-49, 352
The Truth and Error of Darwinism (von Hartmann) **96**:212
"Truth and Perspective" (Ortega y Gasset) **9**:348
"Truth and Politics" (Arendt) **193**:62, 123, 182
Truth and Reality: A Life History of the Human Will (Rank) **115**:222, 262-66, 269, 281, 311, 315, 318
Truth and Right (Tammsaare)
See *Tõde ja õigus*
Truth Is God (Gandhi) **59**:61-2
"The Truth of Masks" (Wilde) **8**:493, 497, 502
"The Truth of the Matter" (Nemerov) **124**:152, 287
"A Truthful Adventure" (Mansfield) **164**:235
Try a Little Tenderness (Osborne) **153**:312, 314

"Try the Girl" (Chandler) **7**:176; **179**:124-28, 168, 170
"Trying Conclusions" (Nemerov) **124**:292
Trying Conclusions: New and Selected Poems, 1961-1991 (Nemerov) **124**:289, 295, 297-302
The Trying Hour (Lagerkvist)
See *Den svåra stunden*
"Trying to Understand Endgame" (Adorno) **111**:185-86
"A Tryst at an Ancient Earthwork" (Hardy) **143**:169
"Tryste Noël" (Guiney) **41**:207
"Tržnice" (Nezval) **44**:247
"Tsar and God! Grant Those Your Pardon" (Tsvetaeva) **35**:395
Le Tsar et la Révolution (Hippius) **9**:161
Tsar' Iksion (Annensky) **14**:17, 21
"Tsar' Solomon" (Remizov) **27**:355
Tsarapina po nebu (Khlebnikov)
See *Carapina po nebu*
Tsar-devitsa (Tsvetaeva) **7**:557, 559, 561, 567-68; **35**:375, 390, 394, 402, 410, 413
"Tsarevna Mymra" (Remizov) **27**:333, 339, 347
The Tsar-Maiden (Tsvetaeva)
See *Tsar-devitsa*
Tschandala (Strindberg) **47**:342
"Tselaya zhizn" (Pilnyak) **23**:203
"Tsep" (Olesha) **136**:58, 103-5, 108, 154, 156
Tseykhenungen (Kahanovitsch) **56**:109
Tsezeyt un tseshpreyt (Aleichem) **35**:306
Tsimshian Mythology (Boas) **56**:81
"Tsoncho's Revenge" (Vazov) **25**:454
Tsugaru (Dazai Osamu) **11**:176-77, 184
Tsuki ni hoeru (Hagiwara) **60**:288-9, 295-6, 298, 311-6
"Tsum barg" (Kahanovitsch) **56**:115
"Tsum shnit" (Kahanovitsch) **56**:115
"Tsuyu dandan" (Rohan) **22**:294, 301, 304-05
Tsuyu no atosaki (Nagai) **51**:86, 92, 96-7
"Tu croyais tout tranquille" (Garneau) **13**:195
Tú eres mi secreto (Villaurrutia) **80**:466
"Tu infancia en Menton" (García Lorca) **197**:201, 217, 278
Tu ne t'aimes pas (Sarraute) **145**:265, 276-81, 288, 311
"Tu Quoque" (Dobson) **79**:5
"Tu tzuch'un" (Akutagawa Ryūnosuke) **16**:27
"Tudor Translations" (Henley) **8**:106
"Tuércele el cuelo al cisna" (Gonzalez Martinez) **72**:154
Túeres la paz (Martinez Sierra and Martinez Sierra) **6**:276, 279-80, 286
"A Tuesday Evening with Stephane Mallarme" (Hartmann) **73**:116
"Le tueur de grenouilles" (Vallette) **67**:278, 319, 321-23
"Tui Hoo" (Borchert) **5**:109
De Tuin der Rotsen (Kazantzakis) **181**:237
Tujci (Cankar) **105**:161
"Tukuhnikivats, the Island in the Sky" (Abbey) **160**:24, 35
Tulio Montalbán y Julio Macedo (Unamuno) **148**:256
Tulip (Hammett) **187**:47, 77, 155, 205, 207
"A Tulip Garden" (Lowell) **8**:233
"La Tulipe" (Huysmans) **69**:8
Tulips and Chimneys (Cummings) **137**:18, 34, 36, 41, 45-47, 50
"Tulsah" (Shiel) **8**:361
Una tumba sin nombre (Onetti)
See *Para una tumba sin nombre*
Tumbling in the Hay (Gogarty) **15**:119-20
"Tumbling-Hair" (Cummings) **137**:41, 61
"Tumma" (Leino) **24**:368
Tündérkert (Moricz) **33**:242-44, 250
Tündérvilág (Mikszath) **31**:167
"Tune the Old Cow Died To" (March) **96**:266
El tungsteno (Vallejo) **56**:299
"The Tungszu Problem" (Yosano)
See "Toshi-sho no mondai"
"Tunk: A Lecture of Modern Education" (Johnson) **19**:210
"The Tunnel" (Crane) **5**:186-87, 190; **80**:82-3, 94, 96, 102-3, 116-8, 126, 140, 147, 166-8, 174, 177-8, 182, 186, 191
"Tunnel" (Verhaeren) **12**:468
The Tunnel (Richardson) **3**:347, 356, 358
Tuomas Vitikka (Leino) **24**:372
Tuonelan joutsen (Leino) **24**:368-71
Túpac Amaru Kamaq Taytanchisman/A nuestro padre creador Tupac Amaru (Arguedas) **147**:30, 89, 95
Tup-i murvari (Hedāyat) **21**:72, 76
"A Turbulent Year" (Andrić)
See "Nemirna godina"
An T-úr-Ghort (Moore) **7**:476, 481, 490-94
"Turjan loihtu" (Leino) **24**:368
"Turja's Spell" (Leino)
See "Turjan loihtu"
"Turkestanski generaly" (Gumilev) **60**:280
"The Turkish Yataghan" (Rohmer) **28**:286
"The Turkman" (Olesha) **136**:155
"Der Turm" (Kandinsky) **92**:67
"Der Turm" (Rilke) **195**:233-37
Der Turm (Hofmannsthal) **11**:298-99, 302-03, 306, 310
Der Turm (Weiss) **152**:246-47, 285-87, 289
"Türmers Töchterlein" (Raabe) **45**:190
The Turmoil (Tarkington) **9**:453, 455-56, 459-60, 463, 467, 472
"Turmoil in a Morgue" (Bodenheim) **44**:59, 62
Turn Back the Leaves (Delafield) **61**:127, 130
The Turn Inward (Hesse)
See *Der Weg nach Innen*
The Turn of the Screw (James) **2**:246, 250-51, 269; **11**:341-42; **24**:314-63; **40**:120; **47**:166, 174, 195-97, 199-200, 206; **64**:156, 171; **171**:151, 180
The Turn of the Year (Grove) **4**:133, 136, 140-41
"Turned" (Gilman) **9**:113, 115; **37**:213
"Turned Down" (Lawrence) **93**:12
"Turning Away: Variations on Estrangement" (Dickey) **151**:98, 102-3, 113, 116-17
"The Turning of the Babies in the Bed" (Dunbar) **12**:110
"Turning Point" (Rilke) **1**:420
The Turning Point (McCoy) **28**:212
"The Turning-Point of My Life" (Twain) **185**:234
"Die Turnstunde" (Rilke) **195**:175
"The Turtle" (Nash) **109**:362
"The Turtles of Tasman" (London) **9**:267
Tuscan Cities (Howells) **41**:263
Tusen är hos Gud (Dagerman) **17**:96-7
"Tuskegee" (Cotter) **28**:43
"Tuti artic" (Anwar) **22**:22-3
"Tuti's Ice Cream" (Anwar)
See "Tuti artic"
The Tutor (Brecht) **1**:112
Tutti i miei peccati (Jovine) **79**:44, 47, 61, 65
Tutti i nostri ieri (Ginzburg) **156**:21, 33, 38-41, 45, 49-50, 71, 104-6, 112
Tutto il miele è finito (Levi) **125**:207, 209, 211
Tutto per bene (Pirandello) **4**:340; **29**:285, 301, 318
"Tutuguri, le rite du soleil noir" (Artaud) **36**:30
"Tutuguri, the Rite of the Black Sun" (Artaud)
See "Tutuguri, le rite du soleil noir"
"Tuulikannel" (Leino) **24**:370-71
"Tuuri" (Leino) **24**:368, 376
"Tüzek" (Babits) **14**:39
"TV" (Nemerov) **124**:260
Två sagor om livit (Lagerkvist) **144**:222
"Två vägar" (Södergran) **31**:290
Tvorenija (Khlebnikov) **20**:148
Tvorimaja legenda (Sologub) **9**:434-38, 447
"Tvrdoglav zavezljaj" (Popa) **167**:156
"Tweed Days in St. Louis" (Steffens) **20**:336-37, 341-42
Tweedles (Tarkington) **9**:465
"Twelfth Anniversary" (Scott) **6**:394
The Twelfth Hour (Leverson) **18**:186, 188, 192-93
The Twelfth Hour: A Night of Horror (Murnau)
See *Die zwölfte Stunden: Eine Nacht des Grauens*
"Twelfth Morning; or, What You Will" (Bishop) **121**:9
"Twelfth Night" (Bishop) **103**:25
"The Twelfth of February" (Ivanov) **33**:138
"The Twelfth Wedding Anniversary" (Brennan) **124**:6
The Twelve (Blok)
See *Dvenadsat*
"The Twelve and the One" (Nemerov) **124**:234
"Twelve Arguments on the Theater" (Jarry) **147**:292
The Twelve Chairs (Petrov)
See *Dvenadtsat stulyev*
Twelve Idyls (Abercrombie) **141**:23
"Twelve Letters" (Pirandello) **4**:349
Twelve Men (Dreiser) **35**:71
Twelve Million Black Voices (Wright)
See *Twelve Million Black Voices: A Folk History of the Negro in the United States*
Twelve Million Black Voices: A Folk History of the Negro in the United States (Wright) **136**:240, 259, 276, 287-88, 305
Twelve Occupations (Bosschere)
See *Métiers divins*
Twelve Poems (Warner)
See *Azrael and Other Poems*
Twelve Poems (Wharton) **129**:363
"Twelve Tone Composition" (Schoenberg)
See "Composition with Twelve Tones"
Twelve Types (Chesterton) **6**:101
The Twelve Words of the Gypsy (Palamas)
See *Ho dodekálogos tou gýphtou*
The Twelve-Pound Look (Barrie) **2**:41; **164**:39
The Twentieth Century (Hecht) **101**:62-3, 77
Twentieth-Century Jamaica (De Lisser) **12**:95, 99
Twenty (Benson) **17**:18
Twenty Bath-Tub Ballads (Service) **15**:411
Twenty Thousand Leagues under the Sea (Verne)
See *Vingt mille lieues sous les mers*
20,000 Leagues Under the Sea, or David Copperfield (Benchley) **55**:14
"Twenty Years After" (Adams) **4**:11
Twenty Years at Hull-House (Addams) **76**:5, 10, 34, 48-9, 51-7, 65, 69, 84, 93, 96-8, 101-03, 133, 135, 141, 143-45, 148
Twenty Years on Broadway (Cohan) **60**:163
Twenty-Five (Gregory) **1**:335-36; **176**:13-14, 16
Twenty-Five Poems (Thomas) **8**:458-59; **45**:399; **105**:305
XXIV Elegies (Fletcher) **35**:98, 100, 102, 106
Twenty-Four Hours (Bromfield) **11**:76, 81, 85-6
Twenty-Four Minds (Papini)
See *Venti quattro cervelli*
"Twenty-Four Years" (Thomas) **45**:362, 399; **105**:336
"The Twenty-Ninth of June" (Chekhov) **96**:33
Twenty-One Poems (Johnson) **19**:240
XXI Poems, MDCCCXCII-MDCCCXCVII: Towards the Source (Brennan) **17**:54-5
Twenty-one Stories (Agnon) **151**:3
Twenty-Six Men and a Girl (Gorky)
See *Dvádtsat' shesti i odná*
Twenty-Six Poems (Thomas) **1**:473
Twenty-Three and a Half Hours' Leave (Rinehart) **52**:282
"Twenty-Two" (Rinehart) **52**:282
"Twice-Done, Once-Done" (Muir) **2**:485; **87**:178
"Twilight" (Apollinaire)
See "Crépuscule"
"Twilight" (Lee-Hamilton) **22**:194
"Twilight" (Montgomery) **51**:203
"Twilight" (Södergran)
See "Skymning"

"Twilight at a Little Harbor" (Anwar)
See "Sendja di pelabuhan ketjil"
Twilight in Italy (Lawrence) **2**:347-48, 358-59; **9**:216, 221; **33**:184; **61**:258
Twilight of a World (Werfel) **8**:470, 479
Twilight of Authority (Nisbet) **117**:315, 326-27, 334, 352, 355, 358, 360, 363, 367, 379
"The Twilight of Disquietude" (Brennan) **17**:41, 43, 54
"The Twilight of Earth" (Baker) **10**:20
"Twilight of Idols" (Bourne) **16**:44, 64, 67
"The Twilight of Rhyme" (Sapir) **108**:250
"The Twilight of the God" (Wharton) **129**:360
The Twilight of the Idols (Nietzsche)
See *Die götzendämmerung; oder, Wie man mit dem Hammer philosophiert*
Twilight of the Philosophers (Papini) **22**:271, 276, 287
The Twilight of the Spirit (Hippius)
See *Sumerki dukha*
"Twilight over Shaugamauk" (Roberts) **8**:321
Twilight Sleep (Wharton) **3**:573, 580; **9**:548; **129**:350, 363
"Twilight Song" (Robinson) **101**:119, 124
Twilight Songs (Tynan) **3**:504-05
"Twilights" (Brennan) **17**:53
"Twilight's Last Gleamings" (Burroughs) **121**:136
"The Twin Soul" (Sharp) **39**:389
"Twin-Flowers on the Portage" (Scott) **6**:393
The Twinkle Tales (Baum) **132**:80
Twinkletoes (Burke) **63**:127, 129
Twins (Nezval)
See *Blíženci*
The Twins of Table Mountain (Harte) **25**:193
"The Twisting of the Rope" (Yeats) **31**:414
"The Twitch" (Nemerov) **124**:231
"The Twitching Colonel" (White) **176**:159-61, 171, 176
The Twits (Dahl) **173**:20
Twixt Earth and Stars (Hall) **12**:194
'Twixt Land and Sea: Tales (Conrad) **6**:120; **43**:100; **57**:78, 100, 116
"The Two" (Hofmannsthal) **11**:294
"Two" (Stein) **48**:235
The Two (Nabokov)
See *Dvoe*
Two (Stein) **28**:332
"The Two Adams" (Gumilev) **60**:280
"The Two Babes" (Buchanan) **107**:15
"The Two Bottles of Relish" (Dunsany) **59**:27
"2 x 2" (Fondane) **159**:240, 245-47
Two Can Play at That Game (Pinero) **32**:412
Two Cheers for Democracy (Forster) **125**:114, 183-84
"Two Clowns" (Coppee) **25**:121
"Two Communists" (Ginzburg) **156**:26
"Two Concepts of Liberty" (Berlin) **105**:8, 19, 67, 69, 74-6, 79-81, 84, 105, 109, 114, 132, 137, 145, 147
Two Concepts of Liberty (Berlin) **105**:40
"Two Couples and a Single" (Tammsaare)
See "Kakspaari ja üksainus"
Two Crimes (Ibarguengoitia)
See *Dos crímenes*
"Two Critics of Poetry" (Flecker) **43**:211
"The Two Devines" (Paterson) **32**:373
"Two Doctors" (James) **6**:216
"The Two Dreams" (Swinburne) **36**:299, 336
"Two Drops" (Herbert)
See "Dwie krople"
"Two Elements in Contemporary Symbolism" (Ivanov) **33**:127-31
"Two Fathers" (Čapek) **6**:84
"Two Figures in Dense Violet Light" (Stevens) **3**:476; **45**:347
The Two Fontiers: A Study in Historical Psychology (Fletcher) **35**:106
"Two Forest Kings" (Tsvetaeva) **7**:572
"Two French Theatrical Critics" (Matthews) **95**:226
"Two Friends" (Cather) **11**:98; **132**:136, 138
"Two Gallants" (Joyce) **8**:170; **35**:141-42, 145, 147, 149, 156, 160, 163, 167, 193, 197; **159**:301, 304
The Two Gardens (Miyamoto)
See *Futatsu no niwa*
"The Two Generations" (Bourne) **16**:69
Two Generations (Grove) **4**:136, 140
"Two Girls" (Nemerov) **124**:177
Two Girls on a Barge (Duncan) **60**:206
The Two Guardians; or, Home in this World (Yonge) **48**:366, 378
"The Two Heavens" (Davies) **5**:202
"Two Hexameters" (Jozsef) **22**:165
"Two Holy Sailing Boats" (Ady) **11**:21
"Two Houses" (Thomas) **10**:455-56
The Two Hundred Tenth Day (Natsume)
See *Nihyakutōka*
"Two Hundred Years Ago" (Drummond) **25**:145
"The Two Hunters" (Arnow) **196**:88-9
"Two Hussars" (Tolstoy) **173**:269
Two Hussars (Tolstoy) **4**:445, 474; **11**:464-65; **17**:413; **79**:376, 383
"Two in One" (Pirandello) **4**:331
"Two Interviews on Science and Literature" (Calvino) **183**:141-42
"Two Irish Peasant Songs" (Guiney) **41**:214
"Two Ivans" (Babel)
See "Ivany"
"The Two Kings" (Yeats) **31**:385
"The Two Kings and Their Two Labyrinths" (Borges)
See "Los dos reyes y los dos laberintos"
"Two Lacquer Prints" (Lowell) **8**:230
"Two Larrykins" (Lawson) **27**:121
"Two Latter-Day Lyrists" (Matthews) **95**:226
"Two Letters" (Bishop) **121**:71
"Two Lights" (Stephens) **4**:412
"Two Listeners" (de la Mare) **53**:39
"Two Little Boots" (Dunbar) **12**:110
Two Little Savages (Seton) **31**:262-64
"Two Little Tales" (Twain) **59**:170
Two Little Wooden Shoes (Ouida) **43**:357
"Two Lives" (Tolstoy) **18**:377
Two Loose Sports (March) **96**:248
"Two Lottery Prizes" (Caragiale)
See "Două loturi"
"Two Lottery Tickets" (Caragiale)
See "Două loturi"
"Two Lowly Tokens of My Grief" (Tsvetaeva) **35**:394
"The Two Matches" (Cahan)
See "Ditsvey shidukhim"
"The Two Matches" (Clark)
See "Ditsvey shidukhim"
Two Memoirs: Dr. Melchior, a Degeated Enemy, and My Early Beliefs (Keynes) **64**:208, 245
Two Memories (Griffith) **68**:245
"Two Men Named Collins" (Runyon) **10**:428
Two Men of Sandy Bar (Harte) **25**:192, 217
The Two Mendicant Students (Mikszath)
See *A két koldusdiák*
"Two Military Executions" (Bierce) **44**:45
"The Two Minutes' Silence" (MacCarthy) **36**:254
"Two Mothers" (Unamuno) **148**:238
Two Mothers (Unamuno)
See *Dos madres*
Two Novellas: Valentino and Sagittarius (Ginzburg)
See *Valentino*
"Le 2 novembre en Lorraine" (Barrès) **47**:65, 68
"The Two Nuts" (Fitzgerald) **52**:63
"Two of a Kind" (O'Faolain) **143**:230, 266
"Two of a Trade" (Somerville & Ross) **51**:351
"The Two Offers" (Harper) **14**:258
"Two Old Men" (Tolstoy) **11**:463; **79**:422
Two on a Tower (Hardy) **4**:149, 159; **10**:217, 227; **18**:46; **32**:281; **53**:90, 95; **143**:78
"Two or Three Ideas" (Stevens) **12**:373, 387; **45**:273, 286, 326
"The Two Painters" (Dobson) **79**:3
"Two Pair" (Nemerov) **124**:259
The Two Paths (Griffith) **68**:186
Two People (Milne) **6**:318; **88**:247
"Two Pewits" (Thomas) **10**:455, 463
Two Phases of Criticism: Historical and Aesthetic (Woodberry) **73**:375
The Two Pierrots (Rostand)
See *Les deux pierrots*
"Two Poems of Going Home" (Dickey) **151**:101, 143, 170
"Two Poets" (Cullen) **37**:167
"Two Points of View" (Korolenko) **22**:169
"Two Portraits" (Chopin) **14**:60, 69
"Two Pounds of Goose Fat" (Calvino) **183**:47
"Two Rivers" (Roberts) **8**:321
"Two Salvation Army Women" (Bodenheim) **44**:71
"Two Scholars Who Lived in Our Town" (Agnon)
See "Sne talmide hakamim sehayu be'ir-enu"
Two Secrets of Russian Poetry: Tiutchev and Nekrasov (Merezhkovsky) **29**:250
Two Shepherds (Martinez Sierra and Martinez Sierra)
See *Los pastores*
Two Shepherds and a Nymph in a Hut (Kuzmin)
See *Dva pastukha i nimfa v khizhine*
Two Sides of a Question (Sinclair) **3**:437; **11**:413
The Two Sides of the Shield (Yonge) **48**:389
"The Two Sisters" (Muir) **87**:239-40
"Two Soldiers" (Himes) **139**:244, 323
"Two Soldiers" (March) **96**:241, 254
"Two Songs from a Play" (Yeats) **11**:519; **18**:448
Two Songs From a Play (Yeats) **116**:272
Two Songs: Song of Prisoner and Song of Malaya (p'Bitek) **149**:23, 31, 36, 42, 44, 89, 97, 112
"Two Sonnets" (Robinson) **101**:123
"Two Sonnets in Memory" (Millay) **169**:268
"Two Sonnets to My Wife" (Bodenheim) **44**:59
"Two Souls With But a Single Thought" (Millay) **169**:237
The Two Sources of Morality and Religion (Bergson) **32**:34, 44-6, 50-2
"Two Speak Together" (Lowell) **8**:234, 236
Two Stories and a Memory (Lampedusa)
See *Racconti*
"Two Streaks of Blood" (Ishikawa) **15**:130
Two Streets (Thomas) **105**:309
"Two Studies from the Life of Goethe" (Sinclair) **11**:407
Two Tales (de la Mare) **53**:16
Two Tales About Life (Lagerkvist)
See *Två sagor om livit*
Two Tales of Life (Lagerkvist)
See *Två sagor om livit*
"Two Thoughts on Death" (Cullen) **37**:160, 166
2001: A Space Odyssey (Kubrick) **112**:127, 129-30, 137, 145, 152-53, 155-56, 159-63, 173-75, 188-91, 195, 204, 214, 225-30, 232, 235-36, 238-39, 252-60, 262, 265, 267, 269, 273
"Two Thousand Stiffs" (London) **9**:281
The Two Towers (Tolkien) **137**:238, 258-60, 296, 299-304, 306, 308, 310, 317, 322, 325, 347, 358-59
"The Two Trees" (Yeats) **31**:410
"Two Tupenny Ones, Please" (Mansfield) **39**:303
The Two Vanrevels (Tarkington) **9**:459-60, 466
"The Two Voices" (Forten) **16**:147, 150
"Two Ways" (Södergran)
See "Två vägar"
"Two Ways of the Imagination" (Nemerov) **124**:172
"Two Who Crossed a Line (He Crosses)" (Cullen) **37**:146, 154
"Two Wives" (Lawrence) **93**:46, 69

"Two Women" (Dickey) **151**:175
"Two Women" (Schreiner) **9**:400
"Two Women and an Infant Gull" (Carr) **32**:119
Two Worlds (Bergelson) **81**:23
Two Worlds and Their Ways (Compton-Burnett) **180**:123-25, 130-31, 142, 147, 171
"Two Worlds in One World" (Cahan) **71**:84
Two Years, Holiday (Verne) **6**:501
Two Years in the French West Indies (Hearn) **9**:122, 128, 133-34, 138-39
Two-faced Herma (Pirandello)
See *Erma bifronte*
"Two-Handed Engine" (Kuttner) **10**:269-70, 276
"The Twonky" (Kuttner) **10**:268-69, 272-73
"Two-Volume Novel" (Parker) **143**:320, 323
The Twyborn Affair (White) **176**:182-83, 186, 188, 192, 194, 196-98, 200-208, 211-16, 219, 231, 246, 249, 252, 306-7, 309, 319, 323, 327, 330
"Ty" (Hippius) **9**:166
Tyazhelye sny (Sologub) **9**:435-36, 440
Tycho Brahe's Way to God (Brod)
See *Tycho Brahe's Weg zu Gott*
Tycho Brahe's Weg zu Gott (Brod) **115**:78, 84-6, 88, 96-7, 101
"The Tyneside Widow" (Swinburne) **8**:427
Tyomnyye allei (Bunin) **6**:55-8
"A Type" (Mayakovski) **4**:292
"A Type of Loss" (Bachmann) **192**:65
"Types of Christian Drama" (Sayers) **15**:388
"Types of Nationalism" (Wirth) **92**:372
"The Typewriter" (West) **108**:309-10
"Typhoon" (Dreiser) **10**:198; **35**:71-2
"Typhoon" (London) **9**:273
Typhoon (Conrad) **1**:213, 221-22; **6**:118; **13**:119-20; **25**:73, 76; **57**:63, 110
Der tyrann (Mann) **9**:320-21, 327, 331
The Tyranny of the Ancestors (Blasco Ibáñez)
See *Los muertos mandan*
"The Tyranny of the Skyscraper" (Wright) **95**:383
"The Tyranny of the Ugly" (Middleton) **56**:192
"The Tyrant" (Mann) **9**:314-15
The Tyrant (Valle-Inclán)
See *Tirano banderas*
The Tyrant: An Episode in the Life of Cesare Borgia (Sabatini) **47**:301
"The Tyrants" (Tolstoy) **18**:377
Tyrants Destroyed, and Other Stories (Nabokov) **108**:216
"Tysjača let" (Pilnyak) **23**:211
Tysk höst (Dagerman) **17**:93-4
The Tysons (Sinclair)
See *Mr. and Mrs. Nevill Tyson*
"Tyyri's Girl" (Leino) **24**:376
"Tzadi" (Fondane) **159**:255
"La tzigane" (Apollinaire) **3**:36
"Tzinchadzi of the Catskills" (Cahan) **71**:13, 28, 71
"Tzvishen Zwee Berg" (Peretz) **16**:392-93, 399, 401
"U bat'ki nashego Makhno" (Babel) **171**:8
"U ćeliji br. 115" (Andrić) **135**:51
"U groba" (Annensky) **14**:32
"U kamina" (Gumilev) **60**:280
"U menja ne zhivut cvety" (Gumilev) **60**:279
"U morja" (Bryusov) **10**:82
"U Nikoly, čto na Belyx Kolodezjax" (Pilnyak) **23**:211, 213
The U. P. Trail (Grey) **6**:183, 187
"U pepljari" (Popa) **167**:154, 175
"U sviatogo Valenta" (Babel) **171**:8, 10-11, 21-24, 37, 61, 77, 83-87
"U uzdahu" (Popa) **167**:154, 176
"U zaboravu" (Popa) **167**:152, 154
U-aggrey um-Afrika (Mqhayi) **25**:327
Über Allen Gipfeln (Heyse) **8**:119
Über allen Gipfeln ist Ruh (Bernhard)
See *Über allen Gipfeln ist Ruh: ein deutscher Dichtertag um 1980*
Über allen Gipfeln ist Ruh: ein deutscher Dichtertag um 1980 (Bernhard) **165**:74, 96, 108
"Über Bühnenkomposition" (Kandinsky) **92**:26
"Uber Charakteranalyse" (Reich) **57**:340, 342
Über das Geistige in der Kunst (Kandinsky) **92**:22, 26, 30-1, 36-7, 39, 48, 51-3, 57-63, 71-2, 75-6, 78-9, 81, 86, 91, 95-98, 102-5, 107-14, 124-5, 134, 140, 143, 146-7
"Über den Marktplatz zu schweifen" (Raabe) **45**:188
Über den nervösen Charakter (Adler) **61**:3, 5, 11, 18, 24, 26-7
"Über die Brücke" (Böll) **185**:139
"Über die Formfrage" (Kandinsky) **92**:24, 53, 81
"Uber die Kreuzung sozialer Kreise" (Simmel) **64**:323
Über die letzten Dinge (Weininger) **84**:290, 327, 352
"Über die Psychogenese eines Falles von Weiblicher Homosexualität" (Freud) **52**:108
"Über einige Motive bei Baudelaire" (Benjamin) **39**:10, 28, 53
"Uber glitzernden Kies" (Lasker-Schueler) **57**:327
"Über Kunst" (Rilke) **195**:288
"Über meiner Zelle" (Toller) **10**:490
"Über mich selbst" (Böll) **185**:19
"Über Neurotische Disposition" (Adler) **61**:5
Uber soziale Differenzierung (Simmel) **64**:317, 319-320, 323, 352
"Über Warheit und Lüge im aussermoralischen Sinn" (Nietzsche) **55**:386-87, 392
"Überfließende Himmel verschwendeter Sterne" (Rilke) **195**:256
"Ubivets" (Korolenko) **22**:179, 181
U-bomi bom-fundisi uJohn Knox Bokwe (Mqhayi) **25**:324
Ubu cocu (Jarry) **2**:280, 282-83, 285; **14**:274, 277, 282-84; **147**:271
Ubu cocu ou l'Archéoptéryx (Jarry) **147**:259, 263
Ubu Cuckolded (Jarry)
See *Ubu cocu*
Ubu enchaîné (Jarry) **2**:280, 282-83; **14**:272-74, 277, 282-84, 286; **147**:259, 261, 272-73, 275-76, 279, 286, 340
Ubu Enchained (Jarry)
See *Ubu enchaîné*
Ubu Rex (Jarry)
See *Ubu Roi*
Ubu Roi (Jarry) **147**:227, 232-33, 235, 247-50, 252-57, 259, 261-62, 264, 266, 269-73, 277-78, 280, 285-87, 290, 296-97, 308, 311, 314, 318-22, 329, 332-33, 335, 337-40
Ubu sur la butte (Jarry) **14**:272; **147**:262, 271
"Übung am Klavier" (Rilke) **195**:227
Uccelli (Saba) **33**:374
"Uchenik" (Tsvetaeva) **7**:560; **35**:392, 411
"Uchilitsa" (Khlebnikov) **20**:136
"Učitel' Slovesnosti" (Chekhov) **3**:153, 165-66; **10**:108
Udaijin Sanetomo (Dazai Osamu) **11**:176, 179, 184, 186
Udekurabe (Nagai) **51**:86, 88, 92-4, 108
UDingiswayo kaJobe (Vilakazi) **37**:403
U-Don Jadu (Mqhayi) **25**:321-22, 324, 327
Ueber de Galgenlieder (Morgenstern) **8**:308
Uedinennoe (Rozanov) **104**:304-5, 317-18, 320, 324, 328, 351, 354-56, 358, 386-90, 392-94, 397-99
Uezdnoe (Zamyatin) **8**:541-43, 546, 551, 557-58; **37**:424, 427-28, 430
"Œufs de grenouilles" (Arp) **115**:6
Ugetsu Monogatari (Mizoguchi) **72**:293-304, 315-20, 323, 325-28, 332, 335-36, 341
The Ugly Duchess (Feuchtwanger)
See *Die hässliche Herzogin*
Uguns un nakts (Rainis) **29**:380-81, 383, 386, 391-92
Die Uhr schlägt eins (Zuckmayer) **191**:306, 328
"Der Uhrmacher" (Meyrink) **21**:232
Uitkomst (Heijermans) **24**:288
Új versek (Ady) **11**:14-15, 17, 22-5
Uj Zrinyiász (Mikszath) **31**:168, 170, 172
"Újabb fény és árnyképek" (Mikszath) **31**:169
Újhold (Radnóti) **16**:418-19
"Újmódi pásztorok éneke" (Radnóti) **16**:418
"Ujujuju kwelakwa nyawuza" (Mqhayi) **25**:320
Ukigumo (Futabatei) **44**:77, 79-81, 83-6, 88-100
Ukigumo (Hayashi) **27**:104, 106-07
Ukishizumi (Nagai) **51**:98
"Ukon lintu ja virvaliekki" (Leino) **24**:371
"Ukradený kaktus" (Čapek) **37**:48
Ukrepa (Remizov) **27**:347
"Ukrotitel' zverej" (Gumilev) **60**:279-80
"Ukuhlwa" (Vilakazi) **37**:404
"Ula and Urla" (Sharp) **39**:377
Üle piiri (Tammsaare) **27**:370-71, 373
Ulick and Soracha (Moore) **7**:497-98
"Ulisse" (Saba) **33**:370, 374
"Ulitsa" (Guro) **56**:142-43, 147-49
"Uljez" (Popa) **167**:156
Ulla Winblad oder Musik und Leben des Carl Michael Bellman (Zuckmayer) **191**:284, 298, 325-26, 331
Ulladu Narpadu (Ramana Maharshi) **84**:259, 261, 271
Últtimos Poemas (Sá-Carneiro) **83**:413
Ulrich und Brigitte (Sternheim) **8**:371
Ulrick the Ready (O'Grady) **5**:352, 354
Ulrike Woytich (Wassermann) **6**:510, 513
"La última guerra" (Nervo) **11**:394
Ultima saggi (Croce) **37**:96, 113
"Ultima Thule" (Galsworthy) **45**:33
"Ultima Thule" (Nabokov) **108**:218
Ultima Thule: Being the Third Part of the Chronicle of the Fortunes of Richard Mahony (Richardson) **4**:373-74, 382-83
L'ultima visita del gentiluomo malato (Papini) **22**:280
"Ultimata" (Stringer) **37**:343
"Ultimate Birth" (Aleixandre) **113**:53
"The Ultimate Poem Is Abstract" (Stevens) **45**:300
"Ultimate Reality" (Lawrence) **93**:53
"Ultimate Religion" (Santayana) **40**:389, 408
Ultime cose (Saba) **33**:366, 370, 373-74
"El último amor" (Aleixandre) **113**:49
"Último capítulo" (Machado de Assis) **10**:290-91
"Ultimo sogno" (Pascoli) **45**:149
Ultimo viene il corvo (Calvino) **183**:213, 223, 237
Ultimos poemas (Huidobro) **31**:132-33
Los últimos románticos (Baroja) **8**:61
Ultramarine (Lowry) **6**:235, 241, 253-54
"Ultra-taedium" (Sá-Carneiro)
See "Além-Tédio"
"Ulysse bâtit son lit" (Bosschere) **19**:56-8, 63
"Ulysses" (Bosschere) **19**:52, 54-5
Ulysses (Fondane) **159**:241, 254
Ulysses (Joyce) **3**:252-66, 268-82; **8**:159-62, 164-5, 167-9, 171-2; **16**:204, 208-9, 211, 213, 219, 221, 224-5, 228, 230-32, 237, 239, 243-5; **26**:386-416; **35**:144-7, 149-51, 153-7, 160-63, 167, 169-70, 173-4, 176-7, 192-5, 197; **52**:198, 200-1, 204, 208, 212-16, 219-20, 222, 225-6, 228-31, 233-4, 237, 239, 241-53; **159**:267-9, 271-2, 275, 279-80, 282-5, 287, 29
"Ulysses Builds His Bed" (Bosschere)
See "Ulysse bâtit son lit"
"Uman" (Naidu) **80**:340
"Umanità fervente sulla sprone" (Campana) **20**:83
"Umbertino" (Svevo) **35**:345, 352
The Umbilicus of Limbo (Artaud)
See *L'ombilic des limbes*
Umbra Vitae (Heym) **9**:144
"Umbrae Puellularum" (Benét) **28**:2

"UmHlekazi uHintsa" (Mqhayi) **25**:322, 327
Umi to dokuyaku (Endo) **152**:167, 176, 185, 189, 198, 202, 207, 213, 215, 230, 234, 237, 240
"Umiltà" (Ouida) **43**:356-57
"Umkhosi wemidaka" (Mqhayi) **25**:322, 327
"Umkhuleko wesiphoxo" (Vilakazi) **37**:397
"Ummm Oh Yeah" (Holly)
See "Dearest"
L'umorismo (Pirandello) **4**:329-32; **29**:282, 308, 313-16; **172**:160, 164, 188
Umozreniie i otkroveniie: Religioznaya filosofia Vladimira Solovyova i drugiie stat'i (Shestov) **56**:260, 262, 264, 277-79
U-Mqhayi Wase-Ntab'ozuko (Mqhayi) **25**:325, 327
The Unabridged Mark Twain (Twain) **161**:252
"Unabsolved" (Campbell) **9**:30-1
The Unadulterated Sexton (Nezval) **44**:241
"Un'amara serenità" (Calvino) **183**:103
Unambo: Roman aus dem jüdisch-arabischen Krieg (Brod) **115**:85-7, 98-104, 106, 111
Unamuno (Barea) **14**:50
"The Unattained Place" (Muir) **87**:307
"Das Unaufhörliche" (Benn) **3**:112
The Unbearable Bassington (Saki) **3**:363-70, 373-75
Das Unbehagen in der Kultur (Freud) **52**:85-6, 120, 125-26
Die Unbekannte aus der Seine (Horvath) **45**:77-8, 93
Der unbekannte Gast (Wassermann) **6**:510
Unbekannte Gedichte (Walser) **18**:426-27
Die Unbekannte Grösse (Broch) **20**:49, 60
"Unbelievable Characters" (Nemerov) **124**:233
"The Unbeliever" (Bishop) **121**:4
"An Unbeliever to the Church" (Fletcher) **35**:108
"Unbelieving, I Believe in God" (Ady) **11**:20
The Unbidden Guest (Hornung) **59**:113
"The Unborn Child" (Sharp) **39**:391-92
"Unbreakable Guarantee" (Morgenstern)
See "Unverlierbare Gewähr"
The Uncalled (Dunbar) **2**:129, 132; **12**:107, 111-13, 118-19, 122-23
Uncanny Stories (Sinclair) **11**:421
The Unchanging Sea (Griffith) **68**:186, 247
The Unclassed (Gissing) **3**:222-23, 226-27, 229, 231-32, 235, 237; **24**:220, 222, 232, 234, 239, 241, 243, 248-49; **47**:130, 134
Unclay (Powys) **9**:368-69, 374-75, 378
Uncle Abner, Master of Mysteries (Post) **39**:338, 343-45, 347-48
"Uncle Ananias" (Robinson) **101**:111
Uncle Bernac (Doyle) **7**:220, 239
"Uncle Chatterton's Gingerbread" (Montgomery) **51**:201
Uncle Dynamite (Wodehouse) **108**:383
Uncle Fred in the Springtime (Wodehouse) **108**:384, 386-87, 392
"Uncle Isaiah" (Kirk) **119**:278, 335-36
"Uncle Jake and the Bell-Handle" (Crane) **11**:167
"Uncle Jim" (Cullen) **37**:143, 146
"Uncle Jim and Uncle Billy" (Harte) **25**:222
Uncle Leonidas Facing the Reaction (Caragiale) **76**:164
Uncle Moses (Asch)
See *Onkel Moses*
"Uncle Remus" (Harris) **2**:209
Uncle Remus, His Songs and His Sayings: Folklore of the Old Plantation (Harris) **2**:214
"Uncle Richard's New Year's Dinner" (Montgomery) **51**:200
Uncle Tom's Children (Wright) **136**:223, 240, 245, 275-77, 284, 314-18, 320-22
Uncle Tom's Children: Four Novellas (Wright) **180**:283, 298
Uncle Vanya (Chekhov)
See *Dyadya Vanya*
"Uncle Wellington's Wives" (Chesnutt) **5**:130-31; **39**:80, 98
"Uncle Willy" (Faulkner) **170**:138
Uncollected Poems (García Lorca) **197**:211
"The Uncommon Prayer-Book" (James) **6**:212, 215-16
The Unconquered (Williams) **89**:398, 402
Unconscious Memory (Butler) **33**:40, 42, 50
"The Unconscious Patterning of Behavior in Society" (Sapir) **108**:286
"Uncovenanted Mercies" (Kipling) **8**:196, 201
The Uncrowned King (Wright) **183**:346, 349, 379
"The Uncultured Rhymer to His Cultured Critic" (Lawson) **27**:139
"Und" (Lasker-Schueler) **57**:312
Und das Krumme wird gerade (Agnon)
See *Vehaya He'akov Lemishor*
"Und ich war fer" (Liliencron) **18**:215
"Und Keiner weiss wohin" (Borchert) **5**:105
Und Pippa tanzt (Hauptmann) **4**:202
Und sagte kein einziges Wort (Böll) **185**:4-6, 9, 16-18, 23, 27-9, 31, 33, 40, 50, 57, 63, 101, 105, 129, 139, 144, 149, 189-90
"Und wie manche Nacht" (Carossa) **48**:21
"The Undefeated" (Hemingway) **115**:143
"Under a Fence: A Revue" (Kahanovitsch)
See "Unter a ployt: Revyu"
Under a Thatched Roof (Hall and Nordhoff) **23**:63, 68
"Under an Evergreen" (Shimazaki Toson) **5**:439
"Under Ben Bulben" (Yeats) **1**:570, 579; **11**:533; **18**:463; **31**:396, 408; **93**:360
"Under Buzzards" (Dickey) **151**:100-101, 113
Under False Pretenses (Hecht) **101**:48
Under Fire (Barbusse)
See *Le feu*
The Under Groove (Stringer) **37**:336
Under høstsjernen (Hamsun) **2**:202, 204-05; **14**:223; **49**:128-29
Under Milk Wood (Thomas) **1**:469-70, 473, 475-76; **8**:452-54, 456-58; **45**:363, 366-69, 371, 378, 390-91, 394, 397-98, 412; **105**:309-10, 313-316, 325, 351-51, 356-57, 362
Under Northern Skies (Balmont)
See *Pod severnym nebom*
Under Our Sky (Vazov) **25**:453
"Under Saturn" (Yeats) **93**:390
Under the Autumn Star (Hamsun)
See *Under høstsjernen*
"Under the Bamboo Tree" (Johnson) **175**:225
"Under the Bell Jar" (Nemerov) **124**:171
"Under the Cypress Tree" (Engel) **137**:123
Under the Deodars (Kipling) **8**:176
"Under the Earth" (Aleixandre) **113**:25-27, 54
"Under the First Snow" (Wright) **136**:301
Under the Greenwood Tree (Hardy) **4**:147-49, 158, 160, 165, 168; **10**:215, 217, 225, 227; **32**:268, 270; **53**:71, 73; **72**:238; **143**:76, 107-8, 154; **153**:100, 106, 108, 110-13, 115-16, 119, 130, 202, 204-6
"Under the Jaguar Sun" (Calvino)
See "Sotto il sole giaguaro"
Under the Jaguar Sun (Calvino)
See *Sotto il sole giaguaro*
"Under the Knife" (Wells) **133**:323
Under the Lamp (Fargue)
See *Sous la lampe*
"Under the Lion's Paw" (Garland) **3**:190, 196
Under the Midnight Heavens (Platonov)
See *Po nebu polunochi*
Under the Moons of Mars (Burroughs)
See *A Princess of Mars*
Under the Net (Murdoch) **171**:221-22, 224, 239, 245-47, 250-52, 255, 266, 279-80, 309, 311-12, 323
"Under the Oak" (Lawrence) **93**:17
"Under the Old Code" (Davis) **6**:154
Under the Open Sky: My Early Years (Nexø)
See *Erindringer*
"Under the primeval light" (Aleixandre) **113**:54
Under the Red Flag (Braddon) **111**:227
"Under the Royal Oak" (Papadiamantis) **29**:272
Under the Sign of Gemini: A Diary about Childhood (Radnóti)
See *Ikrek hava: Napló a gyerekkorról*
Under the Skylights (Fuller) **103**:59, 61-62, 65, 74, 85-86
"Under the Star" (Field) **43**:161
Under the Sun (De Lisser) **12**:95
Under the Sunset (Stoker) **144**:253-55
Under the Tree (Roberts) **68**:294, 297, 301-4, 326, 335-37
Under the Volcano (Lowry) **6**:235-55; **40**:218-86
"Under the Waterfall" (Hardy) **53**:96, 112
Under the Wheel (Garland) **3**:202
"Under the Window: Ouro Prêto" (Bishop) **121**:21, 28, 59-90, 92
"Under the Wood" (Thomas) **10**:463
"Under the World" (Ginsberg) **120**:48
Under the Yoke (Vazov)
See *Pod igoto*
Under Two Flags (Ouida) **43**:342, 348, 360-61, 364, 366-68, 371-73, 375
Under Western Eyes (Conrad) **1**:196, 202-03, 207, 218-19, 221-22; **6**:118, 120-22; **13**:117, 119, 121; **25**:84-6, 90, 111; **57**:39-40, 54, 66, 94, 100, 109, 114-15
"The Under-Dogs" (Service) **15**:412
The Underdogs (Azuela)
See *Los de Abajo: Novela de la revolucion mexicana*
"Underground" (Khodasevich) **15**:209
The Underground City (Verne) **6**:502
"The Underlying Self" (Carpenter) **88**:106
Underneath the Bough (Field) **43**:153-56, 159, 162, 164, 169, 174, 177
The Underpants (Sternheim)
See *Die Hose*
"Undersea Fragment in Collons" (Dickey) **151**:127
"Understand That This Is a Dream" (Ginsberg) **120**:39
"Understanding and Politics" (Arendt) **193**:44, 81, 124, 181-82
Understanding Human Nature (Adler)
See *Menschenkenntnis*
Understood Betsy (Fisher) **87**:72
The Undertaker's Garland (Bishop) **103**:15-6, 18, 26, 31, 45
Undertones (Buchanan) **107**:13-15
"Underwood Girls" (Salinas) **17**:365
Underworld (Hecht) **101**:61, 88
Underworld (Micheaux) **76**:247
The Undesirable Governess (Crawford) **10**:151
Undine (Schreiner) **9**:397-99, 402, 404-05, 407
"Undine geht" (Bachmann) **192**:10, 69-70
"Undines gewaltiger Vater" (Böll) **185**:52
The Undiscovered Country (Howells) **7**:365, 392; **17**:178; **41**:233-34
Undiscovered Country: The New Zealand Stories of Katherine Mansfield (Mansfield) **164**:332
"Undistinguished Americans" (Davis) **6**:154
"Undr" (Borges) **109**:107
Undream'd of Shores (Harris) **24**:272
Undressed Spring (Prishvin) **75**:217-18
The Undying Fire (Wells) **6**:532, 537, 540, 548; **12**:507
"The Undying One" (Hearn) **9**:126
The Undying Past (Sudermann)
See *Es War*
"L'une d'elles" (Sully Prudhomme) **31**:302
Unearthly Evenings (Kuzmin) **40**:191
Uneasy Money (Wodehouse) **108**:335, 369-70
"Uneasy Reflections" (Bodenheim) **44**:59
"The Uneaten Gods" (Bishop) **103**:21
"Unedited Opinions" (Orage) **157**:246, 251
"Unemployed" (Phelps) **113**:342
"Unemployment" (Keynes) **64**:243, 246
The Unending Rose (Borges) **109**:151
"The Unexpected" (Chopin) **14**:69

"The Unexpected Door" (Lindsay) **17**:241
The Unexpected Guests (Howells) **7**:370, 387
Unexpected Island (Lin)
See *Looking Beyond*
The Unexpected Joy (Blok) **5**:90
"The Unexpected Must Happen" (Mansfield) **164**:262
"The Unexplorer" (Millay) **4**:310; **49**:224
"Unexpressed" (Dunbar) **12**:122
"The Unfading Blue" (Balmont) **11**:41
"The Unfair Advantage" (Bennett) **5**:46
"The Unfaithful Married Woman" (García Lorca)
See "La casada infiel"
"The Unfaithful Wife" (García Lorca)
See "La casada infiel"
Unfaithfully Yours (Sturges) **48**:275, 283, 287-88, 291-92, 297, 309, 311, 317-18
Unfettered (Griggs) **77**:146-7, 167-9, 176
Unfinished Business (Erskine) **84**:184
Unfinished Dream (Nagai)
See *Mihatenu yume*
"Unfinished Fragment on the State" (Bourne) **16**:49-50
An Unfinished Journey (Naipaul) **153**:226, 228-30
"An Unfinished Love Story" (Lawson) **27**:119, 148, 150, 152
"Unfinished Portrait" (Wylie) **8**:522, 536
"Unfinished Song" (Dobson) **79**:5
"An Unfinished Story" (Henry) **1**:346; **19**:180, 187-88, 191
Unfinished Tales of Númenor and Middle-Earth (Tolkien) **137**:254
An Unfinished Woman: A Memoir (Hellman) **119**:119-21, 123-25, 132, 140, 142-44, 177, 194-95, 199, 213, 227, 230, 235
"Unfortunate" (Brooke) **7**:122
"The Unfortunate Miller" (Coppard) **5**:177
The Unfortunate One (Couperus)
See *De Ongelv kkige*
An Unfortunate Woman: A Journey (Brautigan) **133**:33
"Unfortunate Coincidence" (Parker) **143**:321
"An Unframed Picture" (Fisher) **87**:73
Ung må verden ennu vaere (Grieg) **10**:206-07, 209
En ung mands kjaerlighet (Grieg) **10**:206, 208
Det unge Tydakland (Brandes) **10**:61-2, 72-3
Ungeduld des Herzens (Zweig) **17**:428, 440, 446, 448, 450, 458-59
"Die ungehaltene Rede vor dem deutschen Bundestag" (Böll) **185**:120
Ungenach (Bernhard) **165**:19-21, 108
De unges forbund (Ibsen) **2**:221, 225; **8**:149-51; **37**:225, 233, 243, 249; **52**:144, 155, 157, 191
"An Ungiven Speech before Parliament" (Böll)
See "Die ungehaltene Rede vor dem deutschen Bundestag"
Ungleiche Welten (Carossa) **48**:33-4
Ungleichzeitigkeit (Bernhard) **165**:119
Unhappy Far-Off Things (Dunsany) **59**:17
"Unhappy Hate" (Lasker-Schueler) **57**:328
Unhappy Love (Giacosa)
See *Tristi amori*
"Unheibar!" (Heyse) **8**:114
"An Unhistoric Page" (Stockton) **47**:313
An Unhistorical Pastoral (Davidson) **24**:159, 182
"Unholy Living and Half Dying" (O'Faolain) **143**:238
The Unhuman Tour (Natsume)
See *Kusamakura*
The Unhushable Tambourine (Remizov)
See *Neuyomny Buben*
"The Unicorn" (Rosenberg) **12**:287-93, 295, 297-301, 303, 307, 309-10
The Unicorn (Murdoch) **171**:221, 225-28, 247, 279, 284-85, 314-16, 318, 321
The Unicorn from the Stars (Gregory) **176**:13
The Unicorn from the Stars, and Other Plays (Yeats) **11**:514; **31**:418
Unicorns (Huneker) **65**:170, 179, 185, 218
"Unidad en ella" (Aleixandre) **113**:11, 49, 56
The Uniform (Abe) **131**:12
"The Unimportance of Being Earnest" (Nathan) **18**:294
"An Unimportant Man" (West) **108**:309-10
"The Union" (Noyes) **7**:513
A Union and Translation of the Four Gospels (Tolstoy)
See *Soedinenie I perevod chetyrex evangelij*
"The Union Buries Its Dead" (Lawson) **27**:121, 128-30, 147
Union Portraits (Bradford) **36**:66
Unions (Musil)
See *Vereinigungen*
"Unison" (Jarrell) **177**:195
"United Dames of America" (Stevens) **12**:381
The United States: An Experiment in Democracy (Becker) **63**:63-4, 67, 71, 80
U.S. Atrocities (Wells-Barnett)
See *Southern Horrors: Lynch Law in All Its Phases*
United West Africa (Casely-Hayford) **24**:132
"Unity in Her" (Aleixandre)
See "Unidad en ella"
"Unity of Figure" (Sarduy) **167**:200
"Unity of Law" (Adams) **80**:13
"Unity of Place" (Sarduy) **167**:200
"Unity Through Diversity: A Baha'i Principle" (Locke) **43**:240
"L'univers solitude" (Éluard) **7**:256; **41**:156
"Universal" (Borges) **109**:57
A Universal History of Infamy (Borges)
See *Historia universal de la infamia*
The Universal Reformer (Bernhard)
See *Der Weltverbesserer*
"The Universe Rigid" (Wells) **19**:436
"The University and the Personal Life" (Frye) **165**:157
Unkist, Unkind! (Hunt) **53**:186, 191, 197
"The Unknowable" (Santayana) **40**:415
"The Unknown" (Masters) **25**:302, 313
"The Unknown Bird" (Thomas) **10**:452, 463
"The Unknown Citizen" (Morley) **87**:123
"An Unknown Friend" (Bunin) **6**:47
"The Unknown Girl Taken from the Seine" (Nezval) **44**:239, 243
"The Unknown God" (Baker) **3**:4; **10**:20
"The Unknown God" (Meynell) **6**:303
The Unknown God (Noyes) **7**:515
The Unknown Land (Ingamells) **35**:129
"The Unknown Poet" (Ady) **11**:15
The Unknown Quantity (Broch)
See *Die Unbekannte Grösse*
The Unknown Star (Housman) **7**:359
The Unknown War: Eastern Front (Churchill) **113**:105, 148
Unkown to History: A Story of the Captivity of Mary of Scotland (Yonge) **48**:377
The Unlit Lamp (Hall) **12**:187, 195, 198
"Unluckily for a Death" (Thomas) **45**:379, 399
"Unmad" (Premchand) **21**:289
Unmade in Heaven (Bradford) **36**:63
Unmei (Rohan) **22**:306-07
Unmei Ronsha (Kunikida Doppo) **99**:299
"The Unnameable" (Lovecraft) **4**:270, 272; **22**:227
The Unnameable (Beckett)
See *L'innommable*
"Unnamed Poem" (McCrae) **12**:210
The Unnatural Death (Sayers) **2**:531, 538; **15**:377-78, 391-93
"The Unnatural Mother" (Gilman) **9**:113
"Unnatural Selection" (Strindberg) **8**:407; **21**:366
"Uno" (Storni) **5**:445
Uno coi capelli bianchi (de Filippo) **127**:294
Uno, nessuno e centomila (Pirandello) **4**:332, 351, 355; **29**:283, 302
An Unofficial Rose (Murdoch) **171**:221, 225-26, 281-82, 312
"The U.N.P.A. Nights" (Calvino)
See "Le notti dell'UNPA"
"Unpacking My Library" (Benjamin) **39**:14, 47
"The Unparalleled Invasion" (London) **9**:269
Unpath'd Waters (Harris) **24**:264
"Unphotographic Paint: The Texture of Impressionism" (Hartmann) **73**:149
The Unpleasantness at the Bellona Club (Sayers) **2**:531; **15**:378, 380-81, 393-94
"The Unploughed Patch" (March) **96**:250, 259, 266
The Unpossessed (Slesinger) **10**:439-46
"Unprofessional" (Kipling) **8**:196
Unprofessional Essays (Murry) **16**:342
Unprofessional Tales (Douglas) **68**:6
An Unpublished Play (Svevo)
See *Una commedia inedita*
Unpublished Writings (Campana)
See *Inediti*
Unpunished (Gilman) **9**:114; **117**:49-53, 125, 164
"The Unquiet Street" (Fletcher) **35**:103
"The Unreality of Time" (McTaggart) **105**:197
Unreliable History (Baring) **8**:37, 41, 44
Unrest (Andrić)
See *Nemiri*
"The Unrest Cure" (Saki) **3**:365, 373
"Unrhyming Poems" (Lawrence) **93**:52
Unruhige Gäste (Raabe) **45**:174, 176-79, 199
"The Unsainting of Kavin" (Carman) **7**:142
"Die Unschuldige" (Mann) **9**:315
"Unscientific Postscript" (Nemerov) **124**:171, 206
An Unseen Enemy (Griffith) **68**:234
The Unselfish Devil (Nervo) **11**:403
"Unser Karl" (Harte) **25**:198, 224-25
"Unser kultureller Notstand—Kultur in der Demokratie" (Böll) **185**:101
"Unsere Gier nach Geschdichten" (Frisch) **121**:192
"Unsere Sorge, der Mensch" (Döblin) **13**:163, 176
Unsere Stadt (Walser) **18**:424
Unsern Täglichen Traum (Arp) **115**:33, 35-6, 46
Unsers Herrgotts Kanzlei (Raabe) **45**:169
"The Unsleeping" (Roberts) **8**:318
"Unsleeping City" (García Lorca)
See "Ciudad sin sueño"
"Unsleeping City (Brooklyn Bridge Nocturne)" (García Lorca)
See "Ciudad sin sueño"
An Unsocial Socialist (Shaw) **3**:379, 388; **9**:410, 422; **21**:318-19, 323
"Unsolved" (McCrae) **12**:210
"The Unspeakable Egg" (Fitzgerald) **157**:190
Unspoken Sermons (MacDonald) **113**:241, 243, 305
Unspoken Sermons. Series One (MacDonald) **113**:311
Unspoken Sermons, Series Two (MacDonald) **113**:222
"Der unsterbliche Mensch" (Döblin) **13**:163-64, 176
"The Unsung Heroes" (Dunbar) **12**:104
"Unsuspecting" (Toomer) **172**:277
The Untamed (Faust) **49**:35, 44-6, 49, 53
"Unter a ployt: Revyu" (Kahanovitsch) **56**:109-17, 122
Unter dem Eisen des Mondes (Bernhard) **165**:95
Unter Flatternden Fahnen (Liliencron) **18**:212
Untergang der Welt durch die Schwarze Magic (Kraus) **5**:285
Der Untergeher (Bernhard) **165**:10-14, 96, 100, 103-4, 111, 117-18
Untersuchungen zur Phänomenologie und Theorie der Erkenntnis (Husserl) **100**:9, 11, 30, 48, 119, 121-22, 125
Der Untertan (Mann) **9**:317-18, 320, 323-25, 327-29

"Unterwegs" (Borchert) **5**:104
"The Unthinking Centralizer" (Kirk) **119**:258
Until after the Equinox (Natsume) **10**:332, 334, 336
Until Break of Dawn (Moricz)
  See *Kivilágos kivirradtig*
Until Daybreak (Moricz)
  See *Kivilágos kivirradtig*
Until the Day Break (Bromfield) **11**:86
"Until the Troubling of the Waters" (Moody) **105**:225, 240, 278
The Untilled Field (Moore)
  See *An T-úr-Ghort*
"Untimely Moment" (Vallejo)
  See "Deshora"
Untimely Observations (Nietzsche)
  See *Unzeitgemässe Betrachtungen*
Untimely Papers (Bourne) **16**:44, 48, 55
Untimely Poems (Palamas) **5**:385
"Untitled" (Levi) **109**:291
Untitled Novel, ca. 1905 (Scott) **6**:400
"Unto Dust" (Bosman) **49**:11-12, 19-20, 29
Unto Dust (Bosman) **49**:3-5, 7-10, 16, 19
Unto the Third Generation (Shiel) **8**:362
Unto This Last (Ruskin) **20**:280, 282, 304-07; **63**:253, 267, 281-82, 291-92, 296, 298, 331
The Untold Adventures of Santa Claus (Nash) **109**:355
"The Untold Lie" (Anderson) **1**:59, 63; **10**:52; **24**:20, 24, 27-8, 34, 37; **123**:16, 36, 82-3
The Untrained Women (Pérez Galdós)
  See *La desheredada*
"UNtsikane" (Mqhayi) **25**:326
"An Unusual Young Man" (Brooke) **2**:60; **7**:127
The Unvanquished (Faulkner) **141**:39, 57-58, 62, 147-49; **170**:107, 109, 128, 134, 164, 244
"Unverändert" (Kandinsky) **92**:67, 69
Die Unvergessliche (Zuckmayer) **191**:304
"Unverlierbare Gewähr" (Morgenstern) **8**:309
Unveröffentlichte Prosadichtungen (Walser) **18**:421-22
"Unwelcome" (Coleridge) **73**:14, 27
The Unwilling Adventurer (Freeman) **21**:56-7, 62
The Unwritten (Sikelianos)
  See "Agraphon"
"Unwritten History" (Davis) **6**:154
"An Unwritten Novel" (Woolf) **101**:300; **128**:371
Unzeitgemässe Betrachtungen (Nietzsche) **10**:356, 359-60, 366-67, 372, 394; **18**:340, 342
"Unzen" (Endo) **152**:203, 214
Das Unzerstörbare (Brod) **115**:103
L'uomo (Saba) **33**:375, 377
"L'uomo che volle essere imperatore" (Papini) **22**:280
L'uomo dal fiore in bocca (Pirandello) **29**:317
L'uomo desireoso (Papini)
  See *Parole e sangue*
L'uomo è forte (Alvaro) **60**:3-4
Uomo e galantuomo (de Filippo) **127**:287, 294
Un uomo finito (Papini) **22**:271, 274, 277-79, 288, 290
L'uomo, la bestia, e la virtù (Pirandello) **4**:340; **29**:282, 301
L'uomo, la bestia, et la virtù (Pirandello) **172**:140
L'uomo nel labirinto (Alvaro) **60**:6-8, 11-2
Un uomo provvisorio (Jovine) **79**:43-4, 49-51, 55, 58, 65, 72-3
Up Against It (Orton)
  See *Up against It: A Screenplay for the Beatles*
Up against It: A Screenplay for the Beatles (Orton) **157**:310, 323
"Up and Down" (Merrill) **173**:172, 218
Up from Earth's Center (Dent) **72**:38
Up from Nowhere (Tarkington) **9**:464
Up from Slavery (Washington) **10**:516, 522, 525, 532-35, 538, 540-43
Up in the Hills (Dunsany) **59**:17
"Up in the Wind" (Thomas) **10**:454, 463
Up Stream (Lewisohn) **19**:262, 264-65, 268, 271-73, 277, 287, 293
"Up the Coulée" (Garland) **3**:190
Up the Country (Franklin) **7**:264-65, 267, 269-73
Up the Ladder of Gold (Oppenheim) **45**:136-37
"Up There" (Gurney) **33**:97
Upadesa Saram (Ramana Maharshi) **84**:261, 270
Upadesa-vundiyar (Ramana Maharshi) **84**:270
"An Upbraiding" (Hardy) **53**:101
Upbuilders (Steffens) **20**:345, 356, 361
"The Upholsterers" (Lardner)
  See "I gaspiri"
Uplands (Chase) **124**:22
Uplands of Dream (Saltus) **8**:349
"Upon a Dying Lady" (Yeats) **31**:401
"Upon a House Shaken by the Land Agitation" (Yeats) **93**:351, 402, 403
"Upon Graciosa, Walking and Talking" (Quiller-Couch) **53**:290
"Upon Payment" (Strindberg)
  See "Mot betalming"
"Upon Returning to the Country Road" (Lindsay) **17**:224
"Upon the Dull Earth Dwelling" (March) **96**:263
"Upon Watts' Picture" (McCrae) **12**:211
"Uppbrottet" (Lagerkvist) **144**:224
"The Upper Berth" (Crawford) **10**:149, 152-54, 157-58
"Uppståndelsemysterium" (Södergran) **31**:295
"Upptäckt" (Södergran) **31**:290
Upptäcktsresanden (Dagerman) **17**:95
"Upriamets" (Balmont) **11**:40
The Uprising (Rebreanu)
  See *Rascoala*
Uprooted by the Storm (Gladkov) **27**:91
"Upstairs in the Wineshop" (Lu Hsun)
  See "Zai jiulou shang"
"The Upturned Face" (Crane) **11**:158
Upward (Kandinsky) **92**:32
"The Upward Movement in Chicago" (Fuller) **103**:106
"Ur 'Lilputs saga'" (Södergran) **31**:291
"Ur Sonata" (Schwitters)
  See "Ursonate"
"Uralte Buddhafigur" (Hesse) **196**:282
"Urania" (Merrill) **173**:157
Urashima-san (Dazai Osamu) **11**:174
"An Urban Convalescence" (Merrill) **173**:171, 208, 211-12, 215, 226-27, 257
"The Urban Mode of Living" (Wirth) **92**:391
"The Urban Pan" (Carman) **7**:150
"Urbane Poem" (Tzara)
  See "Poème mondain"
"Urbanism as a Way of Life" (Wirth) **92**:359, 372, 379-80, 384
Urbanities (Lucas) **73**:159
Urbi et orbi (Bryusov) **10**:80, 86, 90
"The Urchin at the Zoo" (Morley) **87**:127
"Der Urgefährte" (Broch) **20**:54
Úri divat (Molnár) **20**:160, 166, 172
Úri muri (Moricz) **33**:237, 243-44, 246-48, 250
"Uriah on the Hill" (Powys) **9**:372
"Urica" (Heyse) **8**:125
Uriel's Report (Benda)
  See *Le rapport d'Uriel*
Urien's Voyage (Gide)
  See *Le voyage d'Urien*
Urith (Baring-Gould) **88**:20, 38
"Urlandschaft" (George) **14**:199
"Urlautsonate" (Schwitters)
  See "Ursonate"
The Urn (Bely)
  See *Urna*
Urna (Bely) **7**:50
"Ursachen der Schlaflosigkeit im Goethejahr" (Roth) **33**:336
"Ursonate" (Schwitters) **95**:315, 326, 346, 352
Ursprung des deutschen Trauerspiels (Benjamin) **39**:7, 15, 19, 26, 36, 52-4, 61
"Das Urteil" (Kafka) **2**:298, 305-06; **6**:219, 223, 225-30; **13**:266, 275-76, 280, 284, 286; **112**:28-123; **179**:284, 286, 290, 297, 300, 303, 307, 316, 318, 322, 328
Urvasie (Aurobindo) **63**:4, 36
"Us Two" (Milne) **6**:314; **88**:242, 260
"The U.S.A. School of Writing" (Bishop) **121**:44
L'usage de la parole (Sarraute) **145**:263-64, 266, 287-88, 310, 338-39, 341
U-Samson (Mqhayi) **25**:323, 327
The Use of Man (Dunsany) **59**:22, 24
The Use of Speech (Sarraute)
  See *L'usage de la parole*
"The Use Value of D. A. F. de Sade" (Bataille) **155**:97
"Used Car" (Wakefield) **120**:349, 352, 356-59
Useful Knowledge (Stein) **6**:403; **28**:312-13; **48**:214
"Useless Book" (Hagiwara) **60**:288
"The Uselessness of Theater in the Theater" (Jarry) **147**:292
The Uses of Enchantment: The Meaning and Importance of Fairy Tales (Bettelheim)
  See *Kinder Brauchen Märchen*
The Uses of Literature (Calvino)
  See *Una pietra sopra: Discorsi di letteratura e societa*
"The Uses of the Erotic, The Erotic as Power" (Lorde) **173**:56, 59, 62-63, 65, 83, 86, 91, 136-40, 144
"UShaka kaSenzangakhona" (Vilakazi) **37**:407
"Usi politici giusti e sbagliati della letteratura" (Calvino) **183**:101-3, 107, 187
"Les usines" (Verhaeren) **12**:482
Uslovnosti (Kuzmin) **40**:191, 200
"Usomnivshiisia Makar" (Platonov) **14**:409, 417, 424
Uspravna zemlja (Popa) **167**:158-59, 163, 172, 176
"Ustrug Razina" (Khlebnikov) **20**:126-27, 132-33
The Usurer (Griffith) **68**:168
"The Usurpers" (Muir) **87**:168
Utage no ato (Mishima) **161**:51-52, 56
"Utakata no ki" (Mori Ogai) **14**:369, 378-79, 381
Utamaro and His Five Women (Mizoguchi) **72**:306, 322, 335
Utayomi ni atauru sho (Masaoka) **18**:221
Utazás a koponyám körül (Karinthy) **47**:266-67, 269
Utazás Faremidóba (Karinthy) **47**:269, 272
"The Utilization of Human Remains" (Hearn) **9**:127
Az utolsó hajók (Ady) **11**:18, 22, 25
Utopia, Limited; or, The Flowers of Progress (Gilbert) **3**:212, 214, 217-19
Utopia of Usurers (Chesterton) **6**:110
Utro pomeshchika (Tolstoy) **173**:299
Uttarpara Speech (Aurobindo) **63**:29, 36
The Uttermost Farthing (Freeman) **21**:57
The Uttermost Farthing (Lowndes) **12**:201
Az üvegcipő (Molnár) **20**:160-61, 166, 172
Uwasa no Onna (Mizoguchi) **72**:296
Uzushio (Hayashi) **27**:106
V bezbrezhnosti (Balmont) **11**:35, 42
"V bor'be: Proshloe" (Bryusov) **10**:95
"V chiom moya vera" (Tolstoy) **4**:450; **11**:458, 463; **79**:322, 327-8, 332-3, 335, 407, 410-1, 413, 425-7, 431, 437
"V damask" (Bryusov) **10**:93
"V derevne" (Korolenko) **22**:177
"V durnom obshchestve" (Korolenko) **22**:176
"V duxe Francuzskix simvolistov" (Bryusov) **10**:82
"V glavnoj šachte" (Kuprin) **5**:302
"V. Jahrhundert" (Benn) **3**:113
V Kraiu Nepugannykh Ptits (Prishvin) **75**:214, 219

"V Marks the Spot" (Dent) **72**:30
V mire neiasnogo i nereshennogo (Rozanov) **104**:309, 314, 316, 383
"V ogne" (Kuprin) **5**:302
"V okopa" (Vazov) **25**:455
"V otvet" (Bryusov) **10**:93
"V ovrage" (Chekhov) **3**:153; **10**:112, 114, 117; **96**:34, 37
"V parke" (Guro) **56**:143
"V plenu" (Remizov) **27**:338-41
V podzemnoj tjur'me (Bryusov) **10**:83
V pole blakitnom (Remizov) **27**:331, 333-34, 348
"V potmakh" (Kuprin) **5**:303-04
V razdvinutoi dali (Balmont) **11**:38-9, 41-2
"V restorane" (Bryusov) **10**:93
"V sekretnoi" (Remizov) **27**:338
"V shchelochku" (Babel) **171**:7
"V sklepe" (Bryusov) **10**:81
"V starom zamke" (Hippius) **9**:167
"V stenax" (Bryusov) **10**:82, 92
"V Stepi" (Gorky) **8**:67-8
"V trjume" (Bryusov) **10**:81
"V volšebnuju prismu" (Annensky) **14**:27
"V zakrytoi chashe" (Guro) **56**:133, 145
"V zastenke" (Bryusov) **10**:81
"Va' cosí che vi bene" (Calvino) **183**:209
Va et vient (Beckett) **145**:178, 180
Våar aere og vår makt (Grieg) **10**:206-07, 209-11
Vaaren (Undset) **3**:512, 517, 522-23; **197**:300-01, 30
"Vaca" (García Lorca) **49**:93; **181**:28; **197**:186
Vacant Sites (Hrabal)
See *Proluky*
The Vacation of the Kelwyns (Howells) **7**:376-77; **17**:184
"Vacations" (Stephen) **23**:326
"Vacations in the South" (Andrić)
See "Letovanje na jugu"
"A Vacation's Job" (McAlmon) **97**:87-88, 100, 117-18, 120-22
"Vache" (Éluard) **7**:250
La vache tachetée (Mirbeau) **55**:301
"Vacillation" (Yeats) **1**:582; **11**:533; **18**:447, 458; **31**:390, 403, 410; **116**:264
"The Vacuum" (Nemerov) **124**:164
"Vad är i morgon?" (Södergran) **31**:291
"Vademecum—Vadetecum" (Nietzsche) **55**:389
A vadkan (Moricz) **33**:238
"Vaeltaja" (Leino) **24**:371
"Vagabond" (Abbey) **160**:57
The Vagabond (Colette)
See *La vagabonde*
"Vagabond Marko and King Matjaž" (Cankar) **105**:162
"A Vagabond Song" (Carman) **7**:138
Vagabondaggio (Verga) **3**:543
La vagabonde (Colette) **1**:192, 194; **5**:167-68; **16**:115, 117, 122-36, 138
"The Vagabonds" (Carman) **7**:133
"Vagabonds" (Chopin) **127**:9-10, 22-23
"Vagabonds" (Lasker-Schueler)
See "Vagabunden"
Vagabonds (Hamsun)
See *Landstrykere*
"Vagabunden" (Lasker-Schueler) **57**:328-29
"Vägen till Elysium och Hades" (Södergran) **31**:293
Vagh vagh sahab (Hedāyat) **21**:72-3, 75, 77
"Vagrant" (Grove) **4**:144
The Vagrant (Sturges)
See *The Great McGinty*
The Vagrant of Time (Roberts) **8**:321
"Vaila" (Shiel)
See "The House of Sounds"
"A Vain Child" (Beerbohm) **24**:115
Vain Fortunes (Moore) **7**:484
Les vaines tendresses (Sully Prudhomme) **31**:300-01, 306-07
Vainglory (Firbank) **1**:226, 229
Un vainqueur (Rod) **52**:311-12
"Le vaisseau de Thésée" (Larbaud) **9**:201
"Le vaisseau d'or" (Nelligan) **14**:392, 396, 400-01
"Vakok a hídon" (Babits) **14**:39
Valborg (Bjoernson) **7**:100
"Vale" (Pickthall) **21**:243
"Vale, and Other Poems" (Baker) **10**:17
"The Vale of Lost Women" (Howard) **8**:134, 136
"Valedictory on Leaving San Francisco" (Bell) **43**:88
"Valenciennes" (Hardy) **4**:152
Valentino (Ginzburg) **156**:19, 38, 70, 112-13
"Valeria" (Monroe) **12**:214
Valerius (Tey) **14**:459
"Valerys Abweichungen" (Adorno) **111**:177
"Valery's divergences" (Adorno)
See "Valerys Abweichungen"
La valise vide (Drieu la Rochelle) **21**:18
Válka s mloky (Čapek) **6**:86, 92-4; **37**:42, 50, 52-3, 55, 57-9, 61-2, 64-5, 67-8, 70, 72-6; **192**:175, 191, 199, 228-30, 232-36
The Valley Captives (Macaulay) **7**:422
"The Valley Farm" (Gurney) **33**:97, 104
Valley Forge (Anderson) **2**:8; **144**:10, 38, 71, 73
"The Valley of a Thousand Hills" (Vilakazi) **37**:409
"The Valley of Capua" (Vazov)
See "Kapuanska dolina"
"The Valley of Childish Things" (Wharton) **129**:360
The Valley of Decision (Wharton) **3**:551-52, 554, 571; **9**:548; **53**:393, 403; **129**:353, 360; **149**:244, 248, 253, 255-6
The Valley of Fear (Doyle) **7**:220, 228, 232, 237-38
The Valley of Restlessness (Babits)
See *A nyugtalanság völgye*
"The Valley of Silence" (Sharp) **39**:382
"The Valley of the Black Pig" (Yeats) **31**:407
The Valley of the Moon (London) **9**:259-60, 266-67, 273, 278, 280-81; **15**:276
"The Valley of the Spiders" (Wells) **19**:429
The Valley of Vision (Fisher) **140**:149, 155, 157, 186
The Valley Road (Foote) **108**:17
Vallfart och vandringår (Heidenstam) **5**:249-50, 253-56
"Vallorbe" (Kraus) **5**:285
Valmouth (Firbank) **1**:227
"El vals" (Aleixandre) **113**:7-8, 79, 81-3
La Valse des toréadors (Anouilh) **195**:7, 16-17, 26, 28, 33, 48-50
"The Value of the Apparently Meaningless and Inaccurate" (Hartmann) **73**:122
"The Value of Vindictiveness" (Horney) **71**:250
"Value Received" (Freeman) **9**:74
"Values and Imperatives" (Locke) **43**:227-29, 240
"Vámonos, pues, por eso, a comber yerba" (Vallejo) **56**:317
Vampir (Ewers) **12**:135-39
"The Vampire" (Remizov) **27**:353, 355
The Vampire (Reymont) **5**:392-93
The Vampire: His Kith and Kin (Summers) **16**:426, 429, 432
The Vampire in Europe (Summers) **16**:429-30, 432
Vampire's Prey (Ewers)
See *Vampir*
Van Bibber and Others (Davis) **24**:200-01, 209
Van en over mijzelf en anderen (Couperus) **15**:47
"Van Gogh: Le suicidé de la société" (Artaud) **3**:53
"Van Gogh: The Man Suicided by Society" (Artaud)
See "Van Gogh: Le suicidé de la société"
"Van Houten" (Quiroga) **20**:212
Van kusum (Devkota) **23**:49-50
Van oude menschen de dingen de voorbigaan (Couperus) **15**:45-7
"Van Winkle" (Crane) **80**:83, 103, 127, 168, 176, 188, 210
Van Zorn (Robinson) **5**:402; **101**:95, 185
"Vanadio" (Levi) **109**:341
"Vanderbilt" (Sternheim) **8**:368
"Vandmøllen" (Jensen) **41**:308
Vandover and the Brute (Norris) **24**:424, 426-28, 432, 440-41; **155**:259, 269, 282-83, 285, 336
En vandrer spiller med sordin (Hamsun) **2**:202, 204-05; **14**:223, 241; **49**:128, 133-34
"The Vane Sisters" (Nabokov) **108**:218
Vanessa (Walpole) **5**:500
The Vanguard (Bennett) **5**:37; **197**:28
"Vanguard Reaches Menton" (Calvino)
See "Gli avanguardisti a Mentone"
Vanished Arcadia (Graham) **19**:111, 124-25
"The Vanished Race" (Patton) **79**:305
The Vanishing American (Grey) **6**:180-81, 183
"The Vanishing American Hobo" (Kerouac) **117**:266, 271-72
"The Vanishing Gift" (Corelli) **51**:73, 80
The Vanishing Hero (O'Faolain) **143**:271
The Vanishing Lady (Melies) **81**:139,149
The Vanishing Man (Freeman)
See *The Eye of Osiris*
"Vanishing News" (Benchley) **55**:19
Vanishing Point (Weiss)
See *Fluchtpunkt*
"A Vanishing Race" (Graham) **19**:135
"Vanitas" (Symons) **11**:446
The Vanity Case (Wells) **35**:422
The Vanity Girl (Mackenzie) **116**:197, 202, 206, 212, 230
Vanity of Duluoz: An Adventurous Education, 1935-1946 (Kerouac) **117**:214-15, 249, 252
Vanity Square (Saltus) **8**:344, 347
"Vánka" (Chekhov) **10**:112
"Vår" (Obstfelder) **23**:185-86, 189
"Vår nattliga badort" (Dagerman) **17**:89-91
"Det var slik en vakker solskinnsdag" (Bjoernson) **7**:118
Varbis (Ekelund) **75**:94
Varenka Olessova (Gorky) **8**:72
"Varennes" (Gurney) **33**:92
"Varför gavs mig livet?" (Södergran) **31**:292
"The Varia" (Dobson) **79**:20
"Variation" (Khodasevich) **15**:208
"Variations" (Jarrell) **177**:147
"Variations" (Salinas) **17**:369
Variations (Huneker) **65**:185, 218-19
"Variations III" (Jarrell) **177**:147
"Variations on a Seventeenth Century Theme" (Scott) **6**:387, 389-90, 394
"Variations on a Summer Day" (Stevens) **3**:477-78; **12**:361; **45**:272, 281, 285, 288
"Variations on a Theme" (Cullen) **37**:168
"Variations on a Theme" (Zangwill) **16**:461
Variations on a Time Theme (Muir) **87**:174, 186
"Variations on Estrangement" (Dickey)
See "Turning Away: Variations on Estrangement"
"Variations on Sadness" (Radnóti) **16**:418
"Varick Street" (Bishop) **121**:56
Varie e frammenti (Campana) **20**:85
Variété I-V (Valéry) **4**:490, 494; **15**:447, 449, 459
The Varieties of Religious Experience (James) **15**:144, 146, 157, 160-62, 167, 180, 182, 185-86, 192; **32**:345-46, 350
A Variety of People (Marquis) **7**:446-47
A Variety of Things (Beerbohm) **1**:72
Variety, second series (Valéry)
See *Variété I-V*
"The Variety Theatre" (Marinetti)
See "Il teatro di varietà"
Variorum (Yeats)
See *The Variorum Edition of the Poems of W. B. Yeats*

The Variorum Edition of the Poems of W. B. Yeats (Yeats) **93**:358, 360, 362, 364, 366, 367, 399-404; **116**:334
Variorum Plays (Yeats) **93**:364, 371, 372
Variorum Poems (Yeats)
See *The Variorum Edition of the Poems of W. B. Yeats*
De varios colores (Valera y Alcala-Galiano) **10**:501
"Various Kinds of Poetry" (Ishikawa) **15**:131
"Various Kinds of Tanka" (Ishikawa) **15**:125
Various Tendencies in Theatre Art (Stanislavsky) **167**:295, 300
"Vårmysterium" (Södergran) **31**:293
Värt behov au tröst (Dagerman) **17**:96
"Varvary" (Gumilev) **60**:279
Varvary (Gorky) **8**:92-3
"Vasant Panchami" (Naidu) **80**:343
Vasantī (Devkota) **23**:51
"A Vásár" (Babits) **14**:39
Vāsarjan (Tagore) **3**:492
"Le vase brisé" (Sully Prudhomme) **31**:299, 306-08
"The Vase of Roses" (Rilke)
See "Die Rosenschale"
"Vashti" (Abercrombie) **141**:3
"Vashti" (Harper) **14**:259-61, 263
I vasi communicanti (Marinetti) **10**:319
Vasily Suchkov (Tolstoy) **18**:360, 373
"Vassermanova reaktsiia" (Pasternak) **188**:254
The Vast Domain (Schnitzler)
See *Das weite Land*
Vataga (Gladkov) **27**:90-1
The Vatard Sisters (Huysmans)
See *Les soeurs vatard*
"Vater und Sohn" (Werfel) **8**:477
The Vatican Swindle (Gide)
See *Les caves du Vatican*
"The Vats" (de la Mare) **4**:78; **53**:16-7, 23, 36
"Vattenfallet" (Södergran) **31**:295
À vau-l'eau (Huysmans) **7**:408, 410, 415-16; **69**:36, 39, 52, 54
Vayehi Hayom (Bialik) **25**:53-4
"Vdokhnovenie" (Babel) **171**:6
"Vdova" (Babel) **171**:7, 9, 23-25, 45, 47, 70, 73, 76, 81, 87
Věc Makropulos (Čapek) **37**:43, 46, 53, 55, 57-8, 61, 68; **192**:199-202
I vecchi e i giovani (Pirandello) **4**:332, 355; **29**:283, 310
"La vecchia signora in kimona viola" (Calvino) **183**:105
"Vecer" (Babel) **2**:22; **13**:33; **171**:21, 36, 40, 75-77, 85-86
"Vecher" (Babel)
See "Vecer"
Vecherny albom (Tsvetaeva) **7**:559; **35**:380, 382, 389, 407-08
"Vechnoe" (Gumilev) **60**:279
"Vechnost" (Gumilev) **60**:280
"Večoženstvennoe" (Hippius) **9**:166
Ved rigets port: Forspil (Hamsun) **2**:202; **14**:221, 243; **49**:127
"The Vedanta in All Its Phases" (Vivekananda) **88**:362
"Veer-Voices: Two Sisters Under Crows" (Dickey) **151**:152
The Vegetable (Fitzgerald) **157**:189
"The Vegetable King" (Dickey) **151**:104, 199
The Vegetable; or, From President to Postman (Fitzgerald) **1**:234, 241; **6**:159
La veglia funebre (D'Annunzio) **6**:137
Ve-Haya he-Akov le-Mishor (Agnon) **151**:4, 27
Vehaya He'akov Lemishor (Agnon) **151**:36-37, 39
"The Veil" (Buchanan) **107**:19
"The Veil" (de la Mare) **53**:28
The Veil, and Other Poems (de la Mare) **4**:74-5
"The Veil of Isis" (Rohmer) **28**:282
"Veil of Queen Mab" (Darío) **4**:60
Veiled Aristocrats (Micheaux) **76**:265
"Veille" (Apollinaire) **51**:35
"The Veils of Maya" (Baker) **10**:27
Vein of Iron (Glasgow) **2**:178, 183-86, 188, 191; **7**:334-36, 341-43, 346-47
Vēja nestas lapas (Rainis)
See *Klusā grāmata*
"Vejan'e smerti: Proshloe" (Bryusov) **10**:92, 95
"The Veld Maiden" (Bosman) **49**:5, 19-20
"Veleta" (García Lorca) **181**:121
"Velevtovci" (Andrić) **135**:84
"Velga" (Bunin) **6**:54
Velikii blagovest (Sologub) **9**:444
Velitelem města Bugul'my (Hašek) **4**:189-90
"Velká kocicí pohádka" (Čapek) **192**:180
"Velká pohádka doktorská" (Čapek) **192**:180
"Velká policejní pohádka" (Čapek) **192**:179, 181
"Velocity of Money" (Ginsberg) **120**:112
"Velvet Ear-Pads" (Wharton) **129**:363
"Velvet Shoes" (Wylie) **8**:521, 530-33
"Ven ikh bin Roytshild" (Aleichem) **35**:307
"Ven siempre, ven" (Aleixandre) **113**:12, 49
"Ven, ven tú" (Aleixandre) **113**:12
La venda (Unamuno) **2**:570
"Les vendanges de Sodome" (Vallette) **67**:276, 315-16, 319, 334
"Vendémiaire" (Apollinaire) **3**:39; **51**:7, 50, 53-5, 57-9
"The Vendetta at Gojiingahara" (Mori Ogai)
See "Gojiingahara no katakiuchi"
Vendetta! or, The Story of One Forgotten (Corelli) **51**:66-7, 72
"Vendette della luna" (Carducci) **32**:101
Le vendeur du soleil (Vallette) **67**:270-71, 275
"La vendeuse d'ambre" (Schwob) **20**:320, 323
Vendía cerillos (Gamboa) **36**:75
"La vendimia de sangre" (Lugones) **15**:285
"Venerable moon-eggs" (Arp) **115**:24
"Veneta Marina" (Symons) **11**:435
"The Venetian Blind" (Jarrell) **177**:224
"Venetian Comedy" (Lee) **5**:310
The Venetian Glass Nephew (Wylie) **8**:523-28, 530-31, 537-38
Venetian Life (Howells) **7**:365, 368-69, 373, 377, 391; **17**:180
Venetian Madcaps (Kuzmin) **40**:203
"A Venetian Night's Entertainment" (Wharton) **129**:361
"Venganza" (Güiraldes) **39**:190
"Vengeance" (Bunin) **6**:56
La vengeance de la vie (Bourget) **12**:69
"Vengeance Is Mine" (Blackwood) **5**:72
"The Vengeance of Man" (Dunsany) **59**:19
"The Vengeance of Saki" (Campbell) **9**:31
"Vengeance of the Duchess" (Davidson) **24**:163
Vengeance Trail (Faust) **49**:38-9, 46
La Vengence du gate-sauce (Melies) **81**:139
"Veni Creator" (Meynell) **6**:300
"Venice" (Nietzsche) **10**:389
Venice Preserved (Belasco) **3**:86
Venice Preserved (Hofmannsthal)
See *Das Gerettete Venedig*
Venise (Kandinsky) **92**:48
Venise Sauvée (Weil) **23**:386, 388
"Venner" (Obstfelder) **23**:176-77
"Venomous Coral Lips" (Rohan) **22**:299
"The Venomous Viper of the Tragedy" (Lardner) **14**:319-20
"Le vent" (Verhaeren) **12**:466
Le vent dans les moulins (Lemonnier) **22**:199, 201
Vent nocturne (Desnos)
See *Langage cuit*
"Il ventaglino" (Pirandello) **29**:293
Venti quattro cervelli (Papini) **22**:271, 288
Ventre brûlé; ou, la mère folle (Artaud) **36**:25
Le ventre de Paris (Zola) **1**:587, 590; **6**:562; **21**:425, 449; **41**:413, 445
Ventura Allende (Garro) **153**:71
"The Venturers" (Henry) **19**:172
Venus (Crothers) **19**:86
"Venus Anadyomene" (Bishop) **103**:5
"Venus and Mars" (Field) **43**:166
Venus in the Kitchen (Douglas) **68**:15
"Venus, Mercury and Cupid" (Field) **43**:165-66
"Venus, My Shining Love " (Cohan) **60**:169
Venus, The Lonely Goddess (Erskine) **84**:169
"Venus Transiens" (Lowell) **8**:230
Vér (Moricz) **33**:242
"Das Ver botene Epos" (Spitteler) **12**:339
Vér és arany (Ady) **11**:17, 22, 24-5
Ver frem dungseffekt (Brecht) **1**:116-17
Ver y palpar (Huidobro) **31**:126
"Véra" (Merezhkovsky) **29**:230, 246
Vera (Elizabeth) **41**:124, 130-31, 137
"Una vera esistenza" (Ginzburg) **156**:97
Véra; or, The Nihilists (Wilde) **8**:494; **23**:443; **41**:354, 376; **175**:284, 287, 312
Vera the Medium (Davis) **24**:203
Veraneo y otros cuentos (Donoso) **133**:122
Veranilda (Gissing) **24**:222
"Verano" (Lugones) **15**:294
"Verba testamentária" (Machado de Assis) **10**:291, 295
Verbal and Pictorial Art (Lagerkvist)
See *Ordkonst och bildkonst*
"Verbnaja nedelja" (Annensky) **14**:33-5
Verbos y Gerundios (Palma) **29**:255
Vercoquin et le plancton (Vian) **9**:528, 536
Verdad (Pardo Bazán) **189**:197-98
"Verdad, sí, sí" (Jiménez) **183**:334
"Verdad siempre" (Aleixandre) **13**:8
Verdens ansigt (Bojer) **64**:2, 4, 13, 18, 23
Verdi (Werfel) **8**:466-67, 479-81
"The Verdict" (Kafka) **2**:304
"The Verdict" (Wharton) **129**:361
"The Verdict of Posterity" (Middleton) **56**:192
El verdugo afable (Sender) **136**:208
"Verdun belle" (Woollcott) **5**:527
"Das verdunstete Gehirn" (Meyrink) **21**:221, 228
Vereinigungen (Musil) **12**:232, 241, 244-46, 252-53, 261; **68**:264
Verena in the Midst (Lucas) **73**:159
"Verfremdungseffekte in Chinese acting" (Brecht) **169**:12, 19
The Verge (Glaspell) **55**:235-41, 244, 247, 257, 261-62, 266, 268-70, 274-76; **175**:53, 62, 69, 74, 77-82, 98-101, 105-6, 108, 113-14, 116-19, 122, 144, 146-48, 153
"Verger" (Bosschere) **19**:58-9
"Vergine Anna" (D'Annunzio) **6**:144
Le vergini (D'Annunzio) **6**:133
Le vergini delle rocce (D'Annunzio) **6**:127-28, 133, 138-40, 144; **40**:4, 29
"Vergissmeinnicht" (Douglas) **40**:65, 71, 74, 76, 78, 83-5, 91-2, 95
"Vergniaud in the Tumbril" (Guiney) **41**:207
"Das Verhaltnis zum Text" (Schoenberg) **75**:321, 340
"Die Verhaltnisse der Landarbeiter im ostelbischen Deutschland" (Weber) **69**:384
Das verhör des Lukullus (Brecht) **1**:107; **6**:33-4
"Verili my v nevernoe" (Hippius) **9**:164
"La verità" (Svevo) **35**:362-63
La verità (Svevo) **35**:352, 369-70
Vérité (Zola) **1**:587-88; **6**:560; **21**:426, 456; **41**:420-21, 423-24
Vérité et poésie (Éluard) **7**:257
Verklarte Nacht (Schoenberg) **75**:297, 317, 331
Verla démocratie sociale et vers la guerre (Halévy) **104**:111-12
"Verlaine stamning" (Ekelund) **75**:94
"Verloren" (Liliencron) **18**:216
"De verloren huissleutel" (van Ostaijen) **33**:409-10, 412, 417
Die verlorene Ehre der Katharina Blum (Böll) **185**:59, 65, 67, 72-3, 75-7, 88-9, 94, 97-101, 105-07, 128, 131, 148, 179
"Das Verlorene Ich" (Benn) **3**:107
Der Verlorene Sohn (Heyse) **8**:121
"Verlorene Stadt" (Raabe) **45**:188
"Verlorener Sohn" (Broch) **20**:52
Das Vermächtnis (Böll) **185**:103, 128-29
"Vermächtnis" (Musil) **12**:258

Das Vermächtnis (Schnitzler) **4**:387-88, 390
"Vermeer" (Nemerov) **124**:155, 157-58, 181, 250, 296
The Vermilion Box (Lucas) **73**:159
The Vermilion Gate: A Novel of a Far Land (Lin) **149**:326
Vermintes Gelände (Böll) **185**:97, 99, 102, 104
Vermischte Bemerkungen (Wittgenstein) **59**:247, 292, 298, 305
Vermont Tradition: The Biography of an Outlook on Life (Fisher) **87**:96
"Vermouth" (Huidobro) **31**:125
"La verna" (Campana) **20**:86-7
Vernon's Aunt (Duncan) **60**:193-4, 196
"Vernost" (Pilnyak) **23**:213
"Veronica's Napkin" (Yeats) **116**:260, 326
"Veronique Fraser" (Scott) **6**:394, 399
"Die Verrohung der Theaterkritik" (Sudermann) **15**:437
Vers (Jammes) **75**:108, 113, 118
"Vers 4" (van Ostaijen) **33**:414
Vers le soir (Kandinsky) **92**:48
Vers libre (Jiménez) **4**:214
"Versamina" (Levi) **109**:292-93
"Die Verscheuchte" (Lasker-Schueler) **57**:305,316
Die vershobene Antigone (Böll) **185**:95
"Der verschollene" (Kafka) **47**:224; **112**:83, 95
Der Verschollene (Kafka) **179**:249-51, 254, 257, 260, 276, 283, 289-92, 297, 304, 306-8, 310-11, 313-20, 322-24, 326-28
"Verse for Urania" (Merrill) **173**:163, 168, 170, 228, 258
The Verse of Christopher Brennan (Brennan) **17**:42
The Verse of Hilaire Belloc (Belloc) **18**:29
"Verse ohne Worte" (Ball) **104**:29
Verse und Prosa aus dem Nachlass (Lasker-Schueler) **57**:313
"Verse vom Friedhof" (Toller) **10**:480, 489-91
"A Verse with a Moral But No Name " (Pyle) **81**:393
Versek (Ady) **11**:15, 19
"A Verseman's Apology" (Service) **15**:411
Verses (Ady)
See *Versek*
Verses (Burke) **63**:126-27
Verses (Dowson) **4**:84, 90
Verses (Wharton) **129**:360
The Verses about the Beautiful Lady (Blok)
See *Stikhi o prekrasnoi dame*
Verses and Sonnets (Belloc) **7**:32; **18**:28, 30, 40-1
"Verses for a Certain Dog" (Parker) **143**:321
"Verses from the Graveyard" (Toller)
See "Verse vom Friedhof"
"Verses in the Night" (Parker) **143**:323
Verses New and Old (Galsworthy) **1**:296
"Verses on My Soviet Passport" (Mayakovski) **18**:270
"Verses Read at the Dinner of the Omar Khayyam Club" (Dobson) **79**:31
"Verses to a Lord Who, in the House of Lords, Said That Those Who Opposed the South African Adventure Confused Soldiers with Money-Grubbers" (Belloc) **18**:35
"Verses to Blok" (Tsvetaeva) **35**:385
"Verses to Czechoslovakia" (Tsvetaeva)
See "Stikhi k Chekhii"
Versi militari (Saba) **33**:369-70, 372
Die Versicherung (Weiss) **152**:261, 288-89
"The Versifier" (Levi)
See "Il Versificatore"
Versilia (D'Annunzio) **40**:14
"Las versiones homéricas" (Borges) **109**:94, 132
"The Versions of Homer" (Borges)
See "Las versiones homéricas"
"Versos a la tristeza de Buenos Aires" (Storni) **5**:448
Versos viejos (Romero) **14**:433
Het verstoorde leven: Dagboek van Etty Hillesum, 1941-1943 (Hillesum) **49**:171, 173, 176-78, 181, 183, 187
Verstörung (Bernhard) **165**:10-11, 19, 21-22, 50-55, 59, 79, 97, 99-100, 108, 111-16, 119
Versts (Tsvetaeva)
See *Vyorsty I*
Versty I (Tsvetaeva)
See *Vyorsty I*
Versty II (Tsvetaeva)
See *Vyorsty II*
"Versuch einer neuen Religion" (Heym) **9**:142
Versuche (Brecht) **1**:106
Der Versucher (Broch) **20**:68-70
"Die Versuchung" (Werfel) **8**:479
Die Versuchung (Kaiser) **9**:174
Die Versuchung der Stillen Veronika (Musil) **68**:288
"Versuchung des heiligen Antonius" (Ball) **104**:71, 75-76
Die versunkene Glocke (Hauptmann) **4**:193-95
Versus (Nash) **109**:360
Die vertauschten Köpfe: Eine indische Legende (Mann) **2**:431; **168**:155
"Die Verteidigung Roms" (Huch) **13**:253
"Vertical Montage" (Eisenstein) **57**:197
"Vertigral" (Agee) **1**:17
"La vertu" (Sully Prudhomme) **31**:306
Der Veruntreute Himmel (Werfel) **8**:480
Der verwandelte Komödiant (Zweig) **17**:451
Die verwandlung (Kafka) **112**:51, 63, 66-8, 80, 105, 107, 118
"Verwandlung des Bösen" (Trakl) **5**:456
Verwandlungen einer Jugend (Carossa) **48**:16, 20, 25, 30
"Verweilen um Mitternacht" (Toller) **10**:491
Verwirrung der Gefühle (Zweig) **17**:425, 429, 458
Die Verwirrungen des Zöglings Törless (Musil) **12**:232-33, 238, 241-42, 244-46, 252, 254-58, 260-61; **68**:257, 259, 264, 288
Verwisch die Spuren (Brecht) **169**:39
Die Verwundung (Böll) **185**:103
"A Very Dove" (Ginsberg) **120**:8
Very Good, Jeeves (Wodehouse) **108**:392
"The Very Good Mother" (Svevo)
See "La buonissima madre"
"Very Like a Whale" (Nash) **109**:367
Very Like a Whale (Osborne) **153**:323
"A Very Lucky Man" (Caragiale) **76**:176
"A Very Short Story" (Hemingway) **115**:191
A Very Woman (Gourmont)
See *Sixtine: Roman de la vie cérébrale*
Verzamelde werken (Couperus) **15**:47
"Das verzauberte Haus" (Musil) **12**:262
Das verzauberte Haus (Musil)
See *Die Versuchung der Stillen Veronika*
"Der Verzückte" (Ball) **104**:8-9, 41, 77
"Verzweiflung" (Werfel) **8**:477
Verzweiflung und Eeloesung im Werk Kafkas (Brod) **115**:87
"Vešči" (Pilnyak) **23**:211
Vesennee porosh'e (Remizov) **27**:329, 347
"Vesna v Fial'te" (Nabokov) **108**:104
"Vesper" (Ivanov) **33**:138
"Vespers" (Crowley) **7**:208
"Vespers" (Lowell) **8**:227
"Vespers" (Milne) **6**:311, 313; **88**:240
Vespertine Light (Ivanov) **33**:136-41
"The Vest" (Thomas) **105**:334, 337
Vestal Fire (Mackenzie) **116**:228, 230, 232, 254
"Vestalis virgo" (Bryusov) **10**:81
"La veste" (Roumain) **19**:339
The Vested Interests and the Common Man (Veblen) **31**:362, 366
El vestido de boda (Pardo Bazán) **189**:198
"Vestiges: Harlem Sketches" (Fisher)
See "The South Lingers On"
Vestire gli ignudi (Pirandello) **4**:337-39, 351; **29**:283, 285, 300, 318-19
"Veter nam utešen'e prines" (Mandelstam) **6**:267
"The Veteran" (Crane) **11**:167; **17**:71, 73-4; **32**:153, 155-56, 164
"Veteran Sirens" (Robinson) **101**:100, 134
"Veteris Vestigia Flammae" (Hardy) **53**:80
Vētras sēja (Rainis) **29**:391-92
"Vetrogon, sumasbrod, letatel" (Guro) **56**:150
Vetter Gabriel (Heyse) **8**:121
"La veuve Aphrodissia" (Yourcenar) **193**:283, 294-95
Una vez fuí rico (Romero) **14**:434, 442
Via Borealis (Scott) **6**:394, 397
Via crucis: A Romance of the Second Crusade (Crawford) **10**:148, 151-52
La via del male (Deledda) **23**:41-3
"Via et veritas et vita" (Meynell) **6**:300, 303
"I viaggi, la morte" (Gadda) **144**:148
I viaggi la morte (Gadda) **144**:143
"Viaggio a Montivideo" (Campana) **20**:84
"Viaje" (Aleixandre) **113**:62-4
"Viaje" (Jiménez) **183**:259
Viaje a la aldea del crimen (Sender) **136**:209
Viaje a la Habana (Arenas) **191**:219, 239
Un viaje de novios (Pardo Bazán) **189**:205, 222, 237, 224-25, 251, 254, 259, 262
"El viajero" (Pardo Bazán) **189**:226
Vicara-sangraham (Ramana Maharshi) **84**:260
The Vicar's Daughter (MacDonald) **9**:292
"Vice Versa" (Morgenstern) **8**:306
"Vicious Circle" (Machado de Assis)
See "Circulo vicioso"
"The Vicious Negro" (Cotter) **28**:42
The Vicissitudes of Evangeline (Glyn) **72**:127
"Vickery" (Robinson) **101**:112
"Vico and Aesthetic Historicism" (Auerbach) **43**:56, 62
Vico and Herder (Berlin) **105**:11, 71, 118
"Vico und Herder" (Auerbach) **43**:62
"Vicomte" (Proust) **161**:173
La Vicomtesse d'Eristal n'a pas reçu son balai mécanique (Anouilh) **195**:60
"Vico's Contribution to Literary Criticism" (Auerbach) **43**:63-4
"The Victim" (Sinclair) **11**:421
The Victim (Dixon) **163**:166
The Victim (Strindberg)
See *Offret*
"A Victim of Heredity" (Chesnutt) **39**:95, 99
The Victim of Jealousy (Griffith) **68**:249
"Victim of Justice" (Dreiser)
See "Nigger Jeff"
"A Victim to Science" (Pyle) **81**:393
"Víctimas de la opulencia" (Azuela) **145**:21
"La victoire" (Apollinaire) **51**:37
"La victoire de Guernica" (Éluard) **41**:151, 163-64, 167
"The Victor" (Dreiser) **35**:74
The Victor Soul (Benavente) **3**:97
"Victoria" (Campbell) **9**:31
Victoria (Hamsun)
See *Victoria: En kaerligheds histoire*
Victoria (Housman) **7**:358
Victoria and Albert: Palace Plays, third series (Housman) **7**:357
Victoria: En kaerligheds histoire (Hamsun) **2**:202, 208; **14**:222, 224, 226-28, 235, 237, 242, 247-48; **49**:128, 131, 133-34, 159, 168; **151**:232, 234
"Victoria Falls" (Vilakazi)
See "Impophoma yeVictoria"
Victoria Regina (Housman) **7**:357, 361
The Victorian Age in Literature (Chesterton) **1**:184; **6**:101
A Victorian Gentlewoman in the Far West (Foote) **108**:4, 20-30, 36, 38
Victorian Ghost Stories (Summers) **16**:434
A Victorian Village: Reminiscences of Other Days (Reese) **181**:339, 347-48
"The Victorious Sun" (Aleixandre)
See "El sol victorioso"
"Victor-Marie Comte Hugo" (Péguy) **10**:404, 415

The Victors (Bagritsky)
See *Pobediteli*
"Victory" (Graham) **19**:110, 129, 133
Victory (Conrad) **1**:196, 200, 209-11, 217; **6**:121-22; **25**:87, 92; **43**:120; **57**:39, 69
Victory (Huch) **13**:242-43
"Victory Ode" (Carducci) **32**:103
Victory of Women (Mizoguchi) **72**:315, 324
"Victrola" (Morris) **107**:201
Vid lägereld (Lagerkvist) **144**:211
"Vida" (Aleixandre)
See "Life"
"Vida" (Mistral) **2**:478
La vida breve (Onetti) **131**:133, 136, 140, 146-48, 152, 155, 158, 160-63, 165, 167, 169-71, 183, 189, 193-95, 198-99, 203, 207, 214-15, 220, 223, 245-46, 248, 261-63, 268-75, 278, 284, 286, 294, 296
Vida de Don Quijote y Sancho (Unamuno) **148**:229-30, 235, 252-53, 299-301, 337
Vida de Don Quixote y Sancho, según Miguel de Cervantes Saavedra, explicada y comentada por Miguel de Unamuno (Unamuno) **2**:558-59, 563, 567-68; **9**:508, 512, 514
Vida e morte de M. J. Gonzaga de Sá (Lima Barreto) **23**:165-69
"La vida es sueño" (Unamuno) **148**:328
La vida inútil de Pito Pérez (Romero) **14**:433-36, 441-44
"Una vida por una honra" (Palma) **29**:256
Vidas sêcas (Ramos) **32**:419, 424-25, 427-32, 434-37, 439
Vidas sombrías (Baroja) **8**:53, 60
"Le Vide de Torricelli" (Arp) **115**:31
"Videnic" (Zamyatin) **8**:553
"Videniia" (Bryusov) **10**:95-6
"El vidrio roto" (Pardo Bazán) **189**:236
"Vidula" (Aurobindo) **63**:6
"La Vie" (Jammes) **75**:117
"La Vie Artistique" (Huysmans) **69**:27
"La vie cosmique" (Teilhard de Chardin) **9**:481, 487, 491, 494
Vie de Beethoven (Rolland) **23**:268, 276, 280-81
"Vie de bohème" (Symons) **11**:451
La Vie de Guy de Fontgalland (Jammes) **75**:119
Vie de Jeanne d'Arc (France) **9**:44-5, 57
"Vie de Mademoiselle Amandine" (Giono) **124**:103
La vie de Michel-Ange (Rolland) **23**:260
La vie de Samuel Belet (Ramuz) **33**:294-95, 302
Vie de Tolstoï (Rolland) **23**:260, 262
"Vie d'ebène" (Desnos) **22**:61
"La viè des abeilles" (Maeterlinck) **3**:319, 322
La vie en fleur (France) **9**:50
La vie immédiate (Éluard) **7**:254; **41**:150-51, 154, 158, 162
La vie inquiète (Bourget) **12**:73
La vie littéraire (France) **9**:41-2
"La vie passe" (Bourget) **12**:66
"Un vie pleine d'intérêt" (Péret) **20**:201
La vie privée de Michel Teissier (Rod) **52**:310-11, 313-14
La vie secrète (Lemonnier) **22**:204
"La vieille" (Bosschere) **19**:59
Vieille France (Martin du Gard) **24**:384, 386-88, 395-96, 401
La vieja Rosa (Arenas) **191**:136-39
"Una vieja tristeza" (Gonzalez Martinez) **72**:149
"El viejecito del barrio" (Huidobro) **31**:132
"Viejo estribillo" (Nervo) **11**:395
"Der Viele viele Schnee" (Borchert) **5**:109
Les Vieillards (Ghelderode) **187**:5
Viennese Idylls (Schnitzler) **4**:388
"Viennese Waltz" (Wylie) **8**:530
"Viens a la campagne avec moi" (Tzara) **168**:321
"El Viento" (Aleixandre) **113**:3
"Viento de amor" (Jiménez) **4**:214
Viento fuerte (Asturias) **184**:16, 45-47, 87-88
Vientos contrarios (Huidobro) **31**:123
Die vier Jahreszeiten (Wedekind) **7**:582
"Die vier Mondbrüder" (Meyrink) **21**:232
La Vierge et les sonnets (Jammes) **75**:119
"Vierge moderne" (Södergran) **31**:290
"La vierge noire" (Nelligan) **14**:392
"Der vierte Lebenslauf" (Hesse) **148**:160-61
"Vierter Lebenslauf" (Hesse) **148**:159-61, 163
"Vierundzwanzig Stunden aus dem Leben einer Frau" (Zweig) **17**:425, 429
Die vierzig Tage des Musa Dagh (Werfel) **8**:468, 471, 477, 480-82
Vies des hommes illustres (Rolland) **23**:260
Vies imaginaires (Schwob) **20**:322-23, 329
Viet Nam Diskurs (Weiss) **152**:267, 285, 311
Vietnam Discourse (Weiss)
See *Viet Nam Diskurs*
"Le Vieux de la Montagne" (Jarry) **147**:263
Le vieux de la montagne (Bloy) **22**:45, 50
"Les vieux maîtres" (Verhaeren) **12**:465
Vieux ménages (Mirbeau) **55**:281
Le vieux roi (Gourmont) **17**:130-31
"Le vieux temps" (Drummond) **25**:142-43, 151, 157
"A View from a Hill" (James) **6**:206, 213, 215
"The View from an Attic Window" (Nemerov) **124**:179, 227
"The View from Pisgah" (Nemerov) **124**:177-79, 218, 249
"The View from the Northern Ramparts" (Huysmans) **69**:25
The View from the Parsonage (Kaye-Smith) **20**:111-12, 116
"A View of Fujiyama After the War" (Dickey) **151**:225
"View of Teignmouth in Devonshire" (Lowell) **8**:227
"A View of the Burning" (Merrill) **173**:232
"A View of the Woods" (O'Connor) **132**:263, 310, 313-14
A View to a Kill (Fleming) **193**:231
"Viewing of a Painting" (Rohan) **22**:297
Views and Reviews: Essays in Appreciation (Henley) **8**:97-8, 105-06
Views and Vagabonds (Macaulay) **7**:421-22, 428
"Views from a German Spion" (Harte) **25**:225
"Un viex" (Loti) **11**:353
The Vigil of a Nation (Lin) **149**:322
The Vigil of Brunhild (Manning) **25**:263, 275-76
"Vigilance" (Jiménez) **183**:337
"The Vigil-at-Arms" (Guiney) **41**:221
Vigiles de l'esprit (Alain) **41**:7
Vigils (Rilke) **6**:370
"Le vigneron champenois" (Apollinaire) **51**:36
Le vigneron dans sa vigne (Renard) **17**:303
Vignettes in Rhyme and Vers de Société (Dobson) **79**:9, 22, 28, 34
Vignettes of Manhattan (Matthews) **95**:250, 272
Vihar (Babits) **14**:41
The Vikings at Helgeland (Ibsen)
See *Haermaendene på Helgeland*
"Vila i leshy" (Khlebnikov) **20**:131, 134
"A világosság udvara" (Babits) **14**:39
Vildanden (Ibsen) **2**:220, 222-24, 226-32; **8**:148-49, 151-52; **16**:152-98; **37**:242, 258; **52**:143-44, 154, 164
Det vilde Kor (Hamsun) **49**:128
Vilinq ari (Hedāyat) **21**:72, 75
"A Villa and a Wood-Goblin" (Khlebnikov)
See "Vila i leshy"
Villa Aurea (Kaiser) **9**:193
A Villa in Sicily (Kaiser)
See *Villa Aurea*
Villa Magdalena (Santos) **156**:296-97, 300, 306, 317-18
Villa Rubein (Galsworthy) **1**:299-300; **45**:32, 46, 48
Villa Schönow (Raabe) **45**:170-71, 178
Village (Bunin)
See *Derevnya*
Le Village aérien (Verne) **52**:360
Village: As It Happened through a Fifteen-Year Period (McAlmon) **97**:87, 90-91, 118, 121-22
A Village Commune (Ouida) **43**:345-46, 376
Le village dans le montagne (Ramuz) **33**:302, 306
"Village Ghosts" (Yeats) **11**:538
The Village in the Treetops (Verne)
See *Le Village aérien*
"A Village Lear" (Freeman) **9**:65
The Village Magazine (Lindsay) **17**:232, 240
"A Village Mariana" (Symons) **11**:428
"Village Mystery" (Wylie) **8**:521
The Village of Segelfloss (Hamsun)
See *Segelfoss by*
"The Village Olujaci" (Andrić)
See "Olujaci"
"Village Opera" (Lu Hsun) **3**:303
"A Village Shop" (Jewett) **22**:146-47
"A Village Singer" (Freeman) **9**:75-6
"Village Songs" (Naidu) **80**:290
"The Village That Voted the Earth Was Flat" (Kipling) **8**:202
"The Village Wedding" (Sikelianos) **39**:414, 421
"The Village Witch Doctor" (Tutuola) **188**:301
The Village Witch Doctor and Other Stories (Tutuola) **188**:301, 308
Village Wooing (Shaw) **3**:399, 407
Les villages illusoires (Verhaeren) **12**:464, 466, 469
"Villanelle to His Ladye in Which Ye Poore Scribe Complaineth Sorely Because the Cursed Memory of the Thousand Others Doth Poison His Dreams of His Beatrice" (O'Neill) **6**:337
"La ville" (Desnos) **22**:73
La ville (Claudel) **2**:103, 109; **10**:131
Une Ville flottante (Verne) **52**:352
"Les villes" (Verhaeren) **12**:463
Les villes tentaculaires (Verhaeren) **12**:458, 464, 466-67, 469-70, 475-76, 482
"Villon's Straight Tip to All Cross Coves" (Henley) **8**:107
"Villon's Wife" (Dazai Osamu)
See "Buiyon no tsuma"
Le vin est tiré (Desnos) **22**:69
"Le vin perdu" (Valéry) **4**:498
"Vincent van Gogh" (Sternheim) **8**:379
Vincenzo De Pretore (de Filippo) **127**:272
"A Vindication of the Cabala" (Borges)
See "A Vindication of the Kabbalah"
"A Vindication of the Kabbalah" (Borges) **109**:16-17, 148
"The Vines" (Gray) **19**:152
"Viñetas flamencas" (García Lorca) **181**:196-97
"Viney's Free Papers" (Dunbar) **12**:112
Vingt contes nouveaux (Coppee) **25**:126
Les vingt et un jours d'un neurasthénique (Mirbeau) **55**:281, 285, 293
Vingt leçons sur les beaux-arts (Alain) **41**:30
Vingt mille lieues sous les mers (Verne) **6**:497-98, 500, 503, 505; **52**:330, 335, 338, 343-46, 350, 352
Vingt-cinq années de vie littèaire (Barrès) **47**:73
Vingt-cinq poèmes (Tzara) **168**:262
"Viniere el malo" (Vallejo) **56**:312
"Vino generoso" (Svevo) **35**:345, 349, 351
"Vino, primero, pura . . . " (Jiménez) **183**:273-75, 290
"The Vintage" (Gilman) **117**:155
The Vintage Mencken (Mencken) **13**:394
"Vintage Season" (Kuttner) **10**:269, 274-76
"Vinum daemonum" (Johnson) **19**:246
"Viola acherontia" (Lugones) **15**:293
"Violante, or Worldly Vanities" (Proust)
See "Violante ou la mondanitée"
"Violante ou la mondanitée" (Proust) **7**:538; **161**:124, 172-74
The Violent Bear It Away (O'Connor) **132**:229, 231, 246-48, 251, 253, 259, 263, 265, 269,

277, 280, 283, 296, 312, 320, 329, 331-32, 334, 337, 339, 341-42, 361, 366
Violent Night (Dent) **72**:26, 38
"Violet" (Mansfield) **2**:451
The Violet (Molnár) **20**:161
The Violet Apple (Lindsay) **15**:219, 225-30, 234
"La violeta solitario" (Lugones) **15**:289
"Violets" (Lawrence) **93**:2, 3, 46
"Violet's Own" (Green) **63**:142
Der violette Tod, und andrere Novellen (Meyrink) **21**:220
"Violin Sonata by Vincent d'Indy" (Lowell) **8**:234
"The Violin's Enchantress" (Benét) **28**:2
"The Viper" (Tolstoy) **18**:370, 373, 378
The Virago Book of Fairy Tales (Carter) **139**:118-19, 126, 128
Virata; or, The Eyes of an Undying Brother (Zweig)
See *Die Augen des Ewigen Bruders*
"Virgil in Mexico" (Reyes) **33**:318
Virgile (Giono) **124**:114, 138
"Virgilia" (Markham) **47**:285, 287
"The Virgin and the Gipsy" (Lawrence) **2**:364, 371; **48**:102, 118, 121
"The Virgin and the Scales" (Warner) **131**:311
"The Virgin Carrying a Lantern" (Stevens) **45**:334
"The Virgin, Child and St. John" (Field) **43**:166
A Virgin Heart (Gourmont)
See *Un coeur virginal*
The Virgin of the Sun (Haggard) **11**:246
"Virgin Youth" (Lawrence) **93**:43, 44, 69
"Virginia" (Crane) **80**:115
Virginia (Glasgow) **2**:178, 180-81, 184-85, 189-90; **7**:337, 346
Virginia of Elk Creek Valley (Chase) **124**:27
The Virginian: A Horseman of the Plains (Wister) **21**:374-80, 384-85, 387-89, 391-93, 396-401, 403-10
"The Virginians Are Coming Again" (Lindsay) **17**:245
Virginians Are Various (Cabell) **6**:76, 78
"The Virginiola Fraud" (Bramah) **72**:6
The Virgins (D'Annunzio)
See *Le vergini*
The Virgin's Brand (Perutz)
See *St. Petri-Schnee*
"The Virgin's Dream" (Pascoli) **45**:142
"Virtue in War" (Crane) **11**:161
"The Virtues of Getting Drunk" (Middleton) **56**:179
"A Virtuoso" (Dobson) **79**:8
A Virtuous Girl (Bodenheim) **44**:72
The Virtuous Knight (Sherwood) **3**:415
The Visage (Futabatei)
See *Sono omokage*
Les visages de la vie (Verhaeren) **12**:459-60, 464, 469
"Visan från molnet" (Södergran) **31**:291
"Visão 1944" (Drummond de Andrade) **139**:232
"Visée" (Apollinaire) **8**:28; **51**:34-5
De vises sten (Lagerkvist) **144**:189
"Vishnëvaia kostochka" (Olesha) **136**:75, 77, 94-95, 102, 111, 124-26, 132, 136, 154-56
Vishnëvaia kostochka (Olesha)
See *Vishnevaya kostochka*
Vishnevaya kostochka (Olesha) **136**:63, 106, 151, 154
Vishnevy sad (Chekhov)
See *Visňevyi sad*
"Visibilità" (Calvino) **183**:105, 141, 217
"Visibility" (Calvino)
See "Visibilità"
Visibility Good: Essays and Excursions (Lucas) **73**:166
"Visibility in Fiction" (Wharton) **149**:288
"The Visibility of Colour" (Wells) **133**:318
Visible and Invisible (Benson) **27**:8-9, 19
Visible and Invisible (Merleau-Ponty)
See *Le Visible et l'invisible*
Le Visible et l'invisible (Merleau-Ponty) **156**:134, 144-46, 158, 162, 174, 179-80, 183-84, 186, 208, 212, 253, 258, 260, 262, 270-72, 274-77, 280, 287, 291-92
"Vision" (Gibran)
See "Ru'ya'"
"The Vision" (Masters) **25**:315
"The Vision" (Sharp) **39**:380, 392
Vision (Jarry) **147**:309
A Vision (Yeats) **1**:559, 566-71, 577, 582-84; **11**:517, 521-22, 524-25, 528, 531-32; **18**:447-48, 452, 454-55; **31**:390-94, 397, 403-04, 406-11; **93**:339, 340, 344-45, 347, 353-54, 358-69, 371-73, 395, 399, 402-07; **116**:259-62, 264-66, 269, 271, 289, 297-98, 301-02, 310-11, 313, 315, 319, 321-26, 330, 332-33, 337
"Vision And Prayer" (Thomas) **1**:475; **8**:451, 454, 460-62; **45**:363, 372, 377, 380, 402, 406
Visión de Anáhuac (Reyes) **33**:316-18, 322-23, 325
"La visión de la Lluvia" (Villaurrutia) **80**:477
"Vision de prière" (Péguy) **10**:416
La vision du passé (Teilhard de Chardin) **9**:483
"Visioń jivenil desde otros años" (Aleixandre) **113**:50
"The Vision Malefic" (Huneker) **65**:196
Vision of Anáhuac (Reyes)
See *Visión de Anáhuac*
"A Vision of Beauty" (Baker) **10**:27
Vision of Giorgione (Bottomley) **107**:2, 4
"A Vision of Judgment" (Wells) **12**:506
"Vision of Love" (Naidu) **80**:280
Vision of Spangler's Paul (Wolfe) **13**:492
"A Vision of Spring in Winter" (Swinburne) **36**:318, 320
"The Vision of the Dead Creole" (Hearn) **9**:136
"The Vision of the Empire" (Williams) **1**:511
"A Vision of the Garden" (Merrill) **173**:257
"The Vision of the Man Accurst" (Buchanan) **107**:24, 40, 72
"A Vision of the Past" (Wells) **133**:323
The Vision of the Past (Teilhard de Chardin)
See *La vision du passé*
"Vision und Figur" (Kaiser) **9**:185
Visionaries (Huneker) **65**:156-58, 169-70, 195, 216
The Visionaries (Musil)
See *Die schwärmer*
Los visionarios (Baroja) **8**:51-2, 55
"A Visionary" (Yeats) **11**:539
The Visionary (Sikelianos)
See *Alafroiskiotos*
The Visionary; or, Pictures from Nordland (Lie)
See *Den fremsynte*
The Visioning (Glaspell) **55**:241, 243-46; **175**:59, 107
"Visions" (Buchanan) **107**:17
Visions (Ekelund)
See *Syner*
Visions (Lasker-Schueler)
See *Gesichte*
"Visions actuelles et futures" (Jarry) **147**:309, 314, 332
Visions and Beliefs in the West of Ireland (Gregory) **176**:48, 50-56, 61
Visions infernales (Jacob) **6**:202
Visions of Cody (Kerouac) **117**:190-91, 195-197, 200-01, 203-04, 248, 252
Visions of Excess (Bataille) **155**:88-90, 93-98, 104-7, 111
Visions of Gerard (Kerouac) **117**:248, 166
"Visions of the Night" (Bierce) **44**:29
"A Visit" (Borowski) **9**:24
"The Visit" (Dowson) **4**:88
"The Visit" (Jackson) **187**:283
"A Visit from Wisdom" (Gibran) **9**:93
"A Visit of Condolence" (Lawson) **27**:130
"A Visit to America" (Thomas) **105**:356
"A Visit to an Asylum" (Millay) **4**:316
"A Visit to Avoyelles" (Chopin) **14**:58; **127**:112
"A Visit to Grandpa's" (Thomas) **8**:455, 462-63; **45**:412-13; **105**:301, 350
"A Visit to the Asylum" (Millay)
See "A Visit to an Asylum"
"A Visit to Walt Whitman" (Huneker) **65**:161
"Las visitas" (Pereda) **16**:372
"Visitation" (Jacob) **6**:193
"Visitation" (Schulz) **51**:310, 314, 316, 320
"Visitation préhistorique" (Fargue) **11**:200
Visitations (Giraudoux) **7**:322
"Visite" (Cocteau) **119**:107
"Une visite à Don Juan" (Barrès) **47**:58
"The Visiting Sea" (Meynell) **6**:299
"Visiting the Sick" (Pirandello) **4**:329
"The Visitor" (Dahl) **173**:15-16, 18
"A Visitor" (Dazai Osamu) **11**:177
"The Visitor" (Dunbar) **12**:104
"The Visitor" (Muir) **87**:277
"The Visitor" (Thomas) **45**:409-10; **105**:297-98, 300, 318-320, 324-25, 325, 333-34, 336-38, 355, 357
The Visitor (Brennan) **124**:7
"A Visitor in the Piano Warehouse" (Saroyan) **137**:150
"Visitors" (de la Mare) **4**:80; **53**:16, 23, 27
The Visitors (Orton) **157**:344-46
Visitors (Przybyszewski) **36**:289
"The Visitors April '34" (Thomas) **105**:333
"Visitors' Day at the Joke Farm" (Benchley) **55**:11
The Visits of Elizabeth (Glyn) **72**:127, 132
"Visits to St. Elizabeths" (Bishop) **121**:7, 42
Visňevyi sad (Chekhov) **55**:28-80; **96**:8, 16, 35-36, 54; **163**:11, 15, 17, 19, 55, 77, 100-104, 113-14, 116, 120, 128, 133-34
"Víspera de mí" (Aleixandre) **113**:5
Las vísperas de España (Reyes) **33**:322
"Uma vista de Alcebíades" (Machado de Assis) **10**:291
Vistas (Sharp) **39**:360-62, 370-72, 374, 397
Una vita (Svevo) **2**:539-41, 543, 545-48, 553; **35**:332, 334, 336-38, 341-43, 345-49, 351, 355, 364-69
La vita che ti diedi (Pirandello) **4**:338
La vita de nessuno (Papini) **22**:280-81
Vita dei campi (Verga) **3**:539, 541, 543, 545-47
La vita di Cola di Rienzo (D'Annunzio) **40**:11
Vita di Michelangelo (Papini) **22**:288-89
Vita immaginaria (Ginzburg) **156**:103, 110-12
Vita notata. Storia (Gadda) **144**:145
Vita Nova (Barthes) **135**:189
La vita nuda (Pirandello) **29**:282, 291, 295, 300
Vita Nuova (Hrabal) **155**:159, 165
Vita sexualis (Mori Ogai) **14**:369, 379, 385-87
Vita somnium breve (Huch) **13**:241, 243, 245, 247, 251-53
"Vita venturi saeculi" (Johnson) **19**:244
Vital Lies (Lee) **5**:312, 316
The Vital Message (Doyle) **7**:225
Vital Statistics (Drieu la Rochelle)
See *Etat civil*
Vitam impendere amori (Apollinaire) **8**:14
Le vitre d'amour (Artaud) **36**:32
Vitrina pintoresca (Baroja) **8**:63
Vittoria (Meredith) **17**:275; **43**:259
"Vittorini: Progettazione e letteratura" (Calvino) **183**:246
"La viuda Ching, Pirata" (Borges) **109**:40
"Viva!" (Lasker-Schueler) **57**:329, 336
ViVa (Cummings) **137**:27, 34, 47, 49-50
"Viva La France" (O'Faolain) **143**:233
"Viva la Liberta!" (Brod) **115**:94
Viva mi dueño: El ruedo Ibérico II (Valle-Inclán) **5**:477-79, 485, 487-89
Viva Villa (Hecht) **101**:62, 88
Vive le roy (Ford) **15**:87, 90; **172**:53-55
Vive Moi! (O'Faolain) **143**:267, 269
Viventes das Alagoas (Ramos) **32**:433
"Viver!" (Machado de Assis) **10**:280, 290-91
"Vivid Story of the Battle of San Juan" (Crane) **11**:159

Vivis (Gray) **19**:159
"Vivisection" (Pavlov) **91**:150
The Vivisector (White) **176**:138, 143, 145-46, 148, 153, 181-88, 192, 194-96, 199-203, 208, 212, 218-19, 224, 227, 244, 249, 257, 269-70, 272, 274, 278, 280, 301-2, 307, 309-10, 315-17
"Vivre" (Éluard) **7**:250; **41**:159
Vixen (Braddon) **111**:232-36
The Vizier of the Two-Horned Alexander (Stockton) **47**:324, 326-27
Vizio di forma (Levi) **109**:292
"Vladimir Ilích Lenin" (Mayakovski) **18**:248, 255, 257, 266
"Vladimir Mayakovsky" (Mayakovski) **18**:247, 250-52, 254
Vlast' klyuchei: Potestas clavium (Shestov) **56**:260, 264, 276
"Vljublennost'" (Hippius) **9**:166
"Vlom budushchego" (Khlebnikov) **20**:137
"Vlyublyonnost" (Nabokov) **108**:117
"Vnučka Maluši" (Khlebnikov) **20**:130, 139
"A Vocation and a Voice" (Chopin) **5**:157; **127**:9, 23
A Vocation and a Voice: Stories (Chopin) **127**:201, 211
"La vocazione del conte Ghislain" (Svevo) **35**:363
"La voce" (Pascoli) **45**:145, 154
"Voces" (Aleixandre) **113**:3
"Las voces" (Nervo) **11**:399
Voces de gesta (Valle-Inclán) **5**:472, 481, 486
Le Voci de Dentro (de Filippo) **127**:267, 272, 281, 289
Le voci della sera (Ginzburg) **156**:37-39, 42, 63, 74, 105
"Vody mnogie" (Bunin) **6**:58
Der vogel selbdritt (Arp) **115**:6
Der Vogelfreie (Weiss) **152**:284
The Vogelsang Documents (Raabe)
See *Die Akten des Vogelsangs*
"Vöglein Schwermut" (Morgenstern) **8**:309
"The Voice" (Brooke) **2**:59; **7**:124
"The Voice" (Davidson) **24**:186
"The Voice" (Gale) **7**:283-84
"The Voice" (Hardy) **4**:164; **53**:101, 112, 114
"The Voice" (Pascoli)
See "La voce"
"A Voice" (Sarton) **120**:305
"The Voice and the Dusk" (Scott) **6**:393
"The Voice and the Shadow" (Pickthall) **21**:254
A Voice Crying in the Wilderness: Vox Clamantis in Deserto (Abbey) **160**:36, 69, 78, 86
"A Voice from a Chorus" (Blok) **5**:85, 87
"A Voice from a Cloud" (Capote) **164**:199
"A Voice from the Depths" (Zabolotsky) **52**:366
The Voice from the Minaret (Hichens) **64**:131
"A Voice from the Town" (Paterson) **32**:377
"The Voice in the Night" (Hodgson) **13**:235, 237
Voice in the Night (Shepherd) **177**:312
The Voice of Jerusalem (Zangwill) **16**:447, 461-62
"The Voice of Job" (MacDonald) **113**:227
The Voice of the City (Henry) **1**:346
"Voice of the Crow" (Ingamells) **35**:131
The Voice of the Ocean (Hodgson) **13**:237
The Voice of the People (Glasgow) **2**:176, 179, 189; **7**:333, 339, 348
The Voice of the People (Peretz) **16**:396, 398
The Voice of the Turtle (Van Druten) **2**:573-75
The Voice of the Valley (Noguchi) **80**:360
"The Voice of the Waters" (Baker) **10**:17
A Voice through a Cloud (Welch) **22**:439-45, 447, 450-53, 455-62
"Voices" (Aleixandre)
See "Voces"
"The Voices" (Muir) **87**:231
"The Voices" (Rilke)
See "Die Stimmen"
"Voices from the Other World" (Merrill) **173**:241
"Voices From Things Growing in a Churchyard" (Hardy) **53**:100; **143**:156, 192
Voices in the Evening (Ginzburg)
See *Le voci della sera*
The Voices of Marrakesh: A Record of a Visit (Canetti)
See *Die Stimmen von Marrakesch: Aufzeichnungen nach einer Reise*
Voices of the Stones (Baker) **3**:6
Voices of the Tide (Su Man-shu)
See *Ch'ao-yin chi*
"La voie lactée" (Sully Prudhomme) **31**:302
Voina (Sologub) **9**:444
Voina i mir (Tolstoy) **4**:445-48, 451, 453-71, 474-79, 481-83; **11**:458, 460-61, 463-68, 470, 472, 475-76, 478; **17**:373-74, 377-78, 389, 391-93, 399-401, 403, 405, 409-14, 416; **28**:346-404; **44**:334, 349, 355; **79**:325-6, 334, 353-4, 363, 365-6, 368-9, 375-7, 382-3, 387, 389-90, 394, 415-8, 421, 424, 433, 436, 443, 445-7, 452, 455; **173**:271, 275, 280, 295, 301-3, 305
"La Voix" (Huysmans) **69**:30
"Voix" (Lyotard) **103**:267
"La voix dans la vision" (Nelligan) **14**:396
"La voix de Robert Desnos" (Desnos) **22**:60-1
La voix du sang (Vallette) **67**:270, 275
"Vojna" (Gumilev) **60**:282
"Vojna: Opjat'raznogolosica" (Mandelstam) **6**:267
Vol de nuit (Saint-Exupéry) **2**:515-19, 523, 526; **56**:230; **169**:314, 320, 324, 332, 337, 340
"The Volcano" (Lowry) **6**:238
Volcano (Endo)
See *Kazan*
The Volcano (Santos) **156**:296, 317
Volga Country (Tolstoy) **18**:364, 377
La Volga nasce in Europa (Malaparte) **52**:273-74
The Volga Rises in Europe (Malaparte)
See *La Volga nasce in Europa*
"Volgelschau" (George) **14**:203, 205, 208
"Volki" (Pilnyak) **23**:212
"Volksweise" (Rilke) **195**:263
"Vollendung der Liebe" (Musil) **12**:232, 245; **68**:264, 288
Die Vollendung des königs Henri Quatre (Mann) **9**:317-19, 322, 325-29
"Volodja bolšoj i Volodja malen'kij" (Chekhov) **55**:62
"Volodya" (Chekhov) **3**:168
Volpone (Zweig) **17**:453
Volshebnik (Nabokov) **108**:121-24, 126, 135, 180, 205-07, 209
Volshebny fonar (Tsvetaeva) **7**:559; **35**:380, 382, 389, 407
Voltaire (Noyes) **7**:515
"Voltaire Combe" (Rourke) **12**:330
"Voltaire—Goethe" (Mann) **9**:327
Volume Two (Villa) **176**:105, 112, 117-18
"La voluntad" (Quiroga) **20**:212, 216-17
Voluntad de vivir manifestándose (Arenas) **191**:194-96
"Voluntad de vivir manifestándose" (Arenas) **191**:194
Un voluntario realista (Pérez Galdós) **27**:287
"The Volunteers" (Gurney) **33**:81, 86
"Volunteers at Sipka" (Vazov)
See "Opalčenite na Šipka"
"Volupte" (Vallette) **67**:277
Volupteé (Crowley) **7**:211
Les voluptes imprevues (Vallette) **67**:284
"Volver . . ." (Villaurrutia) **80**:489
Vom armen B. B. (Brecht) **169**:37, 41-44
"Vom Attentäter zum Schmock" (Roth) **33**:336
Vom Kaiserhof zur Reichskanzlerei (Goebbels)
See *From the Kaiserhof to the Reich Chancellery*
Vom liebe Gott und Andres (Rilke) **6**:357; **195**:175
"Vom Tagewerk des Todes" (Morgenstern) **8**:309
"Vom Zeitunglesen" (Morgenstern) **8**:306
"El vómito" (Hearn) **9**:134
Von den Königen und der Krone (Huch) **13**:241, 243, 246, 249, 252
"Von der Armut und dem Tode" (Rilke) **195**:320
Von der Pilgerschaft (Rilke) **195**:265, 267
"Von deutscher Republik" (Mann) **168**:154, 176
Von heute auf morgen (Schoenberg) **75**:365, 371
Von Insel zu Insel (Weiss) **152**:282-85, 289
"Von Lust zu Lust" (Carossa) **48**:25
Von Morgens bis Mitternachts (Kaiser) **9**:171-75, 177, 179-81, 184-85, 187-89, 191-93
"Von Zeichnungen aus der Kokoschka-Mappe" (Arp) **115**:5
"The Voodoo of Hell's Half-Acre" (Wright) **136**:283
Voprosy literatury i estetiki (Bakhtin) **160**:135, 138, 183, 213
"Vor dem Föhn" (Morgenstern) **8**:305
"Vor dem gesetz" (Kafka) **47**:237; **179**:255, 289
"Vor dem Laden" (Beer-Hofmann) **60**:38
Vor dem Ruhestand (Bernhard) **165**:65, 71, 108
Vor egen stamme (Bojer) **64**:21, 23-24
Vor Sonnenaufgang (Hauptmann) **4**:192-93, 195-97, 209
La vorágine (Rivera) **35**:282-99
"Vorgefühl" (Rilke) **195**:182, 184
"Vorhang" (Kandinsky) **92**:67
Vorlesungen zur Einführung in die Psychoanalyse (Freud) **52**:84, 95
Vorlesungen zur Phänomenologie des innern Zeitbewusstseins (Husserl) **100**:10-11, 14, 40, 59
Vormorgen (Toller) **10**:480, 489-90
Voronezh Notebooks (Mandelstam) **6**:265
A vörös malom (Molnár) **20**:166-67, 170
"Vorspiel" (George) **2**:151
Vorspiel auf dem Theater zu "Köanig David" (Beer-Hofmann) **60**:34
"Die Vorstadt" (Heym) **9**:147
Vort rige (Bojer) **64**:2, 3-4, 15, 18, 22-23
The Vortex (Asturias) **184**:20
"The Vortex" (Kipling) **8**:201-02
The Vortex (Rivera)
See *La vorágine*
"Vorüber" (Raabe) **45**:189
"Vorüberziehende Wolke" (Broch) **20**:56-7
"Vos heyst 'neshome'" (Peretz) **16**:389-90
Voskhozhdeniia (Sologub) **9**:443
Voskresenie (Tolstoy) **4**:455, 458, 463, 468-69, 476-77, 480, 483; **11**:463, 471, 474-76, 478; **17**:384-85; **44**:334; **79**:338, 386, 398, 422, 440; **173**:278
Vos'mistishiia (Mandelstam) **2**:401
"Vospominanie" (Esenin) **4**:116
"Vospominanie" (Olesha) **136**:155
"Vospominaniya" (Tolstoy) **173**:294, 306, 321
Voss (White) **176**:130, 142-44, 146-48, 150-54, 156, 158, 165, 181-82, 185-93, 219, 235, 238-40, 246-47, 249-50, 301-2, 306-7, 309-11, 315-17
"Votes for Women" (Orage) **157**:251
Vouloir et pouvoir (Rod) **52**:324
Vous les entendez? (Sarraute) **145**:289, 317, 322, 344, 347-48
"The Vow" (Fletcher) **35**:107
"A Vow" (Ginsberg) **120**:39
A Vow Fulfilled (Dazai Osamu)
See *Mangan*
"The Vowels" (Fletcher) **35**:92
"Vox populi" (Söderberg) **39**:428, 437-38
"Voy a hablar de la esperanza" (Vallejo) **56**:300
"The Voyage" (Mansfield) **39**:303-04, 321, 329-30; **164**:266, 301-2, 304, 306, 310, 315-16, 339
"The Voyage" (Muir) **2**:485; **87**:189
The Voyage (Murry) **16**:355

The Voyage, and Other Poems (Muir) **87**:183
Voyage au centre de la terre (Verne) **6**:491-92, 499, 501, 504-05; **52**:333-34, 336-38, 341, 349, 352, 360
Voyage au Pays des Tarahumaras (Artaud)
See *D'un voyage au pays des Tarahumaras*
"A Voyage by Ballon" (Verne)
See "Un Voyage en ballon (réponse à l'enigme de juillet)"
Le Voyage dans la Lune (Verne) **6**:491
"Voyage de découverte" (Péret) **20**:184
Le voyage de Sparte (Barrès) **47**:48, 51, 53, 65, 81
"Le voyage des Dardanells" (Drieu la Rochelle) **21**:27-9
Le voyage d'Urien (Gide) **5**:224-25; **12**:143, 168, 176-77; **177**:4, 12
"Un Voyage en ballon (réponse à l'enigme de juillet)" (Verne) **52**:349
Le Voyage en calèche (Giono) **124**:49, 97
Voyage en Italie (Giono) **124**:115
Le voyage intérieur (Rolland) **23**:277, 282
Voyage musical à travers l'Europe du XVIII siècle (Rolland) **23**:267
Voyage musical aux pays du passé (Rolland) **23**:267
A Voyage of Consolation (Duncan) **60**:226, 230
The Voyage Out (Woolf) **1**:527-28, 531-32, 534-36, 542, 550; **5**:506, 509-10, 514-16; **20**:396-97, 405; **43**:395; **56**:363, 371-72; **128**:318, 327, 331-32, 335, 339, 341, 344, 348-49, 351, 353-54, 356-57, 361, 364-65, 372, 380
The Voyage That Never Ends (Lowry) **6**:241, 247
A Voyage to Arcturus (Lindsay) **15**:216-23, 225-28, 231-34, 236-43
Voyage to Faremido (Karinthy)
See *Utazás Faremidóba*
"Voyages" (Crane) **2**:117, 120, 122-25; **5**:188-94; **80**:97-8
"Voyages" (Jacob) **6**:199
Les voyages extraordinaires (Verne) **6**:497; **52**:337, 343, 348, 350, 352, 355-57, 359-61
"Voyages I: Poster" (Crane) **5**:189, 191-92
"Voyages II" (Crane) **5**:192-93; **80**:182
"Voyages III" (Crane) **5**:192-93
"Voyages IV" (Crane) **5**:193
"Voyages V" (Crane) **5**:193
"Voyages VI" (Crane) **5**:193
"Le voyageur" (Apollinaire) **3**:37, 39, 44; **51**:61
"The Voyageur" (Drummond) **25**:143, 145
Le voyageur sans bagage (Anouilh) **195**:6, 8, 10, 13, 18, 25, 27, 33, 38, 46
Les voyageurs de l'impériale (Aragon) **123**:143
Voyageuses (Bourget) **12**:68
Voyna v myshelovke (Khlebnikov) **20**:137, 140
"Voyna-smert" (Khlebnikov) **20**:131-32
The Voysey Inheritance (Granville-Barker) **2**:192-97, 199
La voz a ti debida (Salinas) **17**:354, 359-63, 365-69
"Voz de esperanza" (Huidobro) **31**:133
"Voz de la sangre" (Pardo Bazán) **189**:290, 292-93
Vozmezdie (Blok) **5**:85
"Vozrashchenie vozhdia" (Tsvetaeva) **35**:412
"Vozvrashchenie" (Gumilev) **60**:280
Vozvrashchenie Chorba (Nabokov) **108**:83, 146
Vozvrashchyonnaya molodost' (Zoshchenko) **15**:492, 502, 504-05, 511-13
Vozvrat: Tretiia simfoniia (Bely) **7**:57-8
"Vracar polje" (Popa) **167**:160
La vraie religion selon Pascal (Sully Prudhomme) **31**:307
Les Vraies Richesses (Giono) **124**:45, 47-48, 93, 95-96, 99, 103-4
"Vrati mi moje krpice" (Popa) **167**:154-55
"Vrazhdebnoe more" (Kuzmin) **40**:216
"Vridar Hunter" (Fisher) **140**:149, 160, 165, 167-68
"Vrolik landschap" (van Ostaijen) **33**:418
"Vrsacka kolica" (Popa) **167**:164
"Vrsacki idol" (Popa) **167**:164
"Vsadnik" (Kuzmin) **40**:216
"Vse napevy" (Bryusov) **10**:81
"A vse-taki" (Mayakovski) **10**:256
"Vstreča" (Zabolotsky) **52**:367
"Vstreča" (Zamyatin) **8**:553
Vtoraia simfoniia: Dramaticheskaia (Bely) **7**:48-9, 57-8
Vtoraya kniga (Mandelstam) **2**:401, 406-09; **6**:259, 265-66
Vtoraya kniga (Zabolotsky) **52**:365
Vtornik Meri (Kuzmin) **40**:200
Vučja so (Popa) **167**:160, 163, 172
"Vucja zemlja" (Popa) **167**:162
"Vucje kopile" (Popa) **167**:162
"Vucje oci" (Popa) **167**:163
"Vucje poreklo" (Popa) **167**:164
La vue (Roussel) **20**:228, 230-31, 234, 240, 243, 253
La vuelta al mundo de un novelista (Blasco Ibáñez) **12**:43
La vuelta al mundo en la Numancia (Pérez Galdós) **27**:283
"La vuelta de la cumbre" (Unamuno) **148**:311
"Vuelta de paseo" (García Lorca) **49**:80, 121; **197**:183, 200, 217, 223, 230, 258, 273, 278-79
"Vuk as a Writer" (Andrić) **135**:40
Vulcani (Marinetti) **10**:317
The Vulgar Streak (Lewis) **2**:386-87, 389, 391; **9**:238, 246; **104**:189-90, 214-16,
"Vultur aura" (Hearn) **9**:133
"Vulture" (Abbey) **160**:43
"Vultures of Whapeton" (Howard) **8**:128
"Vulturne" (Fargue) **11**:194, 196, 200
VV (Cummings)
See *ViVa*
Vyasi and Valmiki (Aurobindo) **63**:26
"Vybor" (Gumilev) **60**:278
Vybor nesty (Kuzmin) **40**:201
Vyorsty I (Tsvetaeva) **7**:557, 559-61; **35**:381, 390, 394, 399, 408-11, 415
Vyorsty II (Tsvetaeva) **35**:410-11, 415
Vzvikhrennaia Rus (Remizov) **27**:348-49
"W" (Schwitters) **95**:346
W (Cummings) **137**:47, 49
W. C. (Bataille) **155**:129
W. C. Fields by Himself: His Intended Autobiography (Fields) **80**:243
W. D. Freund and Sons Dairy Farms . . . (Gardner) **195**:105
W pustyni i puszczy (Sienkiewicz) **3**:424
Wa ga haiku (Masaoka) **18**:230, 236
"Die Waage der Baleks" (Böll) **185**:27-8, 31, 52-3
"Das Wachsfigurenka binett" (Meyrink) **21**:218, 221, 223, 232
"Wading at Wellfleet" (Bishop) **121**:9
Waffen für Amerika (Feuchtwanger) **3**:179, 182-83, 186
"Der Waffengefährte" (George) **14**:201
"Waga Uta" (Yosano) **59**:328
Wagahai wa neko de aru (Natsume) **2**:490-91, 493, 495; **10**:328, 331-32, 336, 338, 344, 347-48
"The Wage Slave" (Service) **15**:406
"Wages" (de la Mare) **53**:22-3
The Wages of Men and Women: Should They Be Equal? (Webb and Webb) **22**:413
"Wagner" (Brooke) **2**:59
"A Wagner Concert" (Cather) **1**:153; **11**:92, 101-02; **99**:266
"A Wagner Matinée" (Cather) **11**:92, 101-02; **99**:266; **132**:132, 147; **152**:16
"Wagner's Aktualitat" (Adorno) **111**:44-5
Wahrheit? (Heyse) **8**:119
Wahrheit und Wissenschaft (Steiner) **13**:454
"Wahrscheinliches, Unwahrscheinliches" (Bernhard) **165**:106
"A Waif of the Plains" (Harte) **25**:213
Waifs (Moricz)
See *Árvalányok*
"Wail" (Parker) **143**:320
"The Wail of the Wandering Dead" (Markham) **47**:278
"Wailing Well" (James) **6**:216
"A Waist" (Stein) **48**:254
"The Waistcoat" (Prus)
See "Kamizelka"
Wait No Longer (Drieu la Rochelle) **21**:39
"Waiting" (Baker) **10**:26
"Waiting" (Davidson) **24**:164
"Waiting" (Ledwidge) **23**:109
"Waiting" (Tynan) **3**:503
"Waiting at the Window" (Milne) **88**:260
"Waiting Both" (Hardy) **143**:148
Waiting for Daylight (Tomlinson) **71**:383, 386, 391, 397, 406
Waiting for Godot (Beckett)
See *En attendant Godot*
Waiting for Supper (Hardy) **4**:217
"Waiting for the Barbarians" (Cavafy) **2**:89, 94; **7**:152-53, 155, 158, 164
"Waiting for the Bugle" (Higginson) **36**:179
Waiting for the Verdict (Davis) **6**:148, 151-53
Waiting on God (Weil)
See *L'attente de Dieu*
"The Waiting Room" (Hansen) **32**:249
"Waiting Rooms" (Nemerov) **124**:210, 259
The Waiting-Room (Feuchtwanger) **3**:178
Wakai (Shiga) **172**:202, 207-10, 212-18
Wakai: Kozo no kamisama (Shiga)
See *Wakai*
"Wakakarishi hi no Toho" (Nishida) **83**:215
Wakanashū (Shimazaki Toson) **5**:434, 438-39
"Wake Up, England" (Bridges) **1**:125
"Wake Up/Ring Out" (García Lorca)
See "Amanecer y repique"
"Wakeupworld" (Cullen) **4**:44
Waking World (Stapledon) **22**:314, 322
"Der Wald" (Walser) **18**:428
"Wald im Winter" (Carossa) **48**:21
Waldo Trench and Others: Stories of Americans in Italy (Fuller) **103**:59, 63, 65, 86
"Waldo Trench Regains His Youth" (Fuller) **103**:114
"Wales" (Johnson) **19**:242
Wales (Thomas) **10**:449
"Wales Visitation" (Ginsberg) **120**:4, 77, 129-30
"The Walk" (Donoso)
See "Paseo"
"The Walk" (Hardy) **53**:105; **143**:197
"The Walk" (Walser) **18**:416, 437-38
"Walk Around My Birthplace" (Ady)
See "Séta bölcső-helyem körül"
"A Walk in the Desert Hills" (Abbey) **160**:41-42
Walk in the Light While There Is Light (Tolstoy) **4**:476
"A Walk in the Night" (La Guma) **140**:206-8
A Walk in the Night, and Other Stories (La Guma) **140**:196-97, 199-200, 202, 209, 211, 215, 220-27, 229, 233-34, 239-41, 244-46, 254, 256, 272-73
"Walk On, Condemned!" (Radnóti)
See "Járkálj csak, halálraitélt!"
Walk On, Condemned! (Radnóti) **16**:414
A Walk to an Ant Hill, and other Essays (Bengtsson) **48**:4, 13
"A Walk up the Avenue" (Davis) **24**:199
Walker, London (Barrie) **2**:42-3; **164**:5
"The Walker of Prague" (Nezval)
See "Pražký chodec"
Walker of the Secret Service (Post) **39**:344-45
"Walking All Night" (Merrill) **173**:256
Walking Back (Stroheim) **71**:339
"Walking Blues" (Johnson) **69**:77
"A Walking Delegate" (Kipling) **17**:209
Walking Down Broadway (Stroheim) **71**:333, 341, 362-363
"Walking Down Main Street" (Allen) **87**:37, 41, 50

"Walking Down Westgate in the Fall" (Nemerov) **124**:259, 302
"Walking on Water" (Dickey) **151**:169
"Walking Out" (Beckett) **145**:202
"Walking the Dog" (Nemerov) **124**:291, 293, 300
"Walking through Meadows . . ." (Warner) **131**:311
Die Walküre (Firbank) **1**:224
The Wall (Andreyev) **3**:21, 23, 26
The Wall (Rinehart) **52**:284, 290, 292, 299, 302-03
"The Wall and the Books" (Borges)
See "La muralla y los libros"
"The Wall and the Shadows" (Sologub) **9**:445-47
"The Wall Street Pit" (Markham) **47**:282
Walled In: A Novel (Phelps) **113**:340-41
Walled Towns (Cram) **45**:15-16, 21
Wallenstein (Döblin) **13**:160, 162, 174, 180
"Waller im Schnee" (George) **14**:210, 213
The Wallet of Kai Lung (Bramah) **72**:2, 4-12
"Wallflower's Lament" (Parker) **143**:334
"The Walls Are Cold" (Capote) **164**:99-100, 102-3
"The Walls of Jericho" (Dunbar) **2**:133; **12**:107
The Walls of Jericho (Fisher) **11**:203-08, 213-14
The Walls of Jericho (Sutro) **6**:419-23
Wälsungenblut (Mann) **2**:429-30, 433; **14**:358-59; **168**:157, 186
"Walt Whitman" (Jiménez) **183**:330
"Walt Whitman" (Robinson) **101**:196
"Walt Whitman, 1819-1919" (Andrić) **135**:79
"Walt Whitman Miniatures" (Morley) **87**:127
"Walt Whitman's Children" (Carpenter) **88**:143
"Walter Knox's Record" (Chesnutt) **39**:98
"Walter Pater" (Johnson) **19**:244
Walter Sickert: A Conversation (Woolf) **128**:326
"The Waltz" (Aleixandre)
See "El vals"
"The Waltz" (Parker) **143**:285, 287-89, 291, 314-15, 332, 334
The Waltz Invention (Nabokov)
See *Izobretenie Val'sa*
The Waltz of the Toreadors (Anouilh)
See *La valse des toréadors*
"Waltzing Matilda" (Paterson) **32**:372-73, 378-80
Wanda (Ouida) **43**:352-53, 357, 366
"Wanda Hickey's Night of Golden Memories" (Shepherd) **177**:304, 308
Wanda Hickey's Night of Golden Memories, and Other Disasters (Shepherd) **177**:295-96, 299, 304-5, 315
Wanderbilder (Haeckel) **83**:147
"The Wanderer" (Brennan) **17**:39-42, 44, 46, 48-53, 55-7, 60
"The Wanderer" (Dobson) **79**:7, 37
"The Wanderer" (Grahame) **136**:38
"The Wanderer" (Leino)
See "Vaeltaja"
"Der Wanderer" (Rilke) **195**:284
The Wanderer (Alain-Fournier)
See *Le grand meaulnes*
The Wanderer (Gibran) **9**:89, 92
The Wanderer (Goebbels) **68**:103
A Wanderer among Pictures: A Companion to the Galleries of Europe (Lucas) **73**:157
The Wanderer and His Shadow (Nietzsche) **10**:367; **55**:369
A Wanderer in Holland (Lucas) **73**:162
A Wanderer in London (Lucas) **73**:157, 162, 165, 170
Wanderer, kommst du nach Spa . . . (Böll) **185**:26
Wanderer of the Wasteland (Grey) **6**:186
A Wanderer Plays on Muted Strings (Hamsun)
See *En vandrer spiller med sordin*
"The Wanderers" (Lewis) **3**:285
"The Wanderers" (Stringer) **37**:341
The Wanderers (Hamsun)
See *Landstrykere*
"The Wanderer's Song" (Hagiwara)
See "Hyōhakusha no uta"
A Wanderer's Songs (Vazov) **25**:453
"Wandering Clouds" (Södergran)
See "Irrande moln"
Wandering Ghosts (Crawford) **10**:149, 152
Wandering Heath (Quiller-Couch) **53**:290
"The Wandering Jew" (Apollinaire)
See "L'Hérésiarque"
"The Wandering Jew" (Robinson) **5**:407, 409, 417; **101**:102, 127, 164, 167-72
The Wandering Jew (Buchanan) **107**:19-20
The Wandering Jew, and Other Stories (Apollinaire)
See *L'hérésiarque et cie*
The Wandering Lady (Baroja)
See *La dama errante*
Wandering Off the Point (Garro)
See *Andarse por las ramas*
Wandering Stars (Aleichem)
See *Blondzhnde shtern*
"Wanderinger Singers" (Naidu) **80**:290
"Wanderings" (Nezval)
See "Procházky"
Wanderings (Grove)
See *Wanderungen*
The Wanderings of a Spiritualist (Doyle) **7**:225
"The Wanderings of Oisin" (Yeats) **11**:513, 526
The Wanderings of Oisin, and Other Poems (Yeats) **11**:507-09, 511; **18**:441-42, 456; **116**:330, 334, 336
"Wanderlied" (Pickthall) **21**:252
Wanderungen (Grove) **4**:143-44
Die Wandlung (Toller) **10**:474, 477, 479-81, 483, 485-87, 489-90, 492
Die Wandlungen Gottes (Barlach) **84**:73
"Wanted by the Police" (Lawson) **27**:132
"Wapping Alice" (Twain) **185**:322
"War" (Apollinaire) **8**:20
"The War" (Heym)
See "Der Krieg"
"A War" (Jarrell) **177**:195
"War" (Sterling) **20**:386
War (Artsybashev) **31**:9-11
War (Sologub)
See *Voina*
"War after War" (Ingamells) **35**:131
The War and Elizabeth (Ward) **55**:437, 442, 446
"War and Peace" (Mayakovski) **18**:261
War and Peace (Neumann) **100**:318-19
War and Peace (Tolstoy)
See *Voina i mir*
War and Self-Determination (Aurobindo) **63**:32, 33
The War and Spiritual Decisions (Simmel) **64**:338
"War and the Intellectuals" (Bourne) **16**:44
"War and the World" (Mayakovski) **4**:288, 291-92, 296
War As I Knew It (Patton) **79**:281, 309
"War Ballad" (Nezval) **44**:249
"War Books" (Gurney) **33**:87-8
War Bulletins (Lindsay) **17**:236
The War Chief (Burroughs) **2**:79-80, 85-6
War Diary (Thomas) **10**:464
War er es? (Zweig) **17**:458
The War for the World (Zangwill) **16**:461
War Games (Morris) **107**:124, 157-98, 203, 206-11
The War God (Zangwill) **16**:445, 461, 466
The War Goes On (Asch)
See *Auf'n opgrunt*
The War in a Mousetrap (Khlebnikov)
See *Voyna v myshelovke*
The War in Eastern Europe (Reed) **9**:387, 389
"War in Ethiopia" (Bishop) **121**:87
War in Heaven (Williams) **11**:487, 489, 493, 496-97
The War in Spain (Sender) **136**:216-17
The War in the Air and Particularly How Mr. Bert Smallways Fared While It Lasted (Wells) **6**:534; **12**:506; **19**:426, 442
"War Is Kind" (Crane) **11**:130
"War Is the Only Cure for the World" (Marinetti) **10**:325
War Memoirs (Churchill) **113**:182-85 87
"War Memories" (Crane) **11**:128, 135, 143; **32**:165
"War of Attrition" (Toller)
See "Stellungskrieg"
The War of the Air (Wells)
See *The War in the Air and Particularly How Mr. Bert Smallways Fared While It Lasted*
The War of the Classes (London) **9**:254, 265; **39**:278, 280
"The War of the Wall" (Bambara) **116**:15
The War of the Worlds (Wells) **6**:523-24, 535, 539, 542-44; **12**:488, 506, 509-10, 514-16; **19**:422, 424-25, 428-29, 434-36, 438-46, 453; **133**:231, 239-40, 244, 284, 299, 303-4, 325, 327, 339
War on the Plains (Ince) **89**:9
War on Venus (Burroughs) **32**:59
War Party (Faust)
See *Call of the Blood*
War, Peace, and Change (Dulles) **72**:77, 115
"War Poems" (Bell) **43**:88
War Poems (Hardy) **53**:100
"War Profit Litany" (Ginsberg) **120**:38, 72
"War Song" (Davidson) **24**:164
"War Song" (Parker) **143**:317
"War Songs" (Palamas) **5**:386
War Stories (Nemerov) **124**:304-5
The War That Will End War (Wells) **12**:503, 515; **19**:451
"The War, the Death" (Khlebnikov)
See "Voyna-smert"
"War to the Knife" (Graham) **19**:112
War with the Newts (Čapek)
See *Válka s mloky*
"The War Wound" (Dickey) **151**:90, 172, 217
"A Ward in the States" (Jarrell) **177**:155
"Ward No. Six" (Chekhov)
See "Palata No. 6"
"Ward O 3 b" (Lewis) **3**:287-89
"A Ward of the Golden Gate" (Harte) **25**:223
"The Wardrobe" (Mann) **14**:353
"The Warf" (de la Mare) **53**:14-5, 27, 31, 33, 36
The Warlord of Mars (Burroughs) **2**:80; **32**:58, 66, 68-70
"A Warm Thought Flickers" (Rosenberg) **12**:299, 311
"Warning" (Baker) **10**:27
"The Warning" (Lindsay) **17**:240
"Warning: Children at Play" (Nemerov) **124**:273
Warning to Hikers (Butts) **77**:106
"A Warning to the Curious" (James) **6**:206, 212
"A Warning to the People" (Lu Hsun) **3**:303-04
Warren Hastings, Gouverneur von Indien (Feuchtwanger) **3**:181
"The Warrior" (Eastman) **55**:170-71
"The Warrior" (McCrae) **12**:211
The Warrior's Barrow (Ibsen) **2**:239; **37**:243
War's Embers, and Other Verses (Gurney) **33**:80-2, 85-7, 90, 94, 96, 107, 109, 112
Wars I Have Seen (Stein) **1**:430-31; **6**:412; **28**:313-14, 329, 335, **48**:249
Warsaw (Asch) **3**:67-8
Warsaw Visitor (Saroyan) **137**:172-81, 186, 188
"The War-Song of Gamelbar" (Carman) **7**:133
Der Wartesaal-Trilogie (Feuchtwanger) **3**:181, 186-87
"Wartime Stories" (Calvino) **183**:224
Wartime Writings (Saint-Exupéry)
See *Ecrits de guerre*
"Warum?" (Kandinsky) **92**:69
"Warum mein Gott" (Werfel) **8**:477
The War-Workers (Delafield) **61**:125, 127
"Was" (Faulkner) **141**:103; **170**:162, 213, 244

"Was bedeutet: Aufarbeitung der Vergangenheit" (Adorno) **111**:51
"Was heute links sein könnte" (Böll) **185**:41
"Was ich in Rom sah und hörte" (Bachmann) **192**:140
"Was It Heaven? Or Hell?" (Twain) **19**:393
Was It Love? (Bourget)
See *Un crime d'amour*
Was soll aus dem Jungen bloß werden? (Böll) **185**:103, 134
Was wird man sagen? (Herzl) **36**:132
"The Washer of the Ford" (Sharp) **39**:375
The Washer of the Ford, and Other Legendary Moralities (Sharp) **39**:354, 362, 364, 373
"The Washerwoman" (Huysmans) **69**:25
"The Washerwoman" (Khlebnikov)
See "Prachka"
"Washerwoman's Day" (Arnow) **196**:88-9
"Washing" (Jarrell) **177**:149
Washington Square (James) **11**:344; **40**:120, 133; **47**:206; **64**:149, 158-59, 184
"Washington's Birth-Day" (Pyle) **81**:390
Wasps (Evans) **85**:5, 12
"Wasser" (Kandinsky) **92**:67, 92
"The Wasserman Reaction" (Pasternak)
See "Vassermanova reaktsiia"
"Waste" (Baker) **3**:9
Waste (Granville-Barker) **2**:194-97, 199-200
"A Wastrel's Romance" (Freeman) **21**:51
"Wasure-enu Hitobito" (Kunikida Doppo) **99**:299, 302, 304
"Wat is er met Picasso" (van Ostaijen) **33**:412
"Watakushi no kojinshugi" (Natsume) **10**:347
"Watakushi no mono" (Endo) **152**:202, 214
"Watakushi no ronri ni tsuite" (Nishida) **83**:323
"Watakushi to nanji" (Nishida) **83**:363
Watashi no aishita shosetsu (Endo) **152**:235, 237-38
The Watch (Levi)
See *L'Orologio*
Watch and Ward (James) **2**:269; **47**:205
"The Watch at Midnight" (Brennan) **17**:47
"Watch at Midnight" (Toller)
See "Verweilen um Mitternacht"
Watch It Come Down (Osborne) **153**:239, 242, 312, 314
Watch on the Rhine (Hellman) **119**:123, 142-43, 146-53, 164-65, 175-76, 178-79, 197, 212, 214, 235
"The Watcher" (Rilke)
See "Der Schauende"
"The Watcher" (Torrence) **97**:158
The Watcher and Other Stories (Calvino)
See *La giornata d'uno scrutatore*
"A Watcher by the Dead" (Bierce) **7**:88-9; **44**:12, 44-5, 47-8
"The Watcher by the Threshold" (Buchan) **41**:73
The Watcher by the Threshold, and Other Tales (Buchan) **41**:35, 37, 73
"Watchers at the Strait Gate" (Kirk) **119**:281, 332, 335, 337
Watchers at the Strait Gate (Kirk) **119**:281, 283, 292-93, 334, 342
Watchers of the Sky (Noyes) **7**:504, 506-07, 513
Watchers of Twilight, and Other Poems (Stringer) **37**:327, 329-30
"Watching Football on TV" (Nemerov) **124**:210, 261
The Watchmaker's Wife (Stockton) **47**:314
"The Watchman" (Colette) **16**:128
"The Watchman" (Millett) **51**:209
The Watchman, and Other Poems (Montgomery) **51**:196, 204, 207
"Watchman, What of the Night?" (Zangwill) **16**:446
"Water" (Abbey) **160**:45, 95
"Water" (Kandinsky)
See "Wasser"
"Water" (Toomer) **172**:273
Water and Dreams: An Essay on the Imagination of Matter (Bachelard)
See *L'Eau et les Reves: Essai sur l'imagination de la matière*
The Water Color Painter (Shimazaki Toson)
See *Suisaigaka*
The Water Hen (Witkiewicz) **8**:507-08, 513-15
"The Water Hyacinth" (Merrill) **173**:257
"The Water Hyacinth" (Naidu) **80**:315
"Water Lilies" (Higginson) **36**:175, 186
Water Lilies (Jiménez)
See *Ninfeas*
"The Water Lily" (Scott) **6**:391-92
"The Water Lord" (Baker) **47**:17
"The Water Mill" (Jensen)
See "Vandmøllen"
"Water Music" (Lewis) **3**:290
"Water Noises" (Roberts) **68**:336
"The Water of the Lake Bay" (Lagerloef) **36**:240
Water on the Brain (Mackenzie) **116**:228, 232-35, 237-39, 248-49
"The Water Ouzel" (Muir) **28**:251
"Water Sleep" (Wylie) **8**:521
"The Water-sprites' Tale" (Čapek)
See "Pohádka vodnická"
Water Street (Merrill) **173**:171, 175, 207-11, 225-27, 251, 257-59
"Water Them Geraniums" (Lawson) **27**:121, 145-47
Water Unlimited (Roberts) **23**:240
Watercolor (No. 13) (Kandinsky) **92**:38
"The Watercress Girl" (Coppard) **5**:181
"The Water-Devil: A Marine Tale" (Stockton) **47**:317, 324
"The Waterfall" (Hardy) **53**:93
"The Waterfall" (Södergran)
See "Vattenfallet"
The Waterfall (Tagore)
See *Muktadhārā*
"Water-Fence" (Coffin) **95**:22
"Waterfront Fanciers" (Hecht) **101**:38
"The Water-Lily" (Lawson) **27**:134, 140
Waterloo Bridge (Sherwood) **3**:410, 412, 415-16, 418
Waterloo Bridge (Whale) **63**:339, 340, 345, 378, 380
"Watermaid" (Okigbo) **171**:356
De Waterman (van Schendel) **56**:238-39
"The Watermelon" (Bagritsky) **60**:16
The Waters of Edera (Ouida) **43**:368
"The Waters of Strife" (Somerville & Ross) **51**:357, 381, 383
"The Watershed" (Meynell) **6**:299
"Watkwenies" (Scott) **6**:393
Watt (Beckett) **145**:77-78, 82, 90, 93-94, 142, 183, 185-88, 190-91, 193-94, 199, 203
Watten: Ein Nachlass (Bernhard) **165**:38
The Watter's Mou' (Stoker) **8**:384
"Wav and the Universe" (Mayakovski) **18**:250-51, 270
The Wave (Blackwood) **5**:71-2
"The Wave of Osiris" (Lagerkvist) **144**:156
"Wave of the Night" (Benn)
See "Welle der Nacht"
"The Wave Song" (Cram) **45**:12
"The Waveless Bay" (Gogarty) **15**:101, 109
"Waverer's tale" (Calvino) **183**:124
Wavering (Kandinsky) **92**:32
The Waves (Woolf) **1**:531, 533, 535, 537-40, 542-46, 550; **5**:509-12, 516-17; **20**:397, 419; **43**:388; **56**:361, 374-75, 379-80, 392; **101**:205, 227, 274, 276, 278, 293, 326; **128**:318, 331-32, 337-38, 340-41, 344, 359, 363-66, 372, 374, 382, 385
Waves Striking the Sky (Rohan)
See *Sora utsu nami*
"The Waxwork Museum" (Leroux) **25**:260
Waxworks (Molnár) **20**:171
"The Way" (Muir) **87**:178
"The Way" (Nemerov) **124**:258
"The Way a Novel Gets Written" (Cary) **196**:196
"The Way Back" (Lewis) **3**:291-92
Way Down East (Griffith) **68**:151, 153, 168-69, 172, 183, 214
"Way Down on Lonesome Cove" (Murfree) **135**:205, 223
The Way Home: Being the Second Part of the Chronicle of the Fortunes of Richard Mahony (Richardson) **4**:373, 382
"The Way I Look at Su Qing" (Chang) **184**:146
"The Way it Came" (James) **47**:200
The Way of a Man (Dixon) **163**:169, 172
"The Way of a Woman" (Dunbar) **12**:120
The Way of All Flesh (Butler) **1**:134-36, 138-39; **33**:26-7, 29-33, 37-8, 41-9, 51-4, 58-63, 70, 73
The Way of Ambition (Hichens) **64**:127
The Way of an Indian (Remington) **89**:300, 311
The Way of Ecben (Cabell) **6**:68
The Way of Evil (Deledda)
See *La via del male*
"A Way of Life" (Nemerov) **124**:148, 177
The Way of the Animal Powers (Campbell)
See *The Historical Atlas of World Mythology*
The Way of the Conquistadors (Gumilev)
See *Put' konkvistadorov*
"Way of the Cross" (Cankar) **105**:162
"The Way of the Earth" (Evans) **85**:11, 22
The Way of the Grain (Khodasevich) **15**:200, 208, 210-12, 214
The Way of the Happy One (Lagerkvist)
See *Den lyckliges väg*
The Way of the Seeded Earth (Campbell)
See *The Historical Atlas of World Mythology*
The Way of the Spirit (Haggard) **11**:253, 256
The Way of the World (Baroja)
See *El mundo es ansí*
The Way of These Women (Oppenheim) **45**:128
The Way Out (Heijermans) **24**:292-93
"The way that Lovers use is this" (Brooke) **7**:122
The Way Things Are (Delafield) **61**:127
The Way through Hell (Tolstoy) **18**:359-60
"The Way through the Woods" (Kipling) **8**:191, 200
"De Way T'ings Come" (Dunbar) **12**:104
The Way to Perfection (Baroja)
See *Camino de perfección*
"The Way to the Churchyard" (Mann) **2**:432
The Way to Victory (Tolstoy) **18**:383
"The Way up to Heaven" (Dahl) **173**:14
"The Wayfarer" (Sharp) **39**:376
The Wayfarer (Natsume)
See *Kōjin*
Wayfarer: A Voice from the Southern Mountains (Dickey) **151**:167-68
Wayfarers (Hamsun)
See *Landstrykere*
"Wayfaring" (Carman) **7**:141
"The Ways of Death Are Soothing and Serene" (Henley) **8**:108
"The Ways of Ghosts" (Bierce) **44**:14, 45
"Ways of War" (Johnson) **19**:230, 241
Wayside Crosses (Čapek)
See *Boži muka*
The Wayside Fire (Sologub)
See *Koster dorozhnyi*
Wayside Grasses (Balmont) **11**:32
A Wayside Lute (Reese) **181**:339, 347
The Wayward and the Seeking: A Collection of Writings by Jean Toomer (Toomer) **172**:265, 310, 313, 315
The Wayward Bus (Steinbeck) **135**:250, 252, 349
The Wayzgoose (Campbell) **5**:119-20, 122-23
We Accept with Pleasure (De Voto) **29**:126
"We and You" (Gibran) **9**:93
"We Are" (Éluard)
See "Nous sommes"

We Are Betrayed (Fisher) **140**:155, 165, 169, 182, 185
"We Are Going to Conserve Soil, Conserve Water, Conserve Life" (Roosevelt) **93**:184
"We Are Going to Win the War and We Are Going to Win the Peace That Follows" (Roosevelt) **93**:184
"We Also Have the Minister of Death" (Arenas)
See "También tenemos el Ministerio de la Muerte"
"We Are Introduced to Winnie-the-Pooh and Some Bees, and the Stories Begin" (Milne) **6**:321
"We Are Marching to Conquer the Future" (Redcam) **25**:330
"We Are Moving Forward to Greater Freedom, to Greater Security for the Average Man" (Roosevelt) **93**:184
We Are Not Alone (Hilton) **21**:97
"We Are on Our Way, and We Are Headed in the Right Direction" (Roosevelt) **93**:184
We Bombed in New Haven (Heller) **131**:22; **151**:320
"We Do All the Dirty Work" (Cohan) **60**:168
We Do Not Know How (Pirandello)
See *Non si sa come*
We Have Always Lived in the Castle (Jackson) **187**:235, 237-38, 241-43, 251, 256-57, 259, 273-74, 280, 284-85, 288, 295-97, 313, 316, 318
"We Have Been Believers" (Walker) **129**:297-98, 305, 327-29
"We Have Come" (Gumilev)
See "My prishli"
"We Jews" (Kolmar)
See "Wir Juden"
We Live Again (Sturges) **48**:285, 311
"We Lying by Seasand" (Thomas) **45**:362
We Moderns (Zangwill) **16**:446
We Moderns: Enigmas and Guesses (Muir) **2**:481; **87**:162
"We moya!" (Vilakazi) **37**:402, 407
"We Must Keep on Striking Our Enemies Wherever and Whenever We Can Meet Them" (Roosevelt) **93**:184
"We Need a Union Too" (Childress) **116**:36
We Others (Barbusse)
See *Nous autres*
"We Refugees" (Arendt) **193**:77, 153-54
"We See the Future through the Binoculars of the People" (Burroughs) **121**:142
We Stand United, and Other Radio Plays (Benét) **7**:77
"We That Were Friends" (Flecker) **43**:194
We Want to Live (Bergelson) **81**:23
"We Wear the Mask" (Dunbar) **2**:129; **12**:121, 124-25
"We were not made for refuges of lies" (Coleridge) **73**:12
"We Who Praise Poets" (Gurney) **33**:97
We Will Never Die (Hecht) **101**:90
The Weakened Fetish (Rozanov) **104**:345
The Weaker Sex (Pinero) **32**:398, 405, 412
"Wealth" (Lawrence) **93**:25
"Wealth Won't Save Your Soul" (Williams) **81**:430
Wealthy Red Shlome (Asch)
See *Reb Shloyme nogid*
"Weaning the Baby" (Guest) **95**:213
"Weariness" (Baker) **10**:27
"Weary Blues from Waitin" (Williams) **81**:428
"A Weary Hour" (Mann) **35**:215
A Weary Hour (Mann)
See *Schwere Stunde*
"The Weary Man" (Jozsef) **22**:160
"Weary was I of toil and strife" (Coleridge) **73**:21
"The Weary Wedding" (Swinburne) **8**:427
"The Weather" (Jerome) **23**:77
"The Weather of the World" (Nemerov) **124**:260
"Weather Prophet" (Bosman) **49**:16
The Weather Shelter (Caldwell) **117**:21
The Weathervane Plant (Miyamoto)
See *Fūchisō*
The Weavers (Hauptmann)
See *Die Weber*
The Web (O'Neill) **49**:274, 284
The Web and the Rock (Wolfe) **4**:513-14, 516, 520, 525, 531-32, 537, 539; **13**:470-71, 473-74, 479, 486, 495; **29**:405, 409; **61**:299, 312
"The Web of Circumstance" (Chesnutt) **5**:131; **39**:70, 83-4, 94, 98
"The Web of Earth" (Wolfe) **4**:519, 526-27; **13**:386, 492
"The Web of Life" (Nemerov) **124**:159, 231
Der Web zur Macht (Mann) **9**:327
Die Weber (Hauptmann) **4**:193-95, 197, 204, 207, 209
"Webster" (Brooke) **2**:53
"Webster Ford" (Masters) **25**:315
The Wedding (Canetti)
See *Die Hochzeit*
The Wedding (Chekhov)
See *Svadba*
"The Wedding" (Dickey) **151**:97
"The Wedding" (Kuprin) **5**:298
"Wedding" (Pasternak) **188**:182, 184-85, 187
The Wedding (West) **108**:314-15, 327-29
Wedding Band: A Love/Hate Story in Black and White (Childress) **116**:18-20, 23, 26-30, 33, 38, 45, 47-8
"A Wedding Chest" (Lee) **5**:319
"A Wedding Dress" (Callaghan) **145**:255-56
"The Wedding Feast" (Moore) **7**:494
The Wedding Feast (Canetti)
See *Die Hochzeit*
The Wedding March (Bjoernson) **7**:105-06
The Wedding March (Stroheim) **71**:330-332, 335-336, 340, 357-358, 361-364, 366
"Wedding Morn" (Lawrence) **93**:45, 46, 49
"The Wedding Morning" (Ledwidge) **23**:112, 117
The Wedding on the Eiffel Tower (Cocteau)
See *Les mariés de la Tour Eiffel*
"The Wedding Party" (Pasternak) **188**:195
"Wedding Preparations" (Kafka) **13**:284
"Wedding Preparations in the Country" (Kafka)
See "Hochzeitsvorbereitungen auf dem Lande"
Weddings in the House (Hrabal)
See *Svatby v domě*
"Wedlock" (Lawrence) **93**:49
Wedlock (Wassermann)
See *Laudin und die Seinen*
Wee Willie Winkie and other Stories (Kipling) **8**:184
"The Weed" (Bishop) **121**:6, 71
The Weedkiller's Daughter (Arnow) **196**:28-9, 38-9, 78-9, 90, 93, 95-9, 101
"Weeds" (Čapek) **37**:45
"Weeds" (Carpenter) **88**:97-8
"Weeds" (Millay) **4**:306
Weeds (Baroja)
See *Mala hierba*
Weedscapes (Santoka)
See *Zasso fukei*
"A Week in Turenevo" (Tolstoy) **18**:367-68, 377
A Week in Turenevo, and Other Stories (Tolstoy) **18**:367
Week-end in Guatemala (Asturias) **184**:16, 45
"A Weekend in the Middle of the Week, and Other Essays on the Bias" (Gogarty) **15**:106
Weekly Chronicles (Prus)
See *Kroniki tugodniowe*
"Weeknight Service" (Lawrence) **93**:44, 46
"Weep Not My Wanton" (Coppard) **5**:176
"Weep, You Zulus" (Vilakazi)
See "Khalani maZulu"
"Weeping beneath Life's Tree" (Ady) **11**:14
Der Weg der Verheissung (Werfel) **8**:469, 473, 479
Der Weg ins Freie (Schnitzler) **4**:391, 394, 398
Der Weg nach Innen (Hesse) **196**:237
"Die weggeworfene Flinte" (Morgenstern) **8**:310
Wegrath (Schnitzler) **4**:389
"Wegweiser" (Arp) **115**:39, 41-2
Wegweiser (Arp) **115**:4
"Der Wegwerfer" (Böll) **185**:27
Der Wegwerfer (Böll) **185**:138-42
Wegwartten (Rilke) **195**:180
"Weibe Nächte" (Huch) **13**:249
"Die Weiblichkeit" (Freud) **52**:107, 109
"Das Weiche" (Kandinsky) **92**:67
"Die weiße Qualle" (Ball) **104**:8, 76
"Weight without love" (Aleixandre) **113**:57
Weights and Measures (Roth) **33**:363
"Weihe" (George) **14**:204
"We-'im yish' al ha-malach" (Bialik) **25**:63
The Weird o' It (Shiel) **8**:361-62
"The Weird of Michael Scott" (Sharp) **39**:353, 374, 379, 389
The Weird of the Wanderer (Rolfe) **12**:273-74, 276
"Der Weise an seine Feinde" (Werfel) **8**:475
Die Weise von Liebe und Tod des Cornets Christoph Rilke (Rilke) **195**:185-91, 320
"Die Weissagung" (Schnitzler) **4**:395
Der weisse Dominikaner (Meyrink) **21**:218, 231
Der Weisse Fächer (Hofmannsthal) **11**:303
"Die Weisse Kultur; oder, warum in die Ferne Schweifen? Aus einer Berliner Zeitung" (Kraus) **5**:290
Weisst du schwarzt du (Arp) **115**:11
Das weite Land (Schnitzler) **4**:390, 401
"Welcome!" (Cankar) **105**:162-63
"A Welcome Circumcision" (Aleichem)
See "An ongeleygter bris"
"Welcome Home" (Hardy) **143**:170
"Welcome Home, Hal" (Aldrich) **125**:13
"Welcome the New South" (Locke) **43**:236
Welcome to Our City (Wolfe) **13**:483-84; **29**:416
"Welcome to Thomas Mann" (Jozsef) **22**:163, 165
Welded (O'Neill) **1**:382, 384-85, 387; **6**:326, 335; **49**:241, 264, 270, 274
"The Well" (Coppard) **5**:178
The Well (Onetti)
See *El pozo*
"Well Done" (Mayakovski) **18**:248
"Well Dressed Man with a Beard" (Stevens) **45**:299
"The Well in the Desert" (Fletcher) **35**:108
The Well of Loneliness (Hall) **12**:185-98
The Well of Romance (Sturges) **48**:310, 316-17
The Well of the Saints (Synge) **6**:425, 427-28, 432, 434, 439, 441-42; **37**:351-53, 358, 365, 377-79, 383, 386, 389, 391
We'll to the Woods No More (Dujardin)
See *Les lauriers sont coupés*
"We'll to the Woods No More, the Laurels Are Cut Down" (Sarton) **120**:261
"Well Water" (Jarrell) **177**:157
"Well . . . All Right" (Holly) **65**:137-38, 143, 145
The Well-Beloved (Hardy) **4**:163, 177; **10**:217, 233; **32**:281; **53**:77, 110; **72**:211, 237-38, 250, 279; **72**:237, 265; **143**:123, 143, 174, 180
"Welle der Nacht" (Benn) **3**:113-14
Well-Known Pictures (Peretz) **16**:389
A Well-Remembered Voice (Barrie) **164**:36-37
Wells Brothers: The Young Cattle Kings (Adams) **56**:3-4, 6-7, 22
"Wells, Hitler, and the World State" (Orwell) **51**:266
The Well-Tempered Critic (Frye) **165**:227-28, 257
"A Well-to-Do Invalid" (Jarrell) **177**:132, 178
"The Welsh Marches" (Housman) **10**:247, 251
"A Welsh Night" (Lewis) **3**:289

"The Welsh Sea" (Flecker) **43**:187
"Die Welt" (Schwitters) **95**:297
"Welt" (Walser)
See "Das Ende der Welt"
Welt im Kopf (Canetti) **157**:38
Welt- und Lebensanschauungen im 19. Jahrhundert (Steiner) **13**:440-41
Die welt von Gestern (Zweig) **17**:429, 438, 458
Weltanschauung (Zuckmayer) **191**:298
"Das Weltbild von Darwin und Lamarck" (Haeckel) **83**:147
Welten (Kolmar) **40**:174-75, 178
"Weltende" (Lasker-Schueler) **57**:299, 302, 305, 330, 334
"Weltflucht" (Lasker-Schueler) **57**:293, 300, 308, 321, 326, 334
Der Weltfreund (Werfel) **8**:475, 477-78
Weltgericht (Kraus) **5**:285
Weltliche Passion (Toller) **10**:489-90
Die Welträtsel (Haeckel) **83**:147
"Weltschmertz" (Dunbar) **12**:104, 111
"Weltschmerz" (Lasker-Schueler) **57**:328, 330, 336
"Der Weltuntergang" (Huch) **13**:249
Der Weltverbesserer (Bernhard) **165**:96-97, 130, 133, 135
"Wen ein Gott" (Raabe) **45**:189
Der Wendekreis (Wassermann) **6**:510
"The Wendingo" (Blackwood) **5**:70, 73-4, 77, 79-80
"Wendung" (Rilke) **1**:420; **195**:323
Wer pa Lawino (p'Bitek) **149**:3-9, 13-14, 16-22, 25, 27, 29, 31, 38-42, 49, 51-52, 54-55, 58-59, 61, 64-66, 68-73, 75-82, 89-91, 93-94, 96, 106-9, 111-12, 114-16, 119-29, 132-34
"Wer weiss wo?" (Liliencron) **18**:213-14
"We're Getting Closer to the Grave Each Day" (Williams) **81**:434
De wereld een dansfeest (van Schendel) **56**:238
Wereldvrede (Couperus) **15**:46
"The Werewolf" (Carter) **139**:139, 142-43
The Werewolf (Summers) **16**:426, 429-30, 432
"Were-Wolves" (Campbell) **9**:30-1
Werkausgabe (Bachmann) **192**:150
Werkausgabe in zehn Bänden (Zuckmayer) **191**:327, 329-30, 333
Werke (Bachmann) **192**:99, 108-10, 113
Werke in sechs Bänden (Weiss) **152**:293, 298
Werke. Kommentierte Ausgabe in vier Bänden (Rilke) **195**:258, 262-64, 266-67, 269-70, 275, 278
Wert, Würde, Recht (Otto) **85**:321-2
"Wertgesetz und Autonomie" (Otto) **85**:322
"Wessex Heights" (Hardy) **53**:114; **143**:188, 192
Wessex Novels (Hardy) **143**:75-77, 167, 175, 207
Wessex Poems, and Other Verses (Hardy) **4**:151-52; **53**:71, 93, 103, 107; **143**:78, 149, 156, 180, 185-86, 194-95
Wessex Tales: Strange, Lively, and Commonplace (Hardy) **4**:159; **143**:72, 107
"The West" (Housman) **1**:353
"West" (Oppen) **107**:266
"The West Coast" (Wen I-to) **28**:415
The West from a Car-Window (Davis) **24**:201
"West Indians and Africans" (Fanon) **188**:8
West Is West (Rhodes) **53**:315, 318, 320-21, 327
The West of Owen Wister (Wister) **21**:405
West of Suez (Osborne) **153**:239, 242, 312, 322-23
"The West That Was" (Rhodes) **53**:314
West to North (Mackenzie)
See *The West Wind of Love*
The West Wind of Love (Mackenzie) **116**:232, 239, 242
"Westcock Hill" (Roberts) **8**:321, 326
Western and Eastern Mysticism (Otto)
See *Mysticism East and West*
"The Western Approaches" (Nemerov) **124**:226, 306
The Western Approaches: Poems, 1973-1975 (Nemerov) **124**:209-11, 225, 257-62, 300, 304-5, 318
"Western Interpreters" (Adams) **56**:10, 21-2
The Western Lands (Burroughs) **121**:137, 147, 171, 181
Western Star (Benét) **7**:75-6, 82, 84-5
Western Union (Grey) **6**:183, 188
Westfront 1918 (Pabst) **127**:345-48, 350-51, 354, 359-60
"Die westküsten" (Morgenstern) **8**:306
"Westward Ho!" (Adams) **56**:7
Westways: A Village Chronicle (Mitchell) **36**:267, 273
"A Wet August" (Hardy) **53**:81
"Wet Saturday" (Collier) **127**:251, 258
"Whale" (Benét) **28**:9
"The Whale Buster" (Williams) **89**:374, 384
"The Whaler" (Williams) **89**:374-5
The Whaler (Rohan)
See *Isanatori*
"Whales Weep Not" (Lawrence) **93**:60, 73-76
"The Wharf of Dreams" (Markham) **47**:279
"What a b what a b what a beauty" (Schwitters) **95**:315
"What a Night" (Fields) **80**:259
What a Way to Go (Morris) **107**:118-19, 124, 126, 128, 130
"What about Future Flying?" (Mitchell) **81**:168
"What About the Jewish Question?" (Ford) **73**:102
"What Am I?" (Tolstoy)
See "Chto ya?"
"What American Catholics Lack" (Guiney) **41**:220
What Are Masterpieces (Stein) **48**:217
"What Are Masterpieces and Why Are There So Few of Them" (Stein) **28**:316, 330; **48**:218, 236
"What Are 'Spiritual' Values?" (Stapledon) **22**:313
"What Are You Thinking About?" (Villaurrutia) **80**:458
What Became of Anna Bolton (Bromfield) **11**:81, 86
"What Became of Our Flappers and Sheiks?" (Fitzgerald) **52**:58
"What Can the Out-of-Doors Do for Children" (Eastman) **55**:164
What Diantha Did (Gilman) **9**:114-15; **37**:177, 216; **117**:49, 75-6, 151-53, 155-57
"What Do I Care" (Teasdale) **4**:425
What Do I Know (Sully Prudhomme)
See *Que sais-je?*
"What Does Africa Want?" (Childress) **116**:34
"What Does Coming to Terms With the Past Mean?" (Adorno) **111**:196
What Every Woman Knows (Barrie) **2**:40, 42, 49; **164**:39, 80
"What Good Are Poems" (Bachmann)
See "Wozu Gedichte"
What Happened: A Five Act Play (Stein) **6**:411; **48**:248, 264
"What I Am Saying Now Was Said Before" (Cullen) **4**:44
"What I Believe" (Einstein) **65**:133
"What I Believe" (Tolstoy)
See "V chiom moya vera"
"What I Don't Have Is Everything" (Hagiwara) **60**:288
"What I Found in My Pockets" (Chesterton) **1**:184
What I Have Done with Birds (Porter) **21**:261
"What I saw and heard in Rome" (Bachmann)
See "Was ich in Rom sah und hörte"
"What I Saw of Antietam" (Bierce) **44**:8
"What I Saw of Shiloh" (Bierce) **44**:14, 21, 48
"What I Shall Teach Bud and Janet about Marriage" (Guest) **95**:211
"What I Will Pay" (Gurney) **33**:97
"What I'd Like to Do" (Ginsberg) **120**:39-40
"What Is a Hokku Poem?" (Noguchi) **80**:386
"What Is a Realist?" (Morrison) **72**:389
What Is American Literature? (Van Doren) **18**:410
"What is Art?" (Tolstoy)
See "Chto takoe iskusstvo?"
What Is Art? (Tolstoy)
See *Chto takoe iskusstvo?*
"What Is Class Consciousness?" (Reich) **57**:350
What is Class Consciousness? (Reich) **57**:350
"What is Epic Theater?" (Benjamin) **39**:29
"What is Existenz Philosophy?" (Arendt) **193**:157
"What Is He Storing Up" (Jozsef) **22**:161
"What Is Historiography" (Becker) **63**:106
What Is Living and What Is Dead in the Philosophy of Hegel (Croce) **37**:80, 123
"What Is Man?" (Twain) **185**:269, 331
What Is Man? (Twain) **6**:460, 466, 469, 472, 477, 485; **12**:432, 434, 436-37; **36**:367, 411; **48**:351; **161**:243; **185**:250, 289, 297-98
What Is Philosophy? (Deleuze)
See *Qu'est-ce que la philosophie?*
What is Philosophy (Ortega y Gasset)
See *Qué es filosofía?*
"What is Political Philosophy?" (Strauss) **141**:251
What Is Political Philosophy? (Strauss) **141**:222-23, 230-31, 233-34, 251-52, 302, 336, 338-39, 341
"What is Postmodernism?" (Lyotard) **103**:146
"What Is Religion, and Wherein Lies Its Essence" (Tolstoy) **79**:429
"What Is Soul?" (Peretz)
See "Vos heyst 'neshome'"
What Is to Be Done (Lenin) **67**:218, 228-29, 251
"What Is to Come" (Henley) **8**:108
"What Is Tomorrow?" (Södergran)
See "Vad är i morgon?"
"What Kind of Guy Was He?" (Nemerov) **124**:275
"What Know We?" (Montgomery) **51**:208-09
"What Lack I Yet?" (Powys) **9**:366, 372
What Life Should Mean to You (Adler) **61**:9, 11, 18, 28, 34
"What Lips My Lips Have Kissed" (Millay) **49**:215
What Maisie Knew (James) **2**:247, 270; **11**:342, 346, 348; **24**:314-15, 323; **40**:120; **47**:158, 163, 206-07
What Might Have Been Expected (Stockton) **47**:325
What Might Have Been: The Story of a Social War (Bramah) **72**:5, 7
What Nietzsche Taught (Van Dine) **23**:351, 357
What Not (Macaulay) **7**:421-22, 426
What Now? (Trotsky) **22**:365
"What Pessimism Is Not" (Saltus) **8**:352-53
"What Pragmatism Is" (Peirce) **81**:200
What Price Glory (Anderson) **2**:1-2; **144**:8, 17, 36-37, 52, 71-72, 76, 78
"What Psychical Research Has Accomplished" (James) **32**:350
What Really Happened (Lowndes) **12**:203
"What Shadows We Pursue" (Kirk) **119**:279, 335
What Shall We Do Now? (Fisher) **87**:79
What Shall We Do Now? A Book of Suggestions for Children's Games and Enjoyment (Lucas) **73**:162
What Shall We Do Then? (Tolstoy)
See *What to Do*
"What Social Objects Must Psychology Presuppose?" (Mead) **89**:170
"What story down there awaits its end?" (Calvino) **183**:133
"What the Buffalo Desires" (p'Bitek) **149**:89
What the Butler Saw (Orton) **157**:296, 298, 302-4, 307-8, 310-11, 316-17, 322, 324, 329, 331-32, 336, 346-48, 352-60

What the "Friends of the People" Are and How They Fight the Social Democrats (Lenin) **67**:219, 222, 231-32
"What the Old Man Said" (Sarton) **120**:266
What the Public Wants (Bennett) **5**:43; **197**:14, 16-18
"What the Shell Says" (Runyon) **10**:437
"What the U.S. Steel Corporation Really Is and How It Works" (Baker) **47**:6
"What Then?" (Yeats) **18**:463
What Then Must We Do? (Tolstoy)
See *What to Do*
"What Theosophy Is" (Besant) **9**:13
"What Thomas Said in a Pub" (Stephens) **4**:409, 416-17
What Times Does a Train Leave for Paris? (Apollinaire)
See *A quelle heure un train partira-t-il pour Paris?*
"What To Do" (Holly) **65**:147, 149, 151
What to Do (Tolstoy) **4**:450; **11**:458, 463, 469; **79**:333, 336-7, 374, 408, 413, 426, 430
"What Was Modern Poetry?" (Nemerov) **124**:214, 218, 317
"What We Have Been Doing and What We Are Planning to Do" (Roosevelt) **93**:184
"What We See Is What We Think" (Stevens) **45**:300
What We Used to Say (Ginzburg)
See *Lessico famigliare*
"What White Publishers Won't Print" (Hurston) **131**:80
"What You Up To?" (Ginsberg) **120**:57
"Whatever Hope We Have" (Anderson) **144**:16
"What's in Time" (Gurney) **33**:87
"What's It All Bloomin' Well For?" (Gill) **85**:98
What's Mine's Mine (MacDonald) **113**:245
What's O'Clock (Lowell) **8**:227-29, 234-35, 237
What's to Become of the Boy? (Böll)
See *Was soll aus dem Jungen bloß werden?*
What's Wrong with the World (Chesterton) **6**:102, 110
"Wheat and Wine" (Crowley) **7**:208
"The Wheatfield" (Morgenstern)
See "Das kornfeld"
The Wheel (Jensen)
See *Hjulet*
The Wheel of Life (Glasgow) **2**:176, 179-80, 182, 184, 186, 189; **7**:332
The Wheel of Time (Kuprin)
See *Kolesno vremeni*
"The Wheelbarrow" (Pirandello)
See "La carriola"
Wheels and Butterflies (Yeats) **93**:342, 364
The Wheels of Chance: A Holiday Adventure (Wells) **6**:536, 547-48; **12**:487-88, 494-95; **133**:228, 315
Wheel-Tracks (Somerville & Ross) **51**:362
"When a Fellow's on the Level with a Girl That's on the Square" (Cohan) **60**:170
When a Man Marries (Rinehart) **52**:281, 288
When a Man's a Man (Wright) **183**:349, 360, 362, 372-75, 381-82
When a Man's Single (Barrie) **2**:45-6
"When All Is Done" (Dunbar) **12**:122
When All Is Said and Done (Bergelson)
See *Nokh Alemen*
"When All My Five and Country Senses See" (Thomas) **45**:362
When All the Woods Are Green (Mitchell) **36**:274
When Authority Went Away (Rozanov) **104**:314, 316, 346
When Blood Is Their Argument: An Analysis of Prussian Culture (Ford) **57**:282; **172**:8, 90-91
"When Bryan Speaks" (Lindsay) **17**:227
When Cherries Ripen (Shimazaki Toson) **5**:435
"When Closing Swinburne" (Stringer) **37**:342
"When de Co'n Pone's Hot" (Dunbar) **12**:104, 108, 121
When Democracy Builds (Wright) **95**:400, 402, 405
"When Democratic Virtues Disintegrate" (Becker) **63**:72
"When Dey Listed Colored Soldiers" (Dunbar) **12**:110, 115
When Dreams Come True (Saltus) **8**:346
"When Everyone Is Panic Stricken" (Crane) **11**:159
When Five Years Pass (García Lorca)
See *Así que pasen cinco años*
"When Gassy Thompson Struck It Rich" (Lindsay) **17**:225
"When God Comes and Gathers His Jewels" (Williams) **81**:419,423
"When Helen Lived" (Yeats) **31**:385
"When I Am Covered" (Gurney) **33**:99
"When I Am Dead" (Bialik) **25**:50
"When I came to know Houghton" (Gilman) **117**:150
"When I First Met Dr. Hickey" (Somerville & Ross) **51**:360
"When I Met Tristan" (Lasker-Schueler) **57**:335
"When I Pounded the Pavement" (McKay) **41**:329
"When I Set Out for Lyonesse" (Hardy) **143**:196, 215
"When I Think of Rilke" (Villa) **176**:96
"When I too long have looked upon your face" (Millay) **49**:232
When I Was a Little Girl (Gale) **7**:283
"When I Was a Witch" (Gilman) **9**:113, 115
When I Was Mad (Pirandello)
See *Quand'ero matto*
"When I Was Thirteen" (Welch) **22**:445, 447, 456
When I Whistle (Endo) **152**:179-80, 186, 189, 213
"When Israel out of Egypt Came" (Housman) **10**:258
When it no longer Matters (Onetti)
See *Cuando ya no importe*
"When Jove, the Skies' Director" (Dobson) **79**:27
When Kings Were the Law (Griffith) **68**:186
When Ladies Meet (Crothers) **19**:76, 78-82, 85
"When Like a Running Grave" (Thomas) **45**:361
"When Malindy Sings" (Dunbar) **12**:106, 108, 126
"When Milking Time Is Done" (Roberts) **8**:318, 320
When No Man Pursueth (Lowndes) **12**:200-01
"When on the Marge of Evening" (Guiney) **41**:221
"When Once the Twilight Locks No Longer" (Thomas) **45**:365, 380, 383
When One Is Somebody (Pirandello)
See *Quando si è qualcuno*
"When Sam'l Sings" (Dunbar) **12**:114
"When She Comes Home Again" (Riley) **51**:285, 291, 303
When Someone is Somebody (Pirandello)
See *Quando si è qualcuno*
"When Spirits Speak of Life" (Bodenheim) **44**:62, 68
"When the Army Prays for Watty" (Lawson) **27**:134
When the Authorities Quit (Rozanov)
See *When Authority Went Away*
"When the Bough Breaks" (Kuttner) **10**:274
"When the Children Come Home" (Lawson) **27**:134
"When the Earth Lived" (Kuttner) **10**:267
"When the Evening" (Villaurrutia) **80**:480
"When the Fishing Boats Go Out" (Montgomery) **51**:209
"When the Frost Is on the Punkin" (Riley) **51**:283, 300-01
"When the Gods Slept" (Dunsany) **59**:19
"When the Grass Grew Long" (Oskison) **35**:280-81
When the Iron Curtain Falls (Lie) **5**:331
"When the Mode" (Ginsberg) **120**:136
"When the Moon Is Last Awake" (Pickthall) **21**:245, 250
When the Mountain Fell (Ramuz)
See *Derborence*
When the New Wine Blooms (Bjoernson)
See *Når den ny vin blomstrer*
"When the Old Century Was New" (Dreiser) **10**:197, 199-200; **35**:72
"When the Red-Haired Imposter, Fell Dimitri" (Tsvetaeva) **35**:394
When the Sleeper Wakes (Wells) **6**:539, 544; **12**:488; **19**:425, 428-31, 437-39
"When the Sun Went Down" (Lawson) **27**:129
"When the Tide Goes Out" (Montgomery) **51**:209
"When the Trees Grow Bare on the High Hills" (Muir) **87**:306
When the Turtle Sings, and Other Unusual Tales (Marquis) **7**:446
When the Vineyards Are in Bloom (Bjoernson)
See *Når den ny vin blomstrer*
When the War Was Over (Frisch)
See *Als der Krieg zu Ende war*
When the Whippoorwill (Rawlings) **4**:363
When the Wicked Man (Ford) **15**:88-90; **172**:52-55, 57, 61
"When the Wind Is in the South" (Rölvaag)
See "Klare morgen og vaate kveld"
When the World Screamed (Doyle) **7**:226
When the World Shook (Haggard) **11**:246
"When the Year Grows Old" (Millay) **4**:306-07
"When Thou Wast Naked" (Powys) **9**:373
"When Under the Icy Eaves" (Masters) **25**:288
"When We Are M-A-Double R-I-E-D" (Cohan) **60**:170
When We Dead Awaken (Ibsen)
See *Når vi døde vågner*
When We Were Very Young (Milne) **6**:307, 309, 311, 316-17, 319-20; **88**:228
When West Was West (Wister) **21**:405
When William Came: A Story of London under the Hohenzollerns (Saki) **3**:367, 370, 373, 375-76
When Women Love (Delafield) **61**:133
"When You Are Old" (Yeats) **11**:512, 526, 529
"When You Are Poor" (Prado)
See "Cuando se es pobre"
"When You Come Back, and You Will Come Back" (Cohan) **60**:171
"When You See a Rattlesnake Posed to Strike You Do Wait Until He Has Struck Before You Crush Him" (Roosevelt) **93**:184
"When Your Pants Begin to Go" (Lawson) **27**:133
"Whence the Song" (Dreiser) **35**:65
"Where and How the Devil Lost His Poncho" (Palma)
See "Dónde y cómo el diablo perdió el poncho"
Where Angels Fear to Tread (Forster) **125**:24-5, 31, 114, 121, 154
"Where Are You" (Bialik) **25**:50
"Where Does the Rose Begin" (Prado) **75**:206
"Where Dream Begins" (Sarton) **120**:267
"Where Is Britain Going" (Trotsky)
See "Kuda idet Angliya?"
"Where is David, the Next King of Israel?" (Lindsay) **17**:224
Where Is My Home? (Balmont)
See *Gde moi dom?*
"Where Is My Iceland Jumper?" (Dagerman) **17**:93-4
"Where Is the Real Non-Resistant?" (Lindsay) **17**:226
Where Love and Friendship Dwelt (Lowndes) **12**:204
"Where, O Where?" (Wylie) **8**:536
"Where Once the Waters of Your Face" (Thomas) **8**:458; **45**:361, 365

"Where Tawe Flows" (Thomas) **8**:463; **45**:394, 396; **105**:344, 357
Where the Battle Was Fought (Murfree) **135**:218, 227
Where the Blue Begins (Morley) **87**:125
Where the Forest Murmurs (Sharp) **39**:368, 373, 377
"Where the Negro Fails" (Micheaux) **76**:264
Where the Sidewalk Ends (Hecht) **101**:75
Where the Wolves Drink (Tzara) **168**:274
"Where Their Fire Is Not Quenched" (Sinclair) **11**:421
Where There Is Nothing (Gregory)
See *The Unicorn from the Stars*
Where There Is Nothing (Yeats) **31**:386, 415, 418; **93**:363-64
"Where There Is Nothing, There Is God" (Yeats) **31**:418
Where There's a Will (Rinehart) **52**:282
Where Will You Fall (Perutz)
See *Wohin rollst du, Äpfelchen . . .*
"Where Your Treasure Is" (Williams) **89**:375
"Where-Away" (Riley) **51**:294
"Wherefore?" (Howe) **21**:107-08
Wherever the Earth (Borowski)
See *Gdziekolwiek ziemia*
Whether a Dove or Seagull (Warner) **131**:310-11, 330
"Whether I Live" (Coleridge) **73**:12
"Whether or Not" (Lawrence) **93**:2, 46, 69
"Which, Being Interpreted, Is as May Be, or, Otherwise" (Lowell) **8**:235, 237
"Which Was It?" (Twain) **185**:327, 329-30
"Which Was the Dream?" (Twain) **185**:327, 329
Which World—Which Way (Toller)
See *Quer Durch*
"While Convalescing" (Wright) **136**:301
"While Drawing in a Churchyard" (Hardy) **53**:100
While Love is New (Moricz)
See *Míg új a szerelem*
While Rome Burns (Woollcott) **5**:522, 524, 527, 529
"While the Auto Waits" (Henry) **19**:173
While the Billy Boils (Lawson) **27**:118-19, 121, 127, 129-32, 148-50
While the Sirens Slept (Dunsany) **59**:18
Whilomville Stories (Crane) **11**:128, 131, 136
A Whimsey Anthology (Wells) **35**:420
"The Whip" (Robinson) **101**:100, 105
"The Whipping" (Bonner) **179**:39, 53, 56, 58-59
A Whirl Asunder (Atherton) **2**:12
"The Whirligig of Life" (Henry) **1**:346
Whirligigs (Henry) **19**:191
"The Whirlpool" (Hedāyat)
See "Girdab"
The Whirlpool (Gissing) **3**:221-23, 228, 232-33; **24**:220-21, 230-31, 235, 239-40, 243
Whirlpools: A Novel of Modern Poland (Sienkiewicz)
See *Wiry*
"The Whirlwind Road" (Markham) **47**:282
Whisky Galore (Mackenzie) **116**:228, 231-32, 234, 243-44, 246
"Whisper of the Wind" (Austin) **25**:34
"The Whisperer in Darkness" (Lovecraft) **4**:267, 270; **22**:217, 238, 241
"Whispering Leaves" (Glasgow) **7**:342-43, 345
"The Whispering Mummy" (Rohmer) **28**:277, 286
Whispering Windows (Burke) **63**:124, 127-28
"Whispers" (Chang) **184**:147-48
"The Whistle" (Saroyan) **137**:181
"The Whistle of Sandy McGraw" (Service) **15**:399
The Whistler Book (Hartmann) **73**:117, 122, 134, 149
"Whistling Dick's Christmas Stocking" (Henry) **1**:348; **19**:178
"A Whistling Girl" (Parker) **143**:323
"The Whistling Room" (Hodgson) **13**:236
"Whistling Sam" (Dunbar) **12**:122
"Whistling Song" (Anwar)
See "Lagu siul"
White and Black (Pirandello)
See *Bianche e nere*
"White Ant" (Bosman) **49**:13
"The White Ape" (Lovecraft)
See "Facts concerning the Late Arthur Jermyn and His Family"
White April and Other Poems (Reese) **181**:339
The White Architect (Balmont)
See *Belyi zodchii*
"White Arrow" (Toomer) **172**:265, 277
A White Bird Flying (Aldrich) **125**:9, 12, 14-15
"The White Birds" (Yeats) **11**:512; **116**:331, 334, 336
White Birds (Bojer) **64**:21, 23
"White Bread" (Gale) **7**:285
White Buildings (Crane) **2**:112, 117, 119-20, 123; **5**:185, 188-90; **80**:79-80, 103, 121
The White Cheyenne (Faust) **49**:37-9, 53
"White Christmas" (Service) **15**:412
"White Chrysanthemums" (Hartmann) **73**:117, 127
"The White City" (McKay) **41**:336
"The White Cliffs" (Noyes) **7**:513
The White Cockade (Gregory) **1**:332, 334; **176**:11, 16, 37, 40
The White Company (Doyle) **7**:215, 217, 220-21, 224, 227-28, 234, 237-39
"White Culture; or, Why Roam Far? From a Berlin Newspaper" (Kraus)
See "Die Weisse Kultur; oder, warum in die Ferne Schweifen? Aus einer Berliner Zeitung"
"White Desert" (Anderson) **2**:10
White Desert (Anderson) **144**:7-8, 13, 34, 71
The White Dominican (Meyrink)
See *Der weisse Dominikaner*
"The White Eagle" (Chopin) **127**:10-11
White Fang (London) **9**:256, 258, 261, 266, 270-71, 273; **15**:267, 274, 276; **39**:263-64, 266, 275
"White Fingers" (Rhodes) **53**:316
The White Flag (Porter) **21**:268, 277
The White Gate (Chase) **124**:21
"White, Gray, Black, Red" (Sologub)
See "Belye, serye, černye, krasnye"
The White Guard (Bulgakov)
See *Belaia gvardiia*
"The White Gull" (Carman) **7**:135, 138, 142, 146, 148
"A White Heron" (Jewett) **1**:369; **22**:122, 124-25, 127, 133-48
"The White Heron" (Jewett)
See "A White Heron"
A White Heron, and Other Stories (Jewett) **22**:147
"The White House" (McKay) **41**:336, 345
"The White Jellyfish" (Ball)
See "Die weiße Qualle"
"The White Lady" (Ady) **11**:15
"The White Ladye" (Cram) **45**:4, 12
"The White Light" (Lu Hsun) **3**:297
"The White Lights" (Robinson) **101**:132
"White Lily of Weardale Head" (Buchanan) **107**:15
White Lines (Kandinsky) **92**:147
"The White Lotus-Flowers" (Ady) **11**:15
White Magic (Phillips) **44**:256-58, 262, 265, 275
The White Man (Endo)
See *Shiroi hito*
White Man, Listen! (Wright) **136**:240-42, 276, 287, 290, 332
"The White Man's Burden" (Kipling) **8**:179
"White Man's Solution for the Negro Problem in America" (Garvey) **41**:188
"The White Medusa" (Ball)
See "Die weiße Qualle"
The White Mice (Davis) **24**:209
The White Monkey (Galsworthy) **1**:298; **45**:46-7, 63
"The White Moth" (Quiller-Couch) **53**:290
"The White Mulberry Tree" (Cather) **132**:126; **152**:13, 20-21, 33, 36, 44, 76-77
White Narcissus (Knister) **56**:152, 156, 159, 165, 168-69, 171
"White Night" (Pasternak) **188**:183, 192-93
"White on Black" (Slesinger) **10**:441
The White Paternoster, and Other Stories (Powys) **9**:374
"The White Peacock" (Millay) **169**:232, 275-76, 280
The White Peacock (Lawrence) **2**:343, 358-60; **9**:211, 222-23, 226; **16**:277, 283, 285, 287, 302; **33**:184; **48**:117, 119
The White People and Other Stories (Machen) **4**:285
The White Plague (Čapek)
See *Bílá nemoc*
The White Princess (Rilke) **6**:370
The White Prophet (Caine) **97**:7-8
"The White Rabbit" (Remizov)
See "Belyi zayats"
The White Rocks (Rod)
See *Les roches blanches*
"A White Rose" (Sterling) **20**:384
The White Rose (Griffith) **68**:170, 217-18, 248
White Rose and Red (Buchanan) **107**:25, 33, 57, 84
White Rose of Weary Leaf (Hunt) **53**:185-88, 190-92, 196-98, 200
The White Sail, and Other Poems (Guiney) **41**:203-04, 206-07, 213
The White Scourge (Čapek)
See *Bílá nemoc*
"The White Shadow" (Chambers) **41**:113
"The White Ship" (Lovecraft) **4**:272; **22**:209
"White Shroud" (Ginsberg) **120**:56
White Shroud, Poems 1980-1985 (Ginsberg) **120**:53
"The White Silence" (London) **9**:268; **39**:284, 287-88
The White Sister (Crawford) **10**:150, 155-56
The White Slaver (Rohmer)
See *Yu'an Hee See Laughs*
White Stains (Crowley) **7**:208, 210-11
"The White Symphony" (Fletcher) **35**:100-01, 103-04
White Teeth (p'Bitek)
See *Lak tar miyo kinyero wi lobo*
"White Teeth Make People to Laugh a Lot on Earth" (p'Bitek)
See *Lak tar miyo kinyero wi lobo*
The White Terror and the Red (Cahan) **71**:26, 30, 32-33, 44
White Threads of the Waterfall (Mizoguchi)
See *Taki no Shiraito*
"The White Tower" (Remizov)
See "Belaya bashnya"
White Velvet (Rohmer) **28**:284, 292
"The White Villa" (Cram) **45**:5
"The White Weathercock" (Powys) **9**:369
The White Wedding (Shiel) **8**:361-62
White Wings (Barry) **11**:47, 50, 52, 54, 64-7
"The White Witch" (Johnson) **3**:244
The White Witch of Rosehall (De Lisser) **12**:96-9
"Whitebear and Graybear" (Rölvaag) **17**:347
"The Whiteboys" (Somerville & Ross) **51**:358, 384
"Whites of the Future" (Ady) **11**:21
"White-Throat" (Gosse) **28**:139
Whither Russia? (Trotsky) **22**:365
"Whither the "New" Art" (Kandinsky) **92**:61
"Whitmania" (Swinburne) **36**:310
"Whitmans Apoteosis" (Jensen) **41**:301
Whitsun Fires (Leino)
See *Helkavirsiä*
"Whitsunday in the Church" (Howe) **21**:107
Who am I? (Ramana Maharshi)
See *Nan Yar?*
"Who are you, standing turned away?" (Lagerkvist) **144**:164

"Who Be Kind To" (Ginsberg) **120**:4, 24, 35
"Who Can Fall in Love after Thirty?" (Fitzgerald) **52**:58
"Who comes is occupied" (Oppen) **107**:345
"Who Crosses Storm Mountain?" (Murfree) **135**:206
"Who Dat Say Chicken in Dis Crowd" (Dunbar) **12**:122
"Who Dealt?" (Lardner) **2**:337; **14**:307
"Who Do You Wish Was with Us" (Thomas) **8**:463; **45**:395; **105**:303, 318, 320-22, 344, 346
Who Doesn't Have His Own Minotaur? (Yourcenar)
See *Qui n'a pas son Minotaure?*
"Who Goes with Fergus?" (Yeats) **1**:578; **18**:445
"Who Killed Kirk Rubin" (Allen) **87**:61
"Who Killed the Student Revolution?" (Nisbet) **117**:306
"Who Knows" (Dunbar) **2**:129
"Who Might Be Interested" (Parker) **143**:331-32
Who Rides on a Tiger (Lowndes) **12**:203
"Who Said Peacock Pie" (de la Mare) **53**:42
"Who Shrieks? Not I" (Jozsef) **22**:160
"Who / threw the silver dollar . . ." (Cummings) **137**:20
"Who Was My Quiet Friend" (Harte) **25**:223
"Whoever Finds a Horseshoe" (Mandelstam)
See "Nashedshij podkovu"
"The Whole Duty of Critics" (Matthews) **95**:237
Whole Family (Phelps) **113**:342
"A Whole Life" (Pilnyak)
See "Tselaya zhizn"
The Whole Motion: Collected Poems 1945-1992 (Dickey) **151**:169, 171, 199, 203
Whom Do We Write For? (Calvino)
See "Senza colori"
"Whom Do We Write For or The Hypothetical Bookcase" (Calvino)
See "Per chi si scrive (Lo scaffale ipotetico)"
Whom God Hath Joined (Bennett) **5**:26, 38, 40-1, 43; **20**:24, 26; **197**:31, 118, 120, 122-23
"Whom I Write For" (Aleixandre)
See "¿Para quién escribo?"
"Whom Mince Pie Hath Joined Together" (Glaspell) **175**:144
"Whores" (Walker) **129**:294, 323, 332-34
Whoroscope (Beckett) **145**:189-90
Whose Body (Sayers) **2**:537-38; **15**:393
"The Whosis Kid" (Hammett) **187**:82, 134-35, 166
"Why" (Carman) **7**:137
"Why" (Tagore) **3**:488
"Why?" (Woolf) **43**:392
"Why and How I Became an Author" (Smith) **25**:389
"Why Did Nellie Leave Her Home?" (Cohan) **60**:169
"Why Did the Young Clerk Swear?" (Crane) **11**:157; **32**:164
"Why Did This Spring Wood" (Wright) **136**:303
Why Do Jews Need a Country? (Aleichem)
See *Oyf vos badarfn yidn a land*
Why Do Men Stupefy Themselves (Tolstoy)
See *Why Do People Intoxicate Themselves?*
Why Do People Intoxicate Themselves? (Tolstoy) **11**:463; **79**:430
"Why Does One Write?" (Levi) **109**:286
"Why Don't You Love Me like You Used to Do?" (Williams) **81**:423
"Why East Wind Chills" (Thomas) **45**:364
Why Europe Leaves Home (Roberts) **23**:228, 238
"Why Girls Go Wrong" (Addams) **76**:38
"Why I Am a Marxist" (Laski) **79**:105
"Why I Am Not a Communist" (Čapek)
See "Proč nejsem komunistou"
"Why I am not a Conservative" (Hayek) **109**:180, 230
"Why I Am Not Editing 'The Stinger'" (Bierce) **44**:45
"Why I Joined the I.L.P." (Orwell) **128**:257
"Why I Live in a Small Town" (Aldrich) **125**:16
"Why I Voted the Socialist Ticket" (Lindsay) **17**:229
"Why I Write" (Orwell) **6**:342; **15**:321, 348; **31**:193; **51**:230, 237, 240, 253, 258-59, 268; **128**:267, 273, 289; **129**:233
"Why I Write Ghost Stories" (Wakefield) **120**:349, 357
"Why I Wrote 'The Yellow Wallpaper'" (Gilman) **37**:200; **117**:95
"Why Ill Words? Sleep Silently" (Jozsef) **22**:160
"Why I'm Such a Sorehead" (Shepherd) **177**:316
Why Is Economics Not an Evolutionary Science? (Veblen) **31**:355
"Why is the Anglo-Saxon Disliked" (Fuller) **103**:106
"Why Muggins Was Kept" (Hawthorne) **25**:247
"Why Only Ten Percent of the Movies Succeed" (Fitzgerald) **55**:225
"Why Particulars Are So Much More Effective Than Generalities" (Jarrell) **177**:225
"Why Read the Classics?" (Calvino) **183**:60, 104
"Why Should Not Old Men Be Mad?" (Yeats) **18**:463
Why Stop Learning? (Fisher) **87**:79
"Why the Chickadee Goes Crazy Once a Year" (Seton) **31**:259
Why the Chisolm Trail Forks (Adams) **56**:11
"Why the Classics" (Herbert) **168**:23, 73, 77
"Why the Clock Stopped" (Bennett) **5**:46
"Why the History of English Law Remains Unwritten" (Maitland) **65**:281
"Why the Mllkman Shudders When He Perceives the Dawn" (Dunsany) **59**:21
"Why the Rose Is Red" (Rolfe) **12**:272
"Why Was I Given Life?" (Södergran)
See "Varför gavs mig livet?"
"Why We Remain Jews" (Strauss) **141**:266, 270
"Why Women Should Write the Best Novels" (Norris) **24**:432
"Wichita Vortex Sutra" (Ginsberg) **120**:4, 23-4, 33, 37, 57-9, 96
Wichita Vortex Sutra (Ginsberg) **120**:57-62
"A Wicked Voice" (Lee) **5**:320
The Wicker-Work Woman (France)
See *Le mannequin d'osier*
The Wide Land (Schnitzler) **4**:393
"The Wide Prospect" (Jarrell) **177**:195
"Wider" (Adorno)
See "Fur und Wider den Jazz"
Widersehen mit Drüng (Böll) **185**:5
"Widmung für Chopin" (Ball) **104**:41
"The Widow" (Babel)
See "Vdova"
"The Widow" (Bosman) **49**:6
"The Widow and Her Son" (Gibran) **9**:85
"The Widow Ching, pirate" (Borges)
See "La viuda Ching, Pirata"
"Widow La Rue" (Masters) **2**:461; **25**:298
"The Widow Mysie: an Idyl of Love and Whisky" (Buchanan) **107**:15, 79
"The Widow of Pisa" (Heyse)
See "Die Wittwe von Pisa"
"A Widow Woman" (Evans) **85**:28-9
"The Widowed House of Cuckoo Songs" (Tynan) **3**:503
"The Widower Turmore" (Bierce) **44**:45
Widowers' Houses (Shaw) **3**:384, 400, 406; **9**:411-12, 414, 425; **21**:323; **45**:226, 241
"Widowhood" (Bialik)
See "Almenut"
"The Widow's Loan" (Blasco Ibáñez) **12**:39
"The Widow's Might" (Gilman) **9**:113, 115; **117**:116, 123
"Wie der alte Timofei singend starb" (Rilke) **195**:215
"Wie der Verrat nach Rußland kam" (Rilke) **195**:215
"Wie die Träumenden" (Sudermann) **15**:433
"Der Wiederkehrende Christus" (Huch) **13**:249
"Wiese im Park" (Kraus) **5**:292
"The Wife" (Chekhov)
See "Žena"
"The Wife" (Rebreanu)
See "Nevasta"
The Wife (Belasco) **3**:88
"Wife and Mistress" (Svevo) **2**:545
"The Wife Blessed" (Riley) **51**:291
"The Wife of a King" (London) **9**:273-74, 277
The Wife of Altamont (Hunt) **53**:192
The Wife of Bringas (Pérez Galdós)
See *La de Bringas*
"The Wife of his Youth" (Chesnutt) **5**:130-31, 133; **39**:70, 79, 99
The Wife of his Youth, and Other Stories of the Color Line (Chesnutt) **5**:131-33; **39**:75, 79-80, 84
"The Wife of King Heleos" (Warner) **131**:311
"The Wife of Llew" (Ledwidge) **23**:111
"The Wife of Palissy" (Robinson) **101**:119
The Wife of Rossetti—Her Life and Death (Hunt) **53**:193-95
The Wife of Sir Isaac Harman (Wells) **6**:528, 539; **12**:495
The Wife of Steffen Tromholt (Sudermann)
See *Die Frau des Steffen Tromholt*
"The Wife of Usher's Well" (James) **6**:213
"The Wife of Yasui Sokken" (Mori Ogai)
See "Yasui Fujin"
The Wife without a Smile (Pinero) **32**:393, 404, 411-12
"The Wife's Story" (Davis) **6**:151, 153-54
"A Wife's Story" (Holley) **99**:328
Wigwam Evenings: Sioux Folktales Retold (Eastman) **55**:167-70, 172-3
Wild Animal Ways (Seton) **31**:258
Wild Animals I Have Known (Seton) **31**:253, 256, 258, 262-63, 266-74, 278
Wild Apples (Gogarty) **15**:100-01, 103, 114
"The Wild Boar" (McAlmon) **97**:97
The Wild Boar (Moricz)
See *A vadkan*
The Wild Body (Lewis) **2**:389, 391, 394-95; **9**:236, 245, 250; **104**:151, 177, 199-200, 285, 288, 296-97
Wild Cherry (Reese) **181**:339, 347
The Wild Choir (Hamsun)
See *Det vilde Kor*
"The Wild Common" (Lawrence) **9**:230; **93**:12, 16, 43, 44, 45, 48, 65, 79
The Wild Country (Bromfield) **11**:86
The Wild Duck (Ibsen)
See *Vildanden*
Wild Eden (Woodberry) **73**:367
"The Wild Geese of Wyndygoul" (Seton) **31**:271
"The Wild Goose" (Moore) **7**:491, 493
The Wild Goose (Mori Ogai)
See *Gan*
"The Wild Goose Chase" (Chesterton) **6**:108
Wild Goslings (Benét) **28**:7, 10
Wild Grass (Lu Hsun)
See *Yeh ts'ao*
Wild Harvest (Oskison) **35**:274-79
Wild Honey (Chekhov)
See *Platonov*
Wild Honey from Various Thyme (Field) **43**:155, 159
"The Wild Horses" (Yourcenar)
See "Les Chevaux sauvages"
The Wild Hunter in the Bush of the Ghosts (Tutuola) **188**:284-86, 288, 290
"Wild Hunting Companions" (Roosevelt) **69**:187
Wild Is the River (Bromfield) **11**:86
Wild Justice (Osbourne) **93**:132
The Wild Knight (Chesterton) **1**:178; **64**:30
The Wild Man of Borneo (Mankiewicz) **85**:109

A Wild Old Man on the Road (Callaghan) **145**:233, 254
"A Wild Old Wicked Man" (Yeats) **18**:447
The Wild One (Fisher) **140**:183
"The Wild Ones" (Williams) **89**:396
The Wild Orchid (Undset)
See *Gymnadenia*
"The Wild Palms" (Faulkner) **141**:49-50, 55, 117-19, 122-23, 125
The Wild Palms (Faulkner) **141**:34, 39, 42, 48-50, 52, 57-58, 117-26, 138; **170**:115, 129, 166, 230, 233, 244
"Wild Peaches" (Wylie) **8**:521, 531-32, 534-35
"The Wild Ride" (Guiney) **41**:204, 213, 217
"Wild Swans" (Millay) **4**:306
"The Wild Swans at Coole" (Yeats) **116**:276, 314
The Wild Swans at Coole (Yeats) **1**:559, 566, 569, 580-81; **11**:521-22, 528, 540; **18**:442; **31**:386-89
"Wild with All Regrets" (Owen) **27**:212, 214
"Wild Wool" (Muir) **28**:250, 257-58
"Wildcat and the Acorns" (Miyazawa) **76**:278
"Ein Wildermuth" (Bachmann) **192**:10-11
"The Wilderness" (Robinson) **5**:400
"Wilderness and Freedom" (Abbey) **160**:54
The Wilderness Hunter (Roosevelt) **69**:175, 250-51, 256
"Wilderness Lost" (Sarton) **120**:305
A Wilderness of Mirrors (Frisch)
See *Mein Name sei Gantenbein*
The Wilderness of Zin (Lawrence) **18**:159
Wilderness Trail (Micheaux) **76**:270
"Wilderspin" (Coleridge) **73**:11
"Wilding Flowers" (Moody) **105**:237, 250, 265
Wilfred Cumbermede (MacDonald) **9**:292, 294, 296-97; **113**:282
"Wilfrid Holmes" (Moore) **7**:491
"Wilhelm Tell für die Schule" (Frisch) **121**:233
"The Will" (Merrill) **173**:163, 168, 170, 173, 176, 187, 241
The Will (Barrie) **164**:37
Will o' the Wisp (Drieu la Rochelle)
See *Le feu follet*
The Will of an Eccentric (Verne)
See *Le Testament d'un excentrique*
"Will Power" (Quiroga)
See "La voluntad"
Will Rogers Says (Rogers) **8**:340
Will Therapy: An Analysis of the Therapeutic Process in Terms of Relationship (Rank) **115**:222-23, 233-34, 237, 262-67, 284-85, 287-88, 311-12, 316, 318, 321, 324-26, 329
"The Will to Believe" (James) **15**:141, 176-77, 184; **32**:348-49, 351-54, 363-64; **171**:179
The Will to Believe, and Other Essays in Popular Philosophy (James) **15**:140-41, 167, 177; **32**:337, 340, 346-47, 350
"The Will to Happiness" (Mann) **35**:210
The Will to Live Manifesting Itself (Arenas)
See *Voluntad de vivir manifestándose*
"The Will to Live Manifesting Itself" (Arenas)
See "Voluntad de vivir manifestándose"
The Will to Power (Nietzsche)
See *Der wille zur macht*
"Will Ulrike Meinhof Gnade oder freies Geleit?" (Böll) **185**:88
Will Warburton (Gissing) **24**:222, 247-48
"Will You Walk into My Parlor?" (Dreiser) **35**:74
Willa Cather in Person: Interviews, Speeches, and Letters (Cather) **132**:151
Willa Cather's Collected Short Fiction, 1892-1912 (Cather) **132**:137
Willard and His Bowling Trophies: A Perverse Mystery (Brautigan) **133**:31
Der wille zur macht (Nietzsche) **10**:362, 370, 377-79, 386, 388; **18**:335, 346; **55**:323, 330, 332-33, 337-38, 369-70, 373-76
"Willem Prinsloo's Peach Brandy" (Bosman) **49**:19
Willemsdorp (Bosman) **49**:24
"Willful Murder" (Hornung) **59**:112, 116, 119
"William and Mary" (Dahl) **173**:14
William Blake (Murry) **16**:336, 338, 355
William Blake (Swinburne) **36**:305, 307, 331
"William Earl Chatham" (Wilson) **79**:484
"William H. Herndon" (Masters) **25**:314
"William Hazlitt" (Woolf) **43**:406
"William II" (Verhaeren) **12**:471
"William Lloyd Garrison" (Cotter) **28**:43
William Lloyd Garrison (Chapman) **7**:189-90
"William Marion Reedy" (Masters) **25**:298
"William Riley and the Fates" (Benét) **7**:81
The William Saroyan Reader (Saroyan) **137**:155
William Shakespeare (Brandes) **11**:66-8, 70
"William the Conqueror" (Kipling) **8**:194
"Williams Mix" (Burroughs) **121**:138
"William's Wedding" (Jewett) **22**:130-31, 135
"Willie Baird" (Buchanan) **107**:15, 25
Willing (Arendt) **193**:30, 32-6, 39
"Willing to Pay the Price" (Walker) **129**:312, 316
"Willingness" (Anwar)
See "Penerimaan"
"Willow" (Merrill) **173**:255
Willow and Leather: A Book of Praise (Lucas) **73**:172
"The Willows" (Blackwood) **5**:70, 72, 74, 77, 79-80
"Willows" (Garneau) **13**:203
"Willows" (de la Mare) **4**:78; **53**:27
"Willow's Forge" (Kaye-Smith) **20**:106
Willow's Forge, and Other Poems (Kaye-Smith) **20**:101, 106-08
Willows Shedding Their Leaves at an Evening Window (Nagai)
See *Gesakusha no shi*
"The Willow-Ware" (Freeman) **9**:73
Will's Boy: A Memoir (Morris) **107**:176, 184-87, 208, 212, 225
"Willy Wet-Legs" (Lawrence) **93**:21
"Wilting" (Rebreanu)
See "Ofilire"
"A Wilting Jonquil" (Wright) **136**:302
"Wiltshire" (Pickthall) **21**:256
"Wimsey Papers—XI" (Sayers) **15**:389
"The Wind" (Bennett) **5**:46
"Wind" (Manning) **25**:278
"Wind" (Pasternak) **188**:184
"Ein Wind" (Rilke) **195**:210
"The Wind among the Poplars" (Forten) **16**:147, 150
The Wind among the Reeds (Yeats) **1**:569; **11**:508-09, 512, 526; **18**:442, 446; **31**:388
"Wind and Fog" (Dunsany) **59**:3
"Wind and Lyre" (Markham) **47**:286
"Wind and Mist" (Thomas) **10**:454, 463
"Wind and Silver" (Lowell) **8**:229
The Wind and the Rain (Burke) **63**:125-30
Wind and Wave (Sharp) **39**:395-96
"Wind at Night" (Symons) **11**:435
"The Wind Blows" (Mansfield) **39**:294, 303, 319, 322; **164**:252-53, 265, 302, 304, 306-7, 309-10
The Wind Blows Over (de la Mare) **4**:78; **53**:27, 35, 38
The Wind from Nowhere (Micheaux) **76**:239, 241, 244, 253
"Wind in the Rocks" (Galsworthy) **45**:33
"The Wind in the Rosebush" (Freeman) **9**:72
The Wind in the Rosebush, and Other Stories of the Supernatural (Freeman) **9**:72
The Wind in the Trees (Tynan) **3**:504
"Wind in the Valley" (Symons) **11**:435
The Wind in the Willows (Grahame) **64**:54-9, 63-4, 66-7, 70-80, 82-3, 85, 87-92, 96-104, 106, 108-10, 114-16; **136**:1-56
The Wind Is Rising (Tomlinson) **71**:400, 406
"Wind of Death" (Wetherald) **81**:413,415
The Wind of Freedom: The History of the Invasion of Greece by the Axis Powers, 1940-1941 (Mackenzie) **116**:228
Wind, Sand, and Stars (Saint-Exupéry)
See *Terre des hommes*
"The Wind Shifts" (Stevens) **45**:297
"The Wind That Lifts the Fog" (Drummond) **25**:150-51
"The Wind, the Shadow, and the Soul" (Sharp) **39**:374
"Windermere" (Johnson) **19**:244
The Windfall (Murfree) **135**:209, 220, 224
"Windflowers" (Miyazawa) **76**:293
"The Windigo" (Drummond) **25**:151
The Winding Stair, and Other Poems (Yeats) **1**:559; **11**:528; **18**:445, 452; **31**:388-89, 401, 403; **116**:261, 301, 314, 317
"Windjam" (Dent) **72**:30
"The Windmill" (Lucas) **73**:170-71
"The Window" (Moore) **7**:493
Window (Chandler)
See *The High Window*
"The Window and the Hearth" (Brennan) **17**:43
The Window at the White Cat (Rinehart) **52**:288-89, 291, 303-094
A Window in Thrums (Barrie) **2**:45; **164**:61, 80
"The Window Is Wide" (Brennan) **17**:53
"The Window of a Clinic" (Ishikawa) **15**:130
"The Window of the Tobacco Shop" (Cavafy) **2**:98
"Windows" (Jarrell) **177**:155
Windows (Galsworthy) **1**:304; **45**:53-4
Windows of Night (Williams) **1**:517; **11**:484
Winds and Wildcat Places (Miyazawa) **76**:277
Winds from Afar (Miyazawa) **76**:277
Winds of Doctrine (Santayana) **40**:376, 381
"The Winds of Orisha" (Lorde) **173**:86
"Winds of the World" (Meynell) **6**:294
"Winds of Winter" (Percy) **84**:198
The Windsor Tapestry (Mackenzie) **116**:228
"A Wind-Storm in the Forests" (Muir) **28**:241, 246
Windswept (Chase) **124**:15-16, 18, 21, 24
"A Windy Corner at Yonge-Albert" (Callaghan) **145**:254
Windy McPherson's Son (Anderson) **1**:35, 53, 55-7, 61; **10**:31-3, 36-8, 44; **24**:30; **123**:48, 57, 102-5
"Wine from These Grapes" (Millay) **169**:249-50, 267-68, 271
Wine from These Grapes (Millay) **4**:313; **49**:208, 210, 220, 222
Wine in Ferment (Moricz) **33**:249
Wine in the Wilderness: A Comedy Drama (Childress) **116**:38-40, 42
"The Wine Menagerie" (Crane) **2**:117, 120-22; **5**:188, 190
"The Wine of Illusion" (Sterling) **20**:387
The Wine of Life (Stringer) **37**:337
"A Wine of Wizardry" (Sterling) **20**:369-73, 377-80, 384, 386-87, 389
A Wine of Wizardry, and Other Poems (Sterling) **20**:371, 373-74, 384
Wine Press (Mistral)
See *Lagar*
"The Wine Worm" (Akutagawa Ryūnosuke) **16**:17, 27
"The Wine-Cups" (Mori Ogai)
See "Sakazuki"
Winesburg, Ohio (Anderson) **1**:35-7, 39, 41, 43-8, 50-61, 63-4; **10**:32-3, 36, 40-5, 50-2, 54-7; **24**:16-21, 23-9, 31-40, 43-4, 46-59; **123**:3-4, 9-13, 15-17, 26-7, 30-2, 37-9, 41-2, 48, 52-4, 56-7, 63-4, 68, 71-3, 75-8, 80, 82-3, 85, 88, 103-7, 109, 112
Winged Chariot (de la Mare) **4**:81
Winged Defense (Mitchell) **81**:159,161
"The Winged Destiny" (Sharp) **39**:396
The Winged Destiny: Studies in the Spiritual History of the Gael (Sharp) **39**:373-74
"Wingless" (Tolstoy) **18**:377
The Wingless Victory (Anderson) **2**:3, 9; **144**:17, 22, 73
Wings (Kuzmin)
See *Krilya*

The Wings (Nezval)
See *Křídla*
"Wings and Blue Flame: A Trilogy" (Villa) **176**:112
"Wings in the Dark" (Gray) **19**:152
"Wings of 'Lias" (Williams) **89**:363, 383, 391, 398
The Wings of the Dove (James) **2**:254, 257-58, 260, 263-64, 266-67, 270-71; **11**:319-20, 335-36, 340-42, 346; **40**:116, 120, 133, 149, 153, 169; **47**:161-62, 164-72, 185-87, 191, 195, 207-08; **64**:156, 171; **171**:142, 174, 180
"The Wings of the Dove: A Modern Sequel" (O'Faolain) **143**:273
Winkelberg (Hecht) **101**:80
Winner Take Nothing (Hemingway) **115**:189
Winnie-the-Pooh (Milne) **6**:309, 317, 320-21; **88**:229, 256-61
The Winning Lady, and Others (Freeman) **9**:73; **47**:84, 86, 103
"The Winning Loser" (Heyward) **59**:92-3
The Winning of Barbara Worth (Wright) **183**:349, 359, 372, 376, 380-81
"The Winning of Pomona" (Benét) **28**:2
"The Winning of the Biscuit-Shooter" (Wister) **21**:406
The Winning of the West (Roosevelt) **69**:175, 180, 182, 185, 188-89, 198-99, 205-09, 227-28, 240, 242, 250, 252-54, 275-76
"The Winnipeg Wolf" (Seton) **31**:270, 278-79
Winona: A Tale of Negro Life in the South and Southwest (Hopkins) **28**:174-75
Winston and Clementine: The Personal Letters of the Churchills (Churchill) **113**:191
"Winter" (Baker) **10**:19
"Winter" (Roberts) **8**:316
Winter (Reymont) **5**:390-91, 397
"The Winter Addresses of Kenneth Burke" (Nemerov) **124**:218
"A Winter Amid the Ice" (Verne)
See "Un Hivernage dans les glaces"
"Winter Beauty" (Gurney) **33**:86
"Winter Bells" (Stevens) **45**:275
"Winter Branch" (Balmont) **11**:41
"Winter Dreams" (Fitzgerald) **1**:262; **6**:169; **157**:126, 142, 189
"A Winter Drive" (Jewett) **22**:140
"Winter Exercise" (Nemerov) **124**:180, 249
"Winter Field" (Coppard) **5**:178
"A Winter Garland" (Sarton) **120**:245
"A Winter Holiday" (Carman) **7**:138
"Winter Hungary" (Ady)
See "A téli Magyarország"
"Winter in a Durnover Field" (Hardy) **53**:81
Winter in Moscow (Muggeridge) **120**:145-46, 148, 180, 182
"Winter in the Abruzzo" (Ginzburg)
See "Inverno in Abruzzo"
"Winter in the Air" (Warner) **131**:321
Winter in the Air, and Other Stories (Warner) **131**:321
"Der Winter ist vergangen" (Raabe) **45**:187
"Winter Lightning" (Nemerov) **124**:205
"Winter Lilies" (Annensky)
See "Zimnie lilii"
The Winter Murder Case (Van Dine) **23**:360
"Winter Night" (Jozsef) **22**:158, 161-62, 164
"Winter Night" (Millay) **169**:293
"Winter Night" (Pasternak) **188**:189, 193, 196, 204
"Winter Night" (Talvik) **87**:319
The Winter Night (Leino)
See *Talvi-yö*
The Winter of Our Discontent (Steinbeck) **135**:286
"Winter on Earth" (Toomer) **172**:265
"Winter Rain" (Davidson) **24**:164
"Winter Rug" (Brautigan) **133**:2-4
"Winter Sleep" (Wylie) **8**:532-33
"Winter Solace" (Lucas) **73**:171, 174
Winter Sonata (Valle-Inclán)
See *Sonata de invierno: Memorias del marqués de Bradomín*
"Winter Song" (Owen) **5**:374
"Winter Songs" (Bialik) **25**:58
Winter Sonnets (Ivanov)
See *Zimnie sonety*
Winter Words: Various Moods and Metres (Hardy) **53**:117; **143**:143, 151, 191, 196-97, 213
"Ein Winterabend" (Trakl) **5**:457, 460
"Winterdämmerung" (Trakl) **5**:456
"Wintergarden" (Arp) **115**:5, 16-18, 20
"Winter's Dregs" (Hardy) **53**:81
"A Winter's Tale" (Gale) **7**:284
"A Winter's Tale" (Lawrence) **93**:17, 117
"A Winter's Tale" (Thomas) **1**:470-71, 473; **45**:363, 377; **105**:334
"Winter's Turning" (Lowell) **8**:236
Winter's Wind (Natsume) **10**:332
"The Winter's Camp—A Day's Ride from the Mail" (Foote) **108**:34
Winterset (Anderson) **2**:3, 5-7, 10-11; **144**:4-7, 10-11, 13, 17-18, 20-24, 26-37, 39, 51-52, 57, 70, 72-73, 75-77
Wintersmoon (Walpole) **5**:496, 498, 503-04
Wintertag (Kandinsky) **92**:49
Winthrop's Adventure (Lee) **5**:314
"Wiosna" (Schulz) **5**:423-24; **51**:308, 316
Wir fanden einen Pfad (Morgenstern) **8**:304-05, 311
"Wir Juden" (Kolmar) **40**:175
Wir müssen wahre Sätze finden. Gespräche und Interviews (Bachmann) **192**:55, 95, 99, 129, 147, 155
Wir sind (Werfel) **8**:475, 477-78
Wir spielen, bis uns der Tod abholt (Schwitters) **95**:341
Wird Hill amnestiert? (Feuchtwanger) **3**:181
The Wire Tappers (Stringer) **37**:335, 337
"Wireless" (Kipling) **8**:202; **17**:209
"A Wireless Message" (Bierce) **44**:45
"Wires" (Tsvetaeva)
See "Provoda"
"A Wire-Walker" (Graham) **19**:129
Wiriamu Morisu kenkyū (Akutagawa Ryūnosuke) **16**:17
Wirtschaft und Gesellschaft (Weber) **69**:296, 314-15, 355, 383
Die Wirtschaftsethic der Weltreligionen (Weber) **69**:355
Wiry (Sienkiewicz) **3**:424-25
"Wisdom" (Parker) **143**:323
"Wisdom" (Zoshchenko)
See "Mudrost'"
Wisdom (Zoshchenko) **15**:492
Wisdom and Destiny (Maeterlinck)
See *La sagesse et la destinée*
"Wisdom Cometh with the Years" (Cullen) **4**:40
"Wisdom Garnered by Day" (McAlmon) **97**:99
The Wisdom of China and India (Lin) **149**:320-21, 346
The Wisdom of Father Brown (Chesterton) **6**:102
"The Wisdom of Life" (Lagerkvist) **144**:216
The Wisdom of Sands (Saint-Exupéry)
See *Citadelle*
"The Wisdom of Silence" (Dunbar) **2**:131, 133; **12**:112
"The Wisdom of the King" (Yeats) **31**:416, 419
The Wisdom of the Sands (Saint-Exupéry)
See *Citadelle*
Wisdom While You Wait (Lucas) **73**:158, 168
Wisdom's Daughter: The Life and Love Story of She-Who-Must-Be-Obeyed! (Haggard) **11**:248, 254-56
"The Wise" (Cullen) **4**:45; **37**:148, 160, 165
Wise Blood (O'Connor) **132**:229, 232, 243, 246-47, 253, 257, 259, 263, 265, 279, 283-84, 290-97, 328, 356, 364-65
Wise Children (Carter) **139**:45, 53-54, 58, 128, 197-200, 217, 219
"The Wise Dog" (Gibran) **9**:82
The Wise King (Garro)
See *El Rey mago*
"The Wise Little Girl" (Carter) **139**:128
"The Wise Men" (Crane) **11**:125, 155
"The Wise Old Dwarf" (Frank) **17**:108, 114
The Wise Tomcat (Heijermans) **24**:293
The Wise Virgins (Undset)
See *De kloge jomfruer*
"The Wise Woman" (Prado)
See "La risa en el desierto"
The Wise Woman (MacDonald)
See *The Lost Princess*
"Wiser than a God" (Chopin) **14**:61, 70; **127**:61, 77, 185, 194, 208
"A Wish" (Cullen) **37**:156, 160
"The Wish" (Dahl) **173**:10
The Wish (Sigurjónsson)
See *Ønsket*
"The Wish House" (Kipling) **8**:194-95, 200-01, 208-09; **17**:207
"The Wish to Be a Red Indian" (Kafka) **179**:307-8
"Wishing" (Holly) **65**:138, 149, 151
"Die wissenschaft" (Morgenstern) **8**:305
Wit and Its Relation to the Unconscious (Freud)
See *Der Wit und seine Beziehung zum Unbewussten*
Der Wit und seine Beziehung zum Unbewussten (Freud) **52**:90
"The Witch" (Coleridge) **73**:4-5, 11, 27
"The Witch" (Jackson) **187**:336-37
"The Witch" (Kolmar) **40**:175
"The Witch" (Tynan) **3**:504
The Witch (Lindsay) **15**:225, 227-30, 232
The Witch (Williams) **1**:518; **11**:499
The Witch from Riga (Rainis)
See *Rīgas ragana*
The Witch-Herbalist of the Remote Town (Tutuola) **188**:306, 308
The Witch of Ellangowan (Chambers) **41**:89
"The Witch of Lecca" (Post) **39**:339, 343
The Witch of Prague (Crawford) **10**:140, 143, 151-52, 157-58
"Witch of the Hours" (Barlach)
See "Stundenhexe"
"A Witch Shall Be Born" (Howard) **8**:133, 136
"The Witch Wife" (Millay) **169**:300
Witch Wood (Buchan) **41**:39, 72-3, 75-6
Witchcraft (Williams) **11**:502
Witchcraft and Black Magic (Summers) **16**:430
"Witchcraft and the Cinema" (Artaud) **36**:36
"Witchcraft—New Style" (Abercrombie) **141**:20-22
The Witchcraft of Salem Village (Jackson) **187**:253
"A Witch-Doctor and Venus" (Khlebnikov)
See "Shaman i Venera"
The Witchery of the Butterfly (García Lorca)
See *El maleficio de la mariposa*
"The Witches" (Papadiamantis) **29**:272-73
The Witches (Dahl) **173**:20, 26, 28
Witchfinder (Buchanan) **107**:30
The Witching Hour (Thomas) **97**:126, 131-32, 134-36, 138-40
"The Witching of Elspie" (Scott) **6**:398
"The Witch-Mother" (Swinburne) **8**:427
The Witch's Head (Haggard) **11**:237-39, 244, 253
"Witch-Woman" (Lowell) **1**:371, 373
"With a Difference (Not Literature)" (Gilman) **117**:100, 102-03, 105, 107, 116, 119-20, 123
"With a Fiery Maur" (Remizov)
See "S ognenoi past'iu"
With a Pen of Gold (Svevo)
See *Con la penna d'oro*
With All My Might (Caldwell) **117**:10, 28
"With an Evening Primrose" (Rhodes) **53**:316
"With 'Buster'" (Harte) **25**:218
With Clipped Eyes (Remizov)
See *Podstrizhennymi glazami*

With Closed Eyes (Arenas)
See *Con los Ojos Cerrados*
With Closed Eyes (Tozzi)
See *Con gli occhi chiusi*
With Fire and Sword (Sienkiewicz)
See *Ogniem i mieczem*
"With French to Kimberley" (Paterson) **32**:374
"With Her in Ourland" (Gilman) **117**:134-35, 37-41
With Her in Ourland (Gilman) **9**:108-09, 115; **37**:183; **117**:49, 75, 78, 114, 124-27, 130-31, 136, 166, 171-74, 177
"With Intent to Steal" (Blackwood) **5**:79
"With Kyushu Students" (Hearn) **9**:129
With Love and Irony (Lin) **149**:317-18
"With Mr Cogito Thinks About Hell" (Herbert) **168**:20
With My Friends: Tales Told in Partnership (Matthews) **95**:271
With Open Eyes (Yourcenar)
See *Les yeux ouverts*
"With or Without Buttons" (Butts) **77**:76
"With Quiet Evening" (Balmont) **11**:41
"With Rue My Heart Is Laden" (Housman) **10**:247, 252
"With Scindia to Delhi" (Kipling) **17**:196
"With Seed the Sowers Scatter" (Housman) **10**:247
With the Band (Chambers) **41**:88
"With the Gypsies" (Gumilev) **60**:272
With the Immortals (Crawford) **10**:144, 151, 157-58
"With the Main Guard" (Kipling) **17**:204
"With the North-West Wind" (Graham) **19**:112
With the Procession (Fuller) **103**:57, 59, 62, 65-66, 68, 70-71, 73-74, 79-82, 84-85, 87, 90, 94-95, 99, 101-06, 108, 117
"With the Rear Guard" (Kipling) **8**:176
With the Russians in Manchuria (Baring) **8**:40
"With These Hands" (Kornbluth) **8**:216-17
With You (Bacovia) **24**:64
Wither China? (Barthes) **135**:173
"The Withered Arm" (Hardy) **4**:159; **143**:77
"Withered Fields" (Akutagawa Ryūnosuke)
See "Karenoshō"
"A Withered Flower" (Chang)
See "Hua diao"
"The Withered Leaf and the Green" (Powys) **9**:377
"Withered Skin of Berries" (Toomer) **172**:305, 308, 310
Within a Budding Grove (Proust)
See *À l'ombre des jeunes filles en fleurs*
"Within a Grove" (Akutagawa Ryūnosuke)
See "Yabu no naka"
"Within an Ace of Greatness" (Warung) **45**:419
Within and Without (MacDonald) **9**:287, 291, 300, 304; **113**:197
Within Life's Limits (Éluard)
See *A l'intérieur de la vie*
Within Our Gates (Micheaux) **76**:245-46, 262
Within the Gates (Phelps) **113**:345
"Within this Arcadian Garden" (Nabokov) **108**:209
"Without Benefit of Clergy" (Kipling) **8**:183, 202, 207; **17**:207-08
Without Dogma (Sienkiewicz)
See *Bez dogmatu*
"Without Fairies or Witches" (Ginzburg) **156**:29
Without Fathers (Chekhov) **31**:99
"Without fear of wind or vertigo" (Calvino) **183**:134
"Without Hope" (Jozsef) **22**:158
"Without Knocking" (Jozsef) **22**:160
"Without Light" (Aleixandre)
See "Sin luz"
Without Love (Barry) **11**:58, 60, 63-5
"Without Name" (Obstfelder) **23**:189
Without Prejudice (Zangwill) **16**:444, 461
"Without Reason but Tired" (Quiroga)
See "Cuento sin razón, pero cansado"
"Without the Nighted Wyvern" (Lowry) **6**:237
"Without Visible Means" (Morrison) **72**:353
"The Witness" (Bergelson) **81**:23
"The Witness" (Petry) **112**:290, 300
"The Witness" (Rilke)
See "Der Schauende"
Witness (Chambers) **129**:2-3, 5-6, 10-13, 15-19, 22-24, 27, 29, 31-32, 40-45, 48-56
Wittgenstein's Lectures, 1932-1935 (Wittgenstein) **59**:298
Wittgensteins Neffe (Bernhard)
See *Wittgensteins Neffe: eine Freundschaft*
Wittgensteins Neffe: eine Freundschaft (Bernhard) **165**:19, 58, 79-83, 85, 95-97, 100, 111
Wittgenstein's Nephew (Bernhard)
See *Wittgensteins Neffe: eine Freundschaft*
"Die Wittwe von Pisa" (Heyse) **8**:113
Wives (Bradford) **36**:57, 59, 67
The Wives' Friend (Pirandello)
See *L'amica delle mogli*
Wives in Exile (Sharp) **39**:373
Wives under Suspicion (Whale) **63**:339
"A Wizard from Gettysburg" (Chopin) **14**:69
The Wizard of Oz (Baum)
See *The Wonderful Wizard of Oz*
The Wizard of Venus (Burroughs) **2**:81
"Wo die strahlen schneil verschleissen" (George) **14**:213
"Wo ist dein Bruder?" (Böll) **185**:188, 192-93
Wo warst du, Adam? (Böll) **185**:4-5, 17-19, 26, 49-50, 57, 129-30
"Woe Water" (Wakefield) **120**:350
The Woggle-Bug Book (Baum) **132**:12-13, 75, 80-81
Wohin rollst du, Äpfelchen . . . (Perutz) **60**:370-71
"Wolf" (Chekhov) **163**:78, 106, 130
The Wolf (Molnár)
See *A farkas*
The Wolf (Norris) **155**:269
"Wolf Alice" (Carter) **139**:135, 142, 204
"The Wolf at the Door" (Gilman) **9**:97
The Wolf Woman (Stringer) **37**:337
Wolfbane (Kornbluth) **8**:215-16
Wolfgang Goethe (Brandes) **11**:68, 71
"Wolf's Head" (Murfree) **135**:208
Wolf's Salt (Popa)
See *Vučja so*
"Wolken" (Ball) **104**:13-15
Die wolkenpumpe (Arp) **115**:8, 10, 28, 31
Wolkenpumpe (Arp) **115**:5, 46
The Wolves (Palamas) **5**:388
"The Wolves of Cernogratz" (Saki) **3**:372, 374
"The Wolves of God" (Blackwood) **5**:71
The Wolves of God, and Other Fey Stories (Blackwood) **5**:71, 77
"Woman" (Bodenheim) **44**:69
"Woman" (Carpenter) **88**:72
"The Woman" (Eastman) **55**:170-71
"Woman Afraid" (Santos) **156**:324-25
"Woman an Opinion" (Twain) **12**:438
"A Woman and Her Son" (Davidson) **24**:163, 169, 189
The Woman and the Man (Buchanan) **107**:85
The Woman and the Priest (Deledda)
See *La madre*
"The Woman and the Wife" (Robinson) **101**:119
"Woman as Type" (Andreas-Salome) **56**:57
"The Woman at Dusk" (Stringer) **37**:329
A Woman at Dusk, and Other Poems (Stringer) **37**:330, 332, 340
"The Woman at the Crossways" (Sharp) **39**:377
"The Woman at the Store" (Mansfield) **2**:451, 458; **8**:286; **39**:293, 301-03, 319, 322; **164**:269, 339-42
"The Woman at the Washington Zoo" (Jarrell) **177**:125, 132, 141, 152, 159, 170, 172-73, 175-77, 181, 183, 207, 211, 218-19, 231-32
The Woman at the Washington Zoo (Jarrell) **177**:131, 139-40, 162, 173, 176-77, 193, 215
"Woman, Death, and Jehovah" (Grieg) **10**:208
"Woman Friend" (Tsvetaeva) **35**:410
The Woman I Abandoned (Endo)
See *The Girl I Left Behind*
"The Woman I Met" (Hardy) **53**:101
"The Woman in his Life" (Kipling) **8**:191, 196
Woman in Moscow (Kandinsky) **92**:37
"Woman in Science" (Roosevelt) **69**:268
The Woman in the Alcove (Green) **63**:152
The Woman in the Dunes (Abe)
See *Suna no onna*
Woman in the Plural (Nezval)
See *Žena v množném čísle*
"The Woman in the Rain" (Stringer) **37**:334, 342
The Woman in the Rain, and Other Poems (Stringer) **37**:329, 341
"The Woman in the Rented Room" (Nagai)
See "Kashima no onna"
A Woman in the Window (Drieu la Rochelle)
See *Une femme è sa fenêtre*
The Woman Interferes (Moricz)
See *Az asszony beleszól*
The Woman Intervenes (Moricz)
See *Az asszony beleszól*
"Woman Looking at a Vase of Flowers" (Stevens) **12**:360; **45**:334-35
The Woman of Dreams (Nagai)
See *Yume no onna*
A Woman of Genius (Austin) **25**:23, 25-7, 30, 33
The Woman of Knockaloe (Caine) **97**:6, 15
A Woman of No Importance (Wilde) **1**:495, 497-98, 502, 504, 506, 508; **8**:490, 494, 499; **23**:409, 411-12, 420, 424, 427, 435, 438; **41**:397; **175**:268, 272-74, 276, 280, 286, 312-13
Woman of Rumor (Mizoguchi) **72**:313, 315
The Woman of Samaria (Rostand)
See *La Samaritaine*
Woman of the Earth (Trambley) **163**:305, 307
Woman of the River (Alegria)
See "A Temple of the Holy Ghost"
Woman of the Rock (Mankiewicz) **85**:149
"The Woman of the Saeter" (Jerome) **23**:83
"The Woman on the Rock" (Andrić)
See "Žena na kamenu"
"A Woman Sang" (Stringer) **37**:331, 342
The Woman Thou Gavest Me (Caine) **97**:3, 8, 10
"The Woman Tramp" (Kolmar) **40**:175
Woman Triumphant (Blasco Ibáñez)
See *La maja desnuda*
"Woman Trouble" (Kunikida Doppo)
See "Jonan"
"Woman Undiscovered" (Kolmar) **40**:175
A Woman Ventures (Phillips) **44**:253, 257, 262, 273, 277
"Woman Wading" (Papadiamantis) **29**:272
"Woman Wants Bread, Not the Ballot" (Anthony) **84**:11, 22-3
"The Woman Who Blamed Life on a Spaniard" (Stevens) **45**:348
The Woman Who Could Not Read, and Other Tales (Zoshchenko) **15**:494
"The Woman Who Lost Her Man" (Hedāyat)
See "Zani-ka mardash ra gun kard"
"The Woman Who Loved Chopin" (Huneker) **65**:169, 198
"The Woman Who Rode Away" (Lawrence) **48**:121, 125; **93**:97, 103
The Woman Who Rode Away, and Other Stories (Lawrence) **2**:354, 357
"The Woman Who Sowed Iniquity" (Evans) **85**:38
"The Woman Who Stole Everything" (Bennett) **5**:46
The Woman Who Was Poor (Bloy)
See *La femme pauvre*
"The Woman Who Wasn't Allowed to Keep Cats" (White) **176**:193, 228, 244
The Woman with the Fan (Hichens) **64**:122-23, 126, 131

"The Woman with the Net" (Sharp) **39**:376
"The Woman with the Velvet Collar" (Leroux) **25**:260
The Woman Within (Glasgow) **7**:342
"The Woman without a Shadow" (Barthes) **135**:125
"A Woman Young and Old" (Yeats) **31**:398; **116**:332
"A Woman's Arms" (Machado de Assis) **10**:288
The Woman's Bible (Stanton) **73**:245-46, 250, 258-63, 265, 268, 270, 274-75
"A Woman's Hand" (White) **176**:159, 190, 229
Woman's Honor (Glaspell) **55**:234, 236, 258-59; **175**:107, 112, 144
"A Woman's Kingdom" (Chekhov)
See "Bab'e carstuo"
A Woman's Reason (Howells) **7**:366, 381; **17**:184-85; **41**:263
"Woman's Rights" (Eddy) **71**:143
A Woman's Secret (Mankiewicz) **85**:158
"A Woman's Sonnets" (Gregory) **176**:61-63, 66
"A Woman's Utopia" (Gilman) **117**:75-6
"A Woman's Voice" (Baker) **3**:2; **10**:28
"A Woman's Wrath" (Peretz) **16**:405
"The Womb" (Zamyatin)
See "Chrevo"
"Wombwell" (Jensen) **41**:307
"The Women" (Apollinaire)
See "Les femmes"
"Women" (Lardner) **14**:307
Women (Tarkington) **9**:459, 461, 469
Women and Economics (Gilman) **9**:98-100, 102-05; **37**:174, 176, 178, 182-83, 187-88; **117**:49, 54-7, 59, 68, 70, 76, 78, 85, 93, 125-27, 131-134, 139-40, 151-56, 167, 167, 169-70
"Women and Education" (Iqbal) **28**:183
"Women and Labour" (Schreiner) **9**:394-95, 397, 399-400, 402-04
Women and Men (Ford) **15**:70, 79; **39**:128
Women and Men (Higginson) **36**:166
Women and the Factory Acts (Webb and Webb) **22**:413
Women Are Like That (Delafield) **61**:133
The Women at the Pump (Hamsun)
See *Konerne ved vandposten*
The Women from Sarajevo (Andrić)
See "Gospodjicd"
Women in a River Landscape (Böll)
See *Frauen vor Flußlandschaft*
Women in Love (Lawrence) **2**:344, 348, 350, 357-61, 366, 368-69, 371-75; **9**:214, 216, 221-22, 226-27, 230; **16**:291, 295, 300, 313; **33**:176-231; **48**:100-02, 113, 115-17, 123, 125-26, 130-32, 134, 136, 142; **61**:183, 186-7, 191, 193, 197-200, 203-4, 210, 215, 217-21, 225, 232, 240, 252-3, 258-9, 277; **93**:21, 23, 48, 68, 97, 103, 127
Women in Love (Sutro) **6**:421
"The Women of Dan Dance With Swords in Their Hands to Mark the Time When They Were Warriors" (Lorde) **173**:83
The Women of Shakespeare (Harris) **24**:262
"The Women of Spain" (Pardo Bazán)
See "La mujer española"
Women of the Night (Mizoguchi)
See *Yoru no Onnatachi*
"Women of Today" (Gilman) **37**:176, 198
"Women Travelling Alone" (Engel) **137**:117-18
"Women's Complete Independence" (Yosano)
See "Joshi no tettei shita bokuritsu"
A Women's Duel (Dazai Osamu)
See *Onna no kettō*
"Women's Speah" (Holley) **99**:315
"Wonder and a Thousand Springs" (Percy) **84**:198
The Wonder Clock (Pyle) **81**:398
The Wonder Effect (Kornbluth) **8**:215-16
The Wonder Hat (Hecht) **101**:37, 73
"The Wonder of It" (Monroe) **12**:216
"Wonder of the World" (Arp) **115**:21-2
"The Wonder of the World" (Lee-Hamilton) **22**:187, 189
"Wonder of Woman" (London) **39**:288
The Wonderful Adventures of Nils (Lagerloef)
See *Nils Holgerssons underbara resa genom Sverige*
Wonderful Fool (Endo)
See *Obakasan*
The Wonderful Lamp (Valle-Inclán)
See *La lampara maravillosa: Ejer cicios espirituales*
"The Wonderful Old Gentleman" (Parker) **143**:314-15, 331, 343
"The Wonderful Story of Henry Sugar" (Dahl) **173**:17
The Wonderful Story of Henry Sugar and Six More (Dahl) **173**:10, 17
The Wonderful Visit (Wells) **6**:542-43, 547; **12**:487-88; **19**:424, 436; **133**:224-25
The Wonderful Wizard of Oz (Baum) **7**:12-17, 19-23, 25-7; **132**:3-5, 7-15, 18-24, 28, 30, 32, 35-6, 43-4, 46-52 , 54-60, 62, 66-8, 74-7, 80-2, 85-9, 91-2, 97-9, 101, 103-8
The Wonders of Life (Haeckel)
See *Die Lebenswunder*
"The Wonder-Worker" (Peretz)
See "Der Kuntsenmakher"
"The Wondrous" (Mann)
See "Das wunderbare"
"The Wondrous Child" (Stoker) **144**:254-55
"The Wood by the Sea" (Scott) **6**:393, 397
The Wood Carver's Wife (Pickthall) **21**:244-45, 251, 254-56, 258
The Wood Demon (Chekhov)
See *Leshy*
"Wood Note" (Dreiser) **18**:51
"Wood, Paper, Stone" (Sarton) **120**:265
"The Wood Peewee" (Scott) **6**:388
"The Wood Thrush" (Reese) **181**:344
Woodbarrow Farm (Jerome) **23**:82
Woodbine Lodge (Bradford) **36**:63
"The Wood-Choppers" (Chopin) **127**:10
Woodcutters (Bernhard)
See *Holzfällen: Eine Erregung*
"Wooden Die" (Herbert)
See "Drewniana kostka"
The Wooden Horse (Walpole) **5**:492, 498, 502
"Wooden Shoes of Little Wolff" (Coppee) **25**:121
"The Woodfelling" (Tolstoy)
See "Rubka lesa"
"Woodford's Partner" (Post) **39**:337-38
"Woodland Anguish" (Khlebnikov) **20**:134
The Woodland Life (Thomas) **10**:449
"The Woodland Orchard" (Coffin) **95**:15
The Woodlanders (Hardy) **4**:149, 153; **10**:217, 227-28, 230, 233; **18**:90, 100; **32**:274, 280-81; **48**:71; **53**:73, 83, 111; **72**:168, 216, 237, 241, 246, 266; **143**:72, 76-78, 81-82, 94, 99, 109, 111, 113, 115, 118, 129, 135, 169-71, 178, 206; **153**:128, 194, 202-4, 207-8
Woodrow Wilson: Life and Letters (Baker) **47**:8
"The Woods" (Gumilev)
See "Les"
"The Woods of Westermain" (Meredith) **17**:256
"The Woodside Way" (Wetherald) **81**:408
"The Woodsman in the Foundry" (Pickthall) **21**:253
"The Woodspring to the Poet" (Scott) **6**:389, 396
"The Wooing of Becfola" (Stephens) **4**:414
"The Wooing of Monsieur Cuerrier" (Scott) **6**:398
"The Wooing of Sir Keith" (Pyle) **81**:390
"The Wooing Pine" (Guiney) **41**:206-07
"Wooing Song for Sir Toby" (Morley) **87**:146
The Woollcott Reader (Woollcott) **5**:523-24
"The Word" (Gumilev) **60**:264, 272-3
"The Word" (Thomas) **10**:452
"Word" (Villaurrutia) **80**:489
The Word (Nabokov)
See "Slovo"
"The Word and Culture" (Mandelstam) **2**:405
Word Art and Picture Art (Lagerkvist)
See *Ordkonst och bildkonst*
"The Word as Such" (Khlebnikov) **20**:151
A Word Child (Murdoch) **171**:284-85, 300-301, 323, 329
"Word for Word" (Bachmann)
See "Simultan"
"The Word of Fu Manchu" (Rohmer) **28**:301
Word-dreams and black stars (Arp)
See *Wortträume und schwarze Sterne*
"The Wordless Touch" (Stringer) **37**:342
"Wordlessness" (Balmont)
See "Bezglagol'nost"
"Words" (Andrić)
See "Reci"
"Words" (Coleridge) **73**:5
"Words" (Douglas) **40**:71
"Words" (Thomas) **10**:456, 464
"Words" (Yeats) **93**:348
"Words and Music" (Cobb) **77**:120
Words and Music (Beckett) **145**:136, 140
Words are stones (Levi)
See *Le parole sono pietre*
Words for Music Perhaps, and Other Poems (Yeats) **1**:580
Words for Pictures (Beerbohm) **24**:115-16, 122
"Words for the Hour" (Harper) **14**:260, 263
Words for the Hour (Howe) **21**:109, 112
"Words of Comfort to the Scratched on a Mirror" (Parker) **143**:322
"Words of Love" (Holly) **65**:138, 140-42, 145, 151-52
"Words of Love and Warmth" (Guro)
See "Slova ljubvi i tepla"
"Words to My Love" (Cullen) **37**:155, 164, 167
The Words upon the Window-Pane (Yeats) **1**:583; **11**:513-14, 523
"Wordsworth" (Forten) **16**:150
"Wordsworth's Ethics" (Stephen) **23**:328
Work and Leisure (Gill) **85**:55, 79, 83, 91
Work & Property &c. (Gill) **85**:89, 91
"Work, Death, and Sickness" (Tolstoy) **11**:463
Work in Progress (Joyce)
See *Finnegans Wake*
Work Is Tiresome (Pavese)
See *Lavorare stanca*
The Work of an Actor on a Role (Stanislavsky) **167**:305
"A Work of Art" (Warner) **131**:317
Work of Art (Lewis) **4**:251-52, 260
The Work of Art in the Age of Mechanical Reproduction (Benjamin)
See *Das Kunstwerk im Zeitalter seiner technischen Reproduzierbarkeit*
The Work of Iron, in Nature, Art and Policy (Ruskin) **63**:242
The Work of the Digestive Glands (Pavlov) **91**:146, 150, 154-5, 157, 162-3
"The Work on Red Mountain" (Harte) **25**:217
The Work, Wealth, and Happiness of Mankind (Wells) **6**:537; **133**:236, 339
Work Wearies (Pavese)
See *Lavorare stanca*
"The Worker" (Gumilev) **60**:263-4, 276
"Worker" (Jozsef) **22**:161
"The Worker in Sandalwood" (Pickthall) **21**:245-46, 248
Workers in the Dawn (Gissing) **3**:227, 229-31, 233, 235-37; **24**:215, 220, 226, 233, 247-49; **47**:134
Workers of All Lands, Unite (Heijermans) **24**:291
The Workhouse Ward (Gregory) **1**:334-37; **176**:14, 17-19, 31-32, 34, 40
"Working Notes" (Merleau-Ponty) **156**:184
Working People (Kielland)
See *Arbeidsfolk*
Working with the Hands: Being a Sequel to "Up from Slavery" Covering the Author's Experiences in Industrial Training at Tuskegee (Washington) **10**:525

"The Workingmen and the Tariff" (Darrow) **81**:66
The Workings of Fate (Machado) **3**:313
"The Workman" (Dunsany) **59**:77
"Workman" (Oppen) **107**:309
"The Workman" (Storni)
See "El obrero"
"A Workman's Budget" (Morrison) **72**:374
Works (Caragiale) **76**:173-74
Works (Ortega y Gasset) **9**:347
Works (Remizov)
See *Sochineniia*
The Works (Ruskin) **63**:251
Works and Days (Field) **43**:165, 170-71, 174-76, 179
The Works of Anne Frank (Frank) **18**:108
Works of Fancy and Imagination (MacDonald) **9**:292, 303
The Works of H. G. Wells (Wells) **133**:315
The Works of John Galsworthy (Galsworthy) **45**:53, 56
The Works of Love (Morris) **107**:95, 97-8, 103, 111, 113, 122, 142-43, 147-49, 156, 174-77, 179-80, 185, 188, 208, 212, 226, 235-37
The Works of Max Beerbohm (Beerbohm) **1**:66-7, 73; **24**:96, 98, 109-10, 115-16
The Works of Theodore Roosevelt (Roosevelt) **69**:255, 267
The Works of Thomas Hardy in Prose and Verse (Hardy) **143**:83, 95
World Alone (Aleixandre)
See *Mundo a solas*
"The World and the Child" (Merrill) **173**:257-58
"The World and the Door" (Henry) **19**:191
"The World and Will as Idea" (Svevo) **2**:547
"The World as Ballet" (Symons) **11**:445, 449
"The World as Breughel Imagined It" (Nemerov) **124**:256, 306
"The World as Meditation" (Stevens) **45**:273, 279-80
The World at War (Brandes) **11**:66
World Brain (Wells) **133**:236
The World Crisis (Churchill) **113**:89, 102, 104, 112-13, 133, 148-49, 152, 162, 182, 184-85
The World Crisis of 1914-1918 (Halévy) **104**:112
The World Does Move (Tarkington) **9**:468
"The World Economic Conference, 1933" (Keynes) **54**:244
"World Harmony" (Khlebnikov)
See "Ladomir"
The World I Breathe (Thomas) **8**:449; **105**:306, 325
A World in a Grain of Sand (Frye) **165**:188, 192
A World in Birth (Rolland) **23**:264
The World in Falseface (Nathan) **18**:303-04, 324
The World in the Attic (Morris) **107**:96, 101, 114, 142-47, 154, 156-57, 203
World in the Head (Canetti)
See *Welt im Kopf*
The World Is Dancing (van Schendel)
See *De wereld een dansfeest*
"World Lines: A War Story" (Nemerov) **124**:292
"The World Movement—Biological Analogies in History" (Roosevelt) **69**:245-47, 262, 268
The World My Wilderness (Macaulay) **44**:124, 126, 133
The World of Action (Nishida) **83**:345
The World of Chance (Howells) **7**:368, 376, 378-79, 397-400; **17**:184-85
The World of Dreams (Ellis) **14**:112, 114, 131
"The World of Grandpa Benchley" (Benchley) **55**:15
The World of Jeeves (Wodehouse) **108**:378
"The World of Life" (Platonov) **14**:420
A World of Light: Portraits and Celebrations (Sarton) **120**:230, 267, 273
A World of Love (Bowen) **148**:9-15, 17-18, 20, 26-28, 30-37, 40-43, 45, 67, 79, 103, 109-11, 115-19, 123-24, 126-27, 129-30, 132
The World of Mr. Mulliner (Wodehouse) **108**:362
The World of Psmith (Wodehouse) **108**:395
"The World of Seven Wells" (Storni)
See "El mundo de siete pozos"
"A World of Sound" (Stapledon) **22**:324
The World of Stone (Borowski) **9**:23-4
The World of the Thibaults (Martin du Gard)
See *Les Thibault*
The World of William Clissold (Wells) **6**:529, 532, 537, 553; **12**:499-500
"The World of Wrestling" (Barthes) **135**:128
The World of Yesterday (Zweig)
See *Die welt von Gestern*
The World Over (Wharton) **129**:364
World Peace (Couperus)
See *Wereldvrede*
The World Reformer (Bernhard)
See *Der Weltverbesserer*
The World Set Free: A Story of Mankind (Wells) **6**:539; **19**:426, 438, 440-41, 453
World So Wide (Lewis) **4**:260; **13**:339
The World Tomorrow (Rogers) **8**:332
The World Upside Down (Khlebnikov)
See *Mirskonca*
The World We Live In (Bromfield) **11**:83
The World We Live In: The Insect Comedy (Čapek)
See *Ze života hmyzu*
"World without Peculiarity" (Stevens) **45**:349
"World World" (Oppen) **107**:263, 361
The World-Improver (Bernhard)
See *Der Weltverbesserer*
"The World-Mother" (Campbell) **9**:31
"The World-Purpose" (Markham) **47**:284
"Worlds" (Masters) **25**:298
Worlds (Kolmar)
See *Welten*
"The World's Desire" (Masters) **25**:298
The World's Desire (Lang) **16**:251, 265
World's End (Wassermann)
See *Der unbekannte Gast*
The World's Illusion (Wassermann)
See *Christian Wahnschaffe*
"The World's May Queen" (Noyes) **7**:513
Worlds of Color (Du Bois) **169**:213
The World's Own (Howe) **21**:109, 112
Worlds within Worlds (Benson) **17**:23-34
Worleys (Reese) **181**:339
"A Worm Fed on the Heart of Corinth" (Rosenberg) **12**:293, 303, 310, 312
The Worm Ouroboros (Eddison) **15**:51-2, 54, 57-63
"The Worms at Heaven's Gate" (Stevens) **12**:365, 376
"Worms of the Earth" (Howard) **8**:137
"Wormwood" (Pilnyak)
See "Polyn"
Wormwood: A Drama of Paris (Corelli) **51**:66-7, 74-5
"Worpswede" (Rilke) **195**:292
"The Worship of Love" (Naidu) **80**:308
The Worship of Nature (Frazer) **32**:203, 234
The Worshipful Lucia (Benson) **27**:9
"Worshipping the Statue of Maupassant" (Nagai)
See "Mōpasan no sekizō o hai-su"
Worstward Ho (Beckett) **145**:91, 115, 121
"Ein Wort" (Benn) **3**:114
"Das Wort" (George) **2**:154; **14**:209
Worte in Versen (Kraus) **5**:285, 291
"Worth a Leg" (Williams) **89**:374, 384
The Worth of a Woman (Phillips) **44**:260, 262, 268, 275
Wortträume und schwarze Sterne (Arp) **115**:3, 13
Wosley (Belloc) **18**:45
"Would Not Green Peppers" (Wright) **136**:302
The Would-be Gentleman (Gregory) **176**:36
"The Wound of Money" (Anouilh) **195**:54
"The Wounded" (Leino)
See "Loukatut"
The Wounded Stag (Santos) **156**:314
Wounds in the Rain: A Collection of Stories Relating to the Spanish-American War of 1898 (Crane) **11**:128, 161
"Wounds of Love" (García Lorca)
See "Llagas de amor"
"Woven" (Yeats) **1**:578
"Wozu Gedichte" (Bachmann) **192**:68
"WPA Blues" (Williams) **81**:428
"Wraith" (Millay) **4**:306
"Wraith of the Red Swan" (Carman) **7**:133
"The Wrath of Fu Manchu" (Rohmer) **28**:301
The Wrath To Come (Oppenheim) **45**:126, 135
"Wratislaw" (Saki) **3**:374
Wreath (Bryusov) **10**:86
The Wreath (Undset)
See *Kransen*
"Wreath for the Warm-Eyed" (Merrill) **173**:238
"The Wreck" (Tomlinson) **71**:395
The Wreck (Tagore)
See *Nouka-Dubi*
"Wreck in the Offing" (Pyle) **81**:398
"The Wreck of the Julie Plante: A Legend of St. Pierre" (Drummond) **25**:142, 148, 151, 157
"The Wreck of the 'Marco Polo'—1883" (Montgomery) **51**:209
"The Wreck of the Sunday Paper" (Benchley) **55**:13
The Wreckage of Agathon (Gardner) **195**:88, 121, 131, 150
The Wren (Tarkington) **9**:465
The Wrench (Levi)
See *La chiave a stella*
The Wrens (Gregory) **1**:333; **176**:11, 20, 24
"The Wrestlers" (Benét) **28**:5
The Wretched of the Earth (Fanon)
See *Les damnés de la terre*
"Wring the Neck of the Swan" (Gonzalez Martinez)
See "Tuércele el cuelo al cisna"
Writ in Barracks (Wallace) **57**:397
"Writ in My Lord Clarendon, His History of the Rebellion" (Guiney) **41**:217
Write it Right (Bierce) **44**:14
"The Writer" (Galsworthy) **45**:33
The Writer and the Absolute (Lewis) **2**:391, 399; **9**:248
Writer Sollers (Barthes)
See *Sollers, écrivain*
"Writers and Leviathan" (Orwell) **15**:329; **51**:238, 243, 259; **128**:290; **129**:235, 237
"A Writer's Credo" (Abbey) **160**:43, 75, 77, 99, 104
"Writer's Diary" (Prishvin) **75**:218
A Writer's Diary (Woolf) **1**:547-48; **20**:412-13; **43**:401, 405, 413, 421; **56**:393, 411; **101**:205, 207-08, 277, 305, 313
"The Writer's Dream" (Lawson) **27**:139
"A Writer's Notes" (Olesha) **136**:58
"Writers of Dialect" (Bierce) **44**:14
"Writers of Plays" (Nathan) **18**:308
"The Writer's Profession" (Canetti)
See "Der Beruf des Dichters"
A Writer's Recollections (Ward) **55**:417, 429, 442
"Writing" (Nemerov) **124**:155, 178, 181, 220, 309
"Writing about Happiness" (Borges)
See "La felicidad escrita"
"Writing and Living" (Wolfe) **13**:495-96
Writing Degree Zero (Barthes)
See *Le degré zéro de l'écriture*
"The writing I/subject" (Bachmann)
See "Das schreibende Ich"
"Writing, Identity, and Copyright in the Net Age" (Acker) **191**:128
"The Writing of a Novel" (Chesnutt) **39**:93
"The Writing of a Poem" (Sarton) **120**:262

The Writing of Fiction (Wharton) **9**:546, 549; **27**:394; **53**:368, 385; **129**:363; **149**:184, 288
"The Writing of God" (Borges)
See "La escritura del Dios"
The Writing of Informal Essays (Chase) **124**:28
"Writing of One's Own" (Chang) **184**:147-48
Writing on a Body (Sarduy)
See *Escrito sobre un cuerpo*
"Writing Organic Fiction" (Morris) **107**:176, 208
Writings in Time of War, 1916-1919 (Teilhard de Chardin)
See *Écrits du temps de la guerre, 1916-1919*
The Writings of E. M. Forster (Macaulay) **7**:424; **44**:126
The Writings of "Robinson" (Petrov) **21**:153
The Writings of Will Rogers (Rogers) **71**:307
Writings on Education (Frye) **165**:256, 259-61
"Writings on the theatre" (Barthes) **135**:163
Writings on Writing (Sarton) **120**:262-63
"Written during My Stay at White Clouds Monastery at West Lake" (Su Man-shu) **24**:456
"Written in a Year When Many of My People Died" (Lindsay) **17**:227
"Written in Our Flesh" (Wakefield) **120**:354
Written on Water (Chang)
See *Liuyan*
Wrong for Wrong (Caragiale)
See *The Bane*
"The Wrong Hand" (Post) **39**:338
"The Wrong House" (Hornung)
See "Willful Murder"
"The Wrong House" (Milne) **6**:313, 319
"Wrong Number, Please" (Benchley) **55**:3
"Wrong Pigeon" (Chandler) **179**:129
"The Wrong Sign" (Post) **39**:336
"Wrong Time" (Jiménez) **183**:330
"Wully" (Seton) **31**:273, 279
"Die Wunde Heine" (Adorno) **111**:56
Wunder in Amerika (Toller) **10**:492
"Das wunderbare" (Mann) **9**:314
"Wunderkind" (McCullers) **155**:179, 234-38
Das Wunderkind (Mann) **2**:432; **60**:358
Wunnigel (Raabe) **45**:201
"Der Wunsch" (Sudermann) **15**:429
"Wunsch und Vorsatz" (Raabe) **45**:188
Die Wupper (Lasker-Schueler) **57**:295
"Wurzel" (Kandinsky) **92**:69
Wurzel-Flummery (Milne) **6**:308, 310
Wuthering Heights (Hecht) **101**:63, 89
Wybór wierszy (Herbert) **168**:18-19
Wyllard's Weird (Braddon) **111**:227, 231
"X Marks the Spot" (Bataille) **155**:92
X=0. A Night of the Trojan War (Drinkwater) **57**:128-29, 140, 143, 145-46
Xaimaca (Güiraldes) **39**:175, 177-78, 182, 186, 189-90
Xaipe: Seventy-One Poems (Cummings) **137**:15, 29-30
"Xalome" (Villa) **176**:101
"Xelucha" (Shiel) **8**:359, 361
Xenophon's Socrates (Strauss) **141**:232
"The Xhosa Calamity—1856" (Vilakazi)
See "Inkelekele yakwaXhoza"
"Xiangjian huan" (Chang) **184**:138
"Xiao ai" (Chang) **184**:138-39
"Xingu" (Wharton) **129**:362, 365
Xingu, and Other Stories (Wharton) **3**:580; **129**:362
"Xinjing" (Chang) **184**:124, 138
Xozjain i rabotnik (Tolstoy)
See *Khozyain i rabotnik*
Xylographies (Kandinsky) **92**:47
Y avait un prisonnier (Anouilh) **195**:38
"Y Después" (García Lorca) **181**:198
"Y la cabeza comenzó a arder" (Storni) **5**:451
Y Matarazo no llamó (Garro) **153**:72
"Y si después de tántas palabras" (Vallejo) **56**:311
Ya (Mayakovski) **4**:291, 293
"Ya es tarde" (Aleixandre) **113**:7
"Ya Mahbub" (Naidu) **80**:314
"Ya mi súplica es llanto" (Villaurrutia) **80**:477
"Ya no es posible" (Aleixandre) **113**:15
"Yablonka" (Remizov) **27**:339
"Yabu no naka" (Akutagawa Ryūnosuke) **16**:19, 36
The Yage Letters (Burroughs) **121**:113
The Yage Letters (Ginsberg) **120**:135
"Yaguai" (Quiroga) **20**:213
The Yale Edition of the Unpublished Works of Gertrude Stein (Stein)
See *The Yale Gertrude Stein*
The Yale Gertrude Stein (Stein) **48**:245, 248
"Yalluh Hammer" (Walker) **129**:271, 331
"Yam Gruel" (Akutagawa Ryūnosuke)
See "Imogayu"
Yama (Kuprin) **5**:297, 299, 307
"Yama no ugoku hi" (Yosano) **59**:332, 346
Yama: The Pit (Kuprin)
See *Yama*
"Yamagata" (Shiga) **172**:202
"Yamamoto Annosuke-kun no 'Shukyo to risei' to iu rombun o yomite shokan o nobu" (Nishida) **83**:227
"Yamamoto Chosui-kun no omoide" (Nishida) **83**:216
"Yamaraja" (Hearn) **9**:138
"Yamashina no kioku" (Shiga) **172**:214
Yang Kwei Fei (Mizoguchi)
See *Yokihi*
"Yangge" (Chang) **184**:138-39
Yangge (Chang) **184**:106
"The Yankee Doodle Boy" (Cohan) **60**:162-3, 167, 169-70
The Yankee Prince (Cohan) **60**:157, 159, 162, 171
The Yankee Princess (Cohan) **60**:166
"The Yankee Trader" (Bishop) **103**:4, 101
"Yanko the Musician" (Sienkiewicz) **3**:430
"Yánnina" (Merrill) **173**:162-63, 166, 169-70, 173, 228
"Yao" (Lu Hsun) **3**:295, 297, 301
"The Yardstick" (Fletcher) **35**:95
Yashin (Nagai) **51**:87, 91
"Yashka" (Korolenko) **22**:181-82
"Yasmin" (Flecker) **43**:190
"Yasui Fujin" (Mori Ogai) **14**:378, 380, 384
"Yasukichi no techōkara" (Akutagawa Ryūnosuke) **16**:36
"Yātrī" (Devkota) **23**:47, 49
"Yawar (Fiesta)" (Arguedas) **147**:67, 72
Yayá Garcia (Machado de Assis) **10**:282, 285
"ydoan o nudn" (Cummings) **137**:64
"Ye Olde Cheshire Cheese" (Pilnyak) **23**:203
"Ye Sad Story Concerning One Innocent Little Lamb and Four Wicked Wolves" (Pyle) **81**:393
"Ye Song of Ye Foolish Old Woman" (Pyle) **81**:392
"Ye Two Wishes" (Pyle) **81**:392
Year Books of Edward II (Maitland) **65**:252
"A Year in Europe" (Fuller) **103**:116
Year In, Year Out (Milne) **6**:316
The Year of Decision: 1846 (De Voto) **29**:124, 127-29
A Year of Famine (Korolenko) **22**:170-71
The Year of Pilár (Riggs) **56**:209
Year of Sweet Illusions (Carossa)
See *Das Jahr der Schönen Täuschungen*
The Year of the Soul (George)
See *Der Jahr der Seele*
"A Year of Their Life" (Pilnyak)
See "God ikh zhizni"
"A Year Off" (Lovecraft) **4**:266
The Year 1794 (Reymont)
See *Rok 1794*
The Yearling (Rawlings) **4**:360-66, 368
"Yearning for the Day" (Aleixandre) **113**:41
"Year-One Atomic Age-A Message" (Einstein) **65**:122
The Years (Woolf) **1**:538-39, 543-44, 546; **5**:508, 510-11, 517-18; **20**:397, 409; **56**:376-78; **101**:227; **128**:319, 323, 326-27, 331, 333, 337, 343-46, 349-50, 352-53, 359-60, 365-67, 373, 381-82
A Year's Letters (Swinburne)
See *Love's Cross-Currents: A Year's Letters*
Years of My Youth (Howells) **7**:398; **17**:162
"Yeats and the Language of Symbolism" (Frye) **165**:165
"Yeghishe Charentz" (Saroyan) **137**:181
Yeh ts'ao (Lu Hsun) **3**:297
Yekl; A Tale of the New York Ghetto (Cahan) **71**:9-11, 15-17, 21, 24-26, 38-39, 41, 45, 55, 67, 71, 87-88
"Yell'ham Wood's Story" (Hardy) **53**:84
The Yellow Claw (Rohmer) **28**:276-77, 282, 284, 295, 301
The Yellow Danger (Shiel) **8**:358, 361-62
"Yellow Dog Blues" (Handy) **97**:40, 45, 47, 50
"Yellow Dog Blues" (Wright) **136**:264
The Yellow Fairy Book (Lang) **16**:272
Yellow Gentians and Blue (Gale) **7**:282-83, 285
"The Yellow Goat" (Hecht) **101**:36-7
The Yellow Man (Endo)
See *Kiiroi hito*
Yellow Man (Endo)
See *Kiiroi hito*
The Yellow Pages: 59 Poems (Merrill) **173**:162, 173
"The Yellow Peril" (Bryan) **99**:116
"The Yellow Peril" (London) **9**:265
The Yellow Peril (Shiel)
See *The Dragon*
"Yellow Petals Gone" (Wright) **136**:301
Yellow Point (Kandinsky) **92**:32
The Yellow Ribbon (Oppenheim) **45**:134
The Yellow Room (Rinehart) **52**:290-91, 300, 303
Yellow Shadows (Rohmer) **28**:282, 301
"The Yellow Sign" (Chambers) **41**:87, 100-01, 103, 105-06, 110
The Yellow Snake (Wallace) **57**:402
The Yellow Sound (Kandinsky)
See *Der Gelbe Klang*
Yellow Sparks (Bacovia) **24**:64
The Yellow Ticket, and Other Stories (Harris) **24**:263
"The Yellow Wallpaper" (Gilman) **9**:101-03, 105-07, 110, 112, 115; **37**:176-77, 188-95, 198-201, 205-07, 209-11, 213; **117**:42-3, 45-7, 56-7, 59, 76-7, 89-96, 99, 106, 108-10, 115, 120, 122, 124-26, 139, 151, 153, 163
The Yellow Wallpaper, and Other Stories (Gilman) **117**:53, 85, 89, 95
The Yellow Wave (Shiel) **8**:362
"The Yellowed Birch Leaf, the Drop of Rain, and the Lower Sky" (Sologub)
See "Poželtevšij berezovy list, kaplja, i nižnee nebo"
"The Yellow-Red Parrot" (Korolenko) **22**:183
The Yeomen of the Guard; or, The Merryman and His Maid (Gilbert) **3**:213, 215, 219
"The Yerl of Waterydeck" (MacDonald) **9**:300
Yerma (García Lorca) **1**:314, 316, 318; **7**:293-96; **49**:74-80, 86-8, 97, 109, 114, 116-18; **181**:17, 44-47, 50, 54, 70-77, 97, 129, 133, 135, 179
El yerro candente (Villaurrutia) **80**:468
"¡Yes!" (Jiménez) **183**:334, 336
"Yes and It's Hopeless" (Ginsberg) **120**:80
"Yes and No" (Caragiale) **76**:166
"Yes, how?" (Nexø)
See "Ja, hvordan?"
"Yes, We Love This Land" (Bjoernson)
See "Ja, vi elsker dette landet"
Yesterday: A Study in One Act, in Rhymes (Hofmannsthal) **11**:293
"Yesterday at the Exposition" (Baum) **132**:80
Yesterday Hertofore (Agnon)
See *Temol shilshom*

"Yesterday Lost" (Gurney) **33**:93
"Yesterday's Mirror: Afterthoughts to an Autobiography" (Muir) **87**:284
"Yesternight" (Lawrence) **93**:69
Yet Again (Beerbohm) **1**:66-7; **24**:98, 115-16
"Yet Do I Marvel" (Cullen) **4**:40-1, 44, 49; **37**:142, 148, 152
Les yeux fertiles (Éluard) **7**:250; **41**:163
Les yeux ouverts (Yourcenar) **193**:262, 308-09, 320-22, 324, 328-29, 355
"The Yew-Tree on the Downs" (Lawrence) **93**:43
"YgUDuh" (Cummings) **137**:56
"A Yiddish 'Hamlet'" (Zangwill) **16**:165
"The Yiddish Theatre and American Novels" (Cahan) **71**:85
Yin Chin Wen (Suzuki) **109**:387
"Yksilön murhe" (Leino) **24**:370-71
"Ylermi" (Leino) **24**:369, 373, 376-78
L'Ymagier (Jarry) **147**:275, 311
"Yo ga tachiba" (Mori Ogai) **14**:379
"Yo y Yo" (Jiménez) **183**:289-90
Yoaké maé (Shimazaki Toson) **5**:432-33, 438
Yoga as Philosophy and Religion (Dasgupta) **81**:91,93
Yoga Philosophy in Relation to Other Systems of Indian Thought (Dasgupta) **81**:93
Yogāyog (Tagore) **3**:495
"Yogisha" (Hagiwara) **60**:312, 315
The Yoke of Life (Grove) **4**:133-34, 140
A Yoke of Thunder (Coffin) **95**:4
Yökehrääjä (Leino) **24**:368
"Yokes" (Vallejo) **3**:529
Yokihi (Mizoguchi) **72**:293, 296, 315-16, 324, 326
"Yokohama Garland" (Coppard) **5**:178
"A Yom Kippur Scandal" (Aleichem) **35**:323, 328
"Yonder See the Morning Blink" (Housman) **10**:247
"La Yonfantayn" (Trambley) **163**:376-79
"Yonjussai no otoko" (Endo) **152**:198, 202
"Yonosuke no hanashi" (Akutagawa Ryūnosuke) **16**:20
Yordim (Bergelson) **81**:24,27-8,32
"Yore" (Nemerov) **124**:160-61, 231, 291
"York Beach" (Toomer) **172**:265
The York Road (Reese) **181**:339
"York Street" (Stephens) **4**:419
Yoru no Onnatachi (Mizoguchi) **72**:306, 313, 324
Yosa Buson: A Poet of Nostalgia (Hagiwara) **60**:303
"Yosele Solovey" (Aleichem) **1**:28
The Yosemite (Muir) **28**:243, 247, 259
Yoshe Kalb (Singer) **33**:381, 384-86, 389-90, 392
"Yotei chowa o tebiki to shite shukyo tetsugaku e" (Nishida) **83**:332, 335
"You" (Kolmar) **40**:176
You and I (Barry) **11**:45-7, 54-5, 60-6, 68
You and I (Monroe) **12**:215-17
"You and the Atom Bomb" (Orwell) **128**:279, 287; **129**:249
"You Are Very Brown" (Webb) **24**:473
"You Aren't Mad, Am I?" (Cummings) **137**:3, 19
"You Can Have Broadway" (Cohan) **60**:168
You Can't Cheat an Honest Man (Fields) **80**:226, 246
You Can't Go Home Again (Wolfe) **4**:514-16, 518-21, 525, 529, 532-34; **13**:472-74, 479, 490, 495-96; **29**:405, 410-11; **61**:290, 312
You Don't Know How (Pirandello)
See *Non si sa come*
You Don't Love Yourself (Sarraute)
See *Tu ne t'aimes pas*
"You foolish little days" (Arp)
See "Im Hoffnungslosen"
"You Frog!" (Hagiwara)
See "Kaeru yo"
"You Have Been Gone So Long" (Reese) **181**:344
"You Have Lost the Strike! And Now What Are You Going to Do about It?" (Sinclair) **160**:247
You Have Seen Their Faces (Caldwell) **117**:9-11, 13, 23, 25, 17, 35-8
"You Have Your Lebanon and I Have Mine" (Gibran) **9**:90
You Know Me Al: A Busher's Letters (Lardner) **2**:326, 329, 332, 335, 337, 339; **14**:290, 293, 297, 301, 303-05, 307, 311-12, 315-16, 320
You Lovely People (Santos) **156**:296, 308
"You Made Me Child" (Jozsef) **22**:162
You Never Can Tell (Shaw) **3**:393; **9**:414; **21**:306, 329
You Only Live Twice (Fleming) **193**:194, 198-99, 201, 208-09, 215, 228, 239
You Too Are Guilty (Abe)
See *Omaenimo tsumi ga aru*
"You Were Perfectly Fine" (Parker) **143**:331
You Who Have Dreams (Anderson) **144**:34, 70
"You Who Never Have Left Your Garden-Land" (Södergran)
See "Du som aldrig gått ut ur dit trädgårdsland"
You Won't Get the Better of Us (Tolstoy) **18**:379
"You Words" (Bachmann)
See "Ihr Worte"
Youma (Hearn) **9**:131, 138
Young Adventure: A Book of Poems (Benét) **7**:69
"The Young Baptist" (Pickthall) **21**:245, 250
"Young Blood" (Benét) **7**:69
"The Young Blood Hungers" (Bonner) **179**:30, 44
The Young Cosima (Richardson) **4**:377-78, 380
"The Young Daimyo" (Fletcher) **35**:95
The Young David (Beer-Hofmann)
See *Der junge David*
"Young Death and Desire—1862" (Bishop) **103**:13, 24
The Young Diana: An Experiment of the Future (Corelli) **51**:75, 77-8
Young Dr. Gosse (Chopin) **5**:148
Young Emma (Davies) **5**:210-11
The Young Enchanted (Walpole) **5**:496
The Young Fate (Valéry)
See *La jeune parque*
Young Folks' History of the United States (Higginson) **36**:165
"The Young Gentlemen" (Wharton) **129**:363
Young Germany (Brandes)
See *Det unge Tydakland*
"The Young Girl" (Mansfield) **8**:282, 289-91; **164**:239
"A Young Girl Can Spoil Her Chances" (Brennan) **124**:5
"A Young Girl's Confession" (Proust)
See "La confession d'une jeune fille"
The Young Guard (Fadeyev)
See *Molodaya gvardiya*
Young Henry of Navarre (Mann)
See *Die Jugend des königs Henri Quatre*
The Young Hilaire Belloc (Lowndes) **12**:205
"The Young Immigrants" (Lardner) **14**:305
The Young Joseph (Mann)
See *Der Junge Joseph*
"Young Lady" (Csáth) **13**:146
"The Young Lady and the Woolworth's" (Mayakovski) **18**:259
"The Young Lioness" (Quiroga)
See "La señorita Leona"
The Young Lovell (Ford) **15**:93; **57**:216; **172**:57
"The Young Maid" (Trakl) **5**:466
"Young Man Axelbrod" (Lewis) **4**:257
A Young Man in a Hurry (Chambers) **41**:95
"Young Man in a Room" (Anderson) **1**:38
"The Young Man under the Walnut Tree" (Coppard) **5**:178
Young Manhood (Tolstoy)
See *Yunost*
A Young Man's Love (Grieg)
See *En ung mands kjaerlighet*
A Young Man's Year (Hope) **83**:173
The Young Master of Hyson Hall (Stockton) **47**:327
The Young Medardus (Schnitzler)
See *Der junge Medardus*
The Young Men Are Coming (Shiel) **8**:360, 363-64
"Young Men Dead" (Bishop) **103**:2, 4, 6
Young Men in Spats (Wodehouse) **108**:366
Young Mrs. Greeley (Tarkington) **9**:463
"The Young Neophyte" (Meynell) **6**:299
"The Young Nietzsche" (Leino)
See "Nuori Nietzsche"
"A Young Pan's Prayer" (Carman) **7**:149
Young People's Pride (Benét) **7**:80
"A Young Poet, in His Twenty-Fourth Year" (Cavafy) **7**:157
"The Young Ravens That Call upon Him" (Roberts) **8**:326
"Young Robin Gray" (Harte) **25**:200
"The Young Sailor" (Warner) **131**:307
Young Souls (Tammsaare)
See *Noored hinged*
The Young Stepmother; or, A Chronicle of Mistakes (Yonge) **48**:374
Young Törless (Musil)
See *Die Verwirrungen des Zöglings Törless*
"Young Wife" (Gilman) **9**:96
Young Wisdom (Crothers) **19**:74
A Young Woman (Leino)
See *Nuori nainen*
A Young Woman Citizen (Austin) **25**:23
"A Young Woman in Green Lace" (Parker) **143**:331
Young Women (Crothers) **19**:86
Young Woodley (Van Druten) **2**:572-73
"Young Worker" (Jozsef) **22**:161
"The Young Writer" (Tolstoy) **18**:377
"Young Writer in a New Country" (Villa) **176**:112
The Younger Generation (Key) **65**:237
"Younger Poets: The Lyric Difficulty" (Nemerov) **124**:175
The Younger Set (Chambers) **41**:92, 95, 101
The Youngest (Barry) **11**:47, 49, 55, 61, 64, 66
"Your Chase Had a Beast in View" (Bishop) **103**:4, 6
"Your Cheating Heart" (Williams) **81**:423,426,436-7,422
"Your Childhood in Menton" (García Lorca)
See "Tu infancia en Menton"
Your City (Thorndike) **107**:380, 419
"Your Last Drive" (Hardy) **53**:101,111
Your Navy (Anderson) **144**:39
"Your Temple, So Stern and So Stately" (Tsvetaeva) **35**:394
"You're the One" (Holly) **65**:138, 148, 150
Yours, Plum: The Letters of P. G. Wodehouse (Wodehouse) **108**:383, 385
"You's Sweet to Yo' Mammy jes de Same" (Johnson) **19**:210
"Youth" (Bourne) **16**:69
"Youth" (Conrad) **1**:200, 202-03; **6**:119, 122; **13**:100-02, 117-18, 133; **43**:139, 142; **57**:71, 85, 101
"Youth" (Kraus)
See "Jugend"
"Youth" (Lasker-Schueler) **57**:334, 336
"Youth" (Ledwidge) **23**:116
Youth (Khodasevich) **15**:208, 210-11
The Youth (Mori Ogai) **14**:375
Youth (Rosenberg) **12**:296, 308-09
Youth (Tolstoy)
See *Yunost*
Youth: A Narrative, and Two Other Stories (Conrad) **1**:202-03, 210; **13**:99-100
Youth and Life (Bourne) **16**:40, 52, 54, 59-63, 68

Youth and the Bright Medusa (Cather) **1**:151-52; **11**:92-3, 95, 101, 114; **132**:128, 133-34, 141
"Youth and Time" (Scott) **6**:385
Youth and Tomorrow (Stapledon) **22**:319, 322
Youth Dying (Erskine) **84**:160
Youth, Egolatry (Baroja)
See *Juventud, egolatría*
"Youth from Vienna" (Collier) **127**:258
Youth Goes West (Knister) **56**:155
Youth in Turin (Calvino)
See "L'italiano, una lingua tra le altre lingue"
"The Youth Linus" (Sologub) **9**:446
The Youth of an Intellectual (Benda)
See *La jeunesse d'un clerc*
The Youth of Washington (Mitchell) **36**:273
Youth Restored (Zoshchenko)
See *Vozvrashchyonnaya molodost'*
Youth Runs Wild (Lewton) **76**:202-03, 210
Youth without God (Horvath)
See *Jugend ohne Gott*
"The Youthful Years" (Chang)
See "Nianqing de shihou"
Youth's Encounter (Mackenzie)
See *Sinister Street*
"You've Got Love" (Holly) **65**:140
"You—You" (Hippius) **9**:163
"Yowa no butō" (Nagai)
See "Butō"
"Ypres" (Verhaeren) **12**:471
Yu'an Hee See Laughs (Rohmer) **28**:284, 295, 301
"Yuan nu" (Chang) **184**:138-39
Yucrshocrsha to nare (Yosano) **59**:337
"Yud" (Fondane) **159**:255
Yugozapad (Bagritsky) **60**:16
Yuki Fujin Ezu (Mizoguchi) **72**:306, 309, 315, 318-19
Yukige (Nagai) **51**:86
"The Yule Guest" (Carman) **7**:135, 138
Yume no onna (Nagai) **51**:87, 91-2
Yunosheskie stikhi (Tsvetaeva) **35**:408-09, 411
Yunost (Tolstoy) **4**:445, 473; **11**:464; **79**:379-80, 415, 445; **173**:265-354
"Yuntas" (Vallejo) **56**:311
Z domoviny (Nezval) **44**:241, 249
"Z legend dawnego Egiptu" (Prus) **48**:161
"Za Russkuiu zemliu" (Remizov) **27**:341
Za volshebnym kolobkom (Prishvin) **75**:215, 219, 222
"Zabludivshijsja tramvaj" (Gumilev) **60**:264, 270-2, 276, 280
Zabur-i ajam (Iqbal) **28**:182
"Zachem" (Balmont) **11**:42
Zagadka Tolstogo (Aldanov) **23**:24
Zagover chuvstv (Olesha) **136**:72, 74, 78, 111, 171, 182
"The Zahir" (Borges)
See "El Zahir"
"El Zahir" (Borges) **109**:37, 40-2, 49, 58, 65-6, 150
"Zai jiulou shang" (Lu Hsun) **3**:295, 303
"Zakat" (Babel) **171**:8, 11, 98-99, 104-7
Zakat (Babel) **2**:23-4; **13**:29-31, 34
Zakkicho (Yosano) **59**:347
"Zaklyatie smekhom" (Khlebnikov) **20**:124, 130, 135, 137-38, 141-42, 149-50
"Zakulisy" (Zamyatin) **37**:425, 428, 430
Zalacaín el aventurero (Baroja) **8**:54-6, 62
Zalacaín the Adventurer (Baroja)
See *Zalacaín el aventurero*
Zami: A New Spelling of My Name (Lorde) **173**:38-46, 50, 57-61, 63-66, 69, 82-83, 86-87, 89-96, 98-110, 118, 123, 125-31
"Zamost'e" (Babel) **171**:25, 35-37, 74, 76, 83, 85, 87-88
La zampa del gatto (Giacosa) **7**:310
Zampogna (Pirandello) **29**:310
La zampogna verde (Tozzi) **31**:321
"Zang tumb tuum" (Marinetti) **10**:324-25
Zangezi (Khlebnikov) **20**:124, 126-27, 137, 140, 146, 150, 152
Zangiku Monogatari (Mizoguchi) **72**:314-15, 323, 325
"Zangwill" (Péguy) **10**:408
"Zani-ka mardash ra gun kard" (Hedāyat) **21**:71
"Zanofa" (Remizov) **27**:341, 348
"Zaočnost" (Tsvetaeva) **7**:560
La zapatera prodigiosa (García Lorca) **1**:309; **5**:292; **7**:292; **49**:88, 105, 107; **181**:17-22, 29-31, 34, 45, 52
"Zapis o versalima na Terazijama 1941" (Popa) **167**:166
"Zapisi o kuci nasred druma" (Popa) **167**:166
Zapiski iunogo vracha (Bulgakov) **16**:76, 80-1, 85, 91, 109, 111
Zapiski na manzhetakh (Bulgakov) **16**:101
"Zapiski sumashshedshego" (Tolstoy) **173**:294-95
Zapiski sumasshedshego (Tolstoy) **11**:463-64, 478; **44**:328; **79**:406, 443
"Zapisky kavalerista" (Gumilev) **60**:283
"Zaporogue" (Apollinaire) **51**:61
Zaragoza (Pérez Galdós) **27**:286-87
Zarb-i kalim (Iqbal) **28**:182-83
"Die Zaren" (Rilke) **195**:181
"Zarina" (Valera y Alcala-Galiano) **10**:505
Zářivé hlubiny (Čapek) **6**:84; **37**:51, 56; **192**:178, 181
Zaščita (Bryusov) **10**:84
Zashchita Luzhina (Nabokov) **108**:52, 55, 83, 104, 108-11, 113, 115, 135, 179, 200, 209, 216, 218, 224
Zasso fukei (Santoka) **72**:418
"Zaswiaty Pana Cogito" (Herbert) **168**:39
Der Zauberberg (Mann) **2**:412-18, 420, 425, 428-31, 433-36, 439, 441; **8**:254-61, 263-65, 269-72; **14**:326, 333, 338, 356; **21**:161-214; **35**:208, 217, 223, 231, 238, 241-42, 265, 268, 270-71; **44**:145-46, 162-63, 165, 168-69, 172, 174-76, 180, 195-96, 198-99, 201-02, 207, 209, 220-21; **60**:322-23, 339, 355-56, 360; **168**:108-9, 111-13, 116-20, 122, 147-48, 150,
Der Zauberlehrling (Ewers) **12**:133-38
Zauberreich der Liebe (Brod) **115**:84, 98, 108
Ein Zauberspiel (Werfel) **8**:479
"Zaveščan'e" (Annensky) **14**:33
"Zavetnye skazki" (Remizov) **27**:339
"Zavety" (Bryusov) **10**:95-6
Zavist' (Olesha) **136**:58, 63-73, 75, 78-80, 83-91, 102, 104-5, 110, 112-13, 120, 124-26, 132, 135-36, 140-46, 148, 152, 154-56, 161-62, 164-69, 173, 181-85, 193-202
"Zavoloč'e" (Pilnyak) **23**:212, 219
"Zavoloch'e" (Pilnyak) **23**:204, 220
"Zavtra" (Zamyatin) **37**:429
"Zayin" (Fondane) **159**:255
Zaza (Belasco) **3**:85
"Zdenko Petersilka" (Cankar) **105**:164
Ze života hmyzu (Čapek) **6**:83-4, 86-7, **37**:40, 42, 46, 50, 53, 56-8; **192**:175, 177, 185, 197, 201-02, 228, 235
The Zeal of Thy House (Sayers) **2**:534; **15**:376, 381, 390
"The Zebras" (Campbell) **5**:126-27
"Zedj" (Andrić) **135**:59-60
Ein zeitalter wird besichtigt (Mann) **9**:322
"Zeitgedichte" (George) **2**:151; **14**:207, 214
"Der Zeitgenosse und die Wirklichkeit" (Böll) **185**:28, 32, 38
"Zeko" (Andrić) **135**:17, 84, 96
Zelënyi vertograd: Slova potseluinye (Balmont) **11**:37
Zella Sees Herself (Delafield) **61**:126-7
Zeltа zirgs (Rainis) **29**:386, 392
Zelyonoye kol'tso (Hippius) **9**:155, 162, 167, 169
"Zemlemer" (Zamyatin) **8**:544, 548
"Zemlja na rukax" (Pilnyak) **23**:213
Zemnaya os (Bryusov) **10**:83
Zemnye primety (Tsvetaeva) **7**:570-71
Zen Buddhism and Its Influence on Japanese Culture (Suzuki) **109**:389
Zen no kenkyu (Nishida) **83**:214, 216, 219, 221-3, 226-8, 231, 233, 235-6, 240-1, 243, 247, 249-50, 268-9, 272, 274-6, 278-9, 281-2, 284, 287-90, 304, 306-7, 309, 311, 351-2, 370, 379-81, 388
"Žena" (Chekhov) **3**:169
"Žena iz slonove kosti" (Andrić) **135**:23, 52, 92
"Žena mašinista" (Platonov) **14**:425
"Žena na kamenu" (Andrić) **135**:90, 93-94
Žena v množném čísle (Nezval) **44**:241, 246-47
"Zendeh be-gur" (Hedāyat) **21**:67, 71, 81
A zenélő angyal (Molnár) **20**:177
Le zénith (Sully Prudhomme) **31**:302
Zeno's Conscience (Svevo)
See *La coscienza di Zeno*
Zenshu (Shiga)
See *Shiga Naoya zenshu*
Der Zentaur (Kaiser) **9**:171, 173
"Zeppelin" (van Ostaijen) **33**:421
Zeppelin Nights: A London Entertainment (Hunt) **53**:187
Der zerbrochene Krug (Bernhard) **165**:109
Zerkala (Hippius) **9**:160
Zerkalo dev (Kuzmin) **40**:201
"Zerline" (Broch) **20**:52
Zero Degree Writing (Barthes)
See *Le degré zéro de l'écriture*
"Zerviah Hope" (Phelps) **113**:355
Zettel (Wittgenstein) **59**:229, 239, 242
"Zev nad zevovima" (Popa) **167**:156
Het zevende gebod (Heijermans) **24**:288, 292, 300
Zhang Ailing duanpian xiaoshuoji (Chang) **184**:107-10
"Zharkoe leto" (Remizov) **27**:339
Zhar-ptitsa (Balmont) **11**:34, 37
Zhemchuga (Gumilev) **60**:260, 262, 269
Zhemchuzhnye zvetila (Sologub) **9**:444
Zhen'-shen': koren' zhizni (Prishvin) **75**:217, 220, 224
"Zhenskoe" (Hippius) **9**:161
"Zhertva" (Remizov) **27**:341, 347-48
"Zhestokoj" (Gumilev) **60**:280
Zhivoy trup (Tolstoy) **4**:453-54; **11**:463, 466
Zhivye litsa (Hippius) **9**:155, 158, 162-63, 169
Zhizń chelovieka (Andreyev) **3**:16, 18-20, 24, 26-30
Zhizn gospodina de Mol'era (Bulgakov) **16**:76, 90, 96, 109-11
"Zhongguo de riye" (Chang) **184**:123, 151
Zhubilei (Chekhov) **31**:80; **163**:17
"Zhufu" (Lu Hsun) **3**:295, 302-03
"Zhuravl" (Khlebnikov) **20**:130-32, 134, 139-40
"Zibn Gite Yor" (Peretz) **16**:398
Zikaden (Bachmann) **192**:9
"Zid" (Popa) **167**:164
Ziemia obiecana (Reymont) **5**:390-91, 393, 396-97
"Zimnie lilii" (Annensky) **14**:32
Zimnie sonety (Ivanov) **33**:117, 127, 132-33, 136
"Ziporeth" (Bialik) **25**:63
Zipper und sein Vater (Roth) **33**:333
"Zir-i buta" (Hedāyat) **21**:75
"Zisneopisanie Pavlicenki, Matveja Rodionyca" (Babel) **13**:33; **171**:8, 20, 37, 40, 61, 72-74, 83, 86
Živi kak chočeš (Aldanov) **23**:22-3
Živo meso (Popa) **167**:163-64, 172, 174, 178-79
Život a dílo skladatele Foltýna (Čapek) **37**:55
Zivotopis trochu jinak (Hrabal) **155**:159
"Zmei" (Remizov) **27**:352
"Zmei poezda" (Khlebnikov) **20**:131
Zmeinye ochi (Sologub) **9**:443
Zmii (Sologub) **9**:443
"Zmija" (Andrić) **135**:84
"Zmure" (Popa) **167**:155
"Znakovi pored puta" (Andrić) **135**:15, 23, 26, 39, 41-42, 44-45, 47, 74, 86, 88
"Znamenja" (Popa) **167**:156

The Zodiac (Dickey) **151**:118-24, 128, 141, 143, 145-46, 149-53, 162-63, 167, 172-73, 203
Zoikina kvartira (Bulgakov) **16**:84, 110-11; **159**:104, 162
"Zoku keiken to shisaku" (Nishida) **83**:327
"Zoku sosaku yodan" (Shiga) **172**:203, 215
Zola (Mann) **9**:328
"Zola as a Romantic Writer" (Norris) **155**:336-39
"The Zola-Bibescu Case of Plagiarism" (Caragiale) **76**:169
"Zolas Vorurteil" (Broch) **20**:57
A zöld huszár (Molnár) **20**:175, 177
"A zóld légy és a sárga mókus" (Mikszath) **31**:167
"Zolotaia parcha" (Balmont) **11**:37
"Zolotistye fei" (Bryusov) **10**:82
Zoloto v lazuri (Bely) **7**:49-50
"Zolotoe iabloko" (Olesha) **136**:183
Zolotoi telenuk (Petrov) **21**:151-53, 157-60
"Zone" (Apollinaire) **3**:33, 35-6, 39, 41, 44; **8**:13, 18-19; **51**:14, 19, 29, 31, 38, 50, 52-4, 56-61
"Zone of Quiet" (Lardner) **14**:307, 312
Zones of the Spirit (Strindberg)
See *En blå bok*
"Zoological Retrogression" (Wells) **133**:230-31, 233, 262
"Zoot Suit Riots are Race Riots" (Himes) **139**:325
Zora Neale Hurston: A Life in Letters (Hurston) **131**:70, 82
Zorba the Greek (Kazantzakis)
See *Bios kai politei'a tou Alexe Zormpa*
Zoroaster (Crawford) **10**:144, 148, 151-52
El zorro de arriba y el zorro de abajo (Arguedas) **147**:8, 12-15, 18, 37-38, 42, 44, 48, 51, 56-62, 80, 83-86, 89-90, 95, 97-103, 109
Zoya's Apartment (Bulgakov)
See *Zoikina kvartira*
"Zpěv miru" (Nezval) **44**:249-50
"Zrelishche" (Olesha) **136**:182
"Zsoltár férfihangra" (Babits) **14**:39
Der Zug war pünktlich (Böll) **185**:4, 18, 26, 29, 50, 56, 107
"Zukunftssorgen" (Morgenstern) **8**:305
Zuleika Dobson; or, An Oxford Love Story (Beerbohm) **1**:67-75; **24**:96, 98-100, 107, 110-14, 116, 118-19, 126-27
"The Zulu Girl" (Campbell) **5**:117, 124, 126
Zulu Horizons (Vilakazi)
See *Amal'eZulu*
Zulu Songs (Vilakazi)
See *Inkondlo kaZulu*
"Zum Begriff der Geisteswissenschaften" (Broch) **20**:57
Zum Lesebuch für Städtebewohner gehörige Gedichte (Brecht) **169**:37-38, 43
"Zum Schillerfest 1859" (Raabe) **45**:187
Zum Tee bei Dr. Borsig (Böll) **185**:24, 27, 31, 50
Zunĩ Mythology (Benedict) **60**:146
"Zur Einführung des Narzissmus" (Freud) **52**:109
Zur Erneuerung und Ausgestaltung des Gottesidenstes (Otto) **85**:313
"Zur Frage unserer Gesetze" (Kafka) **53**:225-26, 229
Zur genealogie der Moral (Nietzsche) **18**:342, 350, 352-54; **55**:330, 352-53, 360, 391
Zur Kritik der deutschen Intelligenz (Ball) **104**:22, 24, 27, 29, 34-36, 43, 45-47, 56-57, 59, 61-67
Zur Logik der Kulturwissenschaften: Fünf Studien (Cassirer) **61**:70, 71, 83-4, 89-91
Zur Phaenomenologie des innern Zeitbewusstseins (Husserl)
See *Vorlesungen zur Phänomenologie des innern Zeitbewusstseins*
Zur Psychologie des Individuums (Przybyszewski) **36**:286
Zur schönen Aussicht (Horvath) **45**:76, 91, 95, 100-01
Zur Soziologie des Parteiwesens in der modernen Demokratie (Michels) **88**:151, 153, 173, 185, 188, 193-200, 203-6, 209-215, 217, 219, 222
"El Zurdo" (Güiraldes) **39**:190
"Zurich Chronicle 1915-1919" (Tzara) **168**:244, 304
Zusammenstoâ (Schwitters) **95**:346-8
Zvenigorod oklikannyi: Nikoliny pritchi (Remizov) **27**:334, 348
"Zverine" (Mandelstam) **6**:267
Zvezda Nadzvezdnaia: Stella Maria Maris (Remizov) **27**:357
"Zvezde izbeglice" (Popa) **167**:158
"Zvezdoubijca" (Hippius) **9**:166-67
"Zvezdoznanceva ostavstina" (Popa) **167**:156
"Zvezdy" (Remizov) **27**:339
"Zvëzdy zakryli resnicy" (Bryusov) **10**:82
"Der Zwang" (Zweig) **17**:444
Das zwanzigste Jahrhundert (Mann) **9**:331
Zwei Gefangene (Heyse) **8**:121
"Zwei Läufer" (Kraus) **5**:291
"Zwei Meilen Trab" (Liliencron) **18**:215
"Die Zweibel" (Schwitters) **95**:317-21, 330, 352
Zweimal Amphitryon (Kaiser) **9**:177-78, 181, 192
"Zweimal Chaplin" (Adorno) **111**:164
Zweimal Oliver (Kaiser) **9**:185
Die Zweite Revolution (Goebbels) **68**:100
"Zwiegespräch an der Mauer des Paradieses" (Werfel) **8**:476, 478
"Die Zwillingsgeschwister" (Liliencron) **18**:215
Zwischen den Rassen (Mann) **9**:323, 325-28, 332
Zwischen neuen und neuen (Perutz) **60**:366-68
Zwischenspiel (Schnitzler) **4**:385, 387, 389, 396
"Zwölf" (Schwitters) **95**:303
"Der zwölf Elf" (Morgenstern) **8**:305
Zwölftausend (Frank) **81**:102
Die zwölfte Stunden: Eine Nacht des Grauens (Murnau) **53**:258